Contents

Introduction

Sunday opening

Pubs in England and almost all of Wales are now allowed to stay open through Sunday afternoon (Scottish pubs have been allowed to do so for years). Our national survey of opening times shows that in most of England and Wales only one in four pubs is taking advantage of this. More than half the pubs in London and other big cities are staying open through Sunday, though; other areas where Sunday afternoon opening is now common, with around half the pubs staying open then, are Hertfordshire, the Isle of Wight, Lancashire, Nottinghamshire and Staffordshire. In Wales, about one-third of pubs are staying open through Sunday. By contrast, all-day Sunday opening is relatively rare in Bedfordshire, Berkshire, Shropshire, Oxfordshire, Somerset and Northumbria – with only about one in ten pubs staying open then.

As we say in the section on Using the Guide, as Sunday afternoon opening is still the exception rather than the rule you should assume that our listed pubs do close then, unless the text says specifically that they stay open on Sunday afternoons.

Children in pubs

The vast majority of pubs in this Guide allow children. Although most specify particular areas for them, over one in three allow them without constraint in any part of the pub.

This does not square up with the letter of the law (see section on Using the Guide). Only pubs which have a Children's Certificate can allow children in any part of the pub – but in fact very few such certificates have been granted. All other pubs are supposed to confine them to parts where there is no drinks servery.

Before Children's Certificates were introduced for England and Wales last year (Scotland had them already), we argued strongly that it would be better to deregulate altogether – leaving the question to be settled in a common-sense way between parents and licensees. If a pub doesn't want children because it wants to preserve a traditional adult atmosphere, then so be it. Equally, parents should be able to judge for themselves whether or not to take their children into any particular pub. And even complete deregulation would keep the ultimate safety net – that licensing authorities can and do simply close down pubs which prove to be sources of potential harm or danger to children.

The advocates of Children's Certificates originally forecast that about 80% of pubs would take them up. The number actually doing so has turned out to be minuscule – around 1% in many areas, less in some. So it's clear that the Children's Certificate scheme has failed to work properly.

The Home Office initially circulated licensing authorities with two general conditions that a pub should meet before being granted a certificate: that the bar area must be suitable for children; and that food must be available. We have always supported this second condition, about food. But the looseness of the wording of the first condition has been a major problem. While some licensing authorities have taken the common-sense view that this means only that a pub should be a decent sort of place rather than a rowdy working men's club or disco bar, others have imposed extraordinarily exacting specific conditions of their own which even a McDonalds does not have to meet. It's quite common for licensing authorities to demand a no smoking area (though other authorities do not believe that they should have a public health role), and to ban games machines. Some go further and ban SkyTV, demanding high chairs, fireguards, baby-changing facilities and electricity plug covers.

An example of the strict approach is Bolton, which imposes stringent requirements on the grounds that they should guard the welfare of children carefully. Their area covers around a thousand pubs. They have had only ten applications in the scheme's first 18 months (and granted five). But even areas which take the broader view, impose no particular conditions and tend to grant all the applications they get, have had very few pubs applying for certificates. An example not far from Bolton is Keighley, covering some 1,100 pubs. They have had only 11 applications (all granted).

From informal discussions we have had with individual licensees, two things are clear. One is that even licensees in 'lenient' areas are under a mistaken impression that magistrates impose fearsomely strict conditions. The second is that in most areas the police, who are responsible for enforcing the licensing laws, will turn a blind eye to the presence of children in a pub so long as that pub is well run in a responsible manner. This is true even in places in which the police are particularly strict about enforcing other aspects of the licensing laws.

As a result, both Children's Certificates and the letter of the law about children in pubs are being very widely disregarded.

It doesn't seem at all sensible for some licensing authorities to be prompting pubs in their areas to become a new breed of creches and day nurseries which happen to sell alcohol. Nor is there any sense in either the wide variation between areas, or the way that present practice – with the great majority of pubs admitting children – simply does not square up with the law. So we think that the Children's Certificate scheme should be dropped, and that while food is being served, if a pub chooses to admit children it should be allowed to do so, without condition.

Having said that, we must emphasise that parents have a real (and in some cases urgent) responsibility to make sure their children don't spoil pubs for everyone else. For every complaint we get about a pub excluding children or treating them as third-class citizens, we hear from a different reader who complains about the thoughtlessness of parents letting hordes of unruly and uncontrolled small children ruin the peace of what would otherwise be a civilised and enjoyable bar. No-one wants to eat and drink in something more like a rowdy school playground than a pub. When licensees make clear to their customers, firmly but kindly, that noisy, badly behaved or crying children are spoiling other people's enjoyment and really shouldn't be allowed to stay in the pub, they certainly have our support – and we believe the sympathy of the great majority of other parents.

Of course, there is a market for really family-oriented pubs – the sort of place that a traditionalist would firmly avoid. Increasingly, the brewery chain pubs are catering quite specifically for families, with high chairs, baby-changing facilities, good children's entertainment or play areas indoors as well as out, special food deals for children, and jolly family events. The Coombe Cellars at Combeinteign-head (Devon), a Whitbreads Brewers Fayre pub, and the Barbridge Inn at Barbridge (Cheshire), a Greenalls Millers Kitchen, are good examples. And on the Channel Islands, it's common for pubs to have a supervised play area for a small charge.

It's much more difficult to combine this sort of approach with the traditional appeal of an individual pub of character. As we've said, most pubs in this Guide do make at least some provision for children. However, four stand out for their strong appeal to families at the same time as the pleasure they give to people who simply want a really good pub. They are the Otter at Weston (Devon), the Wight Mouse at Chale (Isle of Wight), the Old Coach House at Ashby St Ledgers (Northants) and the Ring o' Bells at Compton Martin (Somerset). Of these, the Otter at Weston is **Family Pub of the Year**.

Bad pubs

Every year, we get many thousands of letters about pubs. The overwhelming majority of these are recommendations of individual pubs, and paint a rosy picture of all the best things about British pubs. We'd strongly agree with this generally favourable assessment: pubs which fail to please their customers soon lose them, so don't last long.

However, there are black spots. This year we have had well over a thousand complaints about pubs – people writing about a pub to say that it could never be called 'good', and should never be included in our Guide. So what is it that makes a Bad Pub? To see, we have analysed over 500 of these serious criticisms.

They fall into five main categories – for each, we show the percentage of all complaints:

Complaint . . . . %

bad service or house-keeping 36
disappointing premise 25
poor food 23
poor drinks 9
inflated prices 7

This overall picture shows no general improvement since our last survey four years ago. There are now slightly fewer complaints about food than there were then; but there are now slightly more complaints about bad service and house-keeping.

The real cause for concern lies in some of the detail behind these overall figures.

To start with the main category – bad service and house-keeping. Sheer inefficiency accounts for one-third of such complaints – sluggish or slipshod service, bar staff knowing nothing about the drinks they're serving, understaffing, forgotten orders, leaving fires unlit on cold days, and so forth. There can be no excuse for pubs which accept such a low standard of service as part of their operation. Even more serious, though, is that the most common complaint about service was not mere inefficiency but downright rudeness or indifference. More than half the people who had any complaint about service or house-keeping told us that they felt the pub was unwelcoming, that the licensees or staff were at best inattentive or at worst surly or rude, or that a legitimate complaint was shrugged off with no adequate response – let alone an apology or (where it would have been appropriate) a refund. A happy relationship between customers and staff is absolutely vital to a pub. Fortunately, the great majority of landlords, landladies and staff treat even their most difficult customers with kind and welcoming consideration. The few who do not are a real blot on their profession.

Though it accounts for relatively very few complaints – around five per cent of all those to do with service – one thing which causes great distress to customers is inflexibility over food service times. There are few things more infuriating than turning up at a pub at two minutes past two, hungry after a long walk or even longer journey, to be told that the kitchen closed at two – so there's no possibility of even a sandwich. Perhaps the only thing that's worse is the pub that has a sign outside proclaiming Food All Day – but in fact doesn't start doing lunches until say 12.30, or tells you that they won't be cooking again till 6.

In some ways, of course, this is trying to put right a detail when the big principle is wrong. Although it's growing, the number of pubs which do serve food whenever they're open is still very small indeed. Longer food service, particularly at weekends in holiday areas, is becoming an increasing need as people use their time more flexibly. On the continent, for a pub-equivalent which serves food to stop serving it for some of its opening time would be considered as absurd as for a shoe-shop to stop selling shoes and only sell laces for part of its opening time. We'd like to see many more pubs adopt this sort of sensible put-the-customer-first attitude here.

When people condemn a pub because they don't like it as a place, it's often a simple matter of personal preference – nothing to get anxious about. For each person who finds one pub too smart or lah-di-dah or genteel, there will be two who find another too rough or too full of rowdy young people; for each person who faults a pub for being too crowded, there will be two who fault another for being too quiet.

What customers do unite over is the faceless chain pub. When a pub gets the thumbs-down because of its style, atmosphere, or some other disappointment to do with the building, in over one-third of cases it's because the pub is simply not special – too obviously part of a big chain, or wrecked by thoughtless refurbishment which has destroyed any sense of genuine character or individuality. Pub desecration seems at last to be emerging from its sham olde-worlde phase – the fake beams and timbers, shelves of unreadable books and collections of unuseable rustic tools which have been all the rage with the big breweries' marketing teams. But it's almost a case of out of the frying pan into the fire. This year, their new craze has been for pseudo-Irish pubs, renaming a tired old Coach & Horses Bleary O'Learys or Filthy McGuiltys, stripping out the carpets, taking the cushions off the seats, ditching the Best of Ernest Lush tape and replacing it with loud and jaunty fiddle music, putting in fake handpumps that dispense gassed-up beers with Irish names, and hoping that changing accents from Australian to Irish will endear customers to quaint habits like rinsing out used glasses in the wine-bottle ice-water bucket. We dread to think of what will follow: the Kilt & Ceilidh? Lee's Creole Gumbo Bar? The Virtual Arms and Pickled Internet?

About three per cent of all the complaints we get are about intrusive piped music in pubs. That sounds a small number, but it accounts for some very strong feelings indeed. What really irritates is that all too often the only people who seem to be enjoying it are the bar staff. And to add insult to injury, you're paying for it: a sound system and performing rights fees cost a pub several hundred pounds a year, and that has to be loaded on to the price of your drinks and food. Besides writing to us to let off steam about this, readers might like to know of a well supported campaign against piped music generally, called Pipedown, based at 6 Kingsley Mansions, London W14 9SG.

By far the most common complaint about pub food is simply that it's not good: poor choice, dull, ordinary, too chippy, tough, dried up or overcooked. This has to be set against the high standards for pub food which readers of our Guide now have. Given high expectations, and given the thousands of reports on pub meals which we get each year, it's no surprise that there are at least some disappointments. And as we've said, the proportion of people complaining about pub food has fallen since our last survey.

If there is one villain in the pub kitchen, it's the over-used microwave. Over one in five complaints about food pointed a sternly accusing finger at the microwave. Mostly, people simply dislike a pub's food being obviously bought-in, or coming straight off the freezer-pack company's lorry. One reader objected to the cheek of a pub's calling such stuff 'Our own special game casserole', only to be told by a trading standards officer friend that there was nothing to stop the pub doing that after all, once they'd bought it from the company, it was their own! Another phrase to be wary of is 'home-cooked', which could simply mean a blast on the microwave for a mass-produced catering supply; better to ask 'Is it home-made?'. The most irritating thing of all, of course, is when a pub elies on a microwave but doesn't even use it properly – seven or eight per cent of complaints about pub food are that it's only just warm, or decidedly undercooked, or that dire give-away, cold or even raw in the middle.

Closely allied are those Ugly Sisters of pub catering – the foil-topped tub of UHT milk or cream instead of the real thing, and the foil-wrapped microslug of butter, designed apparently more as a device to grease one's finger-tips than as proper food. Pubs which use these are giving their customers a tell-tale warning – that portion control and staff convenience are more important to them than customer enjoyment.

On the drinks side, we get very occasional reports of short measure being served, but these are now so rare that we believe this problem has been virtually overcome. What is interesting is that we get about ten times as many complaints about the quality of beer in pubs as we do about the quality of wine. These beer complaints split into about two-thirds finding the beer badly kept or served, and about one-third disappointed by a poor or dull choice of beers. This year, the two most deeply felt complaints about beer have been about the increasing use of sparklers to give real ales a thick creamy head (and take up valuable drinking space at the top of the glass), and the way that pubs pass off as real ale new keg beers like Caffreys and Kilkenny which are inert and dead like other keg beers, but fizzed up with nitrogen rather than the usual carbon dioxide.

Knowing that what upsets people more than any other fault in a pub is dirt, we are amazed that so many pubs continue to have such visibly dodgy house-keeping. In 12% of the cases in which people tell us they won't visit a pub again, it's dirt or other poor house-keeping that's to blame. The most common single put-off in this line is just general drabness, dowdiness, scruffiness, lack of care and need for redecoration (accounting for about one-third of this type of complaint); then comes unpleasant lavatories (one in seven of these complaints), dirt or dog mess in the garden (one in seven), dirt in the bar (one in eight) and dirty cutlery, crockery or glasses (one in ten). There are still complaints about cigarette smoke, but nowadays people are far less likely to come out of a pub with their clothes smelling like a used ash tray than just a few years ago.

Reports of prices being too high, running at seven per cent of all complaints about pubs, are pretty much a constant from year to year. The next section shows our analysis of the facts behind these complaints.

Pub prices

In a sample of over 300 pubs' steak and kidney pies and over 600 ploughman's, we found that the average price increase this year has been around 6% for both – over double the general level of price inflation. The most expensive areas for pub meals are Sussex and Hampshire, but it's clear that throughout the country pubs have been cashing in too greedily on the trend to eating out in them. It's now only in Derbyshire, Lancashire, Nottinghamshire, Staffordshire, the West Midlands, London and the Channel Islands that you can still be confident of finding good hot pub main dishes for under £5.

In our view, £6 marks a sensible upper limit for the price of a decent middle-of-the-road pub main dish. It is quite possible for a pub to produce a comprehensive range of dishes profitably, using quality ingredients, within this limit. Good pubs can turn a profit on something more intricate or sophisticated for under £8, though steaks and the more expensive fish can justify a higher price. A handful of pubs can justify prices higher than these levels on the grounds that their cooking is really first-class and is generally recognised to be so good that despite high prices it is good value. Excluding these special places, though, it makes sense to avoid pubs which charge more than the limits we have suggested.

As we do each year, we have also compared what individual pubs are charging this year for beer with prices in those same pubs last year. This analysis of individual price increases in a national sample of 1,166 pubs is the only accurate indicator of how beer prices are changing (other comparisons, which include different pubs each year in their averages, can be unreliable). This year the analysis shows that beer prices have risen by 3.5% only one per cent more than the underlying rate of inflation, which over the same period was about 2.5%. This is the third year running in which we have found that beer price increases have either been no higher than underlying inflation, or have only slightly outstripped it.

The brewing industry and its supporters have gone to great lengths to discredit the regulations introduced a few years ago to weaken the monopoly power of the big national brewing combines. However, in the years before the regulations started having an effect we always saw beer prices increasing at around double the rate of other price increases. The fact that beer prices are now holding as steady as other prices shows clearly that the regulations are indeed having their desired effect, in keeping pub beer prices down – especially given the contrast with pub food prices, which without the restraining effect of the regulations have been shooting up.

This year has also seen the effects of the takeover by Scottish & Newcastle of the Courage brewing combine. There were worries that the sheer monopoly size of this vast new brewing group would make their beers more expensive. But as we said last year the optimistic view was that the takeover would allow production and marketing economies which would moderate their prices. This seems to be what is happening in practice: in pubs tied to the new combined group, beer prices have risen by only 2.8% – less than the national average, and less than in any other major brewing group.

The biggest beer price rises have been in pubs tied to the Carlsberg-Tetleys brewing combine – in which price rises have averaged 4.7%. This group's British breweries have been up for sale for some time, and Bass has made clear it intends to buy them. We believe that the results could again be lower beer prices through economies, as has happened with Scottish Courage (the name of the new S&N/Courage combination). So it's possible that a Bass/Tetleys takeover would help to keep beer prices stable – grounds for some cautious optimism, even though Bass and Scottish Courage would between them control about two-thirds of Britain's brewing capacity. A key factor will be arrangements for limiting the size of the new combined tied pub estate, and we will be watching developments here very closely.

Of course, 'economies' means job losses, and the closing of subsidiary breweries which have been operating well below capacity and therefore unprofitably – with Scottish Courage, for example, shifting production of

Websters Yorkshire from Halifax to Tadcaster, and Home Ales from Nottingham to Mansfield (for contract production by the independent Mansfield Breweries there). Any job loss is regrettable, but in our experience the vast majority of pub customers find no ill effect in the move of a beer from one brewery to another – but do notice the beneficial effects on their pockets of the keener prices that more efficient beer production allows.

This year has also seen Greenalls take over Boddingtons, to create the biggest independent pub chain (both had stopped brewing for themselves some years earlier). Again, in the new combined group's pubs, beer price rises – at 3% – are a little lower than the national average, so in this respect the takeover has worked well for customers.

A vital ingredient of the beer price picture, and of beer choice, is the requirement that pubs tied to the big brewers should be allowed to buy one real ale direct from a different source. A growing number of pubs have taken advantage of this, and in some cases – where they charge a lower price for the guest beer than for their tied beers – it has had a direct influence on price as well as giving customers a wider choice. But it also has an important indirect influence. All the big national brewers, keen not to lose out, have made deals with independent breweries, effectively acting as wholesalers of a portfolio of independent 'guest' beers to their own tied pubs, and to free houses. Though these are not true guest beers in the legal sense of the beer regulations' requirements – because they are bought through the big breweries and not direct – from a customer's point of view they do very nicely, thank you. A far wider choice of independently produced beers is now generally available than was the case a few years ago.

As we go to press, the European Commission has told the UK to change its guest beer rule, on the grounds that it specifies that the guest beer must be a real ale of the traditional cask-conditioned 'bottom-fermented' type, and therefore discriminates against European beers – which are almost invariably 'top-fermented'. We hope that any new rule will continue to prevent mass-produced lagers counting as guest beers, while allowing the small-scale specialist Continental ales which are the equivalent of our own real ales (and naturally we are doing our best to persuade the Corporate and Consumer Affairs Minister about this).

In beer pricing, the real heroes are the smaller local and regional breweries which set far lower prices in their pubs than other pubs in the same area. We list the breweries which came out of our price survey best for this below, showing how much cheaper beer in their pubs is than typical pub prices in their areas:

brewery	savings per pint
Hydes	.41p
Holts	.38p
Donnington	.30p
Clarks	.29p
Fullers	.27p
Hook Norton	.25p
Bathams	.23p
Banks's/Hansons/Camerons	.20p
Batemans	.19p
Belhaven	.16p

Pubs brewing their own beers also save their customers about 20p a pint, compared with the local average. Another brewer, Sam Smiths, can also be counted as cheap: though its beers are not so very much cheaper than the (low) local average in Yorkshire, its home territory, when they are sold at similar prices in Sam Smiths pubs further south they do stand out as bargains.

Beer

Batemans of Lincolnshire, one of the proud band of customer-friendly brewers listed above, does brew particularly fine ales. This year like many other brewers it has been producing additional seasonal ales. The Batemans seasonal ales are really interesting, and well worth seeking out. For this reason, for the fine quality of its regular ales, and for its good record in helping to hold down beer prices in its area, we name Batemans as **Brewer of the Year**.

Fine pubs which stand out particularly for the quality of the beers they serve are the Bhurtpore at Aston (Cheshire), the Quayside in Falmouth and Old Ale House in Truro (Cornwall), the Alexandra in Derby, Old Crown in Shardlow and Derby Tup at Whittington Moor (Derbys), the Prince of Wales at Stow Maries (Essex), the Lytton Arms in Knebworth (Herts), the Taps in Lytham (Lancs), the Rose & Crown at Hose and Swan in the Rushes in Loughborough (Leics), the Vane Arms in Sudborough (Midlands), the Victoria in Beeston and Market Hotel in Retford (Notts), the Richmond Arms at West Ashling (Sussex), the Prince of Wales in Aberdeen, Athletic Arms, Bow Bar, Kays Bar and Starbank in Edinburgh, Bon Accord in Glasgow and Four Marys in Linlithgow (Scotland), and the Open Hearth in Pontypool and Star at Talybont on Usk (Wales). From among these we choose as **Beer Pub of the Year** the Bhurtpore at Aston – a wide choice of constantly changing unusual ales in first-class condition (they've now had over 1,000 different ones), and over 100 interesting bottled beers.

Over three dozen of the pubs in this book brew their own beer, or are supplied by a brewery right beside them. Generally this is cheaper than the surrounding competition; often, it's exceptionally good. Those currently finding wide favour are the Masons Arms on Cartmel Fell and Sun at Dent (Cumbria), the John Thompson near Melbourne (Derbys), the Fountain Head at Branscombe and Mildmay Colours at Holbeton (Devon), the Farmers Arms at Apperley (Gloucs), the Flower Pots at Cheriton (Hants), the Old Brewery at Somerby (Leics), the Brewers Arms at Snaith (Lincs), the Fur & Feather at Woodbastwick (Norfolk), the Plough at Wistanstow (Shrops), the White Hart at Trudoxhill (Somerset), the Burton Bridge at Burton on Trent (Staffs), the Victoria at Earl Soham (Suffolk) and the New Inn at Cropton and Fat Cat in Sheffield (Yorks). Our choice as **Own Brew Pub of the Year** is the Flower Pots at Cheriton (Hants).

Whisky

We've been pleased to see a very real increase in the number of English and Welsh pubs stocking a good range of malt whiskies – there's never been any problem finding good malts in Scotland, but this is a significant change south of the border. It's now fairly common to find around 50 malts in stock (not just the few very widely promoted ones) in English and Welsh pubs – enough for some very happy explorations. Some pubs stand out for going far beyond this, usually because it's a real personal interest of the licensee. The Cragg Lodge at Wormald Green (Yorks) has a legendary collection, the finest in the world – over 1,000, including many great rarities. Others with a remarkable choice include the Crown & Horns at East Ilsley (Berks), the Quayside in Falmouth (Cornwall), the King George IV at Eskdale Green (Cumbria), the Nobody Inn at Doddiscombsleigh (Devon), the Wight Mouse at Chale (Isle of Wight), the Bulls Head at Clipston (Northants), the Victoria in Beeston (Notts), the White Horse at Pulverbatch (Shrops), the Rising Sun at Shraleybrook (Staffs), the Fox & Hounds at Great Wolford (Oxon) and the Dinorben Arms at Bodfari (Wales). It's this last pub, the Dinorben Arms at Bodfari, which we choose as **Whisky Pub of the Year**, for its combination of a very wide general range of malt whiskies with some carefully explored specialities – Islay malts and uncommon Macallan bottlings, for instance.

Wine

Most of the main entries in this Guide now have wine by the glass that is at least respectable – a huge change over the last ten years. By our reckoning between a third and a half of these have wines that aren't just part of the scenery but are a matter of real pleasure. Even many of the more modest pubs now have a small but decent wine list, and house wines that show some thought, using vacuum devices to ensure that bottles stay fresh once opened.

It's increasingly common for a pub to offer ten or more wines by the glass (at least three dozen pubs in this Guide), and we know of quite a few which offer 20 or more.

Pubs with a really exceptional range of wines by the glass, and a helpfully informative approach to choosing among them, are the Knife & Cleaver at Houghton Conquest (Beds), the Five Arrows in Waddesdon (Bucks), the Eagle in

Cambridge, Pheasant at Keyston and Three Horseshoes at Madingley (Cambs), the Grosvenor Arms at Aldford (Cheshire), the Trengilly Wartha near Constantine and Pandora near Mylor Bridge (Cornwall), the Masons Arms at Branscombe, Nobody Inn at Doddiscombsleigh, Barn Owl at Kingskerswell, Castle at Lydford and Cridford at Trusham (Devon), the Spyway at Askerswell and Three Horseshoes at Powerstock (Dorset), the White Hart at Great Yeldham (Essex), the Fox at Lower Oddington (Gloucs), the Red Lion at Boldre and Wykeham Arms in Winchester (Hants), the Ancient Camp at Ruckhall (Herefs & Worcs), the George in Stamford (Lincs), the Crown at Colkirk and Rose & Crown at Snettisham (Norfolk), the Red Lion at Adderbury and Perch & Pike at South Stoke (Oxon), the Fitzhead Inn at Fitzhead (Somerset), the Crown in Southwold (Suffolk), the Plough at Blackbrook (Surrey), the Angel at Hetton and Three Acres at Shelley (Yorks), the Bear at Crickhowell (Wales), and the White Cross in Richmond (London). The landlord of the Fitzhead is a real enthusiast for wine, glad to talk helpfully and knowledgeably about his stock, and willing to open nearly half the wines on his full list of 160 for just a glass or two; so the Fitzhead Inn (Somerset) is our **Wine Pub of the Year.**

Food

The BSE scare has had one very positive result for pub food. This year we have found pub cooks much more careful about the sources of their ingredients. This doesn't just mean meat. Many more pub cooks now tell us of the special efforts they make to find reliable local sources of fresh produce of all sorts – eggs, vegetables, fish, meat. This approach has done wonders for the confidence of their customers. Pubs which have always taken trouble over their buying were able to keep their meaty menus virtually unchanged even at the height of the scare. And a great many other pubs have now joined these, making their careful buying of sound produce both a selling point and a real boost for the quality of their food.

All this means that there is now a very wide choice indeed of good genuine cooking in pubs. Among the best pubs for food, there are two main approaches: on the one hand, proper home cooking at its most enjoyable – a really rewarding stew or pie, fresh fish in good batter with crisp chips, fruit crumbles and pies, and so forth. The other approach is creative cooking to the highest standard by chefs who would be quite at home in the kitchens of some of the country's top restaurants.

For a really enjoyable meal out, both approaches need an extra ingredient – the ambience of the pub itself must be up to a special occasion. This does narrow the field. This year's outstanding dining pubs are the Five Arrows in Waddesdon (Bucks), the Knife & Cleaver at Houghton Conquest (Beds), the Pheasant at Keyston and Three Horseshoes at Madingley (Cambs), the Cholmondeley Arms near Bickley Moss (Cheshire), the Punch Bowl at Crosthwaite (a new main entry), Queens Head at Tirril and Queens Head at Troutbeck (Cumbria), the Castle at Lydford and Cridford at Trusham (Devon), the Fox at Corscombe (Dorset), the White Hart at Great Yeldham (Essex), the Wild Duck at Ewen (Gloucs), the Roebuck at Brimfield and Olde Salutation at Weobley (Herefs & Worcs), the Albion in Faversham (Kent), the New Inn at Yealand Conyers (Lancs), the Chequers at Gedney Dyke (Lincs), the Saracens Head near Erpingham (Norfolk), the Perch & Pike at South Stoke and Lamb at Shipton under Wychwood (Oxon), the Cotley at Wambrook (Somerset), the Beehive at Horringer, Crown at Southwold and Angel at Stoke by Nayland (Suffolk), the Woolpack at Elstead (Surrey), the Crabtree at Lower Beeding and Horse Guards at Tillington (Sussex), the Bulls Head at Wootton Wawen (Warwicks), the George & Dragon at Rowde (Wilts), the Crab & Lobster at Asenby, Three Hares at Bilbrough, Blue Lion at East Witton, Angel at Hetton, Nags Head at Pickhill and Wombwell Arms at Wass (Yorkshire), the Eagle in Farringdon St (London EC1), the Nantyffin Cider Mill near Crickhowell and Walnut Tree at Llandewi Skirrid (Wales), and the Kilberry Inn at Kilberry and Wheatsheaf at Swinton (Scotland).

A meal at any of these is memorable, but shining through above all, with enormous approval from readers, is the Queens Head at Troutbeck in Cumbria, our **Dining Pub of the Year.**

It's good that even inland pubs are now securing supplies of really fresh fish and seafood. Outstanding fish can be had at the Red Lion at Great Kingshill (Bucks), the Trinity Foot at Swavesey (Cambs), the Drewe Arms at Broadhembury, Anchor at Cockwood and Start Bay at Torcross (Devon), the Crown at Blockley and Dog at Old Sodbury (Gloucs), the Dering Arms at Pluckley and Sankeys in Tunbridge Wells (Kent), the Rising Sun at Knapp (Somerset), the Red Lion at Icklingham and Pykkerel at Ixworth (Suffolk), the White Hart at Stopham (Sussex), the George & Dragon at Rowde (Wilts), the Tayvallich Inn at Tayvallich, Crinan Hotel at Crinan and Morefield Motel in Ullapool (Scotland), and the Ferry at Pembroke Ferry (Wales). The Red Lion at Great Kingshill (Bucks) earns the highest praise for serving such perfectly cooked fish so far inland: it is our **Fish Pub of the Year**.

Some pubs are still managing to serve amazing value meals. Prime among them are the Olde Dolphin in Derby (Derbys), the Digby Tap in Sherborne (Dorset), the Hoop at Stock (Essex), the Black Horse at Amberley (Mon-Thurs; Gloucs), the Elephant & Castle at Bloxham (Oxon), the Lion of Morfe at Upper Farmcote (Shrops), the Burton Bridge Inn in Burton on Trent (Staffs), the Six Bells at Chiddingly (Sussex), the Vine in Brierley Hill and Old Windmill in Coventry (W Midlands), the Fat Cat in Sheffield (Yorks), and Bannermans Bar and Kays Bar in Edinburgh and Bon Accord and Horseshoe in Glasgow (Scotland). For its outstanding value we choose the Fat Cat in Sheffield as **Bargain Food Pub of the Year**.

The Three Acres at Shelley (Yorks) shows what can be done with the humble sandwich – an imaginative up-to-the-minute approach which elevates it to a satisfyingly stylish dish. Much more straightforwardly, the new landlord of the Wheatsheaf at Raby (Lancs) is doing an extraordinarily wide range of toasties; the Kings Head at Allendale (Northumberland) has several dozen interesting sandwiches; the massive range of filled rolls at the Hobnails at Little Washbourne (Gloucs) is most impressive; the filled hot granary rolls at the Prince Albert at Frieth (Bucks) are very satisfying. But for sheer value and enjoyment you can't beat the very well filled crisp rolls at the Bell at Aldworth (Berks) – our **Sandwich Pub of the Year**.

The top pubs

For many people, there's nothing to beat a traditional unspoilt pub – no frills, maybe no food to speak of, lots of real character. Shining examples are the Bell at Aldworth and Pot Kiln at Frilsham (Berks), the Red Lion at Chenies, Prince Albert at Frieth and Crown at Little Missenden (Bucks), the Free Press in Cambridge and Queens Head at Newton (Cambs), the White Lion at Barthomley (Cheshire), the Hole in t' Wall at Bowness on Windermere (Cumbria), the Olde Gate at Brassington, Olde Dolphin in Derby and Barley Mow at Kirk Ireton (Derbys), the Fox in Corfe Castle and Square & Compass at Worth Matravers (Dorset), the Flitch of Bacon at Little Dunmow (Essex), the Boat at Ashleworth Quay and Bakers Arms at Broad Campden (Gloucs), the White Horse near Petersfield and Harrow at Steep (Hants), the Fleece at Bretforton and Monkey House at Defford (Herefs & Worcs), the Cap & Stocking at Kegworth (Leics), the Adam & Eve in Norwich (Norfolk), the Falkland Arms at Great Tew and North Star at Steventon (Oxon), the Tuckers Grave at Faulkland, Rose & Crown at Huish Episcopi and Talbot at Mells (Somerset), the Scarlett Arms at Walliswood (Surrey), the Case is Altered at Five Ways (Warwicks), the Birch Hall at Beck Hole, White Horse in Beverley, George at Hubberholme, Whitelocks in Leeds, Farmers Arms at Muker and Laurel at Robin Hoods Bay (Yorks), the Bow Bar in Edinburgh (Scotland) and the Cressely Arms at Cresswell Quay (Wales). From among these, we choose the Harrow at Steep (Hants) as **Unspoilt Pub of the Yea.**

The Yew Tree at Cauldon (Staffs) doesn't quite fit into this unspoilt category; certainly without frills, its unique collections of remarkable objects make it something else – well worth a visit.

This year we've had the bonus of finding over a hundred attractive new entries. Some of these are outstanding. We have particularly enjoyed the Old Harkers Arms in Chester (Cheshire), Earl of St Vincent at Egloshayle and Old Inn at Mullion (Cornwall), White Hart at Bouth (Cumbria), Loders Arms at Loders (Dorset), Prince of Wales at Stow Maries (Essex), Eight Bells at Chipping

Campden and Inn For All Seasons at Little Barrington (Gloucs), Hawkley Inn at Hawkley (Hants), Three Crowns at Ullingswick (Herefs & Worcs), Rose & Crown at Selling (Kent), Old White Hart at Lyddington and Old Brewery at Somerby (Leics), Nickerson Arms at Rothwell (Lincs), Earle Arms at Heydon (Norfolk), Fox & Hounds at Great Brington (Northants), Allenheads Inn at Allenheads (Northumbria), Talk House at Stanton St John (Oxon), Fitzhead Inn at Fitzhead and Woolpack at Beckington (Somerset), Froize at Chillesford and Star at Lidgate (Suffolk), Stephan Langton at Friday Street (Surrey), Cricketers at Duncton and Black Jug in Horsham (Sussex), Owl at Little Cheverell (Wilts), Chapel (N London), Pant-yr-Ochain in Gresford and New Inn at Rosebush (Wales), and Chambers in St Helier (Channel Islands). Most memorable of all of these has been the Fox & Hounds at Great Brington (Northants): it is **Newcomer of the Year**.

A number of pub chains make their mark well in these pages. We are most impressed with the Wetherspoons chain (reliable town pubs with low prices, decent food all day, no smoking areas, a good choice of drinks and often striking architectural character); the English Pub Company (individual country pubs with good food and often comfortable bedroom accommodation); Tynemill (bare-boards real ale pubs with an excellent choice of beers, but also good interesting food and plenty of character); and Pubs Limited, a small family concern responsible for three of the new entries mentioned above (those in Chester, Horsham and Gresford), and two other main entries (in Aldford, Cheshire and Langton Green, Kent). All its pubs that we have seen are civilised, interestingly laid out and well run, with good food and drink and a particularly good atmosphere. So we name Pubs Limited as **Pub Chain of the Year**.

Individual pubs which are currently doing extremely well all round are the Trengilly Wartha near Constantine, Halzephron at Gunwalloe near Helston, Roseland at Philleigh and Ship at Porthleven (Cornwall), Masons Arms on Cartmel Fell, Britannia at Elterwater and Queens Head at Troutbeck (Cumbria), the Cott at Dartington, Castle at Lydford and Cridford at Trusham (Devon), the Bell at Horndon on the Hill (Essex), the Boat at Ashleworth Quay, Wild Duck at Ewen and Fox at Lower Oddington (Gloucs), the Flower Pots at Cheriton (Hants), the Falcon at Fotheringhay (Northants), the Lamb in Burford (Oxon), the Cotley at Wambrook (Somerset), the Beehive at Horringer, Red Lion at Icklingham and Angel in Lavenham (Suffolk), the Bell at Alderminster and Howard Arms at Ilmington (Warwicks), and the Foresters Arms at Carlton and Angel at Hetton (Yorks). In a close-fought finish between the Angel in Lavenham, the Lamb in Burford and the Queens Head at Troutbeck, it's the Angel in Lavenham (Suffolk) which gains the palm as **Pub of the Year 1997**.

Some individual licensees stand out this year, for the warmly welcoming and happy atmosphere that they generate in their pubs: David and Marie Gray of the Maltsters Arms at Chapel Amble, Colin Oakden of the Ship at Porthleven and Graham Hill of the Philleigh at Roseland (Cornwall), Gerry McDonald of the Lantern Pike near Hayfield and Bill and Jill Taylor of the White Horse at Woolley Moor (Derbys), David and Susan Grey of the Cott at Dartington and James Parkin of the Journeys End at Ringmore (Devon), the Barretts of the Marquis of Lorne at Nettlecombe (Dorset), Patricia and Joanna Bartlett of the Flower Pots at Cheriton (Hants), Neil Spiers of the Bewicke Arms at Hallaton (Leics), Colin and Jenny Smith of the Bulls Head at Clipston (Northants), Colin Mead of the Red Lion at Steeple Aston (Oxon), Stephen Waring of the Wenlock Edge Inn (Shrops), Alistair and Sarah Cade of the Notley Arms at Monksilver and David Livingstone of the Cotley at Wambrook (Somerset), and Gerry O'Brien of the Churchill Arms (West London). Colin Mead of Steeple Aston in Oxfordshire exemplifies the classic concerned traditional landlord, welcoming, witty and informed; for 22 years he has preserved the Red Lion there as a bastion of traditional values – he is our **Landlord of the Year**.

What is a Good Pub?

The main entries in this book have been through a two-stage sifting process. First of all, some 2,000 regular correspondents keep in touch with us about the pubs they visit, and nearly double that number report occasionally. The present edition has used a total of just over 46,400 reports from readers, and from users of the electronic version of the book which is available on the Internet, on Compuserve. This keeps us up-to-date about pubs included in previous editions – it's their alarm signals that warn us when a pub's standards have dropped (after a change of management, say), and it's their continuing approval that reassures us about keeping a pub as a main entry for another year. Very important, though, are the reports they send us on pubs we don't know at all. It's from these new discoveries that we make up a shortlist, to be considered for possible inclusion as new main entries. The more people that report favourably on a new pub, the more likely it is to win a place on this shortlist – especially if some of the reporters belong to our hard core of about five hundred trusted correspondents whose judgement we have learned to rely on. These are people who have each given us detailed comments on dozens of pubs, and shown that (when we ourselves know some of those pubs too) their judgement is closely in line with our own.

This brings us to the acid test. Each pub, before inclusion as a main entry, is inspected anonymously by the Editor, the Deputy Editor, or both. They have to find some special quality that would make strangers enjoy visiting it. What often marks the pub out for special attention is good value food (and that might mean anything from a well made sandwich, with good fresh ingredients at a low price, to imaginative cooking outclassing most restaurants in the area). Maybe the drinks are out of the ordinary (pubs with several hundred whiskies, with remarkable wine lists, with home-made country wines or good beer or cider made on the premises, with a wide range of well kept real ales or bottled beers from all over the world). Perhaps there's a special appeal about it as a place to stay, with good bedrooms and obliging service. Maybe it's the building itself (from centuries-old parts of monasteries to extravagant Victorian gin-palaces), or its surroundings (lovely countryside, attractive waterside, extensive well kept garden), or what's in it (charming furnishings, extraordinary collections of bric-a-brac).

Above all, though, what makes the good pub is its atmosphere – you should be able to feel at home there, and feel not just that *you're* glad you've come but that *they're* glad you've come.

It follows from this that a great many ordinary locals, perfectly good in their own right, don't earn a place in the book. What makes them attractive to their regular customers (an almost clubby chumminess) may even make strangers feel rather out-of-place.

Another important point is that there's not necessarily any link between charm and luxury – though we like our creature comforts as much as anyone. A basic unspoilt village tavern, with hard seats and a flagstone floor, may be worth travelling miles to find, while a deluxe pub-restaurant may not be worth crossing the street for. Landlords can't buy the Good Pub accolade by spending thousands on thickly padded banquettes, soft music and luxuriously shrimpy sauces for their steaks they can only win it, by having a genuinely personal concern for both their customers and their pub.

Using the *Guide*

THE COUNTIES

England has been split alphabetically into counties, mainly to make it easier for people scanning through the book to find pubs near them. Each chapter starts by picking out the pubs that are currently doing best in the area, or specially attractive for one reason or another.

Occasionally, counties have been grouped together into a single chapter, and metropolitan areas have been included in the counties around them – for example, Merseyside in Lancashire. When there's any risk of confusion, we have put a note about where to find a county at the place in the book where you'd probably look for it. But if in doubt, check the Contents.

Scotland and Wales have each been covered in single chapters, and London appears immediately before them at the end of England. Except in London (which is split into Central, North, South, West and East), pubs are listed alphabetically under the name of the town or village where they are. If the village is so small that you probably wouldn't find it on a road map, we've listed it under the name of the nearest sizeable village or town instead. The maps use the same town and village names, and additionally include a few big cities that don't have any listed pubs – for orientation.

We always list pubs in their true locations – so if a village is actually in Buckinghamshire that's where we list it, even if its postal address is via some town in Oxfordshire. Just once or twice, while the village itself is in one county the pub is just over the border in the next-door county. We then use the village county, not the pub one.

STARS ★

Specially good pubs are picked out with a star after their name. In a few cases, pubs have two stars: these are the aristocrats among pubs, really worth going out of your way to find. The stars do NOT signify extra luxury or specially good food – in fact some of the pubs which appeal most distinctively and strongly of all are decidedly basic in terms of food and surroundings. The detailed description of each pub shows what its special appeal is, and it's that that the stars refer to.

FOOD AND STAY AWARDS 🍴 🛏

The knife-and-fork rosette shows those pubs where food is quite outstanding. The bed symbol shows pubs which we know to be good as places to stay in – bearing in mind the price of the rooms (obviously you can't expect the same level of luxury at £20 a head as you'd get for £50 a head). Pubs with bedrooms are now mapped and are marked on the maps as a square.

♀

This wine glass symbol marks out those pubs where wines are a cut above the usual run. This should mean that a glass of house wine will be at least palatable. The text of the entry will show whether you can expect much more than this.

◑

The beer tankard symbol shows pubs where the quality of the beer is quite exceptional, or pubs which keep a particularly interesting range of beers in good condition.

£

This symbol picks out pubs where we have found decent snacks at £1.50 or less, or worthwhile main dishes at £3.90 or less.

RECOMMENDERS

At the end of each main entry we include the names of readers who have recently recommended that pub (unless they've asked us not to). Important note: the description of the pub and the comments on it are our own and not the recommenders'; they are based on our own personal inspections and on later verification of facts with each pub. As some recommenders' names appear quite often, you can get an extra idea of what a pub is like by seeing which other pubs those recommenders have approved.

LUCKY DIPS

We've continued to raise the standard for entry to the Lucky Dip section at the end of each county chapter. This includes brief descriptions of pubs that have been recommended by readers, with the readers' names in brackets. As the flood of reports from readers has given so much solid information about so many pubs, we have been able to include only those which seem really worth trying. Where only one single reader has recommended a pub, we have now not included that pub in the list unless the reader's description makes the nature of the pub quite clear, and gives us good grounds for trusting that other readers would be glad to know of the pub. So with most, the descriptions reflect the balanced judgement of a number of different readers, increasingly backed up by similar reports on the same pubs from different readers in previous years (we do not name these readers). Many have been inspected by us. In these cases, LYM means the pub was in a previous edition of the *Guide*. The usual reason that it's no longer a main entry is that, although we've heard nothing really condemnatory about it, we've not had enough favourable reports to be sure that it's still ahead of the local competition. BB means that, although the pub has never been a main entry, we have inspected it, and found nothing against it. In both these cases, the description is our own; in others, it's based on the readers' reports.

Lucky Dip pubs marked with a ✩ are ones where the information we have (either from our own inspections or from trusted reader/reporters) suggests a firm recommendation. Roughly speaking, we'd say that these pubs are as much worth considering, at least for the virtues described for them, as many of the main entries themselves. Note that in the Dips we always commend food if we have information supporting a positive recommendation. So a bare mention that food is served shouldn't be taken to imply a recommendation of the food. The same is true of accommodation and so forth.

The Lucky Dips (particularly, of course, the starred ones) are under consideration for inspection for a future edition – so please let us have any comments you can make on them. You can use the report forms at the end of the book, the report card which should be included in it, or just write direct (no stamp needed if posted in the UK). Our address is *The Good Pub Guide*, FREEPOST TN1569, WADHURST, East Sussex TN5 7BR.

MAP REFERENCES

All pubs are given four-figure map references. On the main entries, it looks like this: SX5678 Map 1. Map 1 means that it's on the first map at the end of the book. SX means it's in the square labelled SX on that map. The first figure, 5, tells you to look along the grid at the top and bottom of the SX square for the figure 5. The *third* figure, 7, tells you to look down he grid at the side of the square to find the figure 7. Imaginary lines drawn down and across the square from these figures should intersect near the pub itself.

The second and fourth figures, the 6 and the 8, are for more precise pin-pointing, and are really for use with larger-scale maps such as road atlases or the Ordnance Survey 1:50,000 maps, which use exactly the same map reference system. On the relevant Ordnance Survey map, instead of finding the 5 marker on the top grid you'd find the 56 one; instead of the 7 on the side grid you'd look for the 78 marker. This makes it very easy to locate even the smallest village.

Where a pub is exceptionally difficult to find, we include a six-figure reference in the directions, such as OS Sheet 102 reference 654783. This refers to Sheet 102 of the Ordnance Survey 1:50,000 maps, which explain how to use the six-figure references to pin-point a pub to the nearest 100 metres.

MOTORWAY PUBS

If a pub is within four or five miles of a motorway junction, and reaching it doesn't involve much slow traffic, we give special directions for finding it from the motorway. And the Special Interest Lists at the end of the book include a list of these pubs, motorway by motorway.

PRICES AND OTHER FACTUAL DETAILS

The *Guide* went to press during the summer of 1996. As late as possible, each pub was sent a checking sheet to get up-to-date food, drink and bedroom prices and other factual information. By the summer of 1997 prices are bound to have increased a little – to be prudent, you should probably allow around 5% extra by then. But if you find a significantly different price *please let us know*.

Breweries to which pubs are 'tied' are named at the beginning of the italic-print rubric after each main entry. That means the pub has to get most if not all of its drinks from that brewery. If the brewery is not an independent one but just part of a combine, we name the combine in brackets. Where a brewery no longer brews its own beers but gets them under contract from a different brewer, we name that brewer too. When the pub is tied, we have spelled out whether the landlord is a tenant, has the pub on a lease, or is a manager; tenants and leaseholders generally have considerably greater freedom to do things their own way, and in particular are allowed to buy drinks including a beer from sources other than their tied brewery.

Free houses are pubs not tied to a brewery, so in theory they can shop around to get the drinks their customers want, at the best prices they can find. But in practice many free houses have loans from the big brewers, on terms that bind them to sell those breweries' beers – indeed, about half of all the beer sold in free houses is supplied by the big national brewery combines to free houses that have these loan ties. So don't be too surprised to find that so-called free houses may be stocking a range of beers restricted to those from a single brewery.

Real ale is used by us to mean beer that has been maturing naturally in its cask. We do not count as real ale beer which has been pasteurised or filtered to remove its natural yeasts. If it is kept under a blanket of carbon dioxide to preserve it, we still generally mention it – as long as the pressure is too light for you to notice any extra fizz, it's hard to tell the difference. (For brevity, we use the expression 'under light blanket pressure' to cover such pubs; we do not include among them pubs where the blanket pressure is high enough to force the beer up from the cellar, as this does make it unnaturally fizzy.) If we say a pub has, for example, 'Whitbreads-related real ales', these may include not just beers brewed by the national company and its subsidiaries but also beers produced by independent breweries which the national company buys in bulk and distributes alongside its own.

Other drinks: we've also looked out particularly for pubs doing enterprising non-alcoholic drinks (including good tea or coffee), interesting spirits (especially malt whiskies), country wines (elderflower and the like) and good farm ciders. So many pubs now stock one of the main brands of draught cider that we normally mention cider only if the pub keeps quite a range, or one of the less common farm-made ciders.

Meals refers to what is sold in the bar, not in any separate restaurant. It means that pub sells food in its bar substantial enough to do as a proper meal – something you'd sit down to with knife and fork. It doesn't necessarily mean you can get three separate courses.

Snacks means sandwiches, ploughman's, pies and so forth, rather than pork scratchings or packets of crisps. We always mention sandwiches in the text if we know that a pub does them – if you don't see them mentioned, assume you can't get them.

The food listed in the description of each pub is an example of the sort of thing you'd find served in the bar on a normal day, and generally includes the dishes which are currently finding most favour with readers. We try to indicate any difference we know of between lunchtime and evening, and between summer and winter (on the whole stressing summer food more). In winter, many pubs tend to have a more restricted range, particularly of salads, and tend then to do more in the way of filled baked potatoes, casseroles and hot pies. We always mention barbecues if we know a pub does them. Food quality and variety may be affected by holidays – particularly in a small pub, where the licensees do the cooking themselves (May and early June seems to be a popular time for licensees to take their holidays).

Any separate *restaurant* is mentioned. We also note any pubs which told us they'd be keeping their restaurant open into Sunday afternoons. But in general all comments on the type of food served, and in particular all the other details about meals and snacks at the end of each entry, relate to the pub food and not to the restaurant food.

Children's Certificates exist but in practice *Children* are allowed into at least some part of almost all the pubs included in this *Guide* (there is no legal restriction on the movement of children over 14 in any pub, though only people over 18 may get alcohol). As we went to press, we asked the main-entry pubs a series of detailed questions about their rules. *Children welcome* means the pub has told us that it simply lets them come in, with no special restrictions. In other cases we report exactly what arrangements pubs say they make for children. However, we have to note that in readers' experience some pubs make restrictions which they haven't told us about (children only if eating, for example), and very occasionally pubs which have previously allowed children change their policy altogether, virtually excluding them. If you come across this, please let us know, so that we can clarify the information for the pub concerned in the next edition. Beware that if children are confined to the restaurant, they may occasionally be expected to have a full restaurant meal. Also, please note that a welcome for children does not necessarily mean a welcome for breast-feeding in public. Even if we don't mention children at all, it is worth asking: one or two pubs told us frankly that they do welcome children but don't want to advertise the fact, for fear of being penalised. All but one or two pubs (we mention these in the text) allow children in their garden or on their terrace, if they have one. Note that in Scotland the law allows children more freely into pubs so long as they are eating (and with an adult). In the Lucky Dip entries we mention children only if readers have found either that they are allowed or that they are not allowed – the absence of any reference to children in a Dip entry means we don't know either way.

Dogs, cats and other animals are mentioned in the text if we know either that they are likely to be present or that they are specifically excluded – we depend chiefly on readers and partly on our own inspections for this information.

Parking is not mentioned if you should normally be able to park outside the pub, or in a private car park, without difficulty. But if we know that parking space is limited or metered, we say so.

Telephone numbers are given for all pubs that are not ex-directory.

Opening hours are for summer; we say if we know of differences in winter, or on particular days of the week. In the country, many pubs may open rather later and close earlier than their details show unless there are plenty of customers around (if you come across this, please let us know – with details). Pubs are allowed to stay open all day Mondays to Saturdays from 11am (earlier, if the area's licensing magistrates have permitted) till 11pm. However, outside cities most English and Welsh pubs close during the afternoon. Scottish pubs are allowed to stay open until later at night, and the Government has said that it may introduce legislation to allow later opening in England and Wales too. We'd be very grateful to hear of any differences from the hours we quote. You are allowed 20 minutes' drinking-up time after the quoted hours – half an hour if you've been having a meal in the pub.

Permitted hours for *Sunday* opening are now 11-10.30, though pubs are allowed to open earlier (for instance to serve breakfast) so long as they don't serve alcohol. We have found that the majority of pubs still close in the afternoon on

Sunday, so unless we say otherwise you should assume that Sunday opening is 12-3 and 7-10.30. In Scotland, a few pubs close on Sundays (we specify those that we know of); most are open 12.30-2.30 and 6.30-11, and some stay open all day. In Wales, pubs in Dwyfor (from Porthmadog down through the Lleyn Peninsula) are not allowed to sell alcohol to non-residents on Sunday, and generally close then. If we know of a pub closing for any day of the week or part of the year, we say so. The few pubs which we say stay closed on Monday do open on bank holiday Mondays.

Bedroom prices normally include full English breakfasts (if these are available, which they usually are), VAT and any automatic service charge that we know about. If we give just one price, it is the total price for two people sharing a double or twin-bedded room for one night. Otherwise, prices before the / are for single occupancy, prices after it for double. A capital B against the price means that it includes a private bathroom, a capital S a private shower. As all this coding packs in quite a lot of information, some examples may help to explain it:

   £50 on its own means that's the total bill for two people sharing a twin or double room without private bath; the pub has no rooms with private bath, and a single person might have to pay that full price

   £50B means exactly the same – but all the rooms have private bath

   £50(£55B) means rooms with private baths cost £5 extra

   £28/£50(£55B) means the same as the last example, but also shows that there are single rooms for £28, none of which have private bathrooms

   If there's a choice of rooms at different prices, we normally give the cheapest. If there are seasonal price variations, we give the summer price (the highest). This winter – 1996-97 – many inns, particularly in the country, will have special cheaper rates. And at other times, especially in holiday areas, you will often find prices cheaper if you stay for several nights. On weekends, inns that aren't in obvious weekending areas often have bargain rates for two- or three-night stays.

MEAL TIMES

Bar food is commonly served from 12-2 and 7-9, at least from Monday to Saturday (food service often stops a bit earlier on Sundays). If we don't give a time against the Meals and snacks note at the bottom of a main entry, that means that you should be able to get bar food at those times. However, we do spell out the times if we know that bar food service starts after 12.15 or after 7.15; if it stops before 2 or before 8.45; or if food is served for significantly longer than usual (say, till 2.30 or 9.45).

   Though we note days when pubs have told us they don't do food, experience suggests that you should play safe on Sundays and check first with any pub before planning an expedition that depends on getting a meal there. Also, out-of-the-way pubs often cut down on cooking during the week, especially the early part of the week, if they're quiet – as they tend to be, except at holiday times. Please let us know if you find anything different from what we say!

NO SMOKING

We say in the text of each entry what if any provision a pub makes for non-smokers. Pubs setting aside at least some sort of no smoking area are also listed county by county in the Special Interest Lists at the back of the book. The Plough at Clifton Hampden (Oxon) and Free Press in Cambridge are completely no smoking.

CHANGES DURING THE YEAR – PLEASE TELL US

Changes are inevitable, during the course of the year. Landlords change, and so do their policies. And, as we've said, not all returned our fact-checking sheets. We very much hope that you will find everything just as we say. But if you find anything different, please let us know, using the tear-out card in the middle of the book (which doesn't need an envelope), the report forms here, or just a letter. You don't need a stamp: the address is *The Good Pub Guide*, FREEPOST TN1569, WADHURST, East Sussex TN5 7BR.

Author's
Acknowledgements

This book would not be possible without the enormous volume of help we get
from several thousand readers, who send us reports on pubs they visit: thanks to
you all. Many have now been reporting to us for a good few years, often in
marvellously helpful detail, and in a number of cases have now sent us several
hundred reports even, in one or two cases, over a thousand. We rely heavily on
this hugely generous help, all of it unpaid, to keep us up to date with existing
entries, to warn us when standards start slipping, to build up a record of reports
on the most promising Lucky Dip entries, and to uncover for us new gems that
we'd otherwise never hear of.

For the exceptional help they've given us, I'm specially grateful to Gwen and
Peter Andrews, Ian Phillips, Richard Lewis, Roger Huggins, Dave Irving, Tom
McLean, Ewan McCall, George Atkinson, Thomas Nott, Colin Laffan, CMW
and JJW, Susan and John Douglas, Richard Houghton, James Nunns, Tony and
Louise Clarke, John Fahy, DWAJ, Peter and Audrey Dowsett, Jenny and Michael
Back, TBB, Derek and Sylvia Stephenson, Jenny and Brian Seller, Joan and
Michel Hooper-Immins, David Carr, Ann and Colin Hunt, Stephen and Julie
Brown, Dave Braisted, Chris Westmoreland, Gordon, David Hanley, John Wooll,
Mike and Wendy Proctor, John Evans, Dr Gerald Barnett, Marjorie and David
Lamb, Mr and Mrs A E McCully, M J Morgan, H K Dyson, Andrew and Ruth
Triggs, Mayur Shah, Anthony Barnes, Basil Minson, Charles Bardswell, A and R
Cooper, PGP, Phyl and Jack Street, Michael A Butler, Sue and Bob Ward, Tony
Martin, Tom Evans, David and Tina Woods-Taylor, Comus Elliott, Joan Olivier,
Richard Gibbs, Malcolm Taylor, Sue Holland, Dave Webster, Lynn Sharpless,
Bob Eardley, Pat and Malcolm Rudlin, J Waller, MDN, P Boot, Joy and Peter
Heatherley, Mark Walker, Meg and Colin Hamilton, M Joyner, Nigel
Woolliscroft, Ted George, R J Walden, Bruce Bird, John Barker, Tim Barrow and
Sue Demont, Vann and Terry Prime, Nigel Norman, Jim and Maggie Cowell,
Simon Collett-Jones, Peter Baker, Chris Raisin, John and Vivienne Rice, Michael
Sargent, John and Wendy Trentham, Mrs K Clapp, E G Parish, John Fazakerley,
Mr and Mrs C H Stride, HNJ, PEJ, Tony and Wendy Hobden, Jim Farmer, John
and Joan Nash, John C Baker, R T and J C Moggridge, David Wallington and
John Bowdler.

A word of special gratitude to Steve and Carolyn Harvey, our Channel Islands
Inspectors; to Frank W Gadbois, a long-standing supporter of the Guide and
great lover of English pubs who after many years over here with the USAF has
been posted back to the United States; and to our mysterious friend 'LM', who
reports so frequently but has never given an address – so that we've never been
able to reply in thanks.

Finally, heartfelt gratitude to the thousands of publicans and their staff who
work so unstintingly and so warm-heartedly to give us so very many Good Pubs.

Alisdair Aird

England

Avon *see* Somerset

Bedfordshire

*This is the first year that the Guide has devoted a separate chapter to
Bedfordshire. By and large, it's a county more noted for its cheerful locals
than for pubs likely to attract strangers from a distance, but if you know
where to look there are quite a few distinctive places to track down. The Bell
at Odell and Three Tuns at Biddenham are both doing particularly well at the
moment, with good value food and an enjoyably homely atmosphere. The
Three Cranes at Turvey, a new main entry, couples decent food with some of
the best beer to be found in the county. On a different plane, the Knife &
Cleaver at Houghton Conquest is a smart eating place which stands out as
the county's Dining Pub of the Year. If you find good British beef elusive
these days, head for the Fox & Hounds at Riseley. In the Lucky Dip section
at the end of the chapter, pubs to watch include the Cock at Broom, Globe in
Linslade, Hare & Hounds at Old Warden, Royal Oak at Potton, Rose &
Crown at Ridgmont, Kings Arms in Sandy and Sow & Pigs at Toddington.
Drinks prices in this county are a little higher than the national average: we
found savings to be made in pubs tied to the regional brewer Greene King.*

BIDDENHAM TL0249 Map 5

Three Tuns

57 Main Road; village signposted from A428 just W of Bedford

Appealingly set in a rather attractive village, this welcoming thatched house is
popular for good very reasonably priced bar food from a fairly short straightforward menu. There are sandwiches (from £1.30), home-made soup (£1.50 – or
with a choice of any sandwich £2.30), pâté (£2), ploughman's (£2.50), burgers
(from £3), salads (£3.50), quiche, lasagne or chilli con carne (£4.50), seafood
platter, home-made steak and kidney pie or chicken casserole (£5.20), and 8oz
sirloin steak (£8); usual children's menu (£1.60) and puddings (£2). The lively
bustling lounge has low beams and country paintings, and there are table skittles,
darts, dominoes and a fruit machine in the public bar; piped music. Well kept
Greene King IPA, Abbot and Rayments kept under light blanket pressure; cheerful,
prompt service. On warm summer days families are drawn to the attractively
sheltered spacious garden. There's a big terrace with lots of picnic tables, white
doves and a dovecote, a very good children's play area with swings for all ages and
a big wooden climbing frame. *(Recommended by Margaret and Nigel Dennis, Arnold and
Maureen East, Michael Marlow, Ian Phillips, G and M Hollis, Piotr Chodzko-Zajko)*

*Greene King ~ Tenant Alan Wilkins ~ Real ale ~ Meals and snacks (not Sun or
Mon evenings) ~ (01234) 354847 ~ Children in small dining room ~ Open 11.30-
2.30, 6-11(12-2.30, 7-10.30 Sun); cl evening 25 Dec*

BOLNHURST TL0859 Map 5

Olde Plough

B660 Bedford—Kimbolton

There's a warmhearted relaxed atmosphere in the comfortably spacious carpeted lounge bar of this pretty 500-year-old black-beamed cottage, with little armchairs around low tables, a leather sofa and armchair and a log fire in the big stone fireplace. The lighthearted landlady is a faith-healer who gives free healing, hosts clairvoyant sessions and psychic suppers and writes cheerful poems and philosophy which appear on the pub walls alongside enlarged naughty postcards and watercolours by a local artist. There's a big woodburning stove, a couple of refectory tables and settles, darts, pool, hood skittles, cribbage, dominoes, Trivial Pursuit and cards in the flagstoned public bar. The dining room has seats around tables ingeniously made from salvaged barn oak and a wooden ceiling made with boards from a Bedford church. The upstairs restaurant (minimum charge £10 a person) has old beams and polished tables. As well as a daily special like liver and bacon casserole or sausage and chips (£4.95), the weekly changing bar and restaurant menu might include soup (£2.50), steak and kidney pie or chicken, ham and mushroom pie (£6.25), fillet of salmon and broccoli pancake, baked avocado and Norwegian prawns in cream and cheese or smoked fish lasagne (£7.95), 8oz fillet steak (£11.95) and puddings like treacle tart, pavlova, spotted dick or apple and blackberry pie (£2.95). Well kept Butcombe or a guest beer, Courage Directors and Ruddles Best on handpump, and seasonal drinks like mulled wine, kir royale or buck's fizz. In summer there may be Morris men or country dancing and bell ringers or carol singers at Christmas. In the lovely tree-shaded garden rustic seats and tables and a long crazy-paved terrace look on to the pond where you can still see the remains of a moat that used to surround the pub. The cats are called Blacky and Titch, the doberman Zeus and the other dog Lica – she likes to fall asleep under the tables; dogs welcome. *(Recommended by Roger Danes, John Saul, Mr and Mrs J Brown, Michael Marlow, Tom Saul, John Fahy)*

Free house ~ Licensee M J Horridge ~ Real ale ~ Meals and snacks (till 10 if busy) ~ Restaurant (Fri/Sat evenings and Sun lunch) ~ (01234) 376274 ~ Well behaved children welcome till 9pm ~ Open 12-2.30, 7-11(12-3, 7-10.30 Sun); cl 25 and 26 Dec

HOUGHTON CONQUEST TL0441 Map 5

Knife & Cleaver 🍴 ♟

Between B530 (old A418) and A6, S of Bedford

Bedfordshire Dining Pub of the Year

The leisurely and comfortable bar – with maps, drawings and old documents on the walls and blazing fire in winter – at this civilised 17th-c brick-built pub is fairly small, as there's quite a restauranty emphasis here. As well as regular sandwiches (from £2.25), they do a very popular home-baked focaccia one with whole chicken breast, bacon and tomato (£5.95), and a baguette filled with fried Scotch fillet steak, smoked Applewood cheese and onions (£6.25). Other smartly stylish bar snacks in moderate helpings from the monthly changing menu might include a soup of the day like walnut and broccoli or mange-tout and fresh mint (£2.25), French fish soup with rouille, croûtons and gruyère (£3), tagliatelle with chicken livers, sherry, nutmeg and bay leaf (£4.50), ciabatta filled with parma ham, black olives, shaved parmesan and tomatoes (£4.95), garlicky Toulouse sausages with mashed potatoes and onion gravy, salmon fish cakes with fresh spinach, fried potatoes and lemon sauce, and fresh fish (£7.95). The dish of the day might be gingered beef casserole, lamb and apricot casserole or Woodland Cobbler – venison, rabbit and wild boar with bacon and onion scone topping (£5.25), and they do a vegetarian dish like pastry parcels of goat's cheese with apples, leeks, walnuts and onions (£5.50). Home-made puddings include steamed lemon pudding, spicy bread pudding with brandy custard or hazelnut meringue ice cream (£2.50); there's a good British cheeseboard (£2.95). There are 24 or more good wines by the glass (or 50cl carafe) including one from a local vineyard, and a fine choice of up to 20 well aged malt whiskies besides well kept Adnams Extra and Batemans XB on handpump; Stowford Press cider; well managed, attentive service and maybe unobtrusive piped classical music. The airy conservatory restaurant has rugs on the tiled floor, swagged curtains, cane furniture and lots of hanging plants.

There are tables out in the neatly kept garden. *(Recommended by David and Mary Webb, Mr and Mrs T F Marshall, Colin McGaughley, Maysie Thompson, Rita Horridge, David Shillitoe, V Green, Michael Marlow, J E Rycroft, Peter Burton)*

Free house ~ Licensees David and Pauline Loom ~ Real ale ~ Meals and snacks (not every Sat evening) ~ Restaurant (not Sun evening) ~ (01234) 740387 ~ Children in restaurant only ~ Themed dinners with jazz or classical music some Fri evenings ~ Open 11.30-2.30(2 Sat), 7-10.30(11 Sat); closed Sun evening and 27-30 Dec ~ Bedrooms: £45B/£59B

KEYSOE TL0762 Map 5

Chequers

B660 N of Bedford

An unusual stone-pillared fireplace divides the two neatly modernised simple beamed rooms at this welcoming village local. One bar is no-smoking and there's a video game, dominoes and piped music. Tasty bar food from the menu and a huge blackboard might include sandwiches, interesting home-made soups, tagliatelle with a creamy mushroom and white wine sauce (£5.25), chicken and ham pancake (£6.50), steak in mustard cream or green peppercorn and brandy sauce (£10), fresh fish on Saturday, and Sunday roast (£4.75); puddings like treacle tart, orange cheesecake or fresh fruit pavlova; children's helpings. Well kept Hook Norton Best and another beer like Jennings Cumberland that changes every couple of months on handpumps on the stone bar counter; some malts. The terrace at the back looks over the garden which has a wendy house, play tree, swings and a sand-pit. There is a surcharge for credit cards. *(Recommended by Jenny and Michael Back, Arnold and Maureen East, Margaret and Roy Randle, Michael Marlow)*

Free house ~ Licensee Jeffrey Kearns ~ Real ale ~ Meals and snacks (12-2, 7-9.30) ~ (01234) 708678 ~ Open 12-2.30, 6.30-11; cl Tuesdays, may be closed in early summer

ODELL SP9658 Map 5

Bell

Horsefair Lane; off A6 S of Rushden, via Sharnbrook

Since last year the cheerfully welcoming interior of this pretty thatched stone village pub has been charmingly redecorated in shades of honeysuckle and mulberry. The five small homely low-ceilinged rooms – some with shiny black beams – loop around a central servery and are furnished with quite a few handsome old oak settles, bentwood chairs and neat modern furniture, with a log fire in one big stone fireplace and two coal fires elsewhere. Very tasty good value bar food includes sandwiches (from £1.85), ploughman's (from £3), omelettes (from £3.50) savoury pancakes or home-made vegetable pie (£4.35), chicken quarter or home-made lasagne (£4.50), steak and kidney pie or turkey, leek and mushroom pie (£5.40) and daily specials from the board such as seafood pasta, fish pie or shepherd's pie (£4.50), beef, bacon and cider casserole or pork slices with bacon, mushroom and vermouth and cream sauce (£6.25), usual children's dishes (from £1.85) and home-made puddings like boozy chocolate mousse or orange cheesecake shortbread (£1.95). Well kept Greene King Abbot, IPA and their seasonal ales and Raymonts on handpump, faint piped music or radio. The friendly licensees have also added a new flower-filled terrace with picnic tables overlooking a beautifully positioned wooded garden that runs down through a wild area to a bridge over the Great Ouse. The garden is full of golden pheasants, cockatiels, canaries, and a goose called Lucy who's rather partial to lettuce leaves. Further along the road is a very pretty church. Controlled dogs in garden only. *(Recommended by Mr and Mrs A W Chapman, R A Buckler, Margaret and Howard Buchanan, Maysie Thompson, Meg and Colin Hamilton, Bob and Maggie Atherton, George Atkinson, Rita Horridge, Andy and Jill Kassube, Lynda Brightman, John Fahy)*

Greene King ~ Tenant Derek Scott ~ Real ale ~ Meals and snacks (not Sun evening in winter) ~ (01234) 720254 ~ Children in eating area of bar only ~ Open 11-2.30, 6-11(all day Sat in summer); cl 25 Dec

RISELEY TL0362 Map 5

Fox & Hounds

High St; village signposted off A6 and B660 N of Bedford

Although we decided not to get caught up this year in discussions about what beef different pubs are serving, it can't really be avoided here as their long-standing speciality is the cabinet of well hung steaks at one end of this cheerful pub's bar counter. The licensees describe their establishment as a patriotic steak-house – needless to say the beef is British. You choose which piece of meat you want yours cut from, say how much you want and how you want it cooked, and you're then charged by weight (price unchanged since last year) – say £8.80 for 8oz rump, £9.60 for 8oz of sirloin and £11.90 for fillet. Alternatively there's a wide choice of other food such as sandwiches (from £1), home-made soups like stilton and broccoli and leek and potato (£1.95), home-made steak burger (£3.95), steak and kidney pie, chicken Monte Christo or marinaded beef pie (£6.95) and peppered steak (£8.95); good puddings. There are plenty of tables spreading around among timber uprights under the heavy low beams, with two candlelit side dining rooms. Well kept Charles Wells Eagle with regularly changing guests like Brains SA, Charles Wells Bombardier and Theakstons XB on handpump, a decent collection of other drinks including several malts and a good range of cognacs; unobtrusive piped Glen Miller or light classics, very friendly, helpful service. There are picnic tables in the huge garden. The landlord is great fun – a real personality. *(Recommended by E J Etheridge, Keith and Cheryl Roe, Mr and Mrs A W Chapman, Philip Brindle, Stephen Brown)*

Charles Wells ~ Managers Jan and Lynne Zielinski ~ Real ale ~ Meals and snacks (12-1.45, 7-10) ~ Restaurant ~ (01234) 708240 ~ Children welcome ~ Open 11.30-2.30, 6.30-11(12-3, 7-10.30 Sun)

TURVEY SP9452 Map 2

Three Cranes

Just off A428 W of Bedford

Dominating one side of a pleasant village triangle, with the church and large houses on another and stone-built cottages on the third, this 17th-c inn is also stone-built, with a striking portico and upper-storey jettied gable added in Victorian times. Its two-level bar is clean, airy and spacious, with a rather genteel atmosphere at lunchtime, lots of pictures and a quiet decor majoring on stuffed owls and other birds; there's a solid fuel stove. A useful range of generous bar food includes good sandwiches (from £1.50), baked potatoes (from £2.50), ploughman's (from £3.25), steak, mushroom and ale pie (£5.75), lasagne (£5.95), gammon (£7.50), rump steak (£8.95), a couple of vegetarian dishes, and blackboard specials like fresh fish (from £6.95), supreme of chicken (£8.50) or rack of lamb (£9); there are plenty of sensible tables with upright seats. Well kept Bass, Black Sheep, Fullers London Pride and ESB and Smiles and a guest beer such as Wadworths 6X on handpump; decent wines and whiskies and coffee, efficient pleasant staff, unobtrusive piped music. There are picnic tables in a neatly kept garden with a climbing frame; in summer the pub's front is a mass of colour from carefully tended hanging baskets and window boxes. *(Recommended by George Atkinson, Mike Sheehan, John Saul, T G Saul, Maysie Thompson, Mary and David Webb, Andy and Jill Kassube, Ian Phillips)*

Free house ~ Mr Alexander ~ Real ale ~ Meals and snacks (till 10 Fri and Sat) ~ Restaurant ~ (01234) 881305 ~ Children welcome in eating area ~ Open 11-3, 6-11(7-10.30 Sun) ~ Bedrooms: £33.50S/£47S

Lucky Dip

Besides the fully inspected pubs, you might like to try these Lucky Dips recommended to us and described by readers (if you do, please send us reports):

☆ **Astwick** [Taylors Rd, signed off A1 northbound; TL2138], *Tudor Oaks*: Open-plan, partly Tudor, with old beams and timbers, exposed brickwork, real fires and woodburner, barometer and lots of brass, banquettes and chesterfields, fresh flowers, friendly service and cat – no dogs alllowed; good generous freshly prepared food inc OAP lunches, seven real ales from independent brewers, local farm cider, upstairs restaurant; tables in courtyard, small play area; bedrooms *(CMW, JJW)*

Bromham [Bridge End; nr A428, 2 miles W of Bedford; TL0050], *Swan*: Comfortable and welcoming beamed village pub with quick service, open fires, lots of pictures, well kept Greene King, decent coffee, popular food inc good value carvery (children allowed here) and salad bar; public bar with darts and fruit machine, pleasant garden *(John Fahy, Michael and Wilma Bishop)*

☆ **Broom** [23 High St; TL1743], *Cock*: Attractive and unusual old-fashioned small-roomed pub with well kept Greene King ales tapped from the cask in corridor servery (no bar counter), wide range of food inc good steaks, traditional bar games, real fire; camping in paddock behind *(Colin McGaughley, Tim Heywood, Sophie Wilne, Roger Danes, Michael Marlow, Dr Jim Cowburn, Robert Bland, Ian Phillips, LYM)*

Cardington [The Green; off A603 E of Bedford; TL0847], *Kings Arms*: Quiet and pleasant Brewers Fayre pub with three real ales, usual old books, garden with picnic tables *(JJW, CMW)*

Chalton [B579 3 miles from M1 junction 12, via Toddington; TL0326], *Star*: Recently smartened up in Brewers Fayre style, nice prints, good ploughman's and lots of steaks, Courage, Flowers and Theakstons ales, big garden with play area; good for families *(the Sandy family)*

Clophill [TL0837], *Green Man*: Attractive bar food, useful for the area *(K H Frostick)*

☆ **Dunstable** [A5183 (old A5) S, 4 miles N of M1 junction 9; TL0221], *Horse & Jockey*: Well done new Chef & Brewer, huge interior divided up into many smaller areas, light pine furnishings, well kept Boddingtons, Flowers and Whitbreads Castle Eden, very friendly staff, good promptly served food; children very welcome, play areas inside and out (huge garden), maybe bouncy castle *(the Sandy family, LYM)*

☆ **Dunstable** [High St], *Old Sugarloaf*: Quaint and hospitable former coaching inn with three busy bars, good friendly service, good range of real ales, good local atmosphere; popular bar and restaurant food *(VC)*

Dunstable [A5183 S, by Kensworth turn], *Packhorse*: Straightforward pub, friendly staff, warming fire, Flowers and Tetleys, beams and exposed brickwork, piped music,

good soup *(George Atkinson)*

☆ **Eaton Bray** [SP9620], *White Horse*: Wide choice of generous well served food and good relaxed atmosphere in rambling old low-beamed dining pub, particularly well run, with timbered dividers, suit of armour in one room, real ales such as Friary Meux Best and Ruddles Best; ranks of tables on back lawn, good walking nearby *(Jenny and Michael Back)*

Felmersham [Grange Rd; SP9857], *Six Ringers*: Thatched village pub in attractive Ouse valley countryside, good value food *(Colin Skevington)*

Harlington [Sundon Rd, off A5120; a mile from M1 junction 12; TL0330], *Carpenters Arms*: Comfortable, quiet and friendly low-beamed village pub with good value bar food, generous Sun lunch in upstairs restaurant (also Weds-Sat evenings), well kept Banks's *(Michael and Alison Sandy)*

Harrold [High St; SP9456], *Magpie*: Well equipped in modern style, friendly atmosphere, efficient service, decent food from usual bar snacks to eg pheasant casserole *(T Saul)*

Hockliffe [A5/A4012; SP9726], *Fox & Hounds*: Friendly free house, well kept Theakstons, food inc good pork and apple sausages *(Dave Braisted)*

☆ **Ireland** [off A600 Shefford—Bedford – OS Sheet 153 map ref 135414; TL1341], *Black Horse*: Welcoming staff and good value food (not Sun evening) in pleasant pub's extensive dining area, Bass and Stones, good coffee, tables in garden; has been closed Mon *(Rita Horridge)*

☆ **Kensworth** [B4540, Whipsnade end; TL0318], *Farmers Boy*: Fine village pub with good value generous food inc vegetarian, well kept Fullers, good lounge bar, excellent old-fashioned dining room (more restauranty evenings and Sun); play area and rabbit hutches in fenced-off garden by fields with horses; children very welcome *(the Sandy family, Mel Smith, Shirley Cannings)*

Lidlington [High St; off A421 not far from M1 junction 13; SP9939], *Green Man*: 17th-c thatched village pub, with comfortable dark-beamed lounge, real fire, good reasonably priced food in raised dining area, friendly and attentive service, Greene King IPA and Abbot; piped music; fruit machine and pool in separate bar; picnic tables outside, boules; handy for walkers *(CMW, JJW)*

☆ **Linslade** [SP9225], *Globe*: Whitewashed canalside pub dating from 1830, lots of rooms – some with flagstones – lots of beams, cosy charm, wing armchair by open fire, canalia, mottoes and couplets; well presented promptly served food inc sizzler dishes (restaurant must be booked), particularly well kept beers such as Courage Directors, Fullers London Pride, Marstons Pedigree, local Tring

Icknield and guests, welcoming service; waterside garden, children's play area; pleasant walks nearby *(Lynda Payton, Sam Samuells, Tony O'Reilly, Andrew Scarr, Mel Smith, Shirley Cannings)*

Luton [Chapel St (bottom end of B4540); TL0921], *Fedora & Firkin*: All the usual Firkin fittings, with own-brewed Fedora, Mad Hatter and Temple of Doom; old-fashioned furnishings, wooden pews etc, roast Sun lunch; very popular with students and office workers *(Michael Sandy)*; [Church St], *Lodge*: Previously the Masons Lodge, now large comfortable Greene King dining pub with wide-ranging American-based food, not cheap but good value and generously served, inc children's *(Michael Sandy)*

☆ Maulden [TL0538], *White Hart*: Freshly cooked food, good value if not cheap, in friendly thatched low-beamed pub with big fireplace dividing bar, lots of tables in separate eating area, pleasant efficient service, Whitbreads-related and other beers such as Morlands and Theakstons *(C H and P Stride, M P Herring, Phil and Heidi Cook)*

Northill [2 Ickwell Rd; TL1546], *Crown*: Welcoming local in attractive village, well kept Charles Wells ales, games room (popular with YFC); not far from the Shuttleworth Collection *(Ian Stanley)*

☆ Odell [Little Odell; SP9657], *Mad Dog*: Cosy old beamed and thatched pub doing well under welcoming new licensees, wide choice of reasonably priced food, well kept Greene King ales, open fire in inglenook, quiet piped music and pleasant garden; handy for Harrold-Odell Country Park *(Tom Saul)*

☆ Old Warden [TL1343], *Hare & Hounds*: Small friendly beamed pub with wide choice of generous food, well kept Charles Wells Fargo, Eagle and Bombardier, simple pleasant decor, open fire, comfortable lounge and dining room – very much geared up for eating; big sloping back garden with scramble net and tyre swings; beautiful village, handy for Shuttleworth Collection *(M Carey, Giles Quick, Cynthia Archer, Carl Lukens, Christopher Gallop)*

☆ Potton [TL2449], *Royal Oak*: Large comfortable bar, spacious dining area opening into restaurant, above-average straightforward bar food (served evenings too) inc bargain lunchtime roasts, very friendly service, well kept Greene King IPA, Abbot and seasonal ales *(Sidney and Erna Wells, P Stallard, Martyn Carey, Jon MacLellan)*

Potton, *Rose & Crown*: Well kept Charles Wells; bedrooms adequate, with good breakfast *(Martyn Carey)*

Pulloxhill [off A6 N of Barton le Clay – OS Sheet 153 map ref 063341; TL0633], *Cross Keys*: Attractive heavily timbered early 17th-c inn hung with about 90 flower baskets and tubs, very friendly licensee and family, good value bar food (dining room often fully booked), Charles Wells; pretty part of village in nice countryside *(Anon)*

☆ Radwell [TL0057], *Swan*: Roomy and

attractive beamed and thatched pub, two rooms joined by narrow passage, woodburner, lots of prints, unobtrusive piped music, wide choice of good food, Charles Wells Eagle on handpump, decent coffee, hospitable landlord, popular evening restaurant; pleasant garden, small quiet village *(Maysie Thompson)*

☆ Ridgmont [handy for M1 junction 13; SP9736], *Rose & Crown*: Consistently good sensible pub food served quickly even when busy, warm welcome, choice of well kept real ales, good coffee, interesting collection of Rupert Annual covers in well laid out lounge; low-ceilinged traditional public bar with open fire, games inc darts and pool; piped music, stables restaurant (not Mon or Tues evenings); long and attractive suntrap sheltered back garden; children allowed in bar eating area; easy parking, good wheelchair access *(L M Miall, F M Bunbury, Nick Holmes, LYM)*

☆ Sandy [Old London Rd; TL1649], *Kings Arms*: Attractive two-bar pub with comfortable banquettes, lots of beams, open fire, wide choice of good reasonably priced food (veg charged separately), friendly relaxed atmosphere, good staff, Greene King IPA and Abbot, decent wines, restaurant; bedrooms in well built chalets *(Tom Saul, Phil and Heidi Cook)*

Sharnbrook [Templars Way, SE of village; SP9959], *Fordham Arms*: Pleasantly refurbished with lots of plates, copper and local paintings, Flowers IPA and Marstons Pedigree, good range of very generous food inc good vegetarian choice, reasonable prices, quick friendly service even when busy, big garden with loose rabbits in play area *(George Atkinson, Harry Whitcher)*; [High St], *Swan with Two Nicks*: Popular smallish local with Charles Wells and guest ales, good food in generous helpings (carpeted dining area), cheerful friendly service, terrace dripping with geraniums *(George Atkinson, John Fahy)*

☆ Silsoe [TL0835], *George*: Obliging service and decent bar food inc good snacks for children (and high chairs) in big pleasant open-plan hotel bar with family ends, well kept Greene King IPA and Abbot, restaurant; big garden with play equipment, pets' corner, maybe a paddling pool (popular with ducks); organist Sat evening; bedrooms *(the Sandy family)*

☆ Southill [off B658 SW of Biggleswade; TL1542], *White Horse*: Well decorated and comfortable lounge, dining room with spotlit well, small public bar with prints, harness and big woodburner; good value food (not Sun evening) inc wide choice of sandwiches and snacks, Whitbreads-related ales; children in eating areas; delightful big garden maybe with children's rides on diesel-engine miniature train, separate sheltered lawn with bird feeders, garden shop and good play area *(the Sandy family, Roger Danes, LYM)*

Steppingley [TL0135], *French Horn*: 16th-c pub with wide choice of real ales, good food in bar and restaurant, garden *(Colin McGaughley)*

Stotfold [Brook St; TL2136], *Stag*: Small but very friendly, with well kept beers inc some brewed on the premises – Abel Brown Brewery *(Richard Houghton)*

☆ Studham [Dunstable Rd; TL0215], *Bell*: Friendly two-bar village pub dating from 16th c, beams, brasses, prints and plates, big helpings of good food with good sauces cooked to order (expect a wait), Benskins, Ind Coope Burton, Tetleys Bitter and Imperial on handpump; booking advised Sat, Sun lunch very popular – service can slow then; handy for Whipsnade and the Tree Cathedral *(Phil and Heidi Cook, Norma and Keith Bloomfield, John Hawkins)*

☆ Toddington [19 Church Sq; handy for M1 junction 12; main street from junction into village; TL0028], *Sow & Pigs*: Welcoming and genuine 19th-c pub named after carving on church opp, with assorted furnishings inc pews, two armchairs and a retired chesterfield, bare boards, lots of old books and knick-knacks inc armless mannequin and amusing pig motifs, well kept Greene King ales, good coffee, wide choice of food (back Victorian-style dining room can be booked for parties), two real fires; picnic tables in small garden, attractive village *(JJW, CMW, Ian Phillips, Richard Hedges)*

Toddington [Station Rd], *Griffin*: Greene King pub with pool, darts and Monopoly machine in small bar, dining area in larger lounge, small patio and garden with swings, decent food with Mexican/American leanings *(CMW, JJW)*

Totternhoe [SP9821], *Cross Keys*: Small friendly bar in picturesque black-and-white pub with lovely garden and orchard views *(Colin McGaughley, BB)*

☆ Turvey [Bridge St, at W end of village], *Three Fyshes*: Some flagstones but now red carpet

too in early 17th-c pub with beams, inglenook, beers brewed on the premises, farm ciders, welcoming staff; good value traditional food, maybe piped local radio; relaxed family atmosphere in garden with access to Great Ouse, summer barbecues, dogs, cats and rabbits; open all day Sat; children and dogs welcome, can get crowded *(Bob and Maggie Atherton, Roger Danes, LYM)*

Westoning [High St/Greenfield Rd; 1½ miles from M1, junction 12: A5120; SP0332], *Bell*: Friendly licensee, obliging service, well kept Greene King and Rayments, decent food inc vegetarian and thoughtful children's options, traditional bar areas, nice dining area with cuckoo clock; boules pitch, lots of tables inc child-sized picnic tables around flowerbeds, big slide and swing *(the Sandy family)*

Whipsnade [B4540 E; TL0117], *Old Hunters Lodge*: 15th-c pub handy for zoo, with generous straightforward food inc children's helpings, pleasant snug area on right, plusher modernised main lounge, sofa by roaring fire, oil paintings and castle prints, subdued piped music, well kept Charles Wells Eagle, Bombardier and Fargo and Websters Yorkshire, tables under cocktail parasols in front garden; spacious old-world restaurant *(Nigel Norman, David Shillitoe)*

☆ Woburn [1 Bedford St], *Black Horse*: Spacious open-plan food pub with wide choice from sandwiches and baked potatoes to steaks and fish cut to order and grilled in the bar, also children's, vegetarian and special orders; well kept real ales; open all day summer Sat and bank hols, summer barbecues in pleasant sheltered garden; children in eating areas *(Keith Algar, Mrs H Ellis, Miss I W Stillman)*

Wootton [Hall End; TL0045], *Chequers*: Warm and cosy 15th-c character local with friendly, helpful service; good food in bar and restaurant *(Colin McGaughley)*

Children welcome means the pubs says it lets children inside without any special restriction. If it allows them in, but to restricted areas such as an eating area or family room, we specify this. Places with separate restaurants usually let children use them, hotels usually let them into public areas such as lounges. Some pubs impose an evening time limit – let us know if you find this.

Berkshire

Some changes to note here include the upgraded bedrooms now in use at the charmingly placed old Bull in Sonning, new licensees bringing a newly pro-family policy to the nice old Bell at Waltham St Lawrence, a new landlord at the fine old Bel & the Dragon in Cookham and (with a different style of food and atmosphere) at the Horns at Crazies Hill, and a new microbrewery behind that delightfully unpretentious country pub, the Pot Kiln at Frilsham. No news is good news from our favourite Berkshire pub, the gloriously unchanging Bell up on the downs at Aldworth – unspoilt as ever, and such good value. The very child-friendly Harrow at West Ilsley gains a Food Award, after a year in which readers have been particularly enthusiastic about its very home-made country food: it's our choice as Berkshire Dining Pub of the Year. Other places we'd pick out for a good meal include the civilised Thatched Tavern at Cheapside, the Water Rat at Marsh Benham, and an interesting new entry, the Crown at Burchetts Green; the Italian-influenced White Hart at Hamstead Marshall can be very good, too. The Crown & Horns at East Ilsley, a traditional all-rounder, is doing well at the moment. Pubs in the Lucky Dip section at the end of the chapter which are currently looking good include the Old Manor in Bracknell, Crown at Bray, Pineapple at Brimpton, Pheasant at Great Shefford, Green Man at Hurst, Bird in Hand at Knowl Hill, Little Angel at Remenham, Old Boot at Stanford Dingley, Winterbourne Arms at Winterbourne, Duke of Edinburgh at Woodside and Rowbarge at Woolhampton; as we have inspected almost all of these we can vouch firmly for their appeal. Good news is that the Swan at Inkpen, which was to have been closed as a private house, has been reprieved and reopened as a pub (too late for us to try); it's a nice old place which should be well worth knowing. More sadly, we have to report the death of Michael Morris who for so long ran the Dew Drop tucked away above Hurley; until its future is more certain, we have placed it in the Dip section too. We have the impression that Reading has never had so many decent pubs as now, with a better variety than in previous years; a good selection in the Lucky Dip is headed by the Sweeney & Todd. Drinks cost significantly more than the national average in this county, but we found real savings to be made this year in free houses getting their beer from local or regional breweries (particularly the Bell at Aldworth); and in the Pot Kiln at Frilsham, supplied by its own new microbrewery.

ALDWORTH SU5579 Map 2

Bell ★ £ ♀ ▨

A329 Reading—Wallingford; left on to B4009 at Streatley

A good mix of customers are attracted to this characterful 14th-c country local (run by the same family for over 200 years) by its marvellously unspoilt atmosphere and the warm welcome you get from the friendly licensees. The cosy bar has beams in the shiny ochre ceiling, benches around its panelled walls, a woodburning stove, an ancient one-handed clock, and a glass-panelled hatch rather than a bar counter for service. Incredibly good value food is confined to hot crusty rolls (apart from winter home-made soup), filled with cheddar (90p), ham, brie, stilton or pâté (£1), smoked salmon, salt beef or ox tongue (£1.50), and particularly good Devon crab in season (£1.90); salad basket and garlic dressing (£1.50). Very well kept and very cheap Arkells BBB and Kingsdown, Morrells Bitter and Mild, and from the local West Berkshire Brewery, Old Tyler on handpump (they won't stock draught lager); particularly good house wines. Darts, shove-ha'penny, dominoes, cribbage, chess, and Aunt Sally. The quiet, old-fashioned garden is lovely in summer, and the pub is handy for the Ridgeway, so popular with walkers on Sundays. Occasional Morris dancing; Christmas mummers. *(Recommended by PHS, TBB, Sandra Kench, Steven Norman, Prof J R Leigh, Andy Jones, Bob and Maggie Atherton, Paul Chaundy, Mark Brock, Jack and Philip Paxton, John and Pam Smith, A T Langton, C A Hall, Mayur Shah, Mr and Mrs J Brown, Mark Hydes, Liz, Wendy and Ian Phillips, Wayne Brindle, Tom McLean, Roger Huggins, Ewan McCall, Stephen, Julie and Hayley Brown, Iain McBride)*

Free house ~ Licensee H E Macaulay ~ Real ale ~ Snacks (11-2.50, 6-10.45; not Mon) ~ (01635) 578272 ~ Well behaved children in tap room ~ Open 11-3, 6-11; closed Mon (open bank hols), 25 Dec

BURCHETTS GREEN SU8381 Map 2

Crown

Side road between A4 and A404, W of Maidenhead

This small country pub has in the last couple of years turned into an interesting eating-out place. There is still a very small plain bar with two or three tables for casual customers, and well kept Charles Wells Bombardier and Morlands Original, but the civilised main bar is emphatically for diners. It's clean, warm and comfortable, with unobtrusive piped music; though booking is recommended and the layout is restaurary, the licensees have succeeded in preserving the informal and very welcoming atmosphere that a good pub should have. The food is a decided cut above normal pub cooking, and dishes that either we or our readers have particularly enjoyed include lunchtime things such as cream of celery with stilton soup (£2.25), a melt-in-the-mouth chicken liver parfait (£3.65), daily specials like chicken napolitaine, wild mushroom risotto or cumberland sausage, mashed potato and onion gravy (£4.25), scrambled egg with smoked salmon and chives (£4.95), two fresh fish dishes (£8), and puddings such as chocolate torte or summer pudding (£3.25); evening meals work up to things like grilled mediterranean vegetables with goat's cheese (£6.95), chicken marinated with fresh herbs and lemon (£8.65), calf's liver with bubble and squeak (£9.25) or rack of lamb (£10.25). Presentation is careful and appetising, with interesting garnishes such as warm potato and onion salad, celeriac dauphinoise, home-made apple and grape chutney; contrary to expectations of this style of cooking, helpings are generous. Service is by friendly attentive waitresses, and there are eight decent wines and champagne by the glass; piped music. There are tables out in a pleasant quiet garden – and plans for an extension to relieve pressure on space. *(Recommended by MA, Mr and Mrs T A Bryan, TBB, Lady Palmer, Ron and Val Broom. P A Baxter)*

Morlands ~ Tenants Ian Price and Alex Turner ~ Real ale ~ Meals and snacks (till 10pm) ~ Restaurant ~ (01628) 822844 ~ Children in restaurant ~ Open 12-2.30, 6-11

CHADDLEWORTH SU4177 Map 2

Ibex

Off A338 Hungerford—Wantage and take second left after reaching summit of downs; village is signposted also, off B4494

In a racing country village (thatched cottages, narrow lanes and signs saying 'Caution – Mares and Foals'), this brick and flint pub is run by licensees who breed thoroughbreds and own and have owned successful racehorses. There's a good country atmosphere in the thoroughly traditional carpeted lounge as well as a big log fire, paintings done by Mr Froome, and properly old-fashioned bench seating and refectory-style tables. The public bar has low settles, and darts, cribbage, dominoes, fruit machine, and piped music. Tables are set for evening meals in the sun lounge (and snug little dining room), and good home-made bar food includes sandwiches, moules (£4.15), ibex pie (£4.25), home-made steak and kidney pie or hotpot (£5.75), lamb in orange and Dubonnet (£8.95), and puddings like peanut butter cheesecake, treacle tart or winter spotted dick (£3). Well kept Bass, Morlands Old Speckled Hen, Theakstons XB, and Charles Wells Bombardier on handpump. Out on a sheltered lawn and on the floodlit terrace are some tables. *(Recommended by PHS, A Jones, HNJ, PEJ, Julie Peters, T R and B C Jenkins; more reports please)*

Morlands ~ Lease: Sylvia and John Froome ~ Real ale ~ Meals and snacks (not winter Sun evenings) ~ Restaurant ~ (01488) 638311 ~ Children welcome ~ Open 11(10.30 Sat)-11; closed winter Tues evening

CHEAPSIDE SU9469 Map 2

Thatched Tavern

Cheapside Road; off B383, which is itself off A332 and A329

Just south of Ascot Gate to Windsor Great Park, this quietly civilised pub (not actually thatched) has polished flagstones, very low gnarled and nibbled beams, small windows with cheerful cottagey curtains, and an old cast-iron range in a big inglenook with built-in wall benches snugly around it. Food is a main attraction (bar food is served lunchtime only), with pretty red gingham tablecloths brightening up the longish carpeted back dining area, and a vast blackboard choice covering such dishes as sandwiches (from £1.50), home-made soup (£3.50), vegetarian dishes (from £5), home- made steak and kidney pudding or slow-roasted half shoulder of lamb (£10), fish that's delivered daily like grilled cod or wild Tay salmon (from around £10.50), and lots of puddings such as fruit crumbles and bread and butter pudding (£3.75); get here early on Saturday evening. Well kept Greene King IPA, Abbot and Sorcerer on handpump, polite, friendly staff, spotless housekeeping, and no games or piped music. Rustic seats and tables are grouped on the sheltered back lawn, around a big old apple tree. Handy for walks around Virginia Water, with the Blacknest car park a mile or so down the road. *(Recommended by Simon Collett-Jones, Julian Bower, Chris Westmoreland, Susan and John Douglas, Mayur Shah, Mrs C Blake)*

Greene King ~ Licensees Robert King, Johnathan Michael Mee ~ Real ale ~ Bar meals and snacks lunchtime only ~ Restaurant ~ (01344) 20874 ~ Well behaved children welcome away from bar ~ Open 11.30-3, 6-11

CHIEVELEY SU4774 Map 2

Blue Boar

2 miles from M4 junction 13: A34 N towards Oxford, 200 yds left for Chieveley, then left at Wheatsheaf pub and straight on until T-junction with B4494; turn right to Wantage and pub is 500 yds on right; heading S on A34, don't take first sign to Chieveley

Handy for the M4, this thatched inn has a beamed bar with three rambling rooms furnished with high-backed settles, windsor chairs and polished tables, and decked out with a variety of heavy harness (including a massive collar); the left-hand room has a log fire and a seat built into the sunny bow window. A lot of space is given over to eating the bar food, which includes soup (£1.80), sandwiches (from £1.95), ploughman's (£3.95), speciality sausages (£4.95), half char-grilled chicken (£6.50), pies like beef in Guinness (£6.95), and puddings; there's a wider range in the civilised oak-panelled restaurant. Well kept Boddingtons, Fullers London Pride, and Wadworths 6X on handpump; several malt whiskies; soft piped music. There are tables among tubs and flowerbeds on the rough front cobbles outside. Oliver Cromwell stayed here in 1644 on the eve of the Battle of Newbury. *(Recommended by Tom McLean, Pauline*

Langley, Julie Peters, Colin Blinkhorn, Nigel Norman, Peter and Joy Heatherley, Gary Roberts, Ann Stubbs, Mayur Shah, Dave Braisted, B J Harding, Margaret Dyke)

Free house ~ Licensee Peter Ebsworth ~ Real ale ~ Meals and snacks ~ Restaurant (closed Sun) ~ (01635) 248236 ~ Children in eating area of bar ~ Open 11-3, 6-11 ~ Bedrooms: £47B/£57B

COOKHAM SU8884 Map 2

Bel & the Dragon

High Street; B4447 N of Maidenhead

Claiming to be one of the oldest licensed houses in England, this civilised and rather smart old place has three peaceful rooms with old oak settles, deep leather chairs, pewter tankards hanging from heavy Tudor beams, and open fires; one room is no smoking. From the low zinc-topped bar counter well kept Brakspears PA is tapped from the cask, there's a good choice of wines, decent ports and champagne, and freshly squeezed orange juice; prompt, professional service. Good bar food includes soup (£2.75), sandwiches (from £2.75), home-made quiche (£3.50), home-made cannelloni (£5), omelettes (from £5.25), home-made steak and kidney pie (£6.50), and home-made puddings (£2.50); the home-made crisps are popular. In summer and good weather, snacks may be served in the garden or on the back terrace. The inn has no car park and street parking can be very difficult. The Stanley Spencer Gallery is almost opposite. *(Recommended by John and Patricia White, James Nunns, Gordon, Simon Collett-Jones, Mayur Shah, Nigel Norman, Piotr Chodzko-Zajko, Nigel Wilkinson, Susan and John Douglas)*

Free house ~ Licensee Malcolm Tall ~ Real ale ~ Meals and snacks (served throughout opening hours) ~ Restaurant (closed Sun evenings) ~ (01628) 521263 ~ Children welcome ~ Open 11-2.30, 6-11

COOKHAM DEAN SU8785 Map 2

Jolly Farmer

Off A308 N of Maidenhead, or from A4094 in Cookham take B4447 and go past Cookham Rise stn, turn left into Mill Lane past a memorial; pub is on right in Church Rd

Some picnic tables out among tubs of flowers in front of this 18th-c pub look across the quiet lane to a little village green and the flint-faced church; there's also a terrace and a big play area on the very long side lawn with swings, slides and a wendy house. Inside, the traditional small rooms have a happy, busy atmosphere and open fires, and the middle one is the main bar serving well kept Courage Best and two guest beers such as Morlands Old Speckled Hen, Ruddles County, Wadworths 6X or Youngs Special on handpump from a tiny counter. At one end is the attractive dining room with its starched pink and white tablecloths, and bar food includes home-made soup (£2.15), warm goat's cheese and tomato salad (£4.50), filled french bread (£2.95), steak and onion £4.95), home-cooked gammon and two eggs (£4.50), home-made steak and kidney or chicken, leek and mushroom pies (£5.95), Dutch calf's liver (£8.95), poached salmon in a dill sauce (£8.95), and lots of puddings. It's quietest on weekday lunchtimes; dominoes, cribbage, and shove-ha'penny. *(Recommended by Chris and Martin Taylor, Heather Martin, Sandra Kench, Steven Norman, Martin and Karen Wake, Nigel Norman, Simon Collett-Jones, Mark Hydes, TBB)*

Free house ~ Licensees Simon and Tracey Peach ~ Real ale ~ Meals and snacks (not Sun or Mon evenings) ~ Restaurant (not Sun evening) ~ (01628) 482905 ~ Well behaved children welcome away from bar ~ Open 11.30-3, 5.30(6 Sat)-11

COOKHAM DEAN COMMON SU8785 Map 2

Uncle Toms Cabin

Hills Lane, Harding Green; village signposted off A308 Maidenhead—Marlow – keep on down past Post Office and village hall towards Cookham Rise and Cookham

The tiled cat's slide roof at the back of this pretty cream-washed cottage is so long that the ceilings in that part slope. There's a chattily informal atmosphere in the friendly series of 1930s-feeling, mainly carpeted little rooms with low beams and joists in the front ones, lots of shiny dark brown woodwork, and old-fashioned plush-cushioned wall seats, stools and so forth; quite a lot of breweryana, and some interesting golden discs. Food (with prices, they tell us, unchanged since last year) includes french bread or granary rolls with a wide choice of good fillings (from £2.55), filled baked potatoes (from £3.15), ploughman's, and home-made hot dishes from soup (£2.50) through pizzas (£4.55), pasta with bacon and mushrooms (£5.25) and steak and Guinness pie (£5.75) to 8oz rump steak (£8.75), with a special such as home-made curries and stir-frys. Well kept Benskins Best and a weekly changing guest such as Adnams Broadside, Fullers London Pride or Shepherd Neame Spitfire on handpump, Addlestones cider, sensibly placed darts, cribbage. Piped music, if on, is well chosen and well reproduced. The two cats Jess (black and white) and Fluffy (black) enjoy the winter coal fire and Oggie the busy black and white dog welcomes other dogs (who get a dog biscuit on arrival). There are picnic tables and a climbing frame in an attractive and sheltered back garden. *(Recommended by Nigel Norman, George Atkinson, GWB, Dr G W Barnett, Mark Hydes)*

Carlsberg Tetleys ~ Tenants Nick and Karen Ashman ~ Real ale ~ Meals and snacks (12-2, 7.30-10; half-hour later Sat/Sun lunchtime; not Sun evening) ~ (01628) 483339 ~ Well behaved children in eating area of bar ~ Open 11-3, 5.30-11

CRAZIES HILL SU7980 Map 2

Horns

From A4, take Warren Row Road at Cockpole Green signpost just E of Knowl Hill, then past Warren Row follow Crazies Hill signposts; from Wargrave, take A321 towards Henley, then follow Crazies Hill signposts – right at Shell garage, then left

A new licensee has taken over this little tiled whitewashed cottage and has made a few changes. There's still no juke box or fruit machine and the bars now have rugby mementoes on the walls as well as exposed beams, open fires and stripped wooden tables and chairs; the barn room has been opened up to the roof like a medieval hall. Good bar food includes home-made soup (£2.95), lunchtime filled french bread, potted shrimps (£3.95), cumberland sausage or pancakes filled with bacon, mushrooms and stilton (£5.95), scampi provençale (£7.95), wild boar steak with calvados and apple sauce (£8.75), puddings and cheeses (£2.95), and daily specials. Well kept Brakspears PA, Mild, SB, Old and OBJ on handpump, a thoughtful wine list, and several malt whiskies. Attractive three-acre garden. *(Recommended by Dr G W Barnett, TBB, Chris Westmoreland, Derek and Sylvia Stephenson, Ted and Jane Brown, Jane and Howard Appleton; more reports on the new regime, please)*

Brakspears ~ Tenant A J Hearn ~ Real ale ~ Meals and snacks (not Sun evening) ~ Restaurant (Fri and Sat evenings, bookings only) ~ (01734) 401416 ~ Children in converted barn attached to pub ~ Jazz/blues Mon evenings ~ Open 11-2.30, 5.30-11; closed 25 and 26 Dec

EAST ILSLEY SU4981 Map 2

Crown & Horns 🚪 🍺

Just off A34, about 5 miles N of M4 junction 13

What readers like about this bustling old pub is its honest mixture of drinking and eating – and the unchanging friendly atmosphere. The walls of the four interesting beamed rooms are hung with racing prints and photographs, emphasising the fact that this is very much horse-training country; and the side bar may have locals watching the latest races on TV. The wide range of regularly changing real ales, all reasonably priced, typically includes Fullers London Pride, Mansfield Old Baily, Morlands Original and Old Speckled Hen, Theakstons Old Peculier and XB, and Wadworths 6X on handpump. There is also an impressive collection of 160 whiskies from all over the world – Morocco, Korea, Japan, China, Spain and New Zealand. Good, interesting bar food includes sandwiches (from £1.75), home-made soup (£2.75), filled baked potatoes (from £3.25), ploughman's (from £4.25), vegetable lasagne or curry (£4.75), pies such as steak and mushroom, game or fish (from £4.75), chicken breast with stilton and mushroom sauce or duck in a port and black cherry sauce (£7.25), steaks (from £7.95), oriental daily specials, and puddings (£3.25); quick, cheerful staff – even when busy. Skittle alley, darts, pool, bar billiards, pinball, dominoes, cribbage, fruit machine, juke box and piped music. The pretty paved stable yard has tables under two chestnut trees. *(Recommended by Tom McLean, G Kernan, Nick and Meriel Cox, Martin and Karen Wake, BJP Edwards, Nigel Norman, Percy and Cathy Paine, J McMillan, Gordon, Wayne Brindle)*

Free house ~ Licensees Chris and Jane Bexx ~ Real ale ~ Meals and snacks (till 10pm) ~ (01635) 281205 ~ Children in eating area, restaurant and TV room ~ Open 11-11; closed evening 25 Dec ~ Bedrooms: £32.50B/£45B

FRILSHAM SU5473 Map 2

Pot Kiln 🍺

From Yattendon take turning S, opposite church, follow first Frilsham signpost, but just after crossing motorway go straight on towards Bucklebury ignoring Frilsham signposted right; pub on right after about half a mile

A microbrewery has been set up behind this unpretentious country pub and the Brick Kiln Bitter is served from a hatch in the panelled entrance lobby – which has room for just one bar stool – along with well kept Arkells BBB, and Morlands Original and Old Speckled Hen on handpump. The timeless bar is not unsmart, with wooden floorboards and bare benches and pews, and there's a good winter log fire, too. Enjoyable, fairly simple food includes good filled hot rolls, home-made soup (£2.20), a decent ploughman's (£3.25), vegetarian dishes such as good pâté and nice lentil bake (from £3.55), excellent salmon and broccoli fishcake (£5.25), sirloin steak (£8.50), and daily specials like steak in ale pie (£5.65) or venison steaks in red wine (£7.45); no chips, and vegetables are fresh. Rolls only on Sundays. The public bar has darts, dominoes, shove-ha'penny and cribbage. The back room/dining room is no smoking. There are picnic tables in the big suntrap garden with good views of the woods and countryside. It's a good dog-walking area and they are allowed in public bar on a lead. *(Recommended by Thomas Neate, PHS, Gordon, TBB, Jamie Pratt, Andy Jones, Bob and Maggie Atherton, Mark and Diane Grist, Mark Brock, Jed and Virginia Brown, Tom McLean, Roger Huggins, Ewan McCall, Iain McBride, Samantha Hawkins, Lesley McEwen, Tracey Anderson)*

Free house ~ Licensee Philip Gent ~ Real ale ~ Meals and snacks (until 9.45pm; limited food Sun and Tues) ~ (01635) 201366 ~ Well behaved children in dining room ~ Irish music most Sun evenings ~ Open 12-2.30, 6.30-11; closed Tues lunchtime

GREAT SHEFFORD SU3875 Map 2

Swan

2 miles from M4 junction 14; on A338 towards Wantage

In summer, this neatly kept and friendly village pub has tables on the terrace by a big willow and sycamore overhanging the River Lambourn, with more seats on the lawn; the restaurant shares the same view. The low-ceilinged rooms of the spacious bow-windowed lounge bar are attractively and comfortably furnished and have old photographs of the village and horse and jockey pictures on the walls; the public side has darts, cribbage, dominoes, pool, a fruit machine, and CD juke box. Good food includes home-made soup (£2.25), king prawns in garlic butter (£4.95), pasta dishes (from £5.95), chicken balti (£6.95), Scotch steaks (from £8.75), and puddings. Well kept Butts Ale (from a microbrewery in the village and not always available), Courage Best, and Wadworths 6X on handpump; attentive service. *(Recommended by Mrs S Wright, Mark Percy, Lesley Mayoh, Peter and Audrey Dowsett, Mark Brock, R W Saunders, HNJ, PEJ, J S M Sheldon)*

Courage ~ Managers Kevin Maul, Sue Jacobs ~ Real ale ~ Meals and snacks ~ Children in eating area of bar ~ Restaurant ~ (01488) 648271 ~ Open 11-2.30, 6-11; all day summer Sats

HAMSTEAD MARSHALL SU4165 Map 2

White Hart 🍺

Village signposted from A4 W of Newbury

It's the good mainly Italian food – at a price – that readers come to this pleasant country inn to enjoy. The cooking is based on meals rather than snacks and includes filling home-made soups with home-made Italian bread (£3.20), pork liver and brandy pâté (£4.50), goat's cheese grilled with garlic and yoghurt (£5.50), various pasta dishes such as quadroni (mushroom and herb-stuffed ravioli with wild mushroom and cream sauce £7.50), fettucine with mussels, saffron and cream (£8.50), fritelli (beef meatballs stuffed with mozzarella, braised in wine sauce or cod fillet with creamy spinach sauce (£9.50), half crispy roast duckling with sweet and sour sauce (£12.50), and puddings (£4.50); the food boards are attractively illustrated with Mrs Aromando's drawings. Badger Best and Wadworths 6X on handpump and decent Italian wines. The L-shaped bar has red plush seats built into the bow windows, cushioned chairs around oak and other tables, a copper-topped bar counter, and a log fire open on both sides. No dogs (their own welsh setter's called Sam, and the pony's called Solo). The interesting walled garden is lovely in summer, and the quiet and comfortable beamed bedrooms are in a converted barn across the courtyard. *(Recommended by Stephen Barney, Verity Kemp, Richard Mills, June and Tony Baldwin, Linda and Brian Davis, Lynn Sharpless, Bob Eardley, Gordon)*

Free house ~ Licensee Mr Nicola Aromando ~ Real ale ~ Meals and snacks (not Sun) ~ Partly no-smoking restaurant (not Sun) ~ (01488) 658201 ~ Children in eating area of bar ~ Open 12-2.30, 6-11; closed Sun ~ Bedrooms: £45B/£70B

HARE HATCH SU8077 Map 2

Queen Victoria

Blakes Lane, The Holt; just N of A4 Reading—Maidenhead, 3 miles W of exit roundabout from A423(M) - keep your eyes skinned for the turning

Once again, readers are happy to report that the atmosphere in this friendly local remains unchanged and is still jaunty and chatty. The two low-beamed rooms have flowers on the tables, decorations such as a stuffed sparrowhawk and a delft shelf lined with beaujolais bottles, and are furnished with strong spindleback chairs, wall benches and window seats; the tables on the right are no smoking. Popular bar food might include sandwiches, mussels in wine and garlic (£3.90), potato shells with creamed stilton and bacon (£4.35), lamb, orange and ginger casserole (£4.50), diced lemon chicken (£4.70), pork escalope in a grain mustard sauce (£7.95), and vegetarian dishes; vegetables are fresh. Well kept Brakspears PA, SB, and Old, and Theakstons XB on handpump; cribbage, fruit machine, video game, and piped music. There's a flower-filled covered terrace with tables and chairs, and a robust table or two in front by the car park. *(Recommended by P J Caunt, Dr G W Barnett, James Nunns, TBB, Mary Bowen Rees, Mark and Diane Grist, Gordon, Ian Phillips)*

Brakspears ~ Tenant Ronald Rossington ~ Real ale ~ Meals and snacks (11.30-2.45, 6.30-10.45) ~ (01734) 402477 ~ Children welcome ~ Open 11-3, 5.30-11

HOLYPORT SU8977 Map 2

Belgian Arms

1½ miles from M4 junction 8/9; take A308(M) then at terminal roundabout follow Holyport signpost along A330 towards Bracknell; in village turn left on to big green, then left again at war memorial shelter

It's hard to believe when sitting in the charming garden looking over the pond towards the village green, that this very popular homely pub is so close to the M4; there's also a pen with a goat and hens. Inside, the L-shaped, low-ceilinged bar has framed postcards of Belgian military uniform and other good military prints on the walls, a china cupboard in one corner, a variety of chairs around a few small tables, and a winter log fire. Bar food includes sandwiches (from £1.60; the toasted 'special' is very well liked: ham, cheese, sweetcorn, peppers, onion and mushroom £1.95), pizzas with different toppings (from £3.95), home-cooked ham and eggs (£5.50), a range of daily specials such as good steak and kidney pie (£4.95), chicken tikka masala or cajun chicken (£6.95), steaks (from £9.95), puddings (from £2.95), and good Sunday lunch; you can also eat in the conservatory area. Well kept Brakspears PA, SB and in winter Old on handpump, and one or two good malts; friendly service. *(Recommended by Jim Reid, TBB, Dr G W Barnett, Ian Phillips, Graham Tayar, Mrs S Wright, Susan and John Douglas, Gary Roberts, Ann Stubbs)*

Brakspears ~ Tenant Alfred Morgan ~ Real ale ~ Meals and snacks (not Sun evening) ~ (01628) 34468 ~ Children in dining conservatory ~ Open 11-3, 5.30 (6 Sat)-11; closed evening 26 Dec

MARSH BENHAM SU4267 Map 2

Water Rat

Village signposted from A4 W of Newbury

The emphasis in this old thatched pub is now firmly placed on the popular food – and the atmosphere very much reflects that. The comfortable bar (set out for eating) has deeply carved Victorian gothick settles (and some older ones), and is attractively decorated with cheerful murals of the *Wind in the Willows* characters. Mainly meals rather than snacks, the bar food might include lentil, bacon and herb soup (£3.25), fresh tagliatelle with spinach, red peppers, baked tomatoes and pine kernels (£4.25), wild rabbit with olives, saffron, basil and tomatoes (£7.75), pot-baked shoulder of lamb with haricot beans, tomato, garlic and rosemary (£8.50), daily specials such as honey roast ham, orange and endive salad (£5.25), garlic sausages with mashed potato and onion gravy (£6.50), steaked skate wing with nut brown lemon and caper butter (£9.75), and puddings such as prune and armagnac tart with an orange sauce (£3.50) or bitter chocolate and bourbon truffle cake with a chocolate sauce (£5); the restaurant is no smoking. Well kept Brakspears PA and Wadworths 6X on handpump, a big wine list, lots of malt whiskies, and quite a few brandies and ports. There are seats on the terrace or on the long lawns that slope down to water meadows and the River Kennet; there's a butterfly reserve, goldfish, and a play area with a climbing frame, sandpit and wooden playhouse for children. *(Recommended by June Bray, Mr and Mrs R A Bryan, Julie and Mike Taylor, AEB, Iain McBride, Samantha Hawkins, Gordon, Ian Phillips, J E Ellis, Roger Byrne, Betty Laker)*

Free house ~ Licensee Ian Dodd ~ Real ale ~ Meals and snacks (12-2.30, 6-10) ~ Restaurant ~ (01635) 42879/582017 ~ Children in eating area and in restaurant ~ Open 11-3, 6-11; closed 25-26 Dec

PEASEMORE SU4577 Map 2

Fox & Hounds ♀

Village signposted from B4494 Newbury—Wantage

From the picnic tables outside this relaxed downland pub there are pleasant views of rolling fields – and on a clear day you can look right across to the high hills which form the Berkshire/Hampshire border about 20 miles southward. It's deep in horse-training country, and this is reflected inside by a full set of Somerville's entertaining Slipper's ABC of Fox-Hunting prints. On another stripped-brick wall there's a row of flat-capped fox masks. The two bars have brocaded stripped wall settles, chairs and stools around shiny wooden tables, a log-effect gas fire (open to both rooms), and piped music. Good bar food includes sandwiches, home-made soup (£1.50), home-made pies, vegetarian dishes like chilli butterbean bake (£4.95), chicken balti (£5.95), steaks (from £7.95), home-made pudings such as baked jam roll or fruit crumble, and daily specials. Well kept Greene King IPA and Abbot, and Marstons Pedigree on handpump, a good few malt whiskies, and a wide range of reasonably priced good wines. Sensibly placed darts, pool, dominoes, cribbage, fruit machine, discreet juke box, and piped music. *(Recommended by HNJ, PEJ, Jeff Davies, Mr and Mrs Colquhoun; more reports please)*

Free house ~ Licensees David and Loretta Smith ~ Real ale ~ Meals and snacks (not Mon) ~ Restaurant ~ (01635) 248252 ~ Children welcome ~ Irish bands monthly ~ Open 11.30-3, 6.30-11; closed Mon

SONNING SU7575 Map 2

Bull

Village signposted on A4 E of Reading; off B478, in village

In a pretty setting, this very attractive inn has two old-fashioned rooms with low ceilings and heavy beams, cosy alcoves, cushioned antique settles and low wooden chairs, and inglenook fireplaces; the back dining area is no smoking. Well kept Gales Best, HSB and BBB and a guest beer on handpump, lots of country wines, and bar food such as filled french sticks, chilli con carne (£6.75), lasagne (£6.95), vegetarian dishes (from £6.95), steak and kidney pudding (£7.25), beef and venison pie (£7.75), seafood thermidor (£8.95), and steak Dorchester (£11.75); darts, shove-ha'penny, fruit machine, trivia, and piped music. The courtyard is particularly attractive in summer with tubs of flowers and a rose pergola resting under its wisteria-covered, black and white timbered walls – though at busy times it may be packed with cars. If you bear left through the ivy-clad churchyard opposite, then turn left along the bank of the river Thames, you come to a very pretty lock. *(Recommended by Gordon, Christine and Geoff Butler, D and D Savidge, Sandra Kench, Steven Norman, Mr and Mrs J R Morris)*

Gales ~ Lease: Mr and Mrs D Mason ~ Real ale ~ Lunchtime meals and snacks ~ (01734) 693901 ~ Children in eating area of bar ~ Open 11-3, 5.30(6 Sat)-11 ~ Bedrooms: £40(£45)/£50(£55)

STANFORD DINGLEY SU5771 Map 2

Bull

From M4 junction 12, W on A4, then right at roundabout on to A340 towards Pangbourne; first left to Bradfield, where left, then Stanford Dingley signposted on right

Under the dark beams in the middle of the tap room in this red brick 15th-c pub are two standing timbers hung with horsebrasses, firmly dividing the room into two parts. The main part is comfortably arranged with red-cushioned seats carved out of barrels, a window settle, wheelback chairs on the red quarry tiles, an old brick fireplace, and an old station clock; the other is similarly furnished but carpeted. There's also a half-panelled lounge bar with refectory-type tables, and a smaller room leading off with quite a few musical instruments. Bar food includes filled baked potatoes (from £2.05), soups like carrot and orange or stilton (from £2.40), garlic bacon and mushrooms on toast (£2.95), ploughman's (from £3.10), cottage pie (£5.45), chicken provençale or turkey with mushroom and yoghurt sauce (£6.75), steaks (from £6.95), and daily specials. Well kept (and very cheap for the area) Archers, Bass, Brakspears, and a beer from the West Berkshire Brewery (very local) on handpump, and elderflower pressé; quick, efficient service. Ring-the-bull, occasional classical or easy listening music. In front of the building are some big rustic tables and benches, and to the side is a small garden with a few more seats. *(Recommended by TBB, PHS, Susan and John Douglas, Bruce Greenfield, Werner Arend, Mayur Shah, M G Hart)*

Free house ~ Licensees Patrick and Trudi Langdon ~ Real ale ~ Meals and snacks (till 10pm; not Mon lunchtime) ~ (01734) 744409 ~ Children in saloon bar; not after 8.30pm; not Sat evening ~ Open 12-3, 7-11; closed Mon lunchtime – except bank hols

WALTHAM ST LAWRENCE SU8276 Map 2

Bell

In village centre

New licensees had just taken over this delightful timbered black and white pub as we went to press and were in the process of refurbishing the dining room to create a family eating area, and have plans to re-open the snug bar. The lounge bar has finely carved oak panelling, a log fire, and a pleasant atmosphere, and the public bar has heavy beams, an attractive seat in the deep window recess, and well kept Adnams, Brakspears PA, Fullers London Pride, Wadworths 6X and guest beers on handpump. Home-made bar food now includes winter soup, sandwiches (from £1.80), ploughman's (from £3), filled baked potatoes (from £3.50), steak in ale, chilli con carne or vegetarian nut roast (£4), daily specials (around £4), and puddings (£2.50). In summer, the hanging baskets in front of the building are very pretty, and the well kept back lawn (sheltered by a thatched barn and shaded by small trees and flowering shrubs) is very popular with walkers. *(Recommended by Ron and Val Broom, Sidney and Erna Wells, Dick Brown, Chris Westmoreland, TBB, Mayur Shah, Nick Holmes, Mark Hydes)*

Free house ~ Licensee Mrs Denise Slater ~ Real ale ~ Meals and snacks (not Sun or Mon evenings) ~ (01734) 341788 ~ Children in eating area of bar and in dining room ~ Open 11-3, 5.30-11

WEST ILSLEY SU4782 Map 2

Harrow 🍽

Signposted at East Ilsley slip road off A34 Newbury—Abingdon

Berkshire Dining Pub of the Year

Readers have been so enthusiastic about the food in this popular white tiled village pub that we have decided to give it a food award this year. Enjoyable meals include granary rolls filled with hot sausage and home-made chutney or stilton, celery and apple (£2), filling home-made soup (£2.95), ploughman's with British farmhouse cheeses (from £5), mushroom and stilton tart with a walnut and herb crumble topping (£5.25), particularly good pies such as lamb and apricot or pork and apple pie in cider (from £5.45; their 'pie nights' are the last Tuesday and Thursday of the month), fillet of salmon with a chive sauce (£7.95), chicken supreme on a bed of oyster mushrooms with a tarragon sauce (£8.25), daily specials such as lamb's liver and bacon, trout baked with fresh herbs and lemon and served with a green yoghurt sauce or green cabbage stuffed with rice and nuts with a coconut sauce (from £5.25), and home-made puddings like treacle tart or sticky toffee pudding (£2.95); children's helpings (and menu). The dining area is no smoking. Well kept Morlands Original and Old Speckled Hen, and a guest like Flowers Original on handpump, and 10 wines by the glass. The open-plan bar has dark terracotta walls hung with many mainly Victorian prints and other ornaments, big turkey rugs on the floor, and a mix of antique oak tables, unpretentious old chairs, and a couple of more stately long settles; there's also an unusual stripped twin-seated high-backed settle between the log fire and the bow window. Darts and fruit machine. This is a lovely spot with lots of nearby walks – the Ridgeway is just a mile away – and the big garden has picnic tables and other tables under cocktail parasols looking out over the duck pond and cricket green, a notable children's play area, and ducks, fowl, and a goat; the stubborn goose still sits in the road and refuses to budge for passing traffic. *(Recommended by Mike and Maggie Betton, Mr Selinger, Mrs J Ashdown, Pauline Langley, PHS, Bruce Bird, Ron and Barbara Watkins, Anthony Barnes, Mark Brock, Nigel Norman, Mayur Shah, Guy Consterdine, J McMillan, Mrs C A Blake, Wayne Brindle)*

Morlands ~ Lease: Mrs Heather Humphreys ~ Real ale ~ Meals and snacks (not winter Sun evenings) ~ (01635) 281260 ~ Children welcome ~ Open 11-3, 6-11; closed evenings 25 and 26 Dec

YATTENDON SU5574 Map 2

Royal Oak 🛏 ♀

The Square; B4009 NE from Newbury; turn right at Hampstead Norreys, village signposted on left

Although most people come to this elegantly handsome inn for its good food, there's a relaxed atmosphere in the comfortable lounge and prettily decorated panelled bar (through at the back), a marvellous winter log fire, and a mechanical wall clock behind the bar counter. Bar food includes home-made soup (£3), mussel, saffron and fennel stew (£5), ploughman's with home-made chutney (£5.25), plaice and chips (£7.75), honey-glazed hock of ham with lentil casserole (£8.50), calf liver and bacon (£9.75), fish daily specials, rump steak (£11.50), and puddings like rhubarb and ginger brûlée (£5); vegetables (£1.50). You must book a table for bar lunches. Well kept Banks's Bitter, West Berkshire Brewery Good Old Boy (from a tiny local microbrewery), and Wychwood Dogs Bollocks on handpump, and a good wine list. The pleasant garden is primarily for the use of residents and restaurant guests, but is available on busy days for those in the bar. The attractive village is one of the few still owned privately, and the pub itself used to be the site of the Yattendon Revels. The bedrooms have been refurbished this year. *(Recommended by TBB, PHS, Christine and Geoff Butler, Nigel Norman, Percy and Cathy Paine, Bob and Maggie Atherton, G C Hackemer, Mayur Shah; more reports please)*

Free house ~ Manager Barry Harpham ~ Real ale ~ Meals and snacks (till 10pm) ~ No-smoking restaurant (not Sun evenings) ~ (01635) 201325 ~ Children welcome ~ Open 11-11; 12-11 Sun ~ Bedrooms: £89.50B/£99B

Lucky Dip

Besides the fully inspected pubs, you might like to try these Lucky Dips recommended to us and described by readers (if you do, please send us reports):

☆ **Aldermaston** [SU5965], *Hinds Head*: Traditional village inn, refurbished but homely and comfortable, with good home-cooked food inc oriental dishes (and special ones for diabetics if requested), good service, well kept ales such as Courage Best, Fullers London Pride and a guest, friendly chunky black cat; children welcome (separate dining room with high chairs); superb enclosed garden; bedrooms – a good place to stay *(Simon Collett-Jones, Gordon, J Palka)*

Aldworth [Haw Lane; B4009 towards Hampstead Norreys; SU5579], *Four Points*: Good generous plain food in thatched family pub, beams, horsebrasses, big log fire, lots of tables, good value Sun roasts, well kept Morlands; neat garden with play area over road *(Jenny and Michael Back, Mr and Mrs Richard Osborne, LYM)*

Ascot [SU9268], *Royal Foresters*: Large pleasantly decorated family dining pub, genuine friendly welcome, relaxed atmosphere, four real ales inc well kept Courage Directors *(Chris Westmoreland)*

☆ **Bagnor** [SU4569], *Blackbird*: Friendly and peaceful country pub in lovely spot nr Watermill Theatre and River Lambourn, good value straightforward food, well varnished old sewing machine tables, cheerful chatty local atmosphere, efficient friendly service, well kept ales such as Fullers London Pride, Marstons Pedigree, Ushers and Websters Yorkshire, sometimes quiet piped music; tables in pleasant side garden *(HNJ, PEJ, TBB)*

Beech Hill [Beech Hill Rd; SU6964], *Old Elm Tree*: Good views from friendly family-run pub with pleasant bar and adjoining restaurant, attentive service, good value food, well kept Brakspears *(D Betts, Dr M I Crichton)*

☆ **Binfield** [B3034 Windsor rd; SU8571], *Stag & Hounds*: Comfortable 14th-c pub with low-beamed bars, open fires, antiques, brass, wide changing choice of good value food from sandwiches up in separate room, consistently affable landlord, daily papers *(Margaret Dyke, Gordon)*

☆ **Binfield** [Terrace Rd North], *Victoria Arms*: Neat no-frills Fullers pub with good choice of seating areas, well kept real ales inc Chiswick, good reasonably priced bar food, children's room, summer barbecues in quiet garden *(G V Price, LYM)*

Binfield [Forest Rd; B4034 Wokingham—Bracknell], *Warren*: Friendly and homely, log fire and beams, good food inc children's, well kept ales; adjoining Tex/Mex restaurant (Tues-Sat), play area in big garden; open all day *(Emma Peek, Nigel Brant)*

Bisham [SU8485], *Bull*: Spacious, with pleasant attentive service, well kept beer, food inc good value Sun roasts *(Basil Minson)*

☆ **Bracknell** [Grenville Pl, High St; SU8769], *Old Manor*: Big open-plan Wetherspoons pub, one of their few that welcome children, with usual good value food, sensibly priced real ales, big no smoking area, good solid decor inc original oak beams, twice-yearly beer festival with up to 30 different beers, three pleasant outside areas; very useful for the M4/M25 short cut via M3 *(Dr Michael Smith, Jane Armstrong, Chris Westmoreland)*

☆ Bray [SU9079], *Crown*: 14th-c pub doing well under latest licensees, lots of low beams, timbers and panelling, leather seats, Courage Best and Wadworths 6X, good well presented food in bar and restaurant, friendly prompt service, log fires; well behaved children allowed, plenty of seating outside inc flagstoned vine arbour *(TBB, Simon Collett-Jones, Susan and John Douglas, Richard Houghton, A C Morrison, Nigel Norman, Mr and Mrs P Smith, LYM)*

☆ Bray [Old Mill Lane], *Fish*: Civilised Georgian pub, formerly the Albion, reopened summer 1996 under new landlady with good GPG track record, emphasis on fresh fish; should be well worth knowing *(Reports please)*
Bray, *Hinds Head*: After long row with villagers who complained about outside drinking (and had pull with local licensing authorities), this 16th-c inn of charm and character has been taken over by new owners who have undertaken to end outdoor drinking and concentrate on food and families *(LYM; reports please)*

☆ Brimpton [Brimpton Common; B3051, W of Heath End; SU5564], *Pineapple*: Friendly thatched and low-beamed country pub with stripped brick and timbering, tiled floor, heavy elm furnishings, open fire, snug and cosy atmosphere; friendly and obliging service, seven well kept Whitbreads-related ales, usual food noon till 9, side games area, maybe piped pop music; lots of tables on sheltered lawn, play area; open all day; children in eating area, folk music first Sun of month *(Bill Scott, Gordon, Simon Collett-Jones, LYM)*

☆ Bucklebury [Chapel Row; SU5570], *Blade Bone*: Warm, friendly and clean, with plush seats and dark tables, tasteful pictures and plates on pastel walls, matching carpets, small dining room with no smoking conservatory overlooking neat garden, wide choice of food from sandwiches up inc good value specials cooked to order – so may be a wait; tables outside, play area *(HNJ, PEJ, F J and A Parmenter)*
Chieveley [East Lane – handy for M4 junction 13 via A34 N-bound; SU4774], *Red Lion*: Spacious old pub, notably welcoming, with roaring log fire in bar area, old world atmosphere, country prints and farm tools; dining area with good range of home-made food and fresh veg (also take-away pizzas till 11pm); Arkells ales, attentive quick service, pool, darts *(HNJ, PEJ)*

☆ Cookham Dean [OS Sheet 175 map ref 872853; SU8785], *Inn on the Green*: Inviting atmosphere, good solid furniture with attractive tables, unspoilt rambling layout, stripped beams, two-sided log fires, good genuine food inc delicious Swiss specialities, several real ales; occasional piped music may obtrude; pleasant restaurant *(Chris and Andy Crow)*

Cookham Rise [The Pound; B4447 Cookham—Maidenhead; SU8984], *Swan Uppers*: Flagstones, low beams, log fire, friendly management, good range of real ales, bar food, unobtrusive piped music; bedrooms *(TBB, LYM)*

☆ Curridge [3 miles from M4 junction 13: A34 towards Newbury, then first left to Curridge, Hermitage, and left into Curridge at Village Only sign – OS Sheet 174 map ref 492723; SU4871], *Bunk*: Stylish but welcoming dining pub with good adventurous food (not Sun evening), smart stripped-wood tiled-floor bar on left, elegant stable-theme bistro on right with wooded-meadow views and conservatory; four well kept real ales, cheerful efficient service, tables in neat garden *(D C and J V Whitman, Jim Reid, PHS, BB)*
Datchet [The Green; not far from M4 junction 5; SU9876], *Royal Stag*: Good friendly atmosphere, good value food esp home-made soups, well kept Tetleys-related ales, handsome well behaved golden retriever; bar partly panelled in claret case lids, occasional juke box *(Ian Phillips, TBB, Richard Houghton)*

☆ East Ilsley [SU4981], *Swan*: Open-plan but comfortably divided and well spaced, with interesting things to look at; wide range of bar food inc vegetarian, well kept Morlands Original and Charles Wells Bombardier, friendly efficient service, daily papers; no smoking restaurant, children allowed; good bedrooms, some in house down road *(Bruce Bird, Wayne Brindle, HNJ, PEJ, Nigel Norman, Alan Skull, LYM)*

☆ Eton Wick [32 Eton Wick Rd; SU9478], *Pickwick*: Welcoming and well kept, with good value food (inc authentic Malay Weds and Sat evenings), pleasant landlord, Youngs ales; maybe piped music *(Dr G W Barnett, TBB)*
Fifield [SU9076], *White Hart*: Pleasant village local, clean and tidy lounge and public bars, well kept Morlands Bitter and Old Speckled Hen, good garden in peaceful setting; aka Fifield Inn *(Simon Collett-Jones)*

☆ Great Shefford [Shefford Woodland; less than ½ mile N of M4 junction 14, by junction B4000/A338; SU3875], *Pheasant*: Good relaxing motorway break, welcoming helpful service in four neat rooms, very wide choice of good food inc home-made dishes and Sun lunches, well kept Brakspears and Wadworths IPA and 6X, decent wines and coffee, log fires; public bar with games inc ring the bull; children welcome, attractive views from garden *(HNJ, PEJ, Dr C E Morgan, Lynda Payton, Sam Samuells, LYM)*

☆ Hampstead Norreys [SU5276], *White Hart*: Friendly and spotless low-beamed Morlands pub with wide range of reasonably priced food inc children's, real ales, decent coffee; darts, pool and fruit machine in public bar; back terrace and garden *(Joan Olivier)*
Holyport [The Green; 1½ miles from M4 junction 8/9 via A308(M)/A330; SU8977], *George*: Generous helpings of reasonably priced real home cooking in busily pubby low-ceilinged open-plan bar with nice old fireplace, friendly efficient service, Courage real ales;

maybe piped pop music, and furnishings not ideal for all; picnic tables outside, lovely village green *(Beryl and Terry Bryan, TBB)*

Hungerford [by Hungerford Common, E edge of town; SU3368], *Down Gate*: Prettily placed and relaxing Arkells pub with friendly efficient landlord, collection of miniature bottles, old coins, blowlamps, oil cans and beer-barrel bushes; two bars overlooking common, small lower room with open fire and three small tables for diners; attractive food *(Gordon, Mark Brock)*

☆ **Hungerford Newtown** [A338 a mile S of M4 junction 14; SU3571], *Tally Ho*: Roomy, well cared for and particularly welcoming, with good well presented home-made food inc beautiful chips and puddings (popular with older people at lunchtime), small no smoking area, well kept Wadworths and decent house wines, chatty yet polite staff, subdued piped music; children if eating *(HNJ, PEJ, John and Wendy Trentham)*

Hurley [A423; SU8283], *Black Boy*: Old-fashioned cottagey pub worth knowing for attractive garden by paddock, picnic tables looking over countryside rolling down to Thames, own serving hatch, shetland ponies and rabbits to watch; welcoming landlord and locals, well kept Brakspears, open fire, affectionate cat called Sooty, tether for visiting horses *(Susan and John Douglas, TBB, BB)*; *Olde Bell*: Handsome and unusual old-fashioned timbered inn with some remarkable ancient features inc Norman doorway and window; small but comfortable bar with decent bar food, fine gardens, very civilised gents', tolerable piped music; restaurant, bedrooms *(TBB, LYM)*; [High St], *Rising Sun*: Doing well under current regime, with good food such as steak and Guinness pie, well kept Brakspears, pleasant atmosphere; restaurant *(P A Baxter)*

☆ **nr Hurley** [just W, off A423 up Honey Lane then right at T], *Dew Drop*: Unchanging country pub in very rustic setting, fine old inglenook, log fires, good simple bar food (not Sun evening or Mon), well kept Brakspears PA and Old, some good malt whiskies, darts; attractive informal sloping garden, play area; a long-standing main entry, but after the sad death of the long-serving landlord his widow was unsure of her plans as we went to press *(LYM; news please)*

☆ **Hurst** [Hinton Rd/Church Hill; SU7972], *Green Man*: Old-fashioned traditional low-ceilinged local, basic though comfortable furnishings with wooden seats and tables and cosy little areas, well kept Brakspears, bar food (not Mon evening), pub games, piped music; pleasant back garden *(Gordon, George Atkinson, Roger and Valerie Hill, LYM)*

Hurst [opp church], *Castle*: Morlands pub done up for diners, warm and clean, with popular food; piped music may obtrude *(J Kirwan-Taylor)*

☆ **Inkpen** [Lower Inkpen; SU 3564], *Swan*: Rambling and attractive beamed pub, homely and comfortable with lovely log fire, reprieved in 1996 from the fate of being sold as private

house – local villager bought it at auction and has reopened it with seven real ales and refurbished bar; new restaurant should be open by the time we publish *(Gordon, LYM)*

☆ **Kintbury** [SU3866], *Dundas Arms*: Clean and tidy with comfortably upmarket feel, bar food (not Mon evening or Sun) from sandwiches to good venison casserole and so forth, well kept real ales from smaller breweries, good wines by the glass and carafe, remarkable range of clarets and burgundies in evening restaurant; pleasant walks by Kennet & Avon Canal, children allowed; comfortable bedrooms opening on to secluded waterside terrace *(GB, LYM)*

☆ **Knowl Hill** [A4 Reading—Maidenhead; SU8279], *Bird in Hand*: Relaxed civilised atmosphere and good home-made food in spacious and attractive beamed main bar and restaurant; splendid log fire, cosy alcoves, much older side bar; well kept Brakspears and Fullers London Pride, wide choice of wines and other drinks, friendly helpful staff, good side garden; no-smoking buffet area where children allowed; clean and tidy modern bedrooms *(R P Daniel, Mike Davies, Nigel Wilkinson, LYM)*

☆ **Knowl Hill** [A4], *Seven Stars*: Simple old-fashioned relaxing place with good honest bar food from sandwiches to steaks at sensible prices, well kept Brakspears (full range), good choice of wines, a lot of panelling, roaring log fire, sleepy dog and cat (alas food may put them on the qui vive); helpful professional service, fruit machine, flowers, big garden with summer barbecue *(Gordon, Nigel Norman, TBB, Mike and Heather Barnes, BB)*

Little Sandhurst [High St; SU8262], *Bird in Hand*: Friendly nicely furnished local with good freshly cooked food (so can be slow when busy), well kept Morlands, welcoming young licensees, Sun bar nibbles *(Margaret Dyke, Maureen Hobbs)*

☆ **Littlewick Green** [3¾ miles from M4 junction 9; A423(M) then left on to A4, from which village signposted on left; SU8379], *Cricketers*: Charming spot opp cricket green, decent food, friendly service, Brakspears and Flowers real ales, neat housekeeping, lots of cricketing pictures; can be very quiet weekday lunchtimes *(Gordon, TBB, LYM)*

Maidenhead [High St; SU8783], *Bear*: Large rambling pub benefiting from pedestrianisation, with tables and flowers outside; food inc good soup and fresh bread, no piped music *(TBB)*; [Queen St], *Hand & Flowers*: Traditional old town pub, good simple food, well kept Brakspears; no piped music, can be crowded weekday lunchtimes *(TBB, Richard Houghton)*

nr Maidenhead [Lee Lane, Pinkneys Green, just off A308 N; SU8582], *Stag & Hounds*: Popular refurbished pub with carpeted dining lounge, small side bar, Gales ales, friendly service *(Chris Westmoreland)*; [Pinkneys Green], *Wagon & Horses*: Friendly Morlands pub overlooking green, quiet back saloon bar *(Chris Westmoreland)*

Newbury [Bartholomew St; SU4666], *Hobgoblin*: Good example of the current bare-boards style of pub, with well kept beer and lots of games (Dr and Mrs A K Clarke); [towpath, nr main st], Lock Stock & Barrel: Spacious wood-floored curved bar with tables out on canalside terrace, friendly helpful service, well kept Fullers ales, good bar food, coffee shop open all afternoon; can be quite busy summer lunchtimes (Tony Dickinson, D J and P M Taylor); [Market Pl], Old Waggon & Horses: Sunny flower-filled riverside terrace, big bright and friendly upstairs family dining bar above it, separate traditional front bar; very friendly staff (Jon Roberts, LYM)

☆ Old Windsor [17 Crimp Hill, off B3021 – itself off A308/A328; SU9874], Union: Tidy L-shaped bar with interesting collection of nostalgic show-business photographs, real ales such as Courage, Everards and Flowers, bar food inc good baked potatoes and steaks and some more interesting dishes, good friendly service even when very busy, woodburner in big fireplace, fruit machine; attractive copper-decorated restaurant, white plastic tables under cocktail parasols on sunny front terrace, country views; comfortable bedrooms (Ian Phillips, Dave Rickell, Mayur Shah, PLB)

☆ Old Windsor [Crimp Hill], Oxford Blue: Well kept beer inc Adnams, good food, welcoming service and atmosphere, interesting airline memorabilia, vast new conservatory extension, nice old benches built into front verandah, tables outside (Ian Phillips, Peter Catley, Mr and Mrs Cox)

Padworth [Padworth Common; SU6166], Round Oak: Warmly welcoming cosy pub, good food with specials such as duck in plum and ginger, well priced wine, Flowers and Wadworths 6X (Anon)

Paley Street [3 miles SW of Bray; SU8675], Bridge House: Small warm clean beamed pub, reasonably priced home-made food, pleasant dining room, welcoming young staff, several real ales; piped pop music, get there early on Sun or book; big garden (TBB)

Pangbourne [Shooters Hill; SU6376], Swan: Attractive riverside pub dating from 1642, good range of bar food all day 7 days a week, good wine list, tea and coffee, Morlands ales on handpump, unobtrusive piped music; picnic tables and moorings; balcony and conservatory reserved for diners (Roberto Villa)

☆ Reading [10 Castle St, next to PO; SU7272], Sweeney & Todd: Warren of small cosy rooms and cubby holes, lots of character, with four well kept real ales upstairs; access via front pie shop – exceptional value home-made pies, adventurous and generously served, such as hare and cherry, peach and pigeon; very busy lunchtime (Andy Cunningham, Paul Bispham)

☆ Reading [Kennet Side], Fishermans Cottage: Fullers pub by lock on Kennet & Avon Canal, lovely big back garden, relaxed atmosphere, modern furnishings of character, pleasant stone snug behind woodburning range, light and airy conservatory; good value pub lunches (very popular then), evening food inc Mexican, well kept ales, small choice of wines, small darts room (TBB, Mark and Diane Grist)

Reading [Forbury Rd], Corn Stores: Well

converted corn warehouse, two bars on split levels; well kept Fullers (Dr and Mrs A K Clarke); [Broad St], Hobgoblin: Real ale pub, former London Inn, interesting layout with several cubicles, well kept Wychwood ales with good range of guest beers, unusual lunchtime filled rolls; occasional live music (Paul Bispham); [Kates Grove Lane – off A4 Pell St/Berkley Ave, off to flyover inner ring rd], Hook & Tackle: Real ale pub with pastiche traditional decor, often full of young people and loud music; good choice of beers, quick service, usual food, maybe smoky; outstanding twice-yearly beer festivals (Nick and Alison Dowson, Mark and Diane Grist); [Southampton St], Hop Leaf: Friendly local refurbished with a modern look by the Hop Back brewery, nice atmosphere, full range of well kept Hop Back beers and some brewed on the premises – maybe even an interesting stout; parking close by is very difficult (John Rawlinson, Mark and Diane Grist); [Rly Stn, Platform 4], Three Guineas: Huge pub with lots of interest, well kept real ale, reasonable value food, good bustle at rush hour, American-style central bar (Mr and Mrs S G Turner, Dr and Mrs A K Clarke)

☆ Remenham [A423, just over bridge E of Henley; SU7683], Little Angel: Good atmosphere, tasty bar meals from sandwiches up, more expensive restaurant food and friendly efficient service in low-beamed dining pub with panelling and darkly bistroish decor; splendid range of wines by the glass, well kept Brakspears, floodlit terrace (TBB, Jenny Garrett, LYM)

Shurlock Row [SU8374], White Hart: Friendly staff in attractive panelled pub, warm, comfortable and relaxing, with inglenook fireplace dividing bar from other rooms; flying memorabilia inc squadron badges, old pictures and brasses, Whitbreads-related ales, decent lunchtime food (Chris and Martin Taylor)

Slough [Albert St; SU9779], Greyhound: Beautifully refurbished, with consistently well kept beer (Dr and Mrs A K Clarke); [Albert St], Wheatsheaf: Spacious but pleasantly pubby, oak beams, well kept Fullers, good value food, smallish suntrap garden (Chris and Martin Taylor)

☆ Stanford Dingley [SU5771], Old Boot: Civilised old country pub, beams, inglenook, pews and other comfortable country furnishings, pleasant views from spacious and attractive suntrap garden, friendly atmosphere, generous and popular food, well kept Fullers Chiswick, ESB and London Pride, adjacent restaurant area; impressive lavatories, no dogs (Mary and Bob O'Hara, Gordon, Dr Ian Crichton, Nigel Wilkinson, LYM)

☆ Swallowfield [S of Reading on Farley Hill lane – OS Sheet 175 map ref 735647; SU7364], George & Dragon: Old country pub attractively modernised, good reasonably priced menu inc imaginative dishes, well kept Wadworths 6X and other ales (staff bring drinks to table), good choice of wines, welcoming young staff, broad appeal; can get very busy, best to book (D D Owen-Pawson,

Nigel Norman, Martin Watson)

☆ **Theale** [Church St; SU6371], *Volunteer*: Open-plan, with flagstones in public bar, comfortable carpeted lounge with historical military prints, nice wooden furniture, well kept Fullers, generous helpings of bar food (not Sun evening), friendly welcome, quiet piped music, free Sun nibbles; children at reasonable times *(Bruce Bird)*

☆ **Upper Basildon** [Aldworth Rd; SU5976], *Red Lion*: Small Victorian pub revamped by Eldridge Pope and under new management, welcoming staff, wide choice of food (still do the good home-made pies, also giant yorkshire puddings etc), well kept ales, decent house wines; no constraints on children *(S J Edwards; more reports on new regime please)*

Warfield [Church Lane/A3095; SU8872], *Yorkshire Rose*: Spanish owners, lively bar staff, beams and open fires, plenty of atmosphere, good bar food, also elegant restaurant; vine-covered conservatory area, garden with summer barbecues *(Dr J Hern)*

White Waltham [Waltham Rd; SU8577], *Beehive*: Friendly local by cricket field, smallish front bar and larger back saloon, Whitbreads-related beers, unpretentious chippy food *(Chris Westmoreland, TAB)*

Wickham [3 miles from M4 junction 14, via A338, B4000; SU3971], *Five Bells*: Friendly and neatly kept local in racehorse-training country, big log fire, decent food inc some individual dishes, Courage-related real ales, garden with good play area; children in eating area, good value bedrooms *(Mark Brock, LYM)*

Windsor [Thames St; SU9676], *Adam & Eve*: Good lunchtime pub by theatre, lots of thespian photographs, friendly courteous staff, juke box and fruit machines; occasional barbecues in little back yard *(Michael Fertig, LYM)*; [Vansittart Rd], *Vansittart Arms*: Welcoming licensees, good reasonably priced healthy food *(Clare Edwards)*

Winkfield [A330, opp church; SU9072], *White Hart*: Neatly modernised Tudor pub popular for food, ex-bakery bar, ex-courthouse restaurant; Courage real ale, sizeable garden *(Gordon, LYM)*

☆ **Winterbourne** [not far from M4 junction 13; formerly the New Inn; SU4572], *Winterbourne Arms*: Nice old building carefully refurbished to point up its interesting features, pleasantly old-fashioned decor, tables in front garden and on green over quiet village lane; friendly local atmosphere early in week (piped pop music may obtrude), more of a dining pub towards the end, with rather restauranty food; good choice of real ales, play area, nearby walks *(Richard Robinson, HNJ, PEJ, Julie and Mike Taylor, Trudi Pinkerton, Gordon Tong, ATRF, LYM)*

☆ **Wokingham** [Gardeners Green, Honey Hill – OS Sheet 175 map ref 826668; SU8266], *Crooked Billet*: Well kept Brakspears in homely country pub with pews, tiles, brick serving counter, crooked black joists; big helpings of popular food, small no smoking restaurant area where children allowed, cosy local atmosphere; nice outside in summer, very busy weekends *(Jeannette Campbell, Mark and Diane Grist, P J Caunt, Mrs C A Blake, LYM)*
Wokingham [Peach St], *Redan*: Well kitted-out town pub with well kept Morlands beers, relaxed atmosphere, comfortable back garden; busy Sat nights *(Nick and Meriel Cox, Simon Minor)*

☆ **Woodside** [signed off A322 Windsor—Ascot; SU9270], *Duke of Edinburgh*: Surprisingly good generous food (not Sun evening) inc a very wide and unusual range of fresh fish dishes in unpretentious pub with cheery obliging service, some attractive furnishings esp in Regency-style back room, well kept Arkells 2B, 3B and Kingsdown, sensible prices; maybe loudish piped music; children welcome, some tables outside *(Robert Crail, Nick Wikeley, Beryl and Terry Bryan, BB)*

☆ **Woolhampton** [Station Rd (off A4 opp Angel); SU5767], *Rowbarge*: Big canalside family dining pub, smart carefully detailed decor featuring pheasants and blowlamps, candlelit tables, beamed bar, panelled side room, small snug, no-smoking back conservatory, tables in big garden with fish pond, well kept Courage Best, Brakspears SB, Fullers London Pride, Greene King Abbot and Wadworths 6X; rather upmarket menu, prices on high side, lots of children, service can lack personal touch *(Gordon, Dr Ian Crichton, Simon Collett-Jones, CPSM, Wilson Carlisle, Dave Braisted, Mr and Mrs J Hall, Mark and Diane Grist, Sandra Kench, Steven Norman, Nigel and Lindsay Chapman, Susan and John Douglas, LYM)*

☆ **Woolhampton** [A4], *Rising Sun*: Unpretentious pub which has had half a dozen or more well kept and interesting real ales, good welcoming service, plentiful home-made food inc huge reasonably priced sandwiches *(Tony and Wendy Hobden, Gordon, John Hazel, MG, DG; reports on new regime please)*

Post Office address codings confusingly give the impression that some pubs are in Berkshire, when they're really in Oxfordshire or Hampshire (which is where we list them).

Buckinghamshire

Quite a few changes this year here include new licensees at the Old Swan at Cheddington, the extraordinary old Royal Standard of England at Forty Green, the Hare & Hounds in Marlow, the Dog & Badger at Medmenham, and the White Hart at Northend (which has been smartened up a bit in consequence). The Pheasant at Brill has a new verandah, to make the most of its unusual views; the Hampden Arms at Great Hampden, one of the best dining pubs here, is doing a lighter style of lunchtime cooking that's proving very popular; and the food at the friendly and old-fashioned Cross Keys in Great Missenden is going all Italian. Entirely new to the Guide, or back among the main entries after a break, are several worthy additions: the enjoyably cheerful Greyhound in Beaconsfield, the civilised Fox at Ibstone (nice countryside though very handy for the M40), the restauranty Rising Sun at Little Hampden (good food in a fine spot), the attractive old Angel in Long Crendon, the busy Two Brewers in Marlow (food all day) and the Chequers at Wooburn Common, an unusually successful combination of pub with hotel. All these in their various very different ways have decent food. Besides the five pubs here which have gained our coveted Food Award, most enjoyable meals may also be had at the Peacock at Bolter End (excellent ingredients), the Seven Stars at Dinton, the Dinton Hermit at Ford, the Red Lion at Whiteleaf near Princes Risborough, the Bull & Butcher at Turville and the Five Arrows at Waddesdon. This year, the three pubs which stand out for memorable meals out are the Mole & Chicken at Easington, the Hampden Arms at Great Hampden and the Red Lion at Great Kingshill. We choose the Red Lion at Great Kingshill as the county's Dining Pub of the Year, for the charming way its Spanish landlord Jose Cabrera has turned quite an unassuming village pub into a remarkably satisfying fish restaurant. In the Lucky Dip section at the end of the chapter, pubs which seem on the verge of a main entry at the moment include the Old Thatched Inn at Adstock, Bull & Butcher at Akeley, Kings Arms in Amersham, Bell at Chearsley, Chequers at Fingest, Yew Tree at Frieth, White Horse at Hedgerley, Crooked Billet at Kingswood, Whip at Lacey Green (the first time we've come across this pub), Greyhound at Marsh Gibbon (for Thai food), Hit or Miss at Penn Street, Polecat at Prestwood, Frog at Skirmett, Seven Stars at Twyford, Red Lion in Wendover and Chequers at Weston Turville. This is one of the most expensive areas in Britain for drinkers, with pub beer prices about 10% over the odds. Of smaller breweries operating in the area, Fullers have much more attractive prices than Brakspears – the Cross Keys in Great Missenden, tied to Fullers, was by far the cheapest of the main entries.

nr AMERSHAM SU9495 Map 4

Queens Head ◄

Whielden Gate; pub in sight just off A404, 1½ miles towards High Wycombe at Winchmore Hill turn-off; OS Sheet 165 map reference 941957

The garden of this unpretentious old brick and tile pub is quite a busy place with bantams running around, an aviary with barn owls, a rabbit in a large run, swings, a climbing frame and slide, and maybe Monty the now elderly dalmatian. Inside, the low-beamed, friendly bar has traditional furnishings, horsebrasses, and lots of brass spigots; flagstones surround the big inglenook fireplace (which still has the old-fashioned wooden built-in wall seat curving around right in beside the woodburning stove – with plenty of space under the seat for logs), and there's also a stuffed albino pheasant, old guns, and a good cigarette card collection. The family room is no smoking. Home-made bar food – using home-grown vegetables from the garden – includes soup (£2.25), ploughman's (£3), sweet pickled trout (£3.50), omelettes (£4), spinach and walnut pancakes (£5), pizzas (from £5; you can take them away as well), wild rabbit pie (£5.50), and venison pie (£6.50). Well kept Adnams, Brakspears, Marlow Rebellion, and Wadworths 6X on handpump, and several malt whiskies; darts, shove-ha'penny, dominoes, cribbage, fruit machine, and piped music. *(Recommended by Dr G W Barnett, SR, PM, Piotr Chodzko-Zajko, Ian Phillips, Gordon, Mr and Mrs G Arbib, Dr Jim Craig-Gray, Miles and Deborah Protter, B M Eshelby, AD)*

Free house ~ Licensees Les and Mary Anne Robbins ~ Real ale ~ Meals and snacks (till 10pm; not Sun evening) ~ (01494) 725240 ~ Children in family room ~ Open 11-3, 5.30(6 Sat)-11

BEACONSFIELD SU9490 Map 2

Greyhound

A mile from M40 junction 2, via A40; Windsor End, Old Town

This pleasant and cosy two-bar former coaching inn has become very popular since the present licensees moved in from their former pub, the Old Hare, at the opposite end of the Old Town. The entertaining landlord gives the atmosphere a light touch, and could scarcely be more welcoming; the rest of the staff are friendly and attentive even in the slightly hectic rush that seems their natural speed. The landlady produces a wide choice of good home-made bar food including filled french bread or granary sandwiches (from £2.95), home-made burgers (from £4.95), interesting pies such as chicken and leek in stilton sauce, pork, apple and cider, a vegetarian garlic mushroom one, seafood, and steak and kidney (from £4.75), popular bubble and squeak with sausage or ham, cheese or beef (from £5.45), and lots of daily specials (5 starters, 5 pastas, 5 main courses and 5 puddings) like crispy duck and spring onion salad or fresh sardines (around £3.45), pasta with all sorts of sauces (£5.95), lots of fresh fish, various chicken dishes, and steak (from £6.95), and good traditional puddings like treacle tart, bread and butter pudding or summer pavlovas (£2.95). There's also a partly no-smoking back bistro-like restaurant. Well kept Courage Best, Fullers London Pride and Wadworths 6X with two regional guest beers on handpump; no piped music and no children. *(Recommended by Dave Everitt, John Curry, Sally Barker, Jan and Colin Roe, GWB, DJW)*

Free house ~ Lease: Jamie and Wendy Godrich ~ Real ale ~ Meals and snacks (till 10pml not Sun evening) ~ Restaurant ~ (01494) 673823 ~ Open 11-3, 5.30-11

BLEDLOW SP7702 Map 4

Lions of Bledlow

From B4009 from Chinnor towards Princes Risborough, the first right turn about 1 mile outside Chinnor goes straight to the pub; from the second, wider right turn, turn right through village

From the door of this mossy-tiled old pub you can walk straight up into the hills and steep beechwoods beyond, and the sheltered crazy-paved terrace and series of neatly kept small sloping lawns are a fine place to quench your thirst afterwards. The attractive low-beamed rooms – one with a woodburning stove – are full of character. The inglenook bar has attractive oak stalls built into one partly panelled wall, more seats in a good bay window (fine views), and an antique settle resting on the deeply polished ancient tiles; log fires. Bar food includes big filled cottage rolls, pasta with creamy mushroom sauce (£4.50), seafood lasagne (£5), spiced fillet of lamb (£5.25), cajun spiced cod (£5.50), and duck breast with satay sauce (£6.25). Well kept Courage Best, Marstons Pedigree, Rebellion IPA, John Smiths, and Wadworths 6X on handpump. One of the two cottagey side rooms has a video game, as well as dominoes and cribbage. *(Recommended by Dr G W Barnett, Jan and Colin Roe, Paul Kitchener, Gordon, Nigel Norman, Tony Dickinson)*

Free house ~ Licensee Mark McKeown ~ Real ale ~ Meals and snacks (not Sun evening) ~ Restaurant (closed Sun evening) ~ (01844) 343345 ~ Children welcome ~ Open 11-3(4 Sat), 6-11; closed winter Sun evenings

BOLTER END SU7992 Map 4

Peacock

Just over 4 miles from M40 junction 5; A40 to Stokenchurch, then B482

The enthusiastic and long-standing licensees here continue to draw locals and visitors alike to this busy and friendly pub. The brightly modernised bar has a rambling series of alcoves, a good log fire, and a cheerful atmosphere; the Old Darts bar is no smoking. And the home-made bar food is very good too, with free-range poultry, Aberdeen Angus steaks and fresh fish specials on Thursdays and Fridays: pasta with tomato and herb sauce (£4.25), mediterranean roast vegetables (£5.10), local butcher pork sausages (£5.50), home-made steak and kidney pie (£5.95), chicken stir-fry with lime and ginger (£6.50), stincotto (lean gammon hock) or poached fresh salmon with a chive sauce (£6.95), steaks (from £11.25), and home-made sponge puddings or fruit crumbles (£2.50). Well kept ABC Bitter, Brakspears PA, Tetleys Bitter, and Wadworths 6X on handpump, decent wines including changing specials, and freshly squeezed orange juice; cribbage and dominoes. In summer there are seats around a low stone table and picnic tables in the neatly kept garden. The 'no children' is strictly enforced here and there is no piped music. *(Recommended by Dr G W Barnett, Mr and Mrs T A Bryan, John Waller, Sandra Iles)*

Carlsberg Tetley ~ Lease: Peter and Janet Hodges ~ Real ale ~ Meals and snacks (till 10pm; not Sun evening) ~ (01494) 881417 ~ Open 11.45-2.30, 6-11

BRILL SP6513 Map 4

Pheasant ♀

Windmill St; village signposted from B4011 Bicester—Long Crendon

The views from this 17th-c pub are marvellous and the newish verandah that overlooks the windmill opposite (one of the oldest post windmills still in working order), is proving very popular. There are also some picnic tables in the small, sheltered back garden. Inside, the quietly modernised and neatly kept beamed bar has refectory tables and windsor chairs, a woodburning stove, and a step up to a dining area which is decorated with attractively framed Alken hunting prints – and which also benefits from the view. Bar food includes home-made soup (£2.20), Greek salad with feta cheese and olives (£3.95), home-cooked ham (£4.95), vegetarian cutlets (£5.40), barbecued ribs or various curries (£5.95), fresh trout (from their own stocked local lake, £6.95), and rump steaks with a choice of seven sauces (£8.50). Well kept Marstons Pedigree and Tetleys on handpump, and seven good wines by the glass; piped music. No dogs (they have two golden retrievers themselves). Roald Dahl used to drink here, and some of the tales the locals told him were worked into his short stories. *(Recommended by D and J McMillan, Howard*

Gregory, K H Frostick, Paul Kitchener, M Sargent, Bob and Maggie Atherton, Steve Goodchild, Ted George)

Free house ~ Licensee Mike Carr ~ Real ale ~ Meals and snacks ~ Restaurant ~ (01844) 237104 ~ Children in eating area of bar and in restaurant ~ Open 11-3, 6-11; 12-10.30 Sun; closed 25-26 Dec

CADMORE END SU7892 Map 4

Old Ship 🍺

B482 Stokenchurch—Marlow

Changes to the garden of this genuinely unspoilt country pub include a new terrace, a large pergola with picnic tables, and an enclosed play area for children (who may not be allowed inside); there are more seats in the sheltered garden. The furnishings in the tiny low-beamed two-room bar (unchanged for decades) are pretty basic – leatherette wall benches and stools in the carpeted room on the right, and on the left scrubbed country tables, bench seating (one still has a hole for a game called five-farthings) bare boards and darts, shove-ha'penny, cribbage, dominoes, shut-the-box, and bagatelle. But what matters is the warmth of the landlady's cheerful welcome, the fine quality of the Brakspears PA, SB and Old tapped directly from casks down in the cellar, and the friendly unhurried atmosphere. Food is simple but decent and carefully prepared: filled french bread (from £1.60; bacon, lettuce and tomato £2.40, steak £2.95), soup (£1.95), stilton mushrooms (£2.75), chilli con carne (£5), daily specials, and evening dishes such as blackened chicken (£6.50), beef casserole with cajun spices (£7.50), and prawn gumbo (cajun spices, £7.75). They do theme evenings on the first Wednesday of the month, a monthly fixed-price curry evening, cream teas on holiday weekends and every summer Sunday until August bank holiday, and summer Sunday lunchtime barbecues. Parking is on the other side of the road. *(Recommended by Ian Phillips, Gordon, Pete Baker)*

Brakspears ~ Tenants Thomas and Julie Chapman ~ Real ale ~ Meals and snacks (not Sun, Mon or Tues evenings) ~ (01494) 883496 ~ Open 12-2.30(3 Sat), 5.30(6)-11

CHEDDINGTON SP9217 Map 4

Old Swan

58 High St

Friendly new licensees have taken over this mainly thatched old pub and readers are happy to report that things are as pleasant as ever. On the right, the quietly civilised bar rooms have old-fashioned plush dining chairs, a built-in wall bench, a few tables with nice country-style chairs on the bare boards, a big inglenook with glass cabinets filled with brass on either side of it, and quite a few horsebrasses and little hunting prints on the walls. On the other side of the main door is a room with housekeeper's chairs on the rugs and quarry tiles and country plates on the walls, and a step up to a carpeted part with stripy wallpaper and pine furniture. Bar food includes sandwiches (from £2), filled baked potatoes (from £2.50), vegetable lasagne (£4.95), gammon and egg (£4.90), daily specials, children's menu, and puddings; the restaurant is partly no smoking. Well kept ABC Best, Greene King IPA, Ridgeway Bitter (from Tring), and guest beers on handpump, quite a few malt whiskies, and decent wines; very pleasant, efficient staff. Fruit machine and piped music. In summer, the pub is attractively decorated with colourful hanging baskets and tubs, and there's a children's play area in the garden. *(Recommended by Ian Phillips, Gordon Tong, Peter and Liz Wilkins, Mel Smith, Shirley Cannings, George Atkinson, Mark and Caroline Thistlethwaite, Pat and Robert Wyatt, Maysie Thompson)*

Carlsberg Tetleys ~ Lease: Maurice and Joyce Cook ~ Real ale ~ Meals and snacks (12-3, 7-9.30 weekdays, 12-4, 7-9.30 weekends) ~ Restaurant ~ (01296) 668226 ~ Children in eating area of bar ~ Live music Sun or Tues ~ Open 11-3, 5-11; 11-11 Sat; 12-10.30 Sun

CHENIES TQ0198 Map 2

Red Lion

2 miles from M25 junction 18; A404 towards Amersham, then village signposted on right;
Chesham Rd

The landlord in this white-painted brick pub likes to keep things simple – no noisy
games machines or piped music, and no children. The unpretentious L-shaped bar
has original photographs of the village and of traction engines, beige or plum-
coloured cushions on the built-in wall benches by the front windows, and traditional
seats and tables; there's also a small back snug and a dining room. Bar food includes
soup (£2.35), filled french bread (from £2.45; bacon and (an unusual) butterscotch
sauce £3; steak and onions £5.25), filled baked potatoes (from £3), pasta and bacon
with blue cheese sauce (£5.25), pies such as rabbit and prune or smoked haddock
and egg (from £5.95), beef curry (£6.50), steak (£9.95), and puddings (from £1.95).
Well kept Benskins Best, Rebellion Lion Pride (brewed for the pub), Vale Notley,
and Wadworths 6X on handpump. The hanging baskets and window boxes are
pretty in summer. *(Recommended by Ken and Jenny Simmonds, Thomas Nott, Gordon,
Christopher Turner, Ian Phillips, Kevin and Tracey Stephens, BKA, Gary Roberts, Ann Stubbs)*

*Free house ~ Licensees Heather and Mike Norris ~ Real ale ~ Meals and snacks
(till 10pm) ~ (01923) 282722 ~ Open 11-2.30, 5.30-11; closed 25 Dec*

DINTON SP7611 Map 4

Seven Stars

Stars Lane; follow Dinton signpost into New Road off A418 Aylesbury—Thame, near
Gibraltar turn-off

Run by warmly friendly people, this pretty old pub is tucked away in a quiet village.
The characterful public bar (known as the Snug here) is notable for the two highly
varnished ancient built-in settles facing each other across a table in front of the vast
stone inglenook fireplace. The spotlessly kept lounge bar, with its beams, joists and
growing numbers of old tools on the walls, is comfortably and simply modernised –
and although these rooms are not large, there is a spacious and comfortable
restaurant area. Good, reasonably priced bar food includes sandwiches (from £1.80;
toasties 25p extra), filled baked potatoes (from £2.80), ploughman's or quiche
lorraine (£3.85), vegetable lasagne (£3.95), beef bourguignon (£4.95), steaks (from
£9), good daily specials, and puddings (from £2). Well kept ABC, Ind Coope Burton,
and Vale Wychert Ale on handpump; darts. There are tables under cocktail parasols
on the terrace, with more on the lawn of the pleasant sheltered garden. *(Recommended
by M Sargent, Mick and Mel Smith, Marjorie and David Lamb, Graham and Karen Oddey, D P
and J A Sweeney, Mrs J Oakes, H Hazzard, Gordon, John Fahy)*

*Free house ~ Licensees Rainer and Sue Eccard ~ Real ale ~ Meals and snacks (not
Sun or Tues evenings) ~ Restaurant (not Sun evening) ~ Children in eating area of
bar ~ (01296) 748241 ~ Open 12-3, 6-11; closed Tues evening*

EASINGTON SP6810 Map 4

Mole & Chicken 🍴 ♀

From B4011 in Long Crendon follow Chearsley, Waddesdon signpost into Carters Lane
opposite the Chandos Arms, then turn left into Chilton Road

Set in rolling open country, this popular dining pub is happy for people to pop in to
enjoy the well kept Hook Norton Best and Morlands Original and Old Speckled
Hen on handpump – but the emphasis is firmly placed on the particularly good food,
and most of the tables are set for meals. Using good ingredients, the changing choice
of food includes home-made soup (£2.95), a few starters that would do as a light
lunch such as baked sweet pepper with mixed cheeses (£4.50), chicken, pork or beef
satay with garlic bread (£4.95), or even home-grown asparagus (from £3.95), and

very generously served main courses including interesting salads like ham and eggs (£5.95), pasta with sweet chilli tiger prawns (£5.95), steak and kidney pie (£6.95), monkfish and bacon salad with pesto dressing (£7.50), piri-piri chicken (£7.95), their speciality half shoulder of English lamb with honey, garlic and rosemary sauce (£10.95), char-grilled steaks (from £11.95), various fresh fish dishes, and puddings; it's essential to book. Decent French house wines (and a good choice by the bottle), and 74 malt whiskies. It's open-plan but very well done, so that all the different parts seem quite snug and self-contained without being cut off from what's going on. The beamed bar curves around the serving counter in a sort of S-shape – unusual, as is the decor of designed-and-painted floor, pink walls with lots of big antique prints, and even at lunchtime lit candles on the medley of tables to go with the nice mix of old chairs. Smiling young neatly dressed staff, a pleasant chatty and relaxed atmosphere with a good mix of different age-groups, unobtrusive piped music, good winter log fires, pistachio nuts and other nibbles on the counter; no dogs. There's a smallish garden with picnic tables under cocktail parasols, with an outside summer bar and maybe lunchtime summer barbecues. *(Recommended by Jim and Maggie Cowell, Mark Gillis, Graham and Karen Oddey, D and J McMillan, Alison Haines, Hugh and Joyce Mellor, Brian White, Heather Couper)*

Free house ~ Licensee Johnny Chick ~ Real ale ~ Meals and snacks (till 10pm; all day Sun) ~ (01844) 208387 ~ Children welcome (until 9.30pm) ~ Open 11-3.30, 6-11; all day Sun

FAWLEY SU7586 Map 2

Walnut Tree 🛏 ♀ 🍴

Village signposted off A4155 (then right at T-junction) and off B480, N of Henley

It's the very good, popular food that draws people to this well run dining pub, surrounded by the Chilterns. In the bar, there might be various ploughman's (£3.75), baked stuffed aubergine (£4.95), home-made steak and kidney pie (£5.75), hot home-baked ham with parsley sauce or chicken oriental (£6.25), salmon and lemon sole goujons (£6.25), and changing specials such as fresh tuna steak (£9.95), roast breast of barbary duck (£10.95) or roast rack of English lamb (£11.95); potatoes are £1 extra and vegetables £1.50. Well kept Brakspears PA on handpump, and a good range of wines (including local English ones); attentive service. The public bar has been refurbished this year, and there's also a no-smoking conservatory, and restaurant. The big lawn around the front car park has some well spaced tables made from elm trees, with some seats in a covered terrace extension – and a hitching rail for riders. *(Recommended by Gwen and Peter Andrews, RJH, Mary and Des Kemp, June S Bray, GWB, Peter Saville, Cyril Brown, Leigh and Gillian Mellor, Piotr Chodzko-Zajko, Mike and Heather Barnes)*

Brakspears ~ Tenants Ben and Diane Godbolt ~ Real ale ~ Meals and snacks ~ Restaurant ~ (01491) 638360 ~ Children in conservatory and in restaurant ~ Open 12-3, 6-11 ~ Bedrooms: £40S/£50S

FORD SP7709 Map 4

Dinton Hermit

Village signposted between A418 and B4009, SW of Aylesbury

Tucked away in pretty countryside, this friendly stone cottage has an attractively traditional partly tiled public bar on the left with scrubbed tables, a woodburning stove in its huge inglenook, and prints of a lady out hunting. The lounge on the right, with a log fire, has red plush banquettes along the cream walls and red leatherette chairs around polished tables, and red leatherette seats built into the stripped stone walls of a small room leading off. Mrs Tompkins cooks the good bar food (with prices unchanged since last year), and at lunchtime, when they don't take reservations, this might include sandwiches (from £1.40), soup (£2), ploughman's (from £3), saucy mushrooms (£3.25), smoked haddock in mushroom and cheese sauce (£4.75), a vegetarian hotpot or kidneys in cognac sauce (£4.95), pancake with stilton and asparagus or curries (£5.75), and puddings such as home-made fruit pie or bread pudding (£2.50); in the evening (when you must book), dishes are slightly more expensive and include more grills and fish. Well kept ABC Best, Adnams, and Wadworths 6X on handpump; darts, shove-ha'penny, cribbage and dominoes. The sheltered and well planted garden opposite (they don't serve food out there in the evenings) has swings, a slide and a seesaw. *(Recommended by Mary and Des Kemp, M Sargent, Karen and Graham Oddey, Gordon, John Fahy)*

Free house ~ Licensees John and Jane Tompkins ~ Real ale ~ Meals and snacks (not Sun or Mon) ~ (01296) 748379 ~ Well behaved children in eating area of bar ~ Open 11-2.30, 6-11; closed Mon lunchtimes

FORTY GREEN SU9292 Map 2

Royal Standard of England

3½ miles from M40 junction 2, via A40 to Beaconsfield, then follow sign to Forty Green, off B474 ¾ mile N of New Beaconsfield

The rambling atmospheric rooms in this historic old pub have huge black ship's timbers, finely carved old oak panelling, a massive settle apparently built to fit the curved transom of an Elizabethan ship, and roaring open fires and handsomely decorated iron firebacks; also, rifles, powder-flasks and bugles, lots of brass and copper, needlework samplers, ancient pewter and pottery tankards, and stained glass. Two areas are now no smoking. Under the new licensees, good bar food includes home-made soups (£2.75), mediterranean beanpot crumble (£4.95), locally-made sausages (£5.20), daily curries (£5.75), home-made pies such as chicken and mushroom or beef in ale (from £5.95), a fresh fish dish, sirloin steak (£10.95), and a popular buffet. Well kept Brakspears, Marstons Pedigree and Owd Rodger (the beer was originally brewed here, until the pub passed the recipe on to Marstons), Morlands Old Speckled Hen, Vale Notely, and guest beers on handpump; country wines and a few malt whiskies. There are seats outside in a neatly hedged front rose garden, or in the shade of a tree. Perhaps at its best in winter when the summer crowds have gone. *(Recommended by Dr G W Barnett, Chris and Martin Taylor, Chris and Andy Crow, John and Phyllis Maloney, Heather Couper, A W Dickinson, Nigel Norman)*

Free house ~ Managers C Cain, Mr and Mrs P Huxley ~ Real ale ~ Meals and snacks (till 10pm) ~ (01494) 673382 ~ Children welcome ~ Open 11-3, 5.30-11

FRIETH SU7990 Map 2

Prince Albert 🍺 ♀

Village signposted off B482 in Lane End; turn right towards Fingest just before village

Standing alone in peaceful wooded countryside with plenty of nearby walks, this pretty little tiled cottage is quietly relaxing, with no noisy machines or piped music – just the buzz of conversation. On the left there's a big black stove in a brick inglenook with a bison's head looking out beside it, copper pots on top, and earthenware flagons in front, hop bines on the mantelbeam and on the low black beams and joists, a leaded-light built-in wall cabinet of miniature bottles, and brocaded cushions on high-backed settles (one with its back panelled in neat squares). The slightly larger area on the right has more of a medley of chairs and a big log fire; magazines, books and local guides to read. Well kept Brakspears Bitter, Special, Mild, Old and OBJ on handpump; Georges Duboeuf house wines, decent whiskies on optic include Smiths Glenlivet and Jamesons, and elderflower pressé. There's an excellent assortment of generous fillings for hot granary bread rolls with salad (around £3.45), such as cheese and onion, giant sausage, black pudding and bacon or pastrami and cucumber, with a handful of robust hot dishes such as ham and eggs, special sausages, boiled bacon with parsley sauce, and pork Normandy. No music, but cribbage and dominoes. The lovely dog is called Leo. A nicely planted informal side garden has views of woods and fields. Please note, children are not allowed inside. *(Recommended by Simon Collett-Jones, Lynda Payton, Sam Samuells, Pete Baker, Jenny Sapp, Peter Hudson, Jack and Philip Paxton, Nigel Norman, Andy Thwaites)*

Brakspears ~ Tenant Frank Reynolds ~ Real ale ~ Meals and snacks (lunchtime only; not Sun) ~ (01494) 881683 ~ Open 11-3, 5.30-11

GREAT HAMPDEN SP8401 Map 4
Hampden Arms 🍴 ♀

Village signposted off A4010 S of Princes Risborough; OS Sheet 165 map reference 845015

It's quite a surprise to find this relaxed and civilised dining pub behind the simple-looking exterior. As well as the serious cooking, a lighter lunchtime menu has been introduced this year: a triple-decker sandwich of garlic mushrooms, bacon and lightly scrambled egg, home-made cannelloni, lancashire hotpot or big baked potato filled with chicken curry (all £4.95), salmon and prawn patty (£5.95), beefburger topped with pâté and onions in puff pastry (£6.95), and roast sirloin of beef with yorkshire pudding (£7.95); from eight blackboards and a set menu there may be home-made soup (£2.95), home-made chicken and brandy pâté (£4.95), seafood pancake (£5.95), chicken and bacon pie (£7.25), home-cooked ham (£7.95), baked stilton avocado or whole trout with herbs (£8.95), prime Scottish steaks (from £16.95; £2.50 extra for sauces), and lovely puddings (from £2.95). A small corner bar has well kept Eldridge Pope Hardy Country, Greene King Abbot, Tetleys, and Wadworths 6X on handpump, Addlestones cider, and decent wines; service is quietly obliging. The cream-walled front room has broad dark tables, with a few aeroplane pictures and country prints; the back room has a slightly more rustic feel, with its pink-cushioned wall benches and big woodburning stove. The gents' has been decorated in French farmhouse theme. There are tables out in the tree-sheltered garden; on the edge of Hampden Common, this has good walks nearby.
(Recommended by Dr G W Barnett, Andrew and Joan Life, Peter Saville, Graham and Karen Oddey, Francis and Deirdre Gevers)

Free house ~ Licensees Terry and Barbara Matthews ~ Real ale ~ Meals and snacks (all day summer Sun) ~ (01494) 488255 ~ Children in small bar ~ Open 12-2.30, 7-11; 12-10.30 Sun; closed Sun evenings Jan-Feb

GREAT KINGSHILL SU8798 Map 4
Red Lion 🍴 ♀

A4128 N of High Wycombe

Buckinghamshire Dining Pub of the Year

If you like fish, then this spotlessly kept dining pub is a must. It's a little brick and flint cottage with unpretentious village pubby furnishings such as shiny brass wall lamps and decorative plates, but the cooking is of an altogether higher order, and all the tables are set for dining, with proper tablecloths. The friendly Spanish landlord is the chef, and there's a tremendous choice all fresh from Billingsgate, and very sensibly priced. Favourite examples include oysters (60p each), fresh calamares or moules marinières (£3.50), haddock (£7.50), skate (£8), brill (£10), dover soles (£12), lobsters (£17), and much more; the chips are freshly cut and good, and there's a bargain Sunday lunch. Tetleys and Tolly Cobbold on handpump, good house wines, and freshly squeezed orange juice; excellent service. *(Recommended by Dr G W Barnett, John Waller, H Kroll, Peter Saville, Ronald Buckler, R Brisbourne, Cyril Brown)*

Pubmasters ~ Tenant Jose Rivero-Cabrera ~ Real ale ~ Meals and snacks ~ Restaurant ~ (01494) 711262 ~ Children welcome ~ Open 12-3, 6-11; closed Sun evening, Mon

There are report forms at the back of the book.

GREAT MISSENDEN SP8900 Map 4

Cross Keys

High St

As we went to press we heard that the food throughout this very friendly and old-fashioned little town pub would shortly be all Italian – but details had not been finalised. The pub is divided inside by wooden standing timbers, and one half of the bar has old sewing machines on the window sill, collectors' postcards, various brewery mirrors, lots of photographs, and horse bits and spigots and pewter mugs on the beams by the bar. The other has a bay window with a built-in seat overlooking the street, a couple of housekeeper's chairs in front of the big open fire, and a high-backed settle. Well kept Fullers Chiswick, London Pride, ESB on handpump and very cheap for the area. The attractive big eating room will soon be an Italian restaurant. Cribbage, dominoes, shove-ha'penny, fruit machine, and piped music. The terrace at the back of the building has picnic tables with umbrellas – and you can eat out here, too. *(Recommended by Ian Phillips, Owen and Rosemary Warnock, Gordon; more reports please)*

Fullers ~ Tenants Martin and Freddie Ridler ~ Real ale ~ Lunchtime meals and snacks ~ Evening restaurant (not Sun evening but they do Sun lunch) ~ Well behaved children in restaurant ~ (01494) 865373 ~ Open 11-3, 5.30-11; closed 25 Dec

George

94 High St

Built as a hospice for the nearby abbey, this 15th-c inn has a cosy two-roomed bar with attractively moulded heavy beams, timbered walls decorated with prints, little alcoves (including one with an attractively carved box settle – just room for two – under a fine carved early 17th-c oak panel), and Staffordshire and other figurines over the big log fire. A snug inner room has a sofa, little settles and a smaller coal fire; shove-ha'penny, cribbage, and dominoes. Bar food as we went to press (a new chef was shortly arriving) includes sandwiches (from £1.75), home-made soup (£2.25), filled baked potatoes (from £2.50), deep-fried crêpes (£3.50), ham and eggs or cod and chips (£4.75), fresh pasta (vegetarian and meat, £5.25), home-made steak and kidney pie (£6.60), and rack of English lamb (£8.95); huge Sunday roast (£6.25), and if you are staying, breakfasts are served until 10am. The restaurant is no smoking. Well kept Adnams, Bass, and Wadworths 6X on handpump kept under light blanket pressure, sangria in summer, mulled wine in winter, and several malt whiskies; prompt and cheerful service. A new terrace has been built and the garden area has plenty of seats. *(Recommended by Gordon, Mrs Jean Dundas, Ian Phillips, Nigel Norman)*

Greenalls ~ Tenants Guy and Sally Smith ~ Real ale ~ Snacks (served all day) and meals; not evenings 25 and 26 Dec ~ Restaurant ~ (01494) 862084 ~ Children in eating area of bar and in restaurant ~ Open 11-11; closed evenings 25-26 Dec ~ Bedrooms: £59.95B/£67.45B

HAMBLEDEN SU7886 Map 2

Stag & Huntsman 🚩

Turn off A4155 (Henley—Marlow Rd) at Mill End, signposted to Hambleden; in a mile turn right into village centre

In summer, the neatly kept garden of this peaceful brick and flint house is a popular place for their huge barbecues – cajun salmon, pork and apple burgers, pork and leek sausages, and various kebabs; maybe live music, too. Inside, the half-panelled, L-shaped lounge bar has low ceilings, a large fireplace, upholstered seating and wooden chairs on the carpet, and a bustling atmosphere. The attractively simple public bar has darts, shove-ha'penny, dominoes, cribbage and a fruit machine, and there's a cosy snug at the front, too; piped music. A wide variety of good home-made bar food includes soup (£2.75), ploughman's (from £3.75), vegetarian quiche (£4.95), home-cooked ham and egg (£5.95), marinated char-grilled chicken or fresh salmon fish cakes (£6.25), smoked and grilled pork loin (£7.95), steaks (from £10.95), and puddings like fresh fruit crumble (£2.50). Well kept Brakspears PA and SPA, Rebellion Mutiny, and Wadworths 6X on handpump, and good wines (they hold seasonal wine appreciation evenings). The pub is set opposite the church in a particularly pretty Chilterns village and the garden is spacious. *(Recommended by RJH, Dr G W Barnett, Helen Pickering, James Owen, TBB, Gwen and Peter Andrews)*

Free house ~ Licensees Hon Henry Smith and Andrew Fry ~ Real ale ~ Meals and snacks ~ Restaurant ~ (01491) 571227 ~ Children in eating area of bar and in restaurant ~ Open 11-2.30(3 in Sat), 6-11 ~ Bedrooms: £38.50S/£48.50S

IBSTONE SU7593 Map 4

Fox

1¼ miles from M40 junction 5: unclassified lane leading S from motorway exit roundabout; pub is on Ibstone Common

Although so handy for the M40, this is very much a friendly old country inn near the village cricket ground, with a neat rose garden prettily lit by old lamps, and views over the common with rolling fields and the Chilterns oak and beech woods beyond. The comfortable lounge bar has low beams, high-backed settles and country seats, old village photographs on the walls, and log fires. In the public bar – which has darts, shove-ha'penny, dominoes, cribbage – the pine settles and tables match the woodblock floor. Good, generously served home-made bar food includes sandwiches (from £1.50), ploughman's (from £3.25), vegetarian dishes (from £5.50), pies such as steak and kidney or chicken and leek (£5.95), salmon steak with hollandaise (£6.25), lamb steak in port and mint sauce (£6.95), whole trout with lemon butter and capers (£7.25), steaks (from £7.95), and traditional puddings (£2.50). The small dining area in the bar is no smoking; there's also a smart restaurant. Well kept Brakspears PA, Fullers London Pride, Rebellion IPA, and Wadworths 6X on handpump or tapped from the cask. *(Recommended by Nigel Norman, George Atkinson, Alec Hamilton, GWG, Robert Gomme, A W Dickinson, Derek and Sylvia Stephenson, Wayne Brindle)*

Free house ~ Licensees Ann and David Banks ~ Real ale ~ Meals and snacks ~ Restaurant (not Sun evening) ~ (01491) 638722 ~ Children in eating area of bar if eating ~ Open 11-3(4 Sat), 6-11 Bedrooms: £59B/£76B

LACEY GREEN SP8201 Map 4

Pink & Lily ♀ ◧

Parslow's Hillock; from A4010 High Wycombe—Princes Risborough follow Loosley signpost, and in that village follow Great Hampden, Great Missenden signpost; OS Sheet 165 map reference 826019

The little taproom in this extended and modernised dining pub has been preserved very much as it used to be, with built in wall benches on the red flooring tiles, an old wooden ham-rack hanging from the ceiling and a broad inglenook with a low mantelpiece (though the fire is not always lit). The airy main bar has low pink plush seats, with more intimate side areas and an open fire, and there's a Spanish-style extension with big arches and white garden furniture. Two open fires in winter. Rupert Brooke liked the pub so much that he wrote about it at the start of one of his poems; the result is framed on the wall (and there's a room dedicated to him). Decent bar food includes sandwiches (from £1.75), ploughman's (£3.95), vegetable curry or leek and stilton bake (£3.95), pies such as steak and kidney or chicken and bacon (£4.25), mixed fish casserole (£4.95), a roast of the day (from £4.95), weekend specials such as chicken with apples and cider or with cream and garlic potatoes (£6.95), and good home-made puddings like bakewell tart, lemon meringue pie or chocolate roulade (£2.25); vegetables are fresh. The good range of well kept real ales on handpump includes Batemans Valiant, Boddingtons, Brakspears PA, Courage Best, and Glenny Hobgoblin; six decent wines by the glass. Dominoes, cribbage, ring-the-bull, and piped music. The big garden has lots of rustic tables and seats. *(Recommended by R Morgan, Nigel Norman, Dave Carter, Gordon, A W Dickinson, Alistair Ferguson, M E Wellington, Jack and Philip Paxton, Heather Couper, George Atkinson)*

Free house ~ Licensees Clive and Marion Mason ~ Real ale ~ Meals and snacks (not Sun evenings) ~ (01494) 488308 ~ Children over 5 if eating, in bottom bar only ~ Open 11.45(11 Sat)-3, 6-11

LITTLE HAMPDEN SP8503 Map 4

Rising Sun ⑪

Village signposted from back road (ie W of A413) Great Missenden—Stoke Mandeville; pub at end of village lane; OS Sheet 165 map reference 856040

In a delightful, secluded setting with tracks leading through the woods in different directions, this smart and comfortable pub is very popular for its imaginative food. Walkers are welcome as long as they leave their muddy boots outside – though there are some tables on the terrace by the sloping front grass. Constantly changing, the food might include deep-fried mushrooms with garlic mayonnaise (£3.95), pasta with a cream, gruyère cheese and smoked sausage sauce (£4.50), grilled sardines with lemon and herb butter (£4.75), poached salmon with white wine and dill (£7.95), barbecued chicken with a sweet and sour sauce and crunchy vegetables (£8.75), roast home-smoked duck with an orange and whisky sauce (£9.75), and puddings such as Jamaican toffee banana pancake, various flummerys, and summer pavlovas (£3.25). Well kept Adnams, Brakspears PA, Marstons Pedigree, Morlands Old Speckled Hen on handpump, with home-made mulled wine and spiced cider in winter and decent wines; efficient service. One part of the interlinked bar rooms is no smoking, and there's also a separate dining room (which enjoys the same food as the bar). *(Recommended by Dr G W Barnett, Mr and Mrs T F Marshall, Andrew and Joan Life, Dave Carter, M A and C R Starling, Graham and Karen Oddey, Mr and Mrs A J Murdoch, Nigel Norman)*

Free house ~ Licensee Rory Dawson ~ Real ale ~ Meals and snacks (not Sun evening, not Mon) ~ (01494) 488393 ~ Children welcome ~ Open 11.30-2.30, 6.30-11; closed Sun evenings and Mon – except for bank hols ~ Bedrooms planned

LITTLE HORWOOD SP7930 Map 4

Shoulder of Mutton

Church St; back road 1 mile S of A421 Buckingham—Bletchley

The rambling and friendly T-shaped bar in this half-timbered and partly thatched 14th-c pub has a huge fireplace at one end with a woodburning stove, and is attractively but simply furnished with sturdy seats around chunky rustic tables on the quarry tiles, and a showcase of china swans; the alsatian is called Benjamin and the black cat, Trouble. Well kept ABC Best and Flowers Original on handpump; shove-ha'penny, cribbage, dominoes, and fruit machine in the games area. Bar food includes sandwiches (from £1.80), filled baked potatoes (from £2.30), chilli con carne or home-made nut cutlet (£4.90), home-made steak and kidney pie (£5.20), Devonshire pork chop (£5.90), and steaks (from £8.50). French windows look out on the pleasant back garden where there are plenty of tables, and the churchyard is next door. From the north, the car park entrance is tricky. *(Recommended by Ian Phillips, Marjorie and David Lamb, GO, KO, S Palmer, John Hazel, Roger and Valerie Hill)*

Pubmaster (Allied) ~ Tenant June Fessey ~ Real ale ~ Meals and snacks (not Sun evening, not Mon) ~ Restaurant (not Sun evening) ~ (01296) 712514 ~ Children in eating area of bar and in restaurant until 9pm ~ Open 11-3, 6-11; closed Mon lunchtime

LITTLE MISSENDEN SU9298 Map 4

Crown 🍺

Crown Lane, SE end of village, which is signposted off A413 W of Amersham

For over 90 years this very popular small brick cottage has been run by the same family – the present helpful and friendly licensees are the third generation. It's all thoroughly traditional and sparkling clean, with its old red flooring tiles on the left, oak parquet on the right, built-in wall seats, studded red leatherette chairs, a few small tables, and a complete absence of music and machines. The atmosphere is very chatty and relaxed, there's a good mix of customers, and the Adnams Broadside, Hook Norton Best, and Morrells Varsity and Dark Mild on handpump are kept particularly well; they also have farm ciders and decent malt whiskies. Bar food is simple but all home-made, majoring on a wide choice of generous very reasonably priced sandwiches (from £1.70), as well as pasties (£3), ploughman's (from £3.50), and Buck's bite (a special home-made pizza-like dish £3.75); darts, shove-ha'penny, cribbage, dominoes. There are picnic tables and other tables in an attractive sheltered garden behind. The village is pretty, with an interesting church. *(Recommended by Paul Kitchener, J Waller, Ian Phillips, Frank Daugherty)*

Free house ~ Licensees Trevor and Carolyn How ~ Real ale ~ Snacks (not Sun) ~ (01494) 862571 ~ Open 11-2.30, 6-11

LONG CRENDON SP6808 Map 4

Angel

Bicester Rd (B4011)

Partly 17th-c, sensitively restored a decade or so ago and since gently refurbished, this friendly and civilised pub is spotless, warm in winter and pleasantly fresh in summer. It is perhaps more restaurant than pub in outlook, but has well kept Brakspears and Flowers IPA on handpump, capacious sofas in a comfortable and pleasantly decorated lounge, and sturdy tables and chairs in another area. Good generous bar food, served quickly despite using fresh ingredients, includes home-made soup (£3.50), filled french bread (from £5.50), smoked salmon and spring onion pasta or crispy duck and bacon salad with a plum dressing (£5.75), a platter of hot grilled provençal vegetables with a pesto dressing (£7.50), baked cod au poivre with a provençal sauce (£9.50), chicken breast stuffed with stilton wrapped in bacon or brochette of beef and lamb with a piquant sauce (£9.75), and lovely puddings such as sunken chocolate soufflé with amaretti prunes, banana and toffee meringue with butterscotch sauce or crème brûlée with fresh fruits (all £4.25). Fish daily specials are a particular strength, with deliveries three times a week, and they do generous Sunday roasts. There's a conservatory dining room at the back, looking out on the garden; young friendly staff; piped jazz. *(Recommended by Paul and Maggie Baker, Andy and Maureen Pickering, M Sargent, Deborah Jackson)*

Free house ~ Licensees Mark and Ruth Jones ~ Real ale ~ Meals and snacks (till 10pm) ~ Restaurant ~ (01844) 208268 ~ Well behaved children welcome ~ Open 12-3, 6-11 ~ Bedrooms: £47.50B/£61B

MARLOW SU8586 Map 2

Hare & Hounds ♀

Henley Rd (A4155 W)

This pretty and neatly kept ivy-clad cottage has carefully refurbished inter-connecting rooms and cosy corners with flowers on the tables, a log fire in the inglenook fireplace as well as two log-effect gas fires, comfortable armchairs, and a big no-smoking area. Under the new licensee food now includes soup (£2.05), filled french bread or filled baked potatoes (from £3.95), chicken and mushroom pie (£6.95), a vegetarian dish (£7.50), various pasta dishes (£7.95), lunchtime specials such as meatballs in spicy sauce or seafood mornay (from £6.95), and puddings like spotted dick or bread and butter pudding (from £2.25); the restaurant is no smoking. Well kept Brakspears, the local Rebellion Smuggler, and a guest beer, as well as good wines by the glass; darts, cribbage, dominoes, and piped music. There's a small garden. *(Recommended by GWB, T R and B C Jenkins, J S M Sheldon; more reports please)*

Whitbreads ~ Lease: Keith Travers ~ Real ale ~ Meals and snacks (till 10pm) ~ Restaurant ~ (01628) 483343 ~ Children welcome ~ Open 11-3, 5.30(6 Sat)-11

Two Brewers

St Peter Street; at double roundabout approaching bridge turn into Station Road, then first right

As well as a sheltered courtyard behind this quietly placed pub with lots of cocktail parasols, there are rustic seats and benches in front that give a glimpse of the Thames. The bustling T-shaped bar has low beams, shiny black woodwork, nautical pictures, gleaming brassware and a pleasant atmosphere. Bar food includes sandwiches (from £1.80), ploughman's (from £4.10), filled baked potatoes (£4.40), goujons of plaice (£6.20), chilli con carne (£6.80), daily specials such as liver and bacon, mushroom stroganoff or steak and kidney pie (from £6.50), and puddings (from £2.50); they serve breakfast from 9.30, lunch from midday, a tapas menu from 2pm, and evening meals. Well kept Brakspears Bitter, the local Rebellion IPA, and Wadworths 6X on handpump, and a good wine list. *(Recommended by Dr G W Barnett, Christine and Geoff Butler, Arnold and Maureen East)*

Whitbreads ~ Licensee Frederick Boxall ~ Real ale ~ Meals and snacks (all day) ~ Restaurant ~ (01628) 484140 ~ Children in eating area of bar and restaurant (no prams) ~ Open 11-11

MEDMENHAM SU8084 Map 2

Dog & Badger

A4155 Henley—Marlow

New licensees have taken over this 14th-c stone and brick timbered pub and apart from changing the menu, hope to keep the cosy, relaxed atmosphere unchanged. The long, busy low-beamed bar is comfortably modernised and neatly kept, with banquettes and stools around the tables, an open fire (as well as an illuminated oven), brasses, a crossbow on the ceiling, and soft lighting. Bar food includes home-made soup (£3.50), french bread with chips (£3.95), daily specials such as curries or stews (around £5.50), a large glorified ploughman's (£5.95), Friday night fish and chips (£6.25), seafood pasta (£6.50), home-made steak and kidney or chicken and ham pies (£6.95), sirloin steak (£9.95), Sunday roast (around £6.95), and proper old-fashioned puddings (£2.80). Well kept Brakspears PA and SB, Flowers Original and local Rebellion IPA on handpump, and an extensive wine list. *(Recommended by Susan and John Douglas, James Macrae, Leigh and Gillian Mellor, Roger and Valerie Hill)*

Whitbreads ~ Tenants Tony and Ann Dunn ~ Real ale ~ Meals and snacks (not Sun evening) ~ Restaurant ~ (01491) 571362 ~ Children in eating area of bar ~ Open 11-3, 5.30(6 Sat)-11

NORTHEND SU7392 Map 4

White Hart

On back road up escarpment from Watlington, past Christmas Common; or valley road off A4155 Henley—Marlow at Mill End, past Hambleden, Skirmett and Turville, then sharp left in Northend itself

In an area popular with walkers, this cosy little 16th-c pub has a charming summer garden full of flowers and fruit trees. Inside has been smartened up under the new licensees, though the quiet bar has good log fires (one in a vast fireplace), some panelling, very low handsomely carved oak beams, and comfortable window seats. Good home-made bar food now includes home-made soup (£3.25), warm salad with stilton, bacon and avocado (£4.75), pasta with mozzarella and a tomato and onion salad (£5.25), cumberland sausage with mash and onion gravy (£6.95), fresh salmon fillet with lime butter or king prawns (£7.50), lemon sole on a creamy spinach sauce (£7.65), various home-made pies, and half roast duck with orange or black cherry sauce (£9.50); fresh vegetables. Well kept Brakspears PA, SB, Old and Mild on handpump, and a fair choice of wines. *(Recommended by Dr G W Barnett, Cicely Taylor; more reports please)*

Brakspears ~ Tenants Derek and Susie Passey ~ Real ale ~ Meals and snacks (till 10pm Fri/Sat; not Sun or Mon evenings) ~ Restaurant ~ (01491) 638353 ~ Children in restaurant ~ Open 11.30-2.30, 5.30-11; all day summer Sat and Sun

nr PRINCES RISBOROUGH SP8003 Map 4

Red Lion

Upper Icknield Way, Whiteleaf; village signposted off A4010 towards Aylesbury; OS Sheet 165 map reference 817040

Tucked away down leafy lanes at the foot of the Chilterns, this friendly 17th-c pub has a pleasantly old-fashioned bar with an informal, chatty local atmosphere. There's a good log fire, antique winged settles, various sporting and coaching prints and pictures on the walls, and quite a collection of antiques which have taken on a nautical theme – including a ship's binnacle that came originally from an old warship. Good home-made bar food includes hot, spicy mushrooms (£2.50), filled french bread (from £1.80; steak and onion £3.25), steak and kidney or chicken, ham and leek pies (£5.50), lamb balti (£5.75), seafood pie (£5.95), chicken on a bed of spinach with stilton, bacon and pepper sauce (£7.95), puddings, popular winter theme evenings, and Sunday lunch. Well kept Brakspears PA, Hook Norton Best, Morlands PA and Wadworths 6X on handpump; dominoes, cribbage, several hand-crafted puzzles, and piped music. Outside there are tables in a small front lawn surrounded by colourful window boxes and hanging baskets, with more in a most attractive large back garden; the pub is close to Whiteleaf Fields (National Trust). *(Recommended by Joan and Andrew Life, Nigel Norman, Gladys Protheroe, Ian Phillips, Gwen and Peter Andrews, Gordon, Marjorie and David Lamb)*

Free house ~ Licensee Richard Howard ~ Real ale ~ Meals and snacks ~ Resaurant ~ (01844) 344476 ~ Children in restaurant ~ Open 11.30-3, 5-11; all day summer Sat and Sun ~ Bedrooms: £29.50B/£39.50B

SKIRMETT SU7790 Map 2

Old Crown 🍴

High St; from A4155 NE of Henley take Hambleden turn and keep on; or from B482 Stokenchurch—Marlow take Turville turn and keep on

Although it's the good food that draws people to this pretty early 18th-c dining pub (now completely no smoking), there's still some pubby atmosphere in the three beamed rooms. Of these, the small central room and larger one leading off have windsor chairs and tankards hanging from the beams, and the little no-smoking white-painted tap room has trestle tables and an old-fashioned settle; also, three open fires (two inglenooks) and over 700 bric-a-brac items, paintings, antiques, bottles and tools. Served by friendly staff, the food might include home-made soup (£3), deep-fried camembert and gooseberry conserve (£4.25), home-made stilton and walnut pâté (£4.20), home-made smoked fish terrine (£5), roast seasonal pheasant (£9), fresh seafood salad (£11), half roast barbary duck in a port and orange sauce (£12.95), and grilled sea bass (£14.25). Well kept Brakspears PA and SB are tapped from casks in a still room, and served though a hatch. A sheltered front terrace has flower tubs, and old oak casks as seats, and the pretty garden has picnic tables under cocktail parasols, and a fish pond. Note that children under 10 are not allowed.

There are two pub alsatians. *(Recommended by Gerald Barnett, John Barker, Mary and Des Kemp, Ian and Liz Phillips, Dr G W Barnett, Jack and Philip Paxton, Nigel Norman, Dan Hayter, TBB, Nigel Wilkinson, Wayne Brindle, Andy Thwaites, Susan and Alan Dominey, Roy and Pat Anstiss, Cyril S Brown, Karen and Graham Oddey)*

Brakspears ~ Tenants Peter and Liz Mumby ~ Real ale ~ Meals and snacks (not Sun evening except July-Sept and not Mon except bank hols) ~ Restaurant ~ (01491) 638435 ~ Open 11-2.30, 6-11; closed Mon except bank hols and Sun evenings except July-Sept

TURVILLE SU7690 Map 2

Bull & Butcher

Valley road off A4155 Henley—Marlow at Mill End, past Hambleden and Skirmett

Set amongst ancient cottages, this pretty black and white timbered pub has a comfortable and atmospheric low-ceilinged bar – partly divided into two areas – with beams from ships seized in the Spanish Armada, cushioned wall settles, and an old-fashioned high-backed settle by one log fire. Good, imaginative bar food includes home-smoked pastrami on rye bread (£4.50), steak and kidney pie (£6.75), balti curries (£7.45), and venison and wild boar mixed grill (£9.95). Well kept Brakspears PA, SB, Old, Mild and OBJ on handpump, and good house wines; efficient service. Darts, shove-ha'penny, dominoes, cribbage, and piped music. This is a fine place to finish a walk, and the attractive garden has tables on the lawn by fruit trees and a neatly umbrella-shaped hawthorn; good summer barbecues. Once a month (Tuesday evenings) the MG car club meet here. It does get crowded at weekends. *(Recommended by A L Ingram, P Goodchild, S Fazackerley, TBB, Dr G W Barnett, Cyril Brown, A Hill, Piotr Chodzko-Zajko, Jack and Philip Paxton, David Craine, Ann Reeder, Nigel Norman, Susan and Alan Dominey)*

Brakspears ~ Tenant Nicholas Abbott ~ Real ale ~ Meals and snacks ~ (01491) 638283 ~ Children in eating area of bar ~ Open 11-3, 6-11

WADDESDON SP7417 Map 4

Five Arrows 🛏 🍷 🍺

A41 NW of Aylesbury

The neat bar in this rather grand small hotel (owned by Lord Rothschild) is an open-plan series of light and airy high-ceilinged rooms with a relaxed but civilised atmosphere. There are family portrait engravings and lots of old estate-worker photographs on the leafy green wallpaper, heavy dark green velvet curtains on wooden rails, mainly sturdy cushioned settles and good solid tables on parquet flooring (though one room has comfortably worn-in armchairs and settees), and copies of *Country Life* in an antique magazine rack. The bar counter is a handsome affair, carved with the five arrows of the Rothschild crest which symbolise the dispersal of the five founding sons of the international banking business. The regular bar menu includes staples such as sandwiches (from £2.95), burgers (£3.95) and salads like home-cooked ham or grilled goat's cheese (from £4.75), but the highlights tend to be found among the wide choice of daily-changing specials: carrot, coriander and cider soup (£3.95), brandied chicken liver parfait with an orange confit (£4.70), Greek char-grilled chicken breast with a yoghurt, cucumber and garlic relish (£7.95), cajun blackened salmon with a remoulade sauce (£8.25), baked cod with a herb crust (£8.50), fillet steak with red shallot butter (£14), and good home-made puddings (£3.95). The restaurant is no smoking. The formidable wine list naturally runs to Rothschild first-growth clarets as well as less well known Rothschild estate wines such as Los Vascos Chilean cabernet sauvignon. Well kept real ales – Chiltern Beechwood, Fullers London Pride and an unusual guest such as Archers Old Cobleigh on handpump; other drinks including many malt whiskies are exemplary. Friendly efficient service, unobtrusive piped music. The sheltered back garden has attractively grouped wood and metal furnishings, with some weekend and bank holiday barbecues. *(Recommended by Gwen and Peter Andrews, Ian Phillips, D and J McMillan Susan and John Douglas, Graham and Karen Oddey, John and Phyllis Maloney, John and Christine Lowe, A McEwen, Iain McBride, JM, PM, Jennie Munro, Jim Wingate)*

Free house ~ Licensees Julian Alexander-Worster, Fabia Bromovsky ~ Real ale ~ Meals and snacks ~ Restaurant ~ (01296) 651727 ~ Children welcome ~ Open 11.30-3, 6-11 ~ Bedrooms:£50B/£65B

WEST WYCOMBE SU8394 Map 4

George & Dragon

High St; A40 W of High Wycombe

With lots of walks all around, this striking 15th-c building does get crowded at weekends, so it's best to get there early then. The comfortable and rambling main bar, cheerfully refurbished, has massive beams, sloping walls, and a big log fire, and the magnificent oak staircase is said to be haunted by a wronged girl. The children's area is no smoking. Popular, promptly served bar food includes home-made soup (£1.85), lunchtime ploughman's (from £3.45) and sandwiches (£4.25; toasties from £1.85), potted stilton (£3.95), vegetable korma (£5.35), very good home-made pies like sweet lamb or game (from £5.75), pigeon pudding (£5.95), chicken boursin (£6.25), grilled halibut steak with smoked salmon butter (£7.55), daily specials, and home-made puddings (from £2.25). Courage Best and Directors and two guests like Gales HSB or Ushers Founders on handpump, and quite a few malt whiskies; cribbage. The arched and cobbled coach entry leads to a spacious, peaceful garden with picnic tables, a climbing frame and slides. Nearby you can visit West Wycombe Park with its fine furnishings and classical landscaped grounds. *(Recommended by Dave Braisted, Dr G W Barnett, Nigel Norman, Neville and Sarah Hargreaves, Wayne Brindle, Simon Collett-Jones, Susan and John Douglas, James Macrae, TBB, Bob and Maggie Atherton, Tony Dickinson, Piotr Chodzko-Zajko)*

Courage ~ Lease: Philip Todd ~ Real ale ~ Meals and snacks (12-2, 6-9.30) ~ (01494) 464414 ~ Children in room set aside for them ~ Open 11-2.30, 5.30-11; 11-11 Sat ~ Bedrooms: £48B/£58B

WOOBURN COMMON SU9187 Map 2

Chequers 🛏

2 miles from M40 junction 2; A355 towards Slough, first right, then right again; Kiln Lane, Widmoor – OS Sheet 175 map reference 910870

The low-beamed partly stripped-brick bar has developed a cheerful traditional atmosphere, with lived-in sofas on its bare boards, a bright log-effect gas fire, standing timbers and alcoves to break it up, and various pictures, plates and tankards; piped music. The bar undoubtedly gets a lot of its custom from the flourishing hotel and restaurant side, but is none the worse for that. There's a tasteful dining room on the left, with good often imaginative bar food that changes twice daily such as soup (£2.35), sandwiches (from £3.25), ploughman's (£4.75), home-made burger (£6.50), strips of chicken with a Thai sauce (£7.25), venison sausages in an onion sauce (£7.50), monkfish and scallops in garlic butter (£9.35), and a platter of smoked fish (£9.50). Well kept Fullers London Pride, Marstons Pedigree, and Timothy Taylors Landlord on handpump, and champagne by the glass; spacious garden away from the road, with cast-iron tables. The attractive stripped-pine bedrooms are in a 20th-c mock-Tudor wing; breakfasts are good. *(Recommended by Mrs Lindsay Healey, Ian and Liz Phillips, Mark Percy, Stephen N Whiteley, Wayne Brindle)*

Free house ~ Licensee Peter Roehrig ~ Real ale ~ Meals and snacks ~ Restaurant ~ (01628) 529575 ~ Children welcome ~ Open 11-11; 12-10.30 Sun ~ Bedrooms: £77.50B/£82.50B

Lucky Dip

Besides the fully inspected pubs, you might like to try these Lucky Dips recommended to us and described by readers (if you do, please send us reports):

☆ **Adstock** [Main St (off A413); SP7330], *Old Thatched Inn*: Beamed and flagstoned pub/restaurant comfortably done up with cosy corners and open fires; generous interesting food inc good snacks, well kept mainly Courage-related ales with guests such as Hook Norton Best, friendly efficient service; piped music; seats out in pleasant back arbour, children in restaurant and eating area *(B J P Edwards, Pat and Derek Westcott, Dr and Mrs A K Clarke, John Fahy, Chris Raisin, Marjorie and David Lamb, Nigel Norman, Roger and Valerie Hill, Karen and Graham Oddey, LYM)*

☆ *nr* **Adstock** [Verney Junction, Addington; SP7327], *Verney Arms*: Now closed

☆ **Akeley** [The Square, just off A413; SP7037], *Bull & Butcher*: Genuine village pub, individualistic landlord, very good value lunchtime buffet (maybe only cold food; not Sun) inc wide range of help-yourself salads, several puddings, also evening steak bar (not Sun or Mon); three good fires in long open-plan beamed bar with red plush banquettes, well kept Fullers London Pride, Marstons Pedigree, Morlands Original and a guest beer, decent house wines, winter spiced wine, traditional games; children allowed in eating area, tables in attractive garden with notable flowerbeds and hanging baskets, occasional live entertainment; handy for Stowe Gardens *(Steve Goodchild, M Sargent, Ann Griffiths, LYM)*

☆ **Amersham** [High St, Old Town (A413); SU9597], *Kings Arms*: Picture-postcard timbered building in charming street, lots of heavy beams and snug alcoves, big inglenook, high-backed antique settles and other quaint old furnishings among more standard stuff; low-priced bar food inc vegetarian, restaurant, pleasant service, well kept Tetleys-related and other ales, children in eating area; open all day, rather a young person's pub evening; nice garden *(SR, PM, LYM)*

☆ **Amersham** [High St], *Eagle*: Friendly low-beamed old town pub, wide choice of good straightforward lunchtime food (not Sun) from sandwiches up inc good fish fresh daily (get there early or book); friendly efficient service, Tetleys-related and guest ales, log fire, maybe soft piped music, fruit machine; more lively young person's pub evenings *(Ken and Jenny Simmonds, GWB)*

Amersham [High St], *Elephant & Castle*: Low beams, china, velvet and brasses in popular food pub with fine U-shaped bar counter, several Whitbreads-related ales; maybe piped music *(James Nunns, LYM)*

Aston Clinton [SP8712], *Bell*: More restaurant than pub, comfortable and smart with nice atmosphere, short choice of good interesting food (very good choice of English farmhouse cheeses), well chosen wines; a comfortable place to stay *(C and M Starling)*; [30 Green End St], *Partridge Arms*: Generous fresh food

at surprisingly low prices, good service, no music *(J A Gardner)*

☆ **Astwood** [off A422; SP9547], *Old Swan*: Attractive, clean, airy and spacious, with well kept Courage-related and guest ales, wine or port by the jug, good bar food esp pies, warm cosy atmosphere; side garden bar *(Mr and Mrs J Brown, Nigel Norman, LYM)*

Aylesbury [Kingsbury Sq (A505); SP8213], *Hobgoblin*: Interesting choice of well kept Wychwood and other real ales, good value snacks, bare boards and church pews and chairs among other wooden furniture, old beer ads, big old fireplace; evenings is very much a young person's pub with loud music, pool, TVs and games machines; live jazz Sun, weekend discos *(JJW, CMW, J Draper)*

☆ *nr* **Aylesbury** [Gibraltar; A418 some miles towards Thame, beyond Stone – OS Sheet 165 map ref 758108], *Bottle & Glass*: Hospitable low-beamed thatched pub, tiled floor, rambling layout, wide choice of good imaginative food, lively atmosphere, well kept Tetleys and Wadworths 6X tapped from the cask, neat garden *(Gordon, George Atkinson, Tim and Ann Newell, LYM)*

☆ **Beaconsfield** [41 Aylesbury End, a mile from M40 junction 2; SU9490], *Old Hare*: Relaxed and civilised dim-lit pub with old-fashioned touches, usual bar food (not Sun evening) inc good fresh fish, well kept Tetleys-related and guest ales, lots of malt whiskies, decent house wines, and good strong coffee, cheerful staff (service can slow when busy), no machines or music; children in eating area, big sunny back garden; open all day *(Gordon, TBB, Simon Collett-Jones, Ian Phillips, N M Baleham, Steve Goodchild, A W Dickinson, Roger and Valerie Hill, LYM)*

☆ **Bellingdon** [about 1½ miles NW of Chesham; SP9405], *Bull*: Concentration on good food – more meals than snacks – in friendly and pleasantly furnished pub with five real ales, decent wines by the glass, keen service; no piped music or machines *(PS, Diana Bishop, R C Hopton, LYM)*

Bennett End [Radnage; SP7897], *Three Horseshoes*: Old beamed pub in pretty countryside, good traditional English food as well as Chinese and Indian dishes *(GWB)*

Bishopstone [Marsh Rd; SP8010], *Harrow*: Country local very much enjoyed by enthusiastic regulars, for food in bar and restaurant, Bass and Flowers IPA, well kept gardens with barbecues *(Anon)*

Bletchley [2 Shenley Rd; SP8733], *Shenley*: Old pub, open all day, with Courage Directors, Ind Coope Burton and Tetleys, restaurant, conservatory, garden/patio, piped music, pool, TV, fruit machine; bedrooms *(CMW, JJW)*

☆ **Botley** [Tylers Hill Rd; narrow lane opp Hen & Chickens; SP9702], *Five Bells*: Friendly, quiet and cosy country local, well off the beaten track and popular with walkers;

inglenook fireplaces, good range of well kept Brakspears and other ales, generous heartening home-made food (not Mon evening, not Sun; kitchen closes at 8 some nights) inc cheap filled rolls, good service, tables outside; well behaved children welcome *(Jan and Colin Roe, Gordon, LYM)*

☆ **Bryants Bottom** [4 miles N of High Wycombe, via Hughenden Valley off A4128; SU8599], *Gate*: Country pub with rather formal beamed plush-seated lounge spreading back from traditional little tiled front bar, very well prepared inexpensive food, well kept ales such as Bass, Greene King Abbot, Morlands Old Speckled Hen and Wadworths 6X, deep fireplace, no piped music, tables in safely fenced garden with cockatiels and play area; popular with walkers and cyclists *(Nigel Norman, Ian Phillips, BB)*

Butlers Cross [Chalkshire Rd; SP8406], *Russell Arms*: Well prepared interesting good value menu, friendly relaxed service *(B Hillyard, Mrs Y Goodwin)*

☆ **Cadmore End** [B482 towards Stokenchurch; SU7892], *Blue Flag*: Wide choice of good value interesting generous food in old-fashioned beamed pub attached to small modern hotel, lots of proper big dining tables; well kept changing real ales, decent wines, good atmosphere, expert unobtrusive service, fascinating vintage MG pictures in side room; attractive little restaurant; bedrooms *(GWB, BB)*

Cadsden [Lower Cadsden; on Ridgeway Path – OS Sheet 165 map ref 826045; SP8204], *Plough*: Friendly pub ideal for Chilterns rambles, good food, Theakstons beers; mind the boots in the entrance *(Dave Braisted)*

Chalfont St Giles [Amersham Rd; SU9893], *Ivy House*: Free house currently doing well, well kept Brakspears, Fullers Mr Harry and Ushers, good range of food from soups and ploughman's to full meals, pleasant welcoming bar staff, coal-effect gas fire; piped pop music may obtrude *(P J Keen, Geoff Abbott, DJW)*; [Deanway], *White Hart*: Friendly licensees and staff, good atmosphere, wholesome food in generous helpings, lovely puddings, big garden; bedrooms in barn at the back *(Abigail Ingram, Paul Goodchild)*

☆ **Chalfont St Peter** [High St; SU9990], *Greyhound*: Spacious yet sometimes crowded traditional beamed bar with usefully long serving counter, well kept Courage-related and guest ales, good value food inc good soups, friendly staff, comfortable separate partly no-smoking restaurant; open all day; bedrooms *(Jan and Colin Roe, Gordon, LYM)*

☆ **Chearsley** [SP7110], *Bell*: Charming old thatched pub on village green, single pleasant bar (locals one end, tables the other), friendly welcome from hard-working licensees, wide choice of good home-made food from sandwiches up, well kept Fullers Chiswick and London Pride, good coffee, summer weekend barbecues in sizeable garden; children and dogs welcome *(John Waller, Roger and Penny Gudge, Mr and Mrs D Johnson, Mark Gillis)*

Cheddington [Station Rd; by stn, about a mile

from village; SP9218], *Rosebery Arms*: Comfortable sofas by roaring log fire, pubbier seats by servery, old photographs on panelled walls, smart restaurant with no-smoking area; good food from sandwiches to imaginative main courses, Charles Wells and guest ales, friendly service; maybe piped music; well spaced picnic tables on back lawn with play equipment and wendy house *(Mel Smith, Shirley Cannings)*

Chenies [TQ0198], *Royal Oak*: Nice relaxed atmosphere, simple decor, good range of beers, interesting food; parking may be a bit of a problem *(Jane Kingsbury)*

☆ **Chesham** [Church St/Wey Lane; SP9501], *Queens Head*: Consistently friendly and increasingly food-oriented, with generous helpings of well cooked good value food (good fish and chips Thurs/Fri); well kept Brakspears PA, SB and Old and Fullers London Pride, small and cosy, with tidy locals' back bar, sparkling brass, interesting pictures and paraphernalia, two coal fires, scrubbed tables; tables in small courtyard; next to River Chess, can be very busy *(Jan and Colin Roe, DJW)*

☆ **nr Chesham** [Chesham Vale – back rd to Hawridge, Berkhamsted and Tring, off A416 as you leave centre], *Black Horse*: Unfailingly welcoming efficient service and big helpings of good value food inc lots of unusual home-made pies and sausages in quietly set and neatly extended country pub with black beams and joists, book-lined converted barn; well kept Tetleys-related and guest ales, lots of well spaced tables out on back grass *(Bill Capper, Paul Coleman, LYM)*

☆ **Chicheley** [A422, quite handy for M1 junction 14; SP9045], *Chester Arms*: Wide choice of generous tasty home-made bar food from sandwiches up inc vegetarian dishes and children's helpings in cosy and pretty two-bar beamed pub with log fire, comfortable settles and chairs, friendly service, Greene King Abbot, darts, fruit machine, quiet piped music; sizeable evening restaurant, picnic tables in garden *(Arnold and Maureen East)*

Colnbrook [High St; nr M4 junction 5; TQ0277], *Olde George*: Very old coaching inn, lots of photographs of old Colnbrook, decent food esp home-made pies (veg cost extra with them), Courage-related ales, friendly atmosphere; upstairs restaurant *(Paul Kitchener)*

Cublington [High St; SP8322], *Unicorn*: Friendly 16th-c pub, supposedly haunted, very old beams, rickshaw, pictures and pine furniture, five changing real ales, very good value food (not Sun evening) inc vegetarian and vegan, picnic tables in garden behind; service can slow *(CMW, JJW)*

Cuddington [Upper Church St; village signed off A418 Thame—Aylesbury; SP7311], *Annie Baileys*: Quiet village pub with big inglenook in discreetly chintzy small lounge, well kept real ales, wide choice of food from snacks to restauranty dishes; piped music, garden with play area *(Shobi, BB)*

☆ **Denham** [¾ mile from M40 junction 1; follow Denham Village signs; TQ0486], *Swan*: Pretty pub in lovely village, quiet midweek lunchtime but pleasant busy atmosphere weekends, with helpful staff, real ales, wide choice of decent straightforward bar food inc good value Sun roast, comfortable seats, open fires, evening candlelight; big floodlit garden behind with play house *(Bob and Maggie Atherton, GWB, Steve Goodchild, Helen Hazzard, LYM)*

☆ **Dorney** [Village Rd; SU9278], *Palmer Arms*: Friendly renovated village pub with wide choice of consistently good food, decent wine list, interesting well kept ales, friendly young staff; plenty of tables in pleasant garden behind *(Simon Collett-Jones, Nigel Norman)*

Dorney [Lake End Rd; off A4 Maidenhead—Cippenham by Sainsburys], *Pineapple*: Old-fashioned rooms with panelling, gleaming bar, simple furniture, wide choice of usual food from sandwiches up, well kept Tetleys-related ales, decent house wine; pleasant open garden, handy for Bressingham Gardens plant centre *(Mark Percy, John Waller)*

Farnham Common [The Broadway (A355); SU9684], *Foresters Arms*: Welcoming landlord and locals in relaxed and civilised two-room dining pub with woodblock floor and panelling, good food, well kept Bass, Fullers and Highgate Mild at a price, two log fires *(Simon Collett-Jones, Dave Uhrich)*; [Collins Wood Rd (A355 a mile S of M40 junction 2)], *Yew Tree*: Well kept ales inc Morlands Old Speckled Hen, good choice of whiskies, friendly atmosphere, darts; really good traditional cooking by landlord (steak and kidney pie, game etc), separate dining room, reasonable prices, log fire in each small room; good value breakfasts from 8am (not Sun); Burnham Beeches within an easy walk *(Dr Jack A Frisch, Nigel Quilter, Dave Uhrich)*

☆ **Farnham Royal** [Blackpond Lane; SU9583], *Emperor of India*: Small pleasant open-plan pub, front so entwined with vines that you have to duck to get in; wide range of interesting food from good choice of sandwiches and baguettes to creole baked crab and honey-roast duck, six or seven Whitbreads-related and guest ales, friendly licensees, well kept garden and barn for summer eating *(Ian Phillips)*

☆ **Fingest** [signed off B482 Marlow—Stokenchurch; SU7791], *Chequers*: Pleasant old-fashioned atmosphere in Tudor pub's several rooms, decor to match, sunny lounge by charming country garden, small no-smoking room, Brakspears PA, SB and Old, popular food from sandwiches to steaks (not Sun evening), romantic restaurant, dominoes, cribbage, backgammon; children in eating area; interesting church opposite, good walks *(S Fazackerly, C Rowan, TBB, S and A Dominey, A Hill, Nigel Norman, GWB, L and G Mellor, J and P Paxton, LYM)*

☆ **Flackwell Heath** [3½ miles from M40 junction 4; A404 towards High Wycombe, 1st right to Flackwell Heath, right into Sheepridge Lane; SU8988], *Crooked Billet*: Old-fashioned 16th-c pub in lovely country setting, pleasant garden with quiet views, good value food, real ale *(Colin Dear, BB)*

☆ **Frieth** [signed off B482 in Lane End], *Yew Tree*: Short but interesting if not cheap choice of well cooked food in civilised candlelit dining pub, well kept real ales such as Brakspears PA, Fullers London Pride and Gibbs Mew Bishops Tipple, pleasant professional service; unobtrusive piped music; walkers with dogs welcome *(Simon Collett-Jones, Heather Couper, Peter Saville, Cyril S Brown, Beryl and Terry Bryan, TBB, GWB, Nigel Peterson, LYM)*

Gayhurst [SP8446], *Sir Francis Drake*: This interestingly Gothick pub has closed, with plans for a private house *(LYM)*

☆ **Great Brickhill** [Ivy Lane; SP9030], *Old Red Lion*: Back lawn with fabulous view over Buckinghamshire and beyond, pub itself (not that big) given over largely to tables for food (not winter Sun eves) from well filled crusty rolls to steaks and Sun roasts; decent house wines, well kept Whitbreads-related ales, maybe unobtrusive piped music; children in eating area *(John Hazel, Roger and Valerie Hill, LYM)*

☆ **Great Horwood** [The Green, off B4033 N of Winslow; SP7731], *Crown*: Attractive two-room Georgian pub doing well under welcoming new tenants, small but frequently changing choice of reasonably priced food all home-made from fresh ingredients, well kept Flowers IPA and Whitbreads Castle Eden and Fuggles, very friendly springer spaniel, attractive front garden and back courtyard *(Graham and Karen Oddey)*

Great Horwood, *Swan*: Front lounge with inglenook fires and dining area, small back bar with pool, games machines and juke box, very wide choice of well prepared straightforward food using good ingredients, particularly well kept ales such as Bass, Greene King IPA, Theakstons Old Peculier and Websters Yorkshire; side garden *(Graham and Karen Oddey, B and K Hypher)*

☆ **Great Kimble** [Risborough Rd (A4010); SP8206], *Bernard Arms*: Plush and popular upmarket pub (where John Major took Boris Yeltsin) with some nice prints, daily papers, good imaginative bar food, four changing Tetleys-related and other ales, decent wines, good range of malt whiskies and bottled beer, good coffee, games room, well kept gardens, interesting food in restaurant; well equipped bedrooms *(Mr and Mrs P W Reeve, Dave Braisted, P Saville)*

☆ **Great Linford** [4½ miles from M1, junction 14; from Newport Pagnell take Wolverton Rd towards Stony Stratford; SP8542], *Black Horse*: Large rambling pub with good range of good value food, well kept Tetleys-related and guest beers, Addlestone's cider, friendly staff, open fire, upstairs restaurant, fresh flowers; just below Grand Union Canal – drinks can be taken out on the towpath (good walks along here), and sizeable lawn with well spaced picnic tables and biggish play area; children allowed away from bar; evenings piped music, games machines and exuberant local youth may be more prominent *(John Fahy, Joe Hill, JJW, CMW, LYM)*

☆ **Great Missenden** [London Rd; old London rd, E – beyond Abbey; SP8901], *Nags Head*: Emphasis on quick straightforward food from sandwiches to good steaks in cosy creeper-covered small pub with well kept Tetleys-related and guest beers, big log fire, no piped music, picnic tables on back lawn *(M J Dowdy)*

☆ **Haddenham** [Church End; SP7408], *Green Dragon*: Spacious pleasantly decorated 17th-c restaurant pub, good food (esp puddings) and service, well chosen wines, well kept real ales, friendly relaxed atmosphere, log fire; tables in quiet walled garden, nr village green and duck pond *(Jan and Colin Roe)*

Hanslope [Castlethorpe Rd; SP8046], *Watts Arms*: Friendly pub with lounge, dining area, public bar with pool and fruit machine; good value food inc takeaways, Charles Wells Eagle and Morlands Old Speckled Hen on handpump; children welcome away from bar, play area in garden *(JJW, CMW)*

☆ **Hawridge** [The Vale; signed from A416 N of Chesham – OS Sheet 165 map ref 960050; SP9505], *Rose & Crown*: Spaciously refurbished open-plan beamed bar with good value straightforward bar food, friendly helpful staff, big log fire, peaceful country views from restaurant area, broad terrace with lawn dropping down beyond, play area; children allowed *(Peter Saville, Jan and Colin Roe, Cyril S Brown, LYM)*

☆ **Hawridge Common** [off A416 N of Chesham; then towards Cholesbury; SP9505], *Full Moon*: Welcoming little country local with snugly comfortable low-beamed rambling bar and spacious common-edge lawn, good friendly service by cheerful young staff, good choice of reasonably priced food, wide choice of changing well kept real ales; children and dogs welcome *(Mark Belcher, LYM)*

☆ **Hedgerley** [SE of M40 junction 2; SU9686], *White Horse*: Welcoming traditional country local with particularly well kept Charles Wells Eagle, Greene King IPA and six unusual changing ales tapped from the cask, very friendly service; relaxed atmosphere in charming small public bar, jugs hanging from beams, open fire, larger lounge with rather intrusive food display unit (usual decent food inc good lunchtime sandwiches; Christmas meals worth booking), occasional barbecues in big pleasant back garden, lovely window boxes, occasional beer festivals; no children, can be very busy; old attractive village, good walks nearby *(Simon Collett-Jones, Richard Houghton, Mark Wilson, Peter Whitehead, Guy Gorton, Helen Hazzard, Nick and Alison Dowson)*

Hedgerley [One Pin Lane, towards Gerrards X; OS Sheet 175 map ref 968863], *One Pin*: Unchanging family-run pub with friendly local atmosphere, Courage-related ales, log fires, decent straightforward food and well kept garden *(Jill Bickerton, GWB)*

High Wycombe [Amersham Rd; Terriers; SU8792], *Beech Tree*: Well kept Courage Best and Directors and Wadworths 6X, cheerful staff even when busy; well equipped children's play area *(A W Dickinson, GWB)*

Hyde Heath [Hyde Heath Rd; village

signposted off B485 Great Missenden—Chesham; SU9399], *Plough*: Prettily placed, with nicely presented reasonably priced food (not Sun evening or Mon) in single chatty bar, well kept Tetleys-related ales, open fires *(Jan and Colin Roe, LYM)*

☆ **Ickford** [E of Thame; SP6407], *Rising Sun*: Pleasant and cosy low-beamed bar in pretty thatched local, reasonably priced hot and cold buffet, over-55s and under-10s discount, admirable starters, separate dining room; well kept ales maybe inc Hancocks HB, decent wine, fresh flowers, woodburner *(A Y Drummond, Gordon)*

☆ **Iver** [TQ0381], *Gurkha*: Gurkha paintings and trophies in pleasant bar, spacious yet cosy and individual; good choice of plain well presented home cooking, wide choice in big restaurant, good service, nice staff *(Nick Holmes)*

Iver [Thorney Lane N], *Fox & Pheasant*: Lively two-bar local with pool, pinball, entertainment most nights, decent food, several guest beers, friendly staff; garden with good play area inc climbing frames, slides, maybe bouncy castle *(Phil Bicknell, Alan Norris)*; [High St], *Swan*: Friendly cottagey two-bar local with wide choice of non-chips bar food, sizeable restaurant, good range of real ales; piped music *(Helen Hazzard, Paul Griffin)*

Iver Heath [Slough rd; TQ0282], *Black Horse*: Attractive inside and out, two-part bar with eating area, good cheerful mix of customers, pleasant service, five real ales, mostly from smaller brewers; conservatory, garden *(Chris and Martin Taylor)*

Kingswood [A41; SP6919], *Crooked Billet*: Pleasantly rambling dining pub, wide and interesting choice of well cooked food under new landlord and chef, Bass and Tetleys-related ales, efficient service, piped classical music; can be busy, and they may not let you use restaurant tables for bar food even if there's no other room to sit down; tables outside, handy for Waddesdon Manor *(George Atkinson, Marjorie and David Lamb, Tim and Ann Newell)*

☆ **Lacey Green** [SP8201], *Whip*: Good range of reliably good bar food inc good lunchtime sandwiches and Sun lunches, well kept beer, welcoming landlord, jolly atmosphere; small restaurant area normally full, garden and terrace *(GWB, Nigel Pritchard, Alison Haines)*

Lane End [SU7991], *Osborne Arms*: Attractive pub, good food, well kept local Marlow Rebellion *(Chris and Andy Crow)*

Lavendon [High St; A428 Bedford—Northampton; SP9153], *Green Man*: Memorable generous puddings and other good value food, tables under cocktail parasols on lovely flower-filled terrace sheltered by pub's stone walls *(Meg and Colin Hamilton)*; [High St], *Horseshoe*: Comfortable village pub bright with hanging baskets and flower tubs, good meals, pleasant decor and service, well kept Badger and Charles Wells Eagle *(Andy and Jill Kassube, Meg and Colin Hamilton)*

Ledburn [off B488 Ivinghoe—Leighton

Buzzard, S of Linslade; SP9021], *Hare & Hounds*: Big country-style bar and adjoining restaurant overlooking garden, wide range of cooked dishes, also ploughman's, baked potatoes etc, Courage-related and guest beers *(Jan and Colin Roe)*

☆ Ley Hill [signed off A416 in Chesham; SP9802], *Swan*: Cosily old-fashioned with snugs and alcoves, heavy black beams and timbers, popular lunchtime bar food from sandwiches up, thoughtful children's menu, no-smoking evening restaurant, well kept Tetleys-related and guest ales; piped music; picnic tables outside with play area, lovely setting by green; children in eating area, open all day at least in summer *(J Sheldon, BKA, David R Shillitoe, Gordon, Dr Jim Craig-Gray, Roger and Valerie Hill, LYM)*

☆ Little Kingshill [Hare La; SU8999], *Full Moon*: Picturesque hidden-away pub with big helpings of reasonably priced food, changing real ales, friendly service, well kept attractive garden *(Dave Carter)*

☆ Little Marlow [Sheepridge Lane; off A4155 at Well End about two miles E of Marlow; SU8786], *Crooked Billet*: Cosy and comfortable low-beamed pub with good choice of lunchtime food (not Sun), separate eating area, friendly efficient service, well kept Brakspears and Whitbreads-related ales, lovely little flower-filled front garden, pleasant views *(Richard Houghton)*

☆ Little Marlow [Church Rd; off A4155 about two miles E of Marlow, pub signed off main rd], *Kings Head*: Flower-covered old free house, warm and clean after open-plan refurbishment, popular reasonably priced bar food promptly served, Whitbreads-related and other ales such as Fullers London Pride *(Simon Collett-Jones, Richard Houghton, GWB, Jenny Garrett, TBB)*

☆ Little Missenden [SU9298], *Red Lion*: Pleasant and popular 15th-c village pub with Tetleys-related and other real ales, decent wines, good value traditional food from sandwiches to robust main courses, sunny garden with pets' corner for children – trout and ducks in the river to feed too *(Paul Kitchener, Peter Watts)*

☆ Little Tingewick [Mere Lane – off A421/B4031 SW of Buckingham; SP6432], *Red Lion*: 16th-c thatched pub with big divided bar and small dining area, well kept Fullers beers, wide choice of good home-made bar food inc vegetarian, magnificent sausage, egg and chips. Jovial Irish landlord and hospitable staff, pleasant piped music; no-smoking area, family garden. *(Jeff Davies, Michael O'Connor Clarke)*

☆ Littleworth Common [Common Lane; 3 miles from M40 junction 2, off A355 towards village then left after Jolly Woodman; SU9487], *Blackwood Arms*: The star landlord here, who earned fame by stocking more than 1,000 different real ales a year, has left, but this friendly pub still has a good bustling family atmosphere, simple food, a roaring log fire and tables outside, and is handy for walkers *(LYM; reports on new regime please)*
Littleworth Common [Littleworth rd; 2 miles

from M40 junction 2, off A355], *Jolly Woodman*: Big busy Whitbreads pub on the edge of Burnham Beeches, beamed and cottagey, wide range of food, usual Whitbreads-related beers, quick pleasant service *(Mr and Mrs R A Bryan, Paul Forbes, LYM)*

☆ Little Crendon [Bicester Rd (B4011); SP6808], *Chandos Arms*: Handsome thatched pub with pleasant low-beamed communicating bars, tasty well presented food, Whitbreads-related and other ales, log fire, lots of brass and copper, friendly efficient service *(Andy and Maureen Pickering)*

☆ Lower Hartwell [Oxford Rd (A418); SP7913], *Bugle Horn*: Lovely rambling 17th-c pub, civilised and comfortable yet unspoilt, with polite friendly service, wide choice of food in bar and restaurant, good range of real ales, big garden *(Gordon, Dr and Mrs A K Clarke)*

☆ Ludgershall [off A41 Aylesbury—Bicester; SP6617], *Bull & Butcher*: Friendly new licensees in quiet little beamed country pub with good range of meals inc home-made pies but no sandwiches in bar or back dining room (where children allowed), Butcombe and Tetleys ales, unobtrusive piped music, front lawn facing green; plans for expansion *(Paul Kitchener, Marjorie and David Lamb)*

☆ Maids Moreton [SP7035], *Wheatsheaf*: Little cosy rooms in small hidden-away thatched local with cosy beamed original part, good food inc interesting specials and superb steaks cooked by landlord and served mainly in quaint home-built conservatory with woodburner, Whitbreads-related and other ales, friendly service, small enclosed garden; piped music, opens noon *(Keith and Gill Croxton, George Atkinson)*
Marlow [High St; SU8586], *Chequers*: Attractive Brakspears pub with heavily beamed cosy front bars, good range of well cooked and presented food from basic fish and chips to more exotic and expensive choices in bright and pleasant restaurant area, friendly service, homely tables on pavement; shame about the piped music; bedrooms; children welcome *(M J B Pearson, Gordon)*; [Quoiting Sq, Oxford Rd], *Clayton Arms*: Newly refurbished but still simple and unspoilt, with good basic lunchtime bar food, well kept Brakspears, no music *(TBB, Pete Baker)*; [West St (A4155 towards Henley)], *Ship*: Lots of interesting warship photographs and nautical equipment in low-beamed town local's small side-by-side bars, straightforward bar lunches from sandwiches upwards, well kept Whitbreads-related ales, good friendly service, piped music, tables on pleasant little back terrace, evening restaurant (children allowed here) *(TBB, LYM)*

☆ Marsh Gibbon [back rd about 4 miles E of Bicester, pub SW of village; SP6423], *Greyhound*: Unusual combination of traditional furnishings (stripped beams and stonework) with good Thai food, half-price for children (no under-6s), in bar and two-room restaurant with oriental statuary; Fullers London Pride, Greene King Abbot and IPA, Hook Norton Best, and McEwans 80/-, handsome woodburner, dominoes, cribbage, and classical piped music, tables outside with play area *(D and J McMillan, Ian Phillips, Paul and Maggie Baker, M A and C R Starling, H O Dickinson, JJW, CMW, Karen and Graham Oddey, Ken and Jenny Simmonds, Gordon, LYM; more reports on atmosphere please)*

☆ Marsworth [Vicarage Rd; village signed off B489 Dunstable—Aylesbury; SP9214], *Red Lion*: Friendly low-beamed partly thatched village pub with well kept ales such as Bass, Hook Norton Best and Wadworths 6X, decent wines, interesting good value food inc good vegetarian dishes, quiet lounge with two open fires, steps up to snug parlour and lively games area; sheltered garden, provision for children; not far from impressive flight of canal locks *(Sidney and Erna Wells, Lynda Payton, Sam Samuells, LYM)*

☆ Marsworth [Startops End (B489)], *White Lion*: Comfortably plush modernised pub notable for position by Grand Union Canal (pleasant walk from Red Lion), nicely planted garden with lily pond, terrace with picnic tables; dining bar, small restaurant, well kept Greene King and guest ales, efficient polite service, good-sized children's room, unobtrusive piped music *(Mel Smith, Shirley Cannings)*

☆ Mentmore [SP9119], *Stag*: Small civilised lounge bar with low oak tables, attractive fresh flower arrangements, open fire; restaurant and public bar leading off; good value well presented bar food from sandwiches to main dishes, with wider evening choice; well kept Charles Wells Eagle, polite well dressed staff, charming sloping garden *(Maysie Thompson, BB)*

☆ Milton Keynes [Broughton Rd, Old Village; SP8938], *Swan*: Handsome and spacious dark-beamed thatched pub with pleasant dining area, inglenook fireplace, no-smoking area; Boddingtons, Courage Best and Marstons Pedigree, vast choice of good generous if not cheap food inc vegetarian, attractive furnishings, friendly attentive service, maybe piped pop music; popular with businesspeople lunchtime, very busy Sun; picnic tables in back garden, footpaths to nearby lakes *(Mary and David Webb)*

☆ Moulsoe [Cranfield Rd; about a mile N of M1 junction 14; SP9041], *Carrington Arms*: Welcoming pub/restaurant with well kept beer and good food, esp steaks and fish chosen or cut to your size and barbecued indoors to order; good service, children welcome, big garden *(Colin Pettit, V Green, Ian and Christina Allen)*

Naphill [SU8497], *Black Lion*: Good choice of food from sandwiches up in comfortable open-plan bar with aircraft pictures (Strike Command HQ nearby), and conservatory dining extension; Courage-related ales with a guest beer, fruit machine, maybe piped music; picnic tables in good-sized garden with swings and slides, nearby Chilterns walks; has been open all day *(Nigel Norman, LYM)*

☆ Newport Pagnell [Tickford St; 2 miles from M1 junction 14; SP8743], *Bull*: Very welcoming traditional 17th-c coaching inn, eight real ales inc rarities for the area, wide range of generous well priced straightforward food, daily papers, chatty Welsh landlord, softly lit low-ceilinged bar and lounge decorated with front pages on famous events; tables in courtyard; next to Aston Martin works, cars on show weekdays; bedrooms *(Darrell Kirsop, George Atkinson)*

Newton Blossomville [4 miles from M1 junction 14, off A428 at Turvey; SP9251], *Old Mill Burnt Down*: Cheery homely beamed open-plan inn, tiled and carpeted, chatty staff, Courage Best, Marstons Pedigree and Ruddles, good ploughman's and sandwiches, extremely friendly cats – Monty and Ginger; bedrooms *(George Atkinson)*

North Marston [minor rd Winslow—Whitchurch; SP7722], *Bell*: Wide choice of good home-made food cooked to order inc fresh fish specials, L-shaped beamed bar, snug and lounge, three real ales; fruit machine, darts, can get a bit smoky; garden with play area, interesting village church nearby *(JJW, CMW)*

Oakley [SP6312], *Chandos*: Small, quiet village pub with peaceful atmosphere *(Andy Pickering)*; [Oxford Rd], *Royal Oak*: Lively village pub with good food and reasonable prices *(Andy Pickering)*

Olney [Mkt Pl; SP8851], *Bull*: Food popular at lunchtime in spacious well placed pub, HQ of the town's famous Shrove Tuesday pancake race; Charles Wells and other ales, nice coffee, log-effect gas fires, very friendly chatty landlord *(Arnold and Maureen East)*; [12 High St, S Olney], *Swan*: Pleasant mix of beamed pub and bistro, good variety of generous home-cooked food, well kept kept beers inc Hook Norton, Jennings and Morrells ales, good competitively priced wine list, keen chatty landlord, friendly helpful staff *(Mark and Liz Slater, Ian and Christina Allen)*; [34 High St (A509)], *Two Brewers*: Very wide choice of generous popular food inc good home-made pies and Sun lunches, big dining area with plenty of different-sized tables, well stocked bar with well kept beer, friendly prompt service, attractive courtyard decorated to show its brewery past, tables in garden too *(Meg and Colin Hamilton, TGS, Stephen Brown)*

Oving [off A413 Winslow rd out of Whitchurch; SP7821], *Black Boy*: Quaint and friendly pub nr Chilterns, great views, good outside areas, magnificent collection of jugs, well kept Whitbreads-related beer, good food inc Sun lunch *(Dr and Mrs A K Clarke, Ann Griffiths)*

Penn [Witheridge Lane; SU9193], *Crown*: Friendly Country Carvery dining pub open all day, perched on high ridge with distant views, attractive gardens with good play area; three low-ceilinged refurbished bars, one with medieval flooring tiles; weekend barbecues, well kept Courage-related ales, friendly service; piped music, popular at lunchtime with businessmen; children in eating areas *(Simon Collett-Jones, GWB, Mel Smith, Shirley Cannings, LYM)*; *Horse & Jockey*:

Friendly, with consistently good range of promptly served daily changing bar food, most home-made, good beers *(GWB)*

☆ Penn Street [SU9295], *Hit or Miss*: Wide range of good generous food from ploughman's to wide range of seafood inc lobster and friendly bustling atmosphere in comfortably modernised low-beamed three-room pub with own cricket ground, good cricket and chair-making memorabilia, welcoming landlord, quick pleasant service, well kept ales such as Brakspears, Fullers and Hook Norton, log fire, no piped music or machines, occasional live music; pleasant setting *(H Hazzard, Chris and Andy Crow, Tony Dickinson, LYM)*

☆ Penn Street, *Squirrel*: Friendly and pubby, with good choice of home-cooked food at attractive prices, well kept Adnams, Bass and other ales, big garden opp cricket green; handy for lovely walks *(Walter and Margaret Ingram)*

☆ Preston Bisset [Pound Lane; SP6529], *White Hart*: Attractive 18th-c thatched and timbered pub with good fresh home-made food inc fish and some unusual dishes, well kept real ale and farm cider, good house wines, kind attractive service, good strong Irish coffee, small dining room; hood skittles, tables in back garden *(Martin Janson, Mr and Mrs G Ricketts, R Thompson, Graham and Karen Oddey)*
Preston Bisset, *Old Hat*: This charming unspoilt country pub closed in 1996 – we hope it will reopen *(News please)*

☆ Prestwood [Wycombe Rd (A4128); SP8700], *Polecat*: Civilised and well appointed old dining pub with quiet corners, charming antique-style furniture, lots of stuffed animals and birds, very wide choice of consistently good imaginative food at modest prices, prompt friendly service, well kept ales such as Marstons Pedigree, Morlands Old Speckled Hen and Ruddles County, decent house wines, open fires; soft piped classical music; nice big garden – handy for walks *(Peter Neate, J Ramage, Simon Collett-Jones, GWB, Nigel Norman)*
Saunderton [Wycombe Rd; SU8198], *Rose & Crown*: Country hotel with nice log fires, big winged leather chairs, good restaurant food, comfortable coffee lounge, friendly staff; bedrooms comfortable *(Nigel Norman, GWB)*
Seer Green [Orchard Rd; SU9692], *Three Horseshoes*: Well run welcoming local with Courage-related ales, good home-made fresh food *(Bernie Tebb)*
Shabbington [off A418 Oxford—Thame; SP6607], *Old Fisherman*: Small riverside inn with Morrells ales, decent food choice, friendly spaniel; garden with play area, small camp site *(Tim and Ann Newell)*

☆ Skirmett [SU7790], *Frog*: Country pub doing particularly well under new licensees, enjoyable atmosphere, good range of good value home-cooked food and of drinks inc local real ales, helpful cheerful service; a pleasant place to stay, in attractive valley *(Mary and Des Kemp, Dave Carter, Dagmar Junghanns, Colin Keane)*
Slapton [SP9320], *Carpenters Arms*: Small pub which doubles as an antique/book shop,with secondhand bookshop and grocery

in car park; inside divided into four, inc a dining room; very friendly staff, local Tring ale *(George Atkinson)*

☆ Speen [Flowers Bottom Lane; road from village towards Lacey Green and Saunderton Stn – OS Sheet 165 map ref 835995; SU8399], *Old Plow*: Restaurant not pub (they won't serve drinks unless you're eating, the bar's tiny compared with the dining room, and atmosphere's rather formal), but relaxing and charmingly cottagey, with good open fires, well kept Adnams and Brakspears, good food and wines (you can have just one course), fine service, log fires, children in eating area, pretty lawns, lovely countryside; cl Sun evening and Mon *(Rod Stacey, Francis and Deirdre Gevers, Mrs Ailsa Wiggans, LYM)*

☆ Stewkley [High St S, junction of Wing and Dunton rds; SP8526], *Carpenters Arms*: Very welcoming indeed, with big helpings of reasonably priced bar food, wide choice from sandwiches up, well kept ales inc Bass and Tetleys, sociable alsatian called Boon; bookcases in extended dining lounge, darts in jolly little public bar, subdued piped music *(George Atkinson, LYM)*

☆ Stewkley [High St N], *Swan*: Old pub with tiled front public bar, comfortable lounge, nice dining area with huge log fire; well kept Courage-related ales, good value food, maybe piped pop music; children's room, extensive gardens inc good big children's play lawn *(Mel Smith, Shirley Cannings)*

☆ Stoke Green [a mile S of Stoke Poges; off B416 signposted Wexham and George Green – OS Sheet 175 map ref 986824; SU9882], *Red Lion*: Rambling small room areas, interesting furnishings and decor, limited range of bar food, well kept Bass and guest ales, decent wines, log fires, no-smoking room, children welcome; tables outside, summer barbecues; has been open all day Fri/Sat *(Chris and Martin Taylor, Dave Braisted, I D Irving, LYM)*
Stoke Hammond [canal, out on A4146 Linslade—Milton Keynes; SP8829], *Three Locks*: Interesting location among locks and associated ponds on Grand Union Canal, stools at chest-high tables built into windows for watching the boats, reasonably priced bar food, family bar with children's activities, Tetleys-related and other ales, stone floor, lots of canal paintings on barrels *(Ian Phillips)*

☆ Stony Stratford [72 High St; SP7840], *Cock*: Quiet and comfortable old-fashioned hotel with leather settles and library chairs on bare floorboards, good bar food served piping hot, very friendly service, six well kept ales such as Fullers London Pride, Morlands Old Speckled Hen and Theakstons; bedrooms *(George Atkinson, LYM)*
Taplow [Rectory Rd; SU9082], *Oak & Saw*: Cosy open-plan local opp attractive village green, interesting pictures, Courage-related and other beers, good food and pleasant lunchtime atmosphere *(Chris and Martin Taylor)*

☆ The Lee [Swan Bottom; back rd ¾ mile N of The Lee – OS Sheet 165 map ref 902055; SP8904], *Old Swan*: Four attractively furnished low-beamed interconnecting rooms, cooking-range log fire in inglenook, relaxed atmosphere, particularly well kept real ales inc interesting guests, decent wines, welcoming long-serving landlord, food from sandwiches up (vegetarian on request); spacious prettily planted back lawns with play area *(Jan and Colin Roe, John and Phyllis Maloney, J Waller, LYM)*

☆ **Thornborough** [just off A421 4 miles E of Buckingham, outside village – pub name on OS165; SP7433], *Lone Tree*: Six interesting quickly changing well kept beers from small breweries, good choice of wines and good coffee in friendly and spotless long stripped-brick bar with old-fashioned tables and chairs, magazines and books in alcove, real fire in inglenook, polite rather than invariably speedy service; wide choice of generous popular food from sandwiches and baked potatoes up, quiet piped music; garden with play area *(George Atkinson, Dave Irving, Marjorie and David Lamb, Frank W Gadbois, Tony Gilbert, John and Phyllis Maloney)*

☆ **Twyford** [Galncott Rd; SP6626], *Seven Stars*: Pleasant and friendly rambling low-beamed country pub popular for varied imaginative food in lounge bar and separate dining area (not Sun evening; fish and meat from London markets daily); welcoming service, well kept Hook Norton Best and Old Hookey with two weekly changing guests, open fires, pictures and old farm tools; pool in games room, tables on pleasant lawn with animals for children, entertainment Sun evening; handy for Claydon House *(Karen and Graham Oddey, Gordon, J McMillan, Mrs J Oakes, Ian Cole)*

Tylers Green [Hammersley Lane; two miles from M40, junction 3; SU9093], *Old Queens Head*: 17th-c, with flagstones and old beams; wide range of good value food in bar and restaurant area (up in former barn eaves), several well kept ales, pleasant atmosphere and service; children in eating area, open all day *(Jan and Colin Roe, Richard Houghton, Steve Hickey)*

☆ **Wavendon** [not far from M1 junctions 13 and 14; SP9137], *Leathern Bottel*: Friendly Charles Wells pub, popular lunchtime for good choice of decent food; good service, log fire *(David and Mary Webb)*

☆ **Wendover** [High St; SP8607], *Red Lion*: Wide choice of good value changing food, generous and imaginative, inc fish specialities and Sun lunch in pleasant bustling refurbished oak-beamed bar and adjacent good value restaurant, ales such as Brakspears, Courage Directors and Hancocks HB, good wines, friendly efficient staff; walker-friendly – on Ridgeway Long Distance Path; comfortable bedrooms *(JM, PM, Kathy Berry, Mr and Mrs R Jacques, Joan and Andrew Life)*

☆ **West Wycombe** [London Rd (A40); SU8394], *Old Plough*: 17th-c National Trust pub with reasonably priced food and real ales; old furniture and quiet piped music in welcoming snug low-beamed downstairs bar; more modern upstairs lounge, restaurant, log fire, darts, winter pool table; barbecue in pretty little garden up behind; interesting village

(CMW, JJW, Ian Phillips)

☆ **Weston Turville** [Church Lane; SP8510], *Chequers*: Wide choice of good interesting food (not Mon) from sandwiches up in flagstoned two-level bar and attractive and characterful beamed restaurant, friendly staff, particularly good range of wines and spirits, well kept Tetleys-related and other ales, open fire, stylish solid wooden furniture; tucked away in attractive part of village, some tables outside *(Nuala Mahoney, M Sargent, Jan and Colin Roe)*

☆ **Weston Underwood** [off A509 at Olney; SP8650], *Cowpers Oak*: Charming old creeper-clad beamed pub with good value interesting bar food in back restaurant area, friendly service, Hook Norton Best and Marstons Pedigree, tropical fish tank, games area with skittles and darts, unobtrusive piped music; tables in garden, attractive surroundings, nearby zoo *(Mrs P J Pearce)*

☆ **Wheelerend Common** [just off A40; SU8093], *Brickmakers Arms*: Homely and friendly, with inglenook log fire, some exposed flintwork, panelling, low beams, elderly settees, kitchen and other tables, shelves of china; good changing bar food, good value upstairs carvery, decent range of beers and wines, welcoming efficient service; good play area in big garden, common opp for walks *(Gordon, Verdun Luck, Nigel Law)*

☆ **Whitchurch** [10 High St; A413 Aylesbury—Buckingham], *White Swan*: Homely and pubby two-bar Fullers local with well kept beer, usual food, picnic tables in rambling garden behind *(John and Phyllis Maloney, Ian Phillips, Roger and Valerie Hill, LYM)*

Winslow [Market Sq; SP7627], *Bell*: Unpretentious former coaching inn with comfortable modernised lounge, efficient landlord, friendly obliging staff, real ales, good bar food, popular good value carvery; bedrooms good value too, dogs allowed *(A Nunnerley, LYM)*; [North Marston rd], *Devil in the Boot*: Bar and areas off decorated with mock Tudor beams etc, real fire, darts, quiet piped radio, lithographs; three well kept ales, good reasonably priced food – may be a wait; picnic tables in sizeable garden *(JJW, CMW)*

Wolverton [Stratford Rd; SP8141], *Wolverton House*: Pleasant Brewers Fayre pub in attractive old building; friendly attentive service *(JJW, CMW)*

☆ **Wooburn Common** [Wooburn Common Rd, about 3½ miles from M40; SU9387], *Royal Standard*: Busy pub with wide choice of enjoyable good value bar food, knowledgeable friendly staff, well chosen wines, well kept Whitbreads-related beers, mix of old and brighter new decor with popular restaurant area; tables outside, boules pitch behind *(Chris and Martin Taylor, LYM)*

☆ **Wooburn Green** [SU9188], *Old Bell*: Light, airy and friendly, good food with emphasis on home-made pies; five real ales *(GWB)*

☆ **Wooburn Green** [14 The Green], *Red Cow*: Old beamed pub with open fires, snug atmosphere, very friendly staff, appetising food *(H Kroll)*

Cambridgeshire

Pubs currently doing particularly well here include the cheerfully idiosyncratic Millstone at Barnack (generous home cooking), the marvellously atmospheric Eagle in Cambridge (19 wines by the glass), the Chequers at Fowlmere (imaginative food at this smart dining pub), the elegantly restored and civilised old Bell at Stilton (another place for imaginative fresh food), the cosily atmospheric Anchor at Sutton Gault (another dining pub with a fresh approach) and the ever-expanding Haycock at Wansford, quite hotelish now but still extremely welcoming (with very good food and wine). Another fine dining pub, the Three Horseshoes at Madingley, is on excellent form at the moment – and our choice as Cambridgeshire Dining Pub of the Year. Two of our Cambridge main entries, the Live & Let Live and the Mill, have new licensees and are now free houses, with relatively low prices; as the Lucky Dip at the end of the chapter shows, there's a growing choice of decent pubs in the city – particularly in the currently fashionable traditional alehouse style. The Pheasant at Keyston has a new chef/patron doing good interesting food; new licensees at the Three Blackbirds at Woodditton are doing more imaginative food; and the Pheasant at Great Chishill joins the main entries this year – a very nice pub, with imaginative dishes of the day. To set against all these major changes is a monument to classic unchanging traditionalism: the landlord of the Queens Head at Newton has just celebrated his 25th year in charge of this fine pub. In the Lucky Dip, pubs currently doing well include the Royal Oak at Barrington, Duke of Wellington at Bourn, Black Horse at Dry Drayton, George & Dragon at Elsworth, Oliver Twist at Guyhirn, Pear Tree at Hildersham, Old Bridge in Huntingdon, Bell at Kennett, Pike & Eel at Needingworth, Lazy Otter at Stretham, White Horse at Swavesey and Tickell Arms at Whittlesford. We have inspected virtually all of these so can vouch for their quality ourselves; the George at Spaldwick, however, sounding very promising from readers' reports, is entirely new to us. Recently both food and drinks prices in the county have been increasing a little more quickly than in most other places, and are now on the high side – for instance, people are typically paying rather more than 10p a pint extra for beer, compared with the national average. A striking exception is the Black Bull at Godmanchester, tied to Whitbreads, where you can save about 25p a pint on prices in other Cambridgeshire pubs.

Post Office address codings confusingly give the impression that some pubs are in Cambridgeshire, when they're really in the Leicestershire or Midlands groups of counties (which is where we list them).

BARNACK TF0704 Map 5

Millstone

Millstone Lane; off B1443 SE Stamford; turn off School Lane near the Fox

Readers are particularly enthusiastic about the natural pubby atmosphere at this friendly village inn, with its excellently kept Adnams, Everards Old Original and Tiger and a good selection of guest beers on handpump. There are also Gales country wines, a good selection of malt whiskies and Scrumpy Jack. Bar food is very popular as well; it's all freshly prepared so there might be a short delay at busy times. Meals served by pleasant, attentive staff include lunchtime sandwiches, toasties and soup (from £1.95), prawn cocktail (£4.25), spare ribs (£3.50), lasagne or ocean pie (£6.25), cajun chicken (£6.75), minted lamb bake (£6.95), stilton chicken (£7.95) and about three vegetarian dishes like vegetable tikka masala (£5.45) or leek and mushroom bake (£5.90); smaller helpings for OAPs; usual children's menu; home-made puddings like sticky toffee or bread and butter pudding (from £1.95). The atmospheric and comfortable timbered bar with high beams weighed down with lots of heavy harness is split into intimate areas with cushioned wall benches on the patterned carpet. The little snug is decorated with the memorabilia of a former regular, including his medals from both World Wars. The snug and dining room are no smoking; piped music. *(Recommended by Tom Evans, Jenny and Michael Back, Erick Locker, John Fahy, Tony Gayfer, George Atkinson, F J Robinson, Edward Storey, John Baker, Stuart Earle)*

Everards ~ Tenant Aubrey Sinclair-Ball ~ Real ale ~ Meals and snacks (not Sun eve) ~ Restaurant (not Sun eve) ~ (01780) 740296 ~ Well supervised children in eating areas ~ Open 11-2.30, 5.30(6 Sat)-11.30; 12-4, 7-10.30 Sun

BYTHORN TL0575 Map 5

White Hart ⑪ ♀

Village signposted just off A14 Kettering—Cambridge

The simple exterior belies a very stylishly run welcoming restauranty pub. Well flavoured and often adventurous food served in generous helpings might include starters like home-pickled salmon, quail eggs or bouillabaisse salad all from the restaurant menu (£4.50), and bar snacks like ploughman's with three cheeses (£4.95), toasted brie with bacon or angel-hair pasta with mushrooms (£5.95), leg of duck with soy sauce and ginger or game casserole (£6.95), crispy loin of pork or squid ink pasta with seafood (£7.50) and sirloin steak (£10); puddings from the restaurant menu include sticky toffee pudding, lemon tart and snow eggs (£4.00). There's plenty to look at in the homely main bar and several linked smallish rooms which are eclectically furnished with a big leather chesterfield, lots of silver teapots and so forth on a carved dresser and in a built-in cabinet, wing armchairs and attractive tables. One area with rugs on stripped boards has soft pale leather studded chairs and stools, and a cosy log fire in a huge brick fireplace. There are cookery books and plenty of magazines for reading, not just decoration. Well kept Greene King IPA and Abbot on handpump; a good, no-nonsense, well chosen wine list including 4 by the glass, free nuts and spicy sausages; pleasant staff and very hospitable professional licensees; no-smoking restaurant *(Recommended by M Sargent, John Fahy, R C Wiles, Maysie Thompson, Mr Brooks, John Saul, John C Baker, Comus Elliott, S G Brown, Michael Marlow)*

Free house ~ Licensees Bill and Pam Bennett ~ Real ale ~ Meals and snacks (till 10; not Sat eve) ~ Restaurant ~ (01832) 710226 ~ Children welcome ~ Open 11-3, 6-11; cl Sun evening, all day Mon

---

Planning a day in the country? We list pubs in really attractive scenery at the back of the book.

CAMBRIDGE TL4658 Map 5

Anchor 🍺

Silver St

This spirited place is really for those who enjoy the lively bustle of foreign and local students; some readers have found the music and atmosphere too loud at times – it's particularly popular in the evening. It's set on four levels with two bars. The area around the entrance is sectioned off to create a cosy atmosphere; there's lots of bric-a-brac and church pews and a brick fireplace at each end. The no-smoking upstairs bar is pubby, with pews and wooden chairs and good riverside views. Downstairs the cafe-bar (open all day) has enamel signs on the walls and a mix of interesting tables, settles, farmhouse chairs, and hefty stools on the bare boards. Steps take you down to a simpler flagstoned room, and french windows lead out to one of the main draws here – the suntrap terrace with picnic tables and some tubs of flowers marvellously set right by the River Cam. You can hire punts here, and in summer they hold occasional events on the river. Inexpensive bar food includes sandwiches (from £1.95), ploughman's (from £3.10), salads (from £3.85) and daily specials like lasagne, steak and kidney pie, fish and chips and a vegetarian choice (£3.95), puddings like apple flan or sticky toffee fudge cake (from £1.95) and Sunday roast (£4.50). Their nine well kept real ales are Boddingtons, Flowers Original, Fremlins, Fullers London Pride, Marstons Pedigree, Morlands Old Speckled Hen, Wadworths 6X, Whitbread Castle Eden and one of the Whitbreads seasonal beers, and there's a good range of foreign bottled beers; cheerful young service, various trivia and fruit machines and a juke box. *(Recommended by JJB, John Fahy, RWD, Amanda Dauncey, John Rudolf, Hanns Golez, James Waller, Anthony Marriott, K Kennedy, J Brown)*

Whitbreads ~ Manager Alastair Langton ~ Real ale ~ Meals and snacks (12-8, till 5 Fri and Sat, 12-2.30 Sun) ~ (01223) 353554 ~ Children in eating area until 7 ~ Open 11-11 (till 10.30 Sun); cl 25 Dec

Eagle ♀

Bene't Street

There's a splendidly relaxed and comfortable atmosphere throughout the five historical rambling bars of this popular old stone-fronted 16th-c building, which was once Cambridge's most important coaching inn and is still probably the town's most interesting pub. Many original architectural features remain; there's the cosy smell of worn wooden floors and plenty of original pine panelling, as well as two fireplaces dating back to around 1600, two medieval mullioned windows and the remains of two possibly medieval wall paintings. The high dark red ceiling has been left unpainted since the war to preserve the signatures of British and American airmen worked in with Zippo lighters, candle smoke and lipstick. The furniture is nicely old and creaky. Hidden behind sturdy wooden gates is an attractive cobbled and galleried courtyard with heavy wooden seats and tables and pretty hanging baskets. There may be a short queue for the good value down to earth bar food which is served from a display counter in a small room at the back. The lunchtime and evening menus differ slightly but might include ploughman's (£4.25), sausage, chips and beans or cornish pasty or vegetarian burger (£3.95), vegetarian quiche (£4.25), lasagne, tuna bake or chilli con carne (£4.50), breaded fillet of plaice or salads (£4.95) and the chef's evening specials like breaded mushrooms with blue cheese dip (£3.95), sweet and sour chicken and vegetable pancake rolls (£4.75) or chicken with orange sauce (£4.95); puddings such as Dutch apple flan, toffee, pecan and apple pie and hot chocolate fudge cake (all £2.25). A neat little booklet lists up to 20 wines, sparkling wines and champagne by the glass which are presented from the bottle with a preservation system that ensures each is delivered in good condition; also jugs of sangria and very well kept Greene King IPA, Abbot, and Rayments and seasonal ales on handpump. This was the local of Nobel Prize winning scientists Crick and Watson, who discovered the structure of DNA. No noisy fruit machines or juke box, no smoking in one area; friendly service from well dressed staff. *(Recommended by John Wooll, Michael Gittins, Stephen and Julie Brown, Julian Holland, G P Kernan, Anthony Marriott, Helen McLagan)*

Greene King ~ Licensees Peter and Carol Hill ~ Real ale ~ Meals and snacks (12-2.30, 5.30-9; not Fri, Sat, Sun eve) ~ (01223) 505020 ~ Children in eating area of bar only ~ Open 11-11; 12-10.30 Sun

Free Press

Prospect Row

Hidden away in a narrow street, this completely no-smoking individual little old inn has been run by the same friendly licensee for nearly 20 years. It's registered as a boat club, so they can display their collection of oars and rowing photographs with more legitimacy than most Cambridge pubs. The civilised and unspoilt rooms are full of character and popular with locals. It's not big, so it's worth getting there early for a seat. Very tasty wholesome home-made bar food served in generous well priced helpings from a fairly short menu (always one vegetarian soup and main course) might include curried parsnip soup or stilton and onion soup (£1.95), up to four hot dishes such as broccoli and butter bean layer, carrot and cumin bake, cod and courgette lasagne, hot Texas chilli, pork and cranberry casserole or beef and beer casserole (all £3.95) and a few cold dishes like vegetarian quiche, nut roast, game pie or lamb, mint and olive pie (£3.95 – £4.75); puddings like chocolate, carrot and apricot cake, lemon torte or date and apricot slice (£1.80). Well kept Greene King IPA and Abbot and a seasonal ale on handpump, with a good selection of malt whiskies and freshly squeezed orange juice; iced coffee in hot weather; cards, cribbage and dominoes behind the bar. The sheltered paved garden at the back is quite a suntrap, and is home for some rabbits who have dug their own burrows there; two friendly cats. *(Recommended by Frank Gadbois, Amanda Dauncey, John Rudolf, Steve and Angela Maycock, Mike Beiley, Brian Horner, Brenda Arthur, John Fahy, David Peakall, Helen McLagan, Anthony Marriott)*

Greene King ~ Tenant Christopher Lloyd ~ Real ale ~ Meals and snacks (12-2, 6-8.30) ~ (01223) 368337 ~ Well behaved children welcome ~ Open 12-2.30(3 Sat and Sun), 6-11(7-10.30 Sun); cl 25 Dec evening, 26 Dec

Live & Let Live £ 🍺

40 Mawson Road; off Mill Road SE of centre

The informal relaxed atmosphere and reasonably priced bar food seem irresistible to students, at this straightforward comfortably busy free house well away from the town centre. The heavily timbered brickwork rooms are furnished with sturdy varnished old pine tables with pale wood chairs on bare boards, alongside lots of interesting old country bric-a-brac and posters about local forthcoming events; piped music. The eating area is no smoking, and basic but generous bar food remains unchanged under the new licensee: sandwiches (from £1.30), filled baked potatoes (from £1.70), ploughman's (from £3), sausage casserole (£3.50), lasagne, chilli or chicken curry (£3.75) and daily specials such as beef and Guinness pie or spinach and feta cheese pie (£3). Friendly bar service and good table clearance; well kept Adnams, Banks & Taylor Shefford and SOS, Everards Old Original and Tiger, Exmoor Stag and Morlands Old Speckled Hen on handpump, local cider and pure orange juice. *(Recommended by Susan and Nigel Wilson, Stephen Brown, Anthony Marriott, K Kennedy; more reports please)*

Free house ~ Peter Gray ~ Real ale ~ Meals and snacks ~ (01223) 460261 ~ Children in eating area till 8.30 ~ Folk group Sun evening ~ Open 11.30-2.30, 6-11

Mill

Mill Lane

Eight handpumps in this popular but small attractive riverside pub serve a constantly changing range of real ales which might include Adnams, Black Sheep Bitter and Special, Daleside Bitter and Monkey Wrench, Marstons Pedigree or Nethergate Bitter, IPA and Growler and often an even more esoteric brew. They also get beers direct from local microbreweries, have farm ciders and 21 country wines. The chatty simple bars – one with an open brick fireplace – attract a mixture of business and college customers. There are kitchen chairs, chunky stools, settles and a mix of wooden tables standing on bare boards and ancient quarry tiles, and lots of display cases filled with clay pipes or brewery taps and slings, photographs of college games teams, and oars with names of past Pembroke College rowers. In summer it gets really busy (bar service can slow down), with crowds sitting out on the expanse of grass that runs down to a bend in the river Cam. Simple bar food includes freshly made sandwiches (from £1.75), filled baked potatoes (from £2.75), ploughman's (£3.95), chilli, ocean pie, chicken and ham pie, beef carbonade, scampi or broccoli and walnut lasagne (£4.50) and daily specials; fruit machine, piped pop music. The main punt station, for hiring them, is next door. *(Recommended by E A Thwaite, JJB, Susan and Nigel Wilson, K Kennedy, Terry Barlow, Anthony Marriott)*

Pubmaster ~ Manager Peter Snellgrove ~ Real ale ~ Lunchtime meals and snacks (till 3; till 7 Sat) ~ (01223) 357026 ~ Children welcome in eating area of bar if eating ~ Open 11-11; Sun 12-10.30

DULLINGHAM TL6357 Map 5
Kings Head

50 Station Road

There is a peaceful old-fashioned atmosphere at this trim pink-washed dining pub. The two cosy relaxed adjoining carpeted rooms (one is no smoking), with well kept ABC Bitter and Flowers IPA on handpump, have small buttonback leatherette bucket seats, windsor chairs, hunting prints, private booths around sturdy wooden tables, and a coal fire at each end in winter. The family/function room across the yard is called the Loose Box. Tasty bar food served by helpful efficient staff includes soup (£1.95), home-made pâté (£3.25), chilli, omelettes or tacos (£4.95), breaded plaice (£5.75), half a chicken, grilled ham and eggs or pizza (£5.95), wiener schnitzel or chicken kiev (£6.95), a good few vegetarian dishes like mushroom and nut fettucine, three-bean chilli, wheat and walnut casserole and vegetable tikka masala (all £6.50) and daily blackboard specials; puddings from (£2.25), lots of ice cream sundaes from (£2.50) and the usual children's menu (from £2.75). It's advisable to book a table for the restaurant. There are sheltered seats under fairy lights on an area of grass above the car park, with more on a terrace overlooking the big sloping village green; swings and an adventure playground, no dogs. *(Recommended by John Fahy, Gwen and Peter Andrews, B and K Hypher, Frank Gadbois, Stephen and Jean Curtis, E A George; more reports please)*

Pubmaster (Carlsberg Tetleys) ~ Tenants Erich Kettenacker and Nigel Sampson ~ Real ale ~ Meals and snacks (till 10pm) ~ Restaurant ~ (01638) 507486 ~ Children welcome in family room and restaurant ~ Open 11-2.30(3 Sun), 6-11(6.30-10.30 Sun); cl 25, 26 Dec

DUXFORD TL4745 Map 5
John Barleycorn

Moorfield Rd; village signposted off A1301; pub at far end of village

This charming thatched and shuttered early 17th-c cottage has the appearance of the perfect English country pub. The small front terrace has delightful hanging baskets, tubs and flowerbeds around picnic tables, and there are more tables surrounded by roses and flowering shrubs in the back garden. The softly lit relaxed bar is attractively furnished with high-backed booth-type oak settles, wheelback chairs, chunky country tables and autumnal-coloured curtains to match the cushions. A couple of standing timbers and a brick pillar break up the room, and below a shotgun on the wall there's a raised brick fireplace. Old prints, decorative plates, photographs of the pub, brass lamps, a ship's clock and horse tack ornament the walls; dominoes and piped (possibly fairly loud) jazz. Well cooked bar food in generous helpings includes winter soup (£3.50), home-made liver pâté (£4.30), open sandwiches (from £4.50), grilled sardines (£5.50), steak and kidney pie or Irish stew with dumplings (£7.20), venison (£7.40), smoked haddock (£7.60), jugged hare (£8.50) or poached salmon (£8.90) and puddings like spicy bread pudding or chocolate orange pudding (£3.30), or you can have a choice of two courses from the above for (£9.80). It's best to book in the evenings. Well kept Greene King IPA, Abbot and seasonal ales under light blanket pressure; decent wines, a range of brandies, and mulled wine in winter. Service is reserved but courteous. There's also a converted barn with ancient timbers and some back-to-back seats, and an attractive brick barbecue and mini bar. *(Recommended by R WD, Brian and Jill Bond, Peter Jowitt, Mick Hitchman, John and Shirley Dyson, David Craine, Ann Reeder, Ian Phillips, Gary Roberts, Ann Stubbs, Susan and Nigel Wilson, J F M West)*

Greene King ~ Tenant Henry Sewell ~ Real ale ~ Meals and snacks (till 10pm) ~ (01223) 832699 ~ Open 12-2.30, 6-11(7-10.30 Sun); cl 25 Dec, 1 Jan

ETTON TF1406 Map 5

Golden Pheasant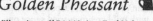

Village just off B1443, just E of Helpston level crossing; and will no doubt be signposted from near N end of new A15 Peterborough bypass

There are always seven very well kept changing real ales on handpump at this tree-surrounded stone-built house, which might include Badger Tanglefoot, Bass, Batemans XXXB, Boddingtons, Butcombe, Courage Directors, Greene King IPA, Timothy Taylors Landlord and Woodfordes Wherry; also lots of malt whiskies. The comfortable homely bar has high-backed maroon plush settles built against the walls and around the corners, an open fire, and prints on the walls. In the airy, glass-walled, no-smoking side room are some Lloyd Loom chairs around glass-topped cane tables. Tasty bar food could include stilton chicken, minted lamb bake and duck with black cherries (£8.50), or enterprisingly filled yorkshire puddings – cumberland sausage with Guinness gravy, or vegetable curry, say. The stone-walled garden looks out across flat countryside, and has an adventure playground, an aviary with about 70 golden pheasants, quail, cockatiels, rosella parakeets and budgerigars, and a big paddock. The golden labrador is called Bonnie. Pool, cribbage, dominoes, fruit machine, video game, and piped music. *(Recommended by M J Morgan, John Baker; more reports please)*

Free house ~ Real ale ~ Meals and snacks (till 10pm) ~ Restaurant ~ (01733) 252387 ~ Children in eating area of bar, in restaurant and family room ~ Open 11-11

FEN DRAYTON TL3368 Map 5

Three Tuns

High Street; village signposted off A14 NW of Cambridge

The cosy, welcoming and unpretentious bar of this pretty thatched country pub has heavy-set moulded Tudor beams and timbers, usually a fire in one of two inglenook fireplaces, and comfortable cushioned settles and an interesting variety of chairs. It's decorated with big portraits, old local photographs, old song-sheets of local folk songs, brass plates, fresh flowers, and old crockery in a corner dresser. There's plenty of drinking space, and helpful staff serve very well kept Greene King IPA, Abbot, Rayments and seasonal ales on handpump as well as a range of malt whiskies. Good value bar food includes sandwiches (from £1.25), home-made soup (£1.80), chicken liver and bacon pâté or Greek dips (£2.50), ploughman's (£3), salads (from £3.50), lasagne or vegetable lasagne (£4.25), chicken curry (£4.50), scampi (£5), gammon with pineapple (£5.50), chicken kiev (£6), and 8oz rump steak (£8); daily specials such as chilli, fisherman's pie, rabbit and bacon pie or moussaka (£4.50), garlic chicken breast or bobotie (£5) or Barnsley chops (£6.50); and puddings like home-made apple pie and good treacle tart. Sensibly placed darts, shove-ha'penny, dominoes, cribbage and fruit machine. A well tended lawn at the back has tables under cocktail parasols, apple and flowering cherry trees, and some children's play equipment. The pub can get very crowded, so it's best to arrive early if you want to eat. *(Recommended by Gordon Theaker, Sidney and Erna Wells, Colin McGaughey, Andrew and Joan Life, Keith and Margaret Kettell, M A Butler, Nigel and Amanda Thorp, F Robinson, Ian Phillips, Maysie Thompson, D Tapper, Julian Holland)*

Greene King ~ Tenants Michael and Eileen Nugent ~ Meals and snacks (not evenings of 24/25 Dec) ~ (01954) 230242 ~ Children in eating area of bar until 8pm ~ Open 11(12 Sun)-2.30, 6.30-11(7-10.30 Sun); cl evening 25 Dec

FOWLMERE TL4245 Map 5

Chequers 🍽 🍷

B1368

The emphasis at this smart 16th-c country house is very much on the excellently prepared imaginative food. Attentive but reserved waiters in black and white serve soup (£2.80), grilled halloumi cheese and aubergine dip (£3.60 starter, £5.60 main course), ploughman's (£3.75), cassoulet (£5.60), loin of pork with raspberry vinegar, cream and berry sauce (£6.90), poached pollack with mild cream curried sauce on stir-fried vegetables (£7.60), puddings (from £3) and Irish farmhouse cheeses (£3.60). There's an excellent choice of very well priced fine wines by the glass (including vintage and late-bottled ports), as well as well kept Tolly Original and Tetleys on handpump, freshly squeezed orange juice and a good choice of brandies. There are two warm and cosy comfortably furnished communicating rooms downstairs with an open log fire – look out for the priest's hole above the bar. Upstairs there are beams, wall timbering and some interesting moulded plasterwork above the fireplace. The pub sign honours British and American pilots who'd made this their second home, with the blue and white chequers of No 19 Sqdn RAF on one side, and the red and white chequers of USAF 339th Fighter Group on the other; there are some interesting black and white photographs in the bar showing the local WW1 and WW2 airfields. There's a light, airy conservatory/function room, overlooking white tables under cocktail parasols among flowers and shrub roses in a pleasant well tended garden. *(Recommended by Nigel and Amanda Thorp, BHP, Paul McPherson, Neil and Angela Huxter, Conor McGaughey, Howard Gregory, Ian Phillips, Susan and Nigel Wilson, Mayur Shah, Gwen and Peter Andrews, Dr Jim Craig-Gray, Jan and Colin Roe, Amanda Dauncey, J Rudolf, Derek and Maggie Washington)*

Pubmaster ~ Lease: Norman Rushton ~ Real ale ~ Meals and snacks (till 10) ~ Restaurant ~ (01763) 208369 ~ Well behaved children welcome ~ Open 12-2.30(3 Sun), 6-11(7-10.30 Sun); cl 25 Dec

GODMANCHESTER TL2740 Map 5

Black Bull

Post St; follow village signposts off A14 (was A604) just E of Huntingdon

This fine old place by the church has plenty of atmospheric character in its heavily beamed bar, with seats built into the inglenook of the enormous fireplace, settles forming booths by leaded-light windows, and quite a bit of glinting brassware; a side room up a step is hung with lots of black agricultural and other rustic ironwork. Friendly staff serve a very wide choice of straightforward but decent food including soup (£1.75), ploughman's (£3.70), steak and ale pie (£6.25), spicy chicken (£7.45), turkey curry (£6.25), mixed grill (£9.25), blackboard specials such as fried whitebait (£3.05), lasagne (£6.25), mixed farmhouse grill (£7.95), seafood platter (£6.45) or half roast duck with black cherry sauce (£8.95) and puddings like apple crumble with toffee and pecan or fresh fruit pavlova from (£1.75); children's menu (£1.95). Well kept Black Bull (made locally for them), Boddingtons, Flowers Original and Whitbreads Castle Eden kept under light blanket pressure; unobtrusive piped pop music; fruit machine. There's a big courtyard and pretty garden behind the car park. *(Recommended by Ian Phillips; more reports please)*

Whitbreads ~ Licensee Colin Dryer ~ Real ale ~ Meals and snacks (till 10pm; all day Sun) ~ Restaurant ~ (01480) 453310 ~ Children welcome till 8.30pm ~ Open 11(12 Sun)-2.30(3 Sat), 6-11(10.30 Sun) ~ Bedrooms: £19/£35

GOREFIELD TF4111 Map 8

Woodmans Cottage 🍴

Main St; off B1169 W of Wisbech

The buoyant personality of the cheery Australian landlady Lucille at this lively village inn shines through in a warm and enthusiastic welcome, and even in her famous array of puddings, which can run to well over 50 at weekends. Very tasty good value bar food in really generous helpings includes toasties (from £1.25), burgers (£2.25), omelettes (£4), steak and kidney pie, gammon, macaroni and seven vegetarian dishes like nut roast, vegetable curry or mushroom stroganoff (£5.75), mixed grill (£6.75), 16oz T-bone steak (£10) and about 20 daily-changing blackboard specials like chicken kiev and lamb vindaloo (£6). The spacious modernised bar, with leatherette stools and brocaded banquettes around the tables on its carpet, rambles back around the bar counter. A comfortable side eating area has a big collection of china plates, as well as 1920s prints on its stripped brick walls. There's space for non-smoking diners called the Cellar, with a display of Lucille's paintings. Beyond is an attractive pitched-ceiling restaurant so popular that it may be booked some three weeks ahead. At the other end of the pub, a games area has darts, dominoes, pool and CD juke box. Well kept Bass, Greene King IPA and Worthington Best on handpump and several Australian wines; piped music, bridge school on Monday evenings. There are tables out in a sheltered back terrace, with a few more on a front verandah. *(Recommended by Jenny and Michael Back, R C Wiles, Terry and Eileen Stott, Mrs Pat Crabb, Anthony Barnes, Stuart Earle, K Kennedy, R C Vincent)*

Free house ~ Licensees Lucille and Barry Carter ~ Real ale ~ Meals and snacks (till 10pm) ~ Restaurant (cl Sun evening) ~ (01945) 870669 ~ Supervised children welcome away from the bar counter ~ Open 11(12 Sun)-3, 7-11(10.30 Sun); cl evenings 25-26 Dec

GREAT CHISHILL TL4239 Map 5

Pheasant

Follow Heydon signpost from B1039 in village

This unassuming little pub offers very well cooked bar food including sandwiches (from £2.40, baguettes from £2.90), ploughman's or filled baked potatoes (£4.95), hot filled baguettes (from £5.95), chilli (£6.50), home-made pie of the day or tortellini with a creamy herb and cheese sauce (£6.75), mixed grill platter (£7.25) and interesting daily specials like bass, grilled calf liver with pine nuts and apple rings, and warm slices of pigeon breast; children's menu (£3.95). The attractive split-level bar has some elaborately carved though modern seats and settles, a few plates on timbered walls, and a stuffed pheasant on the mantelpiece. There are bar stools with decent backs and, at one end, dining chairs around the tables. Well kept Adnams, Marstons Pedigree, Ruddles and two weekly changing guests on handpump; faint piped music, darts, cribbage and dominoes. A rising lawn behind the pub has stout teak seats among flowering cherries and a weeping willow. There is quiet farmland beyond the back rose hedge. *(Recommended by P and D Carpenter, Susan and Nigel Wilson; more reports please)*

Free house ~ Licensee N Clarke ~ Real ale ~ Meals and snacks ~ Restaurant ~ (01763) 838535 ~ Children welcome ~ Open 12-3, 6-11; 12-11 Sat; 12-10.30 Sun(12-3, 7-10.30 Sun in winter)

If we know a pub has an outdoor play area for children, we mention it.

HINXTON TL4945 Map 5

Red Lion

2 miles from M11 junction 9, 3½ miles from junction 10; just off A1301 S of Great Shelford

The mainly open-plan bar of this quaint and busy local is filled with stuffed birds and animals, clocks, mirrors and pictures, grandfather and grandmother clocks, a barometer, some big prints and quite a few smaller rustic pictures on the walls, shelves of china in one corner, and a few beams and timbers hung with horsebrasses. George the chatty Amazon parrot perches above the button-back red brocade wall banquette, and there's a stuffed tarantula, egret and guillemot. Well kept Adnams, Bass, Boddingtons, and Greene King IPA on handpump at the central bar counter, also a useful wine list and fresh orange juice. Good, sensibly priced and well cooked bar food including a reasonable range of fish includes home-made soup (£2.50), stilton and white port pâté or fried camembert with gooseberry sauce (£3.75), chicken kiev (£6.75), fried haddock fillet or scampi (£6.95), gammon steak (£7.95), skate wing (£9.25), roast duck with orange and Grande Marnier sauce (£9.95), beef stroganoff (£13.75), daily specials like chicken curry or home-baked ham salad (£5.25), tuna and pasta bake (£5.50), lamb balti (£7.25) and about six vegetarian dishes such as lasagne, asparagus quiche and curry (from £4.95). A good choice of puddings might include apple tart, treacle sponge pudding or jam roly poly (£2.50). Part of the restaurant is no smoking; trivia and unobtrusive piped classical music. The neatly kept garden has picnic tables and there's a paddock with a small pony and goat; handy for Duxford Aeroplane Museum. *(Recommended by D R Eberlin, Quentin Williamson, Ian Phillips, A W, B W, Sue Rowland, Paul Mallett, Mr and Mrs Tobin, Ann and Bob Westbrook, John Fahy)*

Free house ~ Licensees James and Lynda Crawford ~ Real ale ~ Meals and snacks (till 10pm; 9.30pm Sun and Mon) ~ Restaurant ~ (01799) 530601 ~ Children in eating area of bar and restaurant ~ Open 11(12 Sun)-2.30, 6.30-11(7-10.30 Sun)

HOLYWELL TL3370 Map 5

Old Ferry Boat

Village and pub both signposted (keep your eyes skinned, it's easy to go wrong!) from Needingworth, which is just off the A1123

This rambling old wisteria-covered thatched building is charmingly set in a remote part of the fens, with lazy tables and cocktail parasols on a manicured rose lawn (more on a front terrace) by the Great Ouse – where there's mooring for boats. The six characterful open-plan bar areas (two are no smoking) have window seats overlooking the river, very low beams, and timbered and panelled walls; one also has a pretty little carved settle. One of the four open fires has a fish and an eel among rushes moulded on its chimney beam. A stone in the bar marks the ancient grave of the resident ghost Juliette, said to return every year on 17 March. Good bar food from the imaginative and extensive menu includes home-made soup (£2.50), chicken liver pâté (£3.50), ploughman's (£4.75), tortellini with mixed vegetables in a creamy basil sauce (£5.95), fish and chips (£6.50), steak, mushroom and ale pie (£6.95), diced pork with apples and bacon in a cider and cream sauce (£7.25), knuckle of lamb braised in red wine with orange zest and leeks (£7.75) and grilled tuna steak with crushed black peppercorns (£8.75); real chips and a splendid choice of superb mostly home-made puddings on display (£2.50). Well kept Bass, Nethergate IPA and Websters Yorkshire on handpump, and four interesting guests like Nethergate Umbel or Woodfordes Norfolk Nog that change every week or so; friendly, attentive, efficient service even when it gets very busy in summer and at weekends. Fruit machine, trivia and piped music. *(Recommended by George Atkinson, Jenny and Michael Back, Rita Horridge, Dr and Mrs S Jones, Ted George, Jack Morley, Stuart Earle, Julian Holland, Moira and John Cole, Ian Phillips, Joan and Michel Hooper-Immins, David and Glenys Lawson)*

Free house ~ Licensee Richard Jeffrey ~ Real ale ~ Meals and snacks (till 10pm) ~ (01480) 463227 ~ Well behaved children welcome ~ Open 11.30(12 Sun)-3, 6-11(7-10.30 Sun); cl 25 Dec evening ~ Bedrooms: £39.50B/£49.50B

HORNINGSEA TL4962 Map 5

Plough & Fleece ★

Just NE of Cambridge: first slip-road off A45 heading E after A10, then left at T; or take B1047 Fen Ditton road off A1303

The homely low black-beamed public bar at this small but rambling country pub has comfortably worn high-backed settles and plain seats on the red tiled floor, a stuffed parrot and a fox by the log fire, and plain wooden tables including an unusually long pine one with an equally elongated pew to match. Interesting home-cooked bar food includes lunchtime sandwiches (from £1.45), toasties (from £1.90) and ploughman's (£3) and starters like devilled crab and smoked haddock in creamy sauce on toast (£3.25), vegetarian stilton and broccoli flan (£3.50) and grilled oysters wrapped in bacon and served on toast (£5.25); main courses like shepherd's pie (£5), home-cooked ham in cheese sauce with crispy potato topping (£5.25), cajun fried chicken or salads (£5.25), layers of spinach, tomatoes, onions and roquefort cheese under a puff pastry lid (£5.25), a mixed fish pie flavoured with caerphilly cheese (£5.75), steak and mushrooom pie (£6.25), romany rabbit (£7.25), roast duck with a hot and spicy sauce (£9.50) and beef Wellington (£10.50); puddings include treacle tart, lemon cheesecake, chocolate pudding, plum pudding and home-made ginger and brandy ice cream (all £2.50); in the evening dishes are served with vegetables and are about £1 higher; prompt, cheerful service. There's a good no-smoking dining room with lots of wood and old bricks and tiles, linked by a terrace to the garden; new conservatory at the back. Well kept Greene King IPA and Abbot on handpump, half a dozen good malt whiskies and a couple of vintage ports; dominoes and cribbage. The mix of wild and cultivated flowers in the garden is a nice touch; picnic tables beyond the car park. A reader tells us there is easy disabled access. *(Recommended by J F M West, TBB, Sue Rowland, Paul Mallett, Caroline and Martin Page, Stephen Brown, Dr and Mrs S Jones, Maysie Thompson, Mr and Mrs S R Maycock)*

Greene King ~ Tenant Kenneth Grimes ~ Real ale ~ Meals and snacks (not Sun, Mon eve) ~ No-smoking restaurant ~ (01223) 860795 ~ Children over 5 in restaurant only ~ Open 11.30(12 Sun)-2.30, 7-11(10.30 Sun); cl eve 25 and 26 Dec

KEYSTON TL0475 Map 5

Pheasant 🍴 🍷

Village loop road; from A604 SE of Thrapston, right on to B663

Things appear to be going well under the new chef/patron at this civilised thatched inn, where the emphasis is still on restauranty food of a high standard. The same menu is on offer throughout the building, with linen napkins and bigger tables in the no-smoking Red Room. Very well cooked imaginative dishes from the regularly changing menu could include spinach, watercress and tarragon soup (£3.75), saffron risotto with creamed leeks and parmesan cheese (£4.25), roast quail with a shallot confit and a madeira and pink grapefruit sauce (£4.75), wild boar sausages (£6.95), tomato and black olive tart and green salad or tagliatelle with sun dried tomatoes, basil and parmesan (£7.95), fillet of lemon sole with potato and anchovy bake or roast wood pigeon with celeriac purée (£8.95), tenderloin of pork with beetroot purée (£9.75) and fried bass with fennel and cardamon purée and herb dressing (£12.50), puddings such as lemon parfait with spiced compote of red fruits (£3.50), poached figs in red wine with cinnamon ice cream or a plate of chocolate desserts (£5.95) and a selection of unpasteurised cheeses (£4.95); smaller helpings for children. There's a superb wine list (including fourteen by the glass) as well as well kept Adnams Best and two or three changing guests on handpump. A friendly low-beamed room has old photographs, leather slung stools and a heavily carved wooden armchair; another room, with high rafters, used to be the village smithy – hence the heavy-horse harness and old horse-drawn harrow there. Some tables under cocktail parasols at the front are laid with tablecloths. No dogs. *(Recommended by Graham and Liz Bell, Stephen and Julie Brown, Thomas Nott, John Fahy, Jane Kingsbury, M Sargent, Bob and Maggie Atherton, Simon Cottrell, R C Wiles, D Goodger, Geoffrey and Irene*

Lindley, Dr and Mrs S Jones, Peter Burton, Gordon Theaker, Caroline McAleese, Michael Marlow, Margaret and Roy Randle, Comus Elliott)

Free house ~ Licensee Martin Lee ~ Meals and snacks (12-2, 6-10) ~ Restaurant ~ (01832) 710241 ~ Children welcome ~ Open 12-3, 6-11; cl 25 and 26 Dec evening

MADINGLEY TL3960 Map 5

Three Horseshoes 🍽 ♀

Off A1303 W of Cambridge

Cambridgeshire Dining Pub of the Year

Like the Pheasant at Keysoe (they are both part of the same small group of pubs), the emphasis here is very much on the marvellously imaginative restauranty food and superior wine list. The stylish menu might include pea and mint soup with fried pancetta (£3.75), grilled chicken terrine with roasted courgettes, red onions and salsa verde (£4.50), seared scallops and salmon with braised lentils and coriander pesto (£6.75, main course £14.50), or main courses like spinach and ricotta torte with mixed herb salad, roast tomatoes and pesto (£6.75), fricassee of leeks, asparagus, wild mushrooms, button onions and steamed potatoes flavoured with gewurztraminer (£7.50), grilled lamb's liver with red onion jam, baby leeks and lime (£8.50), char-grilled chicken breast with tarragon cream and pesto (£8.75), grilled fillet of lamb with polenta, braised sweetbreads, kidneys, button onions, peas and broad beans (£12.50), roast beef fillet with potato pancake, oxtail sauce and braised vegetables (£13.50) and roast monkfish (£13.75). Puddings like caramelised lemon tart with mascarpone and mint (£4.50) or warm chocolate tart with marmalade ice cream (£4.75) can be had with a choice of good sweet wines. Well kept Adnams, Everards, Fullers London Pride, Greene King Abbot, Morlands Old Speckled Hen, Theakstons XB, Robinsons, Smiles and Wadworths 6X on handpump, lots of malts and freshly squeezed orange juice. The charming traditional bar is comfortably furnished with an open fire. Service is flexible, efficient and attentive. In summer it's nice to sit out on the lawn, surrounded by flowering shrubs, roses and trees. *(Recommended by Paul and Janet Waring, Stephen and Julie Brown, Frank Gadbois, Maysie Thompson, E D Bailey, R C Wiles, J Sanderson, Patrick Milner, Paul McPherson, M Sargent, Amanda Dauncey, John Rudolf, Dr and Mrs S Jones, John Saul, Julie Peters, Rita Horridge, John Fahy, Ian Phillips, Wayne Brindle, Jane Kingsbury)*

Free house ~ Licensee Richard Stokes ~ Real ale ~ Meals and snacks ~ Children welcome ~ Restaurant (not Sun evening) ~ (01954) 210221 ~ Open 11.30-2.30, 6-11(7-10.30 Sun)

NEWTON TL4349 Map 5

Queens Head ★ ⚑

2½ miles from M11 junction 11; A10 towards Royston, then left on to B1368

In 1996 the erudite and interesting licensee at this down-to-earth authentic old pub celebrated 25 years as landlord. Warmed by a lovely big log fire, the atmospheric well worn friendly main bar has a low ceiling and crooked beams, bare wooden benches and seats built into the walls and bow windows, a curved high-backed settle on the yellow tiled floor, a loudly ticking clock, and paintings on the cream walls. The little carpeted saloon is similar but cosier. Don't expect anything elaborate to eat – food is limited to a good choice of exceptionally good value doorstep sandwiches (from £1.60) including banana and smoked salmon and very good roast beef ones, excellent beef dripping on toast, and mugs of superb home-made soup, or maybe filled baked potatoes (£1.90); in the evening and on Sunday lunchtime they serve plates of excellent cold meat, smoked salmon, cheeses and pâté (from £2.75). Adnams Bitter, Broadside and Extra are tapped straight from the barrel, with Old Ale in winter and Tally Ho at Christmas; country wines and Crone's cider. Darts in a side room, with shove-ha'penny, table skittles, dominoes, cribbage, fruit machine, and nine men's morris. There are seats in front of the pub, with its vine trellis and unusually tall chimney, or you can sit on the village green. Belinda the goose who used to patrol the car park now sits stuffed above the fruit machine, but lives on in the pub sign, painted by the licensee's father and son; no-smoking games room. *(Recommended by Susan and Nigel Wilson, Tony Beaulah, Conor McGaughey, Gervas Douglas, Charles Bardswell, Graham and Karen Oddey, Amanda Dauncey, J Rudolf, Ron Gentry, Jane Kingsbury, John Fahy, Frank Gadbois, Alan and Eileen Bowker)*

Free house ~ Licensee David Short ~ Real ale ~ Snacks (till 10pm) ~ (01223) 870436 ~ Well behaved children in games room ~ Open 11.30 (12 Sat)-2.30, 6-11(7-10.30 Sat); cl 25 Dec

STILTON TL1689 Map 5

Bell 🛏 ♀

High Street; village signposted from A1 S of Peterborough

There is a gently refined atmosphere at this rather elegant old stone coaching inn. The attractive well restored interior has two busy spacious bars. with sturdy upright wooden seats, plush-cushioned button-back banquettes built around the walls and bow windows, big prints of sailing and winter coaching scenes on the partly stripped walls, and a large warm log fire in the fine stone fireplace. Generous helpings of good stylish bar food (there may be a bit of a wait) include soup (£1.95), chunky fish soup (£2.50), herby chicken liver and stilton parfait with home-made red pepper and pear pickle, or a good range of filled baguettes with salad (from £3.25), cultivated and wild mushrooms sautéed with garlic, shallots and meaux mustard in a pastry tartlet (£3.75), smoked salmon with crème fraîche dressing (£4.25), fresh tagliatelle with smoked salmon, sesame oil, shallots, scallops and spinach in lemon cream sauce or stilton, brie and caramelised onions in filo pastry topped with hazelnuts on a bed of continental leaves (£6.95), smoked haddock and beef tomatoes with stilton and caramelised onion bake (£7.50), Indonesian baked chicken with banana and sultanas in cream sauce (£7.95), lamb shank braised with root vegetables, rosemary, redcurrant jelly and red wine (£9.25), and rump steak (£9.50); stilton cheese with plum bread (£3.95), and puddings listed on a blackboard. You can eat outside at tables in a lovely sheltered cobbled and flagstoned courtyard which has the distances to various cities carved on the walls – and a well which is believed to date back to Roman times. Well kept Marstons Pedigree, Ruddles Best and Tetleys and two or three guests a week on handpump, and a broad choice of wines by the glass; good friendly service; dominoes, cribbage, backgammon, chess, Mastermind and Scrabble. Chintzy bedrooms make an elegent stay; no dogs. *(Recommended by Frank Cummins, Tony Dickinson, Carolyn and Michael Hedoin, Geoffrey and Irene Lindley, John Fahy, Gill and Andy Plumb, N B Thompson, June and Malcolm Farmer, Richard Siebert, Christopher Turner, David Peakall, KC, John Tyzack, George Atkinson, L M Miall, J F M and M West, Alan and Heather Jacques, Mrs E D Fryer, Frank Gadbois, Dr and Mrs G H Lewis)*

Free house ~ Licensees John and Liam McGivern ~ Real ale ~ Meals and snacks ~ Restaurant ~ (01733) 241066 ~ Children in eating area of bar till 8pm ~ Open 12-2.30(11-3 Sat), 6-11; 12-3, 7-10.30 Sun ~ Bedrooms: £40B/£55B

SUTTON GAULT TL4279 Map 5

Anchor ★ ⑪ ♀

Village signed off B1381 in Sutton

There is a cosy intimate atmosphere in the four heavily timbered stylishly simple rooms of this family run pub, lit by gas and candles. Antique settles and well spaced scubbed pine tables stand on the gently undulating old floors, with good lithographs and big prints on the walls, and three log fires; three-quarters of the pub is now no smoking. The very imaginative restaurary food is fairly central to the operation – and it's so popular that you may need to book. The daily changing menu might include starters such as home-made tomato, courgette and carrot soup (£3.50), baked avocado with crabmeat or home-made chicken liver and hazelnut pâté

(£4.50), fried pigeon breast and oyster mushroom salad (£4.95), main courses like
fillets of mackerel with caramelised onions on an orange and walnut salad (£7.95),
seafood crumble or steak, kidney and Guinness pie (£9.50), chicken breast and king
prawn kebabs with lemon and tarragon (£9.95), scotch sirloin steak with burgundy
sauce or venison steak with plum and tarragon sauce (£12.20) and maybe two
vegetarian dishes like mushroom and red wine pancake topped with stilton, filo
pastry parcel filled with wild mushrooms, almonds, pine-nuts and sun-dried
tomatoes on a cream and caper pepper sauce (£8.95). They serve real Devon ice
cream in a superb range of flavours (£3.50) and home-made puddings of the day
such as fresh fruit and almond pavlova, chocolate and brandy pot with home-made
brandy snap or hot sticky toffee pudding (£3.95), and a very good daily
cheeseboard; very sensibly, children can have most of their dishes in half-helpings.
There's a very good wine list (including a wine of the week and 10 by the glass),
winter mulled wine, a local cider and freshly squeezed orange juice. A rotating range
of three well kept real ales might include Adnams Best, Ind Coope Burton or
Nethergate IPA tapped from the cask. In summer you can sit outside at the tables or
on the bank of the Old Bedford River watching the swans and house martins; the
river bank walks are lovely. No dogs; piped classical music. *(Recommended by Rita
Horridge, Jane Kingsbury, Stephen and Julie Brown, Andrew and Jo Litten, Ken and Jenny
Simmonds, John Fahy, Gwen and Peter Andrews, Mr Brooks, Karin and Steve Flintoff, Gordon
Theaker, Robin Moore, Paul and Janet Waring, Stephen and Jean Curtis, Hilary Edwards, Viv
Middlebrook, Julian Holland, Mrs C Archer, K Kennedy)*

*Free house ~ Licensee Robin Moore ~ Real ale ~ Meals and snacks (till 9.30 on
Sat) ~ (01353) 778537 ~ Well behaved children in no-smoking rooms (over 5
after 8pm) ~ Open 12-2.30(3 Sun), 7(6.30 Sat)-11(10.30 Sun); cl 25 and 26 Dec
~ Bedrooms: £45B/£55B*

SWAVESEY TL3668 Map 5

Trinity Foot ♀ £

A604, N side; to reach it from the westbound carriageway, take Swavesey, Fen Drayton turn-
off

Fresh fish is delivered here daily direct from the east coast ports and is sold both in
the pub and in their fish shop next door (open Tuesday-Saturday 11-2.30, 6-7.30).
The popular menu includes smoked fish and fresh herb pâté or herring roes on toast
(£3.50), 6 oysters (£5), grilled butterfish, cod or plaice or tuna kebabs (all £7.50),
dressed crab salad (£6.50), grilled fillet of turbot (£9.50), dover sole (£11), and fresh
lobster (£15); other dishes include sandwiches (from £1), ploughman's (£3),
omelettes (£6), mixed grill (£9), and local seasonal things like samphire and soft
fruits. Well kept Boddingtons and Flowers on handpump, lots of wines, freshly
squeezed orange juice and coffee that's constantly replenished at no extra charge.
Service is cheerfully efficient, and there are well spaced tables, fresh flowers, and a
light and airy flower-filled conservatory; no-smoking dining room. There are shrubs
and trees in the big enclosed garden. *(Recommended by David Surridge, N B Thompson,
Pauline Langley, Ian Phillips, Joan Hilditch, Christine Van der Will, J G Cooke)*

*Whitbreads ~ Lease: H J Mole ~ Real ale ~ Meals and snacks (12-2, 6-9.30; till
10 Fri and Sat) ~ (01954) 230315 ~ Children welcome ~ Open 11-2.30, 6-11;
Sun 12-3, cl evening*

WANSFORD TL0799 Map 5

Haycock ★ ⑪ 🛏 ♀

Village clearly signposted from A1 W of Peterborough

The fine flagstoned main entry hall at this smartly civilised and very well run golden
stone hotel has antique hunting prints, seats and a longcase clock. This leads into the
lively panelled main bar with dark terracotta walls, a sturdy dado rail above a
mulberry dado, and old settles. Through two handsome stone arches is another

attractive area, while the comfortable front sitting room has some squared oak panelling by the bar counter, a nice wall clock, and a big log fire. There's an airy stripped brick eating bar by the garden with dark blue and light blue basketweave chairs around glass-topped basket tables, pretty flowery curtains and nice modern prints; doors open on to a big terrace with lots of tables. Friendly helpful staff serve quite smart and tasty bar food which includes home-made soup with ciabattta (£2.95), chicken liver pâté (£4.25), apricot and cheese fritters (£5.25), fresh pasta (from £6.75), grilled Loch Fyne kippers (£7.50), lamb's liver with smoked bacon or lamb hotpot (£7.95), Thai curried chicken (£8.25), grilled rump steak (£10.95). There are a couple of vegetarian dishes like aubergine stew (£7.45). Home-made puddings might include orange tart, fresh fruit meringues or chocolate truffle cake with bitter coffee sauce and cheese (from £3.45). Well kept Bass, Batemans XB, John Smiths, Marstons Pedigree and Ruddles Best and County on handpump, a good range of around 11 good house wines by the glass from an exceptional list, and properly mature vintage ports by the glass; freshly squeezed juices. The sheltered outdoor eating area with its big cream Italian umbrellas is very popular, and the spacious walled formal garden has boules and fishing as well as cricket (they have their own field). The restaurant and part of the dining bar are no smoking. *(Recommended by George Atkinson, Tony Gayfer, Frank Cummins, Hanns P Golez, R C Wiles, Janet Pickles, Susan and Nigel Wilson, John Fahy, Tim and Sue Halstead, S G Brown)*

Free house ~ Licensees Andrew Underwood and Louise Dunning ~ Real ale ~ Meals and snacks (12-10.30) ~ Restaurant ~ (01780) 782223 ~ Children welcome ~ Open all day; cl 25 Dec evening ~ Bedrooms: £72.50B/£115B

WOODDITTON TL6659 Map 5

Three Blackbirds

Village signposted off B1063 at Cheveley

The two comfortably snug and friendly bars at this pretty thatched village pub have high winged settles or dining chairs around fairly closely spaced neat tables, cigarette cards, Derby-Day photographs, little country prints, and winter fires – the room on the left has the pubbier atmosphere. The new licensees have introduced a more imaginative daily changing bar food which is freshly cooked from local produce. As well as two home-made soups of the day (£2.45) it might include starters such as smoked chicken salad (£3.50) and roasted quail on a bed of wild mushrooms with a red wine reduction or asparagus hollandaise (£3.95), and main courses such as a cold roast meat platter of the day (£3.95), roulade of spring chicken filled with smoked chicken mousse with an oyster mushroom sauce (£8.95), rack of English lamb with rosemary and honey sauce (£10.50), at least one fresh fish of the day with three or four at the weekend (from £8.50) and a vegetarian dish like Mediterranean vegetable terrine (£8.95). Home-made puddings might include treacle tart, summer fruit crème brûlée or bakewell tart (£2.45). Two constantly rotating real ales could be Greene King IPA, Flowers Original or Whitbreads Castle Eden well kept on handpump; about six wines by the glass and a wine of the week. The attractive front lawn, sheltered by an ivy-covered flint wall, has flowers, roses, and a flowering cherry, with a muted chorus of nearby farm noises; partly no-smoking restaurant; piped music. *(Recommended by Stephen Brown, Paul and Janet Waring; more reports please)*

Pubmaster (Carlsberg Tetleys) ~ Tenants Mark and Susan Roberts ~ Real ale ~ Meals and snacks ~ Restaurant ~ (01638) 730811 ~ Children welcome till 8pm if eating ~ Open 11.30-3, 6.30-11; Sun 12-3, 7-10.30

People named as recommenders after the main entries have told us that the pub should be included. But they have not written the report – we have, after anonymous on-the-spot inspection.

Lucky Dip

Besides the fully inspected pubs, you might like to try these Lucky Dips recommended to us and described by readers (if you do, please send us reports):

☆ Alconbury [Main St, Alconbury Weston; TL1875], *White Hart*: Friendly and characterful pub in charming village, good value straightforward bar food inc home-made chips, eating areas left and right, back bar with darts, Courage-related ales and an interesting guest beer, very helpful licensees *(Jenny and Michael Back, Norma and Keith Bloomfield, Geoffrey and Irene Lindley)*

☆ Barrington [from M11 junction 11 take A10 to Newton, turn right; TL3949], *Royal Oak*: Rambling thatched Tudor pub, heavy low beams and timbers, lots of character, pleasant no-smoking dining conservatory, tables out overlooking charming green; well kept Greene King IPA and Abbot, prompt friendly staff, food inc wide vegetarian range; maybe piped music, children in one area *(Susan and Nigel Wilson, Nigel Norman, D Horsman, Howard Gregory, Joy Heatherley, Nigel and Amanda Thorp, M Sargent, Dr and Mrs S Jones, S Brackenbury, LYM)*

☆ Bartlow [TL5845], *Three Hills*: Spacious and well established 16th-c family dining pub, neat and tidy, with copper ornaments and olde-worlde pictures, wide choice of bar food inc vegetarian, evening restaurant, Sun lunches, well kept Greene King IPA, decent wines by the glass, very unobtrusive piped music; interesting hill forts nearby *(Ian Phillips, Gwen and Peter Andrews, Richard Balls, A M Bateman)*

☆ Bourn [signed off B1046 and A1198 W of Cambridge; at N end of village; TL3256], *Duke of Wellington*: Consistently good range of generous imaginative food cooked to order in quiet and civilised relaxing bar divided by arches and so forth – where the locals come to dine out; well spaced tables, pleasant attentive staff, well kept Greene King; cl Mon *(Gordon Theaker, Mr and Mrs A J Martin, Maysie Thompson, BB)*

☆ Brampton [Bromholme Lane; off A141 Huntingdon Rd opp Hinchingbrooke House; TL2170], *Olde Mill*: Popular riverside Beefeater, idyllic summer setting – converted mill with working waterwheel and mill race rushing under lounge's glass "tables", usual good value bar food inc nicely garnished sandwiches, upper restaurant, Wl.itbreads-related ales, quick pleasant service, tables out by water *(Ian Phillips, Mrs P J Pearce)*

Buckden [High St, very handy for A1; TL1967], *Lion*: Lovely old coaching inn, comfortable atmosphere with efficient and friendly staff, good food and beers, no piped music, Courage-related ales; bedrooms *(Gordon Theaker)*

☆ Cambridge [85 Gwydir St], *Cambridge Blue*: Well kept Nethergate and frequently changed guest beers, good value food (not Sun evening) inc home-made pies and vegetarian dishes, small and simply furnished – one room no smoking; university sports photographs,

local paintings, friendly pubby atmosphere, sheltered terrace with children's climbing frame and entertaining model train *(David Brazier, Susan and Nigel Wilson, K Kennedy, P Carpenter, Susan and Nigel Wilson, LYM)*

☆ Cambridge [14 Chesterton Rd], *Boathouse*: Carpeted extension with verandah overlooking river (wonderful playground on opp bank), unspoilt relaxed atmosphere, L-shaped main room with varnished wood tables, framed prints and rowing memorabilia inc suspended eights boat, eight or so well kept beers such as Brakspears and Boddingtons, good choice of ciders, decent coffee, generous food, pleasant service; juke box; children welcome, pretty garden with hungry ducks, open all day; no dogs *(Keith and Janet Morris, Sue Grossey, Tim and Sue Halstead, KM, JM, LYM)*

☆ Cambridge [Midsummer Common], *Fort St George*: Picturesque, and very popular for its charming waterside position on Midsummer Common, overlooking ducks, swans, punts and boathouses; extensive but with interesting old-fashioned Tudor core, good bar food and traditional Sun lunches, well kept Greene King real ales, decent wines, games in public bar, intriguing display of historic boating photographs, tables outside *(Clare Wilson, Alice McLerran, K Kennedy, LYM)*

☆ Cambridge [Ferry Path; car park on Chesterton Rd], *Old Spring*: Good individual atmosphere, cosy old-fashioned furnishings and decor, bare boards, gas lighting, lots of old pictures, decent straightforward bar food inc Sun roasts, well kept Greene King IPA and Abbot, two log fires, long back conservatory, summer barbecues; children till 8, has been open all day Sat *(Ian Phillips, LYM)*

☆ Cambridge [Tenison Rd/Wilkin St], *Salisbury Arms*: A dozen or so well kept and well priced real ales and farm ciders in spacious high-ceilinged traditional main bar, good no-smoking area, decent basic lunchtime bar food from separate counter inc vegetarian dishes, friendly licensee, games room, TV, maybe jazz Sun lunchtime; can get very busy, open all day Sat *(Julian Holland, K Kennedy, LYM)*

☆ Cambridge [King St], *Champion of the Thames*: Basic small and cosy pub with friendly welcome, particularly good atmosphere, wonderfully decorated windows, padded walls and seats, painted anaglypta ceiling, lots of woodwork, no music, well kept Greene King IPA and Abbot *(Andy and Jill Kassube, K Kennedy)*

☆ Cambridge [Castle St], *Castle*: Unusual for being an Adnams pub, with their ales and guests such as Courage Directors, Fullers London Pride and Wadworths IPA and Farmers Glory kept well, good value food inc vegetarian; large, airy and well appointed, with easy chairs upstairs, wood grain tables on bare boards in downstairs tap room, no-smoking area, picnic tables in good garden *(Doug Patmore, Terry Barlow)*

☆ Cambridge [129 King St], *St Radegund*: Smallest pub in town, unusual decor with interesting former-student memorabilia, friendly landlord, well kept ales such as Fullers London Pride, Hook Norton Best and Nethergate, good malt whisky collection *(Andy and Jill Kassube, Frank W Gadbois)*
Cambridge [Napier St, next to Grafton Centre], *Ancient Druids*: Big bright air-conditioned modern pub notable for Kite, Merlin and Druids Special ales brewed on premises *(E A Thwaite)*; [19 Bridge St], *Baron of Beef*: Peaceful traditional front bar, old wooden furnishings, scrubbed floor, panelling, lots of old photographs, Greene King ales from uncommonly long counter, buffet food inc good hot beef sandwich *(John Fahy)*; [Clarendon St], *Clarendon Arms*: Very popular local with well kept Greene King and Rayments, friendly staff, wide choice of good cheap but adventurous bar lunches inc giant crusty sandwiches; open all day; bedrooms clean and comfortable *(Frank W Gadbois, E A Thwaite)*; [Regent St], *Fountain*: Replica traditional-style pub specialising in real ales – three Theakstons, Youngs Special, Marstons Pedigree and several interesting guest beers from small breweries; limited but good value traditional pie-style food, good mix of ages *(Bob and Sue Ward, Michael Williamson)*; [Regent St], *Globe*: Popular with business people for good lunchtime food choice, good range of well kept ales and bottled beers *(K Kennedy)*; [17 Bridge St, opp St Johns Coll], *Mitre*: Very friendly attentive service, half a dozen real ales, well priced wines inc some New World ones, attractively priced food from fine sandwiches and hot beef baps up, no-smoking area, log-effect fire, solid wooden country furnishings – aims almost too successfully at the unpretentious alehouse style *(Andy and Jill Kassube, Susan and Nigel Wilson, Kevin and Pam Withers)*; [43 Panton St], *Panton Arms*: Straightforward pub well worth knowing for good interesting quickly served food inc exceptionally fresh help-yourself salads *(Lawrence Pearse, Anthony Barker)*; [New Grange Rd (A603 SW edge)], *Red Cow*: Old-style bare-boards real ale pub with Whitbreads-related and other beers tapped into jugs from the cask; pleasant lively atmosphere, good choice of bar snacks, juke box, helpful staff; seating limited, no children *(Wayne Brindle, Stephen and Julie Brown, Comus Elliott)*; [Dover St (off East Rd)], *Tram Depot*: Unusual former tram stables with bare bricks, flagstones, old furniture, unconventional layout; reasonably priced bar food (not Sat evening), well kept Everards and wide range of other changing ales, seats out in courtyard; can be crowded with students *(P Carpenter, E A Thwaite, Julian Holland)*
Castor [off A47 W of Peterborough; TL1298], *Fitzwilliam Arms*: Long thatched pub, low beams, plush wall banquettes, no-smoking lounge, games machines at one end,

Ind Coope Burton and Tetleys, friendly and obliging service, sensibly priced food, tables outside *(Jenny and Michael Back)*
Chatteris [16 Market Hill; TL3986], *Cross Keys*: Hospitable service in attractive 16th-c building opp church in sleepy fenland town, long bar part public and part comfortable armchairs, pleasant back courtyard, good range of reasonably priced meals and snacks, Greene King beers, inexpensive wine, tea and coffee *(John Wooll)*; [South Pk St], *Honest John*: Friendly local, good bar food served by landlord's mother, well kept real ales inc guest beers (often regulars' requests), also wheat beer on tap; upstairs restaurant *(Alex Nooteboom, Steve Thompson)*
Chittering [Ely Rd (A10); TL4970], *Travellers Rest*: Friendly and efficient, with good generous straightforward food (real chips), well kept ales inc Ind Coope Burton; children in family room, camp site *(R C Vincent, Michael Williamson)*

☆ Conington [Boxworth Rd; signed off A14 (was A604) Cambridge—Huntingdon; TL3266], *White Swan*: Attractive and unpretentious country local with children welcome in several eating areas on right of cheerful traditional bar, games inc bar billiards and juke box on left, good big front garden with play area; good range of popular bar food inc fidgit pie and decent steaks, quick friendly service, well kept Greene King IPA and Abbot tapped from the cask, snuffs; tables outside, play house *(David Campbell, Vicki McLean, Wayne Brindle, Rich Baldry, BB)*

☆ Croydon [TL3149], *Queen Adelaide*: Sizeable beamed dining bar with standing timbers dividing off separate eating area, comfortable sofas, banquettes and stools, good food inc filled yorkshire puddings and steaks, well kept ales such as Boddingtons and Greene King *(M A Hendry)*

☆ Downham [Main St; sometimes known as Little Downham – the one near Ely; TL5283], *Plough*: Charming little traditional fenland village local with constantly changing choice of good value home cooking, friendly staff, lots of old photographs and bric-a-brac, Greene King ales under light top pressure, good choice of malt whiskies, tables outside; bustling atmosphere; the friendly well behaved golden retrievers are called Abbot and Indi *(John and Priscilla Gillett, Richard Balls)*

☆ Dry Drayton [Park St, opp church; signed off A428 (was A45) W of Cambridge; TL3862], *Black Horse*: Unpretentiously straightforward village local with good generous food inc wide vegetarian choice, well kept Greene King and other ales inc weekly changing guests, friendly prompt service, welcoming fire in central fireplace, games area, tables on pretty back terrace and neat lawn; camping/caravanning in meadow behind, maybe geese at end of car park *(Ian Phillips, Ian and Nita Cooper, Miss J Sanderson, E Robinson, Keith and Janet Morris, P and D Carpenter, BB)*

☆ **Eaton Socon** [village signed from A1 nr St Neots; TL1658], *Crown*: Comfortable bustle in old inn, refurbished but keeping the low beams, two open fires and three side areas off bar with separate dining room; good choice of moderately priced food (not Sun) from sandwiches up inc tasty home-made pies, ten or so perfectly kept real ales served in the northern style, friendly service, restaurant (good steaks); piped music may be loud; no T-shirts *(Ian Phillips, Bob and Maggie Atherton, Frank W Gadbois)*

☆ **Eaton Socon**, *Waggon & Horses*: Popular and busy old open-plan pub with lots of low beams and brasses, Bass and Tetleys-related ales, good value quick generous food inc copious fresh veg, delicious home-made puddings, good Sun lunches; friendly Irish landlord, welcoming staff, restaurant; monster marrow competition Sept *(D A Tinley, George Atkinson)*

Ellington [TL1672], *Mermaid*: Wonky old building, friendly local atmosphere *(Barry and Anne)*

☆ **Elsworth** [TL3163], *George & Dragon*: Attractively furnished and decorated panelled main bar and quieter back dining area, emphasis on good range of fresh food but plenty of character and atmosphere, well kept Greene King ales, decent wines, friendly service, open fire; nice terraces, play area in garden, restaurant; attractive village; cl Sun evening and Mon *(Gordon Theaker, Maysie Thompson, Wayne Brindle, E A George, LYM)*

Elsworth [1 Brockley Rd], *Poacher*: Pretty thatched cottage in beautiful surroundings, comfortable lounge, small back bar, lots of carving inc nicely done birds on bar front, loads of brassware and pleasant pictures; friendly staff, well kept Adnams and Everards Tiger, good if not cheap food (no deviations from menu) inc delicious puddings *(Maysie Thompson and others)*

☆ **Eltisley** [signed off A428; TL2659], *Leeds Arms*: Comfortable knocked-through beamed bar overlooking peaceful village green, huge log fire, plenty of dining tables, nicely presented sometimes unusual bar food from sandwiches up, Greene King IPA and Hook Norton Best or Charles Wells Bombardier under light blanket pressure, restaurant; children in eating area, pleasant garden with play area; simple comfortable bedrooms in separate block *(Wayne Brindle, LYM)*

☆ **Ely** [Annesdale, off A10 on outskirts; TL5380], *Cutter*: Lovely riverside setting, with plenty of tables outside and a genuine welcome for children; friendly series of unpretentious bars, decent food, real ales *(Neil and Angela Huxter, John Fahy, JM, PM, Wayne Brindle, LYM)*

☆ **Ely** [Silver St], *Prince Albert*: Cheerfully traditional unpretentious town pub with full range of Greene King ales in peak condition, no juke box, attractive garden below cathedral *(John C Baker, Steve Pickard)*

Ely [2 Brook St (Lynn rd)], *Lamb*: Pleasant hotel nr cathedral, comfortable panelled and

carpeted lounge bar with armchairs and settee, friendly attentive staff, good bar snacks inc warm smoked eel (local delicacy), well kept real ales; popular restaurant; bedrooms *(George Atkinson, W H and E Thomas)*

☆ **Farcet Fen** [Ramsey Rd; B1095 SE of Peterborough; TL2392], *Plough*: L-shaped bar with real fire, pictures, lots of brass and pub games at one end, dining room the other, three real ales; piped radio *(CMW, JJW)*

☆ **Fen Ditton** [High St; TL4860], *Ancient Shepherds*: Well cooked generous bar food inc imaginative dishes in comfortable and immaculate old-world lounge with settees and no music or fruit machines; friendly helpful staff, cosy restaurant (not Sun) *(Margaret Young, Colin Yardley, David Lee)*

☆ **Fowlmere** [High St; TL4245], *Swan House*: Friendly and comfortable local with enormous log fire, good interesting reasonably priced bar food, good choice of well kept real ales, attentive landlord, piano *(John Fahy)*

Girton [89 High St; TL4262], *Old Crown*: Roomy and recently tastefully refurbished, with antique pine, polished floorboards etc; well kept Greene King IPA, good value food, children's garden with pleasant terrace overlooking countryside, real fires, friendly staff; lavatory for the disabled; children welcome *(Richard Donaghy)*

Glinton [Lincoln Rd; TF1505], *Crown*: Good choice of competitively priced food, relaxed atmosphere *(Brian and Jill Bond)*

Grantchester [TL4455], *Red Lion*: Big food pub with sheltered terrace and good-sized lawn (with animals to entertain the many children); comfortable and spacious, busy food counter, restaurant *(Neil and Angela Huxter, Mike Beiley, LYM)*; [junction Coton rd with Cambridge—Trumpington rd], *Rupert Brooke*: Friendly and cosy renovated beamed pub with Whitbreads-related ales, wide choice of bar food inc vegetarian, discreet piped music *(John Fahy, Margaret and Roy Randle)*

Graveley [TL2564], *Three Horseshoes*: Good food, friendly and efficient service *(Mrs P D Denman)*

☆ **Guyhirn** [High Rd (off A47); TF3903], *Oliver Twist*: Comfortable open-plan lounge with well kept sturdy furnishings, real ales such as Bass, Fullers London Pride and Greene King IPA and Abbot on handpump, good range of good value food from sandwiches to steaks inc lots of salads and quite a lot of fish, big open fire, friendly quiet alsatian; restaurant, very popular as lunchtime business meeting place; opp River Nene embankment *(Jenny and Michael Back, E Robinson, Andrew and Janet Bennett, BB)*

Hail Weston [just off A45, handy for A1 St Neots bypass; TL1662], *Royal Oak*: Picturesque thatched and beamed pub in quiet and pretty village nr Grafham Water, with cosy log fire, darts, nice big garden with good play area which children can use even if pub's shut; usual bar food, well kept Charles Wells ales with guests such as Adnams Broadside and Morlands Old Speckled Hen, pleasant service, family room *(George Atkinson, Bob and Maggie Atherton)*

☆ Hardwick [signed off A428 (was A45) W of Cambridge; TL1968], *Blue Lion*: Enjoyably friendly local with fairly priced good food inc quite a lot of fresh fish, well kept beer, very extensive restaurant area, conservatory, Greene King IPA and Abbot, log fires, old farm tools; piped music, unobtrusive ginger tom; pretty roadside front garden *(G Washington, Jane Kingsbury, Michael Walker, Martin Sebborn, BB)*

Heydon [off A505 W of M11 junction 10; TL4340], *King William IV*: No reports of this rambling attractively lit partly 16th-c beamed and timbered pub (with bedrooms) since its 1995 sale, but it was notable for its extraordinary collection of furniture and bric-a-brac, English and continental *(LYM; news please)*

☆ Hildersham [off A604 N of Linton; TL5448], *Pear Tree*: Busy straightforward village local with odd crazy-paved floor, huge woodburner, generous genuine home cooking inc some unusual dishes and good vegetarian ones as well as usual cheery pub dishes, children's helpings and special dishes cooked to order, home-made bread and ice creams; well kept Greene King IPA and Abbot, decent wines, welcoming staff, traditional games, tables in back garden with aviary; children welcome *(Keith and Janet Morris, D A and A M Blackadder, John L Cox, BB)*

☆ Histon [High St; TL4363], *Red Lion*: Friendly local with well kept ales such as Benskins Best, Greene King, Marstons Pedigree and Morlands Old Speckled Hen; good-sized garden *(S R Maycock, Keith Stevens, Wayne Brindle)*

Holme [Station Rd; TL1987], *Admiral Wells*: Well kept ales (up to seven at weekends, esp good Oakham brews), enthusiastic landlord and good interesting food such as smoked eel salad and lavish balti dishes in well refurbished pub with views of Inter-City trains hurtling by; restaurant *(John C Baker, Richard Balls)*

☆ Horningsea [TL4962], *Crown & Punchbowl*: Friendly landlord, particularly well kept Adnams and other ales, obliging service, some emphasis on good food inc wonderful puddings, piped classical music *(Amanda Dauncey, John Rudolf, Comus Elliott)*

Houghton [The Square; TL2872], *Three Horseshoes*: Good cosy local with black beams, inglenook and darts in public bar, french windows into garden from comfortable lounge, well kept Courage-related ales, bar food (not Sun evening) inc good Sun roasts; nr watermill *(Quentin Williamson, LYM)*

☆ Huntingdon [TL2371], *Old Bridge*: Civilised hotel by River Great Ouse, wide choice of good imaginative food inc good value unlimited lunchtime cold table; drinkers just as welcome in charming plush lounge, with good choice of good wine by the glass, fine coffee, afternoon teas, good waitress

service; monthly jazz nights; attractive gardens with terraces and landing stage; bedrooms excellent, if expensive *(E Robinson, D H Tew, John Fahy)*

Ickleton [TL4943], *Red Lion*: Attractive 17th-c village pub with friendly service, clean dining area, good choice of home-cooked food inc OAP bargain lunch, great atmosphere, tables in garden with play area, children welcome *(John Dickerson)*

☆ Kennett [Bury Rd; TL7066], *Bell*: Delightful old heavy-beamed and timbered inn, neatly and plushly refurbished, with wide choice of well cooked and presented generous food inc some creative dishes, well kept Greene King and several other ales, friendly staff; very busy weekends; bedrooms *(Gordon Theaker, George Atkinson, John C Baker, Frank W Gadbois, LYM)*

☆ Kimbolton [20 High St; TL0968], *New Sun*: Character old Charles Wells pub doing well under new licensees, good variety of often imaginative food from chunky sandwiches to ostrich or swordfish, attractive beamed restaurant, conservatory leading to terrace, pleasant service, well kept Bombardier and Eagle and Morlands Old Speckled Hen *(Mr and Mrs A W Chapman)*

☆ Leighton Bromswold [signed off A604 Huntingdon—Kettering; TL1175], *Green Man*: Neatly modernised open-plan village pub with hundreds of good horsebrasses on heavy low beams, inglenook fireplace, original skittle alley; real ales such as Timothy Taylors Landlord, good food and service *(Alan and Heather Jacques, LYM)*

Littleport [Station Rd; TL5686], *George & Dragon*: Reasonably priced home-made food, well kept Charles Wells beers and a guest, farm cider, friendly locals and landlady; quiz night Sun *(Keith Kennedy)*

March [High St; TL4693], *Griffin*: Friendly service, real ale, good range of food *(M J Brooks)*; [High St], *King William IV*: Welcoming licensees, good range of reasonably priced food, small dining room, Courage beers with a guest such as Marstons Pedigree *(E Robinson)*; [Nene Parade], *Ship*: Busy local, open all day, very cheap simple food noon till 10 (small back dining room), Greene King ales, front bar with darts, fruit machine and piped music (can be a bit smoky); picnic tables overlooking River Nene *(JJW, CMW)*; [West End], *White Horse*: On riverside walk, partly thatched with lots of horse pictures in comfortable panelled lounge, Courage-related ales, fairly wide choice of decent food esp baked potatoes (lunchtime, Fri/Sat evening); no dogs *(JJW, CMW)*

Milton [High St; off A10 N of Cambridge; TL4762], *Waggon & Horses*: Friendly pub with L-shaped lounge, attractive garden with slide and swing, apple trees, barbecues, picnic tables and boules pitch; good value food, up to six real ales on handpump, three farm ciders; piped music (may be rather loud), TV, fruit machine *(JJW, CMW)*

☆ Needingworth [Overcote Lane; pub signposted from A1123; TL3472], *Pike &*

Eel: Marvellous peaceful riverside location, with spacious lawns and marina; two separate eating areas, one a carvery, in extensively glass-walled block overlooking water, boats and swans; easy chairs and big open fire in room off separate rather hotelish plush bar, well kept Adnams, Bass, and Greene King Abbot, good coffee, friendly and helpful staff, provision for children; clean simple bedrooms, good breakfasts *(George Atkinson, Julian Holland, Brian and Jill Bond, Dr and Mrs S Jones, LYM)*

Old Weston [off A14; SP7560], *Swan*: Friendly low-beamed old pub with big inglenook, brass and pictures, eight real ales, good value straightforward food from sandwiches up (not Mon/Tues), flowers and encyclopedia in no-smoking dining room, picnic tables outside *(CMW, JJW, LYM)*

Peakirk [12 St Pegas Rd; TF1606], *Ruddy Duck*: Very popular traditional village pub, nicely furnished and well cared for, with good range of generous food inc fresh fish and vegetarian (and late lunches), friendly efficient service, restaurant, terrace; handy for Wildfowl Trust shopping centre; open all day *(Miss P A Wilson, Brian and Jill Bond, M J Brooks)*

☆ Peterborough [Town Bridge; TL1999], *Charters*: Busy pub and restaurant in converted 1907 Dutch barge, interesting well prepared food, good choice of well kept beers from changing independent brewers inc Oakham, friendly atmosphere, tables also out in riverside garden *(John C Baker, Paul Bailey, Reg Nelson)*

☆ Peterborough [17 North St], *Bogarts*: At least six well kept ales such as Adnams and Bass, good simple food, fine mix of customers in basic but genuine pub handy for the Westgate shopping centre; friendly staff, open all day *(Stuart Earle, Reg Nelson, Robert Masters)*

Peterborough [Oundle Rd], *Johnny Byrnes*: Popular and friendly Irish-flavour local with bric-a-brac and memorabilia, well kept Courage-related ales, very quick service in big public bar; games room *(Reg Nelson, Stuart Earle)*; [Eastfield Rd], *Sportsman*: Archetypal backstreet local, comfortable and cosy, well kept ales, extensive sporting memorabilia *(Reg Nelson)*

Reach [off B1102 NE of Cambridge; TL5666], *Kings*: Friendly unpretentious local overlooking village green at N end of Devil's Dyke, landlord's German wife expertly cooks local produce, Elgoods Cambridge on handpump, local pictures for sale, seats outside – a quiet place *(John Fahy)*

☆ Sawston [High St (Cambridge Rd); TL4849], *Greyhound*: Cosy and comfortable L-shaped bar, games room down steps, light and airy high glass-roofed dining room overlooking good big garden, pleasant and obliging staff, good choice of generous prompt food inc vegetarian, open fire, Whitbreads-related real ales, good facilities for children; resident pyrenean mountain dog *(M and J Back)*

☆ Shepreth [12 High St; just off A10 S of Cambridge; TL3947], *Plough*: Changing well

kept ales such as Adnams, Boddingtons, Tetleys and Wadworths 6X and popular well presented home-cooked food from sandwiches and good home-made soup up in very neatly kept bright and airy local; modern furnishings, bow-tied staff, decent wines, side dining room, piped music; well tended back garden with fairy-lit arbour and pond, summer barbecues and play area *(Susan and Nigel Wilson, BB)*

Somersham [Huntingdon Rd (B1086); TL3677], *Windmill*: Panelled bar with windmill pictures, attractive two-part lounge/dining area with brickwork and beams and wooden furniture, helpful friendly staff, decent food inc good puddings, Greene King IPA and Abbot, garden with play area *(Jenny and Michael Back)*

☆ Spaldwick [just off A14; TL1372], *George*: Old village inn with extensive restaurant but keeping pub atmosphere, very friendly, obliging and efficient landlord, good value well presented food (pheasant in asparagus sauce particularly praised), very busy – booking needed Fri/Sat; well kept Charles Wells ales *(Roy and Margaret Randle, Mary and David Webb)*

St Neots [TL1860], *Chequers*: Charming inside, interesting antique furnishings, particularly well kept beers, good varied food, very welcoming staff *(Tim West)*

Stapleford [TL4651], *Rose*: Wide range of good well presented food in dining pub with tap room to left, small bar and big lounge with beams, inglenook and open fire; friendly prompt service, particularly well kept beers inc Fullers London Pride *(Andrew and Ruth Triggs)*

Stibbington [off A1 northbound; TL0898], *Sibson*: Beautifully kept bars and gardens, well kept real ales, friendly staff, tempting if not cheap cooking – handy stop from A1 northbound; bedrooms *(Comus Elliott)*

Stow Cum Quy [Main St; on B1102 follow sign to Angelsey Abbey; TL5260], *White Swan*: Traditional village pub, casual but comfortable and cosy; good value generous food, cooked to order so small delay when busy, inc lots of filled hot baguettes, vegetarian dishes, no-smoking dining room, Adnams and Courage Directors *(Keith and Janet Morris)*

☆ Stretham [Elford Closes; off A10 S of Stretham roundabout; TL5072], *Lazy Otter*: Big family pub well worth knowing for its position on the Great Ouse, with waterside conservatory and neat terrace tables; decent well presented food inc children's, warm fire in bar, friendly service, Greene King, Marstons Pedigree and a guest ale; piped music, can get busy weekends; open all day *(Stephen and Jean Curtis, R C Wiles, Stephen and Julie Brown, Wayne Brindle, R C Vincent, Tom Thomas, JM, PM, K Kennedy, Michael Williamson, Liz and Gil Dudley, LYM)*

☆ Stretham [High St (off A10); TL5374], *Red Lion*: Very neat village pub with wide choice of good generous food inc some unusual dishes, vegetarian and children's food and Sun lunch, solid pine furniture and old village photographs in lounge, marble-topped tables in pleasant no-smoking dining conservatory, five well kept real ales such as Greene King and Nethergate, separate attractive upstairs games room, friendly attentive service; children welcome, picnic tables in garden *(CMW, JJW, Mike Turner, JM, PM)*

Sutton [the one nr Ely; TL4478], *Chequers*: Good atmosphere in simple but bright and attractive bar with good genuine home cooking inc tempting puddings, well kept Greene King and other ales, friendly licensees *(Chris and Andy Crow, Julian Holland)*

☆ Swaffham Prior [B1102 NE of Cambridge; TL5764], *Red Lion*: Welcoming and attractive local in pleasant village, well kept Greene King ales, wide range of generous freshly prepared food from sandwiches and baked potatoes to steaks, comfortable dining area divided into several separate spaces, quick cheerful service; unusually plush gents' *(Alan Kilpatrick, Maysie Thompson, M J Brooks)*

☆ Swavesey [High St/Market Pl; signed off A14 (ex A604) NW of Cambridge; TL3668], *White Horse*: Good fresh home-cooked food from sandwiches to steaks inc vegetarian dishes and notable steak and kidney pie and curries (not Sun evening or Mon lunch) in welcoming village local with attractive traditional furnishings in public bar, more straightforward spacious lounge and no-smoking eating room; three Whitbreads-related ales, enterprising wines and spirits, winter Gluhwein, friendly service, children allowed; maybe discreet piped music *(Peter Carpenter, Simon Durrant, M Thomas, Mr and Mrs David J C Frost, Pauline Langley, BB)*

☆ The Turves [W of March; TL3396], *Three Horseshoes*: Real friendly beamed Fenland local, extended with family conservatory, good original food esp fish, well kept ales, usually one interesting guest and two nationals *(John Baker, Stuart Earle)*

☆ Thorney [A47/B1040; TF2804], *Rose & Crown*: Welcoming pub with wide range of freshly made food (so may be a wait), real ales inc guests, real fire, pleasant lounge, restaurant, pool in public bar; piped music, no dogs, extra charge for credit cards; children welcome, garden with play area *(CMW, JJW, E Robinson)*

Ufford [signed off B1443, which is off A15 N of Peterborough; TF0904], *Olde White Hart*: Old-fashioned 17th-c village pub with interesting features and nice snug (not always open), S&N ales, Wadworths 6X and a weekly guest beer, wide choice of bottled beers, farm cider, traditional games; big garden with terrace and play area, camping;

children welcome, folk music Sun evening, cl Mon lunchtime *(M J Morgan, LYM)*

☆ Upware [off A1123 W of Soham; TL5370], *Five Miles From Anywhere, No Hurry*: Aptly named spacious modern free house, fine riverside site with play area and public slipway, seats on waterside terrace; restaurant, silk flowers, three real ales, pool room, children welcome; live music some nights *(CMW, JJW, LYM)*

West Perry [TL1567], *Wheatsheaf*: Greene King pub on S bank of Grafham Water, handy for picnics, walks, cycle rides etc *(Norma and Keith Bloomfield)*

☆ Whittlesey [North Side; B1040 towards Thorney; TL2799], *Dog in a Doublet*: Comfortable, clean and welcoming riverside pub with bric-a-brac, old prints, well spaced comfortably solid seating; open fire, friendly attentive service, wide choice of reasonably priced bar food inc cheap children's dishes, well kept beer inc Bass, Morlands and Worthington, decent wines; small games room with pool; handy for Hereward Way walks, restaurant has been open all day Sun *(Jenny and Michael Back, Stuart Earle, Anthony Barnes)*

Whittlesey [2 Ramsey Rd], *Boat*: Cleaned up under new landlord, good breakfast, well kept beer *(MJB)*

☆ Whittlesford [off B1379 S of Cambridge; handy for M10 junction 10, via A505; TL4748], *Tickell Arms*: Great character and atmosphere, ornate heavy furnishings, dim lighting, lovely log fires, attractive flower-filled conservatory, beautiful formal garden, wide range of imaginative bar food, friendly service, well reproduced classical music, decent wines, well kept Adnams; cl Mon (exc bank hols), no credit cards *(Frank W Gadbois, John Fahy, L W Guthrie, Conor McGaughey, Richard Siebert, LYM)*

☆ Wisbech [North Brink; TF4609], *Red Lion*: Hospitable and civilised long front bar in lovely Georgian terrace on River Nene, nr centre and NT Peckover House; very popular lunchtime for good range of good value home-cooked food inc several vegetarian and fish, Fri bargain salad bar, well kept local Elgoods beer, decent wines *(M J Morgan, John Wooll)*

☆ Wisbech [53 North Brink], *Rose*: Cosy, friendly and popular little local in same splendid riverside spot, notable for fascinating choice of changing well kept real ales from small often Northern breweries; good value filled french bread, quick service *(PGP)*

Wisbech St Mary [TF4208], *Wheel*: Refurbished under new licensees, good straightforward food, new dining room (booking recommended weekends); comfortable bedrooms *(E Robinson)*

If you enjoy your visit to a pub, please tell the publican. They work extraordinarily long hours, and when people show their appreciation it makes it all seem worth while.

Cheshire

This is an excellent county for pub lovers, with many places of great individuality, lots of good food, some fine attractions on the drinks side, and sensible prices. This year we grant Beer Awards to the Blue Bell at Bell o th Hill (an interesting old place, newly promoted to the main entries) and the friendly and traditional Ship at Wincle. Other new entries here are the welcoming Egerton Arms at Broxton (lovely views) and the unusual and attractive Old Harkers Arms in Chester – the first time for some years that we've had a main entry in the city. Other pubs currently doing particularly well in the county include the Grosvenor Arms at Aldford (most popular for its bistro-style food – it gains a Food Award this year, and is our choice as Cheshire Dining Pub of the Year), the Aston at Bhurtpore (splendid combination of excellent beers with good food and atmosphere), the very simple and unpretentious White Lion at Barthomley, the Cholmondeley Arms at Bickley Moss (outstanding for dining out), the Pheasant at Higher Burwardsley, the smart but very welcoming Sutton Hall Hotel near Macclesfield, the Smoker at Plumley (it's converted its restaurant into a less formal brasserie), the Cheshire Hunt at Pott Shrigley (highly praised for food and service), and the Rising Sun at Tarporley (always busy, never a let-up in its friendly efficiency). The new licensees at Burleydam's Combermere Arms, a local family, are settling in very well. Drinks prices in the area are well below the national average. We even found a pint of Bitter at under £1, in the Jolly Thresher at Broomedge (tied to Hydes of Manchester), and pubs getting their beers from other smaller breweries such as Sam Smiths were also particularly cheap. We found some good brews this year from two small local brewers, Coach House (a rapidly expanding Warrington brewery) and Weetwood (based at an equestrian centre near Tarporley). Pubs currently showing prominently in the Lucky Dip section at the end of the chapter include the Maypole at Acton Bridge, White Lion at Alvanley, Thatch at Faddiley (excellent food, but rather strains the definition of a pub), Lamb in Nantwich, Olde Park Gate at Over Peover, Golden Pheasant at Plumley, Highwayman at Rainow, and both Smallwood entries. We have inspected all of these and can vouch for their appeal; but the Calveley Arms at Handley, another pub on which we've had promising reports, is entirely new to us and we'd be particularly glad of further reports on it. The Spinner & Bergamot at Comberbach has been very popular but was for sale as we went to press.

Post Office address codings confusingly give the impression that some pubs are in Cheshire, when they're really in Derbyshire (and therefore included in this book under that chapter) or in Greater Manchester (see the Lancashire chapter).

ALDFORD SJ4159 Map 7

Grosvenor Arms 🍴 ♀ 🍺

B5130 S of Chester

Cheshire Dining Pub of the Year

Comfortably chatty and enjoyably relaxed, this attractively and individually restyled substantial Victorian inn is gaining quite a reputation for its bistro-style food. But even though you'll have to get there early to be sure of a table, it's not at all the kind of place where eating dominates to the exclusion of all else – indeed the range of drinks at the good solid bar counter is excellent. Well kept beers on handpump might include Boddingtons, Buckleys, Flowers, Jennings Cumberland and Kimberley Classic, they have a couple of dozen malt whiskies, and each of the remarkable collection of wines – largely New World – is served by the glass. They've cleverly combined traditional decor with a spacious open-plan layout, with the best room probably the huge panelled library with floor-to-ceiling book shelves along one wall. Buzzing with conversation and quiet piped pop music, this also has long wooden floor boards, lots of well spaced substantial tables, and quite a cosmopolitan feel. Several quieter rooms are well furnished with good individual pieces including a very comfortable parliamentary type leather settle. Throughout there are plenty of interesting pictures, and the lighting's exemplary. Densely hung with huge low hanging baskets, the airy terracotta-floored conservatory has chunky pale wood garden furniture and opens on to a large elegant suntrap terrace and neat lawn with picnic sets, young trees and a tractor; the summer barbecues are popular. The menu changes every day, but you'll typically find things like home-made soup (£2.25), good value filled rolls (£2.95), peppered mackerel mousse with horseradish fromage frais (£3.50), a choice of ploughman's (£3.95), mushrooms stuffed with black pudding, fried in sesame seed batter and served with apple chutney (£3.95), stir-fried vegetable tortilla with guacamole (£5.45), broccoli, mushroom and brie strudel with spicy sweet pepper and tomato sauce (£6.95), chicken breast filled with sage stuffing with caramelised leeks and onions (£8.45), roast half shoulder of lamb with orange and ginger sauce (£8.95), and chocolate cheesecake with amaretto sauce; pleasant service. Two log fires, dominoes, chess, Scrabble, Trivial Pursuit, shove ha'penny. They take some bookings, but more than half the tables are always left unreserved; they get very busy at peak times. In June they usually organise a Summer Fete and Beer Festival. The family in charge also run half a dozen other pubs around the country; they used to own the Fox Revived in Norwood Hill in Surrey, and the Grosvenor Arms currently has much the same style and atmosphere as they developed down there. (*Recommended by Paul Boot, Peter Neate, Rita and Keith Pollard, KB, DH, Sue Holland, Dave Webster, S L Clemens, Paul Craddock, Dr P D Putwain and others*)

Free house ~ Licensees Gary Kidd and Jeremy Brunning ~ Real ale ~ Meals and snacks (till 10pm) ~ (01244) 620228 ~ Children welcome lunchtime ~ Open 11-3, 5-11; 11-11 Sat; 12-10.30 Sun; closed 25 Dec

ASTON SJ6147 Map 7

Bhurtpore 🍺

Off A530 SW of Nantwich; in village follow Wrenbury signpost

The choice of beers here varies even from day to day, with nine or ten real ales always available, most from little-known breweries. Kept in top condition on handpump, the range on a recent visit included Buffys Polly Folly Extra, Bunces Danish Dynamite, Coach House Gunpowder Mild, Gibbs Mew Bishops Tipple, Hanbys Drawwell, Hop Back Thunderbolt, Kelham Island Pale Rider, and Mordue Workie Ticket. They have dozens of good bottled beers, too, including Belgian fruit beers, keep a changing farm cider, and try to encourage people to try malt whiskies they've not had before (there's a choice of around 60). The pub's unusual name comes from a town in India where local landowner Lord Combermere won a battle, and there's a slightly Indian theme to the decor and the menu. The carpeted lounge bar has a growing collection of Indian artefacts (one statue behind the bar proudly sports a pair of Ray-Bans), as well as good local period photographs, and some attractive furniture. Curries and baltis are a particular feature of the very good bar food, with half a dozen home-made dishes like curried kidneys or chicken dansak (£5.50); other well-liked meals include sandwiches (from £1.60), home-made soup (£1.75), ploughman's (£3.25 – you can have it with a local farmhouse cheshire), tiger prawns in filo pastry with a lime mayonnaise dip (£3.25), sweet and sour Quorn or chicken breast in tarragon sauce (£5.95), braised steak with red wine and onions (£6.50), and good puddings. It can get packed at weekends, but earlyish on a weekday evening or at lunchtime the atmosphere is cosy and civilised. Tables in the comfortable public bar are reserved for people not eating; darts, fruit machine, pool, TV; piped folk, jazz or blues; friendly landlord and staff; tables in garden. Occasional beer festivals (when local trains may make special stops nearby). *(Recommended by Sue and Cliff Wise, Richard Lewis, N E Turner, Norman Huntbach, Nigel Woolliscroft, S L Clemens, Sue Holland, Dave Webster, Sue and Bob Ward, Mairi McArthur)*

Free house ~ Licensee Simon George ~ Real ale ~ Meals and snacks ~ Restaurant ~ (01270) 780917 ~ Well-behaved children in eating area of bar till 8.30 ~ Folk night third Tues of month ~ Open 12-2.30(3 Sat), 6.30-11; closed 25 Dec

BARBRIDGE SJ6156 Map 7

Barbridge Inn

Village signposted just off A51 N of Nantwich; OS Sheet 118 map reference 616566

Friendly and particularly well run, this comfortably modernised open-plan pub benefits from its pretty setting at the junction of the Shropshire Union and Middlewich canals, with a curvy little brick bridge beyond the busy riverside garden. It's especially welcoming to families, with a colouring page on the children's menu (crayons from the bar), baby-changing facilities, and a play house, climber, swings and slide outside; they're happy to help with warming baby food. As at other pubs in the Millers Kitchen chain, bar food includes sandwiches (from £1.85; hot baguettes £3.85), filled baked potatoes (from £2.95), ploughman's (£3.75), steak, kidney and mushroom pie (£4.35), broccoli and hazelnut bake (£4.75), chicken korma (£5.25), steaks (from £6.95), and daily specials such as 1lb lamb joint marinated in mint sauce (£6.30); Sunday roast (£4.95). The balustraded eating area (part of which is no smoking), up steps, overlooks the canal. Well kept Boddingtons and Cains and weekend guest beers on handpump; darts, dominoes, cribbage, shove ha'penny, fruit machine, video game, and quiet piped music. There's a side conservatory and picnic tables (some under cover) from which you can watch the narrow-boats. Good disabled facilities. *(Recommended by Richard Lewis, GT, Mike and Wendy Proctor, Brian and Anna Marsden, Patrick and Mary McDermott)*

Greenalls (Allied) ~ Manager W H Eyre ~ Real ale ~ Meals and snacks (all day) ~ (01270) 528443 ~ Children welcome ~ Jazz Thurs evenings ~ Open 11.30-11; 12-10.30 Sun

BARTHOMLEY SJ7752 Map 7

White Lion ★ £

A mile from M6 junction 16; take Alsager rd and pub is signposted at roundabout

One reader wasn't at all surprised to find himself sharing a pint with Charles I at this delightfully unpretentious black and white timbered pub. He turned out to be one of a group of Civil War re-enactors rather than the much-maligned monarch himself, but the building's unspoilt charms are such that he didn't look at all out of place. The simply furnished main bar has heavy oak beams dating back to Stuart times (one big enough to house quite a collection of plates), as well as attractively moulded black panelling, wobbly old tables, a lovely open fire, Cheshire watercolours and prints on the walls, and latticed windows. Up some steps, a second room has another open fire, more oak panelling, a high-backed winged settle, a paraffin lamp hinged to the wall, and shove-ha'penny, cribbage and dominoes. A third room is very well liked by local societies, and an outside drinking area was added last year. There's a friendly and relaxed atmosphere, with a good mix of people and no noisy games machines or music. The remarkably cheap lunchtime bar food fits in splendidly with the overall style of the place: soup (£1), oatcakes with cheese and beans (£1.30), filled french sticks or hot beef sandwich (£1.50), popular pies such as steak and kidney, and particularly good home-made hotpot (£2); only pies and rolls are available at weekends (when they can get very busy). Very well kept Buccaneer, Burtonwood Bitter, Forshaws, and Top Hat on handpump; the cats have their admirers too. The pub's bedroom is now used for staff accommodation, but as we went to press they were planning to convert an old grain store into hostel-style accommodation for walkers and cyclists. The early 15th-c red sandstone church of St Bertiline across the road is worth a visit. *(Recommended by Esther and John Sprinkle, Nigel Norman, George and Chris Miller, D R Shillitoe, Sue Holland, Dave Webster, Richard Lewis, Nigel Woolliscroft, Ian Williams, Linda Mar, David and Shelia, Paul and Gail Betteley, Alastair Campbell, Alan and Paula McCully)*

Burtonwood ~ Tenant Terence Cartwright ~ Real ale ~ Lunchtime meals and snacks ~ (01270) 882242 ~ Children welcome except in main bar – must be gone by 9pm ~ Spontaneous folk music first Sun lunchtime of month ~ Open 11.30-11 (closed Thurs lunchtime); 12-10.30 Sun

BELL O TH HILL SJ5245 Map 7

Blue Bell 🍺

Signed just off A41 N of Whitchurch

It's been a while since we last featured this characterful black and white timbered country pub as a main entry. The entrance to the building – with its massive central chimney – is through a great oak door by a mounting block; you then find yourself in a small quarry-tiled hallway, with stairs up, and another formidable oak door on your right. This leads into three very heavily beamed communicating rooms, two served by hatch; the main bar is in an inglenook with an attractively moulded black oak mantelbeam. Comfortably plush wall seats among the cheerful mix of furnishings, lots of brass ornaments, and Sunday newspapers to read. Very well kept Hanby Drawwell, All Seasons and Treacleminer on handpump; friendly landlord and staff. Generously served home-made bar food includes sandwiches, soup (£1.35), smoked mussels (£3.25), gammon and egg or a meaty steak and kidney pie (£4.95), various curries or half a chicken with garlic and lime juice (£5.50), local trout (£6.50), and weekend specials such as roasts or chicken tikka; children's helpings. They take pride in being local domino champions. Dogs welcome; their own poodle and great dane are very sociable, and bowls of water and biscuits are offered to other canine visitors. Picnic tables among flowers on the front grass, and maybe cows and a donkey or two in the adjoining field. *(Recommended by Richard Lewis, Paul Boot, Phil Putwain, A Croall, KB, DH)*

Free house ~ Licensees Patrick and Lydia Gage ~ Real ale ~ Meals and snacks ~ (01948) 662172 ~ Children welcome ~ Open 12-3, 6-11

BICKLEY MOSS SJ5549 Map 7

Cholmondeley Arms ★ 🍽 🛏 🍺

Cholmondeley; A49 5½ miles N of Whitchurch; the owners would like us to list them under Cholmondeley Village, but as this is rarely located on maps we have mentioned the nearest village which appears more often

High praise so regularly falls upon this converted Victorian schoolhouse that it's easy to forget how odd it can seem on first acquaintance. After all, the classroom surroundings, with the old school desks above the bar on a gantry, are as far removed from your typical local as the excellent meals are from, well, school dinners. Last year we chose it as our national Dining Pub of the Year, and though the emphasis is very much on eating, you're still likely to see people standing at the bar enjoying the well kept Boddingtons, Flowers IPA and a weekly changing guest beer such as Hanby Treacleminer or Weetwood Old Dog. The daily changing specials are particularly enjoyable, with a typical choice including carrot or celery soup, goat's cheese soufflé with devilled tomato sauce or mussel and leek vol au vents in a saffron sauce (£4.25), salmon and spinach lasagne (£6.95), rabbit braised with wine, mustard and lemon thyme or excellent fishcakes with hollandaise sauce (£7.25), monkfish provençale (£7.50), rump steak with a pepper, cream and brandy sauce (£11.95), and puddings such as rhubarb and ginger crumble or strawberry pavlova; children's dishes. Unless you can spare the time to wait booking ahead is a good idea, especially on a Saturday. The cross-shaped and high-ceilinged bar has a range of seating from cane and bentwood to pews and carved oak, masses of Victorian pictures (especially portraits and military subjects), patterned paper on the shutters to match the curtains, and a great stag's head over one of the side arches. An old blackboard lists ten or so interesting and often uncommon wines by the glass; big (4 cup) pot of cafetiere coffee, teas, and hot chocolate; very friendly, efficient staff. There are seats out on a sizeable lawn, and the Cholmondeley Castle and gardens are close by. *(Recommended by Frank Cummins, KB, DH, T and G Alderman, J F M West, Andrew Shore, David and Fiona Pemberton, Clare Wilson, A R and B E Sayer, Mike and Wendy Proctor, Basil J S Minson, Mr and Mrs C Cole, Martin and Penny Fletcher, W C M Jones, Mr and Mrs E J W Rogers, D Maplethorpe, B Helliwell, David Shillitoe, M Turner, Martin Bromfield, Bernadette Garner, Carl Travis, J and B Gibson, Phil Putwain, SLC, G R Sunderland, Carolyn Reynier, Nigel Woolliscroft, R N Hutton, Roger and Christine Mash, Paul and Maggie Baker, Rita and Keith Pollard, Chris Walling, Mrs J Oakes, Mrs P Abell, Thorstein Moen)*

Free house ~ Licensees Guy and Carolyn Ross-Lowe ~ Real ale ~ Meals and snacks (till 10 Sat) ~ (01829) 720300 ~ Well-behaved children welcome ~ Open 11-3, 7(6.30 Sat)-11; closed 25 Dec ~ Bedrooms: £34.50S/£49S

BRERETON GREEN SJ7864 Map 7

Bears Head ⬅

1¾ miles from M6, junction 17; fork left from Congleton road almost immediately, then left on to A50; also from junction 18, via Holmes Chapel

Masses of heavy black beams and timbers line the rambling open-plan rooms of this civilised timber-framed old pub. It's a relaxed and quietly friendly place, popular with locals coming for a drink and a chat as well as those wanting to eat. A section of wall (under glass for protection) has had the plaster removed to show the construction of timber underneath, and there are some traditional oak panel-back settles and a corner cupboard full of Venetian glass. Only one of the two serving bars is normally in use. Served by smartly dressed staff, popular bar food consists of home-made soup (£1.75), sandwiches (from £2.30), home-made pâté (£3.95), splendid home-made lasagne (£5.95), roast chicken with home-made stuffing or grilled fillet of plaice with banana, lemon and butter sauce (from £6.95) and rump steak (£7.95); also daily specials and a roast of the day (£5.95); very good chips and home-made puddings. Bass, Burtonwood Bitter, Courage Directors and maybe a guest beer on handpump, kept in fine deep cellars, a good range of blend and malt whiskies, fine brandies and liqueurs and decent wines (especially Italian); soothing piped music. Outside a pretty side terrace has white cast-iron tables and chairs under cocktail parasols, big black cast-iron lamp clusters and a central fountain; barbecues are held outside on the terrace in the summer. The pub is handy for the M6. *(Recommended by Joy and Peter Heatherley, Peter and Maris Brigginshaw, Dave Braisted, M L and G Clarke, W C M Jones, John and Pam Smith, Richard Lewis, P Williams, M W Turner)*

Free house ~ Licensee Roberto Tarquini ~ Real ale ~ Meals and snacks (till 10pm) ~ Restaurant ~ (01477) 535251 ~ Children welcome ~ Singers twice a month, usually Fri but some Thurs too ~ Open 12-3, 6-11 ~ Bedrooms: £42B/£56.50B

We say if we or readers have seen dogs or cats in a pub.

BROOMEDGE SJ7085 Map 7

Jolly Thresher

A56 E of Lymm

Tables by the neat bowling green behind this warmly welcoming 16th-c pub look out over the Bridgewater Canal. The bar is spaciously open-plan, with country chairs and tables on stripped boards, prints of some of Lowry's less well known paintings on the papered walls, fresh flowers, two open fires, and swagged curtains. Good value bar food includes lovely soup (£1.25), lunchtime sandwiches (£2; toasties 25p extra), chilli con carne (£3.95), southern fried chicken (£4.95), evening grills like steaks (from £6.25) or barnsley chop (£7.95), and daily specials such as cod and chips or excellent cajun chicken. Well kept Hydes Willy Westwoods (a local brew) on handpump; darts, dominoes, fruit machine, and piped music. *(Recommended by Paul Boot, M A Robisnon, Geoffrey and Brenda Wilson, Richard Lewis, E A Wright)*

Hydes ~ Tenant Peter McGrath ~ Real ale ~ Meals and snacks (not Sun evening or Mon) ~ (01925) 752265 ~ Children in eating area of bar ~ Folk group one Sun of month ~ Open 11.30-3(4 Fri, Sat and Sun), 5.30(6 Sat)-11

BROXTON SJ4754 Map 7

Egerton Arms

A41/A534 S of Chester

Well placed on the old high road, this convenient 19th-c black and white timbered inn gives lovely Cheshire views, as far as the River Dee, from the tables under cocktail parasols on its balcony terrace. Inside, the roomy and attractive dark-panelled bar has well polished old furniture, brasses, antique plates and prints; maybe unobtrusive piped music. The neatly kept dining area, with some no-smoking tables, opens off here. A good choice of generous well presented food includes soup (£1.25), prawn cocktail (£2.75), ploughman's (£3.95), salads, steak and kidney pie or chicken, ham and mushroom pie (£4.50), lasagne (£4.95), gammon steak or tandoori chicken (£5.25), vegetable burritos or grilled trout (£6.25), poached salmon (£7.95), peppered steak (£9.95) and roast rack of lamb (£10.75); good range of children's dishes and half helpings of main dishes are available. Well kept Burtonwood Bitter, James Forshaws, Tom Thumper and Top Hat on handpump; decent wines by the glass; service is consistently welcoming and efficient. Children may be given colouring materials, and the garden, with picnic tables, has a play area with a wendy house; piped music, fruit machine. There are good walks in the surrounding sandstone country. We have not yet had reports on the bedrooms here. *(Recommended by Paul and Maggie Baker, SLC, E G Parish)*

Burtonwood ~ Manager Michael Rothwell ~ Real ale ~ Meals and snacks (12-9.30) ~ Restaurant ~ (01829) 782241 ~ Children welcome till 8.30 ~ Open 10.30-11; 11-10.30 Sun ~ Bedrooms: £40.25S/£45.50S

BURLEYDAM SJ6143 Map 7

Combermere Arms

A525 Whitchurch—Audlem

This friendly 16th-c pub changed hands not long before we went to press but there shouldn't be any major changes – the family that's taken over have lived and farmed in the village all their lives, and early reports suggest they've taken to their new business really well. There's still the same commitment to offering changing guest beers in addition to the regular Bass and Worthingtons on handpump: Fullers London Pride and Saddlers Celebration were proving popular on a recent visit, and they also keep a range of malt whiskies. The traditionally furnished bar has horsebrasses and tankards on the beams, fox masks on standing timbers, and an unusal circular oak bar. Bar food includes soup (£1.50), sandwiches (from £2.25, served with chips and coleslaw so quite a hefty helping), ploughman's (£3.25), various pasta dishes (£3.50), rainbow trout (£5.95), giant vegetarian mixed grill (£6.50), and weekly changing specials such as fillet steak with peppered sauce. Darts, pool, pinball, dominoes, trivia, and piped music. There's a big indoor adventure play complex for children (£1). *(Recommended by Sue and Bob Ward, Mike and Wendy Proctor, Nigel Woolliscroft, Sue Holland, Dave Webster, Richard Lewis, Basil Minson, Paul and Maggie Baker)*

Free house ~ Licensee David Gordon Sutton ~ Real ale ~ Meals and snacks (12-2.30, 5-9.30) ~ Restaurant (all day Sun) ~ (01948) 871223 ~ Children welcome ~ Open 11-11; 12-10.30 Sun

CHESTER SJ4166 Map 7

Old Harkers Arms ♀ ◀

1 Russell St, down steps off City Rd

This attractive and comfortable conversion of an early Victorian canal warehouse is part of the small family-run chain that includes the Grosvenor Arms at Aldford. The lofty ceiling and tall windows give a feeling of space and light, yet the seats and tables are carefully arranged to allow a sense of privacy too. It's comfortably busy at lunchtime, but evenings can be lively; the friendly service remains impressively efficient, regardless. There's a good variety of things to look at, without too much clutter; attractive lamps, sepia nudes, accordion, various books. The bar counter, apparently constructed from salvaged doors, dispenses a good range of malt whiskies, decent well described wines (many from the New World), well kept Boddingtons, Fullers London Pride, Roosters Yankee (which the new landlord tells us is very tasty), Timothy Taylors Landlord and a guest like Weetwood Oast House Gold on handpump. A good changing choice of well presented often unusual food might include soups like cream of broccoli and stilton or cream of tomato and smoked bacon (£2.75), interesting sandwiches like smoked trout, cream cheese and dill or pastrami, gherkin and horseradish (all £2.95), ploughman's (£3.95), chilli in taco shells (£5.45), cumberland sausage in giant bap (£5.65), shepherd's pie or seafood baguette (£5.75), aubergine, courgette and pepper lasagne (£6.25), and fresh salmon on tagliatelle with a tomato vinaigrette (£7.95). Helpings are generous; and high marks for housekeeping – often what lets city pubs down. *(Recommended by Simon and Pie Barker, Richard Lewis, SLC)*

Free house ~ David Harding ~ Real ale ~ Meals and snacks (12-2.30, 5-9.30; not Fri or Sat eve) ~ (01244) 344525 ~ Open 11.30-3, 5-11; 11-11 Sat; cl 26 Dec

COTEBROOK SJ5765 Map 7

Alvanley Arms ⇐

Forest Rd; Junction A49/B5152, N of Tarporley

The pond outside this handsome creeper-covered Georgian inn has been landscaped this year, and they're hoping this will tempt more wildlife to come and join the resident geese. Inside, the main bar has a big open fire, neat high beams, a few hunting and sporting prints, some brasses, and fairly close-set tables (dining-height by the plush wall banquettes around the sides, and lower ones with plush stools in the middle). Well kept Robinsons Mild and Best on handpump from the solid oak bar counter, and several malt whiskies. On the other side of a pleasantly chintzy small hall is a quieter but broadly similar room with more interesting prints and a delft shelf of china; one area is no smoking. Good value waitress-served food includes sandwiches, home-made steak pie (£5.25), cod and chips with mushy peas (£5.45), cumberland sausage (£5.95), duck breast with plum and cointreau sauce (£9.10), and changing blackboard specials such as monkfish or mackerel in orange and tarragon sauce; there may be a wait for food unless you arrive early. The very pleasant garden looks out towards rolling fields and has fairy-lit picnic tables under a small cedar. No credit cards. *(Recommended by Comus Elliott, Paul Bailey, KB, DH, Simon Barber, Olive and Ray Hebson, Mrs P Abell, Karen Eliot)*

Robinsons ~ Tenant Mrs D E White ~ Real ale ~ Meals and snacks ~ Restaurant ~ (01829) 760200 ~ Children in restaurant ~ Open 11.30-3, 5.30(6 Sat)-11 ~ Bedrooms: £25B/£50B

DELAMERE SJ5669 Map 7

Fishpool

A54/B5152

As we hoped last year, nothing has changed at this attractive and well liked pub since the current friendly licensees took over. The four comfortable small room areas (watch out, one of the doors between them is very low) have neatly polished tables and upholstered stools and wall settles, and are bright with polished brasses and china. Well kept Greenalls Bitter, Mild and Original on handpump. Good value bar food includes sandwiches, and hot dishes such as chicken tikka or cumberland sausage in mustard sauce (£5.25), and braised steak with mushroom and onions (£5.50). No games or music; picnic tables outside on the lawn. The pub is so well placed near the pike-haunted lake and Delamere Forest it can be particularly busy at weekends – best to go early, then. *(Recommended by Olive and Ray Hebson, Frank Cummins, Martin Bromfield, Bernadette Garner, Bill and Irene Morley, Mrs P Abell, Graham and Lynn Mason, Mr and Mrs Craig)*

Greenalls (Allied) ~ Tenants Richard and Maureen Lamb ~ Real ale ~ Meals and snacks ~ (01606) 883277 ~ Children welcome ~ Open 11.30-3, 6-11 ~ Bedrooms: £17.50/£35

GREAT BUDWORTH SJ6778 Map 7

George & Dragon 🍺

4½ miles from M6, junction 19; from A556 towards Northwich, turn right into B5391 almost at once; then fork right at signpost to Aston-by-Budworth, Arley Hall & Gardens

Readers enjoy the relaxed atmosphere and well presented bar food at this friendly 17th-c pub, and for those who like pretty buildings in attractive villages it's a must. Popular with a broad mix of people, the rambling panelled lounge has plenty of nooks and alcoves, beams hung with copper jugs, red plush button-back banquettes and older settles, and a fine big mirror with horsebrasses on the wooden pillars of its frame; one area is no smoking. The public bar has darts, pool, dominoes, a fruit machine, video game, and piped music. At busy times families can use the upstairs restaurant, which is no smoking on Sunday lunchtimes. Bar food – with many prices now unchanged for two years – includes soup (£1.75), sandwiches (from £1.95), dim sum (£2.90), ploughman's (£4.25), salads (from £4.75), vegetarian curry (£4.75), fresh fillet of cod or gammon and egg (£4.95), steaks (from £7.95), daily specials such as steak and ale pie (£4.95), lamb and mint fricassee (£5.75), and a curry of the day, and puddings (£2); children's menu (£1.95). Well kept Tetleys and two weekly changing guests on handpump, quite a few malt whiskies, and Addlestones cider. Walkers must leave their muddy boots in the porch. Considered by some to be Cheshire's prettiest, the village is worth exploring. *(Recommended by Derek and Sylvia Stephenson, Martin Bromfield, Bernadette Garner, Alan and Paula McCully, John and Phyllis Maloney, Richard Lewis, Simon Barber, Graham and Lynn Mason)*

Carlsberg Tetleys ~ Lease: Malcolm Curtin ~ Real ale ~ Meals and snacks ~ Upstairs restaurant ~ (01606) 891317 ~ Children welcome til 9pm ~ Open 11.30-3, 6-11; all day Sat and Sun

HIGHER BURWARDSLEY SJ5256 Map 7

Pheasant 🛏️

Burwardsley signposted from Tattenhall (which itself is signposted off A41 S of Chester) and from Harthill (reached by turning off A534 Nantwich—Holt at the Copper Mine); follow pub's signpost on up hill from Post Office; OS Sheet 117 map reference 523566

Good old British beef is something of a speciality at this well placed 17th-c inn. The licensees keep their own herd of Highland cattle, and the walls of the beamed and timbered bar are covered with pictures and rosettes from shows they've won prizes in. There are also plenty of reminders of the landlord's previous career as a ship's pilot, such as his Merchant Navy apprenticeship papers, some ship photographs, and a brass ship's barometer. Even the parrot – who enjoys the splendid view of the Cheshire Plain towards the Wirral and beyond – is called Sailor. Other decorations include a stuffed pheasant, a set of whimsical little cock-fighting pictures done in real feathers, and big colour engravings of Victorian officials of the North Cheshire Hunt. There are some plates above the high stone mantelpiece of the see-through fireplace (said to house the biggest log fire in the county), and around the fire is a tall leather-cushioned fender. Other seats range from red leatherette or plush wall seats to one or two antique oak settles. Good bar food includes sandwiches (from £2.25), home-made soup (£2.25), ploughman's (£4.10), several vegetarian dishes like pasta with leeks in a cream and dill sauce (£5.95), popular fresh fish such as plaice, brill, halibut, john dory and dover sole (from £6.50), a pie of the day (£6), grilled chicken breast stuffed with ginger and leek sausage in a white wine sauce (£8), and their own steaks (from £9.50); popular three-course Sunday lunch (£10.50). Credit cards only accepted for bills over £20 (and watch out for the £1 surcharge for cheques). The pleasant conservatory is no smoking in the daytime. Well kept Bass and a guest such as Butlers or Sadlers on handpump, a choice of over 40 malts and quite a few wines; friendly staff. Fruit machine (not in main bar), dominoes and piped music. The bedrooms are in an attractively and very comfortably converted sandstone-built barn, and all have views; picnic tables on a big side lawn. The pub is well placed for walks along the Peckforton Hills, and the nearby Candle Workshops are quite a draw in summer. *(Recommended by David Shillitoe, Mr and Mrs E J W Rogers, David Gittins, Geoffrey and Irene Lindley, M Turner, Sue Holland, Dave Webster, F A Eames, Mr and Mrs Craig, Don Kellaway, Angie Coles, Paul Robinshaw)*

Free house ~ Licensee David Greenhaugh ~ Real ale ~ Meals and snacks ~ Restaurant ~ (01829) 770434 ~ Children in conservatory till 8pm ~ Horses welcomed, and horse-and-trap rides can be arranged ~ Open 11.30-3, 6.30-11 ~ Bedrooms: £45B/£70B

LANGLEY SJ9471 Map 7

Leathers Smithy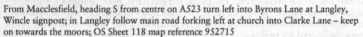

From Macclesfield, heading S from centre on A523 turn left into Byrons Lane at Langley, Wincle signpost; in Langley follow main road forking left at church into Clarke Lane – keep on towards the moors; OS Sheet 118 map reference 952715

Another pub in a lovely setting, the surrounding pastures, hills and pine woods backed by the steep mass of the Teggs Nose country park; benches in front soak up the view. As we went to press the landlord was negotiating to buy the pub from the brewery, but no changes are planned – he's been here 16 years now so already has things pretty much the way he wants them. The room that readers like best is the lively, partly flagstoned right-hand bar with its bow window seats or wheelback chairs, and roughcast cream walls hung with gin traps, farrier's pincers, a hay basket and other ironwork. On the left, there are more wheelback chairs around cast-iron-framed tables on a turkey carpet, little country pictures and drawings of Cheshire buildings, Wills steam engine cigarette cards and a locomotive name-plate curving over one of the two open fires; faint piped music. The family room is no smoking. Well kept Banks, Jennings, Tetleys and a monthly changing guest like Marstons Pedigree on handpump, as well as Addlestones cider. Gluhwein in winter from a copper salamander, and a decent collection of spirits, including around 80 malt whiskies and 10 Irish; dominoes. Bar food includes sandwiches (from £2), black pudding and mushy peas (£3.95), ploughman's, vegetarian dishes such as spinach and walnut pancake (£4.95), lasagne (£5.20), home-made steak pie (£5.50), halibut or gammon and egg (£6.75), steaks (from £8.95), and puddings; they take credit cards. The pub is a popular stop for walkers. *(Recommended by Steve Goodchild, Peter Downes and others; more reports please)*

Carlsberg Tetleys ~ Tenant Paul Hadfield ~ Real ale ~ Meals and snacks (limited Mon lunchtime, not Mon evening; till 8.30 other evenings, though Fri and Sat till 9.30) ~ (01260) 252313 ~ Children in family room Sat and Sun lunchtime only ~ Occasional pianola music ~ Open 12-3, 7(5.30 Fri)-11; all day Sat and Summer Suns

nr LANGLEY SJ9471 Map 7

Hanging Gate

Higher Sutton; follow Langley signpost from A54 beside Fourways Motel, and that road passes the pub; from Macclesfield, heading S from centre on A523 turn left into Byrons Lane at Langley, Wincle signpost; in Sutton (half-mile after going under canal bridge, ie before Langley) fork right at Church House Inn, following Wildboarclough signpost, then two miles later turning sharp right at steep hairpin bend; OS Sheet 118 map ref 952696

Lovely views from this cosy old drovers' pub, looking out beyond a patchwork of valley pastures to distant moors (and the tall Sutton Common transmitter above them). First licensed nearly 300 years ago but actually built much earlier, the pub's three low-beamed rooms are simply and traditionally furnished, and there are big coal fires, a stuffed otter, and some attractive old photographs of Cheshire towns around the walls. Down some stone steps is an airier garden room. Reasonably priced bar food includes soup (£2), sandwiches, and a changing range of hot dishes such as steak and kidney pie, Indian baltis and Mexican chimichangas or spicy meatballs (£5.75). Well kept Courage Directors, Ruddles County and John Smiths on handpump, mulled wine in winter; friendly service. The blue room is no smoking. Dominoes, juke box, seats outside on a crazy-paved terrace. *(Recommended by Mike and Wendy Proctor, Andy Hazeldine, J Muir, Jack Morley, Wayne Brindle, Yolanda Henry, Nigel Woolliscroft)*

Free house ~ Licensees John and Lyn Vernon ~ Real ale ~ Meals and snacks (not Thurs) ~ (01260) 252238 ~ Children in two family rooms ~ Open 12-3, 7-11; closed all day Thurs

LOWER PEOVER SJ7474 Map 7

Bells of Peover ★

The Cobbles; from B5081 take short cobbled lane signposted to church

Tucked away in a beautifully off the beaten track setting, this wisteria-covered pub has long been a lunchtime favourite with readers. The sheltered crazy-paved terrace in front faces a lovely black and white timbered church, and a spacious lawn beyond the old coachyard at the side spreads down through trees and rose pergolas to a little stream. Inside is very neatly kept, and the little tiled bar has side hatches for its serving counter, toby jugs, and comic Victorian prints, while the original lounge has two small coal fires, antique settles, antique china in the dresser, high-backed windsor armchairs, a spacious window seat, and pictures above the panelling. There's a second similar lounge. Good waitress-served bar food includes soup (£1.90), sandwiches with home-cooked meats (from £2.25), filled baked potatoes (£4.25), home-made quiche (£4.95), attractive salads (from £5.25), home-made pies (£5.75), good daily specials, and several puddings (£2.50). Most people wear a jacket and tie in the restaurant. Well kept Greenalls Bitter and Original on handpump and several wines. As it's such an attractive setting the place can get busy, which we trust accounts for the hiccups in food service a couple of readers have encountered this year. Note they don't allow children under 14 except in the restaurant. *(Recommended by Martin Bromfield, Bernadette Garner, Jack and Philip Paxton, RJH, J F M West, John Waller, Paul and Lynn Benny, Roger and Christine Mash, Carl Travis, Mrs P Abell, John Broughton, Kevin and May Bronnsey, Graham and Lynn Mason, John and Pam Smith, Wendy, Liz and Ian Phillips, John Derbyshire, Leith Stuart)*

Greenalls (Allied) ~ Lease: Keith Jones, Philip A Jones ~ Real ale ~ Meals and snacks ~ Restaurant (closed Sat lunchtime, Sun evening, Mon) ~ (01565) 722269 ~ Children in restaurant ~ Open 11.30-3, 5.30(6 Sat)-11

MACCLESFIELD SJ9271 Map 7

Sutton Hall Hotel ★ 🛏

Leaving Macclesfield southwards on A523, turn left into Byrons Lane signposted Langley, Wincle, then just before canal viaduct fork right into Bullocks Lane; OS Sheet 118 map reference 925715

In such grand surroundings you might expect the atmosphere to be a little snooty, but one of the things readers particularly love about this civilised 16th-c baronial hall is the very friendly welcome and congenial atmosphere. The bar (divided into separate areas by tall black timbers) is furnished mainly with straightforward ladderback chairs around sturdy thick-topped cast-iron-framed tables, though there are a few unusual touches such as an enormous bronze bell for calling time, a brass cigar-lighting gas taper on the bar counter itself, a suit of armour by another big stone fireplace, and a longcase clock; also, some antique squared oak panelling, lightly patterned art nouveau stained glass windows, broad flagstones around the bar counter (carpet elsewhere), and a raised open fire. The menu is not unusual but the food is excellently cooked and presented, and there's friendly waitress service; the range includes home-made soup (£1.55), sandwiches (from £2.10), home-made pâté (£3.25), home-made lasagne (£5), home-made steak and kidney pie or spinach pancakes filled with ratatouille with a sour cream dressing (£5.25), daily specials such as venison sausages, smoked quail or monkfish in batter (from £5.35), and puddings (£2). Well kept Bass, Marstons Burton, Stones Best and a guest beer on handpump, 40 malt whiskies, freshly squeezed fruit juice, and decent wines. It's set in lovely grounds with tables on a tree-sheltered lawn; they can arrange clay shooting, golf or local fishing for residents. They recently obtained a licence to hold weddings here. *(Recommended by G R Roberts, Jack Morley, J F M West, J C T Tan, Clare Wilson, C H and P Stride, Thomas Nott, F C Johnston, Kevin and Kay Bronnsey, Nigel Woolliscroft, Mr and Mrs B Hobden)*

Free house ~ Licensee Robert Bradshaw ~ Real ale ~ Meals and snacks (till 10pm) ~ Restaurant ~ (01260) 253211 ~ Children allowed weekends and bank hol lunchtimes only ~ Open 11-11; 12-4, 7-10.30 Sun ~ Four-poster bedrooms: £68.95B/£85B

MARBURY SJ5645 Map 7

Swan

NNE of Whitchurch; OS Sheet 117 map reference 562457

Regular visitors head straight for a seat in the inglenook alcove beside the blazing fire at this creeper-covered white pub. The licensees have been here for more than 25 years now, which perhaps accounts for the buoyantly cheerful atmosphere and good mix of customers; everyone gets an individual welcome. The neatly kept, partly panelled lounge has upholstered easy chairs and other country furniture, a grandfather clock, a copper-canopied fireplace with a good winter fire (masses of greenery in summer), and discreet lighting; half the room is no smoking. Most of the imaginative food is listed on a board, with many dishes changing daily: fine soups (£1.50), chicken liver pâté (£2.65), garlic mushrooms (£3.25), good spinach and garlic mushroom pancake (£5.25), Whitby goujons of plaice (£5.50), smoked haddock and prawn cheesebake or local beef in ale (£5.50), tasty char-grilled lamb chops with orange mint sauce (£6.50), steaks (from £7.95), and puddings like banoffi pie or chocolate and almond torte (£2.50); chips are home-made. Well kept Greenalls Original, Tetleys and in summer a guest on handpump, 40 malt whiskies, Bulmers cider, and friendly service. Darts, dominoes, cribbage; no machines or piped music. Rebuilt in 1884, the pub is in a quiet and attractive village, a half-mile's country walk from the Llangollen Canal, Bridges 23 and 24. The nearby church is worth a visit. *(Recommended by Sue and Bob Ward, George Jonas, Jean and Richard Phillips, Pete Yearsley, Bill Sykes, Nigel Woolliscroft)*

Greenalls (Allied) ~ Lease: George, Ann and Mark Sumner ~ Real ale ~ Meals and snacks (not Mon lunchtime) ~ Restaurant ~ (01948) 663715 ~ Children welcome ~ Open 12-3, 7-11; closed Mon lunchtime (except bank holidays)

MOBBERLEY SJ7879 Map 7

Bird in Hand

B5085 towards Alderley

Seats outside are a useful overflow if the cosy low-ceilinged rooms at this partly 16th-c pub start to get a little too bustling, but it's the kind of place where the number of visitors doesn't really alter the atmosphere – it always feels relaxed and friendly. There are toby jugs and other china on a high shelf, comfortably cushioned heavy wooden seats, warm coal fires, small pictures on the attractive Victorian wallpaper, and wood panelling in the little snug; the top dining area is no smoking. Promptly served home made bar food, in decent helpings, includes sandwiches (from £1.95), welsh rarebit (£4.25), vegetarian bake (£4.50), ploughman's (£4.75), gammon and egg or steak and ale pie (£4.95), several pasta dishes such as spaghetti marinara (£5.25), popular daily specials including good fish, and puddings like home-made fruit pie (£1.95); summer afternoon teas, helpful staff. Well kept Sam Smiths OB and Museum on handpump and lots of malt whiskies; dominoes, cribbage, fruit machine, trivia, and occasional piped music. *(Recommended by Dave and Doreen Irving, Martin Bromfield, Bernadette Garner, Malcolm Taylor, Clare Wilson, Chris Westmoreland, Yolanda Henry, R T and J C Moggridge, Richard Lewis)*

Sam Smiths ~ Manager Guy Richardson ~ Real ale ~ Meals and snacks (served right through till 8.30 on Sun) ~ (01565) 873149 ~ Children in rooms away from the bar ~ Open 11-11; 12-10.30 Sun

OVERTON SJ5277 Map 7

Ring o' Bells £

Just over 2 miles from M56, junction 12; 2 Bellemonte Road – from A56 in Frodsham take B5152 and turn right (uphill) at Parish Church signpost

A couple who emigrated to Canada some 15 years ago recently returned to this early 17th-c local and were delighted to find it exactly as they remembered it. Friendly and characterful, it's very much the sort of place where drinkers stand around the bar chatting, and where the food is good value and tasty rather than particularly unusual or ambitious. There are a couple of nicely old-fashioned little rambling rooms with windows giving a view past the stone church to the Mersey far below; one at the back has some antique settles, brass-and-leather fender seats by the log fire, and old hunting prints on its butter-coloured walls. A beamed room with antique dark oak panelling and stained glass leads through to a darts room (there's also dominoes and cribbage, but no noisy games machines or music). Good value waitress-served bar food is served at lunchtime only, with the most popular dishes typically the sandwiches and toasties (especially the steak and onion), deep-fried camembert (£2.65), home-made chilli, curry or lasagne (£3.35), and chicken balti or home-made steak and mushroom pie (£3.95). Well kept Greenalls Bitter and Original on handpump or tapped from the cask (sometimes kept under light blanket pressure), and around 80 different malt whiskies served from the old-fashioned hatch-like central servery; service is cheerful and friendly, though decidedly unsubtle at closing time. The tabby twins are called Shula and Tilly, and there's another cat, Lottie. The prize-winning hanging baskets in front are quite a sight in summer, and at the back is a secluded garden with tables and chairs, a pond, and lots of trees. *(Recommended by Don Kellaway, Angie Coles, Dr M Owton, Comus Elliott, Dave Thompson, Margaret Mason, Gerry Kelsall)*

Greenalls (Allied) ~ Tenant Shirley Wroughton-Craig ~ Real ale ~ Lunchtime meals and snacks ~ Children welcome away from bar area ~ (01928) 732068 ~ Open 11.30-3(4 Sat), 5.30(6 Sat)-11

PEOVER HEATH SJ7973 Map 7

Dog

Off A50 N of Holmes Chapel at the Whipping Stocks, keep on past Parkgate into Wellbank Lane; OS Sheet 118 map reference 794735; note that this village is called Peover Heath on the OS map and shown under that name on many road maps, but the pub is often listed under Over Peover instead

Two thirds of this rambling and civilised inn are now no smoking. Around the recently refurbished main bar is an engaging series of small areas with seats ranging from a comfortable easy chair, through wall seats (one built into a snug alcove around an oak table), to the handsome ribbed banquettes in the quiet and spacious dining room on the left; logs burn in one old-fashioned black grate and a coal fire opposite is flanked by two wood-backed built-in fireside seats. Well liked bar food includes sandwiches (from £2.40), home-made soup such as carrot and coriander (£2.50), mushrooms in beer batter with garlic dip (£3.95), ploughman's (from £4.45), baked ham and pineapple mornay, haddock and prawn au gratin, roast beef and yorkshire pudding, and rabbit with herbs and mustard (all £7.45), and puddings such as home-made fruit crumble or sticky toffee pudding (£2.50); dishes are 50p more in the evening. Well kept Boddingtons, Flowers IPA, Greenalls Original and a guest on handpump, Addlestones cider, lots of malt whiskies, decent wine list, freshly squeezed orange juice and espresso and cappuccino coffee; darts, pool, dominoes, video game, juke box, and piped music. Friendly service. Weekly quiz night on Thursdays. There are picnic tables out on the quiet lane, underneath the pub's pretty hanging baskets, and an attractive beer garden, nicely lit in the evenings. The licensees also run our main entry in Swettenham, along with a pub in Altrincham. *(Recommended by Ray Cuckow, Harold Harris, R Davies, Jack Morley, Roger and Christine Mash, Simon Barber, Kevin and Kay Bronnsey, Jill and Peter Bickley, K J Phillips, Mr and Mrs Smith-Richards, Mrs B Lemon, Yolanda Henry, L M Miall)*

Free house ~ Licensee Frances Cunningham ~ Real ale ~ Meals and snacks ~ Restaurant ~ (01625) 861421 ~ Children in eating area of bar ~ Pianist Tues, keyboard/guitar vocalist Tues ~ Open 11.30-3, 5.30-11 ~ Bedrooms: £45B/£62.50B

PLUMLEY SJ7175 Map 7

Smoker

2½ miles from M6 junction 19: A556 towards Northwich and Chester

An Edwardian print on the wall capturing a hunt meeting outside shows how little the appearance of this well run thatched pub has changed over the centuries. Named for a favourite racehorse of the Prince Regent some two hundred years ago, it has three well decorated connecting rooms with open fires in impressive period fireplaces. A collection of copper kettles and some military prints punctuate the dark panelling, and there are comfortable deep sofas, cushioned settles, windsor chairs, and some rush-seat dining chairs; one area is no smoking. A glass case contains an interesting remnant from the Houses of Parliament salvaged after they were hit by a bomb in World War II. Good home-made bar food includes soup (£1.95), sandwiches (from £2.20), tasty savoury pancakes or pâté (£3.65), ploughman's (£5.95), fresh plaice (£5.85), kofta curry (£5.95), fresh pineapple filled with nuts and vegetables and topped with cheese (£6.75), steak and kidney pie (£6.75), a splendid beef stroganoff (£6.85), steaks (from £8.60), daily specials and puddings like roly poly with their own raspberry jam (£3.25); children's meals. The restaurant has been transformed into a more informal brasserie, and it now blends more effectively into the pub as a whole. Well kept Robinsons Best, Hatters Mild and Frederics Old Stockport on handpump; 30 malt whiskies and a good choice of wines; friendly service; piped music. Outside there's a sizeable side lawn with roses and flowerbeds, and a children's play area in the extended garden. *(Recommended by Mr and Mrs J A Phipps, George Jonas, W C M Jones, A R and B E Sayer, Charlotte Wrigley, FMH, Mr and Mrs C Cole, S L Clemens, Jack Morley, Mrs Pat Crabb, Simon Barber, Andy Cunningham, Gary*

Roberts, Ann Stubbs, DAV, Mrs B Lemon, Richard Lewis, J and B Gibson, Bronwen and Steve Wrigley)

Robinsons ~ Tenants John and Diana Bailey ~ Real ale ~ Meals and snacks (12-2.30, 6-10; all day Sun) ~ Brasserie ~ (01565) 722338 ~ Children in eating area of bar and in restaurant ~ Open 11-3, 5.30-11; 12-10.30 Sun

POTT SHRIGLEY SJ9479 Map 7
Cheshire Hunt

At end of B5091 in Bollington, where main road bends left at Turners Arms, fork straight ahead off it into Ingersley Road to follow Rainow signpost, then up hill take left turn signposted Pott Shrigley; OS Sheet 118 map reference 945782

Reports on this isolated former farmhouse have become very enthusiastic since the current licensees arrived, bringing with them the enviable skills and reputation they'd built up when they ran the Stanley Arms at Bottom of the Oven. The food in particular stands out, with a good choice including sandwiches, home-made soup (£1.95), white stilton cheese spiced with nutmeg and peppercorns, breaded, deep fried and set on a fresh apple and cinnamon purée (£3.95), black pudding with Irish soda bread (£3.95), locally made spicy sausages (£4.20), pasta with ham, basil, tomato and mushroom (£4.95), vegetable stroganoff (£5.50), baked trout filled with pine kernels, lemon and mediterranean spices (£6.30), steaks (from £7.95), daily specials, and puddings like bilberry pie (£2) or lemon soufflé (£2.20); children's dishes (from £1.95). Booking is recommended for Sunday lunchtime. There are several small rooms that ramble up and down steps with spindleback and wheelback chairs, solidly built small winged settles, sturdy rustic tables, lovely flower arrangements, beams and black joists, and roaring log fires. One room is no smoking. Well kept Boddingtons, Marstons and guest beers on handpump; very good efficient service, no games machines or piped music. Outside, there are seats on three terraces, gardens, and views over pastures. The pub was called the Quiet Woman in the days when it was a weekly cattle-auction house; it got its present name around 1850. *(Recommended by Mrs E Dakin, John Fazakerley, FMH, Jack Morley, Gill and Maurice McMahon, Brian and Anna Marsden, Jill and Peter Bickley, Andrew Ross)*

Free house ~ Licensee Alan Harvey ~ Real ale ~ Meals and snacks (till 10pm; not Mon lunchtime) ~ Restaurant ~ (01625) 573185 ~ Children welcome ~ Open 11.30(12 Sat/Sun)-3, 5.30-11; closed Mon lunchtime

SUTTON SJ9469 Map 7
Ryles Arms 🍺

Off A54 Congleton—Buxton, 2¾ miles E of A523 – signposted Sutton 2¾; or coming into Sutton from Macclesfield, fork right after going under aqueduct; OS Sheet 118 map reference 942694

Surrounded by pleasant countryside with mainly donkeys and ponies as neighbours, this pleasant slated white stone local is very much a popular dining pub – though people do drop in for a drink. The attentive and warmly friendly Irish landlord really puts a lot into running the place, and that comes across in the atmosphere. Consistently reliable food might include sandwiches (from £2), steak and kidney pie or vegetable crumble (£5), game or duck pie (£6), various fish dishes (from £6), and game in season. The section of the pub by the bar is basically two rooms knocked together, with comfortable seats and french windows leading to a terrace with metal and plastic chairs. On the right is a dining area (no smoking at eating times), with some attractively individual furnishings; the family room is no smoking too. Well kept Coach House Best, Marstons Pedigree, and Ruddles Best and County on handpump, and a good choice of whiskies. No music or games. *(Recommended by Andy Hazeldine, J Muir, Mike and Wendy Proctor, Brian and Anna Marsden, Richard Lewis; more reports please)*

Free house ~ Licensee Frank Campbell ~ Real ale ~ Meals and snacks (till 10pm) ~ (01260) 252244 ~ Children in family room and in restaurant (very young ones only till early evening) ~ Open 11.30-3, 7-11; closed 25 Dec

SWETTENHAM SJ8067 Map 7

Swettenham Arms

Village signed off A535 just S of Jodrell Bank or just N of Holmes Chapel – keep following sign; pub behind brick-towered church

A former nunnery used as the resting place for funeral parties travelling to the nearby church, this busy but spacious country pub is popular for its wide choice of generously served food. The heavily beamed bar has three communicating room areas linked by a sweep of fitted turkey carpet, with some interesting and individual furnishings and a variety of old prints – military, hunting, old ships, reproduction Old Masters and so forth. Wherever you eat, you order food from a separate counter in the end no-smoking dining room (where there's a huge inglenook – the pub has several winter log fires). The range of food really is enormous: around 20 starters such as home-made soup (£2.50), whitebait, duck pâté with garlic bread or smoked salmon and prawns (all around £3.95), and just as many main courses, with favourite dishes including steak and kidney pie, baked cod, venison casserole, marinated lamb, and broccoli, brie and hazelnut pie (all £7.95); popular puddings (£2.50). Attentive service from well-trained young staff. The restaurant is no smoking. Well kept Greenalls Original, Jennings and Tetleys on handpump, and a range of malt whiskies. You can sit outside at picnic tables on the quiet neat side lawn surrounded by shrubs and trees; the hanging baskets at the front are pretty. Quiz night on Tuesdays. The pub is run by the same people as the Dog at Peover Heath. *(Recommended by Ray Cuckow, Geoff Kay, R D Kelso, Ena and Rodney Wood, Chris Walling, Richard Lewis, P H and R Sutcliffe)*

Free house ~ Licensees Frances and James Cunningham ~ Real ale ~ Meals and snacks ~ Restaurant ~ (01477) 571284 ~ Children welcome ~ Live music Weds ~ Open 11.30-3, 6-11; all day Sat

TARPORLEY SJ5563 Map 7

Rising Sun

High St; village signposted off A51 Nantwich—Chester

Even on a Monday this cheery village pub seems to be something of a magnet for locals and visitors alike, but however busy it gets the service always remains helpful, efficient, and, most importantly, friendly. The well chosen tables are surrounded by character seats including some creaky 19th-c mahogany and oak settles, and there's also an attractively blacked iron kitchen range (and three open fires), sporting and other old-fashioned prints on the walls, and a big oriental rug in the back room. A wide range of generously served lunchtime bar food includes sandwiches (from £1.75), filled baked potatoes (from £1.95), home-made cottage pie (£2.95), home-made steak and kidney pie (£4.45), gammon and egg or pork and apple in cider (£5.15), and beef in ale (£5.45); more elaborate dishes in the evening from the restaurant menu. Well kept Robinsons Best and Mild on handpump; fruit machine, maybe piped music (usually drowned by conversation). The pub is pretty in summer with its mass of hanging baskets and flowering tubs. *(Recommended by Frank Cummins, George Jonas, Iain Robertson, A R and B E Sayer, David and Shelia, Richard Lewis, F J and A Parmenter, Mrs A Abell)*

Robinsons ~ Tenant Alec Robertson ~ Real ale ~ Meals and snacks (11.30-2, 5.30-9.30) ~ Restaurant ~ (01829) 732423 ~ Open 11.30-3, 5.30-11

Waterside pubs are listed at the back of the book.

WESTON SJ7352 Map 7

White Lion 🛏️

3½ miles from M6 junction 16; A500 towards Crewe, then village signposted on right

This pretty black and white timbered old inn is one of those that passes the powercut test, coping magnificently on a reader's recent visit when the aged rooms were suddenly plunged into darkness. Not only was most of the food service unaffected, but the service was still smiling, and it's hard not to think that the candles used to lighten the proceedings really rather suited the place. The busy low-beamed main room is divided up into smaller areas by very gnarled black oak standing timbers, and has a varied mix of seats from cushioned modern settles to ancient oak ones, plenty of smaller chairs, and a friendly, relaxing atmosphere. In a smaller room towards the left are three fine settles, well carved in 18th-c style. Served by smartly dressed staff, the popular bar food includes home-made soup (£1.50), filled baguettes (from £2.25) or batch cakes (£2.50), smoked salmon pâté (£3), vegetarian quiche or lasagne (£3.95), ploughman's (from £4.50), daily roast (£4.50), poached local Dee salmon (£6.50), steak (£8.25), and big home-made puddings (£1.90). Get there early at lunchtime: it can fill up quickly then. Well kept Bass, Boddingtons, and Flowers IPA on handpump, with a choice of wines by the glass; dominoes, piped music; the restaurant is no smoking – as are some bar areas. Picnic tables shelter on neat grass behind, by the pub's own bowling green. The hotel part is discreetly hidden away at the back. They have a civil wedding licence. *(Recommended by George Jonas, Ian and Villy White, Graham and Karen Oddey, Alan and Paula McCully, Sue Holland, Dave Webster, G S Miller, Richard Lewis, Helen Lowe, Basil Minson)*

Free house ~ Licensee Mrs A J Davies ~ Real ale ~ Meals and snacks (not 25 Dec; from 5.30 weekday eves) ~ Restaurant (not Sun evening) ~ (01270) 500303 ~ Children in eating area of bar and in restaurant ~ Open 11-3, 5(6.30 Sat)-11; closed evening 25 Dec ~ Bedrooms: £49B/£59B

WETTENHALL SJ6261 Map 7

Boot & Slipper 🛏️

From B5074 on S edge of Winsford, turn into Darnhall School Lane, then right at Wettenhall signpost: keep on for 2 or 3 miles

There's quite a chatty and relaxed atmosphere at this attractively refurbished pub. Changes in recent years have left the beamed main bar with a fresh and open feel, along with three shiny old dark settles and more straightforward chairs, white walls, and a fishing rod above the deep low fireplace with its big log fire. The modern bar counter also serves the left-hand communicating beamed room with its shiny pale brown tiled floor, cast-iron-framed long table, panelled settle and bar stools; darts, dominoes. An unusual trio of back-lit arched pseudo-fireplaces forms one stripped-brick wall and there are two further areas on the right, as well as a back restaurant with big country pictures. Good bar food includes sandwiches (from £1.30; steak batch £2.50), home-made soup (£1.40), home-made pie of the week (£3.95), salads (from £4), gammon and egg (£5.50), vegetarian meals, daily specials such as spare ribs (£3.85), peppered cider pork (£4.50) or lamb rogan josh (£4.75), puddings (£1.75), and children's meals (£3). Well kept Highgate Mild and Marstons Bitter and Pedigree on handpump, a decent wine list, and quite a few malt whiskies. Outside a few picnic tables sit on the cobbled front terrace by the big car park. *(Recommended by Thomas Nott, Robert and Ann Lees and others; more reports please)*

Free house ~ Licensee Rex Challinor ~ Real ale ~ Meals and snacks ~ Restaurant ~ (01270) 528238 ~ Children welcome till 8.30 ~ Open 11.30-3, 5.30-11; all day Sat ~ Bedrooms: £26S/£40S

If we know a pub has a no-smoking area, we say so.

WINCLE SJ9666 Map

Ship 🍺

Danebridge

Tucked away in scenic countryside (with good walks all around), this quaint 16th-c pub is said to be one of the oldest in Cheshire. The old-fashioned and simple little rooms have a nice atmosphere, very thick stone walls, a coal fire and consistently well kept Boddingtons Bitter and a weekly changing guest beer on handpump; decent wines. Good bar food includes soup (£1.95), filled french bread with chips (lunchtime only, from £3), grilled Dane Valley trout (£4.75), fresh fish on Wednesday such as haddock in crispy batter (£4.95), well liked gammon and eggs (£5.95), steamed puddings (from £2.50), and children's meals (£1.95); fondue bourguignon is the house speciality and includes a bottle of house red wine. The dining room is no smoking. Friendly welcoming service; dominoes, chess, draughts, Monopoly and cards. *(Recommended by Peter and Joy Heatherley, Jack Morley, J F M West, Nigel Woolliscroft, Mike and Wendy Proctor, Iain Robertson, Mr and Mrs J Tyrer, DC, Wayne Brindle, Roger and Christine Mash)*

Free house ~ Licensees Andrew Harmer and Penelope Hinchliffe ~ Real ale ~ Meals and snacks (till 10pm; not winter Mon) ~ (01260) 227217 ~ Well behaved children in family room ~ Open 12-3(4 Sun), 7-11; closed Monday Nov-Mar ~ One bedroom: £25/£40

WRENBURY SJ5948 Map 7

Dusty Miller

Village signposted from A530 Nantwich—Whitchurch

The lovely setting of this imaginatively converted mill is by no means the only attraction: it's deservedly popular as a place to eat thanks to an imaginative range of thoughtfully prepared food. Relying on local produce where possible, the choice might typically include lunchtime sandwiches, smoked oysters (£3.95), sweet and spicy herring on pumpernickel (£3.75), dim sum (£4.25), vegetarian stuffed peach (£5.55), rainbow trout (£6.95), steaks (from £9.75), good daily specials such as chicken calvados (£7.95), salmon in seafood sauce or kingfish caribbean roulade (£8.50), lots of home-made puddings, and local cheeses; children's menu. The pub is set by the Llangollen branch of the Shropshire Union Canal and next to a striking counter-weighted drawbridge. Picnic tables are set on a gravel terrace among rose bushes by the water, and they're reached either by the towpath or by a high wooden catwalk above the River Weaver; in summer they hold regular barbecues including whole hog roasts. Inside, there's a friendly welcome and the main area is comfortably modern, with a series of tall glazed arches with russet velvet curtains facing the water, long low hunting prints on the white walls, and tapestried banquettes and wheelback chairs flanking dark brown rustic tables. Further in, there's a quarry-tiled standing-only part by the bar counter, which has well kept Robinsons Best and Frederics on handpump; the right-hand side of the lounge bar is no smoking. They concoct a different cocktail every day, and have jugs of Pimms in summer. Dominoes, cribbage, shove-ha'penny, and piped classical music. Good choice of tea and coffees. *(Recommended by Paul and Maggie Baker, Mike and Wendy Proctor, Andrew Rogers, Amanda Milsom, Gordon Theaker, Lynn Sharpless, Bob Eardley, Mark Gillespie, D Deas, Nigel Woolliscroft)*

Robinsons ~ Tenant Robert Lloyd-Jones ~ Real ale ~ Meals and snacks ~ Upstairs restaurant (closed Sun evening) ~ (01270) 780537 ~ Children in restaurant and two tables in corner of bar ~ Open 12-3, 6-11; all day high season; closed evening 25 Dec

Lucky Dip

Besides the fully inspected pubs, you might like to try these Lucky Dips recommended to us and described by readers (if you do, please send us reports):

☆ Acton Bridge [Hilltop Rd; B5153 off A49 in Weaverham, then right towards Acton Cliff; SJ5975], *Maypole*: Big helpings of good varied food in spacious and civilised beamed dining pub, pleasant dining room with lots of brass, copper and china, some antique settles as well as more modern furnishings, two coal fires, friendly service, Greenalls Bitter and Mild on handpump, gentle piped music; attractive outside with hanging baskets and tubs, seats in well kept garden with orchard behind (*Graham and Lynn Mason, Mr and Mrs E J W Rogers, Brian Gregory, Mrs P Abell, LYM*)

☆ Adlington [Wood Lane North, by Middlewood Way – OS Sheet 109 map ref 936818; SJ9381], *Miners Arms*: Clean and comfortable Boddingtons Country Fayre family dining pub in good setting beside Macclesfield Canal, efficient service even when packed, generous standardised sensible food choice from sandwiches to steaks inc vegetarian and smaller helpings, plenty of quiet corners, no-smoking area, well kept Whitbreads-related ales; picnic tables and play area outside (*R Davies, Brian and Anna Marsden, P and M Rudlin, Pete Yearsley, BB*)

Alsager [Sandbach Rd, Lawton Heath; SJ8154], *Horse Shoe*: Big busy open-plan local with comfortable lounge, lunchtime food, well kept Bass, Worthington and Websters Yorkshire, good choice of bottled beers, Sky TV and darts in back room, live organ music, friendly staff (*Richard Lewis*); [Audley Rd; SJ7956], *Manor House*: Part of hotel complex, cosy and charming oak-beamed lounge bar, relaxing atmosphere, good choice of food inc lunchtime salad bar, friendly staff, Flowers Original; comfortable bedrooms (*Richard Lewis*); [Crewe Rd], *Plough*: Recently elaborately refurbished and extended, good food in spacious eating areas, good facilities for children (inside and out) and disabled, superb staff, well kept Ansells, Ind Coope Burton and Tetleys; very busy (*Richard Lewis*); [Sandbach Rd N], *Wilbraham Arms*: Large busy modern pub with comfortable lounge, long bar, restaurant/conservatory, good friendly service, wide choice of good home-cooked food, well kept Robinsons Hatters Mild and Hartleys XB, children welcome; roomy garden with play area and goat, live jazz some nights (*Richard and Anne Lewis*)

☆ Alvanley [Manley Rd – OS Sheet 117 map ref 496740; SJ4974], *White Lion*: Remarkably wide changing choice of generous food from sandwiches up inc vegetarian and children's dishes in comfortable, civilised and very popular dining pub, friendly service, plush seats in low-ceilinged lounge, games in smaller public bar, Greenalls Mild, Bitter and Original, tables and play area outside with some small farm animals (*Derek and Margaret Underwood, Mr and Mrs E J W Rogers, Graham and Lynn Mason, Myke Crombleholme, Mr and Mrs B Hobden, LYM*)

Appleton [B5356 not far from M6 juntion 20; SJ6484], *Thorn*: Cosy and pleasant, wide choice of good generous food (*Martin Bromfield, Bernadette Garner*)

Astbury [off A34 S of Congleton; SJ8461], *Egerton Arms*: Big village local dating from 14th c, in nice spot opp interesting old church in pretty village (though busy main rd), wide choice of usual food with OAP bargains, well kept Robinsons ales, log fires, no-smoking lounge and part of restaurant, tables in back garden with play area; children welcome; bedrooms (*Richard Lewis, Brian Lang*)

☆ Audlem [Audlem Wharf – OS Sheet 118 map ref 658436; SJ6543], *Shroppie Fly*: Beautifully placed canal pub, one bar shaped like a barge, good canal photographs, collection of brightly painted bargees' china and bric-a-brac, seats on waterside terrace; usual food, well kept Boddingtons, friendly staff, mainly modern furnishings, children in room off bar and restaurant; open almost all day summer, closed winter lunchtimes (*SLC, Nigel Woolliscroft, Tony Hobden, LYM*)

Audlem [A525, Audlem Wharf], *Bridge*: Particularly well kept Marstons and guest ales and good food from sandwiches up in friendly unspoilt pub with coal fire, tiled floor, darts, pool, juke box and games machines; dogs allowed, seats out by canal (*SLC, Sue Holland, Dave Webster*)

☆ Beeston [Bunbury Heath; A49 S of Tarporley; SJ5459], *Beeston Castle*: Good value interesting generous food from huge open sandwiches up inc mouth-watering puddings, in clean, comfortable and well restored pub, good friendly service even when busy, short but well chosen wine list, well kept beers; children until 8 (*Mr and Mrs E J W Rogers*)

☆ Bollington [Church St; SJ9377], *Church House*: Wide choice of good value quickly served lunchtime food in corner terrace pub, small and busy but warmly welcoming; well kept Tetleys and Theakstons, furnishings inc pews and working sewing-machine treadle tables, separate dining room, friendly prompt staff; piped music (*C Tan, Tim Boddington*)

Bollington [foot of White Nancy end of Kerridge Hill – OS Sheet 118 map ref 937772], *Redway*: Extended stone pub with large family area inc indoor playroom, very generous good food, well kept beer, warm conservatory, play area outside with sheep and ducks in pets corner (*Dave and Doreen Irving*)

☆ Bosley [Leek Rd (A523); SJ9266], *Harrington Arms*: Cosy roadside pub with wide choice of good generous straightforward home cooking, well kept Robinsons Bitter and Old Stockport on handpump, good decor, friendly landlord, pleasant setting (*Richard Lewis*)

☆ **Bottom of the Oven** [A537 Buxton—Macclesfield, 1st left past Cat & Fiddle – OS Sheet 118 map ref 980723; SJ9872], *Stanley Arms*: Isolated moorland pub with cosy rooms, lots of shiny black woodwork, plush seats, dimpled copper tables, open winter fires, dining room (children allowed here), limited straightforward food from sandwiches up, well kept Marstons Burton and Pedigree, piped music, picnic tables on grass behind; may close Mon in winter if weather bad *(John and Barbara Gibson, Ray Cuckow, Jack Morley, LYM)*

Brownlow [off A34 S of Congleton; SJ8260], *Brownlow Inn*: Fairly big recently expanded spick-and-span Whitbreads dining pub, exposed timbers, popular reasonably priced food from good ploughman's up, Boddingtons and Flowers on handpump, good service *(Ann and Colin Hunt, Ian Phillips)*

☆ **Bunbury** [SJ5758], *Dysart Arms*: Immaculate former farmhouse beautifully placed by village church, cosy and attractive with several nooks and crannies, lots of antique furniture, generally old-fashioned atmosphere, well kept Tetleys and Thwaites, decent wines, very friendly staff, tables in lovely elevated big garden; cl winter weekday lunchtimes *(George Jonas, Sue Holland, Dave Webster, Chris Walling)*

Bunbury, *Yew Tree*: Good lunchtime bar food inc home-made soup *(Margaret and Roy Randle, Jim Smith)*

☆ **Chester** [Upper Northgate St], *Pied Bull*: Attractive and comfortable beamed 16th-c pub, well kept Greenalls and a guest such as Exmoor Gold, warm welcome, staff attentive even when busy, wide choice of generous reasonably priced interesting food even Sun evening, afternoon teas too, no-smoking area; bedrooms *(Dr and Mrs A M Evans, Andrew Shore, SLC, E G Parish, Gordon Theaker, William Cissna)*

☆ **Chester** [Eastgate Row N], *Boot*: Fine position on The Rows, heavy beams, lots of old woodwork, oak flooring and flagstones, black-leaded kitchen range in lounge beyond food servery, no-smoking oak-panelled upper room, good atmosphere, friendly new licensee, cheap well kept Sam Smiths; children allowed *(M A Cameron, Sue Holland, Dave Webster, LYM)*

☆ **Chester** [Lower Bridge St], *Falcon*: Good bustling atmosphere in striking building with beams, handsome stripped brickwork, well kept Sam Smiths OB and Museum, decent basic bar meals (not Sun), fruit machine, piped music; children allowed lunchtime (not Sat) in airy upstairs room; jazz Sat lunchtime, open all day Sat; can get packed *(Richard Lewis, JH, SLC, E G Parish, Simon and Pie Barker, Brian and Anna Marsden, LYM)*

☆ **Chester** [Watergate St], *Old Custom House*: Quiet and civilised old pub with lots of good pottery and brass in three character rooms, good value straightforward food, good range of Marstons ales inc Mild, prompt service, good evening atmosphere, fruit machine in lounge *(Ian Phillips, Brian Wainwright, SLC)*

☆ **Chester** [Tower Wharf, Raymond St; behind Northgate St, nr rly], *Telfords Warehouse*: Interesting pub in former warehouse designed by Thomas Telford, great views over canal basin, well kept ales such as Theakstons and changing guest beers, good unusual food in pub, cellar wine bar and upper restaurant; blond furniture, nightly live music; children welcome *(AA)*

☆ **Chester** [Watergate St], *Watergates*: Wide range of quickly served good food from ploughman's up in lovely medieval crypt – a wine bar, with candlelit tables and good wine choice, but also real ales such as Boddingtons and Cains; can get packed on race days *(Mr and Mrs E J W Rogers, Sue Holland, Dave Webster, Simon and Pie Barker, SLC)*

Chester [Park St, off Albion St], *Albion*: Just below city wall, with three carefully refurbished Victorian rooms; has had lovely welcoming eccentric atmosphere and landlord, masses of WWI, 40s and 50s memorabilia, big helpings of good value home-cooked chip-free lunchtime food inc massive sandwiches and unusual main dishes, Cains and Greenalls beers, quick friendly service, but for sale 1996 *(News please)*; [nr Grosvenor Museum], *Chester Bells*: Pleasant place to eat, with well kept ales such as Boddingtons Bitter and Elgoods Pageant *(William Cissna)*; [Lower Bridge St], *Clavertons*: Popular beamed cellar bar, cosy, comfortable and intimate, with friendly staff, wide choice of food noon-8, well kept ales such as Lees Best and Moonraker *(Richard Lewis)*; [Northgate St], *Coach & Horses*: Lots of woodwork, bric-a-brac and prints, massive range of sandwiches, also baked potatoes, baguettes and fry-ups, two monthly guest ales; piped music, fruit machine *(SLC)*; [Lower Bridge St], *Cross Keys*: Good friendly new landlord, small choice of decent food *(Mrs Braisted)*; [Lower Bridge St], *Olde Kings Head*: Ancient beamed softly lit Greenalls pub, guest beers such as Adnams Broadside and Exmoor Gold, good bar food, restaurant, nice atmosphere *(SLC)*; [Milton St], *Mill*: Popular real ale bar in ex-mill hotel, spacious and comfortable, friendly efficient staff, no piped music or games, decent bar food till late evening, good value Sun lunch, restaurant, well kept house beer from Coach House in Warrington, excellent changing choice of guest and bottled beers; children welcome; bedrooms *(Richard Lewis)*; [Bridge St], *Olde Vaults*: Panelling and leaded lights, well kept Greenalls, upstairs lounge *(SLC)*; [Broughton], *Temperance House*: Pleasantly done out with stripped floorboards, beams and masonry, lots of seating, friendly staff, bar food, good range of well kept ales from unusual servery with handpumps on casks; beer fans will also enjoy nearby Pop Inn off-licence *(Richard Lewis)*; [Francis St/Egerton St], *Union Vaults*: Classic backstreet alehouse with enthusiastic staff, well kept recherché beers and stouts (guest beer suggestions book), bar area with bar billiards, back room with pool; no food, piped music *(Richard Lewis)*; [City Rd], *Westminster*: Large comfortable hotel bar, handy for station, pleasant atmosphere, well kept low-priced Sam Smiths Best and Tetley-Walkers, bar food; open all day; bedrooms *(Richard Lewis)*

☆ **Churton** [Farndon Rd (B5130); SJ4256], *White Horse*: Small village pub with three attractively furnished connecting bars, copper-topped tables, lots of polished bric-a-brac; wide range of reasonably priced home-cooked food, quick efficient service, real ales such as Bass and Burtonwood; pool *(G B Rimmer, E Riley)*

☆ **Comberbach** [off A553 and A559 NW of Northwich, pub towards Great Budworth; SJ6477], *Spinner & Bergamot*: Neat plush beamed bar with log fire, hunting prints and toby jugs, softly lit back dining room with country-kitchen furniture and big inglenook, red-tiled public bar, usual bar food, well kept Greenalls Bitter, Original and Mild; piped music; picnic tables on sloping lawn, lots of flowers, bowling green *(Olive and Ray Hebson, John Broughton, Chris Walling, Martin Bromfield, Bernadette Garner, LYM)*

☆ **Congleton** [High St; SJ8663], *Olde Kings Arms*: Thoroughly renovated former manor house, superb old timbering, small cosy low-beamed separate rooms, open fires, well kept Marstons Best and Pedigree, well priced limited lunchtime bar food *(Steve Goodchild, Richard Lewis)*

Congleton [West St], *Durham Ox*: Comfortable and cosy beamed local, Beartown Bitter, John Smiths and Tetley-Walkers; pool room, juke box *(Richard Lewis)*

☆ **Crewe** [Nantwich Rd (A534) opp rly stn; SJ7056], *Crewe Arms*: Good value attractive bar meals in comfortable and spacious lounge with Victorian pictures, marble-topped tables, alabaster figurines, curtained alcoves, ornate ceiling; good pubby public bar; Tetleys well kept when it's on, friendly staff, open all day; bedrooms *(Richard Lewis)*

Crewe [Pedley St], *Albion*: Popular local with comfortable lounge and bar, lots of railway prints and foreign beer bottles; emphasis on pub games – darts, dominoes, pool and quiz nights; friendly staff, ever-changing well kept beers; piped music, open all day (cl lunchtime Tues and Thurs) *(Richard Lewis)*; [Earle St], *Belle Vue*: Big comfortable open-plan pub, simple bar food, well kept Tetleys and cheap Farrells Folly, friendly staff, pool and snooker tables, Sky TV, seats on terrace; children welcome, bouncy castle, swings and toys *(Richard Lewis)*; [58 Nantwich Rd], *British Lion*: Comfortable partly panelled bar, back snug, well kept Tetleys-related ales and a guest beer, friendly staff; can get smoky when the locals crowd in *(Richard Lewis, Sue Holland, Dave Webster)*; [part of Royal Hotel, Nantwich Rd], *Clancys*: One of the first Irish theme pubs, bare boards and brickwork, panelling and lots of bric a brac; good busy atmosphere but can be noisy and smoky; log fire, live music most nights

(Richard Lewis); [25 Earle St], *Crown*: Original fittings, old-fashioned furnishings and wallpaper; busy main front bar, back games room with pool and juke box, two quietly chatty lounges and drinking corridor; welcoming landlady and locals, well kept Robinsons; handy for Railway Heritage Centre *(Pete Baker, Sue Holland, Dave Webster)*; [Nantwich Rd], *Earl of Crewe*: Lots of railway prints and beer memorabilia, panelling, copper cauldrons; cosy atmosphere, good choice of ever-changing real ales kept well, reasonably priced food *(Richard Lewis, Sue Holland, Dave Webster)*; [56 Earle St], *Kings Arms*: Several friendly rooms, well kept Whitbreads-related ales esp Mild, pool, darts, dominoes and cribbage; very busy lunchtime, no food *(Richard Lewis)*; [Middlewich Rd (A530), Wolstanwood – OS Sheet 118 map ref 673550], *Rising Sun*: Well refurbished, with panelling, prints and comfortable seating, raised eating area, disabled lift, children's facilities; friendly staff, good range of generous food, well kept Greenalls and Stones; bedrooms *(Richard Lewis)*; [Earle St], *Three Lamps*: Smartly refurbished, with lots of woodwork and attractive prints, comfortable seats, back food area, relaxed atmosphere, friendly staff; well kept Banks's Bitter, Mild and Passion, good choice of bottled drinks; piped music, games machines, live music some nights *(Richard Lewis)*

Croft [left just after the Noggin, right at next T-junction; SJ6394], *Horseshoe*: Comfortable and interesting village local, several separate rooms, wide choice of good home-made lunchtime bar food inc fresh fish (and more expensive restaurant), well kept Tetleys *(Karin Postlethwaite)*

Crowton [Station Rd; SJ5875], *Hare & Hounds*: Good varied reasonably priced meals freshly prepared by landlord/chef, warmly welcoming staff and landlady, beautifully appointed restaurant – booking needed for locally famous Sun lunches *(Col and Mrs J Nicholson, Norman Revell)*

Daresbury [Old Chester Rd; SJ5983], *Ring o' Bells*: Recently well refurbished, with roaring log fire, good choice of reasonably priced good food, well kept Greenalls Bitter, Original and Mild and a weekly guest beer, big garden and play area; short walk from canal; village church has window showing all the characters in Alice in Wonderland; bedrooms *(Chris Harrop)*

Disley [Buxton Rd; SJ9784], *Dandy Cock*: 18th-c, by old cock-fighting pit, with bay window, open fire, pictures, ornaments and mirrors, extensive menu, friendly atmosphere, welcoming staff, well kept Robinsons *(Richard Lewis)*

Eaton [School Lane (A536 Congleton—Macclesfield); SJ8765], *Plough*: Pretty 17th-c beamed inn, cosy fires, friendly landlord, imaginative reasonably priced menu, carvery all day Sun, well kept Marstons and guest beers; attractive newly built bedrooms in renovated barn annexe with own bathrooms *(John and Janet Warren, Mrs Gillian Holden)*

Eaton [Beech Lane – the one nr Tarporley; SJ5763], *Red Lion*: Nicely decorated comfortable country pub, wide choice of good generous food inc vegetarian, lots of sandwiches and OAP bargains, good friendly service, no-smoking areas, separate bar with pool and darts, floodlit bowling green, barbecues and play area; well kept Greenalls and Stones, unobjectionable piped music; children welcome, open all day *(Richard Lewis)*

☆ Faddiley [A534 Wrexham—Nantwich; SJ5753], *Thatch*: Attractively cottagey thatched, beamed and timbered dining pub, formerly the Tollemache Arms, now aiming high in the food stakes with a limited restauranty choice which – at a price – often hits the mark; full-sized proper napkins, good home-made bread, excellent friendly service, cosy open fire, well kept ales such as McEwans 70/-, Morlands Old Speckled Hen and Theakstons Old Peculier; children welcome *(Basil Minson, Nigel Woolliscroft, Sue Holland, Dave Webster, LYM)*

Farndon [formerly the Raven; SJ4254], *Farndon Arms*: Nicely decorated, in pretty village; very friendly staff, wide choice of good reasonably priced food, weekend restaurant, good range of well kept beers; dogs welcome *(Jenny and Neil Spink)*

☆ Frodsham [Church St; SJ5278], *Rowlands*: Friendly single-roomed pub with several well kept quickly charging real ales (well over 1,000 in last five years), as well as bottled wheat beers and good choice of wines by the glass; good bar food, children welcome *(Sue and Glenn Crooks, Roger and Susan Dunn)*

Frodsham [Chester Rd], *Netherton Arms*: Recently refurbished and reopened under same management as previous entry, warm welcome, very good imaginative food *(Rod and Jan Rylatt)*

☆ Gawsworth [nr Macclesfield; SJ8969], *Harrington Arms*: Farm pub's two small rooms with bare wooden floorboards, fine carved bar counter, well kept Robinsons Best and Best Mild served in big old enamelled jugs *(Dave Irving, LYM)*

Goostrey [111 Main Rd (off A50 and A535); SJ7870], *Crown*: Extended Marstons dining pub with lots of beams and pictures, cosy and friendly atmosphere, popular landlord, well kept ale; bedrooms *(Richard Lewis, Tony Young, LYM)*; [Station Rd (towards A535)], *Red Lion*: Clean and pleasant modernised open-plan bar and back family restaurant with well kept Boddingtons, Tetleys and a guest beer, friendly efficient service, restaurant, nice garden with play area; piped music, fruit machines; children welcome *(Richard Lewis, Robert and Ann Lees, LYM)*

Grappenhall [nr M6 junction 20; A50 towards Warrington, left after 1½ miles – OS Sheet 109 map ref 638863; SJ6486], *Parr Arms*: Pleasant pub with good lunchtime bar food; nice setting, tables out by church *(Martin Bromfield, Bernadette Garner)*; [Church Lane, off A50], *Rams Head*: Attractive sandstone building not far from Bridgewater Canal, with elaborate wrought-

iron sign and sundial; lots of fine wood panelling, leaded windows, wall seats and carved heads, nice quiet atmosphere, good food, Greenalls *(Martin Bromfield, Bernadette Garner)*

Handforth [Station Rd; SJ8583], *Railway*: Friendly local, cheerful and clean, with enjoyable straightforward lunchtime food, good service (happy to serve sandwich 35 mins after 2pm deadline), well kept Robinsons, fresh flowers, unobtrusive piped music; the airedale who thinks he's a rug (and likes pork scratchings) is Henry; quiz nights *(J S Rutter, Tracey and John Davenport)*

☆ Handley [off A41 Chester—Whitchurch; SJ4758], *Calveley Arms*: Inviting black and white country pub, leaded windows, flower-decked forecourt, alcoves in well furnished beamed lounge, interesting original home-cooked food from imaginative sandwiches to unusual main dishes; friendly service, well kept Boddingtons, Burtonwood, Chesters and guest beers, secluded garden *(E G Parish, R S Fidler, David and Judy Walmsley)*

Hartford [Chester Rd; A559 SW of Northwich opp station; SJ6472], *Coachman*: Former coaching inn done up in old-fashioned style with interconnecting rooms off bar, well cooked reasonably priced food, well kept Greenalls, tables out behind *(Mr and Mrs C Roberts, Michael Gittins)*

☆ Hatchmere [B5152, off A556 at Abbey Arms; SJ5572], *Carriers*: Clean comfortable split-level lounge with bare brickwork, draught horse prints, old brewery photographs and pictures of pike caught nearby, friendly service, reasonably priced food from good sandwiches up inc children's helpings, well kept Burtonwood Bitter, Mild and strong Top Hat; attractive garden leading down to lake, handy for Delamere Forest *(Jenny and Michael Back)*

☆ Hatton [Warrington Rd (B5356, handy for M56 junction 10); SJ6082], *Hatton Arms*: Cosy 18th-c bar with friendly licensees and locals, open fire, two plainer rooms off; bar lunches inc good value soup and sandwiches, real ales, popular restaurant; cobbled pavement outside, local Lewis Carroll connections *(Chris Walling, Alistair Walton)*

Haughton Moss [Long Lane, off A49 S of Tarporley; SJ5856], *Nags Head*: Good atmosphere, warm and friendly, good food and beer, sensible prices; children welcome *(Philip Leay, Sue Holland, Dave Webster)*

Helsby [A56; SJ4975], *Railway*: Big helpings of good value food inc lots of specials, good service, reasonably priced wine and beer *(Mr and Mrs E J W Rogers)*; [164 Chester Rd], *Robin Hood*: Good food and drink, pleasant surroundings; comfortable bedrooms *(T Hughes)*

Henbury [Chelford Rd (A537 W of Macclesfield); SJ8873], *Blacksmiths Arms*: Good Boddingtons Country Fayre family dining pub, usual standard menu and good specials, Whitbreads-related beers inc a guest; open all day at weekends *(L T Lionet)*

Houghton Green [Mill Lane; SJ6292],

Plough: Recently refurbished 19th-c Greenalls pub, pleasant atmosphere, wide choice of good food, new no-smoking dining area, changing guest beers *(Martin Bromfield, Bernadette Garner)*

☆ Kelsall [Chester Rd (A54); SJ5268], *Morris Dancer*: Cosy yet roomy, two bars, wine bar area and restaurant, wide choice of generous imaginatively presented food (Italian chef) inc good fresh veg, efficient genuinely friendly staff, good cross-section of customers, pleasant and relaxing atmosphere; well kept Greenalls, decent wines, sensible prices; live country *(Derek and Margaret Underwood, W D Hollins, John Honnor)*

Kerridge [OS Sheet 118 map ref 937773; SJ9377], *Redway*: Large child-friendly food pub, attentive red-coated waiters serve food and drinks to table, reasonably priced food (beware service charge), Boddingtons ale, Sega machine and good indoors play area for small children, adventure playground and pets corner outside; open all day Sun *(Brian and Anna Marsden)*

Lach Dennis [Allostock; B5082 Northwich rd off A50; SJ7471], *Three Greyhounds*: Generous helpings of well cooked meals, pleasant staff, reasonable prices *(N Revell)*

☆ Little Bollington [the one nr Altrincham, 2 miles from M56 junction 7: A56 towards Lymm, then first right at Stamford Arms into Park Lane – use A556 to get back on to M56 westbound; SJ7286], *Swan With Two Nicks*: Recently extended and refurbished beamed village pub full of brass, copper and bric-a-brac, friendly atmosphere, snug alcoves, some antique settles, popular good value generous food served quickly, log fire, well kept Whitbreads-related real ales, tables outside; attractive hamlet by Dunham Hall deer park *(Geoffrey and Brenda Wilson, R Davies, LYM)*

Little Bollington [A56, about 3 miles E of Lymm], *Olde No 3*: Cosy old beamed pub by Bridgewater Canal, good atmosphere, reasonably priced food in dining area with sensible tables, well kept Courage-related ales, friendly service, coal fire *(Colin and Marjorie Roberts)*

Little Budworth [A54 just N; SJ5966], *Shrewsbury Arms*: Comfortable little pub with welcoming extrovert landlord, nice atmosphere, good well priced food *(Derek and Margaret Underwood)*

Little Leigh [A49, just S of a A533; not far from M56 junction 10; SJ6276], *Holly Bush*: Formerly popular as an unspoilt traditional farm pub, now extended and converted into a carpeted food pub with busy young waitresses, pleasant friendly landlady, well kept Burtonwood and guest beers, no dogs; the old public bar however does survive *(LYM)*

☆ Lower Peover [Crown Lane; B5081, off A50; SJ7474], *Crown*: Good bar food and service and lots of bric-a-brac inc interesting gooseberry championship memorabilia in friendly and attractive L-shaped bar with two rooms off; Boddingtons, dominoes *(Steve Hardy)*

☆ Lower Whitley [SJ6179], *Chetwode Arms*: Very popular and relaxing Millers Kitchen family dining pub with traditional layout, solid furnishings all clean and polished, warm coal fires, Greenalls Mild and Bitter on handpump, good food and service; immaculate bowling area, play area, open all day Sat *(Brian and Anna Marsden, Gary Roberts, Ann Stubbs, W C M Jones, Graham and Lynn Mason, LYM)*

Lymm [Agden Wharf, Warrington Lane; SJ6787], *Admiral Benbow*: Comfortable new canalside pub, nautical theme, separate bar area, well kept Bass-family ales, good range of bottled beers, good value food, jovial friendly atmosphere; live music Sat, organ music Sun pm, canal trips *(Alan Gough)*; [A6144], *Bulls Head*: Particularly well kept Hydes Bitter and Mild in small very friendly local; open all day Sat, seats out behind *(Richard Lewis)*; [Higher Lane], *Church Green*: Pleasant atmosphere, good food esp home-made apple pie, well kept Greenalls *(Iain Taylor, M A Robinson)*; *Golden Fleece*: Pleasant canalside pub with well kept Greenalls Bitter, Original and Mild, comfortable lounge areas, bar with darts and pool, tables out under cocktail parasols, play area; good choice of reasonably priced food, restaurant; open all day Sat *(Richard Lewis)*

☆ nr Macclesfield [A537 some miles out towards Buxton – OS Sheet 119 map ref 001719; SK0071], *Cat & Fiddle*: Worth knowing as Britain's 2nd-highest pub, surrounded by spectacular moorland (though on a trunk road), with magnificent views; otherwise a straightforward spacious roadside pub, with Robinsons real ales, decent bar food, swift friendly service even when busy *(Wendy and Ian Phillips, LYM)*

Marford [SJ4166], *Trevor Arms*: Lovely place to stay for Chester and surrounding area; Stones beer, good restaurant – must book; bedrooms *(Mr and Mrs A Craig)*

Mickle Trafford [Chester Rd; A56; SJ4569], *Shrewsbury Arms*: Good friendly staff, guest beers inc Flowers IPA, Morlands Old Speckled Hen and Wadworths 6X on handpump, good food inc delicious ice creams and puddings, friendly service; tables outside; children welcome *(Mr and Mrs E J W Rogers)*

Middlewich [Lewin St (A533); SJ7066], *Narrowboat*: Pleasant pub not far from canal, decent food with restaurant seating in balcony-like upper area, well kept Burtonwood Bitter, Flowers Original and – new to the Guide – good Tom Thumpers Bitter *(William Cissna)*

☆ Mobberley [opp church; SJ7879], *Church*: Smart but friendly and comfortable, with wide choice of good generous food, great log fire, well kept Greenalls, cheerful service; tables in courtyard, big garden with play area, own bowling green; children welcome *(Chris Westmoreland, Martin Bromfield, Bernadette Garner, R and A Lees)*

☆ Mobberley [Town Lane; down hill from sharp bend on B5185 at E edge of 30mph limit], *Roebuck*: Spacious and pleasant open-plan bar with pews, polished boards, panelling and alcoves; well kept Courage-related real ales, good generously served bar food from lunchtime sandwiches up, good friendly service, upstairs restaurant, seats in cobbled courtyard and garden behind, play area; children welcome *(Chris Westmoreland, LYM)*

Mobberley [Pepper St; Ashley rd out towards Altrincham; SJ7781], *Chapel House*: Small, clean and comfortable, nicely carpeted, darkish woodwork, upholstered stools and wall settles, very friendly landlord, short choice of good value simple lunchtime food (not Sun/Mon), Boddingtons and Scrumpy Jack cider on handpump, real fire, small games room; courtyard seats *(Colin and Marjorie Roberts)*; [Paddock Hill – small sign off B5085 Knutsford—Wilmslow; SJ8179], *Plough & Flail*: Small comfortable three-roomed pub with big helpings of good food inc fish, good toasties, welcoming log fire and dog, well kept Boddingtons; restaurant *(J F M West, Ian Blackwell)*

Mow Cop [Station Rd – OS Sheet 118 map ref 854574; SJ8557], *Cheshire View*: Friendly and simply furnished local with tremendous bird's-eye view of the Cheshire Plain; well kept Marstons Best, Regimental and Pedigree, lots of prints of nearby castle *(Richard Lewis, LYM)*

☆ Nantwich [Hospital St – by side passage to central church; SJ6552], *Lamb*: Civilised hotel bar with leather chesterfields and other comfortable seats, well kept Burtonwood Forshaws, decent malt whiskies, good value nicely served generous home-cooked food inc outstanding fish in bar and traditional upstairs dining room, attentive staff, unobtrusive piped music; bedrooms *(W C M Jones, Sue Holland, Dave Webster, Olive and Ray Hebson, LYM)*

☆ Nantwich [51 Beam St], *Red Cow*: Well renovated former Tudor farmhouse, good relaxed atmosphere, smallish lounge and bar, no-smoking dining area, wide range of good value food esp vegetarian, well kept Robinsons Best, Mild, Old Tom, Frederics and Hartleys XB, back pool table *(SLC, Mrs P J Elfick, Nick and Alison Dowson, Sue Holland, Dave Webster, Gordon Theaker)*

Nantwich [High St; centre almost opp W end of church], *Crown*: Striking Elizabethan inn with rambling comfortably modernised beamed and timbered bar, real ales, bar food, good value attached Italian restaurant, helpful service; comfortable bedrooms *(P D Donoghue, LYM)*; [Mill St], *Wickstead Arms*: Good standard decor with prints, carpeted lounge and lino bar, bar meals inc Sun lunches, Boddingtons; piped music *(SLC)*

No Mans Heath [A41; SJ5148], *Wheatsheaf*: Low beams, lots of pictures, brasses, wrought iron, comfortable seats, cosy fires, friendly staff, well kept Bass, Ruddles County, Theakstons Best and Worthington Best, usual decent food, relaxing atmosphere; piped music; play area in garden *(Richard Lewis, SLC)*

Oakgrove [Leek Old Rd, Sutton; A523 S of Macclesfield; SJ9169], *Fools Nook*:

Welcoming, with well kept Boddingtons ales, several dozen whiskies, lots of brass plates *(C H and P Stride)*

☆ Ollerton [A537 – OS Sheet 118 map ref 775769; SJ7877], *Dun Cow*: Pretty country pub, small-roomed and friendly, with attractive and individual furnishings, two fine log fires, well kept Greenalls Cask and Original, drinkable wine, dominoes, shove-ha'penny and darts in small tap room, interesting bar food from sandwiches up inc vegetarian; open all day (inc restaurant in summer), children in snug and restaurant *(Mrs P J Pearce, LYM)*

☆ Over Peover [off A50 S of Knutsford; SJ7674], *Olde Park Gate*: Pleasant quiet atmosphere in several small black-beamed rooms with some attractive furnishings inc fine Macclesfield oak chairs, well kept Sam Smiths Best, Mild and Stout, good straightforward food from sandwiches up, sensible prices, good friendly service, new lounge with dining area, keen darts team; family room, tables outside *(Richard Lewis, BB)*

Over Peover [Stocks Lane, just off A50], *Whipping Stocks*: Several rooms, good oak panelling and fittings, solid furnishings, well kept Sam Smiths, popular straightforward food (but they allow smoking near diners), children in eating area, picnic tables in garden with safe play area; can be dominated weekday lunchtime by people from nearby Barclays Bank regional HQ, but relaxing evenings; easy walks through nearby parkland *(R Davies, LYM)*

☆ Parkgate [The Parade; village signed off A540; SJ2878], *Boathouse*: Recently attractively refurbished, with cosy alcoves off small bar, efficient young staff, Greenalls Bitter and Mild and Tetleys with guests such as Batemans and Cains, wide choice of usual generous food inc children's, spectacular views over silted Dee estuary to Welsh hills from big conservatory restaurant (booking needed weekends); trad jazz Tues; nearby marshes good for birdwatchers *(W C M Jones, Richard Fairclough, Sue and Bob Ward)*

☆ Parkgate [The Parade], *Red Lion*: Comfortable and welcoming Victorian-feel pub on attractive waterfront with great view to Welsh hills, good value sandwiches and traditional main dishes, well kept Tetleys-related ales, 19th-c paintings and beer-mug collection, good extrovert landlord *(Keith Gilbertson)*

Parkgate [Parkgate Rd], *Old Quay*: Modern single-storey family dining pub in conservation area among parkland, facing Dee and Welsh hills, comfortable banquettes, sensible tables, big picture windows, food all day, several real ales *(E G Parish)*

☆ Plumley [Plumley Moor Lane; off A556 by the Smoker; SJ7175], *Golden Pheasant*: Doing well under current welcoming landlord, with wide choice of often interesting bar food and well kept Lees Bitter and Mild in spacious series of comfortably modernised rooms, good value restaurant, roomy conservatory overlooking back children's garden, pub gardens and bowling green; children welcome, good well equipped bedrooms *(Simon Barber, Paul Gregory, Richard Lewis, LYM)*

☆ **Prestbury** [SJ9077], *Legh Arms*: Striking long heavy-beamed 16th-c building with lots of woodwork, gallery, smart atmosphere, tables laid with cloths and cutlery in main dining bar, good choice of good value inventive food inc vegetarian, cosy comfortable separate lounge bar, well kept Robinsons Best and Frederics, friendly largely Italian service; open all day, children welcome *(Richard Lewis, Steve Goodchild)*

Pulford [Chester Rd (A488); SJ3859], *Grosvenor Arms*: Recently refurbished village pub, quite distinguished exterior, interesting inside too; wide range of beers, tasty rather than speedy food *(Jenny and Neil Spink)*

☆ **Rainow** [NE of village on A5002 Whalley Bridge—Macclesfield; SJ9576], *Highwayman*: Timeless unchanging moorside pub with small rooms, low 17th-c beams, good winter fires (electric other times), plenty of atmosphere, lovely views; Thwaites real ales, bar food inc good sandwiches, rather late opening *(Gwen and Peter Andrews, Gordon, Yolanda Henry, Brian and Anna Marsden, Jack and Philip Paxton, LYM)*

Sandbach [Market Sq; SJ7661], *Lower Chequer*: Attractive recently refurbished 16th-c pub just off cobbled square; choice of eight well kept real ales inc some from small breweries, generous helpings of good value home-made food, friendly jolly landlord *(A Croall)*

☆ **Scholar Green** [off A34 N of Kidsgrove; SJ8356], *Rising Sun*: Good country-pub atmosphere, welcoming service, good choice of well kept ales such as Fullers London Pride, Marstons Best and Pedigree, Robinsons, Thwaites and a changing guest, wide choice of generous interesting home-cooked food, family room, pleasantly refurbished restaurant; darts, unobtrusive piped music *(Dick and Barbara Waterson, Richard Lewis)*

Scholar Green [Congleton Rd N], *Travellers Rest*: Busy, comfortable and cosy, lots of panelling, brass and prints, leather seats, well kept Banks's, Marstons Best and current Brewers Choice, wide choice of good value bar food inc skillet cooking, friendly staff; tables outside *(Richard Lewis)*

☆ **Smallwood** [Knutsford Rd (A50 N of Alsager); SJ8160], *Legs of Man*: Comfortable roadside Robinsons pub with carefully matched chairs, banquettes, carpet, curtains and wallpaper, fin de siecle tall white nymphs on columns, lush potted plants, long rather imaginative menu, well kept Best, Frederics and Hatters Mild, staff friendly and effective even when very busy; restaurant, children truly welcome; well spaced tables on side lawn with play area *(Richard Lewis, Graham Emmett, Helen Lowe, BB)*

☆ **Smallwood** [Newcastle Rd (A50)], *Bulls Head*: Attractive interestingly decorated dining pub with lots of space and particularly good garden with play area; well kept Burtonwood and Tetleys, decent house wines, imaginative range of well presented generous food inc interesting salads and good puddings, good service; piped pop music, children welcome; quite handy for Biddulph Grange (NT) *(K Plant, LYM)*

Sproston Green [A54 nr M6 junction 18; SJ7367], *Fox & Hounds*: Pleasant pub, good food lunchtime and evening *(Graham and Lynn Mason)*

☆ **Styal** [Altrincham Rd (B5166 nr Ringway Airport); SJ8383], *Ship*: Friendly pub in attractive NT village with good service, wide choice of good food all day, well kept Courage-related ales, children allowed; seats out in front, walks in riverside woods *(Dorothee and Dennis Glover)*

Tarporley [50 High St; off A49; SJ5563], *Swan*: Well managed Georgian inn with well kept Harbys Wem and local Weetwood, bistro bar with rather smart food inc superb goat cheeses, restaurant, tables outside, provision for children; comfortable well equipped bedrooms *(Sue and Bob Ward, LYM)*

Tarvin [by-pass; SJ4967], *Village Tavern*: Attractive extensively refurbished pub with cottage-style furnishings, imitation oil lamps, oak beams, big bar with polished tables and chairs, striking stone fireplace, pleasant dining room, good reasonably priced food, well kept beers, decent wines, pleasant garden and terrace with masses of flowers; bedrooms *(Dorothy and Jack Raper)*

Thelwall [Thelwall New Rd; B5157, nr M6 junction 20; SJ6587], *Pickering Arms*: Friendly and attractive low-beamed village pub with cobbled forecourt, good generous reasonably priced bar food lunchtime and evening, friendly service, Greenalls Bitter and Mild; quiz night Thurs, live music Sun, maybe Sat; children welcome if eating *(Iain Taylor, Martin Bromfield, Bernadette Garner)*

☆ **nr Tiverton** [Wharton's Lock; Bates Mill Lane – OS Sheet 117 map ref 532603; SJ5660], *Shady Oak*: Canalside country pub with plenty of seats and good play area in waterside garden and terrace, fine views of Beeston Castle, airy lounge, small carpeted conservatory, pleasant young licensee, well kept Courage/S&N ales, decent Chef & Brewer food, summer barbecues, moorings *(William Cissna, LYM)*

Walgherton [London Rd; A51 between Bridgemere Gdn Centre and Stapeley Water Gdns; SJ6949], *Boars Head*: Country-pub atmosphere, good quick food all day from sandwiches up, very friendly staff, reasonably priced Greenalls, large lounge with dining area, bar with games, prints and boars' heads, very big garden with hens in field and play area; bedrooms *(SLC)*

☆ **Walker Barn** [A537 Macclesfield—Buxton; SJ9573], *Setter Dog*: Warm, clean and civilised extended dining pub with windswept moors view, well kept real ales such as Fullers London Pride, good food inc good value roasts in small bar and restaurant, good friendly service, roaring fire; handy for Teggs Nose Country Park *(Gill and Maurice McMahon)*

☆ **Warmingham** [Middlewich Rd; SJ7161], *Bears Paw*: Good food inc lots of specials and enormous filled baguettes in small plush bar and restaurant, well kept Bass, Boddingtons, Flowers IPA and **Marstons** Pedigree, relaxed atmosphere, friendly staff, pool room, children very welcome; good spot by river and ancient church in small hamlet, seats in front garden *(Helen Lowe, Richard Lewis)*

☆ *nr* **Warrington** [Fiddlers Ferry; leave A562 in Penketh, park in Station rd off Tannery Lane – OS Sheet 108 map ref 560863], *Ferry*: Picturesquely isolated between St Helens Canal and Mersey, four well kept real ales inc very quickly changing guest beers, over 100 whiskies, good home-cooked food in nice upstairs dining room (not Sun evening), cosy and friendly low-beamed bar, log fires, provision for children; tables outside with play area, pets corner, pony paddock, burger trailer *(John McPartland, Peter Hunt, Pete Yearsley, B D Craig, LYM)*

☆ **Waverton** [A41 S of Chester; SJ4663], *Black Dog*: Clean and inviting old Greenalls dining pub recently done out in modern pine and light oak style, with good choice of popular food, real ales inc guests, cordial licensees, big tasteful lounge, small garden; occasional jazz evenings, piped music *(Monroe Mirsky, Gill and Keith Croxton, SLC)*

Whiteley Green [OS Sheet 118 map ref 924789; SJ9278], *Windmill*: Roomy modernised lounge and dining area, good lunchtime bar food from sandwiches up, Tetleys-related ales; provision for children; spacious and attractive garden with summer bar and barbecues, nice countryside with canal and other walks *(Brian and Anna Marsden, Mr and Mrs C Roberts, BB)*

Willaston [Newcastle Rd, Blakelow – OS Sheet 118 map ref 680517; SJ6851], *Horseshoe*: Reliable food inc some imaginative dishes, Robinsons Best, Best

Mild, Old Stockport and Old Tom, panelled lounge with fire, dining room and no-smoking restaurant extension, public bar, well meaning service; garden with swings *(Sue Holland, Dave Webster)*

Willington Corner [Boothdale; off A54 at Kelsall; SJ5367], *Boot*: Friendly welcome, open fires, lots of dining tables, decent bar food (steak sandwich, Norwegian prawns and pheasant casserole all recommended), Greenalls beer *(J Honnor, W C M Jones)*

Wilmslow [Green Ln; SJ8481], *Blue Lamp*: Banks's conversion of high-ceilinged former police station, bare boards, lots of drinking areas, two cosy snugs, interesting interior windows and police artefacts; well kept Bitter and Marstons Pedigree, usual lunchtime food from separate counter, friendly staff, tables outside; games machine, piped music *(Brian and Anna Marsden, Richard Lewis)*; [Altrincham Rd (A538)], *Boddingtons Arms*: Big, modern and comfortable, well kept beer, decent food inc good value restaurant meals *(Mr and Mrs C Roberts)*

☆ **Wistaston** [Nantwich Rd; SJ6853], *Old Manor*: Old manor house recently refurbished by Bass, olde-worlde feel, lots of wood, plenty of comfortable seating, friendly staff, extensive range of food, Bass, Stones and Worthington on handpump; fully supervised Deep Sea Den for children *(Richard Lewis)*

Woodbank [A540; about 1½ miles NW of A5117 roundabout; SJ3573], *Yacht*: In a tiny hamlet, eye-catching family pub with lots of flowers, welcoming service, pleasant garden, well kept beers, good sandwiches and hearty meals inc afternoon food bargains *(E G Parish)*

☆ **Wybunbury** [Main Rd (B5071); SJ6950], *Swan*: Well run pub in charming spot by beautiful churchyard, with seats in garden, well kept beer, reasonably priced genuine home cooking inc interesting dishes, warmly welcoming staff, tasteful furnishings inc some antiques (shop at the back) *(R and A Lees, LYM)*

Stars after the name of a pub show exceptional character and appeal. They don't mean extra comfort. And they are nothing to do with food quality, for which there's a separate knife-and-fork rosette. Even quite a basic pub can win stars, if it's individual enough.

Cornwall

A good crop of new main entries here includes the distinctive Earl of St Vincent at Egloshayle (just outside Wadebridge), the cheerful harbourside Chain Locker in Falmouth, the Halfway House close to the sea at Kingsand, the charming little New Inn at Manaccan with its very friendly Cornish landlady, the Old Inn in Mullion (bags of character), the prettily placed Kings Head at Ruan Lanihorne, and the Victory at St Mawes, a friendly little fishermen's local a few steps from the harbour. All of these in their different ways have worthwhile food, but for an enjoyable pub meal our pick of the county's pubs would now be the Springer Spaniel at Treburley, which gains a Food Award this year – and earns our accolade of Cornish Dining Pub of the Year. Other changes to note here include continuing refurbishments at the very popular Maltsters Arms at Chapel Amble, a new landlady for that thriving ale pub the Quayside in Falmouth (it has a first-class choice of whiskies, too), and the Port William at Trebarwith starting to do bedrooms (but to balance this, the White Hart at St Teath no longer has bedrooms). The enjoyable Eliot Arms at Tregadillett has now boosted its collection of snuffs to 400 – probably the most comprehensive to be found anywhere. Sadly the landlord of the interesting old Bush at Morwenstow has died; we have moved the pub to the Lucky Dip section at the end of the chapter, until its future is more certain. Main entries currently filling our postbag with specially warm praise include the Trengilly Wartha at Constantine (15 wines by the glass – and it's started a mail-order wine business), the happy Halzephron at Gunwalloe south of Helston (gains a Place to Stay Award and a Wine Award this year), the warmly friendly White Hart at Ludgvan, the enjoyably traditional Roseland at Philleigh, the beautifully placed Ship at Porthleven (a free house now), the quietly unchanging Crown at St Ewe (licensees celebrating their 40th year there in 1996), and the very well run Old Ale House in Truro. In the Lucky Dip section at the end of the chapter, front runners include the Borough Arms just outside Bodmin, Napoleon at Boscastle, Dolphin at Grampound, Copley Arms at Hessenford, Ship at Lerryn, Top House at Lizard, Heron at Malpas, Red Lion at Mawnan Smith, Carpenters Arms at Metherell, Royal Oak at Perranwell, Blue Peter at Polperro, Lugger at Polruan, Rising Sun at Portmellon Cove, Who'd Have Thought It at St Dominick, Tree at Stratton and Tinners Arms at Zennor, with several very worthwhile places on the Isles of Scilly. As we have inspected almost all of these, we can vouch for their appeal. Drinks prices in the county used to be low but have been rising rather more than in other places, so are now close to or even a little above the national average. Pubs tied to the local St Austell brewery, however, are still good value, with beer prices generally well below average; their new beer Trelawnys Pride is most enjoyable. The three cheapest pubs we found were the Ship at Mousehole, the Cobweb at Boscastle and (brewing its own unusual beers) the Blue Anchor in Helston.

BOSCASTLE SX0990 Map 1

Cobweb

B3263, just E of harbour

Close to the tiny steeply-cut harbour and pretty village, this cheerfully run pub is welcoming to both locals and visitors alike. The room with the most atmosphere is the lively public bar where hundreds of old bottles hang from the heavy beams, there's a cosy log fire, two or three curved high-backed winged settles against the dark stone walls, and a few leatherette dining chairs. Well kept Bass, St Austell Tinners, HSD, and Shepherd Neame Spitfire on handpump, with occasional guest beers, and several malt whiskies. Quickly served, good value bar food includes sandwiches (from £1.40, crab or prawn £3), fine pasties (£1.60), baked potatoes (from £1.50), sausage, egg and chips (£3.25; the chips are good), meaty or vegetarian lasagne (£4.50), steaks (from £6.50), gammon and egg (£7.50), and daily specials; children's dishes (from £1.25). Darts, pool (keen players here), dominoes, pinball, video game, and fruit machine; the big communicating family room has an enormous armchair carved out of a tree trunk as well as its more conventional windsor armchairs, and another winter fire. Opening off this a good-sized children's room has a second pool table, and more machines. The pub can get crowded in the holiday season. (*Recommended by Clare Wilson, Linda and Mike Proctor, Dr S Savvas, M Martin, Craig and Gillian Brown, R Walden, Alan and Eileen Bowker, Anthony Marriott, M W Turner, R T and J C Moggridge, John Whiting, Jack and Philip Paxton, Brian and Anna Marsden*)

Free house ~ Licensees Ivor and Adrian Bright ~ Real ale ~ Meals and snacks (till 10pm) ~ Restaurant ~ (01840) 250278 ~ Children in own room and in restaurant ~ Live entertainment Sat evening ~ Open 11-11 in summer and on winter Fri and Sat; closed winter weekday afternoons

CHAPEL AMBLE SW9975 Map 1

Maltsters Arms ♀

Village signposted from A39 NE of Wadebridge; and from B3314

The enthusiastic licensees are constantly striving to improve this busy pub by refurbishing rooms, tidying up the small front garden area, planning to extend the sitting area to the right of the stairs, and hoping to rebuild new lavatories. It remains a very popular place with our readers who enjoy the friendly, obliging service, well kept beer, and good food. The attractively knocked-together rooms (one of which is no smoking) have black oak joists in the white ceiling, partly panelled stripped stone walls, heavy wooden tables on the partly carpeted big flagstones, a large stone fireplace, and a nice pubby atmosphere; there's also a side room with windsor chairs and a good upstairs family room with a TV and video (not on all the time). Bar food includes lunchtime sandwiches, filled baked potatoes and ploughman's (£3.50), as well as home-made soup (£1.95), cheesy garlic mushrooms (£3.95), home-cooked ham and egg (£4.25), sizzle dishes such as chicken with ginger or prawns with chilli (from £6), vegetarian dishes (from £6.95), very good fresh fish dishes (from £6.95), daily specials, Sunday hot carvery, and lovely puddings such as fruit crumbles, bread and butter pudding with brandy and cream, and lemon tart; lots of clotted cream. Well kept Bass, Courage Directors, Fullers London Pride, Ruddles County, Sharps Cornish and a beer brewed for the pub by Sharps (who are a local brewery), and a guest beer on handpump kept under light blanket pressure; around 18 wines by the glass (including a proprietor's choice), several malt whiskies, and several brandies. Winter darts, cribbage, dominoes, video game, trivia, and piped music. Benches outside in a sheltered sunny corner. (*Recommended by Howard Clutterbuck, Pete and Rosie Flower, Jenny and Brian Seller, Sharon Hancock, Sue and Bob Ward, John Ledbury, Cdr and Mrs J M Lefeaux, Dr S Savvas, M Martin, Paul and Lynn Benny, R and S Bentley, David and Julie Glover, Rita Horridge, D Horsman, John Woodward, Brian and Anna Marsden, Laurence Bacon, Sue Demont, Tim Barrow*)

Free house ~ Licensees David and Marie Gray ~ Real ale ~ Meals and snacks ~

Restaurant ~ (01208) 812473 ~ Children in restaurant (must be over 8) and family room ~ Open 10.30(maybe 11 Sat)-2.30, 5.30(6 in winter)-11

CONSTANTINE SW7229 Map 1

Trengilly Wartha 🛏 🍷 🍺

Constantine signposted from Penryn—Gweek rd (former B3291); in village turn right just before Minimarket (towards Gweek); in nearly a mile pub signposted left; at Nancenoy, OS sheet 204, map reference 731282

This tucked away, busy inn is a successful combination of local meeting place, popular dining pub, and comfortable hotel. The low-beamed main bar has a wood-burning stove and modern high-backed settles boxing in polished heavy wooden tables, and the lounge has cushioned wall benches, a log fire and some harness. Up a step from the bar is an eating area with winged settles and tables, and there's also a bright no-smoking conservatory family room. Good bar food includes home-made soup (£2.20; the fish one is delicious, £2.40), blue cheese and walnut pâté (£3), leek and cheese soufflé (£4), ploughman's (from £4), spicy vegetable stew (£4.50), smoked fish platter (£5.70), a Moroccan chicken dish with eggs and a cinnamon, almond and sugar paste (£5.80), pork and apricot (£6.20), and lots of daily specials like good mixed fried fish or stilton tartlet (£3.30), spicy Italian sausage (£4.20), steak and kidney pudding (£5.50), baked cod fillet with caramelised onions (£6.70), roast rabbit pie with Dijon mustard sauce (£7), crab cakes with wine sauce (£7.50), and brill fillet with wild mushrooms (£10.80). They keep an unusually wide choice of drinks for the area, such as well kept Fergusons Dartmoor, St Austell XXXX Mild and Sharps Cornish (a local brewery) on handpump with regularly changing ales from smaller brewers tapped from the cask such as Cotleigh Tawny, Exmoor Gold, Gibbs Mew Bishops Tipple, Hook Norton, Otter Bright, Smiles, and so forth. Also, over 40 malt whiskies (including several extinct ones), and lots of interesting wines (with 15 by the glass); they've started selling wine this year by mail order, too. Darts, pool, bar billiards, cribbage, shove-ha'penny, dominoes, fruit machine, and video and trivia machines. The pretty landscaped garden has some picnic tables around the vine-covered pergola, an international sized piste for boules, and a lake garden next door to the inn. This is also in the *Good Hotel Guide. (Recommended by Gwen and Peter Andrews, Colin Draper, David Carr, Wendy Arnold, E A Thwaite, Richard Hearn, Martin and Penny Fletcher, Dr D A Spencer, E D Bailey, Dr G W Barnett, D and B Taylor, Ron Shelton, Molly and Robin Taylor, Jeremy Palmer, P Eberlin, Peter Brimacombe, Anthony Barnes, Mr and Mrs J Woodfield, Jack and Philip Paxton, Sue Demont, Tim Barrow, Andy and Jill Kassube, R and S Bentley, Bob and Maggie Atherton)*

Free house ~ Licensees Nigel Logan, Michael Maguire ~ Real ale ~ Meals and snacks ~ Restaurant ~ (01326) 340332 ~ Children welcome ~ Open 11-3(2.30 winter), 6(6.30 winter)-11 ~ Bedrooms: £37(£40B)/£60B

CROWS NEST SX2669 Map1

Crows Nest £

Signposted off B3264 N of Liskeard; or pleasant drive from A30 by Siblyback/St Cleer rd from Bolventor, turning left at Common Moor, Siblyback signpost, then forking right to Darite; OS Sheet 201 map reference 263692

Tucked away in a small village on Bodmin Moor, this friendly old pub popular with locals and tourists – has lots of stirrups, bits and spurs hanging from the bowed dark oak beams, an interesting table converted from a huge blacksmith's bellows (which still work), and an unusually long black wall settle by the big log fire as well as other more orthodox seats. On the right, and divided by a balustered partition, is a similar area with old local photographs and maybe flowers on the tablecloths. Cheap bar food includes soup (£1.85), lunchtime filled soft rolls (from £1.30), lunchtime ploughman's (£3), chips with ham and egg, sausage or chicken (from £2.75), vegetable lasagne (£4), and children's dishes (£2), with evening grills (from £6); Sunday roast lunch (£3.95; no other food is served then). Well kept St Austell

Tinners and HSD on handpump kept under light blanket pressure; shove-ha'penny, euchre, juke box, and fruit machine. On the terrace by the quiet lane there are picnic tables. This used to be the pay office/company store where tin and copper miners were paid. *(Recommended by James Macrae, Mr and Mrs D E Powell, Andrew and Joan Life, A E and J Toogood, Stephen and Susan Breen, Peter Cornall, Philip and Trisha Ferris, JKW, John Ledbury, R Turnham, Norma Farris, Mr and Mrs J Woodfield, Jack and Philip Paxton, Sue Demont, Tim Barrow)*

St Austell ~ Tenant C R Sargeant ~ Real ale ~ Meals and snacks ~ (01759) 345930 ~ Children welcome ~ Open 11-3, 6-11

EGLOSHAYLE SX0172 Map 1

Earl of St Vincent

Just outside Wadebridge, on A389 Bodmin road

Tucked behind the church, and quite eye-catching in summer with its gorgeous floral displays, this comfortable and civilised pub puts some emphasis on the food side – but there's still a welcome for people who want a quiet pint of their well kept St Austell Tinners, HSD or Trelawnys Pride. A combination of rich furnishings and a fascinating collection of antique clocks gives a cosy and relaxed atmosphere for both drinkers and diners. Generous freshly cooked food includes soup (£1.50), sandwiches (from £1.70), ploughman's or filled baked potatoes (from £3), winter home-made steak and kidney or steak and kidney pies (£4), vegetarian dishes such as mushroom stroganoff or spanish omelette (around £5), king prawns in garlic (£5.75), dover sole (£11.50), speciality steaks (£12), and puddings like sticky toffee and hazelnut meringue or bread and butter pudding (£2); service is consistently friendly and efficient; piped music. There are picnic tables in the lovely garden. *(Recommended by Mark Billings, D and B Taylor, Jack and Philip Paxton, Graham Tayar, Ian Smith, R E Jones, M C F Lloyd)*

St Austell ~ Tenants Edward and Anne Connolly ~ Real ale ~ Meals and snacks ~ (01208) 814807 ~ Well behaved children in eating area of bar if eating ~ Open 11-3, 6.30-11

FALMOUTH SW8032 Map 1

Chain Locker

With Marine Restaurant, on Custom House Quay off Church Street – the main shopping street, parallel to waterfront

Seats in the big corner windows of the bar here have a fine view of fishing boats a few feet away in Falmouth's small central harbour. There's a strong nautical atmosphere – many people working with boats use this as their local – and the plank ceiling is hung with ships' pennants and wheels, there are marine photographs and a collection of ship models, and strip-panelled walls. A bigger communicating inner room has a good separate darts alley. Well kept Bass, Flowers Original, Whitbread Best, and Worthington Best on handpump kept under light blanket pressure; bar food includes sandwiches and snacks as well as scallops (£4.95), local monkfish cooked with prawns and mushrooms (£5.95), steaks (from £5.95), sole (£6.50), and puddings; darts, cribbage, dominoes, fruit machine, and piped music. The dog is called William. *(Recommended by Reg Nelson, E A Thwaite, David Carr)*

Greenalls ~ Manager Trevor Jones ~ Real ale ~ Meals and snacks ~ (01326) 311085 ~ Children welcome until 9pm ~ Parking may be difficult ~ Open 11-11; 12-10.30 Sun

Quayside 🍺

ArwenackSt/Fore St

Under the new licensee, the fine range of real ales here has not diminished: Courage Directors, Flowers Original, Fullers London Pride, Ruddles County, Sharps Doom

Bar, John Smiths, and Tetleys on handpump, with up to 14 tapped from the cask such as Archers Golden, Belhaven 80/-, Black Sheep, Cotleigh Old Buzzard, Exmoor Stag, Gibbs Mew Bishops Tipple, Orkney Raven and Skullsplitter, and Shepherd Neame; they hold beer fesitvals during the spring and autumn half-terms; Old Hazy farm cider. There are lots of beer mats on the panelled walls, book matches on the black ceiling, malt sacks tacked into the counter, a big white ensign, a mix of ordinary pub chairs on the bare boards, a log-effect gas fire in the stripped stone fireplace, and a big barrel of free peanuts (which gives an individual touch to the floor covering); piped music. Upstairs is the lounge bar (which you enter from the attractively bustling street) with comfortable armchairs and sofas at one end, more straightforward tables and chairs at the other, picture windows overlooking the harbour, and huge range of over 219 whiskies (179 are single malts). Bar food includes home-made doorstep sandwiches, good garlic mushrooms, bangers and mash (£3.45), meaty or vegetarian chilli (£3.95), beef in ale pie (£4.55), scallops in white wine sauce (£4.95), and moules marinières (£5.25). There are picnic tables on the tarmac by the Custom House Dock and next to the handsome Georgian harbour-master's office. *(Recommended by David Carr, Ted George, Reg Nelson, E A Thwaite, George Atkinson, David Luke, Peter and Gwyneth Eastwood, Steve Felstead, P and M Rudlin, Alan and Eileen Bowker, Mark Robinson, Nigel Wooliscroft, Sue Holland, Dave Webster, John Lansdown, John Wooll, David and Michelle Hedges)*

Greenalls ~ Manager Miranda Keir ~ Real ale ~ Meals and snacks (not Sun evening) ~ (01326) 312113 ~ Children welcome ~ Duo Fri and Sat evenings, summer brass band and male voice choir ~ Open 11-11; 12-10.30 Sun

HELFORD SW7526 Map 1

Shipwrights Arms

Off B3293 SE of Helston, via Mawgan

In summer, this thatched pub's main draw is its lovely position above a beautiful wooded creek – and you can sit on the terraces, the top part of which is roofed over with Perspex. Inside there's quite a nautical theme with navigation lamps, models of ships, sea pictures, drawings of lifeboat coxswains and shark fishing photographs – as well as a collection of foreign banknotes behind the bar counter. A dining area has oak settles and tables; winter open fire. Well kept Flowers IPA and Whitbreads Castle Eden on handpump, and bar food such as home-made pies and stews (from £5.25), summer buffets and barbecue dishes (from £8.25), evening steaks (£7.75), and puddings (£3.25). It does get crowded at peak times. *(Recommended by David Carr, Mr and Mrs Claude Bemis, David Hillcox, P R White, E A Thwaite, Martin and Penny Fletcher, Christopher Wright, Ian Fraser, D and B Taylor, Adrian and Karen Bulley, A J N Lee, Beverley James, E N Burleton, Nigel Flook, Betsy Brown, Jack and Philip Paxton)*

Greenalls ~ Lease: Charles Herbert ~ Real ale ~ Meals and snacks (not winter Sun or Mon evenings) ~ (01326) 231235 ~ Children in eating area of bar ~ Parking only right outside the village in summer ~ Open 11-2.30, 6-11; closed winter Sun evenings

HELSTON SW6527 Map 1

Blue Anchor £ 🍺

50 Coinagehall Street

Mainly popular with locals (mostly men), this old thatched town pub is the sort of basic place that some people enjoy very much – but it's not to everyone's taste. A series of small, low-ceilinged rooms opens off the central corridor, with simple old-fashioned furniture on the flagstones, interesting old prints, some bared stone walls, and in one room a fine inglenook fireplace. A family room has darts. They still produce their very cheap Medium, Best, `Spingo' Special (the name comes from the Victorian word for strong beer) and Extra Special ales in what is probably the oldest brewing house in the country. At lunchtimes you can usually go and look round the brewery and the cellar; they also sell farm cider. Bar food includes rolls (£1.20), pasties (£1.50), and some pot meals (from £3.25). Past an old stone bench in the sheltered little terrace area is a skittle alley. *(Recommended by James Nunns, Jim Reid, Sue Holland, Dave Webster, Colin Draper, David Carr, Barry Cawthorne, Anne Moggridge, Sian Thrasher, Anthony Barnes, Mark Walker, Jack and Philip Paxton, Alastair Campbell)*

Own brew ~ Licensee Kim Corbett ~ Real ale ~ Snacks (12-4; not Sun) ~ (01326) 562821 ~ Children in family room ~ Parking sometimes difficult ~ Open 11-11; 12-10.30 Sun

Halzephron ♀ 🍴

Gunwalloe, village about 4 miles S but not marked on many road maps; signposted off A3083 Lizard rd by RNAS *Culdrose*

The Thomases and their staff have created a happy, outgoing and friendly atmosphere in this old smugglers' haunt. It's in a lovely spot with Gunwalloe fishing cove just 300 yards away, a sandy beach one mile away at Gunwalloe Church Cove, and lots of unspoilt coastal walks with fine views of Mount's Bay. The quietly welcoming pleasant bar has a warm fire in the big hearth, comfortable seating, copper on the walls and mantelpiece, and maybe the three cats (Millie the tortoiseshell, Humphrey the gentle black one, and a lively marmalade one called Mr Chivers); there's also a family room with toys, games and puzzles. Good, popular bar food includes good sandwiches (lunchtimes), home-made soup (£2.40), fresh pâté (£3.10), grilled goat's cheese on garlic bread (£3.50), ploughman's (from £3.60), daily pasta and vegetarian dishes (£5.60), several delicious platters (from £8; crab £9), enjoyable daily specials, char-grilled sirloin steak (£9.10), and puddings (£3); the restaurant is no smoking. Well kept Furgusons Dartmoor and Sharps Own and Doom Bar on handpump, a good wine list, 50 malt whiskies, and liqueurs, and an interesting wine list; darts, dominoes and cribbage. Small but comfortable and well equipped bedrooms – and huge breakfasts. *(Recommended by Mr and Mrs J Barrett, Michele Gunning, Ron Shelton, C and D Pike, Sybille Weber, Gwen and Peter Andrews, Margaret Dyke, Barry Cawthorne, Anne Moggridge, George and Chris Miller, R P and L E Booth, Sally Andrews, Mick Wood, Bob and Maggie Atherton)*

Free house ~ Licensees Harry and Angela Thomas ~ Real ale ~ Meals and snacks (not 25 Dec) ~ Restaurant ~ (01326) 240406 ~ Children in family room ~ Open 11-3(2.30 winter), 6.30-11 ~ Bedrooms: £35B/£56B

KINGSAND SX4350 Map 1

Halfway House 🍴

Fore St, towards Cawsand

Cosy and softly lit, this attractive old inn's bar, neat and clean, is simply furnished but quite smart, rambling around a huge central fireplace. It's low-ceilinged, and mildly Victorian in style, popular with locals but with a warm welcome for the many summer visitors. A wide choice of good often imaginative bar food majors on well presented fresh local fish and seafood such as grilled sardines (£3.75), scallops with bacon (£4.25), marinated seafood salad (£4.85), sailfish creole (£7.65), hake with leeks, onions and wild mushrooms (£9.25), roast garlic monkfish (£9.50), bass with an orange butter sauce (£13.50), and grilled dover sole (£14.75). Also, staples such as filled french bread (from £2.15), filled baked potatoes (from £2.90), ploughman's (from £4.35), a good breakfast (£4.70), and local home-cooked ham and egg (£4.90), and blackboard specials like spinach soup (£1.95), garlic mushrooms with bacon and cheese (£3.50), sautéed chicken livers with thyme and brandy (£3.95), steak and kidney pie (£6.45), beef carbonnade (£7.45), lamb chops with ratatouille (£8.25), steaks (from £8.25), and puddings such as sticky ginger pudding with brandy sauce, profiteroles with lemon cream and white chocolate sauce (£3); vegetables are fresh and carefully cooked. There are often attractive fresh flowers on the tables. Well kept Bass, Boddingtons, Flowers Original and a guest such as Wadworths 6X on handpump, decent wines and coffee. Service is quick and friendly, and the bar staff add a lot to the enjoyable atmosphere; the landlord himself is a man of strong opinions, not shy of stating them – though always courteous. The piped music is generally unobtrusive; cribbage, dominoes, backgammon, and fruit machine. The inn is quite near the sea and harbour, and this hilly village is well placed for marvellous cliff walks on Rame Head, or for visiting Mount Edgcumbe. *(Recommended by Nicholas Regan, Mr and Mrs M Fletcher, Andrew and Joan Life, R Turnham, Jacky Darville, C E Taylor, Cdr and Mrs W J Soames)*

Free house ~ Licensees Sarah and David Riggs ~ Real ale ~ Meals and snacks ~ Restaurant ~ (01752) 822279 ~ Children welcome ~ Choir Weds evenings, quiz winter Thurs evenings ~ Open 12-4, 6-11; 12-3, 7-11 in winter ~ Bedrooms: £20S/£40S

LANLIVERY SX0759 Map 1

Crown 🍺

Signed off A390 Lostwithiel—St Austell

This pretty 12th-c pub – one of Cornwall's oldest inns – is run by genuinely friendly licensees who keep local ale and are keen to support local producers and fishermen when producing their menu. The bar servery is buried at the heart of a rambling series of rooms – the first of which is the small, dimly-lit public bar with its heavy beams, slate floor, built-in wall settles and attractive alcove of seats in the dark former chimney; darts. A much lighter room leads off here with beams in the white boarded ceiling, some comfortable, if ancient, burgundy plush sofas in one corner, flowery cushioned black settles, a small cabinet with wood-turning stuff for sale, owl and badger pictures, and a little fireplace with an old-fashioned fire; there's also another similar little room. No noisy games machines, music or pool tables. The slate-floored no-smoking porch room has lots of succulents and a few cacti, and wood-and-stone seats. Good bar food includes meaty or vegetarian pasties (from £1.35), sandwiches (from £1.60, double decker £3.10, open sandwiches from £3.95), home-made soup (£2.25), ploughman's (from £2.65), home-made curries (from £4.95), vegetarian dishes (from £5.15), home-made steak and kidney pie (£6.35), an 'under roast' (strips of steak covered with potato and onions and baked, £6.95), steaks (from £7.50), scallops mornay (£9.95), roasted monkfish with herb crust (£10.50), daily specials, puddings with clotted cream (£2.40), and a children's menu (from £1.25). Well kept Bass and Sharps Own on handpump, and farm cider; dominoes, cribbage, shove-ha'penny, and table skittles. In the garden (which has been re-stocked this year) are some white cast-iron furniture and picnic tables sheltered by the black-and-white painted building. *(Recommended by Sean McCarthy, Cdr and Mrs J M Lefeaux, Ian Phillips, Jack and Philip Paxton)*

Free house ~ Licensees Ros and Dave Williams ~ Real ale ~ Meals and snacks ~ Restaurant ~ (01208) 872707 ~ Children in eating area of bar and in restaurant ~ Open 11-3, 6-11 ~ Bedrooms:£23S/£40S

LANNER SW7240 Map 1

Fox & Hounds

Comford; junction A393/B3293; OS sheet 204 map reference 734399

In summer, the front of this attractive old white house is a riot of colour with masses of hanging baskets, flowering tubs, and window boxes; there are picnic tables on the neatly kept back lawn, a big barbecue area, wildlife pond, and swings and a climber for children. Inside, the rambling bar has a relaxed atmosphere, black beams and joists, stripped stonework and dark panelling, some comical 1920s prints by Lawson Wood, and high-backed settles and cottagey chairs. One granite fireplace has a woodburning stove and another has a good log fire. Bar food includes sandwiches and ploughman's, half a dozen vegetarian dishes (from £4), fish dishes and roasts (from £4.10), and genuinely home-made daily specials (from £3.95). Well kept Bass and St Austell Tinners, HSD and Winter Warmer tapped from the cask; around 15

malt whiskies. Pool, shove-ha'penny, cribbage, dominoes, fruit machine, and piped
music. Part of the restaurant is no smoking. *(Recommended by Colin Draper, Alan and
Eileen Bowker, Ian Julian; more reports please)*

*St Austell ~ Tenants Mike and Sue Swiss ~ Real ale ~ Meals and snacks (till 10pm
Fri and Sat) ~ Restaurant ~ (01209) 820251 ~ Children in eating area of bar ~
Open 11-3, 6-11; 11-11 Sat and Sun*

LOSTWITHIEL SX1059 Map 1

Royal Oak 🍺

Duke St; pub just visible from A390 in centre

Seven well kept real ales are kept on handpump in this friendly old town-centre pub:
Bass, Belhaven 90/-, Fullers London Pride and ESB, Marstons Pedigree, Sharps Own,
and St Austell Trelawny – as well as lots of bottled beers from around the world.
Popular bar food includes lunchtime sandwiches and ploughman's, soup (£1.75),
pâté (£2.95), good stuffed mushrooms (£3.15), salads (from £4.75), vegetarian
crêpes (£5.50), scallops in white wine sauce (£7.95), steaks (from £8.10), daily
specials such as beef curry (£5.30), steak and kidney pie (£5.95) or fresh whole
plaice (£7.95), and puddings (£1.75). The neat lounge is spacious and comfortable,
with captain's chairs and high-backed wall benches on its patterned carpet, and a
couple of wooden armchairs by the log-effect gas fire; there's also a delft shelf, with
a small dresser in one inner alcove. The flagstoned and beamed back public bar has
darts, dominoes, cribbage, fruit machine and juke box, and is popular with younger
customers. On a raised terrace by the car park are some picnic tables. *(Recommended
by Graham Tayar, Barry Cawthorne, Anne Moggridge, Jack and Philip Paxton , G Washington,
Peter Williamson, Andy and Jill Kassube, Ron Shelton, Jill Bickerton)*

*Free house ~ Licensees Malcolm and Eileen Hine ~ Real ale ~ Meals and snacks ~
Restaurant ~ (01208) 872552 ~ Children welcome ~ Open 11-11; 12-10.30 Sun
~ Bedrooms: £27.75(£31.75B)/£48.75(£52.75B)*

LUDGVAN SW5033 Map 1

White Hart

Churchtown; off A30 Penzance—Hayle at Crowlas – OS Sheet 203 map reference 505330

Whether you are a local or a visitor, you'll be made to feel at home in this friendly
old pub. The small and snug beamed rooms have lots of atmosphere, masses of mugs
and jugs glinting in cottagey corners, bric-a-brac, pictures and photographs
(including some good ones of Exmoor), soft oil-lamp-style lighting, stripped boards
with attractive rugs on them, and a fascinating mix of interesting old seats and
tables; the two big woodburning stoves run radiators too. Good simple and very
popular bar food includes sandwiches (from £1.20), home-made soup (£1.50),
village-made pasties (£1.60), ploughman's (£2.75), salads (from £3.65; crab £5.76),
omelettes (£3.95), home-made vegetable or meaty lasagne or ham and egg (£4.20),
steaks (from £8), puddings such as home-made crumble or treacle tart (£1.75), and
daily specials such as delicious fresh mackerel, toad in the hole or rabbit casserole; it
is essential to book well in advance. Well kept Flowers IPA, Marstons Pedigree and a
guest beer tapped from the cask, and several whiskies; cribbage, dominoes.
*(Recommended by Molly and Robin Taylor, R and S Bentley, George Atkinson, P and M
Rudlin, DAV, Chris and Sally Blackler, Jill and Patrick Sawdon, S Beele, D Eberlin, Pat and
Roger Fereday, DWAJ, J Ingram, K Stevens, Jack and Philip Paxton, Richard Wood, Fiona
Lewry, Mr and Mrs D Darby, Anthony Barnes, Mrs B Sugarman)*

*Devenish (Greenalls) ~ Tenant Dennis Churchill ~ Real ale ~ Meals and snacks
(not Mon evening Oct-May) ~ (01736) 740574 ~ Children in restaurant ~ Choir
most Mon evenings ~ Open 11-2.30, 6-11*

It's against the law for bar staff to smoke while handling food or drink.

MANACCAN SW7625 Map 1

New

Down hill signposted to Gillan and St Keverne

Run by a warmly friendly Cornish landlady, this unspoilt old thatched local has a cosy and simply furnished double-room bar with a beam and plank ceiling, pictures on the walls, individually chosen chairs, traditional built-in wall seats, and maybe fresh flowers. Good bar food includes home-made soup such as watercress and lettuce or spicy leek and potato or pasties with pickle (£2), sandwiches (from £2, crab £3.75), two sausages with chips (£3), ploughman's (from £3.75), daily specials like chilli con carne (£3.50), chicken balti (£4.50), popular fresh salmon pie (£5), smoked prawns with garlic dip (£6), evening steaks (from £7), and home-made puddings like summer pudding or treacle tart with clotted cream (£2.50). Well kept Flowers IPA and Whitbreads Castle Eden tapped from the cask; winter darts three times a week and euchre once a week (when the pub is very crowded), as well as dominoes, cribbage, and shove-ha'penny. A sheltered lawn with picnic tables slopes up behind the pub. *(Recommended by Molly and Robin Taylor, Ian Fraser, Cliff Blakemore, David Carr)*

Greenalls ~ Licensee Brenda Steer ~ Real ale ~ Meals and snacks ~ (01326) 231323 ~ Well behaved children allowed ~ Parking may be difficult in summer ~ Open 11-3, 6-11

MITHIAN SW7450 Map 1

Miners Arms

Just off B3285 E of St Agnes

The atmospheric small back bar in this 16th-c pub has an irregular beam and plank ceiling, a wood block floor, and bulging squint walls (one with a fine old wall painting of Elizabeth I), and another small room has a decorative low ceiling, lots of books and quite a few interesting ornaments; open fires. Bar food includes sandwiches, good crab bake, pasta bake or chilli (£5.25), nice steak and kidney pie or fish on a bed of spinach with a creamy sauce and cheese crumble topping (£5.50), good butterfly chicken breast in a garlic and cream sauce, and sirloin steak (£9.25). The dining room is no smoking. Bass and Marstons Pedigree on handpump kept under light blanket pressure, and decent wines; friendly service. Dominoes, shove-ha'penny, cars, puzzles, and piped music. There are seats on the back terrace, with more on the sheltered front cobbled forecourt. *(Recommended by James Nunns, John and Moira Hawkes, R Turnham, Mick Hitchman, George Atkinson, Piotr Chodzko-Zajko, Jerry and Alison Oakes, Jack and Philip Paxton, Bob and Maggie Atherton)*

Greenalls ~ Lease: David Charnock ~ Real ale ~ Meals and snacks ~ (01872) 552375 ~ Children welcome ~ Open 12-3, 6-11.30; 12-2.30, 7-11 in winter

MOUSEHOLE SW4726 Map 1

Ship

Follow Newlyn coast rd out of Penzance; also signposted off B3315

In the heart of a lovely village and overlooking the harbour, this traditional fisherman's local is best visited out of season (when you should at least have some chance of parking). The opened-up main bar has a bustling, cheerful atmosphere as well as black beams and panelling, built-in wooden wall benches and stools around the low tables, photographs of local events, sailors' fancy ropework, granite flagstones, and a cosy open fire. Bar food includes sandwiches (crab £3.75), local mussels (£3.75), and local fish dishes and steaks (from £7.25). On 23 December they bake Starry Gazy pie (£5.50) to celebrate Tom Bawcock's Eve, a tradition that recalls Tom's brave expedition out to sea in a fierce storm 200 years ago. He caught seven types of fish, which were then cooked in a pie with their heads and tails sticking out. Well kept St Austell BB, Tinners, HSD and Trelawnys Pride on handpump, and several malt whiskies; friendly staff; darts and dominoes. The elaborate harbour lights at Christmas are worth a visit. *(Recommended by P R White, D and B Taylor, John Ledbury, TBB, Sue Holland, Dave Webster, Bronwen and Steve Wrigley, C P Scott-Malden, Steve Felstead, J C Simpson, Gary Nicholls, Peter and Joy Heatherley, Mark Walker)*

St Austell ~ Tenants Michael and Tracey Maddern ~ Real ale ~ Meals and snacks ~ Restaurant ~ (01736) 731234 ~ Children welcome if kept away from bar ~ Summer parking can be difficult ~ Open 10.30am-11pm; 12-10.30 Sun ~ Bedrooms: /£40B

MULLION SW6719 Map 1
Old Inn

Near centre

This is a lovely thatched village inn with a warm welcome for both visitors and locals. The dark passages and characterful warren of small rooms have lots of brasses, nautical items and old prints and photographs of wrecks, and a big inglenook fireplace with its original bread oven; one room is no smoking. Good bar food includes soup (£1.95), sandwiches (from £1.95), ploughman's (from £3.95), popular beef or oriental chicken sizzlers (£6.50), pasta and broccoli in cheese sauce and topped with three vegetarian cheeses (£6.95), chicken topped with crispy bacon and melted cheese (£7.50), evening steaks (from £8.95), and puddings such as home-made banoffi pie or treacle tart (£2.95). Well kept Bass and two guest beers such as Flowers IPA and Wadworths 6X on handpump; darts, fruit machine, and piped music. There are picnic tables and terraces in the pretty flower-filled garden. Parking is limited but there's a public car park nearby. *(Recommended by Gwen and Peter Andrews, M Wellington, George Atkinson, Barry Cawthorne, Anne Moggridge, George and Chris Miller, Bill and Sylvia Trotter, Ian Phillips, C P Scott-Malden, G Kahan, D Goodger, Dr Venetia Stott, Harry Jackson, Paul and Margaret Baker, Miss P M Gammon)*

Greenalls ~ Manageress Nicola Hull ~ Real ale ~ Meals and snacks (served all day during July and Aug) ~ Children welcome ~ Duo most Fri evenings ~ Open 11-3, 6-11; 11-11 Sat and Sun; 11-11 all day during August ~ Bedrooms: £25B/£40B

nr MYLOR BRIDGE SW8036 Map 1
Pandora ★ ★ ♀

Restronguet Passage: from A39 in Penryn, take turning signposted Mylor Church, Mylor Bridge, Flushing and go straight through Mylor Bridge following Restronguet Passage signs; or from A39 further N, at or near Perranarworthal, take turning signposted Mylor, Restronguet, then follow Restronguet Weir signs, but turn left down hill at Restronguet Passage sign

On a sheltered tidal waterfront, the idyllic setting for this pretty medieval thatched pub is at its best at high tide on a quiet day – and much appreciated from the picnic tables in front or on the long floating jetty. Quite a few people arrive by boat and there are showers for visiting yachtsmen. Inside is splendidly atmospheric, and the several rambling, interconnecting rooms have beautifully polished big flagstones, low wooden ceilings (mind your head on some of the beams), cosy alcoves with leatherette benches built into the walls, a kitchen range, and a log fire in a high hearth (to protect it against tidal floods). Bar food includes home-made soup (from £1.85), sandwiches (from £2.50, local crab £5.50), local sausages in onion gravy (£3.75), pancakes stuffed with mushroom and spinach (£4.75), fish pie (£5.25), evening mixed grill (£5.50), crab thermidor (£8.95), daily specials, puddings like home-made treacle tart (£2.30), Sunday roast, and children's dishes (from £1.60). The refurbished upstairs restaurant is no smoking. Bass, St Austell Tinners, HSD, BB, and Trelawnys Pride on handpump from a temperature controlled cellar, several malt whiskies, 20 good wines by the glass, and farm cider; dominoes, winter pool, and winter weekly quiz. It does get very crowded in summer, and parking is difficult at peak times. *(Recommended by David Carr, D and B Taylor, Canon Michael Bordeaux, M J How, George Atkinson, Cliff Blakemore, E A Thwaite, D Alexander, Ian and Gayle Woodhead, Nick Wikeley, E D Bailey, Pete and Rosie Flower, Mick Hitchman, James Nunns, Steve Felstead, DWAJ, S Beele, Martin Bromfield, Bernadette Garner, J C Aldridge, R J Doe, Gwen and Peter Andrews, Colin Draper, R Walden, G W Stevenson, Andy and Jill Kassube, George and Chris Miller, Jerry and Alison Oakes, Nigel Flook, Betsy Brown, Pat and John Millward, E N Burleton, Ted George, Sue Demont, Tim Barrow, Michael Sargent)*

St Austell ~ Tenant Helen Hough ~ Real ale ~ Meals and snacks (till 10pm in summer) ~ Evening restaurant ~ (01326) 372678 ~ Children in eating area of bar and in restaurant ~ Open 11-11; 12-10.30 Sun; closed winter weekday afternoons

PELYNT SX2055 Map 1

Jubilee 🏠

B3359 NW of Looe

The relaxed, beamed lounge bar in this neatly kept 16th-c inn has a good winter log fire in the stone fireplace, an early 18th-c Derbyshire oak armchair, cushioned wall and window seats, windsor armchairs around oak tables, and mementoes of Queen Victoria, such as a tapestry portrait, old prints, and Staffordshire figurines of the Queen and her consort; the Victorian bar has some carved settles and more mementoes. The flagstoned entry is separated from the bar by an attractively old-fangled glass-paned partition. Bar food includes home-made soup (£2), a good choice of sandwiches (from £1.60), ploughman's (from £2.80), salads (from £4.80), fresh cod (£5.60), gammon and egg (£6.50), sirloin steak (£9.80), and puddings (from £1.80). Well kept Bass and St Austell Trelawnys Pride on handpump, several malt whiskies, and quite a few wines. The quite separate public bar has sensibly placed darts, pool, fruit machine, and piped music. A crazy-paved central courtyard has picnic tables with red and white striped umbrellas and pretty tubs of flowers, and there's a well equipped children's play area. *(Recommended by W F C Phillips, R S A Suddaby, A N Ellis, Dr G W Barnett, M J How, Ian Phillips, Mr and Mrs D E Powell, George Atkinson)*

Free house ~ Licensee Frank Williams ~ Real ale ~ Meals and snacks ~ Restaurant ~ (01503) 220312 ~ Children welcome ~ Open 11-3, 6-11; 11-10.30 Sun ~ Bedrooms: £33B/£56B

PENELEWEY SW8240 Map 1

Punch Bowl & Ladle

Feock Downs, B3289

The cosy rooms in the original part of this old thatched pub have lots of shipwreck paintings and farm implements around the walls, and an open fire. There are several comfortably furnished, modernised dining areas at the back with bar food such as sandwiches (from £2.05; open ones from £3.05), home-made soup (£2.50), filled baked potatoes (from £2.50), spicy ribs (£3.50), ploughman's (from £3.95), salads (from £4.75, crab £9.50), home-made pie (£5.95), beef and stilton casserole (£7.45), Sunday roasts, daily specials, and home-made puddings. Well kept Bass, Courage Directors and Flowers Original on handpump. Darts, shove-ha'penny, cribbage, dominoes, fruit machine, and piped music. The pub is near the King Harry ferry and Trelissick Gardens. *(Recommended by Howard Clutterbuck, Nick Wikeley, M D Davies, David Luke, John Chetwynd-Chatwin, Adrian and Karen Bulley, John Wooll)*

Greenalls ~ Managers Richard and Elizabeth Dearsley ~ Real ales ~ Meals and snacks ~ Restaurant ~ (01872) 862237 ~ Children in eating area of bar and in restaurant until 9pm ~ Middle-of-road live music Fri evenings Sept-May ~ Open 11-11; 12-10.30 Sun; 11-3, 5.30(6.30 Sun)-11 in winter

PENZANCE SW4730 Map 1

Turks Head

At top of main street, by big domed building (Lloyds Bank), turn left down Chapel Street

The atmosphere in this friendly pub is at its best when the chatty main bar is full of locals and visitors. There are old flat irons, jugs and so forth hanging from the beams, pottery above the wood-effect panelling, wall seats and tables, and a couple of elbow rests around central pillars. The menu has quite an emphasis on seafood, with crab soup (£1.70), fish pie (£5.50), crab salad (mixed meat £6.95, white meat £7.80), and cold seafood platter (£9.20), as well as sandwiches (from £1.45), filled baked potatoes (from £1.95), ham and egg (£3.50), ratatouille topped with cheese (£4.25), meaty or vegetarian lasagne (£4.55), popular steak and kidney pie (£4.75), good steaks (from £6.45), and daily specials. Boddingtons, Flowers Original and Marstons Pedigree on handpump, country wines, and helpful service; piped music. The suntrap back garden has big urns of flowers. There has been a Turks Head here for over 700 years – though most of the original building was destroyed by a Spanish raiding party in the 16th c. *(Recommended by P and M Rudlin, SH, DW, S Beele, Phil Putwain, David Carr, P R White, John Ledbury, George Atkinson, Gary Nicholls, Norma Farris)*

Greenalls ~ Tenant William Morris ~ Real ale ~ Meals and snacks (11-2.30, 6-10) ~ Restaurant ~ (01736) 63093 ~ Children in cellar dining room ~ Open 11-3, 5.30-11

PHILLEIGH SW8639 Map 1

Roseland ★

Between A3078 and B3289, just E of King Harry ferry

Readers are very fond of this warmly friendly little 17th-c pub, handy for the King Harry ferry and Trelissick Gardens. The low beamed bar has a nice oak settle and antique seats around the sturdy tables on the flagstones, an old wall clock, a good winter fire, lots of rugby and rowing prints (the landlord's sports), and a good chatty atmosphere; several friendly cats. Good, popular home-made bar food includes soup (£1.30), sandwiches (from £2.60), chicken liver and brandy pâté (£3.95), ploughman's (from £3.95), filled baked potatoes (from £4.25), spare ribs (£4.95), seafood crêpe or lamb navarin (£5.50), fresh local crab salad (£7.35), evening extras such as aubergine gateaux (£7.25), oriental monkfish (£9.65), rack of lamb (£9.75) and fresh local lobster (24 hours' notice); children's dishes (£2.95). Well kept Bass, Greenalls Bitter and Marstons Pedigree on handpump, and quite a few malt whiskies; dominoes, cribbage, shove-ha'penny, and table skittles. The pretty paved front courtyard is a lovely place to sit in the lunchtime sunshine beneath the cherry blossom; the birds are unusually tame. The furniture here too is interesting – one table made from a converted well. *(Recommended by Christopher Wright, M E Wellington, A N Ellis, Nick Wikeley, James Nunns, Penny and Martin Fletcher, D and B Taylor, George Atkinson, David Luke, DJW, Karen Eliot, John Waller, R Walden, Mr and Mrs P Richardson, Kevin and Tracey Stephens, Peter and Joy Heatherley, Cdr and Mrs J Ross, Alan and Eileen Bowker, Stephen and Sarah Pleasance, Jerry and Alison Oakes, R and S Bentley)*

Greenalls ~ Licensee Graham Hill ~ Real ale ~ Meals and snacks ~ Restaurant ~ (01872) 580254 ~ Children welcome ~ Open 11.30-3, 6(6.30 winter)-11; closed evening 25 Dec

POLKERRIS SX0952 Map 1

Rashleigh

Signposted off A3082 Fowey—St Austell

The position here, bordering a lovely beach, is quite a draw in summer and there are fine views from the stone terrace towards the far side of St Austell and Mevagissey bays. Inside, the front part of the bar has comfortably cushioned seats, with local photographs on the brown panelling of a more simply furnished back area; winter log fire and piped classical music. Bar food includes soup (£2.25), sandwiches (from £1.85; open ones from £4.50), ploughman's (from £4), hazelnut and vegetable crumble (£5.25), fish or steak pies (£6), a lunchtime cold buffet (from £6), daily specials such as fresh cod (£4.95), rabbit and bacon pie (£6) and lemon sole (£9.50), and puddings. Bass, Ind Coope Burton, St Austell HSD and a weekly guest beer on handpump or tapped from the cask, decent wine list and several malt whiskies; don't expect warmly personal service at the height of the tourist season. Though parking space next to the pub is limited, there's a large village car park, and there are safe moorings for small yachts in the cove. This whole section of the Cornish coast path is renowned for its striking scenery. *(Recommended by John and Moira Hawkes, Mayur Shah, Piotr Chodzko-Zajko, Romey Heaton, John Ledbury, Cdr and Mrs J G Ross, Jack and Philip Paxton, Barbara and Denis Melling, Mrs B Sugarman, A W Lewis)*

Free house ~ Licensees Bernard and Carole Smith ~ Real ale ~ Meals and snacks (till 10pm in summer) ~ Restaurant ~ (01726) 813991 ~ Well behaved children in eating area of bar ~ Pianist Fri and Sat evenings ~ Open 11(12 Sun)-4.30, 5.30-11; 11.30-3, 6.30-11 in winter

PORT ISAAC SW9980 Map 1

Golden Lion

Fore Street

This 18th-c pub is nice in summer when you can sit on the small back terrace looking down on the rocky harbour and lifeboat slip. Inside, the bar has a fine antique settle among other comfortable seats, decorative ceiling plasterwork, perhaps the pub dog Hollie, and a relaxed, friendly atmosphere – despite the summer crowds. Good home-made food includes sandwiches (lunchtime only, from £1.90; crab £3.75), ploughman's (from £4.50), fish pie or seafood lasagne (£5.95), and fresh seafood platter (£12.75); during the summer, evening meals are served in the bistro. Well kept St Austell Tinners, HSD and Trelawnys Pride on handpump and several malts. Darts, shove-ha'penny, dominoes, cribbage, a fruit machine in the public bar, and piped music. You can park at the top of the village unless you are luckly enough to park on the beach at low tide. The very steep narrow lanes of this working fishing village are most attractive. *(Recommended by Sharon Hancock, R Turnham, Margaret Mason, David Thompson, Ronnie and Joan Fisher, John and Joy Winterbottom, Graham Tayar, David Jones, Ted George, Nigel Clifton, Andy and Jane Beardsley)*

St Austell ~ Tenants Mike and Nikki Edkins ~ Real ale ~ Meals and snacks ~ Evening summer restaurant ~ (01208) 880336 ~ Children in eating area of bar ~ No parking nearby ~ Open 11.30-11; 12-3, 6.30-11 winter Mon-Thurs

nr PORT ISAAC SX0080 Map 1

Port Gaverne Hotel 🛏 ♀

Port Gaverne signposted from Port Isaac, and from B3314 E of Pendoggett

A peaceful place to stay with splendid clifftop walks all round, this early 17th-c inn has big log fires and low beams in the neat bars, flagstones as well as carpeting, some exposed stone, and an enormous marine chronometer. In spring the lounge is filled with pictures from the local art society's annual exhibition, and at other times there are interesting antique local photographs. Bar food includes sandwiches (from £1.50), home-made soup (£2.50), cottage pie (£2.95), ploughman's (from £2.95), aubergine and tomato lasagne (£3.50), home-made beef curry (£4.50), deep-fried local plaice (£4.95) and 6oz steak (£6.95), and is served in the bar or `Captain's Cabin' – a little room where everything except its antique admiral's hat is shrunk to scale (old oak chest, model sailing ship, even the prints on the white stone walls); the restaurant is no smoking. Well kept Bass, Flowers IPA and Sharps Doom Bar on handpump, a good bin-end wine list with 60 wines, a very good choice of whiskies and other spirits. The Green Door Bar across the lane, which has a big diorama of

Port Isaac, is open on summer afternoons. *(Recommended by Sharon Hancock, Sue and Bob Ward, Graham Tayar, Jim Reid, Jenny and Brian Seller, Lawrence Bacon, Nigel Flook, Betsy Brown)*

Free house ~ Licensee Mrs M Ross ~ Real ale ~ Meals and snacks (till 10pm) ~ Restaurant ~ (01208) 880244 ~ Children in eating area of bar and in own area ~ Open 11-11; 12-10.30 Sun; 11-2.30, 6-11 in winter; closed early Jan to mid-Feb ~ Bedrooms: £47B/£94B; restored 18th-c self-contained cottages

PORTHALLOW SW7923 Map 1

Five Pilchards

SE of Helston; B3293 to St Keverne, then village signposted

For 32 years, this robustly stone-built pub has been run by the same licensees. It's set just off the beach with an abundance of salvaged nautical gear, lamps made from puffer fish, and interesting photographs and clippings about local shipwrecks. Well kept Greene King Abbot and three weekly guest beers on handpump kept under light blanket pressure, and lunchtime food such as home-made soup (£1.50), ploughman's (from £3), local crab sandwich (£3.50), daily specials (from £2.25), and prawn platter (£6.95); darts in winter, shove-ha'penny, dominoes, trivia, and piped music. The attractive cove is largely protected against unsightly development by being owned by its residents. Tides and winds allowing, you can park on the foreshore. Please note that children are not welcome. *(Recommended by Debbie Tunstall, Mark Sullivan, David Carr, A J N Lee, Jack and Philip Paxton, Michael Sargent, Anthony Barnes, E N Burleton, S Brackenbury, DJW)*

Free house ~ Licensee David Tripp ~ Real ale ~ Lunchtime snacks ~ (01326) 280256 ~ Open 12-2.30(3 Sat), 7.30-11; closed Mon from Jan-Whitsun ~ Self-contained flat sleeps 6

PORTHLEVEN SW6225 Map 1

Ship ★

Actually built into the steep cliffs, this friendly old fisherman's pub has marvellous daytime views over the pretty working harbour and out to sea, both from the terraced garden and from seats inside, and also fine evening ones too, when the harbour is interestingly floodlit. The knocked-through bar has log fires in big stone fireplaces and some genuine character, and there's a warmly chatty atmosphere and happy mix of locals and visitors; the family room is a conversion of an old smithy and has logs burning in the huge open fireplace. Nicely presented, popular bar food served by friendly staff includes sandwiches (from £1.80; fine toasties; excellent crusty loaf from £3.75), filled oven-baked potatoes (from £2.10), ploughman's (from £4.65), pot meals like vegetable curry, steak and kidney pudding or fish pie (from £5.50), interesting daily specials like fish and tomato bake or chicken tikka, sirloin steak (£8.75), puddings like home-made apple torte, evening extras, and children's meals; the candlelit dining room enjoys the good view. Well kept Greene King Abbot, Fullers London Pride, Sharps Doom Bar, and Ushers Founders on handpump – this year, the landlord has bought the freehold from Ushers; dominoes, cribbage, fruit machine and piped music. *(Recommended by Chris and Sally Blackler, Victoria Regan, Pete and Rosie Flower, Cliff Blakemore, James Nunns, Bronwen and Steve Wrigley, Ian Fraser, Hanns P Golez, David Carr, Steve Felstead, Barry Cawthorne, Anne Moggridge, Chris and Margaret Southon, Martin Bromfield, Bernadette Garner, Colin Draper, Mr and Mrs Bemis, Mark Walker, John and Vivienne Rice, Beverly James, Jack and Philip Paxton, Mr and Mrs Brackenbury, Bob and Maggie Atherton, Peter and Audrey Dowsett, Canon Michael Bourdeaux, Mrs J Jones)*

Free house ~ Licensee Colin Oakden ~ Real ale ~ Meals and snacks ~ (01326) 572841 ~ Children in family room ~ Parking can be difficult in summer ~ Open 11-11 July and August; 11.30-3, 7-11 in winter

SCORRIER SW7244 Map 1

Fox & Hounds

Village singposted from A30; B3298 Falmouth road

Well set back from the road, this friendly white cottage is deservedly popular for its good bar food. Served by uniformed waitresses, it might include home-made soup (£2.15), doorstep, open or toasted sandwiches or filled baked potatoes (from £3.10), omelettes (from £4.20), Lebanese kofta (£4.85), moussaka (£4.90), cumberland sausage (£4.95), Indian vegetable balti (£5.10), fish pie (£5.25), chicken satay (£5.65), sirloin steak (£8.35), daily specials such as avocado in a hot chilli and lemon grass sauce with mozzarella in a filo parcel (£4.95), liver, bacon and onions (£5.25) or Ho Peng pork (£5.45), and puddings such as treacle and fig tart, apple and fresh plum crumble or lovely sticky toffee pudding (£2.25). Well kept Boddingtons and Flowers IPA and Original on handpump; piped music. The long bar is divided into sections by a partition wall and low screens and has creaky joists, vertical panelling, stripped stonework, hunting prints, comfortable furnishings, and big log fires, as well as a stuffed fox and fox mask; there's also more seating in a front extension, formerly a verandah. It's worth noting, that half the premises is no smoking. The long building is prettily decorated outside with hanging baskets and window boxes, and has picnic tables under cocktail parasols in front. *(Recommended by Jim Reid, George Atkinson, R J Herd, Mr and Mrs Jack Pitts, Chris and Margaret Southon, Colin Draper, Tony Wickett)*

Greenalls ~ Tenants David and Linda Halfpenny ~ Real ale ~ Meals and snacks (see below) ~ (01209) 820205 ~ Well behaved children allowed in eating area of bar, subject to landlord's approval ~ Open 11.30-2.30, 6-11; closed Mon evenings 2 Jan-end Mar; 25-26 Dec

RUAN LANIHORNE SW8942 Map 1

Kings Head

Village signposted off A3078 St Mawes road

Opposite the fine old church in a pleasant out-of-the-way village, this attractive and neatly kept pub looks down over the pretty convolutions of the River Fal's tidal estuary – a lovely view, especially from some of the seats outside. The beamed bar is decorated with hanging china, and with framed cigarette cards. A no-smoking family room has a witches-on-broomsticks motif. Besides good open sandwiches (from £3.95), well presented home-made bar food includes soups such as courgette and tomato (£1.95), ploughman's (from £3.75), potted shrimps (£3.95), lots of salads (from £4.25; warm prawn and mango £6.25), fish pie with pasta and leeks in a mustardy cheese sauce or chicken pasta bake in provençale sauce (£5), poached salmon in vodka or with sun-dried tomatoes and yoghurt (£7.50), excellent fillet steak (£10.50), super puddings like sherry trifle, various cheesecakes and popular tiramisu (£2.50), good Sunday roasts, and excellent steaks. Well kept Eldridge Pope Royal Oak and Hardy, and Worthington Best on handpump, very friendly licensees, quick service, and a welcoming local atmosphere. The sunken garden is a real suntrap in summer. *(Recommended by Mr and Mrs J A Goodall, Christopher Wright, G W Stevenson, Peter Cornall, Nick Wikeley, Mr and Mrs R Head, John and Joan Calvert)*

Free house ~ Licensees Peter and Shirley Trenoweth-Farley ~ Real ale ~ Meals and snacks ~ (01872) 501263 ~ Children welcome ~ Open 12-2.30, 7-11; closed winter Mon, closed Mon lunchtime in summer

ST AGNES SW7250 Map 1

Railway

10 Vicarage Rd; from centre follow B3277 signs for Porthtowan and Truro

Part of an unassuming terrace, this friendly little local with its nooks and crannies has a remarkarkable collection of shoes in the older part – minute or giant, made of strange skins, fur, leather, wood, mother-of-pearl, or embroidered with gold and silver, from Turkey, Persia, China or Japan, and worn by ordinary people or famous men; also, some splendid brasswork that includes one of the finest original horsebrass collections in the country – and a notable collection of naval memorabilia from model sailing ships and rope fancywork to the texts of Admiralty messages at important historical moments, such as the announcement of the ceasefire at the end of the First World War. Bar food includes home-made soup (£2.35), sandwiches and ploughman's or filled baked potatoes, and home-made daily specials (£4.25). Well kept Bass, Boddingtons, and Flowers IPA on handpump; darts, pool (popular with young locals), cribbage, pinball, dominoes, fruit machine and juke box. *(Recommended by David Hillcox, George Atkinson, Chris and Margaret Southon, Malcolm and Helen Baxter, Jim Reid, Jack and Philip Paxton)*

Greenalls ~ Tenant Christopher O'Brien ~ Real ale ~ Meals and snacks ~ (01872) 552310 ~ Children in eating area of bar ~ Quiz night Tues, live music Mon/Thurs evenings ~ Open 11-11; 11-3, 6-11 in winter

ST AGNES (Isles of Scilly) SV8807 Map 1

Turks Head 🖙

The Quay

This is Britain's most south-westerly pub and is an easy boat trip from St Marys. It's a little slate-roofed white cottage in a wonderful position just above the sweeping bay, with gorgeous sea views. Across the sleepy lane are a few tables on a patch of lawn above the water, with steps down beside them to the slipway – you can walk down with your drinks and food and sit right on the shore. The simply furnished but cosy and very friendly pine-panelled bar has quite a collection of flags, helmets and banknotes, as well as maritime photographs and model ships; the extension is no smoking, the cats are called Taggart and Lacey, and the collie, Tina. Decent bar food includes legendary huge locally made pasties (though they do sell out; £2.90), open rolls (from £1.85; local crab £3.50), ploughman's (from £3.20), salads (from £4.55), cold roast pork with chips (£4.85), cajun vegetable casserole (£4.95), and puddings (from £2.35), with evening gammon in port wine sauce (£5.65), fresh fish of the day, and sirloin steak (£8.35); children's meals (from £1.95). Ice cream and cakes are sold through the afternoon, and in good weather they do good evening barbecues (£3-7 Tuesday, Thursday and Sunday, July/August only), arranging special boats from St Marys – as most tripper boats leave by 5-ish. Remarkably, they also have real ale which arrives in St Agnes via a beer supplier in St Austell and two boat trips: Fergusons Dartmoor, Flowers Original and IPA, Ind Coope Burton, and St Austell Trelawnys Pride in good condition on handpump, besides decent house wines, a good range of malt whiskies, and hot chocolate with brandy. Darts, dominoes, cribbage, trivia, and piped music. In spring and autumn hours may be shorter, and winter opening is sporadic, given that only some 70 people live on the island; they do then try to open if people ask, and otherwise tend to open on Saturday night, Sunday lunchtime (bookings only, roast lunch), over Christmas and the New Year, and for a Wednesday quiz night. *(Recommended by Robin and Molly Taylor, A Noad, Pete and Rosie Flower, V H and J M Vanstone, David Mead, Douglas Allen, James Davies, Mr and Mrs D Darby, Keith and Janet Morris)*

Free house ~ Licensees John and Pauline Dart ~ Real ale ~ Meals and snacks ~ (01720) 422434 ~ Well behaved children welcome ~ Open 11-11; 12-10.30 Sun (see text for winter) ~ Bedroom: /£43B

ST BREWARD SX0977 Map 1

Old Inn

Old Town; village signposted off B3266 S of Camelford, also signed off A30 Bolventor—Bodmin

Lots of character and a really warm welcome greet you at this small, bustling country pub. The two roomed bar has fine broad slate flagstones, banknotes and horsebrasses hanging from the low oak joists that support the ochre upstairs floorboards, and plates on the stripped stonework. The outer room has fewer tables (old ones, of character), an open log fire in big granite fireplace, a piano and sensibly placed darts. The inner room has cushioned wall benches and chairs around its tables, naif paintings on slate by a local artist (for sale cheaply), a good log fire, and a glass panel showing a separate games room with darts, pool, juke box, video game and fruit machine, where children are allowed; cribbage, dominoes. Big helpings of popular home-made bar food include sandwiches (the large bacon bap is praised) and ploughman's, chicken curry or fresh plaice (£5.25), a pie of the day (£5.50), good smoked seafood salad, two sizes of huge mixed grill (from £7.50), and puddings like good sticky toffee pudding or banoffi pie. Well kept Bass, John Smiths Best, Ruddles County, and Sharps Doom Bar on handpump; the landlord is from the West Highlands and his range of 80 malt whiskies reflects this – only coming from the Highlands and Islands; fast, efficient service. Picnic-table sets outside are protected by low stone walls. There's plenty of open moorland behind, and cattle and sheep wander freely into the village. In front of the building is a very worn carved stone; no one knows exactly what it is but it may be part of a Saxon cross. *(Recommended by Kate and Kevin Gamm, Paul and Judith Booth, A N Ellis, Margaret Mason, David Thompson, Ronnie and Joan Fisher, Graham Tayar, A Preston, John Woodward, Jack and Philip Paxton, Jeff Davies)*

Free house ~ Licensees Iain and Ann Cameron ~ Real ale ~ Meals and snacks (not 25 Dec) ~ Restaurant ~ (01208) 850711 ~ Children in eating areas and games room ~ Open 12-3, 6-11

ST EWE SW9746 Map 1

Crown

Village signposted from B3287; easy to find from Mevagissey

A firm favourite with many of our readers – and some have been regularly visiting this unspoilt cottage for over 20 years (which is half as long as the friendly tenants have now been here). The traditional bar has a relaxed atmosphere, 16th-c flagstones, a very high-backed curved old settle with flowery cushions, long shiny wooden tables, and an ancient weight-driven working spit; the fireside shelves hold plates, and a brass teapot and jug. The eating area has cushioned old church pews and velvet curtains. Popular food includes good, fresh pasties (95p), sandwiches (from £1.65, local crab in season £3.95, open sandwiches £3.75), tasty home-made soup (£1.85), ploughman's or filled baked potatoes (from £2.95), salads (from £4.50, fresh crab in season £6.95), gammon with egg or pineapple (£7.25), tasty steaks (from £7.95), grilled lemon sole (£9.45; evenings only), daily specials, and puddings like home-made fruit or very good mincemeat and brandy pies (from £1.95) and their special Green Mountain ice cream (£3). Well kept St Austell Tinners and HSD on handpump, several malt whiskies and local wine; fruit machine and piped music. Several picnic tables on a raised back lawn. Handy for the Lost Gardens of Heligan nearby. *(Recommended by Mrs C M Elkington, Howard Clutterbuck, A N Ellis, Martin and Penny Fletcher, Christopher Wright, N J Lawless, Karen Eliot, Gwen and Peter Andrews, Graham Rice, Michael Sargent, R and S Bentley, Mr and Mrs J Woodfield, Michael J Boniface, Jack and Philip Paxton, Bob and Maggie Atherton)*

St Austell ~ Tenant Norman Jeffery ~ Real ale ~ Meals and snacks ~ Restaurant ~ (01726) 843322 ~ Children in eating area of bar ~ Open 11-2.30, 6-11; closed 25 Dec ~ Bedrooms: /£36; s/c cottage next door

ST JUST IN PENWITH SW3631 Map 1

Star ➤

Fore Street

This interesting, friendly old inn almost seems to be of a different era with its very relaxed, informal atmosphere and characterful regulars with their long curls, beards and colourful clothes. The dimly lit L-shaped bar has tankards hanging over the serving counter, some stripped masonry, appropriately old-fashioned furnishings, and a good many mining samples and mementoes; there's also a separate snug. Good value bar food includes home-made soup, pasties, cheese melties (£3.20), local crab sandwich (£3.50), home-made pies with herb potatoes or prawn averock (£4.90), vegetarian dishes, and all-day breakfast. Well kept St Austell Tinners, HSD, XXXX Mild, and Trelawnys Pride tapped from the cask, with farm cider in summer, mulled wine in winter, and old-fashioned drinks like mead, lovage and brandy or shrub with rum; shove-ha'penny, cribbage, dominoes, table skittles, fruit machine, and juke box. Attractive back yard with roses, a gunnera, and tables. The bedrooms are simple but comfortably furnished in period style, with notable breakfasts; the pub's not far from the coast path. *(Recommended by Mick Hitchman, Graham and Lynn Mason, M D Davies, Hanns P Golez, Clare O'Connor, S Beele, Pat and Roger Fereday, Colin Draper, D Kudelka, Jack and Philip Paxton, P and M Rudlin, Tom Marshall Corser, Peter and Joy Heatherley, Dave Thompson, Margaret Mason, Bill Sharpe)*

St Austell ~ Tenants Rosie and Peter Angwin ~ Real ale ~ Meals and snacks (11-3, 6-11 unless very crowded) ~ (01736) 788767 ~ Children in snug with toy box ~ Impromptu entertainment any time ~ Open 11-11; 12-10.30 Sun; 11-3, 6-11 Oct-Easter ~ Bedrooms £15/£25(£36B)

ST KEW SX0276 Map 1

St Kew Inn

Village signposted from A39 NE of Wadebridge

Surrounded by pretty countryside, this rather grand-looking old stone building has a big peaceful garden with seats on the grass (one built specifically for children – and there's plenty of space for them to play), a friendly goat called Aneka, and a light jazz band on summer Sunday lunchtimes; there are also picnic tables on the front cobbles. Inside, there's a friendly welcome as well as winged high-backed settles and varnished rustic tables on the lovely dark Delabol flagstones, black wrought-iron rings for lamps or hams hanging from the high ceiling, a handsome window seat, pretty fresh flowers, and an open kitchen range under a high mantelpiece decorated with earthenware flagons. Popular food includes sandwiches, home-made soup (£1.95), filled baked potatoes (£3.75), ploughman's or leeks and bacon in cheese sauce (£3.95), vegetable chilli (£5.50), fresh fish dishes (from £5.50), lasagne (£5.75), good sirloin steak (£9.50), daily specials, and evening extras like seafood provençale (£6.50), king prawns in garlic (£7.25), and roast duck (£8.95); children's menu (from £3.25). Well kept St Austell Tinners and HSD tapped from wooden casks behind the counter (lots of tankards hang from the beams above it); service can suffer under pressure. Parking is in what must have been a really imposing stable yard. The church next door is lovely. *(Recommended by Rita Horridge, P Eberlin, Howard Clutterbuck, Don Kellaway, Angie Coles, Graham Tayar, Margaret and Roy Randle, Mr and Mrs J Jones, Sharon Hancock, Giles Quick, Pete and Rosie Flower, Richard Cole, Paul and Judith Booth, Piotr Chodzko-Zajko, JKW, R and S Bentley, P V Caswell, Sue Demont, Tim Barrow, Jack and Philip Paxton, R T and J C Moggridge, Cdr and Mrs A C Curry, A N Ellis, Lawrence Bacon)*

St Austell ~ Tenants Steve and Joan Anderson ~ Real ale ~ Meals and snacks ~ Restaurant ~ (01208) 841259 ~ Well behaved children in eating area of bar and in restaurant ~ Open 11-2.30, 6-11; closed 25 Dec

ST MAWES SW8433 Map 1

Victory

Tucked away up a steep lane just up from the harbour and Falmouth ferry, this neat little fisherman's local has a relaxed, friendly atmosphere. The talk in the simple bar – full of sailing and other sea photographs – is mainly of the sea and boats, and there's a carpeted back part with comfortable seats, an antique settle and old prints of Cornish scenes. Generous helpings of good bar food include sandwiches (from £2.25; nice fresh crab £4.95), pasties (£3.25), ploughman's (from £4.75), daily specials such as potato, cheese and leek bake or ham and mushroom tagliatelle (£5.50), fresh fish like salmon (£5.95), fillet of plaice (£6.50) or local scallops (£6.95), steaks (£7.95), and puddings (£2.50); the restaurant is no smoking. Well kept Greenalls Original on handpump; courteous service. Dominoes, cribbage, chess and Scrabble. Benches outside on the cobbles give glimpses of the sea. *(Recommended by John Waller, Gwen and Peter Andrews, John and Joan Calvert, George Atkinson, G W Stevenson, Jim Reid, Andy Bryant, Anthony Barnes)*

Greenalls ~ Lease: Andrew Kent ~ Real ale ~ Meals and snacks (not Sun evening) ~ Restaurant ~ (01326) 270324 ~ Children in restaurant ~ Parking in public car park ~ Open 11-11; 12-10.30 Sun (12-3, 7-11 winter Sun)

ST MAWGAN SW8765 Map 1

Falcon

NE of Newquay, off B3276 or A3059

As well as being quite a summer suntrap, the peaceful, pretty garden of this wisteria-covered old stone pub has plenty of seats, a wishing well, play equipment for children, and good views of the village; also, stone tables in a cobbled courtyard. Inside, the big friendly bar has a log fire, small modern settles and large antique coaching prints on the walls, and there's plenty of space for eating the well-presented food, which might include sandwiches (lunchtime only, from £1.65), soup (£1.75; the crab is good £2.35), garlic mushrooms and bacon in white wine and cream (£3.35), home-made steak and kidney pie (£5.25), and steaks (from £8.75), with evening dishes such as fresh cod in a herb batter (£4.85), lamb and cranberry casserole (£4.95), and lemon chicken (£5.50); on summer evenings barbecues are held in the garden. The restaurant is no smoking. Well kept St Austell Tinners, HSD and Trelawnys Pride on handpump; efficient service even when busy. Darts, dominoes. A handsome church is nearby. *(Recommended by Piotr Chodzko-Zajko, R Turnham, John and Moira Hawkes, P Eberlin, John and Joan Calvert, RLW and Dizzy, Norma Farris, Charles E Owens, Catherine C Almond, A Lock, Jack and Philip Paxton, Ian Phillips, S Brackenbury)*

St Austell ~ Tenant Andy Banks ~ Real ale ~ Meals and snacks ~ Restaurant ~ Children in restaurant ~ (01637) 860225 ~ Open 11-3, 6-11 ~ Bedrooms: £15/£40(£48S)

ST TEATH SX0680 Map 1

White Hart

B3267; signposted off A39 SW of Camelford

Sailor hat-ribands and ships' pennants from all over the world (as well as swords and a cutlass) decorate this friendly village pub. And a coin collection is embedded in the ceiling over the serving counter in the main bar, which also has a fine Delabole flagstone floor. Between the counter and the coal fire is a snug little high-backed settle, and leading off is a carpeted room, mainly for eating, with modern chairs around neat tables, and brass and copper jugs on its stone mantelpiece; piped music. Straightforward, popular bar food includes ploughman's (£3.95), filled baked potatoes (from £3.95), home-cooked ham (£4.95), home-made steak pie or beef curry (£5.95), sirloin steak or gammon with pineapple (£9.95), Sunday roasts (£4.50), and children's meals (£1.95); the restaurant is no smoking. Well kept Bass, Ruddles County and Ushers Best on handpump. The games bar has darts, two pool tables, dominoes, and fruit machine. Please note, they no longer do bedrooms. *(Recommended by Graham Tayar; more reports please)*

Free house ~ Licensees Barry and Rob Burton ~ Real ale ~ Meals and snacks (till 10pm) ~ Restaurant ~ (01208) 850281 ~ Children welcome ~ Open 11-2.30, 6-11

TREBARWITH SX0585 Map 1

Port William

Trebarwith Strand

Obviously a main attraction of this converted old harbourmaster's house is the lovely setting, with glorious views over the beach and out to sea from the picnic tables on the terrace. Inside, there's quite a nautical theme with fishing nets and maritime memorabilia decorating the walls, a separate gallery area with work by local artists, and the no-smoking 'captain's cabin' which has a full-size fishing dinghy mounted on the wall. Enjoyable bar food includes home-made soup (£2.25), granary or jumbo rolls (from £2.45, local crab or steak £3.95), pasties (£2.50), platters (from £4.75), home-cooked ham and eggs (£4.95), daily specials such as smoked fish platter (£4.15), steak and kidney pie, mushroom stroganoff or lamb casserole (£5.95), local crab salad (£6.95), redfish in tomato and garlic (£7.75), and whole grilled dover sole (£10.25), evening steaks (from £9.45), puddings, and children's meals (from £2.35). Ruddles County, St Austell HSD, Tinners and Trelawnys Pride, and John Smiths on handpump, kept under light blanket pressure, and summer sangria and rum punch. Darts, pool, cribbage, dominoes, fruit machine, and piped music. *(Recommended by Jenny and Brian Seller, Margaret Mason, David Thompson, Dr S Savvas, M Martin, Margaret and Roy Randle, Hans P Golez, KM, JM, Rita Horridge, R T and J C Moggridge, Jeff Davies)*

Free house ~ Licensee Peter Hale ~ Real ale ~ Meals and snacks ~ Restaurant ~ (01840) 770230 ~ Children in eating area of bar ~ Folk music Fri evening ~ Open 11-11; 12-10.30 Sun ~ Bedrooms:£28.50B/£57B

TREBURLEY SX3477 Map 1

Springer Spaniel 🍴

A388 Callington—Launceston

Cornwall Dining Pub of the Year

Readers have enjoyed the food at this friendly roadside pub so much that we have given them a Food Award this year. From a changing menu, this might include sandwiches or french bread rolls (from £1.75; poached salmon £3.50), freshly-made soup (£2.50; seafood chowder £2.95), mushrooms with bacon, cream, brandy and cheese, ham and banana mornay or sausage and egg (£3.95), cold roast rib of beef with pickle and chips (£4.50), vegetable risotto (£5.50), steak and kidney pie (£5.95), baked fillet of cod with parsely and pinenut crust (£6.95), spiced persian lamb (£7.95), steaks (from £8.95), fillet of sea bass (£9.95), and puddings like crème caramel with exotic fruits or spotted dick (from £2.95). Well kept Furgusons Dartmoor and St Austell HSD and Trelawnys Pride on handpump kept under light blanket pressure, and a good range of spirits; very good service. The bar has a lovely, very high-backed settle by the woodburning stove in the big fireplace, high-backed farmhouse chairs and other seats, and pictures of olde-worlde stage-coach arrivals at inns, and this leads into a room with chintzy-cushioned armchairs and sofa in one corner, a big solid teak table, and dominoes, cribbage, video game and trivia. Up some steps from the main bar is the beamed, attractively furnished, partly no-smoking restaurant; friendly black cat. *(Recommended by James Macrae, Graham Tayar, E Robinson, D J Underhill, Mr and Mrs Jack Pitts, Mr and Mrs J Jones, J Jones, R V L Summers, Jack and Philip Paxton, Jacquie and Jim Jones, Rita Horridge*

Free house ~ Licensee John Pitchford ~ Real ale ~ Meals and snacks ~ Restaurant ~ (01579) 370424 ~ Children in eating area of bar, in restaurant or snug ~ Open 11-3, 5.30-11

TREEN SW3824 Map 1

Logan Rock

Just off B3315 – the back rd Penzance—Lands End

A genuine local with a friendly welcome for visitors too, this bustling pub takes its name from the nearby Logan Rock (an 80-ton boulder); you can walk from the pub to look at it and then on along the wild cliffs. The low-beamed main bar has a series of old prints telling the story of the rock, high-backed modern oak settles, wall seats, a really warm coal fire, a chatty atmosphere, and well kept St Austell Tinners, HSD and Trelawnys Pride on handpump. Popular bar food (with prices unchanged since last year) includes sandwiches (from £1.50, local crab when available £4.25), good pasties (£1.40), wholesome soup (£1.95), salads (from £4.25, crab £7.25), a popular fish and egg dish they call the Seafarer or bacon and pasta bake (£4), lasagne (£4.50), scampi (£5.25), very good char-gilled steaks (from £7.50), and puddings like home-made fruit pie or crumble (£2.10); children's dishes (from £1.40) and afternoon cream teas. They will heat baby foods on request. Lots of games such as darts, dominoes, cribbage, fruit machine, video games, winter pool and another fruit machine in the family room across the way; juke box, piped music. Dogs are allowed in if on a lead. There are some tables in a small wall-sheltered garden, looking over fields, with more in the front court. *(Recommended by Bronwen and Steve Wrigley, George Atkinson, Cliff Blakemore, Mr and Mrs Peter Smith, John Ledbury, Colin Draper, Pat and Roger Fereday, Steve Felstead, Gwen and Peter Andrews, Mrs E Howe, Bill Sharpe, George and Chris Miller, Alan and Eileen Bowker, A J N Lee)*

St Austell ~ Tenants Peter and Anita George ~ Real ale ~ Meals and snacks (from June-Sept all day, otherwise 12-2, 7-9) ~ Restaurant ~ (01736) 810495 ~ Well behaved children in family room only ~ Open 10.30am-11pm; 12-10.30 Sun; 10.30-3, 5-11 in winter

TREGADILLETT SX2984 Map 1

Eliot Arms ★ ★ ♀

Village signposted off A30 at junction with A395, W end of Launceston bypass

The welcoming licensees of this creeper-covered old house have bought what is possibly the largest collection of snuffs in the country – there are nearly 400 on display. And also squashed into the charming series of little softly lit rooms is a collection of 72 antique clocks including 7 grandfathers, hundreds of horsebrasses, old prints, old postcards or cigarette cards grouped in frames on the walls, and shelves of books and china. Also, a fine old mix of furniture, from high-backed built-in curved settles, through plush Victorian dining chairs, armed seats, chaise longues and mahogany housekeeper's chairs, to more modern seats, open fires, flowers on most tables, and a lovely ginger cat called Peewee; inoffensive piped music. The good home-made food comes in very big helpings, and might include open sandwiches (the beef and prawn are recommended), burgers and basket meals (from £3.50), a dozen ploughman's (from £3.95; the stilton is good), shepherd's pie or vegetable pasta bake with nuts (£4.95), fisherman's crunch or steak, kidney and mushroom pie (£5.50), pork steak with barbecue sauce (£6.95), turkey escalope with a creamy stilton sauce (£7.95), whole local lemon sole with parsley and lemon butter (£9.50), and home-made puddings such as chocolate and rum roulade or butterscotch cream pie (£2); enjoyable Sunday lunch. Well kept Flowers Original, Marstons Pedigree, and a guest beer like Morlands Old Speckled Hen or Wadworths 6X on handpump, a fine choice of wines, several malt whiskies, and excellent friendly service; darts, shove-ha'penny, table skittles, dominoes, and fruit machine. A garden beyond the car park has picnic tables, a good climbing frame, swing and playhouse. *(Recommended by Pete and Rosie Flower, Christopher Turner, Malcolm and Pat Rudlin, Moira and John Cole, Graham Tayar, Heather March, M D Davies, Ron Shelton, Mrs R Horridge, Basil J Minson, Brian and Anna Marsden, R W Brooks, S Lonie, S Tait, Jerry and Alison Oakes, Piotr Chodzko-Zajko, Alan and Eileen Bowker, J and J O Jones, Bob and Maggie Atherton, SC, JC, R and S Bentley, Beverley James, Jack and Philip Paxton)*

Free House ~ Licensees John Cook and Lesley Elliott ~ Real ale ~ Meals and snacks (not 25 Dec) ~ (01566) 772051 ~ Children in eating area of bar and in family room ~ Open 11-2.30(3 Sat), 6-11; closed 25 Dec ~ Bedrooms: £24/£38

TRESCO (Isles of Scilly) SV8915 Map 1

New Inn 🍺 ♀

New Grimsby

Once a row of fishermen's cottages, this popular inn has a nice pubby atmosphere, light and airy bars refurbished with lots of washed-up wood from a ship's cargo, and picture windows looking out over the swimming pool. Good bar food includes lunchtime pizza dishes (from £2.90), doorstep sandwiches or filled baked pots (from £3.50), ploughman's (from £4.10), popular fish soup (virtually a meal in itself, £4.80), gammon with egg (£4.90), barbecue ribs (£5.70), and daily specials such as steak in stout pie (£5.80), grilled john dory with a changing sauce (£7.50), tagliatelle milanaise (£6), and crab salad (£8). The well regarded no-smoking restaurant also has a separate children's menu. Bass, Flowers Original, Marstons Pedigree, Wadworths 6X, and Whitbreads Castle Eden and Pompey Royal on handpump, interesting wines, and 20 malt whiskies. Pool and juke box (rarely played), darts, cribbage, dominoes and piped music. There are white plastic tables and chairs in the garden. Many of the people staying here are regular return visitors. *(Recommended by R J Herd, V H and J M Vanstone, Keith and Janet Morris, Pete and Rosie Flower, Dorothee and Dennis Glover)*

Free house ~ Licensee Graham Shone ~ Real ale ~ Meals and snacks ~ Restaurant ~ (01720) 422844 ~ Children welcome in eating area of bar until 9.30 ~ Live music once a month ~ Open 10.30-4, 6-11; 12-10.30 Sun ~ Bedrooms: £62B/£150B – these prices include dinner

TRURO SW8244 Map 1

Old Ale House ★ 🍺 £

7 Quay St/Princes St

There's an appealing bustling and friendly atmosphere in this old-fashioned, back-to-basics pub that quite a cross-section of our readers enjoys very much – plus the fact that they keep up to 24 real ales on handpump or tapped from the cask. Constantly changing, these might include Boddingtons, Bass, Cotleigh Old Buzzard and Tawny, Courage Best and Directors, Exmoor Gold, Ale and Beast, Fullers London Pride, Kings Head Golden Goose, Ma Hussons and Kings Ransom, Morlands Old Speckled Hen, Sharps Own, Shepherd Neame Spitfire, Smiles Exhibition, Tetleys, and Wadworths 6X; interesting wines such as damson and birch. As well as newpapers and magazines to read, the bar has some interesting 1920s bric-a-brac, an engagingly old-fashioned diversity of furnishings that would do credit to any small-town auction room, and a barrel full of monkey nuts whose crunchy discarded shells mix affably with the fresh sawdust on the floor; piped music. The enterprising and varied choice of good food, freshly prepared in a spotless kitchen in full view of the bar and with prices unchanged since last year, might consist of doorstep sandwiches (from £2.15; delicious hot baked garlic bread with melted cheese from £1.25), filled oven baked potatoes (£2.85), ploughman's (£3.25), hot meals served in a skillet pan like oriental chicken, sizzling beef or liver, bacon and onions (small helpings from £3.25, big helpings from £4.50), lasagne or steak and kidney pie (£3.95), daily specials like crab bake, mussels in white wine or beef and stilton pie, and puddings (from £1.65). No dogs, clean lavatories. *(Reeommended by N J Lawless, Chris and Margaret Southon, Karen Eliot, Colin Draper, M E Wellington, Malcolm and Pat Rudlin, Linda and Brian Davis, KM, JM, DAV, David Carr, David Luke, Canon Bourdeaux, Jeff Davies, Peter Williamson, Alastair Campbell, Jack and Philip Paxton, Mrs E Howe, RLW and Dizzy, S Brackenbury, Jeff Davies)*

Greenalls ~ Manager Ray Gascoigne ~ Real ale ~ Meals and snacks (12-2.30, 5-7; not Sat or Sun) ~ (01872) 71122 ~ Children in eating area of bar ~ Live bands Mon/Thurs evenings, solo or duo Sat evening ~ Open 11-11; 12-10.30 Sun; 12-3, 7-10.30 in winter

Lucky Dip

Besides the fully inspected pubs, you might like to try these Lucky Dips recommended to us and described by readers (if you do, please send us reports):

☆ **Albaston** [OS Sheet 201 map ref 423704; SX4270], *Queens Head*: Welcoming pub handy for Cotehele and Tamar Valley railway, well kept Courage, food inc good pasties, low prices, interesting local industrial memorabilia *(JP, PP)*

Altarnun [just N, OS Sheet 201 map ref 215825; SX2182], *Rising Sun*: Basic old farmers' local, not smart but friendly, with flagstoned bar, six real ales, decent simple food *(A N Ellis, JP, PP)*

☆ **Bodinnick** [across the water from Fowey; SX1352], *Old Ferry*: Simple inn with character back flagstoned public bar partly cut into rock, lots of boating pictures, bar food, well kept real ales, lively games room where children allowed; hotel part looking over water, with summer evening restaurant, most bedrooms comfortable and roomy; lovely walk from Polruan *(Cdr and Mrs J M Lefeaux, R and S Bentley, LYM)*

☆ **Bodmin** [Dunmere (A389 NW); SX0467], *Borough Arms*: Neat and friendly, with stripped stone, open fire, lots of railway photographs and posters, well kept Bass, Boddingtons and Whitbreads, decent wines, friendly atmosphere, speedy service and plenty of room even when busy, big helpings of good value straightforward food (no sandwiches), unobtrusive piped music, fruit machine; children in side room, picnic tables out among shady apple trees *(Peter Williamson, P and M Rudlin, Christopher Warner, BB)*

Bolingey [Penwartha Rd, off B3284; SW7653], *Bolingey Inn*: Attractive 16th-c stone village local, interesting home cooking by landlady, well kept Bass, Greenalls Royal Wessex and other real ales, small but good wine list *(Olive and Hugh Duckett)*

☆ **Bolventor** [signed just off A30 on Bodmin Moor; SX1876], *Jamaica Inn*: All sorts of tourist attractions and trunk-road catering, but welcoming, with lots of character in clean, comfortable and cosy oak-beamed bar, log fire, well kept Whitbreads ales, and pretty secluded garden with play area; bleak moorland setting *(John and Wendy Trentham, Gary Nicholls)*

☆ **Boscastle** [upper village, stiff climb from harbour; SX0990], *Napoleon*: Charming 16th-c pub, comfortable and welcoming little low-beamed rooms, interesting Napoleon prints, basic good value food inc vegetarian, well kept Bass and St Austell ales, decent wines, very friendly staff, polished slate floor, big open fire, pool room, children allowed; piped music, maybe folk music; suntrap terrace, second garden too; may close early if quiet *(Stuart Williams, JP, PP, A W Lewis, Jeff Davies, Brian and Anna Marsden, LYM)*

Boscastle [The Harbour], *Wellington*: Long busy bar with popular food, friendly service, Bass and Whitbreads-related ales, cats and dogs, enjoyable Mon folk night; comfortable bedrooms, children welcome *(Clare Wilson, M Sinclair, Richard Cole, BB)*

Botusfleming [SX4061], *Rising Sun*: Cosy bar in pleasant local, good fire *(James Macrae)*

Breage [3 miles W of Helston; SW6128], *Queens Arms*: Popular local with enthusiastic and efficient young landlord, long narrow plate-festooned bar with open fire, no-smoking dining room, decent choice of food worth waiting for inc mammoth grill, vegetarian and children's dishes, Whitbreads-related ales; tables and children's games room outside, another play area and garden over the lane; quiz night Weds; bedrooms *(P and M Rudlin)*

☆ **Bude** [Falcon Terrace; SS2005], *Falcon*: Comfortable locals' bar overlooking canal in impressive 19th-c hotel, lots of quick good value generous food inc daily roast, local fish and home-made puddings, well kept Bass and St Austell Tinners and HSD, pleasant efficient staff, big family room with two pool tables, very efficient and reliable service; bedrooms *(Tony McLaughlin, Dr N Holmes, Mrs R Horridge, Malcolm and Pat Rudlin, Clare Wilson)*

Cadgwith [SW7214], *Cadgwith Cove*: Basic friendly local, roomy and clean, with snack menu in lounge inc sandwiches and ploughman's and lots of well priced plain food with chips; big terrace at front overlooking fish sheds and bay; wide range of food in separate restaurant with different management *(DJW, Ian Fraser, Molly and Robin Taylor)*

Callington [Newport Sq; A388 towards Launceston; SX3669], *Coachmakers Arms*: Old inn with irregularly shaped modernised timbered bar, reliable bar food, Bass, decent wines and efficient service; children in eating area and restaurant; bedrooms *(Tony and Wendy Hobden, LYM)*

☆ **Camborne** [B3303 out towards Helston; SW6440], *Old Shire*: Consistently good value wide-ranging food in bar and restaurant, young efficient staff, good range of beers, lots of comfortable chairs and sofas and great coal fire in homely family pub; garden with summer barbecues, five bedrooms *(Ian Phillips, Malcolm and Pat Rudlin)*

☆ **Camelford** [Main St (A39); SX1083], *Masons Arms*: Unpretentious heavy-beamed stonebuilt pub with St Austell ales, decent value bar food inc children's dishes and good steak and kidney pudding, friendly service, local photographs, advertising mirrors, houseplants; pool and juke box in one bar; children allowed *(Bill and Sylvia Trotter, Mike Beiley)*

Cargreen [off A388 Callington—Saltash; SX4362], *Crooked Spaniard*: Lovely waterside position, with tables on terrace by Tamar – always some river activity, esp at high tide; name change from Spaniards Arms marks internal changes (not all for the best – great carved oak overbar cut down) and apparent push for more lively image, but has kept small panelled bar and huge fireplace in another smallish room; bar food, several real ales, big restaurant *(A N Ellis)*

Carnkie [Piece, E of Camborne; minor rd Pool—Four Lanes – OS Sheet 203 map ref 679408; SW6740], *Countryman*: Well filled sandwiches, good welcoming service, reasonable prices, games room; interesting tin-mining country *(Chris and Margaret Southon)*

Cawsand [The Cleave; SX4350], *Devonport*: Good food inc roasts, well kept ales with lots of guest beers; bedrooms comfortable, good value *(Richard Nemeth)*

Charlestown [SX0351], *Rashleigh Arms*: Large pub with good generous quick straightforward food inc fresh fish and popular puddings, seats out by picturesque little harbour in interesting conservation village, shipwreck museum nearby; good range of real ales, friendly service, good canalside family room; piped music; big restaurant; good value bedrooms *(John and Jill Woodfield, JP, PP)*

☆ Crackington Haven [SX1396], *Coombe Barton*: Huge clean open-plan pub in tiny village, spectacular sea view from roomy lounge/dining area, friendly service, good usual bar food inc local fish, well kept local and other ales, good coffee, back family room, tables on terrace, games room with pool tables; bedrooms *(G T White, D and B Taylor, P and M Rudlin, Nigel Clifton, Jeff Davies)*

☆ Crafthole [SX3654], *Finnygook*: Clean and comfortable much-modernised lounge bar, well cooked and presented straightforward food, friendly quick service, Whitbreads-related beers, good coffee, pleasant restaurant, good sea views from residents' lounge; piped music may obtrude; bedrooms good value *(George Atkinson, Andrew and Joan Life, BB)*

☆ Cremyll [SX4553], *Edgcumbe Arms*: Super setting by ferry to Plymouth, with good Tamar views and seats out by water; recent spacious and comfortable refurbishment, slate floors, big settles, sofa by fire, window seats, nautical feel; good value food, real ales inc Courage and St Austell, quick friendly service; children welcome *(S Parr, P Birch, George Atkinson)*

Devoran [SW7939], *Old Quay*: Friendly idyllically placed seaside local, unpretentious decor, welcoming obliging licensees, generous cheap food, well kept ale; good value bedrooms *(Hazel and David Taylor)*

☆ Duloe [B3254 N of Looe; SX2358], *Olde Plough House*: Good value interesting food in spacious pub with friendly staff, two log fires, cushioned settles, polished sewing-machine treadle tables, good wine, locals' area with pool and darts *(JE, J C Simpson, R Turnham)*

Edmonton [SW9672], *Quarrymans Arms*: Interesting pub part of health/holiday

complex in slate-built former quarrymen's quarters, guns, pictures and antiques, informative landlord, Bass beers, good choice of food inc grilled monkfish; outside seating; sports centre, pool, sauna, small bistro, bedrooms as well as holiday cottages *(Jenny and Brian Seller)*

☆ Falmouth [The Moor; SW8032], *Seven Stars*: Unchanging local with wonderfully entertaining vicar-landlord, tatty furnishings, warm welcome, well kept Bass, Flowers Original and St Austell HSD tapped from the cask, minimal food, tables on roadside courtyard *(Reg Nelson, Sue Holland, Dave Webster, David Carr, BB)*

Falmouth [Prinslow Lane, Swanvale], *Boslowick*: Good value straightforward food and well kept ale in spacious suburban black and white beamed pub, friendly staff, plenty of seats inc plush sofas, log-effect gas fires, family room with games machines; children's play area *(John Wooll, DC)*; [Church St], *Cork & Bottle*: Rambling pub with local prints, memorabilia and bric-a-brac, real ales, good juke box spanning different eras and tastes *(Reg Nelson)*; [Dracaena Ave], *Four Winds*: Big helpings of consistently good value food, pleasant garden, good service *(Mr and Mrs B Hobden)*; [Church St], *Kings Head*: Rambling old pub with plenty of potential (high-backed settles, pews, tubby little casks, old plates and engravings, log fire etc); aimed at diners midweek, more youth-minded weekends (Fri night DJ) *(Alan and Eileen Bowker, David Carr, LYM)*; [Wodehouse Terr], *Seaview*: Convivial maritime local above 111-step Jacob's Ladder, lots of appropriate bric-a-brac, stunning harbour view from picture windows and tables outside, good range of well kept ales; bedrooms *(Reg Nelson, Nick Hughes)*; [High St], *Star & Garter*: Thriving genuine local with fine high views over harbour, clean and tidy but lived-in enough to create atmosphere; well kept real ales, huge collection of teapots, friendly service, reasonably priced bar food, well kept Flowers Original and interesting guest ales *(Sue Holland, Dave Webster, Reg Nelson)*

Flushing [SW8033], *Royal Standard*: Trim and traditional waterfront local, neat bar with pink plush and copper, alcove with pool and darts, simple well done food inc good baked potatoes and home-made pasties, well kept ales such as Bass, Flowers IPA and local Sharps, warm welcome, plenty of genuine characters; unreconstructed outside gents' *(Gwen and Peter Andrews, Sue Holland, Dave Webster)*

☆ Fowey [Town Quay; SX1252], *King of Prussia*: Upstairs bay windows looking over harbour to Polruan, well kept St Austell ales, efficient cheerful service, piped pop music (may obtrude), good value side family food bar with wide choice of fish and seafood, seats outside; bedrooms *(Mike, Ian and Gayle Woodhead, George Atkinson, W F C Phillips, Steve Felstead, LYM)*

☆ Fowey [Fore St], *Ship*: Pubby local, good

value food from sandwiches through local fish
to steak, comfortable cloth-banquette main
bar with coal fire, pool/darts room, family
dining room with big stained-glass window;
St Austell Tinners and HSD, juke box or
piped music (may obtrude), dogs allowed;
bedrooms old-fashioned, some oak-panelled
*(Steve Felstead, Ted and Jane Brown,
Christopher Turner, AW, BW, Lindsley
Harvard, Margaret Whalley, Mike
Woodhead, LYM)*
Fowey [Town Quay], *Galleon:* Well
refurbished with solid pine, terrace
overlooking harbour and estuary, good well
priced bar meals inc fresh fish, well kept and
priced beers inc Bass, friendly efficient service
(P and M Rudlin, BB); Lugger: Unpretentious
locals' bar, comfortable small dining area
popular with older people for good
inexpensive food, tables outside; bedrooms
(Ted and Jane Brown, BB)
☆ **Golant** [off B3269; SX1155], *Fishermans
Arms:* Plain but charming waterside pub local
nice garden, lovely views from terrace and
window; warm welcome, good generous
straightforward home-made food, well kept
Courage-related ales, log fire, interesting
pictures, tropical fish *(Andy and Jill Kassube,
JP, PP)*
Goldsithney [B3280; SW5430], *Crown:*
Straightforward pub with bargain lunches, St
Austell ales, decent house wines, friendly
service; pretty suntrap glass-roofed front
loggia, masses of flowers outside *(G G
Young)*
☆ **Grampound** [Fore St; A390 St Austell—
Truro; SW9348], *Dolphin:* Exceptionally
friendly helpful staff, good value generous
straightforward food inc OAP lunches, St
Austell ales, decent house wines, comfortable
chintzy settees and easy chairs; handy for
Trewithen Gardens; bedrooms *(Gwen and
Peter Andrews, Colin May, Margaret Dyke)*
☆ **Gulval** [SW4832], *Coldstreamer:* Good value
if not cheap food in busy but civilised local,
comfortable dining atmosphere, Whitbreads-
related ales, friendly staff and cat, unusual
high ceilings, cosy restaurant; quiet, pleasant
village *(Robin and Molly Taylor, P and M
Rudlin, JP, PP)*
Gunnislake [lower road to Calstock;
SX4371], *Rising Sun:* Comfortable 17th-c
dining pub with particularly good serious if
not cheap food using seasonal produce,
interesting curios and antiques, friendly
service, garden with play area; live music
Mon *(Richard Weltz, Beverley Mort, R A
Cullingham)*
☆ **Gurnards Head** [B3306 Zennor—St Just;
SW4338], *Gurnards Head:* Good choice of
food inc some really unusual dishes, local fish
and fresh veg, friendly service, well kept
Flowers Original and other ales and decent
wine in unspoilt genuine pubby bar, open fires
each end (family room bleaker); food all day
(at least in summer, when it can get busy),
bedrooms – good base for terrific cliff walks
*(Bronwen and Steve Wrigley, Bill Sharpe, D
and B Taylor, Jeanne Cross, Paul Silvestri)*

☆ **Helford Passage** [signed from B3291;
SW7627], *Ferryboat:* Extensive bar in great
summer spot by sandy beach with swimming,
small boat hire, fishing trips and summer
ferry to Helford, full well kept St Austell
range, bar food, no-smoking restaurant; piped
music, games area with juke box and Sky TV;
suntrap waterside terrace, barbecues, usually
open all day summer (with cream teas and
frequent live entertainment); children allowed;
parking can be difficult *(George Atkinson,
Steve Felstead, James Nunns, David Carr,
John Beeken, JR, A Barnes, Werner Arend, A
and K Bulley, LYM; more reports on service
and atmosphere please)*
Helston [Coinagehall St; SW6527],
Fitzsimmons Arms: Large bar with several
comfortable rooms, well kept Bass,
Boddingtons and Flowers, reliable food,
separate restaurant area; very popular Fri
evening with personnel from nearby naval air
base *(Alastair Campbell, David Carr, G
Washington)*
☆ **Hessenford** [A387 Looe—Torpoint; SX3057],
Copley Arms: Comfortable pub with spacious
and attractive streamside garden and terrace,
good range of generous well priced food from
good sandwiches up in bar and restaurant,
well kept St Austell ales, big family room,
play area; bedrooms *(Ian McCulloch, George
Atkinson)*
Kingsand [village green; SX4350], *Rising Sun:*
Friendly unsmart local, generous food from
sandwiches, pasties and burgers up, good
choice of well kept beer (inc local Sharps) and
wine, open fire; can get packed *(Andrew and
Joan Life)*
☆ **Lamorna** [off B3315 SW of Penzance;
SW4424], *Lamorna Wink:* Simple unspoilt
country local, hardly needs to put itself out
given charming surroundings – short walk
from pretty cove with good coast walks;
cheap food (pasties, baked potatoes, plenty of
fish etc) served briskly from hatch,
Whitbreads-related ales, maybe under blanket
pressure; interesting naval memorabilia and
pictures *(Alan and Eileen Bowker, Sue
Holland, Dave Webster, Jim Reid, Chris and
Margaret Southon, LYM)*
Lanreath [off B3359; SX1757], *Punch Bowl:*
Unspoilt 17th-c inn of great potential,
charmingly traditional flagstoned public bar
and comfortable black-panelled lounge,
games bar, garden bar, food in bars and
restaurant, well kept St Austell ales; bedrooms
(IP, J S Rutter, BB)
Launceston [SX3384], *White Hart:* Big pub,
good lunch break with well priced home-
made food from good sandwiches up inc good
value help-yourself salad bar; good choice of
beers, nice log fires, dining room *(John and
Christine Vittoe, Brian Websdale)*
Lelant [Griggs Quay, Lelant Saltings; A3047
St Ives rd, just off A30; SW5437], *Old Quay
House:* Large pub in marvellous spot
overlooking estuary, car park shared with
RSPB; very efficient servery with usual range
of food, St Austell HSD and Ruddles County;
bedrooms *(George Atkinson)*

☆ Lerryn [signed from A390 in Lostwithiel; SX1457], *Ship*: Busy local, partly no smoking, with popular bar food inc sandwiches and lots of good pies, well kept ales such as Bass, Courage Best, Morlands Old Speckled Hen and Sharps Doom Bar, local farm cider, fruit wines and malt whiskies, games room; can be overrun with children, service – normally speedy – can slow, landlord taciturn; picnic tables outside, play area; famous stepping-stones and three well signposted waterside walks nearby; bedrooms, self-catering flat *(S N T Spencer, W F C Phillips, JE, D and B Taylor, George Atkinson, JP, PP, Mr and Mrs D E Powell, Philip Jackson, Patricia Heptinstall, Gwen and Peter Andrews, CB, Mr and Mrs J Woodfield, MS, Dr and Mrs B D Smith, LYM)*

☆ Lizard [SW7012], *Top House*: Reliably well run and welcoming pub particularly popular with older people; in same family for 40 years, lots of interesting local sea pictures, fine shipwreck relics and serpentine craftwork in neat bar with generous good value bar food inc good local fish and seafood specials, interesting vegetarian dishes, well kept Bass, Whitbreads-related ales and good choice of other drinks, helpful service, roaring log fire, darts, no piped music; fruit machine; tables on terrace, interesting nearby serpentine shop *(Anthony Barnes, Jim Reid, Sue Holland, Dave Webster, Malcolm and Pat Rudlin, Peter and Joy Heatherley, Ian Fraser, Gwen and Peter Andrews, W N Brandes, Margaret Dyke, BB)*

☆ Longrock [old coast rd Penzance—Marazion; SW5031], *Mexico*: Interesting – even adventurous – choice of generous good value food from substantial sandwiches up, no-smoking dining extension, cheerful local atmosphere, welcoming; former office of Mexico Mine Company, with massive stone walls *(P and M Rudlin, Brenda and Derek Savage, Bill Sharpe)*

Looe [SX2553], *Olde Salutation*: Ancient heavy beams, sloping floors, shark-fishing photographs, busy with locals and fishermen; consistently good simple food (not Sat evening) esp crab sandwiches and Sun roasts, also vegetarian dishes, fast friendly service, well kept Ushers Best; handy for coast path *(Dr and Mrs B D Smith)*

Madron [SW4532], *King William IV*: Friendly local, lovely in winter with good fire; food basic but good value; unusual building *(Molly and Robin Taylor)*

☆ Malpas [off A39 S of Truro; SW8442], *Heron*: Straightforward and friendly, in lovely setting above wooded creek; big helpings of decent quick food inc good crab sandwiches, St Austell Tinners and HSD, log fire, lots of local photographs; pool, machines, piped music; suntrap slate-paved terrace; children welcome, can be very busy *(Michael Sargent, P R White, G W Stevenson, George Atkinson, LYM)*

Marazion [The Square; SW5231], *Cutty Sark*: Not far from beach, overlooking St Michaels Mount, with well kept Whitbreads-related ale, decent food, open fire, some stripped stone and nautical bric-a-brac, pleasant separate hotel bar, restaurant; bedrooms comfortable, with shower and sea view *(DAV)*

Marhamchurch [off A39 just S of Bude; SS2203], *Bullers Arms*: Big rambling L-shaped bar, wide choice of generous low-priced food inc some unusual dishes, friendly new licensees and staff, Hook Norton and a guest beer, decent wine by the glass, good choice on CD juke box, darts in flagstoned back part, restaurant; children welcome; tables and play area in sizeable garden, a mile's walk to the sea; bedrooms *(Jeanne Cross, Paul Silvestri, LYM)*

☆ Mawgan [St Martin; SW7323], *Old Courthouse*: Prettily placed open-plan split-level pub, very spacious, clean and comfortable, with good choice of food, well kept Whitbreads-related ales, friendly service, pleasant garden; children welcome *(Nigel Woolliscroft, Adrian and Karen Bulley)*

☆ Mawnan Smith [W of Falmouth, off Penryn-Gweek rd – old B3291; SW7728], *Red Lion*: Generous helpings of good attractively presented food esp seafood (not cheap but restaurant quality) in pleasantly furnished thatched pub, lots of pictures and bric-a-brac in cosy interconnected beamed rooms inc no-smoking room behind restaurant, lots of wines by the glass, well kept Bass and other ales, friendly helpful staff; children welcome *(Mr and Mrs Hall, Sybille Weber, Air Cdr and Mrs A C Curry, Cliff Blakemore, LYM)*

☆ Menheniot [off A38; SX2862], *White Hart*: Stripped stone, red leatherette button-back seats and lots of brass in friendly relaxing bar with well kept Bass and Boddingtons, wide choice of generous good food (can be taken away); bedrooms well equipped and neatly modernised *(Jill Bickerton)*

☆ Metherell [Lower Metherell; follow Honicombe sign from St Anns Chapel just W of Gunnislake on A390; SX4069], *Carpenters Arms*: Heavily black-beamed inn with huge polished flagstones and massive stone walls, cheerful new landlord and pleasant staff, wide choice of decent food inc children's dishes, good Sun roasts and puddings, well kept ales; handy for Cotehele; children welcome, bedrooms *(C A Hall, Andrew and Joan Life, Paul and Heather Bettesworth, LYM)*

☆ Mevagissey [off Fore St by Post Office; SX0145], *Fountain*: Welcoming unpretentious local with good simple food inc fresh fish, well kept St Austell ales, plenty of atmosphere, lots of old local prints and photographs; piano sing-songs some evenings, popular upstairs restaurant *(JP, PP, Eric and Margarette Sibbit, Ted George, John and June Gale, Christopher Wright, N J Lawless)*

Mevagissey [Fore St, nr harbour], *Ship*: 16th-c pub with generous food inc good fish and chips, full range of well kept St Austell beers, welcoming landlord; big comfortable room divided into small interesting areas, ships' memorabilia, open fire, friendly cat; fruit machines, piped music; bedrooms *(Jim Reid, JP, PP, Christopher Wright)*

☆ **Mitchell** [off A30 Bodmin—Redruth; SW8654], *Plume of Feathers*: Rambling bar with lots of bric-a-brac, generous food from sandwiches to hearty grills from open-plan back kitchen, Whitbreads-related ales, flame-effect gas fire; piped music, darts and winter pool; tables outside, with play area and farm animals; children welcome (*P M Rudlin, Bill Sharpe, LYM*)

☆ **Morwenstow** [signed off A39 N of Kilkhampton; SS2015], *Bush*: One of Britain's oldest pubs, part Saxon, with serpentine Celtic piscina in one wall, ancient built-in settles, flagstones, and big stone fireplace, upper bar with interesting bric-a-brac, well kept St Austell HSD and Worthington BB, Inch's cider, simple cheap lunchtime food (not Sun), welcoming service, darts; no piped music, children or dogs; seats out in yard; interesting village church with good nearby teashop; handy for great cliff walks, cl Mon in winter (*Basil Minson, Jeanne Cross, Bruce Bird, Colin Draper, Hanns P Golez, LYM*)

☆ **Mousehole** [SW4726], *Old Coastguard*: Spacious yet cosy and relaxed, with board floor, pine and cane furniture, interesting prints and superb views; friendly attentive staff, good interesting food such as baked tuna with basil and tomato dressing, guinea fowl with sun-dried tomato and tarragon sauce or Thai curry with baked banana, rich puddings, ales such as Bass, Sharps Doom Bar, St Austell Trelawnys Pride; no restrictions on families, piped music, lots of musical events; sizeable gardens and terrace, leading down to rocky beach; bedrooms (*George Atkinson, Sue Holland, Dave Webster, Molly and Robin Taylor*)

Mylor Bridge [SW8137], *Lemon Arms*: St Austell pub with well kept real ales; handy for start or finish of very pretty walk (*David Carr*)

Newbridge [A3071 Penzance—St Just; SW4231], *Fountain*: Friendly and unspoilt stonebuilt pub well done out with attractive old-fashioned decor inc cheery fire in awesome fireplace, good atmosphere; licensee changes prevent a verdict on the food or real ale (both have been good); tables out in garden (*Dr D K M Thomas, Molly and Robin Taylor, TW, PD*)

Newlyn [Fore St (coast rd); SW4628], *Fishermans Arms*: Perfect position above fishing harbour, big inglenook fireplace with real fire, lots of nooks and crannies, good choice of St Austell ales, unpretentious bar food; great place for local gossip (*Sue Holland, Dave Webster*)

Newlyn East [Church Town; SW8255], *Pheasant*: Traditional friendly Cornish village inn in quiet back street, attractive window boxes and tubs, good home cooking; not far from Trerice Gardens (*Mr and Mrs Peter Smith*)

☆ **Newtown** [the one off B3293, SE of Helston; SW7423], *Prince of Wales*: Small stone pub with original food in bar and restaurant, friendly landlady and staff, Whitbreads ales, good coal fire in pretty fireplace; pool, darts,

maybe piped music – popular with young locals; can park caravans behind (*DJW, Mr and Mrs J Barrett, Gwen and Peter Andrews*)

☆ **Notter** [Notter Bridge; just off A38 Saltash—Liskeard; SX3861], *Notter Bridge*: Attractive spot in wooded valley, knocked-through bar/lounge, dining conservatory (can get hot) overlooking river, wide choice of good cheap generous food inc curry evenings, happy bustling atmosphere, friendly service, well kept beer, tables on terrace (*Ted George, Bronwen and Steve Wrigley, Jacquie and Jim Jones*)

☆ **Padstow** [Lanadwell St; SW9175], *London*: Unpretentiously cottagey fishermen's local with lots of pictures and nautical memorabilia, good atmosphere (busy evenings), well kept St Austell ales, good value food in small back dining area; games machines but no piped music; open all day; bedrooms good value too – made to feel one of the family (*Cdr and Mrs A C Curry, Graham and Lynn Mason, George Atkinson, Mike Beiley, LYM*)

☆ **Padstow** [Lanadwell St], *Golden Lion*: Friendly local with pleasant black-beamed front bar, high-raftered back lounge with plush banquettes against ancient white stone walls; reasonably priced simple lunches, evening steaks and fresh seafood; well kept Whitbreads and Cornish Original, piped music, juke box, fruit machines; bedrooms (*M W Turner, Mr and Mrs J Woodfield, P and M Rudlin, BB*)

☆ **Padstow** [South Quay], *Old Custom House*: Airy and spacious open-plan quayside bar with conservatory and big family area, good reasonably priced unpretentious food inc vegetarian from adjoining restaurant, comfortable chesterfields around open fire, lots of prints of old harbour, big beams and timbers; efficient friendly staff, well kept St Austell ales, restaurant; attractive bedrooms (*George Atkinson, Ted George, Andy and Jane Beardsley, Mr and Mrs Pitt, Sandra Kench, Steven Norman, BB*)

Paul [SW4627], *Kings Arms*: Pleasant friendly little inn, carpets, appliqué pictures, good food and service, St Austell HSD; bedrooms (*George Atkinson*)

Pendeen [SW3834], *Radjel*: Simple local with lots of wreck and other photographs on stripped stone walls, St Austell ales, piped music; popular with walkers, nr Cape Cornwall (*George Atkinson, LYM*)

☆ **Penzance** [Barbican; Newlyn rd, opp harbour after swing-bridge; SW4730], *Dolphin*: Welcoming and attractive nautical pub with good harbour views, quick bar food inc good pasties, well kept St Austell ales, great fireplace, big pool room with juke box etc; children in room off main bar; no obvious nearby parking (*G Washington, Colin Draper, Gary Nicholls, Mark Walker, LYM*)

Penzance [Chapel St], *Admiral Benbow*: Elaborately nautical decor, friendly staff, decent food inc good curries, Courage-related ales, children allowed, downstairs restaurant; open all day summer (*Gary Nicholls, David*

Carr, Mark Walker, LYM); [Quay], *Yacht*: St Austell pub with useful children's area *(Gary Nicholls, Mark Walker)*

Perranuthnoe [signed off A394 Penzance—Helston; SW5329], *Victoria*: Comfortable L-shaped bar with coastal and wreck photographs, some stripped stonework, well kept Courage-related ales, bar food, neat coal fire, booth seating in family area, games area; handy for Mounts Bay; bedrooms *(Peter and Joy Heatherley, LYM)*

☆ **Perranwell** [off A393 Redruth—Falmouth and A39 Falmouth—Truro; SW7839], *Royal Oak*: Pleasant unassuming black-beamed village pub, friendly staff and locals, cosy seats, good value bar food inc sandwiches and attractive lunchtime cold table, well kept Whitbreads-related ales and decent wines, good winter fire, provision for children, garden with picnic tables; piped music *(John Wooll, LYM)*

☆ **Pillaton** [off Callington—Landrake back rd; SX3664], *Weary Friar*: Pretty tucked-away 12th-c pub with four tidy but interesting knocked-together rooms (one no smoking), comfortable seats around sturdy tables, easy chairs one end, popular bar food inc lunchtime sandwiches (service stops on the dot), well kept Bass, Courage Directors, Morlands Old Speckled Hen and Wadworths 6X, farm cider, country wines and mulled wine; restaurant (cl Mon), children in eating area; piped music; tables outside; comfortable bedrooms *(J and J O Jones, JP, PP, R J Walden, S Brackenbury, James Macrae, Ted George, John Kirk, LYM)*

☆ **Polgooth** [SW9950], *Polgooth*: Much modernised country local with good big family room and (up steep steps) outside play area; popular food, St Austell real ales, pleasant atmosphere *(JP, PP, John Barr, LYM)*

☆ **Polperro** [The Quay; SX2051], *Blue Peter*: Cosy and unpretentious little low-beamed wood-floored harbourside local with well kept St Austell Tinners and HSD and guest beers, farm cider, log fire, traditional games, piped music, some seats outside; family room, open all day – can get crowded; no food *(L Harvard, M Whalley, M J How, Bryan Hay, David Carr, Jerry and Alison Oakes, George Atkinson, JP, PP, LYM)*

☆ **Polperro** [top of village nr main car park], *Crumplehorn Mill*: Friendly atmosphere and affordable generous food inc local fish in converted mill, separate dark areas inc upper gallery, beams, stripped stone, flagstones, log fire, comfortable seats, well kept Bass and St Austell HSD and XXXX, farm cider; pool area, piped music (can be fairly loud); good value bedrooms *(Bryan Hay, George Atkinson, L Harvard, M Whalley, BB)*

☆ **Polperro** [Quay], *Three Pilchards*: Low-beamed dim-lit fishermen's local high over harbour, generous good value food inc good home-made specials, open fire, neat helpful and chatty staff, Ushers Best and Founders, tables on terrace up 30 steep steps; piped music can be fairly loud, open all day *(L*

Harvard, M Whalley, Ted George, AW, BW, George Atkinson, David Carr)

Polperro [bear R approaching harbour], *Noughts & Crosses*: Cheerful riverside bar, soft lighting, comfortable banquettes, beams, stripped stone and panelling; good value food, real ale (often Ushers), pool, fruit machine, good friendly service, upper family room; unobtrusive piped music; pretty street *(George Atkinson)*

☆ **Polruan** [The Quay; SX1251], *Lugger*: Waterside local reached by passenger ferry from Fowey (or car – nearby parking expensive and limited, steep walk from main car park); beams, high-backed wall settles, big model boats etc, open fires, good views from upstairs partly no-smoking family room, good straightforward bar food inc children's and local fish, wider evening choice, restaurant, St Austell BB, Tinners, HSD and XXXX, pub games; piped music may be obtrusive (live Thurs, maybe Fri/Sat), games machine, well behaved dogs allowed; good walks, self-catering cottage; open all day summer *(Mike Woodhead, Andrew and Joan Life, Norma Farris, Peter and Audrey Dowsett, Michael Sargent, Andy and Jill Kassube, George Atkinson, C Moncreiffe, JE, Martin Bromfield, Bernadette Garner, LYM)*

Port Isaac [The Terrace; SX0080], *Shipwright*: Great clifftop views from small hotel's restaurant, snooker table brings young people to lively public bar, friendly staff, good home-cooked food esp seafood, real ale, warm solid fuel stove; bedrooms *(F Jarman, Graham Tayar)*

Porthleven [SW6225], *Harbour*: Informal local atmosphere, good food and service, wide range of beers; comfortable bedrooms overlooking working harbour *(B and M Beesley)*

☆ **Portloe** [SW9339], *Lugger*: Well presented bar lunches inc children's dishes, simple easy chairs, two fires, good evening restaurant, decent wines, tables on terrace, pretty setting in attractive village above cove; bedrooms (not all with sea view); restaurant licence – you can't just go for a drink; bedrooms *(Stephen Horsley, G W Stevenson, LYM)*

☆ **Portmellon Cove** [SX0144], *Rising Sun*: Fine spot overlooking sandy cove nr Mevagissey, friendly flagstoned nautical bar with unusual open fire, big upper family/games room, decent generous food inc children's and vegetarian, well kept Boddingtons, Marstons Pedigree and Wadworths 6X, seats outside; comfortable beamed bedrooms, most with sea view *(Dr M Robson, N J Lawless, JP, PP, LYM)*

☆ **Portscatho** [SW8735], *Plume of Feathers*: Friendly and comfortable, with thriving atmosphere, good value food in main bar or small eating area, side locals' bar, well kept St Austell, well reproduced loudish pop music, good staff; pretty fishing village, very popular with summer visitors; dogs allowed *(R and S Bentley, LYM)*

☆ **Poughill** [SS2207], *Preston Gate*: Busy welcoming local with pews and long mahogany tables on flagstones, log fires, well kept Tetleys-related ales, bar food (evenings get there early or book), darts, some seats outside; children welcome, dogs looked after well *(Richard Cole, Tony McLaughlin, LYM)*

☆ **Quintrel Downs** [East Rd; SW8560], *Two Clomes*: Attractive la.gely unspoilt former cottage with open fire, apt furnishings, nice mix of customers, well kept ales, reasonably priced food, pleasant landlord; family room *(JP, PP)*

☆ **nr Redruth** [Tolgus Mount; SW6842], *Tricky Dickies*: Well converted isolated former tin-mine smithy, dark inside, with interesting industrial relics, good value food esp pizzas, changing well kept beers, decent wines, efficient service, partly covered terrace with barbecues *(Malcolm and Pat Rudlin, Don and Shirley Parrish)*

Rilla Mill [SX2973], *Manor House*: Wide choice of food inc local fish and home-baked ham, well kept ales such as Shepherd Neame Spitfire, good house wines, cheerful helpful landlord *(John Kirk)*

Saltash [SX4258], *Two Bridges*: Friendly local, good beer, live music Wed and Fri *(James Macrae)*

Sennen [OS Sheet 203 map ref 357255; SW3525], *First & Last*: Comfortable and spacious roadhouse handy for Lands End, well kept real ales (glass panel shows spring-cooled cellar), friendly local atmosphere, decent straightforward food; pool table, piped music can be intrusive, can get noisily busy in summer — popular with teenagers *(Molly and Robin Taylor)*

☆ **Sennen Cove** [SW3526], *Old Success*: Big bustling nautical-theme bar, perhaps best out of season, by clean beach with glorious view along Whitesand Bay; lots of old photographs, well kept Bass, St Austell, Tetleys and Worthington, piped music, bar food, carvery restaurant; gents' past car park; children welcome, attractive bedrooms, good breakfasts *(Mr and Mrs D Fellows, Mrs B Sugarman, Sue Holland, David Webster, James Nunns, C P Scott-Malden, Gwen and Peter Andrews)*

St Austell [98 Victoria Rd, Mt Charles; SX0152], *Duke of Cornwall*: Busy pub in quiet part of town, main bar popular with young locals, small separate lounge area, good food; bedrooms *(Graham and Lynn Mason)*

St Cleer [SX2468], *Market*: Large welcoming village pub with stone fireplace in lounge, pool and fruit machines in bar, well priced nicely presented bar meals; opp church *(Ian Phillips)*

St Columb Major [SW9163], *Silver Ball*: Food inc generous cheap Sun lunch, simple furnishings, character landlord *(Chris and Margaret Southon)*

☆ **St Dominick** [Saltash; a mile E of A388, S of Callington – OS Sheet 201 map ref 406674; SX3967], *Who'd Have Thought It*: Spick and span, with flock wallpaper, tasselled plush seats, Gothick tables, gleaming pottery and copper; reliably good interesting food inc

fresh fish (lunch orders may stop 1.30), well kept Bass and Whitbreads-related ales, decent wines, friendly staff, impeccable lavatories, superb Tamar views from attractively furnished family conservatory; quiet countryside nr Cotehele *(Ted George, Mr and Mrs J Woodfield, Jacquie and Jim Jones, Peter Massocchi, LYM)*

☆ **St Issey** [SW9271], *Ring o' Bells*: Neatly modernised cheerful village inn with consistently good food inc fresh local crab, children's helpings and well served Sun roasts, well kept Courage, friendly staff, open fire; can get packed in summer; bedrooms *(Mr and Mrs B Hobden, J R T Powys-Smith, Howard Clutterbuck, LYM)*

☆ **St Ives** [The Wharf; SW5441], *Sloop*: Simple but charming 14th-c seafront inn, slate floor and beams, enjoyable collection of pictures for sale in cellar bar, good choice of reliable bar food inc good fish pie and chowder, friendly service, Boddingtons and Courage; open all day, very busy in summer, handy for Tate Gallery; bedrooms *(Jenny and Brian Seller, Liz and John Soden, Jim Reid, Sue Holland, Dave Webster, George Atkinson, Martin Bromfield, Bernadette Garner)*

St Ives, *Badger*: 16th-c, wide choice of good value food, garden *(Martin Bromfield, Bernadette Garner)*; [Fore St], *Castle*: Comfortable and friendly two-room local, well priced bar food (may be a wait), Whitbreads-related ales, pine panelling, old local photographs, maritime memorabilia, unobtrusive piped music; best out of season *(Martin Bromfield, Bernadette Garner, Bill and Sylvia Trotter)*; *Peterville*: Non-touristy good food pub, newly decorated, very friendly, good children's room and children's menu *(Piotr Chodzko-Zajko)*

St Just in Penwith [Mkt Sq; SW3631], *Wellington*: Well kept St Austell beers, generous food inc good ploughman's; bedrooms *(Graham and Lynn Mason)*

St Keverne [The Square; SW7921], *White Hart*: Handsome bar, friendly newish licensees, generally good food often with well prepared local fish, refurbished restaurant; comfortable well furnished bedrooms – good value *(John and Moira Hawkes, Eric and Margarette Sibbit, E D Bailey, Mr and Mrs J Hordern, LYM)*

St Kew [St Kew Highway; A39 Wadebridge–Bude; SX0375], *Red Lion*: Friendly local, a welcome for tourists too, good value food, well kept beer *(S N T Spencer, Mr and Mrs Dane)*

☆ **St Mabyn** [SX0473], *St Mabyn Inn*: Good interesting food in sympathetically refurbished pub/restaurant, all cooked freshly so may be a wait *(A N Ellis, Mark Billings, JP, PP)*

☆ **St Mawes** [SW8433], *Rising Sun*: Waterside hotel with pubby front locals' bar, plush hotel bar, attractive conservatory, pretty bedrooms and slate-topped tables on terrace just across lane from harbour wall; reopened 1996 after extensive refit too late for us to gauge success, but has had decent food, well kept St Austell ales and wines and good service; open all day summer *(LYM; reports please)*

☆ St Merryn [SW8873], *Farmers Arms*: Big busy family dining pub with bright and spacious no-smoking dining area, St Austell ales, good value house wine, attentive helpful landlady, quick service, floodlit well, children's games room with videos and so forth, tables on back terrace; bedrooms – handy for Trevose Head and superb walks *(Andy and Jane Beardsley, Jenny and Brian Seller)*

☆ St Merryn [Church Town (B3276 towards Padstow)], *Cornish Arms*: Well kept St Austell ales and usual bar food inc good steaks in firmly run and spotless local with fine slate floor and some 12th-c stonework; good games room, picnic tables outside; children over 6 may be allowed in eating area *(MJVK, A J N Lee, Dave Thompson, Margaret Mason, LYM)*

☆ Stratton [SS2406], *Tree*: Rambling and interesting pub with seats alongside unusual old dovecot in attractive ancient coachyard, very friendly bar rooms, well kept Bass, St Austell Tinners and a guest ale, farm ciders, good range of well priced bar food, great log fires, character evening restaurant; children welcome in back bar, cheap bedrooms with huge breakfasts *(Alan and Heather Jacques, R T and J C Moggridge, P and D Carpenter, BB)*

☆ Stratton, *Kings Arms*: Fine old well kept three-room 17th-c free house, six or more regularly changed real ales, attentive helpful staff, varied tempting food; children welcome *(Malcolm and Pat Rudlin)*

Threemilestone [W of by-pass outside village; SW7844], *Oak Tree*: Spacious yet cosy and cheerful, Whitbreads-related ales, decent wines, wide choice of well presented tasty food, good quick service *(John Wooll)*

☆ Trebarwith [signed off B3263 and B3314 SE of Tintagel – OS Sheet 200 map ref 058865; SX0585], *Mill House*: Under friendly new owners, marvellously placed in steep streamside woods above sea, food inc children's dishes in pleasantly redecorated bar with fine Delabole flagstones, games room with pool table and children's play area, real ales, evening restaurant (not Mon-Weds in winter); dogs welcome, tables out on terrace and by stream; five comfortable bedrooms *(LYM; more reports please)*

Tregony [B3287; SW9245], *Kings Arms*: Good welcoming in plainly refurbished old coaching inn, two bars, dining area, good value bar food, well kept Whitbreads-related ales *(Christopher Wright)*

☆ Trelights [signposted off B3314 Wadebridge—Delabole; SW9979], *Long Cross*: Coastal hotel with fine restored Victorian garden, modern bar with plush-and-varnish furnishings, stained-glass panels, unusual heptagonal bench around small central fountain; family room, further dining bar, good play area; well kept St Austell ales, good value bar food, good afternoon teas, lively folk nights; bedrooms comfortable and well furnished, many with good views *(Pete*

and Rosie Flower, BB)

Trematon [Stoketon Cross; SX3959], *Crooked Inn*: Wide choice of good generous reasonably priced home-cooked food such as lamb stew with apricots, almonds and amaretto, good range of Whitbreads-related ales and cider; well fed goat may roam the bar; comfortable bedrooms *(John Kirk, Mr and Mrs T A Bryan)*

Tresillian [A39 Truro—St Austell; SW8646], *Wheel*: Neatly thatched and friendly, pleasant mix of plush seating with timbering, stripped stone and low ceiling joists, steps between two cosy main areas, generous usual food from large filled rolls to steaks inc children's dishes, well kept Whitbreads-related ales; piped music may obtrude; play area in neat garden stretching down to tidal inlet *(Mr and Mrs J Woodfield, John Ledbury, R T and J C Moggridge, JP, PP, Deborah and Ian Carrington, Piotr Chodzko-Zajko, LYM)*

Treswithian [SW6340], *Cornish Choughs*: Good interesting fresh well cooked food with particularly carefully prepared fish and seafood, welcoming atmosphere, Bass and Flowers; bedrooms *(Murray J Daffern)*

☆ Trevarrian [B3276 NE of Newquay; SW8566], *Travellers Rest*: Good plentiful food, well kept St Austell beers, good friendly service; can get crowded in summer *(Charles Owens, Catherine Almond, R G Bywaters)*

☆ Trevaunance Cove [The Beach; SW7251], *Driftwood Spars*: Good quickly served fresh food from sandwiches up in former tin-mine store nr beach with huge beams, thick stone walls and log fires, decor highlighting smuggling and lifeboats; reasonable prices, big family room, attractive restaurant, well kept ales, lots of malt whiskies; comfortable bedrooms *(Jim Reid, BB)*

☆ Truro [Frances St; SW8244], *Globe*: Comfortable and welcoming, with good choice of reliable generous home-made food inc good value self-help salad bar, well kept Whitbreads-related ales, good service, mix of furnishings inc leather armchairs and sofas, several rooms off central serving area; old panelling and beamery, fine antique prints, bottle-glass screens, taxidermy *(P M Rudlin, Reg Nelson, John and Wendy Trentham)*

☆ Truro [Frances St/Castle St], *Wig & Pen*: Good generous reasonably priced bar food with interesting specials in big neatly kept L-shaped pub, well spaced comfortable chairs and tables, newspapers to read, unobtrusive piped music, pleasant service, well kept St Austell ales, decent house wines in big glasses; tables out on busy street *(M Wellington, David Carr)*

☆ Truro [Kenwyn St], *William IV*: Busy dark-panelled bar with slightly secluded raised areas and lots of bric-a-brac, well kept St Austell beers, decent wine, good value buffet food inc hot dishes in elegantly tiled airy two-level conservatory dining room opening into small flowery garden *(Bill Sharpe, David Carr, Peter Williamson, John Wooll)*

Truro [Pydar St], *City*: Authentic character pub with superior bric-a-brac, particularly well kept Courage ales *(Reg Nelson)*; [Lemon Quay, by central car park], *Market*: Unchanging town local, friendly and simple, with home-made food inc good Cornish pasties, well kept beer *(Anthony Barnes, Bill and Sylvia Trotter, LYM)*

☆ **Veryan** [SW9139], *New Inn*: Wide choice of good value bar food in neat and homely one-bar local, friendly service, well kept St Austell tapped from the cask, quiet seats out behind; bedrooms, lovely village *(Ted George, Christopher Wright, G J Newman)*
Wadebridge [SW9872], *Molesworth Arms*: Comfortably plush main bar with three areas and interesting fireplace, Courage-related and St Austell ales, wide range of bar food, attractive restaurant in former back stables, locals' bar across coach entry; good service, children welcome; bedrooms *(Charles Owens, Catherine Almond, Graham Tayar)*

☆ **Zennor** [SW4538], *Tinners Arms*: Welcoming gently extended country local in lovely windswept setting by church nr coast path, reasonably priced good simple food, well kept St Austell ales from casks behind bar, decent coffee, rather spartan feel with lots of granite and stripped pine; child-free upstairs bar, friendly dogs and lots of cats, no music, tables on attractive terrace *(Pat and Roger Fereday, Stephen Horsley, S Beele, Jeanne Cross, Paul Silvestri, Richard and Anne Ansell, Mike and Heather Barnes, Sue Holland, Dave Webster, George and Chris Miller, LYM)*

Isles of Scilly

☆ **Bryher** [SV8715], *Hell Bay*: Snug low-ceilinged granite-walled bar with sea views from deep window recesses, pleasant atmosphere, friendly staff, good quickly served cheap bar food (new dining room), attractive gardens with sheltered play area, stroll from beaches; keg beers; well equipped bedrooms *(J C Simpson, Keith and Janet Morris, BB)*

☆ **St Marys – Hugh Town** [The Strand; SV9010], *Atlantic*: Big low-beamed L-shaped bar full of interesting nautical bric-a-brac, wreck salvage and photographs, wonderful harbour views from all tables, good cheery atmosphere (esp on live music nights), wide choice of simple reliable generous bar food inc local fish, well kept St Austell Tinners and HSD, great assortment of customers; piped music (may be obtrusive); family room, no-smoking restaurant; good views, esp from small back jetty/terrace; bedrooms in adjacent hotel *(David Mead, A Noad, V H and J M Vanstone, BB)*

☆ **St Marys – Hugh Town** [Silver St (A3110)], *Bishop & Wolf*: Very wide choice of good well presented generous food esp fish, friendly efficient staff, interesting sea/boating decor with gallery above rd, nets, maritime bric-a-brac, lifeboat photographs, attractive upstairs restaurant, popular summer live music *(Keith and Janet Morris, A Noad, Mr and Mrs D Darby, Naomi Badcock)*
St Martins [SV9215], *St Martins*: Really a hotel, with upholstered gilt chairs etc, but friendly bar, delightful surroundings, wonderful views and sunsets; limited choice of very well cooked and presented bar food, extremely friendly staff; beautiful spot overlooking Tresco; comfortable bedrooms *(V H and J M Vanstone)*
Tresco [SV8915], *Island*: Friendly upmarket hotel in beautiful spot, very comfortable bar, excellent reasonably priced food, good atmosphere; fine grounds, tables out on terrace by grass (with badminton); right by shore with superb sea and island views; bedrooms *(V H and J M Vanstone, BB)*

If you have to cancel a reservation for a bedroom or restaurant, please telephone or write to warn them. A small place – and its customers – will suffer if you don't. And recently people who failed to cancel have been taken to court for breach of contract.

Cumbria

One of the best counties for good pubs, this combines generally low prices with places of considerable character, often in wonderful scenery and particularly well sited for walkers; there's plenty of really good food, and excellent local real ales. Pubs currently doing specially well here include the Royal Oak at Appleby, the White Hart at Bouth (an enjoyable new main entry), the Hole in t' Wall at Bowness, the Cavendish Arms at Cartmel (gains one of our Place to Stay Awards this year), the Masons Arms on Cartmel Fell (excellent all round), the Pheasant at Casterton, the Punch Bowl at Crosthwaite (another new entry: first-class food, outclassing most restaurants in the north), the Britannia at Elterwater, the Queens Head in Hawkshead, the Watermill at Ings, the Shepherds at Melmerby, the White Horse at Scales (back into the main entries under its newish local licensees; good food using plenty of local produce), the Queens Head at Tirril, the Mortal Man at Troutbeck, and the Queens Head at Troutbeck. This Troutbeck pub is right on the crest of a wave these days, and has been giving readers enormous plea·:ure: so it's the Queens Head at Troutbeck which is our choice as Cum·:ria Dining Pub of the Year. The King George IV at Eskdale Green gains one of our Place to Stay Awards this year (and has a massive collection of malt whiskies now); the cheerful Sun in Kirkby Lonsdale gains one of our Beer Awards. There are good local beers to be found in many of the area's pubs, from Jennings, Yates, and the newer excellent little Cartmel Brewery (actually in Kendal now, rather than Cartmel itself); Jennings's changing seasonal ales are well worth looking out for. Generally, drinks prices are well below the national average here; cheapest of all (apart from a £1 a pint special offer we found at the Abbey Bridge at Lanercost) was the Blue Bell at Heversham, tied to Sam Smiths of Yorkshire. In the Lucky Dip at the end of the chapter, pubs coming to prominence these days include the New Crown at Ainstable, Barbon Inn at Barbon, Fish at Buttermere, two Cockermouth pubs (the Bush and Bitter End), the Sun at Crook, Posting House at Deanscales, Sawrey at Far Sawrey, Dicksons Arms at Haverthwaite, Old Crown at Hesket Newmarket, Howtown Hotel at Howtown, Farmers Arms at Lowick Green, Middleton Fells at Middleton, Wasdale Head Inn at Wasdale Head and Brown Horse at Winster; we have inspected most of these and can vouch firmly for their appeal.

ALSTON NY7246 Map 10

Angel

Front Street (A689)

Nicely set on the steep cobbled main street of a quaintly old-fashioned Pennine village, this 17th-c stone building is a friendly place. The L-shaped bar has black beams and timbers, logs burning in a big stone fireplace, horsebrasses on the beams, brass pans and a coach-horn on the walls, and wheelback chairs and traditional black wall seats around dimpled copper tables. Good value bar food, quickly served, includes sandwiches, soup (£1.40), ploughman's (£2.95), salads (from £3.30), good cumberland sausage (£3.50), leek and smoky bacon bake (£3.95), mushroom and nut fettucini (£4.15), gammon and egg (£5.75), 8oz sirloin steak (£7.50), and puddings like sticky toffee or pavlova (£1.80); children's meals. Well kept Boddingtons and Flowers IPA on handpump, and darts, dominoes, and piped music. A sheltered back garden has some picnic tables and umbrellas. *(Recommended by L Dixon, R Davies)*

Free house ~ Licensees Nicky and Sue Ashcroft ~ Real ale ~ Meals and snacks (not Tues evening) ~ (01434) 381363 ~ Children in eating area of bar until 9pm ~ Open 11-5(4.30 Sun), 7-11 ~Bedrooms: £14/£28

AMBLESIDE NY3804 Map 9

Golden Rule

Smithy Brow; follow Kirkstone Pass signpost from A591 on N side of town

There's a genuine local atmosphere in this traditional town pub – and you can be sure of a friendly welcome from the landlord and his staff. There are lots of local country pictures and a few fox masks decorating the butter-coloured walls, horsebrasses on the black beams, built-in leatherette wall seats, and cast-iron-framed tables. The room on the left has darts, a fruit machine, and dominoes; the one down a few steps on the right is a quieter sitting room. Well kept Hartleys XB and Robinsons Best, Old Stockport, and Hatters Mild on handpump; local pork pies (35p) and filled rolls (£1.25) only; friendly dog. There's a back yard with tables, a small pretty summer garden, and wonderfully colourful window boxes. The golden rule referred to in its name is a brass measuring yard mounted over the bar counter. *(Recommended by SLC, H Dyson; more reports please)*

Hartleys (Robinsons) ~ Tenant John Lockley ~ Real ale ~ Limited snacks ~ (01539) 433363 ~ Children welcome ~ Nearby parking virtually out of the question ~ Open 11-11; 12-10.30 Sun

APPLEBY NY6921 Map 10

Royal Oak ★ ⑪ 🛏 ⚏ 🍴

Bongate; B6542 on S edge of town

For thirteen years, this very enjoyable old-fashioned coaching inn (a favourite with many readers) has been run by the same diligent and friendly licensees. It's a long low partly 14th-c building, and the beamed lounge has old pictures on the timbered walls, some armchairs and a carved settle, and a panelling-and-glass snug enclosing the bar counter; there's a good open fire in the smaller, oak-panelled public bar; darts. Imaginative, very popular home-made food might include lunchtime sandwiches, soup like roast tomato and fennel (£1.75), home-made pâté such as chicken liver, pork and apple or stilton, port and smoked bacon (from £2.75), ploughman's with home-made bread (£2.95), crab, prawn and cheese crêpe (£3.45), little brown shrimps (£3.75), glazed cumberland sausage with apple sauce or lentil, red pepper and mushroom lasagne (£4.95), Whitby scampi (£5.45), fresh fish of the day such as mussels in white wine and cream (£5.95) or huge whole lemon sole with nut brown butter (£8.95), lamb pudding with sweet leeks (£5.95), prawn and queenie gratin (£6.95), pork fillet with mushrooms, madeira and cream (£8.95), daily specials, puddings such as rhubarb crumble, raspberry sherry trifle or orange steamed pudding with citrus sauce (from £3), and children's meals (from £1.95). One of the dining rooms is no smoking. They keep a fine range of real ales on handpump: Bongate Special Pale Ale (their own beer made locally) and Theakstons Best, with regular visitors such as Black Sheep Bitter and Rigwelter, High Forest XB, Maclays 80/-, Ushers Spring Fever, Yates Bitter, and Youngers Scotch Bitter; several malt whiskies, and a carefully chosen wine list with around 8 by the glass and quite a few half bottles. In summer the outside is very colourful, with seats on the front terrace among masses of flowers in tubs, troughs and hanging baskets. You can get here on the scenic Leeds/Settle/Carlisle railway (best to check times and any possible delays to avoid missing lunch). *(Recommended by H Webb, Walter and Susan Rinaldi-Butcher, Paul Boot, Martin Hickes, Paul Cornock, Chris and Andy Crow, John Fazakerley, Angus Lyon, Andrew and Kerstin Lewis, Richard Holloway, John and Jackie Chalcraft, Malcom Taylor, Mr and Mrs N Evans, Anthony Barnes, Karen Eliot, A W Lewis, Malcolm Taylor, Tony Gayfer, Dr Peter Crawshaw, Jack and Heather Coyle, Steve and Julie Cocking, Pat and John Millward)*

Free house ~ Licensees Colin and Hilary Cheyne ~ Real ale ~ Meals and snacks (12-2, 6-9) ~ Restaurant ~ (017683) 51463 ~ Well behaved children welcome ~ Open 11-3, 6-11 ~Bedrooms: £29.50B/£62.50B

See also entry under nearby BRAMPTON

ARMATHWAITE NY5146 Map 10
Dukes Head 🏠

Off A6 a few miles S of Carlisle

Well run and friendly, this popular inn has a civilised lounge bar with oak settles and little armchairs among more upright seats, oak and mahogany tables, antique hunting and other prints, and some brass and copper powder-flasks above its coal fire. Good bar food includes sandwiches and ploughman's, nice soup, baked smoked haddock (£3.10), hot shrimps (£3.15), deep-fried cod (£5.75), steak and mushroom pie (£5.95), home-cooked ham (£6.50), grilled venison (£9), wonderful roast duckling (£9.75), and home-made puddings like apple pie or bread and butter pudding; the breakfasts are huge. Well kept Boddingtons and Whitbreads Castle Eden on handpump, piped music, and dominoes; separate public bar with darts and pool, two games machines and juke box in back lobby. There are tables out on the lawn behind. *(Recommended by Enid and Henry Stephens, Richard Holloway, David and Margaret Bloomfield, Chris Rounthwaite, Simon and Amanda Southwell, Bob Ellis, Malcolm Taylor, A N Ellis)*

Free house ~ Licensee Peter Lynch ~ Real ale ~ Meals and snacks ~ Restaurant ~ (016974) 72226 ~ Children welcome ~ Open 11-3, 5.30-11; 12-3, 6-10.30 Sun ~ Bedrooms: £25B/£45B

ASKHAM NY5123 Map 9
Punch Bowl

Village signposted on right from A6 4 miles S of Penrith

The setting for this friendly pub – popular with locals and visitors alike – is most attractive and faces the lower village green. The rambling bar has interesting furnishings such as Chippendale dining chairs and rushwork ladder-back seats around sturdy wooden tables, well cushioned window seats in the white-painted thick stone walls, coins stuck into the cracks of the dark wooden beams (periodically taken out and sent to charity), an antique settle by an open log fire, and local photographs and prints of Askham. The old-fashioned woodburning stove, with its gleaming stainless chimney in the big main fireplace, is largely decorative. Generous helpings of bar food include home-made soup (£2.25), lunchtime sandwiches (£2.50), shrimp pot (£2.85), mushroom and tomato lasagne (£5.95), roast duck breast in a raspberry flavoured sauce (£8), and specials such as ginger and garlic chicken (£5.20), baked local trout (£5.80), and venison in a red wine sauce (£6.10), and steaks (from £9.50); children's dishes (£3). Marstons Pedigree, Morlands Old Speckled Hen, and Whitbreads Castle Eden on handpump; dominoes and piped pop music, and in the separate public bar darts, pool, juke box and fruit machine. There are tables out on a flower-filled terrace, and the setting, facing the lower village green, is attractive. *(Recommended by Richard Lewis, RJH, A Preston, H Dyson, Angus Lyon, James and Patricia Halfyard, G O Cook)*

Whitbreads ~ Licensees David and Frances Riley ~ Real ale ~ Snacks (lunchtime) and meals ~ (01931) 712443 ~ Children welcome until 9pm ~ Open 11.30-3, 6-11 ~Bedrooms: £19.50/£39

BASSENTHWAITE LAKE NY1930 Map 9

Pheasant ★ ↝

Follow Wythop Mill signpost at N end of dual carriageway stretch of A66 by Bassenthwaite Lake

Although this is a rather smart and civilised hotel, the little bars here are surprisingly old-fashioned and pubby: Persian rugs on the parquet floor, rush-seat chairs, library seats, and cushioned settles, hunting prints and photographs on the fine ochre walls, and drinks served from a low serving counter. Well kept Bass and Theakstons Best on handpump and quite a few malt whiskies. Good lunchtime bar food includes soup (£2.10), cold roast meat platter or ploughman's (£4.10), smoked local trout with cucumber and dill vinaigrette (£4.85), potted Silloth shrimps (£4.95), smoked venison and breast of duck with cumberland sauce (£5.95), and puddings (£2.95); the elegant restaurant is no smoking. If the bars are full, you might want to move to the large and airy beamed lounge at the back, which has easy chairs on its polished parquet floor and a big log fire on cool days; there are also some chintzy sitting rooms with antique furniture (one is no smoking). The hotel is surrounded by very attractive woodlands, with beeches, larches and Douglas firs, and you can walk into them from the garden. This is a very good walking area. *(Recommended by R WD, Jason Caulkin, Paul Bailey, Val Stevenson, Rob Holmes, C A Hall, Nigel Wooliscroft, Gwen and Steve Walker, SLC, H K Dyson, John and Pam Smith, S Fazackerly, C Rowan, John and Christine Lowe, Jack Morley, John Waller)*

Free house ~ Licensee Barry Wilson ~ Real ale ~ Lunchtime meals and snacks ~ Restaurant ~ (017687) 76234 ~ Open 11-2.30(3 Sat), 5.30-10.30(11 Sat); winter morning opening 11.30; closed 25 Dec ~Bedrooms: £60B/£72B

BASSENTHWAITE NY2332 Map 9

Sun

Village itself, signposted off A591 a few miles NW of Keswick

Set in a charming village, this bustling, welcoming inn was originally a farmhouse. The rambling bar has low 17th-c black oak beams, a good stone fireplace with big logs burning in winter, lots of brasses, built-in wall seats and plush stools around heavy wooden tables, and areas that stretch usefully back on both sides of the servery. The landlady is from the Lakes, while her husband is Italian, and the bar food draws on both their backgrounds: minestrone soup (£1.50), squid in batter (£3), lunchtime ploughman's (£3.50), lancashire hotpot (£4.50), home-made steak pie (£5), home-made lasagne (£5.50), pork steaks in mushroom sauce (£6), sirloin steak (£8), and puddings such as syrup sponge or sticky toffee pudding (£2.25). Well kept Jennings Bitter on handpump; no dogs. A huddle of white houses looks up to Skiddaw and other high fells, and you can enjoy the view from the tables in the pub's front yard, by a neighbour's blackberry bush. *(Recommended by Mayur Shah, Vann and Terry Prime, Richard Holloway, Chris and Andy Crow, C A Hall, Tina and David Woods-Taylor, SLC, Mrs P Abell, MB)*

Jennings ~ Tenants Giuseppe and Josephine Scopelliti ~ Real ale ~ Meals and snacks (12-1.30, 6.30-8.30ish; not Sun evening) ~ (017687) 76439 ~ Children in side rooms whenever possible ~ Open 12-2.30, 6-11; may close earlier winter lunchtimes if very quiet; closed Mon lunchtimes Nov-Mar

BEETHAM SD5079 Map 7

Wheatsheaf ↝

Village (and inn) signposted just off A6 S of Milnthorpe

In the 17th c, this fine old building was a coaching inn for travellers on the main London to Scotland road and its timbered cornerpiece is very striking – a two storey set of gabled oriel windows jettied out from the corner into the quiet village street.

The lounge bar is relaxed and chatty and has lots of exposed beams and joists, attractive built-in wall settles, tapestry-cushioned chairs, a massive antique carved oak armchair, and a cabinet filled with foreign costume dolls. Beyond a little central snug is a tiled-floor bar with darts and dominoes. Good, reasonably priced bar food includes soup (£1.60), sandwiches (from £1.90), home-made hotpot (£3.50), ploughman's (£3.90), home-made pies like cheese or steak and kidney (from £3.40), sausage, liver and bacon (£3.60), steaks (from £7), daily specials, and puddings (from £1.70); courteous, friendly staff. If the bar is too crowded, you can eat in the upstairs no-smoking dining room for the same price. Well kept Boddingtons on handpump, and quite a few malt whiskies. *(Recommended by Mrs R D Knight, Michael and Alison Leyland, Angus Lyon, Gill and Keith Croxton, Prof I H Rorison)*

Free house ~ Licensee Mrs Margaret Shaw ~ Real ale ~ Meals and snacks (11.45-1.45, 6-8.45) ~ Restaurant ~ (015395) 62123 ~ Children welcome till 8.30pm ~ Open 11-3, 6-11; closed evenings 24-26 Dec ~ Bedrooms: £30B/£40B

BOOT NY1801 Map 9

Burnmoor

Village signposted just off the Wrynose/Hardknott Pass road, OS Sheet 89 map reference 175010

As the friendly licensees tell us, this is not a gimmicky place, but a simple inn with Lakeland hospitality and good home cooking – and many of their customers have made lots of return visits over the years. Inside, the beamed and carpeted white-painted bar has an open fire, red leatherette seats and small metal tables. Mrs Foster is Austrian and there are always some speciality dishes on the menu: delicious soup (£1.40), sandwiches (£1.50), lunchtime ploughman's (£3.40), several flans such as cheese and onion or Austrian smoked ham and cheese (from £3.80), home-cooked cold meats (£4), Cumberland game pie (£5.50), Wienerschnitzel (£6.10), sirloin steak (£7.80), and daily specials. They grow a lot of the vegetables themselves, and keep hens and pigs. Well kept Jennings Bitter, Cumberland and Snecklifter on handpump, Austrian wines, and gluhwein in winter; pool, dominoes, and juke box. The inn is surrounded by peaceful fells, there are seats outside on the sheltered front lawn, and it's close to Dalegarth Station (the top terminus of the Ravenglass and Eskdale light steam railway), and a restored watermill said to be the oldest in the country; lots of attractive tracks. *(Recommended by Tony Young, Romey Heaton, H K Dyson, John and Heather Bentley, S Fazackerly, C Rowan, John T Ames, J S M Sheldon)*

Free house ~ Licensees Tony and Heidi Foster ~ Real ale ~ Meals and snacks (12-2, 6-9) ~ Restaurant ~ (019467) 23224 ~ Children welcome till 9pm ~ Open 11-3, 5-11 ~ Bedrooms: £21/£42(£48B)

BOUTH SD3386 Map 9

White Hart

Village signposted off A590 near Haverthwaite

Well placed in good walking country, this small village inn has a thoroughly authentic Lakeland feel. It's on top form under the friendly and energetic landlord who took over at the end of 1994 (but has known and loved the pub for 30 years). Sloping ceilings and floors show its age and add to a mood of intimacy even when the pub's bouncing with vitality, and one of the two roaring log fires is in a fine old kitchen range; the atmosphere is very relaxed as there are no noisy games machines except in the games room (where there are darts, pool, pinball, football, video, and juke box). There are lots of old local photographs and bric-a-brac – farm tools, stuffed animals, a collection of long-stemmed clay pipes. The wide choice of home-made food includes good value sandwiches (from £1.50), ploughman's (from £3.50), tuna and pasta bake (£4.95), mushroom stroganoff or vegetable lasagne (£5), 1lb gammon and egg (£5.95), daily specials like venison or wild boar steaks, lancashire hotpot, pork and pineapple curry or local trout (from around £4.95), steaks (from £8.95), and puddings like blackberry and apple crumble, sticky toffee pudding or rice pudding

(£2.50). Well kept Black Sheep, Boddingtons, Highgate Mild, Jennings Cumberland, and Tetleys on handpump; tables out in the attractively planted and well kept garden, with occasional summer barbecues. We have not yet had reports on the bedrooms, but would expect this to be a most enjoyable place to stay in. *(Recommended by Jack Morley, David Carr, JCW, Gordon Day, Sally Edsall, Andy and Jill Kassube)*

Free house ~ Licensees Dave and Kathleen Trotter ~ Real ale ~ Meals and snacks ~ Restaurant ~ (01229) 861229 ~ Children welcome until 8.30pm in bar and in family room ~ Open 12-3, 6-11; closed Mon lunchtime ~Bedrooms: £20/£30(£40B)

BOWLAND BRIDGE SD4289 Map 9
Hare & Hounds 🛏

Village signposted from A5074; OS Sheet 97 map reference 417895

Set in the pretty Winster Valley away from the crowds, this attractive white-painted pub is run by ex-international soccer player Peter Thompson. The comfortably modernised bar, divided into smaller areas by stone walls, has oak beams, ladder-back chairs around dark wood tables on the spread of turkey carpet, Liverpool and England team photographs and caps, reproduction hunting prints, a stuffed pheasant, and open fires. Bar food includes soup (£1.50), sandwiches (from £1.95), pizzas (from £3.95), ploughman's (£4.75), giant yorkshire pudding filled with cumberland sausage and onion gravy or mushroom stroganoff (£5.50), coq au vin (£5.95), poached halibut steak (£6.75), steaks (from £9.75), daily specials, and 4-course Sunday roast lunch (£8.95); very good, prompt service. Well kept Tetleys and a weekly guest beer on handpump, and several malt whiskies from a long bar counter with a cushioned red leatherette elbow rest for people using the sensible backrest-type bar stools. Dominoes, video game, and piped music. The climbing roses, window boxes and hanging baskets are pretty in summer, and there are picnic tables in the spacious garden at one side, with more by the road. The pub is set by the bridge itself. *(Recommended by Mrs R D Knight, Julie Peters, Colin Blinkhorn, Bill and Irene Morley, Beryl and Bill Farmer, J Finney, H K Dyson)*

Free house ~ Licensee Peter Thompson ~ Real ale ~ Meals and snacks ~ Restaurant (residents only) ~ (015395) 68333 ~ Children welcome ~ Open 11-11 ~Bedrooms: £34B/£48B

BOWNESS ON WINDERMERE SD4097 Map 9
Hole in t' Wall 🍺

Lowside

'A gem' is how several readers have described this bustling and characterful pub, tucked away in a back street. It's Bowness's oldest pub and the friendly licensees welcome regulars and tourists alike. The bar has lots to look at such as giant smith's bellows, old farm implements and ploughshares, and jugs hanging from the ceiling, and a room upstairs has handsome plasterwork in its coffered ceiling. On cool days a splendid log fire burns under a vast slate mantelbeam. The tiny flagstoned front courtyard (where there are sheltered seats) has an ancient outside flight of stone steps to the upper floor. Mrs Mitton decides what to cook each day once she gets into her kitchen. There might be sandwiches (from £1.90), vegetarian ratatouille with cheese topping and garlic bread (£5.25), fresh mussels and king prawns in white wine (£5.10), chicken, rump steak and mushrooms in white wine and cream (£5.50), home-made fish pie (£5.25), popular whole roast pheasant with red wine sauce (£6.50), and puddings like lemon meringue pie or fruit cake and cheese (£2). Hartleys XB and Robinsons Frederics, Best, Old Stockport, and Old Tom on handpump in excellent condition, home-made lemonade and very good mulled winter wine; darts, pool, fruit machine and juke box upstairs. If you'd rather catch it on a quiet day, it's better to visit out of season. *(Recommended by Mike and Wendy Proctor, Mayur Shah, Ian and Gayle Woodhead, Miss K Law, K M Timmins, M Joyner, Richard Lewis, A R and B E Sayer, Val Stevenson, Rob Holmes, Joy and Peter Heatherley, SLC, Christopher Turner, Katie Hornby, Rosemarie Johnson)*

Hartleys (Robinsons) ~ Tenants: Andrew and Audrey Mitton ~ Real ale ~ Meals and snacks (not Sun evening) ~ (015394) 43488 ~ Children in family room off taproom until 9pm ~ Parking nearby can be difficult ~ Open 11-11

BRAITHWAITE NY2324 Map 9

Coledale Inn

Village signposted off A66 W of Keswick; pub then signed left off B5292

On warm days, the garden here is a restful place after a walk (the inn is perfectly placed at the foot of Whinlatter Pass) with tables and chairs on the slate terrace beyond the sheltered lawn, and a popular play area for children. The left-hand bar has fine views of Skiddaw and the much closer bracken-covered hills from the window-seats, a winter coal fire, and little 19th-c Lakeland engravings; the green-toned bar on the right, with a bigger bay window, is more of a dining bar. Simple, reliable food includes home-made soup (£1.40), lunchtime sandwiches (from £1.80), filled baked potatoes (from £3), platters and salads (from £3.50), cumberland sausage (£5.50), gammon and egg (£6.30), sirloin steak (£8.90), and puddings with custard or cream (£2.05); daily specials, and several children's dishes (£1.90). Well kept Jennings Bitter, Theakstons XB, and Yates on handpump; cribbage, dominoes, and piped music. The dining room is no smoking. *(Recommended by Jason Caulkin, Ian and Gayle Woodhead, Roger Davey, SLC, Mike Beiley, P and M Rudlin, J Finney, Simon Watkins, Terry and Eileen Stott, Mrs W E Darlaston, Jon Aldous)*

Free house ~ Licensees Geoffrey and Michael Mawdsley ~ Real ale ~ Meals and snacks ~ (017687) 78272 ~ Children welcome ~ Open 11-11; 12-10.30 Sun ~ Bedrooms: £21.50S/£53S

BRAMPTON NY6723 Map 10

New Inn

Note: this is the small Brampton near Appleby, not the bigger one up by Carlisle. Off A66 N of Appleby – follow Long Marton 1 signpost then turn right at church; village also signposted off B6542 at N end of Appleby

This is an attractively traditional inn with two cosy little rooms decorated with a good range of local pictures (mainly sheep and wildlife), a stuffed fox curled on top of the corner TV, and a red squirrel poking out of a little hole in the dividing wall; nice stripped and polished old pine benches with upholstered cushions and old pine tables. The particularly interesting flagstoned dining room has horsebrasses on its low black beams, well spaced tables, and a splendid original black cooking range at one end, separated from the door by an immensely sturdy old oak built-in settle. Good bar food includes lunchtime sandwiches (from £1.25; steak £2.95), home-made soup (£1.50), potted Morecambe Bay shrimps (£3), pizzas (from £3.30), ploughman's (£3.75), home-made nut roast (£4.95), chicken tikka masala (£5.20), gammon and egg (£5.95), seafood gratinée (£6.50), sirloin steak (£8.30), and puddings (£2.20); 3-course Sunday lunch (£6.50; children £3). Well kept Boddingtons, Theakstons Best, and Youngers Scotch on handpump, and a good choice of whiskies with some eminent malts; friendly service, darts, dominoes and piped music. There are seats on the lawn and a barbecue area. In June, the Appleby Horse Fair tends to base itself here. Incidentally another Brampton near Chesterfield has a pub of the same name. *(Recommended by Val Stevenson, Rob Holmes, Richard Holloway, Roger Davey, David and Margaret Bloomfield, Beryl and Bill Farmer, Malcolm Taylor, Ian Rorison, Christopher Turner, Mark and Caroline Thistlethwaite)*

Free house ~ Licensees Roger and Anne Cranswick ~ Real ale ~ Meals and snacks ~ Restaurant ~ (017683) 51231 ~ Children in eating area of bar until 9pm ~ Open 12-2(3 Sat), 6-11; 12-10.30 Sun; closed 25 Dec ~Bedrooms: £18/£36

Pubs staying open all afternoon are listed at the back of the book.

BUTTERMERE NY1817 Map 9

Bridge Hotel 🛏️

Being in some of the best steep countryside in the county, this inn is naturally
popular with walkers – and the flagstoned area in the bar is good for walking boots.
The beamed bar is divided into two parts and furnished with settles and brocaded
armchairs around copper-topped tables, a panelled bar counter, and some brass
ornaments, and there's also a comfortable lounge bar. Good bar food at lunchtime
includes a large soup (£3.30), filled baked potatoes, and a quiche or pâté (all £3.60),
as well as cumberland hotpot, Borrowdale trout, vegetarian cannelloni or gammon
and egg (£5.95), sirloin steak (£8.95), puddings, and Sunday lunch; the restaurant is
no smoking. Well kept Ind Coope Burton, Marstons Pedigree, Tetleys, and
Theakstons Old Pecuiler on handpump, quite a few malt whiskies, and Addlestones
cider. Outside, a flagstoned terrace has white tables by a rose-covered sheltering
stone wall. The views from the bedrooms are marvellous. *(Recommended by H Dyson,
SLC, Christine Bartley, Ian and Gayle Woodhead, RWD, Richard Holloway, AW, BW, Chris
and Andy Crow, Michael and Alison Leyland, Mark Percy, Jack Morley, K and F Giles, Vicky
and David Sarti, Bronwen and Steve Wrigley, Tony Gayfer, Wayne Brindle, Michael Butler, P H
Roberts)*

*Free house ~ Licensee Peter McGuire ~ Real ale ~ Meals and snacks ~ Evening
restaurant ~ (017687) 70252 ~ Children welcome ~ Open 9am-11pm; 9am-
10.30pm Sun; winter opening 10.30 ~Bedrooms: £38.50B/£77B; also, s/c
apartments*

CARTMEL SD38879 Map

Cavendish Arms 🛏️ 🍺

Off main sq

Readers have enjoyed staying at this popular and friendly pub recently – and after a
day or two, feel more like locals than visitors. As well as a relaxed, welcoming
atmosphere and enjoyable food, the real ales are well kept, too: Bass, excellent
Lakeland Gold (brewed elsewhere by Mr Murray's son), Marstons Pedigree, John
Smiths, and Charles Wells Bombardier on handpump. A fair choice of malt whiskies.
Good bar food includes lunchtime open sandwiches (£2.75), various omelettes
(£4.25), salads (from £4.95), and 6oz steak Canadian (£6.50), as well as black
pudding and kidney with a grain mustard cream sauce (£4.70), vegetarian cannelloni
(£4.95), steak and mushroom pie (£5.95), duck breast with a blackberry and plum
glaze (£10.50), steaks (from £10.50), and Friday fish like skate wing with capers and
black butter or char-grilled marlin with lime and coriander, and Sunday spit-roasts;
helpful staff. The restaurant is no smoking. There are tables in front of the pub, with
more at the back by the stream, and their flower displays tend to win awards. The
landlord will take inexperienced fell walkers on guided treks over the mountains.
*(Recommended by Jack Morley, Ian and Nita Cooper, Mr and Mrs Gardner, Karen A Connolly,
C Reed, Colin Partington, J Gilbert, Marianne Jones, Chris and Andy Crow, Jim and Maggie
Cowell, G Davidson, Ian Coburn, Joy and Peter Heatherley, Mike and Sue Walton, Philip
Johnson, Wayne Brindle, George Atkinson, H K Dyson, Malcolm Taylor, John Scarisbrick)*

*Free house ~ Tom and Howard Murray ~ Real ale ~ Meals and snacks (11-2.15,
6-9.30; all day Sun) ~ Restaurant ~ (015395) 36240 ~ Children welcome until
8.30pm ~ Open 11-11; 12-10.30 Sun ~Bedrooms: £25B/£46B*

CARTMEL FELL SD4288 Map 9

Masons Arms ★ 🍺

Strawberry Bank, a few miles S of Windermere between A592 and A5074; perhaps the
simplest way of finding the pub is to go uphill W from Bowland Bridge (which is signposted
off A5074) towards Newby Bridge and keep right then left at the staggered crossroads – it's
then on your right, below Gummer's How; OS Sheet 97 ref 413895

As always, there have been lots and lots of warmly enthusiastic reports from readers this year for the lovely setting, extraordinary choice of beers, and enjoyable food. On the five handpumps are two beers brewed on the premises – Amazon (light and hoppy but quite strong) and Big Six or Great Northern – and usually Batemans, Thwaites and another guest; Dekoninck and Riva Blanche are guests from Belgium. There's also their own damson beer (depending on the fruit crop) and cider using mainly local apples (called Knickerbockerbreaker). A 24-page booklet clearly describes hundreds of imported beers, most stocked and some even imported, which is now in its 16th edition and, considering its scale, is unique. You can be sure of finding some beers here that simply don't exist anywhere else in the country, and many of the beers have their own particular-shaped glasses. Carefully chosen mainly New World wines, too. Popular wholesome food (lots of vegetarian choices) includes soup (£2.50), sandwiches (from £3.25), hazelnut and lentil pâté (£4.25), Morecambe Bay potted shrimps (£4.50), spicy vegetable burritos or fisherman's pie (£6.50), cumberland sausage and cider casserole or rogan josh (£7.50), home-made puddings like fruit cheesecake or toffee banoffi (£2.95), and daily specials. The main bar has low black beams in the bowed ceiling, country chairs and plain wooden tables on polished flagstones, and a grandly Gothick seat with snarling dogs as its arms. A small lounge has oak tables and settles to match its fine Jacobean panelling, and a plain little room beyond the serving counter has pictures and a fire in an open range; the family room has an old-parlourish atmosphere, and there's also an upstairs room which helps at peak times. The setting overlooking the Winster Valley to the woods below Whitbarrow Scar is unrivalled and a good terrace with rustic benches and tables makes the most of the dramatic view. They sell leaflets outlining local walks of varying lengths and difficulty. As it's such a favourite with so many people, don't be surprised if the bar is extremely crowded; it's often much quieter mid-week. *(Recommended by Mick Hitchman, Jim and Maggie Cowell, N J Lawless, Bill and Irene Morley, Amanda Quinn, Carl Travis, R D Greatorex and family, Mike and Wendy Proctor, Howard Gregory, Joy and Peter Heatherley, AW, BW, Mike Whitehouse, Paul McPherson, Mark Percy, Ian and Gayle Woodhead, Mike and Heather Watson, Brian Wainwright, M J Morgan, John Allsopp, John Zeffertt, John Andrew, Jason Caulkin, Kim and Anne Schofield, Julie Peters, Colin Blinkhorn, Mr and Mrs C Cole, Jack Morley, Ann Reeder, David Craine, Malcolm Taylor, Nigel Woolliscroft, John Scarisbrick, Jenny and Roger Huggins, C M Fox, Tina and David Woods-Taylor, H K Dyson, J H and S A Harrop, Wayne Brindle, R J Walden, David Heath, MJVK, John and Christine Simpson)*

Own brew ~ Licensees Helen and Nigel Stevenson ~ Real ale ~ Meals and snacks (12-2, 6-8.45) ~ (015395) 68486 ~ Children welcome till 9.30pm ~ Open 11.30-11; 12-10.30 Sun; 11.30-3, 6-11 winter Mon-Thurs ~ Four s/c flats and two s/c cottages available

CASTERTON SD6279 Map 10

Pheasant ⊕ ⇔ ♀

A683 about a mile N of junction with A65, by Kirkby Lonsdale; OS sheet 97, map reference 633796

The friendly licensees of this civilised inn go to a lot of effort to make you feel comfortable and welcome. The neatly kept and attractively modernised beamed rooms of the main bar glow with polish and have table lamps and pot plants, padded wheelback chairs, plush wall settles, newspapers and magazines to read, an open log fire in a nicely arched bare stone fireplace with polished brass hood, and souvenir mugs on the mantelpiece; there's a further room (which is no smoking during meal times) across the passage with a piano. Well kept Marstons Pedigree, Morlands Old Speckled Hen, Theakstons Bitter and XB, and Charles Wells Bombardier on handpump kept under light blanket pressure, a small but good wine list from Corney & Barrow, and over 30 malt whiskies. Good, popular bar food includes home-made soup (£2.25), sandwiches (from £2.25), mushroom and garlic pancake with a brandy and parmesan cheese sauce (£4.75), omelettes (£4.95), home-made steak and kidney pie or deep-fried fresh fillet of halibut (£5.75), mixed vegetable pilaff (£5.95), platters (from £5.95), Aberdeen Angus steaks (from £10.95), daily specials such as fresh Loch Fyne cockles provençale style (£4.95), local lamb cutlets with mint (£7.50), fresh loin of sailfish (£9.50), and crispy roast duck with a port and stilton sauce (£10.50); hearty breakfasts. The restaurant is no smoking; darts, dominoes, a popular weekly winter quiz night in aid of the Guide Dogs, and piped music. There are some tables with cocktail parasols outside by the road and the garden has been improved this year. The nearby church (built for the girls' school of Brontë fame here) has some attractive pre-Raphaelite stained glass and paintings. *(Recommended by Paul and Sue Merrick, Dr W S M Hood, A T Rhone, Karen Eliot, T J Bagley, R A Cook, Richard Holloway, Graham Mair, Mrs Pat Crabb, John Allsopp, Michael and Joan Melling, Malcolm Taylor, Sue Holland, Dave Webster)*

Free house ~ Licensees Melvin and May Mackie ~ Real ale ~ Meals and snacks ~ Restaurant ~ (015242) 71230 ~ Children welcome ~ Open 11-3, 6-11; closed 1 week Jan ~Bedrooms: £37B/£64B

CHAPEL STILE NY3205 Map 9
Wainwrights
B5343

This is a lovely spot for walkers – though the less energetic can enjoy the views from the picnic tables out on the terrace of this white-rendered Lakeland house. Inside, there's a relaxed and friendly atmosphere and plenty of room in the characterful slate-floored bar with its old kitchen range and cushioned settles. Good food includes soup (£1.90), sandwiches (from £1.95), filled baked potatoes (from £3.25), ploughman's or quiche (£4.95), broccoli and cream cheese bake (£5.95), good lamb shoulder cooked with honey and mint (£6.95), children's dishes (£2.50), and daily specials; good, prompt service. The dining area is no smoking. Well kept Theakstons Best, XB and Old Peculier with a summer guest beer like Jennings Cumberland or Lakeland Gold on handpump and a decent wine list; darts, dominoes, fruit machine, video game, trivia, and piped music. *(Recommended by Phil and Heidi Cook, Joy and Peter Heatherley, Mayur Shah, Howard Gregory, Mrs P Hare, Bronwen and Steve Wrigley, Jenny and Roger Huggins, Richard Lewis)*

Matthew Brown (S & N) ~ Manager Alan Hurst ~ Real ale ~ Meals and snacks ~ (015394) 37302 ~ Children welcome until 9.30 ~ Quiz night Tues evening ~ Open 11.30-11; 12-10.30 Sun; 11-3, 6-11 in winter

COCKERMOUTH NY1231 Map 9
Trout 🛏
Crown St

If you are staying in this solid 17th-c hotel and are interested in fishing then it's worth knowing that they have fishing rights on the River Derwent behind, and hold fishing weekends for beginners from February to June. The comfortable and friendly bar has an open fire in the stone fireplace, low pink plush sofas and captain's chairs around dark polished tables, some patterned plates on the walls, and several pot plants; the coffee lounge (at lunchtime) and the restaurant are no smoking. Well kept Jennings Cumberland, Marstons Pedigree, and Theakstons Best on handpump, over 50 malt whiskies, wines of the month, and freshly squeezed orange or grapefruit juices; piped music. Bar food includes home-made soup (£1.60), good sandwiches (from £2.35; open ones from £3.45), soup and a sandwich (from £3.65), home-made chicken pâté with brandy (£2.95), filled baked potatoes (from £3.35), cumberland sausage with apple sauce (£5.55), home-roast cold meats (£5.65), sirloin steak (£9.25), and a daily fish and vegetarian dish; courteous staff. In summer you can eat in the pretty, award-winning gardens, next to the river, and William Wordsworth's birthplace is next door. *(Recommended by Ian Rorison, RWD, Ann Bartlett, R J Walden)*

Free house ~ Licensee Gill Blackah ~ Real ale ~ Meals and snacks (not 25 Dec) ~ Restaurant ~ (01900) 823591 ~ Children welcome ~ Open 10.30-3, 5.30-11 ~ Bedrooms: £59.95B/£76.95B

CROSTHWAITE SD4491 Map 9

Punch Bowl ⑪ ♀

Village signposted off A5074 SE of Windermere

Stephen Doherty who ran the Brown Horse at Winster so successfully and who trained under the Roux brothers, is now firmly at the helm of this idyllically placed 16th-c inn. The emphasis, not surprisingly, is very much on the excellent food and wine: lunchtime sandwiches (not Sun), tomato and basil soup (£2.20), pork terrine with home-made chutney (£3.75), Cumbrian air-dried ham with Italian-style marinaded and grilled vegetables (£4.75), fresh tuna niçoise (£4.85), baked cod fillet on creamed spinach topped with a cheese sauce (£6.75), grilled leg of lamb steak provençale (£7.50), fillet of sea bass with a ginger, spring onion and soy sauce (£8.25), sirloin steak (£8.50), and puddings such as chocolate truffle cake, passion fruit crème brûlée or local and British farmhouse cheeses (from £2.50); there will be 'guest chef' evenings in the autumn with the likes of Albert Roux and Gary Rhodes and they plan to have tutorial wine tastings. Well kept Jennings Cocker Hoop and Cumberland, and Theakstons Best on handpump; friendly, helpful service. There are several separate areas carefully reworked to give a lot of space, and a high-raftered central area by the serving counter with an upper minstrels' gallery on either side; several no-smoking areas. Steps lead down into a couple of small dimly lit rooms on the right, and there's a doorway through into two more airy rooms on the left. It's all spick and span, with lots of tables and chairs, beams, pictures, and an open fire. There are some tables on a terrace stepped into the hillside. *(Recommended by Revd and Mrs McFie, Brian and Ursula Kirby, Dr J R Norman, Margaret Dyke, Malcolm Taylor, A Preston, Jack Morley, Roger and Corinne Ball, H K Dyson)*

Free house ~ Licensee Stephen Doherty ~ Real ale ~ Meals and snacks (12-2, 6-9) ~ (015295) 68237 ~ Children welcome ~ Open 12-3, 6-11; winter evening opening 6.30; closed 2 wks Nov/Dec and evenings 25-26 Dec ~Bedrooms: £29B/£35B

DENT SD7187 Map 10

Sun ◗

Village signposted from Sedbergh; and from Barbon, off A683

Surrounded by high fells, this traditional, pretty pub brews its own Dent Brewery real ales just a few miles up in the Dale – and supplies other pubs all over the country with them: Bitter, T'Owd Tup, and Kamikazee Strong Ale on handpump. There's a pleasant atmosphere in the bar and fine old oak timbers and beams studded with coins, as well as dark armed chairs, brown leatherette wall benches, lots of local snapshots and old Schweppes advertisements on the walls, and a coal fire; one of the areas is no smoking. Through the arch to the left are banquettes upholstered to match the carpet (as are the curtains). Good value, straightforward bar food includes home-made soup (£1.55), sandwiches (£1.60), ploughman's (£3.65), home-made pasties (£3.85), home-made steak and kidney pie or vegetarian lasagne (£4.25), cumberland sausage (£4.45), gammon and pineapple (£5.45), rump steak (£5.95), puddings (£1.85), children's helpings (£2.35), and nice breakfasts; prompt service. Darts, pool, bar billiards, dominoes, cribbage, fruit machine, video game, and juke box (in the pool room). There are rustic seats and tables outside. *(Recommended by John Fazakerley, Paul McPherson, Angus Lyon, Peter and Audrey Dowsett, David Varney, J K W)*

Own brew ~ Licensee Martin Stafford ~ Real ale ~ Meals and snacks ~ (015396) 25208 ~ Children welcome until 9pm ~ Open 11-11; 12-10.30 Sun; 11-2, 7-11 in winter; closed 25 Dec ~Bedrooms: £18.50/£33

DOCKRAY NY3921 Map 9

Royal ⇦ ♀ ◗

A5091, off A66 W of Penrith

Run by friendly, helpful licensees, this carefully renovated little white inn is set among lovely low hills and pleasant walks, and was once used by William and Dorothy Wordsworth. The unusually spacious, airy and light open-plan bar is comfortably plush with built-in bays of olive-green herringbone button-back banquettes, a spread of flowery pink and green carpet, and a woodburning stove. For walkers, an area of more traditional seating has stripped settles on flagstones, with darts, cribbage, and dominoes, and there are unusual leatherette-topped sewing-machine tables throughout. Two dining areas (one no smoking) spread beyond the bar, and good home-cooked food includes soup (£1.90), lunchtime filled rolls (from £2.50), baked potatoes (from £2.75) or choice of lunchtime ploughman's (£4.75), omelettes (£5.50), salads (from £5.50), home-made steak and kidney pie (£5.90), grilled barnsley chop (£7.75), 8oz sirloin steak (£8.50), and with particularly good dishes of the day such as various quiches (£5), seafood pie (£6) or roast local herdwick mutton with garlic and rosemary (£6.50), home-made puddings (£2.75), and children's helpings (£3.25). Well kept Boddingtons Bitter, Jennings Cumberland, Marstons Pedigree, Mitchells ESB, and Whitbreads Castle Eden on handpump, a decent range of malt whiskies, and good wines by the glass for this area; unobtrusive piped music. As well as picnic tables on a tree-sheltered lawn, there is now a landscaped garden and field areas with a pond. *(Recommended by Mr and Mrs W B Barnes, Mike Stokes, Kim and Anne Schofield, John Gay, F J and A Parmenter, Ewan and Aileen McEwan, Mike and Wendy Proctor, R and B Davies, Pat and John Millward, Mark Rumsey, Jack Morley)*

Free house ~ Licensees James and Sarah Johnson ~ Real ale ~ Meals and snacks (12-2.30, 6-9.30) ~ Restaurant ~ (017684) 82356 ~ Children in eating area of bar if supervised ~ Open 11-11; 12-10.30 Sun ~ Bedrooms: £26B/£53B

ELTERWATER NY3305 Map 9

Britannia Inn ★ 🛏 🍷

Off B5343

Set right in the heart of the Lake District, this unpretentious and friendly little pub is a favourite with many of our readers. It's obviously popular with walkers with so many tracks over the fells, and walking boots are not barred. At the back is a small and traditionally furnished bar, while the front bar has winter coal fires and settles, oak benches, windsor chairs, a big old rocking chair, and a couple of window seats looking across to Elterwater itself through the trees on the far side; there's also a comfortable no-smoking lounge. Well kept Boddingtons Bitter, Jennings Bitter and Mild, and two guest beers on handpump, quite a few malt whiskies, and a well chosen, good value wine list; good service, even when busy. Popular bar food at lunchtime includes home-made soup (£1.40), filled crusty rolls (£2), ploughman's (£3.75), vegetable tikka masala (£6), pork chop in cider or home-made steak and kidney pie (£6.50), and evening extras like poached fresh salmon with parsley butter (£6.75) or sirloin steak (£8.50); daily specials, puddings like home-made sticky toffee pudding (£2.50), and children's dishes (£3.25); super breakfasts. The restaurant is no smoking; dominoes. The front terrace has chairs and slate-topped tables. At peak times, the inn does get packed, and in summer, people flock to watch Morris and Step and Garland Dancers on the pretty village green opposite. *(Recommended by R and B Davies, Joy and Peter Heatherley, Graham and Karen Oddey, Jack Morley, Howard Gregory, Ian and Gayle Woodhead, Jason Caulkin, Michael and Alison Leyland, Vann and Terry Prime, Tina and David Woods-Taylor, Jenny and Roger Huggins, N H and A H Harris, A R and A J Ashcroft, S Fazackerly, C Rowan, Fiona Wynn, John and Maureen Watt, John and Liz Stevenson, Nigel Woolliscroft, Paul Carter, G S Miller, A Preston, Jack Morley, Dr Diana Terry, George Atkinson, R J Walden, LM, Tommy Payne)*

Free house ~ Judith Fry ~ Real ale ~ Meals and snacks (snacks are sold all afternoon) ~ Restaurant ~ (015394) 37210 ~ Children welcome until 9 ~ Summer parking may be difficult ~ Open 11-11; 12-10.30 Sun; closed 25 Dec and evening 26 Dec ~ Bedrooms: £23.50/£47(£60B)

It's against the law for bar staff to smoke while handling food or drink.

ESKDALE GREEN NY1400 Map 9

Bower House ⇐

½ mile W of village towards Santon Bridge

In summer the neatly kept sheltered garden here is a pleasant place to relax and on Sundays you can watch the cricket on the field alongside the pub. Inside, it's quietly relaxed (no noisy machines or piped music), and the lounge bar has a good winter log fire, and cushioned settles and windsor chairs that blend in well with the original beamed and alcoved nucleus around the serving counter; also, a separate lounge with easy chairs and sofas. Decent bar food comes in generous helpings and includes good soup (£2), good sandwiches (from £2), ploughman's (£3.50), tasty nut loaf with mushroom sauce (£5.50), several game and vegetarian dishes, cumberland sausage or lasagne (£5), steak and kidney pie (£6), sirloin steak, and home-made daily specials. Well kept Courage Directors, Hartleys XB, Theakstons Best and Youngers Scotch on handpump, a reasonably priced wine list, and quite a few malt whiskies; friendly staff; dominoes. Some of the comfortable bedrooms are in the annexe across the garden. *(Recommended by H K Dyson, R and S Bentley, Mayur Shah, Romey Heaton, B Eastwood, John Allsopp, Robert and Ann Lees, Dave Braisted, Wayne Brindle)*

Free house ~ Licensee Derek Connor ~ Real ale ~ Meals and snacks (12-2, 6.30-9.30) ~ Restaurant ~ (019467) 23244 ~ Children in eating area of bar ~ Open 11-11 ~Bedrooms: £47B/£60B

King George IV ⇐

E of village at junction of main rd with rd up to Hard Knott Pass

A good mix of walkers and other visitors fill the refurbished bar of this old pub. There are traditional wall seats for the handful of tables on the flagstones, giving plenty of space out in the room, a comfortable lounge, and a back games room with darts, bar billiards, dominoes, fruit machine, and piped music; warming winter log fire. A wide choice of generously served good bar food includes home-made soup (£1.70), good sandwiches (from £1.60), black pudding in a cider and cream sauce (£4.25), ploughman's or cumberland sausage and egg (£4.95), vegetable lasagne (£5.95), steaks (from £7.50), daily specials such as liver and onions (£4.95), pork fillet with a masala cream sauce or seafood platter (£5.50), and children's meals (£2.50). The restaurant is no smoking. Well kept Bass, Jennings Cumberland, and Theakstons Best, XB and Old Peculier on handpump, and 170 malt whiskies; friendly staff. Fine views from the tables in the garden. *(Recommended by Dave Thompson, Margaret Mason, John Abbott, J Hibberd, Robert and Ann Lees, Paul M Harris, H K Dyson, Neil Townsend, C Driver)*

Free house ~ Licensees Harry and Jacqui Shepherd ~ Real ale ~ Meals and snacks ~ Restaurant ~ (019467) 23262 ~ Children welcome ~ Open 11-11; 12-10.30 Sun; 11-3, 6-11 in winter; closed 25 Dec ~ Bedrooms £21B/£42B

GARRIGILL NY7441 Map 9

George & Dragon 🍺

Village signposted off B6277 S of Alston

Originally a posting inn, this stonebuilt inn is part of a largely 17th-c terrace in a pretty village set in a high Pennine valley (the Pennine Way passes the pub door). Inside on the right, the bar has a lovely stone fireplace with a really good log fire, good solid traditional furnishings on the very broad polished flagstones, and a cosy and relaxed atmosphere; there's a separate tartan-carpeted games room with sensibly placed darts, pool and dominoes; piped music. The very friendly landlord's wife prepares the good value generous bar food, such as soup (£1.40), sandwiches (from £1.45), filled yorkshire pudding (from £1.75), baked potatoes (from £2.10), cumberland sausage and egg (£4.25), home-made steak pie (£4.50), lentil crumble

(£4.75), and sirloin steak (£7.75), and children's dishes (from £1.75). Well kept McEwans 70/-, Theakstons Best, XB and Old Peculier and changing guest beers on handpump. *(Recommended by GSB, Richard Holloway; more reports please)*

Free house ~ Licensees Brian and Jean Holmes ~ Real ale ~ Meals and snacks ~ Restaurant ~ (01434) 381293 ~ Children welcome ~ Open 11.30-4, 6.30-11; 12-3, 7-11 in winter ~ Bedrooms: £15/£30, also very cheap small bunkhouse

GRASMERE NY3406 Map 9

Travellers Rest

Just N of Grasmere on A591 Ambleside—Keswick rd; OS sheet 90, map ref 335089

This welcoming little 16th-c pub is surrounded by wonderful scenery and good walks, and there are picnic tables in the side garden. The comfortable, beamed lounge bar has a warming log fire, banquettes and cushioned wooden chairs around varnished wooden tables, local watercolours, and a relaxed atmosphere; suggested walks and coast-to-coast information on the walls, and piped classical music. The games room is popular with families: pool and darts. Bar food includes home-made soup (£1.95), local trout pâté (£2.95), open sandwiches (from £4.45), ploughman's, char-grilled burger or vegetable brochette (all £4.95), steak and kidney pie (£5.75), coq au vin (£5.95), steaks (from £9.85), children's menu (£2.95), daily specials such as good fresh fish (from £4.95), and puddings (£2.75); the restaurant is no smoking. Well kept Jennings Bitter, Cumberland, Mild and Snecklifter, and Marstons Pedigree on handpump, and at least a dozen malt whiskies. From the picnic tables in the garden you can admire the wonderful views. *(Recommended by Tony Kemp, Rachel Weston, Phil and Heidi Cook, Sue Holland, David Webster, Dave Thompson, Margaret Mason, Roger and Pauline Pearce, R H Rowley, Helen Pickering, James Owen, Mr and Mrs J Watson, Tina and David Woods-Taylor, H K Dyson, Miss M A Watson, John and Joan Nash, James House, Mr and Mrs J A Moors, Nigel Wolliscroft)*

Free house ~ Licensees Lynne, Derek and Graham Sweeney ~ Real ale ~ Meals and snacks (12-3, 6-9.30) ~ (015394) 35604 ~ Children welcome ~ Open 11-11; 11-10.30 Sun ~ Bedrooms: £23.95(£26.95B)/£47.90(£53.90B)

nr HAWKSHEAD NY3501 Map 9

Drunken Duck ★ 🍺

Barngates; the hamlet is signposted from B5286 Hawkshead—Ambleside, opposite the Outgate Inn; or it may be quicker to take the first right from B5286, after the wooded caravan site; OS Sheet 90 map reference 350013

It says a lot for this friendly old pub that it manages to make such a wide mix of people feel so welcome – not any easy task. There are several cosy and traditionally pubby beamed rooms with good winter fires, tub chairs, cushioned old settles, blond pews, ladderback country chairs, and wheelbacks on the fitted turkey carpet, and maybe the multi-coloured cat (sadly, the elderly dog passed away at the ripe old age of 17 and is much missed). Around the walls are pictures, cartoons, cards, fox masks, and cases of fishing flies and lures. Very popular bar food includes soup such as cream of celery (£2.25), lunchtime rolls (£2.50), lunchtime ploughman's with cheese, cold meat or lentil and tomato or chicken liver pâté, (£4.25), Italian artichoke casserole (£5), ricotta and mixed pepper filo (£5.50), cottage pie (£5.95), minted lamb casserole or beef in ale (£6.50), gammon and egg (£6.95), and wild boar steak (£8.75). The dining room is no smoking. Well kept Boddingtons Bitter, Jennings Bitter, Mitchells Lancaster Bomber, Theakstons Old Peculier, Yates Bitter, and a beer brewed for the pub by Yates, called Drunken Duck Bitter, on handpump or tapped from the cask, and 60 malt whiskies; darts and dominoes. Seats on the front verandah look across to Lake Windermere in the distance; to the side there are quite a few rustic wooden chairs and tables, sheltered by a stone wall with alpine plants along its top, and the pub has fishing in a private tarn behind. *(Recommended by Vann and Terry Prime, Jack and Philip Paxton, Phil and Heidi Cook, Kim and Anne Schofield, Alan and Louise*

Duggan, Ian and Gayle Woodhead, Howard Gregory, Jack Morley, Joy and Peter Heatherley, R and S Bentley, SLC, Tina and David Woods-Taylor, Mrs P Hare, Mr and Mrs Richard Osborne, RLW and Dizzy, C M Fox, Nigel Woolliscroft, John and Christine Simpson, S R and A J Ashcroft, John and Christine Lowe, Ann Reeder, David Craine, John Scarisbrick, Bronwen and Steve Wrigley, George Atkinson, K H Frostick, Richard Lewis, Jack Morley, James House)

Free house ~ Licensee Stephanie Barton ~ Real ale ~ Meals and snacks ~ (015394) 36347 ~ Children in eating area of bar ~ Open 11.30-3, 6-11; closed 25 Dec ~ Bedrooms: £43.75B/£59.50B

HAWKSHEAD SD3598 Map 9

Kings Arms 🛏 🍺

Sitting outside on the terrace of this pretty inn is a very pleasant place to be in summer as it overlooks the central square of this lovely Elizabethan village. Inside, the cosy and traditional low-ceilinged bar has comfortable red-cushioned wall and window seats and red plush stools on the turkey carpet, an open fire, and is popular with locals. Bar food includes home-made soup, sandwiches, vegetarian hotpot or mushroom stroganoff (£5.50), spaghetti carbonara (£5.75), steak and mushroom pie (£6), seafood fettucini (£7.50), and Sunday roast (£5.75). The restaurant is no smoking. Well kept Greenalls Original, Tetleys, Theakstons XB and guest beers on handpump, and a good choice of malt whiskies. Darts, dominoes, cribbage, fruit machine, and piped pop music. In keeping with the atmosphere of the rest of the place, the bedrooms have coins embedded in the old oak beams. The village car park is some way away, but if you're staying at the inn, you'll get a free permit. *(Recommended by M J Morgan, Val Stevenson, Rob Holmes, John Allsopp, Michael and Alison Leyland, SLC, John and Chris Simpson)*

Free house ~ Lease: Rosalie Johnson ~ Real ale ~ Meals and snacks (12-2.30, 6-9.30) ~ Restaurant ~ (015394) 36372 ~ Well behaved children welcome ~ Occasional live folk music/country & western ~ Open 11-11; 12-10.30 Sun; closed 25 Dec ~ Bedrooms: £29(£34B)/£48(£58B)

Queens Head

Bustling and friendly, this attractive black and white timbered pub has a good atmosphere in its low-ceiling bar, heavy bowed black beams, red plush wall seats and plush stools around heavy traditional tables, lots of decorative plates on the panelled walls, and an open fire; a snug little room leads off. Tasty bar food includes soup (£2.50), kipper mousseline (£4), smoked salmon tartlet (£4.75), black-eyed bean casserole (£5.50), cumberland sausage with onion gravy (£5.95), black pudding on beans and lentils or mediterranean risotto (£6.25), liver and onions (£6.75), fresh haddock and chips (£6.95), monkfish Italian style or tarragon and smoked chicken (£7.50), braised rabbit (£7.75), pheasant casserole (£8.50), and saddle of lamb (£9.25); helpful staff. The restaurant is no smoking. Well kept Hartleys XB and Robinsons Bitter, Frederics, and Mild on handpump, and quite a few whiskies; dominoes and piped music. Walkers must take their boots off. In summer, the window boxes are most pretty. *(Recommended by SLC, Val Stevenson, Rob Holmes, Kim and Anne Schofield, Vann and Terry Prime, John Waller, M J Morgan, Chris and Andy Crow, Mike and Heather Watson, Richard Lewis)*

Hartleys (Robinsons) ~ Tenant Tony Merrick ~ Real ale ~ Meals and snacks (12-2.30, 6.15-9.30) ~ Restaurant ~ (015394) 36271 ~ Children in restaurant if eating and in snug ~ Occasional live jazz ~ Open 11-11 ~ Bedrooms: £35(£53)/£45(£59.50B)

HEVERSHAM SD4983 Map 9

Blue Bell

A6 (now a relatively quiet road here)

This partly-timbered old country inn has a comfortably civilised bay-windowed lounge bar with warm winter fires, an antique carved settle, cushioned windsor armchairs and upholstered stools on the flowery carpet, pewter platters hanging from the beams, and small antique sporting prints and a display cabinet with two stuffed fighting cocks on the partly panelled walls. One big bay-windowed area has been divided off as a children's room, and the long, tiled-floor, quieter public bar has darts and dominoes. Good bar food based on fresh local produce includes sandwiches, home-made soup, lovely Morecambe Bay potted shrimps, filled giant yorkshire puddings (£4.95), local game casserole (£5.95), vegetarian dishes, good steak and kidney pie (£6.25), and sizzling sirloin steak platter (£8.95). The restaurant is no smoking. Well kept Sam Smiths OB on handpump, with Museum kept under light blanket pressure, several malt whiskies, a decent wine list, and their own cider; helpful staff. Darts, pool, cribbage, dominoes, fruit machine, and piped music. Crossing over the A6 into the village itself, you come to a picturesque church with a rambling little graveyard; if you walk through this and on to the hills beyond, there's a fine view across to the estuary of the River Kent. The estuary itself is a short walk from the pub down the country road that runs by its side. Pets welcome by arrangement. *(Recommended by Christopher Tobitt, Vann and Terry Prime, Enid and Henry Stephens, Mr and Mrs Greenhalgh, S L Clemens)*

Sam Smiths ~ Manager Richard Cowie ~ Real ale ~ Meals and snacks (11-2.30, 6-9.30) ~ Restaurant ~ (015395) 62018 ~ Children welcome ~ Ceilidh 1st/3rd Thurs of month ~ Open 11-11 ~ Bedrooms: £37.50B/£64B

INGS SD4599 Map 9

Watermill 🛏 🍺

Just off A591 E of Windermere

As well as planning to extend the bar next to the River Gowan here, the beer garden is to be moved to the front so everyone can enjoy the sunshine. It's a friendly family-run place with no noisy machines or juke box, and an incredible range of up to 14 real ales on handpump: Black Sheep Bitter, Jennings Bitter, Theakstons Best, XB and Old Peculier and Lees Moonraker, and 8 regularly changing guests such as Bunces Sign of Spring, Fullers London Pride, Greenwood Hop Pocket, Hop Back Summer Lightning, Jennings Cumberland, Moorhouses Black Cat and Pendle Witches Brew, and Roosters Desperado; farm cider, bottled beers, and up to 50 malt whiskies. There's a happy mix of chairs, padded benches and solid oak tables, bar counters made from old church wood, open fires, and amusing cartoons by a local artist on the wall; one room is no smoking. The spacious lounge bar, in much the same traditional style as the other rooms, has rocking chairs and a big open fire. Walkers and their dogs (on leads) are welcome. Bar food includes home-made soup (£1.70), lunchtime sandwiches (from £2), lunchtime ploughman's (£3.50), local cumberland sausage (£4.50), salads (from £4.90), home-made curry (£5.50), Whitby scampi (£5.60), local grilled gammon (£6), and steak (£9.10); they specialise in real ale casseroles and pies (£5.50); children's meals (from £2.50). Darts, table skittles and dominoes. Lots of climbing, fell-walking, fishing, boating of all kinds, swimming and pony-trekking within easy reach. *(Recommended by Jim and Maggie Cowell, Dick Brown, M Joyner, Paul Boot, William Harper, Julie Peters, Colin Blinkhorn, D R Shillitoe, Karen Eliot, SLC, Howard Gregory, David and Helen Wilkins, John and Pam Smith, Sue Holland, Dave Webster, Jeff Davies, Ian Morley, Graham and Lynn Mason, R J Walden, Jenny and Roger Huggins)*

Free house ~ Licensees Alan and Brian Coulthwaite ~ Real ale ~ Meals and snacks (not 25 Dec) ~ (01539) 821309 ~ Children in lounge until 9pm ~ Open 12-2.30, 6-11; closed 25 Dec ~ Bedrooms: £25S/£45S

KIRKBY LONSDALE SD6278 Map 7

Snooty Fox

Main Street (B6254)

At lunchtime, this rambling pub is popular with shoppers and tourists while the evening customers are aiming for a more restful meal. The various rooms are full of stage gladiator costumes, horse-collars and stirrups, mugs hanging from beams, eye-catching coloured engravings, stuffed wildfowl and falcons, mounted badger and fox masks, and guns and a powder-flask. The bar counters are made from English oak, as is some panelling, and there are also country kitchen chairs, pews, one or two high-backed settles and marble-topped sewing-trestle tables on the flagstones, and two coal fires. Good home-made food includes soup with fresh poppy seed and apricot bread (£2), chicken, pork and hazelnut terrine wrapped in smoked bacon with a cumberland sauce or deep-fried crispy duck pancakes with a sweet and sour tomatina coulis (£4.75), leek and brie tart with rich tomato sauce (£5.50), cajun nut and bean risotto with spicy peach purée (£5.95), highland venison ragout in flaky pastry (£7.95), fresh scallops on buttered spinach with brandy cream sauce (£9.50), rump steak with caesar salad (£9.75), daily specials and traditional Sunday lunch; the dining annexe is no smoking. Well kept Hartleys XB, Theakstons Best, and Timothy Taylors Landlord on handpump, several malt whiskies, and country wines; fruit machine and good juke box in back bar only. There are tables out on a small terrace beside the biggish back cobbled stableyard, with more in a pretty garden; small play area for children. *(Recommended by Paul McPherson, Angus Lyon, Ian and Gayle Woodhead, Richard Holloway, Mr and Mrs French, R Hatton-Evans, Sue Holland, Dave Webster, Neil Townend, Paul and Sue Merrick, Peter and Audrey Dowsett)*

Free house ~ Licensee Jack Shone ~ Real ale ~ Meals and snacks (till 10pm) ~ Restaurant ~ (015242) 71308 ~ Children in eating area of bar and in restaurant ~ Open 11-11; 12-10.30 ~ Bedrooms: £29B/£45B

Sun 🛏 🍺

Market St (B6254)

It's the warmly friendly feeling in this bustling, atmospheric little pub that both locals and visitors of all ages like so much. The low beamed, rambling rooms have good winter fires and are filled with a collection of some 500 banknotes, maps, and old engravings; the walls – some of which are stripped to bare stone or have panelled dados – are hung with battleaxes and other interesting antiques, and even a fireplace, and furnishings include window seats and cosy pews. Very well kept Black Sheep Bitter, Boddingtons, Dent Bitter (from the Sun in Dent) and Youngers No 3 on handpump, and 50 malt whiskies; dominoes and piped music. Generous helpings of tasty bar food include home-made soup (£1.75), filled french bread (£3.50), devilled lamb kidneys (£4.25), feta cheese and spinach strudel (£4.95), pizzas with choose-your-own topping (from £4.95; take-away also), home-made steak and kidney or chicken, leek and cheese pies (£5.25), mixed grill (£6.95), and Aberdeen Angus rump steak (£7.95); the restaurant has been attractively refurbished this year. Good personal service and super breakfasts. There's an unusual pillared porch; the steep cobbled alley is also attractive. Some of the bedrooms are in a stone barn with lovely views across the Barbon Fells. *(Recommended by Paul and Sue Merrick, Steve Calvert, Mr and Mrs R P Begg, Angus Lyon, Walter Oston, Sue Holland, Dave Webster, Steve and Julie Cocking, Mr Jackson, B J and J S Derry, Dave McKenzie)*

Free house ~ Licensee Andrew Wilkinson ~ Real ale ~ Meals and snacks (11-2, 6-10) ~ Restaurant ~ (015242) 71965 ~ Children welcome ~ Open 11-11; 12-10.30 Sun ~ Bedrooms: £22.50(£27.50B)/£44(£48B)

LANERCOST NY5664 Map 9
Abbey Bridge Inn 🛏 🍺

Follow brown Lanercost Priory signs from A69 or in Brampton

Set in lovely quiet off-the-beaten-track countryside, this unusual inn sits by a strikingly arched medieval bridge, just down the lane from the great 12th-c priory (well worth a visit). The pub part is in a side building (formerly a smithy) with a relaxed but rather stylish atmosphere, high pitched rafters and knobby whited stone walls, and has an understated rustic decor that includes charming Ashley Boon prints as well as a large woodburning stove. Using fresh produce, the food at lunchtime includes good soup such as tomato, bacon and sweetcorn (£1.75), sandwiches (£1.95), a plate of smoked fish (£3.35), quiche of the day (£4.75), home-made steak or vegetarian pie (£6.50), cajun chicken or salmon steak (£8.99), and puddings (£2.25); in the evenings it's normally served restaurant-style in a no-smoking gallery up spiral stairs. Well kept and well chosen real ales on handpump change every few days: Burton Bridge, Fullers Chiswick, Shepherd Neame and Yates; other good drinks, such as the excellent Fentimans ginger beer and quite a few malt whiskies. Welcoming service; very faint piped pop music, cribbage, and dominoes. There are a few seats outside. *(Recommended by Dave Thompson, Margaret Mason, D and J Tapper, Wayne A Wheeler; more reports please)*

Free house ~ Licensee Philip Sayers ~ Real ale ~ Meals and snacks ~ Evening restaurant ~ (016977) 2224 ~ Children welcome ~ Open 12-2.30, 7-11; closed 25 Dec

LANGDALE NY2906 Map 9

Old Dungeon Ghyll 🛏

B5343

In such a dramatic setting, it's not surprising that this characterful but basic inn is so popular with fell walkers and climbers. It's at the heart of the Great Langdale Valley and surrounded by fells including the Langdale Pikes flanking the Dungeon Ghyll Force waterfall – and there are grand views of the Pike of Blisco rising behind Kettle Crag from the window seats cut into the thick stone walls of the bar. Furnishings are very simple, and straightforward food includes lunchtime sandwiches (£1.75), filled baked potatoes (£2.75), pizzas (£4.20), cumberland sausage (£4.95), chilli con carne (£5.25), puddings, and children's meals (£2.95); if you are not a resident and want to eat in the restaurant you must book ahead. Well kept Jennings Cumberland and Mild, Theakstons XB and Old Peculier, and Yates Bitter on handpump, and farm cider; darts, cribbage and dominoes. It can get really lively on a Saturday night (there's a popular National Trust campsite opposite). *(Recommended by H K Dyson, Ian and Gayle Woodhead, M Joyner, Michael and Alison Leyland, LM, Nigel Woolliscroft, George Atkinson, Dr Diana Terry, David Heath, Wayne Brindle, Bronwen and Steve Wrigley)*

Free house ~ Licensee Neil Walmsley ~ Real ale ~ Meals and snacks (12-2, 6-9) ~ Evening restaurant ~ (015394) 37272 ~ Children welcome ~ Open 11-11; 12-10.30; closed 24-26 Dec ~Bedrooms: £30(£33.50B)/£60(£67B)

LEVENS SD4886 Map 7

Hare & Hounds

From A6 South, take A590 for Barrow and turn immediately right into village; from M6 junction 36 take A590 for Barrow and after 1½ miles turn right into village

On the wall of the low-beamed lounge bar in this attractive little village pub is a brief history of the pub and its licensees dating back to 1714; also, a wicker-backed Jacobean-style armchair and antique settle on its sloping floor, and old-fashioned brown leatherette dining seats and red-cushioned seats built into the partly panelled walls. The snug front tap room has been refurbished and has an open coal fire and darts, cribbage and dominoes; the juke box and fruit machine are in the separate pool room, down some steps. Bar food includes soup (£1.50), lunchtime sandwiches (from £1.70; toasties from £1.90), filled baked potatoes (from £3.15), ploughman's (£3.95), salads (from £3.95), cumberland sausage (£4.75), home-made steak and kidney pie (£4.95), sirloin steak (£8.50), daily specials, Sunday roast, and children's menu (from £2.50); friendly, prompt service. Well kept Vaux Samson and Wards Thorne plus winter guests on handpump. Outside there is a terrace with nice views of the local fells and Kent estuary, and the pub is also close to Sizergh Castle. *(Recommended by Ian Rorison, Howard Gregory, John Scarisbrick, Peter and Audrey Dowsett, Wayne Brindle, Brian and Anna Marsden)*

Vaux ~ Tenants Colin and Sheila Burrow ~ Real ale ~ Meals and snacks ~ Restaurant ~ (015395) 60408 ~ Children welcome ~ Open 11-3, 6-11; 12-4, 7-10.30 Sun

LITTLE LANGDALE NY3204 Map 9

Three Shires 🍺

From A593 3 miles W of Ambleside take small road signposted The Langdales, Wrynose Pass; then bear left at first fork

For 22 years, the same friendly family have run this pleasant stone-built inn. There are lovely views over the valley to the partly wooded hills below Tilberthwaite Fells, and seats on the terrace with more on a well kept lawn behind the car park, backed by a small oak wood. Inside, the comfortably extended back bar has a warm winter fire in the modern stone fireplace with a couple of recesses for ornaments, antique oak carved settles, country kitchen chairs and stools on its big dark slate flagstones, stripped timbers and a beam-and-joist stripped ceiling, and Lakeland photographs lining the walls; an arch leads through to a small, additional area. Bar food includes soup (£1.95), lunchtime sandwiches (from £2), filled baked potatoes (£3.25), home-made pâté (£3.30), ploughman's (from £4.25), good cumberland sausage (£5.50), pie of the day (£5.75), chicken tikka (£6), daily specials, evening dishes such as herb-crusted fillet of cod (£6.50) and pork steak with a grain mustard sauce (£7.50), home-made puddings (£2.50), and children's meals (£3). The restaurant and snug are no smoking. Well kept Black Sheep Bitter, Marstons Pedigree, Ruddles County, and Websters Yorkshire on handpump, and quite a few malt whiskies and wines; darts, cribbage and dominoes. The three shires are Cumberland, Westmorland and Lancashire, which used to meet at the top of the nearby Wrynose Pass. *(Recommended by Michael and Alison Leyland, Phil and Heidi Cook, Chris and Andy Crow, Anthony Barnes, Jack Morley, Steve Playle, Tina and David Woods-Taylor, H K Dyson, Richard Lewis, Gillian and Michael Wallace, Nigel Woolliscroft)*

Free house ~ Licensee Ian Stephenson ~ Real ale ~ Meals and snacks (no evening food Dec and Jan) ~ Evening restaurant ~ (015394) 37215 ~ Children welcome until 9pm ~ Open 11-11; 12-10.30 Sun; 11-3, 8-10.30 in winter; closed 25 Dec ~ Bedrooms: £35B/£60B

LOWESWATER NY1222 Map 9

Kirkstile

From B5289 follow signs to Loweswater Lake; OS Sheet 89, map reference 140210

For some readers, sitting outside on a warm day at the picnic tables on the lawn and admiring the spectacular surrounding peaks and soaring fells, is their idea of heaven; you can also enjoy the view from the very attractive covered verandah and from the bow windows in one of the rooms off the bar. The bar itself is low-beamed and carpeted, with a big log fire, comfortably cushioned small settles and pews, and partly stripped stone walls. Decent bar food includes sandwiches, home-made soup and filled baked potatoes, omelettes (from £4.75), cumberland sausage (£5), and home-made daily specials (from £4.50); big breakfasts. Well kept Jennings Bitter and Cocker Hoop on handpump, a fair choice of malt whiskies, and decent wine list; darts, dominoes, and a slate shove-ha'penny board; a side games room called the Little Barn has pool, video game and juke box. *(Recommended by H K Dyson, Jack Morley, N J Lawless, John Allsopp, A Preston, R and S Bentley, Enid and Henry Stephens, Chris Rounthwaite, Michael and Alison Leyland, Ian Rorison, Phil and Karen Wood, Simon and Chris Turner, John and Liz Stevenson, S R and A J Ashcroft, John and Christine Lowe)*

Free house ~ Licensees Ken and Shirley Gorley ~ Real ale ~ Meals and snacks (12-2.30, 6-9) ~ Restaurant ~ (01900) 85219 ~ Children welcome ~ Open 11-11 ~ Bedrooms: £30(£40B)/£40(£55B)

Pubs close to motorway junctions are listed at the back of the book.

MELMERBY NY6237 Map 10

Shepherds ★ ⑪ ♀

About half way along A686 Penrith—Alston

The star here is not so much for enormous character but for the fact that readers remain consistently delighted with the very good food, hard-working, friendly staff, and well kept beers – it's a tremendous achievement on the part of the licensees. The menu has changed this year but they have kept their fine range of cheeses – 11 North Country and 6 other English cheeses (£4.80 with home-made granary and white rolls and locally made pickles, chutneys and mustards). All produce is supplied locally and as well as favourites such as lovely barbecued spare ribs (£6.90), chicken leoni (£7.20), and very good venison and roquefort crumble (£7.90), they offer daily specials like chicken and leek or cream of venison soup (from £1.80), stilton and walnut pasta bake (£3.60), a quiche of the day (£4.70), good cumberland casserole (£5.40), pies like lamb and apricot (£6.40; their pies recently won them a large calor gas barbecue), red snapper with cajun spices (£7.20), steaks (from £9), and delicious puddings such as ginger surprise or lemon meringue pie (£2.40); half helpings for children. Much of the main eating area is no smoking. Well kept Boddingtons, Jennings Cumberland and Snecklifter, Macklays 80/-, Marstons Pedigree, and Wadworths 6X on handpump, as well as 50 malt whiskies, a good wine list, country wines, and quite a few bottled continental beers. The bar is divided up into several areas; the heavy beamed room to the left of the door is carpeted and comfortable with bottles on the mantelbeam over the warm open fire, sunny window seats, and sensible tables and chairs, and to the right is a stone-floored drinking part with a few plush bar stools and chairs. At the end is a spacious room with a high-raftered ceiling and pine tables and farmhouse chairs, a woodburning stove, and big wrought-iron candelabra, and steps up to a games area with pool and darts; shove-ha'penny, cribbage, dominoes, fruit machine and juke box. Hartside Nursery Garden, a noted alpine and primula plant specialist, is just over the Hartside Pass, and there are fine views across the green to the Pennines. *(Recommended by William Wright and family, William and Edward Stapley, Richard Holloway, Dick Brown, SS, F J Robinson, Paul Cornock, John Prescott, Graham and Karen Oddey, Ann Reeder, David Craine, E Carter, Laura Darlington, Gianluca Perinetti, Joan and Tony Walker, Michael Butler, Pat and John Millward, Malcolm Taylor, John and Chris Simpson)*

Free house ~ Licensees Martin and Christine Baucutt ~ Real ale ~ Meals and snacks (11-2.30, 6-9.45) ~ (01768) 881217 ~ Children welcome away from bar until 9pm ~ Folk music every 2 weeks, Fri evenings ~ Open 10.30-3, 6-11; closed 25 Dec ~ Several holiday cottages

NEAR SAWREY SD3796 Map 9

Tower Bank Arms

B5285 towards the Windermere ferry

As seen in the Peter Rabbit films, this bustling pub backs on to Beatrix Potter's Hill Top Farm (owned by the National Trust) and so can get busy at peak times. The low-beamed main bar has a good traditional atmosphere, high-backed settles on the rough slate floor, local hunting photographs and signed photographs of celebrities on the walls, and a grandfather clock; Emma or Maxwell the pub's labradors may be sitting in front of the big cooking range with its fine log fire. Lunchtime bar food includes soup (£1.90), filled rolls (from £2.25), ploughman's (from £3.80), home-made quiche (£4.90), and a home-made pie of the day (£4.95); more substantial evening main meals such as local trout (£6.75), grilled gammon and eggs (£6.90), venison or duckling (£7), and puddings (from £2.50). Well kept Theakstons Best, XB and Old Peculier, and Mild, and a weekly changing guest beer on handpump, as well as 28 malt whiskies, Belgian fruit beers and other foreign beers, and wine bottled for the pub; darts, shove-ha'penny, cribbage, dominoes, backgammon, chess and Shut-the-box. Seats outside have pleasant views of the wooded Claife Heights. This is a good area for golf, sailing, birdwatching, fishing (they have a licence for two rods a day on selected waters in the area), and walking, but if you want to stay at the pub, you'll have to book well in advance. *(Recommended by R and S Bentley, R Hatton-Evans, Brian and Anna Marsden, Vann and Terry Prime, Jack Morley, H K Dyson, Gwyneth and Salvo Spadaro-Dutturi, S R and A J Ashcroft)*

Free house ~ Licensee Philip Broadley ~ Real ale ~ Meals and lunchtime snacks (not 25 Dec) ~ Restaurant ~ (015394) 36334 ~ Children in eating area of bar at lunchtime, in restaurant in evening ~ Open 11-3, 5.30(6 in winter)-11; closed evening 25 Dec ~ Bedrooms: £32B/£44B

SCALES NY3427 Map 9

White Horse

A66 1½ miles NE of Threlkeld: keep your eyes skinned – it looks like a farmhouse up on a slope

This isolated old farmhouse – under new local licensees since it was in the Guide last – has been partly refurbished, and the cosy little no-smoking snug and old kitchen now have all sorts of farming implements such as a marmalade slicer, butter churns, kettles, and a black range. The comfortable beamed bar has warm winter fires, hunting pictures and local hunting cartoons on the walls. Good, carefully presented bar food includes home-made soup (£1.95), grilled black pudding (£2.75), Flookburgh shrimps in spicy butter (£3.50), lovely mussels in a lemony cream sauce and Thai spices, Waberthwaite sausage with home-made damson chutney (£5.50), salads (from £5.50), good lasagne, Borrowdale trout with lemon and capers (£5.95), ratatouille with garlic bread (£6.75), roast duckling (£8.50), sirloin steak (£9.90), and puddings like sticky toffee pudding (from £2.50). They only serve Cumbrian ales: well kept Blencathra Bitter, Jennings Bitter, and Yates Bitter on handpump; no noisy games machines or music. From the cluster of pub and farm buildings, tracks lead up into the splendidly daunting and rocky fells around Blencathra – which have names like Foule Crag and Sharp Edge. *(Recommended by L Dixon, Tina and David Woods-Taylor, C A Hall, R J and A Parmenter, Paul Bailey, H K Dyson)*

Free house ~ Licensee Bruce Jackson ~ Real ale ~ Meals and snacks (not Mon) ~ (017687) 79241 ~ Children in eating areas; under 5s must eat before 7pm ~ Open 12-2.30, 6.45-10.30(11 Sat); closed Mon

SEATHWAITE SD2396 Map 9

Newfield

Duddon Valley, nr Ulpha (ie not Seathwaite in Borrowdale)

With good walks from the doorstep of this cottagey 16th-c inn, it's hardly surprising that walkers and climbers crowd in at weekends. The slate-floored bar still manages to keep a relaxed and genuinely local atmosphere, and there's a comfortable side room, and a games room with pool, darts, and dominoes. Good value bar food includes filled granary french bread or proper home-made soup (£1.75), big cumberland sausages (£4.95), home-made steak pie or a vegetarian dish (from £4.95), huge gammon steaks with local farm eggs (£6.50), and good steaks; the restaurant is no smoking. Well kept Theakstons Best, XB and Old Peculier and a guest such as Marstons Pedigree or Morlands Old Speckled Hen on handpump, and several Polish vodkas; good service. Tables out in the nice garden have good hill views. The pub owns and lets the next-door cottages. *(Recommended by J Hibberd, Romey Heaton, LM, H K Dyson, Jack Morley, Catharine Driver, John Unsworth, Prof I H Rorison)*

Free house ~ Licensee Chris Burgess ~ Real ale ~ Meals and snacks ~ Restaurant ~ (01229) 716208 ~ Well behaved children welcome ~ Open 11-3, 6-11; 11-11 Sat; 11-3, 7-10.30 Sun ~ S/c flats available

Sunday opening is generally 12-3 and 7-10.30 throughout England, but many pubs stay open all day in summer.

SEDBERGH SD6692 Map 10

Dalesman 🍺

Main St

This nicely modernised old pub is decorated with horsebrasses and spigots, Vernon Stokes gundog pictures, various stuffed animals including a badger and a greater spotted woodpecker, tropical fish, and a blunderbuss. There are cushioned farmhouse chairs and stools around dimpled copper tables, a raised stone hearth with a log-effect gas fire, and lots of stripped stone and beams. Through stone arches on the right a no-smoking buttery area serves good value food such as soup (£1.50), filled rolls and toasties (from £2), filled baked potatoes or ploughman's (from £4), steak and kidney pie (£4.95), and daily specials like gammon and egg (£5.95), local lamb chops or steak and kidney pie, fresh poached salmon (£6.95), half a roast duckling (£8.50), and a huge mixed grill (£12.50); Sunday lunch (£4.95); friendly, helpful service. Well kept Ind Coope Burton, Tetleys Bitter, and Theakstons Best on handpump; dominoes, fruit machine, and piped music. There are some picnic tables out in front; small car park. *(Recommended by John Fazakerley, Paul McPherson, Addie and Irene Henry, Lynn Sharpless, Bob Eardley, Dono and Carol Leaman, George Atkinson, Peter and Audrey Dowsett, JKW)*

Free house ~ Licensees Barry and Irene Garnett ~ Real ale ~ Meals and snacks ~ Restaurant ~ (015396) 21183 ~ Children in eating area of bar and in restaurant ~ Open 11-11; 11-3, 6-11 in winter ~ Bedrooms: £25S/£50B

STAINTON NY4928 Map 10

Kings Arms

1¾ miles from M6 junction 40: village signposted from A66 towards Keswick, though quickest to fork left at A592 roundabout then turn first right

The roomy open-plan bar in this pleasant, modernised old pub has leatherette wall banquettes, stools and armchairs, wood-effect tables, brasses on the black beams, and prints and paintings of the Lake District on the swirly cream walls. Bar food includes home-made soup (£1.35), sandwiches (from £1.80; toasties from £1.95), filled baked potatoes (from £3.30), cumberland sausage with egg (£4.20), home-made steak and kidney pie (£4.70), breast of chicken with sage and onion stuffing (£5.10), vegetable lasagne (£5.80), sirloin steak (£9.45), puddings (from £1.70), children's dishes (£2.50), and daily specials (from £3.75). Well kept Boddingtons, Whitbreads Castle Eden, and guest beers on handpump or electric pump. Sensibly placed darts, dominoes, cards, fruit machine, and piped music. There are tables outside on the side terrace and a small lawn. *(Recommended by Ian Rorison, Roger Bellingham, Anthony Barnes, Roger and Pauline Pearce, Mike and Wendy Proctor, John and Christine Lowe, Gary Roberts, Ann Stubbs, Richard Holloway)*

Whitbreads ~ Tenants James and Anne Downie ~ Real ale ~ Meals and snacks (not 24-25 Dec, not 1 Jan) ~ (01768) 862778 ~ Children in eating area of bar until 9pm ~ Open 11.30-3, 6.30-11; winter weekday evening opening 7pm and closed winter Mon lunchtime

THRELKELD NY3325 Map 9

Salutation

Old main rd, bypassed by A66 W of Penrith

After a day on the fells, this unpretentious little village local is where walkers head for, and the tiled floor is used to muddy boots. The several simply furnished connecting rooms can get quite crowded in summer, but even then there's a good atmosphere and the staff are welcoming. Bar food includes sandwiches (from £2.15), soup (£2.25), basket meals (from £3.50), large ploughman's (from £4.35), Hungarian goulash, sweet and sour pork or good steak and mushroom pie (all

£4.95), daily specials like chicken in red wine, beef curry or king prawns in garlic and ginger, and puddings (from £2.15). Well kept Theakstons Best, XB and Old Peculier and guests like Courage Directors, Jennings Bitter, Mitchells Lancaster Bomber and Morlands Old Speckled Hen on handpump. The spacious upstairs children's room has a pool table and juke box (oldies); there are also darts, cribbage, dominoes, video game and piped music. The owners let a couple of holiday cottages in the village. *(Recommended by J W Jones, H K Dyson, Mike and Wendy Proctor, S L Clemens, Dr Pete Crawshaw, Richard Holloway, Nigel Woolliscroft)*

S & N ~ Tenants Ken and Rose Burchill ~ Real ale ~ Meals and snacks (not 25 Dec) ~ (017687) 79614 ~ Children welcome (must be in family room after 9pm) ~ Open 11-3, 5.30-11; 12-2, 6-11 in winter

TIRRIL NY5126 Map 10

Queens Head 🍴 🛏

3½ miles from M6 junction 40; take A66 towards Brough, A6 towards Shap, then B5320 towards Ullswater

Although the emphasis in this popular and friendly inn is very much on the imaginative food, there's a good local atmosphere, too. The oldest parts of the bar have low bare beams, black panelling, high-backed settles, and a roomy inglenook fireplace (once a cupboard for smoking hams). The floor underneath the carpet is actually raw rock, quarried out for the pub in the early 18th c. Attractively presented, very good food from a menu that serves both the bar and restaurant might include unusual dishes such as kangaroo (£5.95), wild boar goulash (£9.50), charcoal-grilled ostrich steaks (£14.95), alligator, emu, and crocodile, as well as more straightforward dishes like good soup (£2.25), home-made chicken liver and brandy pâté (£2.95), quite a few excellent pasta dishes such as paglia e fieno (green and white noodles with smoked salmon, parmesan and cream, fettucini marinara (noodles in tomato sauce with prawns and tuna in white wine) or lasagne (£3 starter, £5.95 main course), hazelnut and lentil loaf (£7.25), steak in ale pie (£6.95), steaks (from £8.95), beef florianna (£10.95), fresh fish dishes, and children's dishes (£2.95); attentive service. Well kept Deakins White Rabbit, Marstons Pedigree, Morlands Old Speckled Hen, Theakstons Best and Youngers Scotch on handpump; darts, pool, and dominoes in the back bar. The pub is very close to a number of interesting places, such as Dalemain House at Dacre. *(Recommended by John Waller, Tina and David Woods-Taylor, David Heath, John and Phyllis Maloney, Mike and Wendy Proctor, H K Dyson, Neville Kenyon, Johnathan and Ann Tross, G O Cook, Mr and Mrs B Fletcher, Terry and Eileen Stott, Mr and Mrs J Futers, John Barlow)*

Free house ~ Licensees Nunzio and Lynne D'Aprile ~ Real ale ~ Meals and snacks (till 10pm) ~ Restaurant ~ (01768) 863219 ~ Well behaved children welcome ~ Open 12-2.30(3 Sat), 6-11 ~ Bedrooms: /£42B

TROUTBECK NY4103 Map 7

Mortal Man

Upper Rd, nr High Green – OS Sheet 90, map ref 411035

Very well run and spotlessly kept, this relaxing inn is surrounded by marvellous scenery. The bustling, partly-panelled bar has a big roaring fire, a nice medley of seats including a cushioned settle and some farmhouse chairs around copper-topped tables, horsebrasses on its dark beams, a friendly black dog – and no piped music; there's also a small, cosy lounge. Good bar food includes lunchtime things like home-made soup (£2), smoked trout pâté, sandwiches (from £2.25), ploughman's (£4), and vegetable curry (£4) or poached breast of chicken with asparagus sauce (£5.25), as well as smoked wood pigeon with apple sauce and celery sticks (£3.50), vegetarian moussaka (£5.25), turkey stroganoff or lamb liver and smoked bacon casserole (£5.75), pork hotpot (£6), and puddings (£2.50); very good breakfasts and helpful, friendly staff. The restaurant, with its big picture windows, is no smoking.

Well kept Theakstons Best and Youngers Scotch on handpump and on electric pump; darts and dominoes. *(Recommended by Kim and Anne Schofield, RJH, A Preston, Roger Calrow, H K Dyson, Peter and Audrey Dowsett, Gillian and Michael Wallace, Mrs B Lemon; also in Good Hotel Guide)*

Free house ~ Licensee Christopher Poulsom ~ Real ale ~ Meals and snacks (not Mon evening) ~ Restaurant ~ (015394) 33193 ~ Children in eating area of bar until 9pm ~ Open 12-2.30, 5.30-11; closed mid Nov-mid Feb ~ Bedrooms: £35B/£70B

Queens Head ★ (�$) 🛏

A592 N of Windermere

Cumbria Dining Pub of the Year

We have had more enthusiastic reports about this bustling 17th-c coaching inn than any other pub in the Lake District – or for that matter, the country. The bright bar has a massive Elizabethan four-poster bed as the basis of its serving counter, other fine antique carving, cushioned antique settles among more orthodox furniture, and two roaring log fires in imposing fireplaces. The bar rambles through some half-dozen attractively decorated rooms, including an unusual lower gallery, a comfortable dining area and lots of alcoves and heavy beams. Exceptionally good, interesting food includes home-made soup, lunchtime filled french bread, a pastry tart filled with spinach, baked egg and mustard and topped with fresh parmesan or home-made cajun spiced lamb and mint sausage on grated celeriac with lemon scented yoghurt dressing (both £4.25), fresh haddock in a herb crust with garlic mash, tomato coulis and julienne of snow peas and carrots (£4.95), delicious cod steak with curried spices and wild mushrooms and served with a dried fruit sauce or goat's cheese filled with olives and fresh basil in filo pastry with spinach and capers and a pesto beurre blanc garnished with roast hazelnuts (£6.95), good haunch of venison with hotch potch of potato, leek and savoy cabbage with a rich beetroot flavoured jus (£10.95), and beautifully presented puddings such as orange and chocolate tart with a Grand Marnier sabayon (£2.75); other dishes readers have enjoyed include good white cabbage, sage and mustard soup, calvados-flavoured duck mousse with a citrus and mint dressing, lamb noisette with roast parsnips and mint, super turbot on a bed of samphire (and other highly praised fish dishes), and delicious pheasant breast; there will be a wait at busy times. Well kept Boddingtons, XB, Mitchells Lancaster Bomber, Tetleys and two guest beers on handpump; friendly service. Darts, dominoes, cards, chess and piped music. Plenty of seats outside have a fine view over the Trout valley to Applethwaite moors. The bedrooms over the bar can be a bit noisy. *(Recommended by John Waller, A Preston, Paul Boot, Mick Hitchman, LM, C and G Fraser, Darrell and Frances Kemp, Paul Bailey, Roger and Pauline Pearce, Walker and Debra Lapthorne, Mike Beiley, Julie Peters, Colin Blinkhorn, Tina and David Woods-Taylor, Carl Travis, Phil and Heidi Cook, Robert and Ann Lees, Jack Morley, Joy and Peter Heatherley, Dene Caton, R and B Davies, Gwen and Steve Walker, H K Dyson, R L W and Dizzy, Neville Kenyon, Ernest Russell, Wayne Brindle, Mr and Mrs Jacob, Simon Watkins, J S M Sheldon, George Atkinson, R W Saunders, Mrs B Lemon, Gillian and Michael Wallace, Andy and Jill Kassube, F Jarman, Richard Fawcett, Liz and Julian Long, Anne and Brian Birtwistle)*

Free house ~ Licensees Mark Stewardson and Joanne Sherratt ~ Real ale ~ Meals and snacks ~ Restaurant ~ (015394) 32174 ~ Children welcome ~ Open 11-11 ~ Bedrooms: £37.50B/£55B

ULVERSTON SD2978 Map 7

Bay Horse (♥) 🍸

Canal Foot signposted off A590 and then you wend your way past the huge Glaxo factory

The beautifully presented, very good food is what draws people to this rather civilised and very well run inn. In the bar, food is served at lunchtime only and might include filled sandwiches (£1.60), home-made soup such as chilled potato and lovage with cream and toasted almonds (from £1.95), home-made herb and cheese pâté or savoury terrine with cranberry and ginger purée (£4.75; as a main course £7.50), smoked chicken and button mushrooms in a tomato, cream and brandy sauce with puff pastry topping (£5.95), farm chicken with pineapple, shallots and red chilli peppers with honey, marsala and blackcurrant vinegar (£14.50), fillets of lemon sole filled with fresh shrimps and avocado with a white wine and fresh herb cream sauce (£14.95), and puddings such as sticky toffee pudding with butterscotch sauce or apple and strawberry pie (£3.25). There's also the grill with well hung Scotch steaks, and a no-smoking conservatory restaurant (with exceptional views across to Morecambe Bay, and where bookings are essential); the three-course lunch is fine value for £15.75 (separate evening menu). Well kept Boddingtons, Mitchells Lancaster Bomber, Morlands Old Speckled Hen and so forth on handpump, a decent choice of spirits, and an impressive and interesting New World wine list; lovely home-made shortbread with the good coffee. The bar has a relaxed atmosphere and a huge stone horse's head, as well as attractive wooden armchairs, some pale green plush built-in wall banquettes, glossy hardwood traditional tables, blue plates on a delft shelf, and black beams and props with lots of horsebrasses. Magazines are dotted about, there's a handsomely marbled green granite fireplace, and decently reproduced piped music; darts, bar billiards, shove-ha'penny, and dominoes. Out on the terrace are some picnic tables. They hold friendly and informal day cookery demonstrations. The owners also run a very good restaurant at their Miller Howe hotel on Windermere. *(Recommended by Mick Hitchman, David Carr, Neville Kenyon, Robert and Ann Lees, Malcolm Taylor, Kim Maidment, Philip Vernon, Jack Morley, John Derbyshire, M J Brooks, Anne and Brian Birtwistle, John and Chris Simpson)*

Free house ~ Licensee Robert Lyons ~ Real ale ~ Lunchtime bar meals and snacks (not Mon) ~ Separate lunchtime and evening restaurant (not Mon lunchtimes) ~ (01229) 583972 ~ Children under 12 in bar lounge only ~ Open 11-11; 12-10.30 Sun ~ Bedrooms: £65B/£130B inc dinner

YANWATH NY5128 Map 9

Gate 🍴

2¼ miles from M6 junction 40; A66 towards Brough, then right on A6, right on B5320, then follow village signpost

In a quiet area of the Lake District, this bustling village local serves particularly good inventive food. This might include sandwiches, home-made soup (£2.25), good 'black devils' (sliced black pudding in a thin mildly peppery cream sauce – an excellent starter or very light snack at £2.95), mushroom stuffed pancakes (£3.25), smoked fish pie, cumbrian cassoulet, chicken, ham and egg pie or vegetable crumble (all £5.50), sirloin steak (£9.75), excellent gin and lime duck (£10.50), and puddings such as baked chocolate cheesecake with pecan nuts, spiced winter fruit compote or hot sticky toffee pudding (£2.50). The simple turkey-carpeted bar, full of chatting regulars, has a log fire in an attractive stone inglenook and one or two nice pieces of furniture and middle-eastern brassware among more orthodox seats; or you can go through to eat in a more staid back two-level no-smoking dining room which is used as a restaurant on Saturday nights. Well kept Theakstons Best and two changing guest beers such as Flowers IPA and Charles Wells Fargo on handpump, and obliging service; darts, dominoes, and very unobtrusive piped music; the border collie is called Domino. There are a few picnic tables outside. *(Recommended by Richard Holloway, John Prescott, Paul McPherson, Steve and Carolyn, H K Dyson, Mike and Wendy Proctor, Terry and Eileen Stott, David Heath, Gail Swanson)*

Free house ~ Licensees Ian and Sue Rhind ~ Real ale ~ Meals and snacks ~ Restaurant ~ (01768) 862386 ~ Children welcome ~ Open 12-3, 6.30(6 Sat)-11; 12-2.30, 7-11 in winter

Lucky Dip

Besides the fully inspected pubs, you might like to try these Lucky Dips recommended to us and described by readers (if you do, please send us reports):

☆ Ainstable [NY5346], *New Crown*: Reopened in association with Dukes Head at Armathwaite (see main entries); good traditional well cooked food in simple flagstoned bar or small attractive dining room, striking cleanliness, short choice of good value wines; well behaved dogs welcome; comfortable bedrooms *(Richard Holloway)*

☆ Alston [Main St; NY7246], *Turks Head*: Convivial local with good value food, pleasant landlord, well kept Boddingtons and Theakstons, spotless housekeeping; bar counter dividing big front room into two areas, back lounge with cosy fire and small tables; at top of steep cobbled street *(L Dixon)*

☆ Ambleside [Market Sq; NY3804], *Queens*: Neatly comfortable hotel bar, good value food inc vegetarian, generous puddings and good children's menu, prompt friendly service, well kept ales such as Boddingtons, Hook Norton, Jennings, Theakstons XB, separate cellar bar with pool room; shame about the piped music; well equipped bedrooms *(Andy and Penny Scott, Ron Gentry, Simon Watkins)*

Ambleside [just above Mkt Sq], *Royal Oak*: Busy beamed and carpeted local with rolls in main bar area and more substantial meals in another section across courtyard; well kept Theakstons XB and Youngers Scotch, friendly staff, outside seats *(George Atkinson, H K Dyson)*

☆ nr Ambleside [A592 N of Troutbeck; NY4007], *Kirkstone Pass*: Lakeland's highest inn, best out of season, with fine surrounding scenery, not smart but cheery, with lots of old photographs and bric-a-brac, good coffee, wide choice of whiskies, well kept Tetleys, friendly staff, open fire, lively amusements (inc parrot), simple food, maybe piped Classic FM; bedrooms, all with four-posters *(H K Dyson, John and Joan Nash, John and Maureen Watt, LYM)*

Appleby [25 Clifford St; NY6921], *Midland*: Worth knowing especially for railway buffs, as this severe-looking but comfortable building is right by the station on the famous Settle—Carlisle line, with lots of railway memorabilia in its two smallish bars; well kept Jennings, open all day *(Dave Braisted)*

Arrad Foot [SD3180], *Racehorse*: Basic but very welcoming little country local, lovely views across valley, well kept Thwaites *(Jack and Philip Paxton)*

☆ Askham [village crossroads by lower green; NY5123], *Queens Head*: Comfortably pubby two-room lounge, open fire, lots of beams, copper and brass, usual food from sandwiches to steaks, particularly well kept Wards Sheffield Best, wide choice of wines, friendly efficient service; children welcome, pleasant garden; bedrooms comfortable with creaking floorboards *(Richard Holloway, H K Dyson, Angus Lyon, J V Dadswell, LYM)*

☆ Bampton [NY5118], *St Patricks Well*: Pretty little village local, friendly landlord, well kept Jennings Bitter and Mild, bar food inc good shepherd's pie and steaks, big open fire, pool room, darts, juke box; a couple of seats outside; bedrooms good value, huge breakfasts *(Dr B and Mrs P Baker, H K Dyson, BB)*

Bampton Grange [NY5218], *Crown & Mitre*: Enthusiastic welcoming landlady, interesting attractively priced food, Boddingtons ale, darts and quiz teams; bedrooms simple but clean – good value *(Rita and Keith Pollard)*

☆ Barbon [off A683 Kirkby Lonsdale—Sedbergh; SD6383], *Barbon Inn*: Charming village setting below fells, with sheltered garden, some individual furnishings in small somewhat hotelish rooms off plain little bar with big blacked range, well kept Theakstons Best and Old Peculier, decent well served food from sandwiches up inc vegetarian dishes, no-smoking restaurant, homely service; children welcome, attractive old-fashioned bedrooms *(John and Joan Nash, Mrs Hilarie Taylor, Paul and Sue Merrick, R Davies, Sue Holland, Dave Webster, LYM)*

☆ Blencogo [signed off B5302 Wigton—Silloth; NY1948], *New Inn*: Must book for very good food – real serious cooking – in bright and simply modernised former village local, log fire, Mitchells ale, decent wines and whiskies, a few big Cumbrian landscapes, pleasant service; no food Sat-Mon evenings, maybe faint piped pop music *(BB)*

Bowness on Windermere [Rayrigg Rd; SD4097], *Olde John Peel*: Lounge, panelled bar and back family room, hunting memorabilia, good service, bar food, Theakstons ales; TV, darts, fruit machine and piped music; handy for World of Beatrix Potter *(SLC)*

Bowness on Windermere, *Westmorland Arms*: Victorian house, formerly pub, restaurant, then pizza place, now popular and cosy drinkers' pub; friendly staff, good choice of well kept ales eg Jennings Cumberland and Sneck Lifter, Timothy Taylors Landlord, Yates; bar food; open all day *(Richard Lewis)*

Brampton [Wallbankgate; NY5361], *Belted Will*: Cosy cheerful atmosphere, good value generous food, well kept Bass and a guest, friendly staff, dining room, crazy sheepdog called Rob *(Bob Griffiths)*; [old A69, Newcastle Rd], *Sands House*: Generous good value food inc children's, friendly staff; well kept Jennings *(Roger and Pauline Pearce)*; [High Cross St, just off A69], *White Lion*: Warm and friendly old-world Victorian hotel, real ales inc Whitbreads Castle Eden, good home-cooked food, two comfortable well decorated rooms with coal fires, obliging service; bedrooms *(William Irving)*

☆ Broughton in Furness [The Square; SD2187], *Manor Arms*: From outside scarcely looks like a pub, but has wide range of well kept ales such as Bass, Butterknowle Banner, Courage Best, Hopback wheat beer, Timothy Taylors Landlord, Ushers Spring Fever, Worthington BB and Yates; good snacks, comfortable relaxed atmosphere; lovely bedrooms *(Camille Walsh, H K Dyson)*

Broughton in Furness [Princes St], *Black Cock*: Olde-worlde pub dating from 15th c, good value food, friendly service, cosy fireside, well kept Courage-related ales; open all day Tues; bedrooms *(Michael Taylor, H K Dyson)*

nr Broughton in Furness [Broughton Mills, off A593 N; SD2290], *Blacksmiths Arms*: Tucked away in the middle of nowhere, unchanging three-room 18th-c pub, log fires, friendly young landlord, well kept Theakstons; bedrooms *(Jack and Philip Paxton, Gillian and Michael Wallace)*

☆ Buttermere [NY1817], *Fish*: Spacious and smartly refurbished former coaching inn on NT property between Buttermere and Crummock Water, wide range of good value bar food from fresh sandwiches to trout, good range of well kept Jennings and Theakstons and guests such as Charles Wells Bombardier and Morlands Old Speckled Hen; can get crowded; bedrooms *(G O Cook, E A George, H and D Payne, Janet Stephenson, Christopher Warner, HKD, SLC, BB)*

☆ Caldbeck [B5299; NY3239], *Oddfellows Arms*: Comfortable nicely extended village pub doing well under enthusiastic young owner, wide choice of good generous food from overflowing filled rolls up, well kept Jennings and guest ales, friendly staff, pleasant dining room, careful housekeeping *(David and Margaret Bloomfield, Ian and Lynn Brown, Margaret Davis)*

Carlisle [Botchergate; NY4056], *Caledonian Cask House*: Large open-plan pub with lots of seating, prints, railway memorabilia, some flagstones, board ceiling and panelling, wide choice of good value home-cooked lunchtime bar food with two-for-one bargains, Whitbreads-related ales and a couple of interesting guests, Weston's farm cider, busy friendly staff; pool, fruit machine, TV *(Richard Lewis, M Walker, SLC)*; [nr stn], *Coronation*: Large open-plan bar, friendly staff, good range of real ales *(Nigel Hopkins)*; [English St], *Crown & Mitre*: Cosy and comfortable panelled bar in big well equipped hotel, steam railway memorabilia, good lunchtime buffet, friendly staff; bedrooms comfortable *(Richard Lewis)*; [John St, Caldewgate (A595 W)], *Maltsters Arms*: Welcoming down-to-earth little local, very friendly obliging staff, well kept Jennings, wide choice of good value freshly prepared straightforward food (not Sun evening), darts; cl lunchtime Mon-Fri *(Pete Baker)*

☆ Cartmel [The Square; SD3879], *Kings Arms*: Picturesque pub nicely placed at the head of the attractive town square – rambling heavy-beamed bar, mix of furnishings from

traditional settles to banquettes, usual bar food and no-smoking restaurant all day, well kept Whitbreads-related ales, children welcome, seats outside *(H K Dyson, M J Morgan, E A George, Julie Peters, Colin Blinkhorn, Wayne Brindle, LYM)*

☆ Cockermouth [Main St; NY1231], *Bush*: Four welcoming and cosy communicating areas, two with carpets and banquettes, two with bare boards, beams and old tables, attractive decor, well kept Jennings (full range) and guest beers, very friendly bar staff, open fires; cheap and cheerful generous lunchtime food, fairly unobtrusive piped music; children allowed *(Margaret Mason, Dave Thompson, Mike, Ian and Gayle Woodhead, A and R Lees)*

☆ Cockermouth [Kirkgate], *Bitter End*: Interestingly refurbished reopened pub, three main rooms each characterised by different atmosphere, old local pictures and sporting memorabilia, tiny see-in brewery behind back room producing home brews (strength depends on landlord's mood at the time), also Ind Coope Burton, Jennings, Tetleys and guest beers, decent lunchtime bar food *(Mike, Ian and Gayle Woodhead, A and R Lees)*

☆ Cockermouth [Main St], *Huntsman*: Well refurbished Jennings pub, good well priced food inc bargain Sun lunch (queues for this), well kept ales, very friendly landlord, quick service even when busy; interesting local photographs, juke box; open all day *(Mike, Ian and Gayle Woodhead, R J Walden)*

☆ Coniston [Yewdale Rd; SD3098], *Black Bull*: Big welcoming beamed pub with red banquettes and stools, log fires, piped classical music, relaxed atmosphere, filling home-made bar food promptly served all day, well kept S&N ales and own Old Man of Coniston, friendly staff, Donald Campbell photographs; separate bar suiting walkers; restaurant, tables in courtyard; comfortable good value bedrooms, good breakfasts *(Catherine Sawyers, P J S Goward, Neil and Anita Christopher, Mayur Shah)*

☆ Coniston [signed from centre], *Sun*: Attractively placed below mountains (doubling as rescue post), with interesting Donald Campbell and other Lakeland photographs in basic back bar, friendly atmosphere, good log fire, bar food, well kept Jennings, Marstons Pedigree and Tetleys from the deep granite cellar; children in carpeted no-smoking eating area and restaurant, darts, dominoes, maybe piped music; open all day; comfortable bedrooms *(George Atkinson, J Finney, Tina and David Woods-Taylor, G S Miller, LYM)*

☆ Cowgill [nr Dent Stn, on Dent—Garsdale Head rd; SD7587], *Sportsmans*: Fine Dentdale location with good nearby walks; home-made bar food lunchtime and evening, well kept S&N ales, drinkable wine, log fires, plainish bar/lounge with darts in snug at one end and pool room at the other, no piped music; bedrooms overlooking lovely river *(Peter and Audrey Dowsett)*

☆ Crook [B5284 Kendal—Bowness; SD4795],

Sun: Extensive range of first-class food and good value wines, a surprise find in this otherwise quietly straightforward more or less open-plan village local; well kept Jennings and Theakstons, welcoming fire *(Leslie and June Lyon, A Preston, RJH, LYM)*

Dean [just off A5086 S of Cockermouth; NY0825], *Royal Yew*: Very busy modernised village local, good range of good value food, efficient service, well kept Jennings, Stones and Theakstons *(W R Cunliffe)*

☆ **Deanscales** [A5086 S of Cockermouth; NY0927], *Old Posting House*: Homely and friendly comfortable split-level dining pub, very popular for good value generous well presented home-made food from sandwiches to steaks, interesting old fittings surviving from posting and coaching days, lots of brass and copper, Lakeland and heavy-horse prints; well kept Jennings Bitter and Cumberland, no-smoking restaurant *(R Davies, M E A Horler, W R Cunliffe, Jackie Moffat, BB)*

☆ **Dent** [Main St; SD7187], *George & Dragon*: Clean, comfortable and quiet pub/hotel, local Dent Bitter, Ramsbottom and T'Owd Tup, also S&N ales, good generously served bar food, bargain Sun lunch, reasonably priced evening restaurant, no piped music; pleasant staff, pool, darts; bedrooms comfortable *(Peter and Audrey Dowsett, Paul McPherson, D Gardner, J Turner, Warren Beverley)*

Dufton [NY6925], *Stag*: Small, basic pub in lovely unspoilt village on Pennine Way; friendly licensee, good food, four or five well kept ales inc Jennings *(Steve Jennings, DA)*

☆ **Durdar** [NY4151], *Black Lion*: Well kept Theakstons Best, very pleasant staff, no-smoking room, well presented home-made food in huge helpings, all extremely clean; handy for Carlisle racecourse, not far from M6 junction 42 *(Joe Green, Mr and Mrs J H Cookson)*

Eamont Bridge [handy for M6 junction 40; NY5328], *Beehive*: Pleasant roadside pub, seats out under hanging baskets, cosy bar with good straightforward food, open fire, Whitbreads-related ales; big back play area, attractive village *(Angus Lyon)*

Ennerdale Bridge [NY0716], *Shepherds Arms*: Good fresh food, decent coffee, modest prices *(Ian Rorison)*

☆ **Eskdale** [NY1400], *Brook House*: Wide choice of good generous home-cooked food served cheerfully in small family-run hotel, small plush bar, comfortable lounge, open fires, Jennings Cumberland, good views; handy for Ravenglass rly, good bedrooms *(G T and R M Ross)*

Eskdale [Bleabeck, midway between Boot and Hardknott Pass; NY1400], *Woolpack*: Good value simple country inn just below the Pass, popular with walkers ; bedrooms *(H K Dyson)*

☆ **Far Sawrey** [SD3893], *Sawrey*: Simple but comfortable and welcoming stable bar with tables in wooden stalls, harness on rough white walls, big helpings of good simple lunchtime bar food, well kept Black Sheep Bitter and Special and Jennings, pleasant staff;

separate hotel bar, evening restaurant; seats on nice lawn, beautiful setting, walkers, children and dogs welcome; bedrooms comfortable and well equipped *(Gordon Smith, Simon Barber, Ron Gentry, M Joyner, Jack Morley, LM, LYM)*

☆ **Faugh** [off A69 in Warwick Bridge at Heads Nook, Castle Carrock sign; NY5155], *String of Horses*: Welcoming 17th-c coaching inn, several cosy communicating beamed rooms, log fires, some interesting carved furniture, prints and panelling; good bar food from sandwiches to steak; keg beer but wide choice of wines; piped music, darts, pool, dominoes, fruit machine, video game; attractive sheltered lantern-lit terrace; restaurant, children welcome; bedrooms *(R E and P Pearce, E V Walder, Jack and Heather Coyle, LYM)*

Glenridding [back of main car park, top of road; NY3917], *Travellers Rest*: Friendly unpretentious bar with big helpings of food for hungry walkers, well kept Whitbreads-related ales, simple decor; great views from seats outside *(N J Lawless)*

Grange Over Sands [Grange Fell Rd; off B5277; SD4077], *Hardcrag Hall*: Friendly former 16th-c farmhouse, two character panelled rooms and dining rooms, good choice of bar meals with children's helpings, well kept Thwaites and a weekend guest beer, reasonable prices; bedrooms *(John Scarisbrick, P A Legon)*

☆ **Grasmere** [main bypass rd; NY3406], *Swan*: Upmarket but relaxed and individual, with friendly service, lively little public bar, quieter old-fashioned lounge popular with older people (this is where children go), oak beams, armchairs, velvet curtains, prints and swords, inglenook log fires; well prepared bar food, keg beer but good malt whiskies, tables in garden, picturesque surroundings, drying room for walkers; easy parking, comfortable bedrooms *(H and D Payne, LYM)*

Grasmere, *Red Lion*: Ideal spot in lovely village, very friendly staff, tasty bar food in plush lounge bar and cane-chair conservatory, well priced restaurant meals, well kept beers, good range of malt whiskies; good bedrooms *(A Preston)*

Hartsop [A592; NY4113], *Brothers Water*: Walkers' pub in magnificent setting at the bottom of Kirkstone Pass; recently completely refurbished *(H K Dyson)*

Haverigg [Main St; SD1678], *Harbour*: Super cheap sandwiches and enormous cumberland sausage with well kept Boddingtons and Theakstons Best in unpretentious atmospheric pub handy for this unsmart but enjoyable resort's beautiful beaches; great sailing and fishing *(David and Margaret Bloomfield)*

☆ **Haverthwaite** [A590 Barrow rd; SD3284], *Dicksons Arms*: Good generous food inc delicious puddings and well kept Jennings and Marstons Pedigree in pleasant low-beamed bar with woodburner and hunting prints; prompt friendly service, restaurant *(Roger and Christine Mash, Dr J Norman, Margaret and Roy Randle, Catherine and Martin Snelling)*

Haweswater [NY4914], *Haweswater*: On reservoir, away from the crowds – just those here for the walks and spectacular scenery ; bedrooms *(H K Dyson)*

Hawkshead [SD3598], *Red Lion*: Friendly modernised local with some old-fashioned touches, good log fire, well kept Courage-related ales with guests such as Jennings, good range of usual food, piped music; bedrooms *(Richard Lewis, SLC, LYM)*; *Sun*: Useful for serving lunchtime food when others here have stopped; friendly staff, big dining area, well kept Courage-related ales inc takeaway packs; piped music, TV; bedrooms *(Richard Lewis, Chris and Andy Crow, SLC)*

☆ Hesket Newmarket [signed from B5299 in Caldbeck; NY3438], *Old Crown*: Relaxed and homely local in attractive village, decent food inc good curries from spotless kitchen, friendly new landlord, good unusual real ales brewed here *(Patrick Rivett, Ian and Gayle Woodhead, H K Dyson, LYM)*

☆ Howtown [NY4519], *Howtown Hotel*: Stunning setting nr Ullswater, small cosy hotel lounge bar, separate public bar with good lunchtime sandwiches for hungry walkers, restaurant, morning coffee or afternoon tea; book for good Sun lunch; welcoming very long-serving owners, well kept Theakstons Best, decent wines by the glass, pleasant garden; charming old-fashioned bedrooms, early morning tea ladies *(Christine and Geoff Butler, Ian Rorison, Enid and Henry Stephens, Chris Rounthwaite)*

Kendal [Crook Rd (B5284 NW); SD5293], *Gateway*: Former boarding house, now refurbished as pub/restaurant; good food, well kept Thwaites, good service; tables out on terrace, play area; bedrooms *(Mike and Carole Dixon, SLC)*; *Globe*: Civilised but cheerful beamed split-level bar, pleasant decor, good cheap bar food, quick friendly service, separate dining-room upstairs (where children welcome) *(M Joyner, Sue Holland, Dave Webster)*; [39 Kirkland], *Ring o' Bells*: Sensitively refurbished 17th-c pub in grounds of parish church, relaxed genteel atmosphere, cosy panelled lounge with Lakeland prints and banquettes, basic public bar, nice little snug, reasonably priced food, Vaux Samson and Lorimers Scoth, Wards Sheffield Best and a guest beer, no-nonsense service, unobtrusive piped music *(Sue Holland, David Webster)*; [Highgate], *Shakespeare*: Upstairs pub through archway to small close, lots of woodwork, mixed customers, simple food, Theakstons Best *(Sue Holland, David Webster)*; [Strickland Gate], *Woolpack*: Comfortable old coaching inn popular with locals, good choice from lunchtime carvery inc a vegetarian dish, lots of fresh veg and salads; bedrooms *(Arthur and Margaret Dickinson)*

☆ Keswick [Lake Rd, off top end Mkt Sq; NY2624], *Dog & Gun*: Lively and unpretentious town local with some high settles, low beams, partly slate floor (rest carpeted or boards), fine Abrahams mountain photographs, coins in beams and timbers by fireplace, log fire; well kept Theakstons Best

and Old Peculier and guests such as Black Sheep or Gales Harvest, open fires, well presented generous bar food from sandwiches up, friendly efficient staff; piped music may be loud; children if eating, no dogs or credit cards *(Jeanne Cross, Paul Silvestri, SLC, Mr and Mrs R J Foreman, Paul and Gail Betteley, F J and A Parmenter, Nigel Woolliscroft, LYM)*

☆ Keswick [Lake Rd], *Four in Hand*: Cosy and inviting back lounge, stage-coach bric-a-brac, wide choice of good reasonably priced food, decent-sized tables in dining room, full Jennings range on handpump, friendly staff; very busy in summer *(Vann and Terry Prime, Paul and Gail Betteley, Michael Butler, Jason Caulkin)*

☆ Keswick [St John's St], *George*: Attractive traditional black-panelled side room with interesting Wordsworth connection (and good log fire), more straightforward open-plan main bar with old-fashioned settles and modern banquettes under Elizabethan beams, usual bar food inc children's, well kept Theakstons and Yates, smartish restaurant; bedrooms comfortable *(J S M Sheldon, H K Dyson, P and M Rudlin, LYM)*

Keswick [47 Main St], *Bank*: Well kept Jennings, decent bar food, good atmosphere; bedrooms *(SLC)*; [Market Sq], *Keswick Lodge*: Hotel lounge bar with comfortable pubby feel, well kept Theakstons and a guest such as Timothy Taylors Landlord, wide choide of reasonably priced bar food, pleasant service; bedrooms *(SLC)*; [Lake Rd], *Kitchins Cellar*: Ancient timbered building, clean, comfortable and quiet, with wide choice of bar snacks esp sandwiches, Sun roast beef, Jennings Cumberland and Sneck Lifter and a guest such as Morlands Old Speckled Hen, good choice of house wines, good coffee, friendly landlord; children allowed upstairs *(SS)*; [off Market Sq], *Lake Road Vaults*: Old town pub with Victorian fireplace, panelling and old prints in two communicating rooms, Jennings ales, efficient service, substantial helpings of usual food; tables on small terrace *(Neil and Anita Christopher)*; [Main St], *Oddfellows Arms*: Popular, cosy and comfortable panelled pub, well kept Jennings, wide choice of generous low-priced food, efficient service, lots of horse-racing photographs; back family room with TV and fruit machines *(Richard Lewis, SLC, Lesley Macklin)*; [Pack Horse Ct; off Market Sq, behind Lloyds Bank], *Pack Horse*: Lushly refurbished low-beamed pub in attractive alley courtyard, well kept Jennings (full range) and interesting guest beers, reasonably priced food, friendly service, cheery locals – upstairs is an oasis of calm *(R V G Brown, Richard Lewis, LYM)*

☆ nr Keswick [Crosthwaite Rd; by A66, a mile out], *Pheasant*: Small friendly beamed pub with lots of local cartoons, big helpings of good value tasty food, well kept Jennings, particularly friendly prompt service; children if eating; bedrooms *(Michael Butler, SLC, P and M Rudlin)*

☆ *nr* Keswick [Newlands Valley – OS Sheet 90 map ref 242217], *Swinside*: Clean and friendly modernised pub in peaceful valley below marvellous crags and fells, full Jennings range kept well, welcoming new licensees, good fires, good value bar food, restaurant; tables outside with best view, open all day Sat and summer; bedrooms *(Simon Watkins, Tony Gayfer, SLC, H K Dyson, LYM)*

Kirkoswald [NY5641], *Crown*: Friendly local, good home-cooked food *(Anne Crowley)*

Langdale [by car park for Stickle Ghyll; NY2906], *Stickle Barn*: In lovely setting, suiting walkers and mountaineers well, good choice of food inc packed lunches, well kept Courage-related beers; fruit machines, maybe loud piped music; big pleasant terrace, open all day in summer; bunkhouse accommodation, live music in loft *(John and Maureen Watt, RLW and Dizzy)*

Langwathby [A686 Penrith—Alston; NY5633], *Shepherds*: Unpretentious and cheerful, good quickly served reasonably priced food inc good vegetarian choice, comfortable banquettes, well kept Whitbreads-related ales, bar down steps from lounge, games room with pool and darts; tables outside, attractive spot on huge green of Pennines village *(David and Margaret Bloomfield)*

☆ Lazonby [NY5539], *Joiners Arms*: Small pub furnished brewery-style, roaring fire, beautifully presented food inc oriental dishes, well kept Bass and Stones (friendly landlord was a head brewer there) with a guest such as Batemans, pool table in lower bar; clean comfortable bedrooms, excellent breakfasts *(DJW)*

☆ Levens [Sedgwick Rd, by Sizergh Castle gates – OS Sheet 97 map ref 500872; SD5087], *Strickland Arms*: Wide choice of generous imaginative well cooked food in clean if rather plain pub, friendly prompt service even when very busy, well kept Marstons Pedigree, Morlands Old Speckled Hen and Theakstons XB, Best and Old Peculier, log fire; piped music, pool table; no-smoking upstairs restaurant, children allowed, good garden *(R H Rowley, RD, Richard Lewis)*

Levens [on new cut-off from A590, nr A5074 junction; SD4785], *Gilpin Bridge*: Popular for good value bar food; well kept Theakstons, pleasant piped music, dining room *(Arthur and Margaret Dickinson)*

Lindal in Furness [SD2576], *Anchor*: Doing well under current licensees, with good food (though little in the lower price range), plenty of fresh coffee, no-smoking children's room with stickle-brick activity table *(Arthur and Margaret Dickinson)*

Lorton [Low Lorton; B5289 Buttermere—Cockermouth; NY1525], *Wheat Sheaf*: Bar and dining lounge, good food inc huge filled yorkshire puddings and big helpings of other traditional dishes, well kept Jennings, fast service; Sunday lunch; caravan park behind *(Tim Heywood, Sophie Wilne, SLC)*

Lowick Bridge [just off A5084; SD2986], *Red Lion*: Busy family pub with two spacious,

attractive and comfortable areas, well kept Hartleys XB and Robinsons, good choice of generous bar food inc Sun roasts, friendly if not always quick service; charming spot *(LM, IHR, Prof I H Rorison)*

☆ Lowick Green [A5092 SE of village; SD2985], *Farmers Arms*: Charming cosy public bar with heavy beams, huge slate flagstones, big open fire, cosy corners and pub games (this part may be closed winter), some interesting furniture and pictures in plusher hotel lounge bar across yard, tasty well presented food in bar and restaurant inc two-person bargains, well kept Theakstons XB and Youngers IPA and No 3, friendly efficient staff; children welcome, open all day; piped music; bedrooms *(JCW, David Carr, LYM)*

☆ Middleton [A683 Kirkby Lonsdale—Sedbergh; SD6288], *Middleton Fells*: Comfortably plush open-plan oak-beamed bar with lots of brasswork (some made by the friendly landlord), three good fires, good choice of popular sensibly priced home-made food, well kept Boddingtons and Tetleys; games room, juke box, quiz nights; very attractive garden, fine scenery; children welcome *(Peter and Audrey Dowsett, Katie Hornby, LYM)*

Milburn [Gullom; NY6629], *Stag*: 17th-c inn with small bar and dining room, good choice of generous if not cheap well presented bar food inc fine salads and home-made puddings; bedrooms *(anon)*

☆ Mungrisdale [village signed off A66 Penrith—Keswick, a bit over a mile W of A5091 Ullswater rd – OS Sheet 90 map ref 363302; NY3731], *Mill Inn*: Simple pub in lovely valley hamlet, good bar food, well kept Jennings, lots of malt whiskies, plain games room, separate restaurant; children welcome, tables on gravel forecourt and neat lawn sloping to little river; warm pleasant bedrooms (note that there's a quite separate Mill Hotel here) *(A Preston, H K Dyson, LYM)*

Nenthead [NY7843], *Miners Arms*: Friendly relaxing family-run pub, basic decor, genuine home cooking inc good chips, real ale with at least two guests, no piped music *(L Dixon)*

☆ Nether Wasdale [NY1204], *Strands*: Warm and friendly hotel in lovely spot below the remote high fells around Wastwater, spacious bar with big open fires, local pictures and lots of horsebrasses, good range of generous bar food, well kept Hartleys XB and Robinsons Best, friendly helpful service; bedrooms *(Maurice Thompson)*

Newby Bridge [SD3786], *Newby Bridge*: Panelled hotel bar popular with locals and tourists, good value sandwiches and snacks, well kept Jennings ales, games room with pool, cards, dominoes and board games; esp nice in winter; bedrooms *(Paul Bispham)*; *Swan*: Fine setting next to river with waterside picnic tables by old stone bridge, hotelish atmosphere even when very busy, decent food inc Sun roasts, Boddingtons ale; bedrooms *(Ron Gentry, LM)*

☆ Newton Reigny [off B5305 just W of M6

junction 41], *Sun*: Open-plan village inn with
plush seats and velvet curtains, stripped stone
and wrought iron, central open fire, well kept
Courage-related and other ales inc a local
guest, well prepared food, no-smoking
restaurant; darts, dominoes and pool off at
one end, children away from bar, open all day
Sat; piped music, cheap bedrooms, good
breakfast *(Margaret Mason, Dave Thompson,
David Bloomfield, Richard Holloway, Mike
and Wendy Proctor, LYM)*

☆ Outgate [B5286 Ambleside—Hawkshead;
SD3699], *Outgate Inn*: Attractively placed
country pub with three comfortably
modernised rooms, banjoes, trumpets and
tuba hanging from beams, decent food inc
huge mixed grill, well kept Hartleys and
Robinsons, popular jazz Fri; bedrooms *(Mark
Percy, Chris and Andy Crow, David Carr, H
K Dyson, LYM)*
Patterdale [NY3916], *White Lion*: Well kept
Whitbreads-related ales and usual bar food,
busy with walkers in summer; bedrooms *(Rita
and Keith Pollard, H K Dyson)*
Penrith [Cromwell Rd/Castlegate (first
roundabout coming from M6); NY5130],
Agricultural: Popular welcoming local,
friendly chatty landlord, good choice of well
kept Jennings beers, comfortable L-shaped
lounge, wide choice of reasonably priced food
(Richard Lewis); [pedestrianised area off main
st], *General Wolfe*: Friendly and comfortable,
busy all day, well kept ales such as
Boddingtons, Charles Wells Bombardier,
Theakstons Best and Wadworths 6X; juke
box, can be smoky *(Richard Lewis)*; *George*:
Decorous beamed and oak-panelled lounge
hall with fine plasterwork, oak settles and
easy chairs around good open fire, big bow
windows; short choice of reasonably priced
lunchtime bar food, well kept Marstons
Pedigree, lively back bar, restaurant;
comfortable bedrooms *(Frank Davidson,
LYM)*; [Cornmarket], *Gloucester Arms*: Cosy
low-beamed pub, lots of wood and panelling,
comfortable seats, big open fire, friendly
landlord, bar food, well kept Boddingtons
and Whitbreads Castle Eden; open all day
(Richard Lewis); [Bowscar (A6 N); NY5034],
Stoneybeck: Big comfortable cheerful pub,
cheap generous food, Theakstons *(David and
Margaret Bloomfield)*

☆ Penruddock [NY4327], *Herdwick*: Carefully
refurbished old pub with consistently good
well priced food esp Sun roast, good
atmosphere, friendly service, attractive
restaurant – worth booking evenings *(Mike
and Wendy Proctor, Malcolm Taylor)*
Pooley Bridge [NY4724], *Sun*: Warm and
cosy lounge bar with plush settee in front of
open fire, steps past servery to second
interesting room, well kept Jennings ales,
good value generously served simple bar food
inc sandwiches, separate restaurant; tables in
garden *(G O Cook, A Preston, Mike and
Wendy Proctor)*; *Swiss Chalet*: Handy for
glorious scenery around Ullswater and
Martindale, several real ales, wide choice of
popular bar food, separate dining room,

friendly staff; bedrooms comfortable and well
equipped *(H K Dyson, Ian and Gayle
Woodhead)*

☆ Ravenstonedale [signed off A685 Kirkby
Stephen—M6; NY7204], *Black Swan*: Good
bar food with interesting specials in genteel
bar with open fire and some stripped stone,
well kept Hartleys XB, Robinsons,
Theakstons, Worthington, Youngers and a
changing guest, lots of country wines, good
service; dogs welcome, tables in pretty tree-
sheltered streamside garden over road;
comfortable bedrooms inc some for disabled,
good breakfasts, peaceful setting *(Kim and
Anne Schofield, SS, H K Dyson, BB)*
Ravenstonedale, *Kings Head*: Friendly two-
room beamed bar with log fires, button-back
banquettes and dining chairs, good range of
generous food, not cheap but tasty and good
value, well kept Jennings and other ales,
separate games room; bedrooms *(R P Knight,
D Varney, H K Dyson, LYM)*

☆ nr Ravenstonedale [Crossbank; A683
Sedbergh—Kirkby Stephen; SD6996], *Fat
Lamb*: Remote friendly inn with pews in
brightly modernised bar, log fire in traditional
black kitchen range, good local photographs;
cheerful service, usual bar food, well kept
Mitchells, maybe piped classical music,
restaurant, seats out by sheep pastures;
facilities for disabled, children really welcome;
comfortable bedrooms with own bathrooms,
good walks from inn *(Graeme Mew, David
Varney, BB)*

☆ Rockcliffe [signed off A6; NY3661], *Crown
& Thistle*: Comfortable and clean, well
divided so as to be spacious, light and airy yet
cosy, wide choice of attractively priced good
food in huge helpings, quick friendly service
even when busy, well kept Theakstons Bitter
and Mild; locally popular games bar
(Dorothy and David Young)

☆ Rosthwaite [NY2615], *Scafell*: Lots of
walkers and locals in extended slate-floored
bar, lunchtime food from sandwiches to steak
and salmon, children's helpings of most
dishes, full range of Theakstons ales kept
well, afternoon teas, log fire, enthusiastic
licensee, quick friendly service; glassed-in
verandah overlooking river, picnic tables
outside; shame about the piped music; hotel
has cosy sun-lounge bar and dining room;
bedrooms not big but good *(H K Dyson,
Tony Gayfer, David Heath)*

☆ Sandside [B5282 Milnthorpe—Arnside;
SD4781], *Ship*: Spacious modernised pub
with glorious view of estuary and mountains
beyond; friendly staff, decent bar food, well
kept S&N real ales, decent wines, summer
barbecues, tables out on grass by good
children's play area; children allowed in
eating area *(John Fazakerley, LYM)*
Santon Bridge [NY1102], *Bridge*: Good value
food inc children's and friendly service in
relaxed traditional Lakeland
pub; bedrooms *(Sally-Anne Lenton)*

☆ Satterthwaite [SD3492], *Eagles Head*: Small
and unpretentious but friendly, with good
value generous home-cooked lunchtime food

esp soup, sandwiches and home-made pies (also Fri/Sat summer evenings), big log fire, helpful landlord, well kept Thwaites, pool, darts; papers and guidebooks for sale; handy for Grizedale Forest; bedrooms comfortable and clean, shared bathroom; maybe some closures winter esp Mon, but usually open all day at least Thurs-Sat in summer *(Margaret and Roy Randle, LM, Mrs H H Lord)*

☆ Seatoller [NY2414], *Yew Tree*: Well presented imaginative food in good low-ceilinged restaurant at foot of Honister Pass, good beer and choice of whiskies and wines in little bar with wonderful collection of police hats, garden behind; can get crowded, but efficient friendly staff *(Paul McKeever, Richard Holloway)*

Spark Bridge [SD3185], *Royal Oak*: Large riverside food pub with raftered upper bar, relaxed informal atmosphere, friendly service, well kept Hartleys and Thwaites ales, good value food inc wonderful steaks and fresh seafood, good children's menu; large pool room *(Camille Walsh)*

St Bees [Main St; NX9712], *Oddfellows Arms*: Small lively terraced local, wide choice of good value food, well kept Jennings inc Sneck Lifter, friendly service, darts; piped music *(Neil Taylor)*

☆ Staveley [SD4798], *Eagle & Child*: Simple good value home-cooked bar food with fresh veg, well kept Newcastle Exhibition, Tetleys and Theakstons Best, friendly service, bright but comfortable little modern front lounge and more spacious carpeted bar; well kept, with small neat garden; bedrooms inexpensive, good breakfast *(Dr and Mrs B Baker, Sue Holland, Dave Webster, G Washington, BB)*

Stonethwaite [Borrowdale; NY2613], *Langstrath*: Friendly, neat and clean, with good fresh bar food, good service, walkers welcome; delightful peaceful village; bedrooms *(H K Dyson, Nigel Woolliscroft)*

☆ Talkin [village signed off B6413 S of Brampton; NY5557], *Blacksmiths Arms*: Welcoming and cheerful, good generous quick food in bar or dining room, Sun lunch very popular (booking advisable); well kept Youngers ales on handpump, open fire, local pictures; unobtrusive piped music, fruit machine; five well appointed bedrooms, prettily set village nr good walks *(LM)*

Talkin, *Hare & Hounds*: Well kept beer, pleasant staff, decent food; bedrooms *(GSB, LYM)*

☆ Thirlspot [A591 Grasmere—Keswick; NY3217], *Kings Head*: Attractively placed long low beamed bar with wide choice of usual food inc good puddings, well kept Jennings, Theakstons Best, XB and Mild, Yates and guest such as Marstons Pedigree, inglenook fires, tables in garden, games room with pool, maybe live music Fri/Sat; piped music; children welcome, with toy box; good value bedrooms (the hotel part and restaurant is quite separate) *(Tina and David Woods-Taylor, Richard Lewis, H K Dyson, LYM)*

Torver [A593 S of Coniston; SD2894],

Church House: Decent varied food in tidy and civilised low-beamed bar, pleasant service, splendid hill views, good fire, particularly well kept Whitbreads Castle Eden, big garden; children welcome, attractive evening restaurant; open all day at least in summer; bedrooms *(Mrs S Peregrine, LM)*

Uldale [NY2537], *Snooty Fox*: Two simple unpretentious atmospheric rooms, friendly helpful landlord, well kept Theakstons and a beer brewed for them in Hesket Newmarket, good generous food; reasonably priced bedrooms, tiny village *(David Heath)*

☆ Ulverston [King St; SD2978], *Rose & Crown*: Good friendly traditional pub atmosphere, good food, well kept Hartleys XB, Robinsons Best Mild and Bitter, quick service even when busy on Sat market day *(Anne and Brian Birtwistle, M J Morgan)*

☆ Wasdale Head [NY1808], *Wasdale Head Inn*: Mountain hotel doing well under current management, marvellous fellside setting, spacious panelled main bar with cushioned settles on slate floor and great mountain photographs, adjoining pool room, no-smoking snug and children's room; popular if not cheap bar food, well kept Jennings, Theakstons Best and Old Peculier and Yates, decent choice of wines and malt whiskies; open all day, cl much of winter; comfortable bedrooms, well equipped self-catering accommodation *(Brian and Anna Marsden, Ann Reeder, David Craine, John Abbott, Mick Hitchman, A and R Lees, Piotr Chodzko-Zajko, H K Dyson, Nigel Woolliscroft, LYM)*

Windermere [Elleray Rd; SD4109], *Grey Walls*: Comfortable and popular turn-of-the-century former doctor's house, friendly staff, good value meals all day Sat, well kept Theakstons Mild, Best, XB and Old Peculier and guests such as Mitchells Lancaster Bomber and Jennings Cocker Hoop on handpump; open all day; bedrooms *(Richard Lewis)*

☆ Winster [A5074; SD4293], *Brown Horse*: Popular if restauranty dining pub, open-plan, light and comfortable, with small choice of good attractively priced food (the goat's cheese dishes are excellent), prompt friendly smart service, well spaced tables and good log fire, well kept Jennings and Marstons Pedigree, decent wines, children welcome *(Malcolm Taylor, Dr J R Norman, T Large, Miss V Smith, Tina and David Woods-Taylor, A D Robson, Dave Braisted, Mike and Sue Walton, LYM)*

☆ Winton [just off A685 N of Kirkby Stephen; NY7810], *Bay Horse*: Two low-key and low-ceilinged rooms with Pennine photographs and local fly-tying, generous reasonably priced home-cooked food inc fresh veg, well kept Theakstons Best, Jennings Bitter and Cumberland and Youngers Scotch, summer guest beers, pool in games room; may close Tues-Thurs lunchtimes in winter; comfortable modestly priced bedrooms, good breakfasts; peaceful moorland hamlet *(T M Dobby, Alan Dove, LYM)*

Derbyshire

This is a good county for beer lovers, with most of the main entries having a fine choice of well kept ales; a far higher proportion than in most areas have been granted our Beer Award. Drinks prices here are well below the national average, too – saving about 15p a pint. Much the cheapest pub we found was the Brunswick in Derby, charging only £1 for the good beer it brews itself (and it has a splendid range of others); there were also bargain prices at the very unspoilt Barley Mow at Kirk Ireton, the Alexandra in Derby (which now has bedrooms), and – one of the longest-standing own-brew pubs – the John Thompson near Melbourne. Pubs currently gaining the warmest praise from readers here include the Waltzing Weasel at Birch Vale (our choice as Derbyshire Dining Pub of the Year), the surprisingly ancient Olde Dolphin in Derby (promoted to the main entries for this edition), the Chequers at Froggatt Edge (a dining pub that's kept its pubby feel), the outstandingly welcoming Lantern Pike near Hayfield, the Yorkshire Bridge just below the Ladybower Reservoir (another newcomer to the main entries), the Lathkil at Over Haddon (lovely setting), the Old Crown near Shardlow (unusual beers, good dishes of the day) and the White Horse at Woolley Moor (a great all-rounder). Good new licensees are now opening the attractive Old Bulls Head at Little Hucklow every day. Quite a few pubs in the Lucky Dip section at the end of the chapter are earning warm praise these days: the Derwent at Bamford, Devonshire Arms at Beeley, Navigation at Buxworth, Boat at Cromford, Standing Order in Derby, Quiet Woman at Earl Sterndale, Bluebell at Farnah Green, Bulls Head at Foolow, Queen Anne at Great Hucklow, Red Lion at Litton, Colvile Arms at Lullington, Royal Oak at Millthorpe, Bulls Head at Monyash, Little Mill at Rowarth and Bulls Head at Wardlow; we have inspected almost all of these, and give them a clear thumbs-up. This is an area in which breweries' chain family dining pubs are also often well worth trying, notably Marstons' Tavern Tables (the Excavator at Ripley is a good example), and Mansfields' Landlords Tables (such as the Grouse & Claret at Rowsley or Clock Warehouse at Shardlow).

ASHBOURNE SK1846 Map 7

Smiths Tavern

St Johns St; bottom of market place

This well cared for pub at the foot of the market place stretches back a lot further than you might think from the relatively narrow shop-front entrance. The attractive bar seems very much the archetypal old-fashioned town tavern, with horsebrasses and tankards hanging from heavy black beams, a delft shelf of antique blue and white china, old cigarette and drinks advertisements, and a black leatherette wall seat facing the bar counter. Steps take you up to a middle room with leatherette seating around barrel tables, a log-effect gas fire and piano, and beyond that a light and airy end dining room with three nice antique settles among more ordinary seats around simple dining tables. Well kept Marstons Best and Pedigree and a guest on handpump, around 36 malt whiskies, and a range of vodkas. Popular and generously served bar food includes soup (£1.90), sandwiches, ploughman's, home-made pies such as steak and kidney (£4.75), home-made dishes like chicken kiev (£5.85) or veal holstein (£7.65), a couple of vegetarian meals, and an increasing emphasis on fresh fish such as local trout (£4.95), seabass, crab and sole; good fresh vegetables, well-priced three-course Sunday lunch. Very friendly service and atmosphere; dominoes, fruit machine and well chosen and reproduced if not always quiet piped pop music. *(Recommended by Sue Holland, Dave Webster, Ann and Colin Hunt, T and G Alderman, Paul Robinshaw, Anthony Barker)*

Marstons ~ Tenants John and Elaine Bishop ~ Real ale ~ Meals and snacks (12-2.30, 7-9.30) ~ (01335) 342264 ~ Children in dining room ~ Maybe piano singalongs Fri, Sun ~ Open 11-11; 12-10.30 Sun

ASHFORD IN THE WATER SK1969 Map 7

Ashford Hotel 🛏 ♀

Church Street; village signposted just off A6 Bakewell—Buxton

Usefully positioned in a remarkably pretty village, this stone-built inn is clearly a hotel rather than a simple pub, but surprises several readers by being rather more welcoming than that might suggest; those who've arrived in hiking boots and shorts for example aren't made to feel uncomfortable. The cosy refurbished bar has lots of gleaming brass and copper on the stripped brick of the broad stone inglenook fireplace, plush seats and stools around its traditional cast-iron-framed tables on the patterned carpet, and an imposing bar counter. Reliable bar food (served through till 6) comes in good sized helpings, from a choice that includes soup (£1.75), sandwiches (from £2.25), filled baked potatoes (from £2.75), ploughman's (£4.75), chicken, ham and leek pie (£5.75), a casserole and a roast of the day (£6.25), pork fillet in sherry sauce with apricots (£7.50), and daily specials like plaice filled with spinach in a tomato and basil sauce (£6.50); in the evening they do meals such as braised pheasant in port and red berry sauce (£6.95) and pan-fried swordfish steak in lemon and dill butter (£7.50); usual children's menu (£1.95). Friendly neatly dressed staff serve well kept Mansfield Best, Old Baily, Ridings and seasonal brews, and Morlands Old Speckled Hen on handpump; decent wines and lots of malt whiskies. Cribbage, dominoes, fruit machine and piped music (occasionally a little loud). There are tables out in the garden. Comfortable bedrooms, no-smoking lounge and restaurant; highchairs. *(Recommended by Derek and Sylvia Stephenson, Peter and Maris Brigginshaw, David Carr, M Mason, D Thompson, Mike and Wendy Proctor, Ann and Colin Hunt, D and D Savidge, Brian and Margaret Beesley, Mary Roebuck, Jack and Philip Paxton, M W Turner, Jamie and Ruth Lyons, Ben Grose, Sue Holland, Dave Webster, Alan and Eileen Bowker)*

Free house ~ Licensees John and Sue Dawson ~ Real ale ~ Meals and snacks (bar meals 12-6, restaurant 6-9) ~ Restaurant ~ Children in eating area of bar and restaurant ~ (01629) 812725 ~ Open 11-11; 12-10.30 Sun ~ Bedrooms: £50B/£75B

BIRCH VALE SK0286 Map 7

Waltzing Weasel 🛏 ♀

A6015 E of New Mills

Derbyshire Dining Pub of the Year

Quite a few strings to the bow of the licencees who've transformed this winsome place in recent years: the landlord is a former philosophy lecturer, his wife is an artist, and together they used to deal in antiques – an interest that manifests itself in the furnishings in the bar and the smartly individual bedrooms. They work hard to balance the needs of visitors wanting just a drink, a full meal, or a civilised place to stay, with a great deal of success – a reader who's been coming here for 30 years says it's never been better than it is now. The U-shaped bar has comfortably chatty corners, a cheerful fire, a good longcase clock, some handsome oak settles and tables among more usual furniture, houseplants on corner tables, and lots of nicely-framed mainly sporting Victorian prints; there are daily papers on sticks, and a friendly dog, Sam. Well kept Marstons Best, Churchills and maybe Hartingtons on handpump, and a good choice of decent wines and malt whiskies. No games or music. Though not cheap, the food is a strong point, with a lunchtime spread taking in game soup (£2.50), sandwiches (not Sun), duck pâté (£4), crayfish tails in garlic mayonnaise (£5.50), vegetable tart (£6.75), smoked trout (£8.50), and seafood tart (£8.75), with evening extras like chicken curry (£6.75), duck and cherry pie (£8.25), and grilled turbot (£11.50). Puddings and cheeses are excellent. The charming back restaurant has picture-window views of Kinder Scout and the moors, and these are shared by a pretty garden and terrace. Service is obliging and attentive. *(Recommended by Tony Young, K and B Forman, J F M West, Pat and Tony Young, N Duckworth; also in Good Hotel Guide)*

Free house ~ Licensee Mike Atkinson ~ Real ale ~ Meals and snacks ~ Restaurant ~ (01663) 743402 ~ Children in restaurant ~ Monthly singing group ~ Open 12-3, 5.30-11 ~ Bedrooms: £45B/£65B

BIRCHOVER SK2462 Map 7
Druid

Village signposted from B5056

Few places in the area can offer as wide a range of food as this busy creeper-covered dining pub, and considering the choice, it's even more remarkable to find the meals so interesting. The menu is written up on the blackboards that line the long fairly narrow bar (at busy times it can be hard to get close enough to read it let alone make up your mind), and favourite dishes amongst the 100 or so listed currently include prawn, chicken and spare ribs with crispy vegetables in a sweet and spicy hot broth (£4.40 small, £8.60 large), vegetable wellington (£5.90), and honey saddle of lamb with redcurrant and gooseberry sauce (£11.80); readers have also particularly enjoyed the venison casserole with bitter chocolate sauce and the duck and chicken pomodoro. Half-price helpings for children. It's extremely popular so bookings are advisable for evenings and weekends – you probably won't be able to sit down at all if you're not eating. The bustling bar is small and plain, with plush-upholstered wooden wall benches around straightforward tables, and a big coal fire; the Garden Room is reserved for non-smokers. The spacious and airy two-storey dining extension, candlelit at night, is really the heart of the place, with pink plush seats on olive-green carpet, and pepper-grinders and sea salt on all the tables. Well kept Adnams, Mansfield Bitter and Morlands Old Speckled Hen on handpump, along with Belt & Braces or some similarly named ale from the Leatherbritches brewery at Fenny Bentley; good collection of malt whiskies; welcoming service. A small public bar has dominoes; well reproduced classical music. There are picnic tables in front. *(Recommended by Ms C Dyson, Frank Cummins, Ann and Colin Hunt, Neville Kenyon, Kath Wetherill, Margaret and Nigel Dennis, FMH, Mr and Mrs B Langrish, Mike and Wendy Proctor, J E Rycroft, Nigel Woolliscroft, Cathryn and Richard Hicks, John and Christine Lowe, David and Shelia, D Eberlin, Yolanda Henry, Jamie and Ruth Lyons, Jack and Philip Paxton, Jack Morley)*

Free house ~ Licensee Brian Bunce ~ Real ale ~ Meals and snacks ~ (01629) 650302 ~ Children in dining area if eating but must be gone by 8.15 ~ Open 12-2.30, 7-11; winter 12-2, 7-10; closed 25/26 Dec

BRASSINGTON SK2354 Map 7
Olde Gate

Village signposted off B5056 and B5035 NE of Ashbourne

Though the date outside says 1874, this genuinely unspoilt creeper-covered pub was actually built in 1616, partly from timbers salvaged from Armada wrecks and exchanged for local lead. The peaceful public bar is traditionally furnished, with gleaming copper pots on the lovely old kitchen range, pewter mugs hanging from a beam, embossed Doulton stoneware flagons on a side shelf, an ancient wall clock, and rush-seated old chairs and antique settles (one ancient, partly reframed, black oak solid one). Stone-mullioned windows look across lots of garden tables to small silvery-walled pastures. On the left of a small hatch-served lobby, another cosy beamed room has stripped panelled settles, tables with scrubbed tops, and a roaring fire under a huge mantelbeam. Bar food changing day by day includes big open sandwiches, steak and ale pie (£6.95), balti dishes (from £7.95) and a popular summer barbecue, with lamb steaks, cajun chicken, swordfish and tuna; good puddings. No chips. The dining room is no smoking. Well kept Marstons Pedigree and a guest on handpump, and a good selection of malt whiskies; cribbage and dominoes, no games or music. The small front yard has a couple of benches – a nice spot in summer to listen to the village bell-ringers practising on Friday evenings. Five minutes' drive away is Carsington reservoir, ideal for water sports and so forth. *(Recommended by Phil and Sally Gorton, Jack and Philip Paxton, Mike and Wendy Proctor, Peter Marshall, Alex and Betty McAllan, Paul Robinshaw, David Atkinson, Neil and Anita Christopher, A P Jeffreys, Chris Raisin, John and Christine Lowe, D Kudelka)*

Marstons ~ Tenant Paul Burlinson ~ Real ale ~ Meals and snacks (not Mon eve, or Sun eve in winter) ~ (01629) 540448 ~ Children over 10 in eating area and restaurant ~ Open 12-2.30(3 Sat), 6-11; closed Mon lunchtimes in winter

nr BUXTON SK0673 Map 7
Bull i'th' Thorn
Ashbourne Road (A515) six miles S of Buxton, nr Hurdlow; OS Sheet 119 map reference 128665

What earns this solid old place its main entry is the very unexpected historic main bar room, a fascinating medieval hall that's survived since 1472. A massive central beam runs parallel with a forest of smaller ones, there are panelled window seats in the embrasures of the thick stone walls, handsome panelling, and old flagstones stepping gently down to a big open fire. It's furnished with fine long settles, an ornately carved hunting chair, a longcase clock, a powder-horn, and armour that includes 17th-c German helmets, swords, and blunderbusses and so forth. Despite all this, the atmosphere is that of any straightforward roadside pub. No-frills bar food includes sandwiches, soup (£1.20), steak and kidney pie, scampi or roast beef (£4), sirloin steak (£7.50), and puddings (£1.50); Sunday roast (£4.50). An adjoining room has darts, pool, dominoes, fruit machine, juke box; piped music. Robinsons Best on handpump. The simple family room opens on to a terrace and big lawn, with swings, and there are more tables in a sheltered angle in front. Look out for the lively old carvings at the main entrance: one shows a bull caught in a thornbush, and others an eagle with a freshly caught hare, and some spaniels chasing a rabbit. There's a holiday flat and adjacent field for caravans and camping. The pub is handy for the High Peak Trail. Coach parties are welcome. *(Recommended by James Nunns, Mike and Wendy Proctor, David Carr, D G Clarke, Roger and Valerie Hill, Jack and Philip Paxton, Jean Gustavson, Geoffrey and Irene Lindley)*

Robinsons ~ Tenant George Haywood ~ Real ale ~ Meals and snacks ~ Restaurant (only used for big parties) ~ (01298) 83348 ~ Children in family room, pool room and restaurant ~ Occasional weekend live groups and karaoke ~ Open 11.30-3, 6.30-11 ~ Two bedrooms: £16/£32

DERBY SK3435 Map 7
Alexandra £
Siddals Rd, just up from station

The landlord of this solid Victorian town pub is something of a real ale enthusiast. Every year he serves around 600 uncommon and even unheard of beers, with usually six well kept guests at a time alongside the more familiar Bass, Batemans XB and Mild, and Marstons Pedigree; recent brews passing through the handpumps have included Bridgwater Blakes Best, Elsecar Black Heart, Rudgate Maypole, Shefford Bedfordshire Clogger, and Slaters All Mighty. Also rare farm ciders, country wines, around two dozen malt whiskies, a good range of Belgian bottled beers, and changing continental beers on draught. The lively refurbished bar has an attractive 1920s feel, as well as good heavy traditional furnishings on dark-stained floorboards, shelves of bottles, and local railway photographs around the walls. Though this is perhaps a pub more for drinking than for eating, the bar food is so remarkably priced it's an ideal place for an informal snack: popular filled rolls and open sandwiches (from £1), sausage, chips and beans (£1.95), ploughman's (£2.75), yorkshire pudding filled with sausage and vegetables (£3), changing daily specials including a vegetarian dish, and several carefully chosen English cheeses. You can order food by phone so it's ready when you arrive. Quick cheery service; dominoes, cribbage, a soundless fruit machine and piped music. Note they now have bedrooms. *(Recommended by D Eberlin, Richard Lewis, Jack and Philip Paxton, Richard Houghton, Dr and Mrs B Baker, Mr and Mrs P Byatt, David and Shelia, Chris Raisin, A Summerfield)*

Free house ~ Licensee Mark Robins ~ Real ale ~ Lunchtime meals and snacks (not Sun) ~ (01332) 293993 ~ Open 11-11; 11-2.30, 6-11 Sat ~ Bedrooms: £25B/£35B

Brunswick 🍺 £

1 Railway Terrace; close to Derby Midland railway station

As if the previous entry didn't offer enough variety on the beer front, this traditional old railway pub round the corner generally has a choice of fifteen very well kept ales on handpump. Several of these are from their own Brunswick Brewery (the workings of which are visible from a viewing area), including Recession, Second Brew, the highly-praised Railway Porter, Light Dinner Ale, Festival, and others like Rams Return, brewed to celebrate the return of Derby County F.C. to the Premiership; the first of these is only £1 a pint, and a couple more are well below the average beer price for the area. Other beers include Bass (straight from the cask), Batemans Mild, Burton Bridge, Hook Norton Old Hookey, Kelham Island Pale Rider, Marstons Pedigree, Theakstons XB and Old Peculier, and Timothy Taylors Landlord. They have a beer festival in early October; draught farm cider. The very welcoming high-ceilinged serving bar has heavy, well padded leather seats, whisky-water jugs above the dado, and a dark blue ceiling and upper wall, with squared dark panelling below. The no-smoking room is decorated with little old-fashioned prints and swan's neck lamps, and has a high-backed wall settle and a coal fire; behind a curved glazed partition wall is a quietly chatty family parlour narrowing to the apex of the triangular building. Darts, cribbage, dominoes, fruit machine; good friendly service. Daily changing home-made bar food includes pork pies (75p), filled salad rolls with turkey, beef and ham (£1.10), home-made celery and stilton soup (£1.75), hot beef, hot turkey or hot traditional sausage beef cobs (£1.75), ploughman's (£2.95), home-made chicken, leek, mushroom and celery pie (£3); note they only do rolls on Sunday. There are seats in the terrace area behind. *(Recommended by Chris Raisin, Alan Hopkin, Richard Lewis, David Carr, Mr and Mrs P Byatt, Jack and Philip Paxton, David and Shelia, Dorothee and Dennis Glover, John Scarisbrick, Andrew Stephenson)*

Free house ~ Licensee Trevor Harris ~ Real ale ~ Lunchtime meals and snacks 11.30-2.30 (rolls only Sun) ~ Restaurant (Sat only or by reservation) ~ (01332) 290677 ~ Children in family room and restaurant ~ Jazz Thurs evenings ~ Open 11-11; 12-10.30 Sun

Olde Dolphin £

6 Queen St; nearest car park King St/St Michaels Lane

An attractive 16th-c building very close to the cathedral and main pedestrianised area, this friendly and civilised pub has four cosy rooms, two with their own separate street doors. It's traditional and old-fashioned throughout, from the varnished wall benches of the tiled-floor public bar to the little carpeted snug with its brocaded seat; there are big bowed black beams, shiny panelling, cast-iron-framed tables, a coal fire, lantern lights and opaque leaded windows; the atmosphere is friendly and quietly chatty, with no piped music. Well kept Bass, Highgate Dark Mild, Ruddles and Worthington BB on handpump, with interesting guest beers such as Archers Golden, Burton Bridge and Charles Wells Bombardier (cut prices on Monday evening); very cheap food includes sandwiches (from £1.35), filled baked potatoes (from £2), omelettes (from £2.80), all-day breakfast (£2.95), gammon and egg (£3.99) and a generous mixed grill (£3.99), with dishes of the day such as liver and onion or braised steak (£3.75). There is a no-smoking upstairs tearoom (closed on our inspection visit). They have daily papers and board games, and there's said to be a ghost. *(Recommended by John and Christine Lowe, Jack and Philip Paxton, Richard Lewis, Norma and Keith Bloomfield, Alan and Charlotte Sykes, David Carr)*

Bass ~ Manager David Willis ~ Real ale ~ Meals and snacks (11-7.45, Sun 12-7) ~ (01332) 349115 ~ Children allowed in tearoom ~ Live music Sun night ~ Open 10.30-11; Sun 12-10.30

EYAM SK2276 Map 7

Miners Arms ⌂

Signposted off A263 Chesterfield—Chapel-en-le-Frith

At lunchtimes this well organised old place is pretty much given over to the many people who come here to enjoy the good fresh food, though as the evening draws on you'll find the locals arriving to drink; they don't do bar meals then. Well served by attentive staff, the choice of home-made dishes includes light and crispy filled baguettes (£1.95), ploughman's with the area's traditional fruitcake (£3.75) and daily changing blackboard specials like cauliflower and almond soup (£1.95), cumberland sausage in onion gravy (£3.95), braised beef in stout sauce (£4.95), crispy roast duck (£5.25), poached salmon in white wine sauce (£5.50), and puddings like bakewell pudding or pavlova (£1.95); good Sunday roast (no bar food then). There's a pleasant restful atmosphere in the three little plush beamed rooms, each of which has its own stone fireplace. Well kept Stones and Tetleys on handpump. Decent walks nearby, especially below Froggett Edge. *(Recommended by Peter and Jan Humphreys, Alan and Heather Jacques, R D Kelso, M Mason, D Thompson, Peter Marshall, Tony Young, Norma and Keith Bloomfield, C T Harrison, Peter and Anne Hollindale, Prof I H Rorison, KC, John and Christine Lowe, Jack and Philip Paxton, Jack Morley, Cathryn and Richard Hicks)*

Free house ~ Licensees Nicholas and Ruth Cook ~ Real ales ~ Lunchtime meals and snacks (not Sun) ~ Evening restaurant open for Sun lunch ~ (01433) 630853 ~ Children welcome ~ Open 12-3, 7-11; closed Sun night, Mon lunchtime and first 2 weeks Jan ~ Bedrooms: £25B/£45B

FENNY BENTLEY SK1750 Map 7

Coach & Horses

A515 N of Ashbourne

Readers like this welcoming and quietly friendly 17th-c coaching inn for its good value food and pleasant comfortable atmosphere. Popular bar meals, in decent-sized helpings, include soup (£1.75), baps and sandwiches (from £1.30, toasties from £2.75), filled baked potatoes (mostly £3.75), salads (from £4.25), chicken balti (£5.25), steak and kidney pie (£5.45), grilled trout or filled yorkshire puddings (£5.50), lamb liver and onions or well-praised vegetarian meals like mushroom and stilton bake (£5.95), and steaks (from £9.25); children's meals (£2.50). The dining room is no smoking. The little back room has ribbed green built-in wall banquettes and old prints and engravings on its dark green leafy Victorian wallpaper. There are more old prints in the friendly front bar, which has flowery-cushioned wall settles and library chairs around the dark tables on its turkey carpet, waggonwheels hanging from the black beams, horsebrasses and pewter mugs, and a huge mirror; two cosy log fires. Well kept Bass on handpump, along with Black Bull and Dovedale brewed a couple of fields away – recent reports suggest the former especially is quite a draw. Good coffee and service; darts, dominoes and piped music. Picnic tables on the back grass by an elder tree, with rustic benches and white tables and chairs under cocktail parasols on the terrace in front of this pretty rendered stone house. Leave muddy boots outside. *(Recommended by Mike and Wendy Proctor, Derek and Sylvia Stephenson, Joy and Peter Heatherley, Norma and Keith Bloomfield, Richard Houghton, Pat and Roger Fereday, Colin Fisher, Jack and Philip Paxton, Eric Locker, Richard Lewis, Brian Horner, Brenda Arthur, Paul Robinshaw, Basil Minson, D Hanley, Jack Morley, Neil and Anita Christopher, David and Shelia, John Scarisbrick, Geoffrey and Irene Lindley, R H Sawyer)*

Free house ~ Licensee Edward Anderson ~ Real ale ~ Meals and snacks ~ Restaurant ~ (01335) 350246 ~ Children welcome ~ Open 11.30-2.30, 6.30-11; closed 25 Dec

nr FOOLOW SK1976 Map 7

Barrel

Bretton; signposted from Foolow which itself is signposted from A623 just E of junction with B6465 to Bakewell

A popular stop with walkers, this unspoilt old place is perched on the edge of an isolated ridge, offering splendid views of the surrounding five counties. Stubs of massive knocked-through stone walls divide the cosy peaceful beamed bar into several areas – the snuggest is at the far end with an open wood fire, a leather-cushioned settle, and a built-in corner wall-bench by an antique oak table. The pub was in the process of being sold as we went to press, but as the building and surroundings have kept their charms throughout many similar changes of licensee over the years we trust that this occasion won't be any different. Darts, cribbage, dominoes. There are seats on the breezy front terrace. *(Recommended by John Fahy, Ian Rorison, Nigel Norman, Alex and Betty McAllan, FMH, David and Shelia, Jack Morley, Jack and Philip Paxton, Hilary Dobbie, Andy and Jane Bearsdley, Don Kellaway, Angie Coles, Nigel Woolliscroft)*

Free house ~ Real ale ~ Meals and snacks ~ (01433) 630856

FROGGATT EDGE SK2477 Map 7

Chequers 🍽

B6054, off A623 N of Bakewell; Ordnance Survey Sheet 119, map reference 247761

Last year this beautifully placed country inn was our Derbyshire Dining Pub of the Year, and it's proved a popular stop with readers again in recent months. Dishes that sound familiar often have an imaginative spin that transforms them into something slightly more unusual, the prices are very competitive, and though there is some emphasis on eating, there is still a pubby atmosphere in the bar. The fairly smart bar has antique prints on the white walls, partly stripped back to big dark stone blocks, library chairs or small high-backed winged settles on the well waxed floorboards, an attractive, richly varnished beam-and-board ceiling, and a big solid-fuel stove; one corner has a nicely carved oak cupboard. Efficiently served by smartly dressed staff, meals include soup of the day (£1.25), camembert and cranberry parcels (£2.10), big sandwiches served with salad and chips (from £3.55), rabbit and leek pie or pork casserole (£4.75), liver skillet, wild mushroom stroganoff or a roast of the day (£4.95), chicken and coconut curry (£5.65), daily specials, and puddings like whisky bread and butter pudding or traditional bakewell pudding (from £1.75). Well kept Wards Best and Thorne and Vaux Double Maxim on handpump, about 25 malt whiskies and a good wine list. The restaurant is no smoking; piped music. There are seats in the peaceful back garden. Froggatt Edge itself is just up through the woods behind the inn; no boots, dogs or children. *(Recommended by G P Kernan, David Carr,*

Mike and Wendy Proctor, Ian Rorison, Margaret and Nigel Dennis, James Waller, Ken and Joan Bemrose, Neville Kenyon, Mike Gorton, Mike and Karen England, A Preston, DC, R N Hutton, John and Joan Calvert, Wayne Brindle, Jack and Philip Paxton, Elizabeth and Anthony Watts, Sue Holland, Dave Webster)

Wards ~ Lease: E and I Bell ~ Real ale ~ Meals and snacks ~ Restaurant ~ (01433) 630231 ~ Children over 14 in restaurant ~ Open 11-3, 5-11; 12-10.30 Sun ~ Bedrooms: £42B/£54B

GRINDLEFORD SK2478 Map 7

Maynard Arms 🛏

B6521 N of village

Relaxed and civilised, this comfortable hotel in the heart of the Peak District has fine views of the Derwent Valley. Completely refurbished over the last year or so, the smart and spacious high-ceilinged main bar has some dark wood panelling, silver tankards above the bar, and local and cricketing photographs on the walls. Good home-made bar food includes soup (£1.50), sandwiches (from £1.95, with more elaborate deli-style ones from £3.95), smoked chicken, tomato and almond salad (£3.20), lamb and spinach curry or several pasta dishes like wild mushroom tagliatelle (£4.75), popular filled yorkshire puddings (£4.85), all-day breakfast (£5), venison casserole and blackberry sauce (£5.45), daily specials, and puddings such as apricot and kiwi cheesecake or apple and sultana charlotte (£2.35); choice of coffees. The restaurant is no smoking, and overlooks the neatly kept gardens. Well kept Boddingtons and Whitbreads Castle Eden on handpump; piped music. *(Recommended by Mike and Wendy Proctor, Margaret and Nigel Dennis, Janet and Peter Race, FMH, I P G Derwent, Derek and Sylvia Stephenson, Sue Holland, Dave Webster, Mr and Mrs Jones, Prof I H Rorison, Paul Robinshaw)*

Free house ~ Licensees Jonathan and Joanne Tindall ~ Real ale ~ Meals and snacks ~ Restaurant ~ (01433) 630321 ~ Children in restaurant and eating area of bar ~ Open 11-3, 6-11; 12-10.30 Sun ~ Bedrooms: £49B/£65B

HARDWICK HALL SK4663 Map 7

Hardwick Inn

2¾ miles from M1 junction 29: at roundabout A6175 towards Clay Cross; after ½ mile turn left signed Stainsby and Hardwick Hall (ignore any further sign for Hardwick Hall); at Stainsby follow rd to left; after 2½ miles staggered rd junction, turn left

Like the splendid park around it, this charming early 17th-c golden stone house is owned by the National Trust; it was originally a lodge for the nearby Elizabethan Hall. Each of the several separate rooms has a relaxed old-fashioned atmosphere, but perhaps most comfortable is the carpeted lounge, with its varnished wooden tables, comfortably upholstered wall settles, tub chairs and stools, and stone-mullioned latticed windows. One room has an attractive 18th-c carved settle. Big helpings of popular bar food like soup (£1.25), sandwiches (from £2), ploughman's (from £3.35), Lincolnshire sausage with egg (£3.60), home-made steak and kidney pie (£4.50), a daily vegetarian dish (£4.75), grilled trout (£4.85), gammon and egg or pineapple (£4.95) and steaks (from £7.85); puddings (£2), and children's menu (from £2.10). Well kept Marstons Pedigree, Morlands Old Speckled Hen, Theakstons XB and Old Peculier and Youngers Scotch on handpump, 40 or so malt whiskies, and several coffees; friendly staff. The restaurant is no smoking. Tables outside offer a very nice view. The pub can get crowded, especially at weekends. There's a charge for entry to the park, which you can no longer get into from the inn. *(Recommended by Peter and Audrey Dowsett, H E and E A Simpson, Dr and Mrs A H Young, Ian Rorison, David Craine, Ann Reeder, A Preston, A and R Cooper, DC, M W Turner, Stephen and Julie Brown, M D Phillips, Ann and Colin Hunt)*

Free house ~ Lease: Peter and Pauline Batty ~ Real ale ~ Meals and snacks

(11.30-9.30; 12-9 Sun) ~ Carvery restaurant (Tues-Sat, Sun lunchtime) ~ (01246)
850245 ~ Children in restaurant and three family rooms ~ Open 11.30-11; 12-
10.30 Sun

HAYFIELD SK0388 Map 7

Lantern Pike 🛏

Little Hayfield; A624 towards Glossop

In 1959 Tony Warren used to come to this village local at weekends working out the
origins of what became *Coronation Street*. These days it's the outstandingly warm
and friendly service from the landlady and her team that makes it special. It's
unpretentious but cosy, comfortable, and spick and span, with a warm fire, plush
seats, flowers on the tables, lots of brass platters, china and toby jugs. Well kept
Boddingtons, Flowers IPA, Timothy Taylors Landlord and maybe a guest on
handpump, and a good selection of malt whiskies. Well presented home-made bar
food includes soup (£1.95), sandwiches from (£2.35), breaded plaice (£4.80),
lasagne, curry, chilli or vegetarian dishes like leek and mushroom crumble (£5.15),
and several daily specials such as steak and stout pie (£5.50); children's menu
(£2.25), Sunday roast (£5.25). Darts, dominoes, and sometimes piped nostalgic
music. The back dining room is no smoking. Tables on a two-level stonewalled back
terrace, served from a window, look over a big-windowed weaver's house to the
Lantern Pike itself, and the pub's very well placed for walkers. This year a couple of
readers have picked out the ladies' lavatory for particular praise. *(Recommended by
Helen and Keith Bowers and friends, Mike and Wendy Proctor, J E Rycroft, Wallis Taylor,
Dorothy and Leslie Pilson, E J Hawkes, Gwen and Peter Andrews, Mike and Penny Sanders,
Robert and Ann Lees, Harriet and Michael Robinson, Mike Woodhead)*

Free house ~ Licensee Geraldine McDonald ~ Real ale ~ Meals and snacks (12-
2.30, 6-9.30; all day weekends and bank holidays) ~ Restaurant open all day Sun
~ (01663) 747590 ~ Children welcome ~ Open 12-3, 6-11; all day weekends and
bank holidays ~ Bedrooms:£25B/£35B

HOLMESFIELD SK3277 Map 7

Robin Hood

Lydgate; just through Holmesfield on B6054

Footpaths opposite this friendly moorland inn lead off into the Cordwell valley, with
fine views over Chesterfield and Sheffield; it's an ideal stop for assuaging an appetite
worked up whilst exploring the surroundings. Promptly served by smart and
pleasant young staff, the wide choice of popular food might include home-made
soup (£2.25), filled baguettes (from £2.25) or jacket potatoes (from £2.95),
ploughman's (£4.95), lasagne or chilli (£5.45), steak, ale and mushroom pie (£5.95),
honey-glazed ham (£6.95), a good range of changing blackboard specials like fresh
Whitby cod or leek and potato bake (£5.95), marinated chicken (£6.50), or strips of
beef in spring onion and ginger sauce (£9.50), and puddings like home-made apple
and peach crumble or bakewell tart (£2.50); children's menu. It's best to book at
weekends. The neat extended lounge area has exposed beams, chintz and paisley
curtains, plush button-back wall banquettes around wood-effect tables, partly
carpeted flagstone floors, and lovely open fires; piped music. Vaux Samson on
handpump, several malt whiskies. There are stone tables outside on the cobbled
front courtyard. *(Recommended by Michael Butler, K Frostick, Mr and Mrs B Langrish,
FMH, Comus Elliott, A Preston, JP)*

Free house ~ Licensees Chris and Jackie Hughes ~ Real ale ~ Meals and snacks
(11.30-2.30, 6-9.30; all day Sun) ~ (0114) 289 0360 ~ Children welcome if eating
~ Open 11.30-3, 6-11; 12-10.30 Sun

You are now allowed 20 minutes after 'time, please' to finish your drink –
half-an-hour if you bought it in conjunction with a meal.

KINGS NEWTON SK3826 Map 7
Hardinge Arms

5 miles from M1 junction 24; follow signs to E Midlands airport; A453, in 3 miles (Isley) turn right signed Melbourne, Wilson; right turn in 2 miles to Kings Newton; pub is on left at end of village

New owners arrived here just as we went to press, and though they do plan some changes there shouldn't be anything to alter the civilised and friendly feel of the place. They've kept the same manager and staff, as well as the carvery that's proved so popular with readers over the last year. Good value and with a choice of roasts, this is particularly well liked at lunchtimes by the older set and businessmen; there should also be a full menu by the time this Guide hits the shops. The rambling front bar has open fires, beams, a fine panelled and carved bar counter, and blue plush cushioned seats and stools – some in a pleasantly big bow window. At the back is a stately and spacious lounge. Well kept Bass and Ind Coope Burton on handpump, and several malt whiskies. Dominoes; piped music; large car park. *(Recommended by A and R Cooper, Mr and Mrs E M Clarke, Derek and Leslie Martin, Eric Locker, C H and P Stride, Stephen and Julie Brown, Marjorie and Bernard Parkin, James Nunns, Wayne Brindle, Jack and Philip Paxton,)*

Free house ~ Licensee Mel Stevens, same manager as before, all same staff ~ Real ale ~ Meals and snacks ~ (01332) 863808 ~ Children welcome if eating ~ Open 11-2.30, 6-11

KIRK IRETON SK2650 Map 7
Barley Mow 🛏 🍽

Signposted off B5023 S of Wirksworth

When so many pubs change beyond recognition within the space of weeks it's all the more delightful to find ones like this handsomely gabled Jacobean stone house where nothing seems to have changed for centuries. The simple sign outside is almost obscured by a tree branch, time is measured by a 17th-c sundial, and the only games you'll find in the unspoilt little rooms are dominoes, cards and cribbage. The timeless and quietly pubby small main bar has antique settles on the tiled floor or built into the panelling, a coal fire, old prints, shuttered mullioned windows – and a modest wooden counter behind which reposes a tempting row of casks of real ales. They usually have four of these on at once, such as Charles Wells Bombardier, Hook Norton Old Hookey, Marstons Pedigree, Timothy Taylors Landlord or Wadworths 6X, all costing a bit less than you'd usually pay for a pint in this area; also Thatcher's farm cider. Another room has cushioned pews built in, oak parquet flooring and a small woodburner, and a third has more pews, tiled floor, beams and joists, and big landscape prints. One room is no smoking. Popular filled lunchtime rolls; good value evening meals for residents only. Civilised old-fashioned service, a couple of friendly pugs and a somnolent newfoundland. There's a good-sized garden, as well as a couple of benches out in front. The charming village is in good walking country. *(Recommended by Jack and Philip Paxton, Pete Baker, David Carr, John Beeken, Phil and Sally Gorton, Wayne Brindle, A J and M Thomasson, Graham and Lynn Mason)*

Free house ~ Licensee Mary Short ~ Real ale ~ Lunchtime sandwiches ~ (01335) 370306 ~ Children at lunchtime, not in bar ~ Open 12-2, 7-11; closed 25 Dec, 1 Jan ~ Bedrooms:£21.50B/£36.75B

LADYBOWER RESERVOIR SK1986 Map 7
Yorkshire Bridge

A6013 N of Bamford

This substantial late Victorian roadside hotel has been attractively refurbished more or less in period style. One area has sturdy cushioned wall settles, staffordshire dogs and toby jugs on a big stone fireplace with a warm coal-effect gas fire, china on delft shelves, a panelled dado and so forth. A second extensive area, with another fire, is lighter and more airy, with floral wallpaper, pale wooden furniture, good big black and white photographs and lots of plates on the walls, and a small no-smoking conservatory with wicker chairs. All this space is certainly needed: this is good walking country, and the pub can get very busy, especially in summer. Service, however, is invariably pleasant and efficient. Consistently good value home-made bar food, served generously, includes soup (£1.65), ploughman's (£3.75), cod fillet or chicken and mushroom pie (£5.10), steak and kidney pie or lasagne (£5.25), scampi (£5.95) and puddings (from £2.30). Well kept Bass, John Smiths Magnet and Stones on handpump, good coffee with real cream; darts; fruit machine; maybe piped David Bowie or the equivalent. *(Recommended by Victoria Regan, Harold Bramhall, Steve Goodchild)*

Free house ~ Licensees P A and M Herling ~ Real ale ~ Meals and snacks (all day Sun) ~ (01433) 651361 ~ Children welcome ~ Open 11-11; 12-10.30 Sun; cl 25 Dec ~ Bedrooms: £38B/£49.50B

LITTLE HUCKLOW SK1678 Map 7

Old Bulls Head

Pub signposted from B6049

New licensees have taken over this atmospheric little country pub in the last year, and it's once again open throughout the week. In a very pleasant village setting, surrounded by upland sheep pastures, its two spick and span main rooms have old oak beams, thickly cushioned built-in settles, antique brass and iron household tools, and a coal fire in a neatly restored stone hearth. One room is served from a hatch, the other over a polished bar counter. The unusual little 'cave' room at the back has been opened up again, and is fast becoming a popular place to sit. The pub has traditionally had a reputation for gammon, and huge gammon steaks (£6.75) are still the prominent feature of the menu, along with big T-bone steaks (£9.95) and a few other well cooked dishes. Well kept Tetleys, Wards and a guest from carved handpumps; darts, dominoes. There are tables in the neatly tended garden, which is full of an unusual collection of well restored and attractively painted old farm machinery. *(Recommended by Peter Marshall, John Fahy and others; more reports please)*

Free house ~ Licensee Julie Denton ~ Real ale ~ Meals and snacks ~ (01298) 871097 ~ Children welcome ~ Open 12-3, 5(6 Sat)-11

LITTLE LONGSTONE SK1971 Map 7

Packhorse

Monsal Dale and Ashford Village signposted off A6 NW of Bakewell; follow Monsal Dale signposts, then turn right into Little Longstone at Monsal Head Hotel

The Wednesday evening folk singing and Mrs Lythgoe's splendid steak and kidney pie are two of the features that have particularly delighted recent visitors to this snug and atmospheric little 16th-c cottage, and there are plenty more – it's quite a favourite with some readers. The two traditional and cosy rooms are simply furnished with country kitchen chairs, cloth-cushioned settles and a more unusual almost batwinged corner chair under the beam-and-plank ceiling. Around the walls are a collection of prettily hung decorative mugs, brass spigots, attractive landscape photographs by Steve Riley, blow-ups of older local photographs and the odd cornet or trumpet. Good, popular bar food includes baps spread with dripping and generously filled with hot well hung beef or with hot pork, apple sauce and stuffing (£2), soup (£2.25) spare ribs (which are a meal in themselves) or stilton garlic mushrooms (£3.45), ploughman's (£4.50), probably three vegetarian dishes like cheese and spinach cannelloni (£5), or very tasty, filling steak and kidney pie (£5), lamb steak in stilton sauce (£6.60), steaks or chicken with lemon and coriander (£7.95), and puddings like brandy roulade or steamed puddings (£2.45). Warmly welcoming licensees, locals and dog. Well kept Marstons Best or Pedigree on handpump; darts, dominoes, cribbage.

There's a terrace in the steep little garden. The pub can get busy at weekends and some evenings. *(Recommended by Alan and Heather Jacques, Esther and John Sprinkle, Mike and Wendy Proctor, Jack and Philip Paxton, Ann and Colin Hunt, Jenny and Michael Back, A J Payne, Nigel Woolliscroft, Paul Robinshaw, Jack Morley, Derek and Sylvia Stephenson, Comus Elliott, David and Shelia, Bronwen and Steve Wrigley)*

Marstons ~ Tenants Lynne and Mark Lythgoe ~ Real ale ~ Meals and snacks (12-2, 7-9) ~ Restaurant (Thurs-Sat, bookings only) ~ (01629) 640471 ~ Well behaved children in eating area lunchtime and perhaps early eve ~ Live music Wed nights ~ Open 11-3, 5(6 on Sat)-11; closed 25 Dec evening

nr MELBOURNE SK3825 Map 7

John Thompson

Ingleby; village signposted from A514 at Swarkestone

Like the friendly pub itself, the popular own brew here is named after the enthusiastic landlord. He brews the JTS beer himself (home-brew kits are available), as well as a winter Porter, and the lighter Summer Gold in warmer months; they also have Bass on handpump. The big, pleasantly modernised lounge has ceiling joists, some old oak settles, button-back leather seats, sturdy oak tables, antique prints and paintings, and a log-effect gas fire; a couple of smaller cosier rooms open off, with pool, a fruit machine, and a juke box in the children's room, and a no-smoking area in the lounge. Straightforward but good and well priced bar food consists of sandwiches (from £1.20, nothing else on Sundays; the beef is excellent), home-made soup (£1.20), a cold buffet with very good meats or excellent hot roast beef (£5, not Mondays) and well liked puddings (£1.50); friendly efficient service. It's in a lovely setting above the River Trent, with lots of tables on the well kept lawns by flowerbeds, and on a partly covered outside terrace with its own serving bar. *(Recommended by Colin Fisher, Peter and Patricia Burton, CW, JW, Richard Houghton, R & A, Beryl and Bill Farmer, Eric Locker, A and R Cooper, J Honnor, J F M West, Jack and Philip Paxton, Wayne Brindle)*

Own brew ~ Licensee John Thompson ~ Real ale ~ Lunchtime meals and snacks (sandwiches only Sun; cold buffet only, Mon) ~ (01332) 862469 ~ Children in separate room ~ Open 10.30-2.30, 7-11

MONSAL HEAD SK1871 Map 7

Monsal Head Hotel 🛏 🍺

B6465

Dramatic views down over the valley draw a good number of people to this extended Victorian hotel, and especially to the cosy side stable bar, once home to the unfortunate horses that lugged people and their luggage up from the station deep down at the end of the valley viaduct. There's still a bit of a horsey theme, with stripped timber horse-stalls, harness and brassware, as well as flagstones, a big warming woodburning stove in an inglenook, cushioned oak pews around flowery-clothed tables, farm tools, and railway signs and lamps from the local disused station; steps lead up into a crafts gallery. Well kept John Smiths, Marstons Pedigree, Morlands Old Speckled Hen, Ruddles Best and County, Theakstons Best and Old Peculier, and Woodham Old Chopper on handpump, along with farm cider. Service is polite and helpful, but can slow right down when they're very busy; darts, shove ha'penny. Bar food includes sandwiches (from £1.50), Thai stir fry (£4.25), babotie (£4.75), pork piri-piri (£5.25), a vegetarian dish like leek and mushroom au gratin (£4.95) and home-made steak and kidney pie (£5.75); Sunday roast (£5.95); afternoon teas. The back garden has a play area. The spacious high-ceilinged front bar is set out like a wine bar, with dining chairs around big tables; it's partitioned off from a no-smoking restaurant area. The best views are from the front terrace or the upstairs sun lounge. *(Recommended by Jack and Philip Paxton, David Carr, Ann and Colin Hunt, Esther and John Sprinkle, Mike and Wendy Proctor, I P G Derwent, Dennis Stevens, Henry Paulinski, Roger and Valerie Hill, David and Shelia, Phil and Heidi Cook)*

Free house ~ Licensee Nicholas Smith ~ Real ale ~ Meals and snacks (12-9.30) ~ Restaurant ~ (01629) 640250 ~ Children welcome, but not after 7 in Stable bar ~ Irish folk music Fri ~ Open 11-11; 12-10.30 Sun; closed 25 Dec ~ Bedrooms: £30S/£35B; must be dinner and B&B for two nights at weekends)

OVER HADDON SK2066 Map 7

Lathkil 🖙

Village and inn signposted from B5055 just SW of Bakewell

Many would say the little hillside hamlet of Over Haddon is the best situated Derbyshire village, and this comfortable hotel reaps the benefit of its breathtaking views. Steeply down below is Lathkil Dale, one of the quieter dales, with an exceptionally harmonious spread of pastures and copses and plenty to interest the nature lover; paths from the village lead straight into this tempting landscape. Walkers will find a place for their muddy boots in the pub's lobby, and further in some good civilised comforts. The airy room on the right has a warming fire in the attractively carved fireplace, old-fashioned settles with upholstered cushions or plain wooden chairs, black beams, a delft shelf of blue and white plates on one white wall, original prints and photographs, and big windows. On the left is the spacious and sunny family dining area – partly no smoking – which doubles as a restaurant in the evenings; it's not quite as pubby as the bar, but there isn't a problem with shorts or walking gear. At lunchtime the bar food is served here from a buffet and includes home-made soup (£1.95), filled cobs (from £1.95), salads (£4.50), meat or vegetable lasagne (£5.10), steak and kidney pie (£5.60), smoked trout (£5.70), and home-made puddings like treacle tart (£2); evening extras include spicy chicken breast with mango chutney (£7) and lamb cutlets with redcurrant jelly (£7.80). They have a slightly more expensive menu on Friday and Saturday evenings, with meals like duckling breast with orange and brandy sauce (£10.50). Well kept Wards Best, Mild and Thorne Best on handpump; select malt whiskies and new world wine; piped classical music or jazz, shove-ha'penny, dominoes, cribbage. Best to get here early in good weather. If you stay in spring you may be lucky enough to wake up to the bleating of the lambs, perhaps one of the reasons why readers planning to stay just one night often end up staying two or three. *(Recommended by Mike and Wendy Proctor, Ian Rorison, Dennis Stevens, Joy and Peter Heatherley, Gwen and Peter Andrews, J E Rycroft, Christopher Warner, PGP, Esther and John Sprinkle, M Mason, D Thompson, Eddy and Emma Gibson, David Carr, S Palmer, Jack and Philip Paxton, Nigel Woolliscroft, Dorothee and Dennis Glover, Michael and Harriet Robinson, Tony Young, Ian Jones, Helen Pickering, L P Thomas, C J Scott, Basil Minson, John Waller, Dr Peter Donahue)*

Free house ~ Licensee Robert Grigor-Taylor ~ Real ale ~ Lunchtime meals and snacks ~ Restaurant Fri/Sat eves ~ (01629) 812501 ~ Children in dining area if eating ~ Open 11.30-3, 6.30-11; closed evening 25 Dec ~ Bedrooms: £35S/£70B

SHARDLOW SK4429 Map 7

Old Crown 🍺

Cavendish Bridge, 2½ miles from M1 junction 24: A6 towards Derby (pub actually just over the Leicestershire border)

We know quite a few people for whom a trip to this thriving 17th-c coaching inn is a regular lunchtime outing. It's popular not just for the very good food, but for its interesting range of rather unusual well kept real ales, so you need to arrive early to be sure of a seat. The daily specials are the meals to go for, with a good choice of dishes like meatballs in a rich mushroom sauce (£4.75), minced venison covered in mushrooms, onion and creamed potato (£5.75), curried frog legs (£5.95), leg of pork with grapes, dates and apples, pot roasted in red wine (£6.75), fresh cod with mussels and prawns poached in a whisky sauce (£6.95), and breast of duck casseroled with onion, celery and mushrooms in sweet cider (£8.25); other dishes include soup (£1.30), filled rolls or sandwiches (from £1.50), salads (from £4.25), tomato and vegetable tagliatelle (£5), sirloin steak (£7.75) and puddings (£1.70). A good selection of beers (many of them local) includes well kept Bass, Batemans XXXB, Courage Directors, Fullers London Pride, Greene King Abbot, Hook Norton Old Hookey, Natterjack, Rooster, Wadworths 6X, and a couple brewed for them in Leicestershire, Wide Eyed and Crownless and Chancellors Revenge; nice choice of malt whiskies. Obliging service, prompt even when busy. The busy friendly beamed bar is packed with bric-a-brac, including hundreds of jugs and mugs hanging from the beamed ceiling, brewery and railway memorabilia, and lots of pictures. Cribbage and piped music. The pub is next to the River Trent and was once the deportation point for convicts bound for the colonies. *(Recommended by Chris Raisin, Martin and Penny Fletcher, A and R Cooper, Jack and Philip Paxton, GSB, Wayne Brindle, Sue Holland, Dave Webster, Rona Murdoch, Susan and John Douglas, Andrew Stephenson, Alan and Eileen Bowker, Mike Pugh, Andy and Jane Bearsdley, Dr and Mrs J H Hills)*

Free house ~ Licensees Peter and Gillian Morton-Harrison ~ Real ale ~ Lunchtime meals and snacks ~ (01332) 792392 ~ Children in eating area of bar only ~ Open 11.30-3, 5-11; cl evenings 25/26 Dec

WARDLOW SK1875 Map 7

Three Stags Heads

Wardlow Mires; A623 by junction with B6465

Although we're rather fond of this delightfully unspoilt little stone cottage, it's certainly not the sort of place that pleases everyone. Some find it slightly too rough-and-ready, so if you don't like scruffy loos and dogs cheerfully wandering about the bar then it probaby isn't a pub you'll enjoy. But if well worn furnishings and unhurried service aren't likely to spoil your appreciation of the uniquely old-fashioned and idiosyncratic atmosphere, then you should like it very much indeed. The tiny unassuming parlour bar has old leathercloth seats, a couple of antique settles with flowery cushions, two high-backed windsor armchairs and simple oak tables on the flagstones, and a cast-iron kitchen range which is kept alight in winter; one curiosity is the petrified cat in a glass case. Tables in the small, no-smoking dining parlour – where there's an open fire – are bookable. They try to vary the seasonal menu to suit the weather so dishes served on their hardy home-made plates (the barn is a pottery workshop) might include a three-cheese ploughman's (£5), vegetarian dishes like vegetable and apricot casserole or leek and stilton hot pot (from £5), rabbit in mustard and herbs (£6.50), chicken breast in wine with chunky vegetables or rack of lamb (£7). Excellent Kelham Island Pale Rider and Fat Cat (both brewed by our Sheffield main entry – see Yorks chapter), Springhead Bitter from the little Springhead brewery in Sutton-on-Trent, and Hoskins & Oldfields Old Navigation on handpump, and lots of continental and British bottled beers. Cribbage and dominoes, nine men's morris and chess. Walkers, their boots and dogs are welcome; they have four dogs (and some cats) of their own. The front terrace outside looks across the main road to the distant hills. The car park is across the road by the petrol station. *(Recommended by M Mason, D Thompson, Ann and Colin Hunt, Ian and Trish Avis, Esther and John Sprinkle, Nigel Woolliscroft, Addie and Irene Henry, Fiona and David Pemberton, Mike and Wendy Proctor, Barbara Wensworth, Jack and Philip Paxton, David Carr, Jack Morley, R N Hutton, Comus Elliott, Derek and Sylvia Stephenson, Brian and Anna Marsden)*

Free house ~ Licensees Geoff and Pat Fuller ~ Real ale ~ Meals and snacks (12-3, 7-10) ~ Restaurant ~ (01298) 872268 ~ Children may be allowed in room without bar until 8.30pm ~ Live folk, Irish or bluegrass music Sat eve ~ Open 12-3, 7-11; all day weekends and bank holidays

WHITTINGTON MOOR

Derby Tup £

387 Sheffield Rd; B6057 just S of A61 roundabout

The choice of real ales at this straightforward corner pub seems to get bigger every year, these days usually running to eleven at a time. The regulars are Batemans XXXB, Kelham Island Fat Cat, Marstons Pedigree, Tetleys, and Theakstons XB and Old Peculier, with five quickly changing guest beers; our last look turned up Ash Vine Casablanca, Fullers London Pride, Gibbs Mew Bishops Tipple, and Ushers Best and Founders. They also have lots of continental and bottle-conditioned beers, changing ciders, and decent malt whiskies. The unspoiled plain rectangular bar with frosted street windows and old dark brown linoleum has simple furniture arranged around the walls – there's a tremendously long aged red plastic banquette – leaving lots of standing room; two more small unpretentious rooms; fruit machine. Besides good sandwiches, the daily changing bar food, home-made with fresh ingredients, might include mushroom soup (£1.95), spaghetti bolognese or cauliflower cheese (£2.95), chilli con carne or chicken casserole (£3.95) and chicken escalopes in plum sauce or pork steak in juniper and vermouth sauce (£4.50); cheerful relaxed atmosphere, darts, cribbage, dominoes, piped rock and blues. A no-smoking dining area was added last summer. Despite the remote-sounding name, Whittington Moor is on the northern edge of Chesterfield. *(Recommended by Colin Bournes, Tony Sheppard, David Atkinson, Jack and Philip Paxton, Ian Keenleyside)*

Free house ~ Licensee Peter Hayes ~ Real ale ~ Meals and snacks (12-2.30, 5(6 Sat)-7.30; not Sun evening) ~ (01246) 454316 ~ Children in eating area ~ Open 11.30-3(12-4 Sun), 5-11, all day Thurs-Sat

WOOLLEY MOOR SK3661 Map 7

White Horse 🍺

White Horse Lane, off B6014 Matlock—Clay Cross

Set in lovely rolling countryside, this attractive old pub is doing rather well at the moment, with a good many readers singing its praises over the last twelve months. The enthusiastic licensees keep a good balance between the popular food served in the cottagey beamed dining lounge, and the original tap room where the cheerful locals gather to organise their various teams – darts, dominoes, and two each for football and boules. They'll also probably be enjoying the well kept Bass, Jennings and three weekly changing guests from the local Townes brewery, such as Sunshine or Double Bagger. Good value bar food, made with fresh local produce, includes a dozen or so daily specials like feta cheese, cashew nut and grape slice (£4.95), venison sausage bake (£5.25), pork and wild mushroom stroganoff (£5.95), and fresh salmon and asparagus fricassee (£6.25); also sandwiches (from £2.20), ploughman's (£3.50), steak and kidney pie (£3.95), game pie (£4), and puddings like banana and caramel pie or treacle sponge (£2); children's meals come with a puzzle sheet and crayons. Decent wine list, with a couple of wines of the week; piped music in the lounge. There's a small no-smoking room at the side of the dining room. Picnic table sets in the garden have lovely views across the Amber Valley, and there's a very good children's play area with wooden play train, climbing frame and swings. A booklet describes eight walks from the pub, and the landlord is a keen walker; the pub is handy for Ogston Reservoir. They organise a couple of real ale festivals every year. *(Recommended by Norma and Keith Bloomfield, Peter Marshall, Tony Young, John Saul, David and June Harwood, Vicky and David Sarti, David and Fiona Pemberton, P Poole, Alan Hopkin, Derek and Sylvia Stephenson, Jack and Philip Paxton, Joy and Peter Heatherley, Ian Rorison, John and Christine Lowe, Peter and Audrey Dowsett, Geoffrey and Irene Lindley, David and Shelia, Pat and Tony Young, Paul Robinshaw, John Beeken, John Fahy, Ian Jones, Alan and Judith Gifford, Jenny and Brian Seller, R N Hutton, D Kudelka, JJW, CMW)*

Free house ~ Licensees Bill and Jill Taylor ~ Real ale ~ Meals and snacks (11.30-2, 6.30-9; 5.30-8.30 Sun) ~ Restaurant (not Sun evening) ~ (01246) 590319 ~ Children in restaurant and dining area of lounge bar if eating ~ Open 11.30-2.30(3.30 Sat), 6-11

Places with gardens or terraces usually let children sit there – we note in the text the very very few exceptions that don't.

Lucky Dip

Besides the fully inspected pubs, you might like to try these Lucky Dips recommended to us and described by readers (if you do, please send us reports):

Alfreton [High St; SK4155], *Olde McDonalds Farm*: Fun pub in big Edwardian building, wild and wonderful bric-a-brac inc parachuting chickens, sheep, funny farm memorabilia; pinball, pool, football table and video games in games room, separate eating area for bar food; very busy for Thurs, Fri, Sat live entertainment; Theakstons Best and XB and Youngers Scotch *(Mr and Mrs Russell Allen)*

☆ **Ashbourne** [Ashbourne Green (A515 towards Matlock); SK1846], *Bowling Green*: Well kept Bass, Worthington and two other changing ales, wide choice of good value home-cooked food inc vegetarian, friendly atmosphere, straightforward comfort; good bedrooms *(Colin Sims)*

☆ **Ashbourne**, [Victoria Sq], *Horns*: Attractive olde-worlde 18th-c pub with bay window overlooking steep cobbled street, friendly fast service, good range of food inc home-made pies, well kept Bass, decent coffee *(Tracey Hitchcock, Graham Moore)*

Ashbourne [Mkt Pl], *Olde Vaults*: Imposing and attractive old pub recently refurbished by welcoming new licensees; good reasonably priced bar food, particularly well kept Bass, good choice of other ales inc Theakstons XB and Worthington; open all day weekends and summer; bedrooms *(Bill and Irene Morley)*

☆ **Ashford in the Water** [SK1969], *Black Bull*: Cosy and homely comfortable lounge with well kept Robinsons ales, nicely presented home-cooked food from good soup and sandwiches up, reasonable prices, quick friendly service, no piped music; tables out in front *(Dorothy and Leslie Pilson, JP, PP, Keith Croxton, David Carr, John Waller, Ann and Colin Hunt)*

Ashover [Church St; SK3564], *Black Swan*: Decent cheap food inc good range of sandwiches, prompt cheerful service *(Allan Preston)*; [Milltown], *Miners Arms*: Currently doing well, good value food, well kept Mansfield beers, good friendly service; need to book lunchtime *(RAH)*

Bakewell [4 Buxton Rd; SK2168], *Aitchs*: Pleasant food and drink in wine bar/bistro with tables outside *(Paul McPherson)*; [Bridge St], *Castle*: Good value food, newspapers to read, smart wine-bar feel but good choice of ales, friendly staff *(Sue Holland, Dave Webster, Martin Bromfield, Bernadette Garner)*

☆ **Bamford** [A6013; SK2083], *Derwent*: Interestingly varied separate rooms off central hall-servery, big pictures and windows, friendly helpful service, bar food inc vegetarian, well kept Marstons Best and Pedigree and Stones Best, RAF Dambuster photographs, good value restaurant; children welcome, seats in garden; comfortable reasonably priced bedrooms, open all day *(Derek Patey, Wayne A Wheeler, Pat and Tony Young, Lynn Sharpless, Bob Eardley, LYM)*

Barlborough [Church St; on roundabout, junction A616/A619; SK4777], *De Rodes Arms*: Old but modernised Brewers Fayre pub, pleasant friendly atmosphere, good value food, Whitbreads-related beers, picnic tables outside; children away from bar *(Alan and Charlotte Sykes)*

☆ **Beeley** [SK2667], *Devonshire Arms*: Black beams, flagstones, stripped stone and plenty of atmosphere, good range of well kept ales inc Black Sheep, Theakstons XB and Old Peculier, queue at nice dining room's counter to order good though not cheap food from sandwiches up, prompt cheerful service, big log fires, no music; attractive rolling scenery nr Chatsworth – can get very busy; children welcome, with upstairs family room and own menu *(Pat and Tony Young, John and Christine Lowe, Allan Preston, JP, PP, Derek and Sylvia Stephenson, LYM)*

☆ **Biggin** [W of A515; SK1559], *Waterloo*: Hard-working and welcoming newish landlord, wide choice of good value generous food inc help-yourself salads and children's dishes, Bass; dales views *(Paul Robinshaw, JP, PP, D and D Savidge)*

☆ **Birch Vale** [via Station Rd towards Thornsett off A6015; SK0287], *Sycamore*: Thriving four-roomed dining pub with good reasonably priced food inc children's dishes and rich puddings, well kept ales, friendly helpful service, piped music, fountain in downstairs drinking bar; spacious streamside gardens with good play area, pets corner and summer bar; restaurant open all day Sun, children welcome, handy for Sett Valley trail; bedrooms comfortable, good breakfast *(S A Moir, LYM)*

Boylestone [Harehill; signed off A515, N of A50 junction; SK1735], *Rose & Crown*: Friendly traditional country local, oak beams and tiled floor, enthusiastic singing landlord, well kept beers inc guests *(JP, PP, G C Sonhurst)*

Brackenfield [A615 Matlock—Alfreton, about a mile NW of Wessington – OS Sheet 119 map ref 360587; SK3658], *Plough*: Much modernised but welcoming oak-beamed former 18th-c farmhouse in lovely setting, cosy three-level bar, cheerful log-effect gas fire, well kept Bass, Mansfield Old Baily, Tetleys and Worthington, sensibly priced food; big beautifully kept gardens with play area *(A Preston)*

Bradwell [Smalldale; off B6049 at Gore Lane/Townend; SK1781], *Old Bowling Green*: Good views from tables on terrace and garden outside attractive old stone local, much modernised inside, with three real ales, lots of malt whiskies, decent food and games room; fruit machine, unobtrusive piped music *(JJW, CMW, LYM)*

☆ **Brassington** [SK2354], *Miners Arms*: Very welcoming and pubby, with good food, well kept Marstons Pedigree, good-humoured landlord; children welcome, live music some nights; bedrooms *(Ian Jones, JP, PP)*

☆ **Buxton** [Bridge St; SK0673], *Railway*: Large railway-theme food pub under viaduct, very welcoming atmosphere, huge helpings of varied well cooked food, well kept Hardys & Hansons, prompt service *(J C and I F Paterson, Richard Houghton)*

Buxton [37 High St], *Cheshire Cheese*: Big low-ceilinged open-plan local with dark timber and stained glass, good value food, well kept Hardys & Hansons, friendly service, live music Sun, Mon and Weds *(B M and P Kendall, FT)*

☆ **Buxworth** [Silkhill, via B6062 off A6 just NW of Whalley Bridge roundabout – OS Sheet 110 map ref 022821; SK0282], *Navigation*: Busy bright cluttered decor and atmosphere to match in welcoming extended pub by former canal basin (restoration nearly complete), several low-ceilinged rooms, some canalia and brassware, lacy curtains, cheery staff, real coal and log fires, flagstone floors, good value generous food inc vegetarian and children's, four well kept Courage-related and other ales; darts, pool, piped music; tables on sunken flagstoned terrace, play area and pets corner; food all day; bedrooms *(David Carr, Pete Yearsley, Ann and Colin Hunt, Karl Green, Tony Young, Sue Demont, Tim Barrow, C H and P Stride, BB)*

Calver [off A623 N of Baslow; SK2474], *Bridge*: Unspoilt but comfortable, with well kept Hardys & Hansons, quickly served good value generous usual food, pleasant landlord, old brass and local prints; tables in nice big garden by River Derwent *(Comus Elliott, Alan and Heather Jacques)*

Carsington [just N of B5035 Wirksworth—Ashbourne – OS Sheet 119 map ref 252534; SK2553], *Miners Arms*: Reasonably priced usual food, efficient service; pleasant village in good walking and cycling country nr Carsington reservoir *(Allan Preston)*

☆ **Castleton** [Cross St; SK1583], *Olde Nags Head*: Small but solid hotel dating from 17th c, has civilised turkey-carpeted main bar with interesting antique furnishings, coal fire, faint piped music, friendly uniformed staff, well kept Bass and Boddingtons, good coffee, bar food from sandwiches up inc vegetarian dishes, cosy Victorian restaurant; open all day, comfortable bedrooms *(LYM; reports on new regime please)*

☆ **Castleton** [How Lane], *Peak*: Roomy airy bar, dining room with high ceiling and picture window view of Peak hills, wide choice of above-average generous reasonably priced food inc vegetarian, Tetleys and other ales, friendly service *(Peter and Anne Hollindale, B and K Hypher)*

☆ **Castleton** [High St/Castle St], *Castle*: Plush hotel bars with handsome flagstones, beams, stripped stonework, open fires, decent bar food though keg beers; open all day summer, tables outside; good bedrooms *(Martin Bromfield, Bernadette Garner, JP, PP, LYM)*

☆ **Castleton**, *George*: Good atmosphere and good value simple food in roomy bars with friendly helpful staff, well kept Bass; tables on wide forecourt; popular with young people – nr YHA; dogs welcome *(R H Sawyer, JP, PP)*

Castleton, *Olde Cheshire Cheese*: Two communicating bar areas, cheery and cosy, with well kept Wards tapped from the cask, friendly staff, wide choice of reasonably priced food, open fire, sensibly placed darts; bedrooms *(Tracey Hitchcock, Graham Moore, BB)*

Chapel en le Frith [SK0680], *Cross Keys*: Pleasant atmosphere and good food (all day Sun) in old pub with smartly decorated restaurant, well kept beers, very friendly service; children welcome *(S E Paulley, Mike and Wendy Proctor)*

Chellaston [High St; SK3730], *Lawns*: Attractive hotel, thatched servery in oak-beamed main lounge, friendly efficient service, good value carvery, Bass, Marstons Pedigree and a changing guest beer; bedrooms *(Andrew and Ruth Triggs)*

Chesterfield [43 Chatsworth Rd; SK3871], *Royal Oak*: Friendly pub with well kept beers and good atmosphere *(Richard Houghton)*

☆ **Chinley** [off A624 towards Hayfield; SK0482], *Lamb*: Profusely decorated three-room stone-built roadside pub with friendly atmosphere, well prepared quick reasonably priced bar food, well kept Bass and other ales; children till 8.30; lots of tables out in front *(Mike and Wendy Proctor, BB)*

☆ **Chunal** [A624 a mile S of Glossop; SK0391], *Grouse*: Pleasant open-plan but cosy moorland pub, good bar food inc enjoyable home-made pies, excellent chips and interesting specials, friendly service, well kept Thwaites; spectacular views of Glossop, real fires, old photographs of surrounding countryside, traditional furnishings and candlelit tables, unobtrusive piped music; children allowed in upstairs restaurant *(J F M West)*

☆ **Church Broughton** [OS Sheet 128 map ref 205337; SK2033], *Holly Bush*: Neat and attractive village pub, popular for good cheap simple home cooking inc Sun lunch; well kept Marstons Pedigree, friendly labradors *(Chris Raisin, Michael Seals)*

Combs [SK0478], *Beehive*: Comfortable, with well kept Marstons and good food; by lovely valley tucked away from main road; bedrooms *(John and Margaret Batstone)*

☆ **Cromford** [Scarthin; SK2956], *Boat*: Long comfortable bar with bric-a-brac and books, very welcoming staff, two beers brewed for the pub in Chesterfield as well as Bass and Mansfield ales kept well, well priced food from black pudding to wild boar inc good Sun lunch, log fire; TV may be on for sports; children welcome, garden *(Dave Irving, Pete Yearsley, David and Helen Wilkins)*

☆ **Cutthorpe** [NW of Chesterfield; B6050 W of village; SK3273], *Gate*: Picture-window views over eastern Peak District from chatty area around bar, neat dining lounge down steps, decent fair-priced food inc bargain lunches popular with older people, well kept ales such as Bass, Boddingtons, Flowers Original and Mansfield Riding, friendly efficient staff, lots of biggish pictures (*Alan and Heather Jacques, FMH, BB*)

Cutthorpe [B6050], *Peacock*: Neatly kept and comfortable, good straightforward food, good service, Wards Sheffield Best and Vaux Waggledance (*Alan and Heather Jacques*)

Dale [Main St, Dale Abbey; SK4339], *Carpenters Arms*: Olde-worlde picturesque pub, popular with walkers; good value food in bar, lounge and new restaurant, well kept Ind Coope Burton and a guest beer, keen licensee, garden with play area, camping and caravan park behind; pleasant village, Abbey ruins nearby (*Jack and Philip Paxton, Peter Clarke*)

☆ Derby [Irongate], *Standing Order*: Vast Wetherspoons conversion of imposing bank, central bar, booths down each side, elaborately painted plasterwork, pseudo-classical torsos, high portraits of mainly local notables; usual popular food all day, well kept Banks's Mild, Courage Directors, Marstons Pedigree, Theakstons Best and XB, Youngers Scotch, reasonable prices, neat efficient young staff, no-smoking area; shame about the vaulting acoustics (*Chris Raisin, BB*)

Derby [Chapel St], *Blessington Carriage*: Friendly simple town pub, popular freshly cooked lunchtime food, well kept beer, lots of memorabilia, walls panelled with old doors; children in eating area (*David Carr*); [25 King St], *Flowerpot*: Extended real ale pub, friendly staff, comfortable back bar with lots of books and old Derby photographs, pleasant garden (*Richard Lewis, Richard Houghton*); [204 Abbey St], *Olde Spa*: Relaxed old local, well kept Tetleys-related ales, tiled-floor bar, games room, garden with fountain (*Chris Raisin, David Carr*)

☆ Earl Sterndale [signed off B4053 S of Buxton; SK0967], *Quiet Woman*: Friendly little stonebuilt village pub, low-beamed and softly lit, lots of china ornaments, real fires, genuine food from sandwiches up using local (even home-grown) fresh ingredients – may have free-range bantam and goose eggs and local cheese for sale; Marstons Pedigree and Best and a guest such as Banks's Mild; picnic tables out in front, lots of animals (*Derek and Sylvia Stephenson, M Mason, D Thompson, BB*)

☆ Edale [SK1285], *Old Nags Head*: Useful walkers' pub at start of Pennine Way, substantial basic cheap food, open fire, S&N and other ales; can be very busy; children in airy back family room, tables on front terrace and in garden – short path down to pretty streamside cottages (*Victoria Regan, JP, PP, David Carr, LYM*)

Elton [SK2261], *Duke of York*: Homely utterly unspoilt old-fashioned local, like stepping back in time; darts in one of three rooms; cl lunchime, open 8-11 (*JP, PP, D and D Savidge*)

☆ Farnah Green [follow Hazelwood sign off A517 in Blackbrook, W edge of Belper; SK3346], *Bluebell*: Plush smartly run dining pub, good prompt food in relaxing small rooms; sturdy tables out on terrace and in quiet gently sloping spacious side garden, restaurant with inventive cooking, well kept Bass (*John Waller, BB*)

☆ Fenny Bentley [A515 N of Ashbourne; SK1750], *Bentley Brook*: Big open-plan bar/dining room with bare boards, mix of set tables and cushioned settles, bow windows, log fire, communicating airy carpeted restaurant; Marstons Pedigree, Tetleys and own-brewed Leatherbritches Belter and Robert Catesby, usual food from baked potatoes up inc children's bargains, well reproduced piped music, games machines; picnic tables on terrace with proper barbecue area, skittles; open all day, handy for Dovedale; children more than welcome, bedrooms (*John Scarisbrick, David and Shelia, B M Eldridge, Richard Lewis, Derek and Sylvia Stephenson, BB*)

☆ Foolow [SK1976], *Bulls Head*: Attractive moorland village pub, good helpings of interesting and well served if not cheap food in good no-smoking restaurant area, also cheaper bar snacks; Wards and Vaux beers and one or two guests, good welcoming service; bedrooms, fine views (*Mr and Mrs J A Moors, Adrian and Gilly Heft, Ann and Colin Hunt, Mr and Mrs G Archer, Miss A G Drake, LYM*)

Glapwell [The Hill; A617 a mile E of M1 junction 29; SK4866], *Young Vanish*: Small no-smoking dining area, decent standard food, five real ales; fruit machine, piped pop music may be loud; garden with play area in garden (*JJW, CMW*)

☆ Great Hucklow [SK1878], *Queen Anne*: Good range of food inc unusual fish, well kept beer, good atmosphere in comfortable beamed bar with open fire, two other rooms, one with french windows to small terrace and pleasant garden with lovely views; children welcome, handy for walks (*Mike and Wendy Proctor, JP, PP, Alex and Betty McAllan, Neville Kenyon*)

Grindleford [B6001; SK2478], *Sir William*: Relaxed local atmosphere, wide choice of good value food, pool table in spacious room; splendid view, walking nearby (*FMH, Alex and Betty McAllan*)

☆ Hartington [The Square; SK1360], *Devonshire Arms*: Good choice of tasty food at sensible prices, well kept beer, friendly efficient service; bedrooms comfortable (*Wayne A Wheeler, D and D Savidge, John and Joan Calvert*)

☆ Hartington, *Minton House*: Beautifully presented reasonably priced bar food, decent wines, welcoming fire and friendly staff in spick and span hotel – a nice place to stay; bedrooms (*Mrs B H Adams*)

nr Hartington [Newhaven; A515 a mile N of A5012; SK1561], *Jug & Glass*: Low-beamed moorland pub still closed 1996 after fire a year earlier (*LYM*)

Hartshorne [Ticknall Rd; SK3322], *Old Mill Wheel*: Interesting conversion of old screw mill, bar and dining area on ground floor, small bar and more extensive dining area upstairs, Marstons Pedigree and guest beers, good-sized helpings of interesting food, friendly atmosphere and service, mill wheel and machinery in full view *(M Joyner)*

Hassop [SK2272], *Eyre Arms*: Cosy 17th-c inn with good food in small dining area; doing well under courteous friendly newish landlord; good walks nearby *(Mike and Wendy Proctor, Geoffrey and Irene Lindley)*

☆ **Hathersage** [Leadmill Bridge; A622 (ex B6001) towards Bakewell; SK2381], *Plough*: Ex-farm with Derwent-side garden, good helpings of good fresh food in bar and two dining areas, friendly landlord, impressive organisation – cheerful prompt service even when very busy; well kept ales such as Wadworths 6X, decent wines *(M Baxter, FMH, Ian Rorison, Janet and Peter Race, Geoffrey and Irene Lindley, James Waller, John and Joan Calvert)*

☆ **Hathersage** [Church Lane], *Scotsmans Pack*: Big welcoming open-plan local dating from 17th c, good choice of generous nicely presented food (best to book Sun lunch), reasonable prices, well kept Burtonwood Bitter and Forshaws, decent wines; some seats on pleasant side terrace by trout stream; good bedrooms, huge breakfast *(Derek and Sylvia Stephenson, M S Crabtree, James Waller)*

☆ **Hayfield** [Market St; SK0387], *Royal*: Well run 18th-c former vicarage, oak panelling, six well kept ales, cheerful atmosphere, good food from young chef with good ideas; pleasantly decorated bedrooms *(Frank Hughes, Mike and Wendy Proctor)*

Heath [just off M1 junction 29; A6175 towards Clay Cross, then first right; SK4466], *Elm Tree*: Lively pub doing well under new landlord, basic reasonably priced food inc children's, lounge, tap room, games room; children welcome *(P J and S E Robbins)*

Hilton [Main St; SK2430], *Kings Head*: 17th-c ex-coaching dining pub with good value generous food inc good Sun lunch, well kept Marstons Pedigree, pleasant surroundings *(M· Joyner)*

☆ **Hope** [Edale Rd; SK1783], *Cheshire Cheese*: Welcoming 16th-c stonebuilt pub with cosy little up-and-down oak-beamed rooms, interesting good value home cooking, welcoming helpful staff, well kept Stones and Wards, several coal fires; attractive village, children allowed in eating area, walkers welcome; two bedrooms *(Simon and Ann Ward, JP, PP, Malcolm and Pat Rudlin, LYM)*

☆ **Hope** [A625 towards Castleton], *Poachers Arms*: Pleasant relaxed atmosphere in modern but traditionally furnished interconnected rooms, friendly staff, wide choice of popular food from sandwiches up (may be a wait), well kept Courage-related ales, children welcome, back conservatory; darts, dominoes, maybe piped music; the two dogs are Barney and Tina; comfortable bedrooms *(John and Christine Lowe, Anthony Barker, FMH, M W Turner, Prof I H Rorison, D Kudelka, LYM)*

Hope [1 Castleton Rd], *Woodroffe Arms*: Tastefully redeveloped with several rooms inc conservatory, wide choice of good value food inc children's dishes and Sun lunch, four real ales and Addlestone's cider, real fire, polite service; Sun quiz night, garden with swings; bedrooms *(CMW, JJW, FMH)*

Horsley [Church St; SK3744], *Coach & Horses*: Friendly village local, two rooms and a conservatory (where children allowed), big fireplace, brasses; usual pub food inc Sun roasts and cheap basket meals, big garden with tables and play area *(D and D Savidge)*

Ilkeston [Station Rd, Ilkeston Junction; SK4642], *Dewdrop*: Large three-room local by rly in old industrial area, friendly staff, good value bar snacks, Ind Coope Burton, Hook Norton Old Hookey, Kelham Island Pale Rider, Wards Kirby and guests, two coal fires, barbecue; good value bedrooms *(Simon, Julia and Laura Plumbley, Jack and Phil Paxton)*

Knockerdown [1½ miles S of Brassington on B5035; SK2352], *Knockerdown*: Firmly run pub with teacups on beams, pictures and bric-a-brac, extensive reasonably priced menu, good value Sun lunch, well kept Banks's Mild and Marstons Pedigree, no piped music; good views from garden, nr Carsington reservoir; well behaved children may be allowed *(JJW, CMW, Mike and Wendy Proctor, A Preston)*

☆ **Ladybower Reservoir** [A57 Sheffield—Glossop, at junction with A6013; SK1986], *Ladybower*: Fine views of attractive reservoir from unpretentious open-plan stone pub, clean and spacious; reasonably priced popular food, Tetleys-related ales, red plush seats, discreet piped music; children welcome, stone seats outside, good walks *(Prof I H Rorison)*

Lees [just off Langley Common—Longford rd, off B5020 W of Derby; SK2637], *Black Cow*: Particularly good value generous food inc very cheap puddings, quick service by friendly landlord and family, Ansells, Bass and Marstons Pedigree *(Alan and Heather Jacques)*

☆ **Litton** [off A623; SK1675], *Red Lion*: Pretty village pub/restaurant (you can't just have a drink), above-average food esp game in cosy low-ceilinged partly panelled front rooms or bigger back room with stripped stone and antique prints; huge log fires, good friendly service, well kept Boddingtons, decent wine, quiet piped classical music; dogs allowed; cl weekday lunchtimes, Sun/Mon evenings *(Chris Hodgson, LYM)*

Longlane [SK2538], *Ostrich*: Well appointed country pub, formerly a farm, improved by current owners; plenty of tables outside, very popular food inc house speciality curries, well kept Marstons Pedigree, old tractors for children to play on *(Alan and Heather Jacques)*

☆ **Lullington** [SK2513], *Colvile Arms*: 18th-c village pub with basic panelled bar, plush lounge, pleasant atmosphere, friendly staff, piped music, well kept Bass and Marstons

Pedigree on handpump, good value snacks (no cooking), tables on small sheltered back lawn overlooking bowling green; cl weekday lunchtimes *(John Beeken, Graham Richardson, LYM)*

☆ Makeney [Holly Bush Lane; A6 N, cross river Derwent, before Milford turn right, then left; SK3544], *Holly Bush*: Cosy and friendly old-fashioned two-bar pub with five well kept ales brought from cellar in jugs, besides Ruddles County and one named for the pub on handpump – also annual beer festival; three roaring open fires, beams, tiled floors and snug, good value basic meals inc lunchtime snacks, Thurs steak night, dining area; games machines in lobby, can be smoky; children allowed in conservatory, aviary on small terrace *(B Adams, JJW, CMW, David Lloyd-Jones)*

Marshlane [B6056 S of Sheffield; SK4079], *Fox & Hounds*: Jovial new landlord in cosy dark-beamed pub with pictures, plates and brass, fresh flowers, open fire, separate tap room with darts, four well kept Burtonwood ales, good coffee, good value food inc children's, quiet piped music, two friendly dogs; big garden with picnic tables, good play area, good views *(JJW, CMW)*

Matlock [Dale Rd, Matlock Bridge – A6 S edge of town; SK2959], *Boat House*: By River Derwent, between rd and cliff of old limestone quarry, friendly unchanging old-fashioned pub with very wide choice of good value food inc good vegetarian dishes; well kept Hardys & Hansons ales, open all day – tea at teatime; can get smoky, juke box may be loud; interesting walks; bedrooms *(Pat and Tony Young, Norma and Keith Bloomfield)*; [48 Jackson Rd], *Thorn Tree*: Superb views over the Wye Valley and town from the garden; well kept beers usually include one from Whim brewery *(Richard Houghton)*

☆ Melbourne [SK3825], *White Swan*: Welcoming and interestingly restored 15th-c pub with good value imaginative food, friendly service, well kept Marstons Pedigree, comfortable wing armchairs, separate rather austere dining room; can get quite smoky nr bar; pleasant narrow garden; children welcome *(Mr and Mrs B H James, JP, PP, Mr and Mrs A Cooper, LYM)*

☆ Melbourne [222 Station Rd, towards Kings Newton/Islay Walton], *Railway*: Good old-fashioned chatty local, good value basic well cooked food, attractive dining room, well kept Marstons Pedigree, Timothy Taylors Landlord, Wards and guest beers, tiled and wooden floors, cast-iron gas fireplaces; well behaved children allowed; bedrooms *(Wayne Brindle, JP, PP, R and A Cooper)*

☆ Millthorpe [Cordwell Lane; SK3276], *Royal Oak*: Stripped stone, oak beams, relaxed welcome for all inc walkers, cosy snug, real fires, inexpensive simple but interesting home-made lunchtime food, well kept Wards on handpump, good helpful service, no piped music; no children inside, tables out on pleasant terrace; good walks nearby, cl Mon lunchtime exc bank hols *(Norma and Keith Bloomfield, R E Kay, Keith and Sonya Byres, FMH, Chris and Elizabeth Riley, J M Pawson, LYM)*

Milton [just E of Repton; SK3126], *Coach House*: Imaginative range of home-made food, well kept guest beers, pleasant surroundings, occasional entertainment, attractive garden *(Allan Randall, Patricia and Peter Burton)*

☆ Monyash [SK1566], *Bulls Head*: Attractive furnishings in friendly high-ceilinged two-room bar inc oak wall seats and panelled settle, horse pictures, shelf of china, roaring log fire, mullioned windows, good generous low-priced home-cooked food inc vegetarian and good salads, well kept Ind Coope Burton and Tetleys Mild and Bitter, efficient staff; nicely set tables in plush two-room dining room, pool in small back bar, maybe quiet piped music; long pews outside facing small green, friendly ginger cat, children and muddy dogs welcome; simple bedrooms *(Phil and Heidi Cook, Nick and Meriel Cox, Rita and Keith Pollard, Mrs B Sugarman, BB)*

Moorwood Moor [nr South Wingfield; SK3656], *White Hart*: Good choice of reasonably priced food, spacious and comfortable dining area, tables in garden *(Allan Preston, JP, PP)*

Oakerthorpe [B6013 Belper—Claycross; SK3955], *Anchor*: Comfortable dining pub with good choice inc game and lots of puddings; lots of tables in tidy and spacious separate bar (piped music here may be rather loud); can be busy weekends *(Allan Preston)*

Ogston Reservoir [B6014 Stretton—Tansley; SK3761], *New Napoleon*: Basic traditional pub popular with anglers, good value fresh food, gas fire, darts, piano, fresh flowers; tables in garden, view across reservoir *(David Carr)*

☆ Pilsley [off A619 Bakewell—Baslow; SK2471], *Devonshire Arms*: Cosy and welcoming local with limited good value food using fresh Chatsworth ingredients lunchtime and early evening, well kept Mansfield Riding and Old Baily and other ales on handpump; lovely village handy for Chatsworth Farm and Craft Shops *(DC, Peter Marshall, G Washington)*

Ridgeway [SK3551], *Bridge*: Nice setting in pretty village, good service, pleasant beer, food inc good sandwiches *(J S Rutter)*

☆ Ripley [Buckland Hollow; A610 towards Ambergate, junction B6013 – OS Sheet 119 map ref 380510; SK3851], *Excavator*: Welcoming open-plan Marstons Tavern Table with separate family dining area and no-smoking area, wide choice of good value food (all day Sun) inc vegetarian and good children's menu, friendly efficient staff, reasonable prices, particularly well kept Pedigree and other ales *(Mike and Penny Sanders, Mark Elvin)*

☆ Rowarth [off A626 in Marple Bridge or Mellor sign, sharp left at Rowarth sign, then follow Little Mill sign; OS Sheet 110 map ref 011889 – but need Sheet 109 too; SK0189], *Little Mill*: Beautiful tucked-away setting, unusual features inc working waterwheel, vintage Pullman-carriage bedrooms; wide choice of cheap plentiful bar food all day (may be a wait), big open-plan bar with lots of little settees, armchairs and small tables, Banks's, Hansons, Robinsons Best Mild and Bitter and a guest beer, hospitable landlord, pub games, juke box, busy upstairs restaurant; children welcome, pretty garden dell across stream with good play area; bedrooms *(N M Baleham, JP, PP, Geoffrey and Irene Lindley, TBB, LYM)*

☆ **Rowsley** [A6; SK2566], *Grouse & Claret*: Spacious and comfortable Mansfield Landlords Table family dining pub in well refurbished old stone building, good reasonably priced food (all day weekends) from carvery counter with appetising salad bar, friendly helpful efficient service, no-smoking area, decent wines, open fires; tap-room popular with walkers, tables outside; good value bedrooms, caravan and camping site behind *(Patricia Young, David and Mary Webb, JP, PP, Richard Lewis, Geoffrey Lindley)*

☆ **Shardlow** [3½ miles from M1 junction 24, via A6 towards Derby; The Wharf; SK4330], *Malt Shovel*: Friendly 18th-c former maltings attractively set by canal, good changing lunchtime food, well kept Marstons and guest ales; odd-angled walls, good open fire heating two rooms, pleasant service; seats out by water *(Andy and Jane Bearsdley, A and R Cooper, JP, PP, LYM)*

☆ **Shardlow**, *Clock Warehouse*: Handsome 18th-c brick-built warehouse in attractive spot with picture windows overlooking canal basin, a pub for some time and now converted into family dining pub, with reasonable food, Mansfield real ales, play areas indoors and out, tables outside too *(GSB, LYM)*

Shardlow [Aston Rd (old A6)], *Dog & Duck*: Well converted Marstons Tavern Table family food pub, well kept ales in small bar away from the bustle of the dining area *(Chris Raisin)*

☆ **Smalley** [A608; SK4044], *Bell*: Charming three-room village pub, friendly staff, generous straightforward food, well kept ales such as Batemans XB and XXXB, Marstons Pedigree and Ruddles, good choice of wines, keen landlord; lovely garden *(Jack and Philip Paxton)*

South Wingfield [B5035 W of Alfreton; SK3755], *Olde Yew Tree*: Convivial local with interesting panelled corner, well kept Marstons Pedigree and two guests such as Fullers, Jennings Cumberland or Shepherd Neame Spitfire, good food inc good value Sun lunch, real fire *(Derek and Sylvia Stephenson, Ross Fletcher)*

Sparklow [SK1266], *Royal Oak*: Friendly, with well kept Burton Bridge, Mansfield and other guest beers, good food inc vegetarian; children genuinely welcome; on Tissington Trail *(Mr and Mrs Bradford)*

☆ **Sparrowpit** [nr Chapel en le Frith; junction of A623 – B6061; SK0980], *Wanted Inn*:

Friendly and attractive stonebuilt 16th-c inn, two rooms each with real fire, good value home cooking, well kept Robinsons Bitter and Mild, lots of copper; piped music; picnic tables by car park, beautiful countryside *(JP, PP, David Carr)*

☆ **Stanton by Dale** [3 miles from M1 junction 25; SK4638], *Stanhope Arms*: Cosy and attractive rambling pub, friendly staff, well kept Tetleys-related ales, good value generous fresh bar food, upstairs dining room converted from adjoining cottage; unspoilt village *(R Johnson, Dr and Mrs J H Hills)*

Stanton by Dale, *Chequers*: Welcoming pub with decent food inc delicious soups and good cold buffet, friendly service *(J H and S A Harrop)*

Swarkestone [A514/A5132; SK3628], *Crewe & Harpur Arms*: Old inn and stables refurbished as Marstons family dining pub, variety of eating areas, plus indoor and outdoor places for children; welcoming staff, wide choice of popular food served noon till 9, separate bar area, Marstons ales, adequate wines, outside play area; handy for Calke Abbey on Trent and Mersey Canal *(M Joyner, Gordon Theaker)*

Taddington [SK1472], *Queens Arms*: Attractively furnished and decorated, welcoming landlord and staff, varied generous nicely presented food inc good children's dishes, Mitchells and Tetleys; quiet village in good walking country *(S Howe, JP, PP)*

☆ **Ticknall** [7 High St; SK3423], *Staff of Life*: Very neat and friendly local with a dozen or more well kept ales on handpump or tapped from the cask inc ones from distant breweries such as Moorhouses, Pendragon, Shepherd Neame, also wide choice of good popular inexpensive food; magazines to read, open fire, good service even when busy, restaurant, good wine list *(Rona Murdoch, Pete Yearsley, Anthony Barker, Janet Box, JP, PP, Simon Marshall, Eric Locker, Michel Hooper-Immins)*

☆ **Ticknall** [B5006 towards Ashby de la Zouch], *Chequers*: Small, friendly and full of atmosphere, with vast 16th-c inglenook fireplace (maybe with winter roast chestnuts), bright brass, old prints, well kept Marstons Pedigree and Ruddles, very welcoming licensees, good fresh lunchtime baps and ploughman's (not Sun); no machines, seats in sizeable garden *(Allan Randall, JP, PP, Mrs W Bryn Davies, LYM)*

☆ **Tideswell** [SK1575], *George*: Spacious and comfortably refurbished, with simple traditional decor and furnishings, separate room areas, wide choice of good value simple but generous home cooking, well kept Hardys & Hansons, open fires, welcoming staff; tables in front overlooking pretty village, sheltered back garden; children welcome; 60s music Fri, good value bedrooms, pleasant walks *(Norma and Keith Bloomfield, Kay Neville-Rolfe, JP, PP, Derek and Sylvia Stephenson, Mike and Wendy Proctor, A F and J Gifford, BB)*

Tideswell [Four Lanes End; A623 NE],

Anchor: Cosy, with very friendly staff, generous freshly cooked food, panelled dining area *(Ian and Melanie Henry)*

Tintwistle [Old Rd; off A628, N side; SK0297], *Bulls Head*: Good value generous food, well kept ales and reasonable prices in low-beamed character 16th-c pub, suitable decor; may be closed some weekday lunchtimes *(Tony Owens, J F M West)*

Walton [Matlock Rd (B6015 SW of Chesterfield); SK3669], *Blue Stoops*: Former coaching inn with well kept ales, good home cooking; tables in back garden *(Charlie McDowell)*

☆ **Wardlow** [B6465; SK1874], *Bulls Head*: Plushly comfortable country dining pub with short menu of decent food, good specials and steaks, Wards ale, helpful landlord and welcoming staff, provision for children; no dogs or walking boots; simple bedrooms *(Derek and Sylvia Stephenson, A Preston, JP, PP, Geoffrey and Irene Lindley, Comus Elliott, Brian and Anna Marsden, Roger and Christine Mash, LYM)*

Wessington [A615 ¾ mile NW; SK3758], *Plough*: Well kept Marstons Pedigree, nice choice of reasonably priced food in adjoining converted barn; good country views from tables outside *(A Preston)*

Whaley Bridge [Old Rd; SK0181], *Shepherds Arms*: Old-fashioned unspoilt country pub with old-fashioned welcome, low-ceilinged lounge, flagstones, wall benches and scrubbed pine tables in public bar, coal fires, well kept Marstons Bitter and Pedigree and Banks's Mild, traditional games – no piped music, machines or greasy food *(Phil and Sally Gorton, J W Jones)*

Whatstandwell [A6/Crich rd; SK3354], *Derwent*: Pleasant atmosphere, good reasonably priced bar food inc good sandwiches, quick friendly service even when busy, well kept sensibly priced Hardys & Hansons *(Derek Patey, PGP)*

Whittington [Old Whittington; SK3874], *White Horse*: Well refurbished village inn with big lounge, good value food (not Sun evening), well kept Whitbreads-related ales *(FMH)*

☆ **Winster** [B5056 above village; SK2460], *Miners Standard*: Welcoming local, well kept Marstons Pedigree, Theakstons XB and a guest such as Black Sheep, good value food till 10, big open fires, interesting lead-mining photographs and mineral specimes, well placed darts, restaurant, attractive view from garden; children allowed away from bar *(Jamie and Ruth Lyons)*

☆ **Youlgreave** [Church St; SK2164], *George*: Handsome yet unpretentious stonebuilt local opp church, quick friendly service, good range of reasonably priced home-cooked food, comfortable banquettes, well kept S&N ales; flagstoned public bar, games room, juke box; attractive village, roadside tables outside; handy for Lathkill Dale and Haddon Hall, walkers welcome *(Harriet and Michael Robinson, JP, PP, Sue Holland, Dave Webster)*

☆ **Youlgreave** [High St], *Farmyard*: Welcoming local with low ceilings, impressive stone fireplace, old farm tools, friendly landlady, well kept Mansfield Mild and Riding with a guest such as Charles Wells Bombardier, good cheap food, comfortable banquettes, big upstairs restaurant; children welcome, tables in garden *(Gwen and Peter Andrews, Mike and Wendy Proctor, JP, PP)*

Youlgreave, *Bulls Head*: Comfortable old village inn, several cosy cavernous rooms, decent bar food, well kept Marstons ales inc changing Head Brewers Choice *(Sue Holland, Dave Webster)*

Devon

This county is always a special favourite on our inspection circuit: pub after pub of real character and individuality, with getting there half the fun – wonderful very varied countryside. The variety among pubs here is marvellous, too: from simple to very smart, from alehouses concentrating on their beers and farm ciders to dining pubs where food outclasses many restaurants. Of course, one consequence of this richness is that competition for a place among the main entries here is particularly intense – so, despite having so many main entries here (87 at the last count), there are plenty of pubs in the Lucky Dip section at the end of the chapter that are just as appealing in their way. Our current shortlist of these would include the Ship at Axmouth, Anchor at Beer, Cricket at Beesands, Poltimore Arms at Brayford, Coppa Dolla at Broadhempston, Pilchard at Burgh Island, Artichoke at Christow, Linny at Coffinswell, Wild Goose at Combeinteignhead, Royal Oak at Dunsford, Sir Walter Raleigh at East Budleigh, Swans Nest at Exminster, Hartland Quay Hotel at Hartland Quay, Red Cow in Honiton, Hoops at Horns Cross, Boathouse at Instow, Crabshell at Kingsbridge, Ebrington Arms at Knowle, New Inn at Moreleigh, White Hart at Moretonhampstead, Ring of Bells at North Bovey, Sandy Park Inn at Sandy Park, both Stokeinteignhead pubs, Maltsters Arms at Tuckenhay, both Widecombe pubs and Kings Arms at Winkleigh; on the edge of Exmoor the small chain that includes the Old Station House at Blackmoor Gate, Black Venus at Challacombe and Pyne Arms at East Down is good, too. As we have inspected the great majority of all these, we can vouch for their quality; and there's a splendid choice in Exeter and in Topsham. Back among the main entries, pubs currently on sparkling form include the Watermans Arms in its nice waterside setting at Ashprington, the Avon Inn at Avonwick (promoted to the main entries this year for its exceptional Italian-inspired food), the Sloop at Bantham (good food, nice spot), the warmly friendly Coach & Horses at Buckland Brewer, the Anchor at Cockwood (great seafood and fish), the Cott at Dartington (very good all round), the ancient Church House at Harberton (good specials from its Madeiran chef), the relaxing Rock at Haytor Vale, the idiosyncratic Masons Arms at Knowstone, the Who'd Have Thought It at Miltoncombe (character, food), the relaxed and homely Journeys End at Ringmore (its hard-working licensees have gained it one of our Place to Stay Awards this year), the friendly Blue Ball at Sidford, the atmospheric Oxenham Arms at South Zeal, the Kings Arms at Stockland (nice to stay overnight for a meal here), the nicely refurbished Passage in Topsham, the Cridford Inn at Trusham (great all round), the Anchor at Ugborough (very enjoyable food brings it back into the main entries this year). For a really enjoyable meal out, four pubs which have been giving particular pleasure this year are the Castle at Lydford, the Old Rydon at Kingsteignton, the Kings Arms at Stockland and the Cridford Inn at Trusham: of these, we choose the Cridford Inn as Devon Dining Pub of the

Year. There are too many changes – of management, of decor, of food type – to list here this year; but the overall message is that a great deal's happening in Devon's pubs, with a lot of good news. Drinks prices in the county are just a shade higher than the national average: the two cheapest places we found, both brewing their own, were the Beer Engine at Newton St Cyres (refurbished this year, and now doing a Mild alongside its other beers) and the Fountain Head at Branscombe. Dartmoor Best and Legend, incidentally, which used to be brewed in Devon, are now brewed for Carlsberg Tetleys by St Austell, in Cornwall.

ABBOTSKERSWELL SX8569 Map 1

Court Farm

Wilton Way; look for the church tower

Even when busy, the licensees of this attractive old farmhouse remain friendly and efficient. The long bar has a woodburning stove in a stripped red granite fireplace, a nice big round table by an angled black oak screen, a mix of seats on the polished crazy flagstones, a turkey rug in one alcove formed by a low granite wall with timbers above, and a long rough-boarded bar counter; a further small room is broadly similar with stripped kitchen tables and more spindleback chairs; piped music. On the right of the entrance is the two-roomed public bar with a woodburning stove, fruit machine, and a simple end room with darts, cribbage and dominoes. Bar food includes home-made soup (£1.55), doorstep sandwiches (from £1.65), fresh mussels or ploughman's (from £3.25), home-cooked ham and egg or mushroom and stilton tagliatelle (£4.25), home-made steak and kidney pie (£5.35), whole grilled fresh local plaice (£5.95), 12oz rump steak (£9.95), roast rack of lamb with rich madeira sauce (£8.95), and puddings (from £2). Well kept Bass, Boddingtons, Flowers IPA and Wadworths 6X on handpump or tapped from the cask, and several wines by the glass. The pretty garden has a wendy house and toys for children. *(Recommended by Andrew Hodges, H James, Ian Phillips, Joan and Gordon Edwards)*

Heavitree (who no longer brew) ~ Tenant Robin Huggins ~ Real ale ~ Meals and snacks (till 10pm) ~ (01626) 61866 ~ Children in eating area of bar ~ Open 11-3, 5-11; 11-11 Sat, 12-10.30 Sun

ASHBURTON SX7569 Map 1

London Hotel 🍺

11 West St

Roaring log fires and a friendly welcome greet you in the spacious turkey-carpeted lounge of this rather grand 15th-c coaching house – which was up for sale as we went to press (but current reports from readers are still favourable). There are also little brocaded or red leatherette armchairs and other seats around the copper-topped casks they use as tables, and stripped stone walls, and the room spreads back into a softly lit dining area. From their own brewery, they serve Best, Figurehead, Man o' War, Black Velvet Stout, Celebration Porter, and IPA on handpump. Decent bar food includes sandwiches (from £1.70; toasties from £2), ploughman's (from £4), ham and egg (£4.20), omelettes (from £4.50), grilled trout (£7.50), steaks (from £7.60), daily specials and vegetarian meals, and puddings like home-made fruit crumble (£1.80); farm ciders; darts, shove-ha'penny, dominoes, and piped music. There is some connection here to Conan Doyle's *Hound of the Baskervilles*. *(Recommended by June and Malcolm Farmer, Hanns P Golez, Alan and Paula McCully, John and Christine Vittoe, Richard Houghton, Jeanne Cross, Paul Silvestri; more reports please)*

Own brew ~ Manager David Reese ~ Real ale ~ Meals and snacks (not winter Sun evening) ~ Restaurant ~ (01364) 652478 ~ Children welcome ~ Open 11-3, 5.30-11; 12-10.30 summer Sun – 12-3, 7-10.30 winter Sun ~ Bedrooms: £27.50S/£40S

ASHPRINGTON SX8156 Map 1

Durant Arms

Village signposted off A381 S of Totnes; OS Sheet 202 map reference 819571

Friendly new licensees are now running this neatly kept gable-ended dining inn and have settled in well. The open-plan bar has beams, lots of dried flowers, lamps and horsebrasses, several open fires, and a mix of seats and tables on the red turkey carpet; there's a lower carpeted lounge too, with another open fire. Good bar food includes sandwiches, liver and bacon, chicken curry, rabbit or steak and kidney pies, mushroom stroganoff, and haddock and broccoli bake (all £5.25). Well kept Flowers Original, Greenalls Royal Wessex, and Wadworths 6X on handpump; no games machines or piped music. Tables in the sheltered back garden. The church is opposite and this is a pretty village. *(Recommended by Peter Haines, David and June Harwood, John Evans, Viv Middlebrook, S Demont, T Barrow, Roger and Lin Lawrence)*

Free house ~ Licensees Graham and Eileen Ellis ~ Real ale ~ Meals and snacks ~ Restaurant ~ (01803) 732240 ~ Children in restaurant ~ Open 11.30-2.30, 6-11 ~ Bedrooms: £20S/£50S

Watermans Arms 🛏

Bow Bridge, on Tuckenhay road; OS Sheet 202 map reference 812565

The pretty flower-filled garden here won awards last year and you can relax with a drink at the picnic tables – or sit by the river across the road and watch the ducks (or even swans and kingfishers). Inside, this historic place (once a smithy and brewhouse, and a prison during the Napoleonic Wars), has a quarry-tiled and heavy-beamed bar area with a bustling, friendly atmosphere, high-backed settles, built-in wall benches, rustic seats, and candles in bottles; the comfortable eating area has windsor chairs on its red carpet, more beams, and stripped stone walls; log fires. Good bar food includes lots of daily specials as well as soup (£2.25), sandwiches (from £2.50; fresh crab £3.95), mushrooms with bacon, garlic tomato and herbs (£3.95), ploughman's (from £4.95), pasta carbonara or lasagne (£5.50), salads and platters (from £6), prawns piri-piri or home-made steak and kidney pie (£6.95), and steaks (from £10.95); children's menu (£2.75). Part of the restaurant is no smoking. Well kept Bass, Dartmoor Best, Palmers IPA, and Tetleys on handpump, with Flowndes Neck (a cask conditioned cider), a farm cider called Pigsqueal, and Luscombe real apple juice; good, quick service. Darts, dominoes and piped music. *(Recommended by C A Hall, Brian Benjamin, Dennis Glover, JWC, MC, Jim and Maggie Cowell, S N Robieson, Joy and Paul Rundell, Roger and Susan Dunn, Nigel Spence, Kim Greek, George and Jeanne Barnwell, B H Sharpe, David Wallington, Jeanne Cross, Paul Silvestri)*

Free house ~ Licensee Trevelyan Illingworth ~ Real ale ~ Meals and snacks ~ Restaurant ~ (01803) 732214 ~ Children in eating area of bar ~ Open 11-3, 6-11; 12-3, 6-10.30 Sun but winter evening opening then, 7 ~ Bedrooms: £36S/£64S

AVONWICK SX7157 Map 1

Avon Inn 🍴

B3210, off A38 E of Plymouth, at South Brent

Very much a dining pub, this rings some unusual changes on what we've come to expect from Devon pubs. There's a wide range of bar food in the small back bar: open sandwiches (from £2.50; prawn £3.30), an amazing variety of pasta dishes such as chicken and walnut, salmon and mushroom, clams in garlic and tomato sauce and carbonara, vegetarian things like artichokes with gorgonzola cheese or aubergines with peppers, tomato and mozzarella (all from around £4.50), plenty of fish dishes such as dover or lemon soles and bass, seasonal rabbit, venison, and pheasant, fillet of beef with wild mushrooms or chicken stuffed with seafood or lemon sauce (all from around £8.50), outstanding fillet steak (£12), and lovely puddings such as fruit tartlets or crème brûlée (£2.75). Yes, there is an Italian chef/patron at the helm here, so you can also expect interestingly flavoured ice creams and authentic espresso coffee. Moreover, there are decent Italian wines alongside the well kept Badger Best and Bass on handpump; fruit machine and piped music. It's in the big front restaurant, with very good friendly service from neat efficient waitresses, that his cooking really comes into its own, and here it's best to book on Friday or Saturday night. Decor and furnishings are comfortable and pleasant in a fairly modern style. There are tables out in a pleasant garden by the River Avon. *(Recommended by Walker and Debra Lapthorne, Mr and Mrs J Woodfield, DJW)*

Free house ~ Licensees Mario and Marilyn Velotti ~ Real ale ~ Meals and snacks ~ Restaurant (01364) 73475 ~ Well behaved children allowed ~ Open 11.30-2.30, 6.30-11

AXMOUTH SY2591 Map 1

Harbour

B3172 Seaton—Axminster

You can be sure of an enjoyable visit at this popular thatched stone pub. The Harbour Bar has a friendly atmosphere, black oak beams and joists, fat pots hanging from pot-irons in the huge inglenook fireplace, brass-bound cask seats, a high-backed oak settle, and an antique wall clock. A central lounge has more cask seats and settles, and over on the left another room is divided from the no-smoking dining room by a two-way log fireplace. At the back, a big flagstone lobby with sturdy seats leads on to a very spacious and simply furnished family bar. Well kept Bass, Flowers IPA and Original, and Greenalls Royal Wessex on handpump; darts, pool, and winter skittle alley. Good bar food includes sandwiches (from £1.45), ploughman's (from £3.75), vegetarian dishes (from £4.75), fresh fish (from £5.25), puddings (from £1.85), and children's menu (£2.25); friendly, cheerful service even when busy. They have a lavatory for disabled people, and general access is good. There are tables in the neat flower garden behind. The handsome church has some fine stone gargoyles. *(Recommended by David Holloway, Pat and John Charles, A Denman, Mrs A M Fishleigh, Basil Minson, Galen Strawson)*

Free house ~ Licensees Dave and Pat Squire ~ Real ale ~ Meals and snacks (not winter Sun evenings) ~ (01297) 20371 ~ Children in eating area of bar and in family room ~ Open 11-11; 12-10.30 Sun; 11-2.30, 6-11 in winter

BANTHAM SX6643 Map 1

Sloop 🛏 ♀

Off A379/B3197 NW of Kingsbridge

In such a favoured position with a lovely sandy beach (and rock pools) just 300 yards over the dunes, this 16th-c inn does get crowded in summer – but service remains friendly and efficient. The black-beamed bar has country chairs around wooden tables, stripped stone walls and flagstones, and easy chairs in a quieter side area with a nautical theme. Good bar food includes home-made soups such as scrumpy and onion or tomato (from £2.10), sandwiches (from £1.75; crab £3.50), basket meals (from £2.50), home-made pâté (£3.40), ploughman's (from £3.70), local lamb steak (£7.85), steaks (from £8.85), daily specials such as laver bread with ham and cockles (£3.45), barbecued spare ribs (£3.65), liver and onions (£4.35), scallop mornay (£4.85), mediterranean hotpot (£5.25), braised oxtail (£5.50), giant cod (£7.40), crab salad (£8.65), grilled bass with hollandaise sauce (£9.60); hearty breakfasts. Well kept Bass, Blackawton Bitter, Ushers Best and a guest beer on handpump, Churchward's cider from Paignton, 16 fine malt whiskies, and a carefully chosen wine list including local ones. Darts, dominoes, cribbage, table skittles, fruit machine, trivia, and piped music. There are some seats at the back. The bedrooms in the pub itself have the most character. *(Recommended by Bryan Taylor, G W Stevenson, Verity Kemp, Richard Mills, Marianne Lantree, Steve Webb, John and Vivienne*

Rice, G L Brown, Chris and Martin Taylor, Mr and Mrs J Jones, M Clifford, Jon Pike, Julie Murphy, James Macrae, J and J O Jones, Mrs M Lawrence, B Taylor, Roger and Susan Dunn, Owen and Margaret Warnock, Anthony Marriott, Peter Lewis)

Free house ~ Licensee Neil Girling ~ Real ale ~ Meals and snacks (till 10pm) ~ Restaurant ~ (01548) 560489/560215 ~ Children in eating area of bar and in restaurant ~ Open 11-2.30, 6-11; winter evening opening 6.30 ~ Bedrooms: £29.50B/£56B; s/c cottages also

BERRYNARBOR SS5646 Map 1

Olde Globe ★

Village signposted from A399 E of Ilfracombe

In a pretty village, this rambling and atmospheric 13th-c pub happily changes little over the years. The series of dimly lit homely rooms have floors of flagstones or of ancient lime-ash (with silver coins embedded in them), low ceilings, curved deep-ochre walls (bulging unevenly in places), and old high-backed oak settles (some carved) and plush cushioned cask seats around antique tables. Decorations include lots of cutlasses, swords, shields and fine powder flasks, a profusion of genuinely old pictures, priests (fish-coshes), thatcher's knives, sheep shears, gin traps, pitchforks, antlers, and copper warming pans. Well kept Courage Directors and Ushers Best and a guest beer on handpump, and several country wines; sensibly placed darts, pool, skittle alley, dominoes, cribbage, fruit machine, and piped music. Bar food includes sandwiches (from £1.30), ploughman's or vegetarian sausages (£2.60), pasties (£2.65), salads (from £3.10), home-made steak and kidney pie or lasagne (£4.10), steaks (from £6.95), puddings (from £1.50), children's dishes (£1.95), and popular main course Sunday lunch (£3.95; 3-course in restaurant £6.50 – best to book); quick, friendly service. In high season, the restaurant is used as a no-smoking room for bar rather than restaurant meals. There's a children's activity house in the garden and the crazy-paved front terrace has some old-fashioned garden seats. *(Recommended by Lynne Sharpless, Bob Eardley, Dave Irving, Dr G W Barnett, Tony and Wendy Hobden, David Carr, Nick Lawless, Basil Minson, Dorothy and Leslie Pilson, R J Walden, George and Jeanne Barnwell, Ted George, Graham and Sue Price)*

Courage ~ Lease: Phil and Lynne Bridle ~ Real ale ~ Meals and snacks (till 10pm) ~ Gaslit restaurant ~ (01271) 882465 ~ Children in family/function room with toys ~ Live entertainment Thurs evenings July/Aug ~ Open 11.30-2.30, 6-11; winter evening opening 7pm

BISHOPS TAWTON SS5630 Map 1

Chichester Arms

Pub signposted off A377 outside Barnstaple

This thatched pub – and the village – are relatively peaceful in comparison with busy Barnstaple. The rather smart bar has an open fire, low heavy beams and stout supporting timbers, plush wall banquettes and cushioned wheelback chairs on its patterned carpet, a solid old bar counter, and uneven sloping floors. The family room has its own bar: darts, pool, skittle alley, football table, cribbage, dominoes, fruit machine, video game, piped music, and doors out to barbecue area. Bar food (with prices unchanged since last year) includes soup (£1.75), sandwiches (from £1.75), filled baked potatoes (from £2.95), meat or vegetable burgers (£2.95), cod in batter (£3.95), tortellini and prawns (£4.95), steaks (from £7.95), and puddings (£2.75); the restaurant has a no-smoking area. Well kept Bass and Worthington on handpump. There are picnic tables on a flagstoned front terrace, with more in a sheltered back area. *(Recommended by Colin Draper, Rita Horridge, Alan and Charlotte Sykes, Joan and Andrew Life, Peter and Audrey Dowsett, Lynn Sharpless, Bob Eardley)*

Free house ~ Lease: Hugh Johnston ~ Real ale ~ Meals and snacks (till 10pm) ~ Restaurant ~ (01271) 43945 ~ Children in eating area of bar and in restaurant ~ Occasional live entertainment Sun evening ~ Open 11.30-11; 12-10.30 Sun

BLACKAWTON SX8050 Map 1

Normandy Arms 🛏

Signposted off B3122 W of Dartmouth; OS Sheet 202 map reference 807509

The quaint main bar in this solid inn has an interesting display of World War II battle gear and a good log fire, as well as bar food such as home-made soup (£1.95), sandwiches (from £1.80), ploughman's (£3.95), home-made chicken liver pâté (£4.50), home-made steak and kidney pie or vegetable lasagne (£4.95), whole lemon sole or pork in cider (£8.95), steaks (from £8.95), and home-made puddings like tipsy cake or chocolate mousse (from £2.60). Well kept Bass, Blackawton Bitter and Shepherd's Delight, and Wadworths 6X on handpump. Sensibly placed darts, pool, cribbage and dominoes. Some tables out in the garden. *(Recommended by Dr S Willavoys, Paul and Janet Waring, Roger and Susan Dunn, Jack and Philip Paxton, George and Jeanne Barnwell, Phil and Anne Smithson; more reports please)*

Free house ~ Licensees Jonathan and Mark Gibson ~ Real ale ~ Meals and snacks (not winter Sun evenings) ~ Restaurant ~ (01803) 712316 ~ Children in restaurant ~ Open 11.30-2.30, 6.30-11; 12-2.30, 7-11 winter weekdays ~ Bedrooms: £30B/£48B; not 24-26 Dec

BRANSCOMBE SY1988 Map1

Fountain Head 🍺

Upper village, above the robust old church; village signposted off A3052 Sidmouth—Seaton

The end of June beer festival held at this old tiled stone house is very popular: three days of spitroasts, barbecues, cream teas, a balloon race, and over 30 real ales – as well as their own-brewed beers, Branoc, Jolly Geff (named after Mrs Luxton's father, the ex-licensee), summer Summa'that, and winter Olde Stoker. They also keep Green Valley farm cider. The room on the left – formerly a smithy – has a log fire in the original raised firebed with its tall central chimney, forge tools and horseshoes on the high oak beams, and cushioned pews and mate's chairs. On the right, an irregularly shaped, more orthodox snug room has another log fire, white-painted plank ceiling with an unusual carved ceiling-rose, brown-varnished panelled walls, and rugs on its flagstone-and-lime-ash floor; the children's room is no smoking, and the new airedale is called Max. Bar food includes cockles or mussels (£1.50), sandwiches (from £1.75; fresh crab when available £2.75), ploughman's (£3.95), home-made meat or vegetable lasagne (£4.25), home-made steak and kidney pie or home-cooked ham and egg (£4.95), kebabs (£6.25), evening steaks (from £8.50), daily specials like fresh battered cod (£4.95), and children's dishes (from £1.50). Darts, cribbage, dominoes. There are seats out on the front loggia and terrace, and a little stream rustling under the flagstoned path. *(Recommended by David Holloway, Sue Demont, Tim Barrow, Jane Warren, A Preston, Howard Clutterbuck, Jack and Philip Paxton, Mrs A M Fishleigh, Peter Burton, M Richards)*

Free house ~ Licensee Mrs Catherine Luxton ~ Real ale ~ Meals and snacks (not 25 Dec) ~ (01297) 680359 ~ Children in own small room; if over 10 can eat in eating area of bar in evening ~ Folk group last Sun lunchtime of month ~ Open 11.30-3, 6-11; 11.30-2, 7-11 in winter ~ S/c available

Masons Arms ♀ 🛏

Main St; signed off A3052 Sidmouth—Seaton

Run by a hard-working and enthusiastic licensee, this 14th-c inn is being constantly improved. The open log fire in the bar is now used every day for lunch and supper to spit roast legs of lamb or pork, ribs of beef or chicken – and sometimes goose, a whole shark or pig, and turkey, and the kitchen has been reorganised which has helped reduce waiting times. The top dining room is to become a second bar (which will be no smoking) and improvements have been made to the bedrooms. The rambling low-beamed bar has a massive central hearth in front of the roaring log fire, windsor chairs and settles, and a relaxed atmosphere. Good bar food now includes soup (£1.80), lunchtime sandwiches (from £2.95; hot spit roast £3.50; interesting open ones from £3.95), lunchtime ploughman's (from £3.95), cheese and broccoli bake (£4.95), beef and lamb lasagne (£5.95), spare ribs (£6.50), pork in cider (£7.25), baked rack of lamb roasted in cider with a mint and honey glaze or chicken piri-piri (£7.95), breast of duckling with cashew nuts (£9.20), and daily specials such as broccoli, artichoke and mint soup (£2.80), pasta with mushroom, basil, crème fraîche and yoghurt (£5.50), cod in beer batter (£6.95), smoky bacon and honey baked chicken pie (£7.20), large local plaice (£8.55), puddings, and children's dishes (from £2.95); good breakfasts. One of the three rooms of the restaurant is no smoking. Well kept Bass, Dartmoor Best, and Otter Bitter and two guest beers such as Eldridge Pope Royal Oak, Greene King Abbott, and Morlands Old Speckled Hen on handpump, they hold a summer beer festival with over 37 real ales, a December whisky festival (35 malts), 16 wines by the glass and local farmhouse cider in summer. Shove-ha'penny and dominoes. Outside, the quiet flower-filled front terrace has tables with little thatched roofs, extending into a side garden. *(Recommended by Peter and Audrey Dowsett, Sue Demont, Tim Barrow, James Nunns, Jane Warren, J A Snell, Ann and Colin Hunt, Gwyneth and Salvo Spadaro-Dutturi, Peter Burton, Mrs A M Fishleigh)*

Free house ~ Licensee Murray Inglis ~ Real ale ~ Meals and snacks ~ Restaurant ~ (01297) 680300 ~ Children welcome ~ Live entertainment some Fri/Sat evenings ~ Open 11-11; 12-10.30 Sun; 11-3, 6-11 in winter ~ Bedrooms: (some in cottage across road) £22(£32B)/£44(£54B)

BRENDON SS7748 Map 1

Rockford

Lynton—Simonsbath rd, off B2332

Handy for walkers from Lynmouth and Watersmeet, this homely little inn is set by the East Lyn river with its good salmon, brown trout and sea trout fishing. The original stables and hay loft have been converted into bars and on the walls there are lots of old photographs (which the landlord is happy to describe to you). Good bar food includes lunchtime dishes like home-made cottage pie (£2.95), smoked trout (£3.95), or home-made chicken and mushroom pie (£4.50), with evening things such as gammon braised in ale with a honey glaze, salmon with hollandaise sauce or lamb in redcurrant and port (all £6.95); well kept Cotleigh Barn Owl, Courage Best, and Morlands Old Speckled Hen on handpump, and decent wines. Darts, pool, shove-ha'penny, cribbage, dominoes, and piped music. *(Recommended by Dave Irving, Bruce Bird, R and S Bentley, Nigel Clifton, H and D Payne, Mrs C Blake,)*

Free house ~ Licensees D W Sturmer and S J Tasker ~ Real ale ~ Meals and snacks ~ Restaurant ~ (01598) 741214 ~ Children in eating area of bar ~ Local folk every 3rd Sat evening of month ~ Open 12-2.30(2 in winter), 7-11; closed weekday lunchtimes 2 weeks Nov ~ Bedrooms: £18/£36

BROADCLYST SX9897 Map 1

Red Lion ♀

B3121, by church

You can be sure of a peaceful visit to this tiled, ochre-washed old pub as there are no noisy machines or piped music. The long red-carpeted bar has heavy beams, cushioned window seats, some nice chairs around a mix of oak and other tables, and a collection of carpenters' planes; a flagstoned area has cushioned pews and low tables by the fireplace, and at the end of the L-shaped room are big hunting prints and lots of team photographs. Popular bar food includes home-made soup (£1.60), sandwiches (from £1.80), home-made chicken liver pâté (£2.90), lamb kidneys in sherry (£3.60), ploughman's (from £3.80), vegetable lasagne (£4.70), steak and kidney pie or pork and apple in cider casserole (£4.80), rump steak (£7.90), daily specials, children's meals (from £2.40), roast Sunday lunch (£4.50), and puddings (from £2.20). Well kept Bass, Eldridge Pope Royal Oak, Fullers London Pride, Wadworths 6X, and Worthington Best on handpump, 8 wines by the glass, and local farm cider; they sell home-produced honey. Darts and a beamed skittle alley. There are picnic tables on the front cobbles by the wisteria, and more seats in a small enclosed garden across the quiet lane. *(Recommended by Patrick Stewart-Blacker; more reports please)*

Free house ~ Licensees Stephen and Susan Smith ~ Real ale ~ Meals and snacks (till 10pm) ~ Restaurant ~ (01392) 461271 ~ Children in family room, eating area of bar and in restaurant ~ Open 11-3, 5.30-11

BROADHEMBURY ST1004 Map 1

Drewe Arms ★ 🍽 🍷

Signposted off A373 Cullompton—Honiton

In an attractive village of cream-coloured thatched cottages, this pretty 15th-c inn continues to please customers with its particularly good, fresh fish (they do a few meat dishes, too). It's almost essential to book to be sure of a table, and you can eat bar food or a three-course meal anywhere in the pub – or in the flower-filled garden: open sandwiches such as crab, marinated herring, prawns, gravadlax, sirloin steak with stilton, and rare beef (from £4.50), smoked salmon and dill soup (£2.95), cod fillet and fried bacon and mushrooms (£7.50), sea bream and herb butter (£8), excellent salmon fishcakes, monkfish with whole grain mustard sauce (£9.50), half lobster salad (£10.50), fresh langoustines (£12.50), and puddings such as hot lemon pudding or sticky toffee, chocolate and banana pudding; three courses for £19. Well kept Otter Bitter, Ale, Bright and Head (from a tiny brewery a few miles from the pub in Luppitt) tapped from the cask, and a very good wine list (including a wine of the month and 10 by the glass). The bar has neatly carved beams in its high ceiling, and handsome stone-mullioned windows (one with a small carved roundabout horse). On the left, a high-backed stripped settle separates off a little room with three tables, a mix of chairs, flowers on sturdy country tables, plank-panelled walls painted brown below and yellow above with attractive engravings and prints, and a big black-painted fireplace with bric-a-brac on a high mantelpiece. The flagstoned entry has a narrow corridor of a room by the servery with a couple of tables, and the cellar bar has simple pews on the stone floor. There are picnic tables in the lovely garden which has a lawn stretching back under the shadow of chestnut trees towards a church with its singularly melodious hour-bell. *(Recommended by A N Ellis, M R Gorton, Mr and Mrs J Jones, Gethin Lewis, George Jonas, Malcolm Smith, C Hardacre, John Fahy, R Walden, Martin Walsh, R V Ford, J and J O Jones, D E Kent, John and Fiona Merritt, J W Bridge, Sue Demont, Tim Barrow, D I Baddeley, Nigel Flook, Betsy Brown, Jeanne Cross, Paul Silvestri, Mark and Michele Aston, B J Harding)*

Free house ~ Licensees Kerstin and Nigel Burge ~ Real ale ~ Meals and snacks (till 10pm; not Sun evening) ~ Restaurant (not Sun evening) ~ (01404) 841267 ~ Well behaved children welcome ~ Open 11-3, 6-11

BUCKLAND BREWER SS4220 Map 1

Coach & Horses ★ 🛏

Village signposted off A388 S of Bideford; OS Sheet 190 map reference 423206

A comfortable mix of locals and visitors creates a jolly but relaxed atmosphere in this warmly welcoming 13th-c pub. The attractively furnished bar has heavy oak beams, comfortable seats including a handsome antique settle, and a woodburning stove in the inglenook; a good log fire also burns in the big stone inglenook of the cosy lounge. A small back room serves as a children's room; three very friendly cats. Tasty bar food includes home-made soup (£1.75), filled baked potatoes (from £2.30), good home-made pasties (£2.60), ploughman's (from £3.50), home-made Irish stew (£4.75), home-cooked ham and egg, vegetable lasagne or liver and bacon (£4.95), good home-made steak and kidney pie (£5.45), lamb, chicken or beef curries (£5.85), steaks (£8.95), and puddings like treacle tart with lemon and ginger or apple pie (£2.50); children's menu (from £1.50). Well kept Flowers Original, Fullers London Pride, and Wadworths 6X on handpump; friendly and efficient service. Pool, skittle alley, dominoes, shove-ha'penny, cribbage, fruit machine, and video game. There are tables on a terrace in front, and in the side garden. *(Recommended by Joan and Andrew Life, Simon Collett-Jones, Nick Lawless, Graham Tayar, Gerard O'Hanlon, Chris Westmoreland, George Atkinson, Martin Bromfield, Bernadette Garner, Colin Draper, Basil Minson, R Walden, Nigel and Lindsay Chapman, Mr and Mrs Greenhalgh, Roger and Susan Dunn, Philip and Joanne Gavins, Rita Horridge, Jennie Munro, Jim Wingate, L Parikian, Gethin Lewis)*

Free house ~ Licensees Kenneth and Oliver Wolfe ~ Real ale ~ Meals and snacks ~ Restaurant ~ (01237) 451395 ~ Well behaved children welcome ~ Open 11-3, 6-11; closed evening 25 Dec ~ Bedrooms: £20B/£40B

BUDLEIGH SALTERTON SY0682 Map 1

Salterton Arms

Chapel Street

In summer, the flowering tubs and hanging baskets outside this tucked away town pub are very pretty. The L-shaped bar has dark green plush wall seats and solid chairs around plain pub tables on the new dark red carpet, lots of prints on the walls, and small open fires; a very comfortable upper gallery serves as restaurant. Good bar food includes sandwiches (from £1.35, steak £3.95), good soup (£1.75), liver and onions (£3.25), steak and kidney pie or chicken chasseur (£4.25), vegetarian dishes such as roquefort and spinach strudel or crunch nut cutlet (£4.75), lunchtime specials like beef goulash or spaghetti bolognese (£4.25), and evening specials such as cod and prawn mornay or crab platter (£7.25), sea bass (£8.50) and steaks (from £7.50); good fresh vegetables, and puddings like chocolate gunge or banoffi pie (£2); best to book at weekends and for Sunday lunch. Well kept Courage Directors, Marstons Pedigree, and John Smiths on handpump, a good few Irish whiskeys, and neatly uniformed staff; darts and piped music. *(Recommended by David Holloway, F C Smith, Werner Arend, Marjorie and David Lamb, Mark and Heather Williamson; more reports please)*

Free house ~ Licensees Steve and Jennifer Stevens ~ Real ale ~ Meals and snacks (till 10pm; not 25 Dec) ~ Restaurant ~ (01395) 445048 ~ Children welcome ~ Jazz winter Sun evenings ~ Open 11-3, 5.30-11; 11-11 Sat

BUTTERLEIGH SS9708 Map 1

Butterleigh Inn

Village signposted off A396 in Bickleigh; or in Cullompton take turning by Manor House Hotel – it's the old Tiverton road, with the village eventually signposted off on the left

This is an unpretentious village pub with interestingly decorated little rooms: pictures of birds and dogs, topographical prints and watercolours, a fine embroidery of the Devonshire Regiment's coat-of-arms and plates hanging by one big fireplace. One room has a mix of Edwardian and Victorian dining chairs around country kitchen tables, another has an attractive elm trestle table and sensibly placed darts, and there are prettily upholstered settles around the three tables that just fit into the cosy back snug. Bar food includes filled rolls (lunchtimes, £1.75), home-made soup (£2.25), ploughman's (£3.75), good home-made burgers, tuna and pasta bake with a crunchy nut topping or chilli sausage and spinach flan (all £4.95), crab au gratin or bacon chops with plum sauce (£7.95), steaks (£8.95), vegetarian specials such as fennel goulash or tomato and pepper cobbler (£4.25), and puddings like chocolate and brandy pot (£2.25). Well kept Cotleigh Tawny, Barn Owl, and Golden Eagle on handpump; darts, shove-ha'penny, table skittles, cribbage, dominoes, and piped music; jars of snuff on the bar. Outside are tables on a sheltered terrace and neat small lawn, with a log cabin for children. *(Recommended by Jenny and Roger Huggins, P*

and J Shapley, John and Vivienne Rice, Margaret Dyke, John Fahy, JWC, MC, John Hazel, Rich
and Pauline Appleton, Anthony Barnes, Peter and Joy Heatherley, Sally Pidden, George and
Jeanne Barnwell, A P Jeffreys)

*Free house ~ Licensees Mike and Penny Wolter ~ Real ale ~ Meals and snacks ~
(01884) 855407 ~ Children welcome lunchtimes only ~ Open 12-2.30, 6(5 Fri)-
11 ~ Bedrooms: £20/£34*

CHAGFORD SX7087 Map 1

Ring o' Bells

Off A348 Moretonhampstead—Whiddon Down

Bedrooms have been added to this big friendly old pub this year; this has meant they
have had to reduce the size of the servery but have given more space in the bar area
for diners; they still have a small dining room with a fireplace at the back. The oak-
panelled bar has comfortable seats, photographs of the village and local characters
on the walls, a log-effect gas fire, and Tabbie the pub cat (now 17 years old). Good
bar food includes soup (£1.95), big sandwiches (£3), filled baked potatoes (from £3),
vegetarian burger (£3.75), fresh fillet of cod (£4.95), lamb liver and bacon (£5.25),
chicken tikka (£5.50), steak and kidney pie (£5.75), gammon and egg (£6.25), half a
roast duck with orange liqueur sauce (£10.50), daily specials, and puddings like fruit
pie or treacle tart (from £2); Sunday roast (£5) and they do breakfasts for non-
residents. Well kept Butcombe Bitter, Exmoor Ale, St Austells Trelawnys Pride, and
a guest beer on handpump, Addlestones cider, and quite a few malt whiskies. Darts,
shove-ha'penny, dominoes, fruit machine, and piped music. The sunny walled
garden behind the pub has seats on the lawn. Good moorland walks nearby.
*(Recommended by G W Stevenson, John and Vivienne Rice, I Maw, Alan and Paula McCully,
John and Christine Vittoe, P and J Shapley, Helen McLagan, Air Cdr and Mrs A C Curry)*

*Free house ~ Licensee Mrs Judith Pool ~ Real ale ~ Meals and snacks ~
Restaurant ~ (01647) 432466 ~ Well behaved children in eating area of bar ~
Open 11-3(2.30 in winter), 6-11 ~ Bedrooms: £17.50/£35(£50B)*

CHARDSTOCK ST3004 Map 1

George 🛏

Village signposted off A358 S of Chard

The new licensees in this thatched 13th-c inn have incorporated the restaurant into
the main lounge and bar area, thus giving a more homely and relaxed feel. The two-
roomed original bar has massive beams, ancient oak partition walls, character
furnishings, stone-mullioned windows, well converted old gas lamps, and two good
log fires. It's quietly chatty as the piped music is confined to an interestingly laid out
two-level back bar. Generous helpings of good home-made food now include
sandwiches, stilton, walnut and leek pie (£4.50; there are 8 other pies, too), steak
and kidney pudding (£6.45), lamb valentine (£8.95), local trout (£10.50), whole
local crab salad (£11.45), venison steak (£11.95), lots of vegetarian dishes, and
popular home-made puddings (£2.25). Well kept Boddingtons and Otter Ale plus
three other real ales such as Adnams Bitter, Bass, Cotleigh Tawny, Fullers London
Pride, Dartmoor Best, or Smiles on handpump; darts, bar billiards, shove-ha'penny,
cribbage, dominoes, alley skittles, and piped music. There are some tables out in a
back loggia by a flint-cobbled courtyard sheltered by the rather attractive modern
extensions to the ancient inn, with more in a safely fenced grass area with a climber
and swings. The four bedrooms are in a well converted back stable block. The inn
has an interesting booklet about its history. Excellent walks nearby. *(Recommended by
M E Wellington, K S Pike, Margaret and Nigel Dennis; more reports please)*

*Free house ~ Licensee Michael Watkins ~ Real ale ~ Meals and snacks (11-2.30,
6-10) ~ Restaurant ~ (01460) 220241 ~ Children in eating area of bar and in
family room ~ Open 11-3, 6-11; 11-11 Sat ~ Bedrooms: £39B/£49B*

CHERITON BISHOP SX7793 Map 1

Old Thatch

Village signposted from A30

Handy for the A30, this bustling 16th-c pub is a friendly place with very good, enjoyable food. This might include sandwiches, home-made soup (£1.65), home-made pâté (£2.65), devilled mushrooms (£2.70), ploughman's (from £3), gammon and egg (£4.95), steak and kidney pudding (£5.30), pork with apple, cream and calvados (£7.30), steaks (from £7.85), daily specials and vegetarian dishes, puddings such as baked spiced bread pudding or various cheesecakes and tarts (£2.50); best to get there early to make sure of a seat. The rambling, beamed bar is separated from the lounge by a large open stone fireplace (lit in the cooler months). Well kept Badger Tanglefoot, Cotleigh Tawny, and Wadworths 6X on handpump; dominoes, cribbage, and piped music. No children. *(Recommended by R Walden, Mr and Mrs D E Powell, Jenny and Brian Seller, Jeffrey Aspinall, John and Christine Vittoe, Dorothee and Dennis Glover, John Wooll, P V Caswell, R J Walden, R W Brooks)*

Free house ~ Licensee Brian Bryon-Edmond ~ Real ale ~ Meals and snacks ~ (01647) 24204 ~ Open 12(11.30 Sat)-3, 6.30-11; winter weekday opening 7; closed first two weeks Nov ~ Bedrooms: £33B/£45B

CHITTLEHAMHOLT SS6521 Map 1

Exeter Inn 🖙

Village signposted from A377 Barnstaple—Crediton and from B3226 SW of South Molton

In a quiet village, this friendly 16th-c inn has an open woodburning stove in the huge stone fireplace of the bar, cushioned mate's chairs and stools, settles and a couple of big cushioned cask armchairs, and an interesting collection of matchboxes, bottles and foreign banknotes. In the side area there are seats set out as booths around the tables under the sloping ceiling. Good bar food served by attentive staff includes home-made soup (£1.45), sandwiches (from £1.40), filled baked potatoes (from £2.25), ploughman's (from £3.75), hog pudding (like a haggis, £4.95), vegetarian cheese and nut croquettes or local trout (£5.95), excellent local steaks (£8.95), daily specials, children's meals (from £2.75), and home-made puddings with clotted cream (£2); Sunday roast (£4.50; children £3.50). Well kept Dartmoor Best, Tetleys and guest beers on handpump or tapped from the cask; freshly squeezed orange juice and farm ciders; darts, dominoes, cribbage, shove-ha'penny, fruit machine, trivia, and piped music. The dog is called Alice and the cat, Clyde. The terrace has benches and flower baskets. The pub's cricket team play on Sundays. *(Recommended by Alan Pursell, R Walden, Ian and Deborah Carrington, Derek and Iris Martin, R J Walden, Anthony Barnes)*

Free house ~ Licensees Norman and Margaret Glenister ~ Real ale ~ Meals and snacks ~ Restaurant ~ (01769) 540281 ~ Children in eating area of bar ~ Open 11.30-2.30, 6-11 ~ Bedrooms: £25S/£40S; s/c available

CHURCHSTOW SX7145 Map 1

Church House

A379 NW of Kingsbridge

A great stone fireplace in this medieval pub has a side bread oven and the long and cosy characterful bar also has low and heavy black oak beams, cushioned window seats cut into the deep window embrasures of the stripped stone walls, an antique curved high-backed settle as well as lots of smaller red-cushioned ones, and a line of stools – each with its own brass coathook – along the long glossy black serving counter. Bar food, served at the curtained-off end of the bar, includes sandwiches (from £1.80), ploughman's (£3.30), basket meals (from £3.25), vegetarian lasagne (£4.25), home-made fish or steak and kidney pies (£4.65), gammon and egg (£7.50), steak (£8.25), home-made fruit pies (£2.35), children's menu (from £1.35), and popular carvery

(£5.95; 7.95; Wednesday-Saturday evenings and Sunday lunch); the restaurant is no smoking. Well kept Bass and Marstons Pedigree on handpump; cribbage, dominoes, euchre, bridge (Monday evening) and fruit machine. Just inside the back entrance there's a conservatory area with a floodlit well in the centre, and there are seats outside. *(Recommended by Verity Kemp, Richard Mills, TBB, Bryan Taylor, Nick Wikeley, B Taylor, Owen and Margaret Warnock, Mr and Mrs C Roberts)*

Free house ~ Licensees Nick and Vera Nicholson ~ Real ale ~ Meals and snacks (12-1.30, 6.30-9; not 25-26 Dec) ~ Restaurant ~ (01548) 852237 ~ Children welcome ~ Open 10.30-2.30, 6-11

CLYST HYDON ST0301 Map 1

Five Bells

B3176 not far from M5 junction 28

Readers love the cottagey garden in front of this charming and warmly friendly white-painted thatched pub (with reed peacocks on top) as it's filled both in spring and summer with thousands of flowers; the big window boxes and hanging baskets are very pretty, too. Up some steps is a sizeable flat lawn with picnic tables, a waggon filled with flowers, a slide, and pleasant country views. Inside, the long bar is spotlessly kept and very attractive, and divided at one end into different seating areas by brick and timber pillars; china jugs hang from big beams that are studded with horsebrasses, many plates line the delft shelves, there's lots of sparkling copper and brass, and a nice mix of dining chairs around small tables (fresh flowers and evening candles in bottles), with some comfortable pink plush banquettes on a little raised area. Past the inglenook fireplace is another big (but narrower) room with a pine dresser at one end and similar furnishings. Very good home-made bar food includes soup (£1.95), sandwiches (from £1.95), smoked prawns with garlic mayonnaise (£3.75), platters (from £4), cold rare roast beef with chips and pickles or curry (£5.95), daily specials like fresh local mussels cooked in cider and cream, smoked fish platter, roasted vegetables topped with melted brie, venison and apricot casserole, chicken breast with bacon, leek and sherry sauce, and puddings such as treacle tart and filo parcels with apricot and a raspberry coulis; children's dishes (from £2.25). Well kept Cotleigh Tawny, Dartmoor Best, and Wadworths 6X on handpump, and a thoughtful wine list. *(Recommended by Anna Ralph, Heather March, G Shove, Mr and Mrs Greenhalgh, Catherine Pocock, Mr and Mrs G Ricketts, Mr and Mrs J Jones, Timothy Gee, Marian Greenwood, Tony Beaulah, H Beck)*

Free house ~ Licensees Robin Bean and Charles Hume Smith ~ Real ale ~ Meals and snacks ~ Restaurant ~ (01884) 277288 ~ Well behaved children in eating area of bar ~ Open 11.30-3, 6.30(7 in winter)-11

COCKWOOD SX9780 Map 1

Anchor 🍴

Off, but visible from, A379 Exeter—Torbay

Both locals and visitors come to this friendly pub to enjoy the wide choice of good fresh fish. There are 30 different ways of serving mussels (£5.50 normal size helping, £9.75 for a large one), 14 ways of serving scallops (from £5.25 for a starter, from £10.50 for a main course), and 11 ways of serving oysters (from £5.25 for starter, from £11 for main course); other fresh fish dishes might include fried shark steak or locally caught cod (£5.50), whole grilled plaice (£6.50), local crab platter (£6.95), a shellfish platter (£14.95), and red snapper, bream, grouper and parrot fish. Non-fishy dishes feature as well, such as sandwiches (from £2.25), home-made chicken liver pâté (£3.85), ratatouille (£3.95), home-made cottage pie (£4.50), 8oz rump steak (£8.95), and children's dishes (£2.10). The restaurant is no smoking. The small, low-ceilinged, rambling rooms have black panelling, good-sized tables in various alcoves, and a cheerful winter coal fire in the snug. Well kept Bass, Boddingtons, Eldridge Pope Royal Oak, Flowers IPA, Whitbreads Fuggles, Marstons Pedigree, and two guests on handpump or tapped from the cask, with rather a good wine list, country wines, 30 malt whiskies, and Inchs cider; darts, dominoes, cribbage, fruit machine, and piped music. From the tables on the sheltered verandah here you can look across the road to the bobbing yachts and crabbing boats in the landlocked harbour. Nearby parking is difficult when the pub is busy – which it usually is. *(Recommended by James Nunns, Wendy Arnold, Bob Medland, Rip and Pauline Kirby, John and Vivienne Rice, JWC, MC, George Jonas, Rita Horridge, R Walden, R W Flux, Jean Cross, Paul Silvestri, Chris Westmoreland, John Beeken, Mrs Pat Crabb, Adrian Alton, Paul and Janet Waring, Ian Phillips)*

Heavitree (who no longer brew) ~ Tenants T Morean, Miss A L Sanders, Mrs J Wetton ~ Real ale ~ Meals and snacks (till 10pm) ~ Restaurant ~ (01626) 890203 ~ Children in eating area of bar ~ Open 11-11; 12-10.30 Sun

COLEFORD SS7701 Map 1

New Inn ⑪ ⇔ ♀

Just off A377 Crediton—Barnstaple

This 600-year-old inn must be one of the oldest 'new' inns around. It has four interestingly furnished areas that spiral around the central servery: ancient and modern settles, spindleback chairs, plush-cushioned stone wall seats, some character tables – a pheasant worked into the grain of one – and carved dressers and chests, as well as paraffin lamps, antique prints and old guns on the white walls, landscape plates on one of the beams and pewter tankards on another; the resident parrot is chatty and entertaining. The servery itself has settles forming stalls around tables on the russet carpet, and there's a winter log fire. Good bar food might include cream of tomato and basil soup (£2.20), warm pigeon breast and smoked bacon salad with orange vinaigrette (£4.50), grills (from £6.20), pancake with chicken, mushroom and cream filling, fresh pasta with stilton, walnut and mushroom sauce or venison sausages with cumberland sauce (all £6.25), seafood provençale (£8.25), salmon en croûte with a green herb sauce or lamb wellington (£9.25), and lovely puddings like chocolate cups filled with chocolate rum mousse with orange sauce or blackcurrants with a yoghurt and cream topping (£2.75); friendly, helpful staff. Well kept Badger Best, Otter Ale, Wadworths 6X, and a guest beer on handpump, an extensive wine list, quite a range of malt whiskies, and port; fruit machine (out of the way up by the door), darts, and piped music. Big car park. There are some benches and seats outside by the stream. *(Recommended by Pat and Tony Martin, R Walden, Peter Burton, Rita Horridge, Dr and Mrs Brian Hamilton, Anthony Savage, Howard Clutterbuck, R J Walden)*

Free house ~ Licensees Paul and Irene Butt ~ Real ale ~ Meals and snacks (till 10pm) ~ Restaurant ~ (01363) 84242 ~ Children in eating area of bar ~ Open 12-2.30, 6-11; closed 25 and 26 Dec ~ Bedrooms: £38B/£52.50B

COMBEINTEIGNHEAD SX9071 Map 1

Coombe Cellars

Pub signed from village on unclassified road between Shaldon and Newton Abbot station

This is a different sort of pub to the ones readers would normally expect of our Devon entries but it is useful as a big family place with lots to do for children – they have an indoor play area, their own menu, baby-changing facilities, highchairs, parties with face painting and games, and an outside play galleon and fenced-in playground in the garden. There are also fun days with magicians, live music, barbecues and beach parties, quiz nights and darts tournaments, and disabled lavatories and ramped entrances. The estuary setting here is really lovely and at low tide you can watch innumerable wading birds on the mudflats. Pontoons and jetties with tables overlook the water, and there are more tables on big terraces. Lots of water-sports facilities, too – the pub is the base for the South Devon Water Sports Association. There's a pleasure trip service from Teignmouth that takes in this pub. Inside, the long beamed bar has one area with old photographs and pictures of the pub, another with hunting, shooting and fishing items, and yet another with nautical bric-a-brac; comfortable seating, a woodburning stove, and two log-effect gas fires. Darts, dominoes, fruit machine, and piped music. Bar food under the new licensee typically includes sandwiches or baps (from £1.99), chilli with tortilla chips (£3.45), platters (from £3.95), vegetable tikka masala (£4.35), steak and kidney pie (£4.25), fish pie (£4.99), gammon and egg (£5.10), chicken balti (£5.65), steak (£7.99), puddings (£2.10), and children's menu (£3.30). Well kept Boddingtons, Flowers Original, Wadworths 6X, and a guest beer on handpump, and 14 wines by the glass. *(Recommended by Geoff Dibble, Alan and Paula McCully, John Wilson, Adrian Zambardino, Debbie Chaplin; more reports please)*

Whitbreads ~ Manager P J Marsh ~ Real ale ~ Meals and snacks (all day) ~ (01626) 872423 ~ Children welcome away from main bar area ~ Open 11-11; 12-10.30 Sun

CORNWORTHY SX8255 Map 1

Hunters Lodge

Off A381 Totnes—Kingsbridge ½ mile S of Harbertonford, turning left at Washbourne; can also be reached direct from Totnes, on the Ashprington—Dittisham road

In summer, there is plenty of room to sit outside – either at the picnic tables on a big lawn stretching up behind the car park, with swings, a climbing frame and summer barbecues, or at more seats on the flower-filled terrace closer to the pub; several walks start from here. Inside, the two rooms of the little low-ceilinged bar have only around half-a-dozen red plush wall seats and captain's chairs around heavy elm tables, and there's also a small and pretty cottagey dining room with a good log fire in its big 17th-c stone fireplace. Popular bar food includes sandwiches (from £1.95), home-made soup (£2.50), ploughman's (from £3.95), home-cooked honey roast ham (£5.25), grilled sardines (£5.25), home-made steak and kidney pie (£5.95), chicken maryland (£6.25), chicken breast with smoked turkey and smoked cheese in a white wine and cream sauce (£8.95), guinea fowl (£9.25), tandoori halibut (£9.50), seafood grill (£9.75), and puddings (£2.50); three course Sunday roast (£6.75). Well kept Blackawton Special and Forty-four and Ushers Best on handpump and local Pig Squeal cider; darts, dominoes, shove-ha'penny, children's games, puzzles and colouring place-mats, trivia and piped music; they have four dogs (only let loose after closing time). *(Recommended by John Fahy, C and E M Watson, D I Baddeley, B Taylor)*

Free house ~ Licensee Robin Thorns ~ Real ale ~ Meals and snacks (till 10pm) ~ Cottagey restaurant ~ (01803) 732204 ~ Children welcome ~ Open 11-3, 6.30-11; closed evening 25 Dec

DALWOOD ST2400 Map 1

Tuckers Arms

Village signposted off A35 Axminster—Honiton

Reached down narrow high-hedged lanes, this very attractive thatched longhouse has a fine flagstoned bar with 800-year-old stripped beams and a welcoming, friendly atmosphere. Also, a log fire in the inglenook fireplace, a woodburning stove, and a random mixture of dining chairs, window seats, a pew, and a high-backed winged black settle. A side lounge with shiny black woodwork has a couple of cushioned oak armchairs and other comfortable but unpretentious seats, and the back bar has an enormous collection of miniature bottles. At lunchtime, the good bar food includes home-made soup such as carrot and coriander (£1.95), filled french bread (from £3.25), potato skins with interesting dips (from £3.50), ploughman's, fresh fish in beer batter with chops of lamb korma (£3.95), cold beef and pickles (£4.25), warm salad of wild mushrooms and prawns with garlic (£5.25), fresh asparagus with fresh crab salad (£5.45), and puddings such as chocolate brandy mousse, lovely treacle tart or crème brûlée (£2.75); in the evening you can choose between a main course (£8.25), two courses (£10.95), and three courses (£12.95) – though you can choose items from this menu to eat at lunchtime, too: lots of fish such as king scallops with cider, cream, mustard and tarragon, whole lemon sole, skate with capers and lemon butter or sea bass with red wine, tomatoes, olives and fresh basil, and meat dishes like rack of lamb, speciality rib-eye steaks, venison steaks with wild mushrooms and supreme of duck with orange or cherry sauce. The main dining room is no smoking. Well kept Flowers Original, Otter Ale (and quite often Bitter, Head and Bright as well), and Whitbreads Fuggles on handpump, farm cider, and quite a few malt whiskies; skittle alley. In summer, the flowering tubs, window boxes and hanging baskets are lovely. *(Recommended by Desmond and Pat Morris, R Walden, James Nunns, David Wallington, K S Pike, George Atkinson)*

Free house ~ Licensees David and Kate Beck ~ Real ale ~ Meals and snacks (till 10pm; not evenings 25-26 Dec) ~ Restaurant ~ (01404) 881342 ~ Children in eating area of bar, in restaurant and in skittle alley until 9pm ~ Open 12-3, 6.30-11 ~ Bedrooms: £25S/£40S

DARTINGTON SX7762 Map 1

Cott ★ ⑪ 🛏 ♀

In hamlet with the same name, signposted off A385 W of Totnes opposite A384 turn-off

Apart from the marvellous atmosphere – which readers tell us even on a winter Sunday evening remains undimmed – it's the genuinely warm, friendly welcome that makes this lovely thatched 14th-c inn so special. The communicating rooms of the traditional, heavy-beamed bar have big open fires, flagstones, and polished brass and horse-harnesses on the white-washed walls; one area is no smoking. At lunchtime, the good food includes sandwiches and ploughman's and dishes from the hot and cold buffet like quiches, pies and cold meats, a roast, casseroles, and a fish dish (£5.95), and in the evening there is quite an emphasis on fresh fish from Brixham or Plymouth such as local mussels in tomato, garlic and basil (£4.25), fillets of plaice with prawns and pink peppers (£7.95), fillets of john dory with hazelnut and stilton sauce (£10.95), char-grilled fillet of sea bass with an anchovy and lime butter sauce (£11.25), and baked turbot with asparagus and melted gruyère (£12.50); also chick pea and vegetable curry or spicy ginger pork with sweet peppers and tagliatelle (£6.75), steak and kidney pie with a suet crust pastry (£6.95), shank of lamb Green style (£7.95), supreme of duck breast roasted with a plum and ginger purée (£10.95), and calf liver with bacon, roasted shallots and garlic mashed potato (£11.75); quite a few local cheeses, and ample breakfasts. The restaurant is no smoking. Well kept Bass, Butcombe Bitter and Cotts Wallop (see if you can guess what it really is) on handpump, Inch's cider, 12 interesting wines by the glass, and a good selection of malt whiskies. There's a pub cricket team – they'd welcome enquiries from visiting teams. Harvey the cat still likes to creep into bedroom windows in the middle of the night (despite advancing age), and Minnie and Digger the jack russells have been joined by Molly the black labrador and remain keen to greet visitors. The garden has a new terrace and new seating amidst the attractive tubs of flowers. Good walks through the grounds of nearby Dartington Hall, and it's pleasant touring country – particularly for the popular Dartington craft centre, the Totnes—Buckfastleigh steam railway, and one of the prettiest towns in the West Country, Totnes. *(Recommended by Bryan Taylor, Pam and Tim Moorey, Verity Combes, David and June Harwood, R J Isaac, Nigel Clifton, Karen and Chris Nelson, R Morgan, Paul and Janet Waring, Miss R Thomas, Dr G Blackwell, Moira and John Cole, Mr and Mrs A O Meakin, Walker and Debra Lapthorne, S Demont, T Barrow, M V and J Melling, John Waller, Anne Davenport, Ed Southall, Ted George, John Evans, Mr and Mrs J Jones, Revd A Bunnerley, Andrew Hodges, Kees van Kempen, David Wallington, Martin Foss, David Holman, Anthony Marriott, Peter Williamson, Barry Lynch, Mr and Mrs D Clements, H and D Payne, Joan and Gordon Edwards, Paul and Janet Waring, Simon and Debbie Tomlinson, George and Jeanne Barnwell, John and Vivienne Rice, Nigel Spence, Kim Greek, Mrs V Coombs, Mr and Mrs D Clements, George Jonas)*

Free house ~ Licensees David and Susan Grey ~ Real ale ~ Meals and snacks (12-2.15, 6.30-9.30; not 25 Dec) ~ Restaurant ~ (01803) 863777 ~ Children in restaurant ~ Live entertainment Sun evenings and in garden on summer Sun lunchtimes ~ Open 11-2.30, 5.30-11; closed evening 25 Dec ~ Bedrooms: £45B/£55B

DARTMOUTH SX8751 Map 1
Cherub
Higher St

This is Dartmouth's oldest building. It's a fine Grade I listed building dating from 1380 and each of the two heavily timbered upper floors juts further out than the one below. Inside, the bar has tapestried seats under creaky heavy beams, red-curtained leaded-light windows, an open stove in the big stone fireplace, and well kept Flowers Original, Morlands Old Speckled Hen, Wadworths 6X and a guest beer on handpump, 30 malt whiskies, and farm cider; piped music (rather loud at times). Under the new licensee, bar food includes soup (£2.25), filled baked potatoes (from £3.50), ploughman's (from £3.95), smoked haddock in white wine and cheese sauce (£3.95), chilli con carne or beef in ale stew (£4.95), and seafood pasta (£6.55). In summer, the flower baskets are very pretty. *(Recommended by Christopher Turner, Bryan Taylor, Alan and Paula McCully, Miss K Law, K M Timmins, John Fahy, Rip and Pauline Kirby, Paul and Janet Waring, E Carter, Joy and Paul Rundell, G W Stevenson)*

Free house ~ Licensee Alan Jones ~ Real ale ~ Meals and snacks (till 10pm) ~ Restaurant ~ (01803) 832571 ~ Children in restaurant lunchtime only ~ Open 11-11; 12-10.30 Sun; 11-2.30, 6-11 in winter

Royal Castle 🛏
11 The Quay

There's a good welcoming atmosphere and quite a bit of character in this rambling 17th-c hotel, overlooking the inner harbour. The left-hand, local bar is decorated with navigation lanterns, glass net-floats and old local ship photographs, and has a mix of furnishings from stripped pine kitchen chairs to some interesting old settles and mahogany tables; one wall is stripped to the original stonework and there's a big log fire. On the right in the more sedate, partly no-smoking carpeted bar, they may do winter spit-roast joints on some lunchtimes; there's also a Tudor fireplace with copper jugs and kettles (beside which are the remains of a spiral staircase), and plush furnishings, including some Jacobean-style chairs. One alcove has swords and heraldic shields on the wall. Well kept Boddingtons, Blackawton Bitter, Courage Directors, and Flowers Original on handpump, 50 malt whiskies, and local farm cider; welcoming staff. Dominoes, fruit machine, trivia, and piped music. Generous helpings of tasty bar food include lunchtime sandwiches (from £1.45; crab £2.75) and a choice of ploughman's (from £2.45), as well as home-made soup (£1.65), baked potatoes with hot or cold fillings (from £2.70), cauliflower cheese and bacon (£3.25), home-made steak and kidney pie or smoked haddock and mushroom crumble (£4.50), curry of the day or whole plaice (£4.95), steaks (from £9.95), daily specials like spit-roast lamb, pork or beef (£5.25) or chicken kiev (£5.95), and puddings (£2.45). *(Recommended by Alan and Paul McCully, Dave and Doreen Irving, Mr and Mrs R Head, John Fahy, Mr and Mrs C Roberts, Colin and Marjorie Roberts, T H Thomas)*

Free house ~ Licensees Nigel and Anne Way ~ Real ale ~ Meals and snacks (all day) ~ Restaurant ~ (01803) 833033 ~ Children in first-floor library lunchtimes only ~ Jazz Sun lunchtime, country rock 2 nights a week ~ Open 11-11; 12-10.30 Sun ~ Bedrooms: £44.50B/£89B

DODDISCOMBSLEIGH SX8586 Map 1
Nobody Inn ★ ★ 🛏 ♀ ◖
Village signposted off B3193, opposite northernmost Christow turn-off

The two atmospheric rooms of the lounge bar in this very popular inn have a relaxed, friendly atmosphere, handsomely carved antique settles, windsor and wheelback chairs, benches, carriage lanterns hanging from the beams, and guns and hunting prints in a snug area by one of the big inglenook fireplaces. They keep perhaps the best pub wine cellar in the country – 800 well cellared wines by the bottle and 20 by the glass kept oxidation-free; there's also properly mulled wine and twice-monthly tutored tastings (they also sell wine retail, and the good tasting-notes in their detailed list are worth the £3 it costs – anyway refunded if you buy more than £30-worth); also, a choice of 250 whiskies, Gray's and Luscombe's ciders, and well kept Bass and a beer by Branscombe Vale especially for the pub called Nobodys, usually RCH PG Steam, and guest beers from all over the country on handpump or tapped straight from the cask. Tasty bar food includes home-made soup (£1.95), hot wholemeal pitta bread filled with cheese, tomato, onion and herbs (£2.75), sausages and mash with onion gravy (£3), coarse home-made duck liver pâté with port (£3.10), mixed bean, mushroom and barley bake (£4.50), daily specials like smoked fish mornay (£4.20), mushroom and fennel bake (£4.50), chicken in an orange and tarragon sauce (£5.80), pork, ginger and rhubarb pasta (£5.90), puddings such as sticky toffee pudding, orange mousse or warm chocolate tart (£2.90), and a marvellous choice of over 50 West Country cheeses (half-a-dozen £3.50; you can buy them to take away as well). The restaurant is no smoking. There are picnic tables on the terrace, with views of the surrounding wooded hill pastures. The medieval stained glass in the local church is some of the best in the West Country. No children. *(Recommended by John Fahy, R Walden, John and Vivienne Rice, John Waller, Ian Williams, Linda Mar, Mr and Mrs D E Powell, Bryan Taylor, Lynn Sharpless, Bob Eardley, Dr I Maine, Hanns Golez, Jim and Maggie Cowell, John and Christine Vittoe, John and June Gale, JWC, MC, E B Davies, B Taylor, Charlotte Creasy, George Jonas, Chris Westmoreland, Jack and Philip Paxton, Joan and Gordon Edwards, Anthony Marriott, Jane Hosking, Ian Burniston, Nigel Spence, Kim Greek, Martin Foxx, Mike Woodhead)*

Free house ~ Licensee Nicholas Borst-Smith ~ Real ale ~ Meals and snacks (till 10pm) ~ Evening restaurant (not Sun) ~ (01647) 252394 ~ Open 12-2.30, 6-11; winter evening opening 7; closed evening 25 Dec ~ Bedrooms: (some in distinguished 18th-c house 150yds away);£23(£35B)/£59B

DREWSTEIGNTON SX7390 Map 1

Drewe Arms

Signposted off A30 NW of Moretonhampstead

Run by new licensees, this old thatched pub is a very basic village tavern. There's no serving counter and the well kept Flowers IPA, Morlands Old Speckled Hen and Wadworths 6X and local draught cider are kept on racks in the tap room at the back. Bar food now includes sandwiches, a big bowl of home-made soup (£2), home-baked gammon ploughman's (£3.95), and smoked haddock and mushroom bake (£4.95). Darts, dominoes, cribbage and chess. Castle Drogo nearby (open for visits) looks medieval, though it was actually built earlier this century. They hope to open a restaurant and bedrooms. *(Recommended by Gordon, Jonathan Williams, John Fahy, Jeanne Cross, Wendy and Ray Bryn Davies, Jack and Philip Paxton, John Hazel)*

Whitbreads ~ Licensees Janice and Colin Sparks ~ Real ale ~ Meals and snacks (lunchtime) ~ (01647) 281224 ~ Children in eating area of bar ~ Open 11-3, 6-11; 11-11 Sat; 12-10.30 Sun

EXETER SX9292 Map 1

Double Locks ★ ◗

Canal Banks, Alphington; from A30 take main Exeter turn-off (A377/396) then next right into Marsh Barton Industrial Estate and follow Refuse Incinerator signs; when road bends round in front of the factory-like incinerator, take narrow dead end track over humpy bridge, cross narrow canal swing bridge and follow track along canal; much quicker than it sounds, and a very worthwhile diversion from the final M5 junction

This lively place is one of the oldest canal lockhouses in the country. There's always a good mix of people (though a large percentage are, of course, students) and a fine range of beers on handpump or tapped from the cask: Smiles Bitter, Best and

Exhibition with guests like Adnams Broadside, Everards Old Original, Greene King Abbot, Shepherd Neame Spitfire, and Wadworths 6X; Grays farm cider, several malt whiskies, and organic apple juice. Bar food includes soup (£1.90), sandwiches (£2.20), mushrooms on toast (£3.30), filled baked potatoes (from £3.50), ploughman's (£4.20), feta cheese and spinach pie or ham and eggs (£4), ratatouille crêpe (£4.50), breakfast special (£4.90), and puddings like chocolate biscuit cake or sticky toffee pudding (£2.60); summer barbecues (from £1.80). There's quite a nautical theme in the bar – with ship's lamps and model ships – and notably friendly service. Darts, cribbage, dominoes, Scrabble, Monopoly, chess, trivia, volleyball, and piped music. There are picnic tables outside and cycle paths along the ship canal. *(Recommended by R WD, PM, AM, Jack and Philip Paxton, David Carr, Henry Paulinski, John and Vivienne Rice, Steve Felstead, Mike Gorton, Rita Horridge, Werner Arend, George and Jeanne Barnwell, Andy and Jill Kassube, Jerry and Alison Oakes, Chris Westmoreland, Owen and Margaret Warnock)*

Smiles ~ Manager Tony Stearman ~ Real ale ~ Meals and snacks (all day) ~ (01392) 56947 ~ Children welcome ~ Folk Weds evening, Jazz Thurs evening ~ Open 11-11; 12-10.30 Sun

White Hart ★ ⇔ ♀

66 South St; 4 rather slow miles from M5 junction 30; follow City Centre signs via A379, B3182; straight towards centre if you're coming from A377 Topsham Road

For centuries, the atmospheric rambling bar of this well run 14th-c inn has been a popular meeting place. The heavy bowed beams in the dark ochre terracotta ceiling are hung with big copper jugs, there are windsor armchairs and built-in winged settles with latticed glass tops to their high backs, oak tables on the bare oak floorboards (carpet in the quieter lower area), and a log fire in one great fireplace with long-barrelled rifles above it. In one of the bay windows is a set of fine old brass beer engines, the walls are decorated with pictorial plates, old copper and brass platters (on which the antique lantern lights glisten), and a wall cabinet holds some silver and copper. From the latticed windows, with their stained-glass coats-of-arms, one can look out on the cobbled courtyard – lovely when the wisteria is flowering in May. The Tap Bar, across the yard, with flagstones, candles in bottles and a more wine-barish feel, serves soup, sandwiches, cold meats, pasties with bubble and squeak (£2.95), steak and oyster or chicken and chestnut pies (£5.95), and char-grilled chicken with lemon, garlic and tarragon (£6.95) or steaks (from £8.95). There is yet another bar, called Bottlescreu Bill's, even more dimly candlelit, with bare stone walls and sawdust on the floor. It serves much the same food, as well as a respectable range of Davy's wines and pint jugs of vintage port from the wood or tankards of bucks fizz, and in summer does lunchtime barbecue grills in a second, sheltered courtyard. On Sundays both these bars are closed. Bass, Davy's Old Wallop (served in pewter tankards in Bottlescreu Bill's) and John Smiths on handpump. Bedrooms are in a separate modern block. *(Recommended by Andrew Hodges, Jim and Maggie Cowell, David Carr, JWC, MC, R Walden, M E Wellington, P and T Ferris, Ron Gentry, F C Johnston, Werner Arend)*

Free house ~ Licensee Graham Stone ~ Real ale ~ Meals and snacks (till 10pm) ~ Restaurant ~ (01392) 79897 ~ Children in eating area of bar and in lounges ~ Open 11.30-3, 5-11; 11.30-11 Sat ~ Bedrooms: £54.50B/£78B

EXMINSTER SX9487 Map 1

Turf ★

Continue to end of track, by gates; park, and walk right along canal towpath – nearly a mile

It's well worth the effort to get to this attractively isolated pub, set by the last lock of the Exeter Canal before the estuary of the River Exe. You can either walk (which takes about 20 minutes along the ship canal) or take a 40-minute ride from Countess Wear in their own boat, the *Water Mongoose* (bar on board; £3.50 adult, £2.50 child return, charter for up to 56 people £125). They also operate a 12-seater and an 8-seater boat which bring people down the Exe estuary from Topsham quay

(15 minute trip, adults £2.50, child £2). For those arriving in their own boat there is a large pontoon as well as several moorings. From the bay windows of the pleasantly airy bar there are views out to the mudflats – which are full of gulls and waders at low tide – and mahogany decking and caulking tables on the polished bare floorboards, church pews, wooden chairs and alcove seats; big bright shorebird prints by John Tennent and pictures and old photographs of the pub and its characters over the years on the walls; woodburning stove and antique gas fire. Bar food (using local suppliers where possible) includes sandwiches (from £2.25; toasties from £2.70), home-made soup (£2.50), cheesy nut roast (£4.95), ploughman's (£5.50), lasagne and garlic bread (£5.95), daily specials such as fresh pasta with pesto, mushrooms, tomatoes and peppers (£4.95), chilli with tortilla chips and soured cream or local smoked trout platter (£5.95), and puddings like apple crumble or sticky toffee pudding (from £2); the dining room is no smoking. Well kept Eldridge Pope Royal Oak, Dartmoor Bitter and Legend, and Tetleys Bitter on handpump, and Green Valley farm cider; darts, shove-ha'penny, cribbage, dominoes, trivia, and evening/weekend piped music; friendly, efficient service. The garden has a children's play area. *(Recommended by Chris Westmoreland, Jeanne Cross, Paul Silvestri, Mike Gorton; more reports please)*

Free house ~ Licensees Clive and Ginny Redfern ~ Real ale ~ Meals and snacks ~ (01392) 833128 ~ Children welcome ~ Open 11.30-11; 12-10.30 Sun; closed Nov-March ~ Bedrooms: £25/£50

HARBERTON SX7758 Map 1

Church House

Village signposted from A381 just S of Totnes

In a tucked away steep little village, this ancient and atmospheric pub was probably used as a chantry-house for monks connected with the church, and parts of it may, in fact, be Norman. There's some magnificent medieval oak panelling, and the latticed glass on the back wall of the open-plan bar is almost 700 years old and one of the earliest examples of non-ecclesiastical glass in the country (it had been walled off until Victorian times). Furnishings include attractive 17th- and 18th-c pews and settles, candles, and a large inglenook fireplace with a woodburning stove; one half of the room is set out for eating. The family room is no smoking. As well as the standard menu with things such as home-made soup (£1.85), sandwiches (from £1.95), ploughman's (from £3.75), a fry-up (£5.25), grilled whole plaice (£7.75), and super steaks (from £7.95), there are popular daily specials such as deep-fried banana wrapped in bacon with a mild curry mayonnaise dip (£2.95), local mussels (£3.95), pancakes filled with spinach and cottage cheese au gratin (£4.95), stuffed aubergine or steak and kidney pie (£5.95), seafood piri-piri or steak picado (stir-fried rump steak with olives, wine and so forth, £6.95), and lamb steak with a port, rosemary and redcurrant sauce (£9.50), with puddings like bread and butter pudding or tiramisu (from £2.75). Well kept Bass and Courage Best and two weekly-changing guest beers such as Badger Tanglefoot, Dartmoor Bitter and Legend, Eldridge Pope Royal Oak, and Marstons Pedigree on handpump, farm cider, and several malt whiskies; darts, dominoes and cribbage. *(Recommended by Viv Middlebrook, M G Hart, Colin and Marjorie Roberts, Dennis Glover, Mr and Mrs R Head, J H Bell, Jean Cross, Paul Silvestri, Bill Sharpe, Roger Wain-Heapy)*

Free house ~ Licensees David and Jennifer Wright ~ Real ale ~ Meals and snacks (12-1.45, 7-9.30) ~ (01803) 863707 ~ Children in restaurant and family room ~ Occasional Morris men in summer ~ Open 12(11.30 Sat)-3, 6-11; closed evenings 25-26 Dec and 1 Jan

HATHERLEIGH SS5404 Map 1

George ♀

A386 N of Okehampton

In summer, the courtyard here is very pretty with hanging baskets and window boxes on the black and white timbering, and rustic wooden seats and tables on its cobblestones; there's also a walled cobbled garden. Inside, the little front bar in the original part of the building has huge oak beams, stone walls two or three feet thick, an enormous fireplace, and easy chairs, sofas and antique cushioned settles; you can get drinks here all day. The spacious L-shaped main bar was built from the wreck of the inn's old brewhouse and coachmen's loft, and has more beams, a woodburning stove, and antique settles around sewing-machine treadle tables; a quieter no-smoking extension, with more modern furnishings, leads off this; darts, pool, dominoes, fruit machine and piped music. Well kept Bass, Boddingtons, Hook Norton, and Wadworths 6X on handpump, wine and champagne by the glass, Inch's cider, several malt whiskies, and home-made lemonade, ginger beer, and sloe gin. Bar food includes rare beef sandwiches (£1.80), soup (£2.20), fried halloumi with lime vinaigrette (£2.90), ploughman's (£3.25), spinach and ricotta pie or tagliatelle carbonara (£4.50), steak and kidney pie (£5), Sri Lankan curry (£5.95), a mixed grill, steaks (£8.50), daily specials, and puddings. *(Recommended by Colin Draper, R Walden, Rita Horridge, Mr and Mrs Jack Pitts, Moira and John Cole, Jack and Philip Paxton, Derek and Iris Martin, R J Walden, Werner Arend)*

Free house ~ Licensees John Dunbar and Veronica Devereux ~ Real ale ~ Meals and snacks (12-2, 6-9.30) ~ Restaurant ~ (01837) 810454 ~ Children in eating area of bar ~ Folk 3rd Fri of month ~ Open 11-3.30, 6-11 ~ Bedrooms: £28.50(£48B)/£49.50(£69.50B)

Tally Ho

Market St (A386)

The opened-together rooms of the bar in this friendly pub have heavy beams, two woodburning stoves, sturdy old oak and elm tables on the partly carpeted wooden floor, decorative plates between the wall timbers, and shelves of old bottles and pottery; the two cockatiels are called Squeaky and Squashy. Bar food includes lunchtime sandwiches (from £2.35), omelettes (from £2.95), and ploughman's (from £3.50), as well as soup, home-made pâté (from £3.90), trout (£6.50), steaks (from £9.50), daily specials like pasta with smoked salmon, white wine and vodka (£6.25), Thai green curry (£7.75) or cod fillet with beer batter (£8.25); pizzas on Wednesdays and grills or barbecues on Thursdays, with a Swiss fondue on winter Thursdays (£18 per couple); you must book for the restaurant. Through a big window in one building of the former back coach yard you can see the spotless copper brewing equipment where they brew deep-coloured quite strongly hopped Potboiler with its sturdily appetising finish, Jollop (winter only), Tarka Tipple, Thurgia, Nutters, and Master Jack's Mild (summer only); a decent range of wines, and several malt whiskies. Darts, shove-ha'penny, dominoes, cribbage, trivia, winter chess club (all welcome), and piped music. There are tables and an aviary in the sheltered garden. *(Recommended by Moira and John Cole, Mr and Mrs Jack Pitts, Paul Boot, J R T Powys-Smith; more reports please)*

Own brew ~ Licensees Megan and Jason Tidy ~ Real ale ~ Meals and snacks ~ Restaurant ~ (01837) 810306 ~ Well behaved children in eating area of bar and in restaurant ~ Open 11-2.30, 6-11 ~ Bedrooms: £30B/£50B

HAYTOR VALE SX7677 Map 1

Rock ★

Haytor signposted off B3387 just W of Bovey Tracey, on good moorland road to Widecombe

Locals, visitors and walkers alike are welcomed to this rather civilised Dartmoor inn. The atmosphere is very restful with the crackling of logs, the ticking of the clock and the hum of conversation (no noisy games machines or music). The two communicating, partly panelled bar rooms have easy chairs, oak windsor armchairs and high-backed settles, candlelit, polished antique tables, old-fashioned prints and decorative plates on the walls, and good winter log fires (the main fireplace has a fine Stuart fireback); two lounges and the restaurant are no smoking. A wide choice of good bar food includes home-made soup (£2.35), sandwiches (from £2.80), filled baked potatoes (from £4.55), 3-egg omelettes using free range eggs (£4.95), ploughman's (from £4.95), steak and kidney pie (£5.55), local rabbit in a whole grain mustard sauce (£5.65) fresh herb pasta with smoked salmon and a basil and cream sauce or curries (£5.95), steak and kidney pie (£5.55), local rabbit in mustard sauce (£5.65), spinach and mushroom pie (£6.50), local fish in a white wine and chive sauce (£9.95), half a roast duck with orange cinnamon sauce (£11.95), steaks (from £12.55), and puddings like toffee apple crumble pie or treacle and walnut tart (from £3.25); friendly, attentive staff. Well kept Eldridge Pope Royal Oak and Hardy, and Dartmoor on handpump, a decent wine list, and several malt whiskies. In summer, the pretty, well kept large garden opposite the inn is a popular place to sit and there are some tables and chairs on a small terrace next to the pub itself. The village is just inside the National Park, and golf, horse riding and fishing (and walking, of course) are nearby. *(Recommended by Marc and Yvonne Weller, Alan and Paula McCully, G W Stevenson, Sue Demont, Tim Barrow, Mr and Mrs C Roberts, G and M Stewart, Mrs J Beale, P H Roberts, John and Vivienne Rice, John and Christine Vittoe)*

Free house ~ Licensee Christopher Graves ~ Real ale ~ Snacks (not Sun or Bank Hol) ~ Restaurant ~ (01364) 661305 ~ Children in restaurant ~ Open 10.30-3, 5.30-11; winter evening opening 6.30 ~ Bedrooms: £29.95(£45.95B)/£51.90(£71B)

HOLBETON SX6150 Map 1

Mildmay Colours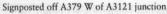

Signposted off A379 W of A3121 junction

You are welcome to look at the brewery in this neatly kept, pleasant pub, and the beers include Colours Best, SP, 50/1, Old Horse Whip, and Tipster on handpump; local farm cider, and a decent wine list. Lots of named tankards hang over the bar counter and there are plenty of bar stools as well as cushioned wall seats and wheelback chairs on the turkey carpet, various horse and racing pictures on the partly stripped stone and partly stripped walls, and a tile-sided woodburning stove; an arch leads to a smaller, similarly decorated family area. The separate plain back bar has pool, sensible darts, dominoes, and fruit machine. Popular bar food includes home-made soup (£2.25), sandwiches (from £2.50), home-made chicken liver and hazelnut pâté (£2.95), sliced pork or beef with pickle (£3.50), home-cooked ham and egg (£3.95), ploughman's (from £4.25), Mexican chicken enchilada (£5.95), rump steak (£8.95), and daily specials such as beef and mustard pie or vegetable korma (£4.95), kidney creole (£5.10) or poached local trout (£7.25), and puddings (£2.75); children's meals (£2.50); helpful service. The well kept back garden has picnic tables, a swing and some guinea pigs and rabbits in a big cage, and there's a small front terrace. *(Recommended by Mr and Mrs N Spink, B Taylor, Nigel Spence, Kim Greek, Andy and Jill Kassube, D Rowe, Richard Houghton)*

Own brew ~ Licensee Andrew Patrick ~ Real ale ~ Meals and snacks (served throughout opening hours) ~ Upstairs carvery restaurant ~ (01752) 830248 ~ Children welcome ~ Open 11-3, 6-11; occasional all day opening summer Sats ~ Bedrooms in two cottages opposite: £20B/£40B

HOLNE SX7069 Map 1

Church House 🛏

Village signed off B3357 2 or 3 miles W of Ashburton

Busy with walkers and those out for a proper meal, this country inn has a lower bar with stripped pine panelling and an 18th-c curved elm settle, and is separated from the atmospheric carpeted lounge bar by a 16th-c heavy oak partition; open log fires in both rooms. There are fine moorland views from the pillared porch (where regulars tend to gather). Bar food includes soup (£1.95), lunchtime sandwiches (from £2.50), home-made pâté (from £2.95), filled baked potatoes (from £3.50), 3-egg omelettes (from £3.75), lunchtime ploughman's (from £3.95), excellent steak and kidney in ale pie (£5.25), local rabbit pie (£5.50), grills (from £5.75), daily specials such as smoked fish or cold meat platters (£4.95), chicken and leek or fish pies (£4.95), cheese and lentil loaf with fresh tomato sauce (£5.75), and lamb pie (£5.95); 3 course Sunday lunch £8.50 in the restaurant (which is no smoking). Well kept Dartmoor Bitter and Legend, Palmers IPA and 2000, and Wadworths 6X on handpump, Grays farm cider, country wines, and decent house wines (several by the glass); darts, dominoes, cribbage, and table skittles in the public bar. The quarter-hour walk from the Newbridge National Trust car park to the pub is rather fine, and there are many other attractive walks nearby, up on to Dartmoor as well as along the wooded Dart valley. Charles Kingsley (of *Water Babies* fame) was born in the village. *(Recommended by R and S Bentley, M G Hart, John and Vivienne Rice, R Walden, Mr and Mrs M Matthews, Ian Dunkin, EHW, RFW, Anthony Marriott, Jeanne Cross, Paul Silvestri, Dr N Holmes, Alan and David Rose, David Mowbray)*

Free house ~ N E and W J Bevan ~ Real ale ~ Meals and snacks ~ Restaurant ~ (01364) 631208 ~ Well behaved children in eating area of bar; over 7 (except residents) in restaurant in evening ~ Local musician last Fri of month, summer Morris dancers ~ Open 11.30-3, 6.30-11; winter Mon-Thurs evening opening 7 ~ Bedrooms: £22.50(£27.50B)/£39(£50B)

HORNDON SX5280 Map 1

Elephants Nest ★ ◪

If coming from Okehampton on A386 turn left at Mary Tavy Inn, then left after about ½ mile; pub signposted beside Mary Tavy Inn, then Horndon signposted; on the Ordnance Survey Outdoor Leisure Map it's named as the New Inn

One couple were very happy to find that after many years, the welcome and enjoyable atmosphere here had not diminished. There are large rugs and flagstones, a beams-and-board ceiling, a good log fire, and cushioned stone seats built into the windows, with captain's chairs around the tables; the name of the pub is written up on the beams in 60 languages. Another room – created from the old beer cellar and with views over the garden and beyond to the moors – acts as a dining or function room or an overspill from the bar on busy nights. Good home-made bar food at lunchtime includes soup (£1.45), good filled granary rolls (£1.50), home-made pâté (£3.20), ploughman's (from £3.20), steak and kidney pie (£5.30), daily specials such as vegetable curry (£4.40), mediterranean chick peas (£4.50), beef with orange and walnut (£6.70), and pheasant casserole (£7), with evening dishes such as garlic prawns or stilton and walnut pâté (£3.20), gammon with pineapple (£5.20), local game pie (£6.90), steaks (from £9.90), and puddings like sherry trifle, apple crumble or steamed plum pudding (£2.20). Well kept Boddingtons Bitter, Palmers IPA, St Austells HSD, and a local and another guest on handpump; farm cider. Sensibly placed darts, cribbage, dominoes, and piped music. On the spacious, flower-bordered lawn in front of the pub are some wooden benches and tables that look over the walls to the pastures of Dartmoor's lower slopes. You can walk from here straight onto the moor or Black Down, though a better start (army exercises permitting) might be to drive past Wapsworthy to the end of the lane, at OS Sheet 191 map reference 546805. They have three dogs, two cats, ducks, chickens, rabbits, and horses; customers' dogs are allowed in on a lead. *(Recommended by John and Vivienne Rice, R Walden, Paul and Heather Bettesworth, Dr and Mrs N Holmes, Andy and Jill Kassube, Andy, Andrew and Friends, Nigel Spence, Kim Greek, George and Jeanne Barnwell, Jack and Philip Paxton)*

Free house ~ Licensee Nick Hamer ~ Real ale ~ Meals and snacks (11.30-2, 6.30-10) ~ (01822) 810273 ~ Children welcome away from bar ~ Folk music 2nd Tues evening of month ~ Open 11.30-2.30, 6.30-11

Most pubs in the *Guide* sell draught cider. We mention it specifically only if they have unusual farm-produced 'scrumpy' or even specialise in it.

HORSEBRIDGE SX3975 Map 1

Royal 🏠

Village signposted off A384 Tavistock—Launceston

New licensees have taken over this prettily-set pub and are continuing the home-brewed beers: Horsebridge Best, Right Royal, Tamar and the more powerful Heller – plus Bass and Sharps Own on handpump, and country wines. The two bar rooms are simple and old-fashioned and there's another small room, called the Drip Tray, for the overflow at busy times; darts, bar billiards, cribbage, dominoes, and piped music. Bar food includes seafood pancakes (£5.75), and beef in beer casserole or chicken tikka masala (£5.95). There's a covered area in the garden and a big terrace with seats, a rose arbour and hanging baskets. The pub was originally called the Packhorse, and got its present name for services rendered to Charles I (whose seal is carved in the doorstep). Children must be over six. *(Recommended by James Macrae, Mr and Mrs J Jones, R and S Bentley; more reports on the new regime, please)*

Own brew ~ Licensees David and Catherine Johnson ~ Real ale ~ Meals and snacks ~ (01822) 870214 ~ Children in eating area if over 6 ~ Open 12-3, 7-11 ~ Bedrooms planned

IDDESLEIGH SS5708 Map 1

Duke of York

B3217 Exbourne—Dolton

This friendly old thatched pub is very much somewhere to come for a relaxing drink or meal and it's usually filled with chatty regulars – no noisy games machines or piped music. The bar has rocking chairs by the roaring log fire, cushioned wall benches built into the wall's black-painted wooden dado, stripped tables, and other homely country furnishings, and well kept Adnams Broadside, Cotleigh Tawny and a local ale called Jollyboat Mainbrace tapped from the cask. Bar food includes sandwiches (from £1.75), home-made soup (£1.95), home-made pâté (£2.10), leek and blue cheese bake (£4.50), tagliatelle with ham, mushrooms in a creamy sauce (£4.75), home-baked ham with two eggs (£4.95), steak and stilton pie (£5.25), a fresh fish of the day, steaks (from £8.25), and puddings such as chocolate mousse with brandy or sticky toffee pudding (£2.10); Sunday roast, and a Wednesday oriental menu. Darts, shove-ha'penny, cribbage, and dominoes. Through a small coach arch is a little back garden with some picnic tables under cocktail parasols. Good fishing nearby. *(Recommended by R Walden, Douglas Dwyer, Paul and Wendy Bachelor, David Wallington, Derek and Iris Martin, Paul and Wendy Bachelor, Joan and Gordon Edwards)*

Free house ~ Lease: Bill Pringle ~ Real ale ~ Meals and snacks (not Mon evening and see opening hours below) ~ Restaurant ~ (01837) 810253 ~ Children in eating area of bar and in restaurant ~ Occasional folk music ~ Open 11.30-3, 6.30-11; closed lunchtimes Mon/Tues/Weds 1 Nov-31 Mar ~ Bedrooms: £20(£27B)/£40(£44B)

KINGSKERSWELL SX8767 Map 1

Barn Owl 🛏

Aller Mills; just off A380 Newton Abbot—Torquay – inn-sign on main road opposite RAC post

A splendidly rustic 16th-c ex-farmhouse with friendly staff, well kept beer, and enjoyable food. The large bar has some grand furnishings such as a couple of carved oak settles and old-fashioned dining chairs around the handsome polished tables on its flowery carpet, an elaborate ornamental plaster ceiling, antique dark oak panelling, and a decorative wooden chimney piece. The other rooms have low black oak beams, with polished flagstones and a kitchen range in one, and an inglenook fireplace in the other; lots more pictures and artefacts this year, and old lamps on the tables. Good, popular bar food includes home-made soup (£2.25), big sandwiches with interesting side salad (from £3.20), filled baked potatoes (from £3.50), a salad of tomato and crab (£3.95), ploughman's (from £4), quite a few cold platters (from £5.95; fresh local crab £7.25), fresh fillet of lemon sole (£6.25), gammon with egg (£6.95), steaks (from £7.50), mixed grill (£10.25), puddings (£2.75), and daily specials like rack of lamb with a redcurrant and rosemary sauce or breast of pheasant wrapped in bacon with red wine, juniper and cranberry sauce (£7.95), and darne of salmon on spinach with a light mustard and cream sauce (£8.75); a different potato dish every day. Well kept Dartmoor, Ind Coope Burton, and Marstons Pedigree on handpump, 15 malt whiskies, and 18 wines by the glass. There are picnic tables in a small sheltered garden. No children. *(Recommended by Ian Phillips, R T Moggridge, Joan and Michel Hooper-Immins, Alan and Paula McCully, Paul and Janet Waring, Andrew Hodges, Michael Butler, R W Flux, Peter and Jenny Quine)*

Free house ~ Licensees Derek and Margaret Warner ~ Real ale ~ Meals and snacks (till 10pm) ~ Restaurant (not Sun) ~ (01803) 872130 ~ Open 11.30-2.30, 6-11; winter evening opening 6.30; closed evening 25 Dec, closed 26-27 Dec ~ Bedrooms: £40B/£60B

KINGSTEIGNTON SX8773 Map 1

Old Rydon ★ ⑪

Rydon Rd; from A381/A380 junction follow signs to Kingsteignton (B3193), taking first right turn (Longford Lane), go straight on to the bottom of the hill, then next right turn into Rydon Rd following Council Office signpost; pub is just past the school, OS Sheet 192 map reference 872739

It's well worth the difficulty in finding this consistently reliable old pub. The small, cosy bar has a big winter log fire in a raised fireplace, cask seats and upholstered seats built against the white-painted stone walls, and lots of beer mugs hanging from the heavy beam-and-plank ceiling. There are a few more seats in an upper former cider loft facing the antlers and antelope horns on one high white wall; piped music. Adventurous, very good food includes sandwiches, filled baked potatoes, and snacks, as well as daily specials such as chicken liver pâté with home-made chutney (£2.95), smoked salmon and egg mayonnaise (£3.25), vegetable pancake topped with tomato, cream, cheese and herb breadcrumbs (£4.65), venison, lentil and mushroom pie or lamb casserole with rosemary (£5.85), grilled marinated chicken with Thai spices, chilli and lemon grass sauce (£6.25), Brixham fish pie (£6.30), seafood platter (£6.95), and home-made puddings (£2.75). Well kept Bass, Wadworths 6X, and a changing guest ale on handpump, and helpful, friendly service. There's also a prettily planted dining conservatory. Seats in a nice biggish sheltered garden, which also has a swing. *(Recommended by C A Hall, James Cowell, John Waller, Simon and Hayley Marks, R T Moggridge, B A Ferris Harms, Alan and Paula McCully, Don and Shirley Parrish, M G Hart, Jim and Maggie Cowell, Barbara Wensworth, Nick Leslie, Alan and Eileen Bowker, D I Baddeley, Kevin Mitchell, Peter and Jenny Quine, Jeanne Cross, Paul Silvestri, Mrs Pat Crabb)*

Free house ~ Licensees Hermann and Miranda Hruby ~ Real ale ~ Meals and snacks ~ Restaurant (closed Sun) ~ (01626) 54626 ~ Children in eating area of bar, but no under 8s after 8pm ~ Open 11-2.30, 6-11.30; closed 25 Dec

KINGSTON SX6347 Map 1

Dolphin

Off B3392 S of Modbury (can also be reached from A379 W of Modbury)

Very helpful, friendly licensees run this peaceful shuttered 16th-c inn. The several knocked-through beamed rooms have a relaxed, welcoming atmosphere (no noisy games machines or piped music), amusing drawings and photographs on the walls, and rustic tables and cushioned seats and settles around their bared stone walls; one small area is no smoking. Very good home-made bar food (with prices unchanged since last year) includes sandwiches (from £1.50), soup such as onion and coriander or lentil (£1.95), ploughman's (from £3.50), chicken with an apple and calvados sauce or leek and pistachio nut lasagne with garlic bread (£4.95), steak and kidney pie (£5.50), fisherman's pie (£5.95), lamb steak with rosemary and garlic (£6.50), steaks (from £7.95), plaice fillets with an apricot and hazelnut stuffing in a wine, apricot and dill sauce (£8.95), puddings such as chocolate pear pudding or treacle tart (£2.25), and children's meals (from £1.50). Well kept Courage Best and Ushers Founders on handpump. Outside, there are tables and swings, and several tracks leading down to the sea. *(Recommended by Marianne Lantree, Steve Webb, Jeanne Cross, Paul Silvestri, H F C Barclay, R W Brooks, B Taylor, Mr and Mrs C C Mathewman, Roger and Susan Dunn, Norma Farris, B J Harding)*

Ushers ~ Tenants Neil and Annie Williams ~ Real ale ~ Meals and snacks (till 10pm) ~ (01548) 810314 ~ Children in eating area of bar and in children's room ~ Open 11-2.30, 6-11 ~ Bedrooms: £37B/£49B

KNOWSTONE SS8223 Map 1

Masons Arms ★ 🛏 ♀

Village signposted off A361 Tiverton—South Molton

As good as ever with its particularly relaxed, characterful atmosphere, this 13th-c thatched pub is in a lovely quiet position opposite the village church. It's run in a very personal way by the friendly licensees, and the unspoilt small main bar has heavy medieval black beams hung with ancient bottles of all shapes and sizes, farm tools on the walls, substantial rustic furniture on the stone floor, and a fine open fireplace with a big log fire and side bread oven. A small lower sitting room has pinkish plush chairs around a low table in front of the fire, and bar billiards. Bar food can be very good indeed: widely praised home-made soup (£1.95) and pâté (£2.75), ploughman's with proper local cheese and butter in a pot or Greek salad (£3.75), fried plaice (£4.25), home-made pies, varying from day to day, like venison, cheese and leek or rabbit (£4.50), home-made curry (£5.50), and home-made puddings like pear and strawberry crunch (£2.25); specials such as piri-piri prawns (£2.95), cashew nut vegetable risotto or stuffed squid (£3.95), chicken with walnuts and tarragon (£4.25), beef bourguignon (£4.50), and cassoulet (£5.50); good value Sunday lunch, popular Thursday curry night, traditional fish and chips on Friday (£4.95), and theme nights about once a month, usually with live music, a special menu and a special drink. The restaurant is no smoking. They often sell home-made marmalades, fruit breads or hot gooseberry chutney over the counter. Well kept Badger Best and Cotleigh Tawny tapped from the cask (and an occasional guest beer), farm cider, a small but well chosen wine list (with around 8 by the glass), and coffee and teas; several snuffs on the counter; darts, shove-ha'penny, bar billiards, dominoes, cribbage, board games, and quiz nights. Maybe weekend evening summer barbecues in the back garden. Charlie the engaging bearded collie likes to join you on a walk – at least part of the way; the cats are called Archie and Allie. The refurbishment of the bedrooms is nearly complete. *(Recommended by Sue Demont, Tim Barrow, Joyce McKimm, Tony and Wendy Hobden, Paul Boot, Ian and Nita Cooper, R Walden, Anna Bramhill, Simon Clarke, Linda and Mike Proctor, James Nunns, Tina and David Woods-Taylor, PM, AM, L Parikian, Jack and Philip Paxton, Dr Peter Donahue, S G N Bennett, Clive Gilbert, N M Baleham, Chris Westmoreland)*

Free house ~ Licensees David and Elizabeth Todd ~ Real ale and snacks ~ Restaurant (not Sun evening) ~ (01398) 341231/341582 ~ Children in eating area of bar and in restaurant ~ Occasional live music ~ Open 11-3, 6-11; winter evening opening 7; closed evenings 25/26 Dec ~ Bedrooms: £21(£37.50B)/£55B; dogs £1.50

LITTLEHEMPSTON SX8162 Map 1

Tally Ho!

Signposted off A381 NE of Totnes

Spotlessly kept and very friendly, this is a grand little pub with very enjoyable food and a relaxed, chatty atmosphere. The bare stone walls in the cosy low-beamed rooms are covered with lots of porcelain, brass, copperware, mounted butterflies, stuffed wildlife, old swords, and shields and hunting horns and so forth; there's also an interesting mix of chairs and settles (many antique and with comfortable cushions), candles on the tables, fresh flowers, panelling, and two ornamental woodburning stoves; no noisy machines or piped music. Very good bar food includes delicious soup (£2.75), sandwiches (from £2.75; lovely crab £3.25), mussels in cream and white wine (£2.95), rabbit casserole or steak and kidney pie (£6.50), whole local plaice (£7.25), pork with cider and apple and cream (£7.75), Brixham fish pie (£8.50), Aberdeen Angus steaks (from £9.25), fresh roast duckling (£11.50), home-made puddings with clotted cream, and daily specials. Well kept Dartmoor, Palmers Tally Ho!, Teignworthy Reel Ale, and Wadworths 6X on handpump from a temperature controlled cellar, and several whiskies. The terrace is a mass of flowers in summer. *(Recommended by DWAJ, Alan and Paula McCully, Dennis Glover, David and June Harwood, David Wallington, John A Barker, Peter Burton, Mrs B Lemon, George and Jeanne Barnwell)*

Free house ~ Licensees Alan and Dale Hitchman ~ Real ale ~ Meals and snacks (till 10pm) ~ (01803) 862316 ~ Children in eating area of bar ~ Open 12-2.30, 6-11; closed 25 Dec

LOWER ASHTON SX8484 Map 1

Manor 🍺

Ashton signposted off B3193 N of Chudleigh

This creeper-covered, unspoilt pub is popular with chaps enjoying the well kept Wadworths 6X tapped from the cask and Shepherd Neame Spitfire, Teignworthy Reel Ale, Theakstons XB and a changing guest ale such as Burton Bridge on handpump, or perhaps the local Green Valley farm cider. This side of things is very much concentrated in the left-hand room, its walls covered in beer mats and brewery advertisements; on the right, two rather more discreet rooms have a wider appeal, bolstered by tasty home-made food including sandwiches (from £1.50), soup (£1.60), ploughman's (from £3.50), filled baked potatoes (from £2.60), vegetable bake (£4.25), steak and kidney pie (£4.95) and steaks (from rump £8.50), with a good choice of changing specials (many topped with melted cheese and served with very garlicky garlic bread) such as mixed bean chilli or vegetable and nut curry (£4.50), lamb goulash (£5.50), chicken curry or seafood pasta mornay (£5.75), beef casserole (£5.25). Service is quick; shove-ha'penny, spoof. The garden has lots of picnic tables under cocktail parasols (and a fine tall Scots pine); it's a charming valley. No children. *(Recommended by Jeanne Cross, Paul Silvestri, Julian McMahon, Chris Westmoreland; more reports please)*

Free house ~ Licensees Geoff and Clare Mann ~ Real ale ~ Meals and snacks (12-1.30, 7-9.30; not Mon) ~ Open 12-2.30, 6(7 Sat)-11; closed Mon exc bank holidays

LUSTLEIGH SX7881 Map 1

Cleave

Village signposted off A382 Bovey Tracey—Moretonhampstead

The neat and very pretty sheltered garden here is lovely in summer and full of cottagey flowers. Inside this friendly old thatched pub, the cosy, low-ceilinged lounge bar has big winter log fires, and attractive antique high-backed settles, pale leatherette bucket chairs, red-cushioned wall seats, and wheelback chairs around the tables on its patterned carpet. The second bar has similar furnishings, a large dresser, harmonium, an HMV gramophone, and prints, and the family room has crayons, books and toys for children. Generously served, the enjoyable bar food includes home-made soup (£2.25), sandwiches (£2.85), ploughman's (from £3.25), home-made chicken liver pâté (£3.95), very good local sausages (£5.25), home-made chicken curry (£5.75), home-made steak, kidney and Guinness pie (£6.45), good roast pork with apple sauce or nut roast with spicy tomato sauce (£6.85), daily specials, and puddings like treacle tart or blackcurrant cheesecake (£2.25), and children's dishes (from £2.95). Well kept Bass, Flowers Original and a guest like Whitbreads Fuggles on handpump, several malt whiskies, and farm ciders; cribbage and pool. The village is most attractive. *(Recommended by Margaret Dyke, Alan and Paula McCully, M G Hart, G and M Stewart, John and Christine Vittoe, Alan Newman, R J Walden, Mr and Mrs C Roberts, A Lock, Joan and Gordon Edwards, Sue Hobley, John and Vivienne Rice, Werner Arend)*

Heavitree (who no longer brew) ~ Tenant Alison Perring ~ Real ale ~ Meals and snacks ~ (016477) 223 ~ Open 11-11; 12-10.30 Sun; 11-3, 6-11 in winter ~ Children in eating areas and in no-smoking family room ~ Parking may be difficult

LUTTON SX5959 Map 1

Mountain

Off Cornwood—Sparkwell road, though pub not signposted from it

From seats on the terrace (and from one room inside) there is a fine view over the lower slopes of Dartmoor. It's a friendly place and the bar has a high-backed settle by the log fire and some walls stripped back to the bare stone, with windsor chairs around old-fashioned polished tables in a larger connecting room. Well kept Dartmoor Best, Marstons Pedigree and a guest beer on handpump, several malt whiskies, and farm cider; darts, cribbage, and dominoes. Generous helpings of good straightforward bar food include pasties (£1.20), sandwiches (from £1.60), soup (£1.70; with a hunk of cheese as well £3), sausage and chips (£2.60), cottage pie (£3.50), ploughman's or ham cooked in cider (£3.80), and chicken kiev (£4.50). *(Recommended by Mervyn Jonas, John Poulter, Roger and Susan Dunn, Mr and Mrs Jones, Andy and Jill Kassube, George and Jeanne Barnwell)*

Free house ~ Licensees Charles and Margaret Bullock ~ Real ale ~ Meals and snacks (till 10 evening) ~ (01752) 837247 ~ Children in eating area of bar ~ Open 11-3, 6-11; winter Mon-Weds evening opening 7

LYDFORD SX5184 Map 1

Castle ★ 🛏 🍽 🍷

Signposted off A386 Okehampton—Tavistock

Some changes to this very popular and friendly pink-washed Tudor inn this year include the addition of a residents' lounge and coffee lounge and two spacious bedrooms. But this won't affect the relaxed atmosphere of the twin-roomed bar which is furnished with country kitchen chairs, high-backed winged settles and old captain's chairs around mahogany tripod tables on big slate flagstones. One of the rooms (where the bar food is served) has low lamp-lit beams, a sizeable open fire, masses of brightly decorated plates, some Hogarth prints, an attractive grandfather clock, and, near the serving-counter, seven Lydford pennies hammered out in the old Saxon mint in the reign of Ethelred the Unready, in the 11th c; the second room has an interesting collection of antique stallion posters; unusual stained-glass doors. Good, enjoyable home-made bar food might include lovely soup (£2.40; Thai chicken and coconut soup £2.50), wild boar pâté (£3.95), Devon cheese platter (£4.10), hot and sour prawns with tomato, fresh chillies and coriander (£4.95), Moroccan vegetable casserole (£5.55), steak and kidney pie (£5.70), local venison pie (£6.25), provençale chicken (£6.35), szechuan prawns (£6.95), salmon and cod plait with a champagne and lemon thyme sauce (£7.50), and lovely home-made puddings like caramelised rice pudding, heavenly apple and blackberry crumble or brandy mousse ice cream (from £2.50); Sunday roast (including boar, £5.70). The partly no-smoking restaurant now has a fixed-price menu with supplemented dishes, and there are Indian and Thai evenings. Well kept Blackawton Bitter, Fullers London Pride, Mildmay Colours (a little brewery at Holbeton), and Wadworths 6X on handpump or tapped from the cask (they keep 3 real ales in winter and 6 in summer), and around 17 wines by the glass from a carefully chosen wine list; sensibly placed darts, cribbage, and dominoes. The terrace in the well kept garden has a pets corner for residents' children with goats and hens. The pub is next to the village's daunting, ruined 12th-c castle and close to a beautiful river gorge (owned by the National Trust; closed Nov-Easter); the village itself was one of the four strongpoints developed by Alfred the Great as a defence against the Danes. *(Recommended by Viv Middlebrook, A and R Cooper, Pete and Rosie Flower, Mr and Mrs J Jones, B J Cox, Clive Hall-Tomkin, Michael and Lynne Steane, Paul Boot, John and Christine Vittoe, Colin Draper, Paul and Lynn Benny, E G Cox, Jonathan Williams, Geoff Dibble, V G and P A Nutt, Mr and Mrs A O Meakin, R Walden, Hanns P Golez, Andy and Jill Kassube, Nigel Flook, Betsy Brown, S Lonie, S Tait, Anthony Marriott, Simon and Debbie Tomlinson, S P Ward, Jack and Philip Paxton, T Cobden Pike, Mike Gorton, Howard Clutterbuck)*

Free house ~ Licensees Clive and Mo Walker ~ Real ale ~ Meals and snacks ~ Restaurant ~ (01822) 820241/820242 ~ Children in restaurant and snug area; must be over 7 in evening restaurant ~ Open 11.30-3, 6-11; closed evening 25 Dec ~ Bedrooms: £28.75(£38.75B)/£44(£55B)

LYNMOUTH SS7249 Map 1

Rising Sun 🛏

Mars Hill; down by harbour

The setting for this extended thatched inn with its 14th-c heart is pretty, with views over the boats in the little harbour and out to sea. The modernised panelled bar has a relaxed atmosphere, as well as cushioned built-in stall-seats on the uneven oak floors, black beams in the crooked ceiling, some stripped stone at the fireplace end, and latticed windows facing the harbour; piped music. Well kept Courage Best, Exmoor Ale, and Ruddles County on handpump, and decent bar food (only available at lunchtime) such as home-made soup (£2.25), filled rolls (from £2.75), filled baked potatoes (from £3.50), ploughman's (£4.75), two jumbo spicy sausages with egg (£4.95), steak, mushroom and Guinness pie (£5.25), local trout (£5.75), and 6oz sirloin steak (£7.25); the attractive restaurant is no smoking. There's a charming terraced garden behind the inn, cut into the hillside. Shelley reputedly spent his honeymoon with his 16-year-old bride, Harriet, in one of the cottages here. The steep walk up the Lyn valley to Watersmeet (National Trust) and Exmoor is particularly pleasant. Most of the business here is on the hotel and restaurant side, and casual visitors to the bar have sometimes felt service could be more helpful to them. *(Recommended by Rip and Pauline Kirby, Simon Collett-Jones, PM, AM, S Demont, T Barrow, Tina and David Woods-Taylor, R Walden, V Kavanagh, John and Christine Vittoe, Gary Gibbon, Mark Berger)*

Free house ~ Licensee Hugo Jeune ~ Real ale ~ Lunchtime meals and snacks ~ Restaurant ~ (01598) 53223 ~ Children in eating area of the bar ~ Open 11-3, 5.30-11; winter evening opening 6.30 ~ Bedrooms: £45B/£79B

MEAVY SX5467 Map 1

Royal Oak

Off B3212 E of Yelverton

Picnic tables and benches outside this traditional, friendly old pub are set by the attractive village green. Inside, the carpeted L-shaped bar has pews from the next door church, red plush banquettes and old agricultural prints and church pictures on the walls, and there's a smaller bar – where the locals like to gather – with a big fireplace and side bread oven, and red-topped barrel seats. Bar food includes sandwiches (£1.80), soup (£1.90), filled baked potatoes (£2.95), ploughman's (£3.50), filled crêpes (£3.95), chicken tikka masala, fish pie or spinach and mushroom lasagne (all £4.75), mussels with cockles, cheese-topped with white wine and garlic sauce (£4.95), home-made steak and kidney pie (£5.50), daily specials, puddings, and roast Sunday lunch. Well kept Bass, Courage Best, Eldridge Pope Royal Oak, and Otter Bitter on handpump kept under light blanket pressure, and three draught ciders. Dominoes and piped music. No children. *(Recommended by James Macrae, Jacquie and Jim Jones, R Walden, G and M Stewart, C A Hall, M J How, Colin Draper, Joan and Michel Hooper-Immins, Mr and Mrs J Woodfield, Jeanne Cross, Paul Silvestri, Bill Sharpe, Andy and Jill Kassube)*

Free house ~ Licensees Roger and Susan Barber ~ Real ale ~ Meals and snacks (11.30-2.30, 6.30-9.30) ~ (01822) 852944 ~ Open 11.30-3, 6.30-11

MILTONCOMBE SX4865 Map 1

Who'd Have Thought It ★

On A386 ¾ mile S of Yelverton, turn W onto signposted country road for 2 miles

You can be sure of an enjoyable visit at this attractive 16th-c pub, handy for Buckland Abbey or the lovely gardens of the Garden House at Buckland Monachorum. The atmospheric, black-panelled bar has cushioned barrel seats and high-backed winged settles around solid, polished wooden tables, colourful plates on a big black dresser, rapiers, sabres and other weapons on its walls, and a woodburning stove in the big stone fireplace; two other rooms (one is no smoking) have seats made from barrels. Generous helpings of popular bar food include sandwiches (from £2.25; the open prawn one is tasty), ploughman's (from £3.10), battered cod (£3.65), platters (from £5.50), steaks (from £8.75), and daily specials such as delicious local salmon, steak and kidney pie or chicken curry (£4.50), good rabbit in honey and mustard (£5.95), grilled trout (£6.95), and lemon sole (£9.50). Well kept Bass, Blackawton Headstrong, Eldridge Pope Royal Oak, Exmoor Ale, and Wadworths 6X on handpump; efficient staff. There are picnic tables on a terrace with hanging baskets by the little stream. No children. *(Recommended by R Turnham, Philip and Trisha Ferris, R Walden, Nigel Clifton, Dennis Glover, Peter Burton, Colin Draper, James Macrae, Andy and Jill Kassube, Anthony Marriott, R W Brooks, Ted George)*

Free house ~ Licensees Keith Yeo and Gary Rager ~ Real ale ~ Meals and snacks ~ (01822) 853313 ~ Folk club Sun evening in lower bar ~ Open 11.30-2.30(3 Sat), 6.30-11

NEWTON ST CYRES SX8798 Map 1

Beer Engine 🍺

Sweetham; from Newton St Cyres on A377 follow St Cyres Station, Thorverton signpost

Popular with locals, this friendly old station hotel brews its own beer: Rail Ale, Piston Bitter, Return Ticket (Mild), and the very strong Sleeper. The spacious main bar (refurbished this year) has partitioning alcoves, windsor chairs and some cinnamon-coloured button-back banquettes around dark varnished tables, and a new brown carpet. Decent bar food includes speciality sausages like pork and garlic or oriental (£4.25), home-made steak and kidney pie (£4.95), chicken in barbecue sauce (£5.25), Brixham plaice (£6.25), and rump steak (£7.50); darts, shove-ha'penny, dominoes and cribbage; fruit machine and video game in the downstairs lobby. There's a large sunny garden on several interesting levels with lots of sheltered seating; you can eat out here, too. *(Recommended by Dr and Mrs J M Coles, R Walden, John Hazel, Jeanne Cross, Paul Silvestri)*

Own brew ~ Licensee Peter Hawksley ~ Real ale ~ Meals and snacks (till 10pm) ~ (01392) 851282 ~ Children in eating area of bar ~ Live music Sat evenings and some Sun lunchtimes ~ Open 11-11; 12-10.30 Sun

NOSS MAYO SX5447 Map 1

Old Ship

Off A379 via B3186, E of Plymouth

A fine setting for a pub (but watch the tide if you park on the slipway) with tables on the terrace overlooking the water; at high tide you can get here by boat – so it's popular with yachtsmen. Inside, the two thick-walled bars have a warm, friendly atmosphere and reliably good bar food that includes sandwiches, good pasties, home-made daily specials, really delicious locally caught fish grilled on the bone (from £4), steaks, and nice puddings with clotted cream; 3-course Sunday carvery (£7.50). The restaurant is no smoking. Well kept Bass and Dartmoor with a changing guest beer on handpump, and several malt whiskies; swift, helpful service; darts, fruit machine, and piped music. *(Recommended by Ted George, Mr and Mrs Peter Smith, Ian and Gayle Woodhead, George Atkinson, A N Ellis, B Taylor)*

Free house ~ Licensees Norman and Val Doddridge ~ Real ale ~ Meals and snacks (till 10.30pm) ~ Restaurant ~ (01752) 872387 ~ Children welcome ~ Open 11-3, 6-11

PETER TAVY SX5177 Map 1

Peter Tavy

Off A386 nr Mary Tavy, N of Tavistock

After two years of hard work – exposing original fireplaces and beams, laying slate floors, adding beams and floorboards using reclaimed timber, moving the bar, searching for old furniture and old pictures relevant to the area, opening bedrooms, and much more – the licensees feel that this 15th-c stone inn is now how it should be. The bar has a lot of atmosphere, as well as low beams, high-backed settles on the black flagstones by the big stone fireplace (a good log fire on cold days), smaller settles in stone-mullioned windows, and a snug side dining area; no-smoking area at weekends. Good bar food at lunchtime includes soup (£1.80), interestingly filled baked potatoes (from £2.25), pâté such as liver and mushroom or cashew and carrot (£2.95), filled french bread (from £3.50), shepherd's pie (£4.10), crab cakes (£4.75), steak and kidney pie or pudding (£5.25), lots of vegetarian dishes (also available in the evening) like lentil cottage pie (£3.95), stuffed red peppers (£5.10) or spicy vegetable and bean tacos (£5.25), scallops (£5.95), and evening dishes such as prawn and pernod crêpe (£3.75), carpaccio (£3.95), a changing Eastern dish (£6.45), sirloin steak (£8.95), and wild boar with wild mushroom sauce (£10.25); puddings like trifle, spotted dick and zabaglione (£2.50), fresh fish and daily specials, and four Sunday roasts (£5.25); Thursday evening themed nights. There are always seven real ales, well kept on handpump or tapped from the cask: Bass, Courage Directors, Dartmoor Best, and St Austell HSD, with changing weekly guest beers such as Exmoor Gold, Gibbs Mew Bishops Tipple, Palmers 200, Shepherd Neame Spitfire, Theakstons Old Peculier, and Wadworths 6X; farm cider, 30 malt whiskies, and country wines. From the picnic tables in the pretty garden there are peaceful views of the moor rising above nearby pastures. There is now a car park behind the pub. *(Recommended by R Walden, M J G Martin, C Hardacre, Andy and Jill Kassube, Jeanne Cross, Paul Silvestri, Jill Bickerton, Andy, Andrew and friends; more reports on all the changes, please)*

Free house ~ Licensees Rita Westlake and John Vaughan ~ Real ale ~ Meals and snacks ~ (01822) 810348 ~ Children in back room ~ Open 11.30-2.30(3 Fri), 6.30-11; winter evening opening 7pm ~ Bedrooms: £25B/£50B

PLYMOUTH SX4755 Map 1

China House ★

Marrowbone Slip, Sutton Harbour, via Sutton Road off Exeter Street (A374)

The position of this carefully converted 17th-c waterside pub (Plymouth's oldest warehouse) is marvellous, overlooking Sutton Harbour; picnic tables and benches on the verandah enjoy the view – and the view from the Barbican across to the pub is lovely, too. Inside, it's lofty and very spacious but partitioned into smaller booth-like areas, with great beams and flagstone floors, bare slate and stone walls, and lots of nets, kegs and fishing gear; there's even a clinker-built boat. On the left is the main bar with plain wooden seats around dark tables in front of a good log fire – all very chatty, comfortable and relaxed. Under the new manageress, food is now served all day and includes doorstep sandwiches (from £2.95), soup (£2.50), filled baked potatoes (£4.25), a vegetarian dish of the day like mushroom macaroni bake (£4.75), lamb cutlets or fish dishes such as cod in white sauce (£4.95), and puddings (£2.75); they serve sandwiches and cream teas (£2.95) from 3 to 5pm, and a tapas menu (£2.95 for crudités, potato wedges with dips, garlic mushrooms and so forth) from 5 to 7, before the no-smoking restaurant starts. Well kept Dartmoor Best, Ind Coope Burton, and Tetleys on handpump; fruit machine, trivia and piped music. *(Recommended by Mr and Mrs P Byatt, Karen Eliot, Mrs P V Burdett, Ian and Gayle Woodhead, James Macrae, Mr and Mrs D S Price, Andrew Hodges, P H Roberts, Mike Woodhead, Jeanne Cross, Paul Silvestri, Peter Williamson, Nigel Spence, Kim Greek)*

Ansells (Allied) ~ Manageress Nicole Quinn ~ Real ale ~ Meals and snacks (all day; all day Sun, too) ~ Restaurant ~ (01752) 260930 ~ Children welcome ~ Open 11-11; 12-10.30 Sun

nr POSTBRIDGE SX6780 Map 1

Warren House

B3212 1¾ miles NE of Postbridge

In a marvellous Dartmoor spot, this remote, friendly place is, not surprisingly, popular with walkers – but even in high season there's quite a local atmosphere as the pub is something of a focus for this scattered moorland community. The cosy bar is simply furnished with easy chairs and settles under a beamed ochre ceiling, wild pictures on the partly panelled stone walls, and dim lighting (fuelled by the pub's own generator); at one end of the bar is a fire that is said to have been kept almost continuously alight since 1845. Bar food includes sandwiches, home-made soup (£1.80), filled baked potatoes (from £2.50), local jumbo sausage (£3.75), good ploughman's with local cheeses (£4), quite a few vegetarian dishes, and home-made pies like rabbit (£5.50) or steak in ale pie (£6). Well kept Badger Tanglefoot, Butcombe Bitter, Flowers Original, and Gibbs Mew Bishops Tipple on handpump, farm cider, and local country wines. Darts, pool, cribbage, dominoes, fruit machine, video game, and piped music. This road is worth knowing, as a good little-used route westward through fine scenery. *(Recommended by Mayur Shah, Mr and Mrs D E Powell, John and Vivienne Rice, R Walden, M G Hart, A N Ellis, Hanns P Golez, Andrew Hodges, Alan Newman, Jack and Philip Paxton, Norma Farris, Jeanne Cross, Paul Silvestri)*

Free house ~ Licensee Peter Parsons ~ Real ale ~ Meals and snacks (noon-9.30 in summer) ~ (01822) 880208 ~ Children in family room ~ Open 11-11; 11-2.30, 6-11 winter weekdays

POUNDSGATE SX7072 Map 1

Tavistock

From A38 at Peartree Cross, follow Two Bridges, Princetown signpost on to Ashburton—Tavistock road, pub about 5 miles from Ashburton; or from central Dartmoor follow B3357 E, keeping on to bear right past Corndon Tor

There's usually a good chatty crowd of locals and walkers in this 13th-c slated white village house. The bar has a friendly atmosphere and the pub has some interesting old features like the narrow-stepped granite spiral staircase, original flagstones, and ancient fireplaces – one with a woodburning stove, the other with logs. Bar food includes home-made soup or mushroom crêpe (£1.95), bacon and eggs (£2.85), burgers (from £3.15), ploughman's (from £3.25), stilton, walnut and leek pie (£3.95), pasta and tuna bake (£4.70), steak and kidney or bacon and onion puddings (£5.25), chicken tikka masala (£5.95), steaks (from £6.95), and puddings (from £1.70). Well kept Courage Best and Ushers Best and Founders from a temperature-controlled cellar, local farm cider, elderflower pressé and fruity schnapps coolers in summer, and mulled wine and brandied hot chocolate in winter; good welcoming service; darts, cribbage, dominoes, and fruit machine. The family room was once the stable. In summer, there are lots of pretty hanging baskets, a lovely back garden with displays of bedding plants, and picnic tables on the front terrace just above the quiet lane. *(Recommended by Mike Gorton, Jonathan Williams, G and M Stewart, Joan and Gordon Edwards, A N Ellis, Alan Newman)*

Ushers ~ Lease: Ken and Janice Comer ~ Real ale ~ Meals and snacks (11.30-2.15, 6-9.30; not 25 Dec) ~ (01364) 631251 ~ Children in family room ~ Open 11-3, 6-11

RATTERY SX7461 Map 1

Church House

Village signposted from A385 W of Totnes, and A38 S of Buckfastleigh

This is one of the oldest pub buildings in Britain and the spiral stone steps behind a little stone doorway on your left as you go in probably date from about 1030. There are also massive oak beams and standing timbers in the homely open-plan bar, large fireplaces (one with a little cosy nook partitioned off around it), windsor armchairs, comfortable seats and window seats, and prints on the plain white walls; the dining room is separated from this room by heavy curtains; Shandy the golden labrador is very amiable. Good bar food includes home-made soup, filled rolls, ploughman's with local cheeses, and daily specials such as tropical chicken with fruit (£6.30), Indonesian beef (£6.40), roast pheasant with black cherry and port sauce (£6.60), and fresh salmon steak with red pepper sauce (£6.95); puddings and children's meals. Well kept Dartmoor Best and Legend, Tetleys Imperial, and a weekly guest beer on handpump, a range of malt whiskies (up to 40 years old), and decent wines; friendly staff and locals. Outside, there are peaceful views of the partly wooded surrounding hills from picnic tables on a hedged courtyard by the churchyard. *(Recommended by Paul and Janet Waring, Hanns P Golez, John Evans, David and Helen Wilkins, Mr and Mrs B Cox, Bryan Taylor, M G Hart, R W Brooks, Jack and Philip Paxton, B J Harding, Barry Lynch, Dorothee amd Dennis Glover, Mr and Mrs Jones, Joy and Paul Rundell)*

Free house ~ Licensees Brian and Jill Evans ~ Real ale ~ Meals and snacks ~ (01364) 642220 ~ Children in eating area of bar and in dining room ~ Open 11-2.30, 6-11

RINGMORE SX6545 Map 1

Journeys End

Off B3392 at Pickwick Inn, St Anns Chapel, nr Bigbury

Several readers so enjoyed staying at this partly 13th-c inn this year that we have given it a Stay Award. The atmosphere is particularly relaxed and friendly, and the licensees take a lot of care to make visitors feel at home. The main bar has a thatched bar counter, bare boards, flagstones and panelling, an unusual partly pitched ceiling, soft lighting from a nice mix of lamps, and a blazing log fire. Good bar food includes sandwiches (from £2; hot bacon and mushroom £3), omelettes (£3.50), ploughman's (from £3.50), lentil and split pea moussaka or lasagne (£4.50), local trout (£5.95), gammon and egg (£6.50), steaks (from £7.95), good daily specials such as crab tartlets, lemon pepper chicken or very good halibut steak with chervil and pink peppercorn sauce, children's meals (£3), and puddings like home-made fruit pies or rum-baked banana syllabub (£2); smashing breakfasts and good value meals in candlelit, no-smoking dining room. Well kept Adnams Broadside, Archers Golden, Butcombe Bitter, Exmoor Ale, Otter Ale, and Shepherd Neame Spitfire on handpump or tapped from the cask, Stancombe farm cider, and winter mulled wine; darts, dominoes, and fruit machine. The big, attractively planted garden has plenty of seats. It's worth a wander around the pretty village, and National Trust coastal walks are only 10 minutes away. *(Recommended by Dave Irving, Tom McLean, Ewan McCall, Marianne Lantree, Steve Webb, Tim Brierly, Jenny and Roger Huggins, Jeanne Cross, Paul Silvester, J Brunel Cohen, Patrick and Lynn Billyeald, David Mowbray, Steve Webb, Marianne Lantree)*

Free house ~ Licensee James Parkin ~ Real ale ~ Meals and snacks (not evening 25 Dec) ~ Conservatory restaurant ~ (01548) 810205 ~ Children in restaurant ~ Live music every other Fri evening ~ Open 11.30-3, 6-11 ~ Bedrooms: £20(£25B)/£40(£45B)

SHEEPWASH SS4806 Map 1

Half Moon 🛏 ♀ £

Off A3072 Holsworthy—Hatherleigh at Highampton

This buff-painted, civilised inn is the place to stay if you love fishing as they have 10 miles of private fishing on the River Torridge (salmon, sea trout and brown trout) as well as a rod room, good drying facilities and a small shop stocking the basic things needed to catch fish. There are lots of fishing pictures on the white walls of the neatly-kept and friendly carpeted main bar, solid old furniture under the beams, and a big log fire fronted by slate flagstones. Lunchtime bar food is attractively straightforward and good, including sandwiches (£1.50, toasties £2), home-made vegetable soup (£1.75), home-made pasties (£2.50), ploughman's (£3.25), home-cooked ham salad (£3.75), and home-made puddings (£2). Well kept Courage Best and Directors, Jollyboat Mainbrace Bitter (brewed locally), Marstons Pedigree, and an occasional guest on handpump (well kept in a temperature-controlled cellar), a fine choice of malt whiskies, and an extensive wine list; darts, fruit machine, and separate pool room. *(Recommended by R Walden, Colin Draper, John and Vivienne Rice; more reports please)*

Free house ~ Licensees Benjamin Robert Inniss and Charles Inniss ~ Real ale ~ Snacks (lunchtime)~ Evening restaurant ~ (01409) 231376 ~ Children welcome lunchtime only ~ Open 11-2.30(3 Sat), 6-11 ~ Bedrooms: £34(£41.50B)/£68B

SIDFORD SY1390 Map 1

Blue Ball ★ 🛏 🍺

A3052 just N of Sidmouth

One reader has known this old thatched inn well for 30 years and still loves it (though it has grown in size considerably) – and indeed, the same family have been in charge for 78 years now. It's a very popular place with locals and holidaymakers, and the low, partly-panelled and neatly kept lounge bar has a bustling, cheerful atmosphere, heavy beams, upholstered wall benches and windsor chairs, lots of bric-a-brac, and a lovely winter log fire in the stone fireplace (there are two other open fires as well); the snug is no smoking. Quickly served bar food includes soup (£1.75), sandwiches with several choices of bread (from £1.80; crab £2.50), filled baked potatoes (£3.50), lots of ploughman's and salads (from £3.50), omelettes or spinach, walnut and leek flan (£4.50), steak and mushroom pie (£5.95), chicken balti (£6.25), steaks (from £8.75), daily specials, children's dishes (£1.99), and puddings (£2.25); friendly seervice. Boddingtons, Flowers IPA, Greenalls Royal Wessex, and Marstons Pedigree on handpump, kept well in a temperature-controlled cellar. A plainer public bar has darts, dominoes, cribbage and a fruit machine; piped music. Tables on a terrace look out over a colourful front flower garden, and there are more seats on a bigger back lawn – as well as in a covered area next to the barbecue; safe swing, see saw and play house for children. *(Recommended by Graham and Lynn Mason, M E Wellington, David Holloway, D Toulson, G J Newman, D Godden, Shirley Pielou, Mrs R Horridge, James Nunns, Clem Stephens, John and Christine Vittoe, V G and P A Nutt, Michael Butler, Nick Wikeley, Werner Arend, George and Jeanne Barnwell, Denzil Taylor, Chris Westmoreland, Don and Thelma Beeson, A Denman, Michael Boniface, Martin Pritchard, Nicolas Corker, Malcolm Taylor, Maj D A Daniells, Mrs A M Fishleigh, Dr C E Morgan)*

Devenish ~ Tenant Roger Newton ~ Real ale ~ Meals and snacks (till 10pm) ~ Well behaved children in family room ~ (01395) 514062 ~ Open 10.30-2.30, 5.30-11; 11-11 in July and August ~ Bedrooms: £24/£40

SOURTON SX5390 Map 1

Highwayman ★

A386 SW of Okehampton; a short detour from the A30

'Unbelievable' is how many readers describe the sheer eccentricity of this pub's design. It doesn't have a lot of the things that people expect from a pub – no real ale and virtually no food – but what it does have is a marvellously well executed fantasy decor that the friendly owners have over 36 years put great enthusiasm and masses of hard work into. The porch (a pastiche of a nobleman's carriage) leads into a warren of dimly lit stonework and flagstone-floored burrows and alcoves, richly fitted out with red plush seats discreetly cut into the higgledy-piggledy walls, elaborately carved pews, a leather porter's chair, jacobean-style wicker chairs, and seats in quaintly bulging small-paned bow windows; the ceiling in one part, where there's an array of stuffed animals, gives the impression of being underneath a tree, roots and all. The seperate Rita Jones' Locker is a make-believe sailing galleon, full of intricate woodwork and splendid timber baulks, with white antique lace clothed tables in the embrasures that might have held cannons. They only sell keg beer, but specialise in farm cider, and food is confined to a range of meaty and vegetarian pasties (£1); service is warmly welcoming and full of character; old-fashioned penny fruit machine, and 40s piped music. Outside, there's a play area in similar style for children with little black and white roundabouts like a Victorian fairground, a fairy-tale pumpkin house and an old-lady-who-lived-in-the-shoe house. You can take children in to look around the pub but they can't stay inside. The period bedrooms are attractive. *(Recommended by George Atkinson, Paul Boot, Graham Tayar, Jim and Judie McGettigan, Pete and Rosie Flower, Anthony Marriott, Jerry and Alison Oakes, S P Ward, John Hazel, Jack and Philip Paxton, John Davies)*

Free house ~ Licensees Buster and Rita Jones and Sally Thomson ~ Snacks (11-1.45, 7-10) ~ (01837) 86243 ~ Open 11-2, 6-10.30 ~ Bedrooms: /£36

SOUTH POOL SX7740 Map 1

Millbrook

Off A379 E of Kingsbridge

At high tide, boating visitors like to make the most of the mooring facilities offered by this tiny pub (one of the smallest in the book) – and opening times tend to be adjusted to suit the tide times; there are seats on the terrace by the stream with its Aylesbury ducks. Inside, the charming little back bar has handsome windsor chairs, a chintz easy chair, drawings and paintings (and a chart) on its cream walls, clay pipes on the beams, and fresh flowers; the top bar has been refurbished this year. Home-made bar food includes home-made soup (£2.25), sandwiches (from £2), good ploughman's (from £3.75), cottage pie (£4), chilli con carne (£4.15), vegetarian dishes, daily specials such as fresh pasta with smoked salmon, cream and dill (pasta dishes from £4.75), popular halibut au poivre (£6.95), seafood paella with monkfish, ling and so forth (£7.25) or Aberdeen Angus sirloin steak (£8.50), and puddings like pavlova with fresh fruit compote (£2.75). Bass, Ruddles Best, Wadworths 6X and a guest ale on handpump, and Churchwards farm ciders; good, friendly service even when busy. Darts and euchre in the public bar in winter. *(Recommended by Peter Lewis, Nick Wikeley, Owen and Margaret Warnock, Mike Gorton, David Eberlin, Roger Wain-Heapy)*

Free house ~ Licensees Jed Spedding and Liz Stirland ~ Real ale ~ Meals and snacks ~ (01548) 531581 ~ Children in top bar ~ Open 11-2.30, 5.30-11 – depending on high tide

SOUTH ZEAL SX6593 Map 1

Oxenham Arms ★ 🛏 ♀

Village signposted from A30 at A382 roundabout and B3260 Okehampton turn-off

Steeped in history, this friendly inn has a lovely relaxed atmosphere. It was first licensed in 1477 and has grown up around the remains of a Norman monastery, built here to combat the pagan power of the neolithic standing stone that still forms part of the wall in the family TV room behind the bar (there are actually twenty more feet of stone below the floor). It later became the Dower House of the Burgoynes, whose heiress carried it to the Oxenham family. The beamed and partly panelled front bar has elegant mullioned windows and Stuart fireplaces, and windsor armchairs around low oak tables and built-in wall seats. The small no-smoking family room has beams, wheelback chairs around polished tables, decorative plates, and another open fire. Popular bar food includes soup (£1.85), sandwiches (from £2.15), good ploughman's (£3.50), home-made steak, kidney, Guinness and mushroom pie (£4.95), fish and chips (£5.25), daily specials such as vegetable stroganoff (£3.75), chicken cacciatore or squab pie (lamb, apple, sultanas, £4.75) or salmon and broccoli mornay (£4.95), evening steaks (£9.25), and puddings (£2.35). Well kept Dartmoor Best and Princetown Jail Ale (a local brew) tapped from the cask, and an extensive list of wines including good house claret; darts, shove-ha'penny, dominoes, cribbage, and trivia. Note the imposing curved stone steps leading up to the garden where there's a sloping spread of lawn. *(Recommended by Mr and Mrs J Jones, A N Ellis, John and Christine Vittoe, Mr and Mrs M Peck, Ian Phillips, Nigel Clifton, R Lewis, R Walden, Helen Pickering, James Owen, David Mowbray, R W Brooks, Canon Michael Bourdeaux, Jon Pike, Julie Murphy, John and Vivienne Rice, Jack and Philip Paxton; also in Good Hotel Guide)*

Free house ~ Licensee James Henry ~ Real ale ~ Meals and snacks ~ Restaurant ~ (01837) 840244 ~ Children in family room ~ Open 11-2.30, 6-11 ~ Bedrooms: £45B/£60B

STAVERTON SX7964 Map 1

Sea Trout 🏠

Village signposted from A384 NW of Totnes

Known as the Church House for several hundred years, this friendly old village pub was renamed by a previous landlord after he caught a sea trout in the River Dart just 400 yards away. The main bar has low banquettes, soft lighting and an open fire, and the neatly kept rambling beamed lounge bar has cushioned settles and stools, a stag's head above the fireplace, and sea trout and salmon flies and stuffed fish on the walls. There's also a public bar with a pool table, darts, trivia, and juke box; the conservatory is no smoking. Good bar food includes home-made soup (£1.85), sandwiches (from £2.50), home-made pâté (£3.25), ploughman's (from £3.75), pork and apple sausages (£3.95), home-cooked ham and egg or mushroom and nut fettucine (£4.75), smoked haddock and prawn crumble (£5.50), whole grilled Brixham plaice (£6.50), lamb cutlets (£7.25), steaks (from £8.50), daily specials, puddings, children's meals (from £2.85), and good Sunday lunch. Well kept Bass, Dartmoor Best, Wadworths 6X, guest beers like Blackawton Best, Mildmay Colours, and Palmers on handpump, and efficient, helpful staff. There are seats under parasols on the attractive paved back garden. A station for the Torbay Steam Railway is not far away. The licensees have now bought the Maltsters Arms at Tuckenhay (previously owned by Keith Floyd) – we would be grateful for reports on this. *(Recommended by B J Cox, Chris Reeve, Peter and Wendy Arnold, Michael Sargent, Don and Thelma Beeson, J H Bell, Peter and Jenny Quine, Joan and Gordon Edwards, Michael Butler, Rich and Pauline Appleton)*

Free house ~ Licensees Andrew and Pym Mogford ~ Real ale ~ Meals and snacks ~ Restaurant ~ (01803) 762274 ~ Children in eating area of bar ~ Spanish guitar every other Fri evening ~ Open 11-3, 6-11; closed evenings 25-26 Dec ~ Bedrooms: £39.50B/£50B

STOCKLAND ST2404 Map 1

Kings Arms 🍽 🏠 ♀

Village signposted from A30 Honiton—Chard

This is a particularly nice pub to visit – whether for an overnight stay or to enjoy the very good home-made food served by smiling, helpful staff. The dark beamed, elegant dining lounge has solid refectory tables and settles, attractive landscapes, a medieval oak screen (which divides the room into two), and a great stone fireplace across almost the whole width of one end; the cosy restaurant with its huge inglenook fireplace and bread oven has the same menu as the bar. Booking is essential. Lunchtime food includes sandwiches (from £1.50), soup (£2), ploughman's or filled pancakes (£3.50), omelettes (from £3.50), steak and kidney pie or gammon and egg (£5.50), and children's dishes (from £3.50); from the blackboard there might be vegetable mousse, various pâtés or Portuguese sardines (£3), mushroom thermidor (£6.50), chicken tikka masala (£7.50), steaks (from £8.50), rack of lamb or whole plaice (£9.50), half a crispy roast duck (£11.50), and puddings like apple and treacle crumble, morello cherry cheesecake or gooseberry crunch gateau (£3); hearty breakfasts. Well kept Exmoor Ale, Otter Ale, Ruddles County, and John Smiths on handpump, over 40 island and west coast malt whiskies (large spirit measures), a good wine list with house wines and special offers by the bottle or glass chalked up on a board, and farm ciders. At the back, a flagstoned bar has captain's-style tub chairs and cushioned stools around heavy wooden tables, and leads on to a carpeted darts room with two boards, another room with dark beige plush armchairs and settees (and a fruit machine), and a neat ten-pin skittle alley; table skittles, cribbage, dominoes, trivia, and quiet mainly classical piped music. There are tables under cocktail parasols on the terrace in front of the white-faced thatched pub and a lawn enclosed by trees and shrubs. *(Recommended by John Bowdler, Ann and Colin Hunt, R Morgan, James Nunns, Clifford Hall, Mr and Mrs R J Parish, Mrs J Oakes, Anthony Barnes, Mr and Mrs J B Merritt, Ian Phillips, Martin Walsh, Pat and Robert Watt, Margaret and Nigel Dennis)*

Free house ~ Licensees Heinz Kiefer and Paul Diviani ~ Real ale ~ Snacks (lunchtime) and meals ~ Restaurant ~ (01404) 881361 ~ Well behaved/supervised children in eating area of bar but must be over 12 in restaurant ~ Lyme Bay folk club first Sat in month (not Jan or Aug), varied music every Sun (and bank hol Mon) ~ Open 12-3, 6.30-11; on 25 Dec only open 11-1 ~ Bedrooms: £25B/£40B

STOKE FLEMING SX8648 Map 1

Green Dragon ♀

Church Rd

This very relaxed and friendly pub has a beamed main bar with two small settles, bay window seats, boat pictures, and maybe Electra or Maia the burmese cats or Rhea the relaxed german shepherd, while down on the right is an area with throws and cushions on battered sofas and armchairs, a few books (20p to RNLI), adult board games, a grandfather clock, a wringer, and cuttings about the landlord (who is a successful long-distance yachtsman) and maps of his races on the walls. Down some steps is the Mess Deck decorated with lots of ensigns and flags, and there's a playbox of children's games; darts, shove-ha'penny, cribbage, and dominoes. Good home-made bar food includes soup (£1.70), sandwiches (from £2), ploughman's with three cheeses (£3.50), seafood pancakes, venison pie and venison sausages (£4.10), minted lamb casserole (£4.50), salmon roulade (£5.10), seafood pie or Italian meatloaf (£5.50), puddings like chocolate whisky cake or treacle tart (£2.20), and around 20 'light bites' on an evening menu (from £3.20); children's menu (from £1.80). Well kept Bass, Boddingtons, Eldridge Pope Royal Oak, and Flowers Original on handpump, big glasses of six good house wines from Australia, California, France and Germany, Luscombe cider, and a good range of spirits; you can take the beer away with you. There's a back garden with swings, a climbing frame and picnic tables and a front terrace with some white plastic garden tables and chairs. The tall church tower opposite is interesting. *(Recommended by Pam and Tim Moorey, Alan and Paula McCully; more reports please)*

Heavitree (who no longer brew) ~ Tenants Peter and Alix Crowther ~ Real ale ~ Meals and snacks (not winter Sun evenings) ~ (01803) 770238 ~ Children in eating area of bar ~ Open 11-3, 5.30-11

STOKE GABRIEL SX8457 Map 1

Church House ★

Village signposted from A385 just W of junction with A3022, in Collaton St Mary; can also be reached from nearer Totnes; nearby parking not easy

Run by helpful people, this early 14th-c pub is a friendly place for both locals and visitors. The lounge bar has a huge fireplace still used in winter to cook the stew, an exceptionally fine medieval beam-and-plank ceiling, a black oak partition wall, window seats cut into the thick butter-colour walls, and decorative plates and vases of flowers on a dresser. The mummified cat in a case, probably about 200 years old, was found during restoration of the roof space in the verger's cottage three doors up the lane – one of a handful found in the West Country and believed to have been a talisman against evil spirits. Home-made bar food includes soup (£1.95), a huge choice of sandwiches and toasties (from £1.75; good cheese and prawn toasties, lovely local river salmon £3.25), filled baked potatoes (from £2.65), ploughman's (from £3.25), daily specials like tuna and broccoli bake or home-made steak, kidney and ale pie (£5.25), fresh Dart salmon (£6.95), and puddings (from £1.95); well kept Bass, Worthington Best, and a weekly guest ale on handpump, and quite a few malt whiskies. Cribbage in the little public locals' bar; maybe piped music. There are picnic tables on the little terrace in front of the building. No children. *(Recommended by Julie and Tony Baldwin, Dr S Willavoys, Peter and Penelope Gurowich, Andrew Hodges, Peter and Jenny Quine, Mr and Mrs C Roberts, B J Harding, Michael Butler, John and Fiona Merritt)*

Free house ~ Licensee Glyn Patch ~ Real ale ~ Meals and snacks (till 10pm) ~ (01803) 782384 ~ Open 11-3.30, 6-11; 11-11 Sat

TIPTON ST JOHN SY0991 Map 1

Golden Lion 🛏

Pub signposted off B3176 Sidmouth—Ottery St Mary

From the outside this village pub might look a bit unprepossessing, but once inside there are lots of fresh flowers, interesting things to look at, and a friendly, bustling atmosphere. The bar has an attractive Gothick carved box settle, a carved dresser, an open fire, a comfortable old settee, red leatherette built-in wall banquettes, and a longcase clock. Decorations include lots of guns, little kegs, a brass cauldron and other brassware, and bottles and jars along a delft shelf. Generous helpings of bar food such as soup (£1.50), sandwiches (from £2.40), ploughman's (from £3.60), vegetarian chilli (£4.25), home-made lasagne (£4.85), steak and kidney pie (£5.25), tipsy pork with mushrooms and cream sauce (£7.45), steaks (from £7.95), puddings like gooseberry and apple crumble with clotted cream (from £2.40), and daily specials at lunchtime like chicken livers with bacon (£3.15) or wild rabbit pie (£5.25), with evening specials such as fillet of lamb with apricot sauce (£8.55), scallops wrapped in bacon flamed in Cointreau (£8.85), and duck breast with cumberland sauce (£9.25); 3-course Sunday lunch (£7.95). The restaurant and children's area are no smoking. Well kept Bass, Boddingtons, Eldridge Pope Hardy and Whitbreads Castle Eden on handpump, farm cider, decent wines, and country wines; darts, shove-ha'penny, and dominoes. There are pretty summer hanging baskets, a few picnic tables on the side lawn, an attractive walled area, and a terrace. *(Recommended by David Holloway, Peter and Audrey Dowsett, Mr and Mrs Turner, Denzil Taylor, George and Jeanne Barnwell, Alan Newman, Mark and Heather Williamson)*

Heavitree (who no longer brew) ~ Tenants Colin and Carolyn Radford ~ Real ale ~ Meals and snacks ~ Small restaurant ~ (01404) 812881 ~ Children in eating areas but must be aged over 7 in evening ~ Open 11-3(4 Sat), 6-11 ~ Two bedrooms: £19.50S/£37S

If we don't specify bar meal times for a main entry, these are normally 12-2 and 7-9; we do show times if they are markedly different.

TOPSHAM SX9688 Map 1

Passage

2 miles from M5 junction 30: Topsham signposted from exit roundabout; in Topsham, turn right into Follett Road just before centre, then turn left into Ferry Road

This waterside pub has been attractively refurbished this year – inside and out. The traditional bar has wall pews and bar stools and is decorated with electrified oil lamps hanging from big black oak beams in the ochre ceiling, and the lower bar area still has its slate floor but is now a bistro area; the atmosphere is bustling and friendly. But it's still the very good fresh fish that most people come here to enjoy: fresh mussels, pollock, grilled monkfish, lemon sole, Dover sole, turbot, cod, halibut, crab and so forth (£6.50-£12); other food includes filled rolls (from £1.75), ploughman's (from £3.75), ham and eggs (£3.95), platters (from £3.95; crab, prawn and smoked salmon £5.95), chicken curry or vegetable lasagne (£4.50), and 4oz rump steak (£5.95); the restaurant is no smoking. Well kept Bass, Flowers IPA, and Marstons Pedigree on handpump. The front courtyard has benches and tables, and there are more seats down on the quiet shoreside terrace. As the car park is small, you can park on the quay and walk the 150 yards to the pub. No children. *(Recommended by John Fahy, Andrew Hodges, DMT, Chris Westmoreland, John and Vivienne Rice, Werner Arend, John and Fiona Merritt, George and Jeanne Barnwell)*

Heavitree (who no longer brew) ~ Tenant David Evans ~ Real ale ~ Meals and snacks ~ Restaurant ~ (01392) 873653 ~ Parking can be a problem ~ Open 11-11

TORBRYAN SX8266 Map 1

Old Church House

Most easily reached from A381 Newton Abbot—Totnes via Ipplepen

In a peaceful setting next to the part-Saxon church with its interesting tower, this inn was built on the site of a very ancient cottage. The bar on the right of the door is particularly attractive, and has benches built into the fine old panelling as well as the cushioned high-backed settle and leather-backed small seats around its big log fire. On the left there are a series of comfortable and discreetly lit lounges, one with a splendid deep Tudor inglenook fireplace with a side bread oven. Bar food includes sandwiches, home-made soup, and dishes such as beef in ale, chicken in a blue cheese sauce, pork steak with bacon and mushrooms, plaice on the bone, prawns in a white wine sauce, and steak and kidney pie (from £5.95); the eating areas are no smoking. Well kept Bass, Brains Dark Mild, Flowers IPA, Morlands Old Speckled Hen, Whitbreads Fuggles Imperial, and a beer named for the pub on handpump or tapped from the cask, up to 20 malt whiskies, and decent wine list; piped music. *(Recommended by Alan and Paula McCully, H Cazalet, Bryan Taylor, Joy and Paul Rundell, Sheila and Gordon Haden, Mr and Mrs J Woodfield)*

Free house ~ Licensee Eric Pimm ~ Real ale ~ Meals and snacks (till 10.30pm) ~ Restaurant ~ (01803) 812372 ~ Children welcome away from bar ~ Open 11.30-3, 6-11 ~ Bedrooms: £35B/£50B

TORCROSS SX8241 Map 1

Start Bay

A379 S of Dartmouth

In a fine spot by the beach, this is an immensely popular dining pub (especially in summer) and there may be queues before the doors open. People continue to enjoy the basic fresh fish and chips but you may be lucky if the landlord has caught some plaice or scallops himself or the local trawler has delivered fresh dover sole, lemon, sole, skate, calamares and so forth – it's always worth asking what is available. The cod and haddock come in three sizes – medium (£3.90), large (£4.90) and jumbo

(£6.10 – truly enormous), skate wing in batter (£5.10), crevettes (£5.95), and fresh local crab (from £7.25). Other food includes sandwiches (from £1.95), ploughman's (from £3), vegetable lasagne (£4.75), gammon and pineapple (£5.50), steaks (from £7.95), puddings (£2.50), and children's meals (from £1.85); they warn of delays at peak times (and you will probably have to wait for a table); the sachets of tomato sauce or tartar sauce are not to everyone's taste. Well kept Bass and Flowers IPA and Original on handpump, Addlestones and Luscombe ciders, and fresh apple juice. The unassuming main bar is very much set out for eating with wheelback chairs around plenty of dark tables or (round a corner) back-to-back settles forming booths; there are some photographs of storms buffeting the pub and country pictures on its cream walls, and a winter coal fire; a small chatty drinking area by the counter has a brass ship's clock and barometer; one area is no smoking as is part of the family room. The good winter games room has pool, darts, shove-ha'penny, cribbage, dominoes, fruit machine, video game, and juke box; there's more booth seating in a family room with sailing boat pictures. Fruit machine in the lobby. On the terrace are some picnic tables looking out over the three-mile pebble beach. The freshwater wildlife lagoon of Slapton Ley is just behind the pub. *(Recommended by Peter Haines, George Jonas, John Fahy, Viv Middlebrook, Bryan Taylor, P and J Shapley, J B Tuckey, Roger Wain-Heapy, B Taylor, Dorothee and Dennis Glover, David Wallington)*

Heavitree (who no longer brew; Whitbreads tie) ~ Tenant Paul Stubbs ~ Real ale ~ Meals and snacks (11.30-2, 6-10; not evening 25 Dec) ~ (01548) 580553 ~ Children in family room ~ Open 11.30-2.30, 6-11; 11.30-11 during school holidays; closed evening 25 Dec

TORRINGTON SS4919 Map 1

Black Horse £

High St

This pretty twin-gabled inn is very much a family concern, with Mrs Sawyer and her son running the very successful catering side of the business, and Mr Sawyer running the bar. It's one of the oldest inns in North Devon and is reputed to have been General Fairfax's headquarters during the Civil War. Generously served and good value, the bar food might include sandwiches (from £1.40; triple deckers £2.65), filled baked potatoes (from £1.70), ploughman's (from £2.95), roast chicken with gravy (£3.60), home-made stilton and leek bake (£3.65), steak and kidney pie (£3.75), hot and spicy prawns with a garlic dip (£4.25), steaks (from £7.25), daily specials, and children's dishes (from £1.75); promptly served Sunday roast lunch, and good vegetables. Well kept John Smiths, Ushers Best and Founders, and a regular changing guest beer on handpump. The bar on the left has an oak counter, a couple of fat black beams hung with stirrups, a comfortable seat running right along its full-width window, and chunky elm tables; on the right, a lounge has a striking ancient black oak partition wall, a couple of attractive oak seats, muted plush easy chairs and a settee. The restaurant is oak-panelled; darts, shove-ha'penny, cribbage, dominoes, fruit machine, and well reproduced piped music; friendly cat and dogs. Handy for the RHS Rosemoor garden and Dartington Crystal. *(Recommended by R Walden, Graham and Lynn Mason, P and J Shapley, K R Harris, Colin Draper, Jeanne Cross, Joan and Andrew Life, K H Frostick, A M Stephenson, Brian and Louisa Routledge, J F Reay, K R Harris, Nigel and Lindsay Chapman, Chris Westmoreland)*

Ushers ~ Lease: David and Val Sawyer ~ Real ale ~ Meals and snacks (not Sun evening) ~ Restaurant (not Sun evening) ~ (01805) 622121 ~ Children in eating lounge and in restaurant ~ Open 11-3, 6-11; 11-11 Sat; 12-4, 7-10.30 Sun ~ Bedrooms: £16B/£28B

If a service charge is mentioned prominently on a menu or accommodation terms, you must pay it if service was satisfactory. If service is really bad you are legally entitled to refuse to pay some or all of the service charge as compensation for not getting the service you might reasonably have expected.

TOTNES SX8060 Map 1

Kingsbridge Inn

9 Leechwell St; going up the old town's main one-way street, bear left into Leechwell St approaching the top

The low-beamed rambling bar here has an elaborately carved bench in one intimate little alcove, comfortable plush seats and wheelbacks around rustic tables, broad stripped plank panelling, and bare stone or black and white timbering. A small area above the bar (usually reserved by diners) is no smoking. Home-made bar food might include soup (from £2.25), sandwiches (from £2.50; melted mozzarella with tomato and fresh basil £2.95), deep-fried aubergine slices with a spicy tomato dip (£2.95), filled baked potatoes (from £3.50), locally made pork and sage sausages (£3.95), various Mexican dishes (from £4.95), creamy leek and stilton bake (£5.95), pork with apples and cider (£6.95), rump steak (£8.95), and locally caught fresh lemon sole with lime butter (£9.95). Badger Best, Bass, Courage Best, Dartmoor Best, and Theakstons Old Peculier on handpump, 7 wines by the glass, and local farm cider. *(Recommended by Cerry Ann Knott, Viv Middlebrook, JWC, MC, Dr S Willavoys, John Knighton, Andrew Hodges; more reports please)*

Free house ~ Licensee David Wright ~ Real ale ~ Meals and snacks ~ (01803) 863324 ~ Children in eating area of bar ~ Folk or rock music Weds or Fri evenings ~ Open 11.30-3, 5.30-11; closed evenings 25-26 Dec

TRUSHAM SX8582 Map 1

Cridford Inn 🍴 🍷 🛏

Village and pub signposted from B3193 NW of Chudleigh, just N of big ARC works; 1½ very narrow miles

Devon Dining Pub of the Year

Tucked away in pretty countryside, this 14th-c longhouse is a friendly, atmospheric place. The bar has window seats, pews and chapel chairs around kitchen and pub tables, stout standing timbers, natural stone walls, flagstones, and a big woodburning stove in the stone fireplace; the very early medieval transept window in the bar is said to be the oldest domestic window in Britain and is Grade I listed. Very good home-made bar food includes soup (£2.25), egg and anchovy mayonnaise (£2.75), excellent chicken liver pâté with cumberland sauce (£3.75), local cheese platter with chutney, pickles and salad or cheese omelette (£4.95), fresh battered cod or pasta with tuna and prawns baked in a cheese sauce (£5.95), cajun chicken with creole sauce (£7.25), darne of salmon with herb and orange butter sauce (£8.50), lamb steak with rosemary (£8.95), lovely roast duckling with port and orange sauce (£10.50), sirloin steak with bearnaise sauce (£11.95), daily specials, and good puddings such as brown sugar meringue with ginger ice cream and apricot sauce, banoffi pie with caramel sauce or chocolate ginger trifle ((from £3.25). The no-smoking restaurant has a mosaic date stone showing 1081 and the initials of the then Abbot of Buckfastleigh; the children's area is no smoking, too. Well kept Adnams Broadside, Bass, Smiles, and a beer they call Trusham Bitter on handpump, 20 wines by the glass from an interesting wine list, and country wines. The cats are called Smudge and Sophie, and the jack russell, Jack; quiet piped music. You can sit on the suntrap front terrace. *(Recommended by Gwen and Peter Andrews, John and Vivienne Rice, Ian and Deborah Carrington, S Demont, T Barrow, Don and Shirley Parrish, Hanns P Golez, Dr I Maine, David Saunders, Marion Nott, John Allsopp, Nick and Meriel Cox, Joan and Gordon Edwards, Mike Gorton, Sue Hobley)*

Free house ~ Licensees David and Sally Hesmondhalgh ~ Real ale ~ Meals and snacks (not winter Mon) ~ Evening restaurant (closed Sun and winter Mon) ~ (01626) 853694 ~ Children in top bar but must be gone by 8.30pm ~ Open 12-2.30, 6-11; 12-2.30, 7-10.30 in winter; closed 25 Dec ~ Bedrooms: £40B/£60B

UGBOROUGH SX6755 Map 1

Anchor

Off A3121 – village signposted from A38 W of South Brent

It's the wide choice of very good food that both locals and visitors like so much at this friendly village pub. And dishes from either the bar or restaurant menus can be eaten anywhere in the pub (apart from Saturday night when there are no bar snacks in the restaurant): unusual choices such as ostrich, alligator, emu, bison, and wild boar, lots of fresh fish, delicious crispy quail with smoky bacon dip, and fantastic peppered steak, as well as home-made soup (£2.65), filled long crusty rolls (from £2.50; hot bacon and mushroom £3.30), ploughman's (from £3.10), omelettes (from £3.25), several pasta dishes (from £4.05), pizzas (from £4.25), mushroom caps stuffed with crab and topped with cheese (£4.50), vegetarian dishes (from £4.95; Thai spiced vegetable schnitzel £7), steak and kidney pie (£5.30), gammon and egg (£5.80), quite a few steaks (from £9.85), duck simmered in kirsch and served with black cherries (£11.50), veal limona (£11.75), and children's meals (from £2.25); courteous service. Well kept Bass, Tetleys Imperial, Wadworths 6X, and two local guest beers on handpump, and several malt whiskies. The oak-beamed public bar has a log fire in its stone fireplace, wall settles and seats around wooden tables on the polished woodblock floor; there are windsor armchairs in the comfortable restaurant (the top area is no smoking). There are seats in the garden. This is an attractive village, unusual for its spacious central square. *(Recommended by Walker and Debra Lapthorne, J Burrage, Mr and Mrs J Brown, Stephen and Susan Breen)*

Free house ~ Licensees Sheelagh and Ken Jeffreys-Simmons ~ Real ale ~ Meals and snacks ~ Restaurant ~ (01752) 892283 ~ Children welcome ~ Jazz alternate Mons ~ Open 11.30-11.30; 12-10.30 Sun; 11.30-3, 5-11.30 in winter ~ Bedrooms: £30B/£40B

WELCOMBE SS2217 Map 1

Old Smithy

Village signposted from A39 S of Harland; pub signposted left at fork; in hamlet of Darracott

In a lovely rural setting, this friendly thatched pub is on a lane which eventually leads to parking down by Welcombe Mouth, which is an attractive rocky cove. The open-plan bar has woodburning stoves at both ends of the room, button-back banquettes and wheelback chairs, little snug windows, and a chatty, informal atmosphere; the restaurant was once the old forge; friendly dog. Bar food, popular with the nearby campers and holiday bungalow visitors, is straightforward (with prices unchanged since last year) and includes sandwiches, good pasties, ploughman's (£2.95), scampi (£3.60), and lasagne (£4.95). Well kept Boddingtons, Butcombe, Flowers IPA, and Marstons Pedigree on handpump. Darts and piped music. The pretty, terraced, sheltered garden has plenty of seats, a summer tea and gift shop, and assorted owls in an animal rescue sanctuary. *(Recommended by Rita Horridge, Jeanne Cross, Colin Draper, George Atkinson, R Walden, D Alexander, Clare Wilson, Mr and Mrs Westcombe, Anthony Barnes, Jack and Philip Paxton, C P Scott-Malden, Philip and Joanne Gavins, R T and J C Moggridge, James Macrae, Gary Gibbon)*

Free house ~ Licensees Geoff Marshall and sons ~ Real ale ~ Meals and snacks ~ (01288) 331305 ~ Children welcome until 8.30 ~ Open 12-11; 12-3, 7-11 in winter ~ Bedrooms: £19.50/£35(£39B)

WESTON ST1200 Map 1

Otter ★ ♀

Village signposted off A30 at W end of Honiton bypass

This is a good place to take a break from the A30 – especially if you have children. There are high chairs (children sitting in them get a free meal), a children's menu (£1, with a picture to colour and free lollipop), a box of toys, rocking-horse, a bike, and a new climbing frame and slide; also, an animal sanctuary with free-ranging cockerels, hens, rabbits and guinea-pigs. The sizeable lawn runs down to the little River Otter, and has picnic tables, pretty climbing plants, hanging baskets and flowering tubs. Inside, the very low-beamed main bar has chamberpots and jugs hanging from beams, comfortable chairs by the log fire (that stays alight right through from autumn to spring), an interesting mix of polished wooden antique tables, wooden chairs, and handsome chapel pews, and candles in bottles; each day a page of the Bible on the lectern that ends one pew is turned, and attractive bric-a-brac includes some formidable arms and armour, horse collar and bits, quite a few pictures, and an old mangle; a veritable library leads off, with quite a few readable books and magazines, as well as board games, darts, shove-ha'penny, cribbage, dominoes, table skittles, a fruit machine, video game, trivia, juke box and piped music; pool and skittle alley, too. Good bar food includes daily-changing soup (£2.45), sandwiches (from £2.50), filled baked potatoes (from £3.10), asparagus and nut mousse (£3.20), mussels with orange, ginger, saffron and cream (£4.15), ploughman's (£4.80), local butcher's sausages with onion gravy and mashed potato (£5.60), pasta with cheese and garlic in a basil and wine sauce (£5.85), steak and kidney pie (£6.35), steaks (£10.65), daily specials like prawn, smoked trout and crab flan (£4.95), grilled skate wing (£5.10), stuffed peppers (£6.95), duck with orange sauce (£8.95), pork in red wine, dijon mustard and tarragon (£9.95), and salmon in an asparagus and white wine sauce (£10.95), and puddings (£2.95); 3-course Sunday lunch (£9.95). Well kept Bass, Boddingtons, and Eldridge Pope Hardy on handpump, good inexpensive wines, farm cider, and freshly squeezed orange juice; good service. *(Recommended by R and S Bentley, Stephen Horsley, Mayur Shah, E M Clague, R Walden, R T and J C Moggridge, Rich and Pauline Appleton, F C Johnston, Peter and Audrey Dowsett, Martin Pritchard, Nicolas Corker)*

Free house ~ Lease: Brian and Susan Wilkinson ~ Real ale ~ Meals and snacks (till 10pm; not 25 Dec) ~ (01404) 42594 ~ Children welcome ~ Piano player Sun and odd times in week ~ Open 11-3, 6-11; only 11-1 on 25 Dec

WONSON SX6790 Map 1

Northmore Arms ♀ ◧

Off A388 2 miles from A30, at Murchington, Gidleigh signpost; then at junction where Murchington and Gidleigh are signposted left, keep straight on – eventually, round Throwleigh, Wonson itself is signposted; OS Sheet 191 map reference 674903

This secluded cottage is a good example of a very simple rural pub tucked away in a nice Dartmoor-edge spot – the sort of place that has died out in most areas. Its two small connected beamed rooms are modest and informal but very civilised, with wall settles, a few elderly chairs, three tables in one room and just one in the other. There are two open fires (only one may be lit), and some attractive photographs on the stripped stone walls. Besides well kept changing ales such as Adnams Broadside, Cotleigh Tawny and Exe Valley Dobs, they have good house wines, and food such as sandwiches (from £1.40), steak and kidney pudding (£3.95), a roast lunch (£4.50), and puddings (£1.75). The small sheltered sloping garden is rustic and very peaceful, with gentle country noises off; excellent walking from the pub (or to it – perhaps from Chagford or Gidleigh Park). *(Recommended by John Wilson, T Treagust; more reports please)*

Free house ~ Licensee M Miles ~ Real ale ~ Meals and snacks ~ (01647) 231428 ~ Well behaved children welcome ~ Open 11-11 ~ Two bedrooms: £15/£25

WOODBURY SALTERTON SY0189 Map 1

Digger's Rest

3½ miles from M5 junction 30: A3052 towards Sidmouth, village signposted on right about ½ mile after Clyst St Mary; also signposted from B3179 SE of Exeter

This busy thatched village pub has been run by the same licensees for over 23 years now. The bar has heavy black oak beams, comfortable old-fashioned country chairs and settles around polished antique tables, a dark oak Jacobean screen, a grandfather clock, and plates decorating the walls of one alcove; at one end of the room is a log fire, and at the other is an ornate solid fuel stove. The big skittle alley can be used for families, and there's a games room with darts and dominoes. Well kept Bass and Dartmoor Best on ancient handpumps, and local farm ciders; sensibly placed darts and dominoes in the small brick-walled public bar. Decent bar food includes home-made soup (£1.65), sandwiches with home-cooked meats (from £2.75; local crab £3.25), ploughman's (from £3.55), home-made vegetarian or meaty curry or home-cooked beef with chips (£4.45), steaks (from £8.95), daily specials, and puddings (£2.45). The terrace garden has views of the countryside. *(Recommended by D Toulson, Alan and Paula McCully, John and Vivienne Rice, George and Jeanne Barnwell, Chris Westmoreland, George Atkinson, Mark and Heather Williamson)*

Free house ~ Licensee Sally Pratt ~ Real ale ~ Meals and snacks (12-1.45, 7-10) ~ (01395) 232375 ~ Children welcome ~ Open 11-2.30, 6.30-11; closed evenings 25-26 Dec

Lucky Dip

Besides the fully inspected pubs, you might like to try these Lucky Dips recommended to us and described by readers (if you do, please send us reports):

Abbotsham [the one nr Bideford; SS4226], *Thatched House*: Extensively refurbished family pub, mix of modern seats and older features, Bass, Butcombe, Courage Directors and John Smiths, attractive food, families welcome; tables outside; handy for the Big Sheep *(Chris Westmoreland)*
Abbotskerswell [SX8569], *Butchers Arms*: Tucked-away little old pub, well kept Whitbreads, pleasant nooks and corners *(John A Barker, Andrew Hodges, Joan and Gordon Edwards)*
☆ **Appledore** [Irsha St; SS4630], *Royal George*: Simple but good fresh food inc local fish in dining room with superb estuary views, cosy and unspoilt front bar (where dogs allowed), well kept ales such as Bass, Ind Coope Burton, Morlands Old Speckled Hen, good friendly service, attractive pictures, fresh flowers; picnic tables outside, picturesque street sloping to sea *(Rip and Pauline Kirby, Nigel and Lindsay Chapman, Chris Westmoreland, PM, AM)*
Appledore [Irsha St], *Beaver*: Light and airy, with raised area overlooking estuary, good imaginative food (esp fish) and service, well kept changing ales such as Bass, Butcombe, Flowers, pool in smaller games room, views from outdoor tables; children welcome *(Chris Westmoreland, Nigel and Lindsay Chapman, Rip and Pauline Kirby)*; [Market St], *Royal*: Simple good value food inc local fish and substantial Sun lunch, well kept Bass and Wadworths 6X, back family room, picnic tables on front cobbles *(Chris Westmoreland)*
☆ **Ashburton** [West St], *Exeter*: Friendly old-fashioned pub with well kept Courage-related ales, good value food *(Joy and Paul Rundell, Jeanne Cross, Paul Silvestri)*
Avonwick [B3210, off A38; SX7157], *Mill*: Good value bar food inc interesting specials in pretty converted mill with play area in big lakeside garden, friendly service, children's helpings (they have high chairs), Bass on handpump; popular lunchtime carvery *(John Evans)*

☆ **Axmouth** [SY2591], *Ship*: Comfortable and civilised, good fresh local fish, well kept Whitbreads-related real ales, good wine and coffee, friendly staff and samoyeds, lots of embroidered folk dolls; attractive garden with sanctuary for convalescent owls *(M E Wellington, A Denman, LYM)*
Aylesbeare [Sidmouth Rd; A3052 Exeter—Sidmouth, junction with B3180; SY0392], *Halfway*: Welcoming, with high views over Dartmoor, pleasant decor, prints, brasses etc; good food choice inc vegetarian, special diets catered for; well kept ales inc changing guest beers *(Eric and June Heley)*
Babbacombe [112 Babbacombe Rd; A379 Torquay—Teignmouth; SX9365], *Masons Arms*: Friendly and comfortable, three rooms with stripped stone and panelling, well kept Bass and Worthington, decent wine, bar food, children treated well; very busy evenings *(N A Morgans, CR)*
☆ **Beer** [Fore St; ST2389], *Anchor*: Good value generous well presented food inc wide choice of superb fresh fish, big helpings, same menu in several simply furnished rooms of bar and restaurant; quick friendly service, well kept beer; spacious garden looking over delightful sheltered cove, charming village; can get crowded, public car park quite a long walk; bedrooms clean and comfortable *(Mrs B Sugarman, Peter and Audrey Dowsett, Don and Thelma Beeson, D G Clarke, A W Lewis, Mrs Greenwood, Mr and Mrs Garrett, Basil Minson)*
☆ **Beesands** [SX8140], *Cricket*: Attractively basic, in good spot on beach with tables outside; good value standard food and good fish dishes, recently decorated dining room, well kept Whitbreads-related real ales, welcoming atmosphere, log fire, unobtrusive piped music; family room *(Roger Wain-Heapy, Jeanne Cross, Paul Silvestri, Roger Wain-Heapy)*
Belstone [a mile off A30; SX6293], *Tors*: Imposing stone building, good choice of reasonably priced generous food, well kept

Butcombe and Otter ales, decent wines and malt whiskies; bedrooms, attractive village well placed for N Dartmoor walks *(John and Vivienne Rice)*

Bickington [SS5332], *Toby Jug*: Distinctive, full of toby jugs (one 3ft tall), good food, friendly service *(Paul and Heather Bettesworth)*

☆ **Bickleigh** [SS9406; A396/A3072 N of Exeter], *Fishermans Cot*: Fishing hotel with good well served food inc popular reasonably priced carvery, well kept Bass, good restaurant, tables in garden by River Exe with small weir and ancient bridge; comfortable bedrooms looking over own terrace to river *(Simon and Debbie Tomlinson, E Robinson, Alan Newman)*

☆ **Bickleigh** [SS9406], *Trout*: Thatched pub with comfortable easy chairs in huge bar and dining lounge, sizeable buffet counter with good choice of food from sandwiches up and tempting puddings cabinet, well kept ales such as Cotleigh Tawny, Bass, Boddingtons, Exmoor Gold, nice coffee, efficient enthusiastic young staff; tables on pretty lawn, car park across rd; five well equipped bedrooms, good breakfast *(Mrs G Teall, E Robinson, LYM)*

Bideford [Mkt Sq; SS4526], *Joiners Arms*: Good value food, friendly service, well kept Bass, Dartmoor and a guest such as Fullers, good collection of joiner's tools, dining area *(Richard Houghton, Chris Westmoreland)*; [The Quay], *Kings Arms*: Well kept Whitbreads-related and other ales, cheerful landlord and customers, unusual Victorian harlequin floor tiles in alcovey front bar, unassuming food from good filled rolls up, back raised family area; pavement tables *(Rita Horridge, Chris Westmoreland, PM, AM)*

☆ **Blackmoor Gate** [SS6443], *Old Station House*: Former station on redundant line interestingly converted into big dining pub; decent food, well kept ales, carved pews, plush dining chairs, soft red lighting, character no-smoking area with grandfather clock; spacious games area with two well lit pool tables, darts and juke box; big garden with good views; skittle alley; children allowed (but under-5s in small family room only) *(Bruce Bird, Ian Shorthouse, PM, AM, BB)*

Blagdon [Higher Blagdon; pub signed off A385 leaving Paignton; SX8561], *Barton Pines*: Spaciously converted mock-Elizabethan 19th-c mansion, quiet out of season, with friendly service, generous food cooked to order (menu truncated out of season), provision for families, grand gardens giving views out to sea and over to Dartmoor; caravan site behind *(Mr and Mrs C Roberts, LYM)*

☆ **Bolberry** [Bolberry Down – OS Sheet 202 map ref 691392; SX6939], *Port Light*: Unlikely building (blocky ex-RAF radar station) alone on dramatic NT clifftop, amazing views; bright, spacious and popular if rather hotelish inside, with decent bar food, well kept Dartmoor, friendly efficient service, restaurant, conservatory, tables in garden with play area; well behaved children

allowed, play area outside; four bedrooms *(Dorothee and Dennis Glover, Nick Wikeley)*

Bovey Tracey [SX8278], *Cromwell Arms*: Over-generous good basic reasonably priced food in well run town local, friendly quick service, good range of well kept well priced beers, several areas with high-backed settles, no piped music *(Paul and Heather Bettesworth, Mr and Mrs M Cross)*

Braunton [Barnstaple Rd; SS4836], *Williams Arms*: Good atmosphere and housekeeping, pleasant staff, wide choice of food inc good carvery with masses of fresh veg *(K R Harris)*

☆ **Brayford** [Yarde Down; 3 miles from Brayford, on Simonsbath rd over Exmoor – OS Sheet 180 map ref 726356; SS6834], *Poltimore Arms*: Chatty and pubby old two-bar local with attractive traditional decor inc inglenook, bar food from sandwiches to steaks, well kept Cotleigh Tawny and Wadworths 6X tapped from the cask, maybe piped music; darts, pool, shove-ha'penny and juke box in plain games room; children allowed in restaurant, picnic tables in side garden; no dogs inside *(Jennie Munro, Jim Wingate, LYM)*

☆ **Bridestowe** [old A38; SX5189], *White Hart*: Unpretentious local, partly flagstoned beamed main bar with grandfather clock and games end, some nice old furnishings in lounge, panelled restaurant; good generous food, well kept Palmers, friendly staff, informal streamside back garden, peaceful Dartmoor village; bedrooms *(Mr and Mrs Westcombe, BB)*

☆ **Broadhempston** [off A381, signed from centre; SX8066], *Coppa Dolla*: Cheerful buoyant atmosphere and good ambitious food in straightforwardly comfortable bar divided by sturdy timber props, well kept ales such as Bass, Dartmoor Best, Palmers and Wadworths 6X, good service, decent wines, log fires, pleasant upstairs restaurant; well spaced picnic tables in attractive garden with pleasant views; two apartments *(Peter and Jenny Quine, C A Hall, Joan and Gordon Edwards, Dennis Glover, Andrew Hodges, BB)*

Broadhempston [The Square], *Monks Retreat*: Black beams, busy decor with lots of copper, brass and china, log fire in huge stone fireplace, no-smoking dining area, very wide choice of straightforward food inc sizzler steaks, well kept Bass and Teignworthy Reel Ale, very cheerful service – but can slow right down when busy; by arch to attractive churchyard, a few picnic tables out in front *(Jeanne Cross, Paul Silvestri, Andrew Hodges, C A Hall, BB)*

Buckfastleigh [Totnes Rd; SX7366], *Dartbridge*: Functional, friendly and efficient, with good reasonably priced food; well equipped for families, opp Dart Valley Rly – very popular in summer; tables outside, ten letting chalets *(John Evans, Wg Cdr G K A Hollett)*

☆ **Buckland Monachorum** [SX4868], *Drakes Manor*: Well kept Courage-related ales, good friendly service, good value food inc good Sun lunches, beams and oak panelling; public bar with games machines *(Mr and Mrs J*

Woodfield, G W Stevenson, Bruce Bird)

☆ Burgh Island [SX6443], *Pilchard*: The star's for the setting, high above sea on tidal island with great cliff walks; not at all smart, but atmospheric, with blazing fire; Courage-related ales, basic food (all day summer, lunchtime only winter), piped music, children in downstairs bistro (Nigel Spence, Kim Greek, ML, SW, Hanns P Golez, Richard Gibbs, Dave and Doreen Irving, JP, PP, John and Vivienne Rice, Anthony Marriott, LYM)

☆ California Cross [SX7052], *California*: 18th-c beamed pub with nicely decorated old-fashioned lounge, well kept Dartmoor and Wadworths 6X, local Churchward's cider, decent wines, wide choice of good value food inc local fish, friendly staff, children's room with toys, restaurant, games room with skittles and pool; craft shop, tables in garden; very popular (Bryan Taylor, Dr and Mrs N Holmes)

☆ Chagford [Mill St; SX7087], *Bullers Arms*: Welcoming local with very wide food range inc vegetarian, darts, three changing ales, decent coffee, collection of militaria, very friendly licensees; can get smoky at night; summer barbecues (Joan and Gordon Edwards, John and Christine Vittoe, LYM) Chagford, *Three Crowns*: Ancient thatched building of great potential though bar furnishings largely modern, popular food, friendly service, Bass and Flowers Original, big fire, stripped-stone public bar with pool and darts; tables on front cobbles and in back garden; good old-fashioned bedrooms (G Washington, BB)

☆ Challacombe [B3358 Blackmoor Gate—Simonsbath; SS6941], *Black Venus*: Good range of generous reasonably priced home-cooked food, Courage-related ales, good friendly service, low 16th-c beams, pews, decent chairs, stuffed birds, woodburning stove and big open fire, separate games room, attractive big dining area (children over 5 allowed here); seats in garden, attractive countryside; bedrooms (Neil and Anita Christopher, D Alexander, BB) Chawleigh [B3042; SS7112], *Chilcott Arms*: Good value interesting food, comfortable surroundings, helpful landlord, Bass and Flowers ales; children welcome, skittle alley (Mr and Mrs Knott) Chip Shop [OS Sheet 201 map ref 436752; SX4375], *Chip Shop*: Friendly local with good value food, welcoming service, well kept Bass, Exmoor and Smiles Best, lots of mirrors, unobtrusive piped music, garden with play house; well placed darts (Richard Houghton, Andy and Jill Kassube, John Hazel, JP, PP) Chittlehampton [SS6425], *Bell*: Welcoming traditional village pub, inexpensive food, well kept Bass and two changing ales (Philip Jewell)

☆ Christow [signed off B3193 N of A38; SX8385], *Artichoke*: Pretty thatched local with open-plan rooms stepped down hill, low beams, some black panelling, flagstones, straightforward food inc decent specials, vegetarian, fish and game, big log fire (2nd one in no-smoking end dining room), mainly Whitbreads-related ales; rather prominent games machine; tables on back terrace, pretty hillside village nr Canonteign Waterfalls and Country Park (Mr and Mrs A P Vogt, Michael and Lynne Steane, Joan and Gordon Edwards, James Nunns, Mary and William Bankes, M S Crabtree, BB) Chudleigh [B3344, off A38; SX8679], *Highwaymans Haunt*: Good well appointed carvery (evenings and Sun lunch) with help-yourself veg (R C Watkins); *Clay Cutters Arms*: Thatched village pub recently reopened with emphasis on interesting choice of above-average good value food in bar and pleasant restaurant; good range of real ales, friendly if not speedy service; bedrooms (B A Ferris Harms, Don and Shirley Parrish, LYM)

☆ Clayhidon [off A38 via Culmstock, Hemyock; ST1615], *Half Moon*: Good well presented food from welcoming newish licensees in civilised pub with simple unfussy decor, well kept Bass and Cotleigh, good house wine; quiet views from picnic tables in garden over road; opens noon (Shirley Pielou, BB) Clearbrook [off A386 Tavistock—Plymouth; SX5265], *Skylark*: Big and busy, popular with walkers, with generous good value food (but doesn't have a no-smoking area), Bass and Courage Best and Directors, simple furnishings and individual decor, log fire, children's room; good Dartmoor and Plymouth Sound views, big back garden (Ted George, Nigel Spence, Kim Greek) Clovelly [SS3225], *Red Lion*: Lots of character in locals' back bar, bar food inc good pasties and crab sandwiches, good fresh fish in restaurant, friendly staff, Marstons Pedigree; simple attractive bedrooms, lovely spot on curving quay (DJW, David Carr) Clyst St Mary [nr M5 junction 30; SX9790], *Blue Ball*: Rejuvenated free house, good choice of beers, locally popular food; back garden, play area (Chris Westmoreland); *Half Moon*: Pleasant old pub next to multi-arched bridge over Clyst, well kept Bass tapped from the cask; bedrooms (Chris Westmoreland) Cockington [SX8963], *Drum*: Olde-worlde pastiche thatched and beamed tavern in quaint Torquay-edge village by 500-acre park, spacious and well run, with Dartmoor Bitter and Legend, wide choice of reasonably priced food in bar and two family eating areas, friendly staff, Weds summer barbecues, winter skittle evenings and live music; juke box or piped music; seats on terrace and in attractive back garden (Peter Morgan, Richard Houghton, Andrew Hodges)

☆ Cockwood [SX9780], *Ship*: Comfortable and welcoming 17th-c inn overlooking estuary and harbour, food from open crab sandwiches inc good evening fish dishes, Ushers beer, reasonable prices, pleasant qick service, good steep hillside garden (V H and J M Vanstone, Chris Westmoreland)

☆ Coffinswell [SX8968], *Linny*: Very pretty 14th-c thatched country pub with big cheerful beamed bar, settles and other cosy old seats, smaller areas off; some concentration on wide choice of good value bar food; well kept Bass, Ind Coope Burton and Morlands Old Speckled Hen, huge open fires, chatty atmosphere, friendly service, children's room, upstairs restaurant; picturesque village *(Alan and Paula McCully, Peter and Jenny Quine, Paul and Janet Waring, Gordon, Jeanne Cross, Paul Silvestri, Andrew Hodges)*

Colaton Raleigh [A376 Newton Poppleford—Budleigh Salterton; SY0787], *Otter*: Welcoming and efficient, with family room, good reasonably priced food, Courage-related beers, lovely big garden *(A Preston, Chris Westmoreland)*

Colyford [Swan Hill Rd; A3052 Exeter—Lyme Regis, by tramway stn; SY2492], *White Hart*: A pub for opera lovers, run by ex-tenor Craig Sullivan; opera memorabilia in small separate no-smoking dining room with good English food and authentic Caruso recipes; good range of wines and spirits, tables on lawn outside; children's games *(Brian A Websdale)*

☆ **Combeinteignhead** [SX9071], *Wild Goose*: Spacious 17th-c beamed pub, lots of hanging jugs and teapots, comfortably well worn furnishings, separate more formal eating area with wide choice of good food, several well kept changing ales, cheerful service, open fire; pool room, darts, weekly jazz *(Colin and Marjorie Roberts, Richard Houghton, Colin McKerrow)*

☆ **Countisbury** [A39, E of Lynton – OS Sheet 180 map ref 747497; SS7449], *Exmoor Sandpiper*: Rambling and friendly heavy-beamed pub with antique furniture, several log fires, good choice of usual food from sandwiches to steaks, well kept Flowers Original and Greene King Abbot, restaurant with weekend smorgasbord and carvery; children in eating area, open all day; comfortable bedrooms, good walks *(Richard Gibbs, R V Ford, Meg and Colin Hamilton, LYM)*

Croyde [B3231 NW of Braunton; SS4439], *Thatch*: Popular rambling thatched pub nr great surfing beaches, with laid-back feel and customers to match; generous bar food, well kept Tetleys-related ales, informal smiling staff, tables outside; restaurant, children in eating area, open all day; piped music may be a bit loud, can be packed in summer; bedrooms *(Jo Rees, Sam, LYM)*

☆ **Croyde** [off B3231], *Whiteleaf*: A guest house not a pub, but has won many GPG friends with peaceful comfortable surroundings, good food, and a landlord who certainly knows his pubs; dogs allowed *(AF)*

☆ **Dartmouth** [Smith St; SX8751], *Seven Stars*: Crowded beamed and panelled local, quick well priced popular food, real ales such as Wadworths 6X, coal fire, cheery service; maybe piped pop music, fruit machine; upstairs restaurant, children's room *(T G Thomas, C A Hall, Dr S Willavoys, John Evans, June and Malcolm Farmer, BB)*

Dartmouth [Mkt Sq], *Dolphin*: Good reasonably priced food, very welcoming atmosphere *(Mr and Mrs D H Burwood)*

Dawlish Warren [SX9979], *Mount Pleasant*: Marvellous view from garden and front window over the Warren, Exe estuary and sea, decent food, Whitbreads-related ales *(Chris Westmoreland)*

☆ **Denbury** [The Green; SX8168], *Union*: Spotless well run low-beamed local on edge of old village green, simple food from good sandwiches to steaks inc vegetarian and lots of puddings, Whitbreads-related ales, good coffee; tables in garden by green, quietly pretty sheltered village *(Joan and Gordon Edwards, Eamonn Kelly, Jeanne Cross, Paul Silvestri, BB)*

☆ **Dittisham** [The Level; SX8654], *Red Lion*: Welcoming well run local with well kept Bass and good value wines, open fires, sleeping dogs, good value innovative food in restaurant, friendly licensees, family room; attractive village *(Michael Weaver, JWC, MC, Bryan Taylor, John and Wendy Trentham, Andrew Hodges)*

☆ **Dittisham**, *Ferry Boat*: Big windows make the most of beautiful waterside spot, nr little foot-ferry you call by bell; new licensees doing good range of low-priced bar food inc fine speciality sausages, well kept Ushers *(Barry A Lynch, DJW, LYM)*

☆ **Down Thomas** [SX5050], *Langdon Court*: Good food in weloming lounge bar and family room, reasonable prices, good fire, country views, Whitbreads-related ales from ornate servery, picnic tables outside; dogs allowed; interesting country-house hotel with comfortable bedrooms *(Brian White, D Batten, Nigel Spence, Kim Greek)*

☆ **nr Drewsteignton** [Fingle Bridge, off A38 at Crockernwell via Preston or Drewsteignton; OS Sheet 191 map ref 743899; SX7489], *Anglers Rest*: Idyllic wooded Teign valley spot by 16th-c pack-horse bridge, lovely walks; tourist souvenirs and airy cafe feel, but has well kept Cotleigh and Courage ales and reliable food inc children's meals (not Sun); good friendly service, waterside picnic tables *(Jeanne Cross, Paul Silvestri, JWC, MC, JP, PP, John and Christine Vittoe, Alan Newman, BB)*

☆ **Dunsford** [just off B3212 NE of Moretonhampstead – OS Sheet 191 map ref 813891; SX8189], *Royal Oak*: Good unusual reasonably priced food and good friendly service in relaxed village inn's light and airy lounge bar, half a dozen well kept changing ales, local farm ciders, woodburner; steps down to games room, provision for children; quiz nights, piped music may be loud; Fri barbecues in sheltered tiered garden, good value bedrooms in converted barn *(Carol Whittaker, John Crompton, John and Christine Vittoe, Jean Cross, Paul Silvestri, LYM)*

☆ **East Budleigh** [SY0684], *Sir Walter Raleigh*: Small neat village inn doing well under current management, with good range of nicely presented hot and cold food inc help-yourself salad bar, friendly staff and locals, cosy charming dining room, Flowers IPA and Marstons Pedigree; the village itself, and its church, are well worth a visit; bedrooms *(Marjorie and David Lamb, J T Bugby, LYM)*

East Budleigh [Oak Hill (A376); SY0684], *Rolle Arms*: Good range of local beers, standard lunchtime menu good value, friendly service *(MW, HW)*

☆ East Down [off A39 Barnstaple—Lynton nr Arlington – OS Sheet 180 map ref 600415; SS5941], *Pyne Arms*: Low-beamed bar with lots of nooks and crannies, attractive furnishings inc high-backed curved settle, small no-smoking galleried loft (where children allowed), flagstoned games area with unobtrusive juke box, wide choice of generally good fresh food from sandwiches up (lunchtime service may stop short of 2) inc take-away pizzas, well kept Bass and Courage-related ales, decent house wines; handy for Arlington Court, good walks *(Steve and Angela Maycock, Julian Lyons, Mr and Mrs Greenhalgh, Steve and Carolyn Harvey, Joan and Andrew Life, LYM)*

Ermington [SX6353], *First & Last*: Beautiful setting, lots of ivy and hanging baskets, friendly service, limited choice of good cheap food with ample veg, well kept Bass and local beers *(John Evans, Simon and Debbie Tomlinson)*

☆ Exeter [223 High St (basement of C&A)], *Chaucers*: Large dim-lit modern pub/bistro/wine bar down lots of steps, candles in bottles, well kept Bass and Tetleys, good range of generous good value food inc adventurous dishes, quick friendly service, pleasant atmosphere *(H G Robertson, Alan Prine, Steve and Carolyn Harvey, Chris Westmoreland, John Atkins)*

☆ Exeter [Martins Lane – just off cathedral close], *Ship*: Pretty 14th-c pub with substantial comfortable furniture in heavy-beamed busy but atmospheric bar, well kept Bass and Boddingtons on handpump, decent generous food, quieter upstairs restaurant *(Chris Westmoreland, M E Wellington, David Carr, LYM)*

☆ Exeter [The Close; bar of Royal Clarence Hotel], *Well House*: Big windows looking across to cathedral in open-plan bar divided by inner walls and partitions; lots of Victorian prints, well kept changing ales, popular bar lunches inc good salads, good service; Roman well beneath (can be viewed when pub not busy); piped music *(Andy and Jill Kassube, David Carr, Andrew Hodges, BB)*

☆ Exeter [14 Exe St, off Bonhay Rd], *Papermakers*: Pub/wine bar/bistro with charming Continental atmosphere, wide choice of good if not cheap unusual food, friendly efficient service, Wadworths 6X and well chosen guest beers, good choice of wines, reasonable prices *(Arthur McCartney, Steve and Carolyn Harvey, Prof and Mrs John Webster, H G Robertson)*

☆ Exeter [The Quay], *Prospect*: Pleasant setting overlooking waterfront nr Maritime Museum, beams, panelling and settles, old safari pictures and local prints, wide range of reasonably priced interesting fresh food inc good fish in big dining area up a few steps,

well kept Bass and Charrington IPA, helpful staff; welcoming feel, but shame about the piped music and machines *(Tony and Wendy Hobden, P and J Shapley, David Carr)*

Exeter [North St], *Crown*: Limited weekend food but good value, inc giant pasties *(PM, AM)*; [Little Castle St], *Hole in the Wall*: Nicely refurbished Eldridge Pope pub *(R J Walden)*; [Bonhay Rd], *Mill on the Exe*: Comfortably done out with old bricks and timbers, good food, St Austell ales, quick friendly service; riverside terrace *(R J Walden, BB)*; [The Quay], *Port Royal*: Nautical theme, generous reasonably priced standard food, good range of beers inc Bass, Boddingtons and a Whitbreads seasonal beer, separate games room *(Steve and Carolyn Harvey)*; [2 Countess Wear Rd], *Tally Ho*: Long comfortable beamed bar with banquettes in bays, good value home-cooked food, cheerful helpful staff, well kept Bass, Flowers IPA and a guest like Morlands Old Speckled Hen, decent wine; interesting spot on River Exe *(Mike Gorton, Arthur McCartney)*

☆ Exminster [just off A379; SX9487], *Swans Nest*: Huge choice of reasonably priced honest self-service food from sandwiches up in very popular and well run high-throughput food pub, handy for M5, character furnishings in inviting well arranged rambling dining bar; no-smoking areas, Bass and Dartmoor, long attractive carvery/buffet, salads and children's dishes, helpful staff; especially good for family groups with children *(Wg Cdr G K A Hollett, V H and J M Vanstone, LYM)*

Exmouth [The Esplanade; SY0080], *Grove*: Roomy pub with well kept ales (up to nine on regular guest beer nights), good reasonably priced food, friendly service, good atmosphere, lots of pictures, attractive fireplace at back; tables in attractive seafront garden *(Roy R Johnson, A and R Cooper)*

☆ Filleigh [off A361 N Devon link rd; SS6627], *Stags Head*: Good food, generous if not cheap, in friendly and attractive 16th-c thatched pub with lake, neat furnishings, well kept Bass and other beers; bedrooms comfortable and good value, good breakfasts *(Nick and Alison Dowson, Mr and Mrs Greenhalgh)*

☆ Fremington [B3233 Barnstaple—Instow; SS5132], *New Inn*: Good choice of popular food in bar and restaurant, well kept beer *(Don and Thelma Beeson, R E and P Pearce)*

Frogmore [A379 E of Kingsbridge; SX7742], *Globe*: Wide range of good food in spacious comfortable dining room, good friendly service, children welcome; good bedrooms *(R D Bubb, Jennifer Sheridan)*

☆ George Nympton [SS7023], *Castle*: Homely yet comfortably stylish two-bar village inn with good range of generous above-average home cooking inc vegetarian, welcoming service, Flowers IPA and a guest beer; bedrooms comfortable too, fishing rights; handy for the attractive market town of South Molton; bedrooms *(A N E Cox, Marion and John Hadfield, Stuart Cook)*

☆ **Georgeham** [Rock Hill; above village – OS Sheet 180 map ref 466399; SS4639], *Rock*: Cheerful character oak-beamed pub, old red quarry tiles, open fire, pleasant mix of country furniture, lots of bric-a-brac; well kept Courage-related ales, local farm cider, good bar food; piped music, darts, fruit machine, pool room; tables under cocktail parasols on front terrace, pretty hanging baskets *(K H Frostick, BB)*

☆ **Hartland Quay** [down toll rd; SS2522], *Hartland Quay*: Outstanding cliff scenery, rugged coast walks, genuine atmosphere and good untouched maritime feel with panelling, fishing memorabilia and shipwreck pictures; good value generous basic home-cooked food (dogs treat you as honoured guests if you're eating), St Austell Tinners, Inch's cider, quick pleasant service, small no-smoking bar, lots of tables outside; good value bedrooms, seawater swimming pool *(Joan and Andrew Life, A M Stephenson, T Treagust, Nigel and Lindsay Chapman, David Surridge, Jeanne Cross, Paul Silvestri, Barry and Anne)*

Hawkchurch [off B3165 E of Axminster; ST3400], *Old Inn*: Recently reopened after comfortable refurbishment, two log fires in long main bar, real ales such as Boddingtons, Cotleigh Barn Owl, Flowers IPA and Original, Websters Yorkshire and a guest; wide variety of straightforward food, darts, fruit machines, maybe piped music, skittle alley; picnic tables and flowers in back courtyard *(John and Moira Hawkes)*

☆ **Highampton** [A3072 W of Hatherleigh; SS4804], *Golden*: Attractive 16th-c thatched pub with Dartmoor views from garden behind, homely low-beamed alcovey lounge, brasses, watercolours, farm tools, stove in big stone fireplace; good value food, well kept Bass tapped from the cask, pool room; well behaved children allowed *(R J Walden)*

☆ **Holcombe Rogus** [ST0518], *Prince of Wales*: Spacious and comfortable, no machines or music, friendly atmosphere, good food (not Sun or Tues eves) in elegant dining room with good fire, well kept Cotleigh ales *(Bryan Wheeler)*

☆ **Honiton** [43 High St; ST1500], *Red Cow*: Busy welcoming local, pleasant seating areas, log fires, good choice of Courage-related and local ales, decent wines and malt whiskies, wide choice of good value home-made food inc tempting specials and some unusual dishes, friendly helpful staff; bedrooms *(John and Pat Charles, K R Harris, Basil Minson, Jim Reid, Ron Wallwork, June and Malcolm Farmer)*

Honiton, *Vane*: Small local tucked down pretty side-street, friendly service and attractively priced simple food *(Ann and Colin Hunt)*

nr Honiton [Fenny Bridges, A30 4 miles W; SY1198], *Fenny Bridges*: Spacious, with big helpings of good standard food, well kept local beer, quick service; restaurant, tables in garden *(Howard Clutterbuck)*

Horns Cross [A39 Clovelly—Bideford – OS Sheet 190 map ref 385233; SS3823], *Hoops*: Attractive much modernised thatched dining pub with wide choice of Whitbreads-related ales and of tasty food, pleasant friendly service, big inglenook log fires, eating area in central courtyard as well as cosy restaurant and bar, decent wines, provision for children and disabled; Easter beer festival; comfortable bedrooms *(B Rivers, David Carr, A B Agombar, R J Walden, Mr and Mrs P Fisk, Rita Horridge, JP, PP, LYM)*

Horns Cross [A39 Bideford—Clovelly; SS3823], *Coach & Horses*: Small friendly family-run country pub, attractive old building with good old-fashioned atmosphere, quickly served good value bar food; low-priced bedrooms in well converted outbuildings *(Brian Websdale)*

☆ **Ilfracombe** [Broad St; SS5147], *Royal Britannia*: Friendly old-fashioned pub in attractive spot above harbour; low seats, armchairs, copper tables and lots of prints in series of connecting rooms; wide choice of good value bar food inc local fish, well kept Courage-related beers; bedrooms *(David Carr, Martin Bromfield, Bernadette Garner)*

Ilfracombe [Bicclescombe Park Rd (off A361)], *Coach House*: Neat and clean, pleasant beamed upstairs restaurant, bar and family room downstairs *(Anon)*; *George & Dragon*: Lots of local and other bric-a-brac, well kept Courage, bar food inc good Sun lunch and lots for vegetarians, piped music *(Mr and Mrs E J W Rogers)*; *Ship & Pilot*: Clean and friendly town pub, decent food *(David Carr)*

☆ **Instow** [Marine Dr; SS4730], *Boathouse*: Very long bar with picture-window views over beach, estuary and Appledore, good choice of beautifully prepared generous good value food inc local fish and delicious puddings, good atmosphere and range of beers, meticulous all-female service, open fire at one end, model ships and boats, series of prints showing America's Cup yacht race incidents from 1899 on; well behaved dogs allowed, popular with families and older people *(Joan and Andrew Life, Mr and Mrs Jacob, R E and P Pearce)*

Instow, *Wayfarer*: Several small plain rooms in free house tucked away near dunes and beach, interesting menu inc local fish, Whitbreads-related beers, lively in summer; families welcome, tables in garden *(Chris Westmoreland)*

☆ **Kenn** [signed off A380 just S of Exeter; SX9285], *Ley Arms*: Extended thatched pub with polished granite floor and beams in attractive public bar, plush black-panelled lounge with striking fireplace, good wines, Bass and Whitbreads-related ales, bar food, sizeable restaurant side; piped music, no-smoking family room, games area *(John Fahy, Mike Gorton, Don and Shirley Parrish, Rich and Pauline Appleton, LYM)*

Kentisbeare [ST0608], *Keepers Cottage*: Friendly pub with decent food and good value wines *(John Fahy)*

☆ **Kilmington** [A35; SY2797], *Old Inn*: Thatched pub with character bar, inglenook lounge with armchairs and sofa, good value bar food and good Sun lunch, well kept Bass and Worthington BB, traditional games, good value food from sandwiches up, small no-smoking restaurant; children welcome, two gardens *(John Hazel, J A Snell, David Roberts, LYM)*

☆ Kingsbridge [quayside, edge of town; SX7344], *Crabshell*: Lovely waterside position, charming when tide in, with big windows and tables outside, wide choice of bar food inc lunchtime shrimp or crab sandwiches; hot food (ambitious, concentrating on local fish) may be confined to upstairs restaurant, with good views; quick friendly staff, well kept Bass and Charrington IPA, decent choice of wines, good farm cider, warm fire; maybe piped music *(Dorothee and Dennis Glover, JT, WT, Wendy Arnold, George Jonas, Stephen Teakle, BB)*

☆ Kingsbridge [Fore St], *Ship & Plough*: Interesting 18th-c pub brewing its own good cheap Blewitts Brains Out, Mild and Trumpet; friendly informative staff, usual food *(Richard Houghton, S Webb, M Lantree)*

Kingsbridge [Mill St], *Hermitage*: Friendly, usual food inc good home-made soup, good coffee, log fire, wide range of well kept ales inc one special to the pub *(Alan Prine, Steve Mammatt)*; [Mill St], *Seven Stars*: Flourishing town pub with good reaonably priced food *(John and Wendy Trentham)*

☆ Kingskerswell [towards N Whilborough – OS Sheet 202 map ref 864665; SX8666], *Bickley Mill*: Rambling converted out-of-the-way mill, comfortable seats, dark wood and brasses, carpet spreading into all the alcoves, popular generous interesting bar food inc vegetarian, well kept ales such as Ansells, Bass, Wadworths 6X, speedy cheerful service; restaurant Weds-Sat evenings; bedrooms *(John Wilson, Andrew Hodges, Mr and Mrs C Roberts)*

Kingswear [Higher St; SX8851], *Ship*: Friendly unpretentious local, good basic quickly served food, well kept Bass; one table with Dart views, a couple outside *(Paul and Mitzi Auchterlonie, Dr S Willavoys)*

☆ Knowle [just off A361 2 miles N of Braunton; SS4938], *Ebrington Arms*: Welcoming and friendly, good food inc vegetarian, well kept Bass and Wadworths 6X, lots of bric-a-brac in comfortable main bar, attractive candlelit dining area; pool room, piped music *(Deborah and Ian Carrington, Steve and Carolyn Harvey, R J Walden, David Carr, LYM)*

Lamerton [A384 Launceston—Tavistock; SX4476], *Blacksmiths Arms*: Good value generous fresh food, friendly efficient service, well kept ales, children very welcome *(Paul and Heather Bettesworth)*

Landkey [Church St; SS5931], *Ring o' Bells*: Small village pub, good home-made food in cosy dining room, Bass *(K R Harris)*

☆ Landscove [Woolston Green – OS Sheet 202 map ref 778662; SX7766], *Live & Let Live*: Friendly, homely and spotless open-plan bar

with popular bar food, well kept ales inc one brewed for the pub at Plympton, woodburner, tables in small orchard facing over moors to Dart valley *(C A Hall, LYM)*

Lapford [A377 Crediton—Barnstaple; SS7308], *Yeo Vale*: Refurbished pub with welcoming licensees, wide choice of good value home-cooked food inc children's, Bass-related ales; children and dogs welcome *(Brian Websdale)*

☆ Lee [SS4846], *Grampus*: Attractive medieval pub short stroll from sea, lots of seats in quiet sheltered garden, wide range of basic but good well presented home-made food, well kept Whitbreads-related ales, decent piped music; two bedrooms; superb coastal walks; bedrooms *(Mr and Mrs Westcombe, LYM)*

Lee Mill [SX6055], *Westward*: Very reasonably priced food, well kept beer, friendly staff *(Ian Phillips)*

Lifton [SX3885], *Arundell Arms*: Substantial fishing hotel (can arrange tuition – also shooting, deer-stalking and riding), rich decor, very agreeable atmosphere, good lunchtime bar food from outstanding chef (good evening restaurant too); bedrooms – a pleasant place to stay *(Caroline Raphael)*

☆ Loddiswell [SX7148], *Loddiswell Inn*: Welcoming landlady, well kept Ushers, good choice of freshly cooked generous food inc local ingredients, log fire, thriving local atmosphere *(Dr and Mrs N Holmes)*

☆ Lympstone [Exmouth Rd (A376); SX9984], *Nutwell Lodge*: Big modern-looking roadside dining pub, surprisingly attractive inside, with sensibly priced popular food inc generous carvery and early lunchtime bargains, well kept Bass and Dartmoor, decent wines, courteous efficient service; children welcome; roadside garden *(Alan and Margaret Griffiths, Chris Westmoreland, LYM)*

Lympstone, *Globe*: Relaxed simply furnished two-room pub, popular food esp seafood, quick friendly service, Flowers IPA, small pleasant restaurant; pretty waterside village *(Chris Westmoreland, BB)*; [The Strand], *Swan*: Recently reopened after olde-worlde refurbishment, scores on atmosphere and staff friendliness, with strong Irish influence; beers such as Boddingtons, Eldridge Pope Thomas Hardy, Flowers IPA and Original, fairly wide choice of well priced food inc good fresh fish; pool and fruit machine in pleasant public bar; piped music can be rather intrusive; pretty flower troughs and hanging baskets *(Malcolm Smith, Richard Armstead)*

Lynmouth [High St; SS7249], *Village Inn*: Looks more like a junior stealhouse than a pub, but cosy and friendly, with well kept beer, quick welcoming service, reasonably priced food; piped pop music may be rather obtrusive, credit card surcharge *(Meg and Colin Hamilton, Dave Irving)*

Lynton [Sinai Hill; SS7249], *Crown*: Clean and comfortable hotel lounge bar, friendly and relaxed, decent reasonably priced food here and in restaurant, well kept beer and cider, helpful staff; good bedrooms *(W H and E Thomas, Michael and Susan Townsend)*;

[Castle Hill], *Royal Castle*: Fantastic coastal views from back terrace and garden, interesting local photographs and bric-a-brac in comfortable lounge, well kept ales such as Adnams Broadside, Badger Tanglefoot, Butcombe and Cotleigh Tawny, friendly service, good range of reasonably priced lunchtime bar food; comfortable bedrooms *(Bruce Bird, David Carr)*

☆ nr Lynton [Martinhoe, Heddon's Gate – which is well signed down narrow hairpin rd off A39 W of Lynton – OS Sheet 180 map ref 654482], *Hunters Inn*: Outstanding remote setting in lovely wooded NT valley, great walks; most of rambling bar set aside for good plain food; well kept Exmoor ale and Stag and St Austell HSD, good farm cider, friendly service, cream teas (unless inn closed for wedding reception), unobtrusive piped music; attractive bedrooms *(Simon Collett-Jones, John Matthews, Bruce Bird)*

☆ Maidencombe [Steep Hill; SX9268], *Thatched*: Picturesque extended thatched pub with lovely coastal views, good range of well priced food inc local fish, well kept Bass and Tetleys-related ales, quick friendly service, big family room, no-smoking areas, restaurant; attractive garden with small thatched huts (dogs allowed out here but not in pub); children allowed; attractive bedrooms in annexe, good breakfast; small attractive village *(Mr and Mrs H Lambert, Andrew Hodges)*

☆ Malborough [SX7039], *Old Inn*: Plain and unpretentious country pub notable for straightforward but really good bar food (esp mussels and puddings); charming quick service, good house wine, pleasant children's room *(H F C Barclay)*

Manaton [SX7581], *Kestor*: Useful modern Dartmoor-edge inn in splendid spot nr Becky Falls, wide range of food, well kept changing ales, farm cider, open fire; piped music; attractive bedrooms *(Mrs Pat Crabb, G and M Stewart)*

Marldon [just W of Paignton; SX8663], *Church House*: Large paved bar with dining area, sensible tables with comfortable chairs, well kept Bass, Boddingtons, Flowers IPA and Original, good food, quick cheerful service *(Colin and Marjorie Roberts)*

☆ Marsh [signed off A303 Ilminster—Honiton; ST2510], *Flintlock*: Welcoming and comfortable 17th-c inn, wide choice of good bar food inc vegetarian, well kept beer and cider, armoury and horsebrasses *(Howard Clutterbuck)*

☆ Mary Tavy [Lanehead; A386 Tavistock—Okehampton; SX5079], *Mary Tavy*: Warm and welcoming unpretentious old pub, log fire, friendly locals, well kept Bass, St Austell HSD and Mild and two guest beers, reasonably priced freshly cooked food inc vegetarian, weekend front carvery; good value bedrooms, big breakfast *(Mrs M Connor, Bruce Bird, Joan and Michel Hooper-Immins, JP, PP)*

☆ Meeth [A386 Hatherleigh—Torrington; SS5408], *Bull & Dragon*: 16th-c beamed and thatched village pub, Tetleys-related ales with a guest such as Butleigh, decent wines, good value straightforward food, helpful service, friendly locals, unobtrusive piped music; children welcome, exemplary lavatories *(R J Walden, A N Ellis, Ron and Sheila Corbett)*

☆ Merrivale [B3357; 4 miles E of Tavistock – OS Sheet 191 map ref 459752; SX5475], *Dartmoor*: Welcoming refurbished pub with high Dartmoor views, nr bronze-age hut circles, stone rows and pretty river; generous reasonably priced lunchtime food, well kept ales inc Bass, Stones and one labelled for the pub, water from their 120-ft well, good choice of country wines, open fire, friendly attentive staff, tables outside – very popular summer evenings; good walks *(Dr and Mrs N Holmes, Gwen and Peter Andrews, John and Vivienne Rice)*

☆ Molland [SS8028], *London*: Unspoilt dim-lit basic Exmoor-edge pub, well worth tackling the narrow country lanes to get there; Bass and Worthington BB tapped from casks behind bar, good value food inc children's meals in big dining room, log fire, welcoming landlord, upper-crust locals; next to wonderfully untouched church *(John and Elspeth Howell)*

☆ Moreleigh [B3207; off Kingsbridge—Totnes in Stanborough, left in village; SX7652], *New Inn*: Busy country local with character old furniture, big inglenook, nice pictures, candles in bottles; limited choice of good wholesome home-cooked food served generously, reasonable prices, well kept Palmers tapped from the cask; may be closed Sat lunchtime/race days *(DJW, Roger Wain-Heapy, LYM)*

☆ Moretonhampstead [A382 N of Bovey Tracey; SX7585], *White Hart*: Attractively furnished big lounge, lively traditional back public bar, log fires, friendly service and standard poodles, wide choice of promptly served popular bar food from sandwiches up, cream teas, Sun roast, no-smoking restaurant and part of eating area, well kept Bass, Boddingtons and Smiles, Luscombe farm cider, traditional games, fruit machine; children welcome, open all day; attractive bedrooms, well placed for Dartmoor, good walks *(David Gittins, Helen Pickering, James Owen, Ian Phillips, LYM)*

☆ Mortehoe [off A361 Ilfracombe—Braunton; SS4545], *Ship Aground*: Open-plan village pub with big family room, well kept Whitbreads-related and guest ales, Hancock's cider in summer, decent wine, friendly staff, bar food inc good pizzas, log fire; massive rustic furnishings, lots of nautical brassware, friendly cross-eyed cat, pool, skittles and other games, tables on sheltered sunny terrace with good views; piped music may be intrusive; by interesting church, wonderful walking on nearby coast footpath *(Jo Rees, Julian Holland, Sue Demont, Tim Barrow, Jill Grain, Tony McLaughlin, LYM)*

Mortehoe, *Chichester Arms*: Warm and welcoming, with lots of old village prints, wide choice of good value usual bar food,

Bass and Courage-related ales, friendly efficient service, no piped music *(Peter and Audrey Dowsett, Rip and Pauline Kirby, Alec and Susan Hamilton)*

☆ Newton Abbot [East St; SX8671], *Olde Cider Bar*: Fat casks of interesting farm ciders and perries in unusual basic cider house, nononsense stools and wall benches, pre-warstyle decor; good country wines, snacks inc venison pasties, very low prices; small games room with machines *(Jeanne Cross, Paul Silvestri)*

☆ nr Newton Abbot [A381 2 miles S, by turn to Abbotskerswell], *Two Mile Oak*: Atractively quiet and old-fashioned, with good log fire, black panelling, low beams, stripped stone, lots of brasses, comfortable candlelit alcoves; wide choice of decent food, cosy little dining room, well kept Bass, Flowers IPA, Eldridge Pope Royal Oak and guest beers, seats on back terrace, attractive garden *(Joan and Gordon Edwards, Gordon, LYM)*

☆ Newton Ferrers [Riverside Rd East; SX5448], *Dolphin*: Friendly pub in lovely village overlooking yachting harbour, good value food *(Mr and Mrs Peter Smith)*

Newton Poppleford [High St; A3052 Exeter—Lyme Regis; SY0889], *Exeter*: Popular local with well kept Whitbreads-related ales, good value food, darts, pool and skittles, tables on terrace; children allowed *(Brian A Websdale)*

☆ Newton Tracey [5 miles S of Barnstaple on B3232 to Torrington; SS5226], *Hunters*: Friendly old pub with good value bar food, four real ales, log fire, evening restaurant, skittle alley/games room; juke box, fruit machines; tables outside, play area; provision for children *(Nigel and Lindsay Chapman)*

☆ No Mans Land [B3131 Tiverton—South Molton; SS8313], *Mount Pleasant*: Traditional country pub with cosy bars, wide range of good inexpensive home-made food from huge sandwiches up, real ales such as Bass and Butcombe, decent wines, friendly service, open fires, ex-forge restaurant; children's room, tables outside *(Paul and Heather Bettesworth)*

☆ North Bovey [SX7483], *Ring of Bells*: Bulgy-walled 13th-c thatched inn, well kept Dartmoor, Ind Coope Burton, Marstons Pedigree and Wadworths 6X, Gray's farm cider, games etc, good log fire, good straightforward bar food, restaurant, friendly staff; children welcome; seats outside by lovely tree-covered village green below Dartmoor; big bedrooms with four-posters *(John and Vivienne Rice, Paul McGrath, LYM)*

☆ Noss Mayo [SX5447], *Swan*: Small pub with charming waterside views, good range of bar food inc fresh fish, well kept Courage Best and Directors, old beams, open fire; can get crowded, with difficult parking; dogs on leads and children welcome, tables outside – picturesque village *(MJH, Elizabeth Jenner)*

☆ Otterton [Fore St; SY0885], *Kings Arms*: Comfortably refurbished open-plan pub, good choice of food inc good value Sun lunch, fresh fish (not Sun or Mon), well kept Bass, friendly landlady, skittle alley doubling as family room; can get crowded during holidays; beautiful evening view from picnic tables in good-sized back garden, charming village *(Jeanne and George Barnwell, F J Willy, D Toulson, Shirley Pielou)*

Paignton [main shopping st; SX8960], *Old Well House*: Comfortable multi-level open-plan pub with wide choice of food from sandwiches to bargain steaks, very quick service; keg beers *(Colin and Marjorie Roberts)*

nr Paignton [Totnes R, off A385 2 miles out; SX8561], *Blagdon Inn*: Friendly and comfortable thatched pub with spacious open-plan beamed bar, some stripped brickwork, family room, home-cooked bar food inc vegetarian dishes, good restaurant and Sunday carvery; tables on terrace, play area *(D Rome)*

☆ Parkham [SS3821], *Bell*: Spacious, friendly and comfortable thatched village pub, good value fresh food, lots of nooks and crannies, log fire, old-fashioned furnishings, choice of real ales *(Nigel and Lindsay Chapman, LYM)*

☆ Plymouth [Citadel Rd/Saltram Pl – back of Plymouth Hoe, behind Moat House], *Yard Arm*: In fine spot overlooking the Hoe, attractive woodwork and some interesting nautical bric-a-brac giving character, three levels and intimate snug feel, well kept Courage-related ales and a guest such as Bass, very cheap generous straightforward food inc children's service, cheerful service; subdued piped music, children allowed in bottom area, tables outside *(Mark Walker, Brian and Anna Marsden, David Yandle, Andrew Hodges, Brian Atkin)*

☆ Plymouth [Old George St; Derrys Cross, behind Theatre Royal], *Bank*: Smart and busy three-level pub interestingly converted from former bank, dark wood balustrades, conservatory area upstairs (children allowed here), tables outside; cheerful service (quickest on the top level, which is quieter), good value food all day, well kept Tetleys-related ales; music nights, lively young evening atmosphere *(David Yandle, Mayur Shah)*

Plymouth [Barbican], *Dolphin*: Simple and lively, with particularly well kept Bass tapped from the cask; Beryl Cook paintings (you may see her here) *(John Poulter, James Macrae)*; [Commercial Rd, Coxside], *Fareham*: Attractively refurbished free house by modern fish quay, friendly staff and regulars, well kept St Austells HSD; no food, but landlady may supply plates for pasties and pies from shop over road *(Paul Stagg, Mike Woodhead)*

Plympton [George Lane/Ridgeway; SX5356], *George*: Two-roomed pub with very big helpings of good value food upstairs, ales inc Dartmoor, Greene King and Wadworths 6X, seats on terrace; dogs welcome *(Mr and Mrs N Spink)*

Plymstock [Radford Pk Rd; SX5152], *Drakes Drum*: Welcoming atmospheric pub adorned with china and bird pictures, good service, comfortable lounge bar with back eating area, good choice of home-made food; quiet piped music, public bar with darts, pool and fruit machines; children welcome (*Mayur Shah*)

☆ Princetown [SX5873], *Plume of Feathers*: Much-extended hikers' pub, good value food inc good pasties, service friendly and friendly even with crowds, well kept Bass and St Austell HSD and Tinners, two log fires, solid slate tables, live music Fri night, Sun lunchtime – can be lively then; children welcome, play area outside; good value bedrooms, also bunkhouse and camping (*M J How, Andy and Jill Kassube, J R Harris*)
Princetown, *Prince of Wales*: Friendly no-nonsense local, wide choice of good value straightforward food, Flowers and Wadworths 6X on handpump, large dog and two cats; two huge open fires, granite walls hung with rugs (*Joan and Gordon Edwards, BB*)

☆ Pusehill [SS4228], *Pig on the Hill*: Newish family dining pub on farm, pig decorations, bar, raised gallery and adjacent room through archways; decent food inc children's, well kept Ind Coope Burton, reasonable prices, children's TV room; big adventure playground, small swimming pool, boules (*B M Eldridge, Chris Westmoreland*)
Pyworthy [SW of Holsworthy; SS3102], *Molesworth Arms*: Popular country pub with attractively priced food inc good curries in bar or restaurant, well kept Bass and a guest beer, friendly staff (*Mrs R Horridge*)

☆ Rackenford [off A361 NW of Tiverton; SS8518], *Stag*: Interesting 13th-c low-beamed thatched pub reopened under friendly new owners; lots of character and atmosphere, original flagstoned and cobbled entry passage, huge fireplace flanked by ancient settles; bedrooms (*Paul and Heather Bettesworth, BB*)

☆ Rockbeare [SY0295], *Jack in the Green*: Good value food showing real flair, inventive recipes, lots of local fish and game, delicious puddings, well kept Bass and Wadworths 6X, good reasonably priced wines, cheerful staff, back restaurant (*John and Vivienne Rice, Kim Dawson, Chris Jaworski*)

☆ Salcombe [off Fore St nr Portlemouth Ferry; SX7338], *Ferry*: Fine spot overlooking water, bottom stripped-stone bar giving on to sheltered flagstoned waterside terrace, top bar opening off street, and between them a popular dining bar; well kept Palmers ales; piped music may be intrusive, can get busy (*June and Malcolm Farmer, Owen and Margaret Warnock, Richard Hathaway, B Taylor, Chris and Martin Taylor, LYM*)

☆ Salcombe [Fore St], *Victoria*: Well placed and attractive, with comfortable lounge, copious good food cooked to order, pleasant eating area, jovial landlord, well kept Bass and Wadworths 6X; segregated children's room, bedrooms (*Moira and John Cole*)
Salcombe [Union St], *Fortescue*: Busy local nr harbour, three bars, terrace, reliable food, well kept Courage Directors; can get busy in summer (*Joy and Paul Rundell, Allan and Philippa Wright*)
Sampford Courtenay [B3072 Crediton—

Holsworthy; SS6301], *New Inn*: Friendly 16th-c thatched pub with good filling food, low-beamed open-plan bar, open fires, real ales such as Bass, Flowers, Wadworths 6X, nice garden with children's play area and playhouse (*I P G Derwent*)

☆ Sandy Park [SX7189], *Sandy Park*: Thatched country local with convivial old-fashioned small bar, stripped oak tables, built-in high-backed wall seats, big black iron fireplace, well kept ales such as Cotleigh Tawny, Eldridge Pope Hardy and Wadworths 6X, decent wines; bar food (not winter Sun/Mon evenings), children in eating area, cosy restaurant; service can slow if busy; simple clean bedrooms (*Werner Arend, James Macrae, Bryn Davies, A R Hards, W Matthews, Joan and Gordon Edwards, Lara Kramp-Chopin, LYM*)
Seaton [Marine Cres; SY2490], *Fishermans*: Cheap tasty food all day inc bargain tasty lunch, smiling welcome, open fire; very basic decor, but sea view (*Jeanne Cross, Paul Silvestri, Brian A Websdale*)
Shaldon [just past harbour; SX9372], *Ferryboat*: Smallish bar, basic but comfortable, with well kept Courage Best and Directors, big helpings of good food, tables over road by beach (*Colin and Marjorie Roberts*)
Shillingford [SS9823], *Barleycorn*: Genuinely welcoming family-run inn handy for Exmoor, good range of real ales, decent choice of reasonably priced fresh generous food inc vegetarian, sheltered back garden; bedrooms comfortable and clean (*M Lycett Green, M Carter*)

☆ Shiphay [off A380/A3022, NW edge of Torquay; SX8865], *Devon Dumpling*: Popular for its country style, with good value straightforward food inc vegetarian, well kept Courage Best, Morlands Old Speckled Hen and Wadworths 6X, cheerful service; plenty of space inc upper barn loft; aquarium, occasional live music, no dogs inside (*Colin and Marjorie Roberts*)

☆ Sidbury [Putts Corner; A375 Sidbury—Honiton; SY1595], *Hare & Hounds*: Roomy lounge bar, wood-and-tiles tap room, two fine old chesterfields and more usual furnishings, stuffed pike; four or five well kept changing ales, very friendly staff, wide choice of bar food, restaurant; big garden, good views of valley below (*C Kyprianou, Howard Clutterbuck*)

☆ Sidmouth [Old Fore St; SY1287], *Old Ship*: Shiny black woodwork, ship pictures, wide choice of fair-priced food inc vegetarian and home-made specials, well kept ales such as Boddingtons, Marstons Pedigree, Wadworths 6X; close-set tables but roomier raftered upstairs bar with family room, dogs allowed; just moments from the sea, so can get crowded in summer, but service good and friendly (*M E Wellington, A and R Cooper, Ann and Colin Hunt, BB*)
Sidmouth [Old Fore St], *Anchor*: Friendly local with good generous reasonably priced food inc unusual daily specials in no-smoking

dining area; tables in good outdoor area, open all day *(Ann and Colin Hunt)*; [opp Radway Cinema], *Radway*: Friendly local with good value food inc vegetarian, good choice of beers; live music during Sidmouth Folk Week *(Ann and Colin Hunt)*; [High St], *Tudor Rose*: This good popular food pub closed in 1996 – we hope only temporarily *(News please)*

☆ Silverton [14 Exeter Rd; SS9502], *Three Tuns*: Enjoyable food inc fine vegetarian dishes in 17th-c inn's old-fashioned bar or cosy restaurant, well kept Courage Best and Directors, welcoming efficient service; good value up-to-date bedrooms, handy for Killerton *(Nick Wikeley)*

Slapton [SX8244], *Tower*: Ancient low-ceilinged flagstoned pub reopened after refurbishment; open fires, family room, good value standard food, enjoyable atmosphere, peaceful garden overhung by romantic ivy-covered ruined jackdaw tower; bedrooms *(Mr and Mrs D M Fishleigh, LYM)*

☆ South Tawton [off A30 at Whiddon Down or Okehampton, then signed from Sticklepath; SX6594], *Seven Stars*: Friendly and unpretentious local in attractive village, good range of well prepared good value food, well kept Bass, Boddingtons and a guest beer, decent wines; pool and other bar games, restaurant (cl Sun and Mon evenings winter); children welcome; bedrooms *(Chris Bartram, Matthew Baker, LYM)*

☆ Spreyton [SX6996], *Tom Cobbley*: Friendly village local, generous cheap home-made food, well kept Cotleigh Tawny and occasional guest beers; darts, cards, attractive garden with summer barbecues, dog-loving licensees; comfortable bedrooms sharing bath, big breakfasts; bedrooms *(Giles J Robinson, JP, PP)*

☆ Sticklepath [off A30 at Whiddon Down or Okehampton; SX6494], *Devonshire*: Warm and cosy 16th-c thatched village inn with low-beamed slate-floored bar, big log fire, some nice old furniture, comfortable armchairs in room off, good low-priced snacks, bookable Sun lunches and evening meals, welcoming owners and locals, St Austell Tinners and HSD, farm cider, magazines to read; open all day Fri/Sat; bedrooms *(Ray and Wendy Bryn Davies, LYM)*

Stockland [a mile or so towards Chard; ST2404], *Longbridge*: Family-run local with reasonably priced usual food *(Ann and Colin Hunt)*

☆ Stokeinteignhead [SX9170], *Church House*: Civilised 13th-c thatched dining pub, character bar, dining lounge and restaurant area, delightful spiral staircase, good if not cheap food, well kept Bass, Flowers IPA and Marstons Pedigree, farm cider, good coffee; nice back garden with little stream, lovely unspoilt village *(John Wilson, Jeanne Cross, Paul Silvestri, Chris Fydler, Andrew Hodges)*

☆ Stokeinteignhead, *Chasers Arms*: Good value often interesting food inc imaginative veg and unusual puddings in busy 16th-c thatched pub/restaurant (you can't go just for a drink,

but they do bar snacks too and the atmosphere is that of a country pub); fine range of house wines, quick friendly service *(Geraldine Bristol, Paul and Janet Waring, John Wilson, Peter and Jenny Quine, D I Baddeley)*

☆ Stokenham [just off A379 Dartmouth—Kingsbridge; SX8042], *Tradesmans Arms*: Tranquil 15th-c thatched cottage with plenty of antique tables neatly set for good simple fresh bar food esp seafood; well kept Adnams and Bass, good malt whiskies, very friendly staff; restaurant, children allowed in left-hand bar, picnic tables outside (nice surroundings), maybe quiet piped classical music; tiny car park, opens noon *(Joy and Paul Rundell, Paul and Janet Waring, LYM)*

☆ Stokenham [opp church, N of A379 towards Torcross], *Church House*: Firmly run open-plan family pub, good food inc fresh fish and other local ingredients, well kept Bass, Eldridge Pope Hardy and Flowers Original, farm cider, decent wines, no-smoking dining room, unobtrusive piped music; children's room with writing/drawing materials, attractive garden with enjoyable play area, fish pond and chipmunks *(Paul and Janet Waring, Norma Farris, RCV, Roger Wain-Heapy, Hanns P Golez, LYM)*

Strete [SX8346], *Kings Arms*: Pleasant service, good choice of good food, sea-view restaurant *(C and E M Watson)*

Tavistock [Okehampton Rd, outside; SX4874], *Trout & Tipple*: Recently taken over by nearby trout farm, now has superb food (emphasis on trout) in pleasant, cosy and friendly atmosphere *(R and J Protheroe)*

Teignmouth [Quayside; SX9473], *Ship*: Upper and lower decks like a ship, good atmosphere, nice mix of locals and tourists, good value food; lovely setting looking up the River Teign *(A and R Cooper)*

Thelbridge Cross [OS Sheet 180 map ref 790120; SS7912], *Thelbridge Cross*: Attractive, clean and well run beamed pub, welcoming attentive staff, good food quickly served, log fires; bedrooms, views across to Dartmoor *(J Anderson)*

Thorverton [SS9202], *Bell*: Friendly free house with Flowers IPA, Fullers London Pride, good food inc dining rooms *(E Robinson)*

Thurlestone [SX6743], *Village Inn*: Well kept Bass, Palmers and Wadworths 6X and good choice of reasonably priced standard food, in convivial, if rather up-market, village pub handy for coastal path; separate dining area *(Jeremy Brittain-Long, Marianne Lantree, Steve Webb)*

☆ Topsham [Fore St; 2 miles from M5 junction 30; SX9688], *Globe*: Good solid traditional furnishings, log fire and plenty of character in heavy-beamed bow-windowed bar of friendly and relaxed 16th-c inn; low-priced straightforward home-cooked food, well kept Bass, Ushers Best and Worthington BB on handpump, decent reasonably priced wine, snug little bar-dining room, separate restaurant, new back extension blending in well; children in eating area, open all day; good value attractive bedrooms *(Chris Westmoreland, Mark Walker, Andrew Hodges, B Taylor, LYM)*

☆ **Topsham** [from centre head towards Exmouth via Elmgrove Rd], *Bridge*: Unchanging and unspoilt 16th-c pub with fine old traditional furnishings in little no-smoking lounge partitioned off from inner corridor by high-backed settle, open fire, bigger lower room open at busy times, cosy regulars' inner sanctum with really too wide a choice of real ales tapped from the cask; lunchtime pasties, sandwiches and ploughman's, children welcome *(Andy and Jill Kassube, JP, PP, LYM)*

☆ **Topsham**, *Lighter*: Spacious and recently comfortably refurbished family pub, with well kept Badger ales, good friendly staff, decent quickly served bar food, panelled alcoves and tall windows looking out over tidal flats; games machines; seats out on old quay, good value bedrooms *(R J Walden, Ann and Colin Hunt, Chris Westmoreland, John Fahy, BB)*

☆ **Topsham** [High St], *Lord Nelson*: Well priced generously served food inc giant open sandwiches, pleasant atmosphere, attentive service Excellent, best in the town *(Alan Newman, Andrew Hodges)*

Topsham [Fore St], *Drakes*: Friendly and welcoming, with Bass, Boddingtons, Devenish Royal Wessex, a beer named for the pub and guest beers, good choice of wines by the glass, tempting food in upstairs intimate restaurant *(Adrian Alton, Brian Websdale, Andrew Hodges)*; [68 Fore St], *Salutation*: Victorian pastiche complete with flagstoned period courtyard; clean and comfortable, happy obliging staff, well kept Bass and Worthington BB, good value freshly cooked food esp local fish *(K R Harris, Andrew Hodges)*; [Monmouth Hill], *Steam Packet*: Cheap bar food, several well kept ales, dark flagstones, scrubbed boards, panelling, stripped masonry, a lighter dining room; on boat-builders' quay *(Chris Westmoreland, Andrew Hodges, Ann and Colin Hunt, LYM)*

☆ **Torquay** [Park Lane; SX9264], *Hole in the Wall*: More emphasis on food under current management in small two-bar 16th-c local nr harbour, low beams and flagstones, well kept Courage, friendly service, lots of naval memorabilia, old local photographs, chamber-pots; open all day *(Mr and Mrs C Roberts, Peter and Jenny Quine, JWC, MC)*

Torrington [The Square; SS4919], *Newmarket*: Reopened under friendly and welcoming management, well served reasonably priced food; pool in separate bar *(Graham and Lynn Mason)*; [Old Station House], *Puffing Billy*: Popular family pub in former station building done out in old Southern Railway colours, well kept ales, decent wines and food inc good value children's dishes, lots of train memorabilia and pictures, garden with pets corner; on Tarka Trail walk/cycle route *(A M Stephenson, Roger Grimshaw, P Johns)*

☆ **Totnes** [Fore St, The Plains; SX8060], *Royal*

Seven Stars: Civilised old hotel, full of character, with late 1960s decor, impressive central hall below sunny skylight and stairs off, Bass and Courage Best, cheerful helpful service, cheap food, tables out in front – ideal on a Tues market day when the tradespeople wear Elizabethan dress; bedrooms, river on other side of busy main road *(Ian Phillips, JWC, MC)*

Totnes [Bridgetown], *Albert*: Doing well under current character landlord, good generous reasonably priced food (not Sun) cooked by his wife, well kept Bass, Brakspears and Worthington BB, welcoming back snug locals' bar, dark-beamed red plush lounge bar with lots of nick-nacks, handsome pub dog Henry, nice garden; hope to brew own beer soon *(C J W Penrose, S Miles, Nigel Ash)*

☆ **Tuckenhay** [Bow Creek; out of Totnes, keep on Ashprington rd past Watermans Arms; SX8156], *Maltsters Arms*: Marvellous position by peaceful wooded creek, with picture windows in airy and comfortably extended dining lounge, character traditional back bar with log fire, waterside tables with barbecue, bedrooms; after a spell of erratic high-priced glory under Keith Floyd, has been bought by the Mogfords of the Sea Trout, Staverton (see main entries), and managed by pre-Floyd owners; first reports suggest it's well on track to being a reliable main entry again, with nice chatty bar atmosphere, simple lunchtime food choice, and more upmarket restaurany evening food *(DJW, LYM; more reports please)*

☆ **Two Bridges** [B3357/B3212 across Dartmoor; SX6175], *Two Bridges*: Gently refurbished old Dartmoor hotel, nice log fire in cosy bar, another in spacious lounge, decent bar food inc useful buffet lunch from restaurant, afternoon tea, own-brewed beer; comfortable bedrooms, good walks – a romantic winter hideaway, but busy with tourists in summer *(John and Christine Vittoe, Dr and Mrs N Holmes)*

Tytherleigh [A358 Chard—Axminster; ST3103], *Tytherleigh Arms*: Spacious and comfortable, with good range of usual food inc local fish, Eldridge Pope ales, small restaurant *(Howard Clutterbuck, M E Wellington)*

☆ **Ugborough**, *Ship*: Well run open-plan dining pub extended from cosy 16th-c flagstoned core, remarkably wide choice of good food inc lots of fresh fish, good fresh veg and farm ice cream, pleasant efficient waitresses, well kept Bass; tables outside *(Bryan Taylor, Mr and Mrs C C Mathewman, MGH, Dr and Mrs N Holmes, George Atkinson)*

Uplowman [not far from M5 junction 27 via Sampford Peverell; ST0115], *Redwoods*: Genuine village pub with good atmosphere, friendly licensee, good value food *(B J Cox)*

Welcombe [off A39; SS2217], *Welcombe Cross*: Restaurant worth knowing for good food and service, good children's menu; welcoming friendly atmosphere, spotlessly clean *(D J Milne)*

☆ **Westleigh** [½ mile off A39 Bideford—Instow;

SS4628], *Westleigh Inn*: Very welcoming
village pub with old local pictures in single
room split by serving bar, well kept Ruddles
County and Ushers, farm cider, good
straightforward home-cooked food esp
cottage and fish pies, family atmosphere,
gorgeous views down over the Torridge
estuary from spacious neatly kept hillside
garden, good play area; may have local
produce for sale *(Simon Starr, Chris
Westmoreland, Nigel and Lindsay Chapman,
David and Michelle James, Mr and Mrs
Westcombe, LYM)*

☆ **Widecombe** [SX7176], *Olde Inne*: Friendly
and cosy, with stripped 14th-c stonework, big
log fires in both bars, some concentration on
wide choice of good reasonably priced food,
prominent restaurant area, well kept Ushers
and other beers, local farm cider, decent
wines, good friendly service; in pretty
moorland village, very popular with tourists
though perhaps at its best out of season; room
to dance on music nights, good big garden;
great walks – the one to or from Grimspound
gives spectacular views *(G and M Stewart,
John and June Gale, JP, PP, Paul and Janet
Waring, Julie Peters, Colin Blinkhorn, John
and Christine Vittoe, John Hazel, LYM)*

☆ **Widecombe** [turning opp Old Inne, down hill
past long church house – OS Sheet 191 map
ref 720765], *Rugglestone*: Cosy unspoilt bar
with woodburner and dozy dog, careful
extension toning in, splendid value simple
home cooking, well kept Butcombe and
Flowers IPA tapped from the cask, good local
farm cider, larger room with space for darts
etc, no piped music; tables in garden,
beautiful quiet streamside setting, wandering
ponies *(P and T Ferris, Gwen and Peter
Andrews, G and M Stewart, John Hazel, Paul
and Heather Bettesworth, JP, PP)*

☆ **Winkleigh** [off B3220; SS6308], *Kings Arms*:

Current owners doing good food inc some
outstanding dishes, also well kept Courage-
related ales and Inch's farm cider, with
beams, flagstones, scrubbed pine tables,
woodburner and big separate log fire, good
efficient service, well reproduced piped music,
no-smoking restaurant; small sheltered side
courtyard with pool *(R J Walden, G
Washington, LYM)*

☆ **Woodbury** [3½ miles from M5 junction 30;
A376, then B3179; SY0187], *White Hart*:
Consistently good generous food all home-
cooked in attractive and comfortable lounge
bar or small homely restaurant, good friendly
service, well kept Bass and Worthington BB;
good locals' bar with many characters, skittle
alley with own buffet, peaceful village
(George and Jeanne Barnwell)

☆ **Woolfardisworthy** [SS3321], *Farmers Arms*:
Small cosy low-ceilinged thatched local,
friendly landlord, decent food, spotless
housekeeping, well kept guest beers *(R
Pottey)*

☆ **Wrafton** [A361 just SE of Braunton; SS4935],
Williams Arms: Large modernised thatched
dining pub, two bars divided into several cosy
areas, interesting wall hangings, wide choice
of good value bar food, unlimited self-service
from good carvery, friendly speedy service,
Bass; pool, darts, piped music, discreet TV in
furthest bar area; children welcome; picnic
tables outside with play area and aviary *(Jane
Basso, Roger and Pauline Pearce)*

Yelverton [by roundabout on A386 halfway
between Plymouth and Tavistock; SX5267],
Rock: Recently refurbished and extended,
spacious lounge bar with family area, smaller
locals' bar and separate bar with games room,
friendly efficient waitress service, good range
of ales and ciders, wide choice of food inc
children's, popular terrace; children's room,
safe play area; open all day *(Paul Redgrave)*

Please tell us if the decor, atmosphere, food or drink at a pub is different from
our description. We rely on readers' reports to keep us up to date.
No stamp needed: *The Good Pub Guide*, FREEPOST TN1569, Wadhurst,
E Sussex TN5 7BR.

Dorset

This county's pubs are much more likely than most to have a good range of decent wines by the glass. This is largely the result of the good example set by Eldridge Pope, one of the area's local brewers, which has a flourishing and well run wine import business, ensuring good value supplies for its own tied pubs. The standard of pub food is very high, too. For an enjoyable meal out, we'd particularly pick out the very relaxed Fox at Corscombe (careful cooking of local ingredients in a staunchly traditional county pub), the Museum at Farnham (distinctively run, with imaginative food), the Scott Arms at Kingston (doing very well all round, good fresh fish from Brixham), the Elm Tree at Langton Herring (currently very popular for its up-to-the-minute dishes of the day – it gains a Food Award this year), and the enthusiastically run Brace of Pheasants at Plush (another pub granted a Food Award for its imaginative cooking). Of these, it's the Fox at Corscombe which wins our accolade of Dorset Dining Pub of the Year. Other pubs doing particularly well at the moment include the Royal Oak in Cerne Abbas (redecorated under new licensees, lots of wines by the glass), the cheerful Sailors Return at East Chaldon, the unhurried and traditional Loders Arms at Loders (a new main entry, with most enjoyable food), the fine old Crown in Marnhull (another pub brought back into the main entries by its present hard-working licensees), the Marquis of Lorne at Nettlecombe (gains a Beer Award this year), the friendly and pretty Thimble at Piddlehinton, and the splendidly traditional old Digby Tap near the abbey in Sherborne (yet another new main entry). In the Lucky Dip section at the end of the chapter, quite a few pubs seem on particularly good form these days (most of these inspected by us, and firmly vouched for): the Gaggle of Geese at Buckland Newton, Kings Arms at East Stour, Acorn at Evershot, Fiddleford Inn at Fiddleford, Avon Causeway at Hurn, Cock & Bottle at Morden, Halfway at Norden Heath (not one we've yet been able to try ourselves, but the Greek Cypriot food sounds well worth knowing), Inn in the Park in Poole, Mitre at Sandford Orcas, Two Brewers in Shaftesbury and Castle at West Lulworth. Dorchester has a good choice of interesting pubs, and we also now include several decent pubs in Bournemouth, which until recently was quite a pub desert. Drinks prices in the area are rather higher than the national average; with the exception of the Smugglers at Osmington Mills, a free house, the cheapest pubs we found here were all tied to the local brewery Palmers of Bridport.

Post Office address codings confusingly give the impression that some pubs are in Dorset, when they're really in Somerset (which is where we list them).

ABBOTSBURY SY5785 Map 2

Ilchester Arms 🛏

B3157

Although this handsome stone inn is very much a hotel these days, there is still a good, cosy atmosphere throughout its rambling beamed rooms. Lanes lead into the countryside from the back of the pub, and it makes a good base for exploring this picturesque old village. The ancient Swannery is well worth a visit, as well as the sheltered 20-acre gardens (closed in winter) not far from the remains of the abbey, with unusual tender plants and peacocks. The bustling main bar has over 1,000 prints on the walls, many depicting swans from the nearby abbey, as well as red plush button-back seats and spindleback chairs around cast-iron-framed and other tables on a turkey carpet, and chesterfield sofas in front of the open log fire. Hunting horns, stirrups and horsebrasses hang from the beams, there's a stag's head, and some stuffed fish. Bass, Flowers Orginal and Wadworths 6X under light blanket pressure, with a few malt whiskies; dominoes, cribbage, fruit machine, Sky TV, winter pool and darts, and piped music. Bar food includes soup (£2), Dorset sausage baguette (£2.60), ploughman's (from £3.25), baked potato with cheese and bacon (£3.95), home-made steak and ale pie (£4.95), roast beef and yorkshire pudding (£6.25), daily specials like stir-fried pork with bean sprouts, seafood such as local lemon sole (£8.95) or red mullet with chive sauce (£9.25), and home-made puddings (all £2.25); children's menu (from £1.95). Big breakfasts are served in the sizeable and attractive no-smoking conservatory restaurant, and there are afternoon teas in the bar. Some readers have found that service can be a little impersonal at times. (Recommended by D L Evans, Ken and Jenny Simmonds, Chris and Kate Lyons, Jenny and Brian Seller, J Sheldon, Neil Townend, Brian and Anna Marsden, Richard Gibbs, David Holloway, Cheryl and Keith Roe, Philip Orbell, Alan Skull, JKW, Basil Minson, George and Jeanne Barnwell, Gordon, A H Denman, Risha Stapleton)

Greenalls ~ Managers Mike and May Doyle ~ Real ale ~ Meals and snacks ~ Restaurant ~ (01305) 871243 ~ Children in eating area of bar and in restaurant ~ Occasional live entertainment ~ Open 11-11; Sun 12-3, 7-10 ~ Bedrooms (not 24-5 Dec): £48.40B/£51.40B

ASKERSWELL SY5292 Map 2

Spyway ★ ♀ £

Village signposted N of A35 Bridport—Dorchester; inn signposted locally; OS Sheet 194 map reference 529933

The cosy and characterful little rooms of this timelessly simple country local have old-fashioned high-backed settles, cushioned wall and window seats, a vast collection of china teacups, harness and a milkmaid's yoke, and a longcase clock; there's also a no-smoking dining area decorated with blue and white china, old oak beams and timber uprights. Shove-ha'penny, table skittles, dominoes and cribbage. The particularly helpful licensee keeps an excellent choice of drinks: Adnams Best and Southwold, Ruddles County and Ushers Best on handpump, 20 very reasonably priced decent wines by the glass, 23 country wines, around 40 whiskies and a big choice of unusual non-alcoholic drinks. Promptly served and reasonably priced, the good bar food includes a range of generous and tasty ploughman's such as hot sausages and tomato pickle or home-cooked ham with pickle (from £3.50), and lots of salads (from £3.95 – the prawn is well liked), as well as three-egg omelettes (£3.25), haddock or plaice (£3.60), evening extras like gammon and egg (£6.25) or 8oz steak (£8.25), and daily specials like vegetable bake (£3.75) or home made steak and onion pie (£4.50). Good views from the big back garden, and plenty of pleasant walks along the paths and bridleways nearby. Eggardon Hill, which the pub's steep lane leads up, is one of the highest in the region, with lovely views of the downs and to the coast. No children. (Recommended by Dr S Willavoys, E A George, Chris and Margaret Southon, Pete and Rosie Flower, Stephen and Julie Brown, Jack and Philip Paxton, Dr and Mrs G H Lewis, K S Pike, Alan Skull, Bill Edwards, Paul and Sue Sexton, Gordon, George and Jeanne Barnwell, Barry A Lynch, John Beeken, J H Bell, JWK)

Free house ~ Licensees Don and Jackie Roderick ~ Real ale ~ Meals and snacks ~ (01308) 485250 ~ Open 11-2.30(3 Sat), 6-11; Sun 12-3, 7-10.30; cl Mon except bank holidays

BISHOPS CAUNDLE ST6913 Map 2

White Hart

A3030

This busy grey slate dining pub makes a welcoming family stop, with crayons and toys in the no-smoking family area. The big prettily floodlit garden has a play area made up of trampolines, a playhouse with slides, and a sandpit, and there's a covered area for sitting outside on those summer days when the weather isn't quite so perfect. The spacious, irregularly shaped bar is furnished with a good variety of seats and tables, dark red curtains, and nice lamps under the handsomely moulded low beams. The ancient panelled walls are attractively decorated with brass trays and farming equipment. Good bar food includes sandwiches (£2.50), a wide range of ploughman's (£4.25), salads (from £5.25), shepherd's pie (£4.95), steak, kidney and ale pie (£5.25), prawn curry (£5.75), trout filled with apple, onion and cheese and poached in dry cider (£7.25), and vegetarian dishes such as lasagne or brie and broccoli en croûte (from £4.95), and daily specials including very good faggots and pork loin; they also do a smaller-appetite menu; puddings (from £2.50). Well kept Badger Best and Tanglefoot on handpump; friendly helpful service; darts, alley skittles on Sundays, fruit machine and piped music. *(Recommended by Marjorie and David Lamb, Cheryl and Keith Roe, Christopher Gallop, Brian Chambers, John Hazel, Gary Roberts, Ann Stubbs, Major and Mrs E M Warwick, Keith Widdowson)*

Badger ~ Manager Gordon Pitman ~ Real ale ~ Meals and snacks ~ (01963) 23301 ~ Children in eating area of bar only ~ Open 11-2.30, 6.30-11 ~ Bedroom: £14/£28

BRIDPORT SY4692 Map 1

George £

South St

We've often wondered why we get so few letters about this lively and unusual town pub, which is a good deal more civilised than first impressions might suggest. Divided by a coloured tiled hallway, the two sizeable bars – one is served by a hatch from the main lounge – are full of friendly old-fashioned charm and atmosphere. There are nicely spaced old dining tables and country seats and wheelback chairs, big rugs on tiled floors, a mahogany bar counter, fresh flowers, and a winter log fire, along with an interesting pre-fruit-machine ball game. The characterful barman, Tim Quirk, serves a good range of drinks including well kept Palmers Best, 200 and IPA on handpump, up to seven brands of calvados, decent wines by the half-bottle or glass, local apple juice and freshly squeezed orange and grapefruit; there's an espresso coffee machine. The wide range of bar food relies heavily on fresh local produce, and includes sandwiches (from £1.75), home-made soup (£1.90), hot sausages and french bread (£2.50), sausages and mash (£3.15), ratatouille or ploughman's (£3.50), omelettes, chicken breast in mushroom and calvados sauce (£3.95), kedgeree (£4.75), kidneys sautéed in madeira or whole grilled fresh plaice (£4.95) and a plate of cold home-cooked meats or entrecote steak (£6.50), and home-made puddings such as apple tart; you can usually see the licensee at work preparing your meal. Two tables are no smoking. You can only have an evening meal out of season if you make a reservation; Radio 3 or maybe classical, jazz or opera tapes. *(Recommended by Stephen and Julie Brown, Jack and Philip Paxton, Paul M Harris, George Atkinson, R C Morgan; more reports please)*

Palmers ~ Tenant John Mander ~ Real ale ~ Meals and snacks (not Sun or bank holidays – and see note above about evening meals) ~ (01308) 423187 ~ Children in restaurant only ~ Open 10am-11pm (8.30am for coffee every day) ~ Bedrooms: £18.50/£37

BURTON BRADSTOCK SY4889 Map 1

Three Horseshoes

Mill St

Readers consistently tell us how enthusiastically welcoming and chatty the licensees and locals are at this well placed family-run thatched inn. The pleasant roomy bar has an enjoyable homely atmosphere, an open fire, comfortable seating, and Palmers 200, Bridport, IPA and Tally Ho kept under light blanket pressure. Nicely presented promptly served bar food includes burgers (from £2.40), lunchtime sandwiches including a good crab one (from £2.10), several lunchtime ploughman's from (£3.70), steak and kidney pie (£4.15), fish and chips (£4.45), lasagne, seafood lasagne or mushroom and nut fettucine (£4.95), chicken breast (£6.75), crab salad (£8.50) and puddings (from £2.30); usual children's meals (£2.70). There are a couple of evening extras like Cantonese prawns (£6.20), beef curry (£6.40) and sirloin steak (£10.35). The menu is quite an achievement – it seems unlikely that so many groan-inducing jokes have ever before been collected together in one place, but we can match them with the words of one of our readers who told us 'jokey menu takes a bit of swallowing'. The dining room is no smoking, and there's an unusual game called carom, an intriguing mix of shove-ha'penny and snooker; table football and pool in family room; sporadic piped music. There are tables on the lawn, and Chesil beach and cliff walks are only 400 yards away. The pretty village is worth strolling around. *(Recommended by PM, AM, C and E M Watson, Eric Locker, Alan Skull, Ian Phillips, Basil Minson, Julia Duplock, Ron Gentry, JM, PM)*

Palmers ~ Tenant Bill Attrill ~ Real ale ~ Meals and snacks ~ (01308) 897259 ~ Children in eating area and small family room adjoining garden ~ Open 11-2.30, 6-11; Sun 12-3, 6.30-10.30 ~ Bedrooms: £19.50B/£31B

CERNE ABBAS ST6601 Map 2

Red Lion ♀

Long St

The bar at this neatly kept, light and cottagey inn has a handsome wooden counter, wheelback chairs on the green patterned carpet, a good deal of china, plants on tables and two more little areas leading off. Parts of the comfortable building are a lot older than the unassuming mid-Victorian frontage suggests; the fine fireplace in the bar for instance is 16th-c work. There's a relaxed and friendly welcome, especially from the white terrier Gemma who's probably warming you up in the hope of titbits. Well cooked food – most of the meals are available in a reduced size for those with a smaller appetite – includes sandwiches (from £2.25), soup (£1.85), filled baked potatoes (from £3.40), good ploughman's (from £4), omelettes (from £4), pancakes (from £4.50), several vegetarian pasta dishes (£4.95), local trout (£6.95), grilled loin of pork (£7.50) and steaks (from £8.95), with puddings such as apricot strudel (from £1.60). Daily specials might include pheasant breasts in cream and sherry sauce, beef ragout, salmon and seafood lasagne, haunch of venison in red wine, cod in ale batter and chicken fricassee in lemon and garlic sauce. Some of the vegetables come from local gardeners and allotments. Well kept Wadworths IPA and 6X and two interesting guests on handpump, and a decent wine list, with several available by the glass; good cheerful service; darts, skittle alley and piped music. There's a secluded flower-filled garden. *(Recommended by Anthony Barnes, Joan and Michel Hooper-Immins, Cheryl and Keith Roe, Brian and Anna Marsden, Mike and Heather Barnes, Jack and Philip Paxton, James House, Jane Basso, Paul Carter, Galen Strawson, A and J Hoadley, Lynn Sharpless, Bob Eardley)*

Free house ~ Licensees Brian and Jane Cheeseman ~ Real ale ~ Meals and snacks ~ (01300) 341441 ~ Children in eating areas and bowling alley ~ Open 11.30-3, 6.30-11 ~ Bedrooms: £22B/£44B

Tipping is not normal for bar meals, and not usually expected.

Royal Oak ♀

Long Street

This cheery Tudor pub has been totally repainted and the fireplaces which were once the home of dried flower arrangements now boast warming winter log fires. Sturdy oak beams line the three friendly flagstoned communicating rooms, the neat courses of stonework are decked out with antique china, brasses and farm tools, and there's lots of shiny black panelling. Well kept Flowers IPA and Original, Morlands Old Speckled Hen and guests like Ringwood Best, Shepherd Neame Spitfire, Tisbury Best or Wadworths 6X on handpump from the uncommonly long bar counter, and 14 wines by the glass. The good range of well cooked straightforward bar meals is especially popular at lunchtimes when the very friendly service may slow down a bit: vegetarian lasagne or kidney beans and vegetables in a spicy sauce with breadcrumbs and cheese or grilled fresh plaice (£4.75), fisherman's pie or steak and kidney pie (£5.25), hot chicken, bacon and mushroom salad or fresh Portland crab (£5.95), rump steak filled with a mild curry stuffing in curry sauce or fish delight – king prawns in filo pastry and butterfly prawns in seafood sauce (£6.50), and puddings such as Jamaican crunch (£2.95); they can produce dishes for special dietary needs, with a little bit of notice if possible. There are seats and tables in the enclosed back garden, and seats at the front where you can watch the world go by. *(Recommended by Joan and Michel Hooper-Immins, Mr and Mrs J Boler, Jane Warren, David Holloway, Anthony Barnes, Lynn Sharpless, Bob Eardley, Basil Minson, Jack and Philip Paxton, Galen Strawson, D Packman, James House)*

Free house ~ Licensees Brendan and Liz Malone ~ Real ale ~ Meals and snacks ~ Children welcome ~ (01300) 341797 ~ Open 11-3, 5.30-11

nr CHIDEOCK SY4292 Map 2

Anchor

Seatown; signposted off A35 from Chideock

The splendid position of this friendly and welcoming pub, just a few steps from a nearly idyllic cove beach, and nestling dramatically beneath the 617-foot Golden Cap pinnacle, makes for quite a bustling holiday atmosphere in summer – not to mention that it almost straddles the Dorset Coast Path. Seats and tables on the spacious front terrace are ideally placed for lovely sea and cliff views, but you'll have to get there early in summer to bag a spot. Our own preference is to visit out of season, when the crowds have gone and the cosy little bars seem especially snug. The two little rooms have warming winter fires, some sea pictures and interesting local photographs, a few fossils and shells, simple but comfortable seats around neat tables, and low white-planked ceilings; the family room and a further corner of the bar are no smoking, and there are friendly animals (especially the cats). Service is charming and obliging whatever time of year you go. Good bar food includes home-made soup (£2.75), sandwiches (from £1.95, crab £3.75), filled baked potatoes (from £3.25), burgers (from £3.75), ploughman's (£3.95), breaded plaice, curry or pizzas (from £4.95), hot spicy chicken breast (£5.95) and specials such as stuffed peppers (£4.95), beef in Guinness (£5.95), venison pie (£6.25), duck breast stir fry (£6.95) or steak with green peppercorns (£8.45); children's dishes (from £2.45), afternoon clotted cream teas in summer. Well kept Palmers 200, Bridport, IPA and Tally Ho on handpump, under light blanket pressure in winter only; freshly squeezed orange juice, and a decent little wine list. Darts, shove-ha'penny, table skittles, cribbage, dominoes, fruit machine (summer only), a carom board, shut-the-box, and piped, mainly classical, music. There are fridges and toasters in the bedrooms so you can make your own breakfast and eat it looking out over the sea. The licensees now also run the Ferry at Salcombe. *(Recommended by Mark Matthewman, Jeremy Condliffe, E A George, M Carr, Niki and Terry Pursey, Giles Quick, Clem Stephens, Stephen and Julie Brown, P Gillbe, Erick Locker, Marjorie and David Lamb, Ted George, D G Clarke, Mr and Mrs D Towle, George Atkinson, Jeanne Cross, Paul Silvestri, K S Pike, S Lonie, S Tait, Christopher Gallop, Jenny and Brian Seller, Basil Minson, Eric Locker, Richard Dolphin, Jeff Davies)*

Palmers ~ Tenants David and Sadie Miles ~ Real ale ~ Meals and snacks (not winter Sun evenings) ~ (01297) 489215 ~ Well behaved children welcome ~ Folk, blues or jazz most Sat evenings ~ Open 11-11; Sun 12-10.30; 11-2.30, 6-11 in winter ~ Bedrooms: £16.50/£33

nr CHRISTCHURCH SZ1696 Map 2

Fishermans Haunt

Winkton: B3347 Ringwood road nearly 3 miles N of Christchurch

Not far from the New Forest, this creeper-covered hotel is a good stop for anglers as the River Avon runs alongside the grounds, and the tranquil back garden with tables among the shrubs, roses and other flowers is close to weirs on the river. The building looks especially good at night when the fairy lights are lit. Order spring water and it may come from the 17th-c well in one of the series of interconnecting rooms, which are filled with a variety of furnishings on a heavily patterned carpet, and eye-catching adornments, from copper, brass and plates to stuffed fish and fishing pictures, and oryx and reindeer heads. At one end of the chain of rooms big windows look out on the neat front garden, and at the other there's a fruit machine and video game; one area is no smoking. Good value straightforward bar food under the new licensee includes sandwiches (from £2; toasties from £2.50), soup (£1.75), sausages, onion rings and chips (£3.50), chicken nuggets (£3.95) and salads or scampi (£4.75), with specials like steak and kidney pie, lasagne or fisherman's pie (from £4.50); children's meals (£2.95); well kept Bass, Gales Best and HSB and Ringwood Fortyniner on handpump, and a wide selection of Gales country wines; cheerful staff, piped music. *(Recommended by D P and J A Sweeney, P Gillbe, Wayne Brindle; more reports please)*

George Gale & Co Ltd ~ Manager Kevin A Crowley ~ Real ale ~ Meals and snacks (till 10) ~ Restaurant ~ Children welcome ~ (01202) 484071 ~ Open 10.30-2.30, 5-11; Sat 10.30-11; Sun 12-10.30 ~ Bedrooms: £32(£36B)/£54(£59B)

CHURCH KNOWLE (Isle of Purbeck) SY9481 Map 2

New Inn ♀

This partly thatched pub was closed when we went to press, for refurbishments after a fire; they'll be open again when this Guide reaches the bookshops. The licensee tells us the beamed interior will look better than ever with restored furniture, new carpets, and all the other little things that gave this inn its charm. A new chef will prepare healthy traditional English dishes from fresh local ingredients, so expect lots of fresh fish, game pies, lasagne and vegetarian dishes, and old-fashioned puddings. Well kept Devenish Royal Wessex, Flowers Original and a guest such as Boddingtons or Whitbreads Castle Eden. Their dozen or so very reasonably priced wines are all available in two sizes of glass. Good range of coffees and other hot drinks. When the local post office closed recently this became the first pub in the county to serve as local village post office and shop, and you can generally buy locally made cheese to take away. You can hire the skittle alley for functions. Plenty of tables in the good-sized garden, which has fine views of the Purbeck hills. No dogs; camping in two fields at the back but you need to book beforehand. *(Recommended by M G Hart, David Holloway, Eric Locker, Hanns P Golez, Richard Siebert, Christopher Gallop, David Mead, Dr and Mrs J H Hills, Andy Thwaites)*

Greenalls (Whitbreads) ~ Tenant Maurice Estop ~ Real ale ~ Meals and snacks ~ Restaurant ~ (01929) 480357 ~ Children in eating area of bar ~ Open 11-3, 6-11, possibly all day Sat and Sun and possibly cl Mon Nov-April

---

If you stay overnight in an inn or hotel, they are allowed to serve you an alcoholic drink at any hour of the day or night.

CORFE CASTLE (Isle of Purbeck) SY9681 Map 2

Fox 🍺

West Street, off A351; from town centre, follow dead-end Car Park sign behind church

The licensees have kept a really traditional feel in this cosy, characterful old inn – no doubt helped by the fact that it's been run by the same family for over 50 years. The pub itself is made from the same stone as the evocative castle ruins that rise up from behind the very pleasant suntrap back garden, and it seems likely they were both built around the same time. The tiny front bar has small tables and chairs squeezed in, a painting of the castle in its prime among other pictures above the panelling, old-fashioned iron lamps, and hatch service. An ancient well was discovered in the lounge bar during restoration, and it's now on display there, under glass and effectively lit from within. There's also a pre-1300 stone fireplace, and another alcove has further ancient stonework and a number of fossils. Promptly served wholesome bar food includes sandwiches (from £1.95), home-made soup (£1.90), filled baked potatoes (from £3.15), well presented ploughman's (from £3.40), ham, egg and chips (£4.20), home-made steak and kidney pie or plaice (£4.75), daily specials like walnut and lentil bake (£4.75), crab salad (£6.55) and sirloin steak au poivre (£8.60), and puddings (from £2.05). Well kept Eldridge Pope Thomas Hardy and Royal Oak, Gibbs Mew Bishops Tipple, Greene King Abbot, Ind Coope Burton and Wadworths 6X tapped from the cask; good dry white wine. Reached by a pretty flower-hung side entrance, the garden is divided into secluded areas by flowerbeds and a twisted apple tree, and really comes into its own in summer. The countryside surrounding this National Trust village is worth exploring, and there's a local museum opposite. *(Recommended by P Stallard, David Holloway, Eric Locker, Hanns P Golez, Chris Westmoreland, Ann and Colin Hunt, D Eberlin, Richard Siebert, B and K Hypher, D P and J A Sweeney, Alan Skull, Nigel Clifton, Jack and Philip Paxton, Andy Thwaites, Marjorie and David Lamb, C A Hall)*

Free house ~ Licensees Miss A L Brown and G B White ~ Real ale ~ Meals and snacks ~ (01929) 480449 ~ Open 11-3(2.30 winter), 6-11; closed 25 Dec

Greyhound

A351

The new licensees here are working hard to offer sightseers everything they might need for a comfortable modern-day visit. Cyclists can leave their bikes in the shed while they wander round the village, and you can read about the village in one of the little history books placed alongside fresh flowers on every table. Children are welcome here, and there's a no-smoking family area. Lots of paintings and brasses have been added to the three small low-ceilinged areas of the main bar, which also have mellowed oak panelling and old photographs of the town on the walls. There are benches outside at the front, and beneath the battlements of the castle and opening on to Castle Bridge a new courtyard at the back has plenty of seating. The landlord is also working on a new garden. The popular menu has been perked up and now includes lots of home-made dishes and some fresh fish: generous helpings of filled baked potatoes (from £2.75, crab £3.75), ploughman's (from £3.25), home-made pizzas (from £3.50), garlic mushrooms (£3.95), chilli (£4), fisherman's pie (£5.25), lasagne (£5.50), steak and ale pie (£5.90), local crab salad (£8.50), seafood platter (£9.50), lobster (£10); puddings like treacle tart, death by chocolate or fresh fruit salad (£2.25); prompt cheery service. Well kept Boddingtons, Flowers Original and local Poole Best on handpump. Sensibly placed darts, pool, cribbage, dominoes, fruit machine and juke box. There are benches outside at the front. Dogs welcome in one area; the pub can get crowded in season. *(Recommended by Hanns P Golez, Derek Patey, David Mead, James and Jojo Newman, Brian and Anna Marsden, Chris Westmoreland, Jack and Philip Paxton, D P and J A Sweeney, John and Joan Nash; more reports please)*

Whitbreads ~ Lease: Mike and Louisa Barnard ~ Real ale ~ Meals and snacks ~ (01929) 480205 ~ Children welcome in family room and other areas ~ Occasional live pop and folk music ~ Open 11-11; Sun 12-10.30; 11-3, 6.30-11, but possibly all day in winter

CORSCOMBE ST5105 Map 2

Fox

On outskirts, towards Halstock

Dorset Dining Pub of the Year

The landlord here is determined that his cosy thatched house should retain a real pubby atmosphere where locals can comfortably consume bubble and squeak and a pint, yet at the same time he does attract a smarter set who come for much more imaginative thoughtfully prepared food. Carefully chosen ingredients are supplied by locals and neighbours, and all food is cooked to order – no microwaves or chips – so at busy times there may be a delay. What's on the specials board each day depends very much on what's freshly available that morning: sardines grilled with garlic butter (£3.50), provençale char-grilled vegetables (£3.95), salmon and leek terrine or devilled crabmeat (£4.25), squid fried with garlic and herbs (£4.50), whole grilled plaice, ham hock with mustard and chives or pork chop braised with cider and rosemary (£6.25), rabbit braised with red wine and mustard (£6.95), venison casserole with red wine and thyme (£7.95), chicken breast marinated in yoghurt, garlic, chilli and ginger or barbary duck leg with honey, lemon and black pepper (£8.95) and roast rack of Dorset lamb (£12.75); very good fish soup and filled baguettes on the menu (£4.95). Puddings might include sticky toffee, caramelised pear tart or home-made ice cream (£2.95). Three well kept real ales on handpump might include Exmoor, Fullers London Pride or Smiles Best, and at busy times possibly a fourth tapped straight from the cask. There's home-made elderflower cordial, damson vodka, sloe gin and lemonade, as well as local cider and a good wine list. The room on the right has lots of beautifully polished copper pots, pans and teapots, harness hanging from the beams, small Leech hunting prints and Snaffles prints, Spy cartoons of fox-hunting gentlemen, a long scrubbed pine table (a highly polished smaller one is tucked behind the door), an open fire and a newly laid old floor. In the left-hand room there are built-in wall benches, candles in champagne bottles on the cloth-covered or barrel tables, an assortment of chairs, lots of horse prints, antlers on the beams, two glass cabinets with a couple of stuffed owls in each, and an L-shaped wall settle by the stove in the fireplace; darts, dominoes, bridge on Thursday, and backgammon. A new conservatory is filled with flowers and roses, and has a huge oak table. Tinker the greyhound and the two labradors Cracker and Bramble love a bit of attention. There's a big table in a covered courtyard with hanging baskets, roses and honeysuckle, and further seats across the quiet village lane, on a lawn by the little stream. This is a nice area for walks. *(Recommended by L M Miall, Stephen and Julie Brown, Roger Price, K S Pike, R Voorspuy, Mrs A Wells, Robert and Jill Maltby, Dr and Mrs J H Hills)*

Free house ~ Licensee Martyn Lee ~ Real ale ~ Meals and snacks (not 25 Dec) ~ (01935) 891330 ~ Well behaved children welcome ~ Occasional piano and saxophone player ~ Open 12-2.30, 7-11; 11-11 Sat; 12-10.30 Sun; cl eve 25 Dec

CRANBORNE SU0513 Map 2

Fleur-de-Lys ⇐

B3078 N of Wimborne Minster

This reliable and warmly welcoming old inn makes a particularly pleasant place to stay, probably more comfortable now than it was in the days when Thomas Hardy stayed here while writing *Tess of the d'Urbervilles* – if you fork left past the church you can follow the pretty downland track that he must have visualised Tess taking home to 'Trentridge' (actually Pentridge), after dancing in what's now the garage. A Gothic arch and a pair of ancient stone pillars are said to have come from the ruins of a nearby monastery, while the walls are lined with historical documents and mementoes of some of the other people who have stayed here over the centuries, from Hanging Judge Jeffreys to Rupert Brooke, whose poem about the pub takes pride of place above the fireplace. The oak-panelled lounge bar is attractively modernised, and there's also a more simply furnished beamed public bar with well kept Badger Best and Tanglefoot on handpump, farm cider, and some good malt whiskies. Well liked reasonably priced bar food, including imaginative vegetarian dishes, might be broccoli or seafood pancake (£3.95), lamb, apricot and leek pie or salmon and broccoli bake (£4.95), steak and kidney pudding or spinach and cream cheese cannelloni (£5.25), breast of chicken filled with stilton and wrapped in bacon (£8.95) and noisettes of lamb with rosemary and redcurrant sauce (£9.95). It's best to arrive early for their good value Sunday lunch. The friendly landlord has been here 19 years now. Darts, shove-ha'penny, dominoes, cribbage, fruit machine, and piped music. There are swings and a slide on the lawn behind the car park. Bedrooms are comfortable and spacious, and it's an ideal base for exploring the area. *(Recommended by John and Mary Bartolf, P and M Rudlin, Joy and Peter Heatherley, Colin Fisher, Ian Jones, Dr and Mrs A H Young, Helen Pickering, Pat and Robert Watt, E G Parish, H T Flaherty, Robert and Jill Maltby, D Marsh)*

Badger ~ Tenant Charles Hancock ~ Real ale ~ Meals and snacks ~ (01725) 517282 ~ Children in eating area of bar and dining room ~ Open 10.30-3, 6(7 winter)-11 ~ Bedrooms: £26(£29B)/£36(£45B)

DORCHESTER SY6890 Map 2

Kings Arms 🛏

High East St

This rather elegant Georgian coaching inn had strong links with Nelson, and the handsome first-floor bow window is memorable from Thomas Hardy's *Mayor of Casterbridge*. There are some interesting old maps and pictures, as well as a historic photograph showing Hardy here with a 1915 film crew. The most popular tables in the spaciously comfortable bar are those around the capacious fireplace, full of eaters enjoying the well presented fairly straightforward bar food: soup (£1.60), sandwiches (from £2.25), ploughman's or chilli (£4.95), lasagne (£5.25), fish and chips (£5.50), half roast chicken, steak, kidney and mushroom pie, chicken pie or beefburger (£5.95), smoked salmon croissant (£6.25), grilled salmon (£6.95), and three vegetarian dishes like mushroom balti (£6.65); puddings like black forest gateau (from £2.25); they also have evening grills and a coffee shop. Lunchtime service can slow down if they're busy but the neatly dressed staff are consistently friendly and obliging. Well kept Boddingtons, Courage Directors and Flowers Original on handpump, a range of malt whiskies and fruit wines from the long mahogany bar counter; fruit machine, piped music. *(Recommended by Brian and Anna Marsden, Mark Matthewman, Stephen and Julie Brown, Anthony Barnes, John and Joan Nash, Sue Lee, Cheryl and Keith Roe, Jack and Philip Paxton, Ian Phillips, Keith Archer)*

Greenalls ~ Manager Stephen Walmsley ~ Real ale ~ Meals and snacks ~ Restaurant ~ (01305) 265353 ~ Children welcome in restaurant ~ Live entertaiment Tues and Thurs evening ~ Open 11-2.30, 6-11; 11-11 Fri and Sat ~ Bedrooms: /£46.45B

EAST CHALDON SY7983 Map 2

Sailors Return

Village signposted from A352 Wareham—Dorchester; from village green, follow Dorchester, Weymouth signpost; note that the village is also known as Chaldon Herring; Ordnance Survey sheet 194, map reference 790834

This delightful long low whitewashed building is always popular, but even on a busy summer day – when it's probably worth booking – the really friendly service and well presented bar food remain as good as ever. It's been sympathetically renovated over the years by its jovial Welsh landlord, but the cheerfully welcoming bar still keeps much of its original character. The newer part has open beams showing the roof above, uncompromisingly plain and unfussy furnishings, and old notices for decoration; the dining area has solid old tables in nooks and crannies. A wide range of very tasty meals generously served on nice big plates takes in sandwiches, soup, filled baked potatoes,

. burgers, vegetarian meals and popular daily specials such as steak and kidney pie (£5.25), pork, apple and stilton casserole (£5.50), ham hock with mandarin and pineapple sauce (£5.75), local plaice (£7.50) and half shoulder of lamb (£8.75); it's worth coming early if you plan to eat, especially on Sunday, when the good value roast is popular. The restaurant is partly no smoking. Well kept Wadworths 6X, Whitbreads Strong Country and Hook Norton Old Hookey on handpump, country wines, farm cider, and malt whiskies. Darts, shove-ha'penny, table skittles, dominoes, and piped music. It's nicely tucked away in a tranquil spot near Lulworth Cove, and benches, picnic tables and log seats on the grass in front look down over cow pastures to the village. From nearby West Chaldon a bridleway leads across to join the Dorset Coast Path by the National Trust cliffs above Ringstead Bay. *(Recommended by Chris and Margaret Southon, Jerry and Alison Oakes, Marjorie and David Lamb, Sue and David Heaton, John and Joan Nash, Ian Phillips, E A George)*

Free house ~ Licensees Bob and Pat Hodson ~ Real ale ~ Meals and snacks ~ Restaurant ~ (01305) 853847 ~ Children welcome in eating area of bar ~ Open 11-2.30, 6-11; Sun 12-2.30, 6-10.30

EAST KNIGHTON SY8185 Map 2

Countryman 🍽 ⌂

Just off A352 Dorchester—Wareham; OS Sheet 194 map reference 811857

The neatly comfortable, long, carpeted main bar of this friendly bustling pub has a fire at either end, a mixture of tables and wheelback chairs and relaxing sofas. It opens into several other smaller areas, including a no-smoking family room, a games bar with pool and darts, and a carvery. Quickly served and in big helpings, the wide range of popular good value bar food includes well filled sandwiches or baguettes (from £1.75), soup (£1.95), ploughman's (from £4.25), a good few vegetarian meals like vegetable crumble (from £4.95), salads (from £5.25), prawns, lemon sole or scampi (£6.10) and gammon (£7.95), also daily specials like pasta with tomato and herb sauce and cheese and chive topping (£5.25), pork steak with creamy cider and apple sauce (£5.95) or rack of lamb with garlic and rosemary (£7.25); home-made puddings (£2.45) and children's meals (from £2.45); they do a good carvery (£9.45, two courses). Well kept Courage Best, John Smiths, Ringwood Best and Old Thumper, Wadworths 6X, and a rotating guest like Morlands Old Speckled Hen on handpump; Scrumpy Jack cider, good choice of wines, and courteous well trained staff; piped music. Well behaved dogs allowed. There are tables and children's play equipment out in the garden as well as some toys inside. *(Recommended by Ann and Colin Hunt, Brian and Anna Marsden, Nigel Clifton, Andrea Carr, Jason Good, R Walden, Mr and Mrs D C Stevens, Jerry and Alsion Oakes, Alan Skull, Bruce Bird, Chris Westmoreland)*

Free house ~ Licensees Jeremy and Nina Evans ~ Real ale ~ Meals and snacks ~ Restaurant ~ (01305) 852666 ~ Children welcome ~ Open 11-3, 6-11; cl 25 Dec ~ Bedrooms: £35B/£45B

FARNHAM ST9515 Map 2

Museum 🍽 ♀ ⌂

Village signposted off A354 Blandford Forum—Salisbury

An unassuming exterior belies this very characterful old place, with an eccentric landlord who dashes out of the kitchen to make a joke, then rushes back to prepare another excellent meal – there may be a short wait during busy times. As well as the usual bar meals there's a wide range of regularly changing dishes such as home-made mushroom soup (£2.75), warm salad of chicory, blue cheese and walnuts (£4.75), scrambled eggs with anchovies (£4.95), Spanish omelette (£5.75), smoked fish pie (£6.50), salmon fishcakes with spicy tomato sauce, warm smoked chicken and asparagus salad, sauté kidneys and bacon or rustic chicken with rigatoni (£6.95). The evening menu is a bit more expensive and might include grilled fillets of red mullet with spinach and bacon or breast of pheasant with Drambuie and pink grapefruit sauce (£11.25), rack of lamb with candied lemons or beef stroganoff (£11.95), grilled dover sole with lemon butter (£12.95), and puddings like marron glacé or Cointreau pancakes (£3.50). There's a calmly civilised feel to the Coopers Bar, which has green cloth-cushioned seats set into walls and windows, local pictures by Robin Davidson, an inglenook fireplace, and piped classical music. Very well kept Wadworths 6X and changing guests such as Bass, Brakspears or Smiles Best on handpump, as well as a large range of decent wines and around two dozen malt whiskies; darts, pool, trivia machine and juke box. There's a most attractive small brick-walled dining conservatory, leading out to a sheltered terrace with white tables under cocktail parasols, and beyond an arched wall is a garden with swings and a colourful tractor. Spotless bedrooms are in converted former stables. *(Recommended by Ian Phillips, J Morris, Dr and Mrs M Beale, Joy and Peter Heatherley, John and Mary Bartolf, Gwen and Peter Andrews, P Gillbe, J H Bell, Paul Bachelor, Robert and Jill Maltby, Guy Consterdine)*

Free house ~ Licensee John Barnes ~ Real ale ~ Meals and snacks (service stops at 1.45 lunchtime) ~ Restaurant ~ (01725) 516261 ~ Children in eating areas and restaurant ~ Occasional live entertainment ~ Open 11-3(12 Sat), 6-11; cl 25 Dec ~ Bedrooms: £40B/£50B

GODMANSTONE SY6697 Map 2
Smiths Arms

A352 N of Dorchester

Time stands still at this 15th-c thatched building which was originally a smithy. It's absolutely tiny – there are only six tables inside, and they couldn't add any more even if they wanted to; one of the smallest pubs in the country, it measures just 12 by 4 m (39 by 14 ft). There are further seats and tables outside on a crazy-paved terrace, or on the grassy mound by the narrow River Cerne. The little bar has some antique waxed and polished small pews hugging the walls (there's also one elegant little high-backed settle), long wooden stools and chunky tables, National Hunt racing pictures and some brass plates on the walls, and an open fire. Well kept Ringwood Best tapped from casks behind the bar; friendly, helpful staff (the landlord is quite a character); dominoes, trivia, cribbage and piped music. Very good value tasty home-made food typically includes sandwiches (from £1.55), ploughman's (from £3.20), giant sausage (£2.85), quiche (£4.15), chilli con carne (£4.15), a range of salads (from £3.95), home-cooked ham (£4.95), scampi (£5.75), daily specials such as curried prawn lasagne or topside of beef and steak and kidney pie (£4.95) and puddings (£1.85). Note they don't allow children inside. A pleasant walk leads over Cowdon Hill to the River Piddle. *(Recommended by David Holloway, Jack and Philip Paxton, James Nunns, Mr and Mrs Bonner, John Hazel, Bill Edwards)*

Free house ~ Licensees John and Linda Foster ~ Real ale ~ Meals and snacks (till 9.45) ~ (01300) 341236 ~ Open 11-3, 6-11; cl Jan

KINGSTON (Isle of Purbeck) SY9579 Map 2
Scott Arms

B3069

One reader told us that even if this was the worst pub in the world it would still be worth visiting for the magnificent view of Corfe Castle from the interesting well kept garden. In fact it's doing very well at the moment, with a good atmosphere, and bar food that we regard very highly. They do get very busy (even in winter), but the rambling warren-like rooms are capable of absorbing more people than you might think. All have old panelling, stripped stone walls, some fine antique prints and a friendly, chatty feel; an attractive room overlooks the garden, and there's a decent extension well liked by families. Very good bar food includes lots of fresh fish from Brixham like lemon or dover sole, john dory or bass (all about £8.95), as well as home-made soup (£2.50), mushrooms in cream and garlic (£3.25), baked avocado with crab and prawn (£3.50), a big proper ploughman's (£3.95), steak and kidney pie (£6.25), quite hot and flavoursome curries and chilli (£5.75), excellent specials such as seasonal dressed crab (£7.95), chicken stuffed with spinach and bacon in red wine and strawberry sauce (£7.95); good puddings (£2.50), and children's meals (£3.50); part of the dining room is no smoking. Well kept Greenalls Original, Ringwood Best and a guest like Flowers Original or Wadworths 6X on handpump; efficient service from pleasant, smiling staff; darts, backgammon, shut the box and dominoes. *(Recommended by Jack and Philip Paxton, David Mead, E G Parish, James and Jojo Newman, Chris Westmoreland, Derek Patey, B and K Hypher, John and Joan Nash, Alan Skull, James House, P Gillbe, Doreen and Brian Hardham, P J Caunt, WHBM)*

Free house ~ Lease: Simon Trevis ~ Real ale ~ Meals and snacks; not 25 Dec ~ (01929) 480270 ~ Children welcome except in one small bar ~ Acoustic blues every other Weds ~ Open 11-2.30, 6-11(maybe all day in Aug); letting room £40 a night

LANGTON HERRING SY6182 Map 2

Elm Tree ⑪

Village signposted off B3157

There's plenty of praise from readers for the very well prepared imaginative up-to-the-minute daily specials they serve at this slate-roofed cottage: creamed home-made tagliatelle with artichokes and black olives or baked aubergines stuffed with sun-dried tomatoes and mozzarella cheese (£4.95), fried scallops with artichoke hearts, pancetta and bacon (£5.75), braised oxtails in Guinness with winter vegetables (£7.75), fritto misto of red mullet and salmon (£8.95) and fried venison fillets with asparagus and fettucini (£11.50). The bar menu has the usual standards alongside more interesting choices: sandwiches (from £1.95), soup (£2.50), filled baked potatoes (from £2.50), ploughman's or ciabatta with goat's cheese and tomatoes (£3.75), hot garlic bread filled with hot roast beef (£3.25), lasagne (£6.50), steak and ale pie (£6.95), cider, pork and apple casserole (£7.50) and baked crab mornay (£7.95), puddings like banana split or butterscotch banana fritters (from £2.75) and the usual children's menu (from £2.25). There may be a bit of a wait for food when they get busy. The Portland spy ring is said to have met in the main beamed and carpeted rooms, which have walls festooned with copper, brass and bellows, cushioned window seats, red leatherette stools, windsor chairs, and lots of tables; one has some old-fashioned settles and an inglenook. The traditionally furnished extension gives more room for diners. Boddingtons and Greenalls Original kept under light blanket pressure, country wines, mulled wine in winter and elderflower spritzer and Pimms in summer. Outside in the pretty flower-filled sunken garden are colourful hanging baskets, flower tubs, and tables; a track leads down to the Dorset Coast Path, which here skirts the eight-mile lagoon enclosed by Chesil Beach. *(Recommended by Kim Maidment, Philip Vernon, Jenny and Brian Seller, D Mead, Brian and Anna Marsden, D Eberlin, Dr S Willavoys, D C Pressey, Basil Minson, P Gillbe, Howard Clutterbuck)*

Greenalls ~ Tenants Roberto D'Agostino, L M Horlock ~ Real ale ~ Meals and snacks ~ (01305) 871257 ~ Children welcome in eating area of bar ~ Open 10.30-3, 6.30-11

LODERS SY4994 Map 1

Loders Arms ⇐

Off A3066 just N of Bridport; can also be reached off A35 E of Bridport, via Uploders

In a pretty stonebuilt village of largely thatched cottages tucked into a sheltered fold of these steep Dorset hills, this pub has been transformed in the last few years. With careful refurbishment, it's kept a friendly and unspoilt atmosphere, with an unhurried and relaxed feel even when it's busy; and grafted on to this traditional background is cooking that's quite out of the ordinary. So for many the small restaurant is now the main attraction here. The smallish long bar, however, still well used by local people, is welcoming and comfortable, with a log fire, maybe piped classical music, and amiable dogs; well kept Palmers Bridport, 200 and IPA, a good choice of wines, good service. The food runs from delicious huge filled baguettes (from £3, smoked salmon and cream cheese £3.50), with lots of generously served fresh fish and a good Sunday roast (£5.95). The menu changes day by day: dishes which we or readers have particularly enjoyed recently include black pudding with home-made banana chutney or devilled kidneys (£3.50), smoked chicken breast with mango salad (£3.95), pork tenderloin with horseradish and sour cream sauce (£8.95), duck breast with anchovy sauce (£9.25) and scallops in fennel purée or flambéed in pernod (£9.50). Vegetables are carefully cooked and served in profusion, and inventive puddings (£3) have included a sticky date toffee one served with butterscotch sauce and yoghurt – a somewhat surprising success. There's a skittle alley. *(Recommended by Paul and Sue Sexton, Roger Price, Deborah and Ian Carrington, Frances Pennell, John and Sheila French, H G Robertson, Mr and Mrs D V Morris, D C and J V Whitman)*

Palmers ~ Tenant Roger Flint ~ Real ale ~ Meals and snacks (not Sun evening) ~ Restaurant ~ (01308) 422431 ~ Open 11(11.30 Mon-Fri in winter)-3, 6-11; Sun 12-10.30 in summer and possibly in winter; cl 25 Dec ~ Bedrooms: £25B/£35S(£45B)

LYME REGIS SY3492 Map 1

Pilot Boat ♀

Bridge Street

This unpretentious seaside inn is handy for a meal after a day on the beach. The light, airy bar is decorated with local pictures, Navy and helicopter photographs, lobster-pot lamps, sharks' heads, an interesting collection of local fossils, a model of one of the last sailing ships to use the harbour, and a notable collection of sailors' hat ribands. At the back, there's a long and narrow lounge bar overlooking the little River Lym; darts, dominoes, cribbage. Bar food includes sandwiches (from £1.35, delicious crab £2.95), home-made soup (£1.95), ploughman's (£3.25), crab pâté (£3.50), salads (from £5.25), avocado and sweetcorn bake (£5.50), steak and kidney pie (£5.95), pork and cider casserole (£6.25), several fish dishes such as local trout (£7.50) or whole grilled lemon sole (£9.50), steaks (from £9.50), specials such as plaice fillets stuffed with asparagus (£7.50), and children's dishes (from £1.95, not just burgers and fish fingers). The restaurant is no smoking. Well kept Palmers Bridport, IPA and Tally Ho on handpump, and a decent wine and liqueur list. The licensees run another Lyme Regis pub, the Cobb Arms, which has bedrooms. There are seats on a terrace outside. *(Recommended by Niki and Terry Pursey, Don and Shirley Parrish, Jane Warren, Joan and Michel Hooper-Immins, Mrs Cynthia Archer, Marjorie and David Lamb, M E Wellington, Judith Reay, David Gittins, Chris and Kate Lyons, David Holloway, Jill and Antony Townsend, Bruce Bird, Ian Phillips, M E Wellington, Nigel Warr, R C Morgan, D P and J A Sweeney)*

Palmers ~ Tenants Bill and Caroline Wiscombe ~ Real ale ~ Meals and snacks (till 10 in summer) ~ Restaurant ~ Lyme Regis (01297) 443242 ~ Children welcome ~ Occasional live entertainment ~ Open 11-3, 6.30-11 (winter 11-2.30, 7-11)

MARNHULL ST7718 Map 2

Blackmore Vale ♀

Burton Street; quiet side street

The wide choice of thoughtfully presented home-made dishes at this warmly welcoming old pub includes sandwiches, soup (£1.95), gammon and egg (£4.95), minced beef pie (£5.45), several vegetarian dishes such as spicy vegetable salsa (£5.60), steak and kidney pie (£5.85), game pie or grilled plaice (£6.95), lamb and mango curry (£7.45), salmon steak (£7.95), tipsy crab pie (£8.75), mixed grill (£10.75), daily specials, and lots of home-made puddings; Friday is fish night, and they generally have three roasts on Sunday. They will bring your food to the garden, where one of the tables is thatched; service can slow down when they're pushed. Parts of the building date back 400 years, when it started out as a brewhouse and bakehouse for the Strangeways Estate; you can still see the entrance to the old bake oven at the end of the bar, near the fireplace. The pub was used by Thomas Hardy in *Tess of the D'Urbervilles* as the model for Rollivers. The comfortably modernised lounge bar is decorated with fourteen guns and rifles, keys, a few horsebrasses and old brass spigots on the beams, and there's a log fire. Well kept Badger Best and Tanglefoot on handpump, farm cider and a good wine list. Cribbage, dominoes, shove-ha'penny, fruit machine, piped music, and a skittle alley; no-smoking dining room. *(Recommended by Joy and Peter Heatherley, C H and P Stride, Derek Wilson, Tony and Wendy Hobden, Anthony Barnes, Mr and Mrs D C Stevens, John Hazel, Keith Stevens, Richard Dolphin)*

Badger ~ Tenants Roger and Marion Hiron ~ Real ale ~ Meals and snacks (till 10pm; 9pm Sun) ~ (01258) 820701 ~ Children over five welcome ~ Open 11.30-2.30(3 Sat), 6.30-11

Crown 🍺 £

B3092

The oak-beamed public bar of this part-thatched 17th-c inn has old settles and elm tables on huge flagstones, window seats cut into thick stone walls, and logs burning in a big stone hearth. The small and comfortable lounge bar has more modern furniture. Reasonably priced bar food under the friendly new licensees includes soup (£2), seafood and mushroom crêpe (£2.50), filled baked potatoes (from £2.80), ploughman's (£3.50), ham, egg and chips (£3.95), chilli, curry, scampi, Chinese sweet and sour with prawn cracker, cheesy leek and potato bake or home-made lasagne (£4.95), salmon en croûte with lemon and parsley filling (£7.95), and daily specials like stir fry duck, sizzling sausage platter, venison in red wine and port, salmon poached in white wine and pork tenderloins in cream, brandy and mushroom sauce; Sunday roasts; children's menu (£2). Well kept Badger Best and Tanglefoot on handpump. Darts, cribbage, dominoes, shove-ha'penny, a skittle alley, fruit machine and piped music. It's very pleasant sitting out by the rose-covered lichened walls looking across to the church, or at picnic tables on the lawn (where there's a swing). This was the model for 'The Pure Drop' at 'Marlott' in *Tess of the d'Urbervilles*. *(Recommended by Derek Wilson, Nick Hawkins, Jacky Andrew, Tony and Wendy Hobden, John Hazel, Brian Chambers)*

Badger ~ Tenants Kevin and Maxine Spragg ~ Real ale ~ Meals and snacks ~ Restaurant ~ (01258) 820224 ~ Children welcome ~ Open 11-3, 6-11 ~ Bedrooms: £15/£30

MILTON ABBAS ST8001 Map 2

Hambro Arms 🍺

This pretty pub nestles in the heart of a late 18th-c landscaped village, its gently winding lane lined by lawns and cream-coloured thatched cottages. The beamed front lounge bar, reached through a maze of stone corridors, has a bow window seat looking down over the houses, captain's chairs and round tables on the carpet, and in winter an excellent log fire. Well kept Boddingtons and Flowers Original on handpump, good wine list and about ten malt whiskies; darts, juke box and fruit machine in the cosy back public bar. Big helpings of bar food include sandwiches (£1.75), soup (£2.25), ploughman's (£3.95) and daily specials like fresh battered or grilled cod (£5.95), grilled whole plaice, fillet of sea bream, poached salmon or pheasant in mushroom and red wine (£6.95), halibut with white wine and mushroom sauce or venison steaks in a rich madeira sauce (£7.95); roast Sunday lunch (£10.50). The outside terrace has some tables and chairs; pool, fruit machine and juke box. *(Recommended by E G Parish, WHBM, P Gillbe, JN, J Muckelt, Andy Jones, Andy and Jill Kassube, John Honnor, M V and J Melling, Dr and Mrs Nigel Holmes)*

Greenalls ~ Tenants Ken and Brenda Baines ~ Real ale ~ Meals and snacks ~ Restaurant ~ (01258) 880233 ~ Children welcome in eating area of bar and restaurant ~ Open 11-11 including Sunday; 11-2.30, 7-11 in winter ~ Bedrooms: £30B/£50B

NETTLECOMBE SY5195 Map 2

Marquis of Lorne 🛏 🍽

Turn E off A3066 Bridport—Beaminster Road 1½ miles N of Bridport. Pass Mangerton Mill and 1 mile after West Milton go straight across the give-way junction. Pub is on left 300 yards up the hill.

Last year the publicans here won our award for licensees of the year, mainly for their splendidly hospitable welcome, but no less for the way they maintain a marvellously traditional atmosphere, serve consistently good food, keep ale very well, and generally run a jolly good pub. Bar food is all listed on blackboard menus and typically includes dishes like home-made soup (£2), sandwiches (from £2.45), ploughman's (£3.75), fresh local asparagus (£3.95), spinach and walnut casserole (£5.95), pork steak marinated in American mustard, yorkshire pudding filled with steak and kidney, spicy vegetable curry or minted lamb chops (£6.25), fresh battered cod (£6.95), lots of fresh fish like local plaice with lime butter (£6.95), salmon, chicken and mackerel with salad and elderflower chutney (£7.25), chicken breast in garlic and herbs (£7.50), and yummy puddings such as treacle tart or sticky toffee pudding; the vegetables are excellent. The bustling main bar has a log fire, mahogany panelling and old prints and photographs around its neatly matching chairs and tables; two dining areas lead off, the smaller of which has another log fire and is no smoking. A wooden-floored snug has darts, dominoes cribbage and table skittles. Well kept Palmers Bridport, 200 or Tally Ho on handpump or tapped straight from the cask, and good wine list with usually around eight by the glass; piped music is mainly classical. Outside, the summer hanging baskets are pretty, and the recently improved big garden has a rustic-style play area among the picnic tables under its apple trees. Good breakfasts include a lovely fruit salad. It's quite a tortuous drive to get to the pub, but you couldn't hope for a more pleasant journey, through lovely peaceful countryside. The earth-fort of Eggardon Hill is close by.
(Recommended by Lynn Sharpless, Bob Eardley, Mrs G W Green, Mr and Mrs J Lyons, Niki and Terry Pursey, Adrian Wood, Dr and Mrs J H Hills, Mr and Mrs M Spring, Gordon, M Gibbons, Ms Egan-Strang, K Guppy, Paul and Sue Sexton, GL and NMS Royal, Mrs G Slade, P J and Avril Hanson, Phillip Orbell, Philip Herbert, D J Taylor)

Palmers ~ Tenants Ian and Anne Barrett ~ Real ale ~ Meals and snacks ~ (01308) 485236 ~ Children welcome in eating area of bar ~ Open 11-2.30, 6(6.30 winter)-11; cl evening 25 Dec ~ Bedrooms: £35S/£55S

OSMINGTON MILLS SY7341 Map 2

Smugglers ♀

Village signposted off A353 NE of Weymouth

Tucked away on the Dorset Coastal Path, with the sea just a short stroll away, this partly thatched stone-built inn gives stunning clifftop views to Weymouth and Portland from its car park. It's easy to see why the pub – known locally as the Smuggs – was considered such a convenient landing place for contraband in the days when it was the refuge of French Peter, King of the smugglers. It's well run and spacious, with shiny black panelling and woodwork dividing the relaxing bar into cosy, friendly areas. Soft red lantern-lights give an atmospheric hue to the stormy sea pictures and big wooden blocks and tackle on the walls, and there are logs burning in an open stove. Some seats are tucked into alcoves and window embrasures, with one forming part of an upended boat. Quickly served by friendly staff, the good reasonably priced bar food includes home-made soup (£2), first-rate filled french sticks (from £3.25), ploughman's (£4), filled baked potatoes (from £4.50), home-made steak and kidney pie (£5.50), and more expensive dishes from the à la carte menu such as wild mushroom and nut stroganoff (£8), pork fillet with chilli, lime and ginger sauce (£9.25), roast duck marinated in ginger and soy sauce with red plum and port wine sauce (£10.75) or rack of lamb (£11.75). Service stays efficient and friendly even when they're busy. Half the restaurant area is no smoking. Well kept Courage Best and Directors, Morlands Old Speckled Hen, Ringwood Old Thumper, Ruddles County and Wadworths 6X on handpump, and about six wines by the glass. Darts, pool and fruit machine are kept sensibly out of the way; also dominoes and shut-the-box – and piped music. There are picnic tables out on crazy paving by a little stream, with a thatched summer bar and a good play area over on a steep lawn; barbecues out here in summer. It gets very busy in high season (there's a holiday settlement just up the lane). *(Recommended by Dr and Mrs A H Young, Eddie Edwards, A Smith, Clive Gilbert, Ian Phillips, PM, AM, J Morris, Joan and Michel Hooper-Immins, J M T Morris, Keith Pollard, Howard and Margaret Buchanan, A Plumb)*

Free house ~ Licensee Bill Bishop ~ Real ale ~ Meals and snacks ~ Restaurant ~ (01305) 833125 ~ Children in restaurant and eating area of bar ~ Occasional Sunday lunchtime jazz or steel bands in summer ~ Open 11-11; 12-10.30 Sun; 11-2.30, 6.30-11 in winter (cl 25 Dec) ~ Bedrooms: £30B/£65B

PIDDLEHINTON SY7197 Map 1
Thimble

B3143

This picturesque thatched pub is approached by a little footbridge over the River Piddle. It's delightfully set in a flower-filled garden with attractive floodlighting at night. The neatly kept and friendly low-beamed bar is simpler than the exterior suggests, although nicely spacious so that in spite of drawing quite a lot of people in the summer it never feels too crowded. There's a handsome open stone fireplace, and a recently discovered deep well. Bar food might include beef, venison and ale pie or chilli (£4.95), pasta or fresh fish (from £5), curries (from £5.50), game pie (£5.95), cajun spiced lamb (£6.30), and steaks (from £9); three very good value Sunday roasts (£5.75). Well kept Badger Hard Tackle, Eldridge Pope Hardy Country, and Ringwood Old Thumper on handpump, along with farm cider and quite a few malt whiskies; friendly service; darts, shove-ha'penny, dominoes and piped music. *(Recommended by Glen Mitton, M L and G Clarke, Joy and Peter Heatherley, R H Rowley, K H Frostick, Stephen and Julie Brown, Jack and Philip Paxton, H E and E A Simpson, James Nunns, Christopher Gallop, Mr and Mrs M Cody, Nigel Clifton, Gordon, John and Sheila French, Bronwen and Steve Wrigley, David Lamb, Julie Peters, Galen Strawson)*

Free house ~ Licensees N R White and V J Lanfear ~ Real ale ~ Meals and snacks ~ (01300) 348270 ~ Children welcome in eating area of bar ~ Open 12-2.30, 7-11

PLUSH ST7102 Map 2
Brace of Pheasants 🍴

Village signposted from B3143 N of Dorchester at Piddletrenthide

This long, low 16th-c thatched cottage has a marvellously relaxed yet civilised atmosphere. Under meticulous licensees the very wide choice of sensibly imaginative bar food might include soup (£2.15), crab savoury (£3.50), ploughman's (from £3.95), asparagus hollandaise or soft herring roes with garlic butter (£3.95), ham, egg and chips (£5.25), venison sausages (£5.75), local plaice (£6.95), pies such as steak and kidney or lamb and rosemary (£6.75), and dishes borrowed from the restaurant menu, such as lemon sole, pork fillet with blue cheese and sherry, rack of lamb with rosemary and redcurrant, and steamed salmon and scallops with watercress sauce (all around £10.50); even the children's menu (from £1.75) is more interesting than the norm. The restaurant and family room are no smoking. The airy beamed bar has good solid tables, some oak window seats as well as the windsor chairs, fresh flowers, a heavy-beamed inglenook at one end with cosy seating inside the old fireplace, and a good log fire at the other. Well kept Flowers Original, Fullers London Pride and Smiles, and they do country wines; darts, alley skittles, and dominoes. The friendly labrador is called Bodger. Behind is a decent-sized play garden with swings, an aviary, a rabbit in a cage and a lawn sloping up towards a rookery. Originally a row of cottages that included the village forge, the pub lies alongside Plush Brook, and an attractive bridleway behind goes to the left of the woods and over to Church Hill. *(Recommended by R H Rowley, James House, Miss B Oakeley, Mr and Mrs D C Stevens, Mr and Mrs J Boler, Stephen and Julie Brown, Dr and Mrs M Beale, M Carr, Christopher Gallop, John and Pat Smyth, Stan Edwards, John and Joan Nash, John and Sheila French, Jerry and Alison Oakes, John Hazel, K S Pike)*

Free house ~ Licensees Jane and Geoffrey Knights ~ Real ale ~ Meals and snacks (till 9.45) ~ Restaurant ~ (01300) 348357 ~ Children welcome in family room ~ Open 12-2.30, 7-11

POWERSTOCK SY5196 Map 2

Three Horseshoes ♀

Can be reached by taking Askerswell turn off A35 then keeping uphill past the Spyway Inn, and bearing left all the way round Eggardon Hill – a lovely drive, but steep narrow roads; a better road is signposted West Milton off the A3066 Beaminster—Bridport, then take Powerstock road

There's quite an emphasis on well prepared fresh fish at this busy stone and thatch pub. Depending on what's available that day the blackboard menu might include moules marinières (£4.95), grilled squid with rocket leaves and chilli oil (£5.50), fish soup (£5.95) or perhaps roast local cod with tomato, onion and basil (£9.50); no-smoking restaurant. Well kept Palmers Bridport and IPA on handpump, about 20 wines by the glass, and freshly-squeezed fruit juice. The comfortable L-shaped bar has country-style chairs around the polished tables, pictures on the stripped panelled walls, and warm fires. Daisy and Jess, the friendly retrievers, or Charlie the springer spaniel may befriend you for titbits. The garden has swings and a climbing frame, and from the neat lawn rising steeply above the pub, there are lovely uninterrupted views towards the sea. *(Recommended by Mr and Mrs J Boler, David and June Harwood, Jerry and Alison Oakes, Ian Dunkin, J W Hill, V H and J M Vanstone, Anthony Barnes, Mark and Michelle Aston, Gordon, Major and Mrs Warwick, K S Pike, Susan Mullins, Barry A Lynch, Bill Edwards, Mrs S A Burrows, F C Johnston)*

Palmers ~ Tenant P W Ferguson ~ Real ale ~ Meals and snacks ~ Restaurant ~ (01308) 485328 ~ Open 11-3, 6-11 ~ Bedrooms: £25(£30B)/£50(£60B)

SHAVE CROSS SY4198 Map 1

Shave Cross Inn ★

On back lane Bridport—Marshwood, signposted locally; OS Sheet 193, ref 415980

This delightful partly 14th-c flint and thatch inn is charmingly set off the beaten track and well worth the effort of tracking it down. Travelling monks once lodged here, when they might get their tonsures shaved in preparation for the last stage of their pilgrimage to the shrine of St Wita at Whitchurch – hence the pubs' name. There's a notably friendly welcome in the original timbered bar, a lovely flagstoned room, surprisingly roomy and full of character, with one big table in the middle, a smaller one by the window seat, a row of chintz-cushioned windsor chairs, and an enormous inglenook fireplace with plates hanging from the chimney breast. The larger carpeted side lounge has a dresser at one end set with plates, and modern rustic light-coloured seats making booths around the tables, and is partly no smoking. Popular, promptly served bar food includes fine ploughman's (from £2.75), good sausages (£2.75), steak sandwich (£3.95), mushroom and spinach lasagne (£3.90), salads (from £3.75), vegetable balti (£4.15), kebabs of sweet and sour pork and spicy lamb (£5.95), mixed grill (£7.95), and daily specials like lasagne (£3.90), tiger prawns in filo pastry (£4.35), chicken, ham and mushroom pie (£4.45), char-grilled swordfish steak (£7.45), puddings such as gooseberry crumble (£2.25), and children's meals (from £1.95). Well kept Badger Best, Bass and Eldridge Pope Royal Oak on handpump, and local cider in summer; cheery and welcoming staff – one barman is quite skilled at juggling. Darts, alley skittles, table skittles, dominoes and cribbage. The pretty flower-filled sheltered garden has a thatched wishing-well, a goldfish pool, a children's play area, and a small secluded campsite for touring caravans and campers. *(Recommended by M E Wellington, Niki and Terry Pursey, Jack and Philip Paxton, B and K Hypher, Marjorie and David Lamb, M Carr, K S Pike, Dr S Willavoys, Galen Strawson, Pete and Rosie Flower, Bill Edwards, Ron Gentry, Alan Skull, Clive Gilbert, G Washington, Gordon)*

Free house ~ Licensees Bill and Ruth Slade ~ Real ale ~ Meals and snacks (not Mon, except bank holidays) ~ (01308) 868358 ~ Children in lounge bar ~ Open 12-3(2.30 in winter), 7-11; cl Mon (except bank holidays)

SHERBORNE ST6316 Map 2

Digby Tap £ 🍺

Cooks Lane; park in Digby Road and walk round corner

Close to the glorious golden stone abbey, this is a splendid example of an old-fashioned town pub. It was deliberately de-smartened in the early 1990s to suit its use in BBC TV adaptations of Le Carré spy thrillers, and its simple uncluttered decor, with flagstone-floored main bar and traditional seating, seems to make for an easy mix of everyone from smart-suited businesswomen to rugby players and retired gardeners. It has plenty of character, and a thriving relaxed lunchtime atmosphere; in the early evening it is popular with older people, but the average age of customers declines perceptibly as the evening wears on. Led by a landlord who seems naturally happy, service is always pleasant and efficient. Huge helpings of very reasonably priced bar food include soup (£1.50), super sandwiches (from £1.25 to bacon and mushroom or tiger prawn £2.75), garlic mushrooms (£2.25), sausage, beans and chips or burger (£2.75), home-made pasty, chips and beans (£3), omelettes (£3.25), and daily specials like spaghetti bolognese or roasts (all £3.50). Five changing well kept real ales on handpump, such as Ash Vine Bitter, Exmoor Ale, Fullers London Pride, Morlands Old Speckled Hen, Ringood Best and Wadworths 6X; several small games rooms with pool, darts, fruit machine, trivia; piped music; there are some seats outside. *(Recommended by Revd A Nunnerley, Ron Shelton, John Hazel, Stephen G Brown, Richard Houghton, Jim Knight)*

Free house ~ Licensee D Parker ~ Real ale ~ Meals and snacks (not evenings or Sun) ~ Open 11-2.30, 5.30(6 Sat)-11; cl 25 Dec

STOKE ABBOTT ST4500 Map 1

New Inn

Village signposted from B3162 and B3163 W of Beaminster

Nestling about six miles from the coast, this friendly 17th-c thatched inn makes an ideal centre for a walk in the surrounding rolling hills. The carpeted bar has around 200 horsebrasses covering its beams, as well as wheelback chairs and cushioned built-in settles around simple wooden tables, and settles built into snug stripped stone alcoves on either side of the big log fireplace; another fireplace has handsome panelling. Well kept Palmers Bridport, IPA and 200 on handpump; darts, table skittles, piped music. Under new licensees the partly home-cooked menu includes soup (£1.75), ploughman's (£3.85), plaice fillet (£4.95), steak and kidney pie, curry or ham and eggs or lasagne (£5.50), chicken kiev (£5.75), scampi or lamb balti (£5.95), rump steak (£6.95); children's meals (£1.90); at the weekend they do a Sunday roast (£4.25), and a few blackboard specials like pork or sirloin steak or roast rib of lamb; no-smoking dining room. Sheltering behind a golden stone wall which merges into an attractively planted rockery, the well kept garden has a long gnarled silvery log to sit on, wooden benches by the tables, swings, and usually a donkey and some sheep in a paddock. *(Recommended by Ron Shelton, Galen Strawson, Mr and Mrs D Carter, Hetty Owen-Smith, Bill Edwards; more reports please)*

Palmers ~ Tenants David and Anita Reynolds ~ Real ale ~ Meals and snacks ~ (01308) 868333 ~ Children welcome till 9pm ~ Open 12-3, 7-11; cl Mon lunchtime ~ Bedrooms: £17.50/£35

SYMONDSBURY SY4493 Map 1

Ilchester Arms

Village signposted from A35 just W of Bridport

Although delightfully tucked away in a peaceful little village, this attractive old thatched inn is very handy for Bridport. There's a really friendly interested welcome in the cosy open-plan low-ceilinged bar, which has rustic benches and tables, seats in the mullioned windows, and a high-backed settle built into the bar counter next to the big inglenook fireplace. Another area, also with an open fire, has candlelit tables and is used mainly for dining in the evening and at weekends; this part of the pub is no smoking. Tasty bar food includes home-made soup (£2.50), filled rolls or baked potatoes (from £2.50), ploughman's (£3.75), salads (from £3.95), cottage pie (£4.95), gammon steak (£5.25), lamb cassoulet (£5.75), whole lemon sole (£6.95), and a very decent range of daily blackboard specials such as rabbit in cider or seafood and potato pie (£5.25), pheasant casserole, cod in cheese and wine sauce or pies like beef and stilton or game (£5.50), smoked haddock au gratin (£5.75), pork steak in orange and ginger (£6.25 and venison in red wine (£6.75). Well kept Palmers Best, Bridport, Tally Ho and 200 on handpump or tapped from the cask, welcoming licensees. Darts, dominoes, cribbage, fruit machine, table and alley skittles, piped music. There are tables outside in a quiet back garden by a stream. The high-hedged lanes which twist deeply through the sandstone behind the village lead to good walks through the wooded low hills above the Marshwood Vale. *(Recommended by A and I Stewart, O and H Steinmann, Mr and Mrs Austen, Jenny and Michael Back, C and E M Watson, Ted George, Romey Heaton, S J Edwards, Dr and Mrs A H Young, Basil Minson, Paul and Sue Sexton, Gordon, Jenny and Gordon Seller)*

Palmers ~ Tenants Dick and Ann Foad ~ Real ale ~ Meals and snacks (not winter Mon) ~ Restaurant ~ (01308) 422600 ~ Children welcome ~ Open 11(11.30 winter)-3, 6(6.30 winter)-11 ~ Bedrooms: £15/£30 (family room)

TARRANT MONKTON ST9408 Map 2

Langton Arms

Village signposted from A354, then head for church

This friendly and very attractive 17th-c thatched inn is a good steady all-rounder. Big helpings of good value bar meals are popular, with extensive blackboard menus offering dishes such as Poole Bay crab soup (£2.45), wild boar and venison sausages in red wine gravy or pasta parcels filled with spinach and ricotta cheese (£4.25), sweet and sour prawn fritters, breast of chicken in a cheese and bacon sauce, fillet of salmon in a prawn and white wine sauce, and puddings like coffee and Tia Maria cheesecake (£2.25); they also have Monday night fish and chips (£2.95), Thursday night steaks (from £4.25), and usual children's meals (2 courses £1.99). They enjoy hunting out unusual ales and as well as well kept Smiles Best (labelled as Langton Arms Best in the pub), three changing guests might be Church End M Reg GTI, Fullers London Pride, Goffs White Knight, Goldfinch Flashmans Clout, Morlands Old Speckled Hen or Shepherd Neame Spitfire; decent wines, some by the glass, helpful staff. The comfortable beamed main bar has settles that form a couple of secluded booths around tables at the carpeted end, window seats, and another table or two at the serving end where the floor's tiled. There's a big inglenook fireplace in the public bar, and an old stable has been converted into a no-smoking restaurant area; dominoes, darts, pool, fruit machine, juke box and piped music. The skittle alley doubles as a family room during the day, and there are children's play areas in here and in the garden, where you may also find summer barbecues and a bouncy castle. Tracks lead up to Crichel Down above the village, and Badbury Rings, a hill fort by the B3082 just south of here, is very striking. *(Recommended by EML, John and Fiona McDougal, Mr and Mrs D C Stevens, Joy and Peter Heatherley, John and Joan Nash, John Hazel, H T Flaherty, Phil and Heidi Cook, Revd A Nunnerley)*

Free house ~ Licensees James Cossins and Michael Angell ~ Real ale ~ Meals and snacks (12-2.30, 6-10) ~ Restaurant (Tues-Sat evening, Sun lunch) ~ (01258) 830225 ~ Children welcome in family room ~ Open 11.30-2.30, 6-11; Sat 11.30-11; Sun 12-10.30 ~ Bedrooms: £39B/£54B

UPWEY SY6684 Map 2

Old Ship ♀

Ridgeway; turn left off A354 at bottom of Ridgeway Hill into old Roman Rd

Generously served bar meals are quite a draw at this friendly little pub: home-made soup (£2.25), sandwiches (from £2.25), three-egg omelettes (from £3.50), creamed garlic mushrooms (£3.95), local sausages (£3.75), cheese and broccoli quiche (£3.95), ploughman's or filled baked potatoes (from £4.25), ham and egg (£4.95), plaice (£6.25), very good help-yourself salad bar with lots of cold meats, fresh crab and game sausage (£7.50), saddle of lamb filled with forcemeat, glazed with rosemary and apricot with red wine and mushroom sauce (£8.50), cajun-style chicken breast (£8.80), steaks (from £10.95), daily specials and Sunday lunches. The several attractive interconnected rooms have a peaceful and welcoming atmosphere, as well as a mix of sturdy chairs, some built-in wooden wall settles, beams, an open fire with horsebrasses along the mantelbeam, fresh flowers on the solid panelled wood bar counter and tables, china plates, copper pans and old clocks on the walls, and a couple of comfortable armchairs. Well kept Bass, Boddingtons and Greenalls Original on handpump, and a good wine list that always includes a dozen or so by the glass; attentive but unfussy service. There are colourful hanging baskets outside, and picnic tables and umbrellas in the garden. *(Recommended by P Devitt, Joan and Michel Hooper-Immins, Peter Toms, Stephen and Julie Brown, D J and P M Taylor, Bill and Sheila McLardy, Ian Phillips, O Carroll, Galen Strawson, Richard Dolphin, John and Val Spouge)*

Greenalls ~ Tenant Paul Edmunds ~ Real ale ~ Meals and snacks (12-2, 6.30-9.30; till 10 Fri and Sat, till 9 Sun) ~ Restaurant ~ (01305) 812522 ~ Children in eating area ~ Open 11-2.30(3 Sat), 6-11; cl 25 Dec evening

WEST BEXINGTON SY5387 Map 2

Manor Hotel ⏥

Village signposted off B3157 SE of Bridport, opposite the Bull in Swyre

This ancient stone hotel is a short stroll from the beach, and you can see the sea from the bedrooms and from the garden, where there are picnic tables on a small lawn with flowerbeds lining the low sheltering walls; a much bigger side lawn has a children's play area. Inside, a handsome Jacobean oak-panelled hall leads down to the busy pubby cellar bar which is actually on the same level as the south-sloping garden. Small country pictures and good leather-mounted horsebrasses decorate the walls, and there are red leatherette stools and low-backed chairs (with one fat seat carved from a beer cask) under the black beams and joists, as well as heavy harness over the log fire. A smart no-smoking Victorian-style conservatory has airy furnishings and lots of plants. Popular but not cheap bar food includes sandwiches (from £2.25), home-made soup (£2.75), ploughman's (£4.75), moules marinières (£5.55), cottage pie (£5.95), lasagne or chilli (£6.95), aubergine crumble, liver and bacon or rabbit or venison pie (£7.45), grilled plaice (£7.75), rack of lamb (£9.95), baked salmon (£10.25), puddings (£3.35), and children's meals (£3.45); good breakfasts. Well kept Dartmoor, Palmers Bridport and Wadworths 6X on handpump, quite a few malt whiskies and several wines by the glass; alley skittles, piped music. Helpful courteous service. *(Recommended by Richard Gibbs, Jane Warren,*

Nigel Norman, Andrea Carr, Jason Good, M G Hart, Mr and Mrs D C Stevens, Julia Duplock, K S Pike, Basil Minson, Mark and Caroline Thistlethwaite, Galen Strawson)

Free house ~ Licensee Richard Childs ~ Real ale ~ Meals and snacks (till 10pm) ~ Restaurant ~(01308) 897616 ~ Children in eating area of bar ~ Open 11-11; cl evening 25 Dec ~ Bedrooms: £47B/£80B

WORTH MATRAVERS SY9777 (Isle of Purbeck) Map 2

Square & Compass 🍺

At fork of both roads signposted to village from B3069

This idiosyncratic and delightfully unchanging little place has been run by different generations of the same family for over 90 years, with very little altered in all that time. Determinedly basic, and running very much at its own bygone pace – don't expect a trendy zealous welcome here – the old-fashioned main bar has simple wall benches around the elbow-polished old tables on the flagstones, and interesting local pictures under its low ceilings. Well kept Badger Tanglefoot, Morlands Old Speckled Hen, Ringwood Fortyniner, and Whitbreads Strong Country are tapped from a row of casks behind a couple of hatches in the flagstoned corridor (local fossils back here, and various curios inside the servery), which leads to a more conventional summer bar; traditional cider. Bar food is limited to Cornish, cheese and onion or pork and chilli pasties (£1), served when they're open; cribbage, shove-ha'penny and dominoes. On a clear day the view from the peaceful hilltop setting is hard to beat, looking down over the village rooftops to the sea between the East Man and the West Man (the hills that guard the coastal approach), and on summer evenings the sun setting out beyond Portland Bill. There are benches in front of the pub to admire the view, and free-roaming hens, chickens and other birds may cluck happily around your feet. There are good walks from the pub. *(Recommended by Ann and Colin Hunt, David Holloway, Gabrielle Coyle, Ian Lock, Chris Westmoreland, Richard Siebert, Jack and Philip Paxton, Jane Warren, D P and J A Sweeney, Derek Patey, Nigel Clifton, Paul and Sue Sexton, P J Hanson, Andy Thwaites, Avril Hanson, James Macrae)*

Free house ~ Licensee Charlie Newman ~ Real ale ~ Snacks ~ (01929) 439229 ~ Children welcome ~ Occasional live music ~ Open 11-3, 6-11; 11-11 Sat

Lucky Dip

Besides the fully inspected pubs, you might like to try these Lucky Dips recommended to us and described by readers (if you do, please send us reports):

☆ nr **Almer** [B3075, just off A31 towards Wareham; SY9097], *Worlds End*: Efficient open-plan thatched family dining pub, lots of room, good decor, comfortable atmosphere, very wide food choice, well kept Badger Best and Tanglefoot, helpful service; picnic tables out in front and behind, plenty of space with good big well equipped play area *(WHBM, the Sandy family, Howard Clutterbuck, Joy and Peter Heatherley, BB)*

Ansty [Higher Ansty; ST7603], *Fox*: Unusual inn with good range of food, friendly helpful service, part of bar set aside for non smokers, fantastic collection of toby jugs and decorative plates, well equipped children's bar, skittle alley, pool table; beautiful countryside *(Keith Widdowson, LYM)*

Ashley Heath [SU1105], *Struan*: Consistently good value spacious pub, genial very efficient long-serving licensees, log fire, good straightforward food in bar and restaurant; bedrooms *(J Morris)*

☆ **Beaminster** [The Square; ST4701], *Pickwicks*: Quaint and comfortable restaurant with bar attached, good atmosphere, interesting real ales, wide choice of good well presented home-cooked food inc good vegetarian dishes; piped opera, friendly landlord; bedrooms *(Prof and Mrs S Barnett)*

☆ **Beaminster** [The Square], *Greyhound*: Friendly relaxing little 18th-c pub, interesting inside, popular for wide choice of good value food inc interesting vegetarian pâté; well kept Palmers IPA and BB, good friendly service, small family room *(Gordon)*

☆ **Bere Regis** [West St; SY8494], *Royal Oak*: Really friendly and unpretentious open-plan modernised local, good value home-cooked food inc takeaways, well kept Whitbreads-related ales, woodburner, bar billiards, sensibly placed darts, cribbage, fruit machine; dining room; open all day Fri and Sat; bedrooms *(Peter Cornall, Chris de Wet, BB)*

Bere Regis [High St], *Drax*: Village local doing well under friendly and attentive new licensees; open-plan refurbishment, reasonably priced home cooking; Badger Tanglefoot and Malthouse ales *(John and Joan Nash)*

Blandford Forum [77 Salisbury St; ST8806], *Nelsons*: Very old dim-lit bar, beams and sawdust, good value interesting food in big or small helpings, good Sun lunch, half a dozen Whitbreads-related and other ales, hospitable landlord, newspapers *(John and Joan Nash, Iain Phillips)*

☆ **Bournemouth** [The Square, Exeter Rd; SZ0991], *Moon on the Square*: Spacious and well fitted Wetherspoons pub, no-smoking upstairs bar, good range of well kept beers, awesome helpings of bar food, friendly service, sensible prices, no piped music; tables on terrace *(Paul Randall, Chris and Margaret Southon, JJB)*

Bournemouth [165 Old Christchurch Rd], *Botlers Crab & Ale House*: Spacious, clean and well furnished in wine-bar style, with decent food running up to steaks, friendly service, Boddingtons from attractive central bar; can be packed at weekends *(JJB)*; [Durley Chine], *Durley*: Very enjoyable pub lunches *(Hugh Spottiswoode)*; [Holdenhurst Rd], *Firefly & Firkin*: Traditional solid alehouse-style decor, good own-brew beers, friendly service, reasonably priced food inc big filled baps to take away, regular live music *(Richard Houghton)*; [West Hill Rd], *Goat & Tricycle*: Basic and well worn, roaring fires, several well kept ales from around the country, good food, friendly service *(Richard Houghton)*; [Old Christchurch Rd], *Jug of Ale*: Open all day, with well kept Whitbreads-related and other changing ales, straightforward food inc good value Sun lunch; busy weekend evenings *(JJB)*

Bourton [off old A303 E of Wincanton; ST7430], *White Lion*: Plushly refurbished as dining pub, beamed bars with sporting equipment, well kept Bass, Courage Best and Fullers London Pride *(Peter Woods, LYM; more reports on current regime please)*

☆ **Bridport** [West Bay; SY4690], *West Bay*: Straightforward pub very popular for good unusual dishes such as bison sausages, lots of fresh local seafood, occasional gourmet evenings; Palmers IPA and Best, friendly landlady, tables in garden *(Jenny and Brian Seller)*

Broadmayne [SY7286], *Black Dog*: Comfortably modernised village pub with good range of reasonably priced food inc good sandwiches, popular Sun lunch; pleasant staff *(David Lamb, Pat and Robert Watt, LYM)*

☆ **Buckland Newton** [ST6904], *Gaggle of Geese*: Comfortable and well run country pub with good atmosphere and attractive decor, well kept Bass, Badger Best, Wadworths 6X and a guest beer, decent wines and spirits, good reasonably priced usual bar food, smartish restaurant, spacious pool/snooker and skittle rooms, sizeable grounds, friendly dogs and a cat *(R G Glover, John Hazel, BB)*

☆ **Burton Bradstock** [Southover; SY4889], *Dove*: 16th-c thatched inn with pleasant atmosphere, interesting beers, good range of food inc fresh seafood *(RS, Prof and Mrs S Barnett, Dr S L Hurst)*

☆ **Cattistock** [SY5999], *Fox & Hounds*: Hidden-away unspoilt village local, maybe Tudor in parts, with open fires, one local and one national beer kept well, bar food *(Gwyneth and Salvo Spatola-Dutturi, BB)*

☆ **Cerne Abbas** [14 Long St; ST6601], *New Inn*: Handsome Tudor inn with comfortable oak-beamed lounge bar, mullioned window seats, tables on sheltered lawn behind old coachyard; quickly served bar food from sandwiches to char-grilled steaks, well kept Eldridge Pope Hardy and Royal Oak, good house wines; piped music; children welcome, restaurant, old-fashioned bedrooms *(Jack and Philip Paxton, Howard Clutterbuck, Mr and Mrs D C Stevens, LYM)*

☆ **Charlton Marshall** [A350 Poole—Blandford; ST9003], *Charlton Inn*: Wide choice of good generous food from sandwiches and lots of baked potatoes up, well kept Badger Best and Tanglefoot and well chosen wine list in smart and tidy oak-beamed food pub, quick friendly service, unobtrusive piped music, small garden *(K Watson)*

Charmouth [SY3693], *Charmouth House*: A hotel, but worth knowing for good bar food and well kept Worthington BB; pleasant gardens, nice spot; bedrooms *(K H Frostick)*

☆ nr **Chedington** [A356 Dorchester—Crewkerne; ST4805], *Winyards Gap*: Spectacular view from tables in front of tastefully modernised pub with wide choice of traditional food inc lots of home-made puddings, children's and vegetarian dishes, popular Sun lunch; well kept Exmoor Stag, Flowers Original, Wadworths 6X and a guest ale, country wines, no-smoking area, skittle alley, also darts, pool etc; children in dining area, self-catering in converted barn; pleasant walks nearby *(D Marsh, Howard Clutterbuck, LYM)*

Chesil [bear right off A354 into Portland, following Chiswell signs; SY6873], *Cove House*: Modest bare-boards pub listed for its superb position just above the miles-long Chesil pebble beach, with three tables out by sea wall; friendly staff, Whitbreads-related ales, usual food; piped music may be obtrusive *(Eric Locker, John Fahy, Christopher Gallop, Clare Wilson, LYM)*

Chickerell [East St; SY6480], *Turks Head*: Busy stonebuilt village pub with pleasant beamed bar and spacious eating area, good freshly cooked food (so may be a wait) inc children's dishes and great puddings, lots of old local photographs, pictures and decorative plates, cheerful service; children welcome, comfortable bedrooms, good breakfasts *(Dr and Mrs S Jones)*

☆ **Child Okeford** [Gold Hill – village signed off A350 Blandford Forum—Shaftesbury and A357 Blandford—Sherborne; ST8313], *Saxon*: Cosy old village pub, quietly clubby bar with log fire and more spacious side room (where children allowed), well kept Bass, Butcombe and a guest beer, country wines, traditional games, simple food (not Tues evening, not winter Sun evening) from wide choice of sandwiches to steaks inc children's dishes; piped music, dry dogs on leads welcome; quite a menagerie in attractive back garden, also friendly golden retrievers and cats; good walks on neolithic Hambledon Hill *(AB, Mark Matthewman, LYM)*

☆ nr **Christchurch** [Ringwood Rd, Walkford; just off A35 by Hants border – OS Sheet 195 map ref 222943; SZ2294], *Amberwood Arms*: Imaginative food in bar and comfortable restaurant, friendly staff; some live music, weekly trivia night, picnic tables and play area; open all day, festooned with hanging baskets and flower tubs in summer *(Cheryl Baker, Phyl and Jack Street)*

☆ **Colehill** [off A31 E of Wimborne; down hill N of village, right at bottom into Long Lane – OS Sheet 195 map ref 032024; SU0201], *Barley Mow*: Very popular extended thatched 16th-c dining pub, wide range of promptly served food, very reasonable prices, well kept Best and Tanglefoot and a guest such as Charles Wells; attractive beamed and panelled core, good log fires, provision for children, folk music Fri, nice garden with play area *(John Hazel, John H L Davies, LYM)*

☆ **Corfe Castle** [SY9681], *Bankes Arms*: Big busy ex-coaching inn on attractive village square, flagstone floors, comfortable traditional decor, subtle lighting, Whitbreads-related ales, decent food, friendly service, tables on terrace and in long garden with big climbing frame, running down to newly opened tourist railway; children welcome; bedrooms *(B and K Hypher, Chris Westmoreland, Miss T Browne)*

Corfe Castle, *Castle*: Smallish pub mentioned in Hardy's *Hand of Ethelberta*, two smartly refurbished yet unpretentious rooms with flagstoned floors shown to good effect; well kept Bass, interesting food *(Chris Westmoreland)*; [A351 towards Swanage], *Morton*: Delightful old building with limited reasonably priced food in small bar, friendly service; bedrooms *(J Morris)*; *New Inn*: Nice fire, good service, tasty food; outside ladies' *(Miss M Oakeley)*

Dorchester [Gt Western Rd; SY6890], *Junction*: Eldridge Pope pub in sight of brewery, straightforward lunchtime bar food, smiling service, well kept Dorchester and Royal Oak; piped pop music may be loud; children allowed in skittle alley; well equipped bedrooms around courtyard *(Joan and Michel Hooper-Immins)*; [High West St], *Old Ship*: Unmodernised but food generous and cheap *(John and Wendy Trentham)*; [20 High West St], *Royal Oak*: Well kept Eldridge Pope Dorchester, Hardy Country and Royal Oak, plentiful hot food, very friendly service, quiet when the piped pop music is switched off; back dining room now a games room; bedrooms *(Marjorie and David Lamb, Alan Newman)*; [Weymouth Ave, by Dorchester Sth Stn], *Station Masters House*: Spacious open-plan railway-theme pub with friendly service, notable for well kept Eldridge Pope ales straight from the handsome adjacent brewery; plush Victorian-style decor, courteous young staff, generous sensibly

priced food; games area with darts, fruit machines and pool tables, piped music can be rather loud; open all day Weds-Sat, busy Weds (market opp) *(Brian Chambers)*; [47 High East St], *Tom Browns*: Two or three beers from the microbrewery you can see at the back, in basic but friendly well run local with simple good value food; juke box *(Gwyneth and Salvo Spadaro-Dutturi, JM, PM)*; [40 Allington Ave (A352 towards Wareham, just off bypass)], *Trumpet Major*: Bright and airy big-windowed lounge bar, emphasis on food inc help-yourself salad bar and speciality apple cake, well kept Eldridge Pope ales; handy for Max Gate (Thomas Hardy's house, now open to the public); garden, children welcome *(Joan and Michel Hooper-Immins)*

East Burton [SY8387], *Seven Stars*: Newly refurbished pub on quiet road, good choice of generous food and of beers, friendly welcome for families, children's play area; handy for Bovington Tank Museum and Monkey World, parking for caravans *(S J Edwards)*

☆ **East Lulworth** [B3070; SY8581], *Weld Arms*: Friendly pub with nice mix of individual furnishings, attractive little snug, good food from well filled rolls upward inc vegetarian and yummy puddings, tables out in big garden; good value bedrooms *(Dave Braisted, R H Brown, Richard Gibbs, D J Milner, S Lancaster, LYM)*

☆ **East Stour** [E Stour Common, A30 W of Shaftesbury; ST7922], *Kings Arms*: Recently well redecorated, with improved eating area for good value fresh home-made food inc interesting specials and good puddings, wide range of well kept ales inc Bass, decent wines, good friendly service, local paintings and drawings, model railway locomotive collection, no piped music; public bar with darts and fruit machine; tables in big garden, children welcome *(R H Martyn, Mr and Mrs R O Gibson, Canon Kenneth Wills, Matthew Haig)*

☆ **Evershot** [off A37 8 miles S of Yeovil; ST5704], *Acorn*: Comfortable low-beamed stripped-stone bar with wide choice of food inc imaginative dishes, interesting changing ales such as Palmers and Branscombe Branoc, decent wines, efficient friendly service from smartly dressed staff, fine old fireplaces; games in quiet separate public bar, piped music; children in skittle alley and restaurant; bedrooms comfortable, pretty village in attractive Hardy walking country *(Keith Pollard, Gwyneth and Salvo Spadaro-Dutturi, David Lamb, Maj and Mrs Warrick, LYM)*

Eype [SY4491], *New Inn*: Warm and friendly, well kept Palmers, decent food inc children's; magnificent views *(Stephen Bayley)*

☆ **Ferndown** [Wimborne Rd E; SZ0700], *Pure Drop*: Large Eldridge Pope pub doing well under new landlord, their beers kept well, sizeable restaurant with enterprising varied food, good wines *(S J Edwards)*

☆ **Fiddleford** [A357 Sturminster Newton—Blandford Forum; ST8013], *Fiddleford Inn*: Comfortable and spacious refurbished pub keeping some nice old touches, good choice of reasonably priced quickly served food in lounge bar, restaurant area and back family area; well kept Courage-related ales, friendly efficient service, unobtrusive piped music, big attractive garden with play area *(Brian Chambers, Jenny and Michael Back, Mr and Mrs R O Gibson, Dorothy and Leslie Pilson, LYM)*

☆ Gillingham [Peacemarsh; ST8026], *Dolphin*: Welcoming licensees and staff, good choice of particularly good value food, well kept Badger ales *(Clifford Sharp)*

☆ Gussage All Saints [signed off B3078 Wimborne—Cranborne; SU0010], *Drovers*: Sturdily furnished country dining pub with peaceful views, generous well presented food inc vegetarian, well kept Bass, Marstons Pedigree and Ruddles County on handpump, country wines, friendly service, tables out on terrace, good play area; children in eating area, in summer has been open all day Sat *(B and K Hypher, LYM)*

Hinton St Mary [just off B3092 a mile N of Sturminster; ST7816], *White Horse*: Straightforward village local but plenty of character, with unusual inglenook fireplace in jovial tiled bar, nicely set dining tables in extended lounge, reasonably priced food (booking advised Sun lunch), cheerful staff, well kept John Smiths, Tetleys and changing guest beers such as Eldridge Pope Royal Oak and Smiles; tables in flower garden *(Brian Chambers, Pat and Robert Watt, Jenny and Michael Back)*

Holt Heath [SU0604], *Cross Keys*: Very cosy and friendly, in pleasant locality, with usual food, Badger ales, plenty of whiskies, games room behind small bar; very colourful garden with good barbecue *(Jenny and Michael Back, WHBM)*

☆ Hurn [village signed off A338, then follow Avon, Sopley, Mutchams sign – OS Sheet 195 map ref 136976; SZ1397], *Avon Causeway*: Good moderately priced food, Wadworths ales and guests such as John Smiths and Ringwood Old Thumper, good choice of wines and spirits, two comfortable and civilised bars, pleasantly enlarged dining area, welcoming staff; interesting railway decorations, Pullman-coach restaurant by former 1870s station platform, maybe bouncy castle in summer marquee; piped music, open all day; bedrooms *(M Joyner, CT, MT, Mr and Mrs Reeves, Audrey and Peter Reeves, LYM)*

Langton Matravers [B3069 nr junction with A351; SY9978], *Ship*: Robust basic local with lively Purbeck Longboard shove-ha'penny, pool, darts, Courage-related ales; children welcome, handy for Putland Farm *(Chris Westmoreland, LYM)*

☆ Longham [A348 Ferndown—Poole; SZ0698], *Angel*: Cosy beamed roadside pub (big car park, can get very busy) well reworked to give children's area away from bar, wide choice of food from sandwiches to steaks inc children's dishes, friendly prompt service, well kept Badger Best and Tanglefoot, unobtrusive piped music; big garden with lots of play facilities *(P Gillbe, Peter Churchill)*

☆ Lyme Regis [25 Marine Parade, The Cobb; SY3492], *Royal Standard*: Lively but cosy local, open-plan but keeping three separate low-ceilinged areas, with well kept Palmers, good value food inc good cream teas with home-made scones, good service, pool table, floodlit suntrap terrace (floodlit at night) leading to beach; three bedrooms *(Neil Williams, JWC, MC, Mr and Mrs J Irving, B R Shiner)*

Lyme Regis, *Harbour*: Simple pub with back food bar, tasty good value food inc good generous fish soup, no piped music, friendly service, Theakstons beers, seats on verandah and a couple of tables on adjacent beach *(John Voos)*

Manston [B3091 Shaftesbury—Sturminster Newton, just N; ST8115], *Plough*: Richly decorated plasterwork, ceilings and bar front, very obliging service, real ales such as Black Sheep, Butcombe and Websters Yorkshire, good choice of good value food from sandwiches up inc vegetarian dishes, quick courteous service; tables in garden, cl Sun evening *(Jenny and Michael Back, C and E Watson)*

☆ Marshwood [B3165 Lyme Regis—Crewkerne; SY3799], *Bottle*: 16th-c thatched country local, inglenook in low-ceilinged bar, Hook Norton and Wadworths 6X, cheap bar food, small games bar, skittle alley; good spacious garden, pretty walking country *(Ian Phillips, Dr and Mrs J H Hills, Gordon, LYM)*

☆ Morden [B3075 between A35 and A31 E of Bere Regis; SY9195], *Cock & Bottle*: Warmly rustic dining pub, beams and timbering carefully set out of true, tables set in pleasantly divided areas (booking recommended), friendly helpful service, good food (esp fish, poultry and game) ordered course by course from bar, nice fire, well kept Badger Best and Tanglefoot with a guest such as Charles Wells Bombardier, busy locals' bar; children welcome, pleasant countryside *(John and Joan Nash, E G Parish, Nigel Flook, Betsy Brown, Chris Westmoreland, Mr and Mrs D Johnson)*

☆ Moreton [SY8089], *Frampton Arms*: Wide choice of good value food, friendly landlord, steam railway pictures in lounge bar, Warmwell Aerodrome theme in public bar; restaurant, conservatory, comfortable bedrooms *(Janet and John Loder)*

Mosterton [High St; ST4505], *Admiral Hood*: Civilised and popular dining pub with neatly furnished spacious L-shaped bar, well kept Courage-related ales, coal fire in handsome stone fireplace, quick welcoming service, simple skittle alley behind the thatched 18th-c stone building *(Edward Pardey, Pat and Robert Watt, BB)*

☆ Mudeford [beyond huge seaside car park at Mudeford Pier – OS Sheet 195 map ref 182916; SZ1891], *Haven House*: Much-extended, best in winter for old-fashioned feel in quaint old part-flagstoned core and lovely seaside walks (dogs banned from beach May-

Sept), very popular summer for position on beach with family cafeteria, tables on sheltered terrace; Whitbreads-related ales, simple bar food, cheerful service *(Rita Horridge, LYM)*

Mudeford, *Rising Sun*: Good imaginative menu with strong Thai and Chinese influence, well kept beer; piano player adds to friendly atmosphere; good friendly staff and landlord – under same regime as Woolpack at Sopley (see Hants main entries) *(Anon)*

☆ **Norden Heath** [Furzebrook; A351 Wareham—Corfe Castle; SY9483], *Halfway*: Really interesting authentic Cypriot dishes (the slow-cooked kleftiko is excllent) among more usual home cooking in unpretentious and very friendly thatched main-road pub, some cosy corners, well kept Whitbreads-related ales with guests such as Ringwood Best and Twelve Bore, simple inexpensive wines, decent coffee, two log fires; garden with pets corner *(G R Sunderland, Mr and Mrs Damien Burke, Chris Westmoreland, David Lamb, Derek Patey)*

☆ **North Wootton** [A3030; ST6514], *Three Elms*: Interesting and still proliferating Matchbox cars and other collections in lively and welcoming pub with wide range of good reasonably priced food esp vegetarian, also well served sandwiches, well kept beers such as Boddingtons and Fullers London Pride; interesting gents', three bedrooms, good breakfasts, big garden *(David Tyzack, S G Brown, Pat and Robert Watt)*

Piddletrenthide [B3142; SY7099], *Piddle*: Village and pub named after the river here, lots of chamber-pots hanging from ceiling, friendly atmosphere, good food, real ale, children's room and pool room; spacious streamside garden with picnic tables and play area; a favourite stop for cyclists *(Lee Kreider, K Flack)*; *Poachers Arms*: Cheerful Yorkshire landlord, three well kept changing guest beers (often unusual), good value restaurant; chalet-style bedrooms around outside pool *(Joan and Michel Hooper-Immins)*

☆ **Poole** [Pinewood Rd, Branksome Park; off A338 on edge of Poole, towards Branksome Chine – via The Avenue; SZ0590], *Inn in the Park*: Consistently warm welcome in very popular pleasantly redecorated small hotel bar, well kept Bass and Wadworths 6X, good value generous bar food (not Sun evening) inc fresh veg, attractive dining room (children allowed), log fire, tables on small sunny terrace; comfortable bedrooms, quiet pine-filled residential area above sea *(Peter Churchill, B and K Hypher, LYM)*

☆ **Poole** [The Quay; SZ0190], *Portsmouth Hoy*: Enjoyable nautical theme, lots of brass, plenty of atmosphere, good choice of reasonably priced food inc generous fish, well kept Eldridge Pope Blackdown Porter, Dorchester, Hardy Country and Royal Oak, smart bar service, nice back dining area, separate no-smoking area; on lively quay, handy for aquarium *(Paul Barstow, Karyn Taylor, G R Sunderland, John and Joan Nash, M E Wellington)*

☆ **Poole** [88 High St], *Old Harry*: Good menu inc lots of fish and seafood in friendly and bustling city local with comfortable seats inc big raised dining area, cheerful service, Bass and Charrington ale *(Basil Minson)*

Poole [Commercial Rd], *Conjurors Half Crown*: Pleasant pub with good range of beers, simple reasonably priced food *(D J and P M Taylor)*; [Market St], *Guildhall*: Good fresh food esp seafood in bright family eating pub *(Nigel Flook, Betsy Brown, LYM)*; [The Quay], *Lord Nelson*: Good value food inc tasty sandwiches in handy quayside pub, lots of nautical memorabilia, good range of beers *(Hugh Spottiswoode)*; [6 Ravine Rd, Canford Cliffs; SZ0689], *Nightjar*: Modern well run pub in quiet spot, friendly helpful courteous staff, well kept Bass, Worthington and a guest such as Fullers London Pride, attractively served reasonably priced bar food inc OAP discount *(W W Burke)*; [Town Quay], *Poole Arms*: Waterfront tavern looking across harbour to Brownsea Island, good lunchtime bar food, well kept real ale, friendly staff; magnificent green-tiled facade *(R J Ward, LYM)*

☆ **Portesham** [Front St (B3157); SY6086], *Kings Arms*: Large pub with considerable recent extensions, good reasonably priced food inc some unusual dishes, welcoming service, sizeable attractive garden with play area, pond and trout stream *(B and K Hypher, Mr and Mrs R O Gibson, Dave Braisted)*

☆ **Portland Bill** [SY6870], *Pulpit*: Comfortable and warmly welcoming food pub in great spot nr Pulpit Rock, short stroll to lighthouse and cliffs; local shellfish and interesting puddings as well as good value usual bar and restaurant food inc vegetarian, four well kept Gibbs Mew ales, good service; piped music *(A H Denman, P Devitt, M Hart)*

Preston [A353 Weymouth—Osmington; SY7083], *Spice Ship*: Big friendly family pub, nautical decor in series of rooms off central bar, good choice of food, ales such as Marstons Pedigree, live music popular with nearby caravan-campers; covered terrace, dogs allowed in garden, inexpensive drinks and novelties from children's shop, children's attractions maybe inc summer Sun conjuror; open all day all week *(Adrian Stopforth, Stan Edwards)*

Puddletown [SY7594], *Prince of Wales*: Well kept Badger Best and Tanglefoot, useful bar food *(David Lamb)*

☆ **Puncknowle** [Church St; SY5388], *Crown*: Good local atmosphere in 16th-c beamed and thatched flint inn's clean and comfortable open-plan lounge, good choice of reasonably priced home-cooked food esp pies and steak sandwiches, good vegetarian choice, well kept Palmers, decent wines, lots of country wines, very friendly staff; family room, locals' bar; attractive garden, pretty setting opp church; bedrooms *(Paul and Wendy Bachelor)*

☆ **Sandford Orcas** [off B3148 and B3145 N of Sherborne; ST6220], *Mitre*: Good value attractively presented food (steak and kidney pie praised by many) in tucked-away country local, cosy and comfortable with a good deal of unpretentious character, good service, well kept John Smiths and Wadworths 6X; bedrooms *(Betty and David Stockwell, D Waters, Stephen Brown, LYM)*

☆ Shaftesbury [St James St; ST8622], *Two Brewers*: Good atmosphere in well divided open-plan turkey-carpeted bar, lots of decorative plates, very wide choice of reasonably priced popular bar food (children's helpings of any dish) freshly prepared inc vegetarian, good puddings and good Sun roasts, very friendly service, well kept Courage Best and Directors, Wadworths 6X and guests such as Adnams Best and Batemans XB; picnic tables in garden with pretty views, pub at bottom of steep famously photogenic Gold Hill *(Colin Walls, John and Jill Woodfield, DP, Alan and Paula McCully, BB)*

☆ Shaftesbury [Bleke St], *Ship*: 17th-c local with black panelling, oak woodwork, traditional layout; well kept Badger Best and Tanglefoot, farm cider, bar food with separate eating area, helpful friendly service, pool and other games in public bar (crowded with young people weekend evenings), tables on terrace, boules *(JP, PP, V G and P A Nutt, David Carr, LYM)*

☆ Shaftesbury [The Commons], *Grosvenor*: Charming old-fashioned coaching hotel, warm and comfortable; good genuine fair-priced bar snacks, well kept beers inc Bass, stylish restaurant; ask Reception if you can see the magnificently carved oak 19th-c Chevy Chase sideboard in the first-floor residents' lounge; good bedrooms *(Alan and Paula McCully)*

☆ Shaftesbury [High St], *Mitre*: Cheerfully unpretentious, with quickly served good generous food from sandwiches up inc vegetarian, Blackmore Vale views from back dining room, well kept Eldridge Pope beers, good choice of malt whiskies and wines, daily papers, small suntrap garden; bedrooms *(Keith and Janet Morris, LYM)*

☆ Sherborne [Horsecastles; ST6316], *Skippers*: Pleasant local bustle, service welcoming and quick in spite of crowds, good range of reasonably priced food, well kept Bass and other ales; just outside centre *(C and E M Watson, Richard Houghton, John Hazel)*

Sherborne [Cheap St], *Cross Keys*: Comfortably refurbished with three distinct bars, extraordinarily wide choice of food, quick service, Eldridge Pope ales; lots of postal pictures, postbox in corridor *(Joan and Michel Hooper-Immins, Hugh MacLean)*

Shipton Gorge [off A35/B3157 E of Bridport; SY4991], *New Inn*: Friendly village pub, huge log fire, good value food inc freshly caught local fish, well kept Palmers *(Michael Richards, Adrian Wood)*

Sixpenny Handley [High St; ST9917], *Roebuck*: Plain village local well worth knowing for such good fish, meat and game cooked by the landlord's French wife, with home-grown veg *(Margaret Owen)*

☆ Studland [SZ0382], *Bankes Arms*: Wonderful peaceful spot above fine beach, outstanding country, sea and cliff views from huge pleasant garden; friendly and easy-going, substantial simple food, well kept Poole and Whitbreads-related ales, attractive log fire, pool table; children welcome, nr Coast Path; can get trippery in summer, parking can be complicated or expensive if you're not a NT member; big comfortable bedrooms, has been cl winter *(Chris Westmoreland, E G Parish, Nigel Flook, Betsy Brown, M Joyner, David Holloway, A Ellis)*

Sturminster Marshall [A350; SY9499], *Black Horse*: Smart but welcoming, with decent bar food inc wide choice of fish, well kept Badger beers, restaurant *(WHBM)*

☆ Sturminster Newton [Market Cross (B3092); ST7814], *White Hart*: Homely 18th-c thatched and black-beamed inn, warm cosy bar, well kept Badger Best and Tanglefoot with a guest such as Charles Wells Eagle, pleasant staff, jolly landlord, short choice of reasonably priced bar food, morning coffee, afternoon teas, garden beyond cobbled coach entry; bedrooms comfortable, though road not quiet *(Joan and Michel Hooper-Immins)*

☆ Sutton Poyntz [off A353 SE of Weymouth; SY7083], *Springhead*: Spacious but cosy, with comfortable furnishings, beams, well kept Eldridge Pope and Marstons Pedigree, decent reasonably priced wines, good choice of tempting food in bar and restaurant, log fires, welcoming attentive staff, newspapers, bar billiards; lovely spot opp willow stream in quiet village, entertaining ducks, good play area in big garden, walks to White Horse Hill and Dorset Coastal Path *(S J Edwards, Peter Churchill, J H and B V Hartland)*

☆ Swanage [Shore Rd; SZ0278], *Mowlem*: First-floor theatre restaurant, not a pub, but good food inc bar lunches, well kept Badger Best and Tanglefoot from downstairs bar, good service, delightful sea views *(Hugh Spottiswoode, Joan and Michel Hooper-Immins, Derek Patey)*

Swanage [High St], *Anchor*: Quiet pub dating from 16th c, well kept locally brewed beer, small range of food inc notable cheap ploughman's; old-fashioned juke box, not loud *(J S M Sheldon)*; [159 High St], *Black Swan*: Quaint old pub with garden nr millpond, well kept beers, decent house wines, tasty home-made bar food, friendly landlady; maybe piped radio, occasional live music, can get crowded and smoky; well priced bedrooms *(Veronica M Brown, P Stallard)*; [High St], *George*: Well kept Ringwood Fortyniner and Whitbreads Bitter and Strong Country tapped from the cask, friendly staff, food *(Gabrielle Coyle, Ian Lock)*; [Bell St, Herston (just off 1st turn into town off A351)], *Globe*: Small simple local, good atmosphere, chatty landlord, well kept Whitbreads-related ales *(Derek Patey, Chris Westmoreland, D P and J A Sweeney)*; [1 Burlington Rd], *Pines*: Big hotel bar popular with older people for reliably good value lunchtime food; well kept beers, good friendly service, excellent views from garden (a long way from bar); bedrooms comfortable *(John Kirk, P Stallard)*; *Red Lion*: Snug two-bar pub, beams densely hung with mugs and keys, lots of blow lamps, decent inexpensive food, well kept Ringwood and Whitbreads, friendly staff; children's annexe, partly covered back terrace *(Peter and Audrey Dowsett, Chris Westmoreland)*; [High St], *Tawnys*: Long-established wine bar with good range of food, strong on pasta and rice, around 100 wines by glass, many from New World, jovial atmosphere – useful alternative to the pubs here *(P Stallard)*

☆ Sydling St Nicholas [SY6399], *Greyhound*: Wide choice of good well prepared food with plentiful properly cooked veg, friendly service, well kept Ringwood and Wadworths 6X; tables in small garden, attractive village *(Galen Strawson)*

☆ Tolpuddle [SY7994], *Martyrs*: Good choice of genuine home cooking in bar and busy restaurant; friendly staff, well kept Badger beers, nice garden with ducks, hens and rabbits *(Mrs Joan Nash)*

☆ Trent [ST5918], *Rose & Crown*: Traditional relaxed old-fashioned pub, with log fire, flagstone floors, comfortable oak settles, nice pictures, fresh flowers, books, no piped music or machines; wide choice of consistently good quickly served food, decent choice of real ales, dining conservatory; picnic tables behind; children welcome *(Gerry Cox)*

☆ Wareham [South St; SY9287], *Quay*: Comfortable, light and airy stripped-stone bars, bar food from soup and sandwiches up, open fire, well kept Whitbreads-related and other ales, friendly staff, children allowed away from main bar; picnic tables out on the quay, parking nearby can be difficult *(John and Joan Nash, Chris Westmoreland)*

☆ Wareham [41 North St; A351, N end of town], *Kings Arms*: Friendly and lively traditional thatched town local, back serving counter and two bars off flagstoned central corridor, well kept Whitbreads-related ales, reasonably priced bar food (not Fri—Sun evenings), back garden *(Tom Espley, LYM)*
Wareham [14 South St], *Black Bear*: 18th-c inn with pleasant bar on right of through corridor, well kept Eldridge Pope Royal Oak and Hardy Country, good choice of well priced bar food, decent coffee, picnic tables in back yard; bedrooms *(Bruce Bird, Ann and Colin Hunt, Chris Westmoreland)*
Wareham Forest [Coldharbour; Wareham—Bere Regis – OS Sheet 195 map ref 902897; SY8683], *Silent Woman*: Well kept Badger ales and wide choice of good value standard food in busy lounge bar extended into stripped-masonry dining area with country bygones; more interesting books than usual on walls, military insignia, access for wheelchairs; good play area outside, walks nearby *(John and Joan Nash, D Illing)*

☆ West Bay [SY4590], *Bridport Arms*: Thatched pub on beach nr harbour and cliff walks, good range of generous good value food esp local fish, friendly staff, well kept Palmers BB, big fireplace in flagstoned back bar, no music;

bedrooms *(Prof and Mrs S Barnett, Dr J R G Beavon, Bill Edwards)*

☆ West Knighton [off A352 E of Dorchester; SY7387], *New Inn*: Biggish neatly refurbished pub, very busy in summer, with interesting range of reasonably priced food, small restaurant, quick friendly staff, real ales, country wines, skittle alley, good provision for children; big colourful garden, pleasant setting in quiet village with wonderful views *(David Lamb, Dr and Mrs S Jones, Stan Edwards)*

☆ West Lulworth [B3070; SY8280], *Castle*: Pretty thatched inn in lovely spot nr Lulworth Cove, good walks; bustling flagstoned public bar with maze of booth seating, cosy more modern-feeling lounge bar, bar food from filled rolls to steaks inc children's meals, popular garden with giant chess boards, boules, barbecues; well kept Devenish Wessex, Flowers Original and Marstons Pedigree, farm cider, pub and board games; piped music; bedrooms, good breakfasts *(Risha Stapleton, Mark Percy, Mr and Mrs L Boyle, D J Milner, S Lancaster, Hanns P Golez, Andy Thwaites, Jenny and Brian Seller, Helen Pickering, James Owen, David Holloway, Anthony Barnes, Ann and Colin Hunt, Annette and Stephen Marsden, LYM)*

☆ West Stafford [SY7289], *Wise Man*: Comfortable 16th-c local nr Hardy's cottage, very busy in summer; thatch, beams and toby jugs, with wide choice of good value generous standard food, charming staff, well kept Whitbreads-related ales, decent wines and country wines, public bar with darts; children not encouraged *(Howard Clutterbuck, R J Walden, Dr and Mrs S Jones)*

☆ Weymouth [Trinity Rd; SY6778], *Old Rooms*: Lovely harbour views over part-pedestrianised street from benches in front of character low-beamed fisherman's pub, well priced straightforward lunchtime food, unpretentious restaurant, friendly staff, well kept Whitbreads-related ales *(Eric Locker)*

☆ Weymouth [Barrack Rd], *Nothe Tavern*: Roomy well run local with good range of food inc fresh fish and children's dishes, friendly service, well kept Eldridge Pope Royal Oak and Hardy, decent wines; distant harbour glimpses from garden *(Marjorie and David Lamb, Joan and Michel Hooper-Immins, BB)*
Wimborne Minster [West St/Victoria Rd; SZ0199], *Pudding & Pye*: Spacious timbered Greenalls pub, comfortable nooks and crannies, lots of pictures and bric-a-brac, about eight real ales, wide food choice inc well presented sandwiches and Sun lunch, no parking but parking areas nearby *(David Dimock)*

☆ Wimborne St Giles [SU0212], *Bull*: Imaginative food inc fish fresh daily from Cornwall in comfortable red-carpetted bar with cretonne-cushioned modern settles; Badger ales *(Patrick Freeman)*
Winfrith Newburgh [A352 Wareham—Dorchester; SY8084], *Red Lion*: Wide range of promptly served meals and snacks in

comfortable dining pub with friendly efficient service, Badger ales; piped music, tables out behind, bedrooms *(Stan Edwards, Chris and Margaret Southon)*

Winterborne Stickland [ST8304], *Shire Horse*: Friendly landlord, cosy atmosphere, horse-theme decor, good moderately priced food *(Mr and Mrs M Cody)*

Winterborne Whitchurch [A354 Blandford—Dorchester; SY8399], *Milton Arms*: Recently refurbished village local, two busy bars, one with no-smoking area, wide choice of food inc good specials, pleasant atmosphere, helpful staff; weekly live music (usually Sat), quiz nights *(Brian Chambers)*

Winterborne Zelston [A31 Wimborne—Dorchester; SY8997], *Botany Bay*: Attractive restaurant-oriented pub with good range of bar snacks inc good ploughman's, well kept beer, friendly atmosphere, decent coffee; tables on back terrace *(A L Rowell, Mark Gregory)*

☆ **Winterbourne Abbas** [A35 W of Dorchester; SY6190], *Coach & Horses*: Big well run roadside pub with extensive lounge bar and long side dining area, cold food counter and hot carvery service, well kept Bass, Eldridge Pope Thomas Hardy and Royal Oak; particularly good well equipped outside play area; bedrooms *(John Sanders, BB)*

Stars after the name of a pub show exceptional character and appeal. They don't mean extra comfort. And they are nothing to do with food quality, for which there's a separate knife-and-fork rosette. Even quite a basic pub can win stars, if it's individual enough.

Essex

Pubs currently doing particularly well here include the handsome old Marlborough Head in Dedham, the Sun at Feering (interesting food and well kept ales – its Maltese landlord propelling it into our main entries for the first time), the welcoming Black Bull at Fyfield (another good place to eat in), the White Hart at Great Yeldham (doing so well under its new management that it earns our accolade of Essex Dining Pub of the Year), the Bell at Horndon on the Hill (good on all counts, gaining both a Food Award and a Place to Stay Award this year), the Flitch of Bacon at Little Dunmow (a new Place to Stay Award for this fine country tavern), and the Prince of Wales at Stow Maries (unspoilt style, good food and excellent real ales – another pub successfully making the leap into the main entries this year). Currently coming to prominence among the pubs in the Lucky Dip section at the end of the chapter are the Wooden Fender at Ardleigh, Queens Head at Boreham, White Harte in Burnham on Crouch, Three Horseshoes at Duton Hill, Sun at Dedham, Seabrights Barn at Great Baddow, Swan near Great Henny, Rainbow & Dove at Hastingwood, Cock at Hatfield Broad Oak, Wheatsheaf at High Ongar, Duck at Newney Green, White Horse at Pleshey, Bakers Arms at Stock and Black Buoy at Wivenhoe. We have inspected almost all of these and can vouch for their quality. There's also a good choice of places in Coggeshall – and the county has one of the finest station buffets in Britain, the one at Manningtree. Prices in Essex are generally around the national average; we found much the cheapest drinks at the very well run Queens Head at Littlebury, while pubs getting their beers from local breweries such as Crouch Vale, Mauldons and Ridleys were cheaper than average.

ARKESDEN TL4834 Map 5

Axe & Compasses ★ ♀

Village signposted from B1038 – but B1039 from Wendens Ambo, then forking left, is prettier; OS Sheet 154 map reference 482344

There's an agreeable combination of welcoming hospitality, a fine old-fashioned atmosphere and good cooking at this rambling thatched country pub, which is set in an attractive village. A comfortable carpeted saloon bar has a warm coal fire, pastel-green-cushioned oak and elm seats, quite a few easy chairs, old wooden tables, lots of brasses on the walls, and a friendly cat called Spikey. The smaller public bar, with cosy built-in settles, has sensibly placed darts and cribbage. Popular meals served with very good vegetables can be eaten in the bar or the restaurant, and might include sandwiches, home-made soup (£2), deep-fried mushrooms with garlic mayonnaise (£3.95), mushroom pancake with a creamy cheesy sauce (£7.25), grilled whole lemon sole (£9.95), steaks (from £11.50), and daily specials such as chicken and spinach terrine (£3.95), scallops with mushrooms and onions in white wine and glazed with cheese sauce (£5.25), chicken, leek and bacon crumble (£6.75), and pork loin in a creamy mushroom sauce and glazed with stilton cheese or stir fry vegetables in a filo pastry case with french mustard (£7.25), monkfish on a roasted red pepper sauce (£9.75) and honey-glazed duck breast with Cointreau gravy or rack of lamb cooked pink on a fresh rosemary sauce (£11.75); impressive pudding trolley; prompt, attentive service. Well kept Greene King IPA and Abbott on handpump under light blanket pressure, a very good wine list, and about two dozen whiskies. There are seats outside on a side terrace with colourful hanging baskets; maybe summer barbecues. *(Recommended by Tina and David Woods-Taylor, Richard Siebert, Gwen and Peter Andrews, John Fahy, Mr and Mrs I Walker, Robin Moore, Roger Byrne)*

Greene King ~ Lease: Themis and Diane Christou ~ Real ale ~ Meals and snacks (not winter Sun evening) ~ Restaurant (not winter Sun evening) ~ (01799) 550272 ~ Children in eating area of bar and in restaurant until 8.30 ~ Open 11-2.30, 6-11

BLACKMORE END TL7430 Map 5

Bull ♀

Signposted via Beazley End from Bocking Church Street, itself signed off A131 just N of Braintree bypass; pub is on Wethersfield side of village

As well as the usual sandwiches (from £2.25), ham egg and chips (£4.25), ploughman's (£4.50) and salads (£5.95), there's an interesting range of adventurous well prepared specials at this comfortable tucked-away dining pub. The menu changes every two weeks and might include potato, onion and sage cream soup (£2.50), chicken liver pâté (£3.50), sweet cured herrings (£3.95), deep fried crab fritters with a mustard fruit pickle mayonnaise (£4.95), fried lamb liver with melted onions and sage (£6.95), collops of chicken with bacon and mushrooms in a red wine sauce (£7.50), breaded escalope of turkey with wilted spinach and lemon butter sauce (£8.95), baked fillet of salmon with sweet mango and mild curry cream sauce and banana rice (£10.25), mignons of fillet steak with stilton and port sauce (£10.95), slices of roast duck with honey-roast vegetables and ginger honey sauce (£10.95) and medaillons of ostrich with compote of wild mushrooms and coarse grain mustard and red wine sauce or seared scallops with bacon, tomato and chive butter sauce (£13.50); good vegetables are served separately. There are lots of tempting home-made puddings such as bread pudding with rum, whipped cream and toasted nuts or coffee and walnut sponge with hot toffee sauce (from £3.50); good value set lunches (two courses £8.50, three £10.50); Sunday lunch (£10.50). The flowery-carpeted dining bar has red plush built-in button-back banquettes, low black beams and lots of menu blackboards. Beyond a massive brick chimney-piece is a prettily cottagey restaurant area (no cigars or pipes). Well kept Adnams, Boddingtons, Greene King IPA, Mauldons Whiteadder and changing guest ales on handpump; ten wines by the glass from a list of about 70 which includes some enterprising bin-ends; picnic tables outside. *(Recommended by Gwen and Peter Andrews, Roy and Margaret Jones, Richard Siebert; more reports please)*

Free house ~ Licensees Christopher and Mary Bruce ~ Real ale ~ Meals and snacks (till 10 Tues-Sat; no sandwiches or snacks Sat evening) ~ Restaurant ~ (01371) 851037 ~ Children in eating area of bar if eating ~ Open 12-3, 6.30-11; cl Mondays (except bank holidays)

CASTLE HEDINGHAM TL7835 Map 5

Bell

B1058 E of Sible Hedingham, towards Sudbury

The cheerful licensee Sandra Ferguson has been here for 30 years now, and this historic old coaching inn really comes to life when she's behind the bar. The friendly beamed and timbered saloon bar remains unchanged over the years, with Jacobean-style seats and windsor chairs around sturdy oak tables, and beyond the standing timbers left from a knocked-through wall, some steps lead up to a little gallery. Behind the traditionally furnished public bar a games room has dominoes and cribbage; piped pop music. One bar is no smoking, and each of the rooms has a good welcoming log fire. Promptly served bar food includes soup (£2), ploughman's (£3), mushrooms in garlic butter (£3.90), ham and broccoli bake, liver and bacon casserole, steak and Guinness pie or Thai chicken curry (all £4.90), trout (£6), sirloin steak (£7.50), and puddings like treacle tart or banoffi pie (£2.20); Greene King IPA and Abbot and an occasional guest beer like Shepherd Neame Master Brew tapped from the cask. In summer, a particular highlight is the fine big walled garden behind the pub – an acre or so, with grass, trees and shrubs; there are more seats on a small terrace. The great dane is called Lucia. The nearby 12th-century castle keep is worth a visit. *(Recommended by Gwen and Peter Andrews, W W Burke, Richard Siebert, Anthony Barker; more reports please)*

Grays (Greene King, Ridleys) ~ Tenant Mrs Sandra Ferguson ~ Real ale ~ Meals and snacks (till 10pm; not Mon evening, except bank holidays) ~ (01787) 460350 ~ Children welcome except in public bar ~ Jazz last Sun lunchtime of month, acoustic guitar group Fri evening ~ Open 11.30-3, 6-11; cl evening 25 Dec

CHAPPEL TL8927 Map 5

Swan

Wakes Colne; pub visible just off A604 Colchester—Halstead

This charming old timbered pub is nicely set, with the River Colne running through the garden and on down to a splendid Victorian viaduct. And in summer, the sheltered suntrap cobbled courtyard, now partly covered by a canopy, has a rather continental feel with parasols, big tubs overflowing with flowers, and French street signs. The friendly spacious and low-beamed rambling bar has standing oak timbers dividing off side areas, banquettes around lots of dark tables, one or two swan pictures and plates on the white partly panelled walls, and a few attractive tiles above the very big fireplace, filled in summer with lots of plants; one bar is no smoking. Popular and good value bar food includes filled french rolls or sandwiches (from £1.50), ploughman's (from £3.25), home-made steak and kidney pie or gammon with pineapple (£4.45), fried cod or rock eel (£4.95), salads (from £4.95), sirloin steak (£8.95), fresh fish dishes, and good puddings (from £2.25). Well kept Greene King Abbot and Rayments on handpump, a good selection of wines by the glass served by cheery helpful staff; cribbage, dominoes, and faint piped music. The nearby Railway Centre (a must for train buffs) is just a few minutes' walk away. *(Recommended by Jill Bickerton, Mrs P Goodwyn, Paul Randall, Marjorie and Bernard Parkin, Mavis and John Wright, C H and P Stride, Gwen and Peter Andrews, S R Maycock, Ian Phillips, Howard Gatiss, David Shillitoe, Tony and Wendy Hobden)*

Free house ~ Licensees Terence Martin and M A Hubbard ~ Real ale ~ Meals and snacks (till 10.15) ~ Restaurant ~ (01787) 222353 ~ Children over 5 welcome in restaurant and eating area of bar ~ Open 11-3, 6-11

CLAVERING TL4731 Map 5

Cricketers

B1038 Newport—Buntingford, Newport end of village

The emphasis at this comfortably modernised dining pub is very much on the seasonally changing menu, which might include starters like soup (£2.80), noodles baked with mushrooms, peppers, tomato, onion and mozzarella (£4), chilled melon with prawns and tomato and basil sorbet (£4.25), warm salad of roasted celery and goat's cheese with walnut vinaigrette (£4.50), coarse terrine of pork and chicken livers with toasted onion and herb bread (£4.75). Main courses might include steak and kidney pie or sautéed lamb kidneys with button onions on a potato and bacon rosti with tarragon sauce (£8.25), slices of marinated venison char-grilled on a wild mushroom and game sauce (£9.50), pink rack of lamb in a rosemary crust with redcurrant and port sauce (£10.75). The roomy L-shaped beamed bar has standing timbers resting on new brickwork, and pale green plush button-backed banquettes, stools and windsor chairs around shiny wooden tables on a pale green carpet, with gleaming copper pans and horsebrasses and dried flowers in the big fireplace (open fire in colder weather), and fresh flowers; one area is no smoking; piped music. Well kept Boddingtons, and Flowers IPA and Original on handpump. The front terrace has picnic tables and umbrellas and colourful flowering shrubs. Pretty new bedrooms in an adjacent house. *(Recommended by Andrew and Joan Life, Maysie Thompson, Michael Boniface, Jack Morley, Mr and Mrs I Walker; more reports please)*

Free house ~ Licensees Trevor and Sally Oliver ~ Real ale ~ Meals and snacks ~ Restaurant ~ (01799) 550442 ~ Children in eating area of bar and in restaurant ~ Open 10.30-3, 6-11; cl 25 December ~ Bedrooms: £55B/£65B

nr COGGESHALL TL8522 Map 5

Compasses

Pattiswick; signposted from A120 about 2 miles W of Coggeshall; OS Sheet 168 map reference 820247

The spacious and attractive beamed bars of this friendly country pub are neatly kept and comfortable, with tiled floors and lots of brass ornaments, and Greene King IPA, Marstons Pedigree and Rayments on handpump; darts. Home-made bar food includes lunchtime sandwiches or filled baguettes (from £3.50), filled baked potatoes (from £3.95), ploughman's (from £5.25), and lunchtime and evening turkey curry, ham, egg and chips, toad in the hole or battered cod (£6.95), liver and bacon, fisherman's pie, lamb kidneys in sherry gravy or steak, boar and kidney pie (£7.95), gammon steak in mustard and mushroom sauce (£9.50), fried chicken strips in a creamy peppercorn sauce (£9.95), red snapper fillet in cream and tarragon sauce (£10.95) and lamb shoulder roasted in rosemary, garlic and black pepper (£11.75). There's a good choice of seven interesting vegetarian dishes like Thai noodle and nut vegetable satay, vegetable and nut curry or mushroom, brie and cranberry pastry (from £7.95). Cold puddings include chocolate orange bavarois, mint and chocolate cheesecake and giant caramel-filled choux pastry. Outside there are seats on spacious lawns, and a new adventure playground. *(Recommended by Quentin Williamson, Pamela Goodwyn, Hazel Morgan; more reports please)*

Free house ~ Licensees Chris and Gilbert Heap ~ Real ale ~ Meals and snacks ~ Restaurant ~ (01376) 561322 ~ Children welcome in eating area of bar and restaurant ~ Open 11-3, 6.30(6 Sat)-11; 12-10.30 Sun in summer; cl 25 and 26 Dec evening

DEDHAM TM0533 Map 5

Marlborough Head 🍺

The long-standing licensees at this nicely old-fashioned inn manage to combine all aspects of their trade in a comfortably easy way. There's a good pubby atmosphere, a warm welcome, a usefully imaginative menu, and nice comfortable bedrooms. The relaxed central lounge has lots of beams and pictures, a wealth of finely carved woodwork, and a couple of roaring log fires; the beamed and timbered bar is set out for eating with lots of tables (which have a numbered pebble for ordering food) in wooden alcoves around its plum-coloured carpet. It's best to get there early to be sure of a table for the popular bar food, which includes sandwiches (from £1.95), soup (£2), filled baked potatoes (from £2.25), fried squid with spicy tomato sauce (£3.75), creamy mushrooms with a warm muffin (£3.95), bacon, mushroom and tomato quiche (£4.60), vegetable sausage in onion gravy (£5.75), braised rabbit in mustard sauce (£6.35), beef curry or creamy turkey with apricots and almonds (£6.45), fried breast of chicken with mushroom sauce (£6.50) and noisettes of lamb wth spring onion sauce (£7.50), and very good home-made puddings such as treacle tart (£2.75), baby almond meringues with butterscotch sauce and cream (£3.10) or sherry trifle (£3.25); they also do morning coffee and afternoon teas. Ind Coope Burton and Greene King IPA on handpump under light blanket pressure. Seats on the terrace or in the garden at the back (part of which is now the car park). The pub is right in the heart of Constable's old village, directly opposite the artist's school, and the handsome flushwork church tower that features in a number of his paintings. When this became an inn in 1704, it was named for the Duke of Marlborough's victory at Blenheim. *(Recommended by Melanie Bradshaw, Derek and Margaret Underwood, Ian Phillips, Gordon Tong, Simon Penny, A Preston, Joan Hilditch, Derek and Maggie Washington, John Beeken, Paul Noble, Mike Beiley)*

Ind Coope (Allied) ~ Lease: Brian and Jackie Wills and Linda Mower ~ Real ale ~ Meals and snacks (all day) ~ (01206) 323250 ~ Children in eating area of bar ~ Open 10-11; 11-10.30 Sun; cl 25 Dec ~ Bedrooms: £32.50S/£50S

FEERING TL8720 Map 5

Sun

3 Feering Hill; before Feering proper, B1024 just NE of Kelvedon

When the cheery Maltese landlord and his wife arrived at this historic place four years ago, it was run-down and boarded-up. Now after lots of hard work, the handsome 16th-c frontage is gleaming, and there's a busily chatty atmosphere in the comfortably refurbished bar. Chief draws are the food and beer, both of which are unusual. Written up on blackboards over the fireplace, the choice of bar meals might include soup (£1.80), smoked salmon terrine (£2.95), Maltese rabbit in red wine and caper sauce (£4.75), pasta in a leek and vegetable sauce (£5.40), paprika pork in cider (£5.50), spicy chicken and mushroom (£5.75), kangaroo escalope in mustard sauce or ostrich steak in brandy, cream and peppercorn sauce (£7.50), and puddings like budina (a Maltese bread pudding, £1.95), or pears poached in red wine (£2.50). The five very well kept real ales usually change every day, with 17 different brews passing through the handpumps each week; on our visit the choice was Courage Best and Directors, Crouch Vale SAS, Cuckmere Haven Hoppy Wanderer, and Hoskins and Oldfield White Dolphin. They also have a changing farm cider, and a good range of malt whiskies. Their Easter and August bank holiday beer festivals have a regional theme, when they'll stock ales from a particular county or area. Standing timbers break up the several areas of the comfortably refurbished beamed and carpeted bar, which has plenty of neatly matching tables and chairs, and green-cushioned stools and banquettes around the walls. Carvings on the beams in the lounge are said to be linked with Catherine of Aragon, and there's a handsome canopy with a sun motif over the woodburning stove; newspapers to read, piped music, fruit machine, chess, cards, backgammon. Quite a few seats and tables on a partly-covered paved patio behind; there may be barbecues out here on sunny weekends, though the rain was so heavy on our inspection a young family of ducks waddled into it for shelter. There are more tables in an attractive garden beyond the car park. *(Recommended by Chris Smith, John C Baker, David Tindal)*

Free house ~ Licensees Charles and Kim Scicluna ~ Real ale ~ Meals and snacks (not 25/6 Dec or 1 Jan) ~ (01376) 570442 ~ Well behaved children welcome ~ Open 11-3, 6-11

FYFIELD TL5606 Map 5

Black Bull

B184, N end of village

There's a really comfortable welcoming atmosphere at this prettily lit vine-covered dining pub. The very tasty bar food includes soft roes (£2.95), green-lip mussels with black bean sauce (£3.50), hot avocado and stilton (£3), steak and kidney pudding (£6.70), skate wing (£7.25) and a seafood selection in garlic butter (£8.50) on the menu, and changing blackboard specials such as tiger prawns cooked with fresh chillies and garlic (£3.95), home-made gravadlax (£4.75), kleftiko (£7.20), pork fillet fried with fresh cranberries (£7.15), and puddings like chocolate trifle cake or bread pudding (from £1.75). Inside, the series of communicating rooms have low ceilings, big black beams, standing timbers, and cushioned wheelback chairs and modern settles on the muted maroon carpet; warm winter fire. Well kept Courage Directors, Ruddles Best and Wadworths 6X on handpump; darts, dominoes, cribbage, piped music, fruit machine. Outside there are lots of barrels for tables, or filled with flowers, and under an arbour by the car park is an aviary with budgerigars and cockatiels. There are picnic tables on a nearby stretch of grass, as well as to the side of the building. Dogs welcome. *(Recommended by S Palmer, Nigel and Lindsay Chapman, Paul Barstow, Karyn Taylor, Ian Phillips, Beryl and Bill Farmer, Mr and Mrs N Spink, Peter and Joy Heatherley, Keith Archer, Stephen and Jean Curtis, Gwen and Peter Andrews, Mayur Shah, Beryl and Bill Farmer, M A and C R Starling, C H and P Stride, R C Morgan)*

Free house ~ Licensees Alan Smith and Nicola Eldridge ~ Real ale ~ Meals and snacks ~ Restaurant ~ (01277) 899225 ~ Children welcome in eating area of bar ~ Open 11-2.30(3 Sat), 6.30-11

GOSFIELD TL7829 Map 5

Green Man 🍽 ♀

3 m N of Braintree

You will need to book a table at this smart well run dining pub, as it's operated very much like a restaurant – with an atmosphere to match. One of the main attractions is the splendid lunchtime cold table which has a marvellous help-yourself choice of home-cooked ham, tongue, beef and turkey, dressed salmon or crab in season, game pie, salads and homemade pickles (£6.95). Other well cooked dishes include soups like game with sherry (£1.90), soft roes on toast with bacon (£3.25), lasagne (£5.95), fresh battered cod (£6), delicious liver and bacon or braised oxtail with dumplings (£6.50), lamb liver and bacon (£6.65), cider-baked hot ham or hot sirloin of beef (£6.85), tender roast shoulder of wild boar (£6.95), rare lamb chops in a port and cranberry sauce (£7.50), pheasant in red wine (£7.95), fresh scallops mornay (£8.20), roast duck with gooseberry sauce (£8.50) or 20oz T-bone steak (£13.50). A fabulous range of puddings might include raspberry pavlova or steamed marmalade pudding (£3); the vegetables are fresh and the chips home-made. The two little bars have a relaxed atmosphere, and the dining room is no smoking. Greene King IPA and Abbot on handpump, and decent nicely priced wines, many by the glass; darts, pool, fruit machine and juke box. *(Recommended by Gwen and Peter Andrews, Tina and David Woods-Taylor, BNF, M Parkin, John Fahy, Thomas Nott)*

Greene King ~ Lease: John Arnold ~ Real ale ~ Meals and snacks (not Sun evening) ~ Restaurant (not Sun evening) ~ (01787) 472746 ~ Well behaved children in eating area lunchtime and early evening ~ Open 11-3, 6.30-11 (midnight supper licence)

GREAT YELDHAM TL7638 Map 5

White Hart 🍽 ♀

Poole Street; A604 Halstead—Haverhill

Essex Dining Pub of the Year

This attractive black and white timbered Tudor house is now run very succesfully by the Huntsbridge Group along the lines they've shown work so well in their two pubs in Cambridgeshire: the Pheasant at Keyston and Three Horseshoes in Madingley. You can make your meal informal or smart by choosing to eat in the bar or restaurant from the same inventive menu which is available throughout the building. Very well prepared snacks might include ploughman's (£4.75), mozarella, plum tomato and salami sandwich (£4.25), fresh pasta with tomato, garlic and rosemary (£4.75), sausages and mash (£4.95), liver and bacon with bubble and squeak (£5.75). Imaginative starters might be hot Thai soup with chicken, coconut milk, ginger, coriander, lemon grass and noodles (£3.95), grilled goat's cheese with oven-dried figs and baby spinach salad (£4.50), smoked haddock and leek fish cakes with a spicy peanut and cucumber sauce (£4.75), and delicious main courses such as tagliatelle with fennel, sun-dried tomatoes, olives and toasted hazelnuts (£6.95), casserole of rabbit with courgette, aubergine, peppers, plum tomatoes and garlic mash (£7.75), fried pigeon breasts with a roasted parsnip purée and rosti potato (£8.50). A very tempting list of about eight original puddings might include praline parfait with caramel sauce and almond wafer, brochette of fruits with a white pepper ice cream or bourbon whisky and maple syrup ice cream with pistachio shortbread (£3-£4.95), and a selection of unpasteurised cheeses (£5.25); smaller helpings for children; Sunday roast (£9.95); no-smoking restaurant. Well kept Adnams Best and Southwold, Fullers London Pride, Everards Tiger, Morrells Varsity and Wadworths 6X on handpump, and a very fine wine list with about 17 wines by the glass including a good selection of pudding wines. The main areas have stone and wood floors with some dark oak panelling especially around the fireplace. The pretty well-kept garden has seats among a variety of trees and shrubs on the lawns. *(Recommended by Gwen and Peter Andrews, Paul Randall; more reports please)*

Free house ~ Licensees Roger Jones and John Hoskins ~ Real ale ~ Meals and snacks (till 10pm) ~ Restaurant ~ (01787) 237250 ~ Children welcome ~ Open 11-3, 6-11

HORNDON ON THE HILL TQ6683 Map 3

Bell 🍴 🍷 🛏

Village signposted off B1007 NW of Stanford le Hope

This lovely flower-decked medieval inn is meticulously run by enthusiastic hard-working licensees who take great care to ensure their guests have a perfectly pleasing visit. The warmly welcoming heavily beamed open-plan bar has some antique high-backed settles and plush burgundy stools and banquettes, with rugs on the flagstones or highly polished oak floorboards. Seats in a bow window at the back give on to views over the fields. Imaginative carefully home-prepared bar food might include cream of celeriac soup (£2.60), goat's cheese and leek parcel (£3.85), chicken liver pâté with plum preserve (£3.55), smoked salmon filled with cream cheese and chives (£5.50), chicken leg stuffed with wild mushrooms, steak and kidney or chicken, leek and mushroom pie (£4.95), braised rump with herb dumplings (£5.85), braised lamb shank with rosemary (£5.95), pigeon breasts with haggis and roast beetroot sauce (£10.25), fried calf liver with tarragon mash and bacon (£10.95), and puddings like white chocolate mousse with dark chocolate sauce or caramelised lemon tart (£3.50). They have a changing choice of about five real ales which might include Adnams Extra, Bass, Fullers London Pride, Gales or Hancocks HB on handpump, and a huge selection of over 100 well chosen wines from all over the world with about 13 by the glass, listed on a blackboard with suggestions on what to drink with your food; you can also buy them off-sales. On the last weekend in June the High Road outside is closed (by Royal Charter) for period-costume festivities and a crafts fair; the pub holds a feast then. Very attractive beamed bedrooms, up the road. *(Recommended by Mrs J A Blanks, Dave Irving, Bob and Maggie Atherton, James Nunns, Dr and Mrs Baker, Richard Siebert, Peter and Joy Heatherley, Ron Gentry, Quentin Williamson, Mavis and John Wright, Mrs S Miller, Stephen Brown, Mr and Mrs J R Morris, M J How, Kenneth and Muriel Holden, Mark Newbould, Nigel Norman, M A and C R Starling, Neville Kenyon)*

Free house ~ Licensee John Vereker ~ Real ale ~ Meals and snacks (12-2, 6.30-10) ~ Restaurant ~ (01375) 673154 ~ Children in eating area of bar and restaurant ~ Open 11-2.30(3 Sat), 6-11 ~ Bedrooms: /£55B

LAMARSH TL8835 Map 5

Red Lion

From Bures on B1508 Sudbury—Colchester take Station Road, passing station; Lamarsh then signposted

The atmospheric bar of this friendly timbered old hunting lodge has been freshly painted soft pink. As well as abundant timbering there are attractive dried flowers and plants, local scenes on the walls, a roaring log fire, and unobtrusive piped music.

Tables and pews in stalls with red velvet curtain dividers look on to broad views over the fields and colour-washed houses of the Stour Valley. Hearty bar food might include soups such as carrot and orange (£2.25), huge filled rolls with a very flexible range of fillings (from £3.35), stilton and walnut bake or chicken, ham and broccoli pie (£4.95), well liked salads such as Greek-style tuna with feta cheese (£5.25), and home-made puddings such as cherry pie (£2.50). Well kept Fullers London Pride and Greene King IPA and Nethergate on handpump, a range of malt whiskies, and decent dry white wine by the glass; friendly staff. Pool, darts, cribbage, fruit machine, video game. There are swings in the biggish sheltered sloping garden. *(Recommended by Gwen and Peter Andrews, MDN, Nigel Norman, Liz, James and Ian Phillips; more reports please)*

Free house ~ Licensees John and Jackie O'Sullivan ~ Real ale ~ Meals and snacks (till 10pm, not Sun evening) ~ Restaurant ~ (01787) 227918 ~ Children in eating area ~ Open 11-3, 6-11; 11-11 Sat; cl evening 25 Dec

LANGHAM TM0233 Map 5

Shepherd & Dog ♀

Moor Rd/High St; village signposted off A12 N of Colchester

Although very much at the centre of an active village community, this wonderfully friendly inn is much more than just a little village local. Newcomers always feel just as welcome as regulars, and the food goes well beyond what you'd expect. The menu changes daily, and as well as good sandwiches might include cream of leek and potato soup (£1.95), mediterranean seafood cocktail (£3.60), green lip mussels in garlic butter (£3.90), nut cutlets or vegetarian lasagne (£4.50), lamb liver with green pepper and brandy sauce (£5.25), gammon hocks in parsley sauce (£5.50), fried fillets of red bream (£5.95), grilled salmon with hollandaise sauce (£6.95), half roast duck with caramel orange sauce (£9.50) and baked tilapia stuffed with lemon grass and ginger (£10.95). They sometimes have maybe Greek, Indian, French or American themed food evenings. Well kept Greene King IPA, Abbot and Rayments and Nethergate Golden Gate and Old Growler on handpump, and a short but decent wine list. The L-shaped bar, with an interesting collection of continental bottled beers, is kept spick and span, and there's often a sale of books for charity. Tables outside. *(Recommended by C H and P Stride, J S Rutter, Gwen and Peter Andrews, A C Morrison, Cheryl and Keith Roe, Nigel Clifton, John Fahy, M A and C R Starling, Gill and Andy Plumb, Pamela Goodwyn)*

Free house ~ Licensees Paul Barnes and Jane Graham ~ Real ale ~ Meals and snacks (12-2.15, 6-10) ~ Restaurant ~ (01206) 272711 ~ Children welcome ~ Open 11-3, 5.30(6 Sat)-11

LEIGH ON SEA TQ8385 Map 3

Crooked Billet 🍺

51 High St; from A13 follow signpost to station, then cross bridge over railway towards waterside

The spring and autumn beer festivals at this inviting old place are quite a novelty, as you can go down to their cellar to choose from about 30 independent cask-conditioned ales. At other times they have well kept Adnams, Benskins, Ind Coope Burton, Tetleys and Youngs Special on handpump or tapped from the cask, and at least three guest beers. The building is braced against the sea wall, up some steps from the narrow street, and the traditional homely lounge bar has two big bay windows with good views out to sea, as well as seats built around the walls, a solid fuel stove, and photographs of local cockle smacks on the shiny, yellowing walls; on the left, the bare-floored public bar has a big coal-effect gas fire and more photographs. Served only at lunchtime, home-made bar food includes soup (£1.95), sandwiches (from £2.10), filled baked potatoes (from £2.35), baguettes (from £2.50), crab or salmon platter (£3.75), vegetarian dishes (from £4.25) and seafood platter (£5.25). Friendly service may be a bit stretched on busy sunny days. You can watch the shellfish boats in the old-fashioned working harbour from seats out on the big terrace, which has an outside servery used on fine afternoons. No children. *(Recommended by Nigel Norman, Tina and David Woods-Taylor, E G Parish, Tim Heywood, Sophie Wilne)*

Taylor Walker (Carlsberg Tetleys) ~ Managers Andy and Mairi Heron ~ Real ale ~ Lunchtime meals and snacks (till 3; not Sunday) ~ (01702) 714854 ~ Live music once a week in winter ~ Open 11-11; Sun 12-10.30

LITTLE BRAXTED TL8314 Map 5

Green Man

Kelvedon Road; village signposted off B1389 by NE end of A12 Witham bypass – keep on patiently

Pleasantly tucked away in a very quiet lane, this brick house is pretty inside and out. There's a cosy welcoming atmosphere in the characterful little lounge – which can get full in winter – with its interesting collection of bric-a-brac, including 200 horsebrasses and some harness, mugs hanging from a beam, a lovely copper urn, and an open fire. The tiled public bar leads to a games room with pool, darts, shove-ha'penny, dominoes, cribbage, and fruit machine. Well kept Ridleys IPA, Rumpus, Spectacular and Witchfinder Porter are dispensed from handpumps in the form of 40mm brass cannon shells, and there are several malt whiskies, home-made lemonade in summer and mulled wine in winter; piped music. Good, hearty home-made bar food includes sandwiches (from £1.80), filled french bread (£2.50), filled baked potatoes (from £2.55), and daily specials like liver and apple casserole (£4.25), tuna and sweetcorn pasta pot, mushroom stroganoff or chicken breast in mushroom sauce (£5.25) and lasagne (£5.50), and puddings like chocolate mousse or blackberry and apple coconut crumble (£1.95). There are picnic tables and a pretty pond in the sheltered garden behind. No children. *(Recommended by Jill Bickerton, Cheryl and Keith Roe, Thomas Nott, Gwen and Peter Andrews, Tina and David Woods-Taylor, Derek Patey, Roxanne Chamberlain, Alan Budden)*

Ridleys ~ Tenants Tony and Andrea Wiley ~ Real ale ~ Meals and snacks ~ (01621) 891659 ~ Regular traditional jazz ~ Open 11.30-3, 6-11; cl evening 25 and 26 Dec

LITTLE DUNMOW TL6521 Map 5

Flitch of Bacon 🛏

Village signposted off A120 E of Dunmow, then turn right on village loop road

Country characters rub shoulders with visiting businessmen at this rural tavern, which is honestly run by nicely welcoming friendly licensees. Modest refurbishments have preserved a traditional atmosphere in the small timbered bar, which is simply but attractively furnished, mainly with flowery-cushioned pews, and has prettily arranged flowers on the tables, and ochre walls. Quietly relaxing at lunchtime during the week, the atmosphere can be vibrantly cheerful in the evenings – especially on one of the Saturdays they're singing through a musical around the piano at the back. The sensibly small range of unpretentious very tasty bar food all freshly cooked by the landlady might include generous sandwiches – including excellent home-carved ham (£1.75), soup (£2.50), cheese and ham ploughman's (£3.25), anchovies on toast (£3.50), ham and eggs with a crusty roll (£4), smoked salmon and scrambled eggs (£5.50), and three or four changing hot dishes such as sausage hotpot (£4.50) or steak and kidney pie (£6.50), and a couple of puddings; good buffet lunch only on Sunday. Greene King IPA, and a guest like Arundel or Woodfordes Wherry under light blanket pressure. Friendly and thoughtful service; cribbage, dominoes. The pub looks across the quiet lane to a broad expanse of green, and has a few picnic tables on the edge; the nearby church of St Mary is well worth a visit. *(Recommended by Gwen and Peter Andrews, C H and P Stride, Mike and Karen England, N G Neate, S D Penn, John Fahy, Nikki Moffat, David Oppedisano, Jim Leven)*

Free house ~ Licensees Bernard and Barbara Walker ~ Real ale ~ Meals and snacks (cold snacks till 5.30 Sun) ~ (01371) 820323 ~ Children welcome in restaurant ~ Open 12-3(3.30 Sat), 6-11; Sun 12-6 only) ~ Bedrooms: £25S/£45S

LITTLEBURY TL5139 Map 5

Queens Head 🛏 ♀ 🍺

B1383 NW of Saffron Walden; not far from M11 junction 9, but exit northbound only, access southbound only

This vibrant bustling old village inn is a must for real ale lovers because as well as John Smiths for just £1 on Monday-Thursday, they have seven other real ales including Bass, Courage Directors, and Youngers Scotch with changing guests like Hancocks HB, Marstons Best, Mansfield Riding, and Mauldons Black Adder, along with helpful tasting notes. There's an Easter real ale festival with over 70 different beers; also interesting bottled beers, and a decent recently expanded wine list. Good value very tasty home-made food changes every day and might include lunchtime sandwiches (from £1.95), soup such as prawn and samphire (£2.20), filled baked potatoes (from £2.50), baked avocado with stilton butter (£2.80), wild boar and apple sausages (£3.10), ploughman's (£4.25), fresh tagliatelle with vegetarian sauces or provençal tarts with garlic pastry (£5.20), gammon with cider and apple (£5.90), pheasant with cranberries (in season, £7.90) and puddings like different treacle tart or banoffi pie (£2.50); they do a two-course weekday lunch (£5), hold winter themed food evenings, and grow lots of herbs (used in the cooking). The pub is carefully refurbished to make the most of its unassuming appeal – flooring tiles, beams, simple but attractive wooden furniture, old local photographs, bunches of dried flowers and plants, and snug side areas leading off the bar; a small area in the restaurant is no smoking; darts, shove-ha'penny, cribbage, dominoes and piped music. Tables out in a nicely planted walled garden, and swings, stepping stumps, a climbing frame and slide for children. *(Recommended by Marjorie and Bernard Parkin, John Fahy, AW, BW, Gwen and Peter Andrews, Wayne Brindle, S Palmer, Joy and Peter Heatherley, Sarah and Ian Shannon, Richard Siebert, Neil Walden, Ruth Davies, Stephen and Jean Curtis, Peter Saville, Susan and Nigel Wilson, P and D Carpenter, H O Dickinson, E D Bailey, Nigel Clifton)*

Free house ~ Licensees Deborah and Jeremy O'Gorman ~ Real ale ~ Meals and lunchtime snacks (not Sun evening) ~ Restaurant ~ (01799) 522251 ~ Children in eating area of bar and in restaurant ~ Open 12-11(10.30 Sun) ~ Bedrooms: £29.95B/£49.95B

MILL GREEN TL6400 Map 5

Viper 🍺

Mill Green Rd; from Fryerning (which is signposted off north-east bound A12 Ingatestone bypass) follow Writtle signposts; OS Sheet 167 map reference 640019

The cottage garden at this quiet old-fashioned country local is a mass of colour in summer, with the pub almost hidden by overflowing hanging baskets and window boxes. Inside the two timeless little lounge rooms have spindleback seats, armed country kitchen chairs, and tapestried wall seats around neat little old tables, and a warming log fire. The parquet-floored tap room (where booted walkers are directed) is more simply furnished with shiny wooden traditional wall seats, and beyond there's another room with country kitchen chairs and sensibly placed darts; shove-ha'penny, dominoes, cribbage and a fruit machine. The landlord will offer helpful hints about his three very well kept, changing real ales such as Cains Bitter, Charles Wells Eagle or Ridleys IPA on handpump, served from the oak-panelled counter. Simple bar snacks include soup (£1.50), good sandwiches (from £1.75), chilli (£3.15), and ploughman's (£3.50). No children. *(Recommended by Andrew Robinson, Mr and Mrs J R Morris, Richard Siebert, Frank Gadbois, John Fahy, Gwen and Peter Andrews, Basil Minson)*

Free house ~ Licensee Fred Beard ~ Real ale ~ Lunchtime snacks ~ (01277) 352010 ~ Open 11-2.30(3 Sat), 6-11

NAVESTOCK TQ5397 Map 5

Plough 🍺

Sabines Rd, Navestock Heath (off main rd at Alma Arms)

There's a very good range of around eight rotating well kept real ales such as Fullers London Pride, Flowers IPA, Nethergate IPA, Marstons Pedigree, Ridleys IPA and Whitbread Castle Eden on handpump at this enjoyable and friendly no-frills pub, as well as traditional cider, and a dozen malt whiskies. Several interconnecting rooms have a mix of dark wood solid chairs with flowery-cushioned seats around polished wood tables, with horsebrasses and dried flowers on the beams, and an open fire. Straightforward bar food from a simple menu includes baguettes (from £2.35), filled baked potatoes (from £2.55), ploughman's (from £3.55), ham, egg and chips (£3.95), scampi (£4.25), roast chicken (£4.45), lasagne (£4.65), fish and chips or steak and mushroom pie (£4.75), as well as a couple of daily specials; puddings (£1.95); two course Sunday roast (£6.95). Darts, cribbage, dominoes and piped music; no-smoking dining area. *(Recommended by Derek Patey, Richard Siebert, Joy Heatherley, JLP)*

Free house ~ Licensee Christopher Innerd ~ Real ale ~ Meals and snacks (12-9) ~ (01277) 372296 ~ Children welcome ~ Open 11-11, Sun 12-10.30

NORTH FAMBRIDGE TQ8597 Map 5

Ferryboat £

The Quay; village signposted from B1012 E off S Woodham Ferrers; keep on past railway

This attractive and unpretentious 500-year-old weatherboarded pub is simply furnished with traditional wall benches, settles and chairs on its stone floor, nautical memorabilia, old-fashioned lamps, and a few historic boxing-gloves. There's a log fire at one end, and a woodburning stove at the other. Good value bar food includes sandwiches (from £1.20), soup (£1.40), ploughman's (from £2.20), deep-fried cod (£2.95), beef and onion pie (£3), ham and egg (£3.50), vegetable chilli (£4), poached halibut (£6), steaks (from £6), venison in port and red wine (£7), puddings made by the landlady's mother (£1.75), and children's meals (£1.50). Well kept Flowers IPA on handpump and guests like Fremlins or Morlands Old Speckled Hen; friendly chatty landlord; shove ha'penny, table skittles, cribbage, dominoes, and piped music. There's a pond with ducks and carp, and seats in the garden. The pub is tucked away in a quiet spot at the end of the lane down by the River Crouch with lovely marsh views. *(Recommended by Richard Siebert, Paul Mason, Gwen and Peter Andrews, Keith and Cheryl Roe, Paul Barstow, Karyn Taylor, Derek Patey)*

Free house ~ Licensee Roy Maltwood ~ Real ale ~ Meals and snacks ~ Restaurant ~ (01621) 740208 ~ Children in family room or dining conservatory ~ Open 11-3, 6-11; all day Sun in summer

PELDON TL9916 Map 5

Rose

B1025 Colchester—Mersea, at junction with southernmost turn-off to Peldon

There is a fine sense of history at this big pink-washed inn where mysterious alcoves conjure up smugglers discussing bygone contraband. In the cosy atmospheric bar one or two standing timbers support the low ceiling with its dark bowed 17th-c oak beams, creaky close-set tables, and some antique mahogany, chintz curtains in the leaded-light windows, and brass and copper on the the mantelpiece of the Gothick-arched brick fireplace; the large conservatory is no-smoking. A wide range of bar food includes lasagne or steak and kidney pie (£5.75), chicken tikka masala (£5.85), chicken in spring onion and mushroom cream sauce (£5.95), and Sunday roasts (£7.25). Two well kept Whitbreads-related beers on handpump; friendly service. The spacious garden is very relaxing with good teak seats and two ponds with geese and ducks. *(Recommended by Gwen and Peter Andrews, Mayur Shah, Richard Siebert, Ian, Liz and James Phillips, Joy Heatherley, Hilary Dobbie; more reports please)*

Free house ~ Licensees Alan and Ariette Everett ~ Real ale ~ Meals and snacks (until 10pm) ~ Restaurant (Fri and Sat evening only) ~ (01206) 735248 ~ Children welcome until 9pm away from main bar ~ Open 11-3, 5.30-11 ~ Bedrooms: £25/£35

RICKLING GREEN TL5029 Map 5

Cricketers Arms ♀

Just off B1383 N of Stansted Mountfichet

The fairly plain Victorian facade of this friendly family-run inn veils a mass of Elizabethan timbering. The licensees have shuffled the interior around slightly since the last edition so that customers don't arrive through the games room – pool, darts, cribbage, dominoes, fruit machine and juke box. Not surprisingly there's lots of cricket memorabilia, with masses of cricket cigarette cards on the walls of the softly lit and comfortable saloon bar, the two bays of which are divided by standing timbers; in winter chestnuts are roasted on the log fire. Bar food includes sandwiches from (£1.50), ploughman's (£3.25), filled baked potatoes (from £2.25), starters like fish soup (£2.95), chicken liver pâté (£2.95), prawn cocktail (£3.95), mussels cooked in various sauces (from £4.95, £6.95 for a main course), smoked fish platter (£5.50) and main courses like cottage pie (£5), liver and bacon or black pudding in mustard sauce (£5.50), chicken in apricot and cream sauce (£5.75), chilli or balti curries (from £5.95), steak and kidney pie (£6.95), beef or lamb kebab (£7.25), beef stroganoff (£8.25), 8oz sirloin (£8.95) and mixed grill (£12.50); five vegetarian dishes (from £4.50), and home-made puddings like banoffi pie, steamed syrup sponge pudding or pineapple fritters (from £2.10), and a sensible children's menu. Well kept Flowers IPA and a monthly changing strong bitter, and about two dozen bottle-conditioned beers from all over Britain as well as 10 wines by the glass. A sheltered front courtyard has picnic tables overlooking the cricket green where Essex CC play once a year. The bedrooms are in a modern block behind and are handy for Stansted Airport, with a courtesy car for guests. *(Recommended by Stephen and Jean Curtis, Gwen and Peter Andrews, JR, CR, Maysie Thompson, John Fahy, Stephen Brown)*

Free house ~ Licensees Tim and Jo Proctor ~ Real ale ~ Meals and snacks (till 10) ~ Restaurant ~ (01799) 543210 ~ Children welcome in restaurant ~ Open 12-2.30(3 Sat), 6-11; all day summer Sat/Sun ~ Bedrooms: £50B/£60B

SAFFRON WALDEN TL5438 Map 5

Eight Bells ♀

Bridge Street; B184 towards Cambridge

There's a pleasant friendly welcome at this handsomely timbered black and white Tudor inn. A big draw is the wide range of tasty bar food which includes home-made soup (£2.10), ploughman's (from £4.25), dressed Cromer crab (£4.75), home-made lasagne (£5.75), mushrooms thermidor (£5.95), skate wing with capers (£7.25), calf liver with smoked ham, mushroom and cream sauce (£8.60), and steaks (from £10.30), as well as daily specials which might be chilli or broccoli and mushrooms in puff pastry (£5.85) or salmon in white wine and mushrooms (£7.55). Well kept Adnams, Friary Meux, Ind Coope Burton, Tetleys, and a changing guest on handpump, and half a dozen decent wines by the glass (with a choice of glass size). The neatly kept open-plan bar is divided by old timbers, with modern oak settles forming small booths around the tables. The bar leads into the old kitchen which is now a carpeted family room with an open fire. The partly no-smoking restaurant is in a splendidly timbered hall with high rafters, tapestries and flags. There are seats in the garden. Nearby Audley End makes a good family outing, and there are good walks around this attractive and interesting village. *(Recommended by John Fahy, M J How, Sarah and Ian Shannon, Stephen Brown, M A Butler, F Tomlin, Dono and Carol Leaman, JKW, Gwen and Peter Andrews, Ian Phillips)*

*Ind Coope (Allied) ~ Manager David Gregory ~ Real ale ~ Meals and snacks (till
10pm Sat) ~ Restaurant ~ (01799) 522790 ~ Children welcome in restaurant and
family room ~ Open 11-3, 6-11; 12-10.30 Sun*

STOCK TQ6998 Map 5

Hoop £ 🍺

B1007; from A12 Chelsmford bypass take Galleywood, Billericay turn-off

This popular local seems to have evolved comfortably with the years, keeping the
best of the old ways without getting stuck in the past. There's a really friendly
atmosphere in the truly classless and happily unsophisticated little bar, as well as a
fine range of about six changing real ales that might be from Adnams, Crouch Vale,
Fullers, Charles Wells or Nethergate, on handpump or tapped from the cask. During
the May Day week they hold a beer festival when there might be around 150 beers;
farm ciders, summer country wines, and winter mulled wine. There are brocaded
wall seats around dimpled copper tables on the left, a cluster of brocaded stools on
the right, and a coal-effect gas fire in the big brick fireplace. Very good value bar
food in generous helpings includes home-made soup (£1), sandwiches (from £1.20),
filled baked potatoes (from £1.80), sausage pie or quiche (from £2.85), ploughman's
(from £3), home-cooked ham and egg (£3.60), lancashire hotpot, vegetable pie,
chicken and ham pie or steak and kidney pie (£3.50); home-made puddings include
spotted dick and custard, apple pie and blackcurrant and apple pie (£1.50). Sensibly
placed darts (the heavy black beams are studded with hundreds of darts flights),
cribbage and dominoes. Lots of picnic tables in the big sheltered back garden are
prettily bordered with flowers. *(Recommended by Gwen and Peter Andrews, Richard
Byrne, Mr and Mrs J R Morris, Mr and Mrs N Spink, Derek Patey, Beryl and Bill Farmer, Tina
and David Woods-Taylor)*

*Free house ~ Licensee Albert Kitchin ~ Real ale ~ Meals and snacks (throughout
opening hours) ~ (01277) 841137 ~ Children in eating area of bar ~ Open 11-11;
12-10.30 Sun*

STOW MARIES TQ8399 Map 5

Prince of Wales 🍺

B1012 between S Woodham Ferrers and Cold Norton

In summer the gap between this simple country pub's white picket fence and the
weatherboarded frontage is filled with beautiful dark red roses, with some scented
pink ones at the side. Other beds are being developed in Victorian style to fit in with
the style of the building. The several cosy low-ceilinged rooms seem unchanged since
the turn of the century, but in fact were carefully restored in genuinely traditional
style only a few years ago; few have space for more than one or two tables or wall
benches on the tiled or bare-boards floors, though the room in the middle squeezes
in quite a jumble of chairs and stools. One room used to be the village bakery, and in
winter the oven there is still used to make bread and pizzas. Posters and
certificates reflect the landlord's knowledge and enthusiasm for beer; he runs a beer
wholesaling business (supplying rare ales for local beer festivals), and changes the
five or six brews in the pub every day. As well as Fullers Chiswick, you might find
beers like Burton Bridge Bitter and Porter, Hop Back Summer Lightning, or the
unusual honey-flavoured Mysicha. They're the only pub in the country to stock the
draught Belpils lager, and they also keep a particularly unusual range of continental
bottled beers, Belgian fruit beers, farm cider, and a good choice of malt whiskies and
vintage ports. Home-made bar food includes blackboard specials like fresh grilled
sardines (£4.50), double lamb chops with herbs and wine (£4.95), swordfish steak or
chicken breast with cheese and bacon (£5.25), and seafood pie (£6.95); the chef is
Greek so expect a proper moussaka or kleftiko. No games or music, just a friendly
chatty atmosphere. There are seats and tables in a garden behind. *(Recommeneded by
Paul Mason, R E Baldwin, Adrian White, Julie King)*

Free house ~ Licensee Rob Walster ~ Real ale ~ Meals and snacks ~ (01621)
828971 ~ Children in family room ~ Live music pm Sun in winter, occasionally
summer too ~ Open 11-11; 12-10.30 Sun; cl evening 25 Dec

TILLINGHAM TL9903 Map 5

Cap & Feathers ★ ◧

B1021 N of Southminster

There's a wonderfully warm and envelopingly snug atmosphere in the low-beamed and timbered bars of this handsome 15th-c tiled house. The old-fashioned rooms are furnished with sturdy wall seats (including a venerable built-in floor-to-ceiling settle), a homely dresser and a formidable woodburning stove, as well as little wheelback chairs with arms and etched-glass brass-mounted lamps; one parquet-floored part has bar billiards (operated by an old shilling, provided at the bar), sensibly placed darts, and table skittles – there's another set in the attractive no-smoking family room. They also have shove-ha'penny, cribbage and dominoes. Very good home-cooked bar food is listed on blackboards and features the distinctively flavoured products of their own smokery, such as smoked fillet of beef (£5.95) or trout (£6.75), as well as soup (£2.20), ploughman's (£3.95), beef in beer pie, Middle Eastern lamb, liver and bacon provençal or lasagne (£5.25) and 12oz sirloin steak (£12), and popular home-made puddings like cider apple crumble and bread and butter pudding (£2.20). Four really well kept real ales include Crouch Vale Best, IPA, Best Dark, and a changing guest on handpump; farm cider and country wines; friendly and efficient service. A small side terrace has picnic tables under birch trees. Just down the lane is the village cricket pitch, and the pub fields its own team. *(Recommended by Quentin Williamson, Mrs P Goodwyn, Richard Siebert, Gwen and Peter Andrews, George Atkinson, Paul Barstow, Karen Taylor)*

Crouch Vale ~ Tenant John Moore ~ Real ale ~ Meals and snacks ~ (01621)
779212 ~ Children in no-smoking family room ~ Open 11.30-3, 6-11 ~ Three
bedrooms: £20/£30

WENDENS AMBO TL5136 Map 5

Bell ◧

B1039 just W of village

This cheery little village pub has a cottagey interior with spotlessly kept small rooms that ramble engagingly round to the back, with brasses on ancient timbers, wheelback chairs around neat tables, comfortably cushioned seats worked into snug alcoves, and quite a few pictures on the cream walls as well as friendly open fires. Good hearty food includes tasty home-made bread, lunchtime filled home-baked rolls (from £1.65, the prawn is recommended), jalapeno peppers stuffed with cream cheese and chilli sauce (£3.25), ploughman's (£3.50), vegetarian dishes (from £4.95), popular curries (from £5.25), beef in ale pie (£5.95), cajun chicken or mixed grill (£6.75), and puddings such as spotted dick or treacle tart (£2); popular winter Sunday lunch. Four well kept real ales include Adnams Southwold and Ansells Dark Mild, as well as two guests like Gales HSB, Marstons Pedigree or Wadworths 6X on handpump or from the cask; darts, dominoes, Monopoly, and piped music; boules. The very extensive back garden is quite special: an informal layout with a big tree-sheltered lawn, lots of flower borders, unusual plant-holders, as well as Gertie the goat, a wooden wendy house, and a sort of mini nature-trail wandering off through the shrubs make plenty of natural distractions for children. The two dogs are called Kate and Samson. *(Recommended by Gwen and Peter Andrews, Stephen Brown, Mrs P J Pearce, Joe Platts)*

Free house ~ Licensees Geoff and Bernie Bates ~ Real ale ~ Meals and snacks (not
Mon evening) ~ Restaurant ~ Children in family dining room ~ (01799) 540382 ~
August bank hol Sat live music festival ~ Open 11.30-3(2.30 winter), 6-11; cl 25
and 26 Dec evenings

WOODHAM WALTER TL8006 Map 5

Cats 🐾

Back road to Curling Tye and Maldon, from N end of village

Prowling stone cats picket the roof of this attractively timbered black and white country cottage, and the feline theme is continued inside where there are shelves of china cats. There's a wonderfully relaxed atmosphere in the rambling low-ceilinged friendly bar which is full of interesting nooks and crannies, and traditionally decorated with low black beams and timbering set off well by neat white paintwork, as well as a warming open fire. Well kept Adnams Southwold and Broadside, Greene King IPA and Abbot and Rayments Special on handpump, and friendly service. The pleasantly chatty landlord would rather we didn't include his pub in the Guide so won't give us any factual information. But of course letting licensees decide for us which pubs not to include would damage our independence almost as much as allowing other landlords to pay for their inclusion, so we have, quite deservedly, included it once more; no children or piped music. *(Recommended by Mike and Karen England, John Fahy; more reports please)*

Free house ~ Real ale ~ Lunchtime snacks (Thurs-Sat but see note above) ~ Open 11-2.30ish, 6.30ish-11; may close if not busy in winter

YOUNGS END TL7319 Map 5

Green Dragon

A131 Braintree—Chelmsford, just N of Essex Showground

Courteous tidily dressed staff serve generous helpings from a wide range of food at this well run dining pub. The bar part has normal pub furnishings in its two rooms, with a little extra low-ceilinged snug just beside the serving counter; turkey carpet sweeps from the main bar room into the restaurant area, which has an understated barn theme – stripped brick walls, a manger at one end, and low beams supporting the floor of an upper 'hayloft' with steep pitched rafters. At lunchtime (not Sunday) you can have bar food down this end, where the tables are a better size than in the bar. The bar food includes soup (£2), filled baked potatoes (from £2.80), ploughman's (from £3.95), cottage pie (£4.30), suffolk hotpot (£4.95), four vegetarian dishes like brown rice and hazelnut roast (£5.65), seafood pie (£5.75) and steak, kidney and mushroom pie or curry (£5.95); fresh vegetables; good puddings like spotted dick or treacle sponge and a pudding trolley (£2.55). Well kept Greene King IPA, Abbot and their seasonal beers; unobtrusive piped music (jazz on our inspection visit). The neat back garden has lots of picnic tables under cocktail parasols, a big green play dragon, climbing frame and budgerigar aviary; summer barbecues. *(Recommended by Mark Walker, John and Val Spouge)*

Greene King ~ Lease: Bob and Mandy Greybrook ~ Real ale ~ Meals and snacks (till 10 Fri and Sat) ~ Restaurant (evenings, Sun lunch) ~ (01245) 361030 ~ Children welcome in eating area of bar till 8pm ~ Open 11.30-3(3.30 Sat), 6(5.30 Sat)-11

Post Office address codings confusingly give the impression that some pubs are in Suffolk, when they're really in Essex (which is where we list them).

Lucky Dip

Besides the fully inspected pubs, you might like to try these Lucky Dips recommended to us and described by readers (if you do, please send us reports):

Abridge [London Rd (A113); TQ4696], *Maltsters Arms*: Largely 18th-c two-bar beamed pub with well kept Greene King IPA and Abbot, open fires *(Nigel Giddons, John Fahy)*

☆ **Ardleigh** [Harwich Rd; A137 – actually towards Colchester; TM0529], *Wooden Fender*: Friendly beamed bar, open-plan but traditional, with good choice of home-cooked food inc Sun lunch, well kept Adnams, Fullers ESB, Greene King IPA and Morlands Old Speckled Hen, friendly character landlord who writes witty messages outside, log fires, restaurant allowing children, a pool in back garden; immaculate lavatories *(Magda and Derek Kelsey, Virginia Jones, E G Parish, LYM)*

☆ **Bannister Green** [off A131 or A120 SW of Braintree; TL6920], *Three Horseshoes*: Popular and comfortable country local, well kept Ridleys, good value food, tables out on broad village green and in garden; children welcome *(Tony Beaulah, LYM)*

☆ **Barnston** [A130 SE of Dunmow; TL6419], *Bushel & Sack*: Friendly staff, pleasant atmosphere, big helpings of good value food, can eat in moderate sized bar or comfortable restaurant, sitting room between *(Tony Beaulah, Cheryl and Keith Roe)*

☆ **Battlesbridge** [Hawk Hill; TQ7894], *Barge*: Weatherboarded pub by art and craft centre nr Crouch estuary, warren of refurbished rooms, interesting pictures, good value bar meals; well kept Tetleys-related ales and a guest such as Adnams, quick friendly service; pervasive piped pop music, busy weekend lunchtimes; children's room *(P Pearce)*

Beazley End [off B1053 N of Braintree; TL7428], *Cock*: Relaxing country pub dating from 14th c, polished tables and open fire in spotless and comfortable beamed lounge, wide range of food inc fish, bar snacks and sandwiches, good choice of beers; cl Mon *(Walter and Muriel Hagen)*

Billericay [Southend Rd, South Green; TQ6893], *Duke of York*: Oak beams, real fire, upholstered settles and wheelback chairs, good value food in bar and modern restaurant, long-serving licensees, Greene King and occasional guest beers *(David Twitchett)*

Blackmore [off A414 Chipping Ongar—Chelmsford; TL6001], *Bull*: Old partly timbered building nr church in quietly attractive village with big antique and craft shop; extensively and tastefully redecorated as dining pub, above-average food inc enterprising dishes, well kept real ale, no music *(Paul Randall)*; [The Green], *Prince Albert*: Several knocked-through rooms around central servery, wide choice of bar food, well kept Bass, Charrington and Hancocks HB, friendly efficient service, fairly unobtrusive piped music *(Joy Heatherley, GA, PA)*

☆ **Boreham** [Church Rd; TL7509], *Queens Head*: Friendly and popular traditional pub with well kept Greene King IPA and Abbot, decent wines, good generous low-priced straightforward food (not Sun evening) inc Weds roast and Sun lunch; snug beamed saloon with stripped brickwork, more tables down one side of long public bar with darts at end; maybe piped music; small garden *(Gwen and Peter Andrews, George Atkinson)*

☆ **Boreham**, *Cock*: Two partly curtained-off no-smoking restaurant areas off beamed central bar, relaxed friendly atmosphere, good value food from sandwiches and ploughman's to generous fish fresh daily from Lowestoft, good puddings, well kept Ridleys, decent wines and coffee, pleasant young staff; piped radio, some traffic/rail noise in family garden *(Gwen and Peter Andrews, Paul Randall)*

Boreham [Colchester Rd], *Six Bells*: Comfortable bar in pleasant dining pub, Greene King ales, emphasis on substantial helpings of good value fish, friendly efficient service even when busy, play area in garden *(George Atkinson)*

Braintree [A120; TL7622], *Fowlers Farm*: Built to resemble an old farmhouse that once stood here, floorboards and old farm equipment, usual food; a handy stop *(Nikki Moffat)*

Broxted [TL5726], *Prince of Wales*: Friendly L-shaped bar with restaurant and conservatory family dining area, food from hearty sandwiches up, particularly good choice of wines by the glass, Tetleys-related ales with a guest such as Mauldons, pleasant service; piped music; good garden with play area *(Gwen and Peter Andrews, John Fahy)*

Bulmer [TL8440], *Cock & Blackbird*: Welcoming bar with smartly set dining extension, Adnams and Greene King IPA, decent wines, food inc bargain midweek lunches and themed evening menus *(Gwen and Peter Andrews)*

Burnham on Crouch [The Quay; TQ9596], *White Harte*: Two high-ceilinged panelled bars in old-fashioned Georgian yachting inn overlooking anchorage, very busy weekends with mix of sailors and locals inc retired captains; oak tables, polished parquet, sea pictures, panelling and stripped brickwork; good value food from sandwiches up, restaurant, well kept Adnams and Tolly, caring landlord, friendly staff, terrace above river; children allowed in eating area; simple bedrooms overlooking water, good breakfasts *(Paul Mason, Colin Laffan, LYM)*

Canfield End [Little Canfield; A120 Bishops Stortford—Dunmow; TL5821], *Lion & Lamb*: Pleasantly refurbished, with welcoming staff, good value food inc children's in bar and spacious restaurant, well kept Ridleys, decent wines and coffee; piped music; back garden with barbecue and play area *(Jez Cunningham, A C Morrison, Gwen and Peter Andrews)*

Chelmsford [TL7006], *County*: Smallish hotel bar with pleasantly pubby atmosphere, well kept Adnams, Greene King IPA and Ridleys, decent wine, good straightforward bar food inc sandwiches, very friendly staff; bedrooms *(Gwen and Peter Andrews)*; [Church Lane, Springfield; TL7208], *Tulip*: Local with very friendly landlady, Greene King IPA and Shepherd Neame, open fire in quiet lounge, games bar with pool and darts *(Gwen and Peter Andrews)*; [Springfield Rd, opp Tesco], *Two Brewers*: Spacious and friendly, beams and exposed brickwork, well kept Courage Directors and Trumans IPA, freshly cooked lunchtime food; piped music *(Gwen and Peter Andrews)*

☆ Chigwell [High Rd (A113); TQ4693], *Kings Head*: Beautiful 17th-c building with interesting Dickens memorabilia, some antique furnishings; Chef & Brewer bar food, quick friendly service, well kept ales, upstairs restaurant; piped music, can get very crowded weekend evenings; attractive garden *(John Fahy, Mrs P J Pearce)*

☆ Coggeshall [West St; towards Braintree; TL8522], *Fleece*: Handsome Tudor pub with thriving local atmosphere, well kept Greene King IPA and Abbot, decent wines, reliable straightforward bar food (not Tues or Sun evenings), cheery service, children welcome, open all day; spacious sheltered garden with play area, next to Paycocke's *(Gwen and Peter Andrews, Gordon Long, LYM)*

Coggeshall [main st], *White Hart*: Lots of low Tudor beams, antique settles among other more usual seats, prints and fishing trophies on cream walls, wide choice of food, Adnams, decent wines and coffee; bedrooms comfortable *(John Fahy, LYM)*

☆ Colchester [East St; TM0025], *Rose & Crown*: Carefully modernised handsome Tudor inn, timbered and jettied, parts of a former gaol preserved in its rambling beamed bar, usual bar food, pricey restaurant, well kept Adnams and Home ale; comfortably functional bedrooms, many in modern extension, with good breakfast; handy for interesting museum and castle *(Paul Mason, Mrs B Sugarman, LYM)*

Colchester [28 Mersea Rd], *Odd One Out*: Unspoilt free house with several cosy if not exactly bright drinking areas, with good ever-changing range of well kept ales *(Paul Mason, Mark Watson)*; [Stockwell St], *Stockwell Arms*: Relaxing real ale pub with good well kept choice inc Marstons Pedigree, Morlands Old Speckled Hen, Nethergate, Ruddles County and Websters Yorkshire *(Mervyn and Zilpha Reed)*; [123 Crouch St], *Tap & Spile*: Refurbished quiet attractive interior, partly flagstone, with cosy separate areas, up to nine changing well kept real ales, small choice of lunchtime food, friendly staff, lots of Essex CC and rugby photographs, woodburner; tables in small back courtyard *(Ian Phillips, Paul Mason, Stuart Earle)*

☆ Crays Hill [London Rd; TQ7192], *Shepherd & Dog*: Spotless bar with low beam-and-plank ceiling, bare boards, soft lighting, good log fire, attractive side conservatory overlooking big nicely lit garden, well kept Tetleys-related ales and a beer brewed for the pub, varied good value straightforward food inc vegetarian and children's, OAP bargains Tues/Thurs, good waitress service; children welcome; fruit machines, quiet piped music, live music Sun pm; good walks *(Paul Barstow, Karyn Taylor)*

☆ Danbury [Runsell Green; N of A414, just beyond green; TL7905], *Anchor*: Lots of beams, timbering, brickwork and brasses, two log fires, separate games bar, attractive dining conservatory, good generous straightforward food, well kept Adnams and Ridleys *(Nigel Norman, Paul Barstow, Karyn Taylor, LYM)*

Danbury [Penny Royal Rd], *Cricketers Arms*: Pleasant pub by common, several beamed rooms and restaurant, friendly bar staff, reasonably quick food service *(George Atkinson)*; [A414], *Griffin*: Quiet and spacious newly refurbished Chef & Brewer, 16th-c beams and some older carved woodwork, well kept Theakstons, decent food, friendly service *(Gwen and Peter Andrews)*

☆ Dedham [TM0533], *Sun*: Roomy and comfortably refurbished Tudor pub, cosy panelled rooms with log fires in huge brick fireplaces, handsomely carved beams, well kept beer, reasonable wines, good range of generous reasonably priced food, cheerful staff, good piped music; tables on back lawn, car park behind reached through medieval arch, wonderful wrought-iron inn sign; panelled bedrooms with four-posters, good walk to or from Flatford Mill *(John and Wendy Trentham, A C Morrison, LYM)*

Dunmow [Churchend; B1057 to Finchingfield/Haverhill; TL6222], *Angel & Harp*: Pleasantly refurbished, with real ales; open all day *(Thomas Nott)*

☆ Duton Hill [off B184 Dunmow—Thaxted, 3 miles N of Dunmow; TL6026], *Three Horseshoes*: Quiet country pub gently updated to keep welcoming traditional atmosphere, decent low-priced food, well kept Flowers Original, Ridleys IPA and a guest such as Eldridge Pope, friendly licensees, homely armchairs in left-hand parlour, interesting theatrical memorabilia and enamel advertising signs; pool in small public bar, fine views from garden where local drama groups perform in summer *(John Fahy, Gwen and Peter Andrews)*

☆ Fiddlers Hamlet [Stewards Green Rd, a mile SE of Epping; TL4700], *Merry Fiddlers*: Long low-ceilinged 17th-c country pub profusely decorated with chamber-pots, beer mugs, brasses and plates; Adnams, Morlands Old Speckled Hen and Tetleys, usual pub food, efficient friendly staff, unobtrusive piped music, occasional live sessions; big garden with play area *(Joy Heatherley)*

Finchingfield [TL6832], *Fox*: Splendidly pargeted late 18th-c pub with Greene King ales and a guest such as Morlands Old Speckled Hen, reasonably priced generous food; tables in garden, very photogenic village *(Gwen and Peter Andrews, John Fahy)*

☆ **Fuller Street** [The Green; off A131 Chelmsford—Braintree, towards Fairstead; TL7416], *Square & Compasses*: Now open-plan, with attentive and friendly new licensees, relaxed atmosphere, good honest food cooked to order inc local game, big log fire, rural decor inc stuffed albino pheasant, well kept Ridleys, good wines and coffee; unobtrusive piped music *(Gwen and Peter Andrews)*

☆ **Furneux Pelham** [TL4327], *Brewery Tap*: Good food esp fish in friendly refurbished bar with well kept Greene King and Rayments; back garden room and terrace overlooking neat attractive garden *(Geo Rumsey)*

Fyfield [Church St (off B184); TL5606], *Queens Head*: Welcoming local, amusing landlord, well kept changing ales such as Adnams Bitter and Broadside, Arundel Bullseye, Morrells Varsity and Ridleys, good value generous food from sandwiches and giant filled baps to freshly cooked hot dishes (may be a wait when busy); low beams and local prints, high-backed upholstered settles forming cosy areas, tabby cat, scottie dog; can be a bit smoky *(Jean, Bill and Sandra Iles, Joy and Peter Heatherley)*

☆ **Gestingthorpe** [signed from B1058; pub at Audley End end; TL8138], *Pheasant*: Cheerfully old-fashioned country pub with its interestingly furnished little bow-windowed lounge bar, traditional games in public bar, log fires, family room, usual bar food, Adnams Best and Broadside, Bass, Greene King IPA and Abbot, maybe piped music; country views from garden with boules, occasional live music *(Gwen and Peter Andrews, LYM; reports on new regime please)*

Goldhanger [B1026 E of Heybridge; TL9009], *Chequers*: Nice old village pub with good variety of food inc extremely fresh Friday fish, well kept Greene King and Tolly; good walks and birdwatching nearby *(Colin Laffan, Mike Beiley)*

Grays [Duck Rd; TQ6178], *Bull*: Big genuinely old white-painted beamed pub, big covered dining terrace, attractive garden, good range of bar food, friendly staff *(Ian Phillips)*; [Lodge Lane (A1306 towards Lakeside)], *Treacle Mine*: Big new Americanised pub with several Bass ales and a guest such as Crouch Vale, competitively priced food, two homely eating areas, one no smoking, lots of woodwork, pictures and mining tools, realistic-looking 'mine' in small garden with play area *(Paul Barstow, Karyn Taylor, PPP)*

☆ **Great Baddow** [Galleywood Rd; or off B1007 at Galleywood Eagle; TL7204], *Seabrights Barn*: Fine Greene King family pub in rustic raftered barn conversion, lots for children though also a spacious child-free bar, good food (all day Sun), good friendly service, well kept real ales, decent wines, summer barbecues *(Derek Howse, LYM)*

Great Braxted [off A12 Witham—Kelvedon; TL8613], *Du Cane Arms*: Clean and friendly bar with dining area, good value food from sandwiches to steaks; restaurant *(K H Frostick)*

☆ **Great Bromley** [Harwich Rd (B1029 just off A120); TM0826], *Old Black Boy*: Attractively refurbished 18th-c pub with wide choice of good value food inc lots of fish in bar and restaurant, real ales, decent wines, no-smoking area; big garden *(Alan Wilkins, Alan Budden)*

Great Burstead [South Green, A129; TQ6892], *Kings Head*: Old pub, small but barn-like, with several well kept ales inc Bass and Charrington IPA, good range of reasonably priced wines, good food, generous coffee *(John A Barker)*

Great Easton [Mill End Green; pub signed 2 miles N of Dunmow, off B184 towards Lindsell; TL6126], *Green Man*: Dates from 15th c, cosy and welcoming beamed bar, good range of food, friendly efficient service, real ales inc Adnams and Fullers London Pride *(Jean, Bill and Sandra Iles)*

☆ **nr Great Henny** [Henny Street; Sudbury—Lamarsh rd E; TL8738], *Swan*: Tables on lawn by quiet river opp cosy well furnished darkly timbered pub with partly no-smoking conservatory restaurant, generous good value bar food (not Sun evening), barbecues, well kept Greene King IPA and Abbot, decent wines, friendly staff; children allowed, maybe unobtrusive piped music *(Gwen and Peter Andrews, Mrs P Goodwyn, LYM)*

☆ **Great Horkesley** [Nayland Rd (A134); TL9730], *Rose & Crown*: Lovely old two-floored pub, clean, cosy and welcoming, good varied food, Greene King and other ales, three bars and restaurant *(Quentin Williamson)*

☆ **Great Saling** [signed from A120; TL7025], *White Hart*: Friendly and attractive Tudor pub with easy chairs in unusual upper gallery, ancient timbering and flooring tiles, lots of plates, brass and copperware, good speciality giant filled baps inc hot roast beef and melted cheese and other snacks served till late, well kept Adnams Extra and Ridleys on handpump, decent wines, good service, restaurant Tues-Sat evenings, well behaved children welcome; seats outside *(Nikki Moffat, John Fahy, LYM)*

☆ **Great Stambridge** [1 Stambridge Rd; TQ9091], *Cherry Tree*: Spacious but cosy beamed country dining pub with wide choice of well served food from sandwiches up inc good fish and lots of traditional puddings, Courage Directors and Flowers IPA, good wine choice, friendly service, coal-effect gas fire, elegant circular dining conservatory, garden; fairly quiet piped music; very popular, can get crowded *(Susan and Alan Dominey)*

Great Wakering [High St; TQ9487], *Red Lion*: Pleasant beamed village inn, log fire, Crouch Vale SAS, Wadworths 6X and Woodham IPA, friendly staff, good value food from hot salt beef rolls to fish, piped music, small garden *(George Atkinson)*

☆ **Great Waltham** [old A130; TL6913], *Beehive*: Cheerful refurbished pub with decent lunchtime food, well kept Ridleys and Wadworths IPA and 6X, useful malt whiskies, good log fire; tables outside, opp attractive church *(Gwen and Peter Andrews)*

☆ **Great Warley Street** [TQ5890], *Thatchers Arms*: Pretty Chef and Brewer in attractive village, reliable food, well kept S&N or Courage-related ales, helpful service *(Quentin Williamson, John Fahy)*

☆ **Hastingwood** [very nr M11 junction 7; follow Ongar sign, then Hastingwood turn; TL4807], *Rainbow & Dove*: Comfortable and very friendly Mway break, low-beamed rooms packed with bric-a-brac, roaring fire, efficient service, well kept ales, generous good value food (children allowed in eating area), jovial landlord does much of the cooking; picnic tables in sheltered garden, barbecue can be booked by parties *(Eric and Jackie Robinson, Tony Beaulah, Wayne Brindle, Quentin Williamson, LYM)*

☆ **Hatfield Broad Oak** [High St; TL5416], *Cock*: Character 15th-c beamed village pub with well kept Adnams Best, Nethergate IPA and four guest beers, Easter beer festival, old-fashioned atmosphere, no-smoking tap room with open fire, music hall song sheets and old advertisements, roaming dog, enjoyable food (not Sun evening) from sandwiches to interesting hot dishes, restaurant; bar billiards, juke box and darts; children in eating area *(Gwen and Peter Andrews, G Brooke-Williams, Joy Heatherley, John Fahy, S G Brown, LYM; more reports on housekeeping please)*

Hatfield Heath [TL5215], *Thatchers*: Spacious beamed and thatched pub with woodburner, copper kettles and brasses, well kept Bass, Greene King IPA and a guest ale, decent house wines, wide choice of generous bar food, friendly licensees; piped pop music; tables out under cocktail parasols *(Gwen and Peter Andrews)*

Henham [Chickney Rd; TL5428], *Cock*: Heavily timbered family pub/restaurant in pleasant village, relaxing views from nice tables outside *(Eddie Edwards)*

☆ **Herongate** [Billericay Rd; A128 Brentwood—Grays; TQ6391], *Green Man*: Good value food inc popular baked potatoes and children's dishes, big bright and welcoming beamed bar area with jug collection, cricket memorabilia, log fires each end, Adnams and Tetleys-related ales, decent wines, helpful staff; unobtrusive piped music, ginger cat called Tigger; children allowed in back rooms, side garden *(Paul Barstow, Karyn Taylor, Mrs J Boyt, Graham Bush)*

Herongate [Billericay Rd, Ingrave], *Boars Head*: Picturesque beamed Chef & Brewer with pleasant nooks and crannies, garden, seats by big attractive pond with ducks and moorhens, Courage Directors and John Smiths; can get crowded at weekends *(George Atkinson)*; [Dunton Rd, off A128 Brentwood—Grays at big sign for Boars Head], *Old Dog*: Friendly and relaxed, with

good choice of well kept ales and of lunchtime bar food inc good sandwiches in long traditional dark-raftered bar, open fire, comfortable back lounge; front terrace and neat sheltered side garden *(Beryl and Bill Farmer, LYM)*

☆ **High Easter** [TL6214], *Cock & Bell*: Friendly timbered Tudor pub with grand old beams, dining area up steps from lounge, log fire in cheery second bar, generous home-cooked straightforward food, well kept ales such as Batemans, Crouch Vale, Fullers London Pride, Morlands Old Speckled Hen, children welcome; piped radio may obtrude; bedrooms *(D Broughton, Gwen and Peter Andrews, Roger and Valerie Hill, Frank Gadbois, LYM)*

☆ **High Ongar** [King St, Nine Ashes – signed Blackmore, Ingatestone off A414 just E; TL5603], *Wheatsheaf*: Comfortable and very welcoming low-beamed country dining pub, some intimate tables in bay-window alcoves, two open fires, fresh flowers, wide choice of home-cooked food (fish and steaks particularly recommended), well kept Whitbreads-related ales and guests such as Crouch Vale, Fullers and Youngs, attentive service, spacious attractive garden with play house *(Walter and Muriel Hagen, MJVK, Dave and Pam Bowell, BB)*

☆ **High Roding** [The Street (B184); TL6017], *Black Lion*: Attractive low-beamed bar dating from 15th c, good food esp authentic Italian dishes, courteous long-serving landlord and cheerful staff, comfortable relaxed surroundings, well kept Ridleys; discreet piped music *(Gwen and Peter Andrews)*

Leigh on Sea [Old Leigh; TQ8385], *Peter Boat*: Chef & Brewer in good spot by sea wall, good views from seats outside and from lounge; usual range of food, Courage Best and Directors, John Smiths and Theakstons Old Peculier; cockle stall in car park *(George Atkinson)*

Lindsell [TL6426], *Green Man*: Delightful beamed country pub, cosy winter retreat, lovely summer garden; food, well kept beers, decent wines *(Nikki Moffat)*

Little Hallingbury [Hall Green; TL5017], *Sutton Arms*: Good changing menu with lots of interesting generous dishes in pleasant beamed and carpeted thatched pub with quick friendly service; close to M11, can get very busy *(Mr and Mrs C J Pink, Stephen and Jean Curtis)*

☆ **Little Walden** [B1052; TL5441], *Crown*: Neat and clean L-shaped bar with big log fire, flowers on tables, Greene King IPA and Abbot and Worthington BB, decent wines, good range of home-cooked food (not Sun evening) with good veg and vegetarian dishes, unobtrusive piped music *(Ian Phillips, Gwen and Peter Andrews, Peter and Joy Heatherley)*

☆ **Little Waltham** [TL7012], *Dog & Gun*: Comfortable banquettes and chairs in spacious timbered L-shaped bar, welcoming attentive staff, very wide choice of generous interesting food, good ingredients cooked with care (so apart from sandwiches may be a wait), well kept Greene King IPA, Abbot and

Rayments, good house wines; piped music usually unobtrusive; garden with elegant willow *(Gwen and Peter Andrews)*

☆ **Loughton** [103 York Hill, off A121 High Rd; TQ4296], *Gardeners Arms*: Country feel in (and outside) traditional low-ceilinged pub with Adnams and Courage-related ales, two open fires, friendly service, good straightforward lunchtime bar food (not Sun) from sandwiches up with hot dishes all fresh-cooked (so can be delays), children in restaurant *(Gwen and Peter Andrews, LYM)*

☆ **Maldon** [Silver St; TL8506], *Blue Boar*: Fine old Forte coaching inn, very pubby atmospheric bar in separate coach house on left, with beams, roaring log fire, Adnams tapped from the cask, keen and friendly young staff, good if not cheap lunchtime bar food; pleasant well equipped bedrooms, good breakfast *(Paul Mason, Christopher Danes)*

☆ **Manningtree** [Manningtree Stn, out towards Lawford; TM1031], *Station Buffet*: Warm glow of nostalgia about this early 1950s long marble-topped bar, well worth a brief encounter; three little tables and a handful of unassuming seats, interesting well kept ales such as Adnams, Greene King, Mauldons and Summerskills, real cheese and ham baps etc, traditional hot dishes, cheerful service *(John C Baker, Thomas Nott)*

Margaretting [B1002; TL6701], *Spread Eagle*: Simple place with friendly licensee, well kept Bass, good value bacon baps and cheap hot dishes, fine array of daily papers; unobtrusive piped music *(Jenny and Brian Seller, John Fahy)*

☆ **Mashbury** [towards the Walthams; TL6411], *Fox*: Friendly beamed and flagstoned lounge, old-fashioned long tables, generous homely food, well kept Adnams and Ridleys tapped from the cask, decent wine; dominoes, cribbage, skittles; quiet countryside *(Beryl and Bill Farmer)*

Matching Green [TL5311], *Chequers*: Lovely drive out here, nice in summer with cricket on pretty green outside, good food, wide choice of beers and wines *(Nikki Moffat)*

☆ **Mill Green** [TL6401], *Cricketers Arms*: Genuine country pub in picturesque setting, comfortable and spruce, doing well under current cheerful licensees; locally popular for its wide choice of well prepared food, with well kept Greene King IPA and Abbot tapped from the cask, good wines *(Clive Rumsey, John Fahy, Tony Beaulah)*

☆ **Moreton** [signed off B184 at Fyfield or opp Chipping Ongar school; TL5307], *Nags Head*: Former Moreton Massey, back to original name under new owners; attractive array of salvaged rustic beams and timbers, nice mix of tables, three big log fires, country nick-nacks, wide choice of reasonably priced standard food, well kept ales such as Brakspears and Hook Norton Best, no machines or juke box; children welcome, picnic tables under cocktail parasols on side grass *(Gwen and Peter Andrews, BB)*

☆ **Moreton**, *White Hart*: Rambling unspoilt local with lovely log fire, cosy rooms on different levels, sloping floor and ceilings, five real ales such as Adnams, Courage Best and Directors, Everards Tiger and Trumans IPA, wide choice of generous briskly served home-cooked food inc properly cooked veg in two dining rooms; bedrooms *(Joy Heatherley, Quentin Williamson, Tony Gayfer)*

☆ **Navestock** [Huntsmanside, off B175; TQ5397], *Alma Arms*: Concentration on generous good value well presented food (may be a wait) in spacious dining area, with good choice of wines, well kept ales such as Adnams, Greene King Abbot and Rayments; low beams, comfortable seats *(H O Dickinson, Joy and Peter Heatherley, P Pearce)*

☆ **Newney Green** [TL6507], *Duck*: Comfortable dining pub with engaging rambling bar full of beams, timbering and panelling; very friendly service, enjoyable food inc good value roasts, drinkers welcomed too with useful range of ales such as Hop Back Summer Lightning and Shepherd Neame Spitfire; attractive garden *(George Atkinson, LYM)*

☆ **Norton Heath** [just off A414 Chelmsford—Ongar; TL6004], *White Horse*: Particularly good bar food with a French slant (Tues-Sat lunchtimes) in comfortably modernised somewhat formal long timbered bar, well kept Courage Directors and Sam Smiths; piped music usually unobtrusive, bar billiards; restaurant (Tues-Sat evening, Sun lunch); garden with play area; cl Mon *(Richard Siebert, Paul Randall, Peter Andrews, John Davison)*

☆ **Pilgrims Hatch** [Ongar Rd; TQ5895], *Black Horse*: Busy olde-worlde low-beamed dining pub with bare boards and red flooring tiles, lots of pictures, photographs and country bygones, small fireplace at either end, large eating areas off small attractive bar, with wide choice of good home cooking (all day Sun) at sensible prices inc fresh veg, vegetarian dishes and huge puddings; Bass and Hancocks HB, also imported Staropramen on tap, friendly service, good garden with play area *(Paul Barstow, Karyn Taylor, Eddie Edwards)*

☆ **Pleshey** [signed with Howe Street off A130 Dunmow—Chelmsford; TL6614], *White Horse*: Cheerful 15th-c pub with nooks and crannies, lots of bric-a-brac, comfortable sofa in snug room by servery, more orthodox tables and chairs in other rooms, big dining room with huge collection of miniatures, bar food from good big hot filled baps upwards, well kept Archers, Batemans, Crouch Vale, Elgoods, Jennings, and Nethergate, local cider, tables out on terrace and in garden with small safe play area; children welcome, fruit machine, cat called Tigger *(Tony Beaulah, Basil Minson, J Mayhew, Thomas Nott, Maysie Thompson, LYM)*

☆ **Purleigh** [TL8401], *Bell*: Cosy rambling beamed and timbered pub up by church, fine views over the marshes and Blackwater estuary; beams, nooks and crannies, big inglenook log fire, well kept Adnams and Benskins Best, good reasonably priced home-made lunchtime food (service may slow on busy weekends), magazines to read, welcoming landlord, friendly dog; picnic tables on side grass *(George Atkinson, S Dominey, Comus Elliott, LYM)*

☆ Radwinter [B1053 E of Saffron Walden – OS Sheet 154 map ref 612376; TL6137], *Plough*: Neatly kept red plush open-plan black-timbered beamed bar with central log fire and separate woodburner; good choice of popular bar food inc vegetarian, well kept Adnams, Greene King IPA and Wadworths 6X, decent wine; maybe piped music; very attractive terrace and garden, open countryside; bedrooms *(Gwen and Peter Andrews, John Fahy, BB)*

☆ Rayleigh [39 High St; TQ8190], *Old White Horse*: Friendly and attractive, with good cheap home-cooked food, well kept Charrington IPA, Fullers London Pride, Worthington and guest beers, friendly staff, lots of sporting memorabilia; back terrace with barbecues; children welcome, open all day, with breakfast from 8 *(R Walmsley, Mr and Mrs C Wragg)*

Rayleigh [14 High Rd], *Paul Pry*: Limited choice of good value food, very friendly service, well kept ales, decent wine; lovely big garden (with summer tuck shop) *(Keith and Cheryl Roe)*

Saffron Walden [10-18 High St; TL5438], *Saffron*: Comfortably modernised former coaching inn, wide choice of waitress-served food in bar and restaurant, tables on terrace; bedrooms *(John Fahy)*

Sandon [TL7404], *Crown*: Village pub carefully upgraded by good new landlord, well kept Bass, Fullers London Pride and so forth *(Simon Bobeldijk)*

☆ Shalford [TL7229], *George*: Well restored, with lots of exposed brickwork, attractive plates and brassware on walls and beams, good solid tables and chairs, log fire in enormous fireplace, good home cooking (worth the wait), well kept Adnams Broadside, Boddingtons and Greene King IPA, decent wines, friendly helpful staff, lots of children at weekends, no music; tables on terrace *(Gwen and Peter Andrews)*

☆ South Weald [Weald Rd (off A1023); TQ5793], *Tower Arms*: Imposing thoughtfully refurbished building opp church, good friendly atmosphere in several small high-ceilinged rooms, conservatory restaurant (not Sun-Tues evenings), decent Chef & Brewer food, well kept Theakstons Best, Old Peculier and XB and John Smiths, friendly staff; children allowed away from bar; extensive secluded garden with boules (you can hire the balls); picturesque village *(Graham Bush, Simon Bobeldijk)*

South Woodham Ferrers [Wickford Rd; TQ8097], *Whalebone*: Friendly landlord and staff, tasty well priced food, wider lunchtime choice inc stir-fries and home-made pies, well kept local Crouch Vale Golden Duck and Wadworths 6X *(Julie King, Adrian White)*

Southend [53 Alexandra St; TQ8885], *Fish & Firkin*: Tasty home-brewed Firkin beers, friendly helpful service; bars on two levels, picnic tables outside *(Richard Houghton)*;

Stapleford Tawney [Tawney Common; about 2 miles N – OS Sheet 167 map ref 500013; TL5001], *Mole Trap*: Unspoilt remote county pub with two long settles for the tables in its small bar, McMullens AK and County, limited basic food, pleasant seats outside; popular with walkers and cyclists *(Roy Williams)*

Stebbing [Stebbing High St; TL6624], *Kings Head*: Cosy and comfortable 17th-c beamed local, barbecues; beautiful walking trails in delightful village *(Nikki Moffat)*; [High St], *White Hart*: Local with lovely beamed interior, lively staff, delicious food *(Nikki Moffat)*

Stock [Common Rd; just off B1007 Chelmsford—Billericay; TQ6998], *Bakers Arms*: Open-plan beamed pub with smart banquettes, well above-average genuine home cooked bar food inc vegetarian, well presented good value set meals in attractive dining room with french windows, pleasant service, no piped music; charming well kept garden *(Paul Barstow, Karyn Taylor, David J Brown, Tina and David Woods-Taylor)*

☆ Stock [The Square (just off main st); TQ6998], *Bear*: Lovely old comfortably unmodernised building with wise old men in front bar, Arrolls 90/-, Friary Meux Best, Tetleys and Youngs, cosy restaurant, good well cooked and presented food esp fish; children's room, cat called Rhythm (don't ask about Blues), nice garden overlooking pond at the back *(M A and C R Starling, Mr and Mrs J R Morris, Keith and Cheryl Roe, Ian Phillips)*

☆ Sturmer [The Street; A604 SE of Haverhill; TL6944], *Red Lion*: Warm and welcoming thatched and beamed dining pub, good choice of generous reasonably priced good food (not Sun evening); well kept Greene King ales, jovial landlord, helpful staff, plenty of tables with solid cushioned chairs, convenient layout if you don't like steps, big fireplace; unobtrusive piped music, children in dining room and conservatory, pleasant garden *(Gwen and Peter Andrews)*

Thaxted [Bullring; TL6130], *Swan*: Tudor pub doing well under new management, revitalised and attractive, with well kept ales inc Adnams and Greene King, warm atmosphere in big bar area, plenty of well spaced tables, restaurant; bedrooms *(Peter Plumridge, John Fahy)*

Tolleshunt Major [TL9011], *Bell*: Pleasant long building, beams, studwork and bay windows inside (inviting the sun), friendly new licensees, good cooking inc Thai chicken curry, well kept Abbot and Greene King IPA, verandah and barbecue area overlooking big rustic pond, immaculate lavatories (inc separate facilities for disabled) *(Colin Laffan)*

☆ Toot Hill [village signed off A113 S of Ongar and from A414 W of Ongar; TL5102], *Green Man*: Good simply furnished country dining pub, remarkable choice of wines from a good variety of merchants, inc dozens of champagnes, well kept Adnams and unusual ales from further afield, friendly staff, uncrowded relaxed feel, pretty front terrace, tables in back garden; no children under 10 *(A J and M Thomasson, H O Dickinson, Lesley Zammit, Wayne Brindle, Warren O'Callaghan, G and T Edwards, Mrs M Starling, MJVK, Tony Gayfer, LYM)*

☆ *nr* Waltham Abbey [very handy for M25 junction 26; A121 towards Waltham Abbey, then follow Epping, Loughton sign from exit roundabout], *Volunteer*: Good genuine chow mein and big pancake rolls (unless Chinese landlady away Mar/Apr) and generous more usual food in big open-plan McMullens pub; attractive conservatory, guest beer, some tables on side terrace, pretty hanging baskets; nice spot by Epping Forest, can get very busy weekends *(C H and P Stride, BB)*

West Bergholt [Nayland Rd; 2 miles from Colchester on Sudbury rd; TL9627], *White Hart*: Old coaching inn with good value food, real ales inc changing guests, big garden, adjacent caravan and camp site; children welcome *(J E Kemp)*

Wethersfield [High St; TL7131], *Dog*: Fine Georgian building, freshly cooked good value food inc home-made Italian ice creams in two spacious pleasantly furnished bars and restaurant, Greene King and other ales, welcoming service, good Italian house wines, muted piped music *(John Fahy, Gwen and Peter Andrews)*

☆ White Roding [TL5613], *Black Horse*: Sprucely well kept plush Ridleys pub with generous home cooking (not Sun evening; fresh fish Thurs), well kept IPA and Best, decent house wines, welcoming attentive service, relaxing atmosphere, bar billiards, very quiet piped music *(Gwen and Peter Andrews)*

Wicken Bonhunt [TL4933], *Coach & Horses*: Attractive partly thatched pub with three small cosy sections, welcoming licensees, beams and brasses, decent food in bar and restaurant, well kept Greene King ales; no music *(Gwen and Peter Andrews)*

☆ Wickham Bishops [TL8412], *Mitre*: Pleasantly refurbished with snug bars and spacious family dining area, reasonably priced food cooked to order inc some unusual dishes and first-class Sun lunch, well kept Ridleys IPA and ESX, decent wines, good fire; service may be slow *(Gwen and Peter Andrews, Colin Laffan)*

Wickham Bishops, *Chequers*: Attractive old-fashioned local, good straightforward food esp fresh fish with juicy real chips, Charrington and Ind Coope Burton; big fenced garden with play area, pretty village; children's play area in fenced in garden *(Julie King, Adrian White)*

☆ Widdington [High St; signed off B1383 N of Stansted; TL5331], *Fleur de Lys*: Unpretentious low-beamed timbered bar with inglenook log fire, seven well kept enterprising real ales, decent wines,

straightforward seating, pleasant food, banknote collection; games in back bar, children in restaurant and no-smoking family room, picnic tables on side lawn *(Jack Davey, Gwen and Peter Andrews, Eddie Edwards, John Fahy, LYM)*

☆ Wivenhoe [Black Buoy Hill, off A133; TM0321], *Black Buoy*: Well kept Greene King and weekly guest ale in charming 16th-c building's spacious open-plan bar, wide choice of good food inc local fish, inventive vegetarian choice and some other unusual dishes, convivial atmosphere, open fires, maybe classical piped music, restaurant; tucked away from water in conservation area, but has river views *(K B Bacon, Mike Harrison, G and M Stewart, Hazel Morgan)*

Wivenhoe [Quayside], *Rose & Crown*: Atmospheric friendly unspoilt inn in delightful spot by Colne river, log fire, low beams, scrubbed floors, well kept reasonably priced Adnams; some jazz nights *(Mick and Hilary Stiffin, Mike Harrison, Hazel Morgan)*

Woodham Mortimer [TL8104], *Hurdlemakers Arms*: Quietly placed country local with picnic tables well spaced among trees and shrubs outside, cottagey feel in simply furnished flagstoned lounge with cushioned settles, low ceiling and timbered walls; well kept Greene King IPA and Abbot and Ridleys, good fresh food, darts alley in public bar; summer barbecues, garden children's room with video games *(Paul Zimmerman, Peter Helsdon, BB)*; [A414 Danbury—Maldon], *Royal Oak*: Promising new licensees, fresh fish daily, well kept Benskins Best and Ind Coope Burton, decent wine, obliging staff; piped music *(Gwen and Peter Andrews)*

☆ Woodham Walter [signed off A414 E from Chelmsford; TL8006], *Bell*: Striking Elizabethan pub with beams and timbers, decorative plates and lots of brass, comfortable alcoves on various levels, log fire, decent bar food (not Mon) from a wide choice of well priced sandwiches to steaks inc vegetarian, pretty dining room in partly panelled upper gallery, Adnams, Friary Meux Best and a guest beer on handpump; children in eating area *(Ian and Nita Cooper, Nigel Norman, Mike and Karen England, Paul Barstow and Karyn Taylor, John Fahy, Thomas Nott, LYM)*

Wormingford [B1508; TL9331], *Crown*: Reasonably priced food and well kept Greene King ales in pleasant and relaxing old pub, no music, friendly service; good big garden *(Mrs P Goodwyn)*

Writtle [TL6706], *New Inn on the Green*: Spacious pub with five well kept ales such as Mansfield, Mauldons and Wadworths 6X, friendly well dressed staff, great choice of good bar food, dining area *(Frank W Gadbois)*; *Wheatsheaf*: Wonderful genuine pub atmosphere, well kept Greene King beers and a guest, friendly knowledgeable landlord *(Frank W Gadbois)*

Gloucestershire

This county has a lot of beautifully placed pubs, both smart and simple. Certainly all the new main entries in this edition have enviable positions: the delightful old Eight Bells in one of the nicest parts of Chipping Campden (a charming small town with an exceptional choice of good pubs), the carefully extended Dog & Muffler tucked away near Coleford in the Forest of Dean, the warmly welcoming Farmers Arms in the conservation village of Guiting Power, the Halfway House at Kineton (another attractive Cotswold local), the very civilised Inn For All Seasons at Little Barrington, the Greyhound at Siddington just outside Cirencester (doing very well under its friendly new tenants), and the venerable Mill by its pretty stream in Withington. Other pubs currently on top form here include the Black Horse at Amberley, the delightfully unspoilt Boat at Ashleworth Quay (gains a Star Award this year), the Village Pub at Barnsley (good food without losing its enjoyable pub atmosphere), the atmospheric Bear at Bisley, the bustling Wild Duck at Ewen (its engaging combination of good food and atmosphere gains it our accolade of Gloucestershire Dining Pub of the Year), the unusual Royal Oak at Gretton, the upmarket but relaxed Fox at Lower Oddington, the Old Lodge at Minchinhampton (doing very well indeed, with worthwhile changes under its newish regime), the Butchers Arms at Oakridge Lynch (a fine all-rounder), the Anchor at Oldbury on Severn (good food in an enjoyable atmosphere), the Dog at Old Sodbury (very popular for food, lots of fresh fish) and the Queens Head in Stow on the Wold (friendly and full of character). Welcoming new people at the Black Horse at Naunton have brightened it up quite a bit, and eager-to-please new licensees for the Horse & Groom at Oddington have among other changes introduced a lobster tank; there are also new people making changes at the Ragged Cot at Hyde and the Green Dragon near Cowley. The popular Golden Heart at Brimpsfield has added bedrooms, and the Boars Head at Aust, one of Britain's handiest motorway stop-offs, is flourishing since changing its tie from Courage to Eldridge Pope. All our main entries here can provide decent food – and the Black Horse at Amberley deserves special mention for its innovative special bargain pricing on some days (£3.50 for anything from the menu). But surprisingly, really outstanding pub food is less common in Gloucestershire than we would have thought the local market would support; only half a dozen places here have qualified for our Food Award this year. By contrast, it's a rewarding county for drinkers, with a relatively high proportion of the pubs here serving good wines by the glass as well as good beers. Moreover, drinks prices are below the national average – we found pubs tied to the local Donnington brewery particularly good value. In the Lucky Dip section at the end of the chapter, particularly rewarding pubs include the Gardeners Arms at Alderton, Lygon Arms in Chipping Campden, Slug & Lettuce in Cirencester, Tunnel House at Coates, Farmers Boy at Longhope, Masons Arms at Meysey Hampton, Rose & Crown at Nympsfield, Royal Oak in Painswick, Daneway at Sapperton,

Snowshill Arms at Snowshill and Crown at Tolldown. Our own inspections confirm how appealing most of these are; and there's an interesting choice in Tewkesbury.

ALMONDSBURY ST6084 Map 2

Bowl 🛏 ♀

1¼ miles from M5, junction 16 (and therefore quite handy for M4, junction 20; from A38 towards Thornbury, turn first left signposted Lower Almondsbury, then first right down Sundays Hill, then at bottom right again into Church Road

You can usually find a quiet corner in this bustling white cottage – even on a busy lunchtime. The long neatly kept beamed bar has a big winter log fire at one end, with a woodburning stove at the other, blue plush-patterned modern settles, pink cushioned stools and mate's chairs around elm tables, quite a few horsebrasses, and stripped bare stone walls. Well kept Courage Best and Directors, Otter Bright, Smiles Best, Wadworths 6X, and Wickwar Merrywood on handpump, several malt whiskies, and freshly pressed fruit juices; friendly service. Popular bar food includes sandwiches (£1.95; toasties from £1.95; filled french bread £2.95; open sandwiches £3.95), soup (£1.95), home-made leek and macaroni (£3.65), ploughman's (£3.95), omelettes (from £4.45), vegetable cottage pie (£4.95), chicken balti (£5.65), beef and beer casserole (£6.45), steak and kidney pie (£6.75), oriental platter (£7.95), daily specials, and puddings (£2.45); they may charge extra to eat from this menu in the attractive little restaurant, part of which is no smoking. The brown spaniel is called Charlie, another dog Corrie, and there's a black and white cat. In summer, the flowering tubs, hanging baskets and window boxes are pretty, a back terrace overlooks a field, and there are some picnic tables across the quiet road.

(Recommended by A and R Cooper, Virginia Jones, H F C Barclay, Simon and Amanda Southwell, Roy and Sue Morgan, Lindsley Harvard, Margaret Whalley, Mike Woodhead, Howard Clutterbuck, Nigel Clifton, R W Brooks, Keith Pollard, Meg and Colin Hamilton, Brian and Anna Marsden)

Courage ~ Lease: John Alley ~ Real ale ~ Meals and snacks (till 10pm) ~ Restaurant ~ (01454) 612757 ~ Children welcome ~ Open 11-3, 5(6 Sat)-11; closed evening 25 Dec ~ Bedrooms: £25B/£39B

AMBERLEY SO8401 Map 4

Black Horse £ 🍺

Village signposted off A46 Stroud—Nailsworth; as you pass village name take first very sharp left turn (before Amberley Inn) then bear steeply right – pub on your left

From inside and out, the views here are really marvellous – but it's not just this that readers enjoy about this friendly, very popular pub. You can be sure of a friendly welcome, the food is most enjoyable, and apart from weekends, there are good value offers such as three real ales on Tuesdays at £1 a pint, and anything from the menu at lunchtime or in the evening for £3.50 (Monday-Thursday). The dining bar has wheelback chairs, green-cushioned window seats, a few prints on the plain cream walls, and a fire in a small stone fireplace, there's a conservatory, and a family bar on the left which is partly no smoking. A fine range of well kept real ales on handpump, such as Archers Best, Dartmoor Best, Hook Norton, Smiles, Wadworths 6X and Youngs Special, and farm cider. Bar food includes sandwiches and other straightforward bar meals, as well as daily specials and a particularly good carvery-style Sunday lunch; good service. Darts, pool, shove-ha'penny, cribbage, and dominoes, with pool and a juke box in a separate building. Teak seats and picnic tables on a back terrace, a new barbecue and spit roast area, and on the other side of the building, a lawn with pretty flowers and honeysuckle has more picnic tables.

(Recommended by S Godsell, Craig Peck, Dave Irving, Tom McLean, Roger Huggins, Ewan McCall, Cherry Ann Knott, Pat and Roger Fereday, James and Patricia Halfyard, G C Brown, Paula Williams, Lt Col E H F Sawbridge, S G Brown)

Free house ~ Licensee Patrick O'Flynn ~ Real ale ~ Meals and snacks ~ (01453) 872556 ~ Children welcome ~ Open 12-3, 6-11; 12-11 summer Sats

AMPNEY CRUCIS SP0602 Map 4

Crown of Crucis 🛏

A417 E of Cirencester

Most people come to this dining pub (popular with older people at lunchtime) for the reliable good value food: sandwiches (from £1.85), a lunchtime daily special such as steak and mushroom pie (£3.75), ploughman's (£4.45), a trio of locally made sausages (£4.60), pasta with finely chopped vegetables in a tomato and herb sauce (£4.90), gammon and egg (£5.60), seared escallope of salmon (£5.70), steaks (from £9.40), good home-made puddings (£1.85), and children's meals (£2.40). It's worth arriving early to be sure of a table; part of the restaurant is no smoking. The spacious and comfortable modernised bar has a pleasant, relaxed atmosphere, well kept Archers Village, Boddingtons, and Ruddles County on handpump, and helpful, friendly service. In summer, you can sit outside at the many tables on the back grass by a stream with ducks and maybe swans. *(Recommended by Dick Brown, David Surridge, Colin Laffan, Pat Crabb, David Holman, Mr ad Mrs J Brown, Andrew and Ruth Triggs, E A George, Marjorie and Colin Roberts)*

Free house ~ Licensee R K Mills ~ Real ale ~ Meals and snacks (till 10pm) ~ Restaurant ~ (01285) 851806 ~ Children welcome until 8pm ~ Open 11-11; closed 25 Dec ~ Bedrooms: £52B/£74B

APPERLEY SO8628 Map 4

Farmers Arms ♀ 🍴

Nr Apperley on B4213, which is off A38 N of Gloucester

Popular locally, this friendly beamed pub has a little thatched brewhouse where they brew their own Mayhems Oddas Light and Sundowner Heavy; also, guests such as Courage Directors, Theakstons Old Peculier, and Woods Wonderful on handpump or tapped from the cask. Inside, the airy extended pub has plenty of room at the bar, though you'll generally find most people in the comfortable and spacious dining lounge. Fresh fish is delivered daily, which leads to several interesting blackboard specials, and there's also open sandwiches (the prawn is good) and ploughman's (£3.75), lasagne (£5.25), lamb in rosemary and red wine or a vegetarian dish (£5.75), chicken in white wine and tarragon or beef in ale pie (£5.95), several steaks, and quite a few puddings; friendly service; coal-effect gas fires, piped music. Decent wines (including a red and a white wine of the month), and a fair range of malt whiskies. Guns line the beams of the bar, and there are old prints, horseshoes and stuffed pheasants dotted about. The neat garden has picnic tables by a thatched well, with a wendy house and play area. *(Recommended by Nigel Clifton, Jeanne and George Barnwell, Dave Irving, Roger Huggins, Ewan McCall, Tom McLean, John and Vivienne Rice, Neil and Anita Christopher, J Roy Smylie, Mr and Mrs C Roberts)*

Own brew ~ Licensees Geoff and Carole Adams ~ Real ale ~ Meals and snacks (till 10pm) ~ Restaurant ~ (01452) 780307 ~ Children welcome ~ Organist Fri evening, Sun lunchtime ~ Open 11-3, 6-11

ASHLEWORTH QUAY SO8125 Map 4

Boat ★

Ashleworth signposted off A417 N of Gloucester; Quay signed from village

'A gem' is how several people describe this gentle, unspoilt old cottage – run by the same family ever since it was first granted a licence by Charles II. It's in a lovely spot on the banks of the River Severn and there's a front suntrap crazy-paved courtyard, bright with plant tubs in summer, with a couple of picnic tables under cocktail parasols; more seats and tables under cover at the sides. It's very much the kind of place where strangers soon start talking with each other and the charming landladies work hard at preserving the unique character. Spotlessly kept, the little front parlour has a great built-in settle by a long scrubbed deal table that faces an old-fashioned open kitchen range with a side bread oven and a couple of elderly fireside chairs; there are rush mats on the scrubbed flagstones, houseplants in the window, fresh garden flowers, and old magazines to read; shove-ha'penny, dominoes and cards (the front room has darts and a game called Dobbers). A pair of flower-cushioned antique settles face each other in the back room where Arkells BBB, Oakhill Yeoman, and Smiles Best and guests like Crown Buckley Reverend James, RCH Pitchfork, and Wye Valley Bitter are tapped from the cask, along with a full range of Westons farm ciders. They do excellent lunchtime rolls (from £1.40) or ploughman's with home-made chutney (£3) during the week, and groups of walkers can book these or afternoon teas. The medieval tithe barn nearby is striking; some readers prefer to park here and walk to the pub. *(Recommended by Dave Irving, Roger Huggins, Tom McLean, Ewan McCall, Meg Bowell, Derek and Sylvia Stephenson, Peter and Audrey Dowsett, AEB, Alan and Paula McCully, Brian Wainwright, David Campbell, Vicki McLean, Sandra Kench, Steven Norman, Pete and Rosie Flower, Jack and Philip Paxton, Sara Nicholls, Keith Stephen, Nigel Clifton, Mrs Pat Crabb, Jeff Davies, Michael Launder, Dr Paul Kitchener)*

Free house ~ Licensees Irene Jelf and Jacquie Nicholls ~ Real ale ~ Lunchtime snacks ~ (01452) 700272 ~ Children welcome till 8pm ~ Open 11-2.30(3 Sat), 6-11; winter evening opening 7pm

AUST ST5789 Map 2

Boars Head

½ mile from M4, junction 21; village signposted from A403

Even on a Monday lunchtime this small-roomed village pub is full of customers. There's a bustling, friendly atmosphere and the neatly kept and comfortable main bar has a big log fire, well polished country kitchen tables and others made from old casks, old-fashioned high-backed winged settles in stripped pine, some walls stripped back to the dark stone, decorative plates hanging from one stout black beam, and big rugs on dark lino. In another room is a woodburning stove, while a third has dining tables with lace tablecloths, fresh flowers and candles. Popular bar food includes good soup, sandwiches and ploughman's, and daily specials like good tagliatelle, smoked haddock and eggs (£5.95), steak and kidney pie or smoked salmon and scrambled eggs (£6.95), fresh whole plaice or roast half pheasant (£7.95), and Sunday roast lunch (£6.25). Part of the eating area is no smoking; piped music. Well kept Courage Best, Eldridge Pope Hardy, Flowers Original, and John Smiths on handpump. There's a medieval stone well in the pretty sheltered garden, which has an aviary and rabbits (including Newbury, an enormous lop-eared one), and even a cheery chipmunk. Also a touring caravan site. *(Recommended by S H Godsell, Dennis Shirley, Heather and Trevor Shaw, Mayur Shah, Simon and Amanda Southwell, Mr and Mrs J R Morris, Ken and Jenny Simmonds, A R and B E Sayer, Pat and John Smyth, C H and P Stride, David Shillitoe, Pat and Richard Tazewell, J M Mogg)*

Eldridge Pope ~ Manageress Mary May ~ Real ale ~ Meals and snacks (not Sun evening) ~ (01454) 632278 ~ Children in Pine Room only ~ Open 11-3, 6-11; winter evening opening 6.30

AWRE SO7108 Map 4

Red Hart

Village signposted off A48 S of Newnham

Tucked away in a remote farming village, this surprisingly tall 16th-c pub has a nice mix of locals and visitors and very friendly licensees. Attractive and immaculately kept, the L-shaped main part of the bar has a deep glass-covered illuminated well, an upholstered wall settle, and wheelback chairs; there are plates on a delft shelf at the end, as well as a gun and a stuffed pheasant over the stone fireplace, big prints on the walls, and a bale of straw swinging from the pitched rafters. Decent bar food includes sandwiches, wholesome home-made soup (£2.25), home-made pâté (£3.50), ploughman's (£3.95), home-made lasagne (£5.45), broccoli and cream cheese bake or cold home-baked ham with egg (£5.75), home-made steak and kidney pie (£6.25), seafood pancake (£6.95), and steaks (from £9.50); service can slow down under pressure; the restaurant is no smoking. Well kept Wadworths 6X and a changing guest beer on handpump, and several malt whiskies; fruit machine and piped music. In front of the building are some picnic tables. *(Recommended by K H Frostick, Alan and Paula McCully, Tom McLean, Roger Huggins, Dave Irving, Ewan McCall, Glenda Jones, Robert Huddleston, A Y Drummond)*

Free house ~ Licensee James Purtill ~ Real ale ~ Meals and snacks (not Sun evenings) ~ Restaurant (not Sun evenings) ~ (01594) 510220 ~ Children welcome ~ Open 11-3, 7-11; closed Mon exc bank hol lunchtimes

BARNSLEY SP0705 Map 4
Village Pub
A433 Cirencester—Burford

This is a very enjoyable and friendly place, much liked by our readers. It's the good food served by helpful staff that attracts most comments: interestingly filled bagels or toasted muffins or filled baked potatoes (from £2.50), smoked trout and cream cheese pâté (£3.25), crispy stuffed pepper (£3.35), ploughman's (£3.50), a quorn dish of the day or steak and kidney pie (£4.95), smoked salmon and dill quiche (£5), chicken curry (£5.50), and daily specials like pasta with vegetables in a sweet and sour sauce (£5), leek and mushroom pie with a puff pastry topping (£5.25), grilled local trout (£6.25), salmon steak with a red pepper sauce (£6.95). Well kept King & Barnes Twelve Bore and Wadworths 6X on handpump, and country wines. The walls of the comfortable low-ceilinged communicating rooms are decorated with country pictures, gin-traps, scythes and other farm tools, and there are several winter log fires, as well as plush chairs, stools and window settles around the polished tables (which have candles in the evening). Darts, cribbage, shove ha'penny, dominoes, and piped music. The sheltered back courtyard has plenty of tables, and its own outside servery. The pub is handy for Rosemary Verey's garden in the village. *(Recommended by Dr and Mrs A H Young, Jean Minner, Dave Irving, Roger Huggins, Tom McLean, Ewan McCall, Sue Lee, Don and Shirley Parrish, Frank W Gadbois, Maysie Thompson, John and Joan Wyatt, Steve Gilbert, Helen Cox, John Broughton, Paul and Sue Merrick, Andrew and Ruth Triggs, John Bowdler, SRP)*

Free house ~ Licensee Mrs Susan Wardrop ~ Real ale ~ Meals and snacks ~ Restaurant ~ (01285) 740421 ~ Children in eating area of bar ~ Open 11-3, 6-11; closed 25 Dec ~ Bedrooms: £30B/£45B

BIBURY SP1106 Map 4
Catherine Wheel 🍺
Arlington; B4425 NE of Cirencester

The atmosphere in this low-beamed Cotswold stone pub is bustling and happy with friendly staff and lots of chatty customers. The main bar at the front dates back in part to the 15th-c, and has lots of old-fashioned dark wood furniture, a good log fire, gleaming copper pots and pans around the fireplace, and newspapers to read; there are also two smaller and quieter back rooms. Generous helpings of straightforward bar food include sandwiches (from £2; sausage and fried onion £2.50; steak £3.75), good soup (£2.25), filled baked potatoes or ploughman's (from £3.50), ratatouille topped with parmesan cheese (£4.50), prawns in garlic butter or home-made cottage pie (£4.75), ham and egg (£5), meat or vegetable lasagne (£5.50), poached salmon (£6.75), steaks (£8.25), and daily specials; children's menu (from £1.50). Well kept Archers Golden, Boddingtons, Courage Best, Flowers Original, and Whitbreads West Country PA on handpump, and a good few malt whiskies; well-behaved dogs (who may be given a Bonio); shove-ha'penny, table skittles, dominoes, cribbage, fruit machine, piped music. There's a good sized and well kept garden behind with picnic tables among fruit trees (and a play area), and some seats out in front. *(Recommended by D G King, Simon Collett-Jones, Dave Irving, Tom McLean, Ewan McCall, Andrew and Ruth Triggs, D K Williams, Peter Woolls, Richard J Raeon, Karen Barnes, Mrs K Neville-Rolfe, Neil and Anita Christopher, SRP, Peter and Audrey Dowsett, George Atkinson, Jennie Munro, Jim Wingate)*

Free house ~ Licensee Carol Palmer ~ Real ale ~ Meals and snacks (all day) ~ (01285) 740250 ~ Children welcome ~ Open 11-11 ~ Bedrooms: /£50S

BISLEY SO9006 Map 4

Bear 🍺

Village signposted off A419 just E of Stroud

Atmospheric and friendly, this elegantly gothic 16th-c inn is popular with a good mix of customers. The meandering L-shaped bar has an enormously wide low stone fireplace (not very high – the ochre ceiling's too low for that), a long shiny black built-in settle, and a smaller but even sturdier oak settle by the front entrance; a separate no-smoking stripped-stone area is used for families. Good, home-made bar food includes filled french sticks (from £2.50; Greek salad £3; garlic and lemon fried prawns £3.80), home-made burgers (from £3.50), fried potatoes and onions with tomato and mature cheddar or bacon and sausage (£4), vegetable pasty filled with fennel, mushrooms and pine kernels in white wine and cream sauce (£5), home-made steak and kidney pie (£5.50), daily specials such as roasted peppers stuffed with pesto ratatouille and topped with parmesan cheese (£3.95), pheasant braised in white wine with celery and thyme (£5.65) or tuna fish steak with capers, olives and garlic (£6.25), and nice puddings (from £1.95). Well kept Bass, Flowers Original, Morlands Old Speckled Hen, Tetleys, and Whitbread Castle Eden on handpump; darts, table skittles, and dominoes. A small front colonnade supports the upper floor of the pub, and the sheltered little flagstoned courtyard made by this has a traditional bench; as well as the garden across the quiet road, there's quite a collection of stone mounting-blocks – and quoits. The steep stone-built village is attractive. *(Recommended by Richard Gibbs, Jim Fraser, Joan and Alex Timpson, Nick and Meriel Cox, Mike Beiley, Roger Huggins, Ewan McCall, Tom McLean, Dave Irving, John and Phyllis Maloney, Don and Shirley Parrish, John and Joan Wyatt, R W Brooks, Marjorie and Colin Roberts, Andrew and Ruth Triggs)*

Pubmaster ~ Tenants Nick and Vanessa Evans ~ Real ale ~ Meals and snacks (not Sun evening; till 10pm) ~ (01452) 770265 ~ Children in family room ~ Open 11-3, 6-11; open all day Sat and Sun if busy in summer; closed evenings 25-26 Dec ~ Bedrooms: £18/£36

BLEDINGTON SP2422 Map 4

Kings Head 🍴 🛏 🍷 🍺

B4450

It is quite a job to combine the benefits of a two-bar pub with a very good restaurant and comfortable accommodation, but this pleasantly up-market 15th-c inn has managed to do just that. The smart but welcoming main bar is full of ancient beams and other atmospheric furnishings, such as high-backed wooden settles, gateleg or pedestal tables, and there's a warming log fire in the stone inglenook (which has a big black kettle hanging in it); the lounge looks on to the garden. From the bar menu, the very good food might include home-made soup (£1.95), ploughman's or sandwiches on granary or ciabatta bread with interesting fillings like crispy bacon and banana, hot pear and stilton or black pudding, onion and mango (all £3.25, with straw potatoes), salads (from £3.50; poached fillet of salmon with lemon mayonnaise £6.95), tartlet of mushrooms with watercress dressing (£3.95), lamb liver with red wine, thyme and parsnip purée (£4.95), steak, mushroom and wine pie (£5.95), daily specials such as omelettes with local free range eggs or lovely mussels (£3.95), popular black pudding, bacon and egg rosti (£4.95), pasta dishes like smoked salmon and dill or curried nutty raisin and lemon (£5.25), baked cod with sweetcorn fritter and lime butter (£6.95), and grilled lemon sole (£8.95), lovely puddings such as rum-flavoured bread pudding, chocolate biscuit cake or treacle tart (£2.25), and good children's dishes (from £1.50); they also do a mix-and-match menu (from £2.95) and a good value 3-course meal (£9.95). It's worth arriving in plenty of time as they stick very firmly indeed to their afternoon closing time, and in the evening a 10% service charge is added to all meals. An antique bar counter dispenses well kept Eccleshall Hi Duck, Hook Norton Best, Judges Gravel Pit, Stanway Old Eccentric, Uley Old Spot, and Wilds Wild Oats, and Inch's ciders in summer, excellent extensive wine list (with eight by the glass), and 50 or so malt whiskies; efficient, friendly service. Part of the restaurant area is no smoking; piped music. The public bar has darts, shove-ha'penny, dominoes, table skittles, and juke box. The back garden has Aunt Sally and tables that look over to a little stream with lots of ducks that locals often greet by name. The bedrooms over the kitchens can be noisy. *(Recommended by Andrew and Ruth Triggs, Pellman familiy, Sue Demont, Tim Barrow, Arnold Day, Coyne and Mills party, Adam and Elizabeth Duff, D C T and E A Frewer, M J Morgan, Julia Doust, Paul Boot, M A and C R Starling, D J Hayman, Don and Shirley Parrish, John C Baker, Richard Baker, Mr and Mrs Peter Woods, Maysie Thompson, D D Collins, Nigel Wilkinson, Peter and Audrey Dowsett, Gillian and Michael Wallace, Margaret Templeton, Bruce Warren, D G King, Jerry and Alison Oakes, John Waller, David Holman, Malcolm Taylor)*

Free house ~ Licensees Michael and Annette Royce ~ Real ale ~ Meals and snacks (12-2, 6.30-10) ~ Restaurant ~ (01608) 658365 ~ Children in garden room extension ~ Open 11-2.30, 6-11; closed evening 24 Dec, 25 Dec ~ Bedrooms: £40B/£60B

BLOCKLEY SP1634 Map 4
Crown ★ ⑪ ♀ ⇔
High Street

Although this smartly civilised Elizabethan inn has long been highly regarded for the marvellous fresh fish served in both the hotel-ish restaurant and back bistro, the bustling bar has a proper pubby atmosphere with a large influx of locals as well as visitors. Here, the food includes home-made soup (£3.25), sandwiches (from £3.25), fish pie (£4.95), home-made hand-raised venison and pigeon pie (£5.25), spiced bacon and lentil casserole of squid with tomatoes, black olives and feta cheese (£6.50), local cod in a beer and chive batter (£6.95), chicken in tomato, garlic and ginger (£7.50), mixed grill (£9.95), daily specials, and home-made puddings like delicious mango and banana fool (£3.95); good Sunday lunch. Well kept Butcombe, Buchanans, Donnington, Jouster, Smiles, and Theakstons ales on handpump, a large choice of wines, and several malt whiskies; friendly staff. There's an antique settle amongst the more recent furnishings, and leading off from the bar is a snug carpeted lounge with an attractive window seat, windsor chairs around traditional cast-iron-framed tables, and a winter log fire; steps lead up into a little sitting room with easy chairs, which in turn leads through to another spacious dining room; piped music. The terraced coachyard is surrounded by beautiful trees and shrubs, and there's a hatch to hand drinks down to people sitting out in front, by the lane. The inn is handy for sights such as Batsford Park Arboretum. *(Recommended by K H Frostick, M A and C R Starling, Dr I Maine, Mr and Mrs H W Clayton, Jenny and Michael Back, Neville Kenyon, Martin and Karen Wake, M J Dowdy, Andrew and Ruth Triggs, Hanns P Golez, M A Robinson, Richard Raeon, Karen Barnes, John and Heather Dwane, Moira and John Cole, P J Caunt, John Waller, Sara Nicholls, Julie Peters, D G King, Alain and Rose Foote)*

Free house ~ Licensees John and Betty Champion ~ Real ale ~ Meals (not in bar Sat evening) and snacks ~ Restaurant ~ (01386) 700245 ~ Well behaved children welcome ~ Piano in bar Weds, Thurs, Fri evenings ~ Open 11-12; 11-11 Sun ~ Bedrooms: £60B/£84B

BRIMPSFIELD SO9312 Map 4

Golden Heart ♀ ◀

Nettleton Bottom; A417 Birdlip—Cirencester

The main low-ceilinged bar in this extended 16th-c country pub is divided into three
cosily distinct areas, with a roaring log fire in the huge stone inglenook fireplace in
one, traditional built-in settles and other old-fashioned furnishings throughout, and
exposed stone, wood panelling, quite a few brass items, and typewriters. A
comfortable parlour on the right has another decorative fireplace, and leads into a
further room opening on to the terrace. Bass, Hook Norton, Marstons Pedigree, and
Timothy Taylors Landlord on handpump or tapped from the cask, and a good range
of wines by the glass. Served by friendly staff, bar food might include sandwiches,
vegetarian dishes (£5.95), a fresh fish of the day, steak in ale or hot bacon, chicken
and avocado salad (all £6.95), and fashionable dishes such as kangaroo and wild boar
(£7.25), and ostrich steak (£10.95). There are pleasant views down over a valley from
the rustic cask-supported tables on its suntrap gravel terrace; good nearby walks.
*(Recommended by Neil and Anita Christopher, Dave Irving, Ewan McCall, Roger Huggins, Tom
McLean, Joan and Alex Timpson, Paula Massey, Mervyn Hall, Jeremy Brittain-Long, Dave
Braisted, F C Johnston, Thomas Nott, R G Watson, Mr Chamberlain, Mrs B Lemon)*

*Free house ~ Licensee Catherine Stevens ~ Real ale ~ Meals and snacks (till
10pm) ~ (01242) 870261 ~ Children welcome ~ Irish folk every 2nd and last
Weds of the month ~ Open 11-3, 6-11.30 ~ Bedrooms: £25B/£35B*

BROAD CAMPDEN SP1637 Map 4

Bakers Arms ★ ◀

Village signposted from B4081 in Chipping Campden

The enthusiastic landlady of this delightfully simple little pub works very hard to
keep the unpretentious atmosphere just right. There are generally seven real ales on
handpump in summer and five in winter (cheap for the area), with regulars including
Courage Best, Donnington BB, Everards Old Original, Hook Norton, Stanway (a
tiny brewery in Stanway House, Winchcombe), and Wickwar Brand Oak. Good and
very reasonably priced food includes ploughman's (from £1.95), cottage pie (£2.95),
chilli (£3.25), vegetable lasagne (£3.95), chicken tikka masala (£4.50), fish pie
(£4.75), steak and kidney pie (£4.95), daily specials such as good salmon and
broccoli tagliatelle, bacon and onion suet pudding or mushroom and nut crumble,
children's menu (from £2, with dishes like chicken madras), and puddings (£1.75);
vegetables and salads are £1.25 extra. Very cosy and friendly, the tiny beamed bar
has a pleasant mix of tables and seats around the walls (which are stripped back to
bare stone), a log fire under a big black iron canopy at one end with a rocking chair
beside it, and another at the other end; several friendly cats. The oak bar counter is
attractive, and there's a big framed rugwork picture of the pub; darts, cribbage,
dominoes. There are white tables under cocktail parasols by flower tubs on a side
terrace and in the back garden, some seats under a fairy-lit arbour, and a play area,
with Aunt Sally and Tippit. The tranquil village is handy for the Barnfield cider mill.
*(Recommended by Terry and Vann W Prime, Jason Caulkin, M L and G Clarke, Martin and
Karen Wake, Alain and Rose Foote, Jerry and Alison Oakes, Andrew and Ruth Triggs, Mr and
Mrs C Moncreiffe, H O Dickinson, Hanns P Golez, D G King, Martin Jones, MDN, John
Waller, Sara Nicholls, Simon Small, Christopher and Maureen Starling, Ted George, Mrs B
Lemon, Kathryn and Brian Heathcote)*

*Free house ~ Licensee Carolyn Perry ~ Real ale ~ Meals and snacks (till 10pm Fri
and Sat) ~ (01386) 840515 ~ Children welcome ~ Folk night 3rd Tues of month ~
Open 11.30-2.30, 6-11; winter evening opening 6.30; closed 25 Dec, evening 26 Dec*

We accept no free drinks or payment for inclusion. We take no advertising,
and are not sponsored by the brewing industry – or by anyone else. So all
reports are independent.

BROCKHAMPTON SP0322 Map 4

Craven Arms ♀

Village signposted off A436 Andoversford—Naunton – look out for inn sign at head of lane in village; can also be reached from A40 Andoversford—Cheltenham via Whittington and Syreford

Very popular, this attractive 17th-c inn is set in an attractive gentrified hillside village with lovely views. There are low beams, thick roughly coursed stone walls and some tiled flooring, and though much of it has been opened out to give a sizeable (and spotlessly kept) eating area off the smaller bar servery, it's been done well to give a feeling of several communicating rooms; the furniture is mainly pine, with some wall settles, tub chairs and a log fire. Good bar food includes home-made soup (£2.10), big ploughman's (£3.75), sausages and egg (£4.50), mussels in pasta with a cream and wine sauce (£4.95), chicken and leek crunchy crumble (£5.75), steak, mushroom and Guinness pie (£5.95), sirloin steak (£9.95), and home-made puddings like treacle tart, sherry trifle or banana and peach crumble (£2.75). Well kept Bass, Hook Norton Best, and Wadworths 6X on handpump; friendly service. Darts, shove-ha'penny. There are swings in the sizeable garden. *(Recommended by Frank W Gadbois, Nick and Meriel Cox, Malcolm Taylor, David and Natalie Towle, John and Joan Wyatt, Frank Cummins)*

Free house ~ Licensees Dale and Melanie Campbell ~ Real ale ~ Meals and snacks ~ Restaurant ~ (01242) 820410 ~ Children welcome ~ Open 11-2.30, 6-11

BROCKWEIR SO5401 Map 4

Brockweir Inn

Village signposted just off A466 Chepstow—Monmouth

In fine walking country this 17th-c pub has a bare-stone-walled main bar with sturdy settles on quarry tiles in the front part, a winter open fire, beams, and brocaded seats and copper-topped tables in a series of carpeted alcoves at the back; pool, cribbage and trivia in the bare-floored and traditionally furnished public bar; the characterful trainhound is called Monty. Well kept Freeminer Bitter (brewed only four miles away), Greene King Abbot, and Hook Norton Best with a changing guest on handpump. Bar food includes sandwiches, tomato and orange soup (£1.80), ploughman's (£3.30), tuna bake (£3.50), lamb balti (£4.80), beef in stout or pork in cider (£4.90), and puddings such as fruit cheesecake or ginger pudding (£2). A covered courtyard at the back opens into a sheltered terrace, and there are picnic tables in a garden behind. As the pub is not too far away from the steep sheep-pastures leading up to Offa's Dyke Path and the Devil's Pulpit, with views over the Wye and Tintern Abbey, it's understandably a popular stop with walkers (no muddy boots); canoeing, horse riding and salmon fishing are available locally. *(Recommended by Barry and Anne, Piotr Chodzko-Zajko, Roger and Jenny Huggins, George Atkinson; more reports please)*

Free house ~ Licensees George and Elizabeth Jones ~ Real ale ~ Meals and snacks (not Tues evening) ~ (01291) 689548 ~ Children in eating area of the bar and in family room ~ Open 12-2.30(3 Sat), 6-11 ~ Bedrooms: £25/£36

CHEDWORTH SP0511 Map 4

Seven Tuns

Queen Street, Upper Chedworth; village signposted off A429 NE of Cirencester; then take second signposted right turn and bear left towards church

The famous Roman villa is only a pleasant walk away from this attractively placed Cotswold pub and there are other nice walks through the valley, too. Inside, the happy mix of locals and visitors can choose between two bars with completely different characters. On the right, the smarter but cosily atmospheric little lounge has sizeable antique prints, tankards hanging from the beam over the serving bar, comfortable seats, decent tables, a partly boarded ceiling, a good winter log fire in the big stone fireplace, and a relaxed, quiet atmosphere; no muddy boots in here. The basic public bar on the left is more lively, and opens into a games room with darts, pool, dominoes, fruit machine and video game; there's also a skittle alley (which can be hired). Bar food includes ploughman's (from £4.50), fresh cod fillets in home-made batter (£4.95), home-made proper pies like Gloucester Old Spot pork pie or cheese, plum tomato and onion, and steak in ale or chicken and ham (£5.95), fresh salmon fillet with watercress sauce or sea bass on minestrone (£6.95), lamb Shrewsbury or halibut steaks with tiger prawns and garlic butter (£7.95), and puddings like fresh lemon tart or home-made spotted dick (£3.25); on Wednesday evenings they have a local prize-winning bangers and mash menu (£4.50), and every Friday there is a curry platter (£6.50; must book). They only use Aberdeen Angus meat for their steaks, and fresh fish and shellfish; there's a new restaurant area this year. Well kept changing real ales such as George's International and Old Ambrose from the Bristol Brewery and Goffs Jouster (from Winchcombe) on handpump; friendly, helpful staff. Across the road is a little walled raised terrace with a stream running through it forming a miniature waterfall, and there are plenty of tables both here and under cocktail parasols on a side terrace. *(Recommended by Tom McLean, Roger Huggins, Ewan McCall, Dave Irving, Sharon Hancock, Alan and Charlotte Sykes, John and Joan Wyatt, Lawrence Pearse, Mr and Mrs J Brown, Dr A Y Drummond, Andrew and Ruth Triggs, Nick and Meriel Cox, G Washington, Marjorie and Colin Roberts)*

Free house ~ Licensee Brian Eacott ~ Real ale ~ Meals and snacks (not Mon, or 25 Dec) ~ (01285) 720242 ~ Well-behaved children in eating area of the bar ~ Open 12(11.30 Sat)-2.30, 6.30-11

CHIPPING CAMPDEN SP1539 Map 4

Eight Bells 🛏 🍴 🍷

Church Street

Dating from the 13th or 14th c, and used then as a hostel for workmen building the nearby church, this handsome old pub now has the style and atmosphere to suit it. Gone are the log-effect gas fires and banquettes of its Whitbreads days in the early 1990s. These days, it has cushioned pews and solid dark wood furniture on its broad flagstones, stripped stone walls (with caricatures of regulars and photographs of pub events), heavy oak beams with massive timber supports, fresh flowers on tables, and log fires in up to three restored stone fireplaces – an enormous one has a painting of the pub in summer. Good generous home-made food includes a whole board's-worth of filled baguettes (from £3), and other daily-changing dishes use fresh often local ingredients; the choice might include an interesting soup such as tomato with orange (£2.75), baked brie with garlic toast, bacon and avocado salad or warm salad with scallops and bacon (£4.75), paella (£5.95), rabbit casserole (£6.25), steak and kidney pie (£6.75), chicken supreme cooked with ginger and spring onions, stir-fried monkfish (£7.50) or sautéed pork fillet with apricot and cream sauce (£7.50), seasonal venison, and 8oz sirloin steak (£9.25); puddings such as a delicious crème brûlée (£2.75). A new dining extension tones in well. Obliging service, with a chatty landlord and friendly knowledgeable staff; four well kept real ales such as Greene King Abbot, Marstons Pedigree and Tetleys, and a changing guest such as Wyre Piddle, Piddle in the Wind, from handpumps on a striking oak bar counter; a good range of changing wines by the glass, good coffee, daily papers; backgammon, dominoes. A fine old courtyard surrounded by roses and climbers has picnic tables. *(Recommended by Martin Jones, Martin and Sarah Constable, Martin and Karen Wake, MDN, Andrew and Ruth Triggs, Linda Norsworthy, George Atkinson, Owen Warnock, Ann and Bob Westbrook)*

Free house ~ Licensees Paul and Patrick Dare ~ Real ale ~ Meals and snacks ~ Restaurant ~ (01386) 840371 ~ Children welcome ~ Occasional live music ~ Open 11-3, 6-11; cl evening 25 Dec ~ Bedrooms: £38B/£44B (continental breakfast)

Kings Arms ♀

You can be sure of a genuinely warm and friendly welcome in this civilised little 16th-c hotel, overlooking the market square. The comfortably old-fashioned bar has handsomely carved black beams, a fine stone inglenook fireplace, maybe fresh flowers, and some big bay window seats; piped music. Good bar food includes lunchtime sandwiches (not Sun), soup (£1.90), quiche (£3.25), ploughman's (£3.75), steak and kidney pie (£4.95), and daily specials; good breakfasts; the restaurant is no smoking. They keep 10 wines by the glass from an extensive list. Children are given crayons and colouring books. There are seats in the gardens behind, and the hotel is handy for the attractive nearby gardens of Hidcote and Kiftsgate Court.
(Recommended by Mr and Mrs B Cox, Andrew and Ruth Triggs, Martin, Jane and Laura Bailey, Owen Warnock, W C Jones, John Bowdler, Martin and Karen Wake, Mrs J Oakes, Peter Lloyd, Ian Rorison, H O Dickinson, Brian and Anna Marsden)

Free house ~ Licensee Stan Earnshaw ~ Meals and snacks (12-3, 6-9.30) ~ Restaurant ~ (01386) 840256 ~ Children welcome ~ Open 11-11 ~ Bedrooms: £40B/£60B

Noel Arms 🛏 ♀

In 1360, this well run and rather smart old inn was reputedly licensed for the wool traders that were making the town's name. The relaxed, friendly bar has old oak settles, attractive old tables, seats and newer settles among the windsor chairs, and is decorated with casks hanging from its beams, farm tools, horseshoes and gin traps on the bare stone walls, and armour; there's a winter coal fire, and a conservatory behind. The small lounge areas are comfortable and traditionally furnished with coach horns, lantern lighting, and some stripped stonework, and the reception area has its quota of pikes, halberds, swords, muskets, and breastplates. Well kept Bass and Hook Norton on handpump, with guest ales such as Fullers London Pride, Hogs Back Rip Snorter, and Jennings Cocker Hoop, 25 malt whiskies, and a good wine list. Generous helpings of good home-made lunchtime bar food include sandwiches (from £2.25), ploughman's (£3.95), mushroom and aubergine tart (£4.85), sausage with mash and onion gravy (£5.10), spaghetti with pesto and bacon (£5.20), Irish stew (£5.50), rump steak (£6.25), and puddings like fruit crumble (£2.95), with evening dishes in the Green Room such as braised oxtails with creamed potatoes and swede (£6.80), king prawn and monkfish brochette with Thai sauce (£7.75), and haunch of venison with blackcurrant and liquorice (£7.80); friendly efficient service. There are seats in the old coachyard. *(Recommended by Martin Jones, Pam Adsley, Andrew and Ruth Triggs, DAV, John Waller)*

Free house ~ Licensee Neil John ~ Real ale ~ Lunchtime bar meals and snacks ~ Restaurant ~ (01386) 840317 ~ Children welcome ~ Open 10-3, 6-11 ~ Bedrooms: £60B/£85B

CLEARWELL SO5708 Map 4

Wyndham Arms 🛏 ♀

B4231, signposted from A466 S of Monmouth towards Lydney

In a lovely setting, this civilised and neatly kept country inn is a comfortable place to stay, with excellent breakfasts, and well placed for exploring the area – and you can stay free on winter Sundays if you eat in the restaurant. Despite being a hotel, it still has a distinctly pubby feel and character, and the smart beamed bar has red plush seats and velvet curtains, a collection of flat-irons by the log-effect gas fire in its spacious stone fireplace, and two big unusual patchwork pictures on its bared stone walls. Well kept Bass on handpump, lots of malt whiskies, a very good range of generously served wines by the glass (12) or half bottle – and maybe gherkins, onions and olives on the counter; good service from smartly turned-out staff. Bar food is pricey but worth the extra: home-made soup (£3.25), sandwiches (from £3.75; open ones from £4.25), ploughman's (£4.75), home-made pâtés like cheese and fresh herb or chicken liver (£4.95), smoked haddock with poached egg (£5.95), a daily pasta dish (£6.95), prawn or vegetable curry (£7.85), a vegetarian dish of the day, local salmon salad, deep-fried lemon sole with home-made tartare sauce or liver and bacon (all £8.25), steaks (from £10.75), and puddings (£3); some of the fruits, vegetables and herbs are grown in the garden; the restaurant is no smoking. There are seats out on the neat terraces; the friendly and characterful flat-coated retriever is called Theo and the huge black newfoundland is called Brian. *(Recommended by Mrs P Goodwyn, M J Morgan, George Atkinson, Dave Irving, Dr C E Morgan, S H Godsell)*

Free house ~ Licensees John, Rosemary and Robert Stanford ~ Real ale ~ Meals and snacks ~ Restaurant ~ (01594) 833666 ~ Children welcome ~ Open 11-11, 12-10.30 Sun ~ Bedrooms: £49B/£65B

COLD ASTON SP1219 Map 4
Plough

Village signposted from A436 and A429 SW of Stow on the Wold; beware that on some maps the village is called Aston Blank, and the A436 called the B4068

A new licensee has taken over this neatly kept and friendly little 17th-c village pub. It's a marvellously unspoilt place and the bar – divided into snug little areas by standing timbers – has low black beams, a built-in white-painted traditional settle facing the stone fireplace, simple old-fashioned seats on the flagstone and lime-ash floor, and a happy mix of customers. Bar food now includes filled rolls (from £2.75), garlic mushrooms coated with stilton (£2.95), ploughman's (£3.95), cauliflower cheese or lasagne (£4.95), steak in ale pie (£5.25), half roast chicken (£5.95), scampi and king prawn platter (£6.95), puddings (from £2.50), and a Sunday roast (£5.50); half helpings for children. Well kept Theakstons Best and Wadworths 6X and Henrys IPA on handpump; quoits, winter darts, and piped music. The small side terraces have picnic tables under parasols, and there may be Morris dancers out here in summer. *(Recommended by Ted George, Don and Shirley Parrish, Dave Irving, Ewan McCall, Roger Huggins, Tom McLean, Nick and Meriel Cox, Frank Cummins, F J and A Parmenter)*

Free house ~ Licensee Ernie Goodwin ~ Real ale ~ Meals and snacks (till 10pm) ~ (01451) 821459 ~ Children over 5 welcome ~ Open 11-2.30, 5.30-11

nr COLEFORD SO5813 Map 4
Dog & Muffler

Joyford, best approached from Christchurch 5-ways junction B4432/B4428, by church – B4432 towards Broadwell, then follow signpost; also signposted from the Berry Hill post office cross-roads; beyond the hamlet itself, bear right and keep your eyes skinned for the pub sign, which may be obscured by the hedge; OS Sheet 162 map reference 580134

Going into this prettily set country pub, which from outside looks like an idealised farmhouse, first of all you pass an 18th-c cider press by the path from the car park, then in the entrance lobby there's an ancient well. All this bodes well. The turkey-carpeted lounge bar, open yet cosy-feeling, has neat tables and comfortably cushioned wall settles and wheelback chairs, under black beams hung with pewter and china. A separate recently built beamed and flagstoned extension has a games area with pool, and a nearby skittle alley. At the back, a pleasant carpeted sun-lounge dining room with raj ceiling fans looks out past more tables on a verandah. A good range of well presented reasonably priced food includes sandwiches (from £2.25), filled baked potatoes (from £2.75), ploughman's (£3.95), steak and kidney pie (£4.85), vegetarian lasagne or leek and haddock bake (£5.25), daily specials such as chicken tikka, minted lamb chops, sweet and sour pork or cottage pie (from £4.80), sizzling platters (from £8.75), and home-made puddings such as apple pie or spotted dick with custard; 4-course Sunday roast lunch (£7.50). Well kept Fullers London Pride, Ruddles County and Sam Smiths on handpump, very pleasant cheerful service. The lawn is well sheltered, with some shade from mature trees, and well spaced picnic tables – some under thatched conical roofs; it has swings and a climbing frame. We have not yet had readers' reports on the bedrooms here, but

would expect this to be a pleasant place to stay in. There are nice walks nearby.
(Recommended by Ted George, Pete Yearsley, Dave Irving, Neil and Anita Christopher, P and M Rudlin, John Hazel)

Free house ~ Licensee Dennis Brain ~ Real ale ~ Meals and snacks (till 10pm) ~ Restaurant ~ (01594) 832444 ~ Children welcome ~ Open 12-3, 7-11 ~ Bedrooms: £30B/£45B

COLN ST ALDWYNS SP1405 Map 4

New Inn 🍴 🛏 ♀

On good back road between Bibury and Fairford

This civilised ivy-covered inn is popular for its beautifully presented restaurant standard food served in a pubby atmosphere, though for walkers – the surrounding countryside is good for walking and readers say the riverside walk to Bibury is not to be missed – helpings are not robust. From a regularly changing menu there might be filled baps, soup (£3.50 or £5), smoked haddock, bubble and squeak and curry sauce (£4.50 or £6.50), whisky and kipper pâté (£4.75 or £6.50), ploughman's or cumberland sausage and mash with onion and ale gravy (£5.95), vegetable moussaka (£6.25), braised shoulder of lamb with mash and rosemary or salmon fishcakes with chive sauce (£6.75), enjoyable boiled bacon with cabbage and gherkin sauce (£6.95), daily specials, children's dishes, and puddings such as warm bakewell tart with clotted cream, rhubarb crumble with ginger anglaise or fruit pudding with marmalade sauce (£3.50); bread, chips and salad are extra. The restaurant is no smoking. The two main rooms are most attractively furnished and decorated, and divided by a central log fire in a neat stone fireplace with wooden mantelbeam and willow-pattern plates on the chimney breast; there are also low beams, some stripped stonework around the bar servery and hops above it, oriental rugs on the red tiles, and a mix of seating from library chairs to stripped pews. Down a slight slope, a further room has a log fire in an old kitchen range at one end, and a stuffed buzzard on the wall. Well kept Hook Norton Best, Morlands Original, Wadworths 6X, and guests on handpump, half-a-dozen good wines by the glass, and several malt whiskies; friendly rather than speedy service. Darts, cribbage, dominoes, cards, chess and draughts. Lots of seats under umbrellas in the split-level terraced garden, and maybe sunny weekend barbecues. The peaceful Cotswold village is pretty.
(Recommended by Nigel Norman, Adam and Elizabeth Duff, Robin and Laura Hillman, Miss A Henry, M A Robinson, Jason Caulkin, Pat and John Millward, Rob Pope, Esther and John Sprinkle, Dorothy and Leslie Pilson, John Waller, D G King, John Bowdler, Andrew and Ruth Triggs, Dr I Maine, Colin Laffan, Roger Huggins, A G C Harper, Dr I H Maine, Peter and Audrey Dowsett, Bronwen and Steve Wrigley; also in Good Hotel Guide)

Free house ~ Licensee Brian Evans ~ Real ale ~ Meals and snacks ~ Restaurant ~ (01285) 750651 ~ Children welcome ~ Open 11-2.30, 5.30-11; 11-11 summer Sats ~ Bedrooms: £55B/£79B

nr COWLEY SO9614 Map 4

Green Dragon 🍴

Cockleford; pub signposted from A435 about 1½ miles S of junction with A436 – or follow Elkstone turn-off; OS Sheet 163 map reference 969142

The licensees of this attractive stone-fronted pub have changed yet again this year. The genuinely old-fashioned bar has antique furnishings including an aged dresser, big flagstones in one tiny room and wooden boards in the other, beams, a spacious stone fireplace, and a woodburning stove; dominoes, cribbage. Bar food now includes soup (£1.95), sandwiches (from £2.20), filled baked potatoes (from £2.95), ploughman's (from £4.25), a daily curry or steak in ale (£4.95), and daily specials such as popular mushroom and stilton bake (£4.25), lamb in cream and mint sauce, fresh local trout or beef braised in red wine (£5.25), and cod mornay (£5.95). A good range of beers includes Smiles Best, Exhibition and Mayfly, Badger Tanglefoot,

Hook Norton Best, Theakstons Old Peculier, and Wadworths 6X on handpump or tapped from the cask. There are terraces outside overlooking Cowley Lake and the River Churn, and the pub is a good centre for the lovely local walks. *(Recommended by Dave Irving, Roger Huggins, Tom McLean, Ewan McCall, Craig Peck, John and Joan Wyatt, Dr and Mrs M Beale, Richard Raeon, Karen Barnes, David Surridge, Neil and Anita Christopher, Dave Braisted, S C King, Tom Gondris, Frank W Gadbois, Thomas Nott, Malcolm Taylor, Mr and Mrs Mullins, Marjorie and Colin Roberts)*

Smiles ~ Managers Lynn James and Beverley Jones ~ Real ale ~ Meals and snacks ~ (01242) 870271 ~ Children welcome ~ Jazz/folk Weds evening ~ Open 11.30-2.30, 6-11

CRANHAM SO8912 Map 4

Black Horse 🍺

Village signposted off A46 and B4070 N of Stroud; up side turning

Dating back to the 17th c, this friendly local is unpretentious and old-fashioned, with welcoming licensees and enjoyable food. A cosy little lounge has just three or four tables, and the main bar is quarry-tiled, with cushioned high-backed wall settles and window seats, and a good log fire. Generous helpings and a wide choice of bar food might include sandwiches (from £1.50; toasties from £2), ploughman's (from £3), and a good changing choice of hot dishes such as homity, steak and mushroom or chicken and leek pies (from £4.95), a daily roast (from £5.50), sausage and bacon toad-in-the-hole (£5.95), fresh salmon (£6.25), lamb casserole with apricots and rosemary or gammon and eggs (£6.50), popular kleftico or roast pheasant, haddock and prawn mornay (£7.50), and puddings like fruit crumbles, lemon shortcake or treacle tart (£2); vegetables are fresh, and because this is not out-of-a-packet cooking most things can be had in small helpings for children. Very well kept Boddingtons, Flowers Original, Hook Norton Best, Whitbreads PA and Wickwar Brand Oak on handpump, Stowford Press cider, and decent wines. Shove-ha'penny, cribbage, and occasional piped music; Truffle the brittany spaniel is quite a character. Tables in the sizeable garden behind (and in the dining room, where it might be wise to book at weekends) have a good view out over the steep village and wooded valley. *(Recommended by LM, Tom McLean, Roger Huggins, Dave Irving, Ewan McCall, D G Clarke, Neil and Anita Christopher)*

Free house ~ Licensees David and Julie Job ~ Real ale ~ Meals and snacks (not Sun evening) ~ (01452) 812217 ~ Children welcome ~ Occasional folk music or Morris men ~ Open 11.30-2.30, 6.30-11

EBRINGTON SP1840 Map 4

Ebrington Arms

Signposted from B4035 E of Chipping Campden; and from A429 N of Moreton in Marsh

This unpretentious alehouse is very much a local rather than the smarter dining pubs so often found in this part of the world, and usually has a good mix of chatty countryfolk and visitors. The little bar has sturdy traditional furnishings, with seats built into the airy bow window, and a slightly raised woodfloored area, and there are some fine old low beams, stone walls, flagstoned floors and inglenook fireplaces – the one in the dining room still has the original iron work. A lower room, also beamed and flagstoned, has stripped country-kitchen furnishings. Decent, simple bar food (chalked up on the beams) is generously served and might include sandwiches (£2.25), egg and chips (£2.50), filled french sticks (from £3.75), ploughman's, lasagne or ratatouille (£3.95), various types of local sausage (£4.95), gammon and eggs or pies such as chicken, ham and mushroom or a good steak and kidney pie (£5.45) and steaks (from £8.50). The landlord has a pottery in the courtyard where he hand throws and fires the crockery used in the restaurant. Well kept Donnington SBA, Hook Norton Best and guests on handpump, and Bulmer's farm cider; absolutely no piped music or games machines – just an old-fashioned harmonium. Trophies bear witness to the success of the pub's dominoes team, and you can also play cribbage, darts and shove-ha'penny. An arched stone wall shelters a terrace with picnic tables under cocktail parasols. No dogs at least at mealtimes, when even the licensees' friendly welsh springer is kept out. Handy for Hidcote and Kiftsgate. *(Recommended by MDN, Jerry and Alison Oakes, Martin Jones, Martin and Karen Wake, Don and Shirley Parrish, Ted George, Barry and Anne, Christopher and Maureen Starling, P R White, Graham Reeve)*

Free house ~ Licensees Gareth Richards and Andrew Geddes ~ Real ale ~ Meals and snacks (not Sun evening) ~ (01386) 593223 ~ Children in dining room ~ Folk music last Mon of each month ~ Open 11-2.30, 6-11; closed 25 Dec ~ Bedrooms: £30/£35B

EDGE SO8509 Map 4

Edgemoor

A4173 N of Stroud

The view looking down over the valley to Painswick from both the terrace and the big picture windows of this busy but friendly dining pub is terrific. If you're here at dusk you'll see the lights in the little cluster of houses come on one by one, watched over by the serenely superior church spire towering above them. Good home-made bar food includes sandwiches, soup (£2.25), smoked salmon pâté (£3.75), stir-fry vegetables and cashew nuts or fried fillet of plaice (£5.50), lamb liver and bacon (£6.50), garlic chicken (£6.95), lamb cutlets (£7.50), mixed grill (£8.50), steaks (from £10.95), daily specials such as fresh fish, steak pie or beef rogan josh, and puddings; the restaurant may be fully booked for their three-course Sunday lunch, but they have the same menu in the bar. Clean and tidy, the main bar is an orderly place, with West Country cloth upholstery and pale wood furniture on the patterned carpet, and neat bare stone walls. Two dining areas are no smoking. Smiles Best, Tetleys and Uley Old Spot and Hogshead on handpump, kept under light top pressure in winter, good wines by the glass, and an interesting range of malt whiskies; piped music. *(Recommended by MH, M Hoyner, Roger Huggins, C Jones, Catherine Hamilton, Christopher and Maureen Starling)*

Free house ~ Licensee Chris Bayes ~ Real ale ~ Meals and snacks (not Sun evening ~ Restaurant ~ (01452) 813576 ~ Children welcome ~ Open 11-3, 6-11; closed Sun evening Oct-Mar

EWEN SU0097 Map 4

Wild Duck ★ ⑪ ♀ ◧

Village signposted from A429 S of Cirencester

Gloucestershire Dining Pub of the Year

This lovely 16th-c inn is doing very well at the moment with readers especially enjoying the lively, welcoming atmosphere and good food from the extensive, varied menu. It's actually more like an old manor house in part than a typical pub, and the high-beamed main bar has a nice mix of comfortable armchairs and other seats, candles on the tables, a fine longcase clock, a talking grey parrot in a cage near the bar, paintings on the coral walls, crimson drapes, magazines to read, and an open winter fire; another bar has a handsome Elizabethan fireplace and antique furnishings, and looks over the garden. Bar food includes soup (£2.95), crab croquettes (£4.75), ploughman's (£4.95), asparagus and hazelnut flan (£5.25), Japanese prawns with cucumber yoghurt (£5.50), cumberland sausage and mash with a giant yorkshire pudding with sage and onion gravy (£6.50), tagliatelle with prawns and mascarpone (£6.95), pork loin wrapped in smoked bacon in a cream and mushroom sauce (£8.50), chicken and duck breast medley with a light orange and rosemary sauce (£9.95), sirloin steak (£12.95), lovely fish such as fish and chips (£6.50), parrot fish (£9.95), bream (£12.95), and dover sole (£14.95), and daily specials like liver, bacon and onion casserole or poached salmon salad (£6.50), and pork loin cooked in cider and cream sauce (£7.50); consistently friendly service. As well as Duckpond, brewed especially for the pub, well kept beers might include

Smiles Best, Theakstons Best, XB and Old Peculier, and Wadworths 6X. Good wines; shove-ha'penny, gentle piped music. The pub does get busy as it's on the edge of an attractive village and is handy for Cirencester – though there are teak tables and chairs in the sheltered and well kept garden. The bedrooms in the newer part perhaps don't have so much atmosphere. *(Recommended by Mrs J Oakes, Dr J R Hilton, Joan and Alex Timpson, S H Godsell, Nick and Meriel Cox, Dr I Maine, Dave Irving, Roger Huggins, Tom McLean, Ewan McCall, Mr and Mrs P Fisk, Miss A Henry, D G King, Mr and Mrs G H Rutter, N H and A H Harris, David Holman, Malcolm Taylor, Stephen, Julie and Hayley Brown, Marjorie and Colin Roberts, John and Chris Simpson, SRP, John Waller)*

Free house ~ Licensees Brian and Tina Mussell ~ Real ale ~ Meals and snacks (till 10pm) ~ Restaurant ~ (01285) 770310 ~ Children in eating area of bar ~ Open 11-11; closed evening 25 Dec ~ Bedrooms: £48B/£65B

FORD SP0829 Map 4

Plough

B4077

As the gallops for local stables are opposite, there's quite a racing feel to this pretty stone pub, particularly on the days when the horse owned by a partnership of locals is running at Cheltenham. The beamed and stripped-stone bar has racing prints and photos on the walls, log fires, old settles and benches around the big tables on its uneven flagstones, oak tables in a snug alcove, and a traditional, friendly feel; dominoes, cribbage, shove-ha'penny, fruit machine, and piped music. Bar food includes good sandwiches, home-made soup (£2.75), home-made pâtés (£3.75), home-cured ham and egg (£5.75), steak, mushroom and Guinness casserole (£6.75), salmon fillet with dill and lemon butter (£8.95), and home-made puddings (£2.75). They still have their traditional asparagus feasts every April-June, when the first asparagus spears to be sold at auction in the Vale of Evesham usually end up here. Well kept Donnington BB and SBA on handpump, Addlestones cider, and a few malt whiskies. There are benches in front, with rustic tables and chairs on grass by white lilacs and fairy lights, and a play area at the back. This used to be the local court house, and what's now the cellar was the gaol. Look out for the Llama farm between here and Kineton. *(Recommended by E Walder, Angus Lyon, Dave Irving, Roger Huggins, T McLean, Ewan McCall, John and Joan Wyatt, Dr and Mrs A K Clarke, Andrew and Ruth Triggs, V Kavanagh, Roger Byrne, Martin and Karen Wake, Martin Jones, D E Kent)*

Donnington ~ Tenant W Skinner ~ Real ale ~ Meals and snacks (not Sun evenings) ~ (01386) 584215 ~ Children welcome ~ Open 11-11; 12-10.30 Sun ~ Bedrooms: £35B/£50B

GREAT BARRINGTON SP2013 Map 4

Fox

Village signposted from A40 Burford—Northleach; pub between Little and Great Barrington

In summer, the seats on the riverside terrace of this simple Cotswold inn, prettily set beside a stone bridge over the Windrush, are a fine place to enjoy a drink – and there are more seats near the landscaped pond in the orchard; maybe summer barbecues. Inside, the low-ceilinged little bar has stripped stone walls, rustic wooden chairs, tables and window seats, and two roaring log fires; sensibly placed darts, pool, shove-ha'penny, dominoes, cribbage, fruit machine, and piped music. Donnington BB, SBA and XXX on handpump, and Addlestones cider. The pub dog is called Bruiser (though he's only little). Bar food includes sandwiches (not Sun), warm chicken, bacon and brie salad (£3.95), home-made fresh salmon fishcakes (£6.25), local trout with an almond and butter sauce or beef in ale pie (£6.50), and very good steaks supplied by the landlord's father; giant breakfasts. There's a skittles alley out beyond the sheltered yard, and they have private fishing. *(Recommended by Ted George, Canon Michael Bordeaux, P R Ferris, P and J Shapley, Roger and Jenny Huggins, Dr A Y Drummond, Andrew and Ruth Triggs, P G Topp, Gordon, Martin Jones, Neil and Anita*

Christopher, Lawrence Pearse, Dave Irving, Ewan McCall, Roger Huggins, Tom McLean)

Donnington ~ Tenants Paul and Kate Porter ~ Real ale ~ Meals and snacks ~ (01451) 844385 ~ Children welcome ~ Open 11-11; 12-10.30 Sun; 12-3, 7-10.30 winter Sun ~ Bedrooms: £22.50/£40

GREAT RISSINGTON SP1917 Map 4

Lamb 🛏 ♀

There's a relaxed, rather civilised atmosphere in this partly 17th-c inn set in an attractive, peaceful village. The cosy two-roomed bar has an interesting collection of old cigarette and tobacco tins, photographs of the guide dogs the staff and customers have raised money to buy (over 20), a history of the village, and various plates and pictures. Wheelback and tub chairs with cushioned seats are grouped around polished tables on the light brown carpet, a table and settle are hidden in a nook under the stairs, and there's a log-effect gas fire in the stone fireplace. Bar food (they tell us prices have not changed since last year) includes sandwiches, home-made soup (£2.25), mushrooms stuffed with stilton or deep-fried brie with redcurrant jelly (£3.95), pasta bake (£6.75), local trout with apricot and almond stuffing (£8.75), sirloin steak with a crushed pepper, mushroom and brandy sauce (£10.50), daily specials like home-made sausages or local asparagus (£4.50), and char-grilled liver and bacon (£4.65), and home-made puddings (£2.50); the restaurant is partly no smoking. Morlands Old Speckled Hen, Smiles Best, and a guest beer on handpump, a good wine list, and several malt whiskies; friendly service. You can sit out in the sheltered hillside garden, or really take advantage of the scenery and walk, via gravel pits now used as a habitat for water birds, to Bourton on the Water. This really is a pleasant place to stay and this year, two new garden suites have been opened by the residents' garden. *(Recommended by John and Jackie Chalcraft, D J Hayman, Peter Neate, Simon Collett-Jones, V Kavanagh, John Waller, DJW, Gwen and Peter Andrews, George Atkinson, R W Brooms, Bronwen and Steve Wrigley, Helen Pickering, James Owen)*

Free house ~ Licensees Richard and Kate Cleverly ~ Real ale ~ Meals and snacks ~ Restaurant ~ (01451) 820388 ~ Children welcome ~ Open 11.30-2.30, 6.30-11; closed 25-26 Dec ~ Bedrooms: /£52B

GREET SP0230 Map 4

Harvest Home

B4078 just N of Winchcombe

Set in good walking country not far from medieval Sudeley Castle, this spick-and-span, civilised pub places much emphasis on its wide choice of good food: home-made soup (£1.75), filled french sticks (from £2.50), ploughman's (from £4.25), home-made lasagne or omelettes (£4.50), king prawns in garlic butter (£5.25), chicken tikka (£5.50), seafood crêpes (£5.70), pies such as duck and bacon (£5.75), fresh local trout (£6.25), pork schnitzel (£7.25), steaks (from £9.75), daily specials such as halibut beurre blanc, wild boar with a shallot and cranberry sauce or chicken breast filled with leek and bacon with creamy tarragon sauce, vegetarian dishes like mushroom stroganoff, puddings such as praline parfait or a special apple cake, and children's menu (from £2.25). The bar has a dozen or so well spaced tables, with seats built into the bay windows and other sturdy blue-cushioned seats; there are pretty flower prints and country scenes on the walls, and several dried-flower arrangements. Boddingtons, Hook Norton Old Hookey, Wadworths 6X and Whitbreads PA on handpump, and decent wines; darts down at one end (the other, with a good open fire, is no smoking), cribbage, dominoes, and unobtrusive piped classical music; helpful and pleasant young staff. There's a big beamed pitched-roof side restaurant (same food, also no smoking). The sizeable garden has a play area and boules, a terrace with access to the restaurant, and a narrow-gauge GWR railway that passes it. The miniature schnauzers are called Oscar and Boris. *(Recommended by Martin Jones, R W Phillips, AH, S Richardson, Lorraine Gwynne, Ian and Sheila Richardson, Michael Green, Brian and Genie Smart)*

Whitbreads ~ Lease: Heinz and Lisa Stolzenberg ~ Real ale ~ Meals and snacks ~
Restaurant ~ (01242) 602430 ~ Children welcome till 9pm ~ Open 10.30-3, 6-11

GRETTON SP0131 Map 4

Royal Oak

Village signposted off what is now officially B4077 (still often mapped and even signed as
A438), E of Tewkesbury; keep on through village

From seats on the flower-filled terrace here you can enjoy the wonderful views over
the village and across the valley to Dumbleton Hills and the Malverns. There are
more seats under a giant pear tree, a neatly kept big lawn running down past a small
hen-run to a play area (with an old tractor and see-saw), and even a bookable tennis
court. The Gloucestershire—Warwickshire Railway that runs from Toddington to
Winchcombe station often stops at the bottom of the garden in summer. There's
quite a friendly atmosphere in the series of bare-boarded or flagstoned rooms – the
pub was once a pair of old stone-built cottages – all softly lit (including candles in
bottles on the mix of stripped oak and pine tables), and with dark ochre walls,
beams (some hung with tankards, hop bines and chamber-pots), old prints, and a
medley of pews and various chairs; the friendly setter is called George. The no-
smoking dining conservatory has stripped country furnishings, and a broad view
over the countryside. Enjoyable bar food includes fried potato skins with garlic
mayonnaise, delicious home-made ratatouille with brie, crab and mushroom pot
(£3.25), mexican beef, gloucester sausages with cumberland sauce (£5.25), chicken
breast wrapped in bacon with stilton and cream sauce, and puddings such as lemon
tart or raspberry mousse. Well kept John Smiths, Marstons Pedigree, Morlands Old
Speckled Hen, Ruddles County, Smiles Best and Wadworths 6X on handpump,
around 70 whiskies, and a decent wine list; friendly service. Shove-ha'penny and
fruit machine. *(Recommended by Martin Jones, D G King, The Goldsons, Dave Braisted, Dr
and Mrs M Beale, Jo Rees, Sara Nicholls, Basil Minson, Brian White)*

Free house ~ Licensees Bob and Kathy Willison ~ Real ale ~ Meals and snacks ~
Restaurant ~ (01242) 602477 ~ Well-behaved children welcome ~ Folk music
Weds evening ~ Open 11-3, 6-11; closed 25-26 Dec

GUITING POWER SP0924 Map 4

Farmers Arms 🍺

Village signposted off B4068 SW of Stow on the Wold (still called A436 on many maps)

In a neat and sensitively restored Cotswold village, this is a busy, friendly creeper-
covered local with a warm welcome for visitors, too. The long bar is partly
flagstoned and partly carpeted, and has some bared stone walls, a good log fire, and
(at the front part) a window seat and a high old settle; lots more seating further
back; the skittle alley which leads off here can be used for children at lunchtime and
there is usually a stack of toys. Particularly well kept Donnington BB and SBA on
handpump, and decent bar food such as chicken or vegetabe soup (£2.20), garlic
mushrooms (£3.50), ploughman's (from £3.75), omelettes (from £4), sausage and
chips (£4.20), home-made butterbean bake (£4.95), ham and egg (£5.50), sirloin
steak (£8.95), daily specials such as faggots and peas (£4.25), liver and bacon
(£4.75), cottage pie (£4.95), chicken breast in stilton sauce on tagliatelle (£5.50), and
puddings like sherry trifle or rhubarb crumble (£2.30); the bread's often home-made.
Darts, pool, cribbage, dominoes, fruit machine, and juke box; service is prompt and
the licensees are very friendly. There are seats (and quoits) in the garden, set
attractively against the backdrop of the village; it may have a bouncy castle over
holiday periods. There are good walks nearby – the pub welcomes both walkers and
dogs. We have not yet had reports from readers on the bedrooms here. *(Recommended
by Diane Bassett, Dennis Murray, Angus Lyon, M Mason, D Thompson, Mr and Mrs
Buckingham, John and Joan Wyatt, Lady Emma Chanter, Dorothy and Leslie Pilson, Martin
and Karen Wake*

Donnington ~ Tenant Martin Macklin ~ Real ale ~ Meals and snacks ~ (01451)
850358 ~ Children welcome ~ Occasional live music in skittle alley ~ Open
11.30-3, 6-11 ~ Bedrooms: £25B/£36(£38B)

HYDE SO8801 Map 4

Ragged Cot 🛏 ♀ ◗

Burnt Ash; Hyde signposted with Minchinhampton from A419 E of Stroud; or (better road)
follow Minchinhampton, Aston Down signposted from A419 at Aston Down airfield; OS
Sheet 162 map reference 886012

New licensees have taken over this chatty old cottage, nicely set beside a row of chestnut
trees in the heart of the Cotswolds. The rambling bar has lots of stripped stone and
black beams, as well as a traditional dark wood wall settle by the end fire, cushioned
wheelback chairs and bar stools, and cushioned window seats; off to the right is a newly
redecorated, no-smoking restaurant area. Bar food now includes sandwiches and rolls
(from £1.20), soup (£1.60), ploughman's (from £3.25), filled baked potatoes (£3.95),
vegetarian dishes, lasagne, steak and kidney pie or a pasta dish (£4.95), a roast (£5.25),
salmon steak (£5.75), sirloin steak (£8.95), daily specials like chicken breast stuffed with
peppers and mushroom in a garlic and cream sauce (£4.95) and pork, sage and apple
hotpot or swordfish (£5.25), home-made puddings, and 3-course Sunday lunch (£7.95).
Well kept Bass, Marstons Pedigree, Theakstons Best, Uley Old Spot, and Wadworths
6X on handpump, and 32 malt whiskies; shove-ha'penny, cribbage, dominoes,
backgammon, Scrabble, and fruit machine. There are picnic tables (and an interesting
pavilion) in the garden, and bedrooms in an adjacent converted barn. *(Recommended by
M J Morgan, Dave Irving, Roger Huggins, Tom McLean, Ewan McCall, Don and Shirley Parrish,
Dorothy and Leslie Pilson, Andrew Shore, Neil and Anita Christopher)*

Free house ~ Licensee N Winch ~ Real ale ~ Meals and snacks ~ Restaurant
(closed Sun evening) ~ (01453) 884643 ~ Children in eating area of bar and
restaurant ~ Open 11-2.30, 6-11 ~ Bedrooms: £35B/£60B

KILKENNY SP0018 Map 4

Kilkeney Inn 🍽 ♀

A436 nr Cheltenham – OS Sheet 163 map reference 007187; if this hamlet is not shown on
your map look for Dowdeswell

It's the imaginative good food that draws people to this popular and comfortable
dining pub. Changing regularly, the menu might include lunchtime filled french
sticks (from £2.50), ploughman's (£3.85), and dishes like local pork sausages (£4.75)
or fish pie (£5.75), as well as soup (£2.25), warm salad of chicken livers with a
stilton and walnut dressing (£3.75), deep-fried filo-wrapped prawns with a black
bean and ginger dip (£4.35), spinach, cheese and tomato pancakes baked in a white
onion sauce (£6.50), supreme of chicken and king prawns with a sweet and sour
sauce (£8.50), steaks (from £10.45), medallions of beef fillet on a croûton, topped
with chicken liver pâté and a Madeira sauce (£10.95), half a crispy roast duck with a
damson wine and apricot sauce (£11.50), and puddings such as lime, lemon and
honey cheesecake, brandy and apricot bread and butter pudding or banoffi pie
(£2.95); good, fresh vegetables. Booking is recommended, especially at weekends.
The extended and modernised bar, quite bright and airily spacious, has neatly
alternated stripped Cotswold stone and white plasterwork, as well as gleaming dark
wheelback chairs around the tables, and an open fire. Up at the other end of the
same long bar is more of a drinking area, with well kept Hook Norton Best, Ruddles
Best, and John Smiths on handpump, an excellent range of decent wines and lots of
malt whiskies. It opens into a comfortable no-smoking dining conservatory.
Attractive Cotswold views, and good parking. *(Recommended by Sandra Kench, Steven
Norman, C and M Starling, David Surridge, Joan and Alex Timpson, Pat and Roger Fereday,
Mr and Mrs Mullins, Thomas Nott, Brian White, Christopher Darwent, Sara Nicholls, Mrs B
Lemon, S Whittingham, Roger Huggins, Tom McLean, Ewan McCall, Dave Irving)*

Free house ~ Licensees John and Judy Fennell ~ Real ale ~ Meals and lunchtime snacks ~ (01242) 820341 ~ Well behaved children in eating areas ~ Open 11.30-2.30, 6.30-11; closed 25-26 Dec, and Sun evenings Jan-March

KINETON SP0926 Map 4

Halfway House

Village signposted from B4068 and B4077 W of Stow on the Wold

Handy for Sudeley Castle and Cotswold Farm Park, this pretty and friendly little stone house has a sheltered back lawn with seats – and more on the narrow flagstoned front terrace (separated from the slow, quiet village lane by tubs of bright flowers on top of a low stone wall). Inside, the unpretentious bar has a warm winter log fire, attractive plates and colourful posters on the walls, and some old ancient farm tools and pictures at one end, with beams at the other; a good mix of customers and well kept Donnington BB and SBA (fresh from the nearby brewery) on handpump. Tasty bar food such as sandwiches (£2.50), ploughman's, steak and stout pie (£5.50), various pasta dishes (£5.75), and local trout (£5.95); they hold regular themed food fortnights throughout the year – French, seafood, Italian and Tex/Mex. *(Recommended by Gwen and Peter Andrews, Peter Phillips, JEB, Martin Jones, Dr A Y Drummond)*

Donnington ~ Tenant Paul Hamer ~ Real ale ~ Meals and snacks ~ (0451) 850344 ~ Children in eating area of bar ~ Open 11.30-2.30, 6.30-11; 11.30-11 Sat; 12-10.30 Sun ~ Bedrooms: £20/£30

KINGSCOTE ST8196 Map 4

Hunters Hall ★ ♀

A4135 Dursley—Tetbury

Even when this civilised, creeper-covered old inn is really busy, the series of bar rooms and lounges ensures that it doesn't feel too crowded. There are fine high Tudor beams, a lovely old box settle, sofas and miscellaneous easy chairs by the stone walls and velvet curtains, and sturdy settles and oak tables on the flagstones in the lower-ceilinged, cosy public bar. Generally served from a buffet in an airy end room, bar food usually includes sandwiches, spinach and gruyère tart (£5.25), pork and leek sausages with onion gravy (£5.50), braised lamb liver in grain mustard (£6.15), fillet of cod in a pesto sauce (£6.25), home-made puddings, and children's meals; there's more space to eat in the no-smoking Gallery upstairs. Well kept Bass, Hook Norton, Marstons Pedigree and Uley Old Spot on handpump, around ten wines by the glass, several malt whiskies and elderberry punch in winter; pleasant and efficient staff. A back room – relatively untouched – is popular with local lads playing pool; darts, shove-ha'penny, and juke box. The garden has seats, and for children, a fortress of thatched whisky-kegs linked by timber catwalks, a climber, and some swings. *(Recommended by Roger Huggins, Nick and Meriel Cox, V H and J M Vanstone, Dr and Mrs A K Clarke, Stephen Brown, Mr and Mrs P Smith, Gwen and Peter Andrews, Dave Irving, Tom McLean, Ewan McCall, Sara Nicholls, Julie Peters)*

Free house ~ Licensee David Barnett-Roberts ~ Real ale ~ Meals and snacks ~ Restaurant ~ (01453) 860393 ~ Children in family area and in restaurant ~ Open 11-3, 6-11; 11-11 summer Sats ~ Bedrooms: £45B/£66B

LITTLE BARRINGTON SP2012 Map 4

Inn For All Seasons 🛏 ♀

Well placed for the Cotswolds, this handsome old inn has a big log fire (with a big piece of World War II shrapnel above it), leather-upholstered wing armchairs and other comfortable seats, country magazines to read, and maybe quiet piped classical music in its attractively decorated mellow and timeless lounge bar. The licensee has a fish business in Brixham, so their half a dozen fresh fish dishes are particularly good: plaice (£6.50), skate (£6.75), red mullet or lemon sole (£8.50). A wide choice of other good generous bar food might include terrine (£4.50), ploughman's (£5.50), steak sandwich (£5.95), steak and kidney or chicken and leek pie (£6.50) and lemon curry (£6.95), with about half a dozen vegetarian dishes. Enjoyable puddings might be summer pudding or hot sticky toffee pudding (£2.95); breakfasts are good, too. They have well kept Wadworths 6X and a second changing ale such as Bass or local Glenny Wychwood Best tapped from wooden casks, seven wines by the glass, and about sixty malt whiskies; welcoming owners, friendly staff. The pleasant garden has tables, and there are walks straight from the inn – if you're staying, you may be asked to take the owners' two well trained dogs along with you. It's very busy during Cheltenham Gold Cup Week – when the adjoining field is pressed into service as a helicopter pad. *(Recommended by Andrew and Ruth Triggs, Jeremy Palmer, Pat Woodward, Peter and Audrey Dowsett, Patricia Heptinstall, Philip Jackson, Simon Collett-Jones)*

Free house ~ Matthew Sharp ~ Real ale ~ Meals and snacks ~ Restaurant (not lunchtimes or Mon-Wed evening) ~ (01451) 844324 ~ Children welcome ~ Open 11-2.30, 6-11; cl 25 and 26 Dec ~ Bedrooms:£42.50B/£77B

LITTLE WASHBOURNE SO9933 Map 4

Hobnails

B4077 (though often mapped still as the A438) Tewkesbury—Stow on the Wold; 7½ miles E of M5 junction 9

For around 254 years, this friendly and characterful 15th-c pub has been run by the same family. The snug and welcoming little front bar has old wall benches by a couple of tables on its quarry-tiled floor, low sway-backed beams hung with pewter tankards, and lots of old prints and horsebrasses, and there's a more modern, carpeted back bar with comfortable button-back leatherette banquettes; open fire. Bar food includes their speciality baps (from £1.55; liver £3; steak in wine £4.95; you can build your bap with extras like fried banana, fried egg, and so forth), soups like parsnip and apple or pumpkin and tomato (£2.65), hazelnut, cashew nut and chestnut stuffed loaf, apricot lamb casserole or lasagne (£6.45), specials like cumberland sausage with bubble and squeak and onion gravy or collar of bacon with parsnip and potato cake and mustard sauce (£4.95), and lamb garam masala or chicken cashew nut moghul (£6.90), puddings like home-made sherry trifle (£2.95), and children's menu (from £1.95); fresh vegetables £2.55. One dining room is no smoking, as is half of a second. Well kept Boddingtons, Flowers Original, Hook Norton, and Wadworths 6X on handpump; shove-ha'penny, quiet piped music. A separate skittle alley (with tables) can be hired weekday evenings. Between the two buildings, and beside a small lawn and flowerbed, there's a terrace with tables, and children's playground. *(Recommended by Mrs J Oakes, Jack Barnwell, Bob Arnett, Judy Wayman, DMT, Gordon, M Joyner)*

Whitbreads ~ Lease: Stephen Farbrother ~ Real ale ~ Meals and snacks (till 10) ~ Restaurant ~ (01242) 620237 ~ Children in restaurant ~ Open 11-2.30, 6-11; closed 25-26 Dec

LITTLETON UPON SEVERN ST5990 Map 2

White Hart 🍺

3½ miles from M4 junction 21; B4461 towards Thornbury, then village signposted

The three atmospheric main rooms in this carefully restored 17th-c farmhouse have flagstones in the front, huge tiles at the back, and smaller tiles on the left, along with some fine furnishings that include long cushioned wooden settles, high-backed settles, oak and elm tables, a loveseat in the big low inglenook fireplace, some old pots and pans, and a lovely old White Hart Inn Simonds Ale sign. By the black wooden staircase are some nice little alcove seats, there's a black-panelled big fireplace in the front room, and hops on beams, fresh flowers, and candles in bottles. An excellent no-smoking family room, similarly furnished, has some sentimental engravings, plates on a delft shelf, and a couple of high chairs, and a back snug has pokerwork seats, table football and table skittles; darts, shove ha'penny, cribbage, dominoes, trivia. Good promptly-served bar food includes soup, ploughman's, crispy potato skins with guacamole and salsa (£4.25), spinach, mushroom and chestnut lasagne or stilton, leek and potato pie (£4.95), and Thai green chicken curry (£6.25). Well kept Smiles Bitter, Best, Exhibition, and summer Mayfly, and guests such as Ashvine Hop and Glory, Gales HSB, and Wadworths 6X on handpump. They often get very busy at weekends, but staff are always pleasant. Picnic table sets sit on the neat front lawn, intersected by interesting cottagey flowerbeds, and by the good big back car park are some attractive shrubs and teak furniture on a small brick terrace. Dogs are allowed if on a lead, and there are quite a few walks from the pub itself. *(Recommended by M G Hart, Andrew Shore, Steve and Carolyn Harvey, Peter and Audrey Dowsett, John and Donna Bush, Pat and John Millward, D G Clarke, C H and P Stride, W Marsh)*

Smiles ~ Manager Philip Berryman ~ Real ale ~ Meals and snacks ~ (01454) 412275 ~ Children in family area ~ Open 11.30-2.30, 6-11; all day Sat ~ Bedrooms: £29.50B/£39.50B

LOWER ODDINGTON SP2325 Map 4

Fox 🍴 ♀

Nr Stow on the Wold

Success has not gone to the heads of the Elliots and they continue to run this consistently enjoyable dining pub with enthusiasm and care. The simply and spotlessly furnished rooms have a relaxed but smart feel, fresh flowers, flagstones, and an open fire, and there's a lovely dining room; piped classical music. Served by very friendly and knowledgeable staff (who have to taste the dishes so they can describe them to customers), the first-rate food might include cream of watercress soup (£2.50), french bread sandwiches (£2.95), twice baked goat's cheese soufflé (£3.50), prawn and cucumber timbale (£3.95), fish pie made with smoked haddock or pasta carbonara (£5.95), Thai chicken curry (£6.95), popular local trout baked in newspaper with a fresh herb sauce (£7.95), rib-eye steak (from £8.50), rack of English lamb with Shrewsbury sauce (£8.95), daily specials, and puddings such as hot walnut tart or rich chocolate mousse (£2.50). The wine list is excellent and shipped in conjunction with a highly regarded wine guru, they keep good Hook Norton Best, Marstons Pedigree and a guest such as Boddingtons or Fullers London Pride on handpump, and do a proper pimms; shove-ha'penny, dominoes, and backgammon. A good eight-mile walk starts from here (though a stroll around the pretty village might be less taxing after a fine meal). *(Recommended by John Bowdler, Mike and Heather Watson, Neville Kenyon, Pam Adsley, Peter Neate, Mike Gorton, Mr and Mrs J R Morris, Sue Demont, Tim Barrow, D C T and E A Frewer, P H Boot, Tom Evans, Tim and Pam Moorey, Martin Jones, M and J Huckstepp, Karen and Graham Oddey, Ian Irving)*

Free house ~ Licensees Nick and Vicky Elliot ~ Real ale ~ Meals and snacks (till 10pm) ~ (01451) 870555 ~ Children welcome ~ Open 12-3, 6.30-11; closed 25 Dec and evening 1 Jan

MINCHINHAMPTON SO8600 Map 4

Old Lodge

Minchinhampton Common; from centre of common take Box turn-off then fork right at pub's signpost

Doing very well at the moment, this former hunting lodge is marvellously placed on the plateau of the National Trust owned Minchinhampton Common, and there are tables on a neat lawn by an attractive herbaceous border that look over grey stone walls to the neatly grazed common and the Iron Age earthworks which surround it. Inside, the small and snug central bar has substantial pine tables and chairs, and a relaxed, friendly atmosphere, and opens into a pleasant bare-brick-walled room and an airy stripped-stone dining area, both of which are no smoking; no noisy games or piped music. The ever-improving bar food includes home-made soup (£2.30), ploughman's, filled french bread, moules marinières, baked goat's cheese with salad and walnut dressing or grilled sardines with a tomato and basil sauce (£3.95), vegetable and pasta bake, good gloucester sausage with a mild mushroom dip, stir-fried vegetables with ginger and black bean sauce, very good strips of monkfish in coconut with apricot sauce, spicy sticky pork with noodles (£5.75), sea bass with sorrel butter (£10.50), puddings like treacle and coconut tart (£2.25), and children's meals (£2.40). Well kept Marstons Pedigree, Thwaites Bitter, and Uley Bitter on handpump, a good range of wines including a wine of the month, country wines, and summer drinks like elderflower spritzer. Service is friendly and helpful. They share car parking with the adjoining golf club, so lots of cars outside doesn't necessarily mean the pub is full. *(Recommended by Roger Huggins, Dave Irving, Tom McLean, Ewan McCall, S Godsell, Tom Tees, D G King, GSB, Janet and Paul Boak, Neil and Anita Christopher)*

Free house ~ Licensees David Barnett-Roberts and Eugene Halford ~ Real ale ~ Meals and snacks (till 10pm; not Mon) ~ (01453) 832047 ~ Children in eating area of bar ~ Open 11-3, 6.30-11; winter evening opening 7; closed Mon (except bank holidays)

NAILSWORTH ST8699 Map 4

Weighbridge

B4014 towards Tetbury

The three cosily old-fashioned rooms of the friendly bar here have a pleasant unchanging atmosphere as well as antique settles and country chairs, stripped stone walls, and window seats; one even has a bell to ring for prompt service. The black beam-and-plank ceiling of the left-hand room is thickly festooned with black ironware – sheepshears, gin traps, lamps, cauldrons and bellows – while up some steps a raftered loft has candles in bottles on an engaging mix of rustic tables, as well as unexpected decorations such as a wooden butcher's block; no noisy games machines or piped music. Bar food includes filled rolls (from £1.60), ploughman's (from £3.40), meaty or vegetarian lasagne (£4.20), a two-in-one pie with cauliflower cheese in one half and steak and mushroom or chicken, ham and leek in the other (small £4.90, big £5.90), and puddings like treacle tart or banoffi pie. Well kept Marstons Pedigree, John Smiths, Smiles, Ushers Best, and Wadworths 6X on handpump, and quite a few wines by the glass. Behind is a sheltered garden with swings and picnic tables under cocktail parasols. Back in the days when the landlord used to run the bridge from which the pub takes its name, it would cost you 3d for each score of pigs you wanted to take along the turnpike. *(Recommended by Gwen and Peter Andrews, Tom McLean, Roger Huggins, Dave Irving, Ewan McCall, Don and Shirley Parrish, Neil and Anita Christopher, Peter Neate)*

Free house ~ Licensee Janina Kulesza ~ Real ale ~ Meals and snacks ~ (01453) 832520 ~ Children in eating area of bar ~ Open 11-2.30, 7(6.30 Sat)-11; closed 25 Dec

NAUNTON SP1123 Map 4

Black Horse 🛏 ♀

Village signposted from B4068 (shown as A436 on older maps) W of Stow on the Wold

Friendly new licensees have taken over this busy old inn, tucked away in an unspoilt little village, and early reports from readers are most favourable. The comfortable bar (brightened up now) has black beams and stripped stonework, simple country-kitchen chairs, built-in oak pews, and polished elm cast-iron-framed tables, and a big woodburning stove. Good food now includes sandwiches (from £1.75), home-made soup (£1.95), ploughman's (from £3.50), jumbo sausage and chips (£4.50), home-cooked ham and egg (£4.95), steak in ale pie (£5.50), fresh trout (£6.95), steaks, daily specials such as delicious butterfly chicken, bubble and squeak (£3.50), lasagne

(£5.50), and whole tail scampi (£5.75), changing puddings like toffee and pecan cheesecake, fresh fruit flan or apple and rhubarb crumble (from £2.75), roast Sunday lunch (£5.50), and children's menu (£2.25). Well kept and well priced Donnington BB and SBA on handpump, and several malt whiskies; sensibly placed darts, shove ha'penny, dominoes, and piped music. Some tables outside. *(Recommended by Mrs J Oakes, MDN, Dr I Maine, Peter Wade, Michael Monday, Simon Collett-Jones, John Waller, Gordon, Michael Richards, D D Collins, DP,LP)*

Donnington ~ Tenants Leo and Carole O'Callaghan ~ Real ale ~ Meals and snacks ~ Restaurant ~ (01451) 850565 ~ children welcome ~ Open 11-3, 6-11; 11-11 Sat ~ Bedrooms: £20/£35

NEWLAND SO5509 Map 4

Ostrich ♀ ◀

B4231 Lydney—Monmouth, OS Sheet 162 map reference 555096

There's a fine range of real ales in this atmospheric and friendly partly 13th-c inn: Exmoor Gold, Freeminers Iron Brew, Hardington Bitter, Oakhill Mendip Tickler, RCH Firebox, Shepherd Neame Spitfire, and so forth on handpump; 30 malt whiskies, Westons Old Rose cider, fresh fruit juice, and several wines by the glass. The spacious but cosily traditional low-ceilinged bar has comfortable furnishings such as cushioned window seats, wall settles, and rod-backed country-kitchen chairs, and a fine big fireplace decorated with a very capacious copper kettle and brass-bound bellows; creaky floors, uneven walls, magazines to read, candles on the tables, and classical music playing quietly in the background. From a wide menu, there might be ploughman's, good soup, steak and oyster pie (£8.50), Libyan-style chicken, pork tenderloin with calvados, salmon en croûte (£9), ostrich steak with oyster sauce (£12), and roasted wild boar (£12.50); good vegetables, and they bake all their own bread. Tables out in the small garden, and walkers are welcome if they leave their muddy boots at the door. No children. *(Recommended by Christine Timmon, Mrs P Goodwyn, Mr and Mrs C J S Pink, Phil and Heidi Cook, Terry and Vann Prime, Neil and Anita Christopher, Helen Pickering, James Owen, George Atkinson, Steven Coughlan, Mrs B M Innes-Ker, P and M Rudlin, Richard Mattick)*

Free house ~ Licensees Richard and Veronica Dewe ~ Real ale ~ Meals and snacks (not 25 Dec) ~ (01594) 833260 ~ Open 12-2.30(3 Sat), 6.30-11; closed 25 Dec ~ Two bedrooms: £25/£40

NORTH CERNEY SP0208 Map 2

Bathurst Arms ♀

A435 Cirencester—Cheltenham

On the edge of the little River Churn, this handsome old inn has a good strong local following – but is warmly welcoming to visitors, too. The atmosphere is relaxed and civilised in the beamed and panelled bar and there's a good mix of old tables and nicely faded chairs, old-fashioned window seats, some pewter plates, and a fireplace at each end, one quite huge, and housing an open woodburner. There are country tables in a little carpeted room off the bar, as well as winged high-backed settles forming booths around other tables; all is highly polished and obviously cared for. A good choice of bar food might include sandwiches (from £2), home-made pâté (£2.95), warm goat's cheese salad (£3.25), moules marinières (£3.95), various pasta dishes (£5), home-made pies (£5.25), gammon topped with mozarella cheese (£5.50), salmon fishcakes in prawn and dill sauce (£6.95), steaks (from £7.95), panfried monkfish or mixed grill (£8.95), and puddings (£2.40). Well kept Arkells BBB, Hook Norton Best, Wadworths 6X and a changing guest on handpump, freshly squeezed fruit juice, good wines; the staff are notably friendly, and there's a very happy feel to the place. The Stables Bar has darts, pool, cribbage, pinball, dominoes, and piped music. The attractive flower-filled front lawn runs down to the river, and there are picnic tables sheltered by small trees and shrubs, as well as summer barbecues in good weather. The bedrooms have been refurbished this year. *(Recommended by Mrs Jean Dundas, Tom McLean, Reece and Mike Gannaway, D M Wilkins, Peter and Audrey Dowsett, Andrew and Ruth Triggs)*

Free house ~ Licensee Mike Costley-White ~ Real ale ~ Meals and snacks ~ Restaurant ~ (01285) 831281 ~ Children welcome ~ Open 11-3, 6-11; closed 25 Dec ~ Bedrooms: £35B/£45B

NORTH NIBLEY ST7596 Map 4

New Inn ★ 🛏 🍺

Waterley Bottom, which is quite well signposted from surrounding lanes; inn signposted from the Bottom itself; one route is from A4135 S of Dursley, via lane with red sign saying Steep Hill, 1 in 5 (just SE of Stinchcombe Golf Course turn-off), turning right when you get to the bottom; another is to follow Waterley Bottom signpost from previous main entry, keeping eyes skinned for small low signpost to inn; OS Sheet 162 map reference 758963; though this is the way we know best, one reader suggests the road is wider if you approach directly from North Nibley

In summer, this peaceful rural brick inn is a fine place to visit as it's set in the heart of pleasant walking country. There are seats on the neatly kept terrace, with the garden beyond, and attractive surrounding pastures and woods. At the far end of the garden is a small orchard with swings, slides and a timber tree-house. Inside, the carpeted lounge bar has cushioned windsor chairs and varnished high-backed settles against the partly stripped stone walls, and sensibly placed darts, dominoes, shove-ha'penny, cribbage, table skittles, and trivia in the simple public bar. Particularly well kept Cotleigh Tawny and WB (a beer brewed specially for the pub), Greene King Abbot, Smiles Best, Theakstons Old Peculier and changing guests are either dispensed from Barmaid's Delight (the name of one of the antique beer engines) or tapped from the cask; the character landlady is quite a real ale expert; over 50 malt whiskies and Inch's cider. Good value bar food includes filled brown baps (from 60p), toasties (from £1.30), ploughman's (from £2.80), home-made egg and bacon quiche (£3.85), steak and onion pie (£3.95), plaice (£4.95), daily specials, and puddings (£1.50); piped music. To stay here you have to book a long way ahead – and best not to arrive outside opening hours. No children. *(Recommended by Stephen Brown, B A Hayward, D Godden, Richard Raeon, Karen Barnes, Vicky and David Sarti, Tom McLean, Roger Huggins, Dave Irving, Ewan McCall, John and Pat Smyth, Jack and Philip Paxton, Thomas Nott, Drs Ben and Caroline Maxwell)*

Free house ~ Licensee Ruby Sainty ~ Real ale ~ Meals and snacks ~ (01453) 543659 ~ Open 12-2.30, 7-11; closed evening 25 Dec ~ Two bedrooms: £20/£35

OAKRIDGE LYNCH SO9102 Map 4

Butchers Arms

Village signposted off Eastcombe—Bisley road, E of Stroud, which is the easiest approach; with a good map you could brave the steep lanes via Frampton Mansell, which is signposted off A419 Stroud—Cirencester

Well worth the effort in finding it, this neatly kept pub is popular locally, both for the splendid food and as somewhere to enjoy well kept real ales. At lunchtime, dishes might include rolls, ploughman's, highly praised hot french sticks filled with things like melted brie and salami (£3.75), garlic prawns (£4.75), haddock in celery sauce (£5.95), rib-eye steak (£7.95), and daily specials (£4.95-£6.95); on Wednesday-Saturday evenings there are starters (from £3.50), and main courses (from £6.95), with weekly specials like sole in spinach sauce (£8.95) or medallions of pork in creamed brandy and peppercorn sauce (£9.95); popular Sunday lunch (£7.95; 3 courses £11.95). Best to book at the weekend. The prominence given to food hasn't in any way made this less of a drinker's pub – in the evening, food is only served in the Stable Room (just off the main bar area) which keeps the atmosphere warm and lively – and diners can enjoy a drink at the bar before or after their meal. The spacious rambling bar has a few beams in its low ceiling, some walls stripped back to the bare stone, three open fires, and comfortable, traditional furnishings like wheelback chairs around the neat tables on its patterned carpet. Well kept Archers Best, Bass, Goffs Jouster, Hook Norton Old Hookey, Tetleys Bitter, and Theakstons Best on handpumps; a little room off the main bar has darts, fruit machine, and trivia. Picnic tables on a stretch of lawn look down over the valley, and you can really appreciate the village's rather odd remote setting; pretty hanging baskets in summer. There are good walks in the valley along the old Thames & Severn canal. Usefully, the pub's car park is up on the level top road, so you don't have to plunge into the tortuous network of village lanes. *(Recommended by Dr M I Crichton, Peter and Audrey Dowsett, Dave Irving, Ewan McCall, Tom MacLean, Roger Huggins, Dr S Willavoys, Don and Shirley Parrish, Lawrence Pearse, Colin W McClerrow, Keith Stevens, Neil and Anita Christopher)*

Free house ~ Licensees Peter Coupe ~ Real ale ~ Meals and lunchtime snacks ~ Restaurant (Weds-Sat evenings, Sun lunch) ~ (01285) 760371 ~ Children in small ante room and in restaurant ~ Open 11-3, 6-11; 12-10.30 Sun

ODDINGTON SP2225 Map 4

Horse & Groom

Upper Oddington; signposted from A436 E of Stow on the Wold

There's been yet another change of licensee here but reports from readers are warmly positive. It's an attractive, partly ivy-covered Cotswold inn (refurbished since the new owners took over) and the welcoming bar has a big log fire, pale polished flagstones, a handsome antique oak box settle among other more modern seats, some horsebrasses on the dark 16th-c oak beams in the ochre ceiling, and stripped stone walls with some harness and a few brass platters; a quarry-tiled side area has a fine old polished woodburner. As well as quite a few fish dishes (they have their own lobster tank, £19), the good bar food might include sandwiches, stilton and whisky mushrooms (£3.25), seafood pancakes (£3.75), garlic scallops or moules (£3.95), stilton and broccoli lasagne (£5.75), steak and kidney pie (£5.95), chicken supreme stuffed with stilton and celery and wrapped in bacon (£6.95), crab cakes or good monkfish wrapped in bacon served with a sauce of creamed mushrooms and white wine (£7.50), lamb steak with stir-fried vegetables with minted hollandaise (£7.95), peppered sirloin steak (£8.95), home-made puddings, and a children's menu; the candlelit dining room is pretty. Well kept Hook Norton Best, Wadworths 6X, and Wychwood Best on handpump, and a decent wines list. Fat trout patrol the little water-garden beyond a rose hedge, and there are picnic tables on the neat lawn below the car park, apple trees, and a fine play area including an enormous log climber and Aunt Sally. *(Recommended by Dr S Willavoys, John Waller, Pam Adsley, E A George, Jenny and Michael Back, Penny and Martin Fletcher, Andrew and Ruth Triggs, Dr D Radley, Moira and John Cole, Bronwen and Steve Wrigley, John and Heather Dwane, Peter and Audrey Dowsett, Ian Irving, John and Shirley Dyson, Gordon)*

Free house ~ Licensees Ben and Jill Sands ~ Real ale ~ Meals and snacks (till 10pm Fri/Sat) ~ Restaurant ~ (01451) 830584 ~ Children welcome ~ Open 11-2.30, 6-11 ~ Bedrooms: £37.50S/£60S

OLD SODBURY ST7581 Map 2

Dog

To enjoy the huge range of popular food at this friendly pub you must get there early to be sure of a seat – it does get crowded. There's quite an emphasis on fresh fish with dishes like plaice, red mullet, halibut, shark or tuna, whole fresh sole, Devon scallops or clam fries, and several different ways of serving mussels (from £3.25) and squid (£4.95). Other dishes include sandwiches (from £1.75), ploughman's (£3.95), cottage pie (£4.75), home-made steak and kidney pie or cheese and onion flan (£4.95), Mexican tamales with chilli sauce (£5.95), sweet and sour pork (£6.25), curries or Hawaiian chicken creole (£6.50), steaks (from £6.95), puddings (from £1.95), children's menu (called 'puppy food', from £1.50), and daily specials. The two-level bar and smaller no-smoking room both have areas of original bare stone walls, beams and timbering, low ceilings, wall benches and cushioned chairs, open fires, and a welcoming, cheery atmosphere. Well kept Boddingtons, Flowers Original, Wadworths 6X, and Wickwar Brand Oak on handpump, decent wine list, pimms and sangria by the glass or jug, vintage port, and malt whiskies; helpful, attentive staff. Darts, skittle alley, cribbage, dominoes, fruit machine, and juke box. Trophy, the border collie, likes playing football with customers. There's a large garden with lots of seating, a summer barbecue area, pets corner with rabbits, guinea pigs and so forth, climbing frames, swings, slides, football net, see-saws and so forth, and bouncy castle most bank holidays. Lots of good walks nearby. *(Recommended by M W Turner, V H and J M Vanstone, the Sandy family, Tom Evans, Simon and Amanda Southwell, Basil Minson, Pat and Richard Tazewell, R T and J C Moggridge, Nigel Clifton, Martin and Karen Wake)*

Whitbreads ~ Lease: John and Joan Harris ~ Real ale ~ Meals and snacks (till 10pm) ~ (01454) 312006 ~ Children welcome until 9.30pm ~ Open 11-11 ~ Bedrooms: £23.50/£36.50

OLDBURY ON SEVERN ST6292 Map 2

Anchor

Village signposted from B4061

Remote but deservedly popular, this attractively-modernised village pub is doing very well at the moment – mainly for the very good, quickly served food and for the cosy and friendly atmosphere. The kitchen has doubled in size to cope with demand and the food changes daily and uses fresh, local produce: no sandwiches but they do offer topside of beef, home-baked ham, pâté or cheeses with wholemeal bread (from £2.50), quite a few salads (from £3.35), lasagne (£3.95), yorkshire pudding filled with roast beef and onion gravy or ratatouille (£4.50), madras beef and cashew nut curry (£4.75), pigeon breasts braised in port (£5.10), locally reared pork and garlic sausages cooked on the charcoal grill (£5.25), fresh salmon in a cream and white wine sauce (£5.60), honeyed Welsh lamb or chicken breast cooked in brandy and apple juice with cream and mushrooms (£5.70), sirloin steak (£7.95), and puddings such as home-made fresh strawberry flan, marvellous sticky toffee pudding with hot butterscotch sauce or banoffi pie (£2.40); no chips and prompt and efficient waitress service in no-smoking dining room. Well kept Bass tapped from the cask, with Black Sheep, Butcombe, Theakstons Best and Old Peculier, and Worthingtons Best on handpump, all well priced for the area. Also over 75 malts, decent choice of good quality wines, and Inch's cider; darts, shove-ha'penny, dominoes and cribbage. The comfortably furnished beamed lounge has a curved high-backed settle facing an attractive oval oak gateleg table, winged seats against the wall, easy chairs, cushioned window seats, and a big winter log fire. There are seats in the pretty garden (where there is a sizeable boules pitch). St Arilda's church nearby is interesting, on its odd little knoll with wild flowers among the gravestones (the primroses and daffodils in spring are lovely), and there are lots of paths over the meadows to the sea dyke or warth which overlooks the tidal flats. *(Recommended by John and Joan Wyatt, Andrew Shore, S H Godsell, Helen Pickering, James Owen, V H and J M Vanstone, Peter Conrall, Dr and Mrs B Smith, Simon and Amanda Southwell, P H Roberts, M G Hart, Mrs B Lemon, Peter and Audrey Dowsett, Paul Carter, R V Ford, Steve and Carolyn Harvey)*

Free house ~ Licensees Michael Dowdeswell, Alex de la Torre ~ Real ale ~ Meals and snacks ~ Restaurant ~ (01454) 413331 ~ Children in restaurant only ~ Occasional pianist ~ Open 11.30-2.30(3 Sat), 6.30(6 Sat)-11; closed 25 Dec

REDBROOK SO5410 Map 4

Boat 🍺

Pub's car park is now signed in village on A466 Chepstow—Monmouth; from here 100-yard footbridge crosses Wye (pub actually in Penallt in Wales – but much easier to find this way); OS Sheet 162 map reference 534097

The friendly licensees here tell us that they are always happy to welcome anyone – be it walker, canoeist, motor cyclist or families – so there is always a lively mix of customers. It's a place of great character set by the River Wye and you can sit on the ancient bench-type seats in the garden (prettily lit at night) with the sound of the water spilling down the waterfall cliffs into the duck pond below. Inside, the cheery bar has fresh flowers, lots of pictures of the pub during floods, landscapes, a wall settle, a grey-painted piano, and a woodburning stove on the tiled floor; some readers have felt the housekeeping could be improved. A fine choice of at least eight well kept beers, tapped straight from casks behind the bar counter, might include Badger Best, Bass, Brains SA, Fullers London Pride, Greene King Abbott, Hook Norton Best, Reverend James, Shepherd Neame Spitfire, Theakstons Old Peculier, and Wadworths 6X; good range of country wines and summer cider. Decent bar food includes filled baked potatoes (from £1.60), soup (£1.75), ploughman's (£3.70), vegetable curry (£4), shepherd's pie (£4.25), rabbit and sausage pie or beef curry (£4.45), brie and haddock pie (£4.95), and puddings (from £1.90). Darts, shove-ha'penny, table skittles, cribbage, and dominoes, with a quiz night every other winter Monday. They do get busy on sunny days. *(Recommended by Pete and Rosie Flower, Piotr Chodzko-Zajko, Michel Hooper-Immins, Christopher Gallop, Joan and Alex Timpson, Keith and Audrey Ward, Sue and Mike Lee, Alan and Paula McCully, Jack and Philip Paxton, N Christopher, Mr and Mrs J Brown, Ted George, P and M Rudlin, Dr R F Fletcher)*

Free house ~ Licensees Steffan and Dawn Rowlands ~ Real ale ~ Meals and snacks ~ (01600) 712615 ~ Children welcome ~ Folk/rock Tues evening, jazz/blues Thurs ~ Open 11-3, 6-11; 11-11 Sat; 12-4, 6.30-10.30 Sun

SAPPERTON SO9403 Map 4

Bell

Village signposted from A419 Stroud—Cirencester; OS Sheet 163 map reference 948033

With good walks all round, this is a straightforward, neatly kept village pub. The spacious but warm and cosy carpeted lounge has stripped stone walls and a good log fire; an extension up a couple of steps makes it L-shaped, with sturdy pine tables and country chairs. Well kept Flowers Original, Tetleys, Wadworths 6X, and Whitbreads West Country PA on handpump, and simple but good value bar food (with prices unchanged since last year) includes sandwiches (from £1.40), soup (£1.75), ploughman's (from £3), good gloucester sausages (£3.25), salads (from £3.25), macaroni cheese (£4.15), half chicken (£4.95), grilled gammon and pineapple (£5.25), and steaks (from £7.90). No credit cards; friendly service. The large public bar has some old traditional wall settles, and well placed darts, cribbage, dominoes, and fruit machine; separate skittle alley/function room. There are tables out on a small front lawn. *(Recommended by Ewan McCall, Tom McLean, Dave Irving, Roger Huggins, Mrs J Turner, W W Burke, Don and Shirley Parrish, Jack and Philip Paxton, Thomas Nott, Andrew and Ruth Triggs, Mrs J M White, D G King)*

Free house ~ Licensees Gordon and Violet Wells ~ Real ale ~ Meals and snacks (till 10pm) ~ (01285) 760298 ~ Children welcome ~ Open 11-2.30, 6.30-11; closed evening 25 Dec

SHEEPSCOMBE SO8910 Map 4

Butchers Arms ♀

Village signposted from B4070 NE of Stroud, and A46 N of Painswick (narrow lanes)

This is just the sort of place where one would hope to find a really nice pub – a quiet village in such a steep valley that the views seem as close as a landscape painting, almost. There are teak seats below the building, tables on the steep grass behind, and a cricket ground behind on such a steep slope that the boundary fielders at one end can scarcely see the bowler. The pub can be quite crowded on summer days and weekends. Inside, there's a good smart chatty atmosphere (no noisy games machines or piped music), and the busy bar is decorated with lots of interesting oddments like assorted blow lamps, irons, and plates; seats in big bay windows, log fires, and flowery-cushioned chairs and rustic benches. Well kept Fullers London Pride, Greene King Abbot, Hook Norton Best, and guest beers on handpump, farm ciders, and a good wine list; darts, cribbage, dominoes, and maybe winter quiz evenings. Good lunchtime bar food includes soup (£1.75), filled baps (from £2.50), filled baked potatoes (from £3.50), home-made ham, cheese and mushroom crêpe (£4), ploughman's (£4.50), vegetable lasagne (£4.80), honey roast ham and chips (£5.25), home-made steak and kidney pie (£5.75), mixed grill (£7.95), and evening extras such as a half rack of pork ribs (£4.50), swordfish steak in garlic butter (£6.50), home-made beef pepperpot (£6.25), and half a fresh roast duck with grand marnier and citrus fruit sauce (£9.80); daily specials and puddings. The restaurant and a small area in the bar are no smoking. *(Recommended by R and S Bentley, Dave Irving, Roger Huggins, Tom McLean, Ewan McCall, Graham Tayar, LM, Peter and Lynn Brueton, Howard Allen, S G N Bennett, James Nunns, R G Watson, Marjorie and Colin Roberts, Moira and John Cole, Thomnas Nott, E J Wilde, Neil and Anita Christopher, Keith Stevens, John and Joan Wyatt, C Smith, David Campbell, Vicki McLean, Simon Warren, Angus Lyon)*

Free house ~ Licensees Johnny and Hilary Johnston ~ Real ale ~ Meals and snacks (till 10pm) ~ Restaurant ~ (01452) 812113 ~ Children welcome ~ Open 11-11; 12-10.30 Sun; 11-2.30, 6.30-11 in winter

SIDDINGTON SU0399 Map 4

Greyhound

Ashton Rd; village signposted from industrial estate roundabout in Cirencester through-traffic system; and from A419 (northbound only)

Very handy for Cirencester, this bustling, friendly pub has new licensees – and reader reports are most favourable. The biggish lounge bar has a happy mix of high-backed winged settles, high dining chairs, chapel seats and so forth on the old herringbone brick floor, good tables – mainly stripped pine, but one fine circular mahogany one – and two big warming log fires. The beams and ochre walls are covered with lots of copper and brass, as well as a few hunting prints, some black-lacquered farm tools, and china and other bric-a-brac. Good, popular bar food includes home-made soup (£2.25), home-made chicken liver pâté or mushroom and bacon kebab (£2.95), sandwiches (from £2.95; they come with chips and salad garnish), ploughman's (from £4.25), stilton, celery and apple pie (£5.75), a daily fresh fish dish like fillet of haddock with a crunchy cheese topping, butterfly lamb chops with minted gravy or home-made steak and kidney pie with suet crust (all £5.95), breast of chicken in a tarragon, cream and white wine sauce (£8.95), beef stroganoff (£9.95), and home-made puddings like bread and butter pudding, crunchy nut plum and apple crumble or chocolate brandy crunch (from £2.25); the cellar is being converted into a dining room. Well kept Wadworths IPA and 6X, and Badger Tanglefoot and a changing guest such as Butcombe Bitter or Youngs Special on handpump, and decent wines; the public bar has darts. There are seats among lilacs, apple trees, flower borders and short stone walls behind the car park. *(Recommended by Dave Irving, Roger Huggins, Ewan McCall, Tom McLean, Pat Crabb, MRSM, Mark Matthewman, Esther and John Sprinkle, Dr I Maine, Peter and Audrey Dowsett, Frank Gadbois, Stephen, Julie and Hayley Brown, Nick and Alison Dowson)*

Wadworths ~ Managers Mike and Louise Grattan ~ Real ale ~ Meals and snacks (till 10pm) ~ (01285) 653573 ~ Children welcome ~ Open 11.30-3, 6.30-11

SOUTH CERNEY SU0497 Map 4

Eliot Arms

Village signposted off A419 SE of Cirencester; Clarks Hay

Becoming a firm favourite locally, this handsome wisteria-draped stone inn has an unusual layout: the solidly done little bar servery is where you might expect to find a reception desk, so a bit of a surprise at first (it grows on you), and lots of separate snug places to sit are linked by short passages lined with decorative plates. It's all been done very well, adding up to a good relaxed atmosphere, with some interesting racing-car pictures from Fangio and Moss to Mansell among all the bric-a-brac in the back room – which has a fine log fire. Decent bar food includes sandwiches (from £1.75), filled baked potatoes, lasagne (£4.75), steak and kidney pie (£4.95), vegetarian dishes like spinach and cream cheese crêpes (from £4.95), chicken stroganoff (£5.75), chicken, ham and leek pie (£5.95), duck breast with black cherry sauce (£9.95), and fillet steak (£10.50); curries on Tuesday evenings, fresh fish on Wednesday evenings, and children's menu (£2.75). As well as the cosily attractive little dining room down a step or two, there's a smart separate no-smoking restaurant, and a coffee shop. Well kept Boddingtons, Flowers Original, and Wadworths 6X on handpump, good range of malt whiskies, German bottled beers, and helpful service; shove-ha'penny, cribbage, dominoes, and tucked-away silenced fruit machine; skittle alley. There are picnic tables and a swing in the neat back garden. *(Recommended by Roger Huggins, Tom McLean, Dave Irving, Ewan McCall, Mr and Mrs P Smith, Esther and John Sprinkle, M L and G Clarke*

Free house ~ Licensees Duncan and Linda Hickling ~ Real ale ~ Meals and snacks ~ Restaurant ~ (01285) 860215 ~ Children welcome till 9pm ~ Open 10am-11pm; 12-10.30 Sun ~ Bedrooms: £35B/£40.50B

SOUTHROP SP2003 Map 4

Swan ♀

Village signposted from A417 and A361, near Lechlade

Although there is quite an emphasis on the enjoyable food in this creeper-covered old pub, there is a friendly public bar in which to enjoy the Morlands Original and guests like Archers Golden and Oakhill Bitter on handpump or tapped from the cask. At lunchtime, good bar food includes stilton and onion soup (£2.80), duck and orange pâté (£2.95), cottage pie (£4.50), gloucester sausages (£5.25), venison or ostrich sausages with mushroom sauce (£5.50), and home-made fish pie (£5.75), with evening dishes like Thai fishcakes (£3.30), buckwheat pancake filled with chicken, bacon and mushrooms (£9.25), and roast duck breast with kumquat sauce (£9.95); a good wine list. The small restaurant is no smoking. The extended low-ceilinged front lounge has cottagey wall seats and chairs, and winter log fires, while beyond it is a spacious stripped-stone-wall skittle alley, well modernised, with plenty of tables on the carpeted part, and its own bar service at busy times. There are tables in the sheltered garden behind. The village is pretty, with lovely spring daffodils. *(Recommended by Frank Gadbois, Pat Crabb, Peter and Audrey Dowsett, Peter Neate, John Bowdler, SRP, Mr and Mrs R J Grout)*

Free house ~ Licensees Patrick and Sandra Keen ~ Real ale ~ Meals (not Sun evening) ~ Restaurant (not Sun evening) ~ (01367) 850205 ~ Children welcome ~ Open 12-2.30(3 Sat), 7-11

ST BRIAVELS SO5605 Map 4

George 🛏

This lovely old pub (not far from Tintern Abbey) has tables on a flagstoned terrace at the back overlooking the grassy former moat of the silvery stone 12th-c castle built as a fortification against the Welsh, and later used by King John as a hunting lodge (it's now a youth hostel); there are more tables among roses and shrubs, and an outdoor chess board. Lots of walks start nearby. Inside, the three rambling rooms have old-fashioned built-in wall seats, some booth seating, green-cushioned small settles, toby jugs and antique bottles on black beams above the servery, and a large stone open fireplace; a Celtic coffin lid dating from 1070, discovered when a fireplace was removed, is now mounted next to the bar counter. A dining area is no smoking. Tasty bar food includes home-made soup (£2.50), deep-fried brie with cranberry sauce (£3.95), home-made chilli or liver and bacon casserole (£5.95), home-made steak and kidney pie, home-made crunchy nut loaf or whole hock of ham glazed with honey and brown sugar (all £6.95), fresh grilled tuna steak (£7.95), steaks (from £7.95), and duck breast in madeira sauce (£8.95); Sunday roast lunch (£6.95); friendly service. The dining room is no smoking. Well kept Boddingtons, Marstons Pedigree, Wadworths 6X, and Wye Valley on handpump, and lots of malt whiskies; cribbage and piped music. *(Recommended by Mr and Mrs C J S Pink, Michael and Alison Leyland, M L Hughes, Geoffrey Lindley, Howard James, D Godden, Alan and Paula McCully, Mr and Mrs P E Towndrow, Pat and Richard Tazewell, Piotr Chodzko-Zaiko)*

Free house ~ Licensee Bruce Bennett ~ Real ale ~ Meals and snacks ~ Restaurant ~ (01594) 530228 ~ Children in eating area of bar ~ Open 12-3, 6.30-11 ~ Bedrooms: £25B/£40B

STANTON SO0634 Map 4

Mount

Village signposted off B4632 (the old A46) SW of Broadway; Old Snowshill Road – take no through road up hill and bear left

This is a beautifully positioned pub with splendid views from seats on the pretty terrace over the picture-postcard golden stone village below and on as far as the Welsh mountains; boules on the lawn. Inside, the atmospheric original bar has black beams, cask seats on big flagstones, heavy-horse harness and racing photographs, and a big fireplace. An older spacious extension, with some big picture windows, has comfortable oak wall seats and cigarette cards of Derby and Grand National winners. A no-smoking extension is used in winter as a restaurant and in summer as a more informal eating bar. Donnington BB and SBA on handpump, and farm cider; darts, shove ha'penny, dominoes, cribbage, backgammon, chess, and piped music. Straightforward bar food includes sandwiches (£2.50; toasties £3.50), ploughman's (£3.95), chicken and broccoli lasagne or leek, cheese and potato bake (£4.75), and puddings (£2); at busy times a PA announces when your meal is ready. *(Recommended by Mrs Jean Dundas, MDN, Alan and Paula McCully, Pam Adsley, Sara Nicholls, Tom Evans, Martin and Karen Wake, Frank Gadbois, George Atkinson, Ted George, Martin Jones)*

Donnington ~ Tenant Colin Johns ~ Real ale ~ Meals and snacks (not Sun evening) ~ (01386) 584316 ~ Well behaved children welcome ~ Open 11-3, 6-11; 11-11 Sat; 12-10.30 Sun; closed 25 Dec

nr STOW ON THE WOLD SP1729 Map 4

Coach & Horses £ 🏠

Ganborough; A424 2½ miles N of Stow; OS Sheet 163 map reference 172292

This pleasant little Cotswold pub is the nearest to the Donnington brewery, so the Donnington XXX, BB and SBA on handpump are well kept. The bar area has a winter log fire in the central chimney-piece, leatherette wall benches, stools and windsor chairs on the flagstone floor, and is decorated with good wildlife photographs on the walls and coach horns on its ceiling joists; steps lead up to a carpeted part with high-backed settles around the tables. Bar food includes home-made soup (£1.95), sandwiches (£2.10), macaroni cheese or cottage pie (£2.50), filled baked potatoes (from £3.25), ploughman's (from £3.50), lasagne (£3.95), home-made steak and kidney pie or grilled Donnington trout (£5.95), mixed grill (£7.50), daily specials, and roast Sunday lunch; one dining room is no smoking. Decent wines and 25 malt whiskies; darts, dominoes, fruit machine and juke box, a popular skittle alley, and piped music. The garden has a waterfall and rockery, as well as seats on a terrace and a narrow lawn. The attached field where the three pub dogs play (one an enormous wolfhound) also has a goat and maybe an occasional horse, and is a site for Caravan Club members; slide and swings for children. *(Recommended by Dr and Mrs A K Clarke, Peter Lloyd, JJW,CMW, Andrew and Ruth Triggs, Derek and Margaret Underwood, Barbara and Dennis Melling, Peter and Audrey Dowsett, Bronwen and Steve Wrigley)*

Donnington ~ Tenant Andy Morris ~ Real ale ~ Meals and snacks ~ (01451)
830208 ~ Children welcome ~ Occasional live music (usually Sun evening) ~
Open 11-3, 6.30-11; closed 25 Dec

STOW ON THE WOLD SP1925 Map 4
Queens Head 🍺

The Square

In a village of charming buildings, this chatty and characterful old local is one of the
best with its colourful climbing rose and hanging baskets. The most atmospheric
part is the traditional flagstoned back bar, with lots of beams and a couple of
interesting high-backed settles as well as wheelback chairs, a big log fire in the stone
fireplace, public school football team colours on a back wall, and several horse
prints (the friendly landlord is quite a racing buff). The music is piped classical or
opera (not in front), and there's shove-ha'penny, a fruit machine, darts, and two nice
dogs. The busy stripped-stone front lounge is packed with small tables, little windsor
armchairs and brocaded wall banquettes. Bar food (they tell us prices are the same as
last year) includes sandwiches, soup (£1.75), filled baked potatoes, omelettes (from
£2.75), ploughman's, steak and kidney or lamb and leek pies (£4.95), and puddings
like apricot crumble; they may not do food some winter evenings. Donnington BB
and SBA are particularly well kept on handpump; they do mulled wine in winter,
and service is quick and helpful. A green bench in front has a pleasant view, and in a
back courtyard there are some white tables. *(Recommended by John Baker, John Bowdler,*
Andrew and Ruth Triggs, Brian Wainwright, Hugh MacLean, Tony and Wendy Hobden, Helen
McLagan, John Waller, Pat and Richard Tazewell)

Donnington ~ Tenant Timothy Eager ~ Real ale ~ Meals and snacks (not Sun, or
Mon evening) ~ (01451) 830563 ~ Children welcome ~ Occasional jazz Sun
lunchtimes ~ Open 11-2.30, 6(6.30 Sat)-11

WITHINGTON SP0315 Map 4
Mill Inn

Village signposted from A436, and from A40; from village centre follow sign towards Roman
villa (but don't be tempted astray by villa signs before you reach the village!)

The setting for this warmly welcoming 17th-c pub (under good new management
and doing very well) is marvellous – it stands virtually alone in a little valley
surrounded by beech and chestnut trees and a rookery, and the small pretty garden
has a stream and bridges; lots of seats on the terrace. The Roman villa is a good
walk away. The rambling carpeted bar is full of little nooks and corners, and has
antique high-backed settles and big cut-away barrel seats under its beams, an
attractive bay window seat, old china and pewter on a high delft shelf, a good log
fire in its stone fireplace, and little side rooms leading off; two no-smoking rooms.
Good bar food includes cheese, a roll and pickle or ham, a roll and mustard (£2.95),
ploughman's (£4.25), very good local goat's cheese rolled in breadcrumbs and poppy
seeds and baked in the oven and served with a tomato coulis (£3.95), pasta with
mixed seafood, cream and dill (£5.25), an enjoyable nut roast with a tomato
provençale or spinach and onion sauce (£5.95), chicken supreme (£6.50), salmon
steak in tomato, tarragon and ginger (£6.75), nice pork in apple, celery and beer
sauce, duck breast (£7.50), and puddings like blueberry and lime cheesecake or
popular bread pudding (£2.25). Well kept Sam Smiths OB on handpump, a decent
wine list, and quite a few malt whiskies; piped music. *(Recommended by John and Joan*
Wyatt, Graham and Karen Oddey, Tom McLean, Ewan McCall, Dave Irving, Roger Huggins,
Mrs J Huntly, Helen Pickering, James Owen)

Sam Smiths ~ Managers Peter Nielson and Robin Collyns ~ Real ale ~ Meals and
snacks (till 10 evening) ~ (01242) 890204 ~ Children in eating area of bar ~
Open 12-3, 6.30-11 ~ Bedrooms: £17.50/£38 – they hope to add en suite
bathrooms soon

WOODCHESTER SO8302 Map 4

Ram 🍺

South Woodchester, which is signposted off A46 Stroud—Nailsworth

From the picnic tables on the terrace of this attractive country pub there are spectacular views down the steep and pretty valley. Inside, the L-shaped beamed bar has country-kitchen chairs, several cushioned antique panelled settles around a variety of country tables, built-in wall and window seats, some stripped stonework, and three open fires; sensibly placed darts. The fine choice of real ales on handpump might include Archers Best, Boddingtons, Buchanan's Best, John Smiths and Uley Old Spot with three changing guest beers such as Banks & Taylor Dragonslayer, Burtonwood Top Hat, and Aberdeen Bronco. Bar food includes sandwiches and ploughman's, and daily specials like lamb and sweetcorn lasagne (£3.95), cauliflower and potato curry or 12oz gammon (£4.95), crab roulade or pork schnitzel (£5.95), venison bourguignon (£6.95), and 16oz rump steak (£7.95). *(Recommended by Frank Gadbois, Roger Huggins, Tom McLean, Ewan McCall, Dave Irving, Joan and Michel Hooper-Immins, Tom Rees, Cherry Ann Knot, Jack and Philip Paxton)*

Free house ~ Licensees Michael and Eileen McAsey ~ Real ale ~ Meals and snacks ~ Restaurant ~ (01453) 873329 ~ Children welcome ~ Occasional Irish band ~ Open 11-3, 5.30-11; 11-11 Sat; 12-10.30 Sun

---

Post Office address codings confusingly give the impression that some pubs are in Gloucestershire, when they're really in the Midlands (which is where we list them).

Lucky Dip

Besides the fully inspected pubs, you might like to try these Lucky Dips recommended to us and described by readers (if you do, please send us reports):

☆ **Alderton** [off B4077 Tewkesbury—Stow – OS Sheet 150 map ref 999334; SP0033], *Gardeners Arms*: Civilised old-fashioned thatched Tudor pub with well kept Hook Norton Best, Theakstons Best and XB and Wadworths 6X, reasonably priced lunchtime sandwiches, soup or ham and eggs, log fire, good antique prints, high-backed settles among more usual seats; interesting restaurant food (evenings not Sun, and weekend lunchtimes; may be booked up), extension keeping bar sensibly separate; swift friendly service, tables on sheltered terrace, well kept garden; children welcome *(Tricia Kelly, BHP, Norman and Mary Phillips, Mr and Mrs W M Stirling, Neil and Anita Christopher, LYM)*

☆ **Aldsworth** [A433 Burford—Cirencester; SP1510], *Sherborne Arms*: Much-extended relaxing modernised dining pub with beams, bric-a-brac and spacious and attractive no-smoking conservatory dining area, wide choice of good fresh food esp fish, Whitbreads-related ales, log fire, service welcoming and attentive without being fussy, lovely garden; fills quickly weekends, lavatory for disabled *(Marjorie and David Lamb, Jill Bickerton, Cherry Ann Knott)*

☆ **Ampney Crucis** [turn left at the Crown of Crucis and veer left at triangle; SP0602], *Butchers Arms*: Lively friendly atmosphere,

well kept Tetleys-related ales with a guest like Marstons Owd Rodger, good value food, enthusiastic licensees, log fire *(T McLean, R Huggins, D Irving, E McCall, T O Eccles)*

☆ **Ampney St Peter** [A417, ½ mile E of village; SP0801], *Red Lion*: Unspoilt traditional 17th-c country local, old-fashioned benches facing open fire, informal counterless serving area (well kept Whitbreads PA), welcoming chatty regulars, hatch to corridor; separate room with wall benches around single table, darts, cards and dominoes; cl weekday lunchtimes *(Roger Huggins, Dave Irving, Ewan McCall, Tom McLean, Pete Baker, BB)*

☆ **Apperley** [village signed off B4213 S of Tewkesbury, go down lane beside PO opp Sawpit Lane; SO8628], *Coal House*: Airy bar notable for its splendid riverside position, with Bass, Wadworths 6X and a guest ale, red plush seats; front terrace with Severn views, play area *(E McCall, R Huggins, T McLean, D Irving, BB)*

☆ **Ashleworth** [signed off A417 at Hartpury; SO8125], *Queens Arms*: Comfortable and friendly, with good choice of bar food inc some unusual dishes, lovely fresh veg; well kept Donnington, attractive restaurant alongside with nice touches like good big mugs of coffee to close; skittle alley *(Keith Stephen, David and Margaret Bloomfield)*

Avening [ST8897], *Bell*: Thriving lively

recently reopened local with at least four well kept ales inc guests such as Timothy Taylors Landlord and Aug bank hol beer festival, wide choice of food, cheery knowledgeable landlord; quiz night, in sleepy valley village nestling below Gatcombe Park *(Dave Irving, T McLean, E McCall, R Huggins)*

Berry Hill [Christchurch – OS Sheet 162 map ref 572129; SO5712], *Kings Head*: Small and friendly, with prints on grey walls, corner pianola, coal-effect gas fire, good value food, Marstons Best and a seasonal beer, Theakstons XB *(Phil and Heidi Cook)*

Bibury [B4425; SP1106], *Swan*: Attractively placed old Cotswold inn, noted for its wonderful spritzers; bedrooms *(PP)*

Birdlip [OS Sheet 163 map ref 926143; SO9214], *Royal George*: Pleasant and spacious, with variously furnished little room areas; Bass and Boddingtons, guest beer tapped from the cask, wide range of reasonably priced lunchtime bar food, separate restaurant; bedrooms *(D G King, John and Phyllis Maloney, Neil and Anita Christopher, Dr and Mrs A K Clarke)*

Bishops Cleeve [Cheltenham Rd; SO9527], *Crown & Harp*: Happy atmosphere, friendly service, good value food, wide choice of Whitbreads-related ales with a guest such as Bunces Old Smoky, big garden and play area, good location; quiz night Thurs *(Joshua Corbion, David Walker)*

☆ **Bisley** [SO9006], *Stirrup Cup*: Spacious but bustling local, good choice of enjoyable food inc sandwiches, hot-filled rolls and good value specials, friendly staff *(D Irving, E McCall, R Huggins, T McLean, Mr and Mrs J Brown, Robert Huddleston)*

☆ **Blaisdon** [off A48 – OS Sheet 162 map ref 703169; SO7017], *Red Hart*: Well kept changing ales from good small breweries in brightly lit beamed and flagstone-floored village local, good value food (not Sun evening) in unobtrusive dining extension, friendly service, spring beer festival; dogs allowed; tables under cocktail parasols in attractive garden *(John Reed, Edwin Field, Ian Phillips)*

☆ **Blockley** [Station Rd; SP1634], *Great Western Arms*: Peaceful, comfortable and spacious modern-style lounge, wide choice of reasonably priced home-cooked food, well kept Flowers, Hook Norton and Marstons Pedigree, welcoming service, no piped music, busy public bar with games room; attractive village, lovely valley view *(Jenny and Michael Back, G W A Pearce, Heinz and Bruni Bauer, F and E Lindemann)*

☆ **Bourton on the Water** [SP1620], *Old New Inn*: Unchanging old hotel next to 1:9 scale model of village built here in 1930s by present landlord's father, comfortably worn and welcoming, with particularly well kept Bass and a weekly guest beer, good changing home-made food inc children's dishes, lovely dining room overlooking ford through River Windrush – a breath of genuine fresh air in this tourist village; bedrooms good *(Robert Whittle, Gary Nicholls)*

Bourton on the Water [Bridge End Walk], *Old Manse*: Lovely setting with front garden overlooking River Windrush, wide range of beers inc well kept Morlands Old Speckled Hen, generous helpings of well cooked food, courteous service, staff helpful and efficient; bedrooms *(Mr and Mrs A G Bennett, Derek and Margaret Underwood)*; *Parrot & Alligator*: Attractive Cotswold stone ex-guest house, wide choice of imaginative well cooked food inc unusual vegetarian dishes, dazzling array of real ales, wide choice of wines, obliging staff; big no-smoking area, children welcome *(John and Joan Wyatt)*

Brimscombe [off A419 SE of Stroud; SO8602], *Ship*: Named for former shipping canal here (its trans-shipment port, England's biggest in 1700s, now an industrial estate); well laid out to combine roominess with feeling of snugness, varied good value food esp steaks, well kept Bass and Boddingtons *(Dave Irving)*

Broadoak [A48 Gloucester—Chepstow; SO7013], *White Hart*: Overlooking Severn with tables out on high terrace by quay, lots of dining tables inside, Boddingtons, Marstons Pedigree and John Smiths *(T McLean, R Huggins, D Irving, E McCall)*

☆ **Broadwell** [off A429 2 miles N of Stow on the Wold; SP2027], *Fox*: Pleasant local opp attractive village's broad green, with well kept Donnington BB, SB and SBA, Addlestone's cider, stripped stone walls, flagstones, quick friendly service even when busy, darts, dominoes and chess, newer pool room extension, Sky TV, piped music; big back garden with wooden tables and Aunt Sally, field behind for Caravan Club members; bedrooms *(Andrew and Ruth Triggs, ML, DL, MJ, Angus Lyon, Pam Adsley)*

Cambridge [A38; SO7403], *White Lion*: Decent choice of food from sandwiches to steaks, Whitbreads-related ales, caravan park behind; handy for Slimbridge *(Jenny and Michael Back)*

☆ **nr Camp** [B4070 Birdlip—Stroud, junction with Calf Way; SO9111], *Fostons Ash*: Quietly isolated Cotswold inn reopened after open-plan refurbishment, well spaced tables, with good value home-made food, well kept Tetleys-related ales with Smiles and Wadworths 6X, efficient obliging service; piped music may be rather obtrusive; children welcome, garden with play area, good walks *(John and Joan Wyatt)*

☆ **Cerney Wick** [SU0796], *Crown*: Roomy modernised lounge bar, neat and clean, opening into comfortable semi-conservatory extension, public bar with pool, darts, fruit machine and log fire, popular straightforward food inc good Sun roasts, well kept Whitbreads-related ales, helpful service; children welcome, good-sized garden with swings, small motel-style bedroom extension *(Mrs P J Peeprose, Neville Kenyon, BB)*

☆ **nr Chalford** [France Lynch – OS Sheet 163 map ref 904036], *Kings Head*: Friendly and attractive old country local, well kept beer, wide range of good bar food, no juke box or fruit machine, garden, great views *(Don and Shirley Parrish)*

Chalford [Chalford Hill – OS Sheet 163 map ref 895032; SO8903], *Old Neighbourhood:* Good generous food under new licensees, welcoming easy-going atmosphere, local real ales, basic wooden floors and tables, open fire, children's play area, views from lovely big terrace and garden *(Alec and Susan Hamilton)*

☆ Charlton Kings [Cirencester Rd; A435; SO9620], *Little Owl:* Clean, friendly and attractive, good range of food in bar and restaurant, Whitbreads-related ales, decent wines, friendly licensees *(Janet and Paul Boak)*

Cheltenham [Bath Rd; SO9422], *Bath:* Basic unspoilt 1920s two-bar layout and simple furnishings, friendly landlady, locals' smoke room, well kept Bass and Uley *(Pete Baker);* [184 London Rd (A40 towards Charlton Kings, nr junction A435)], *Beaufort Arms:* Thriving local atmosphere, well kept Badger and Wadworths ales, decent food in bistro, pool room, obliging friendly service, tables out by road *(John and Joan Wyatt, M Mason, D Thompson, Frank Gadbois);* [Grosvenor/High St], *Restoration:* Long dim-lit open-plan pub with raised dining area, lots of beams, tons of bric-a-brac, simple wooden furniture, good atmosphere, five or more well kept reasonably priced beers *(Thomas Nott, Gary Nicholls)*

☆ Chipping Campden [High St; SP1539], *Lygon Arms:* Good welcoming service, lots of horse pictures (and friendly evening locals) in carpeted stripped-stone bar, well kept Donnington SBA, Hook Norton Best, Wadworths 6X and interesting guests such as Woods Christmas Cracker, open fires, good choice of plentiful food from well filled rolls and good ploughman's up in back dining area, raftered evening restaurant beyond sheltered courtyard with tables; children welcome, open all day exc winter weekdays; good bedrooms *(Andrew and Ruth Triggs, Keith and Janet Morris, George Atkinson, Jason Caulkin, Mr and Mrs Thompson, Terry and Vann W Prime, LYM)*

Chipping Campden [Sheep St], *Red Lion:* Simple good value home-cooked food, upstairs dining room, attractive left-hand bar with well kept Bass from long counter, separate back bar with machines and music, welcoming staff, friendly locals; bedrooms *(E V Walder, Andrew and Ruth Triggs, Martin Jones);* [quiet end of main st], *Volunteer:* Cosy little pub with good friendly atmosphere, good range of well kept beers such as Fullers ESB and Wadworths 6X and of good food, military memorabilia *(Terry and Vann W Prime, Pam Adsley, David E Scott)*

☆ Cirencester [W Market Pl; SP0201], *Slug & Lettuce:* Civilised atmosphere, flagstones, bare boards, lots of woodwork, pleasantly worn furnishings inc good big tables, no-smoking area, big log fires; well kept Marstons Pedigree and other ales, good coffee, wide choice of bar food inc unusual dishes (no chips), friendly helpful staff,

children welcome; tables in inner courtyard; piped pop music, very popular with young people evenings *(Simon Collett-Jones, Marjorie and Colin Roberts, Pat and Richard Tazewell, Alan and Charlotte Sykes, LYM)*

☆ Cirencester [Black Jack St; between church and Corinium Museum], *Golden Cross:* Backstreet 1920s local with longish comfortable bar, sensible tables, simple cheap generous food, three Arkells ales, very friendly service, good beer mug collection; piped music may obtrude; skittle alley, tables in back garden, nr wonderful church *(Marjorie and Colin Roberts, Roger Huggins, Dave Irving, Ewan McCall, Tom McLean, Nick and Alison Dowson, Peter and Audrey Dowsett, Frank W Gadbois, Keith and Janet Morris)*

Cirencester [Dyer St], *Bear:* Lively, esp in french-style pavement tables area, with cheap well kept Moles *(D Irving, R Huggins, Tom McLean, E McCall);* [Dollar St/Gloucester St], *Corinium Court:* Roaring log fire in smart but relaxed and cosy bar, well kept Hook Norton Old Hookey and Wadworths 6X, decent wine, reasonably priced food, attractive restaurant, no piped music; entrance through charming courtyard with tables; bedrooms *(Peter and Audrey Dowsett);* [10-14 Chester St], *Oddfellows Arms:* Cosy backstreet local with good range of well kept strong ales, changing reasonably priced food, friendly service, live music twice weekly *(Nick and Alison Dowson, D Irving, R Huggins, T McLean, E McCall, S G Mullock);* [Lewis Lane], *Twelve Bells:* Friendly and lively open-plan backstreet pub, coal fire in back room, continental prints, particularly well kept Archers Best, Eldridge Pope Hardy Country and two or three other changing ales, bar food *(Tom McLean, Roger Huggins, D Irving, E McCall, Nick and Alison Dowson)*

☆ Coates [follow Tarleton signs from village (right then left), pub up rough track on right after rly bridge, OS Sheet 163 map ref 965005; SO9600], *Tunnel House:* Idyllically placed idiosyncratic beamed country pub by interesting abandoned canal tunnel, very relaxed management style, mix of well worn armchairs, sofa, rustic benches, enamel advertising signs, stuffed mustelids, race tickets, real ales such as Archers Best, Morlands Old Speckled Hen, Wadworths 6X and Youngs, basic bar food, Sunday barbecues, log fires (not always lit), pub games, big juke box much appreciated by Royal Agricultural College students; children welcome (good safe play area), camping facilities *(Andrew and Ruth Triggs, Frank Gadbois, Stephen, Julie and Hayley Brown, Esther and John Sprinkle, Dr and Mrs A K Clarke, Tony and Wendy Hobden, Giles Francis, LYM)*

☆ Codrington [handy for M4 junction 18, via B4465; ST7579], *Codrington Arms:* Fair-sized recently refurbished village pub with wide choice of popular good value food, prompt welcoming service, good range of beers inc Marstons Pedigree, big gardens with good views; piped music *(Meg and Colin Hamilton,*

DGC, Andrew Shore, Peter and Audrey
Dowsett)
Coleford [Christchurch; SO5712], New Inn:
Smallish open-plan stripped-stone pub,
discreetly lit, with big log fire, ales such as
Boddingtons, Flowers IPA, Marstons Pedigree
and local Freeminers, straightforward food;
piped pop music may be loud (Phil and Heidi
Cook)
☆ Colesbourne [A435; SO9913], Colesbourne
Inn: Comfortable old-fashioned panelled inn
with good bar food, efficient staff,
Wadworths ales, country wines, huge log fires
in several rooms, hunting prints, settles and
oak tables, masses of mugs on beams;
comfortable bedrooms (Malcolm Taylor)
Compton Abdale [A40 outside village; former
Puesdown Inn; SO0616], Cotswold Explorer:
Ancient pub completely refurbished by
enthusiastic new licensees, cosy decor, two log
fires, good atmosphere, wide choice of good
fresh home-cooked food inc delicious
puddings, well kept ales and winter mulled
wine; comfortable bedrooms (Judith Wilson,
Steve Jones, A Halliday)
Cromhall [ST6990], Royal Oak: Lots of little
rooms with covered well in centre bar, good
value varied food in separate dining rooms,
tables outside (Meg and Colin Hamilton, John
Sidgwick)
☆ Didmarton [A433 Tetbury rd; ST8187], Kings
Arms: Doing well under new management,
with Bass, John Smiths and local beers, open
fire, wide choice of good interesting food,
candlelit restaurant with white linen and
relaxed atmosphere; children and dogs
welcome (Peter Robinson, D G Clarke)
Duntisbourne Abbots [A417 N of Cirencester
– OS Sheet 163 map ref 978091; SO9709],
Five Mile House: Sadly the long-serving
landlady of this unspoiled country tavern with
Grade I listed drinking rooms has died; moves
are afoot to preserve it, though adding a back
restaurant area (News please)
☆ Dursley [May Ln, by bus stn; ST7598], Old
Spot: Simple, friendly pub with great
atmosphere, well kept Bass, Uley and two
guest beers, friendly landlord, doorstep
sandwiches and quick snacks, lots of pig
paraphernalia; bar billiards, cribbage,
dominoes and boules, no music or machines
(Julian Jewitt)
☆ Eastleach Turville [off A361 S of Burford;
SP1905], Victoria: Charming unpretentious
lounge/dining area, pool in spacious separate
bar, welcoming staff and locals, well kept
Arkells, nice views, straightforward home
cooking; quiet midweek lunchtime, busy
evenings esp Sat (when pianist replaces juke
box); pleasant front garden (John and Joan
Wyatt, D Irving, T McLean, E McCall, R
Huggins, David Campbell, Vicki McLean)
☆ nr Elkstone [Beechpike; A417 6 miles N of
Cirencester – OS Sheet 163 map ref 966108;
SO9610], Highwayman: Well kept Arkells
real ales, good house wines, fair range of
decent standard food, good friendly staff, and
considerable character in rambling 16th-c
warren of low beams, stripped stone, alcoves,

antique settles among more modern
furnishings, log fires, airy dining room; piped
music; outside play area, good indoors
provision for children (Thomas Nott, John
and Joan Wyatt)
Fairford [Market Pl; SP1501], Bull: Friendly
beamed hotel, no-smoking areas at mealtimes,
very wide choice of reasonably priced food,
Arkells 3B and Kingsdown; piped music;
bedrooms (George Atkinson, PD, AD);
[Whelford Rd], Old Rangoon: Popular and
unusual place by power-boat lake, with
Oriental touches, bar food, maybe Tetleys
real ale, big dance floor used mainly for
functions (Peter and Audrey Dowsett)
Forest of Dean [B4226 nearly a mile E of
junction with B4234; SO6212], Speech
House: Forte hotel superbly placed in centre
of Forest, superbly warm interior with lots of
oak panelling, substantial reasonably priced
bar food, well kept Bass, afternoon teas, plush
restaurant; bedrooms comfortable (A E and P
McCully, Dave Irving, W H and E Thomas)
Forest of Dean see: Berry Hill, Coleford,
Lower Lydbrook, Mitcheldean, Parkend,
Viney Hill; and main entries for Clearwell,
Coleford, Newland and St Briavels
☆ Frampton Mansell [off A491 Cirencester—
Stroud – OS Sheet 163 map ref 923027;
SO9102], Crown: Welcoming stripped stone
lounge bar with dark beam-and-plank ceiling,
well kept ales such as Archers Village, Oakhill
Farmers, Wadworths 6X, friendly service,
public bar with darts, good food in bar and
attractive restaurant; lovely views over village
and steep wooded valley; children in eating
area, teak seats outside; comfortable good
value bedrooms (David Surridge, D Irving, R
Huggins, Tom McLean, E McCall, Don and
Shirley Parrish, BB)
Frampton on Severn [The Green; SO7407],
Bell: Pleasantly done-up Whitbreads pub by
cricket pitch, good range of fairly priced
lunchtime food, decent service, real ales inc
interesting guests such as Butcombe (A Y
Drummond, Malcolm Taylor)
☆ Glasshouse [by Newent Woods; first right
turn off A40 going W from junction with
A4136 – OS Sheet 162 map ref 710213;
SO7122], Glasshouse: Carefully preserved
small country tavern with changing well kept
ales tapped from the cask, flagstone floors,
log fire in vast fireplace, limited good value
food (no sandwiches), helpful landlady,
interesting decorations, darts and quoits, seats
on fenced lawn with big weeping willow
loved by children; fine nearby woodland
walks (Edwin Field, LYM)
☆ Gloucester [Llanthony Rd; off Merchants Rd,
S end of Docks], Waterfront: Atmospheric
bare-boards black-beamed waterside bar with
wide range of ales tapped from the cask inc
some specials offers, scrubbed tables, tin
helmets, barrels you can chalk on, free
peanuts (shells go on the floor), beermat
collection, other interesting bric-a-brac; bar
billiards, table football, ninepins etc; generous
cheap food, eating area up a step with back-
to-back cubicle seating; piped music (live

some nights), fruit machine, Sky TV; *(Richard Lewis, M Joyner, T McLean, R Huggins, D Irving, E McCall)*

☆ **Guiting Power** [signed off B4068 SW of Stow on the Wold; SP0924], *Olde*: Quiet beamed main bar with log fire, attractive built-in wall and window seats and small armchairs, flagstoned public bar with darts, cribbage and dominoes, limited choice of hearty bar food with home-made bread, some interesting specials and children's meals, Hook Norton and Theakstons Best and guests such as Bass or Marstons Pedigree, some tables out by back car park, good walks; restaurant *(Margaret Dyke, Mr and Mrs D C Stevens, D Irving, E McCall, R Huggins, T McLean, Jason Caulkin, MM, DT, Maureen Hobbs, Angus Lyon, Frank Cummins, Martin Jones, Philip Orbell, LYM)*

Hardwicke [Sellars Bridge; SO7912], *Pilot*: Worth knowing for lovely canalside setting overlooking lock, with good children's facilities inc nappy-changing room; usual food etc, can get quite crowded *(John and Elisabeth Cox)*

☆ **Hillesley** [ST7689], *Fleece*: Welcoming attractive local with good traditional furnishings, interesting bar food inc good specials and steaks, no-smoking upper dining bar; well kept Whitbreads-related real ales, decent wines and malt whiskies, friendly landlord; small Cotswold village surrounded by lovely countryside, nr Cotswold Way; bedrooms *(M I Ellis)*

Hinton Dyrham [nr M4 junction 18; A46 towards Bath, then 1st right; ST7376], *Bull*: Pretty 16th-c stone-built village pub, two bars each with log fires, good food, well kept Bass and Wadworths IPA, 6X and Old Timer, family room, oak and elm settles in public bar, big garden with picnic tables and swings *(T H Adams)*

Horsley [ST8397], *Bell & Castle*: Wide choice of reasonably priced food with emphasis on fresh Cornish fish, some good vegetarian dishes; friendly service, skittles and darts etc; can get a little smoky *(Margaret Dyke)*

Hucclecote [Hucclecote Rd; SO8617], *Royal Oak*: Lively local with emphasis on games, good range of real ales *(Dr and Mrs A K Clarke)*

Kemble [outside village on A433 Cirencester—Tetbury; ST9897], *Thames Head*: Stripped stone, timberwork, cottagey back area with pews and log-effect gas fire in big fireplace, country-look dining room with another big gas fire, real fire in front area; well kept Arkells Bitter, 2B and 3B on handpump, good value straightforward food, friendly service, seats outside, children welcome *(D Irving, E McCall, R Huggins, T McLean, LYM)*

Lechlade [Park End Wharf; SU2199], *Riverside*: Worth knowing for well furnished garden leading down to river; Arkells and Wadworths 6X, quick low-priced bar food *(SLC)*; [Fairford Rd, Downington; A417 towards Cirencester; SU2099], *Three Horseshoes*: Boddingtons and two Smiles ales

in 17th-c pub slowly being restored to original stone etc; friendly staff, fish motif, landlady specialises in good fish cooking – trout lakes nearby *(Frank W Gadbois)*

☆ *nr* **Lechlade** [St John's Bridge; A417 a mile E], *Trout*: Low-beamed three-room pub dating from 15th c, with some flagstones, stuffed fish and fishing prints, big Thameside garden with boules, Aunt Sally and a simple summer family bar; Courage Best and Directors and John Smiths, popular well presented food from ploughman's through pizzas to steaks (may be a wait at busy times), no-smoking dining room; children in eating areas, jazz Tues and Sun, fishing rights; open all day Sat in summer *(Frank W Gadbois, Dr Peter Donahue, George Atkinson, John Wooll, I Maw, LYM)*

☆ **Leighterton** [off A46 S of Nailsworth; ST8291], *Royal Oak*: Unpretentious pub with appropriately simple decor and matching extension, four well kept interesting ales, decent straightforward home cooking, friendly landlord, nice garden, quiet village; quite handy for Westonbirt Arboretum *(Margaret Dyke)*

☆ **Longhope** [Ross Rd (A40); SO6919], *Farmers Boy*: Good wholesome food inc good range of curries in three big carefully refurbished rooms, one with running water in covered well; stripped stone, farm tools, log fire, relaxed atmosphere, friendly service, well kept Adnams and Wadworths 6X, no juke boxes or machines; attractive garden and terrace *(Neil and Anita Christopher, Dennis Shirley, Mrs B Lemon, S Godsell)*

Longhope [A4136 Gloucester—Monmouth; SO6918], *Yew Tree*: Locally popular for usual food from sandwiches up inc good roast of the day, good-sized helpings, friendly staff, Whitbreads-related ales, big log fire, beams and stripped stone, piped music; no dogs, pub area outside *(Jenny and Michael Back, Dennis Shirley)*

Lower Lydbrook [Vention Lane; pub signed up single-track rd from B4228 NE of village – OS Sheet 162 map ref 604167; SO5916], *Royal Spring*: Very prettily placed, simple and quiet, with pews and high-backed settles in long beamed lounge looking down valley, wide range of bar food, log fire, well kept Wadworths; informal garden around stream dropping down steep coombe, play area, pets corner, muscovy ducks free among the tables (with obvious consequences); children very welcome *(Lawrence Pearse, A Y Drummond, LYM)*

Lower Swell [B4068 W of Stow on the Wold; SP1725], *Golden Ball*: Sprucely furnished local with Donnington BB and SBA from the pretty brewery just 20 mins' walk away, good range of ciders and perry, bar food, evening restaurant (no food Sun evening); simple bar with log fire, games area with fruit machine and juke box behind big chimneystack, small garden with occasional barbecues, Aunt Sally and quoits; no dogs or children, decent simple bedrooms *(P J Keen, G and T Edwards, LYM)*

☆ **Lower Wick** [off A38 Bristol—Gloucester just

N of Newport; ST7196], *Pickwick*: Bright clean two-bar dining pub very popular (particularly with older people) for generous changing home-cooked food, straightforward but interesting; full range of Smiles beers, decent wines, traditional games inc antique table skittles, no music; one room sectioned off with rather close-set tables; garden with play area and country views but some noise from nearby M5 and rly; children welcome *(John and Pat Smyth, D G Clarke, Gwen and Peter Andrews)*

☆ Marshfield [signed off A420 Bristol—Chippenham; ST7773], *Catherine Wheel*: Interesting and busy family-run old pub with plates and prints on stripped stone walls, medley of settles, chairs and stripped tables, impressive fireplace, cottagey back family bar, charming no-smoking Georgian dining room, flower-decked back yard; good food inc Thurs fresh fish, (not Sun), well kept Ruddles County and Wadworths IPA and 6X, farm cider, decent wines; golden labrador called Elmer, darts, dominoes; provision for children *(Pete and Rosie Flower, Peter Neate, Ian Jones, M G Hart, LYM)*
Marshfield [A420], *Crown*: Large busy local with coach entry to yard, big log fire in well furnished beamed lounge, wide choice of competitively priced food esp steaks, well kept Tetleys, Websters and their own Mummers Ale, service quick even when crowded; children welcome, live music Sat, occasional quiz nights *(Pete and Rosie Flower)*
Mayshill [Badminton Rd; A432 Coalpit Heath—Yate; ST6882], *New Inn*: Interesting and well kept real ales, nice drinking area outside, maybe bouncy castle *(Dr and Mrs A K Clarke)*

☆ Meysey Hampton [off A417 Cirencester—Lechlade; SU1199], *Masons Arms*: Welcoming carefully renovated beamed 17th-c village inn with good freshly cooked reasonably priced food, well kept John Smiths, Wadworths 6X and Websters Yorkshire, decent wines inc several ports, commendable service, good solid furnishings, big inglenook log fire at one end, no-smoking restaurant up a few steps; homely and cosy well equipped bedrooms, good breakfasts *(D H and M C Watkinson, Miss R Booth, D G King, Sarah Orchard, David Campbell, Vicki McLean, Matt Richardson, BB)*

☆ Mickleton [B4632 (ex A46); SP1543], *Kings Arms*: Comfortable, clean, relaxed and civilised, popular for good value food inc notable ploughman's and Sun roasts, nice puddings, vegetarian dishes; good service, Whitbreads-related ales, farm cider, decent wines; some tables outside, handy for Hidcote and Kiftsgate *(P J Keen, Anita and Neil Christopher, BB)*
Mickleton [B4632 (ex A46)], *Butchers Arms*: Fair choice of food inc children's in clean, tidy and cosy timbered pub with friendly staff, well kept Bass, Flowers and Tetleys; garden with fish pond *(John and Joan Wyatt)*; [Chapel Lane; B4632, junction with Pebworth

rd], *Three Ways*: Good bar food inc scrumptious puddings, part of hotel (now under enthusiastic new ownership) famous for its pudding club; bedrooms *(Martin Jones)*
Minsterworth [A48 S of Gloucester; SO7716], *Apple Tree*: Friendly and comfortable roadside Whitbreads dining pub based on extended oak-beamed 17th-c farmhouse, decent standard food, open fires, prompt service, unobtrusive piped music, well kept ales; big garden with enclosed play area; open all day – lane beside leads down to the Severn, a good way of avoiding east bank crowds on a Bore weekend *(Thomas Nott, Dennis Shirley)*
Miserden [SO9308], *Carpenters Arms*: Cheerful and relaxed reopened village local, not over-modernised, with two open-plan bar areas, nice old wooden tables on bare boards, exposed stone, open fires, friendly staff, real ales such as Brakspears, Boddingtons and Greene King Abbot, bar food inc original dishes, small dining room with dark wood traditional furniture; tables in garden, idyllic quiet Cotswold village *(Neil and Anita Christopher, Simon Warren, Don Gross, John and Joan Wyatt, Giles Francis)*
Mitcheldean [SO6718], *Lamb*: Two unspoilt bars, recently refurbished restaurant, well kept beer, food that's something special; bedrooms good – well placed for Forest of Dean *(Paul and Heather Bettesworth)*

☆ Moreton in Marsh [High St; SP2032], *White Hart Royal*: Busy and comfortable old-world inn, partly 15th c, with interesting Civil War history, oak beams, stripped stone, big inglenook fire in lounge area just off main bar, particularly well kept Bass and Worthington BB, good value straightforward food changing daily in bar and simple but pleasant restaurant, inc good seafood and Sun lunch, enthusiastic landlord, quick welcoming service; a real welcome for children, can get crowded; good value bedrooms *(Henry Paulinski, Pam Adsley, Mark Ellis, E Walder, Andrew and Ruth Triggs, N W Neill)*
Moreton in Marsh [High St], *Bell*: Pleasant homely pub with Courage-related ales, good value food all day, efficient service; bar covered with banknotes and beermats, tables (some under cover) in garden *(Andrew and Ruth Triggs, Dr and Mrs A K Clarke)*; [Market Pl], *Black Bear*: Good keenly priced home-made food, local Donnington SBA, BB and XX, friendly service, warm, comfortable and relaxing lounge, livelier public bar, back garden *(Joan and Michel Hooper-Immins, Dr and Mrs M N Edwards, Mr and Mrs Carr, Don and Shirley Parrish)*; [High St], *Inn on the Marsh*: Good reasonably priced restaurant-style food, well kept interesting ales, friendly young staff, comfortable armchairs and settles, dining conservatory; bedrooms *(Andrew and Ruth Triggs, Annette and Stephen Marsden)*; [High St], *Redesdale Arms*: Fine old coaching inn with prettily lit alcoves and big stone fireplace in comfortable panelled bar on right, well kept Tetleys-related ales with a guest such as Exmoor Stag,

quickly served generous food inc vegetarian, restaurant, darts and fruit machine in flagstoned public bar, TV in back conservatory; tables in big back garden, comfortable well equipped bedrooms *(Pam Adsley, Mrs B Sugarman, Andrew and Ruth Triggs, George Atkinson, Annette and Stephen Marsden)*

☆ Nailsworth [coming from Stroud on A46, left and left again at roundabout; ST8499], *Egypt Mill*: Attractively converted three-floor mill with working waterwheel in one room, static machinery in second area, Ind Coope Burton and Wadworths 6X on handpump, wide choice of good generous bar food inc fresh veg, quick service, good value meals in civilised upstairs restaurant; can get crowded weekends, occasional loud karaoke or jazz evenings; children welcome, no dogs; lovely gardens, good bedrooms *(D Irving, E McCall, R Huggins, T Mclean)*

☆ Nether Westcote [SP2120], *New Inn*: Good value home-cooked food, well kept Morrells and good service in warmly welcoming pub, pleasantly unpretentious but cosy and clean; can get busy, piped pop music may be loud; sizeable adjoining campsite, pretty village *(James de la Force, Barry Perfect, Peter and Audrey Dowsett, Nicolas Allport)*

☆ North Nibley [B4060; ST7496], *Black Horse*: Straightforward village local with good atmosphere, wide range of generous good value fresh home-made food (service may slow when busy) well kept Whitbreads-related real ales and an interesting guest beer, good log fire, maybe piped music; popular restaurant Tues-Sat evenings, Sun lunchtime, tables in pretty garden; good value cottagey bedrooms, good breakfasts *(Martin and Karen Wake, Margaret Dyke, Pat and Richard Tazewell, LYM)*

☆ Northleach [Cheltenham Rd; SP1114], *Wheatsheaf*: Clean and smartly comfortable, almost more hotel than pub, with pleasantly upmarket atmosphere, quiet piped classical music, very polite friendly staff; good if not cheap lunchtime bar food, real ales inc Marstons Pedigree; restaurant, lovely terraced garden; well equipped modern bedrooms *(John and Joan Wyatt, John and Wendy Trentham)*

☆ Northleach [Market Pl], *Red Lion*: Good value generous food from good sandwiches to Sun roasts in straightforward bar with open fire, well kept Courage-related ales, decent coffee, very friendly service; piped music and fruit machines *(Margaret Dyke)*

☆ Nympsfield [SO8000], *Rose & Crown*: Clean and very hospitable village local nr Coaley Peak viewpoint over Severn Valley, handy for Cotswold walks, wide choice of generous home-cooked food inc huge ploughman's in extended eating area, cosy partly stripped-stone lounge with big fireplace, up to ten or so ales such as Bass, Boddingtons and Uley Bitter and Old Spot, decent wines, good quick service even when busy, separate public bar; terrace and garden, good play area; comfortable well equipped bedrooms, big

breakfasts *(Margaret Dyke, T Dobby, Neil and Anita Christopher, M Joyner, Martin and Karen Wake, G L Jones, Phil Humphris)*

Old Sodbury [junction of A46 with A432; 1½ miles from M4 junction 18; ST7581], *Cross Hands*: Popular and comfortably done-up spacious pub/hotel, extremely obliging staff, subdued piped music, good reasonably priced bar menu (good coffee), log-effect gas fire, Bass, Wadworths 6X and Worthington BB; restaurant, comfortable bedrooms *(Peter and Audrey Dowsett, LYM)*

Olveston [ST6088], *White Hart*: Clean and carefully modernised old village pub with flagstones, stripped stone walls and exposed beams; particularly well kept Ushers Founders, bar food *(Dr and Mrs A K Clarke, BB)*

☆ Painswick [St Mary's St; SO8609], *Royal Oak*: Busy and attractive old town local with bubbly atmosphere, interesting layout and furnishings inc some attractive old or antique seats, good value honest food (bar nibbles only, Sun) from sandwiches to changing hot dishes inc Thurs fresh fish, well kept Whitbreads-related ales, friendly family service, small sun lounge by suntrap pretty courtyard; children in eating area; can get crowded, nearby parking may be difficult *(E J Wilde, M J How, G C Hackemer, LM, Thomas Nott, R Michael Richards, LYM)*

☆ Parkend [Whitecroft, just off B4234 N of Lydney; SO6208], *Woodman*: Relaxing, spacious and comfortable without being plush, two open fires, heavy beams, stripped stone, forest and forestry decorations, mix of furnishings inc some modern seats, well presented food from soup and ploughman's to guinea fowl inc children's meals and Sun lunch, well kept Bass and Boddingtons, decent wines, evening bistro (Thurs-Sat); picnic tables on front terrace, facing green, good walks into Forest of Dean; service can be leisurely, maybe darts, fruit machine, juke box; bedrooms *(Piotr Chodzko-Zajko, Mrs B Sugarman, Dennis Shirley, Neil and Anita Christopher, SRP, LYM)*

Pennsylvania [4 miles from M4 junction 18 – A46 towards Bath; ST7373], *Swan*: Friendly atmosphere, well kept Archers Best, Marstons Pedigree, Morlands Old Speckled Hen and Otter Best, good food *(Roberto Villa)*

Poulton [SP1001], *Falcon*: Renovated under new management, with wide choice of good evening Chinese food as well as usual dishes, Arkells BBB, Hook Norton Best and Theakstons XB *(Frank W Gadbois)*

☆ Prestbury [Mill St; SO9624], *Plough*: Good generous food in well preserved thatched village local's cosy and pleasant oak-panelled front lounge, friendly and comfortable; lots of regulars in basic but roomy flagstoned back tap room with grandfather clock and big log fire, well kept Whitbreads-related ales tapped from casks, pleasant back garden *(D Irving, E McCall, R Huggins, T McLean)*

Purton [SO6904], *Berkeley Hunt*: Basic, friendly local by bridge over Sharpness—Gloucester canal, flagstoned rooms off central servery *(R W Brooks, R Huggins, T McLean, D Irving, E McCall)*

☆ **Quenington** [SP1404], *Keepers Arms*: Cosy and comfortable stripped-stone pub, very friendly, with traditional settles, lots of mugs hanging from low beams, good coal fire, decent food in both bars and restaurant, Whitbreads-related ales, no piped music; bedrooms *(Don and Shirley Parrish)*

Randwick [SO8206], *Vine Tree*: Roomy hillside village pub, wonderful valley views esp from terrace and garden; well kept Whitbreads-related ales, good choice of food (not Tues), beams, timbering, stripped stone, rush matting, copper-topped tables, plates and Lawson Wood prints on walls, warm welcome; children welcome, play area *(R Huggins, D Irving, E McCall, T McLean, Neil and Anita Christopher)*

Rodborough [SO8404], *Bear*: Flagstoned bar with pleasant window seats, welcoming log fire, good value bar food, well kept local beer; children welcome; comfortable Forte hotel – good base for touring Cotswolds; bedrooms *(John Broughton, D Irving, E McCall, R Huggins, T Mclean)*

☆ **Sapperton** [village off A419 Stroud—Cirencester, from village follow Edgeworth, Bisley signpost; SO9303], *Daneway*: Bustling and friendly local, not smart but clean, with amazing floor-to-ceiling carved oak fireplace, sporting prints, short range of generously served food from good value filled rolls and hot dishes to evening steaks, well kept Archers Best, Bass, Wadworths 6X, a well priced beer locally brewed for the pub, a changing guest beer and local farm cider, cheery licensees, small no-smoking family room; traditional games in inglenook snug bar, lovely sloping lawn in charming quiet wooded countryside alongside derelict canal with good walks and interesting tunnel *(Roger and Jenny Huggins, Nick Dowson, Dave Irving, Tom McLean, Ewan McCall, Mike Davies, F J and A Parmenter, Marjorie and Colin Roberts, Jack and Philip Paxton, Peter and Audrey Dowsett, Howard Allen, Andrew and Ruth Triggs, Malcolm Taylor, Dr and Mrs A H Young, Kevin and Tracey Stephens, Thomas Nott, LYM)*

☆ **Shepperdine** [off B4061 N of Thornbury; ST6295], *Windbound*: Well placed on Severn estuary nr Wildfowl Trust Centre, spacious pubby bar with decent straightforward food, well kept beers, attractive pictures, friendly landlord; upstairs room (which has the views) may now be open only for functions; tables on fairylit lawn *(John and Donna Bush, LYM)*

Slad [B4070 Stroud—Birdlip; SO8707], *Woolpack*: Basic village local in splendid setting, lovely valley views, very welcoming landlord, cheap food, well kept Bass and Uley Old Spot, autographed copies of books by Laurie Lee for sale *(Thomas Nott, Roger Huggins, Prof I H Rorison, D Irving, E McCall, T McLean, PN, John and Joan Wyatt)*

Slimbridge [Shepherds Patch – OS Sheet 162 map ref 728042; SO7303], *Tudor Arms*: Character not its strongest point, but very handy for Wildfowl Trust and canal, useful home-cooked food in bar and evening restaurant, three or four real ales, children's room; bedrooms in small annexe *(Tom McLean, Roger Huggins, John Broughton, P A Haywood)*

☆ **Snowshill** [SP0934], *Snowshill Arms*: Handy for Snowshill Manor (which closes lunchtime), with good popular food, well kept Donnington BB and SBA, efficient service, spruce and airy bar, log fire; charming village views from bow windows and from big back garden, friendly local feel midweek winter, can be very crowded other times – get there early; skittle alley, good play area; children welcome if eating, nearby parking may be difficult *(Pam Adsley, SLC, P and M Rudlin, Mrs P J Pearce, Nick and Meriel Cox, Lawrence Pearse, A C Morrison, RP, BP, Maysie Thompson, LYM)*

☆ **Somerford Keynes** [OS Sheet 163 map ref 018954; SU0195], *Bakers Arms*: Homely and traditional partly stripped-stone local in lovely Cotswold village, wide choice of enjoyable food inc good specials, vegetarian and Sun lunch, well kept Bass and other frequently changing ales, knowledgeable and very friendly barman; busy lunchtime (booking recommended), big garden *(M A and C R Starling, D G King, T McLean, D Irving, E McCall, R Huggins)*

☆ **Staverton** [Haydon, W of Cheltenham; B4063 – OS Sheet 163 map ref 902248; SO9024], *House in the Tree*: Not in a tree but a pleasantly busy spick-and-span pub with splendid choice of farm ciders, Bass and Boddingtons, good choice of lunchtime food in big dining lounge, more traditional public bar, obliging service; may get crowded at weekends, plenty of tables in garden with pets corner *(John and Joan Wyatt, D Irving, E McCall, R Huggins, T McLean, David and Alison Walker)*

Stow on the Wold [Digbeth St; SP1925], *Royalist*: One of Britain's most genuinely ancient inns, parts of timber frame around 1,000 years old; good promptly served bar food, not that cheap, but inc some unusual bar snacks *(Mrs P J Pearce)*; [The Square], *Talbot*: Popular local with well kept Wadworths IPA and 6X and a guest such as Maclays 60/-, decent lunches, friendly staff; open all day inc Sun *(Joan and Michel Hooper-Immins)*

Stroud [Nelson St, Rookmoor; just E of centre; SO8504], *Golden Fleece*: Small old terrace pub, fairly dark inside, with daily papers, cheerfully musical decor, unobtrusive piped jazz, well kept beer, unspoilt feel, separate smaller upstairs room *(Dave Irving)*; [top end of High St], *Retreat*: Pink walls, polished wooden floors and tables, well kept Archers Best and Boddingtons, imaginative lunchtime meals and snacks; can get crowded evenings *(Dave Irving)*

☆ **Tetbury** [Gumstool Hill, Mkt Pl; ST8893], *Crown*: Friendly 17th-c town pub with

imaginative choice of good bar food inc some upmarket dishes, well kept Hook Norton Best and Whitbreads-related ales, long oak-beamed front bar with big log fire and attractive medley of tables, efficient courteous service, unobtrusive piped music; back family dining conservatory with lots of plants, picnic tables on back terrace; comfortable bedrooms, sharing bathroom *(Karen and Graham Oddey, Grahame McNulty, LM, D G Clarke, B and K Hyper, Simon Penny)*
Tetbury [Market Pl], *Snooty Fox*: Good food in welcoming modernised hotel lounge and restaurant; bedrooms good value *(Maureen Kayll)*; [A433 towards Cirencester, nr Cherington], *Trouble House*: Pretty 17th-c pub with friendly new landlord, well kept Wadworths beers, open fire, small quiet lounge, more lively bar with bar billiards and darts in room off, usual food, no music *(Karen and Graham Oddey, D Irving, R Huggins, E McCall, T McLean)*
☆ nr Tetbury [Calcot; A4135 W, junction A46; ST8394], *Gumstool*: Smart and busy cafe/bar attached to Calcot Hotel, modern pine tables and seats on flagstones, well kept Bass and Uley Old Spot, good choice of wines by the glass, varied good value food inc interesting dishes, big log fire; bedrooms – handy for Westonbirt Arboretum, lovely walks *(Pat and John Millward, D G King, John and Annette Derbyshire)*
☆ Tewkesbury [52 Church St; SO8932], *Bell*: Plush but interesting hotel bar with friendly helpful service, black oak beams and timbers, some neat 17th-c oak panelling, medieval leaf-and-fruit frescoes, armchairs, settees and tapestries; good choice of decent bar food from sandwiches up inc vegetarian and civilised Sun buffet lunch, comfortable restaurant, well kept Bass and Banks's, big log fire; garden above Severnside walk, nr abbey; good bedrooms *(F M Steiner, Trevor Hing, Andrew and Ruth Triggs, Mr and Mrs J Brown, BB)*
☆ Tewkesbury [High St], *Black Bear*: Extremely picturesque timbered pub, said to be county's oldest, with rambling heavy-beamed rooms off black-timbered corridors, inviting yet not too crowded, five or six ales such as Shepherd Neame Spitfire and Wychwood Dog and Hobgoblin tapped from the cask, reasonably priced bar food inc good children's menu, friendly service, riverside lawn *(Clifford Payton, Sue and Mike Lee, LYM)*
Tewkesbury [9 Church St], *Berkeley Arms*: Pleasant olde-worlde refurbishment in striking medieval timbered pub, well kept Wadworths Henrys, 6X, Farmers Glory and winter Old Timer with a summer guest such as Badger Tanglefoot, friendly staff, open fire in lounge bar, wide range of good value food inc succulent real chips, separate front public bar (can be smoky), raftered ancient back barn restaurant; open all day summer, bedrooms *(Joan and Michel Hooper-Immins, Brian Wainwright, Martin Ennis)*
☆ Thornbury [Chapel St; ST6390], *Wheatsheaf*: It's the good home cooking that counts in this

straightforward 1930s local – the six or so very appetising evening specials do run out early though! Very friendly obliging licensees, wide range of real ales, children's helpings, minimal music *(K R Harris, Pat Woodward, D G Clarke)*
☆ Tockington [ST6186], *Swan*: Spacious pub with beams, standing timbers, bric-a-brac on stripped stone walls, Bass and Boddingtons on handpump, guests such as Smiles and Theakstons Best tapped from the cask, good range of reasonably priced food inc speciality pies and popular chocolate canary pudding, friendly staff; piped music; tables in garden, quiet village *(Simon and Amanda Southwell, Pat and Richard Tazewell, E D Bailey)*
☆ Tolldown [under a mile from M4 junction 18 – A46 towards Bath; ST7577], *Crown*: Surprisingly unspoilt off-motorway pub with usual food inc good steaks with fresh veg in heavy-beamed stripped stone bar, no-smoking area, well kept Wadworths, woodburner, quick friendly service; dominoes, darts and fruit machine, piped music, good garden with play area; no dogs (friendly cat), children in eating area and restaurant; bedrooms *(Philip Coward, Ian and Nita Cooper, LYM)*
☆ Tormarton [handy for M4 junction 18, signed off A46 N; ST7678], *Portcullis*: Good atmosphere, beams and stonework, quick friendly service, generous interesting food from filled baguettes up inc vegetarian and good range of fish dishes, good range of Hartington and other real ales, log fire (sometimes two), attractive panelled dining room; piped music may be rather loud; tables in garden, quiet village; bedrooms *(Jeff Davies, Ian and Nita Cooper, Barry and Anne, Dick Mattick, Pete and Rosie Flower, Meg and Colin Hamilton, Jeff Davies)*
Tormarton, *Compass*: Very extended off-motorway hotel with choice of rooms inc cosy local-feeling bar open all day for wide choice of food, pleasant conservatory, well kept ales inc Archers and Smiles, friendly staff, rather pricey restaurant; children welcome in eating areas, comfortable bedrooms *(Ian and Nita Cooper, LYM)*
☆ Uley [The Street; ST7898], *Old Crown*: Welcoming prettily placed village local with long narrow lounge, good value standard food inc children's, well kept Boddingtons, Hook Norton Best, Uley Bitter and Old Spot (the brewer is a regular) and guest beers, attractive garden; dogs welcome, service may slow when busy; darts and fruit machine, small pool room up spiral stairs, unobtrusive piped music; bedrooms good value with super breakfast, good base for walks *(Tom Potts, Emma Hayes, Joan and Michel Hooper-Immins)*
☆ Upton Cheyney [Brewery Hill; signposted off A431 at Bitton; ST6969], *Upton Inn*: Clean, plush and spacious, with wide choice of good generous reasonably priced home-cooked bar food inc vegetarian, attractive red-decor restaurant, well kept Bass, Smiles and Wadworths 6X, decent wine and coffee, prompt friendly service; delightful

surroundings, lovely Avon Valley views
(*Graham Fogelman, Roy Storm, Andrew
Rogers, Amanda Milsom*)

Viney Hill [off A48 Blakeney—Lydney;
SO6606], *New Inn*: Wide views over Forest
of Dean, Spanish manager, food from tapas to
full meals, well kept real ales, very friendly
atmosphere, comfortably refurbished lounge,
restaurant, pool room; children very welcome,
downstairs disco, some live music (*Chris
Cripps*)

☆ Westbury on Severn [Bell Lane (A48
Gloucester—Chepstow); SO7114], *Red Lion*:
Tiled and timbered pub with comfortable
small front bar and big dining room, old
pews, good genuine interesting food, well
kept ales inc Fullers London Pride and Smiles,
decent wine, very friendly staff, coal stove;
next to churchyard by footpath to Severn,
handy for Westbury Court gardens (NT) (*Mrs
C Watkinson, Dr and Mrs B Baker, Neil and
Anita Christopher, S H Godsell*)

☆ Westonbirt [A433 SW of Tetbury – OS Sheet
162 map ref 863904; ST8690], *Hare &
Hounds*: Well run old-fashioned hotel bar,
comfortable and relaxed, with decent
reasonably priced lunches inc salad bar and
good cheap rolls, John Smiths, Wadworths
IPA and 6X, quick helpful service, pleasant
gardens; handy for Arboretum; limited space
for families; bedrooms (*Dr Ian Crichton*)

Whitminster [A38 1½ miles N of M5 junction
13; SO7708], *Old Forge*: Simple small beamed
pub with welcoming staff, good choice of
beers and wines, food in bar and small
restaurant; children welcome (*H F C Barclay*)

☆ Willersey [nr Broadway – OS Sheet 150 map
ref 106396; SP1039], *Bell*: Civilised 14th-c
golden stone dining pub, comfortable and
spotless, with good interesting food, not
cheap, from well presented sandwiches up;
Whitbreads-related ales and Wadworths 6X,
efficient service; no dogs; overlooks delightful

village's green and duck pond, lots of tables in
big garden (*Moira and John Cole, George
Atkinson*)

☆ Winchcombe [Abbey Terr; SP0228],
Plaisterers Arms: Split-level 18th-c pub with
stripped stonework, beams, good generous
cheapish food inc vegetarian, children's and
good puddings, prompt cheerful service, well
kept Tetleys, Wadworths and local Goffs
Jouster and White Knight, open fire, plenty of
seating inc comfortably worn settles, copper,
brass and old tools, dim-lit lower back area,
dining area, lots of steps; play area in
attractive garden, long and narrow;
comfortable bedrooms (*Neil and Anita
Christopher, C and J Roe, Dr I H Maine,
Michael and Hazel Lyons, DAV, George
Atkinson*)

Winchcombe [High St], *Old Corner
Cupboard*: Quietly refurbished pub at top of
attractive village, with beams, stripped stone
and good inglenook log fire, attractive small
back garden; well kept real ales, good bar
food inc modishly crunchy veg, affable staff,
attractive old English sheepdog; piped music
may be loud; bedrooms in self-contained wing
(*D G Clarke, Alan and Paula McCully; more
reports on new regime please*)

Winterbourne [High St, nr M4 junction 19;
ST6580], *Swan*: Interesting variety of well
kept guest beers (*Dennis Heatley*)

Woodchester [Church Rd, North
Woodchester; SO8302], *Royal Oak*: Small
cosy local, good value standard food; quiet
and friendly (*Cherry Ann Knott*)

☆ Woodmancote [Stockwell Lane; SO9727],
Apple Tree: Wide choice of good popular
food in roomy local with cheerful courteous
staff, Bass, Wadworths and Whitbreads-
related ales, decent wines, restaurant; small
children looked after well; garden – fine
views, secluded setting at foot of hill (*Mr and
Mrs J Brown*)

Children welcome means the pubs says it lets children inside without any
special restriction. If it allows them in, but to restricted areas such as an eating
area or family room, we specify this. Places with separate restaurants usually
let children use them, hotels usually let them into public areas such as lounges.
Some pubs impose an evening time limit – let us know if you find this.

Hampshire

The Wykeham Arms in Winchester deserves special praise for staying right
on the crest of a wave for some years now – an exceptional pub that is doing
very well all round, with most enjoyable food. Other Hampshire pubs
currently generating a lot of enthusiasm include the Milbury's at Beauworth
(good food in a happy atmosphere), the Sun at Bentworth (good food, lots of
character), the Jolly Sailor in its delightful waterside spot at Bursledon (food
all day), the Flower Pots at Cheriton (this fine pub gains a Star Award this
year), the Fleur de Lys at Pilley (excellent under its current licensee, gaining
both a Food Award and a Beer Award this year), and the Still & West right
on the water in Portsmouth (an excellent showing from what could be just
another chain pub). This year we have had to say goodbye to Jack
Eddleston, the Lancashireman who made the White Horse above Petersfield
many people's favourite unspoilt country pub; it's in good hands since his
retirement, though, and the new people have not changed anything that
matters. A warm welcome to some attractive new entries: the simple but
most enjoyable Hawkley Inn at Hawkley (really good country cooking), the
Plough at Longparish (particularly good fish in this friendly dining pub), the
White Lion at Soberton (an attractive village pub run well by its current
licensees), the Fishermans Rest at Titchfield (particularly praiseworthy for a
chain pub) and the White Lion at Wherwell (a most enjoyable honest village
pub). Hampshire scores with a lot of genuine home cooking, both among the
main entries and in the Lucky Dip section at the end of the chapter. For a
really rewarding meal out, pubs that would go to the top of our current
shortlist here are the idiosyncratic Hobler at Battramsley, the Milbury's at
Beauworth, the Sun at Bentworth, the Red Lion at Boldre, the White Hart at
Cadnam (though you may have to book), the simple yet very civilised Dever
Arms at Micheldever, the Fleur de Lys at Pilley, the friendly Rose & Thistle
at Rockbourne, the Vine in Stockbridge (the new licensee is doing well here)
and the Wykeham Arms in Winchester. From among these we select the
Fleur de Lys at Pilley as Hampshire's Dining Pub of the Year. In the Lucky
Dip section, pubs to note particularly (most of them inspected and vouched
for by us, though for a variety of qualities, not necessarily food) include the
Three Tuns at Bransgore, White Buck at Burley, Horse & Jockey at
Curbridge, Chairmakers Arms at Denmead, Hampshire Bowman at
Dundridge, Turf Cutters Arms at East Boldre, George at East Meon, Star at
East Tytherley, Royal Oak at Fritham, Osborne View at Hill Head, Trout at
Itchen Abbas, Trusty Servant at Minstead, Ship at Owslebury, Good Intent
in Petersfield, Fish at Ringwood, Filly at Setley, Plough at Sparsholt, Jekyll &
Hyde at Turgis Green, George at Vernham Dean and Eclipse in Winchester;
there's a good choice both in this town and in Lymington. Prices are
generally higher than the national average here: expect to pay at least 10p
over the odds for a drink. However, you can find real bargains if you know
where to look. We found huge savings to be made at the Flower Pots at

Cheriton, which brews its own beer (and is now supplying some other local pubs), and the Dever Arms at Micheldever also had surprisingly cheap beer. We found pubs tied to Gales (based in Horndean) and Eldridge Pope (from Dorset) rather cheaper than most here, but those tied to Badger (also Dorset) were if anything more expensive – as were those getting their beers from the national breweries.

ALRESFORD SU5832 Map 2

Horse & Groom

Broad St; town signposted from new A31 bypass

Particularly popular on Alresford's Thursday market day, the open plan bar here has a pleasantly secluded feel thanks to its rambling nooks and crannies. There are neat settles and windsor chairs, black beams and timbered walls partly stripped to brickwork, old local photographs, and shelves of earthenware jugs and bottles. Perhaps the nicest place to sit is at the tables in the three bow windows on the right, looking out over the broad street. Bar food includes sandwiches, baked potatoes (from £3.95), warm salads (£4.25), winter liver and bacon (£4.75), steak and kidney pie (£5.25), and steaks (from £7.95). Well kept Bass, Boddingtons, Fremlins, Marstons Pedigree, Whitbreads Castle Eden and Strong Country, and maybe a guest or two on handpump, kept under light blanket pressure; coal-effect gas fire, unobtrusive piped music. Service can slow down at busy periods. *(Recommended by J Sheldon, Ann and Colin Hunt, Pete Yearsley, John Sanders, John and Joan Nash, Mr and Mrs R J Foreman, MCG, Caroline Kenyon, Canon Kenneth Wills, KCW)*

Whitbreads ~ Lease: Robin and Kate Howard ~ Real ale ~ Meals and snacks ~ (01962) 734809 ~ Children welcome ~ Open 11-11; maybe 11-3, 6-11 in winter

BATTRAMSLEY SZ3099 Map 2

Hobler

A337 a couple of miles S of Brockenhurst; OS Sheet 196 map reference 307990

The atmosphere here owes a lot to the landlord's idosyncratic sense of humour, and if you're in tune with that then you should enjoy yourself very much indeed. A particular draw is the above average bar food, which has won several awards in recent months; meat is especially well looked after – the landlord is also the local butcher. The weekly changing menu usually has things like home-made soup (£2.50), ploughman's (£3.95), steak and kidney pie (£4.95), stir fried vegetable salad with edam cheese, mangetout and mango (£6.95, or £8.95 with warm chicken), New Zealand green-lipped mussels topped with smoked bacon and cheese (£8.95), half roasted duck with alcoholic orange sauce (£10.95), fillet steak en croûte (£11.95), and their popular 'Hot Rocks', a hot stone on a plate upon which you cook your own meat; big helpings. They recommend booking in the evening, and even at lunchtime it's worth arriving early, as tables soon fill up. The black-beamed bar – divided by the massive stub of an ancient wall – has a very relaxed feel, and is furnished with pews, little dining chairs and a comfortable bow-window seat. Guns, china, New-Forest saws, the odd big engraving, and a growing collection of customer photographs decorate the walls, some of which are stripped back to timbered brick; the cosy area on the black-panelled and full of books. Well kept Bass, Flowers Original, Wadworths 6X and guest beers from small local breweries on handpump, a good range of malt whiskies (over 75) and country wines. In summer a spacious forest-edge lawn has a summer bar, a huge timber climbing fort in the very good play area, and picnic tables, as well as a paddock with ponies, pigs, donkeys, a peacock and hens. Note children aren't allowed inside. *(Recommended by Dr and Mrs A K Clarke, M Joyner, Brian Hall, Lynn Sharpless, Bob Eardley, D Marsh, C A Hall)*

Whitbreads ~ Licensee Pip Steven ~ Real ale ~ Meals and snacks (till 10) ~ (01590) 623291 ~ Live jazz three Tues eves a month, blues the other ~ Open 10.30-2.30, 6-11

BEAUWORTH SU5624 Map 2
Milbury's 🍺

Turn off A272 Winchester/Petersfield at Beauworth ¾. Bishops Waltham 6 signpost, then continue straight on past village

A great feeling of age seeps through this popular place, thanks mainly to its sturdy beams and panelling, stripped masonry, interesting old furnishings, and massive open fireplaces (with good winter log fires). There's a 600-year-old well cut nearly 300 feet into the chalk; the massive treadwheel beside it used to be worked by a donkey. Well kept Courage Directors, Hampshire King Alfred and Pendragon, and a beer named for the pub on handpump, Addlestones cider, and full range of country wines. Tasty generously served bar food includes home-made soup (£2.25), spare ribs (£3.25), filled baguettes or jacket potatoes (£4.20), chicken tikka or stuffed vegetarian pancake (£4.95), beef and Guinness pie (£5.50), delicious grilled salmon fillet (£5.95), steaks (from £7.95), puddings (£2.45), children's dishes (£2.95), and Sunday brunch (from £3.90). Service is friendly, efficient and cheerful, but slows down at busy periods and can stop promptly; best to book at weekends. There may be two fluffy cats and a big dog; darts, fruit machine, skittle alley. Surrounded by a Bronze Age cemetery – the Mill Barrow, hence the name – the pub has fine views from the garden, and good walks nearby. *(Recommended by Susan and John Douglas, John Sanders, A R and B E Sayer, J Sheldon, Jane Warren, Andy Jones, Martin and Karen Wake, Dave Braisted, Margaret and Nigel Dennis, Lynn Sharpless, Bob Eardley, W George Preston, John and Fiona McDougal, G S Stoney, T Roger Lamblee, J S M Sheldon, Clive Gilbert, N Matthews, JKW, N E Bushby, Miss W E Atkins, M J D Inskip, Canon Kenneth Wills)*

Free house ~ Licensees Jan and Lenny Larden ~ Real ale ~ Meals and snacks (till 10) ~ Restaurant ~ (01962) 771248 ~ Children in eating area of bar and skittle alley ~ Open 11-2.30, 6-11; all day weekends ~ Bedrooms: £22.50/£38.50

BENTLEY SU7844 Map 2
Bull

A31 Farnham—Alton, E of village and accessible from both directions at W end of dual carriageway Farnham bypass

There's a very pleasant relaxed and civilised feel to this little tiled white pub, well placed for woodland walks. The low-beamed, traditionally furnished rooms have plenty of interesting local prints, pictures and photographs on the walls, especially in the snug left-hand room, which also has a dimly lit back alcove with a tapestried pew built around a nice mahogany table, and a log-effect gas fire in a big old fireplace. The restaurant area has several comical prewar Bonzo prints. Good well presented bar food includes sandwiches and ploughman's, and changing daily specials like Thai beef (£8.25), home-made steak and kidney pudding (£8.65), and fresh fish like crab or lobster (around £10.25). Courage Best, Fullers London Pride and Gales HSB on handpump, various wines, and pimms in summer; darts, fruit machine, piped music. Plenty of pretty summer flowering tubs and hanging baskets outside, and tables on the side terrace, by a fairy-lit wendy house on stilts. *(Recommended by James Macrae, Beryl and Bill Farmer, T Roger Lamble, P J Caunt, D Marsh, Clive Gilbert, Stephen Teakle; more reports please)*

Courage ~ Lease: Bill Thompson ~ Real ale ~ Meals and snacks (till 10) ~ Restaurant ~ (01420) 22156 ~ Children in eating area of bar and restaurant ~ Jazz Sun lunchtime ~ Open 11-11; 12-10.30 Sun

---

It's very helpful if you let us know up-to-date food prices when you report on pubs.

BENTWORTH SU6740 Map 2

Sun 🍽 🍺

Sun Hill; from the A339 coming from Alton the first turning takes you there direct; or in
village follow Shalden 2¼, Alton 4¼ signpost

The very good imaginative bar food is one of the major draws to this unspoilt old
cottage, but plenty of people come for the beers and the atmosphere too. The two tiny
communicating rooms are traditional and old-fashioned, with open fires in the big
fireplaces, a mix of seating that takes in high-backed antique settles, pews and
schoolroom chairs, olde-worlde prints and blacksmith's tools on the walls, and bare
boards and scrubbed deal tables on the left; lots of fresh flowers dotted around and
newspapers and interior magazines to read. An arch leads to a brick-floored room
with another open fire and hanging baskets; it's the kind of place that stays deliciously
cool on a hot day. As well as sandwiches (from £1.90; not Friday or Saturday
evenings), the well-prepared food includes soups like asparagus or cauliflower and
mushroom (£2.20), ploughman's (£3.50), filled baked potatoes (from £4), particularly
good cumberland sausage with onion gravy (£4.50), spinach roulade with bacon and
cream cheese (£5), lentil crumble (£5.50), lamb casserole with port and redcurrants,
sweet and sour chicken or pies such as steak and kidney (£6.50), pork stroganoff or
fresh salmon (£7.50), and puddings like pear, honey and almond tart or hazelnut
meringue with apricot sauce (£2.50). Booking is recommended, and pretty much
essential at weekends. Well kept Courage Best, Badger Best, Cheriton Pots Ale,
Marstons Pedigree, Ringwood Best, Ruddles Best, Wadworths 6X, Worldham Old
Dray, and a beer named after the pub (brewed by Hampshire) on handpump; range
of country wines; dominoes. Service is quick and friendly – as are the two dogs,
Honey and Ruddles. Several picnic tables under cocktail parasols look over the quiet
lane. *(Recommended by Peter and Michele Rayment, Dr M I Crichton, Colin and Ann Hunt,
Jerry and Alison Oakes, Malcolm Taylor, Lynn Sharpless, Bob Eardley, Derek and Margaret
Underwood, Andrew Scarr, Margaret Dyke, A G Drake, Joan and Andrew Life, Dr Ronald
Church, Joy and Paul Rundell, Roger Walker, Margaret Dyke)*

*Free house ~ Licensees Richard and Jan Beaumont ~ Real ale ~ Meals and snacks
(not Sun evening Nov-Feb) ~ (01420) 562338 ~ Children allowed in garden
room, no under 10s after 8pm ~ Occasional Morris dancers (26 Dec and odd Fri
nights in summer) ~ Open 12-3, 6-11; closed Sun evening Nov-Mar and 25 Dec*

BOLDRE SZ3298 Map 2

Red Lion ★ 🍽 ♀

Village signposted from A337 N of Lymington

Some readers have been coming here for more than 30 years now, since the days
when the current landlord's father held the licence, and say that standards have been
maintained at the same high level for just about all that time. Nicely set on the edge
of the New Forest, it's bigger inside than it looks, the four warmly atmospheric
black-beamed rooms filled with heavy urns, platters, needlework, rural landscapes,
and so forth, taking in farm tools, heavy-horse harness, needlework, gin traps and
even ferocious-looking man traps along the way; the central room with its profusion
of chamber-pots is no smoking. An end room has pews, wheelback chairs and
tapestried stools, and a dainty collection of old bottles and glasses in the window by
the counter. The very popular bar food changes every week but might include home-
made soup (£2.50), good sandwiches and quite a few ploughman's, avocado pear
with cottage cheese and walnuts (£4.20), unusual and well liked basket meals
ranging from sausages to duck with wine-soaked orange slices (from £4.90; the duck
is £8.90), stuffed aubergine (£5.90), fillet of fresh cod provençale (£6.90), chicken
breast in a minted cream sauce (£7.20), cold home-cooked gammon with poached
eggs or grilled turkey fillet on asparagus sauce topped with sweetcorn (£7.80), daily
specials such as pheasant in red wine or jugged hare (£7.80), and good puddings like
amaretti torte or steamed ginger sponge (£3.20); some meals can seem slightly pricier
than average, but most people agree they're worth any extra. Do get there early,

some days tables go within minutes. Well kept Eldridge Pope Dorchester, Hardy Country and Royal Oak on handpump, a range of malt whiskies, and up to 20 wines by the glass; prompt and friendly service. In summer, the flowering tubs and hanging baskets are lovely and there's a cart festooned with colour near the car park. No children inside. A slight refurbishment should be under way by the time this edition is published. *(Recommended by Vann and Terry Prime, Derek and Margaret Underwood, Jenny and Michael Back, John and Phyllis Maloney, J and D Tapper, W F C Phillips, Dr and Mrs A K Clarke, Lynn Sharpless, Bob Eardley, Phyl and Jack Street, C A Hall, Joan and Michel Hooper-Immins, Mr and Mrs M F Norton, A Y Drummond, D Marsh, R H Rowley, Kim Redling, Tom Gondris, Nigel Flook, Betsy Brown)*

Eldridge Pope ~ Lease: John and Penny Bicknell ~ Real ale ~ Meals and snacks (11.30-2.30, 6.30-10) ~ Restaurant ~ (01590) 673177 ~ Open 11-3, 6-11; cl 25 Dec

BRAMDEAN SU6128 Map 2

Fox ♀

A272 Winchester—Petersfield

A popular choice for a relaxed meal, this white 17th-c weather-boarded dining pub is the kind of place where they don't think twice about specially opening a bottle from the extensive wine list if you're not sure which to choose. Much modernised and neatly cared for, the open-plan bar has black beams, tall stools with proper backrests around the L-shaped counter, and comfortably cushioned wall pews and wheelback chairs; the fox motif shows in a big painting over the fireplace, and on much of the decorative china. At least one area is no smoking. Favourite lunchtime dishes include sandwiches (from £2.25; good cold meat), good soup (£2.95), a choice of ploughman's (£4.25), locally smoked trout (£4.50), king prawns with mayonnaise or mussels and prawns in sherry and garlic butter (£5.95), cauliflower cheese with grilled bacon (£6.50), battered cod (£6.95), beef stroganoff (£8.50), and plenty of fresh fish such as skate, halibut, lobster or salmon; evening meals like chicken breast with asparagus in boursin sauce (£10.95), pork fillet with wild mushrooms in cream and brandy sauce (£11.95), and whole grilled dover sole (£13.95). Well kept Marstons Bitter and Pedigree on handpump; piped music. At the back of the building is a walled-in terraced area, and a spacious lawn spreading among the fruit trees, with a really good play area – trampoline as well as swings and a see-saw. No children inside. *(Recommended by Mr and Mrs Cody, John Sanders, Dennis Stevens, Betty Laker, Dave Braisted, Clive Gilbert, J H Bell, T Roger Lamble, Canon Kenneth Wills, Lynn Sharpless, Bob Eardley)*

Marstons ~ Tenants Jane and Ian Inder ~ Real ale ~ Meals and snacks (not 26 Dec) ~ (01962) 771363 ~ Open 10.30-3, 6-11; closed 25 Dec and evening 26 Dec

BURITON SU7420 Map 2

Five Bells

Village signposted off A3 S of Petersfield

An attractive and genuinely welcoming unpretentious country local, its low-beamed lounge on the left dominated by a big log fire. There are period photographs on the partly stripped brick walls in here, as well as a rather worn turkey carpet on oak parquet; the public side has some ancient stripped masonry, a woodburning stove, and old-fashioned tables. An end alcove with cushioned pews and old fishing prints has board games such as Scrabble (sensibly issued with a referee dictionary). Popular bar food includes lunchtime filled baguettes (£2.75) and ploughman's (£3.75), soup (£2.50), baked brie with toast and preserve (£3.75), moules marinières (£4.75), Indonesian pork or vegetarian dishes like three cheese and asparagus charlotte or nut roast with red wine and mushroom sauce (£5.95), steak and kidney pie or liver and bacon casserole (£6.95), fresh fish like grilled red snapper or swordfish in garlic butter (£7.95), seasonal game such as jugged hare (£8.95) or partridge stuffed with bacon, walnut and stilton (£9.95), and home-made puddings (£2.75). Well kept

Ballards Best, Eldridge Pope Hardy, Friary Meux Best, Ind Coope Burton, Ringwood Old Thumper, and Tetleys on handpump, and decent wines. Prompt, friendly service. Darts, dominoes, cribbage, trivia, piped music. There are a few tables on sheltered terraces just outside, with many more on an informal lawn stretching back above the pub. A couple of readers experienced slight hiccups in the normally flawless cooking last summer, but considering the number of people that can pass through here on the way to the ferry at Portsmouth (especially at weekends) it's amazing they manage to keep standards so consistently high. The stables have been converted into self-catering cottages. The village is pretty, with its duck pond. *(Recommended by Lynn Sharpless, Bob Eardley, Pete Yearsley, Mrs S Peregrine, Dennis Stevens, Martin and Karen Wake, John and Joy Winterbottom, Ann and Colin Hunt, Mike Fitzgerald, Mrs Jane Basso, G R Sharman, JEB, Clive Gilbert, Paula Williams)*

Free house ~ Licensee John Ligertwood ~ Real ale ~ Meals and snacks (till 10) ~ Restaurant (not Sun evening) ~ (01730) 263584 ~ Children over 14 in restaurant ~ Jazz last Mon in month, folk, country or blues each Weds, Bluegrass last Sun in month ~ Open 11-2.30(3 Fri and Sat) 5.30-11 ~ Self-catering cottage from £35S

BURSLEDON SU4809 Map 2
Jolly Sailor

2 miles from M27 junction 8; follow B3397 towards Hamble, then A27 towards Sarisbury, then just before going under railway bridge turn right towards Bursledon Station; it's best to park round here and walk as the lane up from the station is now closed to cars

Yachtsmen will be delighted to know that this charmingly unspoilt pub started opening all day just as we went to press, with meals served throughout the day too. Several readers love the delightfully cosy atmosphere on a winter evening, but we still prefer those balmy days sitting out at the tables under the big yew tree or on the wooden jetty, watching all the goings on in the rather pretty harbour. The nautical theme continues inside, with ship pictures, nets and shells in the airy front bar, as well as windsor chairs and settles on its floorboards. The atmospheric beamed and flagstoned back bar, with pews and settles by its huge fireplace, is a fair bit older. It can seem crowded, but rarely feels touristy. A wide range of generously served bar food includes soup (£2), sandwiches (£2.50), ploughman's (£4.25), devilled whitebait (£3.95), warm lentil salad or fish and tomato bake (£5.60), several vegetarian dishes like macaroni and mushroom loaf or cabbage and nut korma (£5.75), beef and mushroom pie (£5.80), lamb biryani (£5.95) and chicken provençale (£6.95); friendly efficient service. The restaurant is no smoking. Well kept Badger Best and Tanglefoot and Wadworths 6X on handpump, and country wines; fruit machine and piped music. The path down to the pub (and of course back up again) from the lane is steep. *(Recommended by N S Smith, Lynn Sharpless, Bob Eardley, David Carr, Clive Gilbert, John Knighton, Chris and Martin Taylor, D Maplethorpe, B Helliwell, Ann and Colin Hunt, Jack and Philip Paxton, C A Hall, Ian Phillips, Jenny and Brian Seller)*

Badger ~ Managers Stephen and Kathryn Housley ~ Real ale ~ Meals and snacks (12-9.30) ~ Restaurant ~ (01703) 405557 ~ Children in eating area and restaurant ~ Open 11-11;12-10.30 Sun; closed 25 Dec

CADNAM SU2913 Map 2
White Hart

½ mile from M27 junction 1; A336 towards village, pub off village roundabout

The ambitious food here is now so highly regarded that you'll probably have to book ahead even on a chilly winter evening. The pub has been transformed in the last couple of years by the Emberley family, who previously ran a couple of other New Forest main entries with great success; several readers feel the standards here are even higher. The wide choice of good attractively presented food includes sandwiches, soup (£3.25), chicken and spring onion satay (£4.75), home-cured gravadlax or black pudding, bacon and poached egg salad (£5.25), stuffed cabbage in beetroot sauce or a daily pasta or curry (£7.25), chicken fillets in garlic sauce (£8.25), breast of duck with fresh victoria plum sauce (£9.75), half a dozen imaginative daily specials like john dory with olives, sundried tomatoes and capers, and puddings like brioche bread and butter pudding; sauces are delicious, and they do some splendid meals around Christmas. Extensive renovations to the building have created a spacious multi-level dining lounge, with good solid furnishings, soft lighting, country prints and appropriate New Forest pictures and mementoes; it's a place to come to for a relaxing meal rather than just a quick snack. Well kept Courage Best, Flowers Original, King and Barnes Sussex, Morlands Old Speckled Hen and Wadworths 6X on handpump, farm ciders, decent wines, no games machines; efficient service even when it's busy. There are picnic tables under cocktail parasols outside. *(Recommended by Kim Maidment, Philip Vernon, Mrs J A Blanks, Lynn Sharpless, Bob Eardley, Lyn and Simon Gretton, Joan and Dudley Payne, John Sanders, N E Bushby, Miss W E Atkins, F J Willy, Mark and Heather Williamson)*

Free house ~ Licensees Nick and Sue Emberley ~ Real ale ~ Meals and snacks ~ (01703) 812277 ~ Children welcome ~ Open 11-2.30, 6-11 (10.30 winter)

CHALTON SU7315 Map 2

Red Lion ♀

Village signposted E of A3 Petersfield—Horndean

Long before this lovely thatched house won prizes for its gardens and from local newspapers, it was able to claim a title none of its competitors can ever hope to beat – it's the oldest pub in Hampshire, first licensed in 1503, but said to date back as far as 1150. The setting is lovely, beneath the village church and overlooking the South Downs, so don't expect to have its charms all to yourself. Inside the most characterful part is the heavy-beamed and panelled bar, with high-backed traditional settles and elm tables and an ancient inglenook fireplace with a frieze of burnished threepenny bits set into its mantelbeam. Popular bar food includes sandwiches (from £2.50), filled baked potatoes (from £3.65), ploughman's (£3.95) and daily specials such as chicken normande with bacon, celery, apples and cream, marinated venison with redcurrants or pot roasted hare (£6.20), grilled red snapper with chive butter (£6.95), and fresh sea bass in white wine and cucumber sauce (£7.50); families are usually directed to a modern no-smoking dining extension. Gales BBB, Best, HSB, Winter Brew, and a guest beer on handpump, a dozen or so wines by the glass, country wines, and over 50 malt whiskies; efficient service. Fruit machine, piped music, and they run cricket and football teams. Popular with walkers and riders, the pub is fairly close to the extensive Queen Elizabeth Country Park and about half a mile down the lane from a growing Iron Age farm and settlement; it's only about 20 minutes to the car ferry too. *(Recommended by Drs R and M Woodford, Pete Yearsley, John Sanders, Phyl and Jack Street, Ann and Colin Hunt, D Maplethorpe, B Helliwell, Dennis Stevens, Wendy Arnold, T Roger Lamble, Clive Gilbert)*

Gales ~ Managers Mick and Mary McGee ~ Real ale ~ Meals and snacks (not Sun evening) ~ (01705) 592246 ~ Children in family dining room ~ Open 11-3, 6-11; closed 25 Dec evening

CHERITON SU5828 Map 2

Flower Pots ★ ▥

Pub just off B3046 (main village road) towards Beauworth and Winchester; OS Sheet 185 map reference 581282

Last year the Pots Ale produced in the little brewery at this bustling village local won the Best Bitter prize at CAMRA's Great British Beer Festival. The pub has been winning plenty of plaudits from our readers too, with a constant stream of glowing reports dropping through our letterbox in recent months. And what's particularly nice is that it's not the sort of place likely to be affected by all this acclaim – the hard-working licensees will just carry on in the same unfussy style they've been demonstrating for over 25 years. As well as the Pots, their Cheriton Brewhouse also produces Cheriton Best and Diggers Gold, and all three are very well priced and full of flavour; they may let you look at the brewery. The two little rooms both have a really pleasant atmosphere, and the one on the left feels almost like someone's front room, with pictures of hounds and ploughmen on its striped wallpaper, bunches of flowers, and a horse and foal and other ornaments on the mantelpiece over a small log fire; it can get smoky in here. Behind the servery there's disused copper filtering equipment, and lots of hanging gin traps, drag-hooks, scaleyards and other ironwork. Good value straightforward bar food includes sandwiches (from £1.50, toasted from £1.80), filled jacket potatoes (from £2.60), ploughman's (from £3), chilli (£3.60) and beef stew (£3.80); efficient service. Darts in the neat plain public bar (where there's a covered well), also cribbage, shove-ha'penny and dominoes; the family room has a TV, board games and colouring books. There are old-fashioned seats on the pretty front and back lawns – very useful in fine weather as they can quickly fill up inside; they sometimes have Morris dancers out here in summer. Near the site of one of the final battles of the Civil War, the pub once belonged to the retired head gardener of nearby Avington Park, which explains the unusual name. *(Recommended by Kevin and Katharine Cripps, Andy Jones, Joone Fairweather, James Macrae, M L and G Clarke, G S Stoney, Marjorie and David Lamb, John and Joy Winterbottom, Lynn Sharpless, Bob Eardley, Ron Shelton, Ann and Colin Hunt, Bruce Bird, John and Joan Nash, Derek and Sylvia Stephenson, Derek Patey, A R and B E Sayer, Simon Collett-Jones, Canon Kenneth Wills, D A Forsyth, Richard Houghton, Dono and Carol Leaman, Jack and Philip Paxton, Martin and Karen Wake, John and Chris Simpson, Nigel Clifton, Drs Ben and Caroline Maxwell)*

Own brew ~ Licensees Patricia and Joanna Bartlett ~ Real ale ~ Meals and snacks (not Sun evening) ~ (01962) 771318 ~ Children in family room ~ Open 12-2.30, 6-11 ~ Bedrooms: £26B/£43.50B

CRAWLEY SU4234 Map 2

Fox & Hounds

Village signposted from A272 Winchester—Stockbridge and B3420 Winchester—Andover

Even amongst so many other fine houses this striking building stands out – each timbered upper storey successively juts further out, with lots of pegged structural timbers in the neat brickwork (especially around the latticed windows), and elaborately carved steep gable-ends. The scrupulous workmanship continues inside, with oak parquet, latticed windows, and an elegant black timber arch in the small lounge, and neatly panelled upholstered wall benches around the tables of the beamed main bar. There are fires in both spotlessly maintained rooms – real logs in the lounge, log-effect gas in the other. Written up on blackboards, the changing range of good, well presented bar food might include sandwiches (not Sunday), home-made soups (£2.50), mushrooms in garlic butter or home-made trout and smoked mackerel pâté (£3.95), mixed bean casserole or spicy cheese and lentil loaf with tangy tomato sauce (£6.25), home-made steak and kidney pie (£6.50), pork chop with cider and calvados (£6.75), fresh local trout with prawns and mushrooms flamed in brandy (£6.95), plenty of other very good fresh fish like grilled lemon sole or Dorset crab, and rump steak (£8.95); service is friendly and careful, though may slow down on busy Sundays. Well kept Gales BBB and Wadworths 6X on handpump. *(Recommended by Colin Laffan, DC, Prof A N Black, John and Phyllis Maloney, Mike and Heather Watson, Howard Allen, Phyl and Jack Street, Tim Espley, Roger Byrne, Philip and Trisha Ferris, Wayne Brindle)*

Free house ~ Licensees Doreen and Luis Sanz-Diez ~ Real ale ~ Meals and snacks ~ Restaurant (not Sun evening) ~ (01962) 776285 ~ Children in eating area of bar and in restaurant ~ Open 11.30-2.30(3 Sat), 6.30-11 ~ Bedrooms: £45B/£60B

DROXFORD SU6018 Map 2

White Horse

4 miles along A32 from Wickham

The licensee who did so much to develop the rather special atmosphere at this rambling 16th-c coaching inn retired earlier this year, but as the replacements are his own chef and barman things are carrying on in much the same fashion as before, and early indications suggest it's still well worth knowing. The atmospheric lounge bar is made up of a series of small intimate rooms with attractive furnishings, low beams, bow windows, alcoves and log fires, while the public bar is larger and more straightforward: cribbage, dominoes, pool, shove ha'penny, table football and occasionally loudish CD juke box. Well presented, tasty food includes good sandwiches (from £1.80; toasties 25p extra; hot crusty french sticks from £2.75), home-made soup (£2), green-lipped mussels (£3.25), ploughman's (from £3.50), Portuguese sardines in garlic butter (£4.25), vegetable curry (£4.95), gammon and egg (£5.65), a brace of locally smoked quail (£5.95), popular steak, mushroom and Guinness pie (£7.95), steaks (from £9.15), and puddings; children's menu (from £2.10). The restaurant is no smoking. Well kept Badger Tanglefoot, Charles Wells Bombardier, Exmoor Gold, Greene King Abbot, Hampshire Hog, Morlands Old Speckled Hen and Wadworths 6X on handpump, and country wines; prompt professional service. One of the cubicles in the gents' overlooks an illuminated well. There are tables in a secluded flower-filled courtyard comfortably sheltered by the building's back wings. *(Recommended by Lynn Sharpless, Bob Eardley, Ann and Colin Hunt, Phyl and Jack Street, Derek and Margaret Underwood, Mr and Mrs R J Foreman, Andrew Shore, John Sanders, N Matthews, Clarence Shettlesworth, Barry and Anne, Simon Collett-Jones, Sue Ridout, T W Fleckney, Ian Phillips)*

Free house ~ Lease: Paul Young, Darren Moore ~ Real ale ~ Meals and snacks (till 9.45) ~ Restaurant ~ (01489) 877490 ~ Children in family room and restaurant ~ Open 11-3, 6-11; closed 25 Dec ~ Bedrooms: £25(£40B)/£35(£50B)

DUMMER SU5846 Map 2

Queen

Half a mile from M3, junction 7; take Dummer slip road

A very useful retreat from the M3, with the very quiet village lane in front as complete a contrast in roads as you could imagine. Most people inside the tiled white cottage are here to eat, with a good choice of dishes like home-made soup (£2.50), sandwiches (from £2.95), a good range of filled baked potatoes (£3.95), cod in their own beer batter (£5.95 medium, £8.95 large), seven types of burger (from £6.50), lasagne (£6.95), steak and kidney pudding (£9.95), Scotch Angus steaks (from £11.95), daily specials, puddings, and roast Sunday lunch (from £6.95); notably cheery and friendly service. The bar is open-plan, but has a pleasantly alcovey feel, with a liberal use of timbered brick and plaster partition walls, as well as beams and joists and an open fire. There are built-in padded seats, cushioned spindleback chairs and stools around the tables on the dark blue patterned carpet, and pictures of queens, old photographs, small steeplechase prints and advertisements. Well kept Courage Best and Directors, Fullers London Pride and Marstons Pedigree on handpump; fruit machine in one corner, cribbage, and well reproduced pop music. Picnic tables under cocktail parasols on the terrace and in a neat little sheltered back garden. *(Recommended by Mr and Mrs D S Price, Phyl and Jack Street, B N F and M Parkin, KC, Guy Consterdine, Kevin and Tracey Stephens, Gary Roberts, Ann Stubbs)*

Courage ~ Tenants David and Sally Greenhalgh ~ Real ale ~ Meals and snacks (till 10) ~ Restaurant ~ (01256) 397367 ~ Children in eating area of bar and restaurant ~ Open 11-3.30, 5.30(6 Sat)-11

HAWKLEY SU7429 Map 2

Hawkley Inn

Pococks Lane; village signposted off B3006, first turning left after leaving its junction with A325 in Greatham; OS Sheet 186 map reference 746292

Tucked away in attractive countryside still strongly redolent of Edward Thomas's poetry, with plenty of interesting walks all around, this unpretentious pub will appeal strongly to anyone who has enjoyed our popular Sussex entry the Elsted Inn at Elsted. There's a simple airy decor in the opened-up bar and back dining room, with big pine tables, fresh or dried flowers, candles at night, and big posters and prints on the white walls. The atmosphere is warm and welcoming, with a good mixed bunch of customers; parts of the bar can get a bit smoky when it's busy, but there is a no-smoking area. Food which we or readers have particularly enjoyed here includes various types of ploughman's, mussels cooked with white wine and cream, ham and leek pancakes, a goat's cheese flan, and Sussex beef stew. Other promptly served home-made food includes rolls (from £2.50), ploughman's (from £3.75), mushroom and goat's cheese flan (£5.85), grilled black bream (£6.75) or paella (£8.25); puddings like Spanish orange and almond tart or summer pudding (£2.50). Helpings are generous, and service is friendly. Well kept Ballards and Cheriton Flower Pots and four guests like Hampshire Uncle Sam, Hogs Back Hop Garden Gold, Ringwood Fortyniner or Otter on handpump; the piped music raised no hackles. There are tables in the pleasant garden behind, and the pub is on the Hangers Way Path. *(Recommended by Ann and Colin Hunt, Sue Cubitt, JP, PP, Mike Fitzgerald, J O Jonkler, Martin and Karen Wake, Nigel Norman)*

Free house ~ E N Collins and A Stringer ~ Real ale ~ Meals and snacks (not Sun evening) ~ Restaurant ~ (01730) 827205 ~ Children welcome till 8pm ~ Occasional live entertainment in winter ~ Open 12-2.30(3 Sat), 6-11; cl 25 Dec evening

IBSLEY SU1509 Map 2
Old Beams

A338 Ringwood—Salisbury

Efficiency is the watchword of this much extended dining pub, which effortlessly handles the flow of diners that streams through its spacious rooms every lunchtime. From a very wide choice, popular and promptly served meals might include an appetising cold buffet (from £5.90) as well as sandwiches (from £2.40), curries (£5.10), braised oxtail (£5.80), venison in red wine, pork normandie or braised steak (all £6.90), duck with orange or pheasant in port wine (£7.50), char-grilled Scotch steaks (£9), and fresh fish such as dover sole (£11.65); they announce when food is ready over an intercom. Well kept Eldridge Pope Royal Oak, Gales HSB, Gibbs Mew Bishops Tipple, Ringwood Best and Old Thumper, Wadworths 6X, and maybe a guest beer on handpump, and country wines. The main room is divided by wooden panelling and a canopied log-effect gas fire, and there are lots of varnished wooden tables and country-kitchen chairs under the appropriately aged oak beams; the conservatory is popular. Part of the eating area and half the restaurant are no smoking. Fruit machine. *(Recommended by David N Ing, Chris and Margaret Southon, GWB, A Ellis, P Gillbe, Mr and Mrs B Hobden, P J Caunt, Howard Clutterbuck, Ian Phillips, Jack and Philip Paxton, Wayne Brindle, Stephen and Anna Oxley)*

Free house ~ Licensees R Major and C Newell ~ Real ale ~ Meals and snacks (till 10) ~ Restaurant (not Sun evening) ~ (01425) 473387 ~ Children in eating area, restaurant and family room ~ Open 11-3, 6-11

LANGSTONE SU7105 Map 2
Royal Oak

High Street; last turn left off A3023 (confusingly called A324 on some signs) before Hayling Island bridge

The new patio at this delightfully-positioned old pub is ideally placed for watching the goings-on in the adjacent harbour. In summer you'll usually find plenty of people outside soaking up the views and the sun, but a visit here in winter can be just as satisfying, when through the bow windows in the bar you can follow the afternoon sun as it slowly slips away over Hayling Island. The spacious and atmospheric flagstoned bar is simply furnished with windsor chairs around old wooden tables on the wooden parquet and ancient flagstones, and two open fires in winter. The emphasis with the food is increasingly on the daily changing blackboard menu, where the most popular features include moules marinières (£4.50), various pasta dishes (£5.50), a daily curry (£5.95), duck breast with cranberry and rosemary sauce (£9.50), plenty of locally caught fresh fish like lemon sole in hollandaise sauce (£7.50), and puddings like good apricot crumble; friendly, obliging service. Well kept Boddingtons, Flowers Original and Marstons Pedigree on handpump, Bulmer's cider, decent range of wines, and cappuccino machine; bar billiards, cribbage. At high tide swans come right up to here, much as they must have done in the days when it was a landing point for the 18th-c Langstone Gang, a notorious group of smugglers. The garden has a pets corner for children. *(Recommended by Chris and Margaret Southon, Ian Jones, Ian Phillips, Lynn Sharpless, Bob Eardley, David Carr, John Sanders, Colin and Ann Hunt, Christopher Perry)*

Whitbreads ~ Manager Stuart Warren ~ Real ale ~ Meals and snacks (12-9.30) ~ (01705) 483125 ~ Children in eating area of bar till 9.30 ~ Parking at all close may be very difficult ~ Open 11-11; 12-10.30 Sun; closed evening 25 Dec

LOCKS HEATH SU5006 Map 2

Jolly Farmer

2½ miles from M27 junction 9; A27 towards Bursledon, left into Locks Rd, at end T-junction right into Warsash Rd then left at hire shop into Fleet End Rd; OS Sheet 196 map reference 509062

A welcome sight amongst an area of largely modern development, this thriving white-painted inn has an attractively pubby feel, but is really a place where everyone has come to eat. The wide choice of quickly served good value bar food includes filled baps (from £1.95, steak £4.25), soup (£2.95), ploughman's or seafood sandwiches (from £3.25), spicy crisped vegetables (£4.25), home-baked ham and eggs or steak and kidney pie (£5.45) and specials such as moules marinières (£4.95), whole plaice or mixed meat salad (£5.95), ribeye steak (£6.95) and lobster (£16.95); a three-course Sunday lunch is £9.25. The small bar on the right and extensive series of softly lit rooms on the left have nice old scrubbed tables, cushioned oak pews and smaller chairs; their ochre walls and beams are hung with a veritable forest of country bric-a-brac, racing prints, Victorian engravings and so on, making for a very cosy feeling that's amplified by the coal-effect gas fires. One restaurant is no smoking. Well kept Boddingtons, Flowers Original and Gales HSB on handpump, country wines, several malt whiskies; silenced fruit machine, piped music. Neat friendly staff. There are tables under cocktail parasols on two sheltered terraces, one with a play area. *(Recommended by C H and P Stride, Phyl and Jack Street, D Maplethorpe, B Helliwell, Peter and Audrey Dowsett, M J Inskip, Colin and Ann Hunt, N Matthews)*

Free house ~ Licensees Martin and Cilla O'Grady ~ Real ale ~ Meals and snacks (till 10) ~ Two restaurants ~ (01489) 572500 ~ Children welcome ~ Open 10.30-3, 5-11 ~ Bedrooms: £36.50S/£48S

LONGPARISH SU4344 Map 2

Plough

B3048 – off A303 just E of Andover

It was something of a dream come true for the Dales when they took over the licence of this pretty creeper-covered village inn; they'd both lived in the village for most of their lives and tell us it had always been their ambition to run the Plough. The range of meals they offer is huge, with something of an emphasis on fresh local fish; dishes vary every day but typically include cod provençale (£5.95), sea bass, lobster, and their popular Cornish crab salad (£9.95), as well as sandwiches, lots of salads, and daily specials like wild boar sausages (£5.95), vegetable risotto (£7), and prawn balti (£7.95). Waitress service is fast, efficient and friendly. There is a small pubby part, and some hops around the cream-painted walls, but the feel of the place is quite restauranty; the open-plan bar is divided into smaller areas by a series of arches.

Boddingtons, Flowers Original, Hampshire King Alfreds and Wadworths 6X, and a range of country wines. Piped music, Sky TV. There are seats and tables on a side terrace, and maybe barbecues in the garden on summer evenings. *(Recommended by Jenny and Michael Back, John Evans, Carol and Brian Perrin, G Washington)*

Whitbreads ~ Lease: Pauline and Christopher Dale ~ Real ale ~ Meals and snacks ~ Restaurant ~ (01264) 720358 ~ Children in eating area of bar ~ Open 11-3.30, 6-11 ~ Bedrooms: £25/£40

MATTINGLEY SU7357 Map 2
Leather Bottle 🍺

3 miles from M3, junction 5; in Hook, turn right-and-left on to B3349 Reading Road (former A32)

Roaring log fires in inglenook fireplaces add to the cosy feel of this brick and tiled pub in winter, while in summer the wisteria, honeysuckle and roses both at the front and in the attractive tree-sheltered garden are quite a draw. The busy beamed main bar is friendly and relaxed, and has brocaded built-in wall seats, little curved low backed wooden chairs, some sabres on the cream wall, a ticking metal clock over one of the fireplaces, and a good local atmosphere. At the back is the characterful cottagey second bar with lots of black beams, an antique clock, country pictures on the walls (some stripped to brick), lantern lighting, sturdy inlaid tables with seats, and a red carpet on bare floorboards. Generously served bar food includes sandwiches (from £1.80, toasted ham, mushroom and egg £3.50, steak £4.75), soup (£2.30), ploughman's (from £3.95), good sausages (£5.50), ham off the bone with eggs and chips (£5.80), vegetable balti (£6.20), lasagne (£6.90), salmon, cod and mushroom pie (£7.20), steaks (from £12.50), and puddings like treacle tart (from £2.50). Well kept Courage Best and Directors and guest beers such as Badger Tanglefoot, Ringwood Old Thumper, and Wychwood Dogs Bollocks on handpump or tapped from the cask. Prompt friendly service; fruit machine. *(Recommended by Gordon, J Sheldon, Neville Kenyon, KC, Nigel Norman, Henry Winters, T Roger Lamble, Thomas Nott, TBB, Clive Gilbert)*

Courage ~ Lease: Richard and Pauline Moore ~ Real ale ~ Meals and snacks (till 10) ~ (01734) 326371 ~ Children in eating area of bar ~ Open 11-2.30, 6-11

MICHELDEVER SU5142 Map 2
Dever Arms 🍷 🍺

Village signposted off A33 N of Winchester

A good starting point for exploring the Dever Valley (there are lots of good walks nearby), this attractive country pub is a very civilised spot, with interesting food and excellent drinks. The calm and simply decorated bar has beams, chintzy curtains, heavy tables and good solid seats – a nice cushioned panelled oak settle and a couple of long dark pews as well as wheelback chairs; there is a woodburning stove at each end, and a fresh and attractive no-smoking area with lighter-coloured furniture opens off. Most of the generously served bar food changes from day to day, and as well as sandwiches and ploughman's (£4.25), might include soup (£2.25), chilli with salsa and sour cream or crêpe filled with mediterranean vegetables and chilli sauce (£4.50), liver, bacon and onion casserole (£4.95), poached whole trout with caper sauce or rabbit and herb casserole (£6.95), grilled gammon steak with tomato, herbs and melted mozzarella cheese (£7.50), chicken cacciatore (£8.95), and puddings (£3), with winter game. Well kept Badger Best and Tanglefoot, Dorset Best, Hopback Summer Lightning, and Pots Ale (from the Flower Pots at Cheriton) on handpump – the last of these is particularly well priced; choice of malt whiskies, interesting wines by the glass and bottle. Very good quietly friendly and attentive service; bar billiards, shove ha'penny and darts up at one end, well chosen and reproduced piped music. There are white cast-iron tables under cocktail parasols on a small sheltered back terrace, and some more widely spaced picnic tables and a play area on the edge of a big cricket green behind. *(Recommended by A J Stevens, John and Sherry Moate, Phyl and Jack Street, A W Dickinson, Mike Hayes, Joan and John Calvert, George Rodger, Mr and Mrs Hargreaves and others)*

Free house ~ Licensees Mike and Violet Penny ~ Real ale ~ Meals and snacks (not Sun evening) ~ Restaurant ~ (01962) 774339 ~ Children in eating area of bar and family room ~ Open 11.30-3, 6-11

OVINGTON SU5531 Map 2

Bush ♀

Village signposted from A31 on Winchester side of Alresford

Tucked away down a leafy lane, this charming and quietly upmarket little cottage has lots of seats in the garden behind running down to the River Itchen, and more on a tree-sheltered pergola dining terrace with a good-sized fountain pool. The setting is understandably popular on a sunny day, but we prefer visiting on chilly winter weekdays when the atmosphere is undisturbed by lots of people, and the low-ceilinged bar has a warmly cosy feel that immediately makes you feel at home. There's a roaring fire on one side with an antique solid fuel stove opposite, as well as cushioned high-backed settles, elm tables with pews and kitchen chairs, and masses of old pictures in heavy gilt frames on the green walls. Current favourites among the good range of home-made bar food include vegetable goulash topped with sour cream (£5.95), duck and bacon pie (£6.50), braised duck legs in orange and Dubonnet sauce (£7.50), and smoked ham and toulouse sausage with sauerkraut (£8.50); they also do sandwiches, soup, steaks and the like. Well kept Flowers Original, Gales HSB, Wadworths 6X, Whitbreads Strong Country and a guest on handpump; a good choice of wines, country wines, and farm cider. They do get very busy, and service can be a little stretched then. It's handy for the A31, and there are nice walks nearby. *(Recommended by John Fahy, Susan and John Douglas, John and Joan Calvert, Eddie Edwards, Dave Braisted, M L and G Clarke, Lorraine Patterson, Maurice Southon, G C Hackemer, David Luke, J Sheldon, Mr and Mrs R A Broadbent, Richard and Anne Ansell, Michael Clarke, Derek and Margaret Underwood, Jane Warren, Helen Pickering, James Owen, K A Louden, John and Christine Simpson, Mike Fitzgerald, Canon Kenneth Wills, Gwen and Peter Andrews, Martin and Karen Wake, David Rule, A W Dickinson, Mike Hayes, Clive Gilbert, N Matthews, James Macrae, Iain McBride, Samantha Hawkins, BKA, Mr and Mrs Craig, David Rule)*

Free house ~ Licensees Geoff Draper and Victor Firth ~ Real ale ~ Meals and snacks ~ Evening restaurant (not Sun) ~ (01962) 732764 ~ Nearby parking may be difficult ~ Children in eating area of bar, lunchtime only ~ Open 11-2.30, 6-11; closed 25 Dec

nr PETERSFIELD SU7423 Map 2

White Horse ★ 🍴

Priors Dean – but don't follow Priors Dean signposts: simplest route is from Petersfield, leaving centre on A272 towards Winchester, take right turn at roundabout after level crossing, towards Steep, and keep on for four miles or so, up on to the downs, passing another pub on your right (and not turning off into Steep there); at last, at crossroads signposted East Tisted/Privett, turn right towards East Tisted, then almost at once turn right on to second gravel track (the first just goes into a field); there's no inn sign; alternatively, from A32 5 miles S of Alton, take road by bus lay-by signposted Steep, then, after 1¾ miles, turn off as above – though obviously left this time – at East Tisted/Privett crossroads; OS Sheet 197 coming from Petersfield (Sheet 186 is better the other way), map reference 715290

Our old friend Jack Eddlestone has now retired and will be a tough act to follow, but the new licensees seem just as committed to keeping this marvellous old farmhouse as unspoilt as ever, so fingers crossed it will retain its special appeal for a good while yet. The two charming and idiosyncratic parlour rooms have exactly the same relaxing mix of furnishings and bric-a-brac as before – Mr Datchler told us he wouldn't dream of touching a thing. Dotted around are various old pictures, farm tools, drop-leaf tables, oak settles, rugs, stuffed antelope heads, a longcase clock, and a fireside rocking-chair to name a few. Tables are candlelit in the evenings. An excellent range of a dozen or so beers on handpump includes the very strong No Name Bitter and Strong, as well as Ballards Best, Bass, Fullers London Pride, Gales BBB, Best and HSB, Ringwood Fortyniner, Theakstons Old Peculier, and guest beers; cider from a tub behind the bar in summer, mulled wine in winter, and a good choice of country wines. Shove-ha'penny, dominoes, cribbage. A changing range of bar food, all cooked by the landlady, might include sandwiches, soup (£2.30), ploughman's (£3.95), ham and eggs (£4.50), hotpot or liver and bacon (£4.95), cod fillet with prawn sauce (£6.75), and individual legs of lamb (£6.50). They've usually got local eggs for sale, including organic free range ones, and in summer they may have honey too. There are of course times (not always predictable, with Sundays – even in winter – often busier than Saturdays) when the place does get packed. Rustic seats (which include chunks of tree-trunk) and a terrace outside; as this is one of the highest spots in the county it can be quite breezy. They recently came across some long-forgotten bullace trees, and in autumn, after the first couple of frosts, they plan to let customers harvest the fruit from these; it translates very well into jam, jelly and even gin (they'll provide the recipe). A nearby field has caravan facilities, and is regularly used for pony club meetings – as well as a landing place for the odd Tiger Moth plane or hot-air balloon. If trying to find it for the first time, keep your eyes skinned – not for nothing is this known as the Pub With No Name. No children inside. *(Recommended by Pat and Tony Martin, Pete Yearsley, Richard Houghton, Colin and Ann Hunt, J Sheldon, John and Phyllis Maloney, Verity Kemp, Richard Mills, Vann and Terry Prime, A R and B E Sayer, JWC, MC, Lynn Sharpless, Bob Eardley, Wendy Arnold, R Walden, PM, AM, Paul Boot, David Carr, MCG, David Machinek-Tidd, Kevin and Tracey Stephens, Martin and Penny Fletcher, Christopher Turner, T W Fleckney, F C Johnston, Jack and Philip Paxton, Adrian Zambardino, Debbie Chaplin, David Craine, Ann Reeder, Roger and Valerie Hill, Canon Kenneth Wills, Michael J Boniface, Ian Phillips)*

Gales ~ Manager Roger Datchler ~ Real ale ~ Meals and snacks (not Sun lunchtime) ~ (01420) 588387 ~ Open 11-3, 6-11

PILLEY SZ3298 Map 2

Fleur de Lys 🍴 🍺

Village signposted off A337 Brockenhurst—Lymington

Hampshire Dining Pub of the Year

In the two years or so since the energetic current landlord arrived, the food at this characterful old place has quickly come to stand out as being some of the very best in the area. The choice of meals has grown almost as fast as their reputation, and they now have a very wide range of freshly prepared dishes written up on the blackboards and menus, all thoughtfully prepared and presented by a former QE2 chef. Vegetarians are particularly well provided for, with around eight interesting dishes like forest mushrooms and sundried tomatoes in garlic and cream served with steamed rice, stuffed peppers, or spinach pancakes with stilton and walnuts, while other choices might include soup (£2.55), ploughman's (£3.95), big open sandwiches (from £4.45), venison and wild boar sausages or giant mushrooms filled with stilton and garlic (£4.50), pork in stilton and cider (£6.95), roast venison with black cherries and port wine (£8.25), and fresh fish such as Dorset plaice (£6.95), skate wing (£8.25), or fresh lobster (£14.95); vegetables are served on a separate dish, and they're good at adapting meals to diners with special needs. A better than usual children's menu includes 4oz steaks and home-made ravioli (£4.25). Well kept Boddingtons, Brakspears, Flowers Original, Marstons Pedigree, Morlands Old Speckled Hen, and Ringwood Best on handpump or tapped straight from the cask, good wines, country wines, and farm ciders; very good, genuinely caring service. In the entrance-way is a list of landlords that goes back to 1498 – but there's evidence that an inn of some sort existed here in Norman times, making this the oldest pub in the New Forest. The characterful lounge bar has heavy beams, lots of bric-a-brac and a huge inglenook log fire. There are seats in the garden with its waterfall and dovecote, and in summer they put up a marquee around the 14th-c wishing well; on Friday and Saturday evenings then (weather permitting) they barbecue around 10 choices of fresh fish. *(Recommended by Gwen and Peter Andrews, Meg and Colin Hamilton, Jerry and Alison Oakes, Mrs P McFarlane, Sheila and Norman Davies, M J How, Dr and Mrs A K Clarke, D G King, Dave Braisted, Clive Gilbert, Mr and Mrs Craig, D Marsh, R C Hopton, Mr and Mrs M F Norton, James House, Stephen and Anna Oxley)*

Whitbreads ~ Lease: Craig Smallwood ~ Real ale ~ Meals and snacks ~ Restaurant ~ (01590) 672158 ~ Children welcome ~ Open 12-3, 5.30-11

PORTSMOUTH SZ6501 Map 2
Still & West

Bath Square; follow A3 and Isle of Wight Ferry signs to Old Portsmouth water's edge

Breathtaking views from the terrace or upstairs restaurant here can stretch as far as the Isle of Wight, and even when the outlook isn't quite as clear the boats and ships fighting the strong tides in the very narrow mouth of Portsmouth harbour seem almost within touching distance. It's a friendly, cheerful place and the habitual haunt of the clergy who attend diocesan meetings at the cathedral. The bar is comfortably decorated in nautical style, with ship models, old cable, and even a powder drum, and has very well kept Gales BBB and HSB tapped from the cask, with a guest like Everards Tiger, Morlands Old Speckled Hen or Morrells Varsity, along with some aged whiskies and country wines; piped music, fruit machine. Chatty landlord and staff. Popular bar food includes traditional fish and chips (wrapped in newspaper ready to take away if you want, £3.75), a proper ploughman's (£3.95) and perhaps 10-15 cheeses from around the world. There's a wider range of meals upstairs, with eight or so fresh fish dishes; part of the dining area is no smoking. The pub is quite near to HMS *Victory*, and can get busy on fine days; its splendid floral displays have won awards locally. Nearby parking can be difficult. *(Recommended by PM, AM, John Fahy, June S Bray, Steve Felstead, Phyl and Jack Street, David Carr, Ann and Colin Hunt, JJB, Peter and Jenny Quine, Peter and Audrey Dowsett, JWC, MC, M J D Inskip, Thomas Nott)*

Gales ~ Managers Mick and Lynn Finnerty ~ Real ale ~ Meals and snacks ~ Restaurant ~ (01705) 821567 ~ Children in eating area of bar ~ Open 11-11

ROCKBOURNE SU1118 Map 2
Rose & Thistle ♀

Village signposted from B3078 Fordingbridge—Cranborne

The very good bar food is still the main draw at this attractive thatched 17th-c pub, but the smartly civilised atmosphere makes it the kind of place people like returning to. Lunchtime meals might include home-made soup (£2.60), ploughman's (from £4.45), locally-made sausages (£4.45), tagliatelle carbonara (£5.95), steak and kidney pie (£6.45), and specials like broccoli and cheese pancake with almond topping (£3.95), rabbit casserole with a cheese croûte top (£6.25), or sea bass on a bed of fennel with red wine sauce (£10.95), with evening extras such as lamb steak with an orange and mint sauce (£8.95), monkfish wrapped in bacon and creamy prawn sauce (£10.45) or medaillons of beef fillet with a stilton and port sauce (£12.45); lovely puddings like sticky toffee and date pudding (£3.25). A changing range of well kept beers on handpump like Adnams Broadside, Courage Best, Marstons Pedigree and Wadworths 6X, and there's a good range of wines from around the world, some by the glass; friendly attentive service. The public bar has tables arranged like booths, old engravings, sparkling brass and a good log fire, as well as new furnishings such as lovely polished tables and carved benches; darts, shove ha'penny, and dominoes. One small area is no smoking. There are tables by a thatched dovecot in the neat front garden. The charming village has the excavated remains of a Roman villa. *(Recommended by Dr and Mrs A K Clarke, Mark Matthewman, John Le Sage, Howard Allen, J O Jonkler, Rob Holt, Dave Braisted, Jerry and Alison Oakes, Jason Caulkin, J H L Davis)*

Free house ~ Licensee Tim Norfolk ~ Real ale ~ Meals and snacks ~ Restaurant (not Sun evening) ~ (01725) 518236 ~ Children welcome till 9pm ~ Open 11-3, 6-11; winter 12-3, 7-10.30

ROTHERWICK SU7156 Map 2

Coach & Horses 🍺

4 miles from M3, junction 5; follow Newnham signpost from exit roundabout, then Rotherwick signpost then turn right at Mattingley, Heckfield signpost; village also signposted from A32 N of Hook

The two small beamed front rooms at this creeper-covered 16th-c pub have a stripped brick open fireplace, oak chairs and other interesting furniture, and a fine assortment of attractive pictures; one is tiled, the other flagstoned, and one is no smoking. Well kept real ales on handpump at the servery in the parquet-floored inner area include Badger Best, Hard Tackle and Tanglefoot, Gribble Black Adder and Wadworths 6X; cribbage, dominoes, backgammon, and Connect Four. Under the new managers bar food includes soup (£2.25), doorstep sandwiches (from £3.45), home-made lasagne (£5.45), and a home-made pie of the day (£5.95). In summer, there are tubs and baskets of flowers, and rustic seats and picnic tables under cocktail parasols. *(Recommended by Gordon, Neville Kenyon, KC, Gary Roberts, Ann Stubbs, David Wallington, Clive Gilbert, J S M Sheldon)*

Badger ~ Managers Adie and Lyn Thompson ~ Real ale ~ Meals and snacks (till 10, 9.30 Sun) ~ Restaurant ~ (01256) 762542 ~ Children welcome ~ Open 11-11; 12-10.30 Sun

SOBERTON SU6116 Map 2

White Lion

Village signposted off A32 S of Droxford

Doing well under its new licensees, this friendly 16th-c country pub has very pleasant views from its sheltered garden, over the quiet green to the tall trees of the churchyard. There are picnic tables out here as well as swings, a slide and climbing bars, with more tables on a suntrap fairy-lit terrace. Bar food includes sandwiches, home-made soup (£1.95), king prawns in filo pastry with garlic dip (£2.95), potato, cheese and mushroom bake (£4.95), mushroom and walnut stroganoff (£5.25), shepherd's pie with leek and potato topping, a daily curry, and particularly well praised home-made pies (£5.50); children's menu. Vegetables come in a separate dish. The rambling, carpeted bar on the right is simply furnished with red-cushioned pews and scrubbed tables, a woodburning stove, and in a lower area a big photograph of HMS *Soberton*; piped music. The irregularly shaped public bar has more pews with built-in wooden wall seats, and darts, bar billiards and dominoes. Well kept Fremlins, Fullers London Pride and Ringwood Best on handpump, and country wines. It tends to get busy at weekends. *(Recommended by Ann and Colin Hunt, Pete Yearsley, Lynn Sharpless, Bob Eardley, John Evans, A J Netherton)*

Whitbreads ~ Lease: Graham Read ~ Real ale ~ Meals and snacks (12-2.30, 6-10.30) ~ Restaurant (open noon-10.30 Sun) ~ (01489) 877346 ~ Children in eating area of bar ~ Open 11-2.30, 6.30-11; all day Sat

SOPLEY SZ1597 Map 2

Woolpack

B3347 N of Christchurch; village signposted off A338 N of Bournemouth

Among the visitors said to have walked through the thatched porch of this busy old place over the years are Winston Churchill, Eisenhower, and even Greta Garbo. The licensees have changed since our last edition, but all is much the same, even down to the pianist, whose regular evening performances have been delighting readers for quite some time. The rambling low-beamed open-plan bar has a good local atmosphere, red leatherette wall seats and simple wooden chairs around heavy rustic tables, and has both a woodburning stove and a small black kitchen range; there's also a conservatory. Good bar bar food includes lunchtime filled rolls (from £3.50) and ploughman's (£3.95), home-made soup (£2.95), scallop, crab, mushroom and pepper creole (£5.25), vegetable lasagne (£5.95), steak and kidney pudding (£5.25), battered cod or avocado, courgette and red pepper bake (£6.45), Thai chicken curry (£6.75), baked gammon hock in honey, cider and apricot sauce (£7.95), pan fried duck in orange and Cointreau sauce (£10.95), and steaks (from £10.95). Well kept Flowers Original, Ringwood Best and Wadworths 6X on handpump; piped music. The garden has seats from which you can watch the ducks dabbling about on the little chalk stream under the weeping willows, by the little bridge. No children. *(Recommended by John and Joan Nash, Lynn Sharpless, Bob Eardley, Martyn Carey, Anna Groocock, Jerry and Alison Oakes, Joy and Peter Heatherley, J Morris, WHBM)*

Whitbreads ~ Lease: C L and C E Hankins ~ Real ale ~ Meals and snacks ~ (01425) 672252 ~ Children in eating area of bar ~ Pianist most evenings ~ Open 11-11; 12-10.30 Sun ~ Bedrooms: £70B/£75B

SOUTHSEA SZ6498 Map 2

Wine Vaults 🍺 £

Albert Rd, opp Kings Theatre

The decor in this simple pub is fairly basic, but the atmosphere is particularly sociable; it's the kind of place where everyone seems to be enjoying themselves, and people mix together really well. There's an excellent range of real ales, topped off with Spikes Impaled Ale and Stingor from their own little brewery; changing guests might include Brewery-on-Sea Spinnaker Bitter, Hampshire King Alfred's, Hop Back Summer Lightning, and Ringwood Old Thumper. Monday evening sees two separate happy hours, and they hold beer festivals in May and November with up to 70 different ales. The bar, usually full of students, has wood-panelled walls, a wooden floor, Wild West saloon-type swing doors, and an easy-going, chatty feel; pool, table football and piped music. Bar food is good value and served in decent sized helpings, with vegetarian dishes like mediterranean vegetables in pitta bread all priced at £3.65, and all the meat dishes such as pork in ginger and orange costing £3.95; they also have some Mexican meals at £4.55. Friendly staff. The one-eyed black labrador is called Ziggy; other dogs are welcome. *(Recommended by JJB, JWC, MC, Richard Houghton, Ann and Colin Hunt, J A Snell, Clive Gilbert and others)*

Own brew ~ Licensee Mike Hughes ~ Real ale ~ Meals and snacks (12-3, 5.30-9.30) ~ (01705) 864712 ~ Children welcome till 9.30 ~ Open 11-11; 11-10.30 Sun

STEEP SU7425 Map 2

Harrow

Take Midhurst exit from Petersfield bypass, at exit roundabout first left towards Midhurst, then first turning on left opposite garage, and left again at Sheet church; follow over motorway bridge to pub

A charmingly old-fashioned place run by a dedicated family, this little gem particularly delights readers discovering it for the first time. Hops and dried flowers hang from the beams in the little public bar, which also has built-in wall benches around scrubbed deal tables, a tiled floor, stripped pine wallboards, and a good log fire in the big inglenook; cribbage, dominoes. Enormous helpings of good simple home cooked bar food include home-made scotch eggs (£1.50), sandwiches, excellent soups overflowing from old-fashioned bowls (£2.70), huge ploughman's (from £3.70, some come with home-cooked meats), home-made quiches, cottage pie or cauliflower cheese (£5), ham lasagne (£5.25), and puddings made by the landlord's daughter including a delicious treacle tart (£2.60). Well kept Boddingtons, Flowers Original and Whitbread Strong Country tapped from casks behind the counter, country wines, Bulmers cider; polite and friendly staff, even when under pressure. The big garden is left free-flowering so that goldfinches can collect thistle seeds from the grass, and there are lots of tables out here. The Petersfield bypass doesn't intrude on this idyll, and you will need to follow the directions above to find it. No children inside. *(Recommended by M J P Martin, Colin and Ann Hunt, MCG, TBB, Wendy Arnold, Lynn Sharpless, Bob Eardley, KC, Howard Bateman, Christopher Perry, M W Jones)*

Free house ~ Licensee Edward McCutcheon ~ Real ale ~ Meals and snacks ~ (01730) 262685 ~ Open 11-2.30(3 Sat), 6-11

STOCKBRIDGE SU3535 Map 2
Vine
High St (A30)

Doing well under the licensee who took over just after our last edition, this bustling old coaching inn is a popular stop for a good lunchtime meal, but despite the emphasis on food still has a distinctive pubby feel. The comfortable open-plan bar has an interesting combination of woodwork, brickwork and purple papered walls, a delft shelf of china and pewter, and brightly floral chintz curtains; tables are prettily candlelit in the evening. Reliable bar food might include sandwiches (from £2.45), a big, proper ploughman's (£3.75), vegetable bake (£4.75), popular wild boar sausages, beef and ale pie or a roast of the day (£4.95), poached salmon salad (£7.95), and lobster thermidor salad (£9.95); half helpings for children. Well kept Boddingtons, Flowers Original, Ringwood Best and a guest ale on handpump. Very good obliging service; unobtrusive piped music. They now have summer weekend barbecues in the big garden (weather permitting). The pub is handy for Test Valley walks. *(Recommended by June S Bray, John and Phyllis Maloney, Phyl and Jack Street, A R and B E Sayer, Joy and Peter Heatherley, Ian Phillips, Major and Mrs T Savage, John Sanders, Gwen and Peter Andrews, Wayne Brindle, Mr and Mrs Craig, M J D Inskip, Simon Collett-Jones, Ann and Colin Hunt)*

Whitbreads ~ Tenant Kevin Lockstone ~ Real ale ~ Meals and snacks ~ Restaurant ~ (01264) 810652 ~ Children welcome ~ Open 11-11; 12-10.30 Sun ~ Bedrooms: £28/£38

TICHBORNE SU5630 Map 2
Tichborne Arms
Village signed off A31 just W of Alresford

The rolling countryside around this attractive thatched pub is well worth exploring before or after a relaxed meal, and the cheery landlord will happily point you towards the best local walks. The comfortable, square-panelled room on the right has pictures and documents on the walls recalling the bizarre Tichborne Case, when a mystery man from Australia claimed fraudulently to be the heir to this estate, as well as a log fire in an attractive stone fireplace, wheelback chairs and settles (one very long), and latticed windows with flowery curtains. On the left, a larger and livelier room, partly panelled and also carpeted, has sensibly placed darts, cribbage, shove-ha'penny, dominoes and a fruit machine. Good bar food might include sandwiches (from £1.45; toasties from £1.95), home-made soup (£2.25), liver and bacon nibbles with a home-made dip (£2.50), ploughman's or baked potatoes with a fine range of fillings (from £3.50), daily specials such as liver, bacon and onion casserole (£5.25), chicken breasts with apricots in brandy (£6.35), or poached fresh pink trout (£6.95), and puddings like fudge and walnut flan (£2.25). Well kept Flowers IPA, Wadworths 6X, Whitbreads Fuggles and a guest tapped from the cask, and country wines; excellent friendly service. There are picnic tables outside in the big well kept garden. Dogs are welcome, but no children or credit cards. *(Recommended by Sheila and Robert Robinson, John and Joan Nash, A M Pickup, Mark Percy, Tony and Wendy Hobden, G R Sunderland, Ann and Colin Hunt, Lynn Sharpless, Bob Eardley, Joan and John Calvert, G and M Stewart, JKW)*

Free house ~ Licensees Chris and Peter Byron ~ Real ale ~ Meals and snacks (12-1.45, 6.30-9.45) ~ (01962) 733760 ~ Open 11.30-2.30, 6-11

TITCHFIELD SU5305 Map 2

Fishermans Rest ♀

Mill Lane, Segensworth; off A27 W of Fareham at Titchfield Abbey sign

One of the best in Whitbreads' Wayside Inns chain, this clean and comfortably extended dining pub gets off to a good start, with its fine spot by the River Meon, opposite Titchfield Abbey. It's particularly popular with older people at lunchtime, for its wide choice of good freshly cooked food such as cob rolls with chips (from £2.45), filled baked potatoes (from £2.95), ploughman's (from £3.95), fish and chips (£4.75), lasagne (£5.25) and steak and kidney pudding (£5.95). The specials board might offer vegetable pie (£4.95), chicken and leek pie or turkey fricassee (£5.75), beef, celery and rosemary pie (£5.95), salmon steak with lemon and dill or creamy tarragon sauce (£7.50); puddings like sticky toffee pudding, apple pie or banoffi pie (from £1.95). Separate warm cosy rooms including a mellow eating area, and a no-smoking family room lead off the long bar; there are two log fires, light wood furnishings, daily papers, and a good deal of fishing memorabilia including stuffed fish. Real ales include well kept Boddingtons Bitter and Mild, Flowers IPA, Gales HSB, Wadworths 6X and a guest that might be a Whitbreads seasonal ale or perhaps Morlands Old Speckled Hen on handpump; about a dozen decent wines by the glass, cheerful quick service by young smiling staff, no piped music. Tables out behind overlook the river running along the back. *(Recommended by Terry and Eileen Stott, M Inman, Gwen and Peter Andrews, N Matthews, Roger and Corinne Ball, Ann and Colin Hunt, John and Chris Simpson)*

Whitbreads ~ Manager Harry Griffiths ~ Real ale ~ Meals and snacks 12-9.30 ~ Restaurant ~ (01329) 842848 ~ Children welcome in family area ~ Open 11-11; Sun 12-10.30

UPHAM SU5320 Map 2

Brushmakers Arms

Shoe Lane; village signposted from Winchester—Bishops Waltham downs road, and from B2177 (former A333)

It's been a busy year at this neatly attractive old pub – the Cobbs had a baby, Charlotte, and were surprised to be told by their local radio station that the building was haunted. Other than that it was business as usual, which here means creating a notably welcoming and friendly atmosphere that you'll notice as soon as you go in. The comfortable L-shaped bar is divided into two by a central brick chimney with a woodburning stove in the raised two-way fireplace; also, comfortably cushioned wall settles and chairs, a variety of tables including some in country-style stripped wood, a few beams in the low ceiling, and quite a collection of ethnic-looking brushes. Well kept Bass, Fullers London Pride, Ringwood Best, and a weekly guest beer on handpump, several malt whiskies, and Gales country wines. Good reasonably priced bar food includes sandwiches, deep fried camembert with redcurrant sauce (£3.50), salmon and prawn au gratin (£4.50), chicken filled with brie and wrapped in bacon (£4.95), monkfish thermidor (£6.25), pan fried duck breast with black cherry sauce (£7.95), and fillet steak with mustard cream sauce (£9.50); Sunday roasts and occasional themed evenings. Sensibly placed darts, dominoes, and cribbage; the friendly dog is called Rosie. The big garden is well stocked with mature shrubs and trees, and there are picnic tables on a sheltered back terrace among lots of tubs of flowers, with more on the tidy tree-sheltered lawn; Morris dancers occasionally visit in summer. Good walks nearby – though not much parking. *(Recommended by Phyl and Jack Street, Lynn Sharpless, Bob Eardley, John and Chris Simpson, Stephen and Sophie Mazzier, Ann and Colin Hunt, John and Joan Nash, N Matthews, Howard Allen)*

Free house ~ Licensees Sue and Andy Cobb ~ Real ale ~ Meals and snacks ~ (01489) 860231 ~ Children welcome ~ Open 11-2.30(3 Sat), 6(6.30 Sat)-11

WELL SU7646 Map 2

Chequers

5 miles W of Farnham; off A287 via Crondall, or A31 via Froyle and Lower Froyle (easier if longer than via Bentley); from A32 S of Odiham, go via Long Sutton; OS Sheet 186 map reference 761467

Considering how remote this comfortably civilised North Downs pub can seem, it's amazing how many people manage to track it down. The snugly atmospheric rooms are full of alcoves, low beams, wooden pews and old stools, and GWR carriage lamps, and the panelled walls are hung with lots of 18th-c country-life prints, and old sepia photographs of locals enjoying a drink. Promptly served bar food includes bangers, mash and beans or hot chicken and bacon salad (£5.75), scrambled eggs and smoked salmon (£5.85), home-made fishcakes with hollandaise sauce (£5.95), stuffed leg of chicken with red wine sauce (£6.25), and quenelle of pike with seafood sauce (£6.95). While agreeing with the consensus that the meals here are generally a touch above average, a few regular visitors have had unexpectedly disappointing meals in recent months; things should settle down under the new French chef, who plans to introduce a more continental style to the menu. Well kept Boddingtons, Flowers Original, and Whitbreads Strong Country on handpump. In the back garden are some chunky picnic tables, and at the front, there's a vine-covered front arbour. The pub can get busy at weekends. *(Recommended by TBB, Martin and Karen Wake, Lynn Sharpless, Bob Eardley, Jon and Julie Gibson, Brenda and Derek Savage, Susan and John Douglas, J Sheldon, Clive Gilbert, James Macrae)*

Free house ~ Licensees Rupert Fowler and Tommy McGrath ~ Real ale ~ Meals and snacks (till 10) ~ Restaurant (not Sun) ~ (01256) 862605 ~ Children welcome ~ Open 11-3, 5.30-11

WHERWELL SU3941 Map 2

White Lion

B3420, in village itself

This unpretentious 17th-c village pub has built up an enthusiastic following over the last few years, under its present licensees. There's an attractively relaxed and old-fashioned feel in its multi-level beamed bar, decorated with plates on delft shelves, fresh flowers and sparkling brass. There are buttoned plush seats, with cosy nooks and curtained alcoves. Freshly cooked food includes lunchtime sandwiches (from £1.60), filled baked potatoes or ploughman's (from £3.30), salads (from £4), scampi or lasagne (£4.80), and good value daily specials like fish pie (£4.70), breaded seafood platter (£4.80), steak and mushroom pie (£4.90), jumbo cod (£6.25) or fillet steak (£9), with good Sunday roasts (worth booking for these). They take particular care over the quality of their meats, and in season the pheasant casserole (£4.90) is a must. Well kept Boddingtons, Flowers IPA and Whitbreads Castle Eden on handpump, friendly helpful service; there's a good log fire, and the dining room is pleasant; darts, hexagonal pool table, fruit machine, juke box and piped music. The village is well worth strolling through. *(Recommended by Stephen M Jackman, Peter Neate, Ann Cassels-Brown, James Nunns, Gordon, Mr and Mrs J Woodfield, A J Stevens)*

Greenalls ~ Tenants Adrian and Patsy Stent ~ Real ale ~ Meals and snacks (not Sun evening) ~ (01264) 860317 ~ Children welcome in restaurant ~ Folk night Thurs in back barn ~ Open 10-2.30(3 Sat), 7-11; cl evening 25 Dec ~ Bedrooms: £18/£34

nr WHERWELL SU3839 Map 2

Mayfly ♀

Testcombe; A3057 SE of Andover, between B3420 turn-off and Leckford where road crosses River Test; OS Sheet 185 map reference 382390

The tables beside the River Test here are ideally placed to enjoy what must be one of the nicest settings of any pub we know, and watching the swans, ducks and, if you're lucky, plump trout drifting in and out of view is a fine way to spend a warm summer lunchtime. Surroundings like these do draw the crowds, but it's the kind of place that's very much geared up to handling huge numbers of people without any fuss or problems, and staff can often still spare a moment for a chat. The spacious, beamed and carpeted bar has fishing pictures and bric-a-brac on the cream walls above its dark wood dado, windsor chairs around lots of tables, two woodburning stoves, and bow windows overlooking the water; there's also a conservatory. Popular bar food, from a buffet-style servery, includes a wide range of cheeses (around three dozen) served with fresh crusty wholemeal bread or home-made quiche (£3.95), smoked trout (£3.95), chicken tandoori (£6), winter pies, casseroles and so forth, and a splendid selection of cold meats such as rare topside of beef (£4.20); salads are an extra 70p per spoonful, which can bump up the total cost. You'll usually find queues at busy periods. Well kept Boddingtons, Flowers Original, Wadworths 6X and Whitbreads Castle Eden on handpump, 14 wines by the glass, and country wines; fruit machine and piped music. *(Recommended by Cherry Ann Knott, Ron Gentry, Lynn Sharpless, Bob Eardley, G C Brown, A J Stevens, John Voos, Sue Demont, Tim Barrow, A R and B E Sayer, Mrs Cynthia Archer, Jane Warren, K A Louden, Wayne Brindle, Barry A Lynch, P J Caunt, J R Whetton, Anne Parmenter, M J D Inskip, P Gillbe, Martin and Karen Wake, Ian Phillips, Clive Gilbert)*

Whitbreads ~ Managers Barry and Julie Lane ~ Real ale ~ Meals and snacks (11.30-10) ~ (01264) 860283 ~ Children welcome ~ Open 11-11; 12-10.30 Sun

WINCHESTER SU4829 Map 2

Wykeham Arms ★ ★ ⑪ 🛏 ♀

75 Kingsgate Street (Kingsgate Arch and College Street are now closed to traffic; there is access via Canon Street)

You don't have to look much further than the landlord to understand the extraordinary popularity of this marvellous place. Mr Jameson's dedication really is remarkable, and although every year profits are up and his customers are happy, he seems constantly to be looking at ways of making things even better. Oozing an air of sophisticated comfort, the series of busy and stylish rooms radiating from the central bar are furnished with 19th-c oak desks retired from nearby Winchester College (the inkwells imaginatively filled with fresh flowers), a redundant pew from the same source, kitchen chairs and candlelit deal tables and big windows with swagged paisley curtains; all sorts of collections are dotted around. A snug room at the back, known as the Watchmakers, is decorated with a set of Ronald Searle 'Winespeak' prints, a second one is panelled, and all of them have a log fire; several areas are no smoking. Particularly good food at lunchtime might include sandwiches (£2.45; the more expensive hot or cold open sandwiches are popular), delicious soups like carrot and coriander (£2.35), roasted vegetable terrine or coarse country pork pâté with cumberland sauce (£3.95), a platter of mixed cheeses with home-made pickle (£4.75), red pepper, onion and pesto quiche or grilled tuna steaks with sweet and sour vegetables (£5.25), and beef and Guinness casserole or duck confit with rocket salad (£5.95); in the evening they do meals such as pan fried skate wing with anchovy butter, mussels and capers (£9.95), pot-roasted guinea fowl with apple, cider and sage (£11.95), and honey-roasted duck breast with apricot and almond stuffing and a sharp madeira sauce (£12.25); puddings like tipsy raspberry and ratafia trifle (£3.95) or chocolate and Baileys mousse cake (£4.25). Service is welcoming and friendly, though not always flexible. There's an excellent seasonally-changing list of wines including around 20 by the glass and by the 250ml and 500ml carafe, several half-bottles, and helpful tasting notes. Also well kept Eldridge Pope Dorchester, Hardy and Royal Oak on handpump, and a number of cognacs and liqueurs. The Alternative Beverage list (an eclectic range of non-alcoholic drinks taking in Horlicks, Ovaltine and Bovril) is still popular. There are tables on a covered back terrace, with more on a small but sheltered lawn. The lovely bedrooms are thoughtfully equipped, and residents have the use of a sauna. No children.

(Recommended by H L Davis, Bob and Maggie Atherton, Mr and Mrs R J Foreman, Susan and John Douglas, David Carr, Martin and Karen Wake, Major and Mrs T Savage, Pat and Tony Martin, JEB, Phyl and Jack Street, John and Phyllis Maloney, D Horsman, Ian Phillips, A N C Hunt, John and Joan Nash, Ann and Colin Hunt, Kim Maidment, Philip Vernon, Malcolm Taylor, Martin and Penny Fletcher, Mr and Mrs R A Broadbent, Maggie, Jenny and Brian Seller, Lynn Sharpless, Bob Eardley, John Whiting, Prof J R Leigh, Linda and Brian Davis, R V Ford, Thomas Nott, Kim Redling, N Matthews, Kevin and Katherine Cripps, N W Neill, Caroline Kenyon, Wayne Brindle, Mike Hayes)

Eldridge Pope ~ Tenants: Mr and Mrs Graeme Jameson ~ Real ale ~ Snacks (not Sun lunch) and meals ~ Evening restaurant ~ (01962) 853834 ~ If the small car park is full local parking may be difficult – don't be tempted to block up Kingsgate Street itself ~ Open 11-11; 12-10.30 Sun; closed 25 Dec ~ Bedrooms: £67.50B/£77.50B

Lucky Dip

Besides the fully inspected pubs, you might like to try these Lucky Dips recommended to us and described by readers (if you do, please send us reports):

Abbotts Ann [Little Ann; A343 Andover—Salisbury; SU3343], *Poplar Farm*: Spacious well furnished Brewers Fayre divided for families and non-smokers, quick polite cheerful service, usual food nicely cooked and served with choice of veg; spotless in and out (*HNJ, PEJ*)

☆ **Alresford** [The Soke, Broad St (extreme lower end); SU5832], *Globe*: Recently refurbished, with lovely view of 12th-c ponds from patio doors and attractive garden, lots of ducks, swans etc; Courage-related ales with a guest such as Wadworths 6X, lots of decent wines by the glass, cheapish popular food, friendly busy atmosphere, helpful staff, big open fire each end; piped music, board games; open all day, nearby parking can be difficult (*Lynn Sharpless, Bob Eardley, Ann and Colin Hunt, Mike Ledwith, John and Joan Nash, Christopher Warner, N Matthews, Mr and Mrs R J Foreman, BKA, George Hollingbery, KCW*)
Alresford [West St; SU5832], *Bell*: Georgian coaching inn now recovered from early 1996 fire, extended relaxing bar, smallish dining room, quickly served good value food inc children's helpings, well kept Ringwood Best, Old Thumper and maybe March Hare, good coffee, friendly service, pleasant back courtyard; comfortable bedrooms (*KCW, P J and J E F Caunt, Ann and Colin Hunt, Christopher Warner*); [Jacklyns Lane], *Cricketers*: Large pub, cottagey eating area with good straightforward food, unobtrusive piped pop music, garden with play area (*Ann and Colin Hunt*)
Alton [Church St; SU7139], *Eight Bells*: Very basic but comfortable local with good choice of beers, helpful landlord (*Richard Houghton, Derek Patey*)

☆ **Ampfield** [off A31 Winchester—Romsey; SU3923], *White Horse*: Good value generous food but also a welcome for drinkers in comfortably done-up extended open-plan Whitbreads dining pub with period-effect furniture, log fire, well kept ales, decent wine, welcoming efficient service, Victorian prints

and advertising posters in dining room; good play area, pub backs on to golf course and village cricket green; handy for Hillier arboretum (*Andrew and Joan Life, H and D Payne, KCW, B D Craig, Nick Wikeley, John and Chris Simpson*)
Appleshaw [SU3148], *Walnut Tree*: Picturesque pub with attentive staff, good food at affordable prices, nice choice of wines (*Mr and Mrs J M Colvill, A J Stevens*)
Ashmansworth [SU4157], *Plough*: No-frills pub in attractive village, Hampshire's highest; two rooms knocked together, hard-working friendly landlord, simple home-cooked food with good attentive service, well kept Archers ales and changing guest tapped from the cask; seats outside, good walks (*Phyl and Jack Street, Gordon*)
Ashurst [A35 Lyndhurst—S'hamptn; SU3310], *Forest*: Old village pub well done up for the holidaymakers, well kept Whitbreads-related and guest ales, friendly willing staff, good value food (*James Cowell, Roy Johnson*)

☆ **Avon** [B3347; SZ1498], *New Queen*: Well run attractive dining pub with atmospheric different areas and levels, low pitched ceiling, good range of popular reasonably priced food, friendly service, well kept Badger ales, helpful staff; tables out on spacious covered terrace and lawn, bedrooms (*the Sandy family*)

☆ **Ball Hill** [Hatt Common; leaving Newbury on A343 turn right towards East Woodhay; SU4263], *Furze Bush*: Clean and airy decor, pews and pine tables, good helpings of quickly served bar food, well kept Bass and Marstons Pedigree, decent wines by the bottle, log fire, tables on terrace by good-sized sheltered lawn with play area, restaurant; children allowed, no-smoking area in dining-room (*Mrs J Ashdown, David Hawkings, LYM*)
Bank [signed off A35 S of Lyndhurst; SU2807], *Royal Oak*: Cleanly refurbished New Forest pub in attractive untouristy village, good choice of food, country wines, chilled real ales tapped from the cask; piped

music; chipmunks and goats in garden, stunning scenery; very busy evenings *(Mr and Mrs A J Rapley, Frances Pennell)*

☆ **Basing** [Bartons Lane (attached to Bartons Mill Restaurant), Old Basing; SU6653], *Millstone*: Simply decorated converted mill in lovely spot by River Loddon, decent good value food, good choice of Wadworths and other well kept ales tapped from the cask; can sometimes get smoky; big garden, handy for ruins of Basing House *(Jim Reid, Andy Jones)*

☆ **Beaulieu** [almost opp Palace House; SU3802], *Montagu Arms*: Civilised comfortable hotel in attractive surroundings; separate less upmarket Wine Press bar, open all day, has simple lunchtime bar food, well kept Whitbreads-related ales, decent wines, lots of malt whiskies, quick friendly service, picnic tables out on front courtyard, piped pop music; children welcome; comfortable but expensive bedrooms *(Mr and Mrs R J Foreman, LYM)*

☆ **Bighton** [off B3046 in Alresford just N of pond; or off A31 in Bishops Sutton – OS Sheet 185 map ref 615344; SU6134], *Three Horseshoes*: Good simple lunchtime food (maybe just sandwiches in summer) in simple village local with open fire in small lounge, police memorabilia (ex-police landlord), well kept Gales HSB, BBB, winter 5X and Prize Old Ale, lots of country wines, friendly family service; children welcome, geese in garden *(Ian Exton, Martin Quirk, Lynn Sharpless, Bob Eardley, JP, PP)*

Binsted [SU7741], *Cedars*: Lively local with big public bar, quieter sitting-roomish lounge bar, friendly landlord, well kept ales, good freshly prepared food; piped music *(Daniel Suttle, BB)*

☆ **Bishops Sutton** [former A31 Alresford—Alton; SU6031], *Ship*: Pleasantly relaxed local, good quickly served bar food, polite friendly service *(Christopher Warner, D Marsh, Ann and Colin Hunt)*

Bishops Waltham [Church St; SU5517], *Bunch of Grapes*: Unspoilt simple two-room village local run by third family generation; well kept Ushers ales, bar food, plenty of character *(A and C Hunt, Stephen and Jean Curtis)*; *White Swan*: Welcoming village local, courteous staff, simple good value bar food from sandwiches up, Courage-related ales *(A and C Hunt)*

Botley [The Square; SU5112], *Bugle*: Attractive beamed pub with good value straightforward food, Whitbreads-related ales, restaurant; tables in flower-filled yard *(Colin and Ann Hunt, JFS; more reports on new management please)*; [Botley Rd, nr stn; SU5213], *Railway*: Popular good value generous food, fresh veg, quick cheerful service, well priced Marstons with a guest such as Banks's Mild; large comfortable railway-theme bar, extensive restaurant area *(John and Chris Simpson, Phyl and Jack Street, John Sanders)*

☆ **Braishfield** [Newport Lane; SU3725], *Newport*: Particularly well kept Gales HSB, Best and Butser in friendly and unpretentious

unmodernised two-bar village local with simple good value food inc huge sandwiches and good value ploughman's, country wines, decent coffee, down-to-earth licensees, weekend singsongs; good summer garden with geese, ducks and chickens *(John and Chris Simpson, Ann and Colin Hunt, Lynn Sharpless, Bob Eardley, John and Phyllis Maloney)*

Braishfield, *Dog & Crook*: Cottagey, with well kept Whitbreads-related ales, good choice of freshly cooked food inc vegetarian, fish specialities; garden with play area *(David Aarons, Ann and Colin Hunt)*

Bramshaw [SU2615], *Bramble Hill*: Ageing hotel in lovely setting with hunting trophies in bar, an unpretentious return to gentler times; with leisurely service of good food; bedrooms *(Dr and Mrs A K Clarke)*

☆ **Bransgore** [Ringwood Rd, off A35 N of Christchurch; SZ1897], *Three Tuns*: Pretty little thatched whitewashed pub with tasteful low-beamed bar, comfortable dining area, quick friendly service, wide range of good food inc vegetarian and imaginative daily specials, well kept Whitbreads-related ales and others such as Ringwood Fortyniner, fresh flowers, small restaurant; pleasant back garden with play area and open country views, flower-decked front courtyard; bedrooms *(R S Dancey, Mr and Mrs J Jackson, C C Stamp, W W Burke, Sue and Mike Todd)*

☆ **Bransgore** [Ringwood Rd], *Crown*: Clean and comfortable Brewers Fayre pub with quick friendly service, good value generous food from sandwiches up inc children's and lots of puddings, Whitbreads-related ales, big garden with good play area *(J Hibberd, D Marsh)*

Bransgore [Burley Rd], *Carpenters Arms*: Well kept Eldridge Pope beers and interesting food inc children's and OAP specials, well spaced tables, some in alcoves; good garden with play area *(J Hibberd)*

Brockenhurst [SU2902], *Rhinefield House*: Elegant hotel, not a pub, but good bar lunches in spacious comfortable lounge – not cheap, but good value; wonderful surroundings; bedrooms *(Hugh Spottiswoode)*; [Lyndhurst Rd], *Snakecatcher*: Long narrow lounge bar with decent food from sandwiches to steaks inc some interesting dishes and children's food, well kept Eldridge Pope ales, good choice of wines by the glass, good service, candles at night; function room doubling as restaurant; tables outside *(WHBM, K Flack)*

☆ **Broughton** [opp church; signed off A30 Stockbridge—Salisbury; SU3032], *Tally Ho*: Sympathetically renovated local, big plain modern flagstoned bar with darts, comfortable hunting-print lounge, well kept beers tapped from the cask inc those brewed at the Cheriton Flower Pots (it's in the same family as that main entry), simple sensibly priced food, welcoming landlord, decent wines in two glass sizes, tables in pretty garden behind *(Lynn Sharpless, Bob Eardley, Ann and Colin Hunt, Howard Allen)*

Bucklers Hard [SU4000], *Master Builders*:
Original core with beams, flagstones and big
log fire attractive when not too crowded,
Tetleys-related ales, tables in garden; part of a
substantial hotel complex in charming
carefully preserved waterside village, good
bedrooms *(M Joyner, W J Wonham, Dr and
Mrs A K Clarke, LYM)*
☆ Burghclere [Harts Lane, off A34 – OS Sheet
174 map ref 462608; SU4660], *Carpenters
Arms*: Pleasantly furnished small pub with
thriving atmosphere, good country views
from attractively laid-out dining conservatory,
big helpings of bar food from well presented
sandwiches up, well kept Arkells, unobtrusive
piped music; garden; handy for Sandham
Memorial Chapel (NT) *(HNJ, PEJ, R T and J
C Moggridge, D Marsh, Mr and Mrs P
Gregory)*
Buriton [SU7420], *Master Robert*: Friendly
welcome, well kept Flowers IPA, popular
food; good view from car park *(Ann and
Colin Hunt)*
☆ Burley [Bisterne Close, ¾ mile E; SU2003],
White Buck: Plushly elegant high-ceilinged
pub/restaurant in attractive quiet spot, good
choice of reasonably priced food, friendly
service, good choice of well kept beers,
separate dining room, children's room; dogs
allowed, hitching posts, tables on spacious
lawn; well equipped bedrooms *(WHBM, Sheila
and Norman Davies, D Marsh, Ian Grant, J M
T Morris, Jenny and Michael Back)*
Burley [back rd Ringwood—Lymington],
Queens Head: Done-up Tudor pub but still
with some flagstones, beams, timbering and
panelling, wide choice of good generous
straightforward bar meals, well kept
Whitbreads-related real ales on handpump,
maybe piped music; gift/souvenir shop in
courtyard – pub and New Forest village can
get packed in summer; children welcome *(M
Joyner, K Flack, LYM)*
Burley, *Woolpack*: Lovely New Forest spot;
relaxing and atmospheric, good food and beer
(Matthew Baker)
☆ Bursledon [Hungerford Bottom; SU4809],
Fox & Hounds: Included for handsomely
rebuilt ancient back barn with cheerful rustic
atmosphere, immense refectory table, lantern-
lit side stalls, lots of interesting farm
equipment, wide choice from food bar, well
kept Courage-related ales, country wines;
children allowed in conservatory connecting it
to original pub *(JP, PP, A and C Hunt, LYM)*
☆ Cadnam [by M27, junction 1; SU2913], *Sir
John Barleycorn*: Attractive low-slung long
thatched pub with dim lighting, low beams
and timbers, traditional decor, Whitbreads-
related ales, big helpings of competitively
priced standard food, two log fires; can be
very busy; suntrap benches in front *(W J
Wonham, Dr and Mrs A K Clarke, A Y
Drummond, Chris and Margaret Southon,
John H L Davies, K A Louden, BB)*
☆ Canterton [Upper Canterton; off A31 W of
Cadnam follow Rufus's Stone signs (no right
turn westbound); SU2613], *Sir Walter Tyrell*:
Pretty pub by lovely New Forest clearing

often with ponies, ideal base for walks;
restaurant, wide choice of good value bar
food, well kept Courage-related ales, friendly
atmosphere, roomy bar and restaurant; big
play area, sheltered terrace *(Dr and Mrs A K
Clarke)*
Charter Alley [White Hart Lane; off A340 N
of Basingstoke; SU5957], *White Hart*:
Deceptively big, with woodburner in lounge
bar, log fire in no-smoking annexe, skittle
alley in simple public bar, restaurant;
extensive blackboard menu, reasonable choice
of wines, regularly changing guest beers such
as Bunces Sign of Spring, Fullers London
Pride, Greene King Abbot; friendly welcome,
nice local atmosphere *(Andy Jones)*
Chilbolton [SU3939], *Abbots Mitre*: Busy
Whitbreads pub in remote village, guest beers,
big helpings of good food, very friendly staff
and landlord; games room, garden *(P Gillbe)*
Chilworth [A27 Romsey Rd; SU4018],
Clump: Busy dining pub useful for good value
straightforward food, with Whitbreads-
related ales, conservatory, tables in garden
(John and Chris Simpson, Clive Gilbert)
Church Crookham [SU8151], *Wyvern*:
Smartly refurbished suburban pub, pleasant
lunchtime atmosphere, plenty of seats in tidy
garden; handy for Basingstoke Canal *(Clive
Gilbert)*
Colden Common [SU4822], *Fishers Pond*: Big
Whitbreads pub next to attractive pond,
worth knowing about for pretty setting; tables
behind look across water, simple bar food
(Ann and Colin Hunt)
☆ Crondall [The Borough; SU7948], *Plume of
Feathers*: Interesting if not cheap freshly
cooked food (so may be a wait) in cosy and
attractive 17th-c local, well kept Marstons
with guest beers such as Morlands Old
Speckled Hen and Theakstons, entertaining
Irish landlord; two red telephone boxes in
garden, picturesque village *(Robert Duke, P J
Caunt, Miss S E Barnes, J Sheldon, Clive
Gilbert)*
Crondall [SU7948], *Castle*: Has been popular
village local, but closed and for sale in spring
1996 *(news please)*; *Hampshire Arms*:
Unpretentious local, but welcoming to
strangers, and new landlord has widened the
choice of decent food, from sandwiches to
rabbit pie with fresh veg – good value; well
kept Morlands, traditional games, boules *(KC)*
☆ Curbridge [A3051; SU5211], *Horse &
Jockey*: Beautiful setting by River Hamble
tidal tributary at start of NT woodland trail,
well refurbished with separate dining area;
two spotless bars, well presented good value
home-made food inc vegetarian and
imaginative specials, Gales ales, country
wines, cheerful licensees, prompt friendly
service; lovely garden with trees and fenced
play area *(John Sanders, John and Chris
Simpson, Geoff Holt, Ann and Colin Hunt,
Ruth and Alan Cooper, John and Joy
Winterbottom, Ian Phillips)*
Curdridge [Curdridge Lane (B3035); just off
A334 Wickham—Botley; SU5313],
Cricketers: Open-plan country pub with

banquettes in refurbished lounge area, little-changed public part, welcoming licensee, Marstons ales, above-average food inc good specials, nice dining area; quiet piped music, tables on front lawn *(Ann and Colin Hunt, John and Chris Simpson)*

☆ Denmead [Forest Rd, Worlds End; SU6211], *Chairmakers Arms*: Simple, roomy and comfortable country pub surrounded by paddocks and farmland, welcoming staff, fine range of good value well presented food inc superb sandwiches, no-smoking dining area, well kept Gales BBB, HSB and XXXL, decent wine, log fires; no music *(Ann and Colin Hunt, Eric Heley, C Slack, LYM)*

Denmead [School Lane, Anthill Common; SU6611], *Fox & Hounds*: Open-plan bar with restaurant off, cheerful staff, well kept ales such as Bass, Boddingtons, Fullers London Pride, Ringwood Old Thumper and Shepherd Neame Spitfire, decent food *(Ann and Colin Hunt)*

☆ Downton [A337; SZ2793], *Royal Oak*: Wide choice of reliable home cooking esp pies in neat and quiet partly panelled family pub, half no smoking, with well kept Whitbreads-related ales, decent wines, friendly landlady, unobtrusive piped music; huge well kept garden with good play area *(D Marsh, Howard Clutterbuck)*

☆ Droxford [Station Rd; SU6018], *Hurdles*: Good generous home cooking, pleasant mature staff, well kept ales; not at all pubby *(John Sanders)*

Dummer [A30; SU5846], *Sun*: Quiet, pleasant and friendly, with Boddingtons and Courage Best, good sandwiches, interesting hot dishes, log fire in lounge *(John and Vivienne Rice)*

☆ Dunbridge [Barley Hill; SU3126], *Mill Arms*: Emphasis on good well flavoured and presented food inc well prepared veg and home-made bread, in dining area and restaurant; real ales such as Hampshire King Alfred, refurbished bar keeping some character, conservatory, tables in garden *(Howard Allen, D J and P M Taylor)*

☆ Dundridge [Dundridge Lane; off B3035 towards Droxford, Swanmore, then right towards Bishops Waltham – OS Sheet 185 map ref 579185; SU5718], *Hampshire Bowman*: Good atmosphere, not too smart, in friendly and cosy downland pub with well kept Archers Golden, King & Barnes Festive and Ringwood Best and Old Thumper tapped from the cask, decent house wines, country wines, good straightforward home cooking inc vegetarian, sensible prices; children, dogs, vintage motor-cycles and walkers welcome, tables on spacious and attractive lawn *(John and Joy Winterbottom, Colin and Ann Hunt, Lynn Sharpless, Bob Eardley, John and Joan Nash, BB)*

☆ Durley [Durley Street; just off B2177 Bishops Waltham—Winchester; SU5116], *Robin Hood*: Friendly simple two-bar Marstons pub, log fire, impressive choice of good food, cheerful waitresses; back terrace and pleasant garden overlooking field *(Ann and Colin Hunt, Lynn Sharpless, Malcolm and Wendy Butler)*

Durley [Heathen St – OS Sheet 185 map ref 516160], *Farmers Home*: Good genuinely home-cooked food inc fine steaks, also vegetarian and children's dishes, well kept Boddingtons, log fire in small bar, big dining area, relaxed atmosphere, efficient obliging staff; big garden with good play area and pets corner *(Roger and Corinne Ball, Brian Mills)*

☆ East Boldre [SU3700], *Turf Cutters Arms*: Roomy and relaxed dim-lit New Forest pub with good original atmosphere, lots of beams and pictures, two log fires, Flowers Original, Wadworths 6X and a guest such as Gales HSB, several dozen malt whiskies, character landlord, friendly service and very enjoyable food – worth waiting for a table; no children, unusual charity coin-collecting device in gents', live jazz first Sun lunchtime of month; tables in garden; three big old-fashioned bedrooms, huge breakfasts *(Howard West, M Joyner, J V Dadswell, J W Mason)*

East Dean [OS Sheet 184 map ref 269267; SU2626], *Old Brewers*: Unusual pavilion-like building doing well under welcoming new young licensees, bright, neat and tidy beamed lounge and restaurant, log-effect gas fire as well as central heating, good quickly served well presented home-cooked food, good range of real ales *(Phyl and Jack Street, Geoffrey and Penny Hughes)*

East End [back rd Lymington—Beaulieu, parallel to B3054; SZ3697], *East End Arms*: Popular New Forest pub with Ringwood ales tapped from the cask, good value food, curious tree trunk in lounge bar *(Michael Andrews, Derek and Sylvia Stephenson)*

☆ East Meon [Church St; signed off A272 W of Petersfield, and off A32 in West Meon; SU6822], *George*: Friendly and attractive rambling beamy country pub in lovely setting, cosy areas around central bar counter, scrubbed deal tables and horse tack; well kept Badger Tanglefoot, Ballards, Bass, Flowers and Gales HSB, decent wines, substantial straightforward food in bar and restaurant, maybe log fire; children welcome, good outdoor seating arrangements, quiz night Sun; small but comfortable bedrooms, good breakfast *(Dagmar Junghaans, Colin Keane, Pete Yearsley, Gordon Case, Mr Ely, Martin and Karen Wake, Sara Nicholls, Ann and Colin Hunt, J R Smylie, John Sanders, LYM)*

East Meon [High St], *Izaak Walton*: Simple village local with good fresh food inc vegetarian and children's dishes, attractive prices, pleasant welcome, well kept beers inc a guest such as Ironside Best, newly decorated lounge, darts and pool in public bar; children welcome, tables in big garden with unusual rabbits, new side terrace; busy weekends, open all day Sun, quiz night most Weds *(Paul Foster, T W Fleckney, Ann and Colin Hunt)*

☆ East Tytherley [SU2929], *Star*: Charming country pub in lovely surroundings, well priced Courage-related, Gales and Ringwoods ales, good coffee, decent food from sandwiches up with emphasis on 'healthy' eating, log fires, no-smoking lounge bar, cosy and pretty restaurant, smart efficient staff, relaxing pubby atmosphere; giant chess and draughts games on forecourt, skittle alley, play area *(D Marsh, John Knighton, L M Parsons, Phyl and Jack Street, Ann and Colin Hunt, Peter Singleton)*

East Worldham [Caters Land (B3004); TV6199], *Three Horseshoes*: Comfortable and attractive inside, good range of reasonably priced food, Gales ales *(Rob Harrison)*

Easton [SU5132], *Chestnut Horse*: Comfortable rambling beamed dining pub in lovely sleepy village, wide choice of food, Bass, Charrington IPA, Courage Best, Fullers London Pride, good log fire, smart prints and decorations; attractive garden behind, good Itchen valley walks *(Lynn Sharpless, Bob Eardley, J and P A Street, KCW)*; *Cricketers*: Good choice of real ales such as Eldridge Pope Hardy, Mansfield Old Baily, Ringwood Best and Youngs Special, good straightforward food from ploughman's up, polite landlord and good staff; fruit machine, piped music, occasional entertainment *(Ann and Colin Hunt, KCW)*

☆ Ellisfield [Fox Green Lane, Upper Common – OS Sheet 186 map ref 632455; SU6345], *Fox*: Comfortable and interesting two-bar village local with well priced food attracting lunchtime trade from Basingstoke, good choice of beers such as Badger Tanglefoot, Fullers London Pride, Gales HSB, Theakstons Old Peculier and Wadworths 6X, decent wines and country wines, friendly attentive service; restaurant area, pleasant garden *(Tony and Wendy Hobden, Jim Reid, Geoff Kontzle, J V Dadswell)*

☆ Emery Down [village signed off A35 just W of Lyndhurst; SU2808], *New Forest*: Good position in one of the nicest parts of the Forest, with good walks nearby, tables out on three-level back lawn; attractive softly lit open-plan lounge with log fires, Whitbreads-related ales, wide choice of house wines; mixed reports on food, which some have liked a lot; children allowed *(David Holloway, David Shillitoe, Margaret and Geoffrey Tobin, Lynn Sharpless, Bob Eardley, H T Flaherty, Mr and Mrs D J Nash, Clive Gilbert, D Godden, Adrian Zambardino, Debbie Chaplin, LYM)*

Emsworth [South St; SU7406], *Coal Exchange*: Busy little cheerful local, welcoming young licensees, good lunchtime food, a real fire at each end, well kept Gales and a guest beer *(Percy and Cathy Paine)*; [High St], *Crown*: Good range of ales such as Wadworths 6X and Youngs Ram Rod, good food and friendly service in bar and restaurant, competitive prices; bedrooms *(Ann and Colin Hunt, R B Gee)*; [Havant Rd], *Kings Arms*: Cosy and traditional friendly local with good generous well priced food cooked by landlady, fresh veg, well kept Gales and a guest ale, good choice of decent wines; garden behind *(Peter Couch, R B Gee)*; [35 Queen St], *Lord Raglan*: Welcoming and relaxing little Gales pub with log fire, good range of food esp fish, restaurant; children welcome if eating, garden behind nr water

(Ann and Colin Hunt)

Eversley Cross [The Green (A327); SU7861], *Toad & Stumps*: Well kept beer, food inc good vegetarian curries, lots of toys and games, opp cricket green *(Nigel Norman)*

☆ Everton [3 miles W of Lymington; SZ2994], *Crown*: Good cheap food in relaxing traditional bar with log fire (bookable tables), well kept Bass, Ringwood True Glory and Whitbreads-related ales, lots of jugs and china hanging from ceiling, second lively bar with pool, darts, table football, Sky TV and good juke box, welcoming chatty locals and ex-Navy landlord; picnic tables outside, quite handy for New Forest *(SLC)*

Ewshot [off A287; SU8149], *Windmill*: Friendly two-bar pub with well kept Ind Coope Burton and Ushers, popular food inc Sun roast, enormous garden with putting green and Sunday lunchtime barbecues *(Chris De Wet, Tim and Chris Ford)*

Exton [signed from A32; SU6121], *Shoe*: Very attractive outside, bright, clean and comfortable in, with well kept Bass, friendly barman, attractive food, lovely grassed area across road *(Dave Braisted)*

☆ Faccombe [SU3858], *Jack Russell*: New licensees yet again – smart yet comfortably homely bar, attractive and spotless dining conservatory with good value usual pub food inc some imaginative dishes, tables in lovely garden, nice setting opp village pond, by flint church; bedrooms spotless and cheerful *(JS, PAS, HNJ, PEJ)*

☆ Fair Oak [Winchester Rd (A3051); SU4918], *Fox & Hounds*: Busy, comfortable and attractive open-plan family dining pub with exposed brickwork, beam-and-plank ceilings, soft lighting; wide choice of reasonably priced food (all day weekends) in old-world bar and separate modern family area, friendly service, Courage-related ales, decent wines; piped music; children's play area by car park *(Joan and John Calvert, Lynn Sharpless, Bob Eardley, Colin and Ann Hunt)*

Fareham [Porchester Rd (A27), Cams Hill; SU5706], *Delme Arms*: Two-bar Victorian pub with Archers Village and Bass, well priced standard bar meals, friendly service, comfortable lounge; opp splendidly restored Cams Hall *(Ann and Colin Hunt, Colin Turnbull)*

☆ Farnborough [Rectory Rd; nr Farnborough North stn; SU8753], *Prince of Wales*: Good choice of real ales and whiskies in lively and friendly local with three small connecting rooms, good service, lunchtime food; can get very crowded *(KC)*

Farnborough [Cove Rd], *Old Court House*: Doesn't look old from the outside but in fact dates back at least 300 years, full Fullers ale range, prompt efficient service, friendly atmosphere, cheap food from sandwiches up *(Ian Phillips)*

☆ Fawley [Ashlett Creek, off A326; SU4703], *Jolly Sailor*: Plushly modernised waterside pub with good value food inc Sun carvery and good puddings, Whitbreads-related and guest ales, friendly prompt service, restaurant, good liner pictures; piped music (live Fri/Sun), children welcome; by dinghy club overlooking busy shipping channel, handy for Rothschild rhododendron gardens at Exbury *(Dr M Owton, B W Bailey, LYM)*

☆ Freefolk [N of B3400; SU4848], *Watership Down*: Friendly and cosy partly brick-floored bar, lounge and games areas off, five ales such as Archers Best, Brakspears PA and Mild and Bunces Pigswill, popular food with good specials; piped music, Sun quiz night; attractive garden with play area and rabbit pen *(Andy Jones, Ann and Colin Hunt)*

☆ Fritham [SU2314], *Royal Oak*: Thatched New Forest pub in same family for 80 years, no concessions to modernity, well kept Ringwood Best and Fortyniner, maybe Wadworths 6X, tapped from the cask, odd assortment of furniture inc high-backed settles, pots and kettles hanging in wide old chimney, log fires – but there is a video game; tables in garden with climbing frame, all sorts of passing animals; no food beyond crisps, nuts, seafood in jars and occasional barbecues, bring your own sandwiches; children in back room *(JP, PP, David Holloway, Howard Allen, Pete Baker, John Beeken, LYM)*

☆ Froyle [Upper Froyle; A31 Alton—Farnham; SU7542], *Hen & Chicken*: Emphasis on food, straightforward but varied and generous, in cosy 16th-c dining pub with oak beams and pillars, antique settles, oak tables among more orthodox furnishings, log fire in huge inglenook; friendly helpful staff, well kept Fullers London Pride and other ales, unobtrusive piped music; children welcome away from front room, tables in big garden with play area and rabbits *(Hazel Morgan, Paul and Sue Sexton, Peter and Liz Wilkins, LYM)*

Gosport [Fort Rd; SZ6199], *Dolphin*: Nautical theme, well kept beers inc Gales HSB, good wine, popular food, no piped music, big well laid out garden with play equipment; nr sea *(Peter and Audrey Dowsett)*; [Hardway], *Hogshead & Halibut*: Former Jolly Roger now popular for good choice of well kept real ales; friendly staff *(Ann and Colin Hunt)*; [Queens Rd], *Queens*: Popular real ale pub with five well kept beers such as Archers, Black Sheep and Ringwood, basic food, nice atmosphere, family room, good service, parking may be difficult *(John and Chris Simpson, Ann and Colin Hunt)*

Griggs Green [Longmoor Rd; off A3 S of Hindhead – OS Sheet 186 map ref 825317; SU8231], *Deers Hut*: Pleasantly laid out L-shaped bar, welcoming licensees, nice atmosphere, Morlands ales; picnic tables on attractive front lawn with pretty flower beds, touring caravan site behind *(John Sanders)*

☆ Hambledon [West St], *Vine*: Friendly beamed pub, traditional and unpretentious, in pretty downland village, good range of beers such as Charles Well Bombardier, Fullers London Pride, Gales HSB and BBB, Hampshire Hare, country wines, good simple home cooking (not Tues evening) esp fish, welcoming attentive staff, open fire in lounge, old prints,

china, ornaments, farm tools, high-backed settles, well in bar; shove-ha'penny, darts *(Lynn Sharpless, Bob Eardley, Ann and Colin Hunt, John Sanders, Pete Yearsley)*

Hambledon [Hipley; SU6414], *Horse & Jockey*: Welcoming staff, well kept Whitbreads-related beers, good reasonably priced food, good service, delightful garden by stream *(John Sanders, Ann and Colin Hunt)*

Hatch [A30; SU6752], *Hatch*: Nice old roadhouse recently converted to steak house, but still has pleasantly old-fashioned bar area; good garden, children welcome *(Comus Elliott)*

Havant [East St; SU7106], *Bear*: Big smart low-beamed bar, friendly service, good range of ales inc Flowers Original, Ringwood Best and Old Thumper, interesting prints and mirrors; coffee lounge and dining room upstairs; bedrooms *(Ann and Colin Hunt)*; [South St], *Old House At Home*: Fine Tudor two-bar pub, enlarged and much modernised, with low beams, two fireplaces in lounge, well kept Gales BBB and HSB, good choice of bar food inc vegetarian; piped music (live Sun), back garden *(Ann and Colin Hunt, LYM)*

Hazeley [B3011 N of H Wintney – OS Sheet 186 map ref 742591; SU7459], *Shoulder of Mutton*: Popular dining pub with good from speciality burgers to good steaks, good vegetarian choice, efficient friendly service, good fire in cosy lounge, no-smoking area, Courage-related ales, quiet piped music; attractive building, terrace and garden *(Blaine and Kerry Faragher)*

☆ Heckfield [B3349 Hook—Reading; SU7260], *New Inn*: Big well run rambling open-plan dining pub with good choice of food, some traditional furniture in original core, two good log fires, well kept ales such as Badger Tanglefoot, Courage Directors, Fullers London Pride, decent wines, unobtrusive piped music; restaurant (not Sun); bedrooms in comfortable and well equipped extension *(Malcolm Gregory, LYM)*

Hedge End [Shamblehurst Lane, close to M27 junction 8; SU4812], *Shamblehurst Barn*: Recently refurbished big two-level dining pub with generous standard bar food, good range of ales, nice restaurant; children welcome *(A and C Hunt)*

☆ Highclere [Andover Rd; A343 S of village; SU4360], *Yew Tree*: Relaxing comfortably plush small dining bar with good value food, good atmosphere, big log fire, friendly efficient service, well kept ales such as Brakspears, Ringwoods Fortyniner, Wadworths 6X, decent wines, some attractive decorations; restaurant; four comfortable bedrooms *(Gordon, Guy Consterdine, LYM)*

☆ Hill Head [Cliff Rd; SU5402], *Osborne View*: Clean and modern clifftop pub by bird reserve, with good bar food inc Sun roasts, well kept Badger Best and Tanglefoot, good service and exceptional picture-window Solent views (you need field-glasses to see Osborne House itself); evening restaurant; open all day *(June and Eric Heley, Ann and Colin Hunt, N Matthews, John Sanders, E Cowdray, B D Craig)*

Hinton [A35 4 miles E of Christchurch; SZ2095], *East Close*: Particularly good food (meals not snacks) inc some south-east asian dishes, fresh fish and good steaks, well kept Flowers and Wadworths 6X, decent wines and whiskies, convivial owners; no-smoking area; comfortable bedrooms *(Mark Brock)*

☆ **Hook** [London Rd – about a mile E; SU7254], *Crooked Billet*: Smartly refurbished, with lots of tables, wide choice of good attractively presented food all day, swift pleasant service, well kept Courage-related ales, homely open fires, good range of soft drinks, early-evening happy hour, soft piped music; attractive streamside garden with ducks; children welcome *(Simon Collett-Jones, Alan Newman, Eric Locker)*

Horndean [London Rd; SU7013], *Ship & Bell*: Big pub/hotel adjoining Gales brewery, full range of their beers kept well, good relaxed local atmosphere in bar with deep well, comfortable snug lounge with steps up to dining room; bedrooms *(John Sanders)*

☆ **Horsebridge** [about a mile SW of Kings Somborne – OS Sheet 185 map ref 346303; SU3430], *John o' Gaunt*: Plain village local with well kept Adnams, Palmers IPA and Ringwood Fortyniner, friendly landlord; picnic tables outside, by mill on River Test; very popular with walkers for cheap food (not Tues evening), dogs welcome *(Ann and Colin Hunt, Mike Hayes, Lynn Sharpless, Bob Eardley, Martyn and Mary Mullins, Nick Wikeley)*

☆ **Houghton** [S of Stockbridge; SU3432], *Boot*: Friendly and well run, with wide range of tasty well presented food in popular restaurant, well kept Boddingtons and Wadworths 6X, lovely stretch of lawn leading down to river; cl Mon *(Ian Phillips, DP)*

Hursley [A31 Winchester—Romsey; SU4225], *Dolphin*: Good relaxed country atmosphere, decent food, hard-working licensees, well kept beer; tables in garden *(KCW, Mr and Mrs Craig)*

Hurstbourne Tarrant [A343; SU3853], *George & Dragon*: Low beams and inglenook, separate rooms and eating area, real ales inc Wadworths 6X, reasonably priced bar food; bedrooms, attractive village *(Prof A N Black, LYM)*

☆ **Itchen Abbas** [4 miles from M3 junction 9; A34 towards Newbury, fork right on A33, first right on B3047; SU5333], *Trout*: Smallish country pub with discreet partly no smoking lounge bar, chatty public bar with darts and bar billiards, well kept Marstons Bitter and Pedigree, decent wines, good value changing bar food inc some interesting hot dishes, friendly service, restaurant; pretty side garden with good play area; roomy comfortable bedrooms, good breakfast *(Michael Bird, C and E M Watson, Fiona and Paul Hutt, R H Rowley, Colin and Joyce Laffan, BB)*

☆ **Keyhaven** [SZ3091], *Gun*: 17th-c nautical-theme beamed pub overlooking boatyard, popular at lunchtime particularly with older people for wide choice of generous bar food, well kept Whitbreads-related ales; garden with swings and fishpond; children welcome

(Nick Wikeley, Graham and Karen Oddey, D Marsh)

☆ **Kings Worthy** [A3090 E of Winchester, just off A33; SU4933], *Cart & Horses*: Good value renovated Marstons Tavern Table family dining pub with softly lit alcoves, lots of well spaced tables, conservatory, decent home-cooked food, well kept beer, good service, tables in pleasant garden with marvellous play houses *(KCW, Graham and Karen Oddey, LYM)*

Kingsclere [Swan St; SU5258], *Swan*: Old-fashioned and unpretentious 15th-c village local, welcoming atmosphere, well kept Greene King IPA and Abbot with guest ales tapped from the cask such as Gales Gold and Tetleys, prompt service, enjoyable food inc Sun roast, Sunday papers, dresser of crockery *(Simon Collett-Jones)*

☆ **Langstone** [A3023; SU7105], *Ship*: Waterside pub with lovely view from roomy pleasantly decorated bar and upstairs restaurant, good generous food esp fish cooked within sight, obliging service, well kept Gales, country wines, log fire; children's room, seats out on quiet quay *(Wendy Arnold, John and Chris Simpson, T Roger Lamble, John Sanders, JP, PP, Colin and Ann Hunt)*

☆ **Lasham** [SU6742], *Royal Oak*: Welcoming and comfortable country pub in attractive spot nr gliding centre, well kept Hampshire King Alfred and Ringwood Best with guests such as Bunces Benchmark and Hop Back Summer Lightning, good generous home cooking inc vegetarian, log fire, quiet piped music, friendly cat; tables in pleasant garden *(Bruce Bird, H L Davis)*

Lee on the Solent [Broom Way; SU5600], *Wyvern*: Big pub with cottagey frontage, doing well under new owners (and new chef), with decent food, friendly service, well kept Gales; pleasant walks nearby *(J and P A Street)*

☆ **Linwood** [signed from A338 via Moyles Court, and from A31; keep on – OS Sheet 195 map ref 196107; SU1910], *High Corner*: Big rambling pub very popular for its splendid New Forest position, with extensive neatly kept lawn and sizeable play area; bar food from sandwiches to steaks, Whitbreads-related ales, decent wine, restaurant carvery open all day Sun, no-smoking verandah lounge; children and dogs welcome in some parts, open all day Sat; bedrooms *(K Flack, Margaret and Geoffrey Tobin, M Joyner, LYM)*

☆ **Linwood** [up on heath – OS Sheet 195 map ref 186094], *Red Shoot*: Attractive old furniture and rugs on the floorboards, generous decent food inc good sandwiches, well kept Wadworths IPA, 6X and Morrells Varsity on handpump, friendly staff, nice New Forest setting *(Alan Skull)*

☆ **Longstock** [SU3536], *Peat Spade*: Character landlady cooking short choice of good food (can take a time, and is not cheap) in elegantly rural airy dining pub, often fully booked; pot plants and central table with books, adjoining dining room, well kept Ringwood Best and Fortyniner; wines not cheap but unusually wide choice by glass; only well behaved dogs may be allowed (pub dogs Mr Hades and Golly-Gosh in bar); small pleasant garden, handy for Test Way long-distance path, and Danebury hill fort *(Mike Hayes, A J Stevens, Ian Phillips, BB)*

☆ Lower Froyle [signed off A31; SU7643], *Anchor*: Well run, warm and attractive brightly lit pub with wide range of good standard food inc sandwiches and fish, reasonable prices, cheerful informal service, well kept ales; well in one of the two connecting bars, restaurant; piped music; seats outside *(G and M Stewart, R Crail, GSS, J S M Sheldon, KC)*

☆ Lower Wield [SU6340], *Yew Tree*: Reliably good value dining pub, kept spotless, with good choice from soup to steaks, salmon and bass, can eat in dining room or bar; cheerful and friendly, with well kept Marstons Pedigree, fresh flowers; cl Mon *(A J Stevens)*

☆ Lymington [Ridgeway Lane, Lower Woodside, marked as dead end just S of A337 roundabout in Pennington W of Lymington, by White Hart; SZ3294], *Chequers*: Simple but stylish yachtsmen's local with polished boards and quarry tiles, attractive pictures, plain chairs and wall pews; good range of home-made bar food from lunchtime filled french sticks to duck, steak and fresh fish, inc vegetarian, four well kept Whitbreads-related ales, good wines, fine rums; friendly service, well if not quietly reproduced piped pop music, traditional games, tables in neat garden; well behaved children allowed *(D Deas, D Marsh, LYM)*

☆ Lymington [108 High St], *Angel*: Popular but roomy and peaceful dark-decor modernised bar with largely home-made bar food, three well kept Eldridge Pope ales, neat young staff, open all day; tables in attractive inner courtyard, bedrooms *(SLC, Joan and Michel Hooper-Immins, Dr and Mrs A K Clarke, D Marsh, LYM)*

☆ Lymington [Southampton Rd (A337)], *Toll House*: Wide choice of reliably good value food (not Sun or Mon evening) inc children's, good friendly atmosphere, well kept Ringwood, Wadworths 6X, a beer brewed for the pub and several guest ones, pleasant efficient staff, oak beams; piped music; good-sized children's room *(D Marsh, SLC)*

Lymington [The Quay], *Ship*: Waterfront Brewers Fayre family food pub, spacious and well decorated, with some flagstones, open all day from breakfast on, good value usual food, Whitbreads-related ales, some seating outside with boating views *(Hugh Spottiswoode, SLC)*

Lyndhurst [High St; SU2908], *Crown*: Hotel bar worth knowing for good reasonably priced bar food; Courage-related ales, bedrooms *(A R Nuttall)*; [Brockenhurst rd (A337) ½ mile S], *Crown Stirrup*: Good food inc unusual dishes, well kept Whitbreads-related ales, two low-ceilinged rooms, friendly staff, covered terrace and garden; good forest walks *(M Joyner)*; [22 High St], *Fox & Hounds*: Big much modernised dining pub

with lots of exposed brickwork, standing timbers as divisions, family room beyond former coach entry, games room with pool, darts etc, Whitbreads-related and local guest ales, usual food from good ploughman's to steaks *(B and K Hypher)*

Marchwood [off A326; SU3810], *Pilgrim*: Immaculately sprightly decor in smart thatched pub with well kept Eldridge Pope ales, lunchtime food, welcoming open fire; neat garden *(Dr and Mrs A K Clarke, LYM)*

Meonstoke [SU6119], *Bucks Head*: Two-bar Morlands pub with well kept Bass and Old Speckled Hen, country wines, good value substantial bar food with fresh veg, interesting specials and good range of puddings, red plush banquettes, friendly service, log fire, garden; lovely village setting, nearby river *(Lynn Sharpless, Bob Eardley)*

Milford on Sea [High St; SZ2891], *Smugglers*: Big, friendly and efficient, well geared for holiday crowds, with good value generous food, Whitbreads-related ales, children welcome; side play area with boat to play on *(P Gillbe)*

☆ Minstead [SU2811], *Trusty Servant*: In pretty New Forest village with wandering ponies; small bare-boards public bar, unsophisticated back lounge (also small), wide choice of good fresh fish and other bar food inc enormous sandwiches, well kept changing ales such as Hook Norton Best, Hop Back Summer Lightning, Smiles Best and Wadworths 6X, country wines; sizeable attractive restaurant, airy by day, candlelit by night; comfortable bedrooms *(W Wonham, D Marsh, David Sowerbutts, K A Louden, Ron Shelton, Malcolm and Wendy Butler, BB)*

Nether Wallop [signed from A30 or B2084 W of Stockbridge; SU3036], *Five Bells*: Simple village pub with long cushioned settles and good log fire in beamed bar (one end serving as local post office), cheap bar food, well kept Marstons, bar billiards and other traditional games in locals' bar, small restaurant, seats outside, provision for children *(Ann and Colin Hunt, LYM)*

Newnham [Newnham Green, handy for M3 junction 5; SU7054], *Old House At Home*: Peaceful bay-windowed house in secluded hamlet, attractive frontage with flower tubs and carriage blocks; chatty welcome, well kept Courage and Ushers, country food; pleasant walks nearby *(Anon)*

☆ North Gorley [Ringwood Rd, just off A338; SU1611], *Royal Oak*: Comfortable and welcoming 17th-c thatched pub with beam and plank ceiling, flagstones, panelled dado, generous reasonably priced usual food from sandwiches to steaks inc children's dishes, well kept Whitbreads-related ales, welcoming young staff; children in family room, big well kept garden with swings and climber, idyllic New Forest setting nr pond *(Jerry and Alison Oakes, Chris and Margaret Southon)*

North Waltham [signed off A30 SW of Basingstoke; handy for M3 junction 7 – OS Sheet 185 map ref 564458; SU5645], *Fox*: Friendly two-bar village local, attractive and comfortable, with well kept Ushers Best and Founders and guest beers, welcoming licensees, wide choice of food inc lots of seasonal game (landlord an ex-gamekeeper) in bar and recently extended restaurant; darts and juke box in public bar, tables in garden *(Lynn Sharpless, Bob Eardley, Chris and Georgie Brown, Neil Cole)*

☆ North Warnborough [nr M3 junction 5; SU7351], *Swan*: Friendly canalside village pub with good choice of well priced good food, well kept Courage Best, Marstons Pedigree, Wadsworth 6X *(Margaret Dyke)*

Oakhanger [off A325 Farnham—Petersfield – OS Sheet 186 map ref 769359; SU7736], *Red Lion*: Unpretentious old beamed pub with well kept Courage, good food esp fresh fish, big log fire, friendly staff, eating area *(Mr and Mrs R J Foreman, Mike Fitzgerald)*

☆ Odiham [High St (A287); SU7450], *George*: Comfortable old-fashioned inn with well kept Courage-related ales, decent wines by the glass, good value bar food, attentive staff, interesting old photographs, fish restaurant; comfortable little back bar overlooking garden; bedrooms *(Christine and Geoff Butler, J Sheldon, Clive Gilbert, Martin and Karen Wake, LYM)*

☆ Owslebury [SU5123], *Ship*: Small very popular village local with little-changed character public bar, lots of local pictures, extended family area, good value generous home cooking (lunchtime and from early evening, can be a wait – and many tables may be booked), friendly service, Marstons ales; magnificent downland views from two big floriferous garden areas, huge play area, goats, maybe even bowls practice and cricket net; good walks, handy for Marwell Zoo *(M J D Inskip, Ann and Colin Hunt, A J Blackler, Peter and Audrey Dowsett, LYM)*

Pennington [Milford Rd; SZ3194], *White Hart*: Country local with well kept Whitbreads-related ales, good value straightforward food, pleasant atmosphere, terrace and garden *(SLC)*

☆ Petersfield [College St; SU7423], *Good Intent*: Doing well under current regime – now a Gales pub, with IPA, BBB, HSB and Gold; good food changing daily, with big helpings, reasonable prices, and willingness to vary dishes for individual preferences; children in cosy former restaurant area *(A J Blackler)*

☆ nr Petersfield [old coach rd NW past Steep – OS Sheet 186 map ref 726273], *Trooper*: Well kept Bass, Ringwood and guest beers such as Wadworths, interesting good value wines, decent straightforward bar food inc good evening steaks, friendly service, candlelight, scrubbed pine tables and bare boards, good views *(Wendy Arnold)*

Porchester [next to Porchester Castle; SU6105], *Cormorant*: Whitbreads pub in pleasant close handy for the castle, good value food, obliging staff, children in dining area; seats outside, plenty of parking *(David Dimock)*

☆ Portsmouth [Bath Sq, Old Town; SU6501], *Spice Island*: Roomy modernised waterside

Whitbreads pub with seafaring theme, big windows and outside seats overlooking passing ships, well kept ales, food all day inc vegetarian, family room (one of the few in Portsmouth), bright upstairs restaurant; can be very crowded; as with other pubs here nearby parking may be difficult *(T Roger Lamble, David Carr, Colin and Ann Hunt, Thomas Nott)*

☆ Portsmouth [High St, Old Town], *Dolphin*: Spacious and genteel old timber-framed pub with ten or more Whitbreads-related and other ales, wide range of food, good log fire, cosy snug; video games; open all day Sat, children welcome in eating area, small terrace *(Colin and Ann Hunt, KCW, JJB, Martyn Hart)*

☆ Portsmouth [High St, Old Town], *Sally Port*: Spick-and-span, brightly modernised but still interesting with reasonably priced good bar food esp fish, well kept Marstons, good friendly staff, upstairs restaurant; comfortable bedrooms *(Ann and Colin Hunt, David Carr, Shirley Pielou)*

Portsmouth [The Wharf, Camber Dock], *Bridge*: On the wharf, good water views, bar food, upstairs fish bistro, Whitbreads-related ales *(Ann and Colin Hunt)*; [Queens St, nr dockyard entrance], *George*: Recently reopened, welcoming and restful, with brass and copperware, friendly service, ales inc Marstons Pedigree, Theakstons, Wadworths 6X and Youngers No 3, good choice of wines *(Ann and Colin Hunt)*; [Highland Rd, Eastney; SU6899], *Mayflower Beer Engine*: Fairly smart two-bar pub with old pictures and stone jars etc, comfortable tables and chairs, well kept Tetleys and other ales, good cheap straightforward bar food, cheerful licensee, black cat; darts, juke box, garden *(Ann and Colin Hunt)*; [Port Solent marina], *Mermaid*: Very smart pub on exclusive marina with Boddingtons beer and limited bar snacks; plenty of seating inside and out, lots to look at *(Peter and Audrey Dowsett)*; [Victory Rd, The Hard], *Ship & Castle*: Large modernised Whitbreads family pub with big dining area, handy for HMS *Victory* etc *(Ann and Colin Hunt)*; [London Rd, North End], *Tap*: Free house with eight changing well kept ales, thriving atmosphere, genuine service, good choice of bar food inc king-sized sandwiches *(Roger Stroud)*; [Guildhall St], *Yorkshire Grey*: Large Victorian Bass pub with cheap lunchtime snacks, interesting old tile pictures; upstairs function room is said to have ghost of murdered prostitute *(J A Snell)*

Preston Candover [Arlesford Rd; SU6041], *Purefoy Arms*: Welcoming licensees, good range of generous food inc speciality topped garlic breads, interesting salads, vegetarian dishes; get there early for live jazz Thurs and first Sun in month; open all day Sun *(Gill and Mike Grout)*

☆ Ringwood [The Bridges, West St, just W of town; SU1505], *Fish*: Several quiet and cosy areas (some away from bar perhaps a bit dark), intriguing fishy decorations, well kept ales such as Brakspears and Fullers London

Pride, coffee and tea, wide choice of good value generous food maybe inc bargain offers, log fire, good obliging service, eating area allowing children, no dogs; tables on riverside lawn with play area and budgerigar aviary, open all day *(Howard Allen, Nick Wikeley, J Sheldon, A Pring, LYM)*

Ringwood [12 Meeting House Lane, behind Woolworths], *Inn on the Furlong*: Several rooms, with flagstone floors, stripped brick and oak timbering, conservatory restaurant; full range of Ringwood beers inc winter Porter kept well, good value lunchtime bar food; live music some nights, Easter beer festival; other times can be rather sombre *(Bruce Bird, Mark Brock)*; [Mkt Sq], *White Hart*: Real market-square pub, everything centuries old, with pleasant helpful staff, good food inc home-made specials, local and guest beers *(T A and B J Bryan)*

☆ Rockford [OS Sheet 195 map ref 160081; SU1608], *Alice Lisle*: Friendly and pleasant open-plan pub attractively placed on green by New Forest, wide choice of good value food inc good sandwiches and children's helpings in big conservatory-style family eating area, well kept Gales and guest beers, country wines, helpful staff, baby-changing facilities; garden with good play area and pets' corner, ponies wander nearby; handy for Moyles Court *(Mrs Pointon, Candida, BB)*

Romsey [Church St; SU3521], *Abbey*: Plush inn opp abbey, with good choice of food, welcoming efficient service, well served Courage Best and Directors; bedrooms *(Dr and Mrs A K Clarke)*; [Love Lane], *Old House At Home*: Nice-looking thatched pub with long-serving licensee and basic old-fashioned decor; good food *(Mr and Mrs R J Foreman)*; [Middlebridge St], *Three Tuns*: Comfortable atmosphere, good reasonably priced food *(A R Nuttall)*; [bypass, 300 yds from entrance to Broadlands], *Three Tuns*: Deceptively small from the outside, lots of space inside, two bars with old beams and good log fires, beers such as Bass, Flowers, Ringwood, Wadworths 6X, generous well presented home-made food from temptingly filled baguettes up, friendly efficient service, afternoon teas, pleasant terrace *(C A Hall, Phyl and Jack Street)*

☆ nr Romsey [Botley Rd; A27 towards N Baddesley – handy for M27 junction 3; SU3621], *Luzborough House*: Recently refurbished extensive Whitbreads family dining pub with interesting series of smaller rooms leading off high-raftered flagstoned main bar, good generous food all day, well kept ales, big log fire, cheerful staff; piped music; children welcome away from bar, tables and play area in spacious walled garden *(Mr and Mrs Craig, John Sanders, N E Bushby, Miss W E Atkins, LYM)*

nr Romsey [Greatbridge, A3057 towards Stockbridge; SU3422], *Dukes Head*: Attractively decorated dining pub festooned with flowering baskets in summer; wide range of good attractively priced food, smart efficient waitresses, Whitbreads-related ales,

inglenook eating places, charming back garden wth old tractor and rabbits *(Ruth and Alan Cooper, Ian Phillips, Lynn Sharpless, Bob Eardley)*

☆ Rotherwick [High St; SU7156], *Falcon*: Welcoming country local with half a dozen rotating well kept ales such as Brakspears PA, Greene King Abbot, Marstons Pedigree and Wadworths 6X, good reasonably priced food, open fire, smartish public bar with darts, bar billiards, TV, smaller lounge; children welcome *(Simon Collett-Jones, Stephen Teakle)*

Rowlands Castle [SU7310], *Robin Hood*: Decent pub food inc good Fri fish specials and good cheesecake *(R A Cooper)*

Selborne [SU7433], *Queens*: Friendly village pub/hotel with interesting local memorabilia in bar, well kept beer, good value standard food inc children's, open fires; children welcome; bedrooms, very handy for Gilbert White's home *(A J Blackler, Thomas Nott, LYM)*

☆ Setley [A337 Brockenhurst—Lymington; SU3000], *Filly*: Relaxing and comfortable, with two contrasting and attractive bars, interesting choice of generous well presented food inc vegetarian, well kept Bass, Ringwood Old Thumper and Wadworths 6X, decent wines, friendly landlord, quick service – very popular with older people (and children) lunchtime; piped music; some tables outside, handy for New Forest walks *(Howard Clutterbuck, Dr and Mrs A K Clarke, Derek and Margaret Underwood, D Marsh, C A Hall, Lynn Sharpless, Bob Eardley, John and Joan Nash, D Deas, LYM)*

☆ Sherfield on Loddon [SU6857], *White Hart*: Tidily refurbished and welcoming, with wide choice of generous freshly made food from good bacon sandwiches up (can be a wait if busy), huge inglenook fireplace, friendly efficient service, well kept Courage and guest ales, good choice of wines, interesting coaching-era relics, tables outside; soft piped music; handy for The Vyne *(J S M Sheldon, Mr and Mrs T Bryan, LYM)*

Sherfield on Loddon, *Four Horseshoes*: Quiet and friendly, with well kept Courage Best and good value food inc good bacon and egg sandwich, enormous omelettes *(Anon)*

Shirrell Heath [B2177; SU5714], *Prince of Wales*: Staff cheerful even when busy, good food inc OAP weekday bargains, nice restaurant *(John Sanders)*

Southampton [Osborne Rd, opp St Denys Stn; SU4313], *Dolphin*: Done out well in basic bare-boards style with three roaring coal fires, big tables, interesting photographs; six changing ales such as Cains Formidable and Traditional, Gibbs Mew Bishops Tipple, Deacon and Salisbury Best, welcoming staff, enterprising reasonably priced food from hot sandwiches to Sun lunch inc vegetarian, no-smoking area, some live music *(Richard Mason, Ian Phillips, Dr M Owton)*; [36 Bugle St], *Duke of Wellington*: Ancient timber-framed building on 13th-c foundations, bare boards, log fire, bar food inc good home-made soups; very handy for Tudor House Museum *(B and K Hypher)*; [55 High St, off inner ring rd], *Red Lion*: Interesting for its lofty galleried hall, genuinely medieval, with armour and Tudor panelling; open all day, Courage-related ales *(BH, KH, LYM)*; [38 Adelaide Rd, by St Denys stn], *South Western Arms*: A dozen or so real ales inc Badger and Gales, enthusiastic staff, basic food, bare boards, exposed brickwork, toby jugs and stags' head on beams, lots of woodwork, beermats on ceiling, upper gallery where children allowed; popular with students, easy-going atmosphere; picnic tables on terrace, live jazz Sun afternoon *(Jane Warren, Dr M Owton, Gary Smith)*

☆ Southsea [15 Eldon St/Norfolk St; SZ6498], *Eldon Arms*: Big comfortable rambling bar with old pictures and advertisements, attractive mirrors, lots of nick-nacks; half a dozen Eldridge Pope and other changing ales, decent wines, good changing range of promptly served food, sensibly placed darts; pool and fruit machine, restaurant, tables in back garden *(Ann and Colin Hunt, Stephen and Judy Parish, Malcolm Young)*
Southsea [Victoria St], *Fuzz & Firkin*: Usual bare boards and solid furnishings, friendly staff, good beer brewed at the pub, nice atmosphere; loud music and lots of young people Sat night *(Richard Houghton)*
Southwick [just off B2177 on Portsdown Hill; SU6208], *Golden Lion*: Relaxing two-bar local in attractive village, with scenic walks nearby; well kept Boddingtons and Flowers IPA, friendly staff, good value homely food, pleasant restaurant; where Eisenhower and Montgomery came before D-Day; two nice tortoise-shell seats *(Colin and Ann Hunt, Phyl and Jack Street)*

☆ Sparsholt [signed off A272 W of Winchester; SU4331], *Plough*: Airy and comfortable extended bar with some stripped brick and panelling, rustic tools, good changing food (not Sun evening) from sandwiches to interesting main dishes inc unusual vegetarian ones, well kept Wadworths IPA and 6X, good house wines, copes well with children; piped music, wandering dogs, side bar with bar billiards, shove-ha'penny, cribbage and dominoes; tables outside, play area, donkeys and hens; live music Fri *(Lynn Sharpless, Bob Eardley, Ian Phillips, Paul Boot, Howard Allen, D Waters, John and Wendy Trentham, John and Joy Winterbottom, Joy and Peter Heatherley, P J Caunt, Jane Warren, LYM; more reports on new regime please)*

☆ Steep [Church Rd; Petersfield—Alton, signed Steep off A325 and A272; SU7425], *Cricketers*: Spacious carpeted lounge, massively pine-oriented and almost urban-feeling, with lots of cricket prints, good generous food inc outstanding sandwiches, well kept Gales ales, decent wines and malt whiskies, most obliging licensees; restaurant, picnic tables on back lawn with swings and play-house; comfortable good value bedrooms *(Colin Laffan, MW, KW, LYM)*

☆ Stockbridge [A272/A3057 roundabout, E end; SU3535], *White Hart*: Cheerful and welcoming divided bar, oak pews and other seats, antique prints, shaving-mug collection, reasonably priced bar food, Sun lunches, Bass and Charrington IPA on handpump, country wines, courteous service; children allowed in comfortable beamed restaurant with blazing log fire; bedrooms *(Mr and Mrs R O Gibson, Christopher Warner, Lynn Sharpless, Bob Eardley, LYM)*

☆ Stockbridge [High St], *Grosvenor*: Good atmosphere and quick cheerfully courteous service in pleasant and comfortable old country-town hotel's two smallish bars and dining room, decent food, Courage Directors and Whitbreads Best, log fire; big attractive garden behind; bedrooms good value *(Simon Collett-Jones, W H E Thomas, W and S Jones, John and Phyllis Maloney, BB)*
Stockbridge [High St], *Greyhound*: Spacious but cosy, with dark beams, log fires each end, guitars and prints on wall, carved high-backed settles among other seats, wide choice of usual good value food inc good pies and specials, Courage Best, Ushers Founders and a seasonal ale, decent wines, public bar with pool, friendly courteous service; children and dogs allowed *(Lynn Sharpless, Bob Eardley, John and Phyllis Maloney)*

☆ Stratfield Turgis [SU6960], *Wellington Arms*: Elegant small country inn with individual furnishings in restful and attractively decorated tall-windowed two-room lounge bar, part with polished flagstones, part carpeted; well kept Badger Best, Tanglefoot and BXB, orange juice pressed to order, wide choice of good bar food, open fire, garden; comfortable well equipped bedrooms *(J O Jonkler)*
Stubbington [Stubbington Lane; SU5503], *Golden Bowler*: Good choice of reasonably priced food, comfortable dining area *(E Cowdray)*
Swanmore [Hill Grove – OS Sheet 185 map ref 582161; SU5716], *Hunters*: Popular plush dining pub with big family room, wide choice of decent straightforward food inc vegetarian and children's, Courage Directors, good house wine, country wines, lots of carpentry and farm tools, beams and banknotes; plenty of picnic tables, good big play area with fort, swingboats etc; very busy weekends *(Neil and Anita Christopher)*

☆ Swanmore [Hill Pound Rd; SU5716], *Rising Sun*: Welcoming and comfortably pubby, good log fires, good choice of food (booking advised weekends), well kept Whitbreads-related ales, humorous landlord, quick friendly service; garden with play area *(Stephen and Jean Curtis, Kevin Warrington, John and Chris Simpson)*

☆ Sway [SZ2798], *Hare & Hounds*: Well spaced tables in airy and comfortable New Forest pub with hospitable new licensees, urbane staff, good range of generous good value food, real ales, nautical touches, big garden, hospitable new landlord couple, urbane staff, good food, spacious bar with decent furniture, good range of drinks *(David Surridge, Andrew Scarr)*

☆ Tangley [SU3252], *Fox*: Busy little pub with

generous good value imaginative food inc good puddings, well kept Courage-related and guest ales, good choice of wines, two big log fires, friendly and chatty landlord, prompt helpful service, pleasant restaurant *(Sarah and Graham Rissone, John Hazel)*

Thruxton [just off A303; SU2945], *George*: Well spaced tables in big busy dining area, decent, generous food inc sandwiches and good home-made pies *(W H E Thomas)*

☆ **Timsbury** [Michelmersh; A3057 towards Stockbridge; SU3424], *Bear & Ragged Staff*: Very busy Whitbreads country dining pub, airy and comfortable, with wide choice of food all day from good value ploughman's up, several well kept ales, lots of wines by the glass, country wines, tables out in garden, good play area; children in eating area *(Joan and Andrew Life, D Illing, Joan and John Calvert, P J Caunt, Mr and Mrs Gordon Turner, LYM)*

Titchfield [East St, off A27 nr Fareham; SU5305], *Wheatsheaf*: Popular bar food from sandwiches up, well kept Courage and a guest ale such as Bass, small restaurant, tables out behind *(John Sanders, Ann and Colin Hunt)*; [High St], *Bugle*: Pleasant efficiently run old inn, flagstones and blue carpet, Boddingtons, Flowers IPA, Gales 1066 and Wadworths 6X, very popular good bar food, restaurant in old barn behind *(N Matthews, Ian Phillips)*

Totford [B3046 Basingstoke—Alresford; SU5738], *Woolpack*: Friendly pub/restaurant with well kept Gales HSB, Palmers IPA and local Cheriton Pots on handpump, stripped-brick bar, large dining room, good food inc vegetarian and good Sun roast, open fire; tables outside, lovely setting in good walking country; bedrooms *(Martyn and Mary Mullins, Ann and Colin Hunt)*

☆ **Totton** [Eling Quay; SU3612], *Anchor*: Nautical photographs, well kept Bass and good value promptly served basic home-cooked food in interestingly placed little creekside local, no frills but friendly; a few tables by quay, handy for NT Tidal Mill *(Ian Phillips, Clive Gilbert)*

☆ **Turgis Green** [A33 Reading—Basingstoke; SU6959], *Jekyll & Hyde*: Busy rambling black-beamed pub with wide range of good food from sandwiches up, all day inc breakfast; five changing real ales, some interesting furnishings and prints particularly in back room, prompt friendly service; lots of picnic tables in good sheltered garden (some traffic noise), play area and various games; piped music; lavatories for the disabled, children allowed *(Jim Reid, LYM)*

☆ **Twyford** [SU4724], *Bugle*: Friendly open-plan pub done up in rich post-Victorian style, wide choice of generous reasonably priced good food inc good value Sun lunch, well kept Eldridge Pope ales, decent wines by the glass *(Colin and Ann Hunt)*

Twyford [High St; SU4724], *Phoenix*: Roomy open-plan Marstons local with warmly welcoming managers, decent food, pleasant restaurant, garden *(Ann and Colin Hunt, John Knighton)*

☆ **Upton** [the one nr Hurstbourne Tarrant; SU3555], *Crown*: Classic comfortable country pub with friendly and hard-working licensees, good bar food, well kept beer *(Nick Bell, BB)*

☆ **Upton Grey** [SU6948], *Hoddington Arms*: Consistently good value interesting food inc good puddings in unpretentious two-bar local; well kept Morlands and other ales, Australian wines by glass, friendly service, family room, bar billiards; piped music; garden, attractive village *(Jim Reid, Guy Consterdine, T and M Stewart, Christopher Glasson)*

☆ **Vernham Dean** [off A343 via Upton, or off A338 S of Hungerford via Oxenwood; SU3456], *George*: Relaxed and neatly kept rambling open-plan beamed and timbered bar, carefully refurbished, with some easy chairs, inglenook log fire, good value bar food (not Sun evening) from toasties to steaks inc good home-made puddings, well behaved children allowed in no-smoking eating area, well kept Marstons Best and Pedigree; darts, shove-ha'penny, dominoes and cribbage, tables in pretty garden behind *(Mark Matthewman, Marjorie and David Lamb, Gordon, Peter and Audrey Dowsett, Joy and Paul Rundell, Dr and Mrs A K Clarke)*

Wallington [1 Wallington Shore Rd; nr M27 junction 11; SU5806], *Cob & Pen*: Wide choice of good value food, well kept Whitbreads-related ales; large garden *(N Matthews, Ann and Colin Hunt)*; *White Horse*: Neat little well furnished local with pictures of old Fareham, good value lunchtime food popular with executives from nearby industrial estate; pleasant atmosphere, four ales inc well kept Bass tapped from the cask *(June and Eric Heley, Ann and Colin Hunt)*

☆ **Warnford** [A32; SU6223], *George & Falcon*: Spacious and comfortable softly lit country pub, popular generous food in bar and restaurant, quick friendly service, piped light classical music, Courage-related ales *(P Gillbe, John Hobbs)*

Warsash [Shire Rd; SU4906], *Rising Sun*: Waterside Whitbreads pub open all day for well presented food inc good range of fish dishes, efficient service, long bar part tiled-floor and part boards, spiral stairs to restaurant with fine views Hamble estuary and Solent; handy for Solent Way walk and Hook nature reserve *(Phyl and Jack Street)*

☆ **West Meon** [High St; SU6424], *Thomas Lord*: Good atmosphere in attractive cricket-theme village pub, well kept Whitbreads-related ales, good value generous food, friendly new landlord, collection of club ties in lounge; tables in garden *(Joan and Andrew Life, Colin and Ann Hunt)*

West Wellow [nr M27 junction 2; A36 2 miles N of junction with A431; SU2919], *Red Rover*: Warm welcome, wide range of good value food, Whitbreads-related ales, extensive partly no-smoking dining area, friendly staff *(Ann and Colin Hunt, R Pattison)*; [Canada Rd, off A36 Romsey—Ower at roundabout, signed Canada], *Rockingham Arms*: Plush beamed 19th-c pub on edge of New Forest, good food and drinks, friendly atmosphere and service, open fire; dogs on leads allowed, pool and darts, restaurant; children welcome; garden with play area, small caravan park *(D Marsh, Mr and Mrs Craig)*

☆ Weyhill [A342, signed off A303 bypass; SU3146], *Weyhill Fair*: Popular local with six well kept ales inc Gales HSB, Marstons, Morrells and good varied guests, wide choice of good value food inc enjoyable puddings; spacious solidly furnished lounge with easy chairs around woodburner, old advertisements, smaller family room, no-smoking area; children welcome, handy for Hawk Conservancy *(John Watkins, Julian Sore, Bruce Bird, K J Ashby, Richard Houghton, Peter and Lynn Brueton, BB)*

Weyhill, *Star*: Tidy pub with well kept Hampshire King Alfreds, good value simple sandwiches, pasta restaurant, pleasant service *(R T and J C Moggridge)*

Whitchurch [Bell St; SU4648], *Bell*: Friendly little two-bar local in attractive country town, cosy lounge bar with steps leading up to another cosy room, inglenook fireplace, well kept Gales HSB, good coffee, attractive exterior *(Ann and Colin Hunt)*

☆ Whitsbury [follow Rockbourne sign off A354 SW of Salisbury, turning left just before village; or head W off A338 at S end of Breamore, or in Upper Burgate; SU1219], *Cartwheel*: Smart low-beamed country pub with wide choice of well presented reasonably priced food inc good sandwiches, good range of changing real ales with Aug beer festival, horse-racing decorations, friendly service, neat restaurant (children allowed here if it's not being used); dogs allowed, weekly barbecue in attractive secluded sloping garden with play area, pleasant walks *(Jerry and Alison Oakes, Dr and Mrs A K Clarke)*

☆ Whitway [Winchester Rd (old A34); SU4559], *Carnarvon Arms*: Locally very popular for extraordinarily wide choice of good well presented food – walls in main bar too small to cope with menu; well kept Ushers, very friendly service, open fire, OAP bargain lunches Tues-Thurs, fish and chips Fri; bedrooms *(HNJ, PEJ, R T and J C Moggridge)*

Wickham [The Square; SU5711], *Knockers*: Striking Tudor building with lots of beams, vaulted ceiling, flagstones and roaring log fire, upper dining gallery with rustic tables, separate dining room with medieval wall painting, good fresh food inc Thai and more traditional dishes, also sandwiches etc, very wide choice of wines by the glass, Butcombe and Hampshire real ales, tables out in front and on vine-covered terrace; well behaved children and dogs allowed, jazz Weds *(Geoff May)*; [Kingsmead, A32 towards Droxford], *Roebuck*: Generous reasonably priced food in pleasantly divided pub, painstaking landlady, nice secluded back garden *(Phyl and Jack Street)*; [Station Rd], *White Lion*: Well kept Badger Best and Tanglefoot and Hardington, genuine wholesome home cooking in new dining area *(John and Joy Winterbottom)*

☆ Winchester [The Square, between High St and cathedral; SU4829], *Eclipse*: Picturesque little partly 14th-c pub with massive beams and timbers, oak settles, well kept Whitbreads-related ales, Hampshire Pendragon and Ringwood Old Thumper, well done lunchtime bar food inc good value toasties, welcoming service even when very busy; seats outside, very handy for cathedral *(Rona Murdoch, A and C Hunt, Dr and Mrs A K Clarke, John and Joan Nash, LYM)*

Winchester [Wharf Hill], *Black Boy*: Wide range of mainly Whitbreads-related ales, bays of button-back banquettes in main L-shaped bar, plans for barn restaurant, seats outside *(A and C Hunt, LYM)*; [57 Hyde St (A333, beyond Jewry St)], *Hyde*: Unspoilt 15th-c local with hardly a true right-angle, friendly welcome, sensible prices, particularly well kept Marstons Pedigree; a country pub in a nice part of town *(Tom Espley, Dr and Mrs A K Clarke)*; [Kingsgate Rd], *Queen*: Quiet, friendly and comfortable two-bar pub in attractive setting nr College, with well kept Marstons, good value home cooking *(Mike and Caroline Hayes, John and Chris Simpson)*; [Royal Oak Passage, off pedestrian part of High St], *Royal Oak*: Cheerful well kept town pub with ten or so well kept real ales, little rooms (some raised) off main bar, beams and bare boards, simple furnishings, no-smoking areas, well priced straightforward food, cheerful prompt service; the cellar bar (not always open) has massive 12th-c beams and a Saxon wall which gives it some claim to be the country's oldest drinking spot *(A and C Hunt, LYM)*; [Stanmore Lane off Romsey Rd, two miles out], *Stanmore*: Friendly family pub, courteous efficient staff, good food in bar and restaurant, well kept Eldridge Pope ales, family room, pool, table footer etc; tables outside with play area; reasonably priced bedrooms *(John and Chris Simpson, Adam Darbyshire)*; [Durngate], *Willow Tree*: Intimate nicely furnished pub in beautiful riverside setting, well presented generous food inc bargain daily special, well kept Marstons beers, friendly service; can be rather smoky *(A and C Hunt, Mr and Mrs John Baskwell)*

☆ Winchfield [Winchfield Hurst; SU7753], *Barley Mow*: Two-bar local with light and airy dining extension, wide choice of good value generous home-cooked food from sandwiches up, well kept Courage-related ales, decent wine, unobtrusive piped music; dogs welcome, nr Basingstoke canal – lots of good walks *(June and Eric Heley, Betty Laker, J Sheldon, Liz and Ian Phillips)*

Wolverton [Towns End, just N of A339 Newbury—Basingstoke; SU5558], *George & Dragon*: Comfortable rambling pub, opened-up but still with historic timbers and open fires; pictures, mirrors, hops along the low beams, good range of well kept beers, good value food, big garden; no children in bar *(Gordon)*

☆ Woodgreen [OS Sheet 184 map ref 171176; SU1717], *Horse & Groom*: Busy beamed local, good choice of home-cooked food inc lovely puddings; real ale, log fire, eating area off bar *(Joan and John Calvert)*

Hereford & Worcester

This area includes several really unusual old country taverns, often owing their survival in an utterly unspoilt state to very long-serving licensees. The Monkey House at Defford is a fine example among the main entries, and several others can be found in the Lucky Dip section at the end of the chapter – for example, at Brockhampton and Risbury. This individuality spills over into many other pubs here, occasionally as a matter of deliberate policy (the Little Pack Horse in Bewdley is the best of a small local chain of 'Little' pubs in which eccentricity has been raised to a high art). More often, though, it's deeply ingrained in the pubs' past: many have a long and interesting history, and among these the Fleece at Bretforton stands out as a magnificently preserved ancient farmhouse pub, with antique furnishings of great beauty. Other pubs currently doing very well here include the Bear & Ragged Staff at Bransford and Fox & Hounds at Bredon (both very foody), the fine old Feathers in Ledbury, the bustling and rambling Kings Arms at Ombersley, the Olde Salutation in the charming village of Weobley, and the very friendly little Crown at Woolhope. We'd add to these three new main entries: the lively King & Castle at the steam railway station in Kidderminster, the Bell at Pensax (a nice country pub recently taken over by the man who last year gained our Beer Man of the Year award in his former Buckinghamshire pub), and the Three Crowns at Ullingswick (a charming out-of-the-way pub with good food, particularly in the evenings). The Roebuck at Brimfield and the Hunters Inn at Longdon also have very good food; but for a memorable meal out our choice as Hereford & Worcester Dining Pub of the Year is the Olde Salutation at Weobley. In the Lucky Dip section, currently notable pubs include the Penny Farthing at Aston Crews, Riverside at Aymestrey, Halfway House at Bastonford, Duke of York at Berrow, Mug House at Claines, Pandy at Dorstone, Firs at Dunhampstead, Queen Elizabeth at Elmley Castle, Green Man at Fownhope, Old Bull at Inkberrow, Hope & Anchor in Ross on Wye, Country Girl at Stoke Prior and Rhydspence at Whitney on Wye; there's a good choice in and around Tenbury Wells. We have inspected most of these and can vouch for their appeal. Drinks prices in the area are well below the national average, with most of the pubs getting beers from interesting smaller breweries; bizarrely, the cheapest beer we found was at the Roebuck at Brimfield, which is really a smart and expensive dining pub; beer was also very cheap at the Talbot at Knightwick.

Post Office address codings confusingly give the impression that some pubs are in Hereford and Worcestershire, when they're really in the Midlands, Shropshire, Gloucestershire or even Wales (which is where we list them).

BEWDLEY SO7875 Map 4

Little Pack Horse

High Street; no nearby parking – best to park in main car park, cross A4117 Cleobury road, and keep walking on down narrowing High Street; can park 150 yds at bottom of Lax Lane

Full of eccentricities and oddities, this characterful pub has various clocks, wood-working tools, Indian clubs, a fireman's helmet, an old car horn, lots of old photographs and advertisements, and even an incendiary bomb on its walls; a wall-mounted wooden pig's mask is used in the pub's idiosyncratic game of swinging a weighted string to knock a coin off its ear or snout. There are pews, red leatherette wall settles, a mixed bag of tables on the red-tiled floor, roughly plastered white walls, and low beams. Bar food includes home-made soup (£1.95), very substantial sandwiches (weekdays only from £2.25), filled baked potatoes (£2.95), lasagne (£3.95), gammon with pineapple (£4.25), the hefty Desperate Dan pie (in 3 sizes £2.95, £3.95, £4.95), and sirloin steak, with puddings such as jam roly poly with custard (£1.95); friendly service. As well as their own Lumphammer on handpump, they keep Ind Coope Burton and a changing range of guest beers; woodburning stove. *(Recommended by Tony Kemp, Rachel Weston, Lucy James, Dean Foden, DMT, Lawrence Bacon, Martin and Karen Wake, Mrs P J Pearce)*

Free house ~ Licensees Peter and Sue D'Amery ~ Real ale ~ Meals and snacks ~ (01299) 403762 ~ Children in eating area of bar ~ Open 11-3, 6-11; 11-11 Sat; 12-10.30 Sun

BIRTSMORTON SO7935 Map 4

Farmers Arms

Off B4208

Surrounded by plenty of walks, this attractive black and white timbered village pub is neatly kept and friendly, and has a good old-fashioned rural atmosphere. On the right a big room rambles away under low dark beams, with some standing timbers, and flowery-panelled cushioned settles as well as spindleback chairs; on the left an even lower-beamed room seems even snugger, and in both the white walls have black timbering. Popular, good value home-made bar food includes sandwiches, ploughman's, filled baked potatoes (from £3.10), macaroni cheese (£2.80), cauliflower cheese (£3), lasagne (£4.40), steak and kidney pie (£4.95), gammon (£6), steak (£7.25), and puddings (from £1.45. Well kept Hook Norton Old Hookey and guest beers like Hobsons and Woods on handpump; darts in a good tiled area, shove-ha'penny, cribbage, and dominoes. There are seats out on the grass; they have a self-catering cottage. *(Recommended by Dorothy and Leslie Pilson, V Kavanagh, Neil and Anita Christopher, Kay Neville-Rolfe, Ted George)*

Free house ~ Licensees Jill and Julie Moore ~ Real ale ~ Meals and snacks (12-2, 6-10) ~ (01684) 833308 ~ Children in eating area of bar ~ Open 11-2.30(3 Sat), 6-11

BRANSFORD SO7852 Map 4

Bear & Ragged Staff 🍴 ♀

Powick Rd; off A4103 SW of Worcester

It's the particularly good food that draws readers to this stylish dining pub with its proper tablecloths, linen napkins, and fresh flowers: sandwiches (from £2) and ploughman's (from £5.25), with daily specials such as mixed pepper, mushroom and cream cheese pancake (£6.10), nice savoury pesto bread and butter pudding, lamb and apricot cobbler (£6.15), lamb with redcurrant sauce (£6.20), strips of sirloin steak in a black pepper and brandy sauce (£6.75), salmon, halibut and prawn lasagne (£6.95), breast of chicken stuffed with chicken liver pâté (£7.25), fresh fish like john dory, sardines, turbot and sea bass (from £9), and puddings such as sticky toffee pudding, lovely treacle tart or spotted dick (£3.10); best to book. The interconnecting rooms have a relaxed and cheerful atmosphere (the restaurant is no smoking), an open fire, well kept Boddingtons and Flowers Original on handpump kept under light blanket pressure, a good range of wines (mainly New World ones), lots of malt whiskies, and quite a few brandies and liqueurs; willing, helpful service; darts, cribbage, dominoes, and piped music. *(Recommended by Dave Braisted, Gethin Lewis, Joy and Peter Heatherley, T H G Lewis, A Preston, M V and J Melling, E A George, Lucy James, Dean Foden, Christopher and Maureen Starling, W H E Thomas, Paul and Elizabeth Anthony, Michael and Margaret Norris)*

Free house ~ Licensee John Owen ~ Real ale ~ Meals and snacks (till 10pm) ~ Restaurant ~ (01886) 833399 ~ Children in eating area of bar ~ Piano Fri and Sat evenings ~ Open 12-3(4 Sat), 6.30-11; closed Sun evening

BREDON SO9236 Map 4

Fox & Hounds

4½ miles from M5 junction 9; A438 to Northway, left at B4079, then in Bredon follow To church and river signpost on right

Down a quiet lane leading to the river and next to the church, this neat thatched place is almost more of a restaurant now – though there is still a thriving trade at the bar. The comfortable and well-modernised carpeted bar has a friendly atmosphere, dressed stone pillars and stripped timbers, a central woodburning stove, upholstered settles, wheelback, tub, and ktichen chairs around attractive mahogany and cast-iron-framed tables, dried grasses and flowers, a toy fox dressed in hunting scarlet, and elegant wall lamps. A smaller side bar has assorted wooden kitchen chairs, wheelbacks, and settles, and an open fire at each end. The wide choice of popular food might include home-made soup (£2.25), ploughman's (from £3.75), smoked bacon and mushroom bake or king prawns on garlic toast (£4.95), home-made pies like lamb and mint (from £6.25), gammon and eggs (£6.75), vegetarian dishes, cod, salmon and prawn gratin (£6.95), fresh fish dishes (from £7.95), steaks (from £8.95), home-made puddings, and children's menu; roast Sunday lunch; very pleasant service. Well kept Boddingtons, Marstons Pedigree, and Morlands Old Speckled Hen on handpump, freshly squeezed fruit juice and several malt whiskies. The pub is pretty in summer with its colourful hanging baskets, and some of the picnic tables are under Perspex; there's a thatched wendy house. *(Recommended by Frank Cummins, M Joyner, Dorothee and Dennis Glover, Derek and Sylvia Stephenson, Mrs J Oakes, M L and G Clarke, Mrs K Neville-Rolfe, W H and E Thomas, D G King, Dave Braisted, James Macrae, G and M Hollis, Ian Jones)*

Whitbreads ~ Lease: Michael Hardwick ~ Real ale ~ Meals and snacks (till 10pm) ~ Restaurant ~ (01684) 772377 ~ Children welcome ~ Open 11-2.30, 6-11

BRETFORTON SP0943 Map 4

Fleece ★ ★

B4035 E of Evesham; turn S off this road into village; pub is in centre square by church; there's a sizeable car park at one side of the church

This marvellous old pub is best visited on a quiet weekday when you can enjoy the beauty of the place and inspect the antiques at leisure. Originally, this was a farm owned by one family for nearly 500 years, and they first opened it as a pub in 1848 and ran it until 1977 when the last of the line bequeathed it to the National Trust (under the stipulation that no crisps, peanuts and so forth be sold). All the furnishings are original, many of them heirlooms: a great oak dresser holds a priceless 48-piece set of Stuart pewter, there's a fine grandfather clock, ancient kitchen chairs, curved high-backed settles, a rocking chair, and a rack of heavy pointed iron shafts, probably for spit roasting, in one of the huge inglenook fireplaces. There are massive beams and exposed timbers, worn and crazed flagstones (scored with marks to keep out demons), and plenty of oddities such as a great cheese-press and set of cheese moulds, and a rare dough-proving table; a leaflet details the more bizarre items, and there are three warming winter fires. The room with the pewter is no smoking. Well kept Everards Beacon Bitter, M & B Brew XI and Uley Old Spot and Pigs Ear on handpump, country wines, winter mulled wine, and farm cider; the beer festival is usually held in the second half of July. Bar food includes sandwiches (from £1.50), ploughman's (from £3.30), sausages (£3.40), lasagne (£4), steak and kidney pie (£4.50), locally cured gammon (£5.25), and steak (£6.25). Darts, cribbage, dominoes, shove-ha'penny. In summer, when it gets very busy, they make the most of the extensive orchard, with seats on the goat-cropped grass that spreads around the beautifully restored thatched and timbered barn, among the fruit trees, and at the front by the stone pump-trough. There's also an adventure playground, a display of farm engines, an aviary, and an enclosure with sheep, chicken, geese and a goat. They also hold the village fete and annual asparagus auctions at the end of May. *(Recommended by Jerry and Alison Oakes, Dr P Jackson, Martin and Penny Fletcher, Bryan Taylor, MDN, Medwin Bew, Miss K Law, K M Timmins, Denys Gueroult, B J Cox, Michael and Hazel Lyons, JJW,CMW, Paul Boot, Susan and John Douglas, Terry and Vann W Prime, Dave Brown, Martin Jones, Lynn Sharpless, Bob Eardley, Phil and Sally Gorton, Richard Holmes, Fran Reynolds, Jack and Philip Paxton)*

Free house ~ Licensee N J Griffiths ~ Real ale ~ Meals and snacks (not Mon or Sun evenings in winter) ~ (01386) 831173 ~ Children welcome ~ Morris men summer weekends ~ Open 11-2.30, 6-11

BRIMFIELD SO5368 Map 4

Roebuck 🍴 🛏 🍷

Village signposted just off A49 Shrewsbury—Leominster

Very well run and warmly friendly, this smartly civilised dining pub remains popular for its beautifully presented – if pricey – meals. In the bar this might include soup with home-made bread (£2.90), salmon pot with melba toast or black pudding with a purée of potato, apple and celeriac (£5), mushroom and herb risotto (£6), spinach roulade stuffed with cream cheese and onion, served with a tomato sauce (£6.50), baked queen scallops stuffed with a mushroom and garlic butter (£7), fish pie (£7.50), cider chicken pie (£8), confit of duck on a bed of red cabbage with an orange sauce (£9.50), puddings such as banana baked in a paper parcel with a passion fruit sauce, fresh lemon tart with a fresh fruit sauce and chocolate soufflé with a bitter chocolate sorbet (from £5), and an excellent range of unusual British farmhouse cheeses served with home-made oat cakes and walnut and sultana bread (£6); vegetables are £1.50 extra. The quiet and old-fashioned snug has an impressive inglenook fireplace, and another panelled bar has dimpled copper-topped cask tables, decorative plates mounted over dark ply panelling and a small open fire; the big-windowed side restaurant is elegant and modern (but expensive). Caring, pleasant staff serve olives and friandises (good ones) before your bar meal comes. The wine list is enormous and remarkably good, particularly strong on the better burgundy and rhone growers and éleveurs, and New World wines; also Crown Buckley Reverend James, Greene King Abbot, and Morlands Old Speckled Hen on handpump, and several malt whiskies; darts. Incidentally, there's a family connection with the Walnut Tree at Llandewi Skirrid. *(Recommended by Mrs J Huntly, W H and E Thomas, R D Greaves, Christopher Tobitt, Malcolm Taylor, Wayne Brindle, M Holdsworth, Mike Dickerson, Nigel Woolliscroft, F C Johnston, H and D Payne, J C Green)*

Free house ~ Licensee Carole Evans ~ Real ale ~ Meals and snacks (till 10pm; not Sun or Mon) ~ Restaurant (closed Sun and Mon) ~ (01584) 711230 ~ Children welcome ~ Open 12-2, 7-11; closed Sun, Mon and 25-26 Dec ~ Bedrooms: £45B/£60B

BROADWAY SP0937 Map 4

Crown & Trumpet 🍺

Church St, just off High St

There's a pleasant, cheerful atmosphere in this lovely golden stone building, and the cosily unpretentious beamed and timbered bar has dark high-backed settles and a blazing log fire; quiz night on Thursdays, Saturday sing-along duo, and darts, bar billiards, shove-ha'penny, cribbage, dominoes, and ring-the-bull at one end, fruit machine and piped music; also, Evesham quoits. Well kept Boddingtons, Flowers IPA and Original, Morlands Old Speckled Hen, local Stanway Bitter, and Wadworths 6X on handpump, hot toddies and mulled wine in winter, and summer pimms and kir. Good bar food includes soup (£2.45), ploughman's (from £3.95), faggots and mushy peas (£4.45), steak and kidney pie or beef cooked in a local plum sauce (£4.95), 10oz rump steak (£7.95), daily specials (£2.95-£6.95); asparagus menu (from £4.45), and Sunday roast; quick, friendly service; seats out on the front terrace. *(Recommended by SLC, Pat and Roger Fereday, Terry and Vann Prime, Angus Lyon, DAV)*

Whitbreads ~ Lease: Andrew Scott ~ Real ale ~ Meals and snacks ~ (01386) 853202 ~ Children welcome ~ Sing-along duo Sat, occasional jazz ~ Open 11-2.30, 5-11; 11-11 Sat; 12-4, 6-10.30 Sun ~ Bedrooms: /£45B

CAREY SO5631 Map 4

Cottage of Content 🛏 ♀

Village, and for most of the way pub itself, signposted from good road through Hoarwithy

This very pretty and out-of-the-way medieval country cottage is peacefully set by a stream in a quiet little lane, with picnic tables on the flower-filled front terrace and a couple more on a back terrace looking up a steep expanse of lawn. The main bar is a light, airy room with a friendly atmosphere, lots of hops hanging from the beams and over the bar counter, stripped pine tables and country kitchen chairs on the old flagstones, a brick fireplace, and through a partly knocked-through timbered wall on the left, a big table with long pews on either side. An alcove with just one table connects this room with a similarly furnished second bar, and standing timbers lead to the end dining room with elegant spindleback chairs around a mix of old-fashioned tables, a big rug on the stripped wooden floor, and fish prints on the walls. As well as bar food such as home-made pies, Whitby scampi and gammon and pineapple, there are lots of daily specials (especially at weekends when they are very busy) such as marinated anchovies with potato salad or soup (from £1.95), broccoli, cheese and almond bake (£5.50), bison sausage casserole (£6.95), escalope of pork normandy (£7.50), fresh fish and game in season, breast of duck with port and blueberry sauce (£9.50), and puddings (£2.50). Well kept Hook Norton Best and Old Hookey, and Ruddles Best and County on handpump, with a good wine list, and 35 malt whiskies; darts, dominoes, and cribbage, and piped music. The two samoyed dogs are called Shadow and Storm. *(Recommended by Christopher Tobitt, Ted George, Dennis Shirley, Simon Small, Malcolm Taylor, Andrew Stephenson, Nigel Clifton, Nigel Wilkinson, Roger and Christine Mash, Gordon, Jerry and Alison Oakes, Lynn Sharpless, Bob Eardley)*

Free house ~ Licensee Mike Wainford ~ Real ale ~ Meals and snacks (till 10pm Fri-Sat ~ (01432) 840242 ~ Children welcome ~ Open 12-2.30, 7-11; closed 25 Dec ~ Bedrooms: £35B/£48B

DEFFORD SO9143 Map 4

Monkey House

Woodmancote; A4104 towards Upton – immediately after passing Oak public house on right, there's a small group of cottages, of which this is the last

At first you might think this pretty black and white cottage – set back from the road behind a small garden with one or two fruit trees – was just a private house as there's no inn-sign. In fact, it's one of the few remaining absolutely traditional cider-houses, and from a hatch beside the door, very cheap Bulmer's Medium or Special Dry cider is tapped from barrels and poured by jug into pottery mugs. Beer is sold in cans – a concession to modern tastes. They don't do food (except crisps and nuts), but allow you to bring your own. In good weather, you can stand outside with Tess the bull terrier and Tapper the jack russell, and hens and cockerels that wander in from an adjacent collection of caravans and sheds; they have two horses called Murphy and Mandy. Or you can retreat to a small side outbuilding with a couple of plain tables, a settle and an open fire; darts and dominoes. The name came from a drunken customer some years ago who fell into bramble bushes and insisted he was attacked by monkeys. *(Recommended by Chris Raisin, Derek and Sylvia Stephenson; more reports please)*

Free house ~ Licensee Graham Collins ~ (01386) 750234 ~ Open 12-2.30, 6-11; closed Mon evening, all day Tues

HANLEY CASTLE SO8442 Map 4

Three Kings £ 🍺

Pub signposted (not prominently) off B4211 opposite Manor House gates, N of Upton on Severn, follow Church End signpost

Very little has changed in the 80-odd years that this genuinely unspoilt, friendly local has been run by the same family. The little tiled-floor tap room on the right is separated off from the entrance corridor by the monumental built-in settle which faces its equally vast inglenook fireplace. A hatch here serves very well kept Butcombe Bitter, Thwaites and usually three guest beers from small independent breweries on handpump, 50 malt whiskies and farm cider. On the left, another room is decorated with lots of small locomotive pictures, and has darts, dominoes, shove-ha'penny and cribbage. A separate entrance leads to the comfortable timbered lounge with another inglenook fireplace and a neatly blacked kitchen range, little leatherette armchairs and spindleback chairs arounds its tables, and another antique winged and high-backed settle. Straightforward bar food includes soup (£1), sandwiches (from £1), omelettes (from £2.25), sausage and egg or burgers (£2.75), ploughman's (from £2.75), gammon and egg (£4.75), and daily specials; there may be some delay. Bow windows in the three main rooms and old-fashioned wood-and-iron seats on the front terrace look across to the great cedar which shades the tiny green. *(Recommended by Mr and Mrs H M Mortimer, Hugh MacLean, J and P Maloney, Alan and Paula McCully, Donald Clay, P and M Rudlin, Derek and Sylvia Stephenson, Dave Thompson, Margaret Mason, John Bowdler)*

Free house ~ Licensee Mrs Sheila Roberts ~ Real ale ~ Meals and snacks (not Sun evening) ~ (01684) 592686 ~ Children in family room ~ Singer/guitar Sun evening, singalong alternate Sat evenings, folk club alternate Thurs evenings ~ Open 11-3, 7-11; closed evening 25 Dec ~ Bedrooms: £27.50B/£45B

KIDDERMINSTER SO8376 Map 4

King & Castle

Railway Station, Comberton Hill

In the terminus of Britain's most lively private steam railway, this is a loving recreation of a classic station refreshment room. It perfectly conjures up the feel of a better-class Edwardian establishment that has unbent a little to greet the more informal ways of the 1920s. More importantly, however, it functions as a good welcoming pub. Besides well kept Bathams and Bass, two guests might include Holdens Special Bitter or Highgate Saddlers on handpump. A wide choice of straightforward good value bar food runs from filled rolls (£1.50), filled baked potatoes (from £2.25), ploughman's (£3.65), lasagne (£4.25) to beef and beer pie, Cajun chicken or Texan beef (£4.95), with puddings like treacle sponge, rum and raisin pudding or apple pie (£1.95). The cheery good humoured landlady and her friendly staff cope well with the bustle of bank holidays and railway gala days (when it can be very difficult to find a seat). Furnishings are solid and in character (even to the occasional obvious need for a touch of reupholstery), and there is the railway memorabilia that you would expect. The atmosphere is lively and sometimes noisily good-humoured (and again in character can sometimes be rather smoky). With steam trains right outside, some railway-buff readers are quite content to start and end their journeys right here; others have used a Rover ticket to shuttle happily between here and the Railwaymans Arms in Bridgnorth (see Shropshire chapter). *(Recommended by R C Vincent, John C Baker, Henry Brugsch, B M Eldridge, Patrick and Mary McDermott, Nick and Alison Dowson)*

Free House ~ Licensee Rosemary Hyde ~ Real ale ~ Meals and snacks (not Mon-Wed evenings) ~ (01562) 747505 ~ Children welcome ~ Open 11-3, 5-11; Sat 11-4, 6-11, Sun 12-10.30

KNIGHTWICK SO7355 Map 4

Talbot 🛏 ♀

Knightsford Bridge; B4197 just off A44 Worcester—Bromyard

There's a bustling atmosphere in this attractively placed 14th-c coaching inn, just as there would have been when it was the focus for both crossing the ford and changing horses. The lounge bar has heavy beams, entertaining and rather distinguished coaching and sporting prints and paintings on its butter-coloured walls, a variety of interesting seats from small carved or leatherette armchairs to the winged settles by the tall bow windows, and a vast stove which squats in the big central stone hearth; there's another log fire. Well kept (and very cheap for the area) Bass, Hobsons Bitter and Worthingtons Best on handpump, and decent wines by the glass. Enjoyable home-made food (nothing is bought in except the smoked salmon and the local produce is carefully chosen) might include soup made with broad beans, peas, and leeks (£1.95), pasta with pesto sauce (£4.25), pork, orange and cognac pâté (£4.50), liver and bacon (£6.95), steak and kidney pie (£7.50), rabbit fricasee or mushroom pilaff (£8.95), skate wing with fresh lemon dressing and capers (£9.95), wild boar casserole (£10.95), lemon sole (£14.95), and puddings such as rhubarb and ginger flan or spiced lemon and strawberry pudding (£3.50); several varieties of home-baked bread, and good breakfasts. The well furnished back public bar has pool on a raised side area, fruit machine, video game and juke box; dominoes and cribbage. There are some old-fashioned seats outside, in front, with more on a good-sized lawn over the lane by the river (they serve out here too). Some of the bedrooms are above the bar. *(Recommended by W C M Jones, James Nunns, Jack and Philip Paxton, Gordon, Dave Braisted, Lawrence Bacon)*

Free house ~ Licensees Annie and Wiz Clift ~ Real ale ~ Meals and snacks ~ Restaurant ~ (01886) 821235 ~ Children welcome ~ Open 11-11; 12-10.30 Sun; closed evening 25 Dec ~ Bedrooms: £24.50(£31B)/£42(£56.50B)

LEDBURY SO7138 Map 4

Feathers 🍽 🛏 ♀

High Street, Ledbury, A417

It's not always easy to cater for both drinkers and diners harmoniously, but the atmospheric and rather civilised Fuggles Bar in this elegant and striking mainly 16th-c timbered inn manages to do just that. Locals tend to gather at one end of the room or at stools by the bar counter and don't feel at all inhibited by those enjoying the imaginative food and fine wines. And if you want to get away from drinkers there are some very snug and cosy tables with nicely upholstered seats with bays around them off to one side. Also, beams and timbers, hop bines, some country antiques, 19th-c caricatures and fowl prints on the stripped brick chimney breast (lovely winter fire), and fresh flowers on the tables. Very attractively presented, the good food includes home-made soup (£2.95), spinach and ricotta tartlet (£3.95), pasta gratin with three cheeses and leeks (£4.25), home-made burgers (£5.85), fresh salmon and fennel seed cakes with fresh tomato sauce (£5.95), three bean and chick pea chilli with celery salad (£7.50), casserole of local rabbit with rosemary and coarse mustard (£8), grilled breast of chicken with garlic and basil sauce (£9.50), steaks (from £11.75), duck breast with five spice, garlic, and sweet soy (£12.95), and home-made puddings like apricot and brandy syllabub, dark rum and raisin cheesecake or apple charlotte with calvados cream (£3.95); friendly, attentive service.

They do good afternoon teas in the more formal quiet lounge by the reception area with comfortable high-sided armchairs and sofas in front of a big log fire, and newspapers to read. Well kept Bass, Greene King Abbot, Marstons Bitter, Worthington Best, and guest beers on handpump, a fine wine list, various malt whiskies, and farm cider. They have their own squash courts. *(Recommended by Mrs J A Powell, Hugh MacLean, Chris Wheaton, John Bowdler, Dave Braisted, Mr and Mrs T A Bryan, JAH, V Kavanagh, Ted George, Gordon Theaker, Michael Richards, Michele and Clive Platman, JAH, David Peakall)*

Free house ~ Licensee David Elliston ~ Real ale ~ Meals and snacks (till 10pm Thurs-Sat) ~ Restaurant (not Sun evening) ~ (01531) 635266 ~ Children in eating area of bar and in hotel lounge area ~ Jazz/blues/folk jazz Weds evening ~ Open 11-11; 12-10.30 Sun ~ Bedrooms: £59.50B/£79.50B

LONGDON SO8336 Map 4

Hunters ⊕ ♀

B4211 S

Rather grand from the outside, this civilised pub has a relaxed, friendly atmosphere in its bar rooms. On the right as you go in there are two comfortable armchairs in a bay window, one-person pews and wheelbacks around a mix of tables, plates and dried flowers on a delft shelf, a warm open fire, and photographs of the licensees in racing cars, and so forth; on the left is a similarly furnished room with flagstones and a big woodburning stove – a small dining room leads off here, and there's a smart heavily beamed restaurant as well. Good, imaginative bar food includes sandwiches (brown, white or crusty from £1.75; hot open ones from £3.75), home-made soup (£2.25), stilton pâté (£3.70), a proper ploughman's (from £3.95), lambs kidneys in a light dijon mustard sauce (£3.95), mushroom, celery and cashew nut stroganoff (£5.95), steak and kidney pie or gammon and egg (£6.50), lamb madras (£6.95), fresh cod with prawns in a prawn and lobster sauce (£7.50), rack of lamb with a honey and mint glaze (£8.95), half crispy roast duck with orange and grand marnier sauce (£10.95), puddings, and Sunday roast lunch. Well kept Everards Beacon, Ruddles Best and Websters Yorkshire on handpump, and good wine by the glass; piped music. There's always a lot going on in their six acres of grounds, and the attractive back garden has some picnic tables on the crazy-paved terrace, with more on the big lawn; dogs, rabbits and ponies. *(Recommended by Alan and Paula McCully, V Kavanagh, Jo Rees, W L Congreve)*

Free house ~ Licensees Howard and Polly Hill-Lines ~ Real ale ~ Meals and snacks (till 10pm) ~ Restaurant ~ (01684) 833388 ~ Children in eating area of bar ~ Open 11-3, 6-11

LUGWARDINE SO5541 Map 4

Crown & Anchor ♀

Cotts Lane; just off A438 E of Hereford

This is an attractive, enjoyable pub with a warm welcome from the friendly licensees. The several smallish character rooms (one suitable for families) are smart and comfortable, with an interesting mix of furnishings, well kept Bass, Hook Norton Best, Worthington Best, and weekly guest beers on handpump, and decent wines including a clutch of usefully priced bin ends; big log fire. A wide choice of food includes sandwiches (from £1.70; stilton and apple £2), home-made soup (£1.75), herring with tomato and onion marinade or camembert and almond pâté (£2.60), ploughman's (£3.50), aubergine and parmesan bake (£5), courgette and ricotta lasagne (£5.20), rabbit with ginger and garlic (£5.75), fish pie or lamb kidneys in red wine (£6), lemon chicken with sweet pepper sauce or gammon and egg (£6.50), char-grilled venison with huntsman's sauce (£7.50), rump steak with garlic butter (£9), puddings (£2.50), and children's meals (£2.40); main dishes come with a choice of accompaniments – chips, salad, vegetables, rice, even paella. The village has become a dormitory village for Hereford with quite a lot of stylish mainly modern houses. *(Recommended by Peter J King, Lynn Sharpless, Bob Eardley, Chris Wheaton, Trevor Swindells, Kay and Bob Barrow)*

Free house ~ Licensees Nick and Julie Squire ~ Real ale ~ Meals and snacks (till 10pm) ~ (01432) 851303 ~ Children welcome ~ Live music monthly ~ Open 11.30-11; 12-10.30 Sun

MICHAELCHURCH ESCLEY SO3134 Map 6
Bridge

Off back rd SE of Hay on Wye, along Escley Brook valley; or can be reached off B4348 W of Hereford, via Vowchurch, then eventually left at Michaelchurch T-junction, and next left

This is a homely place – tucked away down a steep lane in an attractive valley – with a very relaxed local atmosphere. The simple left-hand bar has dark beams, straightforward pine pews and dining chairs, brocaded bar stools, some paintings of the pub and detailed farm scenes, a TV in one corner, and a very big woodburning stove. The quarry-tiled public bar has sensible darts, two video games, juke box, board games, cribbage, dominoes, and darts. Well kept Courage Directors, Ruddles County, Wye Valley Hereford, and Wadworths 6X on handpump, several farm ciders, country wines, and an unexpectedly good choice of fairly priced wines. Bar food includes sandwiches, home-made soups like cream of watercress or leek and potato (£2), bacon, egg and chips (£2.80), deep-fried camembert (£3.25), filled baked potatoes (£3.80), local sausages with onions and apple (£4.25), salmon and broccoli flan or pasta with various sauces (£4.50), rump steak (£7.50), and puddings like fruit pies or trifle (£2.50); best to book Sunday lunch; the restaurant is no smoking. In summer, you can sit outside watching the muscovy ducks and brown trout, and there's a small riverside campsite with hot showers and changing room. *(Recommended by Pete and Rosie Flower, Katheryn Aldersea, Ivan Smith; more reports please)*

Free house ~ Licensee Jean Draper ~ Real ale ~ Meals and snacks ~ (not Mon) ~ Restaurant ~ (01981) 510646 ~ Well behaved children in eating areas until 9.30 ~ Open 12-2.30(3 Sat); 12-4, 6-10.30 Sun; winter evening opening 7; cl Mon lunchtime

MUCH MARCLE SO6633 Map 4
Slip Tavern

Off A449 SW of Ledbury; take Woolhope turning at village stores, then right at pub sign

This year, there has been some refurbishment to this quiet country pub and the bar has been knocked through into the very neatly kept lounge. The atmosphere is cosy and chatty, it's a popular place with locals, and there are ladder-back and wheelback chairs around the black tables – as well as a similar family area. Well kept Hook Norton Old Hookey, and Whitbreads Castle Eden on handpump, with local farm ciders (the pub is surrounded by Weston's cider-apple orchards), and 6 wines by the glass; pleasant service, muted piped music. At lunchtime, bar food includes soup (£1.70), ploughman's (£3.85), sausages and beans (£4.60), home-cooked ham and salad (£5.30), tomato and vegetable tagliatelle (£5.35), and beef in ale (£5.50), with evening extras such as trout and almonds (£5.95), chicken tikka masala (£7.10), steaks (from £8.10), daily specials like pork and leek casserole, cod in cider or coq au vin, and puddings such as creamy lemon crunch or strawberry and apple crumble. There's more space for eating in the attractively planted conservatory, though it's best to book. The landlord used to be a nurseryman and the gardens that stretch out behind the building are really lovely and full of interesting plants; the hanging baskets and big urns in front are very pretty, too. There's a well separated play area, and maybe summer barbecues. *(Recommended by Mrs B Sugarman, P G Topp, Brian and Barbara Matthews, Joy and Peter Heatherley, Mr and Mrs Blackbourn, Michael Richards, G and M Hollis, Norma Farris, A E and P McCully, Judith and Stephen Gregory, Lynn Sharpless, Bob Eardley)*

Free house ~ Licensee Gilbert E Jeanes ~ Real ale ~ Meals and snacks ~ Restaurant (not Sun) ~ (01531) 660246 ~ Children welcome ~ Charity fun folk night 1st Thurs of month ~ Open 11.30-2.30, 6.30-11; closed 25 Dec

OMBERSLEY SO8463 Map 4

Crown & Sandys Arms 🍺 ♀

Coming into the village from the A4133, turn left at the roundabout in middle of village, and pub is on the left

The enjoyable food remains the draw to this pretty and civilised Dutch-gabled white inn. The lounge bar has black beams and some flagstones, comfortable windsor armchairs, antique settles, a couple of easy chairs and plush built-in wall seats, old prints, maps and ornamental clocks (which are for sale) on its timbered walls, log fires, and maybe daily newspapers; half is no smoking. As well as daily specials which include lots of fresh fish such as sole, hake, tuna, monkfish, and cod, vegetarian dishes, seasonal game, guinea fowl, and pot-roast lamb, the menu has snacks and meals (from £4.95), steaks (£9.50), and puddings (£2.50). Well kept Bass, Hook Norton Best and Old Hookey, Hobsons Best, Woods Special, and guest beers on handpump, 4 wines by the glass, litre or half-litre, and country wines; no noisy games or music. There are picnic tables in the garden behind the building. *(Recommended by JAH, Denys Gueroult, A Lock, Lucy James, Dean Foden, Mr and Mrs Blackbourn, Dr M I Crichton, W H and E Thomas, Bryan Taylor, Dorothy Pilson, Nick and Meriel Cox, Joan and Michel Hooper-Immins, G S and E M Dorey, John Bowdler, A J Morton, Jeff Davies, Gethin Lewis, C Smith, Martin Jones, John and Joan Humphreys, David Shillitoe)*

Free house ~ Licensee R E Ransome ~ Real ale ~ Meals and snacks (till 9.45) ~ Restaurant ~ (01905) 620252 ~ Well behaved children allowed until 7pm ~ Open 10.30-3, 5.30-11; closed 25 Dec and evening 26 Dec ~ Bedrooms: £20(£30S)/£45S

Kings Arms

Although this black-beamed and timbered Tudor pub is quite a big place, the various nooks and crannies and different levels create a cosy atmosphere. The comfortable and informal rambling rooms have have a friendly, bustling feel, and are full of stuffed animals and birds, a collection of rustic bric-a-brac, and four open fires; one room has Charles II's coat of arms moulded into its decorated plaster ceiling – he's reputed to have been here in 1651. Good, popular food includes sandwiches, soup (£2.65), smoked salmon and prawn pâté or crunchy nut brie (£4.95), vegetarian burgers with guacamole (£5.75), fresh cod or haddock (£5.95), pasta with spinach pesto (£6.25), lamb curry (£6.75), beef in beer (£7.50), 10oz sirloin steak (£9.25), jumbo prawns in garlic butter (£9.50), and puddings like cherry pie or treacle sponge (£3.25). Well kept Bass, B & B Brew XI, Morlands Speckled Hen, and Worthingtons Best on handpump, and several Irish malts; quick cheerful service, even when busy. A tree-sheltered courtyard has tables under cocktail parasols, and colourful hanging baskets and tubs in summer, and there's also a terrace. *(Recommended by Jack Barnwell, John Bowdler, Basil Minson, Alan and Paula McCully, Bryan Taylor, David Tristram, David Holman)*

Free house ~ Licensees Chris and Judy Blundell ~ Real ale ~ Meals and snacks (till 10pm, all day Sun) ~ (01905) 620142 ~ No children under 8 and older ones must leave by 8.30pm ~ Open 11-2.45, 5.30-11; 12-10.30 Sun; closed 25-26 Dec

PENSAX SO7269 Map 4

Bell 🍺

B4202 Abberley—Clows Top, S of village

Graham Titcombe who was our Beer Man of the Year in 1996 is now the licensee at this friendly country pub. His passion is tracking down lots and lots of unusual real ales from small independent brewers. Six handpumps will quickly rotate beers from brewers like Green Cucumber, Red Cross and the new Weymouth brewery and others. There are also a couple of stouts from new little Irish brew pubs. They're planning to hold two or three beer festivals in a marquee. A range of good mostly home-made sensibly priced food includes soup (£1.95), garlic mushrooms (£2.75), sautéed mushrooms (£2.95), creamy prawn pot (£3.85), fisherman's platter or vegetable curry (£4.95), scampi provençale, whisky spiced beef and walnuts or beef in Guinness (£6.95), 8oz peppered steaks (£8.95), and about ten specials like seafood tagliatelle (£5.50); puddings like home-made mango ice cream (£1.75) or hot walnut fudge cake (£2.25); no-smoking restaurant. The L-shaped main bar has a restrained traditional decor, with long cushioned pews on its bare boards, good solid pub tables, and a woodburning stove. Beyond a small carpeted area on the left with a couple more tables is a more airy dining room added in the late 1980s, with french windows opening on to a wooden deck that on hot days can give a slightly Californian feel; it has a log fire for our more usual weather. Service is very friendly, There are decent reasonably priced wines and good coffee. In the back garden, picnic tables look out over rolling fields and copses to the Wyre Forest. *(Recommended by Mrs Sarah Blenkinsop, Lawrence Bacon, Jean Scott, Andy Petersen, Alan Skull)*

Free house ~ Licensee Graham Titcombe ~ Real ale ~ Meals and snacks (12-2, 6-9.30) ~ Restaurant ~ (01299) 896677 ~ Children welcome in snug and restaurant ~ Open 11-2.30, 5-11; Sat 11-11; Sun 12-10.30; cl evening 25 December

RUCKHALL SO4539 Map 4

Ancient Camp 🛏 ♀

Ruckhall signposted off A465 W of Hereford at Belmont Abbey; from Ruckhall pub signed down private drive; can reach it too from Bridge Sollers, W of Hereford on A438 – cross Wye, then after a mile or so take first left, then left again to Eaton Bishop, and left to Ruckhall

From seats on the terrace among the roses, there are wonderful country views looking down to the river and beyond. If you're staying try and get the front bedroom which has the same view. The central beamed and flagstoned bar is simply but thoughtfully furnished with comfortably solid green-upholstered settles and library chairs around nice old elm tables. On the left, a green-carpeted room has matching sofas around the walls, kitchen chairs around tripod tables, and a good few sailing pictures. On the right, there are simple dining chairs around stripped kitchen tables on a brown carpet, and stripped stonework; nice log fire. Good lunchtime bar food includes sandwiches, home-cured gravadlax or game terrine with plum chutney (£4.50), and delice of salmon or chicken with braised flageolet beans (£7.50); in the evening you must eat in the restaurant with dishes like mushroom soup (£3.75), fresh tuna oriental with beansprouts (£6.50), sea bass with tomato coulis (£12.75), and rack of Welsh lamb with leeks (£13.75). Well kept Hook Norton Best, Smiles Best, and Woods Parish on handpump, and fine wines and vintage port from the licensee's private collection. *(Recommended by Jim and Maggie Cowell, Chris Wheaton, Greta and Christopher Wells, John Bowdler, Martin and Penny Fletcher, JAH, Mrs S Wright, Joan Olivier, Joy and Peter Heatherley, Dr C E Morgan)*

Free house ~ Licensees Pauline and Ewart McKie ~ Real ale ~ Meals and snacks (not Sun evening except for residents, not Mon) ~ Restaurant (not Mon) ~ (01981) 250449 ~ Children allowed until 7pm ~ Open 12-3, 7-11 ~ Bedrooms: £38B/£58B

SELLACK SO5627 Map 4

Lough Pool Inn ★ ♀

Back road Hoarwithy—Ross on Wye; OS Sheet 162 map reference 558268

Set in countryside full of bridleways and walks, this attractive black and white timbered cottage has plenty of picnic tables on its neat front lawned area, and pretty hanging baskets. The beamed central room has kitchen chairs and cushioned window seats around plain wooden tables on the mainly flagstoned floor, sporting prints and bunches of dried flowers, and a log fire at each end. Other rooms lead off, with attractive individual furnishings and nice touches like the dresser of patterned plates. Bar food includes soup like carrot and coriander (£2.10), stilton and port pâté (£3.10), ploughman's (£3.95), Caribbean fruit curry or home-made steak and kidney pie (£5.95), chicken korma (£7.15), popular Greek-style goat casserole (£8.95), local steaks (from £8.95), daily specials such as wild boar casserole or seafood bake, and puddings like chocolate rum pot or lemon syllabub (from £2.50); the restaurant is no smoking. Well kept Bass, John Smiths and Wye Valley Hereford on handpump, as well as a good range of malt whiskies, local farm ciders and a well-chosen wine list; piped classical music. *(Recommended by Mrs J Crawford, JAH, Malcolm Taylor, Robin Hillman, Keith and Audrey Ward, Dr C E Morgan, Gordon, Frank Cummins, Nigel Wilkinson, Graham and Glenis Watkins)*

Free house ~ Licensees Malcolm and Janet Hall ~ Real ale ~ Meals and snacks ~ Restaurant ~ (01989) 730236 ~ Well behaved children in restaurant and snug ~ Open 11.30-3, 6.30-11; closed 25 Dec, evening 26 Dec

ST OWENS CROSS SO5425 Map 4
New Inn

Harewood End

There are lots of nooks and crannies in this friendly timbered old coaching inn, filled with a happy mix of drinkers and diners. Both the lounge bar and restaurant have huge inglenook fireplaces, as well as settles, old pews, beams, and timbers. Bar food is home-made using local seasonal produce, and might include sandwiches, soup (£2.25), fresh sardines in garlic (£3.50), lasagne (£4.50), fillet of cod (£5.25), steak and kidney pie (£6.45), mushroom and asparagus pancake (£6.75), honey-roast rack of english lamb (£8.95), steaks (from £10.45), puddings, and children's menu (from £1.95). Well kept Bass, Fullers London Pride, Hook Norton Old Hookey, Smiles Best, Tetleys Bitter, Wadworths 6X, and guest beers on handpump, and a fair choice of malt whiskies; darts, shove-ha'penny, cribbage, dominoes, and piped music. The three characterful domermans are called Baileys and her two daughters Tia Maria and Ginnie. There are fine views over rolling countryside to the distant Black Mountains, and the hanging baskets are a fine sight. *(Recommended by Mike Perks, F A Owens, Martyn Hart, N Lawless, Mrs L K Dix, Alan and Paula McCully, Frank Cummins, Nigel Wilkinson)*

Free house ~ Licensee Nigel Donovan ~ Real ale ~ Meals and snacks ~ Restaurant ~ (01989) 730274 ~ Children welcome ~ Open 12-2.30, 6-11 ~ Two bedrooms: £30S(£45B)/£50S(£80B)

ULLINGSWICK SO5949 Map 4
Three Crowns ♀

Village off A465 S of Bromyard (and just S of Stoke Lacy) and signposted off A417; pub at Bleak Acre, towards Little Cowarne

This attractive old country pub, pretty in summer with its well tended hanging baskets, is charming and cosy inside, with hops strung along the low beams of its smallish bar, a couple of traditional settles besides more usual seats, and open fires. The decor, while traditional, has one or two gently sophisticated touches (candles on tables and napkins to match the curtains, for instance), and, in the two or three years they've been there, its licensees have made the carefully cooked and generously served food well worth knowing about. They try to be flexible about the menu, so it's worth asking about a favourite omelette or salad. The light lunchtime menu includes salads (from £2.75), half a pint of peeled prawns with garlic mayonnaise (£3.50), omelettes (from £3.75, spanish £4.50), ploughman's (£4.50), vegetable pasta bake or tuna and ham bake (£4.75), and about four vegetarian dishes such as goat's cheese and courgette lasagne (all £6.50). The evening menu is far more elaborate and might include grilled goat's cheese on a tomato salad, smoked chicken salad or smoked venison salad (£3.95), rabbit pie or stuffed lamb hearts with rich onion gravy (£6.95), kidneys with cream and sherry (£7.25), lamb and leek pie (£7.95), squid and prawn (£8.50), rack of lamb with mint and mustard glaze or lamb kofta with tzatziki (£8.95), peppered rump with cream and brandy (£10.95), and puddings like chocolate and prawn soufflé or crème brûlée with fresh fruit (£2.95). Service is very welcoming; well kept Bass, Ind Coope Burton, Tetleys and a guest like Hobsons Best on handpump; good house wines. There are tables out on the lawn, not large but attractively planted, with good summer views. *(Recommended by Anthony Byers, Mr and Mrs Paul Aynsley, Frank Davidson, John Bowdler, S and S Pines, J and S Holman)*

Free house ~ Licensees Derrick and Sue Horwood ~ Real ale ~ Meals and snacks (not Tues) ~ (01432) 820279 ~ Well behaved children welcome ~ Open 12-3, 7-11; cl Tues

WEOBLEY SO4052 Map 6

Olde Salutation 🍽 ⇔ ♀

Village signposted from A4112 SW of Leominster; and from A44 NW of Hereford (there's also a good back road direct from Hereford – straight out past S side of racecourse)

Herefordshire and Worcestershire Dining Pub of the Year

This is the sort of place that people like to return to again and again – and it isn't just that the food is first-rate, it's also the particularly good, friendly service, and enjoyable atmosphere, too. The two areas of the quiet, comfortable lounge – separated by a few steps and standing timbers – have a relaxed, pubby feel, brocaded modern winged settles and smaller seats, a couple of big cut-away cask seats, wildlife decorations, a hop bine over the bar counter, and logs burning in a big stone fireplace; more standing timbers separate it from the neat no-smoking restaurant area, and there's a separate smaller parquet-floored public bar with sensibly placed darts, and a fruit machine; dominoes and cribbage. Excellent bar food includes home-made filled rolls, soup (£2.20), filled french sticks (from £3.30), mushroom and pasta gratin (£3.85), ploughman's (from £3.95), steak and Guinness pie or lamb liver and bacon (£5.85), roast leg of lamb with honey and rosemary sauce (£5.95), daily specials such as nice home-baked ham in a mustard and parsley sauce, pasta and blue cheese bake (£5.50), venison sausage with redcurrant and onion sauce (£6.50), pheasant in red wine (£6.75), and home-made puddings like good lemon tart, banoffi pie or sticky toffee pudding (from £3.50); lovely breakfasts. The restaurant is no smoking. Well kept Hook Norton Best, Wadworths 6X, and a monthly guest ale on handpump, a good, interesting wine list with lots to explore, quite a good collection of whiskies, and a summer farm cider. On a sheltered back terrace are tables and chairs with parasols. *(Recommended by Dorothee and Dennis Glover, Robin and Laura Hillman, Sarah and Peter Gooderham, Chris Wheaton, Basil Minson, O K Smyth, Mr and Mrs C Cole, R C Hopton, Don Kellaway, Angie Coles, Frank Davidson, Margaret and Nigel Dennis, G and M Hollis, Brian and Barbara Gorton, Gwen and Peter Andrews, Lynn Sharpless, Bob Eardley, Karen Eliot, P Sumner, Thorstein Moen; also in Good Hotel Guide)*

Free house ~ Licensees Chris and Frances Anthony ~ Real ale ~ Meals and snacks ~ Restaurant (not Sun evening) ~ (01544) 318443 ~ Children in eating area of bar ~ Open 11-3, 7-11; 11-11 Sat; 12-10.30 Sun; closed 25 Dec ~ Bedrooms: £34B/£58B

WINFORTON SO2947 Map 6

Sun

This year an 18 hole pitch-and-putt/crazy golf course has been created in the garden of this neatly kept, friendly little dining pub; sheltered tables and a good timbery play area. Inside, there's a really friendly feel to the two beamed areas on either side of the central servery, with an individual assortment of comfortable country-kitchen chairs, high-backed settles and good solid wooden tables, heavy-horse harness, brasses and old farm tools on the mainly stripped stone walls, and two log-burning stoves; partly no-smoking area. The inventive bar food might include sandwiches, soup such as curried parsnip and apple (£2.75), mushroom ravioli with a wild mushroom sauce (£3.50), crab and lobster tartlets (£3.95), a warm salad of wood pigeon, bacon and mushrooms (£3.99), rook pie (£7.99), wild rabbit in cider with flageolet beans (£8.99), maize-fed guinea fowl on spinach noodles with a walnut and sesame sauce or half shoulder of lamb with lentil and mint sauce (£10.25), salami of ostrich in red wine with juniper berries (£11.99), and puddings like a fine chocolate torte or turkish delight charlotte. Well kept Hook Horton Old Hookey, Jennings Cumberland, and Woods Parish and Shropshire Lad on handpump, 18 malt whiskies, and Westons cider; sensibly placed darts, cribbage, dominoes, maybe piped music. (*Recommended by Dr Paul Kitchener, Sally and Bill Hyde; more reports please*)

Free house ~ Licensees Brian and Wendy Hibbard ~ Real ale ~ Meals and snacks (not winter Tues) ~ (01544) 327677 ~ Children in eating area of bar ~ Open 11-3, 6-11; closed winter Tues evening ~ Bedrooms: £28B/£48B

WOOLHOPE SO6136 Map 4

Butchers Arms ★ 🛏

Signposted from B4224 in Fownhope; carry straight on past Woolhope village

As good as ever, this unusually friendly place is popular with a good mixed crowd of people – both locals and visitors. One welcoming bar has very low beams decorated with hops, old-fashioned built-in seats with brocaded cushions, captain's chairs and stools around small tables, old photographs of country people on the walls, and a brick fireplace filled with dried flowers. The other, broadly similar though with less beams, has a large built-in settle and another log fire; there are often fresh flowers. Good bar food includes lots of lunchtime sandwiches (from £1.95), home-made soup (£2.25), leek and hazelnut terrine wrapped in vine leaves (£3.75), sausage and chips (£3.95), ploughman's with home-made pickles and chutney (from £3.95), butterbean and mushroom au gratin (£4.75), smoked haddock with bacon in a cream and cheese sauce (£5.25), very good local wild rabbit in cider (£5.50), steak and kidney pie (£6.25), rump steak (£8.95), and puddings like home-made apple pie; very good, hearty breakfasts; the restaurant is no smoking. Well kept Fullers London Pride, Hook Norton Best and Old Hookey, and Charles Wells Bombardier on handpump, local ciders, quite a few malt whiskies, and decent wines. Friendly cat – dogs not welcome. Sliding french windows lead from the bar to a little terrace with teak furniture, a few parasols and cheerful flowering tubs; there's also a tiny willow-lined brook. The countryside around is really lovely – to enjoy some of the best of it, turn left as you come out of the pub and take the tiny left-hand road at the end of the car park; this turns into a track and then into a path; the view from the top of the hill is quite something. (*Recommended by Ian Jones, Mr and Mrs H M Mortimer, John Bowdler, Graham and Lynn Mason, S G N Bennett, L T Lionet, Chris Wheaton, Iain Robertson, Lynn Sharpless, Bob Eardley, Denys Gueroult, Norma Farris, Dr J A T Saul, DMT, Jerry and Alison Oakes, Sarah and Peter Gooderham*)

Free house ~ Licensees Patrick Power and Lucinda Matthews ~ Real ale ~ Meals and snacks ~ Restaurant ~ (01432) 860281 ~ Well behaved children welcome ~ Open 11.30-2.30, 6.30(7 Mon-Thurs in winter)-11 ~ Bedrooms: £25/£39

Crown ♀

In village centre

The neatly kept lounge bar in this popular old place has open fires, dark burgundy plush button-back built-in wall banquettes and stools, a timbered divider strung with hop bines, and good wildlife photographs and little country pictures on the cream walls. Decent bar food includes home-made soup (£1.90), broccoli and blue cheese quiche (£3), chestnut, onion and apple pie with cumberland sauce (£5), home-made salmon fishcakes (£5.50), sweet and sour chicken or steak and kidney pie (£5.75), Herefordshire steaks (from £8.75), Sunday roast (£5.75; children £3.25), home-made puddings like treacle tart or steamed ginger and marmalade sponge (£2.50), and children's menu (from £3.50); the restaurant is no smoking. Well kept Hook Norton Best, Smiles Best, Tetleys Bitter, and a guest beer on handpump, decent wine list, and farm cider. There are picnic tables under cocktail parasols on the neat front lawn; darts, summer quoits. *(Recommended by Derek and Sylvia Stephenson, S G N Bennett, DMT, Denys Gueroult, Paul and Sue Merrick, Jerry and Alison Oakes, Ardill and Anne Booth)*

Free house ~ Licensees Neil and Sally Gordon ~ Real ale ~ Meals and snacks (till 10pm) ~ Restaurant ~ (01432) 860468 ~ Well behaved children allowed till 8pm – though customers are asked to check beforehand ~ Open 12-2.30, 6.30(6 Sat)- 11; winter evening opening 7(6.30 Sat); closed evening 25 Dec

WYRE PIDDLE SO9647 Map 4

Anchor

B4084 NW of Evesham

In summer, this easy-going, unpretentious pub really comes into its own as there are seats on the spacious lawn that runs down to the River Avon, and views spreading out over the Vale of Evesham as far as the Cotswolds, the Malverns and Bredon Hill; quite a few customers arrive by boat. The big airy back bar shares the same fine view, and there's a friendly and well kept little lounge with a good log fire in its attractively restored inglenook fireplace, comfortably upholstered chairs and settles, and two beams in the shiny ceiling. Decent bar food includes home-made soup (£2.45), open baps (from £2.75), ploughman's (from £3.75), moules marinières (£5.25), mushroom ravioli (£5.95), steak and kidney pie (£6.25), daily specials like home-made venison pâté (£2.95), grilled salmon (£8) and grilled duck breast flamed with calvados, apple and honey sauce (£9.75), and pudding such as apricot crumble or treacle sponge (from £2.35); 3-course Sunday lunch (£10.75), and children's meals (from £3.25). Friendly, obliging service. Well kept Boddingtons, Flowers IPA and Original, Hook Norton Best, and Marstons Pedigree on handpump, a few whiskies, and country wines; fruit machine and piped music. *(Recommended by Mrs J Huntly, Dorothee and Dennis Glover, Lucy James, Dean Foden, Andy Petersen, Paul Boot, G S and E M Dorey, W C M Jones, Lynn Sharpless, Bob Eardley, Jack Barnwell)*

Whitbreads ~ Tenant Michael Senior ~ Real ale ~ Meals and snacks (not Sun evening) ~ River-view lunchtime restaurant (not Sun evening) ~ (01386) 552799 ~ Children welcome ~ Open 11-2.30(12-3 Sat), 6-11

Lucky Dip

Besides the fully inspected pubs, you might like to try these Lucky Dips recommended to us and described by readers (if you do, please send us reports):

☆ Abbey Dore [SO3830], *Neville Arms*: Spotlessly refurbished open-plan local, partly divided by arches, with bays of banquettes in lounge area, real fire, well kept Wye Buckleys and M&B ales, reasonably priced bar food (no sandwiches); nr Norman abbey church, in charming Golden Valley countryside *(Nigel Wilkinson, W H and E Thomas, Mr and Mrs R J Phillips, BB)*
Alvechurch [Red Lion St; SP0272], *Red Lion*: Big beamed lounge with side snugs, big log fire, low lighting, good varied reasonably priced generous food, good service, interesting beers and wines, quiet piped music; big back garden *(Dave and Sue Price, Mike and Emma)*
☆ Aston Crews [SO6723], *Penny Farthing*: Partly 15th-c, roomy and relaxing, with lots of beams, horsebrasses, harness and farm tools, well in bar with skeleton at bottom; interesting good value food, well kept

Marstons, decent wines, easy chairs, two restaurant areas, one with pretty valley and Forest of Dean views (shared by tables in charming garden), subdued piped music; bedrooms *(Mrs D Cross, Neil and Anita Christopher, BB)*
☆ Aymestrey [A4110; SO4265], *Riverside*: Friendly refurbished 16th-c half-timbered inn with well kept Bass, Boddingtons, Flowers Original and Marstons Pedigree, decent malt whiskies, wide choice of generous food cooked to order (so may be a wait) in bar and restaurant, relaxed atmosphere, obliging staff, warren of rooms with low oak beams and open fires, piped classical music, no games machines; booking essential weekends; attractive terrace gardens by River Lugg; bedrooms *(John and Joan Wyatt, Paddy and Marilyn Gibbon, Basil Minson, Trevor Swindells, C R Whitham, Mrs J Hailstone, J M Potter)*
☆ Bastonford [A449 Worcester—Malvern;

SO8150], *Halfway House*: Three-storey turn-of-the-century pub, very welcoming new licensees concentrating on wide choice of nicely prepared generous tasty food (not Tues evening; Sun lunch can be booked), inc well thought-out theme food evenings; sensible tables and chairs in eating area (where children allowed), well kept Marstons Bitter and Pedigree, home-made orange brandy, shove-ha'penny; fruit machine, maybe unobtrusive piped music; open all day Sat in summer *(J H E Peters)*

Baughton [A4104 Pershore—Upton; SO8741], *Jockey*: Real ales such as Adnams Broadside, Banks's, Woods Parish and Gibbs Mew Bishops Tipple, decent Australian wines, good bar and restaurant food, friendly landlord *(Frank Gadbois, Derek and Sylvia Stephenson)*

☆ Belbroughton [High St (off A491); SO9277], *Queens*: Neat and friendly local with good value food inc enjoyable specials, polite staff, well kept Marstons, comfortable alcove seating, bigger tables in family area, fresh flowers; picnic tables on small terrace, quiet village *(Andy Petersen, DMT, W L G Watkins, Jonathan Wynn)*

☆ Berrow [Ryecross, nr junction A438/B4208; SO7934], *Duke of York*: Two linked rooms, 15th-c beams, nooks and crannies, good log fire, new chefs doing wider choice of food from sandwiches to steaks inc children's dishes and good puddings, well kept Boddingtons, Fremlins and Ruddles Best, farm cider, welcoming locals, dominoes, cribbage; piped music; recently extended back restaurant, part no smoking, picnic tables in big back garden; handy for Malvern Hills *(S C King, B Walton, DMT, Dave Braisted, V Kavanagh, LYM; more reports on new regime please)*

☆ Bishops Frome [just off B4214 Bromyard—Ledbury; SO6648], *Green Dragon*: Attractive unspoilt flagstoned pub with plenty of character, good interesting range of well kept beers, fine log fire, reasonably priced simple bar food, games room, seats outside; children welcome, no dogs; open all day Sat *(Dorothy Pilson, Anthony Byers, Gordon, LYM)*

Bournheath [Dodford Rd; SO9474], *Gate*: Attractive country dining pub with popular food inc vegetarian and lunchtime and early evening bargains, in bar and adjoining restaurant, well kept Boddingtons, Smiles Best and Exhibition and a weekly guest beer; nice garden *(Chris Wrigley, Ian Shorthouse)*

☆ Bredenbury [A44 Bromyard—Leominster; SO6056], *Barneby Arms*: Substantial hotel popular for wide range of generous food inc vegetarian and carvery in clean bright busy bar with ceiling joists, horse tack, lots of old woodworking tools; well kept Banks's and Marstons Pedigree, friendly staff; children welcome, big garden, bedrooms *(John Hazel, Richard Gibbs, Philip Jackson, Patricia Heptinstall, Graham Bush)*

Bredon [High St; SO9236], *Royal Oak*: Relaxed country pub, open fire, good choice of real ales, food inc fresh fish and chips Fri, pool, darts, friendly staff; skittle alley *(Derek and Sylvia Stephenson, Andrew Aldridge)*

☆ Broadway [Collin Lane; follow Willersey sign off A44 NW – marked Gt Collin Farm on OS Sheet 150 map ref 076391; SP0739], *Collin House*: Wide choice of good interesting freshly done bar food inc traditional puddings in lovely bar of small country hotel, very relaxed and civilised – good log fires, no machines or piped music (but no sandwiches or ploughman's either), very accommodating; nice restaurant not overpriced (wise to book), good wines, local beers, proper coffee, pleasant staff; tables outside; comfortable bedrooms *(W C Jones, Ian Rorison)*

☆ Broadway [Main St (A44)], *Lygon Arms*: Magnificent old inn (run by Savoy group – far from cheap) with interesting rooms rambling away from attractive oak-panelled bar; sandwiches all day; imaginative bar food in adjoining more intimate Goblets wine bar, with decent wines, wooden tables and pleasant service – does get busy in holiday season; tables in prettily planted courtyard, well kept gardens; children allowed away from bar; bedrooms *(GA, John and Shirley Dyson, LYM)*

Broadway [The Green], *Broadway Hotel*: Popular for bar meals inc good omelettes and good value specials some akin to dishes from its restaurant; bedrooms *(Peter Lloyd)*; [Main St (A44)], *Horse & Hound*: Spacious bay-windowed bar with plenty of woodwork, open fire, china cabinets, dining end with good value food; quick pleasant staff, Whitbreads-related ales with guests such as Hook Norton Old Hookey or Wadworths 6X, Sunday papers *(Neil and Anita Christopher, SLC)*; [Main St], *Swan*: Beefeater with well kept real ale, decent food, good service *(RP, BP)*

☆ Brockhampton [Bringsty Common; off A44 Bromyard—Worcester; SO6955], *Live & Let Live*: Consistently friendly service and well kept beers in basic rustic tavern down rough track over bracken-covered common – only the sign of this black and white half-timbered cottage is visible from the road *(Gordon)*

☆ Bromyard [Sherford St; SO6554], *Crown & Sceptre*: Wide choice of good generous food inc children's dishes in simply decorated 17th/18th-c family pub; good dining room, changing guest beers, daily papers, big woodburner in inglenook; popular at weekends; bedrooms *(Anthony Byers)*

Callow Hill [Elcocks Brook – OS Sheet 150 map ref 010645; SP0164], *Brook*: Busy country inn, well kept Marstons, good value lunchtime food, welcoming fire *(Dave Braisted)*

☆ Castlemorton [Castlemorton Common; B4208 – OS Sheet 150 map ref 787388; SO7838], *Plume of Feathers*: Lovely little low-beamed whitewashed country pub, log fire, warmly welcoming landlady, attractively priced home cooking, Bass, Boddingtons, Hook Norton Best, Morlands Old Speckled Hen and John Smiths, separate darts and dining areas *(A Y Drummond, Mike Dickerson)*

Castlemorton [B4208, 1¼ mile S of Welland crossroads; SO7937], *Robin Hood*: Charming old beamed country pub, relaxed atmosphere, medley of cushioned pews etc, big brick fireplace, lots of horsebrasses, hops, jugs, welcoming landlady, good generous interesting food, well kept Boddingtons, Flowers and Theakstons, local Weston's cider; area with fruit machine and darts, separate small dining room; big lawns and space for caravans behind *(Tom Evans, Colin Fisher)*

Catshill [SO9573], *Royal Oak*: Busy popular Banks's pub *(Dave Braisted)*

Chaddesley Corbett [off A448 Bromsgrove—Kidderminster; SO8973], *Fox*: Spaciously refurbished, with well priced bar food and lunchtime carvery (get there early for a table), welcoming atmosphere, friendly staff, well kept Theakstons, nice dogs *(W H and E Thomas, Moira and John Cole)*; *Talbot*: Attractive timbered pub in quiet village street, welcoming landlord, Banks's Bitter, bar food inc good chunky sandwiches, attractive prices, good service *(Dr M I Crichton)*

Charlton [the one nr Evesham – OS Sheet 150 map ref 012458; SP0145], *Gardeners Arms*: Straightforward local with good generous food, welcoming atmosphere and service, lots of tables in lounge, spartan public bar with darts; attractive village *(P J Ankcorn, Nigel Rendell)*

☆ Claines [3 miles from M5 junction 6; A449 towards Ombersley, then leave dual carriageway at second exit for Worcester; village signposted from here, and park in Cornmeadow Lane; SO8558], *Mug House*: Fine views from ancient basic country tavern in unique churchyard setting by fields below the Malvern Hills, low doorways, heavy oak beams, well kept cheap Banks's Bitter and Mild, minimal choice of basic but generous snacks (not Sun), children allowed in snug away from servery *(Gwen and Peter Andrews, LYM)*

☆ Clent [A491 Bromsgrove—Stourbridge; SO9279], *Holly Bush*: Pleasant country pub very popular midweek lunchtime for good range of freshly cooked bar food esp fish, Holt Plant & Deakins Bitter and Entire *(Dorothee and Dennis Glover)*

Clifton upon Teme [SO7162], *Red Lion*: Civilised and comfortable, with central log fire in big bar, decent food, friendly service; attractive beamed bedrooms, pretty village *(Anthony Byers, Gordon)*

☆ Clows Top [A456 Bewdley—Tenbury; SO7171], *Colliers Arms*: Reliable dining pub, roomy and comfortable, with wide choice of food inc vegetarian, no-smoking restaurant, civilised service, log fires, well kept Theakstons Best and XB, unobtrusive piped music; no dogs *(Frank Cummins)*

Colwall [Walwyn Rd; SO7342], *Oddfellows*: Popular child-friendly family pub with dining and children's area, good bar food inc children's, Theakstons XB and Old Peculier; cheerful piped music; big play area, caravan/camp site *(Ian and Nita Cooper)*

☆ Crowle [SO9256], *Old Chequers*: Smart and busy, with more modern restaurant extension opening off old pubby core of some character, good generous food inc unusual dishes (no sandwiches etc); prompt service, several well

kept ales inc Bass *(Martin Lavery, G S and E M Dorey, Miss M Roberts, David Jones)*

Cutnall Green [SO8768], *Live & Let Live*: Small and unpretentious converted cottages, first-rate service, wide range of good reasonably priced home-made food; small but pretty garden *(Dave Braisted)*

Docklow [A44 Leominster—Bromyard; SO5657], *Kings Head*: Traditional simple pub, food from bacon butties up, Bass and M&B beers *(Dave Braisted)*

Dodford [SO9372], *Dodford*: Greenalls pub with choice of guest beers, good food (not Mon) *(Dave Braisted)*

☆ Dorstone [pub signed off B4348 E of Hay on Wye; SO3141], *Pandy*: County's oldest pub, in pretty countryside, heavy beams, stout timbers, broad worn flagstones, traditional furnishings, alcoves, vast log fireplace, good bar food from sandwiches to interesting and very rewarding main courses and themed food evenings, well kept Bass, Smiles, Wye Valley and guest ales, excellent choice of whiskies, traditional games; piped music; picnic tables and play area in neat garden; children welcome, cl winter Mon lunchtime, winter Tues *(S C King, Ian Williams, Linda Mar, David Morris, Kevin and Tracey Stephens, Anthony Barnes, Sue Demont, Tim Barrow, O K Smyth, Graham and Glenis Watkins, Richard and Jean Phillips, M E Wellington, LYM)*

☆ Doverdale [off A449 Kidderminster—Worcester; SO8665], *Ripperidge*: Good food esp fresh fish, separate restaurant, pleasant service and surroundings *(W H and E Thomas)*

Drakes Broughton [A44 towards Pershore, off M5 junction 7; SO9248], *Plough & Harrow*: Friendly and efficient new licensees, attractive rambling lounge, well kept real ales; tables nicely set behind by old orchard *(Mrs Greenwood)*

Drayton [SO9076], *Robin Hood*: Comfortable dining pub with open fires, low beams, friendly efficient service, well kept Ansells, Bass and Ind Coope Burton, good value varied bar food esp curries and vegetarian dishes; garden with trampoline, good walks nearby *(Steve Gilbert, Helen Cox)*

Droitwich [Smite; 1½ miles outside; SO9063], *Pear Tree*: Civilised surroundings, good bar food inc daily OAP lunch, Bass and other real ales; new bedroom extension *(W H and E Thomas)*; [Kidderminster Rd], *Railway*: Traditional local with canal and river views from extended upper terrace, Banks's Mild, Marstons Pedigree and guest ales, limited choice of home-cooked lunches, friendly landlord and customers, pub games; open all day Fri/Sat *(Dr and Mrs B Baker)*

☆ Dunhampstead [just SE of Droitwich; pub towards Sale Green – OS Sheet 150 map ref 919600; SO9160], *Firs*: Civilised and relaxing country local with good enthusiastic chef, prompt welcoming service, friendly dogs, comfortable conservatory; well kept Banks's and Marstons, flowers on the tables, popular restaurant, tables in garden – a nice spot nr canal *(Pete Yearsley, LYM)*

Dunhampton [A449 S-bound; SO8466], *Old*

Leaking Well: Newly refurbished 17th-c country pub with modern dining extension, well kept Banks's and Marstons, reasonably priced food inc big steaks *(Graham Reeve, AF)*

Eardisland [A44; SO4258], *White Swan*: Interesting old pub in lovely black and white village, with armchairs and enormous fire in cosy inner core, two rooms furnished more suitably for eating, pleasant public bar with pool and fruit machine, good back garden with play house; the former licensees can now be found at the Halfway House at Bastonford *(Lynn Sharpless, Bob Eardley, BB)*

☆ Elmley Castle [village signed off A44 and A435, not far from Evesham; SO9841], *Queen Elizabeth*: Very good genuine cooking using fresh local and more exotic ingredients in new (independently run) restaurant attached to ancient tavern in pretty village below Bredon Hill; pub part has cheap farm cider and well kept Marstons in attractive old-fashioned tap room, haphazard medley of periods in decoration and furnishings, friendly locals and landlord (here for over 30 years), maybe piped classical music *(Don Pawley, Derek and Sylvia Stephenson, LYM)*

Fladbury [Chequers Lane – OS Sheet 150 map ref 996461; SO9946], *Chequers*: Cosy, warm and comfortable, dating back to 14th c, with good value food inc good Sun carvery, well kept Theakstons and other ales, good friendly service; beamed restaurant, comfortable bedroom extension *(Tom and Julie Sobchack)*

☆ Flyford Flavell [½ mile off A422 Worcester—Alcester; SO9754], *Boot*: Unpretentious 18th-c beamed pub with plenty of character, wide range of good generous food (cooked to order so may be a short wait), well kept beer inc Bass, dining conservatory; lovely surroundings *(M R Smith, Dennis Boddington, Geoff and Angela Jaques)*

☆ Fownhope [B4224; SO5834], *Green Man*: Striking 15th-c black and white inn, often very busy (so the friendly service can slow), with big log fire, wall settles, window seats and armchairs in one beamed bar, standing timbers dividing another, popular food from sandwiches to steak inc children's and Sun carvery (no-smoking main restaurant), well kept Courage Directors, Hook Norton Best, Marstons Pedigree, John Smiths and Sam Smiths OB, Weston's farm ciders, attractive prices; children welcome, quiet garden with play area; comfortable bedrooms *(Iain Robertson, Paul and Sue Merrick, Chris Wheaton, Peter Neate, Gordon, P J Keen, Adam Nell, John Hazel, John Bowdler, Ted George, N Lawless, LYM)*

☆ Gorcott Hill [off A435 3 miles S of M42 junction 3; SP0868], *Hollybush*: Quietly placed but lively country pub with wide range of generous good value home-made food inc seafood, well kept Courage-related ales, good service; busy with office people weekday lunchtime *(Dave Braisted)*

Grimley [A443 5 miles N from Worcester, right to Grimley, right at village T – OS Sheet 150 map ref 835592; SO8359], *Camp House*: Pleasant Severnside setting with own landing stage, attractive lawns with swing; food inc massive sandwiches lunchtime and early evening, well kept Whitbreads-related ales, friendly staff, very popular; children welcome *(Ted Townley)*

☆ Hadley [Hadley Heath; A4133 Droitwich—Ombersley; SO8664], *Bowling Green*: Attractively refurbished three-roomed inn under new management, wide range of reasonably priced food inc lots of interesting dishes and popular good value Sun carvery, also lunchtime sandwiches; well kept Banks's Bitter and Mild, Marstons Pedigree and Hook Norton, good value wines, attractive restaurant, comfortable bedrooms; has UK's oldest bowling green *(Bryan Taylor, Denys Gueroult, Stefan Norrman, Dave Braisted, Dorothee and Dennis Glover)*

Hagley [A456/A491; SO9180], *Spencers Arms*: Alehouse theme under new Strongarm Taproom alias, fashionably derenovated with plaster crumbling from brickwork, Banks's, Morrells and other ales, food inc good faggot and gravy sandwich (use a fork) *(Dave Braisted)*

Hampton Bishop [SO5638], *Bunch of Carrots*: Traditional country pub recently redecorated by new landlord, regulars enthusiastic about beers, food and service *(T Ruthven, Mrs W Hyett)*

☆ Hanbury [Woodgate; SO9663], *Gate Hangs Well*: Much extended dining pub alone in farmland, open-plan but well divided, with good value attractively presented generous food inc carvery and fine home-made pies, well kept Bass and Worthington, friendly service; very popular, best to book *(Jean and Richard Phillips, Les Jobson)*

Hereford [Kings Acre Rd; SO5139], *Bay Horse*: Attractive biggish pub with quick friendly service and good food inc enjoyable sandwiches and soup *(Bill and Steph Brownson)*; [just off main sq], *Imperial*: Old-world inn with good value food in several eating rooms, friendly staff; bedrooms *(Mrs Linda Bonnell)*

☆ Howle Hill [coming from Ross fork left off B4228 on sharp right bend, first right, then left at crossroads after a mile – OS Sheet 162 map ref 603204; SO6121], *Crown*: Delightful hidden-away pub with good range of well priced tasty food (not Sun evening, Mon; no sandwiches), well kept Whitbreads-related ales, friendly landlord and labradors (no visiting dogs), padded pews; bar skittles, tables in garden; winter opening may be limited *(Colin Laffan)*

☆ Inkberrow [A422 Worcester—Alcester, set well back; SP0157], *Old Bull*: Photogenic Tudor pub with bulging walls, huge inglenooks, flagstones, oak beams and trusses, and some old-fashioned high-backed settles among more modern furnishings; lots of *Archers* memorabilia (it's the model for the Ambridge Bull), friendly service, good simple home-made food inc vegetarian and Sun roast, good range of Whitbreads-related ales with guests such as Banks's and Bass, good value coffee; children allowed in eating area, tables outside *(Meg and Colin Hamilton,*

Adrian Ward, Anthony R Clemow, Moira
and John Culpan, E W Pitts, Anthony Byers,
Angus Lyon, LYM]
Kemerton [Bredon—Beckford; SO9437],
Crown: Unpretentious 18th-c local with
bustling L-shaped lounge bar, panelled
benches, well kept Whitbreads-related ales,
popular family lunches, maybe free Sunday
sausages *(David Campbell, Vicki McLean)*
☆ **Kempsey** [Green Street – a village, signed off
A38 in Kempsey itself; SO8649], *Huntsman*:
Plain and simply furnished out-of-the-way
local with horsey and hunting prints, county
cricket memorabilia, well kept Banks's Mild
and Bitter and Everards Old Original, friendly
and relaxed landlord and locals, limited food;
children welcome (though no special food for
them, nor sandwiches etc) *(Nigel Clifton,
Philip Jackson, Patricia Heptinstall, Sue and
Mike Lee, Brig J S Green, LYM)*
☆ **Kempsey** [Main Rd (A38); SO8648], *Walter
de Cantelupe*: Good value food (not Mon) inc
sound local produce and some really
adventurous cooking in bar's two small
rooms or intimate and relaxing candlelit
dining room; great atmosphere, log fire,
interesting changing guest beers from very
small breweries, wines imported direct from
Italy – eight by the glass; no music, friendly
labrador, back garden *(Drs Ben and Caroline
Maxwell, Mrs Sarah Blenkinsop)*
Kington [Bridge St; note this is the Herefs
Kington; SO3057], *Queens Head*: Wide
variety of farm ciders and real ales, inc its
good own-brewed Solstice Golden Torc,
Talisman and Capstone; good range of
generous reasonably priced food inc
imaginative dishes *(Dave Irving, Geoffrey and
Irene Lindley, Ronald and Ruth Locke)*
☆ **Ledbury** [New St; SO7138], *Olde Talbot*:
16th-c timbered inn, cheerful and
comfortable, with two bars and a restaurant,
brass and copper hanging from the beams,
well kept beers, good value home-cooked bar
lunches, more interesting evening meals, good
friendly service, open fire, tales of a friendly
poltergeist; decent bedrooms sharing bath
(Peter Lloyd, J and P Maloney)
Ledbury, *Brewery*: Friendly, with genuinely
interested staff *(Peter and Sarah Gooderham)*
☆ **Leintwardine** [SO4174], *Sun*: More private
house than pub, three tables and benches in
red-tiled bar with faded blue wallpaper and
roaring fire; lounge with small settee and a
couple of chairs is octogenarian landlady's
own sitting room – she makes you feel very
much at home; Pitfield PA and Mild drawn
from casks in her kitchen *(Dave Irving,
Wayne Brindle, Jack and Philip Paxton)*
Leintwardine [High St], *Lion*: Well kept
Boddingtons and Morlands Old Speckled
Hen, good choice of nicely presented good
value food in bar and popular restaurant,
efficient friendly staff *(Mr and Mrs D Olney,
Mrs Kennedy)*
Leominster [Broad St; SO4959], *Grape
Vaults*: Consistently welcoming little local
with well kept Marstons Pedigree and Best
and guests, wide range of simple freshly

cooked food, open fire, no games machines or
music *(P Campbell, Roger Thompson)*
☆ **Leominster** [West St; SO4959], *Talbot*:
Comfortable and attractive old coaching inn
with heavy beams and standing timbers,
antique carved settles, log fires with 18th-c
oak-panelled chimneybreasts, sporting prints;
decent straightforward home-made bar food
inc good sandwiches, well kept Courage-
related ales, efficient cheerful service; piped
music; bedrooms *(W H and E Thomas, BB)*
☆ **Leominster** [South St], *Royal Oak*: Generous
cheap home-made food inc good beef
sandwiches and soups in handsome Georgian-
fronted small hotel's bustling locals' bar,
friendly service, big log fire, several well kept
ales inc Hook Norton and Woods; can be
rather smoky, unobtrusive piped music; spotless
genuine Edwardian gents'; simple bedrooms
*(Neil and Anita Christopher, Dr and Mrs A H
Young, Mervyn and Zilpha Reed, BB)*
Letton [SO3346], *Swan*: Friendly atmosphere,
accommodating service, good value home-
made food, well kept cheap beers inc local Wye
Valley, good games room *(Simon Bobeldijk)*
☆ **Lingen** [OS Sheet 149 map ref 367670;
SO3767], *Royal George*: Friendly pub
combined with PO and shop, Bass, Hook
Norton and Morlands Old Speckled Hen,
good value bar food, coal fire, plenty of tables
in big garden with good hill views, play area,
fenced-off water garden; in beautiful country
setting nr Kim Davis's alpine nursery and
garden *(Dorsan Baker)*
☆ **Little Cowarne** [off A465 S of Bromyard,
towards Ullingswick; SO6051], *Three
Horseshoes*: Wide choice of good home
cooking in quarry-tiled bar and spacious
restaurant (lunchtime carvery), well kept Bass
and other ales, decent wines, log fire, mix of
solid tables and chairs, friendly obliging
licensees, disabled access; juke box, pool,
darts and fruit machine; lovely country views
from terrace and simple pleasant garden;
comfortable bedrooms *(A E and P McCully,
Anthony Byers)*
☆ **Lulsley** [signed a mile off A44; SO7455], *Fox
& Hounds*: Tucked-away dining pub with
smallish parquet-floored bar stepping down
into neat dining lounge, pretty little restaurant
on left, wide choice of food from sandwiches
up, Bass and Worthington BB, decent wines,
open fire, colourful enclosed garden with play
area; live jazz some Sats *(JAH, Dave Braisted,
Denys Gueroult, BB)*
Luntley [Dunkertons, Hays Head; off A44 in
Pembridge at New Inn; ST1606], *Cider
House*: An airy country restaurant (not pub)
but with an organic real ale and six excellent
ciders and perries made on the premises; quite
short menu inc cider/perry recipes, cooked to
order (so may be a wait); can taste and buy
from the cider farm *(Joan and Michel
Hooper-Immins, BB)*
☆ **Lyonshall** [SO3355], *Royal George*: Clean and
inviting, with good food, friendly service, three
rooms off central servery, pleasant partly no-
smoking dining room; comfortable bedrooms,
outstanding floral decorations outside *(A J*

Major, Vanessa Vassar, Robert Kopun)

Malvern [SO7845], *Foley Arms*: Good range of food inc vegetarian and popular puddings in bar, hotel lounges or on sunny terrace with splendid views, nice atmosphere in smarter restaurant with good value enterprising menu, Bass and Ushers Founders, friendly efficient uniformed staff; back bedrooms have the views too *(B and K Hypher, Ian and Nita Cooper)*; [Belle Vue Terr], *Mount Pleasant*: Edwardian hotel with glorious views, popular bar with log fire and good value food inc good vegetarian choice, restaurant with Spanish dishes; bedrooms *(Steve Gilbert, Helen Cox)*; [74 Wyche Rd, Gt Malvern], *Wyche*: Clean and comfortable half-timbered pub nr top of Malvern hills so good for walkers; fine view, Morlands, Ruddles and John Smiths, wide choice of reasonably priced well presented food, quick helpful service; bedrooms *(P and M Rudlin, Dave Braisted, Philip Jackson, Patricia Heptinstall)*

Mordiford [just off B4224 SE of Hereford – OS Sheet 149 map ref 572374; SO5737], *Moon*: Good value pub meals in front restaurant inc unusual daily specials, friendly relaxed service, Bass, Boddingtons, Flowers IPA and Wye Valley Bitter, local farm ciders; back bar popular with young locals *(Paul and Sue Merrick)*

Much Dewchurch [SO4831], *Black Swan*: Roomy partly 14th-c pub, attractive and friendly, with good freshly cooked straightforward food (so maybe a short wait), several well kept ales such as Bass, Hook Norton Best, Woods Special and one brewed for the pub; basic lavatories *(Gwen and Peter Andrews, Margaret Dyke)*

Newtown [A4103 Hereford—Worcester, junction with A417; SO6145], *Newtown*: Clean decor, good value attractively presented food, damask tablecloth and napkins, first-class service, well kept Whitbreads-related ales; very popular with older people though not a lot of space *(Margaret Waldron)*

☆ **Pembridge** [Mkt Sq (A44); SO3958], *New Inn*: Ancient inn overlooking small black and white town's church, comfortable and atmospheric three-room bar, elderly and antique traditional furnishings on worn flagstones, substantial log fire, good food from sandwiches up inc some interesting dishes, well kept Ruddles Best and County and guest beers such as Adnams or Wadworths 6X, farm cider, traditional games; small carpeted family dining room (not Sun evening); outside lavatories, simple bedrooms *(John Hibberd, Joan and Andrew Life, Sara Nicholls, D Lorking, Bill Flisher, Neville Kenyon, LYM)*

Peopleton [SO9350], *Crown*: Welcoming local, very pretty and cosy; beamed bar with piano, big inglenook fireplace, well kept Whitbreads-related beers; masses of flowers around tables outside *(Angus Lyon)*

Pershore [Bridge St; SO9445], *Brandy Cask*: Own-brewed beers and several guests usually inc Ruddles, friendly service, good bar food and brasserie, good prices *(R O Goss)*; [Bridge St], *Millers Arms*: Spacious but cosy beamed pub with well kept Wadworths IPA,

6X and Farmers Glory, evening pizzas and jolly evening atmosphere – popular with young people then; more orthodox lunchtime food *(Joan and Michel Hooper-Immins)*

Peterstow [A49 Ross—Hereford, N; SO5625], *Red Lion*: Good food, pleasant welcome, cheerful ex-London landlord *(JAH)*

Rashwood [A38, ½ mile SW of M5 junction 5; SO9165], *Robin Hood*: Log fire, good service, enjoyable food *(Dave and Sue Price)*

Risbury [OS Sheet 149 map ref 560549; SO5654], *Hop Pole*: Classic basic country tavern in old farm buildings, in same family for over a century; knock to be let into tiled hallway leading to small bar with tiny serving area, bus seats lined up in pairs and small fireplace; well kept Woods Parish and Special served by jug from barrel in a back room, crisps – no other food; lively welcoming locals, open 11-5, 6-11 *(Graham Bush, Richard Lewis)*

☆ **Ross on Wye** [Riverside; coming in from A40 W side, 1st left after bridge; SO6024], *Hope & Anchor*: Plain big-windowed family extension looking out on flower-lined lawns leading down to river, plenty of tables out here (and summer ice-cream bar and barbecues), boating theme in cheery if not smart main bar, cosy upstairs parlour bar and Victorian-style dining room, generous competitively priced food inc good choice for children, well kept Bass and Hancocks HB, farm cider, convivial landlord; open all day, can be crowded weekends, summer boat trips *(Lynn Sharpless, Bob Eardley, Ian Rorison, Christopher Glasson, Geoffrey and Irene Lindley, Prof I H Rorison, George Atkinson, Ted George, LYM)*

Ross on Wye [Wilton], *Hereford Bull*: Relaxing riverside pub, lots of panelling, log fire, rods and nets hanging from ceiling, good range of food, real ales, pleasant service, outbuilding for children; prettily placed in small hamlet just outside, lovely view of river and bridge, french windows to garden sloping gently down to it; bedrooms *(Neil and Anita Christopher)*; [8 High St], *Kings Head*: Pleasant comfortable beamed and panelled lounge bar popular with locals, food from good sandwiches and toasties to reasonably priced hot dishes, swift friendly service, evening restaurant; open all day; bedrooms *(Peter Lloyd)*

☆ **Severn Stoke** [A38 S of Worcester; SO8544], *Rose & Crown*: Beautiful 16th-c black and white pub, well modernised keeping low beams, nick-nacks and good fire in character front bar, well kept Courage-related and other ales, good value generous food inc children's dishes and enormous granary rolls, welcoming atmosphere, back room where children allowed; maybe piped local radio; lovely big garden with picnic tables, playhouse and play area *(M A Cameron, Dorothy and Leslie Pilson)*

Sinton Green [SO8160], *New Inn*: Unpretentious unspoilt interior, particularly well kept very cheap ales, lovely village green setting; no food *(Ted Townley)*

☆ Stiffords Bridge [A4103 W of Gt Malvern; SO7348], *Red Lion*: Roomy and busy main-road country local with good cheery atmosphere, log fire, sensible mix of table sizes, good food from rewarding sandwiches to lots of interesting home-made specials, sensible prices, well kept Banks's, Hobsons Best and Marstons Pedigree, local farm cider, pleasant service, tables on trellised terrace; bedrooms (*B and K Hypher, BB*)

☆ Stockton Cross [Kimbolton, off A49; SO5161], *Stockton Cross*: Beautifully kept squat old black and white building, furnishings in keeping, huge log fire adding warmth to atmosphere, well kept beers, decent wines, friendly helpful landlord, efficient service, very wide range of good value food inc interesting specials; can get busy weekends, attractive garden (*Joy and Peter Heatherley, Basil Minson, Mike and Emma*)

Stoke Heath [Hanbury Rd (A38), 2½ miles from M5 junction 5; SO9468], *Hanbury Turn*: Former Grasshopper reopened with good short range of bar food, mainly Tetleys-related ales (*Dave Braisted*)

Stoke Lacy [A465 Bromyard—Hereford, just N of village; SO6249], *Plough*: Attractively modernised beamed pub by Symonds' cider plant, comfortable and clean, with good range of reasonably priced pleasantly served food in separate dining area, log fire, well kept Tetleys and Wethereds, choice of ciders; children welcome (*G and M Hollis, Nigel and Sue Foster*)

☆ Stoke Prior [Hanbury Rd (B4091); the one nr Bromsgrove, SO9468], *Country Girl*: Rustic brickwork, light oak beams, farm tools, soft lighting for Victorian feel, vast choice of good generous food inc huge sandwiches and enterprising specials, reasonable prices, efficient service, good choice of Whitbreads-related ales, unobtrusive piped music; handy for walks on Dodderhill Common (*G S and E M Dorey, Dave Braisted, Jean and Richard Phillips*)

Stoke Wharf [SO9566], *Navigation*: Popular Davenports pub nr Worcs & Birmingham Canal, good value food
Increasingly popular (*Dave Braisted*)

Symonds Yat [Symonds Yat West; SO5616], *Old Ferre*: Lively and attractive black and white timbered pub overlooking Wye, with its own hand-pulled ferry; well kept Wadworths 6X, old local photographs in pleasant lounge, games area with darts and pool, good value meals in separate eating area; good walks, open all day (*Alan and Paula McCully*);
[Symonds Yat E; SO5615], *Saracens Head*: Riverside spot next to ferry, easy-going down-to-earth flagstoned bar popular with canoeists, mountain bikers and hikers, cheerful staff, reasonably priced nourishing food for people with big appetites, Theakstons ales, settles and window seats; cosy carpeted restaurant, games bar with pool, piped jazz and blues, Sky TV, river-view tables outside, live music Thurs; bedrooms (*Pete and Rosie Flower, BB*)

☆ Tenbury Wells [A4112 S; SO5968], *Fountain*: Quaint low timbered pub with lots of black beams in open-plan lounge bar, red and gold flock wallpaper, big brass platters, delft shelf of bright china, masses of artificial flowers, coal-effect gas fire, big dining room beyond, side bar with pool; good choice of well home-cooked food inc fine specials, particularly well kept Bass and Courage-related ales, decent wines by the glass, friendly and courteous service, maybe unobtrusive piped music; picnic tables on side lawn with lots of play equipment (*Joan and Andrew Life, Malcolm Taylor, BB*)

☆ Tenbury Wells [Teme St], *Ship*: Snug old town pub with lots of dark wood inc fine Elizabethan beams, little hunting prints and other pictures, well kept changing ales such as Timothy Taylors Landlord, respectable house wines, good coffee, good imaginative bar food and Sun lunch in bright dining room with fresh flowers, reasonable prices, friendly landlord and staff, good relaxed atmosphere; piped music; picnic tables in coach yard and on neat sheltered back lawn; comfortable bedrooms (*RP, BP, E S Hales, Ann Robbins, D Balmer, BB*)

☆ Tenbury Wells [Worcester Rd; A456 about 1½ miles E – so inn actually in Shrops; SO6168], *Peacock*: 14th-c inn with several separate rooms, heavy black beams, views towards River Teme, cheerful log fires, comfortable kitchen chairs and ex-pew settles, well kept Bass, Ind Coope Burton and Tetleys, decent wines, attractively served food (not cheap), back family room, picnic tables on terrace (*Mike Forrester, Frank Cummins, C Wood, LYM*)

☆ Trumpet [A438 Hereford—Ledbury; SO6639], *Verzons*: Cheerful and welcoming small hotel, good choice of decent food in long comfortable bar-cum-bistro on left, well kept Hook Norton, friendly relaxed staff, restaurant on right; lovely garden with Malvern views, tasteful bedrooms (*J F Risbey, Michael Lloyd*)

Upper Wyche [Chase Rd off Walwyn Rd; off B4218 Malvern—Colwall, 1st left after hilltop on bend going W; SO7643], *Chase*: Fine views from attractive garden and refined and comfortable lounge of genteel rather clubby country two-bar pub on Malvern Hills, well kept Donnington BB, Wye Valley Bitter and HBA and guest ales, limited choice of good bar food – may stop well before 2 (*Philip Jackson, Patricia Heptinstall, Dr J A T Saul, Ian and Nita Cooper*)

☆ Upton Bishop [SO6527], *Moody Cow*: Charming refurbished country pub with good range of ales inc Courage, Hook Norton and Wye Valley, good generous food inc Sun lunch, helpful service, attractive floorboards; live jazz Thurs (*Malcolm Smith, Dr Paul Kitchener, Mike Dickerson*)

Upton Snodsbury [Worcester Rd (A422); SO9454], *Coventry Arms*: Wide choice of good value food in friendly traditional inn, wonderful location, well kept Whitbreads-related ales, wide choice of good value food, pleasant atmosphere; attractive bedrooms (*Mr *and Mrs Hammond)*

☆ **Upton upon Severn** [High St; SO8540], *Olde Anchor*: Picturesque and rambling but neat and tidy 16th-c pub with helpful service, old-fashioned furnishings, black timbers propping its low beams, lots of copper, brass and pewter, good fire in unusual central fireplace; well kept Courage-related ales, straightforward low-priced food; has been open all day summer, can get crowded evenings then *(Ted George, Gordon, LYM)*

Upton upon Severn [Old St, far end main st], *Little Upton Muggery*: Basic pub tricked out with nearly 4,000 mugs festooning walls and ceiling; generous food, well kept ales, rather informal service *(Ted George, PR, MR)*; [High St], *Star*: Spacious rather dark 17th-c coaching inn, with some panelling, good heating, friendly attentive service, cheap Bass, bar food inc vegetarian; well equipped bedrooms *(A Preston)*; [Riverside], *Swan*: Straightforward low-beamed riverside bar, well kept Banks's and Marstons Pedigree, two open fires, boating memorabilia, fruit machine, games machines in anteroom; small smarter bar with sizeable dining room off, good value interesting food; garden with summer barbecues *(JAH, LYM)*

☆ **Upton Warren** [Worcester Rd; SO9367], *Swan*: Good value friendly Greenalls Millers Kitchen dining pub, well kept beers; new bedroom extension *(Dave Braisted)*

☆ **Walterstone** [off A465 at Pandy – OS Sheet 161 map ref 340250; SO3425], *Carpenters Arms*: Particularly welcoming service in lovely traditional unspoilt pub, clean and friendly, with good reasonably priced food, well kept Wadworths and other ales, nice kitchen range; peaceful country setting, children welcome *(Gwyneth and Salvo Spadaro-Dutturi, Gordon)*

☆ **Weatheroak Hill** [Icknield St – coming S on A435 from Wythall roundabout, filter right off dual carriageway a mile S, then in village turn left towards Alvechurch; not far from M42, junction 3; SP0674], *Coach & Horses*: Roomy country pub popular for its wide choice of interesting well kept ales, most from small breweries; plush-seated low-ceilinged two-level lounge bar, tiled-floor public bar, cheap straightforward bar food, modern restaurant, plenty of seats out on lawns and upper terrace; piped music; children allowed in eating area *(Wayne A Wheeler, Dave Braisted, LYM)*

☆ **Wellington Heath** [SO7141], *Farmers Arms*: Good friendly service, reliably good food inc good value Sun lunch, well kept Courage Best and Directors, spacious and comfortable; tables on sunny terrace overlooking pretty wooded valley *(Mr and Mrs P Akitt, Joy and Peter Heatherley)*

West Malvern [W Malvern Rd; SO7646], *Brewers Arms*: Refurbished Marstons local down steep path from the road, with welcoming landlord, well kept beers, good food (not Mon lunchtime), folk and jazz nights; small garden *(Simon Thompson)*

Weston under Penyard [SO6323], *Weston Cross*: Well kept Bass, Boddingtons and Whitbreads, good food, friendly staff, nice garden *(Frank W Gadbois)*

☆ **Whitney on Wye** [SO2747], *Rhydspence*: Good interesting if not cheap food in very picturesque country inn, old-fashioned furnishings, heavy beams and timbers in rambling spick-and-span rooms, pretty dining room, Bass, Hook Norton Best and Robinsons Best, children allowed, tables in attractive garden with fine views over Wye valley; comfortable bedrooms – be on time for breakfast *(Jane Hosking, Ian Burniston, Frank Cummins, Phil Putwain, Ted George, Colin Laffan, LYM)*

Wolverley [B4189 N of Kidderminster; SO8279], *Lock*: Cottagey-looking pub with bay window overlooking a lock on the quaint Staffs & Worcs Canal as it negotiates a red sandstone bluff into which the pub is set; not that smart but comfortable enough, with generous well prepared straightforward food, Banks's and Camerons ales, good prices; lovely spot, some waterside tables *(P and M Rudlin, Gordon)*

☆ **Worcester** [London Rd, about ½ mile from centre], *Little Worcester Sauce Factory*: Fun pub with tiled walls advertising sauces, tiled map of Britain filling ceiling of largest room, lots of stripped pine and sawdust – and lots more sauce; good atmosphere, decent range of hearty good value food, friendly staff, Tetleys-related ales and their own Lumphammer *(JJW, CMW, SLC, Frank W Gadbois)*

Worcester [Fish St], *Farriers Arms*: Pleasantly furnished lounge, basic public bar, relaxed atmosphere, interesting decorations, decent food, cheerful service, well kept ales such as Glenny Hobgoblin and Wychwood; very handy for cathedral *(SLC, Ron Leigh, LYM)*; [Angel St], *Horn & Trumpet*: Carpeted lounge, well laid out airy flagstoned bar, plenty of bric-a-brac, Marstons ales inc Oyster Stout, good food; fruit machines, tables outside *(SLC)*; [50 Lowesmoor], *Jolly Roger*: This formerly popular brew-pub closed in spring 1996, and its stablemate the ancient Cardinals Hat has been bought by Banks's *(Anon)*; *Severn View*: Open fireplaces, black and white timbering, S&N ales, bar food, good service; piped music; views of river beyond main road *(SLC)*; [8-10 Barbourne Rd, The Tything], *Talbot*: Spacious panelled lounge, front bar with small bay window, dance floor tucked, Courage-related ales, oak-panelled restaurant, fruit machines; dances upstairs; bedrooms *(SLC)*

Wythall [Icknield St; SP0775], *Peacock*: Unusual well kept guest beers and good food from baps to char-grilled steaks in reliable old country pub; no-smoking area, open all day *(Jack Barnwell, Dave Braisted)*

☆ **Yarpole** [SO4765], *Bell*: Comfortably smart picturesquely timbered ancient pub extended into former cider mill, lots of brass and bric-a-brac, Whitbreads-related ales, extremely wide choice of food – former skittle alley prettily decked out as country dining area; tables in sunny garden, very handy for Croft Castle *(J Northey, Rebecca and Chris Stanners)*

Hertfordshire

Pubs doing particularly well here at the moment are the Bushel & Strike at Ashwell (nice new back bar and trompe l'oeil dining room), the lively and jolly Boat at Berkhamsted (restored to the main entries after a break), the Lytton Arms at Knebworth (excellent for real ales, but decent food too, in civilised surroundings), the attractively renovated Cock at Sarratt (another new main entry – good food here), and the White Lion at Walkern, a very good pub for family outings (yet another new entry). The Sword in Hand at Westmill has suffered a bad fire, but rebuilding is well under way as we go to press. In the Lucky Dip section at the end of the chapter, pubs to watch these days include the Valiant Trooper at Aldbury, Three Horseshoes at Bourne End, Green Dragon at Flaunden (good new chef), Fox in Harpenden, Silver Cross at Hertford Heath, Three Horseshoes at Letchmore Heath, Nags Head at Little Hadham and Cabinet at Reed (though we hear it's up for sale). We have inspected all of these, so can vouch firmly for their appeal. Prices in the area are close to the national average. The cheapest drinks we found were at the Fox & Hounds at Barley (which brews its own beer); prices were also low at pubs tied to Fullers.

ARDELEY TL3027 Map 5

Jolly Waggoner

This charming little pink-washed inn is peacefully set in a pretty tucked-away village. The sensitively refurbished comfortable bar has lots of open woodwork and a relaxed and civilised atmosphere, while the restaurant (extended into the cottage next door) is decorated with modern prints. Very carefully cooked using good ingredients, the attractively presented bar food includes sandwiches (from £2), french onion soup (£2.75), locally made sausages (£3.50), lunchtime ploughman's (from £3.50) salads (from £5.50), home-made burgers (from £4.75), vegetable and pasta bake (£5.95), Arnold Bennett omelette filled with smoked haddock and cheese (£6.50), calf liver with sage and butter or roquefort cheese and horseradish (£10.95), and delicious puddings; booking is essential for their Sunday lunch, and there's a £1 surcharge for credit cards. Friendly, flexible service. Well kept Greene King IPA, Abbot and a guest tapped from the cask, a good range of wines and freshly squeezed juice in summer; darts, cribbage, dominoes, fruit machine and piped music. They may play boules in the lovely garden on Monday evening. The landlord also runs a main entry pub at Cottered. *(Recommended by K Archard, R S Reid, Bob and Maggie Atherton, Charles Bardswell, Anthony Barnes, Cyril S Brown)*

Greene King ~ Tenant Darren Perkins ~ Real ale ~ Meals and snacks (not Mon) ~ Restaurant ~ (01438) 861350 ~ Well behaved children welcome ~ Open 12-2.30(3 Sat), 6-11; cl Monday lunchtime

ASHWELL TL2639 Map 5

Bushel & Strike

Off A507 just E of A1(M) junction 10, N of Baldock, via Newnham; also signposted off A1 southbound; and off A505 Baldock—Royston; in village turn off High St into Gardiners

Lane, pub is opposite the church (car park can be reached down Swan Lane)

They've effected some rather nice transformations at this cheerful old pub, opposite the village church. The front part is still devoted to eating with a large salad bar and pudding display cabinet as well as neatly laid tables with fresh flowers, attractive hunting and coaching prints, and local colour photographs – this is a pretty village, with some ancient timbered houses. Beyond this, the bar has been given a much more civilised air with leather chesterfields on polished floorboards in front of an open fire. Through a passage the pub opens up into an enchanting trompe l'oeil Edwardian conservatory restaurant – it's actually an old school hall – with abundant painted foliage, horses and rolling hills. The wide choice of popular food (they are flexible about food serving times) includes sandwiches (from £2), filled baked potatoes (£2.95), lunchtime special (£3.50), ham, egg and chips (£4.50), breaded plaice (£4.95), mushroom and pimento stroganoff (£6.25), lasagne or venison, guinea fowl and pigeon in redcurrant, thyme and red wine sauce (£6.95), pork chop with apple sauce (£7.50), rack of ribs or chicken and ribs in barbecue sauce (£8.25), 8oz fillet (£11.50) or 18oz T-bone (£12.50); good three course Sunday buffet lunch (£11.95); the restaurant is no smoking during food serving hours. Well kept Charles Wells Bombardier, Eagle and Fargo and two guests such as Adnams Broadside or Morlands Old Speckled Hen on handpump, as well as cask cider and about ten wines by the glass; very friendly staff. There are tables out on a small terrace and more spacious lawn, under a big apple tree and flowering cherry. *(Recommended by Thomas Nott, Susan and Nigel Wilson; more reports please)*

Charles Wells ~ Tenant Michael Mills-Roberts ~ Real ale ~ Meals and snacks (till 10.30pm) ~ Restaurant ~ (01462) 742394 ~ Children welcome ~ Live music alternate Sunday nights ~ Open 11-3, 5.30(6 in winter)-11; Sat 11-11; Sun 12-10.30

AYOT ST LAWRENCE TL1916 Map 5

Brocket Arms ★ ◗

B651 N of St Albans for about 6 miles; village signposted on right after Wheathampstead and Marshall's Heath golf course; or B653 NE of Luton, then right on to B651

Peacefully set well off the beaten track in lovely countryside and down some very narrow lanes, this white-painted and tiled 14th-c brick pub is delightfully traditional, simple and unspoilt. Two bustling low-ceilinged rooms brimming with atmosphere and genuine character, and complete with ghost story, have orange lanterns hanging from sturdy oak beams. There's a big inglenook fireplace (often too hot to sit in), a big coal fire in the back room, a fishtank in the dining room fireplace, magazines to read, and a long built-in wall settle in one parquet-floored room. Pictures by a local artist are for sale; darts, dominoes, shove ha'penny, piped music. Five real ales on handpump and two on tap behind the bar include Adnams Broadside, Greene King Abbot and IPA, Theakstons Best and Wadworths 6X, with two weekly changing guests like Gibbs Mew Bishops Tipple or Eldridge Pope Royal Oak tapped from the cask or on handpump; about 11 wines by the glass. Big helpings of lunchtime bar food include home-made soup (£2.50), sandwiches or filled baked potatoes (from £2.50), ploughman's (from £4), pies like cold pork and cranberry (£5) and 8oz sirloin steak (£9.50. The evening menu is a bit different with 4oz steak in french bread or scampi (£5), salads (from £5), chicken or halibut steak and lobster sauce (£9.50) and roast duck, pheasant or venison (£9.95). On Sunday they have a cold buffet counter in summer, and a roast in winter. It can get very crowded at weekends. The extensive south-facing suntrap walled garden has a summer bar and a children's play area. Dogs welcome in bar. *(Recommended by I P G Derwent, Graham and Karen Oddey, Gwen and Peter Andrews, Howard Gregory, Thomas Nott, Gareth and Toni Edwards, Michael Sandy, Ian Phillips, Zach Hurst, Colin Steer, James Nunns, M W Turner, Tom McLean, Roger Huggins, Howard James, Nigel Hopkins, Phil and Heidi Cook, Peter and Joy Heatherley, Nigel Norman, Nick and Alison Dowson)*

Free house ~ Lease: Toby Wingfield Digby ~ Real ale ~ Meals and snacks ~ Restaurant (not Sun or Mon evening) ~ (01438) 820250 ~ Children in eating area of bar and restaurant ~ Open 11-11; Sun 12-10.30 ~ Bedrooms: £40/£55(£70B)

BARLEY TL3938 Map 5

Fox & Hounds 🍺

Junction 10 of M11 then A505 towards Royston, then left on to B1368 after 4 miles

A fabulous range of vegetarian dishes, many of which are suitable for vegans, is only one reason why this attractive 15th-c local is doing well at the moment. As well as sixteen vegetarian dishes such as pasta and mushrooms baked with stilton and mozzarella, beefsteak tomatoes stuffed with olives, pine nuts, onion, pimento and beans or cashew nut roast with wild berry and port sauce (£4.95-£6.45), carefully prepared bar food includes soup (£1.95), chestnut and port pâté (£3.45), spare ribs (£3.65), pies such as steak and kidney or venison in red wine (from £5.95), rabbit with mustard and cider casserole (£6.15), lamb fillet or beef stew with dumplings (£6.25), king prawn and mushoom korma (£6.75), breast of chicken in an apricot, brandy and cream sauce or paella (£6.95), salmon fillet stuffed with crab en croûte (£7.95), half a honey roast duck (£7.95), and children's meals (from £1.75). In addition to their own very well priced Nathaniel's Special, well kept beers on handpump include Adnams Broadside and Southwold as well as about six changing guests, with lots more during their real ale festivals. Also farm cider, a good range of wines by the bottle or glass and several malt whiskies. There's a nicely furnished series of atmospheric candlelit low-ceilinged and alcovey rambling rooms, with substantial log fires on both sides of a massive central chimney. The dining area with its odd-shaped nooks and crannies was originally the kitchen and cellar; half of it is no smoking. Friendly staff, locals and cat, and a fine range of games, from darts, bar billiards and dominoes (two schools), to shove-ha'penny, cribbage, fruit machine and skittles; also a league cricket team, and pétanque. They have disabled lavatories and ramp access to a dining room at the back. (*Recommended by Susan and Nigel Wilson, R Turnham, Nigel and Amanda Thorp, Frank Gadbois, David Craine, Ann Reeder, Charles Bardswell, Susan and Nigel Wilson, M E Wellington*)

Own brew ~ Licensee Rita Nicholson ~ Real ale ~ Meals and snacks ~ Restaurant ~ (01763) 848459 ~ Well behaved children welcome until 9pm ~ Open 12-2.30, 6-11 (all day summer Sat and Sun)

BERKHAMSTED SP9807 Map 5

Boat 🍷 🍺

Gravel Path

There's a really jolly, friendly atmosphere at this prettily placed flower-decked canalside pub. The energetic landlord keeps the lively bar full of plants and fresh flowers, and there are little touches like home-made chutneys and pickled onions. A short bar menu includes sandwiches (from £2.50), soup (£2.95), omelettes (from £4.50), burgers (from £5.25); seafood tagliatelle (£5.95), strips of chicken cooked in ginger and garlic with stir fried vegetables or steak, Guinness and smoked oyster pie (£6.25). The evening menu (only Monday and Tuesday) includes pheasant and pecan nut terrine surrounded by fried apple slices (£3.75), poached breast of chicken with a shallot and tarragon sauce oyster mushrooms and cherry tomatoes (£7.50) or fillet of beef stroganoff (£9.75), and puddings like hot apple strudel (£3.75). Very helpful happy staff serve well kept and very reasonably priced Fullers Chiswick, ESB, Hock and London Pride on handpump, and a good wine list with about twenty wines (and champagne) by the glass. Trivia and piped music. (*Recommended by Thomas Nott, Ian Phillips, Gwen and Peter Andrews, Susan Stevens, Craig Turnbull, Peter and Mavis Brigginshaw, Jan and Colin Roe, Nigel and Lindsay Chapman*)

Fullers ~ Tenant Chris Elford ~ Real ale ~ Meals and snacks (not Weds to Sun evening) ~ (01442) 877152 ~ Children welcome till 7pm ~ Open 11-3, 5.15-11; all day Fri-Sun

---

If we know a pub has an outdoor play area for children, we mention it.

BURNHAM GREEN TL2516 Map 5

White Horse

Off B1000 N of Welwyn, just E of railway bridge by Welwyn Station

This smartly refurbished and extended beamed dining pub is popular at lunchtimes for good value bar food, which includes sandwiches (from £1.60), local sausages (£3.25), ploughman's (£3.50), filled baked potatoes (from £3.50), vegetable lasagne or broccoli and cream cheese bake (£3.95), omelettes (£4), fresh burger (£4.95), gammon (£6.95), steaks (from £7.95), and three daily specials like cod florentine (£4.95), chicken, ham and leek pie (£4.75), farmhouse grill (£5.25). There's a more elaborate restaurant menu. The nicest part – get there early for a chance of a seat – is the original black-beamed bit by the bar, with solid traditional furnishings, hunting prints, corner china cupboards and log-effect gas fire in two small communicating areas. There are many more tables in a two-floor extension with pitched rafters in its upper gallery, no smoking downstairs. A back brick terrace by a fountain, with a gentle country view, has neat green garden furniture, large umbrellas and outdoor heaters, so you can eat outside even on cooler evenings; there are rustic benches on grass by a pond beyond. Children under 16 are not allowed in this garden unless they stay seated as the pond is deep, but there is lots of room to play on the broad green in front. Well kept Adnams, Greene King IPA, Ind Coope Burton, Marstons Pedigree, Theakstons Best and Old Peculier and Tetleys on handpump, quick friendly service. *(Recommended by Neil O'Callaghan, Stephen and Jean Curtis; more reports please)*

Free house ~ Licensees Richard Blackett and Nicky Hill ~ Real ale ~ Meals and snacks (12.30-2, 6.30-8) ~ Restaurant (till 9.30) ~ (01438) 798416 ~ Children welcome in restaurant ~ Open 11-3, 6-11

COTTERED TL3129 Map 5

Bull

A507 W of Buntingford

Improvements under the fairly new licensees at this attractive old tree-surrounded inn have opened up the two bars a little, and exposed wooden floors which are now decorated with an attractive rug. There are more antiques in the friendly low-beamed front lounge, which is roomy and comfortable, with lots of horsebrasses, and a good fire. A second bar has darts, shove-ha'penny, cribbage, fruit machine, and trivia; unobtrusive piped music. Well kept Greene King IPA, Abbot and their seasonal ales on handpump, decent wines, and freshly squeezed orange juice in summer; quick pleasant service. Bar food includes sandwiches (from £2), soup (£2.75), ploughman's (from £3.95), filled baked potatoes (£4.25), home-made burgers (£4.50), scampi (£4.95), lasagne (£5), srir fried chicken (£6.95) and smoked salmon (£7.95). The evening menu has one or two more substantial dishes like roast rack of lamb with garlic or rosemary (£8.95) and beef en croûte (£14.50). There's a £1 surcharge for credit cards. The well reworked sizeable garden has boules and a play area. *(Recommended by Michael Taylor, Enid and Henry Stephens, Phil and Heidi Cook, Charles Bardswell; more reports please)*

Greene King ~ Lease: Darren Perkins ~ Real ale ~ Meals and snacks ~ Restaurant ~ (01763) 281243 ~ Children over 7 welcome ~ Open 12-3, 6.30-11; cl evening 25 Dec

FLAUNDEN TL0100 Map 5

Bricklayers Arms

Village signposted from A41; Hogpits Bottom – from village centre follow Boxmoor, Bovingdon road and turn right at Belsize, Watford signpost

There's a comfortably smart atmosphere in the snug cottagey rooms of this Virginia creeper-covered country pub. The warmly decorated low-beamed bar has dark brown painted traditional wooden wall seats, open winter fires, and stubs of knocked-through oak-timbered walls that give a snug feeling to the three areas that used to be separate rooms. The life-size bronze dogs and model gorilla at the bar certainly catch the eye. There's a back dining room. Bar food includes soup (£1.95), sandwiches (from £2.85), filled baked potatoes (from £3.15), ploughman's (from £3.95), local sausages (£5.45), chicken curry or fish pie (£5.95), bricklayer's feast – ribs, chicken wings and potato skins coated with barbecue sauce and garlic dip (£6.95), beef in ale pie (£7.25), steaks (from £11.75), fish, daily specials, and puddings (£3.45). Half a dozen well kept beers on handpump might include Boddingtons, Marstons Pedigree, Shepherd Neame Spitfire, Ushers Founders or Wadworths 6X, and there's a good range of wines; prompt professional service from welcoming staff; dominoes. It gets very busy at the weekends, so arrive early for a table. Just up the Belsize road there's a path on the left, through woods, to more Forestry Commission woods around Hollow Hedge. *(Recommended by Ian Phillips, Kath Wetherill, Howard Gregory, Keith and Cheryl Roe, Heather Couper, Nigel and Lindsay Chapman; more reports please)*

Free house ~ Licensees R C Mitchell and D J Winteridge ~ Real ale ~ Meals and snacks (no sandwiches Sun) ~ Restaurant ~ (01442) 833322 ~ Children welcome in restaurant ~ Open 11-2.30, 6-11; all day Sat and Sun in summer

GREAT OFFLEY TL1427 Map 5

Green Man ♀

Village signposted off A505 Luton—Hitchin

There's an impressive view from the spaciously elegant conservatory at this busy dining pub, across the picturesque garden, pond and waterfall, and beyond to flatter land stretching for miles to the east. The flagstoned terrace around three sides of the conservatory has chairs and tables and a profusion of flowers in hanging baskets and tubs. The neat low beamed bars have lots of antique farm-tool illustrations, wheelback and spindleback chairs around simple country pine scrubbed tables, some stripped brick, an open fire and a woodburning stove. An airier right-hand room has countryside prints, cushioned built-in wall seats, and another big woodburner with a row of brass spigots decorating the chimneypiece. Generously served bar meals include soup (£1.60), sandwiches and large filled rolls (from £2.40), filled baked potatoes (from £2.30), ploughman's (from £3), hot salt beef sandwich (£3.95), yorkshire pudding filled with curry or chilli (£4.65), spaghetti bolognese (£4.65), cottage pie or chicken and mushroom pie (£5.15), vegetarian dishes like leek and potato bake (£5.25), salads from a buffet table (from £6), southern fried chicken (£6.25), scampi or lamb chop (£6.40) and a carvery (£6.50). Boddingtons, Courage Directors, John Smiths, Marstons Pedigree, Ruddles County and Websters on handpump, and a decent choice of wines by the glass; piped music, fruit machine. Children are encouraged to play in the front garden, where there are swings and a slide, rather than the back. *(Recommended by Bob and Maggie Atherton, Barry O'Keefe, the Sandy Family, I P G Derwent, David and Ruth Shillitoe, James Waller, Howard James, Nigel Norman, Susan and Nigel Wilson, Jan and Colin Roe)*

Free house ~ Licensee Raymond H Scarbrow ~ Real ale ~ Meals and snacks (cold food all day) ~ Restaurant ~ (01462) 768256 ~ Children welcome ~ Open 10.30-11; Sun 12-10.30

KNEBWORTH TL2320 Map 5

Lytton Arms

Park Lane, Old Knebworth, 3 miles from A1(M) junction 7; A602 towards Stevenage, 2nd roundabout right on B191 towards Knebworth, then right into Old Knebworth Lane; at village T-junction, right towards Codicote

This simple Victorian pub with its friendly service and unaffected approach is the comfortable home of a fabulous range of about seven well kept guest ales, alongside the regular crew of Bass, Fullers London Pride, Nethergate Old Growler, Theakstons

Best and Woodfordes Wherry. The very enthusiastic licensee also has Staropramen beer from Prague on draught, and about 50 Belgian bottled beers – as well as regular beer festivals. There are also country wines, about 50 malt whiskies, Weston's Old Rosie farm cider, and hot chocolate and herb teas as well as coffee; in the winter, hot gluhwein served by the log fire, with chestnuts roasting. Several solidly furnished big-windowed carpeted rooms, some panelled and each with a slightly different decor (railway memorabilia here, old Knebworth estate photographs there), ramble around the big central servery, ending in a newish no-smoking conservatory with orderly pale tables on its shiny brown tiles; the dining area is also no smoking. Bar food includes sandwiches (from £1.70), soup (£2), filled baked potatoes (from £2.90), ploughman's (£4.30), ham and egg (£4.50), home-made steak and kidney pie (£5.50) and a fine mixed grill (£7.60), with children's dishes (from £2.30); there may be a delay at busy times. There are picnic tables on the front grass, and the back garden has a play area; summer barbecues. Dominoes, shove-ha'penny, maybe piped music; friendly efficient service; Rimau the three-legged cat has now got used to being called Tripod. *(Recommended by Mayur Shah, Richard Houghton, Howard Gregory, Steve Gledhill, John Fahy)*

Free house ~ Licensee Stephen Nye ~ Real ale ~ Meals and snacks ~ Restaurant ~ (01438) 812312 ~ Well behaved children in conservatory till 9pm ~ Open 11-3, 5-11; all day Fri, Sat and Sun; cl 25 Dec evening

RUSHDEN TL3031 Map 5

Moon & Stars

Village signposted from A507 Baldock—Buntingford, about 1 mile W of Cottered

Life in the unspoilt and cottagey little bar at this traditional country local moves at a comfortable and friendly leisurely pace. There's a vast inglenook fireplace beneath the heavy-beamed low ceiling, and leading off is a table-filled no-smoking lounge bar. The straightforward but well liked and good value bar menu includes open sandwiches (from £3.50), soup (£2.95), ploughman's (from £4.50), good fresh fish and chips on Tuesday evening (£4.50), ham and egg (£4.75), steak and kidney pie (£6.25), roast rack of lamb (£8), and 10oz steaks (from £9.95). On Friday and Saturday night they substitute a full blackboard menu which includes starters like smoked salmon and scrambled eggs (£3.95) or Spanish vegetable salad (£3.95) and main courses like chicken breast in orange and horseradish (£7.95). They're particularly proud of the home-made puddings (£3); and they do Sunday roasts (£5.75), and cream teas on summer Sunday afternoons. Well kept Greene King IPA, Abbot and XX Dark Mild on handpump, and a short, decent wine list. Very friendly service; darts, dominoes, shove-ha'penny, cribbage, fruit machine, pétanque, piped music. The two dogs are called Fred and Lucy. There are good views from the tables on the rolling lawns that extend up the hillside and benches at the front. *(Recommended by Gwen and Peter Andrews, Bob and Maggie Atherton; more reports please)*

Greene King ~ Tenants Robbie and Gill Davidson ~ Real ale ~ Meals and snacks (not Mon, or evening Sun) ~ (01763) 288330 ~ Children over 5 in eating area lunchtime only ~ Open 12-2.30, 6(6.30 Sat)-11; Sun 12-5.30(4 in winter), 8-10.30; cl Mon lunchtime ~ Bedroom: £30S/£37.50S

SARRATT TQ0499 Map 5

Cock

Church End: a very pretty approach is via North Hill, a lane N off A404, just under a mile W of A405

The latched door of this cosy white 17th-c country pub opens into a carpeted snug with a vaulted ceiling, original bread oven, bar stools and a television, as well as very well kept Brakspears Old Ale, Fullers London Pride, Shepherd Neame Spitfire and Theakstons Old Peculier on handpump. Through an archway, the partly oak-panelled cream-walled lounge has a log fire in an inglenook, pretty Liberty-style curtains, pink plush chairs at dark oak tables, and lots of interesting artefacts. Long-standing Guide readers will have spotted that this description constitutes quite considerable changes since this pub last appeared in the Guide well over a decade ago – in fact it's been out of operation as a pub for quite a few years, and reopened about a year ago. Well liked freshly cooked bar food includes sandwiches (from £2.95), ploughman's (from £4.25), seafood pasta (£5.75), steak and ale pie (£6.50), and a specials board with imaginative dishes like pork fillet with dijon mustard and cream sauce (£6.95), salmon with asparagus en croûte (£7.95) or grilled shark steak wth asparagus tips (£9.50); lovely puddings like brandy sponge with meringue topping (£3.25); pleasant young staff. Benches in front look across a quiet lane towards the churchyard, and at the back there's an outside summer bar on a terrace, and tables under umbrellas on a small sheltered lawn with open country views. The restaurant is in a nicely restored thatched barn. *(Recommended by Mr and Mrs T E Warr, David English, Keith Archer, Nick Chettle, K L Smart, A L Ingram, P Goodchild)*

Free house ~ Licensees Anthony Power and Julian Thompson ~ Real ale ~ Meals and snacks ~ Restaurant ~ (01923) 282908 ~ Children welcome in restaurant ~ Open 11-3, 5.30-11; Sat 11-11; Sun 12-10.30

ST ALBANS TL1507 Map 5

Fighting Cocks

Off George Street, through abbey gateway (you can drive down, though signs suggest you can't)

Unaffectedly friendly and pubby, this well run place has heavy low beams in its much modernised bar, a good log fire in the inglenook fireplace, some pleasant window alcoves, and other nooks and corners. The stuffed cock in a cabinet alludes to the fact that the sunken area down from the bar, with its ring of comfortable seats, used to be a Stuart cock-fighting pit. In fact there's been some sort of inn on this site for a very long time indeed; and the present building was known as the Round House some 400 years ago because of its rather odd shape. Eight well kept real ales include Ind Coope Burton, Eldridge Pope Royal Oak, Tetleys and Wadworths 6X as well as four guests like Adnams Broadside, Greenalls Original, Jennings Cocker Hoop or Shepherd Neame Spitfire on handpump; farm cider. Sensibly limited bar food includes popular filled wholemeal baps (from £3.15), excellent ploughman's (from £3.40), vegetarian dishes (from £3.95), steak and kidney or chicken and mushroom pie (£4.85), and about ten daily specials like liver and bacon (£4.65) or chicken and ham lasagne (£5.15). Seats in the attractive garden look down towards the river with its ducks. *(Recommended by JJB, Thomas Nott, Lou Gollin, Mark Matthewman, Nigel Hopkins)*

Ind Coope (Carlsberg Tetleys) ~ Manager Cilla Palmer ~ Real ale ~ Meals and snacks (till 3 Sat and Sun; not Sun and Mon evening) ~ (01727) 865830 ~ Children welcome ~ Open 11-11

Garibaldi £ 🍺

61 Albert Street; off Holywell Hill below White Hart Hotel – some parking at end of street

There's a good friendly atmosphere and a nice mix of customers in the refurbished Victorian style bar, which angles round the central island servery at this bustling town pub. Up some steps is a little tiled-floor snug, while a separate food counter on a lower level opens out into a neat and cosy little no-smoking conservatory. Victorian and Edwardian theatrical prints decorate the walls. Very reasonably priced bar food under the new licensee includes lunchtime sandwiches (from £1.40) and daily specials like beef in beer pie, tuna and pasta bake or chicken curry (£3.50). The evening menu has doritos (£3.50), chicken kiev or fisherman's pie (£4.50) and mixed grill (£7.50), and each night of the week they do a different special: Monday fish and chips (£3.75), Wednesday curries (£3.95), Thursday sizzling platters (£4.95), and Friday 10oz T-bone steak (£7.95); Sunday lunch roasts (£4.50). Traditional English puddings like treacle sponge or sticky toffee pudding (£2.20). Well kept Fullers Chiswick, London Pride, ESB and Summer Ale on handpump; darts, cribbage, dominoes, fruit machine, decent piped pop music. The pub has its own cricket team. A side yard has a few picnic tables. *(Recommended by Michael Sandy, BKA, Jan and Colin Roe; more reports please)*

Fullers ~ Manager Rob Potts ~ Real ale ~ Meals and snacks (not Sun evening) ~ Restaurant (cl Sun evening) ~ (01727) 855046 ~ Children in conservatory until 9 ~ Live blues music at least once a month ~ Open 11-11; Sun 12-10.30

Goat 🍺

Sopwell Lane; a No Entry beside Strutt and Parker estate agents on Holywell Hill, the main southwards exit from town – by car, take the next lane down and go round the block

In the 18th c the inn of which this fine old pub is one surviving fragment had the most extensive stables of any in the county; what's left of them now shelters the tables in the back yard. The attractive building has changed enormously over the years, although the several areas rambling around the central bar are full of character, with a profusion of eye-catching decorations: stuffed birds, chamber-pots, books, prints and so forth; there's an open fire in winter. It's a popular place, especially with students, so there's usually a cheery boisterous atmosphere, even more so during their well received live jazz. Adnams, Courage Directors, Greene King IPA, Marstons Pedigree and Worthington Best on handpump; good range of malt whiskies. Home-made bar food includes dishes like filled baked potatoes (from £2.25), big roast beef baguette (£2.95), giant yorkshire pudding with hotpot filling (£3.95), scampi or chilli (£4.25), and home-made pies (from £4.50); Sunday lunch (£4.95). Fruit machine, trivia and piped music. There are tables on the neat lawn-and-gravel smallish back garden, and maybe barbecues out here in summer. *(Recommended by JJB, Michael Sandy, Nigel Hopkins, Susan and Nigel Wilson; more reports please)*

Greenalls ~ Real ale ~ Meals and snacks (till 4 Sun; not evenings Fri, Sat or Sun) ~ (01727) 833934 ~ Children in eating area ~ Jazz Sun lunchtime ~ Open 11.30-11; Sun 12-10.30; cl evening 25 Dec

Rose & Crown

St Michaels Street; from town centre follow George Street down past the abbey towards the Roman town

The beamed public bars at this relaxed and civilised pub are firmly traditional (no games machines or music), with unevenly timbered walls, old-fashioned wall benches, chintzy curtains and cushions and black cauldrons in a deep fireplace; big fires in winter. The friendly American landlord is the originator of the nicely presented speciality American-style gourmet sandwiches served here. They range from straightforward cheese (£1.60), through Royalty sandwiches served with potato salad, crisps and pickled cucumber on a granary or white loaf or bap filled with perhaps chicken, cheddar, pickle and salad (£3.80) to toasted double-deckers like roast beef, horseradish, mustard, tomato, American cheese and salad (£4.25). A few other dishes include soup (£1.95), chilli (£3.75) or lasagne (£4.65). Well kept Adnams and Greenalls Original and changing guests on handpump; a dozen or so malt whiskies; efficient service. Darts (placed sensibly to one side), dominoes, cribbage. Lots of tables and benches along the side and at the back of the pub with shrubs and roses, flowerbeds and hanging baskets. *(Recommended by JJB, Nigel Hopkins and Mark Hydes)*

Greenalls ~ Tenant Neil Dekker ~ Real ale ~ Lunchtime meals and snacks (not Sun) ~ (01727) 851903 ~ Children in lounge area lunchtime only ~ acoustic music Mon night, Irish and Scottish folk Thurs eve ~ Open 11.30-3, 5.30(6 Sat)-11

TEWIN TL2714 Map 5

Plume of Feathers ♀

Village signposted off B1000 NE of Welwyn Garden City; Upper Green Road, N end of village, OS Sheet 166 map reference 273153

There's a good choice of low-ceilinged rooms at this cosy dining pub. We think the nicest part is up some steps at one side, where there's a big oriental rug, easy chairs and sofas, a low table, oak-panelled bookcases covering most of one wall – very snug and clubby. Decor is generally very low key, with just a few carefully chosen prints on the cream walls. Behind the bar is a pretty pink-tablecloth restaurant, and there are well spaced picnic tables in a pleasant back garden overlooking a golf course, with some more tables out in front. Good interesting bar food, all home-made from fresh ingredients, includes soup (£2.95), filled potato skins (from £4.25), salads (from £4.50), tagliatelle (£5.75), steak and kidney pudding (£6.50), with a few changing specials such as avocado and tomato bake (£4.95), liver and bacon or braised cod (£6.25), fillet of brill, or duck fillets with pepper, carrot and leek strips on a sizzler stone (£6.50); they'll do a bowl of olives (£1.25), and sandwiches (£3.25) for two rounds; good Sunday lunch. Well kept Adnams, and up to seven guests such as Bass, Boddingtons, Caledonian 80/- or Marstons Pedigree; decent wines by the glass, including vintage and late-bottled ports. *(Recommended by Neil O'Callaghan, Enid and Henry Stephens, A C Morrison)*

Free house ~ Licensees David Berry and Liz Mitchell ~ Real ale ~ Meals and snacks ~ Restaurant ~ (01438) 717265 ~ Children welcome in restaurant ~ Open 11-2.30(3 Sat), 6-11

WADESMILL TL3517 Map 5
Sow & Pigs

Thundridge (the village where it's actually situated – but not marked on many road maps, which is why we list it under nearby Wadesmill); A10 just S of Wadesmill, towards Ware

The new landlady at this cheerful little village pub has shifted the emphasis a little towards the good generously served bar food, with fresh fish and game alongside their speciality Yorkshire fish and chips (haddock in an unusual batter) (£5.50), several dishes of the day such as beef in Guinness (£5.75), liver and bacon (£5.95) and mixed grills (£8.50); there are lots of home-made puddings (£2.95). They also do sandwiches (from £2.65), soup (£2.75) and ploughman's (from £4.50). They do cream teas on summer afternoons (not Sunday), and if you ring ahead they can make breakfast. The plank-panelled central serving bar has a small ship's wheel and binnacle, a rustic table supported by two barrels in the bay of the cosy window seat, and, as the name of the pub suggests, quite a porcine theme. There are lots of little piggies in a glass cabinet and amusing pictures in this vein on the wall. More spacious rooms lead off on both sides – the dining room on the right has dark beams and massive rustic tables, while the area on the left has a timber part divider, and a couple of steps half way along, helping to break it up. A box of activities should keep children occupied. Well kept Adnams, Shipstones, Wadworths 6X and one or two guests on handpump. There are picnic tables under cocktail parasols, with their own service hatch, on a smallish fairy-lit grass area behind by the car park, sheltered by tall oaks and chestnut trees. Access directly on to the A10 can be difficult; no dogs. *(Recommended by Joy Heatherley, John Fahy, A C Morrison)*

Greenalls ~ Tenant Meriel Riches ~ Real ale ~ Meals and snacks ~ Restaurant ~ (01920) 463281 ~ Children welcome in eating area of bar and restaurant ~ Open 11-11; Sun 12-10.30

WALKERN TL2826 Map 5
White Lion

B1037

In 1711 this sensitively restored 17th-c brick building housed the judges who were the last in this country to condemn a woman to death for witchcraft; her sentence was later commuted to life imprisonment. Its associations are much friendlier these days; it now makes a good friendly family stop with lots to keep the children happy. Through conifers in the pleasant garden there's an exciting wooden play area, a bouncy castle and football nets (the football-playing dog is called Mr Bobby), as well as rabbits (crunchy food supplied by the staff), and satellite cartoon channel on the terrace in summer. Generously served tasty bar food includes soup (£2.45), filled potato skins (£3.75), toasted bacon and goat's cheese salad (£4.25), sausage and mash (£4.95), 8oz burger (£6.95), Swahili hot chicken salad, hot and spicy Jamaican pork (£7.95), spicy cajun chicken (£8.45), cantonese-style fish stir fry (£8.95), steaks (from £8.95), mixed grill (£10.95), daily specials, and puddings (£3.25); Sunday lunch (£6.95); usual children's menu; there is also a small separate no-smoking restaurant. The comfortable open-plan bar (with very low beams where its separate rooms have been knocked together, making cosy little alcoves) has an inglenook fireplace with a good fire in winter, comfortable leatherette banquettes and lots of tables, ticking clocks, and gentle piped music. Well kept Greene King Abbot, IPA and seasonal ales, jugs of pimms in summer; darts, shove-ha'penny, dominoes and cribbage. (Recommended by Kerry Samson, I P G Derwent, Charles Bardswell, Mr and Mrs Peter Gregory, Sidney and Erna Wells, Tony Spring, Jonathan Bridger, M E Wellington)

Greene King ~ Licensees Gary Diaz and Helen Ward ~ Meals and snacks (from 5pm, all day Sat and Sun) ~ Restaurant ~ (01438) 861251 ~ Children welcome ~ Open 11-3, 5-11; Sat 11-11; Sun 12-10.30

WATTON AT STONE TL3019 Map 5

George & Dragon ★ ▮

Village signposted off A602 about 5 miles S of Stevenage, on B1001; High St

This civilised dining pub has country kitchen armchairs around attractive old tables, dark blue cloth-upholstered seats in its bay windows, an interesting mix of antique and modern prints on the partly timbered ochre walls, and a big inglenook fireplace. A quieter room off the main bar has spindleback chairs and wall settles cushioned to match the green floral curtains, a hunting print and old photographs of the village above its panelled dado. Proper napkins, antiques and daily newspapers add to the smart feel; it's not the sort of place where people wear sleeveless T-shirts. Greene King Abbot and IPA under light blanket pressure; several malt whiskies and good house wines by half-pint or pint carafes, and a selected house claret. Bar food includes sandwiches (from £1.20), home-made soup (£1.70), Greek salad (£4.75), pasta with red lentils, spinach, tomato and cheese (£6.75), strips of chicken with mushrooms in cream and brandy or steak roll (£6.75), beef stew with haricot beans (£7.75), poached fresh salmon in pastry with a prawn and sparkling wine sauce (£8.75), rack of lamb (£10.85), fish stew (£10.75), and very reasonably priced daily specials like fresh asparagus (£3.85), liver and bacon or pork chop with whole grain mustard and cream sauce (£4.55) or wing of fresh skate with black butter (£5.25), and nice puddings like summer pudding, treacle sponge and custard (£2.45). They do get busy, so you may have problems finding a table unless you arrive early; a couple of readers have found the service a bit slow at times. Partly no-smoking restaurant. Fruit machine, summer quiz nights, and boules in the pretty extended shrub-screened garden. The pub is handy for Benington Lordship Gardens. (Recommended by Peter Saville, Colin Steer, Maysie Thompson, Michael Gittins, Mayur Shah, Steve Gledhill, R C Wiles, Howard Gregory, M E Wellington, Nigel Norman, Joy Heatherley, Bob and Maggie Atherton, Howard James, Mrs C Archer, Maysie Thompson, G L Tong, Neil O'Callaghan)

Greene King ~ Lease: Kevin Dinnin ~ Real ale ~ Meals and snacks (till 10; not Sun evening) ~ Restaurant (not Sun evening) ~ (01920) 830285 ~ Children in eating area of bar and restaurant until 9pm ~ Open 11-2.30, 6-11(11-11 Sat); cl evening Dec 25 and 26

WESTMILL TL3626 Map 5

Sword in Hand

Village signposted W of A10, about 1 mile S of Buntingford

As we went to press this pretty colour-washed local was closed after a fire, but rebuilding had already started, and with the same landlord in charge – with his eye firmly on reopening in spring 1997 – we're sure this long-standing main entry will be well worth a visit when it does reopen then. But of course it would be wise to telephone, in case there's been a delay. The building is listed, and the friendly licensees are taking this opportunity to expose even more beams in the traditional bar. The sort of food that's likely is garlic and herb prawns, warm avocado and smoky bacon salad, ham, egg and chips, steak and kidney pudding and pigeon breast with port and mustard sauce. Well kept beers have been Greene King IPA and Abbot, and a guest on handpump, with a changing range of wines. There are seats on a terrace surrounded by climbing roses and clematis, and more in the partly crazy-paved side garden running down to the fields, where a play area has a log cabin, slide, and an old tractor to climb on; piped music; nice walks nearby. *(Reports please)*

Free house ~ Licensees David and Heather Hopperton ~ Real ale ~ Meals and snacks ~ Restaurant ~ (01763) 271356 ~ Children welcome in eating area of bar till 9pm ~ Open 12-3, 6(7 Sun)-11; cl evening 25 Dec ~ Bedrooms: /£39.50B

Post Office address codings confusingly give the impression that some pubs are in Hertfordshire, when they're really in Bedfordshire or Cambridgeshire (which is where we list them).

Lucky Dip

Besides the fully inspected pubs, you might like to try these Lucky Dips recommended to us and described by readers (if you do, please send us reports):

☆ Aldbury [Trooper Rd, Aldbury Common – not the prettiest part of this charming village just E of Tring; SP9612], *Valiant Trooper*: Lively beamed and tiled bar with woodburner in inglenook, some exposed brick in carpeted middle bar, far room is no smoking at lunchtime, well kept Bass, Fullers London Pride, John Smiths, Wadworths 6X, Youngs Special and a guest beer, popular simple food (not Sun or Mon evenings; good Sun lunch in restaurant), good prices, traditional games, tables in garden – good walks nearby; children and dogs welcome (the pub's is called Alexander) *(Nigel and Lindsay Chapman, Andrew Scarr, D and J McMillan, P Saville, John and Patricia White, S J Edwards, John Fahy, Jan and Colin Roe, LYM)*

☆ Aldbury, *Greyhound*: Simple old Georgian-faced inn by village duckpond below Chilterns beechwoods, handy for walks and popular with locals for good bar food; cosy snug eating areas with separate drinks and food serveries in passage between them, efficient welcoming service, well kept Tring Brewery beer; children welcome; good value bedrooms *(David Evans, Ted George, LYM)*

Aldenham [TQ1398], *Round Bush*: Good friendly village local, plenty of atmosphere and well kept beer *(Comus Elliott)*

☆ Amwell [village signed SW from Wheathampstead; TL1613], *Elephant & Castle*: Secluded and spacious floodlit grass garden behind low-beamed ancient pub with inglenook fireplace, panelling, stripped brickwork, 200-ft well shaft in bar; bar food (not Sun), well kept Tetleys-related ales; restaurant, children in eating area *(Nigel Norman, LYM)*

☆ Ashwell [High St; TL2639], *Three Tuns*:

Flower-decked 18th-c inn with lots of pictures, stuffed pheasants and antiques in opulently Victorian lounge, old-fashioned hotel atmosphere, wide choice of very quickly served food, Greene King IPA and Abbot, good coffee, friendly staff; more modern public bar with pool; bedrooms *(Brian Horner, Brenda Arthur)*

Ashwell [69 High St], *Rose & Crown*: Comfortable open-plan local, 16th-c beams, lovely log fire, usual bar food, candlelit restaurant, Greene King IPA, Abbot and Rayments, pleasant service, darts and machines at plainer public end of L-shaped bar; tables in big pretty country garden *(Phil and Heidi Cook)*

☆ Ayot Green [off B197 S of Welwyn, nr A1(M) – OS Sheet 166 map ref 222139; TL2213], *Waggoners*: Friendly, good well presented bar food, three cosy well kept areas, lots of mugs hanging from low ceiling, separate eating area, six changing real ales, good service and atmosphere even on a busy Sat night, quiet suntrap back garden with play area, wooded walks nearby *(Fiona and Paul Hutt, Phill Gardiner, Howard Gregory)*

Baldock [Whitehorse St; TL2434], *Rose & Crown*: Former coaching inn doing well under current regime, with tasty good value food, well kept Greene King IPA and Abbot, good atmosphere *(Graham and Karen Oddey, K Glanville)*

☆ Benington [just past PO, towards Stevenage; TL3023], *Bell*: Generous food, efficient service, well kept beer in lovely old pub with unusual stag-hunt mural over big fireplace; secluded village *(M E Wellington)*

Borehamwood [Shenley Rd; TQ1996], *Hart & Spool*: Good atmosphere and four or five well kept ales in Wetherspoons pub, reasonable prices, no-smoking eating area; no music, children or games, can get busy weekends *(Paul Bessell)*

☆ **Bourne End** [Winkwell; just off A41 Berkhamsted—Hemel, by Texaco at E end; TL0206], *Three Horseshoes*: 16th-c pub in charming canal setting by unusual swing bridge, tables out by water, three cosy and homely low-beamed rooms with inglenooks, one with an Aga, bay-windowed extension overlooking canal, good range of well kept Tetleys-related and guest ales, friendly staff, bar food (not Sun evening); children welcome, open all day *(David Shillitoe, K Archard, R S Reid, Nigel and Lindsay Chapman, John Fahy, Thomas Nott, M W Turner, Mr and Mrs Hillman, LYM)*

Bourne End [A4251; TL0206], *White Horse*: McMullens pub doing well since return of previous licensees, wide choice of food (all day Sun) from sandwiches up *(Jan and Colin Roe)*

☆ **Brickendon** [1 Brickendon Lane; S of Hertford – OS Sheet 166 map ref 323081; TL3208], *Farmers Boy*: Roomy refurbished village pub in attractive spot, friendly service, good range of Whitbreads-related and other ales and of wines, wide choice of good value food from sandwiches up, dining area; seats in back garden and over road *(R A Buckler, Howard Gregory, Chris Mawson)*

Bushey [25 Park Rd; turning off A411; TQ1395], *Swan*: Homely atmosphere in rare surviving example of single-room backstreet terraced pub, reminiscent of 1920s *(Pete Baker, LYM)*

Chandlers Cross [TQ0698], *Clarendon Arms*: Friendly traditional country pub with well kept Marstons Bitter and Pedigree, Ruddles County and a guest beer, attractive verandah, lots of tables and cocktail umbrellas; handy for woodland walks, bar lunches (not Sun) *(Jonathan and Helen Palmer, Richard Houghton)*

☆ **Chipperfield** [The Common; TL0401], *Two Brewers*: Country hotel with relaxed and pubby dark-beamed main bar, cushioned antique settles, well kept Bass, Greene King IPA and Abbot, Marstons Pedigree and a guest beer; popular lunchtime bar food in bow-windowed lounge with comfortable sofas and easy chairs, good restaurant; overlooks pretty tree-flanked cricket green; children allowed in lounge and restaurant, open all day Sat; comfortable bedrooms *(John Misselbrook, LYM)*

☆ **Chorleywood** [The Swillet; from M25 junction 17 follow Heronsgate signpost; TQ0295], *Stag*: Open-plan dining pub, but still a welcoming place for a drink, with well kept Tetleys-related ales, good atmosphere, no piped music or fruit machines; popular if not cheap food (not Sun evening) from sandwiches up inc imaginative dishes and lovely puddings, tables on back lawn, children's play area; busy weekends *(Peter Saville, Richard Houghton, SMG, Helena Reid, N M Baleham)*

Darleyhall [nr Luton Airport; TL1422], *Fox*:

Refurbished village local with wide choice of good value freshly cooked food in no-smoking dining area, Greene King IPA and Abbot; fruit machine, TV, piped music may be loud; picnic tables outside, walks nearby *(JJW, CMW)*

Datchworth [formerly Inn off the Green; TL2718], *Tilbury*: Two-bar pub with pleasant atmosphere, polite service, good range of ten or so ever-changing well kept beers, home-made food inc vegetarian in bars and bookable restaurant *(Paul Gatens, Graham Hall, Richard Houghton)*

nr **Datchworth** [Bramfield Rd, Bulls Grn; TL2717], *Horns*: Pretty 15th-c Whitbreads country pub, beams and inglenook log fire, rugs on brick floor, china and pictures, seats out among roses on crazy paving overlooking green; has been relaxed and enjoyable, but plans for extension and refitting under new management *(LYM; news please)*

Digswell [Digswell Hill; TL2314], *Red Lion*: Large and attractive, with wide choice of very promptly served food; very popular with business people from Welwyn *(Charles Bardswell)*

Essendon [TL2708], *Salisbury Crest*: Has now closed, with plans for redevelopment; its former landlord runs the Five Horseshoes at Little Berkamstead *(LYM)*

☆ **Flamstead** [High St; TL0714], *Three Blackbirds*: Cosy low-beamed pub, partly Tudor, with chatty landlady, two real fires, old dark wood and brickwork, pictures, brass and copper; quick service, well kept Courage-related ales, Greene King and Marstons Pedigree, good value food; friendly bull terrier, pool, darts and fruit machine in games area; piped local radio; good walks nearby; children welcome *(JJW, CMW)*

☆ **Flaunden** [TL0100], *Green Dragon*: New chef doing imaginative fresh food inc good puddings in attractive and comfortable Chilterns pub with well kept Greene King IPA and Abbot and Marstons Pedigree, partly panelled extended lounge with small back restaurant area, darts and shove-ha'penny in traditional 17th-c small tap bar; friendly service, fruit machine, quiet piped music; very popular Sun lunchtime; charming well kept garden with summer-house and aviaries, pretty village, only a short diversion from Chess Valley Walk *(CMW, JJW, Kath Wetherill, Maggie and Trevor Stewart-Sweet, LYM)*

☆ **Frithsden** [from Berkhamsted take unmarked rd towards Potten End, pass Potten End turning on right then take next left towards Ashridge College; TL0110], *Alford Arms*: Secluded Whitbreads country local, pleasant old-world atmosphere, good plain bar food from filled rolls up (step down to nicely furnished eating area), quick friendly service, open all day Sat; darts, bar billiards, fruit machine; in attractive countryside, picnic tables out in front; may have ales brewed at the pub *(Maurice Southon, Peter and Maris Brigginshaw, Ted George, Nigel and Lindsay Chapman)*

☆ **Graveley** [TL2327], *Waggon & Horses*:

Former coaching inn with comfortable beamed and timbered lounge, big open fire, very popular lunchtime for good choice of reasonably priced straightforward food, Whitbreads-related ales; locals' snug by door; plenty of seats in secluded attractive garden with big terrace by village duck pond, summer lunchtime barbecues; car park fills quickly *(Charles Bardswell, Mrs P Hare)*
Graveley, *George & Dragon*: Well run old coaching inn, restaurant popular with business people from Stevenage *(Charles Bardswell)*
Great Amwell [TL3712], *George IV*: Quiet spot by church and river, good varied reasonably priced food inc fish and vegetarian and good puddings, friendly service, Adnams ales *(Rev D F Perryman)*; [Pepper Hill], *Wagon & Horses*: Good food, big back garden with play area; children welcome *(R E and P Pearce)*
☆ **Halls Green** [NW of Stevenage; TL2728], *Rising Sun*: Charming 18th-c beamed country pub recently refurbished by friendly new licensees, interesting choice of food in bar or conservatory inc special evenings (booking recommended weekends), convivial atmosphere, well kept McMullens and a guest ale, big open fire in small lounge, good big garden with terrace, summer barbecues and play area *(Jeffery Smith)*
☆ **Harpenden** [Luton Rd, Kinsbourne Green; 2¼ miles from M1 junction 10; A1081 towards town, on edge; TL1015], *Fox*: Pews, beams, antique panelling, lots of bric-a-brac and masses of prints in big but cosy and relaxing lounge bar, good value food, smaller public bar; friendly efficient staff, good choice of Tetleys-related and other well kept ales with March real ale festival, good coffee, log fire in both rooms, board games, daily paper, fresh flowers, no music; children welcome, play area in big garden *(Phil and Heidi Cook, JJW, CMW, Howard Gregory, BB)*
☆ **Harpenden** [Cravells Rd], *Carpenters Arms*: Small and welcoming, with chatty landlord, friendly efficient staff, good cheap home cooking from sandwiches up, well kept Dartmoor and Ruddles, displays of overseas number-plates, miniature cars and special issue bottled beers; neat well planned terrace garden *(Steve and Sue Griffiths, R A Buckler, Howard Gregory, Steve Gledhill)*
Harpenden [Marquis Lane], *Marquis of Granby*: Picturesque pub nr River Lea, with newish seats outside, wide choice of good food, well kept beers, decent wines, hardworking licensees; children and dogs welcome *(R Buckler)*; *Oak Tree*: Good value food and decent choice of beer; straightforwardly refurbished *(Howard Gregory)*
☆ **Hatfield** [Park St, Old Hatfield; TL2308], *Eight Bells*: Quaint and attractive old beamed pub, pleasantly restored, well kept Tetleys-related and a guest ale, decent reasonably priced bar food, couple of tables in back yard, piped music; open all day, occasional live music; best at quiet times, crowded Fri/Sat

nights *(Christopher Turner, JJB, Nick and Alison Dowson)*
☆ **Hertford** [33 Castle St; TL3213], *White Horse*: Small intimate no-frills free house dating from 17th c, very pubby, with open fire between the two bars, interesting furniture in three recently refurbished beamed and timbered no-smoking rooms upstairs, good range of real ales inc good Dark Horse beers brewed nearby by the landlord, wide range of country wines, simple wholesome weekday lunchtime food, friendly service; popular with younger people evenings, opp Castle grounds *(Richard Houghton, Chris Loxley-Ford, Neil O'Callaghan, Andrew W Ellis)*
☆ **Hertford** [The Folly], *Old Barge*: Nicely placed canalside pub, long and low, good service even when hectic, friendly helpful young staff, lots of barge pictures etc, Tetleys-related ales kept well, decent food inc good ploughman's and vegetarian; fruit and games machines *(George Atkinson, LYM)*
☆ **Hertford** [Fore St], *Salisbury Arms*: Relaxing hotel lounge, lots of character, well kept McMullens inc AK Mild, efficient cheerful service, decent food (not Sun evening); splendid Jacobean staircase to bedrooms *(Nicky Letts)*
☆ **Hertford Heath** [B1197, signed off A414 S edge of Hertford; TL3510], *Silver Fox*: Bustling and friendly well kept rather suburban-feeling local, very popular lunchtime (busy most nights too) for sensibly priced food from sandwiches up inc good range of puddings, quick service, particularly well kept Adnams, Tetleys and Theakstons Best and Old Peculier; busy most evenings too; relaxing sheltered back terrace with fountain *(G L Tong, Chris Mawson, Rita Horridge, Neil O'Callaghan, Stephen and Jean Curtis, BB)*
Hexton [signed off B656; TL1230], *Raven*: Large civilised rambling pub with nice dining area, dining lounge and long tidy public bar (pool one end); good well presented food inc two children's menus, Fullers Chiswick, Greene King IPA and Wadworths 6X; pleasant garden with well segregated play area, children allowed inside too (high chairs etc) *(the Sandy family)*
☆ **Hinxworth** [Main St, just off A1(M); TL2340], *Three Horseshoes*: Olde-worlde thatched, beamed and timbered dining pub with friendly atmosphere, wide changing choice of good value food (not Sun evening, Mon) inc children's, fresh fish, local game and Sun roast; big brick inglenook, small dining extension, well kept Greene King IPA and Abbot, decent wines, lots of premium lagers, friendly licensees, no juke box or piped music; children welcome, big garden with swings, climbing frames and maybe friendly wandering pig *(S R Spokes, M and A Sandy)*
Ickleford [107 Arlesey Rd, off A600 N of Hitchin; TL1831], *Cricketers*: Up to 10 real ales, decent choice of reasonably priced food, several areas around friendly smallish single bar, lots of cricket photographs and cigarette

cards, whisky-water jugs hanging from beams, inglenook fireplace, books, TV, darts, fruit machine and piped music; children welcome, small garden and terrace with barbecue; very busy Sun lunchtime; bedrooms *(JJW, CMW)*

☆ **Langley** [off B656 S of Hitchin, on edge of Knebworth Park; TL2122], *Farmers Boy*: Friendly low-beamed and timbered local, huge inglenook fire one end, woodburner at the other, small public bar behind; lots of brasses, old photographs and prints, well kept Greene King IPA and Abbot, wide-ranging bar food from toasties up; garden behind *(Phil and Heidi Cook)*

☆ **Letchmore Heath** [2 miles from M1 junction 5, first left off A41 towards Harrow; TQ1597], *Three Horseshoes*: Cottagey little low-ceilinged local opp duck pond on serenely tree-shaded green, good friendly atmosphere, wide choice of straightforward honest home-made lunchtime food (not Sun, just snacks Sat), well kept Benskins Best and Ind Coope Burton; busy, maybe faint piped music; white tables outside the pretty flower-decked pub *(Comus Elliott, Dr M J Ingram, LYM)*

Lilley [West St, off A505 NE of Luton; TL1126], *Lilley Arms*: Quiet village pub with carpeted bar, flowers in dining room, wide choice of good value food, well kept Greene King IPA and Abbot; quiet piped music, no dogs or boots; tables in garden, chickens and ducks in car park, pot-bellied pig in stable; bedrooms *(CMW, JJW)*

☆ **Little Berkamstead** [1 Church Rd; TL2908], *Five Horseshoes*: 17th-c beams and stripped brickwork, two log fires, well kept Greene King and Tetleys-related ales, decent wines, wide range of good generous bar food inc sandwiches and vegetarian, quick friendly responsive service; good restaurant, and cosy little attic room for private dinners; garden with picnic tables, busy in summer; attractive countryside *(James and Ulrike Henderson, Jon Field)*

Little Gaddesden [B4506; SP9913], *Bridgewater Arms*: Pleasant civilised yet unpretentious atmosphere, good changing food in bar and cosy restaurant, real ales, decent wines, open fires; good walks straight from the pub *(Mrs K A Edwards, BB)*

☆ **Little Hadham** [The Ford, just off A120 W of Bishops Stortford; TL4322], *Nags Head*: Good freshly cooked changing food inc lots of fresh fish in 16th-c country dining pub's cosy and relaxed heavily black-beamed interconnecting rooms, clean and comfortable; well kept Greene King IPA, Abbot, Rayments and a seasonal beer tapped from the cask, decent wines, freshly squeezed orange juice, efficient friendly staff, old local photographs, guns, copper pans; restaurant; children welcome *(Gwen and Peter Andrews, Ben Grose, LYM)*

Little Wymondley [off Stevenage/Hitchin bypass; TL2127], *Bucks Head*: Friendly and pleasantly decorated timbered pub with several well kept real ales, decent food, good staff; attractive garden *(Steve Gledhill, LYM)*;

Plume of Feathers: Welcoming new licensees doing good straightforward food in comfortably refurbished pub *(CB)*

☆ **Much Hadham** [Hertford Rd, about ¼ mile outside; TL4319], *Jolly Waggoners*: Family country pub with friendly animals in huge garden, good home-cooked food inc children's dishes and choice puddings, pleasant efficient service, Greene King ales, good range of malt whiskies, nice window seats; handy for Hopleys nursery *(Joy Heatherley)*

Northchurch [High St; A4251 Berkhamsted—Tring; SP9708], *George & Dragon*: Traditional family-run low-beamed 18th-c coaching inn, log fire, warm welcome, good range of reasonably priced home-cooked lunchtime food (not Sun), well kept Bass and Tetleys-related ales, good choice of bottled beers; tables in big garden with aviary, beautiful floral display in yard; opp church where Peter the Wild Boy is buried *(Peter and Maris Brigginshaw)*

☆ **Nuthampstead** [TL4034], *Woodman*: Out-of-the-way but welcoming thatched and weatherboarded local, good range of well kept ales, tasty reasonably priced food, inglenook log fire, pleasant garden *(Leslie Fryer)*

☆ **Potters Crouch** [leaving St Albans on Watford rd via Chiswell Green, turn right after M10; TL1105], *Holly Bush*: Clean and spacious, with highly varnished good-sized tables, sparkling glassware, particularly well kept Fullers Chiswick, London Pride and ESB, good generous simple lunchtime food, efficient service, decent wines, lots of pictures, plates, brasses and antlers, old-fashioned lighting; busy weekends; good big garden with picnic tables *(Jan and Colin Roe, N M Baleham)*

Puckeridge [TL3823], *White Hart*: Quiet and cosy, with friendly staff, extensive good value menu in rambling bar and dining room, enjoyable specials, massive seafood platter and Thurs bargain OAP lunch, four McMullens ales, log fire, lots of wooden armchairs as well as button-back banquettes, interesting collection of copper utensils hanging from ceiling; children welcome, tables outside *(Les and Pam Leeds, LYM)*

Radlett [14 Cobden Hill; Watling St (opp Tabard RUFC); TL1600], *Cat & Fiddle*: Fine old building converted from cottages, cat theme throughout, lots of china ones; well kept beers, wide choice of good food *(Comus Elliott)*

☆ **Reed** [High St; TL3636], *Cabinet*: Friendly and relaxed tiled and weatherboarded house, a pub for centuries, with helpful welcoming service, log fire in little rustic parlourish public bar, pleasant lounge, five well kept ales, good generous food, helpful staff, tables in charming big garden with pond and flowers; up for sale as we go to press *(Ann Griffiths, Charles Bardswell, LYM)*

Rickmansworth [Uxbridge Rd; TQ0594], *Whip & Collar*: Well kept pub in nice spot backing on to River Colne, lovely flower tubs, big conservatory area, huge helpings of good value food Tues-Fri, tasty puddings *(Diane Rawson)*

☆ Sandridge [High St; TL1610], *Rose & Crown*: Clean and comfortable dining pub with wide range of generous changing straightforward food inc five rich soups and lots of main courses, good service, several Whitbreads-related and other ales *(Helena Reid, Andrew Scarr)*

Sarratt [The Green; TQ0499], *Boot*: Friendly and attractive early 18th-c tiled pub in pleasant spot facing green, cosy rambling rooms, nice inglenook fireplace, well kept Tetleys-related ales, good changing bar food; handy for Chess Valley walks *(Adele Fishleigh, LYM)*; [The Green], *Cricketers*: Busy pub in lovely village setting, well kept Courage Best and Directors, good choice of food esp seafood, friendly service; dining area, tables out by pond; open all day *(David Craine, Ann Reeder, Adele Fishleigh, Ian and Colin Roe)*

Sawbridgeworth [Station Rd, by stn; TL4814], *George IV*: Restaurant recently opened, good value wines, good range of well priced food inc superb swordfish and lamb cutlets, welcoming licensees *(Nikki Moffat)*

St Albans [2 Keyfield Terr; off London Rd; TL1507], *Beehive*: Done up in spit-and-sawdust style, with period photographs, well kept Whitbreads-related ales, bar food (not Fri/Sat evenings, but summer evening barbecues Fri-Sun); piped music may be loud (live Thurs), quiz night Tues, live band Thurs, very busy with young Fri/Sat *(JJB)*; [36 Fishpool St], *Lower Red Lion*: Two very friendly bars, good choice of changing real ales, home cooking live music Weds, log fire, red plush seats; tables in pleasant good-sized back garden; bedrooms *(Richard Houghton, Hortense McQuiggley)*; [Victoria St], *Philanthropist & Firkin*: Converted library, very pleasant in quieter times, can get packed and smoky some evenings; Tetleys and its own Dogbolter, Bookworm and Philanthropist ales, live music upstairs Weds and Sat *(JJB, Nick and Alison Dowson)*

nr St Albans [Tyttenhanger Green; from A414 just under 2 miles E of A6/A1081 roundabout, take B6426 signed St Albans, then first left; TL1805], *Barley Mow*: Completely refurbished and reopened, with spacious and sunny-windowed welcoming

bar, big log fire, well kept ales such as Adnams, Bass, Courage Directors, Fullers ESB and London Pride and Tring Ridgeway, with a guest beer, usual pub food; popular with local sportsmen, quiz nights etc; children welcome, tables in garden with pond overlooking paddocks *(Crispin Driver, David Rollinson, BB)*

Therfield [off A505 Baldock—Royston; TL3336], *Fox & Duck*: Pleasantly refurbished village pub with four real ales, good value food, good children's garden with climbing frames, swings and tree house *(Susan and Nigel Wilson)*

Tring [London Rd (A4521), Wigginton – just outside Berkhamsted; SP9310], *Cow Roast*: Welcoming 17th-c pub with huge inglenook log fire in interesting two-level bar, generous choice of good if not cheap food from huge hot roast-meat baps to steaks, well kept Tetleys-related and guest ales, good coffee, efficient welcoming staff; superb garden with play area, barbecue very popular with families *(Gareth and Toni Edwards)*

Turnford [High Rd; TL3604], *Turnford Massey*: Traditional oak-beamed pub with well kept beers, no juke box or games machines, just a pleasant buzz of conversation *(NW)*

Walkern [B1036; TL2826], *Yew Tree*: Good unpretentious atmosphere in ancient pub doing well under very experienced new licensees, wide choice of genuine well cooked food *(Charles Bardswell)*

☆ Water End [B197 N of Potters Bar – OS Sheet 166 map ref 229042; TL2204], *Old Maypole*: Low ceilings, big inglenook fire, lots of brasses, miniatures and bric-a-brac; good value basic food, well kept Greene King IPA and Abbot, friendly service, family room; outside tables *(Chris Mawson)*

Wheathampstead [Marford Rd, E edge of town; TL1813], *Nelson*: Comfortably refurbished small pub with welcoming new licensees, well kept real ales, good choice of reasonably priced food (not Sun), open fires, lots of Nelson memorabilia, old title deeds and so on; picnic tables out by car park *(Michael Sandy)*

Woolmer Green [London Rd; TL2518], *Chequers*: Doing well under current regime, with good daily-changing food in bar and restaurant, well kept ales such as Marstons Pedigree, Tetleys and Wadworths 6X, friendly efficient staff *(John and Anne Peacock)*

The letters and figures after the name of each town are its Ordnance Survey map reference. *How to use the Guide* at the beginning of the book explains how it helps you find a pub, in road atlases or large-scale maps as well as in our own maps.

Isle of Wight

The Isle of Wight has far more child-friendly family pubs than most places. The Wight Mouse, part of the Clarendon Hotel at Chale, is a particularly fine example, going from strength to strength as a very successful family pub that still manages to keep the locals happy. The Seaview Hotel in Seaview stands out as a most civilised yet very alive place, good for a meal out – we name it Isle of Wight Dining Pub of the Year; it has the bonus of serving drinks at the most attractive prices we found on the island. The prettily set Crown at Shorwell is also doing well at the moment, with good imaginative food and a most enjoyable atmosphere. In the Lucky Dip section at the end of the chapter, current front-runners include the Eight Bells at Carisbrooke, Chequers at Rookley and New Inn at Shalfleet, with the Travellers Joy at Northwood a haven for real ale lovers. There's a wider choice of real ales on the island these days, with Burts and Goddards producing good beers on the island itself, and beers from several smaller mainland breweries to be found alongside the nationals. It's still the national breweries who dominate beer supplies here, though, and drinks prices are about 10p higher than the country-wide average – and have been rising more quickly than on the mainland.

ARRETON SZ5486 Map 2

White Lion

A3056 Newport—Sandown

There's a very welcoming feel in the cosy beamed lounge bar of this white village pub, with its guns, shining brass and horse-harness on the partly panelled walls, and cushioned windsor chairs on the brown carpet; piped music. The new licensees have made the public bar more comfortable since the last edition; fruit machine, shove ha'penny, table skittles and darts. Bar food includes sandwiches (from £1.95), soup (£1.95), ploughman's (from £2.75), filled baked potatoes (from £3.25), smoked haddock pasta (£3.95), chilli (£4.50), steak and kidney pie or chicken korma (£4.95) and steaks (from £5.95), and home-made specials such as vegetarian lasagne or prawn stir fry (£4.95). The restaurant is no smoking until 9pm. Well kept Bass, Boddingtons, Flowers IPA and Goddards Fuggle Dee Dum on handpump or tapped from casks behind the bar, with an interesting cask-levelling device. The pleasant garden has a new children's play area, and you can also sit out in front by the tubs of flowers – you may need to as it does get very busy. *(Recommended by D P and J A Sweeney, Dr and Mrs A K Clarke, D H and M C Watkinson, Jack Barnwell, Simon Collett-Jones)*

Whitbreads ~ Lease: Mark and Rucky Griffith ~ Real ale ~ Meals and snacks (not Mon evening) ~ (01983) 528479 ~ Children welcome in eating area and restaurant ~ Open 11-3, 6(7 in winter)-11; all day Sat and Sun in summer

BONCHURCH SZ5778 Map 2

Bonchurch Inn

Bonchurch Shute; from A3055 E of Ventnor turn down to Old Bonchurch opposite Leconfield Hotel

The little buildings that make up this idiosyncratic pub are set round a courtyard which is dwarfed below a steep rock slope. The best atmosphere is in the chatty furniture-packed Victorian public bar, which conjures up an image of salvaged shipwrecks with its floor of narrow-planked ship's decking, and seats of the sort that old-fashioned steamers used to have; there's a separate entrance to the very simple no-smoking family room. Courage Best and Directors and Morlands Old Speckled Hen tapped from the cask, Italian wines by the glass, a few bottled French wines, and coffee; darts, bar billiards, shove-ha'penny, table tennis, dominoes and cribbage; piped music. Bar food includes sandwiches (from £2), minestrone soup (£1.80), ploughman's (£3), spaghetti bolognese, canelloni with spinach, seafood risotto, or fettuccine carbonara, battered squid rings, grilled fillet of plaice, chicken nuggets (£4.50), duckling with orange sauce (£6.50), and puddings such as zabaglione (£3.50); children's helpings. They don't always open the homely continental little dining room across the courtyard. *(Recommended by Meg and Colin Hamilton; more reports please)*

Free house ~ Licensees Ulisse and Aline Besozzi ~ Real ale ~ Meals and snacks (11.30-2.15, 6-10.30) ~ Restaurant ~ (01983) 852611 ~ Children in family room ~ Open 11-4, 6.30-11; cl 25 Dec ~ Bedrooms: £17.50/£35

CHALE SZ4877 Map 2

Clarendon / Wight Mouse ★ ♀

In village, on B3399; also access road directly off A3055

The enthusiastic licensees at this cheerfully busy pub cleverly manage to retain a good atmosphere for adult visitors (and locals), as well as providing lots of family entertainments. It's an extended, rambling, atmospheric place, the original core hung thickly with musical instruments, and with guns, pistols and so forth hanging over an open log fire. One end opens through sliding doors into a pool room with dark old pews, large antique tables, video game, juke box, dominoes, fruit machine, and pinball. At the other end there's a woody extension with more musical instruments, lots of china mice around a corner fireplace, decorative plates and other bric-a-brac, and even part of a rowing eight hanging from its high pitched ceiling. The turkey-carpeted family room extends beyond a two-way coal-effect gas fire, with quite close-set pews around its tables, hunting prints, and more decorative plates. A very good range of drinks includes well kept Boddingtons, Marstons Pedigree, Morlands Old Speckled Hen, Wadworths 6X and Whitbreads Fuggles Imperial and Strong Country on handpump, an outstanding choice of around 365 whiskies, over 50 wines, and some uncommon brandies, madeiras and country wines. Popular bar food includes sandwiches (from £2, fresh crab £3.50), home-made soup (£1.80), ploughman's (from £3.30), a few vegetarian dishes like a daily pasta bake or quiche (£3.90), salads or burgers (from £3.90), ham and eggs (£4.10), breaded plaice (£5.10) and fisherman's platter (£7.30). Daily specials might be sweet and sour pork, beef in red wine or liver and bacon, with puddings including ice cream made at a farm nearby; children's meals (from £1.60). Despite serving hundreds of meals every day, service is always efficient and smiling; no-smoking dining area. Live music every evening is never too loud for conversation. There are play areas inside and out, pony rides on Sid and Arthur, the well liked Shetlands, a pets corner, and maybe even Punch and Judy shows in the spacious sheltered back garden. More restful souls can soak up the lovely views out towards the Needles and Tennyson Downs. They run a mini-bus service for four or more people (from £3 a person). *(Recommended by Maj and Mrs T Savage, John and Joan Calvert, the Sandy family, Paul and A Sweatman, John Farmer, Joan and Michel Hooper-Immins, Mike Starke, T Roger Lamble, R F and M K Bishop, Phil and Heidi Cook)*

Free house ~ Licensees John and Jean Bradshaw ~ Real ale ~ Meals and snacks (noon-10pm; 9.30 Sun) ~ Restaurant ~ (01983) 730431 ~ Children welcome ~ Live music every night ~ Open 11-midnight; Sun 12-10.30 ~ Bedrooms: £25(£33B)/£50(£66B)

The knife-and-fork rosette distinguishes pubs where the food is of exceptional quality.

nr COWES (EAST) SZ5092 Map 2

Folly

Folly Lane – which is signposted off A3021 just S of Whippingham

The maritime connections at this shipshape old pub go back a long way, as the original building was based around a beached sea-going barge; the roof still includes part of the deck. These days it's a very handy and well known yachting stop, with moorings, a water taxi, long-term parking, and showers; they keep an eye on weather forecasts and warnings. It's prettily set on the bank of the estuary, with big windows and seats on a waterside terrace offering bird's-eye views of the boats. The nautically themed opened-out bar has a wind speed indicator, barometer and a chronometer around the old timbered walls, as well as venerable wooden chairs and refectory-type tables, shelves of old books and plates, railway bric-a-brac and farm tools, old pictures, and brass lights. It can get busy. Bar food under the new licensees includes generously filled sandwiches (from £2.25), soup (£1.85), potato skins (£2.75), ploughman's (£3.95), home-made chilli or steak and kidney pie (£4.65), breaded scampi (£5.35) and 8oz sirloin (£8.85), and children's meals (£2.25). Well kept Boddingtons, Flowers Original, Marstons Pedigree and Morlands Old Speckled Hen on handpump or tapped from the cask; pool, darts, bar billiards, shove ha'penny, table skittles, dominoes, fruit machine, trivia, and sometimes fairly loud piped music. There's a bouncy castle in the landscaped garden in summer, and it's not far to Osborne House. If you're coming by land, watch out for the sleeping policemen along the lane. *(Recommended by D P and J A Sweeney, W F C Phillips, Dr and Mrs A K Clarke, Peter and Audrey Dowsett, Andy Cunningham, R F and M K Bishop)*

Whitbreads ~ Managers Andrew and Cheryl Greenwood ~ Real ale ~ Meals and snacks (from 9am for breakfast till 10pm) ~ (01983) 297171 ~ Children in eating area and restaurant ~ Live entertainment Thurs and Sat evenings ~ Open 11-11 (9 for breakfast); Sun 12-10.30

FRESHWATER SZ3487 Map 2

Red Lion

Church Place; from A3055 at E end of village by Freshwater Garage mini-roundabout follow Yarmouth signpost, then take first real right turn signed to Parish Church

The comfortably furnished and civilised open plan bar of this popular pub has open fires, low grey sofas and sturdy country-kitchen style furnishings on mainly flagstoned floors with bare boards at one end, and a good mix of pictures and china platters on the walls. Well kept Boddingtons, Flowers Original, Goddards Best (brewed on the island) and Wadworths 6X handpump, as well as White Monk cider (cask-conditioned on the island for three years in an oak barrel, to a Carthusian monks' recipe); fruit machine, darts, shove-ha'penny, dominoes, bardo, jenga and shut-the-box. The piped music is mainly classical. As well as a short standard menu with sandwiches (from £1.75), filled baked potatoes (from £3.75), ploughman's (from £3.25), ham, egg and chips (£5.25), the big blackboard behind the bar lists daily specials such as curried parsnip soup (£2.50), chicken liver pâté (£3.95), steak and kidney or fish pie (£6.50), lamb or vegetable curry or chicken tikka masala (£6.95), grilled plaice, salmon steak with orange butter or duck breast with black cherry sauce (£7.95), rump steak with prawns and garlic (£10.50) or lobster and prawn salad (£14.95), and tempting puddings like treacle pudding, bread and butter pudding, strawberry cheesecake and sherry trifle. The pub is prettily set with tables in front beside the church, and more on grass at the back. There are good walks nearby, especially around the River Yar. *(Recommended by D P and J A Sweeney, June and Malcolm Farmer, A Kilpatrick, W F C Phillips, Major and Mrs T Savage, Meg and Colin Hamilton, Simon Collett-Jones, Cathryn and Richard Hicks, Peter and Audrey Dowsett, Mrs C Watkinson, R F and M K Bishop, Jeanne Cross and Paul Silvestri)*

Whitbreads ~ Lease: Michael Mence ~ Real ale ~ Meals and snacks (not winter Sun evening) ~ (01983) 754925 ~ Children over 10 welcome ~ Open 11.30-3, 5.30-11; Sat 11-4, 6-11

NITON SZ5076 Map 2

Buddle 🍺

From A3055 in extreme S of island, take road to St Catherine's lighthouse

For many years this friendly old house was the haunt of notorious local smugglers, and it still retains something of the atmosphere of those days. The characterful modernised bar – which can get very busy – still has its heavy black beams and big flagstones, a broad stone fireplace with a massive black oak mantelbeam, and old-fashioned captain's chairs around solid wooden tables; pewter mugs and so forth hang on the walls. A couple of areas are no smoking; piped music. They generally have seven or eight real ales available, the changing range perhaps including Adnams, Bass, Brakspears, Flowers IPA and Original, Greene King Abbot and Morlands Old Speckled Hen on handpump or tapped from the cask; also a range of wines by the bottle or the glass and local wines and ciders. Service is consistently pleasant and welcoming. Reliable generously served bar food includes winter sandwiches, soup (£1.95), garlic mushrooms (£2.75), vegetable samosas (£2.95), chilli (£4.25), breaded plaice (£4.35), mushroom and kidney bean stroganoff (£4.45), steak (from £8.75), puddings (from £1.95), and children's meals (from £1.75); good chips. The menu may be restricted on bank holidays in an attempt to end long delays. Along one side of the lawn, and helping to shelter it, is what they call the Smugglers' Barn, which doubles as a family dining area and function room with shove ha'penny, cribbage, dominoes, fruit machine, trivia, and juke box. The ancient cat is called Duke and although he likes being stroked prefers not to be picked up; there are friendly dogs. You can look out over the cliffs from the well cared for garden, with its tables spread over the sloping lawn and stone terraces; at night you may be able to see the beam of the nearby lighthouse sweeping round the sea far below. Good walks nearby. *(Recommended by Meg and Colin Hamilton, HNJ, PEJ, D P and J A Sweeney, Sybille Weber, Peter and Audrey Dowsett, T Roger Lamble)*

Whitbreads ~ Lease: John and Pat Bourne ~ Real ale ~ Meals and snacks (11.30-3, 6-9.45) ~ (01983) 730243 ~ Well behaved children welcome in eating area of bar ~ Regular live music in summer ~ Open 11-11; Sun 12-10.30; cl evening 25 and 26 December

SEAVIEW SZ6291 Map 2

Seaview Hotel 🛏 🍷

High Street; off B3330 Ryde—Bembridge

Isle of Wight Dining Pub of the Year

Popular with the yachting set, this is one of the pleasanter towns on the island, with this smartly bustling little hotel as a favourite gathering spot. Set in a quiet road on a steep hill down to the sea, it has a small continental-style terrace – particularly pleasant sitting out in fine weather. Inside, the nautical back bar is a lot pubbier than you might expect, with traditional wooden furnishings on the bare boards, as well as oars, a ship's wheel, porthole cover, and block and tackle around its softly lit ochre walls, and a log fire; it can be busy with young locals and merry yachtsmen. The airier bay-windowed bar at the front is more relaxed and civilised, and has a splendid array of naval and merchant ship photographs, as well as Spy nautical cartoons for *Vanity Fair*, and original receipts fom Cunard's shipyard payments for the *Queen Mary* and the *Queen Elizabeth*; it has a line of close-set tables down each side on the turkey carpet, and a pleasantly chatty civilised atmosphere. The very kind, thoughtful and courteous staff couldn't have been more helpful on our most recent anonymous inspection, when we absent-mindedly locked our keys in the car last summer – thank you! Freshly made bar food is very popular, with particularly praised dishes including soup (£2.25), fresh island crab in rich cream soup (£3.95), fresh island crabmeat baked with cream, tarragon, spices and grilled cheese topping, toasted mushrooms and spinach with new potatoes and garlic bread, hot melted goat's cheese with salad, Greek salad, chicken liver and mushroom pâté or ploughman's (£3.95), seafood quiche (£5.95), scampi (£6.95), fried breast of chicken (£7.95), entrecote steak

(£9.95), and puddings like apple cake and cinnamon crème fraîche or hot treacle
pudding (£2.95); good Sunday roast, and a more elaborate menu in the restaurant.
One restaurant is no smoking. Flowers IPA, Goddards and a guest on handpump,
good wine list, local apple juice, and a choice of malt whiskies; darts, cribbage and
dominoes, piped music. More tables in a sheltered inner courtyard. There are sea
views from some of the bedrooms, a few of which have recently been refurbished with
balconies and new bathrooms. *(Recommended by Glen and Gillian Miller, D H and M C
Watkinson, Shirley Pielou, Jack Barnwell, Simon Collett-Jones)*

*Free house ~ Licensees Nicholas and Nicola Hayward ~ Real ale ~ Meals and
snacks ~ Restaurant ~ (01983) 612711 ~ Children welcome (over 5 in restaurant
in evening) ~ Open 11-3, 6-11 ~ Bedrooms: £45B/£78B*

SHANKLIN SZ5881 Map 2

Fishermans Cottage

Bottom of Shanklin Chine

This unpretentious thatched cottage, picturesquely tucked into the cliffs, enjoys one
of the nicest and most unusual settings of any pub we know. It's only a few minutes'
walk to busy Shanklin's Esplanade, but sitting at one of the tables on the terrace
looking towards the beach and sea with the sound of the surf in the background, it
seems a lot more remote. It's best to go during the day, as the terrace does lose the
sun in the evening, and it is a lovely walk to here along the zigzagged path down the
steep and sinuous chine, the beautiful gorge that was the area's original tourist
attraction. Inside, the clean low-beamed and flagstoned rooms have been cosily
refurbished, with photographs, paintings and engravings on the stripped stone walls.
Decent bar food includes sandwiches (from £1.90), ploughman's (from £3.10),
salads (from £3.70, crab or prawn £6.20), scampi (£4.90), and a pint of prawns
(£6.20). Courage Directors under light blanket pressure, coffee all day, and a range
of local country wines; polite and friendly bar staff. Fruit machine, piped music;
wheelchair access. Do remember before starting that the pub is closed out of season.
(Recommended by D P and J A Sweeney, GWB, Mr and Mrs P C Clark; more reports please)

*Free house ~ Licensees Mrs A P P Springman and Mrs E Barsdell ~ Real ale ~
Meals and snacks (12-3, 6-9) ~ (01983) 863882 ~ Children welcome ~ Live
entertainment Wed, Fri and Sat evenings ~ Open 11-3(4 in July and Aug), 7-11;
cl Nov-Feb*

SHORWELL SZ4582 Map 2

Crown

B3323 SW of Newport; OS Sheet 196 map reference 456829

In an attractive rural setting on the prettier south-eastern side of the island, this
friendly old place draws summer crowds to its peaceful tree-sheltered garden. With a
pretty church steeple in the backgroud, a little steam runs down one side of the lawn,
with quite closely spaced picnic tables and white chairs and tables on grass, and
broadens into a wider trout-filled pool. A decent children's play area blends in
comfortably at the end of the garden. Four atmospheric rooms wander round a
central bar. The characterful, warm and cosy beamed two-room lounge has blue and
white china in an attractive carved dresser, old country prints on the stripped stone
walls, other individual furnishings, a cabinet of model vintage cars, and a winter log
fire with a fancy tilework surround; one area is no smoking. Black pews form bays
around tables in a stripped-stone room off to the left, with another log fire; the stone
window ledges are full of houseplants. Consistently good bar food includes
sandwiches, fisherman's pie (£4.95), steak and kidney pie (£5.50), sea bream with
crab sauce (£7.50), lemon sole (£8.50), duck breast with honey and ginger sauce
(£8.95), and very tasty puddings. Well kept Badger Tanglefoot, Boddingtons,
Flowers Original, Wadworths 6X and Worthington on handpump, local apple juice,
cider and country wines. Efficient service from cheery staff and landlord; darts, fruit

machine, trivia, boules, faint piped music. *(Recommended by Ian Phillips, HNJ, PEJ, Sybille Weber, John Evans, Meg and Colin Hamilton, D H and M C Watkinson, Simon Collett-Jones, Mrs C Watkinson)*

Whitbreads ~ Tenant Mike Grace ~ Real ale ~ Meals and snacks (till 10) ~ (01983) 740293 ~ Children welcome ~ Open 10.30a.m.-11p.m.; 10.30-3, 6-11 in winter

VENTNOR SZ5677 Map 2

Spyglass

Esplanade, SW end; road down very steep and twisty, and parking can be difficult

Wrecked rudders, ships' wheels, old local advertisements, stuffed seagulls, an Admiral Benbow barometer and an old brass telescope are just part of the interesting jumble of memorabilia that fills the snug separate areas of the mostly quarry-tiled bar. Furnishings include pews around traditional pub tables, with a carpeted no-smoking room at one end and a family area (with piped pop music) at the other. A spacious sunny terrace is perched on top of the sea wall with views along the bay. Bar food includes sandwiches (from £1.85), filled baked potatoes (£2.75), ploughman's (£3.35), salads (from £4.25), chilli con carne or several vegetarian meals like vegetable kiev (£4.50), home-made cottage pie (£4.65), seafood lasagne (£5.25), crab (£6.50), a whole fresh local lobster (£11.75), and daily specials like ham and leek bake or beef beaujolais (£6.25). Well kept Badger Best and Tanglefoot on handpump, with a changing guest like Wadworths 6X or Charles Wells Bombardier tapped from the cask; on special occasions such as a lifeboat support week there may be half a dozen or more. Also White Monk cask-conditioned cider. Fruit machine, and a boat rocker for children. They have no objection to dogs or muddy boots. *(Recommended by Derek and Margaret Underwood, Derek and Sylvia Stephenson, Glen and Gillian Miller, D P and J A Sweeney, GWB)*

Free house ~ Licensees Neil, Stephanie and Rosie Gibbs ~ Real ale ~ Meals and snacks; afternoon tea in summer ~ (01983) 855338 ~ Children in family room ~ Live traditional Irish, blues or jazz every night ~ Open 10.30a.m.-11p.m.; 10.30-3, 7-11 in winter ~ Bedrooms: /£35B

YARMOUTH SZ3589 Map 2

Wheatsheaf

Bridge Rd

Don't be put off by the slightly unprepossessing street frontage – inside it's comfortably relaxed and spacious, with four eating areas including a light and airy conservatory. Generously served and reasonably priced meals include sandwiches (from £2), filled baked potatoes or ploughman's (from £3), burgers (from £3.40), salads (from £4.95), home-cooked gammon (£5.95), trout with stilton sauce or chicken kiev (£5.95), steaks (from £7.50), and good blackboard daily specials such as vegetarian kiev (£5.95), crab salad (£6.95), chicken tikka masala or turkey and ham pie (£6.25), roast shoulder of lamb (£7.95), 16oz T bone steak (£10.95), whole lobster (£16.50); Sunday roast (£5.95). Service is very quick and friendly. Four well kept beers include Boddingtons, Flowers Original, Gales HSB, Goddards or Morlands Old Speckled Hen on handpump or under light blanket pressure; fruit machine, pool (winter only) and juke box (in public bar). The pub is particularly handy for the ferry. *(Recommended by Derek and Sylvia Stephenson, D P and J A Sweeney, HNJ, PEJ, Dr and Mrs A K Clarke, Clive Gilbert)*

Whitbreads ~ Lease: Anthony David and Suzanne Keen ~ Real ale ~ Meals and snacks (11-10.30(10 Sun) in summer and winter Saturdays; 11(12 Sun)-2.15, 6-9.30(9.15 Sun) winter weekdays) ~ (01983) 760456 ~ Children in harbour lounge and conservatory ~ Open all day in summer; 11-3, 6-11 Mon-Fri, 11-11 Sat, 12-3, 6-10.30 Sun, in winter

Lucky Dip

Besides the fully inspected pubs, you might like to try these Lucky Dips recommended to us and described by readers (if you do, please send us reports):

☆ Bembridge [Station Rd; SZ6487], *Row Barge*: Tasty pizzas and well kept Whitbreads-related and other ales in open-plan pub with unpretentious nautical decor, farm cider, friendly landlord; children welcome, bedrooms, nr harbour *(S Holder, June and Malcolm Farmer)*

Brading [56-57 High St; A3055 Sandown—Ryde; SZ6086], *Bugle*: Welcoming place with family rather than pubby atmosphere, big helpings of good straightforward food inc four vegetarian choices and children's dishes in three roomy areas, pretty floral wallpaper, quicky friendly service, well kept Whitbreads-related ales; piped music; restaurant, supervised children's room with lots of games and videos, free lollipops for children, baby-changing in gents' as well as ladies', garden *(S Holder)*

☆ Carisbrooke [High St; SZ4888], *Eight Bells*: Refurbished dining pub well set at foot of castle, bigger than it looks inside, with Whitbreads-related and other beers such as the well priced local Goddards, very reasonably priced generous straightforward food with sparkling fresh veg, unfailingly polite staff; charming garden behind running down to lovely lake with lots of waterfowl, also play area; off-street parking *(HNJ, PEJ, Meg and Colin Hamilton)*

☆ Carisbrooke [Park Cross; Calbourne Rd, B3401 1½ miles W; SZ4687], *Blacksmiths Arms*: Quiet and spotless hillside pub, panoramic views from dining room and terraced back garden, friendly helpful staff, Badger, Hampshire Pendragon and Ruddles ales, good value bar food; great for children *(Michael Andrews, D H and M C Watkinson)*

Colwell Bay [A3054 Yarmouth—Freshwater; SZ3387], *Colwell Bay*: Large old-fashioned plush main bar, pubby yet welcoming for families, with well spaced tables, at least eight real ales, cheap spirits, wide choice of good generous standard food with good veg, very cheery helpful staff; quiet piped music, pool room *(HNJ, PEJ)*

☆ Cowes [Watchhouse Lane; SZ4896], *Union*: Small Gales local with good atmosphere, cosy side room, good choice of beers inc interesting guest beer, generous well cooked nicely presented food – good value; bedrooms *(Michael Andrews, Ian Pickard, Dr and Mrs A K Clarke)*

Downend [A3056, at the crossroads; SZ5387], *Hare & Hounds*: Refurbished and extended thatched dining pub with lots of beams and stripped brickwork, separate areas, friendly waitress service, decent straightforward food, Goddards Special and Whitbreads-related ales, good views from terrace, nice spot by Robin Hill Country Park which has good play area *(June and Malcolm Farmer, Simon Collett-Jones, Jack Barnwell, BB)*

Gurnard [1 Princes Esplanade; SZ4795], *Woodvale*: Recently refurbished 1930s Wayside Inn with picture windows overlooking Solent, glass-panelled ceilings, decent range of standard food inc bargain steaks, well kept Whitbreads-related ales and decent wines, obliging staff, smaller bar and billiards room; boules *(Jenny and Brian Seller, HNJ, PEJ, Dr and Mrs A K Clarke)*

Havenstreet [off A3054 Newport—Ryde; SZ5690], *White Hart*: Ancient building, tidy and comfortable, with two clean and pubby bars, well kept Badger ales, varied generous food esp pies with fresh veg and splendid salads, friendly staff; interesting beer-bottle collection *(A Kilpatrick)*

☆ Hulverstone [B3399 – OS Sheet 196 map ref 398840; SZ3984], *Sun*: A pub to look at, with thatch, charming flower-filled garden, even village stocks; friendly informal licensees, well kept Gales BB and HSB tapped from the cask, food inc good home-made steak and kidney pie; piped music; sea views, lovely garden *(J B and P N Bishop, Anne Parmenter, Dr and Mrs A K Clarke)*

☆ Limerstone [B3399 towards Brighstone; SZ4382], *Countryman*: Large brightly lit high-ceilinged open-plan bars and restaurant area, mock dark beams, white paintwork, horse/farming equipment and pictures, lots of tables with candles and flower decorations, usual bar food from filled rolls to steaks, prompt polite service, Badger Best and Tanglefoot, Charles Wells Eagle and Ind Coope Burton on handpump; moderate piped music; front garden with sea view *(Michael Andrews, D P and J A Sweeney)*

☆ Newchurch [SZ5685], *Pointer*: Genuine village local, friendly and unpretentious, with good generous straightforward home cooking, well kept Gales BBB and HSB, good range of country wines; brightly lit plush lounge, flame-effect fires, old photographs, L-shaped games bar on right, spotty dogs, pleasant back garden with floodlit boules area *(June and Malcolm Farmer, BB)*

☆ Newport [St Thomas Sq; SZ4988], *Wheatsheaf*: Inn dating back to 17th c, in attractive old part by parish church; comfortable bare-bricks refurbishment, good atmosphere, friendly helpful staff, generous reasonably priced food, Whitbreads-related ales; piped music may be rather obtrusive; children welcome, comfortable bedrooms *(Eric Phillips, Ian Phillips)*

Newport [91 High St; SZ4988], *Castle*: Well kept Whitbreads-related ales, friendly service, good varied lunchtime food, plenty of local atmosphere, open all day; maybe piped music; behind the beamery, lattice-effect windows, log-effect gas fire and reproduction furniture and brasses, there's a genuinely ancient pub – as the flagstones and massive end wall show; was the last English pub to hold a cock-fighting licence *(Dr and Mrs A K Clarke, HNJ, PEJ)*

☆ Niton [off A3055; SZ5076], *White Lion*: Straightforward food done well in clean, roomy and comfortable pub with good no-smoking section, children's dishes and Sun lunches, welcoming landlord, well kept Greene King Abbot, good atmosphere; children welcome, nice setting *(Anne Parmenter)*

☆ Northwood [85 Pallance Rd; off B3325 S of Cowes; SZ4983], *Travellers Joy*: Not the smartest pub, but this busy local is a boon to serious real ale drinkers on the island, with plenty of interesting well kept mainland guest beers alongside Burts and Goddards; good range of generous reasonably priced simple bar food, friendly staff, old island prints; fruit machine, subdued piped music; family room, garden behind with swings and lots of rabbits; open all day *(Michael Andrews, Derek and Sylvia Stephenson)*

☆ Rookley [Niton Rd; pub signed off A3020; SZ5183], *Chequers*: A straightforward menu, but good cooking using fresh ingredients, with plenty of veg served separately, at most attractive prices; clean and spacious plush refurbished lounge bar looking over road to rolling downland, very helpful service, well kept Courage-related ales, small log fire, partly flagstoned games area on left; Lego in family room, baby-changing, picnic tables out on grass, realistic play house in safely fenced play area; open all day, next to riding stables *(HNJ, PEJ, Anne Parmenter, Jack Barnwell, BB)*

Seaview [Esplanade; B3340, just off B3330 Ryde—Brading; SZ6291], *Old Fort*: This spacious and popular cafe-bar has been reported closed *(News please)*

☆ Shalfleet [A3054 Newport—Yarmouth; SZ4189], *New Inn*: More restaurant than pub, with plenty of good seafood and short choice of other dishes, generous helpings, friendly atmosphere, roaring log fire in traditional panelled bar, pleasantly redecorated carpeted dining lounge and restaurant, no-smoking family area; well kept Gales HSB and island beers on handpump, decent wines, country wines and coffee, service cheerful even when crowded, children in eating area, open all day summer *(Michael Andrews, HNJ, PEJ, D H and M C Watkinson, Anne Parmenter, Dr and Mrs A K Clarke, W F C Phillips, LYM)*

☆ Shanklin [Chine Hill; SZ5881], *Chine*: Tastefully refurbished, with beams and flagstones, separate bright family conservatory, wide choice of decent pub food (not Sun evening, Tues or Sat) inc good value specials, well kept real ales; lovely wooded setting with good sea views *(Martyn and Mary Mullins, L R Stubbington, D P and J A Sweeney)*

Shanklin [Old Village], *Village Pub*: Big helpings of good reasonably priced food, small pleasant back garden with wendy house; children allowed in family area if eating *(M J Stow)*

Totland [Alum Bay Old Rd; SZ3185], *High Down*: A gentle move up market after refurbishment, with fresh well cooked food inc some unusual dishes and good sauces, smart little dining room, good pleasant service; piped music can be a little obtrusive; picnic tables out in raised paddock area; bedrooms *(HNJ, PEJ)*

Ventnor [Victoria St; SZ5677], *Volunteer*: Small old-fashioned local with interesting customers, three well chosen real ales, reasonable prices, darts, the local game of rings, quiz nights, no machines or juke box, no food *(Mr and Mrs C C Crichton, Paul Waterman)*

☆ Whitwell [High St; SZ5277], *White Horse*: Friendly country atmosphere, wide range of good food inc vegetarian, full range of Gales ales, well furnished big interconnected beamed bars with separate comfortable family areas; cheerful quick service, horsebrasses, log fire, muted piped music *(T Harman Smith)*

☆ Wootton Bridge [A3054 Ryde—Newport; SZ5492], *Sloop*: Reliable Whitbreads Brewers Fayre pub, very popular, with good value generous food, lots of tables in huge spacious split-level bar, smart upmarket decor, friendly quick service, subdued piped music; nice setting, fine views over yacht moorings *(HNJ, PEJ)*

☆ Wroxall [Clarence Rd (B3327); SZ5579], *Star*: Welcoming two-bar local, plush and tidy, with good choice of reasonably priced straightforward food, quick friendly service, well kept cheap Burts ales with a guest such as Ringwood, big open fire in cosy tiled public bar *(Derek and Sylvia Stephenson, Jason Reynolds, HNJ, PEJ)*

☆ Yarmouth [St James' Sq; SZ3589], *Bugle*: Peaceful lounge, lively bar with counter tiles galleon stern, dark panelling, food from well filled sandwiches to grills inc children's dishes, well kept Whitbreads-related ales; piped music can be rather loud; restaurant, children's room with pool and video game, sizeable garden, summer barbecues; good big airy bedrooms – make sure you get one that's not over the bar *(Dr and Mrs A K Clarke, LYM)*

Yarmouth [Quay St], *George*: Sizeable hotel with Solent views, big garden running down to shore and comfortable bedrooms; has been good over the years, but we've had no reports since it closed for refurbishment last year *(News please)*

People don't usually tip bar staff (different in a really smart hotel, say). If you want to thank them – for dealing with a really large party say, or special friendliness – offer them a drink.

Kent

A good *few new entries* here include the simple and relaxed Yew Tree tucked away at Barfrestone, the friendly Henry VIII by Hever Castle, the unspoilt Clarendon not far from the sea in Sandgate, the Rose & Crown out in the woods above Selling (one of the year's most enjoyable finds), and, (back in the Guide after an absence) Pearsons in Whitstable included primarily for its little informal upstairs fish restaurant. With newly-wed licensees, the friendly Albion over the creek from Shepherd Neame's Faversham brewery is doing particularly well at the moment: it gains a Food Award this year, and is our choice as Kent Dining Pub of the Year. Other pubs that are particularly enjoyable for meals out are the Dering Arms at Pluckley (another to gain our Food Award for the first time this year), and Sankeys in Tunbridge Wells – both have excellent fish. A small but important piece of good news is that the track down to the Shipwrights Arms at Oare (which is now open all day) has been improved by its new licensee. The Red Lion at Hernhill has been taken over by one of the big changes, and as things were in a state of flux as we went to press we have had to drop this nice pub from the main entries. In the Lucky Dip section at the end of the chapter, other pubs that are doing well these days (most of them inspected by us) include the White Horse at Boughton Street, White Hart at Brasted, Fordwich Arms at Fordwich, Star & Eagle in Goudhurst, Plough at Ivy Hatch (very good, though too restauranty for the main entries), Cock at Luddesdown, Alma at Painters Forstal, Rock near Penshurst, Coopers Arms in Rochester, Black Lion in Southfleet and Bull at Wrotham; the choice in Tunbridge Wells seems to be broadening, too. Down in the Weald, the small Hooden Horse chain is appealing to younger people: see Ashford, Cranbrook, Great Chart and Rolvenden Layne. Drinks prices in Kent are higher than the national average; there are useful savings to be made in pubs tied to the local brewer, Shepherd Neame, whereas our price survey showed that pubs tied to national brewers were even more expensive than the county average.

BARFRESTONE TR2650 Map 3

Yew Tree

Off A2 on B2046 towards Aylesham, first right, then fork right towards Frogham, and keep on until Barfreston signed right

In a pretty little tucked-away hamlet, this relaxed, friendly pub really does have a yew tree in front of it. The chatty main bar has upholstered pine chairs and wall seats around a mix of old pine tables on the bare boards, cream walls with old local photographs, lots of hops draped over a large beam, a delft shelf with an ancient wooden yoke and a few horsebrasses, candles in bottles, and a coal fire; fresh flowers on the bar counter. Well kept Black Sheep Bitter, Fullers ESB, Greene King IPA and Dark Mild, Mansfield Bitter, Mauldons Black Adder, and Timothy Taylors Landlord on handpump, farm ciders, and 7 different fresh coffees; cards, trivia, piped music and a table-top skittles game called daddlums. A second little bar, simply furnished, has french windows onto a terrace, and there's a cosy dining room with just four tables, a piano, and an open fire in the stone fireplace. Decent bar food includes doorstep sandwiches (from £2), soup (£2.25; popular curried parsnip £2.65), ploughman's (£3.50), mushroom, spinach and feta cheese pie (£4.65), boozy beef pie (£5.25), game pies with rabbit, pheasant, pigeon or hare (from £5.25), daily specials such as leek, mushroom and cheese pasta (£4.50), roasted rolled stuffed breast of lamb (£4.95), and pork loin with dijon mustard and cream sauce (£5.50), and a few puddings like home-made apple pie (£2); winter Sunday roast lunch. The church next door with its attractive carvings is very pretty indeed. *(Recommended by L M Miall)*

Free house ~ Licensee Angie McFadyen ~ Real ale ~ Meals and snacks (all through opening hours) ~ (01304) 831619 ~ Irish folk Thurs evening ~ Open 11-3, 6-11 Mon-Thurs; 11-11 Fri and Sat; 12-10.30 Sun

nr BIDDENDEN TQ8538 Map 3

Three Chimneys ♀ 🍺

A262, a mile W of village

The rambling series of small, very traditional rooms in this atmospheric old country pub are huddled under low oak beams with simple wooden furniture and old settles on flagstone and coir matting, some harness and sporting prints on the exposed brick walls, and good winter log fires. The simple public bar has darts, shove-ha'penny, dominoes and cribbage, and the good range of well kept real ales tapped from the cask might include Adnams Best, Brakspears, Fremlins, Harveys Best (and Old in winter), Marstons Pedigree, Morlands Old Speckled Hen and Wadworths 6X, along with Biddenden local cider, and a carefully chosen wine list with a range of half bottles (as well as local wine) and about twenty malt whiskies. Bar food is limited to four starters and main courses each day, though selected from quite a wide-ranging repertoire: carrot and tarragon soup (£2.50), potted stilton in port and walnuts (£3.35), Kentish smokies (£3.85), hot cheese flan (£4.95), mushroom stroganoff (£5.55), lamb pie or rabbit in cream and mustard sauce (£6.50), beef in Guinness and orange sauce (£6.75), scallop and mushroom pie (£6.85), 10oz sirloin steak with horseradish butter (£9.75), and puddings like gooseberry and elderflower tart (£2.80) or date and walnut pudding served with fresh Jersey cream. You can book tables in the garden room. At the back the lusciously growing garden has nut trees at the end, and densely planted curving borders with flowering shrubs and shrub roses. Sissinghurst gardens are just down the road. *(Recommended by Stephen Brown, Tina and David Woods-Taylor, Pam and Tim Moorey, AEB, James Nunns, Dr R Sparks, D Jardine, Thomas Nott, RWD, M Holdsworth, G Garvey, J O Jonkler, Richard and Ruth Neville, D B Stanley, E Carter, Martin Hickes, R G and J N Plumb, Tony and Wendy Hobden, John Fahy, K Burvill, Richard Fawcett, R Misson, Hilary Dobbie, J H Bell)*

Free house ~ Licensees C F W Sayers and G A Sheepwash ~ Real ale ~ Meals and snacks (till 10pm) ~ (01580) 291472 ~ Children in garden room ~ Occasional live entertainment ~ Open 11-2.30, 6-11; closed 25-26 Dec

BOUGH BEECH TQ4846 Map 3

Wheatsheaf 🍺

B2027, S of reservoir

On the walls and above the massive stone fireplaces in this lovely old pub are quite a few horns and heads – as well as a sword from Fiji, crocodiles, stuffed birds, squirrels and even an armadillo; also, lots of hops, cigarette cards, swordfish spears and the only manatee in the south of England. The atmosphere is congenial and welcoming, as are the staff and the old-school landlord, and the neat central bar has unusually high-ceilings with lofty oak timbers; divided from this by standing timbers – formerly an outside wall to the original building – is the snug. Other similarly aged features include a piece of 1607 graffito, 'Foxy Galumpy', thought to have been a whimsical local squire. The public bar has an attractive old settle carved with wheatsheaves, shove-ha'penny, dominoes, and board games. Bar food – served all day – includes good Greek salad, home-baked ham with honey and brown sugar or home-made steak pie (£5.95), curries (from £6.95), and specials deals for those over 55. Service can slow down at busy times. Well kept Boddingtons, Brakspears, Fremlins, Flowers Original, Morlands Old Speckled Hen, and Whitbreads Fuggles on handpump, local wine, summer Pimms, winter mulled wine, and several malt whiskies; piped music. There's a rustic cottage and boat in the garden for children to play on, and flowerbeds and fruit trees fill the sheltered side and back gardens. *(Recommended by A M Pring, Mark Percy, RWD, Michael Grigg, J and P Maloney, Winifrede Morrison, G S B Dudley, Mr and Mrs C Starling, Reece and Mike Gannaway, Dr Michael Smith, Colin Laffan, Simon Pyle)*

Whitbreads ~ Lease: Elizabeth and Peter Currie ~ Real ale ~ Meals and snacks (noon-10pm) ~ (01732) 700254 ~ Children in one part of the bar ~ Folk music Weds evening ~ Open 11-11; 12-10.30 Sun

BOUGHTON ALUPH TR0247 Map 3

Flying Horse 🍺

Boughton Lees; just off A251 N of Ashford

On a warm summer's day, readers enjoy sitting outside this 15th-c pub watching the cricket on the broad village green. The open-plan bar has lots of standing room – as well as comfortable upholstered modern wall benches, fresh flowers, hop bines around the serving area, horsebrasses, stone animals on either side of the blazing log fire, and a friendly atmosphere; two open fireplaces were discovered this year during redecoration. A few clues to the building's age still remain, mainly in the shiny old black panelling and the arched windows (though they are a later Gothic addition), and two ancient spring water wells are illuminated and covered at ground level with walk-over glass. From the back room, big doors open out onto the spacious rose filled garden, where there are seats and tables. Good bar food such as sandwiches, mussels (£3.50), home-made steak and kidney pie (£4.95), good Indonesian nasi goreng or seafood tagliatelle (£5.25), several fish dishes (from £5.25), pork in cider (£5.50), roast pheasant in season (£5.95), and fillet of duck with orange sauce or peppered steaks (£7.50); particularly good breakfasts. Well kept Courage Best, Fullers London Pride, King & Barnes Sussex, Marstons Pedigree, Morlands Old Speckled Hen, and Wadworths 6X on handpump. Shove-ha'penny, cribbage, dominoes, fruit machine, and piped music. The Shuttle is only 8 miles away. *(Recommended by Thomas Nott, R T and J C Moggridge, Mayur Shah, Martin Hickes, Christopher Warner, Roger Davey, James House, Stephen George Brown, Werner Arend, George Jonas, Reece and Mike Gannaway, John Hardie, S G Brown)*

Courage ~ Lease: Howard and Christine Smith ~ Real ale ~ Meals and snacks ~ Restaurant ~ (01233) 620914 ~ Children in restaurant ~ Occasional live music ~ Open 11-11; 12-10.30 Sun ~ Bedrooms: £25/£40

BOYDEN GATE TR2265 Map 3

Gate Inn ★ 🍺

Off A299 Herne Bay—Ramsgate – follow Chislet, Upstreet signpost opposite Roman Gallery; Chislet also signposted off A28 Canterbury—Margate at Upstreet – after turning right into Chislet main street keep right on to Boyden; the pub gives its address as Marshside, though Boyden Gate seems more usual on maps

This is very much an unpretentious rustic local and the cheery licensee has now been here for 21 years. The bar is distinctly pubby and quite a focus for local activities ('MCC' here stands for Marshside Cricket Club), with flowery-cushioned pews around tables of considerable character, hop bines hanging from the beam, a good winter log fire (which serves both quarry-tiled rooms), and attractively etched windows; there are photographs on the walls – some ancient sepia ones, others new. Unfussy but tasty, bar food includes sandwiches (from £1.30, black pudding £1.60), soup (£1.90), quite a few filled baked potatoes (from £2.10), burgers (from £1.65), ploughman's (£3.75), home-made vegetable flan (£4.10), home-cooked spicy hotpots (£4.30), pasta with pesto and bacon mixed grill (£4.60), and puddings; they use organically grown local produce where possible, and you can generally buy local honey and free-range eggs. The eating area is no smoking at lunchtime. Well kept Shepherd Neame Bitter, Spitfire, and Bishops Finger tapped from the cask, with country wines and local apple juice. Shove-ha'penny, dominoes, cribbage, and trivia. On a fine evening, it's marvellously relaxing to sit at the picnic tables on the sheltered side lawn listening to the contented quacking of what seems like a million happy ducks and geese (they sell duck food inside – 5p a bag). *(Recommended by Sue Lee, James Nunns, Dave Braisted, David R Shillitoe, David Hodgkins, Chris Westmoreland, Tommy Payne, Gwen and Peter Andrews)*

Shepherd Neame ~ Tenant Christopher Smith ~ Real ale ~ Meals and snacks ~ (01227) 860498 ~ Children in eating area of bar and in family room ~ Open 11-2.30(3 Sat), 6-11

BROOKLAND TQ9926 Map 3

Woolpack

Just out of village; off A259

The tremendous age of this crooked white cottage is immediately apparent in the ancient entrance lobby with its uneven brick floor and black painted pine panelled walls. On the right, the simple but homely softly lit main bar has basic cushioned plank seats in a massive inglenook fireplace, a painted wood effect bar counter hung with lots of water jugs, and plenty of old-fashioned character. Some of the ships' timbers in the low-beamed ceiling may date from the 12th c. On the newish quarry tiled floor is a long elm table with shove-ha'penny carved into one end, other old and new wall benches (a lazy cat sleeps on one) and chairs at mixed tables around the walls, and characterful photos of the locals (and perhaps their award winning sheep). To the left of the lobby a sparsely-furnished tiny room leads to an open-plan games room with central chimney stack, modern bar counter, and young locals playing darts or pool; dominoes, fruit machine, piped music. Well kept Shepherd Neame Best, Bishops Finger and Spitfire on handpump. Generous helpings of good value, straightforward bar food include sandwiches (from £1.80), soup, ham and egg or ploughman's, a pint of prawns (£3.95), dover sole (£6.50), and mixed grill (£7.45). Tables outside look down the garden to a stream where the pub has fishing rights. *(Recommended by J and D Tapper, L M Miall, R and S Bentley, John Fahy, James Nunns, Stephen George Brown)*

Shepherd Neame ~ Tenants John and Pat Palmer ~ Real ale ~ Meals and snacks ~ (01797) 344321 ~ Children in family bar until 9pm ~ Open 11-2.30, 6-11

CHIDDINGSTONE TQ4944 Map 3

Castle ♀

Village signposted from B2027 Tonbridge—Edenbridge

For 32 years Mr Lucas has been running this rambling old place and it could have been where Anne Boleyn found shelter when she was stranded in a terrible blizzard on her way to nearby Hever. The handsome, carefully modernised beamed bar has an attractive mullioned window seat in one small alcove, latticed windows, well made settles forming booths around the tables, and cushioned sturdy wall benches; it might get busy with visitors in summer so it's worth arriving early for a table. Well kept Harveys Sussex, Larkins Traditional (brewed in the village) and a guest beer on handpump, a good range of malt whiskies, and a very good wine list (the quality is reflected in the prices, though the house wines should suit all pockets). Darts, shove-ha'penny, dominoes and cribbage. Bar food includes home-made soup (£2.95), open sandwiches (from £3.55), home-made pâté (£3.65), filled baked potatoes (from £4.15), a daily pasta dish (£4.80), ploughman's (£5.25), very hot chilli con carne (£5.15), local sausages (£5.40), salads (from £6.95), and puddings (£2.75); there's also a changing two or three course meal (from £9.95), with starters like marinated squid salad, and main courses such as rabbit provençale or roast rack of English lamb. The pretty back garden has a small pool and fountain set in a rockery and tables on a brick terrace and neat lawn. There are more tables at the front opposite the church, and it's worth a walk around the village to look at the marvellously picturesque cluster of unspoilt Tudor houses; the countryside around here is lovely. *(Recommended by R and S Bentley, LM, J and P Maloney, June S Bray, Sue Lee, J S M Sheldon, Jenny and Brian Seller, E D Bailey, Steve Goodchild, Paula Williams)*

Free house ~ Licensee Nigel Lucas ~ Real ale ~ Meals and snacks (until 15 minutes before closing time) ~ Restaurant ~ (01892) 870247 ~ Children welcome (not in public bar) ~ Open 11-3, 6-11; 11-11 Sat; 12-10.30 Sun

DARGATE TR0761 Map 3

Dove

Village signposted from A299

150 years ago, this old-fashioned and peacefully set brick house started life as a home brewhouse – they now serve well kept Shepherd Neame Bitter and Spitfire on handpump, and an unusual strong local cider. The carefully refurbished rambling rooms have photographs of the pub and its licensees throughout the century on the walls, a good winter log fire, and plenty of seats on the bare boards; piped music. Bar food includes sandwiches and ploughman's, welsh rarebit with beer (£2.95), omelettes or bangers and mash (£4.25), leek, celery and pepper crumble (£5.50), lamb cutlets in a creamy mint sauce (£7.95), tuna steak with a piquant salsa (£9), duck breast with summer fruits sauce (£11.95), daily specials such as grilled cod on a bed of spinach, and roast Sunday lunch (2 courses £6.95). The sheltered garden is particularly attractive, with roses, lilacs, paeonies and many other flowers, picnic tables under pear trees, a dovecot with white doves, a rockery and pool, and a swing. A bridlepath leads up from the pub (along the charmingly-named Plumpudding Lane) into Blean Wood. *(Recommended by D R Eberlin, M Miall, John Fahy, Ian Irving, Ian Phillips, David Rule, S G Brown)*

Shepherd Neame ~ Tenant Theresa Anderson ~ Real ale ~ Meals and snacks (not Sun evening) ~ (01227) 751360 ~ Well behaved children welcome ~ Open 11.30-3, 6-11; closed 25 Dec

FAVERSHAM TR0161 Map 3

Albion 🍽️

Follow road through town and in centre turn left into Keyland Road; just before Shepherd Neame Brewery walkway over road turn right over bridge, bear right, first right into public car park

Kent Dining Pub of the Year

A good mix of customers gathers at this attractive weatherboarded cottage overlooking the creek, and big picture windows and open french doors make the most of the view; there are picnic tables out on the walkway and you can stroll along the bank for about an hour. Inside, you can be sure of a warm welcome and the light and airy open-plan room, where locals gather at the central bar, has a relaxed, pleasant atmosphere – as well as simple but solid mixed old pine furniture on wood and sisal flooring; the pale pea green walls have some nautical paraphernalia and old pine mirrors. Very good food includes sandwiches or filled french bread (from £1.95), soup (£2.50), roquefort and nut terrine (£3.25), ploughman's (from £3.75), warm salad of chicken livers and wild mushrooms with raspberry vinegar dressing (£4.25), spinach, mushroom and stilton pancake (£6.25), braised stuffed lamb hearts (£6.85), monkfish with seafood and tomato au gratin (£7.50), chicken stuffed with bacon and mushroom and vermouth sauce (£7.95), duck leg with rich Cointreau and orange suace (£8.50), and puddings such as steamed date and apple pudding or chocolate crunch slice (from £2.75); best to book at weekends. As the Shepherd Neame Brewery is just across the river the Bishops Finger, Bitter, and Spitfire on handpump are just as perfectly kept as you'd expect; a decent French wine list.

(Recommended by Comus Elliott, Ian Phillips, Martyn Golesworthy, Andrew and Ruth Triggs, Stephen and Julie Brown, Belinda Price, Bryn Evans, Mrs M Henderson)

Shepherd Neame ~ Tentants Patrick and Josephine Coevoet ~ Real ale ~ Meals and snacks (till 10pm Fri and Sat) ~ (01795) 591411 ~ Children in eating area of bar ~ Open 11-3, 6.30(6 Sat)-11

GROOMBRIDGE TQ5337 Map 3
Crown ♀

B2110

Set in a pretty row of cottages overlooking the steep green, this quaint and carefully preserved Elizabethan inn has several snug, atmospheric rooms with a relaxed and chatty atmosphere. Logs quietly burning in the big brick inglenook, there are lots of old teapots, pewter tankards, and antique bottles, and usually a crowd of people around the long copper-topped serving bar. The end room, normally for eaters, has fairly close-spaced tables with a variety of good solid chairs, a log-effect gas fire in a big fireplace, and an arch through to the food ordering area. The walls, mostly rough yellowing plaster with some squared panelling and some timbering, are decorated with small topographical, game and sporting prints, and a circular large-scale map with the pub at its centre; some of the beams have horsebrasses. A pretty little parlour serves as an overflow for eaters, and is bookable too. The range of tasty home-made bar food includes duck liver pâté (£3), vegetable and cashew nut curry (£4.50), steak and mushroom pie (£5.50), and pork schnitzel (£6). Well kept Courage Directors, Harveys IPA and Ruddles County on handpump, good value house wines (by the glass as well), and local Biddenden cider; shove-ha'penny, cribbage and scrabble. There are picnic tables on the sunny front brick terrace or on the green. Across the road is a public footpath beside the small chapel which leads, across a field, to moated Groombridge Place (the gardens of which are now open to the public) and fields beyond. *(Recommended by David and Lynne Cure, M Holdsworth, Margaret and Nigel Dennis, Sue Lee, Colin and Joyce Laffan, Mr and Mrs C Starling, Richard Gibbs, W J Wonham, Hilary Dobbie, Keith and Audrey Ward, Stella Knight)*

Free house ~ Licensees Bill and Vivienne Rhodes ~ Real ale ~ Meals and snacks (not Sun evening) ~ Evening restaurant (not Sun) ~ (01892) 864742 ~ Children in eating area of bar and in restaurant ~ Open 11-2.30, 6-11; 11-11 summer Sats ~ Bedrooms: £23/£38

nr HADLOW TQ6352 Map 3
Artichoke

Hamptons; from Hadlow—Plaxtol road take second right (signposted West Peckham), the pub has a new sign on the grass verge; OS Sheet 188, ref 627524

This partly tile-hung and shuttered 13th-c cottage is tucked away in a quiet rural setting, and on a sunny summer day you can sit under the awning on the front terrace, or on the wooden seat built around the lime tree, and gaze across the surrounding countryside. Inside, the two atmospheric little rooms have fairly closely-spaced cushioned high-backed wooden settles, wooden farmhouse-kitchen chairs, upholstered wrought-iron stools matching unusual wrought-iron, glass-topped tables on the turkey carpet, and beams in the low ceilings; there is a woodburning stove and an inglenook fireplace filled with tree trunk sized logs, as well as lots of gleaming brass, some country pictures (mainly hunting scenes), antique umbrellas, old storm lamps, and a fox mask. Home-made bar food includes vegetable soup (£2.25), mushrooms in garlic butter (£2.95), ploughman's (£3.95), lasagne (£5.95), pies such as chicken and mushroom (£6.25), mixed grill (£6.95), steaks (from £10.25), and weekly specials; the restaurant is no smoking. Fullers London Pride, Greene King Abbot, and Youngs Special on handpump, with a good range of spirits. *(Recommended by M Miall, Sue Demont, Tim Barrow, Ian Phillips, Dr S Willavoys, Sue Lee, Nigel Wikeley)*

*ree house ~ Licensees Terry and Barbara Simmonds ~ Real ale ~ Meals ~
Restaurant (not Sun evening) ~ (01732) 810763 ~ Children in eating area of bar
and in restaurant ~ Open 11.30-2.30, 6.30-11; closed winter Sun evenings*

HEVER TQ4744 Map 3
King Henry VIII

The origins of this friendly pub by Hever Castle go back to the 14th c, and there's
some fine panelling and heavy beams, and an inglenook fireplace. Comfortable seats
by the big leaded-light windows look across to the church where Anne Boleyn's
father, the local landlord, is buried, a good mix of tables and chairs sit on the carpet
(woven with pictures of Henry VIII), and there are lots of Henry VIII decorations.
Good bar food includes home-baked rolls (from £1.95), about 20 different summer
ploughman's (from £4.25), lunchtime casseroles, curries and vegetarian dishes like
tortellini with a creamy tomato sauce or tuna and pasta bake (from £4.95), evening
fish such as fresh salmon with lobster sauce, stuffed trout or halibut (£6.75), baked
half duck (£9.95), steaks (from £9.25), and puddings (from £2.25). Well kept
Harveys Best, a beer named for the pub called Old Henry, and a guest beer on
handpump, and around 20 malt whiskies; piped music but no games. There are seats
and umbrellas on the terrace with picnic tables on the grass by the big pond and a
view of rolling fields and distant woods. No dogs. (*Recommended by R Morgan, W
Ruxton, Sue Lee, Quentin Williamson, Peter and Wendy Arnold, Michael Grigg*)

*Free house ~ Licensees Mike and Julie James ~ Real ale ~ Meals and snacks (not
Sun or Mon evenings) ~ (01732) 862163 ~ Children in dining room lunchtime
only ~ Open 11-3, 6-11; winter evening opening 7*

LAMBERHURST TQ6635 Map 3
Brown Trout ♀

B2169, just off A21 S of village nearly opposite entrance to Scotney Castle

The main draw to this popular pub, covered with brilliant hanging baskets in summer
and winter, remains the fresh fish from Billingsgate: mediterranean prawns in garlic
butter (£4.95), 8-10oz cod or fillet of plaice (£5.25), halibut steak (£6.75), dressed
crab with prawns (£8.50), and whole lobster (£14.95); also non-fishy dishes like soup
(£1.95), chicken kiev or 10oz gammon steak (£6.25), and steaks (from £9.50), with
good value three-course meals (£10.95; one menu is vegetarian); friendly, welcoming
service. You may have to book ahead, particularly on Saturday evenings. The small
bar has a big central counter surrounded by russet hessian walls with small country
prints, glowing copper and brass hanging thickly from the beams, and eight or nine
tables – most people tend to eat in the biggish extension dining room which has many
closely set tables and a fish tank. Well kept Harveys IPA and Wadworths 6X on
handpump, and a fair choice of wines; faint piped music. Picnic tables under cocktail
parasols on the sloping front grass to the road and a large, safe garden behind with
swings, slides and trampolines. (*Recommended by Kath Wetherill, M Holdsworth, Dr S
Willavoys, Peter and Pat Frogley, Margaret and Nigel Dennis, Mr and Mrs P Brocklebank*)

*Whitbreads ~ Lease: Joseph Stringer ~ Real ale ~ Meals and snacks (till 10pm) ~
Restaurant ~ (01892) 890312 ~ Children welcome ~ Open 10.30-11; 12-10.30
Sun; shut weekday winter afternoons*

LANGTON GREEN TQ5538 Map 3
Hare ♀

A264 W of Tunbridge Wells

The food in this relaxed dining pub changes twice a day and is very popular with a
good mixed crowd of people. Well prepared and generously served, there might be
light lunchtime dishes such as ploughman's (£4.75), french toast with roast pork,
apple sauce and melted cheese (£5.25), and char-grilled burgers topped with

mozarella cheese and smoked bacon (£6.25), and soups such as mushroom and chestnut or cream of watercress (£2.30), salami and bean salad with lemon dressing and garlic croûtons (£5.25), brie and courgette skewers on vegetable stir-fried rice (£6.95), salads such as prawns, smoked salmon, avocado and citrus fruits (from £8.50), venison and beef pie (£8.95), lemon sole with lemon butter and an orange and coriander sauce (£9.95), and ribeye steak with brandy and black pepper sauce (£11.25); they only take bookings in one room, and your food is brought to you by attentive young waitresses. The knocked-through ground floor of this spacious Victorian inn is light and airy, with good-sized rooms, high ceilings and lots of big windows: dark-painted dados below light walls and dark ceilings, oak furniture and turkey carpets on stained wooden floors, and largely period romantic pastels and bric-a-brac (including a huge collection of chamber-pots). The chatty big room at the back has old books and pictures crowding its walls, two big mahogany mirror-backed display cabinets, and lots of large tables (one big enough for at least 12) on a light brown carpet; french windows open on to a terrace with picnic tables, looking out on to a tree-ringed green (you don't see the main road). Well kept Greene King IPA and Abbot and Rayments on handpump, decent wines, and 40 malt whiskies; piped pop music in the front bar area, shove-ha'penny, cribbage, dominoes, and trivia. *(Recommended by Mrs D McFarlane, Jonathan Nettleton, Julia Lawrence, E V J Rushton; more reports please)*

Greene King ~ Tenant Brian Whiting ~ Real ale ~ Meals and snacks ~ (01892) 862419 ~ Children welcome away from bar ~ Open 11.30-2.30(3 Sat), 6-11; 12-10.30 Sun

NEWNHAM TQ9557 Map 3

George ★ ♀

44 The Street; village signposted from A2 just W of Ospringe, outside Faversham

Although there is quite an emphasis on the very good food in this distinctive and neatly kept 16th-c village pub, the atmosphere remains properly pubby – which pleases readers. The spreading series of atmospheric rooms have prettily upholstered mahogany settles, dining chairs and leather carving chairs around candlelit tables, table lamps and gas-type chandeliers, rugs on the waxed floorboards, early 19-c prints (Dominican negroes, Oxford academics, politicians), a cabinet of fine rummers and other glassware, and a collection of British butterflies and moths; hop bines hang from the beams and there are open fires and fresh flowers. Generously served, the popular food might include dishes such as sandwiches (from £1.60), soup (£2.20), garlic mushrooms (£3), cottage pie (£3.90), ploughman's and salads (from £4.40), pasta of the day (£4.90), steak and kidney pudding (£6.40), salmon with mushrooms, onion, white wine and cream (£8.50), rack of lamb with rosemary and garlic (£8.90), steaks (from £10.45), weekly specials like duck breast and rocket salad with orange vinaigrette, rabbit pudding, liver and bacon casserole, a vegetarian dish such as roasted parsnips in coconut and ginger paste with stir-fried broccoli and mushroom dahl, local skate with black butter and capers, and pork fillet with wild mushrooms and cream, and puddings such as chocolate roulade or an old-fashioned suet pudding (£2.50); vegetables and salads are extra (£1.30 or £1.45), and they do a three-course Sunday lunch (best to book) - food service stops at 1.45 then. No credit cards. Well kept Shepherd Neame Bitter, Best, Bishops Finger and Spitfire on handpump, four wines by the glass and more by the bottle, and unobtrusive, better-than-usual piped music; shove-ha'penny, cribbage, dominoes, fruit machine. There are picnic tables in a spacious sheltered garden with a fine spreading cobnut tree, below the slopes of the sheep pastures. Dogs allowed (drinking bowl in lobby). Good walks nearby. *(Recommended by Pam and Tim Moorey, James Nunns, Frank Ashbee, D Hayman, Joe Jonkler, D R Eberlin, Tina and David Woods-Taylor, J O Jonkler, E D Bailey, Wayne Brindle, Chris Westmoreland, Mrs M Henderson)*

Shepherd Neame ~ Tenant Simon Barnes ~ Real ale ~ Meals and snacks (till 10pm; not Sun evening, not Mon) ~ (01795) 890237 ~ Children welcome ~ Open 10.30-3, 6-11

OARE TR0163 Map 3

Shipwrights Arms

Ham Road, Hollow Shore; from A2 just W of Faversham, follow Oare—Luddenham
signpost; fork right at Oare—Harty Ferry signpost, drive straight through Oare (don't turn
off to Harty Ferry), then left into Ham Street on the outskirts of Faversham, following pub
signpost

Many customers arrive at this splendidly unspoilt 17th-c tavern by boat as it's
marvellously placed in the middle of marshland, 3ft below sea level. Most of us will get
there along a track (the licensees have improved it since the last edition) which is also a
popular destination for bird watchers. Low-roofed, dark and cosy, the three relaxed
and cosy little bars are as traditional and rustic as fans of this type of pub could wish
for. Separated by standing timbers and wood part-partitions or narrow door arches,
they're filled with a medley of seats from tapestry cushioned stools and chairs through
some big windsor armchairs to black wood-panelled built-in settles forming little
booths. Lighting is by generator (and water is pumped from a well), and there are hops
and pewter tankards hanging over the bar counter, boating jumble and pictures, flags
or boating pennants on the ceilings, several brick fireplaces, and a woodburning stove.
Simple bar food such as burgers (from £1.80), good pizzas (from £2.50), steak and
kidney pie (£4.20), and seafood platter (£4.20); part of the eating area is no smoking.
Well kept beers such as Fullers London Pride, Goachers Mild, Shepherd Neame Bitter
and Spitfire, and a guest tapped from casks behind the counter, and a strong local farm
cider; darts, dominoes and cards. Very friendly service. The small front and back
gardens outside the white weather-boarded and tiled building lead up a bank to the
path above the creek where lots of boats are moored. *(Recommended by Stephen Brown,
Ian Phillips, Werner Arend, Mrs M Henderson, Chris Westmoreland)*

*Free house ~ Landlord Rod Carroll ~ Real ale ~ Meals and snacks (possibly all
day) ~ (01795) 590088 ~ Children in eating area ~ Open 11-11; 12-10.30 Sun*

PENSHURST TQ5243 Map 3

Bottle House

Coldharbour Lane, Smarts Hill; leaving Penshurst SW on B2188 turn right at Smarts Hill
signpost, then bear right towards Chiddingstone and Cowden

There's a huge choice of tempting meals at this friendly family-run 15th-c free house,
and the very wide range of daily specials might include mushroom carbonara or
spicy ratatouille (£5.95), chilli, lasagne or cold chicken and ham pie with
cumberland sauce (£6.50), smoked trout with dill and mustard sauce, steak and
kidney pudding or sardines grilled in fresh herbs and garlic (£6.95), whole fried
plaice, chicken balti or Morrocan lamb curry (£7.95), grilled swordfish in garlic, dill
and mustard sauce, baked skate wing with prawn sauce, breast of chicken in cream,
brandy and mustard sauce or char-grilled pork steak with tarragon and mustard
sauce (£8.50), avocado and smoked salmon salad or gammon steak with fried eggs
(£8.95), pheasant supreme wrapped in smoked bacon and filo pastry (£9.50), minted
lamb fillet with redcurrant and lime sauce (£10.50), venison steak with cranberry
and peppercorn sauce (£11.50) or duck breast with fig sauce (£12.95); good
puddings and Sunday lunch. The neatly kept and comfortable low-beamed front bar
quickly fills up, but even when busy service remains efficient and notably welcoming.
The exposed brick floor, smoothed with age, extends to behind the polished copper
topped bar counter. Big windows look to a terrace with climbing plants and hanging
baskets around picnic tables under cocktail parasols, and beyond to views of quiet
fields and oak trees. Down a step, the unpretentious main red-carpeted bar has
massive behopped supporting beams, two large stone pillars with a small brick
fireplace, and stuffed turtle to one side, and old paintings and photographs on
mainly plastered walls. To the far right, an isolated extension forms a small pine
panelled snug hung with part of an extensive collection of china pot lids; the rest are
in the low ceilinged, well appointed dining room. Scattered throughout the pub is the
licensees' collection of old sewing machines. Well kept Harveys, Ind Coope Burton,

and Larkins from nearby Chiddingstone on handpump (they've won awards for their cellar), cider from Chiddingstone too, and local wine; unobtrusive piped music. Dogs welcome (they may offer them biscuits). The affable licensees run another Kent main entry, the George & Dragon at Speldhurst. *(Recommended by Margaret and Nigel Dennis, Nigel Wikeley, Bob and Maggie Atherton, J and P Maloney, James House, Margaret and Nigel Dennis, Keith and Audrey Ward, Ian Jones, Jon Carpenter)*

Free house ~ Licensees Gordon and Val Meer ~ Real ale ~ Meals and snacks (till 10) ~ Restaurant ~ (01892) 870306 ~ Children welcome till 9pm ~ Open 11-3, 6-11

Spotted Dog ♀

Smarts Hill; going S from village centre on B2188, fork right up hill at telephone box: in just under ½ mile the pub is on your left

This quaint old tiled house, perched down on the side of a hill, is one of those places that is perfectly cosy in winter, and with an outdoor setting you couldn't improve in summer. You go down a few steps to enter the neatly kept and heavily beamed and timbered bar, which has some antique settles as well as wheelback chairs on its rugs and tiles, a fine brick inglenook fireplace, and attractive moulded panelling in one alcove. It's quite small, so there may be an overflow into the restaurant at busy times. Outside, twenty miles of untouched countryside stretch away in fabulous views from a series of carefully constructed terraces. Particularly good bar food covers up to five blackboards, the range of meals might change twice a day, with particularly well received dishes over the last year including smoked chicken, avocado and wild mushroom bake or spinach, cream cheese and green peppercorn roulade (£6.25), bass grilled with lime, ginger and coriander butter (£9.25) or half a shoulder of lamb braised in red wine, garlic and rosemary (£9.45), and puddings like cherry strudel or treacle tart; staff stay smiling amidst the cheery bustle. Well kept Adnams, Eldridge Pope Royal Oak and King & Barnes Sussex on handpump, along with Old Spotty – a Best Bitter brewed specially for the pub by Courage. The wine list is good (lots from the New World, even some from Penshurst); unobtrusive piped music. Lots of room for children to play outside. *(Recommended by J and P Maloney, Peter and Wendy Arnold, Dr S Willavoys, Bob and Maggie Atherton, Sue Lee, Mr and Mrs J Jackson, Steve Goodchild, Roger and Valerie Hill, Peter Harrison, Keith and Audrey Ward, Hilary Dobbie, M E A Horler, Nigel Wikeley)*

Free house ~ Licensee Andy Tucker ~ Real ale ~ Meals and snacks ~ Restaurant ~ (01892) 870253 ~ Children in eating area of bar ~ Open 11.45(11.30 Sat)-3, 6-11; 12-11 Sun; cl 25 and 26 Dec

PLUCKLEY TQ9243 Map 3

Dering Arms 🍴 🛏 ♀

Near station, which is signposted from B2077 in village

The rather handsome castle-like exterior of this old hunting lodge has quite an inspiring effect when you first arrive – it hints at a rather special night out. Cleanly cut Dutch gables top massive grey stone blocked walls above heavy studded oak doors. The unusual arched mullioned Dering windows took the family name when a member of the clan escaped from the Roundheads by climbing through one, and subsequently decreed that all houses built on the estate should have similar fenestration – you can still see lots locally. The high ceilinged bar still has something of a baronial feel – it's not hard to imagine huge dogs lounging on the wood and stone floors in front of the great log fireplace – although all this means it can be a bit chilly on really cold winter days. There's a good pubby atmosphere in this part, with a few locals and perhaps the chef/licensee chatting at the bar, and decorations are sylishly simple, with a variety of good solid wooden furniture. A smaller panelled bar has similar furnishings; dominoes, shove ha'penny and cribbage. There is quite some emphasis on very well cooked fresh fish from a sound and not particularly lengthy menu which includes chicken livers with bacon, mushroom and cream sauce (£3.85), pie of the day like pork with apples and cider, lamb and apricot or chicken and banana (£6.95), skate with caper butter (£8.95), local trout with hazelnuts and lemon or fillet of salmon with pernod and lemon butter (£9.65), sirloin steak with green peppercorn sauce (£10.65), alongside very well-presented blackboard specials such as oysters (£4.45), pasta with stilton and basil sauce (£6.95), wild duck casseroled with prunes and new potatoes, crab salad, fillet of red bream meunière, monkfish in creamy bacon and orange sauce or garlic fish stew (£9.65), rack of lamb with herb crust or fillet of halibut meunière (£10.65) grilled dover sole (£12.95), and seafood platter (24 hours' notice required, £18). A few puddings might include fruit crumble or oranges in caramel with Grand Marnier (£2.45). Every six weeks they have gourmet evenings, elaborate black-tie affairs with seven courses. Well kept real ales on handpump are all from Goachers including Dering ale, a beer brewed specially for the pub; very good extensive wine list, home-made lemonade, local cider and about 20 malt whiskies. There's a vintage car rally once a month, and in summer garden parties with barbecues and music from jazz to classical string quartets. Good breakfasts. *(Recommended by Hilary Dobbie, Melanie Bradshaw, Mayur Shah, Hilary Patrinos, John Fahy, Stephen Brown, RAB, J Fane, Dave Braisted, E Carter)*

Free house ~ Licensee James Buss ~ Real ale ~ Meals and snacks (not Sun evening) ~ Restaurant (not Sun evening) ~ (01233) 840371 ~ Children in eating area and restaurant ~ Occasional jazz or string quartet in summer ~ Open 10-3, 6-11; cl 26 and 27 Dec ~ Bedrooms: £28/£36

RINGLESTONE TQ8755 Map 3

Ringlestone ★ ♀ 🍺

M20 Junction 8 to Lenham/Leeds Castle; join B2163 heading N towards Sittingbourne via Hollingbourne; at water tower above Hollingbourne turn right towards Doddington (signposted), and straight ahead at next crossroads; OS Sheet 178 map reference 879558

These days a very wide range of tasty bar food is one of the main draws at this wonderfully characterful 16th-c inn. The help-yourself hot and cold lunchtime buffet is well worth a short queue for meals like herrings in madeira or mussels provençale (£3.95), macaroni with tuna and clams or spinach and ricotta lasagne (£4.50), and cidered chicken casserole (£4.80). The menu includes a thick vegetable and bean soup with sherry (£3.25), filled baked potatoes (£3.35), spinach and cheese quiche (£5.35), lamb, coconut and banana curry (£6.35), lots and lots of very good pies such as turkey, bacon and walnut or game with redcurrant wine or ham, leek and parsnip wine (£7.85), as well as fresh trout (£8.85). You order vegetables and potatoes separately (£2.80). Puddings such as chocolate, plum and elderberry trifle, treacle, orange and nut tart or brandy bread pudding (£3.25); many of these dishes turn up more cheaply as part of the lunchtime buffet. Three or four changing well kept real ales tapped from casks behind the bar or on handpump, and chalked up on a board might include Adnams, Cains Formidable, Fullers London Pride, Marstons Pedigree, Morlands Old Speckled Hen, Shepherd Neame Spitfire or Wadworths 6X; also about two dozen country wines (including sparkling ones), local cider and fresh fruit cordials. The central room has farmhouse chairs, cushioned wall settles, and tables with candle lanterns on its worn brick floor, and old-fashioned brass and glass lamps on the exposed brick and flint walls; there's a woodburning stove and small bread oven in an inglenook fireplace. An arch from here through a wall – rather like the outside of a house, windows and all – opens into a long, quieter room with cushioned wall benches, tiny farmhouse chairs, three old carved settles (one rather fine and dated 1620), similar tables, and etchings of country folk on its walls (bare brick too). Regulars tend to sit at the wood-panelled bar counter, or liven up a little wood-floored side room. Hard-working, friendly staff. There are picnic tables on the two acres of beautifully landscaped lawns, with shrubs, trees and rockeries, and a water garden with four pretty ponds linked by cascading waterfalls, a delightful fountain, and troughs of pretty flowers along the pub walls. Well behaved dogs welcome. *(Recommended by Melanie Bradshaw, D Hayman, AEB, Carole and Philip Bacon, Gill and Bryan Trueman, Julie Peters, Colin Blinkhorn, M J How, E D Bailey, Clive Gilbert, E Carter, Gwen and Peter Andrews, Martin Hickes, Wayne Brindle, Tina and David Woods-Taylor, R G and J N Plumb)*

Free house ~ Licensees Michael Millington-Buck and Michelle K Stanley ~ Real ale ~ Meals and snacks ~ Restaurant ~ (01622) 859900 ~ Children welcome ~ Open 11-3, 6-11; Sat and Sun 11-11; cl 25 Dec

SANDGATE TR2035 Map 3

Clarendon

Head W out of Sandgate on main road to Hythe; about 100m after you emerge onto the seafront park on the road across from a telephone box on the right; just back from the telephone box is an uphill track.

Half way up a steep lane from the sea, this little flower-decked local is run by a homely and friendly couple. Visitors will probably feel most comfortable in the big windowed lounge on the left – you can just see the sea through one window. Decor is unaffected, with copper topped or new pine tables on a light patterned carpet, a few impressions of the pub, and a coal-effect gas fire. There's a very simple chatty atmosphere in the straightforward right hand bar (popular with locals), and the well kept real ales include Shepherd Neame Best, Master Brew, Spitfire and seasonal ales from a rather nice Victorian mahogany bar and mirrored gantry, as well as a surprisingly good chardonnay by the glass; cheery piped Irish folk music when we inspected. Good plain home-cooking includes sandwiches (from £1.80, crab £2.50), simple ploughman's (£3.50), chilli (£3.95), lamb chops (£5.25), beef and beer pie (£5.50), and the editors' recommendation, delicious, simply cooked dover sole (£6.95). *(Recommended by Peter Chamberlain, Derek St Clair-Stannard, Michael Mills, Ian Phillips; more reports please)*

Shepherd Neame ~ Tenant: Dave Smith ~ Real ale ~ Meals and snacks (not Sun and Tues evening) ~ (01303) 248684 ~ Open 11.30-3.30(may be all day in summer), 6(7 Sat)-11

SELLING TR0455 Map 3

Rose & Crown

Coming from M2 junction 7 (see White Lion, next entry), keep right on through village and follow Perry Wood signposts; or from A252 just W of junction with A28 at Chilham follow Shottenden signpost, then right turn signposted Selling, then right signposted Perry Wood

Tucked away up a very quiet lane through ancient woodland, this small 16th-c pub has a chatty and relaxed atmosphere, quietly civilised without being over-smart. The bar winds round a central servery with pretty fresh flowers by each of its sturdy corner timbers; the beams are strung with hop bines, and decorated with an interesting variety of corn-dolly work – there's more of this in a wall cabinet in one cosy side alcove, and much more again down steps in the comfortably cottagey restaurant. Apart from a couple of old-fashioned housekeeper's chairs by the huge log fire (replaced in summer by an enjoyably colourful mass of silk flowers interlaced with more corn dollies and the like), the seats are very snugly cushioned. Good generously served bar food includes steak and kidney pie (£5), chicken tikka masala or China Town platter (£6.50), fisherman's platter (£8), daily specials such as prawn creole, Jamaican chicken and smoky haddock pasta (£6.50), and puddings (on show in a cold cabinet down steps in a small family room) like fresh nectarine bakewell, raspberry torte or lemon meringue pie (£2.50). Well kept changing ales such as Adnams, Harveys Best, Theakstons Best and Charles Wells Bombardier on handpump, decent wines in good measures; informal, friendly and helpful service. The garden has a good play area with bat and trap, and picnic tables on a concrete terrace and on grass under a big apple tree and yew tree; there's a small aviary at the end. *(Recommended by Mr and Mrs S R White, Mr and Mrs C Neame, Chris Westmoreland, L M Miall, Prof Geoffrey Stephenson, K Smith)*

Free house ~ Licensees Richard and Jocelyn Prebble ~ Real ale ~ Meals and snacks (not Sun or Mon evening) ~ Restaurant ~ (01227) 752214 ~ Children in snug area ~ Open 11-2.30, 6.30-11; closed evening 25 Dec

White Lion ♀

3½ miles from M2 junction 7; village signposted from exit roundabout; village also signposted off A251 S of Faversham

Prettily tucked-away down narrow country lanes, this 300-year-old coaching inn is a mass of colour in summer with its riotous hanging baskets. Warmly atmospheric and welcoming, the comfortable bar is decorated with moss and dried flowers, and has two huge brick fireplaces (with a spit over the right-hand one) with fires in winter, pews on stripped floorboards, and an unusual semi-circular bar counter; maybe quiet piped music. Good, generously served bar food includes soup (£2.25), chicken liver pâté (£2.95), ploughman's (from £4.25), steak and kidney pie or beef and onion suet pudding, vegetable curry (£5.50), lasagne (£6.50), mushroom stroganoff or cashew nut paella (from £7.25), hot spicy beef (£7.50), pork fillet in coarse grain mustard and cream sauce (£7.95), fresh salmon, cream and dill en croûte (£8.50), roast duck breast in rich orange sauce (£8.95), 8oz fillet (£12.50), and a range of home-made puddings; smaller helpings for younger and older customers. Monday is curry night, they do Sunday roasts, and cream teas on Saturday and Sunday afternoon. Well kept Shepherd Neame Master Brew and Spitfire on handpump, extensive wine list (with some by the glass), and a good range of malt whiskies. The welcoming landlord is a trumpet-player, and may even play on jazz nights. There are rustic picnic tables in the attractive garden behind. *(Recommended by Steve Goodchild, Mr and Mrs J Randolf, M Holdsworth, D Hayman, E D Bailey, Ian Irving, E G Parish)*

Shepherd Neame ~ Tenant Anthony Richards ~ Real ale ~ Meals and snacks (all day Sat and Sun) ~ Restaurant ~ (01227) 752211 ~ Children welcome (in family room) ~ Live music second and last Tues of month ~ Open 11-3, 6.30-11; 11-11 Sat and Sun

nr SMARDEN TQ8842 Map 3

Bell ★ ♀ ◨

From Smarden follow lane between church and the Chequers, then turn left at T-junction; or from A274 take unsignposted turn E a mile N of B2077 to Smarden

There's a wonderfully historic atmosphere in the snug dimly lit little low beamed back rooms of this pretty peg-tiled blacksmith's forge. Its ancient walls are bare brick or rough ochre plastered, with brick or flagstone floors, pews and the like around simple tables (candlelit at night), and inglenook fireplaces; one room is no smoking. The larger airy white painted and green matchboarded bar has a beamed ceiling and quarry tiled floor, a woodburning stove in the big fireplace, and a games area with darts, pool, cribbage, dominoes, fruit machine and juke box at one end. Straightforward bar food includes home-made soup (£1.95), sandwiches or toasties (from £2.20, rump steak £3.55), home-made pâté (£2.75), pizzas (from £3.25), ploughman's (from £3.75), shepherd's pie (£3.75), salads (from £4.75), plaice (£5.25), steaks (from £8.95), and puddings like home-made chocolate crunch cake (£2.25); usual children's and vegetarian meals. You might have to wait for meals at busy times. Well kept Fremlins, Goacher's Maidstone, Harveys Best and Shepherd Neame Best on handpump, eight wines by the glass, and local Biddenden cider. In summer it's very pleasant sitting in the garden amongst the mature fruit trees and shrubs, looking up at the attractive rose-covered building with its massive chimneys – though on sunny weekends you're hardly likely to have the place to yourself. There's a gathering of vintage and classic cars on the second Sunday of each month. *(Recommended by Jeremy Palmer, Stephen Brown, Kath Wetherill, Colin Laffan, Christopher Warner, Sue Lee, Hilary Dobbie, Jack and Philip Paxton, E N Burleton, Mr and Mrs P Brocklebank, Gordon Milligan)*

Free house ~ Licensee Ian Turner ~ Real ale ~ Meals and snacks (till 10) ~ (01233) 770283 ~ Children in large bar only ~ Open 11.30-2.30(3 Sat), 6-11; cl 25 Dec ~ Bedrooms: £20/£32

SOLE STREET TQ6567 Map 3

Compasses

Back lane between Godmersham (A28) and Petham (B2068); OS Sheet 189 map reference 095493

The big neatly kept garden with rustic tables under fruit trees at this unassuming

15th-c brick tavern is full of distractions to keep the children occupied. The enthusiastic licensees now have miniature horses as well as aviaries, goats and sheep, and a couple of wooden play houses and a steel climbing frame , and on fine summer lunchtimes the landlady might bring out her cockatoo, B Bob. It's very atmospheric inside, particularly in the little room at the back with its narrow wooden wall benches around the big kitchen table on the polished flagstone floor, a carefully restored massive brick bread oven, and enamelled advertisement placards on the walls. The front bar is a long, narrow room with beams in the shiny ochre ceiling, simple antique tables on its polished bare boards, rows of salvaged theatre seats along some walls, and a log fire in winter; bar billiards, piped music. The piano isn't just for decoration – they invite any customer who wants to play to have a go. Very good, popular bar food includes soup (£2.10), filled rolls (from £1.95), large filled french sticks (from £2.95), dim sum (£3.75), ploughman's (from £3.95), filled baked potatoes (£4.95), lentil crumble (£5.30), battered cod (£5.40), scampi, chicken and sweetcorn pie or steak and kidney pie (£5.95), cheese, mushroom and tomato en croûte (£6.50), stir fried Cantonese prawns and vegetables (£6.95), grilled trout (£8.50) and 14oz T bone (£14.95), and lots of ice cream sundaes (from £2.95), as well as lemon brûlée, treacle sponge pudding and banoffi pie (from £2.70). Well kept Boddingtons, Fremlins, Fullers London Pride and ESB and a guest like Timothy Taylor Landlord or Wadworths 6X on handpump, local cider and fruit wines. Service is very friendly, and readers tell us the cheery landlord has a good sense of humour. The area is good for walking, and cobwebbed with footpaths. *(Recommended by Stephen Brown, Christopher Warner, L M Miall, James Nunns, Wim Cock, D B Stanley, W J E Kock, W J Kock)*

Free house ~ Licensees John and Sheila Bennett ~ Real ale ~ Meals and snacks (till 10 Fri and Sat) ~ (01227) 700300 ~ Children in garden room ~ Open 12-3, 6.30-11

SPELDHURST TQ5541 Map 3
George & Dragon ♀
Village signposted from A264 W of Tunbridge Wells

It's well worth a visit here just to take in the marvellously distinguished half black and white timbered building which is based round a 13th-c manorial hall. Massive oak beams were added during modernisation in 1589, and it's not hard to picture Kentish archers returning from their victory at Agincourt resting on the enormous flagstones in 1415. The spacious open-plan bar, part-panelled and part plastered, has as its centrepiece a huge sandstone fireplace with a vast iron fireback that's over three hundred years old, and seating is on high backed wooden benches at several old wood topped cast iron tables. To the left is a partly enclosed panelled and carpeted bar with a comfortable sofa and padded banquettes, exposed beams, rough plaster, a grandfather clock that marks the half hour and a small fireplace. Well kept Bass, Fullers London Pride and Harveys Best on handpump, with lots of malt whiskies and a large wine cellar of around 140 bins; trivia, darts and piped music. Efficiently served bar food includes Speldhurst sausage and chips (£5.50), moules marinières (£5.95), cheese, vegetable and onion pie (£6.50), avocado and smoked salmon salad (£7.95), cajun chicken (£8.50), local trout stuffed with prawns and asparagus (£8.95), minted lamb fillet with port and redcurrant sauce (£10.95) and fillet steak stuffed with Boursin and wrapped in bacon (£11.95). It can get busy at weekends when unfortunately all the tables in the bar may be reserved for eating even though they are unoccupied. The first-floor restaurant under burdensome roof timbers is striking. There are white tables and chairs on the neat little lawn, ringed with flowers, in front of the building. The licensees also run the Bottle House at Penshurst. *(Recommended by David and Lynne Cure, Bruce Bird, Mavis and John Wright, Dr S Willavoys, James Nunns, Richard Gibbs, Alan and Eileen Bowker, Hilary Dobbie, J S M Sheldon, Paula Williams, Keith and Audrey Ward, M A and C R Starling, Winifrede D Morrison)*

Free house ~ Licensees Gordon and Val Meer ~ Real ale ~ Meals and snacks (till 10, 9.30 Sun) ~ Restaurant (not Sun evening) ~ (01892) 863125 ~ Children welcome in restaurant and in saloon bar till 9~ Monthly jazz supper ~ Open 10.30a.m.-11p.m.; Sun 12-10.30

TOYS HILL TQ4751 Map 3

Fox & Hounds

Off A25 in Brasted, via Brasted Chart and The Chart

There are no up to date frills or stylish menus at this down-to-earth and slightly eccentric remote country local which is run by the fairly firm but kind Mrs Pelling who doesn't allow mobile phones, and has little notices by the open fires warning against 'unofficial stoking'. When your eyes have adjusted to the dim lighting you can sit comfortably on one of the homely and well worn old sofas or armchairs which are scattered with cushions and throws, and read the latest *Country Life, Hello* or *Private Eye*. Some of the aged local photographs, letters and pictures on the nicotine-stained walls don't look as if they've moved since they were put up in the 1960s, and it's unlikely that much in the two simple rooms, including the decor, has changed since then. Lunchtime bar food is at an absolute minimum with pre-wrapped filled rolls (from £1.35) and ploughman's (from £3.65). Well kept Greene King IPA and Abbot on handpump; occasional sing-songs around the piano; darts, shove-ha'penny, cribbage and dominoes. The garden is particularly lovely with picnic tables on a good area of flat lawn surrounded by mature shrubs. As you approach this peaceful retreat from the pretty village (one of the highest in the county) you will catch glimpses through the trees of one of the most magnificent views in Kent. There are good walks nearby, and it's handy for Chartwell and for Emmetts garden. *(Recommended by Ian Phillips, LM, John and Elspeth Howell, Jenny and Brian Seller)*

Greene King ~ Tenant Mrs Pelling ~ Real ale ~ Lunchtime snacks ~ (01732) 750328 ~ Children away from bar lunchtime only ~ 11.30-2.30(3 Sat and Sun), 6-11; cl 25 Dec

TUNBRIDGE WELLS TQ5839 Map 3

Sankeys 🍽 ♀

39 Mount Ephraim (A26 just N of junction with A267)

There's a fun, relaxed town pub atmosphere in the pubby downstairs bar of this famous seafood restaurant. As well as lots of sturdy old pine tables on the York stone floor, it's cheerily decorated with old mirrors, prints, enamel advertising signs, antique pub engines and other bric-a-brac (most of which has been salvaged from local pub closures) and french windows leading to a small suntrap terrace with white tables and chairs under cocktail parasols. Fortunately for us all, the excellent restaurant menu is also available in the bar. It includes starters like potted shrimps, salmon and crab roulade or fish soup (£4.50), stuffed clams or local oysters in a shallot dressing (£5), fried scallops or smoked fish selection from Loch Fyne (£6.50), and main courses like seafood paella (£10), grilled monkfish with mozzarella, black olives and garlic, grilled halibut or Cornish crab (£14.50), bass steamed with spring onions, soy and ginger (£15.50), seafood platter (£17.50), and lobster (from £25). The reasonably priced bar menu has filled baguettes (£3), home-made pâté or a daily pasta dish (£4), fish soup, home-made lamb and chilli sausages or a very good charcuterie (£4.50), vegetarian meals (£5.50) and Morroccan lamb, fishcakes or chicken breast filled with crab meat (£6.50). Some combination of Harveys, King and Barnes or Shepherd Neame ales from an antique beer engine, though most people seem to be taking advantage of the superb wine list; they also have quite a choice of unusual teas, running to Black Dragon Oolong and Japanese Sencha. You need to get there early in the evening for a table in the bar. *(Recommended by D Hayman, Heather Martin, Roger and Valerie Hill, Hilary Dobbie)*

Free house ~ Licensee Guy Sankey ~ Real ale ~ Meals and snacks (12-3, 7-10) ~ No smoking restaurant (not Sun) ~ (01892) 511422 ~ Children welcome ~ Live music Sun evenings ~ Open 11-11; 11-3, 6-11 Sat; cl Sun and 25 Dec

---

The details at the end of each main entry start by saying whether the pub is a free house, or if it's tied to a brewery (which we name).

ULCOMBE TQ8550 Map 3

Pepper Box 🍺

Fairbourne Heath (signposted from A20 in Harrietsham; or follow Ulcombe signpost from A20, then turn left at crossroads with sign to pub)

For many the main attraction at this cosy old country inn is the really good bar food, although it's still a nice place for a very well kept pint. The friendly, homely bar has standing timbers, low beams hung with hops, copper kettles and pans on window sills, some very low-seated windsor chairs, wing armchairs, and a sofa and two armchairs by the splendid inglenook log fire. A side area is more functionally furnished for eating, and there's a very snug little no-smoking dining room. The menu is a good length and sensibly imaginative with perhaps thoughtfully prepared duck and orange pâté (£3.20), breaded mozzarella fingers with dijon dip (£3.80), mixed seafood salad (£4), smoked salmon and mushroom tagliatelle or Thai beef with sweet potatoes and green bean curry (£6.50), lemon chicken with olives on cous cous or stir fried duck with ginger and olives (£7.20), poached salmon hollandaise or lamb with rosemary, aubergine and black olives (£7.50), Thai-style prawns with lemon grass or pork with prunes in white wine sauce (£8); they also do lunchtime sandwiches, good puddings, and a Sunday roast. Very well kept Shepherd Neame Bitter, Bishops Finger and Spitfire on handpump or tapped from the cask, and fruit wines and malt whiskies; efficient, courteous service. It's very nicely placed on high ground above the weald, looking out over a great plateau of rolling arable farmland, and if you're in the garden, with its small pond, swing and tables among trees, shrubs and flowerbeds, you may catch a glimpse of the deer that sometimes come up, but if not you're quite likely to meet Jones the tabby tom, the other two cats, or Boots the plump collie. The name of the pub refers to the pepperbox pistol – an early type of revolver with numerous barrels. *(Recommended by D Hayman, Comus Elliott, Mr and Mrs R Buckler, G S B G Dudley, Tony Gayfer, R Suddaby)*

Shepherd Neame ~ Tenants Geoff and Sarah Pemble ~ Real ale ~ Meals and snacks (till 10, not Sun evening) ~ Restaurant (not Sun evening) ~ (01622) 842558 ~ Live music Sun evening ~ Open 11-3, 6.30-11

WHITSTABLE TR1166 Map 3

Pearsons 🍴

Sea Wall; follow main road into centre as far as you can, turning L into Horsebridge Rd; pub opposite Royal Free Fishers & Dredgers; parking limited

We've made an exception in this case, and have included this cheery seafood pub because readers really love the delicious fresh seafood served in the upstairs restaurant: cockles (£1.75), mussels (£4.95), grilled king prawns (£5.75), six local oysters in season (£6), vegetarian meals like spinach and mushroom lasagne (£7.50), seafood platter (£10.25), Pearsons paradise – a huge meal for two involving lobster, crab, prawns, oysters, mussels and more (£36), and changing fresh fish (excellent plaice) or shellfish specials; children's menu (from £3.50). There's a nicely relaxed atmosphere, with lots of tables close together, and fine sea views. They serve a few seaside snacks in the bar downstairs such as rollmops (£2.25), smoked mackerel (£2.50) and platter of prawns (£2.95), as well as the usual reasonably priced bar food. Well kept Boddingtons, Flowers Original, Fremlins, Morlands Old Speckled Hen and a changing guest on handpump; decent house wines; piped pop music, fruit machine. There are some picnic tables outside between the pub and the sea. *(Recommended by Frank Ashbee, Mr and Mrs R A Broadbent, L M Miall, D Bryan, David Shillitoe, Heather Martin, Claude and Bennie Bemis, E D Bailey, Mrs M Henderson, James Macrae)*

Whitbreads ~ Lease: Linda Wingrove ~ Real ale ~ Meals and snacks ~ Restaurant ~ (01227) 272005 ~ Children in restaurant and eating area of bar ~ Open 11-3, 6-11

Planning a day in the country? We list pubs in really attractive scenery at the back of the book.

Lucky Dip

Besides the fully inspected pubs, you might like to try these Lucky Dips recommended to us and described by readers (if you do, please send us reports):

☆ **Addington** [handy for M20 via junctions 2 and 4; TQ6559], *Angel*: 14th-c inn in classic village green setting, plenty of well spaced tables, usual food inc sandwiches and generous ploughman's, quick friendly service, reasonable prices; Courage-related ales *(L M Miall, C R Bridgeman, Mark Percy)*

Aldington [Frith Rd; TR0736], *Good Intent*: Good 17th-c village pub, nice decor, good vegetarian and vegan food, well kept changing ales such as Marstons Pedigree *(Mr and Mrs J Russell)*

Appledore [The Street; TQ9529], *Red Lion*: Friendly pub reopened under new management, with partitioned eating area, good imaginative food esp fish; comfortable bedrooms *(Max and Jan Logan)*

☆ **nr Ashford** [Silverhill Rd, Willesborough; TR0241], *Hooden Horse on the Hill*: Done up cheerfully in unpretentious style, well kept ales served through sparkler inc Goachers and five guests, farm ciders, country wines, good freshly cooked food esp Mexican, friendly local atmosphere and staff *(John C Baker, Richard Stafford, Richard Balls)*

Ashurst [A264, next to railway station; TQ5038], *Bald Faced Stag*: Welcoming pub with well kept Harveys, informal atmosphere despite some emphasis on food, good choice inc good value Sun lunch and interesting South American or Asian spicy snacks, helpful landlord, daily papers, plain decor; pleasant garden with play area, country walks nearby *(G Futcher, John Kimber, Mr and Mrs J Jackson)*

☆ **Aylesford** [handy for M2 junction 3 or M20 junction 6, via A229; 19 High St; TQ7359], *Little Gem*: Tudor pub, Kent's smallest, very cosy and quaint, with tiny front door, lots of atmosphere, interesting upper gallery; good range of interesting ales and farm ciders, bar lunches (can be a wait) and evening snacks, flame-effect gas fire; children welcome, piped radio *(Sheldon Barwick, Bob Happ, LYM)*

Badlesmere [TR0054], *Red Lion*: Character Shepherd Neame pub, beams and panelling, slightly raised front area; garden behind *(Chris Westmoreland)*

Benenden [The Street (B2086); TQ8033], *King William IV*: Low-ceilinged village local with country furnishings, Shepherd Neame ales, reasonably priced food, good log fire; games in public bar, small garden *(Comus Elliott, Michael Grigg, LYM)*

Bidborough [95 Bidborough Ridge; TQ5743], *Hare & Hounds*: Pleasant decor and atmosphere, good value food from lunchtime meals and snacks to good evening menu, good choice of wines, new restaurant *(Lee Brown)*

☆ **Biddenden** [High St; TQ8538], *Red Lion*: Plush but friendly Tudor inn in lovely village, good straightforward food and service, well kept Whitbreads-related ales *(Tim Masters)*

Birling [nr M20 junction 4; TQ6860], *Nevill Bull*: Well run dining pub with good value nicely presented food in black-beamed partitioned bar, friendly service, well kept Whitbreads-related ales; restaurant *(Comus Elliott)*

☆ **Bodsham** [Bodsham Green; TR1045], *Timber Batts*: Attractive and busy, with very wide range of tasty food inc lots of vegetarian dishes, good service, unspoilt country setting *(Comus Elliott, Pauline Langley)*

Bossingham [off B2068 Canterbury rd; TR1548], *Hop Pocket*: Friendly atmosphere and service, good home-cooked food, well kept ales such as Shepherd Neame Spitfire and Timothy Taylors Landlord, home-made country wines; children welcome *(Mr and Mrs P Cornock)*

☆ **Boughton Street** [¾ mile from M2 junction 7, off A2; TR0559], *White Horse*: Carefully restored dark-beamed bars and timbered dining room, well prepared food all day inc early breakfast and good value carvery Fri, Sat and Sun, quick service even when busy, well kept Shepherd Neame beers, decent wines, good tea and coffee; tables in garden, children allowed; good value bedrooms (back ones quieter), good breakfasts *(Steve Goodchild, Mrs M Henderson, Andrew and Ruth Triggs, LYM)*

Boxley [TQ7759], *Kings Arms*: Friendly recently refurbished Whitbreads Wayside Inn, nice building, good choice of ales and of sensibly priced straightforward food inc good sandwiches, good garden for children; pretty village, pleasant walks *(Comus Elliott, E D Bailey)*

☆ **Brabourne** [Canterbury Rd, E Brabourne; TR1041], *Five Bells*: Old beams and inglenook log fire, comfortable banquettes in open-plan bar, helpful staff, wide choice of good fresh food inc Austrian dishes (and good sandwiches), several well kept mainly Courage-related ales, continental beers; tables in garden with play area *(Douglas and Margaret Chesterman, Cyril and Janet Morley and friends, Lyn Browne)*

☆ **Brasted** [A25, 3 miles from M25 junction 5; TQ4654], *White Hart*: Spacious relaxing lounge and extension sun lounge, interesting Battle of Britain bar with signatures and mementoes of Biggin Hill fighter pilots, well kept Bass and Charrington IPA; children welcome, big neatly kept garden; good food in bar and restaurant, very popular with older people – service can slow; bedrooms *(E G Parish, M E A Horler, Christopher Warner, Sue Lee)*

☆ **Bridge** [53 High St, off A2; TR1854], *White Horse*: Good fresh food and very pleasant service in smartly refurbished good value old dining pub with cosy interconnected rooms inc civilised restaurant, good range of well kept ales, interesting wines; attractive village *(D Hayman, P D R Milner)*

☆ **Canterbury** [12 The Friars, just off main St Peters St pedestrian area], *Canterbury Tales*: Small friendly pub, relaxing and civilised in almost a continental way, with books, games and chess table in the clean and airy lounge; well kept Shepherd Neame and more distant ales maybe inc Belgian cherry beer, good bar food inc Mexican and good sandwiches, attentive service by real people; popular lunchtime with local businesspeople, opp Marlow Theatre (*John A Barker, L M Miall, R T and J C Moggridge*)

Challock [Church Lane; TR0050], *Chequers*: Cosy and pleasant 17th-c beamed pub with well kept Greene King IPA, reasonably priced food, some tables on front terrace opp village green, more in garden (*Eddie Edwards*)

Chiddingstone Causeway [Charcott, off back rd to Weald; TQ5247], *Greyhound*: Unchanging country local, very unpretentious, with good choice of cheap beer and food inc outstanding value cheese and pickle sandwich and superb home-made summer pudding; very welcoming to young children (*Cedric and Ruth Reavley*); [B2027; TQ5146], *Little Brown Jug*: Spacious, clean and comfortable even when busy, olde-brick-and-beam-style decor, well kept Harveys and other ales, decent wines, friendly welcome, wide range of promptly served food (no sandwiches), restaurant, no-smoking area; children welcome if eating, attractive garden with play area; bedrooms (*Stephen Harvey, Margaret and Nigel Dennis*)

Chilham [off A28/A252; TR0753], *Woolpack*: Good range of reasonably priced bar food inc vegetarian and good steak sandwiches, cheerful service, pews, sofa, little armchairs, inglenook fires, well kept Shepherd Neame ales; restaurant (children allowed till early evening), unobtrusive piped music; bedrooms, delightful village (*V J Ward, Mike Colquhoun, LYM*)

☆ **Chillenden** [TR2653], *Griffins Head*: Reliable food and good service in attractive beamed, timbered and flagstoned 14th-c pub with three comfortable rooms, big log fire; pleasant small garden surrounded by wild roses (*L M Miall, D Hayman*)

Chipstead [39 High St, handy for M25 junction 5; TQ4956], *George & Dragon*: Dining pub with heavy black beams and standing timbers, very wide choice of good food inc vegetarian choice, good value wines, relaxed friendly service, children welcome in most areas; tables in pleasant garden (*James and Karen Davies, LYM*)

☆ **Cliffe** [Church St; TQ7376], *Black Bull*: Good genuine Malaysian bar food rubbing shoulders with local village atmosphere in friendly cosy pub with good choice of well kept ales, weekday evening basement restaurant, darts/pool room, quiet juke box; very welcoming to children (*Pam and Tim Moorey*)

☆ **Cobham** [B2009, handy for M2 junction 1; TQ6768], *Leather Bottle*: Beautifully laid-out extensive colourful garden with fish pond and play area, masses of interesting Dickens memorabilia, ancient beams and timbers (but extensive modernisation), real ales; quiet, pretty village; bedrooms (*E D Bailey, Sue Lee, LYM*)

Cobham [Redhill Rd], *Inn on the Lake*: New pub set on lake (part of golf club), four real ales, friendly staff, wide choice of good food inc tasty seafood platters (*J D Hearn*); *Ship*: Spaciously refurbished food pub, good fish, good service (*Julie Peters, Colin Blinkhorn*)

☆ **Conyer Quay** [from A2 Sittingbourne—Faversham take Deerton St turn, then at T-junction left towards Teynham, then follow Conyer signs; TQ9664], *Ship*: Rambling collection of cosily nautical little rooms in attractive creekside position, cheery atmosphere; well kept real ales and good range of other drinks, good straightforward food from ploughman's up, friendly new landlord, tables outside facing waterfront – road outside can flood at spring tides (*Dr I Russell Eggitt, Richard Gibbs, Sue Lee, LYM*)

☆ **Cowden** [Cowden Pound; junction B2026 with Markbeech rd; TQ4642], *Queens Arms*: Unspoilt two-room country pub like something from the 1930s, with splendid landlady, well kept Whitbreads, darts; strangers quickly feel like regulars (*Pete Baker*)

☆ **Cowden** [Holtye Common; A264 S of village – actually just over border in Sussex; TQ4539], *White Horse*: Wide choice of good generous attractively priced food esp fish, also vegetarian dishes, in bar and spacious dining room, carp swimming under glass panels in its floor; warm friendly atmosphere, barbecues (*Jill Reeves*)

☆ **Cranbrook** [High St; TQ7735], *Grand Old Hooden Horse*: Good lively atmosphere, friendly courteous staff, good range of beers, fine choice of food inc delicious Mexican meals (*Richard Stafford, Hilary Dobbie*)

Crockham Hill [on Vanguard Way; TQ4450], *Royal Oak*: Wide choice of reasonable food inc some home-grown veg and good value ploughman's, well kept Shepherd Neame Spitfire; handy for walks (*Michael Grigg*)

Darenth [Darenth Rd; TQ5671], *Chequers*: Popular food esp good value home-cooked Sun lunch in warm and friendly traditional local, can book tables in pleasant room behind bar (*Mr and Mrs Hillman, Sue Lee*)

Deal [West St; TR3752], *Alma*: Well kept Shepherd Neame and interesting reasonably priced changing guest beers, good snacks (*D J Hayman*); [Beach St], *Kings Head*: Two-room seafront pub with drawings, pictures and prints, tables overlooking water, attentive staff, wide choice of good value standard food, several real ales (*Jim Clugston, Thomas Nott*)

Doddington [TQ9357], *Chequers*: Lovely old country pub with well kept beer, very friendly landlady, nice log fires; a summer base for vintage motor cycle club (*B Price, B Evans*)

Dungeness [by old lighthouse; TR0916], *Britannia*: Friendly and spotless, handy for Romney Hythe & Dymchurch railway, with good range of modestly priced food inc consistently good fresh local fish; very friendly service *(Stephen Harvey, Vic and Rene Cove)*

☆ Dunks Green [Silver Hill; TQ6152], *Kentish Rifleman*: Cosy early 16th-c local, good choice of freshly cooked bar food, friendly prompt service, well kept real ales such as Fullers and Marstons Pedigree, decent wine, plenty of character, no machines; dogs welcome; plenty of seats in unusually well designed garden behind *(A Quinsee, R C Watkins, John and Elspeth Howell, Robert Huddleston)*

☆ Eastling [The Street; off A251 S of M2 junction 6, via Painters Forstal; TQ9656], *Carpenters Arms*: Pretty and cottagey oak-beamed pub with big fireplaces front and back, friendly service, decent food (not Sun evening), well kept Shepherd Neame, some seats outside; children allowed in restaurant; small but well equipped bedrooms in separate building, huge breakfast *(Mrs M Henderson, Wayne Brindle, Mary and Peter Clark, E D Bailey, LYM)*

☆ Elham [St Marys Rd; TR1743], *Kings Arms*: Good interesting reasonably priced food, reliably good service, attractive lounge bar, good open fire, friendly service (and cats), steps down to big dining area; pool table in public bar; opp church in square of charming village *(L M Miall, Sybille Weber, Alan and Maggie Telford)*

Elham [High St], *Rose & Crown*: Small cosy inn, partly 16th-c, doing well under friendly newish landlord, with well kept ales, good value bar food, evening restaurant, tables in garden; bedrooms *(Robert Bray, P J Brunwin)*

☆ Eynsford [TQ5365], *Malt Shovel*: Spacious dining pub handy for castles and Roman villa, wide range of generous bar food inc lots of good value seafood (lobster tank), Pilgrims ales, quick friendly service, nice atmosphere *(Colin Laffan, Jenny and Brian Seller)*

Eynsford [24 Riverside], *Plough*: Friendly Beefeater, good value food from snacks to full meals, well kept beer, good atmosphere, tables out by river *(David C Thompson, A M Pring)*

Farningham [High St; TQ5466], *Chequers*: Old open-plan village local with full range of Fullers ales and guests such as Shepherd Neame Spitfire, home-made bar food (can take a time), friendly welcome; can be a bit smoky *(Michael Wadsworth, Jenny and Brian Seller)*

☆ Faversham [31 the Mall, handy for M2 junction 6; TR0161], *Elephant*: Very picturesque flower-decked terrace town pub concentrating on good range of food inc imaginative vegetarian dishes; good choice of well kept changing ales, prompt welcoming service, simple but attractive furnishings on stripped boards; summer barbecues *(JP, PP, Frank Ashbee, Mrs M Henderson, BB)*

Faversham [Abbey St], *Anchor*: Smallish friendly two-room Shepherd Neame local nr quay, bare boards and individual furniture, hall with bench seats, a couple of picnic tables outside *(Chris Westmoreland)*; [10 West St],

Sun: Rambling old-world 15th-c town pub with good unpretentious atmosphere, reasonably priced lunchtime bar food, well kept Shepherd Neame; tables in pleasant back courtyard *(Mr and Mrs J Rudolf)*

Folkestone [16 The Stade; TR2336], *Carpenters*: Nicely placed by fishing harbour, good varied food inc super fresh fish in bar and upstairs restaurant (with lovely view); pleasant staff, unobtrusive piped music *(Sybille Weber, Marian Greenwood, B D Craig)*

☆ Fordcombe [TQ5240], *Chafford Arms*: Pretty pub, tastefully extended by long-serving licensees, with charming garden with plenty of shade, well kept Whitbreads-related ales, local cider, interesting food esp good (though not cheap) fish and shellfish *(D D Collins, C Moncreiffe, John and Elspeth Howell)*

☆ Fordwich [off A28 in Sturry; TR1759], *Fordwich Arms*: Generous helpings of decent plain cooking inc fresh veg and vegetarian in civilised and handsome pub with open fire in attractive fireplace, welcoming atmosphere, Whitbreads-related ales, discreet piped music, dining room; spacious garden by River Stour; ancient town hall opposite worth visiting *(Roger Thompson, G S and E M Dorey, David and Margaret Bloomfield, LYM)*

☆ Four Elms [B2027/B269 E of Edenbridge; TQ4648], *Four Elms*: Busy dining pub, welcoming and comfortable, impressive choice of reliably good generous food inc fresh fish, well kept Courage Directors and Harveys, decent wine, good service, two big open fires, some interesting decorations inc huge boar's head, pleasant restaurant; children allowed, tables outside; juke box, fruit machine; handy for Chartwell *(Margaret and Nigel Dennis, Colin and Joyce Laffan)*

☆ Goudhurst [TQ7238], *Star & Eagle*: Attractively timbered medieval inn with settles and Jacobean-style seats in relaxing heavily beamed open-plan bar, good bar food using local produce, well kept Whitbreads-related ales, decent wine, good friendly staff; lovely views esp from tables out behind; children welcome, bedrooms comfortable *(Derek Howse, Hanns P Golez, David Newsome, Lesley Meagher, LYM)*

☆ nr Goudhurst [A262 W], *Green Cross*: Good value genuine home cooking inc Sat night carvery (winter cold cuts, summer roasts), real ales inc some unusual ones, enjoyable if not exactly pubby atmosphere, open fires and friendly staff; beamed dining room for residents; bedrooms light and airy, good value *(Mark Percy, M Holdsworth)*

☆ Great Chart [Chart Rd; TQ9842], *Hooden Horse*: Almost entirely Mexican menu, six changing well kept ales and local farm cider in quarry-tiled two-roomed pub, beams a forest of hop bines; cheap and cheerful furnishings, good lively atmosphere, friendly staff, piped blues *(Jim Penson, Richard Stafford, Hilary Dobbie, BB)*

☆ Hadlow [Ashes Lane (off A26 Tonbridge Rd); TQ6349], *Rose Revived*: Friendly and attractive 16th-c pub with well kept beers inc

Harveys and King & Barnes, good bar food inc well filled fresh sandwiches *(E D Bailey)*

☆ Hawkhurst [Pipsden – A268 towards Rye; TQ7730], *Oak & Ivy*: Immaculately refurbished and extended (perhaps needs time to develop character), with well kept Whitbreads-related ales, friendly efficient staff, generous good value home cooking inc popular Sun roasts, heavy low beams and timbers, dark brown terracotta walls and ceilings, roaring log fires (one in massive inglenook), new dark tables on quarry tiles; farm tools, piped music, fruit machine; tables outside, good play area *(A M Pring, Colin and Joyce Laffan, Charles Gysin, BB)*

Hawkhurst [Rye Rd (A268)], *Queens Head*: Huge log fire, charming barmaid, Harveys and another real ale, quickly produced, well cooked and presented food; bedrooms *(Colin Laffan)*

☆ Heaverham [Watery Lane – OS Sheet 188 map ref 572587; TQ5658], *Chequers*: Impressive choice of good food and friendly service in quietly attractive two-bar country pub with well kept range of beers; lots of birds both caged and free in big garden *(Nick Peacock, E D Bailey, L M Miall)*

Herne Bay [TR1768], *Richmond*: Very clean and friendly, just off sea front, with good home-cooked food in bar and back restaurant, well kept Shepherd Neame ales, three open fires *(Stephen and Julie Brown)*; [seafront], *Ship*: Nautical-style oak pillars, bare boards and screens from old ships, well presented reasonably priced pub food with some more imaginative dishes, good choice of ales and spirits *(F Robinson)*

☆ Hernhill [off A299 at High Street roundabout via Dargate, or off A2 via Boughton Street and Staplestreet; TR0660], *Red Lion*: Pretty Tudor inn by church, densely beamed and flagstoned, pine tables, log fires, upstairs restaurant, garden with boules and good play area; has been a popular main entry with generous helpings of good food and well kept Boddingtons, Fullers London Pride, Morlands Old Speckled Hen and Shepherd Neame, allowing children, but 1996 takeover by Labatts leaves uncertainty as we go to press about future direction; bedrooms *(LYM; news please)*

☆ Hodsoll Street [TQ6263], *Green Man*: Pretty pub on village green, lots of hanging baskets, big garden with play area, aviary and pets corner; quiet inside, with good food (not Sun/Mon pm), well kept beer, cheerful staff, log fires, no music *(E D Bailey, Sue Lee)*

☆ Hollingbourne [Eyhorne St; B2163, off A20; TQ8454], *Dirty Habit*: Dim-lit old pub with lots of different old kitchen and dining tables and chairs, nooks, crannies and uneven floors, interesting food, well kept ales, decent house wines, flame-effect gas fire in big fireplace; games area, unobtrusive juke box, maybe live music Sun lunchtime; on Pilgrims Way, handy for Leeds Castle *(Peter and Joy Heatherley, Steve Goodchild)*

☆ Ickham [TR2257], *Duke William*: Friendly comfortable front bar, more formal seating

behind with restaurant and conservatory, very wide choice of good food, well kept beers such as Adnams, Fullers, Shepherd Neame and Youngs; smart garden *(Stephen and Julie Brown, D Hayman, Chris Westmoreland)*

☆ Ide Hill [off B2042 SW of Sevenoaks; TQ4851], *Cock*: Pretty village-green local, neatly modernised, with well kept Greene King, straightforward bar food (not Sun evening, only sandwiches Sun lunchtime), fine log fire, bar billiards, piped music, some seats out in front; handy for Chartwell and nearby walks – so gets busy, with nearby parking sometimes out of the question *(Dr Michael Smith, Sue Lee, LYM)*

Ide Hill, *Crown*: Simple pub with friendly welcome from locals and dogs, food inc good sandwiches, real ales, unobtrusive piped jazz, darts, small back garden with picnic tables; seats on attractive village green *(Sue Lee)*

Iden Green [pub signed off B2086; TQ8032], *Woodcock*: Small 17th-c country local, relaxed and homely, with beams and bare boards, big inglenook, single bar with cosy alcoves off, couple of steps up to eating area, usual food, very friendly staff; maybe piped pop music; hatch to pleasant garden with mistletoe in big tree *(Mr Cornock, BB)*

nr Iden Green [A262 E of Goudhurst], *Peacock*: Traditional low-beamed lounge with flagstones and massive fireplace, well kept Whitbreads-related ales, simple food inc good ploughman's, friendly staff, plain public bar with music and games, good big garden; packed with young people Sat night *(Comus Elliott, BB)*

Ightham [TQ5956], *Chequers*: Friendly and comfortable, good atmosphere, good range of food (no sandwiches), discreet piped music *(John Evans)*

☆ Ightham Common [Common Rd; TQ5755], *Harrow*: Cosy and unpretentious country local with good fresh food, sparse wooden furniture, roaring log fire, papers to read, pool, darts, board games and jigsaws, well kept Greene King IPA and Abbot, friendly staff; restaurant evenings and Sun; bedrooms *(John and Elspeth Howell, Russell Isaac)*

☆ Ivy Hatch [off A227 N of Tunbridge; TQ5854], *Plough*: More restaurant than pub now, by no means cheap, and you may not get a table if you don't book; but it's good, with fastidious French cooking, good wines (and decent real ales), attractive candlelit surroundings, solidly professional service, and delightful conservatory and garden *(Mrs P D McFarlane, Nigel Wikeley, M Carr, Tony Gayfer, L M Miall, W Ruxton, RWD, N B Thompson, Jason Caulkin, G Kirkland, Mavis and John Wright, Sue Lee, Mrs Olive Oxley, LYM)*

☆ Kingsdown [Cliff Rd; TR3748], *Rising Sun*: Small friendly 17th-c village pub with decent food, well kept real ales, open fire, lovely cottage garden; good walks nearby, nr beach *(Chris Brooker)*

Kingston [TR1951], *Black Robin*: Friendly, with chatty staff, wooden floors, old pine tables, candles, flowers and low lighting; good unusual food inc gorgeous puddings, Shepherd Neame beers *(June Goncalves, Tim Lancefield, Roger Goodsell)*

Kingswood [TQ8450], *Battle of Britain*: Welcoming village pub, with obliging staff, good choice of well cooked food, some covered tables in garden with hanging baskets; good bottled beer range *(M Chaplin, N Simmonds)*

Knockholt [Star Hill; TQ4658], *Harrow*: Great improvements made by new landlord, pleasant beamed dining room, enjoyable atmosphere, good home-cooked food with lots of veg, well kept beer; lovely walks *(Mrs P J Elfick)*

Knox Bridge [A229 N of Cranbrook; TQ7840], *Knox Bridge*: Basic and rustic, flagstoned, but comfortable, homely and friendly, good well priced generous food cooked with flair, well kept Fullers, Shepherd Neame and guest beers, good coffee, tables in garden *(Frank Ashbee)*

Lamberhurst [School Hill; TQ6635], *Chequers*: Friendly service, separate dining area with good choice of specials; bedrooms *(A M Pring)*; [B2100], *Horse & Groom*: Welcoming village local with good variety of well priced well presented generous food, well kept Shepherd Neame, darts, massive tie collection; bedrooms *(Lesley Neville, Comus Elliott)*

☆ nr Lamberhurst [Hook Green (B2169 towards T Wells)], *Elephants Head*: Ancient rambling country pub with wide choice of food inc vegetarian, well kept Harveys, heavy beams, some timbering, brick or oak flooring, log fire and woodburner, plush-cushioned pews etc; darts and fruit machine in small side area, picnic tables on back terrace and grass with play area (peaceful view), and by front green; nr Bayham Abbey and Owl House, very popular with families weekends *(C R and M A Starling, Michael Grigg, LYM)*

☆ Leigh [Powder Mills; the village is pronounced Lye – OS Sheet 188 map ref 568459; TQ5646], *Plough*: Busy, rambling and well kept timbered country pub with good atmosphere, huge log fire, well kept ales inc Harveys, King & Barnes and Youngs, good value generous straightforward food from sandwiches up, Sun lunches in capacious old barn carvery, quick friendly service; juke box; tables in well kept big garden *(Sue Lee)*

Linton [A229 S of Maidstone; TQ7550], *Bull*: Friendly 17th-c beamed pub with well kept Whitbreads-related ales, friendly staff, good if not cheap food esp fresh fish and shellfish, efficient staff; restaurant; superb well kept garden with wonderful views *(Lesley Zammit)*

☆ Littlebourne [4 High St; TR2057], *King William IV*: Straightforward character and decor, but unusual range of good freshly prepared food running up to ostrich and kangaroo, good friendly service, well kept ales, interesting wines inc New World ones; small dining area, good value bedrooms; handy for Howletts Zoo *(Martin Hickes, J Randall, Christopher Warner, Desmond and Gillian Bellew, A Ellis, BB)*

☆ Loose [Old Loose Rd; TQ7552], *Chequers*: Attractive riverside pub with unusual range of good food, good choice of Whitbreads-related ales, warmly welcoming and efficient service *(F Barwell, Marie-Christine Bouilles, Mrs Allerston)*

☆ Luddesdown [Henley Street – OS Sheet 178 map ref 664672; TQ6667], *Cock*: A pub since early 18th c, simple bar with bar billiards and woodburner, more comfortable lounge, log fires, up to ten or more well kept changing real ales with four cider farmers in summer, simple hearty bar food from cheap bread and cheese to seafood collected daily from Billingsgate, bar billiards, darts and shove-ha'penny; no children inside, music or games machines; big secure garden, summer weekend barbecues *(Sue Lee, A R Turner)*

Lympne [Aldington Rd; marked on OS Sheet 189 map ref 118351; TR1135], *County Members*: Comfortable, with exceptionally wide choice of reasonably priced bar food, well kept ales; where Michael Howard did his photocall for all-day Sunday opening *(Thomas Nott)*

☆ Maidstone [King St; TQ7656], *Muggleton*: New Wetherspoons pub in former grand colonnaded Victorian insurance HQ, beautifully converted in conjunction with English Heritage; lovely muted atmosphere, high ceilings, plenty of room; good value food all day, six real ales inc one at 99p *(Comus Elliott)*

Maidstone [9 Fairmeadow, off A20/A229], *Drakes*: Done up as Whitbreads Cask & Cork old-fashioned tavern, with bare woodwork in dark interior; down nr river *(CE)*

Marden Thorn [Pagehurst Lane; TQ7842], *Wild Duck*: Friendly and comfortable, with good well presented food in bar and dining room, real pub atmosphere; good range of beers and of wines *(Frank Ashbee)*

Marshside [TR2265], *Hog & Donkey*: Idiosyncratic small pub with Whitbreads-related ales, no food, cottagey front room with unsmart mix of tables, chairs, sofas and bright cushions strewn around; car park may be full of cars even if pub empty – landlord collects them *(Chris Westmoreland, James Nunns)*

Martin [TR3346], *Old Lantern*: Worth knowing for beautiful setting, with sizeable play area and wendy house in sprawling pretty gardens *(Martin Hickes)*

Matfield [Maidstone Rd; TQ6541], *Standings Cross*: Friendly local with oak beams, panelling, leaded windows, scrubbed tables, rickety chairs and darts in small front bar (can get smoky when busy); cosy inglenook fireplace in lovely old back restaurant, good range of reasonably priced home-cooked food inc good value Sun lunch, pleasant helpful service *(A M Pring)*; *Wheelwrights Arms*: Attractive old beamed and weatherboarded pub, simply furnished, lots of toby jugs and china gravy boats, Whitbreads-related real ales, bar food from big sandwiches and ploughman's to steaks *(Michael Grigg)*

☆ Meopham [Meopham Green; A227

Gravesend—Wrotham; TQ6466], *Cricketers*: Neatly kept 17th-c pub with seats out overlooking green, more in back garden, cricket memorabilia, Tetleys-related ales, usual food, friendly service, tasteful modern restaurant extension; piped music *(Gwen and Peter Andrews)*

Meopham, *George*: Popular with young people, can be smoky and noisy, but friendly, with enormous good sandwiches *(Julie Peters, Colin Blinkhorn)*

☆ Mersham [Flood St – OS Sheet 179 map ref 049341; TR0539], *Farriers Arms*: Smart and attractive three-room local based on early 17th-c forge, wide choice of good value straightforward food, well kept Tetleys-related ales, good friendly service; exceptionally well kept gardens behind, pleasant country views; bedrooms *(Mr and Mrs J Russell, Terry Baylis)*

Molash [TR0251], *George*: Interesting food inc outstanding sandwiches, enormous ploughman's, hot dishes cooked to order (so may be a wait) in 16th-c character country pub up on the downs; friendly helpful service, well kept Whitbreads, old kitchen tables and chairs; pleasant garden, plenty of pets *(Chris Westmoreland)*

☆ Nettlestead [Nettlestead Green; B2015 Pembury—Maidstone; TQ6852], *Hop Pole*: Spacious carpeted bar with interesting prints, copper and brass, wide range of decent food inc good value Sun lunch, well kept ales such as Adnams Extra and Fullers London Pride, decent wine, friendly service, central fire, fresh flowers; tables out in pleasant back area, hops and orchards around *(John and Elspeth Howell, N B Thompson)*

☆ Oad Street [nr M2 junction 5; TQ8662], *Plough & Harrow*: Nice old village pub opp craft centre, friendly landlord, well kept Shepherd Neame and several changing ales, good value home cooking, one small bar, another much larger, light and airy at the back; children welcome; picnic tables in secluded back garden *(Chris Westmoreland)*

☆ Otford [High St; TQ5359], *Crown*: Pretty pub with character beamed bar, opp pond in delightful village with pleasant walks; friendly staff, good sandwiches and some really imaginative home cooking, well kept Tetleys-related ales with a guest such as Wadworths 6X, decent house wines; occasional jazz evenings, lovely garden behind *(James Nunns, Sue Lee)*

☆ Otford [66 High St], *Horns*: Cosy 15th-c pub with big inglenook log fire, lots of Victorian memorabilia, hops on beams, attentive friendly service, short choice of good well presented food, well kept ales inc Harveys and King & Barnes *(E D Bailey, A Pring, Ellis and Norma Myers)*

☆ Painters Forstal [signed off A2 at Ospringe; TQ9958], *Alma*: Friendly, neat and tidy weatherboarded village local, very popular, with wide choice of decent food, largeish dining lounge, small bare-boards public bar, well kept Shepherd Neame inc winter Porter, maybe piped classical music, picnic tables on

lawn *(Chris Westmoreland, June and Tony Baldwin, G Bond, BB)*

☆ Penshurst [centre; TQ5243], *Leicester Arms*: Busy pub in charming village by Penshurst Place, extended eating area (best bit is old dining room up steps, with country views), wide choice of reasonably priced bar food, well kept if very cool real ale, willing young staff; children welcome, economical bedrooms *(Cedric and Ruth Reavley, Colin Laffan, TM, PM)*

☆ nr Penshurst [Hoath Corner – OS Sheet 188 map ref 497431], *Rock*: Charmingly old-fashioned untouristy atmosphere in tiny beamed rooms, wonky brick floors, inglenook, pleasant licensees, good value sandwiches and generous home cooking, well kept local Larkins and other ales, ring the bull; children and dogs welcome (pub dog very shy); tables outside, beautiful countryside nearby *(Keith Widdowson, J and P Maloney, Dr D R Pulsford, Colin Laffan)*

Plaxtol [Sheet Hill; TQ6054], *Golding Hop*: Secluded country pub, good in summer with suntrap streamside lawn; small and simple inside, with real ales tapped from the cask, choice of ciders (sometimes even their own), limited bar food (not Mon evening), woodburner *(Sue Lee, Nicholas Watmough, LYM)*

Pluckley [TQ9245], *Black Horse*: Comfortable and spacious open-plan bar with roomy back dining area in attractive old house, hops on beams, vast inglenook, usual furnishings and food, cheery atmosphere and service, well kept Whitbreads-related ales with a guest such as Brakspears PA; piped music may seem rather loud, fruit machine; children allowed if eating; picnic tables in spacious informal garden by tall sycamores, good walks *(Martin Hickes, Mr and Mrs P Brocklebank, E D Bailey, Michael Butler, BB)*; [Munday Bois], *Rose & Crown*: Welcoming little pub with nicely furnished dining room, good varied food, interesting wines, well kept ales, reasonable prices, good service; friendly dog *(Barbara and Alec Jones, R Misson)*

☆ Rochester [10 St Margarets St; TQ7467], *Coopers Arms*: Quaint and interesting ancient local, good bustling atmosphere with fine mix of customers, friendly licensees, comfortable seating, generous low-priced bar lunches, well kept Courage-related ales; handy for castle and cathedral *(A W Lewis, W J E Kock, W J Kock, Steve Goodchild, Mrs M Henderson)*

Rochester [High St], *Ship*: Tidy, unpretentious and friendly, several changing well kept beers, good basic food; live music *(Chris Westmoreland)*

Rolvenden [1 Regent St; TQ8431], *Bull*: Bass local with good simple home-cooked food inc Sun lunch, children welcome in dining area; tables in garden *(L T Lionet)*

Rolvenden Layne [TQ8530], *Another Hooden Horse*: Beams, hops and candlelight, popular good value home-made food inc Mexican, good range of beers, local ciders and wine, cheery atmosphere; music may be intrusive *(Richard Stafford)*

Ruckinge [B2067 E of Ham Street; TR0233], *Blue Anchor*: Well kept and friendly, with Whitbreads-related ales, good value home-cooked food inc good all-day breakfast, tastefully furnished conservatory; garden with pretty pond *(D B Stanley, John Fahy)*

Sandgate [High St; TR2035], *Ship*: Old-fashioned, not smart but welcoming, quickly changing real ales tapped from the cask, cheap and cheerful food, seafaring theme; seats outside *(Alan and Maggie Telford, Peter Haines, Michael Mills)*

Sandway [TQ8851], *White Horse*: Popular food pub, with imaginative well presented choice in bar and restaurant; pleasant surroundings *(Mrs A Beck, Mrs J A Morgan)*

Sandwich [Cattlemarket/Mote Sole; TR3358], *Red Cow*: Carefully refurbished old pub, small, neat and clean, with welcoming staff, several Whitbreads-related and other real ales, two old fireplaces, old prints and photographs; guide dogs only, garden bar, hanging baskets *(Alan and Eileen Bowker, Mr and Mrs N Spink)*

☆ Sarre [A28 Canterbury—Margate; TR2565], *Crown*: Carefully restored pub making much of its long history as the Cherry Brandy House, pleasant bars, quiet restaurant, good range of reasonably priced home-cooked food, several well kept Shepherd Neame real ales; comfortable bedrooms *(Wim Kock, Jean Minner)*

☆ Selling [Perry Wood; from M2, keep right on through Selling; TR0456], *Rose & Crown*: Attractive 16th-c pub, wonderful garden surrounded by ancient woodland, good play area; enormous log fire, mix of furnishings inc wooden settle, generous good value home-made food in bar and restaurant, welcoming staff and atmosphere, well kept Shepherd Neame and Whitbreads-related real ales; no piped music or machines *(Mr and Mrs S R White, Mr and Mrs C Neame, Chris Westmoreland, L M Miall, Prof Geoffrey Stephenson, K Smith)*

☆ Sevenoaks [London Rd, nr stn; 2½ miles from M25 junction 5; TQ5355], *Halfway House*: Quiet and friendly partly 16th-c local with beams and brasses, well kept Greene King IPA, Abbot and Rayments, wide range of reasonably priced home-made food inc crisp fresh veg, good service, helpful licensees; parking may be difficult *(Pam and Tim Moorey, Sue and Mike Todd)*

☆ nr Sevenoaks [Godden Green, off B2019 just E; TQ5555], *Bucks Head*: Picturesque old village-green local in pretty spot by duck pond, surrounded by cherry blossom in spring; particularly well kept Courage-related and guest beers, friendly atmosphere, decent bar food, cosy furnishings; children really welcome; in attractive walking country nr Knole *(Cedric and Ruth Reavley)*

Shipbourne [Stumble Hill; TQ5952], *Chaser*: Hotel in lovely spot by village church and green, a comfortable place to stay; bar food from ploughman's up, bistro-like end part with candles and stripped pine, cheerful

public bar welcoming walkers, friendly efficient service, well kept Harveys, decent wines, high-vaulted restaurant, tables outside *(E G Parish, Nigel Wikeley, Steve Goodchild, Jenny and Brian Seller)*

Shoreham [High St; TQ5161], *Olde George*: Friendly simply furnished old beamed pub doing well under friendly newish licensee, with roaring open fire, well kept Courage Best and Tetleys, decent sandwiches, ploughman's, home-made soup, children and dogs welcome *(Simon Pyle, A M Pring)*

☆ Sissinghurst [TQ7937], *Bull*: Good food esp (not weekday lunchtimes or Mon eve) authentic pastas and pizzas in roomy welcoming pub with some armchairs, shelves of books and china, big pleasant dark-beamed restaurant area, quick willing service, Whitbreads-related ales, quiet piped music, fruit machine; neat quiet garden *(Comus Elliott, Joy Heatherley, R G and J N Plumb)*

☆ Smarden [TQ8842], *Chequers*: Cosy and relaxed beamed local in lovely village, one small eating area with a good deal of rustic character off main turkey-carpeted bar, another at the back more orthodox; second parquet-floored bar largely laid for diners; good varied freshly made food from a fine filled baguette to quite exotic main dishes inc vegetarian; Bass, Morlands Old Speckled Hen, Ruddles County, Worthington and Youngs Special, decent wines and spirits, log fire, local-interest books, no music or machines; pleasant tables outside; bedrooms simple (and some within earshot of bar) but good value, with huge breakfast *(Marian Greenwood, Hilary Dobbie, BB)*

☆ Snargate [Romney Marsh; B2080 Appledore—Brenzett – OS Sheet 189 map ref 990285; TQ9928], *Red Lion*: Delightfully old-fashioned and unspoilt 19th-c country pub, bare boards and old kitchen furniture, well kept Adnams and Batemans tapped from the cask, no music or food *(Comus Elliott, Thomas Nott, Pete Blakemore)*

Snodland [Ham Hill; TQ7061], *Freemasons Arms*: Well arranged, with long bar, air conditioning, good range of good food pleasantly and efficiently served *(DAV)*

☆ Southfleet [off A2 via A227 S towards Southfleet; or from B262 turn left at Ship in Southfleet then sharp right into Red St; pub about half-mile on right; TQ6171], *Black Lion*: Character two-room local, with good generous bar food from ploughman's up, well kept Courage-related beers, friendly helpful staff, handsome no-smoking restaurant; children in eating area; big shrub-sheltered garden *(N B Thompson, Sue Lee, LYM)*

Southfleet [Red St;], *Ship*: Clean, comfortable and relaxed, with interesting decorations, good reasonably priced homely food, smart efficient friendly staff, nice little dining room *(M F Shaylor)*

St Margarets at Cliffe [High St; TR3644], *Cliffe Tavern Hotel*: Attractive clapboard-and-brick inn opp church with simple bar and larger open-plan lounge, good log fire, well kept Greene King and Shepherd Neame ales, two cats and a singing dog, secluded back walled garden, separate dining room; has been open all day Sat, allowing well behaved children; bedrooms, inc some in cottages across yard *(Sue and Bob Soar, John Fahy, LYM)*

☆ St Margarets Bay [on shore below Nat Trust cliffs; TR3844], *Coastguard*: Tremendous views (to France on a clear day) from very cheery modernised seaside pub, open all day in summer; well kept sensibly priced real ales, good range of food esp vegetarian; children welcome; lots of tables out below NT cliff, summer Sun afternoon teas out here *(R Misson, Mark Thompson, Roger Goodsell, LYM)*

St Mary in the Marsh [TR0628], *Star*: Relaxed remote pub, Tudor but very much modernised; friendly family service, well kept Shepherd Neame inc Mild tapped from the cask; bedrooms attractive, with views of Romney Marsh *(Thomas Nott)*

Staplehurst [Chart Hill Rd – OS Sheet 188 map ref 785472; TQ7847], *Lord Raglan*: Doing well under current owners, comfortable, dark and cool in summer with two log fires in winter, good-sized garden, careful cooking by landlord from generous sandwiches through burgers and fish to delicious big steaks and puddings – good produce, much well kept Goachers and guests such as Shepherd Neame Spitfire and Youngs Special *(Anon)*

Stone in Oxney [TQ9427], *Crown*: Pleasant, old-fashioned country pub, decent choice of bar food, real ale *(Comus Elliott)*; *Stone Ferry*: Former smuggling pub by what used to be the landing for the Oxney ferry – simple old-fashioned cottage with no fuss or frills, pleasantly worn feel; wide choice of decent reasonably priced bar food, big garden *(Comus Elliott)*

☆ Stone Street [by-road Seal—Plaxtol – OS Sheet 188 map ref 573546; TQ5754], *Padwell Arms*: Small relaxed local by orchard, with good choice of genuinely home-cooked food, sensible prices, friendly staff, Badger, Hook Norton Old Hookey and changing guest ales, open fires *(Paul Brown, H W and R Owen)*

☆ Stowting [off B2068 N of M20 junction 11; TR1242], *Tiger*: Character country pub, partly 17th-c, with attractive unpretentious furniture, candles on tables, faded rugs on bare boards, three or more well kept real ales, Biddenden farm cider, good log fire, tables outside with occasional barbecues; well behaved children allowed, good jazz Mon *(Christopher M McNulty, Mr and Mrs R A Broadbent, LYM)*

Sundridge [TQ4854], *Lamb*: Pleasant roomy bar with decent food, cheerful landlord and staff *(R M Macnaughton)*

Tankerton [TR1267], *Tankerton Arms*: Busy convivial pub (bar area of former hotel, now flats) overlooking sea, informal and unsmart, with good food inc good vegetarian and vegan range, well kept beer inc Fullers London Pride, farm cider; pool, live music

Tues; picnic tables out on grass, plenty of play space, summer entertainer; open all day, cl Mon night *(Frank Ashbee)*

☆ Tenterden [High St; TQ8833], *Woolpack*: Striking 15th-c inn with several oak-beamed rooms inc family dining room, inglenook log fires, pleasant modest atmosphere, good generous home-cooked food, friendly service, well kept Whitbreads-related and other ales, decent coffee; open all day; comfortable bedrooms *(Thomas Nott)*

Tenterden [High St], *Eight Bells*: Old building doing well after refurbishment by newish licensee, well kept ales such as Fullers London Pride, Marstons Pedigree, Youngs Special, very promising food *(Colin Laffan)*; [St Michaels,¾ miles towards Biddenden; TQ8835], *Man of Kent*: Wayside country pub recently re-opened by very welcoming new licensees, good bar food with fresh veg in small dining area, garden with play area *(T Miller)*

Tonbridge [St Stephens St; TQ5946], *Punch & Judy*: Attractive surroundings, friendly family service, well kept beer, tasty food *(F Barwell)*

☆ Tunbridge Wells [Tea Garden Lane, Rusthall; TQ5639], *Beacon*: Comfortable sofas, stripped wood, relaxing atmosphere and imaginative food from filled french bread to Sun lunch, interesting wines; live music or theatre downstairs weekends; lovely views from terrace *(Hilary Dobbie)*

Tunbridge Wells [Spa Hotel, Mt Ephraim], *Equestrian Bar*: Stylish and comfortable bar with unusual equestrian floor-tile painting and steeplechasing pictures, good polite helpful service, fine choice of bar food inc excellent bangers and mash, well kept real ales; hotel lounge takes overflow; bedrooms *(E G Parish, Mrs R D Knight, LYM)*; [Chapel Pl/Castle Sq], *Grapevine*: Handy for Pantiles, new management doing good food inc Thai dishes in refurbished cellar restaurant (booking essential Sat night), good range of wines by the glass *(Mrs H Dobbie)*; [The Common], *Mount Edgcumbe*: Pleasantly refurbished bar with lots of bricks, hops and wood, good views over the common, good choice of food inc unusual dishes, obliging service; bedrooms *(Hilary Dobbie, LYM)*; [Mount Ephraim], *Royal Wells*: Well lit hotel bar with comfortable settees and chairs, cosy corners, well kept real ales, good food in lunchtime brasserie – outstanding value, good service by pleasant young staff; bedrooms *(Mr and Mrs Passmore, Chris Rasmussen)*;

Ulcombe [The Street; TQ8548], *Harrow*: Warm and friendly, appealing choice of good value food, good range of real ale and malt whiskies *(D Crofts)*

Under River [SE of Sevenoaks, off B245; TQ5551], *White Rock*: Friendly two-bar pub with several real ales such as Adnams Broadside, impressive choice of good value food, chatty landlord, interesting bar games as well as pool and bar billiards; good big garden, not far from Ightham Mote *(Jenny and Brian Seller, Sue Lee)*

☆ Warren Street [just off A20 at top of North

Downs – OS Sheet 189 map ref 926529; TQ9253], *Harrow*: Quiet and comfortable dining pub neatly extended around 16th-c low-beamed core, generous above-average food, well kept Shepherd Neame and a guest beer on handpump, flowers and candles, big woodburner, faint piped music; restaurant (not Sun evening, and there may be some inflexibility of choice for large parties at busy times) with attractive conservatory extension; good bedrooms, on Pilgrims Way *(Mary and Peter Clark, Wayne Brindle, Comus Elliott, Colin McKerrow, BB)*

☆ Wateringbury [Livesey St, Red Hill; TQ6853], *North Pole*: Small country pub with unusual range of reasonably priced tasty food, friendly staff, well kept beers; beautful garden *(F Barwell)*

☆ West Farleigh [B2010 off A26 Tonbridge—Maidstone; TQ7152], *Tickled Trout*: Good food esp fish in pleasant bar and attractive dining room, well kept Whitbreads-related ales, fast friendly service; Medway views (esp from garden), path down to river with good walks *(E D Bailey, Dr S Willavoys, E D Bailey, LYM)*

Westerham [Grays Rd, Hawley Corner (A233 to Biggin Hill); TQ4454], *Spinning Wheel*: Well appointed Brewers Fayre pub-restaurant, open all day, with good food, pleasant waitresses, family dining room, facilities for disabled *(E G Parish)*

☆ Wingham [Canterbury Rd; TR2457], *Dog*: Medieval beams, lots of character, good range of Whitbreads-related ales, good-sized wine glasses, good food, friendly service, landlord in good voice; comfortable bedrooms *(M A Watkins, Frank Ashbee)*

Wootton [TR2246], *Endeavour*: Quiet pub with pretty garden in sleepy village *(Martin Hickes)*

☆ Worth [The Street; TR3356], *St Crispin*: Friendly and relaxed low-ceilinged refurbished pub with well kept Boddingtons Mild, Marstons Pedigree, Gales HSB, Shepherd Neame and changing guest beers, local farm cider, wide range of sensibly priced food in bar and restaurant, quick cheerful service, central log fire, charming large garden with barbecue; lovely village position not far from beach *(Keith Sanham, Jim Burton)*

Wrotham [signed 1¼ miles from M20, junction 2; TQ6159], *Bull*: Welcoming helpful service in attractive 14th-c inn with good food, log fires, well kept Whitbreads-related ales, decent wines; children welcome, separate restaurant; comfortable bedrooms, huge breakfasts, attractive village *(Pierre Haddad, L T Lionet, LYM)*

☆ Wye [signed off A28 NE of Ashford; TR0546], *Tickled Trout*: Good summer family pub with lots of tables and occasional barbecues on pleasant riverside lawn, spacious conservatory/restaurant; clean tidy modernised rustic-style bar with usual bar food, Whitbreads-related ales; children welcome *(LM, Stephen Brown, Martin Hickes, LYM)*

☆ Yalding [Yalding Hill; TQ7050], *Walnut Tree*: Brightly lit beamed bar on several levels with inglenook and interesting pictures, welcoming staff, good bar food inc some unusual dishes, wide restaurant choice, Fremlins, Harveys and Wadworths 6X; bedrooms *(C R and M A Starling, Mr and Mrs P Brocklebank, Dr S Willavoys)*

Children welcome means the pub says it lets children inside without any special restriction. If it allows them in, but to restricted areas such as an eating area or family room, we specify this. Some pubs may impose an evening time limit.

Lancashire

*Pubs currently doing particularly well here include the distinctive Eagle &
Child at Bispham Green (its interesting food gains it one of our Food
Awards this year – and the accolade of Lancashire Dining Pub of the Year),
the Old Rosins tucked away near Darwen, that unique building the
Philharmonic in Liverpool, the civilised and friendly Inn at Whitewell
(starting extensive work on the public bar), and the New Inn at Yealand
Conyers (excellent food). The Moorcock at Blacko, using its own hill lamb in
the food, now has bedrooms – saving a tortuous drive home at night. The
Lass o' Gowrie in Manchester has joined Whitbreads' chain of Hogshead
real ale pubs, and seems to have been making the most of its possibilities.
The Royal Oak in Manchester, so famous for its cheeses, has a new landlord;
we've detected no change in the quality. Two other Manchester cheese pubs,
the trendier Dukes 92 and Mark Addy, have swapped their managers, and
the change seems to be working well for both. The landlady of the
Devonshire Arms in Mellor has extended its garden, and her Monday
suppers are proving very popular. The Wheatsheaf at Raby has a very
welcoming new landlord, making worthwhile changes. Sadly the Stalybridge
Station Buffet, a long-standing main entry, finally lost its battle against
Railtrack redevelopment plans and closed in the summer of 1996. In the
Lucky Dip section at the end of the chapter, pubs to note particularly (most
of them already inspected and approved by us) include the Coach & Horses
at Bolton by Bowland, Crown & Thistle above Darwen, Globe in
Dukinfield, Strawbury Duck near Entwistle, Farmers Arms at Heskin Green,
Irby Mill at Irby, Ship at Lathom, Cains Brewery Tap in Liverpool, Robin
Hood at Mawdesley and Hark to Bounty at Slaidburn. There's an excellent
choice of pubs in Manchester, particularly for people with a taste for real ale
– who are also catered for well in Preston and Stockport. Incidentally, please
note that we include in this chapter those places around Stockport which
have for the last couple of decades been absorbed into the Greater
Manchester area – and those parts of the Wirral which were at the same time
'pinched' from Cheshire by Merseyside. Food and drinks prices are in general
most attractive in Lancashire, with the Black Dog at Belmont standing out
on both counts (it gains our Bargain Award symbol this year for its cheap
food), and the Manchester brewery Holts setting a splendid example of
keeping drinks prices really low in its tied pubs. In the general run of
Lancashire pubs, drinks cost around 30p less than in comparable places in
the south of England.*

Post Office address codings confusingly give the impression that some pubs are
in Lancashire when they're really in Yorkshire (which is where we list them).

nr BALDERSTONE (Lancs) SD6332 Map 7

Myerscough Hotel

Whalley Rd, Salmesbury; A59 Preston—Skipton, over 3 miles from M6 junction 31

A popular food stop at lunchtime, when it's usually busy with families, businessmen or workers from the British Aerospace plant across the road, this bustling 18th-c pub takes on a more traditionally pubby feel in the evenings, when the softly lit beamed bar has a pleasant relaxed and cottagey feel. There are well made and comfortable oak settles around dimpled copper or heavy cast-iron-framed tables, as well as nice pen and ink drawings of local scenes, a painting of the month by a local artist, and lots of brass and copper. The serving counter has a nice padded elbow rest, and dispenses well kept Robinsons Best and Mild and occasionally Hartleys XB on handpump, and several malt whiskies; darts, shove-ha'penny, dominoes, and fruit machine. Favourite meals on the good-sized menu include stilton and mushroom bake (£3.95) and home-made lamb balti (£4.95), and readers have this year also particularly praised the prawn sandwiches, stuffed sole, and vegetable pasta. The front room is no-smoking. There are picnic tables, bantams and their chicks, and rabbits in the garden. The pub is very handy for the M6. *(Recommended by Carl Travis, David Peakall, Mrs A L Stride, John and Pam Smith)*

Robinsons ~ Tenant John Pedder ~ Real ale ~ Meals and snacks (12-2, 6.30-8.30) ~ (01254) 812222 ~ Well behaved children in front room at mealtimes ~ Weds quiz night ~ Open 11.30-3, 5.30-11 ~ Bedrooms: /£45S

BELMONT (Lancs) SD6716 Map 7

Black Dog £

A675

Ever since we first mentioned that the friendly landlord of this characterful 18th-c farmhouse sometimes whistles along to the softly piped classical music, it seems almost as though readers have been going along specially to catch him in action. Apart from this, what makes the pub such an enduring favourite is the very good value food and drinks, with the well kept Holts Bitter still only £1.02 a pint. The original cheery and traditional small rooms are packed with antiques and bric-a-brac, from railwaymen's lamps, bedpans and chamber-pots to landscape paintings, as well as service bells for the sturdy built-in curved seats, rush-seated mahogany chairs, and coal fires. The atmosphere is perhaps best on a winter evening, especially if you're tucked away in one of the various snug alcoves, one of which used to house the village court. Twice a year they have a small orchestral concert, and on New Year's Day at lunchtime a Viennese concert. Very popular and generously served bar food includes home-made soup (£1; they do a winter broth with dumplings, £1.50), sandwiches from £1.30; steak barm cake £1.90), ploughman's (from £3.30), steak and kidney pie, scampi, gammon or lamb cutlets (£3.90), steaks (from £5.90), well liked salads with various fruits like grape, banana and strawberry, and daily specials like spinach and ricotta cheese lasagne (£4.50), swordfish steak in lemon and herb butter (£6), or venison in red wine (£6.50). We like the way they've kept it pubby by not taking bookings, but it does tend to fill up quickly so get there early for a table; there may be some delays to food service at busy times. An airy extension lounge with a picture window has more modern furnishings; morning coffee, darts, pool, shove-ha'penny, dominoes, cribbage, and fruit machine. From two long benches on the sheltered sunny side of the pub there are delightful views of the moors above the nearby trees and houses; there's a track from the village up Winter Hill and (from the lane to Rivington) on to Anglezarke Moor, and paths from the dam of the nearby Belmont Reservoir. *(Recommended by Andy Hazeldine, Brian Wainwright, Nick Wikeley, Iain Robertson, E M Walton, S R and A J Ashcroft, Gordon Tong, John and Pam Smith, Graham and Lynn Mason, Howard Bateman, Kevin Potts)*

Holts ~ Tenant James Pilkington ~ Real ale ~ Meals and snacks (not Mon or Tues evenings except for residents) ~ (01204) 811218 ~ Children welcome away from bar ~ Open 12-4, 7-11 ~ Bedrooms: £29.50B/£38B

BILSBORROW (Lancs) SD5139 Map 7

Owd Nells 🍺

Guy's Thatched Hamlet, St Michaels Road; at S end of village (which is on A6 N of Preston) take Myerscough College turn

Though this busy pub is the kind of place families flock to as part of a day out, it's still very much somewhere where people like to come for a decent pint – in fact this last year they've added a snug specifically for locals to do so. It's part of a thriving little complex called 'Guy's Thatched Hamlet', which with its expanding hotel, craft and teashops and so forth has transformed a previously neglected stretch of canal into quite a tourist attraction. The three or four spacious communicating rooms of the pub have an easy-going rustic feel, with their mix of brocaded button-back banquettes, stable-stall seating, library chairs and other seats, high pitched rafters at either end, and lower beams (and flagstones) by the bar counter in the middle; a couple of areas are no smoking. Children are made especially welcome; there may be free lollipops and bags of bread for feeding the ducks. Colourful seats out on the terrace, part of which is covered by a thatched roof; a small walled-in play area has a timber castle, and you can play cricket or boules. There may be Morris dancers out here on summer weekends. Generously served bar meals such as soup (£1.30), cheese and pickles (£2.95), steak sandwich (£4.25), ploughman's (£4.40), curried chicken (£4.60), half a BBQ chicken (£4.75), and steak and kidney pudding (£4.95), as well as afternoon sandwiches (from £2.50) and scones (£1.50) and evening finger snacks like fingers of breaded mozzarella with a chilli dip (£1.95), deep-fried sticks of celery (£2), or goujons of fresh fish with a dip (£2.95); children's menu (£2.25). Waitress service is prompt and professional even under pressure – it often gets busy, especially in school holidays. Well kept Whitbreads Castle Eden and weekly changing guests like Boddingtons, Flowers, Jennings, Mitchells, Marstons Pedigree, Timothy Taylors Landlord, and Wadworths 6X on handpump, several wines including a bargain house champagne, tea and cof..e; darts, dominoes, cribbage, shove ha'penny, video game, fruit machine, Connect-Four, and unobtrusive piped pop music. *(Recommended by Carl Travis, Bill and Steph Brownson, Mayur Shah, JWC, MC, Emma Darlington, Rosemarie Johnson, Sarah and Gary Goldson, Graham Bush, Bronwen and Steve Wrigley)*

Free house ~ Licensee Roy Wilkinson ~ Real ale ~ Meals and snacks (all day) ~ Next-door restaurant (all day inc Sun) ~ (01995) 640010/640020 ~ Children welcome ~ Live music Thurs and Fri evenings ~ Open 10.30-11; 10.30-10.30 Sun; cl 25 Dec ~ Bedrooms: £39B/£44B

BISPHAM GREEN (Lancs) SD4914 Map 7

Eagle & Child 🍽 🍺

Maltkiln Lane (Parbold—Croston rd), off B5246

Lancashire Dining Pub of the Year

Quail with rice in vine leaves with wild mushrooms is the kind of meal that readers have particularly enjoyed at this striking three-storey dark brick pub in the last year. Other imaginative daily specials include meals made with goat, alligator, ostrich, kangaroo, mahi-mahi, frogs' legs, goose, or buffalo, with plenty of fresh fish and game, and as the owner's family farm much of the land around Parbold, there may be well hung meat from their herd of pedigree Galloways. More orthodox dishes might include often unusual soups like mushroom and mixed pepper (£1.80), hot smoked fish and bacon brioche (£2.95), smoked chicken salad (£3.75), choice of oriental stir-fries (£4.75), steak and ale pie (£5.30), char-grilled chicken fillet with mascarpone sauce (£5.50), gammon (£5.65), and an interesting choice of cheeses (£2.50); children's meals. They have a curry night the last Monday of each month, for which booking is essential. Rebuilt in an attractively understated old-fashioned style, the civilised bar is largely open-plan, but well divided by stubs of walls. There are fine old stone fireplaces, oriental rugs and some coir matting on flagstones, old hunting prints and engravings, and a mix of individual furnishings including small oak chairs around tables in corners, and several handsomely carved antique oak settles – the finest apparently made partly from a 16th-c wedding bed-head. House plants stand on a big oak coffer. One area is no smoking. A particularly good range of well kept beers on handpump consists of Boddingtons, Coach House Gunpowder Dark Mild, Theakstons Best and Thwaites, with three or four changing guest ales such as Hanby Scorpio Porter, Timothy Taylors Landlord and Worth Alesman. Also farm cider, decent wines, and a good collection of malt whiskies. Friendly and interested service; maybe piped pop radio. There is a neat if not entirely orthodox bowling green behind (with croquet in summer), and the pub garden has recently been restored. Harry the dog is not the most sober individual (especially if there are hot-air balloons around). *(Recommended by Janet Lee, Tony Young, Mrs J Anderton, Mike Meadley, John and Diana Davies, James Cowell, Maurice and Gill McMahon, Tim Kent)*

Free house ~ Manager Monica Evans~ Real ale ~ Meals and snacks (12-2, 6-8.30 weekdays, till 9 Fri and Sat, and 12-8.30 Sun) ~ (01257) 462297 ~ Children in restaurant ~ Monthly live music night ~ Open 12-3, 5.30-11; 12-10.30 Sun

BLACKO (Lancs) SD8541 Map 7

Moorcock

A682; N of village towards Gisburn

One of the pleasures of visiting this isolated stone inn is its splendidly remote setting, high up on the moors, and now that they've started doing B&B we imagine it must be a wonderfully atmospheric spot to spend the night. Another draw has long been the well presented bar meals, all home-made by the landlady using fresh local produce; there's an increasing emphasis on the tasty daily specials, which might include a number of lamb dishes made with meat from their own flock. On a typical day you'll find dishes like their popular meat and potato pie (£4.50), leek and mushroom crumble (£4.95), haddock and smoked salmon mornay or lamb liver with Dubonnet and orange (£5.50), whole ham shank with mustard sauce (£5.95), rack of lamb with barbecue sauce (£6.95), duckling with orange (£7.50), and puddings like chocolate pecan pie or blackberry and apple tart (£2.50); most dishes are served with garlicky cream potatoes. The spaciously comfortable bar has a lofty ceiling, brass ornaments hanging from the cream walls, and breath-taking views from its big picture windows. Well kept Thwaites Bitter on handpump; efficient and cheery service. The attractively landscaped back garden is very busy at weekends, though quieter during the week; there's usually a goat, a couple of lambs, game cocks, and lots of white doves. The pub used to be a farmhouse and the landlord maintains the tradition, often out with his sheep around the Blacko Tower a mile or so across the moors. His collie puppies go to other working farms as far afield as Ireland, Canada and America. *(Recommended by Arthur and Margaret Dickinson, Gwen and Peter Andrews, B A Hayward, David Shillitoe, Mr and Mrs R Hebson, Bronwen and Steve Wrigley, J A Swanson, Roger and Christine Mash, K C Forman, Laura Darlington, Gianluca Perinetti, Wayne A Wheeler)*

Thwaites ~ Tenant Elizabeth Holt ~ Meals and snacks (till 10) ~ (01282) 614186 ~ Children welcome ~ Open 12-2, 6.30-11; 12-10.30 Sun; cl 25 Dec ~ Bedrooms: £15/£30

BLACKSTONE EDGE (Gtr Manchester) SD9716 Map 7

White House

A58 Ripponden—Littleborough, just W of B6138

Even in summer visitors to this imposing 17th-c pub can be greeted by swirling mists and wild moorland winds. It's spectacularly set 1,300 feet above sea level on the Pennine Way, with panoramic views stretching far off into the distance. The busy, welcoming and cheery main bar has a turkey carpet in front of a blazing coal fire and a large-scale map of the area (windswept walkers hardly know whether to head for the map or the fire first). The snug Pennine Room opens off here, with brightly coloured antimacassars on its small soft settees, and there's a new extension. A spacious room on the left has a big horseshoe window looking over the moors, as well as comfortable seating. Good helpings of homely bar food include vegetable soup (£1.30), sandwiches (from £2), cumberland sausage with egg (£3.50), steak and kidney pie, roast chicken breast or vegetarian quiche (£3.95), chilli, beef curry or lasagne (£4.50), daily specials (one reader enjoyed kangaroo not long before we went to press), and home-made apple pie (£1.25); children's meals (£1.50). Prompt friendly service. Two well kept beers on handpump such as Black Sheep, Moorhouses Pendle Witches Brew or Theakstons Best, farm cider, and malt whiskies; fruit machine. Muddy boots can be left in the long, enclosed porch. *(Recommended by M L and G Clarke, Geoffrey and Irene Lindley, Ron and Sheila Corbett, James Macrae; more reports please)*

Free house ~ Licensee Neville Marney ~ Real ale ~ Meals and snacks (11.30-2; 7-10) ~ (01706) 378456 ~ Children welcome till 9pm ~ Open 11.30-3, 7(6 Sat)-11

BRINDLE (Lancs) SD6024 Map 7

Cavendish Arms

3 miles from M6 junction 29; A6 towards Whittle le Woods then left on B5256

Though the current snugly civilised building dates back only 300 years or so, it's thought some sort of public house has stood on this peaceful spot since the 12th c. The friendly licensees are happy to chat about its history, which can turn up a few surprises – you might expect the intricate carvings and fascinating stained glass to be amongst the oldest features, but in fact both were comparatively recent additions. The glasswork has many colourful depictions of medieval warriors and minstrels, with the liveliest scenes commemorating a nasty skirmish between the Vikings and Anglo-Saxons that took place nearby in the year 937. Several cosy little rooms, each with quite a distinct character, ramble around a central servery, and there are lots of pictorial plates and Devonshire heraldic devices in plaster on the walls; comfortable seats, discreet flowery curtains. Well kept Burtonwood Best on handpump, and a good choice of malt whiskies; darts and dominoes. Simple bar food includes soup (£2), open sandwiches (£3.25), peppered prawns or home-made beef pie (£4), breaded haddock (£4.50), spinach and mushroom lasagne (£5), chicken balti (£6), and daily specials. There are white metal and plastic tables and chairs on a terrace by a rockery with a small water cascade, with another table on a small lawn behind. It's nicely set in a tranquil little village, and there's a handsome stone church across the road. They tell us the only days they close are when Blackburn Rovers are playing at home. *(Recommended by Jim and Maggie Cowell, Cyril Higgs, John and Pam Smith, K C Forman; more reports please)*

Burtonwood ~ Tenant Peter Bowling ~ Real ale ~ Meals and snacks (12-2, 5.30-9; not Sun evening) ~ Restaurant (not Sun evening) ~ (01254) 852912 ~ Children in restaurant ~ Open 11-2.30, 5.30-11; cl 25 Dec

CHIPPING (Lancs) SD6243 Map 7

Dog & Partridge ♀

Hesketh Lane; crossroads Chipping—Longridge with Inglewhite—Clitheroe, OS Sheet 103 map reference 619413

In attractive countryside between Longridge and Wolf Fell, this comfortable and relaxed dining pub has quite a snugly genteel feel, as well as consistently good home-made food. The choice typically includes dishes like sandwiches (from £2.25), soup (£2), ploughman's (£5.25), three vegetarian dishes like leek and mushroom crumble (£5.50), steak and kidney pie (£6.50), roast duckling or seasonal game (£7.50) and sirloin steak (£8); the home-made chips are particularly well liked and they do various fish and game specials – the roast pheasant is recommended. Parts of the building date back to 1515, though it's been much modernised since, with the eating space now spreading over into a nearby stable. The main lounge is comfortably furnished with small armchairs around fairly close-set low wood-effect tables on a blue patterned carpet, brown-painted beams, a good winter log fire, and multi-coloured lanterns; service is friendly and helpful. Tetleys and a weekly changing guest on handpump, over 40 wines, and a good range of malt whiskies; piped music. Jacket and tie are preferred in the restaurant. *(Recommended by Carl Travis, RJH, K C and B Forman)*

Free house ~ Licensee Peter Barr ~ Real ale ~ Meals and snacks (12-1.45, 7-9.45, not Sat evening unless prebooked) ~ Restaurant ~ (01995) 61201 ~ Children welcome ~ Open 12-3, 7-11; 12-10.30 Sun

CROSTON SD4818 (Lancs) Map 7

Black Horse 🍺 £

Westhead Road; A581 Chorley—Southport

It's the good range of well priced beers that stands out here; the owners also have the lease of two high-throughput Preston real ale pubs (Fox & Grapes and Market Tavern – see Lucky Dip), so bulk buying gives them a real edge over many other free houses. They keep Theakstons Best, XB and Mild on all the time, with another five rotated from a weekly changing batch of at least 16; recent selections have included unusual local brews like Cartmel Bowling Green, Judges Old Gavel Bender, Springhead Roaring Meg, Bank Top Freds Cap, and Border Old Kiln. The landlord usually offers tastes if you can't decide which to try. The bar has a quietly comfortable Victorianised appeal, with carpets, attractive wallpaper, solid upholstered wall settles and cast-iron-framed pub tables, a fireplace tiled in the Victorian manner and reproduction prints of that period (also a couple of nice 1950s street-scene prints by M Grimshaw), and a remarkable back dining room very heavily furnished in reproduction Victorian. Simple reliable bar food includes soup (£1.20), sandwiches (from £1.50), filled baked potatoes (£1.95), several low-priced meals for pensioners (£2.25 inc coffee), cheese and onion quiche (£2.95), breaded haddock or home-made steak pie (£3.40), gammon and egg (£3.75), and daily specials; children's meals (£1.50). Darts, pool, cribbage, dominoes, fruit machine, juke box, maybe TV. There are picnic tables outside, and a good solid safely railed-off play area; the pub has its own crown bowls green and boules pitch (boules available from the bar). *(Recommended by John Fazakerley, C A Hall; more reports please)*

Free house ~ Licensees John and Anne Welsh ~ Real ale ~ Meals and snacks (12-2.30, 6-8) ~ Restaurant ~ (01772) 600338 ~ Children welcome ~ Open 11-11; 12-10.30 Sun

nr DARWEN (Lancs) SD6922 Map 7

Old Rosins 🍺

Pickup Bank, Hoddlesden; from B6232 Haslingden—Belthorn, turn off towards Edgeworth opposite the Grey Mare – pub then signposted off to the right; OS Sheet 103 map reference 722227

This attractively set hotel isn't the easiest place to find, so it's something of a shock on arriving to see how many other people take the trouble to track it down. Their reasons for doing so quickly become clear – particularly friendly staff, a good pubby atmosphere, and lovely views over the moors and down into the wooded valley. The open-plan bar is comfortably furnished with red plush built-in button-back banquettes, and stools and small wooden chairs around dark cast-iron-framed tables. Lots of mugs, whisky-water jugs and so forth hang from the high joists, while the walls are decorated with small prints, plates and old farm tools; there's also a good log fire. Parts of the bar and restaurant are no smoking. Well kept Boddingtons, Flowers Original, Marstons Pedigree and Theakstons Old Peculier on handpump or tapped from the cask, plenty of malt whiskies, and coffee; maybe piped music. Served all day (right through till 10 o'clock), the good value bar food includes home-made soup (£1.20), sandwiches (from £1.85; open sandwiches from £3.45) and ploughman's (£2.95), vegetable spring rolls (£3.45), salads or home-made pizzas (from £3.95), freshly battered cod (£4.25), delicious beef in Old Peculier (£4.75), and sirloin steak (£7.25); puddings (from £1.70), and children's meals. There are picnic tables on a spacious crazy-paved terrace. Readers have enjoyed their murder weekends and other themed evenings. *(Recommended by Andy Hazeldine, Charlotte Wrigley, K and B Forman, Steven and Denise Waugh, Vicky and David Sarti, Carl Travis, Gary and Sarah Goldson, G L Tong, Bronwen and Steve Wrigley, Graham and Lynn Mason, Laura Darlington, Gianluca Perinetti)*

Free house ~ Licensee Bryan Hankinson ~ Real ale~ Meals and snacks (all day) ~ Restaurant ~ (01254) 771264 ~ Children welcome ~ Open 11-11; 12-10.30 Sun ~ Bedrooms: £39.50B/£49.50B

DOWNHAM (Lancs) SD7844 Map 7

Assheton Arms

From A59 NE of Clitheroe turn off into Chatburn (signposted); in Chatburn follow Downham signpost; OS Sheet 103 map reference 785443

Even early in the week this well-preserved old place fills up fast, so if you're coming to sample the good fresh fish specials it's worth arriving early. The best choice is at the weekend, when they'll usually have delicious potted Morecambe Bay shrimps (£3.95), smoked salmon, gravadlax or roast smoked salmon (£4.95), grilled plaice (£6.95), monkfish with mixed peppercorns and brandy, scallops, smoked fish platter, sea bass and possibly oysters, crab and lobster. A decent range of other generously served bar meals includes tasty home-made ham and vegetable soup (£1.95), sandwiches (not Saturday evening or Sunday lunchtime; from £2.95), stilton pâté (£3.25), cauliflower and mushroom provençale or home-made steak and kidney pie (£5.50), venison and bacon casserole (£6.95), steaks (from £9.95), puddings including a good toffee gateau and French lemon tart (£2.25), and children's dishes (£2.75); the chips are excellent. The rambling, beamed and red-carpeted bar has olive plush-cushioned winged settles around attractive grainy oak tables, some cushioned window seats, and two grenadier busts on the mantelpiece over a massive stone fireplace that helps to divide the separate areas; one area is no smoking. Well kept Boddingtons, Flowers Original and Whitbreads Castle Eden under light blanket pressure; decent wines by the glass or bottle; piped music. The pub is charmingly set in a stonebuilt village spreading along a duck-inhabited stream; picnic tables outside look across to the church. *(Recommended by Alan Griffiths, M Joyner, Mr and Mrs J Tyrer, Bronwen and Steve Wrigley, John Fazakerley, K C Forman; more reports please)*

Whitbreads ~ Tenants David and Wendy Busby ~ Real ale ~ Meals and snacks (till 10pm) ~ (01200) 441227 ~ Children welcome ~ Open 12-3, 7-11

GARSTANG (Lancs) SD4845 Map 7

Th'Owd Tithebarn ★

Signposted off Church Street; turn left off one-way system at Farmers Arms

We're told that only the York Museum has a bigger collection of antique farming equipment than this beautifully set creeper-covered canalside barn. It's a fascinating and quite unique old building, in some ways a bit like an old-fashioned farmhouse kitchen parlour. There's an old kitchen range, prints of agricultural equipment on the walls, stuffed animals and birds, and pews and glossy tables spaced out on the flagstones under the high rafters. Waitresses in period costume with mob-caps complete the vintage flavour. The site gets busy, and is something of a tourist attraction, with the Lancaster Canal Museum and Information Centre upstairs. Sitting on the big stone terrace is particularly pleasant, with plenty of ducks and boats wending their way along the water. Under the new managers bar food includes soup (£1.95), filled cottage loaves (from £3.25, lunchtime only), cauliflower and macaroni cheese or prune, rice and apricot casserole (£4.95), beef stew or hotpot (£5.25), a choice of roasts (£5.30), and children's meals. They do afternoon teas in summer. Well kept Mitchells Original and Lancaster Bomber on handpump; lots of country wines, dominoes, and a fine antique bar billiards machine. *(Recommended by Vicky and David Sarti, Mike and Wendy Proctor, Peter and Audrey Dowsett, Cyril Higgs, Dorothee and Dennis Glover, Rosemarie Johnson, Winifrede D Morrison, MJVK)*

Mitchells ~ Managers Gordon Hutchinson and Jo Thurogood ~ Real ale ~ Meals and snacks ~ Restaurant ~ (01995) 604486 ~ Children in restaurant ~ Open 11-11; 12-10.30 Sun; winter opening 11-3, 7-11

GOOSNARGH (Lancs) SD5537 Map 7

Bushells Arms ⊕ ♀

4 miles from M6 junction 32; A6 towards Garstang, turn right at Broughton traffic lights (the first ones you come to), then left at Goosnargh Village signpost (it's pretty insignificant – the turn's more or less opposite Whittingham Post Office)

It's not just customers who appreciate the licencees' knowledge of food and wine – the Bests regularly contribute columns to newspapers and magazines, and they were recently asked to write a book about pub catering. They really do put tremendous care and attention into their meals, with the highlight the constantly changing specials menu. What's available each day is determined by the availability of good fresh ingredients, often local, but there's usually quite a Mediterranean tendency, so lots of olive oil, beans, garlic and olives. As well as unusual soups like lovage or Dutch pea with ham and garlic sausage, recent dishes have included local black pudding (£1.50), Mediterranean beanpot casserole (£5), thai-style lemon chicken with oriental vegetables, Syrian potato omelette or lamb liver with onions, sausage and bacon in a rich sherry gravy (£5.50), and fresh salmon marinated in lime, balsamic vinegar, garlic and tarragon then poached (£6). The permanent menu includes spring rolls, samosas or falafel (£2), steak and kidney pie (£5.50), and salmon and broccoli parcel, stifatho (a Greek beef stew), or chicken fillet filled with smoked bacon, asparagus, grated cheese in hollandaise sauce and wrapped in puff pastry (£6). Crisp and fresh vegetables include tasty potatoes done with garlic, cream, peppers and parmesan, and there's a good range of puddings like rhubarb and strawberry crumble or orange bread and butter pudding (£2); they do a couple of children's dishes (£1.75). Fresh fish is delivered daily from Fleetwood. There may be delays at peak periods (mainly evenings and weekends), but service is friendly. The spacious, modernised bar has lots of snug bays, each holding not more than two or three tables and often faced with big chunks of sandstone (plastic plants and spotlit bare boughs heighten the rockery effect); also soft red plush button-back banquettes, with flagstones by the bar; fruit machine. Two areas are no smoking. The well chosen and constantly developing wine list is excellent, with some New World ones and several half bottles, as well as changing wines of the month; the list gives useful notes to help you choose which bottle you want. Also well kept Boddingtons and Tetleys on handpump, and several malt whiskies. Tables in a little back garden, and hanging baskets at the front. The signal for opening the doors at lunchtime is the tolling of the church clock, and haunted Chingle Hall is not far away. *(Recommended by Carl Travis, P H Boot, Neil Townend, Esther and John Sprinkle, David Shillitoe, RTM, JCM, Barry Lynch, Sarah and Gary Goldson)*

Whitbreads ~ Tenants David and Glynis Best ~ Real ale ~ Meals and snacks (till 10pm) ~ (01772) 865235 ~ Very well behaved children in eating area of bar until 9pm ~ Open 12-3, 6-11; cl 25 Dec and occasional Mondays

Horns ♀

Pub signed from village, about 2 miles towards Chipping below Beacon Fell

Older than its brightly mock-Tudor facade suggests, this nicely set former coaching inn has an enjoyably thriving atmosphere. The polished but snug rooms haven't changed much since they were built, and all have log fires in winter. Dotted around are a number of colourful flower displays – a good indication of the care and effort the friendly licensees put into running the place. Beyond the lobby, the pleasant front bar opens into attractively decorated middle rooms with antique and other period furnishings. At lunchtime it's mostly popular with people enjoying the tasty bar food such as wholesome soups (£1.95), beautifully presented sandwiches (£2.50), ploughman's (£3.75), steak and kidney pie (£5.75), plaice or roast pheasant (£5.95), a daily roast (the beef is well liked) and fresh fish of the day like halibut or scallops, and sirloin steak with mushrooms (£9.50), all nicely served with freshly cooked, piping hot chips; home-made puddings like sherry trifle or an excellent sticky toffee pudding (£2.75). A very good range of up to ten or so wines by the glass, an extensive wine list, a fine choice of malt whiskies, but keg Tetleys; cheerful and helpful young staff, piped music. *(Recommended by Sarah Bradbury; more reports please)*

Free house ~ Licensees Elizabeth Jones and Mark Woods ~ Meals and snacks (not Mon lunch) ~ Restaurant ~ (01772) 865230 ~ Children welcome if dining ~ Open 11.30-3, 6.30-11; cl Mon lunchtime ~ Bedrooms: £45B/£70B

LIVERPOOL SJ4395 Map 7

Philharmonic ★ ◗

36 Hope Street; corner of Hardman Street

Theatre-goers, students, Scousers and tourists all blend perfectly into the cheery bustle at this marvellously elegant late Victorian gin palace, properly called the Philharmonic Dining Rooms. There's a wonderful opulence to the exquisitely decorated rooms, at the heart of which is a mosaic-faced serving counter, from where heavily carved and polished mahogany partitions radiate under the intricate plasterwork high ceiling. The echoing main hall is decorated with stained glass including contemporary portraits of Boer War heroes such as Baden-Powell and Lord Roberts, rich panelling, a huge mosaic floor, and copper panels of musicians in an alcove above the fireplace. More stained glass in one of the little lounges declares Music is the universal language of mankind and backs this up with illustrations of musical instruments; there are two plushly comfortable sitting rooms. Lavatory devotees may be interested to know that the famous gents' are original 1890s Rouge Royale by Twyfords: all red marble and glinting mosaics, some readers have long felt these alone earn the pub its star. Well kept Ind Coope Burton, Jennings, Marstons Pedigree, Tetleys Bitter and Imperial, and Walkers Best on handpump, some malt whiskies and cask cider; fruit machine, trivia and juke box. Good value home-made bar food includes soup (£1.25), filled baguettes (£2.15, hot £2.35), and various well-priced dishes like lasagne, steak and kidney pie or haddock (all £3.95), gammon, cajun chicken or cod and prawn pie (£4.95), and mixed grill (£8.45); they do a very well-priced three-course Sunday lunch. Friendly service. *(Recommended by Sue and Bob Ward, Thomas Nott, Paul and Ursula Randall, Alice McLerran, B Adams, John O'Donnell, Andrew Stephenson, M W Turner)*

Walkers (Carlsberg Tetleys) ~ Manager Phil Ross ~ Real ale ~ Meals and snacks (not Sun eve) ~ Restaurant ~ (0151) 709 1163 ~ Children in eating area of bar ~ Weds quiz night, karaoke on Tues ~ Open 11.30-11

LYTHAM (Lancs) SD3627 Map 7

Taps ◗ £

A584 S of Blackpool; Henry Street – in centre, one street in from West Beach

Chances are most of the beers you've heard of and quite a few of the ones you haven't have passed through the handpumps of this cheery drinker's pub. The enthusiastic landlord is forever hunting out new beers, and every time he changes a barrel it's to something different; so far he's had over 1,000. There are usually 10 constantly changing ales on at a time, with maybe Everards Chesters Mild, Flowers Original, Marstons Pedigree, Colonel Pepper's Lemon Ale, Timothy Taylors Landlord, and Wadworths IPA; Boddingtons is more or less a regular fixture, and they usually have some country wines. The Victorian-style bare-boarded bar has a really friendly and unassuming atmosphere, as well as plenty of stained glass decoration in the windows, with depictions of fish and gulls reflecting the pub's proximity to the beach; also captain's chairs in bays around the sides, open fires, and a coal-effect gas fire between two built-in bookcases at one end. As well as a TV for special sporting events there's a bit of a rugby theme, with old photographs and portraits of rugby stars on the walls; piped music, shove-ha'penny, dominoes, fruit machine and juke box. Anyone who's taken sampling the beers a little too seriously will appreciate the seat belts on the bar stools, and the headrest in the gents'. The home-made bar food is simple but good value, with the most popular dishes including a good pea and ham soup or hot roast beef sandwich (£2.25), cold platters, beer sausages and mash (£2.50), and daily specials like steak and ale pie or chicken curry; the ham and beef is home-cooked. There are no meals on Sunday, but instead they have free platters of food laid out, with tasty morsels like black pudding, chicken wings or minted lamb. There are a few seats outside. *(Recommended by Michael and Alison Leyland, Paul Swan, Carl Travis, Andy Hazeldine, Simon Barber, Sue Holland, Dave Webster, Rosemarie Johnson)*

Whitbreads ~ Manager Ian Rigg ~ Real ale ~ Lunchtime meals and snacks (no menu on Sun, free snacks only then) ~ (01253) 736226 ~ Children in eating area during meal times ~ Open 11-11; 11-10.30 Sun

MANCHESTER SJ8498 Map 7

Dukes 92 £

Castle Street, below the bottom end of Deansgate

Some of the splendid value cheeses at this lively place are delightfully obscure – one reader recently enjoyed a Lancashire with blackcurrants in. It's under the same ownership as the well established Mark Addy (see below), and has a similar excellent choice of cheeses and pâtés, served in huge helpings with granary bread (£3.20). They also serve a soup in winter, filled baked potatoes and toasted sandwiches (from £2.50), and various salads. You'll find it right in the heart of old industrial Manchester in an area of vigorous redevelopment by the site of the original Roman fort; don't be disheartened by the hulking old warehouses, smoky railway viaduct and disused canals you pass to get there – this neck of the woods is rapidly becoming rather trendy. The spacious building has been stylishly converted from old canal-horse stables, with black wrought-iron work contrasting boldly with whitewashed bare plaster walls, a handsome marble-topped bar, and an elegant spiral staircase to an upper room and balcony. Up here are some modern director's chairs, but down in the main room the fine mix of furnishings is mainly rather Edwardian in mood, with one particularly massive table, and chaises-longues and other comfortable seats. Well kept Boddingtons and a couple of rotated guests on handpump, along with the Belgian wheat beer Hoegarden, and quite a few Belgian fruit beers; decent wines and a large selection of malts, friendly staff; piped music. There are some tables out by the canal basin which opens into the bottom lock of the Rochdale Canal. On bank holiday weekends events in the forecourt may include jazz and children's theatre, and there's a permanent theatre in the function room. *(Recommended by Carl Travis, Brian Wainwright, Liz, Wendy and Ian Phillips, Dr M Bridge)*

Free house ~ Licensee Sara Louise Ratcliffe ~ Real ale ~ Snacks (all day) ~ (0161) 839 8646 ~ Children welcome away from bar till 7pm ~ Theatre in the function room, and on outside stage on bank holiday weekends ~ Open 11.30-11; 12-10.30 Sun

Lass o' Gowrie ◨ £

36 Charles Street; off Oxford Street at BBC

A few changes at this simple and characterful place over the last year, but nothing to alter its appeal or remarkable popularity. At really busy periods (usually only Friday and Saturday nights during term times), the bar may be so full of good-natured university students you'll have to drink your own-brew pint on the pavement outside in true city-centre pub style, and even at other times you're unlikely to have it to yourself. Revamped this year to give a more open look, the long bar with its gas lighting and bare floorboards is one of the distinctive things about the place, but it's the malt-extract beers that people like best. Named for their original gravity (strength), LOG35 is quite lightly flavoured and slips down very easily, while LOG42 is a little meatier. Seats around a sort of glass cage give a view of the brewing process in the micro-brewery downstairs in the cellar. There's also well kept Fuggles IPA, Whitbreads Castle Eden and several guest beers on handpump, and Old Hazy cider; it might take some while to get served at busy periods. Hop sacks drape the ceiling, and the bar has big windows in its richly tiled arched brown facade, as well as mainly stripped walls. As the pub is now part of Whitbread's Hogshead brand, the good value bar food is the same as you'll find at others in the chain: big filled baps (from £1.60), basket meals like cheesy vegetable grills or spring rolls (from £2.50), a good choice of sausages or steak and kidney pie (£2.85), fish and chips (£3.05), gammon with egg or pineapple (£3.25), and lasagne (£3.75); efficient cheery service. The volume of the piped pop music really depends on the youth of the customers at the time; fruit machine, video game. *(Recommended by Nigel and Amanda Thorp, Clare Wilson, Paul Carter, B Adams, Ian Phillips, Dr and Mrs A K Clarke, S R and A J Ashcroft)*

Own brew (Whitbreads) ~ Manager Joe Fylan ~ Real ale ~ Lunchtime meals and snacks ~ (0161) 273 6932 ~ Children over 2 in small side room and raised area until 6pm ~ Open 11.30-11; 12-10.30 Sun; cl 25 Dec

Marble Arch £ 🍺

73 Rochdale Rd (A664), Ancoats; corner of Gould St, just E of Victoria Station

Though the striking decor is a major draw in its own right, it's the range of beers that has long been the most impressive feature at this late Victorian drinking house. Under the new managers the choice isn't quite so huge as we've known it, but the ales are as well chosen and kept as ever. You'll usually find Hopwood Bitter (nicely priced at less than the regional average), Marstons Pedigree, Oak Wobbly Bob, and four or five regularly changing guests like Goachers, Mitchells, Titanic Captain Smith and Lifeboat, and Youngs Special. They also keep a good choice of bottled beers (including Belgian Trappist beers), Biddenden cider, and a selection of country wines. There's a magnificently restored lightly barrel-vaulted high ceiling, and extensive marble and tiling, amongst which the frieze advertising various spirits and the chimney breast above the carved wooden mantelpiece particularly stand out. A mosaic floor slopes down to the bar, and some of the walls are partly stripped back to the glazed brick. Remarkably low-priced bar food, served in the lounge extension at the back, includes soup (£1), sandwiches (£2), stuffed peppers (£2.50), all-day breakfast or chilli (£2.75), vegetable stir-fry or home-made lasagne (£3.50), and beef stroganoff (£4.50); they have a monthly curry night when you can eat as much as you like for £3. Table skittles, chess, cards, pinball, fruit machine, juke box and lively background music. The Laurel and Hardy Preservation Society meet here on the third Wednesday of the month and show old films. *(Recommended by Richard Lewis, PGP, Paul Carter)*

Free house ~ Managers Mark and Mary Dade ~ Real ale ~ Meals and snacks 12-9 (not Sun) ~ (0161) 832 5914 ~ Children welcome ~ Live music Sat evening ~ Open 12-11; 7-10.30 Sun (closed lunchtime); closed Bank Hol lunchtimes, and all day 25/26 Dec and 1 Jan

Mark Addy ♀ £

Stanley Street, Salford, Manchester 3 (if it's not on your street map head for New Bailey St); look out not for a pub but for what looks like a smoked glass modernist subway entrance

They automatically hand out doggy bags with the huge chunks of cheese sold here, and a good thing too – don't be surprised if you can't finish your helping. At any one time they have a choice of up to 50 different varieties from all over Britain and Europe, served with granary bread (£3.20), and there's also a range of pâtés including a vegetarian one (£3.20), and maybe winter soup. Readers have this year also been impressed by huge pieces of chocolate cake. Well converted from waiting rooms for boat passengers, the pub has quite a civilised and trendy atmosphere, especially in the flower-filled waterside courtyard from where you can watch the home-bred ducks. Inside, the series of barrel-vaulted red sandstone bays is furnished with russet or dove plush seats and upholstered stalls, wide glassed-in brick arches, cast-iron pillars, and a flagstone floor; piped music. Well kept Boddingtons and a couple of changing guests like Marstons Pedigree or Timothy Taylors Landlord on handpump; quite a few wines too, with a sign by the entrance recommending which go best with particular cheeses. They get very busy, so it is worth getting there early, and they prefer smart dress. Named after a 19th-c man who rescued over 50 people from drowning in the River Irwell outside, the pub is run by the same people as another Manchester main entry, Dukes 92 (see above); the two recently swapped licensees. *(Recommended by Carl Travis, Tom McLean, JJW, CMW, Paul Carter, M A Cameron, John O'Donnell, Dr M Bridge)*

Free house ~ Licensee Thomas Joyce ~ Real ale ~ Snacks (all day) ~ (0161) 832 4080 ~ Children welcome away from bar till 8pm ~ Open 11.30-11; 12-10.30 Sun

Royal Oak £

729 Wilmslow Road, Didsbury

Manchester's other great cheese pub has a new landlord this year, but that's the only thing that's changed. He's had plenty of time to learn what it is people like about the Oak – for the last 15 years he's held the tenancy of a pub 300 yards down the road. The food consists mainly of a vast array of cheeses, served with a substantial chunk of bread, salad and extras such as beetroot and pickled onions (£3 for a choice of two cheeses). It's unusual to be served with less than a pound of even the rarer ones, so take-away bags are provided; there are also pâtés and winter soup. Well kept Batemans Mild, Marstons Bitter and Pedigree and a fortnightly changing guest beer on handpump, and some sherries and ports from the wood; efficient, friendly service. The interior was very badly damaged by fire a few years ago, but the busy bar has been so well restored you'd never know; antique theatre bills and so forth cover the walls. There are some seats outside (though the exterior is pretty ordinary). *(Recommended by J C T Tan, Jim Cowell, Christopher Cannon, Roger and Christine Mash, Simon Barber, Mark Hydes, Ian Phillips, Brian and Anna Marsden, John O'Donnell, Yolanda Henry, P Yearsley; reports on the new regime please)*

Marstons ~ Tenant Vincent Crolla ~ Real ale ~ Lunchtime snacks (not weekends or bank holidays) ~ (0161) 434 4788 ~ Children over 14 allowed 12-2 ~ Open 11-11; 12-10.30 Sun; cl evening 25 Dec

Sinclairs 🍺 £

Shambles Square, Manchester 3; in Arndale Centre between Deansgate and Corporation Street, opposite Exchange Street

Part of the charm of this timeless 18th-c pub lies in the complete incongruity of its surroundings. It stands proud and unflinching against a tide of modern development, and inside too it keeps its old-fashioned style and atmosphere intact. The delightfully old-fashioned interior is split up into lots of snugs and dining areas, the interesting rooms have low ceilings, squared oak panelling, and traditional furnishings such as small-backed stools that run along a tall old-fashioned marble-topped eating bar. The larger room upstairs has low old-fashioned wall settles, a scrolly old leather settee, pictures of old Manchester, and good home-made bar food such as carrot and orange soup (£1.10), sandwiches (from £1.25), ploughman's (£3), quiche (£3.40), steak pie (£3.60), chicken, leek and cider bake (£3.75), and lamb and apricot casserole or beef and oyster pie (£3.95); on Sunday they only have a choice of roasts, or you can have a three-course lunch with a glass of wine for £7.25. Above the servery a sign still has the pub's full name, Sinclairs Oyster Bar. The small dining room is no smoking. Friendly welcoming service from neatly uniformed barmaids. Very well kept and well priced Sam Smiths OB on handpump; chess, dominoes, cribbage, draughts, fruit machine, and piped music. There are picnic tables outside in the pedestrians-only square, on the fringes of the area devastated by the IRA bomb last summer. *(Recommended by John Fazakerley, E M Walton, Tom McLean, John O'Donnell, Keith Stevens, John and Pam Smith)*

Sam Smiths ~ Manager Darren Coles ~ Real ale ~ Meals and snacks (12-8 weekdays, 11-3 Sat, 12-5 Sun) ~ (0161) 834 0430 ~ Children welcome till 7pm ~ Nearby parking difficult ~ Open 11-11; 12-10.30 Sun

MARPLE (Gtr Manchester) SJ9588 Map 7

Romper

Ridge End; from A626 Stockport Road in Marple, coming in from Manchester side, look out for Church Lane on your right (third turning after railway bridge and just after a garage); once in Church Lane, follow The Ridge signposts; OS Sheet 109 map reference 965966

Standing alone on the steep side of the Goyt valley, this beautifully positioned country dining pub has a fairly smart feel to its oak-beamed rooms. Reliable and generously served home-made bar food includes lots of daily specials such as pork fillets with pepper sauce or char-grilled duckling breast, as well as lunchtime open sandwiches (not Sunday) with freshly sliced turkey, ham and beef, ploughman's (£4.95), six vegetarian dishes (from £5.75), steak and kidney pie or cumberland sausage (£5.95), sirloin steak (£8.95), mixed grill or T-bone steak (£12.95), and home-made fruit pies (£1.95); fresh haddock on Fridays (£5.95), and Sunday roast (£5.95). The four knocked-through rooms have antique settles around the many tables, soft lighting and gentle piped music. A fairly large raised terrace area has good views. Well kept Boddingtons, Marstons Pedigree, Theakstons Old Peculier and Timothy Taylors Landlord on handpump, with about 30 malt whiskies and a decent wine list; efficient service from friendly staff. They don't discourage children, but they're certainly not setting out to be a family pub. There's a pretty walk down towards the Peak Forest Canal from a car park attractively set in hilly common, 100 yards along the Marple road. (*Recommended by C H and P Stride, Meg and Colin Hamilton, Roger and Christine Mash, Bill Sykes, Gordon, Andrew and Ruth Triggs*)

Free house ~ Licensees Geoff and Patty Barnett ~ Real ale ~ Meals and snacks (till 10 Fri and Sat; all day Sun) ~ (0161) 427 1354 ~ Children in eating area, no under-7s after 7pm ~ Open 12-2.30(3 Fri, Sat), 6-11; 12-10.30 Sun

MELLOR (Gtr Manchester) SJ9888

Devonshire Arms

Longhurst Lane; follow Mellor signpost off A626 Marple—Glossop and keep on up hill; note that this is Mellor near Stockport, NOT the other one on the north side of Manchester

The Harrisons take obvious pride in their pub and do their best to make sure strangers feel at home. It's a friendly and unpretentious place, particularly popular for the carefully home-made lunchtime food. Typical dishes might include pea and ham or leek and potato soup (£1.60), potted shrimps or hummus (£3.25), extremely popular mussel chowder (£3.45), steamed fresh mussels (£4), courgettes provençale or ploughman's (£4.25), smoked sausage, egg curry or tortellini (£4.95), seafood pasta, bean curry or spiced chick pea curry (£5.25), diced chicken and peppers in a spicy sherry sauce (£5.25), tarragon salmon, braised oxtail or beef in Guinness (£5.50), and a couple of puddings such as crêpes with orange and Grand Marnier (£3.25). The only evening they do food is Monday. The cheerful little front bar has a couple of old leather-seated settles among other seats, lots of old local and family photographs, and a sizeable Victorian fireplace with a deep-chiming clock above it. A couple of small back rooms, attractively papered and with something of a period flavour, both have their own Victorian fireplaces – the one on the right including an unusual lion couchant in place of a mantelpiece. Robinsons Best and Mild on electric pump, a decent collection of spirits including about 50 malt whiskies, several New World wines, and good coffee; cribbage, shove-ha'penny and dominoes; possibly background radio. There are picnic tables out in front, and behind, where an attractively planted terrace leads back to a small tree-sheltered lawn. Recent extensions and additions out here are the handiwork of Mrs Harrison, a keen gardener. Walkers are welcome if they take their boots off. (*Recommended by J C T Tan, Allan Worsley, Jack Morley, and others*)

Robinsons ~ Tenant Brian Harrison ~ Real ale ~ Meals and snacks every lunchtime and Mon evening ~ (0161) 427 2563 ~ Well behaved children in eating area ~ Trad jazz Thurs evenings ~ Open 11.30-3.30, 5.30-11

NEWTON (Lancs) SD6950 Map 7

Parkers Arms

B6478 7 miles N of Clitheroe

Delightfully set in a bowl of tree-sheltered pastures between Waddington Fell and Beatrix Fell, with the River Hodder below, this pretty black and white pub is very well liked for its particularly friendly atmosphere – even a previous landlord enjoys it so much he's become one of the resident locals. The popular and generously served bar food (now cooked by the landlord) might include soup (£1.70), very generous sandwiches (from £1.95), big ploughman's, and a wide choice of daily blackboard specials like vegetable moussaka with pitta bread (£4.50), home-made beef and ale pie (£4.95), fillet of plaice on a potato cake with a wine and grape sauce (£6.25), and chicken fillet stuffed with mushrooms and bacon wrapped in a cabbage leaf with mushroom sauce (£6.50); excellent service. Some of the joists in the spacious and welcoming bar are from the same oak used to repair the Blitz-damaged Houses of Parliament. Plenty of stuffed animals and paintings on the walls in here, as well as red plush button-back banquettes, a mix of new chairs and tables, and an open fire. Beyond an arch is a similar area with sensibly placed darts, pool, dominoes, shove ha'penny, table skittles, fruit machine, video game and discreet piped music. Well kept Black Sheep Bitter, Boddingtons and Tetleys on handpump, a good range of malt whiskies, and regularly changing wine list. They have an amiable black labrador (who has been known to bring customers a stick to throw) and jack russell, and a couple of vietnamese pot-bellied pigs. Well spaced picnic tables on the big lawn look down towards the river, and beyond to the hills. *(Recommended by Helen Pickering, James Owen, J Honnor, Paul McPherson, Arthur and Margaret Dickinson, Wayne Brindle, Sarah and Gary Goldson, S R and A J Ashcroft, K C and B Forman)*

Whitbreads ~ Tenant Nick Hardman ~ Real ale ~ Meals and snacks ~ Restaurant ~ (01200) 446236 ~ Children welcome ~ Open 11-4, 6-11; 11-11 Sat, 12-10.30 Sun; cl evening 25 Dec ~ Bedrooms: £22/£38

RABY (Merseyside) SJ3180 Map 7

Wheatsheaf 🍺

The Green, Rabymere Road; off A540 S of Heswall

Enjoying something of a renaissance under its friendly new licensee, this half-timbered, thatched and white-washed country cottage (known locally as the Thatch) is a really authentic and traditional local in almost every way. The little rooms are simply furnished and characterful, with an old wall clock and homely black kitchen shelves in the central bar, and a nice snug formed by antique settles built in around its fine old fireplace. A second, more spacious room has upholstered wall seats around the tables, small hunting prints on the cream walls, and a smaller coal fire. Filling up a good chunk of the menu is the enormous range of toasted sandwiches – 46 different varieties are listed (including such flavours as black pudding), and they're happy to put together any other combination that springs to mind. Other food might include soup (£1.50), cumberland sausage (£3.95), chilli or curry (£4.25), and a good mixed grill or pork chops in barbecue sauce (£4.95). A splendid range of well kept beers on handpump includes Courage Directors, Ind Coope Burton, Tetleys, Theakstons Best, Old Peculier and XB, Thwaites and Youngers Scotch, and there's also a good choice of malt whiskies. The landlord (who used to farm the land next door) has added a patio area with picnic table sets behind – as we went to press it had already proved so popular he was thinking of extending it. *(Recommended by P H Boot, D Maplethorpe, B Helliwell, Phil Putwain, S R and A J Ashcroft; more reports please)*

Free house ~ Licensee Thomas Charlesworth ~ Real ale ~ Lunchtime meals and snacks (not Sun) ~ (0151) 336 3416 ~ Children in room without bar until 9pm ~ Open 11.30-3, 5.30-11 Mon-Thurs; all day Fri, Sat and Sun (maybe not in winter)

RIBCHESTER (Lancs) SD6435 Map 7

White Bull

Church Street; turn off B6245 at sharp corner by Black Bull

A popular stop at lunchtime, this stately stone dining pub was built in 1707, but the Tuscan pillars that guard the entrance porch have been in the area for nearly 2,000 years. Good value bar meals include soup (£1.40), open sandwiches (from £2.10), stuffed mushrooms (£2.55), steak and kidney pie (£4.35), meat or vegetable lasagne (£4.50), ploughman's (£4.75), various steaks with a choice of toppings (from £6), braised shoulder of lamb (£7.35), and changing specials such as swordfish with garlic and prawns; children's menu. Service is friendly and attentive, even during busy periods, and children are made particularly welcome. The spacious and attractively refurbished main bar has comfortable old settles, and is decorated with Victorian advertisements and various prints, as well as a stuffed fox in two halves that looks as if it's jumping through the wall; most areas are set out for eating during the day, and you can also eat out in the garden behind. Half the dining area is no smoking. Well kept Boddingtons, Flowers IPA, Theakstons Best and a weekly changing guest beer on handpump, a good range of malt whiskies, and a blackboard list of several wines by the glass or bottle; they also do coffees, tea, and hot chocolate. It can get busy, so it's worth arriving early for a table. Darts, dominoes, fruit machine, piped music. Behind the pub are the remains of a Roman bath house, and there's a small Roman museum close by. *(Recommended by Caroline Lloyd, Louise Miller, Richard Waddington; more reports please)*

Whitbreads ~ Lease: Marilyn and Bob Brooks ~ Real ale ~ Meals and snacks (not Mon evening; 12-9 Sun and bank holidays) ~ (01254) 878303 ~ Children in eating area of bar till 9pm ~ Occasional jazz or folk night ~ Open 11.30-3, 6.30-11; 12-10.30 Sun and bank holidays

TOCKHOLES (Lancs) SD6623 Map 7

Rock ♀

Village signposted from A666 S of Blackburn; OS Sheet 103 map reference 663233

The views from this delightfully welcoming moorland inn are remarkable, on clear days stretching over the rolling well wooded pastures as far as the coast some 20 miles away; you should be able to see Blackpool Tower, and if you're very lucky even the Isle of Man. What really stands out though is the care and dedication the Gallaghers put into their work – it's not unusual for them to be up at six going off to the fish market, or preparing their home-made pies. But they make it all seem a pleasure rather than a chore, happy to chat about things or, provided they've got the ingredients, to whip up something that's not on the menu. The landlord is also something of a wine buff, so will enthusiastically guide you through his constantly changing range; last time we spoke to him he gave us some tips on how best to serve an Argentinian wine he'd just discovered. And as he enjoys finishing a good bottle himself you can try virtually any by the glass. Also well kept Thwaites Bitter and Mild on handpump, a variety of unusual malt whiskies including some Indian ones, and some unusual liqueurs. The two-room beamed bar is cosy, with wall banquettes, moiré curtains, brass ornaments around the neat fireplace, old sporting prints on the cream-coloured walls and plates on a delft shelf, some really old. On the left by the bar counter (which has unusually comfortable swivel bar stools) there's some dark brown panelling. Unobtrusive piped music, fruit machine. Big helpings of tasty bar food such as carrot, herb and onion soup (£1.75), sandwiches (from £1.55), ploughman's (£2.25), cheese and onion pie (£3.85), steak pie (£3.95), sirloin steak (£7.95), and changing specials like mussels in white wine (£3.25), snails in garlic (£3.55), fisherman's pie (£4.95), beef in ale topped with melted cheese (£5.45), and peppered chicken breast or plaice stuffed with scallops and crabmeat (£6.45); lots of puddings (from £1.75). Booking is advisable at weekends, and they do occasional flambé evenings. There are tables out on a small terrace. *(Recommended by Andy Hazeldine, Karen Eliot, Laura Darlington, Gianluca Perinetti, G L Tong, S and J Cumming/Johnson)*

Thwaites ~ Tenants Dominic and Maureen Gallagher ~ Real ale ~ Meals and snacks (not Mon lunchtime, exc bank holidays) ~ (01254) 702733 ~ Children welcome until 8.45pm ~ Open 12-2, 7-11; Sun 12-11; cl Mon lunchtime

WHARLES (Lancs) SD4435 Map 7

Eagle & Child

Church Road; from B5269 W of Broughton turn left into Higham Side Road at HMS *Inskip* sign; OS Sheet 102 map reference 448356

Dotted throughout the neatly kept rooms of this friendly thatched ale house is the landlord's marvellous collection of lovely antique furnishings. The most interesting are in the L-shaped bar, where a beamed area round the corner past the counter has a whole cluster of them. One of the highlights is a magnificent, elaborately carved Jacobean settle which originally came from Aston Hall in Birmingham, carrying the motto *exaltavit humiles*. There's also a carved oak chimneypiece, and a couple of fine longcase clocks, one from Chester, and another with a nicely painted face and an almost silent movement from Manchester. The plain cream walls are hung with modern advertising mirrors and some older mirrors, and there are a few exotic knives, carpentry tools and so forth on the plastered structural beams; even when it's not particularly cold, there should be a good fire burning in the intricate cast-iron stove. Well kept Boddingtons and three regularly changing guests such as Cains Traditional, Wadworths 6X or Wards on handpump; darts in a sensible side area, friendly cat. One or two picnic tables outside. Nothing ever changes, and there's a delightfully timeless atmosphere; it's hard to understand why we don't get more reports on the place. Do please note it's closed on weekday lunchtimes, and there is no food. *(Recommended by Graham Bush; more reports please)*

Free house ~ Licensees Brian and Angela Tatham ~ Real ale ~ No food ~ (01772) 690312 ~ Open 7-11 (and 12-3 Sat and Sun)

WHITEWELL (Lancs) SD6546 Map 7

Inn at Whitewell ★ ★ ⇐ ♀

Most easily reached by B6246 from Whalley; road through Dunsop Bridge from B6478 is also good

If the Queen ever achieves her apparent ambition to retire to the Hodder Valley, this lovely hotel will be her local. Perhaps most dramatically approached from Abbeystead, it's beautifully set deep in the Forest of Bowland and surrounded by well wooded rolling hills set off against higher moors. The atmosphere is so civilised and the furnishings so individual that at times it has the air of a hospitable country house. The inn also houses a wine merchant (hence the unusually wide range of around 180 wines available – the claret is recommended) and an art gallery, and owns several miles of trout, salmon and sea trout fishing on the Hodder; with notice they'll arrange shooting. A real bonus is that although it gets very busy, it's very spacious inside and out, so usually stays peaceful and relaxing. The old-fashioned pubby bar has antique settles, oak gateleg tables, sonorous clocks, old cricketing and sporting prints, log fires (the lounge has a very attractive stone fireplace), and heavy curtains on sturdy wooden rails; one area has a selection of newspapers, dominoes, local maps and guide books. There's a piano for anyone who wants to play. Down a corridor with strange objects like a stuffed fox disappearing into the wall is the pleasant suntrap garden, with wonderful views down to the valley. The public bar is being extended, and will probably be closed for the next year or more. Popular bar food includes soup (£2.50), big sandwiches (from £3), salads (from £5.50), steak and kidney pie (£6), cumberland sausage (£6.60), fish pie (£7), weekend oysters, steaks, home-made puddings like chocolate roulade (£3) and hand-made farmhouse cheeses (from £3); there's an à la carte menu and slightly different evening dishes, and they serve coffee and cream teas all day. The menus have quite a companionable approach, and some readers feel the civility of the staff is unmatched anywhere else.

Well kept Boddingtons and Marstons Pedigree on handpump. Some of the spacious and beautifully refurbished bedrooms even have their own CD players; the gents', incidentally, now have cricketing prints – more decorous than many readers will remember. *(Recommended by Nigel Hopkins, Michael and Alison Leyland, Paul McPherson, T Large, V Smith, James Nunns, Malcolm Taylor, John and Diana Davies, Nick and Meriel Cox, Nigel Woolliscroft, Graham Bush, Laura Darlington, Gianluca Perinetti, R C Foster, Howard Bateman, Helen Pickering, Robert and Ann Lees, Phil and Karen Wood, Wayne Brindle, Jim and Maggie Cowell; also in Good Hotel Guide)*

Free house ~ Licensee Richard Bowman ~ Real ale ~ Meals and snacks (not Sat evening if a big function is on) ~ Restaurant (not Sun lunchtime) ~ (01200) 448222 ~ Children welcome ~ Open 11-3, 6-11 ~ Bedrooms: from £49.50B/£69B

YEALAND CONYERS (Lancs) SD5074 Map 7

New Inn 🍴

3 miles from M6 junction 35; village signposted off A6 N

Since this simple ivy-covered stone pub opened in the early 17th c it has provided nourishment for generations of tired and hungry walkers fresh from the fells, but it's unlikely many of them would have eaten as well as visitors do today; a meal here really can be very special indeed. The blackboard specials are really rather novel, yet not unreasonably priced: typical dishes include diced pork cooked with pineapple, onions, mushrooms and water chestnuts or a whole quail stuffed with bacon, hazelnut and apricot on a redcurrant croûton (£6.50), carrot and cashew nut loaf on a courgette and red pepper purée topped with deep fried leek rings (£7.50), and salmon steak marinated in oriental flavours and served on a bed of beansprouts and water chestnuts with a coconut and soy sauce (£9.95). Readers make particular mention of the really imaginative salads which come with most dishes. Puddings like apple crème brûlée, bilberry jelly topped with vanilla custard, rich creamy macaroni pudding and sticky toffee pudding (from £2.95) are no less creative. For the not so adventurous the short printed menu is more straightforward: filled baps and baked potatoes (from £2.50), and bobotie (an African dish with gently spiced minced lamb, apricots and almonds, topped by a brandied egg custard, quiche of the day or potato bake (£4.95). There is a good friendly and professional reception, though the emphasis is very clearly on dining. On the left is a simply furnished little beamed bar with a log fire in the big stone fireplace, and on the right are two communicating cottagey dining rooms with black furniture to match the shiny beams, an attractive kitchen range and another winter fire. The newly redecorated dining room is no smoking, and they've won awards for their ladies' lavatory. Well kept Robinsons Best, Hartleys XB, Hatters Mild and Old Tom on handpump, a good choice of around 30 malt whiskies, home-made lemonade. Dominoes, cribbage, piped music. A sheltered lawn at the side has picnic tables among roses and flowering shrubs. *(Recommended by Louise Miller, Richard Waddington, Margaret Dyke, Yvonne and Mike Meadley, Rob and Ann Horley, Mrs J Anderton, Mike and Wendy Proctor, Charlotte Wrigley, Angus Lyon, A N Ellis, Nick and Meriel Cox, George Atkinson, P A Legon, Bronwen and Steve Wrigley, Mrs P J Carroll, R J Walden, David and Gill Carrington, Eric Locker)*

Hartleys (Robinsons) ~ Tenants Ian and Annette Dutton ~ Real ale ~ Meals and snacks (in summer all day till 9.30) ~ Restaurant ~ (01524) 732938 ~ Children welcome ~ Open 11-11; 11-10.30 Sun; winter weekdays 11-3, 5.30-11

Please keep sending us reports. We rely on readers for news of new discoveries, and particularly for news of changes – however slight – at the fully described pubs. No stamp needed: *The Good Pub Guide*, FREEPOST TN1569, Wadhurst, E Sussex TN5 7BR.

Lucky Dip

Besides the fully inspected pubs, you might like to try these Lucky Dips recommended to us and described by readers (if you do, please send us reports):

☆ Altrincham Gtr Man [Navigation Rd, Broadheath; junction with Manchester Rd (A56); SJ7689], *Old Packet House*: Pleasantly restored local with attractive Victorianised decor, shiny black woodwork, good solid furnishings, turkey carpet, well kept Boddingtons and Websters, open fires, good bar food inc lots of sandwiches and well presented salads, some fresh-cooked hot dishes, nice plush back dining room, prompt friendly service; fruit machines, juke box; under same ownership as Dog at Peover Heath (see Cheshire main entries); small sheltered back terrace, well equipped bedrooms, good breakfast *(Erik Williams, Dr and Mrs S Taylor, BB)*

Altrincham [Railway St], *Downs*: Big Edwardian hotel, cool lofty interior, separate pool room, steps to own bowling green, pleasant staff; bedrooms *(Ian Phillips)*

☆ Appley Bridge Gtr Man [Station Approach; SD5210], *Old Station House*: Attractively furnished interesting conversion of station buildings, appetising range of home-made bar food inc ten soups, beef and bamboo sizzles, lovely brasserie with generous Sun roasts (children welcome), well kept Holts and Jennings, decent coffee *(Dr and Mrs B Baker)*

☆ Ashton under Lyne [Mossley Rd (A670); SJ9399], *Hartshead*: Panoramic views over Manchester from Brewers Fayre family dining pub with baby changing, children's lavatories, own menu, marvellous outdoor play area, Lego etc inside; generous standard food, can get very busy summer weekends and bank hols, open all day *(J Mayhew)*

Atherton Gtr Man [30 Bolton Old Rd; SD6703], *Bay Horse*: Traditional Tetleys local with 60s/70s decor; tap room, lounge and separate pool room *(Andy Hazeldine)*; [76 Bolton Rd], *Spinners Arms*: Friendly local, well kept Tetleys and guests, popular with young in the evening, outdoor seating; children welcome till 7 *(Andy Hazeldine)*

Bamber Bridge [8 Church Rd; from M6 junction 29 head towards Preston (former A6), right at first traffic lights; SD5625], *Olde Hob*: Good value food in attractive low-beamed thatched pub with four intimate rooms, one with real fire, fruit machines, fishtank, children's books and toys; well kept S&N and a guest beer, efficient service, dining room with tasteful alcoves and cosy areas *(Andy Hazeldine, Ian and Mary Randles)*

Bamber Bridge [Lostock Lane; A582 W of M6 junction 29; SD5728], *Poachers*: Relaxed family area with own entrance, playroom and outdoor play area; wide choice of enterprising food inc vegetarian, good service *(JWC, MC)*

☆ Barnston Mer [Barnston Rd (A551); SJ2883], *Fox & Hounds*: Homely partly flagstoned long lounge bar with lots of atmospheric paraphernalia, good value quickly served straightforward food from ploughman's up

inc very popular Sun lunch, Courage-related and guest ales; pretty summer courtyard and garden with outside bar; by farm and lovely wooded dell *(Jack Morley, Paul Boot)*

☆ Bashall Eaves [SD6943], *Red Pump*: Tucked-away country pub with very relaxed unpretentious atmosphere, friendly service, good imaginative home cooking inc good value Sun lunch, Whitbreads-related ales, two roaring log fires, restaurant; two bedrooms, good breakfast, own fishing on River Hodder *(A and M Dickinson, John and Paula Whybrow, Drs Philip and Jane Davis)*

Bay Horse [Bay Horse Lane, Ellel; just off A6 S of M6 junction 33; SD4952], *Bay Horse*: Pleasant atmosphere with lovely fires in bar and dining room; useful food *(RJH)*

Birkenhead Mer [Lord St; SJ3289], *Commodore*: Very wide choice of well kept S & N and other rarer ales in friendly bare-boards backstreet local with pool, live music nights and good basic food *(Richard Lewis, Joe Cook)*

Blackburn [Livesey Branch Rd; Mill Hill; SD6828], *Moorgate Arms*: Old unrefurbished corner local, particularly well kept Thwaites, friendly staff and border collie *(Andy Hazeldine)*; [Barbara Castle Way], *Uncle Toms Cabin*: Local by Thwaites Brewery, unspoilt and traditional with separate rooms off bar area, well kept beer *(Andy Hazeldine)*; [Accrington Rd, Eanam], *Wharf*: Open-plan canalside pub with well kept Boddingtons and Tetleys, big windows, covered outdoor seating area by water *(Andy Hazeldine)*

☆ Blackpool [204 Talbot Rd; opp Blackpool North stn; SD3035], *Ramsden Arms*: Attractive decor with masses of bric-a-brac and pictures, friendly helpful staff, no-smoking area, well kept cheap house beer, also Boddingtons, Jennings, Tetleys and guest ales, over 40 whiskies, CD juke box, games; good value bedrooms *(Andy Hazeldine, Bill and Beryl Farmer)*

Blackpool [Bonny St], *Pump & Truncheon*: Real ale pub with wooden floorboards, blackboards with old jokes, good range of ales, lunchtime food, occasional beer festivals *(Andy Hazeldine)*; [192 Talbot Rd, opp Blackpool North stn], *Wheatsheaf*: Friendly local, well kept Theakstons *(Andy Hazeldine)*

Bolton Gtr Man [606 Halliwell Rd; SD7108], *Ainsworth Arms*: Unpretentious and friendly, with particularly well kept Tetleys-related and guest beers, basic good value food, quick service, pub games, old-fashioned smoke room; busy evenings, helpful attitude to wheelchairs *(Andy Hazeldine)*; [36 Pool St], *Howcroft*: Good value lunches and well kept Tetleys-related ales in well preserved friendly old local with lots of small screened-off rooms, Addlestone's cider, plenty of games inc pinball, darts, bar billiards; bowling green, occasional live music *(Andy Hazeldine)*; [52

Junction Rd, Deane; SD6808], *Kings Head*:
Attractive local with central servery for
flagstoned bar and two lounges, well kept
Walkers Bitter, Mild, Best and Winter
Warmer, massive stove, good reasonably
priced lunchtime food, pleasant atmosphere;
seats out overlooking church or back bowling
green *(Andy Hazeldine)*; [127 Crook St],
Sweet Green: Friendly local with four small
rooms off central bar, green decor, well kept
Tetleys-related and guest ales, basic lunchtime
food; darts, pool, seats outside *(Andy
Hazeldine, Dave Swanton)*

☆ Bolton by Bowland [SD7849], *Coach &
Horses*: Quietly welcoming comfortable pub
with pleasantly untouristy traditional decor in
lovely streamside village with interesting
church; good fresh well presented food to suit
the season, well kept Whitbreads-related
beers, coal fires, restaurant (where children
may be allowed); get there early weekends for
a table *(Jim and Maggie Cowell)*

☆ Brierfield [Burnley Rd (A682), just off M65
junction 12; SD8436], *Waggon & Horses*:
Comfortable and beautifully restored and
fitted-out late Victorian small-roomed local,
lots of interest, well kept Thwaites Bitter,
Craftsman and Mild on handpump, good
malt whiskies, warm fires; bar food (not
evenings Sun-Weds), children allowed away
from servery, open all day Fri/Sat *(Alan and
Charlotte Sykes, LYM)*
nr Broughton [not far from M6 junction 32
via A6 N; left into Station Lane about a mile
after Broughton traffic lights; SD4937],
Plough at Eaves: Two homely low-beamed
carpeted bars, well kept Thwaites Bitter and
Craftsman, lots of malt whiskies, usual food
inc children's helpings, darts, pool and other
games, piped music, well equipped play area
outside; cl Mon/Tues *(JM, PM, Sarah and
Gary Goldson, LYM)*
Bury Gtr Man [Rochdale Old Rd, Jericho –
B6222 nr Fairfield Hosp; SD8010],
Gamecock: Small neatly kept friendly pub
with well kept Marstons Bitter and Timothy
Taylors Landlord, good range of food inc
good beef in beer and local black puddings,
low prices; dominoes, cards, chess; can get
rather smoky *(Neil Byrne, Brian Wainwright)*;
[Manchester Old Rd; aka Tap & Spile], *Rose
& Crown*: Friendly staff, good food, well kept
real ales inc regular guest *(Ian Phillips)*

☆ nr Bury [Nangreaves; off A56/A666 N under
a mile E of M66 junction 1, down cobbled
track; SD8115], *Lord Raglan*: Notable for its
lonely moorside location, with great views;
lots of bric-a-brac in traditional front bar, big
open fire in back room, plainer blond-
panelled dining room (where children
allowed); well kept mainly S&N real ales,
interesting foreign bottled beers, hearty bar
food *(Laura Darlington, Gianluca Perinetti, P
M Lane, LYM)*
Chatburn [SD7644], *Brown Cow*: Popular for
very varied choice of good value food inc
particularly good home-made cottage pie;
dining room, real ale, attentive staff, tables
outside *(Arthur and Margaret Dickinson)*

Cheadle Hulme Gtr Man [Church
Rd/Ravenoak Rd; SJ8787], *Church*:
Atmospheric old inn run by same family for
20 years, wide range of well kept ales, good
bar food ordered from small hatch and served
by pleasant waitresses *(Jack Morley)*

☆ Churchtown Mer [Botanic Rd; off A565 from
Preston, taking B5244 at Southport; SD3618],
Hesketh Arms: Spacious Victorian-style
dining pub with good value fresh food from
chip butties to roast beef inc children's
helpings; Tetleys Bitter and Mild on
handpump from central servery, open fires,
lively atmosphere, Weds jazz; pleasant tables
outside, attractive partly thatched village nr
Botanic Gardens *(Alan Goadsby, BB)*
Clayton le Woods [Radburn Brow; SD5522],
Lord Nelson: 18th-c inn with oak beams and
nautical paintings, well kept Theakstons,
good generous wholesome food, reasonable
prices *(Mike and Carole Dixon)*
Clifton [SD4630], *Windmill*: Unusual
building incorporating windmill from which it
takes its name, with big restaurant extension,
Mitchells beers, games area in circular mill
part *(Tony Hobden)*
Clitheroe [Chaigley, out on Chipping rd;
SD6941], *Craven Heifer*: Tetleys pub with
open coal fire, personal service, restaurant
with delightful views, substantial helpings of
well prepared food cooked to order – not
cheap, but a fine choice, inc excellent meat,
some veg from the garden; also bar
sandwiches *(John Brennand)*
Conder Green [Cockerham Rd (A588); not
far from M6 junction 33; SD4556], *Stork*:
Rambling 17th-c pub with good views from
outside seats; several cosy panelled rooms,
Morlands Old Speckled Hen and Tetleys,
good coffee, good home cooking inc
vegetarian in bar or separate dining room;
good service even on crowded Sat night;
bedrooms, handy for Glasson Dock *(Dennis
D'Vigne, Tony Hobden, Richard Fawcett)*

☆ Cowan Bridge [Burrow-by-Burrow; A65
towards Kirkby Lonsdale; SD6277], *Whoop
Hall*: Spacious, airy and comfortable open-
plan bar with interesting quick food inc
decent vegetarian choice all day from 8am
from popular buttery, well kept Boddingtons
and Theakstons Best and XB, decent wines,
pleasant restaurant, friendly service; tables in
garden well off road, with play area; children
allowed in eating area; well appointed
bedrooms *(John Davidson, LYM)*
Croston [Town Rd; SD4818], *Grapes*: Good
value home cooking in dining room off bar
(booking advisable weekends), friendly staff,
well kept beers *(Janet Lee, Robert Lester)*;
[Out Lane (off A581) - OS Sheet 108 map ref
486187], *Lord Nelson*: Welcoming and
relaxed old-fashioned local with well kept
Whitbreads-related ales, decent
straightforward food, no juke box or
machines (TV in side family room), Nelson
theme inc the Trafalgar message in flags on a
mast outside *(John Smith)*
Daisy Hill Gtr Man [321 Leigh Rd; SD6504],
Rose Hill: Big traditional Holts pub next to

station, well kept cheap Bitter, food lunchtimes and some evenings, tables outside *(Andy Hazeldine)*

☆ **Darwen** [Roman Rd, Grimehills; SD6922], *Crown & Thistle*: Small and cosy two-room country dining pub with good if not cheap food (all tables set for diners, must book Fri/Sat), friendly accommodating staff, fresh flowers, moorland views, well kept Thwaites Bitter and Mild, lovely log fires *(Bronwen and Steve Wrigley, Neville Kenyon, Nigel and Amanda Thorp)*

Delph Gtr Man [Broad Lane, Heights; SE0009], *Royal Oak*: Opp old moorland church in steep narrow winding lane, good views of surrounding valleys, real fires in three small rooms, comfortable solid furniture, home-made food, interesting choice of well kept ales such as Hook Norton Old Hookey, very friendly welcome *(Chris Westmoreland)*

Denshaw Gtr Man [Oldham Rd; SD9710], *Printers Arms*: Comfortable layout with open fire in lounge, no-smoking room nr bar, above-average reasonably priced home cooking, six well kept real ales, over 70 whiskies inc some rare malts *(K and B Forman)*

☆ **Diggle** Gtr Man [Diglea Hamlet, Sam Rd; village signed off A670 just N of Dobcross; SE0008], *Diggle Hotel*: Modernised three-room hillside pub popular lunchtime and early evening for food from sandwiches up inc generous Sun roasts and children's dishes; well kept Oldham and Timothy Taylors Golden Best and Landlord, decent wines, good choice of malt whiskies, good coffee, prompt friendly service, soft piped music, rustic fairy-lit tables among the trees, quiet spot just below the moors; opens noon *(K and B Forman, Chris Westmoreland, Bill Sykes, BB)*

Dolphinholme [back rds, a couple of miles from M6 junction 33 – can be reached from Forton services; SD5153], *Fleece*: Beamed lounge with comfortably worn seating, bar with darts and table skittles, open fire, well kept Mitchells Best and Special, friendly atmosphere, tasty bar food, dining area (no hot food Mon lunchtime) *(Gregg Davies, Tony Hobden)*

☆ **Dukinfield** Gtr Man [Globe Sq; SJ9497], *Globe*: Welcoming family-run pub with generous and genuine home cooking inc good value Sun lunch, well kept John Smiths and Tetleys, good comfortable atmosphere, games room; children welcome, open all day weekdays, bedrooms clean and comfortable, attractive surroundings nr Lower Peak Forest Canal *(Mike Pugh, J F M West, LYM)*

Dunham Woodhouses Gtr Man [B5160 – OS Sheet 109 map ref 724880; SJ7288], *Vine*: Carefully refurbished to keep olde-worlde atmosphere, with open fires in four small separate rooms; good food inc soup and sandwiches, seats outside; handy for Dunham Massey Park and Hall *(Margaret and Roy Randle)*

☆ **Eccles** Gtr Man [33 Regent St (A57 – handy

for M602 junction 2); SJ7798], *Lamb*: Untouched Edwardian Holts local with splendid etched windows, fine woodwork and furnishings; cheap well kept beer, full-size snooker table *(Andy Hazeldine, Jack and Philip Paxton)*

Eccles [133 Liverpool Rd, Patricroft, a mile from M63 junction 2; SJ7698], *White Lion*: Another classic Edwardian Holts local with drinking corridor, games in lively vaults bar, separate smoke room (with weekend sing-songs) and quiet lounge *(Pete Baker, Jack and Philip Paxton)*

Eccleston [Towngate (B5250, off A581 Chorley—Southport); SD5117], *Farmers Arms*: Big but friendly low-beamed pub/restaurant with decent food all day, well kept largely Whitbreads-related ales, black cottagey furniture, red plush wall seats, rough plaster covered with plates, pastoral prints, clocks and brasses; darts; parking can be a problem when busy; bedrooms *(John Fazakerley)*

Edgworth [Bury Rd; SD7520], *Rose & Crown*: Good reasonably priced pub food in bars and flagstoned dining area; well kept Flowers IPA *(Gordon Tong)*

☆ **Entwistle** [Overshores Rd; village signed off Blackburn Rd N of Edgworth – OS Sheet 109 map ref 726177; SD7217], *Strawbury Duck*: Cosy dim-lit beamed and flagstoned country pub by isolated station – trains from Blackburn and Bolton; well kept Boddingtons, Moorhouses Pendle Witches Brew, Timothy Taylors Best and Landlord and a house beer, popular generous bar food (all day Sat and Sun) inc children's; games room, no-smoking lounge, restaurant, good unobtrusive piped music (live Thurs), tables outside; children till 8.30; cl Mon lunchtime; comfortable bedrooms, big sizzling breakfasts, good Pennine walks *(Dr and Mrs B Baker, Simon and Chris Turner, S R and A J Ashcroft, Chris Pierce, Bronwen and Steve Wrigley, Andy and Jill Kassube, LYM)*

Fence [Cuckstool Lane, Pendle Forest; SD8237], *Forest*: Refurbished pub with well presented unusually good varied food from fresh local ingredients where possible, good choice of wines and beers, friendly helpful service; not cheap but good value *(D and E M Kershaw, F J Robinson)*

Fleetwood [The Esplanade; nr tram terminus; SD3247], *North Euston*: Big comfortably refurbished bar in architecturally interesting Victorian hotel overlooking seafront, decent lunchtime food, well kept mainstream real ales, no-smoking family area (till 7), seats outside; bedrooms *(Sue Holland, Dave Webster, Andy Hazeldine, Brian Wainwright)*; [Marine Hall, Esplanade], *Wyre*: Part of exhibition/entertainment centre, quiet, good views of beach, Morecambe Bay, boats and ships; well kept Moorhouses Premier and Pendle Witches Brew, Timothy Taylors Landlord and two or three guests, seats outside *(Andy Hazeldine)*

☆ **Galgate** [A6 S of Lancaster, handy for M6 junction 33; SD4755], *Plough*: Particularly well kept Boddingtons and several guest beers, good reasonably priced food inc super sandwiches, friendly efficient young licensees; open all day

Garstang [Mkt Pl; SD4845], *Royal Oak*: Comfortably refurbished, with generous bar food (all day Sun) inc good range of home-cooked meats, imaginatively presented specials, children's helpings of any dish; Robinsons on handpump *(A and M Dickinson)*

Glasson [Docks; SD4456], *Dalton Arms*: Tradtional pub, useful snacks, well kept Thwaites *(Tony Hobden)*; [Docks], *Victoria*: Popular dining pub by harbour, Mitchells beers *(Tony Hobden)*

Greasby Mer [Hillbark Rd/Montgomery Hill; SJ2587], *Farmers Arms*: Extended and refurbished country pub with enthusiastic and welcoming new management, eight real ales, substantial sandwiches, enclosed garden with plenty of tables *(E G Parish)*

Great Eccleston [SD4240], *Farmers Arms*: Italian landlord and food, good curries, pies and steaks, four ales such as Boddingtons, Mansfield Old Baily and Whitbreads *(Margaret and Trefor Howorth)*

Great Mitton Gtr Man [Mitton Hall, Mitton Rd; SD7238], *Owd Neds*: Good value generous food all day inc vegetarian, well kept Boddingtons and Jennings, helpful staff, flagstoned bar, big conservatory, tables on terrace, plenty of space for children in informal grounds with stream and woodland; part of mansion which includes restaurant, frequent entertainment, bedrooms *(Arthur and Margaret Dickinson, Simon Woodhouse, Maria Dobson)*

Haskayne [Rosemary Lane, just off A567 – OS Sheet 108 map ref 364082; SD3608], *Ship*: Useful canalside pub confortably refurbished with navigation lights, ship models etc, two cosy rooms, two more airy, prompt courteous service, well cooked usual food *(Olive and Ray Hebson)*

☆ Haslingden [Hud Rake; SD7823], *Griffin*: Brews its own cheap Bitter, Mild, Stout, Porter, Sunshine, and the occasional Special, in the cellar; basic but clean, quiet and friendly, no juke box or games machines; take-home jugs available *(Markus Buckley, Andrew Green, Rosemarie Johnson, Carl Travis)*

☆ Hawkshaw Gtr Man [91 Ramsbottom Rd; SD7615], *Red Lion*: Recently attractively renovated, good reasonably priced home cooking in bar and restaurant (popular with OAPs lunchtime), well kept Thwaites, Timothy Taylors and Charles Wells beers, friendly staff; comfortable bedrooms, quiet spot by River Irwell *(Andy and Jill Kassube, Mr and Mrs D C Stevens, Gordon Tong)*

☆ Heskin Green [Wood Lane; B5250, N of M6 junction 27; SD5214], *Farmers Arms*: Cheerful sparkling clean country pub, spacious but cosy, with wide choice of well kept Whitbreads-related and good guest ales, heavy black beams, brasses and china, very wide choice of good value home cooking in two-level dining area, very friendly staff; picnic tables outside, good play area, pets corner from pigs to peacocks; open 12-11 *(Ray and Liz Monk, Wendy McKenna, Comus Elliott, BB)*

Heywood Gtr Man [87 Rochdale Rd E; SD8510], *Albany*: Small welcoming family-run hotel with well kept beer in big saloon bar done up in rather smart pub style – brasses, prints, swagged curtains; bedrooms reasonably priced and clean *(Nick Wikeley)*

☆ nr Heywood Gtr Man [off narrow Ashworth Rd; pub signed off B6222 on N side of Heywood; SD8513], *Egerton Arms*: Good interestingly prepared food from sandwiches up, imaginative vegetables and vegetarian dishes, lovely puddings, in isolated hillside pub with great views esp from terrace; good service, comfortable sofas and easy chairs in plush lounge by smart restaurant, simpler bar with old farm tools and coal fire even in summer, big-windowed small extension; keg beer, huge car park *(Laura Darlington, Gianluca Perinetti, Ian and Amanda Wharmby, BB)*

High Lane Gtr Man [Buxton Rd (A6 Stockport—Disley); SJ9585], *Red Lion*: Entirely given over to eating, esp fish, but does have well kept Robinsons, and the very wide choice of good food runs from sandwiches up; good friendly service, big dining room; six bedrooms *(Ray Cuckow)*

Hindley Gtr Man [Ladies Lane, next to stn; SD6104], *Edington Arms*: Friendly and busy local with six ever-changing ales such as Holts, Moorhouses Premier, one brewed for the pub; very busy weekends, back pool table *(Andy Hazeldine, Paul Boot)*

☆ Holden [the one up by Bolton by Bowland – OS Sheet 103 map ref 777494; SD7749], *Copy Nook*: Spick-and-span roomy and well renovated roadside pub with efficient obliging staff, wide choice of good food, well kept Tetleys *(John and Joan Wyatt, Michael and Joan Melling)*

Hornby [SD5869], *Castle*: Welcoming new manager, good range of food, Mitchells real ale *(Nigel Hopkins)*

Horwich Gtr Man [Chorley Old Rd; SD6311], *Jolly Crofter*: Popular extended dining pub, good wholesome reasonably priced food, pleasant service, well kept Greenalls and guest ales *(Annette and Stephen Marsden)*

Hurst Green [Longridge Rd (B6243); SD6838], *Punch Bowl*: Very well run, with good choice of food inc imaginative daily specials, nook-and-cranny eating areas off pleasant bar as well as big Jacobean dining room with minstrel gallery, heraldic shields on walls, tables out on spacious lawn *(Arthur and Margaret Dickinson)*; [OS Sheet 103 map ref 685379], *Shireburn Arms*: Quiet comfortable 17th-c hotel in idyllic setting with panoramic Ribble valley views, good reasonably priced food, Thwaites and other ales; separate tea room, occasional pianist; bedrooms *(Jim and Maggie Cowell)*

Inglewhite [3 miles from A6 – turn off nr

Owd Nells, Bilsborrow; SD5440], *Green Man*: Good food at attractive prices, well kept Greenalls, friendly service; unspoilt countryside nr Beacon Fell country park *(Jim and Maggie Cowell, Sian Ellis)*

☆ Irby Mer [Irby Mill Hill, off Greasby rd; SJ2684], *Irby Mill*: Well kept Bass, Boddingtons, Cains Bitter and Dark Mild, Jennings and two interesting weekly guest beers, good house wines and decent generous fresh-cooked lunchtime food (not Sun) in four low-beamed largely flagstoned rooms, comfortable pub furniture, coal-effect gas fire, relaxed local atmosphere, interesting old photographs and history of the former mill, a few tables outside *(Liz and Graham Bell, Maurice and Gill McMahon, Paul Boot, Andrew Pollard, BB)*

Irby, *Shippons*: Newish farmhouse-style Banks's pub, good lunchtime food *(Graham and Lynn Mason)*

Lancaster [Scale Hall (A589 Morecambe rd)], *Farmhouse Tavern*: Former country club attractively converted by new owners, character traditional stone-walled bar with log fire in great arched fireplace, high beams and stained glass, friendly atmosphere, good food, well kept Boddingtons, Chesters Mild and Marstons Pedigree; bedrooms *(Brian Rayner)*; *George & Dragon*: Attractive small pub nr River Lune with interesting snacks, Wards real ale; busy Sun lunchtime *(Tony Hobden)*; [Canal Side; parking in Aldcliffe Rd behind Royal Lancaster Infirmary, off A6 – cross canal by pub's footbridge], *Water Witch*: Cheerful canalside pub attractively converted from 18th-c barge-horse stabling, well kept cheap real ales, flagstones, stripped stone, rafters and pitch-pine panelling; games room, juke box/piped music – can be loud evening; bar food, upstairs restaurant, seats outside; children allowed in eating areas, open all day Sat, very popular with students *(P Lawson, TN, AN, LYM)*; [Quarry Rd, across canal behind magistrates' courts], *White Cross*: Busy, lively pub by canal with outside seating (nice in summer); good varied menu inc yummy puddings and vegetarian choices, friendly staff, no-smoking area upstairs, Bass-related ales; separate restaurant area, children allowed *(Tim and Ann Newell)*

☆ Lathom [Wheat Lane, off A5209; Parbold Rd after Ring o' Bells heading into Burscough; SD4512], *Ship*: Big and busy well run pub tucked below canal embankment, several separate rooms with decor varying from interestingly cluttered canal memorabilia through naval pictures and crests to hunting prints, lots of copper and brass, cheap popular lunchtime food served promptly, friendly staff, ten well kept changing real ales, often interesting; games room *(James Cowell, Mr and Mrs J Tyrer, Mr and Mrs A Craig, Mike Schaffel, Gary and Sarah Goldson, Philip and Carol Seddon, S R and A J Ashcroft, BB)*

☆ Liverpool [Grafton St], *Cains Brewery Tap*: Splendidly restored Victorian architecture with nicely understated decor, wooden floors,

plush snug, lots of old prints, wonderful bar, flame-effect gas fire, newspapers; cosy relaxing atmosphere, friendly staff, good well priced food, and above all well kept attractively priced Cains ales with guest beers from other small breweries; popular brewery tour ending here with buffet and singing; sports TV *(Chris Walling, Peter Rush, Andrew Stephenson, Richard Lewis)*

☆ Liverpool [Albert Dock Complex], *Pump House*: Relaxing multi-level conversion of dock building, good Mersey views, lots of polished dark wood, bare bricks, mezzanine and upper gallery with exposed roof trusses; marble counter with bulbous beer engines and brass rail supported by elephants' heads, tall chimney; wide choice of generous cheeses, some hot food, friendly efficient service; waterside tables, boat trips in season; keg beers, busy weekend evenings *(John Fazakerley)*

Liverpool [A5036 continuation S; promenade drive by former Garden Festival site], *Britannia*: Fantastic view across wide expanse of Mersey; welcoming efficient staff, good reasonably priced food *(Eric Locker)*; [Walton Rd, Kirkdale], *Clock*: No frills – particularly well kept beer, piano; good on football match days *(Eric and Jackie Robinson)*; [13 Rice St], *Cracke*: Attractively basic, bare boards, walls covered with posters for local events and pictures of local buildings, unusual Beatles diorama in largest room, juke box and TV, very cheap lunchtime food, well kept Marstons Pedigree; popular mainly with young people; sizeable garden *(Eric and Jackie Robinson)*; [25 Matthew St], *Grapes*: Lively and friendly, with well kept Boddingtons and Cains, good value lunchtime bar food, open-plan but cottagey decor (flagstones, old range, wall settles, gas-effect lamps); its Beatles associations are still remembered; open all day, can get crowded Fri/Sat, cl Sun *(Chris Raisin)*; [4 Hackins Hey, off Dale St], *Hole In Ye Wall*: Well restored 18th-c pub, several different areas in pleasant high-beamed panelled bar, beer unusually fed by gravity via oak pillars from upstairs cellar *(Eric and Jackie Robinson)*; [67 Moorfields, off Titheborn St], *Lion*: Splendidly preserved ornate Victorian alehouse, etched glass and serving hatches in central bar, two small lounges off, unusual wallpaper, big mirrors, panelling and tilework, fine domed structure behind, well kept Walkers, cheap lunchtime food *(Eric and Jackie Robinson)*; [93 Rice Lane, Walton; SJ3694], *Prince Arthur*: Victorian alehouse, well kept Walkers *(Eric and Jackie Robinson)*; [Roscoe St], *Roscoe Head*: Three tiny rooms, friendly, quiet and civilised, with outstandingly well kept Tetleys and maybe Jennings, huge and growing tie collection *(Andrew Stephenson, Eric and Jackie Robinson)*; [24 Rainford Gdns, off Matthew St], *White Star*: Traditional basic local with well kept Bass-related and other beers such as Cains and Shepherd Neame, lots of woodwork, prints, White Star shipping line memorabilia, friendly service *(Richard Lewis, Eric and Jackie Robinson, Rich Sharp) nr* **Longridge** [Longridge Fell, off B6243 Longridge—Clitheroe above Ribchester – OS Sheet 103 map ref 644391; SD6439], *New Drop*: In lovely countryside, big room overlooking Ribble Valley; attentive family service, relaxed atmosphere, popular food in bar and restaurant, real ales such as Boddingtons, Timothy Taylors Landlord, Wild Boar, Whitbreads Mild *(SLC)*

Lytham [Promenade; SD3627], *Queens*: Victorian pub with outdoor seating overlooking sea and windmill, well kept Theakstons Best and Youngers 70/-; popular with young in evening *(Andy Hazeldine)*

☆ **Manchester** [127 Gt Bridgewater St, Oxford St side], *Peveril of the Peak*: Three traditional rooms around central servery, busy lunchtime but welcoming and homely evenings, with well kept Courage-related ales, cheap basic lunchtime food (not Sun), very welcoming family service; lots of mahogany and stained glass, sturdy furnishings, interesting pictures, pub games inc table football; splendidly lurid green external tilework, seats outside; children welcome, cl weekend lunchtimes – long may it escape refurbishment *(Sarah Cockburn-Price, Andy Hazeldine, Paul Carter, BB)*

☆ **Manchester** [6 Angel St; off Rochdale Rd], *Beer House*: Lively basic real ale pub with ten or so well kept changing ones (extra in summer), also three farm ciders, several Belgian beers on tap, good range of bottled foreign beers, country wines; bare boards, lots of seating, friendly staff, eclectic juke box, bar billiards, darts, robust cheap bar food inc vegetarian lunchtime (bargains Mon) and Thurs/Fri early evening, old local prints *(Richard Lewis, Richard Wood, Fiona Lewry, Howell Parry)*

☆ **Manchester** [50 Great Bridgewater St; corner of Lower Mosley St], *Britons Protection*: Chatty, genuine and well run by long-serving licensees, with fine tilework and solid woodwork in rather plush front bar, attractive softly lit inner lounge with coal-effect gas fire, battle murals in passage leading to it; exceptional choice of whiskies, well kept though not cheap Ind Coope Burton, Jennings and Tetleys, good home-cooked bar lunches, reasonable prices, no juke box or machines, tables outside behind; quiet and relaxed evenings, handy for GMEX centre *(M Cosgriff, BB)*

☆ **Manchester** Gtr Man [Honey St; off Red Bank, nr Victoria Stn], *Queens Arms*: Well preserved Empress Brewery tiled facade for unusually welcoming extended pub with well kept Batemans XXXB, Mitchells Best, Timothy Taylors Landlord and Best, Theakstons Old Peculier and interesting guest beers, several Belgian beers on tap, Weston's farm cider, simple but often unusual lunchtime and evening bar food, coal fire, bar billiards, backgammon, chess, good juke box; children welcome, open all day weekdays; unexpected views of Manchester across the Irk Valley and its railway lines from pleasant garden with good play area, worth

penetrating the surrounding viaducts, scrapyards and industrial premises *(Richard Lewis, Mark Stevens, S G Brown, Andy Hazeldine)*

Manchester [Chapel Rd, Salford], *Albert Vaults*: Useful for well kept Burtonwood *(PGP)*; [86 Portland St], *Circus*: Two tiny rooms with very well kept Tetleys from cramped corridor bar, friendly landlord; cl afternoons, and often looks closed other times (you have to knock) *(Andy Hazeldine, PGP)*; [Kennedy St], *City Arms*: Well kept Ind Coope Burton, Tetleys and maybe Jennings, popular bar lunches, quiet evenings; bare boards, steps down to back lounge, may be cl much of weekend *(PGP)*; [71 Old Bury Rd, Whitefield, nr Besses o' the Barn Stn], *Coach & Horses*: Multi-room coaching inn built around 1830, little changed, very popular and friendly, with well kept Holts, table service, darts, cards *(Pete Baker)*; [Windsor Cresc̄ ct (A6), opp Salford Univ], *Crescent*: Three 18th-c houses converted into beer house in 19th, strange layout and idiosyncratic homely unsmart decor, chatty buzzing atmosphere, two beers brewed on site, several interesting guest ales, good value food, friendly staff, pool room, juke box; popular with students and university staff *(Richard Lewis, Andy Hazeldine, Alan Daly)*; [95 Cheetham Hill Rd (A665)], *Derby Brewery Arms*: Huge showpiece Holts pub with well kept cheap beer from the nearby brewery, cheap lunchtime food from hatch *(S G Brown, PGP)*; [80 Portland St, nr Piccadilly], *Grey Horse*: Cosy little Hydes pub with well kept beer, some unusual malt whiskies, popular lunchtime food; no juke box or machine *(Richard Lewis)*; [St Marys St], *H R Fletcher*: Lively atmosphere, good choice of real ale *(M A Robinson)*; [Whitworth St, by Deansgate Stn], *Head of Steam*: Recently opened, with about ten well kept ales, farm cider, good range of country wines, interesting carefully executed railways theme (with enthusiasts' model and railwayana shop, maybe Sunday auctions inc brewery memorabilia); bargain food all day, friendly staff; children very welcome *(Richard Lewis)*; [47 Ducie St], *Jolly Angler*: Unpretentious backstreet local, small and friendly, with well kept Hydes, pool and darts, informal folk singing Mon, open all day Fri/Sat *(Pete Baker, Andy Hazeldine)*; [Bloom St, Salford], *Kings Arms*: Large unusually shaped Victorian pub, enthusiast landlord with superb range of changing well kept ales; pool and juke box in side games room, friendly staff, good value lunchtime bar food *(Richard Lewis, Andy Hazeldine)*; [520 Manchester Rd (A6), Wardley, W of Swinton], *Morning Star*: Busy Holts local, well kept ales, good value basic food weekday lunchtime, lively games-oriented bar, usually some Sat entertainment in lounge *(Pete Baker)*; [33 Back Piccadilly], *Mother Macs*: Comfortable, with tall etched glass windows, old local photographs, welcoming staff and customers, weekday bar food inc good sandwiches and generous cheap hot dishes,

Boddingtons, Chesters Best and Flowers IPA; piped music, TV *(Alan Gough)*; [Wilmslow Rd, Didsbury], *Old Cock*: A dozen or more changing ales in big bare-boards pub with large wooden benches and happy mix of locals and students; cheapish food, good fruit machine, tables outside, open all day Sun *(Graham Gowland, Martin Bennett)*; [90 Portland St], *Old Monkey*: Two-floor newish but traditional Holts pub, etched glass and mosaic tiling, interesting memorabilia, well kept cheap Bitter and Mild, low-priced food, warm hospitality, wide mix of customers *(Richard Lewis, S G Brown, Howell Parry)*; [Shambles Sq, behind Arndale], *Old Wellington*: Genuinely ancient, with flagstones, gnarled oak timbers, oak panelling; well kept Bass and Stones on handpump, bar food (from noon, not Sun) esp hot beef sandwiches, small upstairs carvery (cl Mon–Weds evenings and all day Sun); often packed lunchtime *(Bas Hollander, BB)*; [Wilmslow Rd, Withington], *Red Lion*: Long low cottage-style Marstons pub opening into huge two-level complex of plush seating with conservatory, friendly staff, popular good value food (not Sun evening), well kept Pedigree, Banks's Mild and an interesting guest beer; tables in garden, bowling green *(Ian Phillips, Howell Parry, Matthew Callaghan, Clare Wilson)*; [126 Grosvenor St], *Scruffy Murphys*: Huge pastiche of Irish pub, several levels, nooks and crannies, loud piped Irish folk music and Gaelic pipes, very well priced bar food, Tetleys and other real ales *(Ian Phillips)*; [Portland St], *White Horse*: Unspoilt city pub with jovial atmosphere, Hyde beers at sensible prices; small bar *(PGP)*; [43 Liverpool Rd, Castlefield], *White Lion*: Busy but friendly and comfortable, with good inexpensive food in nicely decorated dining area, four Whitbreads-related and guest ales, seats out in open square overlooking site of Roman fort; very handy for GMEX and science museum *(Andy Hazeldine, Dave Braisted)*; [139 Barlow Moor Rd, Didsbury], *Woodstock*: Impressive, roomy conversion of large 1920s house hidden from road by trees, Bass (drinks table service after 8pm) and other real ales, good generous food from vegetarian to kangaroo, deep leather sofas and family portraits, friendly even when busy; picnic tables outside *(John O'Donnell, Andrew Perkin, Wendy and Ian Phillips, Clare Wilson)*; [Bury Old Rd, Prestwich, by Heaton Pk main gate], *Woodthorpe*: Huge Victorian pile, former home of Holts brewing family, extensively refurbished 1993 without altering character; main room still has original Gothick fireplace with log fires, exterior has lots of terracotta decoration; well kept cheap Holts and guest beers, friendly fast service, good bar food, good restaurant *(Dennis D'Vigne)*

☆ **Mawdesley** [Bluestone Lane; follow Eccleston sign from village which is signed off B5246 Parbold—Rufford; SD5016], *Robin Hood*: Busy, neat and comfortable open-plan refurbished pub with button-back wall

banquettes, reproduction Victorian prints, decorative plates, stained-glass seat dividers, some stripped stone; good value generous straightforward home cooking with fresh veg and cheap children's helpings, small pretty upstairs restaurant (often booked well ahead), friendly atmosphere and good service, well kept Whitbreads-related and guest ales, decent wines, children's room; piped nostalgic pop music, fruit machine; picnic tables on neat side terrace, good fenced play area *(John Fazakerley, Arthur Wright, BB)*

☆ **Mereclough** [302 Red Lees Rd; off A646 Burnley—Halifax – OS Sheet 103 map ref 873305; SD8730], *Kettledrum*: Friendly and cosy country local with wide choice of good value genuine home cooking, five well kept Courage and Theakstons ales, good service, fine views, extraordinary collections esp gruesome knives, partly no-smoking gaslit upstairs dining room; children allowed away from main bar till 9, seats outside *(Wayne Brindle, LYM)*

Morecambe [19 Bare Lane, Bare; SD4665], *Dog & Partridge*: Traditional interior, ten real ales inc Boddingtons and Timothy Taylors, good freshly cooked bar food; can get crowded weekends *(Dr and Mrs Baker, P A Legon)*

Mossley Gtr Man [Manchester Rd (A635 N); SD9802], *Roaches Lock*: Canalside pub with Whitbreads-related beers, eating area, friendly efficient service, benches overlooking lock and towpath *(Chris Westmoreland)*; [Manchester Rd (A635)], *Woodend*: Friendly new licensee, good changing well priced food, well kept Marstons and guest beers, log fire, big garden *(Alan Rogers)*

☆ **Mottram** Gtr Man [off A57 M'ter—Barnsley; at central traffic lights turn opp B6174 into Broadbottom Rd; SJ9995], *Waggon*: Generous reliable food served very promptly all day in comfortable open-plan local, sensible prices, well kept Robinsons Best and Best Mild on electric pump, friendly waitresses, big central fire, good wheelchair access; picnic tables and good play area outside *(A Preston, BB)*

☆ **Much Hoole** [Liverpool Old Rd; SD4723], *Rose & Crown*: Huge squarish pitched-roof family dining room given its star for good value home-cooked food (not Sun) using fresh ingredients, esp a fine range of interesting fish dishes; locals' bar with banquettes and piped pop music (may be loud, TV may be on too), games area with pool; Greenalls and Tetleys; children not unwelcome *(Janet Lee, Jim and Maggie Cowell, BB)*

Nether Burrow [SD6275], *Highwayman*: Family-run 17th-c inn with well kept real ales, good value homely food, friendly staff, highwayman theme, pleasant restaurant; lovely gardens, pretty Lune Valley countryside *(Geoffrey and Brenda Wilson)*

nr **Oldham** Gtr Man [Ripponden Rd, Grains Bar (A672/B6197); SD9608], *Bulls Head*: Snug two-room moorland pub with good home cooking inc real chips, open fire, Disney plates, fish pictures, live music some evenings, pitch and putt, walks in nearby open country *(Pauline Crossland, Dave Cawley, BB)*

Ormskirk [Grimshaw Lane; SD4108], *Yew Tree*: Clean, warm and cosy, with welcoming staff, bargain food, well kept Boddingtons, Cains, Higsons and guest beers at reasonable prices *(Michael and Sue Griffin)*

Oswaldtwistle [Haslingden Old Rd (A677/B6231); SD7327], *Britannia*: Attractive traditional core with log-burning ranges, reasonably priced bar food with some emphasis on fresh fish, friendly atmosphere, Thwaites Bitter and Mild; sun-trap back terrace and play area; food all day Sun, children in family restaurant *(John Fazakerley, LYM)*

Over Kellet [SD5269], *Eagles Head*: Extended village pub with emphasis on food; Mitchells ales *(Tony Hobden)*

Parbold [Alder Lane (A5209); SD4911], *Stocks*: Relaxed local atmosphere in two rooms off island bar extending into roomy beamed dining area, well kept Tetleys Bitter and Dark Mild and a guest such as Archers; busy evenings *(Comus Elliott, BB)*; [canal], *Windmill*: Convivial, with well kept Greenalls, wide range of good value food, friendly rugby-enthusiast landlord *(Alan Ashcroft, Comus Elliott)*

☆ Pendleton [SD7539], *Swan With Two Necks*: Welcoming olde-worlde village pub below Pendle Hill, good value interesting well presented food with lots of fresh veg, well kept ale *(Mrs Lyn Jones, LYM)*

Pleasington [Victoria Rd – OS Sheet 103 map ref 642266; SD6426], *Butlers Arms*: Comfortable and friendly, with good varied food inc interesting specials, games room, bowling green at back *(RJH)*

Poulton le Fylde [Ball St; SD3439], *Thatched House*: Busy and friendly recently renovated thatched town pub with well kept Whitbreads-related and guest ales, popular weekend meeting-place; no food *(Rosemarie Johnson, Charles Darbyshire)*

Preston [166 Friargate; SD5330], *Black Horse*: Thriving friendly old-fashioned pub with full Robinsons ale range and Hartleys XB, lunchtime food, side rooms, upstairs 1920s-style bar, unusual curved and tiled Victorian main bar, panelling, stained glass, mosaic floor and small rooms off; pictures of old town, lots of artefacts, good juke box, open all day *(Richard Lewis, Andy Hazeldine, Graham Bush)*; [15 Fox St], *Fox & Grapes*: Busy traditional pub with bare boards, basic fittings, old Preston pictures, cheap lunchtime food, friendly staff, well kept mainly S&N ales – huge throughput of Youngers No 3; juke box, pub games, can get smoky, open all day *(Richard Lewis)*; [99 Fylde Rd], *Hogshead*: Former millowner's house superbly restored by Whitbreads as wood-and-bricks real ale pub, a dozen or more at a time kept well, mainly from small breweries, big window into cellar where casks tilt automatically; no music or games, food served 11-7 (not Sun), chef happy to make things not on menu; open all day *(Richard*

Lewis); [Friargate], *Lamb & Packet*: Well kept Thwaites ales in small comfortable two-level pub, pleasant decor, reasonably priced food *(Richard Lewis)*; [6 Heatley St], *New Britannia*: Eight mainly Whitbreads-related ales kept well; no frills, games room off big bar *(Andy Hazeldine)*; [35 Friargate (by Ringway)], *Old Black Bull*: Another big alehouse conversion, almost too many changing beers, good value food, darts and pub games, friendly staff; can get smoky and crowded with students; unmodified prewar green-tiled frontage with original stained glass *(Graham Bush, Richard Lewis)*; [24 Lancaster Rd, by Guildhall], *Stanley Arms*: Fine mirrors, bare boards, four areas, different levels; friendly staff, popular lunchtime food, 16 handpumps with well kept changing ales from small breweries, German and Belgian beers, Bulmer's cider; pool room, TV, open all day, can be packed evenings, weekend bouncers *(Richard Lewis, Graham Bush)*; [185 Fylde Rd], *Tap & Spile*: Lots of prints, brewery artefacts, machinery and railway lamps, comfortable seats, back pool room, friendly staff, constant changeover of beers and ciders all kept well, country wines, homely bar food *(Richard Lewis)*; [1 Fishergate], *Wall Street*: Converted bank, friendly service, well kept Greenalls Bitter and Original, good food; very busy weekend evenings *(J Tyrer-Wilson)*; *Watering Trough*: Recently comfortably refurnished, striking ceiling, original windows, side games bar, friendly service, well kept Jennings Sneck Lifter, Vaux Waggle Dance and Wards Sheffield Best *(Richard Lewis)*

Radcliffe Gtr Man [Coronation Rd; SD7906], *Wilton Arms*: Busy local, no piped music in lounge, well kept Holts *(A and M Matheson)*

Ramsbottom Gtr Man [Twine Valley, signed off A56 N of Bury at Shuttleworth; SD7916], *Fishermans Retreat*: Surrounded by well stocked trout lakes, good interesting well presented reasonably priced food, generous helpings, good choice of changing beers; open all day from 8am *(Aidan J Grimshaw)*

☆ Riley Green [A6061/A675 Preston—Bolton; SD6225], *Royal Oak*: Cosy low-beamed three-room pub nr canal, decent reliable food, Thwaites Bitter and Mild, friendly efficient service; ancient stripped stone, open fires, seats from high-backed settles to red plush armchairs, turkey carpet, soft lighting, impressive woodwork, fresh flowers, interesting model steam engines; can be packed weekends *(Bronwen and Steve Wrigley, RJH, Arthur and Margaret Dickinson, John Fazakerley, BB)*

Riley Green [A675 NW of A674 junction], *Boatyard*: Dining pub done out in pseudo-Victorian-style, food all day every day, Thwaites real ales; on mound by canal with plenty of small boats and narrowboats to watch; tables outside, beached barge in grounds *(JF)*

☆ Rochdale Gtr Man [Cheesden, Ashworth Moor; A680 towards Edenfield; SD8316], *Owd Betts*: Isolated but cosy moorland pub with great views, three low-beamed areas, oak settles, brasses, open fires, stripped stone; well kept Greenalls Bitter and Mild, food inc good sandwiches, efficient friendly service *(J E Rycroft, K H Frostick, BB)*

Roughlee [nr Nelson; SD8440], *Bay Horse*: Old roomily extended village pub in beautiful valley with pleasant restaurant, good value food (not Mon evening) inc fine puddings, well kept Theakstons or Thwaites, good outdoor play area, table tennis *(Arthur and Margaret Dickinson)*

Scarisbrick [B5242; SD3813], *Heatons Bridge*: Unspoilt friendly pub by canal crossing, four smallish rooms and dining room, Tetleys-related ales *(Chris Westmoreland)*

Scouthead Gtr Man [Thurston Clough Rd; just off A62 Oldham–Huddersfield – OS Sheet 109 map ref 973064; SD9706], *Old Original*: Homely and welcoming, open-plan but partitioned, spectacular Pennine and E Manchester views, eating area with reasonably priced meals inc exceptional fish choice, Tetleys-related ales, decent wines, piped music with Italy/Spain slant *(T D G Isherwood)*

☆ **Simonstone** [Trapp Lane, off School Lane – Simonstone—Sabden trans-Pendle rd, OS Sheet 103 map ref 776356; SD7735], *Higher Trapp*: Attractive refurbished bar with relaxing views, well kept Boddingtons and Theakstons, food in bar and restaurant (all day Sun), no-smoking areas, big conservatory; children welcome, comfortable bedrooms *(A and M Dickinson, Wayne Brindle)*

☆ **Slaidburn** [B6478 N of Clitheroe; SD7152], *Hark to Bounty*: Charming Forest of Bowland village, relaxed country atmosphere, friendly service, decor a pleasant mix of old and new, open fire, brasses, lots of tables for the good value interesting food, good range of S&N ales, decent wines; a nice place to stay, pleasant garden behind, good walks *(Alan Griffiths, Richard R Dolphin, John and Joan Wyatt, Bronwen and Steve Wrigley, LYM)*

Stalybridge Gtr Man [SJ9698], *Station Buffet*: Sadly this wonderful little time capsule, for long a main entry but under threat from Railtrack property redevelopment, has now closed *(LYM)*

☆ **Standish** Gtr Man [Platt Lane, Worthington – not far from M6 junction 27; SD5711], *Crown*: Civilised oasis, chesterfields, armchairs, fresh flowers and open fire in comfortable panelled bar, well kept ales such as Bass, Bass Mild and Boddingtons, airy dining extension with wide range of good reasonably priced food, pleasant conservatory; children allowed away from bar *(Ardill and Anne Booth, LYM)*

Standish Gtr Man [Almond Brook], *Charnley Arms*: Modern Greenalls family dining pub, very tidy; reasonable prices, open all day; not far from M6 *(Mr and Mrs E J W Rogers)*

☆ **Stockport** Gtr Man [552 Didsbury Rd (off A5145), Heaton Mersey; SJ8691], *Griffin*: Thriving unspoilt local with cheap well kept Holts Bitter and Mild in four unpretentiously

Victorian rooms off central servery with largely original curved-glass gantry, basic furnishings, no piped music; lunchtime food in dining extension, seats outside *(N P Greensitt, BB)*

☆ **Stockport** [12 Little Underbank; steps from St Petersgate], *Queens Head*: Long narrow late Victorian pub with delightful separate snug and back dining area; good bustling atmosphere, reasonable bar food, well kept Sam Smiths on handpump, rare brass cordials fountain, daily papers, old posters and adverts; no-smoking area, some live jazz, open all day; famous narrow gents' *(Richard Lewis)*

Stockport [23 Millgate St, behind Asda], *Arden Arms*: Traditional and welcoming, with several room areas inc old-fashioned snug through servery, good value limited lunchtime bar food, well kept Robinsons, several grandfather clocks, Dinky toy collection *(Pete Baker)*; [154 Heaton La, Heaton Norris], *Crown*: Well run town local under arch of vast viaduct; partly open-plan but with several cosy areas, stylish decor, wide range of well kept ales, farm cider, reasonably priced lunchtime bar food, no-smoking room, pool, darts, TV; seats outside, open all day *(Martin Tetlow, Richard Lewis)*

☆ **Summerseat** Gtr Man [½ mile from M66 junction 1 northbound, off A56 N via Bass Lane then Cliffe Avenue, then bear right], *Waterside*: Striking conversion of tall 19th-c cotton-mill building, flagstones, tiles, restored machinery, attractive setting with tables outside; good range of well kept ales, decent wine, reasonably priced straightforward bar food (service can sometimes slow); very popular with young people evenings, piped pop music may be loud *(Gordon Tong, Peter Crawshaw, LYM)*

☆ **Uppermill** Gtr Man [Runninghill Gate, off A670 via New St; SD9905], *Cross Keys*: Low-beamed moorland local up long steep lane, flagstones and original cooking range, big fires, local pictures for sale, basic bar food (lunchtime Sun, all day other days), well kept Lees Bitter and Mild, lots of malt whiskies, pub games, children in side rooms, tables out on terraces with adventure playground; lovely setting, lots of walks; clog dancing Mon, folk Weds *(Chris Westmoreland, Wallis Taylor, Jack and Philip Paxton, LYM)*

Uppermill [High St], *Commercial*: Freshly cooked food (so can be a wait), separate dining room, open fire, pool table, Dinky and Matchbox toy collection, friendly staff; canal walks and craft shop nearby, brass band contest May *(Pauline Crossland, Dave Cawley)*

Urmston Gtr Man [Stretford Rd; SJ7695], *Lord Nelson*: No-frills traditional pub, well kept Holts, free sandwiches on quiz night; salesmen may peddle fish, meat and pies here *(James Todd)*

☆ **Waddington** [SD7243], *Lower Buck*: Traditional friendly and busy local with Timothy Taylors Best, Ruddles County and other well kept ales, popular basic home cooking, hatch-service lobby, front bar with built-in dresser, plain back room, pool room; pretty village *(Malcolm Pollard, Wayne Brindle, Arthur and Margaret Dickinson, BB)*

Whalley Gtr Man [Whalley Rd, off A666 Blackburn—Clitheroe; SD7336], *Hogs Head*: Formerly Whalley Arms, converted into beer drinker's pub with stone floors, dark oak beams hung with woodworking tools, tables made from beer barrels, eight real ales *(Simon Woodhouse, Maria Dobson)*

Wheelton [SD6021], *Top Lock*: Cosy, with friendly hard-working staff, canal-related decor, good range of reasonably priced food – even black pudding as starter *(Sue and Mike Todd)*

Whittle le Woods [Preston Rd (A6 not far from M61 junction 7); SD5721], *Sea View*: This comfortable inland pub really does have a sea view (from upstairs); spacious but cosy and friendly, with decent bar food, Theakstons ales, dining rooms (one no smoking), beams, horsebrasses and coach horns, big stone fireplace in extension; piped music *(A Preston)*

☆ **Wiswell** [just NE of Whalley; SD7437], *Freemasons Arms*: Cosy country pub, wide choice of good value well presented interesting fresh food (must book restaurant Fri/Sat evening) in small bar and overflow upstairs dining room, friendly efficient service, good range of beers, lots of malt whiskies; lovely village below Pendle Hill; cl Mon/Tues evening *(Dr and Mrs D E Awbery, Jon Hesketh, Yvonne and Mike Meadley)*

☆ **Woodford** Gtr Man [550 Chester Rd; A5149 SW of BAe entrance; SJ8882], *Davenport Arms*: Unspoilt traditional country pub, simple but comfortable, with small rooms, coal fires, friendly staff (in same family for 60 years), well kept Robinsons Best and Best Mild, good reasonably priced home cooking lunchtime (toasted sandwiches evening), good games room, no-smoking room; children allowed in back no-smoking snug; tables on front terrace and in attractive garden *(Pat and Tony Young, Richard Lewis, P and M Rudlin)*

☆ **Wrea Green** [Station Rd; SD3931], *Grapes*: Busy but roomy open-plan local with well cooked imaginative food in pleasant clean dining area, well kept Boddingtons, Marstons Pedigree and Theakstons, open fire, efficient courteous staff; tables out overlooking village green, picturesque neighbouring church *(Cyril Higgs, Graham Bush)*

Wrightington Bar [9 Wood Lane, handy for M6 junction 27; SD5313], *Scarisbrick Arms*: Doing well under new licensees, with good choice of well presented unusual dishes, generous helpings, delicious home-made puddings *(Euan and Aileen McEwan)*

Real ale to us means beer which has matured naturally in its cask – not pressurised or filtered. We name all real ales stocked. We usually name ales preserved under a light blanket of carbon dioxide too, though purists – pointing out that this stops the natural yeasts developing – would disagree (most people, including us, can't tell the difference!).

Leicestershire
(including Rutland)

This is the first edition of the Guide in which we have devoted a separate chapter each to Leicestershire, Lincolnshire and Nottinghamshire. It does show up what a fine choice of pub food there is in this county. Pubs doing specially well here these days include the White Horse near Rutland Water at Empingham (gaining a Food Award this year), the Old Barn at Glooston (real endeavour here in the kitchen and indeed the kitchen garden gains it a Food Award too), the welcoming Bewicke Arms at Hallaton, the unspoilt (and unsmart) Cap & Stocking at Kegworth, the cheerful Old White Hart at Lyddington (a newcomer to the main entries, with most enjoyable food), the Crown at Old Dalby, Peacock at Redmile and Bakers Arms at Thorpe Langton (all three very popular dining pubs), and two more new entries, the Cock at Peatling Magna (an exemplary village local) and the Old Brewery at Somerby (brewing a fine range of real ales). Against hot competition, the Old Barn at Glooston gains the title of Leicestershire Dining Pub of the Year – but please note that it is not open on weekday lunchtimes. In the Lucky Dip section at the end of the chapter, pubs earning particular praise in recent months include both Stretton entries, the Royal Arms at Sutton Cheney, Black Horse at Walcote, Noel Arms at Whitwell and Kings Arms at Wing – we have inspected and enjoyed most of these ourselves. Leicester has quite a good choice. Drinks prices in the area are lower than average, with the Old Brewery in Somerby particularly good value; the Nevill Arms at Medbourne gains a Beer Award this year, for the quality of its offerings.

BRAUNSTON SK8306 Map 4
Blue Ball ⑪ ♀

Village signposted off A606 in Oakham

Said to be Rutland's oldest pub, this popular place was bought by the Old English Pub Company not long before we went to press, but they're keeping things exactly as before, with the same staff, chef, and charming French manager. It's very much the kind of place where customers leave saying 'I wish I could cook like that', so it's worth pointing out that in winter they run fortnightly cooking demonstrations; you might not leave ready to open your own kitchen, but at the very least you'll have a better appreciation of how they manage to put together such good meals here. As well as sandwiches (£2.50) and soup (£1.95), well presented dishes might typically include a pâté of the day (£3.75), moules marinières, a choice of cheeses with salad and walnut oil dressing, or warm spinach timbale with pine kernels (£4.50), spicy fishcakes (£5.30), stir-fried vegetable curry (£6.50), tagliatelle with tomato, bacon, garlic and basil (£6.95), and puddings such as strawberry bavarois or nougat flavoured with kirsch and mango (£3.75); children's helpings. Service is very good, even when busy. Although much emphasis is obviously placed on the food, there's a very pleasant relaxed and informal atmosphere; the main area preserves its original form of separate rooms, while the furnishings and decorations – not too fussy – are individual and interesting. Well kept Bass, Greene King Abbot, Marstons Bitter and Pedigree, Ruddles County, and Tetleys on handpump, and up to 8 wines by the glass (including one sparkling). Dominoes, shove-ha'penny (not much used), and piped music; one room is no smoking. *(Recommended by Gill and Bryan Trueman, Jane Kingsbury, Eric Locker, Mavis and John Wright, David and Fiona Pemberton, Peter and Patricia Burton, Joan and Michel Hooper-Immins, Brian and Jill Bond, Penny and Martin Fletcher, Jim Farmer, S G Brown, D Goodger, Julie Peters, David and Shelia)*

Free house ~ Manager Jean Berlioz ~ Real ale ~ Meals and snacks (12-2, 6.30-10) ~ Restaurant (closed Mon and Tues) ~ (01572) 722135 ~ Children welcome ~ Open 12-3, 6-11

Old Plough ♀

The kind of place where they'll happily provide several spoons for just one pudding, this attractive pub is well worth knowing for its very good food, but it's not somewhere dominated by meals to the exclusion of all else. The atmosphere is still pubby and friendly, they hold lots of social and sporting events for locals, and the beers are carefully chosen. The menu changes every season, but might include attractively served dishes such as home-made soup (£1.95), really big filled rolls (from £2.75), filled baked potatoes (from £2.95), chicken, bacon and peanut stir fry (£3.95), cauliflower and chick pea curry (£6.95), beef and mushroom pie (£7.25), smoked fish and prawn cannelloni, prime pork ribs, or Loch Fyne kippers (£7.50), chicken breast wrapped in bacon and served on a creamy leek and black pepper sauce (£8.95), and puddings like lemon and cream cheese roulade (£2.95) or black cherry crème brûlée (£3.25); very good service. The traditional bars have upholstered seats around cast-iron-framed tables under the heavy and irregular back beams, and plenty of brass ornaments on the mantelpiece. At the back is a stylish modern no-smoking conservatory dining room. The real ales are generally all local: well kept Oakham Jeffrey Hudson, Ruddles Best, and brews from the Grainstore Brewery. Also a good, interesting well noted wine list, fruit punches in summer, Scrumpy Jack cider, and a choice of teas and coffees. The carpeted public bar has darts in winter; maybe piped music. Picnic tables shelter among fruit trees, and there's a boules pitch. The inn-sign is attractive. *(Recommended by Eric Locker, M and J Back, George Atkinson)*

Free house ~ Licensees Andrew and Amanda Reid ~ Real ale ~ Meals and snacks (till 10) ~ Restaurant ~ (01572) 722714 ~ Children welcome ~ Open 11-3, 6-11; all day summer weekends; closed 25 Dec

EMPINGHAM SK9408 Map 4

White Horse 🍴 🛏

Main Street; A606 Stamford—Oakham

Very close to the edge of Rutland Water, Europe's largest man-made lake, this very well liked old inn is always cheerful and bustling, and the licensees work very hard to make sure they are offering what people want. It's becoming increasingly popular as a place to eat, with the well presented bar food including home-made soup (£2.10), chicken liver or blue cheese pâtés (£2.95), vegetarian pie (£5.75), ploughman's, steak and kidney pie, or moules marinières (£5.95), chicken breast coated in coarse grain mustard and encased in a lattice pastry (£6.25), a daily fresh fish dish, steaks (from £7.95), and children's meals; they also do morning coffee and afternoon tea. Helpings are big (one reader was delighted to find almost a quarter pound of ham and the same amount of stilton in the ploughman's), and vegetables are served separately in a little dish. Recently recarpeted, the open-plan lounge bar has a big log fire below an unusual free-standing chimney-funnel, lots of fresh flowers, and a very relaxed and comfortable atmosphere; the restaurant and the Orange Room are no smoking. Well kept Courage Directors, John Smiths, Ruddles County, and a guest like Crown Buckley Reverend James on handpump, maybe kept under light blanket pressure; fruit machine and piped music. Outside are some rustic tables among urns of flowers. Some of the bedrooms are in a delightfully converted stable block; expect good breakfasts if you're staying. *(Recommended by Melanie Bradshaw, PGP, RJH, Paul McPherson, R M Macnaughton, John Fahy, Gordon Theaker, A and M Dickinson, AMM, CP, Peter Brimacombe, Alan and Heather Jacques)*

S & N ~ Lease: Roger Bourne ~ Real ale ~ Meals and snacks (till 9.45) ~ Restaurant ~ (01780) 460221 ~ Well behaved children in eating area of bar and in Orange Room, no under 10s after 9 o'clock ~ Open 10am-11pm(10.30 Sun) ~ Bedrooms: £32(£42B)/£45(£55B)

EXTON SK9211 Map 8

Fox & Hounds

Signposted off A606 Stamford—Oakham

This strikingly tall stone building is handy for walkers on the Viking Way, and there are seats among large rose beds on the well kept back lawn, overlooking paddocks. Inside, the comfortable high-ceilinged lounge bar has some dark red plush easy chairs as well as wheelback seats around lots of dark tables, maps and hunting and military prints on the walls, brass and copper ornaments, and a winter log fire in a large stone fireplace; readers like the way it's not the sort of pub where drinkers feel less welcome. Bar food includes soup (£2.45), ploughman's (from £3.75), lamb liver and bacon (£5.95), lasagne or home-made steak and kidney pie (£6.75), and local trout (£7.75), with evening extras like scampi (£5.95) or rump steak (£9.50). Well kept Sam Smiths OB and guests like Badger Best or Charles Wells Bombardier on handpump; piped music. The lively and quite separate public bar has darts, pool, cribbage, dominoes, juke box, fruit machine, and video game. Rutland Water is only a couple of miles away. *(Recommended by Chris Raisin, Eric Locker, H Bramwell, John Fahy, RWD, Jim Farmer, J M Wright, L Walker)*

Free house ~ Licensees David and Jennifer Hillier ~ Real ale ~ Meals and snacks ~ Restaurant (not Sun evening) ~ (01572) 812403 ~ Children in eating area of bar ~ Open 11-3, 6-11 ~ Bedrooms: £22/£36

GLOOSTON SP7595 Map 4

Old Barn ★ 🍴 🛏 🍷 🍺

From B6047 in Tur Langton follow Hallaton signpost, then fork left following Glooston signpost

Leicestershire Dining Pub of the Year

So many more people have been coming to eat at this carefully restored 16th-c pub over the last year or so that they've had to treble the size of the kitchen. It's not hard to see why the meals are such a draw – the short monthly changing menu is remarkably inventive, and dishes are prepared with a great deal of care and individual attention. As well as a soup of the day (£2.75), recent selections have included caribbean turkey mousse flavoured with mango, lime and ginger and served with mango salsa, or oven-baked avocado in stilton sauce with port jelly (£3.95), parsnip and pear sauté garnished with almonds and served on a bed of red cabbage cooked in red wine, cloves and apple (£7.95), braised guinea fowl with a beetroot, celery and orange glaze (£8.95), roast leg of lamb in a juniper and garlic sauce (£9.95), poached turbot in anchovy sauce (£11.95), and excellent home-made puddings like grape and vermouth cheesecake (£3.25). Herbs and other produce now come from the pub's own kitchen garden. Due to their busy evenings and remote situation, the pub is closed on weekday lunchtimes; on Saturday lunchtime they only serve snacks – good Sunday lunch (3 courses £9.50). The lower beamed main bar has stripped kitchen tables and country chairs, pewter plates, Players cricketer cigarette cards, and an open fire. Four well kept real ales on handpump rotated from a wide choice of beers like Adnams Broadside, Bass, Boddingtons, Greene King Abbot, Hook Norton Old Hookey, Morlands Old Speckled Hen, Theakstons Best, and Wadworths 6X; good wine list (with half a dozen by the glass). The dining area is no smoking. There are a few old-fashioned teak seats in front, with picnic tables by roses under the trees behind. The french-style shower-and-wash cabinets please readers, but might perhaps suit best those with at least a modest degree of mobility. Well behaved dogs welcome. *(Recommended by Anthony Barnes, Jim Farmer, Stephen, Julie and Hayley Brown, V W Burgess,*

Vicky and David Sarti, Rex and Mary Hepburn, J D Cloud, F Davy, David Atkinson, H Paulinski, Margaret and Roy Randle, Eric Locker, Frank Cummins, A J Morton)

Free house ~ Licensees Charles Edmondson-Jones and Stewart Sturge ~ Real ale ~ Meals and snacks (not weekday lunchtimes or Sun evening) ~ Restaurant ~ (01858) 545215 ~ Well behaved children welcome ~ Open 7-11 during the week; 12-2.30, 7-11 Sat; closed Sun evening ~ Bedrooms: £37.50B/£49.50B

HALLATON SP7896 Map 4

Bewicke Arms ★

On good fast back road across open rolling countryside between Uppingham and Kibworth; village signposted from B6047 in Tur Langton and from B664 SW of Uppingham

Though the setting and views from this old thatched inn are highly praised, what particularly impresses readers is the warm welcome and friendly service, especially from the genial landlord. Recently redecorated, the unpretentious beamed main bar has two small oddly shaped rooms with farming implements and deer heads on the walls, pokerwork seats, old-fashioned settles (including some with high backs and wings), wall benches, and stripped oak tables, and four copper kettles gleaming over one of the log fires; the bottom room is no smoking during the week. Big helpings of popular bar food include basics like sandwiches, ploughman's, and grills, with daily specials such as egg and prawn mayonnaise (£3.95), deep-fried brie with cranberry dip (£4.45), meaty or vegetarian lasagne (£5.85), fresh local trout with dill and lemon butter (£6.80), chicken boursin (£7.60), chicken breast with bacon and mushrooms in a port, cream and fresh rosemary sauce (£8.20), and puddings such as treacle sponge and custard (£2.50); you can book a table most days, otherwise get there early. Service is charming and flexible. Well kept Marstons Pedigree, Ruddles Best and County and a guest beer on handpump, maybe kept under light blanket pressure; darts, fruit machine in the side corridor, and piped music. No dogs. They have a big self-catering apartment to rent. From the front of the whitewashed building you can watch the various activities on the village green, especially entertaining on Easter Monday when there's a 'bottle-kicking' race (they actually use miniature barrels), or in the summer when there may be Morris dancing. Picnic tables on a crazy-paved terrace behind look over the ex-stableyard car park to the hills behind. (Recommended by Thomas Nott, Ted George, Jim Farmer, Rona Murdoch, Brian and Jill Bond, Howard and Margaret Buchanan, Wayne Brindle, Jack and Philip Paxton, D Goodger, Eric Locker, Margaret and Roy Randle)

Free house ~ Licensee Neil Spiers ~ Real ale ~ Meals and snacks (till 9.45) ~ Restaurant ~ (01858) 555217 ~ Well behaved children welcome ~ Open 12-2.30, 7-11

HOSE SK7329 Map 7

Rose & Crown 🍺

Bolton Lane

Still involved in his game of pool as this atmospheric pub was about to close for the afternoon, a reader saw the landlord approaching and expected to be asked to leave – instead he and his friends were offered another drink, and told they could let themselves out whenever they finished. The range of real ales is perhaps the main attraction: there are usually eight on handpump at a time, often including brews you won't often find in this area, from smaller breweries in the west country or in the north. Forthcoming beers are posted up on the walls. Over the past year these have included Archers Golden, Bathams Best, Butterknowle High Force, Caledonian Deuchars IPA, Fullers ESB, Greene King Abbot, Hook Norton Old Hookey, Ruddles Best and County, Shepherd Neame Spitfire, and Youngs Special to name just a few. They also keep around a dozen malt whiskies. The more-or-less open-plan bar has recently been redecorated, and has pool, darts, dominoes, a fruit machine, trivia and juke box; the restaurant and lounge bar are no smoking. Bar food (not quite so well received this year as the pub's other features) might include filled rolls, home-made soup (£2), garlic mushrooms topped with bacon and stilton (£2.50), daily specials such as vegetable biryani, pork, orange and mushroom casserole or venison pie (£4.95), rack of lamb with mint gravy (£6.95), and chicken stuffed with stilton and wrapped in bacon (£7.95). There are tables on a fairy-lit sheltered terrace behind the building and a fenced family area at the rear of the car park. Campers and caravanners are welcome. *(Recommended by Chris Raisin, Jack and Philip Paxton, D R Eberlin, R M Taylor, June and Malcolm Farmer, Keith and Norma Bloomfield, D C Roberts, Joan and Michel Hooper-Immins)*

Free house ~ Licensee Carl and Carmel Routh ~ Real ale ~ Meals and snacks (till 10, 9 Sun) ~ Restaurant ~ (01949) 860424 ~ Children in eating area of bar and restaurant till 9 ~ Open 11.30-3, 7-11; closed 25 Dec

KEGWORTH SK4826 Map 7

Cap & Stocking ★ £ ◖

Under a mile from M1 junction 24: follow A6 towards Loughborough; in village, turn left at chemists' down one-way Dragwall opposite High Street, then left and left again, into Borough Street

The genuinely old-fashioned flavour of this delightfully unpretentious local extends to the Bass being served the traditional way in a jug direct from the cask. Each of the two determinedly simple front rooms has its own coal fire, and a friendly and easy-going feel; on the right there's lots of etched glass, big cases of stuffed birds and locally caught fish, fabric-covered wall benches and heavy cast-iron-framed tables, and a cast-iron range. The back room has french windows to the garden. Well kept beers on handpump include Hancocks HB, M & B Mild, and Everards Tiger, with a guest such as Badger Tanglefoot, Courage Directors, Shepherd Neame Bishops Finger or Vaux Waggle Dance. Good value bar food includes filled rolls (from 80p; hot from £1), soup (£1.25), ploughman's (from £3.20), pizzas (from £3.40), chilli con carne or vegetable curry (£3.50), Hungarian goulash (£4.25), beef stroganoff (£4.95), daily specials such as apricot pork, Sri Lankan chicken or Szechuan meatballs (from £3.95), and puddings like hot treacle sponge (£1). Dominoes, cribbage, trivia and Monday evening quiz, and floodlit boules in the pleasant garden. *(Recommended by Lucy James, C H and P Stride, PM, AM, D Eberlin, David and Fiona Pemberton, Vicky and David Sarti, RT and J C Moggridge, Christopher Turner, Jack and Philip Paxton, Michael Butler, R and A Cooper, AMM, CP, Jane Hosking, Ian Burniston, Peter and Jenny Quine, Jim Farmer, Dr and Mrs J H Hills, Karen Eliot)*

Bass ~ Lease: Graham and Mary Walsh ~ Real ale ~ Meals and snacks ~ (01509) 674814 ~ Children in eating area of bar ~ Open 11.30-3, 6(6.30 in winter)-11

KNIPTON SK8231 Map 7

Red House ⇐ ♀

Village signposted off A607 Grantham—Melton Mowbray

Friendly dogs and cats may welcome you in the hall of this fine, Georgian ex-hunting lodge – much as they might in a private house. The roomy turkey-carpeted bar, divided by a central hearth with a woodburning stove, has sturdy old-fashioned furnishings, hunting pictures, a delft shelf of sporting or game bird decorative plates, and a relaxed, friendly atmosphere. A neatly furnished no smoking conservatory opens off the airy restaurant. A good choice of rewarding bar food might include soup (from £1.95), yorkshire pudding filled with haggis and onion gravy (£2.95), ploughman's (£3.95), deep-filled Rutland pie (four meats, tomato, cheese, potato, spinach - £5.25), smoked chicken, stilton and tarragon pie or confit of guinea fowl on salsa bean salad (£5.65), a good range of imaginative vegetarian dishes like aubergine fritters with sweet spiced vegetables and dried fruits on garlic and turmeric cous-cous, or gnocchi in saffron and cream cheese sauce with roasted peppers, olives and pesto sauce (all £5.65), griddled salmon steak on squid-ink pasta with pesto and peppers (£7.65), and home-made puddings such as poached pears. Well kept Greene King Abbot, Marstons Pedigree, and Tetleys on handpump and electric pump, a good choice of wines including 120 bin-ends, 20 malt whiskies, and quite a few brandies and vintage ports; service is friendly and obliging – though can slow down when they're busy. The public bar area has darts, cribbage, dominoes and fruit machine; there may be unobtrusive piped music. *(Recommended by R and A Cooper, P Stallard, Derek and Sylvia Stephenson, Jack and Philip Paxton, David and Shelia, A and R Cooper)*

Free house ~ Lease: Robin Newport ~ Real ale ~ Meals and snacks ~ Restaurant ~ (01476) 870352 ~ Children welcome till 9 ~ Occasional trad jazz or folk ~ Open 11-3(4 weekends), 6-11; closed evening 25 Dec ~ Bedrooms: £21.50(£32.50B)/£32.50(£46.50B)

LOUGHBOROUGH SK5319 Map 7

Swan in the Rushes 🍺 £

The Rushes (A6)

This chatty pub successfully combines lively down-to-earth informality with a friendly welcome and good food, but the main draw is the fine collection of beers – interesting German, Belgian and other bottled beers, and on handpump well kept Archers Golden, Batemans XB, Boddingtons, Marstons Pedigree, Springhead Roaring Meg, and four regularly changing guests. Also two ciders, a good range of malt whiskies, and country wines. There are several neatly kept separate room areas, each with its own style – though the most comfortable seats are in the left-hand bay-windowed bar (which has an open fire) and in the snug back dining room. It can get very crowded, but service is good. Very reasonably priced, the home-made bar food includes filled rolls, a choice of ploughman's (from £3.50), tagliatelle bolognese or chilli con carne (£3.75), broccoli and cauliflower mornay filled pancakes (£3.95), bobotie, beef in ale or chicken in apple wine (£4.95), 8oz rump steak (£5.25), and puddings like apple strudel (£1.30). Shove-ha'penny, cribbage, dominoes, juke box, and backgammon. The simple bedrooms are clean and cosy, and breakfasts excellent. An outside drinking area with tables was added last year. *(Recommended by Joan and Michel Hooper-Immins, R M Taylor, Stephen and Julie Brown, James Nunns, Bruce Bird, David and Shelia, S G Brown, Jack and Philip Paxton)*

Free house ~ Licensee Andrew Hambleton ~ Real ale ~ Meals and snacks (12-2, 6-8.30; not Sat/Sun evenings) ~ (01509) 217014 ~ Children in dining room ~ Blues or R&B Sat evening, folk every other Sun and occasional Fri ~ Open 11-11; 12-10.30 Sun ~ Bedrooms: £20(£25B)/£30(£35B)

LYDDINGTON SP8797 Map 4

Old White Hart ♀

Village signposted off A6003 N of Corby

Very warm and welcoming, this traditional 17th-c village inn has a good deal of atmosphere, and enterprising good value food. The seasonal choice varies between lunchtime and evening, and might include starters like soup (£2.45), honeyed chicken and almond salad (£3.40), bacon and cream with a caerphilly cheese crust or baked eggs topped with leeks (£3.60), hot prawns in soured cream with lemon juice and grilled with cheddar (£3.65), and main courses such as steak and mushroom pie (£6.25), lamb and apple pie (£6.55), chicken breast with thyme and mushrooms on a creamy sauce with herb croûtons (£6.95), roast quail with cherry stuffing and port sauce (£8.95). The cosy softly lit bar has just three close-set tables in front of the warm log fire, with heavy bowed beams and lots of attractive dried flower arrangements. It opens into an attractive restaurant with corn dollies and a big oak dresser, and on the other side is a tiled-floor room with some stripped stone, cushioned wall seats and mate's chairs, a woodburning stove, and darts; there is a thriving dominoes school. The licensees are very helpful and friendly, as is their long-serving barmaid Chris. Well kept Greene King IPA and Abbot and Marstons Pedigree on handpump, good house wines (a choice of French or Australian); two of the restaurants are no smoking. There are picnic tables in the safe and pretty walled garden – on Thursday you can listen to the church bell ringers – which has ten floodlit boules pitches; good nearby walks; handy for the Bede House. *(Recommended by Grant Wicks, Rona Murdoch, Wayne Brindle, Rev J E Cooper, Roy Collings, W Elderkin)*

Free house ~ Licensees Barry and Diane Bright ~ Real ale ~ Meals and snacks ~ Restaurant ~ (01572) 821703 ~ Children welcome in eating area of bar and restaurant ~ Open 12-3.30, 6.30-11

MEDBOURNE SP7993 Map 4

Nevill Arms 🏠 🍺

B664 Market Harborough—Uppingham

Attractively placed by a footbridge over the duck-filled River Welland, this handsome old mullion-windowed pub has once again proved very popular with readers over the last year. The appealing main bar has an especially cheerful atmosphere, as well as two winter log fires, chairs and small wall settles around its tables, a lofty, dark-joisted ceiling and maybe a couple of dogs or a cat; piped music. A spacious back room by the former coachyard has pews around more tables (much needed at busy times), and there's a conservatory with newspapers – but in summer most people prefer eating at the tables outside on the grass by the dovecote. Well kept Adnams, Ruddles Best and County and two fortnightly changing guests like Greene King Abbot or Hoskins Penns on handpump, and country wines. Bar food includes home-made soup (£2), sandwiches (from £1.60, open sandwiches £3.45), filled baked potatoes (from £2.45), ploughman's (£3.25), chilli con carne (£4.95), daily specials like chicken in stilton, bacon and mushrooms or lamb in mint and redcurrant, and a couple of children's meals (£1.95). Darts, shove-ha'penny, cribbage, table skittles, cribbage, dominoes, with hoop-la, shut-the-box, and Captain's Mistress on request. The winter Tuesday evening Muddlemind quiz is popular with locals. Readers particularly enjoy staying here, and from this Easter rooms will be available in a neighbouring cottage as well as the pub itself. *(Recommended by Rona Murdoch, Cliff Blakemore, Stephen and Julie Brown, Keith Wright, Jim Farmer, Eric Locker, Joan and Michel Hooper-Immins, Robert P Anderson, Angus Lyon, A J Morton, Margaret and Roy Randle, M J Morgan, Philip Orbell, Frank Cummins)*

Free house ~ Licensees E F Hall and partners ~ Real ale ~ Meals and snacks (till 9.45) ~ (01858) 565288 ~ Children welcome ~ Open 12-2.30, 6-11; closed 25 Dec ~ Bedrooms: £40B/£50B

OLD DALBY SK6723 Map 7

Crown ★ 🍴 🍺

By school in village centre turn into Longcliff Hill then left into Debdale Hill

Everyone seems to leave this rather smart creeper-covered ex-farmhouse satisfied, whether they've come for the ambitious food or just for a drink. It's the food you'll probably notice first – there's a lot of style to the menu, and they grow their own herbs and make their own bread, vinegars and ice creams; no microwaves or chips. Dishes might include soup (£2.95), sandwiches and baguettes (from £2.95), vegetarian potato cake filled with stilton or cheddar or potted chicken livers with a herb butter and plum chutney (£5.50), grilled smoked salmon sausage on a tagliatelli of cucumber (£6.95), vegetable strudel or a hefty ploughman's (£7.95), steak and kidney pudding (£9.95), chicken breast filled with crabmeat with a creamy dill and vermouth sauce (£10.50), loin of lamb rolled in a basil and rosemary crumb, on a bed of creamy leeks surrounded by a red wine jus (£10.95), fillet of red sea bream wrapped in tarragon prawns and smoked salmon (£11.95), pan-fried rump steak (£12.95), puddings like autumn fruits soaked in brandy and topped with mascarpone, or baked Austrian strawberry cheesecake (£3.50), and interesting cheeses (£4.50). The prices are a little high, but as one reader put it, you don't mind paying the extra when it's all so classy. The good range of beers might include Adnams, Batemans XB, Black Sheep, Fullers London Pride, Greene King Abbot, Marstons Best and Pedigree,

Morlands Old Speckled Hen, Timothy Taylors Landlord, Wadworths 6X and others, served by staff wearing black and white uniforms and bow ties; they also have an interesting wine list, quite a few malt whiskies, and several brandies and Italian liqueurs. The pub still keeps much of its original layout and feel, and the three or four little rooms have black beams, one or two antique oak settles, William Morris style armchairs and easy chairs, hunting and other rustic prints, fresh flowers, and open fires; the snug is no smoking. One room has darts, cribbage, cards and dominoes, and they also have table skittles. There are plenty of tables on a terrace, with a big, sheltered lawn sloping down among roses and fruit trees; you can play boules out here. No credit cards. The licensees run another main entry, the Martins Arms at Colston Bassett (see Notts chapter). *(Recommended by John Poulter, Chris Raisin, Vicky and David Sarti, SS, Alan Hopkin, Thomas Nott, Eric Locker, Mr McGrath, David and Helen Wilkins, R and A Cooper, A and R Cooper, Anthony Barker, Brian White, Nigel Flook, Betsy Brown, Jane Hosking, Ian Burniston, Jack and Philip Paxton)*

Free house ~ Licensees Lynne Strafford Bryan and Salvatore Inguanta ~ Real ale ~ Meals and snacks (not Sun evening, other nights till 10) ~ Restaurant (not Sun evening) ~ (01664) 823134 ~ Children allowed in games room and dining rooms (away from bar and Tap Room) ~ Open 12-3(2.30 if quiet), 6-11

PEATLING MAGNA SP5992 Map 4
Cock

Village signposted off A50 S of Leicester

A real village local, this chatty place quickly puts strangers under its welcoming spell. On our evening inspection visit we were amazed to be offered free cut-your-own sandwiches, from loaves of good crusty bread and hunks of excellent stilton or red leicester; or there may be free baked potatoes or roast chestnuts. The friendly and energetic landlord keeps his Courage Directors and John Smiths well, and there are decent house wines; maybe piped pop music. The narrow main bar has horsey pictures and plates above the coal-effect gas fire and on some beams, cushioned wall benches and plush stools; there's a neat country dining area in the right-hand room. Good bar food includes home-made soup (£1.95), sandwiches such as local ham and cheese with a salad garnish and chips (£2.75), steak and kidney pie or vegetarian lasagne (£5.95), chicken tikka masala (£7.95), steaks (from £7.95), honey roast duck or halibut steak (£8.95), puddings like hot chocolate fudgecake or sticky toffee pudding (£1.95), and dishes of the day such as haddock in filo pastry parcels or grilled quail with game chips. The very popular Sunday lunch has three bookable sittings. They organise lots of events – curry nights, quiz nights, treasure hunts, golf. *(Recommended by Louise Wordsworth, Comus Elliott)*

Free house ~ Licensee Max Brown ~ Real ale ~ Meals and snacks ~ Restaurant ~ (0116) 247 8308 ~ Well behaved children allowed ~ Open 5.30-11 (closed weekday lunchtimes); 12-3, 6-11 Sat

REDMILE SK7935 Map 7
Peacock 🍽 ♀

Off A52 W of Grantham; at crossroads follow sign for Belvoir Castle, Harlby, and Melton

One of the locals at this friendly village pub has been coming here for nearly 70 years. In fact that's one of the especially nice things about it – although in recent years it's become quite a magnet for people coming to enjoy the smart food, it's still very much the kind of place that locals visit for a lunchtime drink. They aim for a French flavour with the meals, which might include very good lunchtime filled baguettes, delicious soup (£1.90), spicy fishcakes with chutney or baked avocado with stilton sauce (£4.50), tagliatelle with a sauce of smoked bacon, mushroom, tomato and basil (£5.95), venison sausages with onion gravy (£5.50), daily specials such as curried ham with roasted peppers (£3.95), mussels and clam chowder (£4.20), spicy vegetable cous cous (£6.95), duck confit on a ragout of beans and smoked bacon (£7.50), and baked cod with herb crust on cucumber spaghetti with rocket and sun-dried tomato sauce (£9.50), and lots of perfect puddings such as caramelised apple tart or poached meringue and banana flambé; vegetables are very good. Service is friendly and helpful, but can slow right down at busy times; they recommend booking at lunchtimes. There's also a pretty little no-smoking restaurant, with a set menu for £12.95. The range of well kept beers on handpump includes Bass, Marstons Pedigree, Tetleys, nicely priced Theakstons Best, Timothy Taylors Landlord, and maybe a guest, and they have an interesting wine list including fairly priced bottles and some by the glass; occasional special events such as cookery demonstrations or wine tastings. The spotless beamed rooms have an easy-going pubby feel, as well as pews, stripped country tables and chairs, the odd sofa and easy chair, some stripped golden stone, old prints, chintzy curtains for the small windows, and a variety of wall and table lamps; the snug and the conservatory are no smoking. Open fires, darts, cribbage, dominoes, maybe unobtrusive piped music, and tables outside. The pub is in an extremely pleasant tranquil setting near Belvoir Castle. *(Recommended by June and Malcolm Farmer, Paul Boot, C J Darwent, Paul and Janet Waring, Janet Pickles, Vicky and David Sarti, R and A Cooper, Helen and Keith Bowers and friends, Simon Collett-Jones, Simon Morton, J and P Maloney, Roxanne Chamberlain, James Nunns, Mr and Mrs R Head, Wayne Brindle, Viv Middlebrook, David and Shelia, DC, Jack and Philip Paxton, Chris Raisin and friends, Andy and Jane Beardsley)*

Free house ~ Licensees Celia and Colin Craword ~ Real ale ~ Meals and snacks (12-3, 7-10) ~ Restaurant ~ (01949) 842554 ~ Children in eating area of bar and restaurant ~ Open 11-11; 12-10.30 Sun ~ Bedrooms: £50B/£60B

SIBSON SK3500 Map 4
Cock

A444 N of Nuneaton

They like to say that Dick Turpin sheltered in the chimney of this thatched and timbered country pub when pursuers got too close, with his horse hiding out in the cellar. The building dates back to the 13th c, and though it's changed a fair bit over the years, proof of its age can still be seen in the unusually low doorways, ancient wall timbers, heavy black beams, and genuine latticed windows. An atmospheric room on the right has comfortable seats around cast-iron tables, and more seats built in to what was once an immense fireplace. The room on the left has country kitchen chairs around wooden tables, and what was the bar billiards room is now a no-smoking dining area. Generous helpings of good value bar food include home-made soup (£1.60), good sandwiches (from £1.75), home-made pâté (£2.10), steak and kidney pie or beef curry (£5.10), honey roast ham and egg (£5.95), steaks (from £8.25), specials such as vegetable pasta and nut bake, cantonese prawns, or pork medaillons in a cream and mushroom sauce, decent children's meals (£2.50), and home-made puddings (£2.10); on Sunday the only food is roasts in the restaurant, and there are regular gourmet evenings. It can seem cramped at times but that just adds to the cosy atmosphere. Well kept Bass and M & B Brew XI on handpump, good service; fruit machine and piped music. A little garden and courtyard area has tables and maybe summer barbecues. The restaurant (in a former stable block) is popular, the summer hanging baskets are attractive, and they have a caravan field (certified with the Caravan Club). *(Recommended by Jim Farmer, Graham Richardson, Paul and Janet Waring, Thomas Nott, Mike and Wendy Proctor, Jack and Philip Paxton)*

Bass ~ Lease: Graham and Stephanie Lindsay ~ Real ale ~ Meals and snacks (not in bar Sun lunchtime) ~ Restaurant (not Sun evening) ~ (01827) 880357 ~ Children in eating area of bar and restaurant ~ Open 11.30-2.30(3 summer Sat), 6.30(6 Sat)-11

SOMERBY SK7710 Map 4
Old Brewery ♟

Off A606 Oakham—Melton Mowbray, via Cold Overton, or Leesthorpe and Pickwell; can also be reached direct from Oakham via Knossington

The real point about this pub is the interesting range of distinctive beers brewed here by the landlord, from a very full-flavoured and rewarding Mild through Special, Poachers, Somerby Premium, Farm Gold and Parish Porter (sold in aid of the East Midlands Children's Hospice Appeal), to the awesomely alcoholic Baz's Bonce Blower, all well kept on handpump. Groups can book tours of the little brewery in the former stables, ending with supper and unlimited beer. The comfortable L-shaped main bar has red plush stools and banquettes and plush-cushioned captain's chairs, a sofa in one corner, and a good log fire in the big stone fireplace; another bar has bays of button-back red seating. There's a cheerful relaxed atmosphere, with a much broader mix of customers than you might expect, from children to grannies; one of our readers brought a bus-load of academics from Leicester University and couldn't get them out again. Basic simple popular bar food includes soup (£1.95), pâté (£2.75), garlic mushrooms (£2.95), delicious local sausages (£3.95), three minted lamb chops, breaded plaice or 12oz mixed grill (£5.95), breaded lemon sole or trout served with prawns (£6.95) and 8oz sirloin or scotch salmon fillet with asparagus and lobster sauce (£7.95). Dominoes, video game, fruit and cigarette machines, maybe quiet piped pop music, no dogs. A fenced-off area by the car park has white plastic tables and a climbing frame; boules. *(Recommended by Joan and Michel Hooper-Immins, Mr and Mrs B H James, Jack and Philip Paxton, Rona Murdoch, Richard Houghton, J C Cloud)*

Own brew ~ Licensee Baz Parish ~ Real ale ~ Meals and snacks ~ (01664) 454866 ~ Children welcome ~ Open 11.30-11; 12-10.30 Sun; cl 3-6 in winter ~ Bedrooms: £15/£25

THORPE LANGTON SP7492 Map 4

Bakers Arms 🍴

Village signposted off B6047 N of Market Harborough

Tucked away in a small village, this thatched house has been refurbished and extended as a spacious dining pub, and has become very popular indeed in the evenings for its combination of good food and really welcoming warmth. Furnishing is simple, with straightforward seating and stripped pine tables: some draw a parallel with the Peacock at Redmile, though at the Bakers Arms you'll probably find just about all the tables given over to eating. What counts most is the quality of the cooking, with fresh ingredients and good presentation. There's a wide choice of regularly changing meals written up on the blackboards, with dishes such as pan-fried pork fillet with a dijon mustard sauce (£8.95), well liked duck in cider and brandy sauce, and whole baked seabass with herbs and olive oil (£13.95); on Thursday evenings they have an extensive fish menu, with usually around a dozen fish and seafood dishes in addition to meat and vegetarian meals. You'll generally need to book some time ahead. Well kept Ind Coope Burton and Tetleys on handpump, and an extensive wine list with five by the glass; good friendly service, and no games or piped music. The snug is no smoking. There are picnic tables in the garden – the only place where they allow children, and even then only at weekend lunchtimes. Readers tell us the pub is popular with people from Leicester University – but the staff, not the students. *(Recommended by Mr and Mrs D J Nash, Eric Locker, Doug and June Miles, J D Cloud, Jim Farmer, Angus Lyon, D J Etheridge, Mike and Margaret Banks)*

Free house ~ Lease: Kate Hubbard ~ Real ale ~ Meals and snacks (see opening times) ~ Restaurant ~ Children in garden weekend lunchtimes ~ Pianist Fri evenings ~ Open Tues-Fri 6.30-11; 12-2.30, 6.30-11 Sat, 12-2.30 Sun; cl weekday lunchtimes, Sun evening, all day Mon

WOODHOUSE EAVES SK5214 Map 7

Pear Tree

Church Hill; main street, off B591 W of Quorndon

Likely to be beginning some redecoration by the time this edition of the Guide is published, this busy modern-looking pub is a well run and friendly place, with reliable food and a pleasantly chatty landlord. It's the upper flagstoned food area which is special, with pews forming booths around the walls, flagstone floor, and a pitched roof giving a pleasantly airy and open feel at lunchtime; at night, despite low lighting, the atmosphere is pleasantly lively. The end food servery looks straight through into the kitchen, which does generous helpings of good food such as sandwiches (from £1.95), soup (£2.25), deep-fried camembert with cranberry and orange sauce (£3.95), ploughman's (£4.75), several burgers (from £5.75), char-grilled nut cutlets (£6.25), salmon and tuna fishcakes or spit-roast chicken (£6.50), sirloin steak (£9.95), and puddings (£2.50). There's a log fire in an attractive Victorian fireplace (there may be a couple of labradors sitting in front of here), and decent wines. The lower part of the pub is a straightforward comfortable turkey-carpeted local, with well kept Ind Coope Burton, Marstons Pedigree and Tetleys on handpump, several malt whiskies, fruit machine, and an open fire. Outside there are a few picnic tables under cocktail parasols, with a summer bar by an arbour of climbing plants; good nearby walks. (*Recommended by Jenny and Michael Back, R and A Cooper, J Honnor, Stephen, Julie and Hayley Brown, Jack and Philip Paxton*)

Allied ~ Lease: Richard Dimblebee ~ Real ale ~ Meals and snacks (not Sun evening, otherwise till 10) ~ (01509) 890243 ~ Children in eating area of bar ~ Open 11-3(4 weekends), 6-11

Post Office address codings confusingly give the impression that some pubs are in Leicestershire, when they're really in Cambridgeshire (which is where we list them).

Lucky Dip

Besides the fully inspected pubs, you might like to try these Lucky Dips recommended to us and described by readers (if you do, please send us reports):

☆ Acresford [A444 Burton—Nuneaton; SK3113], *Cricketts*: Attractive and well run, with good home-cooked food inc vegetarian, well kept Bass, Marstons Pedigree and regional ales, good range of other drinks, friendly service; attractive garden and setting (*Ian Phillips*)
Ashby de la Zouch [SK3516], *Royal*: Good value lunchtime carvery, well kept sensibly priced Bass, lively evenings (*Graham Richardson*)
Ashby Folville [SK7011], *Carington Arms*: Half a dozen well kept Everards and interesting guest ales and jovial welcoming landlord in attractively placed spacious and comfortable tudor-style country pub, solid rural home cooking inc good chips; children welcome, nice garden, maybe calves or horses in back paddock (*O K Smyth*)
☆ Barnsdale [just off A606 Oakham—Stamford; SK9008], *Barnsdale Lodge*: Extensive conservatory dining bar with attractively presented food, charming decor, comfortable sitting-roomish coffee lounge, real ales such as Morlands Old Speckled Hen, Ruddles County and Tetleys; bedrooms comfortable and attractive, with good breakfasts (*Alan and Heather Jacques, Gordon Theaker, BB*)
Barrow upon Soar [SK5717], *Hunting Lodge*: Two pleasantly decorated rooms, hunting pictures, friendly staff, good value varied food; children welcome, piped music, pool; big garden with swings, boules and barbecues (*A and R Cooper*); [Mill Lane, off South St (B5328)], *Navigation*: Extended split-level

pub based on former barge-horse stabling, attractive and comfortable, with lovely canal view from small back terrace with moorings; good value home-made food (may be limited winter), interesting bar top made from old pennies, central open fire, friendly service; well kept Courage Directors, Marstons Pedigree and Shipstones, skittle alley, piped music, satellite TV (*R and A Cooper, Jim Farmer*); [OS Sheet 129 map ref 573173], *Soar Bridge*: Interesting spot nr busy canal lock, friendly service and atmosphere, flowers in panelled lounge, good value home-cooked food inc several vegetarian dishes (prompt stop to food service), Everards; unobtrusive piped music (*Jim Farmer*)
Barrowden [just off A47 Uppingham—Peterborough; SK9400], *Exeter Arms*: Beautiful rambling pub built with local stone in super setting by village duck pond; long lounge/restaurant, good value food inc good doorstep sandwiches and vegetarian choice, changing real ales, prompt cheery service, lively public bar (*PGP*)
Billesdon [Church St; SK7202], *Queens Head*: Beamed and partly thatched pub with good well priced food in two attractive bars, small conservatory eating area and upstairs restaurant, friendly service, Everards and guest ales; pretty stone village (*John Wooll, J R M Black*)
Branston [Main St; SK8129], *Wheel*: Two cosy and comfortable bars in unpretentious 18th-c pub in splendid countryside nr Belvoir castle, good food inc schnitzels with various

sauces, good game goulash, log fires, friendly
atmosphere, well kept Batemans *(Norma and
Keith Bloomfield)*

☆ Breedon on the Hill [A453 Ashby—Castle
Donington; SK4022], *Holly Bush*:
Comfortably plush, with low black beams,
lots of brass, sporting plates etc, well kept
Marstons Pedigree and Tetleys, bar food
(stops early lunchtime; not Sun), restaurant
(can be fully booked Sat, cl Sun), no-smoking
area, friendly efficient staff; piped music;
some tables outside, nice bedrooms;
interesting village with Anglo-Saxon carvings
in hilltop church above huge limestone face
(Gordon Theaker, R and A Cooper, BB)
Breedon on the Hill [A453], *Three Horse
Shoes*: Separate bars, popular restaurant with
good value carvery, well kept Marstons
Pedigree; motel-style bedrooms *(R and A
Cooper)*
Bruntingthorpe [Cross St; SP6089], *Joiners
Arms*: Good food inc Sun lunch in beamed
dining area, Hoskins ales, lots of china and
brasses, friendly staff; cl weekday lunchtimes;
handy for aviation museum *(George
Atkinson, A R Hipkins)*
Burrough on the Hill [off B6047 S of Melton
Mowbray; SK7510], *Stag & Hounds*:
Friendly and popular village local with good
choice of bar food and real ales, open fires,
children allowed, garden with play area
(LYM; reports on new regime please)
Castle Donington [A453, S end; SK4427],
Nags Head: Beamed dining pub with
beautifully cooked and presented food, wide
choice of specials, well kept beer, decent wine,
friendly service; busy separate no-smoking
restaurant *(R and A Cooper)*
Catthorpe [just off A5 S of Gibbet Island;
SP5578], *Cherry Tree*: Good value food in
attractive well run country local, friendly,
cosy, clean and warm, with pleasant
atmosphere, dark panelling, lots of plates and
pictures, coal-effect fire, attentive service,
particularly well kept Bass and Hook Norton
Best; piped radio; cl Mon/Tues lunchtimes *(B
Adams, Cdr Patrick Tailyour)*
Clipsham [SK9616], *Olive Branch*: Relaxed
village local with changing food inc local
game, trout and veg, well kept beers, friendly
welcoming licensees, open fires; children in
restaurant *(M J Morgan, BB)*
Cossington [Main St (B5328); SK6013],
Royal Oak: Good imaginative home cooking
in recently refurbished pub/restaurant,
pleasant atmosphere, well kept guest beers,
moderately priced wines; has been cl Sun
(Joan Gregory)
Cropston [15 Station Rd (B5328); SK5510],
Bradgate Arms: Much modernised extended
village pub with traditional snug, well kept
Banks's Bitter and Mild and guest beers, wide
choice of standard Milestone Tavern food inc
bargain offers, sunken alley, fruit machines, piped
music, can get crowded; biggish garden with
play area, handy for Bradgate Park *(Graham
Norman, JJW, CMW, Jim Farmer, LYM)*
Croxton Kerrial [1 School Lane; A607 SW of

Grantham; SK8329], *Peacock*: 17th-c pub
with five real ales, good varied choice of
reasonably cheap food (inc takeaways), long
bar with real fire partitioned off at one end,
some nick-nacks, quiet piped music, pool;
children and dogs welcome, picnic tables in
garden *(JJW, CMW, David and Shelia)*
Fleckney [Main St; SP6493], *Dun Cow*:
Pleasant traditional pub, big garden, wide
range of food using local produce, Sun roasts,
John Smiths Extra, Mansfield Riding and
Websters ales *(Nan Axon)*
Foxton [off A6 N of Market Harborough;
SP7090], *Black Horse*: Two bars, one with
conservatory, well kept Marstons Pedigree,
crowded for jazz Weds *(Jim Farmer)*; [Foxton
Locks (park by bridge 60/62 and walk) - OS
Sheet 141 map ref 691897], *Bridge 61*: In
good setting by locks, spartan flagstones and
pine furniture decor, quickly served chippy
food, lots of canalia and boating relics,
Everards and a guest ale, games and family
room; gift and provision shop next door
(Dorsan Baker); *Shoulder of Mutton*: Pleasant
big garden, cosy pine interior, good service,
well kept beers, small restaurant *(Jim Farmer)*
Frisby on the Wreake [Main St; SK6917],
Bell: Friendly roomy pine-beamed local with
brass, oil paintings and real fire, family room
in back extension, good choice of well kept
ales, fair range of wines, decent coffee and
straightforward lunchtime food, different
evening choice - good value and quality;
smaller back family room; piped music; smart
dress required; tables outside *(Joan and
Michel Hooper-Immins)*

☆ Glaston [A47 Leicester—Peterboro, E of
Uppingham; SK8900], *Monckton Arms*:
Attractive stone inn quite handy for Rutland
Water, with three neat little rooms in bar,
well kept Bass and other ales, friendly new
young management, wide range of food inc
good vegetarian choice, picnic tables on
sheltered terrace by sizeable modern
extension, comfortable bedrooms, good
breakfast *(A V Bradbury, HB, MB, M A
Mees, R and A Cooper, LYM)*
Great Bowden [SP7488], *Countryman*: Very
popular for good food at low prices; Everards
real ale *(B A A Heath)*

☆ Greetham [B668 Stretton—Cottesmore;
SK9214], *Wheatsheaf*: Extremely wide choice
of good value generous food served till 11 inc
lots of char-grills and Fri bargain steak
suppers in welcoming newly decorated L-
shaped communicating rooms, well kept
Tetleys and Whitbreads-related ales, attentive
staff, coal fire, soft piped music; pool and
other games in end room, restaurant, tables
on side grass; bedrooms in annexe *(Jenny and
Michael Back, Jim Farmer, BB)*

☆ Grimston [off A6006 W of Melton Mowbray;
SK6821], *Black Horse*: Clean and firmly
upmarket, with good imaginatively presented
straightforward bar food – all freshly cooked,
so takes time; remarkable collection of cricket
memorabilia (landlord happy to talk about
it), well kept Marstons Pedigree, open fire,
discreet piped music; no food Sun, cl Sun

evening and Mon exc bank hols; attractive village with stocks and 13th-c church *(Colin McKerrow, LYM)*

Groby [signed off A50; SK5207], *Brant*: Very wide choice of food inc vegetarian and special offers in bar and restaurant (which has own bar), well kept Everards Tiger, very friendly helpful staff, good atmosphere *(N B Thompson)*

☆ **Hallaton** [North End; SP7896], *Fox*: Warm and friendly local with good value bar food inc fine vegetarian dishes and Sun carvery; well kept Marstons Pedigree and Tetleys, Spanish landlord; children welcome; tables out by village duck pond *(Rona Murdoch, Carole Cox)*

Harby [High St; SK7331], *Bottle & Glass*: Jocular landlord, wide choice of generous food inc good puddings, well kept Bass, Charrington IPA and Youngers No 3 *(David and Ruth Hollands)*

Hathern [Derby Rd; SK5033], *Kings Arms*: Big modernish pub with good service, decent food, well kept Marstons Pedigree *(Stephen Brown)*

Heath End [SK3621], *Saracens Head*: Basic two-room farm pub by Staunton Harold Reservoir visitor centre, handy for Calke Abbey; well kept Bass served by jug from the cask, cosy coal fires, notable very cheap sandwiches *(Jack and Phil Paxton, Julia, Simon and Laura Plumbley)*

Hemington [21 Main St; SK4528], *Jolly Sailor*: Very welcoming village local with well kept Bass, Mansfield, Marstons Pedigree and two guest ales, farm cider, excellent range of malt whiskies and other spirits, good big fresh rolls; good open fire each end, big country pictures, brasses, blow-torches and bric-a-brac, table skittles; beautiful hanging baskets and tables outside *(Pete Storey, Pete Cherrett, Julia, Simon and Laura Plumbley)*

Hoby [SK6717], *Blue Bell*: Attractive thatched pub with friendly landlord, well kept Everards, three spacious rooms, attractive garden with play area; generous fried and other food (not Sun-Tues) *(R and A Cooper, Jim Farmer)*

☆ **Illston on the Hill** [off B6047 Mkt Harboro—Melton; SP7099], *Fox & Goose*: Welcoming and idiosyncratic unspoilt pub full of interesting decorations, well kept Everards Mild, Beacon, Old Original and Tiger, good coal fires; no food *(Jim Farmer, LYM)*

☆ **Kegworth** [towards West Leake – OS Sheet 129 map ref 501268; SK5026], *Station*: Attractively refurbished, with stripped brickwork and open fires, two rooms off small bar area, well kept Bass and Worthington, well served good food, upstairs dining room; tables on big back lawn; bedrooms *(Jack and Philip Paxton, David Eberlin, A and R Cooper)*

Kegworth [High St], *Red Lion*: Friendly and unpretentious, with well kept beer, good home cooking, no juke box; enclosed garden good for children *(David and Shelia, Andrew and Joanne Priestley)*

Kibworth Beauchamp [5 High St; SP6893],

Old Swan: Friendly pub/restaurant with wide range of good value food inc popular Mon/Tues curry nights, well kept Marstons Pedigree *(I C Smith, Jim Farmer)*

☆ **Kibworth Harcourt** [Main St (just off A6); SP6894], *Three Horseshoes*: Unassuming and relaxed village pub with well kept Bass and Marstons Best and Pedigree, decent straightforward generous food (not Sun evening), friendly service, comfortable and spacious plush seating, side eating areas; piped music, children welcome; tables on attractive back terrace *(Rona Murdoch, Brian Atkin, LYM)*

☆ **Kilby Bridge** [A50 S of Leicester; SP6097], *Navigation*: Fine canalside position with waterside garden, several areas, some small and cosy, off central bar, big dining area, generous straightforward food inc massive well presented mixed grill, warm welcome, well kept Tetleys-related ales and Marstons Pedigree on handpump, good coffee; piped music, fruit machines, busy bookable restaurant; children welcome, no dogs *(J Haywood, C H and P Stride, George Atkinson, Roger and Pauline Pearce)*

Knossington [off A606 W of Oakham; SK8008], *Fox & Hounds*: Unspoilt small village pub with coal fire in cosy comfortable lounge, pool room for younger customers, friendly licensees, well kept Courage-related ales, huge choice of malt whiskies, reasonably priced food inc unusual dishes, summer barbecues in big garden *(Jack and Philip Paxton, Anthony Barnes)*

☆ **Leicester** [9 Welford Pl, corner Newarke St/Welford Rd], *Welford Place*: Impressive stone stairs lead to this spacious former gentlemen's club on a busy corner, with semicircular Victorian bar, tasteful restaurant adjoining; quiet, comfortable and clubby but not stuffy by day, more lively some evenings; Ruddles Best and County, good choice of wines and other drinks, obliging management, friendly staff, imaginative changing bar food; same management as Wig & Mitre, Lincoln *(O K Smyth, Mr and Mrs P Byatt)*

☆ **Leicester** [Silver St/Carts Lane], *Globe*: Old-fashioned three-room local with lots of woodwork, gas lighting, coal-effect gas fire, peaceful upstairs dining room with good value simple lunchtime food; well kept Everards and guest beers; juke box in sometimes noisy back room, can be smoky, children allowed in some parts *(Brian and Anna Marsden, Joan and Michel Hooper-Immins, Mr and Mrs P Byatt, John Wooll, BB)*

Leicester [90 High St], *Cafe Bruxelles*: Belgian cafe in former bank, wide range of Belgian, French and Dutch beers (no real ales), short choice of appropriate food, good service; open all day *(Joan and Michel Hooper-Immins)*; [New Walk], *Courthouse*: Long bar overlooking tree-lined walk, useful food, Bass, Morlands Old Speckled Hen and Wadworths 6X, decent house wine *(John Wooll)*; [Loseby Lane], *Fourpence & Firkin*: Plain but pleasant, with wooden tables and settles, good value food; juke box loudish, but good choice (John Wooll); [Pocklingtons Walk], Lamplighters: Interesting modern pub with neon above bar, stained-glass round ceiling, ceiling fans, bric-à-brac piled on shelves; well kept Mansfield beers inc Riding, good well priced lunchtime food inc children's, good atmosphere; piped music (Brian and Anna Marsden, R and A Cooper); [Charles St], Rainbow & Dove: Big open-plan bare-boards bar nr station with convivial new young landlord, well kept Banks's Bitter, Hansons Mild, Camerons Strongarm, Marstons Pedigree and three guest ales, farm cider, limited weekday lunchtime food; students evening, professionals too lunchtime, regular beer festivals (Joan and Michel Hooper-Immins, Mr and Mrs P Byatt)

☆ Loughborough [The Rushes (A6); SK5319], Black Lion: Wide range of Hoskins and other beers, stripped pine and pews, bare boards and sawdust in front bar area, cosier back lounge; very helpful bar service, good value simple food, peaceful at lunchtime but noisy evenings; handy for canal basin (A and R Cooper, PM, AM)
Loughborough [Canal Bank, Meadow Lane], Boat: Picturesque recently refurbished canalside pub with good atmosphere, very obliging service, good food at reasonable prices inc bargain Sun lunch, good range of beers, boating memorabilia; very popular with local office staff weekday lunchtimes (C H and P Stride, R and A Cooper); [Churchgate], Three Nuns: Good range of beers and country wines, good value food the main lunchtime draw (R and A Cooper); [Sparrow Hill], Windmill: Relaxed and welcoming, carefully restored (oldest pub here) with calm atmosphere, no-smoking room; good plain food, also tapas, Marstons Bitter and Pedigree (Ian and Trish Avis)

☆ Lutterworth [34 Rugby Rd (A426 S); very handy for M1 junction 20; SP5484], Fox: Comfortable dining chairs in lounge, decent food inc good vegetarian special, well kept Whitbreads-related ales, good coffee, friendly obliging service, open fires; video game but no piped music; tables in garden (Frank Davidson, Frank Cummins)
Lutterworth [Leicester Rd], Shambles: Thatch and beams, smart attentive bar staff, Banks's ales, clean tables, quiet juke box; good atmosphere Fri night; bedrooms (Andy Black)

☆ Lyddington [off A6003 N of Corby; SP8797], Marquess of Exeter: Well restored after a fire, comfortable series of well furnished decorous rooms, wing armchairs by big inglenook log fire, black beams, neat staff, good bar food, well kept Ruddles Best and County, good coffee, restaurant (children allowed), good bedrooms; in receivership as we go to press (LYM; news please)

☆ Manton [St Marys Rd; SK8704], Horse & Jockey: Unspoilt character pub with big coal fire, warmly welcoming landlord, good range of promptly served food, well kept Mansfield Riding and Old Baily; can get busy even in winter; comfortable bedrooms, not far from

Rutland Water (Jack and Philip Paxton)

☆ Market Bosworth [Mkt Pl; SK4003], Black Horse: Lots of small rooms, wide choice of good food, keen attentive service, well kept Marstons Pedigree and Tetleys; restaurant; bedrooms, nice setting next to alms houses in attractive village (Graham Richardson, Jim Farmer)

☆ Market Bosworth [Mkt Pl], Softleys: Wine bar/restaurant (but it does have well kept Hook Norton Best and Adnams Broadside or Wadworths 6X, with a little space for drinkers by the bar) in fine old building with oak beams, brassware, hanging mugs, grand fireplace; good individually prepared food inc sandwiches and changing hot dishes, some interesting; very friendly service, decent wine, spotless housekeeping, attractive upstairs dining room; cl Mon; bedrooms (Roy Bromell, Dorothee and Dennis Glover, Joan and Michel Hooper-Immins)

☆ Market Harborough [High St; SP7388], Three Swans: Comfortable and handsome coaching inn with fine range of bar food inc good lunchtime ploughman's and toasties in plush and peaceful front lounge bar, conservatory and attractive suntrap courtyard, decent wines, good coffee, very friendly and helpful staff; Courage-related ales, upstairs restaurant; bedrooms (Joan and Michel Hooper-Immins, Jim Farmer)
Market Overton [Teigh Rd, nr church; SK8816], Black Bull: Attractive thatched pub with artificial pool and waterfall by entrance, thriving lounge bar with Ruddles, Theakstons and Youngs, good home cooking in bar and small back restaurant, welcoming landlord and wandering cat; get there early Sun and in summer; pretty village, some tables out in front (Eddie and Iris Brixton, R and A Cooper)
Markfield [A50 just under a mile from M1 junction 22; SK4810], Field Head: Huge beamed lounge/dining area around hotel's central bar, pictures, antiquey bits and pieces, uncounted nooks and corners; good reasonably priced generous food in bar and restaurant, Hoskins and other ales, decent house wine; bedrooms, big breakfasts (George Atkinson, O K Smyth)
Melton Mowbray [Leicester St; SK7518], Fox: Town pub, several adjoining areas round big bar, banquettes and pub furniture, well kept beers inc guests; beer festival end Aug (Chris Raisin)
Morcott [SK9200], White Horse: Attractive country pub, beautiful setting, well kept Morlands Old Speckled Hen (S G Brown)

☆ Mountsorrel [Loughborough Rd, off A6; SK5714], Swan: Two plain low-key whitewashed bars with log fires and red banquettes, notably good home cooking inc vegetarian – all fresh cooked so can be slow, well kept Batemans XB, Theakstons XB and two guest ales, wide choice of good wines by the glass, unusual non-alcoholic drinks; small walled back garden leading down to canalised River Soar; bedrooms; not much nearby parking (Anthony Barnes, Rona Murdoch,

Jim Farmer)

Oadby [Florence Wragg Way; SK6200], *Grange Farm*: Recent sympathetic conversion of attractive early 19th-c farmhouse, old local photographs, newspapers, wide range of imaginative food, no-smoking area, well kept interesting Bass-related ales, good mix of customers *(Rona Murdoch, J D Cloud)*

Oakham [2 Northgate; SK8508], *Wheatsheaf*: Neat and friendly three-room 17th-c pub nr church, spick and span, with Everards and guest ales, decent usual food, open fire; back garden *(George Atkinson, Angus Lyon)*

Osgathorpe [B5324 N of Whitwick; SK4320], *Stock-Yard*: Efficient cattle-theme combination of pub, restaurant and nightclub, plenty of obliging staff, huge pies with pastry horns, split-level bar, piped swing music *(Jenny and Michael Back)*

☆ Preston [Uppingham Rd; SK8602], *Kingfisher*: Attractive flower-decked pub with lots of exposed stone and beams, of plates, jugs, etc, all immaculate; very friendly efficient service, good simple reasonably priced food, Marstons Pedigree, Tetleys and Worthington ales, comfortable chairs and sofas, no piped music; tables in garden, live entertainment Thurs *(Cdr Patrick Tailyour, George Atkinson)*

Redmile [off A52 Grantham—Nottingham; SK8036], *Olde Windmill*: Welcoming and comfortable lounge and dining room, well kept Everards and other ales, good range of reasonably priced bar food, tables outside *(Elizabeth and Anthony Watts)*

Ryhall [Bridge St; TF0310], *Millstone*: Neatly kept and quite spacious, with comfortable plush seats, welcoming helpful service, generous bar food, well kept Mansfield Bitter, Riding and Old Baily, small dining area, separate bar with pool *(Jenny and Michael Back)*

☆ Saddington [S of Leicester between A50 and A6 – OS Sheet 141 map ref 658918; SP6591], *Queens Head*: Welcoming and popular, with enterprising landlord, good food inc good Sun lunch in dining room with lovely view, OAP bargain lunches, well kept Adnams, Everards Beacon and Tiger and Ruddles *(Cdr Patrick Tailyour, Elizabeth and Anthony Watts)*

Scalford [King St; SK7624], *Kings Arms*: Becoming very popular under new licensees for simple food prepared from fresh ingredients, lovely fresh fish, well kept Marstons *(Chris Raisin)*

Shawell [not far from M6 junction 1; village signed off A5/A427 roundabout – turn right in village; SP5480], *White Swan*: Creeper-covered dining pub with good reasonably priced food under pleasant newish licensees *(I Blackwell)*

☆ Shearsby [A50 Leicester—Northampton; SP6290], *Chandlers Arms*: Comfortable village pub with brocaded wall seats, wheelback chairs, flowers on tables, house plants, swagged curtains, dog pictures for sale, popular straightforward food (helpings not too big), Marstons Bitter and Pedigree and Fullers London Pride, good service; piped

pop music may be intrusive; tables in garden *(Jim Farmer, CMW, JJW, BB)*

☆ Sileby [Swan St; SK6015], *White Swan*: Small unspoilt sidestreet pub with comfortable and welcoming dining lounge, interesting good value generous home-cooked food (not Sun eve or Mon lunchtime) inc vegetarian and superb puddings, home-baked bread, well kept Ansells and Marstons Pedigree, three entertaining boxer dogs, small tasteful restaurant (booking needed); children's playroom in converted back bowling alley with closed-circuit TV *(P and J Farrow, Jim Farmer)*

Somerby [Main St; SK7710], *Stilton Cheese*: Welcoming new owners, good range of good value food in bar and upstairs restaurant, calm professional service, Marstons Pedigree, Ruddles County, Tetleys and a guest beer *(Joan and Michel Hooper-Immins)*

South Kilworth [Rugby Rd (B5414); SP6081], *White Hart*: Intimate and cosy old village pub with quaint little dining room, larger bar with real fire, well kept Banks's, freshly cooked bar food inc cheap Sun lunch, family service; piped pop music, skittles, darts and fruit machine *(Eric Locker)*

Stathern [Red Lion St; SK7731], *Red Lion*: Lively extensively renovated pub with big warm homely carpeted lounge, flagstone floors and abundant old woodwork in smaller cosy bar, open fires, wall-mounted candles, well kept Whitbreads-related ales, imaginative bar food; occasional maggot racing draws big crowds *(R M Taylor, Chris Raisin, G Doyle)*

Stoke Golding [High St; SP3997], *George & Dragon*: Very friendly comfortable local, wide range of good value food, good service from alert staff, Ansells, Marstons and Tetleys; short walk from Ashby Canal *(Sue and Mike Todd, John Cox)*

Stoney Stanton [Stoney Cove, off B4114; SP4894], *Cove*: Remarkable spectacular setting on side of huge disused quarry (now a diving centre, decor reflects this); comfortable and spacious bar and restaurant, good food inc nice choice of puddings, tables out on verandah and terraces; live bands summer Thurs *(Andy Black, P Chapman, S Gill)*

☆ Stretton [just off A1; SK9416], *Ram Jam*: Civilised escape from A1, with mix of sofas and neat contemporary seating in airy modern cafe-restaurant, open fire, good imaginative and unusual food, friendly efficient service, good wines, freshly squeezed orange juice, fresh-ground coffee and so forth, daily papers; children welcome, freshly decorated comfortable bedrooms, open all day, food 7am-10pm *(Mark Hydes, Stephen and Julie Brown, Karen and Graham Oddey, R and S Bentley, Chris Westmoreland, Andrew and Ruth Triggs, F C Johnston, Gill and Andy Plumb, Paul Randall, LYM)*

☆ Stretton [just off A1; SK9416], *Jackson Stops*: Informal homely thatched pub in quiet village, well kept Ruddles and Theakstons, decent wines, good range of freshly cooked food, log fire, old farm tools, pleasant atmosphere, bar on left kept for drinkers;

local for three-nation fighter squadron at RAF Cottesmore with lots of relevant memorabilia *(Ian Phillips, Dorothee and Dennis Glover, Stephen and Julie Brown, LYM)*

☆ Sutton Cheney [Main St – off A447 3 miles S of Mkt Bosworth; SK4100], *Royal Arms*: Dining pub with three small low-ceilinged front rooms, big new back extension with upstairs restaurant, friendly local atmosphere, wide choice of good value food with good fresh veg, two open fires, well kept Marstons and changing guest beers, flagstone floors, regal bric-a-brac, piped music; upstairs restaurant, family conservatory with wishing well, lots of picnic tables in big garden with good children's play area; handy for Bosworth Field and Mallory Park, can get busy *(Mike and Wendy Proctor, George Atkinson, Julie Peters, Colin Blinkhorn, Norma and Keith Bloomfield)*

Swannington [E of Ashby, between A50 and A512; SK4115], *Fountain*: Two pleasant bars with good value basic lunchtime food, Marstons Pedigree, real fire, pictures and books, darts; TV, fruit machine, piped music may be rather loud; picnic tables in garden with play area *(CMW, JJW)*

☆ Swithland [SE end of village; between A6 and B5330, between Loughborough and Leicester; SK5413], *Griffin*: Good value local, with Everards and other well kept beers, reasonable choice of food, pleasant decor; gardens by stream with horses, nice setting *(A and R Cooper, LYM)*

Thrussington [Rearsby Rd; SK6415], *Blue Lion*: Pleasant Tudor-style village pub, oak tables and comfortable settles in carpeted lounge, country bric-a-brac, good value food served till late, well kept ales inc Marstons Pedigree, quiet piped music, fruit machine *(CMW, JJW, Stephen and Julie Brown)*

☆ Tugby [signed off A47 E of Leicester, bear right in village; SK7600], *Black Horse*: Wide choice of good generous home-made evening meals in cosy, quaint and attractive black-and-white thatched village pub with small rooms which fill quickly, well kept Ansells and Tetleys, friendly service, log fire; children welcome; cl lunchtime *(Jim Farmer, LYM)*

Tur Langton [off B6047; follow Kibworth signpost from village centre; SP7194], *Crown*: Friendly new landlord, Courage Directors, John Smiths, King & Barnes 12 Bore and Ruddles, decent food in attractively furnished lounge bar, public bar with TV popular with younger customers, separate restaurant with own bar, tables under cocktail parasols on terrace; no food Sun or Mon evenings *(Rona Murdoch, LYM)*

Ullesthorpe [Main St; SP5087], *Chequers*: Big country inn, beamed and flagstoned bar and most of lounge areas with emphasis on very wide choice of reasonably priced food from large servery, good range of beers inc Batemans XXXB, Gales HSB and Theakstons Old Peculier, faint semi-classical music, no-smoking areas; normally prompt service; children welcome, family room and play area; comfortable bedrooms *(George Atkinson, Cdr*

Patrick Tailyour)

☆ Upper Hambleton [village signposted from A606 on E edge of Oakham; SK9007], *Finches Arms*: Outstanding views of Rutland Water from tables on back gravel terrace and picture-window restaurant extension, built-in button-back leatherette banquettes and open fire in knocked-through front bar, friendly staff, well kept Bass and Theakstons, bar food (people have liked the sausages and mash and venison casserole) *(GW, BW, M J Morgan, Wayne Brindle, Bernard and Becky Robinson, BB)*

☆ Uppingham [High Street W; SP8699], *White Hart*: Wide choice of good value simple tasty food using local produce, inglenook fire in panelled front lounge, quite a warren of passages and rooms, two well kept Courage-related ales with a guest such as Morlands Speckled Hen, reasonably priced wines, good service, back restaurant; bedrooms *(George Atkinson, Eric Locker)*

Uppingham [Market Sq], *Vaults*: Attractive pub overlooking square, tables outside; well kept Marstons Pedigree, popular food; bedrooms *(Jim Farmer)*

☆ Walcote [1½ miles from M1 junction 20, A427 towards Market Harboro; SP5683], *Black Horse*: Authentic Thai food (not Mon or Tues lunchtime) cooked by the landlady, in good value big helpings, well kept ales such as Hook Norton Best and Old Hookey, Timothy Taylors Landlord, Judges Old Growler, interesting bottled beers and country wines, no-smoking restaurant; there's been some tidying-up in the bar but it's still not a smart place; no dogs *(H Paulinski, Jim Farmer, David Peakall, Frank Cummins, LYM)*

Walton on the Wolds [Loughborough Rd; SK5919], *Anchor*: Long rambling open-plan pub popular with businessmen for lunch – good steak and kidney pie; Tetleys-related ales *(R and A Cooper)*

☆ Welham [off B664 Mkt Harboro–Uppingham; SP7692], *Old Red Lion*: Popular dining pub (part of small local chain) with several beamed rooms and attractive if rather dark barrel-vaulted back area, limited choice of good food at really low prices inc good steaks, Courage Best and Directors, decent wines, efficient hard-working staff, no-smoking areas, lovely fire; piped music may be loudish *(George Atkinson, Norman Smith, Stephen Brown, S A Moir)*

☆ Whitwell [A606 Stamford–Oakham; SK9208], *Noel Arms*: Young chef trained at George V in Paris doing wide choice of good food (till 10) esp fish and delicious puddings, in spacious plush and decorous dining lounge; cheerful local atmosphere in original unpretentious little front rooms, well kept Ruddles Best and County, friendly efficient staff, afternoon teas (not Mon), suntrap tables outside, occasional barbecues; piped music, can get busy; handy for Rutland Water, children welcome; bedrooms *(Miss P A Wilson, P Stallard, Dr M V Jones, Mike and Gisela Fuller, LYM)*

☆ Whitwick [B587 towards Copt Oak; quite

handy for M1 junction 22; SK4514], *Bulls Head*: Busy but welcoming L-shaped plush beamed bar with splendid views over Charnwood Forest – highest pub in Leics; well kept Tetleys-related ales, quickly served home-made food (lunchtime, not Sun) using good ingredients, friendly efficient service, back games room with piped music, big garden with menagerie of farm animals; children very welcome away from bar *(Jenny and Michael Back, Mr and Mrs E M Clarke, R and A Cooper)*

Wigston [Bull Head St; SK5900], *Horse & Trumpet*: Big friendly local, with bare boards and well kept Everards beers; spotlessly clean, good value generous lunchtime food, skittle alley *(Comus Elliott)*

☆ Wing [signed off A6003 S of Oakham; SK8903], *Kings Arms*: Engaging early 17th-c stone-built village inn, reopened after restoration; small bar, large restaurant, beams, log fires, good helpings of good food, very attentive service, real ales inc unusual ones such as Salem Porter; seats in sheltered yard, good bedrooms with home-made marmalade at breakfast, interesting medieval turf maze just up the road *(Pam and Mike Collett, George Atkinson, LYM)*

Wing, *Cuckoo*: Friendly thatched country pub, open-plan bar split into two, friendly staff and locals, well kept Bass, Marstons Pedigree and

interesting guest beers, midsummer beer festival, good value generous food inc Indian dishes and even ostrich, darts, pool, weekend live music; pretty village with interesting medieval turf maze *(Jack and Philip Paxton, James Lindesay, Geoffrey Hall)*

☆ Woodhouse Eaves [Brand Hill; beyond Main St, off B591 S of Loughborough – OS Sheet 129 map ref 533148], *Wheatsheaf*: Plush and busy open-plan country pub, welcoming efficient service, good home-cooked food inc sandwiches and vegetarian, half a dozen well kept ales, decent wines, log fires; floodlit tables outside, no motor-cyclists *(A and R Cooper, John Broughton, P J Caunt, Mr and Mrs E I Clark, Rona Murdoch, LYM)*

Wymeswold [A6006; SK6023], *Hammer & Pincers*: Extensively refurbished in exposed-beam style, clean, bright and spacious, with pine furniture in four or five rooms on several levels, good value generous food inc vegetarian, well kept Bass, Ruddles County, Marstons Pedigree, Theakstons Best and XB and guest beers, friendly service; tables on terrace, neat garden *(Jim Farmer, David and Shelia, John and Zoe Chamberlain)*

Wymeswold [45 Far St; SK6023], *Three Crowns*: Good welcoming atmosphere, good value food, well kept ales, pleasant character furnishings, couple of dogs *(A and R Cooper, Chris Raisin)*

Stars after the name of a pub show exceptional quality. One star means most people (after reading the report to see just why the star has been won) would think a special trip worth while. Two stars mean that the pub is really outstanding – many that for their particular qualities cannot be bettered.

Lincolnshire

Several new entries here include the Welby Arms at Allington (good food and beer at this friendly local), the distinguished Tally Ho at Aswarby (enterprising food, a nice place to stay in), the engaging Cider Centre at Brandy Wharf (if you like cider, look no further), and the Nickerson Arms up at Rothwell, a veritable oasis for that part of the county. Other pubs doing really well here these days include the Chequers at Gedney Dyke (good all round, super food), the bustling Beehive in Grantham (very cheap food – and it's the only pub with a living inn sign), the Wig & Mitre in Lincoln (useful for its all-day food), and the very civilised old George in Stamford. The pub which we name as Lincolnshire Dining Pub of the Year is the Chequers at Gedney Dyke. In the Lucky Dip section at the end of the chapter, pubs which are on good form these days include the Leagate near Coningsby, Five Bells at Edenham, Bell at Halton Holegate, Brownlow Arms at Hough on the Hill, Vine in Skegness, White Hart at Tetford and Abbey Lodge at Woodhall Spa; we have inspected most of these and can vouch for their appeal. There's quite a good choice in Lincoln. The area scores well for value: food comes in big helpings, and drinks prices are a little below the national average – the Brewers Arms at Snaith has a fine range of attractively priced beers brewed on the premises, though the cheapest pub of all we found for beer was the Black Horse at Donington on Bain. The local brewer Batemans produces notable ales, and their new seasonal beers are more interesting than most – this last year we've enjoyed one delicately flavoured with liquorice, one given a smoky tang by the incorporation of toasted oak chips, and an unusual Chocolate Malt Stout.

ALLINGTON SK8540 Map 7

Welby Arms 🍺

The Green; off A1 N of Grantham, or A52 W of Grantham

This friendly local in a quiet village set in pleasant countryside has a warmly relaxing atmosphere, with a good welcome from the efficient staff; it's an excellent respite from the A1. A stone archway divides the two rooms of the bar. There are comfortable burgundy button-back wall banquettes and stools, some Lloyd Loom chairs, black beams and joists, red velvet curtains, a coal fire in one stone fireplace and logs burning in an attractive arched brick fireplace. One area has lots of signed celebrity photographs (Phil Collins, Gary Lineker etc); the dining lounge off to one side is partly no smoking. The good range of home-cooked food includes home-made soup (£1.95), home-made pâté (£2.50), very fresh Grimsby haddock (£4.30) ham and egg (£4.50), salmon (£5.95), vegetarian dishes, chicken done with herbs and mustard (£6.95) and rack of marinaded lamb (£9.95), with a good value Sunday roast; the restaurant is no smoking. Particularly well kept Bass, John Smiths, Timothy Taylors Landlord and a couple of guest beers such as Brains SA and Championship on handpump, decent wines and a good range of country wines; maybe piped nostalgic pop music. *(Recommended by Tony Gayfer, Keith and Norma Bloomfield, Derek and Sylvia Stephenson, Keith Wright, Colin and Sue Graham, Chris Mawson)*

Free house ~ Licensee R B Dyer ~ Real ale ~ Meals and snacks (not Sun evening) ~ (01400) ~ 281361 Restaurant ~ Children in restaurant ~ Open 12-2.30(3 Sat), 5.30(6.30 Sat)-11

ASWARBY TF0639 Map 8

Tally Ho 🛏 ⏸

Though not large, this 17th-c country inn is imposing, handsomely built of stone, with dark oak beams inside. The bar has built-in wall banquettes and cushioned wall settles, cast-iron-framed tables, a big log fire, some stripped masonry, country prints and handsome flower arrangements. There's a quietly enjoyable civilised atmosphere, and service is friendly, prompt and helpful. Good bar food includes home-made soup (£2), lincolnshire sausages (£3.25), filled freshly baked french bread or ploughman's (£3.50), home-made salmon and spinach fishcakes with a creamy parsley sauce (£6.25), 10oz rump steak (£8.50), and daily specials (3 starters, 6 main courses, 4 puddings); vegetables are cooked to perfection. Well kept Adnams, Batemans XB and a guest beer on handpump, good house wines (with a splendid system of letting you pour from the bottle, and being charged for what you drink); daily papers. At weekends it's wise to book for the attractive pine-furnished restaurant, which has piped classical music. There are tables out behind among fruit trees, and usually sheep in the meadow beyond. The bedrooms are in a neatly converted back block. Over the road, the pretty estate church, glimpsed through the stately oaks of the park, is worth a visit. *(Recommended by John and Zoe Chamberlain, Anthony Barnes, F J and A Parmenter, D Maplethorpe, B Helliwell, June and Malcolm Farmer, Peter Coombs, M Morgan)*

Free house ~ Licensee William Wood ~ Real ale ~ Meals and snacks (till 10pm) ~ Restaurant ~ (01529) 455205 ~ Children in eating area of bar and in restaurant ~ Open 12-3, 6-11; closed 25-26 Dec ~ Bedrooms: £30B/£45B

BRANDY WHARF TF0197 Map 8

Cider Centre

B1205 SE of Scunthorpe (off A15 about 16 miles N of Lincoln)

Alone by a traffic-controlled humpbacked bridge over the canalised River Ancholme, this unusual pub is a shrine to cider. The main bar is a simple room with wheelback chairs and brown plush wall banquettes on brown carpet squares, cheery customer photographs, a good little coal fire, and – the main point, of course – Addlestone's, Scrumpy Jack and Weston's Old Rosie on handpump, and some six dozen other farm ciders and perries – up to 18 tapped from casks, the rest from stacks of intriguing bottles and small plastic or earthenware kegs on shelves behind the bar; they also keep country wines and mead. The friendly landlord's very happy to talk cider, and will on request show you his extraordinary collection of hundreds of different cider flagons, jugs and bottles. A dim-lit lounge bar open at weekends and in summer has all sorts of cider memorabilia and good-humoured sidelights on cider-making and drinking (not to mention the foot of 'Cyril the Plumber' poking down through the ceiling). Good value generous plain food includes sandwiches (£1.40), ploughman's (£2.90), pork and cider sausage (£3.80 or £4.80), vegetable curry (£4.40), home-made steak and vegetable pie (£4.60), and beef curry madras (£4.80), with wonderful real chips. Darts and dominoes; piped pop music may be rather loud. A simple glazed verandah overlooks the river, and there's lots of space outside (including several dozen different sorts of cider-apple and perry-pear tree, a caravan site, moorings and slipway); the landlord lays on quite a few appropriate jolly events. No children. *(Recommended by Jane Kingsbury, Mr and Mrs P A Jones, Andy and Jill Kassube, Arnold and Maureen East)*

Free house ~ Licensee Ian Horsley ~ Meals and snacks (not Tues lunchtime) ~ (01652) 678364 ~ Open 12-3, 7-11; closed Mon lunchtimes Oct-Easter; closed Fri before Christmas-2nd Fri in Jan

COLEBY SK9760 Map 8

Bell 🛏

Far Lane; village signposted off A607 S of Lincoln, turn right and right into Far Lane at church

The three communicating carpeted rooms in this friendly dining pub each has a roaring winter log fire and low black joists, and the lounge is decorated with horsebrasses, a variety of small prints, and lots of number plates from around the world. Generously served and nicely presented food includes snacks such as doorstep sandwiches (from £1.85), sausage and egg (£2.95), prawn omelette (£3.95), and ploughman's (£3.50), as well as home-made soup, brie with orange and Cointreau sauce (£3.25), mushroom stroganoff (£5.25), beef, mushroom and stout pie (£6.25), chicken in tarragon and mushroom sauce (£7.95), salmon steak with parsley sauce (£7.95), steaks (from £9.75), a big mixed grill (£13.95), and home-made puddings (£2.25). Wednesday night is fish night with fresh fish delivered daily from Grimsby, Thursday is vegetarian night, and on Saturday and Sunday morning from 9.30-11.45 they serve a big breakfast with Sunday newspapers. Well kept Bass, Flowers Original, and Tetleys on handpump, and several malt whiskies; friendly service. There's a quite separate pool room, darts, juke box, and baord games. Several picnic tables outside, and walks along the Viking Way. *(Recommended by D Maplethorpe, B Helliwell, F J and A Parmenter, M J Morgan, Frank Cummins, H and C Ingham, Arnold and Maureen East, Caroline Kenyon, M and J Back, Ian Phillips)*

Pubmaster ~ Tenants Robert Pickles and Sara Roe ~ Real ale ~ Meals and snacks (served all day) ~ Restaurant ~ (01522) 810240 ~ Children welcome ~ Live bands Fri evenings ~ Open 11.30-11; 12-10.30 Sun ~ Bedrooms: /£35.50B

DONINGTON ON BAIN TF2382 Map 8

Black Horse

Between A153 and A157, SW of Louth

As this bustling village pub with its views across the rolling Wolds is on the Viking Way, walkers tend to congregate here (muddy boots must be left in the hall); picnic tables in the back garden. Inside, a softly lit little inner room has some unusual big murals of carousing Vikings, while the snug back bar, with cushioned seats by the log fire in the reconstructed brick inglenook, has very low black beams, and antlers around the wall lanterns. There's more room in the main bar area, popular with locals, with some heavy-horse prints and harness, a very twisty heavy low beam under its ceiling joists, and a big woodburning stove. Popular bar food, served in relaxed, cheerful surroundings, includes soup (£1.95), filled baked potatoes (from £1.95), ploughman's (£2.95), sausage and egg (£3.95), macaroni cheese with bacon, egg and cheese topping or a roast of the day (£4.75), fresh haddock or cod (£5.25), rabbit pie (£5.95), steaks (from £5.95), chicken curry (£6.95), puddings, and children's dishes (from £1.95); the restaurant is no smoking. Well kept Adnams, Boddingtons, Courage Directors, John Smiths, and Ruddles Best on handpump; friendly service. the public bar (another log fire) has a games room off, with darts, pool, dominoes, pinball, fruit machine, and juke box; maybe unobtrusive piped music. *(Recommended by Paul and Janet Waring, Peter Coombs, Keith Wright, B D Craig, F C Johnston, Elizabeth and Anthony Watts, PGP, Nigel and Lindsay Chapman, Caroline Kenyon, Julie Peters, Derek and Sylvia Stephenson)*

Free house ~ Licensees Tony and Janine Pacey ~ Real ale ~ Meals and snacks (till 10pm) ~ Restaurant ~ (01507) 343640 ~ Children in eating area of bar and in restaurant – not late in evening ~ Open 11.30-3, 6.30-12 ~ Bedrooms: £25S/£40S

DYKE TF1022 Map 8

Wishing Well

21 Main Street; village signposted off A15 N of Bourne

At the dining end of the long, rambling front bar in this friendly village inn there is indeed a wishing well – as well as lots of heavy beams, dark stone, brasswork, candlelight and a cavern of an open fireplace. The carpeted lounge area has green plush button-back low settles and wheelback chairs around individual wooden tables. The good solid reputation for tasty food continues, and there might be home-made soup (£1.90), sandwiches (from £1.90), filled baked potatoes (from £2.50), ploughman's (from £3.75), sausages and egg (£4.25), pork chops in barbecue sauce (£4.80), several home-made pies (from £4.95), vegetarian lasagne (£5.50), steak (£6.95), children's meals (from £2.25), and popular Sunday lunch (£8.50; children £5.50 – must book); both restaurants are no smoking. Well kept Batemans Jawbreaker, Greene King Abbot, Hartington Bitter (from Whim Brewery in Derbyshire), Morlands Aunt Sally, Tetleys Bitter, and Woodfordes Wherry on handpump. The quite separate public bar, smaller and plainer, has sensibly placed darts, pool, shove-ha'penny, dominoes, fruit machine and juke box. There's a play area by the garden. *(Recommended by Jenny and Michael Back, M J Morgan, F J and A Parmenter, Mark and Caroline Thistlethwaite, Mark Hydes, Edward Storey)*

Free house ~ Licensee Barrie Creaser ~ Real ale ~ Meals and snacks ~ Restaurant ~ (01778) 422970 ~ Children welcome ~ Open 11-3, 6-11 ~ Bedrooms: £19.50S/£39S

GEDNEY DYKE TF4125 Map 8

Chequers ⑪

Village signposted off A17 Holbeach—Kings Lynn

Lincolnshire Dining Pub of the Year

This small Fenland village pub is very popular with readers – not only for its marvellous food, but for the friendly licensees, welcoming and informal atmosphere, enjoyable wine, and well kept real ales. But it's the food that gets the most praise, especially the really fresh fish and seafood, changing day by day, such as grilled plaice, lemon sole, monkfish with herb crust and tomato and chilli salsa, roast salmon with horseradish sauce, skate wing, Cromer crabs and Brancaster scallops. There's a wide choice of other good freshly cooked attractively presented food, too, including home-made soup (£2.50), sandwiches (from £2; Loch Fyne smoked salmon with rillette of Scottish salmon £3.50), ploughman's (£3.50), mushroom omelette (£4.50), smoked chicken breast with honey dressing and fresh herbs (£5.50), chestnut roast with red berry dressing or cajun chicken with redcurrant and onion confit (£6.50), lamb on a pasta and vegetable base with sauce charcutière (£7.95), and breast of Gressingham duck with sage polenta and madeira (£10.95); children's helpings, and good home-made puddings; roast Sunday lunch. Everything's kept spotless, with an open fire in the bar, a small rather old-fashioned no-smoking restaurant area at one end, and an elegantly done new dining conservatory at the other, overlooking a garden with picnic tables. Well kept Adnams Bitter, Bass, Elgood Pageant, Greene King Abbot, and Morlands Old Speckled Hen on handpump, four or five decent wines by the glass, elderflower pressé, and polite attentive service; chess. *(Recommended by Anthony Barnes, F J and A Parmenter, John Wooll, Peter Burton, Viv Middlebrook, Mark and Caroline Thistlethwaite)*

Free house ~ Licensee Judith Marshall ~ Real ale ~ Meals and snacks (12-1.45, 7-9) ~ Restaurant ~ (01406) 362666 ~ Children welcome ~ Open 12-2, 7-11; closed 25-26 Dec

GRANTHAM SK9135 Map 7

Beehive £

Castlegate; from main street turn down Finkin Street opposite St Peter's Place

Outside this friendly pub, mounted in a lime tree is the unique inn-sign: a beehive with live bees. It's been here since at least 1830, and probably the 18th c, making this one of the oldest populations of bees in the world. The bar is comfortably straightforward with a bustling, friendly atmosphere, and Batemans XB, Shepherd Neame Spitfire, and South Yorkshire Barnsley Bitter on handpump. Bar food includes sandwiches (from £1.35), filled baked potatoes and good value basic ploughman's (from £1.65), omelettes or sweet and sour chicken (£2.95), gammon and egg (£3.50), and puddings like spotted dick (£1.55); cheerful service. Fruit machine, trivia, video game, good juke box, dominoes, and piped music. *(Recommended by Comus Elliott, C and G Fraser, Derek and Sylvia Stephenson, Bernard and Marjorie Parkin, Brian White)*

Free house ~ Licensee S J Parkes ~ Real ale ~ Lunchtime meals and snacks (not Sun) ~ (01476) 67794 ~ Children welcome ~ Open 11.30-11; 11.30-5, 7-11 Sat

HECKINGTON TF1444 Map 8

Nags Head

High Street; village signposted from A17 Sleaford—Boston

There's a chatty atmosphere in this rather cosy 17th-c village pub, and the left-hand part of the snug two-roomed bar has a coal fire below the shiny black wooden chimney-piece in what must once have been a great inglenook, curving into the corner and taking up the whole of one end of the small room – it now houses three tables, one of them of beaten brass. On the right there are red plush button-back built-in wall banquettes, small spindleback chairs, and an attractive bronze statuette-lamp on the mantelpiece of its coal fire; also, a lively watercolour of a horse-race finish (the horses racing straight towards you), and a modern sporting print of a problematic gun dog. From an ever-changing menu, bar food might include soup and sandwiches (£2.10), filled baked potatoes (from £2.95), pears and stilton grilled on toast (£3.50), vegetarian pie or liver and bacon (£4.95), boiled bacon and parsley sauce or pork with cider and apple sauce (£5.50), lamb steak with mint sauce or cod grilled with tomatoes and cheese (£5.95), and home-made puddings (£2.50); Sunday roasts (£5.50). Well kept Wards Sheffield Best and Double Maxim, and a guest beer on handpump, and cheery, efficient service; pool, shove-ha'penny, dominoes, fruit machine, and juke box. The garden behind has picnic tables, and it's not far to an unusual eight-sailed windmill. *(Recommended by Janet and Peter Race, B D Craig, Anthony Barnes, Sue Rowland, John Fahy, P R Morley, Howard James, DC, Brian Horner, Brenda Arthur)*

Wards ~ Lease: Bruce and Gina Pickworth ~ Real ale ~ Meals and snacks ~ (01529) 460218 ~ Well behaved children welcome ~ Open 11-3, 5-11 ~ Bedrooms: £22/£32S

LINCOLN SK9872 Map 8

Wig & Mitre ★ ⑪ ♀

29 Steep Hill; just below cathedral

Some of the original 14th-c features have been carefully preserved in this very civilised and friendly old town pub, such as a section of the original lime ash and reed floor, exposed oak rafters, and part of the medieval wattle-and-daub by the stairs. Downstairs, the cheerful, simpler bar has pews and other more straightforward furniture on its tiles, and a couple of window tables on either side of the entrance; the upstairs dining room has settees, elegant small settles, Victorian armchairs, shelves of old books, and an open fire, and is decorated with antique prints and more modern caricatures of lawyers and clerics, with plenty of smart magazines and newspapers lying about – the kind of place you'd feel comfortable in on your own. But it's the incredible range of food that they serve from lots of different menus, some changing twice a day and served non-stop from 8 o'clock in the morning to around midnight that makes this pub special. They're happy to let you mix and match items from the various lists, and however rushed or busy they are service always stays cordial and efficient. The several menus vary in style and price but a rough selection of dishes might include sandwiches (from £2.95), good soup (£3.50), tuna and lemon pâté (£4.75), chicken livers with black pudding and tarragon mustard or baked cheese soufflé with ham, mushrooms and cream (£5.75), chicken and mushroom pie or salmon fishcakes with lemon and chive butter sauce (£7.50), tagliatelle with asparagus, oyster mushrooms and spinach in a cream and white sauce (£8.50), turkey escalopes with parma ham and fresh basil (£12.50), sirloin steak with black pepper, brandy and cream (£14.50), puddings such as raspberry and sherry trifle or banoffi pie (£3.25), and a proper breakfast (£5.75). There's an excellent and extensive, if somewhat pricey, selection of over 95 wines, many of them available by the glass, with an emphasis on South African, Australian, Chilean or other regional wines. Sam Smiths OB on handpump, lots of liqueurs and spirits, and freshly squeezed orange juice. *(Recommended by Alain and Rose Foote, Arnold and Maureen East, Mr and Mrs B Langrish, F J and A Parmenter, B D Craig, R C Wiles, Sue and Bob Ward, A Preston, Nick Zotov, A Morton, F C Johnston, Ian Phillips, Leigh and Gillian Mellor, Susan and Alan Dominey, H K Dyson, Joan and Michael Hooper-Immins, E J Wilde, David and Shelia, Caroline Kenyon, Dr and Mrs A K Clarke)*

Sam Smiths ~ Tenants Michael Hope and Paul Vidic ~ Real ale ~ Meals and snacks (8am-11pm) ~ Restaurant ~ (01522) 535190 ~ Children in restaurant ~ Open 8am-11pm, including Sun; closed 25 Dec

NEWTON TF0436 Map 8

Red Lion ★ ⑨

Village signposted from A52 E of Grantham; at village road turn right towards Haceby and Braceby; pub itself also discreetly signed off A52 closer to Grantham

Impeccably kept, this civilised old place is as popular as ever for its food – especially the range of excellent imaginatively displayed salads. You choose as much as you like, with six different types of fish such as fresh salmon, nine cold meats, and pies; a small helping is £7.95, normal £8.95, and large £9.95, with children's helpings £3.50. The home-made soups are also very good (£1.90), and there's a choice of hot dishes in the winter months including one or two local specialities such as stuffed chine of pork or spicy lincolnshire sausages; they also do rich puddings, a Sunday carvery, and sandwiches on request. The licensee used to be a butcher, and it does show – the meat and fish could hardly taste better. The welcoming communicating rooms have fresh flowers, old-fashioned oak and elm seats and cream-rendered or bare stone walls covered with farm tools, malters' wooden shovels, a stuffed fox, stag's head and green woodpecker, pictures made from pressed flowers, a dresser full of china, and hunting and coaching prints. Very well kept Bass and Batemans XXXB on handpump; friendly service, unobtrusive but well reproduced piped music, a fruit machine, and nice dogs. During the day and at weekends two squash courts run by the pub can be used by non-members. The neat, well sheltered back garden has some seats on the grass and on a terrace, and a good play area. The countryside nearby is ideal for walking, and acccording to local tradition this village is the highest point between Grantham and the Urals. *(Recommended by M Morgan, F J and A Parmenter, Keith Wright, Chris Walling, Stephen Brown, Peter and Gwyneth Eastwood, Brian and Jill Bond, Gordon Thornton, Michael and Susan Morgan, Howard and Margaret Buchanan, E J Wilde, June and Malcolm Farmer)*

Free house ~ Licensee Graham Watkin ~ Real ale ~ Meals and snacks (till 10pm) ~ (01529) 497256 ~ Children welcome ~ Open 11.30-3, 6-11; closed 25 Dec

OLD SOMERBY SK9633 Map 7

Fox & Hounds

B1176 E of Grantham

This spacious, creeper-covered pub has several friendly little rooms with some copper-topped tables, comfortable seating upholstered in a hunting-print fabric, and pictures on the same theme. One area is no smoking. Good bar food includes home-made soup (£1.60), sandwiches or spectacular jumbo rolls (from £2; smoky bacon and egg £2.60, steak £4.60), home-made mackerel pâté (£3), ploughman's (£3.50), home-made lasagne (£4.50), vegetarian dishes (from £4.75), freshly-battered Grimsby haddock, plaice or halibut (from £5.40), steaks (from £8.50), daily specials (from £5), puddings (£2.20), and Sunday lunch (£5); quite a few fresh fish dishes in the restaurant. Well kept Courage Directors, Marstons Pedigree, Morlands Old Speckled Hen, Ruddles Best and County and John Smiths on handpump; darts, fruit machine, trivia, and piped music. There's a large garden with plenty of tables and chairs, and a big car park. *(Recommended by F J and A Parmenter, F C Johnston, Simon Collett-Jones, H and C Ingham, D Maplethorpe, B Helliwell, Peter Coombs, M G Hart)*

Free house ~ Licensees Tony and Karen Cawthorn ~ Real ale ~ Meals and snacks (till 10pm; not Mon) ~ Restaurant (not Sun evening) ~ (01476) 564121 ~ Children welcome ~ Jazz some Thursdays ~ Open 11-3, 7(6.30 Sat)-11.30; closed Mon (except bank holidays)

ROTHWELL TF1599 Map 8

Nickerson Arms 🍺

Village signposted off B1225 S of Caistor, about a mile S of its junction with the A46

Attractively reworked three or four years ago, this convivial place has a pleasant bar divided by a couple of arches with a warm central coal fire, a good balance between standing room and comfortable chairs and tables (with little bunches of fresh flowers), attractive wildlife prints, and heavy beams; there's a spacious dining area. It's a real oasis for this part of the world, with an enjoyably relaxed and civilised atmosphere. Good bar food runs from good plain generous sandwiches and soups such as herby chicken (£2.25) to Greek salad with feta and olives (£3.75), grilled lemon sole, smoked goose breast, rack of lamb with port and redcurrant sauce, and vegetarian nut provençale; two-course Sunday roast lunch (£6.95). Besides well kept Batemans XB, XXXB and a seasonal beer on handpump, and guest ales such as King & Barnes 12 Bore and Woodfordes Wherry, they keep a fine range of Trappist beers and dozens of other interesting bottled beers, decent wines by the glass, and four ciders. The piped jazz may be on the loud side; darts, cribbage, dominoes. There are tables outside the long white-painted building. Take care coming out of the car park: it's a blind bend. If you're up here, Potterton & Martin's plant nursery on the B1205 on the far side of Nettleton is well worth a visit. *(Recommended by Peter Toms, David and Michelle James, Peter Coombs, Nigel and Lindsay Chapman)*

Free house ~ Licensee Les Purdy ~ Real ale ~ Meals and snacks (not Mon-Thurs evenings) ~ Children in eating area of bar ~ Jazz Fri ~ Open 12-2, 7(5 summer Fri)-11

SNAITH SE6422 Map 7

Brewers Arms 🍺

10 Pontefract Rd

The microbrewery – in a quite separate building and you can arrange to look round – is the main focus of attention here, and the fine set of beers is gaining favour in pubs selling them elsewhere: Old Mill Bitter, Mild, Bullion, Old Curiosity, Black Jack, and Nellie Dean on electric pump. Unusually, they also do their own lager; quite a few malt whiskies. This is an attractive conversion of a former mill, with old local photographs, exposed ceiling joists and a neat brick and timber bar counter. The bar food is good, too, including good sandwiches (from £1.95), filled french bread (£2.35), daily specials (around £4.50), and large, fresh haddock (£4.95); friendly, obliging staff. There are good value home-cooked restaurant meals too, with green plush chairs and turkey carpet in a fresh and airy conservatory-style dining area (no smoking) with a pine plank ceiling and lots of plants. Beware of joining the skeleton at the bottom of the old well; fruit machine and piped music. *(Recommended by Derek and Sylvia Stephenson, Comus Elliott, CW, JW, C A Hall)*

Own brew ~ Manager John McCue ~ Real ale ~ Meals and snacks ~ Restaurant ~ (01405) 862404 ~ Children in eating area of bar and in restaurant ~ Open 11-3, 6-11 ~ Bedrooms: £40/£52

STAMFORD TF0207 Map 8

George ★ ★ (♨) ⬛ ♀

71 High St, St Martins

In the 18th and 19th c, this historic building was a busy coaching inn, with 20 trips a day each way from London and York (two of the front rooms are still named after these destinations). It was actually built in 1597 for Lord Burghley, though there are still parts of a much older Norman pilgrims' hospice – and a crypt under the cocktail bar that may be 1000 years old. Nowadays, it's still much loved by travellers on what was the Great North Road as a civilised, but relaxed, place to enjoy a drink or very good meal. There's a medley of seats ranging from sturdy bar settles through leather, cane and antique wicker to soft settees and easy chairs, while the central lounge has sturdy timbers, broad flagstones, heavy beams, and massive stonework. The nicest place for lunch (if it's not a warm sunny day) is the indoor Garden Lounge, with well spaced white cast-iron furniture on herringbone glazed bricks around a central tropical grove, and food such as soup of the day with Italian bread (£3.95), chicken liver pâté with orange and redcurrant sauce (£4.95), pasta and gnocchi dishes (£8.45), fresh haddock from Billingsgate or lamb liver and bacon (£8.95), tuna steak niçoise (£9.95), and 10oz sirloin steak or a splendidly tempting help-yourself buffet (from £12.95); in the York bar there are more snacky dishes such as sandwiches (from £3.50; french stick with sirloin steak, onions, tomato and mushroom £5.95), cheddar and stilton platter with french bread (£5.55), and puddings (£2.95). Adnams Broadside and Ruddles Best on handpump, but the best drinks are the Italian wines, many of which are good value and sold by the glass; also freshly squeezed orange juice, filter, espresso or cappuccino coffee. Friendly, helpful staff. The cobbled courtyard at the back is lovely in summer, with comfortable chairs and tables among attractive plant tubs and colourful hanging baskets; waiter drinks service. Besides the courtyard, there's a neatly maintained walled garden, with a sunken lawn where croquet is often played. *(Recommended by Vicky and David Sarti, James Nunns, R C Wiles, Mavis and John Wright, D Maplethorpe, B Helliwell, Cliff Blakemore, Jane Kingsbury, Andrew and Ruth Triggs, Chris Raisin and friends, Ian Phillips, Jack and Philip Paxton, Gordon Thornton, Lynn Sharpless, Bob Eardley, David and Shelia, Caroline Kenyon, Bernard and Marjorie Parkin, Stuart Earle; also in Good Hotel Guide)*

Free house ~ Licensees Ivo Vannocci and Chris Pitman ~ Real ale ~ Meals and snacks (noon-11) ~ Two restaurants ~ (01780) 755171 ~ Children welcome ~ Open 11-11; 12-10.30 Sun ~ Bedrooms: £72B/£105B

Lucky Dip

Besides the fully inspected pubs, you might like to try these Lucky Dips recommended to us and described by readers (if you do, please send us reports):

Alford [29 West St (A1004); TF4576], *White Horse*: Smartly redecorated, with comfortable plush furnishings, well kept real ales inc guest beers, good value fresh-cooked food in bar and restaurant; bedrooms *(Chris Raisin, A W Lewis, LYM)*

Barkston [The Green; SK9341], *Stags Head*: Good home-made food, tables laid for dining in left-hand bar, well kept Everards Tiger and Beacon, friendly atmosphere, pool *(F J and A Parmenter)*

Barnoldby le Beck [SW of Grimsby; TA2303], *Ship*: Warm well furnished nautical-theme country pub with good sensibly priced food inc fish, game and vegetarian, attentive welcoming staff, good range of wines, comfortable dining room, pleasant setting *(Gordon B Thornton, John Smith)*

Belchford [E of A153 Horncastle—Louth; TF2975], *Blue Bell*: Three well kept interesting guest beers, simple food inc delicious home-

made pies, good local trout and good value Sun lunch, nicely refurbished bar, pleasant atmosphere *(Caroline Kenyon, Derek and Sylvia Stephenson)*

☆ **Bicker** [A52 NE of Donnington; TF2237], *Red Lion*: Simply modernised and relaxing 17th-c pub with masses of china hanging from bowed black beams, huge fireplace, well kept Batemans and other ales, wide choice of good generous food, staff friendly and efficient even when busy; tables on terrace and tree-shaded lawn *(Bill and Sheila McLardy, Gary Carter, BB)*

☆ **Boston** [Wormgate; TF3244], *Goodbarns Yard*: Popular and comfortable, with old beams in original core (former riverside cottages looking up to Boston Stump), modern but matching back extension, plenty of alcoves, terrace overlooking river, well kept Courage-related and guest ales, wide choice of good value food from filled french bread and baked potatoes to steaks inc interesting snacks

(Ian Phillips, A W Dickinson, John Honnor)
Boston [Horncastle Rd (B1183)], _Kings Arms_:
Fine spot by canal opp tall five-sail working
windpump, airy unpretentious front bar, plush
little back bar, well kept Batemans Mild, XB
and XXXB, friendly efficient landlady, low-
priced usual bar food; bedrooms modern and
comfortable with cheery furnishings _(Ian
Phillips, BB)_
Branston Booths [Bardney Rd, off B1190
Lincoln—Horncastle; TF0669], _Green Tree_:
Good basic reasonably priced home-cooked
food and puddings; five well kept real ales
(Sue and Bob Ward)
Castle Bytham [SK9818], _Castle_: Consistently
good generous bar food, friendly service,
Ansells Mild, Boddingtons Bitter and Gold,
Burtonwood Forshaws, Tetleys, Theakstons
Best and Old Peculier, log fire, nicely laid out
side restaurant; piped music _(Jenny and
Michael Back)_
Caythorpe [SK9348], _Red Lion_: 16th-c pub in
pleasant surroundings, wide choice of fair-
priced food from sandwiches to fresh Grimsby
fish, well kept ales inc Boddingtons, Greene
King Abbot, Timothy Taylors Landlord and
Youngs Special, no piped music, good service
(Peter Burton, H and C Ingham)
Cleethorpes [Kingsway; TA3008], _Willys_:
Modern bistro-style pub with cafe tables, tiled
floor and painted brick walls; brews its own
good beers, also well kept guest beers and well
priced basic lunchtime food; quiet juke box,
Humber estuary views; annual beer festival
(Andy and Jill Kassube, Michael Butler)
Coningsby [Boston Rd (B1192); ½ mile NW of
village – OS Sheet 122 map ref 242588;
TF2458], _Leagate_: Dark old heavy-beamed
fenland local with three linked areas, ageing
medley of furnishings inc great high-backed
settles around the biggest of the three log fires;
prompt attractively priced straightforward
food, several Courage-related and other ales;
piped jazz or pop music, fruit machine; rustic
garden with play area; children if eating
(Martin Riddell, Caroline Kenyon, LYM)
Cowbit [Barrier Bank, A1073 S of Spalding;
TF2618], _Olde Dun Cow_: Welcoming 17th-c
local with wide choice of generous good value
bar food, well kept ales such as Crown Buckley
Rev James, Batemans XXXB, Exmoor Gold
and Theakstons Best and XB, pleasant black
and white split-level bar with old oak beams,
antique notices, restaurant one end, family
games area at the other; fairly subdued piped
pop music, satellite TV plans, maybe live music;
tables in garden with play area, bedrooms
(Gwen and Peter Andrews, E Robinson)
Dunston [TF0663], _Red Lion_: Pleasant village
pub hidden in back streets, big beamed lounge
and restaurant, good food inc home-made
curries/pies, good choice of well kept beers _(D
Maplethorpe, B Helliwell)_
Edenham [A151; TF0621], _Five Bells_: Wide
choice of generous usual bar food in neat busy
modernised dining lounge, well kept Bass and
Tetleys, two log fires, dominoes, piped music,
lots of foreign banknotes, soft lighting; back
restaurant/function room, tables in garden

with good play area; children welcome _(M and
J Back, F J and A Parmenter, Mrs J A Blanks,
Mike and Penny Sanders, LYM)_
Epworth [The Square; SE7804], _Red Lion_:
Several separate beamed areas, lively,
welcoming, comfortable and spacious, with
roaring fire, well kept Tetleys and Youngs, wide
choice of good value food inc lots of vegetarian
dishes, friendly efficient waitress service _(Ian and
Freda Millar, JohnPaul Haigh, Peter Coombs)_
☆ Ewerby [TF1247], _Finch Hatton Arms_:
Substantial plushly furnished well decorated
mock-Tudor pub with good atmosphere,
efficient friendly staff, well kept Stones Best and
Wards Sheffield Best on handpump, coal fire,
decent bar food, smart restaurant, comfortable
back locals' bar; bedrooms _(P R Morley, BB)_
Frognall [A16 E of Mkt Deeping; TF1610],
Goat: Geared to food (all day Sun), with wide
choice inc fish and vegetarian, but also
Adnams, Bass and interesting guest beers such
as Butterknowle Porter, Stocks St Leger Leap,
Wilds Oats and Woodfordes Wherry; low
beams, stripped stonework, two dining lounges,
restaurant, friendly service, no piped music; big
garden with play equipment (no children inside)
(Jenny and Michael Back, JJW, CMW)
Fulbeck [The Green; SK9450], _Hare &
Hounds_: Country pub with brightly pleasant
bar and restaurant, wide choice of varied well
served meals, boules pitch (popular on Sun),
no machines _(Gordon B Thornton)_
☆ Gedney [Chapelgate, just off A17 W of Long
Sutton; TF4024], _Old Black Lion_: Good
welcoming service, wide choice of good value
quickly served food inc fresh veg, Whitbreads-
related ales, good house wines _(John Wooll,
Mrs R Finlay, Ray Tunnicliff)_
☆ Grantham [High St; SK9135], _Angel & Royal_:
Remarkable worn medieval carved stone
facade, ancient oriel window seat in upstairs
plush bar on left, massive inglenook in friendly
high-beamed main bar opp, well kept Bass and
occasional guest beers, bar food; bedrooms in
comfortable modern hotel block extending
behind _(George Brisco, Comus Elliott, LYM)_
Grimsby [Alexandra Dock; TA2609], _Lincoln
Castle_: Paddle-steamer now a friendly
bar/restaurant with upper deck bar and lower
deck restaurant, good value food inc 3-course
Sat specials; well kept Old Oak, Theakstons
and Youngers No 3; games machine, piped
music _(JJW, CMW)_
Hagworthingham [TF3469], _George &
Dragon_: Good food inc special weekly theme
nights, welcoming licensees _(Arnold and
Maureen East)_
☆ Halton Holegate [B1195 E of Spilsby;
TF4165], _Bell_: Pretty village local, simple but
comfortable and consistently friendly, with
wide choice of decent home-made food inc
outstanding fish and chips, vegetarian dishes
and Sun lunches, well kept Bass, Batemans and
Mansfield Old Baily, aircraft pictures, pub
games, maybe piped music; children in eating
area and restaurant _(Derek and Sylvia
Stephenson, LYM)_
Hatton [A158 Wragby—Horncastle; TF1776],
Midge: Good changing fresh-cooked food (not

Mon) in bar and restaurant, sensible prices, Bass, Stones and a guest ale *(Arnold and Maureen East)*

Hemingby [TF2374], *Coach & Horses*: Friendly old-fashioned village local, cordial licensees, good plain food at reasonable prices; Sun quiz night *(V E Thompson)*

Horncastle [West St; TF2669], *Fighting Cocks*: Unpretentious oak-beamed local with quick cheerful service, wide range of good value food inc gigantic garnished Yorkshire puddings, Batemans, Courage Directors, Marstons Pedigree and M & B Brew XI, open fire each end *(Chris Mawson, A W Dickinson)*; [North St], *Old Nicks*: Pleasant, warm and friendly, with very good value lunchtime roasts, no-smoking dining area *(Gordon Thornton)*

☆ **Hough on the Hill** [SK9246], *Brownlow Arms*: Wide range of good value well cooked and presented food in attractive pub's relaxing lounge, sofas and comfortable chairs, well kept Marstons Pedigree and changing guest beers, decent wines, friendly efficient service; pubby separate bar, good restaurant; good value pretty bedrooms, good breakfasts, peaceful picturesque village handy for Belton House *(J and P Maloney, R M Taylor)*

Hubberts Bridge [Station Rd; TF2643], *Wheatsheaf*: Family-run, with good food, decent choice of drinks, open fires, good atmosphere; children's facilities, events organised *(K C McLardy)*

Ingham [High St; SK9483], *Inn on the Green*: Wide choice of quickly served good home-made food inc interesting dishes and Sun lunch in well modernised pub on village green; lots of brass and copper in spacious beamed lounge bar, good fire, upstairs dining room; children welcome *(Chris Mawson)*

☆ **Langworth** [A158 Lincoln—Wragby; TF0676], *New Station*: Pleasant pub (station long gone, railway still there) with roomy conservatory, well kept Courage-related ales, reasonably priced wine, generous food esp outstanding fish and chips; Sunday carvery *(Michael Clark, Arnold and Maureen East)*

Leadenham [High St; A17 Newark—Sleaford; SK9552], *George*: Remarkable range of several hundred whiskies, a good choice of wines by the glass inc their own direct German imports, and well kept ales inc Boddingtons, fair-priced and quickly served food from sandwiches to steaks in unassuming bar, side games room, piped music, restaurant; bedrooms plain but good value; good breakfasts, for non-residents too *(M J Gale, C H Daly, D Maplethorpe, B Helliwell, LYM)*

Legbourne [Station Rd; TF3684], *Queens Head*: Good cheap sandwiches and snacks, well kept ales, simple decor, big garden with tables and play area *(Peter Baker)*

☆ **Lincoln** [Bunkers Hill], *Lincolnshire Poacher*: Roomy and comfortable, with old chairs and books, Lincolnshire memorabilia inc interesting prints, big dining part with no-smoking areas, good range of food inc local dishes, Riding and Old Baily real ale, attentive considerate service; play areas inside and (with

video surveillance) outside; open all day Sun *(Gordon Thornton, M Morgan, Mike and Maggie Betton)*

☆ **Lincoln** [Steep Hill], *Browns Pie Shop*: Wide choice of good food inc popular chunky pies; restaurant licence only, but does have Everards Tiger and Ruddles Best as well as decent wines, comfortable seats, friendly staff, pleasant traditional atmosphere *(Gordon Thornton, M J Morgan, D Maplethorpe, B Helliwell)*

Lincoln [25 Lindum Rd], *Adam & Eve*: Civilised pub, one of the oldest here, opp gate to cathedral close; well kept John Smiths and Theakstons, bar food; boules, tree-shaded play area *(Ian Phillips, Dr and Mrs A K Clarke)*; [Langworth Gate], *Bull & Chain*: Popular local with very reasonably priced food, friendly staff, Bass and John Smiths ales, good darts team; children welcome, big garden overlooking tennis court *(Keith Wright)*; [Tritton Rd], *Nosey Parker*: New Tom Cobleigh pub, good range of beers, pleasant atmosphere, interesting themed decor featuring earlier times in the city, varied menu, no-smoking areas, good parking *(Gordon Thornton)*; [6 Union Rd], *Victoria*: Notable collection of well kept ales inc lots of changing guests in classic quaint backstreet Victorian local behind castle, two cosy rooms, country wines, basic cheap lunchtime food, friendly staff; can get crowded lunchtime, lively late evening *(Dr and Mrs A K Clarke, Corry and Simon)*

Long Bennington [just off A1 N of Grantham; SK8344], *Reindeer*: Very hospitable busy local, scrupulously clean, with good choice of generous home-cooked food in bar and more formal dining lounge, well kept ales and good wines, good service *(Robert Jordan, Mrs F Stubbs)*; *Royal Oak*: Popular and comfortable local, well kept Marstons Pedigree, good value home cooking, decent wines, welcoming service, games room, skittle alley, big back garden with barbecue and play area *(Roy Sowden, Helen and Keith Bowers, Stewart Boyd, D G Stentiford)*

Long Sutton [off bypass A17 Kings Lynn—Holbeach; TF4222], *Crown & Woolpack*: Good generous low-priced home cooking (sandwiches only, Mon-Weds) in friendly unpretentious local with panelled back dining room, good Sun lunch (must book), Ansells Mild, Bass and Worthington BB, roaring fire; dominoes, piped music (may be rather loud) *(Jenny and Michael Back)*; [89 London Rd], *Olde Ship*: Welcoming attractive 17th-c black and white inn, log fires; well kept Bass, Boddingtons, Greene King Abbot and sometimes a guest beer, good home-cooked bar food, cosy restaurant with good Sun roasts and some unusual dishes *(Mrs Viv Elce, R H Freeman)*

Mareham le Fen [A115; TF2861], *Royal Oak*: Interesting partly thatched 14th-c building with pleasant interior, well kept Batemans XB and a guest such as John Smiths, friendly atmosphere, limited good value food *(Joan and Michel Hooper-Immins, M Morgan)*

☆ **Market Deeping** [Market Pl; TF1310], *Bull*: Low-ceilinged alcoves, little corridors, interesting heavy-beamed medieval Dugout Bar; well kept Everards Tiger and Old

Original and guest beers, good value bar food
(not Sun or Mon evening), attractive eating
area, no piped music lunchtime, helpful
friendly service, restaurant; seats in pretty
coachyard; children in eating areas; open all
day Fri, Sat *(M J Morgan, LYM)*

☆ Marston [2 miles E of A1 just N of Grantham;
SK8943], *Thorold Arms*: Pleasantly
refurbished, with good food and atmosphere,
friendly service, well kept ales *(Peter Coombs)*

☆ Navenby [High St; SK9858], *Kings Head*:
Small village pub with decent food inc good
varied puddings in pleasant no-smoking area
off bar, interesting nick-nacks, books, quick
friendly service, well kept Bass, no piped music
(Peter Burton, D Toulson)
Nettleham [A46 N of Lincoln; TF0075],
Brown Cow: Pleasant civilised lounge bar,
good varied reasonably priced food, friendly
service; Sun lunch very popular *(Gordon
Thornton)*; [High St], *White Hart*: Simple and
friendly, with good food, in centre of pleasant
village *(Ian Rorison)*
North Kelsey [off B1434 S of Brigg; TA0401],
Royal Oak: Comfortable old village pub with
good value straightforward food from rolls to
home-made pies and Sunday roasts, well kept
ales inc Batemans and Vaux Samson, bar, snug
with TV, games room with darts and pool; real
fire, fruit machine, quiz night Tues *(JJW, CMW)*
North Scarle [off A1133 Newark—
Gainsborough; SK8567], *White Hart*: Good
choice of generous food in bar and restaurant,
well kept beer, live music Sun *(David and
Ruth Hollands)*
North Thoresby [A16/B1201; TF2998],
Granby: Traditional pub with two bars, Bass,
Worthington and weekly guest beers, good
food inc Sun lunch in lounge bar and no-
smoking restaurant, most attractive prices;
tables out on new terrace *(David Lord)*

☆ Norton Disney [off A46 Newark—Lincoln;
SK8859], *St Vincent Arms*: Attractive if not
spacious village pub with well kept Batemans
Mild and XXXB, Marstons Pedigree, three
guest beers, open fire, good value generous
plain food from sandwiches up inc beautifully
cooked veg, pleasant landlord; tables and big
amusing adventure playground out behind
(Sarah and Peter Gooderhay, H and C Ingham)
Oasby [TF0038], *Houblon Arms*: Large and
rambling, with lots of beams, panelling and
stonework, well kept Batemans and a guest
ale, good interesting food *(Peter Burton)*
Pinchbeck [Glenside S, West Pinchbeck;
TF2425], *Packing Shed*: Cosy and friendly,
with beautiful fire and brasses, wide choice of
good food *(Simon and Louise Chappell)*;
[Northgate], *Ship*: Friendly service, good value
food, comfortable small lounge and dining
area, Courage-related ales *(M J Morgan)*
Sandilands [off A52 nr Sutton on Sea; TF5280],
Grange & Links: A hotel, but good bar food
inc good summer salads served in the ballroom,
well kept beer; fine gardens, some 200 yds from
good beach; bedrooms *(Gordon Thornton)*
Saxilby [Canal Side (out on A57); SK8975],
Bridge: Large mock-Tudor canalside pub with
good home-made food inc good fresh fish in

bar and restaurant, well kept changing ales,
friendly helpful staff, neat garden *(David and
Ruth Hollands)*

☆ Scotter [A159 Scunthorpe—Gainsborough;
SE8801], *White Swan*: Expansive well kept
pub comfortably laid out for dining, decent
straightforward food inc children's, John
Smiths, Ruddles Best and County and
Websters Yorkshire, snug panelled area by one
fireplace, neat pleasant staff; piped pop music
may be intrusive; big-windowed restaurant
looking over lawn with picnic tables to duck-
filled River Eau; comfortable bedrooms in big
modern extension *(Gordon Thornton, BB)*

☆ Skegness [Vine Rd, Seacroft (off Drummond
Rd); TF5660], *Vine*: Dating mainly from late
18th c, comfortable well run bar overlooking
drive and own bowling green, imposing
antique seats and grandfather clock in turkey-
carpeted hall, juke box in inner oak-panelled
room; three well kept Batemans real ales, good
value food in bar and restaurant, friendly staff,
tables on big back sheltered lawn with swings;
pleasant bedrooms, peaceful suburban setting
not far from beach and birdwatching *(R and A
Cooper, Christine and Geoff Butler, LYM)*
Skellingthorpe [High St; SK9272], *Stones
Arms*: Friendly local with good inexpensive bar
food, well kept ale, welcoming service, popular
Sun lunch in plush restaurant; opp church and
meadow *(Marcus Underwood, D Toulson)*
Skendleby [Spilsby Rd, off A158 about 10
miles NW of Skegness; TF4369], *Blacksmiths
Arms*: Old-fashioned bar, cosy and quaint,
with open fire, well kept Batemans, limited
range of good value generous food; busy
(Geoff and Jonathan Butler)
Sleaford [Southgate; TF0645], *Bull & Dog*:
Refurbished town pub, good reasonably
priced food; some evenings more of a young
people's meeting place – esp Thurs *(D
Maplethorpe, B Helliwell, Nige and Jake)*
South Ferriby [A1077; SE9921], *Nelthorpe
Arms*: Doing well under present regime – cheap,
very friendly, with popular food and well kept
Batemans Mild, Mansfield Old Baily and
Tetleys; bedrooms good value *(Comus Elliott)*

☆ Spalding [Herring Lane/Double St; TF2618],
Lincolnshire Poacher: Good choice of S&N
and other constantly changing ales, polished
tiles in bar, other rooms off inc dining area,
good home-made food, friendly service, open
fires, old enamel advertising signs everywhere;
seats on green overlooking river, but traffic a
bit intrusive *(Ian Phillips, J Honnor)*
Spalding [Main St], *Crown & Woolpack*:
Generous good food in small bar, roaring log
fire, Ansells Mild, Bass and Worthington
(Jenny and Michael Back)
Stamford [All Saints Pl; TF0207], *Crown*:
Friendly staff, good value food and well kept
Ruddles County in large rambling stone-built
pub's comfortable panelled bar and no-
smoking dining room; bedrooms *(G B
Longden, Michael Gittins)*; [Sheepmarket],
Golden Fleece: Good value food inc generous
roasts, quick pleasant service, no-smoking area
(Mr and Mrs J Brown); [5 Cheyne Lane,
between High St and St Marys St], *Hole in the*

Wall: A pub since 1807, cosy and busy L-shaped room with old tables, chairs and settles, central servery – may have to wait for a table; good lunchtime food, well kept Bass, Courage Directors, Marstons Pedigree and two guest beers, decent reasonably priced wine *(Cdr Patrick Tailyour, Michel Hooper-Immins)*; [19 Maiden Lane], *Kings Head*: Small homely two-room oak-beamed pub with friendly staff, well kept Flowers and Tetleys, coin collection, decent food; open all day *(Tim and Ann Newell, P Stallard)*; [St Peters St], *St Peters*: Well kept Marstons Best and Pedigree and several guest beers, good food inc pasta, oriental and vegetarian, cosy bar and bistro, quiet music, friendly staff *(P Stallard)*, Sturton by Stow [A1500/B1241; SK8980], *Plough*: Quiet, small and decorous pub with two bars and small no-smoking dining area, discreet piped music; wide choice of freshly made good food inc Sun roast, polite service; three well kept Mansfield ales *(JJW, CMW)* Surfleet [A16; TF2528], *Mermaid*: Wide choice of popular food from sandwiches to good value Sun lunch, two dining areas, well kept ales such as Adnams, Buchanans, Robinsons and John Smiths, friendly family service; by river with footpaths, interesting church nearby with leaning tower; garden with play area; bedrooms *(PGP, Winifred Fry)* Surfleet Seas End [Reservoir Rd, off A16 N of Spalding; TF2728], *Ship*: Unspoilt 17th-c riverside pub, flagstone bar, open fires, well kept Marstons Bitter and Pedigree and guests such as Fullers London Pride, good home-cooked food esp seafood, no-smoking dining room *(Mr and Mrs Cocks, M J Morgan)* Swayfield [OS Sheet 130 map ref 991227; SK9922], *Royal Oak*: Friendly family pub, lots of character, good value generous usual food from ploughman's to steaks inc good Sun lunch, well kept Bass, Tetleys and Oakham ales, efficient service *(J and P Maloney, F J and A Parmenter)* Tattershall Thorpe [B1192 Coningsby—Woodhall Spa; TF2259], *Blue Bell*: Attractive pub with decent food inc good Sun roast, small dining room, attentive service even when busy, Adnams Broadside, Marstons Pedigree, Morlands Old Speckled Hen and Tetleys, Sun bar nibbles; piped pop music; tables in garden, impressive lavatera bushes *(JJW, CMW, D Maplethorpe, B Helliwell)*
☆ Tetford [OS Sheet 122 map ref 333748; TF3374], *White Hart*: Early 16th-c pub with good atmosphere, well kept Mansfield Riding and a guest beer, wide choice of interesting food from good value sandwiches to impressive French dishes inc popular Sun lunches and good options for children; old-fashioned settles, slabby elm tables and red tiled floor in pleasant quiet inglenook bar, no-smoking snug, basic games room; seats and swings on sheltered back lawn, simple bedrooms *(Rita and Keith Pollard, Nigel and Lindsay Chapman, MJH, DJ, MJ, LYM)* Thorpe on the Hill [SK9065], *Railway*: Unspoilt country local with Hamilton Ellis LMS prints of pre-1923 railway scenes,

friendly landlord, well kept Mansfield ales *(John C Baker)* Thorpe St Peter [Thorpe Culvert, off B1195 NW of Wainfleet; TF4760], *Three Tuns*: Unusual decor (bedroomish wallpaper), with popular food and two well kept ales *(Sue and Bob Ward)* Threekingham [just off A52 12 miles E of Grantham; TF0836], *Three Kings*: Big entrance hall, bar, lounge and small dining room; warm and comfortable, good service, good value food, well kept Bass, M&B Brew XI and Stones *(M J Morgan)* Waltham [Kirkgate; B1203 Grimsby—Mkt Rasen; TA2603], *Tilted Barrel*: Comfortable bar with leather seats, good food here and in restaurant inc good value Sun lunch served 12-5, Ind Coope Burton, Tetleys Bitter and Imperial and guest beers, enthusiastic friendly service; comfortable bedrooms *(David Lord)*
☆ Wellingore [High St; off A607 Lincoln—Grantham; SK9856], *Marquis of Granby*: Cheerful, attractive and neatly kept old pub in tiny pretty village, concentration on good value bar food inc interesting specials in bar and restaurant, good filled rolls, welcoming service, well kept Theakstons Best and XB and changing guest ales, comfortable button-back banquettes, log fire; bedrooms *(Frank Cummins, D Toulson, H and C Ingham, Richard Loates)* West Deeping [Main St; TF1109], *Red Lion*: Attractive bar, long and low, with plenty of tables, roaring coal fire, old stonework and beams, Ansells, Bass, Ind Coope Burton and a guest such as Shepherd Neame Spitfire, wide choice of generous food from sandwiches up inc vegetarian, prompt welcoming service; games room *(M and J Back)*
☆ Woodhall Spa [Kirkstead; Tattersall Rd (B1192 Woodhall Spa—Coningsby); TF1963], *Abbey Lodge*: Attractively and discreetly decorated food pub, warm, cosy and popular, with some antique furnishings, faultless welcoming service, wide range of consistently good generous bar food, not cheap but good value, inc fine omelettes and Sun lunches, well kept real ale, RAF memorabilia *(Bill and Sheila McLardy, D Maplethorpe, B Helliwell, Arnold and Maureen East)* Woodhall Spa [Stixwould Rd], *Village Limits*: Good home cooking, pink plush banquettes and aeroplane prints; motel bedrooms *(SS)*
☆ Woolsthorpe [the one nr Belvoir, signed off A52 Grantham—Nottingham; SK8435], *Rutland Arms*: Comfortable and welcoming country pub with good value nicely presented food esp fish, separate dining room, well kept Whitbreads-related ales, lounge with some high-backed settles, hunting prints and brasses, family extension, open fire, video juke box, bric-a-brac; two pool tables in annexe; play equipment on big lawn, quiet spot nr restored canal *(Elizabeth and Anthony Watts, Chris de Wet)* Woolsthorpe, *Chequers*: Attractively refurbished and extended village pub with good food, well kept ale, lots of events esp Fri in big entertainments area, boules, own cricket ground; bedrooms *(David and Shelia, N J Stokes, BB)*

Norfolk

A good clutch of new entries in this well favoured county includes the busy low-beamed Kings Head at Bawburgh with its remarkable range of food, the enjoyably unpretentious Italian-run Kings Head at Great Bircham (just known as Bircham to most people in Norfolk), the charming little Earle Arms tucked away in Heydon (very enjoyable food), the Nelson Head out near the sea defences at Horsey (Austrian licensees here), the Angel at Larling (in and out of the same family since 1913, a good trunk-road refuge), the civilised Sculthorpe Mill in its pretty spot outside Sculthorpe, and the bustling Crown in Wells next the Sea, back in these pages after a break. The handsome old Buckinghamshire Arms at Blickling is flourishing under sympathetic new management, and other pubs which have been showing particularly well in recent months include the restauranty Ratcatchers at Cawston (gains one of our Food Awards this year), the Saracens Head at Wolterton near Erpingham (excellent combination of distinctive food and distinctive surroundings – our choice as Norfolk Dining Pub of the Year), the Crown at Mundford (imaginative dishes of the day, pretty bedrooms), the cheery Hare Arms at Stow Bardolph (reliable food), Darbys at Swanton Morley (a farmer-run pub with good food and a surprisingly cosmopolitan atmosphere), the attractive cottagey Chequers at Thompson, the unspoilt Three Horseshoes at Warham and the welcoming and relaxed Fishermans Return at Winterton on Sea (one of very few East Anglian pubs to qualify for our Bargain Food symbol – low drinks prices, too). In the Lucky Dip at the end of the chapter, pubs currently on form (all inspected and vouched for by us) include the Chequers at Binham, Hare Arms at Docking, Crown at Great Ellingham, Hill House at Happisburgh, Hare & Hounds at Hempstead, Kings Head at Hethersett, Swan at Hilborough and Coldham Hall at Surlingham; Cley next the Sea has a couple of worthwhile places, and there's a good choice in Norwich. Drinks prices here are still a little higher than the national average, but have been holding relatively steady recently, with many more pubs getting their cheapest beer from smallish local brewers – most notably Woodfordes, whose 'brewery tap' the Fur & Feather in the idyllic village of Woodbastwick is well worth a visit.

BAWBURGH TG1508 Map 5

Kings Head

Pub signposted down Hats Lane off B1108, which leads off A47 just W of Norwich

A massive choice of food for once really does seem to cater for all tastes in this big well run pub: our inspection visit found its four linked low-beamed rooms bustling with a very mixed but very good-natured crowd – as if a coach-load of the Not So Young had got enjoyably tangled up with the Grateful Dead's fan club. You name it, the menu and specials boards around the big knocked-through central fireplace have it: anything from good sandwiches (£3), bacon and chicken well filled rolls (£3.95) and baked potatoes (£4.45) to alligator, ostrich or even kangaroo (£15.95), via fried chicken livers (£3.95), smoked haddock and mozzarella tartlet (£4.25), squid tagliatelle with a cream and samphire sauce (£4.75), and pigeon with blueberry and orange compote (£13.50). Helpings are generous, and the home-made puddings make an impression; no smoking restaurant. Adnams, Boddingtons, Flowers IPA and Original, Marstons Pedigree and guests like Whitbreads Pompey Royal and Shepherd Neame Spitfire on handpump; good quick service. There are rustic tables and benches on the gravel outside. *(Recommended by MDN, John Whitehouse, Brian and Jean Hepworth; more reports please)*

Free house ~ Licensee A E Wimmer ~ Real ale ~ Meals and snacks (till 10) ~ Restaurant ~ (01603) 744977 or 743210 ~ Children welcome ~ Live music every other Mon ~ Open 11-3, 6-11; cl 25 Dec evening

BLAKENEY TG0243 Map 8

Kings Arms ♛

West Gate St

Just a short stroll from the harbour, this pretty white inn can get crowded in summer, but even at the busiest times the little rooms keep a cheery pubby atmosphere, and service remains efficient and friendly. Relaxed and welcoming, the three simply furnished, knocked-together rooms have some interesting photographs of the licensees' theatrical careers, other pictures including work by local artists, and what's said to be the smallest cartoon gallery in England in a former telephone kiosk; three rooms are no smoking. Tasty bar food in generous helpings includes soup (£2), sandwiches (from £1.50, the crab are very tasty), filled baked potatoes (from £3.20), ploughman's (from £3.90), vegetarian samosas, curry and lasagne (from £4.50), locally caught battered cod, plaice, haddock and scampi (£5.50), steaks (£9.50), and seasonal specials like local whitebait, locally smoked mackerel or soused herrings (£3.50), beef and ale pie (£5.25) or delicious local crab ploughman's (£5.50); puddings such as home-made crumble or bread pudding (from £2.50), and good children's meals (£2.75) – the fish fingers may be home-made. Very well kept Marstons Pedigree, Ruddles County, Websters Yorkshire and Woodfordes Wherry on handpump, freshly squeezed orange juice; darts, cribbage, dominoes, fruit machine. The large garden has lots of tables and chairs and a separate, equipped children's area; there are baby-changing facilities, too. They can supply information on boat trips out to the seals and birds of Blakeney Point. Dogs welcome. *(Recommended by Melanie Bradshaw, M Morgan, Charles Bardswell, Helen and Ian Cookson, Pam and Mike Collett, Anne Morris, M A Mees, Tony Dickinson, Mike and Heather Barnes, Stephen, Julie and Hayley Brown, Rita Horridge, Mr and Mrs Jones, K H Frostick)*

Free house ~ Licensees Howard and Marjorie Davies ~ Real ale ~ Meals and snacks (12-9.30; 9 Sun) ~ (01263) 740341 ~ Children welcome ~ Open 11-11.30; 12-10.30 Sun ~ Bedrooms: £20S/£40S, and self catering flats upstairs £50

White Horse ↤ ♀

4 High Street

From the bottom end of this small hotel's main bar there's a good view of the quay and tidal inlet. It's a long room, predominantly green (despite the Venetian red ceiling), with a restrained but attractive decor (including two big reproductions of Audubon waterfowl prints up at the far end), and a pleasantly chatty atmosphere. Besides cribbage and dominoes, there's a good collection of other games such as Connect-4, backgammon, well kept Adnams, Boddingtons, and Flowers Original, and a good choice of reasonably priced wines, especially from the New World with a couple of nice ones by the glass – the barman may let you taste one or two to find the right one. It does get very busy in the holiday season, but even then there's a good leavening of local people. There's wheelchair access, though a short flight of steps to the back part of the bar. Good value well presented bar food includes sandwiches (from £1.25), soup (£1.95; the cockle chowder is good, £3), salads (from

£4.50), steak and kidney pie or lasagne (£4.95), daily specials like mussels (£3.50), vegetarian stuffed marrow (£4.95) and steak and kidney pudding, crab thermidor, oriental pork or tagliatelle with mushrooms, bacon and pesto sauce (£5.50), local fresh fish, and home-made puddings like treacle tart or bread and butter pudding (£2.25); brisk service by pleasant young staff; no-smoking area. There's a pleasant little dining room with nice pictures on its white-painted flint walls, and tables out in a suntrap courtyard. *(Recommended by Charles Bardswell, P Gillbe, John Beeken, Ken and Jenny Simmonds, George Atkinson, Peter and Pat Frogley, Jonathan and Helen Palmer, Mike and Heather Barnes, Alan and Mary Reid, Frank Davidson)*

Free house ~ Licensee Daniel Rees ~ Real ale ~ Meals and snacks ~ Restaurant (Tues-Sat evening only) ~ (01263) 740574 ~ Children in restaurant and two other rooms ~ Open 11-3, 6-11 ~ Bedrooms: £30B/£60B

BLICKLING TG1728 Map 8

Buckinghamshire Arms

Off B1354 N of Aylsham

We had known the new licensees at this handsome National Trust Jacobean lodge, which stands at the entrance to Blickling Hall, for their previous fabulous work at the Saracens Head near Erpingham – so we've high hopes for the changes they plan to make here. They've already lightened up the decor, and plan to bring the whole operation up a notch or two. The small front snug is simply furnished with fabric-cushioned banquettes, while the bigger lounge has neatly built-in pews, stripped deal tables, and Spy pictures. Continental-style bar food under the new chef includes filled baguettes (from £3), tomato and mozzarella salad (£3.95), taramasalata (£4.25), salami and goat's cheese salad (£4.50), vegetarian lasagne (£5.25), quiches or steak and kidney pie (£5.95) and whole tail scampi, char-grilled local trout or lemon sole (£7.25), and puddings like raspberry and apple pie or rhubarb crumble (£2.75). About six Bass-related real ales with a guest like Marstons Pedigree or Morlands Old Speckled Hen are well kept on handpump, and there's a good range of wines with half a dozen by the glass, freshly squeezed juices and malt whiskies. There are picnic tables under cocktail parasols on the lawn, and they may serve food from an out-building here in summer. Blickling Hall is open from April to October only, and closed Mondays and Thursdays, though you can walk through the park at any time. *(Recommended by Howard Clutterbuck, R C Vincent, John Wooll, Melanie Bradshaw, Simon Penny, John Honnor, Wayne Brindle, Jerry and Alison Oakes, June and Malcolm Farmer, Tim and Sue Halstead; more reports on the new regime please)*

Free house ~ Licensee Robert Dawson-Smith ~ Real ale ~ Meals and snacks ~ Evening restaurant (not Sun or Mon) ~ (01263) 732133 ~ Children in restaurant ~ Open 11-3, 6-11 ~ Bedrooms: £45S/£60S

BURNHAM MARKET TF8342 Map 8

Hoste Arms 🛏

The Green (B1155)

This 17th-c hotel handsomely faces the long green of a lovely unspoilt Georgian village. The boldly decorated bars have massive log fires and a smartly civilised but relaxed atmosphere. The panelled bar on the right has a series of watercolours showing scenes from local walks, there's a bow-windowed bar on the left, and the owner may play the grand piano. Stylish bar food is served in the front lounge, music room and no-smoking conservatory, with a range of dishes such as half a dozen local oysters or marinated salmon with a warm citrus beurre blanc (£4.95), boiled bacon on a green split pea purée (£6.95), baked salmon on spinach pasta and roasted red peppers (£7.95), roast breast of chicken with grilled pancetta (£8.50). Well kept Greene King Abbot and IPA, Woodfordes Wherry and a changing guest like Shepherd Neame Spitfire on handpump, good wine list (with lots by the glass or half bottle), decent choice of malt whiskies, and freshly squeezed orange juice; nice sitting room, and professional service by friendly staff. Morning coffee and afternoon tea in the conservatory. At the back is a pleasant walled garden with tables on a terrace. It can be busy at weekends. *(Recommended by D and J Tapper, Paul Boot, Jo and Den Reeve, John Wooll, Bill and Sheila McLardy, M J Morgan, Melanie Bradshaw, Anthony Barnes, Jack and Philip Paxton, F C Johnston, George Atkinson, R C Vincent, Neil Gordon-Lee, MDN, DJW, D Hayman, Mr and Mrs M J Matthews, David Culley, Frank Gadbois, Stephen, Julie and Hayley Brown, Stuart Earle, Charles Bardswell, Brian Atkin, Wayne Brindle, Amanda Dauncey, J Rudolf; also in Good Hotel Guide)*

Free house ~ Licensees Leigh Diggins and Paul Whittome ~ Real ale ~ Meals and snacks ~ Restaurant ~ (01328) 738777 ~ Children welcome ~ Jazz Fri evenings ~ Open 11-11 ~ Bedrooms: £60B/£70B

BURNHAM THORPE TF8541 Map 8

Lord Nelson ♦

Village signposted from B1155 and B1355, near Burnham Market

This unusual old pub has no bar counter – just a characterful little room with well waxed antique settles on the worn red flooring tiles, and smoke ovens in the original fireplace. Nelson knew this historic place as the Plough, and held a party here before leaving the village to take command of his 64-gun ship the *Agamemnon* in 1793, so it's no surprise to find lots of pictures and memorabilia of the Admiral lining the walls. A no-smoking eating room has flagstones, an open fire, and more pictures of the celebrated sailor. Bar food in generous helpings includes home-made soup (£2), sandwiches (from £1.80), English breakfast (£3.75), ploughman's (from £3.90), salads (from £4), omelettes (from £3.80), a home-made pie of the day (£4.95), with daily specials like warm salad of salmon, onions and mushroom on a bed of winter leaves with croûtons (£3.65), vegetarian dishes like pancakes filled with spinach, leeks, mushrooms and sweetcorn with spicy tomato sauce (all £4.95), roast loin of lamb with garlic and rosemary stuffing on a red wine and rosemary sauce (£7.45), steamed salmon steak with spinach and leek sauce (£7.65) or fried pork loin with apple and calvados sauce (£7.75), and children's meals (from £2.50). It can get busy so it may be necessary to book. Well kept Greene King Abbot and Mild and Woodfordes Nelsons Revenge tapped from the cask in a back stillroom (good prices), and there's an unusual rum concoction called Nelson's Blood; shove-ha'penny, cribbage, dominoes, draughts, chess. It's popular with families – a highchair is available, and there's a play area with football, basketball and a climbing frame outside. *(Recommended by D R Blake, MDN, M J Morgan, John Wooll, Paul Boot, Jack and Philip Paxton, D Hayman, Emily Heading, R D Greaves, H and C Ingham, Charles Bardswell, Wayne Brindle, Stephen, Julie and Hayley Brown, Peter and Pat Frogley, Bob Arnett, Judy Wayman)*

Greene King ~ Lease: Lucy Stafford ~ Real ale ~ Meals and snacks ~ (01328) 738241 ~ Children in eating area ~ Live music once a month ~ Open 11-3, 6-11

CASTLE ACRE TF8115 Map 8

Ostrich £

Stocks Green; village signposted from A1065 N of Swaffham; OS Sheet 144 map reference 815153

There's a very individual atmosphere in this unspoilt no-nonsense village pub. It's very prettily placed overlooking a tree-lined green, and makes a useful stop on the ancient Peddars Way. Wandering around its rooms, you can still see some of its original 16th-c masonry and beams, and trusses in the lofty ceilings, although it was largely rebuilt in the 18th c. The L-shaped low-ceilinged front bar, unfussy and rather local-feeling, has a huge old fireplace with a swinging potyard below its low mantelbeam (which may be used in winter for cooking soups and hams), straightforward furnishings, and big photographs of the local sights on the walls; it may get a little smoky at busy times. Fairly reliable and very good value bar food includes sandwiches (from £1.30), pizzas (from £2.60), ploughman's (from £3), breaded plaice (£2.95), omelettes (£3), deep-fried seafood platter (£3.40) and sirloin steak (£6.75), with specials like ratatouille crumble, chick pea curry or chilli (£3) and bobotie, beef and ale pie, haddock in wine sauce and salmon and prawn mayonnaise (£4.50-£5); children's meals (from £1). Four Greene King beers are well kept on handpump; dominoes, cribbage, fruit machine, and piped music. Picnic-table sets in the sheltered garden, where they're developing a herb garden for use in the kitchen. There's a Cluniac monastery in the village, as well as the remains of a Norman castle, and a nice toy shop next door. *(Recommended by Stephen Barney, Brigid Purcell, John Benjafield, Sue Rowland, Charles Bardswell, John Beeken, Peter and Pat Frogley, Graham and Sandra Poll)*

Greene King ~ Tenant Ray Wakelen ~ Real ale ~ Meals and snacks (till 10.30pm; not 25/26 Dec) ~ (01760) 755398 ~ Children in family room ~ Jazz every 2nd and 3rd Weds of month, Folk last Weds of month ~ Open 12-3, 7-11; cl 25 Dec evening ~ Bedrooms: £15S/£30S

CAWSTON TG1323 Map 8

Ratcatchers 🍴 ♀

Eastgate, 1 mile S of village; heading N from Norwich on B1149 turn left towards Haveringland at crossroads ½ mile before the B1145 turn to Cawston itself

It's best to book a table at this busy pub/restaurant, as the very good freshly prepared food is extremely popular. Real effort and care goes into its preparation – they bake their own bread, make their own herb oils, chutney, purées and stocks, and pickle their own samphire. There may be a 30-40 minute wait as everything is cooked to order, but it is worth it. Dishes are not cheap, with prices reflecting the restauranty atmosphere. The menu includes soups (£2.65), sandwiches (from £2.85), sausage and mash (£5.55), cottage pie or ploughman's (£5.65), lots of salads (from £5.85), over a dozen vegetarian dishes (from £4.95 to £7.95), lasagne or game pie (£6.95), fish pie (£7.45), madras curry (£7.95), spaghetti with basil, garlic, cream, prawns and parmesan (£8.75), chicken breast in brandy with black peppercorns and cream (£9.35) and 10oz sirloin (£12.95 with sauces from £1.95) puddings including white Belgian chocolate cheesecake (£4.95), and children's meals (£4.35). No credit cards. Well kept real ales on handpump are Adnams Extra, Bass, Hancocks HB and a guest, country wines, several malt whiskies. As well as the L-shaped beamed bar with its open fire, interesting solid wood tables and dining chairs, there's a quieter and cosier no-smoking, candlelit dining room on the right. Bedrooms are planned for this spring; darts, cribbage, dominoes, piped music; no vests in the bar. *(Recommended by Anthony Barnes, Helen and Ian Cookson, Bill and Sheila McLardy, Mrs J Huntly, C J Darwent, I P G Derwent, Wayne Brindle, Tom Thomas, Tony Kemp, Rachel Weston, Mrs B Lemon, P Devitt, Peter and Pat Frogley, H O Dickinson)*

Free house ~ Licensees Eugene and Jill Charlier ~ Real ale ~ Meals and snacks (till 10pm) ~ Restaurant (not Sun evening) ~ (01603) 871430 ~ Children welcome ~ Open 11.45-3, 6-11; closed 25/26 Dec

COLKIRK TF9126 Map 8

Crown ♀

Village signposted off B1146 S of Fakenham; and off A1065

There's a lovely alliance here between the very good reasonably priced bar food, and the nice comfortable pubby atmosphere; on top of that, the friendly landlord will happily open any bottle of wine you want from their list of several dozen, even for just a glass – which could make for a very interesting evening. The calmly welcoming public bar and small lounge both have open fires, solid straightforward country furniture, rugs and flooring tiles, and sympathetic lighting; the no-smoking dining room leading off is pleasantly informal. Well kept Greene King beers on handpump, several malt whiskies. Promptly served and sensibly imaginative bar food includes lunchtime soup (£2.05), tomato and mozzarella salad (£2.25), tiger prawns with mushrooms in a hot oriental sauce (£3.95), brunch (£4.95), salads (from £4.95), several vegetarian dishes like spinach and ricotta cheese canelloni (£5.25), goujons of haddock with a mint yoghurt dip (£5.25), gammon steak (£6.10) and breast of chicken with blue cheese sauce (£6.25), with specials which might include skate wing provençal or steak and kidney pie (£5.50), fresh crab salad or lamb and apricot curry (£5.75), fried loin of pork with cumberland sauce (£6.50) and braised steak in cream and garlic sauce or fillet of salmon with lemon sauce (£6.95). Darts, shove ha'penny, table skittles, cribbage, dominoes, fruit machine. There's a garden and suntrap patio, with picnic tables. *(Recommended by Anthony Barnes, Brian and Jill Bond, Frank Davidson, Philip and Susan Philcox, Bill and Sheila McLardy, John Wooll, Rita and Keith Pollard)*

Greene King ~ Tenant P Whitmore ~ Real ale ~ Meals and snacks (12-1.45, 7-9.30); not 25/26 Dec ~ (01328) 862172 ~ Children welcome ~ Open 11-2.30, 6-11

DERSINGHAM TF6830 Map 8

Feathers 🍺

Manor Road; B1440 towards Sandringham

Families are particularly welcome at this handsome Jacobean inn with its exciting log cabin and fort, as well swings, slide and sandpit in its neatly landscaped garden. The terrace from here leads into a relaxed and characterful main bar, comfortably furnished with soft plush seats, wall settles, carved wooden chairs, and dark panelling and carving. One of the fireplaces is still dominated by the Prince of Wales' feathers, as the pub was a favourite with the future Edward VII when he was visiting nearby Sandringham. Another bar is similarly furnished. As well as Adnams and Bass, the quickly changing guest beer might be Morlands Old Speckled Hen well kept on handpump. Generously served bar food includes sandwiches (from £1.25), soup (£1.50), ploughman's (£3.50), chicken and ham pie (£3.95), daily specials such as steak and beer pie or pork in cider sauce (£4.75), leek and stilton bake (£4.95), puddings (from £1.95) and children's meals (£1.99). Darts, pool, bar billiards, fruit machine, trivia, piped music. They can get busy in summer. *(Recommended by John Wooll, David Carr, K H Frostick, F H Collier, J H Bell, Graham and Sandra Poll, Wayne Brindle, Mark and Caroline Thistlethwaite, Geoffrey and Brenda Wilson)*

Bass ~ Lease: Tony and Maxine Martin ~ Real ale ~ Meals and snacks (till 10pm) ~ Restaurant ~ (01485) 540207 ~ Children welcome ~ Live bands in the barn alternate Fri or Sat nights ~ Open 11-2.30, 5.30-11; cl evening 25 Dec ~ Bedrooms: £25/£40

nr ERPINGHAM TG1631 Map 8

Saracens Head 🍽️ 🛏️ 🍷

Address is Wolterton – not shown on many maps; Erpingham signed off A140 N of Aylsham, keep on through Calthorpe, then where road bends right take the straight-ahead turn-off signposted Wolterton

Norfolk Dining Pub of the Year

Excellent inventive bar food – very fairly priced – at this comfortably civilised inn continues to draw really enthusiastic praise from readers. The regularly changing menu is prepared with great care from the best ingredients, and might include starters like pork, venison and apple pâté (£3.50), deep-fried aubergine with garlic mayonnaise (£3.55), mussels with cider and cream or grilled smoked mackerel and chopped nuts (£3.95), sautéed wild mushrooms and ham with sherry (£4.75). Main courses might be ratatouille (£6.50), fried chicken livers and orange tossed in a warm salad, or stir fry of white fish and orange and ginger tossed in a mixed salad (£7.50), chicken breast simmered in white wine, butter and cream (£7.70), grilled trout (£7.75), sautéed monkfish with fresh mango and turmeric (£8.25), brace of roast woodcock with rich game gravy (£8.50), and puddings like brown bread and butter pudding or apple fritters with apricot sauce (£2.95); good value two-course Sunday supper (£5.95), and three-course monthly feasts (£11.50); booking is almost essential. The two-room bar is simple and stylish, with high ceilings and tall windows giving a feeling of space, though it's not large, and around the terracotta walls are a mix of seats from built-in leather wall settles to wicker fireside chairs, solid-colour carpets and curtains, log fires and flowers on the mantelpieces. It looks out on a charming old-fashioned gravel stableyard with picnic tables; they plan to add a bar for light snacks out here. There's a pretty little four-table parlour on the right – cheerful nursery colours, and another big log fire. Very well kept Adnams and guest beers such as Felinfoel Double Dragon, Morlands Old Speckled Hen on handpump; decent malt whiskies. The wine list is really quite interesting, with some shipped direct from a French chateau. There isn't a designated no-smoking area, but ashtrays have to be requested; £1 surcharge for credit cards. *(Recommended by Roger Danes, BHP, Wayne Brindle, Paul Boot, Ian Phillips, Frank Davidson, Rita Horridge, Mrs M Lewis, Dorothy Smith, Simon Penny, David Culley, Mr and Mrs J R Morris, John Wooll, Jason Caulkin, Neil and Angela Huxter, Ken and Jenny Simmonds, Richard Dolphin, Anthony Barnes, Stephen, Julie and Hayley Brown, Paul Craddoug, Mr and Mrs Duncan, John and Moira Cole)*

Free house ~ Licensee Robert Dawson-Smith ~ Real ale ~ Meals and snacks ~ Restaurant ~ (01263) 768909 ~ Well behaved children welcome ~ Occasional jazz nights ~ Open 11-3, 6-11; closed 25 Dec ~ Bedrooms: £40B/£50B

GREAT BIRCHAM TF7632 Map 8

Kings Head ♀ ⇔

B1155, S end of village (which is called and signposted Bircham locally)

Not as grand inside as suggested by its looks (or its use as a lunch place for Sandringham shooting parties), this old-fashioned Victorian country inn has a pleasantly quiet and relaxed atmosphere, with a mix of high and low tables suiting both diners and drinkers in its unassuming lounge bar – basically two room areas, with a good hot fire in a third more homely bit round behind. The white-aproned Italian landlord is attentive and cheerful without ostentation, and his wife equally pleasant and efficient. Reliable and generous bar food includes lunchtime sandwiches (from £2.50), ploughman's (£4), good home-made fishcakes with crab sauce, moules or steak and kidney pudding (£6.50), smoked haddock mornay (£6.95) and quite a few Italian specialities such as fresh spaghetti or tortellini (£5.50) and saltimbocca. Puddings are massively tempting; the dining area is no smoking. Besides well kept Bass, Charrington IPA and Hancocks Bitter, there's a good choice of malt whiskies, freshly squeezed juices and decent wines; maybe unobtrusive piped music, dominoes. The somnolent alsatian is called Brandy. The big side lawn, with a well kept herbaceous border, has picnic tables and play things. The attractive village has Norfolk's most striking windmill and a decent art gallery, and Houghton Hall is not far off. *(Recommended by Charles Bardswell, R Vincent, John Wooll, A K Clemow)*

Free house ~ Licensees Isidoro and Iris Verrando ~ Real ale ~ Meals and snacks ~ Restaurant ~ (01485) 578265 ~ Open 11-3, 6.30-11; cl 25 and 26 Dec evening ~ Bedrooms: £33B/£55B

HEYDON TG1127 Map 8

Earle Arms

Village signposted from B1149 about midway between Norwich and Holt

Completely transformed by the new landlord, this 17th-c village inn is now a rewarding and unusual dining pub – yet if you drop in for just a drink you'll be warmly welcomed by the friendly and enthusiastic owner or his excellent barman. Two carpeted rooms, one with hatch service, open off a small lobby with a handsomely carved longcase clock, and are individually furnished and decorated, with pretty rosehip wallpaper over a stripped dado, china on shelves, deep tiled-floor cupboards with interesting bric-a-brac, attractive prints and good log fires; dominoes, shove-ha'penny, cribbage and chess. There's a tiny homely dining room, and a simple but well heated conservatory beyond; booking is advised for weekends. Food is good fresh home cooking, with separate small blackboard menus for evening and (cheaper) lunchtime: sandwiches (£1.95), home-made broth (£2.95), stilton ploughman's, shepherd's pie, chestnut roast or cauliflower, cheese and onion tart (£4.95), roast rib of organic beef (£5.45), seafood mornay (£5.45), and evening: spinach and stilton tart (£7.95), lamb liver italienne or honey garlic lamb (£8.95), halibut steak with creole sauce (£9.45), sirloin steak au poivre (£10.95), and puddings (£2.95). Well kept Morlands Old Speckled Hen and Woodfordes Wherry and Great Eastern on handpump; about two dozen decent wines and a dozen malt whiskies. The well behaved dogs sometimes in evidence are called Barnaby and Bendoodle. There are picnic tables in a small and prettily cottagey back garden, and on the front wall above the colourful front flower borders is what looks like a figurehead from a ship wrecked in the Dutch Wars. The village, so cut off from the outside world that you might meet partridges wandering up the street, is very special. *(Recommended by Mrs P Holman, Judy Wayman, Bob Arnett)*

Free house ~ Licensees Keith and Sara Holman-Howes ~ Real ale ~ Meals and snacks ~ (01263) 587376 ~ Open 12-3, 7-11

HORSEY TG4522 Map 8
Nelson Head

Signposted off B1159 (in series of S-bends) N of Gt Yarmouth

Owned by the National Trust, this small tiled brick house is actually below sea level, and near a notoriously weak part of the sea defences; besides the beach down the road, it's also handy for interesting walks around Horsey Mill and the Mere – and thus popular with birdwatchers. It's a very genuine country pub, with two unpretentious rooms divided by a slung-back red velvet curtain, simple but comfortable seats (including four tractor-seat bar stools), lots of shiny bric-a-brac and small local pictures for sale, geraniums on the window sill and in all a relaxed cottagey feel. Besides usual dishes such as ploughman's (£3.85), cod (£3.95), vegetarian tagliatelle or home-cooked ham and egg (£4), braised steak (£5.25), 8oz sirloin steak (£7.95) and children's dishes (£2.50), the Austrian licensees do several good specialities such as wiener schnitzel (£6.95), goulash, sachertorte and apple strudel. Woodfordes Wherry and (of course) Nelsons Revenge on handpump, decent coffee, good fire; maybe piped Radio 2. Dogs on leads are allowed, there's a homely family dining room, and the garden has picnic tables. *(Recommended by David and Anne Culley, Dr Andrew Schuman, Anna Brewer, Norman and Keith Bloomfield)*

Free house ~ Licensee Reg Parsons ~ Real ale ~ Meals and snacks ~ (01493) 369378 ~ Children in eating area of bar ~ Open 11-2.30, 6-11

HUNWORTH TG0635 Map 8
Hunny Bell

Village signposted off B roads S of Holt

The pleasantly welcoming L-shaped bar at this cosy village local has windsor chairs around dark wooden tables, comfortable settees (some of which are grouped around the log fire) and Norfolk watercolours and pictures for sale hanging above the panelling dado; one room is no smoking. Well kept Adnams Best, Greene King Abbot and Woodfordes Wherry on handpump, quite a few malt whiskies, and decent wines. Bar food includes sandwiches (from £2.50), soup or home-made pâté (£2.75), ploughman's (£3), local sausages (£4), salads (from £4.50), home-made steak and kidney pie or chicken and ham pie (£4.95), scampi (£5.75) and sirloin steak (£8.50), ice cream sundaes (from £2.75). Darts, dominoes, cribbage and piped music. The garden is an especially pleasant place to sit on a nice day, when there's bar service to the tables on the lawn; children's play area and maybe weekend barbecues. Readers who have in the past enjoyed the warm atmosphere at the Kings Head at Letheringsett will be pleased to know that Sally King's father, retired as landlord there, does help out here now. *(Recommended by Anthony Barnes, J H Bell, BHP, Charles Bardswell)*

Free house ~ Licensee Sally King ~ Real ale ~ Meals and snacks ~ Restaurant ~

(01263) 712300 ~ Children in eating areas until 9.30 ~ Jazz Thurs nights ~ Open 11-3, 5.30-11

KINGS LYNN TF6220 Map 8

Tudor Rose 🏨 🍺

St Nicholas St (just off Tuesday Market Place – main square)

Dating back to the 15th c, this atmospheric town pub has an attractive half-timbered facade with an interesting medieval oak studded door. The delightfully old-fashioned snug little front bar has high beams, reproduction squared panelling, a big wrought-iron wheel-rim chandelier, and newspapers to read. The quite separate back bar is more spacious, with sturdy wall benches, cribbage, fruit machine and juke box. Simple but reliable good value bar food includes soup (£1.65), chilli or sausage and beans (£2.95), sweet and sour crispy vegetables (£3.95), lasagne (£4.99), scampi (£5.50), with more elaborate dishes from the restaurant menu (available in the bar) like venison sausages braised in red wine (£5.95), steak, kidney and mushroom pie (£6.50), pork loin steaks with sherry and wholegrain mustard sauce or creamy mushroom puff (£6.95), chicken and apricot pie (£7.50), poached salmon fillet with ginger and coriander or parsley sauce (£8.25) and venison in blackcurrant sauce (£10.95), and puddings like delicious treacle tart. Well kept Bass, Boddingtons, Woodfordes Wherry and a guest beer on handpump, a fine choice of whiskies, and decent wines. The upstairs raftered restaurant is no smoking. There are seats in the garden. Bedrooms are simple and modern but comfortable, and some have a pretty view of St Nicholas's Chapel. *(Recommended by Mrs Pat Crabb, John Wooll, R C Vincent, Simon Penny, Hanns P Golez, Terry and Eileen Stott, Peter and Pat Frogley, David Carr, Ian Phillips, Ron Leigh)*

Free house ~ Licensees John and Andrea Bull ~ Real ale ~ Meals and snacks (not Sun evening) ~ Restaurant ~ (01553) 762824 ~ Children in eating area of bar ~ Open 11-11 ~ Bedrooms: £30(£38.50B)/£50B

LARLING TL9889 Map 5

Angel 🍺

A11 S of Attleborough

A real surprise on this busy and otherwise largely barren trunk road, the Angel is a welcoming oasis, a proper family-run free house with a comfortably 1930s-style panelled and turkey-carpeted lounge (dimpled glass, and velvet curtains at night, shut out the traffic). Among the decent generous home-made food, dishes people have liked include sandwiches (from £1.95), ploughman's (£3.95), broccoli and cream cheese bake, tagliatelle niçoise or moussaka (£4.95), daily roast or steak and kidney pie (£5.50), chicken supreme in white wine sauce (£5.95), and a vast slice of home-baked gammon (£7.95); the chips come in for special praise. Well kept Adnams and Tetleys on handpump, with a couple of changing guest beers such as Daleside Nightjar and Delight; over 100 malt whiskies, maybe piped local radio; friendly helpful service, very neat housekeeping. The quarry-tiled black-beamed public bar has a good local atmosphere, with dominoes, dice, darts, juke box and fruit machine. A neat grass area behind the car park has picnic tables around a big fairy-lit apple tree, and a safely fenced play area. Peter Beale's old-fashioned rose nursery is nearby. *(Recommended by Frank W Gadbois, John C Baker, A M Pring, Anthony Barnes)*

Free house ~ Licensee Brian Stammers ~ Real ale ~ Meals and snacks (till 10 Fri and Sat) ~ Restaurant ~ (01953) 717963 ~ Occasional live music ~ Open 10-3, 5-11; Sat 10-11; Sun 12-10.30 ~ Bedrooms: £25B/£45B

MUNDFORD TL8093 Map 5

Crown 🏨 🍺

Crown Street; village signposted off A1065 Thetford—Swaffham

This attractive 17th-c posting inn is doing very well at the moment, with consistently good reports about the well prepared imaginative food, and really comfortable prettily decorated four-poster bedrooms. It's set on a quiet village square, and the relaxed and cosy beamed lounge bar has a huge open fireplace in a flint wall, as well as captain's chairs around highly polished tables, interesting local advertisements and other memorabilia. If the pub is full, a spiral iron staircase with *Vanity Fair* cartoons beside it leads up to the club room, an elegant restaurant and the garden – and brings the food down from the upstairs kitchen. There are more heavy beams in the separate red-tiled locals' bar on the left, which has cast-iron-framed tables, another smaller brick fireplace with a copper hood, sensibly placed darts, dominoes, fruit machine, a juke box and a screened-off pool table. Well kept Courage Directors, John Smiths, Sam Smiths, Websters Yorkshire, Woodfordes Wherry, and Celtic Queen from the local Iceni brewery on handpump or electric pump; good choice of malt whiskies, decent house wines (including a barsac by the glass). Kind staff serve bar snacks which include sandwiches (from £1.50), burgers (from £3.25), hazelnut and rice burger (£3.75), local herb sausage (£4.25), honey fried chicken (£4.55), salads (from £4.95), ploughman's (from £5.25), lemon sole (£5.95) and sirloin steak (£9.95). An imaginative range of changing specials might include starters like french onion soup (£1.85), honey-roast quail stuffed with grapes or smoked salmon parcels filled with cream cheese and chives with grapefruit segments, prawns and citrus dressing (£3.95) or king prawns in garlic butter (£4.25), and main courses like leek and mushroom crêpes (£4.95), fillet of plaice stuffed with fresh asparagus with prawn and chive butter sauce (£7.50), fillet of scotch salmon on crispy fried leeks with caviar cream sauce (£7.95). Puddings like hot chocolate chip muffin with rum sauce or treacle and nut tart are delicious (from £2.20); English cheeses (£2.95), and children's helpings of most meals; Sunday lunch (£5.25). *(Recommended by Frank Gadbois, John Fahy, Joyce McKimm, Ian and Christina Allen, George Atkinson, R D Greaves, Simon Penny, Charles Bardswell, Francine Dupre, P Devitt, Jane and Mike Blanckenhagen)*

Free house ~ Licensee Barry Walker~ Real ale ~ Meals and snacks (12-3, 7-10) ~ Restaurant ~ (01842) 878233 ~ Children welcome ~ Open 11-11; 12-10.30 Sun ~ Bedrooms: £29.50B/£45B

NORWICH TG2308 Map 5

Adam & Eve ♀ £

Bishopgate; follow Palace Street from Tombland N of the Cathedral

Just across the road from the law courts, the little old-fashioned rooms of this striking town pub quickly fill at lunchtime with the cheery bustle of lawyers, clerks and litigants. The splendid Dutch gables were added in the 14th and 15th centuries, but the pub itself is much older, thought to date back to at least 1249, when it was a brewhouse for the workmen building the cathedral. Now it's prettily decked out in summer with award-winning tubs and hanging baskets. The traditionally furnished characterful bars are said to be haunted by a number of ghosts (including Lord Sheffield, hacked to death close by in a 16th-c peasant rebellion), though more substantial features include antique high-backed settles, one handsomely carved, cushioned benches built into partly panelled walls, and tiled or parquet floors; the snug room is no smoking. Well-liked generously served lunchtime and afternoon bar food includes sandwiches (from £1.65), granary baps or filled french bread (from £1.85), cheese and ale soup with a pastry top (£2.80), ploughman's (from £3.20), salads (from £3.75), shepherd's pie (£3.80), vegetable pie (£3.85), chilli (£4), fish pie, prawn curry, turkey and ham pie or breaded scampi (£4.10) and game pie (£4.20), puddings like home-made spicy bread and butter pudding (from £1.90), and daily specials such as steak and kidney pie, chicken breasts with almond and apricot, or tiger prawns wrapped in filo pastry (£4.55); very good Sunday roasts (£4.55). Well kept Adnams or Woodfordes Wherry, John Smiths, Morlands Old Speckled Hen, Ruddles County, and Wadworths 6X on handpump or tapped from the cask, a wide range of malt whiskies, about a dozen decent wines by the glass or bottle, and Addlestone's cider. An outside terrace has seats. *(Recommended by Wayne Brindle, M J Brooks, Simon Penny, John Wooll, Ian Phillips, Paul Boot, John and Christine Lowe, Anthony Barnes, Neil O'Callaghan, John T Ames, Sarah and Gary Goldson, Nick and Alison Dowson)*

Courage ~ Lease: Colin Burgess ~ Real ale ~ Meals and snacks (12-7, till 3 Sun) ~ (01603) 667423 ~ Children welcome ~ Open 11-11; 12-10.30 Sun

REEDHAM TG4101 Map 5

Ferry

B1140 Beccles—Acle; the ferry here holds only two cars but goes back and forth continuously till 10pm, taking only a minute or so to cross – fare £2 per car, 25p pedestrians

The ideal way to approach this splendidly placed Broads pub is by boat, either on the interesting working chain ferry or on a holiday hire boat; there are very good moorings (and showers for boaters). Plenty of well spaced tables on the terrace look out over the River Yare and all its traffic, whether that be colourful yachts, graceful swans or even the occasional wherry. The highly praised and generously served menu includes soup (£2.40), game terrine (£3.25), baked avocado with creamy mushroom and stilton sauce (£3.50), lentil, bean and vegetable curry (£5.85), pheasant braised in mushroom and brandy sauce or char-grilled marinated turkey breasts (£6.30), cutlets of lamb on a redcurrant and port sauce (£6.95), salmon, dill and roulade cheese en croûte (£7.95), breaded veal on a white wine and asparagus sauce (£8.50) and 8oz sirloin (£10.25); excellent vegetables; children's menu (from £2). The restaurant is partly no smoking. Well kept Adnams Best, Tetleys and Woodfordes Wherry on handpump, quite a few malt whiskies, country wines, and good cheerful staff. Cool and relaxing even on the hottest day, the secluded back bar has antique rifles, copper and brass, and a fine log fire, while in the long front bar comfortable banquettes line the big picture windows, and there are robust rustic tables carved from slabs of tree-trunk; cribbage, dominoes, fruit machine, video game and piped music. They're well geared up for families, with arrangements for baby food, and changing facilities. The woodturner's shop next door is worth a look. *(Recommended by J E Hilditch, MDN, Anthony Barnes, Geoff and Gary Goldson, Philip and Susan Philcox, D Goodger, David and Julie Glover, Bronwen and Steve Wrigley, Geoffrey and Brenda Wilson, David Nicholls)*

Free house ~ Licensee David Archer ~ Real ale ~ Meals and snacks (till 10) ~ Restaurant ~ (01493) 700429 ~ Children welcome ~ Open 11-3, 6.30(6 Sat)-11; 11-2.30, 7-11 in winter

RINGSTEAD TF7040 Map 8

Gin Trap

Village signposted off A149 near Hunstanton; OS Sheet 132 map reference 707403

In keeping with its name, a big collection of animal traps fills this attractive white painted pub, with a couple of man-traps ingeniously converted to electric candle-effect wall lights. Copper kettles, carpenters' tools, cartwheels, and bottles hang from the beams in the lower part of the well kept friendly bar, there are toasting forks above an open fire (which has dried flowers in summer), and captain's chairs and cast-iron-framed tables on the green-and-white patterned motif carpet. A small no-smoking dining room has quite a few chamber-pots suspended from the ceiling, and high-backed pine settles; you can book a table in here. Well kept Adnams, Bass, Greene King Abbot, Woodfordes Nog, and Gin Trap Bitter brewed by Woodfordes for the pub on handpump; freshly squeezed orange juice; efficient happy staff. Decent bar food includes lunchtime sandwiches (£1.75), ploughman's (from £3), nut cutlet (£4), home-made steak and kidney pie or lasagne (£5.25), 8oz sirloin (£8.35)), daily specials, mainly home-made puddings (£2.40), and children's meals (from £1.95); service may be quite slow. A handsome spreading chestnut tree shelters the car park, and the back garden has seats on the grass or small paved area and pretty flowering tubs. The pub is close to the Peddar's Way; hikers and walkers are welcome, but not their muddy boots. There's an art gallery next door, and boules in the back car park. *(Recommended by David Carr, Gordon Theaker, M J Morgan, D and J Tapper, John Beeken, Chris Mawson, John Wooll, Peter and Pat Frogley, Eric Locker, V G and P A Nutt, Graham and Sandra Poll, R C Vincent, J F Doleman, David Eberlin, Amanda Dauncey, J Rudolf)*

Free house ~ Brian and Margaret Harmes ~ Real ale ~ Meals and snacks (not winter Sun evenings) ~ (01485) 525264 ~ Well behaved children welcome away from main bar area ~ Occasional piano player ~ Open 11.30-3, 7(6.30 Sat)-11

SCOLE TM1579 Map 5

Scole Inn ⇐

A140 just N of A143

This stately old coaching inn with its magnificently rounded Dutch gables is one of only a handful of pubs to have a Grade I listing. It's a fascinating building with a real sense of history, and over the centuries has provided shelter for people such as Charles II and Nelson; it's not hard to visualise the notorious local highwayman John Belcher riding his horse up the huge oak staircase to shelter from the law. There are several magnificent fireplaces (even one in the ladies' lavatory), and the high-beamed lounge bar has a 17th-c iron-studded oak door, antique settles, and leather-cushioned seats and benches around oak refectory tables on its turkey carpets. The spacious bare-boarded public bar has stripped high-backed settles and kitchen chairs around oak tables. Under new management, bar food includes eggy bread with melted cheese and pickle (£2.95), toasted steak sandwiches with chips (£5), pitta bread filled with sausage and bacon topped wtih cheese (£3.85), seafood stir fry (£5.95), and steak, onion and mushroom pie (£6); the restaurant is no-smoking until 9.30pm. Well kept Adnams Best and Worthington on handpump or tapped from the cask; cribbage, dominoes, and piped music. *(Recommended by David Carr, SR, PM, SS, IS, J E Rycroft, J E Hilditch, Eric and Jackie Robinson)*

Free house ~ Licensee Richard Josif ~ Real ale ~ Meals and snacks (till 10pm) ~ Restaurant ~ (01379) 740481 ~ Children welcome ~ Open 11-11; 12-10.30 Sun ~ Bedrooms: £52B/£66B

SCULTHORPE TF8930 Map 8

Sculthorpe Mill

Pub signed off A148 W of Fakenham, opposite village

The three small genteel rooms which make up this converted watermill's bar have soberly attractive furnishings, with good well polished tables, sensible chairs for diners (food is the main thing here), black beams and joists, and generous open fires in winter. The reception desk on the left of the bar and the neatly uniformed staff add a touch of dignity. Quickly served bar food includes sandwiches (from £2.50), ploughman's (£3.95), filled baguettes (£4.25), turkey pie (£6.95) and fish pie (£7.95) and specials such as devilled whitebait or smoked trout (£3.25), fresh crab salad (£4.95), steak and kidney pie (£5.95) and stir fried monkfish or grilled turkey (£6.25). Adnams, Courage Directors, John Smiths Yorkshire and a guest like Greene King IPA on handpump; decent wines; piped music. The inn is in a quiet and pretty spot, with a little millstream emerging from the bridge just in front, and plenty of tables outside – including one virtually out on an island among the mallards. We have not yet heard from readers who have stayed here, but would expect it to qualify for one of our place-to-stay awards. *(Recommended by R C Vincent, M J Morgan, John Wooll, M A Mees, Helen and Ian Cookson)*

Free house ~ Licensees Ken McGranthin and Catherine Cameron ~ Real ale ~ Meals and snacks ~ Restaurant ~ (01328) 856161 ~ Open 11-11 ~ Bedrooms: £40B/£60B

SNETTISHAM TF6834 Map 8

Rose & Crown ♀

Village signposted from A149 bypass S of Heacham; pub in Old Church Rd just N of centre

There's a particularly nice traditional layout to the four bustling bars at this pretty white cottage. The cosy locals' bar at the back has perhaps the nicest atmosphere, along with cushioned seats around cast-iron-framed tables, and a big log fire. At the front is an old-fashioned beamed bar with lots of carpentry and farm tools, cushioned black settles on the red tiled floor, and a great pile of logs by the fire in the vast fireplace (which has a gleaming black japanned side oven). There's also an extensive family room, and a no-smoking airy carpeted small bar with plush seats around tables, decorated with local pictures. Five real ales on handpump include Adnams, Attleborough Wolf, Bass, Greene King Abbot and Woodfordes Wherry. Their 20 or so wines are all available by the glass; also freshly squeezed orange juice, and afternoon teas. Bar food includes soup (£2.10), filled baguettes (from £2.75), ploughman's (£4.25), bubble and squeak or battered cod (£5.50), lasagne (£5.95), chicken curry (£6.50), grilled plaice (£6.95) and 8oz rump steak (£9.50), with daily specials such as chicken with wild mushroom and madeira sauce (£7.95), supreme of salmon with cucumber and fish cream sauce (£8.95), rack of lamb with ratatouille and rosemary sauce (£9.95) and fillet steak with caramelised garlic and port sauce (£11.50); children's meals. Service can be a bit slow. The colourful garden is particularly attractive, with picnic tables among the flowering shrubs, and two spectacular willow trees. Recently much extended and improved, the adjoining adventure playground has forts, a walkway, climbing net, slide, swings and cages of guinea pigs and budgerigars. *(Recommended by M Morgan, Gordon Theaker, John Wooll, M J Morgan, Anthony Barnes, MDN, Margaret Smith, David Carr, Helen Crookston, R D Greaves, Charles Bardswell, Hugh Edwards, D R Blake, Stephen and Jean Curtis, Wayne Brindle, JKW, Roger Byrne, David Eberlin, Chris and Richard Potts)*

Free house ~ Licensee Anthony Goodrich ~ Real ale ~ Meals and snacks ~ Restaurant ~ (01485) 541382 ~ Children in restaurant and garden room, and in the bar when it's not too busy ~ Blues every second Thurs ~ Open 11-11; 12-10.30 Sun; cl 25 Dec ~ Bedrooms: £35B/£55B

STIFFKEY TF9743 Map 8

Red Lion

À149 Wells—Blakeney

There's a very traditional atmosphere at this big, simple old pub, with stairs going up and down between its three fairly spartan interestingly shadowy bars. The oldest parts have a few beams, aged flooring tiles or bare floorboards, open fires, a mix of pews, small settles, built-in wooden wall seats and a couple of stripped high-backed settles, a nice old long deal table among quite a few others, and oil-type or lantern wall lamps. Big helpings of very good well presented bar food made from local produce, such as excellent ham sandwiches as well as soft herring roes on toast (£3.75), moules marinières (£4.95), grilled local cod (£5.50) and game pie (£5.95), and Sunday roast (£6.25). Well kept Adnams Broadside, Greene King Abbot and Woodfordes Wherry and Norfolk Nog on handpump or tapped from the cask; friendly and efficient staff. A games room, detached from the main building, has darts, pool, dice, backgammon, chess, draughts, cribbage and dominoes. The back restaurant leads into a conservatory, and there are wooden seats and tables out on a back gravel terrace, and on grass further up beyond. There's a pretty stream with ducks and swans across the road, and some pleasant walks from this unspoilt village. *(Recommended by John Bowdler, Philip and Susan Philcox, Helen and Ian Cookson, BHP, M Morgan, Jack and Philip Paxton, Mrs Pat Crabb, Charles Bardswell, Jenny and Michael Back, Mrs P Brown, Derek and Sylvia Stephenson, Rita Horridge, Paul Craddock, J Honnor, John Beeken)*

Free house ~ Manager Jo Wishart ~ Real ale ~ Meals and snacks ~ (01328) 830552 ~ Children welcome ~ Live blues every other Fri evening ~ Open 11-3, 6-11

STOW BARDOLPH TF6205 Map 5

Hare Arms ♀

Just off A10 N of Downham Market

There's a comfortably bustling atmosphere in the friendly old rooms of this happy country pub, which has been run by the same licensees for over 20 years. Although it's very popular – service always remains friendly and efficient – it's unlikely to get as busy as the day one capable landlady hosted Queen Victoria's Jubilee celebrations; she fed huge meals to 1,380 customers in two marquees, washed down with tea brewed in the boiler of a steam roller. Nowadays the welcoming bar is decorated with old advertising signs and fresh flowers, and has plenty of tables around its central servery, and a good log fire; two friendly ginger cats and a sort of tabby roam around socialising. It opens into a spacious heated and well planted no-smoking conservatory, and that in turn opens into a pretty garden with picnic tables under cocktail parasols and wandering peacocks and chickens. Very well liked reliable bar food includes sandwiches (from £1.60), ploughman's (from £4.75), salads (from £5.95), and tasty daily specials like lamb and apricot pie, pork steak in peppercorn sauce or goujons of fresh plaice with lime and yoghurt dip (£5.75), steak and mushroom pie or chicken breast with curry sauce (£6.25), and lamb with garlic and rosemary or salmon with prawn, lemon and tarragon sauce (£7.45). Well kept Greene King IPA, Abbot, Rayments and their seasonal ales on handpump, good range of wines and malt whiskies, and maybe cockles and whelks on the bar counter; fruit machine. *(Recommended by Paul and Maggie Baker, John Wooll, Ken and Jenny Simmonds, Brian and Jill Bond, Stephen and Julie Brown, C H and P Stride, Andrew and Jo Litten, John Fahy, M Morgan, Charles Bardswell, Paul Boot, Richard Rockliffe, Tom Thomas, Stephen, Julie and Hayley Brown, Gordon Tong, Mark Hydes, Wayne Brindle, Richard Dolphin)*

Greene King ~ Tenants Trish and David McManus ~ Real ale ~ Meals and snacks (till 10pm) ~ Restaurant (not Sun evening) ~ (01366) 382229 ~ Children welcome in conservatory or Coach House ~ Open 10.30-3, 6-11; cl 25 and 26 Dec

SWANTON MORLEY TG0117 Map 8

Darbys 🍺

B1147 NE of Dereham

A few years ago the local farmer, using traditional methods and materials, skilfully converted two derelict farm cottages into what's now a really cosy beamed country pub – hence the tractor seats with folded sacks that line the long, attractive serving counter. As well as fresh flowers on the pine tables, and a good log fire (with the original bread oven alongside), there are also lots of gin traps and farming memorabilia. It's a really cheery place, that attracts an easy-going cosmopolitan mix of locals and professionals, young and old, rich and famous – no doubt all keen to try the excellent range of perfectly kept real ales: Adnams Bitter, Broadside and Mild, Badger Tanglefoot, Woodfordes Wherry and three unusual changing guests from countrywide. The very tasty freshly cooked daily specials, made from local produce where possible, are no less of a draw, with perhaps generous helpings of cream of vegetable and stilton soup (£1.95), shellfish chowder (£2.50), moules marinières (£3.50), braised sausages with onion and beer gravy (£3.95), baked potato with a Guinness, ham and cheese savoury filling (£4.25), vegetable and pasta bake (£4.85), tagliatelle carbonara or spiced sweet and sour pork (£5.25), fried rainbow trout with almonds and lemon (£5.95), beef and Guinness pie (£6.25), steamed chicken breast with prawn, mussels, cockles, cashew nuts and cream (£6.50), and puddings like bread and butter pudding, orange marmalade mousse or blackberry and apple crumble (all £2.50); the restaurant is no smoking. The staff stay friendly and helpful even when they're busy, and there are two dogs, a labrador and a border collie; darts, dominoes, cribbage, piped music, children's room with toy box, and a really good play area out in the garden. The bedrooms are in carefully converted farm buildings, and there's plenty to do if you're staying – the family also own the adjoining 720-acre estate, and can arrange clay pigeon shooting, golf, fishing, nature trails, and craft instruction. *(Recommended by Bill and Sheila McLardy, D and J Tapper, R C Vincent, John Wooll, Jenny and Michael Back, B N F and M Parkin, Anthony Barnes, Philip and Susan Philcox, Wayne Brindle, George Atkinson, Ian Phillips, Graham and Sandra Poll, Ruben Brage)*

Free house ~ Licensee John Carrick ~ Real ale ~ Meals and snacks (till 9.45) ~ Restaurant ~ (01362) 637647 ~ Children welcome till 8.30 ~ Open 11-2.30, 6-11; 11-11 Sat; cl evening 25 Dec ~ Bedrooms: £20(£21B)/£36(£39B)

THOMPSON TL9196 Map 5

Chequers

Griston Road; village signposted off A1075 Thetford—Watton; OS Sheet 144 map reference 923969

This attractive 14th-c thatched pub has been winning lots of new admirers over the last few months. Nicely placed off the beaten track in good walking country, it has benches, flower tubs and wall baskets outside, and a large garden with picnic tables and a children's play area. Inside, the three main rooms have crooked oak wall timbers completely covered with original brass and copper artefacts, farming tools, Victorian corkscrews and boot-scrapers and so forth, plenty of exposed beams, genuinely old wheelback and spindleback chairs, and uncommonly low doors and ceilings (one is only five feet high). At one end there's an antiques-filled dining bar with a high gabled ceiling and an inglenook fireplace; the small snug is a family room. Bar food includes soup (£1.95), sandwiches (from £2.10), filled baked potatoes (from £2.95), half a pint of prawns (£3.25), big ploughman's (from £3.95), home-made steak and kidney pie (£4.50), six vegetarian dishes including mushroom and nut fettucine (£4.75), half a roast chicken (£5.50) and 8oz sirloin steak (£7.95); puddings like hot chocolate fudge cake (from £2). Well kept Adnams, Bass, Fullers London Pride, Tetleys and two guests on handpump, local farm cider; dominoes, cribbage and piped music. *(Recommended by Mr and Mrs J Brown, Bill and Sheila McLardy, Norman S Smith, Simon Bird, Frank Gadbois, BHP, Paul Randall, Louise Miller, Richard Waddington, Mr and Mrs Jones, Laurie J Todd, Wayne Brindle)*

Free house ~ Licensee Bob Rourke ~ Real ale ~ Meals and snacks (till 10pm) ~ (01953) 483360 ~ Children welcome ~ Open 11-3, 6-11

THORNHAM TF7343 Map 8

Lifeboat

Turn off A149 by Kings Head, then take first left turn

This rambling old white-painted stone pub is perhaps at its best in winter, when the rooms are moodily lit with antique paraffin lamps, and five warming fires keep out the chill from the remote coastal sea flats. The chatty main bar has low settles, window seats, pews, and carved oak tables on the rugs and tiled floor, great oak beams hung with traps and yokes, shelves of china, and masses of guns, swords, black metal mattocks, reed-slashers and other antique farm tools. Under new licensees the bar food has been extended and the seasonal menu might include soup (£2.60), pork and chicken liver pâté (£3.75), open sandwiches (from £4.25), ploughman's (£4.75), 6oz burger, fish pie or fish and chips (£6.95), salmon and dill fishcakes (£7.50), game pie (£7.75), roulade of chicken, honey ham with fresh spinach sauce (£7.80), lamb cutlets with mint and redcurrant gravy (£7.90) and duck breast (£9.25), and children's meals (from £2.95). Adnams, Greene King IPA and Abbot, and Woodfordes Wherry on handpump, a guest like Attleborough Wolf tapped from the cask, and local farm cider. Up some steps from the simple conservatory is a terrace with picnic tables, a climbing frame, and a slide. *(Recommended by Neil and Angela Huxter, Jack and Philip Paxton, David Austin, D R Blake, KM, JM, David Carr, Peter and Pat Frogley, F C Johnston, Joyce McKimm, MN, DN, Dr and Mrs S Jones, M J Morgan, Andrew and Jo Litten, John Wooll, Ken and Jenny Simmonds, Helen Crookston, Eric Locker, M E A Horler, R Clarke, David Eberlin, David Culley, Jane Kingsbury)*

Free house ~ Licensees Charles and Angie Coker ~ Real ale ~ Meals and snacks (till 10pm) ~ Restaurant ~ (01485) 512236 ~ Children welcome ~ Open 11-11 ~ Bedrooms: £50B/£65B

If you see cars parked in the lane outside a country pub have left their lights on at night, leave yours on too: it's a sign that the police check up there.

TITCHWELL TF7543 Map 8

Manor Hotel 🛏

A149 E of Hunstanton

There are wonderful views over the coastal flats to the sea from the the the cheerful end bar here – recently brightened up, with pine tables and seats by the picture windows. In the main part of this comfortable hotel, which is very handy for the nearby RSPB reserve, the tranquil lounge has magazines, an open fire, and a good naturalists' record of the wildlife in the reserve. French windows in the pretty no-smoking restaurant at the other end of the hotel open on to a sheltered neatly kept walled garden with sturdy white garden seats on a sizeable lawn. Very good bar food includes lots of locally caught fish and might include sandwiches or soup (£3), oysters from the creek (£1 each), mussels or crispy whitebait (£5), platter or marinated seafoods (£5), vegetarian dishes like leek and mushroom stroganoff (£7), smoked gammon, ham and cheddar salad or scampi (£8), seabass fillet with samphire (£8) and lobster thermidor or large dover sole (£17); puddings (£3). Greene King IPA and Abbot on handpump; particularly helpful and pleasant licensees and staff. Lots of good walks and footpaths nearby. *(Recommended by David Carr, M J Morgan, Charles Bardswell, John Bowdler, PGP, Anthony Barnes, Mr and Mrs R O Gibson)*

Free house ~ Licensees Ian and Margaret Snaith ~ Real ale ~ Meals and snacks ~ Restaurant ~ (01485) 210221 ~ Children welcome ~ Open 12-3, 6-11 ~ Bedrooms: £39B/£78B

TIVETSHALL ST MARY TM1686 Map 5

Old Ram ♀

Ipswich Rd; A140 15 miles S of Norwich

This pleasant 17th-c family dining pub is popular for very well cooked and generously served bar food. The wide choice of dishes includes filled rolls (from £2.25), ploughman's (£4.95), burgers (from £5.25), home-made steak and kidney pie or aubergine and mushroom bake (£6.95), big cod fillet in home-made batter (£7.50), gammon (£8.50), daily specials such as pork ribs (£8.50), skate in caper butter sauce (£8.95), or duck in an orange and Cointreau sauce (£10.95), steaks (from £10.95), and formidable puddings (from £2.75). Well kept Adnams, Boddingtons, Ruddles County, and Woodfordes Ram on handpump, decent house wines, several malt whiskies, and freshly squeezed orange juice; unobtrusive fruit machine and piped music. The spacious main room, ringed by cosier side areas, has standing-timber dividers, stripped beams and brick floors, a longcase clock, antique craftsmen's tools on the ceiling, and a huge log fire in the brick hearth; other rooms ramble off, and there are pretty lamps and fresh flowers. An attractive, no-smoking dining room has an open woodburning stove and big sentimental engravings; it leads to another comfortable no-smoking dining room and gallery, with Victorian copper and brassware. Seats on the sheltered flower-filled terrace and lawn behind. No dogs. *(Recommended by Bill and Sheila McLardy, J E Rycroft, Beryl and Bill Farmer, David Carr, Paul Boot, SR, PM, Frank Davidson, Hazel Morgan)*

Free house ~ Licensee John Trafford ~ Real ale ~ Meals and snacks (from 7.30 for breakfast – non-residents welcome – till 10pm) ~ Restaurant ~ (01379) 676794 ~ Children in eating area of bar, under 7s must leave by 8pm ~ Open 11-11; 12-10.30 Sun; cl 25 and 26 Dec ~ Bedrooms: £43.45B/£61.90B

WARHAM TF9441 Map 8

Three Horseshoes 🛏 🍴

Warham All Saints; village signposted from A149 Wells next the Sea—Blakeney, and from B1105 S of Wells

There is a marvellously unspoilt traditional atmosphere in the three friendly gas-lit rooms of this basic but cheery and popular local. A sturdy red leatherette settle is built around the yellowing beige walls, with stripped deal or mahogany tables (one marked for shove-ha'penny) on the stone floor, an antique American Mills one-arm bandit still in working order (it takes 5p pieces), a big longcase clock with a clear piping strike, a twister on the ceiling (you give it a twist and according to where it ends up you pay for the next round), and a log fire. The generously served very tasty bar food includes sandwiches (from £2), starters like soused local herrings or stilton mushroom bake (£3), ploughman's (£4.60), cheesy mushroom bake (£4.80), fish pie (£5.80), beef, beer and vegetable pudding with a suet lid (£5.90) and game pie (£6.50); good vegetables. Decent house wines, summer farm cider and home-made lemonade, as well as notably well kept Greene King IPA and Abbot on handpump, and Woodfordes Mardlers Mild, Nelsons Revenge and Wherry tapped from the cask. Darts, cribbage, shove-ha'penny, dominoes, and fruit machine, and one of the outbuildings houses a wind-up gramophone museum – opened on request. There are rustic tables out on the side grass. New lavatories have wheelchair and baby changing facilities. *(Recommended by E Robinson, MDN, John Beeken, Philip and Susan Philcox, Christopher Harper, Ken and Jenny Simmonds, Howard Clutterbuck, Miss D J Hobbs, PGP, Jenny and Michael Back, Helen and Ian Cookson, John Hobbs, Sheila and Brian Wilson, Wayne Brindle, Mrs P Brown, Mr and Mrs Jones, Alan and Mary Reid)*

Free house ~ Licensee Iain Salmon ~ Real ale ~ Meals and snacks (not 25 and 26 Dec) ~ no-smoking restaurant ~ (01328) 710547 ~ Children in eating area of bar ~ Occasional pianola Sat evenings ~ Open 11.30-3(2.30 winter), 6(6.30 winter)-11 ~ Bedrooms: £20/£40(£44B)

WELLS NEXT THE SEA TF9143 Map 8

Crown 🏠

The Buttlands

There's a pleasantly relaxed atmosphere in the nicely bustling pubby front bar of this small town hotel – the bowed beams show that it's a fair bit older than the big black and white Georgian frontage suggests. The two quieter back rooms are quite different, with some interesting pictures on the wall over the roaring log fire, including several big Nelson prints and maps showing the town in the 18th and 19th centuries. Good waitress-served bar food includes sandwiches (from £1.50), soup (£1.95), ploughman's (£4.50), fish and chips (£5.25), seafood tagliatelle or steak and kidney pie (£5.50), grilled trout (£5.75) lamb chops (£6.50), mixed grill (£12.50), and daily specials like salmon and mushroom fusilli (£6.50), crab thermidor or game casserole (£7.50) or sea trout with hollandaise sauce (£8.50). Adnams, Bass and Marstons Pedigree on handpump; good service; darts and piped music. A neat conservatory has small modern settles around the tables. The central square of quiet Georgian houses is most attractive, and archers used to practise on the tranquil village green opposite. *(Recommended by George Atkinson, Roy Bromell, Jo and Den Reeve, F H Collier, Addie and Irene Henry, Charles Bardswell, Wayne Brindle, John Wooll)*

Free house ~ Licensee Wilfred Foyers ~ Real ale ~ Meals and snacks ~ Restaurant ~ (01328) 710209 ~ Children welcome in eating area of bar ~ Open 11-2.30, 6-11 ~ Bedrooms: £35(£45B)/£58(£68B)

WINTERTON ON SEA TG4919 Map 8

Fishermans Return 🏠 £ 🍺

From B1159 turn into village at church on bend, then turn right into The Lane

This traditional brick and flint pub is not far from the sandy beach, with good birdwatching – even from the doorstep of the bar. There's a particularly relaxed and friendly atmosphere in the white-painted panelled lounge bar, which has neat brass-studded red leatherette seats and a winter log fire, while the panelled public bar has low ceilings and a glossily varnished nautical air. Popular home-made bar food includes toasted sandwiches (from £1.50), filled baked potatoes (from £3), cottage pie (£3.50), ploughman's (£3.75), meat, vegetable or even prawn burgers (from

£4.50), omelettes (from £4.50), dover sole (£10.50), and daily specials such as game pâté (£4), spinach and spicy tomato lasagne (£4.50) and smoked haddock mornay or rabbit pie (£5.50); good breakfasts. Well kept Adnams, Attleborough Wolf, Burton Bridge, John Smiths and Wilds Wild Blonde on handpump, various wines including their own label, and around 30 malt whiskies; darts, dominoes, cribbage, pool, fruit machine and juke box. Seats in front by a quiet lane have nice views, as do the sheltered garden and terrace, which opens out from the back bar. There's a new pets corner and pond with ornamental chickens and bantams. The characterful bedrooms, up the steep curving stairs, have low doors and uneven floors; no-smoking garden room. (Recommended by I P G Derwent, David Carr, Philip and Susan Philcox, Simon Penny, David Lingard, Hazel Morgan, Peter and Pat Frogley)

Free house ~ Licensees John and Kate Findlay ~ Real ale ~ Meals and snacks ~ (01493) 393305 ~ Children welcome in small dining room in winter, in garden room in summer ~ Open 10.30-2.30, 6.30(7 winter)-11; 11-11 Saturday ~ Bedrooms: £30/£45

WOODBASTWICK TG3315 Map 8

Fur & Feather 🍺

Village signposted from Horning off A1062; or off B1140

A main draw is the full range of well kept ales tapped from the cask, brewed right next door in the Woodfordes brewery. These interesting brews crop up individually elsewhere (sometimes as other Norfolk pubs' unnamed house brews), but are very rarely found all together: Broadsman, Great Eastern, Wherry, Mardlers Mild, Baldric, Norfolk Nog (a strong dark ale, good for keeping out the winter cold), very strong Head Cracker, Pride, and Nelsons Revenge. Set in a particularly lovely estate village, this row of thatched cottage buildings was carefully converted into a comfortably, roomy pub in 1992 – olde-worlde without being overdone. Bar food is all made with fresh ingredients (even the burgers, £5.25), and is generously served: sandwiches (from £1.95), filled baked potatoes (from £2.95), ploughman's (£4.95), crispy chicken breast, breaded scampi, lasagne or yorkshire pudding filled with giant sausage (£5.95), seafood or ham and mushroom tagliatelle, grilled gammon steak or game pie (£6.50), lemon sole (£8.25) and beef stroganoff or 10oz sirloin (£9.95). The restaurant, and part of the bar, are no smoking. The staff stay friendly and very efficient even when busy; piped music. There are tables out in the garden, with jazz evenings in summer. (Recommended by D and J Tapper, Tony Dickinson, David and Julie Glover, J E Rycroft, Jack and Philip Paxton, Arthur Gunn, David Toulson, R C Vincent, Wayne Brindle, John and Shirley Dyson, Brian Horner, Brenda Arthur)

Woodfordes ~ Tenants John and Jean Marjoram ~ Real ale ~ Meals and snacks ~ Restaurant (Tues-Sat evenings) ~ (01603) 720003 ~ Children welcome in restaurant ~ Open 11-3(12 winter), 6-11

Lucky Dip

Besides the fully inspected pubs, you might like to try these Lucky Dips recommended to us and described by readers (if you do, please send us reports):

☆ Aldborough [signed off A140 S of Roughton; TG1834], Black Boys: Friendly village local opp broad village cricket green, wide choice of generous bar food from sandwiches to steaks, children's helpings, well kept Benskins Best, Flowers Original and Tolly IPA, decent wines, comfortably low-key furnishings, lots of cricket memorabilia, fresh flowers; darts, dominoes, fruit machine, piped music; restaurant, tables in flower-decked courtyard, open all day Sat (George Atkinson, LYM)
Attleborough [London Rd (off A11); TM0495], White Lodge: Very attractive low thatched and beamed cottage, two roaring log fires, Boddingtons, Flowers IPA, Greene King IPA and Morlands Old Speckled Hen, reasonably priced food (Ian Phillips)
Aylsham [Norwich Rd; out on bypass; TG1926], Greens: Wide choice of good value home cooking inc good puddings in spacious modern barn conversion, cheery attentive service, no-smoking area, restaurant, pleasant lawns (Simon Penny, J and P Daggett)
Banningham [Colby Rd; TG2129], Crown: Good changing range of meals, consistently friendly welcome, well kept beer (Simon Penny, Mark Feneron)
Barnham Broom [TG0807], Bell: Good value

home-cooked food, well kept beers, separate dining room; doing well under current family *(Bill and Sheila McLardy)*

☆ Binham [B1388 SW of Blakeney; TF9839], *Chequers*: Long bar with coal fire each end, one in inglenook, sturdy plush seats, ales such as Adnams, Bass, Greene King Abbot, Morlands Old Speckled Hen and Woodfordes Wherry, good value promptly served food inc imaginative dishes (Sun lunch very popular), no-smoking dining area, picnic tables on grass behind; open all day, interesting village with huge priory church *(Mike and Heather Barnes, Philip and Susan Philcox, Derek and Sylvia Stephenson, Mrs Pat Crabb, Charles Bardswell, BB)*

Blakeney [TG0243], *Manor*: Attractive tiled house in own grounds, opp wildfowl reserve and sea inlet, waitress-served food in big refined but cosy hotel bar, sunny seats outside; bedrooms *(Charles Bardswell)*

Bodham Street [TG1240], *Red Hart*: Village local with two small bars, welcoming service, usual bar food, real ales *(Frank Davidson)*

Brancaster [A149; TF7743], *Ship*: Comfortable and relaxing old country inn, big coal fires, good reasonably priced straightforward bar food, well kept beers, no music, obliging staff, restaurant; three good bedrooms *(Jenny Garrett)*

☆ Brancaster Staithe [A149; TF7743], *Jolly Sailors*: Good freshly cooked specials in simple but rather upmarket old-fashioned pub popular with yachtsmen; well kept Greene King, decent wines, distinct sense of style; provision for children, log fire, attractive restaurant, sheltered tables in nice garden with enclosed play area, open all Sun in summer *(M J Morgan, R D Greaves, Charles Bardswell, LYM)*

Brandon Creek [A10 Ely—Downham Market; TL6091], *Ship*: Good summer pub, in lovely spot on confluence of Great and Little Ouse, tables out by the moorings; spacious bar with massive stone masonry in sunken area that used to be a forge, big log fire one end, woodburner the other, friendly staff, five real ales, usual bar food, evening restaurant *(Chris and Andy Crow, JJW, CMW, LYM)*

Brisley [OS Sheet 132 map ref 954215; TF9521], *Bell*: Good spot on edge of green, olde-worlde long beamed bar, Whitbreads-related ales, good service, wide choice of popular food inc fresh veg, small evening fish restaurant; tables out on green; children welcome; bedrooms *(Brenda Crossley, Frank Davidson, John Wooll)*

☆ Briston [B1354, Aylsham end of village; TG0532], *John H Stracey*: Long-standing landlord, friendly service and wide choice of good value food in clean and well run country dining pub, fresh fish Tues, other speciality evenings, well kept Tetleys and a seasonal winter warmer, comfortable seats, log fire, dog and cat; popular restaurant, good value bedrooms with good breakfasts – nice for people who like being part of family *(R C Vincent, Mr and Mrs J Hall)*

Broome [Yarmouth Rd; TM3491], *Artichoke*: Limited but good choice of well cooked food inc good fish, fresh veg; dining area in lounge, good service, well kept beer, good unlimited coffee *(Peter Lloyd)*

Burnham Overy Staithe [A149; TF8442], *Hero*: Pleasant service, good beer and carefully presented food, friendly atmosphere, interesting bygones *(BHP, Janet and Peter Race)*

☆ Castle Rising [TF6624], *Black Horse*: Comfortable and spotless Beefeater family dining pub in pleasant village setting, usual reliable food, mainly Whitbreads-related ales, friendly unhurried service; children welcome, own menu and play packs; no dogs, pleasant tables out under cocktail parasols *(M J Morgan, John Wooll, Graham and Sandra Poll, R C Vincent, Jane Kingsbury, David Carr, JCW)*

☆ Cley next the Sea [Holt Rd, off A149 W of Sheringham; TG0443], *George & Dragon*: Edwardian pub by salt-marsh birdwatching country, cosy locals' bar, comfortable lounge and dining area, St George artefacts, wide choice of generous bar food inc good Cumbrian speciality pan haggerty and good vegetarian choice, well kept Greene King IPA, Abbot and a seasonal ale, attentive staff; sizeable garden over road, with boules pitch; bedrooms *(Eric Locker, Mike and Heather Barnes, John Beeken, R C Hopton, Mr and Mrs C H Phillips, LYM)*

☆ Cley next the Sea [The Green, nr church], *Three Swallows*: Friendly staff, banquettes around long high leathered tables, roaring fire, steps up to second simpler bar, good choice of decent generous quickly served home-cooked food from sandwiches up, well kept Greene King IPA and Tetleys, good wines; dogs welcome, wandering tabbies; on attractive village green, barbecues in large attractive garden with croquet, aviary, goat pen and lovely view of church; bedrooms simple but clean and comfortable, handy for the salt marshes *(Mike and Heather Barnes, Helen and Ian Cookson, M A Mees, Mike Turner, PGP)*

Cockley Cley [TF7904], *Twenty Churchwardens*: Converted former school, well kept Adnams, courteous landlord, friendly helpful waitresses, limited bar food, beams, darts alcove; plenty of worthwhile places to visit nearby *(Graham and Sandra Poll, John Fahy, N F Ollerenshaw)*

Coltishall [Church St (B1354); TG2719], *Red Lion*: Friendly modernised family pub, away from water but pleasant setting; decent straightforward generous food inc good puddings, up to a dozen mainly Whitbreads-related ales inc Weasel brewed for them by Woodfordes, several attractive split-level rooms, restaurant; tables out under cocktail parasols, good play area; bedrooms *(Bob and Sue Ward, David and Julie Glover, John and Shirley Dyson, David Craine, Ann Reeder)*

Coltishall [Church St *Kings Head*: Recently refurbished, with well kept ales inc cheap house beer, John Smiths and Marstons

Pedigree, decent wines, tasty good value imaginative food, personable landlord, moorings nearby *(Christopher Harper, A J Thomas, R Stewart)*; The Common], *Rising Sun*: Useful big Chef & Brewer on pretty bend of River Bure, with moorings; Courage-related ales, food from sandwiches up, waterside and other outside tables, family room, friendly service even when busy; piped music *(David and Julie Glover, SR, PM, Bronwen and Steve Wrigley, LYM)*

☆ Colton [TG1009], *Ugly Bug*: Good home-made food inc vegetarian in friendly, comfortable and attractive family-run lakeside barn conversion, separate dining area, well kept ales inc Adnams Old, sensible choice of wines, good atmosphere and service; children in conservatory, big garden, fishing; two comfortable bedrooms *(Anthony Barnes)*

Cromer [Promenade; TG2142], *Bath House*: Busy but welcoming seafront local with lots of dark wood, well kept Greene King Abbot and guest beer, standard bar food, dining room; plenty of tables out on prom, good bedrooms *(F H Collier)*; [Brook St, off A149], *Red Lion*: Substantial Victorian seafront hotel, stripped-stone carpeted lounge with screened areas, old bottles and chamber-pots, well kept Adnams, M&B Butlers and McMullens Gladstone, pleasant old-fashioned atmosphere, rather like that of the town overall; very wide range of bar food, restaurant with lots of fresh seafood; tables in back courtyard; bedrooms comfortable, with splendid sea views *(George Atkinson, A Goodger)*

☆ Denver Sluice [TF6101], *Jenyns Arms*: Extensive roadhouse-style pub in fine spot by the massive hydraulic sluices which control the Great Ouse, tables out by the waterside, real ales such as Adnams, Boddingtons, Flowers Original, Fullers London Pride, Greene King IPA and Websters Yorkshire, usual food from sandwiches to steaks inc vegetarian; big light and airy games area, piped music; handy for Welney wildfowl reserve *(M Scarratt, Charles Bardswell, BB)*

☆ Dereham [Swaffham Rd; TF9913], *George*: Good cheap home-cooked bar lunches, good carvery, Courage-related and other ales, carefully attentive landlord; bedrooms good *(G Washington)*

Dersingham [nr church; TF6830], *Gamekeepers Lodge*: Comfortably refurbished old building, well cooked and presented generous food inc good value carvery, pleasant dining room (children welcome here); tables outside *(D R Blake, Graham and Sandra Poll)*

☆ Docking [Station Rd (B1153 towards Brancaster); TF7637], *Hare Arms*: Attractively and individually decorated, with lots of entertaining bric-a-brac in several rooms, nice Victorian corners, good open fire, enterprising food, Flowers Original, Ind Coope Burton and Tetleys on handpump; cosy end restaurant *(John Wooll, BB)*

Docking [High St], *Pilgrims Reach*: Good generous straightforward food, friendly staff,

Adnams Bitter and Broadside, small bar (can be busy), quiet restaurant; tables on attractive sheltered back terrace, children's room *(M Morgan)*

East Barsham [B1105 3 miles N of Fakenham; TF9133], *White Horse*: Pleasantly refurbished and extended, long main bar with big log fire, attractive dining area, well kept ales such as Woodfordes Headcracker, reasonably priced food in bar and restaurant; piped music, darts; children welcome; bedrooms *(M J Morgan)*

☆ East Harling [High St (B1111); TL9986], *Nags Head*: Plush seats in three neat bars and no-smoking tiled-floor dining room (children allowed here), wide range of good food inc Sun lunch, prompt friendly service, John Smiths and Whitbreads; juke box; big garden with boules and aviary; not far from Snetterton *(Anthony Barnes)*

☆ East Ruston [Oak St; back rd Horning—Happisburgh, N of Stalham; TG3427], *Butchers Arms*: Big helpings of well presented food in well run comfortable village pub with good range of well kept ales, lots of golf talk, restaurant, attractive garden, pretty hanging baskets *(Tony Kemp, Rachel Weston)*

Fakenham [Bridge St; TF9229], *Wensum Lodge*: Pleasant modern hotel just outside centre, open all day for coffee, tea and sandwiches; quite spacious and relaxing bar, lots of pictures, interesting reasonably priced food, helpful staff, Flowers Original, piped music; comfortable bedrooms *(George Atkinson, Dorothy Smith, Mr and Mrs Simpson, Mrs J Bishop)*

Framingham Pigot [Loddon Rd (A146); TG2703], *Old Feathers*: Comfortable atmospheric well laid-out interior, friendly staff, comfortable airy conservatory restaurant, good value bar food *(A E Horton)*

Fritton [Beccles Rd (A143); TG4600], *Fritton Decoy*: Good choice of food inc children's, high chairs, courteous helpful licensees, Boddingtons, Flowers and Tetleys; tables in garden, opp country park *(A Tyrrell)*

Gayton [B1145/B1153; TF7219], *Crown*: Attractive flower-decked pub, simple yet stylish inside, with some unusual old features, well kept Greene King beers, bar food, comfortable seats, games room; tables in sheltered garden *(LYM; more reports on new regime please)*

☆ Great Cressingham [Water End; just off A1064 Swaffham—Brandon – OS Sheet 144 map ref 849016; TF8401], *Windmill*: Roomy family pub with three beamed bars, cosy nooks and crannies, huge log fireplace, lots of farm tools, conservatory, games room; good value standard food, quick service, well kept Adnams, Batemans, Bass, Sam Smiths and guest beers; well kept big garden, dogs allowed *(Charles Bardswell, G Washington, Anthony Barnes)*

☆ Great Ellingham [Church St; pub signed off B1077, which is off A11 SW of Norwich; TM0196], *Crown*: Neatly kept open-plan bar well divided into quiet alcoves, comfortable plush and other seats, soft lighting, relaxed

atmosphere, decent food inc good interesting choice of fresh fish and seafood, home-made bread and pickles, bargain lunches, three small attractive dining rooms (one for families), well kept Adnams, John Smiths, Woodfordes Wherry and local Wolf, friendly service, tables in garden; no dogs *(P M Lapsley, Bill and Sheila McLardy, BB)*
Great Ryburgh [TF9527], *Boar:* Friendly and comfortable, well kept Adnams, good food in bar and restaurant *(Chris Mawson)*
Great Yarmouth [Havelock Rd; TG5207], *Red Herring:* Welcoming backstreet pub, nice decor, at least six well kept changing ales such as Adnams and Woodfordes Mild, good value food inc wide choice of good local sausages *(K Kennedy, Chris and Pam Dearmun)*; [King St], *White Lion:* Historic building with interesting panelling, friendly landlord, Boddingtons and Flowers Original, lunchtime bar food; near the ancient 'Row' which survived heavy WWII bombing *(Jenny and Brian Seller)*
☆ nr Great Yarmouth [St Olaves; A143 towards Beccles, where it crosses R Waveney; TM4599], *Bell:* Busy riverside pub doing well under hospitable current licensees, attractive Tudor brickwork and heavy timbering but extensively modernised, with good varied bar food, well kept Whitbreads-related ales from long bar counter, decent wines, games and juke box on public side, restaurant where children allowed; garden with good play area and barbecues *(John Brockington, LYM)*
nr Great Yarmouth [Berney Arms Stn (trains from Gt Yarmouth); TG4604], *Berney Arms:* Accessible only by boat, 8-min train ride or long walk across fields; limited choice of decent food, well kept Greene King IPA, welcoming helpful staff, friendly atmosphere, interesting decor, flagstones, woodburner, ex-cask settles; tables out by towpath, cl winter *(Jenny and Brian Seller)*
Haddiscoe [A143; TM4497], *Crown:* Spacious and comfortable bars and dining room, interesting bric-a-brac, good home-made food, well kept Greene King IPA and John Smiths, good service *(John Honnor)*
☆ Hainford [Station Rd; TG2218], *Chequers:* Friendly thatched cottage in charming setting, wide range of well prepared food, real ales such as Adnams, Hook Norton Old Hookey and Morlands Old Speckled Hen, big airy bar area and rooms off, pleasant staff, well laid-out gardens with play area; children welcome *(Mr and Mrs M A Steane)*
☆ Happisburgh [by church; TG3830], *Hill House:* Heavy-beamed village pub with comfortable plush seats, woodburner in big inglenook, open fire other end, bar billiards in games area, well kept changing ales such as Adnams, Fullers London Pride, Tetleys and Woodfordes Wherry, welcoming service, wide choice of popular generous food inc good value sandwiches and original dishes, neat dining area (children allowed here); tables outside front and back; bedrooms, pleasant setting *(Roy Bromell, David Carr, PGP, BB)*
Harpley [off A148 Fakenham—Kings Lynn;

TF7825], *Rose & Crown:* Interesting reasonably priced food inc unusual vegetarian dishes in small comfortable lounge, decent wine, friendly hard-working landlord; high chairs provided; quietly attractive village *(John Wooll)*
☆ Hempstead [signed from A148 in Holt, pub towards Baconsthorpe; TG1137], *Hare & Hounds:* Unspoilt and relaxed country pub with tiled floor, big woodburner, mix of old-fashioned furnishings and lots of pine, well kept ales such as Bass, Adnams, Greene King Abbot, M & B Mild, Stones and Woodfordes Wherry, decent house wine, good straightforward food; a couple of geese patrolling the informal garden, with a pond, rockery and play area *(PC, Philip and Susan Philcox, Frank Davidson, G Washington, LYM)*
☆ Hethersett [Old Norwich Rd; TG1505], *Kings Head:* Cheerful and homely atmosphere in interesting old pub with good value generous lunchtime bar food, half a dozen well kept changing ales such as Courage Directors, John Smiths, Marstons Pedigree, Morlands Old Speckled Hen, Wadworths 6X and Woodfordes Wherry, comfortable carpeted lounge, obliging staff, old chairs and tables, big log-burning stove in inglenook, traditional games in cosy public bar, attractive and spacious back lawn, good play area *(Roger Wain-Heapy, O C Winterbottom, Ian Phillips, LYM)*
☆ Hevingham [B1149 N of Norwich; TG1921], *Marsham Arms:* Roomy modern-feeling roadside pub with well kept Bass, Greene King Abbot and Woodfordes Wherry, country wines and wide range of good straightforward food inc self-serve salads, friendly staff; double family room on right, tables in garden behind; comfortable bedrooms in motel wing behind *(Sue Rowland, Paul Mallett, Mr and Mrs R Thurston, BB)*
☆ Hilborough [A1065 S of Swaffham; TF8100], *Swan:* Welcoming early 18th-c pub with good simple home cooking done to order (so may be a wait), well kept ales such as Bass, Fullers ESB, Greene King IPA and Abbot, Woodfordes Norfolk Nog and interesting guest beers, plenty of old-fashioned pub and board games, friendly landlord, small back restaurant; picnic tables on pleasant sheltered lawn *(Charles Bardswell, Jane and Mike Blanckenhagen, Graham and Sandra Poll, BB)*
Hillington [TF7225], *Folkes Arms:* Large and comfortable, with wide range of beers, popular Sun carvery, good choice of bar food, garden behind; reasonably priced bedrooms in former barn *(M Morgan, Graham and Sandra Poll, D and J Tapper)*
☆ Holkham [A149 nr Holkham Hall; TF8943], *Victoria:* Quiet and simply furnished brick-and-flint inn with communicating bar rooms, well kept Ansells, Greene King IPA and Tetleys, bar food from sandwiches to steaks inc fresh fish and good value specials, dominoes, cribbage, piped music; children allowed in restaurant, tables outside;

bedrooms, handy for coastal nature reserves, open all day Sat *(Mr and Mrs R O Gibson, Anthony Barnes, George Atkinson, Mike and Heather Barnes, M A Mees, Charles Bardswell, M J Brooks, John Beeken, LYM)*

Holme next the Sea [Kirkgate St; TF7043], *White Horse*: Good value straightforward generous food in recently extended dining area, welcoming licensees and locals, big garden; cl Mon lunchtime *(John Wooll, David Carr)*

Holt [6 Market Pl; TG0738], *Feathers*: Bar extended around original panelled area with open fire, attractive entrance/reception area with antiques, friendly efficient staff, generous usual food, well kept ales inc Bass and Greene King, decent wines; bedrooms spacious and comfortable *(David and Ruth Hollands, Addie and Irene Henry)*; [White Lion St], *White Lion*: Praised in previous editions, closed spring 1996 *(News please)*

Honingham [just off A47; TG1011], *Buck*: Beamed pub with food inc huge sandwiches, vegetarian dishes, good choice of puddings; welcoming licensees *(Mike and Claire Squires)*

Horning [Lower St; TG3417], *Swan*: Busy popular Brewers Fayre pub, open all day, with wide choice of reasonably priced food inc cream teas, riverside picnic tables; bedrooms *(A H Denman)*

Ingham [B1151 E of Stalham; TG3826], *Swan*: Olde-worlde low-beamed thatched inn reopened under friendly new licensee, interesting corners in rambling rooms on two levels, traditional furnishings, five well kept ales, good food, family room by small enclosed garden; bedrooms in detached block *(Sue and Bob Ward)*

☆ Itteringham [TG1430], *Walpole Arms*: Delightfully old-fashioned village pub on River Bure, lively atmosphere, big helpings of good food, swift service even when busy, well kept beer *(Anthony Barnes, R M Broadway, Philip and Susan Philcox)*

Kings Lynn [Tuesday Mkt Pl/King St; TF6220], *Globe*: Spacious atmospheric bar with good food and S&N ales, restaurant with OAP bargains; pleasant bedrooms *(R C Vincent)*; [Gayton Rd, Gaywood; TF6320], *Wildfowler*: Comfortable and relaxed even when busy, popular food, well kept Tetleys-related beers, good choice of wines in big glasses, friendly staff *(John Wooll)*

☆ Letheringsett [A148 just W of Holt; TG0538], *Kings Head*: Set well back from the road like a private house, with plenty of tables on spacious lawn, informally furnished bar with interesting decorations, usual food from sandwiches to steaks inc children's, well kept Adnams, Greene King IPA and Abbot and guest beers, small plush lounge, games room with darts, pool, shove ha'penny, dominoes, cribbage, fruit machines; piped music, occasional live, children and dogs welcome, open all day *(Philip and Susan Philcox, LYM; more reports on new regime please)*

Litcham [B1145; TF8817], *Bull*: Big two-bar village pub with no music, good value food, decent wine by the glass, attentive landlord *(Frank Davidson)*

Loddon [just off A146 Norwich—Lowestoft; TM3698], *Swan*: Cosy and pleasant 17th-c coaching inn in attractive village not far from the water, long bar with lounge at one end and upstairs bar with pool table and video games, good choice of generous home-made food, good range of real ales, friendly service, seats in yard outside *(Bronwen and Steve Wrigley, John Brockington)*

☆ Middleton [Fair Green; off A47 Kings Lynn—Norwich; TF6616], *Gate*: Unpretentious creeper-covered village local, well kept Bass, good straightforward bar food, cosy beamed bar with horsebrasses, lots of bric-a-brac, pews, cushioned settle and milk churns, open fire; games bar with pool and machines, pretty side garden with good value barbecues *(R C Vincent, Graham and Sandra Poll)*

☆ Neatishead [Irstead Rd; TG3420], *Barton Angler*: Good reasonably priced straightforward food, well kept Greene King IPA, comfortable and homely bar, friendly staff, well furnished no-smoking restaurant, decent piped music, lovely quiet gardens; good bedrooms, two with four-posters – a nice place to stay, boat hire possible *(Tony Dickinson)*

Neatishead, *White Horse*: Multi-roomed pub popular with boaters, welcoming family service, well kept ales, popular food inc very wide choice of good pies; piped music *(Bob and Sue Ward, D Toulson)*

New Buckenham [Market Pl; TM0890], *Kings Head*: Homely unmodernised pub on green opp medieval market, comfortable candlelit back dining area, relaxed and atmospheric; three well kept beers, friendly landlord, limited choice of inexpensive good home cooking, antiques showroom upstairs *(Christine van der Will)*

North Creake [B1355 N of Fakenham; TF8538], *Jolly Farmers*: New licensee for these two cheerful homely small bars, good log fire, straightforward bar food, well kept Bass, Greene King Abbot and IPA and Ind Coope Burton, good friendly service, small restaurant; children in eating area, bar billiards, cribbage, dominoes, fruit machine; piped music may be obtrusive; tables in sheltered garden, charming village *(LYM)*

☆ North Elmham [B1110/B1145 N of E Dereham; TF9820], *Kings Head*: Welcoming old-fashioned inn, neat and tidy, with good well presented food from sandwiches up served quickly in log-fire lounge or lovely small dining room; friendly service, Courage-related ales and Greene King IPA, unusual hat collection, no-smoking room, restaurant; garden with play area; bedrooms, handy for several tourist attractions *(R Vincent)*

North Tuddenham [off A47 – OS Sheet 133 map ref 040142; TG0414], *Lodge*: Wide choice of good value food; fruit machine *(Frank Davidson)*

☆ Norwich [Wensum St; S side of Fye Bridge], *Ribs of Beef*: Warm and welcoming, with wide choice of Woodfordes and other ales, farm cider; comfortable main room upstairs, attractive smaller downstairs room with river view and some local river paintings, cheap reliable standard food from filled baps up, quick friendly service; can be studenty evenings, but without deafening music *(Ian Phillips, John Wooll, SR, PM)*

☆ Norwich [149 Newmarket St], *Unthank Arms*: Spacious refurbished Victorian with friendly local bustle, open fires, well kept mainly Whitbreads-related ales, decent wines, good interesting inexpensive home-cooked food, candlelit upstairs dining room, friendly service; garden behind *(Bob Arnett, Judy Wayman, Paula and Adrian Le Roux)*

☆ Norwich [King St], *Ferryboat*: Pleasant riverside Greene King pub with a good deal of character, limited generous tasty food, efficient friendly service, traditional beamed old-fashioned front part, steps down through spacious raftered and flagstoned back dining area to riverside garden with play area and barbecue *(John Wooll, LYM)*

Norwich [Riverside Rd, opp Bishops Bridge], *Bridge House*: Red plush banquettes and cast-iron-framed tables, well kept Whitbreads-related ales, big helpings of good plain food at low prices, prompt friendly service, woodburner; juke box may be loud, pool *(Sarah and Gary Goldson, Ian Phillips)*; [61 St Augustines St], *Catherine Wheel*: Tucked-away pub with Adnams and a guest ale, good house wine, bar food inc fresh pasta, lots of beamery, discreet fruit machines, upstairs dining area with big tables, discreet piped classical music *(Ian Phillips, John and Wendy Trentham)*; [Thorpe Rd], *Coach & Horses*: Busy local with pleasant atmosphere, scrubbed tables on bare boards in big rambling open-plan bar, cheap cheerful food, good range of beers inc four from their own on-site Chalk Hill Brewery, regular live music *(Geoff and Linda Dibble, John Wooll)*; [49 West End St], *Fat Cat*: Worth knowing for its splendid range of well kept real ales, up to 20, half tapped from the cask in glass-fronted still room behind bar; masses of brewing memorabilia, good service, minimal food, no music or machines *(Adrian Hennessy, SR, PM, David Twitchett)*; [2 Timber Hill], *Gardeners Arms*: Various small neatly themed attractive areas inc convincing kitchen, more room in glassed-over former yard, real ales inc Murderer (recalling pub's former name), good value food from filled baps up, friendly staff, families welcome *(Ian Phillips, John Wooll)*; [Orford Pl, off SE end of Haymarket], *Lamb*: Central open-plan pub, handy if no longer smart, standard food with nursery puddings, Theakstons and Websters ales, prompt service, satellite TV, seats out in courtyard *(George Atkinson, Jan and Colin Roe)*; [Earlham Rd], *Pickwick*: Good value food in clean spacious bar *(Chris Mawson)*; [10 Dereham Rd], *Reindeer*: No-frills bare-boards smoky-ceilinged pub, now a Firkin pub, still brewing its own beer (you can see the brewery); reasonable range of generous food, relaxed atmosphere, friendly staff, occasional folk bands; not crowded outside University terms *(Jill Palios, SR, PM, Simon Penny)*; [St

Andrews Hill], *Take Five*: Not a pub (in the evenings you can only get in through Cinema City for which it serves as the cafeteria, and you can't go just for a drink), but has real ales inc one brewed for them, also farm cider, good choice of wines, good value very health-and-trend-conscious food, relaxed atmosphere, changing local art, piped classical music, tables in nice old courtyard *(John Wooll)*; [Dove St], *Vine*: Tiny, warm and friendly, loads of bottled beers from all over the world, guest real ales; frequent live music *(Ian Phillips, Peter Smee)*; [St Martin, nr Palace Plain], *Wig & Pen*: Big partly modernised old beamed bar opp cathedral close, lawyer and judge prints, roaring stove with horsebrasses on overmantel, filling cheap bar food, real ales inc guests, good value wine, quick service *(John Wooll)*; [St George St], *Wild Man*: Thriving lunchtime atmosphere in open-plan room with good value food esp roasts served promptly, Tolly ales; very quiet evening *(SR, PM)*

☆ Old Hunstanton [part of L'Estrange Arms Hotel, Golf Course Rd; TF6842], *Ancient Mariner*: Attractively furnished old bar, comfortable and interesting, with lots of dark wood, bare bricks and flagstones, several little areas inc upstairs gallery, good value usual food, up to half a dozen well kept ales inc Adnams and Broadside, Bass and Charrington IPA, decent wines, open fires, papers and magazines, friendly staff; bedrooms *(John Wooll)*

Old Hunstanton [A149], *Lodge*: Comfortable main-road pub with good choice of quickly served food, Bass, Greene King IPA, Abbot and Rayments Special, friendly staff, plenty of seats; bedrooms *(M A Mees)*

Potter Heigham [A1062 Wroxham Rd; TG4119], *Falgate*: Charmingly refurbished, changing ales such as Flowers Original and Greene King Abbot, varied food, friendly service, restaurant; piped music, fruit machine; aviaries at back; bedrooms, not far from river *(David and Julie Glover)*

Reedham [17 The Havaker; TG4101], *Railway*: Friendly and comfortable, with good range of real ales, dozens of whiskies, log fire, good choice of bar and restaurant food, games room with darts, pool etc *(Bryan Tye)*

Reepham [Market Sq; TG0922], *Old Brewery House*: Rambling Georgian inn with big sundial over two-columned porch, imaginative well prepared fresh food inc good fish in roomy eating areas, well kept Adnams and changing guest ales in small cosy inner bar, friendly service, restaurant; comfortable attractive bedrooms *(David and Anne Culley, Mr and Mrs M A Steane, W W Burke)*

☆ Rollesby [A149; TQ4416], *Horse & Groom*: Straightforward renovated pub worth knowing for good value generous home-made food esp seafood; clean and comfortable, with well kept Boddingtons, good friendly service; fish and steak restaurant, decent wines; well equipped bedrooms in motel wing *(D Middleton, G Durrant, D Mason)*

Rushall [TM1982], *Half Moon*: Wide choice of competitively priced food and drink, everything spotless *(Stephen Luxford)*

Salthouse [A149 Blakeney—Sheringham; TG0743], *Dun Cow*: Warmly welcoming straightforward old country local by salt marshes, decent bar food, maybe figs and apples from the big attractive garden (with play area), Flowers Original (and Tetleys in summer); good walks and birdwatching nearby *(MN, DN, Peter and Pat Frogley)*

☆ Sedgeford [B1454, off A149 Kings Lynn—Hunstanton; TF7136], *King William IV*: Happy casual atmosphere, good value bar food inc Sun roast with good veg, warm woodburner, fast friendly service, well kept Bass and Worthington, restaurant; children allowed in lounge if eating, some live music and quiz nights *(John Wooll, Graham and Sandra Poll, David Carr)*

Sheringham [on promenade; TG1543], *Two Lifeboats*: Lovely sea view from comfortable lounge and terrace tables, big helpings of usual bar food inc fresh fish (no-smoking dining area), well kept Greene King ales, friendly service; bedrooms *(George Atkinson, Geoff Lee)*

Skeyton [off A140 N of Aylsham; TG2425], *Goat*: Recently refurbished and extended thatched low-beamed pub with good value food in bar and restaurant (best to book Sat evening), well kept Adnams, Courage and Marstons Pedigree, log-effect gas fire, enthusiastic staff; pleasant terrace and garden *(David and Lesley Elliott, David and Anne Culley, Christopher Harper)*

☆ South Walsham [TG3713], *Ship*: Small friendly village local with traditional brick and beamed bars, well kept Adnams and Woodfordes Wherry, good generous specials inc vegetarian and lovely puddings, gourmet nights (not Sun), good service, welcoming NZ landlord; pool table; tables on front elevated terrace and more in back garden; children's room, play area with friendly goats *(John Beeken, John and Shirley Dyson, Bronwen and Steve Wrigley)*

South Wootton [Grimston Rd (A148/A149), part of Knights Hill Hotel; TF6422], *Farmers Arms*: Olde-worlde conversion of barn and stables, Courage-related ales with a guest such as Marstons Pedigree, wide choice of tasty, reasonably priced food, friendly service; children welcome, open all day; comfortable motel bedrooms, health club *(John Wooll, M J Morgan)*; [Nursery Lane], *Swan*: Good value home cooking in small old-fashioned two-bar pub overlooking village green, duck pond and bowling green; conservatory dining area, well kept Courage-related ales and Greene King IPA, small enclosed garden with slide and swing *(John Wooll)*

☆ Stanhoe [B1155 towards Burnham Mkt; TF8036], *Crown*: Good friendly atmosphere in small bright country local, popular good value home cooking, well kept Elgoods Cambridge, decent wine and coffee, affable service, central log fire, one beam studded with hundreds of coins; well behaved children allowed; tables on side lawn, lots of fancy fowl (and chicks) outside; caravan site, s/c

cottage available *(John Wooll, E J Taylor, Roger Williams, BB)*

Stoke Holy Cross [TG2301], *Wildebeest*: Good French bistro-style food; good wines, espresso coffee *(Roz Waller, Richard Goodenough, Charlotte Beevor, Rowan Gormley)*

☆ Surlingham [village signed off A146 just SE of A47 Norwich ring rd, then Coldham Hall signed; TG3206], *Coldham Hall*: Well kept ales such as Batemans XB, Shepherd Neame Spitfire and Woodfordes Wherry, wide range of food, comfortable high-backed settles, friendly service, woodburner, pool in games area, Broads-view dining area, sensible dress code, well reproduced piped music (also juke box); picnic tables by big well kept waterside lawn with shrubs and weeping willows; children in family room *(John Brockington, W W Burke, BB)*

☆ Surlingham [from village head N; pub on bumpy track into which both village roads fork], *Ferry House*: Lively and enjoyable riverside pub (though no view from the bar), comfortably modernised, friendly and unpretentious, by rowing-boat ferry over Yare; sensibly priced standard food, well kept Adnams and Courage-related ales, central woodburner, traditional pub games, comfortable restaurant; children welcome, with own menu; winter evening opening may be restricted, very busy with boats and visitors in summer – free mooring; handy for RSPB reserve *(Sarah and Gary Goldson, MDN, John Brockington, LYM)*

☆ Sutton Staithe [village signposted from A149 S of Stalham; TG3823], *Sutton Staithe*: In a particularly unspoilt part of the Broads, with cosy alcoves, built-in seats, flagstones, oak beams, an antique settle among more modern furnishings, well kept Adnams and other ales tapped from the cask, usual food inc children's, good puddings and all-day filled long rolls, friendly helpful service, restaurant; children welcome, flower-filled courtyard and grassy areas; good nearby moorings, comfortable bedrooms *(Roy Bromell, Bronwen and Steve Wrigley, Jenny and Brian Seller, LYM)*

Tasburgh [A140; TM1996], *Countryman*: Welcoming main-road pub with reasonably priced food, willing service, well kept Adnams and two other ales, decent wine *(Anthony Barnes, John and Wendy Trentham)*

Thetford [White Hart St], *Thomas Paine*: Friendly hotel bar with a welcome for families, reasonable food, well kept Adnams, decent wines, open fire; bedrooms *(Tony Dickinson, Roger Danes, LYM)*

☆ Thornham [Church St; TF7343], *Kings Head*: Pretty old pub with lots of hanging baskets, low-beamed bars with banquettes in well lit bays, friendly staff, decent food, Greene King IPA and Abbot, Marstons Pedigree and Tetleys, open fire, no-smoking area; dogs allowed; well spaced tables on back lawn, three homely and comfortable bedrooms *(A E Horton, Mr ands Mrs K Tidy, KM, JM)*

☆ Thorpe Market [North Walsham Rd; A149 N

Walsham—Cromer; TG2335], *Green Farm*: Attractive 16th-c farmhouse with big pine-furnished lounge, good value original food inc vegetarian in bar and smart restaurant, friendly service, real ales; children welcome, attractive bedrooms *(David and Ruth Hollands, M J Morgan)*

Thursford [TF9833], *Crawfish*: Smartly refurbished bar and side restaurant, generous good value food, well kept Flowers Original, open fire, helpful service, decent wine; unobtrusive piped music *(K H Frostick, M J Morgan, JW, J and Z Chamberlain)*

Tilney St Lawrence [TF5413], *Coach & Horses*: Neatly refurbished partly 17th-c pub with dark wood tables, chairs and settles, lots of brasses, good range of bar food, Elgoods Cambridge; children welcome in eating area, good garden for them *(M Morgan)*

☆ Titchwell [A149; TF7543], *Three Horseshoes*: Good range of generous bar food and well kept Adnams and Woodfordes Wherry in refurbished bar with rough walls, exposed wood, beams and struts, log fires; friendly new owner, family room, restaurant; play area in garden overlooking RSPB reserve; peaceful and comfortable bedrooms pleasantly furnished in antique pine, handy for beach *(John Beeken, M A Mees)*

Titchwell [Main St], *Briarfields*: Hotel not pub, but attractive and comfortable, with good value meals inc vegetarian, good beer and wine in back bar, terrace overlooking salt marshes, suntrap courtyard with pond; bedrooms *(John Wooll)*

Trowse Newton [just outside Norwich; TG2406], *Crown Point*: Popular old pub, neat and clean, with friendly attentive service, good generous straightforward fresh food *(MDN)*

☆ Upper Sheringham [B1157, off A148 Cromer—Holt or A149 just W of Sheringham; TG1441], *Red Lion*: Two small no-frills bars with stripped high-backed settles and country-kitchen chairs, red tiles and bare boards, no-smoking snug, big woodburner; seems to be settling down after latest change of chef (we'd like more reports), with good if not cheap food using fresh local ingredients (cooked to order so can be slow), well kept Adnams Best, Greene King Abbot and Woodfordes Victory, dozens of malt whiskies, good wine choice, newspapers to read, dominoes and cribbage; well behaved children welcome, bedrooms; cl winter Sun evenings *(Peter and Pat Frogley, Moira and John Cole, Rita Horridge, Philip and Susan Philcox, Ken and Jenny Simmonds, Anthony Barnes, LYM)*

Walcott [B1159 S of village, nr church; TG3532], *Lighthouse*: Friendly and busy, with wide range of good home-made food inc good value pies and puddings and interesting vegetarian dishes, good choice of real ales, helpful attentive service; children in no-smoking dining room and function room, good walks nearby *(David Culley, Roy Bromell, J and P Daggett, Alan Austin)*

☆ Walsingham [Common Place/Shire Hall Plain; TF9236], *Bull*: Good friendly atmosphere and interesting simply furnished interior, with well kept Ind Coope Burton and Tolly Original, decent food, tables out in the busy village square; much used by pilgrims – collects clerical visiting cards *(J and Z Chamberlain)*

Wells next the Sea [Freeman St; TF9143], *Ark Royal*: Pleasant bar area with replica of *Ark Royal* and Woodfordes ales, some concentration on dining area with wide range of reasonably priced food freshly cooked to order (booking advised at busy times), prompt friendly service *(A H Denman)*; [Stn Rd], *Lifeboat*: Good fish and good meals for children (who are welcome), good choice of beer and wine; pleasant garden *(Neil Gordon-Lee)*

☆ West Beckham [Bodham Rd; TG1339], *Wheatsheaf*: Friendly flint pub, homely beamed bar with cottagey doors and banquettes, feature log fire and a coal one, good range of reasonably priced food with good fresh veg, real ales such as Adnams Broadside and Woodfordes Wherry, decent choice of wine in generous measures, children's room, garden, quiz night; bedrooms clean, comfortable and cheap, with good breakfasts *(John Wooll, Geoff Lee)*

West Rudham [TF8127], *Dukes Head*: 17th-c, with good atmosphere, generous fresh home-made food, well kept Adnams, friendly service, plenty of books to read *(Dennis Parberry, Dr and Mrs N Chamberlain)*

Weston Longville [signed off A1067 Norwich—Bawdswell in Morton; TG1115], *Parson Woodforde*: Clean and spacious beamed pub, lots of alcoves, with popular food, willing service, well kept Adnams Extra, Woodfordes Wherry and a Bass beer brewed for the pub *(George Atkinson, Anthony Barnes)*

☆ Wiveton [TG0342], *Bell*: Big open-plan local with lots of Jaguar and other motoring mementos (even an engine in the fireplace), dozens of model planes, usual food with interesting specials, well kept Morlands Old Speckled Hen, Woodfordes Wherry and maybe Reepham Summer Velvet, daily papers, piped music (may be loud); more automania in carpeted conservatory, picnic tables on lawn; dogs welcome; bedrooms *(John Wooll, Helen and Ian Cookson, Frank Davidson, Charles Bardswell, Mr and Mrs M A Steane, BB)*

☆ Wreningham [TM1598], *Bird in Hand*: Polite service in tastefully refurbished dining pub with good varied reasonably priced food inc unusual vegetarian dishes; well kept Whitbreads-related and Woodfordes ales, cosy Victorian-style panelled dining area, local bygones and Lotus car photographs; good friendly service *(R C Morgan, Anthony Barnes)*

Post Office address codings confusingly give the impression that some pubs are in Norfolk when they're really in Suffolk (which is where we list them).

Northamptonshire

Pubs currently doing specially well here include the well organised and friendly Windmill at Badby, the extremely welcoming Bulls Head at Clipston (what a marvellous collection of whiskies), the Falcon at Fotheringhay (interesting food and drink, excellent service), the Spanish-run White Swan at Harringworth (good food, very good friendly service), and the interesting and individual Star at Sulgrave (good all round; gains a Place-to-Stay award this year). To these, we'd add three new entries, the attractively converted new Brampton Halt at Chapel Brampton, the most enjoyable and pleasantly idiosyncratic Fox & Hounds at Great Brington (straight in with both a Food Award and one Star), and the Kings Head in the pretty village of Wadenhoe (new licensees doing really well here). There are new licensees too at the Black Horse at Nassington: the food is very promising indeed, and we have high hopes that the encouraging news in readers' early reports will be confirmed. Food is generally a strong point in the county's pubs: so our choice of the Falcon at Fotheringhay as Northamptonshire Dining Pub of the Year is high praise indeed. Pubs to note for particular appeal in the Lucky Dip section at the end of the chapter include the New Inn at Abthorpe, Bartholomew Arms at Blakesley, Falcon at Castle Ashby, Eastcote Arms at Eastcote, Saracens Head at Little Brington, Lamb at Little Harrowden and Three Conies at Thorpe Mandeville. Drinks prices are close to the national average – rather cheaper in pubs getting beers from smaller breweries instead of the national chains.

ASHBY ST LEDGERS SP5768 Map 4

Olde Coach House 🍺 ♀ 🍴

4 miles from M1, junction 18; A5 S to Kilsby, then A361 S towards Daventry; village is signposted left. Alternatively 8 miles from M1 junction 16, then A45 W to Weedon, A5 N to sign for village.

This handsome creeper-covered stone inn has a very full diary of events throughout the year, with everything from Indian food festivals to firework displays and bank holiday pig roasts. The several comfortable, rambling little rooms have high-backed winged settles on polished black and red tiles, old kitchen tables, harness on a few standing timbers, hunting pictures (often of the Pytchley, which sometimes meets outside), Thelwell prints, and a big winter log fire. A front room has darts, pool, video game, trivia, TV (very popular for sport) and piped music. Well kept Boddingtons, Everards Old Original, Flowers Original, a beer named for the pub, and four guests on handpump, with lots more during their spring beer festivals; also a dozen wines by the glass, farm cider, fresh orange juice, quite a few malt whiskies, and an unusual choice of non-alcoholic drinks. Bar food includes filled rolls (from £1.95), home-made soup (£2.25), chicken liver and cognac pâté with green peppercorns (£3.50), burgers (from £4.75), turkey masala (£6.45), vegetable bourguignon or brie and broccoli pancake (£6.50), seafood tagliatelli (£7.50), lemon and garlic chicken (£8.25), cajun-spiced trout (£9.50), steaks (from £10.50), and puddings; children's menu (from £1.95), and a good Sunday lunch (from £5.75). Between 6 and 7pm on Fridays and Saturdays accompanied children eat free. The dining rooms are no smoking. Most people enjoy eating here very much indeed, but we have to say a few reports in recent months suggest the kitchen can have its off days too. There are seats among fruit trees and under a fairy-lit arbour (maybe summer barbecues), and a marvellous activity centre for children; disabled entrance and baby-changing facilities, too. The pub is well placed in an attractive village full of thatched stone houses, and the nearby manor house was owned by one of the gunpowder plotters. *(Recommended by Vicky and David Sarti, Mr and Mrs B Langrish, Angus Lyon, Eddy and Emma Gibson, Wayne Brindle, Bruce Bird, Mike Whitehouse, Mayur Shah, James Waller, A W, B W, Susan and John Douglas, Stephen and Julie Brown, Mrs P V Burdett, Eric and Jackie Robinson, Peter and Jenny Quine, Martin Wright, K C, David Alcock, Simon Collett-Jones, Sally Pidden, Gordon Theaker, Nigel Flook, Betsy Brown, Andrew and Ruth Triggs, S Marsden, Hilary Dobbie, Derek and Sylvia Stephenson)*

Free house ~ Licensees Brian and Philippa McCabe ~ Real ale ~ Meals and snacks ~ Restaurant ~ (01788) 890349 ~ Children welcome ~ Open 12-2.30, 6-11; 12-11 Sat ~ Bedrooms: £46B/£56B

BADBY SP5559 Map 4

Windmill 🛏 ♀

Village signposted off A361 Daventry—Banbury

Businessmen in need of speedy service can fax their lunch orders to this thatched coaching inn, and their food will be ready as soon as they arrive. That kind of efficiency has become the hallmark of the place, a popular old pub that skilfully combines old-fashioned charm with tasteful modernisation. The two thriving bars have a good friendly feel, as well as beams, flagstones and lace, cricketing pictures and appropriately simple country furnishings in good solid wood; there's an enormous inglenook fireplace in one area and a cosy and comfortable lounge. A pleasant new restaurant area opened last year, and they add a marquee extension in summer. Good promptly served bar food includes home-made soup (£1.75), sandwiches (from £1.75), stilton mushrooms or pork liver, bacon and brandy pâté (£3.25), filled baked potatoes (from £3.25), ploughman's (£3.95), pasta with vegetables and a cheese sauce or lasagne (£5.25), chicken and ham pie (£6.50), char-grilled cajun chicken (£7.25), steaks (from £8.95), daily specials such as green-lipped mussels (£4.25), steak and kidney herb pastry (£6.50), or barbary duck (£10.25), puddings such as lime cheesecake (£2.25), and children's meals (£2.50). Well kept Bass, Boddingtons, Flowers Original, Highgate Dark Mild and Wadworths 6X on handpump, and obliging service from the courteous licensees. Dominoes, video game, piped music. There are tables outside, with a children's play area beyond the car park. *(Recommended by Barry and Anne, C H and P Stride, James Grant, John Bowdler, M L Hughes, Mayur Shah, Nick Wikeley, Bob and Maggie Atherton, N H and A H Harris, Mrs P Wilson)*

Free house ~ Licensees John Freestone and Carol Sutton ~ Real ale ~ Meals and snacks ~ Restaurant (Fri, Sat and Sun lunchtime) ~ (01327) 702363 ~ Children in eating area of bar till 8.30 ~ Live jazz two Sat eves a month ~ Open 11.30-3, 5.30-11; all day Sat and Sun ~ Bedrooms: £39.50B/£52.50B

CHAPEL BRAMPTON SP7266 Map 4

Brampton Halt

Pitsford Road; off A50 N of Northampton

This attractive recently converted Victorian station master's house stands alone by the little Northampton & Lamport Railway. There are Sunday train rides (maybe more frequently in summer), and during the week you may see enthusiasts working on the rolling stock – or the platform-side flower plantings. There's a 14-mile walk and cycle-way along the line, through pretty countryside. Inside, one low-ceilinged area with a woodburning stove has wash drawings of steam trains; by the bar counter, a high-raftered dining area has some stuffed fish, dagging shears and other agricultural bygones; there's Victorian-style floral wallpaper throughout, with matching swagged curtains, and furnishings are sturdily comfortable. There are a few tables in a small sun lounge. Good value food includes sandwiches (from £1.60), soup (£1.95), ploughman's (£4.25), steak and kidney pie (£5.25), and daily specials like chicken wings with barbecue sauce (£2.25), whitebait (£2.95) and lamb chops in redcurrant sauce (£5.25), large local trout, chicken kiev or butterfly chicken breast with white wine, cream, stilton and mushroom sauce (£5.95); three course winter Sunday roast (£7.95). Well kept Adnams, Bass, Everards Old Original and Fullers London Pride on handpump; friendly service; possibly piped music. There may be a playful alsatian called Max out in the neatly kept garden. *(Recommended by K H Frostick, Gill and Keith Croxton)*

Free house ~ Licensee Roger Thom ~ Real ale ~ Meals and snacks (not Sun evening) ~ Restaurant ~ 01604 842676 ~ Well behaved children welcome away from the bar ~ Open 11.30-3, 5-11; cl 25 Dec

CLIPSTON SP7181 Map 4

Bulls Head 🍺

B4036 S of Market Harborough

Reports on this cheery slate-roofed local rarely fail to use the word friendly – it's a notably welcoming place where they greet you as soon as you walk in, and everyone immediately feels comfortable. The black beams glisten with countless coins, carrying on an odd tradition started by US airmen based nearby in World War II – they used to wedge the money waiting for their next drink in cracks and crannies of the ancient woodwork. The bar is cosily divided into three snug areas leading down from the servery, with comfortable seats, sturdy small settles and stools upholstered in red plush, a grandmother clock, some harness and tools, and a log fire. Well kept Batemans, Boddingtons, Flowers Original and IPA, Fullers Chiswick, Morlands Old Speckled Hen, Shepherd Neame Bishops Finger, and Wadworths 6X on handpump, and an incredible choice of malt whiskies – they had 480 varieties at the last count, but it seems to go up all the time. The long back games bar, lively in the evenings, has darts, pool, table skittles, dominoes, fruit machine, video game, juke box, and piped music. Good bar food includes sandwiches and other light snacks, and daily specials such as cumberland sausage (£4.25), Drunken Bull pie, dijon chicken or local trout poached in white wine (£4.95), and T-bone steak topped with stilton (£9.95). There may be a couple of friendly dogs. Slightly saucy pin-ups decorate the gents', and indeed the ladies' (one reader told us they considerably enlivened her visit). Outside, a terrace has a few white tables under cocktail parasols – maybe summer barbecues. *(Recommended by George Atkinson, Sheila Keene, Sue Grossey, Ted George, Eric Locker, Mike and Margaret Banks, Jack Morley, John Fahy, B Adams, Caroline Kenyon)*

Free house ~ Licensees Colin and Jenny Smith ~ Real ale ~ Meals and snacks (not Sun eves or all day Mon) ~ (01858) 525268 ~ Children in eating area and games room ~ Occasional live entertainment ~ Open 11.30-2.30, 6.30-11; closed Mon lunchtime and 25 Dec ~ Bedrooms: £29.50B/£35.50B

CRICK SP5872 Map 4

Red Lion 🍺

A mile from M1 junction 18; A428

The landlord at this comfortable thatched pub has a good eye for faces, and on a return visit is likely to welcome you as an old friend. A very handy refuge from the M1, the pub has a pleasant low-ceilinged bar with stripped stonework, a notably relaxed chatty air, and two roaring log fires (filled in summer with big, bright copper dishes and brassware); it's quietest and snuggest in the inner part of the bar. Well kept Morlands Old Speckled Hen, Ruddles Best, Wadworths 6X and Websters Yorkshire on handpump. No noisy games machines or piped music. Lunchtime snacks include sandwiches, ploughman's, and steak and kidney pie or a roast (£3.75), and in the evening they do things like chicken kiev, gammon, roast duck, trout and different steaks (between £5 and £8.50); no hot food Sunday lunchtimes. In summer, you can eat on a Perspex-roofed sheltered terrace in the old coach yard, with lots of pretty hanging baskets. There are a few picnic tables under cocktail parasols on grass by the car park. *(Recommended by Ted George, TBB, G S Miller, George Atkinson, Roger and Christine Mash, K H Frostick)*

Free house ~ Lease: Tom and Mary Marks ~ Real ale ~ Meals and snacks (not Sun evenings; lunchtime service stops 1.45) ~ (01788) 822342 ~ Children over 14 in snug lunchtime only ~ Open 11.30-2.30, 6.30-11

EAST HADDON SP6668 Map 4

Red Lion 🛏 ⬛

High St; village signposted off A428 (turn right in village) and off A50 N of Northampton

As welcoming whether you're dropping in for a drink, a snack or a restaurant meal, this civilised golden stone hotel has a friendliness you might not have expected from the rather smart surroundings. It's a popular old place, with most people coming for the high quality daily changing bar food: sandwiches or soups (£2.95), ploughman's or home-made pâté (£5.95), steak and kidney pie or home-made salmon fishcake with tomato and basil sauce (£7.95), prawn and bacon risotto, fresh dressed crab or sausage, apple and cider pie (£8.95), and puddings like bakewell tart or lemon syllabub (£3.25); it's worth booking for their three-course set Sunday lunch. The neat lounge bar has oak panelled settles, library chairs, soft modern dining chairs, and a mix of oak, mahogany and cast-iron-framed tables; also, white-painted panelling, recessed china cabinets, old prints and pewter, and little kegs, brass pots, swords and so forth hung sparingly on a couple of beams. The small public bar has sturdy old-fashioned red leather seats. The pretty separate restaurant is good, as are the breakfasts. Very well kept Adnams Broadside, Charles Wells Eagle and Bombardier, Marstons Pedigree, and Morlands Old Speckled Hen on handpump, and decent wines; attentive, friendly service; piped music. The walled side garden is attractive, with lilac, fruit trees, roses and neat little flowerbeds; it leads back to the bigger lawn, which has well spaced picnic tables. There are more tables under cocktail parasols on a small side terrace, and a big copper beech shades the gravel car park. *(Recommended by John Bowdler, James Waller, F C Johnston, Vicky and David Sarti, Maysie Thompson, George Atkinson, Heather Couper)*

Charles Wells ~ Tenants Mr and Mrs Ian Kennedy ~ Real ale ~ Meals and snacks (not Sun evening) ~ Restaurant (not Sun evening) ~ (01604) 770223 ~ Children in eating area of bar; must be over 12 in evenings ~ Open 11-2.30, 6-11; closed 25 Dec ~ Bedrooms: £50B/£65B

FOTHERINGHAY TL0593 Map 5

Falcon ★

Village signposted off A605 on Peterborough side of Oundle

Northamptonshire Dining Pub of the Year

Readers are full of praise for this stylish old place at the moment, singling out its particularly good service, relaxed and friendly atmosphere, and very satisfying food. The comfortable lounge has cushioned slatback armchairs and bucket chairs, antique engravings on its cream walls, winter log fires in stone fireplaces at each end, lovely dried flower arrangements, and a hum of quiet conversation; the landlord prefers to keep the simpler public bar for the locals. The pleasant conservatory is popular for Sunday lunch. Good waitress-served bar food might include soups like pork and bean or french onion (from £2.70), a really excellent proper ploughman's (£3.50), herrings in sour cream (£3.60), quail's eggs with smoked salmon (£4.60), vegetarian lasagne (£4.80), steak and kidney pie or west African boboti (£4.90), barbecued spare ribs (£5.10), rack of lamb with mint sauce (£6), roast ducking with apple and rosemary stuffing (£7.20), and steaks (from £8.80); in summer you can eat on the terrace. It's worth arriving early, they do get busy; the dining room is no smoking. Well kept Adnams Southwold, Bass, Elgoods Cambridge, Greene King IPA, Nethergate IPA, and Ruddles County on handpump, and wines of the month; darts, shove-ha'penny, cribbage and dominoes. Behind is a well liked neat garden with seats under the chestnut tree. The vast church behind is worth a visit, Richard III was born in the village, and the site of Fotheringhay Castle is nearby (where Mary Queen of Scots was executed in 1587). *(Recommended by Jenny and Michael Back, J A Letham, M Morgan, George Atkinson, Maysie Thompson, A Cowell, Ted George, Brian and Jill Bond, Tom Saul, John Bowdler, Mike and Penny Sanders, Bernard and Marjorie Parkin, Comus Elliott, David Tew, Tom Evans, E D Bailey, Arthur and Margaret Dickinson)*

Free house ~ Licensee Alan Stewart ~ Real ale ~ Meals and snacks (not Mon, or 25-30 Dec) ~ Restaurant ~ (01832) 226254 ~ Children welcome ~ Open 10-3, 6-11

GREAT BRINGTON SP6664 Map 4
Fox & Hounds ★ ⑪

Signposted off A428 NW of Northampton, near Althorp Hall; can also be reached via Little Brington, off A45 (heading W from M1 junction 16 it's the first right turn, signed The Bringtons)

This golden stone thatched village inn, carefully restored in 1992, has a delightfully relaxed and informal feel, with good country cooking and a remarkable range of esoteric real ales: Althorp Best (brewed for the pub by Lloyds), Theakstons Best, XB and Old Peculier with about eight guests like Border Noggins Nog, Butterknowle Conciliation, Cottage Normans Cottage, Cropton Scoresby Stout, Hardington Moonshine, Malton Pickwicks Porter, Ridleys Rumpus, Smiles March Hare. Fortnight-long beer festivals in spring and summer get through up to 100 different ales; about twenty country wines. The bar has lots of old beams and saggy joists, an attractive mix of country tables and chairs on its broad flagstones and bare boards, plenty of snug alcoves, some stripped pine shutters and panelling, two fine log fires, and an eclectic medley of bric-a-brac and country pictures – the well reproduced piped music spans just as wide a range of tastes, varying from serious rock music through jazz and nostalgic pop to Mozart and Verdi. A sensibly short changing choice of freshly cooked food might include home-made pâté (£3.25), pheasant casserole or game pie (£6.95), with a vegetarian dish such as stuffed tomatoes (£5.75); our own inspection meal consisted of a good rabbit casserole (the rabbit came from Althorp) and beautifully seasoned liver and bacon, with excellent fresh vegetables, while readers have particularly enjoyed fish and duck here. Service is very friendly; a cellarish games room down steps has pool, darts, table skittles, juke box, bar billiards, shove-ha'penny, dominoes and two fruit machines. A coach entry goes through to an attractive paved courtyard with sheltered tables, and there are more, with a play area, in the side garden; dogs welcome. *(Recommended by George Atkinson, Guy Turner, Tim Newman, Stephen, Julie and Hayley Brown, CMW, JJW, David and Shelia, Martin and Penny Fletcher, Margaret Dyke)*

Free house ~ P Burchell ~ Real ale ~ Meals and snacks ~ Well behaved children welcome ~ (01604) 770651 ~ Live jazz, blues and country Tues and Sun ~ Open 12-2.30, 5.30-11; 12-11 Sat; 12-10.30 Sun

HARRINGWORTH SP9298 Map 4
White Swan 🛏

Seaton Road; village SE of Uppingham, signposted from A6003, A47 and A43

The Spanish owner of this well-set stonebuilt Tudor inn also makes most of the rather good bar food. The menu changes every day, but might typically include soup (£2.50), ploughman's (from £4.25), lasagne or enchiladas (£5.50), chicken burrito or tagliatelle carbonara (£5.95), asparagus au gratin (£6.25), chicken grilled with stilton (£6.95) and sirloin steak (£8.75). The building still shows signs of its coaching days, in the blocked-in traces of its carriage-entry arch. Inside, the recently refurbished central bar area has good solid tables, an open fire, and old village photographs (in which many of the present buildings are clearly recognisable). There are comfortable settles in the roomy and welcoming lounge/eating area, which is decorated with a collection of carpenter's planes and other tools; a quieter no smoking dining room has a number of old rolling pins on the walls. Well kept Greene King IPA and Abbot and a guest beer such as Marstons Pedigree or Theakstons XB; spotless housekeeping, and excellent service from friendly staff happy to chat about local beauty-spots. Darts, dominoes, cribbage, piped music; tables outside on a little terrace. The pub is in a pretty village with a famous 82-arch railway viaduct as backdrop. *(Recommended by Steve, Julie and Hayley Brown, Joan and Michel Hooper-Immins, Alan and Heather Jacques, Bernard and Marjorie Parkin, Mary and David Webb)*

Free house ~ Licensees Christine Sykes and Miguel Moreno ~ Real ale ~ Meals and snacks (till 10) ~ Restaurant ~ (01572) 747543 ~ Children in eating area of bar and restaurant ~ Open 11.30-2.30, 6.30-11; closed 25 Dec and eves of 26 Dec and 1 Jan ~ Bedrooms: £37.50B/£42(£52B)

NASSINGTON TL0696 Map 5

Black Horse ♀

When new licensees took over this civilised 17th-c pub last March they wanted the food to have as local a flavour as possible, so spent hours in local libraries learning about the area's traditional produce and recipes. The resulting chip-free menu has a wide range of well presented dishes like sandwiches, soup or fish chowder (from £2.95), mushrooms with stilton and ham (£3.75), half a dozen or so vegetarian meals such as mediterranean vegetable gateau or the elaborate babacabouche (£7.25), pork fillet with mustard and apples or very popular guinea fowl with spinach, wild mushroom and bacon in red wine gravy (£9.95), several fresh fish dishes like swordfish tapenade (£10.95), sirloin steak with stilton in a rich red wine and shallot sauce (£11.95), and changing specials like lamb cutlets (£8.95) or cajun red bream (£8.95); puddings might include rhubarb and kirsch crumble or whisky and coffee trifle (£3.25), and they do children's helpings of most things. They hold imaginative monthly themed food evenings and events (best to book well in advance). A splendid big stone fireplace in the lounge bar is thought to have come from Fotheringhay Castle (which had been destroyed some time earlier) when the pub was built. There are easy chairs and small settees, a beamed ceiling, and a pleasant, relaxed atmosphere; piped music. The bar servery, with panelling from Rufford Abbey, links the two comfortable rooms of the restaurant. As we went to press they were planning to add two more beers to the Bass, Courage Directors, John Smiths, and Ruddles County already on handpump. They also have a good varied wine list, with several half bottles, and a good few malt whiskies; service is efficient and friendly. You can sit out on the very well tended attractive sheltered lawn, with plenty of flowers and plants. *(Recommended by A Cowell, Maysie Thompson, David and Mary Webb, John Fahy, Brian and Jill Bond, M Morgan, Peter Hartnell, Thomas Nott, John Bowdler, Wayne Brindle, Roger Bellingham)*

Free house ~ Managers Peter and Lisa Waller ~ Real ale ~ Meals and snacks ~ Restaurant ~ (01780) 782324 ~ Children in eating area of bar and restaurant ~ Twice-monthly theme nights with music ~ Open 12-3, 7(6 Fri and Sat)-11; all day summer weekends

OUNDLE TL0487 Map 5

Mill

Barnwell Rd out of town; or follow Barnwell Country Park signs off A605 bypass

Very handy for Barnwell Country Park, this splendidly restored and rather imposing old mill building is popular with diners enjoying the wide choice of food. It's a little pricey, but meals are well served and carefully prepared, from a range that includes sandwiches (not Sunday), home-made soup (£2.95), snails baked with garlic and herbs (£4.35), lots of pizzas (from £5.25), burgers (from £5.55), steak and kidney pie (£7.95), and quite a few Mexican dishes like nachos with vegetable chilli, cheese and sour cream (£7.95), spicy chicken chimichangas (£8.55), or sizzling fajitas (from £9.95). Stairs outside take you up to the most popular part, the Trattoria, which has stalls around tables with more banquettes in bays, stripped masonry and beams, and a millstone feature; its small window looks down over the lower millpond and the River Nene. A ground floor bar has red leatherette button-back built-in wall banquettes against its stripped-stone walls; on the way in a big glass floor panel shows the stream race below the building. Two-thirds of the bar is no smoking. Courage Directors on handpump (again not cheap); top-floor restaurant (more beams, and the corn hoist), bar billiards, piped music. There are picnic tables under cocktail parasols among willow trees by the pond, with more on the side grass, and some white cast-iron tables on a flagstoned terrace. *(Recommended by David and Mary Webb, P J and S E Robbins, Frank Cummins)*

Free house ~ Licensees Noel and Linda Tulley ~ Real ale ~ Meals and snacks (till 10pm) ~ Restaurant (not Sun evening) ~ (01832) 272621 ~ Well behaved children welcome ~ Open 11-3, 6.30-11

Ship 🍺 £

West St

The buoyantly cheerful atmosphere at this well worn and unpretentious local owes a lot to the genuinely welcoming landlord and his sons. The heavily beamed lounge bar is made up of three rooms that lead off the central corridor on the left: up by the street there's a mix of leather and other seats including a very flowery piano stool (and its piano), with sturdy tables and a log fire in a stone inglenook, and down one end a panelled snug has button-back leather seats built in around it. This area is no smoking – if you light up you have to donate £1 to the RNLI. Well kept Bass, Marstons Pedigree, Tetleys and Wadworths 6X on handpump, and a good range of malt whiskies. Bar food includes sandwiches (from £1.30), home-made soup (£1.60), filled baked potatoes (from £1.70), ploughman's or sausages and beans (£2.50), home-made smoked salmon pâté (£2.75), home-cooked ham and egg (£3), fried cod (£3.20), home-made pies such as venison and steak and kidney or vegetable lasagne (£4.50), steaks (from £7.50), daily specials such as pork chop in cider and apple or barnsley double lamb chops, and puddings. Sunday lunchtimes they just do a roast and pies. Smiling, efficient service. Dominoes, maybe free Sunday nuts and crisps on the bar. The tiled-floor public side has darts, pinball, fruit machine, and juke box. A series of small sheltered terraces strung out behind has wooden tables and chairs, lit at night. Several of the bedrooms are in a new extension. The pub can get busy – especially at lunchtimes or Saturday evenings. *(Recommended by David and Mary Webb, J Curtis, G Hughes, George Atkinson, Bernard and Marjorie Parkin, Norma and Keith Bloomfield)*

Free house ~ Licensee Frank Langridge ~ Real ale ~ Meals and snacks (till 10) ~ (01832) 273918 ~ Children welcome ~ Occasional live music ~ Open 11-3, 6-11; 11-11 Sat; 12-10.30 Sun ~ Bedrooms: £27.50B/£35(£45B)

SUDBOROUGH SP9682 Map 4

Vane Arms 🛏 🍺

High St; A6116 Corby—Thrapston

The nine real ales at this thatched country pub vary each week, but you can usually count on finding a couple of unusual brews amongst the selection. A typical visit will turn up Adnams Broadside, Churchills Pride, Eldridge Pope Royal Oak, Elgoods GSB, Oakham Old Tosspot and JHB, Theakstons Old Peculier, Thwaites Craftsman, and Woodfordes Victory. Mr Tookey will happily guide you through what's on offer, but if you're not sure what to have they do a sample tray for about five pounds, with around a third of a pint of each; they also keep a few Belgian fruit beers, farm cider and lots of country wines. The welcoming and comfortable main bar has some stripped stonework, and good inglenook fireplaces with open fires in winter (and perhaps Nelson the dog in front of one of them). There's a small public bar with darts, pool, table skittles, fruit machine, video game, and piped music. A wide range of freshly cooked bar food includes sandwiches, home-made soup (£1.95), mushrooms in stilton sauce (£2.95), good steak and kidney pie (£5.50), breast of chicken with stilton wrapped in bacon and encased in puff pastry (£7), venison steak (£7.50), steaks (from £9), a weekly changing fresh fish dish, lots of popular Mexican dishes like spicy chicken wings (£2.95), tacos (£5.95) and fajitas (£7.95); helpful, friendly service. The lounge, dining area and restaurant are no smoking. *(Recommended by Stephen and Julie Brown, John Fahy, PGP, David and Shelia, S G Brown, Eric Locker, Wayne Brindle, Julian Holland, Joan and Michel Hooper-Immins)*

Free house ~ Licensees Tom and Anne Tookey ~ Real ale ~ Meals and snacks (not Sun evening, or Mon lunch) ~ Restaurant (not Sun evening) ~ (01832) 733223 ~ Children in eating area of bar ~ Open 11.30-3.30, 5.30(6 Sat)-11; closed Mon lunchtime ~ Bedrooms: £35B/£45B

SULGRAVE SP5545 Map 4

Star 🛏

E of Banbury, signposted off B4525; Manor Road

This very hospitable creeper-covered stonebuilt inn is definitely on the up at the moment – all the reports we've had on it in recent months (and there've been quite a few) have warmly sung its praises, and the landlady's recipe for smoked cheese, leek and potato pie was featured in a recent cookery book. The neat bar is divided by a timbered and leaded-light screen, with polished flagstones in the part by the big inglenook fireplace (with a paper skeleton on its side bench) and a red carpet in the other part Furnishings are mainly small pews, cushioned window seats and wall benches, kitchen chairs and cast-iron-framed tables. Lots of things to look at include front pages of newspapers from notable days (Kennedy's assassination, say), collections of this and that, and some rather joky stuffed animals. The staff are welcoming and friendly, as are one or two very regular locals. Seasonal dishes from the changing blackboard menu might include starters like soup (£2.75), hummus and pitta or filo-wrapped tiger prawns (£3.95), and smoked breast of goose with port and cranberry relish (£4.25), main courses like spinach and ricotta flan (£5.95), a really huge steak and kidney pie, various curries (£6.95), baked salmon with a peanut and lime crust, Moroccan lamb and lentil filo pie, or lamb liver and bacon on creamed celeriac and potato topped with onion gravy (£7.95), and puddings such as baklava or toffee crunch cheesecake (£2.75); they also do good double-decker sandwiches (not Friday or Saturday evenings or Sunday lunch) and ploughman's. Well kept Hook Norton Best and Old Hookey and a monthly changing guest beer like Fullers London Pride on handpump. No-smoking back restaurant; piped music. There are some tables outside. Some of the comfortable bedrooms have good views. Note they don't allow children inside. The pub is on the road to George Washington's ancestral home. *(Recommended by Eric Locker, Lynda Payton, Sam Samuels, John Baker, Colin Sansom, Mrs J Box, E and M Corrin, Rona Murdoch, Paul Moore, George Atkinson, Keith Archer, Leith Stuart)*

Hook Norton ~ Tenant Andrew Willerton ~ Real ale ~ Meals and snacks ~ Restaurant ~ (01295) 760389 ~ Open 11-2.30, 6-11 (cl 25 Dec) ~ Bedrooms: £30S/£45S

THORNBY SP6775 Map 4

Red Lion

Welford Road; A50 Northampton—Leicester – very handy from jctn with A14

A friendly place, this stylish cream-painted slated brick roadside pub never seems to change. The bar has logs burning in an open stove, pewter tankards hanging from a beam, decorative plates densely covering the walls, and china jugs and steins on a shelf and hanging over the bar. Their three amiable dogs are much in evidence, so don't bring your own. Carefully chosen furnishings include individual old-fashioned lamps, a lovingly polished big golden table that sits between a couple of pews in one of the bay windows, and deep leather armchairs and sofa in one of two smallish areas opening off; shove-ha'penny, cribbage, dominoes, shut-the-box, chess, bagatelle, and piped music. Good home-made bar food includes sandwiches, home-made soup (£2.25), vegetable stir fry (£5.25), home-made steak in ale pie, well liked curry, or pan fried free range chicken (£5.95), whole grilled lemon sole (£7.95), steaks (£8.95), and daily specials; also quite a few evening extras, Sunday roasts, and children's helpings. Well kept Bass, Greene King IPA, Marstons Pedigree and Robinsons Best on handpump. There are some seats outside. Their monthly quiz nights on Sunday evenings are popular. *(Recommended by John Fahy, M J Morgan, Cdr Patrick Tailyour, Wayne Brindle, L M Miall, George Atkinson, Frank Cummins, Mr and Mrs Hillman)*

Free house ~ Licensee Caroline Baker ~ Real ale ~ Meals and snacks ~ Small restaurant ~ (01604) 740238 ~ Well behaved children welcome ~ Open 11.45-2.30, 5-11; 11.45-11 Sat; 12-10.30 Sun

WADENHOE TL0083 Map 5

Kings Head

Church Street; village signposted (in small print) off A605 S of Oundle

Down one end of this pretty village of up-and-down lanes and thatched stone cottages, the stone-built Kings Head fits in well, with its own roof mixing thatch and enormously heavy slabs of Collyweston slate. It backs on to a rough but extensive swathe of grass which slopes down to the River Nene, with picnic tables among willows and aspens, and boat moorings. The partly stripped-stone main bar has pleasant old worn quarry tiles, solid pale pine furniture with a couple of cushioned wall seats, and a leather-upholstered chair by the woodburning stove in the fine inglenook. The bare-boards public bar has similar furnishings and another fire, with steps down to a games room with dominoes, hood skittles and board games, and there's yet more of the pale pine furniture in an attractive little beamed no-smoking dining room. A short choice of lunchtime bar food includes soup (£1.75), sandwiches (£2.25 – £1 extra with soup), ploughman's (£3.25) and a good hot dish such as beef casserole (£5); a broader evening menu might include chicken liver pâté (£3.75), chorizo and black pudding salad (£4.50), and main courses like steak and kidney casserole (£6.50), venison sausages with garlic mashed potatoes and shallot gravy (£7.50), baked salmon with herb cream sauce (£8) and roast rack of lamb with puréed aubergines and purée of sautéed onions (£10.50); they do good Sunday roasts. Well kept Adnams Bitter and Broadside, and Marstons Pedigree on handpump, and an extensive wine list; magazines to read, no piped music, friendly service from the young licensees. We have not yet had reports on the bedrooms here, but would expect this to be a nice quiet place to stay in. *(Recommended by Oliver Crispin, Mrs J C Crispin, George Atkinson)*

Free house ~ Licensees Catherine and Alasdair Belton ~ Real ale ~ Meals and snacks (not Sun or Mon evening) ~ Restaurant ~ (01832) 720024 ~ Children welcome in eating area of bar ~ Open 12-3, 6(7 Mon-Wed in winter)-11; cl Mon lunchtime; cl Sun evening in winter~ Bedrooms: £30S/£50S

Real ale may be served from handpumps, electric pumps (not just the on-off switches used for keg beer) or – common in Scotland – tall taps called founts (pronounced 'fonts') where a separate pump pushes the beer up under air pressure. The landlord can adjust the force of the flow – a tight spigot gives the good creamy head that Yorkshire lads like.

Lucky Dip

Besides the fully inspected pubs, you might like to try these Lucky Dips recommended to us and described by readers (if you do, please send us reports):

☆ Abthorpe [Silver St; signed from A43 at 1st roundabout S of A5; SP6446], *New Inn*: Partly thatched take-us-as-you-find-us country local in quiet village, rambling dim-lit bars, beams, stripped stone, inglenook log fire, attractively priced home cooking (not Sun/Mon), well kept Hook Norton Best, Old Hookey and Double Stout, good choice of malt whiskies, friendly service, lots of old family photographs etc; big garden with goldfish pool and aviary *(Martin and Penny Fletcher, Dr and Mrs B Baker, BB)*

Apethorpe [Kings Cliffe Rd; TL0295], *Kings Head*: Surprisingly big stonebuilt pub in attractive conservation village, comfortable lounge with real fire, real ales such as Fullers London Pride, Marstons Bitter and Pedigree and Wadworths 6X, obliging landlord, bar food (not Mon), arch to big dining area with separate menu (inc Mon), cosy bar with pool; children welcome, picnic tables in small enclosed garden *(JJW, CMW, George Atkinson)*

☆ Ashton [the one NE of Oundle, signed from A427/A605 island; TL0588], *Chequered Skipper*: Arriving to inspect this potential main entry, we found fire had destroyed much of it the previous week – but rebuilding had already started, so we hope for reopening before the end of 1996: expect well kept Adnams, Marstons Pedigree and other real ales, generous food, friendly staff and a welcome for children; attractive spot on green of thatched Tudor-style Rothschild village *(BB)*

Barnwell [TL0484], *Montagu Arms*: Warm, cosy and welcoming old-fashioned village pub with four well kept ales inc Hook Norton Old Hookey, good choice of bar food; garden has potential *(PGP)*

☆ Blakesley [High St (Woodend rd); SP6250], *Bartholomew Arms*: Cosy beamed pub with lots of dark panelling in bar and two lounge areas (children welcome in one), stuffed birds and bric-a-brac, good food and service under friendly new licensees, well kept Marstons Pedigree and Tetleys, lovely sheltered back garden with summer house; next to interesting little art gallery *(George Atkinson, Martin and Penny Fletcher, Ken and Jenny Simmonds)*

Blisworth [High St (not far from M1 junction 15A); SP7253], *Royal Oak*: 17th-c beamed pub, long and narrowish, with open fire, hospitable licensees, real ales inc Flowers Original, good value food inc tasty sandwiches all day; pool table, piped music; garden, nr Grand Union canal *(George Atkinson, Lynda Payton, Sam Samuells)*

Boughton [Church St, off A508 N of Northampton; SP7566], *Whyte-Melville*: Pleasantly renovated, with wide range of food from good open sandwiches up, Morlands Old Speckled Hen, log fire, Victorian pictures, friendly attentive service, piped music;

spacious, but can get very busy lunchtime *(George Atkinson, Mr and Mrs S Marshall)*

Braunston [Little Braunston; outside village, just N of canal tunnel; SP5466], *Admiral Nelson*: Popular former 1730 farmhouse in lovely setting by lock and hump bridge, with pleasant waterside garden and towpath walks; well kept Batemans and Courage-related real ales, quick bar food inc children's, restaurant *(Geoffrey Pegram)*

Bugbrooke [14 Church St; SP6757], *Five Bells*: Cheerful recently refurbished pub in attractive village, comfortable low-ceilinged areas off bar, one no smoking, wide choice of good value food inc Sun roasts, Courage-related ales, coal-effect gas fire; pool in games room, piped music (may be rather loud); disabled access, children welcome, garden with play area and barbecue *(CMW, JJW, Matthew Adams)*

Bulwick [Main St, just off A43 Kettering—Duddington; SP9694], *Queens Head*: Long bar with small fire each end, wheelback chairs, plush stools, wall seats, a few beams; well kept Bass, Ruddles County and Worthington, good bar food (must book for Sun roasts); can be smoky *(K H Frostick, David Ellis, Michel Hooper-Immins, BB)*

Burton Latimer [Bake House Lane; SP9075], *Olde Victoria*: Comfortable and spotless mock-Tudor pub with Victoriana inc ornate gas lamps and lots of china, good well priced food from sandwiches to steaks, prompt friendly service, well kept ales such as Everards Tiger, Marstons Pedigree, Morlands Old Speckled Hen, John Smiths and Wadworths 6X; quiet piped music, no pub games, garden and terrace with picnic tables under cocktail parasols *(John Waller, Mr and Mrs P Finlay, Mr and Mrs J Taylor)*

☆ Castle Ashby [SP8659], *Falcon*: Stone walls and hop-hung dark beams in 16th-c cellar bar down tricky steps from smart hotel in attractive preserved village, Adnams Extra, welcoming landlord, good food, open fire; restaurant overlooking pretty garden; bedrooms beautifully decorated, good breakfast *(George Atkinson, Andy and Jill Kassube, Margaret and Nigel Dennis)*

Charwelton [A361 S of Daventry; SP5356], *Fox & Hounds*: Big bar elaborately decorated with fox and hunting memorabilia, Bass and Worthington *(Anon)*

Clay Coton [off B5414 nr Stanford Hall; SP5977], *Fox & Hounds*: Popular, friendly and relaxed, well tucked away, with two log fires, interesting well kept ales such as Archers Village and Oak Hill Black Magic, nice range of reasonably priced well prepared generous food inc good sandwiches in dining area; simple but comfortable furnishings, pleasant garden, dogs and cats, chatty licensees, ocasional piped music – landlord chooses by clientele; skittle alley *(George Atkinson, Simon Kellow)*

☆ Collingtree [High St; 1¼ miles from M1
junction 15; SP7555], *Wooden Walls of Old
England*: Thatched pub with stripped
stonework, low black beams, model galleon
and some other nautical memorabilia, well
kept ales such as Mansfield Riding, Red
Squirrel and Wild Boar, friendly staff, well
priced standard food, open fire; table skittles
and fruit machine in one bar; children
welcome, lots of picnic tables, swings and
tuck shop in back garden (*George Atkinson,
CMW, JJW, PGP, Jeffrey Brown, BB*)

☆ Cosgrove [Thrupp Wharf, towards
Castlethorpe; SP7942], *Navigation*: Lovely
canalside setting, good changing range of well
kept beers, usual pub food, chesterfield and
armchairs around open fire, lots of canal
prints and memorabilia, helpful obliging staff
– character landlord can sometimes be
persuaded to play jazz piano; children
welcome, canalside garden and boat moorings
(*Karen and Graham Oddey, Duncan Small,
Lynda Payton, Sam Samuells, BB*)

Cranford St John [42a High St; 3 miles E of
Kettering just off A14; SP9277], *Red Lion*:
Wide choice of reasonably priced food inc
bargain OAP lunches in attractive two-bar
stone pub, well kept Ind Coope and Tetleys,
decent house wine, good service; pleasant
garden, quiet village (*David and Mary Webb,
Comus Elliott, Meg and Colin Hamilton*)

Croughton [High St; B4031 SW of Brackley;
SP5433], *Blackbird*: Friendly old L-shaped
bar with wide choice of good value food from
sandwiches up, cheap Sun lunch, well kept
Wadworths 6X, lots of country wines, pool
table one end, TV, darts, fruit machine,
maybe piped music (*JJW, CMW, Kevin
Shupe*)

Daventry [Mkt Pl; SP5762], *Plume of
Feathers*: Lots of brick, brasses and
woodwork for countrified feel, big real fire,
Theakstons and a guest beer, friendly
landlord, weekday lunchtime food, good
cheap coffee; pool table, fruit machine, TV
(*George Atkinson*)

☆ Duddington [A43 just S of A47; SK9800],
Royal Oak: Wide choice of good popular
food in attractive stone inn, very courteously
and efficiently run, spotless and comfortable,
with plush banquettes, gleaming brass inc
wartime shell cases, lots of pictures, open fire;
Ruddles County, Portuguese wines strong on
the list; nice garden and terrace; bedrooms
(*Bernard and Marjorie Parkin, Frank
Davidson, George Atkinson*)

Eaglethorpe [Peterborough Rd, just off A605
NE of Oundle; TL0791], *Red Lion*: Early
17th c, with cosy and homely low-beamed
lounge bar, winged high-backed settle, well
kept Bass, Highgate Dark Mild and
Worthington, simple generous bar food (not
Sun evening) inc good sandwiches, cheery
helpful service, good log fire, partly no-
smoking dining lounge (children allowed
here), bar with TV; garden with picnic tables,
play area and barbecue (*JJW, CMW, Jenny
and Michael Back*)

☆ Eastcote [Gayton Rd; village signed off A5 3
miles N of Towcester; SP6753], *Eastcote
Arms*: Attractive unspoilt but spotless
traditional layout, two small music-free areas
off bar, well kept ales inc Hook Norton Best,
Jennings and Ushers Best, very friendly new
licensees, generous food (not Sun-Weds
evenings), log fire, small restaurant, pretty
garden (*George Atkinson, Bruce Bird, K H
Frostick, LYM*)

Evenley [The Green; SP5834], *Red Lion*:
Small friendly local with strong cricket
connections, opp attractive village green;
some flagstones, Banks's and Marstons
Pedigree, decent choice of wines, reasonably
priced food inc good sandwiches and Sun
lunch (*Calum and Susan Maclean, George
Atkinson*)

Farthinghoe [just off A422 Brackley—
Banbury; SP5339], *Fox*: Quiet village local
with friendly licensee, stone fireplace, floors
part tiled and part carpet, food inc good filled
french sticks, Charles Wells ales; garden
(*George Atkinson*)

Farthingstone [SP6155], *Kings Arms*:
Comfortable olde-worlde 18th-c village pub,
well kept Hook Norton, wide choice of good
value home-made food in bar or dining area,
good range of beers and wines, welcoming
licensees, games room with darts and skittles,
friendly service; children allowed (*Robert
Thorne*)

Grafton Regis [A508 S of Northampton;
SP7546], *White Hart*: New people
concentrating on interesting food in
bistro/restaurant (former lounge) with open
fire, also in bar; obliging service, big garden
(*George Atkinson*)

Great Billing [SP8162], *Elwes Arms*:
16th-c friendly traditional village pub, food
worth waiting for from good hot snacks to
tempting Sun lunch (*Mrs S Wilkinson, John
Fahy*)

Great Doddington [B573 S of
Wellingborough; SP8865], *Stags Head*: Big
old stone pub, good traditional atmosphere,
welcoming staff, good helpings of home-
cooked food, real fires, Courage-related beers
(*Grainne Walsh*)

Hardingstone [61 High St; SP7657], *Crown*:
Two-bar Chef & Brewer, Courage and
Theakstons, good value food inc Sun roasts,
separate games room; picnic tables in sizeable
garden with play area, dovecot and pets
corner (*CMW, JJW*); [9 High St], *Sun*:
Stripped stone, tankards and jugs hanging
from beams, big helpings of good value basic
food (not Sun evening or Mon), four well
kept ales, quiet piped music, gas fire, fruit
machine; bar with pool, skittles and darts,
benches in lobby, big st bernard (*JJW, CMW*)

Hargreave [Church St; TL0370], *Nags Head*:
Olde-worlde village pub, originally three
thatched 16th-c cottages, well cooked meals
(not Sun evening), no-smoking dining room,
two changing real ales (*E Robinson*)

Harlestone [A428; SP7064], *Fox & Hounds*:
Comfortable old beamed pub with nice
wooden furniture, usual moderately priced
lunchtime food inc good snacks, friendly

service and country atmosphere, Courage-related ales; nr Althorp House *(Gill and Keith Croxton)*

☆ Harpole [High St; nr M1 junction 16; SP6860], *Bull*: Comfortable old-fashioned village pub with cosy lounge and eating area, consistently good value generous food, well kept Courage-related ales, quick friendly service, log fire in big inglenook, basic bar and games room, small terrace; no dogs *(Keith Croxton)*

☆ Harrington [High St, off A508 S of Mkt Harboro; SP7779], *Tollemache Arms*: Civilised beamed Tudor pub in isolated stonebuilt village, Charles Wells ales, very friendly staff, good home-cooked fresh food inc unusual dishes and good soup, open fires, small back garden; children welcome; clean and attractive bedrooms *(K H Frostick)*

☆ Hellidon [off A425 W of Daventry; SP5158], *Red Lion*: Clean, cosy and comfortable lounge and bars in beautiful setting by village green, tables outside, pleasant walks nearby; good value well served food inc good Weds OAP lunch in bar and restaurant, well kept Bass and Worthington, two farm ciders, welcoming landlord, friendly labradors, woodburner and open fires, games room; bedrooms *(George Atkinson)*

☆ Hinton in the Hedges [off A43 W of Brackley; SP5536], *Crewe Arms*: Busy 17th-c pub with two roomy old-fashioned alcovey bars and modern extension, good choice of reasonably priced good food from sandwiches up, well kept beers such as Boddingtons, Hook Norton Best, Marstons Pedigree and Morlands Old Speckled Hen, good coffee, friendly service, games room, restaurant, some picnic tables outside *(Steven Astaire)*

☆ Holcot [Main St; SP7969], *White Swan*: Attractive partly thatched two-bar village inn with Flowers IPA, Fullers ESB, Jennings, Tetleys and Theakstons, good reasonably priced food (not Sun-Weds evening) inc good value Sun lunch, friendly attentive staff, games room with skittles, pool and darts; children welcome; bedrooms *(Meg and Colin Hamilton, Jenny and Michael Back)*

Lamport [Harborough Rd (A508); SP7574], *Lamport Swan*: Imposing stone building with good views, wide range of good value standard food from sandwiches up in busy bar and cosy restaurant, well kept Courage Directors, good service; children welcome *(Stephen and Julie Brown)*

☆ Lilbourne [Rugby Rd; 4 miles from M1 junction 18; A5 N, then 1st right; SP5677], *Bell*: Neat and comfortable modern lounge bar with good value simple bar food, super service even when busy; seats outside, children welcome *(Ted George, LYM)*

☆ Little Brington [4½ miles from M1 junction 16, first right off A45 to Daventry; also signed from A428; SP6663], *Saracens Head*: Spacious extended lounge with alcoves, lots of pictures, books and odds and ends, even a red telephone box, well kept ales such as local Frog Island, Fullers London Pride, Hook Norton Best, Jennings, Morlands Old

Speckled Hen, wide choice of good generous food from cheap filled rolls up, welcoming landlord, no-smoking restaurant area, log fire, games bar; quiet piped music; tables in neat back garden, handy for Althorp House and Holdenby House *(Bruce Bird, George Atkinson, Ken Frostick, DR, LYM)*

☆ Little Harrowden [Main St; SP8771], *Lamb*: Good interesting reasonably priced home-cooked food (not Sun evening) inc game in spotlessly refurbished 17th-c pub, cosy three-level lounge with log fire, brasses on beams, intimate dining area, well kept Charles Wells and two guest ales served through sparkler, decent coffee, friendly attentive staff, quiet piped music; public bar, darts and hood skittles; children welcome; garden, delightful village *(George Atkinson, John C Baker, Douglas Stevens, K H Frostick, John Waller)*

☆ Lowick [off A6116; SP9780], *Snooty Fox*: Spacious two-room open-plan beamed lounge with stripped stonework, old-fashioned prints, big log fire, Courage-related and guest ales, decent wines, fresh coffee, bar food (fish can be good), top-hat fox behind bar; piped music may be loud; popular restaurant with central open fireplace; some live music; nearby church worth a visit *(David and Mary Webb, Roy Bromell, Wayne Brindle, LYM)*

☆ Marston St Lawrence [off A422 Banbury—Brackley; SP5342], *Marston Inn*: Little oak-beamed village pub, looks like a farmhouse from outside, with books on windowsill, lots of interesting bric-a-brac, friendly landlord and cat attached to its usual chair – gives a feeling of visiting friends; food inc generous sandwiches, children's and vegetarian dishes, more elaborate evening choice (not Sun or Mon evening); open fire, good dining room, well kept Hook Norton; big garden, traditional games inc Aunt Sally *(Mrs J Oakes, LYM)*

☆ Marston Trussell [SP6985], *Sun*: More hotel than pub, with comfortable bedrooms, but well worth knowing for wide choice of delicious home-made food, well kept Bass, decent house wines, helpful uniformed staff *(Anthony Barnes, Jim Farmer)*

Mears Ashby [Wilby Rd; SP8466], *Griffins Head*: Quiet pleasantly refurbished country pub with three rooms off central bar, bucolic views, good friendly service, generous food from good sandwiches to good value Sun roasts, attractive pictures, well kept ales such as Black Sheep, Charles Wells Eagle, Frog Island Natterjack and Wadworths 6X; skittles, piped music, seats out in small garden *(Bill Gottschalk, Bruce Bird, George Atkinson)*

Moulton [23 Church St; SP7866], *Artichoke*: Large village pub, wide choice of generous food (not Sun-Weds evenings), sensibly priced Banks's, Courage, Marstons Pedigree and Websters, restaurant; juke box, TV, fruit machines, pool and skittles *(JJW, CMW)*

☆ Northampton [Wellingborough Rd], *Abington Park*: Large handsomely restored Victorian pub visibly brewing its own good beers, several bars, good range of lunchtime bar food, friendly helpful staff, restaurant, family room; piped pop music, games machines; picnic tables outside, handy for cricket ground *(Bruce Bird)*

Northampton [Old Kingsthorpe; SP7464], *Queen Adelaide*: Enjoyable food, well kept ales, interesting warplane photographs *(Philip Orbell, David Watson)*

☆ Old [Walgrave Rd; N of Northampton between A43 and A508; SP7873], *White Horse*: Wide choice of good sensibly priced food inc some interesting snacks, cosy lounge with welcoming log fire, lots of pictures and plates, cheerful service, well kept Banks's and Marstons Pedigree, decent wines, restaurant; ample seating *(K H Frostick, Robert and Sally Thorne, Eric J Locker, George Atkinson)*

☆ Orlingbury [signed off A43 Northampton—Kettering, A509 Wellingborough—Kettering; SP8572], *Queens Arms*: Large, airy and almost clinically clean, with half a dozen well kept ales from small breweries, stylish furnishings, welcoming staff, food inc super sandwiches and ham and egg, cheap coffee, occasional live music; nice garden with play area *(Stephen Brown, Ted George)*

Oundle [52 Benefield Rd; TL0388], *Black Horse*: Small roadside local popular for good value straightforward food, well kept Bass and John Smiths with maybe a bargain guest beer, lots of up-to-date paperbacks to borrow, simple plush seating, piped music, big games room; picnic tables in garden behind, Sat karaoke *(Jenny and Michael Back, C W McKerrow, BB)*

☆ Pytchley [Isham Rd; SP8574], *Overstone Arms*: Interesting changing food inc some exotic specials in long countrified dining room packed every evening, often with big parties; well kept Courage-related beers with a guest such as Batemans XB, pleasant attentive service, children allowed if eating; big orchard garden, weekend barbecue/salad bar in smaller enclosed one, attractive countryside *(Howard and Margaret Buchanan, George Atkinson, Peter Titmuss)*

Raunds [16 Grove St; SP9972], *Globe*: Popular local with well kept beers, competitively priced food, darts and pool in games room, lots of activities; tables in garden *(Mr and Mrs John Hackett, Mr and Mrs D Phillips)*

Ravensthorpe [Church Lane; SP6670], *Chequers*: Wide range of bar food inc good well priced Sun lunch (with booking this), well kept beers such as Jennings Cumberland, Sam Smiths OB, Springhead and Thwaites, lots of bric-a-brac in L-shaped bar, friendly locals, good service; piano, magazines *(Bruce Bird, George Atkinson)*

☆ Sibbertoft [SP6782], *Red Lion*: Cosy and civilised beamed bar with big tables and comfortably cushioned wall seats, huge range of good generous food inc vegetarian, well kept Bass and Tetleys, decent wines, good service, piano, magazines *(Jim Farmer, Dorsan Baker, Mike Etherington, Robert and Sally Thorne)*

☆ Slipton [Slipton Ln; SP9479], *Samuel Pepys*:

16th-c two-bar pub nicely refurbished with old beams, exposed stonework, open fire, watercolours and decorative plates; wide choice of food inc interesting dishes and OAP bargain lunch, prompt friendly service, five well kept ales, decent wines, good coffee, conservatory; good views from garden with play area; children allowed in restaurant *(David and Mary Webb)*

Staverton [SP5361], *Countryman*: Good imaginatively presented food inc Angus beef and unusual specials like bison, boar and kangaroo, booking advisable *(Michael Lenihan)*

☆ Stoke Bruerne [3½ miles from M1 junction 15 – A508 towards Stony Stratford then signed on right; SP7450], *Boat*: Ideal canal location by beautifully restored lock opp British Waterways Museum and shop; little character flagstoned bar by canal, more ordinary back lounge without the views (children allowed in this bit), tables by towpath; well kept ales such as Marstons Best and Pedigree, Sam Smiths OB or Museum, Theakstons XB, Wadworths 6X and guest beers, skittle alley; bar snacks, no-smoking restaurant (not Mon lunchtime) and all-day tearooms, pub open all day summer Sats *(D Deas, Lynda Payton, Sam Samuells, Piotr Chodzko-Zajko, George Atkinson, James Nunns, LYM)*

☆ Stoke Doyle [S of Oundle; TL0286], *Shuckborough Arms*: Limited range of good food inc vegetarian, in peaceful welcoming L-shaped panelled bar or dining room; well kept ales inc guests, log fires, comfortable chesterfields, hospitable landlord, no music or fruit machines, games room with hood skittles; picnic tables in garden with play area; bedrooms good, with own bathrooms *(George Atkinson)*

Sutton Bassett [B664; SP7790], *Queens Head*: Peaceful village pub with good if not cheap food inc children's using herbs from own garden, changing well kept ales such as Tetleys, Marston Moor and Smiles Exhibition, welcoming Irish landlord, upstairs restaurant; some seats out beyond car park *(Joan and Michel Hooper-Immins)*

☆ Thorpe Mandeville [former B4525; SP5344], *Three Conies*: Cosy and attractive, with brasses, low beams, some stripped stone, gin trap over inglenook fireplace, horse-racing photographs and conversation, furnishings to suit the old building; good reasonably priced food, well kept Hook Norton and Old Hookey on handpump, good choice of wines and spirits, friendly efficient service, games room, appealing restaurant; children welcome, lots of seats in big garden *(Geoffrey Pegram, Ted George, Leith Stuart, Janet and Bill Cliverd, David and Marguerite Morgan, LYM)*

Thorpe Waterville [A605 Thrapston—Oundle; TL0281], *Fox*: Pleasantly extended old pub with wide range of food at attractive prices, coal fire, Charles Wells ales, log-effect fire, quiet piped music, no-smoking dining area, friendly outgoing landlord, prompt service; children allowed, no dogs, small garden with play area *(DW)*

Titchmarsh [TL0279], *Dog & Partridge*: Cosy and welcoming village local, good range of beers, nice food *(Comus Elliott)*

☆ Towcester [Watling St; SP6948], *Saracens Head*: Handsomely restored coaching inn, panelled bar with carpets on pine boards, other old features, interesting *Pickwick Papers* connections, Victorian dining room, short but good range of food, Charles Wells Eagle and Bombardier, neat staff; well equipped bedrooms *(Karen and Graham Oddey, George Atkinson, LYM)*

Towcester [104 Watling St], *Brave Old Oak*: Expensively restored, with nice furnishings, lovely panelling, decent food, Banks's ales on electric pump, family room; not sure about the heraldic shields, decorative lighting, fruit machine and piped music; bedrooms *(Stephen and Julie Brown, K H Frostick)*; [Watling St], *Plough*: Fine steaks, well kept Charles Wells Eagle, long-serving licensees *(Stephen and Julie Brown)*

Twywell [off A604 W of Thrapston; SP9478], *Old Friar*: The landlord of this rather foody family pub, formerly a main entry, has moved to the White Horse at Woodford *(LYM)*

Upper Boddington [Warwick Rd; SP4753], *Plough*: Limited choice of good food, fine landlord, lovely Dolls Parlour *(B Adams, Robin Sherwood)*

Wakerley [Main St (off A43); SP9599], *Exeter Arms*: Good range of ales, limited but enjoyable food (not Mon), two connecting rooms with woodburner, local photographs, friendly black labrador; piped music, fruit machine, occasional live music; garden with swings, good views and walks over Welland Valley *(Richard Clarke, Stephen and Julie Brown)*

Walgrave [Zion Hill, off A43 Northampton—Kettering; SP8072], *Royal Oak*: Old ironstone building, bar and dining lounge split into smaller areas (but the no-smoking room has gone), well kept Batemans XXXB, Morrells Oxford and Wadworths 6X, good coffee, wide choice of good food inc vegetarian, friendly efficient service; piped music, pictures for sale; children welcome, tables outside *(Bruce Bird, Anthony Griffiths)*

☆ Weedon [junction A5/A45; SP6259], *Globe*: Usefully placed attractive country hotel with comfortable atmosphere, consistently good freshly prepared bar food inc vegetarian and take-aways, small helpings for children or OAPs, quick friendly service, Marstons Bitter and Pedigree, Websters Yorkshire and a usually northern guest beer, log fire, restaurant; special events, often rugby-oriented; picnic tables outside; bedrooms *(George Atkinson, Sue and Mike Todd, JJW, CMW)*

☆ Weedon [Stowe Hill; A5 S], *Narrow Boat*: Warm and welcoming well worn-in main bar, plain decor with canal prints and big aquarium, high-raftered ex-kitchen family dining room, good range of bar food inc some dishes from the cantonese/Indonesian restaurant (spacious and airy, with canal and country views – booking advised Sat), well kept Charles Wells ales with a guest such as Adnams; fruit machine, skittles and quiet piped music, very busy in summer; spacious terrace, big garden by canal, barbecues; bedrooms in motel extension, narrowboat hire next door *(JJW, CMW, Lynda Payton, Sam Samuells, LYM)*

☆ Welford [High St (A50); SP6480], *Shoulder of Mutton*: Friendly low-ceilinged roadside pub partly divided by standing timbers and arches, plenty of tables and wheelback chairs, copper and brass on walls, sensibly priced straightforward food (not Thurs) inc children's, Batemans XB and Ruddles Best, good coffee, helpful service; piped music; skittle room, exemplary lavatories, good back garden with play area; nr canal marina *(Gordon Theaker, Roger and Pauline Pearce, R N James, C H and P Stride, BB)*

Welton [off A361/B4036 N of Daventry; SP5866], *White Horse*: Friendly little old pub with two beamed bars, cosy dining area, good value food from ploughman's to steaks, Courage-related and guest ales, friendly attentive service, big open fire, pool room, quiet piped music; attractively lit garden with play area, terrace and barbecue *(Peter Phillips)*

☆ Yelvertoft [49 High St; SP5975], *Knightley Arms*: Comfortably refurbished, simple clean lounge divided by log fire, plates, brasses and pictures, solid wooden furnishings, small neat dining area, good home-cooked food inc children's, Bass, Marstons Pedigree and Websters Yorkshire, good coffee, mood skittles; garden, occasional barbecues *(Alan Chantler, Lynda Payton, Sam Samuells)*

Stars after the name of a pub show exceptional quality. One star means most people (after reading the report to see just why the star has been won) would think a special trip worth while. Two stars mean that the pub is really outstanding – many that for their particular qualities cannot be bettered.

Northumberland & Durham

*Enjoyable new entries, or pubs back among the main entries after an absence,
include the welcoming Kings Head in Allendale, the effusively run and unusual
Allenheads Inn up the road in Allenheads, the beautifully set Lord Crewe
Arms at Bamburgh, the civilised Morritt Arms at Greta Bridge, and the
attractive and unpretentious old Wallace Arms in Haltwhistle. Other pubs
currently doing particularly well here include the friendly Manor House at
Carterway Heads (very good food – gaining our title of Northumbria Dining
Pub of the Year), the Dipton Mill at Diptonmill (gaining one of our Beer
Awards this year, and doing its good value food in the evenings now as well as
lunchtime), the busy Milecastle Inn above Haltwhistle (good game pies), the
Cooperage in Newcastle (excellent beers including its own Hadrian brews)
and Crown Posada there (a building for pub connoisseurs), the Cook &
Barker Arms at Newton on the Moor (a fine dining pub with excellent starters
and main courses), the Rose & Crown at Romaldkirk (particularly enjoyable
as a place to stay), and the Olde Ship by the harbour in Seahouses (packed
with interest). In the Lucky Dip section at the end of the chapter, pubs earning
warm praise in recent months (also inspected and given the thumbs-up by us)
include the Duke of York at Fir Tree, General Havelock at Haydon Bridge,
High Force Hotel at High Force (now brewing its own beers – the highest
brewery in England), and Hadrian at Wall; the Tap & Spile in Morpeth is one
of the best of this chain, and there's lots happening among Newcastle's fine
array of pubs. Drinks prices in the area are below the national average, but
how long can this last? Our year-on-year survey shows that beer prices have
been rising almost twice as quickly here as in most places. The cheapest places
we found for beer were the Manor House at Carterway Heads and the
Wallace Arms in Haltwhistle – both getting their beers from local small
breweries; Butterknowle and Hexhamshire both produce good local ales
which we've been pleased to find increasingly widely available. This chapter
includes Tyneside and Teesside pubs, which we've labelled Tyne & Wear and
Cleveland, respectively.*

ALLENDALE (Northumberland) NY8355 Map 10

Kings Head 🛏

Market Place (B6295)

This rambling town square has half a dozen pubs and inns, and the Kings Head
responds splendidly to the keen competition. Originally a coaching inn dating from
the early 18th c, it's the oldest pub in the area, but wears its years lightly, with a
thriving local atmosphere. The spacious refurbished bar/lounge has straightforward
pub furnishings, with a big log fire, friendly obliging service and flowers on the tables.
Theakstons Best, XB and Old Peculier and four or five guest ales such as Ind Coope
Burton, Jennings Cumberland, Morland Old Speckled Hen or Timothy Taylor
Landlord on handpump are kept well in a temperature-controlled cellar; farm cider,
about twenty decent wines by the glass and coffee, daily papers, no music or

machines. Good value fresh home-made food served in the bar or a smallish L-shaped dining area includes a range of about 30 sandwiches (from £1) including a shalmer sandwiches, an idea that the licensee picked up in Saudi Arabia, Jester's chicken – a surprise platter (£3.95), ploughman's or beef and ale pie (£4.50), and daily specials like pork with cider and apples (£4.45), chicken cacciatoria (£5.45), cannelloni romana (£5.75) and occasional specialities such as venison roast with wild berries (£7.45). They will do a small helping of most dishes for children (from £1.50), and enjoyable puddings (from £1.20); they are happy to deal with special diets, and do afternoon teas (with lots of speciality teas). Darts, dominoes and chess; there are two quoits pitches in the back garden, and they lay on quite a few special events in the upstairs function room, from art shows to story-telling nights. Dogs allowed in the bar. There are good walks in the area, and the road through the valley is a fine scenic drive. *(Recommended by JJW, CMW, GSB, Christopher Warner, David and Margaret Bloomfield, Craig and Gillian Brown)*

Free house ~ Licensee Jim Robson ~ Real ale ~ Meals and snacks (11-4, 6-9.30) ~ Children allowed at meal times ~ (01434) 683681 ~ Live music Fri and Sat nights ~ Open 11-11; 12-10.30 Sun; cl 25 Dec ~ Bedrooms: £18.50B/£37B

ALLENHEADS (Northumberland) NY8545 Map 10
Allenheads Inn

Just off B6295

Up towards the wild old lead-mining country on the Durham border, this engaging pub is practically an extension of the heritage centre opposite. In the few years they've been here, the extremely cheerful, entertaining and eccentric licensees have packed every available space with all sorts of really crazy bric-a-brac in a series of loosely themed rooms: stuffed animals, mangles, old radios, typewriters and sewing machines, long-silenced musical instruments, a ship's engine-room telegraph, brass and copper bygones, even nostalgic old tins and postcards. It's all clean and enthusiastically well cared for. The games room (with darts, pool table, cribbage and antique juke box) has perhaps the most effervescent collection, and the car club discs and number plates on the panelling are a symptom of the fact that members of a classic car club try to persuade their vehicles to wend their way up here every other Tuesday. They do huge helpings of good straightforward cheap food such as sandwiches (from £1.40), ploughman's (£2.50), steak pie and chicken pie (£4.50) with daily specials like sweet and sour chicken – although there is a Harley Davidson on one big table in the dining room. Alongside well kept Ind Coope Burton and Tetleys four or five guests might include Calders, Flowers Original, Hodges Best or Original, Mansfield Red Admiral or Youngs on handpump; decent coffee, real fire, friendly alsatian, very warm-hearted service. There are tables outside, flanked by more hardware – the sorts of machinery that wouldn't fit inside, including a vintage Rolls-Royce parked in front; it's on the Sustrans C2C cycle route. *(Recommended by JJW, CMW, David and Margaret Bloomfield, Margaret and Roy Randle)*

Free house ~ Licensees Peter and Linda Stenson ~ Real ale ~ Meals and snacks ~ Restaurant (bookings only) ~ (01434) 685200 ~ Children welcome in the games room ~ Open 11-3, 7-11 (possibly all day); cl Tues lunchtime in winter ~ Bedrooms: £21.50B/£43B

BAMBURGH (Northumberland) NU1835 Map 8
Lord Crewe Arms 🏨

The setting of this comfortable old hotel is lovely, on the village green a short stroll down from the magnificent Norman castle which commands this fine stretch of coast. Just opposite is a good beach of tidal sand, and there are plenty of bracing walks nearby. The back cocktail bar, with comfortably upholstered banquettes, windsor armchairs and the like around cast-iron traditional pub tables, has a bar counter studded with thousands of pre-decimal polished copper coins, and its beams are festooned with swordfish swords, armadillo skins, miners' lamps, lobster pots, fishing nets and lots more; there's a winter log fire. A more modern side bar has hunting murals. Lunchtime bar food includes soup (£1.95), sandwiches (from £2), ploughman's (£3.95), a quiche of the day (£4.25), smoked local kippers (£4.75), and steak in ale pie (£4.95), with evening extras like grilled lamb cutlets (£7.50); an evening restaurant has four-course dinners for £18.50. Bass and Stones on handpump and electric pump; friendly helpful staff. Do please note they're not open in the evening during winter, and you can't stay here then. The castle is still lived in, and has a splendid collection of arms and armour. *(Recommended by Avril Hanson, John and June Gale, Chris Rounthwaite, Martin Hickes, Annette and Steven Marsden, P J Hanson, Gordon, D Stokes, Dorothy and David Young)*

Free house ~ Licensee Malcolm Eden ~ Real ale ~ Meals and snacks ~ Evening restaurant ~ (01668) 214243 ~ Children in eating area of bar ~ Monthly jazz nights in summer ~ Summer opening 11.30-3, 6-11, all day weekends; in winter only open lunchtimes ~ Bedrooms: £34(£46B)/£46(£68B); not available Nov-Easter

BLANCHLAND (Northumberland) NY9750 Map 10

Lord Crewe Arms

One reader remembers as a boy being fascinated by a placemat of his mother's with a picture of this magnificent partly Norman building; vaguely recalling that it was in Blanchland, he recently called in for a visit, and found not only that it was still exactly the same as the picture, but that they still had the same placemats beside the roaring fire. The building was originally attached to the guest house of a monastery – part of the cloister still stands in the neatly terraced gardens. The cosy barrel-vaulted crypt bar has plush bar stools, built-in wall benches, ancient flagstones, and stone and brick walls that are eight feet thick in some places. Vaux Samson on handpump; darts. Upstairs, the quietly welcoming Derwent Room has low beams, old settles, and sepia photographs on its walls, and the Hilyard Room has a massive 13th-c fireplace once used as a hiding place by the Jacobite Tom Forster (part of the family who had owned the building before it was sold to the formidable Lord Crewe, Bishop of Durham). His loyal sister still haunts the place, asking guests to deliver a message to her long dead brother. Lunchtime bar food – reckoned by a good few readers to be not what it was – includes soup (£1.80), filled rolls (mostly £2.90), cheese filled pasta in a creamy sun-dried tomato sauce and glazed with mozarella cheese (£4), ploughman's (£4.50), salmon fishcakes (£4.85), and wild boar and pheasant pie (£5.60), with a shorter evening choice taking in breaded chicken breast with spicy pasta (£8) and smoked salmon and prawn cornets (£8.50). Staff will usually arrange variations of the main menu for children. On Sunday the menu may be limited to soup and a cold buffet, with Sunday lunch served in the restaurant; afternoon teas with home-made cakes. There's a pleasant enclosed garden. *(Recommended by Martin Hickes, George and Chris Miller, Avril Hanson, Val Stevenson, Rob Holmes, Liz and John Soden, Wayne Brindle, Joyce McKimm, P J Hanson, Gordon, Karen and Graham Oddey; also in Good Hotel Guide)*

Free house ~ Licensees A S Todd, Peter Gingell, Ian Press ~ Real ale ~ Meals and snacks ~ Restaurant ~ (01434) 675251 ~ Children welcome ~ Open 11-3, 6-11 ~ Bedrooms: £75B/£105B

CARTERWAY HEADS (Northumberland) NZ0552 Map 10

Manor House ⚑ ♀ ◗

A68 just N of B6278, near Derwent Reservoir

Northumbria Dining Pub of the Year

One of the things that stands out about the very good food at this simple slate-roofed stone house is the way that even familiar-sounding meals have something just that bit different about them. The choice changes every day, with generously served dishes typically including sandwiches, soup such as tomato and mint (£1.95), chicken liver pâté (£2.75), cumberland sausage (£3.75), roast aubergine and pepper moussaka (£5.35), pork casserole with tomato and mustard (£6.95), chicken breast stuffed with spinach and gruyère cheese or cod fillet with leeks, saffron and wild mushroom (£7.50), roast duck breast with cassis and port or calf liver with honey, Pernod and dijon mustard (£8.50), and puddings such as raspberry and gooseberry betty (£2.85) or their own ice creams (£2.10). The very good table d'hôte menu is available throughout the building and might include brill mousseline with tomato and coriander, wild salmon en papillote with lime butter, and honey and mixed spice wafers with raspberries, (£16.50 including coffee); part of the restaurant is no smoking. Attentive service, relaxed atmosphere. There's a changing range of very well kept beers such as Big Lamp, Butterknowle, Oakhill Best, and Freeminer Slaughter Porter on handpump, a farm cider, fresh apple juice, up to 20 malt whiskies, and decent wines. The comfortable refurbished lounge bar has picture windows with fine southerly views over moorland pastures, and a woodburning stove. The beamed locals' bar is furnished with pine tables, chairs and stools, old oak pews, and a mahogany bar. Darts, dominoes and maybe piped music. Rustic tables out on a small side terrace and lawn. *(Recommended by Eric Larkham, M Morgan, M Fryer, Wayne Brindle, Tony Hall, John, Graham and Karen Oddey, Roger Bellingham, GSB, M Borthwick, M J Morgan, Anne Cherry, Margaret and Nigel Dennis, Dr I H Maine, R Heaven)*

Free house ~ Licensee Anthony Pelly ~ Real ale ~ Meals and snacks ~ Restaurant ~ (01207) 255268 ~ Children in eating area of bar and restaurant ~ Open 11-3, 6-11; closed 25 Dec ~ Bedrooms: £22/£38.50

CHATTON (Northumberland) NU0628 Map 10

Percy Arms 🛏

B6348 E of Wooler

Just starting a refurbishment as we went to press, this partly creeper-covered friendly stone local is a popular stop for its generously served bar food and comfortable bedrooms. The menu generally has soup (£1.85), home-made pâté (£2.95), home-cooked ham salad or tuna pasta salad (£4.95), a vegetarian daily special or steak and kidney pie (£5.25), tagliatelle with pesto, sun-dried tomatoes and olives (£5.45), fillet of salmon (£8.75) and roast half duckling (£8.95); children's dishes (£2.75), and puddings like home-made sherry trifle (from £1.95); all meat is locally butchered and dishes are served with fresh vegetables; good breakfasts. The attractively lit comfortable bar is clean and spacious with wooden upholstered wall seats, there's a carpeted lounge area, and a family area through a stone-faced arch. Round on the other side a similarly furnished tiled-floor section leads through to a stripped-stone eating area. Well kept Theakstons XB on handpump, changing wines, and a fine selection of about two dozen malt whiskies; open fire, unobtrusive piped music; public bar with darts, pool, pinball, dominoes, fruit machine, and juke box. There are picnic tables on its small front lawn above the village road, and a holiday cottage is available; large comfortable bedrooms. No dogs in public areas. Residents have the use of 12 miles of private fishing, where there may be salmon, sea trout or stocked rainbow trout. *(Recommended by R C Wiles, M J Morgan, Neil Townend, Avril Hanson, N E Bushby, W Atkins, David and Mary Webb, June and Tony Baldwin, P J Hanson, John Allsopp, James Macrae, Leigh and Gillian Mellor, A N Ellis, Dr and Mrs J H Hills, Jack and Heather Coyle)*

Free house ~ Licensees Pam and Kenny Topham ~ Real ale ~ Meals and snacks (12-1.30, 6.30-9.30) ~ Restaurant ~ (01668) 215244 ~ Children welcome ~ Open 11-3, 6-11 ~ Bedrooms: £20B/£40B

COTHERSTONE (Durham) NZ0119 Map 10

Fox & Hounds

B6277 – incidentally a good quiet route to Scotland, through interesting scenery

The cosy beamed bar at this white-painted old country dining pub has various alcoves and recesses, with comfortable furnishings such as thickly cushioned wall seats, local photographs and country pictures on the walls, and a winter open fire. Home-made bar food – served in the L-shaped lounge – includes sandwiches, soup (£1.95), spicy whitebait or chicken liver pâté (£3.45), ploughman's (£5.25), braised beef in Guinness or vegetable curry with kidney beans (£5.95), deep fried haddock (£6.95), and grilled lamb cutlets (£7.95); one of the restaurants is no smoking. Well kept Hambleton Best, White Boar (from the same supplier as Hambleton), Goldfield and John Smiths Bitter on handpump, a fair choice of malt whiskies, and a useful wine list. No pets. The pub is prettily placed overlooking a picturesque village green, and there are good walks nearby. *(Recommended by Ian S Morley, Anthony Barnes, David Gittins, Basil Minson, Margaret and Roy Randle, Eric and Jackie Robinson)*

Free house ~ Licensees Michael and May Carlisle~ Real ale ~ Meals and snacks (12-3, 6.30-10) ~ Restaurant ~ (01833) 650241 ~ Children welcome ~ Open 11-3, 6-11 ~ Bedrooms: £37.50B/£50B – children must be over 9 to stay here

CRASTER (Northumberland) NU2620 Map 10

Jolly Fisherman £

Off B1339 NE of Alnwick

Fabulous views and delicious crab sandwiches help make this unpretentious local rather more special than it might at first appear. It's perched high in a lovely fishing town, with the best places to sit perhaps the little garden or beside the big picture windows, both of which look out over the harbour to the sea. Workers from the harbour or the kippering shed opposite are regulars in the relaxed and atmospheric original bar (liking especially the snug by the entrance), but strangers will quickly be welcomed into the swing of things. Simple but popular snacks (available all the time the pub is open) include toasties or home-made stottie pizzas (£1.40), soup (£1.50), really excellent local crab and salmon sandwiches (£1.70, smoked salmon £2.70) and maybe a hot dish of the day. Well kept Wards Thornes Best and Vaux Lorimers Best Scotch on handpump, and a range of malt whiskies; friendly service. Darts, pool, shove-ha'penny, dominoes, cribbage, fruit machine, trivia and juke box. The pub can get crowded on sunny days, but unlike places in similar settings never begins to feel like a tourist attraction. There's a splendid clifftop walk to Dunstanburgh Castle close by. *(Recommended by John and June Gale, Darren Salter, Cdr and Mrs J M Lefeaux, Annette and Stephen Marsden, David Austin, GSB, Dr I H Maine, D Stokes, Caroline Wright, Christopher Turner, J H and S A Harrop, Karen and Graham Oddey, M Carey, A Groocock, Gordon)*

Vaux ~ Lease: W P Silk ~ Real ale ~ Snacks (all day) ~ (01665) 576461 ~ Children welcome till 8.30 ~ Open 11-11 (winter 11-3; 6-11)

DIPTONMILL (Northumberland) NY9361 Map 10

Dipton Mill 🍺

Off B6306 S of Hexham at Slaley, Blanchland and Dye House, Whitley Chapel signposts and HGV route sign

A recent report not unreasonably describes this very popular little local as a treasure, and it really is a pleasant place to unwind, especially on the sunken crazy-paved terrace by the restored mill stream, or by the garden's pretty plantings and aviaries. Inside, the homely rooms have a cheerfully relaxed atmosphere, and a good welcome from the friendly landlord; the snug little bar has dark ply panelling, red furnishings and open fires. Besides Theakstons Best, the well kept beers include Hexhamshire Devils Water, Shire and Whapweasel from a local brewery about two and a half miles down the road; also quite a few malt whiskies. Now served in the evenings too, the nicely concise range of tasty, good value bar food features soup (£1.50), well presented sandwiches (the thick rare beef are recommended), a good choice of ploughman's, with some interesting local cheeses (£2.90), smoked salmon or cheese and onion flan (£3.70), steak and kidney pie or mince and dumplings (£4), chicken breast in sherry sauce (£4.50), and puddings like apricot roulade (£1.50); home-made cakes and coffee (£1.50). Darts, bar billiards, shove ha'penny and dominoes. There may be barbecues on summer weekends. It's in a very peaceful wooded valley and there are easy-walking footpaths nearby. *(Recommended by L Dixon, Eric Larkham, Chris Rounthwaite, Ian Wilson, Robin and Gloria Underwood, A L Carr, Mike Pugh, Karen and Graham Oddey)*

Free house ~ Licensee Geoffrey Brooker ~ Real ale ~ Meals and snacks (12-2.30, 6.30-8.30) ~ Children in simple family room ~ Open 12-2.30, 6-11; closed 25 Dec

GREAT WHITTINGTON (Northumberland) NZ0171 Map 10

Queens Head

Village signposted off A68 and B6018 just N of Corbridge

Just north of Hadrian's Wall, this warmly friendly pub is in an attractive and very neatly kept stonebuilt village nestling in partly wooded gently hilly countryside. Behind its simple stone exterior, two comfortable beamed rooms have been refurbished in a gently rustic style, with log fires, a mural over the fireplace near the bar counter, some handsome carved oak settles among other more modern furnishings, old prints and a collection of keys. The wide choice of changing home-made bar food is written up on blackboards: sandwiches and ploughman's, mushrooms in stilton and cream sauce (£2.95), avocado and smoked bacon salad (£3.25), steak and ale pie or goujons of fresh haddock (£5.95), vegetarian dishes like nut, corn and cheese casserole, leg of local lamb or fillet of trout with honey and almonds (£6.95), and good puddings. Well kept Queens Head (brewed for them by the local Hadrian Brewery), Hambleton Bitter and Stud, and a couple of other beers like Boddingtons and John Smiths; decent choice of malt whiskies, friendly attentive service, unobtrusive piped music. An area off the bar is no smoking. Despite the improvements to the food in recent years, the pub is still well used by locals, and hasn't become an out-and-out dining pub. There are six picnic tables on the small front lawn. *(Recommended by Eric Larkham, Dr R H M Stewart, D K Hyams; more reports please)*

Free house ~ Ian Scott ~ Real ale ~ Meals and snacks ~ (01434) 672267 ~ Children in eating area ~ Restaurant ~ Open 12-2.30(3.30 Sat), 6-11

GRETA BRIDGE (Durham) NZ0813 Map 10

Morritt Arms ⇐

Hotel signposted off A66 W of Scotch Corner

Though in places it can seem more like a grandly comfortable country house than a pub, this characterful old coaching inn has a delightfully pubby bar named after Charles Dickens, who stayed here in 1838 on his way to start his research for *Nicholas Nickleby*. Running all the way round the walls in here is a rather jolly Dickensian mural painted in 1946 by J V Gilroy, more famous for his old Guinness advertisements – six of which are displayed on the wall. There are also big windsor armchairs and sturdy green-plush-seated oak settles clustered around traditional cast-iron-framed tables, and big windows that look out on the extensive lawn. The adjacent green bar has dark grey leatherette wall seats, a stag's head and a big case of stuffed black game. Flowers brighten up the rooms, and there are open fires. Well kept Butterknowle Conciliation, Tetleys, Theakstons Best and Timothy Taylors Landlord on handpump, quite a few malt whiskies, and an extensive wine list; friendly staff. There's a proper old shove-ha'penny board, with raisable brass rails to check the lie of the coins, and darts, pool, cribbage, dominoes and a juke box in the separate public bar. Bar food includes sandwiches (from £2.75), soup (£2.95), warm chicken salad or steak, kidney and Guinness pie (£6.95), and several changing daily specials including a vegetarian dish; the restaurant is no smoking. There are some picnic tables in the nice garden, teak tables in a pretty side area looking along to the graceful old bridge by the stately gates to Rokeby Park, and swings, slide and rope ladder at the far end. *(Recommended by Anthony Barnes, James Nunns, John and Joan Nash, Ian Corsie)*

Free house ~ Licensees Peter Phillips and Barbara Anne Johnson ~ Real ale ~ Meals and snacks (11-9.30) ~ Restaurant ~ (01833) 627232 ~ Children welcome ~ Open 11-11; 11-10.30 Sun ~ Bedrooms: £45B/£75B

HALTWHISTLE (Northumberland) NY6860 Map 10

Wallace Arms

Rowfoot, Featherstone Park – OS Sheet 86 map reference 683607

In attractive surroundings just outside the town, the bar of this rambling thick-walled former farmhouse, reopened as a pub in 1995, has simple furnishings and unpretentious decorations in its five interlinked rooms. There's a good log fire in the small beamed main bar, with dark oak woodwork, some stripped stone and comfortable seats; the side games room has another fire (also darts, pool, scrabble and chess), and there's a third in the middle of the big no-smoking dining room (a former barn), which has its own interesting menu. At lunchtime good value bar food made by the landlady includes soup (£1.75), sandwiches (from £2.25), filled baked potatoes (£2.50), lots of ploughman's (from £3.75), vegetarian quiche (£4.50), fisherman's platter (£5.50) and gammon and pineapple (£6.25). The menu changes slightly in the evening, and includes whitebait (£3), Whitby king prawns (£3.25), a vegetarian pasta bake (£4.50), steak and ale pie (£5.50), chicken breast with a sauce of the day, mixed nut stroganoff or baked trout (£6.25) and 8oz sirloin (£8.95); good Sunday roasts; well kept local Hexhamshire Shire, Devils Water and Whapweasel on handpump, some malt whiskies, character landlord, friendly service, welcoming locals. Access for disabled people is fairly easy. Picnic-table sets outside on both sides of the quiet lane have lovely fell views, and you can walk straight from the pub (one good walk, with fine views, is along the former Alston railway line); there's a play area at the back and quoits. We have not yet had reports on the bedrooms here; there is room for touring caravans. *(Recommended by Leonard Dixon, Christopher Warner, John Oddey)*

Free house ~ Licensees John and Mary Stenhouse ~ Real ale ~ Meals and snacks (not Mon or Tues lunchtime or Sun evening) ~ Restaurant ~ (01434) 321872 ~ Children welcome in snug and games room ~ Open 4-11 Mon/Tues; 12-2.30, 4-11 Wed/Thurs; 11-11 Fri/Sat; 12-3.30, 7-10.30 Sun; cl 25 Dec ~ Bedrooms

nr HALTWHISTLE (Northumberland) NY7164 Map 10

Milecastle 🏆

Military Rd; B6318 NE – OS Sheet 86 map reference 715660

In a nicely remote setting on the old military road that runs alongside Hadrian's Wall, this cosily refurbished 17th-c pub is especially well liked for its food, and more particularly the game. You'll usually find this in a selection of imaginative home-made pies such as beef and venison, wild boar and duckling, turkey, ham and chestnut, or pheasant and claret (all £5.95); their coulibiac pie is a tasty combination of salmon, rice, mushroom and parsley. Other popular dishes include soup (£1.75), splendid venison sausages (£5.25), and vegetable curry (£5.50), with half a dozen or so good daily specials such as chicken breast in port and basil sauce. The local meat is well hung and the fresh local vegetables good, as are the puddings like chocolate and orange cake or treacle tart (from £2.25). Lunchtime sandwiches (from £2.30) and ploughman's (£3.95) tend to be dressed up with a great deal of salad. Well kept changing real ales such as Devils Water and Whapweasel from the Hexhamshire Brewery, another local beer, Four Seasons, Ind Coope Burton, and Tetleys on handpump; also a very decent collection of malt whiskies, and a good wine list. The snug small rooms of the beamed bar, decorated mainly with brasses, horsey and local landscape prints and attractive dried flowers, do get very busy in season (or when two dozen local farmers arrive in force); there's a lunchtime overflow into the small comfortable restaurant. Good friendly chatty service; a splendid coal fire, with a welcome for walkers (but no rucksacks allowed). No games or music. There are some white plastic seats and tables outside in a sheltered walled garden with a dovecote. *(Recommended by Ian and Deborah Carrington, Stephen, Julie and Hayley Brown, A and D B, V Green, Pat and Robert Watt)*

Free house ~ Licensees Ralph and Margaret Payne ~ Real ale ~ Meals and snacks ~ Restaurant ~ (01434) 320682 ~ Children over 5 welcome if eating ~ Open 12-2.30, 6.30-11; closed Sunday evenings Dec-Feb

HEDLEY ON THE HILL (Northumberland) NZ0859 Map 10
Feathers

Village signposted from New Ridley, which is signposted from B6309 N of Consett; OS Sheet 88 map reference 078592

One of the particularly nice things about this little stone local is that despite the quality and popularity of her very good bar food, the landlady only serves meals at weekends – she doesn't want anything to alter the traditional feel of the place. The three well kept turkey-carpeted traditional bars have beams, woodburning stoves, stripped stonework, solid brown leatherette settles, country pictures, and a charmingly relaxed and welcoming atmosphere. Well kept Boddingtons and Jennings Cumberland on handpump, along with a couple of interesting local brews such as Mordue or Durham Magus and Canny Lad; around 30 malt whiskies. The changing range of imaginative weekend meals includes soups such as parsnip, lemon and ginger (£1.95), ploughman's (£3.75), smoked salmon, spinach and asparagus pasta or courgette, tomato and fennel crumble (£3.95), smoked cod in cheese sauce wrapped in a pancake or pork in cider with apple (£5.25), lamb casseroled in red wine with herbs and redcurrant jelly (£5.95), and puddings like rhubarb crumble or pecan and honey tart (£1.95). Shove ha'penny, table skittles and dominoes. They usually have a mini beer festival round Easter, which ends with a barrel race on Easter Monday. *(Recommended by John Fazakerley, GSB, Peter and Patricia Burton, JJW, CMW)*

Free house ~ Licensee Marina Atkinson ~ Real ale ~ Weekend meals and snacks ~ (01661) 843607 ~ Children in lounge and family room ~ Open 6-11; plus 12-3 weekends

MATFEN (Northumberland) NZ0372 Map 10
Black Bull

Village signposted off B6318 NE of Corbridge

Readers who've enjoyed visiting a particular pub often tell us they'll go out of their way to make a return visit, but a letter we had about this creeper-covered long stone inn seemed to be making the point more vociferously – its author lives in Rome. Popular with visitors at lunchtime and locals in the evening, the spacious turkey-carpeted main bar has windsor chairs, copper-topped tables, and steeplechasing pictures, and there's a side room with red plush button-back built-in wall banquettes, and attractive 1940s photographs. Well presented bar food includes soup of the day (£2), duck liver pâté with cumberland sauce (£3.75), fillet of haddock (£5), honey glazed breast of chicken with toasted almonds or steak and mushroom pie (£5.25), filled yorkshire pudding (£5.40), oak smoked trout fillets with horseradish sauce (£5.50), and game pie (£7.50); good, fresh vegetables. They will do sandwiches, and you can order from the very good seasonally changing restaurant menu; the restaurant is no smoking. Obliging staff serve well kept Black Bull, John Smiths, Morlands Old Speckled Hen, Theakstons Best, and summer guests on handpump, as well as over 20 malt whiskies; log fires, sensibly placed darts, pool, dominoes, and juke box. No dogs. There are plenty of seats on an outside terrace. Arrive in summer and you'll see why they often win prizes for their hanging baskets, shrubs and bedding plants. *(Recommended by Mrs M Armini, John Allsopp, Stephen, Julie and Hayley Brown, Chris Rounthwaite, Jack and Heather Coyle, Margaret and Nigel Dennis, J P Burke)*

Free house ~ Licensees Colin and Michele Scott ~ Real ale ~ Meals and snacks ~ Restaurant ~ (01661) 886330 ~ Children in eating area of bar ~ Open 11-11(winter 11-3, 6-11); 12-10.30 Sun ~ Bedrooms: £32.50B/£55B

NEW YORK (Tyne & Wear) NZ3370 Map 10

Shiremoor House Farm ★

Middle Engine Lane/Norham Road; from A1 going N from Tyne Tunnel, right into A1058 then next left signposted New York, then left at end of speed limit (pub signed); or at W end of New York A191 bypass turn S into Norham Road, then first right (pub signed)

The remarkable transformation of these once derelict farm buildings into a smartly relaxed and enjoyable pub quite deservedly won its designers an award. There's a delightful mix of interesting and extremely comfortable furniture, a big kelim on the broad flagstones and warmly colourful farmhouse paintwork on the bar counter and several other tables, as well as conical rafters of the former gin-gan, a few farm tools, and good rustic pictures such as mid-West prints, big crisp black-and-white photographs of country people and modern Greek bull sketches. Gentle lighting in several well divided spacious areas cleverly picks up the surface modelling of the pale stone and beam ends. Well kept local Mordue, Stones Best, Theakstons Best and Old Peculier and a guest like Timothy Taylors Landlord on handpump, decent wines by the glass, polite and efficient young staff. No music or games machines; Monday evening quiz. A separate bar serves the equally attractive rather smart restaurant. Favourites amongst the quickly served bar food include the sandwiches, vegetarian stir fry (£3.75), steak and kidney pie (£4.35), and scampi (£4.45); changing specials might include breast of chicken with prawn and garlic sauce or rump steak with pepper sauce, and they do children's helpings. The granary extension is good for families with high chairs, and bottles or baby food are warmed on request. It can get crowded at weekday lunchtimes. There are picnic tables on neat grass at the edge of the flagstoned farm courtyard, by tubs and a manger filled with flowers; no-smoking area. *(Recommended by Richard Dolphin, Eric Larkham, E A Thwaite, GSB, Karen and Graham Oddey, E V Walder, Roger Bellingham)*

Sir John Fitzgerald Ltd ~ Licensee Bill Kerridge ~ Real ale ~ Meals and snacks (12-9) ~ Restaurant ~ (0191) 257 6302 ~ Children in eating areas of bar and in restaurant ~ Open 11-11; 12-10.30 Sun

NEWCASTLE UPON TYNE (Tyne & Wear) NZ2266 Map 10

Bridge Hotel

Castle Square (in local A-Z street atlas index as Castle Garth); right in centre, just off Nicholas St (A6215) at start of High Level Bridge; only a few parking meters nearby, but evening parking easy

This bustling and chatty Victorian bar was just about to emerge from a thorough refurbishment as we went to press. It was closed for quite a while during the summer and the work really was quite extensive, but we're confident that under its new managers the pub will offer the same friendly comforts that have made it so appealing to visitors. As it's next door to the Crown court lawyers rub shoulders with businessmen and shoppers at lunchtime, while in the evening it's popular with a lively younger set. The imposing, neatly kept old-fashioned lounge has high ceilings, a bar counter equipped with unusual pull-down slatted snob screens, decorative mirrors, and a massive mahogany carved fireplace. The public bar has some cheerful stained glass, as well as games and a good selection of beers on handpump. Tables on the flagstoned back terrace are by the remains of the city wall that look down over the Tyne and its bridges. *(Reports please)*

Sir John Fitzgerald Ltd ~ Real ale ~ (0191) 232 6400

Cooperage ◗ £

32 The Close, Quayside; immediately below and just to the W of the High Level Bridge; parking across road limited lunchtime, easy evening

One of the oldest buildings in the city, this wonky waterfront Tudor house used to be a cooperage, but today it's what's in the casks that makes it worthy of attention.

As well as one of three ales from their own Hadrian brewery – Gladiator, Centurion and Emperor – they usually keep Ind Coope Burton, Marstons Owd Rodger and Tetleys, and three guests such as Benskins, Flowers Original, Friary Meux, Fullers ESB, or Timothy Taylors Landlord. The guest beers vary every time they change a barrel, and they're so busy with locals, businessmen and students that they'll generally get through about 15 a week; also hand-pulled Addlestones and Bulmers ciders. The small bustling bar has huge Tudor oak beams and exposed stonework, and there's extra seating in the lounge area by the pool room; dominoes, fruit machine, video game and a juke box. Prepared with fresh seasonal vegetables and home grown herbs, the excellent value lunchtime bar food is written up on a quickly changing blackboard, with dishes typically including ham and lentil broth (£1.20), mushroom, leek and broccoli cheesebake with bubble and squeak or minced lamb curry (£3), prawns and mussels in a garlic, white wine and herb sauce (£3.25), fried lamb liver and bacon (£3.50), chicken and ham pie with potato and vegetable hotpot or fresh fish from the quay like deep fried haddock (£3.95), and home-made puddings like brandy bread and butter pudding or hot apple and lemon sponge (£1.20); Sunday lunch (£4.95). The pub is close to the Sunday outdoor market, and can be noisy in the evenings. *(Recommended by Val Stevenson, Rob Holmes, E A Thwaite, Eric Larkham, Paul and Ursula Randall, Richard Lewis, S G Brown)*

Free house ~ Licensee Michael Westwell ~ Real ale ~ Meals and snacks (11-7; not Sun) ~ Lunchtime restaurant ~ (0191) 232 8286 ~ Open 11-11; 12-10.30 Sun; cl 25 Dec

Crown Posada 🍺 £

31 The Side; off Dean Street, between and below the two high central bridges (A6125 and A6127)

With its pre-Raphaelite stained-glass windows and imposing golden crown, the marvellous facade of this bustling city centre pub could easily be that of a grand old bank or post office. Inside there's lots of architectural charm such as an elaborate coffered ceiling in cream and dusky pink, and delightful oddities including a line of gilt mirrors each with a tulip lamp on a curly brass mount which match the great ceiling candelabra, stained glass in the counter screens, and Victorian flowered wallpaper above the brown dado (with its fat heating pipes along the bottom – a popular footrest when the east wind brings the rain off the North Sea). It's a very long and narrow room, making quite a bottleneck by the serving counter, and beyond that, a long soft green built-in leather wall seat is flanked by narrow tables. Well kept Bass, Boddingtons, Butterknowle Conciliation, Jennings, Theakstons Best and a guest on handpump and tap; lunchtime sandwiches and toasties (£1). Friendly barmen, chatty customers; fruit machine. On some weekday evenings you can find it quiet (as it often is at lunchtime), with regulars reading the papers put out in the front snug, but by Friday it's generally packed. Note that they don't allow children. *(Recommended by Eric Larkham, E A Thwaite, Val Stevenson, Rob Holmes, N Meachen, Richard Lewis, S G Brown)*

Sir John Fitzgerald Ltd ~ Manager Malcolm McPherson ~ Real ale ~ Lunchtime snacks ~ (0191) 232 1269 ~ Open 11-11

NEWTON ON THE MOOR (Northumberland) NU1605 Map 10
Cook & Barker Arms 🍽 🍺

Village signposted from A1 Alnwick–Felton

You can get an idea of how highly the food is regarded at this old favourite by the fact that the restaurant has been known to be fully booked in the evening up to two weeks in advance. Readers really enjoy coming here, particularly for the way that the carefully attentive licensees make visitors feel so special. The very well liked bar food might include hot sandwiches (from £3.25), vegetarian dishes like Tunisian bean salad or filled croissants (£3.95), spaghetti vongole (£4.80), warm wood pigeon salad with bacon and blackberries or a daily pie like chicken, ham and mushroom (£4.95), smoked salmon cakes with a chive and vermouth sauce (£6.50), and grilled lobster tail with a crayfish butter sauce (£7.95). Well kept Courage Directors and Theakstons Best on handpump and two guests like Jennings or Morlands Old Speckled Hen; about 30 good malt whiskies, and a big wine list. Service is friendly, prompt and efficient, even when they're busy. The unfussy, long beamed and gently atmospheric bar has a coal fire at one end with a coal-effect gas fire at the other, stripped, partly panelled walls, brocade-seated settles around oak-topped tables, framed banknotes and paintings by local artists on the walls, brasses, and a highly polished oak servery. What was the old storeroom now has tables, chairs, an old settle, and darts (popular with locals); the games room has scrubbed pine furniture, french windows leading onto the terrace, and dominoes, trivia and juke box. The lounge is no smoking. *(Recommended by Lucy James, Simon Morton, Roger Bellingham, John Oddey, J H and S A Harrop, Neil Townend, Nigel and Amanda Thorp, R H Rowley, GSB, E J Wilde, Ian Phillips, Laura Darlington, Gianluca Perinetti, Adam and Joan Bunting, Julie Peters, John Allsopp, Dr I H Maine, Mr and Mrs J A Stewart, Jack and Heather Coyle, Tim and Sue Halstead)*

Free house ~ Licensees Lynn and Phil Farmer ~ Real ale ~ Meals and snacks (12-2, 6-8) ~ Evening restaurant ~ (01665) 575234 ~ Children in eating area of bar ~ Open 11-3, 6-11 ~ Bedrooms: £30B/£60B

NORTH SHIELDS (Tyne & Wear) NZ3468 Map 10

Chain Locker 🍺 £

New Quay

Close to the pedestrian ferry landing area, this simple and notably welcoming late Victorian pub is almost dwarfed by the surviving 1816 wharfside commercial buildings – now largely flats – around it. There's quite a nautical theme, with seafaring pictures and navigational charts and maps on the walls (some giving a detailed account of the Falklands campaign), as well as stools and wooden wall benches around small tables (the one on your left as you go in, built over a radiator, is prized in winter), an open fire, and local literature and arts information. Six impeccably kept real ales on handpump might include Ind Coope Burton, Tetleys, Timothy Taylors Landlord, and unusual changing local guests like Danish Dynamite or Rudgate Battleaxe; also malt whiskies, farm ciders. Extremely good and very reasonably priced bar food includes lunchtime sandwiches, steak pie (£3.65), and a good amount of fresh local fish including garlic mussels (£2.50), smoked fish pie (£3.55) or salmon (£4.75), and oysters, lobster or crab if you order them in advance. Families are often really surprised at how cheaply – and well – they can all eat here. Dominoes, fruit machine and piped music. *(Recommended by John Prescott, Verity Kemp, Richard Mills, Eric Larkham, John Oddey, Karen and Graham Oddey, J A Stewart)*

Free house ~ Licensee Wilfred Kelly ~ Real ale ~ Meals and snacks (12-2.30, 6-9.30; not Sun evening) ~ Restaurant (not Sun evening) ~ (0191) 258 0147 ~ Children welcome ~ Folk music Fri evening ~ Open 11-4, 6-11; Thurs-Sun 11-11

RENNINGTON (Northumberland) NU2119 Map 10

Masons Arms

Stamford Cott; B1340 NE of Alnwick

Big helpings of good value bar food are what draw people off the beaten track to this well run old coaching inn. The choice includes lunchtime sandwiches, home-made soup (£1.95), home-made chicken liver and brandy pâté (£3.75), fried haddock (£4.95), vegetable bake or lentil and mushroom cannelloni (£5.65), game casserole (£6.55), gammon steak or chicken chasseur (£6.25), steaks (from £9.95), and several daily specials; children's meals. Courage Directors, Ruddles Best and Whitbreads Castle Eden on handpump, served by friendly, helpful staff; and piped music. The comfortably modernised beamed lounge bar has wheelback and mate's chairs around solid wooden tables on the patterned carpet, plush bar stools, lots of brass, pictures and photographs on the walls, and a relaxed atmosphere; the dining rooms have pine panelling and wrought-iron wall lights. There are sturdy rustic tables on the little front terrace, surrounded by lavender. The bedrooms are in recently converted stables. *(Recommended by Peter Bennett, Ian and Deborah Carrington, Martin Hickes, June and Tony Baldwin, Christopher Turner, Mrs P Abell)*

Free house ~ Licensees Frank and Dee Sloan ~ Real ale ~ Meals and snacks ~ Restaurant ~ (01665) 577275 ~ Children in restaurant up to 8pm; no infants in evening ~ Open 12-2, 6.30-11 ~ Bedrooms: /£47B

ROMALDKIRK (Durham) NY9922 Map 10

Rose & Crown 🍴 🛏

Just off B6277

Tables outside this fairly smart old hotel look out over the village green, still with its original stocks and water pump. It's very popular as a peaceful and well run place to stay, and for its good stylish food. The care they take with the meals is demonstrated by the way they dress their salads with toasted sunflowers. The blackboard specials are particularly interesting, and might include mussels with smoked bacon and cider (£3.95), pan fried skate with capers and nut brown bitter (£6.50), lamb kidneys with a port wine sauce (£6.95), char-grilled rump of venison with madeira sauce (£8.95), or pan fried strips of beef fillet with green peppercorns (£9.25). Other dishes at lunchtime include soup (£2.65), filled brown baps (from £2.65), rich chicken liver pâté (£3.50), pasta with cotherstone cheese in fresh tomato sauce (£3.95), sausages, black pudding and onion confit (£4.25), ploughman's with their own pickled onions and chutney (£4.95), sautéed chicken livers, bacon and walnuts with fresh pasta (£5.50), steak and kidney pie with mushrooms and ale (£7.50), and puddings like apple and calvados tart or lime meringue pie (£2.95). In the evening there are additional dishes like pork fillet in sherry and cream sauce with fresh pasta (£7.95) or char-grilled chicken breast with garlic butter (£8.50). The beamed traditional bar has old-fashioned seats facing the log fire, a Jacobean oak settle, cream walls decorated with lots of gin traps, some old farm tools and black and white pictures of Romaldkirk at the turn of the century, as well as a grandfather clock, and lots of brass and copper. The smart Crown Room, where bar food is served, has more brass and copper, original coloured etchings of hunting scenes, and farm implements – it was about to be redecorated as we went to press. The hall is hung with wine maps and other interesting prints; no-smoking oak-panelled restaurant. Theakstons Best, Marstons Pedigree and Morlands Old Speckled Hen on handpump, and about eight wines by the glass; good service. The village is close to the superb Bowes Museum and the High Force waterfall, and has an interesting old church. *(Recommended by Paul and Janet Waring, Ian S Morley, E A Thwaite, Dr T H M Mackenzie, R T and J C Moggridge, T and G Alderman, Margaret and Roy Randle, Maysie Thompson, Jack and Heather Coyle, H B Parker, Christopher Beadle; also in Good Hotel Guide)*

Free house ~ Licensees Christopher and Alison Davy ~ Real ale ~ Meals and snacks (12-1.30, 7-9) ~ Restaurant (not Sun evening) ~ (01833) 650213 ~ Children welcome ~ Open 11-3, 5.30-11; closed 25/26 Dec ~ Bedrooms: £56B/£78B

SEAHOUSES (Northumberland) NU2232 Map 10

Olde Ship ★ 🛏 🍺

B1340 coast road

With so much seafaring memorabilia dotted around, you could almost be in a maritime museum, were it not for the fact that this is still very much a fisherman's local; even visitors without the sea in their blood can't help being charmed by the marvellous atmosphere in the warmly welcoming bar, or swept along by the talk of the local mariners. Everywhere you look there are shiny brass fittings, sea pictures and model ships, including a fine one of the North Sunderland lifeboat and a model of Seahouses' lifeboat *The Grace Darling*, as well as ship's instruments and equipment, and a knotted anchor made by local fishermen; all the items are genuine. Even the floor of the saloon bar, with its open fire, is scrubbed ship's decking. The one clear window (the others have stained-glass sea pictures) looks out across the harbour to the Farne Islands, and as dusk falls you can watch the Longstone lighthouse shine across the fading evening sky. There is another low-beamed snug bar, and a small family area at the back. Popular bar food might include sandwiches, soup (£1.75), cheesy baked haddock, devilled chicken in barbecue sauce, a vegetarian dish, or pork and mussels with tomatoes, onions, garlic and piri-piri sauce (all £5.95), and puddings such as clootie dumpling or raspberry pie (£2.95); children's helpings. Service remains prompt and helpful even when they're busy. A good choice of real ales takes in Boddingtons, Longstone Bitter (a tasty ale from a micro-brewery just along the road at Belford), Marstons Pedigree, Morlands Old Speckled Hen, Ruddles Best, Theakstons Best and Youngers No 3. They also have several malt whiskies, a hot toddy and mulled wine in winter, and some uncommon bottled beers; dominoes, trivia and piped music. Pews surround barrel tables in the back courtyard, and a battlemented side terrace with a sun lounge looks out on the harbour. An anemometer is connected to the top of the chimney. You can book boat trips to the Farne Islands Bird Sanctuary at the harbour, and there are bracing coastal walks, particularly to Bamburgh, Grace Darling's birthplace. *(Recommended by Martin Hickes, Paul and Janet Turner, Eric Larkham, P J Hanson, Janet and Geoff Smart, David Atkinson, T and G Alderman, Ian S Morley, James Nunns, June and Tony Baldwin, J E Rycroft, David Austin, Christopher Turner, James Macrae, Julie Peters, Laura Darlington, Gianluca Perinetti, Gordon, Leigh and Gillian Mellor)*

Free house ~ Licensees Alan and Jean Glen ~ Real ale ~ Meals and snacks (12-2, 7-8.30) ~ Restaurant ~ (01665) 720200 ~ Children in restaurant and Locker room ~ Open 11-3, 6-11 ~ Bedrooms: £35B/£70B

STANNERSBURN (Northumberland) NY7286 Map 10

Pheasant 🛏

Kielder Water road signposted off B6320 in Bellingham

Just a mile from Kielder Water, this unpretentious 17th-c stone farmhouse is beautifully located in a peaceful valley. There are picnic table sets in the streamside garden, a pony paddock behind, and quiet forests all around. The red-carpeted largely stripped-stone lounge is traditional, comfortable and attractive, and the separate public bar, similar but simpler, opens into a games room with darts, pool and dominoes; in the evenings there's a happy mix of locals and visitors. There's a no-smoking carpeted country dining room. Besides sandwiches (the toasted ones are popular), good home-cooked bar food includes meat or vegetarian lasagne, steak and kidney pie or seafood pasta (all £5.50), Indonesian style fried rice (£5.95), and cider baked gammon with cumberland sauce (£6.50), with evening dishes like roast breast of duck in cherry sauce or beef fillets en croûte with madeira sauce (£10.50); there's an excellent range of fresh vegetables, and they do a good Sunday lunch. Well kept Ind Coope Burton, Tetleys and occasional guests on handpump, a very good collection of malt whiskies, decent wines, friendly welcoming service. Breakfasts are good. *(Recommended by Chris Rounthwaite, David and Margaret Bloomfield, John Poulter, Paul and Janet Waring, J D K Hyams, D and J Tapper)*

Free house ~ Licensees Walter and Irene Kershaw ~ Real ale ~ Meals and snacks ~ Restaurant ~ (01434) 240382 ~ Children welcome till 8.30 ~ Open 11-3, 5.30-11; winter weekdays 12-2, 6.30-11; closed 25/26 Dec and Mon and Tues during Jan/Feb ~ Bedrooms: £32S/£54S

WARENFORD (Northumberland) NU1429 Map 10

Warenford Lodge

Just off A1 Alnwick—Belford, on village loop road

It's a shame we don't get more reports on this comfortable stone house – although it isn't open at lunchtimes during the week, it's well worth tracking down at other times for the attractively presented and often imaginative home-made bar food. The rather cosmopolitan menu might include home-made soup (£2.20), dim sum with oriental sauce (£3.70), garlic snails (£3.90), lamb and spinach lasagne (£5.70), Thai-style mushrooms and greens on a bed of steamed rice noodles or tagliatelle with a porcini mushroom sauce (£6.15), grilled trout (£6.75), pigeon casserole or salmon fillet (£6.90), and stincotto, an Italian shank of pork roasted with wine and herbs (£10.90), and puddings like fruit terrine (£2.95); decent selection of wines and malt whiskies; good choice of teas. From the outside it looks like an ordinary small stone house – there's no pub sign – so beware of driving straight past. Although quite old the bar looks modern with cushioned wooden seats around pine tables, some stripped stone walls, and a warm fire in the big stone fireplace; steps lead up to an extension which now has comfortable dining tables and chairs, and a big woodburning stove. *(Recommended by Christopher Turner, Laura Darlington, Gianluca Perinetti; more reports please)*

Free house ~ Licensee Raymond Matthewman ~ Meals and snacks (not lunchtimes, except weekends when lunchtime service stops 1.30, or all day Mon) ~ Evening restaurant ~ (01668) 213453 ~ Children in restaurant ~ Open 7-11 (closed weekday lunchtimes and all day Mon except bank holidays), plus 12-2 Sat and Sun

Lucky Dip

Besides the fully inspected pubs, you might like to try these Lucky Dips recommended to us and described by readers (if you do, please send us reports):

Acklington N'land [B6345 Amble—Felton; NU2302], *Railway*: Old photographs of its days as RAF officers' mess, open fire, friendly new landlord and staff, good well presented fresh generous bar food, restaurant *(Jack and Heather Coyle)*

☆ Allendale N'land [Mkt Pl, B6295; NY8355], *Golden Lion*: Friendly old pub with Flowers and Websters Yorkshire, country wines, wide choice of good value food (not Mon) inc vegetarian, partly no-smoking dining area with more room upstairs, two real fires, pictures, old bottles, willow-pattern plates; games area with pool and darts, piped music; children welcome; bedrooms *(JJW, CMW, Eric Larkham)*

☆ Alnmouth N'land [N'land St; NU2511], *Saddle*: Wide choice of generous well cooked keen-priced food inc fresh fish, good puddings and first-class cheeseboard in clean and friendly old pub rambling through several rooms, unpretentious and homely but lively and inviting; well kept S & N and local ales, decent wines, helpful staff, paintings for sale; comfortable bedrooms, good breakfast *(Mrs P Abell, John Oddey, D T Deas, Eric Larkham, Meg and Colin Hamilton, Nigel and Amanda Thorp)*

Alnmouth, *Schooner*: Georgian coaching inn with one busy bar, another quieter with red plush seats, interesting local and nautical pictures, bar food, changing real ale, conservatory, candlelit Italian restaurant *(Teresa and Nigel Brooks, Eric Larkham)*

☆ Anick N'land [signed NE of A69/A695 Hexham junction; NY9665], *Rat*: Quaint little pub, friendly and nicely refurbished, with good home-cooked food from hot counter inc good fresh veg, Sun roasts and puddings, well kept Courage-related ales and Scrumpy Jack cider, lovely north Tyne views, good service, friendly cat; children welcome, pretty garden with well planted boots *(V Green, Chris Rounthwaite, Joan and Stephen Sloan, Eric Larkham)*

Bamburgh N'land [NU1835], *Mizen Head*: Really a hotel, but welcoming pubby lounge bar popular with locals, good value food, Theakstons and Youngers Scotch; quiet piped music; bedrooms *(Annette and Stephen Marsden)*

Barnard Castle, Dur [Market Pl; NZ0617], *Golden Lion*: Generous good value home-cooked lunchtime food inc children's helpings in two roomy and comfortable unpretentious bars, Camerons real ale, children's room; decent bedrooms *(John Fazakerley, BB)*; [by Market Cross], *Kings Head*: Pleasant and quiet, four or five real ales, good helpings of basic bar food; no piped music *(Tony Gayfer)*; [The Bank], *Old Well*: Friendly landlady, good atmosphere, big helpings of food from sandwiches up, baked potatoes filled to request, extremely good chips, Courage and Tetleys ales, restaurants inc no-smoking room; comfortable bedrooms *(M Borthwick, David Musto)*

☆ Barrasford N'land [NY9274], *Barrasford Arms*: Friendly country local with blazing fires in compact bar, good value generous straightforward home cooking, eager licensees, cheery regulars; keg beer and can be smoky; dining room, residents' lounge, children's room; lovely sandstone building with wonderful views, good value bedrooms handy for Hadrian's Wall, good breakfast (but early-morning quarry traffic passes) *(Annette and Stephen Marsden, C Smith, Laura Darlington, Gianluca Perinetti)*

Beadnell N'land [NU2329], *Craster Arms*: Usual bar food quickly served by friendly young staff in roomy pleasant lounge with emphasis on dining, some real ales, games room; children welcome *(Ian and Deborah Carrington)*

☆ Beamish Dur [NZ2254], *Shepherd &*

Shepherdess: Very useful for its position nr outstanding open-air heritage museum; good range of quick fairly priced straightforward food, standard layout with tables around walls, but comfortable, with good service, well kept Vaux Samson and Wards Sheffield Best, decent wines, coal fires; can get crowded, piped music; children welcome, tables and play area with fibreglass monsters out among trees; has been open all day *(R A Hobbs, John and June Gale, John Fazakerley, LYM)*

Beamish [off A693 signed No Place and Cooperative Villas, S of museum], *Beamish Mary*: Friendly down-to-earth 1960s pub with Durham NUM banner in games room, very assorted furnishings and bric-a-brac in bar with Aga; plentiful good value basic bar food and Sun lunch, Hartleys, Theakstons, a beer brewed for them by Big Lamp and several other changing beers; piped music, two dogs, children allowed until evening; quiet lunchtime, lively evening with live music in converted stables concert room (Weds, Fri, Sat); bedrooms *(CMW, JJW, Neil Whitmore, Justin Kelly)*; [far side of Beamish Open Air Museum – paid entry], *Sun*: Turn-of-the-century pub moved from Bishop Auckland as part of the museum; very basic real period feel at quieter times (it can get packed like sardines), with well kept McEwans 80/-, Theakstons Best and Youngers No 3, filled rolls *(Lesley Sones, LYM)*

Belford N'land [Market Pl; village signed off A1 S of Berwick; NU1134], *Blue Bell*: Good service and welcoming atmosphere in family stable bar (the Belford Tavern) with wide choice of sensibly priced straightforward food inc children's and cut-price OAPs' helpings, keg beer, darts, pool and piped music; separate hotel lounge, pleasantly old-fashioned restaurant; children in eating areas, bedrooms *(Arthur and Liz Burt, M J Morgan, Christopher Turner, LYM)*

☆ **Bellingham** N'land [NY8483], *Cheviot*: Good-natured village local with welcoming and hard-working young licensees, inviting open fire, plentiful well prepared bar food, interesting upstairs dining room with kitchen range; reasonably priced bedrooms, good breakfast *(Wayne A Wheeler, J D K Hyams, Gordon)*

☆ **Berwick upon Tweed** N'land [Dock View Rd, Spittal (Tweedmouth); NT9952], *Rob Roy*: Local fish a speciality, not cheap but very fresh, in quiet and cosy seaview pub, fishing-theme traditional bar with roaring fire and polished wood floor, friendly landlord; keg beers but decent wines and good fresh coffee; bedrooms *(Christopher Turner, John and June Gale)*

Berwick upon Tweed [Bridge St], *Barrels*: Wide choice of real ales, short choice of well cooked inexpensive food, pleasant staff, good juke box *(A Keys)*; *Foxtons*: Two-floor bar with good range of wines and whiskies, Caledonian, Deuchars and Timothy Taylors Landlord, wide choice of food, side restaurant *(N E Bushby, W Atkins)*; [Castlegate], *Free*

Trade: A pub for connoisseurs of the original and unspoilt *(David Carr)*

nr Berwick upon Tweed N'land [B6461 towards Paxton – OS Sheet 75 map ref 959526], *Cantys Brig*: Rather modern attractive bar with yachting decor, real ales, reasonably priced fresh food inc local fish and haggis, efficient friendly service, open fire, upstairs dining room overlooking River Whiteadder, tables out on lawn running down to it; rather modern, but nice *(Kurt and Kiki Angelrath)*

Brandon Dur [NZ2439], *Bay Horse*: Welcoming local, huge helpings of good straightforward food at very low prices; keg beer *(Richard Dolphin)*

☆ **Catton** N'land [B6295 N of Allendale; NY8358], *Crown*: Friendly and cosy traditional pub with good value home-cooked food till 10 inc children's and lots of sandwiches, new dining area, roaring log fire, Butterknowle and Theakstons, good teas and coffee, jovial landlord, pool, darts, piped music; small garden; well behaved children and dogs welcome *(JJW, CMW)*

Cheswick N'land [Gt North Rd; NU0347], *Cat*: Comfortable lounge with gas fire and cat ornaments, freshly prepared good value meals and sandwiches, quiet piped music; keg beer, separate bar with darts, children welcome; open all day, bedrooms *(CMW, JJW)*

☆ **Corbridge** N'land [Middle St; NY9964], *Black Bull*: Roomy low-ceilinged pub with wide range of well kept Whitbreads-related and guest ales, country wines, good house wines, good choice of generous food inc interesting dishes, traditional settles on stone floor, mix of comfortable chairs, roaring fire, pleasant staff, friendly civilised atmosphere; open all day *(J D K Hyams, John Prescott, Ian Phillips, Eric Larkham)*

Corbridge [Watling St – former A69 just N of centre], *Wheatsheaf*: Comfortable open-plan pub with banquettes, wide choice of food in pleasantly decorated dining lounge and big conservatory, well kept Darleys Thorne and Vaux Waggledance, good choice of wines and malt whiskies, friendly new licensees; pub games, piped music, children welcome, some picnic tables outside; bedrooms *(Marti Hickes, Stephen, Julie and Hayley Brown, LYM)*

☆ **Cornforth** Dur [Metal Bridge, off B6291 N; NZ3134], *Poachers Pocket*: Former Wild Boar, comfortable and welcoming, with bric-a-brac in main bar, overhead model railway in big friendly family room, enjoyable good value bar food, upstairs bistro, Bass and interesting guest ales, prompt obliging service; garden with big play area and rides on miniature railway; BR intercity trains run by *(Verity Kemp, Richard Mills)*

Croxdale Dur [Butchers Race; A167 S of Durham; NZ2737], *Coach & Horses*: Pleasant lounge with coaching relics, pool room, good choice of Vaux ales, decent wines, fairly wide range of good value food *(Richard Dolphin)*

Darlington Dur [22 Coniscliffe Rd; NZ2915],

Alehouse & Canteen: Praiseworthy newcomer with eight real ales inc three brewed on the premises, good food, good atmosphere *(Mike and Sue Walton)*

Durham [Saddler St], *Brewer & Firkin*: Closest pub to the castle and cathedral, decent food, six well kept ales, alluring atmosphere, interesting memorabilia *(Jim Brunt, Gwen and Steve Walker, Wayne Brindle)*; [84 New Elvet], *Dirty Nellies*: Formerly the City, newly revamped as Irish theme pub – interesting memorabilia, decent food, Tetleys-related ales *(Gwen and Steve Walker)*; [Court Lane, next to courts], *Court*: Recently extended, with Bass-related ales and cheap generous food inc fine chips all day (not Sun; may be a wait when it's packed); pleasant surroundings *(Eddie Mackenzie, Jim Brunt, John Fazakerley)*; [Darlington Rd; S of Nevilles Cross on A167; NZ2743], *Duke of Wellington*: Busy but spacious Victorian-style local popular for wide range of hearty good value food inc vegetarian – tables in bar a bit low for eating, but there is a restaurant; well kept Bass, Worthington and a guest such as Adnams, attentive service; children welcome *(John Fazakerley, Richard Dolphin, Pat Woodward, M Borthwick, Gwen and Steve Walker, John Allsopp)*; [Old Elvet], *Dun Cow*: Unsmart but engaging traditional town pub in pretty black-and-white timbered cottage, cosy front bar, cheap snacks, well kept Whitbreads Castle Eden; children welcome *(Gordon, Eric Larkham, Gwen and Steve Walker, LYM)*; [New Elvet], *Half Moon*: Well kept Bass, Worthington and an interesting guest beer, politely friendly service, some basic snacks even on Sun; comfortable unpretentious lower bar, bare-boards top one, can be a little smoky *(John Fazakerley, Gwen and Steve Walker)*; [Market Sq], *Market*: Two-level pub done out as 1900s tavern, simple wooden furniture, sepia prints, bare boards, S&N ales with a guest such as Jennings Cumberland, well listed foreign bottled beers (one on draught), good value straightforward food *(Dr Terry Murphy, John Fazakerley, Gwen and Steve Walker)*; [opp university library], *New Inn*: Bass ales, reliable food, good student atmosphere *(Richard Dolphin)*

Ebchester Dur [B6309 outside; NZ1055], *Derwent Walk*: Good home-cooked food, five well kept ales, welcoming service, comfortable dark settles and chairs; superb views *(John Oddey)*; [towards Shotley Bridge], *Raven*: Good reasonably priced bar food from good restaurant menu in modern multi-level pub, well kept and comfortable, with valley views from picture windows; bedrooms *(Mrs K Burvill)*

☆ Egglescliffe Clvd [NZ4214], *Pot & Glass*: Three warmly welcoming panelled rooms with some slabby tree-trunk tabletops, stools and settles, well kept Bass and Tetleys, decent wine, friendly staff and locals, good value food; darts, no music; tables on terrace, lovely setting behind church *(C A Hall, Mike and Karen England)*

☆ Eggleston Dur [off B6278 N of Barnard Castle; NY9924], *Three Tuns*: Attractive pub set charmingly by broad sloping Teesdale village green, log fire and some interesting furniture in locals' relaxing traditional beamed bar, generous straightforward food (not Sun evening) in big-windowed back room, Whitbreads Castle Eden and an occasional guest beer; tables on terrace and in garden; children welcome *(Clive Gilbert, LYM)*

Eglingham N'land [B6346 Alnwick—Wooler; NU1019], *Tankerville Arms*: Village dining pub with some stripped stonework, coal fire each end, well kept Stones and Theakstons XB, decent choice of wines and malt whiskies, children welcome, restaurant; tables in garden *(N Bushby, W Atkins, Chris Rounthwaite, LYM)*

Elwick Clv [¼ mile off A19 W of Hartlepool; NZ4532], *Spotted Cow*: Wide choice of good value popular food in pleasantly plush lounge and dining room, several real ales, pleasant spot on village green *(Eddie Edwards)*

Embleton N'land [NU2323], *Dunstanburgh Castle*: Good value dining room meals – curry, game, fresh fish and so forth – in comfortable hotel attractively placed nr magnificent coastline, good waitress service, nice cocktail bar with real ale, several malt whiskies; bedrooms *(Leonard Dixon, Ian Wilson)*; *Greys*: Friendly local with very cheap home-cooked food in small downstairs restaurant – worth the wait; garden *(Leonard Dixon)*; *Sportsman*: Large pub converted from two guest-houses, big terrace, stunning views to Dunstanburgh Castle, good food; bedrooms *(Leonard Dixon)*

☆ Etal N'land [off B6354 SW of Berwick; NT9339], *Black Bull*: Pretty thatched pub in attractive village nr steam railway by ruins of Etal Castle, nice walks; modernised lounge with well kept Lorimers Scotch, Tetleys and Wards Sheffield Best, usual food, landlord with dry wit; can get a bit crowded *(David and Mary Webb, Chris Rounthwaite, Martin Hickes, LYM)*

☆ Fir Tree Dur [A68 West Auckland—Tow Law; NZ1434], *Duke of York*: Wide choice of reliable food in comfortable roadside pub with dining room of cosy wing-chair bar; Bass, Stones and Worthington, good value house wines, cheerful competent staff, racing prints; children welcome, tables outside; bedrooms *(P J Keen, Anthony Bradbury, BB)*

☆ Framwellgate Moor Dur [Front St; NZ2745], *Tap & Spile*: Fine range of rapidly changing well kept beers, decent food at low prices; child-friendly, one room with board games, another with pool and fruit machine *(Richard R Dolphin, Gwen and Steve Walker)*

Great Stainton Dur [NZ3422], *Kings Arms*: Wide range of enjoyable generous food, well kept Whitbreads-related ales with a guest such as Fullers ESB, friendly service, spotless and comfortable; restaurant *(Peter Guy)*

Guisborough Clv [Bow St; between A171 and A173, E of centre; NZ6016], *Fox*: Comfortably refurbished dining bar in modernised coaching inn, good value quickly served generous food, Theakstons Old Peculier, Youngers Scotch and No 3; handy for priory; children welcome, bedrooms *(Andrew and Ruth Triggs, LYM)*; [end of main st], *Seven Stars*: Welcoming, with friendly staff, good cheap generous lunchtime food in generous helpings; also handy for priory *(D J and P M Taylor)*

Hartlepool Clv [Marina Way; NZ5133], *Jacksons Wharf*: Brand new 18th-c replica pub with heavily themed maritime interior, decent straightforward bar food, well kept Camerons; next to Historic Quay Museum *(GSB)*

☆ Haydon Bridge N'land [NY8464], *General Havelock*: Civilised and individually decorated dining pub with limited choice of lunchtime bar food (not Sun), also atmospheric Tyne-view stripped stone restaurant (evenings exc Sun, and Sun lunch) with good interesting if rather pricey full meals; well kept Tetleys, good wines by the glass, efficient friendly service, children and dogs allowed; cl Mon/Tues, also early Jan and Sept, also week after Easter *(Caroline Wright, Chris Rounthwaite, AB, DB, LYM)*

Hett Dur [off A167 S of Durham, nr Sunderland Bridge; NZ2837], *Village*: Much renovated friendly village local, almost unique in being tied to Northern Clubs Federation, with their Bitter and Mild; food in cafe/restaurant area *(Richard Dolphin)*

Hexham N'land [Battle Hill/Eastgate; NY9464], *Tap & Spile*: Two bars, eight real ales (⅓ pint nips available), country wines, cheap but limited weekday lunchtime food; no dogs *(JJW, CMW)*

☆ High Force Dur [B6277 about 4 miles NW of Middleton; NY8728], *High Force*: Beautifully placed high-moors hotel, named for England's highest waterfall nearby and doubling as mountain rescue post; now brewing its own good value Teesdale Bitter and Forest XB, also good choice of bar food (and of malt whiskies), good service, friendly atmosphere, quiz night Fri; children allowed, comfortable bedrooms *(DC, Roxanne Chamberlain, Bryan Woods, Mike and Sue Walton, BB)*

Holwick Dur [back rd up Teesdale from Middleton; NY9027], *Strathmore Arms*: Quiet and cosy unspoilt country pub in beautiful scenery, good reasonably priced standard food, well kept ales inc local Butterknowle, friendly owners, lovely dog called Bisto, open fire, games, books etc; bedrooms, camp site *(Liz and John Soden, Hugh Becker, Dave and Sue Newton)*

Holy Island N'land [NU1343], *Lindisfarne*: Small red plush bar and simple dining room with usual food from local crab sandwiches up, keg beer but remarkable number of malt whiskies, pleasant friendly staff, morning coffee, teas and high teas; unobtrusive piped music, children welcome, well kept garden; bedrooms good value *(Christopher Turner, VK, RM, Leigh and Gillian Mellor, Dorothy and David Young)*; [Marygate], *Ship*: Former Northumberland Arms, now done out with beamery, bare boards, panelling,

maritime/fishing memorabilia; bar with eating area off (food inc vegetarian and good local fish), friendly service, well kept Courage-related ales, good choice of whiskies; children welcome, nice setting; three comfortable Victorian-decor bedrooms *(Tony Dickinson, Kurt and Kiki Angelrath)*

Holystone N'land [NT9503], *Salmon*: Comfortably furnished Coquet Valley local, good value simple food, Vaux Samson, open fire, lively pool room; in attractive countryside close to venerable Lady's Well, good nearby walks *(JJW, CMW, LYM)*

☆ Lanchester Dur [NZ1647], *Queens Head*: Good generous often interesting food (sandwiches on request), well kept Vaux beers, decent wines and friendly and attentive Swedish landlady in village pub with smallish locals' bar and plushly comfortable dining room *(John Fazakerley)*

Longframlington N'land [NU1301], *Granby*: Comfortably modernised two-room pub very popular for very wide choice of generous food inc good vegetarian dishes, good collection of malt whiskies, decent wines, restaurant; bedrooms in main building good, with big breakfasts *(Laura Darlington, Gianluca Perinetti, LYM)*

☆ Longhorsley N'land [Linden Hall Hotel, a mile N of village; NZ1597], *Linden Pub*: Sprucely converted ex-granary pub behind country house conference hotel in extensive grounds; briskly served limited but generous bar food, a couple of well kept Whitbreads-related ales, gallery restaurant, quite a few old enamel advertising signs; children welcome, bedrooms in main hotel *(Mike Pugh, LYM)*

☆ Lowick N'land [B6353, off A1 S of Berwick; NU0139], *Black Bull*: Busy country pub with comfortable and attractive main bar, small back bar, popular dining room with good choice of food inc vegetarian, McEwans and Theakstons ales, friendly helpful service; on edge of small pretty village; three attractive bedrooms *(David and Mary Webb, Christopher Turner, John and Janine Monaghan)*

☆ Middleton in Teesdale Dur [Mkt Pl; NY9526], *Teesdale*: Clean pleasantly worn in lounge bar with good service, good bar food inc good vegetarian choice, well kept Tetleys, log fire; comfortable bedrooms; now run by former landlord's children *(Jack and Heather Coyle, SS)*

Morpeth N'land [High Church; NZ2086], *Sun*: Bustling stonebuilt local, S&N ales, shelves stacked with books for customers to read, comfortable chairs and settles; good value standard food, friendly welcome, pool *(John Oddey)*; [Manchester St], *Tap & Spile*: Two cosy rooms, easy-going and cheerful, with up to ten well kept ales, farm cider, limited choice of good value food made by excellent landlady, fair prices, stripped pine furniture, interesting old photographs, folk music Sun afternoons, dominoes, cards, darts etc, fruit machine; unobtrusive piped music, children welcome, open all day *(K Kennedy, Gordon Harris, Ian and Nita Cooper)*

☆ Newcastle upon Tyne [33 Shields Rd, Byker],

Tap & Spile: Excellent choice of interesting well kept ales in well run traditional pub with games in front bar, quieter solidly furnished back room, decent lunchtime bar food inc sandwiches *(Jim and Maggie Cowell, E A Thwaite, Eric Larkham)*

Newcastle upon Tyne [14 Newgate St], *Alewrx*: Rather eccentric decor and furnishings, good value food inc vegetarian and children's, four well kept ales inc local guest beer; facilities for the disabled *(Eric Larkham)*; [High Bridge E], *Bacchus*: Well kept Stones, Tetleys, Theakstons XB, Youngers IPA and a guest beer, good value food (not Sun), some lovely old mirrors in big panelled front bar with elbow-height tables, lower-ceilinged narrow back area; cosy and comfortable when not too busy *(John O'Donnell, Eric Larkham, Val Stevenson, Rob Holmes, E A Thwaite)*; [Broad Chare, by river], *Baltic Tavern*: Well kept Whitbreads-related ales in spacious and comfortably converted riverside warehouse, warren of separate areas with lots of stripped brick and flagstones or bare boards (as well as plusher carpeted parts), good value bar food *(David Jackson, Val Stevenson, Rob Holmes, LYM)*; [125 Westgate Rd], *Bodega*: Beautifully refurbished to a high standard, keeping interesting features inc two magnificent stained-glass domes; good home-made lunchtime food inc interesting vegetarian, six well kept local beers tapped from the cask *(Eric Larkham)*; [78 Newgate St], *Bourgognes*: Lavishly refurbished, with air conditioning and facilities for the disabled, traditional pub food, Theakstons XB, Newcastle Exhibition and Best and guest beers, friendly service, sedate daytime music; open all day, children allowed Sun lunchtime, DJ Fri – very lively then *(Russell and Carolynne Allen)*; [Chillingham Rd, Heaton; NZ2866], *Chillingham Arms*: Fine woodwork and furnishings, five well kept ales and a couple of guest beers, occasional mini beer festivals, good cheap lunchtime food inc Sun *(Eric Larkham)*; [High Bridge], *Duke of Wellington*: Small, welcoming L-shaped bar, up to ten well kept ales such as Marstons Pedigree, Tetleys and Timothy Taylors, good range of basic bar food, low prices; lots of 19th-c prints and documents, many connected with Wellington; open all day, next to market so gets very busy *(Peter Todd, Eric Larkham)*; [opp Central Stn], *Durty Murphys*: Done up in Irish-theme style, with good bar snacks and friendly staff *(K Kennedy)*; [City Rd, nr Milk Mkt, opp Keelmans Hosp], *Fog & Firkin*: Striking Victorian-style decor in big open-plan two-level pub overlooking quayside, bare boards, nautical decorations, real ales brewed for the pub (by Fly & Firkin brewpub), friendly service even when busy, basic good value food inc vegetarian; facilities for the disabled *(Ian and Nita Cooper, Eric Larkham)*; T&W [St Peters Basin], *Fog on the Tyne*: Overlooking marina, modern but nicely decorated, with maritime pictures; four or five well kept ales, welcoming helpful staff,

changing choice of bar food inc some impressive dishes and al dente veg; piped music *(John, Karen and Graham Oddey)*; [Old George Yard, off Bigg Mkt], *George*: Interesting original core, two-level extension beyond low-ceilinged central area, pleasant atmosphere *(E A Thwaite)*; [Eldon Sq], *George & Dragon*: Busy two-bar pub open all day, friendly staff, lots of games machines, big screen TV, good value cheap lunchtime food *(Russell Allen)*; [Prudhoe Chare, Eldon Sq], *Northumberland Arms*: Open all day, good value food 9-5 in no-smoking eating area, friendly staff, Theakstons XB *(Russell and Carolynne Allen)*; [Bigg Market], *Pig & Whistle*: Big brash evening pub, weird bric-a-brac, cheap beer Mon, friendly staff, loud and busy during weekend entertainment *(Russell and Carolynne Allen)*; [Akenside Hill, under Tyne Bridge], *Pump House*: Good range of cheeses, real ales such as Timothy Taylors, decent food, quick friendly service, tables outside; open all day, happy hour Mon, weekend live music *(Russell and Carolynne Allen)*; [35 The Close], *Quayside*: Friendly Beefeater in converted old warehouse by Tyne, tables outside *(E A Thwaite)*; [7 Strawberry Pl], *Strawberry*: Busy and friendly, with ten well kept real ales, farm cider, continental bottled beers, bar food, open fires, bar billiards, old juke box, pictures of old Newcastle, Sky TV for sports; open all day *(Russell Allen)*; [Westgate Rd], *Tilleys*: Popular with actors, stage hands and audiences from the Tyne Theatre next door; lots of pâtés and cheeses served with baskets of crusty bread; full Jennings range kept well and occasional guest beers *(Eric Larkham)*; [Quayside, by New Law Courts], *Waterline*: Stylish warehouse conversion by Tyne, lots of oak beams and pillars, nooks and crannies, maritime bric-a-brac, oak tables and chairs; welcoming staff, full Theakstons range kept well and tapped from the cask, good value bar food inc good steaks, Italian restaurant open all day, open fires, magician Tues; children welcome *(John Oddey, Russell and Carolynne Allen)*

☆ **Newton by the Sea N'land** [The Square, Low Newton; NU2426], *Ship*: Good genuine local quaintly tucked into top corner of courtyard of old cottages facing beach and sea, nice licensees and atmosphere, good crab sandwiches and ploughman's, keg beers, coffee, tea, pool table, ices served outside in summer; very busy on a hot day, children welcome, tables out on green *(Gordon, Peter Todd, Leonard Dixon, Ian Wilson)*

☆ **North Shields T&W** [103 Hudson St; NZ3468], *Wooden Doll*: Dozens of paintings by local artists, high view of Shields Fish Quay and outer harbour, informal mix of furnishings in bare-boards bar, ales such as Ind Coope Burton, Tetleys and Timothy Taylors Landlord, usual bar food and fresh fish (not Sun evening), largely no-smoking eating area; children welcome till 8, live music Sat, open all day Sat *(J A Stewart, Eric Larkham, E A Thwaite, LYM)*

North Shields [Camden St], *Magnesia Bank*: Big brightly lit bar in well run Victorian pub overlooking Tyne, half a dozen well kept real ales, vast choice of cheerful food (not Sun evening), pleasant atmosphere, open fire, quiet piped pop music, TV, fruit machines, tables outside; children welcome, live music Thurs and Sat *(CMW, JJW, L Dixon, Ben Anderson)*

Otterburn N'land [NY8992], *Percy Arms*: Useful haven with generous often imaginative bar food, friendly waitresses, splendid roaring fire, Theakstons XB and Youngers Scotch; small front lounge; back bar with juke box popular with young locals and soldiers, can be smoky; comfortable bedrooms *(J Roy Smylie, Leigh and Gillian Mellor, H Bramwell)*; *Tower*: 1830s castellated mansion built around 13th-c peel tower, imposing but friendly, with armour, crossbows, stuffed birds and so forth; a hotel, but worth knowing for morning coffee or afternoon tea in plush lounge with lovely open fires; neat public bar, good value bedrooms *(Chris Rounthwaite, LYM)*

☆ **Piercebridge** Dur [B6275 just S of village, over bridge; NZ2116], *George*: So rambling as not to suit disabled people, three bars with five open fires between them, comfortably worn-in solid furnishings, wide choice of generous bar food from sandwiches to good steaks inc vegetarian dishes, Courage-related ales, decent wines, the famous clock that stopped short never to go again, fine riverside garden; children in eating areas, piped music; open all day, good value bedrooms *(Andrew and Ruth Triggs, Paul and Janet Waring, Basil Minson, John Fazakerley, John Poulter, WAH, LYM)*

☆ **Romaldkirk** Dur [NY9922], *Kirk*: Cosy little two-room pub, well worn but clean, with wide choice of interesting good value food (not Tues), friendly staff, well kept Butterknowle and Whitbreads-related beers, good coffee, 18th-c stonework, good log fire, darts, piped popular classics; picnic tables out by green of attractive moorland village; doubles as PO *(Roxanne Chamberlain)*

Running Waters Dur [A181 E of Durham; NZ3240], *Three Horseshoes*: Pleasant old dining lounge with good reasonably priced home-cooked food, views over Durham, Courage-related ales; drinkers may be gently pressed to use the plain public bar; attractive bedrooms *(Meg and Colin Hamilton, Gwen and Steve Walker, John Allsopp)*

☆ **Saltburn by the Sea** Clvd [A174 towards Whitby; NZ6722], *Ship*: Beautiful setting among beached fishing boats, sea views from tasteful nautical-style black-beamed bars and big plainer summer dining lounge; good range of above-average bar food, usually Tetleys on handpump, quick friendly service, good evening restaurant (not Sun), children's room and menu, seats outside; busy at holiday times, smuggling exhibition next door *(WAH, Basil Minson, LYM)*

☆ **Seaton Sluice** Dur [A193 N of Whitley Bay; NZ3477], *Waterford Arms*: Comfortably refitted dining pub specialising in wide choice of very generously served fresh fish and seafood (all day summer Suns, not winter Sun evenings), partly no-smoking restaurant, Wards Sheffield Best and Thorne, Vaux Samson and Waggle Dance, children welcome; piped music; comfortable bedrooms *(Neil Townend, Richard Dolphin, JJW, CMW, Ian and Nita Cooper, LYM)*

☆ **Sedgefield** Dur [Front St; NZ3629], *Dun Cow*: Large attractive village inn with interesting choice of good if not cheap food in two bars and restaurant, welcoming service, S&N and guest ales, good range of whiskies, pleasantly upmarket feel; children welcome; bedrooms sharing bathrooms *(Richard Dolphin)*

Shincliffe Dur [A177, Durham end; NZ2941], *Rose Tree*: Clean and comfortable, with good friendly bustle, wide range of good value substantial food, well kept Vaux ales with a guest such as Marstons Pedigree *(Mrs K Burvill)*; [A177], *Seven Stars*: Comfortable and welcoming village inn with two smartly redecorated bars, one with remarkable fireplace, well kept Wards and Vaux Samson, friendly new landlord, usual bar food, restaurant, some tables outside; attractive village, bedrooms *(Ian and Nita Cooper)*

South Shields T&W [137 Commercial Rd; B1301/B1302; NZ3766], *Dolly Peel*: Well kept Courage Directors, Timothy Taylors Landlord, Youngers No 3, guest ales and lots of malt whiskies in friendly and busy local named after legendary fishwife; two rooms with old photographs, nautical and railway mementoes, good variety of filled rolls, free Sun bar nibbles, bar billiards, local radio or piped pop; children welcome, open all day (cl Sun afternoon) *(Ian Dixon)*

Stamfordham N'land [off B6309; NZ0872], *Bay Horse*: Large comfortable beamed pub at end of green in attractive village, long bar with harness on walls, mainly Whitbreads-related ales, wide range of bar food, good coffee, friendly service *(Tony Dickinson)*

Stanhope Dur [89 Front St (A689); NY9939], *Queens Head*: Friendly two-room local, well kept Hodges Original, Newcastle Exhibition, Theakstons Bitter and XB, bar meals, Sun lunch; bedrooms *(Mr and Mrs M Thompson)*

☆ **Thropton** N'land [NU0302], *Cross Keys*: Friendly little three-room village local, decent pub food, Bass and Hancocks HB, open fires in cosy beamed main lounge, darts, satellite TV; attractive terraced garden looking over village to the Cheviots, tame cockerel, hens, pig and guinea-pig; open all day at least in summer *(Leigh and Gillian Mellor, JJW, CMW, LYM)*

☆ **Tynemouth** T & W [Tynemouth Rd (A193); ½ mile W of Tynemouth Metro stn; NZ3468], *Tynemouth Lodge*: Particularly well kept ales and farm ciders, cheap lunchtime filled rolls and coal fire in genuine-feeling friendly and quiet little Victorian-style pub *(Eric Larkham, LYM)*

Tynemouth [Front St], *Salutation*: Single long bar in handsome former coaching inn's big split-level lounge, lots of mahogany and brass rails, comfortable settles along some walls, six beautifully kept Whitbreads-related ales, friendly staff, good range of standard food *(John Oddey)*

Ulgham N'land [NZ2392], *Forge*: Comfortable and airy lounge opening on to terrace and sheltered neat lawn with play area, cheery high-ceilinged public bar (former village smithy), well kept S&N ales, welcoming efficient service, good straightforward food in attractive dining room *(John Oddey, LYM)*

Walbottle N'land [Hexham Rd; NZ1767], *Original Masons*: Very friendly staff, Joules and Theakstons Best and XB, very well prepared reasonably priced food in bar and restaurant; easy wheelchair access, children welcome, open all day *(Jim and Maggie Cowell)*

☆ **Wall** N'land [NY9269], *Hadrian*: Solidly cushioned two-room bar with wide choice of good bar food inc some unusual dishes, well kept Vaux ESB and Samson, interesting reconstructions of Romano-British life, friendly helpful staff; Victorian dining room; children welcome; bedrooms – back ones quieter, with good views *(Mr and Mrs D W Moss, Guy Consterdine, John Oddey, Dr S W Tham, BB)*

☆ **Warden** N'land [½ mile N of A69; NY9267], *Boatside*: Pleasant friendly dining pub, good range of good food, good service *(Chris Rounthwaite)*

Warkworth N'land [Bridge St; NU2506], *Black Bull*: Well kept beers inc Wards Darleys Thorne and Vaux Waggle Dance, good Italian food night Thurs *(A Keys)*; [23 Castle St], *Hermitage*: Clean, friendly and well run, with generous well served food from sandwiches up, well kept Courage-related beers, cheerful obliging staff, small plush upstairs restaurant *(John Oddey, Eric Larkham, Verity Kemp, Richard Mills, BB)*; [3 Dial Pl], *Masons Arms*: Welcoming thriving local, slick service, good value generous starters and main dishes, well kept Youngers Scotch and No 3; attractive back flagstoned courtyard *(Verity Kemp, Richard Mills, Tony Dickinson)*; [6 Castle Terr], *Sun*: 17th-c hotel below castle in attractive village not far from sea, friendly helpful staff, homely atmosphere, well kept S&N ales, wide choice of reasonably priced good food inc local fish; children welcome, bedrooms with good views *(Leigh and Gillian Mellor)*

Weldon Bridge N'land [signed just off B6344 nr A697 junction; NZ1399], *Anglers Arms*: Pleasant welcoming pub in splendid location, well kept Boddingtons, rather austere decor featuring fish, generous bar food inc good steak and kidney pie; restaurant booked well ahead; bedrooms *(Andrew and Kerstin Lewis, P D R Milner)*

West Mains N'land [A1 at Holy Island exit; NU0542], *Plough*: Friendly, clean pub with straightforward food; bedrooms *(T and G Alderman)*

☆ **West Woodburn** N'land [NY8987], *Bay Horse*: Welcoming service in clean and simple open-plan bar with red plush banquettes and other seats, open fire, well kept Theakstons XB, usual bar food inc vegetarian and children's, games room; children welcome, airy dining room, a couple of picnic tables in riverside garden; only roasts, Sun lunch; cl Mon/Tues lunchtime in winter; clean and comfortable modernised bedrooms *(Russell Grimshaw, Kerry Purcell, SS, LYM)*

☆ **Whalton** N'land [NZ1382], *Beresford Arms*: Very good genuine home cooking at reasonable prices in pleasant civilised bar or dining room, friendly helpful staff, well kept Vaux Lorimers Scotch and Wards; attractive village *(C A Hall, H E and E A Simpson, Jill and Peter Bickley)*

☆ **Whittonstall** N'land [B6309 N of Consett; NZ0857], *Anchor*: Attractively refurbished village pub, welcoming and comfortable, with three well kept ales, good varied food inc very popular Sun lunch, pleasant dining room *(John Oddey, Jack and Heather Coyle)*

Wylam N'land [Station Rd; NZ1265], *Boathouse*: Eight well kept ales inc Timothy Taylors Landlord, generous helpings of good food at sensible prices *(Stephen, Julie and Hayley Brown, Eric Larkham)*

People named as recommenders after the main entries have told us that the pub should be included. But they have not written the report – we have, after anonymous on-the-spot inspection.

Nottinghamshire

Drinks much cheaper than the national average and – in most pubs – relatively low food prices make this county's pubs really good value. For really cheap drinks, the Market in Retford (a splendid choice of well kept ales) stands out. We've found enjoyable brews this year from a new small local brewery – Bramcote, from just outside Nottingham. People on the lookout for interesting beers will find it worth keeping their eyes open for Tynemill pubs: this relatively young small chain specialises in providing a really good choice from little-known breweries, in a pleasant atmosphere – the Lincolnshire Poacher in Nottingham is a good example. Traditionalists will be pleased to find that the food side rarely swamps pubs' identity here; the county seems to specialise in pubs that serve good value food but remain predominantly locals. The Martins Arms at Colston Bassett is very decidedly a dining pub, doing fine meals (but is far from cheap); the French Horn at Upton is another very good dining pub. The unpretentious Victoria in Beeston (another Tynemill pub) has a good line in interesting vegetarian food (with plenty for meat-eaters).

BEESTON SK5338 Map 7

Victoria 🍺

Dovecote Lane, backing on to railway station

This once-derelict railway hotel was carefully converted by the Tynemill group, a small northern chain that specialises in keeping extensive ranges of unusual, mainly independent real ales, in traditional basic pubby interiors. Ten or so well kept changing real ales on handpump here might include Batemans XB, Belvoir, Brains Dark, Bramcote Elsie Moe, Courage Directors, Enville White, Holdens Special, Sam Smiths OB or Taylor Golden Best, with two traditional ciders like Biddenden or Thatchers, over 120 malt whiskies and 20 Irish whiskies, and several wines by the glass. The three downstairs rooms in their original long narrow layout have stained-glass windows, stripped woodwork and floorboards, unfussy decor, a good chatty atmosphere and simple solid traditional furnishings. The lounge and bar back on to the station, and picnic tables in a pleasant area outside look over on to the station platform – the trains pass within feet. The no-smoking area on the left has now been reworked for very reasonably priced food service: Italian-style meatballs with herb and tomato sauce on wholewheat pasta or lincolnshire sausage, bacon and black pudding (£4.50), sauté of tiger prawns, wild mushrooms and mange tout or fried fillets of whiting with lemon butter sauce (£5.50) and loin of pork with cider, mushrooms and cream or Indian mixed grill (£5.95). They offer a particularly imaginative range of about four daily vegetarian dishes such as stuffed vine leaves with halloumi, peach and pine nuts, roasted pepper and red onion tart or grilled goat's cheese with aubergine and pesto (from £4.25). Puddings like apple and rhubarb crumble, spotted dick, summer pudding on raspberry coulis (from £1.95); dominoes, cribbage and occasional piped music. *(Recommended by D Eberlin, Jack and Philip Paxton, TBB, R M Taylor, Elizabeth and Anthony Watts, Chris Raisin, R and A Cooper, David and Shelia, Jane Hosking, Ian Burniston, Andrew Abbott, Andy and Jane Bearsdley, Gary Siddall)*

Free house ~ Licensee Neil Kelso ~ Real ale ~ Meals and snacks (12-8; not Sun evening) ~ Restaurant ~ (0115) 925 4049 ~ Children welcome in restaurant till 8pm ~ Jazz every 2nd Sunday night, occasional impromptu folk sessions ~ Open 11-11(10.30 Sun)

COLSTON BASSETT SK7033 Map 7

Martins Arms 🍴 ♀

Signposted off A46 E of Nottingham

The emphasis at this civilised place is firmly on the well prepared and imaginative food served by smart uniformed staff. It isn't cheap, but it's carefully prepared from fresh, daily-delivered produce, and served with home-made chutneys, vinegars, and petits fours. The bar menu might include soup or sandwiches (£2.95), speciality sandwiches made with open textured bread with olive oil and Italian flours (£3.95), char-grilled spicy toulouse sausages (£6.95), ploughman's (£7.95), fried medallions of pork on an apple and stilton flapjack with cider and calvados jus (£9.95), marinated lamb steak char-grilled with cous cous and a rosemary and port jus or game pie (£10.50), and fillet of salmon in filo pastry with white wine and grain mustard sauce (£11.50), with home-made puddings like crème brûlée, chocolate bread and butter pudding or rich Belgian chocolate tart (£3.50). They have occasional gourmet or wine tasting evenings. The well laid out restaurant is decorous and smart, with well spaced tables. About seven real ales include Batemans XB and XXXB, Marstons Best and Pedigree, with guests like Bass, Black Sheep, Greene King Abbot, Fullers London Pride or Morlands Old Speckled Hen on handpump, a good range of malt whiskies and cognacs, and an interesting wine list. There's an open fire in one of the comfortable bars, which have recently been refurbished with attractive fabrics, and a proper snug; dominoes, chess, cards and croquet, and they can arranged riding and ballooning. The pub is run by the same people as the Crown at Old Dalby, a main entry in the Leicestershire chapter; sizeable garden; no children. *(Recommended by June and Malcolm Farmer, Keith Wright, MT, Jack and Philip Paxton, SS, Norman Smith, A and R Cooper, Gareth Morgan, Keith Archer, Brian Atkin, David and Shelia, Andy and Jane Beardsley, Malcolm Taylor, Brian White, David Raine)*

Free house ~ Licensees Lynne Strafford Bryan and Salvatore Inguanta ~ Real ale ~ Meals and snacks (till Sun evenings) ~ Restaurant (not Sun evening) ~ (01949) 81361 ~ Open 12-3(3.30 Sunday in summer); 6-11 ~ Bedrooms: £35B/£50B

DRAKEHOLES SK7090 Map 7

Griff Inn 🛏

Village signposted from A631 in Everton, between Bawtry and Gainsborough

This handsome 18th-c brick inn was originally built to serve the Chesterfield canal which now passes under the road through a long tunnel – a map in the lounge shows its route – and there are pleasant views from seats in the neatly kept landscaped garden over the canal basin and the flat valley of the River Idle. The civilised and carefully colour-coordinated main lounge bar has small plush seats around its tables, and little landscape prints on silky-papered walls; one bar is no smoking. Tasty bar food includes soup (£1.75), sandwiches (from £2.50), filled baked potatoes (from £2.95), salads (from £3.95), battered haddock (£4.50), steak and kidney pie (£4.75), mixed grill (£7.25), and daily specials (from £4.95). As well as the no-smoking restaurant, there's a more airy brasserie-style summer restaurant and a cosy cocktail bar. Boddingtons, Flowers, and Whitbreads Castle Eden on handpump; friendly service; trivia. *(Recommended by Peter Hartnell, David Carr, Alan and Charlotte Sykes, Mrs Cynthia Archer, R and C E Nightingale)*

Free house ~ Licensees Michael and Barbara Edmanson ~ Real ale ~ Meals and snacks (till 10) ~ Restaurant ~ (01777) 817206 ~ Children welcome ~ Open 11.30-3, 6-11; 12-10.30 Sun; cl Monday Oct-April ~ Bedrooms: £35B/£50B

KIMBERLEY SK5044 Map 7

Nelson & Railway £ 🍺

2 miles from M1 junction 26; Kimberley signposted from exit roundabout, pub in Sation Rd, on right from centre

The unusual name of this splendid two-roomed Victorian pub comes from a shortening of its original name, the Lord Nelson Railway Hotel, in the days when it stood yards away from two competing railway stations. The friendly beamed bar and lounge have an attractive mix of period Edwardian-looking furniture, and are interestingly decorated with brewery prints and railway signs; it can get busy. The Hardys & Hansons Bitter, Classic, Mild and seasonal ales here are particularly well kept, as the brewery is directly opposite; several malt whiskies. Good value straightforward bar food includes sandwiches (from £1.10; hot rolls from £1.45), soup (£1.20), burgers (from £1.65), filled baked potatoes (from £1.95), cottage pie (£2.50), tomato and vegetable tagliatelle or steak and kidney pie (£3.95), chicken curry (£4.50), gammon and egg (£4.95), sirloin steak (£5.95), puddings (£1.65), and children's meals (£1.50); good housekeeping, efficient service; darts, alley skittles, dominoes, cribbage, fruit machine, chess, Scrabble and juke box (which can be quite loud). There are tables and swings out in a good-sized cottagey garden. *(Recommended by M L and G Clarke, K Frostick, Jeanne and George Barnwell, Alan Hopkin, I P G Derwent, Jack and Philip Paxton, Roy Bromell, Wayne Brindle, Alan and Eileen Bowker, TBB, G P Kernan, Gary Roberts, Ann Stubbs, M Carey, A Groocock, M W Turner, Jane Hosking, Ian Burniston)*

Hardys & Hansons ~ Tenants Harry and Pat Burton ~ Real ale ~ Meals and snacks (12-2.30, 5.30-9; 12-6 Sun) ~ (0115) 938 2177 ~ Children in eating area of bar ~ Folk band once a month on Sat ~ Open 11-3, 5-11 Mon-Weds, all day Thurs-Sun ~ Bedrooms: £19/£33

LAXTON SK7267 Map 7

Dovecote

Signposted off A6075 E of Ollerton

A window in the central room by the bar at this small cosy redbrick house looks out over the village to the church tower. This room is decorated with brocaded button-back built-in corner seats, stools and chairs, and a coal-effect gas fire; it opens through a small bay which was the original entry, into another similar room. Around the other side a simpler room with some entertaining Lawson Wood 1930s tourist cartoons leads through to a pool room with darts, juke box, fruit machine, cribbage and dominoes. The pub is next to three huge uniquely surviving medieval open fields, and as part of this ancient farming system the grass is auctioned for haymaking in the third week of June, and anyone who lives in the parish is entitled to a bid – as well as to a drink. A former stable block behind the pub has a visitor centre explaining it all. Simple but tasty bar food in generous helpings includes sandwiches (from £1.50), home-made soup (£1.70), chilli (£4), cottage pie (£4.10), home-made steak and kidney pie or lasagne (£4.20), mushroom stroganoff (£4.25), lemon chicken (£4.60), paella (£4.70), seafood au gratin (£4.90), steaks (from £6.50), and children's meals (£2); pleasant service. Well kept Charles Wells Bombardier and Mansfield Riding and a couple of guests on handpump or electric pump; helpful service. There are white tables and chairs on a small front terrace by a sloping garden with a disused white dovecote, and a children's play area. *(Recommended by John Prescott, Garry Fairclough, Geoffrey and Irene Lindley, R F Wright)*

Free house ~ Licensees Stephen and Betty Shepherd ~ Real ale ~ Meals and snacks ~ (01777) 871586 ~ Children welcome ~ Open 11.30-3, 6.30-11

NORMANTON ON TRENT SK7969 Map 7

Square & Compass

Signposted off B1164 S of Tuxford

This popular low-beamed village pub has a welcoming and chatty licensee, and you'll probably find a couple of locals discoursing even towards the end of the session. The bar has fresh flowers and an attractive grandfather clock, and is divided by an enormous woodburning stove in a central brick fireplace. There are several more or less separate snug areas, alcoves and bays, mainly with green plush furnishings, farming photographs, a flowery red carpet, red curtains and roughcast shiny cream walls; piped music. Good value bar food includes soup (£1.10), sandwiches (from £1.15), burgers (from £1.50), home-made pâté (£2.45), steak and kidney pie (from £4.10), mushroom and nut fettucine or vegetarian curry (£4.25), chicken kiev (£4.50), 8oz sirloin steak (£7.25), with a couple of blackboard specials like pork in ginger or devilled kidneys (£4.25), puddings (from £1.40), and children's meals (from £1.60); Sunday roast. Well kept Adnams, Stones and a guest on handpump or electric pump. The public side has pool, table skittles, cribbage, dominoes, juke box. Outside, there are seats and a children's play area with wendy house, swings, and Mother Hubbard boot house and you can camp here. *(Recommended by Thomas Nott, R C Wiles, Derek and Sylvia Stephenson, David and Mary Webb, Tony Gayfer, Helen and Ian Cookson, Keith Wright, Mike and Maggie Betton, L R Jackson)*

Free house ~ Licensee Janet Lancaster ~ Real ale ~ Meals and snacks (traditional Sunday lunch only on Sunday) ~ Restaurant ~ (01636) 821439 ~ Children welcome ~ Open 12-3, 6-11, 12-11 Sat ~ Family bedroom: £20S

NOTTINGHAM SK5640 Map 7

Fellows Morton & Clayton £

54 Canal Street (part of inner ring road)

There's a good pubby atmosphere at this carefully converted old canal building, with screens of wood and stained glass over the counter in the softly lit bar, and dark blue plush seats built into alcoves, wooden tables, some seats up two or three steps in a side gallery, and bric-a-brac on the shelf just below the glossy dark green high ceiling; a sympathetic extension provides extra seating. Satisfying and very good value lunchtime bar food includes filled rolls (from 90p), home-made soup (£1.25), ploughman's (from £2.40), burgers (from £2.50), cauliflower cheese (£2.95), home-made steak and kidney pie (£3.25), home-made lasagne (£3.60), freshly battered haddock (£3.95), tandoori chicken (£4.25), and rump steak (£5.95); prompt, friendly service. Well reproduced nostalgic pop music, trivia, fruit machine and maybe newspapers on a rack. From a big window in the quarry tiled glassed-in area at the back you can see the little brewery that makes their own real ales: Samuel Fellows and Matthew Claytons. They also have Boddingtons, Fullers Chiswick, Morlands Old Speckled Hen, Timothy Taylor Landlord, Wadworths 6X and Whitbreads Castle Eden on handpump. Outside there's a terrace with seats and tables. In the evening it's popular with a younger crowd. The canal museum is nearby, and Nottingham station is just a short walk away. *(Recommended by Alan Hopkin, Norma and Keith Bloomfield, R M Taylor, Stephen and Julie Brown, Jack and Philip Paxton, M Joyner, Richard Lewis, Andy and Jane Beardsley, Jane Hosking, Ian Burniston)*

Own brew (Whitbreads) ~ Lease: Les Howard ~ Real ale ~ Lunchtime meals and snacks (11.30-6.30) ~ Restaurant (not Sun evening) ~ (0115) 9506795 ~ Children welcome in restaurant ~ Open 11-11

Lincolnshire Poacher ▟

Mansfield Rd; up hill from Victoria Centre

A splendid arrangement with Batemans allows this cheery town pub to serve Bass, Marstons Pedigree and four guest ales alongside perfectly kept Batemans XB, XXXB, Salem Porter, Valiant, and Victory Ale on handpump; also good ciders, and over 70 malt whiskies and 10 Irish ones. The traditional big wood-floored front bar has wall settles and plain wooden tables, and is decorated with breweriana; it opens on to a plain but lively room on the left, from where a corridor takes you down to the chatty panelled back snug; cribbage, dominoes, cards, piped Irish music. Every day they offer about two dozen generously served interesting daily specials, about half of them vegetarian: the choice might include hummus and pitta bread with olives and salad (£3.50), vegetable pie (£3.75), cajun chicken salad, lincolnshire sausages and mash or smoked trout (£4.25); Sunday roast (£4.75); no chips, and efficient, pleasant service. It can get busy in the evenings when it's popular with a

younger crowd. A conservatory overlooks tables on a large terrace behind.
(Recommended by Chris Raisin, Alan Hopkin, Graham Fogelman, Derek and Sylvia Stephenson, Mr and Mrs Blackbourn, R M Taylor, Jack and Philip Paxton, Jane Hosking, Ian Burrniston, Andy and Jane Beardsley, Richard Lewis, G P Fogelman)

Batemans ~ Lease: Paul Montgomery and Amelia Bedford ~ Real ale ~ Meals and snacks (12-3, 5-8; not evenings Sat or Sun) ~ (0115) 9411584 ~ Children welcome in conservatory till 8pm ~ Occasional live entertainment ~ Open 11-3, 5-11; 11-11 Sat; 12-10.30 Sun in summer

Olde Trip to Jerusalem ★

Brewhouse Yard; from inner ring road follow The North, A6005 Long Eaton signpost until you are in Castle Boulevard then almost at once turn right into Castle Road; pub is up on the left

The name refers to a tradition that 12th-c crusaders used to meet on this site on the way to the Holy Land; the present building is mainly 17th c, though its unique upstairs cavern bar may have served as cellarage for an early medieval brewhouse which stood here. This bar is cut into the sandstone rock below the castle, its panelled walls soaring narrowly into the dark chasm above; unfortunately, this part is often closed at lunchtime. The friendly downstairs bar is also mainly carved from the rock, with leatherette-cushioned settles built into the dark panelling, barrel tables on tiles or flagstones, and more low-ceilinged rock alcoves. Well kept real ales include Hardys & Hansons Kimberley Best, Best Mild and their cellarman's cask (brewed every two months or so), and Marstons Pedigree on handpump. Home-made bar food includes cobs and sandwiches (from £1.25), filled baked potatoes (from £2.50), giant yorkshire puddings with lots of fillings (£4.45), and daily specials such as Chinese chicken or vegetable pasta with a sundried tomato sauce (£5.50) and chicken and broccoli bake (£5.95); cribbage, chess, fruit machine, ring-the-bull; seats outside. No children. *(Recommended by Stephen and Julie Brown, R M Taylor, Vicky and David Sarti, N Gilbourne, Howard James, Andy and Jane Beardsley, Jane Hosking, Ian Burniston, Richard Lewis, Jack and Philip Paxton)*

Hardys & Hansons ~ Manager Patrick Dare ~ Real ale ~ Lunchtime meals and snacks (till 4pm; not Sun) ~ (0115) 9473171 ~ Open 11-11; 12-10.30 Sun; cl Sept-Dec 1996

RETFORD SK6980 Map 7

Market ◗

West Carr Road, Ordsall; follow Retford Leisure Centre sign off A620 W, then after West Carr Road Industrial Estate sign on your right take first left turning up track which – if you look closely – is signed for the pub; or, on foot, from Retford Rly Stn follow footpath under S of frontage, turn R at end

Don't be put off by the unexceptional-looking exterior or the surprising location of this friendly pub, named after the cattle market which had this site before it became a light industrial estate. It's not that easy to find, but well worth the effort for their marvellous range of up to 14 well kept beers with helpful notes detailing each brew: Adnams Broadside and Mayday, Bass, Batemans, Boddingtons, Marstons Pedigree, Theakstons Best and XB, Thwaites White Oak, Theakstons Black Bull, Timothy Taylor Landlord, Youngers No 3 and guest beers on handpump. Very good value and tasty home cooked bar food includes sandwiches, hot beef roll (£1.65), burgers (from £3.10), home-made pie (£4.25), steak (£5.95), and their popular fresh Scarborough haddock weighing over a pound (£8.50); cheery and obliging service. The cosy bar has green plush wall banquettes and dimpled copper or dark wood tables, and pantiles over the bar servery, with an open fire at one end and a little blue plush snug at the other. A spacious conservatory dining room opens off this, and in turn gives on to a small terrace with white tables; dominoes, cribbage and piped music. *(Recommended by Virginia Jones, Nick Alexander, David Carr, CMW, JJW; more reports please)*

Free house ~ Licensee Raymond Brunt ~ Real ale ~ Meals and snacks (till 10) ~ Restaurant ~ (01777) 703278 ~ Children in eating area of bar ~ Occasional live music ~ Open 11-3, 6-11; 11-11 Sat

UPTON SK7354 Map 7

French Horn

A612

This warm and friendly bustling dining pub is popular for a changing range of very well prepared bar food. Most tables are laid for eating, and you may need to book even during the week: sandwiches (from £1.95), soup (£1.55), mushrooms stuffed with stilton in a port and redcurrant sauce (£2.85), steak pie (£4.50), and very good specials like sweet and sour rack of ribs (£5.25), kebabs in chilli sauce (£5.25), grilled sea bream with prawns (£5.65), guinea fowl in a black cherry sauce or duck breast on a warm salad (£7.95), poached salmon in a cream and dill sauce (£7.25), lemon sole with lime and mango butter (£8.95), and lots of puddings like coffee meringue or white chocolate profiterole gateau (£2.85). Usefully they also do a range of sandwiches and hot snacks all afternoon. The neat and comfortable open-plan bar has a nicely relaxed feel, with cushioned captain's chairs, wall banquettes around glossy tables, and watercolours by local artists on the walls. Well kept Vaux Waggle Dance, Wards, Darleys Thorn and a guest like Greene King Abbot on handpump, and several wines by the glass; staff are friendly and efficient; piped music. The big sloping back paddock, with picnic tables, looks over farmland. *(Recommended by Anthony Barnes, Jack Morley, Alan Hopkin, A F and J Gifford, Brian and Jill Bond, Sarah and Peter Gooderham, Jack and Philip Paxton, Phyl and Jack Street, David Caudwell, Alan and Eileen Bowker)*

Wards ~ Licensee Joyce Carter ~ Real ale ~ Meals and snacks (12-2, 6-9.45; light snacks 2-6) ~ Restaurant ~ (01636) 812394 ~ Children welcome ~ Open 11-11; 12-10.30 Sun

WELLOW SK6766 Map 7

Olde Red Lion

Eakring Road; pub visible from A616 E of Ollerton

A fixed feature on the green outside this old 16th-c pub is the tremendously tall brightly spiral-painted maypole which confirms that May Day celebrations are still a lively part of this conservation village's life. Of four well kept real ales, one is always from the local Maypole brewery (usually Lions Pride, brewed specially for the pub), alongside guests such as Courage Directors, Ruddles Best and County or Marstons Pedigree on handpump. The comfortably furnished series of friendly low-beamed rooms have photographs tracing the building's development on the partly panelled walls. Bar food is very good value, and is served in really generous helpings: good sandwiches (from £1.60), scampi tails, pasta with tomato or basil coulis or home-made steak and kidney pie (£4.50), lasagne or cumberland sausage (£4.95), garlic and herb butterfly chicken breast (£5.95), halibut steak (£6.95), steaks (from £8.95), daily specials and children's menu (£1.95); best to book for Sunday lunch; the dining area is no smoking; quick service; dominoes, table skittles. An L-shaped strip of grass above the car park has picnic tables under cocktail parasols, and a set of swings. *(Recommended by R Davies, V Leach, Andrew and Jo Litten, Keith and Margaret Kettell, A and R Cooper, Derek and Sylvia Stephenson, Ants Aug, Jack and Philip Paxton, Gordon Tong, M Joyner, David and Shelia)*

Free house ~ Licensee Richard Henshaw ~ Real ale ~ Meals and snacks (till 10) ~ Restaurant ~ (01623) 861000 ~ Children in eating area and restaurant ~ Occasional folk evenings and summer Morris dancers ~ Open 11.30-3, 5.30-11

Pubs with particularly interesting histories, or in unusually interesting buildings, are listed at the back of the book.

Lucky Dip

Besides the fully inspected pubs, you might like to try these Lucky Dips recommended to us and described by readers (if you do, please send us reports):

Beeston [Derby Rd; SK5338], *Nurseryman*: Open all day for useful range of good value food *(Geoffrey and Irene Lindley)*

Bingham [Church St; SK7039], *Chesterfield Arms*: Large comfortable open-plan pub with semi-enclosed areas for groups, quiet and lively ends, welcoming licensee, reasonable choice of food, Greenalls/Shipstones ales; bedrooms *(Elizabeth and Anthony Watts)*

☆ **Blyth** [SK6287], *White Swan*: Well kept Whitbreads-related ales esp Castle Eden, good food from sandwiches up inc good fresh fish, in cosy neatly kept pub with big open fires, friendly landlord; may be piped music; good A1 break, by duck pond *(Ian Finney)*

Bramcote [Derby Rd; junction A6007/B5010; SK5037], *Sherwin Arms*: Large prewar roadhouse with comfortable banquettes, wide choice of good value food (not Sun evening) inc two-for-one bargains, well kept Boddingtons, Greenalls Original and Shipstones, weekly guest beer often from small brewery, picnic tables outside; piped music can be loud *(JJW, CMW, Dave Tapp, Mike and Penny Sanders)*

Brinsley [Cordy Lane (A608); SK4548], *Yew Tree*: Large well appointed pub with helpful staff, wide-ranging nicely presented good value food, Hardys & Hansons ales *(Geoffrey and Irene Lindley)*

Carlton on Trent [Ossington Rd; signed just off A1 N of Newark; SK7964], *Great Northern*: Large busy local next to railway line, comfortable and welcoming, with lots of railway memorabilia, toys in large family room; Mansfield Riding, local Springhead and guest ales, decent food inc good fish and chips, small dining area, good service; play area in garden *(Jack and Philip Paxton, A M Pring, Chris Westmoreland)*

Clipstone [Old Clipstone; B6030 Mansfield—Ollerton; SK6064], *Dog & Duck*: Good value basic home cooking in three-roomed pub with comfortable blue plush seating, brass, copper, amazing teapot collection, family dining room, well kept Home ales and Theakstons XB, friendly service, daily papers, conservatory, some seats outside *(JJW, CMW)*

Costock [off A60 Nottingham—Loughborough; SK5726], *Red Lion*: Refurbished early 20th-c pub open all day for good value food, Shipstones and Tetleys ales, family room with games machines, popular locals' bar; big garden with trees and play equipment *(CMW, JJW)*

Cuckney [High Croft; SK5671], *Greendale Oak*: Good range of reasonably priced bar food (not weekend evenings) from sandwiches up, swift service even when very busy midweek lunchtime, roomy but cosy and friendly L-shaped bar, good coffee, popular evening restaurant; bedrooms *(Peter and Audrey Dowsett, Geoffrey and Irene Lindley, Denise Smith)*

☆ **East Bridgford** [Kneeton Rd, off A6075; can also be reached from A46; SK6943], *Reindeer*: Popular village local with beamed dining bar, well kept Ruddles Best and County and Charles Wells Bombardier, good generous food cooked to order (so may be a wait), separate restaurant, log-effect gas fires; children welcome *(Mrs K E Nicholson, Derek and Sylvia Stephenson, Andy and Jill Kassube, Elizabeth and Anthony Watts, BB)*

☆ **Elkesley** [just off A1 S of Blyth; SK6975], *Robin Hood*: Big helpings of good food inc imaginative dishes in well furnished lounge/dining room, games machines and pool in public bar; well kept Whitbreads-related ales, friendly efficient service, picnic tables and play area in garden by A1 – though one reader regularly flies here (to Gamston) instead, for lunch *(Christopher Turner, Arnold and Maureen East, JJW, CMW)*

☆ **Epperstone** [SK6548], *Cross Keys*: Friendly old small two-bar village pub, locally popular for good value hearty home-cooked food esp pies and outstanding ham rolls; well kept Hardys & Hansons beers, cheerful service; pretty village, pleasant countryside *(Moira and John Cole, Norma and Keith Bloomfield, Andy and Jill Kassube)*

Farnsfield [A614 Nottingham—Ollerton; SK6456], *White Post*: Spacious well furnished inn, generous bar food at fair prices, good value wine specials, restaurant *(Geoffrey and Irene Lindley)*

Gotham [off A453 S of Nottingham; SK5330], *Cuckoo Bush*: Cosy and friendly 19th-c pub, L-shaped lounge bar with pictures, plates etc, quiet piped music, limited good value food, well kept Bass, sensibly segregated darts and TV (with sofa); picnic tables and barbecue in small garden *(JJW, CMW)*

☆ **Gunthorpe** [Trentside; SK6844], *Tom Browns*: Modern brick bar over road from River Trent, wok cooking in glass booth, decent bar food (not Sat/Sun evening) too, S&N ales and guest beers such as Black Sheep Riggwelter and Woodfordes Wherry and Great Eastern, easygoing atmosphere, log fire; loud well reproduced funky pop music; restaurant, Sun carvery *(Andy and Jill Kassube, Nigel Lawrence, David and Shelia, BB)*

☆ **Lambley** [Church St; SK6245], *Woodlark*: Well preserved and interestingly laid out, careful extension into next house giving extra lounge/dining area, good value lunches and more ambitious evening meals, cheerful welcome, well kept S&N ales, wide range of pub games inc pool room, table skittles and skittle alley; children in annexe *(Alan and Eileen Bowker, BB)*

☆ **Maplebeck** [signed from A616/A617; SK7160], *Beehive*: Snug little unspoiled beamed country tavern, traditional furnishings, open fire, free antique juke box, well kept Mansfield Riding and Old Baily, tables on small terrace with flower tubs and grassy bank running down to small stream – very peaceful; play area with swings *(JJW, CMW)*

☆ Mapperley [Plains Rd (B684); SK6043], *Travellers Rest*: Lots of nooks and crannies in cosy bar with interesting feature curtains, changing ales such as Charles Wells Bombardier, Morlands Old Speckled Hen, Theakstons Best, Mild, Old Peculier and XB and Wadworths XB, wide choice of good value food all day (not after 2 Sun/Mon) inc vegetarian and children's, good ordering system, popular lunchtime no-smoking area, friendly welcoming staff, back family building with adjacent play area, garden; open all day *(R M Taylor)*

☆ Morton [SK7251], *Full Moon*: Rambling 16th-c local, comfortably enlarged but not spoilt, friendly and atmospheric, very popular even midweek for good fairly priced food inc fish, vegetarian, Indian specialities and lots of puddings; well kept Theakstons and guest beers, enthusiastic welcoming landlord; children welcome, delightfully out-of-the-way hamlet *(Geoffrey and Irene Lindley, Jack Morley)*

Nether Langwith [Queens Walk; just off A632; SK5370], *Jug & Glass*: Pleasant and friendly 15th-c pub with picnic tables out facing village stream and paddling pool, lovely hanging baskets; dark-beamed lounge with lots of brass, copper, plates and pictures, wide choice of reasonably priced basic pub food (inc take-aways), Hardys & Hansons ales, piped music, public bar with pool, separate restaurant *(JJW, CMW)*

Newark [19 Kirkgate; SK8054], *Old Kings Arms*: Pleasantly refurbished by Marstons, opened-up vaulted-ceiling bar with extra room at the back, plentiful cheap straightforward food, well kept Marstons ales, upstairs partly no-smoking eating area *(David and Shelia, LYM)*

Normanton on Soar [village signed from A606; SK5123], *Plough*: Popular two-bar mock-Tudor Big Steak pub in beautiful setting by River Soar, nice atmosphere and decorations, well kept Marstons Pedigree and Tetleys, attentive friendly staff – good local atmosphere when the diners have left; family room, play area *(R and A Cooper, Chris Raisin)*

☆ Nottingham [18 Angel Row; off Market Sq], *Bell*: Quaint low-beamed 15th-c pub enjoyed by all ages, Bass, Eldridge Pope Royal Oak, Jennings, Marstons Pedigree, Theakstons Old Peculier and a guest like Mansfield Old Baily kept well in extraordinarily deep sandstone cellar, three bustling timbered and panelled bars (very crowded and maybe smoky late evening), ancient stairs winding up to calmer raftered upstairs room with nice window seats used as lunchtime family restaurant – good value simple well presented lunchtime food; good value wines, friendly hard-working staff; trad jazz Sun lunchtime (rolls only then), Mon and Tues evenings; open all day weekdays

(Norman Smith, Geoffrey and Irene Lindley, Elizabeth and Anthony Watts, R M Taylor, Chris Raisin, LYM)

☆ Nottingham [40 Broad St; corner of Lower Parliament St, on inner ring rd], *New Market*: Austerely neo-classical facade, well kept S&N ales, interesting array of gins from magnificent engraved bottles, comfortable back bar with carved fittings, open fire in snug, occasional Victorian or Edwardian themed entertainment, efficient staff, good value food inc some interesting dishes *(Russell and Carolynne Allen, BB)*

Nottingham [2 Canal St], *Canal*: Stylishly renovated pub with interesting old canal-life photographs, Batemans, Deakins Stag, Everards Beacon, Mansfield Old Baily, Bitter, Riding and Mild and guest beers, good friendly staff, meals, November beer festival *(Richard Lewis, R M Taylor)*; [273 Castle Bvd, Lenton; SK5438], *Grove*: Busy and studenty, upstairs real ale bar with particularly well kept Theakstons XB and sports TV, good food inc big pies and yorkshire puddings, interesting bottled beers and brewery memorabilia, pleasant staff *(Anna Brewer, Russell and Carolynne Allen)*; [North Sherwood St], *Hole in the Wall*: Refurbished by Mansfield as traditional ale house (shiny bare boards etc) with their full range of beers and up to three guests, reasonably priced conventional bar food, friendly landlord *(R M Taylor, Richard Lewis)*; [Trent Bridge], *Larwood & Voce*: On the edge of the cricket ground, with reasonably priced bar food and well kept Theakstons *(Andy and Jill Kassube, N S Smith)*; [Wellington Circus], *Limelight*: Lively bar and restaurant attached to Playhouse theatre, nine constantly changing well kept ales, good choice of reasonably priced food, urbane atmosphere, occasional modern jazz *(Richard Lewis, Derek and Sylvia Stephenson, R M Taylor)*; [Lower Mosley St, New Basford], *Lion*: Recently reopened after major renovation, with good choice of good home-cooked food and sandwiches, very wide range of real ales – an oasis for the area *(Colin Sims)*; [Alfreton Rd], *Red Lion*: A dozen interesting well kept ales, good reasonably priced food with Tues supper bargain, traditional atmosphere, Sun breakfast with papers; open all day, Mon quiz night *(David and Shelia, Leichen A Bauke, Steve Powell)*; [Maid Marion Way], *Salutation*: Ancient back part with beams, flagstones and cosy corners, plusher modern front, cheap cheerful food, up to a dozen changing ales inc interesting ones, sensible prices and good atmosphere *(Keith Stevens, N Gilbourne, Graham Bush, BB)*; [1 Ilkeston Rd (A52 towards Derby)], *Sir John Borlase Warren*: Traditional local with several connecting rooms, lots of old prints, interesting Victorian decorations and fittings, well kept Greenalls Original, Shipstones and Tetleys, cheap lunchtime bar food, no-smoking eating area, tables in back garden with barbecues; children welcome (not Fri/Sat evenings) *(Alan Hopkin, Brian White, Jane*

Hosking, Ian Burniston, LYM); [Sheriffs Way, Queensbridge Rd], *Tom Hoskins:* Real ale pub with good well kept choice inc Hoskins' own range and guest Milds *(Richard Lewis, R M Taylor)*

Nuthall [Nottingham Rd (B600, away from city), off A610 nr M1 junction 26; SK5144], *Three Ponds:* Friendly and tastefully refurbished Hardys & Hansons roadhouse with garden and play area, well kept Best, Best Mild and Classic on handpump, wide range of good value food with cheaper meals for OAPs, good staff, good coffee; piped music may obtrude; big back garden with play area *(JJW, CMW, Kevin Jackson, Mike and Penny Sanders)*

Ollerton [Market Pl; off A614; SK6667], *White Hart:* Welcoming refurbished village local, opp church nr watermill; good choice of reasonably priced food, well kept ales; handy for Sherwood Forest *(Geoffrey and Irene Lindley)*

Orston [Church St; SK7741], *Durham Ox:* Cosy and welcoming split-level open-plan local, tasty rolls, well kept real ales, interesting collection of whisky bottles, local photographs, tables outside (and hitching rails for horses) *(R M Taylor)*

Radcliffe on Trent [Main St; SK6439], *Round Oak:* A dozen mainly Whitbreads-related ales, generous reasonably priced food, comfortable seating *(R M Taylor)*

✩ Ranby [just off A1 by A620 Worksop—E Retford; SK6580], *Chequers:* Nice building in superb canalside spot, delightful waterside terrace, some mooring, weekend boat trips; well kept beer, cheerful service, attractive and comfortable inside, dining room with farm tools and bric-a-brac; children welcome, open all day, reasonably priced food noon-10 *(Mr and Mrs Buckley, David Campbell, Vicki McLean)*

✩ Ravenshead [177 Main Rd (B6020); SK5956], *Little John:* Well organised modern pub with comfortable airy lounge, good value bar food, games in smaller public bar, aquarium between bars, well kept Mansfield, restaurant; weekend barbecues, no dogs *(JJW, CMW, LYM)*

✩ Scaftworth [A631 Bawtry—Everton; SK6692], *King William:* Welcoming country pub, three rooms with old high-back settles and plain tables and chairs, attractive pictures; well kept Whitbreads-related ales, decent home cooking, darts and pool, friendly little dog; big garden, play area *(David Alcock, JJW, CMW, LYM)*

Selston [Church Ln, nr M1 junction 27; SK4553], *Horse & Jockey:* Very traditional (despite the new indoor lavatories and kitchen), with up to ten real ales tapped from the cask, bank hol beer festivals, decent straightforward food, small play area; can be a bit smoky, open all day Mon and Sat *(JP, PP, Derek and Sylvia Stephenson)*

Shireoaks [in grounds of Shireoaks Hall, Thorpe Lane; SK5580], *Hewett Arms:* Attractively modernised 18th-c coach house by two carp lakes, two rooms with

woodburners, plush blue sofas with contrasting white wood tables and chairs, conservatory with assorted greenery, upper room; daily papers, wide range of food, welcoming licensee, four real ales, fresh coffee; quiet piped music, children welcome *(CMW, JJW)*

✩ Southwell [Church St (A612); SK6953], *Bramley Apple:* Friendly prompt service, generous good value food inc two-sitting Sun carvery and fresh fish, very crisp veg, well kept Mansfield and guest ales, attractively worked Bramley apple theme, eating area screened off by stained glass; bedrooms *(Norma and Keith Bloomfield, Miss E Evans, G P Kernan, BB)*

Southwell [Church St], *Hearty Goodfellow:* Good value food (not Weds evening) inc good Sun roast – open all day Sun; Everards ale, garden with play area *(JJW, CMW)*

Staunton in the Vale [SK8043], *Staunton Arms:* Friendly country pub, well kept Marstons Pedigree, good value food with imaginative French touches in cosy bar and restaurant *(Peter Burton, R M Taylor, Nigel Hopkins)*

Strelley [offf A6002 nr M1 junction 26; SK5141], *Broad Oak:* Good value dining pub, Hardys & Hansons Bitter, Classic and Mild, lots of partitioned areas, comfortable banquettes, OAP specials, no piped music, picnic tables outside, play area in back garden; no dogs *(CMW, JJW)*

Sutton in Ashfield [bypass; SK5059], *Snipe:* Well furnished popular family pub, good menu, reasonable prices, good coffee; unobtrusive piped music; play areas inside and out *(Peter and Audrey Dowsett);* [Church Hill], *Staff of Life:* Comfortable, with new dining room, wide choice of reasonably priced food, quick service; quiet piped music *(Peter and Audrey Dowsett)*

✩ Thurgarton [Southwell Rd (A612); SK6949], *Red Lion:* Wide choice of good value generous food, particularly well kept Mansfield ales, lovely fire, roomy bars and restaurant; pleasant garden, children welcome *(Elizabeth and Anthony Watts, M J Radford, Geoffrey and Irene Lindley)*

Toton [Nottingham Rd; SK5034], *Manor:* Good value Tom Cobleigh dining pub with limited choice of well prepared tasty food, friendly efficient service, big no-smoking area, Boddingtons, Flowers IPA, Ruddles County, Worthington and guest ales, several cheap wines by bottle; handy for Attenborough Nature Reserve – good birdwatching, fine walks *(Mike and Penny Sanders)*

✩ Upton [Main St (A612); SK7354], *Cross Keys:* Rambling heavy-beamed bar with good welcoming service, lots of alcoves, central log fire, masses to look at from sporting cartoons and local watercolours to decorative plates and metalwork, interesting medley of furnishings; well kept Batemans XXXB, Boddingtons, Brakspears, Marstons Pedigree and local Springhead, decent wines; friendly dog, unobtrusive piped music, folk evenings; children in back extension with carved pews or dovecote restaurant *(W D Crane, Derek and Sylvia Stephenson, Duncan Small, D R E Berlin, A C Morrison, LYM)*

☆ **Watnall Chaworth** [3 miles from M1 junction 26: A610 towards Nottingham, left on to B600, then keep right; SK5046], *Queens Head:* Tastefully extended old pub with wide range of good value food, well kept Home Bitter and Mild, Theakstons XB and Old Peculier, efficient friendly service; snug bar and dining area, beams and stripped pine, coal fires; fruit machine, piped music; picnic tables in spacious garden with big play area; open all day Fri/Sat *(N Gilbourne, Mike and Penny Sanders)*

Wellow [SK6766], *Durham Ox:* Comfortable, warm and friendly, with several real ales inc interesting guest beer, popular food; handy for Rufford Country Park *(Peter and Audrey Dowsett)*

West Markham [Sibthorpe Hill (B1164, nr A1/A57/A638 roundabout N of Tuxford); SK7272], *Royal Oak:* Mansfield Landlords Table dining pub with standard menu,

modern bar and dining areas; open all day, real ales inc Dark Mild, friendly staff; civilised journey respite, views over wheatfields, play area outside *(David and Ruth Hollands)*

Widmerpool [just off A46/A606; SK6328], *Pullman Diner:* Converted railway station with strong emphasis on bar and restaurant food, Sun carvery, Ruddles Best and County *(Paul and Helen Burrows)*

Worksop [off Mansfield Rd; SK5879], *Manor Lodge:* Old-fashioned no-frills pub in former 16th-c manor house, interesting choice of strong ales, good value food most nights and weekends, no machines or juke box, popular Fri live music *(Bob Ward, Christopher Turner)*

Wysall [off A60 at Costock, or A6006 at Wymeswold; SK6027], *Plough:* Lively and attractive, well kept Bass and guest ales, very welcoming staff, nice mix of furnishings, soft lighting, lovely log fire, dog and cat wandering about, french doors to terrace and good compact garden; no cooked lunches Sun *(Chris Raisin, A and R Cooper)*

Ideas for a country day out? We list pubs in really attractive scenery at the back of the book – and there are separate lists for waterside pubs, ones with really good garden, and ones with lovely views.

Oxfordshire

Not a cheap county, this: both drinks prices and food prices are on the high side. But there are bargains to be found: the Romany at Bampton has very cheap food and charges 40p less than most local pubs for a pint of beer; the Elephant & Castle at Bloxham also has very low prices all round, and the King William IV at Hailey has bargain food. The small local brewery Hook Norton supplies its own tied pubs and lots of free houses with good beer at much lower prices than the area average; their interesting new Double Stout is worth looking out for. The other local breweries, Brakspears, Morlands and Morrells, are not particularly cheap. Pubs currently showing particularly well on sheer quality include the lovely old Lamb in Burford (this year it adds a Food Award, Wine Award and Beer Award to the string of accolades we have already awarded it), the Black Horse at Checkendon (a beautifully unspoilt country tavern, new to our main entries, doing very well under its current landlady), the Clanfield Tavern, an expanding dining pub in Clanfield, the Duke of Cumberlands Head in Clifton (embarking on some interesting restoration), the interesting old Woodman at Fernham (despite its high beer prices), the Falkland Arms at Great Tew (a wonderful old building), the Pear Tree right by the brewery in Hook Norton and the Gate Hangs High outside the town (good home cooking), the cheerful Olde Leathern Bottel at Lewknor, the Nut Tree at Murcott (lovely garden), the Turf in Oxford (still lots of character despite a major refurbishment), the friendly and simple Royal Oak at Ramsden (good generous food), the Bell at Shenington (another friendly place with good food), the Wykham Arms at Sibford Gower (a newcomer for this edition, very friendly, with good cooking – gains a Place-to-Stay Award), the Mason Arms at South Leigh (excellent food under the new owner, with quite an emphasis on evening dining – it gains a Food Award), the Perch & Pike at South Stoke (interesting food, good wines – it too qualifies for a Food Award this year), the fine new Talk House at Stanton St John (straight into our main entries with a Wine Award and Place-to-Stay Award), and the Red Lion at Steeple Aston (this proper civilised country pub is a real favourite). While many of these pubs are most enjoyable for meals out, the pub which we choose as Oxfordshire Dining Pub of the Year is the Lamb at Shipton under Wychwood – a restauranty place that is doing exceptionally well under its new management. In the Lucky Dip section at the end of the chapter, we'd particularly pick out the Maytime at Asthall, Bull in Burford, Horse & Groom at Caulcott, Fox & Hounds at Christmas Common (a long-standing main entry, but losing its long-serving tenant), Kings Arms in Oxford (where there's a fine choice) and Lamb at Satwell; we have inspected most of these and can vouch for their appeal.

ADDERBURY SP4635 Map 4
Red Lion 🛏 ♀

A423 S of Banbury; not far from M40 junction 11

This is a smartly civilised and comfortable inn overlooking the village green. The right-hand bar has a lovely big inglenook, high stripped beams, prints, and comfortable chairs, and the left-hand bar is more for eating, with cosy floral tablecloths, and leads through to the comfortable and prettily decorated residents' lounge. On one of the terracotta walls is a list of all the landlords since 1690, along with various quotations and pithy sayings. The attractive back dining room is no smoking. There's quite an emphasis on the popular – if not cheap – food, which might include home-made soup (£2.50), filled french bread (from £3), stilton and port pâté (£4.25), filled baked potatoes (from £4.25), macaroni in bacon sauce (£7.50), vegetarian crumble (£7.95), chicken fillet in a wild mushroom sauce (£10.50), seafood mornay (£10.95), duck breast in orange and port sauce (£11.95), beef stroganoff (£12.50), and puddings (£3.25). Well kept Hook Norton Best, Ruddles County, and Websters on handpump, and 20 wines by the glass; very friendly, efficient service. Tables out on the well kept garden terrace. *(Recommended by Dave Braisted, Mrs J Oakes, M L and G Clarke, John Waller, David and Shelia, D C T and E A Frewer, John and Christine Lowe)*

Free house ~ Licensees Michael and Andrea Mortimer ~ Real ale ~ Meals and snacks (till 10pm) ~ Restaurant ~ (01295) 810269 ~ Children welcome ~ Open 11-11 ~ Bedrooms: £47.50B/£65B

ARDINGTON SU4388 Map 2
Boars Head 🍴 ♀

Village signposted off A417 Didcot—Wantage, 2 miles E of Wantage

Not surprisingly, the main emphasis in this civilised place is very much on the good, imaginative food. The regularly changing blackboard menu might include toasted bagels (£2.80), creamed chick pea with merguez sausages (£4.50), ploughman's (£5), smoked chicken with mango and jalapenos (£5.25), avocado and lime guacamole with smoked prawns (£4.80), stuffed boneless quail with grapes and tarragon (£8.50), peppered pork with apple and herb mustard sauce (£9.50), duck caesar salad (£9.95), roast seabass, mussels and shitake mushrooms on a roast red pepper sauce, casserole of king scallops with cashew nuts and a Thai flavouring (£12), and imaginative puddings like roasted bananas with a butterscotch sauce and banana ice cream or pistachio mousse and honey biscuits (£4). Well kept Fullers London Pride, Mansfield Riding, and Morlands Original on handpump, and a fine wine list; caring, friendly service. The three simply furnished but smart interconnecting rooms have low beams and timbers, a few notices and pictures on the pale warm apricot walls above the dado, fresh flowers, and a pleasant light-coloured wood block floor. One room's primarily for eating, with pine settles and well spaced big pine tables, the others have smaller country tables and chairs – still with room for drinkers. Dominoes, cribbage, and piped music. In a peaceful and attractive village, the pub is part of the Ardington estate; good walks nearby. *(Recommended by Julia Cohen, R Watkins, Richard Judd, MLC, GC, Sue Demont, Tim Barrow, T R and B C Jenkins, M Popham, Richard Willmott, J W Rayson, Jed and Virginia Brown, A T Langton)*

Free house ~ Tenants Duncan and Liz Basterfield ~ Real ale ~ Meals and snacks (not Sun evening, not Mon) ~ Restaurant ~ (01235) 833254 ~ Well behaved children welcome ~ Open 11.30-2.30, 6-11; closed Mon, 25-26 Dec

BAMPTON SP3013 Map 4
Romany £ 🍽

Bridge St; off A4095 SW of Witney

When it comes to value for money, this unassuming 17th-c local is just the place to head for. The beer is much cheaper that the county average, you'd be hard pushed to find a decent bar meal for less in this area, and even the bedrooms cost half of what you might expect to pay elsewhere. The comfortable bars have plush cushioned windsor chairs and stools around wooden tables, foreign currency notes from all over the world, plates and prints on the partly stripped stone walls, and a winter open fire. The menu includes sandwiches (from £1.10; toasties from £1.30), home-made soup (£1.25), home-made pâté (£1.75), filled baked potatoes (from £2.10), ploughman's (£2.30), sausage, egg, beans and chips (£2.50), salads (from £2.95), home-made pies like steak and kidney or chicken and mushroom (£3.20), a good few vegetarian dishes like mushroom provençale or vegetable curry (from £3.20), braised pork chop (£3.65), and steaks (from £4.35); best to book for their popular 3-course Sunday lunch (£5.25). Friendly, hard-working licensees. The restaurant is no smoking. Well kept Archers Village, Hook Norton Best and Mild, Wadworths 6X, and a guest beer which changes twice a week, handpumped from the Saxon cellars below the bar; cribbage, dominoes, fruit machine, and piped music. The big garden has picnic tables, Aunt Sally, and a children's play area with tree house, see-saw, and mushroom slide and house. *(Recommended by Gordon, Keith Macaulay, Marjorie and David Lamb, Meg and Colin Hamilton, CMW, JJW, David Campbell, Vicki McLean)*

Free house ~ Licensees Bob and Ursula Booth ~ Real ale ~ Meals and snacks (11.30-2.30, 6-9.30) ~ Restaurant ~ (01993) 850237 ~ Well behaved children welcome ~ Open 11-11; 12-4, 7-11 Sun ~ Bedrooms: £21B/£30B

BARFORD ST MICHAEL SP4332 Map 4

George

Lower Street, at N end of village: coming from Bloxham, take first right turn

Very popular with locals, this is a very attractive 17th-c golden stone pub, with a thatched roof and mullioned windows. Inside, the three rambling modernised rooms have open fires, cushioned rustic seats and captain's chairs around the dark wood tables, and quite a few company and regimental ties hanging from the beams, most donated by customers. Over the fireplace there's a big painting of the Battle of Agincourt, using many of the locals as the soldiers. Bar food includes sandwiches, lamb balti or chicken kiev (£4.95), breaded trout with almonds (£5.95), and vegetarian dishes. Well kept Marstons Pedigree and Morlands Original and Old Speckled Hen on handpump, and lots of country wines. Darts, pool, shove-ha'penny, pinball, cribbage, dominoes, fruit machine, video game, trivia and piped music. The pleasant garden has picnic tables, a giant chess set, an adventure playground, and views over fields. Just up the road is a caravan/camp site with trout fishing. *(Recommended by David and Shelia, John Bowdler; more reports please)*

Free house ~ Licensees Spencer and Theresa Richards ~ Real ale ~ Meals and snacks (not evenings Sun and Mon) ~ Restaurant (not Sun evening) ~ (01869) 338226 ~ Children welcome ~ Folk/blues Mon evenings ~ Open 12-2.30, 6-11; 12-11 summer Sat

BARNARD GATE SP4010 Map 4

Boot

Village signposted off A40 E of Witney

An unusual feature here is the growing collection of celebrities' boots which are displayed on the walls. But it's the food that most people come to this dining pub for, with dishes such as soup (£2.95), grilled king prawns with dip and garlic bread (£3.95), pasta with shredded chicken, bacon, shallots, mushrooms, cream and chilli (£7.25), minute steak with pepper sauce (£7.50), steak and kidney pudding (£7.95), casserole of beans and pulses (£8.25), Thai chilli chicken curry (£8.95), scottish salmon with a basil cream sauce (£9.95), Aberdeen Angus steak (£12.95), daily specials (mostly under £7.50 and including lots of fish), and puddings like sticky toffee pudding (£3.50); part of the restaurant is no smoking. The decor is pleasant and civilised in a gently rustic way, with good solid country tables and chairs on bare boards, and stout standing timbers and stub walls with latticed glass breaking up the main area; there's a huge log fire, decent wines, and well kept Hook Norton Best and Morlands Old Speckled Hen on handpump. There are tables out in front of the stone-tiled stone pub, which despite being so handy for the A40 is out of earshot. *(Recommended by M Sargent, John Waller, Tony and Sarah Thomas, T H G Lewis, Lindsay Gregory, Adam Hodge; more reports please)*

Free house ~ George Dailey ~ Real ale ~ Meals and snacks (12-2, 6-10) ~ Restaurant ~ (01865) 881231 ~ Children welcome ~ Open 11-3, 6-11; closed 25 Dec)

BECKLEY SP5611 Map 4
Abingdon Arms

Village signposted off B4027

They have both a summer and a winter menu in this busy food pub, and from a sensibly short winter menu there might be marinated anchovies with potato salad (£3.85), cold ham with tomato and basil salad, delicious bouillabaisse or chicken and mushroom curry (£6.25), baked ham with mustard sauce (£6.75), and puddings such as rich chocolate torte or apple and almond tart (£2.40); summer dishes like filled french bread (from £2.95), pasta with tuna fish, red peppers, stuffed olives and pine nuts and garnished with crispy seaweed (£5.95), sliced smoked chicken with yoghurt and mint sauce (£6.25), fresh crab with ginger dressing (£7.50), and seafood salad for two (£21). No credit cards. Well kept Hook Norton Best and Wadworths 6X on handpump, a good range of wines, and a few malt whiskies. The comfortably modernised simple lounge has neat flower displays on the tables and cloth-cushioned seats built around the wall, and a smaller public bar on the right has a couple of antique carved settles (one for just one person), and bar billiards; dominoes, cribbage, shove-ha'penny. The pleasant garden has a small formal flower-edged lawn just behind the pub dropping quietly and spaciously away into the shadows of groves of fruit trees, willows and other shrubs and trees. There's a gently floodlit terrace, along with well spaced tables, a summer-house, and a little fountain. No children. *(Recommended by Adam and Elizabeth Duff, Hugh Quick, Prof A N Black, TBB, K Chenneour, Alan Skull, A M Rankin, John Waller)*

Free house ~ Licensee Hugh Greatbatch ~ Real ale ~ Meals and snacks (not Sun evening) ~ (01865) 351311 ~ Open 11.30-2.30, 6.30-11; Sunday opening 8

BINFIELD HEATH SU7478 Map 2
Bottle & Glass ★

Village signposted off A4155 at Shiplake; in village centre fork right immediately after Post Office (signposted Harpsden) and keep on for half mile

Happily, very little changes in this idyllic-looking thatched and black and white timbered 15th-c pub. The neatly kept bar has attractive flagstones, low beams, a roaring log fire in the big fireplace, and scrubbed, ancient tables, a bench built into black squared panelling, and spindleback chairs. The smaller, relaxed side room, similarly decorated, has a window with diamond-scratched family records of earlier landlords. Written up on blackboards, the range of promptly served bar food typically includes lunchtime sandwiches, potted shrimps (£4.75), grilled mussels (£4.95), chicken and ham pie or pork and bean cassoulet (£6.25), large fresh cod fillet (£6.95), chicken supreme or fresh salmon fillet with wine and mustard sauce (£7.75), and 10oz rump steak (£9.50); friendly staff. Brakspears Bitter, and seasonal Old or Special on handpump, and quite a few malt whiskies. The lovely big garden has old-fashioned wooden seats and tables under little thatched roofs (and an open-sided shed like a rustic pavilion). No children or dogs. *(Recommended by Sandra Kench, Steven Norman, TBB, Ted and Jane Brown, P J Caunt, Gordon, Simon Collett-Jones)*

Brakspears ~ Tenants Mike and Anne Robinson ~ Real ale ~ Meals and snacks (lunchtime service stops 1.45; not Sun evening) ~ (01491) 575755 ~ Open 11-4, 6-11; 12-4, 6.30-10.30 Sun

BIX SU7285 Map 2

Fox

On A4130 Henley—Wallingford

If you fancy a quiet weekday get-away-from-it-all visit, this friendly and relaxing brick house is set well off the main tourist routes (it does get busier at weekends). The cosy L-shaped lounge bar has panelling, beams, armchairs and settles making the most of the big log fires, and gleaming brasses. There's another log fire and some settles in the connecting wood-floored farmers' bar, with darts, dominoes and a fruit machine. Quickly served, good value bar food includes sandwiches (from £1.65), home-made soup (£2.25), filled baked potatoes (from £3.25), ploughman's (from £3.35), potted shrimps (£3.55), ratatouille (£3.95), lasagne or steak and kidney pie (£4.75), daily specials like steak and mushroom casserole (£5.25), phesant or rabbit casserole (£5.50), 8oz rump steak (£6.75), puddings (£2.25), and Sunday roast (£5.95). Well kept Brakspears Bitter and seasonal Old or Special on handpump, picnic tables in the good-sized garden behind. The friendly dog is called Henry, and there's a much-used hitching rail for horses outside. You can book a horse and cart to bring you here at weekends; see the entry at Hailey for details. No children. *(Recommended by Joan Olivier, A C Morrison, Eric Locker, Dr G W Barnett, Gordon, TBB, Bill Ingham, Marjorie and David Lamb, D D Collins)*

Brakspears ~ Tenants Richard and Sue Willson ~ Real ale ~ Meals and snacks (not Mon evening) ~ (01491) 574134 ~ Open 11-3, 7-11; closed 25 Dec

BLEWBURY SU5385 Map 2

Red Lion

Chapel Lane, off Nottingham Fee; narrow turning northwards from A417

No noisy games machines or music disturb this welcoming downland village pub. The atmospheric and engaging beamed bar has upholstered wall benches and armed seats on its scrubbed quarry tiles, cupboards and miniature cabinets filled with ornaments, foreign banknotes on the beams, and a steadily ticking station clock; in winter you can roast chestnuts over the big open fire. A no-smoking bar is popular with families. Good bar food includes toasties, liver and bacon or loin lamb chops with crispy breadcrumbs in a cheese sauce (£5), pork loin with orange and apricots, and fresh brill, sea bass, plaice and so forth (£5-£8). Well kept Boddingtons and Brakspears Bitter, Old Ale and Special on handpump, decent wines, and a good range of non-alcoholic drinks; attentive service. The extended garden has a terrace with quite a few seats and tables. *(Recommended by Tim Brierly, Gordon, M W Turner)*

Brakspears ~ Tenant Roger Smith ~ Real ale ~ Meals and snacks ~ Restaurant (weekends) ~ (01235) 850403 ~ Children in restaurant until 8pm ~ Open 11-2.30(3 Sat), 6-11; closed evening 25 Dec ~ Bedrooms: £25/£35

BLOXHAM SP4235 Map 4

Elephant & Castle £

Humber Street; off A361, fairly handy for M40 junction 11

This is the sort of warmly welcoming place where you will be remembered – even after only one visit. The relaxed and elegantly simple public bar has a striking 17th-c stone fireplace and a strip wood floor, and the comfortable lounge (refurbished this year) is divided into two by a very thick wall, and has a good winter log fire in its massive fireplace too; sensibly placed darts, dominoes, cribbage, fruit machine, and trivia, and they have been using the same hardy shove ha'penny board for over a century now. Good value straightforward lunchtime bar food includes soup, decent sandwiches, sausage, eggs and beans (£3), and steak and kidney pie, lasagne, or haddock (£3.50). Well kept and extremely well priced Hook Norton Best (11p less than the county average), Old Hookey, summer Haymaker, Twelve Days, and Double Stout, and guest beers; 30 malt whiskies. The flower-filled extended yard has Aunt Sally in summer and maybe weekend barbecues. *(Recommended by Alan and Paul McCully, Tom Evans, TBB, Stephen Brown, Gordon)*

Hook Norton ~ Tenant Chas Finch ~ Real ale ~ Lunchtime meals and snacks (not Sun) ~ Restaurant (not Sun) ~ (01295) 720383 ~ Children in eating area of bar ~ Open 10-3, 6(5 Sat)-11; 12-5, 7-10.30 Sun

BRIGHTWELL BALDWIN SU6595 Map 4

Lord Nelson ⑪ ♀

Brightwell signposted off B480 at Oxford end of Cuxham or B4009 Benson—Watlington

Just the place for a civilised meal, this was originally called the Admiral Nelson, but its name was changed immediately after the celebrated seaman became a baron in 1797. There's still quite a naval theme in the bar on the left, where the plain white walls are decorated with pictures and prints of the sea and ships, and there are some ship design plans. Most tables are laid out for eating, especially at weekends, and may be booked in advance. Popular dishes include smoked mackerel and whisky pâté (£3.50), mixed leaves with avocado, parmesan cheese, bacon and croûtons (£4.75), super lamb liver and bacon, cod with welsh rarebit crust or salmon fishcakes with bisque sauce (£8.25), local venison casserole (£10.25), and roast guinea fowl with creamy cider and onion sauce (£11.25); they do some rather unusual soups, and a good two or three course Sunday lunch. Service is friendly and helpful; one of the barmaids has been here for over 20 years. Ruddles Best and guests like Batemans XXXB and Greene King Abbot on handpump kept under light blanket pressure, and a good wine list. Furnishings are comfortably modernised, with wheelback chairs (some armed), country kitchen and dining chairs around the tables on its turkey carpet, and candles in coloured glasses; piped music. There's a verandah at the front, and tables on a back terrace by the attractive garden or under its big weeping willow, beside the colourful herbaceous border. The village church is worth a look. Now owned by the Old English Pub company, though management and policies remain unchanged. *(Recommended by M Sargent, Keith and Margaret Kettell, James Waller, Sue Demont, Tim Barrow, Nigel Wikeley, Susan and Alan Dominey)*

Free house ~ Licensees Peter Neal, Richard Britcliffe, Jonathan Seaton-Read ~ Real ale ~ Meals and snacks (till 10pm) ~ Restaurant ~ (01491) 612497 ~ Well-behaved children allowed with manager's agreement ~ Open 12-3, 6.30-11

BROADWELL SP2503 Map 4

Five Bells

Village signposted off A361 N of Lechlade, and off B4020 S of Carterton

By the time this book is published, the hard-working licensees of this 16th-c former coaching inn will have added a conservatory which will give better access to the garden. The neatly kept low-beamed lounge has a sizeable dining room off to the right (very busy at weekends), and another separate dining room which overlooks the spacious, well kept and attractive garden – where they play Aunt Sally, and grow some of the vegetables used in the kitchen. There are big log fires and a pleasant mix of flagstones and carpeting; wheelchair access. Consistently good straightforward food freshly cooked to order changes from day to day, and typically might include open sandwiches (from £1.50), home-made soup (£1.95), garlic mushrooms (£3.25), ploughman's (£3.50), vegetable pasta bake (£4.75), salmon and prawn gratin (£4.95), steak and kidney pudding or stilton chicken (£5.50), pheasant in red wine (£6), grilled swordfish (£6.50), steaks (from £8.50), and puddings like fruit crumbles or pavlovas (£2.25). Hook Norton Best, Wadworths 6X, and a guest beer on handpump or tapped from the cask, decent house wine, and pleasant service. The public bar has shove-ha'penny, dominoes, and fruit machine; piped music. *(Recommended by Joan Olivier, D P Bailey, Marjorie and David Lamb, Peter and Audrey Dowsett, Mr and Mrs R J Foreman, K Neville-Rolfe, Calum and Susan Maclean)*

Free house ~ Licensees Trevor and Ann Cooper ~ Real ale ~ Meals and snacks (12-1.45; 7-9.15; not Mon) ~ Restaurant (not Mon) ~ (01367) 860076 ~ Children in lower dining room (must be over 7 on Sat evening) ~ Open 11.30-2.30, 6.30-11; closed Mon except bank holidays ~ Chalet bedrooms: /£40B

BURCOT SU5695 Map 4

Chequers

A415 Dorchester—Abingdon

In summer this pretty black and white thatched pub has lots of colourful flowers in front, and tables and chairs among roses and fruit trees on the neatly kept roadside lawn. Inside, the smartly comfortable and surprisingly spacious lounge has beams, an open fire, and a very relaxed and friendly atmosphere. Well kept Brakspears, Ruddles County, and Ushers Best on handpump, with some good whiskies and unusual spirits and liqueurs. Relying very much on fresh local produce, the home-made bar food might include doorstep sandwiches (£2.75), soup (£2) chicken liver and herb pâté (£3), salads (from £4.25), spinach and sweetcorn pasta (£5.25), seafood pie (£5.50), steak and kidney pudding (£5.75), trout with lemon and tarragon (£7.50), steaks (from £7.75), and puddings (£2.25); they bake their own bread. They have their own decent little no-smoking art gallery. *(Recommended by Nigel Norman, Gordon; more reports please)*

Free house ~ Lease: Mary and Michael Weeks ~ Real ale ~ Meals and snacks (not Sun evening) ~ Restaurant ~ (01865) 407771 ~ Children in eating area of bar and in gallery ~ Grand piano Fri and Sat evenings; brass band concerts ~ Open 11-2.30(3 Sat), 6-11

BURFORD SP2512 Map 4

Angel

14 Witney St, just off main street; village signposted off A40 W of Oxford

New licensees have taken over this partly 14th-c inn and, as we went to press, had made no big changes. The long beamed and panelled bar has antique furnishings and attractive old tables on its weathered flagstones, cushioned wall settles, wheelback chairs and an open fire; it leads out onto a terrace with a pretty walled garden beyond. Steps lead up from the main bar to a no-smoking dining room, and there's another charmingly cosy eating area beyond, with a huge log fire and stripped stone walls. Bar food now includes sandwiches (from £2.25; french bread 70p extra), cheese platter with celery, grapes and biscuits (£4.50), salads (from £5.25), and evening dishes such as moules marinierès (£4.25), spinach tagliatelle with sun dried tomatoes and parma ham (£6.50), loin of pork en croûte with a ginger and tarragon cream sauce (£7.50), and rack of spring lamb with grain mustard crust and dill jus (£9.95). Well kept Bass, and Morlands Old Speckled Hen and IPA on handpump; fine sherries. No children. *(Recommended by R D Greaves, Andrew and Ruth Triggs, David Carr, M Sargent, John Bowdler, Christopher Gallop, Dr S Willavoys; more reports on the new regime, please)*

Free house ~ Licensees John and Sheila Harrington ~ Real ale ~ Meals and snacks (not Sun evening) ~ Restaurant ~ (01993) 822438 ~ Open 11-11; 12-10.30 Sun ~ Bedrooms: /£50B

Lamb ★ ★

Sheep Street; A40 W of Oxford

It's always a pleasure to come to this unchanging and civilised 500-year-old Cotswold inn. The genteel elegance and old-fashioned character appeals a lot to people – as do the very well kept real ales, good wine and enjoyable food. A smashing place to stay, too. The spacious beamed main lounge has a winter log fire under its fine mantelpiece, distinguished old seats including a chintzy high winged settle, ancient cushioned wooden armchairs, and seats built into its stone-mullioned windows, bunches of flowers on polished oak and elm tables, and oriental rugs on the wide flagstones and polished oak floorboards. Also, attractive pictures, shelves of plates and other antique decorations, a grandfather clock, and a writing desk. The public bar has high-backed settles and old chairs on flagstones in front of its fire. Good bar lunches might include sandwiches or filled french bread (from £2.50; fresh crab with chive mayonnaise), home-made soups like cream of asparagus with toasted almonds (£2.95), ploughman's (£4.25), terrine of sole and salmon with a citrus mayonnaise (£4.95), warm ham and mushroom quiche (£5.25), fresh grilled sardines in parsley butter (£5.75), fricassee of wild rabbit in a mustard and peppercorn sauce with tagliatelle verdi (£6.25), steak and kidney pie or grilled gammon steak with glazed apricots (£6.95), and puddings such as gaelic coffee trifle, almond and orange roulade or crème de menthe cheesecake (£2.50). Note they don't do bar meals Sunday lunchtimes (three courses with a bucks fizz to start, £17.50) though there may be free dips then; the restaurant is no smoking. Well kept Hook Norton Best and Wadworths IPA, 6X and winter Old Timer are dispensed from an antique handpump beer engine in a glassed-in cubicle; good wines. A pretty terrace leads down to small neatly-kept lawns surrounded by flowers, flowering shrubs and small trees, and the garden itself can be really sunny, enclosed as it is by the warm stone of the surrounding buildings. *(Recommended by Basil Minson, Dr I Maine, Brian Wainwright, Lynn Sharpless, Bob Eardley, Dave Irving, James Nunns, Andrew and Ruth Triggs, Alan and Paula McCully, Malcolm Taylor, David Carr, Eric and Jackie Robinson, Ian Carpenter, Jane Hosking, Ian Burniston, David R Shillitoe, Dr Ian Crichton, C Driver, Nigel Wilkinson, John Evans, Mr and Mrs Hillman, Nigel Woolliscroft, E B Davies, John Bowdler, Leith Stuart, Mrs B Lemon, Karen and Graham Oddey; also in Good Hotel Guide)*

Free house ~ Licensee Richard de Wolf ~ Real ale ~ Lunchtime bar meals and snacks (not Sun) ~ Evening restaurant ~ (01993) 823155 ~ Children welcome ~ Open 11-2.30, 6-11; closed 25-26 Dec ~ Bedrooms: £57.50B/£95B

Mermaid ♀

High St

Bar food is usefully served all day in this busy dining pub and promptly served by courteous, efficient staff. Using good quality fresh produce, the lunchtime menu might include soup (£2.50), filled french bread (from £3.25), ploughman's (£4.25), filled baked potatoes or omelettes (£4.95), fish of the day (£5.95), a roast of the day or pasta with stilton and broccoli sauce (£6.95), and daily specials, with evening dishes such as peppered mushrooms (£4.95), stuffed baked peppers or their speciality fish and chips (£6.95), gammon with parsley sauce (£7.95), and glazed duck breast in a plum and ginger sauce (£11.95); puddings, children's dishes, and cream teas (served between 3 and 6pm). Well kept Morlands Original, Old Masters, and Old Speckled Hen on handpump; piped music. The attractive long and narrow bar has polished flagstones, brocaded seats in bays around the single row of tables down one side, and pretty dried flowers. The inner end, with a figurehead over the fireplace and toby jugs hanging from the beams, is panelled, the rest has stripped stonework; there's also a no-smoking dining conservatory and upstairs restaurant. The handsome Tudor-style frontage juts out onto the broad pavement of this famously picturesque sloping Cotswold street, and there are picnic tables under cocktail parasols. *(Recommended by KM, JM, Andrew and Ruth Triggs, John Titcombe, Dr S Willavoys, Brian Wainwright, R D Greaves, Alan and Paula McCully, Simon Collett-Jones, David Carr, Pat and Roger Fereday, R and A Cooper, John and Shirley Dyson, Jane Hosking, Ian Burniston)*

Morlands ~ Lease: John Titcombe ~ Real ale ~ Meals and snacks (noon-10pm) ~ Restaurant ~ (01993) 822193 ~ Children in restaurant but no big pushchairs ~ Parking may be difficult ~ Open 11-11; 11-10.30 Sun; closed evening 25 Dec

CHECKENDON SU6684 Map 2

Black Horse

Village signposted off A4074 Reading—Wallingford; coming from that direction, go straight through village towards Stoke Row, then turn left (the second turn left after the village church); OS Sheet 175 map reference 666841

A real boon for walkers, this delightfully old-fashioned country local is tucked into woodland well away from the main village. Warmly and utterly unpretentious, it's been kept by the same family for many decades: very much the sort of place where even shy people feel it's natural to get into conversation with complete strangers. The room with the bar counter has some tent pegs ranged above the fireplace, a reminder that they used to be made here; a homely side room has some splendidly unfashionable 1950s-look armchairs, and beyond that there's a third room; dominoes, cards. Well kept Brakspears and a few local guests like Old Luxters Barn Ale, Rebellion and Good Old Boy from the new West Berks brewery, are tapped from casks in a back still room (the ladies' is back beyond that). They'll usually do fresh filled rolls (from £1.10), and keep pickled eggs. There are seats out on a verandah. Connoisseurs of antiquated lavatories will enjoy the gents' - though given our current climate may be glad to learn that it no longer has to rely on a shower of rain for flushing. (Recommended by Phil and Sally Gorton, Pete Baker, Jack and Philip Paxton, Jenny and Roger Huggins, Dick Brown, Tom McLean, Gordon)

Free House ~ Licensee Margaret Morgan ~ Real ale ~ Snacks ~ (01491) 680418 ~ Children welcome in end room ~ Open 12-2(3 Sat), 7-11; cl 25 Dec evening

nr CHINNOR SU 7698 Map 4

Sir Charles Napier 🍽 ♀

Spriggs Alley; from B4009 follow Bledlow Ridge sign from Chinnor; then, up beech wood hill, fork right (signposted Radnage and Spriggs Alley) then on right; OS Sheet 165 ref 763983

This is a decidedly civilised place – despite its inauspicious plain outside – with excellent food and an outstanding wine list. It's not quite a restaurant, and the comfortable simply furnished rooms are rather traditional (even homely). At quiet moments during the week you'll generally feel quite welcome coming for just a drink, particularly in the cosy little front bar, but at other times you may find the whole place is virtually dedicated to the stylish back restaurant, and there's little point coming unless you want to eat. This is definitely somewhere to come for a treat, and a typical day's bar menu might include crostini of pigeon and mushrooms with truffle oil or augbergine and polenta cake with tomato and mozarella (£5.50), fried baby Cornish squid with red salsa (£6.75), crab cakes with lime and coriander (£7.50), baked cod with butter beans, fennel and aioli (£10.50), crispy Gressingham duck with lime and ginger (£11.50), and saddle of venison with cranberries and port (£12.50); puddings (£5) and English cheese (£6.50), and service is not included. Two-course set lunch (£13), and Sunday lunch is distinctly fashionable – in summer it's served in the crazy-paved back courtyard with rustic tables by an arbour of vines, honeysuckle and wisteria (lit at night by candles in terracotta lamps). An excellent range of drinks takes in well kept Wadworths 6X tapped from the cask, champagne on draught, an enormous list of exceptionally well chosen wines by the bottle (and a good few half-bottles), freshly squeezed juice, Russian vodkas and quite a few malt whiskies. Piped music is well reproduced by the huge loudspeakers, there's a good winter log fire, a smartly relaxed feel and friendly staff. The croquet lawn and paddocks by the beech woods drop steeply away to the Chilterns, and there's a boules court out here too. (Recommended by N M Baleham, B W and S J, Heather Couper, Gordon, Tina and David Woods-Taylor; more reports please)

Free house ~ Licensee Julie Griffiths ~ Real ale ~ Lunchtime bar meals (not Sun) ~ Restaurant ~ (01494) 483011 ~ Children over 5 lunchtimes, over 8 in evenings ~ Open 12-2.30, 6.30-11; closed Sun evening and all day Mon

CHURCH ENSTONE SP3724 Map 4
Crown 🛏

From A44 take B4030 turn-off at Enstone

In an attractive village, this cottagey Cotswold stone inn is a friendly, enjoyable place. The comfortable beamed bar has open fires, gleaming brasses, plush button-back wall banquettes and windsor chairs, and prints on the bare stone walls; the dining area extends into the pleasant conservatory, which leads out into a little back garden. Reasonably priced bar food includes soup (£1.95), garlic mushrooms (£3.10), ploughman's (from £2.95), cheese and onion flan (£3.95), ham and egg (£4.35), home-made steak, kidney and mushroom pie (£4.95), fish pie (£5.25), rump steak (£7.95), and puddings like treacle tart or spotted dick (£2.25); good traditional breakfast. Well kept Boddingtons, Flowers Original and a guest beer on handpump from the horseshoe bar, and a range of malt whiskies; prompt service. The upper bar is no smoking. There are some white metal tables and chairs in front. Lots of nearby walks. (Recommended by Tim Brierly, Marjorie and David Lamb, Ted George, Lynn Sharpless, Bob Eardley, Gordon Smith, H O Dickinson, David Logan, Mr and Mrs Hillman, George Atkinson, John Bowdler, Jenny and Michael Back)

Free house ~ Licensees Peter Gannon and Jean Rowe ~ Real ale ~ Meals and snacks (not 25 Dec) ~ Restaurant ~ (01608) 677262 ~ Children in restaurant ~ Open 12-3, 7-11; closed evening 25 Dec ~ Bedrooms: £30(£32B)/£42(£45B)

CLANFIELD SP2802 Map 4
Clanfield Tavern ♀

A4095 5 miles S of Witney

A lot of work was being carried out on this pretty village inn as we went to press. A new no-smoking conservatory was to be added linking the pub to a barn, and a courtyard with a fountain was to be constructed; a new bar lounge and new lavatories with disabled facilities were being organised, new kitchens (on view) added, and the car park enlarged. But don't be put off by such daunting-sounding changes. This is an extremely popular place with a very nice atmosphere, pleasant, friendly service, and good, interesting food. Several flagstone, heavy-beamed and stone-walled small rooms (one partly no smoking) lead off the busy main bar, furnished with settles and various chairs and seats cut from casks, as well as brass platters, hunting prints, and a handsome open stone fireplace crowned with a 17th-c plasterwork panel. As well as lunchtime sandwiches (from £1.95), and filled baked potatoes and ploughman's (£4.25), there's soup (£2.25), deep-fried brie with cranberry sauce (£3.25), burgers with different toppings (£5.95), avocado and mushroom pancakes (£6.45), king prawn tails with garlic, rosemary and white wine (£6.95), daily specials such as steamed steak and mushroom suet pudding (£7.25) and glazed marinated pork fillet with apricot sauce (£7.95), and puddings (£2.75); the excellent vegetables are served separately, and they do a good Sunday lunch. Well kept Boddingtons, Flowers IPA, and Hook Norton Best on handpump, quite a few bin end wines, and several malt whiskies. It's pretty in summer, with tiny windows peeping from the heavy stone-slabbed roof and tables on a flower-bordered small lawn that look across to the village green and pond.
(Recommended by Peter and Audrey Dowsett, David Rule, M A and C R Starling, Mike and Heather Watson, D C T and E A Frewer, Mr and Mrs Christopher Ball, Mrs Mary Walters, John Waller, Malcolm Taylor, Mr and Mrs G Turner)

Free house ~ Licensee Keith Gill ~ Real ale ~ Meals and snacks (11.30-2.30, 6-10) ~ Cottagey restaurant ~ (01367) 810223 ~ Children welcome ~ Open 11.30-2.30(3 Sat), 6-11 ~ Bedrooms: /£50B

CLIFTON SP4831 Map 4
Duke of Cumberlands Head ♀ 🛏

B4031 Deddington—Aynho

As we went to press, the licensees here were hoping to get planning permission to carry out some restoration work. This is a very popular and pretty pub and much enjoyed by those staying overnight. The food comes in for consistent praise too: sandwiches, soup (£2.75), ploughman's (£4.50), filo-wrapped king prawns (£5.25), local sausages (£5.50), sweet and sour pork (£6), fish pie or Greek beef stew (£6.25), fresh cod or haddock (£6.50), and home-made puddings like apple and raspberry crumble, apricot and almond tart or chocolate mousse (£3.25); summer Sunday evening help-yourself buffet, and excellent breakfasts. The spacious and simple but stylish lounge has a lovely log fireplace and well kept Adnams Southwold, Hampshire King Alfreds, Hook Norton Best, and Wadworths 6X on handpump, a good wine list, and 25 or so malt whiskies. There are tables out in the garden, and the canal is a short walk away. *(Recommended by Catherine and Andrew Brian, John Bowdler, Georgina Cole, Mike Forrester, Mr and Mrs H D Spottiswoode, Richard Gibbs, R T and J C Moggridge, Karen and Graham Oddey, Jim Reid, E A George, Mick Gray, JCW)*

Free house ~ Licensee Nick Huntington ~ Real ale ~ Meals and snacks (not Sun evening) ~ Restaurant (not Sun or Mon evenings) ~ (01869) 338534 ~ Children welcome ~ Open 12-3, 6.30-11; closed Sun evenings Nov-Apr ~ Bedrooms: £25S/£37S

CLIFTON HAMPDEN SU5495 Map 4

Plough 🛏 ♀

On A415 at junction with Long Wittenham turn-off

This is one of the few pubs we know of that is totally no smoking, which makes it popular with quite a few of our readers. The opened-up bar area has beams and panelling, black and red floor tiles, antique furniture, attractive pictures, and a friendly, relaxed atmosphere; it's said to be haunted by a benign presence that neatly upturns empty glasses. It is very much a place people come to for a meal, with a range of tasty dishes such as home-made soup, sandwiches and other light snacks, and smoked chicken salad (£4.95), pasta with chicken and vegetables (£5.50), and steak in ale pie (£5.95); the restaurant has an engaging portrait of the charming licensee. Well kept Courage Best, Ruddles County, and Websters Yorkshire on handpump, plenty of good wines, and a dozen malt whiskies; no games or piped music. Some tables and seats outside. *(Recommended by Gordon, TBB, Mrs S Wright, Chris Wheaton, Mrs J Gubbins, David Carr, Joyce McKimm, Hanns P Golez, D C T and E A Frewer, Dr G W Barnett, Peter Churchill, John Wooll, Heather Couper, John Waller, Mrs K J Putman, V Beynon, M Willcox, Margaret Dyke, Mrs J M Campbell, John and Philip Paxton, Wayne Brindle)*

Courage ~ Lease: Yuksel Bektas ~ Real ale ~ Meals and snacks (served all day) ~ Restaurant ~ (01865) 407811 ~ Children welcome ~ Open 11-11 ~ Bedrooms (one with four-poster): £44.50B/£64.50B

CROPREDY SP4646 Map 4

Red Lion

Off A423 4 miles N of Banbury

In a lovely village, this peaceful and friendly thatched 15th-c pub is a short walk from a pretty lock and the Oxford Canal. It stands opposite a handsome old church with a raised churchyard, some of the graves in which are reminders of the Civil War battle that took place nearby. The simply furnished and old-fashioned bar has ancient low beams, high-backed settles, seats in one of the inglenooks, quite a lot of brass, plates and pictures on the walls, and winter open fires; the two rooms on the right are more for eating. Popular home-made bar food includes sandwiches (from £1.50), soup (£2.25), filled baked potatoes (from £3), ploughman's (from £3.60), home-cooked ham or home-made steak and kidney pie (£4.75), home-made chicken tikka masala (£4.95), and evening dishes such as tortellini bake (£4.95), chicken malibu (£5.95) and steaks (from £7.50); children's menu (from £1.95), and Sunday roasts. Well kept Courage Best and Directors, John Smiths, and Ruddles Best on handpump; darts, pool, cribbage, dominoes, fruit machine, and piped music. Seats in the small back garden. *(Recommended by Rona Murdoch, Alan and Paula McCully, Mrs J Box, D C T Frewer, Karen and Graham Oddey, Paul Robinshaw, A G Drake)*

Courage ~ Lease: John Dando ~ Real ale ~ Meals and snacks ~ (01295) 750224 ~ Children in restaurant only ~ Parking may be difficult in summer ~ Open 12-3, 6-11

CUDDESDON SP5903 Map 4
Bat & Ball

S of Wheatley; if coming from M40 junction 7 via Gt Milton, turn towards Little Milton past church, then look out for signpost

The restaurant extension here has now been completed and the cricketing memorabilia has increased even more. Every inch of wall-space is covered with cricketing programmes, photographs, porcelain models in well-lit cases, score books, cigarette cards, pads, gloves and hats, and signed bats, bails and balls. The comfortable and immaculately kept L-shaped bar is friendly and welcoming, and there are low ceilings, beams, and a partly flagstoned floor. Popular bar food includes home-made soup (£2.75), lunchtime filled french sticks (from £2.50; bacon and mushroom with melted cheese £2.75; not Sunday), home-made chicken liver pâté (£3.75), moules marinierès (£3.75), ploughman's (£4.75), tagliatelle with creamy mushroom and tomato sauce or fresh vegetable casserole (£6.75), pork dijonnaise (£7.75), chilli king prawns or calf liver flamed with Cointreau (£8.75), grilled 8oz sirloin steak (£9.75), baked fillet of seabass with a bloody mary sauce (£10.75), and roasted half duck with apricots and redcurrant sauce (£11.75). Well kept Flowers Original and IPA, and Wadworths 6X on handpump; piped music. A very pleasant terrace at the back has seats, Aunt Sally, and good views over the Oxfordshire plain. *(Recommended by Caroline Raphael, David Campbell, Vicki McLean, Peter and Audrey Dowsett, Walter Reid; more reports please)*

Free house ~ Licensee David Sykes ~ Real ale ~ Meals and snacks ~ Restaurant ~ (01865) 874379 ~ Children in eating area of bar ~ Open 12-2.30, 6-11 ~ Bedrooms: £35S/£40S

CUMNOR SP4603 Map 4
Bear & Ragged Staff

19 Appleton Road; village signposted from A420: follow one-way system into village, bear left into High St then left again into Appleton Road signposted Eaton, Appleton

It's the well presented food from an imaginative – if pricey – menu that customers come to this smart old place to enjoy. Dishes might include spicy Thai duck soup, Cornish crab with brandy mayonnaise, chicken and ginger salad, grilled Cornish scallops with crispy bacon and pesto (£7.95), medaillons of venison, rosti and green peppercorns (£12.95), crispy duck with five spices on red cabbage marmalade, tranche of turbot with clam chowder and bouillabaisse sauce (£15.95), and puddings (£4.95). The comfortably rambling, softly lit bar has a relaxed but decidely civilised atmosphere, roaring log fires, easy chairs, and sofas and more orthodox cushioned seats and wall banquettes; one part has polished black flagstones, another a turkey carpet; one room is no smoking. Well kept Bass and Morrells Bitter and Varsity on handpump, plus up to 10 wines by the glass and quite a few bin ends; piped music. Service is pleasant and obliging and there's a wooden high chair for children. The building is named for the three-foot model of a Warwick heraldic bear which guards the large open fire. *(Recommended by Joan Olivier, Chris and Martin Taylor, Nigel and Amanda Thorp, Gordon, John and Joan Nash, David Carr, Prof A N Black, John Waller, Neville Kenyon, Ewan McCall, Roger Huggins, Dave Irving, Tom McLean, Robin Hillman, R A Buckler, Roger Byrne, Frank Cummins)*

Morrells ~ Tenants Bruce and Kay Buchan ~ Real ale ~ Meals and snacks (till 10) ~ Restaurant ~ (01865) 862329 ~ Children welcome ~ Big band jazz every 2nd Tues ~ Open 11-3, 5.30(6 Sat)-11; closed several days between Christmas and New Year

CUXHAM SU4588 Map 2

Half Moon

4 miles from M40, junction 6; B480

The friendly and comfortable low-beamed bars in this thatched and rather cottagey village pub have country-style furnishings, an inglenook fireplace with winter log fires or summer flower displays, and a few clues to one of the landlord's interests – vintage motorcycles. Bar food includes home-made soup (£2.50), white bean and garlic pâté (£3.25), ploughman's (£3.50), burgers (from £3.95), Tuscan bean crostini (£5.95), gammon and egg (£6.50), fish pie (£6.95), rack of barbecue ribs (£9.95), rump steak (£8.25), and children's menu (£2.75). Well kept Brakspears Bitter, plus a guest such as Special, Old or Mild, Boddingtons Bitter or Theakstons on handpump; darts, shove-ha'penny, table skittles, cribbage, dominoes. There are seats sheltered by an oak tree on the back lawn, as well as a climbing frame and maybe summer barbecues. Across the road, a stream runs through this quiet village. *(Recommended by James Waller, Marjorie and David Lamb, Mr and Mrs Gregory, Gordon, Calum and Susan McLean; more reports please)*

Brakspears ~ Tenant Simon Daniels ~ Real ale ~ Meals and snacks (not Sun evening) ~ (01491) 614110 ~ Children in separate room ~ Open 12-2.30(3 Sat), 6-11

DORCHESTER SU5794 Map 4

George 🛏 ♀

High St; village signposted just off A4074 Maidenhead—Oxford

As good as ever, this lovely old coaching inn has an enjoyably civilised beamed bar with a roaring winter log fire, comfortable seats and some fine old furniture including cushioned settles and leather chairs, fresh flowers on the tables, and copies of *Country Life*. Good bar food includes home-made soup (£2.95), vegetable pâté (£3.50), fish mousse (£3.95), cheese platters, open sandwiches (from £4.50), four different pasta dishes (starter £5.10, main course £7.75), asparagus, artichoke and goat's cheese strudel (£6.95), lamb sausages (£7.95), steaks (from £8.25), mushroom and mustard crusted salmon (£8.50), and puddings (£3.50); roast Sunday lunch (no bar food then). Well kept Brakspears Bitter and Greene King IPA on handpump, good wine by the glass from a quite exceptional wine list of over 130 bin-ends, and a range of malt whiskies. Pleasant and welcoming service. The inn was originally built as a brewhouse for the Norman abbey that still stands opposite. *(Recommended by David Carr, TBB, Chris and Martin Taylor, Jack and Philip Paxton, John Wooll, Professor John White and Patricia White)*

Free house ~ Licensee Brian Griffin ~ Real ale ~ Meals and snacks ~ Restaurant ~ (01865) 340404 ~ Children in restaurant and lounge ~ Open 11-11; 11-10.30 Sun ~ Bedrooms: £52.50B/£65B

EAST HENDRED SU4588 Map 2

Wheatsheaf ♀

Chapel Square; village signposted from A417

As we went to press, the new licensee here had only been in charge for a few weeks. It's a friendly and attractive black and white timbered 16th-c village pub set just below the downs. The bar has high-backed settles and stools around tables on quarry tiles by an inglenook fireplace, some wall panelling, and a tiny parquet-floored triangular platform by the bar; low, stripped deal settles form booths around tables in a carpeted area up some broad steps. What was the restaurant is to be incorporated into the main pub with some old oak standing timbers. The good home-made food now includes sandwiches (from £1.60), filled baked potatoes (from £2.50), sausage, ham, egg and chips (£3.95), steak, kidney and Guinness pie (£4.75), ploughman's (from £4.75), spinach and mushroom lasagne (£4.75), local trout with ginger and spring onions (£7.95), and lovely puddings like treacle tart, raspberry brûlée or white and dark chocolate mousse (£2.50). Well kept Morlands Original, Old Speckled Hen and Smooth String plus a seasonal guest ale on handpump, and 11 wines by the glass; every week there is a bottled beer at £1.50. Darts, dominoes, cribbage and Aunt Sally teams, and piped music. The black labrador is called Bob and the springer spaniel, Harry. The garden behind is colourful with roses and other flowers beneath conifers and silver birch and there's an aviary. The nearby church is interesting – its Tudor clock has elaborate chimes but no hands. *(Recommended by Peter and Audrey Dowsett, M W Turner, Susan and Alan Dominey; more reports on the new regime, please)*

Morlands ~ Tenant Neil Haywood ~ Real ale ~ Meals and snacks (till 10pm) ~ (01235) 833229 ~ Children welcome ~ Open 11-11; 12-10.30 Sun

EXLADE STREET SU6582 Map 2

Highwayman 🛏 ♀ 🍺

Signposted just off A4074 Reading—Wallingford

Although most of this warmly friendly, rambling inn is mostly 17th c, some parts go back another 300 years or so. The two beamed rooms of the bar have quite an unusual layout, with an interesting variety of seats around old tables and even recessed into a central sunken inglenook; an airy conservatory dining room has more seats (mainly for eating) and overlooks the garden. Popular bar food includes sandwiches (from £1.75), soup (£2.95), garlic mushrooms with bacon and white wine (£4.95), lasagne (£6.50), steak, Guinness and mushroom pie or seafood pancake (£6.95), steaks (from £10.95), and weekly changing specials such as grilled sardines (£5.50), a warm salad of tomato and red mullet (£5.95), game casserole (£9.95), and half roast duck (£13.50). Well kept Bass, Boddingtons, Brakspears, Fullers London Pride, and Gibbs Mew Bishops Tipple on handpump, and decent wines. The attractive garden has tables with fine views. The friendly mongrel is called Gurty and the black and white spaniel, Saigon. *(Recommended by Sheila Keene, Jack and Philip Paxton, Mayur Shah; more reports please)*

Free house ~ Licensees Carole and Roger Shippey ~ Real ale ~ Meals and snacks (12-2.30, 6-10.30) ~ Restaurant ~ (01491) 682020 ~ Children in restaurant ~ Open 11-3, 6-11 ~ Bedrooms: £45S/£60S

FERNHAM SU2992 Map 4

Woodman

A420 SW of Oxford, then left into B4508 after about 11 miles; village a further 6 miles on

In winter you can mull your own wine or beer over the big log fire here. It's a friendly, atmospheric old country pub and the heavily beamed rooms are full of an amazing assortment of old objects like clay pipes ready-filled for smoking, milkmaids' yokes, leather tack, coach horns, an old screw press, some original oil paintings and good black and white photographs of horses. Comfortable seating includes cushioned benches, pews, and windsor chairs, and the candlelit tables are simply made from old casks. The former barn is now an over-spill for the restaurant or used for functions. Good bar food includes sandwiches and filled baked potatoes, home-made soup (£1.80), chicken liver pâté (£3.10), mixed vegetable curry (£4.50), home-cooked ham and egg (£4.90), curries (from £5.40), steak and kidney pie (£5.80), and daily specials such as moules marinierès (in season £3.50), chicken supreme (£6.15), and fresh salmon (£7.20), and puddings like home-made bread and butter pudding or apple and sultana flan (£2.30). OAPs who visit regularly get a substantial discount; dominoes, cribbage, piped music, three entertaining cats. Well kept (if not cheap for the area) Bass, Fullers London Pride, Morlands Original and Old Speckled Hen, and Theakstons Old Peculier are tapped from casks behind the bar. Boules in the enclosed car park. *(Recommended by Peter and Nicol Beard, John and Wendy Trentham, Marjorie and David Lamb, David Peakall, Roger and Valerie Hill, Peter and Audrey Dowsett)*

Free house ~ Licensee John Lane ~ Real ale ~ Meals and snacks (available during opening hours) ~ Restaurant ~ (01367) 820643 ~ Children in eating area of bar ~ Open 11-3, 6.30-11

FINSTOCK SP3616 Map 4

Plough 🖙 ♀

The Bottom; just off B4022 N of Witney

This neatly refurbished thatched old pub is very much the hub of the village and you can expect a warm welcome from all the staff. The long, rambling bar is comfortable and relaxed and nicely split up by partitions and alcoves, with an armchair by the open log-burning stove in the massive stone inglenook, tiles up at the end by the servery (elsewhere is carpeted), and a cosy feel under its low oak beams. The licensees are both dog lovers and have decorated the walls with various doggy-related paraphernalia, including rosettes from canine chums they've exhibited at Crufts. Their own llasl apso is called Jumbo, and other dogs are welcome in the garden (on a lead) and public bar; they'll usually be offered water or food. Bar food includes sandwiches, and specials such as hare and walnut pâté (£3.95), king prawns in garlic butter (£5.45), leek, ham and stilton pie (£5.95), rack of lamb with rosemary and redcurrant gravy (£8.95), and strips of beef with port and stilton (£9.45). A comfortable low-beamed stripped-stone no-smoking dining room is on the right. Well kept Adnams Broadside, Badger Tanglefoot, Batemans XXXB, Boddingtons, Hook Norton Best and Old Hookey, and Robinsons Old Tom on handpump (under light blanket pressure in summer), pink fizzy wine by the glass, and pimms and fruit cocktails in summer; a decent choice of wines and malt whiskies; maybe unobtrusive piped music. A separate games area has darts, bar billiards, cribbage, and dominoes. There are tables (and Aunt Sally) in the good, sizeable garden. Good surrounding walks. *(Recommended by Susan and John Douglas, Mr and Mrs Garrett, Robin and Laura Hillman, Tim Brierly, Graham and Karen Oddey, G W A Pearce, DMT, Peter and Audrey Dowsett, Amanda Clement, Andrew Campbell)*

Free house ~ Licensees Keith and Nigel Ewers ~ Real ale ~ Meals and snacks ~ Restaurant ~ (01993) 868333 ~ Children in eating area of bar and in restaurant ~ Open 12-3, 6-11; 12-11 Sat, 12-4, 7-10.30 Sun ~ One bedroom: /£45B

FYFIELD SU4298 Map 4

White Hart

In village, off A420 8 miles SW of Oxford

It's quite a surprise to find an impressive medieval building inside this humble-looking pub. There are soaring eaves, huge stone-flanked window embrasures, and an attractive carpeted upper gallery making up the main room – a grand hall rather than a traditional bar. A low-ceilinged side bar has an inglenook fireplace with a huge black urn hanging over the grate, and a framed history of the pub on the wall. The priests' room and barrel-vaulted cellar are dining areas; most dining areas are no smoking. Well kept Boddingtons, Badger Tanglefoot, Hook Norton Best, Theakstons Old Peculier and Wadworths 6X on handpump or tapped from the cask. Bar food includes lunchtime sandwiches, soup (£2.50), garlic mushrooms (£3.25), curried nut roast or moussaka (£5.95), chicken curry or steak and Guinness pie (£6.25), Mexican pork or gammon steak (£6.95), venison casserole (£8.50), and steaks (from £8.95); friendly, attentive service. Darts, shove-ha'penny, dominoes, cribbage, and piped music. A heavy wooden door leads out to the rambling, sheltered and flowery back lawn, which has a children's playground. *(Recommended by C Moncreiffe, Andy Petersen, Nigel Norman, D C T and E A Frewer, Dave Irving, Tom McLean, Ewan McCall, Roger Huggins)*

Free house ~ Licensees John and Sherry Howard ~ Real ale ~ Meals and snacks (till 10pm) ~ Restaurant ~ (01865) 390585 ~ Children allowed in several rooms ~ Open 11-3, 6-11; closed 25-26 Dec

GREAT TEW SP3929 Map 4

Falkland Arms ★ ★ 🛏

Off B4022 about 5 miles E of Chipping Norton

Great Tew is an enchanting village of untouched golden-stone thatched cottages – of which this lovely pub is one. For many people this is their idea of a perfect English pub – a partly panelled bar with a wonderful inglenook fireplace, high-backed settles and a diversity of stools around plain stripped tables on flagstones and bare boards, one, two and three handled mugs hanging from the beam-and-board ceiling, dim converted oil lamps, and shutters for the stone-mullioned latticed windows. At the bar counter, decorated with antique Doulton jugs, mugs and tobacco jars, you can buy clay pipes filled ready to smoke, some 50 different snuffs, tankards, a model of the pub, and handkerchiefs; the snug (used as a breakfast room in the mornings) is no-smoking. As well as the regular Badger Tanglefoot, Donnington BB, Hook Norton Best and Wadworths 6X, they always have five well kept guest beers, along with 30 or so country wines, 60 malt whiskies, a couple of farm ciders, and hot punch in winter; darts, shove-ha'penny, dominoes, cribbage, and table skittles. Straightforward lunch menu usually includes sandwiches, sausage and pickle (£4.80), and beef and pâté pie or gingered lamb casserole (£5). There are tables outside in front of the pub, with picnic tables under umbrellas in the garden behind – where there's a dovecot. Staying here is delightful (two of the rooms have four-posters), though if you're planning to come at a weekend you may have to book up to three months in advance. Not surprisingly, both the village and the pub itself do get extremely crowded, so weekday lunchtimes are generally your best bet. There's a specially built car park 60 yards or so away from the pub to try to keep the place as unspoilt as possible. *(Recommended by Nigel Wikeley, Joan Olivier, Pam and Tim Moorey, Geoff Dibble, Jack and Philip Paxton, Miss K Law, K M Timmins, Dr S Willavoys, Frank Gadbois, Andrew and Ruth Triggs, Richard J Raeon, Karen Barnes, Paul Boot, Hanns P Golez, J O Jonkler, Alan Skull, Mrs J M Campbell, P and M Rudlin, Dr Peter Donahue, C Moncreiffe, David Campbell, Vicki McLean, D C T Frewer, S G Brown, Lynn Sharpless, Bob Eardley, A G Drake, John Bowdler, Mark Williams, P J Pearce, Karen and Graham Oddey, Meg and Colin Hamilton)*

Free house ~ Licensees John and Hazel Milligan ~ Real ale ~ Lunchtime meals and snacks (not Sun and Mon, except bank holidays) ~ (01608) 683653 ~ Children in eating area of bar at lunchtime ~ Folk music Sun evening ~ Open 11.30-2.30, 6-11; closed Mon lunchtime except bank holidays ~ Bedrooms: £30(£35S)/£45(£50S)

HAILEY SU6485 Map 2

King William IV ★ £

Note – this is the hamlet of Hailey, near Ipsden (not the larger Hailey over in west Oxon); signposted with Ipsden from A4074 S of Wallingford; can also be reached from A423; OS Sheet 175 map reference 641859

Old ploughs and farm wagons sit on the lawn to the side of this 400-year-old pub and the 18 hands high shire horse in the stable is called Duke; views across peaceful, rolling pastures. Inside, the relaxed beamed bar is filled with well restored farm implements and has some good sturdy furniture on the tiles in front of the big winter log fire; the timbered bare brick walls are covered with root cutters, forks, ratchets, shovels, crooks, grabbers, man-traps, wicker sieves, full-size carts, ploughs, and a pitching prong, all with details of their age, use and maker – there's even a couple of dried bladders. Two broadly similar carpeted areas open off. Well kept Brakspears PA, SB, and Old tapped from casks behind the bar, and farm ciders; simple, cheap food consists of lunchtime ploughman's and filled rolls and pies. The perfect way to arrive is by Ian Smith's horse and wagon service; he arranges rides from Nettlebed to the pub where you then have a ploughman's or supper and gently return through the woods and via Stoke Row back to Nettlebed (01491-641324 to book).

(Recommended by Jack and Philip Paxton; more reports please)

Brakspears ~ Tenant Brian Penney ~ Real ale ~ Snacks ~ (01491) 680675 ~
Children in eating area at lunchtime ~ Open 11-2.30(3 Sat), 6-11

HOOK NORTON SP3533 Map 4

Pear Tree ▄

Village signposted off A361 SW of Banbury

Readers very much enjoy this friendly, largely unspoilt village pub and in summer,
the attractive sizeable garden is a popular place to be with its play area, chickens and
rabbits, Aunt Sally, and Sunday barbecues. The knocked together bar area has
country-kitchen furniture, including long tables as if for communal eating, a well-
stocked magazine rack, open fires blazing away merrily, and a friendly and relaxed
atmosphere; maybe locals drifting in with their dogs. The Hook Norton brewery is
barely 100 yards down the lane, so you can rely on them serving perfectly kept
Hook Norton Best, Old Hookey, and Mild along with the seasonal Haymaker or
Twelve Days; a respectable wine list, and quite a few malt and Irish whiskies. Good
bar food includes home-made soups (£1.95), hot bacon and brie or stilton
sandwiches (£3.10), cheesy topped ratatouille (£3.95), lamb liver in marsala wine
(£4.50), stir fries or fish pie (£4.95), rack of lamb with bubble and squeak patties
(£5.45), and puddings like banoffi pie, lemon cheesecake or chocolate roulade.
Welcoming landlord, good service. Shove-ha'penny, cribbage, dominoes, trivia,
Jenga, and quiz nights. More bedrooms are to be added. (Recommended by Margaret
and Roy Randle, Alan and Paula McCully, Robert Gomme, M Benjamin, George Atkinson,
David Campbell, Vicki McLean)

Hook Norton ~ Tenants Steve and Wendy Tindsley ~ Real ale ~ Meals and
snacks (not Sun or Tues evenings) ~ (01608) 737482 ~ Children welcome till 9pm
~ Occasional folk players/piano ~ Open 12-2.30(3 Sat), 6-11; 12-10.30 Sun;
closed winter Sun afternoons ~ Bedroom: £20S/£35S

nr HOOK NORTON SP3533 Map 4

Gate Hangs High ♀

Banbury Rd; a mile N of village towards Sibford, at Banbury—Rollright crossroads

Even though this welcoming country pub is rather tucked away, it does tend to fill
up quickly and has long been a handy find for travellers in the area, as indicated by
the sign outside:

The gate hangs high, and hinders none,
Refresh and pay, and travel on.

There's quite an emphasis on the popular, weekly changing food served by friendly
staff: sandwiches, home-made soup (£2.25), pâté (£2.95), pancakes filled with
mushrooms and celery in a rich tomato sauce (£6.25), lovely fresh smoked haddock
(£7.25), peanut loaf or steak and kidney pie (£6.50), chicken balti (£6.75), loin of
pork with apricot stuffing and orange sauce or honey-baked ham with local
asparagus and cheese sauce (£7.50), and home-made puddings (£2.95). The bar has
joists in the long, low ceiling, a brick bar counter, stools and assorted chairs on the
carpet, and a gleaming copper hood over the hearth in the inglenook fireplace. Well
kept Hook Norton Best, Old Hookey, Haymaker, and Twelve Days on handpump,
a good wine list, and a range of malt whiskies; dominoes. There are now picnic
tables in front of the pub surrounded by wonderful flowering tubs and wall baskets,
and at the back, the broad lawn with holly and apple trees, has swings for children
to play on and fine views. Five miles south-west are the Bronze Age Rollright Stones
– said to be a king and his army who were turned to stone by a witch. (Recommended
by Alan and Paula McCully, Margaret and Roy Randle, John Bowdler, Marjorie and David
Lamb, Rona Murdoch, Mr and Mrs Box, B E Tarver, P and M Rudlin)

Hook Norton ~ Tenant Stuart Rust ~ Real ale ~ Meals and snacks (not Sun
evening) ~ Restaurant (not Sun evening) ~ (01608) 737387 ~ Children in eating
area of bar and in restaurant ~ Open 11.30-3, 6.30-11

KELMSCOT SU2499 Map 4

Plough 🏠

NW of Faringdon, off A417 or A4095

This rather pretty little inn is only a few minutes' walk from the Thames (where there are moorings) and the attractive garden has Aunt Sally, and seats amongst the unusual flowers. Inside, the attractively traditional small bar is homely and warmly welcoming, with ancient flagstones and stripped stone walls, and a relaxed chatty atmosphere; there's also a larger cheerfully carpeted back room with interesting prints on its uncluttered walls; the licensee is happy to offer advice on local walks. A wide choice of home-cooked food includes sandwiches (from £1.70, toasties from £1.95, filled french bread from £3), soup (£2.50), filled baked potatoes (from £2.60), ploughman's (from £3.50), ham and egg (£4.50), filled pancakes (from £5.95), beef in orange (£6.95), chicken in calvados or grilled trout (£7.25), steaks (from £8.95), daily specials such as deep-fried camembert (£4.25), pigeon breasts in red wine (£6.95), and swordfish steak (£7.25), and puddings (£2.75); on Sunday they only serve snacks and a roast. Well kept Morlands Original and Old Speckled Hen, and a guest such as Mansfield Old Baily on handpump; darts, shove-ha'penny, cribbage, fruit machine, trivia, and piped music. *(Recommended by Ted George, DI, Mr and Mrs Peter Smith, Mrs P J Pearce, Peter and Audrey Dowsett, David Campbell, Vicki McLean)*

Free house ~ Licensees Trevor and Anne Pardoe ~ Real ale ~ Meals and snacks ~ Restaurant ~ (01367) 253543 ~ Children welcome ~ Singer or duo Sat evening ~ Open 11-11; 11.30-3, 6-11 in winter ~ Bedrooms: £30B/£45B

LEWKNOR SU7198 Map 4

Olde Leathern Bottel

Under a mile from M40 junction 6; just off B4009 towards Watlington

There's a happy, bustling atmosphere in this neatly kept pub – and you can be sure of a warm welcome from the friendly licensee. The two rooms of the bar have open fires, heavy beams in the low ceilings, rustic furnishings, and an understated decor of old beer taps and the like; the no-smoking family room is separated only by standing timbers, so you don't feel cut off from the rest of the pub – and part of the lounge is also no smoking. Good, popular and generously served bar food includes lunchtime sandwiches and snacks as well as pâté (£3.95), vegetable or chicken curries (£4.50), home-made steak and kidney pie (£4.95), gammon and egg or barbecued spare ribs (£5.95), steaks (from £7.95), daily specials, and puddings like treacle tart or cheesecake (£2); quick, obliging service. Well kept Brakspears Bitter, SB and winter Old on handpump. There are tables on the sizeable lawn alongside the car park; this is a very pretty village. *(Recommended by Jane Bailey, GWB, TBB, Mrs Hilarie Taylor, Neville Kenyon, Dr and Mrs Baker, Dave Braisted, Roger Huggins, M W Turner)*

Brakspears ~ Tenants Mike and Lesley Fletcher ~ Real ale ~ Meals and snacks ~ (01844) 351482 ~ Children in family room and lounge bar ~ Open 10.30-2.30(3 Sat), 6-11

LITTLE MILTON SP6100 Map 4

Lamb

3 miles from M40, junction 7; A329 towards Wallingford

Set in rolling farmland, this pretty 17th-c stone pub has a long thatched roof hanging low over honey-coloured walls. The old-fashioned and simple beamed bar has little windows in the stripped stone walls that are so near the ground you have to stoop to look out, lots of tables with wheelback chairs, soft lighting, and well kept Bass, Benskins, and Ind Coope Burton on handpump; friendly service. As well as sandwiches, snacks and children's meals, daily specials might include first-class grilled Portuguese sardines, baked avocado with smoked salmon and prawns

(£5.45), fillet of salmon with hollandaise sauce (£7.95), medaillons of beef in pepper and cognac sauce (£9.95), and very good sirloin steak. In summer the quiet garden is lovely: hanging baskets, tubs of flowers, roses, a herbaceous border, fruit trees, and swings. It can get quite crowded at lunchtimes. *(Recommended by John Waller, Dave Braisted, Tim and Ann Newell, Keith Stevens, Gordon, Dave Irving, Ewan McCall, Roger Huggins, Tom McLean; more reports please)*

Sycamore Taverns ~ Tenant David Bowell ~ Real ale ~ Meals and snacks (till 10pm; all day Sun) ~ (01844) 279527 ~ Children in eating area of bar ~ Open 11-2.30, 6.30-11; 12-10.30 Sun

MAIDENSGROVE SU7288 Map 2

Five Horseshoes 🍴 ♀

W of village, which is signposted from B480 and B481; OS Sheet 175, map reference 711890

High up in the Chiltern beechwoods, this busy little brick house is mainly popular for its imaginative food: soup (£2.75), ploughman's (£3.95), home-made chicken liver pâté (£4.95), baked potatoes (from £5.75), mixed hors-d'ouevres (£5.95 per person), pancakes filled with smoked chicken and mushroom (£6.50), steak and kidney pie (£6.95), giant mussels grilled with bacon, parmesan and pine nuts or stir-fried vegetables with a tangy sauce (£7.95), cassoulet (£8.75), steaks (from £12.95), and daily specials like deep-fried brie in wholemeal crumbs with redcurrant and chive sauce (£5.75), sole stuffed with smoked salmon with red and black caviar on lemon hollandaise (£9.50), fresh tuna steaks with lime and chive butter, and fresh dover sole; a sizeable barbecue menu, too (from £6.50). Well kept Brakspears Bitter, Special and winter Old, and guests like Boddingtons and Theakstons on handpump, and a dozen wines by the glass. The rambling bar is furnished with mostly modern wheelback chairs around stripped wooden tables – though there are some attractive older seats and a big baluster-leg table, as well as a good log fire in winter; the low ceiling in the main area is covered in banknotes from all over the world, mainly donated by customers. There's a separate bar for walkers where boots are welcome, and a dining conservatory (booking is pretty much essential in here at weekends). The sheltered garden behind has a rockery, some interesting water features, and fine views down over the woods; they have an outside bar where summer barbecues are held. *(Recommended by Dr G W Barnett, June S Bray, Gill and Andy Plumb, M Sargent, D Hayman, Susan and Alan Dominey, Heather Couper, Andy Thwaites, S and P Hayes)*

Brakspears ~ Tenant Graham Cromack ~ Real ale ~ Meals and snacks ~ Conservatory restaurant ~ (01491) 641282 ~ Children in eating area of bar if over 8 ~ Open 11-2.30, 6-11

MURCOTT SP5815 Map 4

Nut Tree ♀

Off B4027 NE of Oxford, via Islip and Charlton on Otmoor

In summer particularly, this civilised low-thatched old house is a real pleasure to visit with its colourful hanging baskets, ducks on a pretty front pond, trim lawns, and usually plenty of animals such as donkeys, peacocks and rabbits; also Aunt Sally, and an unusual collection of ten gargoyles, each loosely modelled on one of the local characters, and carved into a magnificently grotesque form from a different wood. Nine of them hang in the walnut tree and one from a pillar overlooking the well. Inside, the welcoming beamed lounge has a long polished bar with brasses, antiques and pictures all round, fresh flowers on its tables (set for food), and a winter log fire; there's also a small back conservatory-style extension. Enjoyable food includes soup (£2.50), sandwiches (from £2.50), sausages and chips (£3.95), king prawns with garlic mayonnaise (£5.10), vegetarian lasagne (£5.50), salads (from £5.65), fresh plaice, cod or haddock (from £5.95), gammon with curried peach (£6.65), calf liver and bacon (£8.95), steaks (from £10.20), duck breast with madeira sauce (£10.50), and lots of puddings. Well kept Morrells Oxford and guests like Brains, Brakspears,

Boddingtons, Glenny Hobgoblin, Morells Varsity, Wadworths 6X, and Wychert on handpump, a fair number of malt whiskies, and a decent range of wines. Darts, shove-ha'penny, dominoes, and quiz nights. The pub is handy for walks through the boggy Otmoor wilderness. *(Recommended by Ted George, Carolyn and Michael Hedoin, A Preston, M Sargent, Derek and Sylvia Stephenson, Lucy James, Dean Foden, MLC, GC, Brian White, Sue Demont, Tim Barrow, Roger Byrne, Richard Dolphin, T M Dobby)*

Free house ~ Licensee Gordon Evans ~ Real ale ~ Meals and snacks (not Sun) ~ Restaurant (not Sun) ~ (01865) 331253 ~ Children in restaurant ~ Open 11-3, 6.30-11

NUFFIELD SU6687 Map 2

Crown ♀

A423/B481

As we went to press, the licensees of this attractive and friendly little partly 17th-c brick-and-flint pub told us they would probably be leaving in the next few months, but nothing was certain. The heavily beamed lounge has a relaxed atmosphere, country furniture, a roaring log fire in a fine inglenook fireplace, and shelves of golf balls (there's an adjacent golf course); cribbage, dominoes. The public bar has another big log fire, and there's a family room, and a friendly cat. Bar food includes home-made soup (£2.75), mushroom pâté (£4.50), garlic mushrooms with a herb cream cheese filling (£4.75), steak, kidney and ale pie (£5.95), vegetarian cassoulet (£6.75), home-made crab cakes with fresh tartare sauce (£6.95), lamb steaks marinated with lime and pernod (£8.95), steaks (from £9.95), and half Gressingham duck with a plum and ginger glaze (£10.50); service is prompt and friendly. Well kept Brakspears Bitter and Special, and a guest such as Boddingtons on handpump. Tables out in front, or under cocktail parasols in the partly terraced back garden. Very handy for Nuffield Place, the home of the late Lord Nuffield of Morris cars fame, and good surrounding walks (the pub is right on the Ridgeway Long Distance Path). *(Recommended by Mrs H Astley, Professor J R Leigh, Heather Couper, Gordon, R N Carter, Joan Olivier, Dick Brown, R D Knight)*

Brakspears ~ Tenants Ann and Gerry Bean ~ Real ale ~ Meals and snacks ~ (01491) 641335 ~ Children in small room off bar, lunchtimes only ~ Open 11-2.30, 6-11; closed 25-26 Dec, and evening 1 Jan

OXFORD SP5106 Map 4

Turf Tavern

Bath Place; via St Helen's Passage, between Holywell Street and New College Lane

Whitbreads have refurbished and redecorated this pub inside and out this year – but the two little rooms still have a snug feel, dark beams, and low ceilings, and are much as Hardy described them when Jude the Obscure discovered that Arabella the barmaid was the wife who'd left him years before; there's also a bar in one of the courtyards. A changing range of real ales might include Archers Golden, Boddingtons, Brains SA, Flowers Original, Uley Old Spot and Hogshead, Wadworths 6X and so forth on handpump or tapped from the cask; also, country wines and Westons ciders; trivia. Straightforward bar food includes filled baked potatoes (from £2.25), doorstep sandwiches (from £2.45), and chilli con carne or steak in ale pie (£4.75); the top food area is no smoking. This is a pretty place – especially in summer, when there are tables in the three attractive walled-in flagstoned or gravelled courtyards around the old-fashioned building; in winter the braziers in the courtyard are very atmospheric to huddle around. *(Recommended by Hanns P Golez, David Carr, D C T and E A Frewer, Pat and Roger Fereday, Nigel and Amanda Thorp, Chris and Martin Taylor, Jenny and Brian Seller, Gordon, Simon Ludlow, Sue Demont, Tim Barrow, LM, Wayne Brindle, John Wooll, David Campbell, Vicki McLean, Dave Irving, Roger Huggins, Tom McLean, Ewan McCall, Mr and Mrs R J Foreman, Nigel Wooliscroft, Walter Reid)*

Whitbreads ~ Manager Trevor Walter ~ Real ale ~ Meals and snacks (noon-8pm) ~ (01865) 243235 ~ Children in eating area of bar ~ No nearby parking ~ Open 11-11; 12-10.30 Sun

RAMSDEN SP3515 Map 4

Royal Oak 🏠 ♀

Village signposted off B4022 Witney—Charlbury

There are no noisy games machines or piped music to spoil the relaxed, welcoming atmosphere in this unpretentious village inn. The traditional beamed bar is simply furnished and decorated but comfortable, and has a cheery winter log fire and well kept Archers Golden, Brakspears Special, Fullers London Pride, Hook Norton Best and Old Hookey, and Morrells Graduate on handpump; enjoyable house wines and very obliging service. Generous helpings of good bar food include lunchtime sandwiches and daily specials such as five sausages with mash, stilton, leek and mushroom pie (£7.75), Mexican chicken fajitas with tortillas and dips (£8.50), half shoulder of English lamb with a sage and cider sauce (£10.25), and haunch of venison steak with a sauce (£11.50); lovely puddings and good Sunday lunches. The evening dining room is no smoking. The cosy bedrooms are in separate cottages. *(Recommended by John Waller, Deborah Jackson, John C Baker, Peter and Audrey Dowsett, F M Bunbury)*

Free house ~ Licensee Jon Oldham ~ Real ale ~ Meals and snacks (till 10pm) ~ Restaurant ~ (01993) 868213 ~ Children in eating area of bar ~ Open 11.30-2.30, 6.30-11; closed 25 Dec ~ Bedrooms: £30B/£45B

ROKE SU6293 Map 2

Home Sweet Home

Village signposted off B4009 Benson—Watlington

The two smallish rooms of the bar in this rather smart thatched place have a good country atmosphere, heavy stripped beams, leather armed chairs on the bare boards, a few horsey or game pictures such as a nice Thorburn print of snipe on the stone walls, and big log fires – one with a great high-backed settle facing it across a hefty slab of a rustic table. On the right, a carpeted room with low settees and armchairs, and an attractive corner glass cupboard, leads through to the restaurant. Good bar food includes sandwiches, fresh salmon fishcakes with parsley sauce or steak and kidney pudding (£6.95), calf liver with crispy bacon (£7.95), and chicken with gorgonzola, spring onion and sun-dried tomato stuffing (£8.95); friendly service. Well kept Brakspears Bitter and Eldridge Pope Royal Oak on handpump, and a good choice of malt whiskies. The low-walled front garden is ideal for eating on a sunny day; there are lots of flowers around the tables out by the well. *(Recommended by Margaret Dyke, John Waller, June S Bray, Mrs M Lawrence, Nicholas Stuart Holmes)*

Free house ~ Licensees Jill Madle, Peter and Irene Mountford ~ Real ale ~ Meals and snacks ~ Restaurant ~ (01491) 838249 ~ Well behaved children welcome ~ Open 11-3, 5.30-11; 12-4, 7-10.30 Sun; closed evenings 25-26 Dec

SHENINGTON SP3742 Map 4

Bell ♀

Village signposted from A422 W of Banbury

The lucky local junior school have their lunches cooked for them here and although there's quite an emphasis on the interesting food eaten in this old golden stone cottage, the very friendly landlady does not allow this to over-shadow the bar. The heavy-beamed and carpeted lounge has vases of flowers on the tables, old maps and documents on the cream wall, and brown cloth-cushioned wall seats and window seats; the wall in the flagstoned area on the left is stripped to stone and decorated with heavy-horse harness, and the right side opens into a neat little pine-panelled room (popular with locals) with decorated plates on its walls; darts, cribbage, dominoes, coal fire. Favourite dishes (with prices unchanged since last year) still include sandwiches, well-flavoured soups like parsnip, steak and kidney pie or almond, celery and cashew nut bake (£5.75), salmon in cucumber sauce (£7.50), duck in black cherries (£8.95), and puddings such as a good sticky toffee pudding. Well kept Boddingtons and Hook Norton Best on handpump, and a good choice of wines; good, cheery service. There's a tortoiseshell cat called Willow and a west highland terrier, Lucy. The tables at the front look across to the green. *(Recommended by Gordon Tong, Joan Olivier, D C T and E A Frewer, Nigel Clifton, I D Irving, John Bowdler, David Lewis, Maysie Thompson, Jon Carpenter, S C King, George Jonas, Jill and Peter Bickley, Piotr Chodzko-Zajko)*

Free house ~ Licensee Jennifer Dixon ~ Real ale ~ Meals and snacks (till 10) ~ (01295) 670274 ~ Children welcome ~ Open 12(11.30 Sat)-3, 6-11; 12-4, 7-10.30 Sun ~ Bedrooms: £15/£40B

SHIPTON UNDER WYCHWOOD SP2717 Map 4

Lamb ★ 🍽 ♀ 🛏

Just off A361 to Burford

Oxfordshire Dining Pub of the Year

Now owned by the Old English Pub Company, this civilised and stylish old place also has new managers. There's still a strong emphasis on the very good food but most readers are happy to tell us that this is not at the expense of those just wanting a quiet drink. The beamed bar has quite a relaxed feel, as well as a fine oak-panelled settle, a nice mix of solid old farmhouse-style and captain's chairs on the wood-block floor, polished tables, cushioned bar stools, solid oak bar counter, pictures on old partly bared stone walls, and maybe newspapers on rods to read. As well as the popular buffet, the first-rate dishes might include home-made soup (£2.75), home-made duck and orange pâté (£3.50), sandwiches (from £3.50), grilled goat's cheese with bacon (£3.95), vegetable stroganoff (£6.95), excellent seafood tart, popular cotswold pie (£7.50), chicken supreme (£7.95), fresh fish from Cornwall like lemon sole, plaice, crab and lobster (from £7.95), fillet of pork with calvados (£8.95), lovely duck in orange, and puddings such as lemon tart, fruit crumbles and bread and butter pudding (£2.95); enjoyable Sunday lunch. The restaurant is no smoking. Well kept Hook Norton Best and Wadworths 6X on handpump, several malt whiskies, carefully chosen wines and champagne by the glass. In summer, you can sit at tables among the roses at the back. *(Recommended by Mrs Jean Dundas, Douglas Frewer, Robin and Laura Hillman, MDN, John Bowdler, Mr and Mrs Christopher Ball, Andrew and Ruth Triggs, M Sargent, Adam and Elizabeth Duff, Neville and Sarah Hargreaves, C A Hall, Mrs D P Simms, J O Jonkler, M L and G Clarke, Peter and Nicol Beard, Eric and Jackie Robinson, Stephen Brown, A M Rankin)*

Old English Pub Company ~ Managers Michael and Jenny Eastick ~ Real ale ~ Meals and snacks (till 10pm) ~ Restaurant (not Sun evening) ~ (01993) 830465 ~ Children in eating area and restaurant ~ Open 11-3, 6-11 ~ Bedrooms: £58B/£68B

Shaven Crown 🛏 ♀

Despite the slightly imposing reception area, this lovely old place is as welcoming as ever. It was originally a hospice for the monastery of Bruern in the 14th c, and parts of it are said to have been used as a hunting lodge by Elizabeth I. There's a magnificent double-collar braced hall roof, lofty beams and a sweeping double stairway down the stone wall, and the beamed bar has a relief of the 1146 Battle of Evesham, as well as seats forming little stalls around the tables and upholstered benches built into the walls. But perhaps the glory of this striking heavily stone-roofed inn is the medieval courtyard garden behind, little changed since the days when it was used as an exercise yard by monks. A tranquil place on a sunny day, old-fashioned seats are set out on the stone cobbles and crazy paving, with a view of the lily pool and roses. Good bar food includes soup (£2.65), ploughman's (from £3.45), smoked haddock mousse (£3.50), home-baked ham with chips (£5.75), steak, kidney and mushroom pie (£5.95), curried prawns (£6.25), sirloin steak (£8.95), daily specials like mushroom and walnut pancake (£4.50), lamb liver and bacon (£5.25), and venison sausages in red wine (£5.75), and puddings such as chocolate mousse basque, fruit pie or treacle tart (£2.50); the restaurant is no smoking. Well kept Hook Norton Best and two guests such as Greene King Abbot, Morlands Old Speckled Hen, and Wadworths 6X on handpump, well-chosen wine list with a dozen or so half-bottles and a wine of the week, and very good, friendly service. The pub has its own bowling green. *(Recommended by David Campbell, Vicki McLean, Andrew and Ruth Triggs, Alan and Paul McCully, Dr S Willavoys, Marjorie and David Lamb, Joyce McKimm, Tom McLean, Ewan McCall, Roger Huggins, Dave Irving, Moira and John Cole, Frank Cummins, S May)*

Free house ~ Licensees Trevor and Mary Brookes ~ Real ale ~ Meals and snacks (not 25 Dec) ~ Restaurant ~ (01993) 830330 ~ Children in eating area of bar ~ Open 12-2.30, 7-11 ~ Bedrooms: £33B/£66B

SIBFORD GOWER SP3537 Map 4

Wykham Arms 🛏

Village signed off B4035 Banbury—Shipston on Stour

Friendly, enthusiastic new licensees have taken over this pretty and neatly thatched cottage since it was last in this book, and early indications are that it should be quite a hit with readers. Mrs Fisher is an artist and sculptor and apart from producing the pretty menu, has hung the bare stone walls of the comfortable low-beamed lounge with her own pictures. The room spreads through three open-plan areas around the central servery, with brocaded built-in wall seats and windsor chairs, and one table consisting of a glassed-in ancient well. The smaller tap room has an inglenook fireplace, and the attractive, partly no-smoking restaurant was once the stables. Very good bar food now includes soup such as tomato and roast pepper or carrot and coriander (£2.20), sandwiches (from £2.20), salad niçoise (£2.50), ploughman's (from £3.90), piglet pie with cider and cream (£5.90), chicken balti (£6.50), a platter of cold meats with stir fried curried vegetables and curried fruit chutney or extremely popular fresh fishcakes (one salmon, one smoked haddock and one prawn with lemon butter sauce, £6.90), swordfish steak with fresh lime sauce (£8.50), a Wykham wonder (a sort of oblong pizza based on ciabatta bread baked with olive oil and rosemary, £9.90 for two people), and puddings like warm apple pie or lemon brûlée (£2.50). Well kept Bass, Hook Norton Best, Merivales Edgecutter (from the tiny local Edgcote Brewery), Morlands Old Speckled Hen, and Wychwood Fiddlers Elbow on handpump, and lots of country wines; dominoes. The big well planted garden has views over the rolling countryside. *(Recommended by Marjorie and David Lamb, Ted George, Ben and Chris Francis)*

Free house ~ Licensees Sydney and Doreen Fisher ~ Real ale ~ Meals and snacks ~ Restaurant ~ (01295) 780351 ~ Children welcome ~ Open 12-3, 6.30-11; closed Mon lunchtime ~ Bedrooms: £25B/£35B

SOUTH LEIGH SP3908 Map 4

Mason Arms 🍴 🛏 ♀

3m S of A40 Witney—Eynsham

A new licensee has taken over this delightful thatched country pub and has made quite a few changes. The flagstoned bar now has lots of old photographs and hundreds of beaujolais bottles on the walls, attractive antique furnishings, soft lighting from lots of church candles, a panelled bar counter, and log fires in stone hearths at each end of the room. And you can enjoy the food in three eating areas – at the large refectory table in the bar, in an informal dining room, and in a more formal one with white starched cloths and napkins, pictures on the dark red walls, old books, port decanters, cigar boxes (the best Cuban cigars), and a country house atmosphere. The same menu is used everywhere and they use the best produce possible to create the totally home-made food. At lunchtime there might be sandwiches and dishes such as chicken liver pâté (£4.50), lamb and plum casserole or beef curry (£7.50), and in the evening marvellous steaks (14oz sirloin £13) and lots of fresh fish: potted shrimps (£5.50), mussels in vermouth (£6), fresh scallops (£7), wild scottish salmon (£8), and 20oz dover sole (£15). Lovely puddings like chocolate mousse or french apple tart. You can pre-book a leg of lamb, haunch of venison or pheasants and grouse to cook on a spit over the large fire in winter (around £9). Well kept Ind Coope Burton tapped from the cask, fine French wines, and cocktails; friendly, attentive staff. Outside, there are picnic tables in a small grove by some quite bizarrely-shaped trees and little bushes. Dylan Thomas used to pop in here while writing *Under Milk Wood* at the nearby Manor House. No dogs and no credit cards except American Express. *(Recommended by Peter and Audrey Dowsett, Susan and John Douglas; more reports on the new regime, please)*

Free house ~ Licensee Gerald Stonhill ~ Real ale ~ Meals and snacks (not Sun evening or Mon; till 10pm) ~ Restaurant (not Sun evening or Mon) ~ (01993) 702485 ~ Children in restaurant if over 8 and if arranged beforehand ~ Open 11-3, 6-11; closed Sun evening, closed Mon ~ Bedrooms: /£50B

SOUTH STOKE SU5983 Map 2

Perch & Pike 🍽 ♀

Off B4009 2 miles N of Goring

It's the innovative food that draws most people to this attractive flint pub – though it's also a relaxed place to enjoy the well kept Brakspears Bitter and Special or one of the 15 wines by the glass served from the old oak bar counter. Diners have linen table napkins in old napkins rings, and bone-handled cutlery gleaned from antique markets, and the menu changes every couple of weeks, but as well as sandwiches (from £2.75) or ploughman's (£4.75) you might find dishes such as fresh mussels with cream, wine and garlic (£4.75), fillets of spiced red mullet or char-grilled chicken salad with raspberry vinaigrette (£5.50), prawns and melted stilton on french bread (£5.95), pork and leek sausages with mashed potato and a beer and caramelised onion gravy (£7.95), popular casseroles like beef and mushroom topped with garlic bread or pork with cider and apple (£8.95), lamb cutlets with a lime and coriander sauce served with cous cous (£10.50), Aberdeen Angus steaks (from £10.95), and home-made puddings. The relaxing bar has quite a light and spacious feel, as well as open fires, comfortable seats, and a nice assortment of tables. The window boxes are pretty, and there are seats out on the large flower-bordered lawn. The Thames is just a field away. *(Recommended by Sarah Bemrose, Nicholas Holmes, J M M Hill, Colonel A H N Reade, Mr and Mrs P G Wright)*

Brakspears ~ Tenants Michael and Jill Robinson ~ Real ale ~ Meals and snacks (not Sun evening) ~ Restaurant ~ (01491) 872415 ~ Children in room next to bar ~ Open 12-2.30, 6-11; closed 25 Dec

STANTON ST JOHN SP5709 Map 4

Star

Pub signposted off B4027; village is signposted off A40 heading E of Oxford (heading W, the road's signposted Forest Hill, Islip instead); bear right at church in village centre

The little low-beamed rooms in this busy old pub have a relaxed, chatty feel. One has ancient brick flooring tiles and the other quite close-set tables, while up a flight of stairs (but on a level with the car park) is a busy and well refurbished extension with rugs on flagstones, pairs of bookshelves on each side of an attractive inglenook fireplace, old-fashioned dining chairs, an interesting mix of dark oak and elm tables, shelves of good pewter, terracotta-coloured walls with a portrait in oils, and a stuffed ermine. Well kept Badger Tanglefoot, Wadworths IPA, Farmers Glory, 6X and winter Old Timer, and a weekly guest beer on handpump, country wines and hot toddies. Behind the bars is a display of brewery ties, beer bottles and so forth; shove-ha'penny, dominoes, cribbage, and piped music. The family room is no smoking. The wide range of promptly served bar food might include sandwiches and toasties (from £1.75), lovely home-made soup (£1.85), ploughman's (from £3.25), home-made quiche (£4.95), gammon and pineapple or lemon chicken (£6.45), sirloin steak (£8.25), daily specials like corned beef hash, chicken and leek pie, sea trout and turbot or vegetable pie, and pork and cider casserole (all £5.25), around eight home-made puddings like treacle and walnut tart, blackcurrant cheesecake or chocolate, chestnut and brandy pudding, and children's menu (£2.20). The walled garden has picnic tables among the rockeries, and swings and a sandpit. There are annual classic car rallies, and it gets busy then. *(Recommended by TBB, Chris Wheaton, Marjorie and David Lamb, Nigel Norman, Gordon, A M Rankin, Martin, Jane and Laura Bailey, Calum and Susan McLean*

Wadworths ~ Tenants Nigel and Suzanne Tucker ~ Real ale ~ Meals and snacks (till 10pm) ~ (01865) 351277 ~ Children in eating areas and family room ~ Folk music first Sun of month ~ 11-2.30, 6.30-11; closed 25 Dec

Talk House 🛏 ♀

Wheatley Road (B4027 just outside village)

Opened in May 1995, this capacious and splendidly realised series of linked drinking and eating areas is like the full performance that the Mole & Chicken at Easington (see Buckinghamshire chapter) has served as the dress rehearsal for. It's on an altogether grander scale, but similar in style, with flagstoned and tiled floors, stripped 17th-c stonework, lots of oak beams, simple but solid rustic furnishings, and attractive pictures and other individual and often light-hearted decorations. Unlike the original Mole & Chicken, there's more room for people who just want a drink and a chat, though most of the tables are for dining. It's at its best when it's busy (and it does need a lot of people to fill it), with a cheery bustle, and deft service by well trained good-humoured staff. Good interesting food includes unusual starters that would do as a light lunch, such as a skewer of shell-on prawns with garlic bread and chilli dip (£4.95), and main courses: sausage of the week and mash (£6.25), steak and kidney pie or ham and egg (£6.95), smoked chicken, pine nut and banana salad, chicken liver and bacon salad with raspberry dressing and chicken breast madras curry (£7.95), fried calf liver with bacon and sage (£9.50) and Thai king prawn curry or half a duck in orange sauce (£10.95). Well kept Morlands Original, Old Speckled Hen, Tanners Jack and their seasonal ales on handpump, good house wines, no music. The sheltered courtyard has tables around an impressive fountain. *(Recommended by M Sargent, Alan Heather, Graham and Karen Oddey)*

Free house ~ Licensee A S M Heather ~ Real ale ~ Meals and snacks (till 10.30 Sat and Sun) ~ Restaurant ~ (01865) 351648 ~ Supervised children welcome ~ Open 11-3, 5.30-11; 11-11 Sat and Sun ~ Bedrooms: £45.50B/£59.50B

STEEPLE ASTON SP4725 Map 4

Red Lion ♀

Off A4260 12 miles N of Oxford

Readers are terribly fond of this lovely little pub – made extra special by the exceptionally friendly and welcoming landlord who has now been here for 22 years. Whether you are a local or visitor he seems to go out of his way to make everyone feel at home. He is also very keen on his wines – the cellar contains over 100 different bottles. The comfortable partly panelled bar has beams, an antique settle and other good furnishings, and under the window a collection of interesting language and philosophy books that crossword fans find compelling. Enjoyable lunchtime bar food might include tasty stockpot soup (£2), sandwiches (from £2; the rare beef are recommended), excellent ploughman's with nicely ripe stilton (£3.85), home-made pâté (£4), smoked pork, pâté and cheddar with a large roll (£4.95), summer meals like taramasalata with pitta bread (£3.75), fresh crab (£5.25), fresh salmon salad (£5.50), smoked salmon platter (£5.75), various winter hotpots and casseroles (from £4.50), and puddings (from £1.75); the evening restaurant is more elaborate. Well kept (and reasonably priced) Badger Tanglefoot, Hook Norton Best and Wadworths 6X on handpump, and a choice of sixty or so malt whiskies. The suntrap front terrace with its lovely flowers is a marvellous place to relax in summer. *(Recommended by D C T and E A Frewer, J and D Tapper, Mr and Mrs B Pullee, Jan and Colin Roe, M Sargent, Andrew and Jo Litten, Alan Skull, Gordon, Nigel Norman)*

Free house ~ Licensee Colin Mead ~ Real ale ~ Lunchtime bar meals and snacks (not Sun) ~ Evening restaurant (closed Sun and Mon and two weeks late Sept-early Oct) ~ (01869) 340225 ~ Children in restaurant ~ Open 11-3, 6-11

STEVENTON SU4691 Map 4

North Star

The Causeway; central westward turn off main road through village, which is signposted from A34

Happily, very little changes in this marvellously unspoilt and simple pub – named after an 1837 steam engine (which accounts for some of the pictures around the walls). A low half-hidden door leads through a porch into the main bar, where a high-backed settle faces a row of seats around a couple of elm tables; decorations include a polished brass track gauge, and interesting local horsebrasses. There's no bar counter – the Morlands Mild, Bitter and Best are tapped from gleaming casks and surrounded by lots of neatly stacked bottles, bars of chocolate, crisps and so forth; recent reports suggest the beer quality can vary. Cheap ploughman's, and friendly, chatty licensees. There's also a simply furnished dining room, and a small parlourish lounge with an open fire; cribbage. The garden is entered from the road through a small yew tree arch, and grass at the side has some old-fashioned benches. Unfortunately the licensees wouldn't answer any of our questions this year, so we'd be particularly grateful for up-to-date news and prices. *(Recommended by Gordon, Pete Baker, Roger Huggins, Tom McLean, Jack and Philip Paxton; more reports please)*

Morlands ~ Tenant Mr R Cox ~ Real ale ~ Meals and snacks (weekday lunchtimes only) ~ (01235) 831309 ~ Open 10.30-2.30, 6.45-11

SWINBROOK SP2811 Map 4

Swan

Back road 1 mile N of A40, 2 miles E of Burford

This is another genuinely old-fashioned country pub that seems to have remained unaltered for generations. The tiny interior is cosy, peaceful, and dimly-lit, with simple antique furnishings and a woodburning stove in the flagstoned tap room and the back bar; darts, shove-ha'penny, dominoes and cribbage. Popular lunchtime bar food (with prices unchanged since last year) might include sandwiches, fish pie or venison in ale (£5.50), delicious steak and kidney pie, and rabbit cooked with wine, tomatoes and herbs (£5.60), with more imaginative seasonally changing evening dishes such as roast poussin stuffed with stilton, spinach and chopped ham in cream and madeira sauce, lots of game and fresh fish; best to get here early on Friday and Saturday evenings which tend to be busy. Morlands Original and Wadworths 6X on handpump, and farm ciders; there's an old english sheepdog. There are old-fashioned benches outside by the fuchsia hedge, and the pub is not far from the River Windrush and its bridge. No dogs or children and no muddy boots in the carpeted dining room. *(Recommended by Anthony Barnes, J O Jonkler, Andrew and Ruth Triggs, John Waller, Roger and Jenny Huggins, A M Rankin, Dave Irving, Ewan McCall, Tom McLean, Richard Marjoram)*

Free house ~ Licensee H J Collins ~ Real ale ~ Meals and lunchtime snacks (12-1.30, 6.30-8.45; not Sun evening) ~ Restaurant (not Sun or Mon) ~ (01993) 822165 ~ Open 11.30-2.30, 6-11

TADPOLE BRIDGE SP3300 Map 4

Trout

Back road Bampton—Buckland, 4 miles NE of Faringdon

New licensees have taken over this busy but friendly Thames-side pub and are going to move the front door to create more eating space, and refurbish the inside. They also plan to build a dining extension – though were quick to tell us that they very much want to preserve an atmosphere that also caters for drinkers. Changing bar food now includes sandwiches (from £2.50), home-made pies (from £4.95), home-made lamb and mint burger in a home-made onion bread bap or gammon and egg (£6.50), stuffed fillet of chicken with a smoky bacon sauce or grilled trout fillet with cream of fennel and pernod sauce (£7.25), Aberdeen Angus steaks (from £8.95), and rack of lamb with redcurrant and rosemary sauce (£9.25). The small L-shaped bar has plenty of seats on the flagstones, and Archers Village, Gibbs Mew Bishops Tipple, Morlands Original, and Trout (brewed specially for them) on handpump; a small but comprehensive wine list. Darts, dominoes, cribbage, piped music and Aunt Sally. The garden is pretty in summer with small fruit trees, attractive hanging baskets, and flower troughs, and you can fish on a two-mile stretch of the river (the pub sells day tickets); moorings for boaters, too. *(Recommended by Joan Olivier, Marjorie and David Lamb, Dr G W Barnett, Georgina Cole, Roger and Jenny Huggins)*

Free house ~ Licensee Christopher Green ~ Real ale ~ Meals and snacks ~ (01367) 870382 ~ Children in eating area of bar ~ Open 11.30-3, 6-11

TOOT BALDON SP5600 Map 4

Crown

Village signed from A423 at Nuneham Courtenay, and B480

Whenever possible in season, the welcoming licensees here use home-grown herbs and other produce in the enjoyable cooking. It's a bustling and friendly country pub and the simple beamed bar has a log fire, solid furnishings on the tiled floor, and a pleasant atmosphere. Generous helpings of homely food such as home-made soup, sandwiches (from £2.50), mushrooms with bacon and cheese (£3.95), ploughman's or vegetarian pasta (£4.50), a brunch (£5.50), grills (from £5.95), puddings, and daily specials such as pork chop topped with blue cheese (£6.50), salmon steak or lamb and apricot pie (£6.95), and stuffed chicken breast in filo pastry (£7.95); it may be best to book, especially at weekends. Well kept Adnams Broadside, Mansfield Bitter, and Morlands Original on handpump; darts, shove-ha'penny, and dominoes. Aunt Sally, summer barbecues, and tables on the terrace. *(Recommended by M Sargent, Marjorie and David Lamb, A T Langton, T R and B C Jenkins; more reports please)*

Free house ~ Licensees Liz and Neil Kennedy ~ Real ale ~ Meals and snacks (not evenings Sun/Mon) ~ (01865) 343240 ~ Well behaved children welcome ~ Open 11-3, 6.30-11; 12-5, 7-10.30 Sun

WATLINGTON SU6894 Map 4

Chequers

3 miles from M40, junction 6; take B4009 towards Watlington, and on outskirts of village turn right into residential rd Love Lane which leads to pub

Cosily tucked away in a back alley, this cheerful old place has a peaceful rambling bar with a low oak beamed ceiling darkened to a deep ochre by the candles which they still use, a low panelled oak settle and character chairs such as a big spiral-legged carving chair around a few good antique oak tables, and red-and-black shiny tiles in one corner with rugs and red carpeting elsewhere; steps on the right lead down to an area with more tables. A vine-covered conservatory looks out over the garden. A good range of popular bar food takes in lunchtime sandwiches, toasties, ploughman's, and sausage and egg (from £2), as well as king prawns in filo pastry

(£4), lentil and aubergine moussaka (£6), steak and kidney pie (£6.50), chinese chicken stir fry or gammon steak (£7.50), salmon supreme (£8.50), steaks (from £9.50), daily specials, and puddings such as chocolate fudge cake or treacle tart (£3). Well kept Brakspears Bitter and Special on handpump, friendly staff. The cheese shop in Watlington itself is recommended. The garden is notably pretty – quite refreshing after the bustle of the main street – with picnic tables under apple and pear trees, and sweet peas, roses, geraniums, begonias, and rabbits. *(Recommended by TBB, M Sargent, Gwen and Peter Andrews, Gordon, Bill Ingham; more reports please)*

Brakspears ~ Tenants John and Anna Valentine ~ Real ale ~ Meals and lunchtime snacks ~ Restaurant ~ (01491) 612874 ~ Open 11.30-2.30, 6-11; closed 25 Dec

WITNEY SP3510 Map 4
Three Horseshoes ♀
78 Corn Street

The charming bar in this 17th-c Cotswold stone pub has a bustling atmosphere, beams and flagstones, two log fires, a longcase clock, willow-pattern plates on a welsh dresser, attractive oriental rugs, and a good mix of solid old tables with country-kitchen chairs and long benches; the dining room has long refectory tables and settles, and a back no-smoking snug leads off. Good bar food at lunchtime includes sandwiches (from £2.25), soup (£2.50), chicken terrine (£3.25), filled baked potatoes (from £3.50), cheese, cashewnut and vegetable bake (£3.95), and steak and kidney pie or salmon fishcake with watercress sauce (£5.95), with evening dishes such as tortellini filled with herbs and garlic on a bed of spinach with a cheese and onion sauce (£5.25), lamb fritters with a Thai sauce (£5.95), steaks (from £7.25), and grilled lemon sole (£8.95), and puddings like chocolate truffle torte (£2.50); Sunday roast (£5.95), and bargain steaks on Thursday evening. Well kept Morlands Original and guests like Flowers IPA, Ind Coope Burton, and Charles Wells Bombardier on handpump, a nice little wine list, a few malt whiskies, and attentive service. There are teak seats out in front of the stonebuilt inn, well hung with flower baskets, and a small garden with a collection of chickens and other birds – including an african grey parrot who may be whistling Colonel Bogey. *(Recommended by Andrew and Ruth Triggs, John Waller; more reports please)*

Morlands ~ Lease: Ben, Libby and Charles Salter ~ Real ale ~ Meals and snacks ~ Restaurant ~ (01993) 703086 ~ Children in family room till 8pm ~ Open 11-2.30, 6.30-11; closed evening 25 Dec, and 26 Dec

WOODSTOCK SP4416 Map 4
Feathers ⑪ ⇔
Market St

The pubbiest part in this civilised Cotswold stone hotel is the old-fashioned garden bar at the back with a small bar in one corner, oils and watercolours on its walls, stuffed fish and birds (a marvellous live parrot, too), a central open fire, and a relaxed, tranquil atmosphere; it opens on to a splendid sunny courtyard with attractive tables and chairs among geraniums and trees. And although prices are high for drinks and food (£2.35 for a pint of Wadworths 6X, for example) most readers feel the prices are worth it – and service is excellent. First class food from a short but thoughtful and imaginative menu might include tomato and basil soup (£3.95), broccoli with tapenade and parmesan (£4), chicken liver parfait with brioche and sweet onion marmalade (£4.25), grilled tomato, basil and smoked salmon with pesto (small £5.25, large £8.25), honey-baked ham (£6.75), lovely fishcake with sweet and sour chilli sauce (£6.95), delicious duck with braised red cabbage, char-grilled salmon with tartare mayonnaise (£7.25), puddings like toasted marshmallow with berry compote or white and dark chocolate terrine (£3.95); salad and vegetables are £2.25 extra. A good choice of malt whiskies, and freshly squeezed orange juice. Get there early for a table. *(Recommended by Walter Reid, Nigel Wikeley, George Atkinson, Tim Barrow, Sue Demont, Marion and John Hadfield; also in Good Hotel Guide)*

Free house ~ Licensees Tom Lewis, Andrew Leeman, Howard Malin ~ Real ale ~ Bar meals (not Sat/Sun evenings) ~ Restaurant (not Sun evening) ~ (01993) 812291 ~ Children welcome ~ Open 11.30-3, 6-11 ~ Bedrooms: £75B/£99B

WYTHAM SP4708 Map 4

White Hart

Village signposted from A34 ring road W of Oxford

This picturesque creeper-covered pub is a pleasantly traditional place with a fine winter log fire (there's a fine relief of a heart on the iron fireback), high-backed black settles built almost the whole way round the cream walls of the partly panelled, flagstoned bar, and a shelf of blue and white plates; trivia. Well kept ABC Best, Ind Coope Burton, Tetleys, and a guest beer on handpump, and a good choice of malt whiskies. Bar food from the food servery includes cheese or pâté with bread (from £2.35), filled baked potatoes or help-yourself salads (around £2.95), fresh fish like plaice, trout or salmon, swordfish and tuna (from £7.25), steaks (from £7.45), mixed grill (£9.75), daily pasta and vegetarian specials (from £6.95), and puddings (£2.45); barbecues every day in summer except Monday (weather permitting) in the lovely walled rose garden. The pub's name is said to have come from a badge granted to the troops of Richard II after the Battle of Radcot Bridge in 1390. *(Recommended by Alan and Paula McCully, Andrew Rogers, Amanda Milsom, Gordon, David Carr, M Sargent, Sheila Keene, P H Roberts, Joan Olivier, Roger Byrne, A M Rankin)*

Ind Coope (Allied) ~ Manager Louise Tran ~ Real ale ~ Meals and snacks ~ (01865) 244372 ~ Children in eating area of bar and in conservatory ~ Open 11-3 (2.30 winter Fri/Sat), 5.30(6 winter Fri/Sat)-11; 11-11 Sat; normal Sun hours in winter

---

Lucky Dip

Besides the fully inspected pubs, you might like to try these Lucky Dips recommended to us and described by readers (if you do, please send us reports):

☆ Abingdon [St Helens Wharf; SU4997], *Old Anchor*: Lovely riverside position, flagstoned back bar with shoulder-height serving hatch, little front bar looking across Thames, roomy lounge, panelled dining room overlooking neat almshouse gardens; well kept Morlands, warm fire, some comfortable leather armchairs, decent food inc children's, friendly service *(Alan Kilpatrick, TBB)*

☆ Alvescot [B4020 Carterton—Clanfield – OS Sheet 163 map ref 273045; SP2604], *Plough*: Partly 17th-c village pub with good range of good value food inc vegetarian and Sun lunch (must book), quick welcoming service, well kept Wadworths IPA, 6X and guest such as Adnams Broadside, decent wines, good coffee, lounge with end dining area, old maps, log fire (but cool and pleasant on hot days); separate public bar *(Marjorie and David Lamb, G Pearce)*
Ardley [B430 (old A43) just SW of M40 junction 10; SP5427], *Fox & Hounds*: Wide range of food, welcoming staff, two attractive inglenooks, Banks's ales *(Mr and Mrs J Taylor, Dave Braisted)*

☆ Ashbury [B4507/B4000; SU2685], *Rose & Crown*: Comfortable beamed pub nr Ridgeway with highly polished woodwork, settees, pews and oak tables and chairs, traditional pictures, good range of usual food, sensible prices, friendly helpful staff; bedrooms *(HNJ, PEJ, Anne Cargill, Meg and Colin Hamilton)*

☆ Asthall [off A40 at W end of Witney bypass, then 1st left; SP2811], *Maytime*: Genteel dining pub with very wide choice of well served meals and some bar snacks, slightly raised plush dining lounge neatly set with tables, more airy conservatory restaurant (children allowed), Morrells and Wadworths 6X, decent wines, prompt service, interesting pictures, small locals' bar; piped music; in tiny hamlet, nice views of Asthall Manor and watermeadows from garden, big car park; quiet comfortable bedrooms around striking courtyard, attractive walks *(A M Rankin, Marjorie and David Lamb, David Surridge, Ian and Villy White, BB)*
Bablock Hythe [off B4449 S of Stanton Harcourt; SP4304], *Ferryman*: Good straightforward food in cheery riverside eating area, welcoming and helpful landlord (who works a steel ferry-boat for walkers and cyclists), real ales, displays of old ferry equipment; terrace, moorings; well equipped bedrooms with river-view balconies *(GWB)*
Balscott [signed off A422 W of Banbury; SP3841], *Butchers Arms*: Chatty open-plan village local, darts, cards and dominoes at public end, well kept Hook Norton *(Pete Baker)*

☆ Banbury [47 Parsons St, off Market Pl; SP4540], *Reindeer*: Civilised well restored town pub, beams, panelling, lovely carved overmantel for main room's log fire, well kept

Hook Norton Best and other changing ales, country wines, good coffee, friendly staff, good generous food, snuffs, clay pipes; ask to see the gloriously panelled Globe Room *(Ted George, BB)*

Banbury [Parsons Lane], *Wine Vaults*: No frills, plain seating, good range of Morrells and other real ales, lots of bottled bears, cheap basic wholesome food *(Ted George)*

Bessels Leigh [A420 SW of Oxford; SP4501], *Greyhound*: Big family dining pub, comfortable and popular, varied food inc Sun carvery, well kept beers, decent wine, children's room with lots of toys, play area outside; piped music *(Peter and Audrey Dowsett, Brig J S Green)*

Bletchingdon [Station Rd; B4027 N of Oxford; SP5017], *Blacks Head*: Friendly local overlooking village green, good value usual food, well kept Ansells or Flowers IPA, big woodburner, darts, cards and dominoes in public bar, pool room, garden with Aunt Sally; informal singalong Thurs *(Ian and Liz Phillips, Pete Baker)*

☆ Blewbury [London Rd; SU5385], *Blewbury Inn*: Friendly and comfortably character downland village pub with hotch-potch of mellowed old furniture and attractive log fire in cosy beamed bar, unusually good food in small dining room inc fine evening set menu; bedrooms *(Gordon)*

Bloxham [High St; off A361; SP4235], *Joiners Arms*: Homely and bustling local with friendly chatty staff, five S & N ales, good coffee, decent wine, two fires and lots of brasses; piped music, fruit machines *(Gordon, BB)*

Boars Hill [between A34 and B4017; SP4802], *Fox*: Attractive relaxed timbered pub in pretty countryside, dark wood tables and chairs in several 18th-c feel rambling rooms on different levels, good range of reasonably priced food inc vegetarian and children's, good service, real ales inc Tetleys and Wadworths 6X, decent wine, huge log fireplaces, family area, no piped music; restaurant, big garden with play area *(D C T and E A Frewer, Susan and Alan Dominey, Tim Brierly)*

☆ Bodicote [Goose Lane/High St, off A4260 S of Banbury; SP4537], *Plough*: Old, quaint and dark, with well brewed beers inc Porter from own attached brewery, three other well kept ales, country wines, wide choice of well cooked straightforward food, good friendly service; old beams, pictures and brasses, dining area *(George Atkinson)*

Brightwell [signed off A4130 2 miles W of Wallingford; SU5790], *Red Lion*: Small very basic totally unspoilt pub in peaceful village, warmly welcoming traditional landlord, log fires, small choice of standard food inc good soup, Courage-related and Hook Norton beers *(TBB)*

Britwell Salome [B4009 Watlington—Benson; SU6793], *Red Lion*: Good range of freshly prepared food at reasonable prices, quick service, Brakspears PA, separate back restaurant area *(Marjorie and David Lamb)*

☆ Buckland [SU3497], *Lamb*: Plushly refurbished and extended 18th-c stone building in tiny village, good if not cheap food (not Mon), with half-helpings at half price, smart helpful service, real ale, decent wines; pleasant bedrooms, lovely walking country *(Mr and Mrs M Miles, Dr and Mrs R H Wilkinson)*

Bucknell [handy for M40 junction 10; SP5525], *Trigger Pond*: Neat stone-built pub opp the pond, big helpings of popular reasonably priced food, well kept changing ales such as Adnams, Badger Best and Tanglefoot and Hook Norton Best, attentive staff; piped music; pleasant terrace and garden *(Marjorie and David Lamb, George Atkinson)*

☆ Burford [High St (A361); SP2512], *Bull*: Comfortable sofas in interestingly restored long narrow beamed and panelled hotel bar, Courage-related ales and Wadworths 6X, woodburner, good choice of wines by the glass, wide choice of bar food, restaurant; piped music; children welcome, open all day; good value comfortable bedrooms *(Andrew and Ruth Triggs, Gordon, Mrs P J Pearce, David Carr, LYM)*

Burford [Witney St], *Royal Oak*: Stripped stone, generous popular food inc imaginative good value home-made quiches, well kept Wadworths ales, bar billiards, friendly staff *(Jim Reid, David Carr)*

☆ Caulcott [Lower Heyford Rd (B4030); SP5024], *Horse & Groom*: Welcoming part-thatched creeper-covered 16th-c pub, cosy little unspoilt L-shaped bar, good log fire in stone fireplace, beams and brasses, dining end with wide choice of straightforward home cooking by landlord inc good fish, Charles Wells Bombardier, Hook Norton Old Hookey and local Notley ale, friendly landlady; outside lavatories, garden with picnic tables under cocktail parasols, no car park but lay-by opp *(D C T and E A Frewer, D and J McMillan, Joan Olivier, Marjorie and David Lamb, M Sargent, Gwen and Peter Andrews, Chris Halek, Gordon)*

☆ Chadlington [Mill End; off A361 S of Chipping Norton, and B4437 W of Charlbury; SP3222], *Tite*: Comfortable and welcoming rambling local with settles, wooden chairs, prints, well kept changing ales, decent wines, good log fire in huge fireplace, sensibly priced food, rack of guidebooks; children welcome; lovely views, suntrap garden and terrace, pretty Cotswold village, good walks nearby *(D C T and E A Frewer, Derek and Sylvia Stephenson, Jon Carpenter, Tim Brierly)*

☆ Chalgrove [High St; SU6396], *Red Lion*: Pleasantly restored beamed village pub owned by local church trust since 1640, good value generous food cooked to order (so may be a wait), well kept Brakspears, Hook Norton and changing guests such as Fullers London Pride, Glenny Wychwood Best or Tetleys Premium, friendly attentive staff, log fire and woodburner, partly tiled floor, small restaurant, sizeable garden with Sun lunchtime barbecues; lavatory for disabled (but car park some way off); children welcome *(Marjorie and David Lamb, Joan Olivier)*

☆ Charlbury [SP3519], *Bell*: Small and attractive civilised bar, warm and friendly, with flagstones, stripped stonework, huge open fire, short choice of good interesting bar lunches (not Sun) from sandwiches up, well kept Hook Norton and Wadworths real ales, wide choice of malt whiskies, decent if pricey restaurant; children in eating area; comfortable bedrooms, good breakfasts *(Alan and Paula McCully, LYM)*

Charney Bassett [SU3794], *Chequers*: Popular two-room village-green local with some emphasis on decent freshly prepared food (not Mon); well kept Fullers London Pride, Morlands and Theakstons XB; some singalongs (landlady plays spirited piano), pool, piped music; children welcome *(Pete Baker, Peter and Audrey Dowsett)*

Chipping Norton [Goddards Lane; SP3127], *Chequers*: Three nicely old-fashioned beamed rooms, plenty of character, well kept Fullers ales inc Chiswick, straightforward lunchtime food, impressive French-run evening restaurant; tables in courtyard *(David Campbell, Vicki McLean, M Benjamin, P M Dodd)*; [High St], *Fox*: Clean, tidy and quiet, with prompt friendly service, well kept Hook Norton Best, rambling lounge, open fire, upstairs dining room (can be used for sensibly priced lunchtime bar food); soft piped music, fruit machines; children welcome; well equipped good value bedrooms *(Simon Collett-Jones, BB)*

Chislehampton [B480 Oxford—Watlington, opp B4015 to Abingdon; SU5998], *Coach & Horses*: Small comfortable two-bar 16th-c pub, homely but civilised, with good choice of well prepared food in sizeable dining area (polished oak tables and wall banquettes), well kept ales inc Flowers and Hook Norton, big log fire, cheerful licensees; well kept terraced gardens overlooking fields by River Thame; comfortable bedrooms in back courtyard *(Gordon, JCW)*

☆ Christmas Common [signed from B480/B481; SU7193], *Fox & Hounds*: In early autumn 1996 Kevin Moran who had kept this tiny old cottage so unspoilt and timeless retired as tenant, and as we go to press we have no news of Brakspears' plans for it; under him, it's been a good atmospheric stop for Chilterns walkers, with beams, inglenook and nice old seats outside, so we hope for little change *(LYM; news please)*

☆ Clifton Hampden [towards Long Wittenham, S of A415; SU5495], *Barley Mow*: Chef & Brewer a short stroll from the Thames, newly thatched after a fire and famous from *Three Men in a Boat*; still has character, and friendly atmosphere under new licensees, with very low beams, oak-panelled family room, usual food, Courage-related real ales, piped music, restaurant; tables in well tended garden; bedrooms *(Joan Olivier, JP, PP, David Carr)*

☆ Coleshill [B4019 Faringdon—Highworth; SU2393], *Radnor Arms*: Atmospheric high-raftered bar dominated by huge forge chimney, two coal-effect gas fires, lots of smith's tools, two other cosy bars; Flowers tapped from the cask, good choice of reasonably priced food cooked to order inc tasty home-made pies and fresh veg, friendly quick service, small garden behind; piped music; charming preserved village (NT), lots of good walks *(Tim Brierly, HNJ, PEJ, Peter and Audrey Dowsett, D Lawson)*

Cothill [SU4699], *Merry Miller*: Newly done-up restaurant-pub with formal feel, good New World wines, good choice of well kept beers; booking advised *(Stephen Rudge)*

☆ Crawley [OS Sheet 164 map ref 341120; SP3412], *Lamb*: Good lunchtime bar food and wider choice of interesting evening dishes, all home-cooked using good ingredients, in 17th-c stone-built village pub on several levels; well kept Wychwood Shires and Wadworths 6X, decent wines, friendly hard-working licensees, small family area, restaurant; lots of tables in pleasant garden *(Marjorie and David Lamb, John Waller)*

☆ Crays Pond [B471 nr junction with B4526, about 3 miles E of Goring; SU6380], *White Lion*: Clean and welcoming low-ceilinged pub with open fire, attractive conservatory, well kept Courage-related real ales, good inventive if not cheap food (not Tues evening), big garden with play area *(Susan and Alan Dominey)*

☆ Cumnor [Abingdon Rd; SP4603], *Vine*: Busy extended 18th-c pub with original fireplace, carpeted back dining area, no-smoking area in conservatory, remarkably wide choice of enjoyable food inc fish and game, good service, three well kept guest ales, picnic tables in attractive back garden *(Mr and Mrs H W Clayton, Nick Wedd, Joan Olivier, D and E Frewer, Mrs Linda Jordan, Adam and Elizabeth Duff)*

Curbridge [Bampton Rd (A4095); SP3308], *Lord Kitchener*: Good food, quick friendly service *(Peggy and Bill Linfield)*

☆ Deddington [Horsefair; SP4631], *Kings Arms*: Bustling 16th-c coaching inn with nooks and crannies, black beams and timbers, mullioned windows, attractive settles and other country furnishings, fine log fire, well kept Adnams, Tetleys, Wadworths 6X and two guest beers, good choice of wines by the glass, straightforward bar food inc quick pizzas, children in eating area, restaurant; piped music, traditional games (and Sky TV) in side bar; newly done bedrooms, open all day Sat *(Gwen and Peter Andrews, David and Shelia, Meg and Colin Hamilton, LYM)*

Deddington, *Deddington Arms*: Former local now renamed and emphasising food inc good value Sun lunch, spacious restaurant, friendly service *(Cyril Aydon)*; [Mkt Sq], *Forge*: Another name-change, with new look, new management, agreeable pub lunches; tables out in courtyard *(H D Spottiswoode)*; [Oxford Rd (A4260)], *Holcombe*: Good food and well kept beer in pleasant, comfortable and welcoming 17th-c low-beamed stripped-stone hotel bar; sheltered terrace and lawn, restaurant, comfortable bedrooms *(Mr and Mrs H D Spottiswoode)*; [Market Pl], *Unicorn*: 17th-c inn with inglenook bar, reasonable choice of good value food inc inexpensive set lunch in oak-beamed restaurant, family room with separate games area; bedrooms *(Mr and Mrs H D Spottiswoode)*

☆ Denchworth [SU3791], *Fox*: Picturesque old thatched pub with two good log fires in low-ceilinged comfortable connecting areas, welcoming new licensee doing good range of reasonably priced food inc fresh veg (and sandwiches), Morlands Original and Beechnut, quiet piped music, carvery in small beamed restaurant; peaceful garden, isolated ancient village *(Marjorie and David Lamb, HNJ, PEJ, Peter and Audrey Dowsett, Gordon)*

☆ Dorchester [High St; SU5794], *Fleur de Lys*: Small comfortable 16th-c village pub opp abbey, wide choice of good value home cooking, all fresh (not Mon; no sandwiches), Bass, Flowers IPA and Morlands, friendly service; unobtrusive piped music *(Tim and Carol Gorringe, David Carr)*

Dorchester, *White Hart*: New management doing good interesting food in big beamed bar and attached restaurant, good range of beers, very helpful service; decent bedrooms *(Nigel Norman, JP, PP)*

☆ Drayton [A422 W of Banbury; SP4241], *Roebuck*: Comfortable 16th-c creeper-covered pub with fresh imaginative food in cosy bar and evening restaurant, welcoming staff, well kept ales inc Boddingtons, Fullers London Pride and Hook Norton Best, solid fuel stove *(Edward and Anne Good, Frank Salisbury, F M Bunbury)*

Duns Tew [SP4528], *White Horse*: 16th-c beamed pub in pretty village, rugs on flagstones, oak timbers and panelling, stripped masonry, enormous inglenook, settles, sofas and homely stripped tables, decent food in bar and big pretty dining extension, several well kept ales; comfortable bedrooms in former stables *(Joan Olivier)*

East Hanney [SU4193], *Black Horse*: Doing well under newish landlord, now locally very popular for good range of food from speciality baked potatoes up *(I Maw)*

☆ East Hendred [Orchard Lane; SU4588], *Plough*: Enjoyable straightforward bar food in beamed village pub's attractive and airy main bar, Morlands ales with a guest such as Charles Wells Bombardier, quick friendly service, farm tools; occasional folk nights, attractive garden with good play area *(Dick Brown, BB)*

☆ Eaton [SP4403], *Eight Bells*: Low-beamed small-roomed Tudor pub with open fires, horse tack and brasses, decent bar food inc vegetarian, well kept Morlands, welcoming landlord, dining room (children allowed here) off cosy lounge; no dogs, tables in garden, tethering rail for horses *(Joan Olivier, E McCall, R Huggins, T McLean, D Irving,*

Gordon, Dr and Mrs A K Clarke)

☆ Ewelme [off B4009 about 5 miles SW of M40 junction 6; SU6491], *Shepherds Hut*: Simple clean and friendly local, with good value imaginative food, quick service, well kept Morlands Bitter and Old Masters, welcoming staff, pot plants, darts, small restaurant; piped pop music, fruit machine; children welcome; tables and swing in pleasant garden *(Margaret Dyke, Nick Holmes)*

Eynsham [Newlands St; SP4309], *Newlands*: Cosy beamed and flagstone bar, generous good value food inc vegetarian, friendly staff, Tetleys and Worthington, decent wine, big inglenook log fire, stripped early 18th-c pine panelling, character restaurant; very busy and bustling weekends, piped music *(D C T and E A Frewer)*

☆ Faringdon [Market Pl; SU2895], *Bell*: Bustling local atmosphere, comfortable red leather settles, splendid inglenook fireplace with 17th-c carved oak chimney-piece, interesting mural in inner bar, well kept Badger Tanglefoot, Wadworths 6X and a guest beer, straightforward bar food, restaurant; piped music; children welcome, tables out among flowers in attractive cobbled back coachyard; bedrooms *(JN, John Wooll, Tom McLean, Roger Huggins, LYM)*

☆ Faringdon [Market Pl], *Crown*: Unpretentious but civilised old inn comfortably refurbished by new owners, flagstones, panelling, log fires, reasonably priced well presented food, friendly staff, well kept real ales, no piped music; children welcome; good bedrooms, lovely summer courtyard *(Peter and Audrey Dowsett, BB; more reports on new regime please)*

☆ Fifield [Stow Rd (A424); SP2318], *Merrymouth*: Isolated rambling old pub with relaxed atmosphere, flagstones, lots of stripped stone, bay windows, farm tools on low beams, open fires, Donnington and perhaps other ales, unobtrusive piped music, food in bar and restaurant; tables on terrace and in back garden; children allowed one end; bedrooms *(John Waller, LYM)*

Filkins [off A361 Lechlade—Burford; SP2304], *Five Alls*: Old-fashioned Cotswold stone pub with two unpretentious lounges, good value food from ploughman's to carvery meals, Flowers Original, Hook Norton Best and Old Hookey, decent house wine in good-sized glasses, friendly staff, log fires, sizeable restaurant, coffee lounge; cl Mon *(Mr and Mrs Cresswell, Andrew and Ruth Triggs, Marjorie and David Lamb)*; [A361 Burford—Lechlade], *Lamb*: Decent generous food (limited Sun), well kept Morlands Original, Old Masters and Old Speckled Hen and decent house wines in two-bar stonebuilt local, part Elizabethan, warm, friendly and comfortable; no piped music, big garden, pleasant bedrooms; cl Mon *(K H Frostick, Peter and Audrey Dowsett)*

Freeland [Witney Rd; SP4112], *Shepherds Hall*: Pleasantly decorated roadside pub, large comfortable bar with open fire and gleaming copper, long-serving welcoming and caring licensees, good varied food inc huge mixed grill, well kept Flowers IPA and Wadworths 6X, discreet piped pop music, back games room with two pool tables, garden with play area; comfortable bedrooms *(Trevor Moore, K Neville-Rolfe)*

Fulbrook [SP2513], *Carpenters Arms*: Cotswold stone pub with Bass-related ales from long bar serving tap room and lounge, good value food in big restaurant, tables under cocktail parasols in back garden with big play area *(Andrew and Ruth Triggs)*

☆ **Godstow** [SP4809], *Trout*: Creeper-covered medieval pub, much extended and commercialised as big tourist draw, with large snack room, children's area, garden bar and restaurant – midweek out of season sees the charming beamed and flagstoned original core at its best, with three open fires; Bass and Fullers London Pride, mulled wine in winter; the star's for the lovely terrace by a stream full of greedily plump perch, with peacocks in the grounds *(Gordon, Paul Stanfield, D Maplethorpe, B Helliwell, Adrian Zambardino, Debbie Chaplin, E McCall, R Huggins, T McLean, D Irving, David Carr, Mr and Mrs S Talling, LYM)*

Goring [SU6080], *Catherine Wheel*: Enjoyable genuine local in pretty Thames village, good value food in bar and restaurant, friendly licensee, good log fire; notable door to gents' *(M Holdsworth, John and Pam Smith, JP, PP)*

Great Haseley [handy for M40 junction 7; SP6401], *Plough*: Small and friendly, good food esp steaks; quiet area *(Tony Merrill)*

Great Milton [The Green; a mile from M40 junction 7; SP6202], *Bull*: Welcoming and neatly kept, with well kept Morrells Bitter and Varsity, nicely presented above-average simple pub food inc good value generous ploughman's and Sun roast, bustling public bar, picnic tables on back lawn with play area *(Frank Cummins, Margaret Dyke)*

Hailey [Whiteoak Green, B4022 Witney—Charlbury; SP3414], *Bird in Hand*: Large friendly modern country inn with wide range of food in lounge or attractive restaurant, attentive service, Whitbreads-related ales, lots of wood, well chosen pictures and subdued lighting (inc candles on tables), nice views; comfortable cottage-style bedrooms *(Mrs B Sugarman)*; [B4022 a mile N of Witney; SP3512], *Lamb & Flag*: Extremely friendly welcome, good range of reasonably priced food, well kept Morlands Original and Beechnut *(B H H Pullen, Marjorie and David Lamb)*

☆ **Henley** [Friday St; SU7882], *Anchor*: Cosy and relaxing local, cottagey and attractive, almost right on the Thames, with nice mix of homely country furniture and bric-a-brac in softly lit parlourish beamed front bar, huge helpings of reasonably priced food, well kept Brakspears, friendly and obliging landlady; darts, bar billiards, piano and TV in room on right, caged birds in eating area, back dining room, elegant cat; charming back terrace with rabbit hutch; here and there piles of the sort

of stuff you might find dumped around a loosely run family home; children welcome *(Gordon, GWB)*

Henley [North End], *Old White Hart*: Friendly and comfortable beamed pub in nice spot by Thames, good bar staff, good varied food, well kept Boddingtons and Brakspears; pleasant tables in courtyard *(P and J Caunt)*; [West St], *Row Barge*: Friendly simple local, its cosy low-beamed bar dropping down the hill in steps, good value home cooking, well kept Brakspears, darts, big back garden; lively young weekend crowd *(Andy Thwaites, Derek and Sylvia Stephenson)*; [5 Market Pl], *Three Tuns*: Heavy beams and panelling, two rooms opened together around old-fashioned central servery with well kept Brakspears, straightforward generous home-cooked food all day, floodlit back terrace and separate games bar with pinball, juke box and fruit machine; no children *(TBB, LYM)*

☆ **Highmoor** [B481 N of Reading, off A423 Henley—Oxford; SU6984], *Dog & Duck*: Cosy and cottagey low-beamed country pub with chintzy curtains, floral cushions, lots of pictures – not at all twee; relaxing and comfortable bar on left, dining room on right, log fire in each, smaller dining room behind, good food inc good vegetarian dishes, friendly newish landlord, well kept Brakspears Bitter, Old and Special; tables in garden *(Gordon, Vicky Cashell)*

Highmoor [Witheridge Hill; off B481 at Stoke Row sign, then Witheridge Hill signed], *Rising Sun*: Lovely old Brakspears pub in attractive and remote setting, pleasant garden; very popular esp in summer *(Gordon)*

Hook Norton [SP3533], *Sun*: Good food from sandwiches up, well kept Hook Norton ales from the nearby brewery, restaurant, comfortable bedrooms *(Margaret and Roy Randle)*

Islip [B4027; SP5214], *Red Lion*: Wide choice of well presented generous quick food in three cosy and relaxed eating areas inc main tankard-decorated lounge and conservatory, well kept Whitbreads-related ales and Wadworths 6X, decent wine, quick friendly service, billiards in public bar; lavatories for the disabled, good garden with barbecue and play area *(Gwen and Peter Andrews, Mr and Mrs R A Bryan)*

Kidmore End [Chalkhouse Green Rd, signed from Sonning Common; SU6979], *New Inn*: The landlord who earned readers' praise for this pretty black and white country dining pub has moved with his staff to a larger Brakspears pub, the Crown at Play Hatch *(News please)*

Kingston Blount [The Green; long drive off road to Sydenham beware sleeping policemen; SU7399], *Shoulder of Mutton*: Nice quiet spot, food till 3, well kept Brakspears, tables in garden, sensible attitude to children *(Nigel Pritchard)*

☆ **Kingston Lisle** [SU3287], *Blowing Stone*: Small relaxing refurbished lounge bar, tiny snug, large elegant dining conservatory; good generous food from sandwiches to Sun lunch, decent wine, good range of changing ales such as Bass, Mansfield Bitter and Morlands Original, decent wines, cheerful efficient service; roomy traditional-style public bar with pool and piped music; attractive village, handy for Ridgeway walks; pretty garden with fish pond; bedrooms clean and pretty if small *(Peter and Audrey Dowsett, HNJ, PEJ, Marjorie and David Lamb, Joan Olivier)*

Kirtlington [SP4919], *Oxford Arms*: Good varied food, newish landlord with good track record, friendly family service, sunny back garden with barbecues *(David Campbell, Vicki McLean)*

☆ Long Wittenham [SU5493], *Machine Man*: Good choice of genuine food freshly made to order, wide range of ales inc Eldridge Pope Royal Oak and Wadworths Farmers Glory, decent wines, friendly unpretentious local atmosphere, good service, darts; bedrooms *(Marjorie and David Lamb, Ian Gillingham, D and J McMillan)*

☆ Long Wittenham, *Plough*: Good value food in low-beamed recently refurbished lounge with lots of brass, games in public bar, inglenook log fires, welcoming landlord, Ushers ales, pool and children's room; Thames moorings at bottom of long spacious garden; bedrooms *(Marjorie and David Lamb, Margaret Dyke, A Kilpatrick)*

☆ Longworth [SU3899], *Blue Boar*: Newly thatched cosy country local with plenty of character, two good log fires and unusual decor (skis on beams etc); usual food with speciality evenings, well kept Bass and Morrells Best, piped music, friendly quick service *(Marjorie and David Lamb, Gordon)*

Lower Assendon [B480; SU7484], *Golden Ball*: Well restored and extended late 16th-c pub, attractive interior with hops on beams, log fire, quiet atmosphere, black labrador, good food inc interesting specials, well kept Brakspears, decent house wines, log fire; garden behind *(James Nunns, GWB, Gordon)*

☆ Lower Heyford [21 Market Sq; SP4824], *Bell*: Charming and very welcoming beamed pub in sleepy village, good value simple home-cooked food from home-made sausages in a cob up, good range of beers inc Greene King Abbot, stylishly presented coffee; charming building *(Meg and Colin Hamilton)*

☆ Marsh Baldon [the Baldons signed off A423 N of Dorchester; SU5699], *Seven Stars*: Good interesting rather restaurany generous food (no sandwiches; only barbecues some Sat lunchtimes) in big open room; decent wines, good coffee; on attractive village green *(Marjorie and David Lamb)*

☆ Marston [Mill Lane, Old Marston; SP5208], *Victoria Arms*: Attractive grounds by River Cherwell inc spacious terrace, good play area, punt moorings and hire; full Wadworths range and guest beers, generous good value food (not Sun evening in winter) from chunky sandwiches up inc children's dishes, lots of tables in civilised main room and smaller ones off, real fires; soft piped music, children and dogs allowed; lavatory for disabled; beware

vicious sleeping policemen *(David Campbell, Vicki McLean, Bob Goodenough, Joan Olivier, BB)*

Milton [off Bloxham Rd; the one nr Adderbury; SP4535], *Black Boy*: Old-world oak-beamed bar in former coaching inn, inglenook, woodburner, flagstones and bare boards, stripped stonework, plenty of brasses; well kept Bass and Worthington, food using local produce with creole and other exotic dishes, candlelit restaurant very popular Thurs-Sat nights; piped music *(L H King, George Atkinson)*

☆ Milton under Wychwood [High St; SP2618], *Quart Pot*: Good atmosphere in spotless pub with good choice of French-influenced good value home-cooked food, delicious puddings, Fri steak night, Adnams and Morlands Old Speckled Hen, friendly licensees; garden, attractive Cotswold village *(Sue and Bob Ward)*

Minster Lovell [just N of B4047; SP3111], *Old Swan*: Interesting and attractive old inn now under new management, still upmarket hotel feel but with good friendly service, snacks and light meals as well as restaurant, Marstons ales, roaring log fire, deep armchairs, rugs on flagstones, tables in lovely garden; bedrooms *(Joan Olivier, LYM)*; [B4047 Witney—Burford; *White Hart*: Welcoming 17th-c building, cheerful service in big lounge, well kept Donnington BB and SBA and a guest such as Federation Buchanans, bar food inc sandwiches and jacket potatoes, good log fire, big separate restaurant; the ghost has now been exorcised *(Dave Braisted, Anthony Lock)*

Mollington [just off A423 N of Banbury; SP4447], *Green Man*: Lots of brasses, corn dollies, old photographs, low beams (one so low as to need head-padding, friendly attentive landlord, basic menu *(Ted George)*

☆ Moulsford [Ferry Lane, off A329 N of Streatley Too restaurant/hotelish now for our main entries, but chatty atmosphere and excellent though far from cheap food in Boathouse bar/restaurant by the Thames, well kept Adnams Best, Badger Tanglefoot and Wadworths 6X, good wines, exemplary service, pleasant waterside garden; well behaved children welcome, comfortable bedrooms *(Douglas Frewer, Mr and Mrs P Smith, Fhiona Skaife, Dayl Gallacher, LYM)*

☆ Nettlebed [A423; SU6986], *White Hart*: Civilised rambling two-level beamed bar, handsome old-fashioned furnishings inc fine grandfather clock, discreet atmosphere, good log fires, well kept Brakspears, spacious restaurant; children welcome, bedrooms *(JP, PP, Dr and Mrs A K Clarke, LYM)*

Nettlebed [Watlington Rd], *Sun*: Well kept Brakspears, lots of jugs hanging from old beams, good choice of food, dining room; sheltered attractive garden with climbing frame, swing and barbecue *(David Craine, Ann Reeder, Paul McPherson)*

☆ Newbridge [A415 7 miles S of Witney; SP4001], *Maybush*: Low-beamed unpretentious Thameside local, tables set for good range of decent bar food (no sandwiches), well kept Morlands Original and Old Speckled Hen, clothes presses and other bric-a-brac, no piped music; children above toddling age and dogs welcome, moorings, caravan site, pretty and neatly kept waterside terrace *(Mayur Shah, Meg and Colin Hamilton, D H T Dimock, PD, AD, LYM)*

☆ **Newbridge**, *Rose Revived*: Big pub well worth knowing for its lovely lawn by the upper Thames, across the road from our other entry here, prettily lit at night (good overnight mooring free); inside knocked through as Morlands Artists Fayre eatery – promptly served usual food all day inc Sun carvery, Morlands real ales, piped music, fruit machines; children welcome, comfortable bedrooms with good breakfasts *(Peter and Audrey Dowsett, B H H Pullen, Meg and Colin Hamilton, L M Miall, Neil and Angela Huxter, Gordon, LYM)*

Noke [SP5413], *Plough*: Cheerful country pub on edge of Otmoor which has been well liked, with tables in pretty garden, but found closed earlier in 1996 *(LYM; news please)*

North Hinksey [off A34 southbound just S of A420 interchange; SP4805], *Fishes*: Comfortable Victorian-style open-plan lounge and conservatory, good food from sandwiches up inc fresh veg, children's and imaginative vegetarian dishes, well kept Morrells, helpful staff, pleasant conservatory; soft piped music; big streamside garden with play area and two Aunt Sally pitches *(Joan Olivier, Jon Carpenter, Dick Brown)*

☆ **North Newington** [High St, just W of Banbury; SP4139], *Roebuck*: Attractively refurbished dining pub with wide range of good value interesting home-made food, quiet bistro atmosphere, individual furnishings, well kept ales inc Morlands and unusual guests, good wines and country wines, open fires, lovely briards, obliging service, maybe piped classical music; children very welcome, good garden with play area and animals; in quiet village nr Broughton Castle *(John Bowdler)*

Northmoor [B4449 SE of Stanton Harcourt; SP4202], *Red Lion*: Small stonebuilt Tudor village local, heavily beamed bar and small dining room off, welcoming open fire, wide range of home-cooked bar food inc Fri fish and chips and good value Sun lunch, well kept Morlands, friendly staff, garden *(D C T and E A Frewer, Joan Olivier, Margaret Dyke)*

☆ **Oxford** [Holywell St], *Kings Arms*: Big front bar, half a dozen cosy and comfortably worn-in side and back rooms each with a different character and customers, well kept Youngs and guest such as Morlands Original and Wadworths 6X, good choice of wines, no-smoking coffee room, decent bar food, papers provided, tables on pavement; very busy and popular with students, but civilised, with amiable service, no music or games *(Dick Brown, Wayne Brindle, Pat and Roger Fereday, M Joyner, David Carr, Walter Reid, Hugh MacLean, D Irving, E McCall, R Huggins, T McLean, BB)*

☆ **Oxford** [Binsey Lane; narrow lane on right leaving city on A420, just before Self Operated Storage], *Perch*: Lovely thatched pub in pleasant setting with big garden off riverside meadow; big and busy, with low ceilings, flagstones, stripped stone, high-backed settles as well as more modern seats, log fires, no-smoking eating area (children allowed), Tetleys-related ales and Wadworths 6X, decent wine, unobtrusive piped music; good play area, barbecues, landing stage, attractive waterside walks; in running for main entry, but tenants leaving autumn 1996 *(BB; news please)*

☆ **Oxford** [Broad St], *White Horse*: Small, busy and cheerful, sandwiched between bits of Blackwells bookshop; mellow oak beams and timbers, ochre ceiling, beautiful view of the Clarendon building and Sheldonian, good lunchtime food (the few tables reserved for this), well kept Tetleys-related ales and Wadworths 6X, Addlestone's cider, friendly licensees *(Walter Reid, Alan and Paula McCully, Adrian Zambardino, Debbie Chaplin, Tim and Ann Newell, D Irving, E McCall, R Huggins, T McLean, James Nunns, BB)*

☆ **Oxford** [Alfred St], *Bear*: Lots of atmosphere in four friendly little low-ceilinged and partly panelled rooms, often packed; massive collection of vintage ties, simple food most days inc sandwiches (kitchen may be closed Weds), good range of well kept Tetleys-related and other ales from centenarian handpumps on rare pewter bar counter, no games machines, tables outside; open all day summer *(Walter Reid, David Carr, Sue Demont, Tim Barrow, LYM)*

☆ **Oxford** [North Parade Ave], *Rose & Crown*: Friendly and unspoilt old local with character landlord, limited but popular and well priced bar lunches inc Sun roasts, Tetleys-related ales, decent wine, prompt service; ref books for crossword buffs, no piped music or machines, piano available for good players, jazz Tues; traditional small rooms, pleasant back yard with motorised awning and big gas heaters – children not allowed here or inside unless with friends of landlord *(John Waller, Margaret Dyke, N Hardyman, BB)*

☆ **Oxford** [St Giles], *Eagle & Child*: Busy rather touristy pub (tiny mid-bars full of actors' and Tolkien/C S Lewis memorabilia), but students too; nice panelled front snugs, tasteful modern back extension with no-smoking conservatory, well kept Tetleys-related ales and Wadworths 6X, plentiful quickly served food, piped classical music, newspapers *(David and Shelia, David Carr, Keith and Janet Morris, D C T Frewer, Tim and Ann Newell, Nigel Woolliscroft, BB)*

Oxford [Iffley Rd], *Fir Tree*: Proper local – relief from young-dominated central pubs; tempting pizzas *(David and Shelia, John Hedges)*; [39 Plantation Rd, off Woodstock Rd], *Gardeners Arms*: Relaxed local and University atmosphere in comfortable open-plan pub, good value filling home-made food inc vegetarian in back room where children allowed, well kept Morrells, real cider, tables outside *(David Carr, LYM)*; [Banbury Rd, Summertown], *Kings Arms*: Good value simple food from baked potatoes to steaks inc fine salads, friendly fast service; children welcome if well behaved, busy lunchtime *(David Campbell, Vicki McLean)*; [St Giles/Banbury Rd], *Lamb & Flag*: Well kept S&N ales, good food, friendly service; can be packed with students, back rooms with exposed stonework and panelled ceilings have more atmosphere *(N Hardyman, Pat and Roger Fereday, Joseph Biernat, Walter Reid)*; [288 Cowley Rd], *Philosopher & Firkin*: A new Firkin with its own brewery, friendly helpful staff, more restrained atmosphere than some city Firkins *(Richard Houghton)*; [Iffley], *Prince of Wales*: Pleasantly refurbished, with good mix of customers, relaxed feel, well kept Wadworths, regular beer festivals; seats outside *(Jon Carpenter, GWB)*; [Woodstock Rd], *Royal Oak*: Lots of little rooms, low beams, celebrity pictures in front bar, lunchtime food bar with good soup and doorsteps of bread, simple main dishes, ales inc Tetleys and Wadworths 6X, daily papers, open fire, games area with darts, pool etc *(John and Wendy Trentham)*; [Friars Entry, St Michael St], *Three Goats Heads*: Two good-sized friendly and attractive bars, relaxed downstairs, more formal up; well kept cheap Sam Smiths, good choice of quick generous food, dark wood and booths *(M Joyner, Marjorie Foster, Sue Demont, Tim Barrow)*; [129 High St], *Wheatsheaf*: Well kept Marstons Pedigree, Morrells Bitter, Varsity and Graduate and a guest beer tapped from the cask, simple reasonably priced food, bare boards, plain wooden seats, friendly staff *(Dr Peter Donahue, Abigail Ingram, Paul Goodchild)*; [272 Woodstock Rd], *Woodstock Arms*: Quiet, neat little lounge, bar with bar billiards and fruit machines, friendly service, well kept Morrells, good value simple food inc good Sun roast; garden *(R T and J C Moggridge)*

☆ Pishill [B480 Nettlebed—Watlington; SU7389], *Crown*: Ancient country pub with home-cooked bar food (not Sun or Mon evenings) from sandwiches to steaks, three blazing log fires, black beams, standing timbers, well kept Brakspears, Flowers Original and a guest beer, picnic tables on attractive side lawn, nice surroundings; bedrooms in separate cottage; children allowed Sun lunchtime in restaurant *(Helen Hazzard, Gordon, JP, PP, Susan and John Douglas, S J Tasker, S and P Hayes, LYM)*

☆ Play Hatch [just off A4155; SU7476], *Crown*: Spacious rambling 16th-c pub with two bars and several rooms inc big no-smoking conservatory, well kept Brakspears PA, SB and Old tapped from casks in lounge, decent wines, good food inc interesting specials and home-made ice cream, good service *(Gordon)*; [Foxhill Lane], *Shoulder of Mutton*: Unspoilt country pub with friendly landlord, small cosy low-ceilinged cottagey rooms, lovely oak

settle snugly screening the fire, interesting home-made pies and massive array of hot filled rolls, Sun lunch (must book), Morlands ales; well kept garden with old-fashioned roses, real well, horses in meadows beyond *(Gordon)*

☆ Pyrton [SU6896], *Plough*: Clean and cosy 17th-c thatched pub with good generous fresh food inc vegetarian, fine choice of winter casseroles and well priced puddings, well kept Adnams, Brakspears and Fullers ESB, prompt friendly service, spotless old-fashioned stripped-stone beamed main bar with big woodburner, evening dining area; maybe piped local radio, cl Mon evening, picnic tables outside *(Bill Capper, John Barker, P J Keen, GWB, Margaret Dyke, James Waller)*

Rotherfield Greys [SU7282], *Maltsters Arms*: Dining pub with good food, friendly efficient service, lovely country views, well kept Brakspears *(Clifford Hall)*

Rotherfield Peppard [Gallowstree Rd; SU7181], *Greyhound*: Homely, pretty and cottagey country pub with some concentration on good home-made food; friendly landlord, good choice of beers, attractive garden with boules *(Maysie Thompson)*

Sandford on Thames [Henley Rd, off A423 S of Oxford; SP5301], *Fox*: Simple unspoilt locals' bar with darts, cards and dominoes, smaller lounge, coal fire, well kept Morrells Mild and Bitter *(Pete Baker)*

☆ Satwell [just off B481, 2 miles S of Nettlebed; follow Shepherds Green signpost; SU7083], *Lamb*: Cosy and attractive 16th-c low-beamed cottage, very small (so can get cramped), with tiled floors, newish pine furniture, friendly licensees, huge log fireplace, filled baguettes, ploughman's and wide range of good hot food, well kept Brakspears, traditional games, small carpeted family room, tables outside *(W W Burke, Martin and Karen Wake, BB)*

☆ Shilton [SP2608], *Rose & Crown*: Mellow 17th-c low-beamed stonebuilt village local with wide choice of good home-made food from sandwiches up, friendly attentive staff, well kept Morlands Original, Old Masters and Old Speckled Hen on handpump, woodburner, soft piped music, darts in beamed and tiled public bar, tables in sizeable garden; pretty village *(Joan Olivier, Marjorie and David Lamb, Calum and Susan Maclean)*

Shiplake [SU7678], *Plowden Arms*: Neat and friendly open-plan local, good range of home-made food inc good value Sun lunch, well kept Boddingtons and Brakspears, children's room; handy for Thames walk *(P J Caunt, Gordon)*

☆ South Moreton [SU5588], *Crown*: Above-average home-made food inc some interesting dishes in tastefully opened-out family country pub, well kept Wadworths and guest ales tapped from the cask, friendly service; children allowed, discount scheme for OAPs, Mon quiz night, small garden *(Ailsa Wiggans, John Allen, Tony Merrill)*

Stadhampton [Brookhampton, signed off

A329; SU6098], *Bear & Ragged Staff*: Attractively restored in 1995, lively and stylish atmosphere, with log fire, flagstones and polished bar, good food in bar and restaurant, good range of well kept beers, good wine and champagne by the glass, friendly service; tables outside, barbecue; bedrooms *(Dr and Mrs M Parkes)*

☆ Standlake [High St; SP3902], *Bell*: Unusual plush restaurant/bar area and separate lounge bar, consistently good well presented food inc interesting dishes, well kept Morlands, friendly licensees *(Alison Smith, Craig and Gillian Brown, Simon Miles)*

☆ Stanton Harcourt [B4449 S of Eynsham; SP4105], *Harcourt Arms*: More restaurant than pub, good meals in three welcoming, attractive, simply furnished and pleasantly informal dining areas with Spy cartoons and huge fireplaces; good choice of wines; piped music; children welcome *(Mr and Mrs H W Clayton, LYM)*

☆ Steventon [SU4691], *Cherry Tree*: Spacious and relaxing interconnecting rooms, dark · green walls, two or three old settles among more modern furnishings in quiet lounge with film-star pictures and bric-a-brac; well kept Wadworths Farmers Glory and 6X and guest beers, popular quick straightforward food, efficient friendly service, open fire; unobtrusive piped music in public bar, tables outside *(Bruce Bird, Nigel MacGeorge)*

☆ Stoke Lyne [off B4100; SP5628], *Peyton Arms*: Unspoilt tiny snug, bigger public bar with good range of traditional games (no juke box or machines), welcoming landlord, well kept Hook Norton tapped from the cask, pleasant garden with Aunt Sally *(Pete Baker, JP, PP)*

☆ Stoke Row [Newlands Lane, off B491 N of Reading – OS Sheet 175 map ref 684844; SU6884], *Crooked Billet*: Opened-up country pub/restaurant with wide choice of good interesting home-cooked meals, well kept Brakspears tapped from the cask, decent wines, good log fires; big garden, by Chilterns beech woods *(JP, PP, LYM)*

☆ Stoke Row [Kingwood Common, a mile S, signed Peppard and Reading – OS Sheet 175 map ref 692825], *Grouse & Claret*: Well run dining pub with good changing food, pleasant traditional interior with cosy nooks, friendly helpful service, good choice of wines; piped music *(Simon Collett-Jones)*

☆ Stoke Talmage [signed off A40 at Tetsworth; SU6799], *Red Lion*: Unspoilt country tavern, basic, friendly and welcoming, with cards and dominoes in parlour-like lounge, well kept Butcombe and Morlands, great character landlord; pleasant garden *(Pete Baker, JP, PP, Matthew Jones, D Irving, E McCall, R Huggins, T McLean)*

☆ Sutton Courtenay [SU5093], *George & Dragon*: Friendly 16th-c pub, attractive and interesting, with good choice of fair-priced home-made food from sandwiches upwards inc popular Sun lunch, well kept Morlands, good range of decent wines; relaxed atmosphere, candlelit restaurant; no dogs

(even in garden), friendly cat called Orwell (his namesake is buried in the graveyard overlooked by picnic tables on the back terrace) *(Marjorie and David Lamb, Margaret Dyke)*

☆ Sutton Courtenay [Appleford Rd (B4016)], *Fish*: Attractive dining pub with good fresh-cooked food inc fish, vegetarian, starters that can double as interesting bar snacks, well kept Morlands, decent wines, welcoming staff, no-smoking back dining area where children allowed, new garden room, tables out on terrace *(Peter Frederiksen, LYM)*

☆ Sydenham [SP7201], *Crown*: Welcoming rambling low-beamed bar with a little lamp in each small window, unusual choice of good interesting food, Morrells Best and Varsity with a guest such as Adnams, good choice of wines by the glass, friendly service (and cats), relaxed homely atmosphere, children welcome, dominoes and darts; may be piped radio, can be smoky; picturesque village, views of lovely church *(Jenny and Michael Back, JP, PP, Marjorie and David Lamb, Paul Kitchener)*

Tetsworth [A40; SP6801], *Lion on the Green*: Wide choice of good bar food and good Sun lunch, well kept Boddingtons and Brakspears, very friendly new management, real fire, no dogs; bedrooms *(Dave Braisted, Margaret Dyke)*; *Swan*: Rambling 15th-c coaching inn re-opened partly as busy popular restaurant/pub with good upmarket food inc lots of fish and choice of real ales in bar, partly as antiques centre *(S J Edwards, Joan Olivier)*

Thame [Cornmarket; SP7005], *Abingdon Arms*: Good lunchtime pub, generous bar food inc home-made fresh pasta and speciality doorstep sandwiches, attentive friendly service, well kept Bass, Brakspears, Fullers London Pride, good well identified choice of bottled beers, small no-smoking front lounge and no-smoking bar, bright and basic main bar with bare boards and oriental rugs, three real fires; piped music, busier and noisier evenings; tables in garden with swings *(C Aquilino, Peter Worth)*; *Bird Cage*: Quaint black and white beamed and timbered pub, bare boards, some carpet, loads of old nick-nacks, open fires, cigarette cards, homely chairs; short reasonably priced bar lunch menu, well kept Courage-related ales, good bar food, piped music, friendly staff *(Ted George, LYM)*; [High St], *Black Horse*: Traditional old inn with attractive panelled and chintzy back lounge, simple dining area, sunny covered basic back area, good range of standard food, well kept Bass, good coffee, friendly atmosphere – front bar can get smoky and noisy evenings; open for breakfast; bedrooms *(John Waller, LYM)*; [26 High St], *Rising Sun*: Flagstones and bare boards in three linked rooms, well kept Hook Norton and Morlands ales, good varied home-made food inc vegetarian, pleasant local atmosphere, real fire *(John and Phyllis Maloney, Tim and Ann Newell)*

☆ Thrupp [off A4260 just N of Kidlington;

SP4815], *Boat*: Relaxing and friendly little 16th-c stone-built local in lovely canalside surroundings, quick good value home-cooked food, well kept Morrells, no piped music; restaurant, tables in garden *(H D Spottiswoode, Sue Demont, Tim Barrow, Colin and Meg Hamilton)*

☆ Towersey [down drive nr Chinnor Rd/Manor Rd crossroads; SP7304], *Three Horseshoes*: Unpretentious flagstoned country pub with good value food inc nicely presented fresh veg, old-fashioned furnishings in two low-beamed bars, good log fire, well kept Bass and Tetleys-related ales, small restaurant; piped music, darts; biggish garden with fruit trees and play area; children allowed lunchtime *(Bill Capper, Tina and David Woods-Taylor, LYM)*

Wallingford [St Leonards Ln; SU6089], *Little House Around the Corner by the Brook*: Welcoming and comfortable smallish tasteful bar with pews, good well presented home-made food inc imaginative children's dishes, changing real ales, raised dining area with antique furniture, fresh flowers, candles; piped music; next to church in beautiful spot by brook *(GWB, David Dimock)*

Wantage [Market Pl; SU4087], *Bell*: Low beams, open-plan bar with dining area, decent non-vegetarian bar food, Morlands ales, friendly licensee; clean and comfortable bedroom annexe across street *(G Coates)*

Wardington [A361 Banbury—Daventry; SP4845], *Hare & Hounds*: Roomy and comfortable old pub with well kept Hook Norton Best, good limited food, children in games room with pool and darts; no dogs, fruit machine, piped music; largish garden with play area *(Nick Wikeley)*

Wendlebury [a mile from M40 junction 9; signposted from A41 Bicester—Oxford; SP5619], *Red Lion*: Wide choice of good value food in friendly and spacious low-beamed stone-built pub with parquet floor, open fire, Badger and Worthington ales, games room with pool, juke box and fruit machine, restaurant; big garden with play area, grotesque wooden statuary, waterfowl, peacocks and rabbits; service can slow on busy evenings *(Dave Braisted, Lynda Payton, Sam Samuells)*

☆ West Hanney [SU4092], *Plough*: Pretty thatched pub with attractive timbered upper storey, original timbers and uneven low ceilings, homely and welcoming panelled lounge with open fire in stone fireplace, unusual plates, brasses and exotic butterflies, very friendly landlord, good value simple freshly made tasty food, Tetleys-related ales, interesting whiskies, darts in public bar; back garden with aviaries; children welcome *(Marjorie and David Lamb, Gordon)*

☆ West Hendred [Reading Rd, off A417 – OS Sheet 174 map ref 447891; SU4489], *Hare*: Civilised local, homely and welcoming, very popular for generous good value food served till late evening; decent wine, Morlands ale, two bars – one eating, one drinking *(M W Turner, Hugh Spottiswoode, A T Langton)*

☆ Westcott Barton [Enstone Rd (B4030); SP4325], *Fox*: Spacious yet cosy characterful stonebuilt village pub with friendly Italian landlord, good value food inc good Italian dishes as well as traditional English ones and Sun roast, small restaurant (not Sun evening), seven well kept real ales, good wines, plans for brewing own beer; lovely view from garden across sheep meadow to church *(David Campbell, Vicki McLean)*

☆ Weston on the Green [B430 nr M40 junction 9; SP5318], *Ben Jonson*: Thatched pub with wide choice of good value generous food, some very spicy, well kept Bass and Flowers IPA, good house wine, daily papers, enthusiastic young landlord, comfortable dark wood settles in welcoming beamed lounge bar, snug with roaring winter fire, discreet pool room; usually open all day; children very welcome; big sheltered garden with occasional barbecues *(D C T and E A Frewer, RTM, JCM, David Campbell, Vicki McLean)*

☆ Weston on the Green [A43, a mile from M40 junction 9], *Chequers*: Busy thatched pub with interesting bric-a-brac in long comfortably refurbished raftered bar, view of Thai cook producing good value food inc spicy ethnic dishes, well kept Fullers, farm cider, exuberant landlord, cheerful staff; tables under cocktail parasols in attractive garden with animals *(Chris and Chris Ellis, Pete Yearsley, George Atkinson)*

☆ Whitchurch [High St, just over toll bridge from Pangbourne; SU6377], *Greyhound*: Pretty cottage with neat relaxed low-beamed L-shaped bar, bric-a-brac inc signed miniature cricket bats, good value fresh no-chips food, well kept Flowers and Wadworths 6X, polite service, no music or machines; dogs on leads allowed, pleasant garden; nr Thames in attractive village, good walks *(Gordon, GWB, Lucian Gaudoin)*

Witney [Church Green; SP3510], *Angel*: Popular and friendly extended 17th-c pub, roaring log fires, limited bar food, Wychwood ales; piped music may be obtrusive *(Peter and Audrey Dowsett)*

☆ Wolvercote [First Turn; SP5009], *Plough*: Good interesting food in refurbished pub with armchairs and Victorian-style carpeted bays in main lounge, flagstoned dining room opening off, traditional snug, good-sized public bar with pool and games machines; three well kept Morrells ales, decent wines; piped local radio; tables outside looking over rough meadow to canal and woods *(N Hardyman, Adam and Elizabeth Duff, Geoff and Angela Jaques)*

☆ Woodstock [Park St; SP4416], *Bear*: Handsome old inn with pleasant bar on right, cosy alcoves, tasteful medley of well worn wooden antique oak and mahogany furniture, chintz cushions, paintings, sporting trophies, log fire, Bass and Morrells Bitter, good fresh sandwiches and bar lunches, good service; not cheap; restaurant; good bedrooms *(G C Hackemer, Rebecca and Chris Stanners, Gordon, BB)*

☆ Woodstock [A44 N], *Black Prince*: Subtly lit

timbered and stripped-stone 18th-c pub with old-fashioned furnishings, armour, swords, big fireplace, dining room with good simple bar food inc Tex-Mex and pizzas till late, well kept Hook Norton and Theakstons Old Peculier; occasional live music or nostalgic DJ; children allowed; tables out on grass by small river; planning proposals for housing development being stoutly resisted *(David Campbell, Vicki McLean, M Joyner, David and Alison Walker)*

Woodstock [A34 N], *Rose & Crown*: Good value food inc bowl meals, Morrells ales *(Dave Braisted)*; [22 Market St], *Star*: Good quickly served sandwiches and hot food *(Dr T Grant, GO, KO)*

☆ **Woolstone** [SU2987], *White Horse*: Plushly refurbished partly thatched 16th-c pub, two big open fires in spacious beamed and part-panelled room with air of highly polished well cared-for antiquity, quickly served food inc several vegetarian dishes, Arkells BBB and Wadworths 6X poured with a creamy head, decent wines, children allowed in eating area; sheltered garden; four charming good value bedrooms, secluded downland valley village, handy for White Horse *(Colin McKerrow, HNJ, PEJ, M R Roper-Caldbeck, JEB, Rona Murdoch, Peter and Audrey Dowsett)*

☆ **Wootton** [Glympton Rd (B4027) N of Woodstock; SP4320], *Killingworth Castle*:

Striking three-storey 17th-c inn with good local atmosphere, big helpings of good sensibly priced home-cooked food using fresh produce inc delicious puddings, well kept Morrells and other ales, log fire, attentive welcoming service, pleasant garden; bedrooms cosy and comfortable *(Margaret Dyke, Gordon, Caroline Beloe, S Boorne, Mr and Mrs Garrett)*

☆ **Wootton** [Chapel Hill, off B4027], *Kings Head*: Immaculate 17th-c beamed and stripped stone pub with welcoming newish licensees, old oak settles and chintzy sofas, neat spacious restaurant, good interesting food esp fish, sandwiches too, well kept Morlands Original and Old Speckled Hen, decent wines; well behaved children in eating area, quiet piped music; four bedrooms, delightful village *(Nigel and Amanda Thorp, John Bowdler, Mrs J Oakes, Mike and Heather Watson, M Stribbling, Dr R H and Mrs K M Wilkinson)*

☆ **Wroxton** [Church St; off A422 at hotel – pub at back of village; SP4142], *North Arms*: Pretty thatched stone pub with wholesome bar food (not all its eclectic furnishings suit eating), well kept Morrells, cheerful service, log fire, lots of beer mugs; character restaurant (not Mon); piped music, darts, dominoes, fruit machine; attractive quiet garden, lovely village *(Rona Murdoch, LYM)*

The Post Office makes it virtually impossible for people to come to grips with British geography, by using a system of post towns which are often across the county boundary from the places they serve. So the postal address of a pub often puts it in the wrong county. We use the correct county – the one the pub is actually in. Lots of pubs which the Post Office alleges are in Oxfordshire are actually in Berkshire, Buckinghamshire, Gloucestershire or the Midlands.

Shropshire

Shropshire pubs that have been on particularly good form in recent months include the Feathers at Brockton (good restauranty food, pleasant new conservatory), the Crown at Munslow (an interesting new entry, brewing its own ales), the Horse Shoe in its lovely setting at Llanyblodwel (the newish people, settling in well, are doing good food), the very welcoming Unicorn in Ludlow (good food here too), the Boathouse in Shrewsbury (another new entry: one of Whitbreads' Hogsheads pubs, with a fine range of real ales), the cheerful and civilised Wenlock Edge Inn on Wenlock Edge, and the Plough at Wistanstow (good food, excellent cheap beers from the brewery just behind). The Hundred House at Norton also serves very good food these days; but our overall choice as Shropshire Dining Pub of the Year is the Horse Shoe at Llanyblodwel. Drinks prices are below the national average here; we found beer particularly cheap at the Royal Oak at Cardington and Lion of Morfe at Upper Farmcote. In the Lucky Dip section at the end of the chapter, pubs and inns to note particularly include the Three Tuns in Bishops Castle (a fine old brew pub, reopening after a closure as we go to press), Railwaymans Arms among others in Bridgnorth, Lion at Hampton Loade, Bear at Hodnet, Feathers among others in Ludlow, Old Three Pigeons at Nesscliffe, Crown at Newcastle, Dun Cow Pie Shop in Shrewsbury and Stiperstones in the village of Stiperstones.

BRIDGES SO3996 Map 6

Horseshoe £

Near Ratlinghope, below the W flank of the Long Mynd

Delightfully placed by the little River Onny, this attractive old pub is a real oasis in these deserted hills. It's an interesting building (especially the windows), with a good log fire in its single tidily comfortable bar, and local paintings for sale; a small dining room leads off. A particularly good choice of well kept real ales includes Adnams Extra and Southwold, Shepherd Neame Spitfire and two regularly changing guests on handpump; Weston's farm cider. Service is friendly, and the landlord's a real individual; darts and dominoes. Decent home-made bar food (as we say, only available at lunchtimes), has some emphasis on seasonal local produce, with popular toasted sandwiches (from £1.95), a very good value shropshire blue ploughman's (£2.50), vegetable lasagne (£2.65) and chilli con carne (£2.95). There are tables outside, and the pub's very handy for walks on the Long Mynd itself and on Stiperstones – despite its isolation, it can get very busy in summer. *(Recommended by David Sadler, Gwen and Peter Andrews, David and Julie Glover, Nigel Woolliscroft, Dave Braisted, Robin and Molly Taylor, PM, AM)*

Free House ~ Licensee John Muller ~ Real ale ~ Lunchtime meals and snacks ~ (01588) 650260 ~ Children in dining room ~ Open 12-2.30(3 Sat), 6-11, closed Mon lunchtime (and Tues-Thurs lunchtimes too in winter)

BROCKTON SO5894 Map 4

Feathers 🍴

B4378

The landlord at this stylish stone-built pub tells us that they will cook anything on request as long as they have the ingredients in the kitchen – though most visitors should have little difficulty finding several things they like the look of on the blackboard menu. What's available changes all the time and relies on fresh seasonal ingredients, with a typical choice including Greek salad (£3.45), pâté or stuffed mushrooms (£3.75), toasted vegetable and mozarella tartlets or brie parcels wrapped in filo (£5.45), stir fried strips of chicken, steak, peppers and onions served on a sizzle plate (£8.95), lemon sole (£9.75), half a duck or peppered steak (£11.95), puddings like poached cherries in brandy or bread and butter pudding (£2.95), and an excellent Sunday lunch; efficient and friendly waitress service. The charmingly atmospheric beamed rooms have been fashionably updated with stencilling on the terracotta or yellow colour-wash walls, and the overall feel of the place is rather restaurany. One room is no smoking and they have a policy not to sell cigarettes; piped music. Well kept Banks's Bitter and Marstons Pedigree. A new conservatory was added last summer. *(Recommended by Paul and Maggie Baker, P Fisk, Anthony Marriott, J Evans, Wayne Brindle; more reports please)*

Free house ~ Licensee Mr Hayward ~ Real ale ~ Meals and snacks (6.30-9.30) ~ (01746) 785202 ~ Children welcome ~ Open 6.30-11(also 12-3 Sat and Sun; cl Mon)

CARDINGTON SO5095 Map 4

Royal Oak £

Village signposted off B4371 Church Stretton—Much Wenlock, pub behind church; also reached via narrow lanes from A49

Reputedly Shropshire's oldest pub, this wisteria-covered white stone inn is also one of the county's best placed; it's a really pleasant spot on a sunny day. Tables in the rose-filled front courtyard have lovely views over hilly fields, and a mile or so away – from the track past Willstone (ask for directions at the pub) – you can walk up Caer Caradoc Hill which looks over scenic countryside. The friendly rambling bar has low beams, old standing timbers of a knocked-through wall, hops draped along the bar gantry, a vast inglenook fireplace with a roaring winter log fire, cauldron, black kettle and pewter jugs, and gold plush, red leatherette and tapestry seats solidly capped in elm. Home-made bar food (lunchtimes only) includes macaroni cheese (£2.60), cauliflower cheese (£2.80), cottage pie or fidget pie (£3.60), meat or vegetable lasagne (£4.20) and fish and chips (£5). Well kept Bass on handpump under light blanket pressure, and two other beers like Hobsons or Wadworths 6X. Dominoes and cribbage in the main bar, and there's a no-smoking area. Walkers are welcome, and they keep a friendly boxer dog. *(Recommended by MDN, Paul Carter, Nigel Woolliscroft, Dave Braisted, Joan and Andrew Life, Andy and Gill Plumb, SLC)*

Free house ~ Licensee John Seymour ~ Real ale ~ Lunchtime meals and snacks (not Mon) ~ Children welcome lunchtimes only ~ (01694) 771266 ~ Open 12-2.30, 7-11; closed Mon except bank holidays

LLANFAIR WATERDINE SO2476 Map 6

Red Lion 🛏️

Village signposted from B4355 approaching eastwards; turn left after crossing bridge

The new licensees at this atmospheric old place are adding a terrace dining room at the back so visitors can better enjoy the views down to the River Teme, the border of England and Wales. They're putting a bit of effort into relandscaping the garden too, planting several new trees down towards the water. No changes inside though – the very traditional heavily beamed rambling lounge bar has cosy alcoves, easy chairs, some long, low settles and little polished wooden seats on its turkey carpet, and a woodburner. Perhaps even nicer is the small black-beamed tap room, with plain wooden chairs on its flagstoned floor, and table skittles, dominoes, cribbage, shove-ha'penny, and sensibly placed darts. Lunchtime bar meals include sandwiches, a range of pizzas (from £3.50), ploughman's or meat or vegetable lasagne (£4.95), broccoli and cream cheese bake (£5.20), chicken curry (£5.65), and daily specials, with evening extras like poached cod with lemon and mustard sauce (£5.95), pork chop in a crispy herb crust (£6.50), and steak au poivre (£10.95). The restaurant is no smoking. Well kept Marstons Pedigree, Tetleys and a guest like Wye Valley Dorothy Goodbody on handpump, maybe kept under light blanket pressure; good wine list. The area is renowned for beautiful walks (a good stretch of Offa's Dyke is nearby) and designated an area of outstanding natural beauty. The bedrooms are small but comfortable. *(Recommended by P Barrett, Mike and Maggie Betton, Helen Pickering, James Owen, Mike and Penny Sanders, Gwen and Peter Andrews, Basil Minson; reports on the new regime please)*

Free house ~ Licensees Chris and Judy Stevenson ~ Real ale ~ Meals and snacks (12-1.30, 7-9, not Sun evening, or Tues lunch) ~ Restaurant ~ (01547) 528214 ~ Children in eating area of bar and restaurant ~ Open 12-2, 7-11; closed Tues lunchtime ~ Bedrooms: £25(£30B)/£35(£40B)

LLANYBLODWEL SJ2423 Map 6

Horse Shoe

Village and pub signposted from B4936

Shropshire Dining Pub of the Year

The new licensees seem to be making a roaring success of this lovely early 15th-c inn, with the food in particular turning heads. Even if you don't want to eat, it's a lovely spot to relax for a while, next to a delightful stretch of the River Tant, with the water rushing around boulders under a little red stone bridge. You can sit at the tables outside and watch children splash in the water, or there's a mile of fly-fishing for trout, grayling or late salmon (free for residents, day tickets otherwise). As well as lunchtime baguettes (from £2.50), the good bar food includes soup (£2.25), king prawns pan-fried in garlic butter (£4.95), mediterranean bean casserole (£5.50), steak and kidney pie (£5.95), grilled fresh fish of the day with lemon and dill butter (£6.50), game casserole (£6.95), and roast poussin with sherry and brandy sauce, grilled lemon sole or chicken breast in a mushroom, cream and white wine sauce (£8.95), with puddings (£3.25), and children's meals £2.75). The simple low-beamed front bar has an old black range in the inglenook fireplace, traditional black built-in settles alongside more modern chairs around oak tables on a reclaimed maple floor, and lots of brass and china. In the rambling rooms leading off you'll find darts, pool, dominoes, cribbage, a fruit machine, and piped music. The dining room is oak panelled. Marstons Best and Pedigree, and a range of malt whiskies. *(Recommended by Basil Minson, Sue and Bob Ward, Nigel and Lindsay Chapman, JWK, John and Joan Nash, Gill and Maurice McMahon, David and Fiona Pemberton, Jeff Davies)*

Free house ~ Licensees Dennis and Jessica Plant ~ Real ale ~ Meals and snacks ~ Restaurant ~ (01691) 828969 ~ Children welcome ~ Open 11.30-3, 6.30-11; closed winter Monday lunchtimes ~ Bedrooms: £25/£40

LONGVILLE SO5494 Map 4

Longville Arms 🛏

B4371 Church Stretton—Much Wenlock

Readers have particularly enjoyed staying here over the last year, appreciating the fresh flowers and home-made biscuits in the comfortable rooms, and the warmth and friendliness of the licensees. People popping in for just a meal will notice the last feature too, and they're especially welcoming to families. Of the two spacious bars the left one is simpler with sturdy elm or cast-iron-framed tables, leatherette banquettes and a woodburning stove at each end. The right-hand lounge has dark plush wall banquettes and cushioned chairs, with some nice old tables. There's a wide range of good-value homely bar food, including sandwiches, soup (£1.50), deep fried camembert with home-made chutney (£3.50), a vegetarian dish (£4.40), fresh grilled trout with almonds (£5.85), scampi (£5.95), cajun chicken breast (£6.30), sirloin steak (£7.90), and daily specials; children's meals (from £2) and excellent puddings. Well kept Bass and Worthington BB on handpump, with maybe a guest in summer; also a selection of wines from the new world, and Irish whiskies. Darts, cribbage, trivia, piped music. There are picnic tables under cocktail parasols in a neat terraced side garden, with a good play area. Besides the good value bedrooms in the pub itself, there's a self-contained flat in an adjacent converted barn; they do superb breakfasts. The pub is well-placed near to an excellent range of local attractions. *(Recommended by Mr and Mrs A R Corfield, Maureen Hobbs, D O Evans, Nigel Woolliscroft, Ron Leigh, Andy and Gill Plumb, Anne and Sverre Hagen, P and M Kehely)*

Free house ~ Licensee Patrick Egan ~ Real ale ~ Meals and snacks (not Tues) ~ (01694) 771206 ~ Children welcome ~ Occasional live music ~ Open 12-3, 7-11; closed Tues lunchtime ~ No smoking bedrooms: £20S/£35S

LUDLOW SO5175 Map 6

Unicorn 🍴 🛏

Lower Corve St, off Shrewsbury Rd

The kind of delightfully aged place where your table may be a foot lower at one end than at the other thanks to the undulating floor, this beautiful family run 17th-c inn is built in a row of black and white houses along the banks of the River Corve. The atmosphere is relaxed and warmly welcoming, especially when the friendly locals – including lots of well behaved stable lads and jockeys – gather in the single large beamed and partly panelled bar, with its huge log fire in a big stone fireplace. There's a timbered, candlelit restaurant (where they prefer you not to smoke). Written up on blackboards, the bar food (not over elaborate but extremely good), might include sandwiches (from £1.75), home-made soup, filled baked potatoes (from £2.95), bacon, mushroom and cauliflower bake or black pudding in a cider and mustard sauce (£4.95), pasta and blue cheese bake or nut roast with mornay sauce (£5.25), seafood bake (£5.50), and home-made steak and kidney pie (£5.95), with restaurant meals (also available in the bar) like vegetarian meal (£2.50), trout stuffed with lemon and dill (£7.75), smoked lamb noisette in red-fruit coulis (£8.50), red snapper with orange and ginger coulis (£8.75), and wild boar with English wine and mushrooms (£8.95); there's a splendid choice of home-made puddings like chocolate, toffee and rum gateau or sticky gingerbread, and a good value Sunday lunch. Service is attentive, cheerful and willing. Well kept Bass and Worthington BB on handpump; cribbage, dominoes. Beyond the car park is a terrace with tables sheltering pleasantly among willow trees by the modest river. Warm and comfortable timbered rooms are a good size; good breakfasts. *(Recommended by Michael Butler, Andrew Shore, Steve Gilbert, Helen Cox, Lynda Payton, John Samuells, Neville Kenyon, Ray and Wendy Bryn Davies, Sue and Bob Ward, J Honnor, Robert Boote, Basil Minson, Barry Lynch, Gillian Jenkins, Mrs C J Richards, Pat and John Millward, Rona Murdoch, Nan Axon, Sally Barker)*

Free house ~ Licensees Alan and Elisabeth Ditchburn ~ Real ale ~ Meals and snacks ~ Restaurant ~ (01584) 873555 ~ Well behaved children welcome ~ Open 12-2.30(3 Sat), 6-11; closed 25 Dec ~ Bedrooms: £20B/£40B

MUCH WENLOCK SJ6200 Map 4

George & Dragon 🍺

High St

The cosily atmospheric rooms at this bustling and unpretentious town local are full of a delightful collection of pub paraphernalia, with everything from old brewery and cigarette advertisements, through to bottle labels and beer trays, George-and-the-Dragon pictures, and probably the biggest assemblage of water jugs we've ever seen; there are around a thousand of them hanging from the beams. There are a few antique settles as well as conventional furnishings, and a couple of attractive Victorian fireplaces (with coal-effect gas fires) and an old till on the bar. At the back, the quieter snug old-fashioned rooms have black beams and timbering, little decorative plaster panels, tiled floors, a stained-glass smoke room sign, a big mural as well as lots of smaller pictures (painted by local artists), and a little stove in a fat fireplace. As well as sandwiches, the very good freshly prepared bar food includes stilton and walnut pâté (£3.50), sliced smoked halibut with dill sauce (£3.85), home baked ham with parsley sauce (£5.25), venison casserole with orange and juniper (£5.50), chicken in shropshire mead and cream (£6.75), duck breast with red wine and raspberry sauce (£8.25), and puddings such as sticky toffee pudding or home-made ginger ice cream (£2.50). Some dishes may be slightly more expensive in the evening. Well kept Hook Norton Best and three often unusual guest beers like Hobsons Town Crier, Sarah Hughes Dark Ruby, and Wye Valley Supreme on handpump; piped music, usually jazz, and often from a vintage wireless. The bars can get busy and smoky – though the restaurant is no smoking. *(Recommended by Mike and Wendy Proctor, Mike and Maggie Betton, M Joyner, PM, AM, Paul Boot, Simon Groves, Tom Rodabaugh, Nigel Woolliscroft, Richard Lewis, Mike and Penny Sanders)*

Free house ~ Licensee Eve Nolan ~ Real ale ~ Meals and snacks (not Sun evening) ~ Evening restaurant (not Sun evening) ~(01952) 727312 ~ Well behaved children in eating area of bar and restaurant ~ Open 11-2.30(3 Sat), 6-11; cl 25 Dec evening

Talbot 🛏

High Street

Originally a part of Wenlock Abbey, this civilised 14th-c building has kept the same chef for 17 years under several different landlords. There are several neatly kept areas with lovely flowers, comfortable green plush button-back wall banquettes around highly-polished tables, low ceilings, and two big log fires (one in an inglenook); the walls are decorated with prints of fish and brewery paraphernalia. At lunchtime attractively presented bar food includes sandwiches (from £2.50), soup (£2.95), filled baked potatoes or ploughman's (from £3.75), Greek salad (£4.50), omelettes (from £5.95), country wheat casserole (£6.25), chicken supreme (£7.50), grilled lamb chops with mint and garlic butter or poached salmon in white wine sauce (£7.95), local sirloin steak (£10.95), and various fish and daily specials; Sunday roast lunch (£9.45). The restaurant is no smoking. Well kept changing ales might include Courage Directors, John Smiths, Ruddles County and Morlands Old Speckled Hen on handpump; good value wines, a range of malt whiskies, and pimms in summer. Through the coach entry, there are white seats and tables in an attractive sheltered yard. *(Recommended by Mike and Wendy Proctor, Basil Minson, M Joyner, Mr and Mrs K Giles, N Evans, Mrs J Ingram, Janet and Peter Race, Richard Lewis, Roger and Valerie Hill, Anthony Marriott, Colin Laffan)*

Free house ~ Licensees Sean and Cheryl Brennan ~ Real ale ~ Meals and snacks (not 25 Dec) ~ Restaurant ~ (01952) 727077 ~ Well behaved children in restaurant before 8pm (no pushchairs) ~ Open 10.30am-11pm; 10.30-3, 6-11 winter ~ Bedrooms: £45B/£90B

MUNSLOW SO5287 Map 2

Crown 🍺

B4368 Much Wenlock—Craven Arms

For an unusual sight, head straight to the games room of this tall and ancient roadside pub: there you have not just darts, bar skittles and dominoes but a view into the pub's own microbrewery, producing Munslow Boys Pale Ale, Munslow Ale, and sometimes a third brew named after one of the locals; they also keep Banks's Mild and Marstons Pedigree on handpump. The warm and friendly split-level lounge bar has a pleasantly old-fashioned mix of furnishings on its broad flagstones, a collection of old bottles, country pictures, a bread oven by its good log fire, seats in a traditional snug with its own fire, maybe a friendly dog; the eating area has tables around a central oven chimney, stripped stone walls, more beams and flagstones. A very wide choice of generous good value home-made food served with al dente vegetables includes spicy chicken wings (£2.95), ploughman's (£3.50), moules marinières (£3.95/£7.95), half a pint of shell-on prawns (£4.25), steak and kidney pie (£5.25), chilli (£5.95) and lots of fresh fish like plaice (£5.75), haddock (£5.95), trout (£6.95) or salmon (£7.95) which you can have simply grilled or with a sauce. In the evening a card on the table lists additional dishes like tomato salad (£2.50), fish soup or escargot (£4.50), king prawns and prawns au gratin (£5.25), lamb picardi (£7.50), pork dijon (£8.50) or fillet steak stuffed with smoked oysters (£13.95); puddings (from £1.95); usual children's dishes (from £2.25). Relaxed and friendly family service; tables outside. There may be piped pop music. *(Recommended by Wayne Brindle, Judy and Jerry Hooper, Richard Lewis)*

Own brew ~ Licensee Vic Pocock ~ Real ale ~ Meals and snacks ~ Restaurant ~ (01584) 841205 ~ Children welcome ~ Open 12-2.30, 7-11

NORTON SJ7200 Map 4

Hundred House 🍴 🛏

A442 Telford—Bridgnorth

In spring you can walk around the beautiful gardens that surround this comfortably sophisticated old hotel, admiring the unusual roses, trees, herbaceous plants, and big working herb garden. There's a hint of spices inside too, with the bedrooms named after herbs and maybe scented with lavender. The inn is very much a family business, with various members of the Phillips brood helping out. Most popular with readers at the moment is the brasserie style bar food, with a menu that includes soup of the day or griddled black pudding with apple sauce and sage gravy (£3.50), coriander-cured salmon with beansprouts and lime salad (£3.95), steak and kidney pie (£6.95), minced turkey, sweet peppers and onion served with refried beans and tortilla (£8.25), charlotte of roast carrot and coriander mousse wrapped in courgette with tomato coulis and baked shallots (£8.50), and confit of duck with onion mamalade, red wine and thyme sauce (£8.95); if you eat from this menu in the dining room they slap on a £2 surcharge, and there have been occasions when the restaurant has been so busy on Saturday evenings that they've had to stop doing bar meals then. The beautifully appointed rooms are filled with interesting, even elegant, furnishings. The carefully refurbished bar is divided into several spick and span separate areas, with old quarry tiles at either end and modern hexagonal ones in the main central part – which has high beams strung with hop-bunches and cooking pots. Steps lead up past a little balustrade to a partly panelled eating area where stripped brickwork looks older than that elsewhere. Handsome fireplaces have log fires or working Coalbrookdale ranges (one has a great Jacobean arch with fine old black cooking pots), and around sewing-machine tables are a variety of interesting chairs and settles with some long colourful patchwork leather cushions. Well kept Flowers Original on handpump, along with Ailrics Old, and Heritage Bitter (light and refreshing, not too bitter) brewed for them by a small brewery; also an extensive wine list, and lots of malt whiskies. Dominoes, cribbage and piped music; no dogs. There are seats out in the garden. Some of the bedrooms have a swing in them. *(Recommended by John Knighton, Robert Sheard, Mrs I Tooze, Basil Minson, Carolyn Reynier, RP, BP, Peter and Patricia Burton, Heather Couper, Roger Byrne, Malcom Fowlie, Jenny Williams)*

Free house ~ Licensees Henry, David, Stuart and Sylvia Phillips ~ Real ale ~ Meals and snacks (12-2.30, 6.15-10) ~ Restaurant ~ (01952) 730353 ~ Children welcome ~ Open 11-3, 6-11 ~ Bedrooms: £59B/£79B

Cribbage is a card game using a block of wood with holes for matchsticks or special pins to score with; regulars in cribbage pubs are usually happy to teach strangers how to play.

ULVERBATCH SJ4202 Map 6

White Horse

From A49 at N end of Dorrington follow Pulverbatch/Church Pulverbatch signposts, and turn left at eventual T-junction (which is sometimes signposted Church Pulverbatch); OS Sheet 126 map reference 424023

A pleasant country pub in the narrow lanes south of Shrewsbury, this character-filled place surprises quite a few readers by the way it manages to cope so well with so many visitors. Though at lunchtime most people seem to be here for the reliable bar food, there are still usually plenty of locals crowding into the atmospheric bar. The several rambling areas have black beams and heavy timbering, as well as unusual fabric-covered high-backed settles and brocaded banquettes on its turkey carpet, sturdy elm or cast-iron-framed tables, and an open coalburning range with gleaming copper kettles. A collection of antique insurance plaques, big brass sets of scales, willow-pattern plates, and pewter mugs hangs over the serving counter, and there's even a good Thorburn print of a grouse among the other country pictures. Big helpings of bar food such as cullen skink heavily creamed smoked fish soup (£1.50), sandwiches (from £1.40), burgers and omelettes (from £3.25), ploughman's, fresh fish of the day or lasagne (£4.25), gammon and egg (£5.25), vegetarian platter (£5.50), chicken chasseur (£5.75), steaks (from £6.95), and puddings like pecan and treacle pie (£3.25). Well kept Boddingtons, Flowers Original and Marstons Pedigree on handpump, several decent wines by the glass, and well over a hundred malt whiskies. Darts, juke box, friendly efficient service. The quarry-tiled front loggia with its sturdy old green leatherette seat is a nice touch. The entrance is around the back of the pub. *(Recommended by Basil Minson, RP, BP, A J S Bellamy, Nigel and Lindsay Chapman, Steve and Angela Maycock, Roy Bromell, Roger Byrne)*

Whitbreads ~ Lease: Hamish and Margaret MacGregor ~ Real ale ~ Meals and snacks (till 10pm) ~ (01743) 718247 ~ Children welcome ~ Open 11.30-3, 7-11

SHREWSBURY SJ4912 Map 6

Boat House 🏠

New Street; leaving city centre via Welsh Bridge, follow Bishop's Castle A488 signpost into Port Hill Road

In a lovely position beside a park by the Severn, this comfortably modernised pub has a summer bar on a sheltered and attractive terrace, a lawn with roses, and a footbridge that leads across to the park itself. Inside, the long, quiet lounge bar has good views down over the river, rowing photographs and a collection of oars on the panelling, and a 1732 engraving that shows how little the vicinity has changed over the years. A good range of beers includes well kept Boddingtons, Flowers IPA, Fullers London Pride, Hogshead Abroad Cooper, and three guests like Jennings Cumberland, Morlands Old Speckled Hen and Timothy Taylors Landlord on handpump, served by friendly, helpful staff. The menu is the same as in other Hogshead Ale Houses, with generous helpings of soup (£1.20), sandwiches (from £1.95), steak and kidney pie or vegetable moussaka (£3.95), half a roast chicken with sage and onion stuffing and gravy (£4.25), and chicken tikka (£4.95); Sunday roasts (£4.25). Darts, alley skittles, cribbage, dominoes, fruit machine, and piped music. The pub is popular with young people in the evening. *(Recommended by M Joyner, Sue and Bob Ward, Malcolm and Pat Rudlin, SLC, S L Clemens, John Hibberd)*

Whitbreads ~ Manager Michael Roberts ~ Real ale ~ Meals and snacks (12-2.30, 5-8) ~ Children welcome ~ Open 11-11; 12-10.30 Sun

UPPER FARMCOTE SO7792 Map 4

Lion of Morfe £

Follow Claverley 2½ signpost off A458 Bridgnorth—Stourbridge

Popular at lunchtimes for its good value meals, this pleasant country pub is always friendly and efficient. The traditional public bar with wood-backed wall seats on red tiles and a game trophy over the coal fire is quite a contrast to the more modern conservatory behind. The smartly comfortable brown-carpeted lounge bar has pink plush button-back built-in wall banquettes in curving bays, and a good log fire; it opens into the no-smoking conservatory, with cushioned cane chairs around glass tables on its red-tiled floor. There's a big black kitchen range in the carpeted pool room, as well as darts, dominoes and fruit machine. Especially well liked by a value-conscious older set, the lunch menu includes filled baked potatoes (from £2.45), ploughman's (£2.95), steak and kidney pie or cottage pie (£3.15), lasagne, braised steak or pork in cider (£3.35), and a couple of daily specials including a vegetarian dish; in the evening they do dishes like chicken balti (£4.25) or smoked haddock pasta (£4.95). Well kept and priced Banks's Bitter and Mild and Bass on electric pump or handpump, and maybe a couple of guests. The garden has picnic tables under cocktail parasols on a terrace, and a lawn spreading out into an orchard with a floodlit boules pitch. *(Recommended by Basil Minson, Barbara and Denis Melling, Heather Couper; more reports please)*

Free house ~ Licensees Bill and Dinah Evans ~ Real ale ~ Meals and snacks (not eves Fri or Sat, or all day Sun) ~ (01746) 710678 ~ Children in eating area of bar and conservatory ~ Folk club first Sat of the month, jazz night second Thurs of the month ~ Open 11.30-3(4.30 Sat), 7-11

WENLOCK EDGE SO5796 Map 4

Wenlock Edge Inn ★ ⑪ ⇐

Hilltop; B4371 Much Wenlock—Church Stretton, OS Sheet 137 map reference 570962

This chatty stone pub is another where the whole family helps out with the running of the place, and what's more seems to thoroughly enjoy it. The way they cheerfully draw guests into the run of things is probably what explains the really rather special atmosphere, and it usually ensures a flow of interesting conversation too. The cosy feel is perhaps at its best on the second Monday in the month – story telling night, when the right hand bar is packed with locals telling tales, some true and others somewhat taller. In the right hand bar is a big woodburning stove in an inglenook, as well as a high shelf of plates, and it leads into a little dining room. The room on the left has pews that came from a Methodist chapel in Liverpool, a fine oak bar counter, and an open fire. The good fresh home-made bar food includes meals such as honey baked ham or steak and mushroom pie (£5.50), applejack chicken (£6.50) and sirloin steak (£8.60), and puddings like treacle tart (from £2.70); no chips. Breakfasts are excellent (try the sausage). The dining room is no smoking. Well kept local Hobsons Best and Town Crier on handpump, along with a changing beer like Ruddles Best, interesting whiskies, decent wines by both glass and bottle, and no music – unless you count the deep-throated chimes of Big Bertha the fusee clock. Water comes from their own 190 foot well. There are some tables on a front terrace and the side grass. The building is in a fine position just by the Ippikins Rock viewpoint and there are lots of walks through the National Trust land that runs along the Edge. *(Recommended by Gwen and Peter Andrews, Paul and Maggie Baker, John Mark Noone, Mike and Wendy Proctor, R and S Bentley, Mike Begley, John and Phyllis Maloney, Michael Butler, JKW, MDN, Phyl and Jack Street, Bob and Sue Ward, DMT, Richard Lewis, Nigel Woolliscroft, Brian and Margaret Beedham, Barbara and Denis Melling, Nigel Clifton, Mike and Penny Sanders, Paul Carter, G and M Hollis, Anthony Marriott, Phil and Carol Byng, Andrew Stephenson, Martyn Hart, Andrew Shore, Audrey Scaife, David Holman, F Jarman, M Joyner, Basil Minson; also in Good Hotel Guide)*

Free house ~ Licensee Stephen Waring ~ Real ale ~ Meals (not Mon except bank holidays) ~ Restaurant ~ (01746) 785678 ~ Children in eating area of bar and restaurant, under 14s must be eating ~ Open 11.30-2.30, 6.30-11; closed Mon lunchtime except bank holidays; cl 24/25/26 Dec ~ Bedrooms: £45S/£65S

WHITCHURCH SJ5345 Map 7

Willey Moor Lock

Pub signposted off A49 just under two miles N of Whitchurch

You have to cross a little footbridge over the Llangollen Canal and its rushing sidestream to reach this perfectly set lock keeper's cottage, an ideal spot to watch the colourful comings and goings on the water. Inside, several neatly decorated carpeted rooms have low ceilings, a large teapot collection, a decorative longcase clock, brick-based brocaded wall seats, stools and small chairs around dimpled copper and other tables, and two winter log fires. Well kept Theakstons Best and a couple of particularly unusual guests like Butterknowle Conciliation, Hanby All Seasons, or Wychwood Hobgoblin on handpump, and a large selection of malt whiskies; friendly landlady and staff. Generous helpings of bar food such as sandwiches (lunchtime only), pasties (£3.50), chicken curry or vegetable chilli (£4), steak pie or lasagne (£4.85), steaks (from £6.85), and puddings like jam roly poly (£1.50). Food stops one hour before closing. Fruit machine, piped music, and several dogs and cats. There are tables under cocktail parasols on a terrace, and a children's play area with swings and slides in the garden. (*Recommended by Richard Lewis, SLC, Basil Minson, Sue and Bob Ward; more reports please*)

Free house ~ Licensee Mrs Elsie Gilkes ~ Real ale ~ Meals and snacks ~ (01948) 663274 ~ Children welcome away from bar area ~ Open 12-2.30(2 in winter), 6-11; cl 25 Dec

WISTANSTOW SO4385 Map 6

Plough ♀ 🍺

Village signposted off A49 and A489 N of Craven Arms

Though it enjoys a good reputation locally for food, this is best known as the home of the delicious beers from the Wood Brewery, produced in a separate building behind. It will come as quite a surprise to those who expect brew pubs to be all spit and sawdust – with its high rafters and bright lighting, this is rather modern, looking more like a cafe than a traditional local. Perfectly kept beers include Woods Parish, Shropshire Lad, Special, the strong Wonderful and some seasonal brews; they also keep a couple of guests, two farm ciders, and about 16 wines by the glass, and there's a fine display cabinet of bottled beers. Current favourites amongst the well liked home-made bar meals include field mushrooms filled with stilton and leeks (£5.95), honey-baked ham (£6.25), and shark steak with lemon and garlic butter (£7.50); service can sometimes be a little slow. No credit cards. The games area has darts, pool, fruit machine, video game and juke box; maybe piped music. Outside there are some tables under cocktail parasols. (*Recommended by David and Julie Glover, David Shillitoe, Basil Minson, Robin and Molly Taylor, John and Joan Wyatt, PM, AM, Mervyn and Zilpha Reed, J C Green, Martyn Hart, Wayne Brindle, Mr and Mrs D Johnson, David and Rebecca Killick*)

Own brew ~ Licensee Len Brazendale ~ Real ale ~ Meals and snacks ~ (01588) 673251 ~ Children in eating area of bar lunchtime only ~ Open 12-3, 7-11

Please let us know what you think of a pub's bedrooms. No stamp needed: *The Good Pub Guide*, FREEPOST TN1569, Wadhurst, E Sussex TN5 7BR.

Lucky Dip

Besides the fully inspected pubs, you might like to try these Lucky Dips recommended to us and described by readers (if you do, please send us reports):

☆ **All Stretton** [SO4695], *Yew Tree*:
Comfortable beamed bars, good bar food,
well kept Bass and Worthington BB, quick
helpful service, quiet piped music, restaurant;
children welcome, handy for Long Mynd
(DC)

Alveley [A442; SO7684], *Squirrel*: Beamed
and panelled pub well refurbished by new
licensees, log fire in raised grate, tasteful
lighting, furniture and carpets, cottagey
atmosphere, friendly locals; good unusual
food, well kept Banks's Bitter and Mild *(Ron
and Isobel Kearton, Dave Braisted)*

Ash [Ash Magna; SJ5739], *White Lion*:
Village pub with good choice of real ales inc
interesting guest beers, brewery memorabilia
all over ceilings and walls, good atmosphere,
character landlord, friendly service, blazing
log fires, simple food inc sizzle-stone dishes
*(Sue and Bob Ward, Sue Holland, Dave
Webster)*

Astley [A53 Shrewsbury—Shawbury;
SJ5319], *Dog in the Lane*: Tetleys-related
ales, reasonably priced good straightforward
food, beamed lounge with good brass, copper
and china decor; tables outside *(M Joyner,
SLC)*

☆ **Bishops Castle** [Salop St; SO3289], *Three
Tuns*: A very long-standing main entry, with a
good deal of character in its own right but
specially notable for the unique Victorian
tower brewhouse still producing its own ales;
this closed late in 1995 and reopened under
new owners in summer 1996 – too late for us
to assess the changes *(LYM; news and views
please)*

Bishops Castle [Church St], *Boars Head*: Big
old hearths, stone walls and pleasant tables in
comfortable bar with nicely built benches
along walls, cheerful young staff, well kept
Courage Directors and John Smiths, varied
food inc good sandwiches *(D T Deas)*; *Castle*:
Cosy and friendly panelled local with well
kept Whitbreads-related ales, good value
generous food inc good sandwiches, puddings
and Sun roast, tables in front and in big back
garden *(Mr Kennedy)*

Boningale [A464 NW of W'hampton;
SJ8102], *Horns*: Three friendly bars with real
ales such as St Austell HSD as well as more
local Enville and Hook Norton, wholesome
nicely presented food inc magnificent brunch,
panelled dining room *(J Evans, Dave
Braisted)*

☆ **Bridgnorth** [Stn; A458 towards Stourbridge;
SO7293], *Railwaymans Arms*: Particularly
good real ales from changing Black Country
ad other interesting sources in 1940s-style
station bar of Severn Valley steam railway
terminus, lots of atmosphere esp on summer
days; simple summer snacks, coal fire, railway
memorabilia inc lots of signs, superb mirror
over fireplace, seats out on platform; children
welcome; car-parking fee refundable against

train ticket or what you spend here *(Nigel
Woolliscroft, PM, AM, LYM)*

☆ **Bridgnorth** [just past Northgate], *Bear*: Busy,
friendly and relaxed little timbered town pub
with good fresh unusual lunchtime food (not
Sun) inc sandwiches, gourmet nights Thurs,
well priced changing ales such as Bathams
and Holdens, good choice of bottled beers,
decent wines, old photographs and posters;
tables in sheltered enclosed garden; bedrooms
*(K W Grimshaw, M Joyner, W E and E
Thomas, Richard and Jean Phillips)*

Bridgnorth [Salop St (former A458 towards
Shrewsbury, nr cattle market)], *Bell &
Talbot*: Charming old stone building, calm,
cosy and old-fashioned, farm and railway
implements, well kept cheap beers inc
Banks's, log fire *(A P Jeffreys)*; [St Johns St],
Falcon: Atmospheric and comfortable big
beamed lounge bar, Bass and Boddingtons,
display of whisky miniatures; bedrooms
(Andrew Rogers, Amanda Milsom); [Old
Ludlow Rd; B4364, a mile out], *Punch Bowl*:
Unpretentious beamed and panelled 17th-c
country pub, good generous food inc fresh
veg and good carvery, Marstons Pedigree on
handpump, superb views; piped music *(Jeanne
Cross, Paul Silvestri, A P Jeffreys, Wayne
Brindle)*

☆ **Burwarton** [B4364 Bridgnorth—Ludlow;
SO6285], *Boyne Arms*: Friendly country pub
with generous reasonably priced home-made
food, changing well kept ales such as Bass,
Ind Coope Burton and Woods; tables in
garden, bedrooms *(RP, BP)*

☆ **Claverley** [High St; off A454
Wolverhampton—Bridgnorth; SO7993],
Crown: Picturesque heavily beamed and
timbered pub in lovely village, Interesting old-
fashioned bar, really friendly service, good
competitively priced home-made food (not
Sun-Weds evenings) cooked just as you ask,
well kept Banks's, open fires, splendid family
garden; dogs allowed, long Sat opening;
children allowed in eating area *(Wayne
Brindle, LYM)*

Claverley, *Plough*: Popular for modest range
of consistently good food, changing daily;
Tetleys-related ales with a guest such as
Shepherd Neame Spitfire, relaxed atmosphere,
helpful staff, interesting pictures made from
watch parts; separate bistro *(Paul and Sue
Merrick)*

☆ **Cleobury Mortimer** [Church St; SO6775],
Kings Arms: 16th-c inn with pleasant
atmosphere, carefully kept Hook Norton,
Timothy Taylors Landlord and Wye Valley,
varied reasonably priced food inc vegetarian
and good sandwiches; comfortable bedrooms
(Dennis Boddington, P and M Rudlin)

☆ **Clun** [High St; SO3081], *Sun*: Tudor timbers
and beams, some sturdy antique furnishings,
enormous open fire in flagstoned public bar,
well kept ales inc Banks's Bitter and Mild,

Marstons Pedigree and Woods Special, quiet atmosphere, friendly landlord; children allowed in eating area, tables on sheltered back terrace; bedrooms, lovely village *(Wayne Brindle, PM, AM, Colin Laffan, John Evans, LYM)*

☆ Clun [Market Sq], *White Horse*: Well laid out and neatly kept beamed L-shaped bar with inglenook and woodburner, well kept Bass, Worthington and a guest such as Wye Valley, farm cider, good coffee, decent standard food, friendly efficient service, pool table; children welcome, tables in front and small back garden; bedrooms *(P Tetley, RP, BP, P J Sibbett, David Sadler)*

☆ Coalport [off A442 S of Telford at Coalport/Broseley signpost – OS Sheet 127 map ref 702020; SJ7002], *Woodbridge*: Lovely setting with rustic benches on steepish Severnside lawns giving great view of world's second-oldest iron bridge, softly lit beamed and bow-windowed bar with lots of copper and brass, Victorian prints, good open fire, tables on side terrace with barbecue; good food from sandwiches up, no-smoking restaurant, well kept Courage-related ales with a guest beer, good service, piped music not too loud, children in eating areas; coarse fishing; open all day Sat, bedrooms *(C Moncreiffe, LYM)*

Coalport [Salthouse Rd, Jackfield], *Half Moon*: Welcoming new licensees in refurbished pub by Severn nr Maws Craft Centre, seven or eight real ales, decent malt whiskies, bar food inc good stilton soup, nice atmosphere *(Basil Minson)*; *Shakespeare*: Simple friendly cream-washed pub by pretty Severn gorge park, handy for china museum, with good value generous lunches, Tetleys-related ales *(Eddie and Iris Brixton, BB)*

Corfton [B4368 Much Wenlock—Craven Arms; SO4985], *Sun*: Welcoming country local with good value simple home-cooked food inc children's and bargain Sun lunch, well kept Whitbreads-related ales, pleasant lounge, lively and cheery bar, obliging service, dining room; tables on terrace and in good-sized garden with good play area; piped music *(Richard Houghton, BB)*

Coton [Tilstock Rd; B5476 Wem—Whitchurch; SJ5234], *Bull & Dog*: Black and white open-plan Greenalls pub with screened-off dining area, good value food, Tetleys-related ale, pleasant service; piped music *(SLC, Sue and Bob Ward)*

Ellerdine Heath [SJ6122], *Royal Oak*: Known locally as the Tiddlywink, warm and friendly atmosphere (maybe lots of children), eight real ales, interesting food, happy staff *(Sue and Bob Ward)*

☆ Ellesmere [Scotland St; SJ4035], *Black Lion*: Clean, comfortable and attractively refurbished with bare boards, ornaments, prints, high-backed settles etc, decent substantial food inc OAP bargains and children's dishes, very pleasant staff, well kept Banks's Mild and Marstons Pedigree, dining area *(Rita and Keith Pollard, W L G Watkins, SLC, Keith and Janet Morris)*

Ellesmere [Birch Rd], *White Hart*: Attractive little black and white pub, perhaps the oldest in Shrops, with well kept Marstons, friendly landlord; not far from canal *(SLC)*

☆ Hampton Loade [SO7586], *Lion*: Fine old stripped-stone inn with good unusual food, friendly efficient service, well kept beers, lots of country wines, good day-ticket fishing on River Severn; very busy in summer or when Severn Valley Rly has weekend steam spectaculars, quiet otherwise; tucked away at end of road that's not much more than a track for the last 1/4 mile *(Nigel Woolliscroft)*

☆ Harley [A458 NW of Much Wenlock; SJ5901], *Plume of Feathers*: Comfortable, spacious and attractive beamed pub with big open fire, reasonably priced food inc interesting specials, well kept Courage-related and guest ales, good welcoming service even when busy, darts, piped music (Sun evening live); dining room, tables outside; bedrooms with own baths *(B and K Hypher, SLC, RP, BP, J H Bell)*

Hilton [A454 Bridgnorth—Wolverhampton; SO7895], *Black Lion*: Welcoming new licensees, good varied food, pleasant eating areas, woodburner *(Barbara and Denis Melling)*

☆ Hodnet [SJ6128], *Bear*: Welcoming 16th-c pub with good range of reasonably priced food inc imaginative dishes, well kept Courage-related ales, friendly obliging service; sofas and easy chairs in foyer, sizeable refurbished bar wearing in nicely now and popular with locals, restaurant with small no-smoking area and corner alcove with glass-tile floor over unusual sunken garden in former bear pit; six good value comfortable bedrooms, opp Hodnet Hall gardens *(Olive and Ray Hebson, P D Donoghue, Paul Carter, G Washington)*

Hope [Drury Lane, Hopesgate; just off A488 3 miles S of Minsterley; SJ3401], *Stables*: Sadly the Hardings, under whom this pub was such a delight, have had to give it up; though very different now, it's still worth knowing for a good range of guest beers *(C Parsons, LYM)*

☆ Hopton Wafers [A4117; SO6476], *Crown*: Attractive creeper-covered inn with tables out on terraces and in garden running down to stream, cosy warmly decorated beamed bar with big inglenook fire and woodburner, lots of miscellaneous tables and chairs, good choice of bar food, well kept Whitbreads-related ales, good house wines, restaurant with no-smoking area; provision for children, comfortable and pretty timbered bedrooms *(C Smith, Basil Minson, John Hibberd, Gwen and Peter Andrews, Wayne Brindle, LYM)*

☆ Ironbridge [Buildwas Rd; SJ6704], *Meadow*: Popular and welcoming Severnside dining pub done up with old-fashioned beamery, cigarette cards, tasteful prints and brasses; wide choice of good value generous freshly prepared food in lounge and downstairs restaurant (must book Sun lunch), well kept Courage-related ales and Marstons Pedigree, decent wines, attentive service; pretty waterside garden only slightly marred by partly tree-screened power station on opp bank (*SLC, Iris and Eddie Brixton, Sue and Mike Todd, Basil Minson, Denis and Barbara Melling, Susan Christie, John Fazakerley*)

☆ Ironbridge [Blists Hill Open Air Museum – follow brown museum sign from M54 exit 4, or A442], *New Inn*: Rebuilt Victorian pub in this good heritage museum's recreated working Victorian community (shares its opening hours); informative landlord, friendly staff in period dress, well kept Banks's ales, pewter measure of mother's ruin for 2½ dd (money from nearby bank), good pasties, gas lighting, traditional games, good generous home cooking in upstairs tearoom; back yard with hens, pigeon coop, maybe children in costume playing hopscotch and skipping; children welcome (*Sue and Mike Todd, Steve and Angela Maycock, David and Fiona Pemberton, LYM*)

☆ Ironbridge [Waterloo St], *Olde Robin Hood*: Friendly pub in attractive riverside setting by bridge, five comfortable connecting rooms with various alcoves, lots of gleaming brass and old clocks; well kept Bass-related and guest beers, pleasant landlord, good value standard food inc sandwiches; seats out in front, handy for museums complex; good value bedrooms (*John Cox, SLC, Alan and Paula McCully*)

Ironbridge, *Tontine*: Friendly local, not in best area but with good atmosphere, well kept Bass and M&B Brew XI, tasty food, reasonably priced bedrooms (*Sue and Mike Todd*)

Kemberton [SJ7204], *Masons Arms*: Greenalls village pub with super views, Tetleys-related beers, good value food, friendly staff, tables in garden (*M Joyner*)

Ketley [Holyhead Rd (old A5); SJ6810], *Pudding*: One of the 'Little' pubs, popular at lunchtime for pleasant food, well kept Tetleys-related ales and Lumphammer (*P Yearsley, David and Shelia*)

Knockin [NW of Shrewsbury; SJ3422], *Bradford Arms*: Popular and busy, with good fresh standard food inc Sun lunch, well kept Bass-related ales, friendly service, reasonably priced restaurant; maybe piped Radio 2 (*Alex Mazaraki, SLC, P Beams*)

☆ Little Stretton [Ludlow Rd; village well signed off A49; SO4392], *Green Dragon*: Well kept Tetleys, Wadworths 6X, Woods and quickly changing guest beers, reasonably priced straightforward food, pleasant service, decent wines and malt whiskies, children in eating area and restaurant; tables outside, handy for Cardingmill Valley (NT) and Long Mynd (*Mr and Mrs Jones, Nigel Woolliscroft, Nick and Meriel Cox, Joan and Andrew Life, John and Joan Wyatt, Mike and Penny Sanders, LYM*)

Little Stretton [Ludlow Rd], *Ragleth*: Comfortably worn-in bay-windowed lounge, huge inglenook in brick-and-tile-floored public bar, reasonably priced home-made standard food from sandwiches to steaks, quick service, well kept Ansells Mild and Best, Marstons Pedigree, Woods Parish and guest

beers, tables on lawn by tulip tree; children welcome, restaurant (*Andy and Gill Plumb, LYM*)

Little Wenlock [SJ6507], *Huntsman*: Four-square village pub with bar, lounge and restaurant, pleasant quiet atmosphere, horse paintings, ornamental central fireplace, Tetleys and guest beers such as Crown Buckley Best, Timothy Taylors Landlord, Woods; well behaved children welcome, some tables outside; handy for Wrekin walks (*SLC*)

Loppington [B4397; SJ4729], *Dickin Arms*: Cosy two-bar pub with heavy beams, open fire, Bass, Wadworths and Youngers beers, good food inc good value Sun lunch, dining room (*SLC, RP, BP*)

☆ Ludlow [Bull Ring/Corve St; SO5175], *Feathers*: Superb timbered building, striking inside with Jacobean panelling and carving, fine period furnishings; you may be diverted to a side bar with less of a period feel for the good sandwiches and other decent bar food, or a casual drink – well kept Flowers Original and Wadworths 6X; pleasant service, restaurant, good parking; comfortable bedrooms, not cheap (*Gwen and Peter Andrews, J C Simpson, Michael Butler, LYM*)

☆ Ludlow [Broadgate/Lower Bridge St – bottom of Broad St], *Wheatsheaf*: Wide range of good value food inc interesting dishes and cheap Mon/Tues steak nights in nicely furnished traditional 17th-c pub spectacularly built into medieval town gate; Bass, M&B Brew XI and Ruddles County, choice of farm ciders, good friendly service, restaurant; attractive beamed bedrooms, warm and comfortable (*Frank W Gadbois, Mrs J Burgess, Michael Butler, David Peakall*)

Ludlow [Church St, behind Buttercross], *Church*: Comfortable banquettes, attractive prints and paintings, good value straightforward bar food (ploughman's or roast lunch only, Sun), well kept Courage-related and summer guest ales, prompt service, no-smoking restaurant, quiet piped music; children allowed, open all day; comfortable bedrooms, good breakfasts (but don't be late down) (*Mr and Mrs R J Phillips, SLC, LYM*); [Mill St], *Blue Boar*: Cosy, welcoming and attractively decorated, with lots of Festival photographs, well kept Ansells, restaurant; impressively big bedrooms (*Michael Butler*)

Madeley [Coalport Rd; SJ6904], *All Nations*: Spartan but friendly one-bar pub which has been brewing its own distinctive well priced pale ale for many decades, in the same family since the 1930s; good value lunchtime sandwiches, handy for Blists Hill (*Pete Baker*)

Morville [A458 Bridgnorth—Shrewsbury; SO6794], *Acton Arms*: Good food stop, with short choice of home-made food in dining lounge, pleasant newish landlord, well kept Banks's and good choice of wines at sensible prices, big attractive garden (*Robert Whittle*)

☆ Nesscliffe [A5 Shrewsbury—Oswestry; SJ3819], *Old Three Pigeons*: Wide range of good generous food inc fish and good value Sun lunch, welcoming staff, Whitbreads-related ales with changing guest beers, coffee all day, log fires, restaurant; Russian tank and lots of other used military hardware outside, also plenty of seats; opp Kynaston Cave, good cliff walks *(K Frostick, J R Whetton, M Joyner, Andrew Shore, Lawrence Bacon, Martin and Penny Fletcher, SLC)*

☆ Newcastle [B4368 Clun—Newtown; SO2582], *Crown*: Good value usual food in quite spacious lounge bar with log fire and piped music, lively locals' bar with darts, pool and so forth in games room, well kept Tetleys, decent wines, friendly efficient service, friendly great dane called Bruno; tables outside; charming well equipped bedrooms, attractive walks *(Peter and Sarah Gooderham, Nigel Woolliscroft, J C Green, DC, LYM)*

Picklescott [SO4399], *Bottle & Glass*: Early 17th-c country pub tucked away in delightful spot, pleasant quarry-tiled bar with well kept Bass and Worthington, good range of food inc good Sun lunch and home-made puddings, log fire; bedrooms *(Basil Minson, J R Smylie)*

☆ Pipe Gate [A51 Nantwich—Stone; SJ7441], *Chetwode Arms*: Friendly comfortably refurbished family pub with wide choice of good food in bar and attractively priced carvery restaurant, no-smoking area, pleasant efficient staff, Tetleys-related and interesting guest beers, open fire; play area *(SLC)*

Queens Head [just off A5 SE of Oswestry, towards Nesscliffe; SJ3427], *Queens Head*: Some emphasis on good value food from speciality sandwiches to full meals, with quick friendly service, well kept Theakstons and guest beers, two rooms with roaring coal fires, conservatory; by Montgomery Canal (under restoration), country walks *(Pete McMahon, Pete Yearsley, Basil Minson)*

Rodington [SJ5914], *Bulls Head*: Village pub with well kept Burtonwood beers, reasonably priced generous meals inc traditional puddings *(M Joyner, SLC)*

☆ Ryton [the one nr Dorrington, S of Shrewsbury; SJ4904], *Fox*: Smart country pub, very friendly and relaxed, with comfortable lounge bar and dining area, extensive range of good food, lots of interesting pictures, friendly landlord; stunning views of surrounding hills *(Amanda Dauncey)*

Shifnal [11 Market Pl; aka Odfellows; SJ7508], *Star*: Comfortable and welcoming cafe/bar in pretty village, with four well kept Whitbreads-related ales, good interesting food with inventive specialities, fresh veg and choice of potatoes, excellent service, over two dozen wines by the glass, stripped-pine furniture, log fire *(Peter Hobson)*; [High St], *White Hart*: Good value comfortable olde-worlde half-timbered pub, good range of interesting changing well kept ales, good promptly served standard food inc fresh veg, very welcoming staff *(Alan and Paula McCully)*

☆ Shrewsbury [Abbey Foregate; SJ4912], *M A D O'Rourkes Dun Cow Pie Shop*: Zany but homely decor, good range of good value food,

friendly staff, welcoming atmosphere, lots of jugs hanging from ceiling and enjoyably silly meat-pie memorabilia on walls, well kept Tetleys-related ales and Lumphammer; attractive timber-framed building with enormous model cow on porch which looks pure O'Rourke but long predates his 'Little' chain *(Michael Begley, Addie and Irene Henry, David and Shelia, SLC, Sue and Bob Ward, J Honnor, BB)*

Shrewsbury [16 Castle Gates], *Castle Vaults*: Friendly old timbered local popular for well kept changing ales such as Cottage GWR, Sarah Hughes Ruby Dark Mild and Sedgley Surprise, Mansfield Old Baily, Marstons Pedigree, Morrels Graduate, Ridleys Witchfinder Porter, Ruddles Best, Thwaites Big Ben, good choice of wines and other drinks, good chatty landlord; generous helpings of good food in adjoining Mexican restaurant, little roof garden with spiral staircase up towards castle; bedrooms good *(Richard and Anne Lewis)*; [Swan Hill/Cross Hill, nr old Square], *Coach & Horses*: Pine-panelled snug, pleasant bar and restaurant with carvery, well kept Bass and guest beers, good home-made food, attentive service; pretty flower boxes outside *(SLC)*; [Dogpole], *Cromwells*: Pub with wine bar and restaurant, Courage-related beers with a guest such as Bass or Lichfield. Inspired, good value imaginative food, raised garden and terrace behind; piped music; open all day Sat *(SLC)*; [centre], *Hole in the Wall*: Reasonably priced ales, decent food; noisy cellar jazz club, machines and video games *(Sue and Bob Ward)*; [Mardol], *Kings Head*: Pleasant low-beamed timbered pub with well kept Bass, Highgate Mild, M & B Brew XI, Morlands Speckled Hen and Vaux Sampson, lunchtime food, interesting medieval painting uncovered on old chimney breast; open all day *(Richard Lewis, Alan and Paula McCully)*; [Wyle Cop], *Lion*: Grand largely 18th-c inn with cosy oak-panelled bar and sedate series of high-ceilinged rooms opening off, obliging staff, Bass under light carbon dioxide blanket, reasonably priced bar food and bargain Sun lunches; children welcome; bedrooms comfortable *(R C Vincent, LYM)*; [42 Wenlock Rd], *Peacock*: Split-level pub with prints in partly panelled lounge, full Marstons range and Batemans Mild; piped music, golf video *(SLC)*; [Fish St], *Three Fishes*: Extensively refurbished heavy-beamed pub with six well kept changing ales such as Bass, Boddingtons, Flowers IPA, Fullers London Pride, Jennings Sneck Lifter, Morlands Old Speckled Hen, generous reasonably priced bar food inc Sun lunch, quick pleasant service, open all day; juke box; no-smoking throughout *(SLC, Keith and Janet Morris, Alain and Rose Foote)*; [Welshpool Rd (A458) outside city], *Welsh Harp*: Large lounge, dining area and restaurant, some cricket memorabilia, old advertisements in balcony, good quick food, Bass; pool, darts, bowling green *(SLC)*

☆ Stiperstones [village signed off A488 S of

Minsterley – OS Sheet 126 map ref 364005; SO3697], *Stiperstones*: Open all day, with good value simple food inc vegetarian all day too; welcoming little modernised lounge bar with comfortable leatherette wall banquettes, lots of brassware on ply-panelled walls, friendly atmosphere, well kept Flowers IPA and Woods Parish, good service, darts in plainer public bar, maybe unobtrusive piped music; restaurant, tables outside, good walking nearby *(Colin Laffan, Nigel and Lindsay Chapman, Nigel Woolliscroft, BB)*

Stottesdon [SO6783], *Fox & Hounds*: Classic village local, good service and atmosphere, good beers brewed on site; cl weekday lunchtimes *(Richard Houghton)*

Telford [Long Lane (A442); SJ6710], *Bucks Head*: Hotel bar with well kept Tetleys-related ales, good quick food inc children's and good value Sun lunch, family eating area and restaurant; piped music; bedrooms *(M Joyner)*

☆ Tilley [just S of Wem; SJ5128], *Raven*: Well kept dining pub in pretty 18th-c black and white building, bright, clean and attractive, with good service and food, separate restaurant, Fullers London Pride and Marstons Pedigree, log-effect gas fire, prints and bric-a-brac; nice terrace *(Richard J Holloway, Sue and Bob Ward, SLC, Dr and Mrs C D E Morris)*

☆ Tong [A41 just N of M54 junction 3, just beyond village; SJ7907], *Bell*: Reliable reasonably priced food inc children's and good value Sun lunch in friendly and efficient Milestone Tavern dining pub, well kept Banks's and Marstons Pedigree, olde-worlde stripped brickwork, big family room, dining room, unobtrusive piped music, no dogs; pleasant back conservatory, big garden, attractive countryside nr Weston Park *(Paul and Sue Merrick, D and D Savidge)*

Trench [Trench Rd; SJ6913], *Duke of York*: Big welcoming Greenalls pub with split-level lounge, bar with games and piped music; quickly served good food inc Sun lunch *(SLC)*

Uckington [B5061; old A5 E of Atcham; SJ5810], *Horseshoes*: Decent big Brewers Fayre pub with Whitbreads-related ales, children's eating area and play area; good family atmosphere for Sun lunch *(M Joyner, SLC)*

Upper Ludstone [off B4176 bypass; SO8095], *Boycott Arms*: Good value food, Banks's beers *(Dave Braisted)*

☆ Upton Magna [Pelham Rd; SJ5512], *Corbet Arms*: Wide choice of good value food cooked to order, well kept Banks's ales and short but decent choice of wines in big L-shaped lounge bar with armchairs by log fire; darts and juke

box in smaller public bar, good service; handy for Attingham Park (NT), busy at weekends *(Margaret and Peter Brierley, Paul Carter)*

☆ Whitchurch [St Marys St; SJ5341], *Old Town Hall Vaults*: Good value promptly served home-cooked lunchtime food in attractive and civilised 18th-c pub, well kept Marstons Bitter and Pedigree, cheerful service; piped light classics – birthplace of Sir Edward German *(M Joyner, Sue Holland, David Webster)*

Whitchurch [Green End; A41, 4 miles N], *Wheatsheaf*: Welcoming pub with decent food inc fresh veg, Bass and Cains Bitter, good wines; nicely kept garden and play area *(Sue and Bob Ward)*

Whittington [Ellesmere rd, just off A5; SJ3331], *Olde Boot*: Charming pub attractively placed opp 13th-c castle, cosy and relaxing panelled lounge, well kept Robinsons Bitter, Hatters Mild and Frederics, good value food inc popular Sun roast and OAP specials Mon and Tues night, friendly staff, small restaurant area, TV and games in popular friendly bar; bedrooms *(Richard Lewis, WLGW)*

Whixall [Platt Lane; SJ5236], *Waggoners*: Partly partioned into three rooms, good atmosphere, well kept Bass, Worthington and guests like Robinsons Frederics, enterprising range of good food inc Sun lunch; piped music, pool, camp site; tables in garden, short walk from Llangollen Canal *(SLC)*

Wollerton [A53 Shrewsbury—Mkt Drayton; SJ6230], *Squirrel*: Panelled bar, lounge, two open fires, Ansells and guest beers, good range of wines, competitively priced food, tables outside; restaurant; handy for Hodnet Hall gardens *(K Frostick)*

☆ Woofferton [A456/B4362 S of Ludlow; SO5269], *Salwey Arms*: Busy pub popular for wide choice of good food in bars and restaurant, well kept Bass and Tetleys, welcoming efficient service; handy for Forte Travelodge *(Phil and Carol Byng, Ian and Villy White, David Holman)*

☆ Woore [London Rd (A51); SJ7342], *Falcon*: Huge choice of generous good value food in bars and comfortable dining room inc good fresh fish, good friendly service even when busy, well kept Ansells Mild and Marstons Bitter and Pedigree, interesting prints; dining room more comfortable for eating than bars; nr Bridgemere garden centre *(Paul and Gail Betteley, SLC, J Lowe, Alan and Heather Jacques, Liz and Peter Elsey)*

Worfield [aka The Dog – OS Sheet 138 map ref 758957; SO7696], *Davenport Arms*: Friendly, homely and peaceful local in unspoilt stone village; real fire; brews its own beer *(Richard Houghton)*

People don't usually tip bar staff (different in a really smart hotel, say). If you want to thank a barman – dealing with a really large party say, or special friendliness – offer him a drink. Common expressions are: 'And what's yours?' or 'And won't you have something for yourself?'.

Somerset

A fine county for pub lovers, with lots of character and traditional values preserved well in many gloriously unchanging pubs, friendly and genuinely interested licensees and staff, and surrounding countryside that's often a definite plus. Pubs currently on top form here include the Globe at Appley (fine mix of local atmosphere with good food), the Woolpack at Beckington (a new entry, with good if expensive food in charming surroundings), the Wheatsheaf at Combe Hay (a particularly enjoyable country pub), the Strode Arms at Cranmore (good food, with Mrs Phelps back in her own kitchen), the New Inn at Dowlish Wake (good food here too, with the original licensees back in place), the engaging Fitzhead Inn at Fitzhead (another new entry, good all round), the well run Old Crown at Kelston, the cottagey Kingsdon Inn at Kingsdon, the Kings Arms at Litton (on a definite upswing), the Royal Oak at Luxborough (new licensees settling in well), the nice old Talbot at Mells, the consistently good Notley Arms at Monksilver), the Bird in Hand at North Curry (another good all-rounder making its first appearance among the main entries), the wonderful old George at Norton St Philip (warm and friendly, with good food nowadays), the Royal Oak at Over Stratton (on the edge of a Food Award, and gains a Wine Award this year), the Halfway House at Pitney (a new entry, very traditional, with excellent beers), the charming Full Moon at Rudge (gains both a Food Award and a Place to Stay Award this year), the Royal Oak at Winsford (comfortably chintzy, thoroughly recovered from its fire) and the Royal Oak at Withypool on Exmoor. The Cotley at Wambrook is also doing very well; though the food's not elaborate and there are no fancy names, it's a place that people really enjoy for meals out – and is our choice as Somerset Dining Pub of the Year. In the Lucky Dip section at the end of the chapter, pubs doing well these days (almost all inspected and approved by us) include the Lamb in Axbridge, Batcombe Inn at Batcombe, Red Cow at Brent Knoll, Castle in Bruton, Inn at Freshford (new management with a promising track record, but some ground to make up), Greyhound at Staple Fitzpaine, Lion at West Pennard, Rest & Be Thankful at Wheddon Cross and Holman Clavel at Widcombe. There's a very wide choice in Bristol, and (on a much smaller scale) a good choice for walkers around Priddy. Drinks prices in the county are just a shade below the national average; the cheapest beers we found were at the Poulett Arms at Hinton St George (a free house), the White Hart at Trudoxhill (brewing its own good beers), the Highbury Vaults in Bristol (tied to the small Smiles brewery there) and the Black Horse at Clapton in Gordano (tied to Courage). West country farm ciders are well worth looking out for here – with the unusual old Rose & Crown at Huish Episcopi a fitting place to try quite a range.

APPLEY ST0621 Map 1

Globe 🍽

Hamlet signposted from the network of back roads between A 361 and A38, W of B3187 and W of Milverton and Wellington; OS sheet 181 map reference 072215

Although many people come to this friendly old place for the very good food, the licensees have been careful to keep a good pubby atmosphere where locals and visitors can enjoy a drink and a chat. A stone-flagged entry corridor leads to a serving hatch from where Cotleigh Tawny and Barn Owl, and Dartmoor Best are served on handpump, and they have Lanes farmhouse cider. The simple beamed front room is relaxed and chatty, with benches and a built-in settle, bare wood tables on the brick floor, and pictures of magpies. As well as the restaurant, there's a further room with easy chairs and other more traditional ones; alley skittles. Good generously served bar food might include sandwiches, home-made soup (£2.25), mushrooms in cream, garlic and horseradish (£3.25), a light cold egg pancake filled with prawns, celery and pineapple in marie rose sauce (£4.75), chilli con carne (£4.95), home-made steak and kidney pie in stout or savoury vegetable crumble (£5.95), fresh salmon with chive, white wine and cream sauce (£7.95), steaks (from £7.95), breast of local chicken stuffed with pine nuts, bacon, raisins and apricots and served with a madeira sauce (£8.95), puddings, children's dishes (£3.25), and popular Sunday roast (£5.25). The restaurant is no smoking. Seats, climbing frame and swings outside in the garden; the path opposite leads eventually to the River Tone. *(Recommended by Michael and Lynne Steane, Robin Priest, David Gittins, S G N Bennett, Jane and Adrian Tierney-Jones, R V Ford, Mr and Mrs T J Rigby, G S and E M Dorey)*

Free house ~ Licensees A W and E J Burt, R and J Morris ~ Real ale ~ Meals and snacks (till 10pm) ~ Restaurant (not Sun evening) ~ (01823) 672327 ~ Children in eating area of bar and in restaurant ~ Open 11-3, 6.30-11; closed Mon lunchtime, except bank holidays

ASHCOTT ST4337 Map 1

Ashcott Inn

A39 about 6 miles W of Glastonbury

The bar in this attractively refurbished and pleasantly atmospheric old pub has stripped stone walls and beams, good oak and elm tables, some interesting old-fashioned seats among more conventional ones, and a log-effect gas fire in its sturdy chimney. Under the new managers, bar food includes sandwiches, mushrooms au gratin (£3.25), fish pie (£5.25), oriental stir fry (£5.50), beef in ale pie (£5.95), fresh plaice or salmon (from £7.25), and their house speciality, fillet of beef (£10.50). Well kept Butcombe Bitter, Flowers Original and IPA, and guest beers on handpump; cribbage, dominoes, shove-ha'penny, fruit machine, alley skittles, and piped music. Seats on the terrace, and a pretty walled garden which the no-smoking restaurant overlooks. *(Recommended by Mr and Mrs Beck, A Preston, Julie and Tony Baldwin, V H and J M Vanstone, Judith and Stephen Gregory, Neville Kenyon, Margaret Dyke, R W Brooks, Dorothy and Leslie Pilson, Mr and Mrs Jones)*

Heavitree (who no longer brew) ~ Managers Jon and Helen Endacott ~ Real ale ~ Meals and snacks ~ Restaurant (not Sun evening) ~ (01458) 210282 ~ Well behaved children in eating area of bar and in restaurant ~ Open 11-3, 5.30-11; 11-11 Sat; 12-10.30 Sun (12-4, 7-10.30 winter Sun)

nr ASHILL ST3217 Map 1

Square & Compass

Windmill Hill; turn left off A358 when see Stewley Cross Garage on a side road

The sweeping views from this nicely remote pub over the rolling pastures around Neroche Forest can be enjoyed from the upholstered window seats in the cosy little bar; there are also other comfortable seats (with extra room for eating), and an open fire in winter. Bar food includes sandwiches, mixed salami platter (£4.50), aubergine and lentil curry (£4.95), lamb in a yoghurt and mint sauce (£6.95), pork steak with honey and ginger (£7.50), and rump steak with a port and stilton sauce (£9.50). Well kept Exmoor Bitter, Flowers Original, Marstons Pedigree, Wadworths 6X, and Youngs Special on handpump; darts, cribbage, dominoes and piped music. Outside on the grass are picnic tables and a good children's play area with badminton and volleyball. There's a touring caravan site. *(Recommended by Mr and Mrs Beck, Geoff and Linda Dibble, David Crafts, Howard Clutterbuck, D Godden, Helen and Keith Bowers and friends, Revd A Bunnerley, Mr and Mrs Westcombe, M E Wellington)*

Free house ~ Simon and Ginny Reeves ~ Real ale ~ Meals and snacks ~ (01823) 480467 ~ Children welcome ~ Open 12-2.30, 6.30-11

BATH ST7565 Map 2

Old Green Tree 🍺

12 Green St

No noisy games machines or piped music disturb the cosy, chatty, and genuinely old-fashioned atmosphere of the three oak-panelled little rooms here. The main bar can get quite busy (thanks to its size), but service always remains efficient, attentive and friendly; there's a comfortable lounge on the left as you go in, its walls decorated with wartime aircraft pictures, and the back bar is no smoking. The big skylight lightens things up attractively. Good home-made lunchtime bar food includes soup (£3), good ploughman's or large filled rolls (from £3.30), spaghetti with cheese, wine and herbs or tomato and parmesan (£4.50), interesting salads, Thai chicken curry or popular bangers and mash with tomato and onion or apple, cream, mustard and cider sauces (all £4.80), seafood platter (£6), and daily specials. There are usually five well kept beers on handpump at a time, with some emphasis on ales from local breweries such as Bunces Best, Cottage Southern Bitter, Hardington Best, Uley Hogshead, and Wickwar Brand Oak, lots of malt whiskies, and a nice little wine list with helpful notes. The gents, though good, are down steep steps. *(Recommended by Dr and Mrs A K Clarke, J and P Maloney, N J Lawless, Gordon, Veronica M Brown, Roger Wain-Heapy, Simon and Pie Barker, A Reimer, J Drew, K Neville-Rolfe)*

Free house ~ Nick Luke ~ Real ale ~ Lunchtime meals and snacks (not Sun) ~ Children in eating area of bar if over 12 ~ Open 11-11; closed Sun lunchtime

BECKINGTON ST8051 Map 2

Woolpack 🛏️ ♀

Off A36 Bath—Warminster

This welcoming old inn has gained enormously from the bypassing of the village, settling back into a charming relaxed individuality. Well refurbished three or four years ago, it has a calm and attractive no-smoking lounge with antique furnishings and pictures, a lively flagstoned public bar with stripped pine tables and a good log fire, and a cosy candlelit no-smoking dining room. Good food from a short but regularly changing menu, eaten in the bar or dining room, uses a lots of fresh local produce, including fresh fish from Brixham, and might include sandwiches (from £3.95), starters like soup (£3.95), Greek salad or Cornish crab (£5.95), and main courses such as breast of chicken in white wine and cream sauce (£12.50), best end of lamb with leek and rosemary (£13.95), pork tenderloin, oriental-style monkfish or breast of Norfok duck (£14.50). A couple of more reasonably priced daily specials might be marinated scallops with chilli, coriander and ginger, calf liver with devilled mushrooms, coconut curry cream or confit of duck with honey and mustard dressing (£5.95); vegetables (£1.75). Well kept Greene King IPA, Oakhill Best and Wadworths 6X on handpump, good reasonably priced house wines, cheerful helpful service. *(Recommended by Paul and Ursula Randall, Pat and John Millward, Dr and Mrs A K Clarke)*

Free house ~ Licensee Martin Tarr ~ Real ale ~ Meals and snacks (till 10pm) ~
Restaurant ~ (01373) 831244 ~ Open 11-3, 6-11 ~ Bedrooms: £54.50B/£64.50B

BLAGDON ST5059 Map 2

New Inn

Church Street, off A368

By the time this book is published, new licensees will have taken over this neat, old-fashioned pub. It's in a lovely setting, and from the picnic tables at the back there are fine views looking down over fields to wood-fringed Blagdon Lake, and to the low hills beyond. Inside, the two warm and individualistic rooms have lots of character, ancient beams decorated with gleaming horsebrasses and some tankards, and big logs burning in both stone inglenook fireplaces. Also, some comfortable antique settles – one with its armrests carved as dogs – as well as little plush armchairs, mate's chairs and so forth. Enjoyable lunchtime bar food has included home-made soup (£2), sandwiches (£2.25), ploughman's (from £3.80), sausages (£3.60), filled baked potatoes (from £3.60), home-made steak and kidney pie (£4.40), cold meat platters (from £5.95), daily specials, puddings (£2.50), children's meals (£2.75), and evening grills (from £6.75). Well kept Butcombe and Wadworths IPA and 6X on handpump; darts, shove-ha'penny, table skittles, cribbage, dominoes, fruit machine, trivia, and piped music. The pub can get busy at weekends. No children.
(Recommended by Andrew Shore, Gwen and Peter Andrews, F J Willy, Meg and Colin Hamilton, Jenny and Roger Huggins, R W Brooks, Don Kellaway, Angie Coles, P H Roberts; more reports on the new regime, please)

Wadworths ~ Real ale ~ Meals and snacks ~ (01761) 462475 ~ Open 11-2.30, 7-11

BRADLEY GREEN ST2538 Map 1

Malt Shovel 🍺

Pub signposted from A39 W of Bridgwater, near Cannington; though Bradley Green is shown on road maps, if you're booking the postal address is Blackmoor Lane, Cannington, BRIDGWATER, Somerset TA5 2NE; note that there is another different Malt Shovel on this main road, three miles nearer Bridgeware

The homely and neatly kept straightforward main bar in this warmly friendly, family-run local has various boating photographs, window seats, some functional modern elm country chairs and sturdy modern winged high-backed settles around wooden tables, and a black kettle standing on a giant fossil by the woodburning stove. There's also a tiny snug with white walls and black beams, a solid oak bar counter with a natural stone front, and red tiled floor. Decent bar food includes lunchtime sandwiches (£1.55, crusty rolls £1.95) and ploughman's (from £3.10), as well as pasta and spinach mornay (£3.55), lamb and potato provençale (£3.85), filled baked potatoes (£4.10; you can choose any 3 fillings out of 12), salads (from £4.40), home-made steak and kidney pie (£4.65), grilled gammon and egg (£4.90), home-made fish pie (£5.75), steaks (from £8.50), daily specials, and children's dishes (from £1.95); good breakfasts. Well kept Butcombe Bitter, Morlands Old Speckled Hen, John Smiths, and a guest on handpump, and farm cider; sizeable skittle alley, dominoes, and piped music. The family room opens on to the garden, where there are picnic tables and a fish pond. The bedrooms fit in with the comfortable simplicity of the place. West of the pub, Blackmore Farm is a striking medieval building. *(Recommended by Stephen and Julie Brown, Maysie Thompson, D Alexander, M and A Sandy, Brian and Barbara Matthews, Ian Phillips, Richard Gibbs, Anthony Barnes, Paul Randall, Bruce Bird, Andy Thwaites, G W A Pearce)*

Free house ~ Licensees Robert and Frances Beverley, Philip and Sally Monger ~ Real ale ~ Meals (not winter Sun evening) and lunchtime snacks ~ Restaurant (not winter Sun evenings) ~ (01278) 653432 ~ Children in family room and in restaurant ~ Open 11.30-2.30(3 Sat), 6.30(7 winter)-11; closed 25 Dec ~ Bedrooms: £21.50(£30B)/£30(£38B)

BRISTOL ST5872 Map 2

Highbury Vaults £ 🍺

St Michaels Hill, Cotham; main road out to Cotham from inner ring dual carriageway

A good mix of customers gathers in this atmospheric city pub to enjoy its traditional, unchanging atmosphere – no noisy games or piped music. There's a cosy and crowded front bar with the corridor beside it leading through to a long series of little rooms – wooden floors, green and cream paintwork, old-fashioned furniture and prints, including lots of period Royal Family engravings and lithographs in the front room. It's one of the handful of pubs tied to the local Smiles brewery, so has all their beers well kept on handpump at attractive prices, as well as Badger Best and Butcombe Bitter, and guests like Adnams Best, Crown Buckley Reverend James, Fullers London Pride, and Gales HSB. Very cheap bar food includes filled rolls, vegetable and coconut curry (£2.60), chilli con carne (£2.70), pork and apples in cider (£2.80), and beef in ginger wine (£2.90). Darts, dominoes and cribbage – they keep a crossword dictionary for quieter moments. A nice terrace garden has tables built into a partly covered flowery arbour – not large, but a pleasant surprise for the locality; maybe summer barbecues. In early Georgian times it was a lock-up where condemned men ate their last meal, and some of the bars can still be seen on the windows. *(Recommended by Barry and Anne, JJB, Simon and Amanda Southwell, C Smith, Dr and Mrs A K Clarke, Paul Carter)*

Smiles ~ Manager Bradd Francis ~ Real ale ~ Meals and snacks (12-2, 5.30-8.30) ~ (0117) 973 3203 ~ Children welcome until 9pm ~ Open 12-11; 12-10.30 Sun

CATCOTT ST3939 Map 1

King William

Village signposted off A39 Street—Bridgwater

Now owned by Palmers Brewery and with a friendly new licensee, this neatly kept cottagey pub has a spacious bar with one or two rugs on the stone floors, traditional furnishings such as kitchen and other assorted chairs, brown-painted built-in and other settles, window seats, and Victorian fashion plates and other old prints; big stone fireplaces. Decent bar food includes sandwiches (from £1.50), home-made soup (£1.80), ploughman's (from £3.20), vegetable lasagne (£4.45), home-made steak and kidney pie or curry (£4.60), smoked haddock in cider sauce (£4.75), pork chop dijonnaise (£5.95), steaks, daily specials, and puddings. Well kept Palmers Bridport, IPA, 200, and Tally Ho on handpump, with farm cider and a good range of malt whiskies; darts, fruit machine, cribbage, dominoes, and piped music. A large extension at the back includes a skittle alley and a glass-topped well. *(Recommended by M Carr, Tom Evans, Stephen and Julie Brown, S H Godsell)*

Palmers ~ Tenant Phillip Rowland ~ Real ale ~ Meals and snacks ~ Restaurant ~ (01278) 722374 ~ Children in eating area of bar ~ Open 11.30-2.30, 6-11

CHURCHILL ST4560 Map 1

Crown 🍺

Skinners Lane; in village, turn off A368 at Nelson Arms

As well as the unspoilt charm and rural atmosphere in this old cottage, what locals and visitors like is the constantly changing range of well kept real ales: Bass, Butcombe, Eldridge Pope Hardy, Greene King Abbot, Morlands Old Speckled Hen and Palmers IPA all tapped from casks at the back, along with a nice light but well hopped bitter brewed for the pub by Cotleigh; also a range of country wines, and local Axbridge wine. The small and local stone-floored and cross-beamed room on the right has a wooden window seat, an unusually sturdy settle, and built-in wall benches; the left-hand room has a slate floor, and some steps past the big log fire in a big stone fireplace lead to more sitting space. Generously served bar food (with prices and dishes unchanged since last year) includes a good home-made soup (in winter, £2), rare beef sandwich (£2.50), a good ploughman's, various casseroles (£3.50-£5.50), and chilli con carne (£3.95). They can be busy at weekends, especially in summer. There are garden tables on the front and a smallish but pretty back lawn with hill views; the Mendip Morris Men come in summer. Good walks nearby. Some readers have felt the lavatories need attention. *(Recommended by A R and B E Sayer, Barry Cawthorne, Anne Moggridge, S H Godsell, Derek and Sylvia Stephenson, Pete Yearsley, M W Turner, Mr and Mrs J Brown, Roger Wain-Heapy, A C Stone, P H Roberts)*

Free house ~ Licensee Tim Rogers ~ Real ale ~ Lunchtime meals and snacks ~ (01934) 852995 ~ Children in eating area of bar ~ Open 11.30-3.30, 5.30-11

CLAPTON IN GORDANO ST4773 Map 2

Black Horse

4 miles from M5 junction 19; A369 towards Portishead, then B3124 towards Clevedon; in N Weston opp school turn left signposted Clapton, then in village take second right, maybe signed Clevedon, Clapton Wick

This is a genuinely characterful pub that has changed little over the years – which pleases its loyal local following. The partly flagstoned and partly red-tiled main room has winged settles and built-in wall benches around narrow, dark wooden tables, pleasant window seats, amusing cartoons and photographs of the pub, a big log fire with stirrups and bits on the mantelbeam, and a relaxed, friendly atmosphere. A window in an inner snug is still barred from the days when this room was the petty-sessions gaol; high-backed settles – one a marvellous carved and canopied creature, another with an art nouveau copper insert reading East, West, Hame's Best – lots of mugs hanging from its black beams, and plenty of little prints and photographs. There's also a simply furnished children's room, just off the bar, with high-backed corner settles and a gas fire; darts, dominoes, cribbage, and piped music. Good quickly-served bar food includes filled rolls (from £1.30; black pudding and mushrooms £1.85), french sticks (from £1.65), ploughman's, and two daily specials like sausage, bacon and mushroom casserole or garlic and coriander chicken. Well kept Courage Best and Wadworths 6X on handpump or tapped from the cask; farm cider. The little flagstoned front garden is exceptionally pretty in summer with a mass of flowers in tubs, hanging baskets and flowerbeds; there are some old rustic tables and benches, with more to one side of the car park and in the secluded children's play area with its sturdy wooden climber, slide, rope ladder and rope swing. Paths from here lead up Naish Hill or along to Cadbury Camp. *(Recommended by Ian and Gayle Woodhead, Tom Evans, Alan and Heather Jacques, Jack and Philip Paxton)*

Courage ~ Tenants Nicholas Evans and Alfonso Garcia ~ Real ale ~ Lunchtime meals and snacks (not Sun) ~ (01275) 842105 ~ Children in family room ~ Live music Mon evenings ~ Open 11-3, 6-11; 11-11 Fri/Sat

COMBE HAY ST7354 Map 2

Wheatsheaf

Village signposted from A367 or B3110 S of Bath

In a lovely setting on the side of a steep wooded valley, this is a really enjoyable country pub with good food and friendly staff. The pleasantly old-fashioned rooms have low ceilings, brown-painted settles, pews and rustic tables, a very high-backed winged settle facing one big log fire, old sporting and other prints, and earthenware jugs on the shelf of the little shuttered windows. Popular bar food includes home-made soup (£2.75), ploughman's (from £4.50), game terrine (£4.75), quiche (£5), hot baked ham (£5.25), seasonal pheasant or venison, fresh trout (£8.75), daily specials like chicken livers (£5.25), pasta in a creamy mushroom and courgette sauce (£5.95), shredded crispy duck in an orange and pineapple sauce (£6.25), sautéed tiger prawns (£7.95), and puddings (£2.95). Well kept Courage Best and a guest like Wadworths

6X tapped from the cask. There are three dovecotes built into the walls, tables on the spacious sloping lawn looking down to the church and ancient manor stables, and good nearby walks. *(Recommended by A Thistlethwaite, Mrs B Sugarman, Dr and Mrs A K Clarke, C A Foulkes, Howard Clutterbuck, Roger Wain-Heapy, Kevin and Tracey Stephens, Steve and Carolyn Harvey)*

Free house ~ Licensee M G Taylor ~ Real ale ~ Meals and snacks ~ Restaurant ~ (01225) 833504 ~ Children in eating area of bar and in restaurant ~ Open 11-2.30, 6.30-11

COMPTON MARTIN ST5457 Map 2

Ring o' Bells

A368 Bath—Weston

Families are well catered for at this bustling country pub. They have a big no-smoking family room with games and a rocking horse, changing facilities for babies, a children's menu, and large garden with swings, slide, activity unit/climbing frame. The snugly traditional front part has rugs on the flagstones, inglenook seats right by the log fire, and a warmly cosy atmosphere. In summer, you may prefer to go up the step to a cool and spacious carpeted back part, with largely stripped stone walls and pine tables. Bar food includes sandwiches (from £1.25; toasties from £2.05), soup (£1.65), filled baked potatoes (from £2.50), omelettes (£from £2.75), ploughman's (from £3.15), grilled ham and eggs (small £3.30, large £4.10), lasagne or mushroom, broccoli and almond tagliatelli (£4.25), beef in ale (£4.95), generous mixed grill (£8.95), daily specials, and children's meals (or helpings; from 95p). Well kept Bass, Butcombe Bitter, Wadworths 6X and guest beers on handpump; friendly helpful service. The public bar has darts and shove-ha'penny, and a spacious, no-smoking family room has table skittles and fruit machine. The pub is not far from Blagdon Lake and Chew Valley Lake and is overlooked by the Mendip Hills. *(Recommended by A E Brace, Barry Cawthorne, Anne Moggridge, Hugh MacLean, Tom Evans, Jenny and Roger Huggins, Don Kellaway, Angie Coles, E H and R F Warner, Jack and Philip Paxton, R L W and Dizzy)*

Free house ~ Licensee Roger Owen ~ Real ale ~ Meals and snacks ~ Children in family room ~ (01761) 221284 ~ Open 11.30-3, 6.30-11

CRANMORE ST6643 Map 2

Strode Arms ★ 🍴 🍷

West Cranmore; signposted with pub off A361 Frome—Shepton Mallet

Although it's the very good food (and pretty setting by the village duck pond) that readers like so much about this early 15th-c former farmhouse, the smartly relaxed bar is a comfortable place to enjoy a quiet drink – if that is all you want. The same menu is used in both the bar and restaurant (and Mrs Phelps is back in the kitchen – at strong request from regular customers): sandwiches, soup (£2.75), very good egg mayonnaise with prawns, capers, smoked trout, anchovy and asparagus tips (£3.95), lovely scallops and bacon (£5.25), excellent home-made steak and kidney pie (£6.50), pancake filled with spinach and baked with a cheese sauce (£6.75), gammon and egg (£7.25), fresh salmon fishcakes (£7.50), rack of lamb roasted with rosemary (£9.25), steaks (from £9.25), daily specials such as Greek meatballs with spicy tomato sauce, delicious veal rosti with stilton sauce or vegetarian strudel, and puddings like excellent sticky toffee pudding or treacle tart (from £2.40); Sunday roasts; friendly service. There are lovely log fires in handsome fireplaces, charming country furnishings, a grandfather clock on the flagstones, fresh flowers and pot plants, remarkable old locomotive engineering drawings and big black-and-white steamtrain murals in a central lobby, good bird prints, and newspapers to read. Well kept Flowers IPA, Marstons Pedigree and Wadworths 6X on handpump, an interesting choice of decent wines by the glass and lots more by the bottle, farm cider, and quite a few liqueurs and ports. There's a front terrace with some benches and a back garden. On the first Tuesday of each month, there's a vintage car meeting, and the pub is handy for the East Somerset Light Railway. *(Recommended by Jerry and Alison Oakes, Dr and Mrs A H Young, GSB, MRSM, Andrew Shore, Paul and Lynn Benny, David Shillitoe, Jane and Adrian Tierney-Jones, Revd A Nunnerley, M G Hart, Mr and Mrs M J Matthews, Roger Wain-Heapy, Kevin and Tracey Stephens, Mrs C Blake, John Wooll, Tom Evans, Ted George, A D Sherman, R V Ford)*

Free house ~ Licensees Rodney and Dora Phelps ~ Real ale ~ Meals and snacks (till 10 Fri/Sat) ~ Cottagey restaurant ~ (01749) 880450 ~ Children in restaurant ~ Open 11.30-2.30, 6.30-11; closed Sun evening Oct-March

CROSCOMBE ST5844 Map 2

Bull Terrier

A371 Wells—Shepton Mallet

First granted a licence to sell alcohol in 1612, this handsome building has a neat ('Inglenook') lounge bar with attractively moulded original beams, cushioned wooden wall seats and wheelback chairs around neat glossy tables, pictures on its white walls, a log-effect gas fire in a big stone fireplace with a fine iron fireback, and a red carpet on its flagstone floor. A communicating ('Snug') room has more tables with another gas-effect log fire, and there's a third in the parquet-floored 'Common Bar', by the local noticeboard; also, a no-smoking family room. Bar food includes sandwiches (from £1.40), soup (£1.95), ploughman's (from £2.75), pancakes stuffed with spinach and peanuts (£4.95), lasagne (£5.45), home-made steak and kidney pie (£5.95), steaks (from £9.95), daily specials, and puddings such as home-made apple pie or lemon meringue pie (£1.95). Well kept Brains SA, Butcombe Bitter, Greene King Abbot, Hook Norton Old Hookey, and Theakstons XB on handpump; dominoes, cribbage, and shove-ha'penny. At the back is an attractive walled garden. There's a two-mile footpath to Bishop's Palace moat in Wells. *(Recommended by Mike Hayes, John Waller, Nigel and Amanda Thorp, James Macrae, Colin and Ann Hunt, R L W and Dizzy, Roger Wain-Heapy, A D Sherman, Tom Evans, Brig J S Green, Kevin and Tracey Stephens, Stephen Boot, Revd A Nunnerley; more reports please)*

Free house ~ Licensees Barry and Ruth Vidler ~ Real ale ~ Meals and snacks (not winter Sun evenings or all day Mon Oct-March) ~ (01749) 343658 ~ Children in family room ~ Open 12-2.30, 7-11; closed Mon Oct-March ~ Bedrooms: £30B/£46B

DOWLISH WAKE ST3713 Map 1

New Inn

Village signposted from Kingstone – which is signposted from old A303 on E side of Ilminster, and from A3037 just S of Ilminster; keep on past church – pub at far end of village

Although this neatly kept village pub changed hands over the last year, the friendly licensees who ran it for over 10 years with such success, are now back at the helm again. So the good, popular bar food should be back on course: soup (£1.75; good fish soup with garlic croûtons £2.75), sandwiches (from £1.75), omelettes (from £2.95), ploughman's (£3.25), New Zealand mussels with crispy bacon crumbs and cream (£3.50), fresh fillet of plaice, chicken tikka masala or liver and bacon (all £4.75), good spicy sausage in a huge yorkshire pudding (£3.25), grills (from £6.75), paella (£8.75), pork with stilton and cream sauce on tagliatelle (£9.25), fillet steak fondue (£14.50 for two), and children's menu (from £1.75). Well kept Butcombe Bitter and two guest beers on handpump; a decent choice of whiskies, and Perry's cider. This comes from just down the road, and the thatched 16th-c stone cider mill is well worth a visit for its collection of wooden bygones and its liberal free tastings (you can buy the half-dozen different ciders in old-fashioned earthenware flagons as well as more modern containers; it's closed on Sunday afternoons). The bar has dark beams liberally strung with hop bines, a stone inglenook fireplace with a woodburning stove, and old-fashioned furnishings that include a mixture of chairs, high-backed settles, and attractive sturdy tables. In a separate area they have darts, shove-ha'penny, dominoes, cribbage, bar billiards, table skittles as well as alley skittles and a fruit machine and juke box; maybe piped music. The family room is no smoking. In front of the stone pub there's a rustic bench, tubs of flowers and a sprawl of clematis; the pleasant back garden has flowerbeds and a children's climbing frame. *(Recommended by A Preston, Andy Petersen, Revd A Nunnerley, James Nunns, Douglas Allen, Howard Clutterbuck, Mrs J Ashdown, Nigel Wilkinson, Douglas Allen,)*

Free house ~ Licensees Therese Boosey and David Smith ~ Real ale ~ Meals and snacks ~ (01460) 52413 ~ Children in family room ~ Open 11-3, 6-11

DUNSTER SS9943 Map 1

Luttrell Arms 🛏

A396

Full of history, this civilised and imposing old place is based around a great hall built for the Abbot of Cleeve some 500 years ago, and in the gardens there are cannon emplacements dug out by Blake in the Civil War when – with Praise God Barebones and his pikemen – he was besieging the castle for six months. The comfortable back bar is the place to head for, with a relaxed and pleasant atmosphere, high beams hung with bottles, clogs and horseshoes, a stag's head and rifles on the walls above old settles and more modern furniture, and friendly, attentive staff; winter log fires (though one tends to smoke in the wrong weather conditions). Ancient black timber uprights glazed with fine hand-floated glass, full of ripples and irregularities, separate the room from a small galleried and flagstoned courtyard. Promptly served lunchtime bar snacks include home-made soup (£1.95), good sandwiches (from £3.20), filled baked potatoes (from £3.30), filled french sticks (from £3.60), ploughman's (£4.25), chicken curry (£5.25), mushroom lasagne (£5.35), fish and chips (£5.50), home-made pie (£5.65), daily specials, and evening dishes like mushrooms in garlic and cream (£2.75), a roast of the day (£6.35), steaks (from £6.90); both restaurants are no smoking. Well kept Bass, Exmoor Gold, and John Smiths on handpump, and farm cider. The town, on the edge of Exmoor National Park, is pretty. *(Recommended by Peter and Liz Wilkins, Kevin and Katharine Cripps, Chris Ball, J and P Maloney, Geoff and Linda Dibble, David and Ruth Hollands, David Carr, Richard Gibbs, Mr and Mrs Hillman, David R Shillitoe, Peter and Joy Heatherley, H and D Payne, Neville Kenyon, G W Stevenson)*

Free house (Forte) ~ Manageress Margaret Coffey ~ Real ale ~ Meals and snacks ~ Restaurant ~ (01643) 821555 ~ Children in eating area of bar and in lounge ~ Open 11-11; 12-10.30 Sun ~ Bedrooms: £84.50B/£114B

EAST LYNG ST3328 Map 1

Rose & Crown

A361 about 4 miles W of Othery

You can be sure of a friendly welcome and a relaxed unchanging atmosphere in this traditional pub. The open-plan beamed lounge bar has a winter log fire (or a big embroidered fire screen) in its modernised old stone fireplace, a corner cabinet of glass, china and silver, a court cabinet, a bow window seat by an oak drop-leaf table, copies of *Country Life* and impressive large dried flower arrangements. Generous helpings of good bar food include sandwiches (from £1.50), soup (£1.90), enjoyable ploughman's (from £3.20), home-cooked ham and egg (£3.75), omelettes (from £4.20), vegetable crumble or Mexican bean pot (£4.95), salads (from £5), trout (£5.75), steaks (from £9.25), and puddings like home-made treacle tart or sherry trife (£2.50); pleasant waitress service. Well kept Butcombe and Eldridge Pope Royal Oak and Hardy on handpump; skittle alley and piped music. The back garden (largely hedged off from the car park) is prettily planted and there are picnic tables. *(Recommended by Meg and Colin Hamilton, Dave and Doreen Irving, A and J Tierney-Jones, Pete Yearsley, Richard Dolphin, Colin and Ann Hunt)*

Free house ~ Licensee P J Thyer ~ Real ale ~ Meals and snacks (till 10pm) ~ Restaurant ~ (01823) 698235 ~ Children in restaurant ~ Open 11-2.30, 6.30-11; Bedrooms: £26B/£42B

EAST WOODLANDS ST7944 Map 2

Horse & Groom 🍴 ♀ ◧

Signed off Frome bypass off A361/B3092 junction

Both the staff and locals welcome visitors to this small, civilised pub, set on the edge of the Longleat estate. The comfortable little lounge has an easy chair and settee around a coffee table, two small solid dining tables with chairs, a big stone hearth with a small raised grate, and a relaxed atmosphere (no piped music). The pleasant bar on the left with its stripped pine pews and settles on dark flagstones has Batemans XB, Butcombe Bitter, Greene King IPA, and Wadworths 6X tapped from the cask; good wines by the glass. Very well presented food includes filled home-made french bread (from £1.60), ploughman's (from £2.95), lovely liver, bacon and onion (£4.95), asparagus and pesto pasta (£4.80), home-cooked ham with parsley sauce (£4.90), smoked haddock topped with mozzarella (£6), and delicious cod with mussels and prawns (£6); five or six interesting vegetables are served separately on a side plate; helpful service. There's also a big no-smoking dining conservatory. Shove-ha'penny, cribbage and dominoes. You can sit in the nice front garden at some picnic tables by five severely pollarded limes and there are attractive flower troughs and mini wheelbarrows filled with flowers; more seats behind the conservatory. The village is very quiet. *(Recommended by M Hart, Pat and Robert Watt, Paul and Janette Adams; more reports please)*

Free house ~ Licensee Timothy Gould ~ Real ale ~ Meals and snacks (not Sun evening, not Mon) ~ Restaurant (not Sun evening) ~ (01373) 462802 ~ Children in small lounge bar ~ Open 11.30-2.30(3 Sat), 6.30-11

EXEBRIDGE SS9224 Map 1

Anchor 🛏

B3222 S of Dulverton

This is a peaceful place to stay, beside the handsome three-arched bridge over the Exe with its brown trout and salmon, and the licensees have fishing rights and can organise lots of other local sports; many surrounding walks. The sheltered garden overlooking the water has plenty of well-spaced tables, and a play area for children. Inside, the main front bar has individually chosen tables and seats such as a big winged settle and a nice old library chair among more orthodox furnishings, some carpet on its floor tiles, Cecil Aldin hunting prints and Exmoor pictures above the stripped wooden dado, some hunting trophies, and a warm woodburning stove; piped music. Bar food includes good sandwiches, home-made soup and filled baked potatoes, home-made steak and mushroom pie or chicken breast with broccoli and stilton sauce (£4.95), local baked trout with grain mustard sauce (£6.95), steaks, and children's dishes. There's a back games bar with darts, pool, cribbage, dominoes, and trivia and two fruit machines divided by a flexiwall from a no-smoking lounge bar with button-back leather chesterfields, modern oak tables and chairs, and french windows to the garden. Well kept Marstons Pedigree, Morlands Old Speckled Hen, Ruddles County, Ushers Best, and Wadworths 6X on handpump; alley skittles. The inn is mentioned in R D Blackmore's *Lorna Doone*. *(Recommended by John and Christine Vittoe, Tina and David Woods-Taylor, Cheryl and Keith Roe, H F C Barclay, Peter Newman, Jon Pike, Julie Murphy, David R Shillitoe, John Evans, Clive Gilbert, Mr and Mrs Hillman)*

Free house ~ Licensees John and Judy Phripp ~ Real ale ~ Meals and snacks (till 10pm) ~ Restaurant ~ (01398) 323433 ~ Children in big family lounge ~ Open 11-3, 6-11 ~ Bedrooms: £35B/£70B

FAULKLAND ST7354 Map 2

Tuckers Grave £

A366 E of village

This is a warmly friendly, basic cider house that has for many years claimed the title of the smallest pub in the Guide. It's wonderfully atmospheric and homely, and a flagstoned entry opens into a teeny unspoilt room with casks of well kept Butcombe Bitter on tap and Cheddar Valley cider in an alcove on the left. Two old cream-painted high-backed settles face each other across a single table on the right, and a side room has shove-ha'penny. There's a skittle alley and tables and chairs on the back lawn, as well as winter fires and maybe newspapers to read. Food is limited to sandwiches and ploughman's at lunchtime. No children. *(Recommended by Pete Baker, John Poulter, Tom Beaumont, Roger Huggins, Tom McLean, Dave Irving, Ewan McCall, Kevin and Tracey Stephens, Arthur and Annette Frampton)*

Free house ~ Licensees Ivan and Glenda Swift ~ Real ale ~ Lunchtime snacks (not Sun) ~ (01373) 834230 ~ Open 11-3, 6-11

FITZHEAD ST1128 Map 1

Fitzhead Inn ♀ ⬛

Village signposted off B3227 W of Taunton

In the lush and peaceful countryside of the Vale of Taunton Deane, this cosy village pub is doing well under its enthusiastic young licensees, who clearly get a real kick out of the way they run the place. Though the food is now drawing people from some distance, they have resisted the temptation to pack in extra places: once the variously sized polished tables in the main bar are full, they'd rather turn people away than face overcrowding. The well presented food varies day by day, and is consistently good – not a large choice, but an imaginative one, which might include ploughman's (from £4.25), steak and kidney pie (£4.75), game platter with pigeon, venison and pheasant or rack of lamb done to pink perfection (£9.95), ostrich (£10.50), john dory with lobster tails, scallops done with chives and sorrel or succulent giant prawns with chilli and garlic (£10.95) – all well in the running for a Food Award. Well kept Cotleigh Tawny and three guests like Butcombe, Brains and Hook Norton on handpump. There's a particularly good choice of about 160 wines, and the knowledgeable landlord will happily open about 70 of them for just a glass; Bollhayes farm cider; pleasant relaxed atmosphere, genial attentive service, unobjectionable piped music; tables out in the garden. The lavatories are basic village pub standard. *(Recommended by Mrs Joyce Brotherton, Graham Stanton, Dave Williams, Geoff and Linda Dibble, Paul and Wendy Bachelor, John Barker, John and Pat Smyth, Ken and Janet Bracey)*

Free house ~ Licensee Patrick Groves ~ Real ale ~ Meals and snacks ~ (01823) 400667 ~ Children in family room ~ Open 12-3, 7-11; cl 25 Dec evening

HINTON ST GEORGE ST4212 Map 1

Poulett Arms ♀

Village signposted off A30 W of Crewkerne; and off Merriott road (declassified – former A356, off B3165) N of Crewkerne; take care – there is another pub of the same name a mile or so away, at a roundabout on the former A30

This is a pleasant and friendly dining pub in a quiet, largely retirement village. The larger dining room has big black beams, stripped masonry, plush chairs and a couple of high-backed settles, an imposing stone fireplace, a few pistols and brasses, and two cosy smaller rooms opening off – one with a big disused inglenook fireplace. Decent bar food includes sandwiches, home-made soup (£2.50), ploughman's (£3.75), home-cooked ham and egg (£4.50), lasagne (£4.75), fresh trout fillet calypso (£5.95), and venison with green peppercorn sauce (£9.95). Well kept Bass, Butcombe Bitter, and

Otter Ale on handpump, and a compact but carefully chosen wine list; cribbage, dominoes, shove-ha'penny, and piped music. There's also a skittle alley with darts, and a friendly jack russell called Murphy. The prettily planted back garden has some white tables under cocktail parasols, near a real rarity – a massive pelota wall. *(Recommended by Mr and Mrs D C Stevens, Adrian Stopforth, JKW, E M Clague, Jill Bickerton, Margaret and Nigel Dennis, Nigel Wilkinson; more reports please)*

Free house ~ Licensees Sandy and Marian Lavelle ~ Real ale ~ Meals and snacks ~ (01460) 73149 ~ Children in eating area of bar ~ Open 11.30-3, 6.30-11

HUISH EPISCOPI ST4326 Map 1

Rose & Crown £

A372 E of Langport

For around 130 years this marvellously unspoilt old cider house has been in the same family. It is known locally as 'Eli's', after the present landlady's father, who held the licence for 55 years (having taken over from his father-in-law – who also ran the place for 55 years). The atmosphere and character are determinedly unpretentious and warmly friendly, and there's no bar as such – to get a drink, you just walk into the central flagstoned still room and choose from the casks of well kept Bass, Boddingtons, and changing guests, or the wide choice of Somerset farm ciders (and local cider brandy) and country wines which stand on ranks of shelves all around (prices are very low); this servery is the only thoroughfare between the casual little front parlours with their unusual pointed-arch windows and genuinely friendly locals. Food is home-made, simple and cheap: generously filled sandwiches (from £1.50), filled baked potatoes (from £1.90), soups such as mild curried parsnip or tomato and lentil (£2), ploughman's (£2.80), and steak pie or stilton and celery quiche (£3.95); good helpful service. Shove-ha'penny, dominoes and cribbage, and a much more orthodox big back extension family room has darts, pool, fruit machine, trivia, juke box and a pinball machine; skittle alley and popular quiz nights. There are tables in a garden outside, and a second enclosed garden with a children's play area. George the dog will welcome a bitch but can't abide other dogs. A beer and music festival is held in the adjoining field every September, and on some summer weekends you might find the pub's cricket team playing out here (who always welcome a challenge); good nearby walks. *(Recommended by Pete Baker, Stephen and Julie Brown, Mrs C Blake, Mr and Mrs J Woodfield, Gwyneth and Salvo Spadaro-Dutturi, John Hazel, Pete Baker, Rich and Pauline Appleton, S G Brown)*

Free house ~ Licensee Eileen Pittard ~ Real ale ~ Snacks (mainly 12-2.30, 5.30-8 but maybe all day on summer weekends) ~ (01458) 250494 ~ Children welcome ~ Open 11.30-2.30, 5.30-11; all day Fri/Sat; 12-10.30 Sun

KELSTON ST7067 Map 2

Old Crown 🍺

Bitton Road; A431 W of Bath

Readers are fond of this atmospheric old place where little changes and a friendly welcome is assured. The four small rooms are genuinely preserved and have interesting carved settles and cask tables on polished flagstones (all appealingly lit in the evenings by candlelight), beams strung with hops, logs burning in an ancient open range (there's another smaller, open range and a Victorian open fireplace – both with coal-effect gas fires), and lovely tableau photographs. Well kept Bass, Butcombe, Smiles Best, and Wadworths 6X on handpump, and several malt whiskies; shove-ha'penny and dominoes. Enjoyable lunchtime bar food (with prices unchanged since last year) includes home-made soup (£1.85), ploughman's (from £3.65), cottage pie (£4.70), ham and leek pie (£4.90), a daily vegetarian dish, beef and Guinness casserole (£5.90), steaks (from £8.95) and puddings like fruit crumble or sticky toffee pudding (£2.80); helpful service. Picnic tables under apple trees in the neat, sheltered back garden look out towards distant hills; you'd hardly believe you were just four miles from Bath's city centre. The car park is over quite a fast road. No children. *(Recommended by Peter Neate, Don Kellaway, Angie Coles, Barry Cawthorne, Anne Moggridge, Andrew Rogers, Amanda Milsom, Gwen and Peter Andrews, James House, Jon Lyons, J S Rutter)*

Free house ~ Licensee Michael Steele ~ Real ale ~ Lunchtime meals and snacks (not Sun) ~ Restaurant (not Sun) ~ (01225) 423032 ~ Open 11.30-2.30(3 Sat), 5-11; closed evening 25 Dec, all day 26 Dec

KINGSDON ST5126 Map 2

Kingsdon Inn

From A303 take A372 at roundabout, turn right into village, then turn opposite village post office

Well worth a detour off the A303, this pretty and friendly little thatched cottage is doing very well at the moment. On the right are a few low sagging beams, some very nice old stripped pine tables with attractive cushioned farmhouse chairs, more seats in what was a small inglenook fireplace, and an open woodburning stove with colourful dried and artificial fruits and flowers on the overmantel; down three steps through balustrading to a light, airy room with peach-coloured cushions on stripped pine built-in wall seats, curtains matching the scatter cushions, more stripped pine tables, and a big leaf and flower arrangement in the stone fireplace (open fire in winter). Another similarly decorated room has more tables and another fireplace. Very good food from a sensibly short menu and served by efficient, helpful staff, includes at lunchtime, sandwiches, cream of mushroom soup (£1.90), soused herring fillets with dill sauce (£3.80), tagliatelle with ham, cream and mushrooms (£4.20), baked haddock and mushroom mornay (£4.80), lamb liver and bacon or steak and kidney pie (£4.90), grilled cod steak with herb butter (£5.20), and puddings such as treacle tart or chocolate and brandy roulade (£2.20); evening dishes such as mussels with white wine and shallots (£3.80), baked crab and scallops mornay (£3.95), good wild rabbit in dijon mustard sauce (£8.90), pheasant breasts with calvados, apple and cream (£9.60), and half a roast duck with local cider sauce (£9.80). Well kept Boddingtons, Fullers London Pride, Morlands Old Speckled Hen, Oakhill Best, and Smiles Best on handpump, and local cider; table skittles, darts, cribbage, dominoes, and quiet piped music, and they have rugby, cricket and golf teams. Picnic tables and umbrellas on the grass. *(Recommended by Max Johnson, Stephen and Julie Brown, Colin Draper, Mr and Mrs S A Lea, MRSM, Gethin Lewis, Galen Strawson, John Hazel)*

Free house ~ Licensee Duncan Gordon ~ Real ale ~ Meals and snacks (not Sun evening) ~ (01935) 840543 ~ Children in eating area of bar; must be over 6 in evenings ~ Open 11-3, 6-11

KNAPP ST3025 Map 1

Rising Sun ♀

Lower Knapp – OS Sheet 182 map reference 304257; off A38/A358/A378 E of Taunton

Fresh fish and seafood continue to play a big part in drawing people to this lovely 15th-c Somerset longhouse: starters like moules marinières (£3.25 or £4.90), smoked herring mousse (£4.50), and crab and prawn gratin (£4.75), and imaginative main courses such as scallops and mushrooms with a vermouth, dijon mustard and cream sauce (£10.50), salmon with sun-dried tomatoes and prawns in a lemon and cream sauce (£11), and brill topped with a salmon mousse and cucumber with a white wine sauce (£11.50); also, soup (£2.60), ploughman's (£3.50), open sandwiches (from £3.90), ham and egg (£4.50), nut roast with provençale sauce (£6.75), and steaks (from £9.50). The big single room has well moulded beams, woodwork, and some stonework in its massive rather tilting walls, two inglenook log fires, and a relaxed atmosphere. Well kept Bass, Boddingtons and Exmoor on handpump, farm ciders, and a decent wine list. The staff (and dogs – Pepi the poodle and Pompey, who weighs in at nine stone) are very welcoming. There are fine country views from the suntrap terrace. *(Recommended by Colin W McKerrow, Pete Yearsley, Nigel Paine, Major and Mrs Warrick, E H and R F Warner, Anthony Clemow, Michael Boniface, S Brackenbury)*

Free house ~ Licensee Tony Atkinson ~ Real ale ~ Meals and snacks ~ Restaurant ~ (01823) 490436 ~ Children in eating area of bar ~ Open 11.30-2.30, 6.30-11 ~ Bedrooms: £25/£36

LANGLEY MARSH ST0729 Map 1

Three Horseshoes ★

Village signposted off B3227 from Wiveliscombe

After 10 years, the friendly licensees are still running this nice little country pub, tucked away in the Somerset hills. The back bar has low modern settles and polished wooden tables, dark red wallpaper, planes hanging from the ceiling, banknotes papering the wall behind the bar counter, a piano, and a local stone fireplace. Well kept Dartmoor Best, Palmers IPA, Ringwood Best, Wadworths 6X, Youngs Bitter and various guests tapped from the cask, and Perry's farm cider; polite staff. Genuinely home-made food includes filled rolls, soup (£1.50), pizzas (£3 or £3.95; can take away as well), butterbean bourguignon (£3.95), courgette and mushroom bake (£4.50), lamb in pernod or good steak and kidney pie (£4.95), pigeon breasts in cider and cream (£5.10), enjoyable fish pie (£5.25), popular steaks (from £7.95), and lovely puddings such as apple-filled pancake or lemon mousse (£2.10); no chips or fried food and some vegetables come from the garden. The dining area is no smoking. The lively front room has sensibly placed darts, shove-ha'penny, table skittles, dominoes, cribbage and bar billiards; separate skittle alley; piped music. It is small, so they can get crowded. The pub's elderly alsatian is called Guinness and the other is called Ruddles. You can sit on rustic seats on the verandah or in the sloping back garden, with a fully equipped children's play area and a view of farmland. In fine weather there are usually vintage cars outside. *(Recommended by V Kavanagh, Anthony Barnes, Mr and Mrs J Brown, J and P Maloney, Tina and David Woods-Taylor, K H Frostick, George Jonas, GSD, EMD)*

Free house ~ Licensee John Hopkins ~ Real ale ~ Meals and snacks ~ (01984) 623763 ~ Well behaved children allowed away from bar ~ Spontaneous 'fiddle/squeeze box' sessions with local Morris dancing musicians ~ Open 12-2.30(3 Sat), 7-11

LITTON ST5954 Map 2

Kings Arms

B3144; off A39 Bath—Wells

Readers have very much enjoyed this friendly tiled white building over the past year. From a big entrance hall with polished flagstones, the bars lead off to the left with low heavy beams and more flagstones; a nice bit on the right beyond the huge fireplace has a big old-fashioned settle and a mix of other settles and wheelback chairs; a full suit of armour stands in one alcove and the rooms are divided up into areas by standing timbers. It does get busy at weekends but the friendly staff manage to cope cheerfully. Good bar food includes sandwiches (from £2.60), garlic mushrooms (£3.25), lots of platters and salads (from £5.25; marinaded pork ribs with sour cream and barbecue sauces (£7.25), daily vegetarian and pasta dishes, ham and egg (£4.35), battered cod (£4.75), chicken and broccoli bake (£7.25), chicken tikka (£7.50), king prawns in garlic butter (£9.95), and steaks; children's colouring sheet menu with crayons. Well kept Bass, Courage Best, and Wadworths 6X on handpump. The tiered, neatly kept gardens have picnic tables, excellent heavy wooden play equipment including a commando climbing net, and slides and baby swings; the River Chew runs through the bottom of the garden. The pub is reached down a flight of steps from the car park. *(Recommended by Derek Patey, John Abbott, Andrew Shore, Meg and Colin Hamilton, Roger and Lin Lawrence, Wendy and Paul Bachelor, E H and R F Warner, JCW, P H Roberts, Don Kellaway, Angie Coles)*

Free house ~ Licensee Neil Sinclair ~ Real ale ~ Meals and snacks (till 10pm; not 25 Dec) ~ (01761) 241301 ~ Children in two separate rooms ~ Open 11-2.30, 6-11; closed evenings 26 Dec and 1 Jan

LUXBOROUGH SS9837 Map 1

Royal Oak ★ 🛏 🍺

Kingsbridge; S of Dunster on minor rds into Brendon Hills – OS Sheet 181 map reference 983378

New licensees have taken over this characterful pub and have updated the bedrooms. The atmosphere is warm and chatty and full of local banter and the three atmospheric rooms have flagstones in the front public bar, beams and inglenooks, a real medley of furniture, and good log fires. Well kept real ales such as Cotleigh Tawny, Exmoor Gold, Flowers IPA, and guest beers tapped from the cask, and farm cider. Good bar food now includes home-made soup (£1.95), sandwiches (from £2.25), filled baked potatoes (from £3.55), home-made port and stilton pâté (£3.95), various ploughman's (from £3.95), lamb curry (£4.95), spinach and nut lasagne (£5.65), salads (from £4.95), beef and Beamish pie (£5.25), and evening dishes such as fresh local trout pâté (£4.25), fresh fish, venison casserole in a rich three-berry sauce (£8.95), and steaks (from £9.95); puddings like banana and sticky toffee pudding or lemon cheesecake (£2.50), children's meals (£2.75), and good breakfasts. Pool, dominoes, and shove-ha'penny – no machines or music. Tables outside and lots of surrounding walks. *(Recommended by C A Hall, Sue and Bob Ward, Pete and Rosie Flower, Paul McKeever, Anthony Barnes, Sue Demont, Tim Barrow, Rosalyn Guard, Geoff and Linda Dibble, K Flack, Jonathan Williams, Richard Gibbs, John and Elspeth Howell, Nigel Woolliscroft, Ian Williams, Linda Mar, Maureen and Jeff Dobbelaar, Julian Thomas, David Gittins, Dave Thompson, Margaret Mason, Mrs K N Fowler, G W Stevenson, Mrs C Blake, Jack and Philip Paxton, John Hazel, R V Ford, Mr and Mrs P E Towndrow, John Humphreys, R T and J C Moggridge, Paul Randall, Angela Basso)*

Free house ~ Licensees Kevan and Rose Draper ~ Real ale ~ Meals and snacks (till 10pm) ~ Restaurant ~ (01984) 640319 ~ Children in eating area of bar and restaurant ~ Folk music Fri evening ~ Open 11-2.30, 6-11 ~ Bedrooms: £20(£25B)/£35(£45B)

MELLS ST7249 Map 2

Talbot ☕

W of Frome; off A362 W of Buckland Dinham, or A361 via Nunney and Whatley

As this unspoilt and friendly old coaching inn is surrounded by lovely countryside and good walks, it makes a good base for a weekend stay. An attractive room leads off the informally planted cobbled courtyard (where there are cane chairs around tables), and has stripped pews, mate's and wheelback chairs, fresh flowers and candles in bottles on the mix of tables, and sporting and riding pictures on the walls, which are partly stripped above a broad panelled dado, and partly rough terracotta-colour. A small corridor leads to a nice little room with an open fire; piped music. Good food at lunchtime includes home-made soup (£1.95), macaroni cheese (£4.25), Greek salad (£4.50), duck and cherry pie, ratatouille flan or lasagne (all £4.95), and tagliatelle with smoked salmon and prawns in a cream sauce (£5.95), as well as steak and kidney pie or barbecued spare ribs (£7.50), pork escalope with apple and cider sauce (£8.50), and steaks (from £8.95); two-course Sunday roast (£5.95). Well kept Bass, Butcombe Bitter, and a changing weekly guest beer tapped from the cask, and good wines; well chosen staff. The two-roomed public bar has an appealing room nearest the road with big stripped shutters, a high dark green ceiling, a mix of chairs and a tall box settle, candles in bottles on the stubby pine tables, and a rough wooden floor; the locals' room has sports trophies, darts, cribbage, dominoes, and simple furnishings; skittle alley. They hold an Irish music weekend during the second week of September and a Daffodil Weekend with 350 members of the English Civil

War over the Easter weekend. The village was purchased by the Horner family of the 'Little Jack Horner' nursery rhyme and the direct descendants still live in the manor house next door. *(Recommended by BHP, Robert Huddleston, Pat and John Millward, Andy Wilson, Veronica M Brown, John and Pat Smyth, Mr and Mrs Adams, David Leonard, Michael Richards)*

Free house ~ Lease: Roger Elliott~ Real ale ~ Meals and snacks ~ Restaurant ~ (01373) 812254 ~ Children welcome ~ Open 12-3, 6-11; closed evening 25 Dec ~ Bedrooms: £25B/£39B

MONKSILVER ST0737 Map 1

Notley Arms ★ 🍺

B3188

Run by charming licensees, this bustling pub is much liked for its feeling of well-being, its friendly atmosphere – and of course, the very popular and consistently good food. The characterful beamed and L-shaped bar has fresh flowers, small settles and kitchen chairs around the plain country wooden and candle-lit tables, original paintings on the black-timbered white walls, a couple of woodburning stoves, and maybe a pair of cats. Bar food changes daily but might include home-made soup (£2.10), sandwiches (from £2.25), very good ploughman's (from £2.75), filled baked potatoes (from £2.85), pasta with bacon, cheese and cream (£3.95), tomato and mozzarella tart or wild mushroom strudel (£4.50), seafood lasagne (£4.75), creamy mild lamb curry (£5.75), popular Chinese red roast pork (£5.95), beef and Beamish pie or chicken breast with apple and tarragon stuffing (£6.25), trout (£7.75), and puddings like fresh fruit crumbles, summer strawberry cheesecake or home-made ice creams (from £2.25). Well kept Exmoor Ale, Morlands Old Speckled Hen, Ushers Best, and Wadworths 6X on handpump; dominoes and trivia, and alley skittles. Families are well looked after, with colouring books and toys in the bright little family room. There are more toys outside in the immaculate garden, running down to a swift clear stream. *(Recommended by Maureen and Jeff Dobbelaar, W H and E Thomas, Tom Evans, Graham Stanton, Tina and David Woods-Taylor, Richard Gibbs, Peter and Joy Heatherley, Howard Clutterbuck, Paul and Susan Merrick, Dorothy Pilson, Mrs K N Fowler, R V Ford, John and Christine Vittoe, Mrs C Blake, G S and E M Dorey, Mr and Mrs Westcombe, Mr and Mrs Hillman, Mrs C Watkinson, Jim Reid)*

Courage ~ Tenants Alistair and Sarah Cade ~ Real ale ~ Meals and snacks (see below) ~ (01984) 656217 ~ Children welcome ~ Open 11.30-2.30, 6.30-11; closed 25 Dec; 2 weeks end Jan/beg Feb

MONTACUTE ST4916 Map 2

Kings Arms ♀

A3088 W of Yeovil

In winter, blazing log fires welcome customers to this civilised golden stone inn. It's a delightful, airy place with an emphasis on smart but informal dining in a country house-type atmosphere. The very good food includes innovative, tasty meals as well as more traditional pub things: sandwiches, home-made soup (£2.50), scallop and leek bake (£4.75), smoked trout with pear chutney (£5.50), pies such as beef and oyster in ale or turkey, apricot and walnut (£6.95), ham hock with mushy peas (£7.50), and breast of chicken stuffed with crabmeat and red pepper sauce (£8.25); fresh fish such as trout and watercress fishcakes with tomato coulis, good puddings, and nicely presented vegetables. Well kept Bass, Badger Tanglefoot, and Butcombe Bitter on handpump, and an interesting, expanding wine list with quite a few by the glass; helpful staff. Part of the walls at the front of the lounge bar are stripped back to the handsome masonry, and comfortable furnishings include grey-gold plush seats, soft armchairs, chintz sofas, and a high curved settle; there's a further lounge, too. The restaurants are no smoking. The pretty village includes the stately Elizabethan mansion of the same name, and behind the hotel the wooded St Michael's Hill is owned by the National Trust. *(Recommended by John Fahy, Canon Michael Bordeaux, Graham Fice, F J Willy, Wendy Arnold, Nick and Meriel Cox, Michael Boniface)*

Free house ~ Licensees Jonathan and Karen Arthur ~ Real ale ~ Meals and snacks (not Sun evening) ~ Restaurant ~ (01935) 822513 ~ Children welcome ~ Open 11-2.30, 6-11; closed 25 Dec-8 Jan ~ Bedrooms: £49B/69B

NORTH CURRY ST3225 Map 1

Bird in Hand 🍺

Queens Square; off A378 (or A358) E of Taunton

This traditional village local has come up smiling after a slightly troubled period in which it changed hands a couple of times rather quickly (and even changed its name to the Old Coaching Inn for a while). It's been stripped back to original beams and timbers, with flagstones and inglenook fireplaces, candles on tables, a proper public bar with bar billiards, and a separate restaurant area, partly no smoking, with a conservatory. Well presented home-made food from a stylish blackboard menu includes good soups (£1.75), a notable Thai green curry (£5.25), local fish pie (£5.50), fillet of salmon with salsa (£6) and roast breast of duck with plum sauce (£7.95) with a good choice of delicious puddings (£2.50). Well kept Badger Tanglefoot, Butcombe, Cotleigh Barn Owl and Otter and guest beers such as Branscombe Vale Branoc on handpump, a short but wide-ranging choice of wines, Rich's farm cider, good waitress service; piped music. There are tables out in the sizeable garden. *(Recommended by Mary Doxford, Richard Dolphin, Jane and Adrian Tierney-Jones)*

Free house ~ Licensee Jeremy Hook ~ Real ale ~ Meals and snacks (not Sun and Mon evening in winter) ~ Restaurant ~ (01823) 490248 ~ Children welcome ~ Live jazz or blues alternate Fri evenings ~ Open 12-3(4 Sat), 7-11; cl 25 Dec evening

NORTON ST PHILIP ST7755 Map 2

George ★

A366

This remarkable old building has been a pub for nearly 600 years, and was originally built to house merchants buying wool and cloth from the rich sheep-farming Hinton Priory at the great August cloth market. There's a fine half-timbered and galleried back courtyard, an external Norman stone stair-turret, massive stone walls and high mullioned windows. Furnishings are simple: square-panelled wooden settles, plain old tables, wide bare floorboards, and lofty beams hung with hops. A long, stout table serves well kept Bass, and Wadworths IPA, 6X and seasonal beers on handpump; warmly welcoming licensee and staff. A panelled lounge is furnished with antique settles and tables; it's all perhaps even more atmospheric in winter when the fires are lit. Good, popular bar food places most emphasis on daily specials such as wild boar pâté, fresh fish from Cornwall (from £7.95), vegan and vegetarian dishes, steaks (from £9.95), venison steak in a redcurrant glaze (£10.50), and garlic king prawns (£12.95), as well as soup (£2.25), cheese and leek pancakes, filled baguettes or baked potatoes (£3.95), ploughman's (from £4.25), meat or fish platters (from £5.95), tortellini and blue cheese bake with broccoli (£6.95), gammon or trout baked with bananas and almonds (£7.50), and puddings like treacle tart (£3.25); Sunday roast (£7.50). Darts, pool and dominoes. The Duke of Monmouth stayed here before the Battle of Sedgemoor, and after their defeat his men were imprisoned in what's now the Dungeon cellar bar. When a sympathetic customer held the courtyard gate open for them as they were led out to their execution, he was bundled along with them and executed too. A stroll over the meadow behind the pub leads to an attractive churchyard around the medieval church whose bells struck Pepys (here on 12 June 1668) as 'mighty tuneable'. *(Recommended by Andrew Shore, Mark and Heather Williamson, Tim and Ann Newell, James Nunns, Helen Pickering, James Owen, Mr and Mrs C Moncrieffe, Mrs Cynthia Archer, Jack and Philip Paxton, James House, Arthur and Annette Frampton, Howard Clutterbuck, Tom McLean, Roger Huggins, Tom McCall, Dave Irving)*

Wadworths ~ Tenants Andrew and Juliette Grubb ~ Real ale ~ Meals and snacks (not evenings 25-26 Dec) ~ Lunchtime restaurant ~ (01373) 834224 ~ Children welcome ~ Open 11-3, 5.30(5 Sat)-11

OVER STRATTON ST4315 Map 1

Royal Oak ♀

From A303 Yeovil—Taunton road, take Ilminster turning at South Petherton roundabout; pass Esso garage and take first left to village

Readers have been full of praise for this popular dining pub over the last year. The wide choice of food is most enjoyable, service is attentive and friendly, and the wine and beer very good. The cosily extended dark-flagstoned bars have a mixture of pews, settles or dining chairs, scrubbed deal farmhouse kitchen tables, and a stuffed pheasant. The beams have been prettily stencilled with an oakleaf and acorn pattern, the walls are stripped to bare stonework or attractively ragrolled red, and log fires burn, sometimes even in summer. Bar food includes home-made soup (£2.25), lamb kidneys with pasta in a port and cream sauce (£3.95), baby lobster rails with seasonal fruit and a mild tarragon and mustard mayonnaise (£4.25), ploughman's (£4.75), interestingly filled baked potatoes (from £4.75), home-made char-grilled burger with barbecue sauce (hearty helping £5.95, smaller helping £4.50), venison and wild boar sausages (hearty helping £6.25, smaller helping £4.75), salads (from £6.25), spiced crab profiteroles (hearty helping £6.45, smaller helping £4.95), mushrooms stroganoff (£6.95), steaks (from £8.55), pheasant with thyme and brandy cream sauce (£9.25), salmon with lemon butter (£9.95), a thoughtful children's menu (from £2.85), and puddings like poached fresh pear with hot butterscotch sauce (from £2.75). The restaurant is no smoking. Well kept Badger Best and Tanglefoot, and Stratton Ale (brewed for the pub by Badger) on handpump, several malt whiskies, and a decent wine list. On a floodlit reconstituted-stone terrace sheltered by the back wings of the building are quite a few picnic tables, with more on a further sheltered gravel terrace with a barbecue (Friday and Saturday evenings and Sunday lunchtimes during August); a play area for toddlers has swings, slides, climbing frame and a sandpit, and for older children, there's a mini assault course and three trampolines. *(Recommended by Helen and Keith Bowers and friends, Peter and Audrey Dowsett, Rosalyn Guard, Mrs J Ashdown, Cheryl and Keith Roe, Mark and Heather Williamson, Jenny and Brian Seller, Guy Consterdine, Stephen and Julie Brown, Dr and Mrs S Tham, Frank Gadbois, Gethin Lewis, M E Wellington, Major and Mrs E M Warrick, S G Brown)*

Badger ~ Manager Brian Elderfield ~ Real ale ~ Meals and snacks (till 10pm) ~ Restaurant ~ (01460) 240906 ~ Children in restaurant only ~ Open 11-3, 6-11; 11-11 in August

PITNEY ST4428 Map 1

Halfway House

Just off B3153 W of Somerton

This charming old-fashioned pub, sparsely furnished in a sophisticated rather than spartan way, concentrates very successfully on the beer side, with well kept Berrow Topsy Turvey, Butcombe, Cotleigh Tawny, Hop Back Summer Lightning and St Austell Teignworthy Reel Ale on handpump, and several quickly changing guest beers such as Otter, Ringwood Old Thumper and Smiles Exhibition, all tapped straight from the cask. They also keep Czech Pilsners and other European beers, with a good interesting bottled range, as well as local farm cider. It's a friendly and cosy place, with plenty of space; three or four years ago extension brought it a third lounge (all three have good log fires), and the homely feel is underlined by a profusion of books, maps and newspapers – there are no machines or juke boxes. Good simple food includes sandwiches (from £1.75), soup (£1.95), filled baked potatoes (from £1.95) and a fine ploughman's with home-made pickle (from £3.50). In the evening they do filled baked potatoes, and about half a dozen home-made curries to complement their real ales (from £4.95). There are tables outside. *(Recommended by Andy Jones, Arthur and Anne Frampton, Robert Colledge, John Carter)*

Free house ~ Licensees Julian and Judy Litchfield ~ Real ale ~ Meals and snacks (not Sun) ~ (01458) 252513 ~ Well behaved children welcome ~ Open 11.30-2.30, 5.30-11; cl 25 Dec

RUDGE ST8251 Map 2

Full Moon 🍽 🛏 🍺

Off A36 Bath—Warminster

As we went to press, the friendly licensees of this attractive rustic pub were hoping to turn a small field opposite the pub into a village green – the first new one in Somerset for many years. There are wonderful views across the valley to Salisbury Plain and Westbury White Horse. Inside, there's a lot of character in the differently shaped rooms, and a gently upmarket atmosphere. The two rooms on the right have low white ceilings with a few black beams, a woodburning stove in a big stone fireplace with riding boots on the mantelbeam, a built-in settle by the bar, big shutters by the red velvet-cushioned window seats, and wheelbacks and slatback chairs around mainly cast-iron-framed tables. Other rooms are similarly furnished except the smallish flagstoned dining room with stripped pine tables and high traditional settles; there's also a small plush restaurant and a big back carpeted extension alongside the skittle alley; cribbage. Generous helpings of good bar food includes soup (£1.95), filled french bread (£2.75), mushrooms with bacon in a creamy garlic sauce (£3.50), a choice of deep-fried cheeses with fruit chutney (£3.95), ploughman's (from £3.95), fresh fish in their own beer batter with chips or curry (£4.65), ham and eggs or a bargain lunchtime and early evening 3-course set meal which features a roast and home-made steak and kidney pudding (£4.95), mushroom and vegetable stroganoff (£4.95), beef and pepper stir fry or chicken with pineapple in a light korma sauce (£5.25), local trout with herb butter (£6.95), popular mixed grill (£7.95), and home-made puddings (£2.95); Sunday lunchtime roast carvery (£4.95; two sittings). Well kept Bass, Butcombe and Wadworths 6X on handpump, and Thatchers cider. *(Recommended by Howard James, A D Sherman, Dan Mather; more reports please)*

Free house ~ Licensees Patrick and Christine Gifford ~ Real ale ~ Meals and snacks (not winter Sun evening; bar food in summer starts at 6pm) ~ Restaurant (not Sun evening) ~ (01373) 830936 ~ Children welcome ~ Open 12-3, 6-11; 12-11 Sat and Sun ~ Bedrooms: £30B/£45B

SOUTH STOKE ST7461 Map 2

Pack Horse £

Village signposted opposite the Cross Keys off B3110, leaving Bath southwards – just before end of speed limit

This is very much an unpretentious, old-fashioned country local, liked by quite a mix of people. The entrance alleyway that runs through the middle is still a public right of way to the church, and used to be the route along which the dead were carried to the cemetery. It stops along the way at a central space by the serving bar with its well kept Courage Best, and Ushers Best and Founders on handpump. The ancient main room has a good local atmosphere, a heavy black beam-and-plank ceiling, antique oak settles (two well carved), leatherette dining chairs and cushioned captain's chairs on the quarry-tiled floor, a log fire in the handsome stone inglenook, some Royalty pictures, a chiming wall-clock, and rough black shutters for the stone-mullioned windows (put up in World War I); the cupboard in the fireplace used to be where they kept drunks until they sobered up. There's another room down to the left (with less atmosphere). Cheap bar food includes filled rolls, good pasties or sausage plait (£1.20), daily specials (from £1.80), a Wednesday special of roast lunch and pudding (£2.50), ploughman's (£2.90), and two course Sunday lunch (£2.95); friendly staff.

Rather fine shove-ha'penny slates are set into two of the tables, and there's dominoes, a fruit machine, piped music, and Sky TV. The spacious back garden, with swings, looks out over the stolid old church and the wooded valley. *(Recommended by Virginia Jones, Brian Pearson, Peter Neate, Roger Huggins, Dave Irving, Ewan McCall, Tom McLean, Ron Gentry, Roger Wain-Heapy; more reports please)*

Ushers ~ Lease: Colin Williams ~ Real ale ~ Snacks ~ Restaurant ~ (01225) 832060 ~ Children in eating area of bar ~ Open 11-4, 6-11; 11-11 Sat; 12-10.30 Sun

STANTON WICK ST6162 Map 2

Carpenters Arms 🏠 ♀

Village signposted off A368, just W of junction with A37 S of Bristol

This is an efficiently run, very popular place with reliably good food, comfortable bedrooms, and courteous staff. The Coopers Parlour on the right has one or two beams, red-cushioned wall pews around heavy tables, fresh flowers, and swagged-back curtains and houseplants in the windows; on the angle between here and the bar area there's a fat woodburning stove in an opened-through corner fireplace. The bar has a big log fire, wood-backed built-in wall seats and some red fabric-cushioned stools, and stripped stone walls. Diners are encouraged to step down into a snug inner room (lightened by mirrors in arched 'windows'), or to go round to the sturdy tables angling off on the right; most of these tables get booked at weekends. Good bar food includes home-made soup (£1.95), filled french sticks (from £2.75), blue cheese and watercress cheesecake with a plum and orange sauce (£3.65), ploughman's (£3.95), mushrooms and bacon sautéed with sherry, cream and onions in a warm croissant (£4.45), omelettes (£5.60), liver and bacon (£6.75), fish of the day in beer batter (£7.35), ragout of salmon, peppers and pasta in a light tomato and garlic sauce (£7.45), char-grilled breast of chicken on light salad with coriander, crispy noodles, and a peanut and orange dressing (£7.95), steaks (from £9.75), and home-made puddings (£2.75); good breakfasts. Well kept Bass, Butcombe Bitter, Hook Norton Best, and Wadworths 6X on handpump, freshly squeezed orange juice, and a decent wine list. There are picnic tables on the front terrace and pretty flower-filled flowerbeds. *(Recommended by Andrew Shore, Dick Mattick, DP, DC, David Gittins, Don Kellaway, Angie Coles, A R and B E Sayer, DJW, Tom Evans, P H Roberts, John and Priscilla Gillett, Brian Atkin)*

Free house ~ Licensee Nigel Pushman ~ Real ale ~ Meals and snacks ~ Restaurant (not Sun evening) ~ (01761) 490202 ~ Children welcome (though no facilities for them) ~ Pianist occasionally ~ Open 11-11; 12-10.30 Sun ~ Bedrooms: £48.50B/£65.50B

STOGUMBER ST0937 Map 1

White Horse 🏠

From A358 Taunton—Williton, village signposted on left at Crowcombe

Set in a quiet conservation village facing the red stone church, this is a pleasant, friendly pub. The long room is neatly kept and has a warm winter coal fire, old-fashioned built-in settles, other settles and cushioned captain's chairs around the heavy rustic tables on the patterned carpet, and piped classical music. Good, reasonably priced food includes sandwiches (from £1), home-made vegetable soup (£1.50), salmon mousse (£2.40), ploughman's, ham and egg or an omelette (£3.10), seafood lasagne (£3.90), liver and bacon casserole (£4.40), steak and kidney pudding (£5.80), trout with almonds (£6.90), steaks (from £8.80), and puddings like treacle tart or apple crumble (from £1.30); best to book for Sunday lunch, and breakfasts are good; prompt service. Well kept Cotleigh Tawny, Exmoor Ale, and Otter Ale on handpump, and farm cider in summer. A side room has sensibly placed darts and a fruit machine; shove-ha'penny, dominoes, cribbage, and video game – as well as a separate skittle alley. The garden is quiet except for rooks and sheep in the surrounding low hills. *(Recommended by J and P Maloney, John A Barker, James Nunns, Jane and Adrian Tierney-Jones, Bruce Bird, Jim Reid, Paul and Susan Merrick, Roger Wain-Heapy)*

Free house ~ Licensee Peter Williamson ~ Real ale ~ Meals and snacks (11-2, 6-10) ~ (01984) 656277 ~ Children in one room (but best to phone first) ~ Open 11-2.30, 6-11 ~ Bedrooms: £25B/£35B

STOKE ST GREGORY ST3527 Map 1

Rose & Crown 🍴 ♀

Woodhill; follow North Curry signpost off A378 by junction with A358 – keep on to Stoke, bearing right in centre and right again past church

The industrious Browning family are sure to give you a warm, friendly welcome at this popular 17th-c cottage. The rather jolly and neatly kept bar is decorated in a cosy and pleasantly romanticised stable theme: dark wooden loose-box partitions for some of the interestingly angled nooks and alcoves, lots of brasses and bits on the low beams and joists, stripped stonework, and appropriate pictures including a highland pony carrying a stag; many of the wildlife paintings on the walls are the work of the landlady, and there's an 18th-c glass-covered well in one corner. Mrs Browning's two sons are responsible for the good, honest cooking – using fresh local produce and their own eggs: sandwiches in home-made granary bread (from £1.50), soup (£1.75), local ham and egg (£4), omelettes (£4.25), grilled kidneys and bacon (£5.50), scrumpy chicken (£5.95), nut roast or vegetable stroganoff (£6), skate wings (£6.50), steaks (from £8), dover sole (£12.50), and puddings (£2.50); prices are higher in the evening; good breakfasts, three-course evening menu (£12; lots of choice), and a good three-course Sunday lunch (£7.95). Obliging service. One small dining area is no smoking. Well kept Eldridge Pope Hardy and Royal Oak, Exmoor Ale, and a guest beer on handpump, and decent wines; unobtrusive piped classical music and dominoes. Under cocktail parasols by an apple tree on the sheltered front terrace are some picnic tables; summer barbecues and a pets corner for children. In summer, residents have use of a heated swimming pool. The pub is in an interesting Somerset Levels village with willow beds still supplying the two basket works. *(Recommended by Mr and Mrs Perris, Jay Sally, Dan Taylor, S I Collins, Jane Warren, George Atkinson, Dr and Mrs Brian Hamilton, Vera and John Race, Debbie Tunstall, Mark Sullivan, Jane and Adrian Tierney-Jones, John and June Hayward, Mr and Mrs G Abbott, R V Ford, Marion Greenwood, Stella Knight, J Taylor, Brian and Anna Marsden, P H Roberts, A Preston, E H and R F Warner, Lindsey Harvard, Margaret Whalley, Tina Bird)*

Free house ~ Licensees Ron and Irene Browning ~ Real ale ~ Meals and snacks (till 10pm) ~ Restaurant ~ (01823) 490296 ~ Children welcome ~ Open 11-3, 6.30-11 ~ Bedrooms: £22.50(£30B)/£36(£50B); s/c cottage

STOKE ST MARY ST2622 Map 1

Half Moon

2¾ miles from M5 junction 25; A358 towards Ilminster, then first right, then right at T-junction and follow the signs. Westbound turn left at sign

New licensees have taken over this much-modernised village pub and have landscaped part of the garden with plans to develop it into a family-oriented area. Inside, there's a roomy, relaxed feel to each of the five neat open-plan main areas, and furnishings and decor have quite a bit of character. Bar food now includes filled french bread, home-made soup (£1.95), ploughman's (from £3.75), home-cooked ham and egg (£3.95), chilli con carne or mushroms stuffed with celery and stilton (£4.25), spicy Indian chicken (£4.95), and beef and Guinness pie (£5.25). One restaurant is no smoking. Well kept Bass, Boddingtons, Flowers IPA, Fullers London Pride, and Wadworths 6X on handpump, and quite a few malt whiskies; darts, bar billiards, cribbage, fruit machine, and piped music. Picnic tables on a well kept lawn and more tables on a small gravel terrace. *(Recommended by Alan Newman, Cliff Blakemore, John and Wendy Trentham, Geoff and Linda Dibble, Mr and Mrs C Roberts, Prof A N Black, Sue and Bob Ward, Ian and Nita Cooper, Nigel Clifton, M W Turner, Shirley Pielou, J E N Young, CR, Dr C E Morgan, S E Brown)*

Whitbreads ~ Lease: Clive Parsons ~ Real ale ~ Meals and snacks ~ Two restaurants ~ (01823) 442271 ~ Children in family room and in restaurant ~ Monthly folk, Irish, middle-of-road music ~ Open 11-3, 6-11

TRISCOMBE ST1535 Map 1

Blue Ball

Village (and pub) signposted off A358 Taunton—Minehead

In both summer and winter, the narrow terraced lawns built into the steep and peaceful slope here are full of colourful flowers, and from the picnic tables there are fine views of the Brendon Hills; cyclists from the Quantock Hills come here regularly – as do walkers. Inside this pleasant thatched little pub is a neat brown-beamed bar with sporting prints on the white walls, piped light classical music, and barely more than half a dozen tables – one tucked under the mantelbeam of what used to be a monumental brick and stone fireplace; the no-smoking conservatory does relieve the seasonal pressure on space. Well kept Butcombe Bitter, Cotleigh Barn Owl, Exmoor Ale, and Otter Ale on handpump, and Sheppy's farm cider; dominoes, cribbage, skittle alley, cards, and piped music. They have a cocker spaniel, Chadwick, and other dogs (not muddy ones) are welcome on a lead. Quickly served bar food might include sandwiches, filled baked potatoes (from £2.75), ploughman's (£3.85), walnut and lentil bake (£5.50), filled giant pancakes (£3.95), lamb pie (£5.75), home-made fish bake, spinach and nut lasagne (£5.25), lamb goulash (£5.50), steaks, and puddings such as treacle tart or lemon cream torte. The lavatories are in an unusual separate thatched building, and there's a bedroom suite (separate from the pub). *(Recommended by John and Maureen Fletcher, Mr and Mrs Perris, DJW, H F C Barclay, Jane and Adrian Tierney-Jones, Anthony Barnes, Mrs K N Fowler)*

Free house ~ Licensee Nanette Little ~ Real ale ~ Meals and snacks (not Sun evening) ~ (01984) 618242 ~ Children in conservatory ~ Open 12-2.30, 7-11; closed Sun evening Oct-Easter ~ Bedroom: £30B/£35B

TRUDOXHILL ST7443 Map 2

White Hart ◀

Village signposted off A361 Frome—Wells

Just 30 feet from the bar counter of this friendly creeper covered pub is the busy little Ash Vine Brewery – tours are available if they are not too pushed. From here they produce well-flavoured light Ash Vine Bitter through the smooth Challenger and Black Bess Porter to the rich winter Hop & Glory; Wadworths 6X as a guest. Hop & Glory and Black Bess are now bottled; Thatchers cider, and country wines. The long, attractively carpeted, stripped-stone bar, really two room areas, has beams supporting broad stripped ceiling boards and a thriving, relaxed atmosphere. It's mostly table seating, with a couple of easy chairs by the big log fire on the right (there's a second at the other end), and some seats in the red velvet curtained windows; piped music. A very wide choice of food includes sandwiches (from £1.60; toasties from £1.70; pitta bread from £3.10), home-made soup (£1.75), burgers (from £2.10), ploughman's (from £3.50), devilled kidneys (£3.95), vegetable casserole (£4.50), ham and eggs (£4.75), home-made steak and kidney pie or sweet and sour pork (4.95), rabbit pie (£5.75), salmon steak with parsley butter (£6.50), steaks (from £8.50), big mixed grill (£9.25), puddings (from £1.95), and children's meals (from £1.50). There are picnic tables on a flower-filled sheltered side lawn. *(Recommended by Jerry and Alison Oakes, SGNB, Ted George, Derek and Sylvia Stephenson, Dennis Heatley, Peter Woods, Andrew and Ruth Triggs, Colin and Sarah Pugh, George Atkinson)*

Own brew ~ Licensees Robert Viney and Ian Webster ~ Real ale ~ Meals and snacks (till 10pm) ~ Restaurant ~ (01373) 836324 ~ Children in eating area of bar ~ Open 12-2.30, 7(6.30 Sat)-11

WAMBROOK ST2907 Map 1

Cotley 🍴 🛏️

Village signposted off A30 W of Chard; don't follow the small signs to Cotley itself

Somerset Dining Pub of the Year

Readers have been full of warm praise over the past year for this bustling country pub. The caring licensee makes you feel really welcome, the staff are helpful, and the atmosphere relaxed and happy. And the food has been so well received that we have given a Food Award this year – not so much for innovative dishes with fancy sauces, but for true enjoyment of proper home cooking. There is a smart but unpretentious local atmosphere and the simple flagstoned entrance bar opens on one side into a small plush bar, with beyond that a two-room no-smoking dining area; various open fires. An extension is often used for painting sessions, and the results (complete with price-tags in case you see something you like) can be seen around the walls of the various rooms. Good, pleasing bar food (with prices unchanged since last year) includes home-made soup (£1.75), sandwiches (from £2.20), sausage and chips (£2.75), filled baked potatoes (from £3.25), creamed mushrooms with tarragon (£3.50), ploughman's (from £3.65), omelettes (from £4.95), chicken and gammon pie (£5.75), devilled kidneys with port and cream or ham and egg (£5.95), baked fillet of plaice with lemon and herbs (£6.50), whole trout with mustard sauce (£8.50), steaks (from £9.25), fresh water prawns in a sweet and sour sauce (£9.50), good daily specials (for large and small appetites), and puddings (from £1.95). The restaurant is no smoking. Well kept Flowers Original and Oakhill Bitter on handpump kept under light blanket pressure, and a good choice of wines; pool and skittle alley (winter only), and piped music. Out in the garden below are some picnic tables, with a play area and goldfish pool. Lots of lovely walks all around. *(Recommended by Chris Raisin, John Barker, Peter Toms, Clem Stephens, M E Wellington, K R Harris, D Alexander, Gwyneth and Salvo Spadaro-Dutturi, Mr and Mrs D V Morris, Margaret and Nigel Dennis, R T and J C Moggridge)*

Free house ~ Licensee David Livingstone ~ Real ale ~ Meals and snacks (till 10) ~ Restaurant ~ (01460) 62348 ~ Children welcome ~ Open 11.30-3, 7-11 ~ Bedrooms: £20B/£30B

WEST HUNTSPILL ST3044 Map 1

Crossways 🛏️

2¾ miles from M5 junction 23 (A38 towards Highbridge); 4 miles from M5 junction 22 (A38 beyond Highbridge)

A handy stop from the M5, this spacious, comfortable dining pub has a friendly, relaxed atmosphere and considerate, personable licensees. The main part of the bar has dining-room chairs, a mixture of settles, seats built into one converted brick fireplace and good winter log fires in the others. At one end there's more of a dining room, attractively decorated with old farm machinery engravings, Albert and Chic cartoons (chiefly about restaurants), and 1920ish hunting prints – on Friday and Saturday evenings this area becomes a no-smoking bistro. The other end has an area with big winged settles making booths, and there's a family room with bamboo-back seats around neat tables. Bar food includes generous sandwiches (from £1.60; sirloin steak £4), home-made soup (£2), garlic mushrooms (£3), ploughman's (£3.20), curried nut roast (£4.50), local faggots or steak and kidney pie (£4.80), gammon and egg (£6.50), steaks (from £8.50), daily specials such as cashew nut moussaka, curried prawn quiche, squid and mussel provençale, Thai fishcakes or Mexican pork, puddings such as sherry trifle (£2.20), and children's meals (£2); fresh fish from Brixham on Fridays; friendly staff. Well kept Flowers IPA, Eldridge Pope Royal Oak, and Whitbreads Best, with guests such as Butcombe Bitter, Oakhill Yeoman Strong, Palmers Tally Ho!, Smiles Best, and Wadworths 6X on handpump; a good choice of malt whiskies, Rich's farm cider, and a decent wine list. Darts, cribbage, dominoes, shove-ha'penny, fruit machine, video game and skittle alley. There are picnic tables among fruit trees in quite a big garden. If you're staying, the back rooms are quieter.

(Recommended by Andrew and Ruth Triggs, M and A Sandy, Ian Phillips, Tom Evans, Mr and Mrs D S Price, Sue and Bob Ward, Ian Williams, Linda Mar, Jenny and Michael Back, Jane and Adrian Tierney-Jones, Richard Dolphin, Alan and Eileen Bowker, Gareth and Kay Jones, P H Roberts, B J Harding, JCW, E D Bailey)

Free house ~ Licensee Michael Ronca ~ Real ale ~ Meals and snacks (till 10pm) ~ Restaurant (Fri/Sat evenings and Sun lunch only) ~ (01278) 783756 ~ Children welcome except in main bar ~ Open 12-3, 5.30(6 Sat)-11; 12-4, 7-11 Sun; closed 25 Dec ~ Bedrooms: £24B/£34B

WINSFORD SS9034 Map 1

Royal Oak 🛏 ☂

In Exmoor National Park, village signposted from A396 about 10 miles S of Dunster

In lovely Exmoor surroundings, this beautiful thatched inn is a fine place to stay. The cosy lounge bar is attractively furnished with tartan-cushioned bar stools by the panelled counter (above which hang horsebrasses and pewter tankards), the same cushions on the armed windsor chairs set around little wooden tables, and a splendid iron fireback in the big stone hearth (with a log fire in winter); from the cushioned big bay-window seat, you look across the road towards the village green and foot and packhorse bridges over the River Winn. Another similarly old-fashioned bar offers more eating space with built-in wood-panelled seats creating booths, fresh flowers, and country prints; there are several pretty and comfortable lounges. Bar food includes good home-made soup, sandwiches (from £2.50), somerset brie breadcrumbed and fried with a cumberland sauce (£3.50), ploughman's (£3.95), delicious chicken and leek pie or platter of hot meats, sausage and cheddar cheese (£6.75), seafood pancake (£6.95), local trout with parsley and lemon butter or chicken supreme wrapped in bacon (£8.50), and 8oz sirloin steak (£10.50). Well kept Flowers IPA and Original on handpump with a guest beer such as Gales HSB, Greene King Abbot, Marstons Pedigree, Morlands Old Speckled Hen or Wadworths 6X tapped from the cask; friendly staff. They do a useful guide to Exmoor National Park identifying places to visit and there are good nearby walks – up Winsford Hill for magnificent views, or over to Exford. *(Recommended by V Kavanagh, Maurice and Joan George, Nigel Woolliscroft, John and Christine Vittoe, Sir John Stokes)*

Free house ~ Licensee Charles Steven ~ Real ale ~ Meals and snacks ~ Restaurant (not Sun evening) ~ (01643) 851455 ~ Children in eating area of bar ~ Open 11-3, 6-11 ~ Bedrooms: £75B/£90B

WITHYPOOL SS8435 Map 1

Royal Oak 🛏 ☂

Village signposted off B3233

In a particularly lovely part of Exmoor, this tucked away, very welcoming inn has a marvellous unchanging atmosphere. The smartly cosy beamed lounge bar, popular with locals, has a stag's head and several fox masks on its walls, comfortable button-back brown seats and slat-backed chairs, and a fine log fire in a raised stone fireplace; another quite spacious bar is similarly decorated. Good bar food includes home-made soup (£1.95; the pheasant and the duck and mushroom are both very good), sandwiches (from £2), several prawn starters (from £3.45), ploughman's (from £3.80), filled baked potatoes (from £3.90), home-cooked ham and chips (£5.50), two big venison and bacon sausages with two free range eggs (£6.25), good steaks (from £6.50; 8oz fillet £12), half crispy duck (£10.65), and daily specials such as excellent plaice and chips, nice sweet and sour pork, enjoyable salmon gratinée, and succulent lamb chops. Well kept Flowers IPA and Marstons Pedigree on handpump, several malt whiskies, and a fair number of cognacs and armagnacs; helpful, friendly staff. It can get very busy (especially on Sunday lunchtimes), and is popular with the local hunting and shooting types; cribbage and dominoes. There are wooden benches on the terrace, and just up the road, some grand views from

Winsford Hill, with tracks leading up among the ponies into the heather past Withypool Hill. The River Barle runs through the village itself, with pretty bridleways following it through a wooded combe further upstream. For guests, they can arrange salmon and trout fishing, riding (stabling also), clay pigeon shooting, rough shooting, hunting, sea fishing from a boat and trips to see wild red deer. This is another pub with a *Lorna Doone* connection; R D Blackmore stayed here while writing the book. *(Recommended by R C Watkins, Mr and Mrs Bemis, Jill Grain, Maurice and Joan George, V Kavanagh, Kate and Kevin Gamm, Richard Gibbs, R I Hartley, Barry and Anne, James House, H and D Payne, Mr and Mrs Box, S H Godsell)*

Free house ~ Licensee Michael Bradley ~ Real ale ~ Meals and snacks ~ Restaurant ~ (01643) 831506 ~ Children in restaurant only (if over 8) ~ Open 11-3, 6-11; closed 25-26 Dec ~ Bedrooms: £32B/£76B

Lucky Dip

Besides the fully inspected pubs, you might like to try these Lucky Dips recommended to us and described by readers (if you do, please send us reports):

Allerford [the one W of Taunton; ST1825], *Victory*: Friendly and popular extended pub worth knowing for good range of up to 12 well kept ales, mainly local; restaurant, skittle alley *(Rich and Pauline Appleton, John Barker)*

☆ Ashcott [High St; ST4337], *Ring o' Bells*: Wide choice of food inc vegetarian, well kept Bass and Worthington BB, decent wines and helpful service in comfortable and genuine three-room village local; skittle alley, fruit machines, restaurant with soft piped music *(John Hazel, Douglas Allen)*
Ashcott, *Pipers*: Comfortable and roomy, with good range of food in eating area, Courage-related ales, prompt welcoming service, log fire, pleasant roadside garden *(Howard and Lynda Dix)*

☆ Axbridge [The Square; quite handy for M5; ST4255], *Lamb*: Old inn in attractive square, dark beams, rambling odd corners, welcoming atmosphere, good generous food inc good vegetarian choice and lots of puddings, well kept ales such as Bass, Butcombe and Wadworths 6X, Thatcher's farm cider, huge log fire, pub games inc table skittles, pretty little garden, skittle alley; children in eating area; old-world spacious bedrooms, huge breakfast *(John and Elisabeth Cox, Colin and Ann Hunt, Alan and Paula McCully, Stephen Horsley, Martyn Hart, LYM)*
Axbridge, *Oak House*: Pleasant atmosphere, good if not cheap food, no-smoking eating room *(Derek Allpass)*

☆ Backwell [Farleigh Rd; A370 W of Bristol; ST4968], *George*: Former coaching inn with well priced bar food, wide choice in restaurant inc delicious puddings and Sun lunch, well kept Ushers, good choice of wines; children welcome *(Alan and Paula McCully, John Walmsley)*

☆ Barrow Gurney [Barrow St (B3130, linking A370/A38 SW of Bristol; ST5367], *Princes Motto*: Very welcoming unpretentious local, cosier after refurbishment, with well kept Bass and other ales such as Boddingtons, Smiles Best and Wadworths 6X; snug traditional tap room, long room up behind, cheap wholesome lunchtime snacks *(Alan and Paula McCully, LYM)*

☆ Batcombe [off A359 Bruton—Frome; ST6838], *Batcombe Inn*: Low-beamed well furnished 14th-c family pub behind church in pretty village, wide choice of good attractively presented home-made food inc vegetarian, well kept Flowers Original, Marstons Pedigree and Oakhill, attentive service, big log fire and woodburning stoves, copper and brass, games room, comfortable minstrel's gallery; children really welcome, busy with families weekends (playroom, children's videos Sun), tables in walled garden with expanded play area; two bedrooms with own bathrooms *(R H Martyn, John Barker)*

☆ Bath [Mill Lane, Bathampton (off A36 towards Warminster or A4 towards Chippenham)], *George I*: Attractive creeper-covered canalside pub, well run and friendly, with wide choice of good food inc fish and vegetarian, good log fires, well kept Bass and Courage Directors; dining room by towpath, no-smoking family room, tables on quiet safe spacious back terrace with garden bar (traffic noise at front); can get crowded, esp weekends *(Martin W Elliott, Dr and Mrs A K Clarke, Gordon, B and K Hypher, Paul and Ursula Randall, John Hazel, Meg Hamilton)*

☆ Bath [23 The Vineyards, the Paragon, junction with Guinea Lane], *Star*: Genuinely friendly feel in small dimly lit interconnecting rooms separated by glass and panelling, staunchly basic and old-fashioned; particularly well kept Bass, Butcombe and Wadworths 6X in jugs from the cask, enthusiastic landlord, low prices, no piped music *(J and P Maloney, Alan Vann, Pete Baker, BB)*

☆ Bath [Abbey Green], *Crystal Palace*: Cheerfully busy modernised bar, sheltered courtyard with lovely hanging baskets, heated conservatory; changing straightforward food (not Sun evening) inc lunchtime snacks, speedy friendly service, well kept Eldridge Pope Dorchester, Hardys, Royal Oak and Blackdown Porter, log fire; fruit machines, video game, pinball, piped music *(Vann and Terry Prime, Gordon, Marjorie and Colin Roberts, M and A Sandy, Mrs P J Pearce, Judith and Stephen Gregory, Dr and Mrs A K Clarke, Chris Raisin, Marjorie and David Lamb, LYM)*

Bath [Walcot St], *Bell*: A musicians' pub, with well kept Butcombe, Wadworths 6X and guest beers, superb value filled rolls, friendly efficient service; frequent free music *(Dr and Mrs A K Clarke)*; [Newbridge], *Boathouse*: Large riverside pub nr marina on outskirts, rugs on wooden floor, riverside decorations, good range of lunchtime bar food, restaurant, efficient courteous service, decent house wine, usual beer; wicker furniture and potted plants in conservatory on lower level, opening to waterside garden *(Mark and Heather Williamson)*; [Combe Down; ST7662], *Cross Keys*: Locally popular for good pies (best to book Sat); Ushers ales, friendly service *(Meg and Colin Hamilton)*; [1 Lansdown Rd], *Farm House*: Pleasant setting on hill overlooking Bath, good choice of food and beer, jazz some evenings *(JJB)*; [Westgate Rd], *Mulligans*: Small simple Irish bar, good lunchtime snacks, traditional music, impressive choice of whiskeys, pleasant staff *(Dr and Mrs A K Clarke, JJB)*; [1A The Paragon, London Rd], *Paragon*: Tiny bistro with real ale, good food, very friendly atmosphere and staff *(Dr and Mrs A K Clarke)*; [Daniel St], *Pulteney Arms*: Good atmosphere, popular with Rugby players, well kept Ushers, worthy chip baps, good choice of juke box music *(Stephen O'Connor, Dr and Mrs A K Clarke)*; [Upper Borough Walls], *Sam Weller*: Well kept Bass and Wadworths 6X, good food cooked to order inc all-day breakfast, friendly young staff, lively mixed clientele *(Meg and Colin Hamilton, Dr and Mrs A K Clarke)*; [42 Broad St], *Saracens Head*: Useful for decent food, cheaper than in many pubs here, inc generous Sat cold table; well kept Courage, quick service *(Dr and Mrs A K Clarke, Hugh MacLean, Meg and Colin Hamilton)*

☆ **Bathford** [2 Bathford Hill, signed off A363; ST7966], *Crown*: Spacious and attractively laid out, several distinct but linked areas inc no-smoking garden room, good log fire, wide choice of home-cooked food from filled rolls up inc vegetarian, well kept Bass, Marstons Pedigree and Ushers Best, decent wines; tables on terrace, nice garden *(Meg and Colin Hamilton, LYM; more reports on new regime please)*

Bayford [ST7229], *Unicorn*: Beamed and flagstoned, with snug area beyond water feature in former fireplace, big helpings of food, well kept Butcombe, Fullers London Pride and guest ales, end restaurant area; dogs welcome; four good simple bedrooms with own bathrooms, great breakfast *(John and Elspeth Howell)*

Bicknoller [ST1139], *Bicknoller*: New owners doing good value varied food *(G V Stanton)*

Bishops Lydeard [The Gore, off A358 Taunton—Watchet; ST1629], *Lethbridge Arms*: Good food in two charming well kept

bars and restaurant; real ales, malt whiskies; bedrooms *(Peter Skinner)*

Bleadon [Bridgwater Rd; ST3357], *Hobbs Boat*: Spacious and pleasant, usual Brewers Fayre food all day, well kept beers, good young service, separate no-smoking dining area, family room with own entrance, marvellous indoor play area with ball pit etc, substantial wooden outdoor play equipment *(the Sandy family)*

Bradford on Tone [ST1722], *White Horse*: Stonebuilt local in quiet village, recently transformed and now very popular, with pleasant decor, varied reasonably priced good food (worth the wait) in bar and new restaurant, Cotleigh Tawny and decent wines, welcoming obliging service, well laid out side garden, skittle alley; bedrooms planned *(Brent Dale, Joan and Michel Hooper-Immins, Shirley Pielou)*

☆ **Brendon Hills** [junction B3190/Elsworthy— Winsford; ST0434], *Raleghs Cross*: Isolated roadside inn at 1,200 ft, views to Wales on clear days, good walking country; huge comfortably modernised bar with rows of banquettes, plenty of tables outside with play area, wide choice of popular generous food (some tables no smoking), carvery Fri/Sat evening and Weds, well kept Exmoor and Flowers Original; children in restaurant and family room; open all day summer; bedrooms *(Jill Bickerton, M Joyner, R W Brooks, Mr and Mrs Hillman, John Hazel, LYM)*

☆ **Brent Knoll** [2 miles from M5 junction 22; right on to A38, then first left; ST3350], *Red Cow*: Sensibly short choice of good well priced food inc proper veg and beautifully served Sun lunch in warmly welcoming spotless dining lounge where children allowed, with well spaced tables, quick pleasant staff, well kept Whitbreads-related ales, skittle alley, pleasant sheltered gardens *(Elizabeth and Anthony Watts, D A Walker, Andrew Shore, BB)*

☆ **Bristol** [Upper Maudlin St/Colston St], *Brewery Tap*: Civilised and chatty haven from city bustle, tap for Smiles brewery with their beers kept well, also interesting Continental bottled ones; small but clean and attractive, with interesting decor and good atmosphere even when packed; filled rolls, real fire; drinks 11-8, cl Sun *(Barry and Anne)*

☆ **Bristol** [St Thomas Lane, off Redcliff St/Victoria St], *Fleece & Firkin*: Lively atmosphere in lofty dim-lit 18th-c hall stripped back to striking stonework and flagstones, basic furniture, well kept Smiles, lunchtime food (not Sun) inc gigantic filled baps, pleasant staff, live music Weds-Sat, children weekends *(RLW, LYM)*

☆ **Bristol** [Sion Pl, off Portland St], *Coronation Tap*: Friendly bustling old-fashioned low-ceilinged tavern, little changed since some of our more respectably middle-aged readers were cider-swilling students; still has fat casks of interesting farm ciders, Courage Best and Directors, simple lunchtime food *(Richard Gibbs, Don Kellaway, Angie Coles, LYM)*

Bristol [off Boyce's Ave, Clifton], *Albion*:

Friendly and unpretentiously old-fashioned pub with unusual flagstoned courtyard off cobbled alley, well kept Courage ales, simple snacks *(LYM)*; [15 Small St], *Assize Courts*: Smart early 17th-c pub, fine range of ten or so real ales, cheap simple bar food popular with weekday office workers (better mix weekends), with older upstairs assembly room where Elizabeth I is said to have dined; piped music, small garden *(Neil and Elaine Piper)*; [21 Alfred Pl, Kingsdown], *Bell*: Small welcoming panelled bar with good atmosphere and service, good home-made food, well kept Ushers and a guest beer, decent wines, reasonable prices, traditional furnishings *(J Cobban)*; [Regent Street, Clifton], *Clifton*: Well done up in traditional style, clean and comfortable, good food in back bar, well kept beers on electric pump, friendly staff, snugs in front bar with sports TV; bar billiards, board games, no piped music *(Caroline Grant, D J Atkinson)*; [centre], *Commercial Rooms*: Vast Wetherspoons pub with high ceiling, lots of floor space, snug cubicles along one side, comfortable seating in no-smoking quieter back room; reasonably priced Butcombe, Courage Directors and Hop Back Powerhouse, well priced bar food; very busy weekend evenings *(Andy Jones)*; [Gloucester Rd (A38 N)], *Hobgoblin*: Wide range of real ales inc interesting stronger ones in pleasant surroundings, with good lunchtime atmosphere (crowded with young people evening); a few seats outside *(Don Kellaway, Angie Coles, Simon Pyne)*; [80 Victoria St], *Kings Head*: Packed with polished brass and wood, well kept Courage Best, interesting gas pressure gauge behind bar; friendly atmosphere *(Mr and Mrs P Byatt)*; [Gloucester Lane, Old Market; ST5872], *Old Castle Green*: Neatly kept popular local nr Compuserve HQ, with well kept Marstons inc current Head Brewers Choice, bar food inc vegetarian and good value home-made curries, ex-Navy landlord, children welcome; tables in safely walled garden *(David Bassett-Jones, David Williams)*; [45 King St], *Old Duke*: The Duke of the sign is Ellington - inside, the ochre walls and ceiling are festooned with jazz posters, besides one or two instruments, and the side stage has good bands every night, and at Sun lunchtime; usual pub furnishings, decent value simple food, Courage Best and Directors on handpump; in attractive cobbled area between docks and Bristol Old Vic, gets packed evenings *(Andy Jones, Paul Carter, BB)*; [2 Park Pl, Clifton], *Quinton House*: Very small, cosy and friendly, with good sandwiches *(John and Wendy Trentham)*; [foot of St Michaels Hill], *Scotchman & His Pack*: Good value well presented food and attentive landlord in straightforward pub, lively with students and staff from nearby hospitals *(Barry and Anne)*; [Yeomanside Cl/Wells Rd (A37)], *Yeoman*: Modern but welcoming, with the appearance of a well run working man's club; good cheap straightforward food,

children welcome *(John and Wendy Trentham)*
Broadway [Broadway Lane; ST3115], *Bell*: Country pub with strong cricketing links, big open fire, well kept Bass, Boddingtons and Oakhill, reasonably priced spirits and wines, good generous freshly cooked food, small restaurant area *(Maj and Mrs K W Johnson)*
Broomfield [N of village, on Bishops Lydeard—Bridgwater rd; ST2033], *Travellers Rest*: Attractive two-room pub with three separate sitting areas in largest room; attentive staff, Whitbreads-related ales, wide choice of pleasantly served food inc good soups and pies, log fires; tables outside, well placed for Quantocks *(SP)*
☆ Bruton [High St; ST6834], *Castle*: Good value food, changing well kept ales and welcoming landlady in unpretentious chatty town local, small darkish bars, striking mural of part of town in skittle alley, tables in sheltered back garden; children in eating area and skittle alley *(Canon Kenneth Wills, John Barker, LYM)*
☆ Buckland Dinham [A362 Radstock—Frome; ST7551], *Bell*: Rambling old-fashioned 16th-c stone-built local in small Mendip village, keen lively staff, adventurous choice of food, not cheap but good value, big dining area, well kept ales, welcoming character landlord, log fires, frequent theme nights *(Chris and Tricia Hubbard, K R Harris, Sally Thompson, K H Smith)*
☆ Castle Cary [ST6332], *George*: Tranquil old thatched coaching inn, quiet and civilised, with no-smoking lounge, very cosy small front bar with big inglenook, interesting choice of good reasonably priced fresh bar food, attractive dining room (cl Sun), welcoming helpful staff, well kept Bass, Butcombe and guest ales, decent wines inc local ones, good atmosphere; 16 comfortably refurbished bedrooms *(John Knighton, Derek and Sylvia Stephenson, Gwen and Peter Andrews)*
Catcott [ST3939], *Crown*: Comfortable and atmospheric old local, good food inc imaginative dishes, friendly service, well kept beer *(MJVK)*
☆ Charlton Musgrove [B3081, 5 miles SE of Bruton; ST7229], *Smithy*: Neatly refurbished spaciously open-plan 18th-c pub, sparkling clean, with stripped stone, heavy beams, log fires, good range of reasonably priced home-cooked food inc Sun lunch and good vegetarian choice, well kept Butcombe, Fullers London Pride and Wadworths 6X, good welcoming service; arch to small restaurant overlooking garden, skittle alley and pool table *(John Barker, Brian Chambers)*
☆ Chilcompton [Broadway; ST6452], *Somerset Wagon*: Four well kept ales and wide range of consistently good food, very popular with businessmen weekdays, in cosy, friendly and atmospheric pub with lots of settles, log fire, books, stuffed animals and militaria *(R F Wilson, G and M Stewart)*
Chilthorne Domer [ST5219], *Carpenters Arms*: Comfortable and very welcoming, with

good sensibly priced home-cooked traditional food inc good Sun lunch (must book this, no other food then) and lots of puddings, well kept Boddingtons, Marstons Pedigree and Wadworths 6X, friendly efficient service, open fire, fresh flowers; pleasant countryside (Lt Col and Mrs J M G Kay)

☆ Clevedon [Elton Rd; ST4071], Little Harp: Popular promenade pub, taken over and extended by Marstons, views towards Exmoor and the Welsh hills from terrace, conservatory and new no-smoking area, good helpings of food inc vegetarian and substantial sandwiches, well kept real ale (Tom Evans, Alan and Paula McCully)

☆ Clevedon [15 The Beach], Moon & Sixpence: Substantial seafront Victorian family dining pub with good choice of generous food (superb puddings free to OAPs), efficient friendly service, balconied mezzanine floor with good pier and sea views to Brecon Beacons, well kept Marstons Pedigree (Tom Evans, Alan and Paula McCully, A Preston)

☆ Combe Florey [off A358 Taunton—Williton, just N of main village turn-off; ST1531], Farmers Arms: Neatly rebuilt picturesque thatched and beamed pub with popular food, plenty of tables outside, good log fire, well kept Bass (Howard Clutterbuck, BB)

Combe St Nicholas [2½ miles N of Chard; ST3011], Green Dragon: Good reasonably priced food (ex-butcher landlord – always a good sign), welcoming service, well kept Bass, decent wines, open fire; well behaved children allowed; bedrooms (Howard Clutterbuck)

Compton [B3151 S of Street; ST4933], Castlebrook: Small friendly village local, refurbished keeping old flagstones etc, obliging landlord, well kept Bass and Courage Best, good value well presented food inc imaginative dishes and good Sun roasts, skittle alley, tables on lawn behind; can be crowded, caravan campsite behind (John Barker, Mr and Mrs T A Bryan, Richard Burton)

☆ Congresbury [St Pauls Causeway; ST4363], Old Inn: Unpretentious tucked-away family local, friendly and peaceful, with well kept Bass, Marstons Pedigree, Smiles and Wadworths 6X tapped from the cask, decent cheap food, open fire, ancient stove, hundreds of matchboxes on low beams (J Matthews)

Congresbury [Brinsea Rd (B3133)], Plough: Old flagstoned local with three distinctive seating areas off main bar, two open fires, old prints, farm tools and sporting memorabilia; lunchtime filled rolls, well kept Bass, Worthington BB and guest beers, open fire, enthusiastic darts team, table skittles, shove ha'penny and cards, welcoming jack russells called Pepper and Mustard; small garden with boules, aviary and occasional barbecues (Alan and Paula McCully); [Wrington Rd], White Hart & Inwood: Good unusual reasonably priced food and fair range of beers in welcoming modernised pub with Mendip views from terrace and conservatory, big outside play area, aviary (Mr and Mrs Barker, Dr and Mrs B D Smith)

Corfe [B3170; ST2319], White Hart: Friendly new people doing good food inc vegetarian and enjoyable evening meals in attractive small dining room; pleasant comfortable layout, quite smart but welcoming; guest beers such as Whitbreads Pompey Royal, children welcome (Shirley Pielou, Howard Clutterbuck, Jane Warren)

☆ Corton Denham [OS Sheet 183 map ref 634225; ST6322], Queens Arms: Welcoming and attractive old stonebuilt village inn, good fresh reasonably priced food, interesting changing guest beers from small often far-flung breweries, comfortable smallish main bar with woodburner, fresh flowers and brasses; nr Cadbury Castle, clean comfortable homely bedrooms with good views (John and Joan Nash, G D Payne, R C H Dakin)

Crowcombe [ST1336], Carew Arms: Dating back several centuries, doing well under new owners; sensibly priced home-made food, not at all pretentious; refurbished bedrooms (G V Stanton)

Culbone Hill [A39 W of Porlock, opp toll rd from Porlock Weir; SS8247], Culbone Stables: Spruced-up unpubby open-plan place with neat light wood tables and chairs, worth knowing for location – lovely Exmoor views from garden; moderately priced food inc Sunday sandwiches, no-smoking section, well kept Bass, Worthington and an ale brewed for the pub, good farm cider, jovial landlord; bedrooms (John and Elspeth Howell, John and Christine Vittoe)

Curry Rivel [A378 towards Lamport; ST3925], King William IV: Flagstoned bar with covered well, interesting memorabilia and sports trophies, friendly atmosphere and locals, cheery jack russell called Bullet, Ushers ales, toasties (A M Pring)

☆ Doulting [follow Chelynch signpost off A361 in village; ST6443], Poachers Pocket: Modernised black-beamed bar with log fire in stripped-stone end wall, gundog pictures, generous straightforward food from sandwiches up, Butcombe, Oakhill, Wadworths 6X and a guest beer, local farm cider, pub games, children in eating area, back garden with country views (Kevin and Tracey Stephens, Dr and Mrs J Hampton, A D Sherman, LYM)

☆ Dulverton [High St; SS9127], Lion: Good generous food inc interesting specials in comfortable and welcoming old-fashioned country-town hotel with well kept Exmoor and Ushers on handpump, decent wine and coffee, helpful service; children allowed in room off, pleasant setting (J C Simpson, W H and E Thomas, John and Elspeth Howell)

☆ East Coker [ST5412], Helyar Arms: Tastefully extended village pub in attractive setting, good reasonably priced food esp fish, super service, good range of ales, oak beams, nice decor (John and Wendy Trentham)

East Harptree [B3134, SW; ST5655], Castle of Comfort: Mendip coaching inn, in same friendly family for two generations, treetrunk supporting beams in ancient unspoilt bar; wide choice of generous food, good range of real ales, pleasant atmosphere; attractively set out rooms in newish wing *(Veronica M Brown)*

East Horrington [B3139 NE of Wells; ST5948], *Slab House*: Remote and windswept pub, welcoming staff, roaring fire, pleasant decor, limited bar food from sandwiches up, wider choice in small restaurant area; Eldridge Pope ales; play area *(Hilary Aslett)*

East Lambrook [ST4318], *Rose & Crown*: Attractive old stone local opp Margery Fish historic garden and nursery; five real ales, good substantial reasonably priced lunchtime bar food, restaurant, attentive welcoming staff *(Dr and Mrs S Tham)*

☆ **Easton in Gordano** [Martcombe Rd; A369 a mile from M5 junction 19; ST5276], *Rudgleigh*: Bustling roadside pub, attractive in summer with tables in big garden with willows, tamarisks and play area, facing cricket pitch; small nicely laid-out lounge with lots of commemorative mugs, other china, old guns, well kept Courage-related and Smiles ale, wide range of basic good value generous food; rather bleak little family room; open all day weekdays *(Tom Evans, John and Vivienne Rice, Bronwen and Steve Wrigley, LYM)*

☆ **Edington Burtle** [Catcott Rd; ST3943], *Olde Burtle*: Good reasonably priced food inc fresh fish in bar and restaurant, lovely log fire, well kept beer, attractive and friendly local atmosphere *(P H Roberts, Gethan Lewis)*

Enmore [ST2434], *Tynte Arms*: Low beams, open fires, pleasant dining areas; well kept Whitbreads-related ales, wide choice of good bar food inc vegetarian, reasonable prices, friendly service *(Liz and John Soden)*

☆ **Exford** [The Green; SS8538], *Crown*: Traditional old local with pine furniture, log fire and attractive streamside garden, welcoming service, well kept beer, decent wines, wide range of reasonably priced imaginative food *(Debbie Leam, Mrs C Watkinson, Ron Shelton)*

Exford [B3224], *White Horse*: Rustic-style open-plan bar, hunting prints and trophies, very wide choice of food from filled baguettes to venison pie etc, generous Sun carvery, ales such as Bass, Cotleigh Tawny, Exmoor and Worthington, log fire, pleasant safe garden by River Exe; children in eating area, dogs allowed; open all day summer, lovely Exmoor village setting; bedrooms comfortable *(Shirley Pielou, LYM)*

Failand [B3128 Bristol—Portishead; ST5271], *Failand*: Simply furnished country pub, popular for good straightforward food (get there early for a comfortable seat); well kept Bass *(Mrs C Watkinson, Tom Evans)*

☆ **Farleigh Hungerford** [A366 Trowbridge—Norton St Philip; ST8057], *Hungerford Arms*: Attractive smartly furnished pub with good views, very friendly licensee, decent food in main bar, more airy room off, and popular lower-level restaurant, well kept Courage-related ales *(Ted George, W F C Phillips)*

☆ **Freshford** [signed off B3108; ST7960], *Inn at Freshford*: Comfortably modernised interestingly decorated bar, partly no

smoking; friendly obliging staff, well kept Bass, Ruddles County and Ushers, decent wines, open fire, huge choice of food from sandwiches up inc plenty of vegetarian dishes and good fresh trout; restaurant (not Sun evening); children welcome, piped music; pretty gardens, nice spot by River Frome, walks to Kennet & Avon Canal *(Ron Gentry, MH, CH, Roger Wain-Heapy, A D Sherman, CHS, PS, Stephen Luxford, Mark and Heather Williamson, W F C Phillips, LYM; more reports on new regime please)*

☆ **Glastonbury** [Northload St; ST5039], *Who'd A Thought It*: Good often original food esp fish, well kept ales such as Bass, Eldridge Pope Blackdown Porter and Thomas Hardy and Palmers, decent wines, coal fires, pleasant staff, stripped brickwork, flagstones and polished pine, exuberant collection of bric-a-brac and memorabilia, entertaining decorations in lavatories, no-smoking restaurant; bedrooms cosy and comfortable, good breakfasts *(M J How, Annette and Stephen Marsden, Jo Rees)*

Glastonbury [High St], *George & Pilgrims*: 15th-c inn with magnificent carved stone frontage, interesting front bar with heavy tables, handsome stone fireplace (though staff could perhaps be more obliging about lighting the gas fire on cold days) and traceried stained-glass bay window; rest of pub more ordinary; well kept Bass and Wadworths 6X, children in buffet and pleasant upstairs restaurant, occasional live music; good clean bedrooms *(Colin and Ann Hunt, LYM)*; [27 Benedict St], *Mitre*: Good value food inc fresh fish and veg, home-made pies and big puddings, well kept Ushers Founders and other mainly Courage-related ales *(Annette and Stephen Marsden)*; [4 Chilkwell St (A361, SE of centre)], *Riflemans Arms*: Chatty popular local with real ales such as Flowers IPA, Eldridge Pope Royal Oak and Palmers, farm cider, good games room, play area and sunny terrace *(Dr Wolf Thandoy, Veronica M Brown, BB)*

☆ **Hallatrow** [ST6357], *Old Station*: Formidable collection of bric-a-brac from ancient typewriters to beeping car coming through wall, model train running around ceiling, wide changing choice of food, well kept Bass and other ales, lovely staff; garden behind *(Mike Pugh, John Trentham, Alan and Paula McCully)*

Hardway [rd to Alfreds Tower, off B3081 Bruton—Wincanton at Redlynch; pub named on OS Sheet 183 map ref 721342; ST7234], *Bull*: Country dining pub, popular locally esp with older people weekday lunchtimes, warm comfortable bar, character dining rooms, log fire, Butcombe and Wadworths 6X, farm cider; piped music; tables in nice garden over road, handy for Stourhead Garden *(Pat and Robert Watt, Pat and John Smyth)*

☆ **Haselbury Plucknett** [A3066 E of Crewkerne; ST4710], *Haselbury Inn*: Dining pub with candlelit tables and heavy red-cushioned cask seats, one part with chintz armchairs and sofas by the fire, popular bar food from ploughman's to char-grilled steaks with boldly flavoured specials, good wines, wide choice of real ales such as Butcombe, Charles Wells Bombardier, Morlands Old Speckled Hen, Smiles Best, Teignworthy Reel Ale and Spring Tide and Wadworths 6X, German lager on tap, no-smoking restaurant, picnic tables in garden; children welcome, cl Mon *(S G Brown, Rich and Pauline Appleton, Nigel Wilkinson, B E Tarver, LYM)*

☆ Haselbury Plucknett [Merriott Rd; ST4711], *Old Mill*: Friendly country pub with great atmosphere, good food inc interesting dishes in bar and charming dining room (booking advised); duck pond and tables outside *(Penny Elphick)*

☆ Hatch Beauchamp [old village rd, not bypass; ST3220], *Hatch*: Wide choice of good honest food, very welcoming licensees, lots of copper and brass in carpeted lounge bar with attractive bow-window seats, well kept Butcombe and Teignworthy Reel Ale, farm ciders; games room across yard; good value immaculate bedrooms *(S G Pielou, Richard Dolphin, BB)*

Hewish [nr M5 junction 21; A370 towards Congresbury; ST4064], *Full Quart*: Civilised decor and layout, good food generously and stylishly served, real ales inc Eldridge Pope Royal Oak *(K R Harris)*

Hillfarance [ST1624], *Anchor*: Modernised country pub with lots of flower tubs outside, good food inc children's and some adventurous dishes in attractive bar and two good eating areas, good value evening carvery, family room with wendy house, speedy friendly service, garden with play area; bedrooms, caravan site, holiday apartments *(Shirley Pielou, Rich and Pauline Appleton)*

☆ Hinton Blewett [signed off A37 in Clutton; ST5957], *Ring o' Bells*: Charming low-beamed stone-built country local with good value home cooking (not Sun evening), well kept Wadworths and guest ales, log fire, pleasant view from tables in sheltered front yard; children welcome *(Martin Leathers, Hugh MacLean, LYM)*

Hinton Charterhouse [B3110 about 4 miles S of Bath; ST7758], *Rose & Crown*: Attractive panelled bar which has had interesting decor, well kept Bass, Butcombe and Smiles tapped from casks, decent food in bar and restaurant, friendly service (with a welcome for children) and reasonable prices; sold to pub chain 1996 *(News please)*

☆ Holton [ST6827], *Old Inn*: Charming rustic 16th-c pub, unassuming and friendly, with beams, ancient flagstones, log fire, lots of atmosphere; interesting good value food in bar and restaurant (popular weekdays with businessmen and older people), good service, real ales and ciders, tables on terrace *(Maj and Mrs E M Warrick, Dr and Mrs S Jones, James Nunns)*

Holywell Lake [off A38; ST1020], *Holywell*: Good value food inc wide range of puddings, several local real ales, fast friendly service, quiet relaxed atmosphere (no music); cl lunchtime Mon–Weds *(I F Milne, Peter Woolls)*

Howley [ST2609], *Howley Tavern*: Spacious bar with wide choice of imaginative bar food inc vegetarian and popular Sun lunch, Bass, Flowers Original and changing guest beers, decent wines, attractive old-world restaurant; bedrooms *(John Barker)*

Ilminster [ST3614], *Lord Nelson*: Good food and beer, good service *(M J How)*

☆ Keinton Mandeville [off A37; ST5430], *Quarry*: Comfortably done up pub popular for generous reasonably priced straightforward food inc local seafood, welcoming service, well kept ales, cosy restaurant, skittle room, attractive garden *(Adam and Joan Bunting, John Hazel)*

Kenn [B3133 Yatton—Clevedon rd; ST4169], *Drum & Monkey*: Village local pleasantly done up by newish tenants in welcoming shades of pink and red, wall brasses, open fires, well priced bar food *(Alan and Paula McCully)*

☆ Keynsham [Bitton Rd; ST6568], *Lock Keeper*: Now owned by Smiles, with their beers well kept, good varied food, more room out than in – big garden in lovely spot by Avon with lock, marina and weir; as we went to press we had no news of the promisd refurbishment, but they have done their other pubs in a very appealing old-fashioned simple style *(Tom Evans, D G Clarke)*

☆ Kilve [A39 E of Williton; ST1442], *Hood Arms*: The long-serving licensees who made this village inn so popular have left, but it's still a comfortable stop, with woodburner in the bar, cosy little plush lounge, no-smoking restaurant, usual bar food (no sandwiches now), well kept Cotleigh, Exmoor and Flowers Original; gentle piped music, skittle alley, tables on sheltered back terrace by garden; back bedrooms are quietest *(V Kavanagh, LYM)*

Kingsbury Episcopi [ST4321], *Wyndham Arms*: Unspoilt flagstoned country pub with roaring open fires, good range of reasonably priced food inc good big steaks and impressive range of puddings, well kept Bass and Fullers London Pride; tables in garden *(A Preston, Stephen and Julie Brown)*

Langford Budville [off B3187 NW of Wellington; ST1022], *Martlet*: Old pub sensitively done up, good range of food inc unusual hot filled rolls, well kept beer *(John Barker)*

Lansdown [N towards Dyrham; ST7269], *Blathwayt Arms*: Big reliable all-day Whitbreads pub with well kept ales, good value generous food, friendly efficient service *(Mark Williamson, Dr and Mrs A K Clarke)*

☆ Long Sutton [A372 E of Langport; ST4625], *Devonshire Arms*: Friendly and unpretentious village-green pub with good wide-ranging menu inc unusual dishes, lots of fish and good fresh veg, two or three well kept ales, good mainly Australian service, homely back bar, well appointed restaurant; bedrooms spacious and clean, with good breakfasts *(Mr and Mrs S A Lea, Janet and Harvey Tooth, Stephen and Julie Brown)*

Lower Langford [ST4660], *Langford*: Roomy

and attractive family dining pub, enterprising and vibrant, with lots of toys in amazing children's room, good food inc special offers (also smart private dining area), decent wines, accommodating staff; pleasant terrace, popular barbecues *(David Surridge)*

Mark [ST3747], *White Horse*: Spacious 17th-c pub, attractively old-world, with wide choice of home-cooked food, well kept Flowers and guest beers, good friendly service, some decent malt whiskies; good garden with play area *(John Abbott)*

☆ **Midford** [Bath Rd; ST7560], *Hope & Anchor*: Homely and clean, with welcoming service, particularly good interesting food in bar and flagstoned restaurant end, well kept Bass, Butcombe and Smiles, good Spanish wines, good friendly service; tables outside, pretty walks along River Frome *(Roger Wain-Heapy, Mr and Mrs Paul Adams, N C Walker)*

Minehead [Quay West; SS9746], *Old Ship Aground*: Useful tourist pub with good value food esp fish, friendly staff, Courage-related ales, pleasat harbour views *(Cheryl and Keith Roe)*; [Holloway St], *Queens Head*: Nicely modern interior, good range of well kept ales, decent food, very pleasant landlord; piped music *(John Barker)*

☆ **Misterton** [Middle St; ST4508], *White Swan*: Beautifully kept, comfortable and friendly, with charmingly served good food cooked by landlady, good range of beers, framed tapestries, collection of old wireless sets; attractive garden behind, skittle alley *(Mrs C H Drew, Howard Clutterbuck, Douglas Allen)*

☆ **Montacute** [ST4916], *Phelips Arms*: Roomy and airy pub with varied good freshly cooked fair-priced food inc sandwiches and unusual specials such as shark steak or swordfish, friendly efficient service, well kept Palmers; HQ of Yeovil branch of Monster Raving Loony Party, with their correspondence book; skittle alley, tables in appealing garden, delightful village, handy for Montacute House; bedrooms *(Maj and Mrs Warrick, D G Else, S G Brown, A Preston, Dr S Willavoys, Wendy Arnold)*

Moorlinch [signed off A39; ST3939], *Ring o' Bells*: Friendly atmosphere, good hearty food, well kept ales such as Berrow, Bridgwater, Oakhill and Smiles; cosy attractive lounge with log fire; cl Mon-Thurs lunchtime in winter *(Jane and Adrian Tierney-Jones)*

☆ **North Brewham** [ST7236], *Old Red Lion*: Stone-floored low-beamed former farmhouse with good food, pleasant atmosphere, well kept Butcombe, Fullers and Greene King ales, friendly and efficient service; handy for King Alfred's monument *(John Hazel, Derek and Sylvia Stephenson)*

☆ **North Perrott** [ST4709], *Manor Arms*: Attractively modernised 16th-c pub on pretty village green, inglenook, beams and mellow stripped stone, good value imaginative freshly made food from sandwiches up in bar and cosy restaurant, well kept Boddingtons and Smiles, decent wines, cheerful atmosphere,

very welcoming landlord, pleasant garden with adventure play area; two good value comfortable bedrooms in coach house *(A Preston, Canon Kenneth Wills)*

North Petherton [High St, nr M5 junction 24; ST2932], *Walnut Tree*: Friendly welcoming hotel, comfortable bar with good food in eating area, restaurant; bedrooms spacious and well equipped, substantial breakfasts *(Andrew and Ruth Triggs)*

Oldford [N of Frome; ST7850], *Ship*: Neat and clean, with good simple cheap food (may take a while; no sandwiches); good coffee *(John and Wendy Trentham)*

☆ **Panborough** [B3139 Wedmore—Wells; ST4745], *Panborough Inn*: Spacious 17th-c village inn with attentive friendly service, wide range of consistently good generous food inc vegetarian and splendid puddings; several clean, comfortable and attractive rooms, inglenook, beams, brass and copper, real ales, unobtrusive piped music; skittle alley, small restaurant, tables in front terraced garden; bedrooms comfortable *(Mr and Mrs Beck, K R Harris)*

☆ **Pitminster** [OS Sheet 193 map ref 219191; ST2118], *Queens Arms*: Unspoilt village pub with seven real ales, imaginative wines, good bar food from fine crab sandwiches up, wonderful fish restaurant in pleasant dining room; bedrooms with own bathrooms *(Lady Emma Chanter, Shirley Pielou)*

Polsham [A39 N of Glastonbury; ST5142], *Camelot*: Roomy 18th-c dining pub with wide choice of promptly served good food in bar, restaurant and conservatory looking over fields; Palmers and a local beer brewed for the pub, big children's area, terrace; bedrooms *(R V Ford)*

☆ **Porlock** [High St (A39); SS8846], *Ship*: Picturesque thatched huge-chimneyed partly 13th-c pub, traditional low-beamed locals' front bar with flagstones, inglenooks each end, hunting prints, plush back lounge, well kept Bass, Cotleigh, Courage Best and a local guest beer such as Bosuns Tackle, good country wines, easy-going service, bar food, pub games and pool table, garden; children welcome in eating area; bedrooms *(Martin Appleton, Jonathan Williams, Georgina Cole, Simon Collett-Jones, Risha Stapleton, JP, PP, George and Jeanne Barnwell, Dorothy and Leslie Pilson, Mr and Mrs Westcombe, Dave Thompson, Margaret Mason, Don and Thelma Beeson, LYM)*

Porlock, *Castle*: Lively and cheerful, reasonably priced food, well kept beer; bedrooms *(David Carr)*

☆ **Porlock Weir** [separate from but run in tandem with neighbouring Anchor Hotel; SS8547], *Ship*: Prettily restored old inn included for its wonderful setting by peaceful harbour, with tables in terraced rose garden and good walks (but no views to speak of from bars); usual bar food, Courage-related and Exmoor ales and good welcoming service in straightforward Mariners Bar with family room; roaring fire, attractive bedrooms; not to be confused with the Porlock pub of the same name *(Paul Randall, RS, Jenny and Michael Back, Elizabeth and Anthony Watts, David Carr, LYM)*

Portbury [Station Rd, ½ mile from A369 (off M5 junction 19); ST5075], *Priory:* Pleasant main bar, well kept Bass, bar food inc decent baked potatoes (may take a time) *(Dr and Mrs A K Clarke)*

☆ Portishead [High St; ST4777], *Poacher:* New extension to cope with popularity of its wide range of good reasonably priced freshly cooked food, real veg cooked for each session – get there early as many things sell out by one-ish, though they'll do the good trout much later; well kept Butcombe and Ushers Founders, friendly amusing (though not always speedy) service *(K R Harris, John Millward, Tom Evans)*

Portishead [Old Bristol Rd], *Albion:* Food inc good filling sandwiches, well kept Marstons Pedigree *(Tom Evans)*; [Nore Rd], *Hole-In-One:* Originally a golf club house, big rather functional main bar, no-smoking one in former windmill tower; lovely setting with fine Severn estuary and bridge views, welcoming service, usual food inc good value winter meals offers *(D G Clarke, A Kilpatrick)*; [coast rd to Walton in Gordano], *Ship:* Quiet and relaxing, with lovely Severn estuary views, good value usual food lunchtime, real ales inc Bass and Butcombe *(Tom Evans)*

☆ Priddy [from Wells on A39 pass hill with TV mast on left, then next left – OS Sheet 183 map ref 549502; ST5450], *Hunters Lodge:* Welcoming and unassuming walkers' and potholers' inn, well kept local Oakhill ales tapped from casks behind the bar, simple good food inc bread and local cheese and OAP bargain lunches, log fire, flagstones; tables in garden; bedrooms *(R H Martyn, Veronica M Brown, Barry and Anne)*

☆ Priddy [off B3135], *New Inn:* Convivial low-beamed pub, modernised but still traditional, doing well under new licensees, with good log fire, spacious conservatory, good value food inc interesting dishes, well kept Bass, Eldridge Pope Hardy and Wadworths 6X, good local cider and house wines, good welcoming service, skittle alley; motorcyclists made welcome; bedrooms comfortable and homely, on quiet village green *(Paul Nicholson, David Logan)*

Priddy [off B3135], *Queen Victoria:* Relaxed character country pub with flagstones and good open fires, interesting bric-a-brac, friendly staff and cat; Butcombe and Wadworths 6X tapped from the cask, organic beers, farm ciders and perries, standard food; motorcyclists made welcome; good garden for children over road *(Peter and Wendy Begley, S E Paulley)*

Radstock [62 Frome Rd; ST6954], *Fromeway:* Friendly pub, popular locally for good generous food (meat from own butcher's shop), no-smoking restaurant, quick service, well kept beer; bedrooms clean, bright and reasonably priced *(Mrs J Clark)*

Ridgehill [Crown Hill – pub signed from village; ST5262], *Crown:* Interesting old pub, authentically old-fashioned, with attractive restaurant, skittle alley, lovely views from terrace *(Dr and Mrs A K Clarke)*

Rode [A361 Frome—Trowbridge; ST8153], *Bell:* Friendly new landlord, smart decor, huge range of reasonably priced food inc lots of fish, maybe alligator and kangaroo, well kept ales such as Nethergate Bitter and Old Growler, good coffee *(Peter and Audrey Dowsett)*

Roundham [A30 Crewkerne—Chard; ST4209], *Travellers Rest:* Pleasant interior, with friendly staff and cat, decent food, ales such as Butcombe and Worthington BB *(Howard Clutterbuck)*

☆ Rowberrow [about ½ mile from A38 at Churchill; ST4558], *Swan:* Good bar food from fine sandwiches up amd quick courteous service in olde-worlde pub with comic hunting prints and grandfather clock, well kept Bass and Wadworths 6X; good walking country *(Gethin Lewis, Alan and Paula McCully, D A Walker)*

Saltford [Mead Lane; ST6867], *Jolly Sailor:* Welcoming refurbished pub by weir on River Avon; Courage ales, good bar food inc special offers, restaurant, garden – and its own island between lock and pub; children welcome *(John and Nicki Craven)*

☆ Seavington St Michael [signed from E side of A303 Ilminster bypass; ST4015], *Volunteer:* Friendly and comfortable much modernised dining pub with understated decor, simple wholesome good value home cooking, well kept real ales *(Mr and Mrs G Ricketts, Howard Clutterbuck, BB)*

Shepton Mallet [63 Charlton Rd; ST6445], *Thatched Cottage:* Simple but comfortable decor, with good varied reasonably priced food in bar and restaurant; bedrooms with own baths *(Pat Woodward, Meg and Colin Hamilton)*

☆ Shepton Montague [off A359 Bruton—Castle Cary; ST6731], *Montague:* Old-fashioned deep-country pub with new licensees doing really interesting food (generous bar nibbles too), Butcombe, Greene King IPA and Marstons Pedigree, decent wines, sensible prices, log fire in attractive salvaged fireplace, no machines or music, pretty terrace, brilliant views; three comfortable bedrooms with own bathrooms; has been closed lunchtime *(Mr and Mrs A Allom, M Ward)*

Somerton [Mkt Pl; ST4828], *Globe:* Friendly chatty local with log fire, good bar food, well kept Bass and Oakhill, good choice of wine; no music *(John Barker)*

Sparkford [off A303; ST6026], *Sparkford:* Doing well, with friendly young licensees, good range of bar food, attractive carvery, well kept beers; comfortable bedrooms *(Iain Robertson, Canon Kenneth Wills)*

☆ Staple Fitzpaine [ST2618], *Greyhound:* Relaxing sophisticated atmosphere in interesting rambling country pub with antique layout, flagstones and inglenooks; friendly service, well kept Whitbreads and interesting local ales, good food, pleasant individual service (*Richard Dolphin, Tina Bird, Margaret and Nigel Dennis, LYM*)

Staplegrove [junction A358/A361; ST2126], *Cross Keys*: Spacious yet cosy Chef & Brewer, good service, good range of well cooked food, wide choice of mainly Courage-related beers (*Howard Clutterbuck*)

Stathe [ST3729], *Black Smock*: Good local atmosphere, friendly landlord, good choice of well presented reasonably priced home-cooked food, well kept Butcombe; good fishing nearby; bedrooms comfortable (*Joy and Fred Parker*)

Stoke sub Hamdon [ST4717], *Fleur de Lis*: Popular and friendly old village local with good well priced food, well kept beers and local ciders, friendly landlady; bedrooms (*Mrs M Walters*)

Tarr [Tarr Steps – OS Sheet 181 map ref 868322; SS8632], *Tarr Farm*: Nicely set for river walks, very cosy with huge tables made from slabs of wood, pleasant dog called Fatso (though not fat), teas with good home-made scones, good choice of food (*Tina and David Woods-Taylor*)

☆ Taunton [Magdalene St], *Masons Arms*: Fine friendly town pub, often very busy, with good range of well kept ales inc Exmoor, good reasonably priced quick food (not Sun) inc succulent sizzler steaks and interesting soups, comfortably basic furnishings, no music or pool tables; good bedrooms (*Howard Clutterbuck, Veronica Brown, Hugh Donnelly, Peter Skinner, Julian Pyrke, Ian Phillips, Jane and Adrian Tierney-Jones*)

Taunton [Shuttern], *Pen & Quill*: Good value food with good choice of puddings (*Veronica M Brown*)

☆ Thurloxton [ST2730], *Maypole*: Several attractive areas, very wide choice of generous food from filled baps up, quick friendly obliging service, well kept Whitbreads-related ales, biggish no-smoking area, soft piped music, skittle alley; peaceful village (*Pete Yearsley, Shirley Pielou, T Neate*)

Timberscombe [SS9542], *Lion*: Current hardworking landlords doing well, usual bar food at reasonable prices inc good specials, Exmoor ale, dining area just off main bar – and a couple of other rooms if one wants to escape the juke box; bedrooms (*John and Elspeth Howell*)

Tintinhull [Church St; ST4919], *Lamb*: Quiet village pub with increasingly attractive range of food inc midweek bargains and good value Sun lunch (must book for restaurant); well kept Wadworths 6X, welcoming service, nice garden; handy for Tintinhull Manor (NT) (*K R Harris, J Bidgood*)

Trull [Church Rd; ST2122], *Winchester Arms*: Welcoming lively small local, good varied food, well kept Butcombe, obliging service, cosy atmosphere, small dining room (*Derek Patey, Shirley Pielou, John Barker*)

Upper Langford [ST4659], *Langford*: Family dining pub with wide choice of good food from well filled baked potatoes up in charming spacious dining room, decent wines, fantastic children's room with lots of toys,

welcoming service; attractive terrace (*Denis and Barbara Melling*)

Watchet [ST0743], *Star*: Old pub nr seafront, cheery barman, good log fire, straightforward food from sandwiches up (*David Shillitoe*)

Waterrow [A361 Wiveliscombe—Bampton; ST0425], *Rock*: Clean and friendly, with well kept ales inc Cotleigh Tawny and Exmoor Gold, wide choice of home-made food, attractive prices, log fire in smallish bar exposing the rock it's built on, couple of steps up to lunchtime dining room doubling as evening restaurant; good well equipped bedrooms, charming setting in small valley village (*Jill Bickerton*)

☆ Wellow [signed off A367 SW of Bath; ST7458], *Fox & Badger*: Flagstoned bar with snug alcoves, small winged settles, flowers on the tables, three log fires, well kept Boddingtons, Butcombe, Wadworths 6X and bargain-price Exmoor, Thatcher's farm cider, reasonably priced wholesome food from sandwiches up inc good Sun roast, games and piped music in cosy public bar, restaurant, courtyard with barbecues; children in eating areas, open all day Thurs/Fri – can get very busy (*Jenny and Michael Back, Barry and Anne, Meg and Colin Hamilton, S G N Bennett, LYM*)

☆ Wells [High St, nr St Cuthberts; ST5545], *City Arms*: Good choice of good value food inc well prepared sandwiches and unusual dishes in big L-shaped bar and upstairs restaurant of interestingly converted largely early 18th-c building – some parts even older (said to have been a Tudor jail); Butcombe and Smiles ales, decent wines, friendly prompt service (*Howard Clutterbuck, Tony and Wendy Hobden, Chris Ball*)

☆ Wells [St Thomas St], *Fountain*: Good vaue generous original food in pleasantly pubby downstairs bar with roaring log fire and popular upstairs restaurant – worth booking weekends, good Sun lunch; friendly quick staff, well kept Courage-related ales, farm cider, good choice of wines, piped music; right by cathedral; children welcome (*D and B Taylor, Veronica M Brown*)

☆ West Bagborough [ST1633], *Rising Sun*: Welcoming local in tiny village below Quantocks, family service, short choice of fresh generous home-cooked food, well kept Exmoor and Oakhill, wide choice of wines, unobtrusive piped music, darts, table skittles, big log fires; bedrooms comfortable, with own bathrooms (*Graham Stanton, Anthony Barnes*)

West Coker [A30; ST5113], *Castle*: Attractive thatched village pub, well kept Ushers and guest beers, imaginative range of generous food, friendly licensees (*Mr and Mrs T A Bryan*)

West Harptree [B3114, out of village towards Chew Lake; ST5557], *Blue Bowl*: Extended stonebuilt country dining pub with lots of tables in engaging series of separate rooms, food from sandwiches to steaks, well kept Butcombe, Courage Best and Wadworths 6X, tables on back terrace and spacious enclosed lawn; well behaved children allowed; bedrooms *(W F C Phillips, LYM)*

West Hatch [Slough Green, which is signed off A380 and B3170; ST2720], *Farmers Arms*: 16th-c four-room pub, beams, open fires and attractive uncluttered interior, well kept Exmoor and Whitbreads-related ales, good range of reasonably priced food in bar or dining room, Sun lunch, welcoming service; games area with darts and bar billiards, children's room, garden with play area *(Shirley Pielou)*

West Huntspill [ST3044], *Scarlet Pimpernel*: Large roadside inn, well kept real ales *(Dr and Mrs A K Clarke)*

☆ **West Pennard** [A361 E of Glastonbury; ST 5438], *Lion*: Short choice of rewarding subtly flavoured freshly cooked food in three neat dining areas opening off small flagstoned and black-beamed core with log fire in big stone inglenook, second log fire in stripped-stone family area, well kept local ales, welcoming staff; bedrooms comfortable and well equipped, in neatly converted side barn *(Canon Kenneth Wills, C and E Watson, BB)*

Weston Super Mare [seafront, N end; ST3261], *Claremont Vaults*: Large plush dining pub with wonderful views down the beach or across the bay, helped by floor being raised about a foot; good choice of cheap lunchtime bar food inc lots of fish, well priced Bass and Worthington, decent wine, plush furnishings, friendly obliging service; piped music *(Ian Phillips, Peter and Audrey Dowsett, A C Stone)*; [Knightstone Parade], *Pavilion*: Recently stylishly refurbished in dusty pinks and blues for Edwardian look, period framed posters, helpful service, well kept drinks; lots of tables on sea-facing terrace give Continental feel *(Susan and John Douglas)*

☆ **Wheddon Cross** [A396/B3224, S of Minehead; SS9238], *Rest & Be Thankful*: Good range of generous home-cooked food from children's dishes to salmon en croûte and friendly efficient staff in quietly

welcoming comfortably modern two-room bar with buffet bar and restaurant, well kept Courage-related ales with others such as Morlands Old Speckled Hen and Wadworths 6X, hot drinks, two good log fires, huge jug collection, aquarium and piped music; communicating games area, skittle alley, public lavatory for the disabled; bedrooms *(Patrick and Patricia Derwent, Carol and Brian Perrin, Pete and Rosie Flower, John and Elspeth Howell, LYM)*

☆ **Widcombe** [Culmhead – OS Sheet 193 map ref 222160; ST2216], *Holman Clavel*: Simple but comfortable old-fashioned deep-country pub dating from 14th c and named after its massive holly chimney-beam, good cheap home-cooked bar food, welcoming hard-working landlord, well kept Cotleigh and Flowers Original, nice atmosphere; dogs welcome, handy for Blackdown Hills *(John Barker, BB)*

Wincanton [South St; ST7028], *Nog*: Recently extended jovial and welcoming local, generous reasonably priced food, farm cider *(Brian Chambers)*

Windwhistle Hill [A30 Chard—Crewkerne; ST3709], *Windwhistle*: Useful stop, big locals' bar, busy smaller dining room, wide range of food, well kept John Smiths, Tetleys and Wadworths 6X *(Mr and Mrs T A Bryan)*

Witham Friary [signed off A361 – OS Sheet 183 map ref 745409; ST7440], *Seymour Arms*: Welcoming unspoilt local, two characterful rooms, hatch servery, well kept Ushers tapped from the cask, local farm cider; darts, cards, dominoes – no juke box or machines; pleasant garden *(Pete Baker)*

Woolverton [A36 N of village; ST7954], *Red Lion*: Roomy beamed pub, panelling, flagstones and rugs on parquet, smart Regency chairs and chandeliers, well kept Bass and Wadworths 6X, very wide choice of decent wines by the glass, winter mulled wine, straightforward food inc popular filled baked potatoes, friendly service; open all day *(John and Wendy Trentham, LYM)*

If a service charge is mentioned prominently on a menu or accommodation terms, you must pay it if service was satisfactory. If service is really bad you are legally entitled to refuse to pay some or all of the service charge as compensation for not getting the service you might reasonably have expected.

Staffordshire

Three new entries here are the Swan With Two Necks at Longdon (a splendid example of how even straightforward pub food can be quite delicious), the Holly Bush at Salt (perhaps the county's oldest pub) and the Wellington in Uttoxeter (an extraordinary place, with some very interesting Belgian food). Other pubs currently doing particularly well here are the Moat House at Acton Trussell (our choice as Staffordshire Dining Pub of the Year) and the wonderfully welcoming Olde Royal Oak at Wetton. There's good food to be had at the Izaak Walton at Cresswell (with lunchtime bargains). The Jervis Arms at Onecote stands out for its sensible treatment of families, and the very relaxed Yew Tree at Cauldon for its virtually priceless collections of fascinating hardware (and for extremely low drinks prices). The Rising Sun at Shraleybrook, which brews its own beers, also has keen drinks prices; and the Burton Bridge Inn in Burton itself is another pub brewing its own fine ales. Burton is of course the capital of British brewing, housing Bass, Ind Coope and Marstons; and the county has some interesting much smaller breweries such as Enville (using honey from its own bees in some of its ales – you can try it at the Swan With Two Necks) and Lichfield. In general, both beer and food prices are rather lower here than in most other places. In the Lucky Dip section at the end of the chapter, pubs currently showing well (most of them already inspected and approved by us) include the Boat at Cheddleton, Black Lion at Consall, St George at Eccleshall, Plough in Etruria, Cavalier at Grindon (if you're lucky enough to find it open), Meynell Ingram Arms at Hoar Cross, Worston Mill at Little Bridgeford, Red Lion at Newborough, Stafford Arms in Stafford, Mainwaring Arms at Whitmore and Crown at Wrinehill. Perhaps because this is head office territory, the county's brewery-chain dining pubs tend to set a good example.

ACTON TRUSSELL SJ9318 Map 7

Moat House

Village signposted from A449 just S of Stafford; the right turn off A449 is only 2 miles (heading N) from M6 junction 13 – go through the village to find the pub on the W side, by the canal

Staffordshire Dining Pub of the Year

This attractive 14th-c timbered pub is doing particularly well these days, with the very efficient and welcoming staff coping marvellously with the summer crowds – one reader was really surprised to find how really friendly a fairly big place could still be. It's prettily set in six acres of lovely landscaped grounds next to the Staffordshire & Worcestershire canal, with mooring facilities for narrowboats, and plenty of friendly ducks. The family have a 400-acre farm which supplies some produce for the very good bar food; this might include daily specials like broccoli soup with croûtons (£1.95), roast pork, grilled fillet of plaice with tartare sauce or venison, apricot and ginger sausages (£5.25), lamb liver and bacon with onion gravy or cod in beer batter (£5.75), poached breast of chicken in a mushroom and brandy cream sauce (£5.95), entrecote steak topped with stilton and served with madeira cream sauce. Well kept Banks's Bitter and Mild and Marstons Pedigree with two guests such as Morlands Old Speckled Hen and Camerons Strongarm on handpump, a good wine list with about ten by the glass, and a decent range of spirits served in the charming and comfortable oak-beamed bar; pleasant friendly staff; no-smoking restaurant. Fruit machine, piped music. *(Recommended by Carl Travis, Dorothee and Dennis Glover, Chris Raisin, Frank Cummins, Iain Robertson, Mike and Maggie Betton, Addie and Irene Henry, Dick Brown, C H and P Stride, Bronwen and Steve Wrigley, Peter and Jenny Quine, Carole and Philip Bacon, Margaret and Roy Randle, John and Chris Simpson, Basil Minson, FJ and A Parmenter, Dave Braisted, RT and JC Moggridge)*

Free house ~ Licensees John and Mary Lewis ~ Real ale ~ Meals and snacks (not Sat evening or Sun) ~ Restaurant ~ (01785) 712217 ~ Children welcome ~ Open 11-3, 5.30-11; 11-11 Sat in summer; 12-10.30 Sun; cl 25 and 26 Dec

ALSTONEFIELD SK1355 Map 7

George

Village signposted from A515 Ashbourne—Buxton

Locals, campers and hikers gather by the warm fire in the straightforward low-beamed bar of this unaffected 16th-c stone inn – although muddy boots and dogs may not be welcome. There's a collection of old photographs and pictures of the Peak District, and pewter tankards hanging by the copper-topped bar counter. A spacious family room has plenty of tables and wheelback chairs. Generous helpings of straightforward bar food from a printed menu – you order at the kitchen door – include: sandwiches (£1.85), soup (£1.95), ploughman's (from £3.85), meat and potato pie (£4.95), smoked trout or Spanish quiche (£5.30) and lasagne or chicken (£5.50). Well kept Burtonwood Bitter, Buccaneer and Forshaws on handpump; dominoes, cribbage and piped music. The big sheltered stableyard behind the pub has a pretty rockery with picnic tables, and there are some stone seats beneath the attractive inn sign at the front. You can arrange with the landlord to camp on the croft. *(Recommended by Pat and Roger Fereday, Peter Marshall, Nigel Woolliscroft, J E Rycroft, RG, Eric Locker, Jack and Philip Paxton, Harriet and Michael Robinson, John Waller, Paul and Maggie Baker, Dave Irving)*

Burtonwood ~ Tenants Richard and Sue Grandjean ~ Real ale ~ Meals and snacks (till 10pm)~ (01335) 310205 ~ Children welcome in eating area ~ Open 11-2.30, 6(6.30 winter weekdays)-11; 11-11 Sat; 12-10.30 Sun; cl 25 Dec

Watts Russell Arms

Hopedale

This welcoming 18th-c shuttered house is prettily set in a little lane outside the village. The cheerful bar has comfortable brocaded wall banquettes and wheelback chairs and carvers, an open fire below a copper hood, a collection of blue and white china jugs hanging from the ceiling, bric-a-brac around the roughcast walls, and an interesting bar counter made from copper-bound oak barrels. Bar food includes soup (£1.75), filled baps (from £1.75, hot bacon and tomato £3), filled baked potatoes (from £3), English breakfast or ploughman's (£4.50), vegetable lasagne or chilli (£4.75), scampi (£5.25) and gammon (£6.25); children's meals (£2.75). Well kept Mansfield and White Rabbit and Charles Wells Bombardier on handpump, and about a dozen malts; darts, dominoes and piped music. Outside there are picnic tables on the sheltered tiered little terrace, and garden. It's gloriously set in a deep valley of the Peak District National Park, close to Dovedale and the Manifold so is popular with walkers, and busy at weekends; no-smoking area. *(Recommended by Mike and Wendy Proctor, Ron Gentry, Joy and Peter Heatherley, Peter Marshall, Jack and Philip Paxton, Yolanda Henry, Ian Jones, David Atkinson, Paul Robinshaw)*

Free house ~ Licensees Frank and Sara Lipp ~ Real ale ~ Meals and snacks (not winter Sun evenings) ~ (01335) 310271 ~ Children welcome ~ Open 12-3, 7-11; cl Mon Dec-Easter

BURTON ON TRENT SK2423 Map 7

Burton Bridge Inn £ 🍺

24 Bridge St (A50)

This unpretentious and friendly local has beautifully kept own brew beers on handpump – Burton Bridge Bitter, XL, Porter and seasonal ales, all brewed in the brewery at the back in a long old-fashioned yard (you can go round it on Tuesdays if you book in advance). The simple little front bar has wooden pews, and plain walls hung with notices, awards and brewery memorabilia; even when it's quiet people tend to spill out into the corridor. Basic but good bar snacks such as chip or sausage butties (£1.20), good filled cobs (from £1.45, hot roast pork or beef £1.75), and giant filled yorkshire puddings with ratatouille, faggots and mushy peas, a roast of the day or sausages (£1.85-£2.95). The panelled upstairs dining room is open at lunchtime only; there's also a skittle alley (booked well in advance), with gas lighting and open fires; country wines; about a dozen malt whiskies; dominoes. *(Recommended by Richard Lewis, Penny and Martin Fletcher, Alan and Paula McCully, BB, Jack and Philip Paxton, Sue Holland, Dave Webster, John Scarisbrook)*

Own brew ~ Tenant Kevin McDonald ~ Real ale ~ Lunchtime meals and snacks (not Sun) ~ (01283) 536596 ~ Well behaved children in eating area of bar until 8pm ~ Open 11.30-2.15, 5.30-11; cl bank hol lunchtimes till 7pm

BUTTERTON SK0756 Map 7

Black Lion ★ 🛏

Village signposted from B5053

There are plenty of interesting things to look at as you wander around the rambling neat and tidy rooms of this atmospheric and homely 18th-c stone inn. One welcoming bar has a low black beam-and-board ceiling, lots of brassware and china, a fine old red leatherette settle curling around the walls, well polished mahogany tables, and a good log fire. Off to the left are red plush button-back banquettes around sewing-machine tables and Victorian prints, while an inner room has a fine old kitchen range and a loudly squawking parakeet called Sergeant Bilko. Bar food served in generous helpings includes soup (£1.80), sandwiches (from £1.80), ploughman's and salads (£4.25), steak and kidney pie, lasagne, vegetarian lasagne and stroganoff (£4.95), mixed grill (£8.75) and daily specials such as chicken provençale, cheese and vegetable bake, lamb ragout or pork steaks in cider; puddings like spotted dick (£1.95); children's menu (£3.15). The four well kept real ales on handpump might include Batemans XXXB, Charles Wells Bombardier, Courage Directors, Eldridge Pope Hardy Country, McEwans 70/-, Morlands Old Speckled Hen, Theakstons Best or Youngers No 3; several malt whiskies; a cocktail bar is open weekend evenings. Darts, bar billiards, shove-ha'penny, dominoes, cribbage, table football, table skittles, and separate well lit pool room; piped music and television. Outside picnic tables and rustic seats on a prettily planted terrace look up to the tall and elegant spire of the local church of this pretty conservation village; pleasant views over the Peak National Park; bedrooms have just been refurbished. *(Recommended by David Gittins, Peter Marshall, Vicky and David Sarti, Janet and Peter Race, David Rule, Mike and Wendy Proctor, Nick and Meriel Cox, Joy and Peter Heatherley, Colin Steer, Paul Robinshaw, M W Turner, Dave Irving, Mrs C Blake, Jack Morley, S Howe, Nigel Wolliscroft, Alan and Judy Gifford, Celia Minoughan, Jack and Philip Paxton, Mayur Shah)*

Free house ~ Licensee Ron Smith ~ Real ale ~ Meals and snacks ~ Restaurant ~ (01538) 304232 ~ Children welcome ~ Open 12-3, 7-11; cl Weds lunchtime ~ Bedrooms: £35B/£50B

If we know a pub does sandwiches we always say so – if they're not mentioned, you'll have to assume you can't get one.

CAULDON SK0749 Map 7

Yew Tree ★ ★ £

Village signposted from A523 and A52 about 8 miles W of Ashbourne; OS Sheet 119 map reference 075493

Like Aladdin's cave, the unassuming exterior of this roadside local gives no hint to the unique profusion of fascinating treasures that the eccentrically characterful landlord Alan East has lovingly crowded into its dimly lit rooms. One or two readers struggle to see past the somewhat shabby seats, the dust that settles from the cement factory next door, and the lack of elaborate food, but most are enchanted by this world of bizarre, mostly Victorian objects. Perhaps the most impressive are the working Polyphons and Symphonions – 19th-c developments of the musical box, often taller than a person, each with quite a repertoire of tunes and elaborate sound-effects; go with plenty of 2p pieces to work them. But there are also two pairs of Queen Victoria's stockings, ancient guns and pistols, several penny-farthings, an old sit-and-stride boneshaker, a rocking horse, swordfish blades, and even a fine marquetry cabinet crammed with notable early Staffordshire pottery. Soggily sprung sofas mingle with 18th-c settles and a four-person oak church choir seat with carved heads which came from St Mary's church in Stafford; above the bar is an odd iron dog-carrier (don't ask how it works!) As well as all this there's an expanding set of fine tuneful longcase clocks in the gallery just above the entrance, a collection of six pianolas, including a newly acquired electric one, with an excellent repertoire of piano rolls, a working vintage valve radio set, a crank-handle telephone, a sinuous medieval wind instrument made of leather, and a Jacobean four-poster which was once owned by Josiah Wedgwood and still has the original wig hook on the headboard. Remarkably cheap simple snacks like hot pork pies (65p), meat and potato pies, chicken and mushroom or steak pies (70p), hot big filled baps and sandwiches (from 80p), and quiche or smoked mackerel (£2.50). Beers include very reasonably priced Bass, Burton Bridge and M & B Mild on handpump or tapped from the cask, and there are some interesting malt whiskies such as overproof Glenfarclas; spirits prices are very low here, too. Darts, shove-ha'penny, table skittles (taken very seriously here), dominoes and cribbage. Hiding behind a big yew tree, the pub is difficult to spot – unless a veteran bus is parked outside. Dovedale and the Manifold Valley are not far away. *(Recommended by Ann and Colin Hunt, Sue Holland, Dave Webster, Ian and Gayle Woodhead, Joy and Peter Heatherley, Mr and Mrs P Byatt, Mike and Wendy Proctor, Vicky and David Sarti, Chris Raisin, D and D Savidge, David Carr, David and Shelia, Graham Bush, Hilary Dobbie, B Adams, Mike Woodhead, John and Christine Lowe, Jack and Philip Paxton, Nigel Woolliscroft, H K Dyson, Paul Robinshaw, Mrs C Blake, Mayur Shah, Roger and Valerie Hill)*

Free house ~ Licensee Alan East ~ Real ale ~ Snacks (11-3, 6-9.30 but generally something to eat any time they're open) ~ (01538) 308348 ~ Children in Polyphon room ~ Occasional live folk ~ Open 10-3, 6-11

CRESSWELL SJ9739 Map 7

Izaak Walton

Village signposted from Draycott in the Moors, on former A50 Stoke—Uttoxeter

At lunchtime during the week and until seven in the evening all main courses at this smart dining pub are £2 cheaper (not in December) than the prices we show here. Nicely presented tasty bar food includes soup (£2.50), lunchtime baked potatoes (from £2.25), steak and kidney pie or lasagne (£4.95), chicken and broccoli bake (£5.75), poached salmon (£7.70), a choice of seven vegetarian dishes including broccoli and hazelnut bake (£6.50), and daily blackboard specials like lamb and apricot curry (£5.95), game pie or shoulder or rack of lamb with apricot and ginger sauce (£7.95), grilled dover sole (£8.95) and a fish of the day. All eating areas are no smoking. The neatly kept light and airy bar is prettily decorated with little country pictures, dried flowers on walls and beams, pastel flowery curtains, a little settee in one window, lots of uniform solid country-kitchen chairs and tables in polished pale wood, going nicely with the fawn carpet, and gentle lighting at night. Well kept Marstons Pedigree and Best on handpump, and wines of the month on a blackboard; piped music; relaxed friendly service. There's a surcharge of 2% on credit cards. *(Recommended Andy Petersen, M A Robinson, Dr R F Fletcher, Comus Elliott, Simon Morton, Becky and Karen, John Scarisbrick, Henry Barclay, David and Shelia, Sue Holland, David Webster)*

Free house ~ Licensees Anne and Graham Yates ~ Real ale ~ Meals and snacks 12-2; 6-10; not Sun ~ Restaurant ~ (01782) 392265 ~ Well behaved children welcome ~ Open 12-2.30, 6-11; 12-10.30 Sun; cl 25 and 26 Dec

LONGDON SK0714 Map 7

Swan With Two Necks ◖

Brook Road; just off A51 Rugeley—Stafford

On our inspection visit no less than five coal fires poured warmth into this neatly kept pub. Its long quarry-tiled bar is divided into three room areas, with low beams (very low at one end), a restrained decor, and house plants in the windows; there's a two-room carpeted restaurant. The pub fills quickly, people drawn mainly by the good food a straightforward menu, but all cooked freshly and really well. Fish in particular is outstanding: lunchtime sandwiches (from £1.50), soup (£1.60), lunchtime ploughman's (£4.10), seafood platter (£5), ham salad (£5.10), smoked salmon (£6.50), and daily specials such as very good beef, ale and venison casserole (£4.80), roast tenderloin of pork à l'orange (£5), seasonal poacher's casserole (£5) or wild trout, haddock and prawn thermidor (£5), and a very tasty big fresh cod (£5.50). Well kept Ansells, Bathams, Enville and Ind Coope Burton and Burton Bridge on handpump, with two interesting changing guest beers such as Harwoods Porter (from Guinness) and Hartington; decent wines, friendly helpful service. The garden, with an outdoor summer servery, has picnic tables and swings, and the village is attractive. *(Recommended by Eric J Locker, Nigel Hopkins, Jack and Philip Paxton, Colin Fisher)*

Bass ~ Licensees Jacques and Margaret Rogue ~ Real ale ~ Meals and snacks ~ Restaurant (01543) 490251 ~ Children over 10 welcome in restaurant ~ Open 12-2.30(3 Sat), 7-11

ONECOTE SK0555 Map 7

Jervis Arms ◖

B5053, off A523 Leek—Ashbourne

A resident duck and possibly ducklings live on the little brook that runs through the garden of this cheery bustling 17th-c pub. It's in a lovely setting down below the moors on the banks of the River Hamps (the licensee does warn that this isn't safe for children), with picnic tables under cocktail parasols on the ashtree-sheltered lawn, a little shrubby rockery, slides and swings, play trees, and a footbridge leading to the car park. Inside, the irregularly shaped cosy main bar has white planks over shiny black beams, window seats, wheelback chairs, two or three unusually low plush chairs, little hunting prints on the walls, and toby jugs and decorative plates on the high mantelpiece of its big stone fireplace. A similar but simpler inner room has a fruit machine. Without detracting from its character, families are particularly welcome here; there are two family rooms with high chairs, as well as a mother and baby room. Very well kept Bass, Marstons Pedigree, Ruddles County, Theakstons XB, Old Peculier and Mild, and Worthington on hand or electric pump, a fair range of malt whiskies, and Scrumpy Jack cider. Generous helpings of good bar food include soup (£1.20), filled rolls (£1.60), filled baked potatoes (from £3.75), scampi (£3.95), ploughman's (from £4.25), lasagne (£4.50), leek and mushroom crumble (£4.95) and 12oz sirloin (£8.25) and puddings including a selection of hot sponges or banana split (£1.95); usual children's meals (from £1.25); very friendly landlord and staff. Darts, dominoes, cribbage, fruit machine, and piped music. A spacious

barn behind the pub has been converted to self-catering accommodation.
(Recommended by Richard Lewis, David and Shelia, Sue Grossey, Eric Locker, Brian and Peggy Mansfield, John Scarisbrook, Mike and Wendy Proctor, Nigel Woolliscroft, Richard Lewis, Jack and Philip Paxton, Paul Robinshaw, DMT)

Free house ~ Licensees Robert and Jean Sawdon ~ Real ale ~ Meals and snacks (till 10pm) ~ (01538) 304206 ~ Children welcome away from bar ~ Open 12-2.30, 7(6 Sat)-11; 12-10.30 Sun; cl 25 and 26 Dec ~ Self-catering barn (with two bedrooms); £125 a week for the whole unit

SALT SJ9527 Map 7

Holly Bush

Village signposted off A51 S of Stone (and A518 NE of Stafford)

Dating back to the 14th c, the original part of this pretty thatched pub has a heavy beamed and planked ceiling (some of the beams attractively carved), a salt cupboard built in by the coal fire, and some nice old-fashioned touches – the antique pair of clothes brushes hanging by the door, attractive sporting prints and watercolours, the ancient pair of riding boots on the mantelpiece. Around the standing-room serving section several cosy areas spread off, including a modern back extension which tones in well; there are comfortable settees as well as more orthodox seats. Consistently good value food prepared as much as possible from fresh local produce includes lunchtime sandwiches (from £1.50) and filled baked potatoes (from £2.25), as well as soup (£1.60), prawn cocktail (£2.95), fried cod, gammon steak (£4.95), steak and ale pie or Greek lamb (£5.25), mixed grill (£5.75), chicken piri-piri (£5.95), with particularly good dishes of the day such as pork, leek and and stilton sausages or rabbit casserole with herb dumplings (£5.75), red sea bream char-grilled with lime and oregano sauce, grilled fillet of salmon with lemongrass and pink peppercorn sauce or lamb liver with onions in a rich meat sauce (£6.75) and rack of lamb with fresh rosemary (£7.50); puddings (£1.95). Well kept Bass, Burtonwood Bitter and Forshaws on handpump, pleasant attentive staff, maybe piped nostalgic pop music; darts, shove-ha'penny, cribbage, backgammon, jenga, fruit machine. The big back lawn, where they may have traditional jazz and a hog roast in summer, has rustic picnic tables, a rope swing and a busy dovecot; this is an attractive village. *(Recommended by Pat Bromley, David and Shelia, Kate and Harry Taylor, Catherine and Andrew Brian, Chris Raisin)*

Free house ~ Licensee Geoffrey Holland ~ Real ale ~ Meals and snacks (all day Sunday) ~ (01889) 508234 ~ Children welcome in eating area of bar till 8.30pm ~ Open 11.30-3, 6-11; 12-10.30 Sun; all day Sat in summer

SHRALEYBROOK SJ7850 Map 7

Rising Sun 🍺

3 miles from M6 junction 16; from A500 towards Stoke take first right turn signposted Alsager, Audley; in Audley turn right on the road still shown on many maps as A52, but now in fact a B, signposted Balterley, Nantwich; pub then signposted on left (at the T-junction look out for the Watneys Red Barrel)

Connoisseurs of own brew pubs will love the impressive range of beers produced in the brewery behind this lively easy-going pub. Their five appropriately named brews are: Dusk, Flare, Rising, Setting, Sunstroke, maybe a stronger brew called Total Eclipse, which are well kept alongside guests from Burton Bridge, Eldridge Pope, Tomintoul and Wadworths. As well as these, there are around 120 malts, 12 cognacs and 100 liqueurs; and foreign beers from Belgium, Germany, Singapore, Spain, and Australia. Simple bar food includes pizzas (from £3), cheeseburger (£4), 17 different vegetarian pot meals (£6.50) and beef casserole (£7); friendly service. The well worn, casual bar – at times full of a younger crowd – has shiny black panelling and beams and timbers in the ochre walls, red leatherette seats tucked into the timberwork and cosy alcoves, brasses and some netting, dim lighting, curtains made from beer towels sewn together, and a warm open fire. Dominoes, fruit machine and piped music; camping in two paddocks. *(Recommended by Sue Holland, Dave Webster, Richard Lewis, Wayne Brindle, Esther and John Sprinkle, Mike and Wendy Proctor, John Scarisbrook, John and Joan Nash, Peter and Lynn Brueton, Derek and Sylvia Stephenson, Mr and Mrs R J Grout, P Yearsley, Paul and Gail Betteley)*

Own brew ~ Licensee Mrs Gillian Holland ~ Real ale ~ Meals and snacks (till 10pm) ~ Restaurant ~ (01782) 720600 ~ Children welcome ~ Open 12-3, 6.30-11; 12-11(10.30 Sun) Fri and Sat

TUTBURY SK2028 Map 7

Olde Dog & Partridge

A444 N of Burton on Trent

Our foremost reason for including this civilised 15th-c dining pub is the popular carvery restaurant with roast of the day at £6.95 and prime sirloin of beef with big yorkshire pudding £7.95, as well as other usual pub favourites. Much of the extensive softly lit carvery is no smoking, and you need to arrive early to be sure of a table, especially in one of the snugger corners; a pianist plays each evening. There's a separate short bar menu including soup (£1.50), cheddar platter (£2.95), pork and crackling or beef bap (from £2.95) and venison sausage (£3.35); puddings are from the cold counter in the carvery (from £1.95). The stylish but pleasantly pubby bar has two warm turkey-carpeted rooms, one with red plush banquettes, brocaded stools, sporting pictures, stags' heads and a sizeable tapestry, the other with a plush-cushioned oak settle, an attractive built-in window seat, brocaded stools and a couple of Cecil Aldin hunting prints. Well kept Marstons Pedigree and a guest beer such as the strong Bass Brewing Museum 20th Anniversary Commemorative Ale from the oak bar counter, freshly squeezed fruit juices and decent wines (a choice of 125 or 175ml measures); friendly efficient service. The half timbered frontage is prettily hung with hanging baskets and the neat garden has white cast-iron seats and tables under cocktail parasols, with stone steps between its lawns, bedding plants, roses and trees. The pub is near Tutbury Castle, where Mary Queen of Scots was imprisoned on the orders of Elizabeth I. The quiet bedrooms are in a separate building across the drive. *(Recommended by Peter and Patricia Burton, O K Smyth, PGP, John and Doreen Crowder, William Cissna, Peter and Audrey Dowsett, Martin Bromfield, Bernadette Garner, Derek and Sylvia Stephenson, I D Irving, Clive Gilbert, Paul Robinshaw, Derek and Margaret Underwood)*

Free house ~ Licensee Mrs Yvette Martindale ~ Real ale ~ Lunchtime meals and snacks (not Sun) ~ Carvery ~ (01283) 813030 ~ Children welcome ~ Evening and Sunday lunch pianist ~ Open 11-3, 6-11; cl 25 Dec ~ Bedrooms: £55B/£72B

UTTOXETER SK0933 Map 7

Wellington ♀ ▮

High St, opposite cinema

This distinctive pub, which earns high marks for individuality, is one of those places that needs a sprinkling of regulars to show at its best (a weekday evening, say – it can seem rather stark on a quiet Saturday lunchtime). The superficialities are interesting enough, especially the fine collection of antique Waterloo prints in the left-hand room, and the pair of six-pounder cannon. But the landlord, complete with beard and pince-nez, has injected all sorts of intriguing touches that you might not notice at once. The yard behind, with its row of flower-planted lavatory bowls (the Waterloos), house not only a welsh mountain grey (called Copenhagen, after the Iron Duke's mount), and a shetland called Marengo, but also a remarkable sow called Napoleonne who is reputed to get through six pints of Bass a day. Then there's the *Church Times* and a Belgian newspaper alongside the rack of local and other papers, (Dr Miln doubles as an Orthodox Priest and his family hails from Bruges), with a dozen or so Belgian beers alongside the very well kept Bass on handpump. The Belgian connection shows too in the good bar food: rabbit casseroled in beer (£3.50) and mussels with chips (£4.95), as well as small baguette sandwiches (£1.50), soup (£1.70) and chilli or lasagne (£3.25), Belgian white chocolate ice cream or Belgian apple tart (£2), and you can also have food from the upstairs restaurant such as mussels and prawns in white wine (£3.80), eels in white wine, herb and cream sauce, pigeon breasts with blackcurrant, guinea fowl and rabbit stewed in gin or Flemish chicken stew (£6.50) and cassoulet or venison braised in port (£8.50). The house wines are good. Bar furnishings are simple and traditional, with coal fires; unobtrusive piped music (not always on) varies from Classic FM through 1960s country & western to Welsh male voice choirs. The handsome greyhound Josephine keeps a gentle eye on things from her protected seat, whilst General Pitcon, the house feline, is fond of a place by the fire; dominoes, cribbage and boules. Preserving a 17th-c tradition, this is still the home of the Uttoxeter Lunar Society. *(Recommended by Frank Cummins, Pat Bromley, Sue Holland, Dave Webster, Dave Irving, Ian C Hutchieson)*

Carlsberg-Tetley ~ Tenant Revd Dr Peter Miln ~ Real ale ~ Meals and snacks (11.30-2, 6.30-10; not Sun) ~ Restaurant ~ (01889) 562616 ~ Children welcome in restaurant ~ Open 10.30-11; 12-10.30 Sun ~ Bedrooms:£15/£30

WARSLOW SK0858 Map 7
Greyhound 🛏

B5053 S of Buxton

You may have spotted this plain but cheerily welcoming slated stone pub, in its now regular appearances on the television series *Peak Practice* – we can confirm the good taste of those particular doctors. This year they've decorated the cosy long beamed bar, which has cushioned oak antique settles (some quite elegant), a log fire, houseplants in the windows, and quietly restrained landscapes on the cream walls. Big helpings of good home-made bar food include sandwiches (from £1.80), filled baked potatoes (from £3.25), ploughman's (from £4.50), with blackboard specials like soup (£1.90), pâté, breaded butterfly prawns or chicken or sole goujons with a dip (£3), and chicken in leek and stilton sauce, beef in brandy cream sauce, smoked salmon, haddock and prawn mornay or vegetable balti (£5.50); good breakfasts. Well kept Marstons Pedigree and a guest beer such as Black Sheep, Charles Wells Bombardier, Everards Tiger, Jennings Cumberland or Timothy Taylors Landlord on handpump. Pool room, with darts, dominoes, cribbage, and fruit machine; piped classical music at lunchtimes. The simple bedrooms are comfortable and clean. There are picnic tables under ash trees in the side garden, with rustic seats out in front; handy for the Manifold Valley, Alton Towers and Dovedale. The licensees also run the Devonshire Arms in Hartington. *(Recommended by James Waller, Mike and Wendy Proctor, Derek and Sylvia Stephenson, Eric Locker, Dennis Stevens, Mrs C Blake, Paul Robinshaw)*

Free house ~ Licensees David and Dale Mullarkey ~ Real ale ~ Meals and snacks ~ (01298) 84249 ~ Children welcome in Tap room ~ Live bands Sat night ~ Open 12-2.30, 7-11; cl Mon and Tues lunchtime in winter exc bank holidays ~ Bedrooms: £16.50/£33

WETTON SK1055 Map 7
Olde Royal Oak 🍺

On the first Saturday in June they hold the world championship toe wrestling championships – it seems regulars are keen on the sport – at this wonderful old family run pub, and this year Black Bull (in nearby Fenny Bentley) started brewing a beer for them called Ankle Cracker. Also well kept Ruddles County and Rutland, Theakstons XB and a weekly guest beer on handpump, about 18 malt whiskies, and Addlestone's cider. There's a timelessly relaxed atmosphere in the older part of the building which has black beams – hung with golf clubs – supporting the white ceiling boards, small dining chairs sitting around rustic tables, a piano surrounded by old sheet music covers, an oak corner cupboard, and a log fire in the stone fireplace; this room extends into a more modern-feeling area with another fire which in turn leads to a carpeted sun lounge looking out on to the small garden. Hearty bar food includes sandwiches (from £1.40), filled baked potatoes (from £2.35), ploughman's with local cheeses (from £4.15), lasagne (£5.15), local trout (£5.20) and steak (£9.50), puddings like chocolate fudge cake or cheesecake (from £1.95), and children's meals (from £1.95). Darts, dominoes, cribbage, shove-ha'penny and piped music. Places like Wetton Mill and the Manifold Valley are nearby, and behind the pub is a croft suitable for caravans and tents. *(Recommended by Chris and Angela Wells, Gill and Maurice McMahon, Mike Gorton, Jack and Philip Paxton, Ron Gentry, Richard Houghton, Janet and Peter Race, Mike and Wendy Proctor, Paul Robinshaw)*

Free house ~ Licensee George Burgess ~ Real ale ~ Meals and snacks (not winter Sun evenings) ~ (01335) 310287 ~ Children welcome in family room ~ Open 11.30-3, 6.30-11; 12-2, 7-11 in winter ~ Bedrooms: /£33S

Lucky Dip

Besides the fully inspected pubs, you might like to try these Lucky Dips recommended to us and described by readers (if you do, please send us reports):

☆ **Abbots Bromley** [Mkt Pl; SK0724], *Crown*: Very friendly and welcoming, food freshly cooked to order inc vegetarian and even home-made chips, well kept Banks's Mild and Fullers London Pride, spotless much modernised lounge and bright public bar with games, efficient helpful staff; big mural of the pretty village's famous ancient Horn Dance (first Mon after first Sun in Sept); children welcome, good bedrooms *(Dennis D'Vigne, Kate and Robert Hodkinson, C Whittington, William Cissna, Eric Locker, LYM)*

☆ **Abbots Bromley** [Bagot St], *Royal Oak*: Wide choice of good imaginative food in clean, comfortable and attractive dining lounge (worth booking), well kept Marstons and a guest ale, good wine, efficient friendly service, open fire, interesting restaurant *(Nigel Hopkins, Tricia and Geoff Alderman)*

☆ **Abbots Bromley** [High St], *Coach & Horses*: Well run Tudor village pub, comfortable and attractive inside, with good helpings of well prepared food in refurbished beamed bar and restaurant, well kept Bass and related beers, friendly young staff; good value bedrooms *(SLC, J Curtis, G Hughes)*

Abbots Bromley [Bagot St], *Bagot Arms*: Welcoming 18th-c coaching inn recently comfortably refurbished in character; genial landlord, real fire in lounge, Marstons Pedigree and weekly Head Brewers Choice, popular home cooking from ploughman's through liver and bacon etc to steaks and a huge mixed grill, good Sun lunch, sensible prices *(David Austin, R C D Bastin)*

☆ **Alrewas** [High St (off A38); SK1714], *George & Dragon*: Three friendly low-beamed partly knocked together rooms with consistently well kept Marstons Pedigree, good value generous bar food (not Sun) inc children's dishes, efficient staff, attractive paintings; piped music; pleasant partly covered garden with good play area, children welcome in eating area; opens 5 weekdays *(Graham Richardson, LYM)*

☆ **Alton** [SK0742], *Talbot*: Welcoming stone-built pub, small and cosy, with well kept beer, good choice of varied food, consistently friendly service *(Mike and Wendy Proctor)*

Anslow [59 Hopley Rd; SK2125], *Burnt Gate*: Village local expanding its horizons under new licensee, attractive lounge, good fresh home-made food, Ind Coope Burton and Marstons Pedigree *(Philip Jordan)*

Appleby Parva [A444, under a mile from M42 junction 11; SK3109], *Appleby*: Good if hotelish family pub, well run and open all day; good value food in restaurant and spacious lounge (coach parties sometimes); motel bedrooms, six suited to disabled; handy for Twycross Zoo *(Graham Richardson, SB)*

☆ **Ashley** [signposted from A53 NE of Market Drayton; SJ7636], *Peel Arms*: Immaculate plush local with olde-worlde touches such as warming old kitchen range, friendly licensees, well kept Marstons; lovely big garden with swings *(Sue Holland, Dave Webster, Nigel Woolliscroft)*

Audley [Bignall End; SJ7951], *Plough*: Popular real ale pub, well kept Banks's, Camerons Strongarm, Marstons Pedigree, Titanic Stout and guest beers - enthusiastic landlord listens to what customers want when choosing them; good range of food (not Sun evening) in dining area off lounge, lots of flowers outside *(Richard Lewis)*; [Nantwich Rd], *Potters Lodge*: Relaxing and comfortable, with friendly staff, well kept Whitbreads-related ales inc a seasonal special, wide choice of generous food inc children's, no-smoking areas; children very welcome, play area, open all day *(Richard Lewis)*

Burton on Trent [High St; SK2423], *Blue Posts*: Big open-plan showpiece Bass pub nr brewery (their brewing museum is well worth a visit), alcoves, separate dining area, staff friendly and efficient even when busy; good choice of reasonably priced food, well kept Bass, Stone, Worthington Bitter and Best *(Richard Lewis)*; [Cross St], *Coopers Tavern*:

Fine example of highly traditional back tap room with notably well kept Bass, Hardys & Hansons Classic, Best and Mild and Marstons Pedigree straight from imposing row of casks (no serving counter), cheap and nourishing lunchtime hot filled cobs, pie and chips and so forth, comfortable front lounge, very friendly staff *(Richard Lewis, LYM);* [27 Victoria St], *Duke of York:* Character locals' bar, smart back lounge, tables outside; bar food lunchtime and early evening, well kept Marstons Pedigree, Owd Rodger and Best; open all day *(Richard Lewis);* [Station St], *Roebuck:* Cosy local opp Ind Coope brewery with lots of well kept Tetleys-related ales (inc recherché ones such as Devils Kiss real ginger beer) and interesting changing guests such as Ridleys Witchfinder Porter, good value food, friendly staff; piped music, open all day weekdays; decent bedrooms *(Richard Lewis);* [Station St], *Station:* Hotel with good popular bar and lounge, good reasonably priced food, friendly staff, well kept Tetleys-related ales; bedrooms *(Richard Lewis)*

Butt Lane [W outskirts of Kidsgrove; SJ8254], *Crown:* Good wide range of reasonably priced food, staff friendly and obliging *(Mike and Wendy Proctor)*

☆ **Cauldon Lowe** [Waterhouses; A52 Stoke—Ashbourne; SK0748], *Cross:* Unsmart but attractive and friendly, with good range of well kept beers and of decent food inc vegetarian, reasonable prices, scenic setting *(Mike and Wendy Proctor, JP, PP)*

☆ **Cheddleton** [Basford Bridge Lane, off A520; SJ9651], *Boat:* Consistently good value and cheerful local nr canal, neat long bar, low plank ceilings, particularly well kept Marstons and other ales, good cheap waitress-served food, interesting pictures, attractive fireplace in airy extension; handy for North Staffs Steam Railway Museum; children welcome, fairy-lit tables outside *(Bill Sykes, Mike and Wendy Proctor, JP, PP, D G Clarke, LYM)*

☆ **Consall** [Consallforge; best approach from Nature Pk, off A522 - OS Sheet 118 map ref 000491; SJ9748], *Black Lion:* Pleasant new landlady in unusually placed country tavern, tucked away in rustic old-fashioned canalside settlement; smartened up but still traditional, with good generous cheap food, good coal fire, well kept Marstons Bitter and Pedigree, Titanic and other guest beers such as Morlands Old Speckled Hen, traditional games, piped music; children (but not muddy boots) welcome; busy weekends, good walking area *(Bill Sykes, Mike and Wendy Proctor, LYM)*

☆ **Compmere End** [W of Eccleshall; SJ8029], *Star:* Classic simple two-room country local in nice spot overlooking mere, Bass and guest ale, good home-made food from sandwiches up inc fine puddings, very friendly service, picnic tables in beautiful back garden full of trees and shrubs; children welcome *(Nigel Woolliscroft)*

Coven [off A449 Stafford—Wolverhampton; SJ9006], *Rainbow:* Pretty village setting, good

cheap food promptly served, friendly service, well kept Ansells; popular at lunchtimes *(Dave Braisted)*

☆ **Dovedale** [Thorpe—Ilam rd; Ilam signposted off A52, Thorpe off A515, NW of Ashbourne; SK1452], *Izaak Walton:* Refreshingly informal for sizeable hotel, relaxing low-beamed bar, some distinctive antique oak settles and chairs, good log fire in massive central stone chimney; Ind Coope Burton on handpump, bar food and restaurant, morning coffee and afternoon tea; very tranquil spot - seats on lawn by sheep pastures, superb views; bedrooms comfortable *(Mike and Wendy Proctor, JP, PP, Gwen and Peter Andrews, LYM)*

☆ **Eccleshall** [Castle St; SJ8329], *St George:* Comfortable beamed bar with old prints and open fire, good generous home-cooked food in attractive bistro, good wines, interesting guest beers and, brewed here by friendly landlord, good Slaters Bitter and Premium; comfortable individually decorated bedrooms *(Richard Lewis, Sue Holland, Dave Webster)* **Eccleshall** *Royal Oak:* Ancient black and white local with friendly staff and good value meals; very popular and lively *(Richard Lewis, Sue Holland, Dave Webster)*

☆ nr **Endon** [Denford, some way E; SJ9553], *Holly Bush:* Friendly staff, wide range of well kept ale, good value food from sandwiches up; nice rural position on Caldon Canal, very busy in summer *(M F Thomas, Mr and Mrs Jones, Mike and Wendy Proctor)* **Enville** [A458 W of Stourbridge; SO8286], *Cat:* Mainly 17th c, with four bar areas, cheerful fire, very wide choice of ales inc one brewed in the village, mulled wine, decent standard food with unusual specials; has been cl Sun, popular with walkers - on Staffordshire Way *(Martin and Karen Wake, Dave Braisted)*

☆ **Etruria** [Hanley rd (off A53 opp Festival site); SJ8647], *Plough:* Small busy two-room pub, recently refurbished, with nice atmosphere and decor, coal fire, five well kept Robinsons beers inc Old Tom and Frederics, friendly licensees, wide choice of food served till late esp steaks and hot sandwiches, will do anything on request; busy lunchtime and weekends *(John Scarisbrick, Graham LaCourt, Mike and Wendy Proctor, Richard Lewis, Sue Holland, Dave Webster)*

☆ **Fradley** [Fradley Park signed off A38 Burton—Lichfield, OS Sheet 128 map ref 140140; SK1414], *Swan:* Cheery pub in particularly good canalside spot, wide choice of quickly served food inc good value Sun lunch and tempting puddings, well kept Tetleys-related ales inc Mild, traditional public bar and quieter plusher lounge and lower vaulted back bar (where children allowed), lots of malt whiskies, real fire, cribbage, dominoes, piped music; waterside tables, good canal walks *(Paul Robinshaw, Colin Fisher, Dave Braisted, Mrs P J Pearce, M Joyner, G P Kernan, LYM)* **Gnosall** [SJ8221], *Boat:* Charming canalside pub with well kept ales inc Marstons Pedigree in first-floor bar, small waterside seating area (*Anon*)

☆ Grindon [signed off B5033 N of A523; SK0854], *Cavalier*: 16th-c character pub with well kept Wards Best, decent straightforward food, pleasant service; smallish front bar with larger room behind and separate games room, good mix of locals and visitors; pleasant informal garden, attractive countryside; often closed - sure to be open Fri night, weekends and bank hol Mons (*Nigel Woolliscroft, Jack Morley, JP, PP, LYM*)

Hanbury [OS Sheet 128 map ref 174278; SK1727], *Cock*: Welcoming basic village local, straightforward food, lovely walks inc poignant one to the vast crater of the 1944 Fauld bomb dump explosion (which wrecked the pub and everything else in this area) (*Dr and Mrs C D E Morris*)

☆ Hanley [65 Lichfield St; SJ8747], *Coachmakers Arms*: Character unspoilt friendly town pub, three small rooms and drinking corridor, particularly well kept Bass and M&B Mild, skittles (*Sue Holland, Dave Webster, Nigel Woolliscroft*)

Hanley [Tontine St], *Tontine Alehouse*: Good generous lunchtime food, well kept Tetleys and Marstons Pedigree (*Nigel Woolliscroft, Sue Holland, Dave Webster*)

Hartshill [296 Hartshill Rd (A52); SJ8545], *Jolly Potters*: Real unspoilt local, well kept Bass and M&B Mild, simple snacks, four little rooms off a drinking corridor (*Sue Holland, Dave Webster, Nigel Woolliscroft*)

☆ Hednesford [Mount St; SJ9913], *West Cannock*: Wide choice of well kept reasonably priced beers and good value food in cosy Victorian-style pub, very friendly staff, generous OAP offers Sat and Mon lunchtime, good value Sun lunch inc vegetarian choice; tables outside (*John and Chris Simpson, Steve Owen, Stephen Clough*)

Hednesford [Eskrett St, off Market St], *Mrs O'Rourkes Hen House*: One of the 'Little' pubs chain, ceiling dripping with bric-a-brac, sawdust on floor; hums with life, esp Mon (Irish entertainment); hefty Desperate Dan cow pie, interesting Lumphammer ale (*Steve Owen, David and Shelia*)

☆ High Offley [towards High Lea - Bridge 42, Shrops Union Canal; SJ7826], *Anchor*: Unspoilt homely canal pub in same family for over a century, two simple homely rooms, well kept Marstons Pedigree and Owd Rodger and Wadworths 6X tapped in cellar, Weston's farm ciders, sandwiches; children welcome, seats outside, cl Mon-Weds winter; caravan/campsite (*Nigel Woolliscroft*)

Hill Chorlton [Stone Rd (A51); SJ7939], *Slaters*: Comfortable beamed bar, good standard bar food from sandwiches up inc vegetarian and Sun roasts, well kept Banks's, Boddingtons and Marstons Pedigree, decent wines, upstairs restaurant, children's room; tables out in attractive garden, animals in barn; bedrooms (*Nigel Woolliscroft, LYM*)

☆ Hoar Cross [off A515 Yoxall—Sudbury; SK1323], *Meynell Ingram Arms*: Welcoming traditional country pub, log fire in each bar,

good varied reasonably priced food inc popular Sun lunch, well kept Boddingtons and Marstons Pedigree, quick cheerful service, relaxing atmosphere - and the dogs add a certain something (*Dorothee and Dennis Glover, Eric Locker, Jackie Sherrington, Derek and Margaret Underwood*)

☆ Huddlesford [off A38 2 miles E of Lichfield - OS Sheet 139 map ref 152097; SK1509], *Plough*: Pleasant old beamed pub recently refurbished and extended without losing its character, wide choice of good value generous food in four eating areas, well kept Ansells, Greenalls Original and Worthington, good range of wines, friendly efficient staff, games area; attractive hanging baskets, tables out by canal (*M and J Back, Gareth Brentnall, Dorothee and Dennis Glover, Colin Fisher, David R Shillitoe*)

Hulme End [SK1059], *Manifold Valley*: Welcoming country pub nr river, spacious lounge bar with open fire, well kept Wards and generous popular food; Sun lunch in separate dining room; provision for children (*Dennis Stevens, JP, PP, BB*)

Ipstones [B5053; village signposted from A52 and from A523; SK0249], *Red Lion*: Pleasant and comfortable pub overlooking valley, recently reopened by friendly and helpful young family, friendly locals, well kept beer, generous food (*Esther and John Sprinkle, LYM*)

Ivetsey Bank [A5 Telford—Cannock, 5 miles from M6 junction 12; SJ8311], *Bradford Arms*: Well kept Banks's ales, good reasonably priced food esp local steaks, wide vegetarian choice, children's menu, old car prints, interesting specialist magazines, very friendly staff, disabled access; big garden with play area and animals (maybe potted plants for sale in car park); caravan/campsite (*Paul Lasance, Dave Braisted*)

Keele [A525 W of Newcastle under Lyme; SJ8045], *Sneyd Arms*: Solid 19th-c stone building, formerly local court; Tetleys-related ales, wide choice of lunchtime food inc fish, friendly staff, good landlord; cribbage, pool, popular with students and conference delegates (*Richard Lewis*)

Kings Bromley [Manor Rd; SK1216], *Royal Oak*: Good choice of good value food presented generous food inc vegetarian, welcoming attentive setvice, immaculate premises (*Mrs J M Wilson, Geoffrey and Irene Lindley*)

Knighton [B5415 Woore—Mkt Drayton; SJ7240], *White Lion*: Good food with French influence beautifully presented in cosy dining area, conservatory and (not Mon or Sun evening) restaurant; also big bar with well kept Marstons and guests, large adventure playground (*Gail Kendall, Kent Miller, Nigel Woolliscroft, SLC*)

☆ Leek [St Edwards St; SJ9856], *Swan*: Comfortable old three-room pub with reasonably priced lunchtime food, pleasant helpful staff, no-smoking lounge, well kept Bass and guest ales, occasional beer festivals, lots of malt whiskies, choice of coffees; folk club, seats in courtyard *(Richard Houghton, John Scarisbrick, Sue Holland, Dave Webster, Mike and Wendy Proctor)*

Leek [St Edward St], *Wilkes Head*: More character than comfort, but worth knowing for its well kept Whim Magic Mushroom Mild, Hartington and Old Izaak, and two guest beers *(John Scarisbrick, Sue Holland, Dave Webster)*

nr Leek [Abbey Green; Meerbrook rd, off A523 N; SJ9657], *Abbey*: Attractive ex-farmhouse, dated 1702, large choice of reasonably priced food, very friendly service, well kept Bass and interesting guest beer; spacious front terrace and play area, nice surroundings *(RTM, JCM)*

☆ Lichfield [Market St; SK1109], *Scales*: Cosy traditional oak-panelled bar with wooden flooring, screens, imitation gas lights, sepia photographs of old Lichfield; welcoming service, reasonably priced food, well kept Bass, related ales and interesting guest beers, darts; suntrap back courtyard *(Richard Lewis, LYM)*

☆ Lichfield [Tamworth St], *Pig & Truffle*: Nicely decorated panelled dining pub, friendly and enthusiastic landlady, good value well thought out menu (with a pig theme), well kept ales, good coffee, seats in sunny back yard; piped music; no food Fri-Sun evenings when more a younger person's preserve *(Paul and Ursula Randall, Gary Nicholls)*

Lichfield [10 Conduit St, opp central mkt], *Earl of Lichfield Arms*: Popular, welcoming and comfortable town pub, well kept Marstons and Banks's Mild, good range of simple food, quick friendly service; piped music *(DAV, Richard Lewis)*; [Bird St], *Kings Head*: Part 17th c, traditional beamed front rooms, old prints etc, good lunchtime bar food, well kept Marstons Pedigree, Best and Burton Strong, Bathams Dark Mild, conservatory, tables in courtyard; games machines and pool, popular with young people evenings *(Richard Lewis, Barry Grinsell, Gary Nicholls)*; [14 Queen St], *Queens Head*: Busy open-plan pub with lots of comfortable seating, nice decor, friendly staff, short but interesting range of daily specials and vast choice of unusual cheeses with sour-dough bread or muffins, huge helpings (doggy bags provided) at very reasonable prices, good children's menu; well kept ales such as Adnams Best, Fullers London Pride, Marstons Pedigree, Timothy Taylors Landlord and Charles Wells Fargo *(Dr and Mrs M Beale, Richard Lewis, Barry Grinsell)*

☆ Little Bridgeford [nr M6 junction 14; turn right off A5013 at Little Bridgeford; SJ8727], *Worston Mill*: Very popular family dining pub, spacious and welcoming, in attractively converted 1814 watermill, wheel and gear still preserved, ducks on millpond and millstream in attractive garden with adventure playground and nature trail (but nr main rly line), conservatory; lots of oak and leather, well kept Marstons Pedigree and other ales, good value wine, wide choice of reasonably priced good food, polite efficient staff,

children welcome *(Julian Holland, M Joyner, LYM)*

Milwich [Smallrice; B5027 towards Stone; SJ9532], *Red Lion*: Bar at end of farmhouse, Bass tapped from the cask, friendly welcome, log fire *(JP, PP, Nigel Woolliscroft)*

☆ Newborough [OS Sheet 128 map ref 136255; SK1325], *Red Lion*: Unpretentious pub back on form under new licensees, well kept Marstons Pedigree and good choice of wines and spirits in comfortable extended lounge/dining room, good value traditional food, good service, public bar; facing church in quiet village *(Dr and Mrs C D E Morris, LYM)*

☆ Newcastle under Lyme [High St; SJ8445], *Golden Lion*: Good value simple home cooking weekdays in comfortably modernised but old-fashioned unpretentious pub with well kept Bass; handy for open market, haven for rugby players Fri/Sat *(Tony Kemp, Rachel Weston, Sue Holland, Dave Webster, Nigel Woolliscroft)*

Newcastle under Lyme [Liverpool Rd], *Holy Inadequate*: Rock/motorcyclists' pub with unusual murals and decor - Triumph Bonneville on wall; very friendly licensees, good quiz nights, good outside area; no food *(Nigel Woolliscroft)*; [Etruria Rd], *New Victoria*: Theatre bar worth visiting even on non-performance nights, good choice of well kept ales inc uncommon guest beers, nice atmosphere, bar snacks *(Mike and Wendy Proctor, Nigel Woolliscroft)*; [Bridge St], *Old Brown Jug*: Good home-made lunchtime food, good range of well kept Marstons, live music Thurs *(Nigel Woolliscroft)*

Norbury Junction [off A519 Eccleshall—Newport via Norbury; SJ7922], *Junction*: Popular canalside pub, wide range of good reasonably priced home-cooked bar food, good value carvery, well kept beer, friendly efficient service *(SLC)*

☆ Penkhull [Manor Court St; SJ8644], *Greyhound*: Relaxed traditional two-room pub in hilltop 'village', particularly good value filling snacks, well kept Marstons Pedigree and Tetleys; children in eating area, picnic tables on back terrace *(Mike and Wendy Proctor, LYM)*

Penkhull, *Marquis of Granby*: Well kept Marstons in popular village local *(Nigel Woolliscroft)*

☆ Penkridge [Market Pl - handy for M6 junctions 12/13; SJ9214], *Star*: Open-plan but friendly, with pleasant helpful licensees, lots of black beams and button-back red plush, good value generous lunchtime food (extended hours Weds and Sat) with gingham tablecloths in dining area, well kept cheap Banks's and guest ales; piped music; open all day, barbecues *(John and Chris Simpson, C H and P Stride, BB)*

☆ Rolleston on Dove [Church Rd; SK2427], *Spread Eagle*: Attractive old village inn pub with good range of well kept Bass-related ales, good value food all day, small restaurant with fresh fish, popular Sunday carvery; pleasant garden, nice village *(Stephen and*

Jane Asbury, B M Eldridge)

Rushton Spencer [Congleton Rd; off A523 Leek—Macclesfield at Ryecroft Gate; SJ9462], *Crown*: Friendly simple local in attractive scenery, with busy front snug, bigger back lounge, games room, S&N ales, big good value Sun lunch; shame about the piped music *(Clare Wilson, BB)*; [A523], *Royal Oak*: Well kept Burtonwood, bar food, lots of rally photographs *(SLC)*

Sandon [A518/B5066; SJ9429], *Dog & Doublet*: Good straightforward food; beware of hens in the car park *(Dave Braisted)*

☆ **Sandonbank** [SJ9428], *Seven Stars*: Useful dining pub with weekend carvery, well kept Burtonwood, several cosy corners, two big open fires, houseplants; two food tables (winter only), piped music; restaurant, children welcome, seats out behind *(Catherine and Martin Snelling, David and Shelia, Paul and Gail Betteley, LYM)*

Saverley Green [Sandon Rd; Cresswell—Hilderstone rd, off A50 Stoke—Uttoxeter; SJ9638], *Hunter*: Old-fashioned Burtonwood pub cluttered with bric-a-brac, inc collection of model lorries and buses; tiled floor, wooden benches *(Dave Braisted)*

Shebden [N of Newport, nr Harpur Adams Ag Coll; SJ7626], *Wharf*: Wide choice of good value simple food, guest beers such as Eldridge Pope Royal Oak and Morlands Old Speckled Hen, bar billiards, games machines; children welcome, big garden and playground, nr canal *(Nigel Woolliscroft)*

Shenstone [A5127 Lichfield—Sutton Coldfield; SK1004], *Black Bull*: Pleasant atmosphere in roomily refurbished Bass pub with flagstones, bare bricks, panelling, old pine tables and mixed chairs, good value food inc fish and chips, good welcoming food service even when busy, well kept Bass, M&B Brew XI and Highgate Dark; children welcome *(Basil Minson)*; [Main St], *Railway*: Former butcher's shop and chapel, now airy lounge with leather chesterfields, good range of nicely cooked lunchtime food, well kept Marstons ales, friendly efficient staff; barbecue and picnic tables in garden *(Richard Lewis, Gary Nicholls)*

☆ **Stafford** [turn right at main entrance to station, 100 yards down], *Stafford Arms*: Busy but friendly and relaxing real ale pub with well kept Titanic Best, Capt Smiths, Premium, White Star, Lifeboat and Stout and always interesting changing small-brewery guests, farm cider, cheap simple food (all day weekdays; not Sat evening or Sun), chatty staff, wide range of customers (no under-21s); bar billiards, skittle alley; barbecues and live bands during summer beer festivals; can be very busy *(Richard Lewis, John and Chris Simpson, Sue Holland, Dave Webster)*

☆ **Stafford** [A34/A449 central roundabout, take Access Only rd past service stn], *Malt & Hops*: Rambling comfortable beamed pub with several well kept ales inc Exmoor Gold, big helpings of lunchtime food, low prices, good friendly service, provision for children; evenings esp Thurs-Sat becomes lively young

person's place *(Richard Lewis, LYM)*

Stoke on Trent [Hill St; SJ8745], *Staff of Life*: Character Bass city local, welcoming even when packed, unchanging layout of three rooms and small drinking corridor; well kept ales such as GPG95 *(Sue Holland, Dave Webster, Andy, Pete Baker)*; [Shelton], *Tap & Spile*: Great beers; done out like a pub museum *(Nigel Woolliscroft)*; [Hough Hill, Brown Edge; SJ9053], *Varsovia Lodge*: Attractively decorated stone-built inn, beautiful garden, good home-made bar food inc lovely veg, marvellous puddings *(R McGourlay)*; [Newport Lane; off Newcastle St, Middleport], *White Swan*: Welcoming local with two open-plan rooms, open fires, bar food, good range of Vaux/Wards beers; open all day weekdays, darts, cribbage and pool *(Richard Lewis)*

☆ **Stone** [21 Stafford St (A520); SJ9034], *Star*: Welcoming 18th-c canalside pub with canal photographs and exposed joists in intimate public bar, snug lounge and pleasant family room; well kept Banks's, Camerons and Marstons, good value food inc children's (not Sun evening), open fire, nearby moorings; open all day Apr-Oct *(Paul Robinshaw, Colin Buckle, Tony Hobden, LYM)*

Stone [A34 outside], *Wayfarer*: Roadhouse-style pub with Bass beers and reasonable carvery *(Dave Braisted)*

Swindon [in village itself; SO8690], *Old Bush*: Rambling pub with cheap well kept Banks's Bitter, cheap generous snacks; confusingly there's another Old Bush out by the waterworks - also a decent pub, but Greenalls, with good pizzas *(Dave Braisted)*

☆ **Tatenhill** [off A38 W of Burton via A5121, then signed; SK2021], *Horseshoe*: Pleasant garden view from back family area, tiled-floor civilised bar, snug side area with woodburner, cosy partly no-smoking two-level restaurant; quickly served good value bar food (all day Sat) from sandwiches to steaks inc vegetarian and children's, well kept Marstons Pedigree and a guest beer; good play area; the tenant who made this a main entry has left and the pub, friendly as ever, is now under brewery management *(Dennis Glover, T and G Alderman, Michael and Hazel Lyons, Andrew Hodges, LYM; more reports on new regime please)*

Upper Hulme [A53 Leek—Buxton; SK0161], *Winking Man*: Welcoming modern building with well kept Bass-related beers, good range of generous reasonably priced food *(Richard Houghton)*

Uttoxeter [SK0933], *White Hart*: Old pub with decent sandwiches and well kept Ind Coope Burton *(M A Robinson)*

☆ **Waterhouses** [SK0850], *George*: Large three-room dining pub, good sensibly priced generous food from sandwiches up inc children's, Marstons ales, play area; particularly friendly, if not full of character; handy for Manifold cycle trail, two bike hire places *(John Scarisbrick, Chris Walling)*

Waterhouses, *Olde Crown*: Friendly landlord, good value standard food, good beer;

bedrooms *(Paul Robinshaw)*

☆ **Weston** [The Green, off A518; SJ9726], *Woolpack*: Well modernised, open-plan but separate areas with cosy corners, reasonably priced good fresh food, extended dining room, well kept Marstons and guest ales, smart but pleasant staff, antique furniture inc high-backed settle, polished brass, lovely relaxed, secluded and well tended garden *(Peter and Jenny Quine)*

Wheaton Aston [Canalside, Tavern Br; SJ8412], *Hartley Arms*: Pleasant setting just above canal, reasonably modernised, decent food, Banks's beers; seats outside *(Dave Braisted, SLC)*

☆ **Whitmore** [3 miles from M6 junction 15 - A53 towards Mkt Drayton; SJ8141], *Mainwaring Arms*: Popular old place of great character, rambling interconnected oak-beamed rooms, stone walls, four open fires, antique settles among more modern seats; well kept Bass, Boddingtons, Marstons Pedigree, wide range of foreign bottled beers and ciders, friendly service, seats outside, children in eating area, no piped music; open all day Fri/Sat, picturesque village *(D P and M E Cartwright, Richard Gibbs, Anthony Birchall, Nigel Woolliscroft, LYM)*

Whittington [A51 SE of Lichfield; SK1608], *Whittington Arms*: Brewers Fayre pub keeping some individuality, food inc good vegetarian special *(Dave Braisted)*

Wilnecote [91 Watling St; SK2201], *Globe*: Traditional 1950s-style front bar with wall benches and darts, back lounge, very friendly licensee; worth knowing for particularly well kept Marstons Pedigree, Banks's Mild and a changing Marstons ale; piped music, no food; garden behind *(Richard Lewis, John Howell)*; [Watling St], *Queens Head*: Relaxing and chatty old pub, tastefully refurbished, lots of brickwork and beams, cosy seating; good choice of food, well kept Bass, Brew XI, M&B Butlers and Mild *(Richard Lewis)*

☆ **Wombourne** [High St, just off A449; SO8792], *Vine*: Recently tastefully modernised and extended, more emphasis on very popular good value straightforward bar food and inventive more pricey meals, huge helpings; well kept Bass and a guest such as Morlands Old Speckled Hen, unobtrusive piped music *(G Kernan, Paul and Sue Merrick)*

☆ **Wrinehill** [Den Lane; pub signed just off A531 Newcastle—Nantwich; SJ7547], *Crown*: Well kept Marstons Pedigree and Head Brewers Choice, Banks's Mild and several guests such as Timothy Taylors Landlord, wide choice of good generous food inc vegetarian, in busy but cosy neatly refurbished beamed pub with friendly staff, plush seats but olde-worlde feel, interesting pictures, two log fires, well reproduced pop music; children allowed lunchtime, early evening; cl weekday lunchtimes exc bank hols; lovely floral displays in summer *(Richard Lewis, LYM)*

☆ **Yoxall** [Main St; SK1319], *Crown*: Relaxed atmosphere, good value fresh tasty food, well kept Marstons Pedigree, quick friendly service, cosy refurbished lounge with log-effect gas fire, separate raised dining room; children welcome lunchtime *(Addie and Irene Henry)*

If you enjoy your visit to a pub, please tell the publican. They work extraordinarily long hours, and when people show their appreciation it makes it all seem worth while.

Suffolk

A fine crop of new entries here consists of the cosy and civilised old Six Bells at Bardwell (very good food and wines), the Oyster at Butley (an unchanging very friendly country pub), the Froize at Chillesford (excellent food and drink – one of our most rewarding finds of the year), the prettily placed Crown at Hartest (a popular dining pub), the quaint and very enjoyable little Star at Lidgate (very good interesting food), the Ramsholt Arms in its lovely quiet riverside position, the interesting and unspoilt Crown at Snape (very good food and wines), the well refurbished Angel at Wangford (bargain food, a nice place to stay in) and the unpretentious and welcoming White Horse at Westleton (good value food here too). Among old favourites, pubs on particularly good form these days include the bustling and welcoming Queens Head at Blyford (huge helpings of popular food), the pleasantly well worn Butt & Oyster above the barge base near Chelmondiston, the very well run Ship at Dunwich (good fresh fish and chips), the pleasantly old-fashioned Victoria at Earl Soham, the Crown at Great Glemham (a fine all-rounder), the Beehive at Horringer (excellent food, and gains a Wine Award this year), the smart yet relaxed Red Lion at Icklingham (mainly enjoyed for its food, especially fish) and its stable-mate the Pykkerel at Ixworth, the Angel at Lavenham (an excellent all-rounder, adored by readers – our choice as Suffolk Dining Pub of the Year), the calm old Bull at Long Melford, the Crown at Southwold (another tremendous favourite among readers, with perfect beers, super wines, enjoyable food and quite excellent staff), and the civilised and very foody Angel at Stoke by Nayland. The new landlady at the Bell at Walberswick is turning out extremely well. In the Lucky Dip section at the end of the chapter, pubs currently notching up warm reports include the Ship at Blaxhall, White Hart at Blythburgh, Crown at Framlingham, Kings Arms at Haughley, Black Tiles at Martlesham and White Horse at Risby; we have inspected all of these and give them a firm thumbs-up – as we have for the Peacock at Chelsworth, but a new regime taking over just before we go to press leaves us asking for more reports. There's a good choice of pubs in Bury – and an excellent one in Southwold, home of the brewers Adnams. Drinks prices in the county are close to the national average – and remarkably uniform from pub to pub, with much less variation than we find in most places. Besides Adnams, beers to look out for in the area include the local Nethergate and Old Chimneys; the much bigger regional brewer Greene King is doing interesting seasonal ales now, always well worth a try, and Tolly's new Cobbolds IPA is most enjoyable.

Post Office address codings confusingly give the impression that some pubs
are in Suffolk when they're really in Norfolk or Cambridgeshire (which is
where we list them).

ALDEBURGH TM4656 Map 5

Cross Keys 🍺

Crabbe Street

The two communicating rooms in this attractive old pub have a friendly, unchanging atmosphere and a good mix of customers, and are divided by a sturdy central chimney with woodburning stoves on either side. It does get very smoky at times. Very well kept Adnams Bitter, Broadside, and Mild on handpump, and good bar food such as soup (£2.50), open sandwiches (from £3), ploughman's (£4.25), salads (from £4.75), brie and broccoli or fish pies (£6.25), Italian marinated hock of pork or chicken korma (£7.25), and 10oz rump steak (£8.75), seafood platter (£11.75), daily specials, and puddings like jam roly poly (£2.20); fruit machine. A courtyard at the back opens directly on to the promenade and shingle beach, and there are wooden seats and tables out here to take in the view; the hanging baskets are colourful in summer. *(Recommended by Geoffrey and Brenda Wilson, N S Smith, Gwen and Peter Andrews, John Waller, June and Perry Dann, Stuart Earle, Colin McKerrow)*

Adnams ~ Tenant Graham Prior ~ Real ale ~ Meals and snacks (not winter Sun evenings) ~ (01728) 452637 ~ Children in eating area of bar ~ Open 11-11; 11-3, 5.30-11 in winter; 11-11 July/Aug

BARDWELL TL9473 Map 5

Six Bells ♀

Village signposted off A143 NE of Bury; keep straight through village, then fork right into Daveys Lane off top green

The cosy bar of this quietly placed 16th-c pub has a comfortable mix of easy chairs and settees alongside other seats under its low heavy beams; its timbered walls have an attractive collection of decorative china, black and white etchings and old fashion plates, and the big fireplace has a coal-effect fire. On one side is a snug dining room with pine tables, on the other a bigger restaurant with a new conservatory beyond. A wide range of good food includes ploughman's, soup such as tomato and orange (£2.55), black pudding with char-grilled potato and caramelised apple with red onion marmalade (£3.95 starter, £6.50 main course), mushrooms in creamy garlic sauce with toasted foccacia bread (£4.25 starter, £6.50 main course), pork sausages, mash and onion gravy or prawn and pesto pasta (£4.95), chicken and bacon mousseline in filo pastry with tomato sauce or steak and kidney casserole with herb dumplings (£6.95), fillet of smoked haddock on a potato pancake (£7.95), halibut on potatoes, artichoke hearts and bacon with a lemon and parsley dressing (£9.95), grilled dover sole (£12.50), and puddings like bread and butter pudding with proper custard (from £3). Polite service; Adnams Best, John Smiths, and a summer guest beer such as Theakstons on handpump; a good choice of wines including mulled wine in winter; maybe unobtrusive piped classical music. There are picnic tables under cocktail parasols on a small front gravel terrace, and plastic tables on the back lawn, with a small wendy house and lots of young trees. We have not yet had reports on the bedrooms, which are in the converted barn and stables (and were used in a few episodes of *Dad's Army*), but would expect them to be comfortable. *(Recommended by M J Morgan, Gwen and Peter Andrews, Col A H N Reade)*

Free house ~ Licensees Carol and Richard Salmon ~ Real ale ~ Meals and snacks ~ Restaurant ~ (01359) 250820 ~ Children welcome away from bar ~ Open 12-2.30, 7(6.45 Fri/Sat)-10.30(11 Fri/Sat); closed 25-26 Dec ~ Bedrooms: £40S/£55S

BILDESTON TL9949 Map 5

Crown

104 High St (B1115 SW of Stowmarket)

It's quite a surprise to find such a big attractive garden behind this handsome timbered 15th-c inn set in the High Street of this pretty village; there are several picnic tables sheltering among shrubs and trees. Inside, the comfortable bars have dark beams, dark wood tables with armchairs and wall banquettes upholstered to match the floral curtains, latticed windows, an inglenook fireplace (and a smaller more modern one with dried flowers), and old-fashioned prints and facsimiles of old documents on the cream walls. Good food includes home-made soup (£1.95), sandwiches (from £1.95; three-tier ones from £3.95; toasties from £2.25), filled baked potatoes (from £2.50), ploughman's (£3.95), omelettes or roast leg of cajun-spiced chicken (from £4.95), spinach tagliatelle with tomato sauce (£5.25), home-made burger (£5.75), steaks (from £10.95), and daily specials such as mushrooms with stilton (£3.25), duck and pork rillette (£3.50), cod in beer batter (£4.95), vegetable and fruit curry (£5.95), steak braised in ale (£6.25), and poached salmon with dill and prawn sauce (£6.95); part of the restaurant is no smoking. Well kept Adnams, Burtonwood Top Hat, Nethergate Bitter, Wadworths 6X, and Woodfordes Wherry on handpump, several malt whiskies, and James White cider. Darts, bar billiards, shove-ha'penny, cribbage, dominoes, fruit machine, and piped music. *(Recommended by Eric and Jackie Robinson, Gwen and Peter Andrews, Ian Phillips; more reports please)*

Free house ~ Licensees Dinah and Ted Henderson ~ Real ale ~ Meals and snacks ~ Restaurant ~ (01449) 740510 ~ Children welcome ~ Open 11-11 ~ Bedrooms: £25(£35B)/£35(£55B)

BLYFORD TM4277 Map 5

Queens Head

B1123

Locals are fond of this bustling thatched old village pub – always a good sign – and you can be sure of a friendly welcome from the licensees and their staff. The attractively furnished, unfussy low-beamed bar has some antique settles, pine and oak benches built into its cream walls, heavy wooden tables and stools, and a huge fireplace filled with antique lamps and other interesting implements. They still use water from the original well. Huge helpings of popular food includes lunchtime sandwiches, home-made soups such as pheasant and venison or cheese and broccoli (£2.65), spinach and tomato cannelloni (£5.45), fresh large Lowestoft cod in batter (£6.25), very good steak and kidney pie (£6.95), whole roast pheasant with burgundy sauce (£7.65), giant prawns in garlic butter (£8.35), a whole leg of greek-style lamb (£9.15), half a roast duck in a mango, peach and brandy sauce (£9.75), and Sunday roast (£6.25); the restaurant is no smoking. Well kept Adnams Bitter, Mild, and Broadside on handpump or tapped from the cask. There are seats on the grass outside, and a good play area for children. The small village church is opposite, and another church a mile south at Wenhaston has a fascinating 15th-c wall-painting. *(Recommended by W W Burke, Judy Booth, Beryl and Bill Farmer, Sheila Keene, David and Anne Culley, Chris and Kate Lyons, Malcolm Taylor, Bernard and Becky Robinson, J E Hilditch, June and Perry Dann, Gwen and Peter Andrews, Wayne Brindle, Dave Carter, Joan Hilditch, Andy and Jill Plumb)*

Adnams ~ Tenant Tony Matthews ~ Real ale ~ Meals and snacks ~ Restaurant ~ (01502) 478404 ~ Children in restaurant only ~ Open 11-3, 6.30-11 ~ Bedrooms: /£50B

BRANDESTON TM2460 Map 5

Queens Head

Towards Earl Soham

This is a simply decorated country pub with a busy local feel. The open-plan bar has some panelling, brown leather banquettes and old pews, and the room is divided into separate bays by the stubs of surviving walls; shove-ha'penny, cribbage, dominoes, and faint piped music. Good value bar food includes sandwiches (from £1.50; hoagies from £2), home-made soup (£2), fried aubergine with scordalia (delicious garlicky mashed potato dip, £2.95), home-made chilli (£4.50), ploughman's (from £4.25), home-baked gammon and egg (£4.50), home-made nut and mushroom pancake (£4.25), home-made sausage and onion pie or lasagne (£4.95), big toad-in-the-hole (£5.50), evening extras like smoked oysters au gratin (£3.50), tarragon chicken (£7.25) and roast boned duck with orange sauce (£7.50), and puddings (£2.50). Well kept Adnams Bitter on handpump with Broadside, Mild and seasonal ales kept under light blanket pressure; helpful staff. The big rolling garden – delightful in summer – has plenty of tables on the neatly kept grass among large flower beds; also, a play tree, climbing frame, and slide. The inn has a caravan and camping club site at the back. You can visit the nearby cider farm. (*Recommended by Jenny and Brian Seller, Howard Clutterbuck, Mrs P Goodwyn, Bill and Sheila McLardy, John Saul*)

Adnams ~ Tenants Tony and Doreen Smith ~ Real ale ~ Meals and snacks (not Sun evenings) ~ (01728) 685307 ~ Children in family room ~ Jazz 3rd Mon in month ~ Open 11.30-2.30, 6-11 ~ Bedrooms: £17/£34

BUTLEY TM3651 Map 5

Oyster

B1084 E of Woodbridge

Our 1996 inspection visit showed that this cheerful little country pub has hardly changed since we last dropped in some 25 years ago, during the reign of teetotaller Vera Noble (who ran it for 50 years and is still fondly remembered here). There's still a pair of good coal fires in fine Victorian fireplaces, still a medley of stripped pine tables, stripped pews, high-backed settles and more orthodox seats, still the spinning dial hanging below one of the very heavy beams, for deciding who'll buy the next round – the Adnams Bitter, Mild and Broadside on handpump is well kept. The good choice of nicely presented food is all listed on a blackboard and includes chicken liver pâté (£3.25), New Zealand mussels or hot and spicy nibbles (£3.95), ploughman's (from £3.60), cumberland sausage (£4.95), steak and kidney pie (£5.95), lamb kleftiko (£7.95) and lobster or seafood platter (£12.95); children's helpings (£2.95), puddings (£2.25), and Sunday roast (£4.95). Friendly staff, an airy feel and relaxed atmosphere; darts. The back garden has picnic tables and solid wooden tables and chairs, with budgerigars and rabbits in an aviary. (*Recommended by Pamela Goodwyn, P J and S E Robbins, Norman Smith, SM*)

Adnams ~ Licensee Mr Hanlon ~ Real ale ~ Meals and snacks (not Sun evening) ~ (01394) 450790 ~ Children welcome ~ Folk music Sun evening ~ Open 11.30-11; 11.30-3, 7-11 in winter

nr CHELMONDISTON TM2037 Map 5

Butt & Oyster

Pin Mill – signposted from B1456 SE of Ipswich

The setting for this simple old bargeman's pub is marvellous and from the plenty of seats outside, you can watch the boats going and up and down the River Orwell and enjoy the fine views over the water to the wooded slopes beyond. The same views can also be had from the bay window inside, where there's quite a nautical theme to match the surroundings. The half-panelled little smoke room is pleasantly worn and unfussy, with model sailing ships around the walls and high-backed and other old-fashioned settles on the tiled floor; spare a glance for the most unusual carving of a man with a woman over the mantelpiece. Good bar food includes lunchtime sandwiches (from £1.20), ploughman's (£2.75), ravioli (£3.55), tiger prawns in garlic butter (£5.50), honey-roast half duck (£6.95), daily specials like tuna and mushroom crumble, seafood provençale or normandy pork (£4.25-£4.50), and popular hot and cold buffet on weekend lunchtimes. Tolly Cobbolds Bitter, Original, Shooter, and Mild, and occasional guest beers on handpump or tapped from the cask, and decent wines; shove-ha'penny, cribbage, and dominoes. A good time to visit the pub would be when the annual Thames Barge race is held (end

June/beginning July). *(Recommended by C H and P Stride, Mrs P Goodwyn, John Prescott, Paul Kitchener, Paul Mason, PM, AM, Dave Braisted, June and Perry Dann, John Fahy, Mr and Mrs E Head, Jack and Philip Paxton, Stuart Earle)*

Pubmaster ~ Tenants Dick and Brenda Mainwaring ~ Real ale ~ Meals and snacks ~ (01473) 780764 ~ Children welcome except in main bar ~ Open 11-11; 12-10.30 Sun; 11-3, 7-11 in winter

CHILLESFORD TM3852 Map 5

Froize 🍴 ☂ 🍺

B1084 E of Woodbridge

The Shaws were very popular with readers in their time as tenants of the Kings Head in Orford; now they've bought this place they seem to be flourishing as never before. He's in charge of the kitchen (popping out, apron and all, to see that everything's going well), she runs the comfortable open-plan dining lounge (with gentle good humour, and help from the latest in a long succession of courteous young men from one particular village in the Loire valley). The food is excellent, especially the wide choice of fish fresh from Lowestoft such as grilled wing of skate with brown butter (£5.95), grilled whole plaice or scallops in a sherry and mushroom sauce (£8.50), whole grilled john dory with brown butter, caramelised sugar and garlic (£9.95), and delightfully presented seafood ragout (brill, salmon, scallops, prawns and mussels or cockles) and deftly spiced fried king prawns with an enterprising side salad (both dishes £10.25); they grow most of the herbs they use themselves. Other dishes include hearty home-made soup (£3.35), ploughman's or spinach roulade in parsley sauce (£3.85), shell-on prawns with a tangy basil and tomato mayonnaise dip (£4.25), vegetable stroganoff (£5.25), pancake filled with diced supreme of chicken in mushroom, tarragon and white wine sauce (£8.50), and duck breast in a plum and brandy sauce (£8.95). Helpings are very generous, and there's a good choice of puddings including schoolboy treats. A no-smoking restaurant was being built as we went to press. Well kept Nun Chaser (a dry hoppy beer brewed for them by Mauldons – the name, dreamed up by a customer, relates to the tradition that the pub's name recalls its 15th-c days as a friary whose monks fed travellers on pancakes the locals called froizes) and Chillesford Trembler (also brewed for them by Mauldons), Adnams Bitter, plus guests like Batemans, Greene King, Nethergates, Wychwood, and Woodfordes on handpump; a good range of wines by the glass; dominoes and fruit machine. The bar has beams, a turkey carpet, a mix of mate's chairs and red-cushioned stripped pews around the dark tables, and a couple of housekeeper's chairs by the open stove in the big arched brick fireplace. This has a huge stuffed pike over it, and the big room is full of interesting things to look at. A garden which at the time of our visit had not yet been much worked on has lots of picnic tables under cocktail parasols, and a play area. One of our best new finds. *(Recommended by Roy Oughton, Mrs P Goodwyn)*

Free house ~ Licensees Alistair and Joy Shaw ~ Real ale ~ Meals and snacks (not Mon in low season) ~ (01394) 450282 ~ Well behaved children in eating areas ~ Live entertainment winter Sun evenings ~ Open 11-3, 6(6.30 in winter)-11; 11-11 Sat; 12-10.30 Sun; closed Mon in low season ~ Bedrooms: £15(£25B)/£30(£40B)

COTTON TM0766 Map 5

Trowel & Hammer ☂

Mill Rd; take B1113 N of Stowmarket, then turn right into Blacksmiths Lane just N of Bacton

They offer quite a wide range of good bar food in this big and friendly partly thatched and partly tiled white pub. From a daily-changing menu there might be soups such as leek and potato or creamy spinach (£1.95), warm chicken livers (£3.25), salad of chorizo and poached egg (£3.95), cold roast lamb with bubble and squeak (£4.95), ploughman's or tagliatelle with a leek, broccoli and cheese sauce

(£5.25), steak, kidney and Guinness pie (£5.45), grilled lemon sole with herb butter (£6.25), escalope of salmon with chive sauce (£6.75), grilled sirloin steak (£9.25), and puddings. Well kept Adnams, Greene King IPA and Abbot, and maybe Nethergate Bitter and a local guest on handpump, and an interesting wine list; pool, fruit machine, and piped music. The spreading lounge has wheelbacks and one or two older chairs and settles around a variety of tables, lots of dark beamery and timber baulks, a big log fire, and at the back an ornate woodburning stove. The pretty back garden has lots of roses, neat climbers on trellises, picnic tables and a fine swimming pool. Perhaps some refurbishment in the back area might be in order, but the landlady is well embarked on a programme of improvements. *(Recommended by Gwen and Peter Andrews, Janet Pickles, A Albert, Ray Watson, C H and P Stride, Bill and Sheila McLardy, Paul and Maggie Baker)*

Free house ~ Licensees Julie Huff and Simon Piers-Hall ~ Real ale ~ Meals and snacks (12-2, 6.30-10) ~ Restaurant ~ (01449) 781234 ~ Children in eating area of bar ~ Open 11.30-3, 5.30-11; 11.30-11 Sat; 12-10.30 Sun

DENNINGTON TM2867 Map 5

Queens Head

A1120

For centuries – until quite recently – this lovely Tudor pub was owned by a church charity, and inside, you feel it may easily once have been a chapel: the arched rafters of the steeply roofed part on the right certainly give that impression. The main L-shaped room has carefully stripped wall timbers and beams – the great bressumer beam over the fireplace is handsomely carved – new comfortable padded wall seats on the partly carpeted and partly tiled floor, and brick bar counters. Good bar food includes sandwiches (from £1.50) and a choice of ploughman's (from £3.75), as well as soup (£1.95), tiger prawns in filo pastry and garlic dip (£3.25), cheesy pork pot or lamb and courgette bake (all £3.95), very good fisherman's pie (£4.35), sweet and sour pork (£5.25), steak and mushroom pie (£5.50), layered sausage pie (£5.65), curry platter (£5.95), salmon and prawn au gratin (£6.25), steaks (from £8.95), puddings like sticky toffee pudding or almond lemon tart (£2.50), and children's dishes (from £2.60); with some dishes, vegetables and chips are extra; they serve breakfast, too, from 9am. Well kept Adnams Bitter and Broadside and a guest such as Morlands Old Speckled Hen on handpump; friendly, helpful staff, and piped classical music. The side lawn, attractively planted with flowers, is sheltered by some noble lime trees, and has picnic tables; this backs onto Dennington Park where there are swings and so forth for children. The pub, set by the church, is one of Suffolk's most attractive pub buildings. *(Recommended by Caroline and Martin Page, Miss M Joynson, Frank Gadbois, Wayne Brindle, Tony and Wendy Hobden, Donald Rice)*

Free house ~ Licensees Ray and Myra Bumstead ~ Real ale ~ Meals and snacks ~ Restaurant ~ (01728) 638241 ~ Children in family area ~ Open 11.30-2.30, 5.30-11

DUNWICH TM4770 Map 5

Ship ★ ⇌ ◗

Readers continue to very much enjoy this delightful old pub, just a stone's throw from the sea. There's a good bustling atmosphere, especially at lunchtime, but the friendly, helpful staff manage to cheerfully cope with the crowds. The traditionally furnished bar has benches, pews, captain's chairs and candlelit wooden tables on the tiled floor, a woodburning stove (left open in cold weather) and lots of old fishing nets and paintings on the walls. It's the fresh fish (straight from the boats on the beach) with home-made chips that readers love (£4.75 lunchtime, from £7.75 in the evening), but at lunchtime there are also simple dishes like home-made soup (£1.65), cottage pie (£3.25), ploughman's (from £3.90), macaroni cheese (£3.95); in the evening there might be hot garlicky prawns (£4.50), lemon chicken (£7.30), rump steak (£7.75), and home-made puddings (£2.75). Well kept Adnams Bitter, Broadside (in summer) and winter Old, and Greene King Abbot on handpump at the handsomely panelled bar counter. The public bar area has dominoes, cribbage, fruit machine, video game, and piped music. There's a conservatory and attractive, sunny back terrace, and a well kept garden with an enormous fig tree. Dunwich today is such a charming little place it's hard to imagine that centuries ago it was one of England's major centres. Since then fairly rapid coastal erosion has put most of the village under the sea, and there are those who claim that on still nights you can sometimes hear the old church bells tolling under the water. The pub is handy for the RSPB reserve at Minsmere. *(Recommended by Paul Mason, Graham and Liz Bell, John Waller, MN, DN, P Burrows-Smith, Bill and Sheila McLardy, Chris and Kate Lyons, Ian Phillips, John Fahy, Jowanna Lewis, Tom McLean, Nigel Wikeley, Mrs P Goodwyn, D Hayman, June and Perry Dann, James Nunns, Brian and Jenny Seller, G and T Edwards, Nigel Woolliscroft, Dr Peter Crawshaw, MJVK, Nick and Mary Baker, John Beeken, Andy and Jill Plumb)*

Free house ~ Licensees Stephen and Ann Marshlain ~ Real ale ~ Meals and snacks ~ Evening restaurant ~ (01728) 648219 ~ Children welcome away from main bar ~ Open 11-3, 6-11; closed evening 25 Dec ~ Bedrooms: £22/£44(£54S)

EARL SOHAM TM2363 Map 5

Victoria 🍺

A1120 Stowmarket—Yoxford

Doing very well at the moment, this unpretentious pub is warmly friendly and has its own interesting range of beers brewed on the premises. You can visit the microbrewery that produces the Victoria Bitter, a mild called Gannet, and a stronger ale called Albert, and take some home with you. The relaxed bar has kitchen chairs and pews, plank-topped trestle sewing-machine tables and other simple country tables with candles, tiled or board floors, stripped panelling, an interesting range of pictures of Queen Victoria and her reign, and open fires. Enjoyable bar food includes good soup (£1.75), sandwiches (from £1.75), home-made burgers (£2.50), ploughman's (from £3), very tasty corned beef hash, chilli or pizzas (£3.75), vegetable lasagne (£4.50), pork with apple and cider or good beef curry (£4.95), and puddings (from £1.95); decent wine. Darts, shove-ha'penny, cribbage, dominoes, cards and backgammon; seats out in front and on a raised back lawn. The pub is close to a wild fritillary meadow at Framlingham and a working windmill at Saxtead. *(Recommended by Paul Mason, Frank Gadbois, Nick and Hilary Jackson, Graham and Liz Bell, D and J Tapper, M R Hyde, John C Baker, Jack and Philip Paxton, PM, AM, Simon Cottrell, N S Smith, Stuart Earle)*

Own brew ~ Licensees Clare and John Bjornson ~ Real ale ~ Meals and snacks ~ (01728) 685758 ~ Impromptu folk music Tues and occas Fri evenings ~ Open 11.30-2.30, 5.30-11

ERWARTON TM2134 Map 5

Queens Head 🍷 🍺

Village signposted off B1456 Ipswich—Shotley Gate; pub beyond the attractive church and the manor with its unusual gate (like an upturned salt-cellar)

From seats on the terrace here, there are fine views over fields to ships on the Stour and the distant Parkeston Quay. Inside this friendly pub, the comfortably furnished bar has a relaxed, homely feel, bowed 16th-c black oak beams in the shiny low yellowing ceiling, and a cosy coal fire. The same menu is served in both the bar and more modern restaurant and includes sandwiches, good soups like broccoli and stilton or apple, celery and tomato (£1.90), ploughman's (£3.50), home-made lasagne or moussaka, curry, spicy cod with cajun dip or mushroom and nut fettucine (all £4.95), big gammon steak with egg (£6.30), daily specials like vegetable stew with dumplings or liver and onions (£4.95), lamb chump chop with rosemary and port sauce (£5.25), salmon steak with prawns and lemon or steak, kidney and mushroom pudding (£6.50), seasonal game, and puddings such as steamed ginger pudding (£2.20). Well kept Adnams Bitter, Greene King IPA, and Morlands Old Speckled Hen on handpump; a decent wine list with several half bottles, and a wide choice of malt whiskies. Darts, bar billiards, shove-ha'penny, cribbage, dominoes, and piped music. The gents' has a fascinating collection of navigational maps. Handy for Erwarton Hall with its peculiar gatehouse. *(Recommended by Mrs P Goodwyn, Paul and Juliet Beckwith, A Albert, Peter Woolls, M A and C R Starling; more reports please)*

Free house ~ Licensees Mr B K Buckle and Mrs Julia Crisp ~ Real ale ~ Meals and snacks ~ Restaurant ~ (01473) 787550 ~ Children in restaurant ~ Open 11-3, 6.30(6 Sat)-11; winter evening opening 7pm; closed 25 Dec

FRAMSDEN TM1959 Map 5

Dobermann 🍺 🍴

The Street; pub signposted off B1077 just S of its junction with A1120 Stowmarket—Earl Soham

The two spotless and friendly bar areas in this charmingly restored old thatched pub have very low, pale stripped beams, a big comfy sofa, a couple of chintz wing armchairs, and a mix of other chairs, and plush-seated stools and winged settles around polished rustic tables; there's a wonderful twin-facing fireplace, photographs of show rosettes won by the owner's dogs on the white walls, and a friendly tabby, Tinker. Well kept Adnams Bitter and Broadside and guests such as Adnams Mayday, Greene King Sorcerer or Marstons Pedigree on handpump; efficient service. Shove-ha'penny, table skittles, cribbage, dominoes, and piped music. Good bar food (with prices virtually unchanged since last year) includes sandwiches (from £1.45), home-made soup or deep fried squid (£2.95), home-made chicken liver pâté or brown shrimps (£3.45), huge ploughman's (from £4.95), spicy nut loaf with tomato sauce (£5.25), mixed grill or chilli con carne (£6.95), home-made steak and mushroom pie (£7.50), steaks (from £9.95), and puddings (from £2.50). They play boules outside, where there are picnic tables by trees and a fairy-lit trellis, and lots of pretty hanging baskets and colourful window boxes. No children. *(Recommended by Jill Bickerton, Mrs P Goodwyn, John Waller, Sarah and Ian Shannon, Gwen and Peter Andrews, June and Perry Dann, Wayne Brindle)*

Free house ~ Licensee Susan Frankland ~ Real ale ~ Meals and snacks ~ (01473) 890461 ~ Open 11.30-3.30, 7-11; 12-4, 7-10.30 Sun ~ Bedrooms: £25S/£35S

GREAT GLEMHAM TM3361 Map 5

Crown 🍺 🍷 🍴

Between A12 Wickham Mkt—Saxmundham, and B1119 Saxmundham—Framlingham

In a quiet village, this neatly kept pub is much liked by readers for its very good, quickly served food, friendly licensees, and as somewhere to stay overnight – the landlady's breakfasts are quite something. The open-plan beamed lounge has two enormous fireplaces with logs blazing in winter, one or two big casks, brass ornaments or musical instruments, wooden pews and captain's chairs around stripped and waxed kitchen tables, and a chatty atmosphere. Local photographs and paintings decorate the white walls, and there are plenty of fresh flowers and pot plants, with more in a side eating room. Well kept Adnams Bitter, Broadside and winter Old, and Bass from old brass handpumps; good choice of malt whiskies and decent wines. From a changing menu, the good food might include filled rolls, home-made soup (£2.50), baked aubergine with a cream and garlic sauce (£3.25), ratatouille (£5.50), grilled cod fillet with lemon butter or steak and kidney pie (£6.25), pork tenderloin with a creamy mustard sauce or gammon with pineapple (£6.50), roast duck breast with orange sauce (£7.50), steaks (from £8.95), and puddings such as lemon tart, muscat and grape syllabub or pecan pie (£2.50). The restaurant is no smoking. Shove-ha'penny, dominoes, and cribbage. There's a tidy, flower-fringed lawn, raised above the corner of the quiet village lane by a retaining wall, and some seats and tables under cocktail parasols. *(Recommended by Quentin Williamson, Paul Kitchener, Mark Baynham, Miss Ward, Jill Bickerton, Comus Elliott, June and Perry Dann, Colin Pettit, John Fahy, K H Frostick)*

Free house ~ Licensee Roger Mason ~ Real ale ~ Meals and snacks (not Mon) ~ Restaurant ~ (01728) 663693 ~ Children in eating area of bar ~ Open 12-2.30, 7-11; closed Mon (open bank hol Mon) ~ Bedrooms: £25B/£38B

HARTEST TL8352 Map 5

Crown

B1066 S of Bury St Edmunds

A pretty picture by the village green and church (bell-ringing practice Thursday evening), this comfortably modernised and brightly lit pink-washed pub has plenty of space for its many regular dark wood tables. Its strength is reliable reasonably priced home cooking, with good sandwiches (from £1.50), popular changing soups such as cream of cauliflower, chunky fish soup or duck and vegetable (£1.75), a massive ploughman's (£3), a vegetarian dish of the day such as vegetable and pasta bake (£5.50), good fresh fish such as dressed crab, fried brill, whiting done with Abbot ale and salmon in chive and lemon sauce (£5-£7; they also do a take-away fish and chips £3.25), winter steak and kidney pie (£5.50), chicken in a white wine and mushroom sauce (£6), scotch 10oz sirloin steak (£9.50), and puddings such as double chocolate flan or sherry trifle (£2.25); they do a Wednesday lunchtime home-made pie plus pudding and coffee for £5.50, and a Friday lunchtime fresh fish and pudding menu with coffee for £6. Besides two no-smoking dining areas there's a family conservatory. Well kept Greene King IPA, Abbot and Sorcerer on handpump, decent house wines, quick and friendly black-tie staff, a chatty local atmosphere, and quiet piped music. The big back lawn has picnic tables among shrubs and trees, and there are more under cocktail parasols in a sheltered side courtyard, by a plastic play treehouse. *(Recommended by Gwen and Peter Andrews, P Devitt, Pamela Goodwyn, W T Aird)*

Greene King ~ Tenants Paul and Karen Beer ~ Real ale ~ Meals and snacks ~ Restaurant ~ (01284) 830250 ~ Children welcome ~ Open 11-3, 6-11; closed 25-26 Dec

HORRINGER TL8261 Map 5

Beehive 🍴 ♀

A143

This is a particularly well run place with extremely helpful and friendly staff and quickly served, excellent food. As well as nibbles such as olive and tomato bread, a dish of olives or savoury dip with corn chips (from £1.50), the bar food might include soup (£2.50), chicken liver and pistachio pâté (£3.95), ploughman's (£4.75), steak sandwich (£4.95), omelette filled with prawns and double cream lobster sauce (£5.95), grilled breast of chicken with rosemary, lemon and butter (£7.95), and daily specials such as cold smoked duck (£4.95), Florentine sausages with a white onion and nutmeg confit or enjoyable Black Forest ham with sun-ripened tomatoes and black olives (£5.95), tagliatelle with oyster mushroom and tarragon sauce (£6.95), chicken livers in a devilled cream sauce (£7.95), grilled shark steak with lime and ginger butter (£8.95), delicious salmon rosti with a caper sauce, lovely roast duck, and puddings such as sticky ginger pudding with ginger wine sauce and baked banana cheesecake with toffee pecan sauce (£2.95). Well kept Greene King IPA and Abbot on handpump and decent changing wines with half-a-dozen by the glass. The little rambling rooms have some very low beams in some of the furthest and snuggest alcoves, carefully chosen dining and country kitchen chairs with tartan cushions on the coir or flagstones, one or two wall settles around solid tables, picture-lights over lots of 19th-c prints, stripped panelling or brickwork, and a woodburning stove. Their dog Muffin is very good at making friends, though other dogs aren't really welcome. The gents' has a frieze depicting villagers fleeing from stinging bees. A most attractively planted back terrace has picnic tables, with more seats on a raised lawn. *(Recommended by Gwen and Peter Andrews, Helen Crookston, David Regan, Simon Cottrell, Janet Pickles, R C Wiles, Rita Horridge, BNF, M Parkin, Pamela Goodwyn, JKW, Howard and Margaret Buchanan, Jane Kinsbury, John C Baker, Stuart Earle, W T Aird, G Washington, Susan May)*

Greene King ~ Tenants Gary and Dianne Kingshott ~ Real ale ~ Meals and snacks ~ (01284) 735260 ~ Children welcome ~ Open 11.30-2.30, 7-11

HOXNE TM1777 Map 5

Swan ♀

Off B1118; village signposted off A140 S of Diss

As good as ever, this carefully restored late 15th-c house has an extensive lawn behind used for croquet, and hand-made elm furniture sheltered by a willow and other trees and a shrub-covered wall. The front bar has a peaceful and relaxed atmosphere, two solid oak counters, heavy oak floors, and a deep-set inglenook fireplace, with an armchair on either side and a long bench in front of it; you can still see the ancient timber and mortar of the walls. A fire in the back bar divides the bar area and snug, and the dining room has an original wooden fire surround. Well presented good bar food includes daily specials such as courgette and rosemary soup (£2.75), spinach and garlic terrine (£2.95), aubergine slices baked with tomato and mozzarella (£3.95), pasta with a cream, ham and mushroom sauce (£4.95), cod and prawn gratinée or a selection of smoked fish (£5.95), pork satay with peanut sauce (£6.95), and king prawn tails provençale (£7.95); also, sandwiches (from £1.50), ploughman's (from £2.95), omelettes (£3.25), hash browns, bacon and egg (£3.95), pancake filled with mushrooms and cheese (£4.25), and steaks (from £8.50); vegetables, salads, and various potatoes are extra (from 75p each). If you're sitting outside and waiting for your food order, keep your eye on the roof; rather than use a Tannoy, they briefly sound a school bell and then prop scoreboard type numbers up there when your meal is ready. Well kept Adnams Bitter and winter Old and Tally Ho and Greene King Abbot on handpump or tapped from the cask, and decent wines; pool, shove-ha'penny, dominoes, cribbage, and juke box. Nearby is the site of King Edmund the Martyr's execution; the tree to which he was tied for it is now reputed to form part of a screen in the neighbouring church. *(Recommended by PM, AM, Frank Davidson, Ian Phillips, Pat and Tony Martin, J E Rycroft, Anthony Barnes, P H Roberts, Gwen and Peter Andrews, Wayne Brindle, Dr Ronald Church, Pamela Goodwyn)*

Free house ~ Licensees Tony and Frances Thornton-Jones ~ Real ale ~ Meals and snacks in bar (not Sat evening or all day Sun) ~ Restaurant (Sat evening and Sunday lunch) ~ (01379) 668275 ~ Children in eating area of bar ~ Open 12-2.30(3 Sat), 5.30-11; closed 25 Dec

HUNDON TL7348 Map 5

Plough 🛏

Brockley Green; on Kedington road, up hill from village

Behind this extended and modernised pub are five acres of landscaped gardens, part of which are to become a wildlife sanctuary and trout lake. There's also a terrace with a pergola and ornamental pool, croquet, boules, and fine views over miles of East Anglian countryside; the pub's two friendly retrievers may be out here, too. The neat carpeted bar has low side settles with Liberty-print cushions, pine kitchen chairs and sturdy low tables on the patterned carpet, lots of horsebrasses on the beams, and striking gladiatorial designs for Covent Garden by Leslie Hurry, who lived nearby; there's still a double row of worn old oak timbers to mark what must once have been the corridor between its two rooms. Decent bar food includes lunchtime sandwiches, home-made soup, ploughman's, gammon and egg or pasta dishes, and daily specials such as fillet of sole stuffed with seafood and a white wine sauce (£7.25), chicken with barbecue sauce (£7.50), strips of beef in a hot pepper sauce

(£7.95), and salmon steak with bearnaise sauce (£8.50). Well kept Adnams, Greene King IPA, and a guest beer on handpump, quite a few wines, and freshly squeezed orange juice; piped music. Parts of the bar and restaurant are no smoking. It's also a certified location for the Caravan Club, with a sheltered site to the rear for tourers. The pub has been run by the same friendly family for three generations. *(Recommended by Quentin Williamson, Gwen and Peter Andrews, Mr and Mrs Albert, Stephen Boot, W T Aird, Aubrey Bourne, Frank W Gadbois, JLP; more reports please)*

Free house ~ Licensees David and Marion Rowlinson ~ Real ale ~ Meals and snacks ~ Restaurant ~ (01440) 786789 ~ Children in eating area of bar ~ Open 11-2.30, 5.30-11; winter lunchtime opening midday ~ Bedrooms: £39.50B/£55B

ICKLINGHAM TL7772 Map 5

Red Lion 🕮

A1101, Mildenhall—Bury St Edmunds

It's the consistently good food that draws readers to this civilised and rather smart thatched pub – but they also very much like the relaxed atmosphere and friendly service, too. The heavy beamed bar has a nice mixture of wooden chairs, candlelit tables, and fresh flowers, as well as antlers over the inglenook fireplace, old fishing rods and various stuffed animals, piped classical music, and newspapers to read; they sell clay pipes and tobacco. As well as enjoyable daily specials, there might be popular fish dishes such as seasonal mussels (small £4.25, medium £5.95, huge £7.55), tiger bay prawns in garlic butter (starter £4.95, main course £8.50), local trout (£7.45), and fresh lemon sole or grilled plaice (£9.95) – plus, soup (£2.45), home-made pâté (£2.95), a ham or cheese platter (£4.50), a vegetarian dish (£6.25), lamb liver, bacon and onion gravy (£6.70), pork chops with apple and cider sauce (£7.25), warm fillet of chicken and crispy pasta salad (£8.45), and sirloin steak (£8.95). Well kept Greene King IPA and Abbot, and Rayments, and occasional guest beers on handpump, lots of country wines and elderflower and citrus pressé, and mulled wine in winter. Picnic tables on a raised back terrace face the fields – including an acre of the pub's running down to the River Lark, with Cavenham Heath nature reserve beyond. In front (the pub is well set back from the road) old-fashioned white seats overlook the car park and a flower lawn. Handy for West Stow Country Park and the Anglo-Saxon Village. *(Recommended by J F M West, K Neville-Rolfe, Andrew and Jo Litten, James Macrae, Mrs P Goodwyn, Philip and Susan Philcox, Stephen Barney, Frank Gadbois, Rob Hunter, John and Chris Simpson, K H Frostick, Nigel Pawsey, Michael Marlow, Mrs Heather Martin, Tony Gayfer, Rita Horridge, R C Vincent, Ian Phillips, Dr Ronald Church)*

Greene King ~ Lease: Jonathan Gates ~ Real ale ~ Meals and snacks (12-2, 6-10) ~ Restaurant ~ (01638) 717802 ~ Children welcome ~ Open 12-3, 6-11

IPSWICH TM1744 Map 5

Brewery Tap 🍺

Cliff Rd

Nestling below the great Victorian bulk of the Tolly Cobbold brewery, this attractive pink-washed pub houses the ground floor of what was the Cobbold family home in the 18th c. There are fully guided brewery tours every day at midday in May-September and at the same time on Saturday and Sunday during October-April; other tours by arrangement. Inside, several friendly smallish room areas cluster around the main bar, with decently spaced solid small tables, some armchairs, and rugs on polished boards. Some brickwork's been stripped back, and elsewhere some original lathwork exposed. There are pictures of the docks and other local scenes on the walls, and big windows looking out to the boats you can often see passing on the river outside. One room is no smoking. Bar food includes giant filled baps, a dish of the day (£3.95), home-made curry or vegetarian dish (£4.95), and home-made steak, kidney and ale pie (£5.50). Well kept Tolly Mild, Bitter, Original, Tolly-Shooter and

Old Strong in winter, and Cobbolds IPA all on handpump and the full range of Tolly bottled beers; piped music (sometimes a bit intrusive). A games area has darts, bar billiards, cribbage, dominoes, and fruit machine. The back room looks into the brewery's steam-engine room, and a door from the pub leads straight into the brewery. *(Recommended by Ian Phillips, John Fahy, M R Hyde, Neil Calver, C H and P Stride)*

Tolly ~ Managers R Wales and Jill Willmott ~ Real ale ~ Meals and snacks (not Sun or Mon evenings) ~ (01473) 281508 ~ Children in eating area of bar ~ Jazz last Sun of month ~ Parking restrictions daytime ~ Open 11-11; 11-3, 5-11 in winter

IXWORTH TL9370 Map 5

Pykkerel

Village signposted just off A143 Bury St Edmunds—Diss

There's a good relaxed and friendly atmosphere in the neatly kept small rooms of this popular dining pub. Leading off the central servery, they have moulded Elizabethan oak beams, attractive brickwork, big fireplaces, antique tables and chairs, and persian rugs on the gleaming floors; there's a similarly furnished dining area, and a small back sun lounge facing a sway-backed Elizabethan timbered barn across the old coach yard. Much emphasis is placed on the good bar food: sandwiches, soup (£2.10), warmed bacon, prawn and croûton salad (£4.25), cheese, ham or pâté platters (£4.50), king prawn tails in garlic butter or enjoyable local sausages with mash and onion gravy (£4.95), vegetarian dishes (£6.70), home-made steak in ale pie (£6.95), peppered pork loin with a cheese and cider sauce (£7.95), and up to a dozen daily fresh fish dishes (from £8.95). Well kept Greene King IPA and Abbot, and a guest beer on handpump. Some picnic tables sit on a goodish stretch of grass under a giant sycamore. *(Recommended by Ian Phillips, J F M West, Donald Rice, M Borthwick, Simon Penny, Julian and Liz Long, Peter and Joy Heatherley, Michael Marlow, Andrew Scarr)*

Greene King ~ Tenants Ian Hubbert and J Gates ~ Real ale ~ Meals and snacks (12-2.30, 6-10) ~ Restaurant ~ (01359) 230398 ~ Children welcome ~ Open 12-2.30, 6-11

LAVENHAM TL9149 Map 5

Angel ★ 🍽 🛏 🍷 🍴

Market Pl

Suffolk Dining Pub of the Year

The licensees of this civilised and carefully renovated Tudor inn lift it right out of the ordinary with their complete commitment to and involvement in their customers' enjoyment. This means that despite the strong emphasis on particularly good food it's not just another dining pub: the relaxed and buoyantly pubby atmosphere means that people just dropping in for a quick drink feel as welcome as anyone. The long bar area, facing on to the charming former market square, is light and airy, with plenty of polished dark tables. There's a big inglenook log fire under a heavy mantelbeam, and some attractive 16th-c ceiling plasterwork (even more elaborate pargeting in the residents' sitting room upstairs). Round towards the back on the right of the central servery is a no-smoking family dining area with heavy stripped pine country furnishings. Changing twice a day, the carefully cooked food may include cream of mushroom soup (£2.50), salmon and asparagus tart or pasta with chicken and tomato (£3.95), home-made pork pie with pickles or ploughman's (£4.25), a smoked fish selection (they smoke their own food) or shepherd's pie (£4.50), steak in ale pie (£5.95), roast beef or gammon salad (£6.75), lamb casserole (£7.25), skate wing with black butter (£7.95), sirloin steak (£9.95), and puddings such as blackberry and apple crumble, white chocolate roulade or home-made ice cream (£2.95). Well kept Adnams Bitter, Mauldons White Adder, Nethergate Bitter, and Woodfordes Wherry on handpump, quite a few malt whiskies, and decent wines by the glass or part bottle (you get charged for what you drink). They have shelves of books, a good range of board games, and hold a quiz on Sundays (all are welcome); dominoes, cribbage, and trivia. The big ginger cat is called Dilly and the one without a tail is Stumpy. There are picnic tables out in front, and white plastic tables under cocktail parasols in a sizeable sheltered back garden; it's worth asking if they've time to show you the interesting Tudor cellar. *(Recommended by Gwen and Peter Andrews, Susan May, W W Burke, John Evans, Tina and David Woods-Taylor, Sarah and Ian Shannon, Trent and Tina Conyers, Frank Gadbois, C McFeeters, Prof R Orledge, John Baker, Heather and Trevor Shaw, I P G Derwent, Heather Martin, Graham and Liz Bell, Jamie and Ruth Lyons, Eric and Jackie Robinson, Bill and Steph Brownson, J E Hilditch, C H and P Stride, R G and J N Plumb, Miss R M Tudor, Pamela Goodwyn, Jack and Philip Paxton, Bernard and Ann Payne, Tom Thomas, Paul and Ursula Randall, Dominic and Sue Dunlop)*

Free house ~ Licensees Roy and Anne Whitworth, John Barry ~ Real ale ~ Meals and snacks ~ Restaurant ~ (01787) 247388 ~ Children in eating area of bar and in restaurant ~ Classical piano Fri evenings, played by the landlord ~ Open 11-11; 12-10.30 Sun ~ Bedrooms: £37.50B/£60B

Swan ★ 🛏

Several lovely half-timbered buildings, including an Elizabethan house and the former Wool Hall are incorporated into this 15th-c building. It's a rather smart Forte Heritage hotel but has a quietly relaxed atmosphere and an atmospheric little tiled-floor bar buried in its heart, with leather chairs and memorabilia of the days when this was the local for the US 48th Bomber Group in the Second World War (many Americans still come to re-visit old haunts); the set of handbells used to be employed by the local church bellringers for practice. From here it's an easy overflow into the drift of armchairs and settees that spreads engagingly through a network of beamed and timbered alcoves and more open areas. Well kept Courage Best, Greene King IPA, and Morlands Old Speckled Hen on handpump or tapped from the cask; piped music. Overlooking the well kept and sheltered courtyard garden is an airy Garden Bar, where at lunchtime a buffet counter serves home-made soup (£2.95), sandwiches (from £3.50; £4.50 for smoked salmon), British cheeses and biscuits (£4.95), honey-baked ham and roast turkey salad (£6.95), a vegetarian dish, a daily hot dish of the day (£8.95), and home-made puddings (£3.50); also, morning coffee and good afternoon tea. There is also a lavishly timbered no-smoking restaurant with a minstrel's gallery. Amongst the other fine buildings in this once-prosperous wool town is the Tudor Guildhall, which has a small folk museum. *(Recommended by John Fahy, Tina and David Woods-Taylor, Graham and Liz Bell, Gwen and Peter Andrews, W W Burke, Janet Pickles, Mrs Heather Martin, A and M Dickinson, Nigel Flook, Betsy Brown)*

Free house (Forte) ~ Licensee M R Grange ~ Real ale ~ Lunchtime bar meals and snacks ~ Restaurant ~ (01787) 247477 ~ Children welcome ~ Open 11-2.30, 6-11 ~ Bedrooms: £85B/£140B

LAXFIELD TM2972 Map 5

Kings Head 🍺

Behind church, off road toward Banyards Green

As well as a very friendly welcome, the traditional pubby atmosphere here is rather like that of a village local 100 years ago – probably helped by the lack of noisy games machines or piped music. The old-fashioned front room has a high-backed built-in settle on the tiled floor and an open fire, and a couple of other rooms have pews, old seats, scrubbed deal tables, and some interesting wall prints. Decent bar food includes sandwiches (from £1.60), good soup, ploughman's (£3.95), roasts or various dumplings (£5.50), good grilled plaice, and enjoyable puddings like treacle tart or bread and butter pudding (£2.95). Well kept Adnams Bitter, Broadside, Extra and winter Old and Tally Ho, and Greene King IPA on handpump, and good James White cider; darts, shove ha'penny, cribbage, and cards. Going out past the casks in the back serving room, you find benches and a trestle table in a small yard. From the yard, a honeysuckle arch leads into a sheltered little garden and the pub's own well kept and secluded bowling, badminton and croquet green. *(Recommended by Gwen and Peter Andrews, H Turner, Jack and Philip Paxton, Sarah and Ian Shannon, MJVK, Nick and Alison Dowson)*

Free house ~ Managers Adrian and Sylvia Read ·· Real ale ~ Meals and snacks ~ (01986) 798395 ~ Children in family room ~ Old Suffolk songs with washboard Tues lunchtime, Irish folk/local blues band alternate Fri evenings ~ Open 11-3, 6-11

LEVINGTON TM2339 Map 5
Ship

Gun Hill; village signposted from A45, then follow Stratton Hall sign

Surrounded by lovely countryside, this charming traditional inn is popular with ramblers and birdwatchers – and users of the nearby local marina. The rooms have quite a nautical theme with lots of ship prints and photos of sailing barges, beams and benches built into the walls, and in the middle room a marine compass set under the serving counter, which also has a fishing net slung over it. There are also a number of comfortably upholstered small settles, some of them grouped round tables as booths, and a big black round stove. The no-smoking dining room has more nautical bric-a-brac, beams taken from an old barn, and flagstones; another dining area is also no smoking. Generous helpings of tasty home-made bar food include broccoli, tomato and mushroom quiche (£5.25), mussels in white wine and garlic butter (£5.50), pork with black cherry sauce, chicken in mustard sauce, steak and kidney pudding, or salmon and broccoli bake (all £5.95), and puddings like tiramisu flan or banana cream pie (£2.95). Service is friendly and professional. Well kept Flowers IPA and Original, Ind Coope Burton, and Tolly Cobbolds IPA, and a weekly guest like Boddingtons Best or Tetleys Bitter on handpump or tapped from the cask; country wines. Cribbage, dominoes. If you look carefully enough, there's a distant sea view from the benches in front. In summer, the hanging baskets are magnificent. No dogs or children. *(Recommended by Prof M J Salmon, Malcolm Taylor, Mrs P J Pearce, Ian and Nita Cooper, C H and P Stride, Rita Horridge, Keith Archer, Stuart Earle, Pamela Goodwyn)*

Pubmaster ~ Tenants William and Shirley Waite ~ Real ale ~ Meals and snacks (not Sun/Mon/Tues evenings) ~ Restaurant ~ (01473) 659573 ~ Folk music first Tues of month ~ Open 11.30-3, 6-11

LIDGATE TL7257 Map 5
Star ♀

B1063 SE of Newmarket

Both the food and the welcoming atmosphere of this quaint old place owe a lot to the chatty landlady, who comes from Barcelona. The decor is largely archetypal English. The small main room has a lot of character, with handsomely moulded heavy beams, a good big log fire, candles in iron candelabra on polished oak or stripped pine tables, bar billiards, darts and ring the bull, and just some antique Catalan plates over the bar to give a hint of the Mediterranean. It's in the ever-changing menu that crisp and positive seasonings speak more openly of the South: Mediterranean fish soup or hot little garlicky prawns (£4), a beautifully dressed Catalan salad or a massive Spanish omelette (£4.50), monkfish marinières or herby fresh scallops (£8.50), for example. Other dishes enjoyed by us or readers have included scallops in bacon and garlic (£4.50), lasagne or herby roast chicken (£7.50), lamb steaks in blackcurrant or wild boar or venison in port (£8.50), fried sardines, stewed lamb, and venison sausages with red cabbage. Helpings are big, vegetables are well cooked (good dry continental-style chips), and the sorbets and home-made cheesecake are good. Sadly environmental health spoil-sports have stopped the Sunday beef spit-roasts, hugely enjoyed by readers. Greene King IPA, Abbot, and a seasonal beer on handpump, enjoyable house wines, maybe good unobtrusive piped music. Besides a second similar room on the right, there's a cosy simple dining room on the left. There are tables out by the quiet front lane and in a pretty little rustic back garden. *(Recommended by J F M West, Gwen and Peter Andrews, P and D Carpenter, Mrs P Goodwyn, N S Smith)*

Greene King ~ Tenant Teresa Axon ~ Real ale ~ Meals and snacks (not Sun evening) ~ Restaurant ~ (01638) 500275 ~ Children welcome ~ Open 11-3, 5(6 Sat)-11

LONG MELFORD TL8645 Map 5

Bull 🛏

A134

If you want a calm refuge from the bustle of the attractive village with all its antique shops, then this timbered 16th-c building (originally a medieval manorial great hall) is the place to head for. The atmosphere in the front lounge – divided by the remains of an oak partition wall – is friendly and quietly old-fashioned, and there are big mullioned and leaded windows, lots of oak timbering, a huge brick fireplace with log fire, a longcase clock from Stradbrook, a rack of daily papers, and various antique furnishings. Supporting the beautifully carved high main beam is a woodwose – the wild man of the woods that figures in Suffolk folk-tales. A more spacious back bar has armed brown leatherette or plush dining seats around antique oak tables, dark heavy beams, and sporting prints on the cream timbered walls; cribbage, dominoes, trivia, and piped music. The Mylde lounge and the restaurant are no smoking. Bar food includes sandwiches (from £1.75), soup (£2.75), traditional ploughman's (£4.25), sausages, mash and onion gravy or vegetable bake (£5.50), a daily special pie, roast of the day (£6.50), grilled lemon sole (£9.95), and baked stuffed sea bass (£10.95); it can be busy at lunchtimes. Well kept Adnams Best, Greene King IPA, and Nethergate Old Growler and Umbel Ale on handpump, various malt whiskies, country wines, and helpful staff. There are tables in the paved central courtyard. Handy for the Elizabethan Melford Hall and moated Tudor Kentwell Hall which are both fine buildings in attractive grounds. *(Recommended by John Evans, Jamie and Ruth Lyons, Janet Pickles, Frank Gadbois, Graham and Liz Bell, Ian Phillips, A and M Dickinson)*

Free house (Forte) ~ Manager Peter Watt ~ Real ale ~ Meals and snacks (limited menu Sun; not 25 Dec) ~ Restaurant ~ (01787) 378494 ~ Children welcome ~ Live entertainment Fri/Sat evenings ~ Open 11.30-3, 6-11; 11.30-11 summer Sat; 12-10.30 summer Sun; closed 25-26 Dec ~ Bedrooms: £65B/£85B

ORFORD TM4250 Map 5

Jolly Sailor

It's the position that readers really like about this unspoilt old smugglers' inn – right by a busy little quay on the River Ore, opposite Orford Ness and close to marshy Havergate Island, where avocets breed. Inside, there are several cosily traditional rooms served from counters and hatches in an old-fashioned central cubicle, and an uncommon spiral staircase in the corner of the flagstoned main bar – which also has 13 brass door knockers and other brassware, local photographs, and a good solid fuel stove; a small room is popular with the dominoes and shove-ha'penny players, and has draughts, chess and cribbage too. Well kept Adnams Bitter, Broadside, Mild, and seasonal additions on handpump, and bar food such as fish and chips, home-cooked ham and egg, and daily roasts (all £4.25). The dining room is no smoking. Tables and chairs in the big garden. No children. *(Recommended by Nick and Hilary Jackson, David Heath, W W Burke, PM, AM, Frank Cummins, Keble Paterson, June and Perry Dann)*

Adnams ~ Tenant Philip M Attwood ~ Real ale ~ Bar meals (not Tues/Thurs evenings 1 Oct-Easter; not 25-26 Dec) ~ (01394) 450243 ~ Open 11.30-2.30, 7-11 ~ Bedrooms: /£35

RAMSHOLT TM3141 Map 5

Ramsholt Arms

Village signposted from B1083; then take turning after the one to Ramsholt Church

This beautifully placed pub was once a ferryman's cottage and is quite isolated by an old barge quay on the River Deben which winds past to the sea; there is mooring for 200 boats. The uncarpeted riverside bar has comfortable banquettes and chairs, and a good winter log fire, and is open every afternoon in summer, excluding Sundays. The engine bar has a big picture window, some neatly nautical woodwork, tide tables and charts, and simple dark oak brocaded seats on the plain carpet. Well kept Adnams Bitter, Brakspears Bitter, Theakstons, and Wadworths 6X on handpump, and several malt whiskies. Under the new licensee, bar food now includes sandwiches, half pint of prawns (£3.95), Irish oysters (from £4.75), fresh battered cod (£5.75), and pot-roast partridge (£6.50). The restaurant is no smoking. *(Recommended by Dr and Mrs P J S Crawshaw, PM, AM, Mrs P Goodwyn; more reports on the new regime, please)*

Free house ~ Licensees Michael and Kirsten Bartholomew ~ Real ale ~ Meals and snacks (not Sun evening in winter) ~ Restaurant ~ (01394) 411229 ~ Children welcome ~ Steep longish walk down from car park ~ Open 11-3, 6-11; 12-4, 6.30-10.30 Sun ~ Bedrooms: £30/£50

REDE TL8055 Map 5

Plough 🍽 �

Village signposted off A143 Bury St Edmunds—Haverhill

On a sunny summer's day, the sheltered cottagey garden behind this thatched pub is a lovely place to enjoy a drink, and there's a little dovecote and aviary; picnic tables in front. Inside, you can be sure of a friendly welcome from the licensees – as well as good, plentiful food: lamb with almonds and apricots, braised rabbit, prawns in a provençale sauce with feta cheese or guinea fowl with mushrooms, tarragon and red wine (all £6.95), chicken in a tangy lemon and honey sauce (£7.50), poached monkfish in a pernod and cream sauce (£7.95), and good steaks; helpful service and decent wines. The simple and traditional cosy bar has copper measures and pewter tankards hanging from low black beams, decorative plates on a delft shelf and surrounding the solid fuel stove in its brick fireplace, and red plush button-back built-in wall banquettes; fruit machine, unobtrusive piped music. *(Recommended by Brian and Jill Bond, Gwen and Peter Andrews, J F M West, SS, R E and P Pearce, Tony and Wendy Hobden)*

Greene King ~ Lease: Brian and Joyce Desborough ~ Meals and snacks (not Sun evenings) ~ Evening restaurant (not Sun) ~ (01284) 789208 ~ Well behaved children in eating area of bar and restaurant ~ Open 11-3, 6-11

SNAPE TM3959 Map 5

Crown 🍽 ♏

B1069

Doing very well at the moment and back in these pages after a long absence, this unspoilt smugglers' inn is very close to Snape Maltings and is popular with concert-goers. The atmosphere is relaxed and warmly friendly and there are some striking horseshoe-shaped high-backed settles around the big brick inglenook, spindleback and country kitchen chairs, nice old tables, old brick floors, and lots of beams in the various small side rooms. Served by helpful, smiling staff, the well presented and particularly good food might include at lunchtime, salmon and cod fishcakes with lime and tartare sauce, feta, tomato and caramelised onion tart (£5.95), home-made boudin blanc (plump white sausage) with garlic mash and rich gravy (£6.50), steak and kidney suet pudding or shank of lamb on spiced beans (£6.95), with evening dishes like spinach and parmesan roulade (£3.95), grilled baby squid with chilli oil (£4.25), scallops and salmon mousseline (£4.95), a brace of quail with pine nuts, sultanas and a balsamic deglaze (£8.50), popular rack of lamb with a herb crust, red wine and redcurrant sauce (£10.50), 20oz sea bass with roasted provençale vegetables and aioli (£12.95), and home-made puddings; Sunday roast is usually topside of beef, and they do pre- and post-concert suppers. Well kept Adnams Bitter and Broadside and seasonal beers on handpump or tapped from the cask, and a good thoughtful wine list with 12 by the glass (including champagne). There are tables and umbrellas in the pretty roadside garden. No children. *(Recommended by Dr Andrew Schuman, Anna Brewer, Evelyn Sanderson, Anthony Barnes, Phil and Heidi Cook, Nick and Hilary Jackson, Mrs P Goodwyn, A E R Archer, Neil Powell)*

Adnams ~ Tenant Paul Maylott ~ Real ale ~ Meals and snacks ~ Restaurant ~ (01728) 688324 ~ Open 12-3, 6-11; closed 25 Dec, evening 26 Dec ~ Bedrooms: £35B/£50B

Golden Key ★

Priory Lane

This is a quietly elegant and rather civilised inn. The low-beamed stylish lounge has an old-fashioned settle curving around a couple of venerable stripped tables on the tiled floor, a winter open fire, and at the other end, some stripped modern settles around heavy Habitat-style wooden tables on a turkey carpet, and a solid fuel stove in the big fireplace. The cream walls are hung with pencil sketches of customers, a Henry Wilkinson spaniel and so forth; a brick-floored side room has sofas and more tables. Popular bar food includes filled rolls (£1.50), home-made chicken liver pâté (£2.95), prawns in garlic and herbs (£3.95), sausage, egg and onion pie or smoked haddock quiche (£5.95), steak, kidney and Guinness or chicken and leek pies (£6.95), and fresh fish such as bass, brill, plaice, salmon and seasonal crab and lobster; fresh vegetables and good home-made puddings. The full range of Adnams beers on handpump (including the seasonal ones), a good wine list, and several malt whiskies. There's a terrace at the back near the small sheltered and flower-filled garden, and plenty of white tables and chairs from which you can enjoy the view. *(Recommended by PM, AM, D Hayman, Phil and Heidi Cook, Nicola Coburn, Derek Patey, DH, June and Perry Dann, John Fahy, Pat Woodward, Christine Herxheimer)*

Adnams ~ Tenants Max and Susie Kissick-Jones ~ Real ale ~ Meals and snacks ~ (01728) 688510 ~ Children allowed in dining room only ~ Open 11-3, 6-11 ~ Bedrooms: £45B/£55B

Plough & Sail ⑪ ♀

Snape Maltings Riverside Centre

Snape Maltings Riverside Centre stretches out behind this buff-coloured pub and includes the famous concert hall, art gallery, craft shop, and a house and garden shop and so forth. The pub itself is a long narrow building with the bar facing you as you walk through the door; beyond this on the right is a raised airy eating room with attractive pine furniture and – to one side – a settle in front of the open fire; beyond this is the busy little restaurant. To the left of the bar and down some steps is a quarry-tiled room with dark traditional furniture. The atmosphere is relaxed and friendly, and one room is no smoking. Generous helpings of delicious food include sandwiches (from £1.65; open ones from £3.95), home-made soup (£2.95), ploughman's (from £3.50), local smoked sprats (£3.95), local cod (£6.50), plaice fillets stuffed with salmon mousse (£6.75), ostrich (£6.95), and Sunday carvery (£6.95). Well kept Adnams ales plus Greene King IPA and Abbot on handpump, and a fine wine list with a few by the glass; darts and cribbage. The big enclosed back terrace has lots of picnic tables and a giant chess set. *(Recommended by Alan Jarvis, Ray Watson, Susan Moy, A Albert, John C Baker, MN, DN)*

Free house ~ Licensee G D Gooderham ~ Real ale ~ Meals and snacks ~ Restaurant~ (01728) 688413 ~ Children in eating area of bar ~ Open 11-3, 5.30-11

SOUTHWOLD TM5076 Map 5

Crown ★ ⑪ ⇋ ♀ ◧

High Street

Considering how many people come to this smart old hotel to enjoy its marvellous food and drink (and you will be made just as welcome for either), it's quite a feat that the staff seem able to cope with such smiling cheerfulness and efficiency. The elegant beamed main bar has a stripped curved high-backed settle and other dark varnished settles, kitchen chairs and some bar stools, pretty, fresh flowers on the mix of kitchen pine tables, newspapers to read, a carefully restored and rather fine carved wooden fireplace, and a relaxed atmosphere; the small no-smoking restaurant with its white cloths and pale cane chairs leads off. The smaller back oak-panelled locals' bar has more of a traditional pubby atmosphere, red leatherette wall benches and a red carpet; the little parlour on the left is also no smoking. There's a particularly carefully chosen wine list (they have the full Adnams range, well over 300), with a monthly changing choice of 20 interesting varieties by the glass or bottle kept perfectly on a cruover machine; you can get any of them from the cash and carry by the mixed dozen round the corner. Adnams brewery is nearby, and the Crown is understandably their flagship – perfectly kept Adnams Bitter, Broadside, Mild, and winter Old on handpump; also a good choice of malt whiskies, tea, coffee and herbal infusions. The very good, creative bar food changes every day, but might typically include roast vegetable tartlet on a balsamic vinaigrette or vegetable paella with lemon crostini (£3.50 starter, £6.95 main course), terrine of duck with apple and plum chutney (£3.95 starter, £7.50 main course), oriental beef salad with crisp egg noodles and chilli soy dip (£4 starter, £8 main course), steamed plaice fillet with a light lemon and herb butter (£7.25), braised pork knuckle with cabbage and a mint pea sauce (£7.50), chicken supreme with sautéed greens and a caper cream (£7.95), noisettes of lamb with a coriander potato cake and redcurrant and kumquat marmalade (£8.95), and puddings such as spotted dick, pear and filo pastry gateau on a caramel sauce or hot chocolate and banana steamed pudding with a rich chocolate sauce and chantilly cream (£2.95). The restaurant does a good three-course lunch for £15.50. Shove-ha'penny, dominoes and cribbage. There are some tables in a sunny sheltered corner outside. *(Recommended by J F M West, Robert Gomme, Roger Danes, D Hayman, Dr P J S Crawshaw, Sarah and Ian Shannon, Mavis and John Wright, Frank Gadbois, Gwen and Peter Andrews, Helen Crookston, W W Burke, John Waller, Pat and Roger Fereday, Alan Jarvis, Jamie and Ruth Lyons, J E Hilditch, Graham and Liz Bell, Eric and Jackie Robinson, James Macrae, Tom Thomas, G M Donkin, Pat Woodward, Dave Carter, M J Morgan, John and Sheila French, John and Moira Cole, Gill and Andy Plumb, JKW, Dr Ronald Church, Rita Horridge, James Macrae, Nigel Woolliscroft; also in Good Hotel Guide)*

Adnams ~ Manager Anne Simpson ~ Real ale ~ Meals and snacks (12.15-1.45, 7.15-9.45) ~ Restaurant ~ (01502) 722275 ~ Children in eating area of bar ~ Open 10.30-3, 6-11; closed 25-26 Dec, lunchtime 1 Jan, and 2nd week Jan ~ Bedrooms: £40B/£63B

STOKE BY NAYLAND TL9836 Map 5

Angel ⑪ ⇋ ♀

B1068 Sudbury—East Bergholt; also signposted via Nayland off A134 Colchester—Sudbury

Even on a midweek January lunchtime, this civilised and enjoyable old place fills up very quickly with those keen to enjoy the particularly good food. Attractively presented and delicious, there might be home-made soup (£2.55), fishcakes with remoulade sauce or mushroom and pistachio pâté (£3.95), steamed mussels in white wine (£4.50), vegetable filo parcels with fresh tomato coulis (£5.75), liver and bacon with madeira sauce or home-made steamed steak and kidney pudding with onion gravy (£5.95), roast loin of pork with crackling, apple mousse and braised red cabbage (£6.25), chicken and king prawn brochette with yoghurt and mint dip (£8.25), griddled fresh wing of skate (£8.95), honey glazed roast rack of new season's lamb (£9.75), and puddings like steamed apple pudding with vanilla sauce or dark chocolate ganache gateau (£3.25). The comfortable main bar area has handsome Elizabethan beams, some stripped brickwork and timbers, a mixture of furnishings including wing armchairs, mahogany dining chairs, and pale library chairs, local watercolours and older prints, attractive table lamps, and a huge log fire. Round the corner is a little tiled-floor stand-and-chat bar – with well kept Adnams, Greene King IPA and Abbot and a guest beer on handpump, and a thoughtful wine list. One no-smoking room has a low sofa and wing armchairs around its woodburning stove, and Victorian paintings on the dark green walls. There are cast-iron seats and tables on a sheltered terrace. Handy for Holkham Hall. No children. *(Recommended by MDN, M R Hyde, Gwen and Peter Andrews, Eric and Jackie Robinson, John Evans, DAV, Carolyn and Michael Hedoin, Malcolm Taylor, Mr and Mrs J R Morris, Paul and Maggie Baker, Graham and Liz Bell, John Prescott, MN, DN, Pamela Goodwyn, JKW, R W Hillyard, Quentin Williamson, Nicholas Holmes)*

Free house ~ Licensee Peter Smith ~ Real ale ~ Meals and snacks ~ Restaurant ~ (01206) 263245 ~ Open 11-2.30, 6-11; closed 25-26 Dec ~ Bedrooms: £45B/£59B

THORNHAM MAGNA TM1070 Map 5

Four Horseshoes

Off A140 S of Diss; follow Finningham 3¼ signpost, by White Horse pub

Re-thatched and refurbished recently, this friendly handsome pub has an extensive and rambling bar that is well divided into alcoves and distinct areas. There are very low and heavy black beams, some tall windsor chairs as well as the golden plush banquettes and stools on its spread of fitted turkey carpet, country pictures and farm tools on the black-timbered white walls, and logs burning in big fireplaces; the area with the inside well is no smoking. A wide choice of good food, quickly served by uniformed waitresses, might include sandwiches (from £2.25), ploughman's (from £4.65), vegetarian lasagne (£5.25), fillet of plaice (£5.95), a large mixed grill (£7.95), daily specials such as chicken curry (£6.25), fillet steak and stilton burger (£6.95), and cold poached salmon with mussels and a fruity herb vinaigrette (£8.75), and puddings (from £1.95). The restaurant is no smoking. Well kept Adnams Bitter, Courage Best, Shepherd Neame Spitfire, and Theakstons Best and XB on handpump, some malt whiskies and country wines, and piped music. In summer, you can sit at the picnic tables beside the flowerbeds on a sheltered lawn. Thornham Walks nearby consists of nearly 12 miles of permissive footpaths on the beautiful and privately owned Thornham Estate and there is a half mile hard-surfaced path through the parkland, woodland and farmland which is suitable for wheelchairs and pushchairs as well as those with walking difficulties. The thatched church at Thornham Parva is famous for its ancient wall paintings. *(Recommended by Ian Phillips, Bill and Sheila McLardy, Keith Archer, Richard Balls, Davie Craine, Ann Reeder)*

Free house ~ Licensees Peter and Pam Morris ~ Real ale ~ Meals and snacks ~ Restaurant ~ (01379) 678777 ~ Children in eating area of bar ~ Open 12-3, 6.45(6.30 Sat)-11 ~ Bedrooms: £35B/£50B

TOSTOCK TL9563 Map 5

Gardeners Arms

Village signposted from A14 (former A45) and A1088

Even when this charmingly unspoilt pub is very busy, you can be sure of a warm welcome from the friendly licensees. It's a popular place with locals of all ages, and the smart lounge bar has a bustling villagey atmosphere, low heavy black beams, and lots of carving chairs around the black tables. Enjoyable bar food includes sandwiches, soup, ploughman's, nice chicken livers, spicy bean bake (£4.95), Thai king prawn green curry or chicken piri-piri (£6.75), lamb chops with redcurrant sauce (£7.25), duck breast with ginger sauce and stir-fried vegetables (£9.25), and good salmon with dill and a crème fraîche sauce. Very well kept Greene King Abbot and IPA and seasonal beers on handpump. The lively tiled-floor public bar has darts, pool, shove-ha'penny, dominoes, cribbage, juke box, and fruit machine. The picnic table sets among the roses and other flowers on the sheltered lawn are a lovely place to sit. *(Recommended by Phillip Fox, John Saul, J E Hilditch, Ron Nightingale, Neville Kenyon, Charles Bardswell, David and Mary Webb, Gordon and Clare Phillips, Richard Fawcett, Ian Phillips, Joan Hilditch)*

Greene King ~ Tenant Reg Ransome ~ Real ale ~ Meals and snacks (not Mon or Tues evenings or Sun lunchtime) ~ (01359) 270460 ~ Children in eating area of bar ~ Open 11.30(11 Sat)-3, 7-11

WALBERSWICK TM4974 Map 5

Bell

Just off B1387

As we went to press, a new licensee had just taken over this unpretentious old place. The characterful, rambling bar has the flooring bricks and oak beams that it had 400 years ago when the sleepy little village was a flourishing port, curved high-backed settles on the well worn flagstones, tankards hanging from oars above the bar counter, and a woodburning stove in the big fireplace; the other bar has a very large open fire. Bar food now includes home-made soup (£2.20), sandwiches (toasted brie and cranberry £3, toasted bacon, avocado and peanut butter or smoked chicken and watercress £3.50, smoked salmon and tomato bagel £4.25), ploughman's (from £3.75), good local fish and chips or fried haloumi cheese with Greek salad (£5.25), mushroom stroganoff (£5.50), and chicken stir fry or green beef curry (£6). The restaurant is no smoking. Well kept Adnams Bitter, Broadside and Extra on handpump, and darts, shove-ha'penny, and fruit machine; three resident boxer dogs. Most of the bedrooms look over the sea or the river. This is a nice spot close to the beach, with a well placed hedge sheltering the seats and tables on the sizeable flower-filled lawn from the worst of the sea winds. To really make the most of the setting, it's worth taking the little ferry from Southwold, and then enjoying the short walk along to the pub. *(Recommended by Susan May, Anne Morris, June and Perry Dann, Paul Kitchener, S Holdsworth, Dr B and Mrs P Baker, D Hayman; more reports on the new regime, please)*

Adnams ~ Tenant Sue Cutting ~ Real ale ~ Meals and snacks ~ Evening restaurant ~ (01502) 723109 ~ Children welcome in own room ~ Folk music first Sun of month ~ Open 11-3, 6-11; 11-11 summer Sat; 12-10.30 summer Sun ~ Bedrooms: /£50(£60B)

WANGFORD TM4679 Map 5

Angel 🛏 🍴 £

High St; village signposted just off A12 at junction of B1126 to Southwold

This solid 17th-c village inn was handsomely refaced in Georgian times – and has now been thoroughly refurbished in sympathetic traditional style. There's a feeling of relaxed solidity about the light and airy bar, with some sturdy elm tables, cushioned winged wall benches and other substantial furniture, and a splendid old bar counter. It's all kept spick and span. Bar food includes particularly good value dishes of the day such as locally caught fresh fish, liver and kidney casserole (£3.50), half a roast chicken (£3.95), steak and mushroom or cheese and broccoli pie (£4.50) and haddock (£4.75), besides regular dishes such as soup (£1.50), omelettes (from £2.50), filled baked potatoes (from £2.75), ploughman's (from £3.75), gammon and pineapple (£5.90), grilled lemon sole (£6.25), 8oz sirloin steak (£8.50), puddings (£1.50), children's menu (£1.95), and Sunday 3-course lunch (£4.95). The restaurant is no smoking. Well kept Adnams, Courage Best, Morlands Old Speckled Hen, Theakstons Best and Youngs Special on handpump, decent house wines, good generous coffee; pleasant staff, but maybe piped pop music (local radio on our inspection visit); trivia. The garden behind has picnic tables under cocktail parasols. *(Recommended by Dr and Mrs Nick Holmes, Michael Johnson)*

Free house ~ Licensee Richard Pearson ~ Real ale ~ Meals and snacks ~ Restaurant ~ (01502) 578636 ~ Children in eating area of bar ~ Open 11-11; 12-10.30 Sun ~ Bedrooms: £40B/£45B

WESTLETON TM4469 Map 5

White Horse

Village on B1125 Blythburgh—Leiston; pub just up side road off green

Altogether less smart and considerably cheaper than the Crown, the popular dining pub down the road (see Lucky Dip section), this friendly Victorian village pub does good generous straightforward bar food in huge helpings. Fresh local fish such as plump plaice or cod (£4.95) is particularly praised, and other dishes might include duck pâté or smoked kippers (£2.20), king prawns in garlic butter (£3.20), home-made vegetable quiche (£3.95), chilli or spicy vegetarian burgers (£4.25), chicken and stilton or steak and kidney pie (£4.50), Cromer crab salad (£5.50), puddings (from £1.90), evening steaks (from £7.95), and children's menu (from £1.70). The small high-ceilinged two-room bar is simply furnished with heavy red leatherette settles, library chairs and the like, and has an agreeably busy decor; there's also an attractive Victorian back dining room (no smoking). Well kept Adnams Bitter and Broadside and seasonal ales on handpump, quiet but well reproduced piped music (maybe classical or traditional Scottish – the friendly bearded landlord is Scots), a shelf of local-interest books. There are picnic tables in a small cottagey back garden with a climbing frame (and also out beside the village duck pond), and the hanging baskets and window boxes win awards. Handy for the Minsmere bird reserve, and almost next door to Fisks clematis nursery. We have not yet had reports on the bedrooms here but expect them to be good. *(Recommended by Gill and Andy Plumb, John and Barbara Spencer, Paul Mason, M A Mees, MDN)*

Adnams ~ Tenant Martin Hall ~ Real ale ~ Meals and snacks (not winter Tues) ~ (01728) 648222 ~ Children in eating area of bar and in restaurant ~ Open 12-3(4 Sat and Sun), 6.30-11; winter evening opening 7pm ~ Bedrooms: £25B/£42B

Lucky Dip

Besides the fully inspected pubs, you might like to try these Lucky Dips recommended to us and described by readers (if you do, please send us reports):

☆ Aldeburgh [Market Pl; opp Moot Hall; TM4656], *Mill*: Friendly nautical atmosphere, local fishermen in bar, cosy separate no-smoking eating area, view of sea and boats; good food cooked to order inc local fish; good service, well kept Adnams ales, sensible prices; can get rather full in summer *(M Catterick, June and Perry Dann, Norman Smith)*

☆ Badingham [TM3068], *White Horse*: Old-fashioned pub with attractive stripped brickwork and beams, longcase clock by huge open range with woodburner, wholesome reasonably priced straightforward bar food inc vegetarian and children's, well kept Adnams, relaxing atmosphere, well reproduced piped music in public bar; neat bowling green, nice rambling garden *(Gwen and Peter Andrews, John Beeken, LYM)*

Barham [Old Norwich Rd; TM1451], *Sorrel Horse*: Attractive pink-washed pantiled country pub, nicely refurbished bar with lots of beams, lounge and two dining areas off, particularly well kept Tolly ales inc Cobbolds IPA, decent usual bar food, prompt friendly service; good garden with play area and barbecue, timber stables opp; well placed for

walks *(John Baker, Brian and Jenny Seller, Paul Deasy)*

☆ Barton Mills [A11, by Five Ways roundabout; TL7173], *Bull*: Rambling bar with big fireplaces, well kept Adnams, Bass, Worthington BB and a guest beer, decent wines, good local atmosphere, reasonably priced standard bar food served noon-10 (not Sun) and good summer salad bar, separate grill area, piped music; children allowed in eating area; bedrooms *(Roy Bromell, BB)*

Beccles [New Market; TM4290], *Kings Head*: Hospitable central hotel, handy for coffee or afternoon tea; Tudor behind 18th-c front, lounge and bar areas, Robinsons on handpump, good value bar food with fresh veg (two-for-one evening bargains), Sun carvery 12-5; bedrooms *(June and Perry Dann)*; [town centre], *Swan House*: Several comfortable rooms and courtyard, good attentive service, chilled glass for unusual bottled beers from around the world, bar nibbles, short choice of imaginative well prepared food *(Fleur and John Cannadine)*

☆ Blaxhall [off B1069 S of Snape; can be reached from A12 via Little Glemham; TM3657],

Ship: Low-beamed traditional country local, log fire, generous home cooking with fresh veg in unassuming dining lounge, well kept Tolly and Marstons Pedigree on handpump, piped music, pool in public bar; children in eating area; self-catering cabins available *(June and Perry Dann, LYM)*

☆ **Blythburgh** [A12; TM4575], *White Hart*: Open-plan family dining pub with good reasonably priced food inc cold buffet, fine ancient beams, woodwork and staircase, big open fires, well kept Adnams Bitter, Old and Broadside, decent wines, quick conscientious service; children in eating area and restaurant, open all day Fri/Sat; spacious lawns looking down on tidal marshes, magnificent church over road *(June and Perry Dann, G M K Donkin, Alan J Pegg, N S Smith, Hazel Morgan, LYM)*

☆ **Boxford** [Broad St; TL9640], *Fleece*: Unpretentious partly 15th-c pub with cosy panelled bar on right, airy lounge bar with wonderful medieval fireplace, armchairs and some distinctive old seats among more conventional furnishings; good home cooking, well kept Tolly, welcoming landlord, good live jazz Fri *(John Prescott, LYM)*

Boxford, *White Hart*: Attractive exterior, pleasant interior, good choice of food inc properly cooked Indian dishes, interesting variety of fish *(JP)*

Bradfield Combust [Sudbury Rd; TL8957], *Manager*: Interesting Tudor inn, already a century old when the word used for its present name was coined; well kept Greene King ales, friendly staff, restaurant *(Frank W Gadbois)*

☆ **Bramfield** [A144; TM4073], *Queens Head*: Friendly pleasantly refurbished high-beamed lounge bar, cheery atmosphere, good service, good fresh food, big log fire, well kept Adnams Bitter, Old and Broadside, piped music; darts in public bar; restaurant *(F J and P A Apicella, Rosemary Woodburn, Pamela Goodwyn, June and Perry Dann, Dr Ronald Church)*

Brampton [A145 S of Beccles; TM4382], *Dog*: Friendly pub now doing well under former tenant of Eels Foot at Eastbridge, reasonably priced good food, well kept beers, good live music Thurs *(June and Perry Dann)*

Bungay [Broad St; TM3491], *Green Dragon*: Comfortable small town local brewing its own fine well priced ales (Chaucer is particularly good), food inc very good filled baked potatoes and good value specials, liberal attitude towards children; piped music may be loud, very popular with young people – side room quieter *(G Washington, John Baker, Keith and Janet Morris)*

Bures [TL9033], *Eight Bells*: Pleasant old-fashioned pub with good value well served food in simple but attractive bar, smiling service; popular with card-players *(John Prescott)*

☆ **Bury St Edmunds** [7 Out Northgate St, Station Hill; TL8564], *Linden Tree*: Good bustling yet relaxed atmosphere and wide choice of generous cheap food in busy attractively renovated family dining pub with stripped pine bar, friendly quick service, well kept Greene King IPA and Rayments, wines in two

glass sizes, freshly squeezed orange juice, popular conservatory restaurant (worth booking), good well kept garden *(J F M West, Dr Andrew Shuman, Anna Brewer, Rick and Carol Mercado, Stuart Earle, Sheryl Bailey)*

☆ **Bury St Edmunds** [Whiting St], *Masons Arms*: Particularly good value home-made food from really good snacks up, three well kept Greene King ales and prompt friendly service in busy but comfortable and relaxing dining lounge with lots of oak timbering; more of a local evenings *(Mrs P J Pearce, Frank W Gadbois, Nigel Woolliscroft, PGP)*

Bury St Edmunds [Angel Hill], *Angel*: Thriving long-established country-town hotel with popular food in Regency dining room and terrace rooms, friendly service, well kept Adnams, cellar grill room; bedrooms comfortable *(A Albert, J F M West)*; [Guildhall St], *Black Boy*: Big open-plan pub with side game and sitting areas, Greene King beers, welcoming landlord, reasonably priced food and drink *(PGP)*; [Crown St – park in back yard off Bridewell Lane], *Dog & Partridge*: Rambling town pub with bar, snug and several lounge areas – old, very old and new linked together; well kept Greene King from nearby brewery, usual food, friendly efficient service; games room, restaurant area; more a young people's pub evenings *(PGP, J F M West)*; [Mount Rd; minor rd towards Thurston, parallel to A143; TL8967], *Flying Fortress*: Former farmhouse HQ of USAF support group, on edge of Rougham ex-airfield – the original for the film *Twelve O'Clock High*, with WWII bomber models and evocative black and white pictures; big comfortable modern lounge area, well kept Adnams, Flowers, Whitbreads and Worthington from long bar, wide range of food cooked here (not cheap) inc carvery, friendly staff, take-away wines, tables outside, old fire-engine for children to play on *(Frank W Gadbois, Steve Reynolds, John C Baker)*; [Traverse, Abbeygate St], *Nutshell*: Attractive corner pub, perhaps the country's smallest inside (though it's said 102 people once squeezed in), friendly and cosy, with particularly well kept Greene King IPA and Abbot, lots of odd bric-a-brac – an interesting tourist attraction; cl Sun and Holy Days *(Michael Marlow, PGP, Cdr Patrick Tailyour)*; [39 Churchgate St], *Queens Head*: Much modernised 18th-c coaching inn, half a dozen interesting real ales, cheap food, very quick service, restaurant; busy with professionals at lunchtime and young people Fri/Sat evening; open all day all week *(Tony and Wendy Hobden, Mark Flack)*; [St Johns St], *Wolf*: Comfortable and roomy Wetherspoons pub with decent food and well kept beer; despite high quality prices are low *(John C Baker)*

Buxhall [Mill Green; signed off B1115 W of Stowmarket, then L at Rattlesden sign; TM0057], *Crown*: Tucked-away country pub with snug little bar and side room, fair choice of bar food, Adnams Broadside and Greene King IPA, open fires, games in separate public bar, restaurant; children allowed if eating, pleasant garden *(Stuart Earle, BB)*

Carlton [Rosemary Lane; just N of Saxmundham; TM3864], *Poachers Pocket*: Welcoming country pub completely and carefully refurbished by new owners, scrupulously clean, with well kept changing ales, well presented generous food inc lots of good puddings in bar, small dining area or garden with lovely country views *(John and Barbara Spencer)*

☆ **Cavendish** [High St (A1092); TL8046], *Bull*: Friendly and attractive 16th-c beamed pub locally popular for wide range of good value food; thriving atmosphere, good service, well kept Adnams, nice fireplaces; bar, dining area, garden with barbecue; fruit machines, darts and pool, no piped music; children welcome, reasonably priced bedrooms *(Nick Holmes, Oliver Richardson, Richard and Valerie Wright)*

☆ **Chelsworth** [The Street; near Bury St Edmunds; TL9848], *Peacock*: Genteel dining pub with lots of Tudor brickwork and exposed beams, big inglenook log fire, fairly intimate not over-smart attractively pubby decor, well spaced comfortable tables; new manager/chef since early summer 1996 doing wide choice of good food inc unusual dishes, interesting sauces and good fresh veg (presentation veers towards the robust); good service, well chosen wines, several well kept changing ales, decent coffee, nice small garden; open all day Sat; bedrooms – the two at the back are quieter; pretty village *(MDN, LYM; more reports on new regime please)*

☆ **Clare** [Market Hill; TL7645], *Bell*: Timbered inn with food inc children's dishes in dining conservatory opening on to terrace, rambling lounge bar with splendidly carved black beams, old panelling and woodwork around the open fire, side rooms (one with lots of canal and other prints), well kept Nethergate ales, decent wines; darts, pool, fruit machine; bedrooms, open all day, interesting village *(Gwen and Peter Andrews, Pat and Tony Martin, Tom Thomas, PM, AM, LYM)*

Clare [Nethergate St], *Clare Hotel*: Smart but pleasantly pubby L-shaped bar with enjoyable food, well kept beer, decent service, conservatory/restaurant, attractive garden with shady areas; bedrooms *(MN, DN, BB)*; [High St], *Swan*: Straightforward village pub dating from early 17th c, huge log fire, friendly landlord, good straightforward home-made food from huge bargain huffers *(W T Aird, J A Howl)*

Cretingham [TM2260], *Bell*: Comfortable pub mixing striking 15th-c beams, timbers and big fireplace with more modern renovations and furnishings, Adnams and changing guest beers, bar food inc vegetarian and children's; no-smoking lounge and restaurant with Sun lunch, traditional games in public bar, family room, may open all day in summer; seats out in rose garden and on front grass *(June and Perry Dann, Ricardo Littrell, LYM)*

Darsham [just off A12; TM4169], *Fox*: Friendly new licensees, good reasonably priced bar food with fresh veg and home-made puddings; restaurant *(June and Perry Dann)*

☆ **East Bergholt** [Burnt Oak, towards Flatford Mill; TM0734], *Kings Head*: Well kept attractive beamed lounge with comfortable sofas, interesting decorations, quick willing pleasant service, good value home-made usual bar food, well kept Tolly, decent wines and coffee, piped classical music (juke box in plain public bar); lots of room in pretty garden, flower-decked haywain, baskets and tubs of flowers in front *(Pamela Goodwyn, E A George)*

☆ **Eastbridge** [TM4566], *Eels Foot*: Country pub in pretty village, handy for Minsmere bird reserve and heathland walks, refurbished under new licensee, with new back restaurant, wide choice of reasonably priced bar food, well kept Adnams and other ales, a welcome for walkers, tables on quiet front terrace, children in eating area *(Chris and Kate Lyons, June and Perry Dann, LYM)*

☆ **Easton** [N of Wickham Mkt, Earl Soham rd; TM2858], *White Horse*: Quaint and neatly kept pink-washed two-bar country local with open fires, well kept Adnams, food in bar and homely dining room, welcoming staff, children in eating area, garden with good play area – nice to hear bell practice in next-door church Fri evening *(Graham and Liz Bell, LYM)*

Exning [TL6165], *White Horse*: Unsmart 17th-c local with log fires, good cheap generous home-made food in separate dining room, well kept Whitbreads-related ales, friendly staff *(Frank W Gadbois)*

Felixstowe Ferry [TM3337], *Victoria*: Riverside pub reopened a couple of years ago, friendly landlord, good pub food emphasising local seafood, competitively priced Adnams and guest beers, sailing charts in gents' *(Keith Sale)*

Finningham [TM0669], *White Horse*: Decent lunch, pleasant atmosphere; handy for walkers *(Mrs P Goodwyn)*

Flempton [TL8169], *Greyhound*: Beautifully located spotless village pub, good service, reasonably priced bar food, well kept Greene King ales *(W H and E Thomas)*

Fornham all Saints [TL8367], *Three Kings*: Smart and spotless, nicely modernised in traditional style, Greene King ales, good value popular bar food inc six daily specials, separate dining room, friendly efficient service even though busy *(DAV)*

☆ **Framlingham** [Market Hill; TM2863], *Crown*: Traditional small inn with old-fashioned heavy-beamed public bar opening into hall and comfortable character lounge with armchairs by log fire, worthwhile bar and restaurant food (not cheap) from good newish chef, Adnams on handpump, lively atmosphere on Sat market day, help-yourself morning coffee; comfortable period bedrooms *(John Evans, Ricardo Littrell, N S Smith)*

Framlingham [Castle Approach], *Castle*: Friendly old small pub with Whitbreads and other ales, wide range of good bar food from toasties to steaks; children welcome *(Quentin Williamson)*

☆ **Friston** [B1121; just off A1094 Aldeburgh—Snape, 4.5 m NE of Aldeburgh; TM4160], *Old Chequers*: Welcoming dining pub with simple country pine furnishings, airy decor, pleasant new tenants, good choice of food inc carefully prepared lunchtime buffet, well kept Adnams, good value wines (*Norman Smith, Keith Archer, F Tomlin, LYM*)

Great Barton [A143 NW of Bury; TL8967], *Bunbury Arms*: Spacious and well appointed open-plan L-shaped bar and separate restaurant revitalised by new licensees, buzzing at lunchtime, with well kept Greene King ales, interesting well prepared home-made food from good sandwiches up, big helpings, darts at public end; play area (*Richard Balls, W H and E Thomas*)

☆ **Great Wenham** [The Row, Capel St Mary Rd; TM0738], *Queens Head*: Country pub with creative Indian food (not Mon evening) among other dishes, comfortably traditional pubby atmosphere, friendly licensees, well kept Adnams Bitter and Broadside, Greene King Abbot and a guest beer, good value wines; families welcome in cosy snug (*John Baker, Richard Balls*)

Grundisburgh [TM2250], *Dog*: Good bar food inc bargain OAP Mon lunches in well run carefully extended elegant period pub, good range of well kept beers (*Mrs P Goodwyn*)

Halesworth [Thoroughfare; TM3877], *Angel*: 16th-c coaching inn doing well under new tenants, interesting interior courtyard with 18th-c clock and vines trained round the walls, traditional bar food, well kept ales, decent wines, good Italian restaurant; seven well equipped bedrooms (*R J Sinfield, Nick and Carolyn Carter*); [Thoroughfare], *White Hart*: Pleasant open-plan town pub, wide range of good food inc fresh veg (*June and Perry Dann*)

☆ **Haughley** [centre; TM0262], *Kings Arms*: Friendly new licensees, interesting choice of good value home-made bar food inc good Greek dishes (landlady's mother comes from Cyprus), clean and peaceful beamed dining lounge with lots of shiny dark tables, smaller lounge and busy public bar with games, log fire, well kept Greene King IPA, Abbot and Rayments, piped music; tables and play house on back lawn (*David Frostick, Mrs P Goodwyn, BB*)

☆ **Haughley** [Station Rd – towards Old Newton by level crossing], *Railway*: Tastefully redecorated traditional country local with no frills, good value food esp steak pie, particularly well kept Greene King ales with a couple of guest beers such as Nethergate and Woodfordes Broadsman or Everards and Marstons Pedigree, sometimes tapped from casks in the cellar, log fire, welcoming locals; children in neat back room (*John Baker, Paul Kidger, Richard Balls, BB*)

Hawkedon [Rede Rd; between A143 and B1066; TL7952], *Queens Head*: Lots of character, good sensibly priced home-made food inc unusual dishes, well kept beers inc unusual guests such as the strong Mauldons Crouch Valley, friendly new landlady (*Frank W Gadbois*)

Hepworth [A143 Bury—Diss; TL9874], *Duke of Marlborough*: Simple but often adventurous food at sensible prices, four well kept Adnams,

Greene King and Old Chimneys (from nearby Mkt Weston), spic and span comfort – suburban sitting-room rather than country cottage (*John C Baker*)

Hitcham [The Street; B1115 Sudbury—Stowmarket; TL9851], *White Horse*: Friendly local with good home cooking inc perfect veg in bar and dining room, obliging service, well kept Greene King Abbot (*Margaret and Michael Norris, Stuart Earle*)

☆ **Holbrook** [Ipswich Rd; TM1636], *Compasses*: Good value food inc interesting dishes in bar and restaurant, welcoming staff, log fire, well kept ales inc Flowers and Tolly, garden with play area (*A Albert*)

Horringer [TL8261], *Six Bells*: Comfortably renovated and extended, well spaced tables, good range of reasonably priced food, well kept Greene King, quick cheerful service (*W T Aird*)

Hulver Street [TM4687], *Hulvergate Lodge*: Large pub in pleasant countryside, good food in bar or restaurant, big terrace and garden with weekend barbecues (*June and Perry Dann*)

Huntingfield [TM3374], *Huntingfield Arms*: Neat pub overlooking green, light wood tables and chairs, pleasant combination of beams and stripped brickwork, good range of attractively presented bar food inc good fresh fish, well kept Adnams, friendly service, restaurant, games area with pool beyond woodburner (*Gwen and Peter Andrews*)

☆ **Icklingham** [62 The Street; TL7772], *Old Plough*: Attractively decorated country pub with pleasant atmosphere, well kept Adnams, Greene King IPA and a couple of guests such as Wadworths 6X, good range of home-made food, lots of cricketing memorabilia and books, subdued piped music; big garden with play area (*Frank W Gadbois*)

Ipswich [Henley Rd/Anglesea Rd; TM1744], *Greyhound*: Comfortable Victorian-style decor, well kept Adnams and guest ales, good home cooking inc unusual bar snacks at reasonable prices, spotless housekeeping (*Mary Williamson, Gordon and Clare Phillips*); [76 St Helens St], *Tap & Spile*: Six or more real ales from outside the area, big lounge, snug, games room (*PM, AM*)

Kersey [signed off A1141 N of Hadleigh; TL9944], *Bell*: Quaint flower-decked Tudor building in picturesque village, low-beamed public side with tiled floor and log fire divided from red plush lounge by brick and timber screen, very wide choice of bar food, well kept ales such as Ind Coope Burton, Ruddles County and Nethergate Old Growler, decent house wines, restaurant, polite service, sheltered back terrace with fairy-lit side canopy; open all day (afternoon teas), children allowed, small caravan site (*Gwen and Peter Andrews, Frank Cummins, Graham and Liz Bell, Tony and Wendy Hobden, LYM*)

Kettleburgh [Easton Rd; TM2660], *Chequers*: Once a brewery, with well kept Whitbreads-related ales and others such as Marstons Pedigree, Greene King IPA and Tolly Mild (these last two mix well), unspoilt lively bar

with open fire, good reasonably priced home-cooked food inc fresh fish and local quail served efficiently in panelled dining room *(Jenny and Brian Seller, Dr P J S Crawshaw)*
Knodishall [TM4261], *Butchers Arms*: Warmly refurbished old local with cheery atmosphere, well kept Adnams, pleasant airy dining room, good reasonably priced home-cooked food; SkyTV, karaoke nights *(N S Smith)*
☆ Layham [Upper St, Upper Layham; TM0240], *Marquis of Cornwallis*: Beamed 16th-c pub with plush lounge bar, nicely prepared straightforward food inc good ploughman's and fresh veg, popular lunchtime with businessmen and retired locals, well kept beers such as Marstons Pedigree; good valley views, picnic tables in extensive riverside garden, open all day Sat in summer; bedrooms handy for Harwich ferries *(O K Smyth, R G and J N Plumb)*
☆ Lindsey [Rose Green, signed from Kersey; TL9744], *White Rose*: Pleasantly refurbished half-timbered country dining pub, lovely log fire, wide choice of generous rather sophisticated food, well kept local and national beers, range of wines, welcoming service *(John and Brenda Gibbs, R G and J N Plumb, MDN, T Gondris, Jeremy and Louise Kemp)*
Long Melford [TL8645], *Black Lion*: Very much a hotel/restaurant, but it does have good stylish bar food, and interesting decor inc toby jugs and other china; good wines, well kept beer; bedrooms *(J F M West, F C Johnston)*; [Hall St], *Cock & Bell*: Attractive pink-washed pub, busy and cheerful, with five real ales and a weekly guest, good fresh food cooked to order, friendly service; bedrooms *(Mrs T A Uthwaitt, Frank W Gadbois)*; *Crown*: Attractively renovated, with friendly service, good value food, well kept Bass, Greene King and Hancocks, good open fire, dining room; bedrooms *(Frank W Gadbois, BB)*; [N end of village], *Hare*: Popular pub with good choice of reasonably priced mainly home-made food inc some unusual dishes, good choice of ales, friendly service, log fire in small back bar, larger front bar, dining area, upstairs dining room; attractive garden *(Brian and Louisa Routledge, David Dimock)*; *Scutchers Arms*: Good food and service, pleasant bar *(N S Holmes)*
Market Weston [Bury Rd; TL9877], *Mill*: Old pub recently refurbished and reopened under new licensee, civilised atmosphere, well kept Adnams, Greene King IPA and Old Chimneys Great Raft from the village brewery, reasonably priced interesting food *(John C Baker, Frank W Gadbois)*
☆ Martlesham [off A12 Woodbridge—Ipswich; TM2547], *Black Tiles*: Spotless and spacious family pub with pleasantly decorated bistro-style garden-room restaurant (children allowed here), big woodburner in characterful old bar, wide choice of good inexpensive generous quick home-made food, quick service from smart helpful staff, well kept Adnams Bitter and Broadside and a guest beer, tables in garden; open all day every day *(C H and P Stride, Norman S Smith, LYM)*
Mellis [The Common; TM0974], *Railway*:

Warmly friendly local, open fires, very relaxed licensees, enjoyable food inc fresh fish and good value Sun lunch, well kept Adnams and Nethergate Old Growler; curry and folk nights *(Trevor Moore)*
☆ Melton [Wilford Bridge; TM2851], *Wilford Bridge*: Light and roomy country pub with good value food inc local fish in bar and restaurant, steak nights Mon/Tues, takeaways, prompt friendly service, decent wines; nearby river walks *(Mary and David Webb, Malcolm Taylor, Andrew Day)*
☆ Mendham [TM2782], *Sir Alfred Munnings*: Good cheerful atmosphere in big comfortable open-plan bar with good value neatly served bar food, well kept Adnams and other real ales, unobtrusive piped music, restaurant; children welcome, bedrooms, swimming pool for residents *(Pamela Goodwyn, LYM)*
Mettingham [B1062 Bungay—Beccles; TM3589], *Tally Ho*: Attractive pub, clean, comfortable, unpretentious and roomy, with good reasonably priced home-made food inc good sandwiches, Courage-related beers, pleasant quick service *(David Carr)*
Mildenhall [Main St; TL7174], *Bell*: Well kept Courage Best and Directors in old inn's spacious beamed bar, open fires, friendly obliging service, good value generous food; darts, juke box; comfortable bedrooms *(Sue Rowland, Paul Mallett, Frank W Gadbois)*; *Riverside*: Beautiful extensively refurbished hotel, good atmosphere in spacious attractive lounge, well kept Bass and Ruddles County, attractively presented creative cooking, dining area overlooking lawn down to River Lark; good bedrooms *(Frank W Gadbois)*; [134 High St], *White Hart*: Attractively renovated old hotel opp church, decent reasonably priced home-made food inc good carvery in back dining area and front restaurant, three Tetleys-related real ales, friendly staff, log fires, neat housekeeping; bedrooms *(Frank W Gadbois)*
☆ Monks Eleigh [The Street; B1115 Sudbury—Stowmarket; TL9647], *Swan*: Clean and comfortably modernised lounge bar with good range of home-cooked food, three real ales, open fire, welcoming efficient service, pleasant dining extension; bedrooms *(MN, DN, R Turnham)*
Needham Market [B1113 Ipswich rd; TM0855], *Lion*: Popular welcoming local with wide range of usual food (not Sun evening), friendly staff, Whitbreads-related beers, plenty of space *(Gwen and Peter Andrews)*
Newbourne [TM2643], *Fox*: Very popular lunchtime for straightforward home cooking using fresh local produce and home-grown herbs, well kept Tolly tapped from the cask, genial landlord, cosy unspoilt oak-beamed drinking area around log fire, separate family room; pretty hanging baskets, lots of tables out in front *(C H and P Stride, Martin Hardy, Mrs P Goodwyn)*
North Cove [A146 Worlingham—Barnby; TM4789], *Three Horseshoes*: Cosy, with bare bricks, brasses and rustic timberwork, open fire, generous food inc home-made pies, well

kept ales, restaurant *(Mick and Mel Smith)*

Norton [Ixworth Rd (A1088); TL9565], *Dog*:
Cheerful old pink-washed local with pretty
hanging baskets, good value basic food inc
good curries in functional eating areas,
relatively unspoilt lounge bar, Greene King
ales, handsome dog *(MDN, Mike Simmonds,
Charles Bardswell)*

☆ Orford [Front St; TM4250], *Kings Head*:
Wholesome food from sandwiches up with an
emphasis on fresh fish in cleanly refurbished
bar and restaurant, Adnams ales, decent
wines, welcoming landlord and friendly locals,
military memorabilia, nice dog; bedrooms
now have own bathrooms *(John Evans, David
Heath, David Dimock, Dave Braisted, N S
Dury, LYM)*
Orford, *Crown & Castle*: Very pleasant and
unassuming, with comfortable lounge *(Brian
Horner)*

Pakenham [signed off A1088 and A143 S of
Norwich; TL9267], *Fox*: Friendly village local
with good mix of ages, well kept Greene King
IPA, Abbot and Rayments, cheerful quick
service, wide choice of decent food; beamed
lounge with attractive Skegness advertising
posters and so forth, flame-effect gas stove,
games room, small dining room; tables in
streamside garden with ducks, fieldful of motley
animals behind; children welcome *(Phill Unti)*

Rattlesden [off B1115 via Buxhall or A45 via
Woolpit; TL9758], *Brewers Arms*: Our choice
as Suffolk Dining Pub of 1996, but the Coles
who brought such unexpectedly fine
restaurant-quality cooking (and so many very
happy customers) to this simple two-bar
Greene King village pub with its attractive
garden move on in autumn 1996; they will be
a very hard act to follow *(LYM; reports on
new regime please)*; [High St], *Five Bells*:
Friendly traditional village pub, well worn in,
with perfectly kept Adnams, Charles Wells
Eagle and Bombardier, Wadworths 6X and a
guest beer; famous for its big dog Beamish,
who really does drink his namesake stout; live
music Sat *(John Baker)*

Redgrave [TM0477], *Cross Keys*: Friendly
village local with comfortable lounge bar, well
kept Adnams, popular Sun quiz night *(Pamela
Goodwyn, DC, AR)*

☆ Risby [slip rd off A14; TL7966], *White Horse*:
Well kept Courage and guest beers, decent
generous food inc some adventurous dishes,
log fire, beams, brickwork and panelling, mats
on flagstones, attractive and interesting decor
and furnishings, smart restaurant area, hard-
working licensees *(C H and P Stride, Pat
Crabb, John Baker, LYM)*
Risby, *Crown & Castle*: Congenial Greene King
pub, well kept ales, friendly staff, interesting
WWII intelligence map, reasonably priced home-
cooked food inc good sandwiches and specials;
attractive village *(Dr B and Mrs P B Baker)*

☆ Rumburgh [TM3481], *Buck*: Pretty and
popular country local, clean, tidy and
rambling, with several rooms inc restaurant,
cheap good food inc generous Sun roasts and
fresh veg, lots of character, well kept ales such
as Adnams Extra, friendly atmosphere, cards,

juke box, fruit machine and pool table in end
room; quiet back lawn *(June and Perry Dann)*

☆ Saxtead Green [B1119; TM2665], *Old Mill
House*: Nicely placed across green from
working windmill, attractively refurbished
with neat country look, brick servery, wooden
tables and chairs, pretty curtains, good
reasonably priced home-made food inc carvery
in bar and restaurant, well kept ales, friendly
staff; sizeable garden, pretty back terrace,
good new play area *(Graham and Liz Bell,
June and Perry Dann, Mr and Mrs Newby,
Wayne Brindle, Mrs P Goodwyn, LYM)*

Shottisham [TM3144], *Sorrel Horse*: Good
food, homely surroundings, Tolly ales, log fire,
garden *(Dr Peter Crawshaw, Jack and Philip
Paxton)*

Sizewell [TM4762], *Vulcan Arms*:
Comfortable friendly pub opp entrance to
Sizewell nuclear power plant, handy for visitor
centre; good value lunchtime food, well kept
Adnams *(Paul Mason)*

☆ Southwold [7 East Green; TM5076], *Sole Bay*:
Homely but spotlessly polished little Victorian
local opp brewery (and the lighthouse sharing
its name), moments from the sea; very
welcoming, with particularly good value
simple lunchtime food (not Sun in winter) esp
local smoked sprats, well kept full Adnams
range, chatty landlord, friendly locals and dog
(other dogs allowed), lots of seafaring
memorabilia, unobtrusive piped music,
conservatory with cockatoos, tables on side
terrace *(John Waller, Wayne Brindle, Geoff
and Linda Dibble, M J Morgan, Paul Mason,
Mr and Mrs J Woodfield, PGP, Stuart Earle,
Gwen and Peter Andrews, Gill and Andy
Plumb, MJVK, Keith and Janet Morris, BB)*

☆ Southwold [42 East St], *Lord Nelson*: Bustling
cheerful little local nr seafront, very smoothly
run, with low ceilings, panelling and tiled
floor, with random old furniture and lamps in
nice nooks and crannies, particularly well kept
Adnams Mild, Bitter, Broadside and Old,
good basic lunchtime food, attentive service,
sheltered back garden; open all day, children
welcome *(A J Thomas, Nigel Woolliscroft,
MJVK, PGP, Derek Patey, Tom McLean,
Stuart Earle, John Waller, BB)*

☆ Southwold [Blackshore Quay; from A1095,
right at Kings Head – pass golf course and
water tower], *Harbour*: Popular basic local by
the black waterside net-sheds, tiny low-
beamed front bar, upper back bar with lots of
nautical bric-a-brac – even ship-to-shore
telephone and wind speed indicator; simple
but imaginative food (not Sun evening, just
fish and chips in newspaper Fri evening/Sat
lunch), well kept Adnams Bitter and
Broadside, coal fires, solid old furnishings,
friendly service (though can slow at busy
times), darts, table skittles, tables outside with
play area, ducks and animals – can be a bit
untidy out here *(MJVK, LYM)*

Southwold [Market Pl], *Swan*: Old-fashioned
Georgian hotel with good choice of interesting
fresh bar food (not cheap) in quiet
comfortable back bar, chintzy and airy front
lounge, good polite service, well kept Adnams

and Broadside with the full range of their bottled beers, decent wines and malt whiskies; ambitious restaurant; good bedrooms inc garden rooms where (by arrangement) dogs can stay too *(Peter Woolls, John Waller, Gwen and Peter Andrews, LYM)*; [High St], *Kings Head*: Spacious family dining pub with lots of maroon and pink plush, very wide choice of promptly served good interesting food esp fish with good fresh veg, well kept Adnams, decent house wines, friendly staff; comfortable family/games room with well lit pool table; jazz Sun night, decent bedrooms in house across road *(MJVK, Dr and Mrs B Baker, Derek and Maggie Washington, BB)*

Stoke by Nayland [TL9836], *Crown*: Spacious, quiet and comfortably modernised, decent straightforward food, Tolly ales, restaurant; good with children; bedrooms *(AJ, JJ, LYM)*

☆ Sudbury [Acton Sq; TL8741], *Waggon & Horses*: Comfortable welcoming local with interesting decor, great atmosphere, character landlord, good plain food even Sun afternoon, well kept Greene King ales, bar billiards *(Frank W Gadbois)*

Sweffling [B1119 Framlingham—Saxmundham; TM3463], *White Horse*: Traditional beamed country pub handy for walkers, woodburner in both bars, well kept Adnams, nicely served food, very friendly atmosphere; children welcome, extensive garden; two attractive bedroom suites *(D and J Howl, Pamela Goodwyn)*

Thelnetham [Hopton Rd; village signed off B1111 in Hopton; TM0178], *White Horse*: Civilised and friendly village pub, open fires in bar and dining room (where children welcome), good varied well presented home-made food, Adnams, Greene King IPA and local Old Chimneys, separate games room with pool, darts *(Mrs Marjorie Heath)*

Thorington Street [B1068 Higham—Stoke by Nayland; TM0035], *Rose*: Friendly and enthusiastic new young licensees, good home-made food inc good value Sun lunch and delicious puddings, well kept Adnams, decent house wines, big garden with view of Box valley; bedrooms *(Jeremy and Louise Kemp, Mrs M A Burton)*

☆ Thorndon [off A140 or B1077, S of Eye; TM1469], *Black Horse*: Friendly and individual country pub with good well presented food from sandwiches to unusual main dishes inc good puddings and restaurant Sun lunch; beams, timbers, stripped brick, ancient floor tiles, several well kept ales, tables on spacious lawn with country views; well behaved children in eating areas *(Pamela Goodwyn, LYM)*

Trimley St Martin [TM2736], *Hand in Hand*: Popular and welcoming extended local, good generous food inc vegetarian and fish and bargain special, quick friendly service, good atmosphere, restaurant *(Mrs J M Deale)*

Walberswick [TM4974], *Anchor*: Comfortably modern well furnished hotel bar, reasonably priced food inc good range of seafood, well kept Adnams tapped from the cask, decent wines, quick pleasant service, cosy log fires; bedrooms *(John Waller, P Burrows-Smith, D and J Tapper)*

☆ Wenhaston [TM4276], *Star*: Unpretentious country pub with limited choice of good reasonably priced home cooking (not Sat or maybe Mon – landlady's day off), well kept Adnams, pleasant views; suntrap lounge, games in public bar, tables on sizeable lawn *(Gwen and Peter Andrews, Derek Patey, Keith Archer, Pamela Goodwyn, LYM)*

West Row [NE of Mildenhall; TL6775], *Judes Ferry*: Well renovated pub in beautiful riverside spot with waterside picnic tables, good food from sandwiches up, well kept Adnams Broadside and two guest beers, lots of local photographs *(Frank W Gadbois)*

☆ Westleton [B1125 Blythburgh—Leiston; TM4469], *Crown*: Upmarket extended country inn with country chairs, attractive stripped tables, good local photographs and farm tools in smallish decorous bar area, six interesting real ales, lots of malt whiskies, good wines, farm cider, log fire, pleasant if not always speedy service, piped classical music; wide range of generally good home-made food inc good vegetarian choice in big dining area opening off on left (children allowed) and in roomy no-smoking dining conservatory, pretty garden with aviary and floodlit terrace, peaceful setting, good walks nearby; 19 bedrooms, comfortable if not large, with good breakfasts *(Richard Balls, M J Morgan, John Fahy, Pamela Goodwyn, MJVK, Liz and Gil Dudley, Jamie and Ruth Lyons, Bernard and Ann Payne, David and Anne Culley, Mr and Mrs J Brown, Paul Kitchener, Paul Mason, LYM)*

Wingfield [TM2277], *De La Pole Arms*: Reopened after restoration as interesting pastiche of old ale house, no juke box or machines; good food, small restaurant specialising in local fish and seafood *(Mrs P Goodwyn)*

Witnesham [TM1851], *Barley Mow*: Character old pub with nice atmosphere, home-made food inc good fresh fish Fri in separate dining room, Greene King IPA and Tolly Bitter and Mild, interesting local photographs *(David and Mary Webb)*

☆ Woodbridge [73 Cumberland Rd; opp Notcutts Nursery, off A12; TM2749], *Cherry Tree*: Enjoyable generous fresh straightforward food inc vegetarian doorstep sandwiches, circular bar, lots of partitions for privacy, open fire, stuffed fox, motley collection of books, Flowers Original, Tetleys and Tolly, good pleasant service, 60s piped music, fruit machines; no dogs, garden with swings etc *(Sheila Keene, JCW)*

☆ Woodbridge [Seckford St], *Seckford Arms*: Interesting pub with Mexican accent in decor and good food, well kept Adnams and often unusual guest beers, extrovert landlord, children welcome in garden lounge; open all day *(JP, PP)*

Woodbridge [opp quay], *Anchor*: Good value food inc sandwiches, baked potatoes and well priced fresh local fish, Greene King IPA and Abbot *(Pat and Tony Martin)*

Surrey

Horrifically expensive, Surrey's pubs typically charge over 20p more for a drink than the national average; pub food is generally high-priced, too. So in selecting pubs for the main entries here we've been particularly keen to look for value – which means that in pubs where prices are high, quality has to be outstanding. A general rule to follow is that we found pubs here tied to small brewers such as King & Barnes, Morlands or Youngs generally had much lower drinks prices than pubs tied to the big national brewers, or free houses. Among the main entries, pubs currently on fine fettle include the Drummond Arms at Albury (enormous helpings of decent food), the Plough at Blackbrook (good all round, excellent wines), the genuinely old-fashioned Donkey at Charleshill, the Woolpack at Elstead (huge helpings of good unusual food), the Ram at Farncombe (an unusual cider house, very popular with families – a new main entry), the unspoilt Stephan Langton in lovely surroundings at Friday Street (another newcomer), the King William IV at Mickleham (an informal place with first-class food, especially for vegetarians), the cheerful Dog & Duck at Outwood (back in these pages after an absence), the interesting old Skimmington Castle at Reigate Heath (hard-working licensees winning back its place among the main entries), the Fox & Hounds at South Godstone (new young owners gaining the first main entry ever for this atmospheric pub), and the lovely old Scarlett Arms at Walliswood. As we've said, the King William IV does have excellent food, but for that extra sense of occasion we'd rate the Woolpack at Elstead even better for an enjoyable meal out: for the second year running, it is our choice as Surrey Dining Pub of the Year. In the Lucky Dip section at the end of the chapter, pubs which have been showing particularly well in the last few months include the Crown at Chiddingfold, Villagers at Chilworth, Sun at Dunsfold, Windmill above Ewhurst, Cricketers Arms at Ockley and Punch Bowl just outside, Bell at Outwood, Three Horseshoes at Thursley and White Hart at Witley (we have inspected all these, and can confirm their appeal).

ALBURY TQ0547 Map 3

Drummond Arms 🖙

Off A248 SE of Guildford

In the centre of a delightfully strollable village, this well run pub has a lovely streamside garden overhung with branches and leaves, where ducks and pheasant wander among the tables. There's a friendly, civilised atmosphere in the wood panelled bar with soft seats and alcoves, and in the pleasant conservatory which overlooks the garden. Popular bar food includes sandwiches (from £1.75, toasties from £1.85), soup (£1.95), sausages (£2.95), ploughman's or filled baked potatoes (from £3.95), salads (from £4.95), gammon and pineapple (£6.95), and sirloin steak (£9.95), with a good few daily specials such as soft roes in garlic (£3.95), home-cured salmon or traditional home-made pies (from £4.95), Thai and Indian dishes, and pheasant breast filled with stilton and wrapped in ham (£8.95); helpings can be so big several readers have needed doggy bags. On Sunday lunchtimes in summer they spit roast a large pig on the covered terrace. Well kept Courage Best and Directors, King & Barnes Broadwood, Festive and Sussex, and Youngs on handpump, maybe kept under light blanket pressure; friendly service. Piped music. *(Recommended by Wayne Brindle, DWAJ, D Miles, Ed Birch, G W Jensen, M L and G Clarke, James Nunns, Mayur Shah, Anthony Byers, Andy and Jill Plumb, John Pettit, Sue and Bob Ward, Mr and Mrs D Simons, Ian Phillips)*

Free house ~ Licensee David Wolf ~ Real ale ~ Meals and snacks (till 10pm Fri/Sat) ~ Restaurant (not Sun evening) ~ (01483) 202039 ~ Children over 5 welcome in restaurant ~ Open 11-3, 6-11 ~ Bedrooms: £38B/£50B

ALBURY HEATH TQ0646 Map 3
William IV

Little London; off A25 Guildford—Dorking to Albury, first left to Albury Heath; go over railway and take first left to Peaslake, then right towards Farley Green; OS Sheet 187 map reference 065468

Lovely walks surround this busy and unspoilt pub, right in the heart of the county. The main stone-floored bar has a big chunky elm table with a long pew and a couple of stools, beams in the low ochre ceiling, an enormous basket of dried flowers in the big brick fireplace (with a hearty log fire in winter), and an ancient baboon dressed in a jacket and hat in one corner. A tiny room leading off one end squeezes in an L-shaped elbow rest with a couple of stools in front, a table and settle, and darts, while up a few steps at the other end of the main bar is a simple dining room with gingham-clothed tables, two glass cases with stuffed owls, and a piano. The first Saturday of each month they have a special seafood night, with various fish bought fresh that day from Billingsgate, and on every third Saturday they spit-roast a whole lamb, pig or venison. The rest of the time the small but selective menu includes sandwiches (from £1.80), generous ploughman's, and home-made dishes like mutton casserole with dumplings (£4.95), pheasant in red wine and garlic (£5.20), and steak and kidney pudding (£5.50); some dishes can run out quickly so it's worth getting there early. Changing real ales (all £2 a pint) might include well kept Boddingtons, Fullers London Pride, Greene King Abbot, Whitbreads Castle Eden and local Hogs Back; shove-ha'penny and cards. The little garden in front has some picnic tables under umbrellas, and old cast-iron garden furniture. Several readers have this year felt the pub could do with a tidy-up, with the lavatories perhaps most in need of attention. *(Recommended by G R Sunderland, MLC, GC, R Lake, G W Jensen, Ian Phillips, Jenny and Brian Seller, Nigel Flook, Betsy Brown, Helen Morton, Mr and Mrs B Matthews, Andy and Jill Plumb, Anthony Byers, A J N Lee)*

Free house ~ Licensee Mick Davids ~ Real ale ~ Meals and snacks (not Sun evening) ~ (01483) 202685 ~ Children welcome ~ Open 11-3, 5.30-11 (cl 25 Dec)

BETCHWORTH TQ2049 Map 3
Dolphin

The Street; 2½ miles W of Reigate on A25 turn left into Buckland, then take the second left

The unaffected and genuinely friendly atmosphere here really stands out, and though the pub does get busy, there always seems to be just enough space. The homely front room is furnished with kitchen chairs and plain tables on the 400-year-old scrubbed flagstones, and the carpeted back saloon bar is black-panelled with robust old-fashioned elm or oak tables; nostalgic touches include three coal fires and a well chiming longcase clock. Well priced Youngs Bitter, Special, Ram Rod and seasonal brews on handpump, and a cruover machine guarantees that most wines can be served by the glass; efficient service. Bar food includes soup (£1.95), ploughman's (from £3.35), filled baked potatoes (from £3.45), sausage and egg (£3.15), meat or vegetable lasagne (£4.85), scampi (£4.95), gammon steak (£5.95), daily specials, and puddings like spotted dick or apple pie (£1.95). Darts, dominoes, cribbage, fruit machine and shove-ha'penny. There are some seats in the small laurel-shaded front courtyard and picnic tables on a lawn by the car park, opposite the church and on the back garden terrace. Get there early, the pub fills up fast, sometimes with a lively younger crowd. No children inside. *(Recommended by Pat Booker, P J Caunt, Dorsan Baker, J S M Sheldon, Jack Taylor, John Pettit, David Peakall, DWAJ, G R Sharman, Jenny and Brian Seller, Alison Ball, David Norris, P Gillbe, Jamie and Ruth Lyons, Mayur Shah)*

Youngs ~ Managers: George and Rose Campbell ~ Real ale ~ Meals and snacks (12-2.30, 7-10) ~ (01737) 842288 ~ Open 11-3, 5.30-11; cl 25 Dec evening)

BLACKBROOK TQ1846 Map 3

Plough ♀

On byroad E of A24, parallel to it, between Dorking and Newdigate, just N of the turn E to Leigh

A blaze of colour in summer, this civilised white-fronted pub has recently won a prize for its carefully planted garden. The friendly licensees put a great deal of effort into everything they do, and that comes across particularly in the range of drinks and food, and the affable attentive service. Well kept King & Barnes Sussex, Broadwood, Festive, and seasonal beers on handpump, freshly squeezed orange juice, 13 good wines by the glass (including a wine of the month), vintage port by the glass, and about 20 country wines. There are fresh flowers cut from the garden on the tables and sills of the large linen-curtained windows in the partly no-smoking saloon bar. Down some steps, the public bar has brass-topped treadle tables, a formidable collection of ties as well as old saws on the ceiling, and bottles and flat irons; piped music. They're constantly experimenting with new and original daily specials, with recent dishes including spinach and mushroom soup (£2.45), stilton and port wine pâté (£2.95), avocado baked with crab and cheese sauce (£3.45), spinach and ricotta roulade with tomato coulis (£5.25), Hungarian pork goulash with sauerkraut and noodles (£5.75), spiced lamb hotpot with dumplings (£5.95), and baked cod with leek and cheese sauce (£6.95); the regular menu includes filled baked potatoes (from £3.45), ploughman's or popular bagels (£3.95), ratatouille niçoise (£5.45), lasagne (£5.75), prawn curry (£5.95) and sirloin steak (£10.45). Tess the blind black labrador puts in an appearance after 10pm. At the back is a sizeable secluded cottage garden with a good few tables and children can play in the prettily painted Swiss playhouse furnished with tiny tables and chairs. In summer the white frontage is decked with bright hanging baskets and window boxes. The countryside around here is a particularly good area for colourful spring and summer walks through the oak woods. They usually have a wonderfully atmospheric carol concert the Sunday before Christmas. No credit cards. *(Recommended by Margaret and Nigel Parker, R V G Brown, Margaret and Nigel Dennis, Ron Gentry, Helen Morton, John Evans, John Pettit, Cathryn and Richard Hicks, Derek and Maggie Washington, Winifrede D Morrison, Neville Kenyon, Jamie and Ruth Lyons, Tina and David Woods-Taylor)*

King & Barnes ~ Tenants: Chris and Robin Squire ~ Real ale ~ Meals and snacks (not Mon evening) ~ (01306) 886603 ~ Children over 14 in bar if eating ~ Open 11-2.30(3 Sat), 6-11; cl 25, 26 Dec and 1 Jan

CHARLESHILL SU8944 Map 2

Donkey

Near Tilford, on B3001 Milford—Farnham; as soon as you see pub sign, turn left

A reminder of a more civilised age, this charmingly old-fashioned 18th-c cottage has been in the same family for three generations. Lots of polished stirrups, lamps and watering cans decorate the walls of the brightly cheerful saloon, furnished with prettily cushioned built-in wall benches and wheelback chairs, while the lounge has a lovely old high-backed settle and a couple of unusual three-legged chairs, as well as highly polished horsebrasses, a longcase clock, some powder pouches, swords on the walls and beams. Reasonably priced home-made bar food – in helpings suitable for people with smaller appetites – includes sandwiches and toasted sandwiches (from £2), filled baked potatoes (from £2.30) and four home-made daily specials like broccoli, mushroom and walnut bake, curry, fish pie or lasagne (all £4.95). A no-smoking conservatory with blond wheelback chairs and stripped tables, fairy lights and some plants, has sliding doors into the garden. During the week the pub is a popular lunchtime stop for the ladies of the county. Well kept and priced Morlands IPA and Old Speckled Hen, and Charles Wells Bombardier on handpump, maybe under light blanket pressure, and Gales country wines; shove-ha'penny, dominoes and cribbage, and perhaps quiet piped music. The garden is very attractive, with bright flowerbeds, white garden furniture, a tiny pond, an aviary with cockatiels and a big fairy-lit fir tree. There's a children's play area out here too. *(Recommended by Pat and Tony Martin, Andy and Gill Plumb, J Sheldon, M L and G Clarke, B and K Hypher, Winifrede D Morrison, Mr and Mrs T A Bryan)*

Morlands ~ Lease: Peter and Shirley Britcher ~ Real ale ~ Meals and snacks (not Sun evening) ~ (01252) 702124 ~ Children in conservatory ~ Open 11-2.30, 6-11; cl 25, 26 Dec evening

COBHAM TQ1060 Map 3

Cricketers

Downside Common; 3¾ miles from M25 junction 10; A3 towards Cobham, 1st right on to A245, right at Downside signpost into Downside Bridge Rd, follow road into its right fork – away from Cobham Park – at second turn after bridge, then take next left turn into the pub's own lane

Pleasantly set overlooking the broad village green, this bustling old pub has a delightfully neat back garden with standard roses, dahlias, bedding plants, urns and hanging baskets. The spacious open plan interior has crooked standing timbers – creating comfortably atmospheric spaces – supporting heavy oak beams so low they have crash-pads on them. In places you can see the wide oak ceiling boards and ancient plastering laths. Simple furnishings, horsebrasses and big brass platters on the walls, and a good winter log fire. At lunchtime most people are here to eat, with dishes listed on the blackboards including moules marinières (£4.95), duck à l'orange (£5.25), and poached salmon brioche, steak and kidney pie or grilled wing of skate (£5.95); they also do sandwiches, and a good range of salads. It's worth arriving early to be sure of a table – especially on Sunday. Well kept (though not cheap) Ruddles County, Theakstons Best and Websters Yorkshire on handpump. Dogs welcome. *(Recommended by G W and I L Edwards, Simon Penny, J Sheldon, Clem Stephens, John and Joan Calvert, G W Jensen, Ron Gentry, Thomas Nott, G R Sunderland, John Pettit, S G Brown, Jamie and Ruth Lyons, G W and I L Edwards, Andy Cunningham, Christopher Gallop, Giles Quick, Adrian Zambardino, Debbie Chaplin, Piotr Chodzko-Zajko, Dave Irving, George Atkinson, Martin and Karen Wake)*

Courage ~ Lease: Wendy Luxford ~ Real ale ~ Meals and snacks (till 10pm) ~ Restaurant (not Sun evening, or all day Mon) ~ (01932) 862105 ~ Children in Stable Bar ~ Open 11-2.30, 6-11

COLDHARBOUR TQ1543 Map 3

Plough 🍺

Village signposted in the network of small roads around Abinger and Leith Hill, off A24 and A29

At 800 feet up, this remote pretty black-shuttered white house is the highest pub in south east England. It's a characterful place, busy with a true mix of customers and types, all of whom feel at ease in the well worn rooms and easy going atmosphere. A huge draw has long been the ten very well kept real ales, which might include Adnams Broadside, Badger Best and Tanglefoot, Batemans XB, Fullers London Pride, Ringwood Old Thumper, Shepherd Neame Spitfire and Wadworths 6X. They also have a short but interesting wine list, country wines and Biddenden farm cider. The two bars have stripped light beams and timbering in the warm-coloured dark ochre walls, with quite unusual little chairs around the tables in the snug red-carpeted room on the left, and little decorative plates on the walls and a big open fire in the one on the right – which leads through to the restaurant. Decent home-made bar food includes soup (£2.95), ploughman's (£3.50), filled baked potatoes (from £3.95), fresh haddock with spicy tomato crust (£5.95), chicken breast in leek and stilton sauce (£6), stuffed peppers (£6.50), salmon with rocquefort cheese in pastry, pork and cider casserole with apple and sage dumplings, or rabbit and bacon pie (£6.95), and puddings like cranberry and almond tart. The games bar on the left has darts, pool, cribbage, shove-ha'penny, dominoes, and there is piped music. Outside there are picnic tables by the tubs of flowers in front and in the terraced garden with fish pond and waterlilies. Dogs are allowed if on a lead but not in the restaurant (which is no smoking). Good walks all around. *(Recommended by Tom Hall, Piotr Chodzko-Zajko, James Nunns, Mr and Mrs D Carter, Simon Skinner, J Sheldon, Wayne Brindle, H Gregory, Steve Felstead, Jenny and Brian Seller, Sue Demont, Tim Barrow, S G N Bennett, Tom and Rosemary Hall, Dick Brown, John Davies, Jon Carpenter)*

Free house ~ Licensees Richard and Anna Abrehart ~ Real ale ~ Meals and snacks ~ Restaurant ~ (01306) 711793 ~ Children in eating area of bar ~ Open 11.30-3, 6.30(7 winter weekdays)-11; all day summer weekends ~ Bedrooms: /£50S

COMPTON SU9546 Map 2

Harrow

B3000

Prices at this cheerful dining pub certainly tend towards the top end of the range, but then so does the quality. Recent highlights from the excellent menu have included cauliflower, leek and blue cheese gratin (£7.25), lamb rogan josh (£8.50), Indonesian-style chicken with spicy peanut sauce (£9.25), venison, mushroom, apple and cider pie (£9.50), seafood brochette (£9.75), rack of lamb with red wine, rosemary and thyme jus (£11.25), and puddings like sticky toffee and date pudding or treacle tart (£3.50); they do sandwiches and salads all day. You'll probably need to book on Friday and Saturday evenings. Well kept Greene King IPA, Ind Coope Burton, and Harveys Sussex on handpump. The brightly lit main bar has interesting racing pictures below the ancient ceiling – mostly portraits of horses, jockey caricatures and signed race-finish photographs. Opening off here are more little beamed rooms with latched rustic doors, and nice touches such as brass horse-head coat hooks, photographs of the area, and a bas relief in wood of the pub sign; piped music. Breakfast is available to non-residents. There are some seats outside by the car park, looking out to gentle slopes of pasture. In the pretty village the art nouveau Watts Chapel and Gallery are interesting, and the church itself is attractive; Loseley House is nearby too. *(Recommended by Ed Birch, Derek and Margaret Underwood, G W Jensen, Hilarie Taylor, J Sheldon, Margaret and Nigel Parker, John and Vivienne Rice, Jonathan Nettleton, Mr and Mrs G Turner, DC, Adrian Zambardino, Debbie Chaplin, Thomas Nott, MS)*

Allied ~ Lease: Roger and Susan Seaman ~ Real ale ~ Meals and snacks (12-3, 6-10; breakfast 7.30-12) ~ (01483) 810379 ~ Children welcome ~ Open 11-3, 5.30(6 Sat)-11 ~ Bedrooms: /£35B

Withies

Withies Lane; pub signposted from B3000

The emphasis here is very much on the smart and rather pricey restaurant, but there's still a tiny and genuinely pubby low beamed bar that makes it worth a look, and the garden is delightful on a sunny day. The massive inglenook fireplace is lit with a roaring log fire even on summer evenings, there are some attractive 17th-c carved panels between the windows, and one of the settles is splendidly art nouveau. A short and straightforward choice of bar food includes soup (£2.50), sandwiches (from £3), a choice of pâté (£3.25), good ploughman's (from £3.50), cumberland sausages (£3.90), filled baked potatoes (from £4) and seafood platter (£6.50). Well kept Bass, Friary Meux, and King & Barnes Sussex on handpump. The immaculate garden, overhung with weeping willows, has tables under an arbour of creeper-hung trellises, more on a crazy-paved terrace and yet more under old apple trees. The neat lawn in front of the steeply tiled white house is bordered by masses of flowers. *(Recommended by Mark Stevens, Gill and Andy Plumb, Hilarie Taylor, Barbara Wensworth, Mrs P F Raymond-Cox, MW, HW, Helen Morton, Mayur Shah)*

Free house ~ Licensees Brian and Hugh Thomas ~ Real ale ~ Meals and snacks (12-2.30, 7-10) ~ Restaurant (not Sun evening) ~ (01483) 421158 ~ Children welcome ~ Open 11-3, 6-11; cl evenings 25/26 Dec

EFFINGHAM TQ1253 Map 3

Sir Douglas Haig

The Street; off A246 W of Leatherhead

Almost completely rebuilt a few years ago, this busy roomy free house is a reliable place for a good value lunch. In big helpings with a choice of up to five fresh vegetables, the straightforward home-cooked bar food includes good filled baguettes, daily specials (from £4), steak and kidney pie (£4.95), and a range of steaks (from £6.50); Sunday roast (£4.95). At one end of the long room there's an eating area with an open fire, small settles, banquettes and kitchen chairs, and at the other end, another open fire, a wood-stained floor, stools, an armchair, and shelves of books. Well kept Boddingtons, Fullers London Pride, Gales HSB and Wadworths 6X on handpump; quick, friendly service. There's a back lawn and terraced area with seats and tables; fruit machine, video game, juke box, and a TV in the corner of the lounge. *(Recommended by Mike Gilbert, G W Jensen, J Sheldon, John Pettit, DWAJ, Andy and Jill Plumb, Anthony Byers, Brian and Jenny Seller, Jamie and Ruth Lyons)*

Free house ~ Licensee Laurie Smart ~ Real ale ~ Meals and snacks ~ (01372) 456886 ~ Children over 14 only ~ Open 11-3, 5.30-11(11-11 Sat) ~ Bedrooms: £45B/£55B

ELSTEAD SU9143 Map 2

Woolpack ⑪

The Green; B3001 Milford—Farnham

Surrey Dining Pub of the Year

We know a couple who occasionally visit this cheerfully old-fashioned place for both lunch and dinner on the same day. How they manage it we're not sure, as the main courses are often so big it can be a challenge to finish one of the splendid home-made puddings, let alone start thinking about the next meal. The deliciously creative food varies all the time, depending on what recipes the chef has devised to suit his ingredients, but might include ploughman's (from £3.95), mussels in herb and garlic butter (£4.50), hot breaded blue cheese with cranberry and port (£4.50), a good selection of vegetarian dishes such as mushroom stroganoff (£4.75), Thai fish cakes with peanut, chilli and cucumber sauce or pies such as chicken and ham or cod and prawn (£6.95), whole poussin in orange, coriander and gin sauce (£7.50), turkey escalopes in vermouth, mushroom and tarragon sauce (£8.95) and goose breast with gooseberry, sherry and sage sauce (£8.95). Tastily prepared fresh vegetables include beetroot in creamy sauce or leeks with a crunchy topping, and there's a glorious range of home-made puddings like crème brûlée, pavlovas, rum truffle cake and date and toffee cake (all £2.95). If you haven't booked for Sunday lunch, get there early. Though the pub is frequently busy, there's always a lovely relaxed and informal atmosphere; good attentive service. There's a fair amount of wool industry memorabilia, such as the weaving shuttles and cones of wool that hang above the high-backed settles in the long airy main bar, which also has window seats and spindleback chairs around plain wooden tables. There are fireplaces at each end. The large dog basket tucked into a corner is the home of Taffy, a golden retriever.

Leading off here is a big room decorated with lots of country prints, a weaving loom, scales, and brass measuring jugs; the fireplace with its wooden pillars lace frill is unusual. In the family room there are nursery-rhyme murals and lots of dried flowers hanging from the ceiling, and a door that leads to the garden with picnic tables and a children's play area. A changing range of real ales might include Adnams, Greene King Abbot and Ind Coope Burton tapped from the cask; quite a few wines by the glass and bottle. Dominoes, cribbage, backgammon, fruit machine. *(Recommended by M Clarke, B A Hayward, Derek and Margaret Underwood, Graham and Karen Oddey, E D Bailey, M L and G Clarke, Bob and Maggie Atherton, JEB, Peter Burton, Ed Birch, G W Jensen, Alan Skull, G and M Stewart, Ailsa Wiggans, G C Hackemer, Guy Consterdine, Mike Fitzgerald, Paul Carter, G and M Stewart, Rhoda and Jeff Collins, Clive Gilbert, Mr and Mrs R O Gibson, Ian Phillips)*

Ind Coope (Carlsberg Tetleys) ~ Lease: J A Macready and S A Askew ~ Real ale ~ Meals and snacks (till 9.45) ~ Restaurant ~ (01252) 703106 ~ Children in family room and two rooms off restaurant, or restaurant proper if well behaved ~ Open 11-2.30, 6-11; closed eve 25 Dec, all day 26 Dec

ENGLEFIELD GREEN SU9970 Map 2

Fox & Hounds

Bishopsgate Road; off A328 N of Egham

This smart 17th-c pub backs on to a riding stables, so there's quite a coming and going of riders if you're sitting out at the picnic tables on the neat and pretty front lawn. Inside is simple but civilised in a well mellowed countrified way, popular without being overcrowded, with good sturdy wooden tables and chairs, prints in sets of four, a big fireplace, some stuffed animals and fading red gingham curtains. The bar has sandwiches (from £2), baguettes (Saturday and Sunday only, from £2.50) with a great range of fillings and good salad garnishes, soup (£3.50), and pâté (£5.25). More substantial – and expensive – dishes can be found in the attractive back dining room, candlelit at night, with a blackboard menu brought to your table and more choice on further wall boards: lots of starters (from £5), home-made steak and kidney pudding (£10), fresh fish like wild salmon or tuna in a lime and tarragon butter (£11.50), whole sea bass with garlic basil oil (£14.50), and rack of English lamb, calf liver with bacon and onion or half a roast duckling with orange sauce (all £12.50); they do a three-course Sunday lunch (£16.50). Prompt friendly service. Well kept Courage Best and Directors, John Smiths and a guest such as Greene King IPA on handpump, decent wines. There are more tables on a back terrace. The pub is on the edge of Windsor Park and a very short stroll from the main gate to the Savile Garden. *(Recommended by Ian Phillips, Susan and John Douglas, Simon Collett-Jones, John and Joan Calvert, Mayur Shah, Donald J Arndt)*

Courage ~ Licensees John Mee and Bobby King ~ Real ale ~ Meals and snacks ~ Restaurant ~ (01784) 433098 ~ Well behaved children welcome ~ Jazz Mon evening ~ Open 11-3, 6-11; closed 25 Dec

FARNCOMBE SU9844 Map 3

Ram

Catteshall Lane; behind Catteshall industrial estate on outskirts of Godalming beyond Sainsburys; after Farncombe boathouse take second left, then first right, followed by first left

The charms of this 16th-c cider house seem even greater after the inauspicious drive to find it. It's especially appealing in summer, when the big back garden proves very popular with families; a softly rippling stream runs through the middle, and there are a good few picnic tables and tables and chairs beside the trees on the grass, and on a covered patio. Morris dancers and mummers call here throughout the year, and they have barbecues on summer weekends; there's a small play area, as well as a big carved wooden ram. Though you can get well kept Fullers beers (and maybe Brakspears in winter), cider is the speciality, with around 30 different types in bottles or on handpump, including Bulmers and Westons Old Rosie; also a range of country wines. Bar food might include filled rolls (from 80p) and sandwiches (from £1.80), ploughman's (£3.90), spinach and mushroom lasagne (£4.20), tipsy beef stew (£5.20), and Sunday roasts with wild boar or ostrich. Obliging service from friendly staff. The three simple small rooms have coal-effect fires in old brick hearths, heavy-beams, and wooden tables and pews; there's a talking parrot in the public bar (which can be smoky), and maybe a huge german shepherd, Yum-Yum. The pub gets very popular with a younger set later in the evening. *(Recommended by Gill Cory, Wayne Brindle)*

Free house ~ Licensees Harry Ardeshir and Carolyn Eley ~ Real ale ~ Meals and snacks ~ (01483) 421093 ~ Children welcome ~ Folk music Mon and Weds eves ~ Open 11-3, 6-11 weekdays, all day weekends (and weekdays too in summer)

FRIDAY STREET TQ1245 Map 3

Stephan Langton

Village signed off B2126, or from A25 Westcott—Guildford

In a particularly idyllic spot, this welcoming country local takes its name from a 12th-c Archbishop of Canterbury, who grew up nearby. The village is so unspoilt they prefer you to leave your car in a free car park just outside, but if you don't fancy the lovely stroll there are a few spaces in front of the pub itself. Dotted around the comfortable bar and parlour-like lounge are prints of various historic figures and events, as well as a couple of old-fashioned musical instruments, a stuffed bird in a case, fresh flowers, and pictures of the licensee's dogs; these don't generally appear in the bar until late evening, though other dogs are welcome. There are some handsome vases in front of the fireplace, which has a seat fashioned from a beer barrel amongst the mix of furnishings around it. The popular bar food is listed above here: soup (£2.45), filled baguettes (from £2.50, squid and lemon or avocado and cheese £3.50), vegetable pie (£4.95), game casserole (£5.95), and half a dozen or so specials like dressed crab (£5.25) or braised lamb in rosemary and basil sauce (£5.75). The children's menu includes squid and pasta dishes. Well kept Bass, Fullers London Pride, Harveys Sussex and a guest like Hogs Back on handpump; piped music. Prompt and efficient service. Plenty of tables in a front courtyard, with more on a back terrace. Good walks nearby, with Leith Hill particularly rewarding. *(Recommended by Richard Edwards, Tina and David Woods-Taylor, Dick Brown, Peter Lewis, J Sheldon)*

Free house ~ Licensees Jan and Maria Walaszkowski ~ Real ale ~ Meals and snacks (not eves Sun or Mon) ~ Restaurant ~ (01306) 730775 ~ Children welcome ~ Open 11-3, 6-11, all day weekends

HASCOMBE TQ0039 Map 3

White Horse

B2130 S of Godalming

Tucked away among lovely wooded country lanes, this comfortable rose-draped inn has a good many tables on its spacious sloping back lawn, ideally placed to savour the sunsets on a sunny summer night. There are more on a little terrace by the front porch. Inside, the rooms are simple but characterful, with a very relaxed and comfortable atmosphere. The cosy inner beamed area has a woodburning stove and quiet small-windowed alcoves that look out onto the garden, and there's a conservatory with light bentwood chairs. Written up on blackboards, the popular bar food varies every day, but might typically include huge sandwiches (£2.75), home-made soup (£2.25), ploughman's (from £4), vegetable au gratin (£5.95), home-made pies (£6.95), lamb and mint kebabs (£7.25), swordfish steaks or salmon fish cakes (£7.50), chicken curry or roast pheasant (£7.95), steaks (from £9.50), and puddings like treacle and walnut tart or chocolate truffle cake (£3.50); best to get there early for a table at lunchtime, especially at weekends. Quick cheerful service. Well kept Badger Best, King and Barnes Sussex and Wadworths 6X on handpump;

quite a few wines. Darts, shove-ha'penny, dominoes, and fruit machine. The village is pretty, and the National Trust's Winkworth Arboretum, with its walks among beautiful trees and shrubs, is nearby. *(Recommended by Susan and John Douglas, G W Stevenson, Alan Skull, Mr and Mrs Damien Burke, Chris and Inky Hoare, Keith and Audrey Ward, Brian and Jenny Seller)*

Ind Coope ~ Lease: Susan Barnett ~ Real ale ~ Meals and snacks (12-2.30, 7-10) ~ Restaurant (not Sun evening) ~ (01483) 208258 ~ Children in eating area of bar and restaurant ~ Open 11-3, 5.30-11; all day Sat and Sun; closed 25 Dec and 26 Dec eve

LEIGH TQ2246 Map 3

Plough

3 miles S of A25 Dorking—Reigate, signposted from Betchworth (which itself is signposted off the main road); also signposted from South Park area of Reigate; on village green

Somehow this pretty and welcoming tiled and weatherboarded cottage keeps its brightly coloured hanging baskets looking as fresh as they did in summer right through to the end of October. On the right is a very low beamed cosy white walled and timbered dining lounge and on the left, the more local pubby bar has a good bow-window seat and an extensive choice of games that takes in darts, shove-ha'penny, dominoes, table skittles, cribbage, trivia, a fruit machine and video game, Connect 4, Jenca, chess and Scrabble; piped music. Popular bar food includes sandwiches (from £1.75), soup (£1.95), pâté (£2.50), garlic mussels or ploughman's (from £3.95), filled baked potatoes (from £3.25), ham, egg and chips (£4.50), lasagne (£4.75) and sirloin steak (£9.50), and tasty daily specials including good seafood, and puddings like hot chocolate fudge cake, apple pie and blackberry and apple pancake rolls (from £1.95). Booking is recommended, especially at weekends when it can get a bit cramped. Well kept King & Barnes Bitter, Broadwood, Festive and seasonal ales on handpump, some maybe kept under light blanket pressure, and quite a few wines by the glass. There are picnic tables under cocktail parasols in a pretty side garden bordered by a white picket fence. Parking nearby is limited. Attractively set overlooking the village green, the pub is handy for Gatwick airport. The licensees run another pub at Ifield in West Sussex. *(Recommended by Brian and Jenny Seller, B and M Kendall, Bob and Maggie Atherton, Anthony Byers, Jerry Bemis, Mayur Shah, Keith and Audrey Ward, Wayne Brindle)*

King & Barnes ~ Tenant Sarah Broomfield ~ Meals and snacks (till 10) ~ Restaurant ~ (01306) 611348 ~ Children in restaurant ~ Open 11-2.30 (3 Sat), 5-11

MICKLEHAM TQ1753 Map 3

King William IV 🍽

Byttom Hill; short but narrow steep track up hill just off A24 Leatherhead—Dorking by partly green-painted restaurant, just N of main B2289 village turnoff; OS Sheet 187 map reference 173538

It's a long time since we heard even a hint of criticism of the food at this rather unusually placed 18th-c inn. The wide range of blackboard specials is quite a draw, with a good choice for vegetarians; as well as sandwiches (weekdays only), you'll usually find meals like spinach and aubergine lasagne (£4.95), lamb hotpot or sausages like pork and leek, lamb and apricot or mustard and honey (£5.25), Thai vegetable curry (£5.50), cajun chicken salad (£5.75), spinach and nut bake or brie and leek in filo pastry (£5.95), steak and kidney pie (£6.50), poached salmon with tomato and herb dressing (£7.25), seafood casserole (£7.50), breast of chicken with stilton and bacon (£8.50), sirloin steak with wild mushroom sauce (£9.25), and puddings like hot chocolate fudge cake or caramel apple tart (£2.50). The choice is more limited on Sundays and bank holidays, or if the weather is very hot. Relaxed and unpretentious, the pub is cut into the hillside – so there's quite a climb – with panoramic views back down again from the snug plank-panelled front bar. The more spacious back bar is quite brightly lit with kitchen-type chairs around its cast-iron-framed tables. There are decent log fires, fresh flowers on all the tables and a serviceable grandfather clock. Well kept Adnams, Badger Best, Hogs Back, Hop Garden Gold, and a monthly changing guest on handpump; quick and friendly service; good coffee. Dominoes, and noticeable piped radio. The lovely terraced garden is neatly filled with sweet peas, climbing roses and honeysuckle and plenty of tables (some in an open-sided wooden shelter). A path leads straight up through woods where it's nice to walk after lunch. *(Recommended by J Sheldon, W D Monceux, Ron Gentry, Margaret and Nigel Parker, Simon Penny, Tom Hall, Jean Minner, M Mason, D Thompson, Stephen and Sophie Mazzier, Mr and Mrs J A Phipps, Peter and Wendy Arnold, Patricia and Anthony Daley, John Pettit, David Shillitoe, Tom and Rosemary Hall, Adrian Zambardino, Debbie Chaplin, LM, Eddie Edwards, F Jarman, R A Buckler, Derek and Maggie Washington, Mayur Shah, Andy and Jill Plumb, A G Drake)*

Free house ~ Licensees C D and J E Grist ~ Real ale ~ Meals and snacks (not Mon evening, other nights till 9.45) ~ (01372) 372590 ~ Children over 14 allowed, maybe limited space for younger children in winter ~ Occasional folk/country groups in summer ~ Open 11-3, 6-11; closed 25 Dec

OUTWOOD TQ3245 Map 3

Dog & Duck

From A23 in Salfords S of Redhill take Station turning – eventually after you cross the M23 the pub's on your left at the T-junction; coming from the village centre, head towards Coopers Hill and Prince of Wales Road

This is a very relaxing spot on a sunny day, when picnic tables under cocktail parasols on the grass outside look over a safely fenced-off duck pond to the meadows. Particularly friendly and welcoming, the comfortable and spacious bar has a good choice of well kept real ales on handpump, including Badger Best and Tanglefoot, Charles Wells Eagle and IPA, and Wadworths 6X. As well as sandwiches, the popular promptly served bar food has things like locally made sausages with onion gravy (£5.25), steak and kidney pie or cashew nut and parsnip bake (£5.65), chicken, leek and stilton pie (£5.95), and gammon steak or pan fried chicken in garlic and herbs (£6.25); Sunday roast lunch. The rambling bar has a good log fire, comfortable settles, oak armchairs and more ordinary seats, ochre walls, stripped dark beams, rugs on the quarry tiles, and daily newspapers to read. There's another huge fireplace in the eating area which leads off the bar, and a comprehensive range of games that takes in darts, shove-ha'penny, table skittles, ring-the-bull, cribbage, backgammon, chess, draughts, shut the box, dominoes, Scrabble, backgammon, chess, trivia, and draughts. Happy staff, unobtrusive piped music. There are three cats, Stan and Stella, who are rarely seen, and more sociable Trevor, who may try and sit on your knee. It's a nice walk to the village, with its old windmill, if you have an hour spare for the round trip. *(Recommended by Niki and Terry Pursey, Jenny and Brian Seller, Alan Wright, Peter and Wendy Arnold, John and Elspeth Howell, G Simpson)*

Badger ~ Manager Stephen Slocombe ~ Real ale ~ Meals and snacks (all day) ~ (01342) 842964 ~ Children welcome except in main bar ~ Open 11-11; 12-10.30 Sun

OXTED TQ3951 Map 3

George

High St, Old Oxted; off A25 not far from M25 junction 6

Relaxed and welcoming even at its busiest, this very well run pub has the thriving chatty and contented feel that you seem to get only in places which have done away with games machines and piped music. Furnishings are neat, tidy and comfortable, with attractive prints on the walls and a pleasant restaurant area. A wide choice of generously served bar food includes sandwiches (from £2; bacon £2.75), burgers or vegetarian dishes (from £4.95), cheese platter (£5.95), steak and kidney pie (£6.50), fresh fish and chips (£6.95), well hung steaks cut to the size you want (from £8.95), fresh seafood such as oysters, halibut, salmon, dover sole and giant prawns, daily specials such as oriental lamb or spare ribs, and puddings (from £2.95). Well kept Adnams Bitter, Bass, Boddingtons, Fullers London Pride, Harveys Sussex, and Wadworths 6X on handpump, decent house wines, efficient friendly service; tables outside. *(Recommended by B and M Kendall, Wayne Brindle, G Simpson, Jason Reynolds, G R Sharman, Hugh and Peggy Colgate, Mr and Mrs J Irving)*

Free house ~ Licensees John and Helen Hawkins ~ Real ale ~ Meals and snacks (12-9.30) ~ Restaurant ~ (01883) 713453 ~ Children in restaurant if over 8 ~ Open 11-11; 12-10.30 Sun

PIRBRIGHT SU9455 Map 2

Royal Oak 🍺

Aldershot Rd; A324S of village

The colourful front gardens of this neatly kept Tudor cottage regularly win Guildford's annual Pub in Bloom competition, and look particularly attractive on fine evenings when the fairy lights are switched on. The big back garden is popular too, and less affected by noise from passing traffic; there may be barbecues out here in summer. One of the main attractions is the excellent choice of real ales, with seven well kept beers rotated from a range that includes Adnams, Badger Best and Tanglefoot, Boddingtons, Crown Buckley Reverend James, Flowers Original, Fuggles IPA, Greene King Abbot, Marstons Pedigree, Shepherd Neame Spitfire, and Youngs Special; they also have around 15 wines by the glass and bottle, and several malt whiskies. There's a rambling series of snug side alcoves with heavy beams and timbers, ancient stripped brickwork, and gleaming brasses set around the three real fires. Furnishings include wheelback chairs, tapestried wall seats and little dark church-like pews around the trim tables, and there are plenty of fresh flowers in summer. Bar food (not reckoned by readers to be a particular draw this last year) includes filled baguettes (£2.95, lunchtimes only), steak and ale pie (£5.45), pork in cream sauce with apples (£5.50), vegetable kiev or chicken stuffed with stilton and apricots (£5.95), and steaks (£7.95). The dining area is no smoking. Good walks lead off in all directions, and the licensees are usually happy to let walkers leave their cars in the car park if they ask first. *(Recommended by George Atkinson, Guy Consterdine, KC, Wayne Brindle, H West, Thomas Nott, Paul Carter, Martin and Karen Wake)*

Whitbreads ~ Manager John Lay ~ Real ale ~ Meals and snacks (all day Sun) ~ (01483) 232466 ~ Children in dining area ~ Open 11-11; 12-10.30 Sun

REIGATE HEATH TQ2349 Map 3

Skimmington Castle

3 miles from M25 junction 8: through Reigate take A25 Dorking (West), then on edge of Reigate turn left past Black Horse into Flanchford Road; after ¼ mile turn left into Bonny's Road (unmade, very bumpy track); after crossing golf course fork right up hill

At the end of a delightfully undeveloped bumpy track, this quaint country local has developed quite a reputation for its food in the two years since the current licensees arrived. The blackboard menu changes every day, and as well as sandwiches, ploughman's, and filled baked potatoes, you might find soup (£2.50), duck and port pâté (£2.95), stir-fried vegetable curry (£4.50), cream cheese and broccoli bake (£5.50), cajun chicken, steak and ale pie, or grilled lamb cutlets with honey and rosemary sauce (£5.95), grilled salmon steak with herb and prawn sauce, red snapper with a lime and butter sauce or guinea fowl in apricot and sultana sauce (£6.95), and pan fried duck breast on a bed of blackberries (£7.95). Every other week they do special themed menus (Thai or Mexican food for example), and there are a variety of events and activities throughout the year, taking in everything from Morris dancers and sausage festivals to clairvoyants and Caribbean barbecues and bands. The bright main front bar leads off from a small central serving counter with dark simple panelling. There's a miscellany of chairs and tables, shiny brown vertical panelling decorated with earthenware bottles, decorative plates, brass and pewter and a brown plank ceiling. A changing range of beers might include Fuggles Imperial, Ind Coope Burton, and Tolly Original, and they have a dozen or so malt whiskies, and a varying wine list. Derek the stuffed fox still sits among the crisp packets. The cosy back rooms are partly panelled too, with old-fashioned settles and windsor chairs; one has a big brick fireplace with its bread-oven still beside it – the chimney is said to have been used as a highwayman's look-out. A small room down steps at the back has shove-ha'penny and dominoes; piped music. There are nice views from the crazy-paved front terrace and tables on the grass by lilac bushes, with more tables at the back overlooking the meadows and the hillocks; you can play boules out here. There's a hitching rail outside for horses. The surrounding wooded countryside is easily reached by winding paths. *(Recommended by Helen Morton, Simon Penny, Pam and Tim Moorey, AW, BW, W Wonham, Roger and Jenny Huggins, James Nunns, J S M Sheldon)*

Allied ~ Tenants Guy and Rena Davies ~ Real ale ~ Meals and snacks ~ (01737) 243100 ~ Children in back family room ~ Folk club second Sun in month ~ Open 11-2.30(3 Sat), 5.30-11; 12-10.30 summer Suns

SHAMLEY GREEN TQ0343 Map 3
Red Lion

B2128 S of Guildford

Much smarter than it looks from the unassuming facade, this very pleasant dining pub has a good mix of furniture in its cosy bar, including a handsome panel-back armed settle, red-brocaded high-backed modern settles forming booths around tables, some kitchen chairs and a couple of antique clocks. Under the red glossed ceiling are rows of books on high shelves, and the cream walls have old photographs of games of cricket on the opposite village green. Most tables are laid for meals with a fairly big choice from the menu and blackboard which might include sandwiches, soups such as ham and lentil, grilled stuffed mushrooms topped with brie (£6.75), ham, egg and chips or spinach, mushroom and seafood crêpe (£6.75), dijon peppered chicken or steak and Guinness pie (£9.65), plenty of fresh fish such as sea bass, cod fillet in tarragon sauce, or lemon sole with parsley (£10.65), steaks (from £11.75), and puddings such as raspberry roulade or sticky toffee pudding (£3.25); they do children's helpings, and most weeks a Sunday lunch, though not always in summer. You'll probably need to book at weekends. Well kept Ansells, Flowers Original, and Tetleys Imperial on handpump, and a good selection of wines. Handmade wooden tables outside. *(Recommended by John Barker, Wayne Brindle, Derek and Margaret Underwood, Ed Birch, Guy Consterdine, Ian Phillips, R Sinclair-Taylor)*

Pubmaster ~ Lease: Ben Heath ~ Real ale ~ Meals and snacks (12-3, 6.30-10) ~ Restaurant ~ (01483) 892202 ~ Children welcome ~ Open 11-11; 12-10.30 Sun ~ Bedrooms: £40B/£45B

SOUTH GODSTONE TQ3648 Map 3
Fox & Hounds

Tilburstow Hill Rd; just outside village, turn off A22 into Harts Lane, pub is at the end; handy for M25 junction 6

Though parts of this genuinely old-fashioned place were built in 1368, most of what you see today is 17th-c, with even some of the high-back settles in the cosy low-beamed bar thought to date back at least that far. A couple more were made only last year, but you won't be able to tell the difference. A big kettle constantly simmers away on the woodburning stove, and there are racing prints on the walls, prettily arranged dried hops, and cushioned wall-benches and a window seat around the few low tables; piped classical music. You might not want to go any further than this snugly atmospheric little room, but there are a couple more seats and tables around the tiny bar counter, up a step and beyond some standing timbers. Popular home-made bar food (not cheap but good value) might include soup (£3.50), open sandwiches (from £4), ploughman's (£4.50), prawn, samphire and pasta gratin (£6), specials like lamb and mint sausages with bubble and squeak (£5.50) or steak, mushroom and ale pie (£7), and well liked fresh fish dishes such as wing of skate with black butter (£6.50); the chips are very highly praised. You can reserve tables in the restaurant, which is the only part of the pub where food is served in the evening. Greene King IPA and Abbot on handpump; the very extensive restaurant wine list is usually also available in the bar. Friendly licensees and staff. There are a good few picnic tables out in the garden. Note they don't allow children inside. *(Recommended by TBB, Jonathan Nettleton, BHP, Dr and Mrs S Pleasance)*

Greene King ~ Tenants David and Lorraine McKie ~ Real ale ~ Meals and snacks (not evenings Sun or Mon, and limited Mon lunch) ~ Restaurant ~ (01342) 893474 ~ Open 11-3, 6-11

WALLISWOOD TQ1138 Map 3

Scarlett Arms ★

Village signposted from Ewhurst—Rowhook back road; or follow Oakwoodhill signpost from A29 S of Ockley, then follow Walliswood signpost into Walliswood Green Road

Readers returning to this unspoilt little country pub are often welcomed as old friends; it's the kind of place where locals and visitors blend together to create a warmly friendly and comfortable feel. The red-tiled white building was once a pair of labourers' cottages, and the original small-roomed layout has been carefully preserved. The three neatly kept communicating rooms have low black oak beams, deeply polished flagstones, simple but perfectly comfortable benches, high bar stools with backrests, trestle tables, country prints, photographs of locals, and two roaring winter log fires. The notably good value homely meals have made it a particularly popular stop for lunch, with the menu including sandwiches and ploughman's (lunchtimes only), ham, egg and chips (£4.50), liver and bacon, ham and cheesy leek bake, steak and kidney pie, oxtail stew, rabbit pie or stilton, broccoli, mushroom and cauliflower bake (all £4.75), pheasant casserole (£5.50), and puddings like treacle sponge (£1.85); they do a lunchtime roast on Thursdays and Sundays (£4.75). Most meals come with a selection of five freshly cooked vegetables. Well kept King & Barnes Sussex, Broadwood and Festive on handpump. Darts, bar billiards, cribbage, shove-ha'penny, table skittles, dominoes and a fruit machine in a small room at the end. There are old-fashioned seats and tables with umbrellas in the pretty well tended garden. Note they don't allow under-14s inside. *(Recommended by DWAJ, G R Sunderland, G W Jensen, James Nunns, Bob and Maggie Atherton, Margaret and Nigel Dennis, N H and A H Harries, G W and I L Edwards, Peter Lewis, P Gillbe, J S M Sheldon, Keith and Audrey Ward, Anthony Byers)*

King & Barnes ~ Tenant Mrs Pat Haslam ~ Real ale ~ Meals ~ (01306) 627243 ~ Open 11-2.30, 5.30-11

WARLINGHAM TQ3658 Map 3

White Lion

B269

Full of nooks and crannies and tales of ghosts and secret passages, this delightfully unspoilt Tudor coaching inn comes as quite a surprise so close to the outskirts of London. The marvellously aged warren of low-beamed dark-panelled rooms has plenty of deeply aged plasterwork, as well wood-block floors and high-backed settles, and an impressive old inglenook fireplace. A side room decorated with amusing early 19th-c cartoons has darts, cribbage, and a trivia and fruit machine. Bar food is served in the bigger, brighter room at the end of the building, from a range including sandwiches, vegetarian dishes (£3.95), curries or scampi (£4.25), roasts (£4.50), daily specials, and steaks (£4.95); good service. Bass, Fullers London Pride, Hancocks HB and a changing guest on handpump, and as we went to press they were planning to introduce a range of country wines. Piped music in the eating area, which is no smoking at lunchtimes. The well kept back lawn, with its rockery, is surrounded by a herbaceous border; there may be outside service here in summer. *(Recommended by Niki and Terry Pursey, Jenny and Brian Seller; more reports please)*

Bass ~ Manager Julie Evans ~ Real ale ~ Meals and snacks (not Sun eve) Restaurant ~ (01883) 624106 ~ Children in restaurant and away from bar areas till 8pm ~ Open 11-11; 12-10.30 Sun

WEST CLANDON TQ0452 Map 3

Onslow Arms

The Street (A247)

When this handsome country pub was built in the early 17th c visitors turned up mostly on foot, with the flasher customers arriving on horseback; these days most people have their own horsepower (there's parking space for 200 cars) so anyone really wanting to make an entrance comes by helicopter – the pub has its own pad. The spacious rambling rooms have heavy beams, polished brass and copper, leaded windows, carved settles on the flagstones or thick carpets, and log fires in inglenook fireplaces (one has an unusual roasting spit). There's a quietly comfortable atmosphere with fresh flowers, soft lighting, and courteous, friendly and professional service. A fine choice of around eight well kept real ales might include Bass, Boddingtons, Courage Best and Directors, Fullers London Pride, King & Barnes Sussex, Marstons Pedigree, Wadworths 6X and Youngs Special; they also keep a very good German keg lager, and a range of wines and malt whiskies. The carvery with its hot and cold meats, fish and help-yourself salads has proved so popular that they've had to double the space given over to it; work should be completed by the time this edition hits the shops. Other well-presented meals include sandwiches, coquille st jacques (£3.85), tagliatelle niçoise (£4.50), chicken and mushroom pie (£5.25), steak, kidney and oyster pie (£5.85), and puddings, with a wide range of more elaborate dishes in the stylish candlelit (partly no-smoking) restaurant. In summer the hanging baskets, flower filled tubs, shrubs and flower-laden cart outside on the flagged courtyard are a marvellous sight. *(Recommended by M L and G Clarke, Wayne Brindle, Ian Phillips, Susan and John Douglas, Gillian and Michael Wallace, J S M Sheldon, TBB, John and Shirley Dyson, Paul Carter, June and Malcolm Farmer, Thomas Nott)*

Free house ~ Licensee Alan Peck ~ Real ale ~ Meals and snacks (not Sun evening) ~ Restaurant ~ (01483) 222447 ~ Children welcome ~ Open 11-11; 12-10.30 Sun

Lucky Dip

Besides the fully inspected pubs, you might like to try these Lucky Dips recommended to us and described by readers (if you do, please send us reports):

Abinger Common [Abinger signed off A25 W of Dorking – then right to Abinger Hammer; TQ1145], *Abinger Hatch*: Lovely country setting nr pretty church and duck pond in clearing of rolling woods, with tables in nice garden; character bar with lots of potential – heavy beams, flagstones, basic furnishings, log fires, half a dozen interesting ales, farm ciders, country wines; pool table by entrance, quick food, piped music; big restaurant; provision for children; may have Sun afternoon teas, open all day bank hols and for village fair – around second weekend June *(Nigel Harris, Ian Phillips, Winifrede D Morrison, Ron Gentry, R Lake, J Sheldon, Gill and Andy Plumb, LYM)* Addlestone [Chertsey Rd (handy for M25); TQ0464], *George*: Old three-bar beamed pub listing licensees since 1786, Courage Best and

Fullers London Pride, food in bar and pleasant restaurant area (popular with business people); some tables outside *(Jenny and Brian Seller)*; *Magnet*: Friendly Greene King pub with good atmosphere *(Peter and Lynn Brueton)*
Ashford [Staines Rd W; TQ0870], *Spelthorne*: 1930ish corner pub worth noting for good basic home cooking in back Kiwi Restaurant, very cheap and friendly *(Ian and Liz Phillips)*
☆ Banstead [High St, off A217; TQ2559], *Woolpack*: Busy but spotless Chef & Brewer with consistently good value food from sandwiches up inc children's dishes, good friendly service, well kept Courage-related ales, cosily decorated lounge, good no-smoking area; occasional free jazz, open all day *(DWAJ, John Pettit)*

Banstead [Park Rd; back rd from High St towards Kingswood/B2032], *Mint*: Recently comfortably refurbished, decent home-made food (not Sun evening) from sandwiches up inc vegetarian (may be a wait when busy), garden with play area *(DWAJ)*

☆ Beare Green [A24 Dorking—Horsham; TQ1842], *Dukes Head*: Good atmosphere and generous straightforward food in attractive roadside pub with good service, open fires, Tetleys-related real ales; pleasant garden *(G Washington, LYM)*

Bletchingley [2 High St, 2½ miles from M25 junction 6, via A22 then A25 towards Redhill; TQ3250], *Plough*: Generous helpings of good value food (not Sun evening) in spacious bar or (same price) restaurant of extended pub with well kept ales such as King & Barnes, Tetleys and Wadworths 6X; friendly efficient staff, tables in big garden *(Doreen and Brian Hardham, David Voice, DWAJ)*; *Prince Albert*: Good choice of food in attractive pub with several nooks and corners, fast friendly service, well kept beer, tables on terrace and in small pretty garden *(K Watson)*

☆ Bramley [High St; TQ0044], *Jolly Farmer*: Cheerful and lively, with wide choice of good freshly prepared food (so may be a wait), Theakstons Old Peculier and Pilgrim Talisman served by sparkler, two log fires, beer-mat collection, big restaurant; bedrooms *(B A Hayward, LYM)*

Brockham [Brockham Green; TQ1949], *Dukes Head*: Wide range of good food in friendly pleasantly old-fashioned pub, polite attentive service, several real ales, log fire; in pretty spot by village green *(Dorsan Baker)*

Burstow [Antlands Lane; TQ3140], *Shipley Bridge*: Popular carvery with reasonably priced food and good service, big dining area *(A H Denman)*

☆ Byfleet [104 High Rd; TQ0661], *Plough*: Medley of furnishings in friendly and lively pub with good value straightforward bar food, well kept Courage and guest ales, lots of farm tools, brass and copper, log fire, dominoes; prices low for Surrey; picnic tables in pleasant back garden *(Richard Houghton, Ian Phillips)*

Capel [signed off A24 at Beare Green roundabout; TQ1740], *Crown*: Pleasantly rustic village pub with cosy and comfortable lounge bar and restaurant area, partly no smoking, well kept Friary Meux Best and Marstons Pedigree, good varied menu, friendly staff; pool in two-level public bar *(Keith Ward)*

☆ Charlton [142 Charlton Rd, off B376 Laleham—Shepperton; TQ0869], *Harrow*: Delightfully unexpected thatched 17th-c pub, comfortable, friendly and carefully modernised, with short choice of generous interesting no-frills food (tables can be booked), particularly good service even when crowded, well kept Fullers London Pride and Morlands Old Speckled Hen, plenty of seats *(Ian Phillips, James Nunns)*

Charlwood [Church Rd; TQ2441], *Half*

Moon: Plainly modernised old local in attractive village handy for Gatwick, limited choice of cheap home-made food, friendly staff, bar billiards and other pub games *(Tina and David Woods-Taylor, BB)*

Chelsham [Vanguard Way, over the common; TQ3759], *Bull*: Traditional village-green country pub, home-cooked food Tues-Sat and Sun lunch, table service, tables outside *(E G Parish)*

☆ Chertsey [Ruxbury Rd, St Anns Hill (nr Lyne); TQ0267], *Golden Grove*: Busy local with lots of stripped wood, cheap straightforward home-made food from sandwiches up (not Sat-Mon evenings) in pine-tabled eating area, well kept Adnams and Tetleys-related ales, cheerful service; piped music, fruit and games machines; big garden with friendly dogs and goat, play area, wooded pond - nice spot by woods *(Rhoda and Jeff Collins, Ian Phillips, Clem Stephens)*

☆ Chertsey [London St (B375); TQ0466], *Crown*: Friendly and relaxed Youngs pub with button-back banquettes in attractively renovated high-ceilinged bar, well kept ales, good choice of reasonably priced food, back dining area, restaurant, good service; neatly placed darts, discreet fruit machines; separate garden bar with conservatory, tables in courtyard and garden with pond; children welcome; smart 30-bedroom annexe *(R B Crail, Simon Collett-Jones)*

☆ Chiddingfold [A283; SU9635], *Crown*: Picturesque old inn in attractive surroundings, afternoon teas in hotel side with fine carving, massive beams, big inglenook and tapestried handsomely panelled restaurant; simpler side family bar with well kept ales such as Badger Tanglefoot and Charles Wells, decent food using fresh herbs etc, tables out on verandah; children allowed in some areas; has been open all day, very crowded 5 Nov (fireworks out on green); bedrooms *(Margaret and Nigel Dennis, Steve Goodchild, LYM)*

Chiddingfold [A283 S], *Swan*: Very helpful service in cheery country local with spacious bar and tables set closely in small dining room, wide range of well kept ales, good choice of food, Sun bar nibbles, lovely old dog *(David Dimock, LYM)*

☆ Chilworth [Blackheath; off A248 across the level crossing, SE of Guildford; TQ0247], *Villagers*: Attractive pub with timbers dividing it into cosy nooks and corners, old pews and other tasteful furnishings, good generous interesting home-cooked food from superb sandwiches up, well kept ales inc one brewed for the pub, decent wines and port, very friendly and eager-to-please young staff; lovely garden, cricket green, pretty village, good walks; (table mats show these); bedrooms *(Mr and Mrs B Matthews, G W Stevenson, Ian and Liz Phillips, Mrs W D Morrison, Stephen and Judy Parish, BB)*

☆ Chipstead [B2032, Chipstead Valley - OS Sheet 176 map ref 273575; TQ2757], *Ramblers Rest*: Recently converted pub in collection of partly 14th-c buildings, extensive range of different drinking areas with different atmospheres, panelling and low ceilings, wide range of well kept mainly Whitbreads-related ales, bar food inc generous ploughman's, restaurant popular with families weekends; big pleasant garden behind, decent walks nearby; pervasive piped music; open all day inc Sun, no dogs *(Jenny and Brian Seller, Helen Morton, Simon Ludlow, Eddie Edwards, David Peakall, BB)*

Chipstead [3 miles from M25, junction 8; A217 towards Banstead, right at second roundabout], *Well House*: Cottagey and comfortable partly 14th-c pub with lots of atmosphere, simple lunchtime food (not Sun) from sandwiches up, welcoming staff, log fires in all three rooms, well kept Bass and guest beers, good pot of tea; dogs allowed; attractive garden with well reputed to be mentioned in Doomsday Book (collect your own food if you eat out here), delightful setting *(David Peakall, Jenny and Brian Seller, LYM)*; [Hazelwood Lane], *White Hart*: Fullers London Pride and Worthington, simple good value food, cheery staff, tables outside, maybe a summer bouncy castle *(DWAJ, Mark Coughlin, Simon Ludlow)*

Claygate [TQ1563], *Foley Arms*: Solid Victorian two-bar local, real fires, good value hot meals and giant sandwiches; Youngs ales *(Tony Hobden)*; *Hare & Hounds*: Enjoyable straightforward food, comfortable seating *(DWAJ)*

☆ Cobham [Plough Lane; TQ0960], *Plough*: Cheerful easy-going atmosphere in pretty black-shuttered local with comfortably modernised low-beamed lounge bar, well kept Courage ales, helpful staff, pine-panelled snug with darts, lunchtime food; piped pop music may be rather loud some evenings; seats outside *(John Pettit, B L Sullivan, G W Stevenson, LYM)*

Cobham [Riverhill], *Old Bear*: Large pub, wide range of real ales, good range of bar food *(Ian Phillips)*; [A245 Pains Hill/Byfleet Rd, by Sainsburys], *Snail*: Primarily a brasserie, but cottagey, attractive and comfortable, with well kept ales, efficient friendly staff, good food; handy for Painshill Park *(Mrs J A Blanks, Anthony Byers, James Nunns)*

Cranleigh [Bookhurst Rd; Parkmead estate – towards Shere; TQ0638], *Little Park Hatch*: Friendly landlord, wide choice of good food cooked largely by landlady, well kept Flowers IPA and Original, recent renovations inc small dining area, huge garden with pet fun and adventure play area *(Neil Wood)*; *Onslow Arms*: Friendly open-plan pub with log fires, rural implements, good straightforward quickly served food, well kept Tetleys-related ales, games in public bar *(M Carey, Miss A Groocock)*

☆ Dorking [81 South St; TQ1649], *Cricketers*: Bustling little Fullers pub, very neat and tidy, with solidly comfortable furniture, cricketing memorabilia on stripped brick walls, limited choice of no-nonsense food (not Fri, Sat evening or Sun lunch), well kept Chiswick, London Pride and ESB, low prices, helpful friendly service, pleasant back terrace with barbecues; open all day *(Jeff and Rhoda Collins, G W Stevenson, Dr H Huddart, John Pettit, LYM)*

Dorking [Horsham Rd just out of town], *Bush*: Simple no-frills pub, quiet and cosy, with well kept ales such as Boddingtons, Brakspears, Fullers and Thwaites, good value lunches, friendly unobtrusive service; partly covered terrace, small garden *(Dr H Huddart, Adrian Davis)*; [45 West St], *Kings Arms*: 16th-c half-timbered pub in antiques area, part-panelled low-beamed lounge divided from bar by timbers, quiet black dining area, nice lived-in old furniture, warm relaxed atmosphere, good choice of home-cooked usual food, friendly service, King & Barnes, Marstons Pedigree, Tetleys and Wadworths 6X; open all day *(John Beeken, Tony and Wendy Hobden, Alistair Scott)*; *Surrey Yeoman*: Pleasant local, busy evenings; well kept Fullers London Pride, King & Barnes *(James Nunns)*

Dormansland [Plough Rd, off B2028 NE; TQ4042], *Plough*: Warm traditional atmosphere in old building in quiet village, many original features, real ales inc well kept Flowers Original, popular generous food inc traditional puddings, cheerful staff; busy weekday lunchtime *(E G Parish, J R Tunnadine)*

☆ Dunsfold [TQ0036], *Sun*: Consistently good reasonably priced food inc interesting dishes in elegantly symmetrical 18th-c beamed pub on attractive green, friendly old-fashioned atmosphere, scrubbed pine furniture, helpful staff, well kept Tetleys-related ales, log fires; separate cottage dining room; children welcome *(Rhoda and Jeff Collins, June and Malcolm Farmer, LYM)*

East Clandon [TQ0651], *Queens Head*: Now a Big Steak pub (the specials are home-cooked still), with timbers, small connecting rooms, big inglenook log fire, fine old elm bar counter, bookcases, pictures, copperware, affable service; well kept ales, no lunchtime piped music; tables in quiet garden *(John Evans, E G Parish)*

☆ Effingham [Orestan Lane; TQ1253], *Plough*: Characteristic commuter-belt Youngs local with consistently well kept ales, good value honest home cooking (fresh veg and potatoes may be extra) in enjoyable Sun lunch, two coal-effect gas fires, beamery, panelling, old plates and brassware in long lounge, no-smoking extension, efficient staff; popular with older people – no dogs, children or sleeveless T-shirts inside, no music or machines, lots of tables in big informal garden with play area and out in front; convenient for Polesdon Lacey *(Sue and Mike Todd, David Gregory, A M Pickup, Terry Watkins, Christopher Gallop, John Pettit, John Ashley, P Gillbe, Alan Kilpatrick)*

Elstead [Farnham Rd; SU9143], *Golden Fleece*: Straightforward pub included for good reasonably priced authentic Thai food; busy, with good atmosphere, tall plants adding a faint touch of the exotic *(Martin and Karen Wake, Dr N Kennea)*

Englefield Green [Northcroft Rd; SU9970], *Barley Mow*: Courage pub overlooking green, decent choice of reasonably priced food, back dining area with no-smoking section; tables outside *(Tony and Wendy Hobden)*; [Wick Lane, Bishopgate], *Sun*: Well kept Courage-related ales and Youngs Special, decent wines, good choice of food from sandwiches up, reasonable prices, daily papers, roaring log fire; biscuit and water for dogs, handy for Savile Garden and Windsor Park *(Ian Phillips)*

Epsom [High St; TQ2160], *Bank*: Spacious former bank, plenty of wicker and upholstered chairs, long bar and standing area, spacious back dining area, wide choice of reasonably priced food, Badger Best, Brakspears, Theakstons XB, Youngs Special and other ales; piped music, can be noisy when busy, but quiet at weekends *(John Pettit)*; [Pikes Hill], *Barley Mow*: Friendly Fullers local, attractive decor, decent food *(Robin Cordell, Trevor Thornton)*; [Downs Rd, Epsom Downs], *Derby Arms*: Popular and reliable refurbished Toby dining pub with reasonably priced food in bar and added restaurant, inc carvery; friendly helpful service, open all day Sun *(A H Denman, Simon Ludlow, Mr and Mrs Denman)*; [opp racecourse], *Tattenham Corner*: Big reliable Beefeater, prompt friendly service, good range of usual food, changing ales such as Marstons Pedigree; play area and barbecues in garden *(R C Vincent)*

Esher [71 High St; TQ1464], *Bear*: Spacious and well kept, with good fresh food, good choice of beers *(G R Sunderland)*

Ewell [1 London Rd; TQ2262], *Spring*: Spacious Bass pub with sofas and armchairs in new lounge, sporting pictures, Fullers London Pride and Worthington BB, popular food inc children's dishes, friendly service, jazz pianist in restaurant some Sunday lunchtimes (must book then); live music some evenings *(G W and I L Edwards, DWAJ)*

☆ Ewhurst [Pitch Hill; a mile N of village on Shere rd; TQ0940], *Windmill*: Spacious series of hillside lawns give beautiful views, as does conservatory restaurant; smart modern bar behind, good interesting food in bar and restaurant, half a dozen well kept ales inc Hogs Back, welcoming atmosphere; occasional live music; lovely walking country *(Gwen and Peter Andrews, Chris Kings, Ian and Liz Phillips, LYM)*

☆ Farleigh [Farleigh Common; bus route 403 from Croydon; TQ3659], *Harrow*: Stripped-flint former barn doing well after refurbishment, rustic decor with country bric-a-brac, even an owl high in the rafters; good lunchtime food from good sandwiches up, raised no-smoking area, well kept Bass, Fullers London Pride and Hancocks HB, cheerful efficient staff; separate locals' bar, tables on big lawn with pasture behind; no dogs, popular with younger people evening *(Niki and Terry Pursey, Jenny and Brian Seller, Christopher Wright)*

Farnham [Frensham Rd, Lower Bourne;

SU8544], *Fox*: Open-plan local with good food in small raised back dining section, accommodating new licensees *(Colin Draper)*; [Tilford Rd, Lower Bourne], *Spotted Cow*: Welcoming rural local with wide choice of good food inc lots of fish, well kept Adnams, Courage and Hogs Back TEA, decent wine, attentive friendly service, reasonable prices; play area in big garden – former sandpit now completely rehabilitated *(Mr and Mrs R J Foreman, Vann and Terry Prime, John and Vivienne Rice)*

☆ Felbridge [Woodcock Hill – A22 N; TQ3639], *Woodcock*: Busy little flagstoned bar opening on to richly furnished room a bit like a film props department, spiral stairs up to another opulent room, candlelit and almost boudoirish, nice small Victorian dining room off; also big seafood restaurant; well kept Harveys, Ringwood Old Thumper, Charles Wells Bombardier, piped music (can be loud and late), relaxed atmosphere – service can be very leisurely; children in eating area, open all day, some tables outside *(Dr Paul Kitchener, R C Watkins, Alan Skull, BHP, Adrian Zambardino, Debbie Chaplin, A C Morrison, L M Miall, LYM)*

☆ Forest Green [nr B2126/B2127 junction; TQ1240], *Parrot*: Quaint rambling country pub, pleasant and comfortable, with pervasive parrot motif, well kept Courage ales, good often interesting food (many tables reserved, giving it something of a restaurant feel in the evening), good cheerful service even when crowded; children welcome, open all day; plenty of space outside by cricket pitch, good walks nearby *(A H Denman, Ian Phillips, Winifrede D Morrison, LYM)*

Godalming [5 Wharf St; SU9743], *Old Wharf*: Whitbreads Hogshead pub refurbished using old wood, changing well kept ales such as Flowers Original, Fullers London Pride, Gibbs Mew Bishops Tipple, Ringwood Porter and Old Thumper, four-pint jugs for the price of three, friendly service; piped music; open all day every day, very busy weekends – lively young mixed crowd, occasional live jazz *(Steve Felstead, Scott Reynolds)*

☆ Godstone [128 High St; under a mile from M25 junction 6, via B2236; TQ3551], *Bell*: Extensively refurbished 14th-c pub, comfortable beamed bar with lots of old prints, pictures and artefacts, smaller snug, bigger alcovey restaurant with good interesting food inc Malaysian and other exotic meals; Tetleys-related ales, Victorian-style conservatory, garden; lavatories with disabled access and nappy-changing; bedrooms *(E G Parish, D and A Walters, LYM)*

Godstone [Bletchingley Rd], *Hare & Hounds*: Unpretentious country pub, well kept Greene King IPA and Abbot, wide choice of good food inc ploughman's with three local cheeses, welcoming relaxed atmosphere *(Jenny and Brian Seller, D Deas)*

☆ Gomshall [Station Rd (A25); TQ0847], *Compasses*: Attractive and welcoming, well kept Gibbs Mew Bishops Tipple and Wiltshire, good value wines, good well presented food (not cheap but good value), quick friendly service, lots of tables, well designed restaurant; spacious pleasant garden over duck stream with abundant weeping willows; walkers welcome *(G R Sharman, JEB, B and B Matthews, R B Crail, John Pettit, James Nunns)*

Grayswood [A286 NE of Haslemere; SU9234], *Wheatsheaf*: Good value interesting food in modernised bar and restaurant with neo-classical frescoes, reasonably priced wines; conference rooms etc, bedrooms *(Paula Williams, C Perry)*

Guildford [Woodbridge Rd; SU9949], *Forger & Firkin*: Brewing its own interesting beers inc strong Dogbolter, maybe a strong home-made cider, wide range of other well known beers; weekend live bands *(Chris O'Prey, Steve Felstead)*; [Millbrook, across car park from Yvonne Arnaud Theatre, beyond boat yard], *Jolly Farmer*: Big two-level riverside pub with extensive terrace and moorings, lots of picnic table sets, lower picture-window lounge decorated with boating stuff, food counter upstairs, Ind Coope Burton, Wadworths 6X and Tetleys, friendly young staff, decent food *(G C Hackemer, Wayne Brindle, Ian Phillips, Mark Percy)*; [Quarry St/Stoke Rd], *Kings Head*: Wide choice of seating from spacious banquettes to discreet snugs, lots of beams and stripped brickwork, cosy inglenook fire, subdued piped music, polite service, well kept Courage-related ales, decent wines, good value popular pies etc, tables on flower-filled terraces *(Dr M Owton, David Rashleigh, Ian Phillips)*; [Old Portsmouth Rd], *Olde Ship*: Well kept Morlands, good pizzas and puddings 7 days a week, obliging service; no music *(Roy Shutz)*; [Millmead], *White House*: Recently opened refurbished Fullers pub with well kept beers, pretty riverside setting, pleasant helpful staff, hot and cold food, small upstairs no-smoking bar; for over-25s *(Dr M Owton, Kim Barden, Derek Patey)*

Headley [Church Lane, village signed off B2033 SE of Leatherhead; TQ2054], *Cock Horse*: A former favourite, now redeveloped (and renamed) as Maltsters Table family dining pub, light and airy (difficult to detect signs of its 15th-c origins – photographs in the public bar show how it used to be), with usual food (banners out advertising special meals), Tetleys-related and guest ales, efficient friendly service *(DWAJ, John Evans, LYM)*

Hersham [67 Molesey Rd; TQ1164], *Barley Mow*: An S&N chain dining pub, but cottagey and largely unspoilt with beams, timbers and comfortable modern kitchen chairs; limited choice of decent food, pleasant atmosphere, well kept Theakstons *(Christine Hobson, Jenny and Brian Seller)*; [6 Queens Rd], *Bricklayers Arms*: Friendly atmosphere in well kept pub with wide choice of good value home-made food from back servery, good wines, separate bar with pool; small secluded garden, comfortable bedrooms

(Michael Sage); [Hersham Rd], *Royal George*: Friendly and comfortable, with well kept Youngs, lunchtime food inc wide range of crusty bread sandwiches, good home-cooked specials, two-person bargains, Sun seafood *(Ed Birch)*

Holmbury St Mary [TQ1144], *Kings Head*: Friendly and cosy, in popular walking country, with food worth waiting for, well kept Ringwood Best and Fortyniner, local farm cider, obliging service, amiable golden retriever, slight 70s feel; pretty spot on village green, informal sloping back garden; pool, Sky TV, can be smoky *(Jenny and Brian Seller, Peter and Liz Wilkins)*

Horley [Brighton Rd; TQ2842], *Air Balloon*: Big Tetleys steak house, good adjoining children's indoor play barn; good value Sun roast and tasty puddings, reasonable choice of beers, quick service, small outdoor play area; handy for Gatwick *(R C Vincent)*

Horsell [Horsell Birch; SU9859], *Cricketers*: Tetleys dining pub with wide choice of popular food inc Sun lunch, spacious well kept grounds with barbecues; good range of beers, friendly staff *(Lee Jones, Chris and Martin Taylor)*; [123 High St], *Red Lion*: Good helpings of cheap food in welcoming well renovated pub with pleasant terrace, picture-filled converted barn where children allowed; good walks nearby *(Chris and Martin Taylor)*

Horsell Common [Chertsey Rd; The Anthonys; A320 Woking—Ottershaw; SU9959], *Bleak House*: Welcoming and cheerful, with decent food, Tetleys-related ales, comfortable seats, picnic tables and barbecues on back lawn; good walks to the sandpits which inspired H G Wells's *War of the Worlds (Ian Phillips, Chris and Martin Taylor)*

☆ Hurtmore [just off A3 nr Godalming by Hurtmore/Shackleford turn-off; SU9545], *Squirrels*: Roomy, comfortable, fresh and airy, with upmarket feel, sofas, country-kitchen furniture, partly no-smoking restaurant and conservatory, children's playroom, books for adults and children, decent food in bar and restaurant, good friendly service, well kept Courage-related ales, facilities for disabled people; good bedrooms *(G R Sunderland, Wayne Brindle, LYM)*

☆ Irons Bottom [Sidlow Bridge; off A217 – OS Sheet 187 map ref 250460; TQ2546], *Three Horseshoes*: Friendly country local, rather sophisticated feel, with new landlord doing well – he's a careful cook using good ingredients, and the menu reflects his time abroad; five or six excellently kept Fullers London Pride and interesting guest ales, quiz or darts night Tues, summer barbecues *(Jim Bunting, Mike and Heather Watson, Jenny and Brian Seller)*

Kingswood [Waterhouse Lane; TQ2455], *Kingswood Arms*: Big and busy, with wide variety of reasonably priced popular food, cheerful quick service (announcements when orders are ready), Courage-related ales, conservatory dining extension; spacious rolling garden with play area *(Chris Jackson, Helen Medhurst, Niki and Terry Pursey, P Gillbe)*

Knaphill [Bagshot Rd; SU9658], *Hunters Lodge*: Spacious, attractively renovated and comfortable, good open fire, well presented generous food, enthusiastic friendly staff, big garden; lavatory for the disabled *(Clem Stephens)*; [Anchor Hill], *Royal Oak*: Welcoming characterful local, good honest food inc all-day breakfast, Courage-related ales; small restaurant area *(Ian Phillips, Alison Dowdeswell)*

☆ **Laleham** [B376, off A308 W of M3 junction 1; TQ0568], *Three Horseshoes*: Popular and plushly modernised, but dating back to 13th c, with flagstones, heavy beams, interesting history, lots of tables in enjoyable garden, and easy stroll to Thameside lawns; generous usual bar food (not cheap), well kept Fullers London Pride and Websters Yorkshire, decent wines, efficient service, piped music, restaurant; children in no-smoking conservatory, open all day *(Ian Phillips, Ron and Sheila Corbett, M Carey, A Groocock, Wayne Brindle, Clem Stephens, Margaret and Nigel Dennis, Jeff and Rhoda Collins, D Tapper, Clive Gilbert, Stephen Barney, LYM)*
Laleham [The Broadway], *Feathers*: Friendly old cottage, surprisingly roomy inside, with bar in single-storey front extension, traditional decor, lots of hanging pewter mugs, beamed dining lounge with reasonably priced generous straightforward food from well filled baps up, well kept Courage ales usually with a guest beer from a small independent brewery; piped music; tables outside *(Richard Houghton)*; [Staines Rd], *Lucan Arms*: Two huge roaring log fires in popular family pub, generous tasty bar food and roasts all day, fresh veg, good choice of puddings, good coffee *(Pam Deeprose)*

Leatherhead [57 High St; TQ1656], *Dukes Head*: Busy and friendly, with good range of bar food from separate servery, beams, timbers and open fire, good coffee, small front bar with pool and games machine; piped music; handy for good riverside walks *(John Pettit, J Sheldon)*; [5 North St], *Penny Black*: Busy Whitbreads Hogshead in converted post office, big partitioned beamed bar, framed stamp collections on exposed brick walls, bare boards, lots of tables and chairs, solid fuel stove, wide choice of Whitbreads and guest ales, straightforward reasonably priced cheerfully served bar food; some seats outside, live entertainment some evenings *(John Pettit, Damien Brennan, Jonathan Kearley)*

Limpsfield Chart [TQ4251], *Carpenters Arms*: Friendly much modernised pub in delightful setting by common, lovely walks, within easy reach of Chartwell; good straightforward food, Tetleys-related ales, prompt friendly service *(Dave Braisted)*

☆ **Lower Kingswood** [Buckland Rd; just off A217; TQ2453], *Mint Arms*: Family-run, with decent bar food all day inc Sun, wider restaurant choice, friendly service, wide

choice of ales such as Courage Best, Fullers London Pride, Gales HSB, King & Barnes, Theakstons Old Peculier, Wadworths 6X and Youngs, lots of brasses and copper, pool and darts in games area, big garden with play area *(DWAJ, Mr and Mrs G W Edwards)*
Lower Kingswood [Brighton Rd; A217, 1½ miles from M25 junction 8], *Fox on the Hill*: Spacious refurbished bar, popular lunchtime for well presented straightforward good value food; friendly attentive staff *(DWAJ)*

☆ **Martyrs Green** [Old Lane, handy for M25 junction 10 – off A3 S-bound, but return N of junction; TQ0957], *Black Swan*: Lively low-beamed country local, extensively enlarged, with simple furnishings, well worn back bar, fine range of a dozen or more well kept ales, good service, log fires, lots of brass blowlamps, generous bar food, restaurant; can get crowded with young people evenings, piped pop music may be loud then, maybe live entertainment; children welcome, open all day every day, plenty of tables in big woodside garden with play area and maybe summer barbecue and bouncy castle; handy for RHS Wisley Garden *(G W and I L Edwards, D B Close, Andy Cunningham, Tony Haines, Steve Felstead, G W Stevenson)*

☆ **Mickleham** [Old London Rd; TQ1753], *Running Horses*: Popular refurbished 16th-c beamed village pub attractively placed nr Box Hill, interesting choice of food, well kept Tetleys-related ales, friendly staff, two lovely open fires, comfortable dining extension/conservatory; nice view from pretty courtyard garden *(John Pettit, Chris and Martin Taylor, G W and I L Edwards, J S M Sheldon)*

Mogador [from M25 up A217 past 2nd roundabout, signed off; TQ2452], *Sportsman*: Interesting and welcoming low-ceilinged local, quietly placed on Walton Heath, a magnet for walkers and riders; well kept Hogs Back Hop Garden and Wadworths 6X, darts, bar billiards; the cold snacks are popular; dogs welcome if not wet or muddy; tables out on common, on back lawn, and some under cover *(JS, BS)*

Newdigate [TQ2042], *Six Bells*: Popular local with good range of well kept ales inc Marstons Pedigree, usual food, very helpful staff, plenty of tables in pleasant garden *(Jenny and Brian Seller, J R Tunnadine, Mrs C Watkinson, G W Stevenson)*

Normandy [Guildford Rd E (A323) – OS Sheet 186 map ref 935518; SU9351], *Duke of Normandy*: Discreetly refurbished Greene King pub, well kept IPA, Abbot and a seasonal ale, good variety of food inc reasonably priced fish, friendly service *(R B Crail)*

Norwood Hill [Leigh—Charlwood back rd; TQ2343], *Fox Revived*: Attractive cottagey old-fashioned furnishings in spacious bare-boards country pub, big double dining conservatory, Tetleys-related ales, good vintage port, daily papers and magazines, pleasant atmosphere, spreading garden *(Jason Caulkin, Simon Penny, LYM)*

Oatlands [Oatlands Dr; junction St Marys Rd; TQ0965], *Pickled Newt*: Well refurbished, with Bass, Boddingtons, Greene King Abbot and Websters, friendly service, limited range of good cheap substantial food, live music Thurs *(James Nunns)*

☆ Ockham [Ockham Lane – towards Cobham; TQ0756], *Hautboy*: Red stone Gothick small hotel, pubby feel and good food in character upstairs brasserie bar, darkly panelled and high-raftered, with oil paintings and minstrels gallery; friendly service, table on cricket-view terrace and in secluded orchard garden; chintzy bedrooms *(Susan and John Douglas, LYM)*

☆ Ockley [Stane St (A29); TQ1439], *Cricketers Arms*: Pretty 15th-c stonebuilt village local with Horsham slab roof, flagstones, low beams, inglenook log fires, shiny pine furniture, good simple generous bar food inc good value Sun roast, well kept ales such as Fullers London Pride and Ringwood Best, country wines, friendly staff, quiet piped music, darts area, small attractive dining room with cricketing memorabilia; seats in back garden with duck pond and play area *(Tony and Wendy Hobden, BB)*

Ockley [Stane St (A29)], *Kings Arms*: Smartly refurbished 17th-c beamed country inn, inglenook log fire, imaginative fresh food from good vegetarian to giant steak, good service, small restaurant; discreetly placed picnic tables in pleasant well kept back garden; bedrooms *(Margaret and Nigel Parker)*; [Billingshurst Rd (A29)], *Red Lion*: Former 17th-c beamed coaching inn, refurbished, with good lively evening atmosphere, King & Barnes ale, family room *(Steve Goodchild, BB)*

☆ nr Ockley [Oakwoodhill – signed off A29 S; TQ1337], *Punch Bowl*: Friendly, welcoming and cosy country pub with huge inglenook log fire, polished flagstones, lots of beams, well kept Badger Best and Tanglefoot and Wadworths 6X, wide choice of decent bar food, lots of traditional games, juke box (can be loud); children allowed in dining area, tables outside with flower tubs and maybe weekend barbecues; has been open all day *(Mr and Mrs D Carter, J Sheldon, Winifrede D Morrison, DWAJ, LYM)*

☆ Ottershaw [222 Brox Rd; TQ0263], *Castle*: Comfortable and friendly local, with plethora of farm tools etc, stripped brick and beamery, good home-cooked food (popular for business lunches), wide range of well kept changing Tetleys-related and other ales, Addlestone's cider, log fire, no-smoking dining area; garden with tables in pleasant creeper-hung arbour *(Graham Arnold, Alan Browne, Ian Phillips)*

☆ Outwood [off A23 S of Redhill; TQ3245], *Bell*: Friendly and attractive extended 17th-c country dining pub, olde-worlde main bar, wide choice of food which can be eaten here or in sparser restaurant area, indoor barbecues, summer cream teas, good choice of well kept ales, log fires, children welcome, has been open all day; pretty garden with country views *(E G Parish, Brian and Jenny Seller,*

Mrs K I Burvill, Margaret Dyke, LYM)

Oxshott [Leatherhead Rd (A244); TQ1460], *Bear*: Busy yet relaxed Youngs pub with well kept beer, big conservatory dining room, friendly courteous staff, usual pub food with fresh veg, good log fire, teddy bear collection, occasional barbecues in small garden *(Ian Phillips, M Wheeler, Mike and Heather Watson, JS, BS)*

Oxted [High St, Old Oxted; TQ3951], *Old Bell*: Attractive and popular Country Carvery pub/restaurant, food inc all-day Sun carvery (must book weekends); friendly welcome, comfortable seating, garden *(A H Denman)*

☆ Peaslake [TQ0845], *Hurtwood*: Small prewar country hotel in fine surroundings, friendly bar popular with locals, good freshly made bar food (worth the wait), well kept local Hogs Back ale, attentive staff; popular restaurant, comfortable bedrooms *(E N Burleton, Derek and Margaret Underwood, Stephan Freeman, BB)*

Puttenham [Seale Lane; SU9347], *Good Intent*: Friendly and atmospheric country local, good range of attractively presented reasonably priced food, constantly changing range of ales, Inch's farm cider, roaring log fire; dogs allowed, no children *(Ian Phillips, Tom Attenborough)*

☆ Pyrford Lock [Lock Lane; 3 miles from M25 junction 10 – S on A3, then take Wisley slip rd and go on past RHS Garden; TQ0458], *Anchor*: Busy modern pub starred for its position by bridge and locks on River Wey Navigation; big terrace, conservatory, picture-window bar, upstairs room with narrow-boat memorabilia; Courage Best and Directors, Theakstons Best and XB, usual food inc vegetarian and children's (may be queues and Tannoy announcements), juke box and machines etc; open all day in summer *(Clive Gilbert, V Green, IP, David Shillitoe, A J and G Jackson, DWAJ, P Gillbe, Chris and Martin Taylor, Ron Gentry, Mr and Mrs D Simons, Peter and Joy Heatherley, LYM)*

☆ Ripley [High St; TQ0556], *Ship*: Welcoming and comfortable 16th-c local with wide choice of reasonably priced well prepared mainly home-made lunchtime bar food from sandwiches up, low beams, flagstones, cosy nooks, log fire in vast inglenook; well kept Courage-related beers, very friendly efficient service, small raised games area with bar billiards, window-seats and stools rather than chairs; small high-walled terrace *(Ian Phillips, P D Grimes, Michael Launder, J Sheldon, Bill Capper)*

Ripley [High St], *Half Moon*: Friendly Fullers local in attractive village, well kept ales inc guests such as Adnams and Marstons Pedigree, lunchtime food, quiet piped music *(Gilly Strachan-Gray, Mike Davies)*

☆ Rowledge [Cherry Tree Rd; SU8243], *Cherry Tree*: Cheerful prettily refurbished two-bar 16th-c village pub with several well kept Bass and Morlands, good freshly made food inc imaginative dishes, good range of seafood and fine puddings, interesting landlady, restaurant area, big well kept garden with play area; juke box; very popular, handy for Birdworld and Alice Holt Forest *(Sian Thrasher, G and M Stewart, Colin Barclay, G C Hackemer)*

☆ Sendmarsh [Marsh Rd; TQ0454], *Saddlers Arms*: Friendly and atmospheric local, low beams, toby jugs, brassware etc, well kept Tetleys-related ales, good value straightforward food inc vegetarian and Sun lunch; notable Christmas decorations, tables outside *(Ian Phillips, DWAJ, G W and I L Edwards)*

Shackleford [Pepperharrow Lane; SU9345], *Cyder House*: Wide range of well kept ales inc Piston Broke and Old Shackle brewed here, farm ciders, log fire, good food inc children's, very friendly staff, families welcome; utilitarian furnishings, piped pop music; picnic tables on back lawn; nice village setting *(D J Underwood, Angela Mackintosh, Lesley Sones)*

☆ Shepperton [Church Sq (off B375); TQ0867], *Kings Head*: Immaculate old pub in quiet and attractive square, inglenook fireplace, neat panelling, oak beams, highly polished floors and furnishings, various discreet little rooms, big conservatory extension; good value unpretentious bar food, well kept Courage-related and other ales, attentive service, sheltered back terrace; children welcome, open all day Sat *(James Nunns, LYM)*

☆ Shepperton [152 Laleham Rd], *Bull*: Small local, unassuming but comfortable and very well kept, with good simple generous food at sensible prices inc bookable Sun lunch (food area themed as teddy bears' picnic), well kept Courage, Tetleys and Morlands Old Speckled Hen, friendly helpful staff, tables outside; live music some nights; bedrooms with own bathrooms *(Ian Phillips, Margaret and Nigel Dennis, W L G Watkins)*

☆ Shepperton [Russell Rd], *Red Lion*: Attractive old wisteria-covered local in nice spot across rd from Thames, plenty of tables on terrace among fine displays of shrubs and flowers, more on lawn over road (traffic noise) with lovely river views and well run moorings; wide choice of food in spacious bar and restaurant, well kept Courage-related ales with guests such as Fullers London Pride, restaurant, very friendly staff *(Nigel Flook, Betsy Brown, D P and J A Sweeney)*

Shepperton [47 Upper Haliford Rd], *Goat*: Large chain dining pub with brisk professional service, good self-service starters and generous carvery *(Ron and Sheila Corbett)*

☆ Shere [village signed off A25 3 miles E of Guildford; TQ0747], *White Horse*: Striking half-timbered medieval pub in beautiful village, uneven floors, massive beams, oak wall seats, two log fires, one in a huge inglenook, Tudor stonework – very ancient and atmospheric and a delight to look around; tables outside, children in eating area *(G R Sharman, Helen Morton, Ian Phillips, Nigel Wikeley, John Pettit, LYM)*

Shottermill [Liphook Rd; SU8732], *Mill*: 17th-c pub reopened under enthusiastic new young licensees, good generous food, good choice of wines and beers, small restaurant *(David Lupton)*

South Nutfield [Stn Approach; TQ3049], *Railway*: Well kept old-fashioned village pub with good choice of real ales and good reasonably priced home-made food inc proper pies and marvellous steak and kidney pudding; lots of interesting memorabilia, pleasant gardens *(John Wills)*

☆ Staines [The Hythe; S bank, over Staines Bridge; TQ0471], *Swan*: Recently pleasantly refurbished, in splendid Thameside setting, with well kept Fullers, good choice of food in bar and restaurant, friendly helpful staff, tables on pleasant riverside verandah, conservatory; can be very busy Sun lunchtime and summer evenings; moorings, comfortable bedrooms *(Sandra Kench, Steven Norman, Ron and Sheila Corbett, LYM)*

Staines [124 Church St], *Bells*: Well kept Courage-related ales, wide choice of popular simple promptly served food, friendly staff, cosy traditional furnishings and central fireplace, darts, cribbage, fruit machine, quiet juke box; plenty of seats in big garden *(Ian Phillips, Simon Collett-Jones)*; [London Rd (A30 bypass)], *Crooked Billet*: Comfortable split-level Beefeater, decent food and beer *(Tony and Wendy Hobden)*; [Moor Lane], *Swan on the Moor*: Welcoming pub on green, well kept ales such as Adnams, Boddingtons, Camerons and Wadworths 6X, good range of decent bar food, cosy fire, polite staff, good garden with lots of picnic tables and big aviary *(Ian Phillips, Sandra Kench, Steven Norman)*; [1 Penton Rd], *Wheatsheaf & Pigeon*: Welcoming pub locally known by regulars as the Wee & Pee, well kept Courage-related ales, good fresh food esp fish in largish bar/lounge and small dining area – evenings may be booked weeks ahead *(Ian Phillips)*

Sunbury [64 Thames St; TQ1068], *Magpie*: Pleasantly refurbished, with good views from street-level upper bar, nice terrace overlooking river and boat club, well kept Gibbs Mew, decent wine, reasonably priced food; bedrooms *(Ian Phillips, Bob and Maggie Atherton)*; [Green St, Lower Sunbury], *Three Fishes*: Two welcoming low-ceilinged bars, reasonably priced food inc doorstep sandwiches from small servery, Courage-related ales *(Ian Phillips)*

☆ Sutton [Raikes Hollow; B2126 – this is the Sutton near Holmbury St Mary; TQ1046], *Volunteer*: Attractive good-sized terraced garden in lovely quiet setting, low-beamed traditional bar with bric-a-brac and military paintings, Tetleys and Courage-related ales, decent wines inc port; food usually good and quickly served (hard to hear the numbers being called if you're out on the front terrace; no sandwiches); comfortable bedrooms *(Winifrede D Morrison, Tom Hall, Mark Percy, RBC, DWAJ, G W Stevenson)*

Tadworth [Dorking Rd; TQ2256], *Blue Anchor*: Cosily refurbished, with log fires, subdued decorations, homely feel; varied good value generous food, well kept Bass, Fullers London Pride and Worthington, decent wine *(Keith Ward)*; [Box Hill Rd], *Hand in Hand*:

Roomy extended pub, handy for Box Hill, with well kept Courage, good value simple bar food inc Sun lunch, friendly service, small restaurant *(John Pettit, M A Mees)*

☆ Tandridge [off A25 W of Oxted; TQ3750], *Barley Mow*: Roomy refurbished bar, log fires, good welcoming service, interesting bar food inc good ploughman's, well kept Marstons, Shepherd Neame and Wadworths tapped from the cask, restaurant with strong Italian leanings, Sun bar nibbles; no music or games machines, big garden; interesting church nearby, good walks to Oxted or Godstone *(M D Hare, Jenny and Brian Seller)*

☆ Tandridge [Tandridge Lane, off A25 W of Oxted], *Brickmakers Arms*: Good atmosphere in popular and pretty country dining pub, dating from 15th century but much extended and modernised, with good range of freshly made food inc some German dishes and lots of fish (no cold snacks Sun), well kept Whitbreads-related ales, decent wines inc local ones, restaurant with good log fires, prompt friendly service *(J R Tunnadine, Gordon Smith, Margaret and Nigel Dennis)*

Tatsfield [Westmore Green; TQ4156], *Old Ship*: Big bar with lots of interesting pictures and bric-a-brac, Bass, Charrington IPA and Worthington, good value varied food inc Sun lunch in restaurant with log fire, prompt friendly service; opp village duck pond, with play area in big garden *(G W and I L Edwards, Paul McKeever)*

Thames Ditton [Hampton Court Way, Western Green; TQ1567], *Greyhound*: Refurbished as food-oriented Wayside Inn, with Whitbreads-related ales, helpful staff, pleasant atmosphere, big pine tables in airy rooms *(D P and J A Sweeney)*

Thorpe [Ten Acre Lane; TQ0268], *Red Lion*: Handy for Thorpe Park, with pleasant atmosphere, friendly staff, beamed bar, Theakstons XB, back terrace and orchard garden; piped music, fruit machines, snooker *(George Atkinson)*

☆ Thursley [just off A3 SW of Godalming; SU9039], *Three Horseshoes*: Civilised country pub, lovingly restored, cosy and polished, with two good log fires, well kept Fullers London Pride and Gales HSB and BBB, country wines, good malt whiskies, well presented food inc first-class puddings, prompt smiling service, no piped music, tables in lovely big back garden with barbecues; not really a place for children inside, no dogs, restaurant; has been open all day Sat *(Ian Phillips, C Perry, Charles Hobbis, Guy Consterdine, Jenny and Brian Seller, Robert Crail, LYM)*

☆ Tilford [SU8743], *Barley Mow*: Lovely setting between river and geese-cropped cricket green nr ancient oak, with waterside garden; decent mainly home-made food, good service, well kept Courage ales, good log fire in big inglenook, comfortable traditional seats around scrubbed tables, interesting prints; small back eating area, weekend afternoon teas; darts, table skittles, no children *(Joy and Paul Rundell, Mark Stevens, G and M Stewart,*

Martin and Karen Wake, G R Sunderland, G C Hackemer, Jenny and Brian Seller)

Walton on Thames [Riverside, off Manor Rd; TQ1066], *Anglers Tavern*: Unassuming pub tucked away on Thames towpath, generous bar food from filled baguettes to good fish dishes, oilcloth tablecloths, Courage-related beers and Wadworths 6X, first-floor river-view seafood restaurant, some peaceful tables out by the boats; moorings; boat hire next door *(Ian Phillips, Nigel Harris, Mr and Mrs T A Bryan)*; [50 Manor Rd, off A3050], *Swan*: Three-bar riverside Youngs pub under new tenant, lots of interconnecting rooms, huge neatly kept garden leading down to Thames, food in bar and attractive restaurant, well kept ales; moorings, riverside walks *(RBC, Ed Birch)*

☆ Walton on the Hill [Chequers Lane (fairly handy for M25 junction 8); TQ2255], *Chequers*: Pleasant mock-Tudor Youngs pub with several rooms rambling around central servery, well kept ales, good value quick lunchtime bar food, restaurant (children allowed here), friendly service, terrace and neat sheltered garden with good summer barbecues; evenings busy with younger people; trad jazz Thurs *(Adrian Zambardino, Debbie Chaplin, LYM)*

☆ Walton on the Hill [Walton St], *Fox & Hounds*: Decent food esp puddings in chatty bar and pleasant adjoining restaurant (must book), well kept Bass, Fullers London Pride and two other ales, brisk service, nice surroundings; open all day Sun *(Andy and Gill Plumb, Dianne Parkyns, LYM)*

Walton on the Hill [pub signed down dirt track, N end], *Bell*: Two-bar oddly townish pub at end of track through woodland and heath; friendly landlord, settles and horse paintings in carpeted lounge, games in parquet-floor bar, well kept Bass, M&B Brew XI and Worthington from connecting servery, bar food; tables in garden, good walking area – ramblers welcome *(Jenny and Brian Seller)*

☆ Warlingham [Limpsfield Rd, Worms Heath; T857], *Botley Hill Farmhouse*: Converted farmhouse, more restaurant than pub, but limited choice of good generous reasonably priced bar food too, and well kept ales such as Boddingtons, Flowers, Greene King, Pilgrims and Shepherd Neame Spitfire; friendly efficient service, children welcome, with attractions for them; cream teas, wonderful North Downs views, good walking country; very busy weekends, with live music *(G Simpson, Mrs H M Cook, Paul Randall, Duncan Forsyth, Gareth Woodward-Jones)*

☆ West Clandon [The Street; TQ0452], *Bulls Head*: Friendly and comfortably modernised 16th-c country local, small lantern-lit bar with open fire and some stripped brick, old local prints, raised inglenook dining area very popular esp with older people lunchtime for good value enjoyable straightforward food (same food evenings), bookable Sun lunch, genial landlord, efficient service, Courage Best, Marstons Pedigree and Wadworths 6X, good coffee, games room with darts and pool; lots of tables and good play area in garden, convenient for Clandon Park, good walking country *(DWAJ, John Pettit, G W and I L Edwards, G W Jensen, R B Crail, KC)*

☆ West Horsley [The Street; TQ0753], *Barley Mow*: Small village local, attractively traditional, with flagstones, beams, extraordinary collection of pig ornaments, well kept ales inc Greene King, decent wines and spirits, well cooked lunchtime food at modest prices, small restaurant *(Anthony Byers, Robert Crail)*

West Horsley [The Street], *King William IV*: Comfortable and relaxing, very low beams but plenty of space, well kept Courage Directors and Best and Harveys, log fire, welcoming staff, decent food inc children's *(Matthew Duckworth, John Pettit, P J Keen)*

Weybridge [Thames St; TQ0764], *Farnell Arms*: Consistently good cheap food inc generous roasts, well kept Badger Best and Tanglefoot and Charles Wells Bombardier *(Robert Crail)*; [Princes Rd], *Jolly Farmer*: Warm and cosy small pub opp picturesque cricket ground, interesting reasonably priced food, well kept and priced Fullers London Pride; lovely garden with terrace, tented extension and barbecue *(Maurice Southon, Ian Phillips)*; [Thames St], *Lincoln Arms*: Comfortable newly decorated extended family pub with good inexpensive food, friendly helpful staff under new licensees; tables in garden, water for dogs *(Christine and Geoff Butler)*; [83 Thames St], *Old Crown*: Friendly old-fashioned three-bar waterside pub, nice and clean, very popular lunchtime for reasonably priced generous straightforward food esp fish (served evening too); Courage-related and other ales, Rugby-fan landlord, no music or machines; children welcome, suntrap garden *(DWAJ, Ian Phillips, David Dickson, R B Crail, P Gillbe, J Sheldon)*; [Oaklands Dr], *Pickled Newt*: Cosy free house with limited choice of reasonably priced food inc vegetarian and steak bargains, four real ales, small back garden; piped music *(Alec and Marie Lewery, James Nunns)*; [Cross Rd/Anderson Rd, off Oatlands Dr], *Prince of Wales*: Attractively restored, with relaxed country-local feel, good choice of reasonably priced bar food, well kept ales such as Adnams, Boddingtons, Fullers London Pride, Tetleys and Wadworths 6X, ten wines by the glass, coal-effect gas fires, imaginative restaurant menu *(Ian Evans, James Nunns)*

☆ Windlesham [Chertsey Rd; SU9264], *Brickmakers Arms*: Popular well run dining pub with good interesting freshly made food esp fish, not cheap but good value, cheerful busy bar, well kept Courage and other ales, wide choice of wines, very friendly service,

daily papers; well behaved children allowed in restaurant, attractive garden with boules and barbecues, lovely hanging baskets *(Ian Phillips, Jill Thompson, Guy Consterdine, Dan Deery, Bob Atkinson, Joy and Paul Rundell)*

☆ Windlesham [A30/B3020 junction], *Windmill*: Very popular for its ten or more interesting well kept ales changing weekly, two or three beer festivals a year with massive choice and live music; one long bar, separate side room, busy welcoming atmosphere, youngish customers; friendly landlord, good range of country wines, decent food, unobtrusive piped music; some seats outside *(Dr M Owton, Richard Houghton, Vincent Parry, Joy and Paul Rundell, Alistair Williams)*

Windlesham [Church Rd], *Half Moon*: Big lively friendly local, good range of well kept ales inc Fullers London Pride, Wadworths 6X and many quickly changing guest beers, country wines, good value straightforward food inc good Sun family lunch, cheerful quick service, modern furnishings, log fires, piped music, silenced fruit machine, interesting WWII pictures; huge beautifully kept garden popular with families *(Chris and Martin Taylor, R B Crail, Mrs C Blake, Mike Davies)*; [Chertsey Rd], *Surrey Cricketers*: Popular Fullers pub, lots of neat small tables on bare boards, bar food inc fish, garden, skittle alley *(Ian Phillips)*

☆ Witley [Petworth Rd (A283); SU9439], *White Hart*: Tudor beams, good oak furniture, log fire in cosy panelled inglenook snug where George Eliot drank; good range of well kept ales, very wide choice of good value food in bar and restaurant from new kitchen, friendly licensees, public bar with usual games; seats outside, play area *(Mrs J Beale, G Washington, Charles Hobbis, LYM)*

Woking [51 Chertsey Rd; TQ0058], *Wetherspoons*: Former Woolworths, well converted with lots of intimate areas and cosy side snugs, good range of food and reasonably priced beers inc interesting guest ales *(Ian Phillips)*

Worcester Park [Cheam Common Rd; TQ2266], *Old Crown*: Good value generous varied food inc sandwiches and vegetarian in comfortable recently refurbished beamed pub with Courage-related ales, friendly staff, restaurant; garden *(G W and I L Edwards, DWAJ)*

Wrecclesham [Sandrock Hill Rd; SU8245], *Sandrock*: Good range of well kept ales mostly from smaller breweries, often Midlands ones, in simply converted local with friendly knowledgeable staff, real fire, no piped music, games room and garden *(G C Hackemer, Ben, Lucienne Suter, Steve Merson)*

Post Office address codings confusingly give the impression that some pubs are in Surrey when they're really in Hampshire or London (which is where we list them). And there's further confusion from the way the Post Office still talks about Middlesex – which disappeared in 1974 local government reorganisation.

Sussex

New entries here include the civilised Anchor tucked away by the river at Barcombe, the unpretentious Cricketers Arms in its lovely unspoilt setting at Berwick, the cheerful and attractive Cricketers at Duncton (good food), the neatly restored Foresters Arms at Fairwarp on the edge of the Ashdown Forest, the Black Jug in Horsham (an exemplary town pub, with good food and drinks and plenty of character), the Queens Head at Icklesham (a good all-rounder with marvellous views from its garden), and the Peace & Plenty at Playden, a welcoming and charmingly decorated dining pub. Other pubs on fine form here include the Ash Tree at Brownbread Street and George & Dragon at Burpham (good food and beers in both), both pubs at Elsted (good food, plenty of interest), the enthusiastically run Griffin at Fletching, the attractive and interesting Gun at Gun Hill, the Crabtree at Lower Beeding (top quality food), the fine old Middle House in Mayfield, the Gribble at Oving (good beer brewed here – and you can pick apples in the garden), and the Horseguards at Tillington. The Horseguards is a well run dining pub of real distinction, with excellent food and drink: it's our choice as Sussex Dining Pub of the Year. In the Lucky Dip section at the end of the chapter, pubs currently on good form include the Market Cross at Alfriston, Black Horse at Amberley, Swan in Arundel, Anchor Bleu at Bosham, Royal Oak near Chilgrove, George & Dragon near Coolham, Old Vine at Cousleywood, Boars Head at Boarshead, Red Lion at Fernhurst, Anglesey Arms at Halnaker, Sussex Ox at Milton Street, Cock at Ringmer, Lamb at Ripe, Horse & Groom at Rushlake Green, Salehurst Halt at Salehurst, Hare & Hounds at Stoughton, Best Beech near Wadhurst and Lamb at West Wittering; we have inspected and can vouch directly for the great majority of these. There's a good choice in Brighton. Drinks cost substantially more than average in Sussex pubs; the cheapest pubs we found were the Bull near Ticehurst, the Golden Galleon at Seaford (brewing its own), and the Old House At Home at Chidham. The two main local brewers are Harveys and King & Barnes (we found them no cheaper than 'foreign' brewers). Beards, who have quite a few fine tied pubs in the county, have not brewed themselves since a brewery fire nearly 40 years ago, but have now started having beer brewed for them to their original recipe by the good small Arundel brewery.

ALCISTON TQ5005 Map 3

Rose Cottage

Village signposted off A27 Polegate—Lewes

A warmly traditional place, this rustic little wisteria-covered cottage is a real favourite with some readers. Aside from the genuinely old-fashioned atmosphere, the main draw is the wholesome food, made with fresh, local ingredients. Many of the vegetables are grown organically a quarter of a mile up the road, the eggs come from their own chickens, and the landlord (licensed to deal in game) shoots the pheasants himself. Promptly served dishes might include a hearty soup, ploughman's (from £4.25), ham and egg (£4.50), big salads (from £4.50, prawn with avocado £7.50), Thai-style curries (£5.95), excellent pies like chicken and ham or their very popular rabbit and bacon (£5.25), courgette and rice strudel (£6.95), a couple of daily specials like wild rabbit casserole (£7.50), venison braised in port and Guinness (£7.95), or lamb stroganoff with port, rosemary and mushrooms (£8.50), large steaks (from £7.95), and evening extras such as half a roast duckling with a sauce of orange and green peppercorns (£9.50); Sunday roasts (£6.95). Small and cosy, the relaxed and friendly bar soon fills up, so get there early for one of the half-dozen tables with their cushioned pews – under quite a forest of harness, traps, a thatcher's blade and lots of other black ironware, with more bric-a-brac on the shelves above the dark pine dado or in the etched glass windows. In the mornings you may also find Jasper, the talking parrot (it can get a little smoky for him in the evenings). There's a lunchtime overflow into the no-smoking restaurant area. Service is generally welcoming and efficient, but they do tend to stick very rigidly to serving times. Well kept Harveys (sold as Beards) and a monthly changing guest like Marstons Pedigree on handpump; Merrydown cider and decent wines, including a wine of the month – often English; log fires, darts, maybe piped classical music. There are some seats under cover outside, and a small paddock in the garden has ducks and chickens. A family of house martins regularly returns to its nest above the porch, seemingly unperturbed by the people going in and out beneath them. A once-common Sussex tradition now lives on only at this pub, when every Good Friday lunchtime you can still see locals long-rope skipping to make the crops grow faster. *(Recommended by Sue Demont, Tim Barrow, R and S Bentley, Hugh MacLean, JEB, R Walden, M Holdsworth, Colin Laffan, John Beeken, Mr and Mrs B Pullee, Alan Skull, Tony Hobden, Dave Braisted, E N Burleton, Ian Phillips, E G Parish, Norma Farris)*

Free house ~ Licensee Ian Lewis ~ Real ale ~ Meals and snacks (12-2, 7-10, to 9.30 Sun) ~ Evening restaurant (not Sun) ~ (01323) 870377 ~ Children in eating area ~ Open 11.30-3, 6.30-11; closed 25/26 Dec

ALFRISTON TQ5103 Map 3

Star 🛏

The facade of this 15th-c inn is particularly worth a look, as it's studded with curious medieval carvings, mainly religious. The striking red lion on the corner – known as Old Bill – is more recent, and was probably the figurehead from a wrecked Dutch ship. These days the Star is a fairly smart Forte hotel, but the front part remains wonderfully atmospheric and welcoming, and much as it must have been when built as a guest house for Battle Abbey. Amongst the antiquities in the bustling heavy-beamed bar is a wooden pillar that was once a sanctuary post; holding it gave the full protection of the Church, and in 1516 one man rode a stolen horse from Lydd in Kent to take advantage of the offer – and avoid the death penalty. Elegant furnishings include a heavy Stuart refectory table with a big bowl of flowers, antique windsor armchairs worn to a fine polish and a handsome longcase clock; the fireplace is Tudor. The simple bar menu includes home-made soup (£2.20), sandwiches from (£2), filled baked potato (from £2.95), ploughman's (from £4.25), salads (from £3.50) and blackboard specials. There's also a no-smoking lounge. Bass on handpump, a good range of wines by the glass and malt whiskies; service is excellent, with nothing too much trouble. The comfortable bedrooms are in an up-to-date part at the back. Board games are available, and if you're staying they can arrange a wide range of activities. *(Recommended by E G Parish, Steve Goodchild)*

Free house (Forte) ~ Manager John Tomblin ~ Real ale ~ Meals and snacks (snacks only Sun) ~ Restaurant ~ (01323) 870495 ~ Children in lounge ~ Open 11-3, 6-11 ~ Bedrooms: £76.75B/£106B

If we know a pub has a no-smoking area, we say so.

ASHURST TQ1716 Map 3

Fountain ◗

B2135 N of Steyning

Don't let the Georgian facade here fool you – behind it is a delightfully unspoilt 16th-c country pub, quite foody at times, but with a strong local following that makes sure it never loses its relaxed traditional feel. The charmingly rustic tap room on the right is the one to head for, with its scrubbed old flagstones, a couple of high-backed wooden cottage armchairs by the log fire in its brick inglenook, two antique polished trestle tables and, depending on the season, between three and seven well kept real ales on handpump or tap. The range might include Adnams Broadside and Extra, Courage Best and Directors, Fullers London Pride, John Smiths, and Youngs Special. A bigger carpeted room with its orginal beams and woodburning stove is where most of the popular home-cooked bar food is served: fresh cod or quiche (£5.55), vegetables in light pastry (£6.45), steak and kidney pie or suet and bacon pudding (£6.95) and poached salmon in light pastry (£8.45). They do Sunday roasts (£6.95). Service is cheery and efficient, but can slow down at busy periods; booking is advisable in the evenings. A gravel terrace has picnic tables by an attractive duck pond, and there are swings and a see-saw (and regular barbecues) in the pretty enclosed garden with fruit trees and roses. Shove-ha'penny. They've recently extended the restaurant, and an adjoining barn has been converted into a function room with skittle alley. *(Recommended by David Holloway, Gwen and Peter Andrews, Ron Gentry, Jenny and Brian Seller, Alan Jarvis, James Nunns, R Walden, Romey Heaton, Margaret and Nigel Dennis, Winifrede D Morrison)*

Free house ~ Licensee Maurice Caine ~ Real ale ~ Meals and snacks ~ Restaurant (not Sun evening) ~ (01403) 710219 ~ Children in restaurant till 8pm ~ Open 11-2.30, 6-11; closed evenings 25, 26 Dec

BARCOMBE TQ4114 Map 3

Anchor

From village follow Newick, Piltdown sign, then after a humpbacked bridge a very narrow, long lane is signposted to the pub

The remote riverside setting and beautifully kept waterside lawns and fairy-lit terrace (lovely on a summer night) are what earn this cheerful little pub its place in the Guide. You can hire boats on an unspoilt three-mile stretch of the River Ouse as it winds through the meadows (£3 an hour) – reckon on about two hours if you're going all the way to the fish ladder Falls near Sutton Hall and back. A riverside kiosk serves cream teas and cold drinks, and there are barbecues most summer weekends. The original bar is one of the very smallest we have come across, so that your best chance of a seat would be at a really quiet time – hardly a fault, in what is so clearly a summer sunshine pub. The landlord's late father won a good few motor racing trophies, several of which are still on display in here and in a second bar (converted from some of the bedrooms a couple of years ago), along with some car models, and other racing and RAF memorabilia. There's an intimate candle-lit restaurant. Bar food might include sandwiches (from £2.10), soup (£2.50), filled baguettes (from £3.75), omelettes or filled baked potatoes (from £4.25), ploughman's (from £4.75), sausage egg and chips (£4.75), pasta bake with mushrooms, peppers, shallot onions and sun-dried tomatoes (£4.95), giant mushrooms covered in stilton, apple and walnuts (£5.25), lamb and apricot pie (£6.25), poached brill with citrus butter (£7.50), mixed grill (£8.95), children's meals (£3), and puddings such as their pagoda pudding – a rich moist sponge made with nutmeg and ginger, and served with sticky toffee sauce and fresh cream (£2.75); some of the ingredients come from the organic farm across the road. Well kept Badger Best and Tanglefoot, Ballards Wye Gold and Harveys Best on handpump; one of the two house wines is from the local vineyard, Barkham Manor. Good friendly service; dominoes, shut the box, scrabble, chess and draughts. The family room has toys and children's videos. In winter the approach road can flood and cut the pub off – they leave out a boat or two then, though some customers cheerfully wade through the water. It's been run by the same family for the last 30 years. *(Recommended by M Martin, Dr S Savvas, Mrs R D Knight, Eddie Edwards, Matthew de la Haye)*

Free house ~ Licensee Graham Bovet-White ~ Real ale ~ Meals and snacks (not 25 Dec; 12-3, 6-9.30) ~ Restaurant ~ (01273) 400414 ~ Children in restaurant and family room ~ Open 11-11; 12-10.30 Sun; 11-3, 6-11 winter weekdays ~ Bedrooms: £30/£45(£65B)

BERWICK TQ5105 Map 3

Cricketers Arms

Lower Rd, S of A27

This is a charming and unspoilt old flint cottage in a quiet rural spot surrounded by a pretty, old-fashioned garden with mature flowering shrubs and plants, lots of picnic tables in front of and behind the building, and little brick paths – idyllic on a sunny summer's day. Inside, the three little rooms are similarly furnished with simple benches against the half-panelled walls, a happy mix of old country tables and chairs, burgundy velvet curtains on poles, a few bar stools, and some country prints; quarry tiles on the floors (nice worn ones in the middle room), two log fires in little brick fireplaces, a huge black supporting beam in each of the low ochre ceilings, and (in the end room) some attractive cricketing pastels; a relaxed and friendly atmosphere and helpful, friendly staff – even when really busy. Good bar food includes home-made soup (£2.50), ploughman's (from £3.25), filled baked potatoes (from £3.50), nice scampi (£4.25), ham and egg (£3.95), tasty steaks (from £6.75), daily specials such as steak and kidney pudding, Thai prawns in garlic and vegetable bolognese, puddings like enjoyable home-made treacle tart or bread and butter pudding (£2.50), and children's menu (£1.95); winter themed food evenings. Well kept Harveys Best, PA and seasonal ales tapped from the cask, and decent wine; darts, dominoes, cribbage, and an old Sussex game called toad-in-the-hole. *(Recommended by Andrew Partington, LM, Peter Christmas, Mavis and John Wright, Sue Demont, Tim Barrow, Paul and Heather Bettesworth, Stephen Harvey, Tom and Rosemary Hall, Mrs R D Knight)*

Harveys ~ Tenant Peter Brown ~ Real ale ~ Meals and snacks ~ (01323) 870469 ~ Children at landlord's discretion ~ Open 11-3, 6-11; 12-3, 6.30-10.30 Sun; closed 25 Dec

nr BILLINGSHURST TQ0925 Map 3

Blue Ship 🍺

The Haven; hamlet signposted off A29 just N of junction with A264, then follow signpost left towards Garlands and Okehurst

There's nothing elaborate or particularly spectacular about this remote and friendly little pub – it stands out because of its simple and delightfully peaceful atmosphere, and its genuinely unspoilt charms. Tucked away down a country lane, it's very nice in summer, when you can relax at the tree-shaded side tables or by the tangle of honeysuckle around the front door. In winter the beamed and brick-floored front bar is a cosy haven, with a blazing fire in the inglenook fireplace and hatch service; a corridor leads to a couple of similar little rooms. Well kept King & Barnes Broadwood, Sussex and seasonal beers tapped from the cask. A games room has darts, bar billiards, shove-ha'penny, cribbage and dominoes. It can get crowded with a pleasant mix of the educated middle aged, country locals and pleasant young people, particularly at weekends; there may be a couple of playful cats. Straightforward bar food includes sandwiches (from £1.75), ham and vegetable soup (£2.45), ploughman's (from £3.50), macaroni cheese (£4.10), cottage pie (£4.30), and steak and kidney pie or scampi (£5.70). There's a large beer garden with a play area. They have a gun club and run their own shoot. *(Recommended by Richard J Raeon, Karen Barnes, Paul Kitchener, Peter Lewis, John Fahy, J S M Sheldon, A M Pickup, Bruce Bird; more reports please)*

King & Barnes ~ Tenant J R Davie ~ Real ale ~ Meals and snacks (not evenings Sun or Mon) ~ (01403) 822709 ~ Children in two rooms without bar ~ Open 11-3, 6-11; closed 25 Dec evening

BLACKBOYS TQ5220 Map 3

Blackboys

B2192, S edge of village

This 14th-c weatherboarded house is particularly popular in summer, when the gardens come into their own. There's masses of space, with rustic tables in the back orchard, some seats overlooking the pretty front pond, a play area with a challenging wooden castle and quite a few animals, and a barn with a big well equipped playroom. The pub itself has a string of old-fashioned and unpretentious little rooms, warmly atmospheric with dark oak beams, a good inglenook log fire, bare boards or parquet and masses of bric-a-brac and antique prints. Good waitress-served food includes soup (£1.90), ploughman's with good home-smoked ham (from £3.50), Celonese fish curry, tagliatelle carbonara or chilli con carne (£4.95), seafood pancakes with scallops, prawns and mussels (£5.50), steak and kidney pie (£5.95), summer crab salad (£6.95) or lobster salad (£7.95), steaks (from £7.95), daily specials, and winter game. Well kept Harveys Armada, BB and seasonal brews on handpump; welcoming service, and darts, shove-ha'penny, dominoes, table skittles, cribbage, fruit machine, video game, juke box, and a novel version of ring-the-bull – ring-the-stag's-nose. *(Recommended by R and S Bentley, Dr S Savvas, M Martin, Mr Grant, Alan Skull, Colin Laffan)*

Harveys ~ Tenant Patrick Russell ~ Real ale ~ Meals and snacks (12-2.30, 6.30-10) ~ Restaurant ~ (01825) 890283 ~ Children in eating area and restaurant ~ Occasional Morris dancers and singers ~ Open 11-3, 6-11

BROWNBREAD STREET TQ6715 Map 3

Ash Tree 🍺

Village signposted off the old coach road between the Swan E of Dallington on B2096 Battle—Heathfield and the B2204 W of Battle, nr Ashburnham

Sunday lunch is particularly well liked at this warmly welcoming 16th-c local, and the rest of the time too the food is rather better than average. Favourites on the changing menu might include sandwiches, cottage pie (£3.50), home-made prawn or crab mousse (£3.95), crab salad (£5.75), steak and kidney pie (£5.75), half a roast guinea fowl (£6.50), and half a duckling in orange and brandy sauce (£8.95); on Sundays there's a choice of roasts (from £5.75). They may do only full meals at some of their busiest times. Very well kept Brakspears, Fullers London Pride, Harveys Best and Morlands Old Speckled Hen on handpump; cheerful, friendly service. The cosy beamed bars – candlelit at night – have three inglenook fireplaces, stripped brickwork, and nice old settles and chairs; darts, bar billiards, shove-ha'penny, fruit machine, and a discreet juke box in the simple games room on the left. The black labrador cross is a little shy and keeps out of the way – the elderly ginger cat isn't quite so reticent. There's a pretty garden with picnic tables, and the pub is tucked away down narrow country lanes in a delightfully isolated hamlet. *(Recommended by R and S Bentley, Dr S Savvas, M Martin, Colin Laffan, Pam and Tim Moorey, Mr and Mrs R D Knight, Robert Huddleston)*

Free house ~ Licensees Malcolm and Jennifer Baker ~ Real ale ~ Meals and snacks (not Mon) ~ Restaurant ~ (01424) 892104 ~ Children in eating area ~ Open 12-3, 7-11; closed Mon

---

Sunday opening is generally 12-3 and 7-10.30 throughout England, but many pubs stay open all day in summer.

BURPHAM TQ0308 Map 3

George & Dragon

Warningcamp turn off A27 a mile E of Arundel, then keep on up

Pretty walks along the Arun or off the downs will build up an appetite for the meals at this smart and comfortable pub, though the standard of cooking is so high you really don't need an excuse to enjoy them. The daily specials are what really stand out, with well prepared dishes like wood pigeon with red wine and bacon sauce (£6.25), braised lamb shanks or loin of pork with apple and calvados sauce (£6.95), skate wing and capers (£7.95), and whole black bream (£9.25); other food includes sandwiches (from £2.40, club sandwiches £4.25), soup (£2.60), ploughman's (£3.60), filled baked potatoes (from £3.65), poached chicken breast with dijon cream and white wine sauce (£7.25), and delicious home-made puddings like white chocolate mousse, raspberry crème brûlée, and syrup roly-poly (£2.95). Many of the tables get booked up in advance. Spacious and civilised, the immaculately kept open plan bar has good strong wooden furnishings and constantly changing beers such as Arundel Gold, Ash Vine, Cotleigh Tawny, Courage Directors and Harveys Best on handpump; lots of Irish whiskey. Smiling helpful service. No dogs. The pub is charmingly set in a remote hill village of thatch and flint, and a short walk away there are splendid views down to Arundel Castle and the river. The nearby partly Norman church has some unusual decoration. *(Recommended by Pam and Tim Moorey, Mrs P Boxford, Winifrede Morrison, David Holloway, Nick Dunnell, Jane Talbot, Hanns P Golez, Mavis and John Wright, Ian Jones, R Walden, Colin Laffan, T J Moorey, Romey Heaton, John Fahy, Tina and David Woods-Taylor, A H Denman)*

Belchers Pubs ~ Tenants James Rose and Kate Holle ~ Real ale ~ Meals and snacks (till 9.45; not Sun evening in winter) ~ Restaurant (not Sun evening) ~ (01903) 883131 ~ Children in eating area of bar (no babies or pushchairs) ~ Occasional live music ~ Open 11-2.30, 6-11; closed Sun evenings 1 Nov until Easter

BURWASH TQ6724 Map 3

Bell

A265 E of Heathfield

Mentioned in Kipling's *Puck of Pook's Hill*, and handy for Batemans, the lovely Jacobean ironmaster's house the writer made his home, this is a pleasant village local with a relaxed and well cared for feel in its two genuinely pubby bars. The L-shaped room on the right has an armchair by its big log fire (two fires if it's cold), all sorts of ironwork, bells and barometers on its ochre anaglypta ceiling and dark terracotta walls, and well polished built-in pews around tables. The room on the left is broadly similar, but quieter (and greener). Well kept Batemans XB, Harveys Best and seasonal brews, Morlands Old Speckled Hen and Youngs Ramrod on handpump, a range of malt whiskies, and some new world wines; mulled wine in winter. Darts, bar billiards, shove-ha'penny, ring-the-bull, table skittles, cribbage, dominoes, trivia and maybe unobtrusive piped music. Bar food includes sandwiches and ploughman's, filled baked potatoes (from £3.50), vegetarian pasta dishes or gammon with pineapple (£4.95), chicken breast with mustard and apricot (£5.50), tiger prawns in garlic butter (£6.95), and seasonal fresh fish. The meals – about which we've heard mixed views recently – can take rather a long time to arrive. The bedrooms (oak beams, sloping floors) are fairly basic and the road can be noisy at night. Seats in front of the flower-covered mainly 17th-c building look across the road to the pretty village church. Car park at the back. *(Recommended by Dr S Savvas, M Martin, R A and J A Buckler, Alan and Eileen Bowker, A and J Hoadley, Norma Farris)*

Beards ~ Lease: Colin and Gillian Barrett and Sarah Jennings ~ Real ale ~ Meals and snacks (not Sun evening) ~ Restaurant (not Sun evening) ~ (01435) 882304 ~ Children welcome till 9.30 ~ Open 11(12 winter)-3, 6-11; 11-11 Sat; closed 25 and evening 26 Dec ~ Bedrooms: £20/£40

BYWORTH SU9820 Map 2

Black Horse 🍺

Signposted from A283

The lovely informal gardens are one of the main draws to this unspoilt old pub, and the current licensees are putting a lot of effort into improving them. The top tables on a steep series of grassy terraces, sheltered by banks of flowering shrubs, look across a drowsy valley to swelling woodland, and a small stream runs along under an old willow by the more spacious lawn at the bottom. There's a relaxed and informal atmosphere in the simple bar with basic scrubbed wooden tables, open fires, pews and bare floorboards. Bar food might include large filled baguettes (£3.65), soup (£2.75), filled baked potatoes or ploughman's (£3.95), and daily specials such as vegetarian pasta (£5.50), grilled chicken supreme in a lemon and tarragon sauce (£7.25), pan-fried skate wings in nut brown butter (£7.50), or fillet of red bream in a prawn and caper sauce (£8.50); children's meals (£3.75), and puddings like their popular treacle tart. Well kept changing beers like Badger Best, Flowers Original, Fullers London Pride, Youngs Ordinary and maybe a guest or two on handpump, and good wines. It can be busy at weekends, especially in summer. Darts, shove ha'penny, dominoes. *(Recommended by Peter Wade, Hugh MacLean, Keith Ward, MCG, Tom and Rosemary Hall, John and Mavis Wright, Tor.y Hobden, Alan and Eileen Bowker, Philip and Trisha Ferrris)*

Free house ~ Licensees Neil Gittins and Michael Courage ~ Real ale ~ Meals and snacks ~ Restaurant ~ (01798) 342424 ~ Children in restaurant ~ Occasional live music ~ Open 11-3, 6-11; closed evenings 25/26 Dec

CHIDDINGLY TQ5414 Map 3

Six Bells ★ £

Village signed off A22 Uckfield—Hailsham

Take careful note of the days listed below when there's live music at this idiosyncratic country pub – some would say that's when it really comes into its own. The music is carefully segregated in the bareboarded barn-like bottom bar, but while it's playing might not be the best time to come for a quiet meal; the atmosphere can seem really spirited then. On Sunday lunchtimes the mood is something like that of a London jazz venue, and at other times too there's a remarkably cosmopolitan feel to the place. That might have something to do with the extraordinary mix of customers: bikers, pensioners, well-heeled Porsche drivers and local pig farmers are among the locals and visitors of all ages and types that find their way to such a beautifully remote part of the countryside. The characterful beamed rooms have solid old wood furnishings including some pews and antique seats, log fires, lots of fusty artefacts and interesting bric-a-brac, and plenty of local pictures and posters. A sensitive extension provides some much needed family space; darts, dominoes and cribbage. The friendly landlord loves to chat, and will certainly remember your face the next time you visit. A big draw is the remarkably low-priced bar food, straightforward but tasty, with dishes such as french onion soup (90p), a delicious selection of grilled french breads (from £1.10), meat or vegetarian lasagne (£1.85), steak and kidney pie (£2.40), filled jacket potatoes (from £2.70), ploughman's (from £3), cheesy vegetable bake or vegetable korma (£3.10), chicken curry or spicy prawns mexicano (£3.60), and spare ribs in barbecue sauce (£3.75); vegetables are an extra 60p. Well kept Courage Best and Directors and Harveys on handpump or tap. Outside at the back, there are some tables beyond a big raised goldfish pond, and a boules pitch; the church opposite has an interesting Jeffrey monument. Vintage and kit-car meetings outside the pub once a month. This is a pleasant area for walks. *(Recommended by Dr S Savvas, M Martin, John and Mavis Wright, Ian Phillips)*

Free house ~ Licensee Paul Newman ~ Real ale ~ Meals and snacks (11-2.30, 6-10) ~ (01825) 872227 ~ Children welcome ~ Jazz, blues and other live music in the barn Tues, Fri, Sat and Sun evenings (from 9), and jazz Sun lunch ~ Open 10-3, 6-11

CHIDHAM SU7903 Map 2

Old House At Home

Cot Lane; turn off A27 at the Barleycorn pub

Part of a cluster of farm buildings in a very quiet country lane, this cosy out-of-the-way old pub is a friendly place, very good for a meal but just as welcoming if you only want a drink. The extensive range of generously served meals includes sandwiches (from £1.75), soup (£2.50), filled baked potatoes (from £3.25), ploughman's (from £3.50), salads (from £4.50), spicy bean tortilla pie (£5.25), pies such as steak and kidney, game or lamb and apricot (£5.75), grilled trout with almonds (£6.25), steaks (from £9.75), and a good range of daily specials including fish, game and poultry. Booking is recommended for summer evenings. Well kept real ales such as Badger Best, Ringwood Best and Old Thumper, Old House (Burts Nipper), and a weekly changing guest beer on handpump, as well as a good selection of country wines and several malt whiskies; cheery service. The homely timbered and low-beamed bar has windsor chairs around the tables, long seats against the walls, a welcoming log fire and a large friendly german shepherd. It's quite handy for good walks by Chichester harbour, and in summer has a couple of picnic tables on its terrace, with many more in the garden behind. *(Recommended by N P Smith, Dennis Stevens, Lynn Sharpless, Bob Eardley, Hugh MacLean, John Fahy, John Sanders, Ann and Colin Hunt, Derek and Margaret Underwood, Kevin and Katherine Cripps, Lesley McEwen, Nigel Clifton, Peter Lewis, Mr and Mrs R O Gibson, Keith Stevens, Rita Horridge, R T and J C Moggridge)*

Free house ~ Licensees Mike Young and Terry Brewer ~ Real ale ~ Meals and snacks ~ (01243) 572477 ~ Children in eating area of bar ~ Open 11.30(12 Sat)-2.30, 6-11; closed evening 25 Dec

COWBEECH TQ6114 Map 3

Merrie Harriers

Village signposted from A271

This white-clapboarded village pub was once a farmhouse, and it still has something of the cheery atmosphere of an old-fashioned farm parlour in the friendly public bar. Beamed and panelled, this has a traditional high-backed settle by the brick inglenook, as well as other tables and chairs, and darts. A wide range of lunchtime bar food includes sandwiches (from £2), home-made soup (£2.25), filled cottage rolls, ploughman's (from £4.25), vegetarian dishes (£5.25), steak and kidney pie (£6.95), various fresh local fish like grilled lemon sole (£10.50), and puddings like apple pie or summer pudding; in the evening they add dishes such as mixed grill or steaks (from £9.65), and they do a good Sunday roast. Well kept Flowers IPA and Harveys Best on handpump, good choice of wines; charming, professional service. The brick-walled and oak-ceilinged back restaurant is no smoking. Rustic seats in the terraced garden. *(Recommended by Colin and Joyce Laffan, J H Bell, Bob Arnett, Judy Wayman, Mr and Mrs J A Phipps, Dr S Savvas, M Martin, Christopher Turner)*

Free house ~ Licensees J H and C P Conroy ~ Real ale ~ Meals and snacks ~ Restaurant ~ (01323) 833108 ~ Children in restaurant ~ Open 11-2.30, 6-11

CUCKFIELD TQ3025 Map 3

White Harte ♨ £

South Street; off A272 W of Haywards Heath

Well liked for its bargain lunches, this pretty partly medieval tile-hung pub has a rather appealing traditional feel, with its beams, polished floorboards, some parquet and ancient brick flooring tiles, standing timbers, and small windows looking out on to the road. Furnishings in the public bar are sturdy and comfortable with a roaring log fire in the inglenook, and sensibly placed darts. The more comfortable partly carpeted lounge has a few local photographs, padded seats on a slightly raised area, some fairly modern light oak tables and copper-topped tables, and a brick bar counter. The straightforward meals include regular dishes like ploughman's (from £3), salads, and scampi, but most people tend to go for the five or so very good value home-cooked specials: pies like chicken and mushroom, fish, or steak and kidney, turkey breast in mushroom sauce, smoked haddock bake, or stilton and celery quiche (all £3.90). These often go by around 1.30 (and the tables may be snapped up even earlier), so it pays to arrive early. Well kept King & Barnes Bitter and Broadwood on handpump, and pleasant friendly service, particularly from the cheery landlord; fruit machine, shove-ha'penny. The village is attractive. *(Recommended by DWAJ, David Holloway)*

King & Barnes ~ Tenant Ted Murphy ~ Real ale ~ Lunchtime meals and snacks (not Sun) ~ (01444) 413454 ~ Well behaved children welcome in eating area of bar at lunchtime ~ Open 11-3, 6-11

DONNINGTON SU8502 Map 2

Blacksmiths Arms

Left of A27 on to A286 signed Selsey, almost immediate left on to B2201

This homely little white roadside cottage stands out for its particularly friendly welcome, especially from the character landlord. Readers who've entered the pub to find him discussing the day's races with locals have been delighted when upon spotting them, he's not only broken off his conversation, but offered his hand in greeting, and sometimes even introduced the barmaid. The small down-to-earth rooms are completely crammed with bric a brac: the low ceilings densely hung with hundreds of jugs, pots and kettles (each scrupulously cleaned by the landlord every week), the walls crowded with Victorian prints and a grandfather clock, and an interesting old cigarette vending machine on the sill of one of the pretty little windows. Solid and comfortable furnishings on the patterned carpet include several 1950s sofas; shove ha'penny, dominoes, fruit machine and maybe piped music. Well kept real ales usually include Bass, Badger Best, Fullers London Pride, Morlands Old Speckled Hen, Ringwood Best and Wadworths 6X on handpump or tapped from the cask, sometimes kept under light blanket pressure. Bar food includes sandwiches (from £1.75), soup (£1.80), ploughman's (£3.95), a vegetarian dish of the day (£6.95), lasagne or steak and kidney pie (£7.25), Selsey crab salad (£8.75), 10oz sirloin steak (£9.95), and quite a choice of children's meals (£2.50). The big garden isn't quite as spic and span as inside, but children will find it hard to tear themselves away from the well fenced play area where the grass is virtually obscured by ride-on-toys (some of them have seen better days); there's also a plastic tree house, swings, and trampolines. *(Recommended by RTM, JCM, Alec and Marie Lewery, Ann and Colin Hunt, Bruce Bird, N E Bushby, Miss W E Atkins, Keith Stevens)*

Free house ~ Fergus and Gill Gibney ~ Real ale ~ Meals and snacks (till 10, not winter Sun eves or 25 Dec) ~ Restaurant (not winter Sun eve) ~ (01243) 783999 ~ Children welcome ~ Open 11-2.30, 6-11

DUNCTON SU9617 Map 3

Cricketers

Set back from A285 N

Pretty little white house with lovely flowering baskets and tubs, set back from the road. The jovial landlord and his staff make both visitors and regulars feel very welcome, and the atmosphere is cheerful and relaxed. The bar has a few standing timbers giving the room an open-plan feel, there's an inglenook fireplace at one end with a large summer dried flower arrangement and some brass pots and warming pans on either side of the grate, local photographs on the mantelpiece, half-a-dozen bar stools and a mix of country tables and chairs, and green-cushioned settles; wildlife pictures and a cartoon of the licensee and his wife. Down a couple of steps a similarly furnished room is set for eating and is decorated with farming implements, pictures, and cricketer cigarette cards; doors from here lead out into a charming back garden with a proper barbecue (summer Sunday lunchtime barbecues), picnic tables, and an attractive little creeper-covered seating area. Good, popular bar food includes soup (£2.50), garlic mushrooms (£3.95), chicken liver pâté (£4.25), boeuf bourguignon (£5.95), cod in batter (£6.95), chicken breast on ratatouille (£7.25), veal chop with masala and mushrooms or grilled whole lemon sole (£7.50), crab salad or swordfish steak (£7.95), local trout (£8.95), and best end of lamb with redcurrants and rosemary (£9.95). Well kept Archers Golden, Friary Meux, Ind Coope Burton, and Wilds on handpump, lots of malt whiskies, and decent wines. Darts, dominoes and cribbage – no piped music or games machines. A separate skittle alley at the front to one side of the building, and more picnic tables and a rope swing for children. *(Recommended by Leslie Payne, Tony and Wendy Hobden, Jan and Colin Roe, MCG, Peter Lewis, Michael Grigg)*

Free house ~ Licensee Philip Edgington ~ Real ale ~ Meals and snacks (not Sun or Mon evenings) ~ (01798) 342473 ~ Children in dining area ~ Open 11-3, 6-11; closed evenings 25-26 Dec and 1 Jan

EARTHAM SU9409 Map 2

George

Signposted off A285 Chichester—Petworth; also from Fontwell off A27 and Slindon off A29

Prettily set in a lovely part of the county, this bustling country pub has a really friendly and personal welcome. The well presented bar food is popular, with the choice running over three blackboards, and perhaps including filled baked potatoes (from £2.95), big farmhouse cottage rolls (from £3.35), at least five vegetarian dishes like mushroom stroganoff (£5.20), interesting old-fashioned pies such as lamb and orange or rabbit and juniper, poached salmon with prawn and champagne sauce (£7.95), breast of duck in caramelised orange marmalade (£9), rack of lamb (£9.95), and steaks with various sauces; it's worth booking at busy periods. Well kept Gales Best, Butser and HSB, and maybe a guest on handpump; quick service by very helpful, courteous staff. The cosy lounge is pleasantly comfortable without being fussily overdecorated, and there's a pubbier public bar; both have a relaxed atmosphere even at the busiest times. Darts, shove-ha'penny, cribbage, fruit machine and piped music. The restaurant has a no-smoking area. *(Recommended by DWAJ, Bruce Bird, Christopher Warner, R T and J C Moggridge, Paul Robinshaw)*

George Gale ~ Manager James Crossley ~ Real ale ~ Meals and snacks ~ Restaurant ~ (01243) 814340 ~ Children welcome in eating area of bar and restaurant ~ Open 11-11; 12-10.30 Sun; winter opening 11-3, 6-11

EAST LAVANT SU8608 Map 2

Royal Oak

Signed off A286 N of Chichester

A profusion of mature shrubs and flowers is crammed into the tiny little terraced front garden at this pretty little white house, perched steeply above the narrow lane. Rambling around the back and side are more captivating little terraced, bricked or grassed areas with some metal furniture, picnic tables, a pergola, and tubs and baskets spilling with flowers and roses. This year they've added a fountain, and repainted some of the tables and chairs an unusual dark green. Gloriously peaceful, the very relaxed and spacious open plan bar with modest wood furniture is refreshingly cool in summer and wonderfully cosy with two open fires and a woodburner in winter. It's simply and cleanly decorated relying on the good natural structure and substance of the building. Thick black skirting provides a pleasingly clean line between the almost bare cream and exposed brick walls and the turkey rugs on the mellow wood, brick and tiled floor. Particularly good bar food includes mixed cheese platter, tuna and pasta crumble or vegetarian ratatouille and pasta bake (£5.50), smoked trout (£6.50), steak and kidney pie or big salads like tandoori chicken or seafood (£8.50), and fresh fish like mackerel, hake or crab, depending on what the fishmonger brings that morning. They don't have a specific children's menu, but are happy to whip up suitable meals, and though the friendly landlord isn't a great fan of chips, he doesn't mind serving them if that's what people want. Well kept Gales Butser and HSB and maybe a guest chosen by the brewery, from handpumps on the brick bar. The car park is across the road. The pub is very handy for Chichester. *(Recommended by Viv Middlebrook, J H L Davies, J A Snell, A J Blackler, Dr and Mrs A K Clarke, Jonathan Phillips)*

Gales ~ Tenant Stephen Spiers ~ Real ale ~ Meals and snacks ~ (01243) 527434 ~ Children welcome if eating ~ Open 11-2.30(3 Sat), 6-11; cl 25 and 26 Dec

EASTDEAN TV5597 Map 3

Tiger ♀

Pub (with village centre) signposted – not vividly – from A259 Eastbourne—Seaford

This low-beamed old-fashioned local is beautifully positioned on the edge of a secluded, sloping green lined with low cottages, most of them like the pub itself – bright with climbers, roses and other flowers. It's on the South Downs Way, so does get busy in summer – especially since the closure of the roads around the green has left the area more idyllic than ever. Seats outside let you make the most of the setting, though the green itself can act as an overflow. Inside, the smallish rooms have low beams hung with pewter and china, traditional furnishings including polished rustic tables and distinctive antique settles, old prints and so forth. The only music you're likely to hear will be from Morris dancers, who visit every bank holiday. Regularly changing beers might include well kept Badger Tanglefoot, Flowers Original, and Harveys Best on handpump; also a decent choice of wines with several interesting vintage bin-ends, and some from a local vineyard. A short but good choice of home-made bar meals, listed on a blackboard, might include local sausage ploughman's (£3.95), warm chicken liver salad with apple and bacon (£4.75), macaroni cheese topped with melted stilton and tomato (£4.95), fillet of local fish and chips (£5.25), and local game stew with horseradish dumplings (£5.95). Efficient service from helpful staff. The family room is no smoking. The lane leads on down to a fine stretch of coast culminating in Beachy Head. *(Recommended by Isabel de Alayo Rimmer, S Pyle, E G Parish, John Fahy, Keith Stevens, RLW and Dizzy)*

Free house ~ Licensees Jonathan Steel and Nicholas Denyer ~ Real ale ~ Meals and snacks ~ (01323) 423209 ~ Children in separate family room ~ Open 11-3, 6-11; all day (inc Sun) July/Aug

ELSTED SU8119 Map 2

Elsted Inn ★ 🍽 🍺

Elsted Marsh; from Midhurst left off A272 Petersfield Rd at Elsted and Harting sign; from Petersfield left off B2146 Nursted Rd at South Harting, keep on past Elsted itself

The licensees at this warmly traditional and friendly country pub describe their much-loved food as 'granny cooking', by which they mean (we hope) the sort of deliciously old-fashioned and wholesome meals that clearly rely on the most natural and fresh local ingredients. Anything that isn't hand-made in the kitchen usually comes from somewhere just as distinctive; for example the bread and sausages come from the National Trust bakery at Slindon, their flour is ground at the mill in the Weald and Down Museum, the eggs, chickens and ducks are free range from a local farm, and the mutton comes from the landlady's aunt's herd of sheep. The generously served meals change all the time, but might include sandwiches (from £2.15), ploughman's or filled baked potatoes (from £4.75), spinach and walnut roulade or artichoke and butterbean bake (£6.50), braised oxtail, Sussex bacon pudding or beef in beer pie (£7), rabbit in mustard sauce or game pie (£7.50), duck confit, grilled lemon sole or local trout (£7.75), and puddings like blackcurrant cheesepots or treacle tart (£2.75), and their delicious home-made ice creams (from £2); children's helpings. During the week they do a two set course lunch (£6.50), and on winter Wednesday evenings might have themed menus and special dishes. As there isn't much space, they now reluctantly advise booking for meals. The range of beers includes Fullers London Pride and a couple of guests, and all four locally brewed Ballards beers. Not so many years ago these were actually brewed here, and there's still a close connection, demonstrated best perhaps on L'Ale Nouveau Night, when a beer cask is rolled down the road from the brewery to the pub. Amongst the wines are some from a nearby Hampshire vineyard. The two friendly and cosy bars have simple country furniture on wooden floors, local photographs on the cream walls, an open fire in the Victorian fireplace, and two big friendly dogs, Sam and Truffle (some of their friends may have dropped by, too); darts, dominoes, shove-ha'penny, cribbage, backgammon. There's a separate cottagey dining room. Children are made very welcome, as are visiting dogs, though one area of the lovely big enclosed garden (with tables and boules) is kept dog free. *(Recommended by Peter Wade, Howard Allen, Ann and Colin Hunt, R and S Bentley, Wendy Arnold, Dr S Savvas, M Martin, Lynn Sharpless, Bob Eardley, Bruce Bird, J F Reay, Mrs J A Blanks, Viv Middlebrook, Tony and Susan McDonald, Tony and Wendy Hobden, Peter Lewis, Ian Jones, Howard West)*

Free house ~ Licensees Tweazle Jones and Barry Horton ~ Real ale ~ Meals and snacks (12-3, 7-9.30) ~ Restaurant ~ (01730) 813662 ~ Children in eating area and restaurant ~ Folk music first Sun evening of the month ~ Open 11-3, 5.30(6 Sat)-11; closed evening 25 Dec ~ Bedrooms: £20S/£40S

Three Horseshoes ★ 🍺

Village signposted from B2141 Chichester—Petersfield; also reached easily from A272 about 2 miles W of Midhurst, turning left heading W

A delightful spot on a sunny day, the prettily-planted and recently smartened up garden at this cosily old-fashioned 16th-c pub has free-roaming bantams and wonderful views over the South Downs. The snug little rooms are full of rustic charm, with enormous log fires, antique furnishings, ancient beams and flooring, attractive prints and photographs, and night-time candlelight. Good home-made food, in big helpings, includes soups (£2.95), avocado with stilton and mushroom sauce topped with bacon (£4.95), generous ploughman's with a good choice of cheeses (£5), chicken and bacon casserole with celery and fennel, rabbit and pigeon casserole, or steak, kidney and ale pie (£7.95), Scotch sirloin steak with spring onions, shallots and a red wine sauce, and puddings like delicious treacle tart (you can take it away) or raspberry and hazelnut meringue (£3.50). Well kept changing ales racked on a stillage behind the bar counter might include Ballards Best, Cheriton Pots and Diggers Gold, Hampshire King Alfreds and Hook Norton Best to name a few – they tend to concentrate on brews from smaller breweries; also farmhouse ciders and summer pimms. Service is usually friendly and obliging, even when the pub gets busy – as it often does in summer, especially at weekends. Darts, dominoes and cribbage. *(Recommended by Christopher Warner, Judith Reay, Stephen Goodchild, Howard West, Mr and Mrs D E Powell, Wendy Arnold, Peter and Lynn Brueton, Peter Wade, Ann and Colin Hunt, T Roger Lamble, K G Mather, John Evans, Nigel Wikeley, Clive Gilbert)*

Free house ~ Licensees Andrew and Sue Beavis ~ Real ale ~ Meals and snacks (not winter Sun evenings) ~ Restaurant ~ (01730) 825746 ~ Well behaved children in eating area and restaurant ~ Open 11-2.30(3 Sat), 6-11; closed Sun night from October to Easter

FAIRWARP TQ4626 Map 3

Foresters Arms

Set back from B2026, N of northern Maresfield roundabout exit from A22

At the south end of Ashdown Forest, this is prettily set on a small green among oak trees – a tempting sight from the road, with its newish cream stucco nicely setting off the gleaming red and gold name lettering across its front. Inside, it's homely and welcoming, with a comfortable lounge bar and a big aquarium in the public bar – the size of its main inhabitant, and the shape of the pub's two friendly spaniels, suggest that they are not stingy with the food here, and indeed the bar food is served in generous helpings. It's good home cooking, with fresh vegetables, and includes sandwiches (from £3.25), ploughman's (£3.75), home-made pies (from £5.25), lamb fillet in mustard sauce (£7.25), steaks (from £9.50) and daily specials like lamb and mint curry (£5.50) or steak and Guiness pie (£6.25); good popular Sunday lunch. Well kept King & Barnes Bitter, Festive, Old and Broadwood on handpump, decent wines, efficient service; darts and pool. It's handy for walkers, being near the Vanguard Way and Weald Way; some tables outside. *(Recommended by Colin and Joyce Laffan, Alan Skull, H R Taylor, Stella Knight, John Kimber)*

King & Barnes ~ Licensees ~ Real ale ~ Meals and snacks ~ (01825) 712808 ~ Children welcome in eating area of bar ~ Open 11-3, 6-11

FIRLE TQ4607 Map 3

Ram

Signposted off A27 Lewes—Polegate

Simple and unfussy, this family-run village pub is well placed for exploring a particularly fine stretch of the South Downs. The bustling bars are still mainly unspoilt, with comfortable seating, soft lighting, log fires in winter, and a nice, convivial feel; the snug is no smoking. Well kept Harveys Best and Armada, Otter Bitter, and Rebellion Mutiny on handpump, and decent wines (including three produced locally). Darts, shove-ha'penny, dominoes, cribbage and toad in the hole. The gents' has a chalk board for graffiti, and there are tables in a spacious walled garden behind. They have a magnificent ginger cat. With an emphasis on local ingredients, the concise range of bar food (not reckoned by readers to be such good value these days) might include leek and mushroom soup (£2.50), ploughman's with local cheeses or free-range ham (from £4.90), leek and stilton tart (£6.95), seafood lasagne (£8.15), pork, apple and dijon mustard pie (£9.65), and puddings like chocolate roly-poly (£2.95). Nearby Firle Place is worth visiting for its collections and furnishings, and the pub is handy for Glyndebourne. *(Recommended by John Beeken, Sue Demont, Tim Barrow, Ian Jones, SRP, F M Steiner, JM, PM, Margaret and Nigel Dennis, Dick Brown, LM, D S Cottrell)*

Free house ~ Licensees Michael and Keith Wooller and Margaret Sharp ~ Real ale ~ Meals and lunchtime snacks ~ (01273) 858222 ~ Children in snug bar and courtroom ~ Traditional music second Mon and first Weds of month ~ Open 11.30-3, 7-11; closed evening 25 Dec ~ Bedrooms: /£50(£60S)

FLETCHING TQ4223 Map 3

Griffin ★ ⑪ 🛏 ♀

Village signposted off A272 W of Uckfield

Some readers like this civilised old country inn best on damp, foggy days when the roaring log fires make the rooms especially cosy; others prefer it in summer when tables in the beautifully arranged back garden offer lovely rolling Sussex views. At either time a major draw is the imaginative daily changing menu, which might include dishes like celery, leek and stilton soup (£3.25), stuffed mussels with tarragon and dill butter (£3.95), focaccia pizza with tomatoes, red onions, olives and mozzarella (£4.25), pasta with roast aubergines, pesto and goat's cheese (£5.95), veal and herb meatballs with tagliatelle (£6.50), roast mediterranean vegetable flan or winter game pie (£6.95), Moroccan-spiced lamb shank with cous-cous or fish pie with squid, mussels, cod and red mullet (£7.95), and puddings like sticky toffee pudding or tarte tatin (£3.50); all the ingredients are fresh from local suppliers. They have regular fish nights, and on summer weekends rather better than average barbecues, when they might do local lamb or even poussin. Well kept Badger Tanglefoot, Fullers London Pride, Harveys Best and a changing guest like Hogs Back on handpump, a very good wine list including some English ones and several New World, and various cognacs and malt whiskies; pleasant friendly service. The beamed front bar has a relaxed 1930s feel – straightforward furniture, squared oak panelling, some china on a delft shelf, a big corner fireplace, and a small bare-boarded serving area off to one side. The landlord may be playing the piano. A separate public bar has darts, pool, pinball, fruit machine, video game, juke box and chess and backgammon. Besides those in the garden, there are tables on a sheltered gravel terrace used for dining on warm evenings. Three of the four attractively individual bedrooms have four-posters, and the breakfasts are recommended – several readers have enjoyed wild boar sausages. They can get terribly busy at weekends (even in winter), and the standards of food and service can wobble a little then. The pub is in a pretty spot just on the edge of Sheffield Park. *(Recommended by Bob and Maggie Atherton, Tina and David Woods-Taylor, Hugh MacLean, James Nunns, Margaret and Nigel Dennis, C Barrett, HD, Eric and Jackie Robinson, David Holloway, Derrick and Shirley Thomas, Brenda and Derek Savage, Dr S Savvas, M Martin, R and S Bentley, John Beeken, Alan Skull, Julie Peters, Colin Blinkhorn, Jill Bickerton, Alan and Eileen Bowker, Cathryn and Richard Hicks, SRP, E D Bailey, Richard Bowden, Jamie and Ruth Lyons, Winifrede D Morrison, John and Mavis Wright, J S M Sheldon, Colin Laffan, Mr and Mrs Heron)*

Free house ~ Licensees James and Nigel Pullan and John Gatti ~ Real ale ~ Meals and snacks (till 10 Fri, Sat) ~ Restaurant (not Sun evening) ~ (01825) 722890 ~ Children welcome ~ Piano Fri/Sat evenings and Sun lunchtime, and jazz band in garden summer bank holidays ~ Open 12-3, 6-11; 11.30-11 summer Sats; closed 25 Dec ~ Bedrooms: /£55B

FULKING TQ2411 Map 3

Shepherd & Dog

From A281 Brighton—Henfield on N slope of downs turn off at Poynings signpost and continue past Poynings

Very popular with walkers – a path leads straight up to the South Downs Way – this charmingly atmospheric little pub used to sell illicit liquor to thirsty shepherds on their way to Findon sheep fair. The partly panelled cosy bar still has shepherds' crooks and harness on the walls, as well as antique or stoutly rustic furnishings around the log fire, and maybe fresh flowers on the tables. A changing range of well prepared bar food might include sandwiches (from £3, smoked salmon £4.95), moules marinières (£4.50), a wide choice of ploughman's, with a good selection of carefully picked cheeses (from £4.25), a vegetarian dish like vegetable pancakes or lasagne (£5.25), big summer salads (£5.95), beef and Guinness pie (£6.50), trout (£6.95), wing of skate with capers (£7.50), tender sirloin steak (£9.50), and delicious home-made puddings like banoffi pie (£2.75). Try and get there early, especially if you want a prime spot by the bow windows, as all year round the pub can get crowded; service can slow down at the busiest times (summer weekends, maybe). Well kept Harveys Best, Flowers Original, and three changing guests like Boddingtons, Eldridge Pope and Wethereds on handpump; toad-in-the-hole. There are good views across to the sweeping downs from the series of pretty planted grassy terraces, some fairy-lit, as well as a little stream running down to the big stone trough, and an upper play lawn sheltered by trees. *(Recommended by LM, Dr S Savvas, M Martin, John Beeken, David Holloway, Hanns P Golez, Michael and Alison Leyland, Helen Morton, John and Mavis Wright, Ian Jones, T Roger Lamble, Dr Keith Clements)*

Free house ~ Licensees Anthony and Jessica Bradley Hull ~ Real ale ~ Meals and snacks ~ (01273) 857382 ~ Open 10-3(winter 2.30), 6-11; Sat 11-11; 12-10.30 Sun; closed 25 Dec

GUN HILL TQ5614 Map 3

Gun 🖙

From A22 NW of Hailsham (after junction with A267) turn N at Little Chef; also signed off A267 itself

In a corner of the warren of rooms at this big country inn is an Aga, which they still use for cooking in the winter, and there are several open fires, one in a fine inglenook. Readers very much like visiting in the autumn and winter, though in summer the lovely garden is quite a draw. The Wealden Way runs through it, past plenty of flowers, tables and fairy-lit trees; there's a big play area and some seating in a recently refurbished barn. They don't mind muddy boots, and indeed that sort of customer-comes-first thinking is very much the keynote of the place. Most of the furnishings in the busy, well-run and friendly rooms are aimed at diners, but there are some more individual pieces, with brasses, copper, pewter, prints and paintings on the panelled walls, and alcoves under the oak beams; a couple of areas are no smoking. Well kept Adnams Extra, Flowers Original, Harveys Best and Larkins Chiddingstone on handpump, a good choice of wines by the glass, farm ciders, country wines and freshly squeezed fruit juice. Cheery young service, with a good mix of ages among the many customers (they don't mind small children). Tasty good value food includes soup (£2.80), filled french bread (from £3.60), local sausages or steak and kidney pie (£4.90), meat or vegetable lasagne (£5.50), a popular help-yourself salad buffet (from £4.90), specials like three cheese pasta and broccoli bake (£5.90), or local rabbit pie (£6), fresh fish from Newhaven such as haddock, plaice, lobster or crab, and children's meals (from £3); they mark the healthiest dishes on the menu, and use wholesome, low-fat ingredients wherever possible. There may be a slight delay at busy periods. Cream teas in the afternoon. They now take credit cards. If you're staying they leave breakfast on a tray outside your door the night before; useful for those getting up early to reach the ferry at Newhaven. *(Recommended by Bob Arnett, Judy Wayman, Hugh MacLean, David and Ruth Hollands, Mrs R D Knight, Mike and Julia Evans, George Atkinson, Eddie Edwards, Ian Phillips, Colin Laffan, James House, S G N Bennett, Dick Brown)*

Free house ~ Licensees R J and M J Brockway ~ Real ale ~ Meals and snacks (12-10; winter 12-2, 6-10) ~ (01825) 872361 ~ Children in two no-smoking rooms furthest from bar till 9pm ~ Open 11-11; 12-10.30 Sun; winter weekdays open 11-3, 6-11; cl 25 and 26 Dec ~ Bedrooms: £28(£30B)/£34(£36B)

HARTFIELD TQ4735 Map 3

Anchor 🍺

Church Street

By the time this edition of the Guide reaches the shops, they should have converted the restaurant at this welcoming old local into a new bar, with an inglenook fireplace and beers served straight from the barrel. On the edge of Ashdown Forest, the pub has a very relaxed and friendly feel, and a delightful mix of all types of customers. Old advertisements and little country pictures decorate the walls above the brown-painted dado in the original heavy-beamed bar, and there are houseplants in the brown-curtained small-paned windows, and a woodburner which rambles informally around the central servery. There's a good choice of beers, with very well kept Boddingtons, Flowers Original, Fremlins, Fullers London Pride, Harveys Best, Marstons Pedigree and Wadworths 6X on handpump. Good bar food includes sandwiches (from £1.50), soup (£2.25), filled baked potatoes (from £3), ploughman's (from £3.50), deep-fried brie with redcurrant jelly (£3.75), stir-fry vegetables with cashew nuts, sausage and chips, or cheese and spinach pancakes (£4), tagliatelle with scallops and ginger in a cheese sauce (£4.75), prawn and crab curry (£5.75), pork and lemon brochette (£7.50), lamb kebab marinated in yoghurt and mint (£8.50), puddings (from £2), and children's meals (£2.50); quick friendly service. Darts in a separate lower room; shove-ha'penny, cribbage, dominoes, and piped music. The front verandah soon gets busy on a warm summer evening. It's only been a pub since the last century, but dates back much further, with spells as a farmhouse and women's workhouse. There's a play area in the popular garden and dogs are welcome. *(Recommended by Colin and Joyce Laffan, LM, R and S Bentley, David Peakall, Nigel Wikeley; more reports please)*

Free house ~ Licensee Ken Thompson ~ Real ale ~ Meals and snacks (till 10) ~ (01892) 770424 ~ Children welcome ~ Open 11-11; 12-10.30 Sun; closed evening 25 Dec ~ Bedrooms: £30S/£40S

nr HEATHFIELD TQ5920 Map 3

Star

Old Heathfield – head East out of Heathfield itself on A265, then fork right on to B2096; turn right at signpost to Heathfield Church then keep bearing right; pub on left immediately after church

Though this ancient pub has many charms, one of the main ones must be the imaginatively planted sloping garden, recently equipped with new furniture. Turner painted the lovely view of rolling oak-lined sheep pastures you get from it, and it really is impressive. There's usually garden service in summer. Prettily placed and well out of Heathfield itself, the Star has been an inn ever since it was built in 1328 as a resting place for pilgrims on their way along this high ridge across the Weald to Canterbury. You get a sense of the building's history in the L-shaped beamed bar, which has rustic furniture, some panelling, murals depicting a connection with the founding of Jamestown in America, and window seats and tables by a huge inglenook fireplace. A wide range of bar food includes ploughman's, home-made pies and lasagne (all around £5.50), mussels in saffron, white wine, garlic and cream (£5.50), half shoulder of lamb (£7.95), and fresh local crab or lobster (£10); good service from the warmly welcoming licensees and staff. One area is no smoking. Well kept Fullers London Pride, Harveys Best and a couple of weekly changing guests like Black Sheep or Hopback Summer Lightning, as well as a choice of malt whiskies and farm cider; darts, bar billiards, shove-ha'penny, cribbage, dominoes and piped music. The two dogs wear labels asking visitors not to feed them. The neighbouring church is rather interesting, with its handsome Early English tower. *(Recommended by Margaret and Nigel Dennis, Dr S Savvas, M Martin, Keith Ward, John Collard, Hilary Dobbie, Roger Price, Jill Bickerton)*

Free house ~ Lease: Mike and Sue Chappell ~ Real ale ~ Meals and snacks (not Sun evening) ~ Restaurant ~ (01435) 863570 ~ Children welcome ~ Jazz some Sundays ~ Open 11.30-3, 5.30-11

HORSHAM TQ1730 Map 3

Black Jug

31 North St

This very relaxed town pub is part of a small chain that's doing particularly well in the Guide, and like the Hare at Langton in Sussex the expansive refurbished interior is turn of the century in style, with lots of exposed dark wood and muted colours. Big windows light the airy open plan room which runs around a large central bar, with a nice collection of heavy dark wood sizeable tables, and comfortable chairs on a stripped wood floor. Above dark wood panelling, the cream walls are crammed with interesting old prints and photographs, and the cornice is painted dark green like the old-fashioned radiators. A spacious dark wood conservatory has similar furniture and lots of hanging baskets. Alongside Courage Directors, John Smiths, Wadworths 6X and Youngs Special and a guest like Boddingtons, all well kept on handpump, they serve decent bin ends, and nine chilled vodkas from Poland and Russia. The changing bar menu, densely written on a blackboard, is very popular so you may need to book on weekend evenings. It might include carrot and coriander soup (£2.95), open sandwiches (from £3.50), ploughman's (£3.95), tagliatelle provençale or toad in the hole (£3.75), smoked duck breast with orange and ginger sauce or lasagne (£5.95), steak and kidney pie (£7.95) and chicken breast with honey, ginger and spring onion sauce (£9.75). There are quite a few tables sheltered under a pagoda outside on a back terrace; no children; dominoes, cribbage. *(Recommended by Simon Hurst, Anne Painter-Ellacott, Don and Thelma Anderson, Mr and Mrs David Lee, Peter Walters, Peter Carne, Susan Lee, Richard Lewis, Derek and Margaret Underwood*

Free House ~ Licensee Neil Stickland ~ Real ale ~ Meals and snacks (till 10pm) ~ (01403) 253526 ~ Open 11-11; cl 25 Dec evening

ICKLESHAM TQ8816 Map 3

Queens Head ♀ ◖

Small sign partly obscured by plants off A259

There are broad views over the vast gently sloping plain of the Brede valley from wooden picnic sets in the little garden at this comfortably relaxed old pub. Inside three open plan areas work round a very big serving counter, which stands under a vaulted beamed roof, and where the friendly licensee greets customers and chats to locals. The high beamed walls and ceiling of the easy-going bar are covered with lots of farming implements and animal traps, with well-used pub tables and old pews on the brown patterned carpet. Two other areas (one no smoking) are popular with diners – the bar food is very reasonably priced – and have big inglenook fireplaces. The generously served food is listed on a blackboard on a lofty exposed brick chimney, and includes sandwiches (from £1.75), pâté (£2.50), steak baguettes (£3.95), lasagne (£5.25), scampi (£6.50), and daily specials like macaroni cheese (£4.95), aubergine and tomato pasta (£5.25), grilled haddock (£5.75), pork and apple pie (£5.95), calf liver and bacon (£6.75) and dover sole (£7.25). Four very well kept real ales take in Courage Directors, Greene King Abbot, Old Forge (established locally in 1995) Brothers Best with a guest like Woodefordes Nelsons Revenge, and two additional weekend guests such as Fullers London Pride or Ringwood Old Thumper; about a dozen wines by the glass. Children's play area at the back, fruit machine and boules. *(Recommended by Ernest M Russell, George Bingham, D B Stanley, Bruce Bird, G S and E M Dorey)*

Free House ~ Licensee Ian Mitchell ~ Real Ale ~ Meals and snacks (12-2.45, 6.15-9.45) ~ (01424) 814552 ~ Well supervised children welcome till 9pm ~ Open 11-11; 12-5, 7-10.30 Sun

KINGSTON NEAR LEWES TQ3908 Map 3

Juggs ◖

The Street; Kingston signed off A27 by roundabout W of Lewes, and off Lewes—Newhaven road; look out for the pub's sign – may be hidden by hawthorn in summer

One of the impressive things about this pretty 15th-c tile-hung cottage is the way they manage to cope so well with so many visitors on warm summer days and evenings. Service remains speedy and efficient (aided by a rather effective electronic bleeper system to let you know when meals are ready), and despite the crowds you don't get the processed feel that's all too common in a good few similarly popular pubs. The rambling beamed bar has an old-fashioned country feel, as well as a particularly interesting medley of furnishings and decorations, with especially good prints, pictures and postcards on the walls. Bar food includes open sandwiches (from £3.50), ploughman's or local sausages (£3.95), pitta bread layered with mushrooms and ham or chicken tikka and topped with cheese (from £5.25), a vegetarian dish (£5.75), good steak and kidney pudding (£8.75), daily specials like mushroom roast with tomato sauce or chicken curry, and puddings such as cheesecake or chocolate brownie (£2.95); children's meals. On Sunday lunchtime food is limited to a cold buffet. The restaurant and one of the family rooms are no smoking. Particularly well kept Harveys Sussex, King & Barnes Broadwood and a guest on handpump, with a wider choice than usual of non-alcoholic drinks, and a red and white wine of the month. Log fires, dominoes, shove-ha'penny. There are a good many close-set rustic teak tables on the sunny brick terrace; a neatly hedged inner yard has more tables under cocktail parasols, and there are two or three out on grass by a timber climber and commando net. Covered with roses in summer, the pub was named for the fish-carriers who passed through on their way between Newhaven and Lewes. *(Recommended by Tim Locke, Mavis and John Wright, K Flack, Steve Goodchild, Bruce Bird, LM, Alan Skull, Andrew Partington)*

Free house ~ Licensees Andrew and Peta Browne ~ Real ale ~ Meals (not Sun lunchtime) and snacks ~ Restaurant (not Sun lunchtime) ~ (01273) 472523 ~ Children in two family rooms ~ Open 11-3, 6-10.45(Sat 11); cl 26 Dec, and evening 1 Jan

KIRDFORD TQ0126 Map 3

Half Moon

Opposite church; off A272 Petworth—Billingshurst

The good fresh fish is still what stands out at this 17th-c family run inn. Carefully chosen by the licensees (whose links with Billingsgate go back 130 years), they may have such rarities as tile fish, porgy, parrot fish, soft shell crabs, Morton Bay bugs, scabbard fish, razor shells, mahi mahi, and baramundi (all from around £10, though higher for some of the more unusual dishes). Do remember though that fresh fish is seasonal, so there may be times when the range isn't as big as you might hope. They also do less exotic fish like sword fish, bass, lobster, tiger prawns and snapper, and more ordinary dishes like sandwiches (from £1.90), home-made soup (£2.80), ploughman's (£4.80), salads, lasagne or steak and kidney pie (£6.50). Well kept Arundel Best, Boddingtons, Flowers Original, Fullers London Pride and Wadworths 6X, some under light blanket pressure; local wine and apple juice. Service can slow down when they get busy. The simple partly quarry-tiled bars are kept ship-shape and very clean; darts, pool, cribbage, dominoes, piped classical music. The restaurant is partly no smoking. There's a back garden with swings, barbecue area, tables, and big boules pitch, and more tables in front facing the pretty village's church. *(Recommended by Philip Vernon, Kim Maidment, Dr S Savvas, M Martin, Mavis and John Wright, Vann and Terry Prime, R Walden, J Sheldon, J S M Sheldon, Winifrede D Morrison, Joan G Powell, Michael J Boniface, LM, Ron Gentry)*

Whitbreads ~ Lease: Anne Moran ~ Real ale ~ Meals and snacks (not Sun evening or winter Mons) ~ Restaurant ~ (01403) 820223 ~ Children welcome till 9pm ~ Occasional live music ~ Open 11-3, 7(6 summer Sats)-11; closed evening 25 Dec ~ Bedrooms: £20/£38(£42B)

LEWES TQ4110 Map 3

Snowdrop

South Street; off Cliffe High Street, opp S end of Malling Street just S of A26 roundabout

The atmosphere at this unique place isn't so much relaxed as positively laid-back; it's something of an alternative main entry, like a little piece of Glastonbury transported to Sussex. The interior is a decided oddity, its decor what you'd get if you crossed the Steptoes' living room with a ship's cabin, with a glorious profusion of cast iron tables, bric-a-brac and outlandish paraphernalia that no doubt owes much to the next-door antique shop. Unfolding the rather dreamlike maritime theme, downstairs there are three ships' figureheads dotted around, walls covered with rough sawn woodplank and upstairs a huge star chart painted on a dark blue ceiling, and a sunset sea mural with waves in relief. The pub is quiet at lunchtime but a young people's preserve, and lively to match, in the evenings, when the loudish juke box plays anything from Bob Dylan or Ella Fitzgerald to Indian chants. They serve no red meat, and the good value light hearted menu includes sandwiches, burritos or large home-made pizzas (from £2, seafood pizza £6), garlic prawns (£5), fresh fish like trout, smoked salmon, and lots of well priced and unusual vegan and vegetarian dishes like brown rice with stir fried vegetables (£3.50) or Sicilian salad (£4.50); free range chicken is the Sunday roast, and they do children's helpings. The tapas-style snack dishes are well liked (from £1). Five (occasionally up to seven) well kept real ales such as Gales HSB, Harveys Best, Hop Back Summer Lightning, Ringwood Old Thumper and Shepherd Neame Spitfire on handpump, good coffee, friendly licensees and staff; pool, chess, cards, cribbage, dominoes, and a giant chess board in the car park. There are a few tables in the garden. Dwarfed below a great chalk cliff, the pub is named for something much grimmer than you'd imagine – the Christmas Eve avalanche of 1836, when hundreds of tons of snow falling from the cliff demolished several houses on this spot, burying nine people alive. You can see a dramatic painting of the event in Anne of Cleves House (Southover High Street). *(Recommended by Ann and Colin Hunt, P Simms; more reports please)*

Free house ~ Licensees Tim and Sue May ~ Real ale ~ Meals and snacks 12-3(2.30 Sun), 6(7 Sun)-9 ~ (01273) 471018 ~ Children welcome ~ Live jazz Mon evening and other live music some weekends ~ Open 11-11; 12-10(9.30 Sun); closed 25 Dec and evening 26 Dec

LICKFOLD SU9226 Map 2

Lickfold Inn

The characterful garden at this elegantly-restored Tudor inn spreads over a good few interestingly planted levels, each with a couple of private little seating areas; there may be barbecues out here in summer. In winter big log fires in the enormous brick bar fireplace create a cosy atmosphere and cast subtly flickering shadows on the antique furnishings. In summer the fires are replaced by more tables, but at any time you'll still find the smart Georgian settles, heavy Tudor oak beams, handsomely moulded panelling, and ancient herringbone brickwork under rugs. Five or six well kept beers are rotated from a range that might include Adnams, Ballards Best, Harveys Best, Hopback Summer Lightning, and Tongham Tea and Hop Garden Gold; good coffee. Chalked up on a blackboard, changing home-made bar food might include lunchtime sandwiches (from £1.75, weekdays only), steak and kidney pie or lasagne (£6.25), chicken tikka, poached halibut in a prawn and white wine sauce or mussels in garlic, cream and wine (£6.75), and puddings like ginger pear dumpling (£2.50) or local ice cream. Note they don't allow children. *(Recommended by John Fahy, Hugh MacLean, R and S Bentley, G C Hackemer, R W Flux, Guy Consterdine, Keith and Audrey Ward, J S M Sheldon, Howard West, Ian Phillips, J F Reay; more reports please)*

Free house ~ Licensees Ron and Kath Chambers ~ Real ale ~ Meals and snacks (not Sun or Mon evenings) ~ (01798) 861285 ~ Open 11-2.30(3 Sat), 6-11; closed Mon evenings, and 25 Dec ~ Bedrooms: £25B/£50B

LODSWORTH SU9223 Map 2

Halfway Bridge ★ ⑪ ♀ ◫

Just before village, on A272 Midhurst—Petworth

Some readers think nothing of driving 40 miles to this well run and smartly civilised family run pub, and others love coming in early December when the scent of mulled wine wafts through the air. A particular draw is the inventive home-cooked food, from a range that might include elaborate lunchtime open sandwiches (from £3.95), chicken and vegetable broth (£2.95), black pudding and crispy bacon salad (£3.50), fish soup with rouille and croûtons (£4.50), local garlic sausages (£5.25), vegetable tikka (£5.50), lamb kidneys in dijon mustard and fromage frais (£6.25), confit of duck with honeyed cabbage or home-smoked chicken and avocado salad (£6.95), poached salmon with carrot and ginger butter (£8.95), red snapper with olives and tomatoes (£9.50), local game in season, and puddings like gooseberry and honey crumble or banana bread and toffee cream (£3.50). Home-made puddings like walnut treacle tart or gooseberry and cinnamon crumble (£3), and various Sunday roasts. Booking is advisable at weekends and other busy periods, when service can slow right down. With a decidedly upmarket feel, the three or four comfortable rooms have good oak chairs and an individual mix of tables (many of them set for dining), and use attractive fabrics for the wood-railed curtains and pew cushions. Down some steps the charming country dining room has a dresser and longcase clock. Log fires include one in a well polished kitchen range (this area is no smoking), and paintings by a local artist line the walls. A good range of well kept beers includes Cheriton Pots Ale, Fullers London Pride, Gales HSB, and guests like Hampshire Ironside or Harveys Best; farmhouse cider and a select but very good range of wines, with several by the glass and a few bin-ends. Dominoes, shove ha'penny, cribbage, backgammon, and other games like scrabble, shut the box and mah jong. At the back there are attractive blue wood tables and chairs on a terrace with a pergola. This year not all readers have found the service up to its usual high standards, and in particular motorcyclists are generally banned, however smartly dressed. *(Recommended by J A Blanks, Tony and*

Wendy Hobden, Andrew Shore, Linda and Brian Davis, Dennis Stevens, John Evans, Ann and Colin Hunt, Peter Wade, John Fahy, R A Buckler, Angela and Alan Dale, J O Jonkler, J S M Sheldon, Dave Braisted, M A Gordon Smith, Clive Gilbert, Mrs J A Banks, Paul Williams, Larry Hansen, Peter Lewis, G C Hackemer, Sue Demont, Tim Barrow, Dr Keith Clements, Simon Small, Kevin and Katherine Cripps, Guy Consterdine)

Free house ~ Licensees Sheila, Edric, Simon and James Hawkins ~ Real ale ~ Meals and snacks (till 10) ~ Restaurant ~ (01798) 861281 ~ Children over 10 in restaurant ~ Open 11-3, 6-11; cl winter Sun evenings, plus 25 Dec and evening 26 Dec

LOWER BEEDING TQ2227 Map 3

Crabtree 🍽 ♀

A281 S of village, towards Cowfold

The imaginative lunchtime bar meals here are still among the very best you'll find for many a mile. The daily changing menu isn't huge, but the quality and presentation reflect the real thought and care that's gone into putting it together. As well as sandwiches (from £1.95) and ploughman's (from £3.50), both using their home-made bread, the choice might include fish soup with fennel, ginger, fresh dill and tomatoes or salad of pigeon and chicken with roasted pear, baby corn, and a walnut and balsamic vinaigrette (£4.95), lamb liver and bacon with mustard sauce (£8.50), beef stew with red wine, parsley and dumplings (£9.25), breaded pork chops with apple and cumin sauce (£9.50), salmon marinated in lemon and chervil with rocket and fennel (£9.90), and puddings like toffee pudding or lemon syllabub (£3); they do a set two-course lunch for £9.50. The cosy beamed bars have an air of civilised simplicity, and there's plenty of character in the back no-smoking restaurant (the only place where they do food in the evening). Well kept King and Barnes Sussex, Festive and seasonal brews on handpump (cheaper in the public bar), and good wines, including a wine of the month; prompt, friendly service. Darts, bar billiards, and piped music. A pleasant back garden has seats, and there may be barbecues and live music out here on summer evenings. The pub is very handy for Leonardslee Gardens, which are closed in winter. *(Recommended by Mr and Mrs G Turner, Mavis and John Wright, Graham Tayar, David Shillitoe, M Holdsworth, R Walden, Michael and Alison Leyland, John Beeken, Dr S Savvas, M Martin, E G Parish, Martin and Catherine Horner, Mrs J A Blanks, R and S Bentley, Cathryn and Richard Hicks, Christoper Glasson, Debbie Leam)*

King & Barnes ~ Tenants Jeremy Ashpool and Nick Wege ~ Real ale ~ Lunchtime meals and snacks ~ Restaurant (not Sun evening) ~ (01403) 891257 ~ Children in restaurant ~ Occasional live entertainment summer weekend evenings ~ Open 11-3, 5.30-11

LURGASHALL SU9327 Map 2

Noahs Ark

Village signposted from A283 N of Petworth; OS Sheet 186 map reference 936272

Spectacularly decked with flower baskets in summer, this welcoming 16th-c pub is in a lovely setting overlooking the village green; tables on the grass in front are ideal for watching the cricket matches out there in summer. The two neatly furnished bars have fresh flowers or warm log fires (one in a capacious inglenook), depending on the season, as well as darts, shove-ha'penny, table skittles, dominoes, and cribbage. Well kept Greene King Abbot, IPA and Rayments on handpump; friendly service. Bar food includes sandwiches (from £3, toasties such as bacon and mushroom £3.75), ploughman's (from £4.25), tuna and pasta bake or tomato and vegetable tagliatelle (£5.50), steak and kidney pudding (£5.95), lamb cutlets (£7.25), calf liver and bacon (£7.75), smoked salmon salad (£8.50), and fillet steak (£12.25). Plans are in hand to modernise the lavatories. *(Recommended by R J Bland, John Fahy, R Lake, James Nunns, John and Mavis Wright, R D Knight, M Judd, Chris Duncan, S G N Bennett, Roger Price, J A Snell, Ian Phillips, G C Hackemer)*

Greene King ~ Lease: Kathleen G Swannell ~ Real ale ~ Meals and snacks (not Sun evening) ~ Restaurant (not Sun) ~ (01428) 707346 ~ Children welcome ~ Occasional bands, theatre or concerts in garden marquee on summer evenings ~ Open 11.30-3, 6-11; all day summer Sats, and Sunday too if there's home cricket

MAYFIELD TQ5827 Map 3

Middle House 🏠

High St; village signposted off A267 S of Tunbridge Wells

Villagers have warmly welcomed the return of the ancient sign at this beautiful black and white timbered inn; it was blown down and severely damaged in a gale three years ago, but has now been fully restored, and not long before we went to press went back to its original position. Unusually for a pub, the building, built in 1575, is Grade I listed. The cosiest place to head for on a winter evening before your meal is the group of comfortable russet chesterfields in the tranquil lounge area, gently lit by the flickering log fire in an ornately carved fireplace (disputedly by Grinling Gibbons). Comfortable and chatty, the largely original and uncluttered L-shaped beamed main bar is dominated by a massive fireplace surrounded by menu boards at one end, and as this is still very much a friendly village local, there's a TV at the other end. The wide choice of regularly changing bar food might not seem that cheap, but the standard is excellent, and the helpings are generous – readers have praised their meals very highly indeed over the last year; you might find dishes like chicken and brie soup (£2.75), ploughman's (£4.75), pastry parcels filled with leek and ham or chicken and Barbadian spices (£4.95), home-made pitta bread with fillings like creole mixed meats or stir fried vegetables in korma sauce (£5.50), lots of salads (from £6.50), pies such as steak and kidney or venison and mushroom (£6.50), specials like a pineapple shell filled with almonds, sultanas, rice and curry sauce, and grilled with a cheese and yoghurt topping (£7.25), pasta with salmon and prawns (£7.95), rack of lamb with honey and ginger (£9.50), or black bream fillets sautéed in Chinese black bean and spring onion sauce (£9.95), and puddings like fruit crumbles or banoffi pie (£3.50). They do a three-course Sunday lunch for £13.95, a Monday night carvery, and special menus on their Wednesday Jazz Evenings; friendly service. One of the restaurants has some handsome panelling, and another room was once a chapel. Well kept Greene King Abbot, Harveys Best, and a guest like Fullers ESB or Morlands Old Speckled Hen on handpump; shove-ha'penny, and piped music. Afternoon tea is served in the fairly formal terraced back garden which has picnic tables, white plastic sets with cocktail parasols, nice views, and a slide and a log house for children; bedrooms are attractive and comfortable. *(Recommended by K A C Jeffery, Mrs Sandison, Simon Gardner, Paul Casbourne, Miss A M Phillips, Mike and Heather Watson, Jeremy Collins, Colin Laffan; more reports please)*

Free house ~ Licensee Monica Blundell ~ Real ale ~ Meals and snacks ~ Two restaurants (not Sun evening) ~ (01435) 872146 ~ Children welcome ~ Live jazz every Weds ~ Open 11-11 ~ Bedrooms: £35(£45B)/£45(£55B)

Rose & Crown

Fletching Street; off A267 at NE end of village

Several bars wander round the tiny central servery at this pretty weatherboarded 16th-c inn, but it's the two cosy little front rooms – often packed with locals – that are the most atmospheric. There are low beams, benches built in to the partly panelled walls, an attractive bow window seat, low ceiling boards with coins embedded in the glossy ochre paint, and a big inglenook fireplace which gets the place really roasting in winter. Popular bar food includes soup (£2.50), parma ham and mozzarella salad (£3.50), cottage pie (£3.95), chilli prawns (£4.25), beef stew with herb dumplings (£4.95), plenty of pies such as lamb and apricot or spicy bean and vegetable (from £5.75), slices of aubergine baked with tomato, herbs and mozzarella (£5.95), salmon and spring onion fishcakes (£6.50), filled yorkshire pudding or chicken and spinach curry (£7.95), lamb fillets with redcurrant and rosemary (£8.75) and strips of steak with hot chilli and coriander sauce (£8.95). Well kept Flowers IPA and Original, Harveys Best, Ind Coope Burton and Marstons Pedigree on handpump, many new world wines, a sizeable bin-end list, and a range of malt whiskies; shove-ha'penny, dominoes and cribbage, piped music at lunchtime. The bedrooms are very pretty and comfortable although there may be a little noise from the restaurant below. The building looks especially appealing in summer, with the little windows peeping out from behind the colourful baskets and tubs, and rustic tables in front. *(Recommended by Brenda and Derek Savage, Mavis and John Wright, Claude and Bonnie Bemis, John Rhodes, Margaret and Nigel Dennis, Norma Farris, Sue Demont, Tim Barrow)*

Free house ~ Licensee Sean McCorry ~ Real ale ~ Meals and snacks (11.30-2.30, 7-9.30 – 10 Fri and Sat) ~ Restaurant ~ (01435) 872200 ~ Children welcome ~ Open 11-3, 5.30-11 (all day Sat and in summer) ~ Bedrooms: £38B/£48B

MIDHURST SU8821 Map 2

Spread Eagle 🛏

South St

The atmosphere at this smart old hotel is one of restful luxury, but despite the opulence it's a friendly, welcoming place. Most of it dates from the 17th c, but some parts of the original 1430 building still remain. Best of all is is the spacious massively beamed and timbered lounge, with its dramatic fireplace, imposing leaded-light windows looking out on the most attractive part of this old town, and handsome yet quite unpretentious old armchairs and settees spread among the rugs on the broad-boarded creaking oak floor. There's apparently a secret room six feet up one chimney. A concise lunchtime bar menu consists of vegetable soup (£4.50), warm broccoli and smoked bacon tart, a hot daily special or lentil pâté with toasted brioche, sun-dried tomatoes and olive oil dressing (£5.25), and smoked haddock topped with welsh rarebit (£5.50). The highly regarded restaurant is no smoking. They do good cream teas at weekends. The lounge opens onto a secluded courtyard. Fullers London Pride on handpump, not cheap but well kept, an extensive wine list; shove-ha'penny, cribbage, dominoes, trivia, maybe piped music. This was described by Hilaire Belloc in *The Four Men* as 'the oldest and most revered of all the prime inns of this world'. *(Recommended by Hugh MacLean, Graham and Karen Oddey, Mrs M Rice, Paul Carter; more reports please)*

Free house ~ Licensees Pontus and Miranda Carminger ~ Real ale ~ Lunchtime meals and snacks (not Sun) ~ Restaurant ~ (01730) 816911 ~ Well behaved children welcome ~ Open 11-2.30, 6-11; closed 26 and 31 Dec and 1 Jan ~ Bedrooms: £74B/£89B

NORMANS BAY TQ6805 Map 3

Star 🍺

Signposted off A259 just E of Pevensey; and from Cooden, off B2182 coast road W out of Bexhill

Not the best place to bring someone who finds it hard to make up their mind, this busy pub has a daunting choice of food and drink. There are rarely less than 10 well kept real ales on handpump, with beers like Adnams, Batemans, Charles Wells Bombardier, Harveys Best, Hopback Summer Lightning, Marstons Owd Rodger, and Morlands Old Speckled Hen amongst the range, which usually varies even from day to day. They also do lots of continental bottled beers, good country wines (the local apple is recommended), and a wider range of lagers and ciders than you'll usually come across. The menu has around 100 different dishes, some served in very big helpings – they hand out doggy bags, and mark on the menu with a little elephant picture the things that might defeat even a smuggler-sized appetite. You'll generally find ploughman's (from £3.95), half a dozen or so vegetarian meals such as hot Boston beans, harvest pie, nut roast or pastas (from £4.75), a choice of fresh local fish (from £4.50 – the fishermen's huts are just down the road), ham and eggs (£4.50), scampi or half a roast chicken with a jumbo sausage (£6.50), pork chops (£6.75), half shoulder of lamb (£7.50), a good selection of steaks (from £8.75), a few blackboard specials like lemon sole (£6.95) or beef wellington (£10.95), and masses of puddings (from £2.50), with their large waffles especially popular (£4.25); children's dishes (£2.25). The atmosphere is welcoming and relaxed, especially in the spaciously modernised bar, with comfortably cushioned seats spreading over the carpet of a brick-pillared partly timbered dining lounge; piped music, games in the children's room. Friendly staff cope admirably during the busiest periods. It's incredibly popular in summer, when you can relax in the garden which has a good play area, and there's more white plastic tables on a small front terrace; there may be barbecues in summer. Paths inland quickly take you away from the caravan sites into marshy nature reserve. *(Recommended by R Walden, M P Evans, E G Parish, Dr S Savvas, M Martin, Hanns P Golez, David Lamb, Tim and Pam Moorey, John Beeken, Colin Laffan)*

Free house ~ Licensee Francis Maynard ~ Real ale ~ Meals and snacks (all day weekends) ~ (01323) 762648 ~ Children in own room ~ Jazz Tues evening ~ Open 11-11; 12-10.30 Sun

NUTHURST TQ1926 Map 3

Black Horse 🏆

Village signposted from A281 SE of Horsham

Old-fashioned and welcoming, the main bar of this relaxing black-beamed country pub has big Horsham flagstones in front of the inglenook fireplace, interesting pictures on the walls, and magazines to read. At one end it opens out into other carpeted areas including a dining room. A good range of well kept beers on handpump includes Adnams, Eldridge Pope Hardy Country, King & Barnes Sussex, Ringwood Old Thumper and Wadworths 6X, and they also have Gales country wines and a fair wine list. Popular promptly served bar food such as soup, doorstep sandwiches and ploughman's, filled baked potatoes (from £3.95), a pie of the day or cannelloni romagna (£5.95), and changing specials like chicken panang or prawns piri-piri; children's menu. The restaurant is no smoking. Service is friendly and efficient, and there are two amiable labradors, Jasper and Chaos; cribbage, dominoes, piped music. They're just as welcoming if you turn up wet and muddy after sampling one of the area's lovely walks. The attractive streamside back garden borders some woods. *(Recommended by Andrew and Jo Litten, C B and C H, LM, R J Walden, Michael Grigg, Bruce Bird, Clive Gilbert, Wayne Brindle, G Washington)*

Free house ~ Licensees Trevor Jones and Sue Bradley ~ Real ale ~ Meals and snacks (12-2.30, 6.15-10) ~ Restaurant (not Sun evening) ~ (01403) 891272 ~ Children welcome ~ Open 11-3, 6-11; all day summer weekends

OVING SU9005 Map 2

Gribble 🏆

Between A27 and A259 just E of Chichester, then should be signposted just off village road; OS Sheet 197 map reference 900050

They let you pick apples in season from the trees in the lovely garden at this delightfully pretty rose covered red brick and thatched cottage. It's best known though for the tasty range of rather strong beers brewed in the pub's own microbrewery, which includes the enduring favourites Gribble Ale, Reg's Tipple, Black Adder II, Pluckling Pheasant, Pigs Ear and winter Wobbler, and the more recent Ewe Brew (originally produced as a VE-Day special); they also have Badger Best on handpump, with lots of country wines and farm cider. From the outside, save for the chunky wood furnishings and covered seating area, it looks more like a private house than a pub, as indeed it was until comparatively recently. But the friendly bar could have been a pub for centuries, full as it is of heavy beams and timbering, and old country-kitchen furnishings and pews. On the left, a family room with a toy box and pews provides one of the biggest no-smoking areas we've so far found in a Sussex pub, and also has shove-ha'penny, dominoes, cribbage, a fruit machine and a separate skittle alley. Home-cooked bar food includes open sandwiches (from £2.50), burgers (from £3.75), ploughman's (from £3.95), ham and eggs, oriental vegetables or ratatouille au gratin (£4.75), steak and mushroom pie (£5.25), fisherman's pie (£5.45), Mexican chicken with kidney beans and sweetcorn in a tomato and chilli sauce, or chicken and ham in cider and cheese sauce (£5.95), seafood platter (£6.45), and sirloin steak (£9.45); they do smaller helpings of most meals, as well as children's dishes (£2.45). The pub can get busy. *(Recommended by Bruce Bird, Nigel Kendrick, John Beeken, Sally Cooke, Stephen Harvey, Alec and Marie Lewery, Brian Dodsworth, David Holloway, Jonathan Phillips, R T and J C Moggridge, Clive Gilbert, Lynn Sharpless, Bob Eardley, Winifrede Morrison, Paul Carter)*

Own brew (Badger) ~ Managers Ron and Anne May ~ Real ale ~ Meals and snacks ~ (01243) 786893 ~ Children in family room and eating area ~ Open 11-2.30(3 Sat), 6-11

PLAYDEN TQ9121 Map 3
Peace & Plenty

A268/B2082

There is a calm atmosphere at this cottagey dining pub with its gentle classical piped radio and very attentive but relaxed service from young staff. The main draw here is the traditional very well prepared (but not cheap) bar food such as cream of broccoli soup or half a pint of very tasty prawns (£2.95), bangers and mash (£6.50), a couple of vegetarian dishes including leek and potato pie, beefburger, steak and kidney pie or lamb pie (£6.95), roast beef or delicious steak and kidney pudding (£7.95), salads (from £8.50), good crisp scampi (£10.25), dover sole (£13.95); puddings (£2.95), and children's dishes (£2.95). The intimate bar, with deep pink walls and shelves nicely crowded with lots of little pictures, china and lamps, is well lit by a big bay window with a long comfortable cushioned seat. There are mixed tables on a light brown carpet, and a woodburner in a big inglenook at one end has comfortable armchairs either side. Well kept Greene King IPA, Abbot and Rayments from a small counter. There are two similarly cosy cottagey dining areas. The bar staff say they are happpy to keep an eye on children in their own friendly little room which has a comfy sofa for watching TV and lots of toys scattered on the floor. There are seats in the pretty flowery garden though there is traffic noise. *(Recommended by John T Ames, Lin and Roger Lawrence, Tony McLaughlin, Joy and Graham Eaton, Simon Evans)*

Free house ~ Licensee Yvonne Thomas ~ Real ale ~ Meals and snacks (all day, limited menu 9.30-10.30pm) ~ (01797) 280342 ~ Children welcome ~ Open 11-11; 12-10.30; cl 25 Dec

nr PUNNETTS TOWN TQ6220 Map 3
Three Cups ▪

B2096 towards Battle

Though it's warmly inviting to visitors, it's nice to see that this unspoilt and traditional place is still very much a local, with regulars making up teams for cribbage, darts (men's and women's), and clay pigeon shooting. The peaceful and friendly long low-beamed bar has attractive panelling, and comfortable seats including some in big bay windows overlooking a small green. Burning in the big fireplace under a black mantelbeam dated 1696 are logs that one could just as easily describe as tree trunks. A back family room leads out to a small covered terrace, with seats in the garden beyond – where you'll find chickens and bantams and a good safe play area. Good value unassuming food includes sandwiches, filled baked potatoes (from £2.75), prize-winning local giant sausages (£3.25), home-made steak or chicken pie (£4.50), half a roast chicken (£6.75) and steaks (from £7.50); part of the eating area is no smoking. Four well kept changing beers such as Beards Best, Butcombe, Harveys Best and Shepherd Neame on handpump. Darts, table skittles, shove-ha'penny, cribbage and quiet piped music. There's space for five touring caravans outside. Good walks lead off from here, on either side of this high ridge of the Weald. *(Recommended by Vann and Terry Prime, Dave Braisted, F A Noble)*

Beards ~ Tenants Leonard and Irenie Smith ~ Real ale ~ Meals and snacks ~ (01435) 830252 ~ Children in eating area of bar and family room till 8.30 ~ Open 11-3, 6.30-11

ROWHOOK TQ1234 Map 3

Chequers

Village signposted from A29 NW of Horsham

A recent timber-frame survey established that this characterful old place was built around 1590. Pleasantly rustic and genuinely old-fashioned, it's the kind of pub that manages to weather unscathed any number of changes that go on around it, and even in it: though we've now listed the names of four different sets of licensees in as many years, readers' enthusiasm for the Chequers remains undimmed. The snugly unpretentious front bar has black beams in its white ceiling, upholstered benches and stools around the tables on its flagstone floor, and an inglenook fireplace; up a step or two, there's a carpeted lounge with a very low ceiling. Changing blackboard bar food might include lunchtime sandwiches, moules marinières (£3.95), popular pies (£5.95), chicken breast filled with brie and wrapped in crispy bacon (£10.95), half shoulder of lamb with french mustard, honey and rosemary glaze (£14.95), and children's meals; they grow their own herbs. Well kept Boddingtons, Flowers Original, Fullers London Pride, Morlands Old Speckled Hen and guests on handpump, maybe kept under light blanket pressure; friendly service. Shove-ha'penny, dominoes, cribbage and piped music. A sunny little front terrace borders the quiet lane, and there are a good few tables in the peaceful and prettily planted side garden, with more on another crazy-paved terrace; good children's play area with swings, see-saw, wendy house, slide and climbing frame. *(Recommended by J Sheldon, Mrs W D Morrison, Bruce Bird, Peter and Lynn Brueton, Mr and Mrs P A King, Sally Cooke, Stella Knight, Clive Gilbert, Chris and Chris Ellis, Peter Walters, Alan Whiting, George Atkinson)*

Whitbreads ~ Tenants Joe and Jane Wright ~ Real ale ~ Meals and snacks (till 10 weekends) ~ Restaurant ~ (01403) 790480 ~ Children in eating area of bar and restaurant till 8 ~ Occasional live music Sun ~ Open 11-3, 6-11

RYE TQ9220 Map 3

Mermaid

Mermaid St

All that's really changed in the last couple of hundred years at this ancient smugglers' inn is the advent of electricity. And the beautiful black and white timbered facade, with its distinctive sign hanging over the steeply cobbled street, has barely altered since the hotel was built in the 15th and 16th centuries. It used to be a favourite with gangs of notorious smugglers, who kept their loaded pistols by the side of their tankards while drinking. The ghost of a serving maid who lost her heart to one of those smugglers is said to return just before midnight. Fine panelling, antique woodwork and rare frescoes fill the civilised rooms, and there are some unusual intricately carved antique seats, one in the form of a goat, as well as an enormous fireplace. The cellars that hold the well kept Bass, McEwans and Morlands Old Speckled Hen date back seven centuries; good wine list, ports and sherries. Bar food is served in the recently redecorated function room, the choice typically including soup (£3), filled baguettes (from £3.50), moules marinières (£4.50), quite a few vegetarian dishes, and a big seafood platter with crab, prawns and mussels (£11). Piped music, hearty breakfasts. There are seats on a small back terrace, and on the odd occasion in summer you might come across Morris dancers or Shakespearean players in the car park. *(Recommended by Jacquie and Jim Jones, Hanns P Golez, R T and J C Moggridge, Chris and Martin Taylor, KB, DH, PN, Linda and Brian Davis)*

Free house ~ Licensee Robert Pinwill ~ Real ale ~ Restaurant ~ (01797) 223065 ~ Children in eating area of bar ~ Open 11-11; 12-10.30 Sun ~ Bedrooms: £49.50(£63.80B)/£96.80(£118.80B)

nr SEAFORD TV4899 Map 3

Golden Galleon ♀ 🍴

Exceat Bridge; A259 Seaford—Eastbourne, near Cuckmere

Ay any one time there will be between eight and twelve real ales on handpump at this expanding inn, including up to six from their own little microbrewery. Brewed by the landlord's brother, these might include Cuckmere Haven Best, Guv'nor, Golden Peace, Gentleman's Gold and an old fashioned cask conditioned stout, Saxon King. The balance is made up of ales from other smaller brewers, which might include Harveys Armada, and Greene King Abbot and IPA, on handpump or tapped from the cask; there's also freshly squeezed orange juice, farm cider, a decent selection of malts, continental brandies and Italian liqueurs and cappuccino or espresso coffee. Having said that it's really the excellent food that draws most people here, and as the very chatty landlord is Italian you can expect lots of properly prepared Italian dishes amongst the generously served meals. Recent menus have included soup (£2.45), bruschetta (from £2.75), diced chicken with lettuce and home-made garlic mayonnaise (£3.35), a splendid choice of ploughman's (from £3.80), Italian seafood salad (£3.95), filled baked potatoes (lunchtimes only, from £4.50), breaded chicken (£5.75), fried or steamed fish of the day (£5.95), swordfish steak (£9.25), stincotto – a large pork joint cooked on the bone with wine and herbs (£9.95), and specials like lasagne, spaghetti carbonara, or chicken in tomato and ginger sauce; children's helpings, and various theme nights. No credit cards. At most times of the year there's a cheery bustle that some feel is more reminiscent of an Italian trattoria than a typical pub, and it does get very busy at weekends and holidays. The high trussed and pitched rafters create quite an airy feel, and there's a nice little side area with an open fire; piped music. The conservatory, new river room, and dining area with its neat rows of tables are no smoking. Tables in the sloping garden have good views towards the Cuckmere estuary and the Seven Sisters Country Park; you can walk from here to the sea (a half hour or so's stroll), or inland to Friston Forest and the Downs. The new bedrooms are in a converted bungalow behind, and more are planned. *(Recommended by LM, Frank Gadbois, E G Parish, Sue Demont, Tim Barrow, H D Spottiswoode, Alan Skull, John Fahy, P J Guy, R and S Bentley, Dr Keith Clements, Richard Houghton)*

Own brew ~ Licensee Stefano Diella ~ Real ale ~ Meals and snacks (not Sun eves Sept-May) ~ (01323) 892247 ~ Children welcome ~ Open 10.30-3, 6-11; 11-11 Sat, 12-10.30 Sun ~ Bedrooms: £17.50S/£39.50S

STOPHAM TQ0218 Map 3

White Hart ♀

Off A283 between village turn-off and Pulborough

In summer Morris dancers regularly visit this idyllic spot, at the meeting of the Arun and Rother rivers. The tables and play area are across the road from the pub itself, and really make the most of the setting, beside a graceful seven-arched early 14th-c bridge. Back inside, one of the highlights is the fabulous fresh fish restaurant menu which you can also choose from in the bar: seafood salad (£3.95), sole and salmon roulade (£4.95), medaillons of monkfish fried in garlic and herbs (£5.50), smoked eel fillets (£5.95), baked salmon with broccoli and cheese or plaice fillets filled with salmon mousse in a champagne sauce (£9.95), and fried fillets of tuna in a tangy lemon sauce, maritime mixed grill or shark steak in a peppercorn sauce (£10.50). Other popular bar food includes good home-made sandwiches (from £1.55), soup (£1.90), ploughman's (from £3.50), spicy sausage made to their own recipe (£3.95), meat or vegetable lasagne or tagliatelle with stilton and apple sauce (£4.75), haddock mornay (£4.95), specials like char-grilled cornfed chicken with a spiced apricot and tarragon sauce (£6.75) or half shoulder of lamb with redcurrant gravy (£8.50), and children's meals (£1.90). They do theme nights in winter. The three relaxing cosy and comfortable beamed rooms are quite a draw in their own right with well kept Flowers Original, King and Barnes Sussex, and Morlands Old Speckled Hen on handpump, about 25 bottled beers from around the world, and decent wines including a good few by the glass and half-bottle; darts, shove-ha'penny, cribbage, dominoes, video game, trivia and piped jazz or big band music. The beamed candlelit restaurant and usually one bar are no smoking. There are tree-lined grass walks down by the river. *(Recommended by Hanns P Golez, Alan Jarvis, John Beeken, R J Walden, Peter Plumridge, Dr S Savvas, M Martin, R H Martyn, John Beeken, Tony and Wendy Hobden, John and Mavis Wright, David Holloway, T Roger Lamble, R T and C E Moggridge, John Fahy, J S M Sheldon)*

Whitbreads ~ Lease: John Palmer and Linda Collier ~ Real ale ~ Meals and snacks (not Sun evenings Oct-Easter) ~ Restaurant ~ (01798) 873321 ~ Children welcome ~ Bands in garden some summer eves and bank holiday Mons ~ Open 11-3, 6.30(7 winter Mon-Thurs)-11

nr TICEHURST TQ6830 Map 3
Bull 🍺

Three Legged Cross; coming into Ticehurst from N on B2099, just before Ticehurst village sign, turn left beside corner house called Tollgate (Maynards Pick Your Own may be signposted here)

The core of this peaceful old pub is a 14th-c Wealden hall, and it's this original part with its huge log fire that most people head for. A series of small flagstoned, brick-floored or oak parquet rooms run together, with heavy oak tables and seats of some character; it's a popular place, well liked by locals in the evening, when the friendly very low beamed rooms soon fill up. Well kept Boddingtons, John Smiths, Harveys Best, Morlands Old Speckled Hen, locally brewed Rother Valley Level Best and a changing guest; friendly efficient service. The garden is delightful on a lovely summer evening, with tables beside an ornamental fish pond looking back at the building, covered in climbing roses and clematis. There might be an outside bar and barbecue, and at weekends they usually have a bouncy castle for children. Bar food might include soup, baguettes with fillings like sausage and bacon or smoked salmon (from £2.35), lamb liver and bacon (£5.50), cod steak (£7.25), and a rib of roast beef for two (£16.95). The popular restaurant extension has a fuller menu. There's an unusual round pool table, as well as darts, bar billiards, table skittles, dominoes, cribbage and piped music, and a couple of boules pitches. Tucked away in little country lanes, the pub is handy for visiting the lovely gardens of Pashley Manor. *(Recommended by Mavis and John Wright, Sue Lee, Richard Fawcett, Tom McLean, Roger Huggins, Mr and Mrs Jones, Mrs C A Blake, Sue Demont, Tim Barrow, J H Bell)*

Free house ~ Licensee Mrs E M Wilson-Moir ~ Real ale ~ Meals and snacks (not Sun or Mon evenings) ~ Restaurant ~ (01580) 200586 ~ Children welcome ~ Live entertainment one Sun a month ~ Open 11-3, 6.30-11

TILLINGTON SU9621 Map 2
Horse Guards 🍽 🛏 🍷

Village signposted from A272 Midhurst—Petworth

Sussex Dining Pub of the Year

Tremendous care and attention to detail go into the splendid meals at this neat and friendly inn, and though it's very much a place for eating it's the not just the food that makes it so well liked by readers - the excellent service and smartly relaxed atmosphere come in for high praise too. As well as sandwiches (from £2.50), soup (£3.25), and ploughman's (£4.50), the changing range of bar meals might include courgette and cheddar mousse or game terrine with an apricot and rhubarb chutney

(£4.50), grilled goat's cheese on a citrus fruit salad (£4.95), lamb and mint sausages (£5.25), mushroom stroganoff or herb and honey roasted lamb cutlets with a garlic tomato cream (£5.95), lamb liver with bacon or various salads (£6.95), chicken and broccoli fricassee (£7.25), pigeon breast with bacon and shallots on a port sauce (£7.95), fillet of red bream in cajun spices (£8.75), venison steak with blueberry sauce (£10.25), and excellent puddings. Most ingredients come from local producers, and fresh fish is delivered five times a week. The good wine list usually has a dozen by the glass; well kept Badger Best and King & Barnes Sussex on handpump, good coffee. There's a lovely view beyond the village to the Rother Valley from the seat in the big black-panelled bow window of the cosy beamed front bar which has some good country furniture and a log fire; darts, cribbage, piped music. There's a terrace outside, and more tables and chairs in a sheltered garden behind. The church opposite is 800 years old. The pub got its name in the 1840s and 50s when Horse Guards regiments were billeted in nearby Petworth Park to guard French prisoners of war; in those days the pub was called the Old Star, but the soldiers spent so much time there that the locals rechristened it after them. *(Recommended by Peter Lewis, Margaret and Nigel Dennis, Diane Edmond, Ann and Colin Hunt, J O Jonkler, David Lupton, Viv Middlebrook, Jane Thompson, A S Brown, Fred and Liz Onslow)*

Free house ~ Licensees Aidan and Lesley Nugent ~ Real ale ~ Meals and snacks (till 10) ~ Restaurant ~ (01798) 342332 ~ Children in eating area of bar ~ Open 11-3, 6-11; cl 25 Dec ~ Bedrooms: /£57.50B

WEST ASHLING SU8107 Map 2

Richmond Arms 🍺

Mill Lane; from B2146 in village follow Hambrook signpost

This notably friendly and unpretentious out-of-the-way village pub stands out particularly for its excellent choice of ten well kept real ales, which usually includes brews like Boddingtons, Brakspears, Greene King Abbot, Marstons Pedigree, Morlands Old Speckled Hen, Timothy Taylors Landlord, and Youngs Special; also farm ciders, country wines, Belgian fruit beers and continental bottled beers. The main bar is dominated by the central servery, and has a 1930s feel with its long wall benches, library chairs, black tables and open fire (maybe with a couple of black cats in front of it); it can get smoky. Readers like the good choice of well priced non-nonsense food such as sandwiches, excellent ploughman's, five or so vegetarian meals like home-made spinach and mushroom lasagne or cannelloni (£4.60), and the Texas brunch – a 6oz rump steak on garlic bread, with two fried eggs on top (£6.20); Sunday lunch (£4.60). Service is obliging and flexible, even when the pub is busy, as it often is, especially at weekends. Darts, shove-ha'penny, dominoes, and cribbage; the skittle alley doubles as a function and family room, and is used at weekends for eating (when it's no smoking). There's a pergola, and some picnic tables by the car park. *(Recommended by Bruce Bird, Alan and Eileen Bowker, Ann and Colin Hunt, Karen and Graham Oddey; more reports please)*

Free house ~ Licensee Bob Garbutt ~ Real ale ~ Meals and snacks (till 10) ~ (01243) 575730 ~ Children in skittle alley ~ Tues quiz night ~ Open 11-2.30, 5.30-11; all day Sat and Sun in summer; closed evening 26 Dec

WINEHAM TQ2320 Map 3

Royal Oak 🍺

Village signposted from A272 and B2116

Run by the same family now for over 50 years, this delightfully old-fashioned place never changes – there are no smart tills, fruit machines or even beer pumps, and the emphasis is still on drinking rather than eating. The layout and style are commendably traditional, with ancient corkscrews decorating the very low beams above the serving counter, racing plates, tools and a coach horn on the walls, simple furnishings, and logs burning in an enormous inglenook. Well kept beers tapped from the cask in a still room on the way to a little snug include Flowers Original, Harveys Sussex, Wadworths 6X and Whitbreads Pompey Royal; darts, shove-ha'penny, dominoes, cribbage. The limited range of bar snacks includes fresh-cut or toasted sandwiches (from £1.25, roast beef £1.75 or lovely smoked salmon £2.25), home-made soup in winter (£1.50) and ploughman's (£2.95). It gets very busy at weekends and on summer evenings. Service can be a little slow, but is good and courteous, and in a timeless place like this you rarely feel in a hurry. The charming frontage has a lawn with wooden tables by a well. On a clear day sharp-eyed male readers may be able to catch a glimpse of Chanctonbury Ring from the window in the gents'. *(Recommended by R and S Bentley, Greta and Christopher Wells, Alec and Marie Lewery, Alan Skull; more reports please)*

Whitbreads ~ Tenant Tim Peacock ~ Real ale ~ Snacks (available during opening hours) ~ (01444) 881252 ~ Children in family room ~ Open 11-2.30, 5.30(6 Sat)-11; cl evening 25 Dec

WITHYHAM TQ4935 Map 3

Dorset Arms

B2110

Set well back from the road, and with white tables on a brick terrace raised well above the small green, this 16th-c inn is much older than its Georgian facade suggests. There's a short flight of outside steps up to the L-shaped bar, which at the end of the climb has sturdy tables and simple country seats on the wide oak floorboards, a good log fire in the stone Tudor fireplace, and a traditional welcoming atmosphere. Good bar food includes sandwiches (from £1.70), soup (£2.20), ploughman's (from £3.60), filled baked potatoes (£3.65), ham, egg and chips (£4.40), fresh baked trout (£6), and specials like steak and ale pie or roast pheasant, with a fuller menu featuring vegetables baked in cream and white wine sauce topped with cheese and parsley (£7.55), breaded lemon sole (£7.95), fried strips of chicken breast with garlic and white wine (£8.45), and half a roast duckling with nut stuffing and a brandy and orange sauce (£10.35). They recommend booking, especially in the pretty restaurant. Well kept Harveys BB, IPA and seasonal beers on handpump, and a reasonable wine list including some local ones and a wine of the month. Darts, dominoes, shove-ha'penny, cribbage, fruit machine, cards and piped music. The countryside around here is nice, and the nearby church has a memorial to Vita Sackville-West. *(Recommended by Colin and Joyce Laffan, Tom Wild, Margaret and Nigel Dennis, P Gillbe; more reports please)*

Harveys ~ Tenants John and Sue Pryor ~ Real ale ~ Meals and snacks (not Mon evening) ~ Restaurant (not Sun evening) ~ (01892) 770278 ~ Children in restaurant ~ Open 11.30(11 Sat)-3, 5.30(6 Sat)-11

Lucky Dip

Besides the fully inspected pubs, you might like to try these Lucky Dips recommended to us and described by readers (if you do, please send us reports):

Adversane, W Sus [TQ0723], *Blacksmiths Arms:* Attractive old beamed pub, well kept and spacious but cosy, well cooked food, friendly service, nice log fire; restaurant *(Steve Goodchild)*

☆ Alfriston E Sus [TQ5103], *Market Cross:* Olde-worlde atmospheric low-beamed white-panelled bar with smuggling mementoes, good value bar food from sandwiches to steaks (snacks only, Sun lunch), well kept Courage Best and Directors, good choice of wines by the glass, friendly staff, tables in garden; children allowed in eating area and conservatory; can get crowded *(Keith Stevens, LYM)*

Alfriston [High St], *George:* 14th-c timbered inn, roomy heavy-beamed bar with huge fireplace (can be smoky), intimate candlelit dining area, comfortable attractive bedrooms; has had wide choice of food inc lots of fish, efficient service, well kept Harveys and Smiles, but up for sale 1996 *(E G Parish, John Beeken, Steve Goodchild)*

☆ Amberley W Sus [off B2139; TQ0111], *Black Horse:* Attractive flagstoned village pub, up a flight of steps, its beams festooned with sheep and cow bells; wide choice of good simple home-cooked bar food from ploughman's to steaks, fine real chips, charming licensees, well kept Friary Meux Best and Ind Coope Burton, farm cider, log fire each end, no-smoking lounge with high settles, nice garden; children in eating area and restaurant, occasional folk music, two big dogs, sleepy cat *(John Beeken, Guy Consterdine, Mrs P Boxford, LYM)*

☆ Amberley [Houghton Bridge, B2139], *Bridge*: Attractive, busy open-plan dining pub with pretty riverside terrace garden, good range of fresh food inc local fish, well kept Flowers Original, decent wines, country wines, friendly staff, interesting pictures, unobtrusive piped music; provision for children; bedrooms *(Maureen and Jeff Dobbelaar, Peter Lewis, R T and J C Moggridge)*

☆ Amberley [Rackham Rd, just off B1239], *Sportsman*: Off the beaten track, three small rooms, conservatory and garden, lovely views from balcony, genuine home-cooked food from sandwiches up inc good vegetarian and Sun roasts, decent wines and country wines, well kept ales, friendly welcome *(Julie Peters, Colin Blinkhorn, Tony and Wendy Hobden, Robert W Buckle, Elly Peckham)*

Amberstone E Sus [Amberstone Corner; TQ5911], *Waldernheath*: A restaurant, but has a bar with bar snacks; splendid reasonably priced food with home-grown veg, good wine list *(D J Boddington)*

Angmering W Sus [The Square; TQ0704], *Lamb*: Good range of attractively presented well priced food, well kept King & Barnes, pleasant service *(R T and J C Moggridge)*

Angmering, *Spotted Cow*: Good range of well kept ales such as King & Barnes, Marstons Pedigree, Morlands Old Speckled Hen, Youngs Special and guests like Ringwood Best, generous helpings of good value bar food (very popular weekdays with older people), restaurant; roomy garden, good play area; lovely walk to Highdown hill fort *(Ian Phillips, Tony Hobden, Bruce Bird)*

Apuldram W Sus [Birdham Rd; SU8403], *Black Horse*: Comfortably modernised 18th-c pub with wide choice of reasonably priced food inc specialities each night – fish Fri, curries Sat etc; slide and swings in big garden *(Alec and Marie Lewery)*

☆ Ardingly W Sus [B2028 2 miles N; TQ3429], *Gardeners Arms*: Cheerful olde-worlde dining pub with good choice of home-made food inc fresh fish and good value specials, welcoming and attractive if not exactly pubby bar with big log fire in inglenook, cheerful staff, well kept Boddingtons, Harveys and Theakstons, morning coffee and tea, maybe soft piped music, no children; well spaced tables out among small trees, handy for Borde Hill and Wakehurst Place *(John Pettit, Gordon Smith, Mr and Mrs Jones)*

Ardingly [Street Lane], *Ardingly Inn*: Comfortable pub with wide choice of good quick generous food with good veg, OAP discounts, welcoming helpful staff, decent wines, attractive restaurant; bedrooms reasonably priced *(F M Furlonger, Margaret and Nigel Dennis, Don and Thelma Beeson, D and J Tapper, Mr and Mrs P A King)*; [Street Lane], *Oak*: Beamed 14th-c dining pub,

Courage-related and guest ales, quick service, lots of brass and lace curtains, magnificent old fireplace (they could perhaps use it more); bright comfortable restaurant, pleasant tables outside *(Ron Gentry, Mr and Mrs Jones, M A Mees)*

☆ Arlington E Sus [Caneheath, off A22 or A27; TQ5407], *Old Oak*: 17th-c, with big cosy L-shaped beamed bar, dining room, popular reasonably priced food (not Mon), well kept Badger, Harveys and usually a guest beer tapped from the cask, pleasant staff, log fires, peaceful garden, children allowed, handy for Bluebell Walk *(R and S Bentley, Dr S Savvas, M Martin, J H Bell)*

☆ Arlington, *Yew Tree*: Neatly modernised two-bar village local, reliable generous home cooking inc children's, well kept Fullers London Pride, Harveys, Morlands Old Speckled Hen and Worthington BB, log fires, efficient cheery service, subdued piped music, darts; dining area with french windows to good big garden and play area, by paddock with farm animals *(John Beeken, Dr S Savvas, M Martin, Keith Ward, Mrs Allerston)*

☆ Arundel W Sus [High St; TQ0107], *Swan*: Spotless refurbished open-plan L-shaped bar, good choice of food inc vegetarian in bar and restaurant, full range of good Arundel beers with a guest such as Fullers London Pride, all well kept; good bedrooms *(Bruce Bird, John and Chris Simpson, Chris and Anne Fluck, Clive Gilbert, LYM)*

Arundel [Mill Rd – keep on and don't give up!], *Black Rabbit*: Big touristy pub, plenty of provision for families, included for its position in this peaceful spot, with lots of riverside tables looking across to bird-reserve watermeadows and castle; useful bar food, restaurant specialising in fish, Badger Best and Tanglefoot and guest ales, open all day in summer *(T Roger Lamble, David Holloway, Dr Keith Clements, Brig R Silberrad, Romey Heaton, D Maplethorpe, B Helliwell, Miss A G Drake, LYM)*; [London Rd, by cathedral], *St Marys Gate*: Quiet comfortable open-plan bar with alcoves, lots of horse-racing caricatures, generous good value home-cooked food inc interesting Badger Best and Tanglefoot and guest beer, good service, restaurant, no-smoking area; unobtrusive piped music; bedrooms quiet and good value *(Bruce Bird, Mrs M Rice)*; [3 Queen St], *White Hart*: Two spacious but cosy lounges with old settles and books, comfortable dining area, quick friendly service, three well kept ales, bar food *(Chris and Anne Fluck)*

Barns Green W Sus [TQ1227], *Queens Head*: Opened up, with jovial landlord, well kept Flowers Original, filling ploughman's *(PGP)*

Battle E Sus [Mount St; TQ7416], *Olde Kings Head*: Friendly well kept old pub, two narrow rooms and games room, chatty staff, usual food, open fire, real ales such as Archers Village and Harveys; children welcome *(George Atkinson)*

Bexhill E Sus [Little Common Rd, Little Common; A259 towards Polegate; TQ7107], *Denbigh*: Attractive and friendly small bar and dining area, good choice of real ales, good generous well priced food inc fish and daily roast, pleasant staff; pretty floral decorations *(Christopher Turner, A R Milton)*; [Turkey Rd], *Rose & Crown*: Unpretentious suburban local with good range of decent food inc Sun lunch, old-fashioned rather domestic atmosphere, well kept Harveys Best *(Stephen Harvey)*

☆ Binstead W Sus [Binstead Lane; about 2 miles W of Arundel, turn S off A27 towards Binstead – OS Sheet 197 map ref 980064; SU9806], *Black Horse*: 17th-c, with ochre walls and open fire in big bar, good range of real ales, darts and pool one end, welcoming young licensee, good choice of food in bar and reasonably priced restaurant; idyllic garden with country views; bedrooms *(Bruce Bird)*

☆ Boarshead, E Sus [Eridge Rd, just off A26 bypass; TQ5332], *Boars Head*: Unspoilt cosy old dim-lit stone-floored place next to pleasant farmyard, welcoming log fire, simple good value food, well kept ales, low 16th-c beams; very peaceful weekday lunchtimes (piped music turned down then if asked) *(Mrs R D Knight, Andrew Hamilton, Peter Coward, BB)*

Bodiam E Sus [TQ7825], *Castle*: Given its position so near the castle, useful that this has been reopened after refurbishment; neat and clean, with good usual bar food, summer barbecues, Shepherd Neame ales, friendly young New Zealand licensees *(A M Pickup)*

Bognor Regis W Sus [56 London Rd; SZ9399], *Alex*: Friendly, warm, cosy and clean, good value generous food inc hot pork in home-baked bread (Sat) and Sun lunch, Courage-related and King & Barnes ales, huge mug and jug collection *(Jan and Colin Roe, John and Chris Simpson)*

Bolney W Sus [The Street; TQ2623], *Eight Bells*: Friendly, clean and comfortable, with two Harveys beers and Flowers Original, attentive staff, promptly served food *(S W Whytehead, CL, JL)*

☆ Bosham W Sus [High St; SU8003], *Anchor Bleu*: Lovely sea and boat views from low-beamed waterside pub, in attractive village; well kept Courage-related beers, log-effect gas fire, decent fresh if pricey buffet (some dishes sell out early), seats outside; very popular with tourists, service can take a while in summer *(Jill Franklin, John Sanders, Peter and Audrey Dowsett, MCG, Colin and Ann Hunt, LYM)*

Bramber W Sus [TQ1710], *Bramber Castle*: Very efficient helpful staff, pleasant and roomy old-fashioned quiet lounge, wide choice of reasonably priced food, pretty back garden *(Andrew Rogers, Amanda Milsom, Hugh MacLean)*

☆ Brighton E Sus [15 Black Lion St; TQ3105], *Cricketers*: Bustling and atmospheric down-to-earth town pub with Victorian furnishings and lots of bric-a-brac – even a stuffed bear; usual well priced bar food inc vegetarian and fresh veg (all day Weds-Sat, not Sun or Mon evening), well kept Courage Directors, Morlands Old Speckled Hen and Youngs Special tapped from the cask, efficient service, restaurant (where children allowed), courtyard bar; open all day, piped music may be loud *(Linda and Brian Davis, Dr Keith Clements, John and Mavis Wright, Ann and Colin Hunt, M L and G Clarke, JM, PM, Jenny and Roger Huggins, Mrs C A Blake, Val Stevenson, Tony Hobden, LYM)*

Brighton [The Lanes], *Bath Arms*: Several tall rooms with wood panelling and old fireplaces, lots of old photographs and cartoon prints, good value basic bar food, decent beer and coffee *(Neil and Anita Christopher)*; [Black Lion St], *Black Lion*: Big open-plan pub with sofas, prints, cheap Boddingtons and Flowers Original, video juke box, fruit machine; tables outside *(Jenny and Roger Huggins)*; [10 New Rd, off North St], *Colonnade*: Vibrant theatrical atmosphere, velvet, mirrors, posters and lots of signed photographs, good friendly service even when very busy, some snacks esp salt beef sandwiches, Boddingtons, Flowers and Harveys (early-evening weekday happy hour), tiny front terrace; next to Theatre Royal, they take interval orders *(Ian Phillips, Dr Keith Clements, Val Stevenson)*; [County Oak Ave, Hollingbury; TQ3108], *County Oak*: Recently refurbished, with limited choice of cheap food, Whitbreads-related ales, children welcome *(Alec and Marie Lewery)*; [Surrey St], *Evening Star*: Very popular for up to a dozen well kept interesting changing ales inc two brewed here; bare boards, simple furnishings, friendly service; no food Sun *(Bruce Bird, David Holloway, Richard Houghton)*; [Union St, The Lanes], *Font & Firkin*: Clever church refurbishment (still has pulpit and bell pulls, alongside Sunday comedians and other live entertainment; mezzanine floor, pleasant service, good choice of real ales inc some brewed here, bar food inc good value Sun roasts *(Richard Houghton, Richard Beatty)*; [13 Marlborough Pl], *King & Queen*: Medieval-style lofty main hall with well kept Theakstons Best and XB from long bar, generous good value food, friendly service, pool table, flagstoned courtyard; good free jazz most evenings (when parking tends to be difficult) and Sun lunchtime; open all day Sun, good roasts *(Ann and Colin Hunt, LYM)*; [Market St, Lanes], *Pump House*: Friendly, lively and relaxed, light and airy but cosy, with very mixed age groups, good choice of wines *(John Wooll, Tony Hobden)*; [Guildford Rd], *Sussex Yeoman*: Friendly town pub with eight or so real ales, several dozen different sausages inc six vegetarian *(David Dale, Adrian and Gilly Heft)*

☆ Broad Oak E Sus [A28/B2089 – the one N of Brede; TQ8220], *Rainbow Trout*: Wide range of well cooked food esp fish served by pleasant waitresses in attractive bustling old bar and big adjacent restaurant extension; gets very crowded but plenty of room for drinkers, with wide range of beers, wines and spirits *(J H Bell, C H and P Stride)*

Burwash Weald E Sus [A265 two miles W of Burwash; TQ6624], *Wheel*: A very useful stop – good home cooking all day in well kept open-plan pub with big log fire, well kept Harveys and other ales, friendly and obliging service; tables in back garden under apple trees, along with two goats, hens and kittens *(Jason Caulkin, BB)*

Bury W Sus [off A29 Pulborough—Arundel – OS Sheet 197 map ref 014132; TQ0113], *Black Dog & Duck*: Rustic unpretentious country pub tucked away among thatched cottages, tiny beamed front snug with open fire, walkers welcome in flagstoned public bar, tables out on lawn, good fresh plentiful food in bars and restaurant, particularly well kept King & Barnes, bar billiards, welcoming staff; small pleasant garden with play area; good walking country *(LM)*

Chailey E Sus [A275 9 miles N of Lewes; TQ3919], *Five Bells*: Well run, with good mix of locals, visitors and families, interesting changing choice of home-made food all day inc vegetarian, big log fire, Whitbreads-related ales, good service; picnic tables in big garden with play area *(A H Denman, JEB, Steve Goodchild)*; [South St (A275)], *Horns Lodge*: Simple and unpretentious but pleasant and welcoming, enjoyable food *(Mrs R D Knight)*

Chalvington E Sus [signed off A27 and A22, then follow Golden Cross rd; TQ5209], *Yew Tree*: Isolated proper country pub, low beams, stripped bricks and flagstones, inglenook fireplace, simple good bar food, well kept Harveys and Fremlins; popular with young people Fri and Sat evenings; attractive little walled terrace, and extensive grounds inc own cricket pitch *(Mavis and John Wright, BB)*

Charlton W Sus [off A286 Chichester—Midhurst; SU8812], *Fox*: Cosy old rooms with low beams, no-smoking family extension and restaurant, attractive sheltered garden with Downs views, bar food, Ballards Best, Gales HSB and several S & N ales *(PC, R T and J C Moggridge, Ann and Colin Hunt, LYM)*

Chelwood Gate E Sus [A275; TQ4129], *Red Lion*: Good quickly served bar food, well kept King & Barnes and Courage-related ales, green plush furnishings, small coal fire, dining room; delightful big sheltered garden with well spaced tables; children welcome *(Mavis and John Wright, BB)*

Chichester W Sus [Little London; SU8605], *Jacksons Cellar*: Interesting conversion of three curved cellars, well kept ales served cool from the barrel such as Harveys Armada, Hop Back Summer Lightning, Thwaites and guests such as Brewery on Sea Spinnaker and Kelham Island, also Belgian beers; good food often cooked with beer, piped music; open all day, cl Sun *(Bruce Bird)*

☆ **Chilgrove** W Sus [just off B2141 Petersfield—Chichester; SU8214], *White Horse*: More smart restaurant than pub, lunches cheaper than evening, good food in bar too; remarkable list of outstanding wines, welcoming landlord; idyllic downland setting with small flower-filled terrace and big pretty garden *(Dr Brian Hamilton, MCG)*

☆ **nr Chilgrove** [Hooksway; off B2141 Petersfield—Chichester, signed Hooksway down steep track; SU8116], *Royal Oak*: Smartly simple country tavern in very peaceful spot, beams, brick floors, country-kitchen furnishings, huge log fires; home-made standard food inc vegetarian, several well kept ales, games, attractive seats outside; provision for children, has been cl winter Mons *(Keith Stevens, Hugh MacLean, Jill Geser, LYM)*

☆ **Cocking** W Sus [A286 S of Midhurst; SU8717], *Blue Bell*: Welcoming young chef/patron doing tempting choice of beautifully presented home-made food from ample filled baked potatoes and ploughman's to Sun roasts inc fresh veg and children's helpings, in neatly kept unspoilt country local just off South Downs Way; well kept Boddingtons and other ales; bedrooms *(Mrs Nora Kingbourn, Tom and Rosemary Hall)*

Colemans Hatch E Sus [signed off B2026, or off B2110 opp church; TQ4533], *Hatch*: Basic but welcoming rustic pub with Ashdown Forest views from tables on bluff of grass by quiet lane; good straighforward lunches, well kept Harveys, pub games *(John Davis, LYM)*

☆ **Compton** W Sus [SU7714], *Coach & Horses*: Friendly and spotless, with well kept Fullers ESB, King & Barnes and Gales HSB and Mild, traditional walkers' bar, plusher beamed lounge, good range of food in bars and restaurant; Flemish landlady *(Colin and Ann Hunt, T Roger Lamble, Michael Grigg)*

Coolham W Sus [TQ1423], *Selsey Arms*: Friendly and unspoilt traditional local, open fires, good food, well kept King & Barnes and guest ales, charming garden behind *(Peter Lewis)*

☆ **nr Coolham** [Dragons Green], *George & Dragon*: Charming small and ancient pub with good straightforward food inc exceptional handcut chips, well kept King & Barnes Festive and Broadsword, big inglenook, unusually low beams, pub games; children in eating areas; well spaced tables out in big orchard garden *(Colin Laffan, Winifrede Morrison, LYM)*

Cootham W Sus [TQ0714], *Crown*: Recently refurbished, with conservatory, welcoming staff, good choice of changing food – helpful with special diets *(Miss D Hobbs)*

☆ **Couslewood** E Sus [TQ6533], *Old Vine*: Smooth transfer to new owners in attractive dining pub with lots of old timbers and beams, wide range of generously served modestly priced decent food (jazz suppers Mon), good house wine, four well kept ales; rustic pretty restaurant on right, rather more pubby brick-floored area with woodburner by bar, a few tables out behind *(Colin and Joyce Laffan, Stephen Goodchild, F Barwell, BB)*

Cowfold W Sus [TQ2122], *Hare & Hounds*: Pleasant part-flagstoned pub with Adnams, Harveys and Wadworths, amiable landlord, attractive food *(Comus Elliott)*

Crawley W Sus [Broadwalk; TQ2636], *Hogs Head*: Interesting 17th-c former gaol, good at lunchtime (and for breakfast) with inexpensive wholesome food inc filled baps, good range of well kept ales inc Marstons Pedigree – three-pint jugs for the price of four pints *(John Lawrence, Ian Phillips)*; [High St], *Jubilee Oak*: Wetherspoons pub with good range of food and beer, excellent prices, big no-smoking area *(Alec and Marie Lewery)*;

[Horsham Rd, outside], *Swan*: Country pub with quiet garden, good sandwiches, real ales *(John Lawrence)*

Crowborough E Sus [Beacon Rd (A26); TQ5130], *Blue Anchor*: Taken over by Shepherd Neame, with well kept Bitter, Bishops Finger and Spitfire, good food; refurbishment of pub and sizeable garden under way *(Colin Laffan)*; [Lye Green, Groombridge Rd], *Half Moon*: Pretty and cottagey recently refurbished country pub on edge of Ashdown Forest, tables out in front and in extensive back area with play area, boules and room for caravans (live bands out here some summer evenings, maybe hot air balloons); French chef doing impressive food (not cheap) inc Sun lunch, wider range evenings, Flowers IPA, Harveys, Wadworths 6X and a guest such as Brakspears, good service, friendly labrador *(Colin Laffan, Andrea Woods)*; [Crowborough Hill], *White Hart*: Large Edwardian pub doing well under new young owners, food in comfortable bar and good-sized dining room, real ales, English wines; play area *(Colin Laffan)*

Dallington E Sus [Woods Corner, B2096 E; TQ6619], *Swan*: Country local with good log fires in both traditional front bars, far views from no-smoking back eating room, well kept Harveys and other ales, decent food; tables in back garden with boules *(Doug Edworthy, Tarquin Bell, LYM)*

☆ Danehill E Sus [School Lane, Chelwood Common; off A275; TQ4128], *Coach & Horses*: Consistently good home-cooked food inc vegetarian, well kept Harveys, Greene King and guest beers, hard-working licensees, good atmosphere, pews in bar, decent house wine; ex-stables dining extension, neat gardens *(Ron Gentry)*

☆ Ditchling E Sus [B2112/B2116; TQ3215], *Bull*: Interesting beamed 14th-c inn with attractive antique furnishings in civilised main bar, old pictures, inglenook fireplace, usual bar food inc vegetarian dishes, well kept Whitbreads-related ales, good choice of malt whiskies, comfortable family room, no-smoking restaurant, fairly good wheelchair access; picnic tables in good-sized pretty garden and on suntrap terrace, comfortable bedrooms, charming old village just below downs *(Recommended by R J Walden, Eddie Edwards, J Sheldon, M L and G Clarke, Jane Bailey, Peter Burton, LYM)*

☆ Ditchling [West St], *White Horse*: Popular local, very busy weekends, with well kept Harveys and changing guest beers, unpretentious food from sandwiches up, quick service, log fire, bar billiards, shove-ha'penny etc, unobtrusive piped jazz, live alternate Thurs/Fri *(JM, PM, J Sheldon, Ian and Colin Roe, John Laws)*

Donnington W Sus [Selsey Rd (B2201); SU8502], *Selsey Tram*: Brewers Fayre pub worth noting for big children's area inside and out – slides, swings, race track, bouncy castle *(Alec and Marie Lewery)*

Duncton W Sus [SU9617], *Barbers*: Good solid traditional refurbishment, good food,

well kept beer; shame about the piped pop music *(Peter Lewis)*

☆ Easebourne W Sus [SU8922], *Olde White Horse*: Cosy local with promptly served generous food inc fresh veg, good friendly service, Greene King IPA and Abbot, small log fire, traditional games in tap room, tables on back lawn and in courtyard *(R A Buckler, G C Hackemer, Mr and Mrs R O Gibson, LYM)*

East Ashling W Sus [SU8207], *Horse & Groom*: Good popular food and friendly service in pleasantly refurbished pub; some tables outside *(Colin and Ann Hunt, T Roger Lamble, Keith Stevens)*

East Chiltington E Sus [Chapel Lane, 2 miles N of B2116; TQ3715], *Jolly Sportsman*: Basic pub nice in summer for its lovely garden with rustic furniture, play area and South Downs views; nice spot next to small nursery run by landlord's father-in-law, good walks; well kept King & Barnes, John Smiths and Wadworths 6X, bar food, pool room *(John Beeken, Ron Gentry)*

East Dean W Sus [signed off A286 and A285 N of Chichester; SU9012], *Hurdlemakers*: Charmingly placed by peaceful green of quiet village, with rustic seats and swing in pretty walled garden; great variety of good value food, friendly staff, pleasant atmosphere and staff; handy for South Downs Way (and Goodwood), children welcome *(P Gillbe, LYM)*

☆ Eastbourne E Sus [The Goffs, Old Town; TV6199], *Lamb*: Two main heavily beamed traditional bars off pretty Tudor pub's central servery, spotless antique furnishings, good inglenook log fire, well kept Harveys Best, Armada and Old, friendly polite service, well organised food bar, upstairs dining room (Sun lunch), no music or machines; dogs seem welcome, children allowed in very modernised side room; by ornate church away from seafront; popular with students evenings *(E B Davies, Beryl and Bill Farmer, Dave Braisted)*

☆ Eastbourne [Holywell Rd, Meads; just off front below approach from Beachy Head], *Pilot*: Lively, comfortable and friendly, prompt food inc good crab salad in season, pleasant landlady, well kept real ales, good ship photographs; garden *(Keith Stevens, E D Bailey)*

Eastbourne [Grange Rd], *New Inn*: Recently refurbished, pleasant helpful staff, appetising reasonably priced food, Bass, Courage Directors, Harveys, John Smiths and a guest such as Tolly; restaurant *(E Robinson, Stephen Gilbert)*

Ewhurst Green E Sus [TQ7925], *White Dog*: Extensive and attractive partly 17th-c village pub in fine spot above Bodiam Castle with tables in big garden making the most of the view, interesting choice of food, well kept ales inc Harveys, decent wines; bedrooms *(D Bardrick, P J Howell, Roger Crowther, LYM)*

Faygate W Sus [TQ2134], *Cherry Tree*: Lovely old place, pity about the dual carriageway nearby; obliging landlord, King & Barnes real ales, nice atmosphere, reasonable food *(Comus Elliott)*

Felpham W Sus [just S of A259 E of Bognor;

SZ9599], *George*: Glorious garden with pond, lovely oak-beam decor, friendly staff, good food inc lots of puddings in separate dining room *(Brian Hutton)*

☆ Fernhurst W Sus [The Green, off A286 beyond church; SU9028], *Red Lion*: Heavy-beamed old pub tucked quietly away by green nr church, good reasonably priced food inc interesting specials, attractive layout and furnishings, friendly quick service, several well kept ales, no-smoking area, good relaxed atmosphere; children welcome, pretty garden *(G C Hackemer, J Sheldon, Hugh MacLean, BB)*

☆ Findon W Sus [off A24 N of Worthing; TQ1208], *Gun*: Civilised low-beamed village pub doing well under friendly new licensees, good range of food from generous ploughman's up, quick service, well kept Whitbreads-related ales; attractive sheltered lawn, pretty village in horse-training country below Cissbury Ring; busy weekends *(PGP, J C Brittain-Long, BB)*

☆ Findon [High St], *Village House*: Good food from home-made soup to fish and local game in welcoming converted 16th-c coach house, oak tables, lots of racing silks and pictures, big open fire, changing well kept beers, first-class service, restaurant popular for Sun lunch, small attractive walled garden; bedrooms *(Ron Gentry)*

Fishbourne W Sus [just off A27 Chichester—Emsworth; SU8404], *Bulls Head*: Welcoming landlord, full range of Gales ales kept well, with guests such as Fullers London Pride and Youngs Special; good choice of bar food (not Sun evening), log fires, no-smoking area, children's area, skittle alley, boules pitch, restaurant *(Bruce Bird, J A Snell, Keith Stevens)*

☆ Fittleworth W Sus [Lower St (B2138); TQ0118], *Swan*: Prettily placed 15th-c inn with big inglenook log fire in friendly and comfortable lounge, good bar food with unusual specials and good Sun lunch in attractive panelled side room with landscapes by Constable's deservedly less-known brother George, well kept Boddingtons; piped music, games inc pool in public bar; well spaced tables on big sheltered back lawn, good walks nearby; open all day Thurs-Sat, children in eating area; good value well equipped bedrooms *(Winifrede D Morrison, D Hunter, LYM)*

Forest Row E Sus [TQ4235], *Brambletye*: Long bar at side of hotel with drinks one end, good value self-service food buffet the other, well kept Harveys; restaurant, children welcome; bedrooms *(LM)*

Framfield E Sus [B2012 E of Uckfield; TQ5020], *Hare & Hounds*: Unpretentious but comfortable and pleasant, with good home-cooked food, good range of real ales, helpful and friendly landlord and staff; no music *(Mrs R D Knight and others)*

Frant E Sus [A267 S of Tunbridge Wells; TQ5835], *Abergavenny Arms*: Sprawling but cosy pub dating from 15th c, reasonably priced popular wholesome food (can be a wait at peak times), up to a dozen changing well

kept ales tapped from casks in unusual climate-controlled glass-fronted chamber, friendly helpful staff; log fire, bar billiards, children welcome; piped music *(Simon Gardner, Gwen and Peter Andrews)*

Funtington W Sus [SU7908], *Fox & Hounds*: Extensively refurbished beamed pub with Courage-related ales, farm cider, real ginger beer, reasonably priced wines, good coffee, huge log fire, no music, vast choice of food inc good roasts, comfortable and attractive dining extension, welcoming service *(Viv Middlebrook, MCG)*

☆ Graffham W Sus [SU9217], *White Horse*: Pleasant family pub with good South Downs views from conservatory, small dining room, terrace and big garden; good wide choice of well served food, friendly service, a welcome for walkers *(Sylvia and Lionel Kopelowitz, David Dimock)*

Graffham, *Foresters Arms*: Smallish traditional two-bar pub, peaceful midweek lunchtime, may be crowded weekends, with good reasonably priced food, well kept Gales HSB, big log fire, no music, walkers welcome; pretty restaurant (can be fully booked) *(R D Knight, Martin and Karen Wake)*

Hadlow Down E Sus [A272 E of Uckfield; TQ5324], *New Inn*: Odd 1950s feel in roadside bar with junked machinery outside, snacks on shelves, Harveys beers inc Mild, pool room, very friendly family with plenty of stories to tell; houses the post office *(Tom McLean, Roger Huggins, Jason Caulkin)*

Hailsham E Sus [South Rd; TQ5909], *Kings Head*: Friendly local with well kept beer, Sun quiz night; welcoming to strangers *(Adrian and Gilly Heft)*

☆ Halnaker W Sus [A285 Chichester—Petworth; SU9008], *Anglesey Arms*: Quickly cooked genuine food with occasional interesting Spanish specialities in bright welcoming bar with traditional games, well kept King & Barnes and Tetleys-related ales, good wines (again inc direct Spanish imports); simple but smart candlelit dining room with stripped pine and flagstones (children allowed), tables in garden *(T Roger Lamble, Hugh MacLean, Ron Shelton, John H L Davies, Betty Weaver, LYM)*

Hammerpot W Sus [A27 4 miles W of Worthing; TQ0605], *Woodmans Arms*: Welcoming new landlady in low-beamed 16th-c pub with interesting prints, horsey bric-a-brac, well kept Gales HSB and a guest such as Marstons Pedigree, good bar food; piped music (except in no-smoking snug), seats in pleasant garden *(Bruce Bird)*

Hartfield E Sus [Gallipot St; B2110 towards Forest Row; TQ4735], *Gallipot*: Comfortable L-shaped bar with charming new landlady, a couple of well kept ales, wide range of home-cooked food (may be a wait), no music or machines, log fire, restaurant; can be smoky; on edge of attractively set village, good walks nearby *(Colin and Joyce Laffan)*; [A264], *Haywaggon*: Spacious and welcoming beamed pub, very popular with OAPs lunchtime for reliable low-priced simple bar food (profuse

use of herbs) in attractive dining room (doubles as evening restaurant), well kept ale, prompt friendly long-serving staff *(Margaret and Nigel Dennis, Colin Laffan)*

☆ Hastings E Sus [14 High St, Old Town; TQ8109], *First In Last Out*: Good reasonably priced beers brewed here, farm cider, friendly landlord, chatty atmosphere, attractive booths formed by pews, no games or juke box; interesting simple lunchtime food, free Sun cockles, central log fire *(Chris Fluck, Christopher Turner, Friedolf Joetten)*

Henfield W Sus [A281; TQ2116], *White Hart*: 16th-c village pub with tools hanging from low beams, horsebrasses, paintings, prints and photographs, log fire, Flowers Original and other ales, large popular dining area with good straightforward food and good friendly service, tables on terrace and in garden *(G W and I L Edwards, Brian and Jenny Seller)*

☆ Hermitage W Sus [36 Main Rd (A259); SU7505], *Sussex Brewery*: Cosy atmosphere and good log fires in small friendly pub done out with bare bricks, boards and flagstones; well kept Archers Golden, Badger Best, Tanglefoot and Hard Tackle, Charles Wells Bombardier, Wadworths 6X and an ale brewed for them, good value simple food from sandwiches up inc masses of speciality sausages, neat back restaurant up a few steps, no machines or piped music, small garden; can get very busy, open all day Sat *(Ann and Colin Hunt, P K Broomhead)*

Holtye E Sus [A264 East Grinstead—Tunbridge Wells; TQ4539], *White Horse*: Unpretentiously refurbished old village pub with friendly and helpful young staff, well kept ales inc Brakspears, popular carvery restaurant with illuminated aquarium set into floor; good facilities for the disabled; bedrooms *(Mrs R D Knight)*

☆ Hooe E Sus [A259 E of Pevensey; TQ6809], *Lamb*: Prettily placed dining pub, extensively refurbished with lots of stripped brick and flintwork, one snug area around huge log fire and lots of other seats, very wide choice of generous popular food from well filled sandwiches up, well kept Harveys, quick friendly service *(G Washington, Mr and Mrs Jones)*

Horsham W Sus [Guildford Rd, Bishopric; TQ1730], *Kings Arms*: Comfortable pub with villagey atmosphere, popular with workers from nearby King & Barnes brewery – their beers, good food *(Richard Lewis)*; [29 Carfax], *Stout House*: Small friendly unpretentious local with well kept King & Barnes Festive, Sussex and Broadwood, good lunchtime rolls; cl Tues evening *(Richard Lewis, Mark Chitty)*

☆ Houghton W Sus [B2139; TQ0111], *George & Dragon*: Fine old timbered pub with civilised rambling heavy-beamed bar, nice comfortable mix of furnishings inc some antiques, decent straightforward food inc good puddings, well kept Courage Directors, Tetleys, a beer brewed locally for the pub and a guest ale, log fire, efficient staff, no-smoking room, charming garden with pretty views;

children (and maybe dogs) welcome *(Margaret and Nigel Dennis, John Fahy, Giles Francis, Clive Gilbert, R M Macnaughton, John Beeken, G R Sunderland, LYM)*

Icklesham E Sus [TQ8816], *Oast House*: Friendly 17th-c pub, good range of popular straightforward food, well kept Adnams and Youngs, free Sun seafood nibbles, silk flower arrangements (for sale); attractive garden *(J Baker, Mick and Mel Smith)*

Isfield E Sus [Rose Hill (A26); TQ4516], *Halfway House*: Clean, welcoming and well polished, with well kept Harveys Bitter and Old, good reasonably priced food; decent service *(Adrian and Gilly Heft)*

Kingsfold W Sus [A24 Dorking—Horsham, nr A29 junction; TQ1636], *Dog & Duck*: Comfortable old country pub, well kept King & Barnes and other ales, good value nicely presented food (not after 2 lunchtime) inc popular lunches *(DWAJ, Dave Irving, Alan Whiting)*

☆ Lambs Green W Sus [TQ2136], *Lamb*: Quaint old beamed pub well refurbished to give more space, friendly helpful staff, well kept beers such as Wadworths 6X and Youngs, good varied changing food, good value considering helping size, restaurant; nice log fire *(Steve Goodchild, Doreen and Brian Hardham, LYM)*

Lavant W Sus [Lavant Rd (A286); SU8508], *Earl of March*: Spacious village pub with welcoming and helpful staff, good range of well kept ales such as Ballards Best and Ringwood Fortyniner, farm cider, generous home-cooked food inc vegetarian *(Bruce Bird)*

☆ Lewes E Sus [Castle Ditch Lane/Mount Pl; TQ4110], *Lewes Arms*: Charming unpretentious street-corner local below castle mound, cosy front lounge and two larger rooms (one with pool), particularly well kept Harveys, newspapers and tatty old books, no music – great place for conversation; comically small garden, so people migrate to pavement and street; basic lunchtime food *(Tim Locke, Alan Skull, Richard Gibbs)*

☆ Lewes [22 Malling St], *Dorset Arms*: Good bar food esp fresh fish Fri lunchtime in popular, civilised and friendly 17th-c pub with well kept Harveys, well equipped family room, restaurant, outside terraces; comfortable bedrooms *(Alan Skull, Andrew Partington)*

☆ Lindfield W Sus [98 High St (B2028); TQ3425], *Bent Arms*: Good bar food inc spit-roasted beef (lunchtime Mon, Tues, Fri, Sat) turned by model steam-engine, other interesting bric-a-brac, antique and art deco furnishings and stained glass; good choice of well kept ales, farm cider, prompt friendly service, reasonable prices; attractive garden, children in restaurant and eating area; bedrooms *(Basil Minson, LYM)*

Litlington E Sus [between A27 Lewes—Polegate and A259 E of Seaford; TQ5201], *Plough & Harrow*: Cosy beamed front bar in attractively extended flint local, six well kept changing real ales, decent wines by the glass; good home cooking (may be a long wait at busy times), dining area done up as railway dining car (children allowed here); back lawn with children's bar, aviary and pretty views; live music Fri *(Colin Laffan, LYM)*

Little Common E Sus [TQ7108], *Wheatsheaf*: Doing well under present regime, with wide choice of lunchtime food (has had free starter with specials), Courage Directors and Harveys, garden with fish pond, slide, swings and roundabout; children very welcome in restaurant *(Alec and Marie Lewery)*

☆ **Littlehampton** W Sus [Wharf Rd; westwards towards Chichester, opp rly stn; TQ0202], *Arun View*: Comfortable and attractive 18th-c inn right on harbour with river directly below windows, Whitbreads-related ales, wide choice of reasonably priced decent bar food, restaurant (wise to book), flower-filled terrace; summer barbecues evenings and weekends; bedrooms *(Ruth and Alan Cooper)*

Littleworth W Sus [signed off A272 southbound, W of Cowfold; TQ1920], *Windmill*: Small King & Barnes local with open fires in compact but cosy lounge and memorably rustic public bar decorated with lots of farm tools, local photographs and posters; standard bar food (not Sun eve), well kept ales, friendly staff; darts, dominoes, cards and bar billiards *(Pete Baker)*

☆ **Lodsworth** W Sus [SU9223], *Hollist Arms*: Relaxed welcoming atmosphere in two small cosy bars and big cheerful dining room, good value food, well kept Ballards and Arundel guest beer, two log fires, darts, shove ha'penny etc; whole lamb barbecues *(Howard West, Anne Watson)*

Loxwood W Sus [B2133; TQ0431], *Onslow Arms*: Recently extensively smartened up, with lively young staff, well kept full King & Barnes range, good house wines, big helpings of good value simple food, picnic tables in garden sloping to river and nearby canal under restoration *(Stephen Goodchild, Mike Davies)*

Maplehurst W Sus [TQ1924], *White Horse*: Quiet friendly family-run beamed country local with at least six real ales inc Harveys, King & Barnes and far-flung guest beers; pub cat *(Paul Comerford, Caroline Lewis)*

Mayfield E Sus [A267 S; TQ5524], *Five Ashes*: Old beamed pub with stocks in back garden, pleasant service, good food – a useful stop *(A M Pring)*

Midhurst W Sus [North St; SU8821], *Angel*: Recently smartly refurbished 16th-c coaching inn with good if not cheap bar food, splendid brasserie and dining room, pleasant efficient service, well kept beer; comfortable bedrooms *(Colin Laffan)*; [opp Spread Eagle], *Bricklayers Arms*: Good reasonably priced home-cooked food inc good value Sun roast, well kept Greene King IPA and Abbot, two cosy bars, sturdy old oak furniture, 17th-c beams, old photographs and bric-a-brac *(G W and I L Edwards)*

Milland W Sus [Portsmouth Rd (old A3); SU8328], *Black Fox*: Three or four well kept ales, tasty good value food esp steaks and fish; big garden with play area *(Peter Jowitt)*

☆ **Milton Street** E Sus [off A27 Polegate—Lewes, ¼ mile E of Alfriston roundabout; TQ5304],

Sussex Ox: Attractive family country pub beautifully placed below downs, big lawn and marvellous play area; good atmosphere inside, well kept Harveys and a guest such as Greene King Abbot, reliable food inc good puddings, pleasantly simple country furniture, brick floor, woodburner, one lively and one quieter family room; can camp in nearby field, lots of good walks, busy weekends *(Andrew Partington, Nick Dunnell, Jane Talbot, Jonathan Fry, LYM)*

Newick E Sus [A272 Uckfield—Haywards Heath; TQ4121], *Bull*: Welcoming, comfortable and peaceful for a midweek lunch, lots of beams and character, reasonable choice of moderately priced food esp fresh Newhaven fish quickly served in sizeable eating area, well kept mainly Courage-related ales; no music *(Alan Kilpatrick, Colin Laffan, Mrs R D Knight)*

Nutbourne W Sus [the one nr Pulborough; TQ0718], *Rising Sun*: Friendly service, Badger and other ales such as Fullers London Pride, generous good value food; children and dogs allowed, some live music; tables on small back terrace under apple tree *(LM, Mary Kitcher)*

Nyetimber W Sus [Pagham Rd; SZ8998], *Lamb*: Warm, welcoming pub beautifully kept by Portugese couple, good value food inc fresh seafood in bar and restaurant (must book Sat), good range of beers, decent wines *(M Judd, P J Howell)*

☆ **Pagham** W Sus [Nyetimber Lane; SZ8897], *Lion*: Cosy 15th-c pub with two bars, wooden seating, uneven flooring, low beams, good value imaginatively prepared food, well kept Ringwood beers and good malt whiskies, cheerful service, small restaurant, big terrace; very popular in summer *(Ian and Colin Roe, David and Rebecca Killick, Mark Parsons)*

Pease Pottage W Sus [by M23 junction 11; TQ2533], *James King*: Welcoming and genuine, with good log fire, decent bar food, friendly willing service, well kept ale *(J S Rutter, BB)*

☆ **Pett** E Sus [TQ8714], *Two Sawyers*: Friendly old country pub with character main bar, small public bar, back snug, small oak-beamed back restaurant where children allowed; well kept ales inc two from neighbouring Olde Forge microbrewery, log fires, welcoming staff, good choice of food; tables in big relaxing garden with swings and boules pitch; bedrooms *(Richard Houghton, M P Evans, D B Stanley)*

Petworth W Sus [Coultershaw Bridge, just off A285 1½ miles towards Chichester; SU9719], *Badger & Honeyjar*: Victorian pub in idyllic riverside setting, cottagey feel, attentive staff, good choice of music and of beers, eclectic choice of tempting food; tables outside *(R Wilson)*; [North St], *Stonemasons*: Well refurbished under friendly newish owners, good food, pubby bar, traditional dining area, pleasant garden; bedrooms *(Richard J Raeon, Karen Barnes)*; [A283 towards Pulborough], *Welldiggers*: Stylishly simple low-ceilinged stripped stone dining pub with very friendly atmosphere, well kept Ballards and Youngs, decent wines, no music or machines; plenty of tables on attractive lawns and terraces, lovely views (*G C Hackemer, BB*)

☆ **Plumpton** E Sus [Ditchling Rd (B2116); TQ3613], *Half Moon*: Picturesque and cosy, with wide choice of reasonably priced food (not Sun evening) inc all sorts of quiches, well kept King & Barnes, John Smiths and Wadworths 6X, prompt friendly service, log fire, interesting painting of over 100 regulars; well behaved children welcome, evening restaurant, rustic seats in big garden with downs view, big play house and two retired tractors (*Alec and Marie Lewery, John Beeken*)

Poundgate E Sus [A26 Crowborough—Uckfield; TQ4928], *Crow & Gate*: Well refurbished, with pleasantly busy beamed bar, popular new back dining extension, wide choice of reasonably priced food, good value family Sun lunches, well kept Flowers Original and Ruddles County, efficient service, restaurant; children welcome, tables outside, play area (*Colin and Joyce Laffan*)

Poynings W Sus [TQ2612], *Royal Oak*: Varied popular bar food inc vegetarian and good fish, well kept Courage-related ales and a guest such as Harveys, cosy but plenty of room, good staff, attractive side garden – very popular in summer (*Winifrede D Morrison*)

Rake W Sus [Portsmouth Rd (A3 S of Liphook); SU8027], *Sun*: Comfortable dining pub with wide choice of generous home-made food inc good Sun lunches, quick friendly service, log fires, Bass, Gales BBB and HSB (*G C Hackemer, Gentian Walls*)

☆ **Ringmer** E Sus [Old Uckfield Rd; blocked-off rd off A26 N of village turn-off; TQ4412], *Cock*: Heavily beamed country pub with welcoming landlord, good inglenook log fire, piped music, modernised no-smoking lounge, restaurant, well kept Greene King Abbot and Harveys Best and Mild, wide range of good food, piped music, seats out on good terrace and in attractive fairy-lit garden; children allowed in overflow eating area (*John and Mavis Wright, Colin and Joyce Laffan, John Beeken, LYM*)

☆ nr **Ringmer** [outside village; A26 Lewes—Uckfield, S of Isfield turnoff], *Stewards Enquiry*: Good varied food inc good vegetarian and reasonably priced Sun roasts in tastefully refurbished olde-worlde beamed pub; good service, well kept Harveys, children welcome; some outside tables, play area (*Alec Lewery, Tony and Wendy Hobden, Alan Skull*)

☆ **Ripe** E Sus [signed off A22 Uckfield—Hailsham, or off A27 Lewes—Polegate via Chalvington; TQ5010], *Lamb*: Interestingly furnished snug little rooms around central servery, attractive antique prints and pictures, nostalgic song-sheet covers, Victorian pin-ups in gents'; good generous home-made food inc children's and Sun roast, well kept Courage-related ales and a guest such as Harveys, several open fires, friendly service; pub games ancient and modern, pleasant sheltered back garden with play area and barbecues (*Adrian and Gilly Heft, Tony and Wendy Hobden, LYM*)

Rogate W Sus [SU8023], *Wyndham Arms*: Welcoming village local with well kept Ballards, King & Barnes and Ringwood ales tapped from the cask, wide range of good home-cooked food inc interesting specials, polite staff; dogs and well behaved children welcome (*J O Jonkler, Keith Stevens, Mrs L C Robertson, M B Griffith*)

Rotherfield E Sus [TQ5529], *George*: Attractive village pub with hanging baskets and window boxes, nice old bars, well kept ales, home-cooked food at well spaced tables, friendly staff; pool table in one bar (*Colin Laffan*)

☆ **Rushlake Green** E Sus [signed off B2096; TQ6218], *Horse & Groom*: Done-up country pub overlooking quiet village green, beams and timbers, big log fire, friendly new landlord really trying hard with the food, welcoming atmosphere, well kept Harveys, tables on front lawn (*S N Robieson, Jason Caulkin, LYM*)

☆ **Rusper** W Sus [signed from A24 and A264 N and NE of Horsham; TQ2037], *Plough*: Padded very low beams, panelling and big inglenook, good value straightforward food, good range of well kept ales, lovely log fire, bar billiards and darts in raftered room upstairs; fountain in back garden, pretty front terrace, occasional live music; children welcome (*DWAJ, Nick Davy, G W and I L Edwards, LYM*)

☆ **Rye** E Sus [Gun Gdn, off A259; TQ9220], *Ypres Castle*: Pronounced WWI-style, as Wipers, basic and friendly, in fine setting up towards the tower, with great view, big lawn; good value filled baguettes and wide choice of good home cooking esp fish, well kept changing ales such as Hook Norton and Youngs Special, old yachting magazines, local event posters, piped music; open all day in season (*Bruce Bird, R T and J C Moggridge, John T Ames*)

Rye, *Hope & Anchor*: Agreeable hotel, bar snacks not cheap but good value meals esp fresh fish in roomy and tasteful dining room, attentive landlady, well kept Harveys Best; bedrooms (*Stephen Harvey*)

Rye Harbour E Sus [TQ9220], *Inkerman Arms*: Friendly unpretentious local nr nature reserve, good food inc fresh local fish and old-fashioned puddings, well kept Whitbreads-related ales and one from local microbrewery, interesting painted frieze; boules (*Marian Greenwood, Stephen Harvey*)

☆ **Salehurst** E Sus [½ mile off A21 T Wells—Battle – OS Sheet 199 map ref 748242; TQ7424], *Salehurst Halt*: Cosy and very friendly L-shaped local in station building by dismantled line, good plain wooden furnishings, good log fire, old prints and photographs, well kept Harveys and Wadworths IPA and 6X, decent wines, sensibly short choice of imaginative generous food, pleasant garden, pretty village with 14th-c church; bedrooms (*Mr and Mrs A Park, Hugh MacLean, TBB, BB*)

☆ **Scaynes Hill** E Sus [Freshfield Lock; off A272, via Church Lane signpost; TQ3623], *Sloop*: Tucked-away country pub with sofas and armchairs, games room off basic public bar, lots of tables out in neat garden by derelict Ouse Canal; good choice of generous bar food inc children's, well kept Harveys Best and guest beers, lots of country wines; piped music, relaxed service; children in eating area, handy for Bluebell steam railway, not far from Sheffield Park *(Tony Walker, Simon Pyle, Keith and Audrey Ward, John and Mavis Wright, Stella Knight, LYM)*

Sedlescombe E Sus [TQ7718], *Queens Head*: Clean and comfortable country local opp village green, pleasant and welcoming with big inglenook log fire, Doulton toby jugs, hunting prints, limited good value bar food, Flowers, decent coffee; restaurant, attractive garden *(Michael Grigg)*

Selham W Sus [S of A272 – OS Sheet 197 map ref 935206; SU9320], *Three Moles*: Former railway station below downs converted to peaceful very welcoming country local, well kept King & Barnes *(R J Bland)*

☆ **Shoreham by Sea** W Sus [Upper Shoreham Rd, Old Shoreham; TQ2105], *Red Lion*: Dim-lit low-beamed 16th-c pub with series of alcoves, generous well cooked bar food inc popular Sun lunch, no-smoking dining room, well kept Courage-related ales, King & Barnes, Wadworths 6X and several interesting guest beers, occasional beer festivals, decent wines, farm cider, log fire in unusual fireplace, food in bar and no-smoking dining room (more reports on new chef please), pretty sheltered garden; piped music may obtrude; river walks, good South Downs views *(Jim and Maggie Cowell, John Beeken, Ian Phillips, David Holloway, M Carey, A Groocock, R H Martyn, Bruce Bird)*

Shoreham by Sea [High St], *Marlipins*: Planked ceilings giving nautical feel, bric-a-brac, old local photographs, welcoming licensee, good choice of tasty bar food, well kept Bass, Worthington BB, Fullers London Pride and Harveys Best; piped music, can get busy at weekends; back terrace *(Bruce Bird)*

Shortbridge E Sus [Piltdown – OS Sheet 198 map ref 450215; TQ4521], *Peacock*: Attractive 16th-c beamed and timbered pub which has had good food, well kept ales, pleasant furnishings and sizeable garden with playhouse, but closed for rebuilding after 15-engine fire late 1995 *(News please)*

☆ **Sidlesham** W Sus [Mill Lane, off B2145 S of Chichester; SZ8598], *Crab & Lobster*: Old country local very much enjoyed by those in tune with its uncompromising individuality, log fire in chatty traditional bar, no-smoking plusher side dining lounge, charming back garden looking over to the bird-reserve of silted Pagham Harbour; limited choice of good meals (not Sun evening) inc summer seafood platters, well kept Archers Village and Gales Best and BBB, decent wines, country wines, traditional games; dogs welcome, no music or machines *(John Beeken, Lynn Sharpless, Bob Eardley, C E Ward, Nicholas Semple, K Baxter-Wright, James Cull, Phyl and Jack Street, LYM)*

Sidlesham [Selsey Rd], *Anchor*: Free house

with good food, plenty of tables; handy for wildlife centre *(John and Joy Winterbottom)*

Singleton W Sus [SU8713], *Fox & Hounds*: Welcoming new licensee doing well, relaxed feel in two small bars, real fires, friendly locals; handy for Weald & Downland Open Air Museum *(Ann and Colin Hunt)*

Slaugham W Sus [TQ2528], *Chequers*: Recently plushly extended dining pub with well kept King & Barnes Sussex and Festive, good food inc cheaper lunchtime bar snacks, emphasis on seafood; enormous wine list; tables on front terrace, opp church among pretty cottages by bridleway to Handcross; bedrooms *(F H Keens, James House)*

☆ **Slindon** W Sus [Slindon Common; A29 towards Bognor; SU9708], *Spur*: Smallish attractive 17th-c pub, good choice of reasonably priced food changing daily inc vegetarian, two big log fires, well kept Courage-related beers, friendly staff and dogs; children welcome, games room with darts and pool, sizeable restaurant, pleasant garden *(Doreen and Brian Hardham, Miss D Hobbs, John Davis)*

Slinfold W Sus [TQ1131], *Kings Head*: Peaceful pub with good country food, Whitbreads-related ales, polite attentive staff, tables in big garden; bedrooms *(Jason Caulkin, W D Morrison)*

Sompting W Sus [West St; TQ1605], *Gardeners Arms*: Handy and friendly stop just off main coast rd, generous good value lunches inc curries, Courage-related ales; bedrooms *(Dave Irving)*

☆ **South Harting** W Sus [B2146; SU7819], *White Hart*: Attractive unspoilt pub with good generous home cooking (may be a wait) inc vegetarian and sandwiches, lots of polished wood, hundreds of keys, big log fire in cosy snug, cheerful service, well kept Tetleys-related ales, good coffee, restaurant, separate public bar; well behaved dogs allowed, children welcome (toys in games room); good garden behind for them too, with spectacular downs views *(Dr Brian Hamilton, N E Bushby, W Atkins, Alison and Mike Stevens, Ann and Colin Hunt, MCG)*

South Harting, *Ship*: Very wide choice of good value food in informal unspoilt 16th-c local with Palmers and Eldridge Pope ales, good coffee, unobtrusive piped classical music, dominoes, maybe chestnuts to roast by public bar's log fire; nice setting in pretty village *(Colin and Ann Hunt, N E Bushby, W Atkins, John Evans, MCG)*

Staplefield W Sus [Warninglid Rd; TQ2728], *Victory*: Charming whitewashed pub opp village cricket green, dovecote in roof, picnic tables outside with play area; well kept Gales and King & Barnes beer, decent wines, vast choice of food inc bar snacks worth waiting for, welcoming licensees; popular, get there early *(R Walden, Steve Moore, John Kimber)*

☆ **Steyning** W Sus [41 High St; TQ1711], *Chequer*: Largely Tudor, with labyrinth of bars and seating areas, friendly staff, good range of well kept Whitbreads-related beers, wide choice of generous food from good snacks up, friendly efficient service *(R T and J C Moggridge, Niki and Terry Pursey)*

☆ **Steyning** [130 High St], *Star*: Flagstoned front bar, carpeted back one furnished in pine, rural memorabilia, no-smoking room, friendly service, well kept Whitbreads-related and guest ales, wide choice of good home cooking (can sometimes be a wait); piped music, regular live music; nice gardens, one with climbing frame and rabbits *(Bruce Bird, Ian Carter, Tony and Wendy Hobden, Susan Lee)*

Storrington W Sus [Main St; TQ0814], *Anchor*: Large friendly family-run beamed pub with very wide choice of good competitively priced food, spacious dining area, good atmosphere, well kept Whitbreads-related and guest ales, unobtrusive piped music, separate games room *(M Carey, Miss A Groocock, K Frostick)*

☆ **Stoughton** W Sus [signed off B2146 Petersfield—Emsworth; SU8011], *Hare & Hounds*: Much modernised pub below downs with reliably good home-cooked food in airy pine-clad bar, big open fires, half a dozen changing well kept ales such as Adnams Broadside and Gibbs Mew Bishops Tipple, friendly staff, restaurant, back darts room, tables on pretty terrace; nr Saxon church, good walks nearby; children in eating area and restaurant *(Keith Stevens, Ann and Colin Hunt, Chris McGivern, LYM)*

☆ **Sutton** W Sus [nr Bignor Roman villa; SU9715], *White Horse*: Unspoilt ivy-clad traditional pub, simple and clean, island servery separating bare-boards bar from dining area, good choice of good plentiful food inc local game and fish, flowers on tables, Batemans, Courage, Youngs and guest beers, log fire, friendly staff; tables in garden, pretty downs-foot village; good value bedrooms, comfortable and well equipped *(LM, Mr and Mrs P G Wright, G Washington, Peter Lewis)*

Uckfield E Sus [Framfield Rd; TQ4721], *Alma Arms*: Comfortable and brightly renovated, with good range of well kept beers, friendly staff and customers *(Adrian and Gilly Heft)*

Upper Beeding W Sus [TQ1910], *Kings Head*: Attractive back garden with beautiful downland views, play area and access to River Adur; well kept beer, attractive food *(David Holloway)*

☆ **Wadhurst** E Sus [Mayfield Lane (B2100 W); TQ6131], *Best Beech*: Well run dining pub, pleasant bar on left with wall seats, quiet but individual decor and coal fire, eating area with lots of pictures and china on right, well done fresh bar food (not Sun/Mon evenings) from sandwiches to juicy steaks, well kept Harveys and other ales, decent wines, quick service; back restaurant, good value bedrooms *(Jill Bickerton, BB)*

Wadhurst [St James Sq (B2099)], *Greyhound*: Pretty and neatly kept village pub with wide choice of usual bar food (hot carvery Mon evening instead) and set Sun lunch in neat restaurant or pleasant beamed bar with big inglenook fireplace, real ales such as Bass, Fullers, Harveys, Ruddles County and Tetleys,

good service, no piped music; tables in well kept back garden *(S Barrow, BB)*

☆ **Walderton** W Sus [Stoughton rd, just off B2146 Chichester—Petersfield; SU7810], *Barley Mow*: Pretty village pub with warm and cosy flagstoned bar, comfortable and attractive lounge, two log fires, huge helpings of good bar food inc notable ploughman's and Sun lunch, well kept Gales and country wines, cheerful staff, popular skittle alley; children welcome, fine garden *(MCG)*

☆ **Waldron** E Sus [Blackboys—Horam side rd; TQ5419], *Star*: Lively village local with big inglenook log fire in panelled bar, restaurant off, fair range of standard pub food with some interesting specials, Bass, Charrington IPA, Harveys and Charles Wells Bombardier, no music, friendly service *(P Saville, Roger Price, Tony Watson)*

Warbleton E Sus [TQ6018], *Warbil in Tun*: Friendly extended dining pub with beams and red plush, big log fire, well kept Flowers IPA and Harveys, good coffee, relaxed civilised atmosphere; tables on roadside green *(RDK, SRK, Alan Skull)*

Warnham W Sus [Friday St; TQ1533], *Greets*: 15th-c family-run pub with beams, uneven flagstones and inglenook log fire, lots of nooks and corners, well kept Whitbreads-related ales, decent wines, wide choice of good though not cheap straightforward home cooking (not Sun evening – and worth getting there early as some things run out); convivial locals' side bar, tables in garden *(Jason Caulkin, F H Keens, G W and I L Edwards, Margaret and Nigel Dennis, Charles Parry, Jim Povey, Howard Gregory)*

☆ **Washington** W Sus [just off A24 Horsham—Worthing; TQ1212], *Franklands Arms*: Well kept, roomy and welcoming, with wide choice of good food esp pies and seafood mornay, several well kept ales, decent house wines, prompt service; big bar, smaller dining area, games area with pool and darts; tables in neat garden, quiet spot yet busy weekends *(Mrs J A Blanks, Cathryn and Richard Hicks, Guy Consterdine)*

☆ **West Chiltington** W Sus [Church St; TQ0918], *Elephant & Castle*: Friendly pub behind ancient church, good range of reasonably priced food freshly cooked by South African landlord, good chips, well kept King & Barnes ales, no music; good garden *(Shelagh and Denis Dutton, Tony and Wendy Hobden, Barbara and Alec Jones)*

☆ **West Chiltington** [Smock Alley, just S], *Five Bells*: Consistently good reasonably priced fresh food, well kept King & Barnes and other ales from small breweries, enthusiastic landlord, big sun lounge, pleasant garden *(Bruce Bird)*

☆ **West Hoathly** W Sus [signed off A22 and B2028 S of E Grinstead; TQ3632], *Cat*: Ancient pub delightfully placed in pretty hilltop village, with fine views; heavy beams and timbers, lots of character, very welcoming new licensee and staff, spotless tables with candles and flowers, simple choice of bar food, well kept Beards (brewed for them by

Arundel), good coffee, big log fire *(Heather Martin, W Ruxton, Michael and Alison Leyland, Susan and John Douglas, LYM; more reports on food please)*

West Itchenor W Sus [SU8001], *Ship*: Large pub in good spot nr Chichester Harbour, cheery welcome and service, well kept Courage-related ales, good range of food in bar and restaurant, spotless parquet floor and panelling, tables out under cocktail parasols; said to be able to get supplies for yachtsmen (nearest shop is two miles away) *(Pete Yearsley)*

West Marden W Sus [B2146 2 miles S of Uppark; SU7713], *Victoria Arms*: Good value home-made food inc interesting dishes and good sandwiches in pleasant rustic surroundings, well kept Gibbs Mew, decent house wines, quick service, restaurant *(G and M Stewart, MCG)*

☆ **West Wittering** W Sus [Chichester Rd; B2179/A286 towards Birdham; SU7900], *Lamb*: Immaculate 18th-c country pub, several rooms neatly knocked through with tidy new furnishings, rugs on tiles, well kept ales such as Ballards, Bunces Benchmark, Harveys Old, Hop Back Summer Lightning and Ringwood Fortyniner, decent wines, interesting reasonably priced food from separate servery, big log fire, prompt attentive service; tables out in front and in small sheltered back garden – good for children, with outside salad bar on fine days; busy in summer *(Tim and Sue Halstead, Bruce Bird, Ann and Colin Hunt, John and Wendy Trentham, BB)*

Westbourne W Sus [North St; SU7507], *Good Intent*: Friendly two-bar local with well kept Tetleys-related ales, real fires, darts, juke box, monthly live music; barbecues *(Colin and Ann Hunt)*

☆ **Wilmington** E Sus [just off A27; TQ5404], *Giants Rest*: Simple attractive furnishings in small chatty rooms, good choice of imaginative sensibly priced home-made food inc devastating puddings, well kept ales such as Adnams, Fullers and Harveys, farm ciders, friendly service; very popular lunchtimes; picnic tables outside *(E G Parish, Alan Skull, Paul and Beverley Edwards, M Martin, Dr S Savvas)*

☆ **Winchelsea** E Sus [German St; TQ9017], *New Inn*: Variety of solid comfortable furnishings in well decorated bustling rambling beamed rooms, some emphasis on wide choice of food inc good fresh fish (sandwiches too), well kept changing ales such as Everards Tiger, Harveys, Wadworths 6X and one brewed for them by Adnams, decent wines and malt whiskies, friendly though not always speedy service; separate public bar with darts, children in eating area, pretty bedrooms (some sharing bathrooms), delightful setting *(George Atkinson, J R Whetton, Michael Sargeant, Gerry Z Pearson, Mr and Mrs J Jackson, Angeline Chan, Hanns P Golez, LYM)*

☆ **Wisborough Green** W Sus [TQ0526], *Three Crowns*: Big clean and polished open-plan bar stretching into dining room, stripped bricks and beams, good reasonably priced food inc

big ploughman's and popular Sun lunch, well kept ales such as Greene King Abbot, quick attentive service, sizeable back garden *(John and Elspeth Howell, Colin Laffan, David Dimock, Christopher Warner, Howard West)*

Woodmancote W Sus [junction of B2116 and Wineham Lane; TQ2414], *Wheatsheaf*: Friendly and relaxed, with well kept ales inc Batemans, Harveys and Shepherd Neame, good food from sandwiches to full meals inc locally smoked Newhaven fish, helpful service, family area, garden *(Anon)*

Woodmancote W Sus [the one nr Emsworth; SU7707], *Woodmancote Arms*: Simple village local with reasonably priced bar food, well kept Gibbs Mew; restaurant *(Ann and Colin Hunt)*

☆ **Worthing** W Sus [High St; W Tarring; TQ1303], *Vine*: Good friendly unpretentious local, small, cosy and comfortable, with six well kept ales inc Ballards Best, Hop Back Summer Lightning, Village Bitter brewed for the pub and guests, October beer festival, good home-made food, daily special and other food; can get smoky when crowded, occasional live music; attractive garden *(Dave Irving, Bruce Bird, Peter Sweet)*

Worthing [Portland Rd, just N of Marks & Spencer], *Hare & Hounds*: Friendly and busy extended pub with well kept Whitbreads-related ales, good choice of reasonably priced food, wide range of customers, pleasant staff; no car park but three multi-storeys nearby *(Tony and Wendy Hobden, Robert Marshall, Chris and Anne Fluck)*; [Warwick St], *Hogshead*: Long narrow beamed bar with lots of banquettes, unusual decorations, around a dozen well kept ales, mostly Whitbread-related but some unusual ones too, also farm ciders; an unpretentious place, good for serious drinking (the food is plain, though tasty enough); well behaved children allowed *(Michael Sandy, M Carey, Miss A Groocock, Robert Heaven)*; [Old Brighton Rd, A259 nr Beach House Park], *Royal Oak*: Good helpings of bar food (may be a wait), pleasant staff, nice atmosphere, picnic tables on sunny front terrace *(Chris and Anne Fluck)*; [Richmond Rd], *Wheatsheaf*: Popular open-plan pub, nicely furnished front lounge with open fire, plainer back bar, well kept Bass and Charrington IPA, good choice of decent food, welcoming atmosphere; weekly quiz nights *(Michael Sandy, Tony and Wendy Hobden, Chris and Anne Fluck)*

Yapton W Sus [North End Rd; SU9703], *Black Dog*: Village local with good choice of food and well kept ale in appropriately simple surroundings; nice terrace with covered outdoor seating, children's play area *(Miss A G Drake)*; [Maypole Lane, signed off B2132 Arundel rd], *Maypole*: Friendly staff and customers, two log fires in lounge, generous helpings of reasonably priced home-cooked food (not Sun or Tues evenings), well kept Flowers Original, Ringwood Best, Youngers IPA and four guest ales from small breweries, beer festivals Easter and August bank hol *(Bruce Bird)*

Warwickshire

Pubs currently on particularly good form in this county (given its own chapter for the very first time in this edition of the Guide) include the Bell at Alderminster (a civilised dining pub with a good welcome for families), the relaxed and friendly Fox & Hounds at Great Wolford (gains a Star for all-round quality this year), the cosy old Howard Arms at Ilmington (imaginative good food), the cheerfully eccentric Little Dry Dock in Netherton, the Blue Boar at Temple Grafton (a newcomer to this edition, good food and drink under the newish licensees), the timeless and relaxed Plough in the attractive village of Warmington (another pub back in these pages after an absence), the Pheasant at Withybrook (a reliable dining pub) and the interesting old Bulls Head at Wootton Wawen. The Bulls Head is doing such enjoyable food these days, including a fine range of fresh fish, that it gains a Food Award, and is our choice as Warwickshire Dining Pub of the Year. In the Lucky Dip section at the end of the chapter, four pubs we'd rate highly (all inspected and approved by us) are the Castle on Edge Hill, Black Swan and Garrick in Stratford and Royal Oak at Whatcote. The recently reopened Dun Cow at Dunchurch should also be well worth a visit. Birmingham and Wolverhampton both have a reasonable choice of pubs, especially for people rating real ale as the most important feature; and there's a good choice in Warwick. Drinks prices are significantly lower than the national average here – particularly so in pubs in and around the West Midlands conurbations (which we have included in this chapter). The Case is Altered at Five Ways stands out as one of the cheapest free houses we've come across; the Crooked House in Himley (tied to Banks's) and Brewery in Langley (a Carlsberg Tetleys offshoot with its own ales) were also very cheap indeed. In general we found pubs tied to smaller regional or local breweries cheaper than those getting their beers from the national combines. A new local brewery which we have found worth looking out for has a very easy name to remember – Warwickshire.

ALDERMINSTER SP2348 Map 4
Bell ⑪ ♀

A3400 Oxford—Stratford

You do need to book, or at least arrive early for a table at this friendly and fairly smart dining pub, and as it's only four miles from Statford you could fit in a very pleasant supper here before the theatre. Using fresh produce, the imaginative menu changes monthly. Very well prepared dishes might include carrot and coriander soup (£2.65), fillets of herring in madeira sauce (£3.95), fresh scallops sautéed with leeks, ginger and garlic (£5.50), cashew nut roast or grilled plaice (£7.25), mild chicken curry with cashew nuts (£7.95), grilled lamb liver with smoked bacon or crispy topped lamb in cider (£8.25), casserole of beef with kumquats or steak and kidney pie (£8.95) and fried pork with sage and onions (£9.50), there is also a specials board which includes a catch of the day; two-course lunch (weekdays; £6.50). The communicating areas of the neatly kept spacious bar have plenty of stripped slatback chairs around wooden tables on the flagstones and wooden floors, little vases of flowers, small landscape prints and swan's-neck brass-and-globe lamps on the cream walls, and a solid fuel stove in a stripped brick inglenook; no-smoking restaurant. Flowers IPA on handpump with two guests such as Flowers Original, Fullers London Pride, Hook Norton Old Hookey or Marstons Pedigree kept under light blanket pressure, a good range of wines by the glass, and freshly squeezed juice. Civilised and friendly waitress service, and readers with children have felt particularly welcome here – they have high chairs, and although they don't do a children's menu one reader's child was very happy with the balloon she was given. A conservatory and terrace overlook the garden and Stour Valley. *(Recommended by David Shillitoe, Maysie Thompson, Sharon Hancock, Lawrence Bacon, Roy Bromell, Henry Paulinski, C and M Starling, Paul and Janet Waring, Christine van der Will, Kay Neville-Rolfe, Nigel Wilkinson, Martin Jones, Moira and John Cole, David Shillitoe, Pam Adsley, Mrs J Oakes, Peter Lloyd)*

Free house ~ Licensees Keith and Vanessa Brewer ~ Real ale ~ Meals and snacks ~ (01789) 450414 ~ Children welcome ~ Occasional opera or music nights ~ Open 12-2.30, 7-11; cl evenings 24-27 Dec and 1-2 Jan

BRIERLEY HILL (W Midlands) SO9187 Map 4

Vine £ 🍽

Delph Rd; B4172 between A461 and A4100, near A4100

This lively local is the tap for the next-door Batham brewery, so the Bitter and Mild, and Delph Strong in winter, are well kept and very reasonably priced. It's a popular place and can get crowded. The warmly welcoming front bar has wall benches and simple leatherette-topped oak stools, the extended and refurbished snug on the left has solidly built red plush seats, and the back bar has brass chandeliers as well as darts, cribbage, dominoes, fruit machine and trivia. Good fresh lunchtime snacks include really tasty sandwiches (£1), chicken tikka (£1.20), faggots and peas or steak and kidney pie (£1.70), marvellous-value salads from a cold table (from £1.70) and curry (£1.80). The pub is known in the Black Country as the Bull & Bladder, from the good stained-glass bulls' heads and very approximate bunches of grapes in the front bow windows. *(Recommended by Mike Begley, W L G Watkins, Stephen George Brown, W L G Watkins, Anthony Marriott; more reports please)*

Bathams ~ Manager Melvyn Wood ~ Real ale ~ Lunchtime snacks (not Sun) ~ (01384) 78293 ~ Children welcome in own room ~ Blues Sun evening ~ Open 12-11; cl 25 Dec evening

COVENTRY (W Midlands) SP3379 Map 4

Old Windmill £

Spon Street

All the best city buildings to have survived the blitz have gradually been transplanted to this unusual street. This attractive and unpretentious timber-framed 15th-c pub is the odd one out, as this is its original site. One of the rambling series of tiny cosy old rooms is little more than the stub of a corridor, another has carved oak seats on flagstones and a woodburner in a fine ancient inglenook fireplace, and another has carpet and more conventionally comfortable seats. There are exposed beams in the uneven ceilings, and a back room preserves some of the equipment which used to be used in the days when a former landlady, Ma Brown, brewed here. Nowadays the beers are well kept Courage Directors, John Smiths, Marstons Pedigree, Morlands Old Speckled Hen, Websters and then a couple of guests like Crown Buckley Reverend James and Oakhill Best, all kept under light blanket pressure. Bulmer's cider; dominoes, fruit machine, juke box. Food passed out straight from the kitchen door: filled batches (from £1.10) and cottage pie, steak pie, faggots and mushy peas, gammon or lasagne (£3.25). The pub is popular with students, extremely busy on Friday and Saturday evenings, and handy for the Belgrave Theatre. No children. *(Recommended by Stephen and Julie Brown, Hazel Morgan; more reports please)*

Courage ~ Lease: Lynne Ingram ~ Real ale ~ Lunchtime meals and snacks ~ (01203) 252183 ~ Occasional ceilidhs ~ Open 11-3, 6-11; 11-11 Fri and Sat; cl 25 Dec

FARNBOROUGH SP4349 Map 4

Butchers Arms

Off A423 N of Banbury

This creeper-covered country pub with its matching stable block opposite is set well back from the village road, and there's a safely fenced-in front lawn, with seats on another flower-edged lawn which slopes up behind. The pleasant main lounge bar has been carefully renovated with lots of oak furniture and fittings, flagstone floors and some carpet, piped Classic FM, and well kept Bass, Boddingtons and Marstons Pedigree with weekly guests such as Batemans, Charles Wells Bombardier, Flowers, Frog Island, Oakhill Best or Wadworths 6X; decent wine list, too. There's a prettily countrified dining extension with big timbers, and a front public bar with darts, dominoes and fruit machine. Bar food includes sandwiches (from £1.85), soup (£2.35), filled baguettes or toasted bread filled with ham and cheese and topped with a fried egg (£2.85), home-made pâté (£3.85), lots of ploughman's (£4.35), omelettes, ratatouille lasagne or lamb curry (£4.85), steak and kidney pie (£5.65), children's dishes (£1.85), and home-made puddings like banoffi pie, treacle tart or fruit crumble (£2.85); Sunday roast; friendly staff. It's handy for Farnborough Hall. *(Recommended by George Atkinson, Richard Houghton, Jill and Peter Bickley; more reports please)*

Free house ~ Licensee Kathryn Robinson ~ Real ale ~ Meals and snacks (till 10) ~ Restaurant ~ (01295) 690615 ~ Children welcome away from bar ~ Live music Fri evenings ~ Open 12-3, 7-11

FIVE WAYS SP2270 Map 4

Case is Altered

Follow Rowington signposts at junction roundabout off A4177/A4141 N of Warwick

This marvellously unchanging cottage has been licensed to sell beer for over three centuries. There's no food, no children or dogs, and no noisy games machines or piped music – but you can be sure of a delightfully warm welcome from the landlady, cheery staff and regulars. The small, unspoilt simple main bar is decorated with a fine old poster showing the Lucas Blackwell & Arkwright brewery (now flats) and a clock with its hours spelling out Thornleys Ale, another defunct brewery; there are just a few sturdy old-fashioned tables, with a couple of stout leather-covered settles facing each other over the spotless tiles. From this room you reach the homely lounge (usually open only weekend evenings and Sunday lunchtime) through a door lit up on either side. A door at the back of the building leads into a modest little room, usually empty on weekday lunchtimes, with a rug on its tiled floor and a bar billiards table protected by an ancient leather cover (it takes pre-decimal sixpences). Well kept Ansells Mild and Traditional, Flowers Original, well priced Sam Smiths OB and a guest like Warwickshire Kings Champion served by rare beer engine pumps mounted on the casks that are stilled behind the counter. Behind a wrought-iron gate is a little brick-paved courtyard with a stone table under a chestnut tree. *(Recommended by Pete Baker, Jenny and Roger Huggins, P J Hanson, Wayne Brindle, B Adams, Ted George, Pete Baker)*

Free house ~ Licensee Gwen Jones ~ Real ale ~ (01926) 484206 ~ Open 11.30-2.30, 6-11 (cl evening 25 Dec)

GREAT WOLFORD SP2434 Map 4

Fox & Hounds ★

Village signposted on right on A3400 3 miles S of Shipston on Stour

Readers report with unanimous high praise for this characterful and inviting 16th-c stone pub, where locals relax comfortably alongside visitors in the friendly welcoming atmosphere. The cosy low-beamed old-fashioned bar has a nice collection of chairs and candlelit old tables on spotless flagstones, as well as a window seat with delightful views, old hunting prints on the walls, and a roaring log fire in the inglenook fireplace with its fine old bread oven. A small tap room serves a tremendous choice of eight weekly changing beers like Adnams Broadside, Bass, Black Sheep, Fullers London Pride, Hook Norton Best, Morlands Old Speckled Hen, Shepherd Neame Spitfire, Smiles Best or Wychwood Dogs Bollocks on handpump, and about 160 malt whiskies. Tasty virtually all home-made bar food includes soup (£1.95), garlic mushrooms (£2.95), brie and smoked bacon parcels (£3.50), chicken liver pâté (£3.95), shell-on prawns or lasagne (£5.95), chicken and mushroom pie (£6.50), pork in cider (£6.95) and 8oz fillet (£14.95); good value Sunday lunch with fresh vegetables. There's a well on the terrace outside. *(Recommended by Angus Lyon, Dr and Mrs M Beale, Alan and Paula McCully, Dr J R Hilton, Mrs J Crawford, Martin Jones, Henry Paulinski, Brian White, John Bowdler, Michael Heald, Charlotte Creasy, George Atkinson, Martin Jones, H O Dickinson)*

Free house ~ Licensees Graham and Anne Seddon ~ Real ale ~ Meals and snacks ~ (01608) 674220 ~ Children in eating area of bar ~ Open 12-3, 7-11 ~ Bedrooms: /£35S

HIMLEY (W Midlands – though see below) SO8889 Map 4

Crooked House ★

Pub signposted from B4176 Gornalwood—Himley, OS Sheet 139 map reference 896908; readers have got so used to thinking of the pub as being near Kingswinford in the Midlands (though Himley is actually in Staffs) that we still include it in this chapter – the pub itself is virtually smack on the county boundary

Remotely situated on an old mine shaft at the end of a private road, this crooked old house has shifted considerably over the years, and really does evoke the nursery rhyme. Getting the doors open is an uphill struggle, and as you go into the cosy atmospheric bar you lose all sense of balance – it would spoil the fun to tell you exactly why. On one table a bottle on its side actually rolls 'upwards' against the apparent direction of the slope. For a 10p donation you can get a big ball-bearing from the bar to roll 'uphill' along a wainscot. At the back is a large, level and more modern extension with local antiques. Very reasonably priced Banks's Bitter and Marstons Pedigree on hand or electric pump; dominoes, cribbage, fruit machine and piped music. Good value bar food includes sandwiches (not Sunday), a smokie (£3.25), steak and kidney pie (£3.85) and jumbo cod (£4.35). The conservatory is no smoking at lunchtimes, and there's a spacious outside terrace. *(Recommended by Mark Hughes, S G Brown, Gordon; more reports please)*

Banks's ~ Manager Gary Ensor ~ Real ale ~ Meals and snacks (lunchtimes and Sat evenings till 8.30) ~ (01384) 238583 ~ Children welcome in conservatory at lunchtime ~ Open 11-11; 12-10.30 Sun; 11.30-2.30, 6.30-11 in winter

ILMINGTON SP2143 Map 4

Howard Arms ⓘ ♀

Village signposted with Wimpstone off A34 S of Stratford

Although there is quite an emphasis on the very delicious food at this neatly kept attractive golden-stone inn, there's still a lovely cosy atmosphere in the friendly heavy-beamed bar; this has rugs on polished flagstones, comfortable seats, highly polished brass, and open fires (one is in a big inglenook, screened from the door by an old-fashioned built-in settle). A snug area off here is no-smoking. The imaginative bar food is very popular and it can get busy, but the welcoming and efficient staff cope well: soup (£2.25), chicken liver parfait (£3.50), butterfly prawns with garlic dip (£3.95), lamb and rosemary or steak and kidney pie (£5.95), spiced chicken balti (£6), seafood thermidor (£7.25), filo parcel of wild mushrooms with creamy sherry sauce (£7.95), poached supreme of chicken with dill cream sauce or salad with barbecued king prawns (£8.50) and noisettes of venison with prunes and brandy (£9). Well kept Everards Tiger, Marstons Pedigree and a guest on handpump, decent wines, and excellent freshly pressed apple juice; friendly, polite service, and nice labrador; shove-ha'penny and Aunt Sally on Thursday evenings; piped music. The garden is lovely in summer with fruit trees sheltering the lawn, a colourful herbaceous border and well spaced picnic tables, with more tables on a neat gravel terrace behind. It's nicely set beside the village green, and there are lovely walks on the nearby hills (as well as strolls around the village outskirts). *(Recommended by Dorothee and Dennis Glover, E Walder, Pam Adsley, John Bowdler, Martin Jones, George Atkinson, Maysie Thompson, Henry Paulinski, Peter Lloyd, M J Radford, Moira and John Cole, Dr I H Maine, Mrs J Oakes, Nigel Hopkins)*

Free house ~ Licensee Alan Thompson ~ Real ale ~ Meals and snacks (not winter Sun evenings) ~ Restaurant (not winter Sun evenings) ~ (01608) 682226 ~ Well behaved children welcome ~ Open 11-2.30, 6-11 ~ Bedrooms: £30B/£50B

KENILWORTH SP2871 Map 4

Virgins & Castle

High St; opposite A429 Coventry Rd at junction with A452

This atmospheric and dimly lit old-fashioned town pub has several separate rooms opening off the inner flagstones-and-beams servery, and there's a couple of simply furnished small snugs (one with flagstones, the other with rugs on its bare boards) flanking the entrance corridor; down a couple of steps, a large room has heavy beams, a big rug on ancient red tiles, and matching seat and stool covers. Also, a carpeted lounge with more beams, some little booths, hatch service, and a good warm coal fire, and a new upstairs bar with darts, juke box, bar billiards, pool table, pin table and football table, fruit machine and big TV. Bar food includes good value sandwiches (from £1.20), ploughman's (£2.95), and daily specials like steak and kidney pie or beef stew (£4.25); traditional Sunday roast. Well kept Bass, Davenports, Greenalls Original and guest beers on hand or electric pump. Seats outside in a sheltered garden. *(Recommended by Stephen and Julie Brown, Alan and Paula McCully, Dave Thompson, Margaret Mason, John Allsopp)*

Davenports (Greenalls) ~ Manager Adrian Roberts ~ Real ale ~ Meals and snacks (not Sun or Mon evening) ~ Restaurant ~ (01926) 853737 ~ Children welcome in eating area of bar till 9pm ~ Live music Sun, Wed and Thurs evenings ~ Open 12-11(10.30 Sun)

LANGLEY (W Midlands) SO9788 Map 4

Brewery ★ £ 🍺

1½ miles from M5, junction 2; from A4034 to W Bromwich and Oldbury take first right turn signposted Junction 2 Ind Estate then bear left past Albright & Wilson into Station Rd

It's hard to believe that this welcoming cottagey Victorian reproduction pub was built only in 1984, it's been so lovingly put together. From tractor seats in a back corridor you can see through a big picture window into the brewhouse here – a charmingly think-small subsidiary of the Carlsberg Tetleys brewing empire, where they produce their Entire – full-flavoured, quite strong and much loved by beer-drinkers. The simple Tap Bar serves this and the ordinary Holt, Plant & Deakins Bitter, brewed up in Warrington, and has lots of plates and Staffordshire pottery, and a coal-effect gas fire. The parlour on the left has plates and old engravings on the walls, a corner china cabinet, brass swan's neck wall lamps, a coal fire in a tiled Victorian fireplace with china on the overmantel, and dining chairs or sturdy built-in settles around four good solid tables. A red-tiled kitchen, divided off by shelves of Staffordshire pottery and old books, is similarly furnished, with the addition of lots of copper pans around its big black range; darts, cribbage, dominoes, quiz night every other Tuesday, and piped big band and classical music. Straightforward bar food (written up rather jokingly on a blackboard) includes very good value doorstep sandwiches with hot roast beef, roast ham and cheese, roast pork and stuffing, even black pudding and onion (£1.60), and a home-made dish of the day such as steak and kidney pie, macaroni cheese, chicken curry or Cornish pasties (£2); friendly service. *(Recommended by S G Brown, David and Shelia, Christopher Darwent, Mike and Wendy Proctor, B Adams, John and Christine Simpson, Brian and Anna Marsden, Ian and James Phillips)*

Holt, Plant & Deakins (Carlsberg Tetleys) ~ Manager Tony Stanton ~ Real ale ~ Lunchtime meals and snacks (not Sun) ~ (0121) 544 6467 ~ Children in eating area lunchtimes and early evenings ~ Open 11-2.30, 6(7 Sat)-11

LAPWORTH SP1670 Map 4

Navigation

Old Warwick Rd (B4439 Warwick—Hockley Heath)

This simple bustling canalside local really comes into its own in summer, with canal-users and locals sitting on seats on a back terrace, or on the sheltered flower-edged lawn running down to the water. It's all prettily lit at night, and they might have barbecues, jazz, Morris dancers or even travelling theatre companies out here, and outside hatch service. The friendly flagstoned bar is decorated with some brightly painted canal ware and cases of stuffed fish, and has high-backed winged settles, seats built around its window bay and a coal fire in its high-manteled inglenook. A second quieter room has tables on its board-and-carpet floor. A new extension provides a snug and a large dining area. Generously served bar food includes lunchtime sandwiches (from £1.95), chicken or prawn balti (from £5.75), beef, Guinness and mushroom pie (£6.25), 16oz cod in beer batter (£6.50), steaks (from £7.50), grilled duck breast with plum sauce (£8.95), puddings made by the licensee's mother (£2.25). Well kept Bass, Highgate Dark Mild, M&B Brew XI, and two guests like Walsall Saddlers and Warwickshire Kings Champion on handpump, and farm cider; fruit machine, dominoes, shut-the-box, shove-ha'penny. *(Recommended by RTM, JCM, Rona Murdoch, Gary Roberts, Ann Stubbs, D Alcock, Dave Thompson, Margaret Mason, Stephen Brown, Wayne Brindle, David R Shillitoe, George Atkinson, Roger and Jenny Huggins)*

M&B (Bass) ~ Lease: Andrew Kimber ~ Real ale ~ Meals and snacks ~ (01564) 783337 ~ Children welcome in eating area until 9 ~ Occasional jazz evenings, Morris dancing and canal theatre in summer ~ Open 11-3, 5.30-11; 11-11 Sat; 12-10.30 Sun

LITTLE COMPTON SP2630 Map 4

Red Lion 🛏 ♀

Off A44 Moreton in Marsh—Chipping Norton

This pleasantly friendly pretty 16th-c stone inn is a handy base for exploring the Cotswolds. The simple but civilised and comfortable low-beamed lounge has snug alcoves and a couple of little tables by the log fire. Bar food includes soup (£2), chicken liver pâté (£2.95), filled baguettes (from £2.95), ploughman's (£3.95), filled baked potatoes (from £3.50), ham and egg (£4.95), breaded scampi, tagliatelle niçoise or lasagne (£5.75), seafood pie (£6.50), marinated swordfish steak (£7.75), steaks up to 32oz (8oz £8.95), roast duck with black cherry, peach and orange curaçao sauce (£10.50), and daily specials like fresh sardines cooked in olive oil with garlic and lemon (£4.95), fresh cod/haddock fillet (£6.50), salmon fillet with watercress sauce (£7.95) and very tasty puddings; smaller helpings for children. Booking is recommended on Saturday evenings especially; no-smoking restaurant. The plainer public bar has another log fire, and darts, pool, cribbage, fruit machine and juke box. Well kept Donnington BB and SBA on handpump and an extensive wine list; good service; piped music. The bedrooms are good value. No dogs – even in garden (where there's a children's play area with climbing frame), and Aunt Sally. *(Recommended by Sharon Hancock, H O Dickinson, Andrew and Ruth Triggs, Martin Jones, Pam Adsley, Mr and Mrs P Smith)*

Donnington ~ Tenant David Smith ~ Real ale ~ Meals and snacks ~ Restaurant ~ (01608) 674397 ~ Children welcome in eating area of bar ~ Occasional folk music ~ Open 11-2.45, 6-11 ~ Bedrooms: £24/£36 (no under 8s)

LOWSONFORD SP1868 Map 4

Fleur de Lys ♀

Village signposted off B4439 Hockley Heath—Warwick; can be reached too from B4095 via Preston Bagot

This rather smart and civilised canalside pub is particularly popular on sunny days, when people gather at picnic tables down on the grass among tall weeping willows by the Stratford-upon-Avon Canal; there's a well equipped play area too. The comfortable spreading bar has lots of low black beams in the butter-coloured ceiling, brocade-cushioned mate's, wheelback and dining chairs around the well spaced tables, and rugs on the flagstones and antique tiles. Down steps on the right is a log fire and a couple of long settles; newspapers, magazines and unobtrusive piped music. Bar food might include stilton mushrooms (£2.65), sandwiches (with a bowl of soup as well, £3.95), ploughman's (from £3.95), bangers and mash (£4.45), plaice and chips (£4.55) fish and chips or steak and kidney pudding (£4.95), pie of the day (from £5.75), salads like hot chicken and bacon (from £5.95), pork steak with apple and dijonnaise sauce (£6.35), sirloin steak (£8.95), and puddings (from £1.95); there may be delays when busy; no-smoking dining area. Well kept Boddingtons, Flowers IPA and Original and Wadworths 6X on handpump, and decent wines including good New World ones (lots by the glass). *(Recommended by Karen Eliot, Stephen and Julie Brown, Mike Begley, Alan and Paula McCully, Nigel Clifton, M L and G Clarke, P J Hanson, Wayne Brindle, KC, Mayur Shah, Roy Bromell, K Chenneour, James Macrae)*

Whitbreads ~ Manager David Tye ~ Real ale ~ Meals and snacks ~ (01564) 782431 ~ Children welcome in eating area of bar ~ Open 11-11; 12-10.30 Sun; cl 25 Dec evening

MONKS KIRBY SP4683 Map 4

Bell 🍽 ♀

Just off B4027 (former A427) W of Pailton; Bell Lane

What makes this timbered old pub special is the surprisingly comprehensive and very tasty Spanish menu: you can make a splendid meal from the good range of garlic-drenched tapas dishes served in little frying pans, such as grilled sardines, prawns in white wine, garlic and chilli, Spanish salami cooked in garlic and white wine, squid fried in butter or cooked modizo-style, king prawns in garlic and chilli, and scallops cooked with white wine, tomato, lemon juice and breadcrumbs (£3.75-£4.75). Main courses include a vegetable paella (£6.25), grilled loin of pork with garlic, white wine, lemon and parsley (£8.25), paellas (from £7.75), honey-roasted saddle of lamb with red wine sauce (£9.95), steak flamed with port and topped with pâté (£11.75), and plenty of fish such as salmon in creamy seafood sauce (£8.75), tuna in an iron pan cooked with tomatoes, white wine and prawns (£9.95) and mixed sea grill (£11.75). There's a comfortably informal southern European atmosphere in the dusky flagstoned bars, where the landlord's little girl plays cheerfully with the friendly big alsatian, while locals chat with the friendly Spanish licensees; no-smoking dining area. As well as well kept Boddingtons, Flowers Original and IPA and a guest on handpump there's a very good wine list, ports for sale by the bottle and a healthy range of brandies and malt whiskies. The plain little back terrace has rough-and-ready rustic woodwork and a pretty little view across a stream to a buttercup meadow. Fairly loud piped music. *(Recommended by Mike Begley, Stephen and Julie Brown; more reports please)*

Free house ~ Licensees Paco and Belinda Maures ~ Real ale ~ Meals and snacks (till 10.30pm) ~ (01788) 832352 ~ Children welcome ~ Open 12-3, 7-11 (cl Mon lunchtime)

NETHERTON (W Midlands) SO9387 Map 4

Little Dry Dock

Windmill End, Bumble Hole; you really need an A-Z street map to find it or OS Sheet 139 map reference 953881

This tiny but lively and eccentric canalside pub – painted in red, white and blue, with a red-planked ceiling – is particularly good fun on a Monday night, when they have live Irish folk music. An entire narrow-boat is squeezed into the right-hand bar and used as the servery (its engine is in the room on the left), and there's also a huge model boat in one front transom-style window, winches and barge rudders flanking the door, marine windows, and lots of brightly coloured bargees' water pots, lanterns, jugs and lifebuoys; fruit machine, trivia, and piped music. They have their own Little Lumphammer ale as well as Holt, Plant & Deakins Entire and Ind Coope Burton, and fruit wines; friendly service. Simple bar food in generous helpings includes sandwiches, soup (£1.75), black pudding thermidor (£2.10), faggots and peas (£4.45), home-made lasagne (£4.65), gammon and egg (£5.20), steak and kidney in Guinness pie (£5.25), rump steak (£6.25), and puddings (from £1.75). There are pleasant towpath walks nearby. *(Recommended by Mike and Wendy Proctor, Lucy James, Dean Foden, Peter and Jenny Quine, Anthony Marriott, Howard West, Pat and John Millward)*

Carlsberg Tetleys ~ Tenant Frank Pearson ~ Real ale ~ Meals and snacks (till 10pm) ~ (01384) 235369 ~ Children welcome ~ Irish folk music Mon evenings ~ Open 11-3, 6-11

NEWBOLD ON STOUR SP2446 Map 4

White Hart

A34 Shipston on Stour—Stratford

This welcoming 15th-c pub has been generally smartened up with a lick of paint and some re-upholstering. As part of the improvements they've also put giant draughts and boules in the garden. The atmospheric airy beamed main bar – partly divided by stub walls and the chimney – has modern high-backed winged settles, seats set into big bay windows, a fair amount of brass, and a gun hanging over the log fire in one big stone fireplace. A wide range of good, reasonably priced food includes home-made soup (£1.95), home-made chicken liver pâté or garlic mushrooms in cream and white wine (£3.50), home-baked ham and eggs or grilled fresh local trout with almonds (£5.85), chicken breast poached in cider with rosemary and fresh cream (£6.95), steaks (from £6.95), and daily specials like fried lamb kidneys with garlic, sherry and cream or seafood pie (£5.85) and knuckle of lamb braised in wine with garlic and herbs (£6.95); two-course Sunday lunch (£7.95); best to book weekend evenings and Sunday lunch. The roomy back public bar has pool, dominoes, fruit machine and juke box; Bass and Worthingtons Best on handpump. There are some picnic tables under cocktail parasols in front of the pub, with its well tended hanging baskets. *(Recommended by Peter Lloyd, Colin Fisher, Michael Butler, Derek Allpass; more reports please)*

M & B (Bass) ~ Lease: Mr and Mrs J C Cruttwell ~ Real ale ~ Meals and snacks (not Sun evening) ~ Restaurant (not Sun evening) ~ (01789) 450205 ~ Children welcome ~ Open 11-2.30, 6-11; 11-11 Sat

SAMBOURNE SP0561 Map 4

Green Dragon

A435 N of Alcester, then left fork onto A448 just before Studley; village signposted on left soon after

Nicely placed by a historic village green, this friendly pub is a pretty place in summer with its climbing roses around the shuttered and timbered facade, and picnic tables and teak seats among flowering cherries on a side courtyard, by the car park. Inside, the cheery modernised beamed communicating rooms have little armed seats and more upright ones, some small settles, and open fires; piped music. Good food includes nice sandwiches, home-made soup (£2.25), home-made pâté (£2.50), sausage and mash, home-made steak and kidney pie and very good curry (all £4.95), five interesting vegetarian dishes like vegetable tagliatelle with a saffron cream sauce (from £5.50), fried tuna steak teriaki (£8.95), steaks (from £9.25), roast duckling with port and redcurrant sauce or prawns and scallops in filo (£9.95) and beef en croûte with a lemon stuffing in a madeira sauce (£11.75), puddings (£2.25), and children's menu (from £2.50). Well kept Bass, Hobsons, and M & B Brew XI on handpump; cheerful, attentive service. *(Recommended by Alan and Paula McCully, K Neville-Rolfe; more reports please)*

M & B (Bass) ~ Lease: Phil and Pat Burke ~ Real ale ~ Meals and snacks (till 10; not Sun) ~ Restaurant (not Sun) ~ (01527) 892465 ~ Children welcome in eating area of bar ~ Open 11-3, 6-11

SHUSTOKE SP2290 Map 4

Griffin 🍺

5 miles from M6, junction 4; A446 towards Tamworth, then right on to B4114 and go straight through Coleshill; pub is at Furnace End, a mile E of village

Among the ten or so real ales served by the cheery licensee at this friendly and unpretentious village local, one or two will always be from their own micro-brewery which produces very tasty Church End, Choir Boy, Cuthberts, Old Pal, Vicars Ruin or perhaps Pews Porter. These are served alongside interesting guests such as Bathams, Exmoor Gold, Holdens, Otter Bright, Theakstons Mild and Old Peculier, Timothy Taylors Landlord, all from a servery under a very low, thick beam; country wine, mulled wine and hot punch also. The simple low-beamed L-shaped bar has an old-fashioned settle and cushioned cafe seats (some quite closely packed), sturdily elm-topped sewing trestles, lots of old jugs on the beams, beer mats on the ceiling, and log fires in both stone fireplaces (one's a big inglenook); the conservatory is popular with families. Lunchtime bar food includes sandwiches (from £1.50), steak cob (£2.25), steak pie, curry of the day or chilli (£4.25), cod (£5.50), 8oz sirloin steak (£6.50) and a few blackboard specials. It may get busy at lunchtime so you do need to get there early. There are old-fashioned seats and tables on the back grass, a children's play area, and a large terrace with plants in raised beds. *(Recommended by E McCall, R Huggins, T McLean, D Irving, Graham Richardson, Dorothee and Dennis Glover, Mrs J Oakes, Kate and Robert Hodkinson)*

Own brew ~ Licensee Michael Pugh ~ Real ale ~ Lunchtime meals and snacks (not Sun) ~ (01675) 481205 ~ Children welcome in conservatory ~ Open 12-3, 7(6 Thurs and Fri)-11; cl evenings 25/26 Dec

STRATFORD UPON AVON SP2055 Map 4

Slug & Lettuce ♀

38 Guild Street, corner of Union Street

This lively bustling town pub is a handy stop for an early evening meal before the theatre, and as it can get very crowded with a smart young crowd later this (or lunchtime) is probably the best time for a visit. You can see some of the meals being prepared at one end of the long L-shaped bar counter, with dishes like home-made cream of pea, leek and ham soup (£2.55), hot creamy garlic mushrooms (£4.55), baked chicken pieces with mild curry sauce, pork and chive sausages in tomato sauce topped with melted mozzarella, sautéed chicken livers with bacon, garlic and brandy cream sauce or baked mackerel in a prawn, caper, bacon and herb butter sauce (£5.95), escalopes of turkey in white wine, mushroom, chive and cream sauce, grilled supreme of scotch salmon with lemon, smoked salmon, prawn, white wine and cream sauce or navarin of lamb in a mushroom, red wine, garlic, herb and tomato sauce (£9.95); helpful staff. The nicely furnished open plan bar has old pine kitchen tables and chairs on rugs and flagstones, a few period prints on stripped squared panelling, a newspaper rack, and a solid fuel fire; cribbage, piped music, and a few no-smoking tables at one end although the whole place can get quite smoky. Well kept beers such as Ansells, Ind Coope Burton, Tetleys and a guest beer on handpump, and decent wine. There's a small flagstoned back terrace, floodlit at night, with lots of flower boxes and sturdy teak tables under cocktail parasols, with more up steps. *(Recommended by M Holdsworth, Derek and Margaret Underwood, Clifford Payton, Dr I H Maine, Ted George, Maury Harris, David and Shelia, Dr and Mrs A K Clarke, Sara Nicholls, Lawrence Pearse)*

Ansells (Allied) ~ Manager Andy Cooper ~ Real ale ~ Meals and snacks (12-2, 5.30-9; 12-9 Thurs-Sat) ~ (01789) 299700 ~ Children welcome in eating area of bar ~ Open 11-3, 5.30-11; 11-11 Thurs-Sat; 12-10.30 Sun

TEMPLE GRAFTON SP1255 Map 4

Blue Boar ♀

Off A422 W of Stratford; a mile E, towards Binton

Unusually for the area, this popular beamed dining pub still preserves much of the more traditional appeal of the early 17th-c country tavern on which it's based. Consistently good lunchtime bar food from a good menu includes minestrone soup or soup of the day (£2.35), pâté (£3.15), lamb kidneys au poivre (£6.75), mushroom stroganoff, plaice or very good steak and kidney pie (£6.95), seafood tagliatelle (£7.25), salmon steak (£7.75), lamb kleftico (£7.95), venison steak (£8.95) and 8oz sirloin (£10.75). There are a few more things on offer in the evening, when dishes are quite a bit more pricey with soup of the day at £2.65 and venison steak at £10.95; daily specials and home-made puddings. Well kept Courage Directors, Hook Norton Best and Theakstons XB on handpump, and nearly 40 different wines. There are several good log fires in the comfortable atmospheric rooms, with cast-iron-framed tables and built-in wall and bow-window seats, and cribbage, dominoes and sensibly placed darts in a flagstoned side room stripped back to golden Binton stone. The comfortable stripped-stone restaurant, with its own log fire and a glass-covered old well, is very popular, with excellent service. It's set in a lovely position with picnic tables overlooking the rolling countryside of the Vale of Evesham. *(Recommended by John and Christine Vittoe, Genie and Brian Smart, Sharon Hancock, John Bowdler, Mike Gorton, Dr and Mrs M Beale, Moira and John Cole, Mrs P Woodward, Peter Lloyd)*

Free house ~ Licensee Sean Brew ~ Real ale ~ Meals and snacks (till 10 Mon-Sat) ~ Restaurant ~ (01789) 750010 ~ Children welcome ~ Open 11.30-3, 6-12

TIPTON (W Midlands) SO9592 Map 4

M A D O'Rourkes Pie Factory

Hurst Lane, Dudley Rd towards Wednesbury (junction A457/A4037) – look for the Irish flag

One reader described the interior of this friendly and rather eccentric pub as Disneyesque. It's a pastiche of a 1940s butcher's, with all sorts of meat-processing equipment from the relatively straightforward butcher's blocks to the bewilderingly esoteric (part of the fun is trying to guess what it's all for), not to mention strings of model hams, sausages and so forth hanging from the ceiling. Labels for pigs' heads mounted on the walls tell you about the dogs and abbots that are alleged to go into their recipes. In fact the food's good solid value with black pudding thermidor (£2.25), the gargantuan Desperate Dan cow pie complete with pastry horns, minted lamb pie, fish pie or vegetable pie (£5.25), mixed grill (£6.95), about four daily specials like ham in parsley sauce (£5.75), sirloin steak in port and stilton (£8.75), and puddings such as spotted dick or gateaux (from £2.25); children's dishes (£2.50). A simpler menu is available all afternoon, with baguettes or filled baked potatoes (from £2.50) and salads (from £4.75); Sunday roast (£4.95). The atmosphere is buoyant, and service is cheerful. They have their own variable but generally good Lumphammer ale, as well as Ansells Mild, Holt Plant & Deakins Entire and a guest like Morlands Old Speckled Hen on electric pump; fruit machine and piped music. Though it's roomy, with more space upstairs, it can get very busy (packed on Friday and Saturday evenings), especially if there's a party from a Black Country coach tour wandering around in a state of tickled shock. *(Recommended by Mike Begley, Ian Phillips, Mike and Wendy Proctor)*

Carslberg Tetleys ~ Manager Peter Towler ~ Real ale ~ Meals and snacks (till 10pm, Pantry menu all day) ~ 0121 557 1402 ~ Children welcome ~ Irish folk Tues-Fri ~ Open 11-11; 12-10.30 Sun; cl 25 Dec

WARMINGTON SP4147 Map 4

Plough £

Village just off B4100 N of Banbury

This isn't an ambitious place, but what they do, they do well, with pleasant unaffected service from the cheery licensees, a nice relaxed local atmosphere and good straightforward bar food. The warmly cosy bar has old photographs of the village and locals, an old high-backed winged settle, cushioned wall seats and lots of comfortable Deco small armed chairs and library chairs, and good winter log fires. Well kept Hook Norton Best and Marstons Pedigree on handpump, a guest like Hook Norton Haymaker, and several malt whiskies; darts, dominoes, cribbage and piped pop music. Simple but very generously served meals include soup (£1.95), very good sandwiches (from £1.25), cottage pie or chilli (£3.95), flavoursome home-baked ham (£4.95), a couple of home-cooked daily specials like quiche or steak and kidney pie (from £3.95), and a popular Sunday lunch. It's very well placed in a delightful village a few yards up a quiet lane from a broad sloping green with duck pond and ducks, and it looks especially pretty in the autumn, when the creeper over the front of the building turns a striking crimson colour. *(Recommended by Brian and Anna Marsden, Andrew and Jo Litten, Ted George, Susan and John Douglas, John Bowdler, Alan and Paula McCully)*

Free house ~ Licensee Denise Willson ~ Real ale ~ Meals and snacks (till 8.30pm); not Sun evening ~ (01295) 690666 ~ Children in eating area ~ Occasional live music ~ Open 12-3, 6-11; cl evening Dec 25

WEST BROMWICH (W Midlands) SP0091 Map 4

Manor House

2 miles from M6, junction 9; from A461 towards Wednesbury take first left into Woden Rd East; at T-junction, left into Crankhall Lane; at eventual roundabout, right into Hall Green Rd. Alternatively, 5 miles from junction 7.

This suburban local, serving an extensive built-up area, is housed in a (much modified) small 14th-c manor house. There is a whole lot of enthusiastically themed medieval paraphernalia, but behind all that the building itself well rewards anyone who wanders about with their eyes open. You enter through the ancient gatehouse and across a moat. The main room is actually a great flagstoned hall, where massive oak trusses support the soaring pitched roof (the central one, eliminating any need for supporting pillars, is probably unique). Around the walls there are a few lifesize medieval effigies, including an unusual knight in armour as a centrepiece, who turns round on his neighing horse every 40 minutes or so. This is mainly a no-smoking dining area. A fine old sliding door opens on to stairs leading up to a series of smaller and cosier timbered rooms, including a snug medieval Solar bar, which again have lovely oak trusses supporting their pitched ceiling beams. There are blue carpets and plenty of comfortably cushioned seats and stools around small tables, with the occasional settle. The emphasis is very much on family dining, and it's all rather jolly. Bar food is served in really huge helpings, and their chips are home-made: from the menu battered cod, scampi or steak and kidney pie (£4.45) or mixed grill (£6.99), with half a dozen daily specials like haddock and prawn pasta or chicken and tarragon (£5.95) and salmon hollandaise or chicken curry (£6.50), and a few vegetarian dishes like vegetable tikka masala or broccoli and cream cheese bake (£3.95); good value Sunday lunch; they put sparklers in their home-made ice cream for children. Well kept Banks's Bitter and Mild on electric pump, and Scrumpy Jack cider; fruit machines, piped music. Efficient, courteous staff. A broad stretch of grass leads away behind the moat, towards the surrounding modern houses; a car park is sensitively tucked away behind some modern ancillary buildings. *(Recommended by John and Elizabeth Cox, Mike Begley, Roy Bromell, Joy and Peter Heatherley, Andrew Stephenson, Mike Woodhead, M W Turner, Gary Nicholls)*

Banks's ~ Managers Michelle Jones, Craig Goodwin ~ Real ale ~ Meals and snacks (till 10pm Sat; 12-9 Sun) ~ Restaurant ~ (0121) 588 2035 ~ Children welcome ~ Open 12-2.30(3 Sat), 6(5.30 Sat)-11

WITHYBROOK SP4384 Map 4

Pheasant

4 miles from M6, junction 2; follow Ansty, Shilton signpost; bear right in Shilton towards Wolvey then take first right signposted Withybrook – or, longer but wider, second right into B4112 to Withybrook

There's a warmly welcoming atmosphere in this well run cosy old timbered village pub, which is popular for a good range of nicely cooked bar food served in generous helpings: home-made soup (£1.35), sandwiches (£1.75), lentil and mushroom au gratin (£5.25), very good ploughman's (£5.25), steak and kidney pie, braised liver and onions, cajun style chicken breasts or fish pie (£6.50), venison pie (£6.75), braised pheasant (£7.95), mixed grill (£8.50), fresh fish of the day, and puddings such as lemon meringue or chocolate fudge cake (£2.25). The spacious lounge has a serving counter flanked by well polished rocky flagstones, lots of plush-cushioned wheelback chairs and dark tables on the patterned carpet, a few farm tools on its cream walls. Good open fires in the atmospheric bar are particularly inviting in winter. Well kept Courage Directors and John Smiths under light blanket pressure; fruit machine in the lobby, and piped music (sometimes quite loud). There are tables under lantern lights on a brookside terrace, and the bank opposite is prettily planted with flowers and shrubs. Parking can be difficult at busy times. *(Recommended by Bronwen and Steve Wrigley, Janet Pickles, David Peakall, Michael Butler, Howard and Margaret Buchanan, Thomas Nott, Virginia Jones, Mayur Shah, David and Shelia, JJW, CMW, Cdr Patrick Tailyour)*

Free house ~ Licensees Derek Guy, Alan and Rene Bean ~ Real ale ~ Meals and snacks (till 10) ~ (01455) 220480 ~ Children welcome ~ Open 11-3, 6.30-11; cl 25 and 26 Dec

WOOTTON WAWEN SP1563 Map 4

Bulls Head 🍽

Stratford Road; A34 N of Stratford

Warwickshire Dining Pub of the Year

The very sensible length of the seasonally changing menu at this charming black and white Elizabethan timbered pub is one indication that the deliciously imaginative bar food is all home-made. There's a daily choice of about seven, often unusual, fresh fish dishes such as squid, marlin, strawberry grouper, tilapia or john dory all priced according to the day's market (that tends to mean double figures). Other dishes include soup (£2.95), soft herring roes on toast (£4.95), wild mushrooms in a creamy dill sauce on brioche or seafood tartlet (£5.75), roasted red peppers filled with mushroom and pinenut risotto (£7), escalope of pork saltimbocca (£8.75), char-grilled chicken breast with chilli butter (£9.95) and char-grilled sirloin steak (£10.95), and puddings such as rich chocolate mousse, summer pudding, berry pavlova (£3.25), and unusual British cheeses (£4.95). The attractive low-ceilinged L-shaped lounge has massive timber uprights, fairly smart decorations and furnishings that go well with the building, and rugs setting off the good flagstones; there's also a rather austere tap room with pews and a sawdusted floor, and a handsome restaurant. There are fresh flowers, and service by the notably friendly enthusiastic young staff is quick. Well kept Adnams, Fullers London Pride, Marstons Bitter and Pedigree, Morlands Old Speckled Hen and Wadworths 6X on handpump, and several wines by the glass; dominoes, shove-ha'penny. There are tables out in the garden, with some in a vigorous young vine arbour. It's handy for walks by the Stratford Canal. *(Recommended by Paul Leather, Gethin Lewis, Susan and John Douglas, Fhiona Skaife, Dayl Gallacher, Sue Holland, Dave Webster, Julian Kirwan-Taylor, Alan and Paula McCully, S Palmer, Mike and Wendy Proctor, Mike Begley, Dorothee and Dennis Glover, George Atkinson, Leith Stuart, Roy Bromell)*

Free house ~ Licensee John Willmott ~ Real ale ~ Meals and snacks (12-2.30, 6-10) ~ Restaurant ~ (01564) 792511 ~ Children welcome ~ Jazz Mon ~ Open 12-3.30, 6-11; cl 25 Dec

---

Lucky Dip

Besides the fully inspected pubs, you might like to try these Lucky Dips recommended to us and described by readers (if you do, please send us reports). We have also included pubs in and around the W Midlands conurbations, picking them out with the abbreviation W Mid.

Alcester [Kings Coughton (A435 towards Studley); SP0859], *Moat House*: Clean, comfortable and very well run, with welcoming service, good choice of good generous food and of well kept ales *(A H Thomas, Jack Barnwell)*; [34 High St], *Three Tuns*: Unspoilt single room, flagstone floors, low ceilings, plain furniture, own-brew beer not unlike Bathams, other well kept ales such as Fullers London Pride, friendly service, cheery customers, no food *(Richard Houghton, Paul Bray, Rona Murdoch)*
Amblecote W Mid [Collis St; SO8985], *Robin Hood*: Cosy and informal open-plan local, good changing range of particularly well kept ales inc Bathams, the unique honeyed Enville and a Mild, farm ciders, good value food in dining area, friendly staff, children allowed till 8.30 if eating; comfortable bedrooms *(Steve Spinks, Ian Jones, Chris Wrigley)*
Ansty [B4065 NE of Coventry; SP3983], *Rose & Castle*: Nr canal, some canal-theme decorations, low beams, decent food, friendly licensee, well kept Bass and other ales; linked to Virgins & Castle in Kenilworth *(Dave Braisted, Dan Cooke)*
☆ **Ardens Grafton** [towards Wixford – OS Sheet 150 map ref 114538; SP1153], *Golden Cross*: Pleasant L-shaped room lined with cases of teddy bears, also Shakespearean murals, photographic magazines (local society meets here); good generous bar food, well kept ales such as Badger Tanglefoot, Bathams, Hook Norton and Tetleys, very welcoming efficient service, unobtrusive piped music, fruit machine, restaurant with antique doll collection; seats outside, nice views *(Dave Braisted, Dr and Mrs M Beale)*
Barford [A429, handy for M40; SP2760], *Joseph Arch*: Well kept Flowers and Theakstons and good reasonably priced generous food in pub named for founder of agricultural workers' union *(Dave Braisted, Neville Kenyon)*
Barnacle [signed off B4029 in Shilton, nr M6

junction 2; SP3884], *Red Lion*: Unchanging no-frills two-room pub with good range of substantial good value food (not Sun lunchtime), well kept Bass and M&B ales; pleasant staff, seats out in covered front area *(Geoff Lee, Ted George)*
Barston W Mid [from M42 junction 5, A4141 towards Warwick, first left, then signed; SP2078], *Bulls Head*: Attractive partly Tudor village local, oak-beamed bar with log fires and Buddy Holly memorabilia, comfortable lounge with pictures and plates, dining room, friendly relaxed service, good value basic food, well kept Bass, M&B Brew XI and Tetleys, secluded garden, hay barn behind *(CMW, JJW, Pete Baker)*
☆ **Birmingham** W Mid [Cambridge St], *Prince of Wales*: Good traditional local in lovely old building behind Symphony Hall, welcoming long-serving Irish landlord, genuine hatch-served snug, two quiet and comfortable back parlours one of them frozen in 1900, ochre walls, bare boards, lively friendly atmosphere, fine service, particularly well kept Ansells Bitter and Mild, Ind Coope Burton, Marstons Pedigree and Tetleys; wide choice of good cheap food, piped Irish music, can get packed *(Jack Barnwell, SLC, Douglas Smart, Richard Lewis)*
☆ **Birmingham** [144 High St, Aston (A34) - easily reached from M6 junction 6], *Bartons Arms*: Magnificent specimen of Edwardian pub architecture, with inventive series of richly decorated rooms from the palatial to the snug; well kept M&B ales, limited food *(Frances Fox, Richard Green, LYM)*
Birmingham [308 Bradford St, Digbeth], *Anchor*: Perfectly preserved three-room Edwardian pub, carefully restored art nouveau glass, long high-ceilinged bar with basic seating, well kept Ansells Mild, Everards Tiger and Tetleys, interesting quickly changing guest beers such as Church End, Hogs Back Ripsnorter, Wye Valley Supreme, occasional beer festivals; well priced food inc

huge chip butties, friendly staff, pool, juke box *(Richard Lewis)*; [1 Price St, Aston, off A34], *Bulls Head*: Unspoilt side-street local with displays of guns, bullets etc, open all day, breakfast from 7am, good cheap food, variety of Tetleys-related ales *(Steve Jennings)*; [Church St (nr Eye Hospital)], *Cathedral*: Comfortable well divided lounge, carved ceiling, lots of prints, back eating area, bar with games machine, friendly staff, decent food inc balti bargains, well kept Bass; open all day *(Richard Lewis)*; [22 Gt Hampton St, Hockley], *Church Tavern*: Comfortable and friendly, well known for huge helpings of good value food; well kept Tetleys-related ales inc Holt Plant & Deakins Entire *(David Tyzack, Wayne A Wheeler)*; [Fighting Cocks, St Marys Row, Moseley], *Fieldmouse & Firkin*: Typical Firkin interior with bare boards and brewery bric-a-brac, decent service, some pleasant own brew beers *(Richard Houghton)*; [Cambrian Wharf, Kingston Row – central canal area], *Flapper & Firkin*: Popular canalside pub behind Symphony Hall, typical Firkin features, lots of wood, own brew and other Tetleys-related ales, reasonably priced food, friendly staff; piped music may be loud, some live entertainment, skittles Weds, tables outside *(Richard Lewis, Paul and Ursula Randall)*; [176 Hagley Rd, Edgbaston], *Hagley Duck*: Masses of bric-a-brac in front bar, wide choice of real ales behind, farm cider; smart dress required *(Gary Nicholls, E A Thwaite)*; [Gas St Basin], *James Brindley*: Good lunchtime pub, well furnished and comfortable, with interesting design, good value food esp sandwiches, real ale; evenings gets loud and young, maybe with live jazz; lovely setting overlooking canal boats *(Paul and Ursula Randall)*; [9 Margaret St], *Keys*: Club with pubby atmosphere and good range of particularly well kept ales such as Buchanan, Eldridge Pope, Everards, Morlands Old Speckled Hen, M&B Highgate Mild and Walsall Saddlers, themed brewery events alternate Mons; comfortable bar, larger room with pool, eating area, friendly staff, good menu; open 12-10 Mon to Fri, 3-10 Sat *(Richard Lewis)*; [157 Barford St, Digbeth], *Lamp*: Two small well furnished rooms, cosy and intimate, lunchtime food, well kept ales such as Boddingtons Mild and Bitter, Marstons Pedigree, Stanway Stanney and Wadworths 6X; open 12-11(11.30 Sat) *(Richard Lewis)*; [King Edwards Rd, Brindley Pl], *Malt House*: Handsomely renovated spacious building with lots of wood, windows on to canal, some balcony tables, usual bar food and some interesting specials, live music some nights, well kept Greenalls; handy for National Indoor Arena, Convention Centre and Symphony Hall *(Rona Murdoch, Paul and Ursula Randall)*; [Palisades, New St], *Newt & Cucumber*: Large two-bar pub with lots of comfortable seating, cosy intimate areas, bric-a-brac, friendly staff, extensive well priced menu, well kept ales such as Bass, Crown Buckleys Reverend James, Morlands

Old Speckled Hen, Theakstons XB, Worthington Best, cut prices 5-7.30 *(Richard Lewis)*; [176 Edmund St], *Old Contemptibles*: Spacious and comfortable Edwardian pub with lofty ceiling and lots of woodwork, popular with office workers for good value food lunchtime and early evening (not Sat eve or Sun); well kept Bass, M&B Brew XI, Highgate Dark Mild and changing guest beers such as Jennings and Wadworths Henrys, occasional beer festivals, friendly staff; piped music, pinball, open all day *(Richard Lewis, SLC, Wayne A Wheeler, BB)*; [Broad St], *Some Place Else*: Wine bar cum pub with friendly attentive staff, reasonably priced daily specials, decent wine and cocktails, outside tables; can get crowded but waiting is unusual *(Peter and Jenny Quine)*; [Temple Ct, Corporation St], *Square Peg*: Lots of seating in massive newish Wetherspoons, nicely decorated with pictures of Birmingham's past, long bar, various areas inc no smoking, friendly staff, good choice of well kept beers at attractive prices, food all day *(Richard Lewis)*; [Streetly Rd, Erdington], *Stockland*: Very big nicely decorated split-level M&B pub, bar meals; piped music can be loud, fruit machines *(S L Clemens)*; [Bennets Hill], *Wellington*: Old-style roomy high-ceilinged pub with comfortable seating, lots of prints, friendly staff, wide choice of cheap food from sandwiches up, lunchtime dining area, well kept ales such as Courage Best Bitter and Directors, Mauldons Best, Smiles Best and Summerskills Best; piped music, games machine *(Richard Lewis, Ray)*; [Bradford St, Digbeth], *White Swan*: Unfussy but clean and comfortable friendly local with Victorian tiles esp in corridor, big bar, fire in small lounge, charming staff, lovely fresh rolls, well kept Ansells *(Douglas Smart)*; [Edmund St], *White Swan*: Comfortable pub with lots of seating in lounge areas, L-shaped bar, back dining area with good choice of food from sandwiches to sizzler dishes, well kept Bass and M&B Brew XI, friendly staff; games machine, TV, piped music; open all day *(Richard Lewis)*; [Grosvenor St W], *White Swan*: Ansells pub with roomy lounge, good value bar food, good atmosphere; TV, piped music *(SLC)*

Bodymoor Heath [Dog Lane; SP2096], *Dog & Doublet*: Cosy canalside pub with well kept Bass, Stones and M&B Mild, good value limited food popular with businessmen at lunchtime, beams, brasses, bargees' painted ware, several open fires, tables in pleasant garden; can get a bit crowded; nr Kingsbury Water Park *(Liz and John Soden)*

☆ **Brinklow** [Fosse Way; A427, fairly handy for M6 junction 2; SP4379], *Raven*: 15th-c beams and open fire in dark-panelled lounge, more basic bar with alcoves and plants, collection of mugs and frog curios, well kept Marstons, good friendly service, almost too wide a choice of usual food inc vegetarian – popular and good value; piped local radio; tables on lawn with various pets; said to be haunted *(Dorothy and Leslie Pilson)*

Coleshill [Station Rd; SP1989], *Wheatsheaf*:

Spotless M&B pub with interesting exterior, traditional interior, relaxing friendly atmosphere, good staff, wide choice of usual food inc vegetarian, well kept beer *(Dave Braisted)*

Coventry W Mid [Hill St, by S end of Leigh Mills car park; SP3379], *Gatehouse*: Particularly well kept Bass and Brew XI, good home-cooked food from giant doorstep sandwiches up, friendly atmosphere; converted gatehouse for the Leigh Mills worsted factory *(Brian Randall)*; [252 Foleshill Rd], *Prince William Henry*: Relaxing pub with well kept Bass, extremely friendly service and good value authentic balti dishes, cooked individually so as not to become bland *(Dean Onno)* [Bond St, behind Coventry Theatre], *Town Wall*: Compact unspoilt Victorian pub, with engraved windows, open fire in small T-shaped lounge, simple bar with TV for big sports events, tiny clubby snug and flower-filled back yard; well kept Bass and M&B Brew XI, good value home-cooked food inc generous doorstep sandwiches *(Brian Randall)*

☆ **Deppers Bridge** [4 miles N of M40 junction 12; B4451; SP4059], *Great Western*: Roomy and airy family pub, non-stop model train clattering round overhead, interesting train photographs, generous helpings of promptly served food inc lots of children's specials, Ansells and Holt Plant & Deakins Entire from new-fangled dispensers, decent wines, good service; play area, tables on terrace *(Ted George)*

Dorridge W Mid [Grange Rd (A4023); SP1775], *Railway*: Small largely unspoiled local, well kept Bass and M&B Brew XI, friendly family service, limited choice of good value food (10p extra for thick-sliced sandwiches), no music or machines; small garden *(Dave Braisted)*

Dudley W Mid [Black Country Museum; SO9390], *Bottle & Glass*: Splendid reconstruction of old Black Country alehouse in extensive open-air working Black Country Museum (well worth a visit for its recreated assortment of shops, cinema, fairground, school, barge wharf and tram system); friendly staff in period clothes, two roaring fires, Holt Plant & Deakins Entire, good filled rolls, children welcome in two separate rooms off passage *(Andy Jones, LYM)*; [George Rd, Woodsetton; SO9293], *Park*: Well kept cheap ales from next-door Holdens Brewery, welcoming staff, good low-priced lunchtime food inc hot beef, pork and chicken sandwiches, very busy then; happy hour 4-7pm *(Dave Braisted, Colin Fisher)*

☆ **Dunchurch** [handy for M45 junction 1; SP4871], *Dun Cow*: Fine old coaching inn with handsome central courtyard, reopened late 1995 after major refurbishment; heavy beams, warm fires in inglenooks, panelling, pleasant traditional pubby decor and furnishings, separate no-smoking room, good choice of good value generous bar food, good range of Bass beers; bedrooms *(Ian Irving, LYM)*

Earlswood W Mid [past the Lakes; SP1274], *Red Lion*: Useful dining pub, open all day, with decent range of generous food inc OAP menu, friendly helpful service, Bass and a guest ale, skittle alley *(Jack Barnwell)*

☆ **Easenhall** [SP4679], *Golden Lion*: 16th-c inn with attractively decorated comfortable lounge, beams and dark panelling, commendably short choice of good value generous food inc good Sun carvery, efficient welcoming service even when busy, Boddingtons, Flowers Original and Theakstons Best, log fire; spacious attractive garden with terrace, barbecue, pet donkey; well equipped bedrooms, attractive village *(H Beaufoy)*

☆ **Eathorpe** [car park off Fosse Way; SP3868], *Plough*: Big helpings of good food inc some bargain meals in long neat and clean split-level lounge/dining area with matching walls, carpets and table linen, huge fish in tank by bar, good friendly chatty service; good cappuccino *(George Atkinson)*

☆ **Edge Hill** [SP3747], *Castle*: Interesting and well renovated 18th-c battlemented folly perched on steep hill, with good value proper pub food from sandwiches up, well kept Hook Norton Best, Old Hookey and Double Stout, Stowford Press cider, friendly efficient service, roaring log fire in interesting main bar with armoury and battle paintings, pool in separate room, drawbridge to turreted lavatories; children welcome; thoughtfully placed play house in pretty garden, terrace with fabulous views through trees *(Susan and John Douglas, Richard Lewis, Angus Lyon, Ted George, LYM)*

☆ **Ettington** [A422 Banbury—Stratford; SP2749], *Chequers*: Quickly served cheap usual food (not Mon evening) inc OAP lunches Tues and Thurs and reasonably priced Sun roasts, bright simply refurbished dining lounge with sporting prints, roomy conservatory, changing ales such as Bass, Hook Norton Best and M&B Brew XI, good service, basic front public bar with games and piped music, pool room; tables in good-sized back garden with Aunt Sally; children over 5 if eating *(F J and A Parmenter, Ted George, Nigel and Sue Foster, JB, K H Frostick, LYM)*

☆ **Ettington** [A422 towards Stratford; SP2550], *Houndshill House*: Neat dining pub with modestly priced decent food in pleasant surroundings, very popular with families and OAPs; S&N ales, stripped stone and beams, good service, tables in big attractive garden, good views from front; good well equipped bedrooms *(Thomas Nott)*

Grandborough [off A45 E of Dunchurch; SP4966], *Shoulder of Mutton*: Pleasant creeper-covered pub with lots of flowers outside, beamed and panelled lounge with pine furniture, friendly staff, no music, usual food, Marstons Pedigree and Whitbreads Fuggles Imperial; garden with play area and pets, inc goats *(George Atkinson)*

Halesowen W Mid [Manor Way; SO9683], *Black Horse*: Bigger than it looks, very popular for good value hearty food, efficient ordering system and service; Ansells Mild, Tetleys and Ind Coope Burton *(Howard and Margaret Buchanan)*; [21 Stourbridge Rd], *Waggon & Horses*: Fairly basic, with very welcoming locals, friendly service, well kept Bathams, a house beer and eight or so interesting changing ales from small independent brewers; no food *(Richard Houghton, Bob Mucklow)*

☆ Hampton in Arden W Mid [1½ miles from M42 junction 6 via village slip rd from exit roundabout; SP2081], *White Lion*: Unpretentious inn with unfussy beamed lounge, real fire, nautical decor inc navigation lights, welcoming staff, quick cheap food (not Sun) from sandwiches to steaks inc children's dishes, well kept Bass, M&B Brew XI and John Smiths, decent wine, public bar with cribbage and dominoes, back dining room; children allowed; attractive village, handy for NEC *(Keith Pollard, Malcom Fowlie, Jenny Williams, Martin Wright, LYM)*

☆ Hampton Lucy [E of Stratford; SP2557], *Boars Head*: Welcoming old beamed local, traditional decor, log fire, lots of brasses, well kept ales inc Theakstons and Youngers, prompt friendly service, well presented straightforward food; small enclosed garden, pretty village nr Charlcote House *(George Atkinson, P J Hanson)*

Harbury [Mill St; just off B4451/B4452 S of A425 Leamington Spa—Southam; SP3759], *Shakespeare*: Popular dining pub with linked beamed rooms, stripped stonework, reliable individually cooked food, well kept Whitbreads-related ales with guests such as Fullers London Pride and Timothy Taylors Landlord, good hospitable service, inglenook log fire, horsebrasses, bright and airy garden room, separate pool room; children welcome; tables in back garden with aviaries *(George Atkinson, Jenny and Michael Back)*

Hatton [Birmingham Rd (B4100); SP2467], *Falcon*: Isolated roadside low-beamed pub with big inglenook fireplace, small cosy dining room, very friendly service, good well priced food, well kept Bass, big back garden and walled terrace *(Allison and Geoffrey Wiggin)*

☆ Hawkesbury W Mid [close to M6 junction 3, exit past Novotel northwards on Longford Rd (B4113), 1st right into Black Horse Rd, cross canal and into Sutton Stop; SP3684], *Greyhound*: Cosy pub brimming with stuffed birds, toby jugs, ties and other nick-nacks, good interesting pies and other generous food with delicious proper chips, good puddings with custard, well kept Bass and Banks's Mild, happy staff, coal-fired stove, unusual tiny snug; booking essential for the Pie Parlour – lots of canalia and quite private olde-worlde atmosphere; tables on attractive terrace with safe play area by junction of Coventry and N Oxford Canals; children welcome *(Lynda Payton, Sam Samuells)*

Henley in Arden [High St; SP1466], *Three Tuns*: Small intimate pub, well kept Theakstons ales; weekday happy hour 5-7 *(Dr and Mrs A K Clarke)*

☆ Hockley Heath W Mid [Stratford Rd (A34 Birmingham—Henley-in-Arden); SP1573], *Wharf*: Friendly modernised Chef & Brewer, quick good value generous straightforward food inc first-class hot meat rolls, Courage-related ales, plenty of seats; darts, TV, games machines, piped pop music; children welcome; attractive garden with adventure playground by Stratford Canal, interesting towpath walks *(I Blackwell)*

☆ Kenilworth [High St; SP2871], *Clarendon House*: Comfortable traditional hotel, welcoming and civilised, with partly panelled bar, antique maps, prints, copper, china and armour, well kept Flowers IPA and Original and Hook Norton Best and Old Hookey, decent wines, good value simple bar food, interesting restaurant specials, friendly helpful staff; bedrooms good value *(Martyn E Lea, Tony Walker)*

Kenilworth [Warwick Rd], *Earl Clarendon*: Welcoming neatly refurbished local *(Dr and Mrs A K Clarke)*

Ladbroke [signed off A423 S of Southam; SP4158], *Bell*: Cosy Davenports pub with good range of well served good value grilled and fried food, friendly staff, nice atmosphere; tables in garden, pleasant surroundings – very busy weekends *(F M Bunbury)*

Lapworth [Old Warwick Rd (B4439); SP1670], *Boot*: Nicely placed canalside pub with friendly new management, two small bars, good atmosphere, decent range of beers, reasonable prices; small cosy restaurant upstairs, pleasant walks *(Phil and Julia Wigley, P R Ferris, David Suggitt)*

Leamington Spa [Chandos St; SP3165], *Carpenters Arms*: Restored early Victorian pub, open all day, with Tetleys-related ales, good choice of sandwiches and other freshly made food, coal fire, darts etc; small back terrace *(Terence Finn)*; [Campion Terr], *Somerville Arms*: Neat and cosy character local with tiny unspoilt Victorian back lounge, several well kept Tetleys-related ales, friendly staff, some memorabilia; no food *(Stephen and Jean Curtis)*

Leek Wootton [Warwick Rd; SP2868], *Anchor*: Busy and welcoming, with bookable dining lounge and smaller bar, good choice of tasty food (all day Sat, not Sun), friendly efficient service, particularly well kept Bass and a guest ale such as McMullens Gladstone; welcoming to walkers, popular with older people, picnic-table sets in pleasant garden behind *(George Atkinson, Thomas Nott, Geoff Lee)*

☆ Long Compton [A3400; SP2832], *Red Lion*: Stripped stone, bare beams, panelling, flagstones, old-fashioned built-in settles among other pleasantly assorted old seats and tables, old local photographs and prints, good food inc steak sizzlers in bar and restaurant, well kept Bass, M&B Brew XI and Worthington, obliging friendly staff, log fires and woodburners, separate more spartan bar with pool; garden with swings; bedrooms *(Alan and Paula McCully, LYM)*

☆ Long Itchington [Church Rd; SP4165],

Harvester: Efficiently served good value straightforward food in neat and tidy pub with three well kept Hook Norton ales and a guest, small relaxed restaurant, friendly staff *(Ted George)*

Long Lawford [1 Coventry Rd (A428); SP4776], *Sheaf & Sickle*: Small cosy lounge, biggish bar with darts and dominoes, four or five well kept ales, good value straightforward freshly made lunchtime bar food (so may be a wait), more extensive restaurant choice, friendly staff; tables in garden by cricket ground, open all day Sat *(Alain and Rose Foote, JJW, CMW)*

☆ **Lower Brailes** [B4035 Shipston on Stour—Banbury; SP3039], *George*: Pleasant old inn in lovely village setting, airy front bar with big stripped pine tables and woodburner in inglenook, panelled oak-beamed back bar, attractive country-style flagstoned restaurant, sizeable sheltered garden; well kept Hook Norton beers, pub games, provision for children, and bedrooms – but the tenants who did such good food left suddenly in early 1995, and as we went to press the new people had not yet had a chance to settle in *(LYM; news please)*

☆ **Lower Quinton** [off A46 Stratford—Broadway; SP1847], *College Arms*: Wide range of generous fresh food inc good Sun roasts, well kept Whitbreads-related ales, welcoming efficient service, spacious open-plan lounge with stripped stone and heavy beams, unusual highly polished tables inc one in former fireplace, leather seats, partly carpeted parquet floor; games in public bar; on green of pretty village *(Martin Jones)*

Meer End W Mid [A4147 Warwick—Brownhills; SP2474], *Tipperary*: Low ceilings, open fire, enormous goldfish in piano-aquarium, friendly courteous staff, good service even when busy, reasonably priced varied food inc good choice of puddings, children welcome with own menu, Greenalls ales; picnic-table sets in garden *(Tricia and Geoff Alderman, LYM)*

Meriden W Mid [Main Rd; SP2482], *Bulls Head*: Very wide choice of good value generous bar food in large, busy pub dating from 15th c, agreeable atmosphere, efficient staff; well kept Adnams Broadside and Bass, ancient staircase to restaurant *(Noel Lawrence, Margaret and Howard Buchanan)*; *Queens Head*: Tucked away, with reasonably priced food, M&B Brew XI with a guest ale such as Wadworths 6X, magazines to read *(Dave Braisted)*

Middleton [SP1798], *Green Man*: Busy extended beamed family dining pub with good standard food all day, M&B beers *(SLC, Maurice Drew, Jack Barnwell)*

Newbold on Avon [B4112; canalside; SP4777], *Barley Mow*: Busy local with good value promptly served straightforward food inc children's dishes and Sun lunch, horse-racing pictures, dining conservatory, well kept beer, helpful efficient service; big spacious garden with play area *(Alain and Rose Foote, C H and P Stride, Mayur Shah)*

Nuneaton [SP3592], *Fettlers & Firkin*: Recently opened, with bare boards, high ceiling, long bar, brewery memorabilia and posters, good value food, staff friendly even when busy; brewing own Buffer, Guard, Fettler and Dogbolter; piped music, open all day *(Richard Lewis)*; [Bond St, nr stn], *Railway*: Good choice of well kept mainly Whitbreads-related ales, comfortable lounge, beams and railway posters, partly tiled bar, pool room *(Richard Lewis)*

☆ **Offchurch** [off A425 at Radford Semele; SP3565], *Stags Head*: Low-beamed thatched dining pub doing well under current landlord, wide choice of good sensibly priced generous food inc good vegetarian dishes, friendly service, well kept Bass and Morlands Old Speckled Hen, unobtrusive piped music; tables in good-sized garden with play area *(Nigel and Sue Foster, Shaun O'Brien)*

Old Hill W Mid [A459 Halesowen—Dudley; SO9685], *Victoria*: Nice etched windows, pleasant prints, well priced basic food *(Dave Braisted)*; [132 Waterfall Lane, off Station Rd, between A4099 Gorstyhill Rd and A459 Halesowen Rd], *Waterfall*: Genuine down-to-earth local with well kept Bathams, Everards and Hook Norton and three or four interesting guest beers, farm cider, popular plain food from good filled rolls to Sun lunch, tankards and jugs hanging from boarded ceiling; piped music *(Dave Braisted)*; [Waterfall Lane], *Wharf*: Popular chatty drinking pub with eight or so well kept largely S&N ales, cheap food (not Sun) inc children's dishes, pool, juke box, pinball and other games, family area, tables in canalside garden with play area; occasional live music *(Dave Braisted, LYM)*

Old Swinford W Mid [157 Hagley Rd; SO9283], *Retreat*: Bistro/pub that's a real oasis for its good informal largely Mediterranean-inspired food inc bargain lunches (not Sun), in big-windowed bare-boards dining area *(Simon Cottrell)*

☆ **Oldbury W Mid** [Church St, nr Savacentre; SO9888], *Waggon & Horses*: Impressive Edwardian tiles and copper ceiling in busy town pub with well kept changing ales such as Bathams Best, Enville Bitter and Yellow Belly, Everards Tiger, Morlands Old Speckled Hen and Woods Special, wide choice of food inc balti dishes in bar and bookable upstairs bistro, decent wines, friendly staff, simple furnishings inc high-backed settles and big tables, Black Country memorabilia, tie collection *(Richard Lewis, Andy Petersen)*

Oldbury [Church St], *White Hart*: Nicely refurbished, with comfortable separate areas, friendly staff, lunchtime food, well kept Banks's Bitter, Mild and Timewarp and Camerons Strongarm *(Richard Lewis)*

Pailton [B4027 Coventry—Lutterworth; SP4781], *White Lion*: Biggish nicely furnished 18th-c pub/restaurant popular for wide range of quickly served decent food inc two-sitting Sun lunch and children's dishes, good range of wines, well kept beers; play area in garden; cl Mon; bedrooms *(Geoff Lee)*

Portway [by A435, just off M42 junction 3; SP0872], *Rose & Crown*: Much extended Greenalls pub with large conservatory, food inc good lunchtime toasted baguettes, evening restaurant *(Dave Braisted)*

☆ Princethorpe [High Town; junction A423/B4453; SP4070], *Three Horseshoes*: Friendly old coaching inn with lots of brass, beams, plates, pictures, comfortable settles and chairs; Judges Barristers, Marstons Pedigree, Ruddles County and John Smiths, country wines, good value freshly prepared food inc children's, vegetarian and Sun lunch, good service, no-smoking eating area, open fire; pleasant big garden with play equipment *(JJW, CMW, George Atkinson)*

☆ Priors Hardwick [SP4756], *Butchers Arms*: Medieval oak beams, flagstones, panelling and antiques in good friendly upmarket pub/restaurant (not cheap), good service; log fire and keg beer in small welcoming inglenook bar, country garden *(T M Dobby, Mr and Mrs H G Blenkinsop, D Marsh)*

☆ Priors Marston [Hellidon Rd; village signed off A425 in Southam, and off A361 S of Daventry; SP4857], *Falcon*: Civilised, neat and friendly rambling bar, log fire in high stone fireplace, high-backed winged settles, country pictures, generous popular bar food from sandwiches to prime Scotch steaks, well kept Adnams and Everards Beacon and Old Original, no-smoking area; children welcome, bedrooms *(Thomas Nott, Mrs J Oakes, LYM)*

☆ Priors Marston [follow Shuckburgh sign, then first right by phone box], *Holly Bush*: Character golden stone pub, small rambling rooms, beams and stripped stone, old-fashioned pub seats, up to three fires in winter, good bar food from sandwiches to steaks inc children's and Sun roasts, well kept Bass, Hook Norton Best, Marstons Pedigree and two guest beers, restaurant; darts, pool, games machines, juke box, piped music; children welcome, bedrooms *(Michael Jeanes, George Atkinson, LYM)*

Quarry Bank W Mid [Saltwells Lane; signed off Coppice Lane (A4036) nr Merry Hill Centre – OS Sheet 139 map ref 934868; SO9386], *Saltwells*: At end of rough lane past factory through nature reserve, popular with OAPs and families for good value lunches inc steak bargains; main lounge with bookshelves, family room, garden with play area; can be busy on sunny days; simple clean bedrooms *(Graham and John Mason)*

☆ Ratley [OS Sheet 151 map ref 384473; SP3847], *Rose & Crown*: Handsome old beamed local of golden stone, cosy atmosphere, Badger Tanglefoot and Charles Wells Eagle and Bombardier, good home-cooked food inc superb puddings, friendly family service, woodburning stove in flagstoned area on right, big log fireplace in carpeted area on left; three lively roan cocker spaniels; tables in small garden, nr lovely church in small sleepy village *(George Atkinson)*

Red Hill [off A422 W of Stratford; SP1355], *White Hart*: Useful bar food, pleasant

surroundings, attentive staff; part of a hotel complex, in attractive countryside *(D G King)*

Rugby [Sheep St; SP5075], *Fitchew & Firkin*: Impressive bare-boards refurbishment with plenty of seating, lots of brewery memorabilia, good choice of reasonably priced food, friendly staff, well kept beers brewed on the premises, Addlestone's cider, newspapers, some live music *(Richard Lewis)*; [The Green, Bilton; A4071 SW edge; SP4873], *George*: Largish open-plan pub with pool and skittles at one end, quite good value dining the other, well kept ales inc Ansells; piped pop music may be rather loud *(JJW, CMW)*; [Dunchurch Rd], *Raglan Arms*: Friendly pub with roomy comfortable lounge, basic bar with darts, dominoes and pool, well kept ales such as Batemans Mild, Fullers London Pride, Greene King Abbot, Marstons Pedigree, Best and Monks Habit, Robinsons Best and Timothy Taylors Landlord, sensible prices; no music *(Richard Lewis)*; [centre], *Rugby Tavern*: Cosy lounge with lots of old railway prints, friendly staff, good choice of reasonably priced food, well kept ales such as Marstons Pedigree, Theakstons XB, Wadworths 6X and Websters; bar with pool, TV and games machine *(Richard Lewis)*; [Sheep St], *Three Horseshoes*: Very well kept ales such as Boddingtons, Bunces Old Smoky and Fullers London Pride in plush hotel's cosy olde-worlde bar, usual food from sandwiches up, popular eating area, relaxed atmosphere, friendly staff; bedrooms *(Richard Lewis)*

☆ Sedgley W Mid [Bilston St (A463); SO9193], *Beacon*: Unspoilt local brewing its own good well priced Sarah Hughes Surprise Bitter and Dark Ruby Mild in restored tower brewery, two or three other well kept ales from tiny circular serving area with hatches to several Victorian rooms, family room and conservatory; outside lavatories, seats on terrace *(Mike Begley)*

☆ Shipston on Stour [Station Rd (off A3400); SP2540], *Black Horse*: Ancient thatched and beamed pub with good value home cooking inc Mon-Thurs bargain meals, well kept Home, Ruddles, Theakstons XB, Websters and a guest beer, properly pubby atmosphere, friendly staff and locals, inglenook log fire, small dining room, back garden with terrace and barbecue, newfoundland dog and a couple of cats *(Peter Lloyd, Dr and Mrs J H Hills, Alan and Paula McCully)*

Shipston on Stour [Church St], *Horseshoe*: Pretty timbered inn with open-plan largely modern bar, lots of maroon plush, generous straightforward bar food with good chips, big fireplace with copper pans above, enjoyable chintzy evening restaurant; Courage-related ales with a guest such as Butcombe, decent coffee, darts, no piped music; small flower-decked back terrace; bedrooms pretty, bright and clean *(Pam Adsley, LYM)*; [High St], *White Bear*: Massive settles, good range of beers and cheerful atmosphere in traditional front bar, simple comfortable back lounge, interesting good value generous food, tables in small back yard and benches on street;

bedrooms *(Michele and Clive Platman, LYM)*

Shuttington [SK2505], *Wolferstan Arms*: Well run friendly family pub with imaginative reasonably priced menu, well kept Marstons Pedigree, long-serving staff, wide views from restaurant and garden, play area *(Graham Richardson)*

Snitterfield [Smiths Lane/School Rd; off A46 N of Stratford; SP2159], *Fox Hunter*: Attractive and comfortable, with banquettes and hunting pictures in L-shaped bar/lounge, wide range of well presented and reasonably priced standard food inc Sun roasts, Bass and M&B Brew XI; piped music (turned down on request), fruit machine, children allowed; tables outside *(Dorothy and Leslie Pilson, JJW, CMW)*

☆ **Southam** [A423, towards Coventry; SP4161], *Old Mint*: 14th-c pub open all day Sat, considerable potential in two character heavy-beamed rooms, well kept Bass, Hook Norton Best, Marstons Pedigree, Timothy Taylors Landlord, Wadworths 6X and guest ales, country wines, winter hot punch, open fire; darts, fruit machine, piped music *(David Shillitoe, LYM)*

Stockton [High St; SP4363], *Crown*: Friendly village inn, two real fires, brasses and copper pans, assorted furniture inc armchairs and settee, at least six real ales (some unusual), good reasonably priced straightforward home-made food inc sandwiches and vegetarian; pool, darts and other games one end, piped music or juke box; restaurant in ancient barn, boules *(CMW, JJW)*

☆ **Stonnall** W Mid [Main St, off A452; SK0703], *Old Swann*: Wide choice of good food inc fine sandwiches and bargain OAP meals (booking advised for Sun lunch), friendly and efficient service, particularly well kept Bass and a guest such as Youngs *(Jack Barnwell, Cliff Blakemore, Dorothee and Dennis Glover)*

Stourbridge W Mid [Red Hill, Old Swinford; SO9283], *Labour in Vain*: 1940s wartime theme, good faggots, peas and chips, Banks's *(Dave Braisted)*

☆ **Stratford upon Avon** [Southern Way; SP0255], *Black Swan*: Great atmosphere, mildly sophisticated, in neat 16th-c pub nr Memorial Theatre – still attracts actors, lots of signed RSC photographs; wide choice of plainly served bar food at moderate prices, Flowers and other Whitbreads-related ales, quick service, open fire, bustling public bar (little lounge seating for drinkers), children allowed in small dining area; attractive terrace looking over the riverside public gardens – which tend to act as summer overflow; known as the Dirty Duck *(Gary Nicholls, Peter and Audrey Dowsett, James Hanson, Michael Butler, Ralph Hunter, Greg Grimsley, Buck and Gillian Shinkman, LYM)*

☆ **Stratford upon Avon** [High St, nr Town Hall], *Garrick*: Fine ancient building, with bare boards, lots of beams and timbers, stripped stone, lively evening theatrical character, cosy front bar, busier back one, central open fire, well kept Whitbreads-related ales with guests

such as Fullers London Pride, sensibly priced bar food inc good puddings (popular with office workers lunchtime), friendly service, thoughtfully chosen piped music; children allowed away from bar *(Ted George, Michael Butler, Dr and Mrs A K Clarke, Angus Lyon, Andy and Gill Plumb, SLC, Gary Nicholls, LYM)*

Stratford upon Avon, *Arden*: Hotel not pub, but closest bar to Memorial Theatre, Courage Best and Directors, good baguettes, tasty bread and butter pudding, smart evening bouncer; very popular, get there early; bedrooms good, not cheap *(Christopher and Maureen Starling, Sue Holland, Dave Webster)*; [Arden St/Greenhill St], *Froth & Elbow*: Spacious, with flagstones, bare boards and beams, well kept Flowers, Wadworths 6X and other ales, reasonably priced bar food, welcoming staff; small terrace *(Nigel and Sue Foster)*; [Rother St/Greenhill St], *Old Thatch*: Friendly lively local, decent wine, well kept Brains and Flowers, decent straightforward food *(John and Christine Vittoe)*; [Ely St], *Queens Head*: Cheerful authentic local with decent cheap food inc unusual snacks and Sun lunch, well kept M&B Brew XI and varied guest beers, long-serving staff *(Mike Steveni, SLC)*; [Warwick Rd, opp Midland Red bus depot], *Red Lion*: Large friendly Brewers Fayre pub by canal, reasonably priced standard food, good range of real ales, modern pub games; children welcome, play area *(Dr and Mrs A K Clarke, Alain and Rose Foote)*; [Evesham Rd], *Salmon Tail*: Doing well under hard-working new licensees, with well kept interesting beers, reasonably priced bar food *(Peter Lloyd)*; [Chapel St], *Shakespeare*: Smart hotel based on handsome lavishly modernised Tudor merchants' houses, comfortable lounge with plush settees and armchairs, huge log fire, tables in sheltered courtyard; bedrooms comfortable and well equipped, though not cheap *(John and Christine Vittoe, LYM)*; [Rother St], *White Swan*: Comfortable old-fashioned beamed hotel bar with 16th-c wall painting of Tobias and the Angel, leather armchairs, antique settles, fine oak panelling, lunchtime bar snacks, quick friendly service; children in eating area; bedrooms *(John and Christine Vittoe, LYM)*; [Church St], *Windmill*: Cosy and welcoming old pub beyond the attractive church, wide choice of reasonably priced bar food inc vegetarian, well kept Whitbreads-related and interesting guest ales; shame about the fruit machine *(Geoffrey and Irene Lindley, Sue Holland, Dave Webster, John and Christine Vittoe)*

Stretton on Dunsmore [Brookside, off A45 and A423; SP4172], *Oak & Black Dog*: Friendly pleasant long room with bar and dining area at opp ends, lots of beams and china, fire, tasty good value food, good service from cheerful chatty staff, evening restaurant area, unusual real ales *(George Atkinson)*; *Shoulder of Mutton*: Friendly village local with coal fire in snug Victorian panelled public bar, particularly well kept

M&B Mild and Brew XI on handpump, cards and dominoes, pictures of old Coventry, spotless furniture; spacious 1950s lounge with fancy tiled floor, grand piano and two darts boards; cl Mon-Thurs lunchtime, erratic opening Sat lunchtime *(Pete Baker)*

Stretton on Fosse [just off A429; SP2238], *Plough*: Large lounge and smaller bar with darts and fruit machine, good value pub food, Flowers Original and Theakstons Old Peculier *(George Atkinson)*

☆ Studley [Icknield St Dr; left turn off A435, going N from B4093 roundabout; SP0763], *Old Washford Mill*: Attractive ivy-covered converted watermill, different levels, quiet alcoves, three different restaurants in varying styles, provision for children, real ales tapped from the cask (some brewed on the premises), country wines, internal millstream and interesting old mill machinery; pretty waterside gardens with good play area, ducks and black swan *(Patricia Tovey, LYM)*

Studley, *Barley Mow*: Toby Inn with popular carvery – have to book Sun lunch; staff friendly and efficient, Bass, decent wines *(Dave Braisted)*

Sutton Coldfield W Mid [Slade Rd, Roughley; SP1296], *Plough & Harrow*: Friendly roadhouse with well kept Bass and decent straightforward food with some surprises *(Pete Yearsley)*; [Chester Rd (A452), New Oscott], *Tailors*: Large 1930s country-house-style pub, tall bar stools along long high counter, small tables, leaded lights and prints, good reasonably priced food in bar and restaurant, Courage real ale; piped music may be rather loud; open all day *(Ian Phillips, Lynn Fellows)*

Tanworth in Arden [SP1170], *Bell*: Roomy lounge with well kept Whitbreads-related ales, bar food inc good dish of the day, outlook on peaceful village green and lovely 14th-c church; children in eating area and restaurant *(Dave Braisted, LYM)*

Tipton W Mid [Park Lane W; SO9592], *Boscobel*: Banks's pub popular for good value substantial lunches *(Dave Braisted)*

☆ Ufton [White Hart Lane; just off A425 Daventry—Leamington, towards Bascote; SP3761], *White Hart*: Friendly old hilltop pub with big lounge/dining area, good choice of usual food, well kept Greenalls and Wadworths 6X, quick friendly service; hatch service to garden with boules and fine views (Tannoy food announcements out here) *(Rona Murdoch, J H Bell, George Atkinson)*

Walsall W Mid [Wolverhampton Rd; SP0198], *Bridge*: Handy for M6, good value basic meals, M&B beers *(Dave Braisted)*

☆ Warwick [11 Market Pl; SP2865], *Tilted Wig*: Pleasant bustling Georgian town pub, neat and clean, big airy interior divided into three areas, some stripped stone, scattered rugs on bare boards, country-kitchen furniture, good views over square; well kept Tetleys-related and interesting guest ales such as Judges Barrister, good range of wines, wide choice of good value home-made food (not Sun evening), quick friendly service; tables in

garden, live jazz and folk Sun evening, open all day Fri/Sat and summer *(George Atkinson, Andrew Tilley, Joan and Tony Walker, SLC)*

☆ Warwick [11 Church St], *Zetland Arms*: Pleasant town pub with limited choice of cheap bar food (not weekend evenings), well kept Davenports, friendly quick service, functional bar, comfortable lounge; small conservatory, interestingly planted sheltered garden; children may be allowed; bedrooms, sharing bathroom *(Owen Warnock, SLC, LYM)*

Warwick [Crompton St, nr racecourse], *Old Fourpenny Shop*: Friendly M&B pub with well kept guests like Adnams or Butterknowle, bar meals *(SLC)*; [Guy's Cliffe – A429 just N], *Saxon Mill*: Converted mill with long history, wheel turning slowly behind glass, mill race under glass floor-panel, tables in lovely setting by broad green wooded river, delightful views; inside is straightforward Harvester family eating pub, with beams and flagstones, well kept Courage-related ales, summer weekend barbecues, good play area; open all day every day *(AEM, JD, SD, LYM)*; [West St], *Tudor House*: Attractive and popular old coaching inn, lots of black timber, parquet floor, suits of armour; good promptly served food inc ploughman's and yorkshire puddings, decent wine, reasonable prices; piped music *(James Nunns, Peter Neate)*; [West St, towards Stratford], *Wheatsheaf*: Well laid out, with well kept Tetleys-related and guest ales, wide range of good value food from sandwiches to steaks, attractive bric-a-brac, good staff; pool, fruit machine, two friendly cats; bedrooms, handy for castle *(Mr and Mrs R C Watson, SLC)*

☆ Welford on Avon [High St (Binton Rd); SP1452], *Bell*: Dim-lit dark-timbered low-beamed lounge, flagstoned public bar with darts, pool and so forth, open fires, good friendly staff, well kept Whitbreads-related ales, generous straightforward food inc good value Sun lunch, dining conservatory (children allowed here); piped music; tables in pretty garden and back courtyard; attractive riverside village *(Peter Williams, Marjorie and David Lamb, Martin Lavery, Thomas Nott, Jenny and Michael Back, LYM)*

Wellesbourne [SP2755], *Kings Head*: Pleasantly updated high-ceilinged lounge bar, lively public bar, well kept real ales, tables in garden facing church; bedrooms – handy for Stratford but cheaper *(Dr and Mrs A K Clarke, LYM)*

West Bromwich W Mid [Sandwell Rd; SP0091], *Old Crown*: New licensees doing authentic home-cooked curries, balti, bhuna and tikka dishes inc speciality chicken tikka masala *(Anon)*

☆ Whatcote [SP2944], *Royal Oak*: Dating from 12th c, quaint low-ceilinged small room, huge inglenook, Civil War connections, lots to look at, animal skins on wall; wide choice of decent straightforward bar food (not usually quick unless you ask specially), welcoming service, well kept Bass and Marstons Pedigree,

picnic-table sets outside; children welcome
(*Mrs J Oakes, Nigel and Sue Foster, LYM*)

Whitacre Heath [Station Rd, off B4114 at
Blyth End E of Coleshill; SP2192], *White
Swan*: Recently refurbished, with good value
food, well kept Charles Wells and M&B;
being renovated (*Dave Braisted*)

☆ **Willey** [just off A5, N of A427 junction;
SP4984], *Old Watling*: Polished flagstones,
stripped masonry and plenty of cosy corners,
neatly kept furnishings, open fire, quick
cheerful service, generous good value well
presented enterprising bar food (most tables
may be booked), well kept Adnams, Banks's
and Courage-related beers (*Thomas Nott*)

Willoughby [just off A45 E of Dunchurch;
SP5267], *Rose*: Friendly small beamed pub
with popular lunchtime food from good
toasties to Sun carvery, OAP Tues and Thurs,
evening restaurant, Marstons Pedigree and
Websters Dark, cheerful staff, garden with
play area; cl Mon and Weds lunchtimes
(*George Atkinson*)

Wilmcote [The Green; 3 miles NW of
Stratford, just off new A46 bypass; SP1657],
Swan House: Genteel country hotel with
glass-topped well in 18th-c beamed lounge,
smiling efficient service, good home-made
food inc game and sizzle steaks in bar and
restaurant, well kept Bass, Hook Norton Best
and Theakstons XB; comfortable bedrooms,
front terrace overlooking Mary Arden's
cottage, tables in back garden; bedrooms
(*Joan and Michel Hooper-Immins*)

☆ **Wixford** [SP0954], *Three Horseshoes*: Roomy
pub with consistently good generous food inc
interesting specials (not cheap), charming
landlord and staff, good range of well kept
ales (*W H and E Thomas, Peter Lloyd, Moira
and John Cole*)

☆ **Wolverhampton W Mid** [Sun St, behind old
low-level stn; SO9198], *Great Western*:
Classic three-bar backstreet pub with
particularly well kept Bathams and Holdens,

very promptly served good value plain food
inc huge cheap filled cobs and local
specialities, lots of railway memorabilia,
friendly staff, tables in yard with good
barbecues and extension marquee; parking
limited lunchtime (*Richard Lewis, John
Winterbottom, Addie and Irene Henry*)

Wolverhampton [Penn Wood Lane, Penn
Common (off A449, actually just over Staffs
border); SO9094], *Barley Mow*: Tiny 17th-c
free house tucked away in rural setting
beyond a housing estate, sensibly limited
range of good home-made food using meat
from local butcher, huge helpings, friendly
welcome, unusual real ales and cider,
reasonable prices; children's play area (*Mrs L
M Peach, Wendy Proctor, A P Jeffreys*);
[Dudley Rd], *Brewery Tap*: Very refurbished
and busy, low-priced food, well kept Holt
Plant & Deakins (*Dave Braisted*); [9 Princess
St], *Feline & Firkin*: Large comfortable bare-
boards pub with lots of brewery memorabilia,
big tables, friendly staff, good value food,
well kept own-brewed ales and Addlestone's
cider, back pool table; very busy weekends
(*Richard Lewis, Jared Warner*); [53 Lichfield
St], *Moon Under Water*: New Wetherspoons
in well transformed former Co-op, lots of
seating, panelling and prints, wide choice of
reasonably priced food all day, good choice of
particularly well kept ales inc two guests,
friendly staff (*Richard Lewis*)

Wolvey Heath [SP4390], *Axe & Compass*:
Very good value food from sandwiches up,
well kept Bass, Hook Norton Best, M&B
Brew XI, several guest beers and decent
wines, genial landlord, good neat staff –
friendly even on busy evenings; restaurant;
piped music, seating could be more spacious
(*Michael Jeanes, Genie and Brian Smart*)

Wootton Wawen [A34; SP1563], *Navigation*:
Pleasant spacious dining pub by Stratford
Canal, Boddingtons and Flowers, good value
bar food inc children's, restaurant (*D Stokes*)

We mention bottled beers and spirits only if there is something unusual about
them – imported Belgian real ales, say, or dozens of malt whiskies; so do
please let us know about them in your reports.

Wiltshire

This favoured county has a lot of pubs of real character which do good food – sometimes exceptionally good – without losing their essential charm as places where people enjoy dropping in for a drink and a chat. Pubs which have recently been generating particular enthusiasm among readers include the Red Lion at Axford (very popular food, especially fish), the Quarrymans Arms on its hillside near Box (so steep that they are having to put their new restaurant on stilts), the very busy Cross Guns near Bradford on Avon (popular food in a great setting), the Three Crowns at Brinkworth (doing exceptionally well, with some really unusual food), the charming little Horseshoe at Ebbesbourne Wake, the White Hart at Ford (an excellent all-rounder), the George at Lacock (a real credit to this lovely village), the friendly and relaxed Hop Pole at Limpley Stoke (back in these pages after a long absence), the Owl at Little Cheverell (another newcomer – a sweet little place), the Raven at Poulshot (good food, perfectly kept beer), the George & Dragon at Rowde (exceptional food, especially fish but a proper pub, not just a dining place), the Lamb at Semington (now completely no smoking), the picturesque Golden Swan at Wilcot (a new main entry), and the Royal Oak at Wootton Rivers, very popular for its enormous range of food. This year the George & Dragon at Rowde is our choice as Wiltshire Dining Pub of the Year, for its combination of delicious food with a properly welcoming pubby atmosphere. Drinks prices in the county are close to the national average, though our price survey showed that pubs supplied by Wadworths, the Devizes brewer, often had much cheaper beer than others. In the Lucky Dip section at the end of the chapter, pubs on particularly good form in recent months include the Crown at Alvediston, Crown at Bishops Cannings, Crown at Broad Hinton, Mermaid at Christian Malford, Dove at Corton, Bell at Great Cheverell, Linnet at Great Hinton, Jolly Tar at Hannington, Spread Eagle at Stourton and Poplars at Wingfield (we have inspected all these, and can confirm their appeal). Salisbury has a good interesting choice.

AXFORD SU2370 Map 2

Red Lion 🛏 ♀ ◖

Off A4 E of Marlborough; on back road Mildenhall—Ramsbury

It's the blackboard specials and more especially the fresh fish that have particularly delighted visitors to this pretty flint-and-brick pub over the last year. The emphasis is very much on the food, but drinkers are made just as welcome as those coming for a meal – and you're quite likely to be welcomed like a local on your first visit. A typical day's menu might include sandwiches, courgette and tomato soup, lovely smoked salmon roulade, good potted stilton in port, smoked prawns (£3.75), smoked trout (£4.50), lovely sardines or plaice (£7.25), river trout, mullet (£9), crayfish (£8.50), lamb fillet (£10.50), lemon sole (£10.95), steaks (from £10.25), local game such as pheasant or partridge (£10.50), dover sole (£13.50), and fresh lobster (£18.75); salads and vegetables are very fresh and crisp, and they do excellent sauté potatoes. There are comfortable cask seats and other solid chairs on the spotless parquet floor of the bustling beamed and pine-panelled bar, with picture windows for the fine valley view; the restaurant is no smoking. The well kept beers change all the time, but might include Greene King Abbot, Hook Norton Best, Shepherd Neame Spitfire and Wadworths 6X on handpump; local and New World wines. Darts, shove-ha'penny, cribbage, dominoes, fruit machine, and unobtrusive piped music; prompt, pleasant service. The sheltered garden has picnic tables under cocktail parasols, swings, and lovely views. *(Recommended by D Clarke, Lynda Payton, Sam Samuels, Alan Griffiths, M L and G Clarke, Philip Orbell, Mr and Mrs Cresswell, Michael and Hazel Lyons, Kevin and Kay Bronnsey, Alan and Paula McCully, Pat and Robert Wyatt, Mr and Mrs Smith, S C King, Colin Laffan)*

Free house ~ Licensees Mel and Daphne Evans ~ Real ale ~ Meals and snacks (till 10) ~ Restaurant ~ (01672) 520271 ~ Children welcome ~ Open 11-3.30, 6.30-11 ~ Bedrooms: £30B/£45B

BARFORD ST MARTIN SU0531 Map 2
Barford

Junction A30/B3089

Outstandingly well maintained and cared for, this nicely old-fashioned pub has various chatty interlinking rooms and bars, all with dark wooden tables and red cushioned chairs. Generally busier in the evenings than at lunchtime, the front bar also has some interesting squared oak panelling, and a big log fire in winter. Their Friday evening Israeli barbecues (all year round, from 7pm) are well liked, and other reliable food includes soup (£2.25), filled baked potatoes or big sandwiches (£2.95), ploughman's (from £4.25), falafel with hummous (£4.50), ham and two eggs (£4.95), broccoli and mushroom casserole or cottage pie (£5.25), steak and kidney pie (£6.50), steaks (from £8.95), children's dishes (£2.95), and puddings (£2.25); friendly attentive service. Well kept Badger Best and Tanglefoot on handpump, and quite a few country wines; darts, cribbage, and piped music. Part of the restaurant is no smoking. They've recently added access for wheelchairs, and a lavatory for the disabled. There are tables on an outside terrace, and more in a back garden. The bedrooms may well deserve our stay award, so we'd be particularly interested to hear from readers who've stayed here. *(Recommended by Mayur Shah, Stephen Harvey, R Walden, Sheila Edwards, Stephen and Julie Brown, Dr and Mrs A K Clarke, John and Christine Vittoe, Gordon)*

Badger ~ Tenant Ido Davids ~ Real ale ~ Meals and snacks (11.30-3, 7-10) ~ Restaurant ~ (01722) 742242 ~ Children welcome ~ Summer folk duets and Morris dancers ~ Open 11.30-11; 11.30-3, 7-11 winter ~ Bedrooms: £28B/£40B

BERWICK ST JOHN ST9323 Map 2
Talbot

Village signposted from A30 E of Shaftesbury

Tables are candlelit in the evenings at this well run and friendly Ebbe Valley pub, a popular place for eating. The single long, heavy beamed bar is simply furnished, with cushioned solid wall and window seats, spindleback chairs, a high-backed built-in settle at one end, heavy black beams and cross-beams (nicely shaped with bevelled corners), and a huge inglenook fireplace with a good iron fireback and bread ovens. Carefully prepared bar food includes home-made soups like chicken and mushroom (£2.95), garlic mushrooms or sliced smoked trout (£4.50), excellent ploughman's, pasta with a stilton and walnut sauce, steak and kidney pie (£7.50), good curries (£7.95), chicken tikka (£8.50), steaks (£13.50), and home-made puddings like treacle tart or bread and butter pudding (£3.25); note there is no food on Sunday lunchtimes. Adnams Best and Broadside, Bass, and Wadworths 6X on handpump, and good wines; cribbage and dominoes. The landlord is particularly helpful. There are some tables on the back lawn. The village is pretty and peaceful, and full of thatched old houses. *(Recommended by Joy and Peter Heatherley, G and M Stewart, Gordon, Howard Allen)*

Free house ~ Licensees Roy and Wendy Rigby ~ Real ale ~ Meals and snacks (not Sun) ~ Restaurant ~ (01747) 828222 ~ Children in eating area of bar; no under 7s in evening ~ Open 11.30-2.30, 6.30(7 Mon)-11; closed Sun evening

BOX ST8369 Map 2

Quarrymans Arms

Box Hill; coming from Bath on A4 turn right into Bargates 50 yds before railway bridge, then at T-junction turn left up Quarry Hill, turning left again near the top at grassy triangle; from Corsham, turn left after Rudloe Park Hotel into Beech Rd, then third left onto Barnetts Hill, and finally right at the top of the hill

This popular place isn't the easiest pub to find, but really is well worth tracking down for its excellent food. A typical day's menu might include sandwiches, tasty home-made soup (£2.25), stilton and asparagus pancake (£3.25), excellent mussels and prawns baked in white wine and garlic (£4.50), spinach and ricotta cannelloni (£5.25), chicken supreme with noodles and a brandy, cream and mushroom sauce (£7.25), duck breast with honey and thyme (£8.50), wild boar fillet with blueberry, maple syrup and whisky sauce (£9.95), and specials such as steamed sea bass with tarragon and grain mustard sauce (£9.25) or venison with a blackcurrant sauce and woodland berries (£11.50). Servce is helpful and friendly, though it can be rather slow. Well kept Bass, Butcombe, Wadworths 6X, and guests like Wickwar Brand Oak on handpump, good wines, 40 malt whiskies, and ten or so vintage cognacs. Darts, shove-ha'penny, cribbage, dominoes, fruit machine, video game, boules, cricket, and piped music. Despite the emphasis on food the much-modernised bar is still the kind of place you can come to for just a drink. Interesting quarry photographs and memorabilia cover the walls, and there are dramatic views over the valley; the snug is no smoking. Picnic-table sets outside. The pub is ideally situated for cavers, potholers and walkers, and runs interesting guided trips down the local Bath stone mine. As we went to press they were about to start work on a new restaurant on stilts overlooking the valley, and were planning to add ensuite bathrooms to the bedrooms. *(Recommended by John and Wendy Trentham, A Board, M G Hart, Dr and Mrs A H Young, Meg and Colin Hamilton, Robert Huddleston, Gwen and Peter Andrews, S A Moir)*

Free house ~ Licensees John and Ginny Arundel ~ Real ale ~ Meals and snacks (12-3, 7-10.30) ~ Restaurant ~ (01225) 743569 ~ Children welcome away from bar ~ Open 11-11; 12-10.30 Sun ~ Bedrooms: £20/£30

nr BRADFORD ON AVON ST8060 Map 2

Cross Guns

Avoncliff; pub is across footbridge from Avoncliff Station (road signposted Turleigh turning left off A363 heading uphill N from river in Bradford centre, and keep bearing left), and can also be reached down very steep and eventually unmade road signposted Avoncliff – keep straight on rather than turning left into village centre – from Westwood (which is signposted from B3109 and from A366, W of Trowbridge); OS Sheet 173 map reference 805600

The pretty terraced gardens of this idyllically set country pub, floodlit at night, have splendid views down to the wide river Avon, taking in the maze of bridges, aqueducts (the Kennet & Avon Canal) and tracks that wind through this quite narrow gorge. It's very well liked by readers at the moment, as much for the food as for the location, with the meals extraordinarily good value considering the quality. All home-made, generously served dishes might include sandwiches (from £1.70), pâté (£2.50), very good stilton or cheddar ploughman's (from £3.20), steak and kidney pie (£4.95), various fish dishes, steaks (from £4.50; 32oz £12.50), trout (£4.90), lemon sole (£6.25), and duck in orange sauce (£5.95), with delicious puddings (from £1.95). Well kept Courage Best and Directors, John Smiths, Ushers Best and a guest beer on handpump; good service. There's a nice old-fashioned feel to the bar, with its core of low 17th-c. rush-seated chairs around plain sturdy oak tables (most of which are set for diners, and many of them reserved), stone walls, and a large ancient fireplace with a smoking chamber behind it; piped music. There may be a system of Tannoy announcements for meal orders from outside tables. Walkers are very welcome, but not their muddy boots. The pub gets very busy, especially at weekends and summer lunchtimes, so if you want to eat it's probably best to book. *(Recommended by Andrew Shore, Gordon, Stephen G Brown, Peter and Audrey Dowsett, Dr and Mrs A H Young, Tony and Wendy Hobden, Meg and Colin Hamilton, Richard Dolphin, Andrew Partington, Mrs E M Astley Weston, Dr Diana Terry, Ron Gentry, Roger Wain-Heapy)*

Free house ~ Licensees Dave and Gwen Sawyer ~ Real ale ~ Meals and snacks (till 9.45) ~ (01225) 862335 ~ Children in eating area ~ Open 11-3, 6.30-11; closed 25 and evening 26 Dec

BRINKWORTH SU0184 Map 2
Three Crowns 🍴 ♟

The Street; B4042 Wootton Bassett—Malmesbury

The bar food here really is very good indeed – more expensive than you'd find elsewhere, but with a corresponding leap in quality and flavours; many readers reckon it's among the best food they've eaten in any pub or restaurant. Changing every day, the imaginative choice covers an entire wall and can take some time to read through properly; as well as very good crusty filled rolls they might have home-made pies like steak and kidney (£8.50) or pork and venison (£9.50), an elaborate mushroom stroganoff (£9.95), medaillons of pork with mushrooms, onions and smoked bacon, flamed with apricot wine and served with cheese dumplings (£10.95), tuna en croûte with fresh chervil and brie (£12.45), half a crispy roast duck with orange marmalade sauce (£12.95), whole black-banded bream stuffed with leek, apricot, tomato and basil (£13.45), crocodile tail with chopped shallots and mushrooms, flamed in brandy with a hint of ginger, and served in a filo pastry basket with rice, capers and anchovies (£14.95), and ostrich in peppercorn and marsala sauce, or pan fried kangaroo with sweet roast garlic, flamed in cherry wine (£15.95). Most meals are accompanied by a goodly selection of fresh vegetables. It's worth arriving as early as you can in the evening as they don't take bookings. Particularly nice is the way that this has remained very much a pub, despite its appeal to diners; most people choose to eat in the elegant no-smoking conservatory, so that the rambling bar is busy with drinkers too. There's a lovely traditional feel in all its little enclaves, as well as big landscape prints and other pictures on the walls, some horsebrasses on the dark beams, a dresser with a collection of old bottles, tables of stripped deal (and a couple made from gigantic forge bellows), green-cushioned big pews and blond chairs, and log fires; sensibly placed darts, shove-ha'penny, dominoes, cribbage, chess, fruit machine, piped music. Well kept Archers Village, Bass, Boddingtons, Wadworths 6X and Whitbreads Castle Eden on handpump, an ever-expanding wine list, and mulled wine in winter; prompt efficient service. The garden stretches around the side and back, with well spaced tables, and looks over a side lane to the village church, and out over rolling prosperous farmland. *(Recommended by Mr and Mrs T F Marshall, Andrew Shore, Lynn Sharpless, Bob Eardley, M L and G Clarke, Dave Irving, Ewan McCall, Tom McLean, Roger Huggins, Neville Kenyon, David Saunders, Marion Nott, Steve and Angela Maycock, Philip Orbell, Pat Crabb, Cherry Ann Knott, Andy Petersen, Ian Phillips, D G Clarke, Dr Diana Terry, M G Hart, E Carter, Nabil Tarazi)*

Whitbreads ~ Lease: Anthony and Allyson Windle ~ Real ale ~ Meals and lunchtime snacks ~ (01666) 510366 ~ Children in eating area of bar until 9pm ~ Open 10-2.30(3 Sat), 6-11; closed 25 Dec

CHICKSGROVE ST9629 Map 2
Compasses 🛏 ♟

From A30 5½ miles W of B3089 junction, take lane on N side signposted Sutton Mandeville, Sutton Row, then first left fork (small signs point the way to the pub, in Lower Chicksgrove; look out for the car park); OS Sheet 184 map ref 974294

Reassuringly unchanging and peaceful, this lovely thatched house has the kind of atmosphere that takes centuries to develop. The characterful bar has old bottles and jugs hanging from the beams above the roughly timbered bar counter, farm tools, traps and brasses on the partly stripped stone walls, and high-backed wooden settles forming snug booths around tables on the mainly flagstone floor. It's very pleasant sitting in the quiet garden or the flagstoned farm courtyard. All home-made, the bar food might include sandwiches, soup or pâté (£2.95), mussels with bacon, garlic and cream (£3.75), steak and Guinness pie (£5.95), salmon in tarragon sauce (£6.95), venison (£8.95), sirloin steak (£9.95), and good puddings like lemon flan (£2.75). Well kept Adnams, Bass, Tisbury Old Wardour and Wadworths 6X on handpump; welcoming hard-working licensees. Darts, shove-ha'penny, table skittles, cribbage, dominoes, and shut-the-box. The pub is well placed in a delightful hamlet, with lots to do nearby. *(Recommended by David Surridge, Nigel and Elizabeth Holmes, Stephen and Julie Brown, David Shillitoe, David and Brenda Tew, Eddie Edwards)*

Free house ~ Licensees Tony and Sarah Lethbridge ~ Real ale ~ Meals and snacks ~ (01722) 714318 ~ Children welcome ~ Open 11-3, 6.30-11; closed Mon, except bank hols when closed following Tues ~ Bedrooms: £25B/£45B

CORSHAM ST8670 Map 2

Two Pigs 🍺

A4, Pickwick

This old-fashioned and characterful place is a splendidly quirky example of what's fast becoming a dying breed. They don't serve any food whatsoever, and under 21s aren't allowed – instead the emphasis is firmly on drinking, with well kept Pigswill (from local Bunces Brewery), and four changing guest beers like Badger Tanglefoot, Bridgewater Sunbeam, Foxleys Barking Mad, Hop Back Summer Lightning, and so forth, mostly from smaller independent breweries; also a range of country wines. The very narrow long bar has stone floors, wood-clad walls and long dark wood tables and benches; a profuse and zany decor includes enamel advertising signs, pig-theme ornaments, and old radios, a bicycle and a canoe. The atmosphere is lively and chatty (no games machines and only blues piped music), the landlord entertaining, and the staff friendly, and there's a good mix of customers, too. A covered yard outside is called the Sty. You have to time your visit carefully – the pub is closed every lunchtime, except on Sunday. *(Recommended by Dr and Mrs A K Clarke; more reports please)*

Free house ~ Licensees Dickie and Ann Doyle ~ Real ale ~ (01249) 712515 ~ Live blues Mon evenings ~ Open 7-11, plus 12-2.30 Sun

DEVIZES SU0061 Map 2

Bear 🛏 🍺

Market Place

George III stayed at this rambling 17th-c hotel on his way to Longleat, though the address of welcome that local big-wigs had prepared for the stopover was a little spoilt when the borough Recorder due to deliver it became so overwhelmed by the occasion that he suddenly lost his voice. The old-fashioned main bar has big winter log fires, fresh flowers, black winger wall settles, muted red button-back cloth-upholstered bucket armchairs around oak tripod tables, old prints on the walls and a pleasantly chatty atmosphere. The traditionally-styled Lawrence room (named after Thomas Lawrence the portrait painter, whose father once ran the inn), separated from the main bar by some steps and an old-fashioned glazed screen, has dark oak-panelled walls, a parquet floor, shining copper pans on the mantelpiece above the big open fireplace, and plates around the walls; part of this room is no-smoking. Straightforward bar food includes sandwiches (from £1.75), home-made soup (£1.95), filled baked potatoes, three-egg omelettes or ploughman's (from £2.95), ham, egg and chips (£3.25), 8oz sirloin steak (£7.50), and home-made puddings (£1.95); there's a wider range of meals in the Lawrence room with dishes such as steak and kidney pudding or hotpot with herb dumplings (£3.95) – you can eat these in the bar too. On Saturday nights they have a good value set menu. Well kept Wadworths IPA and 6X and a guest beer are served on handpump from an old-fashioned bar counter with shiny black woodwork and small panes of glass, along with freshly squeezed juices, decent wines, and a good choice of malt whiskies; especially friendly and helpful service. Wadworths beers are brewed in the town, and from the brewery you can get them in splendid old-fashioned half-gallon earthenware jars. *(Recommended by M Clifford, Jane Warren, A R and B E Sayer, Gordon, Philip Orbell, A D Sherman, John Hazel, Tom McLean, Ewan McCall, Roger Huggins, Dave Irving, John and Christine Vittoe, Gwen and Peter Andrews)*

Wadworths ~ Tenant W K Dickenson ~ Real ale ~ Meals and snacks (not Sun lunch) ~ Restaurant (not Sun evening) ~ (01380) 722444 ~ Children welcome ~ Open 11-3, 6-11; all day Sat; closed 25/26 Dec ~ Bedrooms: £50B/£75B

EBBESBOURNE WAKE ST9824 Map 2

Horseshoe 🛏️ 🍺

On A354 S of Salisbury, right at signpost at Coombe Bissett; village is around 8 miles further on

Particularly welcoming to visitors and locals alike, this lovely pub really is a characterful place, and it's not hard to see why it's such an enduring favourite with readers. The pretty little garden has seats that look out over the steep sleepy valley of the River Ebble, and a paddock at the bottom with four goats, and a vietnamese pot-bellied pig. There are fresh flowers from the garden on the tables in the beautifully kept bar, which also has lanterns, farm tools and other bric-a-brac crowded along its beams, and an open fire. Simple but well cooked home-made bar food might include sandwiches (£2.95), fresh trout pâté (£4.95), a very good ploughman's, locally made faggots (£5.95), fresh battered cod or liver and bacon (£6.25), pies such as steak and kidney or venison (£6.95), duckling with gooseberry sauce (£11.95), and excellent home-made puddings; good breakfasts and three course Sunday lunch (£8.95). Well kept Adnams Broadside, Ringwood Best, Wadworths 6X and a couple of guests tapped from the row of casks behind the bar, farm cider, country wines, and several malt whiskies; friendly service. Booking is advisable for the small no-smoking restaurant, especially at weekends when they can fill up quite quickly. The barn opposite is used as a pool room with darts and a fruit machine. There may be a couple of entertaining dogs. *(Recommended by Mike and Heather Watson, Mayur Shah, Jerry and Alison Oakes, James Nason, Percy and Cathy Paine, Michael and Hazel Lyons, Tom and Rosemary Hall, Dr Diana Terry, G W Stevenson)*

Free house ~ Licensees Anthony and Patricia Bath ~ Real ale ~ Meals and snacks (not Mon evening) ~ Restaurant ~ (01722) 780474 ~ Children in restaurant ~ Open 11.30-3, 6.30-11; closed evening 25 Dec ~ Bedrooms: £25B/£40B

FORD ST8374 Map 2

White Hart ★ 🍴 🛏️ 🍷 🍺

A420 Chippenham—Bristol; follow Colerne sign at E side of village to find pub

The symbols above make clear what we think of this stone country inn, and the list of names below shows how many readers are completely in agreement. One couple tell us they often make the 256-mile round trip from Fulham to Ford just to have lunch here, and our postbag turns up plenty more stories in a similar vein. It's a combination of factors that makes it so special: the splendid food, the atmospheric bar, the friendly licensees, and the range of well kept beers. On top of all that the setting is something of a bonus, even though on a sunny day it's hard to think of anywhere more pleasant than the pub's terrace by the stone bridge and trout stream. The weekly-changing menu might include sandwiches, soups such as leek and potato or chicken and vegetable (from £1.50), ploughman's (from £3.95), a couple of well-priced specials such as broccoli and blue cheese crumble (£4.50) or beef stroganoff (£4.75), and more elaborate meals like tagliatelle with spinach, sun-dried tomatoes, pesto and pecarino cheese or onion tart with grilled goat's cheese and roasted peppers on a watercress sauce (£8.50), oven-roasted pork tenderloin with caramelised apples, marinated sultanas and a cider cream sauce (£8.95), supreme of salmon on a bed of spinach with a light saffron cream sauce (£10.50), slow braised shanks of lamb (£10.95), breast of duck with port and black cherries (£12.75), and excellent puddings. There are heavy black beams supporting the white-painted boards of the ceiling, tub armchairs around polished wooden tables, small pictures and a few advertising mirrors on the walls, and an ancient fireplace (inscribed 1553). Despite the number of people eating it's still a place to come to just for a drink; they keep fine wines, farm ciders and a dozen malt whiskies, and well kept Badger Tanglefoot, Bass, Boddingtons, Black Sheep, Flowers IPA, Fullers London Pride, Hook Norton, Smiles Exhibition, and Theakstons Old Peculier on handpump or tapped from the cask. Piped music. It's a particularly nice place to stay and there's a secluded swimming pool for residents. *(Recommended by Susan and John Douglas, Viv Middlebrook, Ian Phillips, John and Wendy Trentham, Don Kellaway, Angie Coles, Mr and Mrs J Liversidge, Andrew Shore, Paul Boot, BJP Edwards, G U Briggs, Dr and Mrs A H Young, Ian and Villy White, RJH, Eric and Jackie Robinson, Stephen and Julie Brown, Simon Collett-Jones, C H and P Stride, Dr I Maine, Dr and Mrs M Beale, D G Clarke, PM, AM, A R and B E Sayer, Brian and Anna Marsden, Kevin and Kay Bronnsey, Peter and Joy Heatherley, Brian Pearson, TBB, Roger and Susan Dunn, Dr and Mrs A K Clarke, Jeff Davies, M W Turner, Mayur Shah, D G King, Alan and Paula McCully, Pat and Jon Millward)*

Free house ~ Licensees Chris and Jenny Phillips ~ Real ale ~ Meals and snacks (till 10) ~ Restaurant ~ (01249) 782213 ~ Children in restaurant ~ Open 11-3, 5-11 ~ Bedrooms: £45B/£65B

HINDON ST9132 Map 2
Lamb

B3089 Wilton—Mere

Lots of readers like to make annual trips to this civilised solidly built old inn, and it's the kind of place where you know nothing is likely to change between visits. Dating back in part to the 13th c, it has a roomy long bar, split into several areas, with the two lower sections perhaps the nicest. There's a long polished table with wall benches and chairs, and a big inglenook fireplace, and at one end a window seat with a big waxed circular table, spindleback chairs with tapestried cushions, a high-backed settle, brass jugs on the mantelpiece above the small fireplace, and a big kitchen clock; up some steps, a third, bigger area has lots of tables and chairs. Good bar food includes sandwiches, pigeon pie or lamb stew with rosemary dumplings (£5.95), venison and wild boar casserole (£6.50), and seafood au gratin (£6.95), with plenty of fresh fish, and a roast Sunday lunch; the restaurant is no smoking. They usually do cream teas throughout the afternoon. The three real ales vary but might include local or unusual brews such as Ash Vine, Mendip Gold, or Oak Hill alongside more familiar ales like Eldridge Pope Hardy and Wadworths 6X; a range of whiskies includes all the malts from the Isle of Islay. Service can slow down when they get busy, but remains helpful and friendly. There are picnic tables across the road (which is a good alternative to the main routes west). No dogs. The lavatories are rather basic. *(Recommended by John Evans, R C Watkins, Gwen and Peter Andrews, Pam and Tim Moorey, John and Vivienne Rice, Colin Laffan, Mr and Mrs G Turner, John and Christine Vittoe, D H and B R Tew, Anthony Barnes, Paul Randall, Ian Phillips, Mrs J A Blanks, Gordon, Peter and Audrey Dowsett, F C Johnston, A R Hands, W Matthews)*

Free house ~ Licensee John Croft ~ Real ale ~ Meals and snacks (till 10pm) ~ Restaurant ~ (01747) 820573 ~ Children welcome ~ Open 11-11; 12-10.30 Sun ~ Bedrooms: £38B/£55B

KILMINGTON ST7736 Map 2
Red Lion 🖙

Pub on B3092 Mere—Frome, 2½ miles S of Maiden Bradley; 3 miles from A303 Mere turn-off

One reader was delighted to see horses tethered to the fruit trees in the pretty garden of this unpretentious old local. It's very popular with walkers, and you can buy the locally made walking sticks that fill up a part of the busy bar. Cosy, comfortable, and rather individual, this also has a curved high-backed settle and red leatherette wall and window seats on the flagstones, photographs on the beams, and a couple of big fireplaces (one with a fine old iron fireback) with log fires in winter. A newer no-smoking eating area has a large window and is decorated with brasses, a large leather horse collar, and hanging plates. It's very much a pub that serves food rather than a place where dining is the main priority; good value simple bar meals include home-made soup (£1.50), filled baked potatoes (from £2.40), toasted sandwiches (from £2.50), ploughman's (from £3.25), steak and kidney or lamb and apricot pie (£3.75), meat or vegetable lasagne (£4.65), a daily special such as very good home-cooked ham, and evening extras like grilled gammon steak. Bass, Butcombe and Wadworths 6X on handpump (maybe under light blanket pressure), along with a guest like Hopback

Summer Lightning or Tisbury Best; also farm cider, elderflower pressé, and monthly changing wines. Sensibly placed darts, dominoes, shove-ha'penny and cribbage. Picnic table sets in the big garden, and maybe Kim, the labrador. A gate leads on to the lane which leads to White Sheet Hill, where there is riding, hang gliding and radio-controlled gliders. Stourhead Gardens are only a mile away. *(Recommended by Guy Consterdine, Stephen Goodchild, Hugh MacLean, David Surridge, R H Martyn, J H Bell)*

Free house ~ Licensee Chris Gibbs ~ Real ale ~ Meals and snacks (not evenings Mon-Thurs and Sun, or 25 Dec) ~ (01985) 844263 ~ Children in eating area of bar till 9pm ~ Open 11.30-2.30, 6.30-11 ~ Bedrooms: £25/£30

LACOCK ST9168 Map 2

George

Village signposted off A350 S of Chippenham

Dating back in part to 1361 (and so one of the oldest buildings in this much-loved National Trust village), this atmospheric and very popular pub has been licensed continuously since the 17th c, when it was known as The Inn. The subsequent arrival of several other alehouses necessitated a name change to avoid confusion, but this is still the pub in Lacock that locals and visitors like best. One of the talking points has long been the three-foot treadwheel set into the outer breast of the magnificent central fireplace. This used to turn a spit for roasting, and was worked by a specially bred dog called, with great imagination, a Turnspit. Often very busy indeed, the bar has a low beamed ceiling, upright timbers in the place of knocked-through walls making cosy corners; there are armchairs and windsor chairs, seats in the stone-mullioned windows and flagstones by the bar. The well kept Wadworths IPA, 6X, and Farmers Glory on handpump are very reasonably priced, and there's a decent choice of wines by the bottle. The good value bar food might include sandwiches, home-made soup (£2.10), lasagne or moules bonne femme (£5.50), pork and leek sausages, broccoli and cream cheese bake (£5.75), beef teriyaki (£5.95), local rainbow trout or chicken stu:fed with stilton in a leek sauce (£6.95), steaks (from £7.95), children's meals (£2.75), and puddings like spotted dick or apple and blackberry pie (from £2.75); prompt and friendly service. Darts, shove-ha'penny, cribbage, dominoes and piped music. There are picnic tables with umbrellas in the back garden, as well as a play area with swings, and a bench in front that looks over the main street. It's a nice area for walking. The bedrooms (very highly praised by readers this year) are up at the landlord's farmhouse, and free transport to and from the pub is provided. *(Recommended by Nigel and Amanda Thorp, Andrew Shore, John and Christine Vittoe, Mark and Heather Williamson, Romey Heaton, Ron Shelton, Peter Neate, Janet Pickles, Peter and Audrey Dowsett, M Clifford, Tim Dobby, Nigel Norman, Philip Orbell, Dave Braisted, Tom McLean, Roger Huggins, Dave Irving, Ewan McCall, TBB, Andrew and Ruth Triggs)*

Wadworths ~ Tenants John and Judy Glass ~ Real ale ~ Meals and snacks (till 10pm) ~ Restaurant ~ (01249) 730263 ~ Children welcome ~ Open 10-2.30, 5-11, all day Sat and Sun ~ Bedrooms – see above – £25B/£35B

Red Lion

High Street

Tourists passing this tall brick Georgian inn often recognise it from the recent TV adaptation of *Pride and Prejudice*. Plain from the outside but spacious once in, the pub has a long bar divided into separate areas by cart shafts, yokes and other old farm implements, and old-fashioned furnishings including a mix of tables and comfortable chairs, turkey rugs on the partly flagstoned floor, and a fine old log fire at one end. Plates, paintings, and tools cover the walls, and there are stuffed birds, animals and branding irons hanging from the ceiling. Bar food includes sandwiches, ploughman's and basket meals (usefully available most of the afternoon in summer), vegetarian dishes (£5.50), pies such as steak and kidney and beef and stilton (£5.95), and a choice of Sunday roasts (£5.50); children's helpings. Well kept and priced Wadworths IPA and 6X on handpump; darts, shove ha'penny, table skittles, cribbage, dominoes, fruit machine, and piped music. The pub can get busy, and towards the latter half of the evening especially is popular with younger people. Close to Lacock Abbey and the Fox

Talbot Museum, this is generally the only pub in Lacock open all day. *(Recommended by Mark Matthewman, June and Tony Baldwin, Tony and Wendy Hobden, Nikki Moffat, Marjorie and David Lamb, TBB, Andrew and Ruth Triggs, John and Wendy Trentham)*

Wadworths ~ Managers Peter and Ann Oldacre ~ Real ale ~ Meals and snacks (not Tues evening) ~ Restaurant ~ (01249) 730456 ~ Children welcome ~ Live music every other Fri night ~ Open 11(11.30 Sat)-11, 12-10.30 Sun; winter opening 11-3, 7-11 ~ Bedrooms: £35B/£60B

LIMPLEY STOKE ST7861 Map 2

Hop Pole

Coming S from Bath on A36, 1300 yds after traffic-light junction with B3108 get ready for sharp left turn down Woods Hill as houses start – pub at bottom; if you miss the turn, take next left signposted Limpley Stoke then follow Lower Stoke signs; OS Sheet 172 map reference 781610

Marvellously relaxed and unchanging, this cream stone-built pub is a wonderful place to unwind. Dating back to 1350, when it was a monks' wine lodge, it has its name deeply incised in the front wall. Welcoming and atmospheric, the dark-panelled room on the right has red velvet cushions for the settles in its alcoves, some slat-back and captain's chairs on its turkey carpet, lantern lighting, and a log fire. The spacious left-hand bar (with an arch to a cream-walled inner room) also has dark wood panelling, and a log-effect gas fire. Well cooked and presented bar food includes sandwiches, trout pâté (£2.95), mushrooms in stilton and basil sauce (£3.85), several very well liked pies such as steak and kidney, lamb and apricot or pork and stilton (£4.95), whole local trout (£5.95), daily specials, and local game like guinea fowl and pheasant in season; friendly, courteous service. Part of the restaurant is no smoking. Bass, Butcombe, Courage Best and a changing guest on handpump, with a range of malt whiskies; darts, shove ha'penny, cribbage, dominoes, and piped music. There's an attractive garden behind with a pond and boules, and it's only a few minutes' walk to the Kennett & Avon Canal. *(Recommended by Meg and Colin Hamilton, Chris Foulkes, Gordon)*

Free house ~ Tenant David John Williams ~ Real ale ~ Meals and snacks ~ Restaurant ~ (0225) 723134 ~ Children in restaurant and games room ~ Open 11-3, 6-11

LITTLE BEDWYN SU2966 Map 2

Harrow ♀

Village signposted off A4 W of Hungerford

A couple of hundred yards from the Kennet & Avon Canal, this welcoming village pub is well liked by walkers and canal users amongst others. Free from music or games machines, the three rooms have quite a relaxed and chatty feel, as well as a massive ship's wheel on the left, a mixture of country chairs and simple wooden tables on the well waxed boards (one table in the bow window), a bright mural of scenes from the village, and a big woodburning stove; the two inner rooms have a fine brass model of a bull and locally done watercolours and photographs for sale. There might be newspapers and local guides to read. Well kept Hook Norton Best and three monthly changing guests like Bass, Greene King IPA and Marstons Pedigree on handpump, and lots of changing New World wines by the glass. There are seats out in the small, pretty garden. Well presented meals might include sweet potato and parsnip soup (£2), popular crab cakes or mussels in tomato, garlic and white wine (£4.95), smoked chicken and avocado salad (£5.50), Tuscan rabbit or oxtail in a rich wine sauce (£9.95), and puddings like lemon torte (£2.95); the restaurant is no smoking. The current managers (who are in the process of buying the pub from the consortium of locals that's owned it for the last few years) run another canalside pub, the Pelican at Froxfield. *(Recommended by Phyl and Jack Street, Rex and Mary Hepburn, Sam Samuells, Lynda Payton, Dr M J Harte, David Rule, Iain McBride, Samantha Hawkins, J E Ellis, Pat Crabb, Anthony Byers, J A and E M Castle, J M M Hill, M E A Horler, Kevin and Kay Bronnsey, N C Walker)*

Free house ~ Licensees Claude Munro and Mita Bhatt ~ Real ale ~ Meals and snacks (not Sun eve or Mon lunch) ~ Restaurant ~ (01672) 870871 ~ Children welcome ~ Open 11-3, 5.30(6 Sat)-11; closed Mon lunchtime ~ Bedrooms: £25B/£50B

LITTLE CHEVERELL ST9853 Map 2
Owl 🍺

Low Rd; just off B3098 Westbury—Upavon, W of A360

This delightfully cosy little local is in such a tranquil spot that at times the only sound might be the cooing woodpigeons in the lovely garden behind. Lined with tall ash and willow trees, the long lawn has quite a few rustic picnic tables, and runs down over two levels to a brook; there are plastic tables and chairs on a terrace above here. Very comfortable and relaxing, the peaceful and neatly traditional bar seems a lot bigger than it really is thanks to plenty of chairs, stools, high-backed settles and tables; a piano separates the main area from a snugger room at the back. There are fresh flowers on the tables, local papers and guides to read, a gently ticking clock, two or three stuffed owls behind the bar, a few agricultural tools on the walls, and noticeboards advertising local events and activities. Well kept Wadworths 6X on handpump, along with a couple of interesting guests such as Foxley Howling Wolf and Oakhill Best; a blackboard lists forthcoming brews, and there's usually a beer festival every April. They also have country wines, and maybe farm cider; friendly smiling service. Good value bar food, written up on a blackboard above the fireplace, might include ham, egg and chips (£3.95), a pie like steak and kidney or pork and apple, and changing dishes like cheesy leek and potato bake (£4), pork chop with mustard and pepper covered in melted cheese (£4.75), local trout (£5.50), and lamb en croûte (£6.75); children's meals and helpings. They do a particularly well priced Sunday lunch (£3.75), as well as mixed grills on Wednesday nights (£5.95), and a two-course set midweek lunch (£3.95). Dogs are welcome (they have their own, and a cat). The pub is at its busiest on sunny weekends, though rarely gets crowded, and on some weekday lunchtimes you might have it almost to yourself. *(Recommended by Colin and Joyce Laffan, Gwen and Peter Andrews)*

Free house ~ Licensee Mike Hardham ~ Real ale ~ Meals and snacks (not Mon) ~ (01380) 812263 ~ Well-behaved children welcome ~ Occasional live entertainment ~ Open 12-2.30(3 weekends), 7-11; closed Mon

LOWER CHUTE SU3153 Map 2
Hatchet

The Chutes well signposted via Appleshaw off A342, 2½ miles W of Andover

This neat and friendly thatched 16th-c house is one of the county's most attractive pubs. The beams seem especially low, and look down over a mix of captain's chairs and cushioned wheelbacks set around oak tables. There's a splendid 17th-c fireback in the huge fireplace, with a big winter log fire in front. Good bar food includes sandwiches, home-made soup (£2.50), ploughman's (from £3.75), good moules marinières (£4.45), salads (from £3.95), mushroom stroganoff (£4.95), steak and Guinness pie (£5.25), tiger prawns in filo pastry (£6.25), and tasty puddings. Well kept Adnams, Greene King Abbot, Marstons Pedigree, and Timothy Taylor Landlord on handpump, and a range of country wines. Darts, shove-ha'penny, dominoes, cribbage, and piped music. There are seats out on a terrace by the front car park, or on the side grass, as well as a children's sandpit. *(Recommended by Lynn Sharpless, Bob Eardley, Dr S Willavoys, Gordon, Kevin and Kay Bronnsey)*

Free house ~ Licensee Jeremy McKay ~ Real ale ~ Meals and snacks ~ Restaurant ~ (01264) 730229 ~ Children welcome ~ Open 11.30-3, 6-11 ~ Self-contained flat available, prices on request

---

If you enjoy your visit to a pub, please tell the publican. They work extraordinarily long hours, and when people show their appreciation it makes it all seem worth while.

LOWER WOODFORD SU1235 Map 2
Wheatsheaf

Leaving Salisbury northwards on A360, The Woodfords signposted first right after end of
speed limit; then bear left

An unusual feature of this well refurbished old pub is the indoor pond with goldfish
in the heart of the bar; to get from one part to the other you have to cross a
miniature footbridge. There's a welcoming and rather cosy feel to the place, and
though many of the tables are busy with people eating, the front bar is still used
mainly by drinkers. The very wide choice of food includes home-made soups like
spinach and broccoli (£1.90), open sandwiches (£3.75), ploughman's (£3.95), filled
baked potatoes (from £4.35), cod mornay or country vegetable pie (£4.95), prawn
korma or jalapeno peppers filled with cream cheese and coated in a crispy crumb
(£5.25), mushroom and nut fettucini or chicken, ham and mushroom pasta bake
(£5.75), steak and kidney pie (£5.95), stuffed plaice or grilled chicken breast with
garlic and herb butter (£6.95), steaks (from £9.25), and children's meals (from
£1.75); part of the dining room is no smoking. Well kept Badger Best and
Tanglefoot and Dorset IPA on handpump, promptly served by helpful, friendly staff;
dominoes and cribbage. Good disabled access, and baby-changing facilities. The big
walled garden has picnic tables, a climber and swings, and is surrounded by tall
trees; there are barbecues out here in summer. *(Recommended by Mrs J Huntly, Don and
Shirley Parrish, Joy and Peter Heatherley, Phyl and Jack Street, S Jones, Clive Gilbert, Nigel
Wikeley, L M Miall, Jerry and Alison Oakes, Don and Thelma Beeson)*

*Badger ~ Tenants Peter and Jennifer Charlton ~ Real ale ~ Meals and snacks (till
10pm) ~ (01722) 782203 ~ Children in eating area of bar ~ Open 11-2.30,
6.30(6 Sat)-11(10.30 winter Mon-Thurs); closed 25 Dec*

NORTON ST8884 Map 2
Vine Tree

4 miles from M4 junction 17; A429 towards Malmesbury, then left at Hullavington, Sherston
signpost, then follow Norton signposts; in village turn right at Foxley signpost, which takes
you into Honey lane

Cosy and pubby, and seeming much more remote than its proximity to the motorway
would suggest, this converted 18th-c mill house is an attractive building in an equally
nice setting. It's well liked at the moment for its food, with bar snacks including
ploughman's (from £2.65), basket meals (from £2.90), filled baked potatoes (from
£3.70), home-made beefburger or nutburger (£4.60), and home-made lasagne
(£5.25), and a fuller menu featuring things like home-made soup (£2.60), a warm
quiche of duck and fennel on a tangerine coulis (£2.90), fennel, vermouth and potato
hotpot (£4.25), braised red snapper with tomato and dill sauce (£8.75), chicken
breast filled with cream cheese, garlic and tomato with an oyster mushroom sauce
(£8.95), steaks (from £9.40), honey-roast duckling breast with an apricot and coconut
cream sauce (£9.75), puddings like toffee apple and pecan pie (from £2.25), and
children's meals (£2.05). Best to book, especially at weekends, and there's a 5%
discount if you pay with cash. The three smallish rooms open together with plates,
small sporting prints, carvings, hop bines, a mock-up mounted pig's mask (used for a
game that involves knocking coins off its nose and ears), lots of stripped pine, candles
in bottles on the tables (the lighting's very gentle), and some old settles. Well kept
Wadworths 6X and a beer named for the pub on handpump, along with a couple of
guests like Archers Golden or Ruddles County; service is efficient and chatty. There
are picnic tables under cocktail parasols in a vine-trellised garden with young trees
and tubs of flowers, and a well fenced separate play area with a fine thatched fortress
and so forth; they have stables at the back. *(Recommended by Jenny and Roger Huggins,
G U Briggs, Comus Elliott, Colin and Alma Gent, Peter Neate)*

*Free house ~ Licensee Ken Camerier ~ Real ale ~ Meals and snacks (till 10pm) ~
Restaurant ~ (01666) 837654 ~ Children in eating area of bar and in restaurant ~
Open 12-2.30, 6.30-11; closed Tues*

PITTON SU2131 Map 2

Silver Plough ♀

Village signposted from A30 E of Salisbury

A farmhouse until the Second World War, this civilised dining pub has jugs, glass rolling pins and other assorted curios hanging from the beamed ceilings in the main bar, paintings and prints on the walls, and comfortable oak settles. The emphasis is very much on the food, with regularly changing menus typically including soup (£2.75), big sandwiches (£3.75), ploughman's (from £3.95), salad or quiche of the day (£4.25), green-lipped mussels in a tomato, chilli, garlic and coriander sauce or pasta with a choice of sauces like smoked chicken and thyme (£4.50), medley of grilled and char-grilled vegetables with ricotta cheese (£7.25), pan-fried red snapper with grilled aubergine and a tomato and pepper salsa (£8.25), free-range chicken with a fondue of gingered leeks, and sirloin steak with a confit of roast garlic and red onion (£12.95); three-course Sunday lunch. Well kept Courage Directors, Eldridge Pope Hardy, John Smiths and Wadworths 6X on handpump, a fine wine list including 10 by the glass and some well priced and carefully chosen bottles, a good range of country wines, and a worthy choice of spirits. There's a skittle alley next to the snug bar; piped music. Service is generally friendly and efficient, but can be a little disinterested at times. There are picnic tables and other tables under cocktail parasols on a quiet lawn, with an old pear tree. *(Recommended by M V and J Melling, Stephen Goodchild, H L Davis, Mayur Shah, Gwen and Peter Andrews, Jerry and Alison Oakes, Dr and Mrs N Holmes)*

Free house ~ Licensee Michael Beckett ~ Real ale ~ Meals and snacks ~ Restaurant (not Sun evening) ~ (01722) 72266 ~ Children in eating area ~ Open 11-3, 6-11

POTTERNE ST9958 Map 2

George & Dragon 🛏 🍺

A360 beside Worton turn-off

During the Civil War Cromwell billeted troops in Potterne, and made the landlord of this 15th-c thatched cottage responsible for feeding them; six years later the poor chap was still vainly trying to get someone to pay for all the beef and beer he'd provided. Originally built for the Bishop of Salisbury, the pub is the kind of place where visitors instantly feel at home. There's a convivial atmosphere in the traditional bar, which has old bench seating and country-style tables, banknotes from around the world, and pictures of customers by a local cartoonist. You can still see the fireplace and old beamed ceiling of the original hall. Under the new tenants bar food includes sandwiches, soup (£2.25), baked potatoes (from £3.25), omelettes (from £3.30), ploughman's (from £3.75), pork and leek sausages (£3.95), gammon steak (£4.95), local trout stuffed with onion and mushroom (£5.25), mixed grill (£6.95), sirloin steak (£7.95), daily specials, and puddings like spotted dick (from £2.25); three-course Sunday lunch. The dining room is no smoking. Well kept and nicely priced Wadworths IPA, 6X and seasonal beers on handpump. A separate room has pool, darts, shove-ha'penny, cribbage, dominoes, and a fruit machine, and through a hatch beyond here is a unique indoor .22 shooting gallery (available for use by groups, though they need notice to arrange marshals and insurance); there's a full skittle alley in the old stables. At the back of the pub is a small museum of hand-held agricultural implements. There's a pleasant garden and a suntrap yard with a grapevine. *(Recommended by Frank Cummins, Tom McLean, Ewan McCall, Roger Huggins, Dave Irving, Jan and Colin Roe; reports on the new regime please)*

Wadworths ~ Tenants David and Jenny Wood ~ Real ale ~ Meals and snacks (not Mon, except bank hol lunchtime) ~ (01380) 722139 ~ Children in eating area of bar and restaurant ~ Folk night Mon ~ Open 12-3, 6.30(6 Sat)-11; closed Mon lunchtimes Oct-Apr ~ Bedrooms: £19.50/£35

Real ale to us means beer which has matured naturally in its cask – not pressurised or filtered.

POULSHOT ST9559 Map 2

Raven 🍺

Village signposted off A361 Devizes—Seend

One reader arrived at this splendid tucked-away pub as part of a group of 24 hungry walkers, but while at some places this would no doubt have sent the staff into panic and confusion, here the efficiency of the service wasn't affected one bit. Neat enough from the outside, especially in contrast to the long rather shaggy nearby village green, it's spick and span inside, the two cosy and intimate rooms of the black-beamed bar well refurbished with sturdy tables and chairs and comfortable banquettes; there's an attractive no-smoking dining room. The landlord keeps personal charge of the kitchen, and his slightly unusual touch gives a distinctive edge to the cooking and presentation of even quite regular dishes. A typical menu might include sandwiches (from £2.25), minestrone and other soups (£2.30), ploughman's (from £2.95), interesting salads and deft fresh pasta dishes, vegetable bake (£5.45), steak and kidney pie (£5.95), seafood crumble (£6.50), grilled lamb steaks with red wine and cranberry sauce (£7.05), poached fresh salmon with tarragon and dill sauce (£7.20), daily specials like spicy pork meatballs in barbecue sauce (£5.70) or chicken parcels with pork and sage stuffing braised in tomato and vegetable sauce, and puddings like crème brûlée (£2.50); good fresh vegetables. Given its value, the food's becoming very popular with older people at lunchtime. Particularly well kept Wadworths IPA, 6X and seasonal brews tapped straight from the cask, and priced a fair bit less than the county average; smiling staff, and a thriving chatty atmosphere. The gents' are outside. *(Recommended by M Hart, Colin and Joyce Laffan, Gwen and Peter Andrews, Meg and Colin Hamilton, Tony and Wendy Hobden, Tony Beaulah, G Washington)*

Wadworths ~ Tenants Susan and Philip Henshaw ~ Real ale ~ Meals and snacks (not 25 or 26 Dec) ~ Restaurant ~ (01380) 828271 ~ Children in restaurant ~ Open 11-2.30, 6.30-11; closed evening 25 Dec

RAMSBURY SU2771 Map 2

Bell 🍺

Village signposted off B4192 (still shown as A419 on many maps) NW of Hungerford, or from A4 W of Hungerford

Victorian-stained glass panels in one of the two sunny bay windows at this comfortably civilised pub look out onto the quiet village street, and a big chimney breast with a woodburning stove divides up the smartly relaxed and chatty bar areas, nicely furnished with polished tables. Well kept Wadworths 6X and IPA and a couple of guests like Hook Norton Best on handpump, decent wines, and 20 malt whiskies; fresh flowers on the tables, evening piped music. Well presented and cheerfully served bar meals might include lunchtime sandwiches (from £1.75) and ploughman's (£3.95), soup (£2.45), king prawns wrapped in filo pastry with a chilli dip (£4.25), venison sausages with onion marmalade (£5.75), mushrooms filled with ratatouille and topped with brie or mushroom and cashew nut curry (£5.95), seafood fettucine (£6.95), beef and ale pie (£7.95), grilled lamb cutlets with a port and redcurrant sauce (£8.25), children's meals (from £1.95), and home-made puddings like apricot crumble. Tables can be reserved in the restaurant, though the same meals can be had in the bar; one section is no smoking. There are picnic tables on the raised lawn. Roads lead from this quiet village into the downland on all sides. *(Recommended by Alan and Paula McCully, Roger Wain-Heapy, Gordon, J M M Hill, Kevin and Kay Bronnsey, R C Morgan, Mr and Mrs Jenkinson, Annabel and Chris, Dr M Ian Crichton)*

Free house ~ Licensee Graham Dawes ~ Real ale ~ Meals and snacks (not winter Sun evenings) ~ Restaurant ~ (01672) 520230 ~ Children welcome in restaurant and room between bar and restaurant ~ Open 12-2.30(3 Sat) 6.30-11

The knife-and-fork rosette distinguishes pubs where the food is of exceptional quality.

ROWDE ST9762 Map 2

George & Dragon 🍽

A342 Devizes—Chippenham

Wiltshire Dining Pub of the Year

The food at this interesting old pub is so exceptional that several readers can't remember when they last had something quite so good at a pub. Ingredients are fresh and well chosen, cooking is light and deft, and unusual tastes perk up familiar dishes (mint, honey and strawberry transforming a melon starter, for example). Cornish fish fresh daily is a special highlight, used to good effect in dishes like provençale fish soup (£4.50), fried squid with lemon, garlic and parsley (£5.50), skate with capers and black butter (£8.50), whole grilled lemon sole or crab pancakes (£10), monkfish with bacon and mustard cream or red mullet with orange and anchovy (£13), and fried turbot with tomatoes and balsamic vinegar (£14). Other dishes might include curried parsnip soup (£3), grilled goat's cheese with onion marmalade (£4.50), ploughman's (£5.50), cheese soufflé baked with parmesan and cream or wild rabbit risotto (£7), grilled guinea fowl with lime (£10), and excellent puddings such as chocolate torte with coffee bean sauce (£4), served with a jug of help-yourself cream. Several dishes come in two sizes, and there's a good value two or three-course set lunch; booking is a good idea at busy times, and virtually essential on a Saturday evening. The dining room is no smoking. Though its emphasis is primarily on food, the pub has kept admirably to its roots, and you'll be just as welcome if the only thing you want to eat is a packet of crisps. The bar has some interesting furnishings, plenty of dark wood, and a log fire (with a fine collection of brass keys by it), while the bare-floored dining room has quite plain and traditional feeling tables and chairs. Well kept Wadworths IPA, 6X and winter Old Timer on handpump. The atmosphere is leisurely and relaxed, and service is friendly and efficient. Shove ha'penny, cribbage, dominoes, trivia, and piped music. *(Recommended by Chris Ball, A V Neal, Mr and Mrs M Clifford, Dr and Mrs A H Young, Gwen and Peter Andrews, F J and A Parmenter, John Hazel, G P Kernan, Mr and Mrs Peter Woods)*

Wadworths ~ Licensees Tim and Helen Withers ~ Real ale ~ Meals and snacks (not Sun or Mon; other days till 10) ~ Restaurant ~ (01380) 723053 ~ Children welcome ~ Open 12-3, 7-11; closed Mon lunchtime

SALISBURY SU1429 Map 2

Haunch of Venison ★ 🍺

1 Minster Street, opposite Market Cross

The characterful old building itself is what makes a visit here special; it can be a pleasure just to sit and pass the time. Built some 650 years ago as the church house for St Thomas's, just behind, it has massive beams in the ochre ceiling, stout red cushioned oak benches built into its timbered walls, genuinely old pictures, a black and white tiled floor, and an open fire; a tiny snug opens off the entrance lobby. A quiet and cosy upper panelled room has a small paned window looking down onto the main bar, antique leather-seat settles, a nice carved oak chair nearly three centuries old, and a splendid fireplace that dates back to the building's early years; behind glass in a small wall slit is the smoke-preserved mummified hand of an unfortunate 18th-c card player. Well kept Courage Best and Directors on handpump from a unique pewter bar counter, with a rare set of antique taps for gravity-fed spirits and liqueurs; over 150 malt whiskies, decent wines (including a wine of the week), and a range of brandies. Bar food, served in the lower half of the restaurant, includes sandwiches (from £2.25), venison sausages (£2.95), ploughman's (from £3.95), vegetarian quiche (£3.95), a venison cottage pie toppped with bubble and squeak or yorkshire pudding filled with strips of roast venison (£4.50), steak and kidney pudding (£4.75), and grilled tuna fish melt. The pub can get a little smoky. *(Recommended by Frank Gadbois, Barry and Anne, Hanns P Golez, Lynn Sharpless, Bob Eardley, Rupert Willcocks, Stephen and Julie Brown, David Carr, Dr and Mrs A H Young, Jerry and Alison Oakes, Andrew and Ruth Triggs, JM, PM, Kevin and Kay Bronnsey, Gordon, Dr Diana Terry)*

Courage ~ Tenants Antony and Victoria Leroy ~ Real ale ~ Meals and snacks (not winter Sun evenings) ~ Restaurant ~ (01722) 322024 ~ Well behaved children in eating areas ~ Nearby parking may be difficult ~ Open 11-11; closed evening 25 Dec

SEEND ST9361 Map 2

Barge

Seend Cleeve; signposted off A361 Devizes—Trowbridge, between Seend village and signpost to Seend Head

When we first knew this canalside pub it was tiny, but its size has increased at the same speed as its popularity, and it's now very well geared up to dealing with the stream of visitors that flock to this pretty spot in summer. The picnic tables among former streetlamps in the neat waterside gardens are the perfect place for idly watching the barges and other boats on the Kennet and Avon Canal, and there are moorings by the humpy bridge. Inside, there's a strong barge theme in the friendly and relaxed bar, perhaps at its best in the intricately painted Victorian flowers which cover the ceilings and run in a waist-high band above the deep green lower walls. A distinctive mix of attractive seats includes milkchurns and the occasional small oak settle among the rugs on the parquet floor, while the walls have big sentimental engravings. The watery theme continues with a well stocked aquarium, and there's also a pretty Victorian fireplace, big bunches of dried flowers, and red velvet curtains for the big windows. Smartly dressed staff serve big helpings of food such as soup (£1.95), open sandwiches (from £2.95), filled baked potatoes (from £3.25), ploughman's (£3.95), lasagne or pancakes filled with spinach, mixed nuts and mushrooms (£5.95), prawns and oriental vegetables with noodles (£5.85), daily specials like cabbage and nut stroganoff (£5.25), spare ribs in barbecue sauce (£6.55), or roast spring chicken with a thyme and mushroom sauce (£6.95), and children's dishes (£1.95); the restaurant extension is no smoking. They recommend booking for meals, especially at weekends. Well kept Wadworths IPA and 6X, and a fortnightly changing guest beer like Badger Tanglefoot on handpump; mulled wine in winter. Good service; trivia. Barbecues outside on summer Sundays. At the busiest times you may find queues to get in the car park. *(Recommended by Nigel and Lindsay Chapman, Frank Cummins, Peter and Audrey Dowsett, Peter Neate, Meg and Colin Hamilton, R C Watkins, Tony and Wendy Hobden, Colin Laffan, F J and A Parmenter, R H Rowley, Ron Gentry, Jerry and Alison Oakes)*

Wadworths ~ Tenant Christopher Moorley Long ~ Real ale ~ Meals and snacks ~ Restaurant ~ (01380) 828230 ~ Well behaved children welcome ~ Open 11-2.30(3 Sat), 6-11

SEMINGTON ST9461 Map 2

Lamb 🍴 ♟

99 The Strand; A361 a mile E of junction with A350, towards Devizes

It's been on the cards for some time, but this civilised creeper-covered eatery has finally taken the plunge and is now completely no smoking; trade is up as a result. Readers love coming here for a meal, and not just because the standard of food is so high – there seems to be that extra bit of attention with the service and welcome too. It really is somewhere to come to eat rather than for a casual drink, especially on Saturday evenings or Sunday lunchtimes when you might find the latter impossible; booking is recommended for meals then. From a changing menu, the food might include sandwiches, home-made soup (£2.50), herrings in a madeira sauce (£2.95), lamb casserole with apricots or braised steak with mushrooms and sherry (£6.95), barbary duck with sherry sauce (£7.50), guinea fowl with orange and port sauce or salmon with a wine and cream sauce (£7.95), seasonal game, fresh fish from Cornwall, and excellent home-made puddings like white chocolate flan or butterscotch fruit and nut pudding (£3.25); vegetables are good – you may come across nuts mixed with the carrots. A series of corridors and attractively decorated separate rooms radiate from the serving counter, with antique settles, a woodburning stove, and a log fire. Well kept Eldridge Pope Hardy and Dorchester on handpump, and good, reasonably priced wines. Very friendly, helpful staff; maybe piped classical music. There is a pleasant colourfully planted walled garden with tables, and outside service when the weather is fine. *(Recommended by George Atkinson, Colin Laffan, Andrew Shore, W G Rhodes, Frank Cummins, Gwen and Peter Andrews, Pete and Rosie Flower, Peter Neate, A D Sherman, Mr and Mrs E H Warner, James*

and Patricia Halfyard, Pat and John Millward, S H Godsell, Mrs B Davidson, R C Watkins, Mrs
L Powell, G W A Pearce, Dan Mather)

*Free House ~ Licensee Andrew Flaherty ~ Real ale ~ Meals and snacks ~
Restaurant (not Sun evening) ~ (01380) 870263 ~ Children welcome ~ Open 12-
2.30, 6.30-10.30(11 Sat); closed Sun evening*

SEMLEY ST8926 Map 2

Benett Arms ♀

Turn off A350 N of Shaftesbury at Semley Ind Estate signpost, then turn right at Semley
signpost

Right on the Dorset border, this attractive and characterful village inn is in a lovely
setting just across the green from the church, with pretty countryside in all directions.
Friendly and welcoming, the two cosy and hospitable rooms are separated by a flight
of five carpeted steps, and have one or two settles and pews, a deep leather sofa and
chairs, hunting prints, carriage lamps for lighting, a pendulum wall clock, and
ornaments on the mantelpiece over the log fire. Down by the thatched-roof bar
servery, the walls are stripped stone; upstairs, there's a dark panelling dado.
Attractively presented bar food includes sandwiches (from £1.50), home-made soup
(£2.65), ploughman's (£3.95), fresh trout or good leek and cheese bake (£4.95),
home-made steak and kidney pie (£5.25), gammon with pineapple (£6.25), 8oz rump
steak (£9.95), fresh fish and game, specials such as rabbit casserole (£5.95) or smoked
eel with lumpfish and raspberry vinaigrette (£6.95), and puddings like lemon and
ginger crunch or chocolate mousse with rum (£2.95); big breakfasts. Well kept Gibbs
Mew Bishops Tipple, Deacon and Salisbury Best on handpump, kept under light
blanket pressure, farm cider, four chilled vodkas, 18 malt whiskies, lots of liqueurs,
and a thoughtfully chosen wine list, including a good few by the glass; helpful chatty
landlord. Dominoes and cribbage, but no machines or music. There are seats outside.
Well behaved dogs welcome. *(Recommended by Stephen Goodchild, James Nunns, Marjorie
and David Lamb, Peter Burton, M G Hart, P Reeves, David Surridge, Roger and Jenny Huggins,
F C Johnston, Mrs S A Mackenzie, Gordon, Mr and Mrs Smith)*

*Gibbs Mew ~ Tenant Joe Duthie ~ Real ale ~ Meals and snacks (till 10pm) ~
Restaurant (not Sun evening) ~ (01747) 830221 ~ Children in eating area of bar
~ Open 11-2.30, 6-11; closed 25/26 Dec ~ Bedrooms: £31B/£48B*

SHERSTON ST8585 Map 2

Rattlebone

Church St; B4040 Malmesbury—Chipping Sodbury

This year the licensees are celebrating their tenth anniversary at this busy 16th-c pub.
There are several rambling rooms and nooks and crannies with pink walls, pews and
settles, country kitchen chairs around a mix of tables, big dried flower arrangements,
lots of jugs and bottles hanging from the low beams, and plenty of little cuttings and
printed anecdotes; the atmosphere is cheery and relaxed, with maybe piped classical
music. The public bar has a hexagonal pool table, darts, table football, shove
ha'penny, fruit machine, cribbage, dominoes and juke box; also table and alley skittles.
The good bar food is very popular, with a wide choice including lunchtime filled rolls
(from £2.25) and ploughman's (from £3.50), home-made soup (£2.25), grilled goat's
cheese with nut dressing (£3.95), vegetable crêpes (£5.75), mushroom and chestnut
stroganoff or steak and kidney pie (£6.25), generous prawn salad (£6.50), escalope of
turkey with smoked cheese, apple and cream (£8.50), pork tenderloin with stilton and
cream sauce topped with cashew nuts (£8.75), steaks (from £8.75), and puddings like
fruit crumble (£2.50). They hope to have more of their well liked fish specials this year.
Part of the dining area is no smoking. Well kept Bass, Smiles Best, Wadworths 6X, a
beer named for the pub, and a regularly changing guest on handpump, 65 malt
whiskies, 20 rums, fruit wines, Westons cider, decent wines, and quick obliging service.
The smallish garden is very pretty with flowerbeds, a gravel terrace, and picnic tables
under umbrellas. There are four boules pitches (Sherston apparently has the biggest

one day boules competition in the country). The pub takes its name from local hero John Rattlebone, who fought bravely to help Edmund Ironside defeat Canute in the Battle of Sherston in 1016. He received a mortal wound during the fracas, but covered it with a tile until the battle was won, so stemming the flow of blood; he then died on this spot. The old core of the village is very pretty. *(Recommended by John and Annette Derbyshire, Janet Pickles, Mr and Mrs Claude Bernis, KC, Andrew Shore, Peter and Audrey Dowsett, Peter Neate, Michael Richards, D G Clarke, Barry Gibbs)*

Free house ~ Licensees David and Ian Rees ~ Real ale ~ Meals and snacks (till 9.45) ~ (01666) 840871 ~ Children in eating area ~ Open 11-3, 5.30-11; 11-11 Sat; 12-11 Sun; closed evening 25 Dec

WILCOT SU1360 Map 2
Golden Swan 🛏️

Village signposted off A345 N of Pewsey, and in Pewsey itself (forking right past hospital)

In a quiet village of other thatched houses, this steeply gabled old thatched inn is very pretty, with tables out on its neat flower-edged front lawn, and more in the attractive back garden. Inside its two main rooms are unpretentiously welcoming. The larger, with a dining area at one end, has lots of decorative jugs and mugs hanging from its beams, comfortable chairs, a collection of brass shell cases and other brassware on the mantelpiece, and attractive pen and wash drawings of local scenes; there's an aquarium at the dining end. A third room has a fruit machine, sensibly placed darts and bar billiards. A short choice of good value home-made bar food includes warm baguettes (from £2.50), a huge ploughman's or faggots and peas (£4) and fish and chips (£4.50), with a couple of extra dishes at the weekend like lasagne or cottage pie (£4.95); no-smoking dining room. Well kept Wadworths IPA and 6X and in winter perhaps Old Timer on handpump, maybe unobtrusive piped music, a friendly golden retriever and a prize-winning cat. Bedrooms are simple but big and airy – good value; there's a field for camping. The restored Kennet & Avon Canal is about 300 metres away – a few minutes' walk. *(Recommended by Meg and Colin Hamilton, Gordon, D G Clarke, Phyl and Jack Street, Ron Shelton)*

Wadworths ~ Tenant Terry Weeks ~ Real ale ~ Meals and snacks (not Sun evening or Mon) ~ (01672) 562289 ~ Occasional weekend jazz or folk ~ Open 11.30(12 winter)-3.30, 6.30-11; 11.30-11 Sat; 12-10.30 Summer Sun; cl 25 Dec evening ~ Bedrooms: £17.50/£35

WOOTTON RIVERS SU1963 Map 2
Royal Oak ♀

Village signposted from A346 Marlborough—Salisbury and B3087 E of Pewsey

A short stroll from the Kennet & Avon Canal, this pretty 16th-c thatched pub is popular mainly for its very extensive range of home-made bar food. As well as lunchtime sandwiches (£1.95) and ploughman's (from £4.50), the choice might include soup (£1.75), basket meals (from £2.75), lots of salads (from £3.50; avocado and prawn £5.50), baked goat's cheese with sweet peppers and anchovies (£4.50), ratatouille topped with toasted brie (£5.50), local trout (£6.50), steak and Guinness pie (£6.50), gammon and egg or chicken with cajun spices (£8), specials like lamb and spring vegetable casserole with butter beans and rosemary (£7.50), wing of skate with capers and prawns (£8), or venison with cranberry and orange (£9.50), steaks (from £11), and puddings such as sticky treacle and almond tart or sherry trifle (£2.85); they do a three-course Sunday lunch (£10). Booking is recommended in the evenings, when some customers may be quite smartly dressed. The friendly L-shaped dining lounge has slat-back chairs, armchairs and some rustic settles around good tripod tables, a low ceiling with partly stripped beams, partly glossy white planks, and a woodburning stove. The timbered bar is comfortably furnished, and has a small area with darts, pool, cribbage, dominoes, chess, Monopoly, fruit machine, trivia and juke box. Well kept Boddingtons, Wadworths 6X and a monthly changing guest like Archers Village on handpump or tapped from the cask, interesting whiskies, and a good wine list (running up to some very distinguished vintage ones). They do seem to be more interested in diners than drinkers, and service can slow down at busy times. There are tables under cocktail parasols in the back gravelled yard. The thatched and timbered village is worth exploring, particularly the 13th-c church. The family also run the True Heart at Bishopstone, and the Pheasant at Shefford Woodlands. *(Recommended by Phyl and Jack Street, Stephen Barney, D and D Savidge, Michael and Alison Leyland, A R and B E Sayer, Cherry Ann Knott, Mrs S Miller, Margaret Dyke, Guy Consterdine, Annabel and Chris, M Carey, A Groocock, R J Herd)*

Free house ~ Licensees John and Rosa Jones ~ Real ale ~ Meals and snacks ~ Restaurant ~ (01672) 810322 ~ Children welcome ~ Open 11-3, 6(7 winter)-11, all day Sat; closed 25 Dec and evening 26 Dec ~ Bedrooms (in adjoining house): £27.50B/£35(£40B)

WYLYE SU0037 Map 2
Bell

Just off A303/A36 junction

Nicely set in a peaceful village, this cosy country pub is very handy for Stonehenge. The neatly kept and black-beamed front bar has one of the inn's three winter log fires, and sturdy rustic furnishings that go well with the stripped stonework and neat timbered herringbone brickwork. Eldridge Pope Dorset Best, Wadworths 6X and a guest beer on handpump, a good range of country wines, and wines from a local vineyard. The back area – partly no smoking – has dominoes, and there are plenty of tables in a side eating area, used to serve bar meals such as a big mixed grill (£8.95), daily specials including game like wild boar, venison and pheasant (from £7.50), children's dishes, and a Sunday roast (£5.95); though some readers like it very much, the food isn't generally considered to be the pub's main attraction. The friendly alsatian can leap from behind the bar counter into the public bar without any running start. There are seats outside, some on a pleasant walled terrace. *(Recommended by James Macrae, Jim Reid, Hugh MacLean, Howard Clutterbuck, D J and P M Taylor, Colin Laffan, MRSM, John and Vivienne Rice, Peter Woods, Clive Gilbert, Stephen Brown, A Lilley, N Virgo, Mr and Mrs R O Gibson, Ian Phillips, A J N Lee)*

Free house ~ Licensees Steve and Ann Locke ~ Real ale ~ Meals and snacks (till 10 Fri/Sat) ~ (01985) 248338 ~ Children welcome till 9pm ~ Open 11.30-2.30, 6-11 ~ Bedrooms: £25B/£39.50B

Lucky Dip

Besides the fully inspected pubs, you might like to try these Lucky Dips recommended to us and described by readers (if you do, please send us reports):

☆ **Aldbourne** [The Green (off B4192); SU2675], *Blue Boar*: Ancient Tudor public bar as core of busy extended dining pub on pretty village green (shame about the cars parked), nice furnishings with homely feel, well kept Archers Village, Wadworths IPA and 6X, friendly attentive staff, good choice of food from generous sandwiches up, fresh veg; children allowed, neatly kept small back country garden *(Mr and Mrs P Smith, HNJ, PEJ)*

☆ **Aldbourne**, *Crown*: Spacious well kept village pub with friendly quick service, pleasant atmosphere, good value straightforward food, well kept Courage-related ales, huge log fire, interesting bric-a-brac, quiet piped music; tables under cocktail parasols in neat courtyard *(Colin Laffan)*

☆ **Alvediston** [ST9723], *Crown*: Welcoming thatched low-beamed country inn carefully extended behind without spoiling the comfortable and attractive rather upmarket main bar, generous helpings of unusual food, well kept Courage, Ringwood and Wadworths, good prices, friendly efficient service, pretty garden, peaceful location; good bedrooms *(Susan May, WHBM, W Marsh, Gordon, LYM)*

Amesbury [High St; SU1541], *New Inn*: Comfortable and welcoming, with good food from sandwiches up, well kept ales, big curving bar with restaurant area, simple decor *(Phyl and Jack Street, Brian White)*

Ashton Keynes [High Rd; SU0494], *White Hart*: Smart and friendly village local with well priced homely cooking, well kept Whitbreads-related ales, good log fire, efficient service; piped music; garden, delightful village *(Keith Astin, Mrs K Neville-Rolfe, A and M Matheson)*

☆ **Avebury** [A361; SU0969], *Red Lion*: Much-modernised thatched pub in the heart of the stone circles; pleasant original core, friendly staff, usual food from unpubby restaurant extension, well kept Whitbreads-related ales *(John and Christine Vittoe, Ralph Lee, Anne Cargill, LYM)*

Badbury [off A345 S of Swindon; SU1980], *Bakers Arms*: Quiet, clean and comfortable village local with central fire, Arkells Bitter and BBB, decent simple food (not Mon) from big well priced sandwiches up, pleasant service; piped music, darts and games machine; children welcome, garden *(Peter and Aubrey Dowsett, R T and J C Moggridge)*

☆ **Beckhampton** [A4 Marlborough—Calne – OS Sheet 173 map ref 090689; SU0868], *Waggon & Horses*: Friendly stone-and-thatch pub handy for Avebury and open all day, full range of Wadworths ales and a guest beer kept well, good coffee, old-fashioned unassuming atmosphere, understated Dickens connections, wide choice of good value bar food, teas, family room (and children's helpings on request), pub games and machines, CD juke box, pleasant garden with good play area; parking over road, no dogs; bedrooms *(PM, AM, Kevin and Kay Bronnsey, Gwen and Peter Andrews, Dick and Peggy Stacy, G Washington, LYM)*

☆ **Biddestone** [The Green; ST8773], *White Horse*: Busy local, traditional and relaxing rather than smart, small cosy carpeted rooms, wide choice of cheap well cooked food and filled rolls, well kept Courage ales, friendly helpful staff, shove-ha'penny, darts and table skittles; overlooks duck pond in picturesque village, tables in good garden with swings and pen of birds and rabbits; bedrooms *(Bill and Peggy Gluntz, Robert Huddleston, Dr and Mrs A K Clarke)*

☆ **Bishops Cannings** [SU0364], *Crown*: Welcoming and enthusiastic new licensees (with fine track record) widening the range of generous food and wines in enjoyable local next to handsome old church in pretty village; well kept Wadworths IPA and 6X; walk to Kennet & Avon Canal *(John and Chris Simpson, Marjorie and David Lamb, Chris De Wet, C Stokoe, F J and A Parmenter, BB)*

Bishopstone [High St; signed off A419/B4192 at Wanborough; SU2483], *True Heart*: Spacious old country pub doing well under new regime (linked to Royal Oak at Wootton Rivers and Pheasant at Gt Shefford), pleasant service, wide choice of good reasonably priced food inc children's, Flowers and Wadworths tapped from the cask, light and airy main bar, corridors to other rooms, restaurant; in beautiful village, handy for the Ridgeway; bedrooms *(HNJ, PEJ)*; *White Hart*: Good evening food, well kept Gibbs Mew, welcoming licensee *(Dr and Mrs N Holmes)*

☆ **Box** [A4, Bath side; ST8268], *Northey Arms*: Yet another change of management at this popular and welcoming open-plan pub with its deep red walls, relaxing decor and lovely view; standards maintained, with wide choice of well prepared food at sensible prices, well kept ales, decent wines, good service,

restaurant; children welcome; nice garden, and bedrooms now *(John and Wendy Trentham, David Johnson, June and Tony Baldwin)*

☆ **Bradford on Avon** [Silver St; ST8261], *Bunch of Grapes*: Atmospheric wine-bar style decor though definitely a pub, on two levels in picturesque steep street, with good choice of reasonably priced food, well kept Smiles and other ales, good service *(Meg and Colin Hamilton)*

Bratton [B3098 E of Westbury; ST9052], *Duke*: Part of small Moles Brewery chain, well refurbished, with comfortable lounge bar, public bar and nice small dining room, wide choice of good home-cooked reasonably priced food inc good sandwiches, welcoming service, Moles Best and Ushers, amiable labrador; ancient whalebone arch to garden; bedrooms *(Colin and Joyce Laffan, Mr and Mrs Peter Smith)*

☆ **Broad Chalke** [SU0325], *Queens Head*: Wide range of home-made food from sandwiches to unusual dishes at reasonable prices, welcoming service, well kept beer, decent wines and country wines, good coffee, attractive furnishings, log fire; maybe piped music; wheelchair access from back car park, tables in pretty courtyard; comfortable well equipped bedrooms *(John and Christine Vittoe, Christopher Warner, Mr and Mrs K Goodale, Nigel and Elizabeth Holmes)*

☆ **Broad Hinton** [High St; off A4361 about 5 miles S of Swindon; SU1076], *Crown*: Unpretentious welcoming local doing well under newish landlord, light and airy open-plan bar, plush and roomy eating area, well kept Arkells BB, BBB, Kingsdown and Mild, good home-cooked food esp salads and puddings, friendly service, lots of interesting bric-a-brac, unobtrusive piped music; unusual gilded inn sign, spacious garden; bedrooms *(Jenny and Michael Back, June and Tony Baldwin, LYM)*

☆ **Bromham** [ST9665], *Greyhound*: Good food esp fish and puddings in two thriving attractively lit bars, beams hung with lots of enjoyable bric-a-brac, two blazing log fires, even a well; interesting real ales, decent wines, small intimate restaurant; skittle alley, pool and darts; big garden *(Mr and Mrs Parmenter, Jeff Davies, John Hazel, Ray Watson)*

☆ **Broughton Gifford** [ST8763], *Bell on the Common*: Lovely old stone-built Wadworths pub with traditional furnishings, generous good value straightforward food in bars and pleasant restaurant, big coal fire, copper bar counter with handpumps on back wall, very friendly service, darts, pool etc, children welcome; garden, bowls club next door *(David Jones, Ian Phillips)*

Burcombe [SU0730], *Ship*: Clean and comfortable, very popular for wide range of good reasonably priced food; country wines *(S Jones)*

Burton [B4039 Chippenham—Chipping Sodbury; ST8179], *Old House At Home*: Spacious stone-built dining pub, wide choice of good if not cheap home-cooked food, big helpings, attractive dining area, log fire, well kept Wadworths; piped music can be loud, steep steps, cl Tues lunchtime *(Margaret and Nigel Dennis)*

☆ **Castle Combe** [signed off B4039 Chippenham—Chipping Sodbury; ST8477], *Castle Inn*: Old-world country inn in famously picturesque village, clean and attractive, lounge overlooking village street, separate locals' bar, new conservatory, tables on terrace; open fires, good home-made food inc all-day snacks, efficient service, Courage-related ales, coffee and cream teas; children welcome, bedrooms *(Andrew and Ruth Triggs, D G King)*

☆ **Castle Combe** *White Hart*: Pretty stone-built pub, attractive inside, with beams, flagstones and big log fire, Wadworths Henrys, Farmers Glory and 6X and a guest such as Adnams, pleasant service, interesting choice of decent food inc good cream teas, family room, games room and tables in sheltered courtyard *(Andrew and Ruth Triggs, R Murmann, Barry and Anne, LYM)*

nr **Castle Combe** [The Gibb; B4039 Acton Turville—Chippenham, nr Nettleton – OS Sheet 173 map ref 838791], *Salutation*: Good choice of attractively served bar food, Whitbreads-related ales, decent wines, comfortable lounge bar, welcoming and pubby locals' bar, raftered restaurant *(R Murmann)*

Charlton [A342 W of Upavon; SU1156], *Cat*: Useful stop, with food from baked potatoes to evening restaurant, Bunces Pigswill, Ushers and Wadworths 6X, reasonably priced wines, beams, pink walls, cat decor, medley of plain furniture; pool and machines in public bar, piped music; garden with picnic tables and climbing frame *(PR, UR)*

Cherhill [A4 E of Calne; SU0370], *Black Horse*: Beamed dining pub under same management as Cross Guns nr Bradford on Avon (see main entries), so popular that it has one sitting at 7 and another at 8.30 – lunchtime less busy; series of well refurbished connecting eating areas, partly no smoking; huge fireplace, wide range of generous well priced food, good service, four Ushers ales, children welcome *(Alan Piesse, Colin and Joyce Laffan)*

☆ **Chilmark** [B3089 Salisbury—Hindon; ST9632], *Black Dog*: Well kept Adnams and Brakspears and good value bar food in comfortably modernised 15th-c local with armchairs by lounge log fire, fossil ammonites in the stone of another bar, games in third bar; decent coffee *(Colin and Ann Hunt, LYM)*

Chiseldon [A345 just S of M4 junction 15; SU1879], *Plough*: Friendly efficient service, well kept Arkells BBB, wide choice of food inc good home-made soup *(R T and J C Moggridge)*

☆ **Christian Malford** [B4069 Lyneham—Chippenham, 3½ miles from M4 junction 17; ST9678], *Mermaid*: Long bar pleasantly divided into areas, good food inc some interesting dishes, well kept Bass, Courage

Best, Wadworths 6X and Worthington BB, decent whiskies and wines, some attractive pictures, bar billiards, darts, fruit machine, piped music (live Thurs), tables in garden; bedrooms *(John and Wendy Trentham, BB)*

Colerne [ST8171], *Vineyard*: Restaurant rather than pub, but you can have just a drink in the lounge bar; good value bar lunches, sandwiches too, in ancient stone building, no smoking, very obliging landlady; cl Sun evening and bank hols *(Mr and Mrs R Payne)*

Collingbourne Ducis [off A338 Marlborough—Salisbury; SU2453], *Blue Lion*: Wide range of beers, decent wines, friendly staff and large choice of reasonably priced food; comfortable and popular; pretty village *(Peter and Audrey Dowsett)*; [A338], *Last Straw*: Cottagey thatched pub with good value food in separate dining room and comfortable bar area, real ales, good open fire *(D G Clarke, M Joyner)*

☆ **Coombe Bissett** [Blandford Rd (A354); SU1026], *Fox & Goose*: Tasty reasonably priced food (interesting vegetarian, fine puddings) and Wadworths 6X and other ales in thriving spacious neatly kept open-plan pub by delightful village green; welcoming staff, rustic refectory-style tables, coal fires, old prints, hanging chamber-pots; piped music (classical at lunchtime), children catered for, evening restaurant; picnic tables on terrace and in garden with play area, good access for wheelchairs *(Stan Edwards, Kate Murley, E A George, Gordon, Ian Phillips, Sue and Mike Todd, John and Elizabeth Chaplin)*

Corsham [High St; ST8670], *Methuen Arms*: Cosy and friendly old-world inn, formerly a priory; good food in bar and pricier restaurant, Gibbs Mew Wiltshire, good atmosphere with locals in bar; tables in courtyard with outside staircase and dovecot in wall; skittle alley; bedrooms comfortable *(Meg and Colin Hamilton)*

☆ **Corton** [off A36 Warminster—Wilton; ST9340], *Dove*: Welcoming and attractive country pub, handsomely refurbished, with good choice of sensible food; brewing its own beer now, with well kept local guest beers; bedrooms *(Patrick Freeman, Richard Houghton, LYM)*

Crudwell [A429 N of Malmesbury; ST9592], *Plough*: Quiet lounge, bar with darts and juke box, pool room, dining area with comfortable well padded seats and more in elevated part; wide range of reasonably priced food, well kept ales such as Bass, Boddingtons, local Foxley, Morlands Old Specked Hen and Wadworths 6X, quick friendly service, maybe open fires, pleasant side garden *(R Huggins, D Irving, T McLean, E McCall, Ian Phillips, JKW)*

☆ **Devizes** [Long St; SU0061], *Elm Tree*: Welcoming heavy-beamed local with wide choice of good food, well kept Wadworths IPA and 6X, decent house wines, no-smoking area; piped music; restaurant, clean and tidy bedrooms *(John and Chris Simpson, John Hazel, Jason Reynolds)*

Devizes [New Park St], *Castle*: Tastefully refurbished, with well kept Wadworths IPA, 6X and Henrys, good straightforward food with fresh veg; open all day, bedrooms *(John and Chris Simpson, A R Cobb)*

☆ **Donhead St Andrew** [off A30 E of Shaftesbury, just E of Ludwell; ST9124], *Forester*: Small old country pub with inglenook fireplace, very friendly staff, good choice of well kept beers, reasonably priced food inc good sandwiches; interesting locals, live music weekends *(Dr and Mrs A K Clarke, John Hazel)*

☆ **East Knoyle** [The Green; ST8830], *Fox & Hounds*: Lovely out-of-the-way setting, superb views from manicured green opp, good choice of enjoyable food inc unusual game and venison, very reasonable prices, comfortable seats and pleasant layout, six well kept ales such as Shepherd Neame Bishops Finger, farm cider, enviable range of malt whiskies, friendly efficient landlord, smart courteous young staff *(Phyl and Jack Street, R H Martyn, Pat and Robert Watt, Klaus D Baetz)*

☆ **Farleigh Wick** [A363 Bath—Bradford; ST8064], *Fox & Hounds*: Clean and welcoming low-beamed rambling bar, highly polished old oak tables and chairs, gently rural decorations; good fresh food, attractive garden; can get packed weekends *(Meg and Colin Hamilton, MRSM, A D Sherman)*

☆ **Fonthill Gifford** [2 miles from A303; ST9232], *Beckford Arms*: Relaxed and welcoming old stone-built pub with huge log fire in attractive relaxing lounge bar, wide range of moderately priced food inc inventive dishes in bar and pleasant restaurant, well kept Courage, good value wines, local country wines, nice conservatory; in lovely countryside; comfortable good value bedrooms, good walks on doorstep *(Michael and Hazel Lyons, Stephen Goodchild)*

Foxham [NE of Chippenham; ST9777], *Foxham*: Small, friendly and cosy, extensive views from front, broad food choice cooked by landlady inc good vegetarian dishes and SE Asian curries; piped music; well behaved children welcome, peaceful village *(Peter and Wendy Begley)*

Froxfield [A4; SU2968], *Pelican*: Nice relaxed atmosphere, good welcome and service, some emphasis on tasty good value food *(Christopher Ball)*

Great Bedwyn [SU2764], *Cross Keys*: Spacious old village pub with comfortable chairs and settles, friendly licensees and locals, good range of well kept ales such as Fullers London Pride, Greene King Abbot and Hancocks HB, wide choice of reasonably priced food quickly served; can be lively evenings; nr Kennet & Avon Canal; bedrooms *(Brian Wilkinson, Beverley Daniels)*

☆ **Great Cheverell** [off B3098 Westbury—Mkt Lavington; ST9754], *Bell*: Spaciously extended dining pub in same hands as Cross Guns nr Bradford on Avon (see main entries), very popular for hearty good value food on big plates with lots of trimmings, at low

prices; comfortable chairs and settles, cosy little alcoves, well kept Courage-related ales and Wadworths 6X, upstairs dining room, friendly attentive service, attractive village *(Colin and Joyce Laffan, A D Sherman, BB)*

☆ **Great Hinton** [3½ miles E of Trowbridge, signed off A361 opp Lamb at Semington; ST9059], *Linnet*: Pleasantly refurbished village local with good value home-made food from sandwiches up inc vegetarian, children's dishes and good Sun lunch, well kept Wadworths IPA and 6X, decent house wines, keen young licensees, friendly efficient service, three dining areas off bar, walking-sticks for sale, unobtrusive piped music; children welcome, picnic tables on new front terrace, pretty village *(Frank Cummins, G Washington, John Hazel, Colin Laffan, Don Ainge, BB)*

☆ **Great Wishford** [SU0735], *Royal Oak*: Very wide choice of food in pleasant old pub in pretty village, well kept Courage-related and other ales, friendly landlord, big family dining area, log fires, public bar with pool alcove, restaurant; pretty village *(Dr Diana Terry, Gwen and Peter Andrews, J C Brittain-Long, LYM)*

☆ **Hannington** [SU1793], *Jolly Tar*: Wide choice of good value honest food, well kept Arkells BB, BBB and Kingsdown, decent wine, welcoming ex-sailor landlord, big log fire in relaxing lounge bar, ships' crests on beams, stripped stone and flock wallpaper; games bar, skittle alley, upstairs grill room; maybe piped music; good robust play area in big garden, tables out in front too; pretty village *(D M Futcher, R Huggins, T McLean, D Irving, E McCall, Peter and Audrey Dowsett, BB)*

Heddington [ST9966], *Ivy*: Simple thatched village local with good inglenook fireplace in low-beamed bar, timbered walls, well kept Wadworths tapped from the cask, bar food, children's room; seats outside the picturesque house *(Roger Huggins, John Hazel, T McLean, D Irving, E McCall)*

☆ **Heytesbury** [High St; ST9242], *Angel*: Wide choice of consistently good interesting food in well kept and attractively refurbished 16th-c inn, charming dining room opening on to secluded garden behind, Ash Vine, Marstons Pedigree and Border and Ringwood (the lovely dog's called Marston, too), friendly helpful service; popular with army personnel and can sometimes be a bit noisy, though not off-putting; bedrooms comfortable and attractive, home-baked bread and cakes for sale *(P and P Fullerton, DP, Peter Brimacombe)*

☆ **Highworth** [Market Pl; SU2092], *Saracens Head*: Comfortable and relaxed rambling bar, several distinct interesting areas around great central chimney block, friendly service, wide choice of good value straightforward bar food (limited Sun) inc vegetarian and children's, well kept Arkells BB and BBB; piped music (may be loud), public bar with TV; children in eating area, tables in sheltered courtyard, open all day weekdays; comfortable bedrooms *(Peter and Audrey Dowsett, LYM)*

Highworth [Swanborough; B4019, a mile W on Honnington turning; SU1891], *Freke Arms*: Airy and friendly, with ample comfortable seating in four connecting rooms on different levels, Ansells ales, good menu at reasonable prices, quick service; subdued piped music; small play area *(Peter and Audrey Dowsett)*

Horton [SU0463], *Bridge*: Long refurbished canalside pub, four partly separated areas, waterside garden; well kept Badger Tanglefoot and Wadworths IPA and 6X, lunchtime bar food, more expensive imaginative evening menu, prompt friendly service; lavatories for the disabled *(F J and A Parmenter)*

Kington Langley [handy for M4 junction 17; Days Lane; ST9277], *Hit or Miss*: Clean bar with big no-smoking area, darts in room off, restaurant with good log fire; well kept Courage and a guest ale, decent generous food; attractive village *(Meg and Colin Hamilton)*; *Plough*: Spacious and pleasant, friendly landlord, good food; also handy for M4 junction 17 *(Janet Pickles)*

Kington St Michael [handy for M4 junction 17; ST9077], *Jolly Huntsman*: Characterful, roomy, scrubbed tables and old-fashioned settees, well kept changing ales inc Marstons Head Brewers Choice (friendly obliging landlord interested in them), good range of fresh-cooked food; maybe sports on TV *(Jeff Davies)*

☆ **Lacock** [Bowden Hill, Bewley Common—back rd to Sandy Lane, OS Sheet 173 map ref 935679; ST9367], *Rising Sun*: Lovely spot with gorgeous distant views, interesting pub (mix of old chairs and basic kitchen tables on stone floors, stuffed animals and birds, country pictures, open fires) and good range of Moles ales, with bar food from sandwiches up and provision of children; rather frequent management changes, though, and may not open promptly at 6 *(LYM; reports on latest regime please)*

Liddington [just off A419, a mile from M4 junction 15; SU2081], *Sun*: Public bar and conservatory dining area, pleasant attentive service, standard home-made food, well kept Ushers Best and Courage-related ales *(R T and J C Moggridge)*; [Bell Lane], *Village Inn*: Comfortable traditional decor in split-level bar, wide choice of good value quick lunchtime bar food, Arkells ales, friendly homely service, log fire, atmosphere that may appeal to older people, no piped music; bedrooms simple but clean, also handy for M4 junction 15 *(J Bliss, Mr and Mrs P Smith)*

Lockeridge [signed off A4 Marlborough—Calne just W of Fyfield; SU1467], *Who'd A Thought It*: Good choice of food, well kept Wadworths IPA and 6X and an interesting guest beer, separate public bar, log fire, family room, pleasant back garden with play area; interesting village *(Marjorie and David Lamb)*

Longbridge Deverill [A350/B3095; ST8740], *George*: Simple village pub, spacious and quiet, with good modestly priced bar food,

small restaurant, well kept Gales *(Hilary Aslett)*

☆ **Luckington** [High St; off B4040 SW of Malmesbury; ST8383], *Old Royal Ship*: Traditional 17th-c roadside country pub with spacious bar and dining area, good range of rather sophisticated food inc some bargains, several well kept ales, farm cider, decent wines (two glass sizes), good coffee, darts, no piped music; attractive garden with play area, bedrooms *(Anne Morris, M J Morgan, Peter and Audrey Dowsett, Jerry and Jan Fowler)*

Malmesbury [Abbey Row; ST9287], *Old Bell*: Fine ancient inn looking across churchyard to Norman abbey, good service, limited choice of good food in Great Hall hotel bar, log fires, Ushers Best and Wadworths 6X, decent wines; not cheap; attractively old-fashioned garden providing well for children; bedrooms *(Rosie and Peter Anguin, PN, LYM)*; [High St], *Smoking Dog*: Cosy if sometimes smoky beamed and stripped stone local with changing well kept ales such as Archers, Courage Best, Greene King Abbot, Smiles Best and Wadworths 6X, farm ciders, decent wines and food (service friendly if not always quick), log fires, daily papers, board games, reference books; bistro, garden, bedrooms *(John Lawton, Peter Neate, Michael Richards, Roger Huggins, Tom Mclean, Dave Irving, D M Futcher)*; [B4014 towards Tetbury], *Suffolk Arms*: Softly lit recently refurbished knocked-through bar with interesting comfortable furnishings, panelled dining room, well kept Wadworths IPA and 6X and a changing guest beer, log fire, usual food; children welcome *(Cherry Ann Knott, Basil Minson, Ian Phillips, D Irving, LYM)*; [Market Cross], *Whole Hog*: Pleasantly modernised, piggy theme throughout, friendly staff, half a dozen well kept ales such as local Goffs Jouster as well as Flowers and Wadworths, decent wine, tea, coffee, big helpings of reasonably priced food, daily papers *(Paul and Sue Merrick)*

☆ **Manton** [High St; SU1768], *Up The Garden Path*: Good interesting country cooking using the best fresh ingredients in very friendly extended village pub with largish beamed bar and no-smoking restaurant; well kept ales, decent wines; gets its name from steep path *(Mrs C Watkinson)*

Manton [High St], *Oddfellows Arms*: Fairly small local, well kept Wadworths, country wines, good straightforward food, big garden *(N and D Clifton, K and K Bronnsey)*

☆ **Marlborough** [High St; SU1869], *Sun*: Heavy 16th-c beams, parquet floor and shiny black panelling, plainer lounge on left (children allowed here), well kept Bass and Hook Norton Best, good coffee, tasty well priced food esp fresh fish, log fire, friendly staff; seats in small courtyard; piped music, live some nights; bedrooms simple but comfortable and reasonably priced *(David Griffiths, W W Burke, Hugh Spottiswoode, PM, AM, LYM)*

☆ **Marlborough** [1 High St], *Bear*: Large Victorian inn with impressive central log fire, well kept Arkells Bitter, BBB, Kingsdown and Yeomanry, good often interesting home-cooked food in old-fashioned side bar, small front lunchtime tapas bar (evening restaurant), medieval-style banqueting hall for special occasions, skittle alley; bedrooms inc good value family room *(Annabel and Chris, Lynda Payton, Sam Samuells)*

Marlborough [High St], *Green Dragon*: Bustling well run town pub with full Wadworths range kept well, good value lunchtime bar food (plenty of eating areas), big coal-effect gas fire, stripped brickwork, lots of blue and white plates, leatherette wall banquettes, pine furniture, steps down to back games room, skittle alley, back terrace; bedrooms, pretty little breakfast room *(Lynda Payton, Sam Samuells, Brian Wilkinson, Beverley Daniels)*

☆ Marston Meysey [SU1297], *Old Spotted Cow*: Big well laid out open-plan Cotswold stone pub, good value generous bar food, well kept Flowers IPA, Wadworths 6X and guest beers such as Fullers London Pride and Hook Norton Best, welcoming landlord, comfortable chairs, raised stone fireplace; fruit machine, piped music; spacious garden with lots of play equipment, picturesque village *(Frank W Gadbois, D Irving, E McCall, T McLean, R Huggins, Dr and Mrs A K Clarke)*

Mere [Castle St; ST8132], *Old Ship*: Interesting 16th-c building with log fires, cosy hotel bar, food and well kept ales in spacious separate more pubby bar across coach entry divided into cosy areas by standing timbers, pub games and piped music, good value timber-walled restaurant; children allowed in eating area; good value bedrooms *(S Crockett, J S M Sheldon, Mr and Mrs P Bradley, James Nunns, LYM)*; *Talbot*: 16th-c inn, very much modernised but friendly, comfortable and cosy with open fire, enjoyable bar food inc good Sun lunch, cream teas, well kept Badger; comfortable bedrooms *(H E and E A Simpson, BB)*

Netherhampton [SU1029], *Victoria & Albert*: Cosy low-beamed pub with antique furniture on polished flagstones, nice long garden behind with own serving hatch; has had well kept Courage-related ales, good choice of wines and consistently good food *(J Sanderson; reports on new regime please)*

☆ Newton Tony [off A338 Swindon—Salisbury; SU2140], *Malet Arms*: Very popular nicely placed local opp footbridge over chalk stream, good imaginative food in cosy bar and restaurant, well kept Badger, Bass, Butcombe and Hampshire King Alfred, pleasant mix of business people, locals and Army officers, efficient polite staff *(Phyl and Jack Street, Tom McLean, Dr and Mrs N Holmes, Jerry and Alison Oakes)*

North Newnton [A345 Upavon—Pewsey; SU1257], *Woodbridge*: Open all day for eclectic world-wide food inc imaginative vegetarian dishes, also afternoon teas; well kept Wadworths 6X, good wines and coffee, friendly service, log fire, newspapers and magazines; big garden with boules, fishing

available; bedrooms, small camping/caravan site *(Joseph Steindl, Peter Brimacombe)*

Nunton [A338 S of Salisbury; SU1526], *Radnor Arms*: Good food inc enormous crab salad, friendly helpful staff, cheerfully busy bar and staider restaurant, very friendly dog, attractive garden popular with children *(Martin and Karen Wake, Jerry and Alison Oakes)*

Oaksey [ST9893], *Wheatsheaf*: Honest village local with dining end, well kept Whitbreads PA, games room with pool and darts *(R Huggins, T McLean, D Irving, T McCall)*

☆ Odstock [SU1526], *Yew Tree*: Fine old thatched country dining pub, bewildering choice of good value wholesome food esp fresh fish and game, good range of real ales, welcoming unpretentious atmosphere *(D R Blake)*

Ogbourne St George [A345 Marlboro—Swindon; SU1974], *Old Crown*: In small village off Ridgeway path, good welcoming service, well kept ales, good imaginative food from thick crusty bread sandwiches up to restaurant meals, tasteful cosy decoration, one table a glass-covered well *(Michael Gidding, Lynda Payton, Sam Samuells)*

Pewsey [A345 towards Marlborough; SU1560], *French Horn*: Good choice of traditional food, well kept Wadworths 6X, log fire, good welcoming service, cheerful furnishings; interesting village *(A R and B E Sayer)*

Ramsbury [Crowood Lane/Whittonditch Rd; SU2771], *Crown & Anchor*: Friendly relaxed beamed village pub, new landlord doing enjoyable well presented food, well kept Bass, Tetleys and usually a guest beer, pool in public bar; no piped music, children welcome, garden *(Mr and Mrs Peter Smith, John Scott)*

☆ Salisbury [New St; SU1429], *New Inn*: No smoking throughout; heavy beams and timbering, quiet cosy nooks and crannies in small eating area off main bar, good range of food, friendly staff, well kept Badger beers, log fires; pleasant garden, bedrooms, handy for cathedral *(John and Christine Vittoe, Dr Diana Terry, BB)*

☆ Salisbury [Town Path, W Harnham; SU1328], *Old Mill*: Cathedral view from former mill as in Constable's paintings, a lovely ten-minute stroll across the meadows; simple but comfortable beamed bars, over 500 china and other ducks, usual bar food, also lots of fresh fish, well kept Boddingtons, Flowers Original, Hop Back GFB and Summer Lightning and a guest beer, decent malt whiskies and wines, floodlit garden by millpond; children in eating area, restaurant, comfortable bedrooms *(John and Christine Vittoe, JM, PM, Peter and Audrey Dowsett, Barry and Anne, Dr and Mrs A H Young, LYM)*

☆ Salisbury [Castle St], *Avon Brewery*: Old-fashioned city bar, long, narrow, busy and friendly, with dark mahogany, frosted and engraved curved windows, friezes and attractive pictures, two open fires; competitively priced food (not Sun evening), well kept Eldridge Pope ales, decent wines, maybe classical piped music; long sheltered garden running down to river; open all day *(Ron Shelton, LYM)*

☆ Salisbury [Milford St], *Red Lion*: Mix of old-fashioned seats and modern banquettes in two-roomed nicely local-feeling panelled bar opening into other spacious and interesting areas, medieval restaurant, well kept Bass, Ushers, Wadworths 6X and a strong guest beer, lunchtime bar food, loggia courtyard seats; children in eating areas; bedrooms comfortable *(JM, PM, G Pearce, LYM)*
Salisbury [St John St], *Kings Arms*: Creaky old Tudor inn, darkly panelled and heavily beamed, with friendly staff, comfortable furnishings, good choice of wines and real ale, food in bar and restaurant; well furnished bedrooms *(John and Christine Vittoe, David Carr, LYM)*; *Old Ale House*: Tasteful refurbishment, lots of guest ales *(Dr and Mrs A K Clarke)*
Seend [A361; ST9461], *Bell*: Recently refurbished country local, prompt friendly service, well kept Wadworths IPA and 6X, good value well cooked food (not Mon evening), cosy lounge with dining section, good views from upstairs restaurant, no music *(John Hazel, Dennis Heatley, Dennis Johnson, Gwen and Peter Andrews)*; [Sells Green; A365 towards Melksham], *Three Magpies*: Unspoilt partly 18th-c pub with well kept Wadworths IPA and 6X, wide range of unusual food (even kangaroo) inc good vegetarian choice – worth the wait; some outside seating *(Joan and Michel Hooper-Immins)*
Semington [A350 2 miles S of Melksham; ST8960], *Somerset Arms*: 16th-c coaching inn with heavy-beamed long bar, real and flame-effect fires, high-backed settles, plenty of tables, lots of prints and brassware, niches with stuffed woodpeckers and the like, some farm tools, huge range of efficiently served generous food inc OAP bargains, real ales, good coffee; piped music; garden behind *(Mrs S Peregrine)*

☆ Sherston [B4040 Malmesbury—Chipping Sodbury; ST8585], *Carpenters Arms*: Cosy beamed village pub with extraordinarily wide choice of food inc lots of fresh fish and children's dishes, well kept Whitbreads-related ales tapped from the cask, shiny tables on carpeted floors, log fire, friendly efficient staff, dining area; TV in locals' bar can be intrusive; tables in pleasant garden *(Peter Cornall, Paul and Sue Merrick, Margaret and Douglas Tucker, Dave Irving, Roger Huggins, Tom McLean)*
South Marston [SU1987], *Carpenters Arms*: Olde-worlde farmhouse-style spaciously but sensitively extended pub with good value generous wholesome food, well kept Arkells and Marstons, friendly landlord and staff; animals in big back garden *(Alan and Paula McCully, T McLean, R Huggins, D Irving, E McCall, Jeff Davies)*; *Carriers Arms*: Two comfortable bars with well kept Ushers, decent wine, good choice of reasonably priced bar food; no piped music *(Peter and Audrey Dowsett)*

South Newton [A36; SU0834], *Bell*: Quiet but friendly 17th-c inn, dining area filled with badger pictures and ornaments, decent food, piped music from the Seekers to Pavarotti; in pleasant countryside with nice walks; bedrooms *(Georgina Cole)*
Staverton [B3105 Trowbridge—Bradford on Avon; ST8560], *Old Bear*: Wide choice of good food in stone pub's long bar divided into sections, big fireplace, friendly helpful staff; booking recommended Sun lunchtime *(Meg and Colin Hamilton)*

☆ Stibb Green [SU2262], *Three Horseshoes*: Friendly and spotless old-world pub with inglenook log fire in small beamed front bar, second smaller bar, wide range of good food, well kept Wadworths ales, country wines, farm cider, lively landlord *(Kevin and Kay Bronnsey)*

☆ Stourton [Church Lawn; follow Stourhead signpost off B3092, N of junction with A303 just W of Mere; ST7734], *Spread Eagle*: NT pub in lovely setting at head of Stourhead lake (though views from pub itself not special), pleasant cool and spacious back dining room popular mainly with older people; standard food till 3, and evening, Ash Vine, Bass and Wadworths 6X, friendly waitress service (can slow when busy), open fire in parlour bar, tables in back courtyard; bedrooms *(G Washington, S Jones, Wendy Arnold, David Lamb, Nick and Meriel Cox, LYM)*
Sutton Benger [ST9478], *Wellesley Arms*: Large Cotswold stone country pub with rural atmosphere, good menu and range of beers, separate dining room *(K R Harris)*
Swindon [Wood St, Old Town; SU1485], *Kings Head*: Lively bar, good reasonably priced plain food, full range of Arkells ales, friendly landlady; big comfortable bedrooms *(G Coates)*; [Upper Stratton; SU1687], *Kingsdown*: Opp Arkells Brewery, pleasantly refurbished, with energetic helpful staff, good food *(Neville Kenyon)*; [Fleet St], *Mail Coach*: Long narrow low-beamed room with high-backed back-to-back settles, plenty of dark wood, well kept Courage-related ales, food servery, further drinking room, back conservatory and nice terrace *(Jenny and Roger Huggins)*; [Regent St], *Rat & Carrot*: Part of a small chain, three or four real ales, big helpings of good value food; nr shops *(Tom McLean)*; [Regent St], *Savoy*: Massive new pub in converted cinema, four to six real ales, reasonably priced food; popular with younger people *(D Irving, E McCall, T McLean, R Huggins)*; [Manchester Rd], *Tap & Barrel*: Lively Irish pub nr railway station, well kept ales *(Dr and Mrs A K Clarke)*
Teffont Magna [ST9832], *Black Horse*: Stonebuilt two-bar pub much improved by friendly new landlord, enjoyable food, Boddingtons and Wadworths 6X, new play area in pretty garden, attractive village *(Anna Ralph, Keith Widdowson, LYM)*
Tilshead [A360 Salisbury—Devizes; SU0348], *Rose & Crown*: Nice little well cared for pub, welcoming and attentive family service, well

kept beer, good value simple wholesome food inc some unusual dishes *(D G King, Colin Laffan)*

Upton Lovell [ST9440], *Prince Leopold*: Civilised dining pub with imaginative food in nicely decorated candlelit restaurant, Wadworths 6X, decent good value wines, cheerful staff; lovely riverside garden, comfortable quiet bedrooms *(Patrick Freeman)*

Wanborough [2 miles from M4 junction 15; Callas Hill, former B4507 towards Lower Wanborough and Bishopstone; SU2083], *Black Horse*: Down-to-earth country local with lovely downland views, limited generous cheap food from doorstep sandwiches up (snacks only, Sun lunchtime), well kept low-priced Arkells BB and BBB, in winter Kingsdown tapped from the cask, welcoming landlord (and Bill and Ben the golden retrievers), beams, tiled floor, antique clock, serious darts and cribbage; lounge doubling as homely Mon-Sat lunchtime dining room; piped music, Sat theme nights; informal elevated garden with play area; children very welcome *(Peter and Audrey Dowsett, Lynda Payton, Sam Samuells, Alan and Paula McCully)*; [High St, Lower Wanborough], *Plough*: Long low thatched stone pub, three genuinely old rooms done out in ye-olde style, huge centrepiece log fire in one, another more or less for evening dining; well kept Archers Village, Bass, Flowers Original, Fullers London Pride and Wadworths 6X, good home-cooked food (not Sun), bar billiards; open all day Sat *(Lynda Payton, Sam Samuells, Cherry Ann Knott)*

West Dean [SU2527], *Red Lion*: After a reprieve this excellent country pub closed again in Nov 1995 and seems unlikely to reopen *(LYM)*

West Lavington [Church St; SU0053], *Bridge*: Long dim-lit pink dining bar, big log fire, pleasant country pictures and the like, well kept Gibbs Mew ales, decent wines, welcoming service, wide choice of locally popular home-cooked food inc interesting fish and vegetarian dishes; pretty flower-filled garden *(Gwen and Peter Andrews)*; *Wheatsheaf*: Hard-working licensees doing very good food at attractive prices; pleasant good value bedrooms *(Colin Laffan)*

Wilton [the village S of Gt Bedwyn; SU2661], *Swan*: Good plain food, friendly service, Fullers London Pride, Hook Norton Old Hookey and Wadworths 6X, pool table; garden with small play area, attractive small village *(Dr Douglas Coombs)*

☆ **Wingfield** [ST8256], *Poplars*: Clean and friendly country local with decent food inc splendid snacks, well kept Wadworths, quick pleasant service, enjoyable atmosphere, no juke box or machines; own cricket pitch *(Geoff Summers, Dr and Mrs A H Young, LYM)*

☆ **Woodborough** [Bottlesford, towards Pewsey – OS Sheet 173 map ref 112592; SU1159], *Seven Stars*: Thatched country pub with roaring log fires, attractive panelling, well kept Badger Tanglefoot, Wadworths 6X and guest beer, food not cheap but often very good indeed (French chef/patron gets regular supplies direct from France), good wine list, two restaurant areas; pretty garden, in 7 acres *(Neville Burrell, Nick Clifton, David Clifton, Ian Harding, Peter Brimacombe)*

Bedroom prices normally include full English breakfast, VAT and any inclusive service charge that we know of. Prices before the '/' are for single rooms, after for two people in double or twin (B includes a private bath, S a private shower). If there is no '/', the prices are only for twin or double rooms (as far as we know there are no singles).

Yorkshire

Quite a change-around among the county's top pubs this year, with a number of old favourites not quite making the main entries (after licensee changes and so forth), but quite a lot of good newcomers to make up. As always, Yorkshire stands out above all other areas for the really welcoming atmosphere which makes so many of its pubs deeply enjoyable. Pubs gaining the warmest approval from readers these days include the Crab & Lobster at Asenby (excellent food, lots of character), the George & Dragon at Aysgarth (a new main entry, fine old welcoming inn), the Birch Hall at Beck Hole (utterly idiosyncratic, great fun, in a lovely spot – another newcomer), the well placed Strines near Bradfield (hard-working new licensee since last in the Guide), the Buck in its lovely setting at Buckden, the Foresters Arms at Carlton (good all round), the Royal Oak at Dacre Banks (friendly young owners gaining a first main entry with their good chip-free food), the Blue Lion at East Witton (good civilised upmarket food, though very unpubby now), the extremely well run Angel at Hetton (super food, tremendous choice of wines by the glass), the unspoilt George beautifully placed at Hubberholme, the Sands House near Huddersfield (reliably good value food and very cheerful service – a new main entry), the George & Dragon at Kirkbymoorside (good all round), the Fountaine at Linton in Craven (gaining a Star Award this year for its all-round excellence), the Will's o' Nat's at Meltham (reliably good food, well kept ales), the ancient Black Swan in Middleham (another good all-rounder, gaining its first main entry), the friendly and well run Nags Head at Pickhill (good food), the White Hart at Pool (no-nonsense good food, interesting furnishings), the charming little Laurel in the lovely village of Robin Hoods Bay (very popular new landlord), the interesting Golden Lion in Settle (gaining its main entry under the son of the couple who run the successful Royal Oak there), the cheery little Fat Cat in Sheffield (good very cheap food and fine ales including ones brewed at the pub), the civilised if unpubby Three Acres in Shelley (excellent food including magnificent sandwiches), the Hare & Hounds at Stutton (enjoyable food, good family garden – another newcomer to the Guide), the attractive Wombwell Arms at Wass (excellent food, very courteous service) and the White Swan at Wighill (new licensees doing good food in this nice old place). For the title of Yorkshire Dining Pub of the Year – hotly contested in this favoured county – we choose the Foresters Arms at Carlton, a very genuine pub, with food that's not at all pretentious but is thoughtfully and skilfully prepared using good often interesting local ingredients. In the Lucky Dip section at the end of the chapter, several pubs have been showing really well in recent months: the Falcon at Arncliffe, Cadeby Inn at Cadeby, Cross Keys at East Marton, Boot & Shoe at Ellerton, Black Horse in Grassington, Queens Head at Kettlesing, Forresters Arms at Kilburn, Shoulder of Mutton at Kirkby Overblow, Red Lion at Langthwaite, Golden Lion in Leyburn, Beehive at Newholm, Star at North Dalton, White Horse just above Rosedale

Abbey, Boat at Sprotbrough, Tan Hill Inn on Tan Hill and Ring o' Bells at Thornton. We have inspected almost all of these and unhesitatingly recommend them for the qualities outlined in the Dip. There's an excellent choice of pubs for all tastes in York; and a good choice in Leeds and in Hull. Yorkshire's pubs charge much less for drinks than the national average; we found particularly low prices in pubs tied to the local brewers Sam Smiths and Clarks. We've been pleased to see the good Black Sheep beers from Masham increasingly widely sold in (and beyond) the area; they are produced by a member of the Theakston brewing family who decided to go independent after Theakstons was swallowed up by the Scottish & Newcastle empire. Other local beers well worth tracking down are Malton and Barnsley.

ALDBOROUGH (N Yorks) SE4166 Map 7

Ship 🍺

Village signposted from B6265 just S of Boroughbridge, close to A1

Run by friendly licensees, this neatly kept old pub is well liked by readers. The heavily beamed bar has a coal fire in the stone inglenook fireplace, some old-fashioned seats around heavy cast-iron tables, and sentimental engravings on the walls. Ample bar food includes home-made soup (£1.60), well filled sandwiches (from £1.95; open ones from £3.75), garlic mushrooms (£2.75), ploughman's or giant yorkshire pudding with roast beef (£4.50), home-made steak and kidney pie, lasagne or home-made chicken curry (£4.95), battered cod (£5.95), steaks (from £7.25), and specials such as king prawns in garlic or liver and bacon (£4.50), ham and mushroom tagliatelle (£5.50), chicken curry (£5.75), and bacon chop (£6.95); good breakfasts. Well kept John Smiths, Tetleys Bitter, and Theakstons Old Peculier on handpump, and quite a few malt whiskies; shove-ha'penny, dominoes, and piped music. There are seats on the front terrace or on the spacious lawn behind. Handy for the ancient church opposite and near the Roman town with its museum and Roman pavements. *(Recommended by Tony Gayfer, Janet and Peter Race, Tony Kemp, Rachel Weston, Martin Hickes, Peter and Patricia Burton, Neil and Angela Huxter, T M Dobby, R A Hobbs)*

Free house ~ Licensee Duncan Finch ~ Real ale ~ Meals and snacks (not Sun evening) ~ Restaurant (not Sun evening) ~ (01423) 322749 ~ Children in eating area of bar ~ Open 11-2.30, 5.30-11; 11-11 summer Sat (12-3, 5.30-11 winter Sat) ~ Bedrooms: £31S/£43S

APPLETREEWICK (N Yorks) SE0560 Map 7

Craven Arms ♀ 🍴

Village signposted off B6160 Burnsall—Bolton Abbey

The view from the picnic tables in front of this creeper-covered country pub is splendid and looks south over the green Wharfedale valley to a pine-topped ridge; there are more seats in the back garden. Inside, the small cosy rooms have roaring fires (one in an ancient iron range), attractive settles and carved chairs among more usual seats, beams covered with banknotes, harness, copper kettles and so forth, and a warm atmosphere; the landlord is quite a character. Generous bar food includes home-made soup (£1.80), sandwiches (from £1.80), potted shrimps (£2.90), ploughman's (£3.80), cumberland sausage and onion sauce (£4.55), home-made steak and kidney pie (£4.65), ham and eggs (£5.65), steaks (from £8.50), and daily specials such as a vegetarian dish (£4.80) and game dishes (£5.25); quick table service in the charming small dining room. Well kept Boddingtons, Black Sheep Bitter, Tetleys Bitter, Theakstons Best, Old Peculier, and XB, and Youngers Scotch on handpump, and decent, keenly priced wines; darts, shove-ha'penny, cribbage, and dominoes – no music. The pub is popular with walkers. *(Recommended by Prof and Mrs S Barnett, WAH, Martin Hickes, Geoffrey and Irene Lindley, M Joyner, Jim and Maggie Cowell, David Sadler, J E Rycroft, Gwen and Peter Andrews)*

Free house ~ Licensees Jim and Linda Nicholson ~ Real ale ~ Meals and snacks ~ (01756) 720270 ~ Children welcome ~ Open 11.30-3, 6.30-11; closed 25 Dec

ASENBY (N Yorks) SE3975 Map 7

Crab & Lobster ★ 🍴 ♀

Village signposted off A168 – handy for A1

People are happy to drive many miles to enjoy the excellent, imaginative food in this very popular thatched dining pub. The menu is chalked over all the dark beams and joists in the characterful rambling L-shaped bar and might include sandwiches such as crispy bacon, lettuce, tomato and mayonnaise (from £3.95), shellfish bisque with crab tortellini (£4.25), baked goat's cheese and hazelnuts in filo, burnt onions, and honeycomb salad or spiced crab cakes with mustard and coriander (£4.95), potted prawns, tomato butter and chilli toast (£5.50), Thai beef pancakes (£5.95), fish pie (£8.95), braised shank of lamb with a hot pot of vegetables (£9.50), crispy confit of duck with caramelised oranges (£9.95), fresh tuna salad niçoise (£10.50), and char-grilled entrecote steak with crispy onions (£12.95); delicious puddings, and there are usually nibbles on the bar counter. Black Sheep, John Smiths, Theakstons Best, Timothy Taylors Landlord, and Youngers No 3 on handpump, and good wines by the glass, with interesting bottles. The cosily cluttered bar has an interesting jumble of seats from antique high-backed and other settles through settees and wing armchairs heaped with cushions to tall and rather theatrical corner seats and even a very superannuated dentist's chair; the tables are almost as much of a mix, and the walls and available surfaces are quite a jungle of bric-a-brac, with standard and table lamps and candles keeping even the lighting pleasantly informal; well reproduced piped music. There are rustic seats on a side lawn, and out on a front terrace by tubs of flowers; wood-stove barbecues every Friday evening and Sunday lunchtime with entertainment during the spring and summer, weather permitting. A permanent marquee is attached to the restaurant. *(Recommended by Susan and John Douglas, John and Chris Simpson, Ian Morley, David and Fiona Pemberton, Peter Marshall, Martin Hickes, J O Jonkler, Jason Caulkin, Walter and Susan Rimaldi-Butcher, Allan Worsley, T Large, Miss V Smith, Peter Bell, Mr and Mrs Chapman, David Stafford, Mr and Mrs C Cole, Robert and Ann Lees, Tim and Sue Halstead, S Head)*

Free house ~ Licensees David and Jackie Barnard ~ Real ale ~ Meals and snacks (not Sun evening) ~ Restaurant (not Sun evening) ~ (01845) 577286 ~ Children welcome ~ Jazz/blues evenings ~ Open 11.30-3, 6.30-11; closed Sun evening

ASKRIGG (N Yorks) SD9591 Map 10

Kings Arms 🛏 ♀

Village signposted from A684 Leyburn—Sedbergh in Bainbridge

Once a well known horse-racing stud and then a coaching inn, this Georgian manor house has three atmospheric, old-fashioned bars with lots of mementoes and photographs of the filming of James Herriot's *All Creatures Great and Small* – the inn itself, in the series, is the Drovers Arms. The very high-ceilinged central room has an attractive medley of furnishings that includes a fine sturdy old oak settle, 19th-c fashion plates, a stag's head, hunting prints, and a huge stone fireplace; a curving wall with a high window shows people bustling up and down the stairs and there's a kitchen hatch in the panelling. The small low-beamed and oak panelled front bar has period furnishings, some side snugs, and a lovely green marble fireplace. A simply furnished flagstone back bar has yet another fire, a fruit machine and juke box. Darts, shove-ha'penny, dominoes, and cribbage. Enjoyable bar food includes Yorkshire specialities such as a hearty broth (£2.95), peat bog pie (shepherd's pie topped with black pudding and oatmeal) or delicious panacalty (grated potato with bacon and onions topped with poached eggs and melted cheese £5), 16oz local trout with home-made tomato chutney (£6.50), and honey-roasted local lamb ribs (£7.95), as well as sandwiches (from £1.95; lemon chicken french bread £3.50; steak danish open £4), soup (£2.50), stir-fried vegetables with citrus fruit (£4), salmon steak with a lemon and mushroom butter (£6), steak in ale pie (£6.25), gammon and egg (£6.50), traditional home-made puddings (£2.75), and children's dishes (from £1.95). The restaurants are no smoking. Well kept Dent Bitter, Theakstons XB, and Youngers Scotch and No 3 on handpump, quite a few malt whiskies, and a very good wine list (including interesting champagnes); pleasant, helpful staff. The two-level courtyard has lots of tables and chairs. *(Recommended by Marianne Lantree, Steve Webb, Paul Boot, Peter and Patricia Burton, R White, Mark and Caroline Thislethwaite, Eddie Edwards, Roger and Corinne Ball, JKW, John Fazakerley, Sara Nicholls, J Royce)*

Free house ~ Licensees Raymond and Elizabeth Hopwood ~ Real ale ~ Meals and snacks ~ Restaurant (not Sun evening) ~ (01969) 650258 ~ Children in eating area of bar and in restaurant ~ Live entertainment monthly Fri evening ~ Open 11-3(5 Sat), 6.30-11 ~ Bedrooms: £50B/£89B

AYSGARTH (N Yorks) SE0088 Map 10

George & Dragon

A684 W of Leyburn

In fine countryside, this bustling inn has a small, cosy and attractive bar with a big open fire, lots of bric-a-brac, portraits of locals by the landlord, a carved wooden bar, and well kept real ales on handpump such as Black Sheep Bitter, John Smiths, and Theakstons Best; there's also a polished hotel lounge with antique china, and a grandfather clock; friendly obliging service, and a welcome for children and dogs. There's quite an emphasis on the popular home-made food in the spacious eating area with its cast-iron and wooden tables: soup (£1.95), sandwiches (from £2), garlic mushrooms (£3.25), ploughman's (£4.95), vegetable tikka masala or cumberland sausage (£5.50), asparagus and mushroom crêpes (£5.95), gammon with two eggs (£6.95), puddings such as apple pie or sticky toffee pudding (£2.50), and evening extras like stuffed chicken with prawns (£7.95), venison casserole or roast duckling (£8.75), and fillet steak in a port and stilton sauce (£11.50). Dominoes, cribbage, piped music, and a grey and white cat called Smokey. Outside on the gravelled beer garden are some picnic tables and tubs of pretty flowers. *(Recommended by Richard Houghton, Angus Lyon, Ian Morley)*

Free house ~ Licensees Nigel and Joan Fawcett ~ Real ale ~ Meals and snacks (12-2, 6-9) ~ (01969) 663358 ~ Children welcome ~ Open 11-3, 6-11 ~ Bedrooms: £25B/£50B

BECK HOLE (N Yorks) NZ8202 Map 10

Birch Hall

Off A169 S of Whitby: take northernmost Goathland signed turning, then first right; a very pretty but long-winded approach is to park at the Goathland steam railway station and walk along the line

Set in a beautiful steep valley village by a bridge over a river and close to Thomason Fosse waterfall and the steam railway, this is a unique, unchanging pub-cum-village shop. There are two rooms with the shop selling postcards, sweeties and ice creams in between, and hatch service to both sides. Furnishings are simple – built-in cushioned wall seats and wooden tables and chairs on the floor (flagstones in one room, composition in the other), and well kept ales such as Black Sheep Bitter, Theakstons Best, XB and Mild, and a couple of guest beers from all over the country on handpump. Bar snacks such as sandwiches (£1.75), locally-made pies (£1.15), and home-made scones and cakes including their lovely beer cake (from 55p); winter darts and dominoes; friendly, welcoming staff. Outside, an ancient mural hangs on the pub wall, there are benches out in front, and steep steps up to a charming little steeply terraced side garden with a nice view. *(Recommended by R Borthwick, S Clegg, JP, PP, Chris Westmoreland, E A Thwaite, Michael Williamson, Eddie Edwards, Andy and Jill Kassube)*

Free house ~ Licensee Colin Jackson ~ Real ale ~ Snacks (available throughout opening hours) ~ (01947) 896245 ~ Children welcome ~ Parking is difficult, so park in the nearest car park ~ Open 11-11; 12-10.30 summer Sun; 11-3, 7.30-11 in winter; closed winter Mon evenings and evening 25 Dec

BEVERLEY (E Yorks) TA0340 Map 8
White Horse ('Nellies')

Hengate, close to the imposing Church of St Mary's; runs off North Bar Within

For those who love determinedly traditional and unspoilt old pubs, then this is the place to be – indeed, little can have changed since the days in the 18th c when John Wesley preached in the back yard; even then the building was over 350 years old. The basic but very atmospheric little rooms are huddled together around the central bar, with antique cartoons and sentimental engravings on the nicotine-stained walls, brown leatherette seats (with high-backed settles in one little snug), basic wooden chairs and benches, a gaslit pulley-controlled chandelier, bare floorboards, a deeply reverberating chiming clock, and open fires – one with an attractively tiled old fireplace. Well kept and very cheap Sam Smiths OB and Museum on handpump. Cheap, simple, quickly served food might include sandwiches (£1.40), filled baked potatoes (£2), and a vegetarian dish or fresh huge haddock (£3.75). A separate games room has darts, cribbage, dominoes, pinball, fruit machine, juke box, and two pool tables – these and the no-smoking room behind the bar are the only modern touches. Those whose tastes are for comfortable modern pubs may find it a little spartan, anyone else will quickly feel at home. *(Recommended by Pete Baker, JJW, CMW, Andy and Jill Kassube; more reports please)*

Sam Smiths ~ Manager John Southern ~ Real ale ~ Lunchtime meals and snacks (not Mon, apart from bank holidays) ~ (01482) 861973 ~ Children welcome except in bar ~ Poetry and music night 1st Thurs of month – all poets/musicians welcome ~ Open 11-11; cl 25 Dec

BILBROUGH (N Yorks) SE5346 Map 7
Three Hares

Off A64 York—Tadcaster

Most people come to this smartly refurbished dining pub to enjoy the very good, imaginative food – but the beer is well kept and you can be sure of a warm welcome from the licensees and their staff. Bar food, using top quality local produce, is served in the lounge bar and might include sandwiches, home-made soup (£1.95), grilled fresh sardines with pesto and lime (£2.95), good deep-fried vegetables in a crisp batter with a sweet and sour sauce or crostini of chicken liver pâté with a red onion marmalade (£3.25), venison sausages with a celeriac mash and red wine sauce (£5.95), loin of local pork steak roasted with red peppers and hoi sin barbecue sauce (£6.50), pasta with smoked Whitby cod, gruyère cheese and spinach and topped with crème fraîche (£6.75), goujons of fresh sole in crisp batter (£6.95), char-grilled fillet of salmon with eastern spices and coriander oil (£7.25), grilled sirloin steak (£9.95), and home-made puddings like yorkshire curd cheesecake with an apple and cinnamon compote, baked ginger and syrup pudding, and terrine of chocolate and amaretti with a biscuit cream (£2.95). They sell the recipes over the counter for charity. Well kept Black Sheep Bitter and Timothy Taylors Landlord, and changing guests like Black Sheep Special, Fullers London Pride, Marstons Pedigree, Theakstons XB, and Wadworths 6X on handpump, and a good, interesting and sensibly priced wine list (Mr Whitehead's wholesale wine business is thriving). The old village smithy forms part of the no-smoking restaurant and the old forge and implement hooks are still visible; the prettily papered walls of the traditional bar are hung with pictures of the village (taken in 1904 and showing that little has changed since then), and there's plenty of polished copper and brass. The churchyard close to the pub is where Sir Thomas Fairfax, famous for his part in the Civil War, lies buried. *(Recommended by J V Dadswell, Martin Bromfield, Bernadette Garner, Jason Caulkin, Gill and Andy Plumb, Syd and Wyn Donald, David and Fiona Pemberton, Neville Kenyon, Janet Pickles, Eric and Shirley Broadhead, Pat and Tony Martin, Carole and Philip Bacon, Keith and Margaret Kettell, Viv Middlebrook, Lawrence Bacon, Tim and Sue Halstead, Bill and Beryl Farmer, Nick Wikeley)*

Free house ~ Lease: Peter and Sheila Whitehead ~ Real ale ~ Meals and snacks (not Mon) ~ Restaurant (not Sun evening or Mon) ~ (01937) 832128 ~ Well behaved children in eating area of bar and those over 10 in restaurant; must be

gone by 8pm ~ Open 12-2.30, 7(6.30 Fri/Sat)-11; closed Mon (except bank holidays), and evenings 26 Dec and 1 Jan

BLAKEY RIDGE (N Yorks) SE6799 Map 10

Lion 🖴 🍺

From A171 Guisborough—Whitby follow Castleton, Hutton le Hole signposts; from A170 Kirkby Moorside—Pickering follow Keldholm, Hutton le Hole, Castleton signposts; OS Sheet 100 map reference 679996

The views from here are stunning and this isolated 16th-c inn is said to be the fourth highest in England (1325 ft up). The cosy and characterful beamed and rambling bars have a bustling, friendly atmosphere, warm open fires, a few big high-backed rustic settles around cast-iron-framed tables, lots of small dining chairs on the turkey carpet, a nice leather settee, and stripped stone walls hung with some old engravings and photographs of the pub under snow (it can easily get cut off in winter). Big helpings of bar food include soup (£1.95), lunchtime sandwiches (£2.25) and ploughman's (£4.45), home-made steak and mushroom pie, home-cooked ham and egg, spinach and mushroom lasagne, cod in batter or home-made lasagne (all £5.45), steaks (from £8.95), and puddings like sticky toffee pudding or jam roly poly (£2.25); good breakfasts, and quick service even when busy – which it usually is. One of the restaurants is no smoking. Well kept John Smiths, Tetleys Bitter, Theakstons Best, Old Peculier, XB and Mild, and Youngers No 3 on handpump; dominoes, fruit machine and piped music. *(Recommended by Eddie Edwards, Addie and Irene Henry, Martin Jones, Mr and Mrs R P Begg, R N Hutton, M Borthwick, R M Macnaughton, Bronwen and Steve Wrigley, Andy and Jill Kassube)*

Free house ~ Licensee Barry Crossland ~ Real ale ~ Meals and snacks (11-10) ~ Restaurant ~ (01751) 417320 ~ Children welcome ~ Open 10.30am-11pm; 12-10.30 Sun ~ Bedrooms: £16.50(£26.50B)/£45(£53B)

nr BRADFIELD (S Yorks) SK2692 Map 7

Strines Inn

Strines signposted from A616 at head of Underbank Reservoir, W of Stocksbridge; or on A57 heading E of junction with A6013 (Ladybower Reservoir) take first left turn (signposted with Bradfield) then bear left

Local people know well that this corner of Yorkshire – virtually unknown to outsiders – can easily hold its own with the more familiar areas of the Peak District, the Dales and the North Yorkshire Moors. And here in its heart, looking out on the forests, the moorland pastures, the Dark Peak itself, and the glint of water from Strines Reservoir below, is a handsome stone-built inn. There's a 16th-c coat of arms over the door, but the pub probably dates back 300 years before that. The best views are from the picnic tables outside, though you can peer out of the bar windows; swings and some rescued animals – Gideon the old donkey, pigs, goats, geese, hens, sheep and a rabbit called Budweiser. Inside, there's a warmly welcoming and relaxed atmosphere, and the main bar has black beams liberally decked with copper kettles and so forth, quite a menagerie of stuffed animals, homely red-plush-cushioned traditional wooden wall benches and small chairs, and a coal fire in the rather grand stone fireplace; there's a good mixture of customers. A room off on the right has another coal fire, hunting photographs and prints, and lots of brass and china, and on the left, a similarly furnished room is no smoking. Genuinely home-made bar food includes sandwiches (hot roast pork or beef cut straight from the joint £2.25 and £2.70), soup (£1.95), filled baked potatoes (from £2.80), pâté (£2.95), garlic mushrooms (£3.95), ploughman's or giant yorkshire pudding filled with vegetables in a cheese sauce (£4.50), steak, kidney and ale pie (£5.50), honey-roast gammon with egg (£5.95), trout with almonds (£6.50), rump steak (£7.95), daily specials like popular carrot, tomato, cheese and herb bake (£3.95), salmon steaks in lemon parsley butter, steaks with garlic or peppered sauce, rabbit and pheasant dishes, and puddings like treacle sponge, strawberry flan and apple pie; four or five fresh vegetables, and most meals can be adapted to children's appetites (at half price). Well kept

Boddingtons, Flowers IPA, Marstons Pedigree, Wadworths 6X, and Whitbreads Castle Eden on handpump, quite a choice of malt whiskies, and particularly good coffee; good service, and piped music. We've had no up-to-date reports on the bedrooms but would expect them to be good – three have four-poster beds and two have open log fires; they will serve breakfast here if you want. *(Recommended by Dave and Karen Turner, Geoffrey and Irene Lindley, Eric Locker, A J Hilton)*

Free house ~ Licensee Jeremy Stanish ~ Real ale ~ Meals and snacks ~ (0114) 285 1247 ~ Children in eating area of bar ~ Open 11-11; 10.30-3, 7-11 winter weekdays ~ Bedrooms: £35B/£45B

BRANDESBURTON (E Yorks)TA1247 Map 8

Dacre Arms

Village signposted from A165 N of Beverley and Hornsea turn-offs

This old inn was once one of the most important posting stations in the East Riding. Travellers weren't the only people to enjoy some kind of hospitality – a snug area on the right once housed the local Court of Justices, while a long-since vanished secret room provided a hiding place for fugitive Jacobites. The rambling rough-plastered modernised bar is vividly furnished with plenty of tables, and has a roomily comfortable feel. Under the new licensees, the wide choice of bar food includes home-made soup (£1.60), filled baked potatoes (from £2.25), steak and kidney casserole (snack size £3.20, king size £4.60), chicken curry (snack size £3.45, king size £4.85), filled yorkshire puddings (from £4.25), salads (from £4.95), smoked salmon and asparagus omelette (£5.45), steaks (from £7.95), house specials like salmon and broccoli pasta bake (£5.45), pork stroganoff (£5.75), and seafood gratin (£6.45), and puddings (from £2.10). Well kept Tetleys, Theakstons Old Peculier and a weekly guest beer on handpump; video game and piped music. *(Recommended by I Maw, C A Hall, KC, R Suddaby; more reports please)*

Free house ~ Lease: Jason and Liza Good ~ Real ale ~ Meals and snacks (12-2, 6.30-10 Mon-Thurs; 12-2, 5.30-10.30 Fri/Sat; 12-10 Sun) ~ Restaurant ~ (01964) 542392 ~ Children welcome ~ Open 11.30-2.30, 6.30(5.30 Fri)-11; 11.30-11 Sat; 12-10.30 Sun; closed 25 Dec

BREARTON (N Yorks) SE3261 Map 7

Malt Shovel 🍽 ♀

Village signposted off A61 N of Harrogate

The friendly licensees here work really hard to get things just as they want them. Apart from installing a new kitchen this year with a large char-grill which will be used for vegetables and fruit as well as steaks and so forth, they try hard to support small local breweries, keep a small but interesting and reasonably priced wine list with a wine of the week and quite a few others by the glass, and serve their house coffee (and a guest coffee) in cafetieres. Several heavily-beamed rooms radiate from the attractive linenfold oak bar counter with plush-cushioned seats and a mix of tables, an ancient oak partition wall, both real and gas fires, and lively hunting prints; they plan to make one area no smoking. The very good food might include goat's cheese and leek tart or fresh mussels with garlic, tomatoes, coriander and white wine with home-baked bread (£3.95), spicy bean pot (£4.50), tagliatelle with mushrooms, sun-dried tomatoes, spinach, basil and cream or home-cooked, honey-baked ham with grain mustard and honey sauce (£4.95), steak in ale pie (£5.25), fresh haddock with real ale batter (£5.50), local wild venison (£5.95), char-grilled tuna steak with green chilli and coriander pesto (£7.25), sirloin steak (£7.50), and puddings like chocolate bread and butter pudding, lemon flan and fresh fruit brûlée (£2.25). Well kept Black Sheep Riggwelter, Durham Sanctuary, Daleside Nightjar, Old Mill Traditional, and Theakstons Best on handpump, and a fair choice of malt whiskies; darts, shove-ha'penny, cribbage, and dominoes. There are tables behind, on the terrace and the grass. *(Recommended by Marian and Andrew Ruston, Syd and Wyn Donald, Walter and Susan Rinaldi-Butcher, Mr and Mrs Chapman, M Heys, Derek and Sylvia Stephenson, David Watson, Paul Boot, Viv Middlebrook, Geoffrey and Brenda Wilson, Dorothy and David Young, Janet and Peter Race, S Thompson, Christine and Christopher Challis, Bob and Maggie Atherton, Andrew and Ruth Triggs, R A Whitehead, Tim and Sue Halstead)*

Free house ~ Licensees Leslie and Charlotte Mitchell ~ Real ale ~ Meals and snacks (not Sun evening, not Mon) ~ (01423) 862929 ~ Children welcome ~ Open 12-2.30, 6.45-11; closed Mon

BUCKDEN (N Yorks) SD9278 Map 7

Buck ♀

B6160

One reader who has known this bustling inn for 20 years feels that it is doing particularly well at the moment. The modernised and extended open-plan bar has upholstered built-in wall banquettes and square stools around shiny dark brown tables on its carpet – though there are still flagstones in the snug original area by the serving counter – local pictures, hunting prints, willow-pattern plates on a delft shelf, and the mounted head of a roebuck on the bare stone wall above the log fire. Very helpful uniformed staff quickly serve the popular bar food which includes home-made soup with home-made roll (£2.45), sandwiches (from £2.95), wild boar pâté (£3.75), ploughman's (from £5.95), braised shoulder of char-grilled pork loin medaillons on black pudding risotto with a grain mustard and brandy sauce (£6.75), poached salmon on celeriac rosti, fresh spinach and a bearnaise sauce (£7.95), a proper cassoulet (£9.50), 16oz rump steak (£10.95), and puddings like caramelised orange and Cointreau tart, steamed vanilla sponge with a red berry sauce and crème anglaise or sticky toffee pudding (£3.25); the dining area and restaurant are no smoking. Well kept Black Sheep Bitter, Special, and Riggwelter, and Theakstons Best, Old Peculier and XB on handpump; a fair choice of malt whiskies and decent wines. Darts, dominoes, cribbage, and piped music. The pub is in a glorious setting in upper Wharfedale with fine moorland views, and lots of surrounding footpaths and lanes. *(Recommended by R N Hutton, E George, Chris Wheaton, Andrew and Ruth Triggs, Dr P Jackson, I Maw, F J Robinson, M Morgan, J E Rycroft, K Frostick, Anthony Marriott, Anne and Brian Birtwistle, J C Simpson, Prof S Barnett, Mike and Ruth Dooley, Jack and Heather Coyle)*

Free house ~ Licensee Nigel Hayton ~ Real ale ~ Meals and snacks ~ Evening restaurant ~ (01756) 760228 ~ Children welcome away from bar ~ Open 11-11; 12-10.30 Sun ~ Bedrooms: £34B/£68B

BURNSALL (N Yorks) SE0361 Map 7

Red Lion ⇒ ♀

B6160 S of Grassington, on Ilkley road; OS Sheet 98, map reference 033613

In the 16th c this popular place was a ferryman's inn, and tables on the front cobbles and most of the bedrooms have views of the River Wharfe and village green; there are more seats on a big back terrace, lots of fine surrounding walks, and fishing permits for 7 miles of river. Inside, the bustling main bar has sturdy seats built in to the attractively panelled walls (decorated with pictures of the local fell races), windsor armchairs, oak benches, rugs on the floor, and steps up past a solid fuel stove to a back area with sensibly placed darts (dominoes players are active up here, too). The carpeted, no-smoking front lounge bar, served from the same copper-topped counter through an old-fashioned small-paned glass partition, has a log fire. Good bar food includes home-made soup (£2.75), lunchtime sandwiches (from £3.25; open sandwiches £5.25), Cumbrian air-dried ham cured in molasses and served with their own chutney (£4.25), ratatouille and blue wensleydale cheese (£6.75), ploughman's, lamb liver and bacon, steak, kidney and ale pie, and gammon with free range eggs (all £6.95), Herdwick lamb or fresh cod baked with tomatoes and fresh basil (£7.95), sirloin steak (£9.25), daily specials such as hake, monkfish, lemon sole, crab, and seasonal game (pheasant, mallard, pigeon and partridge), and puddings such as lemon tart with raspberry coulis or caramelised rice pudding with stewed rhubarb; the restaurant is no smoking. Well kept Tetleys Bitter, Theakstons Best and guest beers on handpump, malt whiskies, and a very good wine list with an interesting choice by the glass. *(Recommended by Norma Hardy, Ian and Christina Allen,*

Tim Davidson, Prof and Mrs S Barnett, Jim Bedford, D Goodger, C H and P Stride)

Free house ~ Licensee Elizabeth Grayshon ~ Real ale ~ Meals and snacks (12-2.30, 6-9.30) ~ Restaurant ~ (01756) 720204 ~ Children in eating area of bar ~ Open 11.30-11; 12-10.30 Sun ~ Bedrooms: £45B/£74B

BYLAND ABBEY (N Yorks) SE5579 Map 7

Abbey Inn ⑪ ♀

The Abbey has a brown tourist-attraction signpost off the A170 Thirsk—Helmsley

It's the good and extremely popular food that continues to draw people to this busy dining pub. Its popularity is such that you have to book a table in advance – not a policy we whole-heartedly agree with (especially if people turn up early on the off-chance to find booked but empty tables). The rambling, characterful rooms have big fireplaces, oak and stripped deal tables, settees, carved oak seats, and Jacobean-style dining chairs on the polished boards and flagstones, bunches of flowers among the candles, various stuffed birds, cooking implements, little etchings, willow-pattern plates, and china cabinets, and some discreet stripping back of plaster to show the ex-abbey masonry. In a big back room an uptilted cart shelters a pair of gnomelike waxwork yokels, and there are lots of rustic bygones; piped music. Served by neat and friendly waitresses, bar food at lunchtime might include sandwiches (from £2.75), home-made chicken liver or hazelnut, mushroom and lentil pâté (£4.25), mixed meat salad (£6.25), turkey, chicken and apricot pie or ratatouille bake (£6.50), roast pork with apple sauce (£7), goujons of salmon (£7.50), with evening dishes like stilton and apple tartlets (£3.80), beef in ale pie (£7), smoked haddock mornay (£7.50), lamb rumps in a mint and mushroom sauce (£8.50), grilled halibut and prawns (£9), breast of duck in orange and caramel sauce (£10), and puddings like lemon ginger crunch cheesecake, chocolate roulade or rhubarb crumble; they only do a roast lunch on Sunday. Well kept Black Sheep Bitter and Theakstons Best on handpump, and an interesting wine list. There's lots of room outside in the garden. The setting, opposite the abbey ruins, is lovely. *(Recommended by David and Fiona Pemberton, Peter and Patricia Burton, Paul and Ursula Randall, Mr and Mrs W B Draper, Chris Mawson, Geoffrey and Irene Lindley, Steve and Julie Cocking, Simon Chappell, Louise Chappell, R F Grieve, Anthony Barnes, Tim and Sue Halstead, Martin Hickes, R N Hutton)*

Free house ~ Licensees Peter and Gerd Handley ~ Real ale ~ Meals and snacks (not Sun evening, not Mon) ~ (01347) 868204 ~ Children welcome ~ Open 11-2.30, 6.30-11; closed Sun evening and all day Mon

CARLTON (N Yorks) SE0684 Map 10

Foresters Arms ⑪ ♀ ⇔

Off A684 W of Leyburn, just past Wensley; or take Coverdale hill road from Kettlewell, off B6160

Yorkshire Dining Pub of the Year

Praise for this comfortable ex-coaching inn has been very warm this year. There's a good, relaxed atmosphere, open log fires, low beamed ceilings, friendly locals, and cheerful, quick service. And food is particularly good and enjoyable: lunchtime specials such as soup (£2.25), ham and garlic terrine (£2.95), baked sweet onion and coverdale cheese tart (£3.95), roast black pudding with dijon sauce (£4.75), sausages and mash with onion gravy (£5.95), seafood tagliatelle (£6.50), and braised chicken in red wine (£6.50). Also, parfait of chicken liver (£3.25), ravioli of squat lobster with a shellfish sauce (£5.50), char-grilled vegetable kebab (£7.95), haunch of venison with a leek and potato cake and red wine and juniper berry sauce (£9.95), saddle of hare with shallot confit (£10.25), and lots of fish dishes like scallops with dressed salad or a ginger butter sauce (£1.95 each), moules marinières (£3.95), char-grilled salmon with pesto (£8.95), fillet of sea bass with rosemary sauce (£10.50), monkfish kebab with bacon on a bed of spinach and a cider butter sauce (£12.50); puddings such as hot baked hazelnut soufflé, tarte tartin with ginger ice cream or treacle tart with vanilla sauce (from £2.95). Well kept John Smiths, Tetleys Bitter, Theakstons Best, and two guest beers on handpump, a good restaurant wine list, 40 malt whiskies, freshly squeezed orange juice, and fresh fruit coulis with spring water. The partly no-smoking restaurant has been refurbished this year and they now have hand-made cigars. Darts, dominoes, and piped music. There are some picnic tables among tubs of flowers. *(Recommended by Mrs S M Halliday, E A Thwaite, Walter and Susan Rimaldi-Butcher, Andrew and Ruth Triggs, Jess Parrish, David and Fiona Pemberton, A Morton, JKW, Ian Morley, Caroline Kenyon, Viv Middlebrook, E J Wilde, J Royce)*

Free house ~ Licensee Barrie Higginbotham ~ Real ale ~ Meals and snacks (not Sun evening, not Mon) ~ Restaurant (not Sun evening, not Mon) ~ (01969) 640272 ~ Children welcome away from bar ~ Open 12-3, 6.30-11; closed Mon lunchtime ~ Bedrooms: £30S/£55S

CARTHORPE (N Yorks) SE3184 Map 10

Fox & Hounds ★ ⑪

Village signposted from A1 N of Ripon, via B6285

Neatly kept and friendly, this pretty little extended village house has a cosy L-shaped bar with quite a few mistily evocative Victorian photographs of Whitby, a couple of nice seats by the larger of its two log fires, plush button-back built-in wall banquettes and chairs, plates on stripped beams, and some limed panelling; piped light classical music. An attractive high-raftered restaurant leads off with lots of neatly black-painted farm and smithy tools. The menu is the same in the bar and no-smoking restaurant (best to book for the restaurant – they don't take bookings in the bar) and might include stilton and onion soup (£2.25), terrine of duckling with home-made apple chutney (£3.95), seafood hors d'oeuvres (£4.95), baby chicken cooked in Theakstons beer (£7.95), fillet of salmon with hollandaise sauce (£7.95), rack of english lamb (£9.95), fillet steak stuffed with mushrooms and garlic (£10.95), daily specials such as salmon and halibut fishcakes (£3.95), queen scallop and prawn mornay (£4.95), steak and kidney pie (£6.95), chicken curry (£7.45), whole fresh crab salad (£7.95), and seafood kebab with sweet and sour sauce (£8.95). Well kept John Smiths Bitter on handpump, and decent wines with bin-ends listed on a blackboard. *(Recommended by David and Julie Hart, Fiona and David Pemberton, Ian Morley, Mrs D Cross, Adrian Jackson, Cynthia Waller, W A and S Rinaldi-Butcher)*

Free house ~ Licensee Howard Fitzgerald ~ Real ale ~ Meals and snacks (not Mon) ~ Restaurant (not Mon) ~ (01845) 567433 ~ Children welcome but no small ones after 8.30 ~ Open 12-2.30, 7-11; closed Mon and first week of the year from Jan 1

COXWOLD (N Yorks) SE5377 Map 7

Fauconberg Arms ★ ♀

This old stone inn is named after Lord Fauconberg, who married Oliver Cromwell's daughter Mary. The two cosy, knocked-together rooms of the lounge bar have cushioned antique oak settles and other fine furniture, a marvellous winter log fire in an unusual arched stone fireplace, and gleaming brass; there's also an old-fashioned back locals' bar for those wanting an informal drink and a chat. From a menu that serves both the bar and restaurant, there might be lunchtime dishes such as home-made soup (£1.95), sandwiches (from £2.60), chicken liver and ham terrine with home-made fruit chutney and tomato and apple salad (£3.35), stuffed aubergine with red lentils, cumin and apricots (£5.35), steak and kidney in ale pie (£5.85), lamb with a mint and apple gravy (£6.75), and sirloin steak (£8.95), with evening meals like hot buttered shrimps (£3.75), breast of chicken Barbados style (£5.85), pink trout fillets in breadcrumbs with almonds and a crème fraîche sauce (£6.25), spinach roulade (£9.95), and monkfish with rosemary and garlic (£10.45). Puddings like home-made coffee, whisky and walnut cheesecake or fresh fruit crumble (£2.95), and children's menu (from £1.35); they do a take-away menu (not winter Monday evenings). Well kept John Smiths, Tetleys Bitter, and Theakstons Best on handpump, and an extensive wine list with blackboard bin ends available by the glass. Darts, dominoes, fruit machine, and piped music. *(Recommended by Mr and Mrs R P Begg, Bill and Sheila McLardy, Dr and Mrs A H Young, R L Gorick, Janet Pickles, Iain Bennett, Fiona*

Haycock, Martin Hickes, Chris and Andy Crow, Bronwen and Steve Wrigley, Michele and Clive Platman, Bob and Maggie Atherton, John and Sheila French, Andy and Jane Beardsley)

Free house ~ Lease: Robin and Nicky Jaques ~ Real ale ~ Meals and snacks (not Mon evening in winter) ~ Restaurant (not winter Mon evening) ~ (01347) 868214 ~ Children welcome ~ Open 11-3, 6-11; winter evening opening 7pm ~ Bedrooms: £24/£40

CRACOE (N Yorks) SD9760 Map 7

Devonshire Arms

B6265 Skipton—Grassington

The cheerful licensees of this honest and comfortable long white pub, set in the middle of a small dales village, make it an enjoyable place to visit. The bar has little stable-type partitions to divide the solidly comfortable furnishings into cosier areas, low shiny black beams supporting creaky white planks, polished flooring tiles with rugs here and there, and gleaming copper pans round the stone fireplace. Above the dark panelled dado are old prints, engravings and photographs, with a big circular large-scale Ordnance Survey map showing the inn as its centre. Enjoyable bar food includes home-made soup (£1.75), sandwiches (from £1.75), garlic mushrooms (£3.75), vegetable and cheese strudel (£4.50), large yorkshire pudding filled with beef in Guinness (£5.25), home-made steak and mushroom pie (£5.45), good steak and kidney pudding, evening steaks (from £8.95), daily specials, and home-made puddings such as cheesecakes or sticky toffee pudding (£2.75); folding doors lead to a snug no-smoking restaurant where bar meals can be eaten during the week. Well kept Tetleys, Theakstons Best, and guest beers on handpump, and several malt whiskies; darts, dominoes, shove-ha'penny, table skittles, and piped music. There are picnic tables on a terrace flanked by well kept herbaceous borders, with more seating on the lawn; and a small dog called Juno may watch you coming and going from his position on the roof (his large airedale friend Jasper does not follow him up there, luckily). Every second Wednesday of the month the Lotus Club of Great Britain meets here and the Morgan Club have frequent rallies around the dales.
(Recommended by Andrew and Ruth Triggs, G Dobson, WAH, Mr and Mrs C Roberts, Gwen and Peter Andrews, Wayne Brindle)

Free house ~ Licensees John and Jill Holden ~ Real ale ~ Meals and snacks (not 25 Dec) ~ Restaurant ~ (01756) 730237 ~ Children welcome ~ Open 11-3, 6-11; winter weekday opening 6.30; 11.30-3, 6-11 Sun ~ Bedrooms: £25B/£40B

CRAY (N Yorks) SD9379 Map 7

White Lion 🍺

B6160, Upper Wharfedale N of Kettlewell

The highest pub in Wharfedale (1,100 ft up by Buckden Pike), this former drovers' hostelry has picnic tables above the very quiet, steep lane, or on the great flat limestone slabs in the shallow stream which tumbles down opposite. Inside, the simply furnished bar has a traditional atmosphere, seats around tables on the flagstone floor, shelves of china, iron tools and so forth, a high dark beam-and-plank ceiling, and a warming open fire; there's also a no-smoking family snug. Good honest bar food includes soup (£2), sandwiches (from £2.75), filled yorkshire puddings (from £2.95), vegetable lasagne or deep-fried chicken (£5.25), ham and mushroom tagliatelle or home-made steak and mushroom pie (£5.95), evening dishes such as garlic mushrooms (£2.50), home-made chicken liver pâté (£2.95), salads (from £6.50), and steaks (from £10.50), puddings (£2.10), and children's dishes (£2.95); good breakfasts. Well kept Ind Coope Burton, Moorhouses Pendle Witches Brew, and Tetleys Bitter on handpump; dominoes. *(Recommended by Geoffrey and Brenda Wilson, David and Judy Walmsley, E J and M W Corrin, Eddie Edwards, Anthony Marriott, Keith J Smith, Lynn Sharpless, Bob Eardley)*

Free house ~ Licensees Frank and Barbara Hardy ~ Real ale ~ Meals and snacks ~ (01756) 760262 ~ Children in dining room ~ Limited parking ~ Open 11-11; 12-10.30 summer Sun; 11-2.30, 6.30-11 winter weekdays ~ Bedrooms: £25(£30S)/£35(£45S)

CROPTON (N Yorks) SE7588 Map 10

New Inn ¶

Village signposted off A170 W of Pickering

The no-smoking downstairs conservatory in this neatly kept and comfortably modernised village inn has been converted into a visitor centre for the Cropton Brewery, and there are take-home bottles of their own beer, a range of merchandise, and art-work showing life in the village from Roman times till present days. Their ales consist of Two Pints, King Billy, Special Strong and Scoresby Stout (brewery trips are encouraged), with guests like Backwoods Bitter and Tetleys Bitter on handpump; several malt whiskies. The airy lounge bar has Victorian church panels, terracotta and dark blue plush seats, lots of brass, and a small open fire. Substantial helpings of good bar food include lunchtime sandwiches (not Sunday), home-made soup and pâté, nut roast with barbecue sauce, giant filled yorkshire puddings (£4.95), chicken burgundy or steak and kidney in ale pie (£5.75), chicken tikka (£6.50), their speciality whole leg of lamb (£7.50), and steaks (from £8.50; 24oz rump £14.50); friendly staff. The elegant small no-smoking restaurant is furnished with genuine Victorian and early Edwardian furniture. Pleasant service; darts, dominoes, fruit machine, piped music, and pool room. There's a neat terrace and garden with pond. Comfortable, good value bedrooms. *(Recommended by R N Hutton, Nigel Hopkins, Basil Minson, David Heath, Andy and Jill Kassube, David and Rebecca Killick, Mike Pugh)*

Own brew ~ Licensee Michael Lee ~ Real ale ~ Meals and snacks ~ Restaurant ~ (01751) 417330 ~ Children in conservatory, restaurant, and pool room ~ Open 11-4, 6-11; 11-11 Sat ~ Bedrooms: £35B/£53B

DACRE BANKS (N Yorks) SE1962 Map 7

Royal Oak

B6451, off B6165 Harrogate—Pateley Bridge

'A hidden gem' is how several readers have described this peaceful old stone pub in a village just above the River Nidd and with beautiful views. Inside, it's open-plan and the two comfortable lounge areas have interesting old photographs, an open fire in the front part, and well kept Black Sheep, John Smiths, Tetleys, and guests like or Youngers Scotch on handpump, and a good house wine; friendly young owners. A wide choice of good chip-free, home-made food always includes local game such as rabbit and bacon pie (£5.95), venison casserole (£6.25), and braised pheasant (£7.25), as well as a couple of daily roasts (pork, beef or lamb, £5.25), coq au vin or navarin of lamb (£6.25), spiced ox tongue in burgundy (£6.95), and traditional puddings like bread and butter or sticky toffee pudding (from £1.95); darts, pool, cribbage, and unusual piped music. Seats, and boules, outside. *(Recommended by Geoffrey and Brenda Wilson, Klaus D Baetz, J A Penny)*

Free house ~ Licensee Lee Chadwick ~ Real ale ~ Meals and snacks ~ Restaurant ~ (01423) 780200 ~ Well behaved children welcome away from bar ~ Open 12-2.30, 7-11; closed 25 Dec

EAST WITTON (N Yorks) SE1586 Map 10

Blue Lion ¶ ⇐

A6108 Leyburn—Ripon

Some changes to this rather smart and stylish place this year include a new kitchen extension, the extending of the bar into the old kitchen, and the conversion of outbuildings into more bedrooms. This remains very much somewhere to enjoy a civilised meal but it pays to get there early as you can't book a table in the busy bar (though you can, of course, in the restaurant) and there may be quite a wait. The big squarish bar has high-backed antique settles, old windsor chairs and round tables on the turkey rugs and flagstones, ham-hooks in the high ceiling decorated with dried wheat, teazles and so forth, a delft shelf filled with appropriate bric-a-brac, a couple of prints of the Battle of Omdurman, hunting prints, sporting caricatures and other pictures on the walls, a log fire, and daily papers; the friendly black labrador is called Ben. Particularly good and very popular, the bar food might include sandwiches, home-made soup (£2.75), char-grilled vegetables with anchovies and black olives (£3.95), deep-fried queen scallops wrapped in bacon with oriental vegetables and a soy and lime sauce (£5.50), home-made tagliatelle carbonara (£5.75), smoked haddock, mackerel and mussel fishcake topped with gruyère and served with macaroni cheese (£7.75), steak and kidney pudding (£7.95), home-made meatloaf with a masala sauce (£8.50), fillet of red mullet scented with walnut oil and oranges (£9.25), breast of Gressingham duck with a ginger, soy and grapefruit sauce (£9.75), jugged hare with parsnip mash (£10.25), and sirloin steak (£10.95); lovely puddings such as bread and butter pudding or a cold pancake filled with sliced banana and creamed toffee and served with a honey and almond crème anglaise (from £2.95), and good breakfasts. Well kept Black Sheep Bitter and Riggwelter, and Theakstons Best and Black Bull on handpump, and decent wines. Picnic tables on the gravel outside look beyond the stone houses on the far side of the village green to Witton Fell, and there's a big pretty back garden. *(Recommended by Susan and John Douglas, Richard Dolphin, Anthony Barnes, J E Rycroft, David and Judy Walmsley, Paul Boot, M J Morgan, J H and S A Harrop, Simon and Amanda Southwell, Mr and Mrs Carrera, J Royce, Martin Chapman, John and Chris Simpson, Gwen and Peter Andrews, S Head, Paul J Cornerford, Ian Morley, Martin Hickes, Jack and Heather Coyle, Dr I H Maine, C Wilson, Michael and Susan Morgan, Jean Gustavson, David and Ruth Hollands)*

Free house ~ Lease: Paul Klein ~ Real ale ~ Meals and snacks ~ Restaurant (closed Sun evening) ~ (01969) 624273 ~ Children welcome ~ Open 11-11; 12-10.30 Sun ~ Bedrooms: £39.50B/£70B

EGTON BRIDGE (N Yorks) NZ8105 Map 10

Horse Shoe 🛏

Village signposted from A171 W of Whitby; via Grosmont from A169 S of Whitby

In summer, the position of this charmingly placed inn is quite a draw, and there are some comfortable seats on a quiet terrace and lawn beside a little stream with ducks and geese. Inside, the bar has a warm log fire, high-backed built-in winged settles, wall seats and spindleback chairs around the modern oak tables, a big stuffed trout (caught near here in 1913), and a fine old print of a storm off Ramsgate and other pictures on the walls. Decent bar food includes home-made soup (£2), lunchtime sandwiches (from £2.30), stilton mushrooms (£2.95), vegetable bake (£5.95), lasagne (£6.45), ham and egg (£6.50), fillet of duck with plum and port sauce (£8.95), sirloin steak (£10.25), daily specials such as home-made pies or fresh fish, puddings (£2.50), and children's meals (£2.75). Well kept Tetleys Bitter, Theakstons Best, Old Peculier and XB on handpump, and a weekly guest beer; darts, dominoes, and piped music. Perhaps the best way to reach this beautifully placed pub is to park by the Roman Catholic church, walk through the village and cross the River Esk by stepping stones. Not to be confused with a similarly named pub up at Egton. *(Recommended by Ian Irving, RB, SC, Jim and Maggie Cowell, Val Stevenson, Rob Holmes, Phil and Heidi Cook, R N Hutton, Michael Butler, Nick Lloyd, Enid and Henry Stephens, Dr and Mrs Frank Rackow, Carol and Dennis Clayson, Bronwen and Steve Wrigley)*

Free house ~ Licensees David and Judith Mullins ~ Real ale ~ Meals and snacks (not 25 Dec) ~ Restaurant ~ (01947) 85245 ~ Children in side room and restaurant ~ Open 11-3.30, 6.30-11; closed evening 25 Dec ~ Bedrooms: £26(£30B)/£38(£46B)

FLAMBOROUGH (N Yorks) TA2270 Map 8

Seabirds ⚑

Junction of B1255 and B1229

Bustling and friendly, this straightforward village pub has quite a shipping theme in its cheerful public bar. Leading off here the comfortable lounge has a whole case of stuffed seabirds along one wall, as well as pictures and paintings of the local landscape, and a woodburning stove; there's a good mix of visitors and locals. The fresh fish daily specials are still the meals to go for (from £4.70), though the other dishes are well liked too, with a range that includes sandwiches, soup (£1.60), prawns in garlic butter (£3.70), yorkshire pudding filled with three cumberland sausages (£3.95), home-made steak and mushroom pie (£4.70), salmon steak mornay (£6.95), and evening extras like broccoli and cream cheese bake (£4.95), pork topped with ham and cheese, breadcrumbed and deep fried (£5.95), and grilled lamb chops (£7.95). Well kept John Smiths, Theakstons Best, and a weekly changing guest on handpump, good reasonably priced wine list, and a wide range of whiskies and liqueurs. Friendly, hardworking staff; darts, dominoes, fruit machine, and piped music. *(Recommended by Susan and Nigel Wilson, David and Fiona Pemberton, Chris Westmoreland, Andy and Jane Beardsley, Ian Rorison, Roger A Bellingham, David Eberlin, R N Hutton, E J Wilde, DC)*

Free house ~ Licensee Jean Riding ~ Real ale ~ Meals and snacks (not Sun or Mon evenings in winter) ~ Restaurant ~ (01262) 850242 ~ Children in eating area of bar ~ Open 11-3, 7(6.30 Sat)-11

GOOSE EYE (W Yorks) SE0340 Map 7
Turkey

High back road Haworth—Sutton in Craven, and signposted from back roads W of Keighley; OS Sheet 104 map ref 028406

It's worth the trip to reach this pleasant pub tucked away down high-walled lanes at the bottom of a steep valley. The various cosy and snug alcoves have brocaded upholstery and walls covered with pictures of surrounding areas, and the restaurant is no smoking. Decent bar food includes sandwiches such as hot beef (£2.50), egg and tuna mayonnaise (£2.30), cheese and onion quiche (£4.40), fillet of breaded haddock (£4.70), good steaks (from £6.90; 32oz rump £14), daily specials like filled yorkshire puddings (£3.80), and puddings (from £2.10). Well kept (and much liked) Gooseye Bitter (brewed by a local man), Ind Coope Burton, and Tetleys on handpump, and 26 malt whiskies; piped music. A separate games area has darts, dominoes, cribbage, fruit machine, trivia, and juke box. *(Recommended by WAH, PM, AM, Mike and Ruth Dooley, Jenny and Brian Seller, Jamie and Ruth Lyons)*

Free house ~ Licensees Harry and Monica Brisland ~ Real ale ~ Meals and snacks (not Mon) ~ Restaurant ~ (01535) 681339 ~ Children welcome until 8.30 ~ Open 12-3, 5.30-11; 12-4, 7-11 Sat; closed Mon lunchtime

GRANGE MOOR (W Yorks) SE2215 Map 7
Kaye Arms 🍽 ♀

A642 Huddersfield—Wakefield

This civilised and busy dining pub has been a family run affair for the last 25 years. Mr and Mrs Coldwell are the licensees and the food side of the business is run by their daughter Niccola and her husband (and chef) Adrian, and other daughter Sarah who is in charge of the puddings. It's very much somewhere to come for a special occasion and people tend to dress accordingly. The good, imaginative, totally home-made food changes regularly but might include sandwiches, home-made soup (£1.95), warm home-smoked chicken with spiced pear salad (£3.95), queen scallops grilled with gruyère cheese and garlic (£4.20), ploughman's (£4.95), mature cheddar cheese soufflé with a waldorf salad (£5.10), hand-breaded Whitby scampi (£6.25), wild boar and ale sausages with a sage and onion sauce or a vegetarian dish of the day (£6.75), chicken breast in a filo pastry parcel with a wild mushroom sauce (£8.95), good sirloin steak (£11.20), daily specials like roast plum tomato and artichoke tart or baked spicy crab and prawns (£3.95), home-made steak and kidney pie (£7.95), and large french duck leg confit on warm home-made apple chutney or roast fillet of fresh salmon on spinach with a lemon butter sauce (£8.95); puddings such as raspberry and almond tart or sticky toffee pudding with butterscotch sauce (£3.10), lovely home-made bread and fine vegetables (extra with some dishes). A thoughtful wine list with exceptional value house wines, 10 by the generous glass and wines of the month, and decent malt whiskies. The U-shaped dining lounge has black mate's chairs and black tables, panelled dado, quiet pastel-coloured wallpaper with decorative plates, a high shelf of hundreds of malt whisky bottles, and a brick fireplace; one area is no smoking. The Yorkshire Mining Museum is just down the road. *(Recommended by Geoffrey and Brenda Wilson, Neil Townend, Michael Butler, R Borthwick, S Clegg, Andrew and Ruth Triggs)*

Free house Licensees Stuart and Brenda Coldwell ~ Meals and snacks (till 10pm) ~ (01924) 848385 ~ Children allowed at lunchtimes only ~ Open 11.30-3, 7(6.30 Sat)-11; closed Mon lunchtime (inc bank holidays)

HARDEN (W Yorks) SE0838 Map 7
Malt Shovel

Follow Wilsden signpost from B6429

This handsome dark stone building is in a lovely spot by a bridge over Harden Beck, and the big garden is open to the public. Inside, the three spotlessly clean rooms (one is no smoking at lunchtime) have kettles, brass funnels and the like hanging from the black beams, horsebrasses on leather harness, blue plush seats built into the walls, and stone-mullioned windows; one room has oak-panelling, a beamed ceiling, and an open fire. Good value bar food includes hot beef sandwiches, giant yorkshire pudding with sausages or beef and gravy (£3.50), home-made steak pie or chilli (£4.50), omelettes (from £4.50), and fresh haddock (£4.95). Well kept Tetleys on handpump, and efficient service; dominoes and Monday evening quiz. *(Recommended by J E Rycroft, A Preston, Nigel Hey, M J Brooks)*

Carlsberg Tetleys ~ Managers Keith and Lynne Bolton ~ Real ale ~ Lunchtime meals and snacks (not Sun) ~ (01535) 272357 ~ Children in side room until 8pm ~ Open 12-11; 12-10.30 Sun; 12-3, 5.30-11 in winter; 12-4, 7-10.30 winter Sun

HATFIELD WOODHOUSE (S Yorks) SE6808 Map 7
Green Tree

1 mile from M18 junction 5: on A18/A614 towards Bawtry

This year, the front car park here had been converted into a pretty garden with a walkway up to the door, the side car park has been enlarged, and a beer garden constructed by the carvery room. The comfortably modernised series of connecting open-plan rooms and alcoves have been attractively refurbished, and bar food now includes home-made soup (£2.20), pâté (£2.95), sardines in garlic butter (£3.50), vegetables au gratin (£6.25), chicken provençale (£8.95), steaks (from £9.75), grilled halibut steak or pork normandy (£9.95), and puddings (£2.65); Sunday carvery (£5.95) and Sunday afternoon tea. The restaurant is no smoking. Well kept Jennings Snecklifter, Shepherd Neame Bitter, and Thorne Best on handpump; prompt service; fruit machine and piped music. *(Recommended by FMH, David and Fiona Pemberton, Derek and Sylvia Stephenson, Andrew and Joan Life, A N Ellis, E J Wilde, JJW, CMW; more reports on the changes, please)*

Wards (Vaux) ~ Managers Peter and Avril Wagstaff ~ Real ale ~ Meals and snacks (all day) ~ Restaurant ~ (01302) 840305 ~ Children in eating area of bar, in restaurant and in carvery room ~ Open 11-11; 12-10.30 Sun ~ Bedrooms: £25S/£35S

HEATH (W Yorks) SE3519 Map 7
Kings Arms

Village signposted from A655 Wakefield—Normanton – or, more directly, turn off to the left opposite Horse & Groom

Once again, new licensees have taken over this old-fashioned pub. It's in a fine setting – which is a surprise being so close to Wakefield – with picnic tables on a side lawn, and a nice walled flower-filled garden; more seats along the front of the building facing the village green. Inside, the original bar has dark panelling, a fire burning in the old black range (with a long row of smoothing irons on the mantelpiece), and plain elm stools and oak settles built into the walls. A more comfortable extension has carefully preserved the original style, down to good wood-pegged oak panelling (two embossed with royal arms), and a high shelf of plates; there are also two other small flagstoned rooms, and the conservatory opens onto the garden. The restaurant is partly no smoking. Good value bar food includes home-made soup (£1.40), sandwiches (from £1.65; hot sausage and onion £1.75), ploughman's (£3.95), omelettes (from £3.25), home-made lasagne, gammon and egg or battered haddock (all £3.95), puddings (£1.95), and children's meals (£2.25). As well as cheap Clarks Bitter and Festival, they also serve guests like Tetleys Bitter and Timothy Taylors Landlord on handpump. *(Recommended by Derek and Sylvia Stephenson, JJW, CMW, Michael Butler, Ian Phillips, Mike and Maggie Betton, Wayne Brindle, MKP, JLP, S Thompson, D M Parsloe, MJVK)*

Clarks ~ Manager Terry Ogden ~ Real ale ~ Meals and snacks ~ Gas-lit restaurant ~ (01924) 377527 ~ Children welcome ~ Modern jazz trio Weds evening ~ Open 11.30-3(4 Sat), 5.30-11; 12-10.30 Sun; closed winter Sun afternoons

HECKMONDWIKE (W Yorks) SE2223 Map 7

Old Hall

New North Road; B6117 between A62 and A638; OS Sheet 104, map reference 214244

It's a surprise to find this interesting 15th-c building perched on the edge of a disused railway cutting and surrounded by 50s and 60s housing. There are lots of old beams and timbers, latticed mullioned windows with worn stone surrounds, brick or stripped old stone walls hung with pictures of Richard III, Henry VII, Catherine Parr, and Joseph Priestley (this was once his home), and comfortable furnishings. Snug low-ceilinged alcoves lead off the central part with its high ornate plaster ceiling, and an upper gallery room, under the pitched roof, looks down on the main area through timbering 'windows'. Decent, straightforward waitress-served bar food (unchanged since last year) includes sandwiches (not Sunday), pie of the day (£3.95), chicken kiev (£4.25), gammon and egg (£4.75), and mixed grill (£6.50). Well kept (and cheap) Sam Smiths OB on handpump; fruit machine, piped music, and sports or music quizes on Tuesday night and a general knowledge one on Thursday evening. *(Recommended by Ian Phillips, Peter Marshall, David and Linda Barraclough, JJW, CMW, Michael Butler, Laura Darlington, Gianluca Perinetti, Monica Shelley)*

Sam Smiths ~ Manager Keith Dunkley ~ Real ale ~ Meals and snacks ~ (01924) 404774 ~ Children welcome ~ Open 11.30-2.30, 6(5 Sat)-11; 12-10.30 Sun

HELMSLEY (N Yorks) SE6184 Map 10

Feathers ♀

Market Square

Readers like the atmospheric older core in this handsome inn: heavy medieval beams and dark panelling, unusual cast-iron-framed tables topped by weighty slabs of oak and walnut, a venerable wall carving of a dragonfaced bird in a grape vine, and a big log fire in the stone inglenook fireplace. The main inn has its own comfortable lounge bar with a pleasant, relaxed atmosphere, and mouseman furniture. Bar food includes sandwiches (from £2.50), soup (£1.95), ploughman's (£3.95), salmon pâté (£3), vegetarian or meaty sausages (£3.50), home-made lasagne (£4.95), home-made steak pie (£6.25), deep-fried battered prawns in sweet and sour sauce (£6.50), gammon and egg (£6.75), steaks (£10.50), and daily specials. Well kept Batemans XXXB, Black Sheep Bitter, Morlands Old Speckled Hen, John Smiths, Theakstons Best and Old Peculier, and Youngers Scotch on handpump, and a large choice of wines chalked on a blackboard; friendly service, darts, dominoes, and piped music. There's an attractive back garden with seats and tables. Rievaulx Abbey (well worth an hour's visit) is close by. The pub does get very busy on Friday (market day) and Sunday lunchtime. *(Recommended by Toby Carlson, Andrew and Joan Life, Dr Jim Craig-Gray, Andrew and Ruth Triggs)*

Free house ~ Licensees Lance and Andrew Feather ~ Real ale ~ Meals and snacks ~ Restaurant (not Sun evening) ~ (01439) 770275 ~ Children welcome ~ Open 10.30-11; 12-10.30 Sun; closed 25 Dec ~ Bedrooms: £25(£35B)/£50(£60B)

HETTON (N Yorks) SD9558 Map 7
Angel ★ ⑪ ♀

Just off B6265 Skipton—Grassington

Few pubs in the country offer as many wines by the glass (twenty-five) as this particularly well run and friendly dining pub. But it's still the marvellous food that draws people from miles around – and to be sure of a table, you must arrive almost as the doors open. Served by hard-working uniformed staff, there might be home-made soup (£2.60; lovely rustic fish soup with aioli £3.85), queen scallops baked with garlic and gruyère (£4.20 starter, £6.30 main course), terrine of Tuscan vegetables with tapenade crostini (£4.50), an open sandwich of smoked salmon, cream cheese, smoked bacon and home-made chutney (£4.95), tagliatelle with smoked salmon and broccoli (£5.95), smoked haddock (£6.75), pork fillet marinated and roasted with honey and served on braised winter cabbage (£7.80), shoulder of lamb slowly braised in its own juices with garlic jus, pesto oil, olive mash and red wine (£8.50), salmon en croûte with lobster sauce (£8.95), confit of duck with braised normandy red cabbage and orange and thyme sauce (£9.90), daily specials and fish dishes, and puddings like crème brûlée, sticky toffee pudding or rich chocolate marquise with orange compôte (from £3.50). Well kept Black Sheep Bitter and Special, and John Smiths on handpump, over 300 wines, and 36 malt whiskies. The four timbered and panelled rambling rooms have lots of cosy alcoves, comfortable country-kitchen chairs or button-back green plush seats, Ronald Searle wine snob cartoons and older engravings and photographs, log fires, a solid fuel stove, and in the main bar, a Victorian farmhouse range in the big stone fireplace; the snug is no smoking. Sturdy wooden benches and tables are built on to the cobbles outside. *(Recommended by M Holdsworth, Ian and Christina Allen, Patrick Milner, Gwen and Peter Andrews, Jim and Maggie Cowell, Paul Boot, J E Rycroft, Kenneth and Muriel Holden, WAH, RJH, Prof and Mrs S Barnett, Chris and Martin Taylor, Anni Fentiman, Mr and Mrs J Tyrer, Wayne Brindle, Lynn Sharpless, Bob Eardley, Bernard and Marjorie Parkin, Simon Barber, Darren and Clare Jones, Geoffrey and Brenda Wilson, MJVK, Dr and Mrs M Locker, Dr and Sue Griffin, Neville Kenyon, Robert and Ann Lees, Janet and Peter Race)*

Free house ~ Licensees Denis Watkins and John Topham ~ Real ale ~ Meals and snacks (till 10pm) ~ Restaurant ~ (01756) 730263 ~ Well behaved children welcome ~ Open 12-2.30(3 Sat), 6-11; 12-3, 6-10 Sun

HUBBERHOLME (N Yorks) SD9178 Map 7
George

Village signposted from Buckden; about 1 mile NW

Friendly licensees run this unspoilt old inn near the ancient church where J B Priestley's ashes are scattered (this was his favourite pub). The two neat and cosy rooms have heavy beams supporting the dark ceiling-boards, walls stripped back to bare stone and hung with antique plates and photographs, seats (with covers to match the curtains) around shiny copper-topped tables on the flagstones, and an open stove in the big fireplace. Good bar food includes sandwiches, cumberland sausage (£5.25), gammon and egg (£5.85), spinach and mushroom lasagne or steak and kidney pie (£5.95), vegetable and cheese parcel (£6.75), chicken in peanut sauce or cod and salmon mornay (£7.75), pheasant in calvados and cream sauce or sirloin steak (£8.95), and daily specials. Very well kept Black Sheep Bitter, Ruddles County, Theakstons Black Bull, and Youngers Scotch on handpump, quite a few malt whiskies, and decent wines. Darts, dominoes, cribbage, and a game they call 'pot the pudding'. There are seats and tables overlooking the moors and River Wharfe – where they have fishing rights. *(Recommended by Andrew and Ruth Triggs, Gwen and Peter Andrews, K Frostick, Brenda and Derek Savage, David and Judy Walmsley, Paul McPherson, T Dobby, John Allsopp, Lynn Sharpless, Bob Eardley, JKW, John Le Sage, Prof and Mrs S Barnett, Eddie Edwards, Caroline Kenyon, Anthony Marriott)*

Free house ~ Licensees Jerry Lanchbury and Fiona Shelton ~ Real ale ~ Meals and snacks ~ Restaurant ~ (01756) 760223 ~ Children in eating area of bar ~ Open 11.30-3, 6(6.30 winter)-11; 11.30-11 Sat; 12-3, 6.30-11 winter Sat ~ Bedrooms: £25/£36(£45B)

HUDDERSFIELD (W Yorks) SE1115 Map 7

Sands House

Crosland Moor; off A62 W

The licensee in this very popular dining pub has a line in friendly repartee which quickly makes strangers feel part of the local scene. The oblong bar has a good buoyant atmosphere and is full of contemporary clocks and watches, lots of woodwork, and well kept Boddingtons, Courage Directors, Ruddles Best, and John Smiths on handpump; there's a downstairs dining room. The wide choice of good, imaginative bar food that changes every two weeks includes sandwiches (from £1.90; butties with hot beef, onion and mustard £2.30 or bacon and brie £2.95), vegetarian dishes like cheese, onion and apple pie (£4.90) or mushroom, courgette and spinach roulade (£5.10), prawn and tuna pasta bake with tomato sauce (£5.50), chicken breast marinated in pesto and lemon (£5.80), red bream fillets en papillote (£6.25), pork fillet in a creamy red wine and pepper sauce (£6.90), and puddings such as peach and almond meringue or chocolate squidgy cake (£2.50); thoughtful children's dishes, too. Piped music. The garden has swings, a play area and wooden seats and tables. *(Recommended by H K Dyson, Neil Townend, Andrew and Ruth Triggs, Malcolm and Nancy Watson-Steward)*

Carlsberg Tetleys ~ Lease: Louise Sykes ~ Real ale ~ Meals and snacks (11.30-2.30, 5-9.30) ~ Restaurant ~ (01484) 654478 ~ Children welcome away from bar ~ Open 11.30-11; 12-10.30 Sun; closed 25 Dec

HULL (E Yorks) TA0927 Map 8

Minerva 🍺

From A63 Castle Street/Garrison Road, turn into Queen Street towards piers at central traffic lights; some metered parking here; pub is in pedestrianised Nelson Street, at far end

From the microbrewery at this picturesque Georgian pub, they brew Pilots Pride and occasional other brews such as Sea Fever (kept under light blanket pressure), and keep Tetleys and a couple of guest beers on handpump; you can visit the brewery (best to phone beforehand). The pub is in the heart of the attractively restored waterfront and bustling marina, so is a great spot from which to watch the harbour goings-on; you might prefer to do this from inside as the tables on the pavement outside can be a little breezy. The several rooms ramble all the way round a central servery, and are filled with comfortable seats, quite a few interesting photographs and pictures of old Hull (with two attractive wash drawings by Roger Davis) and a big chart of the Humber. A tiny snug has room for just three people, and a back room (which looks out to the marina basin) houses a profusion of varnished woodwork. Good sized helpings of straightforward bar food such as soup (£1.25), hot or cold filled baguettes (from £1.95), filled baked potatoes (from £2), ploughman's (£3.75), home-made steak and potato pie (£3.85), home-made curry (£4.25), popular huge battered haddock (£4.50), and rump steak (£6.45), daily specials (several are vegetarian), and puddings (£1.75); Sunday roast. The lounge is no smoking when food is being served. Darts, dominoes, cribbage, fruit machine, video game, and piped music. *(Recommended by Chris Westmoreland, Thomas Nott, M Walker)*

Own brew (Tetleys) ~ Managers Eamon and Kathy Scott ~ Real ale ~ Meals and snacks (not Sat or Sun evenings) ~ (01482) 326909 ~ Children in eating area of bar at mealtimes only ~ Open 11-11; 12-10.30 summer Sun; closed 25 Dec

Olde White Harte ★ £

Off 25 Silver Street, a continuation of Whitefriargate (see previous entry); pub is up narrow passage beside the jewellers' Barnby and Rust, and should not be confused with the much more modern White Hart nearby

Tucked away in a cosy courtyard amongst narrow alleyways is this beautifully preserved ancient tavern – and despite its heritage, this is very much a bustling and friendly working pub. Perhaps you can best appreciate the fascinating interior on a quiet weekday evening. In the downstairs bar attractive stained-glass windows look out above the bow window seat, carved heavy beams support black ceiling boards, and two brocaded Jacobean-style chairs sit in the big brick inglenook with its frieze of delft tiles. The curved copper-topped counter serves well kept Youngers IPA and No 3, Theakstons Old Peculier and XB and a guest, as well as several malt whiskies. The second bar is very similar; dominoes, cribbage, shove-ha'penny, table skittles, fruit machine, and trivia. Simple, traditional bar food such as sandwiches, roasts and nursery puddings, and friendly service. Seats in the courtyard outside. It was in the heavily panelled room up the oak staircase that in 1642 the town's governor Sir John Hotham made the fateful decision to lock the nearby gate against Charles I, depriving him of Hull's arsenal; it didn't do him much good, as in the Civil War that followed, Hotham, like the king, was executed by the parliamentarians. *(Recommended by M Walker, Chris Westmoreland, N Haslewood, I Pocsk, David and Shelia)*

Youngers (S & N) ~ Managers Brian and Jenny Cottingham ~ Real ale ~ Lunchtime meals and snacks ~ Lunchtime restaurant ~ (01482) 326363 ~ Children in restaurant ~ No nearby parking ~ Open 11-11; 12-10.30 Sun

KIRBY HILL (N Yorks) NZ1406 Map 10

Shoulder of Mutton 🛏

Signposted from Ravensworth road about 3½ miles N of Richmond; or from A66 Scotch Corner—Brough turn off into Ravensworth, bear left through village, and take signposted right turn nearly a mile further on

Quite a social centre for the locals, this creeper-covered ex-farmhouse is warmly welcoming to visitors, too. There's a stone archway between the lounge and public bar, green plush wall settles around simple dark tables, local turn-of-the-century photographs of Richmond, and open stone fireplaces. Good bar food includes lunchtime sandwiches, egg mayonnaise with prawns (£2.50), salmon and broccoli mornay (£5.50), gammon and egg (£6.50), steaks (from £8), vegetarian dishes, daily specials such as giant yorkshire puddings filled with beef, lamb or pork (£3.75), steak and mushroom pie or steak braised in beer (£4.75), good haddock (£5.50), and puddings (£1.95). Well kept Black Sheep Bitter and Riggwelter, John Smiths, and Websters Yorkshire on handpump, and quite a few malt whiskies; darts, dominoes, cribbage, and piped music. The yard behind has picnic tables and fine views, and the tree-shaded church opposite has an unusually tuneful bell. *(Recommended by J H and Dr S A Harrop, Wayne Brindle, R H Rowley, A N Ellis, Andrew and Joan Life, Mr and Mrs A G Pollard, SS)*

Free house ~ Licensees Mick and Anne Burns ~ Real ale ~ Meals and snacks (not Mon lunchtime) ~ Restaurant ~ (01748) 822772 ~ Children in eating area of bar until 9pm ~ Sing-along Mon evenings ~ Open 12-3, 7-11; closed Mon lunchtime ~ Bedrooms: £25S/£39S

KIRKBYMOORSIDE (N Yorks) SE6987 Map 7

George & Dragon 🍽 🛏 ♀

Market place

Apart from being a comfortable place to stay with enjoyable food and friendly owners, what readers also like about this particularly civilised 17th-c coaching inn is the pubby atmosphere in the front bar room. The walls are entertainingly covered with lots of photographs, prints, shields and memorabilia connected with cricket and rugby (the landlord's own interest), and there are fresh flowers and daily newspapers, panelling stripped back to its original pitch pine, brass-studded solid dark red leatherette chairs set around polished wooden tables, horsebrasses hung along the beams, and a blazing log fire; no games machines, pool or juke boxes, and the piped music is either classical or jazz, and not obtrusive. The very good bar food might include sandwiches in home-baked buns, home-made vegetable or curried parsnip soup (£2.25), chicken and apricot terrine (£2.95), black pudding with apple, onion and crispy bacon (£3.95), seafood hotpot (£4.90), good butcher's sausages with mash, mushroom and pasta bake (£5.95), home-made salmon fishcakes (£6.50), rabbit and bacon pie (£7.50), minted lamb casserole (£7.90), pork fillet with a herb crust and cider sauce (£8.50), steaks (from £10.95), halibut with cucumber, white wine and cream sauce (£12.90), and home-made puddings like sherry trifle, wildberry cheesecake and chocolate fruit and nut slice; the game and fish are local, breakfasts are delicious, and they offer children's helpings. The attractive no-smoking restaurant was the old brewhouse until the early part of this century. Well kept Black Sheep Bitter, John Smiths Bitter, Timothy Taylors Landlord, and Theakstons XB on handpump, a fine wine list including up to 12 by the glass, and over 30 malt whiskies; dominoes, and shove-ha'penny. There are seats under umbrellas in the back courtyard and a surprisingly peaceful walled garden for residents to use. The bedrooms are in a converted cornmill and old vicarage at the back of the pub. Wednesday is Market Day. *(Recommended by Paul and Ursula Randall, Alan Griffiths, John and Joan Wyatt, Allan Worsley, Michael and Janice Gwilliam, Dr Jim Craig-Gray, Caroline Jarrett, Roger Bellingham, F M Bunbury; also in Good Hotel Guide)*

Free house ~ Licensees Stephen and Frances Colling ~ Real ale ~ Meals and snacks ~ Restaurant ~ (0751) 433334 ~ Well behaved children welcome until 9pm ~ Open 10-3, 6-11 ~ Bedrooms: £49B/£83B

KIRKHAM SE7466 (N Yorks) Map 7
Stone Trough
Kirkham Abbey

This attractively situated inn is handy for Kirkham Abbey and Castle Howard, there's a good outside seating area with lovely valley views, and fine nearby walks. Inside, it's neatly kept and attractive, and the several beamed, cosy and interesting rooms have warm log fires, a friendly atmosphere, and well kept Bass, Black Sheep Riggwelter, Jennings Cumberland, Tetleys, Theakstons, and Timothy Taylors Landlord on handpump; farm cider. Good bar food includes yorkshire puddings filled with steak and Guinness, gammon and egg, huge Whitby haddock, chicken breast stuffed with asparagus and cream cheese or chicken, leek and mushroom pie (all £5.95). The no-smoking farmhouse restaurant has a fire in an old-fashioned kitchen range. Darts, pool, bar billiards, shove-ha'penny, cribbage, dominoes, fruit machine, video game, and piped music. *(Recommended by Andrew and Joan Life, Christopher Turner, David Heath, Ian Irving, Prof S Barnett, C A Hall, Roger Bellingham)*

Free house ~ Licensee Holly Dane ~ Real ale ~ Meals and snacks (not winter Mon lunchtime) ~ Restaurant ~ (01653) 618713 ~ Well behaved children welcome ~ Open 12-2.30, 6(5.30 Sat)-11; 12-3.30, 6-10.30 Sun; closed Mon lunchtime Sept-April

KNARESBOROUGH (N Yorks) SE3557 Map 7
Blind Jacks ⌂
Market Place

The two downstairs rooms in this listed Georgian building have stripped brick on the left and dark panelling on the right, bare floor boards, pews (the one on the right as you go in has a radiator built in behind, which is lovely on a cold day), cast-iron long tables, brewery posters mainly from the south (Adnams, Harveys, Hook Norton, Shepherd Neame), lots of framed beermats, and nice old-fashioned net half-curtains; no noisy games machines or piped music – just a chatty atmosphere and half a dozen real ales on handpump: Ind Coope Burton and White Bear Bitter (brewed locally) plus four guests; farm cider and foreign bottled beers. The licensee has changed again and lunchtime bar food now includes soup (£1.95), sandwiches (from £1.95), creamy garlic mushrooms in pastry (£3.25), and risotto of crab (£3.95). No children. *(Recommended by P Powell, Anthony and Anne Gilligan, Prof S Barnett, Tim and Ann Newell, Drs A and A C Jackson)*

Free house ~ Licensee David Llewellyn ~ Real ale ~ Meals and snacks (not Sun evening or Mon) ~ Evening restaurant ~ (01423) 869148 ~ Open 11.30-11; 12-10.30 Sun; closed Mon till 5.30

LEDSHAM (W Yorks) SE4529 Map 7

Chequers

Claypit Lane; a mile W of A1, some 4 miles N of junction M62

This is a neatly kept and bustling village pub with an enjoyable atmosphere and a friendly welcome. The old-fashioned little central panelled-in servery has several small, individually decorated rooms leading off, with low beams, lots of cosy alcoves, a number of Toby jugs, log fires; well kept John Smiths, Theakstons Best, Youngers Scotch and Number 3 on handpump. Good, straightforward bar food includes home-made soup (£2.20), sandwiches (from £2.75), ploughman's (£4.50), scrambled eggs and smoked salmon (£4.95), lasagne (£5.20), pasta bake (£5.70), generous grilled gammon and two eggs (£7), steaks (from £7.50), a few popular daily specials, and puddings (£2.50); there may be a loaf of crusty bread with bowls of dripping and sliced onion on the bar to help yourself to. A sheltered two-level terrace behind the house has tables among roses and is liked by families. *(Recommended by M W Turner, Thomas Nott, Sue and Bob Ward, I P G Derwent, David Atkinson, M D Phillips, Tim and Sue Halstead, K H Frostick, Roger Bellingham, Roy Bromell, John and Sheila French, Caroline Wright)*

Free house ~ Licensee Chris Wraith ~ Real ale ~ Meals and snacks (not Sun) ~ Restaurant (not Sun) ~ (01977) 683135 ~ Children in separate room ~ Open 11-3, 5.30-11; 11-11 Sat; closed Sun

LEEDS (W Yorks) SE3033 Map 7

Whitelocks ★ £

Turks Head Yard; alley off Briggate, opposite Debenhams and Littlewoods; park in shoppers' car park and walk

If you want to appreciate the unchanging Victorian decor in this marvellously preserved and atmospheric pub, it's best to come here outside peak times (it does get packed). The long and narrow old-fashioned bar has polychrome tiles on the bar counter, stained-glass windows and grand advertising mirrors, and red button back plush banquettes and heavy copper-topped cast-iron tables squeezed down one side. Good, reasonably priced lunchtime bar food includes cornish pasties (95p), sandwiches (from £1.25), chilli or good meat and potato pie (£2.25), and jam roly poly or fruit pie (£1); staff remain very cheerful and pleasant, even when under pressure. Well kept McEwans 80/-, Theakstons Bitter, and Youngers IPA, Scotch and No 3 on handpump. At the end of the long narrow yard another bar is done up in Dickensian style. *(Recommended by Chris Westmoreland, Reg Nelson, Thomas Nott, David Carr, Christopher Turner, George Atkinson, G P Kernan, Amanda Dauncey, Basil Minson, Martin Hickes, J Royce)*

Youngers (S & N) ~ Manager Colin Birks ~ Real ale ~ Meals and snacks (11-8; not Sun evening) ~ Restaurant (not Sun evening) ~ (0113) 245 3950 ~ Children in top bar at lunchtime and in restaurant ~ Open 11-11; 12-10.30 Sun

LEVISHAM (N Yorks) SE8391 Map 10

Horseshoe

Pub and village signposted from A169 N of Pickering

On warm days, the picnic tables on the attractive village green are a fine place to enjoy a drink. Inside, the neatly kept bars have brocaded seats, a log fire in the stone fireplace, a friendly welcome from the licensees. Good bar food includes home-made soup (£2), sandwiches (from £2.65; the steak one is good, £4.95), egg mayonnaise using free range eggs (£2.95), ploughman's (£4.95), fresh Whitby haddock (£5.95), prawn thermidor (£5.80), steak and kidney pie or beef curry (£5.95), gammon and egg (£5.90), cajun chicken (£6.95), steaks (from £10.25), daily specials, vegetarian dishes, children's menu (£3.25), and puddings (£2.50); the dining room is no smoking. Well kept Malton Double Chance (summer only), Tetleys Bitter, and Theakstons Best, XB and Old Peculier on handpump, and over 30 malt whiskies.

Three to five times a day in spring and autumn, and seven times in summer, two steam trains of the North Yorks Moors Railway stop at this village. *(Recommended by R N Hutton, Gill and Andy Plumb, Nigel Hopkins, Eddie Edwards, Andrew and Ruth Triggs, C A Hall, Chloe Gartery, David Surridge, M Borthwick, Bob and Maggie Atherton, Anne and Sverre Hagen, John Allsopp)*

Free house ~ Licensees Brian and Helen Robshaw ~ Real ale ~ Meals and snacks (not 25 Dec) ~ (01751) 460240 ~ Children welcome ~ Open 11-3, 6-11; winter evening opening 7; closed evening 25 Dec ~ Bedrooms: £23(£24B)/£46(£48B)

LEYBURN (N Yorks) SE1191 Map 10

Sandpiper

Market Place – bottom end

This neatly kept and rather charming little stone cottage is said to be the oldest building in Leyburn, dating back to 1640. There's a cheerful bustling atmosphere, and the bar has a couple of black beams in the low ceiling, a stuffed pheasant in a stripped-stone alcove, antlers, and just seven tables – even including the back room up three steps, where you'll find attractive dales photographs, toby jugs on a delft shelf, and a collection of curious teapots. Down by the nice linenfold panelled bar counter there are stuffed sandpipers, more photographs and a woodburning stove in the stone fireplace. There's also a spic-and-span dining area on the left; dominoes and piped music. Carefully cooked good bar food includes home-made soups like celery and wensleydale cheese or cabbage and apple (£1.75), sandwiches (from £1.75), ploughman's (£3.95), meaty or vegetarian lasagne (£4.75), sweet and sour pork or chicken curry and pies like fresh fish or steak and onion (all £4.95), puddings (£2.50), and evening dishes like smoked haddock with poached eggs (£5.95), pork tenderloin with brandy and orange sauce (£7.50), and fresh plaice with parsley butter (£7.95). Well kept Black Sheep Bitter, Dent Bitter, John Smiths, and Theakstons Best on handpump, around 100 malt whiskies, and bin-end wines. The friendly English pointer is called Sadie. There are lovely hanging baskets, white cast-iron tables among the honeysuckle, climbing roses, cotoneaster and so forth on the front terrace, with more tables in the back garden. *(Recommended by Mr and Mrs Greenhalgh, J E Rycroft, M J Morgan, Wayne Brindle, M Morgan, Michael and Susan Morgan, John and Chris Simpson, J H and S A Harrop, Dono and Carol Leaman)*

Free house ~ Licensees Peter and Beryl Swan ~ Real ale ~ Meals and snacks (not 25 Dec) ~ Evening restaurant ~ (01969) 622206 ~ Well behaved children welcome ~ Open 11-2.30, 6.30-11 ~ Bedrooms: £25B/£40B

LINTHWAITE (W Yorks) SE1014 Map 7

Sair 🍺

Hoyle Ing, off A62; 3½ miles after Huddersfield look out for two water storage tanks (painted with a shepherd scene) on your right – the street is on your left, burrowing very steeply up between works buildings; OS Sheet 110 map reference 101143

It's the fine range of own-brewed ales that draws people to this unspoilt place – and if Mr Crabtree is not too busy, he is glad to show visitors the brewhouse: pleasant and well balanced Linfit Bitter, Mild and Special, Springbok Bier, Old Eli, Leadboiler, Autumn Gold, and the redoubtable Enochs Hammer; there's even stout (English Guineas), a porter (Janet St), and occasional Xmas Ale and Smokehouse Ale. Thatchers farm cider and a few malt whiskies. The quaint cluster of rooms is furnished with pews or smaller chairs, bottle collections, beermats tacked to beams, rough flagstones in some parts and carpet in others, and yorkshire ranges in two of the four big stone fireplaces; one room is no smoking. The room on the right has shove-ha'penny, dominoes, and juke box; piano players welcome. There's a striking view down the Colne Valley – through which the Huddersfield Narrow Canal winds its way; in the 3½ miles from Linthwaite to the highest and longest tunnel in Britain, are 25 working locks and some lovely countryside. No food. *(Recommended by Robert Ross, R WD, Jack and Philip Paxton; more reports please)*

Own brew ~ Licensee Ron Crabtree ~ Real ale ~ (01484) 842370 ~ Children in three rooms away from the bar ~ Open 7-11 only on weekdays; 12-4, 7-11 Sat (10.30 Sun); closed 25 Dec

LINTON IN CRAVEN (N Yorks) SD9962 Map 7

Fountaine ★

On B6265 Skipton—Grassington, forking right

The licensees here have worked really hard to create a genuinely warm and friendly atmosphere in which to enjoy the well kept real ales and good food, and readers have appreciated this so much this year, that we have decided to give the pub a star. The spruce little rooms are furnished with stools, benches and other seats, and lots of original watercolours and prints, several with sporting themes. Quite a lot of emphasis is placed on the popular bar food now, with lots of daily specials such as broccoli, almond and blue shropshire or carrot, orange and Grand Marnier soups (£2.50), deep-fried camembert fritters with home-made ginger chutney or mousseline of salmon and oyster mushrooms with lemon and dill mayonnaise (£3.50), mushroom stroganoff (£5.25), delicious haddock with parsley butter sauce, fillet of lincolnshire pork with a cider and apple sauce (£7.65), whole sea bream filled with smoked salmon mousse (£8.95), and roast duckling breast with a blackberry and cassis sauce (£10.45), as well as open sandwiches (from £4.85), lamb, ham and apple pie or bacon chops with a fried egg (£6.45), Whitby scampi (£6.50), and puddings. Well kept Black Sheep Bitter, and Theakstons Best and XB on handpump; decent malt whiskies. Darts, dominoes, cribbage, ring the bull, and piped music. The Linton Room is no smoking. The setting is very pretty and there are seats outside looking over the village green to the narrow stream that runs through this delightful hamlet; you can eat out here on fine days. The pub is named after the local lad who made his pile in the Great Plague contracting in London to bury the bodies. *(Recommended by E A George, Derek and Sylvia Stephenson, Gwen and Peter Andrews, Ian and Christina Allen, Martin Hickes, Angus Lyon, Mr and Mrs C Roberts, Prof and Mrs S Barnett, Roger and Christine Mash, Wayne Brindle, Helen McLagan, J R Whetton, Mike and Ruth Dooley, Caroline Kenyon)*

Free house ~ Licensee Francis Mackwood ~ Real ale ~ Meals and snacks (not Sun or Mon evenings) ~ (01756) 752210 ~ Children welcome away from main bar area ~ Open 11.30-3, 7-11; closed winter Mon

LITTON (N Yorks) SD9074 Map 7

Queens Arms

From B6160 N of Grassington, after Kilnsey take second left fork; can also be reached off B6479 at Stainforth N of Settle, via Halton Gill

At the head of Litton Dale, this inn has an attractive two-level garden with stunning views over the fells; there are fine surrounding walks, too – a track behind the inn leads over Ackerley Moor to Buckden and the quiet lane through the valley leads on to Pen-y-ghent. Inside, the main bar on the right has a good coal fire, stripped rough stone walls, a brown beam-and-plank ceiling, stools around cast-iron-framed tables on the stone and concrete floor, a seat built into the stone-mullioned window, signed cricket bats, and a large collection of cigarette lighters. On the left, the red-carpeted room has another coal fire and more of a family atmosphere with varnished pine for its built-in wall seats, and for the ceiling and walls themselves. Decent bar food includes sandwiches (from £2.35; hot or cold crusty rolls from £2.95), filled baked potatoes (from £2.70), ploughman's (£3.65), meaty or vegetable lasagne (£3.95), home-made pies such as rabbit or steak, kidney and Guinness (£5.30), and gammon and egg (£5.50), with a larger evening menu, and children's meals (from £2). Well kept Youngers Scotch on handpump; darts, dominoes, shove-ha'penny, and cribbage. *(Recommended by Neil and Angela Huxter, David Varney, Philip and Elizabeth Hawkins, Gwen and Peter Andrews; more reports please)*

Free house ~ Licensees Tanya and Neil Thompson ~ Real ale ~ Meals and snacks (not Mon except bank holidays) ~ (01756) 770208 ~ Children in eating area of bar only ~ Open 12-3, 7-11 ~ Bedrooms: £21.50(£21.50B)/£33(£39B)

LOW CATTON (E Yorks) SE7053 Map 7

Gold Cup

Village signposted with High Catton off A166 in Stamford Bridge or A1079 at Kexby Bridge

You can be sure of a warm and friendly welcome in this comfortable white-rendered house. The three communicating rooms of the lounge have open fires at each end, plush wall seats and stools around good solid tables, flowery curtains, some decorative plates and brasswork on the walls, and a very relaxed atmosphere. Generous helpings of good home-cooked food might include soup (£1.75), lunchtime sandwiches (from £1.65; not Sun), crusty rolls (from £2.70), and ploughman's (£3.75), steak and mushroom pie (£4.75), and good fisherman's pie or spicy cajun chicken (£4.95); the restaurant has pleasant views of the surrounding fields. Well kept John Smiths and Tetleys on handpump. The back games bar is comfortable, with a well lit pool table, darts, dominoes, fruit machine, video game, and well reproduced music. There may be fat geese in the back paddock. *(Recommended by Beryl and Bill Farmer, Sheila and Robert Robinson, Roger Bellingham, H Bramwell, Rita and Keith Pollard, Ian Phillips)*

Free house ~ Licensees Ray and Pat Hales ~ Real ale ~ Meals and snacks (all day weekends) ~ Restaurant ~ (01759) 371354 ~ Children welcome ~ Open 12-2.30, 6-11; 12-11 Sat; 12-10.30 Sun; closed Mon lunch (except bank holidays); closed evening 25 Dec

MASHAM (N Yorks) SE2381 Map 10

Kings Head 🛏

Market Square

This is a lovely village and on market day (Wednesday), the two opened-up rooms of the neatly kept and spacious lounge bar here are a bustling and friendly place to be. One room is carpeted and one has a wooden floor, and there are green plush seats around wooden tables, a big War Department issue clock over the imposing slate and marble fireplace, and a high shelf of Staffordshire and other figurines. Bar food includes home-made soup (£1.30), eggs with a spicy mango and curried mayonnaise (£1.95), lamb liver and bacon or three cheese and broccoli bake (£4.95), cajun chicken, Whitby cod or rack of lamb (£5.95), steaks (from £6.95), roasts of the day and daily specials, and puddings (£1.95); friendly, helpful service. Well kept Theakstons Best, XB and Old Peculier and seasonal ales on handpump; fruit machine, dominoes, piped music. The handsome inn's hanging baskets and window boxes are most attractive, and there are picnic tables under cocktail parasols in a partly fairy-lit coachyard. *(Recommended by R N Hutton, Roberto Villa, Ian Phillips, David and Fiona Pemberton, R T and J C Moggridge, John and Chris Simpson, David and Judith Hart, Mrs B Sugarman, Caroline Jarrett, Clive Gilbert)*

Scottish & Newcastle ~ Manager Paul Mounter ~ Real ale ~ Meals and snacks ~ Restaurant ~ (01765) 689295 ~ Well behaved children welcome until 9.30pm ~ Open 11-11; 12-10.30 Sun ~ Bedrooms: £39B/£58B

White Bear 🍺

Signposted off A6108 opposite turn into town centre

Not surprisingly, the Theakstons Best, XB, Old Peculier, and Mild on handpump here are very well kept – Theakstons old stone headquarters buildings are part of the pub and the brewery is on the other side of town; tours can be arranged at the Theakstons Brewery Visitor Centre (01765 89057, extension 4317, Weds-Sun); morning visits are best. The traditionally furnished public bar is packed with bric-a-brac such as copper brewing implements, harness, pottery, foreign banknotes, Fairport Convention and Jethro Tull memorabilia, and stuffed animals – including a huge polar bear behind the bar. A much bigger, more comfortable lounge has a turkey carpet. Bar food includes sandwiches, home-made soup, ploughman's, salad platters (£3.95), beef in Old Peculier or fish pie (£4.95), and daily specials. Shove-ha'penny, dominoes, cribbage, fruit machine and CD juke box. In summer there are seats out in the yard. *(Recommended by R T and J C Moggridge, Neil and Angela Huxter, Simon and Amanda Southwell, R N Hutton, J E Rycroft, Val Stevenson, Rob Holmes)*

*Scottish & Newcastle ~ Tenant Mrs Lesley Cutts ~ Real ale ~ Meals and snacks
(not Sat or Sun evenings) ~ (01765) 689319 ~ Children welcome until 9pm ~
Blues Sat evenings ~ Open 11-11 ~ Two bedrooms: /£35*

MELTHAM (W Yorks) SE0910 Map 7

Will's o' Nat's ♀

Blackmoorfoot Road; off B6107; a couple of miles out of village to north west

Reliably good food, well kept real ales, and a relaxed friendly atmosphere continue
to draw people to this popular pub – quite alone in a fine spot up on the moors.
From a wide choice, bar food might include soup (£1.35), lots of sandwiches (from
£1.40; home-cooked tongue £1.50; bacon and black pudding £2), garlic mushrooms
(£2.95), ploughman's (from £3.25), deep-fried fresh haddock (£3.75), wild boar
sausage with onion sauce or hot and spicy bean casserole (£3.95), steak and kidney
pie or tagliatelle in a ham and mushroom sauce (£4.10), roast pork with apple sauce
and stuffing (£4.60), fresh salmon with parsley butter (£5.35), steaks (from £7.45),
puddings like bakewell tart or lemon meringue pie (from £2.05), and children's
dishes (from £1.85); cheeses are traditionally made and are farmhouse or from a
small dairy (£2.45). Well kept Old Mill Bitter and Tetleys Bitter and Mild on
handpump, a good little wine list, and a large collection of malt whiskies. By the bar
there are comfortably cushioned heavy wooden wall seats around old cast-iron-
framed tables, and the cream walls have lots of interesting old local photographs and
a large attractive pen and wash drawing of many local landmarks, with the pub as
its centrepiece. A slightly raised, partly no-smoking dining extension at one end, with
plenty of well spaced tables, has the best of the views. Dominoes, fruit machine and
piped music (not obtrusive). The pub is situated on both the Colne Valley and
Kirklees circular walks and close to Blackmoorfoot reservoir (birdwatching). The
name of the pub means 'belonging to, or run by, William, son of Nathaniel'.
*(Recommended by Neil Townend, Mike and Wendy Proctor, Bronwen and Steve Wrigley, Syd
and Wyn Donald, Andrew and Ruth Triggs, CW, JW, H Dyson, M C and B Forman, Dave
Braisted, Drs A C and A Jackson, M Borthwick, Laura Darlington, Gianluca Perinetti, John and
Elizabeth Cox)*

*Carlsberg Tetleys ~ Lease: Kim Schofield ~ Real ale ~ Meals and snacks (till
10pm; not 25 Dec) ~ Restaurant ~ (01484) 850078 ~ Children welcome until
8pm ~ Open 11.30-3.30, 6(6.30 Sat)-11; closed evening 25 Dec*

MIDDLEHAM (N Yorks) SE1288 Map 10

Black Swan

Market Pl

In a rather steep and pretty village, this 17th-c stone inn has a very friendly, cheerful
local atmosphere in its immaculately kept heavy-beamed bar; also, high-backed
settles built in by the big stone fireplace, racing memorabilia on the stripped stone
walls, horsebrasses and pewter mugs, and well kept John Smiths Bitter and
Theakstons Best, Old Peculier, and XB on handpump; lots of malt whiskies and
decent little wine list. Reasonably priced bar food includes lunchtime snacks such as
sandwiches (from £1.85), filled baked potatoes (from £1.95), and ploughman's
(from £3.50), as well as home-made soup (£1.70), egg mayonnaise (£1.95), battered
haddock (£4.75), vegetable lasagne or home-cooked ham or beef (£4.95), lasagne or
chicken with a creamy and spicy coconut sauce (£5.25), and evening gammon with
pineapple (£7.50), and steaks (from £10.25); children's dishes (from £2.95), and
substantial breakfasts. Dominoes and piped music. There are tables on the cobbles
outside and in the sheltered back garden. Good walking country. *(Recommended by
John and Lianne Smith, R F Orpwood, Chris Reeve, John and Chris Simpson, Carol and Dennis
Clayson, Neil and Angela Huxter)*

*Free house ~ Licensees George and Susan Munday ~ Real ale ~ Meals and snacks
(not evening 25 Dec) ~ Restaurant ~ (01969) 622221 ~ Children welcome until
9pm ~ Open 11-4, 6-11; 12-3.30, 6.30-10.30 Sun; closed evening 25 Dec ~
Bedrooms: £25B/£44B*

MOULTON (N Yorks) NZ2404 Map 10

Black Bull ⑨⑨

Just E of A1, 1 mile S of Scotch Corner

Happily unchanging, this decidedly civilised place has a lot of character and is much loved by its regular customers. The bar has a huge winter log fire, fresh flowers, an antique panelled oak settle and an old elm housekeeper's chair, built-in red-cushioned black settles and pews around the cast iron tables (one has a heavily beaten-copper top), silver-plate Turkish coffee pots and so forth over the red velvet curtained windows, and copper cooking utensils hanging from black beams. A nice side dark-panelled seafood bar has some high seats at the marble-topped counter. Excellent bar snacks include lovely smoked salmon: sandwiches (£3.25), pâté (£4.50), and smoked salmon plate (£5.25); they also do a very good home-made soup served in lovely little tureens (£2), fresh plump salmon sandwiches (£3.25), fresh pasta carbonara (£3.95), black pudding and pork sausage with caramelised apple (£4.25), welsh rarebit and bacon (£4.50), hot tomato tart with anchovies and black olives or memorable seafood pancakes (£5.25), and puddings (£2); you must search out someone to take your order – the bar staff just do drinks. In the evening (when people do tend to dress up), you can also eat in the polished brick-tiled conservatory with bentwood cane chairs or in the *Brighton Belle* dining car; they also do a three-course Sunday lunch. Good wine, and a fine choice of sherries. Service can seem a little unbending to first-time visitors, but most people quickly come to appreciate the dry humour and old-fashioned standards. There are some seats under trees in the central court. *(Recommended by SS, Beryl and Bill Farmer, Susan and John Douglas, R J Robinson, Jack and Heather Coyle, R J Walden)*

Free house ~ Licensees Mrs A Pagendam and Miss S Pagendam ~ Real ale ~ Lunchtime bar meals and snacks (not Sun) ~ Restaurant (not Sun evening) ~ (01325) 377289 ~ Children in eating area of bar if over 7 ~ Open 12-2.30, 6-10.30(11 Sat); closed Sun evening and 24-29 Dec

MUKER (N Yorks) SD9198 Map 10

Farmers Arms

B6270 W of Reeth

This unpretentious and remote dales pub is useful for walkers (there are plenty of rewarding nearby walks), and there are interesting drives up over Buttertubs Pass or to the north, to Tan Hill and beyond. The cosy bar has a warm open fire and is simply furnished with stools and settles around copper-topped tables. Bar food includes lunchtime baps and toasties (£1.95), filled baked potatoes (£2.65), home-made cottage pie, vegetable lasagne or coconut beef curry (£4.50), gammon and pineapple (£5.35), steaks (from £7.30), children's dishes (from £2.50) and puddings (£2.10). Butterknowle Bitter, John Smiths Bitter, and Theakstons Best, XB and Old Peculier on handpump; darts and dominoes. They have a self-catering studio flat to rent. *(Recommended by R T and J C Moggridge, Viv Middlebrook, Richard Hathaway, JKW, Eddie Edwards, Lesley Sones; more reports please)*

Free house ~ Licensees Chris and Marjorie Bellwood ~ Real ale ~ Meals and snacks ~ (01748) 886297 ~ Children welcome ~ Open 11-3, 6.30-11; 11-11 Sat; 12-10.30 Sun; winter evening opening 7

NUNNINGTON (N Yorks) SE6779 Map 7

Royal Oak ⑨⑨

Church Street; at back of village, which is signposted from A170 and B1257

It's very much the consistently good food that draws customers to this spotlessly kept and attractive little dining pub. Served by friendly and efficient staff, there might be sandwiches (from £2.25), home-made vegetable soup (£2.50), spicy mushrooms or stilton pâté (£3.75), egg mayonnaise with prawns (£4.50), ploughman's or lasagne (£6.50), black-eyed bean casserole, chicken in an orange and tarragon sauce or ham and mushroom tagliatelle (£7.50), enjoyable fisherman's pot or steak and kidney casserole (£7.95), sirloin steak (£10.95), daily specials such as leek and pine kernel pasta (£7.50), rack of lamb (£8.95), and fillet steak au poivre (£13.95), and puddings like home-made apple pie or chocolate fudge cake (£2.50). Well kept Ind Coope Burton, Tetleys, and Theakstons Old Peculier on handpump. The high black beams of the bar are strung with earthenware flagons, copper jugs and lots of antique keys, one of the walls is stripped back to the bare stone to display a fine collection of antique farm tools, and there are open fires; the carefully chosen furniture includes kitchen and country dining chairs or a long pew around the sturdy tables on the turkey carpet, and a lectern in one corner. Handy for a visit to Nunnington Hall (National Trust). *(Recommended by Mr and Mrs W B Draper, R White, Tim and Sue Halstead; more reports please)*

Free house ~ Licensee Anthony Simpson ~ Real ale ~ Meals and snacks (not Mon) ~ (01439) 748271 ~ Children in restaurant only, if over 8 ~ Open 12-2.30, 6.30-11; closed Mon

nr OTLEY (W Yorks) SE2047 Map 7
Spite

Newall with Clifton, off B6451; towards Blubberhouses about a mile N from Otley, straight up hill after crossing bridge and past the hospital – and in fact just inside N Yorks

This popular and welcoming place has a good mix of visitors and locals and a cheerfully straightforward atmosphere. Also, beamed ceilings, plain white walls hung with some wildfowl prints and a collection of walking sticks, traditional pub furniture, and a good log fire. Good, straightforward bar food includes sandwiches (from £1.85; hot beef £4.20), home-made steak pie (£4.30), roast beef, pork, lamb or turkey (from £4.50), fresh salmon salad (£5), roast duckling breast (£6.95), and daily specials. Well kept John Smiths Bitter, Theakstons Best, and Websters Yorkshire, with guests like Greene King Sorcerer or Mitchells Lancaster Bomber on handpump; dominoes. The neat, well-lit little rose garden has white tables and chairs. *(Recommended by J E Rycroft, David and Helen Wilkins, Neville Kenyon, F J Robinson, Joy and Peter Heatherley, Gwen and Peter Andrews, Mike and Ruth Dooley, Ben Grose)*

Courage ~ Lease: Philip Gill ~ Real ale ~ Meals and snacks (not Sun or Mon evenings) ~ Restaurant ~ (01943) 463063 ~ Children in eating area of bar until 9pm ~ Open 11.30-3, 6-11; 11.30-11 Sat

PENISTONE (S Yorks) SE2402 Map 7
Cubley Hall

Mortimer Road; outskirts, towards Stocksbridge

A bedroom extension has been added to this interesting place – originally a grand Edwardian villa – and all the rooms refurbished. The spreading bar has panelling, an elaborately plastered ceiling, and lots of plush chairs, stools and button-back built-in wall banquettes on the mosaic tiling or turkey carpet. Leading off this spacious main area are two snug rooms and a big new no-smoking conservatory which gives a nice view beyond the neat tree-sheltered formal gardens to pastures in the distance. Efficiently served by neat waitresses, the food includes sandwiches, home-made soup (£1.95), mushroom fricassee (£3.25), chicken liver parfait (£3.75), king prawns in garlic butter (£4.95), a choice of three roasts (£6.95), chicken and pasta or tuna steak with a tomato and anchovy salsa (£8.95), sirloin steak (£9.95), and puddings like home-made bakewell tart (£2.95). Well kept Ind Coope Burton, Tetleys Bitter and Imperial, and guest beers on handpump, and a fair choice of wines; piped music. Out on the terrace are some tables and the attractive garden has a good children's play house and adventure playground. *(Recommended by NAB, Martin Aust, George Atkinson; more reports please)*

Free house ~ Licensee John Wigfield ~ Real ale ~ Meals and snacks (served all day) ~ Restaurant (all day on Sunday) ~ (01226) 766086 ~ Children in restaurant and conservatory ~ Open 11-11 ~ Bedrooms: £40B/£57.50B

PICKHILL (N Yorks) SE3584 Map 10

Nags Head 🍺 ♟

Take the Masham turn-off from A1 both N and S, and village signposted off B6267 in Ainderby Quernhow

This is a most enjoyable place to visit and is deservedly popular with a nice mix of locals and visitors. The busy tap room on the left has masses of ties hanging as a frieze from a rail around the red ceiling, and the beams are hung with jugs, coach horns, ale-yards and so forth. The smarter lounge bar has deep green plush banquettes on the matching carpet, and pictures for sale on its neat cream walls, and another comfortable beamed room (mainly for restaurant users) has red plush button-back built-in wall banquettes around dark tables, and an open fire. Particularly good food served by friendly, efficient staff includes sandwiches, soup (£2.25), wild boar terrine or stilton and mushroom tartlet with blackcurrant sauce (£3.75), cottage pie (£4.95), tandoori chicken (£5.95), salmon and halibut fishcake with shellfish sauce (£6.50), large cod and chips (£6.80), steak and oyster pie (£7.95), poached king scallops on a spinach and watercress sauce (£10.95), daily specials like medaillons of pork fillet with an anchovy and thyme sauce (£8.95) or very good roast saddle of hare with bramble and a port wine sauce (£10.95), and puddings such as apple and honey crumble, banoffi pie or squidgy chocolate roll (£2.95); the restaurant is no smoking. Well kept Hambleton Bitter and Goldfield (the brewery is a couple of miles away), and Theakstons Best, XB and Old Peculier on handpump, a good choice of malt whiskies, and good value wines (several by the glass). One table's inset with a chessboard, and they also have cribbage, darts, dominoes, shove-ha'penny, and faint piped music. *(Recommended by Esther and John Sprinkle, John and Chris Simpson, Ian Morley, Eddie Edwards, Ian Rorison, David Stafford, David Heath, Andrew and Ruth Triggs, A Morton, R N Hutton, Hilary Edwards, John Allsopp, Mr and Mrs D S Price; also in Good Hotel Guide)*

Free house ~ Licensees Raymond and Edward Boynton ~ Real ale ~ Meals and snacks (till 10pm) ~ Restaurant (closed Sun evening) ~ (01845) 567391 ~ Well behaved children welcome but small ones must be gone by 7pm ~ Open 11-11; 12-10.30 Sun ~ Bedrooms: £34B/£48B

POOL (W Yorks) SE2445 Map 7

White Hart

Just off A658 S of Harrogate, A659 E of Otley

Although this friendly and popular family dining pub started life as a farmhouse in the 18th c, it was rebuilt internally just a few years ago and now seems as if it's always been this way: four rooms with a restrained country decor, a pleasant medley of assorted old farmhouse furniture on the mix of stone flooring and carpet, and a quiet and comfortable atmosphere; there's a log fire in the main bar, and a no-smoking area. Generous helpings of good bar food include lunchtime sandwiches (not Sunday), soup (£1.95), savoury bacon and cheddar melt (£2.50), gammon and egg (£4.95), lemon chicken or beef and ale pie (£5.25), seafood salad (£5.95), rump steak (£6.95), daily specials such as liver and bacon (£4.75), broccoli and brie pastry with sherry, cream and tomato sauce (£5.50) or pork fillet with wild mushroom sauce and caramelised apple rings (£8.25), and puddings like treacle tart or spotted dick (from £1.95); roast Sunday beef (£5.95). Hardworking staff, well kept Bass, Stones, Timothy Taylors Landlord, and Worthington on handpump, and a well priced wine list (several by the glass) including bin ends. Fruit machine, dominoes, and piped jazz or classical music. There are tables outside, with a play area well away from the road. This part of lower Wharfedale is a pleasant walking area, and despite the emphasis on dining walkers don't feel at all out of place here. *(Recommended by Mike Whitehouse, Andrew Hodges, Mr and Mrs Derwent, Martin Hickes, Lynne Gittins, Ben Grose)*

Bass ~ Manager David McHattie~ Real ale ~ Meals and snacks (all day) ~ (0113) 284 3011 ~ Children welcome away from bar ~ Open 11-11; 12-10.30 Sun; closed evening 25 Dec

RAMSGILL (N Yorks) SE1271 Map 7

Yorke Arms 🛏

Take Nidderdale rd off B6265 in Pateley Bridge; or exhilarating but narrow moorland drive off A6108 at N edge of Masham, via Fearby and Lofthouse

This small country hotel was the shooting-lodge of the Yorke family's Gouthwaite Hall, which now lies drowned under the nearby reservoir named after it. The bars have two or three heavy carved Jacobean oak chairs, a big oak dresser laden with polished pewter and other antiques, and open log fires. Nicely presented bar food includes sandwiches (from £2; fresh salmon £3.75), home-made soup (£2.30), black pudding and bacon mornay (£3.95), ploughman's (from £4.95), vegetable kiev (£5.95), salads (from £5.95), home-made steak in ale pie (£6.25), baked local ham with parsley sauce (£6.50), fresh salmon with a tarragon and lime butter sauce (£7.25), a huge mixed grill (£8.95), sirloin steak (£12.50), and puddings (£3.25). Theakstons XB on handpump, and friendly staff. They prefer smart dress in the no-smoking restaurant in the evening. The inn's public rooms are open throughout the day for tea and coffee, and shorts are served in cut glass. You can walk up the magnificent if strenuous moorland road to Masham, or perhaps on the right-of-way track that leads along the hill behind the reservoir, also a bird sanctuary. *(Recommended by Greta and Christopher Wells, M A Butler, Andrew and Ruth Triggs, Robert and Ann Lees)*

Free house ~ Licensees Mr and Mrs MacDougall ~ Real ale ~ Lunchtime bar meals and snacks ~ Restaurant ~ (01423) 755243 ~ Children welcome ~ Open 11-11; 12-10.30 Sun; closed evening 25 Dec ~ Bedrooms: £40B/£70B

REDMIRE (N Yorks) SE0591 Map 10

Kings Arms 🍺

Wensley—Askrigg back road: a good alternative to the A684 through Wensleydale

From the tables and chairs in the pretty garden here there's a superb view across Wensleydale; fishing nearby. Inside this friendly and unassuming village local the simply furnished bar is neatly kept and has a long soft leatherette wall seat and other upholstered wall settles, red leatherette cafe chairs or dark oak ones, round cast-iron tables, a fine oak armchair (its back carved like a mop of hair), and a woodburning stove. Popular bar food includes good soup (£1.95), sandwiches (from £2.15), omelettes (£4.95), meaty or good vegetarian lasagne (£5.75), vegetarian dishes (£5.95), steak and kidney pie (£6.95), grilled local trout (£6.95), chicken with garlic (£7.75), half a roast duck (£9.95), and steaks (from £10.95); Sunday roast; the restaurant is no smoking. Well kept Redmire Brew (brewed for the pub by Hambleton Ales), as well as Black Sheep Special, Richardson Brothers Four Seasons, John Smiths, and Theakstons Black Bull and Lightfoot on handpump, 56 malt whiskies, and decent wines. The staffordshire bull terrier is called Kim. Darts, pool, dominoes, and cribbage; quoits. Handy for Castle Bolton where Mary Queen of Scots was imprisoned. *(Recommended by Darren Staniforth, Jane Evans, David Hilton, M Morgan, Chris Reeve, JKW, J H and S A Harrop, Ray and Liz Monk, Lesley Sones, Richard Hathaway)*

Free house ~ Licensee Roger Stevens ~ Real ale ~ Meals and snacks ~ Restaurant ~ (01969) 622316 ~ Children in eating area of bar and in restaurant until 9 ~ Open 11-3, 6-11 ~ Two Bedrooms: £18/£34

RIPPONDEN (W Yorks) SE0419 Map 7

Old Bridge 🍷

Priest Lane; from A58, best approach is Elland Road (opposite Golden Lion), park opposite the church in pub's car park and walk back over ancient hump-backed bridge

For 33 years Mr Beaumont has run this friendly old place, set by the medieval pack horse bridge over the little River Ryburn. The three communicating rooms are each on a slightly different level and have oak settles built into the window recesses of the thick stone walls, antique oak tables, rush-seated chairs, a few well-chosen pictures, a big woodburning stove, and a relaxed atmosphere. Bar food includes a popular weekday lunchtime cold meat buffet which always has a joint of rare beef, as well as spiced ham, quiche, scotch eggs and so on (£7.50 with a bowl of soup and coffee); also, sandwiches, home-made soup (£1.85), deep-fried camembert (£3.50), smoked haddock and spinach crumble, lamb in cider or chicken, broccoli and stilton pie (all £4.50), and puddings (£2.25). Well kept Black Sheep Special, Ryburn Best, Timothy Taylors Best and Golden Mild, and a weekly guest beer on handpump, several malt whiskies, and interesting wines with half a dozen by the glass. The popular restaurant is over the bridge. *(Recommended by M L and G Clarke, Greta and Christopher Wells, Monica Shelley, James Macrae, Laura Darlington, Gianluca Perinetti)*

Free house ~ Licensee Ian Beaumont, Manager Timothy Walker ~ Real ale ~ Meals and snacks (till 10pm; no bar meals Sat or Sun evening) ~ Restaurant ~ (01422) 822595 ~ Children welcome until 7pm ~ Open 12-3, 5.30-11; 12-11 Sat; 12-10.30 Sun

ROBIN HOODS BAY (N Yorks) NZ9505 Map 10
Laurel

Village signposted off A171 S of Whitby

A new licensee has taken over this charming little white pub, set in the heart of one of the prettiest and most unspoilt fishing villages on the North East coast. The friendly beamed main bar bustles with locals and visitors, and is decorated with old local photographs, Victorian prints and brasses, and lager bottles from all over the world; there's a roaring open fire. Bar food consists of lunchtime sandwiches (from £1.40) and winter soup. Well kept John Smiths and Theakstons Old Peculier with guests like Marstons Pedigree, Ruddles Best, and Theakstons Black Bull on handpump; darts, shove-ha'penny, dominoes, and cribbage. In summer, the hanging baskets and window boxes are lovely. *(Recommended by Mike and Wendy Proctor, Fiona and David Pemberton, R N Hutton, Gill and Andy Plumb, Mrs Kathy Newens, James Nunns, Jack and Philip Paxton)*

Free house ~ Lease: Brian Catling ~ Real ale ~ Lunchtime snacks ~ (01947) 880400 ~ Children in family room ~ Open 12-11; 12-10.30 summer Sun ~ Bedrooms planned

ROSEDALE ABBEY (N Yorks) SE7395 Map 10
Milburn Arms 🛏 ♀

The easiest road to the village is through Cropton from Wrelton, off the A170 W of Pickering

Both the licensee and his staff will ensure you get a warmly friendly welcome in this 18th-c pub. There's a good atmosphere and log fire in the neatly kept L-shaped and beamed main bar (refurbished this year), and good Bass, Black Sheep Special and Riggwelter, Stones, and a fortnightly guest well kept on handpump; 20 malt whiskies, and seven good house wines by the glass. Enjoyable bar food includes fresh fish and shellfish (sent down overnight from Scotland), as well as super lunchtime sandwiches, grilled queen scallops with leeks and gruyère (£5.25), saffron tagliatelle with roasted peppers (£6.95), good roast lamb shank with rosemary and garlic (£8.50), shellfish platter (£9.50), and banana bread and butter pudding (£2.50); huge breakfasts. The restaurant is no smoking. Darts, shove-ha'penny, cribbage, dominoes, fruit machine, and piped music. There are picnic tables on the terrace and in the garden, and the steep surrounding moorland is very fine. *(Recommended by David Heath, Sue and Bob Ward, Val Stevenson, Rob Holmes, Alison Turner, Barry and Anne, Frank Cummins, David Surridge, Duncan Redpath, Lorraine Milburn, Martin Hickes)*

Free house ~ Licensee Terry Bentley ~ Real ale ~ Meals and snacks ~ Restaurant ~ (01751) 417312 ~ Well behaved children in eating area of bar till 8.30 ~ Open 11.30-3(3.30 Sat), 6.30-11; 12-3, 6.30-10.30 Sun; closed 25 Dec ~ Bedrooms: £44.50B/£74B

If we know a pub does sandwiches we always say so – if they're not mentioned, you'll have to assume you can't get one.

SAWLEY (N Yorks) SE2568 Map 7

Sawley Arms ♀

Village signposted off B6265 W of Ripon

The lovely gardens, flowering tubs and baskets have won the Britian in Bloom competition three times now – quite a feat. This is a rather smart and well managed place (run by Mrs Hawes for 28 years), and the series of small turkey-carpeted rooms have log fires and comfortable furniture ranging from small softly cushioned armed dining chairs and comfortable settees, to the wing armchairs down a couple of steps in a side snug; there may be daily papers and magazines to read, and two small rooms are no smoking. Good bar food includes lunchtime sandwiches, home-made pea, mint and lemon soup with croûtons (£2.30; special seafood £3.50), salmon mousse or stilton, port and celery pâté (£4.10), steak pie or chicken in a mushroom and herb sauce (£5.95), plaice mornay on a bed of leeks (£7.20), and puddings such as lovely bread and butter pudding (£3.50); good house wines and quiet piped music. The pub is handy for Fountains Abbey (the most extensive of the great monastic remains – floodlit on late summer Friday and Saturday evenings, with a live choir on the Saturday). *(Recommended by Geoffrey and Brenda Wilson, Gwen and Peter Andrews, R L Gorick, M A Butler, Donald and Mollie Armitage, Andrew and Ruth Triggs, Mrs P J Pearce, F J Robinson, Neville Kenyon, Dorothy and David Young)*

Free house ~ Licensee Mrs June Hawes ~ Meals and snacks (not Mon evenings except bank holidays) ~ Restaurant ~ (01765) 620642 ~ Well behaved children allowed if over 9 ~ Open 11.30-3, 6.30-11; closed Mon evenings except bank holidays

SAXTON (N Yorks) SE4736 Map 7

Greyhound

Village signposted off B1217 Garforth—Tadcaster; so close to A1 and A162 N of Pontefract

Unchanging over the years, this pleasant village local is next to the church – where Lord Dacre who fell at the Battle of Towton in 1461 is buried upright on his horse. The unspoilt, cosy and chatty tap room on the left has a coal fire burning in the Victorian fireplace in the corner, a cushioned window seat by the mouth of the corridor as well as other simple seats, and ochre Anaglypta walls and a dark panelled dado; an etched glass window looks into the snug with its sturdy mahogany wall settle curving round one corner, other traditional furniture, fancy shades on the brass lamps, and browning Victorian wallpaper. Down at the end of the corridor is another highly traditional room, with darts, shove-ha'penny, and dominoes. Well kept (and very cheap) Sam Smiths OB tapped from casks behind the counter; during the week, they will make sandwiches on request – at the weekends they are on offer. In summer the pub is very pretty with a climbing rose, passion flower, and bedding plants, and a couple of picnic tables in the side courtyard. This is also the community Post Office (Monday, Tuesday and Thursday 8.45am to 10.45am). Lotherton Hall Museum is nearby. *(Recommended by Chris Westmoreland, David Watson)*

Sam Smiths ~ Manager Colin McCarthy ~ Real ale ~ Sandwiches (lunchtime) ~ (01937) 557202 ~ Children in tap room ~ Open 12-3, 5.30-11; 11-11 Sat; 12-10.30 Sun

SETTLE (N Yorks) SD8264 Map 7

Golden Lion

A65

This rather grand looking coaching inn has been taken over by the son of the licensees of our other main entry here, the Royal Oak. The spacious, high-beamed hall bar has a surprisingly grand staircase sweeping down into it, an enormous fireplace, comfortable settles and plush seats, brass, prints and Chinese plates on dark panelling, and a happy atmosphere. Well presented, good bar food includes soup (£2), sandwiches (from £2.50), home-made burgers (£3.50), ploughman's (from £5), and daily specials such as oriental vegetable stir-fry (£5), smoked duck with tagliatelle (£5.85), home-made steak and kidney pudding (£6.10), chicken in a leek and stilton sauce (£6.50), salmon in seafood sauce (£6.75), and puddings such as banoffi pie (£2.45). Well kept Thwaites Bitter and Craftsman, and a monthly guest beer on handpump; friendly, helpful staff. The lively public bar has pool, shove-ha'penny, fruit machine, and piped music; the labrador-cross is called Monty, and the black and white cat, Luke. *(Recommended by Mr and Mrs C Roberts, Chris and Martin Taylor, K and F Giles)*

Thwaites ~ Licensee Phillip Longrigg ~ Real ale ~ Meals and snacks (12-2.30, 6-10; all day Sat/Sun) ~ Restaurant ~ (01729) 822203 ~ Children welcome ~ Open 11-11; 12-10.30 Sun ~ Bedrooms: £21.50/£43(£52B)

Royal Oak 🛏

Market Place; town signposted from A65 Skipton—Kendal

A chatty and bustling atmosphere is created by the good mix of customers in this large stone market town inn. The bar is almost open-plan – though enough walls have been kept to divide it into decent-sized separate areas. There are plenty of comfortably cushioned chairs at brass-topped tables, plates and horsebrasses on the walls, dark squared oak or matching oak-look panelling, and a couple of elegantly carved arches with more carving above the fireplaces. Lights vary from elaborate curly brass candelabra through attractive table lamps and standard lamps with old-fashioned shades to unexpectedly modernist wall cubes. Bar food includes home-made soup (£2), sandwiches (closed, danish or french bread from £2.55), breaded mushrooms with garlic dip (£3.30), popular filled yorkshire puddings (from £4.90), tagliatelle with a mushroom and cream sauce (£4.95), cottage pie (£5.50), steak and kidney pie (£6), calf liver and onions (£6.95), steak and Guinness pie (£6), gammon and egg (£6.60), children's dishes (£3.75), and puddings (from £2). Well kept Boddingtons Bitter, Flowers IPA, Timothy Taylors Landlord, and Whitbreads Castle Eden on handpump; courteous service. Readers say the Settle & Carlisle railway (only 5 minutes away) is worth a trip, and the Tuesday market here is very good. Some road noise (absurdly heavy quarry lorries cut through the attractive small town – they should certainly be kept out). *(Recommended by Andrew and Ruth Triggs, M Holdsworth, Barry and Anne, Brian Ellis, Chris and Martin Taylor, Neil and Anita Christopher, Richard Dolphin, Lynn Sharpless, Bob Eardley, Mr and Mrs R Hebson, JKW)*

Whitbreads ~ Tenants Brian and Sheila Longrigg ~ Real ale ~ Meals and snacks (noon-10pm) ~ Restaurant ~ (01729) 822561 ~ Children welcome ~ Open 11-11 ~ Bedrooms: £33B/£55B

SHEFFIELD (S Yorks) SK3687 Map 7

Fat Cat £ 🍺

23 Alma St

The fine range of beers here is consistently well kept and the bar food is outstanding value. As well as their own-brewed (and cheap) Kelham Island Bitter (named after the nearby Industrial Museum), they also serve well kept Marstons Pedigree, Timothy Taylors Landlord, and seven interesting guest beers on handpump (usually including another beer from Kelham Island), and keep foreign bottled beers (particularly Belgian ones), country wines, and farm cider. Enjoyable bar food includes sandwiches, soup (£1.30), vegetable cobbler, ploughman's, Mexican mince, leek and butter bean casserole, and pork and pepper casserole (all £2.50), and puddings such as apple and rhubarb crumble or jam roly poly (80p); Sunday lunch. The two small downstairs rooms have coal fires and simple wooden tables and burgundy-coloured seats around the walls, with a few advertising mirrors and an enamelled placard for Richdales Sheffield Kings Ale; the one on the left is no-smoking; cribbage and dominoes. Steep steps take you up to another similarly simple room (which may be booked for functions) with some attractive prints of old Sheffield; there are picnic tables in a fairylit back courtyard. *(Recommended by David Carr, R N Hutton, Terry Barlow, Mike and Wendy Proctor, JJW, CMW, Christopher Turner, David and Fiona Pemberton, David and Shelia, Jack and Philip Paxton)*

Own brew ~ Licensee Stephen Fearn ~ Real ale ~ Lunchtime meals and snacks ~ (0114) 249 4801 ~ Children allowed upstairs if not booked, until 8pm ~ Open 12-3, 5.30-11; closed 25-26 Dec

SHELLEY (W Yorks) SE2112 Map 7

Three Acres 🍴 🛏 ⚲

Roydhouse; B6116 and turn left just before Pennine Garden Centre; straight on for about 3 miles

Over the years, this civilised former coaching inn has been very much enjoyed by readers – although it is not, in the strictest sense, a pub. The roomy and relaxed traditional lounge bar has old prints and so forth, and well kept changing ales such as Holt, Plant and Deakin Deakin's Downfall, Mansfield Bitter, Riding and White Rabbit, Morlands Old Speckled Hen, and Timothy Taylors Landlord on handpump, and a good choice of malt whiskies. Very good bar food includes a wide range of really interesting sandwiches such as hot home-made cumberland sausage with fried onions and mild mustard mayonnaise or roast breast of fresh chicken with sage and onion stuffing and apple sauce (£2.95), toasted ciabatta with roasted tomatoes, aubergines, basil, mozarella and spinach salad (£3.25), poached fresh scottish salmon with cucumber and watercress (£3.50), toasted hot smoked ham with grain mustard and gruyère cheese (£3.75), and Whitby crab with lemon and ginger dressing (£4.95); also, soup or yorkshire pudding with caramelised onion gravy (£2.95), coarse pâté with toasted walnut bread and red onion marmalade (£4.95), fettucine with ceps, broccoli and pecorino cheese, a roast of the day or home-made steak, kidney and mushroom pie (£6.95), Thai stir-fry of king prawns on thread noodles (£7.95), and daily specials such as tempura of monkfish with mustard and coriander mayonnaise or fresh dressed Whitby crab (£10.95), and stir-fried fillet of beef in oyster sauce (£12.95). The choice of wines, admittedly not cheap, is exceptional, service is good and friendly even when busy, and the relaxing atmosphere may be helped along by a pianist playing light music. There are fine views across to Emley Moor, occasionally livened up by the local hunt passing. Breakfasts are excellent. *(Recommended by Michael Butler, D and D Savidge, A Preston, Neil Townend, Susan Scanlan, David R Shillitoe)*

Free house ~ Licensees Neil Truelove, Brian Orme ~ Real ale ~ Meals and snacks ~ Restaurant ~ (01484) 602606 ~ Children welcome ~ Open 12-3, 6-11; closed Sat lunchtime ~ Bedrooms: £47.50B/£57.50B

SICKLINGHALL (N Yorks) SE3648 Map 7

Scotts Arms

Leaving Wetherby W on A661, fork left signposted Sicklinghall

Stubs of the old dividing walls give the friendly main bar here a less open-plan feel – the building was originally several cottages. Seats are built into cosy little alcoves cut into the main walls, there's a a lot of bric-a-brac, a curious sort of double-decker fireplace with its upper hearth intricately carved, and a big inglenook fireplace. Bar food includes sandwiches, soup (£1.55), burgers (from £2.65), vegetable lasagne (£4.95), steak and mushroom pie or fish and chips (£4.85), gammon and pineapple (£5), and puddings (£1.95). Well kept Theakstons Best, XB and Old Peculier, and a guest beer on handpump; darts, dominoes, pinball, fruit machine, video game, CD juke box and unobtrusive piped music, and down steps a separate room has pool. In summer, the hanging baskets, flowering tubs and neat garden here are a riot of colour; there are seats and tables, a children's play area with slide, climbing frame and wooden animals, and summer barbecues. *(Recommended by Martin Hickes, Michael Butler, Roy Bromell, Mayur Shah, Mrs P J Pearce, David Varney)*

S & N ~ Manager Carl Lang ~ Real ale ~ Meals and snacks (not 25 Dec) ~ Restaurant (not Sun evening) ~ (01937) 582100 ~ Children in eating area of bar ~ Open 12-3, 6-11; 12-11 Sat; 12-10.30 Sun

We say if we or readers have seen dogs or cats in a pub.

STARBOTTON (N Yorks) SD9574 Map 7

Fox & Hounds 🍽 🛏

B6160 Upper Wharfedale rd N of Kettlewell; OS Sheet 98, map reference 953749

It's still the very good, popular food that most people come to this prettily placed little Upper Wharfedale inn for, and at weekends, particularly, the pub tends to be crowded. Served by friendly staff, there might be lunchtime dishes like ploughman's filled french bread (from £2.50), and shepherd's pie or giant yorkshire pudding (£4.50), as well as carrot and orange soup (£2), double baked cheese soufflé or smoked haddock and egg terrine (£2.75), salad of stilton, sun-dried tomato and sugar-roasted pecan nuts (£3.75), chicken and coriander burger (£5.25), parsnip, chestnut and tomato crumble (£5.75), steak and mushroom pie (£6), Moroccan-style lamb (£7.25), evening extras such as chicken supreme in a creamy white wine and stilton sauce (£8.50), baked salmon with a wine, cream and dill sauce (£10.50), aberdeen angus sirloin steak (£11.50), and puddings such as sticky toffee pudding, whisky marmalade bread and butter pudding or dark chocolate pudding with white chocolate orange sauce (£2.25); the dining area is no smoking. The bar has traditional solid furniture on the flagstones, a collection of plates on the walls, whisky jugs hanging from the high beams supporting ceiling boards, a big stone fireplace (with an enormous fire in winter), and a warmly welcoming atmosphere. Well kept Black Sheep Bitter, and Theakstons Best, XB and Old Peculier on handpump, and quite a few malt whiskies. Dominoes, cribbage, and well reproduced, unobtrusive piped music. There are seats in a sheltered corner that enjoy the view over the hills. *(Recommended by J E Rycroft, Ian and Christina Allen, Neil and Angela Huxter, Chris Wheaton, John Allsopp, I Maw, David and Judy Walmsley, John Honnor, Wayne Wheeler, John and Chris Simpson)*

Free house ~ Licensees James and Hilary McFadyen ~ Real ale ~ Meals and snacks (see below) ~ (01756) 760269 ~ Children in eating area of bar ~ Open 11.30-3, 6.30-11; closed all day winter Mon, closed summer Mon evening; closed Jan-mid-Feb ~ Bedrooms: /£50S

STUTTON (N Yorks) SE4841 Map 7

Hare & Hounds

Off A162 just S of Tadcaster

In summer, the lovely long sloping garden of this stone-built pub is quite a draw for families, and there are toys out here for children. Inside, there's a friendly welcome and cosy low-ceilinged rooms unusually done out in 1960s style; well kept Sam Smiths OB on handpump, decent wine, and good, helpful service. The wide choice of very popular, good imaginative food set out on a huge blackboard in the lounge bar includes up to ten starters and twenty main courses: home-made soup (£1.65), home-made pâté or deep-fried brie with raspberry sauce (£3.50), lunchtime haddock or home-made steak and mushroom pie (£4.95), lamb steak (£5.50), breast of chicken in a cheese and ham sauce (£5.95), and evening extras such as barnsley chops (£9.25), and fillet steak in a stilton and cream sauce (£13.50). Occasional piped music. It does tend to get crowded at weekends. *(Recommended by Chris Westmoreland, Janet Pickles, Tim and Sue Halstead, Gill and Andy Plumb, K R Fell)*

Sam Smiths ~ Tenant Mike Chiswick ~ Real ale ~ Meals and snacks (11.30-2, 6.30-9.30; not Sun or Mon evenings) ~ Restaurant ~ (01937) 833164 ~ Children in eating area of bar and in restaurant ~ Open 11.30-3.30, 6.30-11

SUTTON UPON DERWENT (E Yorks) SE7047 Map 7

St Vincent Arms 🍺

B1228 SE of York

A fine range of around eight well kept real ales is on handpump in this old and cosy family-run pub. Very well priced, too, there might be Courage Directors, Fullers London Pride, ESB, and Chiswick, Old Mill Bitter, John Smiths, Timothy Taylors Landlord, and Charles Wells Bombardier; also a range of malt whiskies, and very reasonably priced spirits. Good friendly service. Nicely presented, home-made bar food includes sandwiches (from £1.55), soup (£1.80), filled baked potatoes (from £1.95), chicken liver pâté (£2.60), ploughman's (from £3.50), fillet of haddock in their own batter (£5.20), steak and mushroom pie (£6), stir-fry of the day (£8.20), steaks (from £10.40), and puddings like treacle tart or apple pie (£2.20). One eating area is no smoking. The parlour-like, panelled front bar has traditional high-backed settles, a cushioned bow-window seat, windsor chairs and a coal fire; another lounge and separate dining room open off. No games or music. An attractive garden has tables and seats, and there are pleasant walks along the nearby River Derwent. The pub is named after the admiral who was granted the village and lands by the nation as thanks for his successful commands – and for coping with Nelson's infatuation with Lady Hamilton. *(Recommended by Jeff Seaman, Roger A Bellingham, Ann and Colin Hunt, C A Hall; more reports please)*

Free house ~ Licensee Phil Hopwood ~ Real ale ~ Meals and snacks ~ Restaurant ~ (01904) 608349 ~ Children welcome (must be well behaved in restaurant) ~ Open 11.30-3, 6-11

TERRINGTON (N Yorks) SE6571 Map 7
Bay Horse

W of Malton; off B1257 at Hovingham (towards York, eventually sigposted left) or Slingsby (towards Castle Howard, then right); can also be reached off A64 via Castle Howard, or via Welburn and Ganthorpe

The hardworking and cheerful licensees in this charming country pub have created a really friendly and relaxed atmosphere. The cosy lounge bar has a roaring log fire, country prints, china on delft shelves and magazines to read, and a traditional public bar has darts and an enthusiastic dominoes school; shove-ha'penny and table skittles. There's a dining area handsomely furnished in oak, and a back family conservatory with farm tools. Good generously served food includes lunchtime sandwiches, baps or crusty bread (from £1.65), filled baked potatoes (£2), and ploughman's (£4.95), as well as home-made soup (£1.75), cockles and mussels poached in white wine and cream (£3), fish crumble or hazelnut and vegetable loaf with green pepper sauce (£5.45), home-made steak and kidney pie (£5.50), venison sausages (£5.75), spiced lemon chicken with leek and stilton sauce (£6.85), steaks (from £9.25), daily specials, puddings like home-made coffee, cream and brandy trifle (£2.35), and children's dishes (from 90p); on Tuesday lunchtimes, they only serve soup and sandwiches. Well kept Theakstons Best, Black Bull and XB, and Youngers Scotch and No 3 on handpump, and 65 whiskies. There are tables out in a small but attractively planted garden. *(Recommended by Mr and Mrs R P Begg, Ann and Colin Hunt; more reports please)*

Free house ~ Licensees Robert and Jill Snowdon ~ Real ale ~ Meals and snacks (not Sun or Tues evening) ~ (01653) 648416 ~ Children welcome ~ Open 12-3, 6.30-11; closed 25 Dec

THORNTON WATLASS (N Yorks) SE2486 Map 10
Buck 🍴 🛏 🍺

Village signposted off B6268 Bedale—Masham

Sunday is a popular day to visit this very friendly country pub – part of a row of low stone cottages. The sheltered garden with its equipped children's play area and barbecues is a draw for families, the quoits team practise then, and they have monthly jazz at lunchtime. The hanging baskets are lovely and the inn looks past a grand row of sycamores to the village cricket green (they have a team). Trout fishing is available on the Ure, and there are plenty of good surrounding walks – their walking holidays remain well liked. The pleasantly traditional right-hand bar has handsomely upholstered old-fashioned wall settles on the carpet, a fine mahogany bar counter, a high shelf packed with ancient bottles, several mounted fox masks and brushes (the Bedale hunt meets in the village), a brick fireplace, and a relaxed atmosphere. Good, popular food at lunchtime might include light dishes such as mushroom rarebit with wensleydale cheese, Theakstons Ale, and a rasher of bacon or locally smoked kipper and scrambled egg (£3.25), and melon, ham, pâté, salad and french bread (£4.25), as well as soups like celery and potato, carrot and apple or cheese and ale (£1.95), red bean and green vegetable stir-fry (£5.50), Whitby cod or lasagne (£5.75), fillet of salmon with a light tarragon and cream sauce (£7.50), breast of duck with a honey and soy sauce (£8.95), and a traditional Sunday roast (£5.50); good vegetables and super breakfasts. The restaurant is no smoking. Well kept Black Sheep, John Smiths, Tetleys, Theakstons Best, and a guest beer on handpump, and around 40 malt whiskies. The beamed and panelled dining room is hung with large prints of old Thornton Watlass cricket teams. A bigger plainer bar has darts, pool, and dominoes. *(Recommended by Chris and Andy Crow, David and Fiona Pemberton, Angus Lyson, Anthony Barnes, R N Hutton, E A Thwaite, Ian Phillips, Viv Middlebrook, J R Whetton, Allen Sharp)*

Free house ~ Licensees Michael and Margaret Fox ~ Real ale ~ Meals and snacks (not 25 Dec) ~ Restaurant ~ (01677) 422461 ~ Well behaved children welcome ~ Organ sing-along Sat/Sun evenings, jazz monthly Sun lunchtime ~ Open 11-2.30, 6-11; 11-11 Sat; 12-10.30 Sun; closed evening 25 Dec ~ Bedrooms: £26(£32S)/£40(£48S)

THRESHFIELD (N Yorks) SD9763 Map 7

Old Hall 🍴 🍺

B6265, just on the Skipton side of its junction with B6160 near Grassington

People like to come back to this friendly pub again and again – it's that sort of place. The three communicating rooms have a good, bustling atmosphere, a mix of locals and visitors, simple, cushioned pews built into the walls, a high beam-and-plank ceiling hung with lots of chamber-pots, unfussy decorations such as old Cadburys advertisements and decorative plates on a high delft shelf, and a tall well blacked kitchen range. Using fresh, seasonal ingredients, the good bar food might include sandwiches, fresh home-made pasta filled with sun-dried tomatoes, cheese and herbs and a tomato sauce (£3.50), Thai crab spring rolls with a mango mayonnaise or grilled brie topped with apple purée and bacon (£3.75), Italian seafood salad (£4.45), jumbo battered haddock (£6.50), ostrich sausages casseroled with baby onions and bacon (£7.45), sweet and sour prawns (£7.50), fillet of fresh sea bass with a crab and white wine sauce (£8.25), chicken breast stuffed with mozarella with a port and mushroom sauce (£8.45), and 12oz fillet steak (£11.50); puddings such as iced tiramisu parfait, sticky toffee pudding or lemon tart (£2.50). Well kept Theakstons Best and Mild, Timothy Taylors Bitter and Landlord and summer guest beers on handpump, and quite a few malt whiskies. Darts, dominoes, and piped music. A neat side garden, partly gravelled, with young shrubs and a big sycamore has some tables and an aviary with cockatiels and zebra finches. This is, of course, a fine base for dales walking; there are two cottages behind the inn for hire. *(Recommended by Andrew and Ruth Triggs, J E Rycroft, James Todd, Gwen and Peter Andrews, Robert and Ann Lees, JKW, Bob and Maggie Atherton, Wayne Brindle, M Joyner)*

Free house ~ Licensees Ian and Amanda Taylor ~ Real ale ~ Meals and snacks (not Mon) ~ Restaurant ~ (01756) 752441 ~ Children welcome (but not in restaurant in evening) ~ Open 11.30-3, 5.30-11; closed Mon lunchtime

WAKEFIELD (W Yorks) SE3321 Map 7

Tap & Spile 🍺

77 Westgate End

New licensees have taken over this traditional gas-lit pub yet again this year, but have kept the fine range of real ales on handpump. As well as their regulars like Tap & Spile Premium (brewed for them by Ushers) and Original (brewed for them by Youngs), there are guests like Big Lamp Bitter, Marston Moor Cromwell Bitter, Morlands Old Speckled Hen, Roosters Cream and Special on handpump. The main bar has flagstones, leatherette cushioned built-in wooden wall seats with high backs, snob-screens, Victorian-style flowery wallpaper, honey-coloured vertical-planked dado, and brewery mirrors; several little rooms leading off the corridor; attractive

Victorian fireplaces with tiled surrounds. Cheap bar snacks include sandwiches (£1.30), filled baked potatoes (from £1.50), and ploughman's or haddock and chips (£2.70). No children. *(Recommended by Roger Bellingham, Michael Butler, Wayne Brindle; more reports please)*

Free house ~ Licensees Alan and Christine Coles ~ Real ale ~ Lunchtime meals and snacks (12-2) ~ (01924) 375887 ~ Open 12-11

WASS (N Yorks) SE5679 Map 7

Wombwell Arms 🍽 🛏 ♀

Back road W of Ampleforth; or follow brown tourist-attraction sign for Byland Abbey off A170 Thirsk—Helmsley

Even on your first visit you can be sure of a warm welcome from the friendly and courteous licensees. The little central bar is spotlessly kept and cosy, and the three low-beamed dining areas are comfortable and inviting and take in a former 18th-c granary. It's the fine choice of very appetising food that most people come here to enjoy: at lunchtime, there might be sandwiches (from £2.25; open ones from £3.90), lovely ploughman's with home-made pickles (£3.95), grilled sardines (£4.50), mushroom florentine or spiced prawns (£4.75), and lamb liver and bacon, venison sausages or salmon fishcakes (£5.75), with evening dishes such as pot roasted lamb shank (£7.25), lamb cutlets on leeks (£7.95), pork fillet with mushroom and a dijon mustard sauce (£8.25), sea bass (£8.50), and halibut fillet (£8.75). Well kept Black Sheep Bitter, Timothy Taylors Landlord, and a guest such as Durham Pagan, Rising Sun Sun Stroke, Shepherd Neame Spitfire or Wadworths Old Timer on handpump, decent malt whiskies, and around 8 wines by the glass. They may open on some winter Sunday evenings for live music. *(Recommended by Mr and Mrs R P Begg, Paul Boot, R Borthwick, S Clegg, Greta and Christopher Wells, Barry and Anne, Allan Worsley, Andy and Jane Beardsley, John and Chris Simpson, Bob and Maggie Atherton, John and Pippa Stock, SRP, David Surridge, W Rinaldi-Butcher)*

Free house ~ Licensees Alan and Lynda Evans ~ Real ale ~ Meals and snacks ~ (01347) 868280 ~ Children in eating area of bar (no under-5s evening) ~ Open 12-2.30, 6.30(7 Sat)-11; winter weekday opening 7; closed Sun evening and all day Mon Oct-Apr, and 10 days in Jan ~ Bedrooms: £24.50B/£49B

WATH IN NIDDERDALE (N Yorks) SE1467 Map 7

Sportsmans Arms 🍽 🛏 ♀

Nidderdale rd off B6265 in Pateley Bridge; village and pub signposted over hump bridge on right after a couple of miles

Although there is a bar where locals do drop in for just a drink in this delightful 17th-c inn, it is the marvellous food that people come to enjoy. Using only fresh produce, local where possible, the carefully presented and prepared food might include sandwiches, cream of parsnip and apricot soup (£2.95), chicken liver terrine with apple chutney (£4.60), Scottish king scallops glazed with garlic and gruyère (£4.95), fresh Nidderdale trout with bacon and capers (£7.25), roasted Scottish salmon with a sesame crust and hollandaise sauce (£7.50), Scarborough woof in a mustard and garlic crust (£7.80), fillet of Whitby cod on a bed of leeks glazed with a cheese sauce (£7.85), baked loin of local pork in a mushroom and tarragon sauce (£8.20), monkfish provençale (£8.50), breast of duckling cooked pink in a blackcurrant and orange sauce or local sirloin steak (£9.50), and puddings like chocolate roulade, raspberry crème brûlée or ginger sponge (from £3). The restaurant is no smoking. There's a very sensible and extensive wine list with an emphasis on the New World, good choice of malt whiskies, several Russian vodkas, and attentive service; open fire, dominoes. Benches and tables outside. *(Recommended by Janet and Peter Race, Gwen and Peter Andrews, Bob and Maggie Atherton; more reports please)*

Free house ~ Licensee Ray Carter ~ Meals and snacks (not 25 Dec) ~ Evening restaurant ~ (01423) 711306 ~ Children welcome ~ Open 12-3, 6.30-11; closed 25 Dec ~ Bedrooms: £35(£39S)/£55(£60S)

WIDDOP (W Yorks) SD9333 Map 7

Pack Horse

The Ridge; from A646 on W side of Hebden Bridge, turn off at Heptonstall signpost (as it's a sharp turn, coming out of Hebden Bridge road signs direct you around a turning circle), then follow Slack and Widdop signposts; can also be reached from Nelson and Colne, on high, pretty road; OS Sheet 103, map ref 952317

Considering its isolation high up on the moors, this friendly, traditional walkers' pub is remarkably popular. The bar has window seats cut into the partly panelled stripped stone walls that take in the moorland view, sturdy furnishings, and warm winter fires. Generous helpings of good bar food include sandwiches, tasty soup, cottage hotpot, ploughman's, home-made steak and kidney pie, steaks, and specials such as haddock mornay (£5.95), grilled salmon steaks (£6.95), and grilled halibut or sea bass and rack of lamb (£8.95). Well kept Theakstons XB, Thwaites Bitter and Craftsman, and Youngers IPA on handpump, around 100 single malt whiskies, and some Irish ones as well, and New World wines; efficient service. There are seats outside. *(Recommended by Dave Braisted, Karen Eliot, PGP, RTM, JCM, Laura Darlington, Gianluca Perinetti)*

Free house ~ Licensee Andrew Hollinrake ~ Real ale ~ Meals and snacks (see below) ~ (01422) 842803 ~ Children welcome until 8pm ~ Open 12-3, 7-11; closed weekday lunchtimes and Mon Oct-Easter ~ Bedrooms: £28B/£40B

WIGHILL (N Yorks) SE4746 Map 7

White Swan

Village signposted from Tadcaster; also easily reached from A1 Wetherby bypass – take Thorpe Arch Trading Estate turn-off, then follow Wighill signposts; OS Sheet 105 map reference 476468

As we went to press, new licensees had been here just a few weeks and were finding their feet. They don't plan to make any major changes to this unspoilt village pub – except perhaps to the menu. There's a tiny characterful front bar (popular with locals), a bar opposite with lots of racing prints, a small lobby that's also a favoured place for locals to gather, and a back bar with a mix of old chairs and tables, and quite a few decorative plates, old theatrical memorabilia, and sporting prints on the wall; a dining room leads off this. Open fires in most rooms, and well kept Tetleys, Theakstons Best, and a guest beer on handpump. Bar food now includes sandwiches (from £1.95), roasted stuffed pepper with sun-dried tomato risotto (£4.25), steak and mushroom pie (£4.75), pasta with ham and wild mushrooms (£4.95), salmon with lime and ginger butter (£7), and puddings (£2.25). There's a terrace overlooking the garden where there are lots of seats. *(Recommended by Dr A C and Dr A Jackson, Beryl and Bill Farmer, Chris Westmoreland, Tim and Sue Halstead; more reports on the new regime, please)*

Free house ~ Licensees Julie and Chris Williams ~ Real ale ~ Meals and snacks (not Mon evenings) ~ Restaurant ~ (01937) 832217 ~ Children in restaurant or family room ~ Open 12-3, 6-11

WORMALD GREEN (N Yorks) SE3065 Map 7

Cragg Lodge £

A61 Ripon—Harrogate, about half way

This comfortably modernised dining pub keeps what is probably the widest choice of malt whiskies in the world. There are nearly 1,000 of them, including two dozen Macallans going back to 1937. They have 16 price bands, between £1.15 and £6.50, depending on rarity – with a 17th 'by negotiation' for their unique 1919 Campbelltown. Also, well kept Tetleys Bitter and Theakstons Best, XB and Old Peculier on handpump, several distinguished brandies, and mature vintage port by the glass. The big open-plan bar is laid out for eating and has Mouseman furniture as well as little upholstered chairs around dark rustic tables, horsebrasses and pewter tankards hanging from side beams, a dark joist-and-plank ceiling, and a coal fire. Bar food at lunchtime includes home-made soup (£1.30), sandwiches (from £1.35), ploughman's (£2.80), cottage pie or home-made steak and kidney pie (£3.50), vegetarian nut cutlets or lasagne (£3.90), gammon and egg (£4.50), steaks (from £7.50), and a daily roast; in the evenings, there's a larger, more elaborate menu, with more emphasis on fish such as halibut bretonne (£6), fish pie (£6.50), and salmon and plaice in a white wine and grape sauce (£6.80). The restaurant is partly no smoking. Shove-ha'penny, cribbage, dominoes and piped music. There are picnic tables under cocktail parasols on the side terrace, with more in a sizeable garden and pretty hanging baskets in summer. The pub is popular with older people. *(More reports please)*

Free house ~ Licensee Garfield Parvin ~ Real ale ~ Meals and snacks ~ Restaurant (not Sun evening) ~ (01765) 677214 ~ Children in restaurant ~ Open 11.30-2.30, 6-11 ~ Bedrooms: £30B/£50B

YORK (N Yorks) SE5951 Map 7
Black Swan

Peaseholme Green; inner ring road, E side of centre; the inn has a good car park

Said to be haunted by three different ghosts, this is a surprisingly unspoilt pub – and deservedly popular. The busy black-beamed back bar (liked by locals) has wooden settles along the walls, some cushioned stools, and a throne-like cushioned seat in the vast brick inglenook, where there's a coal fire in a grate with a spit and some copper cooking utensils. The cosy panelled front bar, with its little serving hatch, is similarly furnished but smaller and more restful. The crooked-floored hall that runs along the side of both bars has a fine period staircase (leading up to a room fully panelled in oak, with an antique tiled fireplace). Good bar food includes sandwiches, filled french sticks, generously filled giant home-made yorkshire puddings (£2.25), and home-made steak pie, lasagne or vegetable curry (all £3.95). Well kept Bass, Stones, Timothy Taylors Landlord and Worthington Best on handpump; they have a happy hour on Sunday-Thursday between 4.30 and 7pm (not December); dominoes, fruit machine, trivia, and piped music. If the car park is full, it's worth knowing that there's a big public one next door. The timbered and jettied facade here and original lead-latticed windows in the twin gables are very fine indeed. *(Recommended by Chris Westmoreland, M Walker, Jamie and Ruth Lyons, Ann and Colin Hunt)*

Bass ~ Manager Pat O'Connell ~ Real ale ~ Meals and snacks (not Fri or Sat evenings) ~ (01904) 625236 ~ Children in separate room ~ Folk Thurs evening ~ Open 11-11; 12-10.30 Sun ~ Bedrooms: /£50B

Olde Starre

Stonegate; pedestrians-only street in centre, far from car parks

It's not surprising that this pub is so popular, as this is one of Yorks's prettiest streets – but even when really busy, staff remain friendly and helpful. It is the city's oldest licensed pub (1644), and the main bar has original panelling, green plush wall seats, a large servery running the length of the room, and a large leaded window with red plush curtains at the far end. Several other little rooms lead off the porch-like square hall – one with its own food servery, one with panelling and some prints, and a third with cream wallpaper and dado; the tap room is no smoking. Well kept Ruddles County, John Smiths Best, and Theakstons Best and XB on handpump, and decent whiskies – most spirits are served in double measures for a single's price; piped music, fruit machine and CD juke box. Good bar food includes sandwiches (from £2.50), generous ploughman's (£3.95), steak and kidney pie or chicken with lemon and tarragon (£3.95), lamb stew, sweet and sour pork or cumberland sausage (£4.25), and puddings (£1.95). Parts of the building date back to 900 and the cellar was used as a hospital in the Civil War. *(Recommended by Esther and John Sprinkle, Mark Walker, Gill and Andy Plumb, A and R Cooper, M Borthwick, John Fazakerley, Andrew and Ruth Triggs, Ann and Colin Hunt, Jamie and Ruth Lyons, J R Whetton)*

S & N ~ Managers Bill and Susan Embleton ~ Real ale ~ Meals and snacks (11.30-3, 5.30-8) ~ (01904) 623063 ~ Children in three areas away from bar ~ Open 11-11; 12-10.30 Sun

Spread Eagle ▮

98 Walmgate

A friendly new licensee has taken over this enjoyable, bustling pub, and as well as Mansfield Riding, Bitter and Old Bailey on handpump, they have guests such as Theakstons XB, Timothy Taylors Landlord, and Yongers No 3; country wines and malt whiskies. The main bar is a dark vault and two smaller, cosier rooms lead off – lots of old enamel advertisements and prints on the walls, and a relaxed atmosphere. Large helpings of good value bar food might include sandwiches (from £1.50), various pasta dishes with different sauces (from £3.50), and daily specials such as pork and pepper stir-fry (£3.95), chicken breast with smoked cheese in a cream and wine sauce (£6.95). Fruit machine, trivia, juke box, and piped music. (*Recommended by Esther and John Sprinkle, Dr A C and Dr A Jackson, P R Morley, Gary Nicholls*)

Mansfield Brewery ~ Manager Mike Dandy ~ Real ale ~ Meals and snacks (noon-10pm Mon-Sat) ~ Restaurant ~ (01904) 635868 ~ Children welcome ~ Live Blues Sun lunchtime ~ Open 11-11

Tap & Spile £ ▮

Monkgate

Just north of the city walls, this traditionally furnished pub is as popular as ever for its marvellous choice of up to eleven well kept real ales: Tap & Spile Premium and Bitter (brewed for them by Youngs), Old Mill Bitter and Theakstons Old Peculier, and seven constantly changing guests on handpump; five ciders, country wines, and some malt whiskies. The big split-level bar has bare boards, green leatherette wall settles right around a big bay window, with a smaller upper area with frosted glass and panelling; darts, shove-ha'penny, cribbage, dominoes, fruit machine, video game, and piped music. Simple cheap bar food includes sandwiches (from £1.55), filled baked potatoes (from £1.80), filled giant yorkshire puddings (from £2.95), and daily specials (around £3.20); popular Sunday roast lunch (£3.25). There are a few picnic tables outside. (*Recommended by Carole and Philip Bacon, PM, AM, Drs A and A C Jackson, Chris Westmoreland, Jamie and Ruth Lyons*)

Pubmaster ~ Manageress Carole Rutledge ~ Real ale ~ Meals and snacks ~ (01904) 656158 ~ Well behaved children welcome ~ Open 11.30-11

Lucky Dip

Besides the fully inspected pubs, you might like to try these Lucky Dips recommended to us and described by readers (if you do, please send us reports):

☆ Aberford W Yor [Old North Rd; best to use A642 exit off A1; SE4337], *Swan*: Huge choice of good value food in attractively refurbished dining place, lots of black timber, prints, pistols and cutlasses, cosy layout, Sun carvery, well kept Whitbreads-related ales, generous glasses of wine, polite uniformed staff, more upmarket upstairs restaurant; separate ticket system for each course; comfortable bedrooms (*Mark Gillis, Roy Bromell, L Sovago*)

Aberford [Old North Rd], *Arabian Horse*: Relaxed down-to-earth beamed local with comfortable lounge area, friendly staff, lunchtime food, good fire, well kept Theakstons Best; open all day Sat (*Mark Gillis, Martin Hickes*)

Addingham W Yor [SE0749], *Craven Heifer*: Pleasant modernised lofty beamed lounge, two fireplaces, dark green plush, lots of country prints; good choice of usual food (not Mon lunchtime), Tetleys-related ales, piped music; steep steps from car park (*WAH*)

Aislaby N Yor [SE7886], *Huntsman*: Carefully refurbished characterful old inn, tables well laid out, very efficient cheerful service, good value food, well kept beers, friendly locals; busy weekends and holidays (*M Borthwick*)

☆ Aldbrough St John N Yor [off A1 signed to Piercebridge, then signed off to left; NZ2011], *Stanwick Arms*: Lovely country pub with happy staff, good food with Barbados influence in bar, bistro and restaurant, Black Sheep and John Smiths Magnet, good log fire, all clean and tidy; seats outside; children welcome, bedrooms (*Nichola Watson, Anthony Barnes, J A Rae*)

☆ Allerthorpe E Yor [off A1079 nr Pocklington; SE7847], *Plough*: Cheery two-room lounge bar with snug alcoves, hunting prints, WWII RAF and RCAF photographs, open fires, wide choice of good value food from sandwiches to steaks inc vegetarian and children's, well kept Tetleys and Theakstons XB and Old Peculier, restaurant, games extension with pool, juke box etc; pleasant garden, handy for Burnby Hall (*John and Sheila French, Roger Bellingham, Ian Phillips, David and Julie Glover, LYM*)

Appleton Roebuck N Yor [SE5542], *Shoulder*

of Mutton: Cheerful and attractive pub/steak bar overlooking village green, wide choice of good value food, Sam Smiths OB and Museum, quick service; can be crowded with caravanners summer; bedrooms *(Michele and Clive Platman)*

☆ **Appletreewick** N Yor [SE0560], *New Inn*: Welcoming stonebuilt pub with good value simple food inc good sandwiches, well kept beers inc Daleside, willing service, interesting photographs, pub games, family room, no music; in fine spot, lovely views, garden, good walking; bedrooms *(Bernard and Marjorie Parkin, Gwen and Peter Andrews, LYM)*

☆ **Arncliffe** N Yor [off B6160; SD9473], *Falcon*: Classic old-fashioned haven for walkers, ideal setting on moorland village green, no frills, Youngers tapped from cask to stoneware jugs in central hatch-style servery, generous plain lunchtime bar snacks, open fire in small bar with elderly furnishings and humorous sporting prints, airy back sunroom (children allowed here lunchtime) looking on to garden; run by same family for generations – they take time to get to know; cl winter Thurs evenings; bedrooms (not all year), good breakfasts and evening meals – real value *(Neil and Angela Huxter, Sally Johnson, LYM)*

☆ **Askwith** N Yor [3 miles E of Ilkley; SD1648], *Black Horse*: Biggish family pub in lovely spot, good views from terrace, good choice of well cooked food (best to book Sun lunch), well kept ales inc Theakstons Best and XB, pleasant helpful staff, open fire *(Prof S Barnett)*

Atwick E Yor [The Green; B1242 N of Hornsea; TA1950], *Black Horse*: Two comfortable rooms with old photographs, three real ales, straightforward food; TV, piped music and fruit machines; dogs and children welcome *(JJW, CMW)*

☆ **Bainbridge** N Yor [A684 Leyburn—Sedbergh; SD9390], *Rose & Crown*: Ancient inn overlooking moorland village green, charming old-fashioned beamed and panelled front bar with big log fire, locals' bar with pool, juke box etc, John Smiths Magnet and Websters Yorkshire, bar food from sandwiches up, restaurant, children welcome, open all day, bedrooms *(JKW, LYM)*

☆ **Bardsey** W Yor [A58 – OS Sheet 104 map ref 363429; SE3643], *Bingley Arms*: Ancient pub with decor to match, very wide range of good value bar food (stops 8) inc interesting hot sandwiches and children's dishes in spacious lounge divided into separate areas inc no-smoking, well kept Black Sheep, Tetleys Bitter and Mild, pleasant speedy service, smaller public bar, picturesque upstairs brasserie, charming quiet terrace with interesting barbecues inc vegetarian; bedrooms comfortable *(David Craine, Ann Reeder, Martin Hickes, Drs A and A C Jackson)*

☆ **Barkisland** W Yor [Stainland Rd; SE0520], *Griffin*: Welcoming and tastefully refurbished cottagey rooms inc cosy oak-beamed parlour, open fires, lots of woodwork, good value food, well kept Bass, Ryburn and Worthington BB, restaurant *(Geoffrey and Brenda Wilson, Ann and Bob Westbrook, Anselm Bassano)*

Barkston N Yor [A162 Tadcaster—Sherburn; SE4936], *Ash Tree*: Thriving roadside dining pub with bar, dining area and restaurant (need to book); wide choice of decent food, well kept Black Bull, Theakstons and Youngers No 3, games machine, garden with picnic tables, swings and fruit trees *(JJW, CMW, Chris Westmoreland)*

☆ **Barnsley** S Yor [Cundy Cross; Grange Lane (A633); SE3706], *Mill of the Black Monks*: Former watermill said to date from 12th century, lovely old stonework in split-level bar and restaurant, five well kept S&N/Courage ales, candlelight, saucy ghost; shame about the piped pop music, live music most nights; big garden with picnic tables, mature trees, swings, pens of ducks and small animals, maybe bouncy castle *(Richard Holmes, Fran Reynolds, Michael Butler)*

nr **Barnsley** S Yor [Park Dr, Stainborough; nr Northern College, about 2½ miles NW of M1 junction 36 – OS Sheet 110 map ref 325038; SE3203], *Strafford Arms*: Pretty stone-built village pub with L-shaped bar and restaurant, sporting photographs, china and pennants, darts, dominoes, cribbage and games machine, Vaux Samson and Waggle Dance, decent food, nice log fire; piped music; garden with play area *(JJW, CMW)*

Bawtry S Yor [Gainsborough Rd; SK6593], *Ship*: Good value bar food under new landlord *(E Robinson)*

☆ **Beverley** E Yor [TA0340], *Beverley Arms*: Spacious traditional oak-panelled bar in comfortable and well run long-established hotel with well kept ales, choice of several decent places to eat inc interesting former coachyard (now enclosed) with formidable bank of the ranges that were used for cooking; good bedrooms, some with Minster view *(Roger Bellingham, Andy and Jill Kassube, LYM)*

Beverley [Wednesday Market], *Queens Head*: Cosy, with well kept Wards, Vaux Mild and guest beers, good value food (evenings too), dining area, efficient prompt service; pool room *(Q Williamson, M Walker)*; [North Bar Without], *Rose & Crown*: Fast courteous service, decent straightforward food inc good speciality giant haddock; bedrooms *(I Maw)*; [1 Flemingate], *Tap & Spile*: Bare boards and exposed brick, open all day every day, reasonable food (service can slow), eight real ales, no-smoking area, darts, fruit machine *(JJW, CMW)*

Bielby E Yor [SE7943], *College Arms*: Floral prints and red plush, good solid Yorkshire food, Tetleys ales, games room and nice back garden; children welcome, cl weekday lunchtimes *(H Bramwell)*

Bingley W Yor [Ireland Bridge; B6429, just W of junction with A650; SE1039], *Brown Cow*: Genuine and unpretentious, open-plan but snugly divided, with easy chairs, toby jugs, lots of pictures, panelling; bar food from sandwiches to steaks, no-smoking restaurant, well kept Timothy Taylors Bitter, Best, Landlord and winter Ram Tam; maybe piped music; children welcome, tables on sheltered terrace, pleasant spot; jazz Mon *(Steve Harvey,*

C *Westmoreland, LYM; reports on new regime please);* [Gilstead Lane, Gilstead], *Glen*: Open all day, with good choice of reasonably priced food from good sandwiches to steaks, well kept Tetleys Mild, Bitter and a guest ale, pleasant staff, railway memorabilia; garden with play area, rural setting *(Pat and Tony Martin, J E Rycroft)*

Birstall W Yor [Church Lane, off Bradford—Dewsbury rd at church – OS Sheet 104 map ref 218262; SE2126], *Black Bull*: Old building opp ancient Norman church, low beams, lots of panelling, former upstairs courtroom, Whitbreads-related ales, well priced home-made food inc bargain early meals, old local photographs; recent small extension *(Michael Butler)*

Bishopthorpe N Yor [SE5947], *Ebor*: Popular and lively local nr main entrance to Archbishop of York's Palace (hence name), beautiful hanging baskets and big well planted garden; lounge opening into dining area, good standard food esp steaks, friendly quick service, Sam Smiths; children welcome *(Thomas Nott, Shirley Pielou)*

☆ Bolton Percy N Yor [SE5341], *Crown*: Basic unpretentious country local, well kept Sam Smiths, generous simple food (not Mon or Tues), low prices, friendly dogs, tables on sizeable terrace with ageing pens of ornamental pheasants, quiet setting nr interesting 15th-c church and medieval gatehouse; children welcome *(Nick Wikeley, Janet Pickles)*

☆ Boroughbridge N Yor [St James Sq; SE3967], *Black Bull*: Lovely old pub in attractive village, well kept Black Sheep and John Smiths, decent wines and coffee, good range of well presented food in bar and restaurant, attentive friendly service; cosy and attractive rooms leading off bar; newish bedrooms wing, good breakfast *(Eric and Shirley Broadhead, Colin and Ann Hunt, James Nunns)*

Bradfield S Yor [High Bradfield, NW of Sheffield – OS Sheet 110 map ref 268927; SK2692], *Old Horns*: Friendly old inn, not spoilt by recent refurbishment – open-plan with divisions, inc a no-smoking area; good choice of reasonably priced food, efficient friendly staff, ales such as Boddingtons, Courage Directors, John Smiths Magnet and Stones; garden with play area, interesting hill village with stunning views *(Alan and Heather Jacques)*

☆ Bradford W Yor [Preston St (off B6145); SE1633], *Fighting Cock*: Busy bare-floor basic alehouse with good choice of particularly well kept ales such as Black Sheep, Exmoor Gold, Sam Smiths, Timothy Taylors, Theakstons, also farm ciders, foreign bottled beers, snacks, coal fires; low prices *(Susan and Nigel Wilson, Reg Nelson, LYM)*

Bradford [Low Moor, Huddersfield Rd], *British Queen*: Unspoilt unpretentious working-class local, well kept Tetleys, coal fire in idyllic back room *(Reg Nelson)*; [Grattan Rd/Barry St], *Castle*: Plain town local owned by group of small independent brewers, distinguished by its good collection of cheap well kept unusual ales such as Goose Eye Bitter and Wharfedale, Griffin Lions, Merry Marker, Riding Bitter and

Mild, Ryburn, Timothy Taylors Golden Pale; basic cheap food, well reproduced piped music (maybe some live) *(Pat and Tony Martin, Susan and Nigel Wilson, BB)*; [Heaton Rd], *Fountain*: Popular and pleasant with good staff, hard-working landlord, good food and beer; probably one of the most civilised pubs in the first town where the police offered their services to pubs as paid security guards *(J E Rycroft)*; [off City St], *Office*: Congenial warmly welcoming corner free house extended into former working men's club, big lounge area, raised pool area, glitzy dining room, wide range of interesting inexpensive food, Boddingtons, Stones, Tetleys and Theakstons *(Ian Phillips)*; [Kirkgate/Ivegate], *Rams Revenge*: Bare boards, basic good value food, well kept Theakstons XB; can be very warm *(G P Kernan)*

Bramham W Yor [The Square; just off A1 2 miles N of A64; SE4243], *Red Lion*: Former Gt North Rd coaching inn substantially well refurbished and opened up by Sam Smiths, quiet understated decor, usual food from good choice of sandwiches up *(Thomas Nott, K H Frostick)*

Bramhope W Yor [SE2543], *Fox & Hounds*: Popular civilised two-roomed pub with well kept Tetleys Mild and Bitter, lunchtime food, open fire; children welcome, has been open all day *(David Watson, Martin Hickes, J E Rycroft)*

Breighton E Yor [SE7134], *Olde Poachers*: Farmyard conversion tucked away in deep countryside, front courtyard gives coaching-inn impression but inside seems more medieval and gothic; comfortable roomy main bar with sofas and easy chairs, big medieval-style dining hall with heraldic shields and minstrels' gallery, good choice of generous bar and restaurant food; cl most weekday lunchtimes *(Ian Morley, H Bramwell)*

Brighouse W Yor [Brookfoot; A6025 towards Elland; SE1524], *Red Rooster*: Real ales such as Old Mill, Marstons Pedigree, Moorhouses Pendle Witches Brew, Timothy Taylors Landlord and several guests in homely smallish pub divided into separate areas inc one with books to read or buy; brewery memorabilia, knowledgeable landlord, open fire *(JP, PP)*

☆ Broughton N Yor [SD9351], *Bull*: Smartly modernised pub popular for good food inc children's meals in bar and restaurant; cosy and comfortable, pleasant busy atmosphere, friendly service, well kept John Smiths and Tetleys *(J E Rycroft, LYM)*

☆ Burnt Yates N Yor [B6165, 6 miles N of Harrogate; SE2561], *Bay Horse*: Friendly 18th-c dining pub with log fires, low beams, brasses; wide range of bar food, pleasant restaurant, traditional atmosphere; bedrooms in motel extension *(S Barclay)*

☆ Burton Leonard N Yor [off A61 Ripon—Harrogate; SE3364], *Hare & Hounds*: Good generous reasonably priced food inc fresh veg and good chips in cheerful spotless beamed bar and spacious restaurant, well kept Black Sheep, Tetleys and Theakstons, decent wines, quality service, paintings, copper and brass on walls, big fairy-lit beech branch over ceiling, cosy coffee lounge, no games or juke box *(Kathryn and Brian Heathcote, Prof and Mrs S Barnett, David Watson, Klaus D Baetz, Dorothy and David Young)*

Burton Salmon N Yor [just off A162 N of Ferrybridge; SE4927], *Plough*: Well kept ales usually inc a southern guest such as Ridleys, intimate yet spacious bar opening on to nice walled garden, side restaurant *(Chris Westmoreland)*

☆ **Cadeby** S Yor [off A1(M) via A630, then Sprotbrough turn; SE5100], *Cadeby Inn*: Biggish, with open fire, gleaming brasses and lots of house plants in back lounge, quieter front sitting room, no-smoking snug, separate games area; generous food from good hot beef sandwich to carvery, well kept Courage Directors, John Smiths and Magnet, Sam Smiths OB and Tetleys, over 200 malt whiskies, good service even when busy, seats out in front; children in eating area, open all day Sat *(L Dixon, F J Robinson, Peter Marshall, Lawrence Pearse, LYM)*

Calder Grove W Yor [just off M1 junction 39; A636 sign Denby Dale, then 1st right; SE3017], *Navigation*: Useful motorway break – cheery waterside bar full of canalia, with well kept Tetleys and Timothy Taylors Landlord, low prices, good simple food, tables outside *(P M Lane, LYM)*

Caldwell N Yor [NZ1613], *Brownlow Arms*: Small friendly pub in isolated village, landlord was the vicar; good home-cooked food, well kept local beer *(F C Johnston)*

Camblesforth N Yor [3 miles S of Selby; SE6426], *Comus*: Friendly, modernised with carpets and soft furnishings, well kept Tetleys and guest beers; popular lunchtime for huge helpings of reasonably priced food – the only pub with the same name as this reader-reporter, who holds the world record for the number of pubs he's visited *(Comus Elliott)*

☆ **Cawood** N Yor [SE5737], *Ferry*: Smallish comfortable rooms cleaned up by new landlord, massive inglenook, stripped brickwork, bare boards, well kept Adnams, Mansfield Riding and a good range of other ales tapped from the cask, good reasonably priced food from refitted kitchen, tables out on grass by river with swing bridge and flagstone terrace above *(Thomas Nott, Chris Westmoreland)*

Cawthorne S Yor [off A635 W of Barnsley; SE2808], *Spencer Arms*: Stone-built low-beamed pub in attractive village by Cannon Hall, lots of cosy alcoves, separate dining area, Whitbreads-related ales *(Michael Butler)*

☆ **Chapel le Dale** N Yor [B6655 Ingleton—Hawes, 3 miles N of Ingleton; SD7477], *Old Hill*: Basic stripped-stone flagstone-floor moorland bar with potholing pictures and Settle railway memorabilia, roaring log fire in cosy back parlour, well kept Dent and Theakstons Bitter, XB and Old Peculier, generous simple home-made food in separate room inc good beef sandwiches and pies, plenty of vegetarian; juke box; children welcome; bedrooms basic but good, with good breakfast – wonderful isolated spot, camping possible *(Donna Lisa Brackenbury, LYM)*

Chop Gate N Yor [Bilsdale; SE5699], *Buck*: Hospitable old-world stone pub with red plush seating, restaurant and garden, good range of meals and sandwiches, well kept Vaux ales; big garden with children's play area and Bilsdale views, good new bedrooms, handy for walks *(E J Cutting)*

Clapham N Yor [off A65 N of Settle; SD7569], *New Inn*: Riverside pub with small comfortable panelled lounge, Dent, John Smiths, Tetleys and Youngers No 3, public bar with games room, popular food in bar and restaurant; handy for walks *(J H and S A Harrop, Paul McPherson)*

☆ **Clifton** W Yor [Westgate; off Brighouse rd from M62 junction 25; SE1623], *Black Horse*: Comfortably smart dining pub, locally popular for enormous choice of good generous traditional food in recently redesigned restaurant; cosy oak-beamed bars, well kept Whitbreads-related beers, friendly service, open fire; bedrooms comfortable *(Michael Butler, Mrs P Tullie, Andrew and Ruth Triggs, RJH)*

☆ **Cloughton** N Yor [N of village; TA0096], *Hayburn Wyke*: Good reasonable priced food inc good value Sun carvery in attractive old rose-covered pub nr NT Hayburn Wyke and Cleveland Way coastal path, lots of tables outside, red-cushioned settles in beamed L-shaped bar, restaurant and eating area beyond; well kept John Smiths, Theakstons Best and Youngers, friendly new management, well behaved children welcome; bedrooms *(M Borthwick, Mike and Wendy Proctor)*

☆ **Cloughton Newlands** N Yor [A171; TA0196], *Bryherstones*: Several interconnecting rooms, well kept Youngers, over 50 whiskies, decent generous food, plenty of atmosphere, welcoming locals and new management; pool room, quieter room upstairs; children welcome, delightful surroundings *(M Borthwick, T M Dobby, Mike and Wendy Proctor)*

Coley W Yor [a mile N of Hipperholme; Lane Ends, Denholme Gate Rd (A644 Brighouse—Keighley); SE1226], *Brown Horse*: Popular for good interesting sensibly priced home cooking, prompt quietly welcoming service by smart staff, well kept Courage-related ales, decent house wines, open fires in three bustling rooms, golfing memorabilia, pictures, delft shelf of china and bottles, no-smoking restaurant *(Geoffrey and Brenda Wilson, Jonathan Harrison)*

☆ **Crayke** N Yor [off B1363 at Brandsby, towards Easingwold; SE5670], *Durham Ox*: Relaxed old-fashioned flagstoned lounge bar with antique settles and other venerable furnishings, interestingly carved panelling, enormous inglenook log fireplace, bustling public area with darts and fruit machine, good usual bar food (not Sun evening) from sandwiches up, well kept Banks's, Camerons Bitter and Crown, and Marstons Pedigree; restaurant, children welcome, bedrooms *(Malcolm and Nancy Watson-Steward, Tim and Sue Halstead, P Sumner, Ian Morley, Peter and Anne Hollindale, Roger Bellingham)*

☆ **Danby** N Yor [NZ7109], *Duke of Wellington*: Roomy and popular, with wide choice of good value well cooked food inc vegetarian, friendly

efficient service, well kept ales such as
Camerons Ruby and Ruddles Best, good coffee;
bedrooms very well appointed *(Bruce and
Maddy Webster, Val Stevenson, Rob Holmes,
Bob Ellis, A N Ellis)*

Danby Wiske N Yor [off A167 N of
Northallerton; SE3499], *White Swan*: Handy
pub for coast-to-coast walk, friendly and
informal, with good value home cooking inc
own free range eggs, well kept beer; bedrooms
undistinguished but cheap and comfortable,
camping in back garden *(Ben Anderson)*

Denby Dale W Yor [A635 to Barnsley;
SK2208], *Dunkirk*: Cosy and low-ceilinged,
comfortable and friendly, good atmosphere,
several rooms inc games room, good freshly
cooked food *(Michael Butler)*

Dewsbury W Yor [Chidswell Lane, Shaw
Cross; SE2523], *Huntsman*: Cosy converted
cottages alongside urban-fringe farm, friendly
atmosphere, lots of brasses and bric-a-brac,
well kept Bass-related ales; no food evening or
Sun/Mon lunchtime, busy evenings *(Michael
Butler)*; [Station, Wellington Rd], *West Riding
Refreshment Rooms*: Attractively converted
station building, good food from nutritionist
licensee, wide variety of constantly changing
real ales, often from interesting small breweries;
occasional beer festivals *(Laura Anderson, H
Cooper)*

Driffield E Yor [Market Pl; TA0258], *Bell*:
Elegant and popular 18th-c inn with delightful
old-fashioned restaurant, long spaciously
comfortable red plush bar, former Corn
Exchange used as stripped-brick eating area
with lots of leafy-looking hanging baskets,
good bar food and splendid imaginative salad
bar; comfortable bedrooms *(Gordon Thornton,
Roger Bellingham)*

Dunford Bridge S Yor [Windle Edge Lane; off
A628 Barnsley—M'ter – OS Sheet 110 map ref
158023; SE1502], *Stanhope Arms*: Cheerful
family pub below the moors around Winscar
Reservoir, friendly attentive service, good value
straightforward food from sandwiches to big
Sun lunch, OAP lunches (not Sat-Mon),
afternoon teas summer Suns, well kept Timothy
Taylor Landlord, Mansfield Riding and Bitter
and a guest ale, pool room (with fruit machine);
piped music can be a bit loud; sizeable garden
with camping ground, occasional live music
(JJW, CMW, LYM)

Dunswell E Yor [Hull Rd; TA0735], *Ship*:
Pleasant, popular old pub open all day, good
food until 7pm inc 3 Sun roasts, five real ales,
long nautical-theme bar; piped music, games
machine; tables out in front and in garden
(JJW, CMW)

Easington N Yor [N Church Side; TA4019],
Granby: Modernised early 19th-c pub, long bar
with pool, darts, machines one end (pop music
may be rather loud), wide choice of reasonably
priced food, Bass and Theakstons; open all day
(JJW, CMW)

Easingwold N Yor [Market Pl; SE5270],
George: Smart pleasantly furnished bar areas in
market town hotel popular with older people,
good generous food inc good Sun roasts, well
kept ales inc North Yorkshire Flying Herbert,

friendly enthusiastic service; bedrooms *(Walter
and Susan Rinaldi-Butcher)*

East Keswick N Yor [Main St; SE3644], *Duke
of Wellington*: Tasty generous home-cooked
straightforward food (not Mon) inc good veg
and traditional puddings, big ornate Victorian
dining room, convivial bar with big open fire
(maybe loud juke box and lots of local youth
Sat night), friendly staff *(David Varney)*

☆ **East Marton** N Yor [Marton Bridge; A59
Gisburn—Skipton; SD9051], *Cross Keys*:
Roomy and comfortable old-fashioned pub
attractively set back behind small green nr
Leeds & Liverpool Canal (and Pennine Way),
log fire, interesting decor and furnishings, good
range of generous food at tempting prices inc
fine salads, wide choice of well kept ales inc
Black Sheep and Theakstons, decent wines,
quick friendly helpful service, children's area
(where the food counter is), evening restaurant;
tables outside *(Jack Hill, Sue and Mike Todd,
Gill and Keith Croxton, Bronwen and Steve
Wrigley, JF, Brian Ellis, LYM)*

East Morton W Yor [SE1042], *Busfeild Arms*:
Attractive country cottage with ivy around
door, impressively run as good value food pub
(popular with lunchtime businessmen), well
kept Bass, Stones and Worthington, good range
of wines, warmly friendly atmosphere,
interesting local historical prints; pleasant
village setting *(Geoffrey and Brenda Wilson, B
M Eldridge, D Stokes)*

Egton N Yor [NZ8106], *Horseshoe*: Traditional
low-beamed moorland village pub with good
value basic food such as pizzas and yorkshire
puddings, good choice of starters, well kept
Tetleys and Theakstons Bitter and Old Peculier,
warm welcome, open fire; may be closed some
winter lunchtimes; not to be confused with the
Horse Shoe down at Egton Bridge *(M
Borthwick, Andy and Jill Kassube, BB)*

Egton Bridge N Yor [signed off A171 W of
Whitby; NZ8005], *Postgate*: Moorland village
local with relaxed and informal atmosphere,
plenty of character, Camerons Lion and
Strongarm, Flowers IPA, Ind Coope Burton and
Tetleys, good value house wine, traditional
games in public bar, discreet piped music, bar
food, tables on sunny flagstoned terrace; can
get a bit smoky; open all day *(R Borthwick, S
Clegg, F M Bunbury, Andrew and Joan Life)*

Ellerby N Yor [just off A174 Whitby rd;
NZ8015], *Ellerby Inn*: Opened-up country
village inn with nice moorland strolls nearby,
good range of bar food (or choose from fancier
restaurant menu), John Smiths and Tetleys ales
and good choice of malt whiskies, lovely
secluded back garden surrounded by flowery
rockeries; bedrooms *(Bronwen and Steve
Wrigley, Michael Butler)*

☆ **Ellerton** E Yor [signed off B1228 – OS Sheet
105 map ref 705398; SE7039], *Boot & Shoe*:
Low-beamed 16th-c cottage, comfortable and
friendly, with very friendly new licensees doing
good generous reasonably priced food from
sandwiches to busy Sun lunches, interesting
puddings, well kept Old Mill and John Smiths;
children welcome, obliging service *(Mrs P J
Pearce, Derek and Sylvia Stephenson, LYM)*

Elslack N Yor [just off A56 Earby—Skipton; SD9249], *Tempest Arms*: The French landlord who made this comfortable pub so popular for good food has now left, and it's been taken over by Jennings, with a manager; it's still a restful stop, with separate areas, comfortable chintzy seats as well as all the tables, log fire, well kept ales, sheltered tables outside; children welcome, restaurant, comfortable bedrooms *(PGP, LYM)*

☆ **Embsay** N Yor [Elm Tree Sq; SE0053], *Elm Tree*: Civilised well refurbished open-plan beamed village pub with good bar food inc good-sized children's helpings, good service, old-fashioned prints, log-effect gas fire; half a dozen interesting well kept changing ales, games area, juke box; busy weekends esp evenings; comfortable bedrooms; handy for steam railway *(M Joyner, Mr and Mrs I B White, J E Rycroft)*

☆ **Escrick** N Yor [E of A19 York—Selby – OS Sheet 105 map ref 643425; SE6343], *Black Bull*: Warm cosy unpretentious village pub, well spaced tables in bar, good imaginative if not cheap freshly prepared food in good-sized comfortable and relaxed dining area, well kept beer, decent wines, very friendly staff; very popular weekends *(Roger Bellingham, Ann and Peter Shaw, John T Ames, Janet Pickles)*

☆ **Etton** E Yor [3½ miles N of Beverley, off B1248; SE9843], *Light Dragoon*: Roomily refurbished country local with wide range of decent bar food, well kept Youngers Scotch and IPA, inglenook fireplace, pleasant atmosphere and service, garden with play area *(RAB, Andy and Jill Kassube, E J Wilde, LYM)*

Fairburn N Yor [just off A1; SE4727], *Bay Horse*: Spacious and comfortable, with good generous cheap food inc good value roasts, pleasant staff, lake views from terrace; keg beer *(Douglas and Margaret Chesterman, Neil and Anita Christopher)*

☆ **Farndale East** N Yor [Church Houses; next to Farndale Nature Reserve; SE6697], *Feversham Arms*: Friendly pub in lovely daffodil valley (very busy then), two unspoilt but bright smallish rooms with flagstone floors and real fires, well kept John Smiths, good value home-cooked food, open fire, smart beamed and stripped-stone restaurant, high standard of service; very popular weekends; walkers with wet boots and dogs not welcome; nice small garden, good bedrooms, big breakfasts *(Chris Westmoreland, Dr Wallis Taylor, A M Pring)*

☆ **Felixkirk** N Yor [SE4785], *Carpenters Arms*: Comfortable old-world 17th-c dining pub in picturesque small village, big helpings of well presented good value food, well kept Tetleys, good friendly service, cosy bar, smart restaurant with own menu inc popular Sun lunch (should book), pleasant service *(H E and E A Simpson, Mike Ellis)*

Ferrensby N Yor [A6055 N of Knaresboro; SE3761], *General Tarleton*: Friendly staff, big open fire, cosy atmosphere, good reasonably priced home cooking in bar and restaurant, particularly well kept Black Sheep, Boddingtons, Tetleys, Theakstons, Timothy Taylors Landlord; reasonably priced good

bedrooms *(Deyrick Blake, Klaus D Baetz)*

☆ **Finghall** N Yor [Akebar Park, off A684 E of Leyburn; SE1890], *Friars Head*: Good imaginative fresh food in attractively converted barn, Black Sheep, John Smiths and Theakstons, good coffee, pleasant service, log fire, attractive stonework and beams, cosy nooks, big conservatory; looks over bowling green and pay-as-you-play golf, adjacent caravan site *(Michael and Susan Morgan, Dono and Carol Leaman, J H and S A Harrop)*

Firbeck S Yor [SK5688], *Black Lion*: Enjoyable free house in attractive village; generous reasonably priced meals *(Richard Cole)*

Flamborough N Yor [junction B1255/B1229; TA2270], *Royal Dog & Duck*: Friendly local with two homely comfortable beamed rooms, well kept Bass, usual food esp local fish; bedrooms *(Chris Westmoreland, LYM)*

Follifoot N Yor [SE3452], *Lascelles Arms*: Interesting reasonably priced food, good open fires, small and cosy lounge area, well kept Sam Smiths OB, decent wines *(J E Rycroft)*

Friendly W Yor [SE0524], *Brothers Grimm*: Well kept Tetleys, good value food at low prices *(PM, AM)*

☆ **Gargrave** N Yor [Church St/Marton Rd; SD9354], *Masons Arms*: Friendly and busy well run local, attractive and homely, well kept Whitbreads-related ales, generous quick bar food inc vegetarian and good sandwiches, copper-canopied log-effect gas fire dividing two open-plan areas; tables in garden, bowling green behind; children if well behaved; on Pennine Way, between river and church *(Wayne Brindle, WAH, P M Lane, A Preston)*

Gargrave N Yor [A65 W], *Anchor*: Big Brewers Fayre catering well for children and worth knowing for all-day food service (from 7.30 b'fast) and superb play area, with canalside tables; welcoming competent service, Whitbreads-related real ales, good wheelchair access; piped music; economically run bedrooms in modern wing *(F R Fell, George Atkinson, WAH, Richard Booth, LYM)*

Gate Helmsley N Yor [A166 York—Bridlington; SE6955], *Duke of York*: Good reasonably priced food inc some unusual dishes such as wild boar and kangaroo, bargain early suppers and OAP meals, friendly staff; small, rather smart and attractively decorated; open all day *(H Bramwell)*

Giggleswick N Yor [Brackenbar Ln; A65 Settle bypass; SD8164], *Old Station*: Handy stop on Settle bypass, generous straightforward home-made food inc excellent black pudding in L-shaped bar with brasses, railway prints and dining end, no-smoking restaurant, friendly staff, well kept John Smiths and Tetleys Mild and Bitter; bedrooms *(John Allsopp)*

Gilberdyke E Yor [B1230 just W; SE8329], *Rose & Crown*: Comfortable roadside pub with pool, games machine and TV in bar, comfortable lounge with pictures and old mirrors, and well kept Mansfield Riding and a guest ale such as Hoskins, decent food inc carvery, separate bar with pool and games machine; play area and a few picnic tables outside *(JJW, CMW)*

☆ **Goathland** N Yor [opp church, off A169; NZ8301], *Mallyan Spout*: Ivy-clad stone hotel, popular from its use by TV's *Heartbeat* series cast, with three spacious lounges (one no smoking), traditional relaxed bar, good open fires, fine views, well kept Malton Double Chance, good malt whiskies and wines; children in eating area, usually open all day, handy for Mallyan Spout waterfall; comfortable bedrooms *(Andy and Jill Kassube, R N Hutton, Phil and Heidi Cook, Frank Cummins, Derek and Sylvia Stephenson, Susan and Walter Rinaldi-Butcher, E A Thwaite, LYM)*

Goathland, *Goathland*: Welcoming big softly lit bar, huge log fire, brasses, old photographs etc, well kept Camerons Bitter and Strongarm, simple quickly served reasonably priced food, friendly staff, smaller plush lounge, stripped-stone restaurant; seats out in front, has doubled as pub in *Heartbeat*; comfortable bedrooms *(Phil and Heidi Cook, Andy and Jill Kassube, Dr Wallis Taylor)*

☆ **Grassington** N Yor [Garrs Lane; SE0064], *Black Horse*: Comfortable and cheerful open-plan modern bar, very busy in summer, with well kept Black Sheep Bitter and Special, Tetleys and Theakstons Best and Old Peculier, open fires, generous straightforward home-cooked bar food inc children's and vegetarian, darts in back room, sheltered terrace, small attractive restaurant; bedrooms comfortable, well equipped and good value *(Bill Sharpe, Prof and Mrs S Barnett, Dave and Karen Turner, Gill Cambridge, M Joyner, Mrs E Howe, BB)*

☆ **Grassington** [The Square], *Devonshire*: Busy and comfortable hotel, good window seats overlooking sloping village square, interesting pictures and ornaments, open fires, good range of well presented food inc good Sun lunch in big well furnished dining room, good family room, attentive Italian landlord, well kept McEwans 80/- and full range of Theakstons ales, tables outside; well appointed good value bedrooms, good breakfasts *(Gwen and Peter Andrews, Mr and Mrs C Roberts, J E Rycroft, LYM)*

Grassington [20 Main St], *Foresters Arms*: Unpretentious but friendly, with pleasant atmosphere and no music *(Prof and Mrs S Barnett)*

☆ **Great Broughton** N Yor [High St; NZ5405], *Wainstones*: Good value varied food and well kept Tetleys in pleasantly unpretentious hotel bar, friendly efficient staff, good restaurant, children welcome; bedrooms *(B B Watling, G Neighbour)*

Great Ouseburn N Yor [SE4562], *Three Horseshoes*: Four spotlessly kept areas, two for eating, low beams hung with vast collection of teapots and jugs, open fires, well kept Black Sheep, John Smiths and Theakstons Best, children welcome *(Angus Lyon)*

☆ **Grenoside** S Yor [Skew Hill Lane; 3 miles from M1 junction 35 – OS Sheet 110 map ref 328935; SK3293], *Cow & Calf*: Neatly converted farmhouse, three friendly connected rooms, one no smoking, high-backed settles, brass and copper hanging from beams, plates and pictures, good value hearty home-made bar food (not Sun evening) inc sandwiches and

children's, well kept Sam Smiths OB and Museum, tea and coffee; piped music; family room in block across walled former farmyard with picnic tables; splendid views over Sheffield, disabled access, open all day Sat *(JJW, CMW, G Washington, KCH, LYM)*

Grenoside [Main St], *Old Harrow*: Open-plan, with comfortable banquettes, plates, pictures and old photographs, adjoining flagstoned former tap room, good value basic lunchtime food, Boddingtons, Stones and Whitbreads Castle Eden; fruit machine, TV, darts, maybe loud piped music; small garden with picnic tables; children and dogs allowed *(JJW, CMW)*

☆ **Grinton** N Yor [B6270 W of Richmond; SE0598], *Bridge*: Attractive riverside inn in lovely spot opp charming church, two bars, very friendly service, well kept Black Sheep Special, John Smiths Magnet and Theakstons, decent wines, good range of good value simple well prepared food inc good steaks; attractive tables outside, front and back; bedrooms with own bathrooms; open all day *(Patrick and Lynn Billyeald, F M Bunbury)*

☆ **Halifax** W Yor [Paris Gates, Boys Lane – OS Sheet 104 map ref 097241; SE0924], *Shears*: Hidden down steep cobbled lanes among tall mill buildings, dark unspoilt interior, welcoming landlord, well kept Marstons Pedigree, Timothy Taylors Landlord and unusual guest beers; very popular lunchtime for good cheap food from hot-filled sandwiches to home-made pies, curries, casseroles etc; sporting prints, local sports photographs, collection of pump clips and foreign bottles; seats out above the Hebble Brook *(Mike, Ian and Gayle Woodhead)*

Halifax [Horsfall St, Savile Pk], *Big 6*: Old-fashioned Victorian mid-terrace pub with snugs, memorabilia, interesting bottle collection; quick friendly service, well kept Ind Coope Burton, Flowers and Tetleys *(Pat and Tony Martin)*; [New Rd, nr stn], *Pump Room*: No-frills pub very popular for its dozen or so well kept changing ales; clean and friendly *(Mike, Ian and Gayle Woodhead, Carl Travis)*; [Lee Lane, Shibden]; steep cobbled lane off A647 Queensbury rd], *Sportsman*: Fine Calderdale views from prominent hilltop which this friendly and comfortable 17th-c pub shares with dry ski slope and squash court; cheap lunches inc good value carvery, fine choice of real ales inc Old Mill, Timothy Taylors Landlord, Tetleys and guests, family extension *(Pat and Tony Martin)*; [Clare Rd], *Tap & Spile*: About eight changing well kept real ales, good usual bar food inc sandwiches and basket meals, solid furnishings, traditional games, no-smoking room; open all day *(Pat and Tony Martin)*

☆ **Hampsthwaite** N Yor [Main St; about 5 miles W of Harrogate; SE2659], *Joiners Arms*: Good food esp well presented good value Sun lunch, good atmosphere, well kept Courage-related ales, decent wines, smallish bar, well spaced dining room tables, and friendly staff; nice village setting *(Geoffrey and Brenda Wilson, F J Robinson)*

Harden W Yor [Long Ln, off B6165; SE0838],

Golden Fleece: Quietly welcoming lounge bar with local prints and plates on racks, small pool room, well kept Tetleys-related ales, bar food *(WAH)*

Harewood W Yor [SE3245], *Harewood Arms*: Busy former coaching inn opp Harewood House, three attractive, comfortable and spacious lounge bars with wide choice of good food from sandwiches up, friendly prompt service, well kept ales inc Sam Smiths OB, decent house wines; coffee and afternoon tea *(Janet Pickles)*

Harome N Yor [2 miles S of A170, nr Helmsley; SE6582], *Star*: Delightful little thatched pub of great character, a long-standing main entry, unfortunately closed towards the end of 1995, awaiting sale; we look forward to its reopening *(LYM)*

☆ **Harrogate** N Yor [Whinney Lane, Pannel Ash, off B6162 W; OS Sheet 104 map ref 287525; SE2852], *Squinting Cat*: Rambling big-brewery chain pub with dark oak panelling, beams, brasses and copper, stone-walled barn-like restaurant extension, well priced usual bar food from sandwiches to steaks inc popular Sun lunch, well kept Tetleys and guest beers, good range of New World wines, pleasant young staff, tables outside; piped music; open all day, handy for Harlow Carr gardens *(H Bramwell, H and D Payne, Karen Eliot, Gordon Thornton, Jack Morley, Andrew Hodges, LYM)*

☆ **Harrogate**, [Crimple Lane; A59/B6161 towards Skipton], *Travellers Rest*: Country pub in pleasant valley setting, beamed locals' bar, shiny woodwork in main bar, conservatory, two real fires, friendly service; good freshly but quickly prepared cheap food inc fish and Sun roasts, well kept Theakstons Best and XB and Youngers Scotch; children welcome, side play area *(Andrew and Ruth Triggs, C A Hall)*

Harrogate [Montpellier Gdns], *Drum & Monkey*: Not a pub but well worth knowing for downstairs fish bar, eat at bar or pub-style tables, good wines; busy, noisy and friendly *(Neville Kenyon)*

☆ **Hartoft End** N Yor [Pickering—Rosedale Abbey rd; SE7593], *Blacksmiths Arms*: Immaculate and civilised 16th-c wayside inn by moors, originally a farmhouse and gradually extended, lots of original stonework, brasses, cosy nooks and crannies, relaxing atmosphere, good bar food inc good fish and fresh veg, attractive restaurant with cane furnishings; bedrooms *(Enid and Henry Stephens, Bronwen and Steve Wrigley)*

Hatfield S Yor [High St, nr M18 junction 5; SE6609], *Bay Horse*: Small, bustling and friendly, with country furnishings, lots of china, good value food lunchtime and early evening, good service; children welcome *(Richard Cole)*

☆ **Hawnby** N Yor [SE5489], *Hawnby Inn*: Good choice of well cooked generous food in spotless inn, lovely location in village surrounded by picturesque countryside, a magnet for walkers; Vaux beers, friendly helpful service, owl theme; tables in garden with country views; well equipped bedrooms *(Addie and Irene Henry)*

Haworth W Yor [Main St; SE0337], *Black Bull*: Was Branwell B's main drinking place,

now a rather touristy open-plan Whitbreads pub, open all day, with focus on good value food noon-8.30; six real ales, quiet piped music and games machines; some no-smoking tables, children welcome; three bedrooms *(JJW, CMW, Michael Butler)*; [Main St], *Fleece*: Small partly panelled rooms, not too touristy, with flagstones, some carpeting, plants in pots and hanging baskets, well kept Timothy Taylors ales, coal fires in stone fireplaces, tasty reasonably priced food most lunchtimes, friendly staff; maybe piped disco/pop music *(Andrew Baren)*; [Main St], *Kings Arms*: Cosy and friendly ancient local with well kept Tetleys and several guest beers, bar food inc good home-made pies and casseroles, restaurant, Sun lunches *(Arnold Day)*; [West Lane], *Old White Lion*: Very good value food, well kept Websters and Wilsons, good popular restaurant (booked up Sat), friendly staff; warm and comfortable, very handy for museum; spotless comfortable bedrooms *(Arnold Day, Jenny and Brian Seller)*; [Bingley Rd, Lees Moor; off A629 N in Cross Roads village, towards Harden – OS Sheet 104 map ref 054381], *Quarry House*: Converted former farmhouse on high moors, almost more of a restaurant but has small interesting bar with upholstered settles and highly polished wood originally from pulpit in Beverley baptist chapel; well kept Ind Coope Burton, Theakstons Best, Timothy Taylors Landlord and Tetleys, good bar food inc notable soups, good steak sandwiches, pies and puddings, friendly staff; cricket ground next door *(Frank Cummins)*

Hebden Bridge W Yor [Thistle Bottom, a mile W; SD9927], *Stubbings Wharf*: Warm and friendly, in good spot by Rochdale canal, reasonably priced food, good-sized helpings; Whitbreads Castle Eden, good pool room *(A Morton)*; [nr clog factory], *Tythe Barn*: They will cook you anything you like (providing they have the ingredients); good waitress service, lovely surroundings *(SB)*

☆ **Helmsley** [Market Pl], *Black Swan*: Smart and attractive hotel, not a pub, but pleasant beamed and panelled bar with carved oak settles and windsor armchairs, cosy and comfortable lounges with a good deal of character, attentive staff, charming sheltered garden; good place to stay – expensive, but comfortable and individual *(Owen and Margaret Warnock, BB)*

Helmsley [Market Pl], *Royal Oak*: Friendly inn with three well decorated and comfortable rooms, antiques, good food inc superb roasts and filled yorkshire puddings, well kept Camerons; bedrooms good *(Andy and Jill Kassube, Ian and Margaret Borthwick)*

Helperby N Yor [Main St; SE4470], *Golden Lion*: Five interesting changing ales from smaller often distant brewers, good simple bar food, cosy atmosphere, friendly staff, no juke box or games; two beer festivals a year *(Charlie Brook, Chris Atkinson)*

Hemingfield S Yor [Beech House Rd, off A633 SE of Barnsley; SE3901], *Lundhill*: Early 19th-c, now considerably enlarged, with several areas off bar, dark beams, lots of brass, very friendly atmosphere, well kept ales inc Barnsley and both John and Sam Smiths, weekend bar food, upstairs no-smoking restaurant, picnic tables outside *(JJW, CMW, Jonathan Lees)*

Hepworth W Yor [38 Towngate, off A616 SE of Holmfirth – OS Sheet 110 map ref 163069; SE1606], *Butchers Arms*: Friendly L-shaped bar, jovial landlord, partly panelled stone walls, open fire, Boddingtons, Tetleys and Timothy Taylors Landlord, bar food, evening restaurant; pool and darts at one end; open all day Fri/Sat *(JJW, CMW)*

☆ **Holme** W Yor [SE1006], *Fleece*: Cosy pleasant L-shaped bar, lots of lifeboat memorabilia, well kept Tetleys, Theakstons and Youngers, good coffee, popular fresh pub food inc special offers, very welcoming landlord, efficient staff, real fire; conservatory with nice flowers, pool/darts room, quiet piped music; attractive village setting below Holme Moss TV mast, great walks *(Chloe Gartery, J E Rycroft, Gwen and Peter Andrews, Martin Hickes)*

Holme on Spalding Moor E Yor [SE8038], *Red Lion*: Well run village pub, clean and comfortable L-shaped bar, good food with fish emphasis in bar and restaurant, friendly staff, eclectic range of wines, sunny terrace with koi carp; comfortable bedrooms in cottages behind *(H Bramwell)*

Holmfirth W Yor [Victoria Sq – OS Sheet 110 map ref 143082; aka Rose & Crown; SD1408], *Nook*: Character local, tiled floor, low beams and basic furnishings, friendly atmosphere, Timothy Taylors and other well kept ales; fruit machine, video game; streamside seats outside *(JP, PP)*

☆ **Holywell Green** W Yor [handy for M62 junction 24; SE0820], *Rock*: Comfortably refurbished in Victorian style, with cosy bar areas, conservatory, well kept Black Sheep, Theakstons and Youngers, open fire, decent bar food, massive choice of good restaurant food; pleasantly decorated bedrooms *(Andy and Jill Kassube)*

Horbury W Yor [Quarry Hill; SE3018], *Quarry*: Popular with smart middle-age crowd, old photographs of stone quarry on stripped stone walls, relaxed affluent atmosphere, very satisfying well priced lunchtime bar meals, range of Bass beers *(Michael Butler)*

☆ **Hovingham** N Yor [SE6775], *Worsley Arms*: Smart atmosphere (linen even on tables out by stream), good value though not cheap well prepared food, interesting choice esp vegetarian, friendly and welcoming back bar, well kept Malton Double Chance and other ales, good coffee, kind staff, lots of Yorkshire cricketer photographs esp from 1930s and 40s; pleasant bedrooms *(R M Macnaughton, G J McGrath, BB)*

Howden E Yor [Mkt Pl; SE7530], *White Horse*: Comfortable banquettes, brass and pictures in U-shaped bar, pool, darts and two fruit machines, good value food inc Sun roast, children's helpings, four real ales *(JJW, CMW)*

Huddersfield W Yor [Chapel Hill, just outside ring rd – OS Sheet 110 map ref 143162; SE1416], *Rat & Ratchet*: Bare-boards two-room local brewing its own Experimental Ale alongside well kept ales inc Marstons Pedigree,

Smiles, Timothy Taylors Landlord and Best and lots of changing guest beers; two more comfortable rooms up steps, basic well cooked cheap bar food inc Weds curry night; opp public car park *(Tony and Wendy Hobden, A Preston)*; [Colne Bridge; B6118 just off A62 NE – OS Sheet 110 map ref 178201], *Royal & Ancient*: Spacious, comfortable and popular, with log fires, good interesting bar food, Bass and Whitbreads ales, plenty of atmosphere, welcoming service, restaurant *(Michael Butler)*; [1 Halifax Old Rd], *Slubbers Arms*: Warmly welcoming landlord in friendly V-shaped pub with good range of simple food (no chips), excellently kept Marstons Pedigree, Timothy Taylor Landlord and a guest beer, a dozen good malt whiskies *(John Allsopp)*

Huggate E Yor [SE8855], *Wolds*: Attractively refurbished small 16th-c pub popular for good inventive food, reasonable prices, friendly staff, benches out in front and pleasant garden behind with views, popular restaurant; cl Mon; lovely village, good easy walks *(H Bramwell)*

☆ **Hull** E Yor [Land of Green Ginger, Old Town; TA0927], *George*: Handsomely preserved traditional long Victorian bar, open all day; lots of oak, mahogany and copper, good choice of cheap, generous and tasty freshly cooked lunchtime food inc good fish, well kept Bass, Bass Mild and Stones, good service; quiet piped music, fruit machines, can get very busy – get there early; handy for the fine Docks Museum; children allowed in plush upstairs dining room *(Chris Westmoreland, JJW, CMW, Andy and Jill Kassube, Thomas Nott, LYM)*

Hull [Peel St], *Duke of Wellington*: Superior back-street local, finely decorated with interesting mirrors; efficient friendly staff, Timothy Taylors, Tetleys and many guest beers; pool, darts, weekly quiz *(Martin Walker)*; [9 Humber Dock St], *Green Bricks*: Early 19th-c inn overlooking marina, open all day, lunchtime and early evening meals, Bass and Stones, seating outside *(JJW, CMW)*; *King William III*: Large open rooms, Rugby League decor, real ales inc a house beer brewed for them in Cropston *(Thomas Nott)*; [77 Charles St], *New Clarence*: Big U-shaped bar partitioned for some cosiness, dark panelling, stone floors, four mainly Tetleys-related changing ales, pool, games machines, juke box, good value; open all day, handy for New Theatre *(JJW, CMW, Chris Westmoreland)*; [193 Cottingham Rd], *Old Gray Mare*: Former Newland Park, refurbished by Tom Cobleigh in country pub image, substantially extended; friendly efficient service, good range of well prepared good value food and ales inc Theakstons XB *(Roger Bellingham)*; [150 High St], *Olde Black Boy*: Tap & Spile in Old Town conservation area, little black-panelled low-ceilinged front smoke room, lofty 18th-c back vaults bar, good value upstairs dining room with very friendly if not speedy service, eight real ales, about 20 country wines, interesting Wilberforce-related posters etc, old jugs and bottles, quiet piped local radio, darts, piano *(JJW, CMW, BB)*; [Spring Bank], *Tap & Spile*: Usual bare boards and brick but comfortable banquettes in no-smoking area; framed brewery posters, eight real ales and Old Rosie farm cider, reasonably priced though not speedy food; piped music, fruit machine; small back terrace *(JJW, CMW)*; [nr Hessle Rd shops], *Whittington & Cat*: Beautifully restored, with many pictures of docks in their heyday, fine brasswork, leather banquettes, quality fittings; well kept cheap Mansfield *(Comus Elliott)*

Hunton N Yor [Leyburn Rd; SE1992], *New Inn*: Small friendly country local with very wide choice of changing food inc good vegetarian choice, using fresh produce inc home-made chips; helpful efficient service *(Mr and Mrs J Thompson, K Bowers)*

Hutton le Hole N Yor [SE7090], *Crown*: Friendly local with good service and food, well kept Tetleys, lots of whisky-water jugs, busy friendly atmosphere; children welcome; small pretty village with wandering sheep *(Chris and Andy Crow)*

Ingleby Cross N Yor [NZ4501], *Blue Bell*: Cosy country local, friendly service, well kept John Smiths Magnet and Theakstons Best, wide choice of good value often interesting bar food from sandwiches to steaks; simple but good bedrooms in converted barn, handy for coast-to-coast walk *(Rita and Keith Pollard)*

Ingleton N Yor [A65 towards Clapham; SD7170], *Goat Gap*: Welcoming and comfortable 17th-c inn with good value food, good range of beers, proper coffee, open fire, children welcome; picnic tables out among trees, play area; bedrooms *(Mr and Mrs D Irving)*

Jackson Bridge W Yor [Sheffield Rd; off A635 Holmfirth—New Mill; SE1607], *Red Lion*: Particularly well kept Tetleys and guests such as Bass, Black Sheep, Fullers London Pride and Theakstons, decent wines, good food from basic bar meals to more elaborate dishes, three friendly cosy rooms with dark wooden tables and chairs, red wall seats, plates and *Last of the Summer Wine* pictures, open fire, frequent jazz nights *(Jenny Wilson)*; [Scholes Rd, signed off A616], *White Horse*: Low-ceilinged small-roomed pub with blue plush wall seats and dining chairs, simple home-cooked early lunches, well kept Bass and Stones, coffee from 9am, friendly landlord, more *Last of the Summer Wine* pictures, pool room looking out on charming waterfall and ducks behind *(JJW, CMW)*

☆ **Kettlesing**, N Yor [signed off A59 W of Harrogate; SE2256], *Queens Head*: Friendly dining with nicely presented good food in wide price range, popular weekday lunchtimes with older people, lots of quite close-set tables, well kept Theakstons Best and XB, Youngers Scotch, good house wines, quick service, unobtrusive piped music, attractive and interesting decorations *(F J Robinson, Martin Hickes, J E Rycroft, BB)*

☆ **Kettlewell** N Yor [SD9772], *Racehorses*: Comfortable and civilised, with good well presented food, Black Sheep, John Smiths and Theakstons, good choice of wines, log fires, attentive service; well placed for Wharfedale walks; bedrooms good, with own bathrooms *(M Joyner, BB)*
Kettlewell, *Bluebell*: Roomy simply furnished

knocked-through local with snug areas and flagstones, friendly landlord, well kept beers (mainly S&N), good simple food; pool room, piped music, children's room, tables on good-sized back terrace; well placed for Upper Wharfedale walks; decent plain bedrooms *(Dr P Jackson, LYM)*; *Kings Head*: Lively and cheerful old character local away from centre, well kept ales such as Black Sheep, Tetleys, Timothy Taylors, good value food; pool room, bedrooms *(Neil and Angela Huxter, BB)*

☆ **Kilburn** N Yor [SE5179], *Forresters Arms*: Next to 'mouseman' Thompson furniture workshops (visitor centre opp), largely furnished by them; big log fire, good food, friendly staff, well kept Black Sheep and Theakstons Best, games and piped music; restaurant, well behaved children allowed, open all day; suntrap seats out in front, pleasant village; bedrooms clean, cheerful and bright *(Martin Hickes, John Allsopp, Dono and Carol Leaman, LYM)*

Kilnsea E Yor [TA4216], *Crown & Anchor*: Two bars, dining room and family room, Bass Bitter and Mild and Tetleys, horsebrasses and china; picnic tables in front facing Humber estuary, and in back garden; open all day *(JJW, CMW)*

☆ **Kilnsey** N Yor [Kilnsey Crag; SD9767], *Tennant Arms*: Good bar food, well kept Tetleys and Theakstons Best and Old Peculier, open fires, interesting decorations; piped music; views of spectacular overhanging crag from restaurant; comfortable bedrooms all with private bathrooms, good walks *(Neville Kenyon, MJ)*

Kirkby Malham N Yor [SD8961], *Victoria*: Pleasantly understated Victorian decor, friendly new licensees, good value food, well kept Theakstons; lovely village with interesting church, quieter spot than nearby Malham though busy with walkers at lunchtime; bedrooms *(Prof and Mrs S Barnett)*

☆ **Kirkby Overblow** N Yor [off A61; SE3249], *Shoulder of Mutton*: Attractive layout and decor, two log fires; very popular with older people for wide choice of good traditional food using fresh local produce, interesting puddings; friendly service, well kept Tetleys, good wines, new upstairs seafood restaurant, children welcome, tables in lovely garden with play area by meadows *(Arthur and Margaret Dickinson, Michael Butler, BB)*

Kirkby Overblow, *Star & Garter*: Cosy welcoming local with generous good value standard bar food, dining room for evening meals; well kept Camerons and Everards *(Mr and Mrs E J W Rogers)*

Knaresborough N Yor [High Bridge, Harrogate Rd; SE3557], *Yorkshire Lass*: Big pub-restaurant in fine riverside position, close to Mother Shipton's Cave with picturesque views from terrace; lively decoration, friendly Scottish landlord, good spacious food, comfortable dining room, five well kept Courage-related and guest ales, several dozen malt whiskies, daily papers; live jazz/blues some nights; good bedrooms and breakfast *(C Maclean, A Marsh, Martin Hickes)*

Knottingley W Yor [2 Racca Green; SE5023], *Steam Packet*: Big and friendly with well kept beers, some brewed on the premises; next to canal *(Richard Houghton)*

Langdale End N Yor [off A170 at East Ayton; or A171 via Hackness – OS Sheet 101 map ref 938913; SE9491], *Moorcock*: Simple moorland village pub, refurbished after long closure to keep its unusual traditional layout – hatch service (no bar counter), three rooms, one allowing children, another with music and pool; changing well kept interesting real ales such as Whitby Wobble *(Derek and Sylvia Stephenson, BB)*

Langsett S Yor [A616 nr Penistone; SE2100], *Waggon & Horses*: Spotless comfortable pub on moors main road, welcoming helpful staff, blazing log fire, stripped stone and woodwork, good if not cheap home cooking inc good value Sun lunch, well kept Bass and Stones, magazines to read, friendly small dog; dining room *(James Waller, CMW, JJW)*

☆ **Langthwaite** N Yor [just off Reeth—Brough rd; NZ0003], *Red Lion*: Unspoilt, individual and relaxing, in charming dales village, with local books and maps for sale, basic cheap nourishing lunchtime food, Black Sheep, Theakstons XB and Youngers Scotch, country wines, tea and coffee; well behaved children allowed lunchtime in very low-ceilinged (and sometimes smoky) side snug, quietly friendly service; good walks all around, inc organised circular ones from the pub *(Maurice Thompson, J H and S A Harrop, Richard R Dolphin, Ray and Liz Monk, Geoff and Angela Jaques, LYM)*

☆ **Lastingham** N Yor [off A170 W of Pickering; SE7391], *Blacksmiths Arms*: Attractively old-fashioned village pub opp ancient church, log fire in oak-beamed bar's open range, traditional furnishings, no-smoking dining area with food from sandwiches to steaks (breakfasts for campers etc), Courage-related ales and a good house beer, separate games room with pool etc; well behaved children welcome, bedrooms, lovely surrounding countryside; open all day Sat *(Dr and Mrs A H Young, Nigel Hopkins)*

☆ **Leeds** [Gt George St; SE3033], *Victoria*: Well preserved ornate Victorian pub with grand etched mirrors, impressive globe lamps extending from the ornately solid bar, smaller rooms off; well kept Tetleys inc Mild, friendly smart bar staff, reasonably priced food in luncheon room with end serving hatch popular for decades with politicians and lawyers *(Chris Westmoreland, Reg Nelson, M Walker)*

☆ **Leeds** [Hunslet Rd], *Adelphi*: Well restored handsome Edwardian tiling, woodwork and glass, several rooms, impressive stairway; particularly well kept Tetleys (virtually the brewery tap), prompt friendly service, good spread of cheap food at lunchtime, crowded but convivial then; live jazz Sat *(PGP)*

☆ **Leeds** [North St (A61)], *Eagle*: Well kept reasonably priced Timothy Taylors and several guest beers usually from distant smaller breweries in 18th-c pub with choice of basic or plush bars, sensible food, helpful staff; pleasant for lunch, good bands in back bar weekends,

occasional beer festivals; bedrooms *(PGP, Reg Nelson, Salim Ali, LYM)*

☆ **Leeds** [9 Burley Rd, junction with Rutland St], *Fox & Newt*: Interesting choice of mainly Whitbreads-related ales as well as several brewed in the cellar here, good value limited standard lunchtime food inc cheap Sun lunch, cheery neo-Victorian decor, well reproduced piped music; open all day, children welcome, pub dog called Buster – other dogs allowed evening; occasional quiz nights *(Tom Eggleston, PM, AM, LYM)*

☆ **Leeds** [37 Waterloo Rd, Hunslet], *Garden Gate*: Ornate but thoroughly down-to-earth Victorian pub with various rooms off central drinking corridor, well worth a look for its now near-unique style and intricate glass and woodwork; Tetleys Bitter and Mild foaming with freshness, farm cider, no food; open all day, can be boisterous evenings *(Chris Westmoreland, David Carr, LYM)*

Leeds [86 Armley Rd, by Arkwright St], *Albion*: Very jolly, with three well restored interesting rooms, well kept Boddingtons and Tetleys from superb brass handpumps, good service, good value filling snacks, separate pool room; the original for the 00-gauge model railway pub *(David Campbell, Vicki McLean)*; [121 Woodhouse St], *Beer Exchange*: Eight well kept ales inc many from smaller breweries, no-smoking area, decent food; popular with young people *(Andy and Jill Kassube, Dr and Mrs A K Clarke)*; [Civic Ct, Calverley St], *Carpe Diem*: Recently opened in basement of former Education Board offices, extensively refurbished in Victorian style with stone floor and wooden fittings; Marstons, Tetleys and guest beers, imaginative well presented but not cheap food *(Lynne Gittins)*; [Mabgate, nr E end of inner ring rd], *City of Mabgate*: Cosy and friendly, with well kept Whitbreads-related and interesting guest beers, interesting old photographs and beer-mat collection, plainer back room with pool and TV; handy for the Playhouse *(Reg Nelson)*; [Headrow, Kirkgate, by indoor mkt], *Duck & Drake*: No-frills big pub with a dozen or more well kept reasonably priced ales inc obscure local brews, bustling friendly atmosphere, simple substantial food, open fire; loud live music Sun, Tues and Thurs nights, quieter back room *(Chris Westmoreland, Tricia Thomson, Paul Alford)*; [Merrion St, by Merrion Shopping Centre], *Edwards*: Big airy wine bar/pub, reasonable range of well presented home-made food, decent big glass of wine, friendly efficient service *(John Wooll)*; [Woodhouse Moor], *Feast & Firkin*: Firkin range of real ales in big former library, friendly staff, big helpings of plain filling food; open all day *(Pat and Tony Martin)*; [Farsley], *Fleece*: Tetleys' oldest pub, recently refurbished in Victorian style; hard-working landlord, perfectly kept Tetleys; used by cast of TV's *Emmerdale* *(Martin Hickes)*; [Great George St], *George*: Well preserved, with friendly service, well kept Tetleys, basement dining area (food in bar too, enjoyably busy weekday lunchtimes) *(PGP)*; [main rd Headingley—Kirkstall], *Old Bridge*:

Pubby upstairs bar with good value food, downstairs done up with flagstones and scrubbed pine tables leading out to riverside garden with barbecues; Boddingtons and Tetleys, handy for Kirkstall Abbey *(R Borthwick, S Clegg)*; [W Yorks Playhouse], *Playhouse Theatre Bar*: Modern and roomy, marvellous views over city, good friendly service, reasonably priced drinks, occasional live music *(Andrew Stewart)*; [Abbey Rd, Kirkstall], *West End House*: Big open-plan bar with raised dining area, friendly service, generous menu inc sandwiches, well kept Boddingtons and Flowers Original; handy for Kirkstall Abbey *(PGP)*; [38 Wellington St], *West Riding*: Big busy pub with bustling friendly service, good range of generous hot and cold food from separate counter, well kept Tetleys *(PGP)*; [alley off Boar Lane, parallel to Duncan St], *Whip*: Worth knowing for particularly well kept Ansells Mild, Ind Coope Burton, Tetleys Mild, Bitter and Imperial; friendly helpful staff, lively mixed customers *(Chris Westmoreland, Dr and Mrs A K Clarke)*; [Merrion St/Briggate], *Wrens*: Relaxing pub with well kept Tetleys and Imperial, good snacks, theatre posters (opp Grand Theatre, used by actors), no-smoking room; lovely summer hanging baskets *(William Gaskill, Chris Westmoreland)*

☆ **Leyburn** N Yor [Market Pl; SE1191], *Golden Lion*: Relaxing bay-windowed two-room panelled bar, quite light and airy, with log-effect gas fire in eating area, good value generous straightforward bar food esp puddings, evening restaurant; good beer brewed to their own recipe in Harrogate as well as Theakstons Best and Youngers No 3, decent coffee, friendly efficient service, tables out in front; open all day, dogs allowed; bedrooms good value *(Andrew and Ruth Triggs, M J Morgan, Simon and Amanda Southwell, BB)*

☆ **Linton** W Yor [Main St; SE3947], *Windmill*: Polished affluent feel in small rooms with pewter tankards for the locals, antique settles, oak beams, longcase clock; generous helpings of good food (not Mon or Sun evening, very busy Sun lunchtime), well kept Theakstons Best and XB and Youngers Scotch, friendly staff, affluent feel; tables in pleasant garden, car park through coaching entrance *(Geoffrey and Brenda Wilson, Martin Hickes, LYM)*

Low Row N Yor [B6270 Reeth—Muker; SD9897], *Punch Bowl*: Friendly youth-hostelish family bar, open all day in summer, with well kept Theakstons Best, XB and Old Peculier and guests, Easter beer festival, rows of malt whiskies, wide choice of good value food, log fire, games room; fine Swaledale views; popular tea room 10-5.30 with home-made cakes, small shop, bicycle and cave lamp hire, folk music Fri; good basic bedrooms, also bunkhouse, big breakfast *(John Unsworth)*

Lund E Yor [off B1248 SW of Driffield; SE9748], *Wellington*: Village pub refurbished by new owners, good food in dining room – already so popular that Sat booked well ahead *(D Hancock)*

☆ **Malham** N Yor [SD8963], *Lister Arms*: Friendly easy-going open-plan lounge, busy weekends, relaxed attitude to children, very generous food inc Mexican, well kept changing ales such as Black Sheep, Moorhouses Pendle Witches Brew and Wadworths 6X, even Liefmans fruit beers in summer, lots of malt whiskies, well worn-in furnishings and fittings, roaring fire, restaurant famous for steaks, games area with pool and maybe loudish piped music; seats outside the substantial stone inn overlooking green, more in back garden – nice spot by river, ideal for walkers; bedrooms *(Marianne Lantree, Steve Webb, Prof and Mrs S Barnett, Neil Calver, Paul McPherson, J A Swanson, Dr J A Spencer, D Goodger, Peter and Audrey Dowsett)*

Malham, *Buck*: Big village pub, wide range of generous home-made food, Black Sheep and Theakstons Best, log fires, comfortable lounge and big bar welcoming walkers, separate candlelit dining room, picnic tables in small garden; decent well equipped bedrooms, many good walks from the door *(Neil Calver, Marianne Lantree, Steve Webb, Geoffrey Stait, Pat Westbury)*

Malton N Yor [Yolkersgate; SE7972], *George*: Plush comfort, six wall clocks showing world times, modern panelling, Tetleys, bar food, friendly service; juke box *(M Walker)*; [Yolkersgate], *Mount*: Interesting local with lots of pictures etc, good choice of good value food, John Smiths, Tetleys and guest beers *(C Turner)*; *Spotted Cow*: Charming little unspoilt town pub overlooking cattle and sheep markets and popular with local farmers on market days, small traditional rooms, well kept Tetleys and occasional guest beers *(Alan Mitchell)*

Market Weighton N Yor [SE8742], *Londesborough Arms*: Two old-fashioned real ale bars with brass footrail along counter, John Smiths and Tetleys, interesting ambitious bar and restaurant food, decent wine, good civilised atmosphere, friendly staff; comfortable well equipped bedrooms *(Tony Gayfer, BB)*

Marsden W Yor [Manchester Rd (A62); SE0612], *Olive Branch*: Bar/brasserie decor, but informal pubby atmosphere and Bass and Stones ales; well presented generous food inc fish and game, good value wines, staff helpful even though busy *(Lawrence Bacon)*

☆ **Marton Cum Grafton** N Yor [signed off A1 3 miles N of A59; SE4263], *Olde Punch Bowl*: Interesting well presented food in attractive old pub with comfortable and roomy heavy-beamed open-plan bar, open fires, brasses, framed old advertisements and photographs; Tetleys and Youngers Scotch and No 3, decent wines, no piped music, welcoming service, restaurant; children welcome, good play area and picnic tables in garden *(Viv Middlebrook, LYM)*

Masham N Yor [Silver St, linking A6168 with Market Sq; SE2381], *Bay Horse*: Comfortable banquettes in split-level lounge, good range of good value straightforward bar food inc choice of Sun roasts, friendly staff, Black Sheep and Theakstons (both produced in this village), real fire, darts and fruit machine in separate bar; piped music; children allowed *(CMW, JJW)*;

Bruce Arms: Local with very pleasant service, attractive menu, particularly well kept Black Sheep *(R T and J C Moggridge)*

Middleham N Yor [Mkt Pl; SE1288], *Richard III*: Big bustling friendly local, horsey pictures, quick service, open fire in front bar, side pool area, back bar with tables for reasonable range of food inc good cheap sandwiches; well kept Tetleys, Theakstons and John Smiths; good value bedrooms *(PGP)*; [Market Pl], *White Swan*: Character village local with homely dining room, new licensees aiming to raise the profile of the food – already good value, with original vegetarian dishes; bedrooms *(D Stokes)*

Middlesmoor N Yor [up at the top of the Nidderdale rd from Pateley Bridge; SE0874], *Crown*: Friendly little inn reopened 1995, with coal fires in small rooms, homely dining room, beautiful view over stone-built hamlet high in upper Nidderdale, particularly well kept Theakstons XB; bedrooms *(Tony and Jenny Hainsworth)*

☆ **Midhopestones** S Yor [off A616; SK2399], *Midhopestones Arms*: Cosy and friendly character 17th-c pub, flagstones, stripped stone and pine, three small rooms, woodburner, pictures, assorted chairs, tables and settles; eight well kept ales inc Courage-related ones, Barnsley, Timothy Taylors Landlord and Wards, friendly staff, log fires, good value home cooking (not Sun evening, restricted Mon/Tues lunch) esp Sun lunch, breakfasts too; restaurant, seats outside; children welcome *(David and Julian Lambley, Peter Marshall)*

Mirfield W Yor [212 Huddersfield Rd; A644; SE2019], *Railway*: Two-bar pub with welcoming staff, well priced Bass, Stones, Worthington and guest beers, wide variety of good value food from double-decker sandwiches to tasty evening dishes; a few tables out in front *(PGP, P M Lane)*

Mytholmroyd W Yor [Cragg Vale; SE0126], *Hinchcliffe Arms*: Remote old stonebuilt country pub on road that leads only to a reservoir, very popular with walkers; plenty of character, good value food in bar and restaurant inc carvery, S&N beers *(PM, AM)*

Nether Silton N Yor [off A19; SE4692], *Gold Cup*: Good food in bar and attached restaurant, Black Sheep and Theakstons ales, pine decor, relaxed friendly welcome; lovely quiet village; bedrooms, good breakfast *(A Keys)*

☆ **Newholm** N Yor [signed off A171; NZ8611], *Beehive*: Long and attractive 16th-c pub with low black beams in two snug bar rooms, several well kept S&N ales, good value food inc local seafood in bar and upstairs restaurant, log fire, very welcoming service; seats outside; children allowed in back room *(Martin Walker, LYM)*

Newton le Willows N Yor [off A684 W of Patrick Brompton; SE2289], *Wheatsheaf*: Very cheap chippy food and well kept Theakstons Best in idiosyncratic pub run by motorcycle enthusiast; juke box may be loud and opening hours seem variable; pleasant service; children in extension with pool table *(Anon)*

Newton on Ouse N Yor [signed off A19 N of York; SE5160], *Dawnay Arms*: Attractive 18th-

c inn nr Benningbrough Hall, with neat lawn running down to moorings on River Ouse, tables on terrace, play area; comfortably plush inside, with lots of beamery, brass and copper, and good bedrooms; has had good food, a fine range of well kept ales and decent wines, and a welcome for children, but in receivership as we go to press *(LYM; news please)*

☆ **North Dalton** E Yor [SE9352], *Star*: Good choice of decent bar food from soup and generous open sandwiches up in comfortably refurbished lounge bar with welcoming coal fire, obliging young staff, well kept real ales, character restaurant; a striking sight, one wall rising straight from sizeable pond; charming well equipped good value bedrooms *(Julie Peters, Colin Blinkhorn, A V Bradbury, BB)*

North Grimston N Yor [SE8468], *Middleton Arms*: Friendly local in good spot on edge of Yorkshire Wolds, lovely garden, well kept Tetleys, good food in bar and restaurant *(Alan Mitchell)*

North Stainley N Yor [SE2977], *Staveley Arms*: Old country pub with decent generous bar food, popular carvery Thurs-Sat evening and Sun lunch, friendly helpful staff, nice chatty atmosphere, rustic bric-a-brac; handy for Lightwater factory outlet, village etc; bedrooms comfortable and well priced *(Andy and Jill Kassube, Mrs B Slater)*

☆ **Nosterfield** N Yor [B6267 Masham—Thirsk; SE2881], *Freemasons Arms*: Friendly and civilised open-plan bar and dining area, two log fires, beams and flagstones, Empire theme with interesting curios, well kept Black Sheep and Theakstons, decent wines, good interesting food (not Mon evening), smiling service; tables outside, very pleasant surroundings *(David and Judith Hart, H J Sharp)*

Nun Monkton N Yor [off A59 York—Harrogate; SE5058], *Alice Hawthorn*: Modernised down-to-earth beamed village local with lots of brass etc, big brick inglenook fireplace, Tetleys and other ales, freshly prepared basic food, keen darts players; on broad village green with pond and lovely avenue to church and Rivers Nidd and Ouse *(Viv Middlebrook, Tim and Sue Halstead, BB)*

☆ **Oakworth** W Yor [Harehills Lane, Oldfield; 2 miles towards Colne; SE0038], *Grouse*: Comfortable, interesting and spotless old pub packed with bric-a-brac, gleaming copper, lots of prints and china, attractively individual furnishings; good lunchtime soup, filling sandwiches and cold dishes (not Mon), charming evening restaurant, well kept Timothy Taylors, good range of spirits, entertaining landlord, good service, good Pennine views *(A and M Dickinson, WAH)*

☆ **Osmotherley** N Yor [SE4499], *Three Tuns*: Concentration on wide choice of interesting fresh food worth the price and the wait in roomy and comfortable back dining room, small simple but atmospheric front bar, well kept Theakstons Best, XB and Old Peculier, smart friendly service, attractive coal fire; tables out in pleasant back garden with lovely views; children welcome; comfortable bedrooms, handy for Mount Grace Priory, good walks nearby (*John and Chris Simpson, R T and J C Moggridge, Martin Hickes, Andrew and Ruth Triggs, M D Phillips, R F Grieve, Dr Terry Murphy*)

Osmotherley, *Pied Piper*: Pleasant old pub with stripped stone, beams and open fires in main lounge area, nice staff, games room with pool, TV and fruit machine, well kept Theakstons and a guest beer, well presented good interesting food in bar and restaurant; good well priced bedrooms (*Eric and Shirley Broadhead*)

★ **Ossett** W Yor [Low Mill Rd/Healey Lane – OS Sheet 104 map ref 271191; SE2719], *Brewers Pride*: Friendly basic local of character, wide range of well kept changing ales mainly from small independent brewers, cosy front room and bar both with open fires, small games room, tasty reasonably priced weekday lunchtime food, generous Sun bar nibbles, big back garden with local entertainment summer weekends; quiz night Mon, country & western Thurs, open all day Fri/Sat (*Richard Houghton, H Cooper, M A Butler*)

Ossett [The Green], *Masons Arms*: Plain exterior, smart interior, lively tap room for darts and dominoes, friendy landlady, well kept John Smiths, small car park (*Michael Butler*); [Manor Rd], *Victoria*: Wide-ranging reasonably priced food inc Sun carvery, even kangaroo steaks, changing well kept ales; cl Mon-Thurs lunchtime (*Michael Butler*)

★ **Oswaldkirk** N Yor [signed off B1363/B1257 S of Helmsley; SE6279], *Malt Shovel*: Former small 17th-c manor house, heavy beams and flagstones, fine staircase, simple traditional furnishings, huge log fires, two cosy bars (one may be crowded with well heeled locals), family room, interestingly decorated dining room, unusual garden; has had well kept and priced Sam Smiths OB and Museum and good fresh simple food, but no reports since new landlord spring 1996 (*S E Paulley, Darren Salter, LYM; news please*)

Otley W Yor [Bondgate; SE2045], *Rose & Crown*: Comfortable stonebuilt pub with friendly staff, wide range of mainly Whitbreads-related ales, good menu (not Fri/Sat evenings); can be busy lunchtime (*Lynne Gittins, Ben Grose*)

Outlane W Yor [A640 Huddersfield—Rochdale; SE0717], *Nonts Sarahs*: Moorland pub with Websters and Theakstons, big helpings of decent food, good views from big back windows; children's room full of toys (*Chris Westmoreland*)

Owston S Yor [A19 3 miles S of Askern; SE5511], *Owston Park Lodge*: Thoroughly refurbished Tom Cobleigh dining pub, attractive and comfortable, with usual food all day, well kept beers (*Thomas Nott*)

★ **Oxenhope** W Yor [A6033 Keighley—Hebden Bridge; SE0335], *Waggon & Horses*: Welcoming stripped-stone moorside pub with good views, good range of generous food till late evening, Tetleys and Theakstons, open fires, pleasant simple decor, friendly efficient service, separate dining room; children welcome (*WAH, LYM*)

Oxenhope [nr Leeming, off B6141 towards Denholme; SE0434], *Dog & Gun*: Well kept Timothy Taylors Landlord and Best in roomy bar with beamery, copper, brasses and delft shelves of plates and jugs, open fire each end, padded settles and stools, a couple of smaller rooms; warm welcome, good varied bar food from sandwiches up inc lots of fish, attractive bistro-style restaurant, nice views (*Mr and Mrs Newby, WAH*)

Pateley Bridge N Yor [SE1666], *Crown*: Cosy lounge with railed-off dining area alongside, stripped stonework and horsebrasses (but not too many), good choice of food, John Smiths and Theakstons, public bar with pool room, good chatty bar service (*Mr and Mrs C Roberts*)

Patrick Brompton N Yor [A684 Bedale—Leyburn; SE2291], *Green Tree*: Friendly old stone local, particularly well kept Black Sheep, Hambleton and Theakstons beers, open fire, wide choice of good value food (not Sun), pleasant service; public bar, separate dining lounge with waitress service (*Dorsan Baker*)

★ **Pecket Well** W Yor [A6033 N of Hebden Bridge; SD9929], *Robin Hood*: Warmly welcoming jovial landlord, two rooms with lots of sporting prints, attractive stone fireplace in separate pool room, banquettes in stripped-stone vaulted-ceiling dining area, careful home cooking inc good veg, well kept Tetleys and Theakstons Best and Old Peculier, decent wines, friendly dog called Kiwi (*Cynthia Waller, Mrs E Howe*)

Pickering N Yor [Market Pl; SE7984], *Bay Horse*: Welcoming heavy-beamed red plush bar with old-fashioned prints and horsey bric-a-brac, big fire, well kept John Smiths, generous good value food, bigger back public bar, upstairs restaurant (*Colin and Ann Hunt, LYM*); [18 Birdgate], *Black Swan*: Attractive hotel keeping pubby atmosphere in smart plush bar, good service, good value tasty food, well kept Black Smith and Courage-related beers; well furnished restaurant; bedrooms (*Ann and Colin Hunt, Andy and Jill Kassube, Q Williamson*); [Market Pl], *White Swan*: Attractive stone coaching inn with two small bars, good traditional well priced bar food inc vegetarian, well kept Camerons and Theakstons, friendly helpful staff, busy but comfortable family room, good restaurant with interesting wines; bedrooms comfortable, good breakfast (*John T Ames, Ian Irving, Andy and Jill Kassube, Willie Bell*)

Pocklington N Yor [5 Market Pl; SE8049], *Feathers*: Roomy open-plan lounge with banquettes (busy Tues market day), well kept Theakstons Best and Youngers Scotch, helpful landlady, usual bar food; children welcome, timbered restaurant, no-smoking conservatory, quiz and jazz nights, comfortable motel-style bedrooms (*Christopher Turner, Eric and Shirley Broadhead, Julie Peters, LYM*)

Pontefract W Yor [Swales Yard; corner Cornmarket/Beastfair, SE4622], *Counting House*: New pub on two floors of carefully restored medieval building, restrained fittings to match original structure; usual food, limited range of beers (*Thomas Nott*)

Pool W Yor [A658 towards Harrogate; SE2445], *Hunters*: Good atmosphere, up to eight well kept ales, balcony for warm weather, open fires for cold, pool, dominoes, table skittles; a popular young meeting place *(Chris Westmoreland, Tina Elson)*

Preston E Yor [Main St; TA1930], *Cock & Bell*: Busy friendly pub, lounge, small pool room, restaurant, good value food esp curries, seven well kept ales, plastic tables and chairs out on terrace, big garden with adventure playground *(JJW, CMW)*

Queensbury W Yor [Mountain; A644 Brighouse—Denholme; SE1030], *Mad Ma Jones's*: Well kept changing ales such as Black Sheep, Morlands Old Speckled Hen and Theakstons, bright cheerful landlord who knows about beer, old kitchen-style bar, imitation hams, old linen press and memorabilia, enjoyable low-priced food esp cow pie *(Jenny and Brian Seller, Janice and Peter Rush)*

Rainton N Yor [under a mile from A1 Boroughbridge—Leeming Bar, N of A168; SE3775], *Bay Horse*: Three rooms off central bar, low beams, open fires, horsebrasses, farm tools and photographs; big helpings of good value food, well kept Theakstons (full range), very friendly owners and staff; good value bedrooms *(John Allsopp)*

Raskelf N Yor [SE4971], *Three Tuns*: Well kept Tetleys and Theakstons XB in vibrant and friendly local, good plentiful home-made food, darts, dominoes *(C A Hall)*

Rawdon W Yor [SE2139], *Emmett Arms*: Good straightforward bar food *(Walter and Susan Rinaldi-Butcher)*

☆ **Reeth** N Yor [Market Pl (B6270); SE0499], *Kings Arms*: Popular dining pub by green, with oak beams, pine pews around walls, huge log fire in big 18th-c stone inglenook, warm plum carpet, quieter room behind; good reasonably priced food, friendly service, well kept Theakstons, John Smiths and Tetleys; children very welcome; bedrooms *(Gwen and Peter Andrews, A Jeffreys)*

Reeth [just off B6270], *Black Bull*: Friendly local in fine spot at foot of broad sloping green, traditional dark beamed and flagstoned L-shaped front bar, well kept John Smiths and Theakstons, reasonably priced usual bar food, open fires, children welcome; piped music in pool room; comfortable bedrooms, good breakfast *(Gwen and Peter Andrews, A Jeffreys, Chris and Andy Crow, James Nunns, LYM)*

Riccall N Yor [A19 10 miles S of York; SE6238], *Hare & Hounds*: Very cheap straightforward bar food from sandwiches up (not Mon or Tues evening, bargain supper for two Weds-Fri), good Sun lunches, well kept John Smiths, decent wines *(Janet Pickles)*

Richmond N Yor [Finkle St; NZ1801], *Black Lion*: Atmospheric well used coaching inn with well kept Camerons and guest ales, friendly staff, several separate rooms inc no-smoking lounge, dark traditional decor, briskly served no-frills food; bedrooms reasonably priced *(Ben Grose, Mr and Mrs M Thompson, R T and J C Moggridge, GSB)*

☆ **Ripley** N Yor [off A61 Harrogate—Ripon; SE2861], *Boars Head*: Beautiful old hotel with long flagstoned bar, neat and well run, with tables in series of stalls, good value bar food, well kept Archers, Theakstons Best and XB and other guest beers, smart friendly service, plenty of tables in charming garden; good restaurant; charming bedrooms *(Andrew and Ruth Triggs, Tim and Sue Halstead, David and Ruth Hollands, Colin and Ann Hunt)*

Ripon N Yor [Bridge Lane, off Bondgate Green (itself off B6265); or cross bridge nr cathedral and turn left along path; SE3171], *Water Rat*: Pleasantly bustling, unassuming but well furnished, prettily set by footbridge over River Skell with ducks and weir, charming view of cathedral and weir from riverside terrace (shame about the air vent noise out here); friendly service, Vaux and related ales, wide choice of food *(Dr and Mrs D Awbery, PJH, Colin and Ann Hunt, Barry and Anne)*

Rishworth W Yor [Oldham Rd (A672) nr M62 junction 22; SE0216], *Turnpike*: Very clean pub with fine view of Booth Wood reservoir and surrounding moorland, big bar area, small dining room, large restaurant; polite friendly staff, good value bar food, well kept Marstons Pedigree and Tetleys *(Michael Butler)*

Rivelin Reservoirs S Yor [A57 W of Sheffield; SK2687], *Norfolk Arms*: Friendly stonebuilt Victorian-style pub in pleasant countryside, lovely views, panelling and comfortable banquettes in two bars, Wards, good value food, lots of nearby walks *(CMW, JJW)*

Robin Hoods Bay N Yor [The Dock, Bay Town; NZ9505], *Bay*: Included for the fine sea views from cosy picture-window bar; Courage-related ales, log fires, food in bar and separate dining area; maybe piped music, well behaved children may be allowed in room up steps; tables outside, bedrooms *(Chris and Andy Crow, Mike and Wendy Proctor)*; [King St, Bay Town], *Olde Dolphin*: Roomy 18th-c inn stepped up above sea front in attractive little town; unpretentious furnishings, friendly service, convivial atmosphere, well kept cheap Courage and a guest such as Batemans XXXB, good open fire, good value bar food inc local seafood, popular back games room; dogs welcome in bar if well behaved, piped music, can get smoky and crowded weekends, long walk back up to village car park; Fri folk club, bedrooms basic but cheap *(Mike and Wendy Proctor, Nigel Hopkins)*

Roecliffe N Yor [SE3766], *Crown*: Thriving village inn, good food, good family service *(Janet and Peter Race)*

☆ **Rosedale Abbey** N Yor [300 yds up Rosedale Chimney; SE7395], *White Horse*: Cosy and comfortable farm-based country inn in lovely spot above the village, local feel in character bar with lots of stuffed animals and birds, well kept Tetleys and Theakstons, quite a few wines and good choice of malt whiskies, friendly service, good generous reasonably priced home-made bar food esp range of pies, restaurant, grand views from terrace (and from bedrooms); children allowed if eating, open all day Sat; bedrooms – a nice place to stay *(Nigel Hopkins,*

Bronwen and Steve Wrigley, Ian S Morley, LYM)

Rotherham S Yor [Broom Valley Rd; SK4393], *New Broom*: Quite spacious, but cosy, big collection of glassware in lounge, friendly new management, good home cooking *(Nigel Brewitt)*; [35 Bridgegate], *Rhinoceros*: Once an old shop, now a very pleasant welcoming Wetherspoons pub, traditional interior, good value food all day, friendly staff *(Linda Howell)*

☆ **Runswick Bay** N Yor [NZ8217], *Royal*: Super setting, lovely views over fishing village and sea from welcoming big-windowed plain front lounge with interesting marine fishtank, limited choice of good value food inc huge helpings of fresh local fish, cosy bustling atmosphere, well kept John Smiths, nautical back bar, terrace; bedrooms *(Michael Butler, Mike and Wendy Proctor, LYM)*

Saltergate N Yor [A169 N of Pickering; SE8594], *Saltergate*: Classic moorland walkers' pub close to scenic Hole of Horcum, surrounded by bleak heather moors; spartan bar with centuries-old ever-burning fire and wildlife sketches, austere atmosphere; family room with pool and moorland views; cheap home-cooked bar meals, keg beers; seats outside *(Eddie Edwards)*

☆ **Saxton** N Yor [B1217 Towton—Garforth about a mile outside; SE4736], *Crooked Billet*: Tidy and well run extended pub doing a huge trade in reasonably priced food esp giant sandwiches, pies and enormous yorkshire puddings – get there early for a seat, it's quite a cult; friendly comfortable atmosphere, well kept John Smiths, efficient service *(Chris Westmoreland, Janet Pickles)*

☆ **Saxton** [Headwell Lane], *Plough*: Smart dining pub, small bar with blackboard over blazing coke fire, good choice of food (not Sun evening) inc interesting specials, good veg and beautifully presented puddings in adjacent dining room, well kept Theakstons, decent house wine, good coffee; cl Mon *(Roy Bromell, BKA)*

Scammonden Reservoir W Yor [A672; SE0215], *Brown Cow*: Dramatic views over M62, reservoir and moors in old-fashioned pub with long bar, reasonably priced food and interesting range of changing guest beers *(H K Dyson)*

Scarborough N Yor [Vernon Rd; TA0489], *Hole in the Wall*: Lively atmosphere and well kept Malton Double Chance, Theakstons BB, XB and Old Peculier and good changing guest beers in friendly three-roomed local with one long central bar, country wines, no piped music or machines; cheap basic lunchtime food *(Dave Braisted)*; [seafront, Scalby Mills; TA0390], *Scalby Mills*: Fine views over North Bay towards the castle from small two-room seafront pub, half a dozen reasonably priced well kept local ales like Cropton; handy for sealife centre *(Tony Leslie)*

☆ **Scawton** N Yor [SE5584], *Hare*: Low and pretty, much modernised, with a couple of cosy settees, simple wall settles, little wheelback armchairs, air force memorabilia; friendly service, well kept Black Sheep, Theakstons Best

and XB, good value generous food inc good vegetarian range, two friendly dogs, eating area, pool room; tables in big back garden with caged geese, nice inn-signs; children welcome, handy for Rievaulx *(Darren Salter, BB)*

☆ **Scorton** N Yor [B1263 Richmond—Yarm, just outside village off A1 just N of Catterick; NZ2500], *St Cuthberts*: New owners doing interesting good food in very clean neatly furnished and decorated dining room, well kept John Smiths and Theakstons Best *(Paul and Ursula Randall)*

Seamer N Yor [Main St; TA0284], *Londesborough Arms*: Warm family welcome, good value usual bar food; good reasonably priced bedrooms *(Mr and Mrs R Hillman)*

☆ **Sheffield** S Yor [601 Penistone Rd, Hillsborough; SK3290], *Hillsborough Barracks*: Up to nine interesting changing well kept ales in old pub, refurbished under new owners (coming from two Guide main entries), comfortable lounge with red leather banquettes, old pine floors, gas fire, plate and bottle collection, bar area with two small rooms off, one with TV and darts; good value freshly made food noon-7 (may take a while), friendly service, newspapers and magazines; quiet piped radio, country music Thurs; children welcome, tables out at back, open all day Fri/Sat; plans for own microbrewery *(CMW, JJW, Terry Barlow)*

Sheffield [537 Attercliffe Common (A6178)], *Carbrook Hall*: Dating from 1620, only surviving part of even older building, popular with ghost-hunters; no-smoking dining room (children welcome here) with armour, helmets and Civil War artefacts, pool room with old bread ovens, Oak Room with panelling, beautiful carved fireplace and Italianate plaster ceiling (games machines, piped music etc); good value bar food and Sun roasts, John Smiths Magnet and Stones, small garden with play area; open all day Sat *(CMW, JJW, Phil Skelton)*; [1 Henry St], *Cask & Cutler*: Small pub in rather bleak area, five well kept changing ales from small breweries, food inc unusual sausages, lots of posters, friendly landlord, sensibly placed pool table, no juke box; annual beer festival *(Simon, Julia and Laura Plumbley, JP, PP)*; [Cobden View Rd, Crookes], *Cobden View*: Friendly local popular with students, well kept Boddingtons and guest beers, pool room, juke box *(A J Hilton)*; [Worksop Rd, just off Attercliffe Common (A6178)], *Cocked Hat*: Largely open-plan, tasteful dark colours, brewery memorabilia, well kept Marstons Burton and Pedigree, good value lunchtime food *(J A Waller)*; [Poole Rd, Darnall, off Prince of Wales Rd; not far from M1 junctions 33/34], *Kings Head*: Good-natured atmosphere, incredible choice of cheap but good basic bar food, much home-made; Stones and Tetleys *(JJW, CMW)*; [94 Crookes], *Noahs Ark*: Good choice of mainly Whitbreads-related ales and of generous good cheap food (not Sun evening) in friendly pub, open all day all week; Addlestone's cider, disabled lavatory; pool, fruit machines *(CMW, JJW, M Porter)*; [3 Crookes/Lydgate Lane], *Old*

Grindstone: Busy Victorian pub with good cheap food inc lots of pies and good Sun roast, Timothy Taylors Landlord, Vaux Waggle Dance and Wards, teapot collection, obliging service, friendly black cat, games room with pool etc, no piped music; open all day all week, jazz Mon *(JJW, CMW, M Porter, D and D Savidge)*

☆ Shelf W Yor [Stone Chair; A644 Brighouse—Queensbury; SE1029], *Duke of York*: Popular and welcoming 17th-c dining pub, beams, vast array of antique brass and copper, almost equally vast menu inc daily Scottish fish and seafood, even ostrich and kangaroo; well kept ales inc Timothy Taylors and Whitbreads, open fires; booking advised evenings *(M R Rimmer, Geoffrey and Brenda Wilson)*

Shepley W Yor [Station Rd, Stocksmoor; Thunderbridge and Stocksmoor signed off A629 N; SE1810], *Clothiers Arms*: Good atmosphere in softly lit rooms inc games room, conservatory extension, polite helpful staff and friendly landlord; bar food (not Sun or Mon evenings), downstairs carvery, Tetleys and Theakstons, tables out on balconies; quiet countryside *(M A Butler)*

Shepley W Yor [44 Marsh Lane; links A629 and A635, from village centre by Black Bull; SE2010], *Farmers Boy*: Converted beamed cottages with new back barn restaurant, doing well under new licensees; Bass-related beers, interesting food, simple new country furnishings and woodwork, flower pictures, pleasant homely atmosphere; very popular with youngish locals *(P R Morley, Michael Butler)*; [Penistone Rd], *Sovereign*: Very popular welcoming open-plan L-shaped dining lounge with low beamery, red carpets and upholstery, yucca plants, restaurant leading off, generous unpretentious good value fresh food, Bass and Worthington BB, moderately priced wines, good atmosphere, attentive service; garden, provision for children *(M A Butler)*

Shipley W Yor [Saltaire Rd; SE1537], *Victoria*: Tastefully redecorated Victorian local with friendly landlord, regularly changing guest beers, usual food *(J E Rycroft)*

☆ Sinnington N Yor [SE7586], *Fox & Hounds*: Two clean and welcoming bar areas, nice paintings and old artefacts, cosy fires, good choice of home-cooked food inc interesting veg, well kept Bass and Camerons, dining area, separate pool room; attractive village with pretty stream and lots of grass; cosy well equipped bedrooms *(Enid and Henry Stephens, Elizabeth and Anthony Watts, M J Morgan, Rita and Keith Pollard)*

☆ Skerne E Yor [Wansford Rd; TA0455], *Eagle*: Quaint and unspoilt village local with two simple rooms either side of hall, coal fire, well kept Camerons from rare Victorian cash-register beer engine in kitchen-style servery, chatty locals, friendly landlord brings drinks to your table; no food, open 7-11 Mon-Fri, 12-2 weekends *(Pete Baker, Jack and Philip Paxton)*

Skidby E Yor [Main St, off A164; TA0133], *Half Moon*: Pleasantly old-fashioned partly panelled front tap room, airy back rooms inc partly no-smoking eating area, John Smiths and Marstons Pedigree, plenty of malt whiskies, usual bar food noon-10 inc loaf-sized yorkshire puddings, pub games, garden with play area and summer children's bar; children in eating area, open all day, live music Tues *(Brian Horner, Brenda Arthur, A Barnes, Helen Winfield, LYM)*

☆ Skipton N Yor [Canal St; from Water St (A65) turn into Coach St, then left after canal bridge; SD9852], *Royal Shepherd*: Busy old-fashioned local in pretty spot by canal, well kept Whitbreads-related ales and guests such as Cains, decent wine, friendly service, unusual sensibly priced whiskies, open fires, low-priced standard quick food, photographs of Yorks CCC in its golden days; big bar, snug and dining room, tables outside, games and juke box; children welcome in side room *(Prof and Mrs S Barnett, Mr and Mrs C Roberts, Ray and Liz Monk)*

Skipton [Market Pl], *Black Horse*: Bustling and friendly beams-and-stripped-stone coaching inn opp castle, popular with cavers, climbers and Saturday-market people; good choice of usual food served quickly, S&N ales, huge log-effect gas fire in big stone fireplace; open all day, children welcome; bedrooms with own bathrooms *(Roberto Villa)*; [Sheep St], *Woolly Sheep*: Series of beamed bars with exposed brickwork, stone fireplace, lots of sheep prints and old photographs, old plates and bottles, Black Sheep and Tetleys, good changing range of food inc good home-made puddings *(Neil and Anita Christopher)*

☆ Slaithwaite W Yor [B6107 Meltham—Marsden; SE0813], *White House*: Friendly and attractive moorland inn with good views, unusual home-cooked food, Tetleys and Timothy Taylors Landlord, good choice of wines by the glass, small bar with log fire, comfortable lounge on right, attractive restaurant area on left, tables out on front flagstones; children welcome; two bedrooms sharing bath, huge breakfast *(Andrew and Ruth Triggs, Derek and Liz Snaith)*

Sleights N Yor [180 Coach Rd; NZ8707], *Plough*: Pleasant two-bar stonebuilt pub with emphasis on tasty food; good views, well kept John Smiths and Theakstons *(WAH)*

Slingsby N Yor [Railway St; off B1257 Malton—Hovingham; SE7075], *Grapes*: Stone-built village local, quiet and clean, with straightforward popular food (not Mon lunchtime) inc Sun roast, well kept Camerons and Tetleys, friendly service, children in room off bar, no-smoking dining room, pool and darts; tables in garden behind *(JJW, CMW, LYM)*

Sneaton N Yor [Beacon Way; NZ8908], *Sneaton Hall*: Comfortable old-fashioned decor, good bar food with emphasis on meat, vegetarian dishes, good chips, restaurant; bedrooms *(M Borthwick)*; [Beacon Way], *Wilson Arms*: Good value generous food from sandwiches up inc good Sun menu, Barnsley, Black Sheep and Theakstons, friendly atmosphere, good open fires, pleasant dining room; bedrooms *(M Borthwick, Mike and Wendy Proctor)*

☆ South Dalton E Yor [SE9645], *Pipe & Glass*: Quiet friendly dining pub prettily set by Dalton Park, well kept Theakstons Best, Morlands Old Speckled Hen and Youngers IPA, some high-backed settles, old prints, log fires, beams and bow windows, conservatory, restaurant, children welcome, tables in garden with play area (*Keith and Rita Pollard, Karen and Graham Oddey, LYM*)

☆ Sowerby W Yor [Steep Lane; SE0423], *Travellers Rest*: Several cosy little rooms, open fire, wide choice of good generous reasonably priced food, friendly service; fine country setting, good view over Halifax and Calderdale Valley from garden (lovely at night) (*Ian and Amanda Wharmby, PM, AM*)

Sowerby Bridge W Yor [off Bolton Brow (A58) opp Java Restaurant; SE0623], *Moorings*: Attractively converted ex-canal warehouse, big windows overlooking canal basin, high beams, stripped stone, canal pictures, no-smoking family room; bar food (not Sun evening) from filled cobs to steaks inc children's and Sun roast, Moorhouses, Theakstons Best and XB, Youngers Scotch and guest beer, lots of bottled beers, pub games; new Belgian-style grill room, tables out on terrace, open all day Sat (*M L and G Clarke, PM, AM, LYM; more reports on new regime please*); [nr canal], *Navigation*: Nr canal, house beers Navigator and No 2, friendly staff, books and magazines to read, good value freshly cooked food (*P M Lane*)

Spennithorne N Yor [SE1489], *Old Horn*: Small cosy low-beamed 17th-c inn, renovated but not spoilt, with well kept Marstons Pedigree, John Smiths and Theakstons Best, decent wine, good home cooking, games area, busy dining room, unobtrusive piped music; two bedrooms with own bathrooms (*M J Morgan*)

☆ Sprotbrough S Yor [Lower Sprotbrough; 2¾ miles from M18 junction 2; SE5302], *Boat*: Interesting roomy stonebuilt ex-farmhouse with lovely courtyard in charming quiet spot by River Don, three individually furnished areas, big stone fireplaces, latticed windows, dark brown beams, good value bar food inc generous hot dishes (no sandwiches), well kept Courage-related beers, farm cider, helpful staff; piped music, fruit machine, no dogs; big sheltered prettily lit courtyard, river walks; restaurant (Tues-Sat evening, Sun lunch); open all day summer Sats (*Alan and Charlotte Sykes, M W Turner, Brian Nicholds, LYM*)

☆ Staithes N Yor [NZ7818], *Cod & Lobster*: Superb waterside setting in unspoilt fishing village under sandstone cliff, well kept beers inc Camerons Best and Strongarm, good crab sandwiches, friendly service, lovely views from seats outside; quite a steep walk up to top car park (*Dr and Mrs A H Young, Mike and Wendy Proctor, LYM*)

Staithes, *Royal George*: Small and friendly, nr harbour, with locals' bar on right, three plusher interconnected rooms, straightforward food, Camerons Bitter and Strongarm, children welcome; piped music, darts (*Phil and Heidi Cook, Mike and Wendy Proctor*)

☆ Stamford Bridge E Yor [A166 W of town;

SE7155], *Three Cups*: Spacious friendly family pub with stripped brickwork, beams, panelling and library theme, country furnishings and kitchen range in dining room, popular food – particularly the generous carvery (Tues-Sun), with friendly uniformed waitresses; well kept Bass and Tetleys, decent wines; children welcome, good play area behind; bedrooms (*H Bramwell, LYM*)

Stanbury W Yor [SE0037], *Old Silent*: Clean and up-to-date moorland village pub with conservatory, games room, juke box; well kept Theakstons, straightforward food, open fire, welcoming service, friendly restaurant; bedrooms (*J E Rycroft, Mark and Rachel Hirst, LYM*)

☆ Staveley N Yor [signed off A6055 Knaresborough—Boroughbridge; SE3663], *Royal Oak*: Prettily laid out beamed and tiled-floor pub locally popular for unusual home-cooked food in bar and restaurant, Tetleys-related ales, welcoming service, broad bow window; tables on front lawn (*Dorothy and David Young, LYM*)

Stokesley N Yor [1 West End; NZ5209], *White Swan*: Simple market-town pub with several regularly changing interesting ales in well worn-in split-level panelled bar, bar food inc tremendous choice of cheeses, hat display, welcoming staff, friendly ridgeback called Bix and little black dog called Titch; live blues Thurs (*Val Stevenson, Rob Holmes*)

☆ Sutton on the Forest N Yor [B1363 N of York; SE5965], *Rose & Crown*: Picturesque two-room dining pub with good fresh food inc excellent steaks, Theakstons ales, interesting wines, smart customers, helpful staff (*H Bramwell, W Rinaldi-Butcher, Andrew Argyle*)

☆ Sutton under Whitestonecliffe N Yor [A170 E of Thirsk; SE4983], *Whitestonecliffe*: Beamed 17th-c roadside pub with wide range of good value traditional generous bar meals (can be eaten in small restaurant) inc fresh fish and good puddings, open fire in relaxing and comfortable front lounge, back pool/family room with juke box and fruit machine, pleasant tap room with traditional games; John Smiths, Tetleys and Theakstons Best, decent wines, very friendly service; children welcome; back bedroom wing (*Martin Hickes, Brian and Peggy Mansfield*)

☆ Tadcaster N Yor [1 Bridge St; SE4843], *Angel & White Horse*: Tap for Sam Smiths brewery, cheap well kept OB and Museum, friendly staff, big helpings of good simple lunchtime food (not Sat) from separate counter; big often under-used bar with alcoves at one end, fine oak panelling and solid furnishings; restaurant (children allowed there); piped music; the dappled grey dray horses are kept across the coachyard, and brewery tours can be arranged – tel (01937) 832225; open all day Sat (*Chris Westmoreland, Gill and Andy Plumb, LYM*)

☆ Tan Hill N Yor [Arkengarthdale (Reeth—Brough) rd, at junction with Keld/W Stonesdale rd; NY8906], *Tan Hill Inn*: Simple furnishings, flagstones, big open fires and a cheery atmosphere in Britain's highest pub, on the Pennine Way, nearly five miles from the nearest neighbour; well kept Theakstons Best, XB and Old Peculier (in winter the cellar does chill down – for warmth you might prefer coffee or whisky with hot water), inexpensive hearty food from sandwiches up, some good old photographs; children welcome, open all day at least in summer; bedrooms, inc some in newish extension; often snowbound, with no mains electricity (juke box powered by generator); Swaledale sheep show last Thurs in May *(Bronwen and Steve Wrigley, M Morgan, Lesley Sones, Nigel Woolliscroft, D Tolson, Barry A Lynch, LYM)*

Thirsk N Yor [Market Pl; SE4382], *Golden Fleece*: Comfortable two-room bar with good reasonably priced food from sandwiches up, well kept Whitbreads-related ales, pleasant service, view across square from bay windows; restaurant, bedrooms *(Dono and Carol Leaman)*

Tholthorpe N Yor [SE4767], *New Inn*: Unspoilt no-gimmick pub with friendly staff, giant helpings of good value food, well kept Boddingtons and Theakstons; bedrooms *(John Knighton)*

Thoralby N Yor [SE0086], *George*: Lively and spotless little dales village local with limited but generous good value food, Black Sheep, John Smiths and Websters, great landlady, darts, dominoes; good value bedrooms, excellent breakfast *(Richard Hathaway, Tim Dobby, Ray and Liz Monk)*

Thornhill W Yor [B6117 Dewsbury—Horbury; SE2518], *Savile Arms*: Friendly old-fashioned Tetleys pub in 16th or 17th-c building, four comfortable and unpretentious small rooms, relaxed atmosphere, well kept Black Sheep and Old Mill ales *(Thomas Nott)*

☆ Thornton W Yor [Hill Top Rd; SE0933], *Ring o' Bells*: Spotless moortop dining pub noted for its success in pub catering competitions, wide choice of well presented good home cooking inc fresh fish, meat and poultry specialities, pleasant bar, popular air-conditioned restaurant; good range of Courage-related and other ales, very welcoming service, wide views towards Shipley and Bingley *(Geoffrey and Brenda Wilson, Sheila and Brian Wilson, F J Willy, K H Frostick, Mrs Pam Deeprose)*

Thornton le Clay N Yor [SE6865], *White Swan*: Friendly old-fashioned dining pub with popular food inc vegetarian, well kept ales such as Black Sheep and Youngers Scotch, decent wines, log fires, tables on terrace; good view from impeccable ladies'; cl Mon lunchtime *(Mrs J Bean)*

Thorpe Hesley S Yor [Smithy Wood Rd, very nr M1 junction 35; SK3796], *Travellers*: Early Victorian, stuffed birds, brass, pictures and fresh flowers, good value food, three well kept ales, restaurant, public bar with fruit machine and piped music; disabled lavatory; family room in garden with swings and pets; live music Thurs; woodland walks nearby *(CMW, JJW)*

Thruscross N Yor [off A59 Harrogate—Skipton or B6255 Grassington—Pateley Bridge; SE1558], *Stone House*: Moorland pub with beams, flagstones, stripped stone, dark panelling and warm fires; generous bar food,

well kept ales, traditional games, sheltered tables outside; children welcome *(Prof and Mrs S Barnett, LYM)*

Thurcroft S Yor [Woodhouse Green; SK4989], *Double Barrel*: Recently tastefully refurbished, with friendly staff, good value home-made food Thurs-Sat; well kept Wards *(Nigel Brewitt)*

Thurlstone S Yor [A628; SE2303], *Huntsman*: Well run old stone-built pub with good range of well kept ales inc Flowers and Marstons, welcoming atmosphere, lunchtime bar food, coal fire *(Michael Butler)*

Tickhill S Yor [Sunderland St; A631 Bawtry rd; SK5993], *Scarbrough Arms*: Cheerful pub with lots of brass and barrel tables, decent food, well kept Ruddles County; swings out behind *(Simon Chappell, Louise Chappell, Margaret Watson)*

Tickton E Yor [Hull Bridge, off A1035; TA0642], *Crown & Anchor*: Busy friendly Mansfield pub with good food choice inc vegetarian and children's, play area and picnic tables in riverside garden, riverside walks *(JJW, CMW)*

Towton N Yor [A162 Tadcaster—Ferrybridge; SE4839], *Rockingham Arms*: Bright and friendly extended pub with popular plentiful food esp fish and chips, good range of sandwiches, horse-racing memorabilia, welcoming efficient service, well kept Vaux Bitter and Samson, good coffee, revolving back pool table *(Chris Westmoreland, Roy Bromell)*

Ugthorpe N Yor [NZ7911], *Black Bull*: Small-roomed atmospheric old local, pleasantly decorated no-smoking restaurant overlooking back garden, good value Sun lunch, friendly service *(M Borthwick)*

☆ Ulley S Yor [Turnshaw Rd; 2 miles from M1 junction 31 – off B6067 in Aston; SK4687], *Royal Oak*: Friendly and cosy stone-built pub in lovely countryside by church, very popular for good range of good value bar food served till late, attractive and intimate inexpensive restaurant (must book); well kept cheap Sam Smiths OB, stable-theme beamed lounge with rooms off, helpful service, quiet piped music, good children's room, big garden; can get packed on warm summer evenings, esp Sat *(GSB, WAH, Paul Robinshaw)*

☆ Upper Poppleton N Yor [A59 York—Harrogate; SE5554], *Red Lion*: Consistently good value well presented food inc good vegetarian in dark and cosy olde-worlde bars and dining areas, quiet, sparkling clean and welcoming – popular with older people and businessmen; pleasant garden; bedroom extension *(Mr and Mrs I B White, F J Robinson)*

Wainstalls W Yor [Lower Saltonstall – Pellon Lane/Pellon New Rd from Halifax, then left into Wainstalls Lane; SE0428], *Cat i' th' Well*: Three cosy rooms with lots of bric-a-brac and interesting pictures, wide range of beers, food lunchtime and weekends, very cheerful licensees, good atmosphere, pleasant tree-sheltered garden with play area *(PM, AM)*; [Warley Moor Rd], *Withens*: Stunning views from one of highest pubs in the county, good homely well priced food, real ale, good landlord, open fire *(Jonathan Harrison)*

Wakefield W Yor [Newmillerdam (A61 S); SE3315], *Dam*: By reservoir dam, attractive walking country – so busy in summer; neatly kept L-shaped stripped-stone bar with usual furnishings, adjoining Toby carvery/restaurant, well kept Stones and Worthington, pleasant coffee lounge, prompt service, generous usual food *(Thomas Nott, Michael Butler)*; [Horbury Rd, Westgate], *Redoubt*: Cosy traditional city pub, four separate rooms off long corridor, Rugby League photographs, well kept Tetleys and interesting guest beers *(Jack and Philip Paxton)*

Warley W Yor [SE0525], *Maypole*: Friendly farmhouse-style refurbishment, country furniture on flagstones, enormous choice of good value generous food, well kept Marstons Pedigree *(Mrs P Tullie, Howard Bateman)*

Weaverthorpe N Yor [SE9771], *Star*: Comfortable little inn in relaxing village setting, good straightforward food, well kept ales, exceptionally welcoming staff; nice bedrooms, good breakfast; cl weekday lunchtimes *(Bob Ellis)*

Welburn N Yor [SE7268], *Crown & Cushion*: Tidy stonebuilt village pub with good home cooking inc good Sun lunch and puddings, friendly staff, decent wine, Camerons Bitter and Strongarm and Tetleys, games in public bar, restaurant; piped music; attractive small back garden with terrace; children in eating areas, has been closed Mon lunchtime in winter *(Jason Caulkin, LYM)*

☆ **Wentworth** [3 miles from M1 junction 36; B6090, signed off A6135; SK3898], *Rockingham Arms*: Good traditional furnishings, hunting pictures, open fires, stripped stone, rooms off inc a dining room and family room, good choice of reasonably priced food (not Sun evening) inc inventive specials, several well kept S&N ales, cheerful service; piped music; tables in attractive garden with own well kept bowling green; has been open all day; bedrooms *(G P Kernan, LYM)*

☆ **West Burton** N Yor [off B6160 Bishopdale— Wharfedale; SE0186], *Fox & Hounds*: Clean and cosy unpretentious local on long green of idyllic dales village, simple generous inexpensive fresh food inc children's, well kept Black Sheep and Theakstons ales, chatty budgerigar, residents' dining room, children welcome; nearby caravan park; good modern bedrooms, lovely walks and waterfalls nearby *(Richard Hathaway, Frank Hughes, Marianne Lantree, Steve Webb, James H Emery)*

☆ **West Tanfield** N Yor [A6108 N of Ripon; SE2678], *Bull*: Open-plan but the feel of two smallish rooms, comfortable pub furniture, popular food all day inc good sandwiches, well kept Black Sheep Best, Tetleys and Theakstons Best, decent wines, welcoming service, small restaurant; shame about the piped music; tables in attractive garden sloping steeply to river *(BB)*

West Witton N Yor [A684 W of Leyburn; SE0688], *Wensleydale Heifer*: Comfortable genteel dining pub with low-ceilinged small interconnecting areas in front lounge, big attractive bistro, separate restaurant, good food inc interesting dishes and seafood (generous though not cheap), good log fire, attractive prints, pleasant decor; small bar with decent wines, Black Sheep, John Smiths and Theakstons Best; back bedrooms quietest, good breakfast *(Keith Croxton, Dr P Jackson, M Morgan, Gwen and Peter Andrews)*

Westow N Yor [SE7565], *Blacksmiths Arms*: Good local with warm country atmosphere, decent food, John Smiths and Tetleys *(Christopher Turner)*

☆ **Whitby** N Yor [Church St; nr 199 Steps, East Side; NZ9011], *Duke of York*: Bustling comfortable beamed pub down by harbour entrance, lovely views from lounge, friendly atmosphere (perhaps more than can be said for the cat), well kept Courage Directors and John Smiths Magnet, good value local cod and wide range of usual food all day, fishing memorabilia, family room; piped music, fruit machine; bedrooms *(Sue and Bob Ward, Andy and Jane Bearsdley, M Borthwick, Andy and Jill Kassube, Chris Mawson, JJW, CMW, Peter Bullen, M Borthwick)*

Whitby [Bridge St; just over bridge to E/Old Whitby], *Dolphin*: Pleasant atmosphere, wide range of bar food inc generous local fish and filled yorkshire puddings, well kept Tetleys and Theakstons *(Andy and Jill Kassube, Dr and Mrs B Baker)*; [New Quay Rd], *Tap & Spile*: Well decorated bare-boards pub, no-smoking area, good bar food inc local cod noon-7, up to eight well kept ales, country wines, farm cider, traditional games; open all day *(Andy and Jill Kassube, JJW, CMW)*; [Church St], *White Horse & Griffin*: Well priced food inc good choice of local fresh fish (you can't have just a drink), cosy candlelit ambience *(Mike and Wendy Proctor)*

☆ **Wigglesworth** N Yor [B6478; SD8157], *Plough*: Little rooms off bar, some spartan yet cosy, others smart and plush, inc no-smoking panelled dining room and snug; popular bar food inc huge sandwiches, good specials and children's dishes (though some find the pit barbecue approach more suited to a chain pub), conservatory restaurant with panoramic dales views, well kept Boddingtons and Tetleys, decent wines, good friendly service; attractive garden, pleasant bedrooms *(Joan and Tony Walker, Steve and Julie Cocking, K H Frostick, John Allsopp, LYM)*

Withernsea E Yor [TA3427], *Commercial*: Good very low-priced food from generous saandwiches to sizzler dishes, friendly staff *(Jackie Moffat)*

Worsborough Bridge S Yor [Park Rd (A61); SE3504], *Ship*: Huge plush lounge, friendly staff, well kept Tetleys; handy for country park *(Dr and Mrs A K Clarke)*

Wortley S Yor [A629 N of Sheffield; SK3099], *Wortley Arms*: Stonebuilt coaching inn brewing its own Earls Ale, also Reindeer, Stones and Youngers, with big lounge, no-smoking area, tap room and dining room, good value food, very good service; piped pop music, tricky car park; open all day, children welcome, bedrooms *(JJW, CMW, Richard Houghton)*

Wragby W Yor [A638 nr Nostell Priory – OS

Sheet 111 map ref 412172; SE4117], *Spread Eagle*: Four homely and friendly traditional low-beamed rooms with well kept Bass and Sam Smiths, good simple generous food, evening restaurant; atmospheric tap room with photographs of regulars as youngsters; quiz night, popular weekends *(M A Butler, Alan Kerry)*

Wykeham N Yor [the one nr Scarboro; SE9783], *Downe Arms*: Good choice of generous food, family room and play area *(Mrs Kathy Newens)*

☆ **York** [High Petergate], *Hole in the Wall*: Good atmosphere in rambling open-plan pub handy for Minster, beams, stripped brickwork, turkey carpeting, plush seats, well kept Mansfield beers, good coffee, cheap simple food noon-8 inc generous Sun lunch, friendly prompt service; juke box, piped music not too loud; open all day *(M Walker, Chris Westmoreland, Esther and John Sprinkle, John Fazakerley, LYM)*

☆ **York** [18 Goodramgate], *Royal Oak*: Cosy black-beamed 16th-c pub with big helpings of good value imaginative bar food (limited Sun evening) served 11.30-7.30, quick friendly service, well kept Ind Coope Burton, Tetleys, Whitbreads Castle Eden, wines and country wines, good coffee; prints, swords and old guns, no-smoking family room; handy for minster, can get crowded *(Chris Westmoreland, BB)*

☆ **York** [26 High Petergate], *York Arms*: Snug little basic panelled bar, big modern no-smoking lounge, cosier partly panelled room full of old bric-a-brac, prints, brown-cushioned wall settles, dimpled copper tables and an open fire; quick friendly service, well kept Sam Smiths OB and Museum, good value simple food lunchtime and early evening, no music; by minster, open all day *(M Walker, Keith and Cheryl Roe, Michele and Clive Platman, BB)*

☆ **York,** [7 Stonegate], *Punch Bowl*: Attractive local with small dim-lit rooms off corridor, helpful service, good generous lunchtime food, well kept Bass, Stones, Worthington Best and a guest such as Timothy Taylors Landlord; piped music may obtrude; open all day all week, some live music and quiz nights, good value bedrooms *(Graham and Lynn Mason, Mark Walker, Chris Westmoreland, Jamie and Ruth Lyons)*

York [55 Blossom St], *Bay Horse*: Basic but pleasant rambling pub, lots of nooks and alcoves, nice back room with button-back leather seats, original old cash register; food inc good value seafood platter *(Martin Hickes, BB)*; [Hull Rd (A1079)], *Black Bull*: Comfortable atmosphere, good mix of chairs and tables, brisk friendly service, reasonably priced Worthington and wine by the glass, generous food; handy for York University; 40 bedrooms in modern back block *(Roger Bellingham)*; [53 Fossgate], *Blue Bell*: Two small friendly Edwardian panelled rooms, coal fires, several well kept Vaux ales, fresh lunchtime sandwiches and pickled eggs, chatty locals *(Chris Westmoreland, Pete Baker, M Walker)*; [29 Bootham], *Bootham Tavern*: Popular untouristy drinkers' pub with well kept

Tetleys Bitter and Mild, cosy lounge, friendly landlord, tap room with darts and games *(Richard Lewis)*; [Monkgate, far end by roundabout], *Brigadier Gerard*: Elegant Georgian exterior, comfortable and friendly in, memorabilia of the great racehorse, good solid Yorkshire food *(H Bramwell)*; [Goodramgate], *Golden Slipper*: Dating from 15th c, quaint series of rooms much favoured by locals, old and young; wide food choice inc OAP bargains, nothing too much trouble *(H Bramwell)*; [23 Market St], *Hansom Cab*: Dark panelling, wall seats, wing chairs, side alcoves, good value quick food counter, Sam Smiths *(Michele and Clive Platman, M Walker)*; [Kings Staithe just below Ouse Bridge], *Kings Arms*: Fine riverside position with lots of picnic tables out on cobbled waterside terrace; bowed black beams and flagstones inside, straightforward furnishings, good lunchtime food from sandwiches up; CD juke box can be loud, keg beers; open all day *(Esther and John Sprinkle, Mark Walker)*; [Lendal], *Lendal Cellars*: Broad-vaulted medieval cellars carefully spotlit to show up the stripped masonry, hand-crafted furniture and cask seats on stone floor, interconnected rooms and alcoves, well kept Whitbreads and a guest ale *(Chris Westmoreland, LYM)*; [Tanners Moat/Wellington Row], *Maltings*: Vast range of well kept beers from small breweries, good choice of continental ones, decent well priced honest food, welcoming service, interesting salvaged fittings like suburban front door for ladies', plenty of atmosphere, friendly staff, daily papers in gents'; handy for Rail Museum, some live entertainment *(J Royce, Tony Hall, Mick Popka, A Summerfield, Mark Walker)*; [Goodramgate], *Old White Swan*: Victorian, Georgian and Tudor themed bars, delightful covered courtyard, bar food, Bass and Worthington, friendly staff; juke box, piped music, games machines, popular with younger people at night *(Martin Hickes, Mark Walker)*; [North St, opp Viking Hotel], *Tap & Spile*: Three smallish rooms, good reasonably priced changing local beers, good simple wholesome food; relaxed and friendly *(Chris Westmoreland)*; [Merchantgate, between Fossgate and Piccadilly], *Red Lion*: Low-beamed rambling rooms with some stripped Tudor brickwork, relaxed old-fashioned furnishings, well kept Courage-related ales, bar snacks and summer meals, tables outside, good juke box or piped music *(Chris Westmoreland, LYM)*; [Goodramgate], *Snickleway*: Snug little old-world pub, lots of antiques, copper and brass, good coal fires, cosy nooks and crannies, good simple wholesome lunchtime snacks (not Sun) inc good value sandwiches, unobtrusive piped music, prompt service, well kept John Smiths *(Shuni Davies, Mark Walker, Giles Bird)*; [Museum St], *Thomas's*: Plush and ornate Victorian-style pub, assorted sports bric-a-brac, popular straightforward food, cheerful efficient service, John Smiths Bitter and Magnet *(M and C Platman, M Walker)*

London
Scotland
Wales
Channel Islands

London

Pubs generating particular enthusiasm among readers this year include, in Central London, the Argyll Arms (lots of well kept beers), the Grapes (Shepherd Market's best pub, back in these pages after a break), the big, busy, atmospheric Cittie of Yorke, the snug little Grenadier, the classic Lamb, the cosy old-fashioned Nags Head (our London-based Research Officer's favourite), the hugely stylish new Fullers pub the Old Bank of England (a new entry), the charming tucked-away Olde Mitre, the friendly Orange Brewery (brewing its own beers), and the striking Princess Louise; in North London, the Chapel (a new entry, with good wines and much better food than the general London rule) and the villagey Olde White Bear (very competitive drinks prices); in South London, the Cutty Sark, the Fire Station (a most unusual new entry), the riverside Ship and the similarly attractively placed White Cross; in West London, the lively Churchill Arms, the well placed Dove, and the chatty Ladbroke Arms (very good food); and in East London, the Town of Ramsgate (an interesting riverside pub new to the main entries). Food tends to be cheap rather than special in most London pubs, but there are some fine exceptions such as the Eagle and Front Page (Central) and the Ladbroke Arms (West); it's the Ladbroke Arms which we choose as London Dining Pub of the Year. Drinks prices are generally much higher than the national average. Pubs in the Wetherspoons chain such as Hamilton Hall by contrast price their drinks well below the national average, as do most pubs tied to Fullers, the West London brewer; and pubs tied to Youngs of South London are generally less expensive than most. London has been hit harder than anywhere else by the big brewers' current craze for Irish-theme pubs; one of the most acceptable we've found is O'Connor Don in W1, in the Lucky Dip section at the end of the chapter. That section does contain a good many worthwhile genuine pubs. Ones which have recently been giving readers particular pleasure include, in Central London, the Hand & Shears and Pheasant & Firkin (EC1), Grouse & Claret, Lord Moon of the Mall and Red Lion in Crown Passage (SW1), and Coopers Arms (SW3); North, the Flask (N6) and Crockers (NW8); South, the Woodman (SW11), Greyhound (SW16) and White Swan (Richmond) – and there are some nice riverside pubs in SE1 and SE16; West, the Sporting Page (SW10), the Strand on the Green pubs (W4) and Plough (Norwood Green); and in East London, Hollands (E1).

CENTRAL LONDON
Covering W1, W2, WC1, WC2, SW1, SW3, EC1, EC2, EC3 and EC4 postal districts

Parking throughout this area is metered throughout the day, and generally in short supply then; we mention difficulty only if evening parking is a problem too. Throughout the chapter we list the nearest Underground or BR stations to each pub; where two are listed it means the walk is the same from either

Albert ▪ (Westminster) Map 13

52 Victoria Street, SW1; ✆ St James's Park

The handsome staircase that leads up to the restaurant at this splendid Victorian pub is lined with portraits of former Prime Ministers, and it's quite likely that several of those pictured would have enjoyed a drink here at some stage – it's not that far to Westminster (they even sound the Division Bell). The mix of customers is wonderfully diverse, and the building itself is one of the great sights of this part of London, handsome, colourful and harmonious; it's rather dwarfed by the faceless cliffs of dark modern glass around it, but still towers above them in architectural merit. The ground floor is a huge open-plan bar, with good solid comfortable furniture, gleaming mahogany, original gas lamps, and by day a fresh and airy feel however busy it gets, thanks to great expanses of heavily cut and etched windows along three sides. Despite the space, on weekday lunchtimes it can be packed with civil servants. Service from the big island counter is swift and friendly (particularly obliging to overseas visitors), with well kept Courage Directors, John Smiths, Ruddles Best, Theakstons Best and XB, Wadworths 6X and Websters Yorkshire on handpump. The separate food servery is good value, with sandwiches (from £1.40), salads (from £3.50) and five home-cooked hot dishes such as cottage pie, steak pie, quiche or lasagne (all £4.25). The upstairs restaurant does an eat-as-much-as-you-like carvery, better than average (all day inc Sunday, £13.95). Piped music is never obtrusive, and noticeable only at quiet times. *(Recommended by C Walker, Robert Lester, John and Wendy Trentham, Wayne Brindle, Robert C Ward Jr, Mary Sikorski, John Ames, Mark Walker, Richard Waller)*

Scottish & Newcastle ~ Managers Roger and Gill Wood ~ Real ale ~ Meals and snacks (11-10.30) ~ Restaurant ~ (0171) 222 5577 ~ Children in eating area and restaurant (except lunchtimes Mon and Fri) ~ Open 11-11; 12-10.30 Sun; cl 25-26 Dec

Argyll Arms ▪ (Oxford Circus) Map 13

18 Argyll St W1; ✆ Oxford Circus, opp tube side exit

Easy to spot by the profusion of plants and flowers that festoon its frontage, this bustling place is a welcome retreat from the hordes of shoppers around Oxford Circus. It's especially nice to find it so traditional, with the three cubicle rooms at the front the most atmospheric and unusual. All oddly angular, they're made by wooden partitions with distinctive frosted and engraved glass, with hops trailing above. A good range of changing beers typically has Adnams, Brains SA, Coachmans Beacon, Hook Norton Best, Tetleys and various other guests on handpump; also Addlestone's cider, malt whiskies, and freshly squeezed orange juice. A long mirrored corridor leads to the spacious back room, with the food counter in one corner; this area is no smoking at lunchtime. Chalked up on a blackboard (which may also have topical cartoons), the choice of meals includes good and unusual sandwiches like generously filled stilton and grape (£2.50) or roast chicken, bacon and melted cheese (£3.50), and main courses such as salads or a pie of the day. Welcoming, efficient staff; two fruit machines, piped pop music. The quieter upstairs bar, which overlooks the busy pedestrianised street (and the Palladium theatre if you can see through the foliage outside the window), is divided into several snugs with comfortable plush easy chairs; swan's neck lamps, and lots of small theatrical prints along the top of the walls. The gents' has a copy of the day's *Times* or *Financial Times* on the wall. Like everywhere else in this area, the pub can get crowded, though there's space for drinking outside. *(Recommended by Wayne Brindle, Hanns P Golez, Christopher Gallop, Bob and Maggie Atherton, Thomas Thomas, John and Anne Peacock, David Carr, Richard Lewis, Per Ness, John Fazakerley, Ian Phillips, Gordon)*

Nicholsons (Allied; run as free house) ~ Managers Mike and Sue Tayara ~ Real ale ~ Meals (11.30-7.30) and snacks (till 9.30) ~ Restaurant ~ 0171-734 6117 ~ Children welcome ~ Open 11-11; 12-10.30 Sun

Black Friar ▪ (City) Map 13

174 Queen Victoria Street, EC4; ✆ Blackfriars

The decor at this unique pub is so impressive that one reader says he wouldn't even mind paying a nominal admission fee. It's the inner back room that stands out, with some of the best fine Edwardian bronze and marble art-nouveau decor to be found anywhere – big bas-relief friezes of jolly monks set into richly coloured Florentine marble walls, an opulent marble-pillared inglenook fireplace, a low vaulted mosaic ceiling, gleaming mirrors, seats built into rich golden marble recesses, and tongue-in-cheek verbal embellishments such as Silence is Golden and Finery is Foolish. The whole place is much bigger inside than seems possible from the delightfully odd exterior, and that's quite a good thing – they do get very busy, particularly after work; lots of people spill out onto the wide forecourt in front, near the approach to Blackfriars Bridge. See if you can spot the opium smoking-hints modelled into the fireplace of the front room. Lunchtime bar food includes filled rolls (£2.50), baked potatoes or ploughman's (£2.95), and a daily hot dish like chicken curry (£3.95); service is obliging and helpful. Well kept Adnams, Brakspears, Tetleys, Wadworths 6X and an Allied beer named for Nicholsons on handpump; fruit machine. If you're coming by Tube, choose your exit carefully – it's all too easy to emerge from the network of passageways and find yourself on the other side of the street or marooned on a traffic island. *(Recommended by Chris Westmoreland, Eric and Jackie Robinson, Christopher Gallop, David Carr, Mark Baynham, Rachael Ward, Karen and Graham Oddey)*

Nicholsons (Allied) ~ Manager Mr Becker ~ Real ale ~ Lunchtime meals (11.30-2.30) ~ 0171-236 5650 ~ Open 11.30-10(11 Thurs/Fri); closed weekends and bank holidays

Chandos (Covent Garden) Map 13

29 St Martins Lane, WC2; ⊖ Leicester Square

They start their working day early at this busy pub, serving breakfasts between 9am and 10.30. That's probably about the only time you can catch it when it's quiet, as later in the day (and especially in the evenings) it can seem all of London is meeting in the bare-boarded downstairs area. It's really the more comfortable upstairs Opera Room that makes it worth knowing: quieter and more atmospheric, it's rather like a cross between a typical pub and a chattily civilised salon, with secluded alcoves, low wooden tables and panelling, and comfortable leather sofas. Opera memorabilia is dotted around the walls, and the small orange, red and yellow leaded panes of glass in the windows give the place a slightly theatrical hue – as well as rather effectively distancing the bustle outside. Most of the food is up here (though they serve pretty much everything but the main meals downstairs too), with a very wide choice of snacks like sandwiches (from £1.80), prawn and pineapple kebabs (£3.50), and stilton mushrooms, deep fried camembert or Thai nibbles (£3.95), full meals like steak and kidney pie or gammon (£4.95), and seafood crêpes (£5.95), and daily specials such as chicken and almond casserole or steak and stilton stew; they do Sunday roasts. Well kept Sam Smiths OB on handpump (maybe under light blanket pressure in summer), at a delightfully un-London price; darts, pinball, fruit machines, video game, trivia and piped music. Even at busy times the atmosphere is cheery and relaxed, and the service friendly and helpful. On the roof facing the National Portrait Gallery they have an automaton of a cooper at work (working 10-2 and 4-9). Lots of attractions and theatres are within easy walking distance of here, with the Coliseum (home of the English National Opera) just around the corner; several readers dash back for a quick pint during the interval, though it's quite a gamble – if you're even a minute late back they'll make you stand up for the whole of the next act. *(Recommended by Gordon Prince, John C Baker, D J and P M Taylor, Mayur Shah, John Fahy, Susan and Nigel Wilson, Helen Pickering, James Owen, Hanns P Golez, Mick Hitchman, Steve Harvey, Gill and Andy Plumb, Neil and Anita Christopher, Susan and Nigel Wilson, Chris Westmoreland, Mike Davies)*

Sam Smiths ~ Manager Neil Park ~ Real ale ~ Meals and snacks (11.30-2.30, 5.30-9, plus breakfast) ~ 0171-836 1405 ~ Children in eating area of Opera Room till 6pm (7 Sun-Weds) ~ Open 11-11; 12-10.30 Sun; closed 25 Dec

Cittie of Yorke 🍺 (Holborn) Map 13

22 High Holborn, WC1; find it by looking out for its big black and gold clock; ⊖ Chancery Lane

One of the many letters of praise we've had recently about this busy old place likens its main back room to the inside of a medieval castle. It really is quite amazing when seen for the first time, the extraordinarily extended bar counter (the longest in Britain) stretching off into the distance, vast thousand-gallon wine vats resting above the gantry, and big bulbous lights hanging from the soaring high raftered roof. It gets packed at lunchtime and in the early evening, particularly with lawyers and judges, but most people tend to congregate in the middle, so you should still be able to bag one of the intimate, old-fashioned and ornately carved cubicles that run along both sides. The unique triangular Waterloo fireplace, with grates on all three sides and a figure of Peace among laurels, used to stand in the Grays Inn Common Room until barristers stopped dining there. Well-priced Sam Smiths OB on handpump, and some unusually flavoured vodkas such as chocolate orange or pear and ginger; fruit machine, video game and piped music. A smaller, comfortable wood-panelled room has lots of little prints of York and attractive brass lights, while the ceiling of the entrance hall has medieval-style painted panels and plaster York roses. There's a lunchtime food counter in the main hall with more in the downstairs cellar bar: the choice typically includes filled baps, ploughman's and salads, and several daily changing hot dishes like Tuscan bean and garlic crostini (£4.25), and steak and kidney pie or fish and chips (£5). A pub has stood on this site since 1430, though the current building owes more to the 1695 coffee house erected here behind a garden; it was reconstructed in Victorian times using 17th-c materials and parts. *(Recommended by Ted George, Val Stevenson, Rob Holmes, Mark Baynham, Rachael Ward, Mr Satterlee, Eric and Jackie Robinson, John Fahy, Chris Westmoreland, R J Bland, Mick Hitchman, Jens Arne Grebstad, E A Thwaite, David Carr, GSB, Gordon)*

Sam Smiths ~ Manager Stuart Browning ~ Real ale ~ Meals and snacks (12-10) ~ 0171-242 7670 ~ Children in eating area ~ Open 11.30-11; closed all day Sun

Dog & Duck (Soho) Map 13

18 Bateman St, on corner with Frith Street, W1; ● Tottenham Court Rd/Leicester Square

A good mix of people squeeze into this delightful little corner house, right in the heart of fashionable Soho. On the floor by the door is a mosaic of a dog, tongue out in hot pursuit of a duck, and the same theme is embossed on some of the shiny tiles that frame the heavy old advertising mirrors. The little bar counter is rather unusual, and serves well kept Eldridge Pope, Timothy Taylors Landlord, Tetleys, and a couple of guests on handpump; doorstep sandwiches (from £1.80). The chatty main bar really is tiny, and it's mostly standing room only, with some high stools by the ledge along the back wall, though there are seats in a roomier area at one end, and in a very pleasant upstairs bar overlooking the street. There's a fire in winter, and newspapers to read. In good weather especially there tend to be plenty of people spilling onto the bustling street outside. No machines or piped music – though if you fancy a few tunes Ronnie Scott's Jazz Club is near by. *(Recommended by Gerry Christie, Steve Harvey, David Carr, Maggie and Bob Atherton, Chris Westmoreland)*

Nicholsons (Allied) ~ Manageress Mrs Gene Bell ~ Real ale ~ Snacks (not weekends) ~ 0171-437 4447 ~ Open 12-11; closed Sat and Sun lunchtimes, opening 6 Sat evening

Eagle 🍴 🍷 (City) Map 13

159 Farringdon Rd, EC1; opposite Bowling Green Lane car park; ● Farringdon/Old Street

Still standing out like a beacon amongst London pubs serving food, this stylish place is well known for its highly distinctive mediterranean-style meals. Made with the finest quality ingredients, the choice changes at least once every day, with typical dishes including pea soup with chorizo and mint (£3.50), butternut squash and sage risotto (£6.50), wholewheat spaghetti with sardines, parsley, black pepper and onion (£7), roast duck with rocket salad, sweet roast onions and sherry vinegar (£7.50), fabada (a stew with butter beans, pork, saffron, chorizo, morcillas and pancetta) or Portuguese baked saltcod (£8), and red mullet baked with tomatoes, capers, olives and basil (£9); they also do Spanish and Italian cheeses (£4.50), and Portuguese custard tarts. They may run out of some dishes fairly early, and the tables go incredibly quickly, so it's worth getting here as early as you can, especially at lunchtimes. The open kitchen forms part of the bar, and furnishings in the single room are simple but stylish – school chairs, circular tables and a couple of sofas on bare boards, modern paintings on the walls (there's an art gallery upstairs, with direct access from the bar). The atmosphere is lively and chatty and although there's quite a mix of customers, it is popular with media folk (*The Guardian* is based just up the road). Well kept Boddingtons, Marstons Pedigree and Wadworths 6X on handpump, decent wines including a dozen by the glass, good coffee, and properly made cocktails; piped music. In the evenings it's more traditionally pubby, though seats and tables are just as fiercely coveted. *(Recommended by James Macrae, Maggie and Bon Atherton, Dave Braisted, Andrew Stephenson, Chris Westmoreland, Ian Phillips)*

Free house ~ Licencees Michael Belben and David Eyre ~ Real ale ~ Meals (12.30-2.30, 6.30-10.30) ~ 0171-837 1353 ~ Children welcome ~ Open 12-11; closed Sun, bank hols, Easter Sat, and 2 weeks at Christmas

Front Page (Chelsea) Map 12

35 Old Church Street, SW3; ⊖ Sloane Square, but some distance away

Written up on big blackboards at both ends of the bar, the bistro-style food at this smartly stylish place is well worth sampling: carrot and coriander soup (£2.60), prawns, spinach and pinenuts in a filo parcel, topped with a creamy mushroom sauce (£4.95), grilled avocado filled with crab, smoked salmon and cream cheese (£5), penne tossed with smoked chicken and mange tout in a creamy pesto sauce (£5.95), spicy monkfish stir fry on a bed of crispy noodles (£6.50), cheese fondue (for two, £8.75), and puddings like baked bananas (£3). Huge windows with heavy navy curtains and big ceiling fans give the place a light and airy feel, and one cosy area has an open fire; lighting is virtually confined to brass picture-lights above small Edwardian monochrome pictures, and there are newspapers to read. It can get full in the evening (on Fridays especially), but fills up rather slowly, so that if you arrive around six o'clock you may have the place almost to yourself. Even at its busiest it's never too crowded, and there's a good mix of people around the heavy wooden tables or pews and benches. Well kept Boddingtons, Ruddles County and Websters Yorkshire on handpump; decent wines. Major sporting events may be shown on a big TV screen. Outside, there are big copper gaslamps above pretty hanging baskets. The same people run the Sporting Page not too far away (see dips), and a couple of other pubs, including the Chequers at Well (see Hampshire main entries). *(Recommended by David Carr, James Macrae, Richard Gibbs, Dr and Mrs A K Clarke; more reports please)*

Courage ~ Lease: Thomas Watt, Richard Colthart ~ Real ale ~ Meals (12-2.30, 7-10) ~ Children welcome lunchtimes only ~ 0171-352 2908 ~ Open 11-11, 12-10.30 Sun; closed 25/26 Dec

Glassblower (Piccadilly Circus) Map 13

42 Glasshouse Street, W1; ⊖ Piccadilly Circus

Recently refurbished, this useful pub is a handy place for lunch, or to escape from nearby Piccadilly Circus. An enormous gently-flickering gaslight hangs from the centre of the ceiling in the busy main bar, with more gaslight-style brackets around the walls. Furnishings are simple and unfussy, though there are more comfortable seats and tables in the upstairs lounge, which is generally quieter and less smoky too. Real ales on handpump include Courage Best and Directors, Greene King IPA, and Theakstons Best, Old Peculier and XB; they also have a good few malt whiskies and Scrumpy Jack cider. Food such as filled baguettes (from £2.85), a choice of sausages like cajun or pork and leek (£2.85), ploughman's (£3.95), popular fish and chips (£4.95), and lemon and pepper chicken (£5.95). Fruit machine, video game, trivia, and juke box. The downstairs bar can get a little crowded. *(Recommended by Steve Harvey, Bob and Maggie Atherton, Mick Hitchman, Hanns P Golez, Ian Phillips, Chris Westmoreland, John Fazakerley, Gordon, David Craine, Ann Reeder, Neil and Anita Christopher, Mark Walker)*

S & N ~ Managers Mervyn and Julie Wood ~ Real ale ~ Meals and snacks (all day) ~ 0171-734 8547 ~ Children in eating area of bar till 9pm (5pm Fri and Sat) ~ Open 11-11; 12-10.30 Sun; closed 25 Dec

Grapes (Mayfair) Map 13

Shepherd Market, W1; ⊖ Green Park

Traditional and friendly, this busy pub is bang in the bustle of civilised Shepherd Market, and on sunny evenings you'll generally find the square outside packed with smart-suited drinkers. The dimly lit bar is cheery and old-fashioned, with plenty of stuffed birds in glass display cases, and a snug little alcove at the back. Bar food might include sandwiches (from £2.50), seafood platter or half roast chicken (£3.95), ploughman's

(£4.95), and steak and mushroom pie (£5.25). A good range of six or seven well kept beers on handpump usually takes in Boddingtons, Brakspears, Flowers IPA and Original, Fullers London Pride and Wadworths 6X; fruit machine. *(Recommended by Peter Todd, Wayne Brindle, Tim Barrow, Sue Demont, Eric and Jackie Robinson)*

Free house ~ Licensees Gill and Eric Lewis ~ Real ale ~ Meals and snacks ~ Restaurant ~ 0171-629 4989 ~ Children welcome if eating ~ Open 11-11; 12-10.30 Sun; closed 25 Dec

Grenadier (Belgravia) Map 13

Wilton Row, SW1; the turning off Wilton Crescent looks prohibitive, but the barrier and watchman are there to keep out cars; walk straight past – the pub is just around the corner; ⊖ Knightsbridge

Famous for its Bloody Marys and well-documented poltergeist, this snugly characterful place is one of the London main entries that readers like best, and it's easy to see why. Nestling in a smartly peaceful mews behind Knightsbridge, it was used for a while as the mess for the officers of the Duke of Wellington, whose portrait hangs above the fireplace, alongside neat prints of Guardsmen through the ages. The bar is tiny (some might say cramped), but you should be able to plonk yourself on one of the stools or wooden benches, as despite the charms of this engaging little pub it rarely gets crowded. Friendly, helpful staff serve well kept Courage Best, Theakstons Best, Morlands Old Speckled Hen and Youngs Special from handpumps at the rare pewter-topped bar counter – or they can shake you a splendid Bloody Mary from their own long-kept-secret recipe. Bar food includes burgers, hot steak sandwiches and scampi (all £5.25), though they're also happy to serve snacks like a bowl of chips or nachos. The little back restaurant is quite pricey, but good for a cosy candlelit dinner with someone special. It's lovely standing outside in summer, watching the sky slowly darken behind the pub's patriotically painted red, white and blue frontage, and forgetting for a while that you're anywhere near the centre of London; if you get there first you may be lucky enough to bag the bench. *(Recommended by Richard Gibbs, David Carr, P Williamson, Ted George, Scott and Patti Frazier, Steve Harvey, Peter Plumridge, James Macrae, Liz and Benton Jennings)*

S & N ~ Managers Paul and Alexandra Gibb ~ Real ale ~ Meals and snacks (12-2.30, 6-10) ~ Restaurant ~ 0171-235 3074 ~ Children in restaurant ~ Open 12-11; closed 24/25/31 Dec and 1 Jan

Hamilton Hall (Bishopsgate) Map 13

Liverpool Street Station, EC2; ⊖ Liverpool St

Once the ballroom of the Great Eastern Hotel (currently enjoying a multi-million pound refit), and still with a great deal of the original stunning Victorian baroque decor, this is pretty much the flagship of the Wetherspoons chain. Plaster nudes and fruit writhe around the ceiling and fireplace, and there are fine mouldings, chandeliers, and mirrors; the upper level was added during the exemplary conversion, and a good-sized section is no smoking. Comfortable small armchairs and stools are grouped into sensible-sized areas, and filled by a varied mix of customers; it can get very crowded indeed early in the evening, when tables will be at a premium. As at other pubs in the chain, reliable bar food, brought to your table, includes hot or cold filled baguettes (from £1.95), soup (£1.95), filled baked potatoes (from £2.45), burgers (from £3.45), fish and chips (£3.65), brie and broccoli crumble (£4.45), pies like steak and mushroom (£4.65), chicken balti or salmon en croûte (£4.95), daily specials, and puddings like toffee crunch pie (£1.95); Sunday roast (£4.95). Drinks prices are so low for this part of the country that visitors new to Wetherspoons will think they've been undercharged – the Youngers Scotch is usually just £1.09 a pint; other beers on handpump include Courage Directors, Theakstons Best and XB, and changing guests such as Greene King Abbot. Fruit machine, video game. There are plenty more Wetherspoons houses dotted around the Lucky dips – most share the same standards of food, beer and service. Now they've conquered virtually all parts of London they're slowly but surely expanding around the rest of the country too. *(Recommended by Thomas Nott, John Fahy, AB, Christopher Gallop, Eddie Edwards)*

Free house ~ Licensee Dave Chapman ~ Real ale ~ Meals and snacks (11-10pm) ~ 0171-247 3579 ~ Open 11-11; 12-10.30 Sun; closed 25/26 Dec, 1 Jan

Lamb ★ 🍺 (Bloomsbury) Map 13

94 Lamb's Conduit Street, WC1; ⊖ Holborn

We had a letter this year from someone who claims that as soon as he leaves his office his feet automatically propel him towards this old favourite, an unspoilt and atmospheric place where Victorian London lives on. It's famous for its cut-glass swivelling 'snob-screens' all the way around the U-shaped bar counter, but sepia photographs of 1890s actresses on the ochre panelled walls and traditional cast-iron-framed tables with neat brass rails around the rim very much add to the overall effect. Decimal currency doesn't quite fit in, and when you come out you almost expect the streets to be dark and foggy and illuminated by gas lamps. Sandwiches, ploughman's and quite a few salads may be available through till evening, and at lunchtime they do hot dishes such as cauliflower cheese and onion with leek and apple, chicken and sweetcorn in cider pie, stuffed lamb hearts in three-mustard sauce, fish tart, or turkey burger in cranberry and red wine sauce (all £3.95); Sunday carvery in restaurant (£5.25). Consistently well kept Youngs Bitter, Special and Ram Rod on handpump, and around 40 different malt whiskies; prompt service, and a good mix of customers. There are slatted wooden seats in a little courtyard beyond the quiet room which is down a couple of steps at the back; dominoes, cribbage, backgammon. No machines or music. A snug room at the back on the right is no smoking. It can get very crowded, especially in the evenings. *(Recommended by Stephen and Jean Curtis, Mark Baynham, Rachael Ward, Richard Lewis, Alice Ridgway, David Carr, Roger and Pauline Pearce, Paul Byatt, Gordon, Chris Westmoreland, B J Harding)*

Youngs ~ Manager Richard Whyte ~ Real ale ~ Lunchtime meals and snacks ~ 0171-405 0713 ~ Children in eating area till 7pm ~ Open 11-11; 12-10.30 Sun; closed evening 25 Dec

Lamb & Flag 🍺 (Covent Garden) Map 13

33 Rose Street, WC2; off Garrick Street; ⊖ Leicester Square

Even in winter you'll find plenty of people drinking and chatting in the little alleyways outside this historic old pub. Still very much as it was when Dickens described the Middle Temple lawyers who frequented it when he was working in nearby Catherine Street, it's a well liked place for Londoners to meet after work. The busy low-ceilinged back bar has high-backed black settles and an open fire, and in Regency days was known as the Bucket of Blood from the bare-knuckle prize-fights held here. It fills up quite quickly, though you might be able to find a seat in the upstairs Dryden Room. There may be darts in the tiny plain front bar. Very well kept Courage Best and Directors, John Smiths, Morlands Old Speckled Hen and Wadworths 6X on handpump, and a good few malt whiskies. Lunchtime bar food includes a choice of several well kept cheeses and pâtés, served with hot bread or french bread, as well as doorstep sandwiches (£3.50), ploughman's (£3.50), and, upstairs, hot dishes like shepherd's pie or bangers and mash (£3.95). It was outside here on a December evening in 1679 that Dryden was nearly killed by a hired gang of thugs; despite several advertisements in newspapers he never found out for sure who was behind the dastardly deed, though the most likely culprit was Charles II's mistress the Duchess of Portsmouth, who suspected him of writing scurrilous verses about her. They still celebrate Dryden Night each year. The pub is very handy for Covent Garden. *(Recommended by Mick Hitchman, Val Stevenson, Rob Holmes, RWD, Bob and Maggie Atherton, Chris Westmoreland, Susan and Nigel Wilson, C Smith)*

Courage ~ Lease: Terry Archer and Adrian Zimmerman ~ Real ale ~ Lunchtime meals (till 2.30) and snacks (12-4.30); limited Sun ~ (0171) 497 9504 ~ Live jazz Sunday evening ~ Open 11-11(10.45 Fri and Sat); 12-10.30 Sun; closed 25-6 Dec and 1 Jan

Museum Tavern 🍺 (Bloomsbury) Map 13

Museum Street, WC1; ⊖ Holborn or Tottenham Court Rd

This old-fashioned little Bloomsbury pub was being refurbished as we went to press, with new carpets and seat coverings, and extra seating in the area where they used to have a fruit machine. It may be the presence of the British Museum just over the road that accounts for the civilised and even rather bookish feel you might find here in quiet moments (late afternoon, say). Karl Marx is fondly supposed to have had the odd glass here, and it's tempting to think that the chap scribbling notes or earnestly studying at the next table is working on a similarly seminal set of ideas. The single room is simply furnished and decorated, with high-backed benches around traditional cast-iron pub tables, and old advertising mirrors between the wooden pillars behind the bar. A good range of well kept (though even for this area not cheap) beers includes Courage Best and Directors, John Smiths, Theakstons Best and Old Peculier, Wadworths 6X, and a couple of guests like Brakspears and Greene King IPA on handpump; they also have several wines by the glass, a choice of malt whiskies, and tea, coffee, cappuccino and hot chocolate. Available all day from a servery at the end of the room, bar food might include cold pasties, pie or quiche with salads (£3.95), and hot dishes like steak and ale pie, Thai chicken, and vegetable goulash (£4.95). Tables may be hard to come by at lunchtime, when it's very popular with tourists and visitors to the museum, but unlike most other pubs in the area, it generally stays pleasantly uncrowded in the evenings. It gets a little smoky when busy. There are a couple of tables outside under the gas lamps and 'Egyptian' inn sign. *(Recommended by Jens Arne Grebstad, Steve Harvey, Tim Barrow, Sue Demont, Mick Hitchman, Hanns P Golez, Hugh MacLean, David Carr, Gordon, Chris Westmoreland, Ian Phillips)*

Scottish & Newcastle ~ Managers Lachlan Mackay and Alison Hughes ~ Real ale ~ Meals and snacks (11-10) ~ 0171-242 8987 ~ Children welcome ~ Open 11-11; 12-10.30 Sun; closed 25/26 Dec

Nags Head 🍺 (Belgravia) Map 13

53 Kinnerton St, SW1; ⊖ Knightsbridge

This snug little gem is the kind of place where they greet you when you come in and say goodbye as you leave – not exactly the norm in this neck of the woods. Hidden away in an attractive and peaceful mews, it's one of those pubs that claims to be the capital's smallest, though it really doesn't feel like London at all; you could be forgiven for thinking you'd been transported to an old-fashioned local somewhere in a sleepy country village, right down to the friendly regulars chatting around the unusual sunken bar counter. Cosy, homely and warmly traditional, it's rarely busy, even at weekends, and the atmosphere is always relaxed and welcoming. One reader tells us it's places like this that make his trips to London worth while. The small, panelled and low-ceilinged front area has a wood-effect gas fire in an old cooking range (seats by here are generally snapped up pretty quickly), and a narrow passage leads down steps to an even smaller back bar with stools and a mix of comfortable seats. There's a 1930s What-the-butler-saw machine and a one-armed bandit that takes old pennies, as well as rather unusual piped music, generally jazz, folk or show tunes. The well kept Adnams, Tetleys and guest are pulled on attractive 19th-c china, pewter and brass handpumps. Decent food includes sandwiches (from £2.90), filled baked potatoes (from £3.50), ploughman's or plenty of salads (from £3.95), real ale sausage, mash and beans, chilli, or steak and mushroom pie (£4.25) and specials like roasts or cod mornay; there's a £1 service charge added to all dishes in the evenings. There are a few seats and a couple of tables outside. *(Recommended by Peter Plumridge, Dave Irving, Roger Huggins, Ewan McCall, Tom McLean, Steve Harvey, Hanns P Golez, Virginia Jones, Hugh MacLean, Bob and Maggie Atherton, Wayne Brindle, David Carr, S G Brown, Susan Douglas)*

Free house ~ Licensees Kevin and Peter Moran ~ Real ale ~ Meals and snacks (12-9) ~ 0171-235 1135 ~ Children welcome ~ Open 11-11; 12-10.30 Sun

Old Bank of England 🍷 (City) Map 13

194 Fleet St, EC4; ⊖ Temple

So grand is the bar here that customers have been known to order their drinks in rather hushed tones, as if overawed by the opulent surroundings. Until the mid-1970s the rather austere Italianate building was a subsidiary branch of the Bank of England built to service the nearby Law Courts; it was then a building society until its splendid conversion by Fullers in 1995. Three gleaming chandeliers hang from the exquisitely plastered ceiling high above the unusually tall island bar counter, and the green walls are liberally dotted with old prints, framed bank notes and the like. Though the room is quite spacious, screens between some of the varied seats and tables create a surprisingly intimate feel, and there are several cosier areas at the end, with more seats

in a galleried section upstairs. The mural that covers most of the end wall looks like
an 18th-c depiction of justice, but in fact was commissioned specially for the pub and
features members of the Fuller, Smith and Turner families. Fullers Chiswick, ESB and
London Pride on handpump, along with a monthly changing guest like Marstons
Pedigree, and around 20 wines by the glass. Bar food includes sandwiches (from
£2.75), sausages and mash (£4.95), four pies like chicken and bacon or lamb and
rosemary (£5.25), a vegetarian dish, and specials like poached salmon (£4.95);
efficient service from smartly uniformed staff. The entrance is up a flight of stone
steps, and Olympic-style torches burn outside in winter. Note they don't allow
children. *(Recommended by Richard Gibbs, Mark Brock, Chris Westmoreland)*

*Fullers ~ Manager Peter Biddle ~ Real ale ~ Meals and snacks (12-8) ~ Restaurant
~ 0171-430 2255 ~ Open 11-11; closed all day weekends*

Old Coffee House (Soho) Map 13

49 Beak Street, W1; ✚ Oxford Circus

Now that so many pubs line their rooms with bought-in bric-a-brac, it's easy to forget
how impressive the effect can be when it's done properly, as at this friendly little
cornerhouse. The downstairs bar is a busy jumble of stuffed pike and foxes, great brass
bowls and buckets, ancient musical instruments (brass and string sections both well
represented), a good collection of Great War recruiting posters, golden discs, death-of-
Nelson prints, theatre and cinema handbills, old banknotes and so forth – even a nude
in one corner (this is Soho, after all). Upstairs, the food room has as many prints and
pictures as a Victorian study. It's a useful place to know about for a decent well priced
lunch, and can be surprisingly peaceful too. The choice of meals is rather wider than
you'll find in most other pubs in the area, including sandwiches, filled baked potatoes
(from £2.25), burgers (£3), various platters (£4), lots of hot dishes like chicken, ham
and leek pie, macaroni cheese, chilli, lasagne, tuna and pasta bake, or winter stews and
casseroles (all £4), and puddings like toffee apple and pecan pie (£1.75); on Sundays
and in the evenings they do only toasted sandwiches. Well kept Courage Best and
Directors and Marstons Pedigree on handpump; helpful friendly service. *(Recommended
by Virginia Jones, David Carr, Wayne Brindle, Ian Phillips, Gordon)*

*Courage ~ Lease: Barry Hawkins ~ Real ale ~ Lunchtime meals and snacks (12-3;
evenings and Sun toasted sandwiches only) ~ (0171) 437 2197 ~ Children in
upstairs food room 12-3pm ~ Open 11-11*

Olde Cheshire Cheese (City) Map 13

Wine Office Court; off 145 Fleet Street, EC4; ✚ Blackfriars

Its cellar vaults dating back to before the Great Fire, this 17th-c former chop house is
one of London's most famous old pubs. Over the years Congreve, Pope, Voltaire,
Thackeray, Dickens, Conan Doyle, Yeats and perhaps Dr Johnson have visited its
unpretentious little rooms, a couple of them probably coming across the famous
parrot that for over 40 years entertained princes, ambassadors, and other
distinguished guests. When she died in 1926 the news was broadcast on the BBC and
obituary notices appeared in 200 newspapers all over the world; she's still around
today, now stuffed and silent. Up and down stairs, the various bars and rooms have
bare wooden benches built in to the walls, sawdust on bare boards, and on the
ground floor high beams, crackly old black varnish, Victorian paintings on the dark
brown walls, and a big open fire in winter. Surprisingly untouristy, it's been extended
in a similar style towards Fleet St. Lunchtime bar food includes sandwiches, filled
jacket potatoes (£2.95), and ploughman's (£3.50), and several weekly changing hot
dishes such as steak, ale and vegetable pie, chicken korma, or vegetarian quiche
(around £4.25). Well kept (and, as usual for this brewery, well priced) Sam Smiths
Old Brewery on handpump, friendly service. The Cellar bar is no smoking at
lunchtimes. *(Recommended by RWD, Chris Westmoreland, Mark Baynham, Rachael Ward, R
T and J C Moggridge, Karen and Graham Oddey, Jamie and Ruth Lyons, John Ames)*

*Sam Smiths ~ Licensee Gordon Garrity ~ Lunchtime meals and snacks (not
weekends) ~ Evening restaurant (not Sun) ~ 0171-353 6170 ~ Children in eating area
of bar and restaurant ~ Open 11-11; 12-5 Sun; closed Sun evening and bank hols*

Olde Mitre £ (City) Map 13

Ely Place, EC1; there's also an entrance beside 8 Hatton Garden; ⊖ Chancery Lane

Finding this quaint little pub can be quite a challenge, but well worth it; every year we hear from people visiting it for the first time who can hardly believe how friendly and helpful the service is. Tucked away rather incongruously on the edge of the City, the carefully rebuilt tavern carries the name of an earlier inn built here in 1547 to serve the people working in the nearby palace of the Bishops of Ely. The dark panelled small rooms have antique settles and – particularly in the back room, where there are more seats – old local pictures and so forth. An upstairs room, mainly used for functions, may double as an overflow at peak periods; on weekdays, the pub is good-naturedly packed between 12.30 and 2.15, with an interesting mix of customers. It fills up again in the early evening, but by around nine becomes a good deal more tranquil. Popular bar snacks include really good value sandwiches such as ham, salmon and cucumber or egg mayonnaise (£1, including toasted), as well as pork sausages (40p), and pork pies or scotch eggs (75p). Well kept Friary Meux, Ind Coope Burton and Tetleys on handpump; notably chatty staff; darts. There are some seats with pot plants and jasmine in the narrow yard between the pub and St Ethelreda's church. The iron gates that guard Ely Place are a reminder of the days when the law in this distrit was administered by the Bishops of Ely; even today it's still technically part of Cambridgeshire. *(Recommended by John Fazakerley, D Hunter, Chris Westmoreland, David Carr, R J Bland, Christopher Gallop, Ian Phillips, A W Dickinson, Tim Heywood, Sophie Wilne)*

Taylor-Walker (Allied) ~ Manager Don O'Sullivan ~ Real ale ~ Snacks (11-10) ~ 0171-405 4751 ~ Open 11-11; closed weekends and bank hols

Orange Brewery 🍺 (Pimlico) Map 13

37 Pimlico Road, SW1; ⊖ Sloane Square

We've had a good few warmly enthusiastic reports on this lively and friendly pub over the last year, with perhaps the most succinct describing it as being like a posher version of a Firkin pub. Every week they produce over 500 gallons of their popular ales – SW1, a stronger SW2, Pimlico Porter, and Victoria lager; they may also have a couple of guest beers, and some bottled Trappist beers. Readers like the way the cheery staff make sure they find the right kind of glass for each drink. Bar food is built around the beers too, with dishes such as sausages with beer and onion gravy (£3.25) or beef and beer pie flavoured with their SW2; they also do sandwiches (£2.30), ploughman's, and fish and chips (£5.25). Above the simple wooden chairs, tables and panelling are various examples of vintage brewing equipment and related bric-a-brac, and there's a nicely tiled fireplace; fruit machine, piped music. A viewing area looks down into the brewery, and you can book tours for a closer look. There may be times when it's hard to find anywhere to sit – though seats outside face a little concreted-over green beyond the quite busy street. *(Recommended by Susan and John Douglas, David Carr, Val Stevenson, Rob Holmes, Frank W Gadbois, Richard Lewis, Mark Baynham, Rachael Ward, Tom McLean, Ewan McCall, Dave Irving, Roger Huggins, James Macrae, Christopher Trueblood, James House, A W Dickinson, Andy Thwaites)*

Own brew (though tied to S & N) ~ Manager Billy Glass ~ Real ale ~ Meals and snacks (12-11; limited choice Sun) ~ 0171-730 5984 ~ Children welcome ~ Open 11-11; 12-10.30 Sun

Princess Louise 🍺 (Holborn) Map 13

208 High Holborn, WC1; ⊖ Holborn

Some people find this old-fashioned gin-palace too big and too crowded – and the relaxed and cheery bustle that ensues is one of the main reasons they like it. Another is the way it's managed to keep its genuinely old-fashioned appeal intact; even the gents' has its own preservation order. The elaborate decor includes etched and gilt mirrors, brightly coloured and fruity-shaped tiles, and slender Portland stone columns soaring towards the lofty and deeply moulded crimson and gold plaster ceiling. Quieter corners have comfortable green plush seats and banquettes. The long main bar serves a fine range of regularly changing real ales, such as Bass, Brakspears PA,

Courage Best, Gales HSB, Greene King Abbot, Theakstons Best, Wadworths 6X, Youngs Special and maybe a couple of more unusual guests; also several wines by the glass – including champagne. Neat, quick staff. They do good sandwiches (from £1.75) just about all day. Fruit machine. The quieter upstairs bar has excellent authentic Thai meals (quite a draw in themselves), though these are now served weekday lunchtimes only. Lively, invigorating, and full of a richly diverse assortment of people, this grand old place has so much in common with London itself that it's easy to see why it's sometimes described as the quintessential City pub. *(Recommended by Eric and Jackie Robinson, David Carr, James Macrae, Wayne Brindle, Chris Westmoreland, Steve Harvey, E A Thwaite, Sue Demont, Tim Barrow, Ian Phillips, Andy Thwaites, Gordon)*

Free house ~ Licensee Joseph Sheridan ~ Real ale ~ Snacks and weekday lunchtime meals ~ 0171-405 8816 ~ Open 11-11; 12-3, 6-11 Sat; closed 25/26 Dec

Red Lion 🍺 (Mayfair) Map 13

Waverton Street, W1; ⊖ Green Park

In a peaceful and especially pretty part of Mayfair, this relaxed and civilised place has something of the atmosphere of a smart country pub; only the presence of so many suited workers reminds you of its true location. The main L-shaped bar has small winged settles on the partly carpeted scrubbed floorboards, and London prints below the high shelf of china on its dark-panelled walls. A good range of well kept beers includes Courage Directors, Fullers London Pride, Greene King IPA, Morlands Old Speckled Hen, Theakstons Best and XB and Wadworths 6X on handpump, and they do rather good Bloody Marys (though we've yet to hear from anyone who's braved the Very Spicy option). Bar food, now served from a corner at the front, includes sandwiches and salads, and one or two hot dishes like cumberland sausage, stilton and leek quiche or meatloaf with capiscum sauce (all £4.95); they home-cook all their meats, and, unusually for the area, serve food morning and evening seven days a week. It can get crowded at lunchtime, and immediately after work. The gents' has a copy of the day's *Financial Times* at eye level. *(Recommended by Christopher Wright, Mike and Karen England, Mark Walker, P R Morley, Hugh MacLean, Bob and Maggie Atherton, Adrian Zambardino, Debbie Chaplin)*

S & N ~ Manager Raymond Dodgson ~ Real ale ~ Meals and snacks (12-2.45, 6-10) ~ Restaurant ~ 0171-499 1307 ~ Children in eating areas and restaurant weekends only ~ Open 11-11 weekdays; 11-3, 6-11 Sat; closed 25 Dec

Seven Stars £ (City) Map 13

53 Carey St, WC2; ⊖ Holborn (just as handy from Temple or Chancery Lane, but the walk through Lincoln's Inn Fields can be rather pleasant)

A unique and timeless gem, this tranquil little pub faces the back of the Law Courts. We're not using the word little lightly – on our last visit it was hard to tell whether the customers (barristers and legal folk on the whole) were standing in the peaceful street outside because it was sunny, or because of the shortage of space inside. The door, underneath a profusion of hanging baskets, is helpfully marked General Counter, as though you couldn't see that the simple counter is pretty much all there is in the tiny old-fashioned bar beyond. Lots of caricatures of barristers and other legal-themed prints on the walls, and quite a collection of toby jugs, some in a display case, the rest mixed up with the drinks behind the bar. Courage Best and Directors on handpump, several malt whiskies, and very good value bar snacks such as sandwiches (from £1.30), pork pies and sausages, with maybe a couple of hot dishes like lamb curry, goulash or cottage pie (£2.95); you'll probably have to eat standing up – the solitary table and stools are on the left as you go in. A cosy room on the right appears bigger than it is because of its similar lack of furnishings; there's a gas-effect fire, and shelves round the walls for drinks or leaning against. Stairs up to the lavatories are very steep – a sign warns that you climb them at your own risk. *(Recommended by Thomas Nott, Richard Davies, Chris Westmoreland, W T Aird)*

Courage ~ Lease: Mr and Mrs G Turner ~ Real ale ~ Snacks (all day) ~ 0171-242 8521 ~ Open 11-11 weekdays only, may close earlier if not busy; closed weekends except Sat of Lord Mayor's Show

Star (Belgravia) Map 13

Belgrave Mews West – behind the German Embassy, off Belgrave Sq; ⊖ Knightsbridge

Lots of London pubs really go to town with their flowering tubs and hanging baskets, but few end up with such an impressive result as this warmly traditional place. Though it can get busy at lunchtime and on some evenings, it's another of those places that seems distinctly un-London, and there's a pleasantly quiet and restful local feel outside peak times. One reader feels it's the sort of pub you might see in an old black and white film. Service is very obliging and helpful; they're quite happy being flexible with the menu or providing something slightly different if they can. The small entry room, which also has the food servery, has stools by the counter and tall windows; an arch leads to a side room with swagged curtains, lots of dark mahogany, stripped mahogany chairs and tables, heavy upholstered settles, globe lighting and raj fans. The back room has button-back built-in wall seats, and there's a cosy room upstairs. Good value bar food might include sandwiches (£1.30), vegetarian quiche (£3.90), barbecue chicken or grilled ham and egg platter (£4.90), smoked salmon salad (£5.50), and Scotch rib-eye steak (£6.30); they do sandwiches on Saturdays, but otherwise there's no food at weekends. Very well kept and priced Fullers Chiswick, ESB and London Pride. *(Recommended by Mark Baynham, Rachael Ward, E A Thwaite, Jasper Sabey, Wayne Brindle, John Fazakerley, M L and G Clarke, Virginia Jones, LM, B J Harding)*

Fullers ~ Managers Bruce and Kathleen Taylor ~ Real ale ~ Meals and snacks (not Sat or Sun) ~ 0171-235 3019 ~ Children welcome ~ Open 11.30-3, 5(6.30 Sat)-11; 11.30-11 Fri, and every day for two weeks before Christmas; closed Dec 25/26

Westminster Arms (Westminster) Map 13

Storey's Gate, SW1; ⊖ Westminster

The main draw at this busy local – handily placed near Westminster Abbey and Parliament Square – is the range of real ales on handpump, typically including Adnams, Bass, Brakspears PA, Theakstons Best, Wadworths 6X, Westminster Best brewed for them by Charringtons, and a monthly changing guest; they also do decent wines. Furnishings in the plain main bar are simple and old-fashioned, with proper tables on the wooden floors and a good deal of panelling; there's not a lot of room, and they can get crowded, so come early for a seat. Pleasant, courteous service. Most of the bar food is served in the downstairs wine bar, with some of the tables in cosy booths; typical dishes include filled rolls (from £2.50), salads and ploughman's, lasagne or steak and kidney pie (£5), and fish and chips or scampi (£5.50). Piped music in this area, and in the more formal upstairs restaurant, but not generally in the main bar; fruit machine. There are a couple of tables and seats by the street outside. *(Recommended by Dr and Mrs A H Young, Hanns P Golez, Jan and Colin Roe, Tim Barrow, Sue Demont, Wayne Brindle)*

Free house ~ Licensees Gerry and Marie Dolan ~ Real ale ~ Meals and snacks (11-9.30; not Sunday evening) ~ Restaurant (not Sun) ~ 0171-222 8520 ~ Children in eating area ~ Open 11-11; 12-10 Sun (6 in winter); closed Dec 25-6

NORTH LONDON

Parking is not a special problem in this area, unless we say so

Chapel ♀ (Marylebone) Map 13

48 Chapel St, NW1; ⊖ Edgware Rd

This attractively refurbished pub is one of several recent conversions rather reminiscent of the Eagle (see above), and is in similarly incongruous surroundings. Light and spacious, the cream-painted main room is dominated by the open kitchen, which produces generously served dishes like leek and mussel soup (£3.50), aubergine and goat's cheese tart (£6), minute steak with grain mustard (£6.50), fishcakes with sorrel sauce (£7.50), braised lamb with mushrooms (£7), orange tillapia and salmon with fennel cream (£8), and puddings such as rhubarb crumble or treacle tart (£3.50). Prompt and efficient service from helpful staff, who may bring warm walnut bread to your table while you're waiting. Plenty of simple wooden tables around the bar, with more in a side room with a big fireplace, and on a sheltered terrace outside. A table has newspapers to read, and the pictures on the walls are all for sale; soft piped music. At lunchtime most people are here to eat (it fills up quite quickly then, though you can book), but in the evening trade is usually more evenly split between diners and drinkers. Well kept Highgate IPA and Mansfield Bitter on handpump, a good range of wines (several by the glass), and a choice of teas such as peppermint or strawberry and vanilla. *(Recommended by Paris Hills-Wright, Kim Inglis, C Leach)*

Bass ~ Tenant Lakis Chondrogiannis ~ Real ale ~ Meals ~ 0171-402 9220 ~ Children welcome ~ Open 12-11

Compton Arms (Canonbury) Map 12

4 Compton Avenue, off Canonbury Rd, N1; ⊖ Highbury & Islington

A tiny pub hidden away up a mews, this peaceful place has beautiful hanging baskets in front, and a delightfully relaxing little crazy paved terrace behind, with benches and cask tables among flowers under a big sycamore tree. Well run by friendly staff, the unpretentious low-ceilinged rooms are simply furnished with wooden settles and assorted stools and chairs, with local pictures on the walls; free from games or music, it has a very personable, village local feel. Well kept Greene King Abbot, IPA, Rayments and Sorcerer on handpump, and around 22 wines by the glass. Good value bar food includes sandwiches, soup and the like, but now majors on sausages, with a choice of around ten different types, all served with mashed potato and home-made gravy (£3.55). *(Recommended by David Carr, JEB, Eric and Jackie Robinson)*

Greene King ~ Manager Derek Richards ~ Real ale ~ Meals and snacks (12-3.30, 6-9, all day weekends; not Tues eve) ~ 0171-359 6883 ~ Children welcome ~ Open 12-11; 12-10.30 Sun

Holly Bush (Hampstead) Map 12

Holly Mount, NW3; ⊖ Hampstead

Real Edwardian gas lamps light the atmospheric front bar of this cheery old local. The walk up to it from the tube station is delightful, along some of Hampstead's most villagey streets and past several of its more enviable properties; London seems so far away you'd hardly think you were so close to Hampstead High Street. There's a dark sagging ceiling, brown and cream panelled walls (decorated with old advertisements and a few hanging plates), open fires, and cosy bays formed by partly glazed partitions. Slightly more intimate, the back room, named after the painter George Romney, has an embossed red ceiling, panelled and etched glass alcoves, and ochre-painted brick walls covered with small prints and plates. During the week bar food includes toasted sandwiches (from £1.75), filled baguettes (£1.95), a choice of ploughman's (£2.95), and a daily special like pasta or shepherd's pie (around £4.50), with maybe home-made scouse at winter weekends (the cheery licensees are from Liverpool), and traditional Sunday roasts (£4.50). Benskins, well-priced Eldridge Pope, Ind Coope Burton, Tetleys and a frequently changing guest on handpump; darts, shove-ha'penny, cribbage, dominoes, fruit machine, and video game. Good friendly service. *(Recommended by Hugh MacLean, Mick Hitchman, Mark Baynham, Rachael Ward, Christopher Wright, Don Kellaway, Angie Coles)*

Taylor-Walker (Allied) ~ Manager Peter Dures ~ Real ale ~ Meals and snacks (12.30-3, 5.30-11) ~ 0171-435 2892 ~ Children in coffee bar till 9 ~ Live jazz Sun night, 60s guitarist Weds ~ Nearby parking sometimes quite a squeeze ~ Open 12-3(4 Sat), 5.30(6 Sat)-11; closed evening 25 Dec

Olde White Bear (Hampstead) Map 12

Well Road, NW3l; ⊖ Hampstead

All sorts of people feel at home in this relaxing and almost clubby neo-Victorian pub, from the young chap in the corner doing the crossword, to the old gentleman reading his magazine with a monocle. Friendly and traditional, it's been described by some of our most-travelled readers as the best pub they've been to in London, not least because of the very well priced range of beer: the cheapest usually costs £1.35 a pint, practically a giveaway in this part of the world. The choice includes Adnams, Ind Coope Burton, Greene King Abbot, Tetleys, Wadworths 6X and Youngs Bitter on handpump; they also have a dozen or so malt whiskies, and maybe winter mulled wine. The dimly-lit main room has lots of Victorian prints and cartoons on the walls, as well as wooden stools, cushioned captain's chairs, a couple of big tasselled armed chairs, a flowery sofa, handsome fireplace and an ornate Edwardian sideboard. A similarly-lit small central room has Lloyd Loom furniture, dried flower arrangements and signed photographs of actors and playwrights. In the brighter end room there are elaborate cushioned machine tapestried pews, and dark brown paisley curtains. Good bar food includes soup (£1.80), filled baguettes (£2.25), lasagne or all-day breakfast (£3.50), ploughman's or Mexican chicken salad (£3.95), steak and kidney pie (£4.50), and in summer the very popular Greek platter – a huge salad with olives, dips, pitta bread and feta cheese (£4.50). Darts, cribbage, fruit machine, piped music. Note they don't allow children inside, and parking may be a problem – it's mostly residents' permits only nearby. *(Recommended by Ian Phillips, R Sheard, Tom McLean, Roger Huggins)*

Taylor Walker (Allied) ~ Lease: Peter and Peggy Reynolds ~ Real ale ~ Meals and snacks ~ 0171-435 3758 ~ Open 11-11; 12-10.30 Sun

Spaniards Inn 🍺 (Hampstead) Map 12

Spaniards Lane, NW3; ⊖ Hampstead, but some distance away; or from Golders Green station take 220 bus

Comfortable and authentically old-fashioned, this charming former toll-house has open fires, genuinely antique winged settles, candle-shaped lamps in pink shades, and snug little alcoves in the low-ceilinged oak-panelled rooms of the attractive main bar. Named after the Spanish ambassador to the court of James I (who is said to have lived here), it also has a very nice sheltered garden behind, with slatted wooden tables and chairs on a crazy-paved terrace opening on to a flagstoned walk around a small lawn, with roses, a side arbour of wisteria and clematis, and an aviary. Popular daily changing bar food includes stilton ploughman's (£3.95), ratatouille (£4.95), home-made quiche or vegetable lasagne (£5.25), lamb moussaka (£5.75), and chicken and mushroom pie (£5.95); the food bar is no smoking at lunchtime. A quieter upstairs bar may be open at busy times. Well kept Bass, Fullers London Pride, Hancocks BB and a guest like Adnams Extra on handpump; friendly service, piped classical music. It's very handy for Kenwood, and indeed during the 1780 Gordon Riots the landlord helped save the house from possible disaster, cunningly giving so much free drink to the mob on its way to burn it down that by the time the Horse Guards arrived the rioters were lying drunk and incapable on the floor. The pub and a similar little whitewashed outbuilding opposite are responsible for the slight bottlenecks you sometimes come across driving round here; they jut out into the road rather like King Canute holding back the tide of traffic, and cars all have to slow down to squeeze past. Dogs welcome. *(Recommended by Michael and Hazel Lyons, Ian Phillips, JSMS, Nigel Flook, Betsy Brown, Gordon, Roger Huggins, Tom McLean)*

Charringtons (Bass) ~ Manager D E Roper ~ Real ale ~ Meals and snacks (12-9.30) ~ 0181-455 3276 ~ Children in eating area of bar, upstairs room, and various small snug areas ~ Open 11-11; 12-10.30 Sun

Waterside (King's Cross) Map 13

82 York Way, N1; ⊖ King's Cross

All the more rewarding considering the fact that King's Cross isn't what you'd call an appealing area for visitors, this friendly little oasis has an unexpectedly calm outside terrace overlooking the Battlebridge Basin; you might find a barbecue out here on sunny days. The building really isn't very old but it's done out in firmly traditional style, with stripped brickwork, latticed windows, genuinely old stripped timbers in white plaster, lots of dimly lit alcoves (one is no smoking), spinning wheels, milkmaids' yokes, and horsebrasses and so on, with plenty of rustic tables and wooden benches. Some of the woodwork was salvaged from a disused mill. Adnams, Boddingtons, Flowers IPA, Marstons Pedigree and a guest on handpump, as well as wines on draught; bar billiards, pinball, fruit machine, and sometimes loudish juke box. The menu is these days a standard Berni one, with things like sandwiches, soup (£1.10), steak and mushroom pudding (£3.95), vegetable mexicana (£4.95), cajun chicken (£5.25), and lots of steaks (from £4.95). No dogs inside. *(Recommended by*

David Carr, Chris Westmoreland, Graham Tayar, Steve Harvey, S R and A J Ashcroft, James Macrae, N C Walker, Nigel Flook, Betsy Brown)

Whitbreads ~ Manager Ann Davie ~ Real ale ~ Meals and snacks (12-2.30, 5-8.30) ~ (0171) 837 7118 ~ Children in eating area till 7pm ~ Open 11-11; 12-10.30 Sun

SOUTH LONDON

Parking is bad on weekday lunchtimes at the inner city pubs here (SE1), but is usually OK everywhere in the evenings – you may again have a bit of a walk if a good band is on at the Bulls Head in Barnes, or at the Windmill on Clapham Common if it's a fine evening

Alma ♀ (Wandsworth) Map 12

499 York Road, SW18; ⇌ Wandsworth Town

Not entirely unlike a French cafe-bar, this stylish and civilised place has an air of chattily relaxed bonhomie. There's a mix of chairs around cast-iron-framed tables, lots of ochre and terracotta paintwork, gilded mosaics of the Battle of the Alma, an ornate mahogany chimney-piece and fireplace, bevelled mirrors in a pillared mahogany room divider, and pinball and a fruit machine. The popular but less pubby dining room has a fine turn-of-the-century frieze of swirly nymphs; there's waitress service in here, and you can book a table. Even when it's very full with smart young people – which it often is in the evenings – service is careful and efficient. Youngs Bitter, Special and seasonal brews on handpump from the island bar counter, decent house wines (with several by the glass), freshly squeezed orange juice, good coffee, tea or hot chocolate, newspapers out for customers. Unusual and tasty, the good value bar food typically includes sandwiches (from £1.40), soup (£2.50), croque monsieur (£2.45), mussels with garlic, parsley, cream and Scrumpy Jack cider (£3.20), filo parcels stuffed with tofu, spring onion, baby corn and mushrooms (£3.90), vegetable cous-cous or toasted muffins with ham and poached egg (£4.50), chicken breast with a creamy ginger, coriander and cashew nut sauce, daily fresh fish, and steak (£9.25); the menu may be limited on Sunday lunchtimes. If you're after a quiet drink don't come when there's a rugby match on the television. Cribbage, pinball, dominoes, fruit machine. Charge up their 'smart-card' with cash and you can pay with a discount either here or at the management's other pubs, which include the Ship at Wandsworth (see below). Travelling by rail into Waterloo you can see the pub rising above the neighbouring rooftops as you rattle through Wandsworth Town. *(Recommended by James Macrae, Richard Gibbs, P Gillbe, Ian Phillips)*

Youngs ~ Tenant Charles Gotto ~ Real ale ~ Meals and snacks (12-11) ~ Restaurant ~ 0181-870 2537 ~ Children welcome ~ Open 11-11; 12-10.30 Sun; closed 25/26 Dec

Anchor (South Bank) Map 13

34 Park St, Bankside, SE1; Southwark Bridge end; ⊖ London Bridge

Shakespeare, Dickens and Pepys are all reputed to have supped at this atmospheric riverside spot over the years, though it's now destined to be known as the pub where Tom Cruise enjoys a pint at the end of the film version of *Mission: Impossible*. A maze of little rooms and passageways, it has an unbeatable view of the Thames and the City from its busy front terrace. Inside are creaky boards and beams, black panelling, old-fashioned high-backed settles, and sturdy leatherette chairs. Even when it's invaded by tourists it's usually possible to retreat to one of the smaller rooms. Courage Best and Directors, Greenalls Best, Youngs Special, a beer named for the pub, and four rapidly changing guest beers on handpump or tapped from the cask; they also do jugs of pimms and sangria. Cribbage, dominoes, three fruit machines, and fairly loud piped music. Bar food includes sandwiches (from £2.95) and salads, winter soup, and five daily changing hot dishes like steak and kidney pie, vegetable lasagne, or fish and chips (£4.50); they do a Sunday roast in the restaurant. The pub can get smoky, and service can slow down at busy periods. The mid-18th-c building was built to replace an earlier tavern, possibly the one that Pepys came to during the Great Fire of 1666. 'All over the Thames with one's face in the wind, you were almost burned with a shower of fire drops,' he wrote. 'When we could endure no more upon the water, we to a little ale-house on the Bankside and there staid till it was dark almost, and saw the fire grow.' Good places to visit nearby, with the Clink round the corner particularly worth a look. *(Recommended by Jens Arne Grebstad, GWB, Tim Barrow, Sue Demont, Paul Randall, Jim Honohan, Don Kellaway, Angie Coles)*

Greenalls ~ Licensees Barry and Jane Jackson ~ Real ale ~ Meals and snacks (12-9) ~ Restaurant ~ 0171-407 1577 ~ Children in eating areas and restaurant till 8.30 ~ Open 11-11; 12-10.30 Sun

Bulls Head ♀ £ (Barnes) Map 12

373 Lonsdale Road, SW13; ⇌ Barnes Bridge

An imposing building facing the Thames, this busy place is a very highly regarded music venue, with top-class modern jazz groups performing every night. You can hear the music quite clearly from the lounge bar (and on peaceful Sunday lunchtimes from the villagey little street as you approach), but for the full effect and genuine jazz club atmosphere it is worth paying the admission to the well equipped music room. Back in the bustling bar alcoves open off the main area around the island servery, which has Youngs Bitter, Special and Ramrod on handpump, around 80 malt whiskies, and decent wines. Around the walls are large photos of the various jazz musicians and bands who have played here; dominoes, cribbage, Scrabble, chess, cards, and fruit machine in the public bar. All the food is home-made, including the bread, pasta, sausages and ice cream, and they do things like soup (£1.70), sandwiches (from £1.95), and pasta, pies, or a popular carvery of home-roasted joints (all £3.80); service is efficient and very friendly. Bands play 8.30-11 every night plus 2-4.30 Sundays, and depending on who's playing prices generally range from £3.50 to £6. *(Recommended by John H L Davis; more reports please)*

Youngs ~ Tenant Dan Fleming ~ Real ale ~ Meals and snacks (12-3, 6-9.30) ~ Evening restaurant (not Sun evening, though they do Sun lunch) ~ 0181-876 5241 ~ Children welcome ~ Jazz every night and Sun lunchtime ~ Nearby parking may be difficult ~ Open 11-11; 12-10.30 Sun; closed evening 25 Dec

Crown & Greyhound (Dulwich) Map 12

73 Dulwich Village, SE21; ⇌ North Dulwich

One of the things readers particularly like about this grand place is the way that the family areas are no different in style or character from the rest of the pub, so visitors with children aren't left feeling like second-class citizens. In fact it's very well geared up for families, with baby changing facilities, and a summer ice cream stall in the very pleasant big two-level back terrace, which also has a good many picnic tables under a chestnut tree. Inside is imposing and astonishingly spacious – it gets very busy in the evenings but there's enough room to absorb everyone without any difficulty. The most ornate room is on the right, with its elaborate ochre ceiling plasterwork, fancy former gas lamps, Hogarth prints, fine carved and panelled settles and so forth. It opens into the former billiards room, where kitchen tables on a stripped board floor are set for the good bar food. Changing every day (the friendly landlady likes to try out new recipes and ideas), the lunchtime choice might include enormous doorstep sandwiches and toasties (from £2.20), ploughman's (£3.60), and a range of specials like chicken, leek and mushroom crumble, steak and onion pie, good lamb and fennel casserole, asparagus and cottage cheese pancakes, and a vegan ratatouille bake (all £5.25); in the evening they do curry or vegetable lasagne (£4.95), and à la carte dishes like cashew nut paella (£7.65), or salmon with spinach and smoked salmon mousse, wrapped in puff pastry (£8.50). Best to arrive early for their popular Sunday carvery (£6.25), they don't take bookings. A central snug leads on the other side to the saloon – brown-ragged walls, upholstered and panelled settles, a coal-effect gas fire in the tiled period fireplace, and Victorian prints. Well kept Ind Coope Burton, Tetleys, Youngs Bitter and unusual monthly changing guests like Arrols 80/- on handpump; they have a wine of the month too. Fruit machines, video game, and piped music. Known locally as the Dog, the pub has long-established links with poetry groups (they still have well regarded readings today), and is handy for walks through the park. *(Recommended by Christopher Gallop, Sue Demont, Tim Barrow, Andy Thwaites)*

Taylor Walker (Allied) ~ Managers Barney and Sandra Maguire ~ Real ale ~ Meals and snacks (12-2.30, 5.30-9; not Sun evening) ~ Restaurant (not evenings Sun) ~ 0181-693 2466 ~ Children in eating area and no-smoking family room ~ Open 11-11; 12-10.30 Sun

Cutty Sark (Greenwich) Map 12

Ballast Quay, off Lassell St, SE10; ⇌ Maze Hill, from London Bridge, or from the river front walk past the Yacht in Crane St and Trinity Hospital

Across the narrow cobbled lane from this attractive late 16th-c white-painted house is a waterside terrace with tables offering fine views along the river and across to the Isle of Dogs. The same views can be had inside through the big upper bow window, which as you approach is particularly striking for the way it jetties out over the pavement. Conjuring up images of the kind of London we imagine Dickens once knew, the atmospheric bar has flagstones, rough brick walls, wooden settles, barrel tables, open fires, low lighting and narrow openings to tiny side snugs; various pithy sayings are chalked up on the old slates. Well kept Bass, Worthington Best and a fortnightly changing guest on handpump, several malt whiskies, and a decent wine list. An elaborate central staircase leads up to an upstairs area; fruit machine, trivia, juke box. A roomy eating area has sandwiches and promptly served meals like plaice (£4.95), lasagne, and steak and Guinness pie (£5.95). A real favourite with some readers, the pub can be very busy with young people on Friday and Saturday evenings. *(Recommended by Robert Gomme, Jenny and Brian Seller, John Fahy, RWD, GWB)*

Free house ~ Manager Harry Parsons ~ Real ale ~ Meals and snacks (not eves Fri/Sat/Sun) ~ 0181-858 3146 ~ Children upstairs till 9pm ~ Various live music Tues eve, jazz Thurs eve ~ Open 11-11; 12-10.30 summer Suns; 11-3, 5.30-11 winter weekdays

Fire Station (Waterloo) Map 13

150 Waterloo Rd, SE1; ⊖ Waterloo

Though this bustling place is hardly your typical local, it does a number of traditionally pubby things far better than anywhere else in the area. A remarkable conversion of the former LCC central fire station, it's perhaps best known for the imaginative food served from the open kitchen in the back dining room, but the two vibrantly chatty rooms at the front are very popular with people who only want a drink. The decor is something like a cross between a warehouse and a schoolroom, with plenty of wooden pews, chairs and long tables (a few spilling out onto the street outside), some mirrors and rather incongruous pieces of dressers, and brightly red-painted doors, shelves and modern hanging lightshades; the fiercely contemporary art around the walls is for sale, and there's a table with newspapers to read. Well kept Adnams Southwold, Brakspears, Youngs, and a beer brewed for them by Hancocks on handpump, as well as a number of bottled beers, and several wines by the glass; helpful service. They recently introduced a short range of bar meals served between 12.30 and 6, which might include filled baguettes (from £2.50), carrot and coriander soup (£3.25), spinach and ricotta cannelloni with wild mushrooms (£7.25), and a selection of British cheeses (£4.25), but it's worth paying the extra to eat from the main menu. Changing every lunchtime and evening, this has things like lemon sole (£9.50), char-grilled smoked cod with parsley mash and tomato and chilli salsa (£9.75), guinea fowl with risotto verde and courgette flowers (£9.95), and puddings such as peach and almond tart with custard sauce (£3.25); they don't take bookings, so there may be a slight wait at busy times. Piped modern jazz and other music fits well into the good-natured hubbub. *(Recommended by Dr and Mrs A K Clarke, Andy Thwaites)*

Free house ~ Manager Peter Nottage ~ Real ale ~ Snacks (12.30-6) and meals ~ Restaurant ~ 0171-620 2226 ~ Children welcome away from bar ~ Open 11-11; 12-5 Sun

Fox & Grapes (Wimbledon) Map 12

Camp Rd, SW19; ⊖ Wimbledon

Since our last edition there's been yet another change of licensee at this well set pub. It's ideally placed on the edge of Wimbledon Common, and is especially pleasant on summer evenings when the doors are open and you can sit out on the grass. The neatly comfortable main bar has no surprises – traditional pub furniture, a bit of beamery, log-effect fire and so forth, with a good chatty atmosphere at lunchtimes; there's a step or two down to a rather cosier area. Bar food includes sandwiches (from £2.25), soup (£2.25), ploughman's (£4.50), scampi, steaks, and other hot dishes (around £5.95), and daily specials like lamb chops or tortellini; Sunday roast (£6.25). Well kept Courage Best and Directors, John Smiths, Wadworths 6X and Websters on handpump; maybe mulled wine in winter, piped music. *(Recommended by Jens Arne Grebstad, David and Margaret Bloomfield, Stephen and Julie Brown, Per Ness, A J N Lee, David Peakall)*

Courage ~ Lease: Billy Murphy ~ Real ale ~ Meals and snacks (12-9.30) ~ 0181-946 5599 ~ Children welcome till 7 ~ Open 11-11; 12-10.30 Sun

George ★ 🍺 (Southwark) Map 13

Off 77 Borough High Street, SE1; ● Borough or London Bridge

Preserved by the National Trust, this splendid looking 17th-c coaching inn is such a London landmark that it's easy to forget it's still a proper working pub, and a good one too. It was noted as one of London's 'fair inns for the receipt of travellers' in 1598, and rebuilt on its original plan after the great Southwark fire in 1676. For a while it was owned by Guys Hospital next door, and then by the Great Northern Railway Company, under whose stewardship it was 'mercilessly reduced' as E V Lucas put it, when the other wings of the building were demolished. The remaining wing is a unique survival, the tiers of open galleries looking down over a cobbled courtyard with plenty of picnic tables, and maybe in summer Morris men or performing players from the nearby Globe Theatre. It's just as unspoilt inside, the row of simple ground-floor rooms and bars all containing square-latticed windows, black beams, bare floorboards, some panelling, plain oak or elm tables and old-fashioned built-in settles, along with a 1797 'Act of Parliament' clock, dimpled glass lantern-lamps and so forth. The snuggest refuge is the simple room nearest the street, where there's an ancient beer engine that looks like a cash register. They use this during their regular beer festivals (generally the third week of each month), when they might usually have ten unusual real ales available; the ordinary range includes Boddingtons, Brakspears, Flowers Original, Whitbread Castle Eden and a changing guest on handpump. Also farm cider, country wines, and mulled wine in winter; bar billiards and trivia. Bar food might include club sandwiches (£2.50), ploughman's (£3.25), cumberland sausage (£3.50), pasta with tomato and garlic sauce (£3.75), and home-cooked gammon or home-made steak and mushroom pie (£4); pleasant service. A splendid central staircase goes up to a series of dining rooms and to a gaslit balcony. One room is no smoking. Unless you know where you're going (or you're in one of the many tourist groups that flock here during the day in summer) you may well miss it, as apart from the great gates there's little to indicate that such a gem still exists behind the less auspicious looking buildings on the busy high street. *(Recommended by Janice Smith, David Carr, William G Hall Jr, Tim Barrow, Sue Demont, Simon Penny, RWD, Mark Baynham, Rachael Ward, James Macrae, A W Dickinson, Gordon, Mark Walker, Buck, Claire and Paul Shinkman)*

Whitbreads ~ Manager John Hall ~ Real ale ~ Meals and snacks (12-9) ~ Restaurant (not Sun; often used for groups only – check first) ~ 0171-407 2056 ~ Children in eating area of bar and in restaurant ~ Nearby daytime parking difficult ~ Folk night first Mon of month (except bank hols); Globe Players, Morris dancers and Medieval Combat Society during summer ~ Open 11-11; 12-10.30 Sun; closed 25/26 Dec, 1 Jan

Horniman (Southwark) Map 13

Hays Galleria, Battlebridge Lane, SE13; ● London Bridge

Like the surrounding area much busier during the day than beyond early evening, this elaborate and rather smart-looking pub has wonderful views of the Thames, HMS *Belfast* and Tower Bridge from the picnic tables outside. The spacious and gleaming bar is rather like a cross between a French bistro and a Victorian local – and something else besides. The area by the sweeping bar counter is a few steps down from the door, with squared black, red and white flooring tiles and lots of polished wood. Steps lead up from here to various comfortable carpeted areas, with the tables well spread so as to allow for a feeling of roomy relaxation at quiet times but give space for people standing in groups when it's busy. There's a set of clocks made for tea merchant Frederick Horniman's office showing the time in various places around the world. Bar food includes filling triple-decker sandwiches (from £3.20), ploughman's, and daily changing hot dishes like steak and mushroom pie or a couple of vegetarian meals (£5); they do a four-course carvery in the evening restaurant (£13.50). Well kept Eldridge Pope, Ind Coope Burton, Morlands Old Speckled Hen, Ringwood Old Thumper, Tetleys, and Timothy Taylor Landlord on handpump. A tea bar serves tea, coffee, chocolate and other hot drinks, and danish pastries and so forth; a hundred-foot frieze shows the travels of the tea. Pinball, fruit machine, trivia, unobtrusive piped music. The pub is at the end of the visually exciting Hays Galleria development, several storeys high, with a soaring glass curved roof, and supported by elegant thin cast-iron columns; various shops and boutiques open off. *(Recommended by Mark Baynham, Rachael Ward, Wayne Brindle, Bob and Maggie Atherton, Niki and Terry Pursey)*

Nicholsons (Allied) ~ Managers Bette Bryant and Dennis Hayes ~ Real ale ~ Lunchtime meals and snacks (12-3) ~ Carvery restaurant (not Sun evening) ~ 0171-407 3611 ~ Children welcome till 8pm ~ Occasional live entertainment ~ Open 10am-11pm (till 4 Sat, 3 Sun); closed 25 Dec, and maybe some evenings Christmas week

Market Porter ♠ (Southwark) Map 13

9 Stoney Street, SE1; ⊖ London Bridge

Busy and pubby, this friendly place is where the market workers and porters traditionally came for a drink at the start or the end of the day. It's particularly well liked today for its range of well kept beers, one of the most interesting and varied in London. As well as the Market Bitter and Special brewed for them, the choice of eight ales on handpump might include a combination of Fullers London Pride, Harveys Sussex, Spinnaker Buzz, Wadworths 6X and Youngs Bitter. The main part of the atmospheric long U-shaped bar has rough wooden ceiling beams with beer barrels balanced on them, a heavy wooden bar counter with a beamed gantry, cushioned bar stools, an open fire with stuffed animals in glass cabinets on the mantelpiece, several mounted stag heads, and 20s-style wall lamps. A decent choice of promptly served bar food includes sandwiches or filled rolls (from £1.95), ploughman's, vegetarian dishes like deep fried jalapeno peppers stuffed with cream cheese, burgers or all-day breakfast (£3.95), steaks (from £4.95), and changing daily specials; Sunday lunch. Obliging service; darts, shove-ha'penny, cribbage, dominoes, fruit machine, video game, pinball, and piped music. A small partly panelled room has leaded glass windows and a couple of tables. Part of the restaurant is no smoking. The company that own the pub – which can get a little full and smoky – have similar establishments in Reigate and nearby Stamford St. *(Recommended by RWD, David Carr, Thomas Nott, Mark Baynham, Rachael Ward, Don Kellaway, Angie Coles, Michael Boland)*

Free house ~ Licensee Steve Turner ~ Real ale ~ Lunchtime meals and snacks (not Sat) ~ Restaurant (not Sun evening) ~ 0171-407 2495 ~ Children in eating area of bar ~ Open 11-11 (11-3, 7-11 Sat)

Phoenix & Firkin ★ (Denmark Hill) Map 12

5 Windsor Walk, SE5; ⇌ Denmark Hill

This vibrant place is an interesting conversion of a palatial Victorian railway hall, but the atmosphere, rather than the architecture, is what draws so many people in. Lively, loud, and crowded with young people in the evenings (when it can be a little smoky), it's a real favourite with some readers. A model railway train runs back and forth behind the food bar, and there are paintings of steam trains, old-fashioned station name signs, a huge double-faced station clock (originally from Llandudno Junction in Wales), solid wooden furniture on the stripped wooden floor, old seaside posters, Bovril advertisements, and plants. At one end there's a similarly-furnished gallery, reached by a spiral staircase, and at the other arches lead into a food room; fruit machine, video game, pinball. Their own Phoenix, Rail and Dogbolter on handpump, and maybe one or two guest beers. Straightforward food includes big filled baps, jacket potatoes (from £2), a good cold buffet with pork pies, salads, quiche and so forth, and daily hot dishes like omelettes

(£3.30), fish and chips (£4.30) or mixed grill (£4.50). Though the piped music can be loud later in the day, the pub is much quieter at lunchtimes. There are a couple of long benches outside, and the steps which follow the slope of the road are a popular place to sit. *(Recommended by RWD, Nigel Wikeley, Dr and Mrs A K Clarke, Andy Thwaites)*

Own Brew ~ Manager Brian Ribbans ~ Real ale ~ Meals and snacks (12-8.30) ~ 0171-701 8282 ~ Children in eating area of bar till 6pm ~ Live music Thurs evenings ~ Open 11-11; 12-10.30 Sun

Ship ♀ (Wandsworth) Map 12

41 Jews Row, SW18; ⇌ Wandsworth Town

Splendid food and service are the trademarks of this smartly bustling pub. With a Thames barge moored alongside, the extensive two-level riverside terrace really comes into its own in summer, when it has picnic tables, pretty hanging baskets and brightly coloured flowerbeds, small trees, and its own bar. Inside, only a small part of the original ceiling is left in the main bar – the rest is in a light and airy conservatory style; wooden tables, a medley of stools, and old church chairs on the wooden floorboards, and a relaxed, chatty atmosphere. One part has a Victorian fireplace, a huge clock surrounded by barge prints, and part of a milking machine on a table, and there's a rather battered harmonium, old-fashioned bagatelle, and jugs of flowers around the window sills. The basic public bar has plain wooden furniture, a black kitchen range in the fireplace and darts, pinball and a juke box. Youngs Bitter, Special and Winter Warmer on handpump, freshly squeezed orange juice, and a wide choice of wines, a dozen by the glass. The sensibly short range of very good, unusual bar food (made with free-range produce) might include sandwiches, soup (£3), green-lipped mussels in a rich cheese and brandy sauce (£4.25), smoked haddock and red leicester cheese fishcakes with a mixed leaf salad and a tangy orange and fennel coulis (£5.50), beef and Guinness en croûte (£6.50), chicken breast with blue cheese sauce, glazed walnuts, and apple potato spiced with mace (£7.50), and lamb steak marinated in garlic and rosemary (£8.50); there's an al fresco restaurant on the terrace. Service is friendly and helpful. The pub's annual firework display draws huge crowds of young people, and they also celebrate the last night of the Proms. Barbecues and spit roasts every weekend in summer, when the adjacent car park can get full pretty quickly. *(Recommended by Bob and Maggie Atherton, R Vernon, P Gillbe, James Macrae)*

Youngs ~ Licensees Charles Gotto, Desmond Madden and Lendre Macnamara ~ Real ale ~ Meals (12-3, 7-10.30) and snacks (all day) ~ Restaurant ~ 0181-870 9667 ~ Children in restaurant ~ Open 11-11; 12-10.30 Sun

White Cross ♀ (Richmond) Map 12

Cholmondeley Walk; ⊖ ⇌ Richmond

The big tree in front of this lovely riverside pub was not so long ago identified by a couple of gardeners from nearby Kew as a rare Greek whitebeam. Prettily fairy-lit in the evening, it shelters a good few of the seats and tables in the paved front garden, which in summer takes on the flavour of a civilised and rather cosmopolitan seaside resort; there's an outside bar at this time of year. Inside, the two chatty main rooms still have something of the feel of the hotel this once was, as well as comfortable long red banquettes curving round the tables in the deep bay windows, local prints and photographs, and a good mix of variously aged customers; the old-fashioned wooden island servery is on the right. Two of the three log fires have mirrors above them – unusually, the third is underneath a window. The views of the river are some of the nicest along the Thames, especially from the balcony of a big bright and airy room upstairs, which has lots more tables and a number of plates on a shelf running round the walls. From a servery at the foot of the stairs, good bar food – all home-made – might include tasty soups like pea or celery and almond (£1.95), sandwiches (from £2.25), ploughman's (£3.95), salads (from £5, with home-cooked meats), and several daily changing hot dishes like banana and cashew nut curry (£5.25), pasta with herbs, squid and tomatoes or turkey, vegetable and bacon pie (around £5.50), rabbit casseroled with prunes, wine and garlic (£6.25), and puddings such as summer fruit bavarois or apple crumble (£2.50); they generally do sandwiches or pasties up to 7 o'clock. Youngs Bitter, Special and Ramrod on handpump, and a good range of thirty or so carefully chosen wines by the glass, including three or four wines of the month; efficient, friendly service. No music or machines – the only games are backgammon and chess (they have a Tues chess night). Boats leave from immediately outside to Kingston or Hampton Court. Bonzo the flat coat retriever loves fetching sticks that customers throw for him, even if this means taking a dip in the river. Make sure when leaving your car outside that you know the tide times – it's not unusual for the water to rise right up the steps into the bar, completely covering anything that gets in its way. At times like this you might end up trapped in the pub for an hour or so – though it's a rather nice place to be marooned in. *(Recommended by A M M Hodges, Donald Boydell, Val Stevenson, Rob Holmes, Helen Pickering, James Owen, M L and G Clarke, ERW, Nigel Williamson)*

Youngs ~ Managers Quentin and Denise Thwaites ~ Real ale ~ Snacks (till 7) and lunchtime meals ~ 0181-940 6844 ~ Children in big upstairs room (high chairs and changing facilities) ~ Very occasional live music (jazz or a harpist on the balcony for example) ~ Open 12-10.30; 12.30 Sun; closed evening 25 Dec

Windmill ♀ (Clapham) Map 12

Clapham Common South Side, SW4; ⊖ Clapham Common/Clapham South

There are times in summer when this bustling Victorian inn seems to serve all the visitors to neighbouring Clapham Common, but it's such a spacious place that however lively it gets you should be able to find a quiet corner. The comfortable and smartly civilised main bar has as its centrepiece an illuminated aquarium, surrounded by colourfully upholstered L-shaped banquettes, and plenty of prints and pictures on the walls, including several of Dutch windmills. Bar food such as sandwiches and baguettes (from £1.60), soup (£1.95), ploughman's (from £3.95), vegetable kiev (£4.75), chicken satay (£4.95), beef stroganoff (£5.95), daily specials, and char-grilled sirloin steak (£8.95); service is friendly and cheerful. Youngs Bitter, Special and Ramrod on handpump, a good choice of wines by the glass and plenty more by the bottle; fruit machine and video game. There's a barbecue area in the secluded front courtyard with tubs of shrubs. The entertaining Monday opera evenings in the no-smoking conservatory now take place only once a month, when the genre's rising stars perform various solos and arias; they also have good jazz in here, all nicely segregated from the main bar. A painting in the Tate by J P Herring has the Windmill in the background, shown behind local turn-of-the-century characters returning from the Derby Day festivities. It's a particularly nice place to stay – a good deal of time and effort has been spent upgrading the accommodation side over the last few years. *(Recommended by Tim Barrow, Sue Demont, Val Stevenson, Rob Holmes, James Macrae, Christopher Gallop, Angeline Chan, Mark Walker)*

Youngs ~ Managers James and Rachel Watt ~ Real ale ~ Meals and snacks (till 10) ~ Restaurant (not Sun evening) ~ 0181-673 4578 ~ Children in no-smoking conservatory ~ Live opera first Mon evening of month, jazz second Thurs ~ Open 11-11; 12-10.30 Sun ~ Bedrooms: £80B/£90B, around £20 less at weekends

WEST LONDON

During weekday or Saturday daytime you may not be able to find a meter very close to the Anglesea Arms or the Windsor Castle, and parking very near in the evening may sometimes be tricky with both of these, but there shouldn't otherwise be problems in this area

Anglesea Arms (Chelsea) Map 13

15 Selwood Terrace, SW7; ⊖ South Kensington

Considering the surrounding affluence you might expect this chatty pub to be slightly snooty, but nothing could be further from the truth; it's a very friendly and unpretentious place, that somehow manages to feel both smart and cosy at the same time. The bar has central elbow tables, leather chesterfields, faded turkey carpets on the bare wood-strip floor, wood panelling, and big windows with attractive swagged curtains; at one end several booths with partly glazed screens have cushioned pews and spindleback chairs, and down some steps there's a small carpeted room with captain's chairs, high stools and a Victorian fireplace. The genuinely old-fashioned mood is heightened by some heavy portraits, prints of London, a big station clock, bits of brass and pottery, and large brass chandeliers. It can get so busy in the evenings that customers spill out onto the terrace and pavement. Well kept Adnams, Boddingtons, Brakspears SB, Fullers London Pride, Harveys, Marstons Pedigree and Youngs Special on handpump, and several malt and Irish whiskies. Food from a glass cabinet includes doorstep sandwiches (from £1.50), ploughman's (£3), broccoli and cheese bake or pies such as steak and mushroom (£3.90), maybe sirloin steak (£6), and a Sunday roast (£4.95); in the late evening, you may get sandwiches for £1 or less. Good, quick service. The pub is very popular with well-heeled young people, but is well liked by locals too; perhaps that's because many of the locals are well-heeled young people. *(Recommended by Mayur Shah, Tim Barrow, Sue Demont, Andy Thwaites, Yolanda Henry, John Fazakerley, Michael J Lumia)*

Free House ~ Licensee Patrick Timmons ~ Real ale ~ Meals and snacks (not Sun evening) ~ 0171-373 7960 ~ Children welcome till 7pm ~ Daytime parking metered ~ Open 11-3, 5(7 Sat)-11; closed 25/26 Dec

Churchill Arms 🍴 (Kensington) Map 12

119 Kensington Church St, W8; ⊖ Notting Hill Gate/Kensington High St

One reader has been coming to this wonderfully friendly pub every month for the last 30 years. Like the other people who've written to us about it this year, he puts the credit for its atmosphere and popularity squarely on the shoulders of the good-natured Irish landlord, who works hard and enthusiastically to give visitors an individual welcome. One of his hobbies is collecting butterflies, so you'll see a variety of prints and books on the subject dotted around the bar. There are also lamps, miners' lights, horse tack, bedpans and brasses hanging from the ceiling, a couple of interesting carved figures and statuettes behind the central bar counter, prints of American presidents, and lots of Churchill memorabilia. It feels very much like a bustling village local, with lots of effort put into organising special events, especially around Halloween or the week leading up to Churchill's birthday (November 30th), decorating the place with balloons, candles and appropriate oddities, serving special drinks and generally just creating a lively carefree atmosphere. St Patrick's Day and Christmas are also marked with gusto. The spacious and rather smart plant-filled dining conservatory may be used for hatching butterflies, but is better known for its big choice of really excellent Thai food: chicken and cashew nuts (£4.95) or Thai noodles, roast duck curry or beef curry (£5.25). They also do things like lunchtime sandwiches (from £1.75), ploughman's (£2.75), home-made steak and kidney pie (£2.95), and Sunday lunch (£4.95). Well kept (and nicely priced) Fullers ESB, London Pride, Chiswick and Hock Mild on handpump; cheerful service. Shove-ha'penny, fruit machine, and unobtrusive piped music; they have their own cricket and football teams. *(Recommended by Frank Ashbee, Thomas Thomas, LM, Maggie and Bob Atherton, Neville Vickers, Ian Phillips, Bob Shearer, Mimi O'Connor, David Peakall)*

Fullers ~ Manager Gerry O'Brien ~ Real ale ~ Meals and snacks (12-2.30, 6-9.30; not Sun evening) ~ Restaurant (not Sun evening) ~ 0171-727 4242 ~ Children welcome ~ Open 11-11; 12-10.30 Sun; closed evening 25 Dec

Dove ★ (Hammersmith) Map 12

19 Upper Mall, W6; ⊖ Ravenscourt Park

'Rule Britannia' is said to have been composed at this old-fashioned Thameside pub, and its author James Thomson also wrote the final part of his less well-known 'The Seasons' in an upper room, whilst dying of a fever he'd caught travelling to Kew in bad weather. It's the nicest of the clutch of pubs that punctuate this stretch of the river, and in summer most people head for the the tiny terrace at the back, where the main flagstoned area, down some steps, has a few teak tables and white metal and teak chairs looking over the low river wall to the Thames reach just above Hammersmith Bridge; a very civilised spot. In the evenings you'll often see rowing crews practising along this part of the water. By the entrance from the quiet alley, the main bar has black wood panelling, red leatherette cushioned built-in wall settles and stools around dimpled copper tables, old framed advertisements, and photographs of the pub; very well kept Fullers London Pride and ESB on handpump. Up some steps, a room with small settles and solid wooden furniture has a big, clean and efficiently served glass food cabinet, offering sandwiches, filled baked potatoes (£3.50), salads (£3.95), cottage pie (£4.50), steak and kidney pie or smoked haddock pasta (£4.95), and lots of changing daily specials; they also do a range of Thai meals, particularly in the evening (from £5.50). No games machines or piped music. Perhaps the best time to visit is at lunchtime when it's not quite so crowded, but even at its busiest, the staff remain briskly efficient. A plaque marks the level of the highest-ever tide in 1928. *(Recommended by Wayne Brindle, Stephen and Julie Brown, Gill and Andy Plumb, SK, Peter Marshall, Gordon, M L and G Clarke, Dave Irving, Ewan McCall, Roger Huggins, Tom McLean, A W Dickinson, James Macrae)*

Fullers ~ Tenant Brian Lovrey ~ Real ale ~ Meals and snacks ~ 0181-748 5405 ~ Open 11-11; 12-10.30 Sun

Eel Pie 🍺 (Twickenham) Map 12

9 Church Street; ⇌ Twickenham

This busy and unpretentious pub is well liked for its range of well kept real ales on handpump, generally including Badger Best, Hard Tackle and Tanglefoot, Gribble Black Adder and Wadworths 6X; they also keep around 14 malt whiskies. Sandwiches are usually served all day (not Sunday), and at lunchtime there might be ploughman's, and three or four changing hot dishes like mushroom and nut fettucine (£3.50) or steak in stout (£4.25). Seats at the front window of the simply furnished downstairs bar, decorated in Laura Ashley style, look out to the quiet village street; bar billiards, dominoes, scrabble, chess, fruit machine, juke box, pinball, and maybe Brady, the irish wolfhound. There are benches outside on the cobbles. It can be very popular at weekends, especially if there's a rugby game on. *(Recommended by Steve Felstead, M L and G Clarke, Liz and Benton Jennings, James Macrae, MS)*

Badger ~ Manager Colin Clark ~ Real ale ~ Lunchtime meals and snacks (not Sun, or rugby days) ~ 0181-891 1717 ~ Children welcome till 6pm ~ Open 11-11; 12-10.30 Sun; they close at 8pm on days with major rugby games

Ferret & Firkin 🍺 (Fulham) Map 12

Lots Road, SW10; ⊖ Fulham Broadway, but some distance away

Like the other Firkin pubs this unusually curved corner house has always had something of an infectiously cheery atmosphere, and at the moment this seems more the case than ever – late on Friday nights you may find customers and staff dancing along to their well liked pianist, sometimes on the tables. Popular with a good mix of mostly young, easy-going customers, the bar is determinedly basic, with traditional furnishings well made from good wood on the unsealed bare floorboards, slowly circulating colonial-style ceiling fans, a log-effect gas fire, tall airy windows, and plenty of standing room in front of the long curved bar counter. Several readers have described it as a sort of anglicised Wild-West saloon. Well kept beers brewed in the cellar include the notoriously strong Dogbolter, Balloonastic, Ferret, and Golden Glory; with 24 hours' notice you may be able to collect a bulk supply. Good friendly service. A food counter serves heftily filled giant meat-and-salad rolls (from £2.50) and one or two hot dishes like chilli con carne, steak and kidney pie or casseroles (£3.95); Sunday roast (£4.95). Good – and popular – juke box, pinball, dominoes, fruit machine, and trivia. It's handy for Chelsea Harbour, which, to continue the Western analogies, at times feels rather like a ghost town. *(Recommended by David Carr, Steve Felstead, Richard Houghton, Dr and Mrs A K Clarke)*

Own brew ~ Manager Guy Davy ~ Real ale ~ Lunchtime meals (12-3); snacks all day (12-78) ~ 0171-352 6645 ~ Daytime parking is metered and may be difficult ~ Pianist Fri evening, occasional other live music ~ Open 12-11(10.30 Sun); closed 25 Dec

Kings Arms (Hampton Court) Map 12

Hampton Court Rd, next to Lion Gate; ⇌ Hampton Court

With its white-painted frontage nicely spruced up in recent months, and floodlit in the evenings, this comfortable and notably welcoming pub is right on the edge of the grounds of Hampton Court. The bar leading off to the right has black panelling, some seats and tables made from casks, and fine stained glass around the serving counter, while the lounge bar on the left, mainly given over to food, has one or two settles, bunches of dried flowers over an old cooking range and walls stripped back to the brick. Well kept Badger Best, Hard Tackle and Tanglefoot, and Gribble Ale and Black Adder on handpump; service is friendly and efficient. They also have a little tea shop, with several unusual varieties of the brew and light snacks. From an efficient servery, the well liked bar food includes sandwiches, good soup (£2.25), filled baked potatoes (£3.75), popular ploughman's (£4.25), battered cod (£5.25) and chicken and mushroom pie (£5.95). The public bar at the end is properly old-fashioned and very relaxed, with good games – an old pin-ball machine that takes two-pence pieces (proceeds to the RNLI), and a decent darts area; sawdust on the floor, dried hops hanging from the beams, a few casks, a fireplace with a stuffed pheasant above it, unobtrusive piped music, and some enamel adverts, one for Camp coffee. They can be busy in summer. There are several picnic tables on the cobbled front terrace near the road. Dogs are welcome, and may be offered free biscuits – not to mention beer, according to a recent report. Parking is metered nearby. *(Recommended by Susan and John Douglas, Peter Burton, John Ames, Jamie and Ruth Lyons, Yolanda Henry; more reports please)*

Badger ~ Manager Niall Williams ~ Real ale ~ Lunchtime meals (12-3) Snacks (all day) ~ Upstairs restaurant; closed Sun evening, Mon ~ 0181-977 1729 ~ Children welcome till 8pm ~ Open 11-11; 12-10.30 Sun; closed evening 25 Dec

Ladbroke Arms 🍴 (Holland Park) Map 12

54 Ladbroke Rd, W11; ⊖ Holland Park
London Dining Pub of the Year

There aren't many pubs in London that we can say stand out for their food, but happily this stylish place is one of them. Few of its peers offer meals this impressive, and it comes as quite a bonus that the pub itself would still be worth a stop even if the only food was a curled-up sandwich or packet of roasted peanuts. Chalked up on a couple of blackboards on the right hand side of the central servery, the imaginative range of home-made dishes might typically include grilled goat's cheese and bacon salad (£5.25), pasta with pesto and sun-dried tomatoes (£5.50), beef goulash (£6.95), salmon fishcakes with hollandaise sauce or chicken breast stuffed with avocado and garlic (£7.95), escalope of turkey filled with mozzarella and bacon on a bed of noodles (£8.95), rack of lamb with barlotti beans (£9.50), steak in a pink peppercorn sauce (£9.95), and freshly delivered fish such as baked cod with coriander; friendly staff bring french bread to the table, and even the mustards and other accompaniments are better quality than average. There's a warm red hue to some parts of the immaculate bar (especially up in a slightly raised area with a fireplace), as well as simple wooden tables and chairs, comfortable red-cushioned wall-seats, several colonial-style fans on the ceiling, some striking moulding on the dado, colourful flowers on the bar, newspapers and *Country Life* back numbers to read, and a broad mix of customers and age-groups; soft piped jazz blends in with the smartly chatty atmosphere. The landlord deals in art so the interesting prints can change on each visit. Courage Directors, John Smiths, Eldridge Pope Royal Oak and Wadworths 6X on handpump, and over a dozen malt whiskies. Lots of picnic tables in front, overlooking the quiet street. *(Recommended by Dr and Mrs A K Clarke, Mrs J A Blanks, C Leach, Tim Haigh, Wayne Brindle, Elizabeth Ibbott)*

Courage ~ Lease: Ian McKenzie ~ Real ale ~ Meals and snacks (till 10) ~ 0171-727 6648 ~ Children welcome ~ Open 11-11; 12-10.30 Sun; winter open 11-3, 5.30-11; closed evening 25 Dec

White Horse 🍷 🍴 (Fulham) Map 12

1 Parsons Green, SW6; ⊖ Parsons Green
Careful and efficient management explains the success of this chatty and all-round excellent pub. The drinks, food and smiling service all stand out, and though it's usually busy, there are enough helpful staff behind the solid panelled central servery to ensure you'll rarely have to wait to be served. Particularly well kept and often unusual beers might include Adnams Extra, Bass, Harveys Sussex, Highgate Mild and a guest on handpump, with some helpful tasting notes; they also have 15 Trappist beers, a guest foreign lager on draught, a dozen malt whiskies, and good, interesting and not overpriced wines (a new Cruover machine should increase the choice by the glass).

Well liked weekday lunches might include sandwiches, soup (£2.50), pasta with artichokes, peppers and mushrooms (£4.25), braised sausages in beer and onion gravy (£4.50), and Chinese spiced pork (£5.25), with evening dishes like spaghetti with sun-dried tomatoes, coriander, roasted peppers and black olives (£5.95), and Thai stir-fried monkfish or warm chicken salad with satay sauce (£6.50). They also do a very good Sunday lunch in the old billiard room upstairs. Redecorated this year, the spacious and tastefully refurbished U-shaped bar has big leather chesterfields and huge windows with slatted wooden blinds; to one side is a plainer area with leatherette wall banquettes on the wood plank floor, and a tiled Victorian fireplace. Several of the high-backed pews on the right hand side may be reserved for eating. Dominoes, cribbage, chess, cards, fruit machine. It's a favourite with smart young people, who on summer evenings relax at the white cast-iron tables and chairs on the rather continental front terrace overlooking the green, so earning the pub its well known soubriquet 'the Sloaney Pony'. They organise several themed beer evenings and weekends (often spotlighting regional breweries) – the best known is for strong old ale, held on the last Saturday in November; lively celebrations too on American Independence Day or Thanksgiving. It's odd we don't hear more from readers about this place, to our minds one of the best pubs in London. *(Recommended by Richard Houghton; more reports please)*

Bass ~ Managers Mark Dorber, Rupert Reeves ~ Real ale ~ Meals and snacks (12-2.45, 5.30-10) ~ 0171-736 2115 ~ Children in eating area ~ Occasional jazz nights ~ Open 11-11; closed 25-28 Dec

Windsor Castle (Holland Park/Kensington) Map 12

114 Campden Hill Road, W8; ⊖ Holland Park/Notting Hill Gate

An attractive summer feature at this unusual pub is the big tree-shaded back garden, which has lots of sturdy teak seats and tables on flagstones, high ivy-covered sheltering walls, and soft shade from a sweeping, low-branched plane tree, a lime and a flowering cherry. There's a brick garden bar out here too, though be warned – on a sunny evening you won't find it easy grabbing a table. It's said that when the pub was built in the early 19th c you could see the real Windsor Castle from the top of this hill, and though the surroundings and view have changed almost beyond recognition since then, the pub has stayed very much the same. The series of small unspoilt dark-panelled rooms have time-smoked ceilings, soft lighting, and sturdy built-in elm benches. Bar food typically includes sandwiches (from £2.25), seafood chowder (£2.95), salads such as riccotta and aubergine (from £3.25), vegetable cous cous (£4.75), salmon fishcakes or moules marinières (£4.95), half a dozen oysters (£5), and steak and kidney pudding or rabbit pie (£5.95). They sell sausages made by the landlord's brother, who has a sausage shop nearby. Adnams Extra, Bass, Charringtons IPA, and a monthly guest like Stones on handpump, along with decent house wines, various malt whiskies, and maybe mulled wine in winter; a round of drinks can turn out rather expensive. Usually fairly quiet at lunchtime, the pub can be packed some evenings, often with smart young people; one room is no smoking. We've had a couple of complaints about the service in the last year, and indeed on our last visit not all the staff shared the same interest in their customers. *(Recommended by Tim Barrow, Sue Demont, Wayne Brindle, JO, Adrian Carter, Andy Thwaites)*

Charringtons (Bass) ~ Manager Matthew O'Keefe ~ Real ale ~ Meals and snacks (12-11) ~ (0171) 727 8491 ~ Children in eating area of bar ~ Daytime parking metered ~ Open 12-11; 12-10.30 Sun

EAST LONDON

Grapes (Limehouse) Map 12

76 Narrow Street, E14; ⊖ Shadwell (some distance away) or Westferry on the Docklands Light Railway; the Limehouse link has made it hard to find by car – turn off Commercial Rd at signs for Rotherhithe tunnel, Tunnel Approach slip-road on left leads to Branch Rd then Narrow St

Nicely off the tourist track, this characterful 16th-c pub was used by Charles Dickens as the basis of his 'Six Jolly Fellowship Porters' in *Our Mutual Friend*: 'It had not a straight floor and hardly a straight line, but it had outlasted and would yet outlast many a better-trimmed building, many a sprucer public house.' Not much has changed since, though as far as we know watermen no longer row out drunks from here, drown them, and sell the salvaged bodies to the anatomists as they did in Dickens' day. It was a favourite with Rex Whistler who came here to paint the river (the results are really quite special). The back part is the oldest, with the recently refurbished back balcony a fine place for a sheltered waterside drink; steps lead down to the foreshore. The partly panelled bar has lots of prints, mainly of actors, some elaborately etched windows, and newspapers to read. Friary Meux, Ind Coope Burton, Tetleys and a guest beer on handpump, and a choice of malt whiskies. Bar food such as soup (£2.50), prawn or crab mayonnaise (£2.95), ploughman's (£3.95), moules marinières or a pint of prawns (£4.25), bangers and mash with a thick onion gravy (£4.75), daily fresh fish like plaice or cod or home-made salmon fishcakes with caper sauce (£5.25), and a Sunday roast (no other meals then). The upstairs fish restaurant (with fine views of the river) is highly praised – booking is recommended. Shove-ha'penny, table skittles, cribbage, dominoes, backgammon, maybe piped classical or jazz; no under 14s. *(Recommended John Fahy, R J Bland, Eddie Edwards)*

Taylor-Walker (Allied) ~ Manager Barbara Haigh ~ Real ale ~ Meals and snacks (not Sun evening) ~ Restaurant (closed Sun) ~ 0171-987 4396 ~ Open 12-3, 5.30; 7-11 Sat (closed lunchtime)

Town of Ramsgate (Wapping) Map 12

62 Wapping High St, E1; ⊖ Wapping

This old pub has an evocative old-London setting, overlooking King Edward's Stairs (also known as Wapping Old Stairs), where the Ramsgate fishermen used to sell their catches. Inside, an enormous fine etched mirror shows Ramsgate harbour as it used to be. The softly lit panelled bar is a fine combination of comfort and good housekeeping on the one hand with plenty of interest on the other: it has masses of bric-a-brac from old pots, pans, pewter and decorative plates to the collection of walking canes criss-crossing the ceiling. There's a fine assortment of old Limehouse prints. Bar food includes sandwiches (from £1.95, steak £3.95), filled baked potatoes (£2.75), pizzas (from £3.75), ploughman's (£3.95) and cumberland sausage and mash (£4.95), with three or four daily specials like sweet and sour chicken (£4.95); well kept Bass and Fullers London Pride under light blanket pressure; friendly service; cribbage, trivia, unobtrusive piped music; good sociable mix of customers. At the back, a floodlit flagstoned terrace and wooden platform (with pots of flowers and summer barbecues) peeps out past the stairs and the high wall of Olivers Warehouse to the Thames. *(Recommended by Martin Gorrod, Gordon, Dave Kitchenham, Tim Barrow, Sue Demont, David Lamb)*

Charringtons (Bass) ~ Manager Alison Keep ~ Real ale ~ Meals and snacks (11.30-3, 6.30-10; 12-4, 6.30-9 Sun)~ (0171) 488 2685 ~ Children welcome, Open 11.30-11; 12-10.30 Sun

Lucky Dip

Besides the fully inspected pubs, you might like to try these Lucky Dips recommended to us and described by readers (if you do, please send us reports). We have split them into the main areas used for the full reports – Central, North, and so on. Within each area the Lucky Dips are listed by postal district, ending with Greater London suburbs on the edge of that area.

CENTRAL LONDON
EC1
[Bunill Row], *Artillery Arms*: Good prompt friendly service, particularly well kept Fullers, darts in small unspoilt public bar – rest kitted out in standard 'character' style; don't be put off by the surrounding estate *(Tim Heywood, Sophie Wilne)*
[Smithfield], *Barley Mow*: Frequently changing real ales, good value varied lunchtime food; lively evenings, popular with Barts staff *(Mark Baynham, Rachael Ward)*;
☆ [115 Charterhouse St], *Fox & Anchor*: Good reasonably priced food esp tender meat in long,

narrow all-wood bar with narrow tables, small back snugs, interesting paintings, period prints and Edwardian photographs, well kept Greene King Abbot, Tetleys and other ales, friendly service; opens early for Smithfield workers' breakfasts *(Ian Phillips, Chris Westmoreland)*
☆ [1 Middle St], *Hand & Shears*: Traditional Smithfield pub with three rooms around central servery, hubbub of lively conversation, Courage and Theakstons Best, quick friendly service, interesting bric-a-brac, reasonably priced food – evening too; open all day but cl weekends *(Ian Phillips, Gordon, R J Bland, BB)*
[33 Seward St], *Leopard*: Good range of beers,

reasonably priced well prepared food; picnic-tables on big terrace *(Ian Phillips, MR)*

☆ [166 Goswell Rd], *Pheasant & Firkin*: Concentrates on good beer (own cheap light Pluckers, also good value Pheasant and powerful Dogbolter brewed here), and basic food at very reasonable prices – bare boards, no glitzy trimmings; good cheery service, congenial company from all walks of life, daily papers, good cheap CD juke box *(PGP, Ian Phillips, LYM)*
[Rising Sun Ct; Cloth Fair], *Rising Sun*: Recently antiquated, with elaborate carved dark woodwork, lots of little tables, stools and benches, books in ornate carved bookcase, friendly staff and youngish atmosphere, piped music, good value well kept Sam Smiths, good choice of food, chess, dominoes, cribbage; piped music and Sky TV may be loud, quieter upstairs (not always open) *(C Gallop, Mark Baynham, Rachael Ward, Tim Heywood, Sophie Wilne)*
[4 Leather Lane], *Sir Christopher Hatton*: Newish pub at base of new office block, in wide pedestrian area festooned with tables and chairs; big cellar bar sensibly split into separate areas by pillars and changes of floor level, well kept Bass, Worthington BB and other ales, popular lunchtime bar food; has been cl Sat evening and Sun *(Chris Westmoreland, Brian O'Keefe)*

EC2

[Masons Ave], *Old Dr Butlers Head*: 17th-c City pub with dark wood, cream paint, bare boards, small-paned windows, a few small tables around big irregularly shaped room, raised back area with old leather and dark wood benches and bar billiards, quick service, lunchtime food, upstairs bar *(Christopher Gallop)*
[Ship Tavern Passage, Gracechurch St], *Swan*: Tiny bar, making up in character and atmosphere what it lacks in space *(C Gallop)*
[St Mary Axe], *Underwriter*: Welcoming, with good value sandwiches *(C Gallop)*

EC3

☆ [St Michaels Alley, Cornhill], *Jamaica Wine House*: Long upstairs bare-boards bar known as the Jampot, benches and partitions, wine bottles and intriguing collection of copper vessels behind bar; downstairs livelier with young city gents, on hot days spilling into alleys and adjacent St Michaels churchyard; good lunchtime sandwiches esp beef and hot dishes, champagne by the glass, friendly atmosphere *(C Gallop, Eddie Edwards)*
[10 Grand Ave; Leadenhall Mkt], *Lamb*: Old-fashioned stand-up bar with plenty of ledges and shelves, spiral stairs to mezzanine with lots of tables, light and airy top-floor no-smoking carpeted lounge bar overlooking market's central crossing, with plenty of seats and corner servery strong on cooked meats inc hot sandwiches; well kept Youngs; also smoky basement bar with shiny wall tiling and own entrance *(Christopher Gallop, Richard Nemeth, Ian Phillips)*
[just off Cornhill], *Simpsons Tavern*: Not a pub, but wonderful tavern atmosphere, good pub food, long-serving waitresses, panelling etc; no real ale *(William G Hall Jr)*
[27 The Minories], *Three Lords*: Typical City corner pub, Youngs, lunchtime sandwiches,

baked potatoes, shepherd's pie etc, lots of prints, satellite TV and games machine *(Ian Phillips)*

EC4

☆ [Fleet St, nr Ludgate Circus], *Old Bell*: Unusually small and cosy for a City pub, largely unspoilt flagstoned front bar with trap door to cellar, stained-glass window, nice window seat; back bar with cast-iron tables and three-legged triangular stools on sloping bare boards; particularly well kept beer; rebuilt by Wren as commissariat for his workers on former church behind *(Mark Baynham, Rachael Ward, Andy Thwaites)*
☆ [Ludgate Circus], *Old King Lud*: 10 to 15 changing reasonably priced real ales in busy beams-and-sawdust style pub, no music, knowledgeable and helpful staff; yesterday's sports page from *The Times* framed in the gents' *(Mark Baynham, Rachael Ward)*
[29 Bow Lane], *Olde Watling*: Well kept Bass and Charrington IPA in heavy-beamed and timbered pub built by Wren in 1662 as a site commissariat for his new St Pauls Cathedral; lunchtime bar food, games room *(Dr and Mrs A K Clarke, BB)*
☆ [99 Fleet St], *Punch*: Warm, comfortable, softly lit Victorian pub, not too smart, fine mirrors, dozens of Punch cartoons, ornate plaster ceiling with unusual domed skylight, good bar food, Tetleys-related and other ales such as Marstons and Wadworths *(C Westmoreland)*

SW1

☆ [Eaton Terr], *Antelope*: Bustling upmarket panelled local, well kept Tetleys-related and guest ales, decent wines, decent food – quiet and relaxed upstairs weekday lunchtimes, can get crowded evenings; open all day, children in eating area *(Gordon, David, David Carr, LYM)*
☆ [62 Petty France], *Buckingham Arms*: Congenial Youngs local close to Passport Office and Buckingham Palace, unusual long side corridor fitted out with elbow ledge for drinkers, well kept ales, decent simple lunchtime food, reasonable prices, service friendly and efficient even when busy *(Derek and Sylvia Stephenson, LYM)*
☆ [14 Little Chester St, just off Belgrave Sq], *Grouse & Claret*: Smart, well run and discreetly old-fashioned, but welcoming, with attractive solid furnishings, well kept ales such as Boddingtons, Brakspears, Greene King IPA, Wadworths 6X and Youngs Special, games area, decent bar food; basement wine bar with three-course lunches, swish upstairs restaurant; children in eating area, open all day weekdays, cl Sun evening and bank hols *(E A Thwaite, LYM)*
[Whitehall], *Lord Moon of the Mall*: Huge and very ornate new Wetherspoons pub in former Williams & Glyns bank, usual range of beers, food all day; so popular with civil servants and tourists that in the evenings they sometimes have to restrict entry *(Sue Demont, Tim Barrow, Helen Pickering, James Owen, BB)*
☆ [58 Millbank], *Morpeth Arms*: Roomy Victorian Youngs pub handy for the Tate, old books and prints, photographs, earthenware jars and bottles; busy lunchtimes, quieter evenings – well kept ales, good choice of wines, food, helpful staff; seats outside (a lot of traffic)

(John Fazakerley, BB)

[37 Whitehall], *Old Shades*: Bright panelled pub with long narrow bar between front and back seating areas, staff friendly, welcoming and efficient even when busy, Bass, Fullers London Pride and Worthington on handpump, food all day, real fire *(Mark Walker)*

[Page St], *Paviours Arms*: Good Thai and other food, well kept Fullers, comfortable – modern, with chrome, but not overdone; packed with civil servants lunchtime, dining area can get cramped *(E A Thwaite, Mike Frost)*

☆ [23 Crown Passage; behind St James's St, off Pall Mall], *Red Lion*: Small cosy local, one of West End's oldest, tucked down narrow pedestrian alley nr Christies; friendly relaxed atmosphere, panelling and leaded lights, decent lunchtime food, unobtrusive piped music, real ales such as Fullers and Ruddles *(Walter Reid, Hugh MacLean, BB)*

☆ [D of York St], *Red Lion*: Busy little pub notable for dazzling mirrors, crystal chandeliers and cut and etched windows, splendid mahogany, ornamental plaster ceiling – architecturally, central London's most perfect small Victorian pub; decent sandwiches, snacks and hot dishes, well kept Tetleys-related ales *(Hugh MacLean, LYM)*

[Montpelier Pl], *Tea Clipper*: Handy for Harrods, with usual bar food and Courage-related ales *(Ian Phillips)*

☆ [Victoria Stn], *Wetherspoons*: Warm, comfortable and individual, a calm haven above the station's bustle, with cheap ever-changing real ales, wide choice of reasonably priced decent food all day, good furnishings, staff and housekeeping – and heaven for people-watchers, with glass walls and tables outside overlooking the main concourse *(Paul McKeever, Tim Barrow, Sue Demont, Anthony Barnes)*

[14 Vauxhall Bridge Rd], *White Swan*: Good service even if busy, well kept Theakstons XB, stuffed white swan by door, something of a rustic feel with sanded and scrubbed tables and real flowers in the tubs outside; handy for the Tate *(Tom McLean, Dave Irving, R Huggins, E McCall, BB)*

SW3

☆ [87 Flood St], *Coopers Arms*: Relaxed atmosphere, interesting style with country furnishings and lots of stuffed creatures, good food (not Sat/Sun evenings) inc some inventive hot dishes and attractive show of cheeses and cold pies on chunky deal table; well kept Youngs Bitter and Special, good choice of wines by the glass; under same management as Alma and Ship in South London (see main entries) *(Richard Gibbs, David Carr, LYM)*

[2 Lawrence St], *Cross Keys*: Reopened as interesting bar/restaurant, wonderful collage of paint-sprayed pots and implements in reworked eating area behind central island bar *(David Carr, LYM)*

[43 Beauchamp Pl], *Grove*: This formerly enjoyable pub has been reopened as an Irish theme bar, renamed J J Murphys – though still with Whitbreads-related ales *(BB)*

☆ [50 Cheyne Walk], *Kings Head & Eight Bells*: Attractive location by gardens across (busy) road from Thames, some tables outside; particularly welcoming local feel, clean and comfortable, with decent food at reasonable prices in bar and restaurant, three well kept ales inc Brakspears; well behaved dogs allowed *(M Walker, Robert E Jankowski, Tim Barrow, Sue Demont, BB)*

[Christchurch Terr], *Surprise in Chelsea*: Pleasantly tucked-away local with well kept Bass and related ales, decent food, friendly service, often surprisingly quiet evenings, cosy and warm; not overly done up considering location, attractive stained-glass lanterns, mural around top of bar *(Tim Barrow, Sue Demont, BB)*

W1

[54 Old Compton St], *Admiral Duncan*: Bright and friendly drinking pub with well kept Theakstons Best and Old Peculier, quick service, bare bricks and beams, good busy atmosphere, piped music, fruit machine *(M Walker)*

☆ [41 Mount St], *Audley*: Roomy and solid, with fine woodwork and panelling, clock hanging from ornate ceiling in lovely carved wood bracket, well kept Courage Best and Theakstons, good service; upstairs dining room *(Gordon, LYM)*

[Kingly St], *Clachan*: Popular and comfortable well kept pub behind Libertys, wide changing range of real ales, ornate plaster ceiling supported by two large fluted and decorated pillars; smaller drinking alcove up three or four steps; can get very busy *(Sue Demont, Tim Barrow)*

[5 Bruton St], *Coach & Horses*: Lovely little timbered pub stuck between modern buildings, small bar with upstairs dining room (not always open), Theakstons Best and Youngers IPA, sandwiches *(James Nunn)*

[Marlborough St/Poland St], *Coach & Horses*: Small *Private Eye* local, with friendly staff, good choice of real ales such as Greene King Abbot, Marstons Pedigree, Morlands Old Speckled Hen and three or four others, good coffee and house wines *(Nigel Woolliscroft, Peter Todd, BB)*

[Romilly St], *Coach & Horses*: Unchanged for years, no piped music, landlord may be playing chess in bar, prices good for London, guest ale; crowded and lively with its irregular regulars in the evening, lots of G Bernard-related cartoons *(L Dixon, BB)*

[27 Great Portland St], *Cock*: Large Sam Smiths corner local with landmark lamps over picnic tables outside, Victorian tiled floor, lots of wood inc good carving, some cut and etched glass, ornate plasterwork, velvet curtains, coal-effect gas fire; popular lunchtime food in upstairs lounge with coal-effect gas fire each end *(Ian Phillips)*

[43 Weymouth Mews], *Dover Castle*: Relaxing and friendly, some panelling and old prints, cosy back area; taken over by Sam Smiths, with OB and Museum ales *(Paul Mason, Gordon)*

[16 Charlotte St], *Fitzroy*: Tidy Sam Smiths pub with photographs of Augustus John and Dylan Thomas, George Orwell's NUJ card and so forth, bare-boards downstairs bar with white-painted brickwork, wooden settles and a couple of snugs, comfortable upstairs bar, OB and Museum, good value food, expert friendy staff; maybe piped music; plenty of outside seating, popular in summer *(Thomas Nott, BB)*

[55 Great Portland St], *George*: Solid old-fashioned BBC local, lots of mahogany and engraved mirrors, friendly atmosphere, well kept Greene King ales, straightforward food; open all day, cl 6 Sat *(David Carr, Ian Phillips, LYM)*

☆ [30 Bruton Pl], *Guinea*: Well kept Young beers, amazing meal-price sandwiches such as steak and anchovy or char-grilled chicken with bacon, olives and mascarpone, both in ciabata bread; summer overflow into mews off Berkeley Sq *(Adrian Zambardino, Debbie Chaplin, LYM)*

[Portland Pl], *Langham Hotel*: Entertaining Tsar Bar here has charming staff in Cossack outfits, very good nibbles in big Russian dolls, enjoyable tasting trio of vodkas on crushed ice; bedrooms *(Bob and Maggie Atherton)*

[Piccadilly Circus], *Long Island Iced Tea Bar*: Good value cocktails and burgers, good choice of loud piped pop music, big-screen TV sports *(Bob and Maggie Atherton)*

[Wardour St], *Moon & Sixpence*: Wetherspoons pub with decent food inc good Sun roast, well kept ales inc changing guest beers, good prices, no music – just chat; busy evenings *(Barry Riley)*

[23 Rathbone St, corner Newman Passage], *Newman Arms*: Both Fullers and Youngs (unusual combination) in small panelled bar, good home-made pies upstairs *(Ian Phillips)*

[Marylebone Lane], *O'Connor Don*: Better than most of the current crop of Irish-fad pubs, good sandwiches and other freshly made bar food, waitress drinks service (to make sure the Guinness has settled properly), Irish landlord, busy atmosphere; good upstairs restaurant *(Richard Gibbs, Simon Davies)*

[118 Marylebone High St], *Prince Alfred*: Smallish old-fashioned bar, friendly and comfortable when it's not too packed, in well worn typical Victorian pub with polished wood floor, dark green walls; Tetleys-related and other ales, interesting memorabilia of this son of Queen Victoria, two satellite TVs, jazz nights *(Gordon, Thomas Nott)*

☆ [Kingly St], *Red Lion*: Friendly, solidly modernised without being spoilt, with well kept Sam Smiths OB and Museum at sensible prices, reasonably priced food upstairs; video juke box *(M Walker, Susan and Nigel Wilson, BB)*

[50 Hertford St, Shepherds Mkt], *Shepherds Tavern*: Good speciality shepherd's pie *(George and Chris Miller)*

[Wardour St], *Ship*: Well kept Fullers, service always friendly, some concentration on lunchtime food, busier pub atmosphere evenings; largely no smoking, but piped music can be loud *(Frank Ashbee)*

[Hilton Hotel, Park Lane], *Trader Vics*: Hotel bar with properly made cocktails, good value despite the price, ditto the well presented bar snacks; good atmosphere; bedrooms *(Bob and Maggie Atherton)*

[8 Mill St], *Windmill*: Refurbished Youngs pub worth knowing for good value food in well run upstairs restaurant *(Richard Gibbs)*

[Woodstock St; off Oxford St, nr Selfridges], *Woodstock*: Small, cosy and busy, with well kept Theakstons Old Peculier and guest beers such as Robinsons Old Tom, wide range of

strong imported beers, welcoming landlord and staff, satisfying lunchtime food (can be rather crowded then), pleasant open fire, no noisy music *(Jens Arne Grebstad, Per Ness, D J Vogl)*

W2

[Bathurst St, opp Royal Lancaster Hotel], *Archery*: Well kept Badger and other ales and good helpings of decent food in homely early Georgian three-room pub with pots and hanging baskets of dried flowers and herbs in pleasant front rooms, darts etc in back room, horses stabled in the yard behind; tables outside *(Stephen and Jean Curtis)*

[57 Ossington St], *Leinster*: Interesting art deco pub, decor worth a visit *(Dr and Mrs A K Clarke)*

[10a Strathearn Pl], *Victoria*: Unusual corner local, lots of Victorian royal and other memorabilia, interesting little military paintings, two cast-iron fireplaces, mahogany panelling, friendly managers, Bass and Charrington IPA, well priced generous food, picnic tables on pavement; upstairs (not always open) replica of Gaiety Theatre bar, all gilt and red plush *(Janette Manson, BB)*

WC1

[St Giles High St], *Angel*: Friendly, busy, atmospheric, interestingly varied customers; well kept Courage Best *(Paul Byatt)*

[252 Grays Inn Rd], *Calthorpe Arms*: Consistently well kept Youngs Bitter, Special and Porter at sensible prices in relaxed and unpretentious pub with plush wall seats, big helpings of popular food upstairs *(Paul Byatt)*

[New Oxford St], *Crown*: Terrace out on small shady square looking down Shaftesbury Ave (an entrance from this side too); comfortable, usually reasonably quiet with relaxed atmosphere, good pub food, good range of beers inc Sam Smiths OB, Museum, Dark Mild and sometimes Taddy Porter *(James Nunns)*

[Northington St], *Dickens*: Clean and pleasant, cheap and cheerful, tucked away enough to escape overcrowding; food supports the Dickens theme (he lived nearby for a while) *(Quentin Williamson)*

[38 Red Lion St], *Enterprise*: Splendidly done out in traditional style, with tiled walls, big mirrors, bare boards; good choice of Bass-related and guest ales, good value food inc Mexican, friendly staff, small back garden; gets busy evening *(Geoff Coe, David Blackledge)*

[nr Staples Inn], *Melton Mowbray*: Newish Fullers pub nr Staples Inn, sensibly laid out with nooks and crannies, good street view and unobtrusive tables outside; particularly well kept Fullers, reasonably priced *(Chris Westmoreland)*

[1 Pakenham St], *Pakenham Arms*: Informal unspoilt split-level bar, generally quiet at lunchtime; well kept ales such as Adnams, Brakspears and unusual guest beers, big helpings of good value food *(Tim Barrow, Sue Demont)*

[63 Lambs Conduit St], *Sun*: Sadly this very popular pub with its uncommonly wide range of real ales has now been turned into another of those Irish theme pubs, and renamed Finnegans Wake *(LYM)*

WC2

☆ [31 Endell St], *Cross Keys*: Festooned with hanging baskets and window boxes, friendly and cosy, with lots of photographs, posters, brasses and bric-a-brac, good comfortable feel; basic lunchtime food, fruit machine, small upstairs bar, tables outside *(Gordon)*

[Betterton St/Drury Lane], *Hogshead*: Good range of well kept Whitbreads-related and other ales, very basic cheap food, pleasant bustling atmosphere *(Tim Barrow, Sue Demont)*

[39 Bow St], *Marquess of Anglesey*: Too transient a clientele to be anyone's favourite, but quiet and roomy, with wide choice of reasonably priced food inc vegetarian upstairs where bar-style seating looks over window boxes to street below, excellent service even when busy (they try to serve quickly if you're going to the theatre or opera), Youngs ales; no loud music *(Frank Ashbee, L Dixon, M Walker, Hanns P Golez)*

[28 Leicester Sq], *Moon Under Water*: Typical Wetherspoons pub conversion beside Odeon, Courage Directors, Theakstons XB, Wadworths 6X and Youngers Scotch on handpump, food always available, prices very reasonable for the area *(Robert Lester)*

[10 James St], *Nags Head*: Etched brewery mirrors, red ceiling, mahogany furniture, some partitioned booths, popular lunchtime food, friendly service, well kept McMullens – unusual here; often crowded *(Thomas Nott)*

[St Martins Ct], *Round Table*: Busy and cheerful, with good range of real ales (sparkler removed on request), also bottled German wheat beers, Belgian beers, real Czech Budweiser; can get very crowded despite high prices *(John C Baker)*

☆ [90 St Martins Lane], *Salisbury*: Sumptuous Victorian pub with sweeps of red velvet, huge sparkling mirrors and cut glass, glossy brass and mahogany; decent food (confined to right-hand side evening; even doing Sun lunches over Christmas/New Year), well kept Tetleys-related ales, decent house wines, no-smoking back room, friendly service; shame about the piped music and games machines *(Martin Hickes, John Fazakerley, Hanns P Golez, BB)*

[Judd St], *Skinners Arms*: Busy but cosy, with lots of comfortable seating, glass, brass and polished wood; well kept Greene King IPA, Abbot, Raven and Rayments, lunchtime food, island bar, friendly staff; picnic-tables outside, open all day *(Richard Lewis, BB)*

☆ [66 Long Acre], *Sun*: Well kept Courage-related ales, several dozen malt whiskies and a good many blends, chatty landlady, decent food inc Sun lunches, good old photographs of Covent Gdn market, first-floor wine bar; not as smart as many pubs round here, but less touristy and more enjoyable *(Andy Thwaites, BB)*

NORTH LONDON

N1

☆ [10 Thornhill Rd], *Albion*: Rather countrified and unspoilt (despite the Front Bench faces), horsebrasses and tack recalling the long-distance coach which was named after it; low ceilings, various snug nooks and crannies inc room behind bar furnished like someone's drawing room, cosy back hideaway on the right, some old photographs of the pub, open fires, some gas lighting, real ales, food, very friendly landlord; big back terrace with vine canopy, interesting Victorian gents' *(Adam Nell, Roberto Villa, BB)*

[115 Hemingford Rd], *Huntingdon Arms*: Informal, comfortable and friendly, with good food and wines *(Hugh Geddes)*

☆ [87 Noel Rd], *Island Queen*: Good freshly made and often unusual food in amiable character pub with eccentric life-size caricature fancy-dress figures floating from ceiling, well kept Bass and Worthington BB, upstairs restaurant; lively welcoming atmosphere, good juke box; handy for Camden Passage antiques area; children welcome *(Tim Barrow, Sue Demont, LYM)*

[115 Upper St], *Kings Head*: Wide choice of real ales, good spot opp antiques area, live music Sat; good theatre in back room (but hard seats there) *(Ian Phillips)*

[Upper St], *Slug & Lettuce*: Good if not generous food inc interesting skillet dishes, also various fish; bare boards and air conditioning, Courage-related ales, good wine list, pleasant staff, tables outside; spacious, but can be crowded evenings *(G J McGrath)*

N4

☆ [Stroud Green Rd], *White Lion of Mortimer*: One of the first Wetherspoons pubs, and still the same good value for all-day food and drink, with good choice of both inc well kept real ales, country wines and farm cider, pleasantly solid frnishings, restful back conservatory; part no smoking *(Mick Hitchman, David Carr, LYM)*

N5

[26 Highbury Pk], *Highbury Barn*: Particularly well kept beers, good value food; recently refurbished, handy for Arsenal FC *(Nigel Woolliscroft)*

N6

☆ [77 Highgate West Hill], *Flask*: Hospitable and comfortable Georgian pub, largely modernised but still has intriguing up-and-down layout, sash-windowed bar hatch, panelling and high-backed carved settle tucked away in snug lower area (this original core open only weekends and summer); usual food all day inc salad bar, Tetleys-related and Youngs ales, coal fire, well behaved children allowed, tables out in attractive front courtyard with big gas heater-lamps *(Graham Tayar, Dave Braisted, Ian Phillips, Gavin May, David Littlejohn, Mick Hitchman, LYM)*

N11

[36 Friern Barnet Rd, nr New Southgate Stn], *Bankers Draft*: Good example of modern traditional-style design *(John Barker)*

N12

[749 High Rd], *Tally Ho*: Imposing landmark pub comfortably renovated, with old local photographs, Courage Best and Directors, Greene King Abbot and Theakstons XB, sensible prices, useful food all day; one of the relatively few Wetherspoons pubs to allow children, if eating *(Robert Lester)*

N16

[Allan Rd], *Shakespeare*: Pleasant friendly bare-boards local with theatrical element – classical figures dancing on walls, central Victorian bar with Flowers, Ind Coope Burton, exotic draught beers such as Budvar and Weissbier, wide choice of bottled beers; good juke box, lots of young people *(Jan Pancheri, Mick Hitchman)*

N20

[1446 Whetstone High Rd], *Black Bull*: Very big Big Steak dining pub, good reasonably priced hot food swiftly served, from filled baguettes to huge steaks *(Alan Newman)*

NW1

[87 Albany St], *Chester Arms*: Run by two lively Americans, with good southern states menu of hickory-smoked ribs and chicken breasts, keg beers; reminiscent of the *Cheers* TV pub *(Frank W Gadbois)*

[corner of Arlington Rd/Delancey St], *Crown & Goose*: Good value home cooking from burgers and steak sandwiches to full meals, good atmosphere, nice clean nouveau-traditional decor; handy for Camden Mkt *(David Carr)*

[1 Starcross St], *Exmouth Arms*: Friendly and cosy local nr Euston Stn, good cheap bar food inc lots of sandwiches, baked potatoes, pies, well kept Courage-related ales, juke box, games machine; despite high ceiling can get smoky when busy late evening; quick service, seats outside *(Richard Lewis)*

[Euston Stn Concourse], *Head of Steam*: Large busy comfortably refurbished bar with lots of railway memorabilia, also models and magazines for sale; eight or nine interesting well kept ales on handpump, most from little-known small breweries, also Biddenham farm cider, friendly staff; open all day *(Richard Lewis)*

[11 Princess Rd], *Prince Albert*: Pleasant split-level pub with well kept beer, most attractive back garden *(Dr and Mrs A K Clarke)*

[141 Albert St], *Spread Eagle*: Typical Youngs pub with well kept beer, convivial hospitality and good decorative order *(Dr and Mrs A K Clarke)*

NW3

[North End Rd], *Duke of Hamilton*: Friendly Fullers local with good choice of beers inc a guest such as Shepherd Neame Spitfire, spirits bargains, maybe free jellied eels Sat afternoon *(Mark Baynham, Rachael Ward)*

☆ [14 Flask Walk], *Flask*: Well kept Youngs, decent coffee, friendly staff, good value food inc baked potatoes and several hot dishes more interesting than usual, in bustling and relatively unspoiled Hampstead local with carved wooden archway and stained glass panels dividing the two front bars, interesting back part, partly arched and vaulted stone; popular with actors and artists as it has been for 300 years; friendly helpful service *(Graham Tayar, Christopher Wright, LYM)*

☆ [32 Downshire Hill], *Freemasons Arms*: Big pub with spacious but busy garden right by Hampstead Heath, good arrangements for serving food and drink outside; several comfortable rooms inside, well spaced variously sized tables, leather chesterfield in front of log fire; usual bar food inc Sun roast beef (no-smoking eating area, at lunchtime), Bass and Charrington IPA; children allowed in dining room, dogs in bar, open all day summer *(Don Kellaway, Angie Coles, LYM)*

[154 Haverstock Hill], *Haverstock Arms*: Lively, with good mix of customers inc actors and musicians, good weekday food, endearing long-serving Irish tenant, good free Eddie Condon-style jazz Sun evening *(GT, BB)*

[68 Heath St], *Horse & Groom*: Classic Youngs pub with exceptional range of Youngs ales on handpump, wonderfully friendly landlord, friendly atmosphere to match; cosy decor, home-made food at good prices *(Mark Baynham, Rachael Ward, BB)*

[Hampstead High St], *King William IV*: Long a gay pub, but by no means exclusively, with good atmosphere, welcoming landlord, well kept real ale *(Graham Tayar, BB)*

☆ [North End Way], *Old Bull & Bush*: Family-oriented pub attractively refurbished in Victorian style, comfortable sofa and easy chairs, nooks and crannies, side library bar with lots of bookshelves and pictures and mementoes of Florrie Ford who made the song about the pub famous; friendly landlord, efficient staff, good food bar inc good Sun specials, decent wines and mulled wine *(Tim Heywood, Sophie Wilne, Gordon, BB)*

[28 Heath St], *Three Horseshoes*: Pleasant Wetherspoons pub in nice location, well kept sensibly priced beers, good staff, food always available, no-smoking area *(Hugh MacLean)*

[Kentish Town Rd], *Vultures Perch*: Good lunchtime food in pleasant pub with hospitable and likeable licensees and good free jazz Sun evening *(GT)*

[30 Well Walk], *Wells Tavern*: Cosy and villagey Hampstead local handy for the Heath, great atmosphere with roaring fires; can sometimes be a bit smoky, and keeping the outer door open to avoid this can make it draughty; tables outside *(Don Kellaway, Angie Coles, BB)*

NW5

[51 Leverton St], *Pineapple*: Small, peaceful and civilised oasis *(Graham Tayar)*

NW8

☆ [24 Aberdeen Pl], *Crockers*: Magnificent original Victorian interior, full of showy marble, decorated plaster and opulent woodwork; relaxing and comfortable, with well kept Bass and wide range of other sensibly priced ales, friendly service, decent food inc vegetarian and good Sun roasts, tables outside *(Stephen, Julie and Haley Brown, LYM)*

NW10

Coliseum: Wetherspoons pub in former cinema still showing original shape, with mock screen and suitable prints; bright clean pine-partitioned layout, friendly staff, good range of pub food all day, well kept Courage Directors, Theakstons XB and Best, very cheap Youngers Scotch, good guest beers, occasional beer festivals, no music; quieter eating area, busy elsewhere *(Ann Reeder, David Craine)*

Arkley

[A411 W of Barnet], *Arkley*: Big Steak chain

pub, seats outside or in attractive conservatory, food inc wide choice of good value filling lunchtime baguettes and lots of specials; pleasant service *(Anon)*

Barnet

☆ [18 Hadley Highstone, towards Potters Bar], *King William IV*: Cosy and well tended old local with real fires, nooks and corners, some antique Wedgwood plates over fireplaces, home-cooked food inc good fresh fish Fri, friendly staff, flower-framed front terrace *(GB, CH)*

☆ [58 High St], *Olde Mitre*: Small early 17th-c local, bay windows in low-ceilinged panelled front bar with fruit machines, three-quarter panelled back area on two slightly different levels, bare boards, lots of dark wood, dark floral wallpaper, open fire, pleasant atmosphere, friendly service, well kept McMullens and other ales; cl afternoon *(Michael Kentish, BB)*

Enfield

Jolly Farmer: Big modern family pub with welcoming atmosphere, plenty of dining space, well kept McMullens, enormous choice of food from sandwiches up, very efficient staff *(Gwen and Peter Andrews)*

[White Webbs Lane; A10 from M25 junction 25, right at 1st lights, right at left-hand bend], *King & Tinker*: Typical country pub opp riding stables, not over-modernised, busy and friendly, with good choice of well kept ales, good lunches inc huge filled rolls, authentic character, interesting old local photographs, well kept Tetleys-related and guest ales, decent wines, welcoming staff; can be rather smoky; attractive garden with fenced play area, occasional Morris men *(Michelle, Mrs P J Pearce, Joy and Peter Heatherley)*

SOUTH LONDON
SE1

[67 Kennington Rd], *Brendan O'Gradys*: Another of the current crop of Irish theme pubs, but well done, very friendly, and handy for Imperial War Museum *(Dr and Mrs A K Clarke)*

[Tower Bridge Rd], *Coppers*: Good value food all day, just outside the pricy tourist zone *(Dave Braisted)*

☆ [Bankside], *Founders Arms*: Sparkling view of Thames and St Pauls from spacious glass-walled plush-seat modern bar and big waterside terrace; well kept Youngs Bitter and Special, reasonable food, pleasant service, genuine feel *(Annette and Stephen Marsden, David Carr, LYM)*

☆ [5 Mepham St], *Hole in the Wall*: No-frills drinkers' pub in railway arch virtually underneath Waterloo Stn – rumbles and shakes when trains go over; not a place for gastronomes or comfort-lovers but well worth knowing for wide range of regularly changing well kept ales such as Adnams, Bass, Boddingtons, Everards Tiger, Greene King IPA, King and Barnes, Wadworths 6X and Youngs Ordinary and Special, also good malts and Irish whiskeys; loudish juke box, pinball and games machines; basic food all day (afternoon closure weekends) *(Tony Dickinson, Owen Walker, RWD, Tom McLean, D Irving, R Huggins, E McCall, LYM)*

[89 Upper Ground], *Mulberry Bush*: Attractively done sympathetically lit new Youngs pub, open-plan with slightly raised balustraded area and back conservatory, decent wines, good service, well priced bar food, spiral stairs to bistro with wider choice inc steak and salmon; handy for the South Bank complex *(Frank Ashbee, Gill and Andy Plumb)*

[29 Cornwall Rd], *White Hart*: Comfortable backstreet pub with well kept ales, marked NZ influence *(Dr and Mrs A K Clarke)*

SE3

[49 Tranquil Vale], *Crown*: Old and unspoilt, with very pleasant welcome, open fire, good imaginative reasonably priced bar food, S&N ales *(W Ruxton)*

☆ [1a Eliot Cottages], *Hare & Billet*: Nicely matured Victorian refurbishment, good solid furniture and open fire, view over Blackheath, popular food, well kept Whitbreads-related and other ales inc Fullers, good atmosphere esp weekends *(Richard Stokes, Andy Thwaites)*

☆ [1 Montpellier Row], *Princess of Wales*: Roomy pub with pleasant front prospect of Blackheath, well kept Bass, Fullers London Pride, Harveys, Wadworths 6X and Worthingtons, occasional beer festivals, good basic snacks and hot meals, brisk service, back conservatory and sheltered garden *(Tony Gayfer)*

SE5

[149 Denmark Hill], *Fox on the Hill*: Good choice of sensibly priced ales, food all day, tables in sizeable garden; one of the relatively few Wetherspoons pubs to allow children, if eating *(Dr and Mrs A K Clarke)*

SE6

☆ [Bromley Rd/Southend Ln], *Tigers Head*: Pleasant Wetherspoons pub festooned with flowers in hanging baskets, tubs and window boxes, picnic tables on attractive front terrace, small lawn with conifers; comfortable and roomy inside, with decent inexpensive bar meals, impressive choice of ales (one very cheap), pleasant service, no music or machines *(E G Parish, AT)*

SE10

[338 Tunnel Rd], *Mitre*: Old-fashioned Victorian pub by St Alphege's church and handy for *Cutty Sark*, RN College, Maritime Museum, Greenwich Theatre etc; recently refurbished with Irish flavour (also known as Sullevans); well kept Bass and Fullers London Pride, cheap food inc basic sandwiches, quick friendly service; lots of locals at lunchtime *(Andrew and Ruth Triggs)*

SE16

☆ [Bermondsey Wall East], *Angel*: Superb Thames views to Tower Bridge and the City upstream, and the Pool of London downstream, esp from balcony supported above water by great timber piles; straightforward bar food, Courage-related and other ales, upstairs restaurant where children allowed *(David Carr, LYM)*

☆ [117 Rotherhithe St], *Mayflower*: Friendly and cosy riverside local with black beams, high-backed settles and open fire, good views from upstairs and atmospheric wooden jetty, well kept Bass and Greene King IPA, Abbot and Rayments, decent bar food (not Sun night), friendly staff; children welcome, open all day; in unusual street with beautiful church (*David Carr, Nigel and Amanda Thorp, LYM*)

SE21

[Park Hall Rd], *Alleyns Head*: Comfortable well spaced seating, book-lined walls giving the saloon a collegey touch, bargain two and three-course meals, accommodating service (*EGP*)

SE22

☆ [Dartmouth Rd, Forest Hl], *Bird in Hand*: Civilised Wetherspoons pub, attractive glass-topped panelled recesses, marble-topped tables in no-smoking food area, spotless throughout; very pleasant staff, good moderately priced food all day, four real ales (*E G Parish*)
[Barry Rd, Peckham Rye], *Clock House*: Friendly and popular local, two rooms with dark woodwork, carpets, plenty of ornaments inc lots of clocks and measuring instruments; some seating outside, lots of colourful flower baskets, tubs and window boxes; well kept Youngs, nice mixed crowd esp evenings and Sun lunchtime, no music, decent home cooking (*Christopher Gallop, Andy Thwaites, Jenny and Brian Seller*)
[522 Lordship Lane], *Grove*: Harvester pub/restaurant with big front bar, friendly staff; suited mainly to families and people out for meals, but pleasant for just a drink too (*A M Pring*)

SE23

[35 Dartmouth Rd], *Bird in Hand*: Nice clean Wetherspoons pub with food all day, real ales, friendly service; quite a few OAP regulars (*EGP, A M Pring*)

SE26

☆ [39 Sydenham Hill], *Dulwich Wood House*: Consistently welcoming Youngs pub in Victorian lodge gatehouse complete with turret, well kept ales, food popular at lunchtime with local retired people, lots of tables in big pleasant back garden with barbecues (*Andy Thwaites, E G Parish*)

SW2

☆ [2 Streatham Hill, on South Circular], *Crown & Sceptre*: Ornate and substantial Wetherspoons pub, good traditional decor, sensible-sized areas inc no smoking, well kept reasonably priced ales inc some unusual ones, good value well organised food, good service (*Tim Barrow, Sue Demont*)
[Acre Lane], *Hope & Anchor*: Large Youngs pub with big colourful garden, good food inc well priced daily pie and salads, friendly landlord, games machines; often live busking-style music (*Tim Barrow, Sue Demont*)
[New Park Rd], *Sultan*: Unpretentious backstreet local with well kept Courage Best, Directors and Theakstons XB, friendly service, delightful secluded and peaceful fairy-lit back garden; can get rather noisy and smoky inside (*Sue Demont, Tim Barrow*)

SW8

[83 Lansdowne Way], *Priory Arms*: Friendly chatty local, landlord enthusiast for real ales with half a dozen particularly well kept inc

changing guests from small breweries; also excellent choice of continental bottled beers, fruit wines, farm ciders such as Thatcher's and Westcroft; good value food 12-5 weekdays, snacks Sat, comfortable seats, open all day; comedy upstairs Sat (*Richard Lewis*)
[169 South Lambeth Rd], *Rebatos*: Consistently good authentic food in front tapas bar and pink-lit mirrored back restaurant – which has great atmosphere, and frequent evening live music; lots of Spanish customers, real Spanish feel, always full and never short of ambience (*Susan and John Douglas, BB*)
[43 St Stephens Terr, off S Lambeth Rd], *Royal Albert*: In handsome Regency square in unpropitious area, well kept beer, good friendly staff, friendly and relaxed old-fashioned atmosphere, lunchtime bar food, pool room; garden (*Tim Barrow, Sue Demont, Dave Urwin, BB*)
☆ [16 Southville], *Surprise*: Quintessential small London local, friendly to all; big collection of framed caricatures, well kept Youngs and cheap wholesome food in two cosy rooms decorated in colourful Liberty prints; dried flowers, real fire, friendly dog and cat, pin table, tables out under leafy arbour overlooking small park (*Christopher Gallop, BB*)

SW11

Castle: Another Gotto pub (they also run the Alma and Ship, SW18, and Coopers Arms, SW3), quieter than the others; pleasant inside, with restaurant (good Sun roast beef), good wine list (*Richard Gibbs*)
[503 Battersea Park Rd], *Latchmere*: Sofas and easy chairs among other seats in imposing corner pub, Bass-related and Greene King ales; good upstairs theatre (*Sue Demont, Tim Barrow*)
[opp Battersea Pk BR stn], *Masons Arms*: Newly refurbished, with interesting mainly Italian food cooked in open-plan bar/kitchen; youngish customers, occasional art shows (*Richard Gibbs*)
☆ [60 Battersea High St], *Woodman*: Busy, friendly and individual young people's local, with little panelled front bar, long main room, log-effect gas fires, lots of enamel advertising signs; tied to Badger, with their beers and those from their own-brew pub at Oving in Sussex, also several guests such as Wadworths 6X, at fair prices, cappuccino coffee; food inc Sun breakfast from 9.30, bar billiards, darts and games machines at one end, picnic tables on partly covered back terrace with barbecue; they're good with children (*James Macrae, Tim Barrow, Sue Demont, BB*)

SW12

☆ [97 Nightingale Lane], *Nightingale*: Welcoming, comfortable and civilised local, good bar food, well kept Youngs, sensible prices, very friendly staff, timeless cream and brown decor with gallery of sponsored guide-dog pictures on one wall, attractive back family conservatory; children in useful small family area (*Tim Barrow, Sue Demont, BB*)

SW13

☆ [7 Church Rd], *Sun*: Several spacious traditionally renovated areas around central servery, pleasant atmosphere, six Tetleys-related and guest ales, usual home-cooked food, benches and tables over road overlooking duck pond; very popular in summer *(Peter Bull)*

SW14

[Ship Lane], *Ship*: Thames-side pub by Mortlake Brewery (and Boat Race finish), with good river view; comfortable Chef & Brewer with raised seating area and well presented straightforward food, tables out on terrace (not on river side) *(Graham Tayar)*

SW15

☆ [8 Lower Richmond Rd], *Dukes Head*: Classic Youngs pub, spacious and grand yet friendly, in great spot by Thames, well kept ales, 20 wines by the glass; main bar light and airy with big ceiling fans, very civilised feel, tables by window with great Thames view, smaller more basic locals' bar, good fresh lunchtime food; plastic glasses for outside, service can slow right down on sunny days *(BB)*

☆ [Wildcroft Rd], *Green Man*: Friendly old local on the edge of Putney Heath, with cosy main bar, quiet sitting room, attractive garden with barbecues most days, straightforward food (not winter evenings), well kept Youngs; open all day *(LYM)*

☆ [14 Putney High St], *Slug & Lettuce*: Bright, spacious, smart and tasteful, with mix of Shaker-style decor and comfortable sofas, delicious food esp risottos, home-baked bread, real ales and wide range of premium bottled beers, proper coffee, freshly squeezed fruit drinks, chatty staff, piped classical music lunchtime, quiet pop evenings; others recommended in this useful chain in Warwick Way (SW1), Islington Green (N1), Alma Lane (SW18), Water Lane (Richmond) and Fulham Rd (SW6) *(Chris Hunter, BB)*

SW16

☆ [151 Greyhound Lane], *Greyhound*: Fine three-bar Victorian local with several beers brewed on the premises, food all day, efficient staff, well equipped games bar, spacious and attractive family conservatory, sizeable garden *(Richard Houghton, LYM)*

[498 Streatham High Rd], *Pied Bull*: Large open-plan bar with many sofas, a couple of sofas and Youngs beer; reasonably priced food *(Mike Frost)*

SW18

[East Hill], *Beehive*: Small neat Fullers local, very popular evenings esp weekend, friendly efficient service, well kept ales, good mix of customers, unobtrusive piped music *(Tim Barrow, Sue Demont, LM, BB)*

[68 Wandsworth High St], *Brewery Tap*: Tap for Youngs Brewery, with their full range kept very well, lots of comfortable seating, genuinely Victorian decor with Youngs prints and artefacts, good choice of food inc lots of specials, good friendly staff; piped music; open all day *(Richard Lewis, Dr Paul Cadman, Dr and Mrs A K Clarke, BB)*

[39 Fairfield St], *Grapes*: Small welcoming single-bar Youngs local with friendly landlord, well kept ales, comfortable seats, weekday lunches, sporting trophies; piped music, Sky TV;

open all day *(Richard Lewis)*

SW19

☆ [6 Crooked Billet], *Hand in Hand*: Very well kept Youngs, good straightforward food inc home-made pizzas and burgers, relaxed and cheerful U-shaped bar serving several small areas, some tiled, others carpeted, log fire; rather spartan no-smoking family annexe with bar billiards, darts etc; tables out in courtyard with vine and hanging baskets, benches out by common; can be very crowded with young people esp summer evenings *(Christopher Gallop, David Peakall, BB)*

[1 Hartfield Rd], *Prince of Wales*: Large handsomely furnished pub with good reasonably priced food inc buffet, well kept Theakstons Old Peculier and other ales, German beer on draught, good range of bottled beers *(Per Ness, Jens Arne Grebstad)*

[Merton Abbey Mills, Merantum Way; next to Savacentre], *William Morris*: Lively and popular two-floor modern pub on site of the old Wm Morris/Liberty mills by R Wandle, lots of corners, seats outside; interesting Wm Morris materials and old bicycle posters, good range of ales inc Youngs, good choice of reasonably priced food inc Thai dishes and traditional puddings (just filled rolls Sat), brisk service; open all day, can get crowded, handy for market and waterwheel *(Stuart Michaels)*

Carshalton

[17 West St], *Racehorse*: Popular, with good reasonably priced honest food and interesting real ales *(Jenny and Brian Seller)*

Cheam

Bell: Clean and pleasantly refurbished, with good value enjoyable home-made food from doorstep sandwiches up, well kept Bass *(DWAJ)*

Chislehurst

☆ [High St], *Queens Head*: Charming comfortable and friendly local by attractive pond on green, pleasantly modernised inside keeping its quiet separate public bar (can be busy evenings), food inc superb value ploughman's, well kept ales inc Adnams and more unusual ones, good service; tables in garden *(Jenny and Brian Seller, David Thompson, Phil Hearn)*

Coulsdon

[Coulsdon Rd (B2030), Old Coulsdon; edge of Common], *Fox*: Handy for North Downs walks, and hugely geared to families, with good big enclosed play garden inc summer bouncy castle and ball pool and maybe a magician; good value usual food done to order, generous helpings, well kept real ale, interesting displays; popular with ramblers and footballers weekends, no dogs *(Christopher Gallop, Brian and Jenny Seller)*

Croydon

[Junction Rd, off Brighton Rd], *Crown & Sceptre*: Small, friendly one-bar pub, clean and nicely furnished, old brewery advertisements, well kept Fullers, big front garden, small back terrace, some floral decoration *(NP, TP)*

[Shirley Hills Rd], *Sandrock*: Good food, nice spot next to Shirley Hills, friendly staff, well kept Bass and Charrington ales *(Christopher Wright)*

Cudham

☆ [Cudham Lane], *Blacksmiths Arms*: Decent reasonably priced food inc interesting soups, huge helpings, well kept ales such as Courage, King & Barnes and Morlands Old Speckled Hen, good coffee, friendly service; nearly always busy yet plenty of tables, with cheerful cottagey atmosphere, soft lighting, blazing log fires, low ceiling; big garden, pretty window boxes, handy for good walks *(Jenny and Brian Seller)*

Downe

[High St], *Queens Head*: Authentic village pub now redecorated and refurbished, under friendly and helpful new management; bar food, well kept ales inc Burts, comfortable seating, well equipped children's room; pleasant greenery all around the pub *(E G Parish)*

Kingston

[Portsmouth Rd], *Harts Boatyard*: Vast Beefeater in good spot on Thames, full of character and endless boating paraphernalia – even whole boats serving as seats; two shaded balconies overlooking river and Hampton Court grounds, seats out in sun, Boddingtons, Wadworths 6X *(Ian Phillips)*

[off Richmond Pk], *Wych Elm*: Good recently decorated Fullers local with food inc decent sandwiches and rolls, well kept Chiswick, London Pride and ESB, reasonable prices, good service, Spanish landlord, no blarey music, pleasant little back garden *(Tim Cherry, M Tews)*

Malden Rushett

☆ [A243 just N of M25 junction 9], *Star*: Busy dining pub with well cooked reasonably priced generous food inc vegetarian, jovial long-serving ex-sea captain landlord, helpful quick friendly service; well kept King & Barnes and Courage-related ales, decent wines, maybe a splendid locally made elderflower champagne, big log fire; handy for Chessington World of Leisure, quickly fills at lunchtime *(Paul and Ursula Randall, J Sheldon, John Sanders, DWAJ, TBB)*

New Malden

[Coombe Rd], *Royal Oak*: Huge Edwardian suburban local with lots of original fittings, stained or etched glass, partitions and decorative tiles; attractive atmosphere, wide range of reliably good home-made lunchtime food inc big helpings of fresh veg, good choice of well kept Tetleys-related ales, big garden *(Christopher Gallop, G W and I L Edwards)*

Orpington

[Green St Green], *Queens Head*: Nicely refurbished as Big Steak pub, friendly service; quiz night Mon *(A Pring)*

Petts Wood

Sovereign of the Seas: Good Wetherspoons pub, wide choice of beers, very friendly atmosphere; gets crowded – lots of young people but no trouble *(Paul McKeever)*

Richmond

[5 Church Ct – alley by Owen Owen], *Angel & Crown*: Interesting Fullers pub with lovely frontage, hanging baskets, covered picnic tables; cosy and comfortable, with lots of prints and woodwork, big lounge, good reasonably priced

food from sandwiches up in side eating area, friendly staff, games machine; open all day *(Richard Lewis)*

[Upper Ham Rd], *Hand & Flower*: Friendly new licensees doing well in attractive commonside pub with spacious and comfortable lounge leading to lower snugs and eating area, coaleffect gas fire and china on walls, smart tiled verandah opening into big sheltered pretty garden, banks of greenery with grotto, waterfall and pond; good food, Courage-related ales, piped music *(Graham Tayar)*

[345 Petersham Rd; Ham Common], *New Inn*: Cleanly refurbished pub in good spot on Ham Common, with friendly atmosphere, comfortable banquettes and stools, good choice of lunchtime food, decent evening meals in pleasant dining area, well kept Marstons Pedigree, Morlands Old Speckled Hen, Theakstons Best and XB *(James Nunns)*

☆ [45 Kew Rd], *Orange Tree*: Interesting main bar with fine plasterwork, big coaching and Dickens prints, fine set of 1920s paintings; open all day, with theatre club upstairs, well kept Youngs, friendly service, decent food all day (not Sun evening) in civilised and spacious cellar bar; pleasant tables outside *(Liz and Benton Jennings, BKA, LYM)*

☆ [Petersham Rd], *Rose of York*: Comfortable seats inc leather chesterfields, Turner prints on stripped pine panelling, old photographs, attractive layout inc no-smoking area; good choice of reasonably priced Sam Smiths ales, pleasant helpful service; high chairs, bar billiards, fruit machines, TV, piped pop music; lighting perhaps a bit bright; bedrooms *(G W Stevenson, GWB)*

[17 Parkshot, just off shopping centre], *Sun*: Rows of cased rugby shirts around walls just below ceilings, also rugby posters, cartoons and photographs – even the day's rugby reports from *The Telegraph* as well as the front page in the gents'; warm friendly atmosphere, Fullers Chiswick, London Pride and ESB, reasonably priced food *(JJB, Kim Edwards)*

[former Prince of Wales], *Triple Crown*: Convivial and comfortable drinking pub, small and friendly, with wide choice of well kept ales inc Timothy Taylors Landlord, not overpriced; darts; popular after rugby matches – a haven from the bar of the London Scottish / Richmond Rugby Club bar nearby *(Comus Elliott, Mr Dallywater)*

☆ [25 Old Palace Lane], *White Swan*: Pleasant setting for little rose-covered cottage with pretty paved garden, barbecues, easy welcoming feel in dark-beamed open-plan bar, well kept Courage beers, good coal fires, good bar food; children allowed in conservatory *(Sara Jessop, David Carr, Graham Tayar, LYM)*

South Norwood

☆ *Goat House*: Delightful art deco pub, not too noisy, with full range of Fullers ales kept well, snugs, real fires, public bar with public-bar prices, pair of goats out behind *(Andy Barber, Martin Kay, Andrea Fowler)*

Surbiton

[1 Surbiton Hill], *Waggon & Horses*: Spacious

and welcoming Victorian panelled Youngs local, well run by long-serving traditional licensees; extensive reasonably priced lunchtime menu, well kept beers, central saloon, galleried upper lounge leading to attractive grapevine courtyard with popular summer weekend barbecues, separate small lounge by small character public bar with TV; efficient staff inc full-time potboy, no piped music or juke box *(J K Ives, Roger and Andrew McBride)*

Sutton
[5 Hill Rd], *Moon on the Hill:* Huge Wetherspoons pub with good choice of beer, reasonably priced decent food; absolutely packed some nights eg Fri *(Tony Hobden)*

West Wickham
☆ [Pickhurst Lane], *Pickhurst:* Big dining pub with good food inc good value Sun lunches (two sittings), double-sitting evening meals too, worth booking Apr-Oct; very pleasant helpful staff *(W L G Watkins)*

WEST LONDON

SW5
[209 Earls Ct Rd], *Blackbird:* Big comfortably furnished pub, dark panelling, plenty of nooks and corners, decent lunchtime food esp home-made pies and freshly carved roasts in barm cakes, full range of Fullers ales kept well, up-to-date atmosphere (music can be loud) *(Paul Mason, Kevin Noll)*

SW6
Anglesea Arms: Newly refurbished, with open fire, no juke box or machines, well kept Courage Directors, good food all week *(J Flitney)*
[617 Kings Rd], *Jim Thompsons:* Oriental-theme bar with South East Asian food inc set menus and vegetarian, jazz Sun evening; oriental items for sale eg Indonesian face masks *(Anon)*

SW7
[10 Fairholt St], *Swag & Tails:* Attractive mix of pubby and continental style, well kept ales such as Courage Directors and Marstons Pedigree, moderately priced good food *(James Nunns)*

SW10
Slug & Lettuce: Great place to meet before a Chelsea FC home game – packed, with a huge sound system, but great atmosphere *(Nigel Norman)*
☆ [6 Camera Pl], *Sporting Page:* Unusual civilised and upmarket pub off Kings Rd, one of the few in London to have genuinely good interesting food; well kept Courage-related and a guest ale, decent house wines, one or two seats outside *(David Carr, LYM)*

W4
☆ [72 Strand on the Green], *Bell & Crown:* Big busy pub with lovely river-view terrace, very friendly feel, local paintings and photographs, simple good value food inc sandwiches and lunchtime hot dishes, well kept Fullers, log fire, no piped music or machines; good towpath walks *(P A Chodzko-Zajko, Tim Barrow, Sue Demont)*
☆ [15 Strand on the Green], *Bulls Head:* Lovely Thames-side spot for this unpretentious well worn in old pub with little rambling rooms,

black-panelled alcoves, simple traditional furnishings, Courage-related ales, good food in no-smoking eating area (not Sun or Mon evenings), no piped music, back games bar; picnic tables by river, children allowed in back conservatory *(Chris Shaw, LYM)*
☆ [27 Strand on the Green], *City Barge:* Small panelled riverside bars in picturesque partly 15th-c pub (this original part reserved for diners lunchtime), also airy newer back part done out with maritime signs and bird prints; usual bar food (not Sun), well kept Courage Best and Directors, back conservatory, winter fires, some tables on towpath *(Richard Gibbs, Christopher Wright, Christopher Round, LYM)*
[80 Chiswick High Rd], *J J Moons:* Wetherspoons pub, with the usual virtues and interesting local historical information *(Helen Pickering, James Owen)*
[110 Chiswick Lane S, by Gt West Rd at Fullers Brewery], *Mawson Arms:* Fullers brewery tap recently refurbished, with lots of seating, bare boards, nice minimalist decor, settee at one end, papers to read, decent food, well kept ESB, London Pride and IPA, also full range of their bottled beers; personable landlady and helpful friendly staff; open all day *(Richard Lewis, Michel Hooper-Immins)*

W5
☆ [124 Pitshanger Lane], *Duffys:* Attractive and civilised, soft lighting, stripped floor, chessboard tables, well kept Brakspears, Fullers London Pride and Wadworths 6X, good value bar food, good friendly staff, slightly separate small restaurant – appetising aromas *(Mark Percy, Alba Siletti)*
[St Marys Row just S of Ealing Broadway, opp BBC Ealing Film Studios], *Red Lion:* Good quiet Fullers local, welcoming to visitors, with well kept London Pride and ESB, simple lunches, single small unspoilt bar with wooden floor and seating in low-backed booths, photographs of BBC studio stars *(Greg Kilminster)*
☆ [Church Pl; off St Marys Rd], *Rose & Crown:* Good food and atmosphere in 1920s/30s pub with small public bar, fairly big lounge and conservatory, well kept Fullers ales, smart efficient staff; games machines, unobtrusive piped country music; tables in back garden *(P A Chodzko-Zajko)*

W6
☆ [2 South Black Lion Lane], *Black Lion:* Chef & Brewer with cosy and welcoming local atmosphere, helpful staff, food reasonably priced and quite imaginative, served evenings too; big log-effect gas fire separating off area with pool tables, machines etc *(Helen Pickering, James Owen, BB)*
[Goldhawk Rd], *Stamford:* Good new bar/restaurant with plain wooden tables on stripped wood floor, small yard, good bar food, well kept beer, good more expensive restaurant *(Helen Pickering, James Owen)*

W8
[1 Allen St; off Kensington High St], *Britannia:* Friendly and peaceful local little changed since the 60s, good value fresh home-cooked food inc

notable bacon rolls, well kept beer, friendly helpful landlady, no music; attractive indoor 'garden' *(BHP)*

☆ [40 Holland St], *Elephant & Castle*: Basic two-bar open-plan pub, bigger than it looks, with friendly staff, well kept Bass and Worthington BB, good food inc pizzas (busy at lunchtime); good seats on small suntrap terrace with very pretty hanging baskets *(George Schaff)*

[24 Hillgate St; behind Gate cinema], *Hillgate*: Quiet two-bar local, well Victorianised, cosily partitioned high-ceilinged main bar, lots of pictures in cottagey room off, good lighting, well kept Fullers and Ruddles, pleasant service, lovely hanging baskets *(Dr and Mrs A K Clarke)*

☆ [23a Edwardes Sq], *Scarsdale Arms*: Busy Chef & Brewer (not the local it used to be) in lovely leafy square, stripped wooden floors, two or three fireplaces with good coal-effect gas fires, lots of nick-nacks, ornate bar counter; Courage-related ales, decent wines, back food servery with reasonably priced food; tree-shaded front courtyard with impressive show of flower tubs and baskets *(Gordon, BB)*

W9

☆ [93 Warrington Cres], *Warrington*: Lusciously decorated Victorian pub (said once to have been a brothel – hence the murals); well kept Fullers, good pub food, solid tables in garden, Thai restaurant upstairs; nr Little Venice *(Roger Wills, Gary Gibbon)*

W11

[14 Blenheim Cres], *Hogshead*: Former Blenheim Arms revamped in basic rustic style with wooden floors, vast range of real ales *(Dr and Mrs A K Clarke)*

W14

[187 Greyhound Rd], *Colton Arms*: Villagey but upmarket U-shaped bar, with lots of dark carved wood, gleaming brass, even a high-backed settle; good housekeeping, well kept Courage-related ales – ring bell for service; pretty back terrace with rose arbour, next to Queens Club *(Dr and Mrs A K Clarke)*

Greenford

[Western Ave (A4)], *Bridge*: Good value food inc good Sun lunch, well kept Youngs, good service *(P A Hubble)*

Hampton

[122 High St], *Dukes Head*: Open-plan local doing well under new licensees, with Courage and other real ales, good value food (not Mon, all day Sun), imaginative and beautifully presented, inc fine anglicised tapas and vegetarian dishes, even kangaroo, ostrich and crocodile, served throughout opening hours; dogs allowed, tables in small yard *(M J Gale, C H Daly, A D Nicholson, Trevor Meacham)*

☆ [70 High St], *White Hart*: Well kept Boddingtons, Flowers, Greene King Abbot and five changing guest ales, helpful knowledgeable staff, usual decent lunchtime food, warm log fire and quiet relaxed atmosphere; subdued lighting, good staff, small front terrace *(Roy Shutz, Dr M Owton, Alain and Rose Foote)*

Harefield

[Hill End Rd – lane to Springfield Lock, just N of hospital], *Plough*: Pleasant atmosphere, no music, welcoming landlord and staff, good service, simple food; worth knowing for the nine or so well kept real ales – landlord keen on trying new ones *(Marjorie and David Lamb)*

☆ [Shrubs Rd/Harefield Rd; Woodcock Hill, off A404 E of Rickmansworth at Batchworth], *Rose & Crown*: Warm welcoming staff, well kept Tetleys-related and Youngs ales and good choice of efficiently served food in attractively refurbished low-ceilinged country local; beautiful garden *(J S M Sheldon)*

Isleworth

Town Wharf: Well appointed riverside pub, splendid views from upstairs bar with lunchtime hot food and good range of beers, good service; good waterside seating area; can be crowded, esp summer Fri lunchtimes *(Mark Williamson)*

Norwood Green

☆ [Tentelow Lane (A4127)], *Plough*: Attractive old-fashioned low-beamed decor, cheerful villagey feel, well kept Fullers ales inc Chiswick, congenial attentive service, cosy family room, even a bowling green dating to 14th c; decent if limited straightforward lunchtime food, flame-effect gas fire; fairly compact and does get crowded weekends; occasional barbecues in lovely garden with play area, open all day, lavatories for the disabled *(Tom Evans, Annabel and Chris Holmes, Jenny and Brian Seller)*

Osterley

[Windmill Lane; B454, off A4], *Hare & Hounds*: Large open-plan suburban Fullers pub in nice setting opp beautiful Osterley Park, lots of tables in good mature garden; soft lighting, reasonably priced straightforward bar lunches, prompt friendly service; darts, piped music *(Ian Phillips)*

Sipson

[Bath Rd (A4); N side, between Sipson Lane and Hatch Lane], *Blue Horizon*: Promising new wine bar/restaurant with attractive decor, friendly service, good food and plenty of beers on tap, also exotic bottled beers *(John and Elisabeth Cox)*

Teddington

[Adelaide Rd], *Adelaide*: Friendly local with good food, well kept ales such as Wadworths 6X *(James Macrae)*

[Broom Rd], *Anglers*: Good spot on Thames at Teddington Lock, big garden very popular summer evenings and weekends, with barbecues; well kept Tetleys-related and guest ales, good pub food from sandwiches up, upstairs restaurant; well placed for footpath walk from Hampton Court *(Larry F Still)*

Twickenham

[39 Church St], *Fox*: Very good value lunches, good helpings *(Tony Pickup)*

☆ [Cross Deep], *Popes Grotto*: Very spacious and solid well run suburban pub, sedate and relaxing, with helpful staff, good value lunchtime bar food from sandwiches to Sun roasts, well kept Youngs, good range of other drinks, no music, games in small public bar; tables in own garden, and attractive public garden over rd sloping down to Thames (cl at night); children in eating area *(M L and G Clarke, P Gillbe, LYM)*

☆ [Riverside], *White Swan*: Relaxed country-style pub tucked away in very quiet spot by Thames, pleasant balcony overlooking it and tables outside right down to the water's edge; attractive lunchtime buffet with reasonably priced hot food, real ales, big rustic tables, walls packed with rugby memorabilia (other sports banned on TV), blazing fire; very busy Sun lunchtime and for events such as barbecues, raft races *(Liz and Benton Jennings, Richard Patterson, LYM)*

Uxbridge

☆ [Villiers St; off Clevedon Rd opp Brunel University], *Load of Hay*: Popular small local with wide choice of good value freshly made generous food, friendly staff, well kept Courage-related and genuine guest beers, choice of teas inc Earl Grey and Darjeeling, impressive fireplace in no-smoking back lounge area used by diners, more public-bar atmosphere nearer serving bar, another separate bar, local paintings; dogs welcome, back garden *(Ian Hill, R J Ward)*

[28 High St (A4007)], *Three Tuns*: Old beams and flagstones, former coach entrance now a drinking area – well kept Tetleys-related ales; mainly diners lunchtime, more relaxed evening *(R Houghton)*

EAST LONDON
E1

[St Katharines Way], *Dickens Inn*: Worth knowing for splendid position above smart docklands marina, well kept Courage-related ales and interesting baulks-and-timbers interior *(John Fazakerley, LYM)*

☆ [9 Exmouth St], *Hollands*: Well worth penetrating the surrounding estates for this unspoilt Victorian gem, friendly and entirely genuine, with lots of original fittings inc bar snob-screens and fine mirrors, interesting bric-a-brac, Youngs ales, simple bar food, darts; open all day *(Eric and Jackie Robinson, Prof J R Leigh, LYM)*

[57 Wapping Wall], *Prospect of Whitby*: Glorious site overhanging Thames with tables outside, well kept Courage, bare boards and flagstones, back part raised with panoramic views towards Docklands; basic pub food such as roasts and salads (5 each); on evening tourist coach trips, can be crowded then; usually fairly

quiet at lunchtime *(Sue Demont, Tim Barrow, Darren Thake, Gordon, BB)*

[8 Artillery Lane], *Williams*: Friendly tucked-away City pub with good choice of Whitbreads-related beers, wide choice of good food *(Geoff Coe, David Blackledge)*

E10

[557 Lea Bridge Rd], *Drum*: Comfortable split-level Wetherspoons pub, their fourth-oldest, with a more local flavour than some; well kept ales such as Greene King IPA and Theakstons XB, good value food *(Robert Lester)*

E17

☆ [off Whipps Cross Rd], *Sir Alfred Hitchcock*: More atmosphere than usual round here, rather countrified, with well kept ales such as Boddingtons, Flowers, Fullers ESB, enthusiastic Irish landlord, large open fires, Chinese bar meals and restaurant, reasonable prices; TV in bar; dogs welcome, sunny terrace *(Tim Wood, Neil and Jenny Spink, Mark Baynham, Rachael Ward)*

Barking

[61 Station Par], *Barking Dog*: Large Wetherspoons pub in former Gateway store, Courage Best and Directors and Youngers Scotch; very popular esp Sat *(Robert Lester)*

Ilford

[308 Ley St, nr A123], *Bell*: Well kept Courage Best and Hunters, recent smart bright refurbishment, old local photographs in saloon; live music *(Robert Lester)*

Romford

[Dagenham Rd (A112)], *Eastbrook*: Unspoilt, roomy and comfortable panelled pub, with restaurant, big public bar, Bass, Courage Best, Fullers ESB and Websters Green Label; bedrooms *(Robert Lester)*

[Dagenham Rd (off A112)], *Farmhouse*: Friendly open-plan pub with Courage Best and Directors, Fullers London Pride, panelling, garden; quiz night Sun *(Robert Lester)*

☆ [South St], *Moon & Stars*: Comfortable and roomy Wetherspoons pub, a real oasis for the area, with booths down one side, raised end area, usual range of beers with a regular guest, decent food all day *(Eddie Edwards, John Fahy)*

[Shafter Rd/Rainham Rd], *Railway*: Massive pub with contrasting bars, lots of panelling, Tetleys; popular with young people, DJ Sun *(Robert Lester)*

Please keep sending us reports. We rely on readers for news of new discoveries, and particularly for news of changes – however slight – at the fully described pubs. No stamp needed: *The Good Pub Guide*, FREEPOST TN1569, Wadhurst, E Sussex TN5 7BR.

Scotland

Outside the big towns, genuine pubs are less common than in England or Wales; especially in the more remote areas, hotels tend to double as pubs, often with a basic locals' public bar that's quite separate from the hotel side. Over the last few years many of these hotels' public bars have become rather more comfortable and approachable by passing visitors. We now include quite a number of them. In towns, the same sort of trend has meant that what used to be rather daunting locals' bars are now altogether more welcoming to visitors. The results are plain from our postbag – readers' reports on Scottish pubs and inns are now generally very enthusiastic. This last year, places that are doing particularly well are the Prince of Wales in Aberdeen (a classic town pub), the Old Inn in a fine spot by the sea loch (and Talisker distillery) at Carbost on Skye, the Clachan Seil at Tigh an Truish on Seil, the well run Creebridge House Hotel at Creebridge (enjoyable food), Bannermans Bar (lots of character, good cheap food), the classic Bow Bar, the handsome Guildford Arms and the Starbank (all in Edinburgh; the Starbank gains a Beer Award this year), the cheerful Lock in Fort Augustus (the publican owns the next-door fish shop – good news on the food front), the civilised but informal Eilean Iarmain at Isle Ornsay on Skye, the Kilberry Inn at Kilberry (takes some getting to, but really worth it), the well refurbished Killiecrankie Hotel just outside Pitlochry, the idyllically placed Plockton Hotel at Plockton, the warmly welcoming Lion & Unicorn at Thornhill (good food), and the cheery Ferry Boat in Ullapool. There's a lot of very good food in Scottish pubs now – particularly fine fish and seafood on the coasts. But it's an inland pub, the Wheatsheaf at Swinton, which this year gains the accolade of Scottish Dining Pub of the Year. In the Lucky Dip section at the end of the chapter, current front-runners include the odd Drovers Inn at Inverarnan and the Settle Inn in Stirling (Central), Black Bull and Moffat House in Moffat (Dumfries & Galloway), Cluanie in Glen Shiel, Clachaig in Glencoe and Letterfinlay Lodge near Spean Bridge (Highland), Wagon at Aberlady and Drovers at East Linton (Lothian), Ardentinny Hotel at Ardentinny, Hungry Monk at Gartocharn, Rab Ha's and Cask & Still in Glasgow, George at Inveraray and Taychreggan at Kilchrenan (Strathclyde), Kenmore Hotel at Kenmore and Drovers at Memus (Tayside), Sligachan Hotel on Skye and Pollachar Hotel on South Uist; we have inspected the great majority of these and can firmly vouch for them. Cask-conditioned beers are becoming much more generally available in Scotland now, though less so in the northern parts – and beer prices are generally higher than in England. However, you're far more likely to find a really good range of malt whiskies up here without having to pay an arm and a leg for them. Local government reorganisation is splitting much of Scotland into unitary authorities – many of them too small to be much help in locating pubs in unfamiliar areas. So for location we use instead the names of the regions which have become familiar over the last 20 years.

ABERDEEN (Grampian) NJ9305 Map 11

Prince of Wales £ ◑

7 St Nicholas Lane

This is a very likeable old city centre tavern set in the heart of the shopping centre, with Union Street almost literally overhead. A bustlingly cosy unspoilt flagstoned area has the city's longest bar counter and is furnished with pews and other wooden furniture in screened booths, while a smarter main lounge has a fruit machine; there are plans to create an upstairs wine bar. Popular, good value and generously served home-made lunchtime food includes chicken in cider sauce or lasagne (£3.30) and steak and Guiness pie (£3.50). A fine range of particularly well kept beers includes Bass, Buchan Gold, Caledonian 80/-, Courage Directors, Orkney Dark Island, Theakstons Old Peculier, Youngers No 3 on handpump and tall fount air pressure. No children. *(Recommended by Tom McLean, Esther and John Sprinkle, Graham Reeve, Angus Lyon, George Atkinson, Mark Walker, Chris Raisin, Susan and John Douglas)*

Free house ~ Licensee Peter Birnie ~ Real ale ~ Lunchtime meals and snacks (not Sun) ~ (01224) 640597 ~ No nearby parking ~ Open 11-midnight; 12.30-12 Sun

APPLECROSS (Highland) NG7144 Map 11

Applecross Inn ⑪

Off A896 S of Shieldaig

After an elating drive over the 'pass of the cattle' (one of the highest in Britain), it's rewarding to reach this beautifully located pub to find such a friendly welcome from the lively Yorkshire landlord. Despite some refurbishment, they are happy to be described as 'decidedly unsmart' and the simple bar is quite comfortable, and popular with the cheerful locals. Good, popular food includes home-made vegetable soup (£1.50), sandwiches (from £1.50), garlic mushrooms (£2.50), nice venison or cheese burgers (£2.15), fresh deep-fried cod or haddock or home-made macaroni cheese (£4.95), half-a-dozen local oysters (£5.95), queen scallops in a cream wine and mushroom sauce or dressed local crab salad (£7.50), sirloin steak (£9.50), and puddings like home-baked apple crumble (£1.95); you must book for the seafood restaurant. Darts, dominoes, and juke box (unless there are musicians in the pub); a good choice of around 50 malt whiskies, and efficient service. There is a nice garden by the shore with tables. Bedrooms are small and simple but adequate, all with a sea view. Mountain bikes for hire. *(Recommended by Andy Hazeldine, Mark and Diane Grist, Vicky and David Sarti, Tony and Joan Walker, Dr and Mrs Peter Kemp, N C Walker, Dave Braisted, Christine and Malcolm Ingram)*

Free house ~ Licensee Judith Fish ~ Meals and snacks (12-9 in summer; 12-2, 7-9 in winter) ~ Restaurant ~ (01520) 744262 ~ Children welcome until 8.30pm ~ Open 11-11(midnight Fri, till 11.30 Sat); 12.30-11 summer Sun; 11-2.30, 5(7pm Sun)-11 winter weekdays; cl 1 Jan ~ Bedrooms: £22.50/£45

ARDFERN (Strathclyde) NM8004 Map 11

Galley of Lorne

B8002; village and inn signposted off A816 Lochgilphead—Oban

From seats on the sheltered terrace here there are marvellously peaceful views of the sea loch and yacht anchorage. The same views can be enjoyed from the cosy main bar, which also has a log fire and is decorated with old Highland dress prints and other pictures, big navigation lamps by the bar counter, and an unfussy assortment of furniture, including little winged settles and upholstered window-seats on its lino tiles. Good bar food includes home-made soup (£1.80), lunchtime filled baked potatoes (from £2.75) and ploughman's (from £4.50), moules marinières (£4.50; large £8.50), burgers (from £4.75), home-made steak pie (£5.75), fresh battered sole fillets (£7.50), daily specials like poached salmon with pesto cream sauce (£8.25) or Loch Craignish langoustines, and puddings (from £2.25); children's menu (from £1); spacious restaurant. Quite a few malt whiskies; darts, pool, dominoes, and fruit machine. *(Recommended by Vicky and David Sarti, A F Ford)*

Free house ~ Licensee Susana Garland ~ Meals and snacks ~ Restaurant ~ (01852) 500284 ~ Children in eating area of bar ~ Open 11-2.30, 5-11; 11-midnight Sat and Sun ~ Bedrooms: £37.50B/£65B

ARDUAINE (Strathclyde) NM7910 Map 11

Loch Melfort Hotel 🖙

On A816 S of Oban and beside Luing

From the wooden seats on the front terrace outside this comfortable hotel, there's a magnificent view over the wilderness of the loch and its islands, and it's only a short stroll through grass and wild flowers to the rocky foreshore, where the licensees keep their own lobster pots and nets. The airy and modern bar has a pair of powerful marine glasses which you can use to search for birds and seals on the islets and on the coasts of the bigger islands beyond, the creamy pink walls are papered with nautical charts, and there are wooden tables and chairs, and a woodburning stove. Bar food might include home-made soup or sandwiches (£2.25), Aberdeen Angus burger (£4.50), ploughman's (£4.75), tagliatelle provençale (£5.25), half-a-dozen Ardencaple oysters or Ormsary venison sausages with caramelised onions (£5.95), local langoustines (£7.95), their own cured gravadlax with dill and sweet mustard sauce (£8.75), Aberdeen Angus steaks (from £10.75), half a local lobster (from £11.75), and daily specials like kidneys in a rich cream and wine sauce (£6.75) and freshly made seafood ravioli with a herby tomato sauce (£8.50); home-made puddings (£2.50). The main restaurant is no smoking; good wine list and selection of malt whiskies. Passing yachtsmen are welcome to use the mooring facilities. From late April to early June the walks through the neighbouring Arduaine woodland gardens are lovely. The comfortable bedrooms have sea views. *(Recommended by Mark and Diane Grist, J E Rycroft, Christine and Malcolm Ingram, Walter Reid; also in the Good Hotel Guide)*

Free house ~ Licensee Philip Lewis ~ Meals and snacks ~ Restaurant ~ (01852) 200233 ~ Children welcome ~ Open 9.30-11(11.30 Fri and Sat) ~ Bedrooms: £60B/£95B

ARDVASAR (Isle of Skye) NG6203 Map 11

Ardvasar Hotel 🖙

A851 at S of island; just past Armadale pier where the summer car ferries from Mallaig dock

The licensees of this comfortably modernised white stone inn will be sure to make you most welcome – and there's a good mix of both locals and holidaymakers in the evening. The simple public bar has stripped pews and kitchen chairs, and the cocktail bar is furnished with plush wall seats and stools around dimpled copper coffee tables on the patterned carpet, and Highland dress prints on the cream hessian-and-wood walls. In a room off the comfortable hotel lounge there are armchairs around the open fire (and a large TV); darts, dominoes, bar billiards, pool table, pinball, video game, juke box and fruit machine. Particularly good home-made bar food includes purée of lentil, carrot and ham soup (£2.50), basket meals (from £3.50), smoked duckling breast with mango and orange salad (£4.50), vegetarian pine nut and spinach jalousie with tomato and onion sauce (£6), roast rib of beef and yorkshire pudding with a bordelaise sauce (£6.10), home-baked game and port pie (£6.50), and puddings like apple and blueberry tart or sticky toffee pudding with fudge sauce (£2.20). Morlands Old Speckled Hen and a guest beer tapped from the cask, and lots of malt whiskies. The views across the Sound of Sleat – an area often referred to as the Island's garden – and to the dramatic mountains of Knoydart are very fine. Handy for the Clan Donald centre. *(Recommended by Andrew and Kerstin Lewis, Walter and Susan Rinaldi-Butcher, Eric and Jackie Robinson, N H and B Ellis, G C Brown)*

Free house ~ Licensees Bill and Gretta Fowler ~ Real ale ~ Bar meals and snacks (12-2, 5-7) ~ Restaurant ~ (01471) 844223 ~ Children in lounge bar ~ Open 12-11; 12.30-11 Sun; closed afternoons in winter, and all day Mon in Jan and Feb ~ Bedrooms: £35B/£65B

BRIG O TURK (Central) NN5306 Map 11

Byre

A821 Callander—Trossachs

Obliging new licensees have taken over this carefully converted 18th-c place, set on the edge of a network of forest and lochside tracks in the Queen Elizabeth Forest Park; lots of walking, cycling, and fishing. The cosy, spotless beamed bar has prints and old photographs of the area, some decorative plates, stuffed wildlife, comfortable brass-studded black dining chairs, an open fire, and rugs on the stone and composition floor. Bar food now includes home-made soup (£1.95), haggis, neeps and tatties (£2.25), sandwiches (£2.95), mussels in garlic and parsley cream or filled baked potatoes (£3.25), pasta in a tomato and basil sauce or smoked fish pie (£5.25), ploughman's, home-made steak pie or chicken, bacon and haggis with a whisky and grain mustard sauce (all £5.95), and puddings (£2.95); the evening bar menu is similar, and there is no bar food on Saturday evening, though you can eat from the restaurant menu in the bar (best to book, then). The restaurant is no smoking. Well kept Broughton Special Bitter and Black Douglas on handpump, and quite a range of whiskies; piped music. There are tables and parasols outside. *(Recommended by Susan and John Douglas, Mr and Mrs J R Morris, RWD, Ian Rorison)*

Free house ~ Lease: Elizabeth and Eugene Maxwell ~ Real ale ~ Meals and snacks ~ Restaurant ~ (01877) 376292 ~ Children in eating area of bar ~ Open 12-11; 12.30-11 Sat; closed winter Tues and 3 weeks in Jan

BROUGHTY FERRY (Tayside) NO4630 Map 11

Fishermans Tavern 🛏 🍺

12 Fort St; turning off shore road

They still have an impressive range of well kept real ales at this friendly town pub, including Belhaven Sandy Hunters and St Andrews Ale, Boddingtons Bitter, and Maclays 80/- and lots of quickly rotating guest beers on handpump and tall fount air pressure; there's also a good choice of malt whiskies, some local fruit wines, and quite a few Belgian and German beers. The little brown carpeted snug has light pink soft fabric seating, basket-weave wall panels and beige lamps, and on the left is a secluded lounge area. The carpeted back bar (popular with diners) has a Victorian fireplace; dominoes and fruit machine, and an open coal fire. Straightforward lunchtime bar food includes filled rolls, soup, and home-made leek and mushroom bake, lamb hotpot or sweet and sour pork (£4.10); enjoyable breakfasts, and comfortable bedrooms. The nearby seafront gives a good view of the two long, low Tay bridges. Bicycle hire available. Disabled lavatories. The licensee also runs the Speedwell Bar in Dundee. *(Recommended by Dave Braisted, Susan and John Douglas, Audrey Jackson)*

Free house ~ Licensee Jonathan Stewart ~ Real ale ~ Lunchtime meals and snacks (though in summer they also do food between 5 and 7pm; snacks only Sun) ~ Restaurant ~ (01382) 775941 ~ Children welcome ~ Folk music Thurs evening ~ Open 11-midnight; 12.20-midnight Sun ~ Bedrooms: £19/£34

CANONBIE (Dumfries and Galloway) NY3976 Map 9

Riverside 🍽 🛏 🍷

Village signposted from A7

Happily for us, the Phillipses are still running this civilised place and it remains the lovely food and wine that readers enjoy so much. The comfortable communicating rooms of the bar have a mix of chintzy furnishings and dining chairs, pictures on the walls for sale, some stuffed wildlife, and a relaxing atmosphere; half of the bar and the dining room are no smoking. Tables are usually laid for dining and the seasonal bar menu is chalked up on two blackboards and might include soups such as parsnip and broccoli or carrot and sage with home-made breads like tomato and pumpkin seed or Guinness and treacle cobs (£2.20), starters such as hot and spicy creel prawns, chicken liver parfait or baked garlic oysters (£3.95-£4.55), stilton and broccoli tart or tomato, mustard and parmesan flan (£5.25), fresh haddock in beer batter (£5.95), home-made hand-raised pork and venison pie (£6.55), home-cooked confit of duck (£6.95), char-grilled chicken in rosemary and lemon (£6.95) or fine steaks (from £8.95), poached wild salmon with watercress sauce (£7.25), poached fillet of plaice with brown shrimps (£7.55), and puddings such as rhubarb crumble ice cream, toffee apple bake or dark treacle pudding (£2.95). They have always used top quality ingredients and suppliers – Aberdeen Angus beef, free range chicken and pork, local roe deer, free range eggs, organic breads and unpasteurised cheeses, fresh fish three times a week from a fine supplier in Carlisle, and they only use fresh, seasonal vegetables. Lunchtime service can stop quite promptly. Well kept Yates Bitter and guests such as Cains and Holts on handpump, a good range of properly kept and served wines, quite a few malt whiskies, and farm cider. In summer – when it can get very busy – there are tables under the trees on the front grass. Over the quiet road, a public playground runs down to the Border Esk (the inn can arrange fishing permits), and there are lovely walks in the area. *(Recommended by SS, John and Phyllis Maloney, G McGrath, Mrs G Bishop, Peter Bell, J M Potter, Vann and Terry Prime, John Fazakerley, Lucy Herring, R M MacNaughton, Dr and Mrs and Hilary Forrest, Brian and Anna Marsden, Leith Stuart, Jack Hill, Mike and Wendy Proctor, W J Uzielli; also in the Good Hotel Guide)*

Free house ~ Licensee Robert Phillips ~ Real ale ~ Meals and snacks (not Sun lunchtime) ~ Children welcome ~ Restaurant (closed Sun) ~ (013873) 71512/71295 ~ Open 11-2.30, 6.30-11; closed Sun lunchtime, 2 weeks in Feb and Nov, 25-26 Dec and 1-2 Jan ~ Bedrooms: £55B/£75B

CARBOST (Isle of Skye) NG3732 Map 11

Old Inn

This is the Carbost on the B8009, in the W of the central part of the island

From the terrace outside this properly pubby, straightforward stone house there are fine views of Loch Harport and the harshly craggy peaks of the Cuillin Hills – and the place is popular with walkers and climbers. The Talisker distillery is only 100 yards away, where there are guided tours, with free samples, most days in summer. The pub stocks the whisky from here, plus a good few more more malts. The three simple areas of the main, bare-board bar are knocked through into one, and furnished with red leatherette settles, benches, and seats, amusing cartoons on the part-whitewashed and part-stripped stone walls, and a peat fire; darts, pool, cribbage, dominoes, and piped traditional music. A small selection of sustaining bar meals includes leek and stilton soup (£1.40), sandwiches, sausage hotpot, burgers, venison casserole (£5.75), and fresh salmon salad (£6.75); children's play area. Non-residents can come for the breakfasts if they book the night before, and the bedrooms in a separate annexe have sea views. *(Recommended by A P Jeffreys, John and Joan Nash, Mrs Olive Oxley, Tim Heywood, Sophie Wilne, R J Bland, David Atkinson, Nigel Woolliscroft)*

Free house ~ Licensee Deirdre Cooper ~ Meals and snacks (till 10pm) ~ (01478) 640205 ~ Children welcome ~ Occasional live music ~ Open 11-midnight(11.30 Sat); 12-10.30 Sun; 11-2.30, 5-11 in winter ~ Bedrooms: £23.50B/£47B

CAWDOR (Highland) NH8450 Map 11

Cawdor Tavern

Just off B9090 in Cawdor village; follow signs for post office and village centre

It's a surprise to find inside this pebbledash slated bungalow, a surprisingly eclectic and stately appearance to the substantial lounge and furnishings, largely due to the oak panelling and chimney breast salvaged from the nearby castle. The public bar on the right has elaborate wrought-iron wall lamps, chandeliers laced with bric-a-brac, and imposing pillared serving counter, and the lounge has green plush button-back built-in wall banquettes and bucket chairs, a delft shelf with toby jugs and decorative plates (chiefly game), small tapestries, attractive sporting pictures, and a log fire. Decent bar food includes sandwiches, home-made soup (£1.75), chicken liver pâté with home-made apple jelly (£2.95), haggis dumplings with a grain mustard sauce (£3.25), venison burgers with redcurrant jelly (£5.75), lamb tikka masala (£6.95), tagliatelle with sun-dried tomatoes, mushrooms and pesto sauce (£5.95), whole Mallaig sole (£7.65), steaks (from £11.95), daily specials such as fresh fillet of haddock (£5.50), pork steak with basil and orange jus (£6.75), and fresh salmon with lemon and herb butter (£7.50), puddings like home-made cheesecake (from £2.50); the restaurant is partly no smoking. Darts, pool, cribbage, dominoes, fruit machine, juke box, piped music, and board games. There are tables on the front terrace, with tubs of flowers, roses, and creepers climbing the supports of a big awning. *(Recommended by Joan and Tony Walker, G Washington, Mr and Mrs G Arbib, Peter and Lynn Brueton)*

Free house ~ Licensee Norman Sinclair ~ Meals and snacks (12-2, 5.30-9) ~ Restaurant ~ (01667) 404316 ~ Children welcome away from public bar until 9.30 ~ Open 11-3, 5-11(midnight Fri); 11-11.30 Sat; 12.30-11 Sun; closed 25-26 Dec, 1-2 Jan

CLACHAN SEIL (Highland) NM7718 Map 11

Tigh an Truish

This island is linked by a bridge via B844, off A816 S of Oban

Next to the handsome old bridge which joins Seil Island to the mainland of Scotland, this traditional 18th-c inn is also close to a lovely anchorage, popular with yachtsmen. There is a thriving local pubby atmosphere in its unpretentious and informal L-shaped bar which has a solid wood feel, with pine-clad walls and ceiling, some fixed wall benches along with the wheelback and other chairs, tartan curtains for the bay windows overlooking the inlet, prints and oil paintings, a woodburning stove in one room, and open fires in the others. Tasty bar food includes home-made soup (£1.60), sweet pickled herring (£3.15), home-made nut burgers (£3.75), lasagne (£4.95), game pie or salmon steak with a lemon, chive and cream sauce (£6.50), locally caught prawns with garlic mayonnaise (£6.95), and puddings such as chocolate pudding or treacle tart (from £1.50). Well kept McEwans 80/- and a summer guest such as Fullers ESB, Theakstons Old Peculier or Youngers No 3 on handpump, and a good choice of malt whiskies; darts and dominoes. There are some seats in the small garden, and they have their own filling station just opposite. *(Recommended by Neil Townend, Mark and Diane Grist, GSB, Andrew and Kerstin Lewis, Roberto Villa, Mrs Olive Oxley, S R and A J Ashcroft, G C Brown)*

Free house ~ Licensee Miranda Brunner ~ Real ale ~ Meals and snacks (12-2, 6-8.30) ~ (01852) 300242 ~ Children in dining room ~ Open 11-11.30(midnight Sat); 12.30-11.30 Sun; 11-2.30, 5-11 Mon-Thurs in winter ~ Self-catering flats: £25B/£40B

CLEISH (Tayside) NT0998 Map 11

Nivingston House 🛏

1½ miles from M90 junction 5; follow B9097 W until village signpost, then almost immediately inn is signposted

This smartly plush and comfortable country house hotel is set in twelve acres of landscaped gardens with benches looking out over a lawn sweeping down to shrubs and trees, with hills in the distance. There's a restful warmly decorated, mainly modern L-shaped bar with bold wallpaper and a log fire, and a library; the main lounge is no smoking. Well presented lunches (with prices unchanged since last year) might include tomato and orange soup (£1.95), home-made pâté with oatcakes (£3.95), venison burger (£4.95), tagliatelle carbonara (£4.95), hot smoked trout (£5.35), chicken tikka or croque madame (£5.45), Scotch smoked salmon and prawn platter (£5.95), minute steak (£5.95) and daily specials; home-made puddings (from £2). No bar snacks in the evening when meals are a bit more formal. Carlsberg-Tetley Alloa Calders tapped from the cask, a good choice of malt whiskies, and a decent wine list; snooker. *(Recommended by Christine and Malcolm Ingram, Susan and John Douglas; more reports please)*

Free house ~ Licensee Allan Deeson ~ Real ale ~ Meals and snacks ~ Restaurant ~ (01577) 850216 ~ Children in eating area of bar ~ Restaurant ~ Open 11-2.30, 5-11 ~ Bedrooms: £75B/£95B

CREEBRIDGE (Dumfries and Galloway) NX4165 Map 9

Creebridge House 🛏️

Minnigaff, just E of Newton Stewart

It's the food that customers particularly like in this sizeable country house hotel, and
feel it's worth travelling for: home-made soup (£1.95; cullen skink £2.50), home-
made chicken liver pâté (£2.95), lunchtime sandwiches (from £2.50; filled croissants
from £3.50) and ploughman's £5.95), steak pie with mushy peas or broccoli cream
cheese bake (£5.95), local scampi (£6.10), gammon and egg (£6.50), Indonesian-
style pork (£7.95), local salmon with creamed leek and asparagus (£9.10), and good
steaks (from £9.25); daily specials, excellent fresh fish on Fridays, and Sunday
lunchtime carvery in the comfortable no-smoking restaurant. Meats are local and
well hung, presentation is careful with good attention to detail. The welcoming and
neatly kept carpeted bar has that great rarity for Scotland, a bar billiards table – as
well as Boddingtons, Ind Coope Burton and Orkney Dark Island on handpump,
about 40 malt whiskies, dominoes, and comfortably pubby furniture; maybe
unobtrusive piped music. In fine weather, tables under cocktail parasols out on the
front terrace look across a pleasantly planted lawn. *(Recommended by Julian Holland,
Neil Townend, MKP, JLP; more reports please)*

*Free house ~ Licensees Susan and Chris Walker ~ Real ale ~ Meals and snacks
(12.30-2, 7-8.30) ~ Restaurant ~ (01671) 402121 ~ Children welcome ~ Open
12-2.30, 6-11(11.30 Sun) ~ Bedrooms: £40B/£75B*

CRINAN (Strathclyde) NR7894 Map 11

Crinan Hotel 🍽️ 🛏️

A816 NE from Lochgilphead, then left on to B841, which terminates at the village

You can choose from quite a number of bars in this beautifully positioned large
hotel – many with marvellous views of the village, lighthouse, and busy entrance
basin of the Crinan Canal, with its fishing boats and yachts wandering out towards
the Hebrides. The simpler wooden-floored public bar (opening onto a side terrace)
has a cosy stove and kilims on the seats, and upstairs there are two stylish and much
smarter glass enclosed roof bars both with stunning panoramic views of the loch.
The cocktail bar has a nautical theme with wooden floors, oak and walnut panelling,
antique tables and chairs, sailing pictures and classic yachts framed in walnut on a
paper background of rust and green paisley, matching the tartan upholstery. The
Gallery bar done in pale terracotta and creams has a central bar with stools, Lloyd
Loom tables and chairs and lots of plants. Popular bar food (lunchtime only)
includes soup, smoked haddock (£5.75), local sea loch mussels (£6.25), cold ham
salad (£8.50), pastry boats filled with fresh seafood (£9.50), locally smoked wild
salmon (£10.50), seafood stew (£12.50), and a pudding of the day such as lemon
tart or chocolate roulade (£3.75); Scottish farmhouse cheddar (from a 75lb cheese)
with oatcakes (£3.75); you can get sandwiches and so forth from their coffee shop.
There's a good wine list, and about 20 malt whiskies and freshly squeezed orange
juice. The restaurants are very formal and are no smoking until after dinner.
(Recommended by Walter Reid, Nigel Wikeley; more reports please)

*Free house ~ Licensee Nicholas Ryan ~ Lunchtime meals ~ Restaurants ~ (01546)
830261 ~ Children welcome ~ Open 11-11 (winter 11-2.30, 5-11) ~ Bedrooms:
£75B/£190B – these prices also include dinner*

CROOK OF ALVES (Grampian) NJ1362 Map 11

Crooked Inn

Burghead Rd, just off A96 Elgin—Forres

This bustling village inn is so popular with regulars that to be sure of a table, you
must book in advance. One room has built-in high-backed brocaded settles, dining
chairs and bar stools in the same fabric on the patterned carpet, lots of prints on the
walls, beams painted with snappy sayings, and an open fire with horse bits and so

forth hanging from the planked ceiling above it; beyond, a lower room has another open fire in the stone wall, similar furnishings, and golf clubs and prints and posters on the walls. Served in huge helpings (the starters are big enough to serve people with light appetites as main courses), the enjoyable food might include filled hogies (on request), garlic mushrooms (£3.40), seafood pancake with white fish, prawns and mussels (£3.75), smoked salmon coronet filled with prawns (£4.95), vegetarian dishes such as stuffed peppers or mushroom pancakes (from £5.25), fresh salmon fillet (£6.50), lamb provençale (£6.60), lots of good steaks (from £9.50), and puddings like sticky toffee pudding, chocolate pudding with a brandy sauce, and home-made apple pie (£2.50); good Sunday roasts. Well kept Theakstons Best on handpump, decent wines, friendly service; piped music and chess. *(Recommended by Spider Newth, RLW, Dizzy, Mr and Mrs M V Wright; more reports please)*

Free house ~ Licensee M Kenna ~ Real ale ~ Meals and snacks (5-9 Mon-Thurs, 12-2.15, 5-9 Fri/Sat, 12.30-8 Sun) ~ (01343) 850646 ~ Children in eating area of bar ~ Open 5-11 Mon-Thurs (closed lunchtime then); 11.45-3, 5-midnight Fri/Sat; 12.30-10.45 Sun

EDINBURGH (Lothian) NT2574 Map 11

The two main areas here for finding good pubs, both main entries and Lucky Dips, are around Rose St (just behind Princes St in the New Town) and along or just off the top part of the Royal Mile in the Old Town. In both areas parking can be difficult at lunchtime, but is not such a problem in the evenings.

Abbotsford

Rose St; E end, beside South St David St

Something of a long-standing institution for city folk, this small gently formal single bar pub has dark wooden half panelled walls, a highly polished Victorian island bar counter, long wooden tables and leatherette benches, and a welcoming log effect gas fire; there are prints on the walls and a notably handsome ornate moulded plaster high ceiling. Well kept Batemans XB, Boddingtons Bitter, Courage Directors, McEwans 70/- and 80/-, and Morlands Old Speckled Hen on handpump or tapped from the cask, and around 50 malt whiskies. Good, reasonably priced food includes soup (£1.25), ploughman's (£4.15), haggis, tatties and neeps (£4.20), vegetarian curry (£4.50), chicken cajun style (£4.60), a roast of the day (£4.95), smoked haddock (£5.10), sirloin steak (£6.05), and puddings such as rhubarb and pear crumble (£1.95); efficient service from dark-uniformed or white-shirted staff. *(Recommended by David Carr, Mark Walker, Liz and Benton Jennings; more reports please)*

Free house ~ Licensee Colin Grant ~ Real ale ~ Lunchtime meals and snacks ~ Restaurant ~ (0131) 225 5276 ~ Children in eating area of bar and restaurant ~ Open 11-11; closed Sun

Athletic Arms 🖤 £

Angle Park Terr; on corner of Kilmarnock Rd (A71)

Also known as the Diggers, thanks to its earlier popularity with workers from the nearby cemetery, this thoroughly unpretentious, old fashioned, plain but bustling pub is at its busiest when football or rugby matches are being played at Tynecastle or Murrayfield, when they may have a team of up to 15 red-jacketed barmen serving. It's the official home of McEwans 80/-, so you'll find it exceptionally well kept, and dispensed from a gleaming row of eleven tall air-pressure fonts which also serve guests like Courage Best, Exmoor Gold, and Hopback Summer Lightning, and Orkney Raven; several malt whiskies. Opening off the central island servery there are some cubicles partitioned in glossy grey wood with photographs of Hearts and Scotland football teams – a side room is crowded with keen dominoes players; fruit machine, cribbage and darts; predominantly young customers. Good value toasties or rolls (75p), pies (from 80p), and stovies (£1.20) are served all day. No children. *(Recommended by David Carr, Lawrence Eckhardt; more reports please)*

S & N ~ Manager Scott Martin ~ Real ale ~ Snacks all day ~ 0131 337 3822 ~ Live folk some Wed evenings ~ Open 11-midnight; 12.30-6 Sun

Bannermans Bar 🍺 £

212 Cowgate

Deep in the bowels of some of the tallest buildings in the Old Town, is this unique warren of simple crypt-like flagstoned rooms. There are barrel-vaulted ceilings, bare stone walls and bright strip lighting, wood panelling and pillars at the front, and theatrical posters and handbills in the rooms leading off. A huge mixture of purely functional furnishings includes old settles, pews and settees around barrels, red-painted tables and a long mahogany table. A no-smoking back area, with tables and waitress service, is open when they're busy. It's popular with students, and one of the best times to visit is during the Festival when there's even more atmosphere. Well kept Caledonian 80/- and Deuchars IPA, Theakstons Best, Youngers No 3, and regular guests from smaller Scottish breweries on handpump, with plenty of malt whiskies and Belgian fruit beers. Good value, popular food includes toasties (from £1), particularly good soup (from £1.40), french bread filled with things like brie and black grape or salami, radicchio and avocado (£3.45), sausage and bean casserole (£3.65), mushroom tortellini pasta or crêpes stuffed with smoked fish and parsley cream (£3.85), and puddings (from £1.65); budget lunch (soup and bread plus a hot main course £2.75), and popular weekend breakfasts (11-3.45; from £3.25). Dominoes, cribbage, trivia, cards and board games. *(Recommended by Peter Todd, Peter Marshall, Ian Williams, Linda Mar, David Carr, Ian Phillips, Terry Barlow, John A Baker)*

Free house ~ Licensee Douglas Smith ~ Real ale ~ Lunchtime meals and snacks, evening snacks ~ (0131) 556 3254 ~ Children welcome until 7pm ~ Live music Tues/Weds/Thurs evenings ~ Open 11-midnight (Sat till 1am); 11(licensed from 12.30)-midnight Sun

Bow Bar ★ £ 🍺

80 West Bow

Impressive tall founts made by Aitkens, Mackie & Carnegie, Gaskell & Chambers, and McGlashan, dating from the 1920s, serve the 12 perfectly-kept real ales rotated from a range of about 80 in this strongly traditional drinking pub: Bass, Caledonian 70/-, 80/-, Deuchars IPA, Courage Directors, Exmoor Gold, their own Edinburgh Real Ale, Greenmantle, Ind Coope Burton, Mitchells Mild, ESB and Bitter, Orkney Dark Island and Raven, Tetleys, and Timothy Taylors Best and Landlord. The grand carved mahogany gantry has an impressive array of malts (over 140) including lots of Macallan variants and 'cask strength' whiskies. The pub is an exclusive supplier of Scottish Still Spirit, with a good collection of vodkas (nine) and gins (eight), and, particularly, rums (24). Splendidly redesigned a few years ago to catch the essence of the traditional Edinburgh bar, the spartan rectangular room has a fine collection of appropriate enamel advertising signs and handsome antique trade mirrors, sturdy leatherette wall seats and heavy narrow tables on its lino floor, cafe-style bar seats, an umbrella stand by the period gas fire, a (silent) prewar radio, a big pendulum clock, and a working barograph. Look out for the antiqued photograph of the bar staff in old-fashioned clothes (and moustaches). Simple, cheap bar snacks – mince pies (90p), filled rolls or steak pies (£1), and forfar bridies (£1.15); no games or music – just relaxed chat, and the clink of glasses; quick and helpful service and friendly landlord. It's conveniently located just below the Castle. They also run another pub, Cloisters in Brougham Street. *(Recommended by M Walker, Vicky and David Sarti, Wayne Brindle, David Carr, Andy Schweizer, Bjorn Vondras, John Baker)*

Free house ~ Licensee Bill Strachan ~ Real ale ~ Lunchtime snacks ~ (0131) 226 7667 ~ Open 11am-11.15pm; closed Sun lunchtime

Cafe Royal Circle Bar

West Register St

The interesting Victorian-style cafe rooms here have quite a sophisticated feel, and a series of highly detailed Doulton tilework portraits (although sadly they are partly obscured by the fruit machines) of historical innovators Watt, Faraday, Stephenson, Caxton, Benjamin Franklin and Robert Peel (famous as the introducer of calico printing). The gantry over the big island bar counter is similar to the one that was here originally, the floor and stairway are laid with marble, there are leather covered seats, and chandeliers hanging from the fine ceilings. Well kept Courage Best, McEwans 80/-, Theakstons Best, and a weekly guest beer on handpump (some kept under light blanket pressure); about 25 malt whiskies. There is a lunchtime carvery in the bar with hot roast beef, pork and lamb rolls carved to order (£1.50-£2.20). Good choice of daily newspapers; fringe productions in the building during festival week. *(Recommended by Mark Walker, David Carr, Wayne Brindle, John A Baker, Susan and John Douglas, R L W and Dizzy)*

S & N ~ Manageress Maureen Diponio ~ Real ale ~ Lunchtime snacks (no carvery Sunday) ~ Restaurant ~ (0131) 556 1884 ~ Children in restaurant only ~ Open 11-11(till midnight Thurs and Fri, and 1am Sat; 12.30-11.30 Sun)

Guildford Arms 🍺

West Register St

A good mix of customers create a bustling, friendly atmosphere in this well preserved Victorian city pub. The main bar has lots of mahogany, glorious colourfully painted plasterwork and ceilings, big original advertising mirrors, and heavy swagged velvet curtains at the arched windows. The snug little upstairs gallery restaurant gives a dress-circle view of the main bar (notice the lovely old mirror decorated with two tigers on the way up), and under this gallery a little cavern of arched alcoves leads off the bar. A fine choice of real ales on handpump, six of which are usually Scottish, might include Bass, Belhaven 60/-, Caledonian R & D Deuchers IPA and 80/-, Orkney Dark Island, and around four guest ales (three English). During the Edinburgh festival they may hold a beer and folk festival. Good choice of malt whiskies; fruit machine, lunchtime piped jazz and classical music. Bar food includes soup (£1.35), fresh mussels steamed in tomato and basil (£2), local salmon, cheese tortellini with spinach and mushroom sauce or burgers (£4.25), steak and Guinness pie or fresh breaded haddock (£4.50), and sirloin steak (£8). It is very poular, but even at its busiest you shouldn't have to wait to be served. No children. *(Recommended by Mark Walker, Wayne Brindle, John Fazakerley, David Carr, Ian Williams, Linda Mar, Neil Townend, Esther and John Sprinkle, Susan and John Douglas, Richard Lewis, Stephen and Jean Curtis, John A Baker, Ian Phillips, George Atkinson)*

Free house ~ Licensee John Durnan ~ Real ale ~ Snacks and lunchtime meals ~ (0131) 556 4312 ~ Open 11-11(midnight Sat); 12.30-11 Sun

Kays Bar £

39 Jamaica St West; off India St

There's bags of atmosphere in this cosy and comfortable reproduction of a Victorian tavern – and a good range of constantly changing and interesting real ales, too: well kept Belhaven 80/-, Boddingtons, Exe Valley Devon Glory, Exmoor Ale, McEwans 80/-, Theakstons Best and XB, Tomintoul Wild Cat, and Youngers No 3; up to 70 malts, between eight and forty years old and 10 blended whiskies. The cosy little bar is bigger than the exterior suggests and has casks, vats and old wine and spirits merchant notices, gas-type lamps, well worn red plush wall banquettes and stools around cast-iron tables, and red pillars supporting a red ceiling. A quiet panelled back room leads off, with a narrow plank-panelled pitched ceiling; very warm open coal fire in winter. Simple lunchtime bar food (with prices unchanged since last year) includes soup (85p), haggis, neaps and tatties, chilli or steak pie (£2.60), filled baked potatoes (£2.75) and chicken balti, lasagne or mince and tatties (£3); dominoes and cribbage. *(Recommended by David Carr, Ian Phillips, Pat Gray; more reports please)*

S & N ~ Tenant David Mackenzie ~ Real ale ~ Lunchtime meals and snacks ~ (0131) 225 1858 ~ Children in back room until 5pm (must be quiet) ~ Open 11-11.45; 12.30-11 Sun

Starbank 🍷 🍺

67 Laverockbank Road, off Starbank Road; on main road Granton—Leith

From the picture windows in the neat and airy bar of this comfortably elegant pub there are marvellous views over the Firth of Forth. It's also an excellent place for a wide range of rotating beers, with around ten well kept real ales on handpump:

Adnams Extra, Belhaven 60/-, 80/- and 90/-, St Andrews Ale and Sandy Hunters Traditional Ale, Boddingtons Bitter, Broughton Special Bitter, Courage Directors, Marstons Pedigree, and Timothy Taylors Landlord. A good choice of wines too, with usually around 12 by the glass, and 25 malt whiskies. Well presented good bar food includes home-made soup (£1.20), madeira herring (£2.50), a vegetarian dish (£4.25), lasagne (£4.50), ploughman's (£4.75), baked haddock mornay or lamb rogan josh (£5), mixed seafood salad (£5.50), and poached salmon with lemon and herb butter (£6.75); puddings (£2.50). Service is helpful and friendly, the conservatory restaurant is no smoking, and there are no noisy games machines or piped music; sheltered back terrace. *(Recommended by Angus Lyon, David Carr, Dave Braisted, Neil Townend, Keith Steven, Pat Gray, Gerry Pearson)*

Free house ~ Licensee Valerie West ~ Real ale ~ Meals and snacks ~ Restaurant ~ (0131) 552 4141 ~ Children welcome till 8pm ~ Open 11-11(till midnight Thurs-Sat); 12.30-11 Sun

ELIE (Fife) NO4900 Map 11

Ship

Harbour

In summer this welcoming and cosily old-fashioned harbourside pub really comes into its own as its gardens are prettily set above the beach which at low tide is mostly sand – and on summer Sundays provides a pitch for the pub's cricket team. There are views across the water to the grassy headland which swings round the bay, to the pier and the old stone fish granary on the left, and to the little town on the right – or you can look more closely through a telescope positioned on the balcony of the restaurant. In summer there's a bar and barbecues in the garden, both lunchtime and evening (not Sunday evening). The villagey, unspoilt beamed bar with friendly locals and staff has a lively nautical feel, as well as coal fires and winged high button-back leather seats against the partly panelled walls that are studded with old maps; there's a simple carpeted back room. Good bar food includes dishes such as soup (£1.40), garlic mushrooms (£3.80), fresh local haddock and chips (£4.30), seafood crêpes or home-made steak pie (£5.50), poached salmon with lime mayonnaise (£6), daily specials such as carrot and butterbean soup, delicious poached halibut with cream and caper sauce, good mushroom stroganoff or tasty fish pie, steaks (from £11.95), puddings (£2.95), and children's dishes (£3.25); roast Sunday lunch (£7.95; children £3.95). Well kept Belhaven Best and 80/-, and Theakstons Best on handpump; darts, dominoes, captain's mistress, cribbage and shut-the-box. *(Recommended by E A Thwaite, Eric Locker, R M Macnaughton, M Carey, A Groocock, Eric Locker, Susan and John Douglas)*

Free house ~ Licensees Richard and Jill Philip ~ Real ale ~ Meals and snacks 12-2.30(3 Sun), 6-9.30(9 Sun) ~ Restaurant (not Sun eve) ~ (01333) 330246 ~ Children welcome (not in front bar) ~ Summer jazz bands and August festival ~ Open 11-midnight(till 1am Sat); 12.30-11 Sun; closed 25 Dec

FORT AUGUSTUS (Highland) NH3709 Map 11

Lock

If it's fresh fish you're after, then this is the place to come as Mr MacLennen, the hospitable and characterful landlord, has his own fishmonger's shop next door; the restaurant specialises in fish and with 24 hours' notice, anything can be provided. This homely and comfortable place, with a gently faded decor and some stripped stone, has a properly pubby atmosphere and is set at the foot of Loch Ness, and right by the first lock of the flight of five that start the Caledonian Canal's climb to Loch Oich. The atmosphere is lively and cheerful – crowded in summer, when it can be packed in the evenings with a good mix of locals and boating people (it can get a bit smoky then). Good value plain substantial food, with good helpings of chips, includes a pint of mussels (£4.50), seafood chowder or fresh Mallaig haddock (£4.95), terrine of wild salmon mousseline (£5.25), seafood stew (£5.95), game casserole (£6.50), grilled sea trout (£7.95), salmon steak in filo pastry (£10.50), venison (£11.25), and daily specials; quite a bit of the space is set aside for people eating. McEwans 80/- and Theakstons Best kept under light blanket pressure, a fine choice of about 100 malt whiskies (in generous measures), and big open fire; there's often unobtrusive piped traditional Scottish music. Upstairs the restaurant is no smoking. *(Recommended by Liz and Benton Jennings, R M Watt; more reports please)*

Free house ~ James MacLennen ~ Real ale ~ Meals and snacks (12-3, 6-9.30) ~ Evening restaurant ~ (01320) 366302 ~ Children in eating area of bar and in restaurant ~ Live music Mon-Weds evenings ~ Open 11-midnight(11.45 Sat); 12.30-11 Sun

GIFFORD (Lothian) NT5368 Map 11

Tweeddale Arms 🛏

High St

Probably the oldest building in this lovely village, this civilised old inn looks across the peaceful green to the 300-year-old avenue of lime trees leading to the former home of the Marquesses of Tweeddale. The comfortably relaxed lounge bar has cushioned wall seats, chairs and bar chairs, dried flowers in baskets, big Impressionist prints on the apricot coloured walls, and a big curtain that divides off the eating area. The tranquil hotel lounge has antique tables and paintings, chinoiserie chairs and chintzy easy chairs, an oriental rug on one wall, a splendid corner sofa and magazines on a table. Sandwiches are available all day, and the lunchtime bar food includes soup (£1.30), a bowl of mussel and onion stew (£3.50), assorted cold meats, deep-fried battered haddock or vegetarian stroganoff (£5.25), poached supreme of salmon with white wine and leek sauce or steak and Guinness pie (£5.50), noisettes of lamb with onion and mushroom sauce (£5.75), Aberdeen Angus steak (£8.50), and puddings (£2.30). In the evening you may be able to order dishes in the bar from the restaurant. Belhaven Best, Greenmantle, and St Andrews Ale, and a guest beer such as Broughtons Merlin Ale, Morlands Old Speckled Hen, and Orkney Dark Island on handpump, quite a few malt whiskies, and charming, efficient service; dominoes, fruit machine, cribbage, and piped music. *(Recommended by P W Taylor, Ian Phillips, Christopher Turner, Roger A Bellingham, Mr and Mrs R M Macnaughton, Frank Davidson, Mrs W E Darlaston)*

Free house ~ Licensee Mrs W Crook ~ Real ale ~ Meals and snacks ~ Restaurant ~ (01620) 810240 ~ Children welcome ~ Open 11-11(midnight Sat and Sun) ~ Bedrooms: £47.50B/£65B

GLASGOW (Strathclyde) NS5865 Map 11

Babbity Bowster 🍴 🍷

16-18 Blackfriars St

Much enjoyed by readers, this lively but stylish 18th-c town house is more like a continental cafe than a traditional pub, and has a good mix of customers. The simply decorated light interior has dark grey stools and wall seats around dark grey tables on the stripped floorboards, an open peat fire, fine tall windows, and well lit photographs and big pen-and-wash drawings in modern frames of Glasgow and its people and musicians. The bar opens onto a small terrace with tables under cocktail parasols and boules; dominoes. They serve breakfast from 8am to10.30 (till 12.30 Sunday) when you can have a bacon roll (£1.45), Loch Fyne kipper (£1.95), Arbroath smokie (£2.50), and a cooked breakfast (£3.65); all day food includes home-made soup (from £1.75), croque monsieur (£2.95), haggis, tatties and neeps (£3.60; they also do a vegetarian version), mixed bean hotpot (£3.65), cassoulet (£3.95), spiced chicken stovies (£4.25), steamed Loch Fyne mussels in a white wine and cream sauce (£4.95), and daily specials. There are more elaborate meals in the airy upstairs restaurant. Well kept Deuchars IPA and Maclays 80/- and Broadsword, and changing guest beers on air pressure tall fount, a remarkably sound collection of wines, malt whiskies, freshly squeezed orange juice and good tea and coffee. Enthusiastic service is consistently efficient and friendly, taking its example from the energetic landlord. Piped Celtic music in the restaurant. Car park. *(Recommended by Ian Phillips, R Morgan, Mr and Mrs B Langrish, David and Michelle James, Val Stevenson, Rob Holmes, Walter Reid, Alan and Paula McCully, Leith Stuart, John Scarisbrick, Mark Walker, Calum and Susan Maclean, Mike and Penny Sanders, RLW and Dizzy, E Carter)*

*Free house ~ Licensee Fraser Laurie ~ Real ale ~ Meals and snacks (12-11) ~
Restaurant ~ 0141 552 5055 ~ Children in eating area of bar and in restaurant ~
Folk music in evenings ~ Open 8-midnight; 12.30-midnight Sun; closed 25 Dec
and 1 Jan ~ Bedrooms: £40B/£60B*

Bon Accord 🍺 £

153 North St

It's the fine range of real ales served from tall founts that draws people to this busy
friendly and basic traditional pub, done up in the style of a Victorian kitchen:
Marstons Pedigree, McEwans 80/-, Theakstons Best and Old Peculier, Youngers No
3, and half-a-dozen guest beers on handpump; a decent choice of malt whiskies.
Tasty well priced bar food includes snacks like filled french bread (£1.95), steak in
ale pie (£2.25 or £3.25 depending on size), filled baked potatoes (£2.50), breaded
haddock (£3.35), basket meals (from £3.50), and puddings (£1.75). There may be
only light snacks weekday evenings. No children. *(Recommended by Paul Kerr, Michael
Hanna, John Scarisbrick, Mike and Penny Sanders; more reports please)*

*S & N ~ Manageress Anne Kerr ~ Real ale ~ Meals and snacks (12-9) ~
Restaurant ~ (0141) 248 4427 ~ Daytime parking restricted ~ Open 11am-
11.45pm; 12.30-11 Sun*

Horseshoe £

17-19 Drury Street

The Guinness Book of Records lists the bar counter in this bustling and friendly pub
as the longest in Britain. There's a great deal of fine Victoriana such as glistening
mahogany and darkly varnished panelled dado, a mosaic tiled floor, a lustrous pink
and maroon ceiling, standing height lean-on tables, lots of old photographs of
Glasgow and its people, antique magazine colour plates, pictorial tile inserts of
decorous ladies, and curly brass and glass wall lamps; the bar has authentic old-
fashioned brass water taps and pillared snob-screens. The horseshoe motif spreads
through the place from the opposite promontories of the bar itself to the horseshoe
wall clock and horseshoe-shaped fireplaces (most blocked by mirrors now). Bass,
Belhaven Best, and Broughton Greenmantle on handpump, and a large selection of
malts; fruit machines, trivia and piped music. Amazingly cheap food is served in the
upstairs bar which is less special with seating in rows, though popular with young
people: from a choice of 12 main courses, there's a 3-course lunch (£2.40); part of
the lounge is no smoking and may have piped music. Not far from Central Station.
*(Recommended by Richard Lewis, Ian Williams, Linda Mar, Val Stevenson, Rob Holmes,
Walter Reid, Calum and Susan Maclean)*

*Tennents (Bass Taverns) ~ Manager David Smith ~ Real ale ~ Meals and snacks
(11-7; not Sun) ~ 0141 221 3051 ~ Children in restaurant until 7pm ~ Karaoke
every evening ~ Open 11-midnight; 12.30-12 Sun; closed 1 Jan*

GLENDEVON Tayside NN9904 Map 11

Tormaukin 🛏 ♀

A823

Beautiful countryside surrounds this smallish, remote hotel and there are good walks
over the nearby Ochils or along the River Devon – plus over 100 golf courses (including
St Andrews) within an hour's drive. It's a comfortable and neatly kept place, and the
softly lit bar has plush seats against stripped stone and partly panelled walls, ceiling
joists, and maybe gentle piped music. Good bar food includes soup (£1.90), Arbroath
smokie pâté (£3.85), hot and sour prawns (£3.95), fresh battered haddock with home-
made tartare sauce or roasted vegetable moussaka (£5.95), local venison sausage
(£6.25), hot chilli meatballs with a tomato sauce (£6.50), pasta with smoked salmon,
mushrooms and cream or baked ham with honey and mustard with salad (£6.85),
Highland game cassoulet (£8.25), herb-crusted supreme of salmon (£8.50), steaks (from
£8.75), puddings like gooseberry pie or sticky gingerbead pudding (from £2.95), and
children's menu (from £2.65); good breakfasts. Well kept Harviestoun 80/-, Montrose,

Ptarmigan 85/- and Schiehallion, Ind Coope Burton, and guest beers on handpump, a good wine list, and quite a few malt whiskies. Some of the bedrooms are in a converted stable block. Loch and river fishing can be arranged. *(Recommended by SR, PM, Sue Rowland, Mrs G Bishop, Ian Wilson, John T Ames, Neville Kenyon, Gerry Z Pearson)*

Free house ~ Licensee Marianne Worthy ~ Real ale ~ Meals and snacks (12-2, 5.30-9.30; all day Sun) ~ (01259) 781252 ~ Restaurant (not Sun lunch) ~ Children welcome ~ Occasional live music winter Fri evening ~ Open 11-11; 12-11 Sun; closed two weeks mid Jan ~ Bedrooms: £49B/£70B

HOUSTON (Strathclyde) NS4166 Map 11
Fox & Hounds

Main Street; B790 E of Bridge of Weir

An exemplary local in the older part of the village, this comfortable place – evidently three old cottages knocked into one – has well kept real ales, reliable food and exceptional service, quick and warmly welcoming. The neatly kept plush lounge has appropriate hunting pictures and so forth (the local hunt does sometimes meet here), with snug seats by the fire – quiet and civilised by day, busy most evenings; there are a couple of no-smoking areas. Besides sandwiches (from £1.75, with soup £3), a wide range of food can be eaten in the relatively sophisticated upstairs restaurant. It includes cumberland sausage (£3.95), battered haddock or haggis sprinkled with whisky and served with tatties and neeps (£4.95), fresh mussels (£5.50), cold poached salmon (£5.95), home-made steak and Guinness pie (£6.50), skate wing or shark steaks (around £7.50), steaks (from £7.75), and puddings (from £2.95). Well kept Heather Fraoch Ale, Isle of Skye Red Cuillin, Moorhouses Premier Bitter, and Tomintoul Wildcat on handpump. The separate more lively public bar has pool, fruit machine, and a video game; piped music. *(Recommended by Walter Reid, B A Hayward, Calum and Susan Maclean, Angus Lyon)*

Free house ~ Licensee Carl Wengel ~ Real ale ~ Meals and snacks (12-2.30, 5.30-10) ~ Restaurant ~ (01505) 612448 ~ Children welcome ~ Open 11-midnight; 12-midnight Sun

INNERLEITHEN (Borders) NT3336 Map 9
Traquair Arms 🛏

Traquair Rd (B709, just off A72 Peebles—Galashiels; follow signs for Traquair House)

Readers have enjoyed staying in this pleasantly modernised inn – the breakfasts are quite something. The simple little bar, popular locally, has a warm open fire, a relaxed atmosphere, and well kept Broughton Greenmantle Ale and maybe Traquair Bear Ale on handpump; several malt whiskies. Enjoyable bar food served by friendly staff includes sandwiches, home-made soup (£1.40), filled baked potatoes (from £2.15), omelettes (from £3.50), vegetable moussaka (£4.35), braised oxtails (£4.90), steak pie (£5.15), ploughman's (£5.20), fresh haddock fillets (£5.25), steaks (from £11.50), and puddings (from £2.10). A pleasant roomy no-smoking dining room has an open fire and high chairs for children if needed. Welcoming licensees, no music or machines. *(Recommended by Mark Walker, Wayne Brindle, Dr D A Spencer, J M Potter, M J Morgan, Brian and Anna Marsden, Mike and Wendy Proctor, Cathryn and Richard Hicks)*

Free house ~ Licensee Hugh Anderson ~ Real ale ~ Meals and snacks (12-9) ~ Restaurant ~ (01896) 830229 ~ Children welcome ~ Open 11-midnight ~ Bedrooms: £42B/£64B

ISLE ORNSAY (Isle of Skye) NG6912 Map 11
Tigh Osda Eilean Iarmain 🛏 ♀

Signposted off A851 Broadford—Armadale

Apart from the fine position overlooking the sea in a picturesque part of Skye, what readers like so much about this civilised and attractive inn is the friendly, informal and very relaxed atmosphere. Gaelic is truly the first language of the charming staff

(even the menus are bilingual) – many of whom have worked here for some years.
The big and cheerfully busy bar has a swooping stable-stall-like wooden divider that
gives a two-room feel: good tongue-and-groove panelling on the walls and ceiling,
leatherette wall seats, brass lamps, a brass-mounted ceiling fan, and a huge mirror
over the open fire. There are about 34 local brands of blended and vatted malt
whisky (including their own blend, Te Bheag, and a splendid vatted malt, Poit
Dhubh Green Label, bottled for them but available elsewhere), and an excellent wine
list; darts, dominoes, cribbage, and piped music. Bar food includes home-made soup
(£1.50), lunchtime sandwiches (from £1.50), avocado and prawn mousse (£1.75),
baked potatoes (£3.75), vegetable schnitzel (£4.50), lamb stovies (£5), chicken curry
(£5.50), fried Mallaig haddock or herring in oatmeal (£5.95), grilled lamb chops
with shrewsbury sauce (£6.50), sirloin steak (£10.50), puddings (£1.75), and
children's menu (£3.50). The pretty, partly no-smoking dining room has a lovely sea
view past the little island of Ornsay itself and the lighthouse on Sionnach (you can
walk over the sands at low tide). Some of the bedrooms are in a cottage opposite.
The most popular room has a canopied bed from Armadale Castle. *(Recommended by
Paul and Ursula Randall, R and S Bentley, Scott J Macdonald, Jackie Moffat, Andrew and
Kerstin Lewis, Mark and Diane Grist, Walter and Susan Rinaldi-Butcher, John and Joan Nash,
Lucy James, Christine and Malcolm Ingram, N H and B Ellis; also in the Good Hotel Guide)*

*Free house ~ Licensee: Sir Ian Noble ~ Meals and snacks ~ Restaurant ~ (01471)
833332 ~ Children welcome (but only till 8.30 in the bar) ~ Occasional live
music some Fri/Sat evenings ~ Open 12-2.30, 5-midnight(11.30 Sat) ~ Bedrooms:
£65B/£86B*

ISLE OF WHITHORN (Dumfries and Galloway) NX4736 Map 9

Steam Packet 🛏 £

The position here is quite special, and the big picture windows of this comfortably
modernised inn look out on to a picturesque natural working harbour with yachts,
inshore fishing boats, fishermen mending their nets, and boys fishing from the end of
the pier. Inside, the cheery low-ceilinged bar is split into two: on the right, plush
button-back banquettes and boat pictures, and on the left, green leatherette stools
around cast-iron-framed tables on big stone tiles, and a woodburning stove in the
bare stone wall. Bar food can be served in the lower beamed dining room, which has
a big model steam packet boat on the white walls, excellent colour wildlife
photographs, rugs on its wooden floor, and a solid fuel stove, and there's also a small
eating area off the lounge bar. Bar food includes soup (95p), filled rolls (from £1.10;
steak and onion £2.70), venison pâté (£1.85), pork schnitzel (£2.40), haggis (£3.10), a
daily special or battered fish (£3.25), vegetable lasagne (£3.75), fried chicken and
bacon (£3.95), and evening dishes like salmon and broccoli cutlet (£5.20), chicken
breast with coriander and garlic (£7.35), and steaks (from £10.50); children's dishes
(from 60p). Well kept Boddingtons and Theakstons XB on handpump, and two
dozen malt whiskies; pool and piped music. White tables and chairs in the garden.
Every 1½ to 4 hours there are boat trips from the harbour; the remains of St Ninian's
Kirk are on a headland behind the village. *(Recommended by Vann and Terry Prime,
Margaret Mason, Dave Thompson, Chris Wheaton, James and Patricia Halfyard)*

*Free house ~ Licensee John Scoular ~ Real ale ~ Meals and snacks ~ Restaurant ~
(01988) 500334 ~ Children welcome ~ Occasional live folk music ~ Open 11-
11(midnight Sat); 12-11 Sun; closed winter Mon-Thurs lunchtimes, 25 Dec ~
Bedrooms: £22.50B/£45B*

KILBERRY (Strathclyde) NR7164 Map 11

Kilberry Inn 🍴 🛏

B8024

Apart from the lonely and lovely position, it's the friendly welcome and the food that
customers like so much about this white painted croft post office. This might include
home-made malted granary garlic bread (£1.65), cream of broccoli soup with home-
made bread (£2.50), port and stilton pâté, popular country sausage pie (£7.50), home-

pickled cold beef (£7.95), salmon and walnut pie, venison in red wine, beef in ale, puddings such as freshly baked apple and raspberry pie, chocolate fudge pudding, and banana shortcake (£3.65); lovely home-made cakes, marmalade and shortbread for sale. They appreciate booking if you want an evening meal. The small relaxed dining bar is tastefully and simply furnished but warmly welcoming, with a good log fire. No real ale, but bottled beers and plenty of malt whiskies; the family room is no smoking. The pub is on a delightful slow winding and hilly circular drive over Knapdale, from the A83 S of Lochgilphead, with breathtaking views over the rich coastal pastures to the sea and the island of Gigha beyond. *(Recommended by Vicky and David Sarti, Dr and Mrs J J Brown, J E Rycroft, Dr and Mrs P Martin, Mr and Mrs J Tyrer, Nicky Bennison, Mark Jobling)*

Free house ~ Licensee John Leadbeater ~ Meals and snacks ~ (01880) 770223 ~ Well behaved children in family room ~ Open 11-2; 5-11; closed Sun and mid-Oct-Easter ~ Bedrooms: £34.50S/£59B

KIPPEN (Central) NS6594 Map 11

Cross Keys 🛏

Main Street; village signposted off A811 W of Stirling

This little family-run 18th-c inn is warmly welcoming and the licensees are particularly courteous. The relaxed and straightforward lounge has been refurbished this year and has a good log fire, there's a coal fire in the painted stone walled family dining room, and a separate public bar. Good value food using fresh local produce includes home-made soup (£1.45), home-made blackberry, liver and port pâté (£2.50), omelettes (from £2.75), ploughman's (£3.85), haddie pancakes (£3.95), home-made lasagne (£4.65), fresh haddock (£5.30), steak pie (£5.85), fresh salmon poached with a ginger and lime sauce (£5.90), Aberdeen Angus sirloin steak (£11.25), and puddings like home-made apple pie (from £2.35); smaller helpings for children. Well kept Broughton Greenmantle Ale and Youngers No 3 on handpump, and quite a few malt whiskies; darts, pool, dominoes, fruit machine, juke box, and board games. The garden has tables and a children's play area; simple bedrooms. *(Recommended by Carolyn and Michael Hedoin, GSB, Paul and Sue Merrick, R M McNaughton, R H Rowley, J M Hill)*

Free house ~ Licensees Angus and Sandra Watt ~ Real ale ~ Meals (12-2, 5.30-9.30 ~ Restaurant ~ (01786) 870293 ~ Children in restaurant ~ Open 12-2.30, 5.30-11(midnight Sat); 12.30-11 Sun; closed evening 25 Dec, 1 Jan ~ Bedrooms: £19.50/£39

KIRKTON OF GLENISLA (Tayside) NO2160 Map 11

Glenisla Hotel 🛏

B951 N of Kirriemuir and Alyth

Run very much as an extension to the friendly licensees' own home, this 17th-c former posting inn is set in one of the prettiest of the Angus Glens. The simple but cosy carpeted pubby bar has beams and ceiling joists, wooden tables and chairs, a roaring log fire, decent prints, and a rather jolly thriving atmosphere. The lounge is comfortable and sunny, and the elegant high-ceilinged dining room has rugs on the wooden floor, pretty curtains, candles and fresh flowers, and crisp cream tablecloths. Good, carefully prepared bar food using fresh local ingredients includes soup (£1.95), Orkney herrings in dill or sherry (£2.60), ploughman's or fresh battered haddock (£4.95), home-baked ham with a mustard crust (£5.25), steak and kidney pie (£5.90), seafood kebabs (£6.65), and evening dishes like mussels with garlic and cream (£2.80), king Orkney scallops with white wine and shallots (£3.95), lamb liver and bacon or mushroom and artichoke crêpe (£6.35), three lamb chops with mint sauce (£8.80), duck breast with morello cherry sauce (£9.95), steaks (from £10.80), and puddings like sticky toffee and bread and butter pudding. Boddingtons, McEwans 80/- and Theakstons Best on handpump, a fair range of island malt whiskies, and caring and attentive service. A refurbished stable block has skittles, also darts and pool; cribbage and dominoes. The bedrooms are attractively individual, and the hotel has fishing and skeet shooting. *(Recommended by Dr M J S Scorer, J F M West, John and Kathleen Potter, Johanna King, Bruce Lawrence, Susan and John Douglas, SRP, Stephen Black)*

Free house ~ Licensees Simon and Lyndy Blake ~ Real ale ~ Meals and snacks ~ Restaurant ~(01575) 582223 ~ Children welcome ~ Traditional Gaelic and ceilidh band monthly ~ Open 11-11(midnight Sat); 11-10.30 Sun; 11-2.30, 6-11 in winter; closed 25-26 Dec ~ Bedrooms £37.50B/£65B

LINLITHGOW (Lothian) NS9976 Map 11

Four Marys 🍺

65 High St; 2 miles from M9 junction 3 (and little further from junction 4) – town signposted

Mary Queen of Scots was born at nearby Linlithgow Palace, and this atmospheric and friendly pub is named after her ladies-in-waiting. The L-shaped, comfortable bar has masses of mementoes of the ill-fated queen, such as pictures and written records, a piece of bed curtain said to be hers, part of a 16th-c cloth and swansdown vest of the type she'd be likely to have worn, and a facsimile of her death-mask. Seats are mostly green velvet and mahogany dining chairs around stripped period and antique tables, there are a couple of attractive antique corner cupboards, and an elaborate Victorian dresser serves as a bar gantry, housing several dozen malt whiskies (they stock around 100 altogether). The walls are mainly stripped stone, including some remarkable masonry in the inner area. A very good choice of around eight constantly changing, very reasonably priced well kept real ales includes Boddingtons, Belhaven 80/-, Broughton Ghillie, Butterknowle Conciliation, Caledonian Deuchars IPA, Harviestoun Schiehallion, Orkney Dark Island, and Theakstons Best on handpump, and 100 malt whiskies; friendly and helpful staff. Enjoyable waitress-served bar food includes soup such as cream of watercress (£1.40), smoked mackerel and cream cheese pâté (£2.65), and beef goulash or chicken basque (£4.65). Parking difficult. *(Recommended by David Carr, T and G Alderman, Vann and Terry Prime)*

Free house ~ Licensee Gordon Scott ~ Real ale ~ Meals and snacks (not Sun evening) ~ (01506) 842171 ~ Children in eating area of bar ~ Open 12-2.30, 5-11.30; 12-11.30 Sat

LYBSTER (Highland) ND2436 Map 11

Portland Arms 🛏

A9 S of Wick

This staunch old granite hotel is our most northerly main entry and was built as a staging post on the early 19th-c Parliamentary Road. The knocked-through open plan bar is comfortable and attractively furnished, and there's also a small but cosy panelled cocktail bar. Good bar food includes soup (£1.80), chicken liver pâté (£2.95), macaroni cheese (£4.95), fillet of haddock (£5.95); fresh salmon salad, a roast of the day or mild beef curry (£5.95), cajun chicken (£8.95), steaks (from £11.95), and puddings (£2.95); friendly and obliging staff. They keep 40 or more malt whiskies (beers are keg). They can arrange fishing and so forth, and the inn is a good base for the area with its spectacular cliffs and stacks. *(Recommended by Alan Wilcock, Christine Davidson, Karen Eliot; more reports please)*

Free house ~ Licensee Gerald Henderson ~ Meals and snacks (11-2.30, 5-9) ~ Restaurant ~ (01593) 721208 ~ Children welcome ~ Open 11-11; 12-11 Sun ~ Bedrooms: £38B/£58B

MELROSE (Borders) NT5434 Map 9

Burts Hotel 🍴 🛏

A6091

This rather smart and comfortable old hotel, in an attractive 18th-c market square, is a popular place for lunch. Served by helpful, cheerful staff there might be smoked salmon pâté with cucumber vinaigrette (£3.45), ploughman's (£4.75), fillet of haddock (£5.75), fried fillet of pink trout in breadcrumbs and almonds with remoulade sauce (£6.75), sirloin steak (£11.75), and puddings (from £3), with daily specials such as creamy halibut mousse or parfait of wild local game (£3.75), vegetable casserole (£5.25), tandoori chicken (£5.65), lamb casserole (£5.85), cold rare roast Scottish beef (£6.25), and breast of chicken stuffed with haggis in oatmeal (£7.25); extremely good breakfasts. Try and get there early, as the food's popularity means tables will go quickly. The comfortable and friendly L-shaped lounge bar has lots of cushioned wall seats and windsor armchairs on its turkey carpet, and Scottish prints on the walls; the Tweed Room is no smoking. Belhaven 70/-, 80/- and Sandy Hunters Traditional Ale, Courage Directors, and Timothy Taylors Landlord on handpump, 50 malt whiskies, and a good wine list; dominoes. There's a well tended garden (with tables in summer). An alternative way to view the abbey ruins is from the top of the tower at Smailholm. *(Recommended by Sharon Hancock, R M Macnaughton, R H Sawyer, Mark Walker, Chris Rounthwaite, Wayne Brindle, Brian and Anna Marsden, Mrs J M Deale, Neville Kenyon, Richard Davies, LB CB, J M Potter, Anne and Sverre Hagen)*

Free house ~ Licensee Graham Henderson ~ Real ale ~ Meals and snacks ~ Restaurant ~ (01896) 822285 ~ Children welcome ~ Open 11-2.30, 5-11; closed 26 Dec ~ Bedrooms: £46B/£78B

MOUNTBENGER (Borders) NT3125 Map 9
Gordon Arms

Junction A708/B709

Planning permission has been granted to erect six pine log cabins in the grounds of this welcoming and remotely set little inn; they also offer lots of outdoor activity holidays, too. The warmly welcoming and comfortable public bar has an interesting set of period photographs of the neighbourhood, one dated 1865, some well illustrated poems, and a warm winter fire. Well kept Broughton Greenmantle, Jennings Oatmeal Stout, and various summer guest beers on handpump, 56 malt whiskies, and a fair wine list. Bar food includes sandwiches, vegetarian dishes, and home-made steak pie or yorkshire pudding with roast lamb (£5.95); children's dishes and smaller helpings at reduced prices for pensioners, and summer high teas in the dining room. Pool, dominoes, and trivia. In addition to the hotel bedrooms, there's a bunkhouse which provides cheap accommodation for hill walkers, cyclists and fishermen, all of whom should find this area particularly appealing. The resident family of bearded collies are called Jura, Misty and Morah. *(Recommended by Wayne Brindle; more reports please)*

Free house ~ Licensees Harry Mitchell ~ Real ale ~ Meals and snacks ~ Restaurant ~ (01750) 82232 ~ Children in eating area of bar until 8pm ~ Accordion and fiddle club third Weds every month ~ Open 11-11(midnight Sat); 12.30-11 Sun; closed Tues end Oct-Easter ~ Bedrooms: £25/£40

OBAN (Strathclyde) NM8630 Map 11
Oban Inn

North Pier, between Stafford St and Oban

The main attraction of this bustling late 18th-c inn is the views from the windows of both bars over the harbour. The beamed downstairs bar has small stools, pews and black-winged modern settles on its uneven slate floor, blow-ups of old Oban postcards on the cream walls, and unusual brass-shaded wall lamps. The smarter, partly panelled upstairs bar has button-back banquettes around cast-iron-framed tables, a coffered woodwork ceiling, and little backlit arched false windows with heraldic roundels in aged stained glass. Well kept McEwans 80/-, a large selection of whiskies. Good straightforward lunchtime bar food includes sandwiches (from £1), home-made soup (£1.25), garlic mushrooms (£1.75), lasagne or vegetable lasagne (£3.75), steak in ale pie (£4.20), haddock in batter (£4.35), daily specials such as trout grilled in garlic butter (£5.75), and puddings (£1.85); high tea (£5.45); juke box or piped music can be loud; trivia, fruit machine, dominoes and chess. *(Recommended by Mrs Olive Oxley, S R and A J Ashcroft; more reports please)*

S & N ~ Manageress Jeanette McLean ~ Real ale ~ Meals and snacks (12-2.30, 5-8) ~ (01631) 562484 ~ Children in small area of lounge at mealtimes only ~ Open 11-12.45 nr PITLOCHRY (Tayside) NN9162 Map 11

Killiecrankie Hotel 🍺 🛏️

Killiecrankie signposted from A9 N of Pitlochry

Well run and comfortable, this relaxing country hotel is splendidly set in lovely peaceful grounds with dramatic views of the mountain pass, a putting course, a croquet lawn – and sometimes roe deer and red squirrels. The attractively furnished bar (newly carpeted) has some panelling, upholstered seating and mahogany tables and chairs, as well as stuffed animals and some rather fine wildlife paintings; in the airy conservatory extension there are light beech tables and upholstered chairs, with discreetly placed plants and flowers. Popular home-made food served by friendly staff might include home-made soup (£2), smoked salmon pâté (£3.25), sweet cured herrings (£3.75), ploughman's (£4.95), deep-fried fresh haddock in beer batter (£6.95), home-made steak burger (£7.25), poached salmon mayonnaise or smoked chicken breast with mango and papaya compote (£7.95), and daily specials such as terrine of Arbroath smokie mousse (£3.75), navarin of lamb or braised pheasant (£6.95); puddings like tiramisu or banoffi pie (£2.95). The restaurant is no smoking. Decent wines and about 20 malt whiskies, coffee and a choice of teas. Some bedroom and bathroom refurbishment has taken place this year. *(Recommended by A P Jeffreys, June and Perry Dann, Mr and Mrs W M Graham, Lucy James, T and G Alderman, R M Macnaughton, Cathryn and Richard Hicks, Tony Walker, E Carter, SRP; also in the Good Hotel Guide)*

Free house ~ Licensees Colin and Carole Anderson ~ Meals and snacks ~ Evening restaurant ~ (01796) 473220 ~ Children welcome ~ Open 11-2.30, 5.30-11; closed 10 days Dec, all Jan/Feb ~ Bedrooms: £50.50B/£100B

PLOCKTON (Highland) NG8033 Map 11

Plockton Hotel

Village signposted from A87 near Kyle of Lochalsh

This friendly little hotel – in the centre of a lovely Scottish National Trust village – is so popular that you have to book well in advance for either an evening meal or for a bedroom. It's set in a row of elegant but pretty houses with a delightful outlook across the palm trees and colourful flowering shrub lined shore and sheltered anchorage across to the rugged mountainous surrounds of Loch Carron. The comfortably furnished and lively lounge bar has window seats looking out to the boats on the water, as well antiqued dark red leather seating around neat Regency-style tables on a tartan carpet, three model ships set into the woodwork, and partly panelled and partly bare stone walls. The separate public bar has pool, shove-ha'penny, dominoes, cribbage, and piped music. Very well liked bar food includes home-made soup (£1.50), sandwiches (from £1.75), home-made chicken liver and whisky pâté (£2.95), a vegetarian dish of the day (£4.75), fresh fillet of haddock in beer batter or home-made lasagne (£4.95), fresh salmon mayonnaise (£5.25), Plockton bay prawns (starter £5.65, main course £10.95), local scallops (£9.65), monkfish and prawn thermidor (£9.85), and steaks (from £11.25); usual children's menu (£1.95); good breakfasts; small no-smoking restaurant. Tennents 70/- and 80/- on tall fount air pressure, a good collection of malt whiskies, and a short wine list. *(Recommended by Eric Locker, Dr and Mrs S Jones, Mrs Olive Oxley, Mark and Diane Grist, Dr and Mrs Peter Kemp, Karen Eliot, Mr and Mrs G Arbib, N C Walker, G Washington, Joan and Tony Walker)*

Free house ~ Licensee Tom Pearson ~ Real ale ~ Meals and snacks ~ Restaurant ~ (01599) 544 274 ~ Children welcome (away from public bar) ~ Occasional local ceilidh band ~ Open 11-2.30, 5-midnight(11.30 Sat); open all day July/Aug ~ Bedrooms: £27.50B/£45B

PORTPATRICK (Dumfries and Galloway) NX0154 Map 9

Crown ★ 🛏️

The bustling, rambling old-fashioned bar in this atmospheric harbourside inn has lots of little nooks, crannies and alcoves, and interesting furnishings such as a carved settle with barking dogs as its arms, an antique wicker-backed armchair, a stag's head over the coal fire, and shelves of old bottles above the bar counter. The partly panelled butter-coloured walls are decorated with old mirrors with landscapes painted in their side panels. With quite an emphasis on seafood, the popular bar food might include herring in oatmeal (£4.35), mussels with a cream and chive sauce (£4.85), delicious grilled scallops wrapped in bacon (£5.15), dressed local crab (£7.10), fillet of plaice with anchovy butter (£9.50), whole grilled jumbo prawns (£12.15), and local lobster (from £20), as well as sandwiches, home-made soup (£2), omelettes (from £4.60), vegetarian pancake (£8.45), grilled lamb cutlets (£8.75), steaks (from £12.50), and puddings (£2.80); good breakfasts. Carefully chosen wine list, and quite a few malt whiskies; maybe piped music. An airy and very attractively decorated early 20th-c dining room opens through a quiet no-smoking conservatory area into a sheltered back garden, and you can sit outside on seats served by a hatch in the front lobby and make the most of the evening sun. *(Recommended by Carolyn and Michael Hedoin, Carolyn Reynier, S H Godsell, M A Cameron; more reports please)*

Free house ~ Licensee Bernard Wilson ~ Meals and snacks (till 10) ~ No-smoking conservatory restaurant ~ (01776) 810261 ~ Children welcome ~ Open 11-11.30; 12-11 Sun ~ Bedrooms: £38B/£72B

SHERIFFMUIR (Central) NN8202 Map 11
Sheriffmuir Inn

Signposted off A9 just S of Blackford; and off A9 at Dunblane roundabout, just N of end of M9; also signposted from Bridge of Allan; OS Sheet 57 map reference 827022

One of the oldest inns in Scotland, this early 18th-c drovers' inn is remotely set in the middle of lonely moorlands with wonderful views. The welcoming L-shaped bar is surprisingly popular for such an isolated spot, and is basic but comfortable with pink plush stools and button-back built-in wall banquettes on a smart pink patterned carpet, polished tables, olde-worlde coaching prints on its white walls, and a woodburning stove in a stone fireplace. Well kept Arrols 80/-, Ind Coope Burton, and Marstons Pedigree on handpump, kept under light blanket pressure, and a good choice of whiskies; friendly, neatly uniformed staff, and piped music. Promptly-served lunchtime bar food includes spicy chicken (£4.95), steak pie (£5.10), and scampi (£5.95). There are tables and a children's play area outside. *(Recommended by Julian Holland, Graham Bush, J F M West, Susan and John Douglas; more reports please)*

Free house ~ Licensee Roger Lee ~ Real ale ~ Lunchtime meals and snacks ~ Restaurant ~ (01786) 823285 ~ Children welcome ~ Open 11.30-2.30; 5.30-11; 11.30-11 Sat; 12-11 Sun; closed Mon Oct-Mar

SHIELDAIG (Highland) NG8154 Map 11
Tigh an Eilean 🛏

Village signposted just off A896 Lochcarron—Gairloch

Of all our Scottish entries, this friendly hotel is in one of the best settings. It looks over the Shieldaig Island – a sanctuary for a stand of ancient Caledonian pines – to Loch Torridon and then out to the sea beyond. It's a usefully comfortable place to stay with easy chairs, books and a well stocked help-yourself bar in the neat and prettily decorated two-room lounge, and an attractively modern comfortable dining room specialising in good value local shellfish, fish and game. Quickly served, simple well priced bar food includes sandwiches, home-made soup (£1.10), mackerel pâté (£2.40), crab salad starter (£3.25), coq au vin (£4.65), fresh monkfish in batter or wild hare (£4.85), venison salad (£4.95), and puddings like apple crumble or crème caramel (£1.50). The smallish bar, which is popular with locals, is very simple with red brocaded button-back banquettes in little bays, picture windows looking out to sea and three picnic tables outside in a sheltered front courtyard. Winter darts. They have private fishing and the National Trust Torridon estate or the Beinn Eighe nature reserve aren't too far away. *(Recommended by Mrs Olive Oxley, Lucy James, Mark and Diane Grist, Christine and Malcolm Ingram; also in the Good Hotel Guide)*

Free house ~ Licensee Mrs Elizabeth Stewart ~ Meals and snacks (12-2.15, 6-8.30) ~ Evening restaurant summer only with advance booking ~ (01520)

755251 ~ Children welcome till 8pm ~ Open 11-11; 11-2.30, 5-11 in winter; closed winter Sun evenings ~ Bedrooms: £41.50B/£90B

SKEABOST (Isle of Skye) NG4148 Map 11

Skeabost House Hotel ★ ⛺

A850 NW of Portree, 1½ miles past junction with A856

Twelve acres of secluded woodland and gardens surround this very civilised and friendly family-run hotel, with glorious views over Loch Snizort (said to have some of the best salmon fishing on the island). The bustling high-ceilinged bar has a pine counter and red brocade seats on its thick red carpet, and a fine panelled billiards room leads off the stately hall; there's a wholly separate public bar with darts, pool, fruit machine, trivia, dominoes, and juke box (and even its own car park); piped music. Lunchtime bar food includes a popular buffet (vegetarian £4.80, cold meats £7.10, salmon £7.20), as well as home-made soup or haggis with oatcakes (£1.50), good filled baked potatoes (£1.95), home-made pizza (£3.70), minute steak in french bread (£4.70), fillet of haddock (£6.10), smoked salmon platter (£7), cold puddings (from £1.75), and children's dishes (£2). The spacious and airy conservatory has a much larger choice, and there's a main dining room, too; all the eating areas (plus a lounge) are no smoking. A fine choice of over 100 single malt whiskies, including their own and some very rare ones. *(Recommended by Joan and Tony Walker, Dr and Mrs Peter Kemp, Eric and Jackie Robinson)*

Free house ~ Licensee Iain McNab ~ Meals and snacks (12-1.30, 6.30-9.30) ~ Restaurant ~ (01470) 532202 ~ Children in eating area of bar ~ Accordion in public bar Sat evening ~ Open 12-2, 6-11(midnight Sat); closed end Nov-beg Mar ~ Bedrooms: £46B/£94B

ST MARY'S LOCH (Borders) NT2422 Map 9

Tibbie Shiels Inn ⛺

'When I'm dead and gone this place will still be ca'ed Tibbie Shiels's,' predicted the redoubtable woman who kept house here for 75 years until she died in 1878, aged 96. The wife of the local mole-catcher, she was a favourite character of Edinburgh literary society during the Age of Enlightenment. Her photograph hangs in the cosy stone back bar with its well cushioned wall benches or leatherette armed chairs. Good value straightforward waitress-served lunchtime bar food includes home-made soup (£1.50), ploughman's (£3.10), cashew nut loaf with tomato and herb salad (£3.85), fried haddock (£4.20), spicy chicken (£3.90), chilli or Yarrow trout (£4.60), daily specials such as venison sausages (£4), and bacon and onion pudding or seafood pancakes (£4.25), and puddings like home-made cloutie dumpling (£2). The lounge bar is no smoking. Well kept Belhaven 80/- and Broughton Greenmantle on handpump, and 58 malt whiskies; shove-ha'penny, cribbage and dominoes. This down-to-earth inn is in a fine quiet setting beside a beautiful loch, and the Southern Upland Way – a long-distance footpath – passes close by; the Grey Mare's Tail waterfall is just down the glen. Day members are welcome at the sailing club on the loch, with fishing free to the inn's residents; it's very peaceful – except when low-flying jets explode across the sky. *(Recommended by Carolyn and Michael Hedoin, M J Morgan, Mike and Penny Sanders, Sharon Hancock, Mike and Wendy Proctor, Nigel Woolliscroft, Brian and Anna Marsden, Dr S W Tham, Mr and Mrs I B White, Mrs J M Deale)*

Free house ~ Licensee John Brown ~ Real ale ~ Meals and snacks (12.30-2.30, 6.30-8.30) ~ Restaurant ~ (01750) 42231 ~ Children welcome ~ Open 11-11(midnight Sat); 12.30-11 Sun; closed Mon/Tues Nov-Mar ~ Bedrooms: £26B/£46B

nr STONEHAVEN (Grampian) NO8493 Map 11

Lairhillock ♀

Netherley; 6 miles N of Stonehaven, 6 miles S of Aberdeen, take the Durris turn-off from the A90 (old A92)

Of course customers do drop into this smart but friendly and relaxed country pub for just a drink, but it would be a shame to miss out on the very popular, good food. In the bar, this might include soup (£2.05; cullen skink £3.05), a changing terrine or pâté (£3.95), filled french stick (£4.25), seafood filled pancakes (£4.50), ploughman's (£5.15), wild mushroom canelloni (£6.50), wholemeal broccoli and stilton quiche or whole baked haddock (£6.95), chicken and chestnut lasagne (£7.50), grilled salmon fillet (£8.95), Aberdeen Angus steak (from £12.25), several vegetarian dishes, and home-made puddings (from £2.85); Sunday buffet lunch. There are countryside views from the bay window in the cheerfully atmospheric beamed bar, as well as panelled wall benches and a mixture of old seats, dark woodwork, harness and brass lamps on the walls, and a good open fire. The spacious separate lounge has an unusual central fire; the traditional atmosphere is always welcoming, even at its busiest. Well kept Boddingtons, Courage Directors, Flowers IPA, McEwans 80/-, Thwaites Craftsman and a changing guest ale all on handpump, lots of malt whiskies, and an extensive wine list; friendly efficient staff; darts, cribbage, dominoes, trivia, and maybe piped music. The restaurant in a converted raftered barn behind is cosy, with another log fire. Panoramic southerly views from the conservatory. *(Recommended by Chris Raisin, Neil Townend, Mark Walker)*

Free house ~ Licensee Frank Budd ~ Real ale ~ Meals and snacks ~ Restaurant ~ (01569) 730001 ~ Children in eating area of bar, dining room or conservatory ~ Occasional live music in snug Fri nights ~ Open 11-2.30, 5-11(midnight Fri/Sat)

STRACHUR (Strathclyde) NN0901 Map 11

Creggans 🛏

A815 N of village

Close to the spot where Mary Queen of Scots landed in 1563 is this decidedly smart little hotel, surrounded by beautiful countryside. The cosy and attractively tweedy cocktail bar (partly no smoking) has wooden ceilings, signed showbusiness photogrpahs, and panoramic views overlooking the loch to the hills on the far side; there are more seats in a no-smoking conservatory. The public bar, lively with locals, has a central stove, and pool in separate room; fruit machine, dominoes, juke box, satellite TV, and piped music. There's a good selection of malt whiskies, including their own vatted malt, a thoughtful wine list, and a cappuccino bar and gift shop with home-baked produce. Popular, good value bar food includes Loch Fyne oysters (£1.10 each), sandwiches (from £1.95), toasties from £2.35; open ones from £4.50), home-made soup (£2.35), home-made game pâté (£3.65), haggis (£3.85), half pint of fresh Oban prawns (£4.15), pasta with four cheeses (£4.50), curry of the day (£4.95), Loch Fyne mussels (£5.50), venison casserole (£6.25), Scotch sirloin steak (£9.25), and puddings (£2.95). In front are some white tables. *(Recommended by Lucy James, Capt E P Gray, Dorothy and David Young; more reports please)*

Free house ~ Meals and snacks ~ Restaurant ~ (01369) 860279 ~ Children welcome ~ Monthly live entertainment in the bar in summer ~ Open 11-midnight; 11-1am Sat/Sun ~ Bedrooms: £45B/£80B

SWINTON (Borders) NT8448 Map 10

Wheatsheaf 🍽 🛏

A6112 N of Coldstream

Scottish Dining Pub of the Year

Apart from being a most enjoyable place to stay, with a warm welcome from the friendly licensees, what customers like most in this smart, very well run place is the superb food. At lunchtime, this might include soup such as cream of leek and asparagus (£1.95), marinated herring fillets in a mustard sauce (£3.60), fresh quail salad in Thai dressing (£3.95), spinach and basil pancake (£4.85), braised oxtails with root vegetables (£6.45), roasted monkfish tails wrapped in bacon provençale (£8.95), roast gressingham duckling in an orange liqueur sauce (£9.85), and evening dishes like spinach and quail egg tartlet on a warm butter and tomato sauce (£3.45), deep-fried prawns in filo pastry with a soya and chilli sauce (£4.45), courgette and aubergine provençale served in roasted peppers (£6.85), breasts of wild woodpigeon on a potato and celeriac rosti with a port and raisin sauce (£10.85), and fillet of venison in a sloe gin and juniper berry sauce with a poached pear and a redcurrant tartlet (£12.90); local seafood every day, and delicious puddings. Booking is advisable, particularly from Thursday to Saturday evening. Well kept Broughton Greenmantle and Merlins Ale, Whim Magic Mushroom Mild, and a guest such as Caledonian 80/- on handpump, a decent range of malt whiskies, good choice of wines, and cocktails. The friendly service and careful decor all indicate tremendous attention to detail. The main area has an attractive long oak settle and some green-cushioned window seats as well as the wheelback chairs around the tables, a stuffed pheasant and partridge over the log fire, and sporting prints and plates on the bottle-green wall covering; a small lower-ceilinged part by the counter has pubbier furnishings, and small agricultural prints on the walls – especially sheep. At the side is a separate locals' bar; no-smoking front conservatory with a vaulted pine ceiling and walls of local stone; dominoes. The garden has a play area for children. *(Recommended by A J Morton, Chris Rounthwaite, Arthur and Lliz Burt, Heather Couper, R C Hopton; also in the Good Hotel Guide; more reports please)*

Free house ~ Licensees Alan and Julie Reid ~ Real ale ~ Meals and snacks (not Mon except for residents) ~ Restaurant ~ (01890) 860257 ~ Children welcome till 8pm ~ Open 11-2.30, 6-11; closed Mon, closed Sun evening Dec-April; closed last two weeks Feb and last week Oct ~ Bedrooms: £28(£42S)/£42(£60S)

TAYVALLICH (Strathclyde) NR7386 Map 11
Tayvallich Inn 🍽

B8025, off A816 1 mile S of Kilmartin; or take B841 turn-off from A816 two miles N of Lochgilphead

There's a relaxed and happy atmosphere in this pleasant, simply furnished pub – and as the sheltered yacht achorage and bay of Loch Sween is just across the lane, there should be good fresh seafood caught by local fishermen on the menu. In the bar, the menu might include home-made soup (£1.60), moules marinières (£3.25), fillet of haddock (£4.50), stir-fried vegetables (£4.75), fried scallops (£4.90), beef curry (£5.10), cajun chicken (£5.50), half-a-dozen Loch Sween oysters (£6), locally smoked salmon (£7), sirloin steak (£10.50), delicious seafood platter (£12.50), and home-made puddings (£3); half helpings for children; decent wines and several malt whiskies. Service is friendly and helpful and people with children are very much at home here. The small bar has cigarette cards and local nautical charts on the cream walls, exposed ceiling joists, and pale pine upright chairs, benches and tables on its quarry-tiled floor, and extends into a no-smoking dining conservatory; sliding glass doors open onto the terrace with picnic tables and lovely views, and there's a garden, too. *(Recommended by Neil Townend, Vicky and David Sarti, A F Ford, R Macnaughton, Karen Kalaway)*

Free house ~ Licensee John Grafton ~ Meals and snacks (12-2, 6-8) ~ Restaurant ~ (01546) 870282 ~ Children welcome ~ Open 11-11(1am Sat); 11-midnight Sun

THORNHILL (Central) NS6699 Map 9
Lion & Unicorn

A873

Readers have very much enjoyed their visits to this well run and particularly welcoming inn. The freshly cooked food on the changing blackboard plays quite a big part in drawing customers in – and might include soup such as carrot and coriander (£1.75), mushrooms stuffed with cream cheese in a garlic and chive batter (£3.50), smoked venison with chestnut cream (£4), open sandwiches (from £4), home-smoked ostrich with raspberry vinegar (£4.75), steak, mushroom and Guinness pie (£5.75), roast rib of Aberdeen Angus beef with yorkshire pudding (£6.50), wild mushroom stroganoff (£7.25), fillet of River Teith salmon with lemon and herb sauce or breast of duck in black grape and kirsch sauce (£9.75), Aberdeen Angus steaks (from £11.50), puddings like banoffi pots, strawberry parfait or bread and butter pudding (from £2), and children's helpings (from £3). Well kept

Broughton Merlin's Ale, Greenmantle, and Special Bitter, and guests like Caledonian 80/- and Deuchers IPA, Moulin Brewery Braveheart, and Orkney Red Macgregor on handpump, with a fine range of malt whiskies, and a good choice of wines. The open-plan front room has comfortable seats on the wooden floors, beams and stone walles, and a warm fire. The beamed public bar with stone walls and floors has a parrot, darts, pool, cribbage, and dominoes. The no-smoking restaurant is in the original part of the building which dates from 1635 and contains the original massive fireplace (six feet high and five feet wide). In summer it's pleasant to sit in the garden where they have summer Sunday barbecued spit-roasted whole pig, lamb or venison (weather permitting), and watch the bowling on the pub's own bowling green – it can be used by non-residents. *(Recommended by Mrs B Oliver, Roger Bellingham, Ian and Deborah Carrington, Esther and John Sprinkle, Lawrence Bacon, Paul and Sue Merrick, Susan and John Douglas, R H Rowley, J M Hill)*

Free house ~ Licensee Walter and Ariane MacAulay ~ Real Ales ~ Meals and snacks (12-10pm) ~ Restaurant ~ (01786) 850204 ~ Children welcome ~ Monthly live music ~ Open 12-12 (1am Fri and Sat) ~ Bedrooms: £25/£37.50

TURRIFF (Grampian) NJ7250 Map 11
Towie

Auchterless; A947, 5 miles S

Handy for Fyvie Castle (Scottish National Trust) and Delgatie Castle, this extended white pebble-dash dining pub has a carefully and comfortably furnished series of warmly welcoming rooms, including an elegant no-smoking dining room. Good, reasonably priced seasonal home-made food from a daily changing blackboard menu includes a wide range of starters, main courses, and puddings: smoked haddock and prawn pasta or steak and mushroom pie (£5.95), and fresh scampi tails or supreme of chicken with a grain mustard and cream sauce (£6.95); helpful service. Well kept Theakstons Best and a weekly changing guest on handpump, a decent wine list, and lots of malt whiskies; darts, pool, shove-ha'penny, cribbage, dominoes, trivia, and piped music. *(Recommended by Neil Townend; more reports please)*

Free house ~ Licensee Douglas Pearson ~ Real ale ~ Meals and snacks (all day Sun) ~ Restaurant ~ (01888) 511201 ~ Children welcome until 8pm ~ Open 11-2.30, 6-midnight; 11-midnight Sat; 12.30-11 Sun

TUSHIELAW (Borders) NT3018 Map 9
Tushielaw 🛌

Ettrick Valley, B709/B7009 Lockerbie—Selkirk

Originally the site of a toll house and drovers' inn, this traditional country hotel has pretty views over Ettrick Water – it's a good base for walkers or for touring, with its own fishing on Clearburn Loch up the B711. The unpretentious but comfortable little bar has decent house wines, a good few malts, and an open fire, and opens on to a terrace with tables for those who are lucky with the weather; darts, shove-ha'penny, cribbage, dominoes, and piped music. Welcoming young owners, and a good range of home-cooked food such as lunchtime filled french bread (£3.50) and ploughman's (from £3.95), as well as home-made soup (£2.25), marinated Orkney herring fillets or mushrooms stuffed with stilton (£3.25), cheese and haggis fritters with home-made cumberland sauce (£3.50), vegetarian lasagne or deep-fried haddock fillets (£4.95), home-made steak and stout pie (£5.25), grilled Aberdeen Angus steak (£9.50), daily specials such as creamy smoked haddock crumble (£2.95) or roast rack of lamb with a cranberry and orange sauce (£9.50), and home-made puddings (£2.95); Sunday roast. The restaurant is no smoking; Broughton 80/- on tall fount air pressure, and some malt whiskies. *(Recommended by A N Ellis, Chris Rounthwaite, M J Morgan, Wayne Brindle, T G Brierly, Andrea and Peter Peirson, Ian Parsons)*

Free house ~ Licensees Steve and Jessica Osbourne ~ Real ale ~ Meals and snacks (all day Sun) ~ Restaurant ~ (01750) 62205 ~ Children in eating areas ~ Open 12-2.30, 7(6 Sat)-11; 12.30-10.30 Sun; closed Mon, Tues, Wed lunchtime Nov-Mar ~ Bedrooms: £22B/£38B

TWEEDSMUIR (Borders) NT0924 Map 9

Crook 🏠

A701 a mile N of village

As well as being an historic inn, this early 17th-c place is also a craft centre, with displays and demonstrations of glassblowing in the old stable block. The pub has been extended and modernised over the years, but there's still a cosy, old-fashioned look and feel, and the flagstoned back bar is simply furnished, with local photographs on its walls; one very thick wall, partly knocked through, has a big hearth, and opens into a large airy lounge with comfortable chairs around low tables and an open log fire; beyond is a sun lounge. The pub's various art-deco features are most notable in the lavatories - superb 1930s tiling and cut design mirrors. Decent bar food includes home-made soup (£1.65), home-made chicken liver pâté with oatcakes (£3.25), ploughman's (£4.25), deep fried breaded haddock (£4.75), lamb liver with bacon (£4.95), home-made steak in ale pie (£5.75), home-made pine nut roast with a piquant tomato sauce (£5.95), poached salmon with a creamy dill sauce (£7.25), steaks (from £8.95), puddings like home-made apple pie (from £2.95), and children's menu (£2.95); friendly service. Well kept Broughton Greenmantle on handpump and a good choice of malt whiskies. A separate room has darts, dominoes, cribbage, shove-ha'penny, and fruit machine. There are tables on the grass outside, with a climbing frame and slide, and across the road the inn has an attractive garden, sheltered by oak trees; maybe pétanque here in summer. Trout fishing permits for about 30 miles' fishing on the Tweed and its tributaries are available from the pub at about £5 a day. (Recommended by Chris Rounthwaite, M J Morgan, Vann and Terry Prime)

Free house ~ Licensee Stuart Reid ~ Real ale ~ Meals and snacks (12-9) ~ Restaurant ~ (01899) 880272 ~ Children welcome ~ Open 11-midnight; 11-11 Sun ~ Bedrooms: £36B/£52B

ULLAPOOL (Highland) NH1294 Map 11

Ceilidh Place

West Argyle St

There's usually quite a lot going on in this pretty rose draped white house and the atmosphere is rather like that of a stylish arty cafe-bar, but with a distinctly Celtic character. There's an art gallery and regular jazz, folk, ceilidhs, and classical music, a bookshop, and a coffee shop. It's set in a quiet side street above the small town, there are tables on a terrace looking over the other houses to the distant hills beyond the natural harbour. Inside, there are bentwood chairs and one or two cushioned wall benches among the rugs on its varnished concrete floor, spotlighting from the dark planked ceiling, attractive modern prints and a big sampler on the textured white walls, piped classical or folk music, magazines to read, venetian blinds, houseplants, and mainly young upmarket customers; woodburning stove, dominoes, and piped music. The side food bar – you queue for service at lunchtime – does good hot dishes from fresh ingredients such as pies (£1.25), stovies (£3), haggis (£4.25), and mince tart (£4.50); there's always a good choice for vegetarians. Though the beers are keg they have decent wines by the glass, an interesting range of high-proof malt whiskies, and a choice of cognac and armagnac that's unmatched around here. There's an attractive no-smoking conservatory dining room and the bedrooms are comfortable and pleasantly decorated. (Recommended by Roberto Villa, K Archard, R S Reid, Monica Shelley, Anthony Marriott)

Free house ~ Mrs Jean Urquhart ~ Meals and snacks (12-9.30pm) ~ Evening restaurant ~ (01854) 612103 ~ Children in eating area of bar and restaurant ~ Regular ceilidhs, folk, jazz and classical music ~ Open 11-11; 12.30-11 Sun; 12.30-2.30, 6.30-11 winter Sun ~ Bedrooms: £40(£55B)/£80(£110B)

Ferry Boat

Shore St

This very friendly traditional pub keeps a good range of well kept, changing real ales on tall founts. From quite a list, there may be Boddingtons, Broughton Greenmantle,

Exmoor Gold, Fullers London Pride, Jennings, Orkney ales, various Shepherd Neame ales, Red Cuillin and Black Cuillin, Thaites, and Wadworths 6X. The simple two-roomed pubby bar has brocade-cushioned seats around plain wooden tables, quarry tiles by the corner serving counter and patterned carpet elsewhere, big windows with nice views, and a stained-glass door hanging from the ceiling. The quieter inner room has a coal fire, a delft shelf of copper measures and willow-pattern plates. Straightforward, tasty bar lunches include home-made tomato, bacon and garlic soup (£1.45), sandwiches (from £1.80), filled baked potatoes (£3.75), ploughman's (£3.95), venison burgers (£4.75), aubergine bake (£5.25), pork and pineapple curry (£5.95), fresh local haddock (£6.25), and lamb and leek casserole (£6.75); the restaurant is no smoking. Fruit machine. In summer you can sit on the wall across the road and enjoy the fine views to the tall hills beyond the attractive fishing port with its bustle of yachts, ferry boats, fishing boats and tour boats for the Summer Isles. *(Recommended by K Archard, R S Reid, Mike and Penny Sanders, John Abbott, Karen Eliot, Anthony Marriott, Eric Locker)*

Free house ~ Licensee Richard Smith ~ Real ale ~ Lunchtime meals and snacks ~ Evening restaurant ~ (01854) 612366 ~ Children in eating area of bar and restaurant ~ Folk music Thurs evening ~ Open 11-11; 12.30-11 Sun ~ Bedrooms: £30B/£58B

Morefield Motel ⑪

North Rd

This year, a conservatory has been added to this very popular dining inn, which should help with the summer crowds. It remains the wonderful fresh fish and seafood that people from all over the world come here to enjoy, and the owners (themselves ex-fishermen and divers) have a ship to shore radio in the office which they use to corner the best of the day's catch before the boats have even come off the sea; there's also a lobster tank in the cellar from which customers can take their pick. Depending on availability, the generous helpings of food might include a platter of six local oysters (£3.95), a basket of langoustines (£4.75), crisp battered haddock (£6.50), moules marinières or dressed crab (£7.50), char-grilled salmon (£7.25), locally caught scallops (£8.50), Lochinver sole (£9.95 – it is huge), lobster royale (cooked with scallops and prawns; from £13.50), and a marvellous seafood platter (£15.50); non-fishy dishes also feature, such as thinly sliced smoked venison or haggis fritters (£3.95), various vegetarian choices (£5.75), quite a few interesting chicken dishes (from £7.50), fine steaks (from £9.50), and venison steak with rich madeira and sliced mushroom gravy. You can also eat in the smarter Mariners restaurant which has a slightly more elaborate menu; enjoyable breakfasts. In winter (from November to March) the diners tend to yield to local people playing darts or pool, though there's bargain food then, including a very cheap three-course meal. Well kept Caledonian 80/-, Orkney Dark Island, and Wadworths IPA and 6X on handpump, and over 100 malt whiskies, some nearly 30 years old; decent wines and friendly tartan-skirted waitresses. The L-shaped lounge is mostly no smoking, and there are tables on the terrace. The bedrooms are functional and popular with hill-walking parties, for whom the licensees have erected a drying shed – and for others caught in the rain while out and about. *(Recommended by Jackie Moffat, Carolyn and Michael Hedoin, Anthony Marriott, Monica Shelley, E J Wilde, Karen Eliot)*

Free house ~ Licensee David Smyrl ~ Real Ale ~ Meals and snacks (12-2, 5.30-9.30) ~ Evening restaurant ~ (01854) 612161 ~ Children welcome ~ Occasional live music winter Fri ~ Open 11-11; 11-2.30, 5-11 in winter; 12-11 summer Sun; closed 25 Dec-3 Jan ~ Bedrooms: £30B/£45B

WEEM (Tayside) NN8449 Map 11

Ailean Chraggan 🖙

B846

As enjoyable as ever, this small, friendly inn is set in two acres with a lovely view across the flat ground between here and the Tay to the mountains beyond, sweeping up to Ben Lawers (the highest in this part of Scotland); there are two outside terraces. The good food remains a big draw for customers. From a changing menu, there might be soup (£1.95; cullen skink £3.45), home-made chicken liver pâté (£3.35), warm stilton and mixed nut roulade (£3.95), mushroom tagliatelle (£6.25), cod au gratin (£6.95), venison casserole (£7.50), grilled whole lemon sole (£8.25), duck breast with madeira sauce (£8.50), sirloin steak (£10.50), lovely Sound of Jura fresh prawn platter (£12.50), and puddings such as strawberry cheesecake or hazelnut and chocolate tart (£3.25). The menu is the same in the restaurant; a good wine list and lots of malt whiskies. The modern lounge has long plump plum-coloured banquettes, and Bruce Bairnsfather First World War cartoons on the red and gold Regency striped wallpaper, and maybe piped music, and winter darts and dominoes. *(Recommended by Susan and John Douglas, Neil Townend, Pat and Derek Westcott, Bob Ellis, A N Ellis)*

Free house ~ Licensee Alastair Gillespie ~ Meals and snacks ~ Restaurant ~ (01887) 820346 ~ Children welcome ~ Open 11-11; 11-2.30, 5-11 winter weekdays; closed 25-26 Dec, 1-2 Jan ~ Bedrooms: £28B/£56B

WESTRUTHER (Borders) NT6450 Map 10
Old Thistle

B6456 – off A697 just SE of the A6089 Kelso fork

The three rooms here are the real core of village life in the evenings – during the week this unpretentious, friendly local is closed at lunchtime. Local farmers, fishermen, gamekeepers and shepherds all come down from the hills then, and may even break into song when Andrew strikes up on the accordion. There's a tiny, quaint bar on the right with some furnishings that look as if they date back to the inn's 1721 foundation – the elaborately carved chimney piece, an oak corner cupboard, the little bottom-polished seat by the coal fire; some fine local horsebrasses. A simple back room with whisky-water jugs on its black beams has darts, pool, dominoes, fruit machine and video game, and doors from here lead out onto the terrace; there's a small, plain room with one or two tables on the left. On the food front, what really stands out is the quality of the evening steaks – fine local Aberdeen Angus, hung and cooked to perfection (8oz sirloin £9, 8oz fillet £10, 20oz T-bone £13); the weekend lunchtime menu is very simple, with soup, sandwiches, sausages, and haddock. A more conventionally comfortable two-roomed lounge has flowery brocaded seats, neat tables and a small coal fire, leading into the restaurant; piped music. *(Recommended by John and Margaret Priestley, Syd and Syn Donald, Gerry Pearson)*

Free house ~ Licensee David Silk ~ Meals and snacks (5-9 Mon-Fri, 12.30-9 Sat, Sun) ~ Restaurant ~ (01578) 740275 ~ Children welcome ~ Open 5-11; 12(12.30 Sun)-11 Sat-Sun ~ Bedrooms: £22.50B/£45B

Lucky Dip

Besides the fully inspected pubs, you might like to try these Lucky Dips recommended to us and described by readers (if you do, please send us reports):

BORDERS

☆ **Bonchester Bridge** [A6088; NT5812], *Horse & Hound*: Wide range of good home cooking, well kept changing ales such as Ansells Mild and Orkney Dark Island, interesting building, splendid open fire in each bar, welcoming landlord, evening restaurant, children's area; bedrooms; cl Tues in winter *(Wayne A Wheeler, Mr Robbins)*

Clovenfords [1 Vine St; A72/B710 W of Galashiels; NT4536], *Clovenfords*: Interestingly refurbished 18th-c coaching inn locals' bar and banquette-lined lounge with open fire and prints; varied menu inc vegetarian, decent wine list; five bedrooms *(John Pickup)*

Denholm [NT5718], *Fox & Hounds*: Small bar lounge, dining room, seats on sheltered terrace

and lawn, Boddingtons, Belhaven 80/- and McEwans ales, bar food; bedrooms *(M J Morgan)*

Duns [NT7954], *Whip & Saddle*: Clean varnished woodwork, ales such as Caledonian Deuchars IPA, Theakstons XB and Wadworths, tasty bar food; handy for Jim Clark museum and popular with local farming community *(O K Smyth)*

☆ **Eddleston** [A703 Peebles—Penicuik; NT2447], *Horseshoe*: Civilised old stone pub, well prepared bar and restaurant meals served by pleasant helpful staff, soft lighting, gentle music, comfortable seats, well kept ale, good choice of wines and whiskies *(G Washington, Simon Morton, LYM)*

Ettrickbridge [NT3824], *Cross Keys*: Nice

welcome, helpful and friendly staff; bedrooms
(A N Ellis)

Greenlaw [NT7146], *Castle*: Lovely outside,
straightforward in, with decent food inc good
value Sun lunch; well kept Greenmantle,
friendly landlords and dogs *(Heather Couper)*

Jedburgh [NT6521], *Pheasant*: Welcoming and
efficient service, good range of generous food
inc amazing value pheasant in season, S&N
ales, decent wines *(Mike and Penny Sanders)*

☆ Kelso [7 Beaumont St; NT7334], *Cobbles*: Small
recently refurbished two-room dining pub with
wall banquettes, some panelling, warm log and
coal fires, good value food inc good home-made
soups and puddings; real ales such as
Boddingtons, Caledonian 70/- and McEwans
80/-, decent wines and malt whiskies; piped
music; disabled lavatory *(John Pickup, M J
Morgan, Mrs Jane Hansell)*

☆ Kelso [Bridge St (A699)], *Queens Head*: Old
coaching inn with good mix of modern and
traditional, pleasant big back lounge, small
front locals' bar with pool, efficient courteous
staff, wide choice of good generous imaginative
food, reasonable prices, well kept ales such as
Boddingtons, Greenmantle, McEwans 70/- and
Theakstons; children welcome; good value
bedrooms, bright and clean *(Neville Kenyon,
Nigel Woolliscroft, Mrs W E Darlaston, Brian
and Anna Marsden)*

Melrose [High St; NT5434], *Kings Arms*: Late
18th-c, with old chairs, interesting ornaments
and cosy log fire in welcoming beamed bar,
well kept Tetleys-related and other ales, good
choice of malt whiskies, good varied reasonably
priced largely home-made food inc fine
Aberdeen Angus steaks and good children's
menu; can get busy Sat; bedrooms *(Mike and
Penny Sanders)*

☆ Oxton [A697 Edinburgh—Newcastle, by
junction with A68; NT5053], *Carfraemill*:
Attractive oak-beamed bar with log fire in
substantial red sandstone hotel, good value
food, good service, two real ales, separate games
room, restaurant; big comfortable bedrooms *(R
C Davey, BB)*

Peebles [High St; NT2540], *Tontine*: Old-
fashioned hotel with small bar and big
comfortable lounge, good bar food, relaxing
atmosphere, obliging staff, Greenmantle ale;
bedrooms *(O K Smyth)*

Selkirk [Market Pl; NT4728], *Cross Keys*: Well
kept Caledonian 80/- and Tetleys, small bar
area with US number plates, larger lounge area
behind, attentive helpful licensees; can get
packed Sat evening *(Mr Robbins, Brian and
Anna Marsden)*

☆ St Boswells [A68 just S of Newtown St
Boswells; NT5931], *Buccleuch Arms*: Restful
Georgian-style plush panelled bar, no-smoking,
in well established sandstone inn, wide choice of
imaginative well prepared bar food (not Sun),
sandwiches all day, restaurant, tables in garden
behind; children welcome; bedrooms *(Susan and
John Douglas, Gordon Smith, LYM)*

West Linton [NT1551], *Gordon Arms*:
Comfortable recently refurbished two-room
lounge bar with Theakstons Best, decent bar
food *(Peter Hitt)*

CENTRAL

☆ Callander [Stirling Rd (A84 a mile outside);
NN6507], *Myrtle*: Interesting food inc good
vegetarian choice and outstanding puddings in
smart and attractive old dining pub; small front
bar leading to two cosy prettily decorated
restaurant rooms inc no-smoking area, keg beer
but sensibly priced wine, herbal tea, decaf
coffee, obliging service; can get very busy – may
have to book *(Paul and Sue Merrick, Gerry Z
Pearson, Bob and Moira Tildsley)*

Crianlarich [Main St; NN3825], *Rod & Reel*:
Good food, good service, well kept McEwans
70/- and 80/-, enjoyable malt whiskies *(Dr and
Mrs P J S Crawshaw)*

☆ Dollar [Chapel Pl; NS9796], *Strathallan*: Good
bar food esp fresh fish in pleasant, clean and
welcoming pub with well kept local
Harviestoun ales, also Belhaven 80/- and lots of
malt whiskies; good service, thriving friendly
atmosphere; bedrooms *(Gerry Z Pearson)*

☆ Drymen [The Square; NS4788], *Clachan*: Great
atmosphere in small cottagey pub, licensed since
1734, friendly and welcoming; original fireplace
with side salt larder, tables made from former
bar tops, former Wee Free pews along one wall;
good fresh food in lounge, well kept Belhaven,
hard-working friendly licensee; on square of
attractive village *(Dr and Mrs Peter Kemp,
Richard and Chris Worsley)*

Drymen [The Square], *Winnock*: A hotel but
has a popular and attractive L-shaped bar
dating from 17th c, reasonably priced food,
three or four real ales, big garden with picnic
tables; bedrooms – friendly place to stay *(Ian
Baillie)*

Dunblane [NN7801], *Stirling Arms*: Relaxed
and friendly, with good range of good value
food in comfortable lounge bar, generous
glasses of wine; good panelled restaurant
downstairs with river views *(Heidi Williamson,
T and G Alderman)*

☆ Inverarnan [A82 N of Loch Lomond; NN3118],
Inverarnan Drovers Inn: Sporting trophies, other
stuffed animals, armour, deerskins slung over the
settles, haphazard decaying fabric and
furnishings, Hogarthian candle-light, peat or log
fires, some very stray customers and animals;
readers with a taste for the unusual (and a blind
eye to the niceties of housekeeping) like it a lot,
probably much closer to what inns were really
like 200 years ago than the usual anaemic
imitations; Scots music, great collection of malt
whiskies, well kept McEwans 80/-, farm cider,
well behaved children allowed, open all day;
creaky ageing bedrooms (look before you sleep),
late breakfast *(Nigel Woolliscroft, Susan and
John Douglas, John and Joan Nash, Tom Espley,
Peter and Lynn Brueton, Barry A Lynch, LYM)*

☆ Kilmahog [A821/A84 just N of Callander;
NN6108], *Lade*: Proper well run pub with wide
range of good straightforward food inc
vegetarian and children's in bar and restaurant,
cheerful service, well kept ales inc a guest, good
range of wines by the glass, real ales, no-smoking
area, pleasant garden with summer evening
barbecues; bedrooms, beautiful surroundings
(Jeremy Brittain-Long, A J Netherton)

☆ Stirling [91 St Mary's Wynd; from Wallace

Memorial in centre go up Baker St, keep right at top; NS7993], *Settle*: Early 18th c, restored to show beams, stonework, great arched fireplace and barrel-vaulted upper room; bar games, snacks till 7, Belhaven 70/- and 80/- and Maclays on handpump, friendly staff; piped music, open all day *(Bobby Paterson, Mark and Diane Grist, LYM)*

☆ nr Stirling [Easter Cornton Rd, Causewayhead; off A9 N], *Birds & the Bees*: Convivial and interestingly furnished dim-lit ex-byre, Caledonian 80/-, Tennents Special and 80/-, guests such as Alloa 80/-, Harviestoun, Marstons Pedigree, good range of food, helpful staff; decor includes milk churns, iron sculptures and re-fleeced sheep; live bands most weekends, open all day till 1am – very popular with young people, reliably well run; children welcome *(Heidi Williamson, Julian Holland, LYM)*

DUMFRIES AND GALLOWAY

Annan [High St; NY1966], *Blue Bell*: Welcoming local with Scots pictures, maps and ornaments on panelled walls, games area on different level, well kept Belhaven, St Andrews, Theakstons and a guest beer *(Pete Baker)*; [41 Scotts St; coming from E, on right as you enter town], *Firth*: Locals' bar in sandstone hotel, decent good value food pleasantly served, real ales, exotic beers, hundreds of whiskies; comfortable bedrooms *(Stuart Vivers, Richard Holloway)*

☆ Auchencairn [about 2½ miles off A711; NX8249], *Balcary Bay*: Lovely spot for eating outside with terrace and gardens in peaceful seaside surroundings, idyllic views over Solway Firth, civilised but friendly bar, honest reasonably priced food from soup and open sandwiches up (inc huge child's helpings), good service even when busy; keg beers; comfortable bedrooms *(David and Margaret Bloomfield, Ian Rorison)*

Bladnoch [NX4254], *Bladnoch*: Small fairly plain bar and dining area with dog pictures, well kept Theakstons, limited reasonably priced lunchtime food, friendly service; children welcome and well catered for *(Dave Thompson, Margaret Mason)*

☆ Canonbie [NY3976], *Cross Keys*: Attractive old coaching inn with fishing in River Esk; wide choice of good food in spacious and comfortable lounge bar, good weekend carvery, staff courteous and friendly even when very busy, friendly locals; bedrooms clean, spacious and well equipped, good breakfast *(Chris Rounthwaite, DMT)*

☆ Dalbeattie [1 Maxwell St; NX8361], *Pheasant*: Good choice of interesting food from help-yourself buffet in simply modernised but comfortable upstairs lounge/restaurant, and has had Youngers No 3; long downstairs bar can be rather noisy; open all day, food till late; bedrooms *(Dave Thompson, Margaret Mason, LYM)*

☆ Gatehouse of Fleet [Ann St], *Masonic Arms*: Well run clean relaxing local, welcoming comfortably refurbished bar, cheerful staff, bustling atmosphere, generous reasonably priced good food served quickly even when busy; conservatory and garden *(MKP, JLP, Mr and Mrs John Fowles, MJVK)*

Gatehouse of Fleet, *Bank of Fleet*: Friendly welcome, good food, S&N beers, doubles as community hall; bedrooms *(Dave Braisted)*; *Murray Arms*: Small hotel with well kept ale such as Theakstons XB, lots of malt whiskies, interesting layout of mainly old-fashioned comfortable seating areas, friendly staff, games in quite separate public bar, rather upmarket restaurant; one part with soft easy chairs open all day for food, children welcome; comfortable bedrooms *(Richard Holloway, James and Patricia Halfyard, LYM)*

☆ Kirkcudbright [Old High St; NX6851], *Selkirk Arms*: Quiet modern decor in cosy and comfortable partly panelled lounge with good local flavour; good food in bar and restaurant, friendly efficient service, tables in good spacious garden; fishing; children in restaurant and lounge; good value bedrooms *(Maysie Thompson, LYM)*

Lockerbie [High St; NY1381], *Blue Bell*: Rambling old building, good range of bar food, friendly staff, Belhaven and Tennents *(Dave Braisted)*

☆ Moffat [1 Churchgate; NT0905], *Black Bull*: Quick friendly service, generous hearty food, friendly public bar with railway memorabilia and good open fire (may be only bar open out of season), plush softly lit cocktail bar, simply furnished tiled-floor dining room, side games bar with juke box; children welcome, open all day; bedrooms comfortable *(Wayne Brindle, LYM)*

☆ Moffat [High St], *Moffat House*: Well run extended Adam-style hotel with good range of good value food in spacious plush lounge, relaxed and quiet; prompt friendly service, real ale; comfortable bedrooms with good breakfast *(Paul and Sue Merrick, Neil Townend, Chris Rounthwaite)*

Moniaive [High St (A702); NX7790], *George*: 17th-c inn with interesting no-frills old-fashioned flagstoned bar of considerable character; friendly staff and locals, simple bedrooms *(Mark and Diane Grist, LYM)*

Portpatrick [NX0154], *Harbour House*: Modern glittery bar with friendly service, lively karaoke night popular with young locals; restaurant, children welcome, good value bedrooms *(Dave Thompson, Margaret Mason)*

FIFE

☆ Anstruther [Bankwell Rd; NO5704], *Craws Nest*: Well run popular hotel with good variety of reliably good generous food inc outstanding haddock and other fresh fish in straightforward lounge; good service, keg beer; bedrooms *(Paul and Ursula Randall)*

☆ Ceres [Main St; NO4011], *Meldrums*: Pleasant spacious bars and clean and attractive beamed dining lounge with good choice of well prepared and presented reasonably priced bar lunches, prompt friendly service even when busy; bedrooms *(Eric Locker, E A Thwaite)*

Craigrothie [NO3710], *Kingarroch*: Long-established small dining pub, really a restaurant with bar, doing imaginative reasonably priced meals *(Gordon Smith)*

☆ Crail [4 High St; NO6108], *Golf*: Welcoming landlord, small unpretentious bar, restrained lounge, restaurant with views over Firth of Forth, well kept S&N ales, good range of malt whiskies, good service, coal fire, above-average food, quaint fishing-village atmosphere; simple comfortable bedrooms, good breakfast *(H Bramwell)*

☆ **Lower Largo** [The Harbour; NO4102], *Crusoe*: Friendly harbourside inn with good food from servery in beamed family bar, stripped stonework, settees in bays, open fire, S&N beers, quick service; separate lounge bar with Crusoe/Alexander Selkirk mementoes, restaurant; bedrooms spacious and comfortable, with good sea views *(Christine and Malcolm Ingram)*

Markinch [High St; NO2901], *Town House*: Well kept town pub, pleasant prompt service, good value imaginative food in comfortable lounge – popular weekends; bedrooms *(Margaret and Nigel Dennis)*

☆ **North Queensferry** [NT1380], *Queensferry Lodge*: Useful motorway break with good views of Forth bridges and the Firth from light and airy hotel lounge, tastefully decorated with lots of wood and plants; McEwans real ale, good value bar food inc good buffet 12-2.30, 5-10; bedrooms good *(Neil Townend)*

☆ **St Monance** [16 West End; SO5202], *Cabin*: Old pub comfortably and tastefully refurbished, with good choice of interesting fresh food for much of the day esp seafood, efficient cheerful staff, well kept Belhaven ales, interesting characters in bar, restaurant, coffee all day; small sheltered terrace with fine views over harbour and Firth of Forth *(Paul Randall, Ken Smith)*

Wormit [NO4026], *Sandford*: Elegant and comfortable yet friendly bar of golfing hotel, cushioned window seat overlooks pretty garden as does the terrace, friendly waitresses in Highland dress; bedrooms good *(Susan and John Douglas)*

GRAMPIAN

☆ **Aberdeen** [Bon Accord St; NJ9305], *Ferryhill House*: Four well kept S&N ales and well over 100 malt whiskies in well run small hotel's comfortable communicating spacious and airy bar areas, friendly staff, generous lunchtime bar food, wide choice in restaurant; lots of well spaced tables on neat sheltered lawns; open all day, children allowed in restaurant; bedrooms comfortable *(Graham Reeve, Mark Walker, LYM)*

Aberdeen [centre], *Blackfriars*: Pleasant atmosphere, good soups, well kept beers *(Esther and John Sprinkle)*; [121 Gallowgate], *Blue Lamp*: Friendly and unsmart flagstoned bar with a couple of well kept ales such as Caledonian Deuchars, basic snacks, free nostalgic juke box, fruit machine, TV, occasional band *(Graham Reeve, Mark Walker)*; [504 Union St], *Cocky Hunters*: Busy lively bare-boards pub, lots of alcoves, dark panelling and bric-a-brac, well kept ales inc Boddingtons and Caledonian 80/-, neat friendly staff, usual lunchtime food (not Sun), big-screen sports TV, piped music, machines, live rock band Fri, disco dancing nights *(Mark Walker, Graham Reeve, J Randy Davis, Tom McLean)*;

[Union St], *Grill Bar*: Old-fashioned well kept pub with polished dark panelling, attractive traditional features, several well kept S&N and other ales in top condition, enormous range of whiskies, unpretentious food; no ladies' *(Tom McLean)*; [Little Belmont St], *Ma Camerons*: Dark cosy intimate snug, back bar, well kept ales inc Orkney Dark Island *(Tom McLean)*; [55 Castle St], *Tilted Wig*: Recently renovated open-plan pub with Tetleys-related and other ales such as Caledonian Deuchars and Marstons Pedigree, reasonably priced usual food 11-9, friendly staff; fruit machine, juke box or piped music, TV *(Graham Reeve, Mark Walker)*

Aboyne [Charleston Rd; NO5298], *Charleston House*: Relaxed and friendly, with well kept beer, welcoming retriever, obliging service even when busy *(Esther and John Sprinkle)*

Banchory [Main St, West End; NO6995], *Burnett Arms*: Comfortable hotel lounge popular for reasonably priced simple bar lunches, well kept beer inc a guest ale; bedrooms *(Chris Raisin)*

☆ **Braemar** [NO1491], *Fife Arms*: Well refurbished big Victorian hotel, comfortable sofas and tartan cushions, reasonably priced reliable pub food, particularly friendly helpful staff, huge log fire; children and dogs welcome, piped music; on the coach routes, used by school ski trips, appropriate entertainment; bedrooms warm and comfortable with mountain views, pleasant strolls in village *(George Atkinson, Liz and Benton Jennings, Susan and John Douglas, Esther and John Sprinkle)*

☆ **Catterline** [NO8778], *Creel*: Cosy bar with real fire, big lounge with friendly cat and plenty of tables, good generous food in bar and seaview restaurant, well kept Maclays 70/- and Tennents 80/-, welcoming landladies; bedrooms *(Ian Rorison)*

☆ **Craigellachie** [Keith Rd; NJ2845], *Fiddichside*: Tiny fishing pub in pretty spot on banks of Fiddich Burn at its confluence with River Spey, virtually unchanged over past 40 years with old bar and fireplace intact, very long-serving licensees, good choice of malt whiskies, keg beer, immaculately kept riverside garden *(George Hollingbery)*

Garlogie [NJ7805], *Garlogie*: Dining pub in pleasant setting overlooking Deeside, generous varied reasonably priced food *(E A Eaves)*

Milltimber [B9077 SW of Aberdeen; NJ8501], *Old Mill*: Smart but friendly hotel with good food in lounge inc fine steaks, well kept Boddingtons and guest beer; bedrooms *(Chris Raisin)*

Monymusk [signed from B993 SW of Kemnay; NJ6815], *Grant Arms*: Comfortable well kept inn with good fishing on the Don, log fire dividing dark-panelled lounge bar, lots of malt whiskies, S&N real ales, games in simpler public bar, wide choice of bar food, restaurant; children welcome, open all day weekends; bedrooms *(B A Hayward, LYM)*

Oldmeldrum [Kirk Brae; NJ8128], *Redgarth*: Comfortably refurbished with banquettes and prints, wide choice of good generous food inc fish and game in lounge bar and more intimate restaurant, welcoming licensees, a well kept house beer from Caledonian, good range of malt whiskies, gorgeous views to Bennachie; immaculate bedrooms *(Rod Hensman)*

☆ Stonehaven [Shorehead; NO8786], *Marine*: Welcoming basic harbourside pub with good cheap food, five real ales inc McEwans 80/- and guests, coffee and tea, polite service, upstairs lounge and restaurant, superb view – in summer people drink out on the harbour wall; lively downstairs, piped music may compete with TV, dogs allowed here; juke box, games machines and pool table in room past bar; open all day; bedrooms *(Sandy Henderson, Mark Walker, Chris Raisin)*

HIGHLAND

Aviemore [Coylumbridge Rd; NH8912], *Olde Bridge*: Well kept friendly inn, small but busy, with good bar food inc four-course meals (with whisky for the haggis), some live entertainment; pleasant surroundings *(Dono and Carol Leaman, TBB, G Washington, Gerry Z Pearson)*

Badachro [B8056 by Gair Loch; NG7773], *Badachro*: Welcoming pub in superb waterside setting, helpful landlord, nice atmosphere – locals and yachtsmen (two moorings, shower available); decent basic food in simple public bar, more comfortable than usual, friendly and relaxing; good log fire, children welcome; Nov-March open only Weds and Fri evenings, Sat lunch and evening; nice garden and tables on terrace over loch; homely bedrooms *(Mrs Olive Oxley)*

Ballachulish [Oban Rd, S; NN0858], *Ballachulish*: Pleasant lounge bar with beautiful view, very friendly staff, good food inc vegetarian and children's, wide range of malt whiskies, McEwans 80/- and Theakstons ales; basic public bar; comfortable bedrooms *(Neil Townend)*

Beauly [The Square; NH5246], *Priory*: Worth knowing for good cheap meals, quite restaurantly; popular with locals, always busy; bedrooms *(Christine and Malcolm Ingram, Neil Townend)*

☆ Carrbridge [nr junction A9/A95 S of Inverness; NH9022], *Dalrachney Lodge*: Consistently good food and friendly staff in pleasant shooting-lodge-type hotel with simple bar, comfortable lounge with books and log fire in ornate inglenook, decent malt whiskies, McEwans 70/-, old-fashioned dining room; very busy with locals weekends; bedrooms, most with mountain and river views; open all year *(Neil Townend, Mark and Diane Grist)*

☆ Cromarty [Marine Terr; NH7867], *Royal*: Small hotel doing well under very friendly new management, good value food, beautiful view across Cromarty Firth to Ben Wyvis; bedrooms – very popular in summer *(Christine and Malcolm Ingram, Euan and Aileen McGinty, Mark and Diane Grist, I S Thomson)*

☆ Dores [B852 SW of Inverness; NH5934], *Dores Inn*: Reasonably priced popular bar food inc good seafood, well kept beer and friendly staff in attractive traditional country inn; stripped stone, low ceilings, basic public bar, more comfortable lounge with open fire; beautiful views over Loch Ness, front garden and tables out behind *(Peter and Lynn Brueton)*

Dornoch [Church Rd; NH8089], *Mallin House*: Good well priced food inc tasty local fish and superb langoustine in welcoming lounge or restaurant, well kept Theakstons Best and other S&N beers, good range of malt whiskies, friendly service, interesting collections of whisky-water jugs and golf balls; comfortable bedrooms *(Mike and Penny Sanders, Mick Hitchman)*

Fort William [66 High St; NN1174], *Grog & Girvel*: Interesting new pub done out in traditional spit and sawdust style, four or five well kept real ales, efficient friendly staff, upstairs restaurant with wide range of good food inc pizzas, pasta, Mexican and vegetarian *(John Abbott, Andy Hazeldine)*; *Nevisport*: Friendly and informal, modern but cosy, used by walkers and climbers among others; lots of maps and climbing photographs *(Tim and Chris Ford)*

Gairloch [just off A832 near bridge; NG8077], *Old Inn*: Usefully placed over rd from small harbour, nr splendid beach; dimpled copper tables and so forth in two small rooms of comfortable lounge, a good few malts, up to eight real ales inc several English ones in summer, popular bar food, games in public bar; piped music may be loud, and does catch the tourist coaches; picnic tables out by stream, open all day; bedrooms *(Andy Hazeldine, BB)*

Garve [A835 some miles N; NH3969], *Inchbae Lodge*: Snug bar with lots of dark woodwork, good generous food from ploughman's with choice of cheeses to imaginative main dishes here and in attractive dining room, good wines, sitting room with velvet chairs and sofas, friendly accommodating staff; comfortable bedrooms, beautiful setting *(Lucy James)*

☆ Glen Shiel [A87 Invergarry—Kyle of Lochalsh - OS Sheet 33 map ref 076117; NH0711], *Cluanie*: Hotel in lovely wild setting by Loch Cluanie (good walks), big helpings of good simple freshly prepared bar food in three knocked-together rooms with dining chairs around polished tables, overspill into restaurant; friendly efficient staff, good fire, well kept ales such as McEwans, Tomintoul and Wild Cat, no pool or juke box; children welcome; interesting gift shop, big comfortable modern bedrooms nicely furnished in pine, stunning views and good bathrooms – great breakfasts for non-residents too *(John and Joan Nash, Mr and Mrs C Nethercott, Nigel Woolliscroft)*

☆ Glencoe [on old Glencoe rd, behind NTS Visitor Centre; NN1256], *Clachaig*: Tremendous setting, surrounded by soaring mountains, inn doubling as mountain rescue post and cheerfully crowded with outdoors people in season, with walkers' bar (two woodburners and pool), pine-panelled snug, big modern-feeling lounge bar; simple snacks all day, wider evening choice, lots of malt whiskies, half a dozen well kept ales such as Arrols 80/-, Maclays 80/-, Marstons Pedigree, Theakstons Old Peculier, Tetleys and Youngers No 3; children in no-smoking restaurant; frequent live music; bedrooms, good breakfast *(D J Atkinson, John and Joan Nash, Mark and Diane Grist, Calum and Susan Maclean, S R and A J Ashcroft, Barry A Lynch, Dave Braisted, Tom Espley, LYM)*

☆ Glencoe [off A82 E of Pass; NN1058], *Kings House*: Alone in a stupendous mountain landscape, with simple bar food inc children's, well kept McEwans 80/- and a guest such as Orkney Dark Island or Shipstones; basic back climbers' bar with loud pop music, pool and darts, central cocktail bar with cloth banquettes and other seats around wood-effect tables, suntrap lounge with scenic windows and log fire; open all day; comfortable bedrooms, also cheaper dormitory-style bunkhouse *(D J Atkinson, Karen Eliot, LYM)*

☆ Glenelg [unmarked rd from Shiel Bridge (A87) towards Skye; NG8119], *Glenelg*: Overlooking Skye across own beach and sea loch; bright public bar/snack bar with blazing fire even in summer, plain solid furnishings, pool table, piped music, homely pictures; good simple fresh food, lots of whiskies, decent wine list, fine set menu in nice restaurant (maybe residents only, Sun out of season), tables on terrace; steep narrow road to inn has spectacular views of Loch Duich – there's a short summer ferry crossing from Skye, too; bedrooms good, superb views *(Mr and Mrs C Nethercott, J G Wilkinson)*

Inverness [93 Academy St; NH6645], *Blackfriars*: Exceptional choice of beer, colourful local atmosphere *(J V Dadswell, Esther and John Sprinkle, Dr Paul McGowan)*; [Academy St], *Phoenix*: Four regular well kept ales and two guest beers, friendly and inviting atmosphere, bar food, stained-glass windows *(Esther and John Sprinkle)*

Kinbrace [B871 8 miles NW; NC8732], *Garvault*: Isolated fishing hotel (good base for walkers too) in wild bleak scenery, quirky little bar with lots of whiskies, full of interesting characters in the evening; bedrooms *(Mick Hitchman)*

Kinlochewe [NH0262], *Kinlochewe*: Welcoming public bar and lounge, good food from toasties and ploughman's up, open fire, piped classical music, Tennents 80/-; stupendous scenery all around, especially Loch Maree and Torridon mountains; attractive bedrooms *(N C Walker)*

Kyle of Lochalsh [NG7527], *Lochalsh*: Useful stop with food inc tasty sandwiches in comfortable hotel lounge by bar, pleasant views of Skye; bedrooms *(Lucy James)*

☆ Kylesku [A894; S side of former ferry crossing; NC2234], *Kylesku*: Useful for this remote NW coast (but in winter open only weekends, just for drinks), rather spartan but pleasant local bar (unusual in facing the glorious view, with seals often in sight), friendly helpful service, short choice of reasonably priced wonderfully fresh local seafood, also sandwiches and soup; sea-view restaurant, five comfortable and peaceful if basic bedrooms, good breakfast; boatman does good loch trips *(Christopher Beadle, P W Taylor, G Washington)*

Mey [ND2873], *Castle Arms*: 19th-c former coaching inn, tastefully refurbished in understated stripped pine and so forth; shortish choice of good usual bar food, wider choice for high teas and dinners in dining room, very pleasant helpful service; photographs of Queen

Mother during her Caithness holidays; bedrooms in back extension, well placed for N coast of Caithness *(K Archard, R S Reid)*

☆ Plockton [Innes St; NG8033], *Creag Nan Darach*: Fresh substantial well cooked food with real chips and veg done just right, McEwans 80/- and Theakstons, good range of malt whiskies, pleasant staff, busy with locals and visitors even in winter; comfortable bedrooms *(Neil Townend, Dr and Mrs S Jones)*

Salen [B8009/A861; NM6864], *Salen*: Useful pub in pleasant spot with seats outside overlooking village, food inc good home-made soups, friendly if not always speedy service; bedrooms *(Andrew and Kerstin Lewis)*

☆ Spean Bridge [A82 7 miles N; NN2491], *Letterfinlay Lodge*: Well established hotel, extensive comfortably modern main bar with popular lunchtime buffet and usual games, small smart cocktail bar, no-smoking restaurant; good malt whiskies, friendly service, children and dogs welcome, pleasant lochside grounds, own boats for fishing; clean and comfortable bedrooms, good breakfasts; gents' have good showers and hairdryers – handy for Caledonian Canal sailors *(Christine and Malcolm Ingram, LYM)*

Strathcarron [NG9442], *Strathcarron*: Reasonably priced traditional bar food, well kept real ales introduced by English owner; bedrooms *(N C Walker, Mark and Diane Grist)*

Struy [B831; NH3939], *Struy*: Pleasantly refurbished small inn, good home-made food inc vegetarian and fish dishes, keg McEwans, good range of malt whiskies, friendly service; good area for fishing and walking; bedrooms *(I S Thomson)*

Tain [A836 W, past bridge; NH7584], *Dornoch Bridge*: Former station buildings with cosy atmosphere, good reasonably priced food, wide range of real ales *(Neil Townend)*

LOTHIAN

☆ Aberlady [Main St; A198 towards Edinburgh; NT4679], *Wagon*: Well run, friendly and attractive bar and restaurant, distant sea and Fife views from airy high-ceilinged back extension and tables in clematis-sheltered yard, wide range of decent food in bar and restaurant, well kept McEwans 80/-, reasonable wine list *(Ian Phillips, Chris Rounthwaite, LYM)*

☆ Cramond [Cramond Glebe Rd; NT1876], *Cramond*: Softly lit little rooms with comfortable brown-and-brass decor, traditional English-style pub furnishing but Scottish bric-a-brac, good coal and log fires, prompt friendly service, Sam Smiths OB, emphasis on good generous well priced salads, grills etc; very popular with retired couples at lunchtime; in picturesque waterside village *(EPG, M Walker, Victor Brilliant, LYM)*

☆ Cramond Bridge [A90 N of Edinburgh; NT1875], *Cramond Brig*: Well run family stop done out in neo-Victorian books style, with family rooms, play area, video and children's menu; bar food all day, well kept McEwans 80/-, restaurant, helpful staff; bedrooms *(Brian and Louisa Routledge, LYM)*

Dalkeith [Lothianbridge (A7 S); NR3367], *Sun*: Single long bar with dining room off, friendly service, big helpings of good value bar food; simple good value bedrooms *(T and G Alderman)*

☆ Dirleton [village green; NT5184], *Castle*: Limited choice of good generous food inc sandwiches and fish in small unpretentiously comfortable bar, well kept ales such as Belhaven or McEwans 80/-, friendly service, restaurant; attractive spot in pretty village on green opp castle, tables in garden; bedrooms *(Ian Phillips, T and G Alderman)*

☆ Dirleton, *Open Arms*: Small comfortable hotel, not a place for just a drink, but good for bar food inc huge open sandwiches and well presented hot dishes such as tender venison casserole with good fresh veg; welcoming service, lovely little sitting room with good open fire, fine position facing castle; comfortable bedrooms *(Chris Rounthwaite)*

☆ East Linton [5 Bridge St; NT5977], *Drovers*: Small dining pub dating from 18th c, cleanly refurbished in an attractive style that gives it something of a wine-bar atmosphere, inventive well presented bistro-style food inc fresh local fish and well cooked veg, interesting changing well kept ales such as Redemption Rye, Old Yellowbelly and Thwaites Craftsman, friendly helpful service, upstairs restaurant; closed as we go to press – would otherwise probably have been a main entry *(F J and A Parmenter, O K Smyth, BB)*

☆ Edinburgh [8 Leven St], *Bennets*: Elaborate Victorian bar with wonderfully ornate original glass, mirrors, arcades, panelling and tiles, well kept McEwans 80/- and other ales from tall founts, lots of rare malt whiskies, bar snacks and simple lunchtime hot dishes, children allowed in eating area lunchtime; open all day, cl Sun lunchtime *(Ian Phillips, Jon Wood, David Carr, LYM)*

☆ Edinburgh [James Ct, by 495 Lawnmarket], *Jolly Judge*: Interesting and comfortable basement of 16th-c tenement, recently brightened up, with traditional fruit-and-flower-painted wooden ceiling, quickly served lunchtime bar meals and afternoon snacks from new kitchen, Caledonian 80/- and a guest beer, changing malt whiskies, hot drinks, friendly service, lovely fire; piped music, games machine; children allowed at lunchtime in eating area; cl Sun lunchtime; space outside in summer *(Ian Phillips, Peter Todd, M Walker, LYM)*

☆ Edinburgh [The Causeway, out below Arthurs Seat at Duddingston], *Sheep Heid*: Old-fashioned rather upmarket ex-coaching inn in lovely spot beyond Holyroodhouse, relaxed pubby atmosphere, interesting pictures and fine rounded bar counter in main room, well kept Caledonian 80/-, Bass and Worthington BB, newspapers, children allowed; piped music; restaurant, pretty garden with summer barbecues, skittle alley; open all day, can get crowded *(Brian and Anna Marsden, Mark Walker, LYM)*

☆ Edinburgh [55 Rose St], *Rose Street Brewery*: Malt-extract beer brewed on the premises, mild-flavoured though quite potent Auld Reekie 80/- and stronger sticky 90/- – tiny brewery can be seen from upstairs lounge (cl at quiet times); back-to-basics downstairs bar open all day, with well reproduced pop music from its CD juke box, machines; good usual bar food, good service, tea and coffee, live music some evenings *(David Carr, Liz and Benton Jennings, Stephen and Jean Curtis, Esther and John Sprinkle, Sue and Mike Todd, Mark Walker, BB)*

☆ Edinburgh [Rose St, corner of Hanover St], *Milnes*: Large bar with another downstairs, dark wood, bare floorboards, cask tables and old-fashioned decor; lots of S&N real ales with a guest or two such as Burton Bridge and Marstons Pedigree, good range of snacks and hot food (not Sun evening) inc various pies charged by size; very busy but cheerful quick aproned staff; mixed customers, lively atmosphere *(Esther and John Sprinkle)*

Edinburgh [1 Princes St], *Balmoral*: Certainly no pub, but this corner lobby of a landmark hotel is a relaxing refuge in its comfortable clubby armchairy way (despite the piped music); welcoming staff, good hot rolls filled with daily roast (not cheap); bedrooms *(Walter Reid, Stephen and Jean Curtis, Mark Walker, Peter Todd)*; [Young St], *Cambridge*: Small quiet rooms, Caledonian Deuchars and Tetleys-related ales, decent snacks, daily papers, dominoes *(Walter Reid, Ian Phillips)*; [Cumberland St], *Cumberland*: If you like the Bow Bar you'll like this, done up in similar highly traditional style, with collection of antique cigarette advertisements, well kept ales, plenty of malt whiskies, friendly staff, no music; packed Fri afternoon/evening *(John Wallace, Mr Hislop)*; [435 Lawnmarket], *Deacon Brodies*: Entertainingly commemorating the notorious highwayman town councillor who was eventually hanged on the scaffold he'd designed; limited decent food inc some unusual home-made dishes, Arrols 80/-, comfortable leather-chair upstairs lounge; piper outside can be a little wearing after a while *(Peter Todd, Mark Walker, David Carr, Stephen and Jean Curtis, BB)*; [159 Rose St], *Dirty Dicks*: Pleasant ambience, decent bar food *(Ian and Villy White)*; [19 Cockburn St], *Drew Nicols*: Panelling, bare boards, friendly efficient staff, decent reasonably priced lunchtime food, well kept Caledonian Deuchars and changing guest ales, Belgian bottled beers, horse-racing theme; no children, open all day *(Mark Walker, Tim Steward)*; [Royal Mile], *Ensign Ewart*: Charming old-world pub handy for Castle, lots of interesting memorabilia relating to Ewart and Waterloo, Alloa, Caledonian Deuchars and 80/-, Orkney Dark Island, wide range of whiskies, usual food lunchtime and some summer evenings, friendly efficient staff; juke box, fruit machine, piped Scottish music, folk music Thurs/Sun; no children, open all day *(Liz and Benton Jennings, Peter Todd, Mark Walker)*; [152 Rose St], *Kenilworth*: Friendly Edwardian pub with ornate high ceiling, carved woodwork, etched mirrors and windows, not many seats; central bar with Tetleys-related and a guest ale, hot drinks inc espresso, good generous bar food lunchtime and evening, quick friendly service, back family room; piped music, games machine, TV; space outside in summer, open all day *(Ian Phillips, David Carr, Mark Walker, LYM)*; [Cockburn St], *Malt Shovel*: Lots of panelling, long serving bar, Caledonian 60/-, 70/- and 80/-, Broughton Greenmantle, Orkney Dark Island and Tetleys, good value basic food popular with students; piped music, TV, occasional folk music; open all day *(Richard Lewis, Mark Walker)*; [30 Wrights Houses], *Olde Golf Tavern*: Dating from 1456 though does not seem old, overlooking Bruntisfield Links (where golf first played here – it's still a sort of unofficial clubhouse for this free public golf course); good atmosphere, consistently good food all day, McEwans 80/-, Theakstons Best and two other beers on handpump, leather chesterfields, old golf prints, newspapers, moderate prices, prompt friendly service, upstairs restaurant; fruit and quiz machines; piped music *(Mark Walker, Christine and Malcolm Ingram, Ian Phillips, BB)*; [8 Young St], *Oxford*: Friendly unspoilt pub with busy front bar, quieter back room, lino floor, Belhaven, Courage and St Andrews ales, mutton pies, pickled eggs, Forfar bridies, lots of interesting characters *(Walter Reid, Bob Kelly, John A Baker)*; [Rose St], *Paddys*: Fair-sized open-plan pub with friendly service and locals, food all day, tables outside; popular with younger people evenings – juke box, machines; cl Sun *(Mark Walker)*; [1 High St], *Royal Archer*: Friendly bar/bistro with masses of prints and other bric-a-brac, good all-day bar snacks inc cheap Scotch broth *(Dave Braisted, David Carr)*; *Smithies*: Attractive genuinely gaslit Victorian pub, good atmosphere, welcoming regulars *(Vann and Terry Prime)*; [118 Biggar Rd (A702)], *Steadings*: Popular modern pub with good choice of Scottish beers and Timothy Taylors Landlord, very varied good generous food 10am-10pm in bar, restaurant and conservatory, friendly staff *(Norma Hardy, B A Hayward)*; [W Register St], *Tiles*: Exquisite tiling from floor to ceiling, good reasonably priced fresh food, prompt obliging service *(Susan Wood)*

Gifford [Main St; NT5368], *Goblin Ha'*: Neatly kept village pub, welcoming and pretty, with very good value home cooking, well kept Bass and an S&N beer such as Theakstons in plainly furnished bar, quick service, jolly atmosphere; boules in good garden with Sat evening jazz; bedrooms *(F J and A Parmenter)*

Haddington [Sidegate; NT5174], *Maitlandfield House*: Pleasant conservatory, good choice of generously served well cooked food, well kept Belhaven; bedrooms *(Andy Morris)*

Haddington [Waterside; NT5174], *Waterside*: Bistro-style riverside pub, locally very popular, often crowded; snug main bar, separate lounge and restaurant, friendly staff, wide range of fresh food, real ales such as Caledonian Deuchars, Courage Directors and Marstons Pedigree, good house wines; tables outside in summer *(M S Saxby)*

North Berwick [Dirleton Ave; NT5485], *Nether Abbey*: Good range of good value food in bar and restaurant; comfortable reasonably priced bedrooms *(Andy Morris)*

☆ Queensferry [South Queensferry; NT1278], *Hawes*: Featured famously in *Kidnapped*, now comfortably modernised, with fine views of the Forth bridges, friendly staff, well kept Arrols 80/-, Ind Coope Burton and guest beers such as Caledonian 80/- from tall founts, wide range of standard food from efficient servery, games in small public bar, no-smoking family room, restaurant, children welcome; tables on back lawn with play area; bedrooms *(Ian Baillie, Mark Walker, David Carr, LYM)*

☆ Ratho [NT1370], *Bridge*: Very welcoming extended 18th-c pub enjoyed by all ages, decent range of food inc vegetarian, good children's dishes and tactful choice of food for those with smaller appetites, well kept Belhaven, pleasant helpful and chatty staff; garden by partly restored Union Canal, good well stocked play area, own canal boats (doing trips for the disabled, among others); open all day from noon *(Roger Bellingham)*

STRATHCLYDE

☆ Ardentinny [NS1887], *Ardentinny Hotel*: Comfortable family hotel with lovely views of Loch Long from waterside bars and garden (dogs allowed out here), friendly helpful staff, consistently good often inventive home-made bar food inc local seafood, Belhaven ale, own moorings, Harry Lauder bar with appropriate memorabilia; no-smoking evening restaurant, children allowed in eating area; decent bedrooms, cl winter *(Karen Kalaway, Walter Reid, LYM)*

Ayr [Burns Statue Sq; NS3321], *O'Briens*: Irish bar with wooden floors, bric-a-brac and coal fire, good mix of customers, friendly service, daytime snacks; popular folk nights Weds, Fri and Sun *(Julian Holland)*

Balloch [just N of A811; NS3881], *Balloch Hotel*: Very pleasant atmosphere, helpful barman, wide choice of particularly well kept ales such as Caledonian Deuchars, Ind Coope Burton and Timothy Taylors Landlord; big bar by retstaurant area, broken up by pillars, many small tables, scattering of fish tackle; bedrooms *(Dave Irving, Kevin Spealman)*

Bearsden [Station Rd; NS5471], *Beefeater*: Former rly stn, now a pub-restaurant with attractive lounge bar full of railway memorabilia; reliable bar food, well kept Whitbreads-related real ales *(Ian Baillie)*

Bishopton [Old Inchinnan Rd; NS4371], *Bishopton*: Neatly kept, with friendly helpful staff, easy access for wheelchairs, good reasonably priced food, at least four real ales inc Bass and Maclays 80/- *(Kenny Grant)*

☆ Bothwell [27 Hamilton Rd (B7071); a mile from M74 junction 5, via A725; NS7058], *Cricklewood*: Smartly refurbished dining pub with good bar food, S&N real ale, pleasant restful atmosphere, neat decorations inc old carved wooden trade signs on stairway, complete sets of cigarette cards in gents'; open all day; bedrooms *(G Washington)*

Bridge of Weir [Main St; NS3966], *Gryffe Inn*:

Pleasant and well decorated, with fast friendly service, good low-priced lunchtime food inc children's, tables outside *(Calum and Susan Maclean)*

Cairnbaan [B841, off A816; NR8390], *Cairnbaan*: Hotel overlooking busy canal lock and swing bridge, with walk to four central locks; attractive small bar with bare boards and restful green walls, good spread of food inc cold buffet in eating annexe, tables on verandah; good bedrooms *(Walter Reid, Andrew and Kerstin Lewis)*

Colintraive [opp the Maids of Bute; NS0374], *Colintraive*: Clean, bright and friendly small family-run hotel in lovely spot overlooking the Maids of Bute, by ferry to Rhubodach on Bute; straightforward food inc nice puddings; bedrooms immaculate and attractive, with huge baths and good breakfast *(Nigel Woolliscroft)*

☆ Connel [North Connel; NM9134], *Lochnell Arms*: Attractive hotel with cosy public bar, small lounge, conservatory extension; good value food inc good seafood, friendly service, bric-a-brac, plants, beautiful views over Loch Etive; waterside garden; bedrooms *(J M Renshaw)*

Erskine [Bridgewater Centre; NS4571], *Bridgewater*: Friendly, with no-smoking conservatory, good service and good lunchtime food (also 4-8 Thurs-Sat; no food Sun) *(Calum and Susan Maclean)*

Ford [B840, end of Loch Awe; NM8603], *Ford*: Archetypal Highland hotel in tiny village, good informal atmosphere, genial landlord, traditional bar with photographs of fishing customers with prize catches, snug bar with piped fiddle music, good food esp fresh fish, seafood and venison; fishing permits; bedrooms *(Vicky and David Sarti, R Macnaughton)*

Furnace [NN0200], *Furnace*: Friendly old stone inn, welcoming locals, good generous food, good choice of whiskies *(Vicky and David Sarti)*

☆ Gartocharn [NS4286], *Hungry Monk*: Lavishly reproduced ornate Victorian decor, plenty of friendly staff, good food inc vegetarian and children's, good choice of beers, lots of whiskies, log fire, unobtrusive Scottish folk music, big dining area, attractive restaurant, pleasant seats outside; nice walks in lovely countryside nr Loch Lomond; bedrooms comfortable and inexpensive *(Calum and Susan Maclean, BB)*

☆ Glasgow [83 Hutcheson St], *Rab Ha's*: Same family as Babbity Bowster – see main entries; civilised dark-panelled bar in sensitively converted Georgian town house, well cooked seafood in bar and basement restaurant, informal atmosphere, candle-light, friendly young staff, newspapers for customers, well kept McEwans 80/-; intermittent robust live music but otherwise relatively quiet; bedrooms elegant and immaculate *(Ian Phillips)*

☆ Glasgow [154 Hope St], *Cask & Still*: Comfortable and welcoming, with bare boards, big carpets, good lounge seating, reasonably priced food all day (menu limited evenings) with well kept Caledonian Deuchars, Merman XXX and 80/-, McEwans 80/-, Theakstons Best and Youngers No 3, lots of interesting bottled beers, over 200 malt whiskies, friendly staff, interesting

prints, good piped music *(Mike and Penny Sanders, Richard Lewis, Ian Phillips, LYM)*

☆ Glasgow [12 Ashton Lane], *Ubiquitous Chip*: Great atmosphere, minimal decoration apart from some stained glass, real ale, wide choice of malt whiskies, some decent wines by the glass, daily changing home-cooked lunchtime food in upstairs dining area inc vegetarian dishes, peat fire; wider choice in downstairs restaurant opening on to courtyard, with outstanding wines; often packed with university staff and students *(Walter Reid)*

Glasgow [Dumbarton Rd, by Kelvin Hall arena], *Hogshead*: Wide choice of Whitbreads-related and other well kept ales on handpump or tapped from cask, simple food, friendly service, well reproduced piped blues music, games machines; opp art galleries, can get busy – popular with students *(Alastair Campbell, Angus Lyon, David Williamson)*; [11 Exchange Pl], *Rogano*: Not a pub, but a fine drinking place, lovingly restored and preserved 1930s art deco interior, good cocktails in ground-floor oyster bar (Guinness too), good well priced wines; good if slightly pricy restaurant, downstairs cafe cheaper but good too – emphasis on fish *(Walter Reid)*; [Airport], *Tap & Spile*: Sometimes seems packed to the gills with homesick Englishmen – well done in the style of a traditional pub, bright yet peaceful, with well kept Arrols 80/- and guest beers such as Ind Coope Burton and Greenmantle, decent malt whiskies, good snacks inc fresh sandwiches, no-smoking area *(Alan and Paula McCully, Ian Phillips, Mike and Penny Sanders, Walter Reid)*; [Byres Rd], *Tennents*: Big busy high-ceilinged pub with Caledonian 70/- or 80/-, Greenmantle, Theakstons Best and lots of interesting changing guest ales, also plenty of good malt whiskies; cheerful atmosphere, usual bar food *(Michael Hanna, S Crosier)*

Glendaruel [NR9985], *Glendaruel*: Plain but friendly, in lovely countryside; bar meals, small lounge, separate bar with darts; outside seats *(Diane Devine, Walter Reid)*

☆ Inveraray [Main St E; NN0908], *George*: Pleasant old-fashioned pub, very popular locally, interesting old Highland feel to friendly low-beamed public bar with real fires, stone walls and fine flagstones; good value pub food served noon to 9pm, friendly helpful staff, Tennents 80/- and occasional guest beers, good choice of whiskies, reasonably priced wines, bar games; children welcome; bedrooms reasonably priced, quieter at the back *(Capt E P Gray, Chris Bax, Dr and Mrs Peter Kemp, LYM)*

☆ Johnstone [High St; NS4263], *Coanes*: Thriving atmosphere in old-fashioned oak-balustered bar with enterprising range of well kept real ales, good malt whiskies inc malt of the month, hard-working friendly family service, above-average food; larger plush lounge popular with young *(Walter Reid)*

☆ Kilchrenan [B845 7 miles S of Taynuilt; NN0322], *Taychreggan*: Friendly airy hotel bar in beautiful setting, easy chairs and banquettes around low glass-topped tables, stuffed birds and fish and good local photographs; wide range of reasonably priced and well served lunchtime bar food inc local fish, well kept beers inc Aitkens (bar service stops 2), polite efficient staff, Sun lunch in no-smoking dining room, unusual lochside garden (good fishing), pretty inner courtyard, children welcome; cl Nov-March, comfortable bedrooms *(Revd A Nunnerley, John Knighton, LYM)*

☆ Kilmelford [NM8412], *Cuilfail*: Former coaching inn in attractive setting, cheerful stripped-stone pubby bar, welcoming family service, good value food in inner eating room with light wood furnishings, well kept McEwans and Youngers No 3, good range of malt whiskies, charming garden across road; bedrooms *(Walter Reid, LYM)*

Langbank [NS3873], *Langbank Lodge*: Incredible Clyde views from welcoming and well designed modern split-level pub with wide range of sensibly priced food inc afternoon tea and scones; keen young staff; handy for wonderful Finlaystone gardens *(Ian Phillips)*

Luss [A82 about 3 miles N; NS3593], *Inverbeg*: Across road from Loch Lomond, lounge often crowded for decent straightforward waitress-served food (also restaurant), well kept real ales, games in simple public bar; bedrooms *(D J Atkinson, LYM)*

Oban [Cologin, Lerags; off A816 S – follow Ardoran Marine sign; NM8526], *Barn*: Very friendly converted barn in lovely quiet countryside nr sea, donkeys, rabbits and hens all around, wide choice of good changing chip-free home-made food esp Fri seafood, Calders and Tetleys ales, wooden tables and settles, Scottish accordion Sun, ceilidh Thurs and folk group Sun; part of chalet holiday complex *(Mrs Olive Oxley, June and Perry Dann)*

Renfrew [Ferry Rd; NS5067], *Ferry*: Four or more well kept changing ales at reasonable prices; straightforward decor, quiet atmosphere, prints of the old ferry *(Kenny Grant)*

Straiton [NS3804], *Black Bull*: Small and attractive two-bar whitewashed stonebuilt village local, warm welcome, good bar food, coal fire in front room, sizeable garden; keg beers *(Ian Williams, Linda Mar)*

☆ Symington [Main St; just off A77 Ayr—Kilmarnock; NS3831], *Wheatsheaf*: Charming and cosy 18th-c pub in pretty village, consistently good original food esp fish and local produce, Belhaven beers, friendly quick service; tables in garden *(DMT, Walter Reid)*

Tarbert [A83 1 mile S; NR8467], *West Loch*: Enthusiastically decorated and immaculately kept old inn overlooking sea loch, convenient for Islay ferry; McEwans beers, good choice of reasonably priced food in bar and restaurant inc interesting dishes and emphasis on local seafood, friendly service; bedrooms *(Walter Reid, LYM)*

Taynuilt [a mile past village, which is signed off A85; NN0030], *Polfearn*: Pleasant lounge bar with picture windows making most of setting by loch with Ben Cruachan towering over, well kept beers, relaxed atmosphere, welcoming landlord, good food esp local mussels and fish soup; bedrooms *(Revd A Nunnerley)*

TAYSIDE

Aberargie [B966; NO1616], *Baiglie*: Good food,

friendly service and atmosphere, immaculate housekeeping, good choice of whiskies and wines; two eating areas, one in cosy room with black stone fireplace, the other conservatory-style *(Sue Rowland)*

☆ Alyth [NO2548], *Alyth*: Family run 18th-c hotel overlooking market town, good home-cooked food in bar and restaurant inc wild salmon, teas and high teas (home-baked bread), well kept ales, good range of malt whiskies, obliging owners; folk music last Fri of month; bedrooms, good value golf breaks *(G Maxwell)*

Bridge of Cally [NO1451], *Bridge of Cally*: Good atmosphere in straightforward friendly and comfortable bar, sensible choice of good value food inc outstanding ploughman's; bedrooms, attractive area *(Ian Rorison)*

Broughty Ferry [behind lifeboat stn; NO4630], *Ship*: Good generous food in pretty nautical-theme upstairs dining room with fantastic view; downstairs bar handsomely refurbished with burgundy and dark wood, stately model sailing ship *(SD, JD)*

Crieff [N, signed off A85, A822; NN8562], *Glenturret Distillery*: Not a pub, but good adjunct to one of the best whisky-distillery tours; good value whiskies in big plain bar/dining area with tasty sandwiches, good generous Highland soups, stews and pies, and knock-out Glenturret ice cream from self-service food counter *(Susan and John Douglas, Mark and Diane Grist)*

☆ Dundee [Brook St; NO4030], *Royal Oak*: Friendly and unusual, with sombre dark green decor and surprising range of interesting reasonably priced food esp curries in bar and restaurant; well kept Tetleys-related ales, courteous friendly staff *(Neil Townend)*

☆ Errol [The Cross; NO2523], *Old Smiddy*: Good food inc fresh local ingredients and interesting recipes, well kept Belhaven 80/-, lots of country wines, attractive heavy-beamed bar with assorted old country furniture, farm and smithy tools inc massive bellows; open all day Sun, cl Mon/Tues lunchtime *(Susan and John Douglas)*

Glenfarg [A912; nr M90 junction 9; NO1310], *Bein*: Beautifully placed, in quiet spot; big comfortable lounge bar, well kept McEwans and Theakstons, good varied food in bar and restaurant, welcoming service; can be crowded weekends; bedrooms *(Margaret and Nigel Dennis)*

☆ Kenmore [NN7745], *Kenmore Hotel*: Civilised and quietly old-fashioned small hotel beautifully set in pretty 18th-c village by Loch Tay, long landscape poem composed here written in Burns' own handwriting on residents' lounge chimneybreast, clean, friendly and smart back bar, lively separate barn bar, lovely views from back terrace; good bar food, helpful staff, restaurant, Tay fishing, fine walks; comfortable bedrooms *(Walter Reid, Susan and John Douglas, LYM)*

☆ Kinnesswood [NO1703], *Lomond*: Well appointed and friendly small inn with lovely sunset views over Loch Leven, good value bar and restaurant food strong on fresh local produce, delicious puddings, well kept Belhaven, Jennings and guest beers, helpful landlord, log fire; bedrooms comfortable (*Andy and Jill Kassube, Margaret and Nigel Dennis, Kerry Barnes*)

☆ Kinross [49 The Muirs; NO1102], *Muirs*: Carefully refurbished, with small plain standing bar with rare original Edwardian bar fittings and mirrors, second panelled bar with small pot still, lounge and supper room with banquettes; good traditional Scottish food and up to eight well kept ales such as Belhaven, Caledonian, Greenmantle and Orkney Dark Island; superb choice of malt whiskies, interesting bottled beers; lavatory for the disabled; bedrooms (*Andy and Jill Kassube*)

☆ Meiklejour [on A984; NO1539], *Meiklejour*: Two lounges, one with stripped stone, flagstones and armour, another more chintzy, both with open fires (shame about the fruit machines); helpful friendly service, good bar food inc fine range of open sandwiches and lunchtime snacks, well kept Maclays 70/-, back public bar; charming garden with tall pines and distant Highland view; nr famous 250-yr-old beech hedge over 30 m (100 ft) high (*Susan and John Douglas, Walter Reid*)

☆ Memus [NO4259], *Drovers*: Pretty little rose-covered cottage with tables out in sheltered orchard, simple and friendly inside, with roaring old-fashioned fire, Maclays IPA, McEwans 80/- and Oatmeal Stout on tall fount, choice of wines and whiskies, good choice of food inc vegetarian, pleasant service in small dining area which can be busy (*Nick and Meriel Cox, P Burvill*)

Perth [15 South St; NO1123], *Greyfriars*: Welcoming simply decorated bar with unusual guest beers on handpump, reasonably priced bar food, daily papers, prints of Perth; small restaurant upstairs (*Walter Reid*)

Pitlochry [11 Kirkmichael Rd, Moulin; NN9459], *Moulin*: Good reasonably priced food in pleasant bar and restaurant, prompt friendly service, well kept Boddingtons and a beer brewed in the pub's own microbrewery (*June and Perry Dann, Andrew Stewart*)

THE ISLANDS

Islay

☆ Port Askaig [NR4268], *Port Askaig Hotel*: Glorious sea views, buzz of ferry activity, two basic bars, one a cosy snug, with full range of the island's malt whiskies, good food inc local dishes and produce from the garden, tables out on big stretch of grass; good bedrooms (*Walter Reid*)
Port Charlotte [NR2457], *Port Charlotte*: Now fully renovated, friendly hotel with warm peat fire, well kept McEwans and Theakstons ales, several malt whiskies, good bar food, prints of sailing ships; piped music; lovely lochside views; bedrooms (*Huw and Carolyn Lewis*)

North Uist

☆ Claddach Kirkibost [NF7766], *Westford*: Very old inn in windswept desolate spot, good original home-made food inc local seafood in two small pine-fitted rooms, enterprising dinner

menu; big back public bar, local traditional music; handy for RSPB reserve at Dalranald, landlord helpful about local walks and archaeology; bedrooms (*Nigel Woolliscroft*)

Orkney

Stromness [HY2509], *Royal*: Friendly, warm and inviting, with helpful and efficient waitresses despite being busy, wide choice of food inc many local dishes, generous helpings, reasonable prices; stained-glass panels inside (*S R Spokes*)

Skye

Ardvasar [Armadale; A851 towards Broadford; NG6203], *Clan Donald Centre*: More cafeteria/restaurant than pub (part of museum with lovely woodland gardens and walks), but does have a bar, as well as good food, efficient friendly service and attractive design; good family day out (*Walter and Susan Rinaldi-Butcher, Mrs Olive Oxley*)
Portree [NG4843], *Cuillins View*: Smart-looking hotel in big grounds on outskirts, fabulous view, wide choice of good reasonably priced bar food in conservatory, S&N ales; bedrooms (*Eric Locker*); *Tongadale*: Crowded friendly bar, lively fun atmosphere, accommodating and relaxed licensees, variety of real ales; bedrooms (*Esther and John Sprinkle*)

☆ Sligachan [A850 Broadford—Portree, junction with A863; NG4830], *Sligachan Hotel*: Remote inn with almost a monopoly on the Cuillins, capacious and comfortable, with well laid-out huge modern pine-clad bar (children's play area, games room, red telephone box) separating the original basic climbers' and walkers' bar from the plusher more sedate hotel side; well kept McEwans 80/- and two ales brewed on Skye, dozens of malt whiskies on optic, quickly served bar food inc particularly fresh seafood, fine log fire, good meals in hotel restaurant, good home-made cakes and coffee; very lively some nights, with summer live entertainment and big campsite opp; bedrooms good value, cl winter (*David Atkinson, AM, Nigel Woolliscroft, RJB, Peter and Lynn Brueton, Mark and Diane Grist, John and Joan Nash, BB*)

Uig [NG3963], *Ferry*: Tiny but friendly, with very comfortable atmosphere, reasonably priced limited food inc good fresh fish and seafood; clean and comfortable bedrooms, mix of Laura Ashley and 1970s teak, overlooking pier and water (*Nigel Woolliscroft, Jackie Moffat, Mrs W E Darlaston*)

South Uist

☆ Pollachar [NF7414], *Pollachar*: Recently comfortably modernised and extended 17th-c inn in glorious setting on seashore with dolphins, porpoises and seals; big public bar, new residents' bar, separate dining room, good bar meals; very helpful friendly staff and locals (all Gaelic speaking), fantastic views to Eriskay and Barra; 12 well renovated bedrooms with own bathrooms, good breakfast (*Mrs Olive Oxley, Nigel Woolliscroft*)

Wales

Pubs which are on top form here include the very civilised Bear in Crickhowell, the Nantyffin Cider Mill just outside (excellent food), the timeless old Blue Anchor at East Aberthaw (new upstairs dining room), the Pant-yr-Ochain in Gresford (a new entry – stylish refurbishment, good food and wine), the Swan overlooking the sea at Little Haven, the Walnut Tree at Llandewi Skirrid (superb restauranty food, the best we've found in Wales), the Queens Head near Llandudno Junction (particularly good food in a quite straightforward pub), the reopened Leyland Arms at Llanelidan (another new entry, good food in relaxing surroundings), the Druid at Llanferres (good all round), the interesting old Cerrigllwydion Arms at Llanynys (real home cooking, nothing too fancy), the pleasantly old-fashioned Griffin at Llyswen (refurbished bedrooms this year), the lively Grapes at Maentwrog, the Clytha Arms outside Raglan (gaining a Food Award and Place to Stay Award this year), the New Inn at Rosebush (good food and drink in charming surroundings gain it a first main entry) and the Armstrong Arms at Stackpole (good value for a civilised meal out). As Welsh Dining Pub of the Year we choose the Nantyffin Cider Mill near Crickhowell: interesting food using good fresh ingredients, in an enjoyable pub atmosphere. The Lucky Dip section at the end of the chapter is so long that it will help if we pick out some current front-runners: in Clwyd, the Sportsmans Arms at Bylchau, West Arms at Llanarmon DC and White Lion at Llanelian yn Rhos; in Dyfed, the Druidstone Hotel at Broad Haven, Dyffryn Arms at Cwm Gwaun, Denant Mill at Dreenhill, Stanley Arms at Landshipping and Wolfe at Wolfs Castle; in Glamorgan, the Llangeinor Arms at Llangeinor (Mid), Bear in Cowbridge and Plough & Harrow at Monknash (South), Joiners Arms at Bishopston and King Arthur at Reynoldston (West); in Gwent, the Rock & Fountain at Clydach, Hunters Moon at Llangattock Lingoed, Gockett near Monmouth and Carpenters Arms at Shirenewton; in Gwynedd, the Llew Coch at Dinas Mawddwy, George III at Penmaenpool, Ship in Porthmadog, Golden Fleece at Tremadog and Lion at Tudweiliog; and in Powys, the Glansevern Arms above Llangurig, Coach & Horses at Llangynidr and Harp at Old Radnor. We have inspected and can heartily recommend the great majority of these. Drinks are now rather cheaper here than in most other parts of Britain, with the big national breweries who still dominate supplies here competing quite hard on price. However, we found pubs tied to smaller breweries such as Burtonwood and Lees particularly cheap – as was the Penhelig Arms in Aberdovey.

Local government reorganisation is splitting the principality into numerous small unitary authorities – too small to be much help in locating pubs in unfamiliar areas. So for location we use instead the names of the county-sized areas which have become familiar over the last 20 years. Some readers have suggested even broader groupings – north, south, mid and west – and we'd be interested to hear if readers generally would find this best.

ABERDOVEY (Gwynedd) SN6296 Map 6

Penhelig Arms 🍽 ⏰

Opp Penhelig railway station

The bar food at this mainly 18th-c hotel is particularly popular, and in summer you can eat out by the harbour wall while you take in the lovely views across the Dyfi estuary. Reasonably priced lunchtime dishes include soup (£1.95), sandwiches (from £1.95), duck liver pâté (£3.95), omelettes (from £4.50), lamb curry, lasagne, or whole brill (£5.95), guinea fowl cooked in burgundy with mushrooms and shallots (£6.25), as well as some fresh fish such as lemon sole fillets steamed with prawns and served with hollandaise (£6.75), and puddings like chocolate apricot frangipane tart or treacle tart (£2.20); children's helpings. Prices are a little higher in the evenings, when there may be one or two additional dishes. The excellent wine list has over 40 half bottles, champagne by the glass, two dozen malt whiskies, fruit or peppermint teas, and coffee. The small original beamed bar has a warmly cosy feel, cheery locals and winter fires, and changing real ales such as Brains SA, Marstons Pedigree or Tetleys (nicely priced below the Welsh average) on handpump; friendly, helpful service; dominoes. *(Recommended by Sue and Bob Ward, RJH, D W Jones-Williams, E Holland, Dr M Owton, David Wallington, Pearl Williams, Christopher Turner)*

Free house ~ Licensees Robert and Sally Hughes ~ Real ale ~ Meals and snacks ~ Restaurant ~ (01654) 767215 ~ Children welcome ~ Open 11-3(4 Sat), 6-11; cl 25 Dec ~ Bedrooms: £39B/£68B

ABERGORLECH (Dyfed) SN5833 Map 6

Black Lion

B4310 (a pretty road roughly NE of Carmarthen)

This pleasant old black and white pub is well placed in the beautiful Cothi Valley with the Brechfa Forest around; picnic tables and wooden seats and benches across the quiet road luxuriate in the views. The garden slopes down towards the River Cothi where there's a Roman triple-arched bridge; the licensee has fishing rights and the river is good for trout, salmon and sea trout. Many of the locals speak Welsh in the plain but comfortable atmospheric stripped-stone bar, which is traditionally furnished with plain oak tables and chairs, high-backed black settles facing each other across the flagstones by the log-effect gas fire, horsebrasses on the black beams, and some sporting prints; a restaurant extension has light oak woodwork. Bar food includes crispy coated camembert (£2.75), king prawns with seafood dip (£3.50), vegetable tikka masala (£4.30), lamb balti (£4.95), salmon in lobster and brandy sauce (£6.95) and children's meals; in summer there may be afternoon teas with a selection of home-made cakes, and Saturday barbecues. Well kept Buckleys and Worthingtons Best on handpump, and Addlestone's cider; good friendly service; sensibly placed darts, cribbage, dominoes, trivia, and unobtrusive piped music. Remy the jack russell loves to chew up beer mats. Lots of good walks nearby. *(Recommended by Richard Siebert, John and Joan Nash; more reports please)*

Free house ~ Licensee Mrs Brenda Entwistle ~ Real ale ~ Meals and snacks (not Mon evenings, and limited Mon lunch except bank holidays) ~ Restaurant ~ (01558) 685271 ~ Children welcome ~ Open 11.30-11

nr ABERYSTWYTH (Dyfed) SN6777 Map 6

Halfway Inn ★

Pisgah (not the Pisgah near Cardigan); A4120 towards Devil's Bridge, 5¾ miles E of junction with A487

This enchanting old place with its panoramic views down over the wooded hills and pastures of the Rheidol Valley is full of genuine old-fashioned charm. The friendly atmospheric beamed and flagstoned bar has stripped deal tables and settles, bare stone walls, and a dining room/restaurant area where tables can be reserved. Darts, pool and piped music (classical at lunchtimes, popular folk and country in the evenings), and well kept Felinfoel Double Dragon, Whitbreads Castle Eden and a guest like Morlands Old Speckled Hen on handpump, several draught ciders, and Welsh wines. Very tasty generously served bar food includes soup (£1.50), filled baked potatoes (from £1.75), sandwiches (from £2.25), leek and double gloucester filo tartlet in a mustard sauce or chicken liver pâté (£3.45), pork sausages (£3.75), ploughman's (£4.25), breaded plaice (£4.95), brie and broccoli pithivier (£5.50), gammon steak (£6.95), char-grilled scotch steaks (from £8.50), daily specials like vegetable lasagne (£5.25) and very tasty steak and kidney, chicken, gammon and leek and vegetable pies (£6.95); children's meals (£2.75). Outside, picnic tables under cocktail parasols have fine views; there's a very simple play area, free overnight camping for customers, and a paddock for pony-trekkers. It's particularly busy in summer, when there may be special events such as sheep shearing contests and Welsh choirs. (*Recommended by E Eastwood, Dr and Mrs S A Jones, M Joyner, Christopher Gallop, Ken and Jenny Simmonds, Jerry and Alison Oakes, John Hazel, John and Joan Nash, Jed and Virginia Brown, Liz and Roger Morgan, Tim and Tina Banks*)

Free house ~ Licensee Sally Roger ~ Real ale ~ Meals and snacks ~ Restaurant ~ (01970) 880631 ~ Children welcome in eating area of bar and restaurant ~ Live music Fri ~ Open 11.30-2.30, 6.30-11; cl for 3 weeks in Jan

BEAUMARIS (Anglesey) SH6076 Map 6

Olde Bulls Head ★ ♀ ◨

Castle Street

The quaintly old-fashioned rambling bar at this smart but cosy old place is full of reminders of its long and interesting past: a rare 17th-c brass water clock, a bloodthirsty crew of cutlasses, even the town's oak ducking stool. There's also lots of copper and china jugs, snug alcoves, low beams, low-seated settles, leather-cushioned window seats and a good open fire. The entrance to the pretty courtyard is closed by the biggest single hinged door in Britain. Very good daily changing lunchtime bar food might include sandwiches (from £1.80), home-made split pea and vegetable broth (£2), good ploughman's with welsh cheeses (£3.60), feta, olive and rocket salad (£4.25), cold poached salmon with mayonnaise (£4.95), roast chicken with tandoori spices (£5), braised ham shank with rosemary and root vegetables, smoked salmon or broccoli quiche or baked fillet of cod with garlic and herb crust (£5.25), and puddings such as lemon tart, apple, pear and walnut crumble or parfait banana and rum (£2). There is a smart restaurant. Very well kept Bass, Worthington Best and a guest on handpump, a good comprehensive list of over 180 wines (with plenty of half bottles), and freshly squeezed orange juice; cheerful, friendly service; draughts and cards. The charming bedrooms (with lots of nice little extras) are named after characters in Dickens's novels. (*Recommended by Dr W M Owton, WAH, KB, DH, the Goldsons, Andy and Jill Kassube, J R Whetton, Martin and Penny Fletcher, J Roy Smylie*)

Free house ~ Licensee David Robertson ~ Real ale ~ Lunchtime meals and snacks (not Sun – but restaurant open then) ~ Restaurant ~ Beaumaris (01248) 810329 ~ Children in eating area of bar and restaurant, no under 7s in dining room in evening ~ Open 11-11, Sun 12-10.30; cl evening 25 Dec ~ Bedrooms: £45B/£75B

BETWS-Y-COED (Gwynedd) SH7956 Map 6

Ty Gwyn ★

A5 just S of bridge to village

This cottagey family-run coaching inn is well placed for the area's multitude of attractions, but manages to maintain a nice personally welcoming atmosphere. The terms of its licence mean that you do have to eat or stay overnight if you want a drink, but the tasty bar food is imaginative, well presented and generously served. Promptly served dishes from the daily changing menu might include good soup (£2.25), lunchtime sandwiches (from £2.25), black pudding with mustard (£2.95), frog legs in garlic butter (£3.50), aubergine and mushroom stroganoff or spicy bean tortilla (£5.50), home-made curry, welsh lamb kebab or a very good huge grilled plaice (£5.95), dressed crab salad (£6.25), chicken stuffed with lobster and prawns or fresh skate (£6.95), fresh Conwy salmon with a dill and Dubonnet sauce (£7.95), local pheasant in a beaujolais and wild mushroom sauce (£8.50), individual roast lamb joint with mint and honey (£9.25), whole fresh lobster thermidor (£15.50), and puddings like plum pudding (£1.95) or from the sweet trolley (£2.50); children's menu (high chair and lots of toys available); excellent three-course Sunday lunch (£11.50). Theakstons Best on handpump, maybe two friendly cats; piped music. The beamed lounge bar has an ancient cooking range worked in well at one end, and rugs and comfortable chintz easy chairs on its oak parquet floor. The interesting clutter of unusual old prints and bric-a-brac reflects the fact that the owners run an antique shop next door. *(Recommended by Basil Minson, Mr and Mrs C Cole, J C T Tan, Barbara and Denis Melling, Phil and Heidi Cook, John and Christine Vittoe, C Smith, KC, Mike and Penny Sanders, Michael J Boniface, Pat Crabb)*

Free house ~ Licensee James Ratcliffe ~ Real ale ~ Meals and snacks ~ Restaurant ~ (01690) 710383/710787 ~ Children welcome ~ Open 12-3, 7-11 ~ Bedrooms: £19(£25B)/£35(£54B)

BODFARI (Clwyd) SJ0970 Map 6
Dinorben Arms ★ ♀

From A541 in village, follow Tremeirchion 3 signpost

The lunchtime smorgasbord is a big draw here. You help yourself and eat as much as you like from a changing range of hot soups, main courses and puddings (£8.50). Other dishes include home-made steak and kidney pie or chicken, ham and mushroom pie (£4.45), lasagne (£5.50), scampi (£5.25), grilled salmon (£5.95), seafood mornay (£6.50), sirloin steak or Welsh lamb chops (£7.95). One child can eat free if both parents are dining (except on Saturday nights). A no-smoking area in the upstairs Badger Suite has a carvery on Friday and Saturday (£12.95) and a good help-yourself farmhouse buffet on Wednesday and Thursday (£8.95). As well as a glassed-over well, the three warmly welcoming rooms which open off the heart of this carefully extended building have plenty of character, with beams hung with tankards and flagons, high shelves of china, old-fashioned settles and other seats, and three open fires; there's also a light and airy garden room; piped music. They have an impressive range of drinks: as well as Ind Coope Burton, Tetleys and a guest on handpump, they keep around 200 whiskies (including the full Macallan range and a good few from the Islay distilleries), plenty of good wines (with several classed growth clarets), vintage ports and cognacs, and quite a few unusual coffee liqueurs. There are lots of tables outside on the prettily landscaped and planted brick-floored terraces, with attractive sheltered corners and charming views, and there's a grassy play area which – like the car park – is neatly sculpted into the slope of the hills. *(Recommended by KC, Mr and Mrs A Craig, Bill and Irene Morley, Mr and Mrs E J W Rogers, J E Hilditch, Marjorie and Ken Hardcastle, Mrs J Oakes, David Peakall)*

Free house ~ Licensee David Rowlands ~ Real ale ~ Meals and snacks (12-3, 6-10.30; Sun lunchtime smorgasbord only, till 4pm) ~ Restaurant ~ (01745) 710309 ~ Children welcome ~ Open 12-3.30, 6-11; 12-11 Sun

BURTON GREEN (Clwyd) SJ3458 Map 6
Golden Grove

Off A483 N of Wrexham: heading N, turn left into B5102 from roundabout, then first right, through Burton, and at T-junction after a little over a mile turn right into Lydir Lane; OS sheet 117 map reference 354587

This peaceful old-fashioned half-timbered 13th-c coaching inn is the kind of place where everyone is welcomed as though they were a familiar local. Standing timbers and plaster separate the knocked-together rooms, which have two open fires, comfortable settees, settles and copper-topped tables, collections of plates and horsebrasses, figures carved in the beams, and a friendly, relaxed atmosphere. Very good home-made bar food changes daily and might include cream of broccoli soup (£2.50), sandwiches (from £2.50), pork and apricot terrine or chicken, leek and smoked bacon mousse (£2.95), vegetarian chilli, beef and spinach lasagne, garlic sausages and mash or spicy lamb liver casserole (£5.95), Hungarian beef with pasta, steak in ale, chicken in tarragon and cream (£6.95) and sirloin steak in peppercorn sauce (£8.95), with puddings like hot pecan pie or ginger and lemon pudding (from £2.50); summer weekend barbecue. Well kept Marstons Best and Pedigree on handpump, country wines; piped music. The big back streamside garden has a children's adventure playground with a plane, train and ship, and climbing frame. *(Recommended by Dr Jim Craig-Gray, Stephen and Julie Brown, B Eastwood, Allan Worsley, Brian and Anna Marsden; more reports please)*

Marstons ~ Tenant Steve Sharpe ~ Real ale ~ Meals and snacks ~ Restaurant ~ (01244) 570445 ~ Children welcome ~ Jazz Thurs nights ~ Open 12-3(4 Sat in winter), 6-11; 12-11 Sat in summer

CAERPHILLY (Mid Glam) ST1484 Map 6
Courthouse

Cardiff Road; one-way system heading N, snugged in by National Westminster Bank – best to park before you get to it

There are splendid views of the adjacent castle and its peaceful lake from tables out on the grassy terrace behind this 14th-c longhouse, or from the light and airy modern cafe/bar at the back (there may be exterior piped music). Much of the original age and character of this ancient place survive in the stone walls and roof and the raftered gallery. The long bar has pews, comfortable cloth-upholstered chairs and window seats, rugs on ancient flagstones, shutters and curtains on thick wooden rails for the small windows and a formidably large stone fireplace. Lunchtime bar food includes home-made filled baked potatoes (£2.25), steak baguette (£3.95), chicken or beef curry (£4.45), chicken breast with mustard and honey sauce or white wine and mushroom or beef and burgundy, chicken and mushroom or steak and ale pie (£4.95), breaded plaice (£5.45), poached salmon or seafood basket (£5.95), and children's meals (from £1.30); on the evenings when they do serve food there are a couple of extra dishes like beef wellington (£7.95). Part of the restaurant is no smoking. Well kept Courage Best, Federation Buchanans Original and Wadworths 6X on handpump, good coffee; cribbage, fruit machine and piped pop music (even outside). Note that children may not be allowed even in the garden in the evening. *(Recommended by Comus Elliott, M and A Sandy; more reports please)*

Courage ~ Lease: James Jenkins ~ Real ale ~ Meals and snacks (Mon, Fri and Sat 9.30-5.30, Tues-Thurs 9.30-9.30, Sun 12-4.30) ~ Restaurant ~ (01222) 888120 ~ Children welcome in restaurant during food serving times ~ Open 11-11, Sun 11-11; cl 25 Dec

CAREW (Dyfed) SN0403 Map 6
Carew Inn

A4075 just off A477

In spite of its fairly touristy location opposite the imposing ruins of Carew Castle, this old inn still has a thriving local atmosphere, a notably friendly welcome and a good deal of character. The snug little panelled public bar and comfortable lounge both have old-fashioned settles and scrubbed pine furniture, and interesting prints and china hanging from the beams, while a no-smoking upstairs dining room has an elegant china cabinet, a mirror over the tiled fireplace and sturdy chairs around the well spaced tables. Generously served and very reasonably priced bar food includes sandwiches (from £1.95), ploughman's (£3.50), mussels provençale (£3.50), spaghetti bolognese or chilli (£3.95), chicken, leek and mushroom or seafood pie (£5.95) and 10oz sirloin (£8.95) with daily specials such as half a pint of prawns (£2.25), home-made salmon fishcakes or chicken liver pâté (£3.50), salmon steak with tarragon sauce or seafood casserole (£6.95), orange-glazed lamb steaks or pork tenderloin with cream and mushroom sauce (£7.50) or bass (£9.95); puddings (from £1.95) and usual children's meals (from £2.25); two-course Sunday lunch (£5.95). The local mackerel can be caught and served within two hours. Well kept Crown Buckley Reverend James and Worthington Best and a summer guest such as Courage

Directors or Shepherd Neame Spitfire on handpump (£1 a pint during their 4.30-7 pm happy hour), as well as local wines and mineral waters; sensibly placed darts, dominoes, cribbage, piped music. Dogs in the public bar only. This year they've made some considerable improvements to the garden which now has a wheelchair ramp and is safely enclosed, with a sandpit, climbing frame, slide and other toys, as well as a remarkable 9th-c Celtic cross. More seats in the little flowery front garden look down to the river, where a tidal watermill is open for afternoon summer visits. *(Recommended by Mrs S Wright, M D Davies, Nick and Meriel Cox, J G Quick, Sarah Bradbury, Allan Worsley, Stuart Earle)*

Free house ~ Licensees Rob and Mandy Hinchliffe ~ Real ale ~ Snacks (not Sun lunch) and meals ~ Restaurant ~ (01646) 651267 ~ Children welcome in eating area of bar and restaurant ~ Live music Thurs evening and summer Sun evenings outside with barbecue ~ Open 11-11, 12-10.30 Sun; 12-2.30, 4.30-11 weekdays, 12-3, 7-10.30 Sun in winter ~ Bedrooms: £15/£25

CILCAIN (Clwyd) SJ1865 Map 7

White Horse

Village signposted from A494 W of Mold; OS Sheet 116 map reference 177652

This creeper-covered and flower-decked little place forms part of an idyllic cluster of stone houses, and is marked out by its attractive inn-sign. The homely parlour by the bar has exposed joists in the low ochre ceiling, mahogany and oak settles, a shelf of china and copper and a snug inglenook fireplace; there are Lloyd Loom chairs, old local photographs and a goldfish tank in the room on the right, and beyond a further little room with a piano and grandfather clock. A separate quarry-tiled bar at the back allows dogs; the whole place can fill very quickly in the evening. Well presented home-made food such as omelettes (from £4.80), spring vegetable or steak and kidney pie (£5.80), pasta dishes (from £5.90) and game pie or ham and eggs (£6.50). The chatty landlord keeps three well kept changing real ales on handpump such as Marstons Pedigree, Morlands Old Speckled Hen or Timothy Taylors Landlord. Darts, dominoes, cribbage and fruit machine. There are picnic tables at the side. Note they don't allow children inside. *(Recommended by E Holland, Iain Robertson, Graham and Lynn Mason, Elizabeth Kew, Peter Lewis; more reports please)*

Free house ~ Licensee Peter Jeory ~ Real ale ~ Meals and snacks ~ (01352) 740142 ~ Open 12-3, 7-11

CILGERRAN (Dyfed) SN1943 Map 6

Pendre

Village signposted from A478

One of the oldest pubs in West Wales, this medieval inn has massive stripped 14th-c stone walls above a panelled dado, with armchairs and settles on a beautifully polished slate floor. Good value bar food includes soup (£1.95), filled rolls (£2.40), home-made salmon and fresh herb terrine (£2.45), ploughman's (£2.70), lasagne or tortellini with mushrooms and cheese or filled yorkshire puddings (£4.50), and daily specials like mackerel (£3.00), fresh trout or cottage pie (£4.50) or crab (£4.95), with more elaborate dishes from the attractive little no-smoking restaurant menu, and cook-your-own summer barbecues; puddings (£2.50); Sunday lunch (£5.95). Bass, Worthington BB and possibly a summer guest on handpump; pool. There are seats outside, with an enclosed play area. The other end of the town leads down to the River Teifi, with a romantic ruined castle on a crag nearby, where coracle races are held on the Saturday before the August bank holiday. There's a good local wildlife park nearby, and this is a good area for fishing. *(Recommended by David Wallington, D M Wilkins, Malcolm Taylor; more reports please)*

Free house ~ Licensee Bob Lowe ~ Real ale ~ Meals and snacks (12-3, 6-9) ~ Restaurant (not Sun lunchtime) ~ (01239) 614223 ~ Children welcome ~ Open 11.30-11; 12-10.30 Sun

COLWYN BAY (Clwyd) SH8578 Map 6

Mountain View £

Mochdre; take service-road into village off link road to A470, S from roundabout at start of new A55 dual carriageway to Conwy; OS Sheet 116 map reference 825785

This very friendly neatly kept plush pub is good value for big helpings of promptly served bar food such as chilli (£2.95), cod and chips (£3.50), 8oz home-made burger (£4.95), salmon with asparagus and cheese sauce (£6.95) and joint of lamb baked in cranberry and mint sauce (£7.25). Near the entrance is a big picture of the Aberglaslyn Pass, and several others of Conwy Castle are hung throughout the spreading carpeted areas divided by arched walls, with quite a few houseplants (and bright window boxes in the large windows). Well kept real ales include Burtonwood Bitter, Buccaneer, Top Hat and Mild on handpump, as well as a good few malt whiskies and various winter warmers – hot and tasty alcoholic drinks; darts, pool, pinball, dominoes, fruit machine, table football, juke box and unobtrusive piped music (in the lounge). *(Recommended by KC, Mr and Mrs Hobden; more reports please)*

Burtonwood ~ Tenant Paul Andrew Sutherland ~ Real ale ~ Meals and snacks *(not Sun evening)* ~ (01492) 544724 ~ Children welcome in eating area ~ Karaoke Thurs night ~ Open 11.30-3.30, 6-11; 11.30-11 Sat; cl evening 25 Dec

CRESSWELL QUAY (Dyfed) SN0406 Map 6

Cresselly Arms

Village signposted from A4075

This marvellously traditional Welsh-speaking creeper-covered local is beautifully set facing the tidal creek of the Cresswell River. There are seats out by the water, and if the tides are right you can get here by boat. There's a relaxed and jaunty feel in the two simple comfortably unchanging communicating rooms, which have red and black flooring tiles, built-in wall benches, kitchen chairs and plain tables, an open fire in one room, a working Aga in the other, and a high beam-and-plank ceiling hung with lots of pictorial china. A third red-carpeted room is more conventionally furnished, with red-cushioned mate's chairs around neat tables. Well kept Flowers Original is tapped straight from the cask into glass jugs by the landlord, whose presence is a key ingredient of the atmosphere; fruit machine and winter darts. *(Recommended by Peter and Michele Rayment, Pete Baker, Martin Pritchard, Mr and Mrs Steve Thomas, Stuart Earle)*

Free house ~ Licensees Maurice and Janet Cole ~ Real ale ~ (01646) 651210 ~ Children welcome in back room ~ Open 11-3, 5-11; 11-11 Sat; 12-10.30 Sun in summer

CRICKHOWELL (Powys) SO2118 Map 6

Bear ★ ⑪ ⇔ ♀ ◗

Brecon Road; A40

The food, service, drinks and atmosphere at this civilised old coaching inn all blend together in a comfortably natural way, making this one of the best (and most popular) pubs in the Principality. Beautifully presented bar meals might include substantial Thai toasts with chilli dip (£3.95), locally smoked salmon with scrambled egg and chives, creamed garlic mushrooms with sherry and herbs, mussels with onions and lardons of smoky bacon in garlic butter or laverbread and cockle cakes with grilled bacon (£4.95), smoked haddock fishcakes (£5.50), smoked salmon salad (£5.95), chicken in tarragon and lime (£6.50), Moroccan-style lamb (£6.95), Welsh lamb hock with thyme and rosemary (£8.50), and very good puddings like bread, banana and butter pudding, treacle or lemon sponge, and home-made rum and brown bread ice cream (from £2.95). Well kept Bass, John Smiths, Ruddles Best and County on handpump; malt whiskies, vintage and late-bottled ports, and unusual wines and liqueurs, with some hops tucked in among the bottles. The heavily beamed lounge has lots of little plush-seated bentwood armchairs and handsome cushioned antique settles, and a window seat looking down on the market square. Up by the great roaring log fire, a big sofa and leather easy chairs are spread among the rugs on the oak parquet floor; antiques include a fine oak dresser filled with pewter and brass, a longcase clock and interesting prints. This year a sympathetic extension has added a separate dining area. It can get terribly busy, but service remains welcoming and friendly; piped music. The back bedrooms – particularly in the quieter new block – are the most highly recommended, though there are three more bedrooms in the pretty cottage at the end of the garden. Lovely window boxes, and you can eat in the garden in summer. *(Recommended by Verity Combes, John and Joan Nash, Phil Putwain, Gavin May, Margaret and Nigel Dennis, PM, AM, Jane and Adrian Tierney-Jones, A R and B E Sayer, Mrs P Goodwin, A P Jeffreys, Rob Holt, James House, Gwen and Peter Andrews, E Carter, Adam Neil, J Honnor, Graham and Glenis Watkins, TBB, William Russell, Howard James, David Shillitoe, G Washington, Pat and John Millward, Mike Pugh, John Hibberd)*

Free house ~ Licensee Mrs Judy Hindmarsh ~ Real ale ~ Meals and snacks (till 10pm) ~ Restaurant (not Sun evening) ~ (01873) 810408 ~ Children welcome in eating area of bar ~ Open 11-3, 6-11; cl 25 Dec ~ Bedrooms: £42B/£56B

nr CRICKHOWELL (Powys) SO2118 Map 6
Nantyffin Cider Mill 🍴 ♀
1½ miles NW, by junction A40/A479
Wales Dining Pub of the Year

The beautifully presented food at this handsome pink-washed inn is easily restaurant standard, but the smartly traditional pubby atmosphere leaves the place feeling more like a brasserie. Relying heavily on local produce and with fresh fish and seafood from Cornwall, the changing range of meals might include starters such as Thai style chicken (£4.35) or roast pepper with parma ham, basil pesto and goat's cheese (£4.45) and main courses such as salmon and spinach fishcakes, lamb, leek and potato pie or lasagne (£6.50), ragout of fish and shellfish (£6.95) and provençal casseroled chicken joints or char-grilled marinaded pork steak (£7.50), with daily specials like char-grilled squid with chilli (£4.95), squab braised in cider (£10.50) or john dory on a fennel and orange casserole (£10.95), rump of lamb with bubble and squeak (£11.25), and puddings like pecan pie or white chocolate cheesecake (£3.30); children's meals or helpings. The look of the place is smartly traditional, with a woodburner in a fine broad fireplace, warm grey stonework, cheerful bunches of fresh and dried flowers, and good solid comfortable tables and chairs. The bar at one end of the main open-plan area has well kept Arkells William Spenser, Bass and Brains SA well kept on handpump, with draught ciders, and good wines, several by the glass or half bottle. A raftered barn with a big cider press has been converted into quite a striking restaurant. The building faces an attractive stretch of the River Usk, and has charming views from the tables out on the lawn above its neat car park. A ramp makes disabled access easy. *(Recommended by Mrs P Goodwyn, Margaret and Nigel Dennis, Ian Williams, Linda Mar, A R and B E Sayer, Caroline Raphael, M D Davies, R C Morgan, Mrs Brenda Calver, W Marsh, Colin McKerrow)*

Free house ~ Licensees Glyn Bridgeman, Sean Gerrard ~ Real ale ~ Meals and snacks (till 10pm) ~ Restaurant (not Sun evening) ~ (01873) 810775 ~ Children welcome ~ Open 12-3, 6-11; cl Mon

EAST ABERTHAW (South Glamorgan) ST0367 Map 6
Blue Anchor ★ 🍺
B4265

This wonderfully unspoilt old thatched inn can barely have changed since it was built in the late 14th c. Low-beamed cosy rooms, nooks and crannies still wander through massive stone walls and tiny doorways (watch your head!), and there are open fires everywhere, including one in an inglenook with antique oak seats built into its stripped stonework. Other seats and tables are worked into a series of chatty little alcoves, and the more open front bar still has an ancient lime-ash floor; darts, dominoes, fruit machine. At lunchtime very good value tasty bar food includes sandwiches (from £1.95), soup (£2.25), filled baked potatoes (from £2.75), salads (from £4.65), roast pork, chicken, ham and mushroom pie or tagliatelle with peppers, onions and mushrooms (£4.75), with half a dozen dishes of the day such as grilled fillet of hake with prawns, tomato and tarragon or supreme of chicken marinated in lemon and honey (£5.50) or grilled monkfish in pesto sauce (£5.75); puddings (£2.10), and children's meals (£2.25). The evening menu is pricier but more elaborate, for example warm salad of black pudding, smoked bacon and calf liver (£3.95), roast duck with blackcurrant, apple and calvados (£11.95) and medaillons of beef on an onion and horseradish galette with crushed peppercorn and red wine sauce (£12.95). There is a newly opened restaurant upstairs. Carefully kept Boddingtons, Buckleys Best, Flowers IPA, Marstons Pedigree, Theakstons Old Peculier, Wadworths 6X and a frequently changing guest on handpump. Rustic seats shelter peacefully among tubs and troughs of flowers outside, with more stone tables on a newer terrace. From here a path leads to the shingly flats of the estuary. The pub can get packed in the evenings and on summer weekends, and it's a shame the front seats are right beside the car park. *(Recommended by Jason Aspinall, E Holland, A R and B E Sayer, Jonathan Davies, John and Joan Nash, Howard James, Risha Stapleton, Mr and Mrs Steve Thomas, Nigel Clifton)*

Free house ~ Licensee Jeremy Coleman ~ Real ale ~ Meals and snacks (not Sat evening or Sun) ~ Evening restaurant (not Sun) ~ (01446) 750329 ~ Children welcome till 8pm if eating ~ Open 11-11; 12-10.30 Sun

ERBISTOCK (Clwyd) SJ3542 Map 6

Boat

Village signposted from A539 W of Overton, then pub signposted

This busy dining pub is enchantingly set virtually alone by a country church, looking out over the sleepy River Dee, with ducks, grebes and maybe a heron on the water and more birds singing in the steep woodland opposite. Old-fashioned seats by tables under cocktail parasols on a gravel terrace are surrounded by flowers and charming informal up-and-down lawns, with hanging baskets adorning the pub itself, and in early summer what amounts to a curtain of flowers on the low sandstone cliff behind it. Inside the character of the place is almost that of a restaurant, and drinkers (most of them going on to eat) really have just the one small bar with oak tripod tables on crazy-paved flagstones, spindleback chairs, and a fire in an open-grate kitchen range. Tasty lunchtime bar food includes sandwiches (from £2.25), soup (£2.75), fried liver, kidneys and bacon in red wine (£3.50), ploughman's (£3.95), steak and kidney pie, cumberland sausage ring, gammon steak, pasta with mushrooms and broccoli in cheese sauce or cold poached salmon with lemon mayonnaise (£5.95), lamb chops with redcurrant sauce (£6.95) and baked cod fillet in tomato sauce (£7.45). The comfortable beamed no-smoking dining room, with plush seats around antique oak tables, has small windows overlooking the river. New licensees since this pub last appeared in the Guide have introduced two well kept real ales which might be Burtonwood, Cains, Hook Norton or Plassey, alongside a good range of malt whiskies; piped music. *(Recommended by Gail Kendall, Kent Miller, Bob and Sue Ward, Paul Weston)*

Free house ~ Licensee J Williams ~ Real ale ~ Lunchtime meals and snacks ~ Restaurant ~ (01978) 780143 ~ Children welcome in restaurant, over 5 in evenings ~ Open 12-3, 6.30-11; 12-11.30(10.30 Sun) Sat; cl Sat afternoon and Sun eve in winter

GRESFORD (Clwyd) SJ3555 Map 6

Pant-yr-Ochain ♀

Old Wrexham Road (B5445 N of Wrexham)

This roomy pub has been most attractively decorated, with a wide range of interesting prints and bric-a-brac on its walls and on shelves, and a good mix of individually chosen country furnishings including comfortable seats for chatting as well as more upright ones for eating. There are good open fires, and the big dining area is set out as a library, with books floor to ceiling. Consistently good interesting food from a menu that changes about every three months might include parsnip and fennel soup (£2.45), chicken liver terrine or chicken satay (£3.95), ploughman's (£4.95), feta cheese, spinach and pine kernel strudel with tomato sauce (£7.75), marinated chicken breast on a bed of stir fried vegetables (£8.25), poached salmon supreme with fresh asparagus and lemon and tarragon butter (£8.95) and braised half shoulder of lamb with port wine and redcurrant sauce (£9.45). They have a good range of decent wines, strong on up-front New World ones, as well as Boddingtons, Flowers Original, Plassey Bitter, Timothy Taylor Landlord and a guest like Plassey Dragon Breath under light blanket pressure, and a good collection of malt whiskies. Service is polite and efficient. This is in the same small family of pubs as the Grosvenor Arms at Aldford (see Cheshire main entries), and not dissimilar in style and gently up-market atmosphere; one room is no smoking; piped music. *(Recommended by Dr Andrew Schuman, Anna Brewer, P H Boot)*

Free house ~ Licensee Duncan Lochead ~ Real ale ~ Meals and snacks (12-9.30 Sun) ~ (01978) 853525 ~ Children welcome at lunchtime ~ Open 11.30-3, 5.30-11; 12-10.30 Sun; cl 25 Dec evening and 26 Dec

HALKYN (Clwyd) SJ2172 Map 6
Britannia

Pentre Rd, off A55 for Rhosesmor

On a fine day the fabulous views from the partly no-smoking dining conservatory and terrace of this cosy old place stretch to Liverpool and the Wirral, and you may even be able to pick out Blackpool tower and Beeston Castle; it's best to book if you want a window table. Although much extended, the recent new additions to this handy north coast stop blend well with the original 15th-c farm building. The cosy unspoilt lounge bar has some very heavy beams, with horsebrasses, harness, jugs, plates and other bric-a-brac; there's also a games room with darts, pool, dominoes, juke box, fruit machine and piped music. Reasonably priced bar food includes soup (£1.10), sandwiches (from £2.35), black pudding or barbecue spare ribs (£2.50), cumberland sausage (£3.95), lasagne (£4.35), minted lamb and barley casserole or steak and kidney pie (£4.95), curry of the day (£5.25), garlic and herb chicken breast (£5.65), pork steak with pepper sauce (£6.25) and barbecue loin of lamb (£7.25); puddings (£1.95), usual children's menu (£1.95). Well kept Lees Bitter, Moonraker and Mild on handpump, a dozen or so malt whiskies, and a choice of coffees. *(Recommended by Phil Putwain, KC, B A and R Davies, Mr and Mrs A E McCully, Andy and Jill Kassube; more reports please)*

J W Lees ~ Tenant Keith Pollitt ~ Real ale ~ Meals and snacks (till 10pm) ~ Restaurant ~ (01352) 780272 ~ Children welcome ~ Open 11-11; 10.30-3, 5-11 in winter; 12-10.30 summer Sun

HAY ON WYE (Powys) SO2342 Map 6
Old Black Lion 🛏 ♀

26 Lion St

This lovely old hotel sits on the town wall and was once the gatehouse to this civilised little medieval town, now internationally famous for the plethora of secondhand and antiquarian bookshops that line its steep twisting streets. The smartly civilised and attractive bar has low beams, some black panelling, old pine tables, an oak and mahogany bar counter and two old timber and glass screens; it's candlelit at night. A wide choice of thoughtful and very carefully prepared bar meals includes sandwiches (from £2.75), smoked duck salad with plum sauce (£4.95), ploughman's (from £4.95), home-made venison burger or turkey and herb lasagne (£5.95), grilled smoked fish on toasted brioche with horseradish sauce (£6.40), lamb moussaka (£6.95), seafood vol au vent (£7.35), Welsh lamb stew (£7.40), spicy venison casserole (£7.65), 8oz sirloin steak (£10.55), and half a dozen imaginative dishes of the day such as braised shank of lamb with kashmiri spices or duck supreme on fennel and chicory flavoured with rosemary. In the evening there are lots more dishes such as goat's cheese salad (£4.70), mousseline of sole (£4.95), roast monkfish with garlic on a pepper sauce or tenderloin of pork wrapped in filo pastry filled with fennel, garlic and rosemary (£11.25). Eight imaginative vegetarian dishes include Thai coconut stir fry, tagliatelle with wild mushrooms, bacon and chick peas or penne with a spicy tomato sauce (from £5.55); puddings include steamed lemon and rhubarb with citrus custard and fresh fruit salad (£3.25). The cottagey restaurant, also candlelit, is no smoking. Well kept Flowers Original and Wye Valley Hereford Supreme on handpump (the cellar's air-conditioned) – as well as an extensive good value wine list and lots of liqueur coffees. A sheltered back terrace has some tables. The inn has trout and salmon fishing rights on the Wye, and can arrange pony trekking and golf. If you plan to stay we recommend booking well in advance. *(Recommended by Revd A Nunnerley, RJH, Gwen and Peter Andrews, KB, DH, Gill and Maurice McMahon, Sue Demont, Tim Barrow, Barry Watling, GWB, Barry and Anne, W C M Jones, Geoff and Angela Jacques, Karen Eliot, Nigel Clifton, Nigel Wilkinson)*

Free house ~ Licensees John and Joan Collins ~ Real ale ~ Meals and snacks ~ Restaurant ~ (01497) 820841 ~ Children over 5 in eating area of bar and over 8 in restaurant ~ Open 11-11; 12-10.30 Sun; breakfasts from 8.30am ~ Bedrooms: £20.95B/£45.90B

KENFIG (Mid Glamorgan) SS8383 Map 6

Prince of Wales £ 🍺

2¼ miles from M4 junction 37; A4229 towards Porthcawl, then right when dual carriageway narrows on bend, signposted Maudlam and Kenfig

Most unusally for a pub, this unspoilt and unpretentious old local houses the local Sunday school, as well as the alderman's mace, a relic from the days when this scatter of houses among windswept dunes was an important medieval port. With its walls stripped back to the stone, the friendly relaxed main bar has heavy settles and red leatherette seats around a double row of close-set cast-iron-framed tables, a warming open fire, and small storm windows. A very good range of well kept real ales might include Bass, Brains SA, Morlands Old Speckled Hen, Wadworths 6X and guests, some tapped from the cask, others on handpump; a good selection of malt whiskies. Simple home-made bar food is very tasty and quickly served, with large filled rolls or sandwiches (from £1.10 – the home-roasted meat is well done) and home-made steak pie, chicken and mushroom pie and roast of the day (£4.95). In summer all the vegetables and potatoes come from the garden, and the eggs are from their own hens. Dominoes, cribbage and card games. There's a nature reserve just across the road, and plenty of rewarding walks nearby. *(Recommended by F A Owens, John and Pat Smyth, David Holloway, John and Joan Nash, Mr and Mrs A Plumb, Stuart Earle, Eddy Street)*

Free house ~ Licensee Jeremy Evans ~ Real ale ~ Meals and snacks (till 10pm) ~ Restaurant ~ (01656) 740356 ~ Children welcome ~ Open 11.30-4, 6-11; cl evening 25 Dec

LITTLE HAVEN (Dyfed) SM8512 Map 6

Swan

This welcoming place gives lovely views across the broad and sandy hill-sheltered cove from seats in its bay window, or from the sea wall outside (just the right height for sitting on). The two communicating rooms have quite a cosily intimate feel, as well as comfortable high-backed settles and windsor chairs, a winter open fire, and old prints on walls that are partly stripped back to the original stonework. Cooked by the landlord, the compact choice of well liked lunchtime bar food includes home-made soup (£2.25), sandwiches (from £1.50), ploughman's (from £3.75), crab bake (£4.25), sardines grilled with spinach, egg and mozzarella (£4.50), chicken curry (£4.95), ham salad (£5.75) and locally smoked salmon (£6.95), and home-made puddings (from £2.50). No credit cards. Well kept Felinfoel Double Dragon, Wadworths 6X and Worthington BB on handpump from the heavily panelled bar counter, and a good range of wines and whiskies; pleasant, efficient service. Little Haven is one of the prettiest coastal villages in west Wales, and the pub is right on the coast path. *(Recommended by Christopher Turner, Ian Rorison, Drs R and M Woodford, Dr G W Barnett, E J Wilde, W H Cooke, Richard Siebert, Professor I H Rorison)*

James Williams (who no longer brew) ~ Tenants Glyn and Beryl Davies ~ Real ale ~ Lunchtime meals and snacks ~ Tiny evening restaurant (Weds-Sat, bookings only in winter) ~ (01437) 781256 ~ Open 11-3, 6(7 winter)-11; cl evening 25 Dec

LLANBEDR-Y-CENNIN (Gwynedd) SH7669 Map 6

Olde Bull

Village signposted from B5106

There is a lovely big wild garden with a waterfall and orchard, a fish pond, and plenty of seats at this prettily set 16th-c drovers' inn. Inside, the knocked-through rooms are full of massive low beams (some salvaged from a wrecked Spanish Armada ship), elaborately carved antique settles, a close crowd of cheerfully striped stools, brassware, photographs, Prussian spiked helmets, and good open fires (one in an inglenook); there might be some subdued classical music or opera in the background. Well kept Lees Bitter and Mild on handpump from wooden barrels, and several malt whiskies; friendly service. The good changing bar food might include soup (£1.50), sandwiches (from £1.95), filled baked potatoes (from £2.80), sausage, egg and black pudding (£3.45), an elaborate danish open sandwich (£3.75), ploughman's (£3.95), steak and kidney pie (£4.95), mushroom tagliatelle or plaice filled with prawns and mushroom sauce (£5.75), and evening dishes like salmon or chicken pancakes (£8) or duck breast with orange, damson and port sauce (£8.65). The pub is popular with walkers. Darts, dominoes, cribbage, cards, chess and dominoes. Lavatories are outside. *(Recommended by Barbara Wensworth, Roger Byrne, Beryl and Bill Farmer, A and J Tierney-Jones, Liz and Roger Morgan, Tim and Tina Banks, Paul Bailey, John A Barker, Dave Thompson, Margaret Mason, J Roy Smylie)*

Lees ~ Tenant Paavo Alexander Salminen ~ Real ale ~ Meals and snacks (not winter Sun evenings or Mon) ~ Restaurant ~ (01492) 660508 ~ Children welcome ~ Open 12-3, 7(6.30 Sat)-11; closed winter lunchtimes

nr LLANBERIS (Gwynedd) SH6655 Map 6

Pen-y-Gwryd 🖙 ◗

Nant Gwynant; at junction of A498 and A4086, ie across mountains from Llanberis – OS Sheet 115 map reference 660558

This magnificently set old inn, isolated high in the mountains of Snowdonia, has for generations been a great favourite among mountaineers. The rugged slate-floored climbers' bar is like a log cabin, and doubles as a mountain rescue post; there's also a smaller room with a collection of illustrious boots back from famous climbs, and a cosy panelled smoke room with more climbing mementoes and equipment. Like many other mountaineers, the team that first climbed Everest in 1953 used the inn as a training base, leaving their fading signatures scrawled on the ceiling. A snug little room with built-in wall benches and sturdy country chairs lets you contemplate the majestic surrounding mountain countryside – like precipitous Moel-siabod beyond the lake opposite. There's a hatch where you order lunchtime bar meals: good robust helpings of home-made food such as soup (£1.80) and pâté or ploughman's with home-baked french bread or quiche (£3.50). In the evening residents sit down together for the hearty and promptly served dinner (check on the time when you book); the dining room is no smoking. As well as Bass under light blanket pressure, and mulled wine in winter, they serve sherry from their own solera in Puerto Santa Maria; friendly, obliging service. This is a particularly enjoyable place to stay: residents have their own charmingly furnished, panelled sitting room, a sauna out among the trees, and table tennis, darts, pool, bar billiards, table skittles, dominoes, and shove-ha'penny. Bedrooms are clean and sensible rather than luxurious; one has an unusual Edwardian bath in it, and another an older Victorian one colourfully decked out with raised fruit and flowers – the V & A apparently say they've never seen anything like it. *(Recommended by Mr and Mrs B Langrish, Mr and Mrs C Cole, Martin Howard Pritchard, Jenny and Brian Seller, Nigel Woolliscroft, John and Joan Nash; also in Good Hotel Guide)*

Free house ~ Licensees Jane and Brian Pullee ~ Real ale ~ Lunchtime meals and snacks ~ Evening restaurant ~ (01286) 870211 ~ Children welcome in eating area of bar ~ Open 11-11; no drinks on Sun except to residents; cl Nov ~ Bedrooms: £20(£25B)/£40(£50B)

LLANCARFAN (South Glamorgan) ST0570 Map 6
Fox & Hounds

Village signposted from A4226; also reached from B4265 via Llancadle or A48 from Bonvilston

There are tables under flowering trees beside a little stream overhung by a thicket of honeysuckle at the back of this prettily set dining pub. Rambling through arches, the neatly kept comfortably modernised carpeted bar has high-backed traditional settles as well as plush banquettes around its copper-topped cast-iron tables, a coal fire in winter, and a weekly changing real ale such as Fullers London Pride; bin ends. Bar food includes things like spicy wedges with sour cream and salsa (£2.50), beef carbonnade (£4.75), Thai spiced prawns with rice (£5.25) and supreme of chicken marinated in ginger, lemon, honey and garlic (£5.75). There's also a candlelit bistro. Darts, fruit machine, unobtrusive piped music. The neighbouring church and churchyard are interesting. *(Recommended by R M Richards, Gareth and Kay Jones, Richard Mattick, Nigel Clifton; more reports please)*

Free house ~ Licensee Michael Ashmore ~ Real ale ~ Meals and snacks ~ (01446) 781297 ~ Children welcome ~ Open 11.30-3, 6-11; 11-11 Sat; 12-10.30 Sun

LLANDEWI SKIRRID (Gwent) SO3416 Map 6
Walnut Tree ★ ⓊⒾ ♀

B4521

This splendid place is best thought of as a restaurant, but unlike many pubs that have excluded themselves from our pages by taking on the atmosphere and style of a restaurant (complete with sniffy intolerance of people who just want a drink or a snack), the Walnut Tree sets a fine example with its warmly relaxed and informal atmosphere, and easy tolerance of those who do pop in for just a drink or a one-course meal. The excellent imaginative food combines strong southern European leanings with an almost fanatical pursuit of top-class fresh and often recherché ingredients. It includes carefully prepared soups such as asparagus and tarragon (£3.95), crispy crab pancakes (£5.45), bruschetta with seafood (£6.75), home-made Italian sausages with butter beans (£6.95), black and white fettucine with smoked salmon and dill (£8.95), half-a-dozen oysters (£8.75), vegetarian platter (£9.95), panache of skate and scallops with balsamic dressing (£10.65), lamb sweetbreads with wild mushrooms, parma ham and marsala (£11.95), escalope of salmon with rhubarb and ginger (£12.85), pigeon with lentils, sausage and bacon (£12.95), roast monkfish with scallops, prawns and laverbread sauce (£14.95) and seafood platter (£23.90); vegetables are £2.75 extra. Puddings are delicious – just try that toulouse chestnut pudding (£5.55); no credit cards, and £1 cover charge. The attractive choice of wines is particularly strong in Italian ones (they import their own), and the house wines by the glass are good value. The small white-walled bar has some polished settles and country chairs around the tables on its flagstones, and a log-effect gas fire. It opens into an airy and relaxed dining lounge with rush-seat Italianate chairs around gilt cast-iron-framed tables. There are a few white cast-iron tables outside in front. *(Recommended by David Peel, Christopher Gallop, Pat and John Millward, Gwen and Peter Andrews, Verity Combes, Mike and Ruth Dooley, BW, SJ, A J Bowen, R W Saunders, Andrew Stephenson, Nigel Wilkinson)*

Free house ~ Licensees Ann and Franco Taruschio ~ Meals and snacks (12-3, 7-10.15, not Sun or Mon) ~ Restaurant (not Sun or Mon) ~ (01873) 852797 ~ Children welcome ~ Open 12-4, 7-12; cl Sun and Mon

LLANDRINDOD WELLS (Powys) SO0561 Map 6
Llanerch £ 🍺

Waterloo Road; from centre, head for station

There is a really cheerful atmosphere in the busy bar of this highly individual 16th-c town local, which has peaceful mountain views looking over the Ithon Valley from tables on a back terrace. This leads on to a garden (with boules), and a front play area and orchard give it all the feeling of a country pub. The squarish beamed main bar has old-fashioned settles snugly divided by partly glazed partitions, and a big stone fireplace that's richly decorated with copper and glass; there are more orthodox button-back banquettes in communicating lounges (one of which is no smoking at lunchtimes and early evenings). Very good value straightforward bar food includes soup (£1.75), sandwiches (from £1.75), filled baked potatoes (from £2.25), vegetable pancake rolls (£2.95), fisherman's pie, lasagne, or meat and potato pie (£3.25), salads (from £4.50), steak and kidney pie (£4.75), and children's meals (from £1.75), and evening extras like chicken bonne femme or beef bourguignon (£5.50). Well kept Hancocks HB and two guests like Timothy Taylors Landlord and Worthington Best on handpump. Service is prompt and generally friendly, though visitors won't be treated as anything special; fruit machine, video game, trivia and piped music, while a separate pool room has darts, cribbage and dominoes. *(Recommended by Joan and Michel Hooper-Immins, George Atkinson, Peter and Audrey Dowsett, Howard James, N J Clifton)*

Free house ~ Licensee John Leach ~ Real ale ~ Meals and snacks ~ Restaurant ~ (01597) 822086 ~ Children welcome away from main bar area ~ Occasional live music Sat in summer ~ Open 11.30-3(2.30 winter), 6-11 ~ Bedrooms: £32.50B/£49B(cheaper at weekends)

nr LLANDUDNO JUNCTION (Gwynedd) SH8180 Map 6
Queens Head 🍽 🍷

Glanwydden; heading towards Llandudno on A546 from Colwyn Bay, turn left into Llanrhos Road as you enter the Penrhyn Bay speed limit; Glanwydden is signposted as the first left turn off this

It's quite a surprise to find the very good food at this modest-looking village pub, and as the secret isn't that well kept you do need to get there early to be sure of a table. Carefully prepared and generously served home-made meals might include soup such as fresh pea and mint (£1.95), open rolls (from £3.50), home-made pâtés such as smoked trout (£3.75), smoked goose breast with kiwi fruit (£4.35), baked black pudding with apple and brandy (£4.50), lasagne (£5.25), local mussels in garlic butter and topped with smoked local cheese (£6.25), salads (from £5.75), salmon and pasta bake (£6.45), sautéed lamb sweetbreads (£6.75), chicken, ham and mushroom pie (£6.50), grilled lamb cutlets with fresh raspberry and amaretto sauce (£8.50), peppered monkfish with mustard sauce (£8.75) and half a lobster (£11.50). The evening menu has extra dishes like steamed breast of chicken filled with sun-dried tomatoes, coated with a spinach and nutmeg cream (£8.75), or medaillons of beef in Guinness and pickled walnuts (£8.95). Delicious puddings include bread and butter pudding, treacle tart and orange and liqueur trifle (£2.50). Fresh local produce is firmly in evidence, and even the mints with the coffee might be home-made. Well kept Benskins, Ind Coope Burton, Tetleys and maybe a guest like Youngs on handpump, decent wines, several malts, and good coffee, maybe served with a bowl of whipped cream. The spacious and comfortably modern lounge bar has brown plush wall banquettes and windsor chairs around neat black tables and is partly divided by a white wall of broad arches and wrought-iron screens; there's also a little public bar. There are some tables out by the car park. No dogs. *(Recommended by Jane and Adrian Tierney-Jones, Mike and Wendy Proctor, J E Hilditch, KC, AW, BW, J R Whetton, Maysie Thompson, Mr and Mrs Jones, F C Johnston)*

Ansells (Carlsberg Tetleys) ~ Lease: Robert and Sally Cureton ~ Real ale ~ Meals and snacks ~ (01492) 546570 ~ Children over 7 only ~ Open 11-3, 6-11; cl 25 Dec

LLANELIDAN (Clwyd) SJ1150 Map 6
Leyland Arms

Village signposted from A494, S of Ruthin; pub is on B5429 just E of village; OS Sheet 116, map reference 110505

This unusual and very relaxing pub is part of a cluster of former farm buildings by a country church, separated by a stretch of quiet fields from the village itself. In fact it's what used to be the dairy of the original village inn (the much grander building in front, which you see first as you approach). Reopened after several years' closure, it's been sensitively refurnished in an attractive country style, with little bunches of flowers on dark wood tables, and mugs hanging from the beams of the smaller room by the servery; pool, juke box and fruit machine in the games room. Very good food might include lunchtime sandwiches (from £2.65), ploughman's (from £4.25), deep fried camembert (£5.25), chicken balti (£6.95), hot and spicy cajun prawns, cod in lemon sauce or smoked ham and continental cheese salad (£7.25), dimsum or steak and kidney pie (£7.50) and venison steak in juniper berry sauce (£10.95), and a more elaborate evening menu with filo pasty basket with leeks and caerphilly (£3.75), chicken in wild mushroom, cream and brandy or lamb cutlets in redcurrant jelly (£8.50), pork in cream, apple and brandy (£8.95) and salmon in Pernod or sirloin steak in pepper or stilton sauce (£9.25). Their home-baked soda bread is delicious, and the midweek lunches (three courses for £7, decent choice) are a bargain. Welcoming licensees, good friendly service, good coffee plus well kept Bass and Worthington on handpump. Though the food is a powerful draw, this isn't just a dining pub; the atmosphere gains a lot from local people dropping in for a drink (and from the absence of piped music). Tables out in the charming garden, with a dozy background of bird and animal noises. *(Recommended by KC, John and Anne Heaton)*

Free house ~ Licensee Elizabeth Meikle ~ Real ale ~ Meals and snacks (till 10 Fri and Sat; not Mon) ~ (01824) 750502 ~ Children welcome ~ Open 11-2.30, 7-11; 12-4, 6-10.30 Sun; cl 25 Dec evening

LLANFERRES (Clwyd) SJ1961 Map 7

Druid 🍺

A494 Mold—Ruthin

The very satisfying combination of consistently good imaginative food, a lovely welcoming atmosphere and delightful location in good walking country make this extended 17th-c inn a good choice for a weekend break. Tables outside sheltered in a corner of the building by a low wall with rock-plant pockets make the most of the view looking down over the road to the Alyn valley and the Craig Harris mountains beyond, as does the broad bay window in the civilised and sympathetically refurbished smallish plush lounge. You can also see the hills from the bigger beamed back bar, also carpeted (with quarry tiles by the log fire), with its two handsome antique oak settles as well as a pleasant mix of more modern furnishings. The attractive dining area, two rooms newly opened together, is relatively smoke-free, and service is very obliging. The interesting range of good bar food includes tomato and coriander or chicken and lemon grass soup (£1.95), delicious granary baps filled with mozzarella and mushroom, sirloin steak, chicken fillet and lemon mayonnaise or pepperoni and mozzarella (£2.95), black pudding with redcurrant jelly or apple sauce (£1.95), stilton-stuffed mushrooms or mussels and mozzarella cheese in a creamy pesto sauce with garlic bread (£2.95), steak and mushroom pie with good pastry (£5.25), tagliatelle with lots of prawns (£5.55), fillet of chicken in a creamy chilli sauce (£7.95), duck breast with oyster sauce (£8.25), fillet steak with bearnaise sauce (£11.50), and good vegetarian dishes such as baked mushrooms and sweet peppers with mozzarella; vegetables are fresh and generous. Well kept Burtonwood Best and Forshaws on handpump, decent malt whiskies and wine list; games area with darts and pool, also dominoes, bagatelle, Jenga and other board games; maybe unobtrusive piped music. *(Recommended by Robert Woodward, Ian Jones, Andrew Shore, KC, Peter and Jan Humphreys, J S M Sheldon, Mrs J Jones, Mr and Mrs M St-Amour)*

Burtonwood ~ Tenant James Dolan ~ Real ale ~ Meals and snacks (when open, till 10pm) ~ Restaurant ~ (01352) 810225 ~ Children welcome ~ Traditional piano sing-along one Sat a month ~ Open 12-3(4 Sun), 5.30-11; 12-11 Sat and bank hol Mon ~ Bedrooms: £18.75/£34.50

Planning a day in the country? We list pubs in really attractive scenery at the back of the book.

LLANFIHANGEL CRUCORNEY (Gwent) SO3321 Map 6

Skirrid

Village signposted off A465 nr Abergavenny

This ancient dark brown stone inn makes the most of its ancient past. It served as the area's courthouse, and between 1110 and the 17th c nearly 200 people were hanged here; you can still see the scorch and drag marks of the rope on the beam above the foot of the stairs which served as the traditional scaffold. The inn still has some medieval windows, oak beams made from ship's timbers, and panelling in the dining room that's said to be from a British man o' war. The high-ceilinged bar has settles and wooden tables on its flagstones, walls stripped back to show ancient stonework, and a big open fire with winter roast chestnuts in the stone hearth. Good bar food in substantial helpings includes sandwiches, home-made soup, vegetarian loaf (£5.95), welsh cheeses with bread and home-made pickles (£5.25), venison sausages with warm home-made apricot and raisin chutney (£6.95) and local lamb chops glazed with an apple and rosemary jelly (£7.25). Well kept Ushers Best, Founders and seasonal brews on handpump, a range of malt whiskies; darts, pool and piped music. It's possible they won't serve food if they are expecting a coach party. A crazy-paved back terrace has white seats and tables, and there are more rustic ones on a small sloping back lawn. *(Recommended by Neil and Anita Christopher, R A and E B Sayer, S H Godsell, Gavin May, Barry and Anne, Gwyneth and Salvo Spadaro-Dutturi, M G Hart, Mike and Ruth Dooley, Rick and Vicki Blechta, Nigel Clifton, Mr and Mrs E H Warner, Mike and Wendy Proctor, Chamberlain)*

Ushers ~ Lease: Heather Gant ~ Real ale ~ Meals and snacks (snacks only Sun eve) ~ Restaurant ~ (01873) 890258 ~ Children welcome ~ Occasional folk singer ~ Open 11-3, 6-11 ~ Bedrooms: £25B/£50B

LLANFRYNACH (Powys) SO0725 Map 6

White Swan 🍺

Village signposted from B4558, just off A40 E of Brecon bypass

There is an enjoyably tranquil atmosphere in the rambling lounge bar of this pretty black and white pub, friendly and relaxed with its series of softly lit alcoves, plenty of well spaced tables on the flagstones, partly stripped stone walls, a roaring log fire and maybe piped classical music. A secluded terrace behind with plenty of stone and other tables is attractively divided into sections by roses and climbing shrubs, and overlooks peaceful paddocks. Very good bar food in generous helpings from a sensible menu includes french onion soup (£2.50), ploughman's (from £4.25), lasagne or macaroni and broccoli cheese (£4.50), two eggs on garlic sausage with chorizo, ham, peppers and green beans (£5.50), fisherman's pie (£6.50), chicken curry (£6.75), Welsh-style grilled trout with bacon (£8.75), lamb chops marinated in garlic and herbs or beef and mushroom pie (£9.25), well hung steaks (from £10.50), puddings such as trifle (£2.25), children's dishes (£3.75), and maybe weekend specials; nicely cooked vegetables. Service is courteous and efficient; well kept Brains Bitter and Flowers IPA on handpump. The churchyard is across the very quiet village lane. *(Recommended by Michael Rowe, Margaret and Nigel Dennis, GWB, Dr G W Barnett, Liz and Peter Elsey, A J Bowen, Mrs Brenda Calver, Tony and Sarah Thomas, Michel Sargent, R C Morgan)*

Free house ~ Licensees David and Susan Bell ~ Real ale ~ Meals and snacks ~ (01874) 665276 ~ Children welcome ~ Open 12-3, 7-11; cl Mon and last three weeks of Jan

LLANGATTOCK (Powys) SO2117 Map 6

Vine Tree

A4077; village signposted from Crickhowell

The fresh fish at this friendly well run dining pub comes twice a week from Cornwall, and they use local meat and vegetables in the wide range of carefully prepared dishes such as stockpot soup (£1.75), prawn cocktail or smoked venison with cranberry sauce (£4.10), roast chicken, lasagne, steak and kidney pie or home-boiled ham (£4.75), half a dozen vegetarian dishes like lasagne or curry (all £5.75), lamb kidneys in sherry sauce (£6.90), scampi or chicken curry (£6.95), rabbit in a wine, celery and almond sauce (£7.60), pork stuffed with apricots in a tangy orange sauce (£7.95), pheasant in cream, grape and white wine sauce (£8.90), very tasty monkfish in white wine, Pernod and leek sauce (£8.95), and steaks (from £9.45). The front part of the bar has soft seats, some stripped stone masonry, and brass ornaments around its open fireplace. The back is set aside as a dining area with windsor chairs, scrubbed deal tables, and decorative plates and Highland cattle engravings on the walls; most of the tables are set out for eating. Well kept Boddingtons, Flowers Original and Wadworths 6X on handpump. Tables under cocktail parasols give a view of the splendid medieval stone bridge over the River Usk, and a short stroll takes you to our Crickhowell main entry, the Bear. *(Recommended by A R and B E Sayer, Andrew Shore, Neil and Jenny Jackson, Mr and Mrs A Plumb, Mrs Brenda Calver, Nigel Clifton, Neil and Jenny Jackson)*

Free house ~ Licensee I S Lennox ~ Real ale ~ Meals (till 10pm) ~ Restaurant ~ (01873) 810514 ~ Children welcome ~ Open 12-3, 6-11

LLANGYNWYD (Mid Glamorgan) SS8588 Map 6
Old House

From A4063 S of Maesteg follow signpost Llan ¾ at Maesteg end of village; pub behind church

This lovely thatched pub dates back to 1147, making it one of the most aged in Wales. It's been much modernised, but there are still comfortably traditional touches in the two cosy rooms of its busy bar, which have high-backed black built-in settles, lots of china and brass around the huge fireplace, shelves of bric-a-brac, and decorative jugs hanging from the beams; piped music. They've built up quite a reputation for well cooked fresh fish – the landlord goes to the local fish market regularly – and for their particularly reasonably priced bar food such as generously served soup (£1.80), filled baked potatoes (from £1.80), pâté (£2.50), aubergine lasagne (£4.25), salads (from £4.25), steak and kidney pie, lasagne or beef curry (£4.50), scampi (£4.80), plaice (£5.40), battered cod (£5.50), gammon and eggs (£6.40), trout and almonds (£6.80), poached salmon (£8.30), steaks (from £10.75), puddings such as raspberry charlotte (£2), daily specials like lamb supreme (£5.50), and children's meals (from £1.25). Well kept Bass, Brains SA, Flowers Original and IPA and Morlands Old Speckled Hen on handpump; good range of whiskies, and a choice of wines by the glass. An attractive conservatory extension (half no smoking) leads on to the garden with good views, play area, and a soft ice cream machine for children. At Christmas they still go in for the ancient Mari Lwyd tradition, which involves parading around a horse's skull on a stick decorated with ribbons, calling at each house and singing impromptu verses about occupants. *(Recommended by Nigel Clifton, David Holloway; more reports please)*

Whitbreads ~ Lease: Richard David ~ Real ale ~ Meals and snacks (till 10.30pm) ~ Restaurant ~ (01656) 733310 ~ Children welcome ~ Open 11-11

LLANNEFYDD (Clwyd) SH9871 Map 6
Hawk & Buckle

Village well signposted from surrounding main roads; one of the least taxing routes is from Henllan at junction of B5382 and B5429 NW of Denbigh

In very clear weather you can see as far as the Lancashire coast, possibly even Blackpool Tower 40 miles away, from most of the bedrooms at this welcoming little hotel perched over 200 m (700 ft) up in the hills. The bar food is well above average, with a choice of home-made dishes like toasted sandwiches (from £1.85), soup (£1.95), ploughman's (£3.95), steak and kidney pie or various vegetarian dishes like mushroom and nut fettucine (£4.95), chicken madras, lasagne or turkey and ham pie (£5.25), lemon sole (£6.95) and sirloin steak (from £8.45); the dining room is no smoking. The long knocked-through black-beamed lounge bar has comfortable modern upholstered settles around its walls and facing each other across the open fire, and a neat red carpet in the centre of its tiled floor, while a lively locals' side bar has darts, pool and piped music; good Spanish house wines. Friendly licensees; two cats and a dog. There's an attractive mosaic mural on the way through into the back bedroom extension; the modern rooms here are comfortable and well equipped. *(Recommended by Anne and Sverre Hagen, Maysie Thompson, KC, Margaret Dyke, D W Jones-Williams; more reports please)*

Free house ~ Licensees Bob and Barbara Pearson ~ Meals and snacks (lunch service stops 1.30 and see opening times) ~ Restaurant ~ (01745) 540249 ~ Children welcome till 8.30 ~ Open 12-2, 7-11; cl lunchtimes Mon; cl winter lunchtimes except Weds and weekend; cl 25 Dec ~ Bedrooms: £38B/£50B

LLANTHONY (Gwent) SO2928 Map 6
Abbey Hotel

The enchantingly peaceful setting of this fascinating old place is one of the most unusual and atmospheric of any pub in Britain; it's surrounded by and indeed really part of a Norman abbey's graceful ruins, with lawns among the lofty arches and tranquil views towards the border hills. The dimly lit vaulted crypt bar is basic and simply furnished with half-a-dozen wooden tables, spindleback chairs and wooden benches on the flagstone floor. It serves well kept Bass, Flowers Original, Ruddles County and Wadworths 6X on handpump or tapped from the cask, and farm cider in summer. Simple lunchtime bar food includes toasted sandwiches, good home-made soups (£2.25), spicy bean dip (£2.95), home-made meat and nutburgers (£3.95) and a lamb dish (£6.25). Note they don't allow children inside; no credit cards. *(Recommended by R C Hopton, John and Joan Nash, Gwyneth and Salvo Spadaro-Dutturi, Nigel Clifton, Leslie and Dorothy Pilson)*

Free house ~ Licensee Ivor Prentice ~ Real ale ~ Meals and lunchtime snacks ~ (01873) 890487 ~ Occasional live music ~ Open 11-3, 6-11; 11-11 Sat; 12-10.30 Sun; Nov-March only open 6-11 Fri, 11-11 Sat, 12-2.30 Sun ~ Bedrooms: /£43.50

LLANYNYS (Clwyd) SJ1063 Map 7
Cerrigllwydion Arms

Village signposted from A525 by Drovers Arms just out of Ruthin, and by garage in Pentre further towards Denbigh

Parts of this wonderfully remote, lovely old place date back to the 15th c, when the vicar allowed construction of the pub partly within the churchyard, so that it wouldn't spoil the view of Denbigh Castle from the vicarage. It looks quite small from the outside but once through the door actually rambles about delightfully, the maze of atmospheric little rooms filled with dark oak beams and panelling, a good mix of seats, old stonework, interesting brasses, and a collection of teapots. Well kept Bass and Tetleys on handpump, and a good choice of malt whiskies and liqueurs; darts, dominoes and unobtrusive piped music. Carefully home-made bar food shows the benefits of using well chosen fresh local ingredients. Besides sandwiches and standard bar snacks, it includes home-made soup (£1.70), and changing dishes of the day such as baked pork chops in apple and cider sauce (£5.90), lamb cutlets in honey and mustard (£6.65), duck in port and brandy sauce (£7.85), local venison in red wine and shallot sauce (£8.25), and a big mixed grill (£9.25); the restaurant is no smoking. Dogs welcome. Across the quiet lane is a neat garden with teak tables among fruit trees looking across the fields to wooded hills; the church is interesting. *(Recommended by KC, B Eastwood, J and B Gibson, Sue and Bob Ward, Dave Thompson, Margaret Mason)*

Free house ~ Licensee Brian Pearson ~ Real ale ~ Meals and snacks ~ Restaurant ~ (01745) 890247 ~ Children welcome ~ Open 11.30-3, 7-11

LLWYNDAFYDD (Dyfed) SN3755 Map 6
Crown 🏆

Coming S from New Quay on A486, both the first two right turns eventually lead to the village; the side roads N from A487 between junctions with B4321 and A486 also come within signpost distance; OS Sheet 145 map reference 371555

This is a popular choice for a family lunch, so it's best to get there early if you want a seat at the weekend – even out of season it can get busy. The pretty tree-sheltered garden has won several awards, and there are picnic tables on a terrace above a small pond among shrubs and flowers, as well as a good play area for children. Home-made bar food includes decent lunchtime sandwiches (from £1.70), as well as soup (£2.30), garlic mushrooms (£2.95), pizzas (from £5.45), vegetarian lasagne (£5.65), steak and kidney pie (£5.65), salads (from £5.95), local trout (£5.95), steaks (from £7.55), and daily specials such as lamb pie or chicken, stilton and broccoli pie (£5.95) and fresh salmon with roast pepper butter or fresh plaice with watercress, orange and aioli (£6.25); children's meals (from £2); the choice may be limited at Sunday lunchtime, when they do a roast. Well kept Flowers IPA and Original and Wadworths 6X and guests on handpump, a range of wines, and good choice of malt whiskies. The friendly, partly stripped-stone bar has red plush button-back banquettes around its copper-topped tables, and a big woodburning stove; piped music. The side lane leads down to a cove with caves by National Trust cliffs. *(Recommended by Mrs S Wright, Christopher Gallop, W H Cooke, RJH, M E Wellington, Ian Phillips, Mike and Wendy Proctor, H D Spottiswoode, Stella Knight)*

Free house ~ Licensee Keith Soar ~ Real ale ~ Meals and lunchtime snacks ~ Restaurant ~ (01545) 560396 ~ Children welcome ~ Open 12-3, 6-11; cl Sun evening Nov-Easter

LLYSWEN (Powys) SO1337 Map 6

Griffin ★ ⇔ ♀

A470, village centre

This attractive ivy-covered inn is run with real enthusiasm by its welcoming licensees. The menu stays up to date, and this year they've refurbished their cottagey bedrooms – for all the years we've known it, it's been a lovely place for a stay. A good range of hearty country cooking relies firmly on local produce, some from their own gardens. Most days after Easter they serve brown trout and salmon, caught by the family or by customers in the River Wye just over the road, and they're well known for very good seasonal game such as pheasant or jugged hare. In the evenings you may find a range of tapas, and they do regular wine tasting nights. Excellent lunchtime meals might include delicious home-made soup such as carrot and sweetcorn (£2.95), pâté or terrine (£4.35), ploughman's, cold mixed seafood salad, smoked haddock and salmon fishcakes or Cornish mussels in white wine and garlic (£4.95), warm duck breast salad or chicken chasseur (£5.95), char-grilled salmon, char-grilled pork chop with honey and mustard or fillets of trout with smoky bacon and mushrooms (£8.95). In the evening the menu is more elaborate, with dishes such as lemon sole with garlic sauce (£9.90), sirloin steak with char-grilled vegetables (£11.50) or rack of lamb with rosemary and shallots (£13). Boddingtons, Flowers IPA and guests on handpump, and a good varied wine list with several half bottles. The Fishermen's Bar is popular with chatty locals; it's decorated with old fishing tackle, and has a big stone fireplace with a good log fire, and large windsor armchairs and padded stools around tables; at lunchtime there's extra seating in the no-smoking dining room for bar meals. Quoits, and a huge mastiff, Amber; other dogs are allowed. You can shoot or fish here – they have a full-time ghillie and keeper. Service is friendly and helpful, though can slow down at busy times. *(Recommended by R Morgan, Bill and Steph Brownson, Miss E Evans, Gwen and Peter Andrews, Karen Eliot, John and Joan Nash, Mrs J Jones, Norma Farris, Frank Cummins, Dr Paul Kitchener, Andrew Stephenson, Chamberlain)*

Free house ~ Licensees Richard and Di Stockton ~ Real ale ~ Meals and snacks (roast only Sun lunchtime, no food Sun evening except for residents) ~ Restaurant ~ (01874) 754241 ~ Children welcome ~ Open 12-3, 7-11 ~ Bedrooms: £34.50B/£60B

MAENTWROG (Gwynedd) SH6741 Map 6

Grapes ★ ⇔ ♀ ◑

A496; village signposted from A470

This warmly welcoming and lively pub is well geared for families, but at the same time is quite a favourite with locals: you'll often hear Welsh speakers among the visitors here for the reliable bar food. Home-made, wholesome, and served in hearty helpings, it includes lunchtime sandwiches (not Sun, from £1.50), soup (£1.75), deep-fried potato wedges with dips (£3.25), burgers or salads (from £5.25), several vegetarian dishes like stilton and mushroom bake or vegetable tikka (from £5.25), steak and kidney pie or leek and ham bake (£5.75), rack of Welsh lamb (£7.75), and children's meals (from £2.50), and good specials tending to concentrate on fresh fish. Quick friendly service even at the busiest times, with well kept Bass, Cambrian Best, Dyffryn Clwyd Four Thumbs and a guest such as Morlands Old Speckled Hen on handpump, good house wines, decent selection of malt whiskies, and good coffee. All three bars are attractively filled with lots of stripped pitch-pine pews, settles, pillars and carvings, mostly salvaged from chapels. Good log fires – there's one in the great hearth of the restaurant where there may be spit-roasts. Dominoes, cribbage and interesting juke box in the public bar, where there's also an intriguing collection of brass blowlamps. The good-sized sheltered verandah (they serve the Sunday carvery from the shellfish counter at one end) catches the evening sunshine and has lovely views over a pleasant back terrace and walled garden; there's a fountain on the lawn, and magnificent further views. The dining room is no smoking; disabled lavatories. *(Recommended by the Goldsons, J E Hilditch, Dr M I Crichton, KB, DH, J A Pickup, Caroline Raphael, MRSM, E Holland, J C T Tan, Gordon Theaker, Roger Byrne, Basil Minson, Peter and Audrey Dowsett)*

Free house ~ Licensees Brian and Gill Tarbox ~ Real ale ~ Meals and snacks ~ Restaurant (not Sun evening) ~ (01766) 590208/365 ~ Children in dining room and verandah ~ Open 11-11; 12-10.30 Sun ~ Bedrooms: £25B/£50B

MARIANGLAS (Anglesey) SH5084 Map 6
Parciau Arms
B5110

There's plenty to look at around the gleaming bar at this cosy and welcoming pub, with local colour photographs on the dark red hessian walls of the inner area, and miners' lamps, horse bits, lots of brass (especially car horns), a mounted jungle fowl and other bric-a-brac dotted around. The main seating area has comfortable built-in wall banquettes and stools around elm tables, a big settee matching the flowery curtains, spears, rapiers and so forth on the elaborate chimney-breast over the coal fire, and antique coaching prints. An airy family dining room with little bunches of flowers on the tables has a series of prints illustrating the rules of golf. Decent bar food includes sandwiches (from £1.75), home-made soup (£1.95), lots of pizzas (from £2.75), filled baked potatoes (from £2.65), ploughman's (from £3.95), cottage pie (£4.50), local plaice with parsley sauce (£5.65), scampi (£5.75), and daily specials like lamb in cider or pork szechuan (£6.50) and beef in red wine (£6.95), with a vegetarian dish of the day like mushroom stroganoff (£3.95), and a fish of the day like halibut with wild mushroom and prawn sauce (£7.50); children's meals (from £2.10). Also morning coffee and afternoon tea. Three well kept rotating beers might be Bass, Ind Coope Burton and Marstons Pedigree on hand or electric pump, various New World wines, and whiskies, freshly squeezed orange juice, milk shakes; obliging, cheery service. Darts, pool, cribbage, shove-ha'penny, dominoes, fruit machine, video game, TV, juke box and piped music; boules area. There are picnic tables on a terrace, with pews and other tables under cocktail parasols in a good-sized garden; it also has a good play area including a pensioned-off tractor, a camel-slide, a climber and a children's play tree and boat. *(Recommended by Alan and Paula McCully, WAH, Andy and Jill Kassube, Roger Byrne)*

Free house ~ Licensee Philip Moore ~ Real ale ~ Meals and snacks (all day) ~ Restaurant ~ (01248) 853766 ~ Well behaved children welcome till 9pm ~ Open 11-11; 12-10.30 Sun

MONMOUTH (Gwent) SO5113 Map 6
Punch House
Agincourt Square

Attractively positioned in the centre of town, this 17th-c market-town pub, handsomely decked out with colourful hanging baskets in summer, has tables out on the cobbles overlooking the square. There is a particularly good relaxed and chatty atmosphere in the spreading open-plan beamed bar, which has red leatherette settles, lots of copper, brass and horse tack, bound copies of early issues of *Punch* (even the dog is called Punch), a big fireplace, and the original oak gate from the town gaol; one area is no smoking. Big helpings of straightforward bar food such as home-made soup (£1.90), chilli (£4.25), steak and kidney pie (£4.75), vegetable stir fry (£5), grilled trout (£6), four roasts (£6.75); the restaurant has a wide range of elaborate dishes prepared by their Italian chef. Prompt, friendly service; well kept Bass, Hancocks HB, Wadworths 6X and Worthington Best on handpump, decent range of wines. *(Recommended by Colin Laffan, Joan and Michel Hooper-Immins, George Atkinson, Piotr Chodzko-Zajko)*

Free house ~ Licensee John Wills ~ Real ale ~ Meals and snacks ~ Restaurant ~ (01600) 713855 ~ Children welcome in eating area of bar and restaurant ~ Occasional live entertainment ~ Open 11-11; 11-3, 5-11 Sun; cl 25 Dec

MONTGOMERY (Powys) SO2296 Map 6
Dragon ♥

The Square

The short but steep walk to the ruined castle up the hill from this timbered 17th-c hotel is rewarded by panoramic views of the countryside, and many of the beams and much of the masonry here are reputed to have come from the castle after it was destroyed by Cromwell. It's popular for eating, with bar meals such as sandwiches and toasties (from £1.95), filled baked potatoes (from £2.85), ploughman's (from £3.65), deep-fried chicken breast with peanut-flavoured batter and a spring onion and ginger dip, roast leg of lamb, fried lamb liver with a spicy dip, filled yorkshire pudding or grilled plaice with capers and lemon (£6.75), sirloin steak or roast duck (£7.95), and children's meals (£2.75); three-course Sunday lunch (£7.50, more in restaurant). Non-residents can have free use of the hotel swimming pool by ordering a full meal – the food will be ready when you come out. The carpeted lounge bar has a window seat looking down to the market square and the peaceful old town hall, tapestried stools and wall benches around dimpled copper tables, game bird and old England prints, and willow-pattern plates on a high shelf, up by the colonial ceiling fan. Efficient service, well kept Woods Special Bitter and one or two guests on handpump, and good coffee; chess, draughts, and jigsaws in winter, and maybe unobtrusive piped music. *(Recommended by Mike and Wendy Proctor, Gwen and Peter Andrews, G Washington)*

Free house ~ Licensees Mark and Sue Michaels ~ Real ale ~ Meals and snacks (limited choice after 7.30pm Sat) ~ Restaurant (lunchtime bookings essential) ~ (01686) 668359 ~ Children welcome in restaurant till 9.30 ~ Open 11-11; 12-10.30 Sun ~ Bedrooms: £42B/£69B

PEMBROKE FERRY (Dyfed) SM9603 Map 6
Ferry

Nestled below A477 toll bridge, N of Pembroke

You won't find this former sailors' haunt by the new ferry, but attractively set by the water's edge below the Cleddau Bridge where the old ferry used to stop years ago. There's a very good combination of a relaxed yet buoyant pubby atmosphere, and particularly good fresh fish – the choice and price depending on market supplies. It's simply cooked so as not to mask the delicacy of its freshness, and might include cod, crab thermidor or plaice (£4.50), brill or turbot (£6.95) or lobster (from £8.95), as well as dover sole, crayfish or salmon. Other meals could include vegetable kiev or leek and bacon pie (£3.50), garlic tiger prawns (£3.95), schnitzel with a creamy mushroom sauce (£4.95) and steak (£8.25). Booking is virtually essential for Sunday lunch. There's a nautical decor to suit its past, with good views over the water. Well kept Bass and Hancocks HB on handpump, and a decent choice of malt whiskies. Efficient service, fruit machine, unobtrusive piped music. There are tables out on the waterside terrace. *(Recommended by W H Cooke, Mike and Karen England, Drs R and M Woodford, Christopher Turner, A J nd M Thomasson, Howard and Lynda Dix)*

Free house ~ Licensee David Henderson ~ Real ale ~ Meals and snacks (till 10) ~ Restaurant ~ (01646) 684927 ~ Children welcome in restaurant ~ Open 11.30-2.45, 6.30-11

PONTYPOOL (Gwent) ST2998 Map 6

Open Hearth ◗

The Wern, Griffithstown; Griffithstown signposted off A4051 S – opposite British Steel main entrance turn up hill, then first right

Although there is some emphasis on dining at this cheery and well run welcoming local, they do keep an excellent range of up to nine changing real ales – much better than you'll find anywhere else in the area – such as Archers Best and Golden, Boddingtons, Bull Mastiff Brindle and Thoroughbred, Cottage Wheeltappers Ale, Hancocks HB, Shepherd Neame Spitfire and Worthington Best on handpump; as well as a good choice of wines and malt whiskies. Reliably tasty good value bar food includes filled rolls (from £1.30), soup or pâté (£1.95), filled baked potatoes (from £2.85), various curries (from £4.25), vegetable stir fry (£4.50), scampi, plaice or cod (£5.15), steak and ale pie (£5.25), pork in stilton, wine and mushroom sauce (£5.95), sirloin steak cooked in a Mexican sauce (£8.45) and venison sautéed in butter with peppers, onion, mushroom, flamed in brandy and finished in cream (£8.50). They do their best to suit you if you want something not on the menu, and the downstairs restaurant is something of a local landmark; decent coffee, cheap tea, very friendly and efficient service. You can watch the comings and goings on a stretch of the Monmouthshire & Brecon Canal from seats outside. The comfortably modernised smallish lounge bar has a turkey carpet and big stone fireplace, and a back bar has leatherette seating. Cribbage, dominoes, and piped music; boules in summer. There are picnic tables, swings, and shrubs in the recently tidied-up garden. (*Recommended by Gwyneth and Salvo Spadaro-Dutturi, PM, AM, Howard James, Nigel Clifton, Mike Pugh, Nick and Helen Hilton*)

Free house ~ Licensees Gwyn Philips and Joeanne Lawrence ~ Real ale ~ Meals and snacks (till 10) ~ Restaurant ~ (01495) 763752 ~ Children in eating area and restaurant ~ Open 11.30-3.30, 6-11; 11.30-11.30 Sat

PRESTEIGNE (Powys) SO3265 Map 6

Radnorshire Arms 🛏

High Street; B4355 N of centre

Although this rambling timbered place has been sold by Forte to the Regal Group, the welcoming manager remains the same, and its old-fashioned charm and atmosphere never seem to change. Renovations have revealed secret passages and priest's holes, with one priest's diary showing he was walled up here for two years. It's now a good deal more comfortable than he'd remember, with discreetly modern furnishings, though he might recognise the venerable dark oak panelling, latticed windows and elegantly moulded black oak beams, now decorated with horsebrasses. Reasonably priced bar food might include good sandwiches (from £1.80) or filled baguettes (from £3.50), home-made soup (£1.95), cumberland sausage and mash (£4.20), popular ploughman's (£3.65), vegetable lasagne (£4.95), steak, kidney and mushroom pie (£5.50), gammon steak with fried egg (£5.95) and puddings (£2.95); children's helpings (about £2.10), as well as dishes of the day such as breast of chicken with mushrooms and tarragon (£5.95) and poached salmon with lobster and prawn sauce (£6.50). Well kept real ales include a brew from Banks's and Marstons Pedigree on handpump, with English wines by the glass, several malt whiskies, and welcoming attentive service; separate no-smoking restaurant, morning coffee, afternoon tea. There are some well spaced tables on the sheltered flower-bordered lawn, which used to be a bowling green. The building was constructed by the brother of one of the men who signed Charles I's death warrant, though it wasn't actually licensed until 1792. This is a nice area for a quiet weekend. (*Recommended by Basil Minson, Barbara and Denis Melling, Sarah and Peter Gooderham, David and Brenda Tew*)

Free house ~ Manager Aidan Treacy ~ Real ale ~ Meals and snacks ~ Restaurant ~ (01544) 267406 ~ Children welcome ~ Open 11-11; cl 25 Dec evening ~ Bedrooms: £61B/£82B

Waterside pubs are listed at the back of the book.

nr RAGLAN (Gwent) SO3608 Map 6

Clytha Arms 🍺 ⇐ 🍴

Clytha, off Abergavenny road – former A40, now declassified

This fine old inn is going very well at the moment – hence the Place to Stay and Food
Awards, added this year to their Beer Award for very well kept Bass, Brains Bitter,
Hook Norton Best and three guest beers such as Badger Tanglefoot, Felinfoel
Double Dragon and Nethergate Old Growler all on handpump; also Weston's farm
ciders and freshly squeezed orange juice. The changing choice of fresh food is well
prepared and presented, and as well as sandwiches (from £1.65, open sandwiches
from £2.95) and ploughman's (£4.75), faggots and mushy peas (£3.30), black
pudding with apple and mustard sauce (£3.95), salmon burger with tarragon and
mayonnaise (£4.95), wild boar sausage with potato pancakes (£4.35), leek and
laverbread rissoles (£3.75), might include asparagus and goat's cheese soufflé with
cummin pancakes (£8.65), grilled tuna with tomato and basil sauce (£9.50), kebab
of pork tenderloin and black pudding (£9.95), fillet of beef with shallot and red wine
sauce (£12.95), delicious home-made puddings (£3.30); good value three-course
Sunday lunch in the no-smoking restaurant. The tastefully refurbished bar has a
good traditional atmosphere, with solidly comfortable furnishings and a couple of
log fires. The cheerful helpful staff are warmly welcoming; darts, shove-ha'penny,
boules, table skittles, cribbage, draughts and chess – no music or machines. The well
cared for grounds are a mass of colour in spring. *(Recommended by David Luke, F J
Willy, KB, DH, Nigel Clifton, Ian Rorison, Gwyneth and Salvo Spadaro-Dutturi, A R and B E
Sayer, Paul Noble, Mike Pugh)*

*Free house ~ Licensees Andrew and Beverley Canning ~ Real ale ~ Meals and
snacks (not Fri or Sat evening, restaurant meals only Sun lunch) ~ Restaurant ~
(01873) 840206 ~ Children welcome till 8.30 ~ Open 11.30-3, 6-11; 11.30-11
Sat; cl Mon lunchtime except bank holidays ~ Bedrooms: £40B/£45B*

RED WHARF BAY (Anglesey) SH5281 Map 6

Ship 🍴

Village signposted off B5025 N of Pentraeth

You do need to arrive early for a table at this very popular solidly built 16th-c house.
Lovely fresh sea views from tables on the front terrace look down over ten square
miles of treacherous tidal cockle-sands, with low wooded hills sloping down to the
broad bay. Inside is old-fashioned and interesting, with a big room on each side of
the busy stone-built bar counter, both with long cushioned varnished pews built
around the walls, glossily varnished cast-iron-framed tables, and quite a restrained
decor including toby jugs, local photographs, attractive antique foxhunting cartoons
and coal fires. Enterprising and well presented daily changing bar food might
typically include cream of celery and stilton soup (£2.40), minted melon and
strawberry cocktail (£3.95), baked black pudding with brandy and apple sauce
(£4.10), venison sausage braised in red wine (£5.90), grey mullet on a bed of mussel
stew (£6.30), baked shoulder of lamb with garlic and rosemary (£8.90), and
puddings like rhubarb and ginger crumble (£2.60) or crème brûlée (£2.65). There
may be delays at busy times (it can be quite crowded on Sundays, when food service
stops promptly at 2), but service is always friendly and smiling; the cheery licensees
have been here now for over 20 years. The dining room and cellar room are no
smoking. Well kept Friary Meux, Ind Coope Burton and Tetleys Mild and Bitter are
drawn by handpump with a sparkler; a wider choice of wines than usual for the
area, and about 30 malt whiskies. Pool, darts and dominoes in the back room, and a
family room; piped music. There are rustic tables and picnic tables by an ash tree on
grass by the side. *(Recommended by Alan and Paula McCully, WAH, Margaret and Roy
Randle, Wayne Brindle, D Goodger, R A Hobbs, A and J Tierney-Jones, J R Whetton, Julie
Peters)*

*Free house ~ Licensee Andrew Kenneally ~ Real ale ~ Meals and snacks ~
(01248) 852568 ~ Restaurant ~ Children welcome ~ Open 11-11; 12-3.30, 7-11
in winter*

ROSEBUSH (Dyfed) SN0630 Map 6

New Inn ♀

Off B4329 Haverfordwest—Cardigan

Recently reopened, this welcoming outpost on the edge of the unspoilt Preseli Hills has been most attractively restored in tune with its origins as a 17th-c drovers' inn, and later a combined farm and coaching inn. The cosy rooms of its small bar have interesting stripped stonework, antique oak country furniture on handsome slate flagstones or red and black diamond Victorian tiles, and a couple of coal fires – one in a quite cavernous fireplace. All this gives a cosy and cottagey feel, and the atmosphere is quiet and relaxed. There is a small garden room. Good wide-ranging bar food using carefully chosen local ingredients might include soup (£2.50), garlic mushrooms (£3.85), cockle, bacon and laverbread gratin (£4.25/£5.25), warm salad of goat's cheese (£4.60/£5.60), rabbit casserole or lasagne (£5.25), steak and kidney pie, lamb tagine, and outstanding Thai green chicken curry or Thai pork curry (£6.50) and venison casserole with juniper berries (£7), as well as puddings such as bread and butter pudding (£2.75); they keep good local cheeses. As the food is freshly prepared there may be a wait. Up to six well kept and changing real ales might include Caledonian Deuchars IPA, Crown Buckley Best and Reverend James and Everards Old Original on handpump, well chosen wines (with two separate lists, under and over £12 and half a dozen by the glass), Weston's farm cider, friendly staff. There are tables outside, and plenty of good walks nearby. *(Recommended by Ian Phillips, Mr and Mrs J R Morris, Robert and Sarah Connor, John and Pat Smyth, R Michael Richards)*

Free house ~ Licensee Diana Richards ~ Real ale ~ Meals and snacks (12-2.30, 6-9.30) ~ Restaurant (evenings, not Mon; also Sun lunch) ~ (01437) 532542 ~ Children welcome ~ Folk music Mon, harp music Tues ~ Open 11-11; 12-3, 7-10.30 Sun; cl 25 Dec evening

ST HILARY (S Glamorgan) ST0173 Map 6

Bush £

Village signposted from A48 E of Cowbridge

This very friendly and genuinely old-fashioned 16th-c thatched pub, tucked away behind the village church, is still said to be haunted by a notorious local highwayman, and very close to Stalling Down, a hill rich in Welsh history. The comfortable and snugly cosy low-beamed lounge bar has walls stripped to the old stone, and windsor chairs around copper-topped tables on the carpet, while the public bar has old settles and pews on aged flagstones, and darts; subdued piped music. Good bar food, using fresh ingredients, includes sandwiches (from £1.50), french onion soup (£1.95), laverbread and bacon (£2.35), welsh rarebit (£2.95), spinach and cheese pancake (£3.35), ploughman's (£3.60), liver or sausages with onion gravy (£3.95), salads (from £3.95), daily roast (£4.25), steak and ale pie (£4.75), gammon (£5.25), mixed grill (£6.75) and good daily specials; the restaurant menu is available in the bar in the evenings, with meals like trout pan fried in sherry with toasted almonds (£7.95) or medaillons of pork normandy (£8.50); they will do smaller helpings for children. A weekday three-course set lunch is £5.95, and three-course weekday set supper (not Friday) £8.95; three-course Sunday lunch (£8.95). Well kept Morlands Old Speckled Hen on handpump, with a range of malt whiskies; efficient service. There are tables and chairs in front, and more in the back garden. *(Recommended by Miss E Evans, C A Hall, Mrs S Wright, David Holloway, the Sandy family, Nigel Clifton, Michael Richards, Mr and Mrs Steve Thomas, M Joyner)*

Bass ~ Lease: Sylvia Murphy ~ Real ale ~ Meals and snacks (till 10; not Sun evenings) ~ Restaurant ~ (01446) 772745 ~ Children welcome in eating area of bar ~ Open 11-11

All *Guide* inspections are anonymous. Anyone claiming to be a *Good Pub Guide* inspector is an fraud, and should be reported to us with name and description.

STACKPOLE (Dyfed) SR9896 Map 6

Armstrong Arms 🍴

Village signposted off B4319 S of Pembroke

You do need to book for a meal at this delightful, rather Swiss-looking building on the Stackpole estate, as it's quickly built an enviable reputation for very fairly priced good changing food, all freshly cooked, and served by cheerful black and white uniformed waitresses. At lunchtime there might be creamy garlic mushrooms (£3.75), moules marinières (£4.50), croissant filled with smoked salmon and egg mayonnaise (£4.75), nan bread filled with chicken tikka masala with tomato and onion salad or battered haddock (£4.95), fresh penne with tomato and basil sauce with focaccia, smoked rosti cakes with toasted sweetcorn salsa or mushrooms stuffed with spinach and stilton cream (£5.25), goujons of lemon sole with fresh tartare sauce (£5.45) and beef and mushroom pie (£5.95), with more elaborate evening dishes such as kidneys dijonnaise (£5.95), grilled supreme of chicken wrapped in parma ham with red wine sauce (£7.75), fillet of salmon with prawn hollandaise (£8.25) and confit of duck with buttered spinach and cumberland sauce (£8.75); vegetables are delicious, with a choice of potatoes. Tasty puddings include crème brûlée, oranges in Grand Marnier with brown sugar meringues or tiramisu (£2.75); coffee is good. Well kept Worthingtons Best and a couple of guests such as Fullers London Pride, Greene King IPA or Marstons Pedigree on electric pump, and quite a few malt whiskies. One spacious area has darts and pool, but the major part of the pub, L-shaped on four different levels, is given over to diners, with neat light oak furnishings, and glossy beams and low ceilings to match. There are tables out in the attractive gardens, with colourful flowerbeds and mature trees around the car park; no credit cards or dogs. *(Recommended by Sarah Bradbury, Mrs M Boulson, W H Cooke, Rob Holt, M E Wellington, Christopher Turner, Heather Martin, Sarah Bradbury, Mr and Mrs Blackbourn, Ian and Lynn Brown, Drs R and M Woodford, Arthur Mole, A J Miller)*

Free house ~ Licensees Senga and Peter Waddilove ~ Real ale ~ Meals and snacks ~ Restaurant ~ (01646) 672324 ~ Children welcome in restaurant till 9.30 ~ Open 11-3, 6-11

TALYBONT ON USK (Powys) SO1122 Map 6

Star £ 🍺

B4558

One reader was amazed that this little canalside pub could keep so many changing real ales – the highlight here, about a dozen, from familiar brews such as Bass, Boddingtons, Felinfoel Double Dragon, Marstons Pedigree, Theakstons and Wadworths, to more unusual ones such as Bullmastiff and Freeminers. They keep a farm cider on handpump too. Several plainly furnished pubby rooms – unashamedly stronger on character than on creature comforts – radiate from the central servery, including a brightly lit games area with pool, fruit machine and juke box; cosy winter fires, one in a splendid stone fireplace. Good value bar food includes sandwiches (from £1.50), soup (£2.25), ploughman's (£3), faggots, peas and chips (£3.50), chilli (£4), lasagne or home-made chicken curry (£4.50), lamb liver casserole (£4.95), Cantonese pork casserole (£5.25), pork steaks in piquant white wine sauce or carbonnade of beef (£5.50), 8oz sirloin with red wine sauce (£7.95), and half a dozen vegetarian dishes such as vegieburger, chilli or spinach and leek pasta bake (from £3); children's meals (£1.80). Friendly service. You can sit outside at picnic tables in the sizeable tree-ringed garden, and the village, with both the Usk and the Monmouth & Brecon Canal running through, is surrounded by the Brecon Beacons national park. The pub was refurbished a couple of years ago after a canal breach. *(Recommended by John and Joan Nash, A P Jeffreys, John Abbott, Ian Mabberley, Gwyneth and Salvo Spadaro-Dutturi, BH, John and Joan Wyatt, Phil Putwain, Mr and Mrs A Plumb)*

Free house ~ Licensee Mrs Joan Coakham ~ Real ale ~ Meals and snacks (till 9.45) ~ (01874) 676635 ~ Children welcome ~ Live blues Weds evening ~ Open 11-3, 6-11, 11-11 Sat, 12-10.30 Sun ~ Bedrooms: £20B/£35B

TY'N Y GROES (Gwynedd) SH7672 Map 6

Groes

B5106 N of village

The new bedrooms at this charmingly situated family-run pub have magnificent views over the mountains or scenic reaches of the Conwy River, as do the no-smoking airy verdant conservatory, and seats on the flower decked roadside frontage. The homely series of rambling, low-beamed and thick-walled rooms have antique settles and an old sofa, old clocks, portraits, hats and tins hanging from the walls – and a good welcoming atmosphere. A fine antique fireback is built into one wall, perhaps originally from the formidable fireplace which houses a collection of stone cats as well as winter log fires. Well liked traditional country cooking includes sandwiches (from £2.95), ploughman's (£5.25), soup and sandwich or smoked haddock in light cream sauce (£5.50), lasagne or scampi (£5.95), pie of the day (£6.25), garlic mushrooms with stilton (£6.50), daily specials such as lancashire hotpot with home-made red pickled cabbage or roast gammon on a wild damson sauce (£5.95), game casserole with herb dumplings or roast of the day (£6.25), poached salmon with hollandaise (£6.95) and seafood platter (£7.50), lots of tasty puddings like banoffi pie, treacle tart or lemon and apple pudding (£2.75), and tempting home-made ice creams like lemon curd or caramelised pears with maple syrup (£2). Well kept Banks's and Marstons Pedigree on handpump, a good few malt whiskies, and a fruity fresh pimms in summer; cribbage, dominoes and light classical piped music at lunchtimes (nostalgic light music at other times). It can get busy, but this shouldn't cause any problems with the efficient friendly service. There are seats in the pretty back garden with its flower-filled hayricks. *(Recommended by Phil Putwain, J E Hilditch, Barbara Wensworth, E Holland, A W, B W, Roger Byrne, Roger and Christine Mash, Gordon Theaker, Mrs J Oakes, John Evans, Martin and Penny Fletcher, Paul Bailey, Pearl Williams)*

Free house ~ Licensees Dawn, Tony and Justin Humphreys ~ Real ale ~ Meals and snacks ~ Restaurant ~ (01492) 650545 ~ Well behaved children may be allowed in eating areas (no pushchairs); in restaurant if over 10 ~ Open 12-11 every day ~ Bedrooms: £40B/£55B

USK (Gwent) SO3801 Map 6

Royal 🍺

New Market Street (off A472 by Usk bridge)

There's usually a good mix of people filling up the two open-plan rooms of the homely old-fashioned bar at this lively Georgian country-town pub. Many come for the tasty bar meals, served in big helpings from a range that might include ploughman's (£2.95), fresh haddock (£4.75), lamb chops (£5.25) or beef burgundy (£5.75) with additional evening dishes like fresh local salmon or chicken in white wine sauce (£7.95) and lovely tender steaks (from £9.95); they do a popular Sunday lunch (£6.75) (when the ordinary menu isn't available). Service can slow down at busy times. The left-hand room is the nicer, with a cream-tiled kitchen range flush with the pale ochre back wall, a comfortable mix of tables and chairs, a rug on neat slate flagstones, plates and old pictures on the walls, china cabinets, and a tall longcase clock. Particularly well kept Bass, Felinfoel Double Dragon, Hancocks HB and a guest such as Adnams Broadside on handpump; open fires, dominoes, cribbage, cards, and piped music. At seats out in front facing a cedar tree, you may be serenaded by canaries. *(Recommended by A R and B E Sayer, Ian Williams, Linda Mar, Peter and Audrey Dowsett; more reports please)*

Free house ~ Licensees Anthony Lyons and Michael Corbett ~ Real ale ~ Meals and snacks (not Sun evening or Mon lunchtime, roasts only Sun lunch) ~ (01291) 672931 ~ Children welcome ~ Open 11-3, 7-11

Post Office address codings confusingly give the impression that some pubs are in Gwent or Powys, Wales when they're really in Gloucestershire or Shropshire (which is where we list them).

Lucky Dip

Besides the fully inspected pubs, you might like to try these Lucky Dips recommended to us and described by readers (if you do, please send us reports):

ANGLESEY

Cemaes Bay [High St; SH3793], *Stag*: Popular straightfoward village local, small, warm and cosy; good value bar food, well kept Burtonwood, real fire; lounge, bar and pool room *(Jeanne Cross, Paul Silvestri, Alan and Paula McCully)*; [High St], *Vigour*: Homely traditional layout, smoke room, bar, lounge and commercial rooms off covered passage, fairly basic but clean, with good value food, well kept Worthington Best *(Alan and Paula McCully)*

☆ **Menai Bridge** [St Georges Pier, by Straits; SH5572], *Liverpool Arms*: Unpretentious old-fashioned four-roomed local with cheerful relaxed atmosphere, low beams, interesting mostly maritime photographs and prints, conservatory with plastic terrace furniture, tasty straightforward good value bar food inc fresh home cooking, panelled dining room, well kept Greenalls Special and Best, welcoming landlord, good service; no music *(David Lewis, N Gilbourne, Jeanne Cross, Paul Silvestri, Andy and Jill Kassube)*

Valley [A5; SH2979], *Bull*: Busy and can be smoky, but worth it for wide choice of good value food and well kept beer *(Roger Byrne, B A Hobbs)*

CLWYD

Broughton [The Old Warren; old main rd towards Buckley; SJ3263], *Spinning Wheel*: Busy pub in pleasant by road now closed to through traffic, traditional freshly prepared good value food, welcoming atmosphere, good choice of beers and malt whiskies; restaurant area *(Basil Minson)*

☆ **Bylchau** [A543 3 miles S; SH9863], *Sportsmans Arms*: Wide views from highest pub in Wales, reliable straightforward food with all fresh veg and vegetarian dishes, well kept Lees Traditional and Best Dark Mild, drinks cheaper than usual; Welsh-speaking locals, cheerful and welcoming prompt service, good log fire, old-fashioned high-backed settles among more modern seats, darts and pool, no piped music, harmonium and Welsh singing Sat evening; children allowed in eating area, cl Mon/Tues lunchtimes in winter (and maybe other lunchtimes then) *(B A and R Davies, KC, LYM)*

Chirk [Chirk Bank (B5070 S); SJ3028], *Bridge*: Unpretentious old local worth knowing for cheap generous home-made food in back eating area, well kept Banks's Mild and Bitter and Marstons Pedigree (summer); water-jugs on beams, children welcome, below Llangollen Canal nr aqueduct *(Ian and Nita Cooper)*

Graig Fechan [signed off B5429 S of Ruthin; SJ1554], *Three Pigeons*: 17th-c inn with good food in bar or dining room *(Graham and Lynn Mason)*

☆ **Gwaenysgor** [just S of Prestatyn; SJ0881],

Eagle & Child: Welcoming and spotless early 19th-c pub, shining brasses and plates, generous freshly cooked good value food, Bass, good service, exemplary lavatories; attractive floodlit gardens, in hilltop village with fine views *(Chris Shelley)*

Gwytherin [B5384 W of Denbigh; SH8761], *Lion*: Well run small pub with roaring log fire, well kept beer, wide choice of good food, attractive restaurant with another log fire, very welcoming licensees; bedrooms *(Jerry and Alison Oakes, D W Jones-Williams)*

☆ **Llanarmon DC** [SJ1633], *West Arms*: Warm welcome and roaring log fires in extended 16th-c beamed and timbered inn, good base for walking; picturesque upmarket lounge bar full of antique settles, sofas, even an elaborately carved confessional stall, well kept Boddingtons, good range of wines and malt whiskies, more sofas in old-fashioned entrance hall, comfortable back bar too; food inc good fresh fish; pretty lawn running down to River Ceiriog (fishing for residents); children welcome; bedrooms comfortable *(Sue and Bob Ward, LYM)*

☆ **Llanelian Yn Rhos** [S of Colwyn Bay; signed off A5830 (shown as B5383 on some maps) and B5381; SH8676], *White Lion*: Family-run 16th-c inn, wide choice of good reasonably priced bar food from sandwiches and big tureen of home-made soup up, neat spacious dining area, broad steps down to traditional flagstoned snug bar with antique settles and big fire; well kept Marstons Pedigree, Tetleys Mild and a guest beer, good range of wines, lots of malt whiskies; dominoes, cribbage, piped music; rustic tables outside, good walking nearby; children in eating area; bedrooms *(Ann and Bob Westbrook, LYM)*

☆ **Llangedwyn** [B4396; SJ1924], *Green*: Very old country dining pub, clean and well run, with lots of nooks and crannies, oak settles, roaring log fire, impressive range of good home-cooked food esp fish in bar and pleasant upstairs evening restaurant, friendly quick service, well kept Whitbreads-related and guest ales, good choice of malt whiskies and wines; lots of tables in beautiful garden over rd, lovely Tanat Valley surroundings, own fishing *(S E Paulley, Nigel Woolliscroft, Paddy Moindrot, KB, DH)*

nr Llangollen [Horseshoe Pass (A542 N); SJ2045], *Britannia*: Included for position, with lovely Dee Valley views from picturesque though much extended pub, two quiet bars and brightly cheerful dining areas (one no smoking), Whitbreads-related ales; well kept garden; good value attractive bedrooms *(RP, BP)*

Llanrhaeadr Ym Mochnant [SJ1326], *Wynnstay Arms*: Small lounge, locals' bar, back games room, good value food, good service, well kept Banks's ale; reasonably priced bedrooms, good walking country *(Gwyneth and Salvo Spadaro-Dutturi)*

Mold [A541 Denbigh rd nr Bailey Hill; SJ2464], *Bryn Awel*: Good choice of satisfying food inc vegetarian, good service, pleasant atmosphere *(KC)*

nr Mold [Loggerheads; A494 3 miles towards Ruthin; SJ1962], *We Three Loggerheads*: The managers who lifted this interestingly furnished wayside Bass pub right out of the ordinary with their unusual cooking have now left *(LYM)*

Northop [SJ2569], *Boot*: Wide choice of good home-made food, well kept Greenalls, friendly service *(Margaret and Trefor Howorth, Mr and Mrs M St-Amour)*

☆ **Overton Bridge** [A539; SJ3643], *Cross Foxes*: Warm and friendly 17th-c coaching inn in attractive setting on Dee, lots of little rooms, one with river views, good value generous straightforward home cooking with some interesting specials *(Graham and Lynn Mason)*

☆ **Pontblyddyn** [A5104/A541 3 miles SE of Mold; SJ2761], *Bridge*: Cosy old traditional bar, sympathetically restored, with good log fire, bar food cooked to order inc some interesting dishes, attractive dim-lit dining area with sensible tables and chairs and another huge log fire, good Sun lunches, real ales, attentive staff; tables on roadside terrace, pleasant gardens by River Alyn with ducks, good for children so long as you keep an eye on the geese *(KC, Karen Burgess, Dylan Hawkings)*

Pontfadog [SJ2338], *Swan*: Good food, inc interesting restaurant dishes Fri/Sat evenings; well kept Cains and Tetleys *(Dave Braisted)*

Prestatyn [A548 4 miles E; SJ0783], *Bells of St Marys*: Useful Brewers Fayre pub, open all day, with Whitbreads-related ales, nooks and crannies in big dining areas, rendered brickwork, leaded lights, prints, bric-a-brac and tools; piped music, Sky TV, fruit machine; play areas inside and out *(SLC)*

Rhewl [the one on A525 Ruthin—Denbigh; SJ1160], *Drovers Arms*: Old-fashioned low-beamed pub with decent food inc children's in three roomy and spotless eating areas, pleasant staff, well kept beer, no piped music, pool room; attractive garden *(KC)*

☆ **Rhewl** [the one off A5 W of Llangollen; OS Sheet 125 map ref 176448; SJ1744], *Sun*: Friendly and unpretentious little cottage in good walking country just off Horseshoe Pass, with relaxing views from terrace and garden; simple good value food from sandwiches to good Sun lunch, well kept Felinfoel Double Dragon and cheap Worthington BB, malt whiskies, old-fashioned hatch service to back room, dark little lounge, portakabin games room – children allowed here and in eating area *(J and B Gibson, KB, DH, Dave Thompson, Margaret Mason, D Maplethorpe, B Helliwell, LYM)*

Rhos on Sea [Rhos Rd; SH8481], *Rhos Fynach*: Picturesque stone-built pub opp small harbour, big lounge with low beams, flagstones, two open fires, prints, brassware, ales inc Banks's and Marstons Pedigree, good bar food, friendly service, upstairs evening restaurant; piped music *(E G Parish, SLC)*

Ruthin [Clwyd Gate; SJ1258], *Clwyd Gate*: Motel not pub, but a useful stop for Offa's Dyke walkers; fairly priced tasty bar meals, terrific view; bedrooms *(Geoffrey and Irene Lindley)*

☆ **St George** [off A55 nr Abergele; SH9576], *Kinmel Arms*: Clean and comfortable pub/restaurant with good interesting freshly cooked food using carefully chosen and often unusual local ingredients (plenty of time needed, as everything cooked for you); reasonable prices, good range of real ales with weekly guest; bedrooms, attractive village *(Colin Francis, J E Hilditch, Nathan Bird, Don Mills)*

☆ **Tremeirchion** [off B5429 up lane towards church; SJ0873], *Salusbury Arms*: Lovely log fires in beamed pub with some 14th-c panelling, comfortable attractive furnishings, well kept Marstons Bitter and Pedigree and three guest beers, well equipped games room, restaurant; children welcome, pretty garden with under-cover barbecue, open all day summer *(Richard Lewis, Paul Boot, Martin and Penny Fletcher, LYM)*

☆ **Trofarth** [B5113 S of Colwyn Bay; SH8470], *Holland Arms*: Good value food inc lunchtime bargains in old-fashioned 17th-c former coaching inn, warm cosy atmosphere, prompt friendly service, Tetleys and Ansells Mild, farm tools in one room, stuffed owls in the other, raised dining area open when busy; some tables outside with valley and mountains views; handy for Bodnant *(Roger Byrne)*

Wrexham [Chester Rd, Garden Village; SJ3450], *Acton*: Pleasant local, well kept and clean, good range of beers, lunchtime bar food; can get busy *(Jenny and Neil Spink)*

DYFED

Aberystwyth [Mill St; SN6777], *Mill*: Friendly local open all day, several well kept Tetleys-related ales with a couple of guests such as local Dinas and Felinfoel Double Dragon, good simple lunchtime cold snacks, pool table, friendly staff and locals inc rugby players *(Richard Lewis, Joan and Michel Hooper-Immins)*

☆ **Amroth** [SN1607], *New Inn*: Traditional beamed local by lovely beach, wide choice of good generous home cooking inc good soups, local seafood, real chips and children's dishes; three small rooms with open fires, no music and good atmosphere, upstairs lounge bar, games room with pool tables and machines (children allowed); well kept ales inc Ind Coope Burton, friendly staff; picnic tables in good garden, holiday flat *(Gwyneth and Salvo Spadaro-Dutturi, A J Bowen)*

Bosherston [SR9694], *St Govans*: Welcoming open-plan bar, useful food (all day Sun in summer), Worthington BB on handpump, piped music, bar billiards, bedrooms; the eponymous hermit's chapel overlooking the sea is worth getting to, as are the nearby lilyponds *(Mr and Mrs Steve Thomas, LYM)*

☆ **nr Broad Haven** [N of village on coast rd, bear L for about 1½ miles then follow sign L to

Druidstone Haven – inn a sharp left turn after another ½ mile; OS Sheet 157 map ref 862168, marked as Druidston Villa], *Druidstone*: Very unusual and for people it suits a favourite place to stay in; its club licence means you can't go for just a drink and have to book to eat there (the food is inventively individual home cooking, with fresh ingredients and a leaning towards the organic; restaurant cl Sun evening); a lived-in informal country house alone in a grand spot above the sea, with terrific views, spacious homely bedrooms, erratic plumbing, a cellar bar (good food here too) with a strong 1960s folk-club feel, well kept Worthington BB and good wines, country wines and other drinks, ceilidhs and folk jamborees, chummy dogs (dogs welcomed), all sorts of sporting activities from boules to sand-yachting; cl Nov and Jan; bedrooms (*J Giles Quick, Dr G W Barnett, LYM*)

Broad Haven, *Galleon*: Good cooking by ex-sea-captain landlord in popular and friendly seafront pub's softly lit small bar, rooms and alcoves leading off, Ansells, Tetleys and Worthington BB; SE Asian dishes Thurs night (*Christopher Turner*)

Burry Port [Colbey Rd; SN4400], *Pemberton Arms*: Sporting theme in well restored pub, well kept beer (*Dr and Mrs A K Clarke*)

☆ Caio [off A482 Llanwrda—Lampeter; SN6739], *Brunant Arms*: Unspoilt chatty village local popular for well kept changing ales; good layout of pews etc, good bar food (best to book evenings for small eating area), interesting egg cup collection, pool table, quiz nights (*R C Morgan, Thomas L Wollensack, M E Hughes, Howard James*)

Cardigan [leaving centre southwards on right after bridge; SN1846], *Eagle*: Very popular lively local, bright and cheerful, rugs on tiled floor, hop-festooned beams, thousands of beer mats on ceiling, lots of bric-a-brac, entertaining verses in poet's corner, well kept Crown Buckley, good straightforward food from outstanding ham rolls to real blowouts (*DJW*)

Cenarth [A484 Cardigan—Newcastle Emlyn; SN2641], *Three Horseshoes*: Welcoming family-run village pub with friendly attentive staff, good choice of generous reasonably priced food – most people here to eat; medieval alehouse at the back (*P and J Daggett, Mr and Mrs J R Morris*)

☆ Cwm Gwaun [Pontfaen; Cwm Gwaun and Pontfaen signed off B4313 E of Fishguard; SN0035], *Dyffryn Arms*: Very basic and idiosyncratic Welsh-speaking country tavern known locally as Bessie's, run by same family since 1840; plain deal furniture, well kept Bass and Ind Coope Burton served by jug through a hatch, good sandwiches if you're lucky, Great War prints, draughts-boards inlaid into tables, very relaxed atmosphere; pretty countryside (*Andy Jones, LYM*)

Cwmdu [5 miles N of Llandeilo, a mile W of B4302 (Talley rd); SN6330], *Cwmdu*: In row of cottages, shop and post office, now owned by National Trust; flagstones, huge log

fireplace, basic furnishings; idiosyncratic service, sophisticated menu inc good leek soup with brown rolls, good range of real ales, attractive setting by bridge (*Anne Morris*)

Dale [SM8006], *Griffin*: Lively friendly local, good range of seafood, good view of boats in estuary, can sit out on sea wall; children allowed when eating (*Keith Archer*)

Dinas [A487; SN0139], *Ship Aground*: 18th-c smugglers' pub done up with nautical trappings, some interesting ropework; friendly staff and locals, good value limited lunchtime bar food, wide evening choice inc local fish and seafood, well kept Crown Buckley; open all day in summer (*John Allsopp, BB*)

☆ Dreenhill [Dale Rd (B4327); SM9214], *Denant Mill*: Welcoming 16th-c converted watermill with great atmosphere, well kept changing ales, inexpensive wines, decent coffee, good informal stripped-stone restaurant with often exotic freshly cooked food inc authentic Goan dishes; remote setting down narrow lane, big safe garden with ducks on millpond, extensive wood behind; simple clean bedrooms (*Andy Jones, Karen Burgess, Dylan Hawkings, Ken and Jenny Simmonds*)

Dreenhill [Dale Rd], *Masons Arms*: Popular friendly cottage local with simple choice of good value food inc good Sun lunch, well kept Bass and Worthington tapped from the cask; children welcome (*Dr G W Barnett*)

☆ Fishguard [Lower Town; SM9537], *Ship*: Cheery landlord and lots of atmosphere and seafaring locals in dim-lit red-painted local nr old harbour, well kept Worthington BB and Dark Mild tapped from the cask, homely bar food (not weekends), coal fire, lots of boat pictures, model ships; children welcome, toys provided (*Ian Phillips, Andy Jones, LYM*)

Fishguard [The Square, Upper Town], *Royal Oak*: Low-beamed long narrow front bar with woodburner and military prints and pictures commemorating defeat here of second-last attempted French invasion, steps down to big picture-window dining extension, Bass, Hancocks HB and Worthington (*Phil and Heidi Cook; more reportts on new regime please*)

☆ Haverfordwest [24 Market St; SM9515], *Georges*: Unusually wide choice of generous home-made food using fresh veg and good meat in attractive bar with character stable-like furnishings, informal relaxed atmosphere and good choice of well kept ales such as Bass, Ind Coope Burton and Marstons Pedigree; more sophisticated evening restaurant, good friendly service; no dogs (*Howard and Lynda Dix*)

Lamphey [SN0100], *Dial*: Has had good home-made food inc local seafood and vegan dishes, Bass, Hancocks HB and guest beer, big public bar, family room, games room and eating area, friendly attentive staff (*Stuart Earle, T and R Rees, Anne Jappie; more reports please*)

☆ Landshipping [SN0111], *Stanley Arms*: Friendly ex-farmhouse local on lovely estuary (moorings), wide choice of good inexpensive food inc vegetarian, children's and imaginative salads, well kept ales such as Fullers Hock, Smiles Best and Worthington BB, farm cider, good coffee, two cats, hand-made clocks for sale; unobtrusive sensible piped music, weekend live music; tables on lawn under ancient chestnut, colourful window boxes and flower baskets, afternoon cream teas *(S A and L M Taylor, Drs R and M Woodford, John Hamilton-Cowburn)*

☆ Little Haven [SM8512], *Castle*: Good fresh local fish and other meals quickly served in friendly well placed pub by green, view over sandy bay, Worthington BB, good service; big oak tables, stone walls, oak beams in bar lounge and restaurant area, collection of castle prints, outside seating; children welcome, good facilities for them; the village has a paying car park *(Dr Michael Smith, Christopher Turner, Dr G W Barnett)*

☆ Little Haven [in village itself, not St Brides hamlet further W], *St Brides*: A short stroll from the sea, with Worthington BB and guest beers such as Theakstons Old Peculier, pews in stripped-stone bar and communicating dining area (children allowed here), quite a wide choice of food, piped music; interesting well in back corner may be partly Roman; big good value bedrooms, some in annexe over rd *(J Giles Quick, LYM)*

☆ Llanarthne [B4300 E of Carmarthen; SN5320], *Golden Grove Arms*: Interestingly laid-out inn with roomy lounge, open fire, well kept ales inc local Crown Buckley BB and Rev James, huge choice of good food inc some sophisticated dishes, very pleasant prompt service, children's play area; many Welsh-speaking customers, Tues folk night; bedrooms *(Anne Morris, LYM)*

☆ Llanarthne [B4300], *Paxton*: Dim-lit bar crammed floor to ceiling with bric-a-brac and collectibles, balloons, flashing lights, more restrained restaurant, most obliging friendly service (character extrovert landlord may wear velvet tails), wide choice of generous bar food, well kept Worthington BB and a guest such as Theakstons, good local farm cider, decent malt whiskies; very music-oriented jazz, folk, blues and poetry, with occasional beer and music festivals; opp wood leading to Paxtons Tower (NT); cl lunchtime exc Sun, may be cl Weds evening *(Anne Morris, Pete Baker, C A Hall, Howard James)*

Llanddarog [SN5016], *Butchers Arms*: Good generous home cooking from sandwiches up inc quite sophisticated daily specials, well kept Felinfoel Double Dragon and other ales tapped from the cask, tiny low-beamed central bar with woodburner, brasses and old photographs, two mainly dining areas off, friendly very helpful staff; tables outside *(A J Bowen)*

Llandeilo [Pentrefelin; A40 towards Carmarthen; SN6222], *Nags Head*: Extensively refurbished dining pub, roomy open-plan bar with log fire and lots of horsey prints and brasses, good choice of bar food, well kept ales such as Boddingtons, Flowers IPA and Worthington BB, friendly service, interesting restaurant with local fish and game;

piped music *(Howard James)*

Llandovery [SN7634], *Kings*: Town hotel doing well under new owners, roomy bars with carpeted comfort or bare boards and oak panelling, back bar with pool; bedrooms comfortable *(Howard James)*

☆ Llandybie [6 Llandeilo Rd; SN6115], *Red Lion*: Wide choice of generous fresh food inc good fish and Sun lunch in attractive inn's tastefully modernised, spacious and comfortable bar and restaurant; several well kept Whitbreads-related ales, welcoming efficient service, local pictures for sale; bedrooms *(Howard James, J A and R E Collins)*

Llangranog, *Ship*: In pretty fishing village, with tables under canopy by beachside car park giving continental feel in summer; interesting varied home-cooked food inc vegetarian, good Sun carvery, well kept Whitbreads-related ales, open fire; can get busy summer, may be cl Mon in winter; bedrooms *(DJW)*

Llansawel [SN6136], *Angel*: Friendly, with freshly made food, log fire, Whitbreads Strong Country, Worthington BB, darts, pool; small restaurant *(C A Hall)*

Llanwnnen [A475 Lampeter—Newcastle Emlyn; SN5346], *Grannell*: Roomy and comfortably refurbished, with good personal service, well kept Worthington BB, good value largely home-made straightforward food in bar and restaurant; good value bedrooms *(DU, MU)*

Lydstep [SS0898], *Lydstep*: Warm, appealing and well decorated main bar and clean, tidy family room; good home-made food, friendly service, well kept Tetleys and Worthington *(Tim and Tracy Clark, Mr and Mrs Blackbourn)*

Mathry [off A487 Fishguard—St Davids; SM8732], *Farmers Arms*: Welcoming local with happy atmosphere, good generous home-cooked food inc local fish and seafood, well kept Bass and Worthington BB, small garden; has been open all day, at least in summer *(James and Linda Skinner)*

Milton [just off A477; SN0303], *Milton Brewery*: Cosy ex-brewery with attractively unfussy olde-worlde decor, panelling and stripped stonework, popular food, well kept Bass and Worthington BB, friendly staff, open fire each end; seats outside *(H and C Ingham)*

Mynydd Y Garreg [NE of Kidwelly, follow signs to Industrial Museum; SN4308], *Gwenllian Court*: Friendly but busy riverside hotel with good value bar food, well kept Hancocks HB, John Smiths and a guest beer, big bar with cane furniture, good carvery; by old tin-working museum, tables out by water, good walks; good value bedrooms *(Steve Thomas, Huw and Carolyn Lewis)*

☆ Nevern [B4582; SN0840], *Trewern Arms*: Extended inn in lovely setting nr notable church and medieval bridge over River Nyfer, stripped-stone slate-floored bar, rafters hung with rural bric-a-brac, high-backed settles, plush banquettes, usually several well kept Whitbreads-related ales, usual bar food from sandwiches to steaks inc children's, separate lounge, restaurant, tables in pretty garden; loudish games room, lunchtime service can stop too promptly; comfortable bedrooms, big breakfast *(Ron and Sheila Corbett, J Giles Quick, G Washington, LYM)*

☆ Newcastle Emlyn [Sycamore St (A475); [SN3040], *Pelican*: Friendly 17th-c inn with reasonable choice of well priced bar food, real ales, helpful service, pews and panelling, and fireplace with bread oven still recognisable as the one where Rowlandson in 1797 sketched a dog driving the roasting spit; tables in garden, children welcome; bedrooms in adjoining cottage *(Mike and Wendy Proctor, LYM)*

Newcastle Emlyn [Bridge St], *Bunch of Grapes*: Solid oak round tables and chairs in roomy and welcoming bar, well kept Bass and other beers, food inc good cawl and genuinely home-cooked vegetarian dishes (and takeaways or delivered lunches), covered yard with grape vines; in attractive main street leading to bridge *(J Honnor, Michael Richards)*

Newport [East St; SN0539], *Llwyngwair Arms*: Friendly straightforward local with good food inc genuine Indian dishes (takeaways too), well kept Worthington and a cheap house beer, coal fire, lots of rugby and rowing mementoes; copes well with the busy holiday season *(Michael Richards, J Lloyd Jones, Dr and Mrs S A Jones, Maj and Mrs T Savage, Roger Brett)*

Pembroke [High St; SM9801], *Old Kings Arms*: Very pleasant atmosphere, good food at modest prices, quick courteous service, real ale; bedrooms *(Richard and Barbara Philpott)*

☆ Pont Ar Gothi [A40 6 miles E of Carmarthen; SN5021], *Cresselly Arms*: Cosy low-beamed restaurant overlooking river, step up to tiled bar area with fishing memorabilia and copper-topped tables around the edges, another step to relaxing lounge area with woodburner and TV; good value bar food, well kept Whitbreads-related ales, welcoming service, riverside walks *(Michael Richards, Derek and Margaret Underwood, Peter Churchill, Howard James)*

Pont Ar Gothi, *Salutation*: Good friendly atmosphere in traditional pub with promptly served plentiful bar food and good value Sun lunch, well kept Felinfoel Swift and Double Dragon, log fire, big settles in small flagstone-floored rooms, restaurant; bedrooms *(A J Bowen, Joan and Michel Hooper-Immins)*

Pontarsais [A485 Carmarthen—Lampeter; SN4428], *Stag & Pheasant*: Welcoming and unpretentious, with good range of reasonably priced food from cawl to more substantial meals, decent choice of real ales, pleasant decor *(Kathryn and Brian Heathcote)*

☆ nr Ponterwyd [A44 nearly 2 miles E; SN7781], *Dyffryn Castell*: Homely friendly atmosphere, good value bar food and well kept Marstons Pedigree, John Smiths and Worthington BB in unpretentious but comfortable inn beautifully placed below the mountains; bedrooms clean, comfortable and good value *(D Jones-Williams, LYM)*

☆ Porthgain [SM8132], *Sloop*: Largely unspoilt old pub in interesting village, close to old harbour; friendly relaxing local atmosphere, dark bare stone, lots of alcoves, character old furniture, nautical and wreck memorabilia, newer family/eating extension; well kept Felinfoel Double Dragon and Hancocks HB, wide range of good value food inc nice full crab sandwiches, afternoon teas, small seating area outside *(Mike and Wendy Proctor, S Hassrip, John Allsopp)*

Pwll [A487; SN4801], *Colliers Arms*: Useful refreshment stop on holiday route, cheap beer, pleasant terrace *(S Thomas)*

☆ Rhosmaen [SN6424], *Plough*: Deep-cushioned comfort and good value fresh bar food inc good puddings in smart lounge with picture-window views, well kept Bass, tiled front bar, separate less cheap popular restaurant; long-serving friendly licensees *(Howard James, DU, MU, LYM)*

Robeston Wathen [B4314 S; SN0815], *Bridge*: Cottagey pub with comfortable welcoming bar, well kept beer, good food, separate dining room; weekend live entertainment *(T H Adams)*

☆ Saundersfoot [Wogan Terr; SN1304], *Royal Oak*: Very popular friendly and unspoilt local, well kept Bass, Boddingtons and Flowers Original, many dozen malt whiskies, no music or machines, local's bar, two rooms used for tasty food esp fresh fish (booking advised in season), tables outside *(Steve Turner, Rob Holt)*

Solva [Lower Solva; SM8024], *Cambrian Arms*: Attractive and interesting dining pub with pleasant atmosphere, popular bar food inc authentic pasta and huge mixed grill, decent Italian wines, well kept Tetleys-related ales, log fires; no dogs or children *(H D Spottiswoode, Dave Braisted, Dr G W Barnett)*

St Davids [Goat St; SM7525], *Farmers Arms*: Cheap and cheerful genuine pub, busy and well patronised, with good food, well kept Worthington BB, cathedral view from tables in tidy back garden *(Prof I H Rorison, N Gilbourne)*; [centre], *Old Cross*: Good basic food inc delicious ploughman's with local cheese, sensible prices, polite service, genteel atmosphere, good position – get there before the tourist coaches arrive; pleasant garden, bedrooms – some people have been coming for 50 years *(Miss E Evans, Ian Rorison, Heather Martin)*

St Dogmaels [SN1645], *Ferry*: Old stone building with modern additions overlooking Teifi estuary, friendly character bar, pine tables, nice clutter of bric-a-brac inc many old advertising signs; Wadworths 6X, generous bar food, children welcome, tables out on terrace Popular waterside family pub, simply furnished *(Michael Sargent, Mr and Mrs J R Morris, D M Wilkins, LYM)*; *Teifi Netpool*: Run by rugby enthusiast, well kept Llanelli real ale, food inc outstanding dressed crab, spotless oak tables; lovely walk to Poppitt sands *(Patrick Freeman, Mr and Mrs J R Morris)*

St Florence [SM0801], *Sun*: Friendly small pub

with well kept Crown Buckley, decent usual food; children welcome (*Drs R and M Woodford*)

☆ Tenby [Upper Frog St; SN1300], *Coach & Horses*: Comfortable lounge with wide choice of home-made food in at least two fresh locally caught fish dishes, three well kept Whitbreads-related ales, good choice of bottled beers, good service, lively separate bar with games machines and CD juke box; open all day (*Martin Bevan, M E Wellington, Simon Penny*)

Tenby [Quay Hill], *Plantagenet House*: Unusual richly renovated ancient building with marvellous old chimney, three floors with several bar rooms and restaurant, unusual not cheap food inc fine soups, fresh local crab and fish, welsh cheeses; real ales; cl lunchtime out of season (*Shirley Pielou, J A and R E Collins*)

Trapp [now often spelled Trap; SN6518], *Cennen Arms*: Attractive small country pub by bridge, good choice of simple but well cooked food, proper sandwiches, well priced Hancocks HB or Worthington BB, local pictures; picnic tables in small garden, pretty hanging baskets; nr Careg Cennen castle, good walks and lovely countryside (*Jeff and Rhoda Collins, Anne Morris*)

Tresaith [SN2751], *Ship*: Tastefully decorated bistro-style pub on Cardigan Bay with magnificent views of sea, beach and famous waterfall; reasonably priced interesting generous home-made food inc local specialities and children's menu, good range of beers inc Crown Buckleys and a guest such as Wychwood Dr Thirstys (*Deborah Bradley, Catherine McGee*)

☆ Wolfs Castle [A40 Haverfordwest—Fishguard; SM9526], *Wolfe*: Wide choice of good popular home-made food (not Sun or Mon evenings in winter) in comfortable dining lounge, garden room and conservatory, well kept Flowers IPA and Original, decent wines, welcoming staff, attractively laid-out garden; simpler public bar with darts, restaurant; children welcome; bedrooms (*H and A McFarlane, Howard and Lynda Dix, Ken and Jenny Simmonds, Gary Roberts, Ann Stubbs, Peter Churchill, LYM*)

GLAMORGAN – MID

Creigiau [ST0781], *Caesars Arms*: Fine display of good value fish, cooked in open kitchen, with tasty starters and tempting puddings; good wine and coffee, very busy (*David Graham*)

☆ Llangeinor [nr Blackmill; SS9187], *Llangeinor Arms*: Partly 15th-c beamed pub with terrific views from front conservatory (children allowed here), lounge with old Welsh china and bygones, coal fire, friendly helpful staff, decent usual bar food, well kept Bass, Hancocks HB and Brains SA, evening restaurant (*John and Joan Nash, Nigel Clifton, LYM*)

Miskin [Mwyndy, outside village; A4119 nr M4 junction 34; ST0581], *Castell Mynach*: Big pub doing huge lunches (*Dr and Mrs A K Clarke*)

☆ Nottage [Heol y Capel (off A4229); handy for M4 junction 37; SS8178], *Rose & Crown*: Useful Chef & Brewer family dining pub in comfortably modernised old inn not far from coast, flagstones and beams, good choice of usual food in bar and restaurant, friendly service, well kept Courage-related ales, unobtrusive piped music, fruit machine; open all day Sat; children in eating area and restaurant; comfortable well equipped bedrooms (*Dr and Mrs A K Clarke, Judith and Stephen Gregory, LYM*)

Nottage Swan: Attractive old pub with bustling comfortable bar, well kept Bass, Courage Best and Wadworths 6X, pleasant staff, generous lunchtime food inc big filled rolls (*John and Joan Nash*)

☆ Ogmore [B4524; SS8674], *Pelican*: Friendly and comfortable old country local above ruined castle, functional main bar leading back to snug, cosy side area and pretty little bistro, well kept Courage-related ales, welcoming staff, cheap bar food; side terrace with swings beside, quite handy for the beaches (*Nigel Clifton, M and A Sandy, LYM*)

Pontneddfechan [SN9007], *Angel*: Welcoming new landlord in 16th-c inn handy for the waterfalls and good walks around here, well kept Bass and Boddingtons, nicely furnished flagstoned hikers' bar, tables laid for good value food in light and airy main bar; tables on terrace; bedrooms (*John and Joan Nash, Salvo and Gwyneth Spadaro-Dutturi*)

GLAMORGAN – SOUTH

Cardiff [St Marys St, nr Howells], *Cottage*: Popular for well kept Brains SA, Bitter and Dark Mild and good value home-cooked lunches, long bar with narrow frontage and back eating area, lots of polished wood and glass, good cheerful service, decent choice of wines; open all day (*Steve Thomas*); [Atlantic Wharf], *Wharf*: Big newish Victorian-look pub in pleasant setting, now largely residential, on edge of old dock, lunchtime bar food, Brains and changing guest ales, paddle-steamer prints and memorabilia downstairs, small lounge bar, maybe restaurant upstairs, family room tricked out like station platform; local bands Fri/Sat, sometimes Thurs (*M G Hart, Joan and Michel Hooper-Immins*)

☆ Cowbridge [High St, signed off A48; SS9974], *Bear*: Neatly kept old coaching inn with Brains Bitter and SA, Hancocks HB, Worthington BB and a guest beer, decent house wines, friendly young bar staff, flagstones, panelling and big log fire in beamed bar on left, pool and pin table in back games area, quieter room with plush armchairs on right, log-effect gas fires, usual lunchtime bar food from sandwiches up; children welcome; bedrooms quiet and comfortable, good breakfast (*Shelton Little, Ian Williams, Linda Mar, LYM*)

☆ Craig Penllyn [SS9777], *Barley Mow*: Welcoming, with good value food and well kept varied real ales; bedrooms comfortable (*Barbara Davies, Nigel Clifton, Chris Morgan*)

Dinas Powis [Station Rd; ST1571], *Star*: Well kept Brains and good choice of food inc fish and curries in spacious well run four-room village pub, stripped stonework and attractive panelling, heavy Elizabethan beams, two open fires, plainer no-smoking room, juke box elsewhere; friendly licensees, cheerful locals, decent wines by the glass; best to book Sun lunch (*S Thomas, LYM*)

Llancadle [signed off B4265 Barry—Llantwit just E of St Athan; ST0368], *Green Dragon*: Peaceful country pub reopened after fire restoration, flagstone floors, high rafters (still showing scorch marks), old-fashioned atmosphere, lots of bric-a-brac, attractively priced home-cooked bar food popular lunchtime with older people, well kept ales such as Hancocks HB, Hardington Moonshine and a changing guest beer, public bar, tables in garden (*Noel Austin, LYM*)

Llandaff [Cardiff Rd; A4119; ST1578], *Maltsters Arms*: Local atmosphere in cheerful and spacious recently refurbished downstairs bar, more comfort upstairs, well kept Brains ales, good quick lunchtime food; busy later with students and BBC people (*Miss E Evans, BB*)

☆ Monknash [Marcross, Broughton sign off B4265 St Brides Major—Llantwit Major, then left at end of Water St; SS9270], *Plough & Harrow*: Unspoilt and untouched isolated country pub, welcoming and very basic – flagstones, old-fashioned stripped settles, logs burning in cavernous fireplace with huge side bread oven, simple choice of good value food inc vegetarian, up to six ales such as Bass, Hancocks HB, Worthington and maybe some from the Whitbreads family tapped from the cask, daily papers, children welcome; pool, juke box and fruit machine in room on left, picnic tables on grass outside the white cottage (*David Lewis, Mr and Mr S Thomas, Stuart Joy, BB*)

Penarth [Esplanade; ST1871], *Chandlers*: Busy pub/bistro, good value fish and meat barbecues, salad bar (*David Graham*)

Pendoylan [2½ miles from M4 junction 34; ST0576], *Red Lion*: Friendly village pub next to church in pretty vale, well kept Flowers IPA and Original, good food in bar and restaurant; good garden with play boat, tractor and tree house/slide (*Simon Bobeldijk*)

Penllyn [village signposted from A48 Cowbridge—Bridgend; SS9776], *Red Fox*: Good choice of real ales, bargain pub lunches, obliging service, evening restaurant (*Christopher Morgan, BB*)

☆ Sigingstone [SS9771], *Victoria*: Quickly served good food in good veg, not cheap but beautifully presented and good value, in welcoming and spotless neo-Victorian country pub/restaurant; well kept Bass (though not the sort of place to go to for just a drink), pleasant surroundings, good service (*C A and B Bristow, John and Joan Nash*)

GLAMORGAN – WEST

☆ Bishopston [50 Bishopston Rd, off B4436; SS5789], *Joiners Arms*: Thriving local, clean and welcoming, with quarry-tiled floor, traditional furnishings, local paintings and

massive solid fuel stove; cheap simple food lunchtime and early evening, particularly well kept Courage-related ales with guests such as Brains Dark Mild and Marstons Pedigree, children welcome, open all day Thurs-Sat – the rugby club's local on Sat nights; parking can be difficult (*John and Joan Nash, Michael Launder, LYM*)

Glais [625 Birchgrove Rd, off A4067 a mile from M4 junction 45; SN7000], *Old Glais*: Traditional old two-bar pub in lovely surroundings, warm welcome, good atmosphere, good range of well kept beers, interesting varied reasonably priced food, quite a few antiques (*Mrs S Wright*)

Gowerton [by traffic lights junction B4296/B4295; SS5896], *Welcome*: Spacious pub with cheery atmosphere and comfortable plush banquettes, well kept Buckleys, good value generous bar food inc good pizzas, big panelled dining room; high chairs etc for children (*the Sandy family*)

☆ Kittle [18 Pennard Rd; SS5789], *Beaufort Arms*: Attractive old pub below ancient chestnut tree, plenty of character in carefully renovated saloon with stripped beams and stonework, comfortably cushioned settles, shortish choice of good food esp fresh fish, also sandwiches, quick friendly service, well kept Crown Buckley Rev James, similar public bar though with less seating (*Anthony Marriott*)

Mumbles [Park Rd; SS6287], *Park*: Cosy little backstreet pub with wide range of interesting well kept beers, good home-cooked food inc popular Sun lunch, lots of photographs of old Mumbles Railway, attractive plate collection (*Brian Thomas, Phil Davies*)

☆ Oldwalls [SS4891], *Greyhound*: Reasonably priced popular bar food inc good local fish and ploughman's with choice of welsh cheeses in busy but spacious and comfortable beamed and dark-panelled lounge bar, half a dozen well kept ales, some tapped from the cask, inc Bass and Hancocks HB, good coffee inc decaf, decent wine, roaring coal or log fires, friendly service; back bar with display cases; restaurant popular at weekends, folk club Sun; big tree-shaded garden with play area and good views (*Richard Startup, Chris Brown*)

Pontardulais [A48 to Pontlliw; SN5903], *Glamorgan Arms*: Pleasant bar with little side rooms, nice prints and good range of ales such as Courage, Shepherd Neame Spitfire, good value interesting food; remarkably big play area outside, with cafe-style building, summer bar, terrace and picnic tables (*the Sandy family*)

Pontlliw [A48 towards Pontardulais from M4 junction 47; SN6100], *Buck*: Useful stop – chain dining pub, some tables on grassed area with slides and swing by little river at end of car park (*HM*)

☆ Reynoldston [SS4789], *King Arthur*: Prettily set overlooking green and common, in good walking country (discounts for YHA members), spacious and airy bar with big log fire, rugs on floorboards, prints, warming pans, interesting displays eg bullets, delft shelf;

plusher dining lounge, back games bar; interesting food changing daily inc fresh fish, well kept Bass and Felinfoel Double Dragon, cheerful staff, quiet piped music; back garden with play area, bedrooms *(Dave Braisted, Dorothy and Leslie Pilson, A J Bowen, Nigel Clifton, John and Joan Nash)*

Swansea [Oystermouth Rd; A4067 towards Mumbles; SS6593], *Fisherman & Firkin*: Massive cleaned-up Victorian-looking building, newly refurbished in traditional style, efficient helpful staff, house beers, lots of standing room around the pillars, plenty of tables, games area one end; very popular esp with younger people *(Michael Sandy)*

Ynystawe [634 Clydach Rd; A4067 just N of M4 junction 45; SN6800], *Millers Arms*: Well decorated cottagey pub with welcoming staff, Marstons Pedigree, generous food inc good lunchtime special *(Mrs S Wright)*

GWENT

☆ Abergavenny [Mkt St; SO3014], *Greyhound*: Particularly good interesting food at sensible prices, Boddingtons, decent wines, good service, comfortable friendly surroundings; good evening meals – more restauranty then *(Mrs Linda Bonnell)*

Abergavenny [Flannel St], *Hen & Chickens*: Small local with tidy bar and cosy back room, good choice of wholesome cheap home-cooked food and thick lunchtime sandwiches, well kept ales inc Bass, friendly staff; can be smoky *(Mike Pugh, Keith Jones)*; [3 miles out on Brecon Rd (A40)], *Lamb & Flag*: Refurbished pub with big helpings of good value food in bar or two dining rooms, well kept Brains Bitter, SA and Mild in big bar, good service; children welcome, high chairs; open all day in summer, looks out to Brecon Beacons – tables outside with play area; comfortable bedrooms *(Joan and Michel Hooper-Immins)*; [Brecon Rd (A40 halfway to Crickhowell)], *Llanwenarth Arms*: Beautifully placed 16th-c riverside inn with views of hills, good restaurant, several real ales, conservatory; 18 well equipped bedrooms *(Margaret and Nigel Dennis)*

Bettws Newydd [SO3606], *Black Bear*: Pleasant and welcoming, good varied changing food, good choice of ales and wines *(Paul Fry, Miss M Desmond)*

Caerleon [Llanhennock, N; ST3592], *Wheatsheaf*: Friendly country pub with cosy bar and snug, good collection of small plates and mugs, three well kept beers inc Bass, good value food (not weekend evenings); children welcome *(Mike Pugh, Ian Williams, Linda Mar, Emma Kingdon, A R and B E Sayer)*

☆ Chepstow [ST5394], *Bridge*: Civilised low-ceilinged pub beautifully placed opp Wye bridge, flagstoned entrance, carpeted main room with light pine tables and chairs, prints on walls, open fire; attractively served bar food, quietly friendly staff, well kept real ales; tables out in delightful garden with castle view *(Mike Pugh)*

☆ Clydach [Old Black Rock Rd, signed off A465; SO2213], *Rock & Fountain*: Good

generous fresh food inc vegetarian at attractive prices, unusual bar with integral rock 'waterfall' in big plush dining area, lovely mountainside spot, very welcoming owners, well kept Bass, Brains and Theakstons; dogs and children welcome, good value clean bedrooms, good traditional breakfasts *(Gwyneth and Salvo Spadaro-Dutturi, John and Elisabeth Cox, BB)*

Clydach, *Drum & Monkey*: Old pub in scenic spot, cheerful helpful staff, good rather upmarket reasonably priced food in pretty bar and restaurant, real ale *(Margaret and Nigel Dennis, A R and B E Sayer)*

Cross Ash [B4521 E of Abergavenny; SO4119], *Three Salmons*: Small, warmly comfortable and friendly, with wide choice of good cheap food, changing real ales, efficient service *(Paul and Heather Bettesworth, Barry Watling)*

Gilwern [High St; SO2414], *Bridgend*: Good range of well kept changing beers and of nicely presented food in small welcoming canalside pub with canal-related prints, friendly staff, sleepy red setter; children welcome; tiled terrace on grassy rise above moorings *(Nigel Clifton)*

Grosmont [SO4024], *Angel*: Simple friendly 17th-c village pub on attractive steep single street – nice to sit out, next to ancient market hall and not far from castle and 13th-c church; welcoming atmosphere, usual bar food, well kept Crown Buckley *(R T and J C Moggridge, BB)*; [B4347 N], *Cupids Hill*: An essential for collectors of unspoilt pubs, basic cottage bar on very steep hill in pretty countryside, old settles by fire, low white ceiling, one keg beer, table skittles, dominoes, cribbage; in same family for 80-odd years *(Gordon, BB)*

Hollybush [A4048 S of Tredegar; SO1603], *Hollybush*: Simple well presented bar food, good Sun lunches, small bistro restaurant, well kept Ansells, Bass and Tetleys, log fire, lovely country location *(A R and E B Sayer)*

☆ Llangattock Lingoed [SO3620], *Hunters Moon*: Attractive beamed and flagstoned country pub nr Offa's Dyke, two character bars dating from 13th c, very friendly atmosphere, well kept Bass; landlord plays the bagpipes, wife does the cooking, very welcoming dog *(Gwyneth and Salvo Spadaro-Dutturi, KB, DH, BB)*

☆ Llantarnam [Newport Rd (A4042 N of M4 junction 26); ST3093], *Greenhouse*: Welcoming and roomy, lots of dark wood, big civilised good value dining room (children welcome, anything from good sandwiches to kangaroo), well kept Courage-related ales, beautiful big tree-sheltered garden with terrace and play area *(the Sandy family)*

Llantilio Crosseny [SO3915], *Halfway House*: Comfortable 16th-c local with flagstones and log fire, well kept Bass and Felinfoel Double Dragon, friendly staff, good food inc sandwiches, some unusual specials and vegetarian, no-smoking area, darts, children welcome; well kept cricket field *(Paul and Heather Bettesworth, Salvo and Gwyneth Spadaro-Dutturi)*; *Hostry*: Relaxing 15th-c pub in very quiet pretty village; beams, flagstones, log fire, lots of character (you can believe it's haunted), interesting ales such as Wye Valley Hereford, simple home-cooked bar food inc good vegetarian choice and cheap Sun lunches, dining room; children welcome, bedrooms comfortable *(Karen Burgess, Dylan Hawkings, A R and E B Sayer)*

☆ **Llantrisant** [off A449; ST3997], *Greyhound*: Good hill views from attractive country pub with well presented reasonably priced reliable home-cooked bar food inc vegetarian, spacious open-plan rooms, friendly service; bedrooms in small attached motel – lovely setting *(A R and B E Sayer)*

☆ **Llanvapley** [B4223 Abergavenny—Monmouth; SO3714], *Red Hart*: Nicely placed by cricket pitch in interesting village with Saxon church, good log fire, lunchtime snacks and good extensive evening menu inc vegetarian and good value steaks, ales such as Crown Buckley Rev James, Hogs Back, Smiles and Tetleys, darts, skittles, pool; tables outside *(A R and B E Sayer, Alan Baird)*

Mathern [ST5291], *Millers Arms*: Good generous food at reasonable prices, choice of real ales *(M E Tennick)*

☆ **Monmouth** [Lydart; B4293 towards Trelleck; SO5009], *Gockett*: Old carefully extended pub, pleasant lounge bar with eating areas and small restaurant, good range of generous hot food inc good Sun lunch and puddings, real ales such as Bass and Hardington, good welcoming service; tables in attractive garden; children welcome; bedrooms with own bathrooms, good breakfast *(A Y Drummond, Revd A Nunnerley, Richard and Alison Evans, Mrs S Thursfield, John Champion)*

Nantyderry [between A4042 and B4598 (former A471) N of Pontypool and Usk – OS Sheet 161 map ref 332061; SO3306], *Foxhunter*: Comfortable and spotless country pub with wide range of good food inc vegetarian in bar and restaurant, well kept Bass and other ales, quick service; good garden with fountain, lawn and swing *(Sylvia Jones, M E Tennick)*

nr **Pontypool** [Coed-y-paen; ST2998], *Carpenters Arms*: Pretty country pub with reasonably priced food, pleasant seating outside, play area *(Salvo and Gwyneth Spadaro-Dutturi)*

☆ **Rhyd Y Meirch** [up cul-de-sac off A4042 S of Abergavenny – OS Sheet 161 map ref 289073; SO2807], *Goose & Cuckoo*: Tiny unspoilt country pub run by very friendly Scottish couple, lots of malt and blended whiskies, good home-cooked food esp vegetarian, well kept Bullmastiff, Wadworths 6X and more esoteric ales; near hill walks, vietnamese pot-bellied pigs in field behind; dogs allowed if on lead *(Anne Morris, Mike Pugh)*

Rogerstone [Cefn Rd; A467 nr M4 junction 27; ST2688], *Tredegar Arms*: Rather unexpected for the area, with low beams, cosy and friendly feel, good food, well kept ale *(Dr and Mrs A K Clarke)*

☆ **Shirenewton** [B4235 Chepstow—Usk; ST4893], *Carpenters Arms*: Four small nicely

decorated rooms off central bar, flagstone floors, two good log fires, welcoming staff, seven well kept ales inc guests such as Bass, Hook Norton Best, Theakstons XB, wide choice of good value food from sandwiches to Sun lunch; still has the huge bellows used when this was a smithy; beautiful hanging baskets and little flowerbeds in summer; children may be allowed *(Nigel Clifton, Emma Kingdon, Peter Hesketh, A R and B E Sayer)*

☆ **Talycoed** [B4233 Monmouth—Abergavenny; SO4115], *Halfway House*: Well run unspoilt 16th-c character inn in lovely setting, good fresh home-cooked food (not Sun evening), friendly service, well kept real ale, log fires, timbers and stripped stone; tables in well kept garden, charming views; bedrooms *(Malcolm Taylor, Paul and Heather Bettesworth)*

The Narth [off B4293 Trelleck—Monmouth; SO5206], *Trekkers*: Unusual and welcoming, esp for children, like a log cabin high in valley, lots of wood with central fireplace, helpful licensee, good generous food inc fun ice creams, good range of well kept ales, facilities for the disabled; long back garden, skittle alley *(LM)*

Tintern [Devauden Rd, off A446 Chepstow—Monmouth; SO5301], *Cherry Tree*: Quaint unspoilt country pub, well kept Hancocks PA and farm cider, charming garden; children welcome *(Paul and Heather Bettesworth)*; [A466], *Moon & Sixpence*: Attractively furnished small pub, well kept real ale, decent food, friendly service, natural spring feeding indoor goldfish pool; tiny windows, but nice view over River Wye *(Dennis Heatley)*; [A466], *Rose & Crown*: Unpretentious inn opp abbey with good value generous food; comfortable bedrooms *(Geoffrey Lindley, BB)*

☆ **Trelleck** [B4293 S of Monmouth; SO5005], *Village Green*: Comfortable and welcoming beamed restaurant/bistro in sensitively preserved old building, cosy little bar, well kept Bass and Worthington, good wines, prints, lots of dried flowers, good changing food using local produce; piped Radio 1; bedrooms in well converted former stables *(R C Morgan, Kevin Gray)*

☆ **Trelleck Grange** [minor rd St Arvans—Trelleck; SO4902], *Fountain*: Welcoming 17th-c inn with cheerful landlord, good home-made food from sandwiches up, well kept beers, interesting range of malt whiskies, decent wines, courteous non-intrusive service, restaurant; attractive garden, lovely countryside; bedrooms simple but clean and comfortable *(Richard and Alison Evans, W L Clarke, Mrs S Thursfield)*

Usk [The Square; SO3801], *Castle*: Useful for food all day; Whitbreads-related ales *(Anne Morris)*; [The Square], *Nags Head*: Relaxed and pleasant, unusual food esp home-made pies and game in season, interesting decor, well kept ales *(Mike Pugh, Dr and Mrs A K Clarke)*

GWYNEDD

☆ **Barmouth** [Church St; SH6116], *Last*: Welcoming 15th-c harbourside local, once a cobbler's cottage, with low beams, flagstones, ship's lamps, little waterfall down back bar's natural rock wall, wide choice of good cheap bar lunches inc local crab, well kept Marstons Pedigree, friendly service *(Joan and Michel Hooper-Immins, Stuart Courtney)*

☆ Beddgelert [SH5948], *Prince Llewelyn*: Plush hotel bar with log fire and raised dining area, simpler summer bar, good atmosphere, helpful staff, wide choice of good value generous bar food, well kept Robinsons, rustic seats on verandah overlooking village stream and hills – great walking country; busy at peak holiday times, children allowed at quiet times; bedrooms pleasant, with good breakfast *(Peter and Audrey Dowsett, R Morgan, BB)*

Betws Y Coed [Holyhead Rd; SH7956], *Glan Aber*: Hotel with two lounges and restaurant, good friendly service, well kept Ansells Bitter and Mild, Dyffryn Clwyd Druids, Marstons Pedigree and Tetley Walkers Bitter and Dark Mild, very wide choice of good food from good sandwiches up, high chairs; comfortable bedrooms *(Richard Lewis)*; *Royal Oak*: Much more hotel than pub, but good range of food esp local fish in civilised grill bar or more upmarket restaurant, also big side stables bar with pool, juke box and TV one end, eating area the other, reasonably priced menu, Whitbreads-related ales, lots of tables out in courtyard; friendly staff, open all day; bedrooms *(Roger Byrne, Phil and Heidi Cook, E G Parish, John A Barker)*

Caernarfon [Northgate St; SH4863], *Black Boy*: Bustling local by castle walls, beams from ships wrecked here in 16th c, bare floors, cheery fire, homely and cosy atmosphere, good choice of ales inc Bass, good value well presented food in bar and restaurant, pleasant service; TV in main bar *(KB, DH)*

☆ Capel Curig [SH7258], *Bryn Tyrch*: Good choice of hearty food esp vegetarian dishes, well kept ales such as Marstons Pedigree and Whitbreads Castle Eden, cheery young staff, cosy pleasantly informal beamed bar with old pews and faded leather easy chairs, big restaurant, good summer mix of walkers and holiday people; basic good value bedrooms *(M Mason, D Thompson, John A Barker, Ron Leigh, Neville and Sarah Hargreaves)*

☆ Capel Curig, *Cobdens*: Civilised feel, with good varied satisfying food inc home-made bread and interesting vegetarian dishes, well kept Courage-related beers, good pleasant service, friendly old english sheepdog and border collie cross; so close to mountain that back bar has bare rockface, lovely river scene across road, good walks all around; bedrooms *(N Gilbourne, KC)*

☆ Capel Garmon [signed from A470 just outside Betwys y coed, towards Llanrwst; SH8255], *White Horse*: Low-beamed inn dating from 16th c, comfortable and homely, with welcoming licensees, log fires, well kept Bass, Stones and Worthington BB, wide choice of food inc local salmon and game, prettily refurbished cottage restaurant, games in public bar; bedrooms simple but comfortable (quietest in new part), fine countryside with magnificent views *(K H Frostick, John A Barker, Peter Titchmarsh, Dave Thompson, Margaret Mason, D W Jones-Williams)*

Conwy [Quay; SH7878], *Liverpool Arms*: Outside walls by water, with some parking and seating on quay; warm inside, with dark panelling, stained glass, settles, tables and stools, open fire, nautical prints; well kept Bass, Bass Mild and Worthington BB, good atmosphere, can be packed with friendly locals; Sky TV music channel, open all day *(Richard Lewis)*

☆ Dinas Mawddwy [just off A470; SH8615], *Llew Coch*: Genuine country local with charming timbered front bar dripping with sparkling brasses, well kept Bass, friendly staff, food inc trout or salmon from River Dovey just behind; plainer inner family room lively with video games, pool and Sat evening live music, tables out on quiet lane; surrounded by steep fir forests, good walks *(John Hazel, KB, DH, Dave Thompson, Margaret Mason, BB)*

Dyffryn Ardudwy [SH5823], *Ael-y-Bryn*: Nicely placed hotel with public bar, conservatory, friendly landlord, good food inc home-made soup, Courage-related real ales; bedrooms *(W H and E Thomas)*

Edern [Lleyn Peninsula; SH2839], *Ship*: Decent main-road pub with good food inc locally caught fish, well kept beers; bedrooms, holiday cottage *(the Goldsons)*

Gellilydan [off A543; SH6839], *Bryn Arms*: Good good-value food, friendly landlord *(D W Jones-Williams)*

☆ Llandudno [Old St; SH7883], *Kings Head*: Friendly rambling pub, much extended around 16th-c core, spaciously open-plan, with comfortable traditional furnishings, red wallpaper, dark pine, wide range of generous food, changing Tetleys-related real ales, smart back dining room up a few steps; children welcome, open all day in summer, seats in front overlooking quaint Victorian tramway's station *(Nigel and Sue Foster, Mike and Wendy Proctor, Mike and Penny Sanders, LYM)*

Llandudno [1 Market St], *Cottage Loaf*: Pleasant atmosphere, good lunchtime bar snacks, several well kept mainly Courage-related real ales, big open fire, flagstones and bare boards, salvaged ship's timbers, good piped music, some live music *(Richard Lewis)*

☆ Llandwrog [aka Ty'n Llan; ½ mile W of A499 S of Caernarfon; SH4456], *Harp*: Attractive pub in pretty village, friendly locals, happy staff, good value food inc Sun roast, well kept Whitbreads-related real ales, comfortable straightforward furnishings; good bedrooms *(B A and R Davies, M A Cameron, D W Jones-Williams, Dave Thompson, Margaret Mason)*

Llanwnda [signed off A499 S of Caernarfon; SH4758], *Goat*: Friendly village local with back bar divided by traditional small-paned hatch servery, coal fire, games room with pool, genteel front room; tables outside, children welcome, cheap good value bedrooms *(D Thompson, M Mason, LYM)*

☆ Morfa Nefyn [A497/B4412; SH2840], *Bryncynan*: Welcoming modernised pub concentrating (particularly in summer) on quickly served well presented good value bar food inc good vegetarian choice, local fish and seafood; quiet in winter with good log fire; above-average summer choice of well kept Tetleys-related ales, restaurant, rustic seats outside, children allowed; cl Sun *(Mr and Mrs D J Brooks, LYM)*

☆ Penmaenpool [SH6918], *George III*: Attractive inn with cheery 17th-c beamed and flagstoned bottom bar and civilised partly panelled upstairs bar opening into cosy and chintzy inglenook lounge; lovely views over Mawddach estuary, sheltered terrace, good walks; good unpretentious home-cooked food in bar and restaurant, efficient service, Courage-related ales under light CO2 blanket, good choice of wines by the glass, children in eating area, open all day; good bedrooms inc some in interesting conversion of former station on disused line *(Monica Shelley, Sharon Hancock, F C Johnston, Peter and Sarah Gooderham, Mrs C Watkinson, Miss E Evans, LYM)*

Pentir [SH5767], *Vaynol Arms*: Good food inc children's helpings in bar and new extension restaurant, friendly service, children very welcome; Theakstons Old Peculier and a guest ale *(Alan Ashcroft, Michael Wadsworth)*

☆ Porth Dinllaen [beach car park signed from Morfa Nefyn, then a good 15-min walk – which is part of the attraction; SH2741], *Ty Coch*: Right on curving beach, far from the roads, with stunning view along coast to mountains; pub itself full of attractive salvage and RNLI memorabilia; keg beer, decent coffee, usual food; may be closed much of winter, but open all day summer *(John Evans, LYM)*

☆ Porthmadog [aka Y Llong; Lombard St, behind playing fields in centre, nr harbour; SH5639], *Ship*: Peaceful welcoming backstreet local with wide choice of mostly fresh generous nicely cooked bar food inc Chinese, popular upstairs evening Cantonese restaurant, well kept Ind Coope Burton, Tetleys and a weekly guest beer, beer festival early Oct; huge open fireplace in lounge (mainly eating in here), nautical decor, long comfortable public bar, Welsh-speaking regulars; children may be allowed in small back room with video games/fruit machines, beyond pool room *(Joan and Michel Hooper-Immins, J C T Tan, David Lewis, Jim Brickley)*

Tal Y Bont [B5106 6 miles S of Conwy, towards Llanwrst; SH7669], *Lodge*: Hotel doing good value meals esp fish and seafood, some home-grown veg; very friendly staff, good bedrooms *(D W Jones-Williams, KC)*; *Ysgethin*: Wide range of bar meals, wet walkers welcome *(Peter and Sarah Gooderham)*

Tal Y Cafn [A470 Conway—Llanwrst; SH7972], *Tal y Cafn*: Good reasonably priced bar food worth the wait in cheerful and comfortable lounge bar with big inglenook, friendly staff, Greenalls, spacious garden; children welcome; handy for Bodnant *(M A Cameron, LYM)*

Talyllyn [SH7209], *Ty'n y Cornel*: Pleasant gloriously placed fishing inn with big lounge looking out over the lake, helpful service, good reasonably priced bar food, more expensive restaurant; decent bedrooms with own bathrooms *(W H and E Thomas)*

Trefriw [SH7863], *Princes Arms*: Pleasant atmosphere, friendly licensee, good food, attractive view; children allowed, bedrooms *(D W Jones-Williams)*

☆ Tremadog [SH5640], *Golden Fleece*: Busy stonebuilt inn on attractive square, friendly attentive staff, good value generous bar food inc vegetarian, well kept Bass, Mild and Marstons Pedigree, decent wines, cosy partly partitioned rambling beamed lounge with open fire, nice little snug, separate bistro (children allowed here and in small family room), games room, intriguing cellar bar, tables in sheltered inner courtyard; cl Sun *(Gordon Theaker, E H and R F Warner, LYM)*

Tremadog [The Square], *Union*: Decent plentiful well served food in attractively decorated restaurant behind clean and tidy traditional stone-built pub *(Dr M I Crichton)*

☆ Tudweiliog [Nefyn Rd; B4417, Lleyn Peninsula; SH2437], *Lion*: Cheerily unpretentious village inn with wide choice of decent straightforward food inc well prepared vegetarian dishes and good puddings in bar and no-smoking family dining conservatory (small helpings for children); fast helpful service, well kept Boddingtons, Marstons Pedigree, Ruddles Best and Theakstons Best and Mild, lots of whiskies, games and juke box in lively public bar; pleasant garden, recently refurbished bedrooms *(Mr and Mrs D J Brooks, Roger Byrne, the Goldsons, Keith and Maureen Barnes, LYM)*

POWYS

Beguildy [B4355 Knighton—Newtown; SO1979], *Radnorshire Arms*: Beautifully set pretty little black and white pub with very small lounge and dining area, immaculately kept, reasonably priced food and Tetleys *(Dorothy and Leslie Pilson)*

Berriew [SJ1801], *Lion*: Black and white timber-framed country inn in interesting attractive village, good home-cooked food in bar and restaurant, Bass and Worthington with guest beers such as Greene King and Shepherd Neame, decent house wines, fairly smart atmosphere, friendly attentive service, separate public bar; good bedrooms *(D Jones-Williams, Peter Gooderham, Paul and Maggie Baker, John and Joan Wyatt)*

☆ Bleddfa [A488 Knighton—Penybont; SO2168], *Hundred House*: Welcoming country local with comfortable and attractively furnished stripped-stone lounge bar, big inglenook log fire, good home cooking, well kept Flowers Original and Worthington Best, big separate bar and games room – walkers welcome; tables in garden

with barbecue, lovely countryside; bedrooms simple but comfortable, good breakfast *(Dorsan Baker, G R Sunderland)*
Brecon [SO0428], *Three Horseshoes*: Log fires, good choice of food in relaxed restaurant area with friendly attentive service, well kept beers, wide choice of malt whiskies *(Sue Lee)*

☆ **Carno** [A470 Newtown—Machynlleth; SN9697], *Aleppo Merchant*: Plushly modernised stripped stone bar, small lounge with open fire, unusual tapestries, no-smoking area, games in public bar, wide choice of usual food from sandwiches to steaks, well kept Boddingtons, Brains SA and an occasional guest beer, welcoming staff, restaurant (children allowed here), tables in garden; piped music; good value refurbished bedrooms *(Thorstein Moen, W H and E Thomas, Sue and Bob Ward, I M Kirk, Miles and Deborah Protter, G Washington, Mr and Mrs G M Pierce, Dr M V Jones, Mike and Wendy Proctor, LYM)*

☆ **Coedway** [B4393 W of Shrewsbury; SJ3415], *Old Hand & Diamond*: Roomy and pleasant, with well kept beers, log fire, good reasonably priced food in dining area and restaurant, smaller back bar, friendly service, no music *(RP, BP)*

☆ **Crickhowell** [New Rd; SO2118], *Bridge End*: Good-humoured and attractive roomy local in good spot by many-arched bridge over weir of river Usk, good straightforward food, gleaming furniture, well kept Bass and Worthington BB on handpump; open all day *(Barry and Anne)*
Crickhowell, *Gliffaes*: Informal and peaceful country-house hotel worth knowing for good bar meals (also restaurant); terrace with glorious view over Usk valley, two attractive lounges, nice conservatory, very willing staff; good bedrooms *(CR)*
Cwm Owen [B4520 S of Builth Wells; SO0144], *Griffin*: Gaslit drovers' inn with good home-cooked food in flagstoned bar and restaurant, friendly licensee; three comfortable bedrooms *(M E Jones)*

☆ **Derwenlas** [A487 Machynlleth—Aberystwyth; SN7299], *Black Lion*: Quaint but smart 16th-c country pub, huge log fire in low-beamed cottagey bar divided by oak posts and cartwheels, good home-cooked food inc vegetarian in dining area, well kept Boddingtons, decent wines, attentive service, unobtrusive piped music; garden up behind with adventure playground and steps up into woods *(DJW, Peter and Sarah Gooderham, J A Collins)*

☆ **Dolfor** [inn sign up hill off A483 about 4 miles S of Newtown; SO1187], *Dolfor Inn*: Generous good value above-average bar food and friendly service in much modernised hillside inn with easy chairs in beamed lounge opening into neatly modern dining area, well kept ales, unobtrusive piped music, good views from behind; bedrooms comfortable and good value *(M Owton, LYM)*
Elan Valley [B4518 below reservoir; off A44/A470 in Rhayader; SN9365], *Elan Valley*: Small hotel with enthusiastic new

owners, good lunches, teas and suppers, well stocked bar, good wine list; attractively placed, handy for the lakes; bedrooms *(Anon)*
Garthmyl [SO1999], *Nags Head*: Good choice of generous home-cooked food (even properly cured home-cooked ham for the sandwiches), real effort made in presentation and service, well kept beers, open fire in lounge; handy for Montgomery Canal, good towpath walks *(Pete Yearsley)*

☆ **Gladestry** [SO2355], *Royal Oak*: Relaxing unpretentious beamed and flagstoned village local handy for Offa's Dyke Path, friendly service, well kept Bass and Felinfoel Double Dragon, low-priced claret, simple home cooking; refurbished lounge, separate bar, children allowed, picnic tables in lovely secluded garden behind, safe for children; lunch opening 12-2; cheap well refurbished bedrooms, good breakfast *(Geoffrey Lindley, Drs Sarah and Peter Gooderham, KB, DH)*
Glasbury [B4350 towards Hay, just N of A438; SO1739], *Harp*: Snug log-fire lounge and airy games bar with picture windows over garden sloping to River Wye, usual bar food inc children's (children very welcome), well kept Robinsons and Whitbreads-related ales; good value simple bedrooms, good breakfast *(RJH, LYM)*
Guilsfield [3 miles N of Welshpool; SJ2212], *Kings Head*: Clean and shiny old pub with well kept Boddingtons and Flowers IPA, wide choice of genuine home cooking inc vegetarian, chatty landlady, beautiful big garden with tubs and hanging baskets; walkers welcome *(Pete Yearsley)*

☆ **Hay on Wye** [Bull Ring; SO2342], *Kilvert Court*: Small well furnished hotel bar popular with young people, flagstones and candles, friendly staff, well kept Boddingtons and Whitbreads Castle Eden, decent house wines, good range of food in bar and restaurant; live music some Thurs, quiz Sun; outside tables overlooking small town square; bedrooms immaculate and well equipped *(Mrs C Watkinson, Ian Williams, Linda Mar, Sarah and Peter Gooderham)*
Hay on Wye [off Castle St], *Blue Boar*: Ancient stone building nr castle, engaging jumble of tables, chairs, settles and sofas on flagstones, ancient log fireplace, nooks and crannies, lots of bric-a-brac, informal friendly atmosphere and service, well kept ales inc Bass, Boddingtons and Morlands Old Speckled Hen, decent wines, good value generous lunchtime bar food from long buffet counter, Thai evening meals (authentic but not cheap), front dining room *(Sue Demont, Tim Barrow, Ian Williams, Linda Mar, Annette and Stephen Marsden, Nigel Woolliscroft, KB, DH)*; *Three Tuns*: One for lovers of the unspoilt, tiny little quarry-tiled bar with chatty landlady, wall benches and Edwardian bar fittings; no food *(KB, DH)*
Knighton [SO2972], *Horse & Jockey*: Good food and service, well kept beer, tables in pleasant courtyard *(Gill and Maurice McMahon)*; *Red Lion*: Generous well cooked cheap meals *(Geoffrey Lindley)*

Libanus [Tai'r-Bull; A470 SW of Brecon; SN9925], *Bull*: Popular local with well kept Welsh Bitter, decent fairly cheap plain food, very friendly staff *(Dick Brown, Dr G W Barnett)*

Llandrindod Wells [Temple St (A470); SO0561], *Metropole*: Big Edwardian hotel's comfortable front bar with glassed-in terrace, useful for all-day snack service; well kept Whitbreads-related ales; bedrooms *(Joan and Michel Hooper-Immins)*

Llanfihangel Nant Melan [SO1858], *Fforest*: Lounge bar with beams and 16th-c stripped stone, welcoming new licensees, good home cooking, good range of beers; restaurant in former cow byre *(Peter and Sarah Gooderham)*

Llanfyllin [High St (A490); SJ1419], *Cain Valley*: Old coaching inn with welcoming helpful staff, good food inc fresh veg and well kept beers in hotelish panelled lounge bar; handsome Jacobean staircase to comfortable bedrooms, good breakfast *(A N Ellis, KB, DH)*

☆ Llangurig [Pant Mawr; A44 Aberystwyth rd, 4½ miles W; SN8482], *Glansevern Arms*: Very civilised, by main road but quite alone up in the mountains – a fine place to stay, with big warm clean bedrooms; cushioned antique settles and log fire in high-beamed bar (used by locals too), well kept Bass and Worthington Dark Mild, decent malt whiskies and wines, lunchtime sandwiches and hot soup (not Sun) with maybe cold wild salmon in season; good value seven-course dinners (not Sun evening; must book, and courses served to fairly strict timing), comfortable residents' lounge *(G Nagle, N J Clifton, Heather Martin, Philip Moses, LYM)*

☆ Llangynidr [B4558, Cwm Crawnon; SO1519], *Coach & Horses*: Friendly and spacious, with wide choice of good generous uncomplicated food, well kept Crown Buckley and Hancocks HB, open fire, pub games, restaurant; children welcome, safely fenced pretty sloping waterside garden by Brecon—Monmouth Canal across road, lovely views and walks *(M B Crump, Mrs P Goodwyn, LM, LYM)*

Llangynidr [off B4558], *Red Lion*: Creeper-covered 16th-c inn, attractively furnished bow-windowed bar with Theakstons Best and XB and a guest ale, good sandwiches and wide range of hot dishes, lively games room, sheltered pretty garden; comfortable bedrooms *(Mr and Mrs A Plumb, Ian Mabberley, LYM)*

Llanyre [SO0462], *Bell*: Old but modernised inn, comfortable and well kept, with wide choice of good food, efficient warmly welcoming service, stylish restaurant; bedrooms *(Frank Cummins)*

☆ Machynlleth [Heol Pentrerhedyn; A489, nr junction with A487; SH7501], *White Lion*: Welcoming mix of locals and visitors in roomy bar with dark oak and copper-topped seats, dark pink plush seats, well kept Banks's Bitter and Mild and Marstons Pedigree, big log fire, wide range of food inc good vegetarian and

children's choices, side dining area, service brisk and cheerful even on busy Weds market day; best to book for 3-course Sun lunch; pretty views from picnic tables in attractive garden; neatly modernised stripped pine bedrooms *(J B and C N Ennion, Mervyn and Zilpha Reed, M Joyner, PG)*

New Radnor [SO2160], *Eagle*: Good food, hospitable licensee *(Kate Langdon-Mead)*

☆ Old Radnor [SO2559], *Harp*: Superb peaceful hilltop position, with lovely views and good walks nearby (despite the quarries), fine inglenook and elderly seats in slate-floored lounge, stripped-stone public bar with a smaller log fire and old-fashioned settles, limited but generous bar food (not Mon), real ales inc Woods, decent wines, character dining room with antique curved settle and other high-backed seats, friendly service, interesting nick-nacks for sale, three sleepy amiable cats; seats outside with play area, pleasant bedrooms, good breakfast *(A E and P McCully, PG, SG, Liz and Roger Morgan, Tim and Tina Banks, G R Sunderland, Lynn Sharpless, Bob Eardley, Chris and Tricia Hubbard, T R and B C Jenkins, Peter and Lynn Brueton, LYM)*

Pencelli [B4558 SE of Brecon; SO0924], *Royal Oak*: Reopened under welcoming new licensees, fine polished wood floor in big whitewashed bar, second small cosy bar, well kept Boddingtons, bar food, charming terrace backing on to canal and fields, lovely canal walks *(John and Joan Nash)*

Penderyn [off A4059 at Lamb to T-junction then up narrow hill; SN9408], *Red Lion*: Old stonebuilt Welsh local high in good walking country, open fires, dark beams, antique settles, blazing log fires, well kept ales such as Bass, Brains, Everards and Marstons Pedigree, welcoming licensees; children tolerated if they sit quietly; great views from big garden *(Gwyneth and Salvo Spadaro-Dutturi, LYM)*

Rhayader [West St; SN9668], *Cornhill*: Welcoming small unspoilt bar with woodburner, three or four real ales inc interesting guests, two farm ciders, good service, friendly chatty Cornish landlord, good cheap generous freshly made bar food, separate atmospheric dining room; cl Jan, Feb *(Karen Burgess, Dylan Hawkings, Phil Shulkind)*

St Harmon [B4518; SN9973], *Sun*: Largely 17th-c, interconnecting rooms with partitions, beams, flagstones, woodburner, obliging service, real ales such as Hook Norton *(RP, BP)*

☆ Talybont on Usk [Usk]: Decidely old-fashioned and unspoilt character inn, one bar with log fire, flagstones with scattered rugs, panelling and sporting prints, another with fishing prints and memorabilia – fishing available; varied homely food inc game, quiet pleasant staff, antiques shop; good value well equipped bedrooms, big breakfast; bedrooms *(Margaret and Nigel Dennis)*

Channel Islands

The Fleur du Jardin at Kings Mills on Guernsey is doing very well at the moment, with fine food from its new chef: it is our choice as Guernsey Dining Pub of the Year. The civilised Hougue du Pommier at Castel on Guernsey is also flourishing, under a new manager who has made some worthwhile changes. On Jersey, we welcome three fine new entries: the large and stylish Chambers in St Helier, the very genuine Royal in St Martin, and Les Fontaines in St John – much more family-oriented than when it was last in the Guide, but with a charmingly unchanged snug locals' bar at the back. The Rozel Bay Inn at Rozel is earning warm praise for its innovative evening meals (and is putting in a new upstairs dining room); it's on the strength of this evening food that it earns the title of Jersey Dining Pub of the Year. (Lunchtime food at the Rozel Bay has been more ordinary, but there may be changes....) Fresh fish and seafood can be a bargain on the islands, and drinks are generally cheap by mainland standards – particularly so in the case of beer at the Star & Tipsy Toad in St Peter and Tipsy Toad Town House in St Helier, which brew their own. Pubs on Guernsey close on Sundays. Those on Jersey have had a break between 1 and 4.30 that day, but in 1996 the States of Jersey (the island's parliament) changed the law to allow all-day opening; we say in the text which main entries are taking advantage of this. Pub/restaurants there have always been allowed to serve drinks with meals: Sunday is a real family day for the islands' residents, so it's wise to book if you want lunch then.

CASTEL (Guernsey) Map 1

Hougue du Pommier 🛏️

Route de Hougue du Pommier, off Route de Carteret; just inland from Cobo Bay and Grandes Rocques

They've extended the gardens at this civilised and friendly well equipped hotel this year, and have changed the main entrance. The name (Apple Tree Hill) commemorates the fact that a cider mill stood here in the 18th c, and plenty of fruit trees still stand shading the tables on the neatly trimmed lawn, as well as by the swimming pool in the sheltered walled garden, and in a shady flower-filled courtyard. Inside, the most prized seats are perhaps those in the snug area by the big stone fireplace with its attendant bellows and copper fire-irons. The rest of the oak-beamed bar is quite roomy, with leatherette armed chairs around wood tables, old game and sporting prints, guns, sporting trophies and so forth. Bar food includes sandwiches (from £1.60), soup (£1.50), local crab salad (£3.60) four cheese quiche (£4.40), mushroom stroganoff (£4.60), salmon fishcakes on a bed of pesto noodles or char-grilled swordfish steak glazed with mozzarella (£4.80), and local mussels in a lemon and lime bouillon or beef, oyster and stout pie (£5.95); decent wines. Pool, darts, dominoes, cribbage and maybe unobtrusive piped music; part of the bar is no smoking. Good leisure facilities include a pitch-and-putt golf course and a putting green (for visitors as well as residents). For residents there's free temporary membership to the Guernsey Indoor Green Bowling association (the stadium is next door and rated as one of the best in Europe), and a daily courtesy bus into town. No dogs. *(Recommended by Bob and Maggie Atherton, Steve and Carolyn Harvey, Mike Dickerson, Major and Mrs E M Warrick)*

Free house ~ Licensee Stephen Bone ~ Meals and snacks (not Sun eve) ~ Restaurant ~ (01481) 56531 ~ Children welcome ~ Singer/guitarist Fri eves ~ Open 11-2.30, 6-11.45; 12-2.30 Sun ~ Bedrooms: £39B/£78B

GREVE DE LECQ (Jersey) OS 583552 Map 1

Moulin de Lecq

Centre of attention at this serenely placed black-shuttered old mill is the massive restored waterwheel turning outside, with its formidable gears remorselessly meshing in their stone housing behind the bar. What's particularly nice is that while some pubs might develop this into a touristy gimmick, here it blends in perfectly with the more traditional features of the place; this is a very proper pub, with plenty of local custom and a warm and pleasant atmosphere. Well kept Ann Street Ann's Treat and Old Jersey and Guernsey Bitter on handpump. There's a good log fire, toasting you as you come down the four steps into the cosy bar, as well as plush-cushioned black wooden seats against the white-painted walls; piped music. Good generously served bar food might include soup, local favourite bean crock (£3.50), steak and kidney pie (£4.95), rabbit casserole, or king prawns in garlic (£6.95); they do children's meals, and there are barbecues from May to September. Most people eat in the former granary upstairs. Service is welcoming and helpful. The terrace has picnic tables under cocktail parasols, and there's a good children's adventure playground. The road past here leads down to pleasant walks on one of the only north-coast beaches. *(Recommended by Steve and Carolyn Harvey, Wayne Brindle, Richard Dolphin, Stephen and Julie Brown)*

Ann Street ~ Manager Shaun Lynch ~ Real ale ~ Meals and snacks (12-2.30, 6-8.30, not Sun eve) ~ (01534) 482818 ~ Children welcome till 9pm ~ Open 11-11 (inc Sun)

KINGS MILLS (Guernsey) Map 1

Fleur du Jardin 🍴 🛏 🍷

Kings Mills Rd

Guernsey Dining Pub of the Year

Those in the know rate this old-fashioned inn as the very best on Guernsey. A bonus is that it's in one of the prettiest spots on the island, in a delightful conservation village, and with its own two acres of beautiful gardens. The food has always stood out, and it's become even more imaginative under the current chef, who until its recent demise was the head chef at Keith Floyd's pub at Tuckenhay in Devon. As well as sandwiches (from £1.95, hot char-grilled steak £4.95), a typical menu might include soups like courgette or mussel (from £1.95), stilton and pear terrine with fresh tomato coulis (£2.50), burgers (from £4.45), stuffed mushroom provençale gratin (£4.50), steak, kidney and beer pie (£4.75), pigeon breast with a wild mushroom sauce or roast leg of lamb with a confit of roast garlic (£7.50), pork fillet with roast apples (£7.95), duck breast with a honey and raspberry vinegar sauce or langoustine with a red pepper jus (£8.50), and puddings like lemon cheesecake or raspberry sable with a red fruit coulis (from £2.75). The cosy and sensitively refurbished rooms have low-beamed ceilings and thick granite walls, with cushioned pews and a good log fire in the friendly public bar, and individual country furnishings in the lounge bar on the hotel side. Well kept Guernsey Sunbeam and their winter or summer ale on handpump, and maybe other guest beers, decent wines by the glass or bottle; friendly efficient service; darts, unobtrusive piped music. Part of the restaurant is no smoking. Outside picnic tables are surrounded by flowering cherries, shrubs, colourful borders, bright hanging baskets, and unusual flower barrels cut lengthwise rather than across; play area. *(Recommended by H K Dyson, Steve and Carolyn Harvey, Bob and Maggie Atherton, D J Underhill, Spider Newth, Tina and David Woods-Taylor, Mr and Mrs Box, J S Rutter, Mike Dickerson)*

Free house ~ Licensee Keith Read ~ Real ale ~ Meals and snacks (12-2, 6-9) ~ Restaurant ~ (01481) 57996 ~ Children welcome ~ Open 11-2.30, 5-11.45; 12-2, 7-10 Sun; closed evenings 25/26 Dec ~ 11.45 ~ Bedrooms: £37.50B/£75B

ROZEL (Jersey) Map 1

Rozel Bay

Jersey Dining Pub of the Year

On the edge of a sleepy little fishing village, just out of sight of the sea and the delightful harbour, this idyllic little pub has been turning heads recently thanks to the landlady's splendid evening meals. The imaginative menu usually includes lots of fresh fish, and might feature starters like gateaux of cod tossed with potatoes and shallots and tomato vinaigrette (£4.20), or warm salad of scallops set on caramelised orange dressed with pesto (£4.50), main courses such as cornfed chicken with creamed oyster mushrooms and a langoustine sauce (£8.90), nage of sole with smoked salmon and leek beurre blanc (£9.40), roast turbot, baby carrots and wild mushrooms with a ginger broth or assiette of lamb with courgette ribbons, tomato and thyme jus (£9.80), and puddings like glazed lemon tart with thick Jersey cream (£3.95). Booking is recommended, sometimes up to two weeks in advance. As we went to press they were building a new dining area upstairs, which should create slightly more space in the bar. They also plan to extend the range of lunchtime meals; this had been very much traditional pub food, but should now be a little more like what you'd find later in the day. Snug and cosy, the small dark-beamed back bar has an open fire, old prints and local pictures on its cream walls, dark plush wall seats and stools around tables. Leading off is a carpeted area with flowers on big solid square tables; pool, darts, cribbage and juke box in the games room. Well kept Bass on handpump. Award winning flower displays flank tables under cocktail parasols by the quiet lane, and there are more tables in the attractive steeply terraced hillside gardens behind. *(Recommended by Steve and Carolyn Harvey, Georgina Cole)*

Randalls ~ Tenant Mrs Eve Bouchet ~ Real ale ~ Meals and snacks (not Sun) ~ (01534) 863438 ~ Children welcome ~ Open 10am-11.30pm; Sun 11-1, 4.30-11.30

ST AUBIN (Jersey) OS 607486 Map 1

Old Court House Inn 🛏

The new conservatory at this charming 15th-c inn makes the most of its prime setting overlooking the tranquil harbour, with views stretching past St Aubin's fort right across the bay to St Helier. The restaurant still shows signs of its time as a courtroom and the front part of the building used to be the home of a wealthy merchant, whose cellars stored privateers' plunder alongside more legitimate cargo. The three main bars are rather individual: upstairs the Mizzen Mast bar is elegantly (and cleverly) crafted as the aft cabin of a galleon, while the Westward bar is constructed from the actual gig of a schooner, with the ceiling made from old ship beams. The atmospheric main basement bar has cushioned pale wooden seats built against its stripped granite walls, low black beams and joists in a white ceiling, a turkey carpet and an open fire; it can get crowded and smoky at times. A dimly lantern-lit inner room has an illuminated rather brackish-looking deep well, and beyond that is a spacious cellar room open in summer. Well-priced bar food includes soup (£1.50), open sandwiches (from £2.75), ploughman's (from £2.95), pizzas (£4.25), moules marinières (£4.70), prawn salad (£5.95), other fresh fish such as monkfish and red mullet, and a huge seafood platter for two with a whole crab and lobster, and oysters, moules, whelks, winkles and gambas (£50); children's meals. Plenty more fresh fish in the restaurant. Marstons Pedigree and Theakstons XB on handpump; cribbage, dominoes, scrabble, chess, shut the box, piped music, and darts in winter. The bedrooms, individually decorated and furnished, are small but comfortable, and you might get one on the harbour front. *(Recommended by Steve and Carolyn Harvey, Wayne Brindle, Martin Wight)*

Free house ~ Licensee Jonty Sharp ~ Meals and snacks (not Sun evening) ~ Restaurant ~ (01534) 46433 ~ Children welcome ~ Sun night folk and blues band ~ Open 11am-11.30pm; 11-1, 4.30-11 Sun; closed 25 Dec ~ Bedrooms £40B/£980B

ST BRELADE (Jersey) OS 603472 Map 1

Old Portelet Inn

Portelet Bay

Commanding magnificent views across Portelet, Jersey's most southerly bay, this characterful 17th-c clifftop farmhouse has been extensively redeveloped in recent years to make it more appealing to families. The atmospheric low ceilinged, beamed downstairs bar has a stone bar counter on bare oak boards and quarry tiles, a huge open fire, gas lamps, old pictures, etched glass panels from France and a nice mixture of old wooden chairs. It opens into the big timber-ceilinged family dining area, with standing timbers and plenty of highchairs. Outside there are picnic tables on the partly covered flower-bower terrace by a wishing well, with more in a sizeable landscaped garden with lots of scented stocks and other flowers (the piped music may follow you out here). Right below, there's a sheltered cove, reached by a long flight of steps with glorious views on the way down. Reliable bar food includes soup (£1.50), dimsum with honey and chilli dip (£3.20), ploughman's (£3.25), tuna and pasta bake, cannelloni or lasagne (£3.90), vegetable curry (£4), moules marinières or steak and mushroom pie (£4.95), poached salmon with parsley butter (£5.95), children's meals (including baby food), and Sunday cream teas; some kind of food is now usually available all day. Friendly neatly dressed staff are quick and well drilled. Well kept Boddingtons and a weekly changing guest like Marstons Pedigree on handpump, and reasonably priced house wine; plenty of board games in the wooden-floored loft bar. No-smoking areas, disabled and baby changing facilities, and a superior supervised children's play area (entrance £1). *(Recommended by Steve and Carolyn Harvey, John Evans, Wayne Brindle, Mark Hydes, Richard Dolphin)*

Randalls ~ Manageress Tina Lister ~ Real ale ~ Meals and snacks (12-2.15, 6-9; small snacks all day) ~ (01534) 41899 ~ Children in family dining room, over 14s only in Loft Bar ~ Live music most nights in summer ~ Open 10am-11pm

Old Smugglers

Ouaisne Bay; OS map reference 595476

In a pretty position overlooking Ouaisne Bay and Common, this popular extended pub was originally a pair of old fishermen's cottages. There's a genuinely relaxed, pubby atmosphere, as well as thick walls and black beams, open fires, and cosy black built-in settles. A good range of beers might include Bass, Ringwood Best and Old Thumper, Gibbs Mew Bishops Tipple, Theakstons Best and Wadworths 6X; sensibly placed darts as well as cribbage and dominoes. Promptly served bar food includes home-made soup (£1.20; local seafood chowder £1.95), home-made pâté (£2.50), lunchtime filled baked potatoes (from £2.75) and ploughman's (£3.25), burgers (from £3.95), dressed crab claws with spicy dip (£4.25), steak and mushroom pie or cod in beer batter (£4.50), oriental vegetable stir fry (£4.95), ragout of seafood with a herb and lemon sauce or chicken satay (£5.95), king prawns in black bean sauce (£6.25), steaks (from £6.75), and daily specials like Thai beef or local lobster; children's menu (with a couple of puzzles). A room in the restaurant is no smoking. Close by are some attractive public gardens. *(Recommended by John Evans, Steve and Carolyn Harvey, E D Bailey, P A Legon, Wayne Brindle)*

Free house ~ Licensee Nigel Godfrey ~ Real ale ~ Meals and snacks (12-2, 6-8.45; not winter Sun evening) ~ Restaurant ~ (015534) 41510 ~ Children welcome till 9pm ~ Sunday folk night ~ Open 11am-11.30pm

ST HELIER (Jersey) Map 1

Admiral £

St James St

Particularly well liked for its excellent value lunchtime food, this big and atmospheric candlelit pub has been carefully renovated with dark wood panelling, attractive and solid country furniture, and heavy beams, some of which are inscribed with famous quotations. Interesting decorations include old telephones, a clocking-in machine, copper milk churn, enamel advertising signs (many more in the small back courtyard which also has lots of old pub signs), and nice touches such as the daily papers to read and an old penny 'What the Butler Saw' machine. With some emphasis on local produce, the menu changes every day, and might include jacket potatoes with fillings such as chilli or half a spit-roast chicken (£3.25), stir fried cajun chicken (£3.75), and fresh scallops in black bean sauce (£4.25); four course Sunday lunch (£7.95). Well kept Boddingtons on handpump; efficient, friendly staff; dominoes, cribbage and chess. There are plastic tables outside on a flagged terrace – quite a suntrap in summer. The pub is busier in the evenings, when it is well liked by a younger set. *(Recommended by Steve and Carolyn Harvey, Mark Percy, Wayne Brindle)*

Randells ~ Manager Craig Dempster ~ Real ale ~ Meals and snacks (12-2, 6-8; not Fri evening or all day Sat) ~ (01534) 30095 ~ Children welcome ~ Open 11am-11.30pm; 11-1, 4.30-11 Sun; closed 25 Dec evening

Chambers

Mulcaster Street

Opened in late 1993 by the owner of the Admiral (see previous entry), this impressive place has quickly become packed with local office workers at lunchtime, attracted by the generous helpings of good value food, and with a lively spread of rather younger customers in the evenings – especially late on, with its hotel licence (inherited from its predecessor here, the Hotel de l'Europe) letting it stay open later than most competitors. But even at its loudest it always stays civilised, with a no-trainers rule after 7pm, and bouncers on the door. It's well designed around a law-courts theme, partly divided into separate room areas, with heavy beams (decorated with apt quotations), lots of imposing paintings, prints and mirrors, and a careful mixture of heavy dark wood furniture with more individual antique and ornate mahogany pieces, a clubby-feeling library room, and an oak-panelled room with deep leather armchairs and daily papers. The massively long bar counter dispenses well kept Boddingtons, Flowers Original, Marstons Pedigree, Theakstons XB and a guest on hand or electric pump, and under light blanket pressure, decent wines; a couple of huge cut-glass chandeliers, gentle wall lamps, candlelit tables, and a mix of bare boards and stone floors add to the atmosphere. The choice of bar food changes daily, and besides filled baked potatoes (from £2.50) might include interesting soups such as leek and butter bean or cream of cauliflower and stilton (£1.75), mushrooms stuffed with pâté with spicy creole sauce (£1.85), vegetarian lasagne (£3.40), tuna and prawn fishcakes with lobster sauce or steak and onion pie (£3.60) and poached chicken supreme with provençale sauce (£3.90); set Sunday menu (£9.50). The neatly uniformed waistcoated staff are well drilled and hard-working. There is a separate gallery dining room up a few steps at the back. A few old penny slot machines cock a gentle snook at fruit-machine culture, and there are log-effect gas fires. *(Recommended by Steve and Carolyn Harvey, Mark Percy)*

Randalls ~ Manager Stephen Jones ~ Real ale ~ Meals and snacks (12-2.30, 5.30-9.30; not Fri, Sat, Sun evenings) ~ Restaurant ~ (01534) 35405 ~ Supervised children welcome till 8pm ~ Live entertainment every evening ~ Open 11-1 am (inc Sun); cl 25 Dec

Tipsy Toad Town House ◗

New Street

They like to refer to this as the Biggest Little Brewery in the World, and certainly the monster on-site microbrewery is one of the largest we've ever come across. It's very much the centrepiece of the attractive 1930s corner building, the gleaming copperwork highly visible through glass panels in the various rooms built around it. The pub is on two floors, and downstairs is mostly quite traditional, with old photographs on the walls, solid furnishings, some attractive panelling and stained glass, and heavy brass doors between its two main parts; there's wheelchair access. The very wide choice of decent food includes filled baguettes (from £1.85), macaroni cheese, local sausages and mash or warm salads such as chicken liver or bacon lardons (£4.95), haggis (£5.95), very popular fajitas with salsa, guacamole and cream dips (from £6.50), char-grilled steaks (from £8.95), lots of fresh fish on the blackboard, children's meals (from £2), and specials like steak avocado and mushroom stroganoff (£5.75), pan-fried entrecote steak with cajun spices on a bed of sizzling peppers and onions (£9.50), or duck breast in calvados and mild mushroom sauce (£9.75). But the main point is the beer: their own Horny Toad, Jimmys, and well priced Tipsy Toad, with maybe two or three guest ales from independent mainland breweries. The house wines are sound, and the whole place is immaculate, running like clockwork; it can get busy in the evenings. Upstairs has at least as much space again as downstairs, very well planned with a lot of attention to detail, rather more toadery and a garden room; one area is no smoking. What was the Hop Shop next door has now become the Mighty Mouse Internet Cafe, with bookable computer terminals offering immediate access to on-line sites around the world. The pub is owned by the same people as the Star and Tipsy Toad in St Peter. *(Recommended by Steve and Carolyn Harvey, John Evans)*

Own brew ~ Manager Colin Manning ~ Real ale ~ Meals and snacks (12.30-2.30, 6.30-10; not Mon evening or all day Sun) ~ Restaurant ~ (01534) 615000 ~ Children welcome till 9pm ~ Live music most nights ~ Open 11-11; closed 25/26 Dec, 1 Jan

ST JOHN (Jersey) OS 620564 Map 1
Les Fontaines

Le Grand Mourier, Route du Nord

Quite a few changes here in the last couple of years, with a major refurbishment aimed at making the place more rewarding for families. A particularly popular new feature is the supervised play area for children, Pirate Pete's (entry £1), though children are also made welcome in the other rooms of the bar. The main bar is clean and carpeted, with plenty of wheelback chairs around neat dark tables, and a spiral staircase leading up to a wooden gallery under the high pine-raftered plank ceiling. But the place to head for is the distinctive public bar – and particularly the unusual inglenook by the large 14th-c stone fireplace. There are very heavy beams in the low dark ochre ceiling, stripped irregular red granite walls, old-fashioned red leatherette cushioned settles and solid black tables on the quarry-tiled floor, and for decoration antique prints and Staffordshire china figurines and dogs; look out for the old smoking chains and oven by the granite columns of the fireplace. This part of the building is easy to miss; either look for the worn and unmarked door at the side of the building, or as you go down the main entry lobby towards the bigger main bar slip through the tiny narrow door on your right. A wide range of changing bar food includes soup (£1.25), sandwiches (from 1.50), large cod and chips (£4.75), plenty of seafood and steaks, daily specials like rack of lamb or chicken and asparagus pie, and children's meals (£2). One area is no smoking; dominoes and piped music. Black Bull on handpump. The pub is attratcively set on the northernmost tip of the island, where the 300-feet-high granite cliffs face the distant French coast, and there are good coastal walks nearby. *(Recommended by Steve and Carolyn Harvey; more reports please)*

Randalls ~ Manager Georgina Berresford ~ Real ale ~ Meals and snacks (12-2.30, 5.30-9.30) ~ (01534) 862707 ~ Children welcome ~ Open 10am-11pm

ST LAWRENCE (Jersey) Map 1
British Union

Main Rd

This bustling roadside pub is right in the centre of the island, opposite St Lawrence church. The busy friendly lounge bar is decorated in a cottagey style with pretty wallpaper, beams and panelling, *Punch*-style cartoons, and royal prints, and a large ceiling fan; leading off here is an interconnecting snug, largely set out for diners, with a wood burning stove, and toy cupboard full of well loved toys, books and games. Locals tend to favour the quieter little bar with cigarette card collections, gun cartridges, and brass beer spigots on the walls, and darts. Children are welcome in the plainly furnished games room with pool, trivia and video games, cribbage and dominoes and juke box and there is even a child-sized cat flap leading out to a small enclosed terrace with a playhouse. Good bar food includes soup (£1.50), filled baked potatoes (from £3.25), ploughman's, lasagne or spicy chicken breast (£4.50), steak and ale pie (£5), 9oz rump steak, and children's meals. Well kept Ann Street Sunbeam on handpump; efficient, thoughtful service; piped music. *(More reports please)*

Ann Street ~ Manager: Mary Boschat ~ Real ale ~ Meals and snacks (not evenings Sun or Mon) ~ (01534) 861070 ~ Children welcome ~ Live entertainment Sun evenings ~ Open 10am-11.30pm; 11-1, 4.30-11.30 Sun

ST MARTIN (Jersey) Map 1
Royal

Grande Route de Faldouet (B30)

This big family pub by the church in an attractive and untouristy village gives a good taste of the 'real' Jersey. It has a snug straightforward public bar, a cosy and comfortable lounge recently extended with a sizeable partly no-smoking eating area, a little children's room off that with toys and video games (children in pushchairs are not allowed in the bar area), and an attractive upstairs restaurant (where you can have lunchtime bar food at no extra charge), with interesting old pine tables and fittings, country-kitchen chairs, and attractive antique prints and bric-a-brac. The wide choice of bar food includes ploughman's (from £3.75), good filled baked potatoes (from £4), chicken curry or chilli (£4.50), lasagne (£4.75), pie of the day (£5), grilled trout or local plaice (£6.50) and 8oz sirloin (£7.50); children's meals (£2.25). Sunday lunch here is popular – as are the set-price restaurant meals (best to book). Helpings are generous, the Boddingtons and a guest on handpump are well kept, and service is quick and friendly; open fire. There are tables out on a large terrace, with a small enclosed play area; pool, darts, bar billiards, cribbage, pinball, dominoes, video game, piped music. *(Recommended by Steve and Carolyn Harvey, Mary Reed, Rowly Pitcher)*

Randalls ~ Tenant: John Alan Barker ~ Real ale ~ Meals and snacks (12-2.30, 6-8; not Sun am) ~ (01534) 856289 ~ Children welcome away from public bar till 9) ~ Open 9.30am-11.30pm; Sun 11-1, 4.30-11.30 (maybe all day Sun)

ST PETER (Jersey) OS 595519 Map 1
Star & Tipsy Toad 🍺

In village centre

Sharp-eyed readers say that visitors arriving in Jersey by air can clearly see this popular brew pub from the plane just as it's about to land. Busy and friendly, it has tours and tastings every day at the on-site microbrewery – and at other times you can see the workings through a window in the pub. As well as their own brews, Horny Toad, Jimmys, and the bargain priced Tipsy Toad (£1 a pint) on handpump, they might have two or three guest ales from smaller mainland breweries. Sensitively refurbished, the cottagey bar has plenty of panelling, exposed stone walls, tiled and wood-panelled floors, a good family conservatory, and children's playground and terraces. Tasty bar food includes home-made soup (£1.60), filled rolls (from £2), home-made pâté with cumberland sauce (£3), ploughman's (£3.50), burgers (from £3.95), vegetable samosas or fresh cod in their own beer batter (£4.75), chicken au poivre or various salads (£4.95), steak and ale pie (£5.25), provençal nut wellington (£5.60), steaks (from £5.95), specials like coq au vin on a bed of tagliatelle(£5.25), and children's meals (£1.75). A small games room has darts, pool, cribbage, pinball, dominoes, fruit machine, video game, trivia, and piped music; wheelchair access and disabled lavatories. Friendly staff. They often have a well regarded World Music Festival. See also the Tipsy Toad Town House in St Helier. *(Recommended by John Evans, Steve and Carolyn Harvey)*

Own brew ~ Manager John Dryhurst ~ Real ale ~ Meals and snacks (12-2.15, 6-8.15; not Sun, or winter Mon evenings) ~ (01534) 485556 ~ Children welcome ~ Live bands Fri, Sat and Sun eves ~ Open 10am-11pm; 11-1, 4.30-11 Sun

Lucky Dip

Besides the fully inspected pubs, you might like to try these Lucky Dips recommended to us and described by readers (if you do, please send us reports):

ALDERNEY

☆ Newtown, *Harbour Lights*: Varied good bar food esp fresh local fish and seafood at (for mainlanders) ridiculously low prices, in welcoming, clean and well run hotel/pub in a quieter part of this quiet island; pleasant garden; caters particularly for families with children; well kept Guernsey Bitter, terrace; children welcome; bedrooms *(D Godden)*

☆ St Anne [Victoria St], *Georgian House*: Small hotel bar, relaxing and civilised, with very accommodating owners and staff, Ringwood Best and Old Thumper, good interesting food in bar and restaurant, charming staff; nice back garden with barbecue and summer food servery; comfortable bedrooms *(Keith Taylor)*

GUERNSEY

Ancresse Bay, *Rockwell*: A good place to sit outside, enjoy the sun and look at the beaches; friendly helpful staff *(Bob and Maggie Atherton)*

Castel [Yazon Bay], *Crabby Jacks*: Simple coastal place popular with families; friendly service, good seafood and ice cream sundaes, decent wines and coffee, English beers *(J S Rutter)*

Forest [Le Bourg], *Deerhound*: Simple stonebuilt country inn with wide choice of good food inc huge sandwiches, evening restaurant, Theakstons Best and Old Peculier, children welcome, friendly black labrador; big garden with play area; bedrooms *(Mike Dickerson, Steve and Carolyn Harvey)*; [Torteval rd, La Villiaze], *Venture*: Friendly landlord and staff in spotless two-bar Randalls pub with good food and well kept ale *(Frank W Gadbois)*

☆ St Martin [Jerbourg, nr SE tip of island], *Auberge Divette*: Glorious view of coast and Herm from fairy-lit garden high above sea; unpretentious picture-window saloon and lounge both with button-back banquettes, sensibly placed darts and bar billiards in back public bar; well kept Guernsey Bitter and Mild, basic food inc children's (may be a wait); spectacular cliff walk to St Peter Port *(Spider Newth, Steve and Carolyn Harvey, Norma and Keith Bloomfield, H K Dyson, LYM)*

St Martin [La Fosse], *Bella Luce*: Former 12th-c manor with lovely gardens, more hotel than pub, but has a super small bar, old-world atmosphere, good service, decent wines and reasonably priced food in bar and restaurant; keg beer; bedrooms *(Mike Dickerson, J S Rutter, Steve and Carolyn Harvey)*

☆ St Peter Port [North Esplanade], *Ship & Crown*: Lively town pub very popular with yachting people and smarter locals, sharing building with Royal Guernsey Yacht Club; good harbour view from bay windows, interesting photographs (esp concerning WWII German occupation, also boats and ships), good value food from sandwiches to steak, well kept Guernsey Bitter, welcoming service *(Spider Newth, Norma and Keith Bloomfield, Bob and Maggie Atherton, H K Dyson, LYM)*

St Peter Port [Trinity Sq], *Britannia*: Interesting bikers' pub with Harley Davidson motif, three well kept real ales on handpump, friendly licensee *(Frank W Gadbois)*; [Le Charroterie], *Drunken Duck*: Well kept beer, pleasant young Irish landlord, bar billiards; live music inc Irish folk *(Matthew Parker, Bob and Maggie Atherton)*; [Glategny Esplanade], *Salerie*: Friendly open-plan bar with well polished nautical brassware, model ship, well kept Guernsey Bitter and Mild, good food and service - good value *(H K Dyson)*

St Peters [Rue de Longfrie; SO8439], *Longfrie*: Well run family food pub based on 16th-c farmhouse, service good even when busy, several well kept Guernsey ales, wide choice of straightforward food, indoor play area, pleasant garden; bedrooms *(Mike Dickerson, Norma and Keith Bloomfield, Steve and Carolyn Harvey)*

St Sampsons [Grand Fort Rd, Les Capelles], *Pony*: Very cheap straightforward food in friendly modern local, lounge done up in shades of brown, with russet plush armchairs and booth seats; well kept Guernsey Mild and Bitter; public bar with games and juke box; tables out by front car park *(Mike Dickerson, LYM)*

JERSEY

☆ Gorey [The Harbour; OS map ref 714503], *Dolphin*: Basic fishing theme (nets etc), unpretentious pubby atmosphere, good fish and seafood inc scallops, big prawns, grilled sardines, seafood platter; restaurant, children in eating area; very busy indeed Sun lunchtime; piped music, Iberian waiters; comfortable bedrooms *(Georgina Cole, LYM)*

Jersey Airport [Departures building], *Aviator Bar*: Up in the lift to glass-walled view of uncommon propeller aircraft buzzing around busily; very wide choice of reasonably priced spirits, conventional airport decor, agreeable restaurant *(John Evans, BB)*

☆ St Helier [Mulcaster St], *Lamplighter*: Good gas-lit atmosphere in pub with admirable facade, heavy timbers, rough panelling and scrubbed pine tables; good value simple lunchtime food inc children's, well kept Bass, Boddingtons, Marstons Pedigree, Theakstons Old Peculier and a guest beer; open 14 hours a day *(Steve and Carolyn Harvey, LYM)*

St Mary, *St Marys*: Neat and well kept, with usual food, some original dishes of the day, lounge with piped music, family room/dining room, real fire, well kept Bass, Stones and Worthington BB, no smoking family conservatory with video games, separate bar with pool and darts; tables on terrace;

bedrooms *(Steve and Carolyn Harvey)*
St Ouens Bay [S end, Five Mile Rd - OS map
ref 562488], *La Pulente*: Across road from
the island's longest beach; reasonably priced
food, well kept ales such as Bass or Fullers
London Pride, green leatherette armchairs in
smallish lounge, sailing ship prints,
leatherette-topped tables; fairy-lit side terrace
(P A Legon, BB)
Trinity [OS map ref 663539], *Trinity Arms*:
Large cheap basic meals and well kept
Guernsey and Old Jersey ale in cheery Jersey
country local, spacious and comfortable
Turkey-carpeted lounge and rambling quarry-
tiled public bar with pool, video game and
juke box or piped music; tables outside *(Mike
Dickerson, BB)*

SARK
☆ *Stocks*: Welcoming family-run hotel with
wide choice of pleasant food served quickly in
good conservatory cafe/bistro, in sheltered
courtyard and on poolside terrace;
comfortably snug and friendly stone-and-
beams bar with stormy sailing-ship prints;
good cream teas, good value good fresh set
evening meals in candlelit partly no smoking
restaurant; comfortable bedrooms in elegant
old extended country house *(Mike Dickerson,
LYM)*; *Bel Air*: First tourist stop (where the
tractors climb to from the jetty): big
woodburning stove in comfortable Boat Bar
with plank ceiling, easy chairs and settees,
model ship, boat-shaped counter; old boat
pictures in simpler Pirate Bar; snacks, darts,
piped pop music, tables on terrace outside this
pretty cottage *(Steve and Carolyn Harvey,
BB)*; [Beau Regard], *Falles Barn Bar*: A
curiosity with decor from the 50s or earlier,
Guernsey beers under high pressure, home-
made sloe gin, very basic chippy food,
welcoming local atmosphere *(Norma and
Keith Bloomfield)*; *La Moinerie*: Splendid
setting, good lunchtime food from hotel bar,
big garden; bedrooms *(Steve and Carolyn
Harvey)*

Please keep sending us reports. We rely on readers for news of new
discoveries, and particularly for news of changes – however slight – at the fully
described pubs. No stamp needed: *The Good Pub Guide*, FREEPOST
TN1569, Wadhurst, E Sussex TN5 7BR.

Overseas Lucky Dip

We're always interested to hear of good bars and pubs overseas – or, more desirably, their genuine local equivalents. These are ones recently recommended by readers. We start with ones in the British Isles, then work alphabetically through other countries. We mark with a star the few pubs that we can be confident would qualify as main entries.

IRELAND

☆ Belfast [Gt Victoria St; opp Europa Hotel], *Crown*: Bustling 19th-c gin palace with pillared entrance, opulent tiles outside and in, elaborately coloured windows, almost church-like ceiling, handsome mirrors, individual snug booths with little doors and bells for waiter service, gas lighting, mosaic floor – wonderful atmosphere, very wide range of customers (maybe inc performers in full fig from Opera House opposite); good lunchtime meals inc oysters, Hilden real ale, open all day; National Trust *(Johnny Saunderson, Mark and Diane Grist)*

Cork [S Main St], *An Spailpin Fanach*: Perhaps Ireland's oldest pub (as opposed to hotel), with intimate nooks and crannies, old-world charm, traditional wood and brass fittings; traditional music sessions *(Ian Williams, Linda Mar)*

Crawfordsburn [Main St], *Crawfordsburn*: Mainly a hotel (actually Ireland's oldest) but has basic function as a pub; quaint and unspoilt, very clean and cosy, with open peat fire, very good food often inc local fish, Bass; thatched roof, small back garden; bedrooms *(W G Hall, Jr)*

Dublin [East Essex St, Temple Bar], *Fitzsimons*: Fairly new friendly bar and restaurant, lots of varnished wood, polished floor and bar counter, good bar food, regular traditional Irish music and set dancing (free) *(Chris Raisin)*; [17 Anglesea St, Temple Bar], *Old Dubliner*: Very popular and friendly, well kept and served Guinness, traditional interior, wall settles, round cast-iron-framed tables; handy for Gallaghers Boxty House restaurant *(Chris Raisin)*

Kilcrohane [Sheeps Head Peninsula], *Fitzpatricks*: Traditional real Irish pub where wellies and dogs are welcome, attentive landlady, excellent Guinness, sandwiches, cards, darts; children welcome, lovely walks and scenery nearby *(Gwyneth and Salvo Spadaro-Dutturi)*; [Sheeps Head Peninsula], *Old Bay View*: Family-run pub with new eager-to-please landlords, meals in summer, excellent Guinness, children welcome; views over Dunmanus Bay *(Gwyneth and Salvo Spadaro-Dutturi)*

Kilkenny [19 John St], *Langtons*:

Comfortable chairs and sofas, older-style decor and elaborate panelling in large divided back area well lit by glass let into roof, front bar, good range of lunchtime bar meals, local beer; possibly a short wait for a table at lunchtime *(M G Hart)*

Waterford [Gt Georges St; SK0850], *T & H Doolan*: Dark old pub said to include fragment of 1,000-year-old city wall, leaded windows, flagstones, friendly welcome, fine Guinness; Irish music Thurs *(Ian Williams, Linda Mar)*

ISLE OF MAN

Castletown [Quayside; aka The Gluepot; SC3584], *Castle Arms*: Overlooks the harbour, good value standard food, Okells Bitter and their better but rarer Wheel, also guest beers such as Cains Mild and Tetleys *(Derek and Sylvia Stephenson)*

Douglas [Harris Promenade; part of Sefton Hotel, with separate entrance; SC3876], *Tramshunters Arms*: Nicely presented reasonably priced food inc superb beef bap, almost too wide a choice of real ales *(Derek and Sylvia Stephenson)*

Glenmaye [just off A27 3 miles S of Peel – OS Sheet 95 map ref 236798; SC2480], *Waterfall*: Named for the waterfall nearby; very popular, with good service, reasonably priced usual food, Cains, Tetleys and maybe Okells ale *(Derek and Sylvia Stephenson)*

☆ Laxey [Tram Station – OS Sheet 95 map ref 433846; SC4484], *Mines Tavern*: Beamed pub in lovely woodland clearing where Manx electric railway and Snaefell mountain railway connect, just below the Lady Isabella wheel (largest working water wheel in the world); splendid old tram photographs, advertisements and other memorabilia in one bar with counter salvaged from former tram, other bar dedicated to mining; fresh sandwiches and reasonably priced home cooking, well kept Bushys, Okells and Tetleys ales; piped music, darts, fruit machines (public bar not lounge); lovely sitting outside watch Victorian trams *(David Campbell, Vicki McLean, Peter and Patricia Burton, Derek and Sylvia Stephenson)*

Port St Mary [Atholl St; SC2167], *Albert*: Basic public bar, nice comfortable lounge, second lounge beyond, good reasonably priced sandwiches and other straightforward meals, good range of beers inc Bushy's, Cains, Okells and Tetleys *(Derek and Sylvia Stephenson)*

Ramsey [West Quay nr swing bridge; SC4594], *Trafalgar*: Food inc excellent local scallops; Bushys and Cains beers *(Derek and Sylvia Stephenson)*

Sulby Glen [A14 below Snaefell; NX3793], *Tholt-e Will*: Attractive and welcoming Swiss chalet by stream in richly wooded glen below Snaefell, good choice of local and other beers inc Smithwicks, good bar food inc good generous Manx cheese with the ploughman's; very popular with the locals *(Rosemarie Johnson, Daniel Travis, Peter and Patricia Burton)*

LUNDY

☆ *Marisco*: One of England's most isolated pubs, great setting, atmospheric roomy interior with lifebelts from local shipwrecks, brews its own beer, also others and Lundy spring water on tap, good value house wines, welcoming staff, good if not cheap range of home-cooked food using island produce, with lots of seafood and vegetarian; children welcome, tables outside, self catering and camping available; souvenir shop, and doubles as general store for the island's few residents *(Ian Christie, Judy Jones, K Flack)*

AUSTRALIA

Prospect [Reservoir Rd], *Royal Cricketers Arms*: One of Australia's oldest pubs, restored two years ago after spell as office of drive-in cinema; character atmosphere, log fires, good food, Bass on tap, other British bottled beers, landlord from Britain, pickled eggs made by loyal customer; handy for Eastern Creek Raceway; open all day (till 6 Sun, cl Mon), seats on verandah and in big garden *(E V Walder)*

☆ Sydney [Argyle Pl, The Rocks], *Lord Nelson*: Solid stone, with beams and bare floorboards – the city's oldest pub; brews its own Nelsons Revenge, Three Sheets, Trafalgar and Victory, and has tastings first Weds of month (not Jan); good choice of other Australian beers, great easy-going service, interesting reasonably priced home-made food, nautical theme, upmarket atmosphere, pine furniture; open all day, gets touristy; delightful bedrooms *(Neville and Sarah Hargreaves)*

Sydney [Lower Fort St, The Rocks], *Hero of Waterloo*: Another stone building, also old – touristy, but good atmosphere, genuine and uncontrived (even in the haunted basement function room, scene of several murders in the old days); ten beers on tap inc Bass and Guinness, English sing along Sun evening, strolling cat; as close to a typical British pub as you'll find abroad *(Beryl and Bill Farmer)*;

[Mercantile Hotel; George St, The Rocks], *Molly Malones*: Almost under S end of Harbour Bridge; green tiles outside, Irish decor in, with good unpretentious atmosphere, some Irish staff, Irish bands most nights; good value bar food inc wiener schnitzel, steaks *(Dr and Mrs A K Clarke)*;

[Harbour], *Sydney Cove Oyster Bar*: Small waterfront bar nr Opera House, stunning bridge views, interesting Carlton Sparkling Ale *(Dr and Mrs A K Clarke)*

AUSTRIA

Seefeld [on plateau above; short bus ride from centre], *Wildmoosalm*: Picturesque bar alone in the winter snowfields, two big rooms with nature displays and striking stuffed birds of prey, fresh flowers on the tables, really friendly bustling atmosphere – wait for a seat may be rewarded by a free schnapps *(John and Joan Nash)*

BELGIUM

Beersel [Herman Teirlinckplein 3; just off E19 junction 14], *Dree Fonteinen*: One of the few microbreweries producing lambic beer, the Gueuze and Kriek made in the cellar going well with excellent choice of tasty food eg guineafowl in Kriek beer sauce; patron in his 80s keeps careful eye on his beers and his two large rooms – restaurant packed at weekends *(Joan and Michel Hooper-Immins)*

☆ Brussels [R Montagne aux Herbes Potageres], *Mort Subite*: A local institution, producing its own good traditional Gueuze, sweet Faro and fruit Kriek and Framboise ales; long Belle Epoque room divided by two rows of pillars into nave with two rows of small tables and side aisles with single row, mirrors on all sides, leather seats, swift uniformed waiters and waitresses scurrying from busy bar on right; good snacks such as omelettes and croques monsieur *(Joan and Michel Hooper-Immins, Ian Phillips)*

Brussels [6 Impasse Schuddeveld; off 21 Petite Rue des Bouchers], *De Toone*: Really a puppet theatre at least at night, down dark passage; good quite large bar area with huge log fire, puppets for sale (some huge) hanging from ceiling, stage room with retractable seating, no-smoking area; good interesting beers, some food *(Ian Phillips)*

BERMUDA

Hamilton [Hamilton Princess Hotel], *Colony*: English-style panelled hotel theme bar useful for decent snacks and food inc pasties and very good steaks; evening pianist; not cheap, service charge added to food orders and drinkers expected to tip barman *(John Evans)*

St Georges [Kings Sq], *White Horse*: Good atmosphere in very large popular pub right on the waterfront in beautiful old square, Bermudan/American tilt to food and service ('please wait to be seated'), many local seafood specialities, not too expensive, Watneys and other beers; nice to feed the fish from the verandah – and watch the local lads fishing *(John Evans, June and Malcolm Farmer)*

CANARY ISLANDS

Lanzarote [Costa Teguise], *Fiddlers Arms*: Truly Irish, with good Guinness, Irish

barmaid and folk singer, Walkers crisps
(Anon)

CAYMAN ISLANDS
Grand Cayman [off 7 Mile Beach], *Lone Star*:
Wide choice of good generous food, friendly
service, good cocktails; interesting array of
divers' T-shirts with autograph messages
(Elaine Pugh)

CYPRUS
Lara, *Viklari*: Worth the bumpy ride for the
glorious bay view from the stone-topped
tables – the owner and his two great danes
sleep out here under the grape trellises; nr
Avakas Gorge *(Roger and Jenny Huggins)*

FIJI
Nadi, *Regent*: Cheap and entertaining happy
hour 5.30-6.30 in big hotel's main bar, local
singers, sunset ceremony, free snacks; Fiji
Bitter and wide range of Australian and NZ
beers *(David Forsyth)*
Savu Savu [waterfront], *Copra Shed*: Classic
South Seas setting for small yachting complex,
Fiji Bitter and Australian lagers, friendly staff,
interesting customers; restaurant, dinghy hire
(David Forsyth)

FRANCE
Antibes [Marche Provencal], *Da Cito*: Very
friendly little bar/cafe with good moules and
pizzas, lots of mainly bottled foreign beers esp
Belgian, inc the Mort Subite range *(Ian
Phillips)*
Paris [116 rue St Denis], *Frog & Rosbif*:
Panelled English-style pub with real ales, bare
boards, rugby shirts, English dailies; beer very
expensive *(JJB)*

MADEIRA
Portela [nr Machico], *Casa da Portela*: A
restaurant, but with a really pubby feel; three
attractive dark pine-panelled front rooms
with incredible view down to coast, centre
one with bar, two cosy side ones for eating,
with quarry-tiled floors, green shutters and
log fire on left; simple dark pine furniture,
good choice of drinks inc local Coral lager
brewed by English firm, speciality steak
kebabs on 5ft skewers *(Susan and John
Douglas)*
Ribeiro Frio, *Old Trout*: Single-storey
wooden building in cool and attractive
mountain woodland setting opp trout
hatchery, by stream; very pubby log-cabin
atmosphere, snug little candlelit Victorian-
style bar with open fire, rugs, cosy sofas, lots
of flowers; rustic softly lit restaurant area
with pine furnishings on quarry tiles, big
windows overlooking stream, very trout-
based food; open 9-5 *(Susan and John
Douglas)*

MAJORCA
☆ **Cala D'Or** [carrer Den Rito 12], *Fowlers*:
Exquisitely furnished, lots of marble busts,
wonderful paintings, oriental rugs, objets,
extravagant flower arrangements, candles
everywhere, glossy magazines, colourful
lanterns; excellent choice of drinks inc
remarkable range of Spanish brandies, well
reproduced opera or jazz (if landlady not
playing light classics or musical comedy on
the corner grand piano); terrace with pretty
balcony overlooking marina *(Susan and John
Douglas)*

MALTA
Bugibba [St Simon St], *Crown & Thistle*:
Very clean, with plenty of fans, local bottled
beers and draught Lowenbrau, friendly
landlord and wife; football and Naval theme,
Sky TV *(Phil and Anne Smithson)*

NETHERLANDS
Amsterdam [Platform 2, Central Stn], *1er
Klasse*: Grand bar/restaurant in the great
tradition of continental stations, good beers
(Dr and Mrs A K Clarke); [66 Prins Hendrik
Kade], *Bizonder*: Elegant cafe with 60 beers,
peanut shells on the floor, smart helpful staff
(Dr and Mrs A K Clarke); [2 Gravenstraat],
Cafe Belgique: Up to 80 Belgian beers in
pleasant small traditional bar *(Dr and Mrs A
K Clarke)*; [Nieuwe Zijdskolksteeg 5], *In De
Wildeman*: 17 draught beers, 150 or more
bottled, in former gin distillery, run by same
firm for over 300 years; two bars, one no
smoking, with no music or machines – plain
drinking house with very welcoming
managers; cl Sun *(Colin West, Dr and Mrs A
K Clarke)*

NEW ZEALAND
Christchurch [opp Victoria Park], *Oxford on
the Avon*: Busy bar and cafeteria, good range
of plain food inc outstanding value and
quality lamb from carvery, good range of
nicely served local beers, quite a pub-like
atmosphere; food all day from good value
breakfasts on (bar opens later), tables outside
(A Albert)
Dunedin [George St], *Albert*: English-style
pub furniture inc high-backed booths, well
presented local beers, usual pub food; big
screen TV can be obtrusive (esp when
England is losing) *(A Albert)*
Harewa Falls [Waitangi, N Island], *Twin
Falls*: Friendly pub brewing its own lager and
dark ale, usual NZ meals and snacks; handy
for Waitangi Treaty House *(A Albert)*
Rangiri [State Highway 1, N Island],
Rangiriri Hotel: Vast pub on main
Auckland—Hamilton highway (but gets locals
too), with good choice of NZ beers and a
local cider, freshly prepared food inc superb
meat dishes *(A Albert)*

SINGAPORE
☆ **Singapore** [Beach Rd], *Raffles*: Magnificent
national monument, lavishly restored: Long
Bar well worth a visit for its atmosphere,
Singapore slings and underfoot peanut shells,
sedate Billiards Bar, Tiffin Room with
elaborate changing buffets, more expensive
meals in the Writer's Room, and five other
food outlets each with its own style of

cooking; cultural and Raffles displays; prices can be astronomical if you stay *(Dr and Mrs A K Clarke)*

OMAN
Muscat [Intercontinental Hotel], *Al Ghazal*: Terrific atmosphere, two pool tables, lots of little booths, Guinness and various keg beers, drinkable wines, long early-evening happy hour, good friendly service; this very heavily Indian-influenced country is not strictly Moslem, so there's the unusual sight of very happy men in full Arab dress downing pints of lager *(Mike and Karen England, Dr and Mrs A K Clarke)*

TURKEY
Istanbul [Taksim; off Istiklal Caddesi], *Andons*: Fairly upmarket three-storey pub with food throughout, pool table upstairs, restaurant above *(JJB)*; [Taksim], *Aramafen*: Live jazz late evenings, food, Efes on tap; fairly upmarket *(JJB)*; [Levent; off Nispetiye Caddesi], *Cheers*: English pub pictures but atmosphere more exotic; Efes on tap at a price *(JJB)*; [Arnavutkoy], *Churchills*: Quiet and not very English-looking, though has some whiskies and canned Heineken and Guinness, as well as Efes on tap *(JJB)*; [Taksim; off Istiklal Caddesi], *Guitar Rock Bar*: Weekend live bands on top floor, lower floor quieter with darts; cheap Efes on tap *(JJB)*; [Levent; off Nispetiye Caddesi], *North Shield*: English pub lookalike, with tables outside, wide choice of whiskies, Efes on tap, canned S&N beers *(JJB)*

USA
Boston [Massachusetts], *Back Bay*: Brewpub doing decent lunches and excellent Burton-style Bitter *(Anon)*
Hamilton [Bay Rd (Rt 1-A); Massachusetts], *Black Cow*: Former Hunters Inn, renovated and reopened, bar area with high tables separated by open fire in massive two-way fireplace from dining room with good food from bar snacks to bistro cooking inc several fish dishes; 25 beers inc Fullers ESB and Red Hook from Seattle, cider, 40 bottled beers, moderate prices, efficient friendly staff; piped music (mostly light jazz); open lunch-midnight, noisy when full – as on weekend nights *(William A Harper)*
Jackson Hole [Wyoming], *Million Dollar*: Huge very lively cowboy bar, bar stools are Western saddles complete with stirrups; live country & western music *(Richard Gibbs)*
Milford [61 Bridge St; New Jersey], *Ship*: All food home-made, very reasonably priced; cheerful informal service, two or three home-brewed ales on handpump and imported UK

keg beers, good atmosphere, original beams and tin ceiling, sturdy furnishings inc tables made from Liberty ship hatch covers; live entertainment Fri/Sat evenings; bedrooms in two self-contained apartments *(Arnold Day)*
Monterey [479 Alvarado St; California], *Mucky Duck*: Ex-Portsmouth licensees have created a charming slice of pub life here, topping local polls for food, atmosphere and above all beers, inc British, Irish and American microbrews on draught; moderate prices, live music weekends, quiz night, British comedy night, darts; open 11.30 am to 2 am all week *(Jim and Justine Finlen)*
New York [15 East 7th St], *McSorleys*: Decor substantially unchanged since this reader first went in 1949 – still an outstanding pub, a landmark for well over a century *(John Roue)*; [56 W 31st St], *O'Reillys*: Traditional Irish decor and staff – very pleasant and attentive; well cooked reasonably priced food from smoked salmon to Boston scrod, good choice of beers inc Guinness; handy for Macys *(Joan and Peter Hurren)*
Richmond [3 Chopt/Ridge, W end of Richmond; Virginia], *Melitos*: Friendly long-established neighbourhood bar/restaurant with good choice of beers, good value American and Italian food; traditional dark panelling with classic mirror; compact booth-style panelled restaurant *(Dr J D Morris)*
San Francisco [2030 Union St; California], *Betelnut*: Perhaps the first of a new post-tapas trend, busy spotlit cafe tables for small dishes of authentic Thai and other SE Asian street-stall and beer hall food, good with beer; also sidewalk tables, back restaurant in chic shades of red (book well ahead); open all day *(Anon)*
San Rafael [1533 Fourth St; California], *Mayflower*: Dark panelling, Courage and Guinness, authentic bangers and mash, ploughman's and other English food, darts and ping-pong downstairs, small shop with English candies, teas and condiments; English manager – his father started the pub in 1971 *(Dick and P J Carlson)*
Sandwich [Massachusetts], *Daniel Webster*: Very atmospheric and cosy heavy-beamed bar over 200 years old, Boston beer, excellent food in bar and restaurant esp sea bass from own fish farm; bedrooms superb *(Steve Goodchild)*
Stowe [Mountain Rd; Vermont], *Mr Pickwicks Polo Club*: Ski lodge transformed by Englishman into Olde English pub, excellent food, over ten English keg beers; bedrooms good *(Steve Goodchild)*; [Mountain Rd], *Shed*: Brewpub producing five or six good real ales from light gold IPA to dark heavy Bitter, cheaper than local average *(Steve Goodchild)*

Special Interest Lists

NO SMOKING AREAS

So many more pubs are now making some provision for the majority of their customers – that's to say non-smokers – that we have now found it is worth listing all the pubs which have told us they do set aside at least some part of the pub as a no smoking area. Look at the individual entries for the pubs themselves to see just what they do: provision is much more generous in some pubs than in others.

Bedfordshire
Keysoe, Chequers

Berkshire
East Ilsley, Crown & Horns
Frilsham, Pot Kiln
Hamstead Marshall, White
  Hart
Hare Hatch, Queen Victoria
Marsh Benham, Water Rat
Sonning, Bull
West Ilsley, Harrow

Buckinghamshire
Amersham, Queens Head
Bolter End, Peacock
Cheddington, Old Swan
Fawley, Walnut Tree
Forty Green, Royal Standard of
  England
Great Missenden, George
Ibstone, Fox
Little Hampden, Rising Sun
Marlow, Two Brewers
Skirmett, Old Crown
Waddesdon, Five Arrows
West Wycombe, George &
  Dragon

Cambridgeshire
Barnack, Millstone
Bythorn, White Hart
Cambridge, Anchor
Cambridge, Eagle
Cambridge, Free Press
Cambridge, Live & Let Live
Dullingham, Kings Head
Etton, Golden Pheasant
Gorefield, Woodmans Cottage
Hinxton, Red Lion
Holywell, Old Ferry Boat
Horningsea, Plough & Fleece
Keyston, Pheasant
Newton, Queens Head
Sutton Gault, Anchor
Swavesey, Trinity Foot
Wansford, Haycock
Woodditton, Three Blackbirds

Cheshire
Barbridge, Barbridge
Broxton, Egerton Arms
Cotebrook, Alvanley Arms

Great Budworth, George &
  Dragon
Higher Burwardsley, Pheasant
Langley, Leathers Smithy
Marbury, Swan
Mobberley, Bird in Hand
Peover Heath, Dog
Plumley, Smoker
Pott Shrigley, Cheshire Hunt
Sutton, Ryles Arms
Swettenham, Swettenham Arms
Weston, White Lion
Wincle, Ship
Wrenbury, Dusty Miller

Cornwall
Chapel Amble, Maltsters Arms
Constantine, Trengilly Wartha
Helston, Halzephron
Lanlivery, Crown
Mithian, Miners Arms
Mullion, Old Inn
Mylor Bridge, Pandora
Port Isaac, Port Gaverne
Ruan Lanihorne, Kings Head
Scorrier, Fox & Hounds
St Agnes, Turks Head
St Mawes, Victory
St Mawgan, Falcon
St Teath, White Hart
Trebarwith, Port William
Treburley, Springer Spaniel
Tresco, New Inn

Cumbria
Appleby, Royal Oak
Bassenthwaite, Pheasant
Beetham, Wheatsheaf
Braithwaite, Coledale
Cartmel, Cavendish Arms
Cartmel Fell, Masons Arms
Casterton, Pheasant
Chapel Stile, Wainwrights
Cockermouth, Trout
Crosthwaite, Punch Bowl
Dent, Sun
Dockray, Royal
Elterwater, Britannia
Eskdale Green, King George IV
Grasmere, Travellers Rest
Hawkshead, Drunken Duck
Hawkshead, Kings Arms
Hawkshead, Queens Head
Heversham, Blue Bell
Ings, Watermill
Kirkby Lonsdale, Snooty Fox
Lanercost, Abbey Bridge
Levens, Hare & Hounds
Little Langdale, Three Shires
Melmerby, Shepherds
Scales, White Horse
Seathwaite, Newfield
Sedbergh, Dalesman
Troutbeck, Mortal Man
Ulverston, Bay Horse
Yanwath, Gate

Derbyshire
Ashford in the Water, Ashford
Birchover, Druid
Brassington, Olde Gate
Derby, Brunswick
Fenny Bentley, Coach & Horses
Froggatt Edge, Chequers
Grindleford, Maynard Arms
Hardwick Hall, Hardwick
Hayfield, Lantern Pike
Kirk Ireton, Barley Mow
Ladybower Reservoir,
  Yorkshire Bridge
Melbourne, John Thompson
Monsal Head, Monsal Head
Over Haddon, Lathkil
Wardlow, Three Stags Heads
Whittington Moor, Derby Tup
Woolley Moor, White Horse

Devon
Ashprington, Durant Arms
Ashprington, Watermans Arms
Axmouth, Harbour
Berrynarbor, Olde Globe
Bishops Tawton, Chichester
  Arms
Branscombe, Fountain Head
Branscombe, Masons Arms
Churchstow, Church House
Cockwood, Anchor
Combeinteignhead, Coombe
  Cellars
Dalwood, Tuckers Arms
Dartington, Cott
Dartmouth, Royal Castle
Doddiscombsleigh, Nobody
Exminster, Turf
Harberton, Church House
Haytor Vale, Rock
Holne, Church House
Kingston, Dolphin
Knowstone, Masons Arms
Lustleigh, Cleave
Lydford, Castle
Lynmouth, Rising Sun
Miltoncombe, Who'd Have
  Thought It
Noss Mayo, Old Ship
Peter Tavy, Peter Tavy
Plymouth, China House
Ringmore, Journeys End
Sidford, Blue Ball
Sourton, Highwayman
South Zeal, Oxenham Arms
Staverton, Sea Trout
Tipton St John, Golden Lion
Topsham, Passage
Torbryan, Old Church House
Torcross, Start Bay
Totnes, Kingsbridge
Trusham, Cridford
Ugborough, Anchor

Dorset
Abbotsbury, Ilchester Arms
Askerswell, Spyway

Bishops Caundle, White Hart
Bridport, George
Burton Bradstock, Three
    Horseshoes
Chideock, Anchor
Christchurch, Fishermans
    Haunt
Church Knowle, New Inn
Corfe Castle, Greyhound
Dorchester, Kings Arms
East Chaldon, Sailors Return
East Knighton, Countryman
Kingston, Scott Arms
Marnhull, Blackmore Vale
Nettlecombe, Marquis of Lorne
Osmington Mills, Smugglers
Plush, Brace of Pheasants
Powerstock, Three Horseshoes
Shave Cross, Shave Cross
Stoke Abbott, New Inn
Symondsbury, Ilchester Arms
West Bexington, Manor

Essex
Castle Hedingham, Bell
Chappel, Swan
Clavering, Cricketers
Fyfield, Black Bull
Great Yeldham, White Hart
Lamarsh, Red Lion
Littlebury, Queens Head
Navestock, Plough
Peldon, Rose
Rickling Green, Cricketers
    Arms
Tillingham, Cap & Feathers

Gloucestershire
Almondsbury, Bowl
Amberley, Black Horse
Ampney Crucis, Crown of
    Crucis
Aust, Boars Head
Awre, Red Hart
Bisley, Bear
Bledington, Kings Head
Chipping Campden, Kings
    Arms
Clearwell, Wyndham Arms
Coln St Aldwyns, New Inn
Edge, Edgemoor
Great Rissington, Lamb
Greet, Harvest Home
Gretton, Royal Oak
Hyde, Ragged Cot
Kilkenny, Kilkeney
Kingscote, Hunters Hall
Little Washbourne, Hobnails
Littleton upon Severn, White
    Hart
Old Sodbury, Dog
Oldbury-on-Severn, Anchor
Sheepscombe, Butchers Arms
South Cerney, Eliot Arms
Southrop, Swan
St Briavels, George
Stanton, Mount
Stow on the Wold, Coach &
    Horses
Withington, Mill

Hampshire
Boldre, Red Lion
Bramdean, Fox
Bursledon, Jolly Sailor
Chalton, Red Lion

Droxford, White Horse
Ibsley, Old Beams
Locks Heath, Jolly Farmer
Micheldever, Dever Arms
Portsmouth, Still & West
Rockbourne, Rose & Thistle
Titchfield, Fishermans Rest
Winchester, Wykeham Arms

Hereford & Worcester
Bransford, Bear & Ragged Staff
Bredon, Fox & Hounds
Michaelchurch Escley, Bridge
Ombersley, Crown & Sandys
    Arms
Pensax, Bell
Sellack, Lough Pool
Weobley, Olde Salutation
Winforton, Sun
Woolhope, Crown

Hertfordshire
Ashwell, Bushel & Strike
Ayot St Lawrence, Brocket
    Arms
Barley, Fox & Hounds
Burnham Green, White Horse
Knebworth, Lytton Arms
Rushden, Moon & Stars
St Albans, Garibaldi
Walkern, White Lion
Watton at Stone, George &
    Dragon

Isle of Wight
Arreton, White Lion
Chale, Clarendon (Wight
    Mouse)
Cowes, Folly
Niton, Buddle
Seaview, Seaview
Shorwell, Crown
Ventnor, Spyglass

Kent
Boyden Gate, Gate
Hadlow, Artichoke
Oare, Shipwrights Arms
Smarden, Bell
Ulcombe, Pepper Box

**Lancashire (inc Greater
    Manchester, Merseyside)**
Balderstone, Myerscough
Bilsborrow, Owd Nells
Bispham Green, Eagle & Child
Chipping, Dog & Partridge
Darwen, Old Rosins
Downham, Assheton Arms
Goosnargh, Bushells Arms
Manchester, Sinclairs
Ribchester, White Bull
Tockholes, Rock
Yealand Conyers, New Inn

Leicestershire
Braunston, Blue Ball
Braunston, Old Plough
Empingham, White Horse
Glooston, Old Barn
Hose, Rose & Crown
Knipton, Red House
Lyddington, Old White Hart
Old Dalby, Crown
Redmile, Peacock
Sibson, Cock

Lincolnshire
Allington, Welby Arms
Donington on Bain, Black
    Horse
Dyke, Wishing Well
Gedney Dyke, Chequers
Old Somerby, Fox & Hounds
Snaith, Brewers Arms

Norfolk
Bawburgh, Kings Head
Blakeney, Kings Arms
Blakeney, White Horse
Blickling, Buckinghamshire
    Arms
Burnham Market, Hoste Arms
Burnham Thorpe, Lord Nelson
Cawston, Ratcatchers
Colkirk, Crown
Great Bircham, Kings Head
Kings Lynn, Tudor Rose
Norwich, Adam & Eve
Reedham, Ferry
Ringstead, Gin Trap
Scole, Scole
Snettisham, Rose & Crown
Stow Bardolph, Hare Arms
Swanton Morley, Darbys
Titchwell, Manor
Tivetshall St Mary, Old Ram
Warham, Three Horseshoes
Winterton-on-Sea, Fishermans
    Return
Woodbastwick, Fur & Feather

Northamptonshire
Ashby St Ledgers, Olde Coach
    House
Fotheringhay, Falcon
Harringworth, White Swan
Nassington, Black Horse
Oundle, Mill
Oundle, Ship
Sudborough, Vane Arms
Sulgrave, Star
Wadenhoe, Kings Head

**Northumberland, Durham,
    Tyneside & Teesside**
Carterway Heads, Manor
    House
Cotherstone, Fox & Hounds
Great Whittington, Queens
    Head
Greta Bridge, Morritt Arms
Haltwhistle, Wallace Arms
Matfen, Black Bull
Newton on the Moor, Cook &
    Barker Arms
Romaldkirk, Rose & Crown
Stannersburn, Pheasant

Nottinghamshire
Beeston, Victoria
Drakeholes, Griff
Wellow, Olde Red Lion

Oxfordshire
Adderbury, Red Lion
Bampton, Romany
Barnard Gate, Boot
Blewbury, Red Lion
Broadwell, Five Bells
Burcot, Chequers
Burford, Angel
Burford, Lamb
Burford, Mermaid

Church Enstone, Crown
Clanfield, Clanfield Tavern
Clifton Hampden, Plough
Cuddesdon, Bat & Ball
Cumnor, Bear & Ragged Staff
East Hendred, Wheatsheaf
Fyfield, White Hart
Lewknor, Olde Leathern Bottel
Oxford, Turf Tavern
Ramsden, Royal Oak
Shipton-under-Wychwood, Lamb
Shipton-under-Wychwood, Shaven Crown
Sibford Gower, Wykham Arms
Stanton St John, Star
Witney, Three Horseshoes
Wytham, White Hart

Shropshire
Brockton, Feathers
Cardington, Royal Oak
Llanfair Waterdine, Red Lion
Ludlow, Unicorn
Much Wenlock, George & Dragon
Much Wenlock, Talbot
Upper Farmcote, Lion of Morfe
Wenlock Edge, Wenlock Edge

Somerset
Appley, Globe
Ashcott, Ashcott
Bath, Old Green Tree
Beckington, Woolpack
Compton Martin, Ring o' Bells
Croscombe, Bull Terrier
Dowlish Wake, New Inn
Dunster, Luttrell Arms
East Woodlands, Horse & Groom
Exebridge, Anchor
Langley Marsh, Three Horseshoes
Montacute, Kings Arms
Over Stratton, Royal Oak
Stoke St Gregory, Rose & Crown
Stoke St Mary, Half Moon
Triscombe, Blue Ball
Wambrook, Cotley

Staffordshire
Acton Trussell, Moat House
Alstonefield, George
Alstonefield, Watts Russell Arms
Cresswell, Izaak Walton
Tutbury, Olde Dog & Partridge
Uttoxeter, Wellington

Suffolk
Bildeston, Crown
Blyford, Queens Head
Chillesford, Froize
Erwarton, Queens Head
Great Glemham, Crown
Hartest, Crown
Hundon, Plough
Ipswich, Brewery Tap
Lavenham, Angel
Lavenham, Swan
Levington, Ship
Long Melford, Bull
Orford, Jolly Sailor
Ramsholt, Ramsholt Arms
Snape, Plough & Sail

Southwold, Crown
Stoke by Nayland, Angel
Thornham Magna, Four Horseshoes
Walberswick, Bell
Wangford, Angel
Westleton, White Horse

Surrey
Blackbrook, Plough
Charleshill, Donkey
Coldharbour, Plough
Pirbright, Royal Oak
Warlingham, White Lion

Sussex
Alciston, Rose Cottage
Alfriston, Star
Barcombe, Anchor
Cowbeech, Merrie Harriers
Eartham, George
Eastdean, Tiger
Firle, Ram
Gun Hill, Gun
Heathfield, Star
Icklesham, Queens Head
Kingston near Lewes, Juggs
Kirdford, Half Moon
Lodsworth, Halfway Bridge
Midhurst, Spread Eagle
Nuthurst, Black Horse
Oving, Gribble
Punnetts Town, Three Cups
Seaford, Golden Galleon
Stopham, White Hart

Warwickshire
Alderminster, Bell
Himley, Crooked House
Ilmington, Howard Arms
Little Compton, Red Lion
Lowsonford, Fleur de Lys
Monks Kirby, Bell
Stratford upon Avon, Slug & Lettuce
West Bromwich, Manor House

Wiltshire
Axford, Red Lion
Box, Quarrymans Arms
Brinkworth, Three Crowns
Devizes, Bear
Ebbesbourne Wake, Horseshoe
Hindon, Lamb
Kilmington, Red Lion
Limpley Stoke, Hop Pole
Little Bedwyn, Harrow
Lower Woodford, Wheatsheaf
Poulshot, Raven
Ramsbury, Bell
Rowde, George & Dragon
Seend, Barge
Semington, Lamb
Sherston, Rattlebone
Wilcot, Golden Swan
Wylye, Bell

Yorkshire
Askrigg, Kings Arms
Beverley, White Horse
Bilbrough, Three Hares
Blakey Ridge, Lion
Bradfield, Strines
Buckden, Buck
Burnsall, Red Lion
Carlton, Foresters Arms
Carthorpe, Fox & Hounds

Cracoe, Devonshire Arms
Cray, White Lion
Cropton, New Inn
Goose Eye, Turkey
Grange Moor, Kaye Arms
Harden, Malt Shovel
Hatfield Woodhouse, Green Tree
Heath, Kings Arms
Hetton, Angel
Hull, Minerva
Kirkbymoorside, George & Dragon
Kirkham, Stone Trough
Levisham, Horseshoe
Linthwaite, Sair
Linton in Craven, Fountaine
Meltham, Will's o' Nat's
Penistone, Cubley Hall
Pickhill, Nags Head
Pool, White Hart
Ramsgill, Yorke Arms
Redmire, Kings Arms
Rosedale Abbey, Milburn Arms
Sawley, Sawley Arms
Sheffield, Fat Cat
Starbotton, Fox & Hounds
Sutton upon Derwent, St Vincent Arms
Thornton Watlass, Buck
Wath-in-Nidderdale, Sportsmans Arms
Wormald Green, Cragg Lodge
York, Olde Starre

London, Central
London EC2, Hamilton Hall
London EC4, Olde Cheshire Cheese
London W1, Argyll Arms
London WC1, Lamb

London, North
London N1, Waterside
London NW3, Spaniards

London, South
London SE21, Crown & Greyhound
London SW4, Windmill

London, West
London W8, Windsor Castle

Scotland
Applecross, Applecross
Arduaine, Loch Melfort
Brig o Turk, Byre
Canonbie, Riverside
Cawdor, Cawdor Tavern
Cleish, Nivingston House
Creebridge, Creebridge House
Edinburgh, Starbank
Fort Augustus, Lock
Glasgow, Horseshoe
Innerleithen, Traquair Arms
Isle Ornsay, Tigh Osda Eilean Iarmain
Kilberry, Kilberry
Melrose, Burts
Pitlochry, Killiecrankie
Plockton, Plockton
Portpatrick, Crown
Skeabost, Skeabost House
St Mary's Loch, Tibbie Shiels
Strachur, Creggans
Swinton, Wheatsheaf

Thornhill, Lion & Unicorn
Turriff, Towie Tavern
Tushielaw, Tushielaw
Ullapool, Ferry Boat
Ullapool, Morefield Motel

Wales
Aberdovey, Penhelig Arms
Bodfari, Dinorben Arms
Caerphilly, Courthouse
Carew, Carew
Crickhowell, Bear
Erbistock, Boat
Gresford, Pant-y-Ochain
Hay on Wye, Old Black Lion
Llanberis, Pen-y-Gwryd
Llandrindod Wells, Llanerch
Llanferres, Druid
Llangynwyd, Old House
Llannefydd, Hawk & Buckle
Llanynys, Cerrigllwydion Arms
Llyswen, Griffin
Maentwrog, Grapes
Presteigne, Radnorshire Arms
Raglan, Clytha Arms
Red Wharf Bay, Ship
Rosebush, New Inn
Tyn y Groes, Groes

Channel Islands
Castel, Hougue du Pommier
Greve de Lecq, Moulin de Lecq
St Brelade, Old Portelet
St Brelade, Old Smugglers
St John, Les Fontaines
St Martin, Royal

PUBS WITH GOOD GARDENS
The pubs listed here have bigger or more beautiful gardens, grounds or terraces than are usual for their areas. Note that in a town or city this might be very much more modest than the sort of garden that would deserve a listing in the countryside.

Bedfordshire
Bolnhurst, Olde Plough
Riseley, Fox & Hounds

Berkshire
Aldworth, Bell
Chaddleworth, Ibex
Cookham Dean, Jolly Farmer
Hamstead Marshall, White Hart
Holyport, Belgian Arms
Marsh Benham, Water Rat
West Ilsley, Harrow

Buckinghamshire
Amersham, Queens Head
Bledlow, Lions of Bledlow
Bolter End, Peacock
Fawley, Walnut Tree
Ford, Dinton Hermit
Hambleden, Stag & Huntsman
Lacey Green, Pink & Lily
Little Horwood, Shoulder of Mutton
Northend, White Hart
Skirmett, Old Crown
Waddesdon, Five Arrows
West Wycombe, George & Dragon

Worminghall, Clifden Arms

Cambridgeshire
Fowlmere, Chequers
Great Chishill, Pheasant
Horningsea, Plough & Fleece
Madingley, Three Horseshoes
Swavesey, Trinity Foot
Wansford, Haycock

Cheshire
Aldford, Grosvenor Arms
Barbridge, Barbridge
Brereton Green, Bears Head
Broomedge, Jolly Thresher
Lower Peover, Bells of Peover
Macclesfield, Sutton Hall
Swettenham, Swettenham Arms
Weston, White Lion

Cornwall
Helford, Shipwrights Arms
Manaccan, New Inn
Philleigh, Roseland
St Agnes, Turks Head
St Kew, St Kew
St Mawgan, Falcon
Tresco, New Inn

Cumbria
Bassenthwaite, Pheasant
Bouth, White Hart
Cockermouth, Trout
Eskdale Green, Bower House

Derbyshire
Birch Vale, Waltzing Weasel
Buxton, Bull i'th' Thorn
Grindleford, Maynard Arms
Little Longstone, Packhorse
Melbourne, John Thompson
Woolley Moor, White Horse

Devon
Avonwick, Avon
Berrynarbor, Olde Globe
Broadhembury, Drewe Arms
Clyst Hydon, Five Bells
Cornworthy, Hunters Lodge
Dartington, Cott
Exminster, Turf
Haytor Vale, Rock
Lower Ashton, Manor
Lydford, Castle
Poundsgate, Tavistock
Sidford, Blue Ball
South Zeal, Oxenham Arms
Torbryan, Old Church House
Welcombe, Old Smithy
Weston, Otter

Dorset
Christchurch, Fishermans Haunt
Corfe Castle, Fox
Farnham, Museum
Kingston, Scott Arms
Nettlecombe, Marquis of Lorne
Osmington Mills, Smugglers
Plush, Brace of Pheasants
Shave Cross, Shave Cross
Stoke Abbott, New Inn
Tarrant Monkton, Langton Arms
West Bexington, Manor

Essex
Castle Hedingham, Bell
Chappel, Swan

Coggeshall, Compasses
Great Yeldham, White Hart
Littlebury, Queens Head
Mill Green, Viper
Peldon, Rose
Stock, Hoop
Wendens Ambo, Bell
Woodham Walter, Cats

Gloucestershire
Amberley, Black Horse
Ampney Crucis, Crown of Crucis
Bibury, Catherine Wheel
Brockhampton, Craven Arms
Chipping Campden, Kings Arms
Coleford, Dog & Muffler
Ewen, Wild Duck
Great Rissington, Lamb
Greet, Harvest Home
Gretton, Royal Oak
Guiting Power, Farmers Arms
Kilkenny, Kilkeney
Kineton, Halfway House
Kingscote, Hunters Hall
Minchinhampton, Old Lodge
North Nibley, New Inn
Oddington, Horse & Groom
Old Sodbury, Dog
Redbrook, Boat
Southrop, Swan
Withington, Mill

Hampshire
Battramsley, Hobler
Bramdean, Fox
Longparish, Plough
Ovington, Bush
Petersfield, White Horse
Steep, Harrow
Stockbridge, Vine
Tichborne, Tichborne Arms

Hereford & Worcester
Bretforton, Fleece
Much Marcle, Slip Tavern
Sellack, Lough Pool
Ullingswick, Three Crowns
Woolhope, Butchers Arms

Hertfordshire
Ayot St Lawrence, Brocket Arms
Great Offley, Green Man
Tewin, Plume of Feathers
Walkern, White Lion

Isle of Wight
Chale, Clarendon (Wight Mouse)
Niton, Buddle
Shorwell, Crown

Kent
Biddenden, Three Chimneys
Bough Beech, Wheatsheaf
Boyden Gate, Gate
Chiddingstone, Castle
Dargate, Dove
Groombridge, Crown
Newnham, George
Penshurst, Bottle House
Ringlestone, Ringlestone
Selling, Rose & Crown
Smarden, Bell
Sole Street, Compasses
Toys Hill, Fox & Hounds

Ulcombe, Pepper Box

Lancashire (inc Greater Manchester, Merseyside)
Darwen, Old Rosins
Newton, Parkers Arms
Whitewell, Inn at Whitewell

Leicestershire
Braunston, Old Plough
Exton, Fox & Hounds
Medbourne, Nevill Arms
Old Dalby, Crown

Lincolnshire
Newton, Red Lion
Stamford, George of Stamford

Norfolk
Castle Acre, Ostrich
Great Bircham, Kings Head
Reedham, Ferry
Sculthorpe, Sculthorpe Mill
Stow Bardolph, Hare Arms
Titchwell, Manor
Woodbastwick, Fur & Feather

Northamptonshire
Ashby St Ledgers, Olde Coach House
East Haddon, Red Lion
Wadenhoe, Kings Head

Northumberland, Durham, Tyneside & Teesside
Blanchland, Lord Crewe Arms
Diptonmill, Dipton Mill
Greta Bridge, Morritt Arms

Nottinghamshire
Colston Bassett, Martins Arms
Drakeholes, Griff
Kimberley, Nelson & Railway
Upton, French Horn

Oxfordshire
Beckley, Abingdon Arms
Binfield Heath, Bottle & Glass
Brightwell Baldwin, Lord Nelson
Broadwell, Five Bells
Burford, Lamb
Chinnor, Sir Charles Napier
Clifton, Duke of Cumberlands Head
Finstock, Plough
Fyfield, White Hart
Hook Norton, Gate Hangs High
Hook Norton, Pear Tree
Kelmscot, Plough
Maidensgrove, Five Horseshoes
Shipton-under-Wychwood, Shaven Crown
Sibford Gower, Wykham Arms
South Leigh, Mason Arms
South Stoke, Perch & Pike
Stanton St John, Star
Tadpole Bridge, Trout
Watlington, Chequers
Woodstock, Feathers

Shropshire
Norton, Hundred House
Upper Farmcote, Lion of Morfe

Somerset
Ashcott, Ashcott
Bristol, Highbury Vaults
Combe Hay, Wheatsheaf
Compton Martin, Ring o' Bells

Dunster, Luttrell Arms
Exebridge, Anchor
Litton, Kings Arms
Monksilver, Notley Arms
Over Stratton, Royal Oak
South Stoke, Pack Horse
West Huntspill, Crossways

Staffordshire
Acton Trussell, Moat House
Onecote, Jervis Arms
Salt, Holly Bush
Tutbury, Olde Dog & Partridge

Suffolk
Bildeston, Crown
Brandeston, Queens Head
Dennington, Queens Head
Hoxne, Swan
Lavenham, Angel
Lavenham, Swan
Laxfield, Kings Head
Rede, Plough
Walberswick, Bell
Westleton, White Horse

Surrey
Albury, Drummond Arms
Charleshill, Donkey
Coldharbour, Plough
Compton, Withies
Farncombe, Ram
Hascombe, White Horse
Mickleham, King William IV
Outwood, Dog & Duck
Pirbright, Royal Oak
Warlingham, White Lion

Sussex
Ashurst, Fountain
Barcombe, Anchor
Berwick, Cricketers Arms
Blackboys, Blackboys
Byworth, Black Horse
Eartham, George
Elsted, Three Horseshoes
Firle, Ram
Fletching, Griffin
Fulking, Shepherd & Dog
Gun Hill, Gun
Heathfield, Star
Kirdford, Half Moon
Lickfold, Lickfold
Oving, Gribble
Rowhook, Chequers
Seaford, Golden Galleon
Stopham, White Hart
Wineham, Royal Oak

Warwickshire
Farnborough, Butchers Arms
Ilmington, Howard Arms
Lowsonford, Fleur de Lys
Stratford upon Avon, Slug & Lettuce
West Bromwich, Manor House

Wiltshire
Bradford-on-Avon, Cross Guns
Brinkworth, Three Crowns
Chicksgrove, Compasses
Ebbesbourne Wake, Horseshoe
Lacock, George
Little Cheverell, Owl
Lower Woodford, Wheatsheaf
Norton, Vine Tree
Seend, Barge
Wilcot, Golden Swan

Yorkshire
East Witton, Blue Lion
Egton Bridge, Horse Shoe
Heath, Kings Arms
Penistone, Cubley Hall
Stutton, Hare & Hounds
Sutton upon Derwent, St Vincent Arms
Threshfield, Old Hall

London, Central
London W1, Red Lion

London, North
London N1, Waterside
London NW3, Spaniards

London, South
London SE21, Crown & Greyhound
London SW18, Ship

London, West
London W6, Dove
London W8, Windsor Castle

Scotland
Ardfern, Galley of Lorne
Arduaine, Loch Melfort
Cleish, Nivingston House
Creebridge, Creebridge House
Edinburgh, Starbank
Gifford, Tweeddale Arms
Pitlochry, Killiecrankie
Skeabost, Skeabost House
Strachur, Creggans
Thornhill, Lion & Unicorn
Tweedsmuir, Crook

Wales
Aberystwyth, Halfway
Bodfari, Dinorben Arms
Burton Green, Golden Grove
Caerphilly, Courthouse
Crickhowell, Bear
Crickhowell, Nantyffin Cider Mill
Llancarfan, Fox & Hounds
Llandrindod Wells, Llanerch
Llanelidan, Leyland Arms
Llanfrynach, White Swan
Llanthony, Abbey
Llwyndafydd, Crown
Marianglas, Parciau Arms
Presteigne, Radnorshire Arms
St Hilary, Bush
Stackpole, Armstrong Arms
Tyn y Groes, Groes

Channel Islands
Castel, Hougue du Pommier
Kings Mills, Fleur du Jardin
Rozel, Rozel Bay

WATERSIDE PUBS
The pubs listed here are right beside the sea, a sizeable river, canal, lake or loch that contributes significantly to their attraction.

Bedfordshire
Odell, Bell

Berkshire
Great Shefford, Swan

Cambridgeshire
Cambridge, Anchor
Cambridge, Mill
Holywell, Old Ferry Boat

Sutton Gault, Anchor
Wansford, Haycock

Cheshire
Barbridge, Barbridge
Wrenbury, Dusty Miller

Cornwall
Falmouth, Chain Locker
Falmouth, Quayside Inn & Old
  Ale House
Helford, Shipwrights Arms
Mousehole, Ship
Mylor Bridge, Pandora
Polkerris, Rashleigh
Port Isaac, Port Gaverne
Porthallow, Five Pilchards
Porthleven, Ship
St Agnes, Turks Head
Trebarwith, Port William
Tresco, New Inn

Cumbria
Cockermouth, Trout
Ulverston, Bay Horse

Derbyshire
Shardlow, Old Crown

Devon
Ashprington, Watermans Arms
Avonwick, Avon
Brendon, Rockford
Combeinteignhead, Coombe
  Cellars
Dartmouth, Royal Castle
Exeter, Double Locks
Exminster, Turf
Lynmouth, Rising Sun
Noss Mayo, Old Ship
Plymouth, China House
Topsham, Passage
Torcross, Start Bay
Weston, Otter

Dorset
Chideock, Anchor
Lyme Regis, Pilot Boat

Essex
Chappel, Swan
Leigh on Sea, Crooked Billet

Gloucestershire
Ashleworth Quay, Boat
Great Barrington, Fox
Redbrook, Boat
Withington, Mill

Hampshire
Bursledon, Jolly Sailor
Langstone, Royal Oak
Ovington, Bush
Portsmouth, Still & West
Wherwell, Mayfly

Hereford & Worcester
Knightwick, Talbot
Michaelchurch Escley, Bridge
Wyre Piddle, Anchor

Hertfordshire
Berkhamsted, Boat

Isle of Wight
Cowes, Folly
Seaview, Seaview
Shanklin, Fishermans Cottage
Ventnor, Spyglass

Kent
Faversham, Albion

Oare, Shipwrights Arms
Whitstable, Pearsons Crab &
  Oyster House

**Lancashire (inc Greater
  Manchester, Merseyside)**
Bilsborrow, Owd Nells
Garstang, Th'Owd Tithebarn
Manchester, Dukes 92
Manchester, Mark Addy
Whitewell, Inn at Whitewell

Lincolnshire
Brandy Wharf, Cider Centre

Norfolk
Reedham, Ferry
Sculthorpe, Sculthorpe Mill

Northamptonshire
Oundle, Mill
Wadenhoe, Kings Head

**Northumberland, Durham,
  Tyneside & Teeside**
North Shields, Chain Locker

Oxfordshire
Tadpole Bridge, Trout

Shropshire
Llanyblodwel, Horse Shoe
Ludlow, Unicorn
Shrewsbury, Boathouse
Whitchurch, Willey Moor Lock

Somerset
Exebridge, Anchor

Staffordshire
Acton Trussell, Moat House
Onecote, Jervis Arms

Suffolk
Aldeburgh, Cross Keys
Chelmondiston, Butt & Oyster
Ipswich, Brewery Tap
Ramsholt, Ramsholt Arms

Sussex
Barcombe, Anchor
Stopham, White Hart

Warwickshire
Lapworth, Navigation
Lowsonford, Fleur de Lys
Netherton, Little Dry Dock

Wiltshire
Bradford-on-Avon, Cross Guns
Seend, Barge

Yorkshire
Hull, Minerva

London, North
London N1, Waterside

London, South
London SE1, Anchor,
  Horniman
London SE10, Cutty Sark
London SW13, Bulls Head
London SW18, Ship
Richmond, White Cross

London, West
London W6, Dove

London, East
London E1, Town of Ramsgate
London E14, Grapes

Scotland
Ardfern, Galley of Lorne

Arduaine, Loch Melfort
Carbost, Old Inn
Clachan Seil, Tigh an Truish
Crinan, Crinan
Edinburgh, Starbank
Elie, Ship
Fort Augustus, Lock
Isle Ornsay, Tigh Osda Eilean
  Iarmain
Isle of Whithorn, Steam Packet
Plockton, Plockton
Portpatrick, Crown
Shieldaig, Tigh an Eilean
Skeabost, Skeabost House
St Mary's Loch, Tibbie Shiels
Strachur, Creggans
Tayvallich, Tayvallich
Ullapool, Ferry Boat

Wales
Aberdovey, Penhelig Arms
Abergorlech, Black Lion
Cresswell Quay, Cresselly Arms
Erbistock, Boat
Little Haven, Swan
Pembroke Ferry, Ferry
Pontypool, Open Hearth
Red Wharf Bay, Ship

Channel Islands
St Aubin, Old Court House

PUBS IN ATTRACTIVE
  SURROUNDINGS
These pubs are in unusually
attractive or interesting places –
lovely countryside, charming
villages, occasionally notable
town surroundings. Waterside
pubes are listed again here only
if their other surroundings are
special, too.

Berkshire
Aldworth, Bell
Frilsham, Pot Kiln
Waltham St Lawrence, Bell

Buckinghamshire
Bledlow, Lions of Bledlow
Brill, Pheasant
Frieth, Prince Albert
Hambleden, Stag & Huntsman
Ibstone, Fox
Little Hampden, Rising Sun
Littleworth Common,
  Blackwood Arms
Northend, White Hart
Turville, Bull & Butcher

Cambridgeshire
Dullingham, Kings Head

Cheshire
Barthomley, White Lion
Great Budworth, George &
  Dragon
Langley, Leathers Smithy
Lower Peover, Bells of Peover
Marbury, Swan
Sutton, Ryles Arms
Swettenham, Swettenham Arms

Cornwall
Boscastle, Cobweb
Chapel Amble, Maltsters Arms
Helston, Halzephron
Manaccan, New Inn

Penelewey, Punch Bowl &
   Ladle
Porthallow, Five Pilchards
Ruan Lanihorne, Kings Head
St Agnes, Turks Head
St Breward, Old Inn
St Kew, St Kew
St Mawgan, Falcon
Tresco, New Inn

Cumbria
Alston, Angel
Askham, Punch Bowl
Bassenthwaite, Pheasant
Boot, Burnmoor
Bouth, White Hart
Braithwaite, Coledale
Cartmel, Cavendish Arms
Chapel Stile, Wainwrights
Crosthwaite, Punch Bowl
Dent, Sun
Dockray, Royal
Elterwater, Britannia
Eskdale Green, King George IV
Garrigill, George & Dragon
Grasmere, Travellers Rest
Hawkshead, Drunken Duck
Hawkshead, Kings Arms
Ings, Watermill
Lanercost, Abbey Bridge
Langdale, Old Dungeon Ghyll
Little Langdale, Three Shires
Loweswater, Kirkstile
Melmerby, Shepherds
Scales, White Horse
Seathwaite, Newfield
Troutbeck, Mortal Man
Troutbeck, Queens Head
Ulverston, Bay Horse

Derbyshire
Ashford in the Water, Ashford
Brassington, Olde Gate
Froggatt Edge, Chequers
Hardwick Hall, Hardwick
Hayfield, Lantern Pike
Holmesfield, Robin Hood
Kirk Ireton, Barley Mow
Ladybower Reservoir,
   Yorkshire Bridge
Little Hucklow, Old Bulls Head
Little Longstone, Packhorse
Monsal Head, Monsal Head
Over Haddon, Lathkil
Woolley Moor, White Horse

Devon
Blackawton, Normandy Arms
Branscombe, Fountain Head
Brendon, Rockford
Broadclyst, Red Lion
Chagford, Ring o' Bells
Exminster, Turf
Haytor Vale, Rock
Holbeton, Mildmay Colours
Holne, Church House
Horndon, Elephants Nest
Horsebridge, Royal
Iddesleigh, Duke of York
Kingston, Dolphin
Knowstone, Masons Arms
Lower Ashton, Manor
Lustleigh, Cleave
Lydford, Castle
Lynmouth, Rising Sun
Meavy, Royal Oak

Peter Tavy, Peter Tavy
Postbridge, Warren House
Rattery, Church House
Wonson, Northmore Arms

Dorset
Abbotsbury, Ilchester Arms
Askerswell, Spyway
Burton Bradstock, Three
   Horseshoes
Corfe Castle, Fox
Corscombe, Fox
East Chaldon, Sailors Return
Farnham, Museum
Kingston, Scott Arms
Loders, Loders Arms
Milton Abbas, Hambro Arms
Osmington Mills, Smugglers
Plush, Brace of Pheasants
Powerstock, Three Horseshoes
Worth Matravers, Square &
   Compass

Essex
Leigh on Sea, Crooked Billet
Little Dunmow, Flitch of Bacon
Mill Green, Viper
North Fambridge, Ferryboat

Gloucestershire
Amberley, Black Horse
Ashleworth Quay, Boat
Bibury, Catherine Wheel
Bisley, Bear
Bledington, Kings Head
Brockhampton, Craven Arms
Brockweir, Brockweir
Chipping Campden, Eight Bells
Chedworth, Seven Tuns
Cold Aston, Plough
Coleford, Dog & Muffler
Coln St Aldwyns, New Inn
Great Rissington, Lamb
Guiting Power, Farmers Arms
Minchinhampton, Old Lodge
Nailsworth, Weighbridge
Newland, Ostrich
North Nibley, New Inn
Sapperton, Bell
St Briavels, George
Stanton, Mount
Stow on the Wold, Queens
   Head

Hampshire
Crawley, Fox & Hounds
Hawkley, Hawkley
Micheldever, Dever Arms
Ovington, Bush
Petersfield, White Horse
Soberton, White Lion
Tichborne, Tichborne Arms

Hereford & Worcester
Broadway, Crown & Trumpet
Hanley Castle, Three Kings
Kidderminster, King & Castle
Knightwick, Talbot
Michaelchurch Escley, Bridge
Much Marcle, Slip Tavern
Pensax, Bell
Ruckhall, Ancient Camp
Sellack, Lough Pool
Weobley, Olde Salutation
Woolhope, Butchers Arms

Hertfordshire
Ashwell, Bushel & Strike

Sarratt, Cock
St Albans, Fighting Cocks
Westmill, Sword in Hand

Isle of Wight
Chale, Clarendon (Wight
   Mouse)

Kent
Boughton Aluph, Flying Horse
Brookland, Woolpack
Chiddingstone, Castle
Groombridge, Crown
Hever, Henry VIII
Lamberhurst, Brown Trout
Newnham, George
Selling, Rose & Crown
Sole Street, Compasses
Toys Hill, Fox & Hounds

**Lancashire (inc Greater
Manchester, Merseyside)**
Blacko, Moorcock
Blackstone Edge, White House
Downham, Assheton Arms
Marple, Romper
Newton, Parkers Arms
Whitewell, Inn at Whitewell

Leicestershire
Exton, Fox & Hounds
Glooston, Old Barn
Hallaton, Bewicke Arms

Lincolnshire
Aswarby, Tally Ho

Norfolk
Blakeney, White Horse
Blickling, Buckinghamshire
   Arms
Burnham Market, Hoste Arms
Castle Acre, Ostrich
Great Bircham, Kings Head
Heydon, Earle Arms
Horsey, Nelson Head
Thornham, Lifeboat
Woodbastwick, Fur & Feather

Northamptonshire
Chapel Brampton, Brampton
   Halt
Harringworth, White Swan

**Northumberland, Durham,
Tyneside & Teesside**
Allenheads, Allenheads
Bamburgh, Lord Crewe Arms
Blanchland, Lord Crewe Arms
Craster, Jolly Fisherman
Diptonmill, Dipton Mill
Great Whittington, Queens
   Head
Haltwhistle, Milecastle
Haltwhistle, Wallace Arms
Matfen, Black Bull
Romaldkirk, Rose & Crown
Stannersburn, Pheasant

Nottinghamshire
Laxton, Dovecote

Oxfordshire
Ardington, Boars Head
Brightwell Baldwin, Lord
   Nelson
Burford, Angel
Burford, Mermaid
Checkendon, Black Horse
Chinnor, Sir Charles Napier

Cropredy, Red Lion
Great Tew, Falkland Arms
Hailey, King William IV
Kelmscot, Plough
Maidensgrove, Five Horseshoes
Oxford, Turf Tavern
Shenington, Bell
Shipton-under-Wychwood,
  Shaven Crown
Swinbrook, Swan

Shropshire
Bridges, Horseshoe
Cardington, Royal Oak
Llanfair Waterdine, Red Lion
Wenlock Edge, Wenlock Edge

Somerset
Appley, Globe
Blagdon, New Inn
Combe Hay, Wheatsheaf
Cranmore, Strode Arms
Luxborough, Royal Oak
Stogumber, White Horse
Triscombe, Blue Ball
Wambrook, Cotley
Winsford, Royal Oak

Staffordshire
Alstonefield, George

Suffolk
Dennington, Queens Head
Dunwich, Ship
Lavenham, Angel
Levington, Ship
Long Melford, Bull
Ramsholt, Ramsholt Arms
Snape, Plough & Sail
Walberswick, Bell

Surrey
Albury, Drummond Arms
Blackbrook, Plough
Cobham, Cricketers
Englefield Green, Fox &
  Hounds
Friday Street, Stephan Langton
Mickleham, King William IV
Reigate Heath, Skimmington
  Castle

Sussex
Barcombe, Anchor
Billingshurst, Blue Ship
Brownbread Street, Ash Tree
Burpham, George & Dragon
Burwash, Bell
Eartham, George
Eastdean, Tiger
Fletching, Griffin
Fulking, Shepherd & Dog
Heathfield, Star
Kirdford, Half Moon
Lickfold, Lickfold
Lurgashall, Noahs Ark
Mayfield, Middle House
Seaford, Golden Galleon
Wineham, Royal Oak

Warwickshire
Himley, Crooked House
Warmington, Plough

Wiltshire
Axford, Red Lion
Bradford-on-Avon, Cross Guns
Ebbesbourne Wake, Horseshoe
Wootton Rivers, Royal Oak

Yorkshire
Appletreewick, Craven Arms
Askrigg, Kings Arms
Beck Hole, Birch Hall
Blakey Ridge, Lion
Bradfield, Strines
Buckden, Buck
Burnsall, Red Lion
Byland Abbey, Abbey
Cray, White Lion
East Witton, Blue Lion
Heath, Kings Arms
Hubberholme, George
Kirby Hill, Shoulder of Mutton
Levisham, Horseshoe
Linton in Craven, Fountaine
Litton, Queens Arms
Masham, Kings Head
Meltham, Will's o' Nat's
Middleham, Black Swan
Muker, Farmers Arms
Ramsgill, Yorke Arms
Robin Hoods Bay, Laurel
Rosedale Abbey, Milburn Arms
Shelley, Three Acres
Starbotton, Fox & Hounds
Terrington, Bay Horse
Thornton Watlass, Buck
Wath-in-Nidderdale,
  Sportsmans Arms
Widdop, Pack Horse

London, Central
London EC1, Olde Mitre

London, North
London NW3, Spaniards

London, South
London SE1, Horniman
London SE21, Crown &
  Greyhound
London SW4, Windmill
London SW19, Fox & Grapes

London, West
Hampton Court, Kings Arms

Scotland
Applecross, Applecross
Arduaine, Loch Melfort
Brig o Turk, Byre
Clachan Seil, Tigh an Truish
Crinan, Crinan
Kilberry, Kilberry
Mountbenger, Gordon Arms
Pitlochry, Killiecrankie
Sheriffmuir, Sheriffmuir
St Mary's Loch, Tibbie Shiels
Strachur, Creggans
Tushielaw, Tushielaw
Tweedsmuir, Crook

Wales
Abergorlech, Black Lion
Aberystwyth, Halfway
Caerphilly, Courthouse
Carew, Carew
Cilcain, White Horse
Crickhowell, Nantyffin Cider
  Mill
Erbistock, Boat
Kenfig, Prince of Wales
Llanbedr-y-Cennin, Olde Bull
Llanberis, Pen-y-Gwryd
Llanelidan, Leyland Arms
Llanthony, Abbey
Maentwrog, Grapes

Monmouth, Punch House
Red Wharf Bay, Ship

Channel Islands
St Brelade, Old Portelet
St Brelade, Old Smugglers
St John, Les Fontaines

PUBS WITH GOOD VIEWS
These pubs are listed for their
particularly good views, either
from inside or from a garden or
terrace. Waterside pubs are
listed again here only if their
view is exceptional in its own
right – not just a straightforward
sea view, for example.

Berkshire
Chieveley, Blue Boar

Buckinghamshire
Brill, Pheasant

Cheshire
Higher Burwardsley, Pheasant
Langley, Hanging Gate
Langley, Leathers Smithy
Overton, Ring o' Bells

Cornwall
Ruan Lanihorne, Kings Head
St Agnes, Turks Head

Cumbria
Braithwaite, Coledale
Cartmel Fell, Masons Arms
Eskdale Green, King George IV
Hawkshead, Drunken Duck
Langdale, Old Dungeon Ghyll
Loweswater, Kirkstile
Troutbeck, Queens Head
Ulverston, Bay Horse

Derbyshire
Foolow, Barrel
Monsal Head, Monsal Head
Over Haddon, Lathkil

Devon
Postbridge, Warren House

Dorset
Kingston, Scott Arms
West Bexington, Manor
Worth Matravers, Square &
  Compass

Gloucestershire
Amberley, Black Horse
Cranham, Black Horse
Edge, Edgemoor
Gretton, Royal Oak
Kilkenny, Kilkeney
Sheepscombe, Butchers Arms
Stanton, Mount
Woodchester, Ram

Hampshire
Beauworth, Milbury's

Hereford & Worcester
Pensax, Bell
Ruckhall, Ancient Camp
Wyre Piddle, Anchor

Hertfordshire
Great Offley, Green Man

Isle of Wight
Niton, Buddle
Ventnor, Spyglass

Kent
Penshurst, Spotted Dog
Ulcombe, Pepper Box

Lancashire (inc Greater Manchester, Merseyside)
Blacko, Moorcock
Blackstone Edge, White House
Darwen, Old Rosins
Marple, Romper
Tockholes, Rock

Leicestershire
Knipton, Red House

Northumberland, Durham, Tyneside & Teesside
Haltwhistle, Wallace Arms
Seahouses, Olde Ship

Somerset
Blagdon, New Inn

Suffolk
Erwarton, Queens Head
Hundon, Plough
Levington, Ship

Sussex
Byworth, Black Horse
Elsted, Three Horseshoes
Fletching, Griffin
Icklesham, Queens Head

Wiltshire
Axford, Red Lion
Box, Quarrymans Arms

Yorkshire
Appletreewick, Craven Arms
Blakey Ridge, Lion
Bradfield, Strines
Kirby Hill, Shoulder of Mutton
Kirkham, Stone Trough
Litton, Queens Arms
Meltham, Will's o' Nat's
Shelley, Three Acres

Scotland
Applecross, Applecross
Ardvasar, Ardvasar
Crinan, Crinan
Edinburgh, Starbank
Isle Ornsay, Tigh Osda Eilean Iarmain
Kilberry, Kilberry
Pitlochry, Killiecrankie
Sheriffmuir, Sheriffmuir
Shieldaig, Tigh an Eilean
St Mary's Loch, Tibbie Shiels
Strachur, Creggans
Tushielaw, Tushielaw
Ullapool, Ferry Boat
Weem, Ailean Chraggan

Wales
Aberdovey, Penhelig Arms
Aberystwyth, Halfway
Bodfari, Dinorben Arms
Caerphilly, Courthouse
Halkyn, Britannia
Llanbedr-y-Cennin, Olde Bull
Llanberis, Pen-y-Gwryd
Llanferres, Druid
Llangynwyd, Old House
Llannefydd, Hawk & Buckle
Ty y Groes, Groes

Channel Islands
St Aubin, Old Court House

PUBS IN INTERESTING BUILDINGS
Pubs and inns are listed here for the particular interest of their building – something really out of the ordinary to look at, or occasionally a building that has an outstandingly interesting historical background.

Berkshire
Cookham, Bel & the Dragon

Buckinghamshire
Forty Green, Royal Standard of England

Derbyshire
Buxton, Bull i'th' Thorn

Devon
Dartmouth, Cherub
Harberton, Church House
Rattery, Church House
Sourton, Highwayman
South Zeal, Oxenham Arms

Hampshire
Beauworth, Milbury's

Hereford & Worcester
Bretforton, Fleece

Lancashire (inc Greater Manchester, Merseyside)
Garstang, Th'Owd Tithebarn
Liverpool, Philharmonic Dining Rooms

Lincolnshire
Stamford, George of Stamford

Norfolk
Scole, Scole

Northumberland, Durham, Tyneside & Teesside
Blanchland, Lord Crewe Arms

Nottinghamshire
Nottingham, Olde Trip to Jerusalem

Oxfordshire
Fyfield, White Hart

Somerset
Norton St Philip, George

Suffolk
Lavenham, Swan
Long Melford, Bull

Sussex
Alfriston, Star
Rye, Mermaid

Warwickshire
Himley, Crooked House
West Bromwich, Manor House

Wiltshire
Salisbury, Haunch of Venison

Yorkshire
Hull, Olde White Harte

London, Central
London EC2, Hamilton Hall
London EC4, Black Friar
London WC1, Cittie of Yorke

London, South
London SE1, George
London SE5, Phoenix & Firkin

Scotland
Edinburgh, Cafe Royal
Edinburgh, Guildford Arms
Glasgow, Horseshoe

Wales
Llanfihangel Crucorney, Skirrid
Llanthony, Abbey

PUBS THAT BREW THEIR OWN BEER
The pubs listed here brew their own brew on the premises; many others not listed have beers brewed for them specially, sometimes to an individual recipe (but by a separate brewer). We mention these in the text.

Cornwall
Helston, Blue Anchor

Cumbria
Cartmel Fell, Masons Arms
Dent, Sun

Derbyshire
Derby, Brunswick
Melbourne, John Thompson

Devon
Ashburton, London
Hatherleigh, Tally Ho
Holbeton, Mildmay Colours
Horsebridge, Royal
Newton St Cyres, Beer Engine

Gloucestershire
Apperley, Farmers Arms

Hampshire
Cheriton, Flower Pots
Southsea, Wine Vaults

Hertfordshire
Barley, Fox & Hounds

Lancashire (inc Greater Manchester, Merseyside)
Manchester, Lass o' Gowrie

Leicestershire
Somerby, Old Brewery

Lincolnshire
Snaith, Brewers Arms

Norfolk
Woodbastwick, Fur & Feather

Nottinghamshire
Nottingham, Fellows Morton & Clayton

Shropshire
Munslow, Crown
Wistanstow, Plough

Somerset
Trudoxhill, White Hart

Staffordshire
Burton on Trent, Burton Bridge
Shraleybrook, Rising Sun

Suffolk
Earl Soham, Victoria

Sussex
Oving, Gribble
Seaford, Golden Galleon

Warwickshire
Brierley Hill, Vine
Langley, Brewery
Shustoke, Griffin

Yorkshire
Cropton, New Inn
Hull, Minerva
Linthwaite, Sair
Sheffield, Fat Cat

London, Central
London SW1, Orange Brewery

London, South
London SE5, Phoenix & Firkin

London, West
London SW10, Ferret & Firkin

Channel Islands
St Helier, Tipsy Toad Town House
St Peter, Star & Tipsy Toad

PUBS CLOSE TO MOTORWAY JUNCTIONS
The number at the start of each line is the number of the junction. Detailed directions are given in the main entry for each pub. In this section, to help you find the pubs quickly before you're past the junction, we give in abbreviated form the name of the chapter where you'll find them in the text.

M1
18: Crick (Northants) 1 mile; Ashby St Ledgers (Northants) 4 miles
24: Kegworth (Leics) under a mile ; Shardlow (Derbys) 2½ miles
26: Kimberley (Notts) 2 miles
29: Hardwick Hall (Derbys) 4 miles

M2
7: Selling (Kent) 3½ miles

M3
5: Mattingley (Hants) 3 miles; Rotherwick (Hants) 4 miles
7: Dummer (Hants) ½ miles

M4
9: Holyport (Berks) 1½ miles
12: Stanford Dingley (Berks)

4 miles
13: Chieveley (Berks) 3 ½ miles
14: Great Shefford (Berks) 2 miles
18: Old Sodbury (Gloucs) 2 miles
21: Aust (Gloucs) ½ mile; Littleton upon Severn (Gloucs) 3½ miles
37: Kenfig (Wales) 2¼ miles

M5
2: Langley (Warwicks) 1½ miles
9: Bredon (Herefs & Worcs) 4½ miles
16: Almondsbury (Gloucs) 1½ miles
19: Clapton in Gordano (Somerset) 4 miles
23: West Huntspill (Somerset) 2¾ miles
25: Stoke St Mary (Somerset) 2¾ miles
28: Broadhembury (Devon) 5 miles
30: Topsham (Devon) 2 miles; Woodbury Salterton (Devon) 3½ miles; Exeter (Devon) 4 miles

M6
2: Withybrook (Warwicks) 4 miles
9: West Bromwich (Warwicks) 2 miles
13: Acton Trussell (Staffs) 2 miles
16: Barthomley (Cheshire) 1 mile ; Shraleybrook (Staffs) 3 miles; Weston (Cheshire) 3½ miles
17: Brereton Green (Cheshire) 2 miles
19: Plumley (Cheshire) 2½ miles; Great Budworth (Cheshire) 4½ miles
29: Brindle (Lancs etc) 3 miles
31: Balderstone (Lancs etc) 2 miles
32: Goosnargh (Lancs etc) 4 miles

35: Yealand Conyers (Lancs etc) 3 miles
40: Yanwath (Cumbria) 2¼ miles; Stainton (Cumbria) 3 miles; Tirril (Cumbria) 3½ miles; Askham (Cumbria) 4½ miles

M9
3: Linlithgow (Scotland) 2 miles

M11
10: Hinxton (Cambs) 2 miles

M18
5: Hatfield Woodhouse (Yorks) 2 miles

M25
8: Reigate Heath (Surrey) 3 miles; Betchworth (Surrey) 4 miles
10: Cobham (Surrey) 3¾ miles
18: Chenies (Bucks) 2 miles; Flaunden (Herts) 4 miles

M27
1: Cadnam (Hants) ½ miles
8: Bursledon (Hants) 2 miles
9: Locks Heath (Hants) 2½ miles

M40
2: Wooburn Common (Bucks) 2 miles; Beaconsfield (Bucks) 2 miles; Forty Green (Bucks) 3½ miles
5: Ibstone (Bucks) 1 mile; Bolter End (Bucks) 4 miles
6: Lewknor (Oxon) ½ mile; Watlington (Oxon) 3 miles; Cuxham (Oxon) 4 miles
7: Little Milton (Oxon) 2½ miles
8: Worminghall (Bucks) 4½ miles

M56
12: Overton (Cheshire) 2 miles

M90
5: Cleish (Scotland) 1½ miles

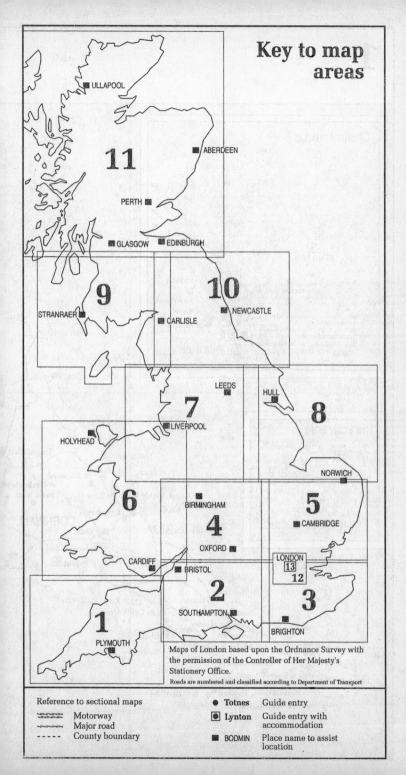

Key to map areas

11
ULLAPOOL
ABERDEEN
PERTH
GLASGOW EDINBURGH

9
STRANRAER
CARLISLE

10
NEWCASTLE

7
LEEDS
HULL
LIVERPOOL

8

HOLYHEAD

NORWICH

6
BIRMINGHAM

4
OXFORD

5
CAMBRIDGE

CARDIFF
BRISTOL

LONDON
13
12

2
SOUTHAMPTON

3
BRIGHTON

1
PLYMOUTH

Maps of London based upon the Ordnance Survey with
the permission of the Controller of Her Majesty's
Stationery Office.

Roads are numbered and classified according to Department of Transport

Reference to sectional maps

⋯⋯⋯ Motorway
⋯⋯⋯ Major road
- - - - County boundary

● **Totnes**   Guide entry

◉ **Lynton**   Guide entry with
                accommodation

▣ BODMIN   Place name to assist
                location

1

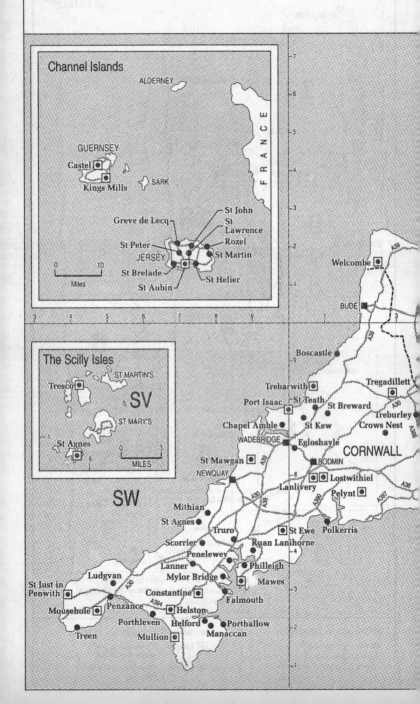

Channel Islands

ALDERNEY

GUERNSEY

Castel

Kings Mills

SARK

F R A N C E

St John

Greve de Lecq

St Lawrence

Rozel

St Peter

St Martin

JERSEY

St Brelade

St Helier

St Aubin

0   10

Miles

The Scilly Isles

ST MARTIN'S

Tresco

SV

ST MARY'S

St Agnes

0   3

MILES

SW

Welcombe

BUDE

Boscastle

Tregadillett

Trebarwith

St Teath

Port Isaac

St Breward

Treburley

Chapel Amble

St Kew

Crows Nest

WADEBRIDGE

Egloshayle

CORNWALL

St Mawgan

BODMIN

NEWQUAY

Lanlivery

Lostwithiel

Pelynt

Mithian

St Agnes

Truro

St Ewe

Polkerris

Scorrier

Ruan Lanihorne

Penelewey

Lanner

Phalleigh

Ludgvan

Mylor Bridge

Mawes

St Just in Penwith

Constantine

Falmouth

Mousehole

Penzance

Helston

Porthleven

Helford

Porthallow

Treen

Mullion

Manaccan

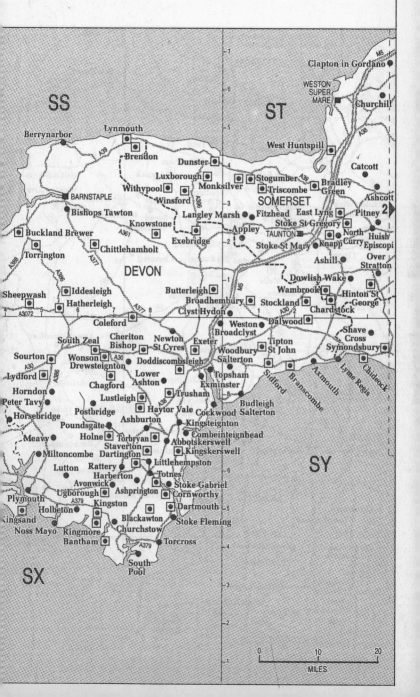

1

SS

ST

Clapton in Gordano

WESTON
SUPER
MARE

Churchill

Catcott

Berrynarbor

Lynmouth

Brendon

Dunster

West Huntspill

Luxborough

Stogumber

Bradley
Green

Ashcott

Withypool

Monksilver

Triscombe

SOMERSET

BARNSTAPLE

Winsford

Langley Marsh

Fitzhead

East Lyng

Pitney

Bishops Tawton

Knowstone

Appley

Stoke St Gregory

North
Curry

Huish
Episcopi

Buckland Brewer

Exebridge

TAUNTON

Knapp

Torrington

Chittlehamholt

Stoke St Mary

Ashill

Over
Stratton

A361

DEVON

Butterleigh

Dowlish Wake

Sheepwash

Iddesleigh

Broadhembury

Wambrook

Hinton St
George

Hatherleigh

Clyst Hydon

Stockland

Chardstock

Coleford

Weston
Broadclyst

Dalwood

Shave
Cross

South Zeal

Cheriton
Bishop

Newton
St Cyres

Exeter

Tipton
St John

Symondsbury

Chideock

Sourton

Wonson

Doddiscombsleigh

Woodbury
Salterton

Sidford

Axmouth

Lyme Regis

Drewsteignton

Lower
Ashton

Topsham

Branscombe

Lydford

Chagford

Exminster

Budleigh
Salterton

Horndon

Lustleigh

Trusham

Peter Tavy

Haytor Vale

Cockwood

Horsebridge

Postbridge

Ashburton

Kingsteignton

Poundsgate

Combeinteignhead

Meavy

Holne

Torbryan

Abbotskerswell

SY

Miltoncombe

Staverton

Kingskerswell

Lutton

Dartington

Littlehempston

Rattery

Totnes

Avonwick

Harberton

Stoke Gabriel

Ugborough

Ashprington

Cornworthy

Plymouth

Kingston

Dartmouth

Holbeton

Blackawton

Stoke Fleming

Kingsand

Noss Mayo

Ringmore

Churchstow

Bantham

Torcross

South
Pool

SX

0   10   20
MILES

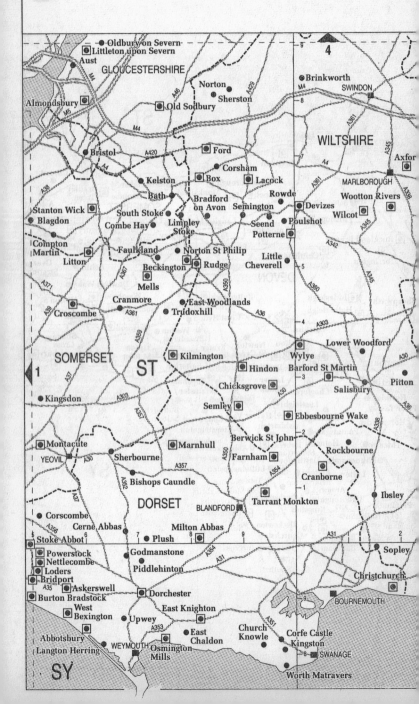

2

Oldbury on Severn
Littleton upon Severn
Aust
GLOUCESTERSHIRE
Almondsbury
Norton
Sherston
Old Sodbury
Brinkworth
SWINDON
Bristol
Ford
Corsham
WILTSHIRE
Kelston
Box
Lacock
Axfor
Bath
Rowde
MARLBOROUGH
Bradford on Avon
Semington
Devizes
Wootton Rivers
Wilcot
Stanton Wick
South Stoke
Limpley Stoke
Seend
Poulshot
Blagdon
Combe Hay
Potterne
Compton Martin
Faulkland
Norton St Philip
Little Cheverell
Litton
Beckington
Rudge
Mells
Cranmore
East Woodlands
Croscombe
Trudoxhill
SOMERSET
Kilmington
Wylye
Lower Woodford
ST
Hindon
Barford St Martin
Kingsdon
Chicksgrove
Salisbury
Pitton
Semley
Ebbesbourne Wake
Montacute
Marnhull
Berwick St John
Rockbourne
YEOVIL
Sherbourne
Farnham
Corscombe
Bishops Caundle
Cranborne
Ibsley
DORSET
Tarrant Monkton
BLANDFORD
Cerne Abbas
Milton Abbas
Stoke Abbot
Plush
Sopley
Powerstock
Godmanstone
Nettlecombe
Piddlehinton
Christchurch
Loders
Bridport
Askerswell
Dorchester
Burton Bradstock
West Bexington
East Knighton
BOURNEMOUTH
Upwey
Church Knowle
Corfe Castle
Abbotsbury
East Chaldon
Kingston
Langton Herring
WEYMOUTH
Osmington Mills
SWANAGE
SY
Worth Matravers

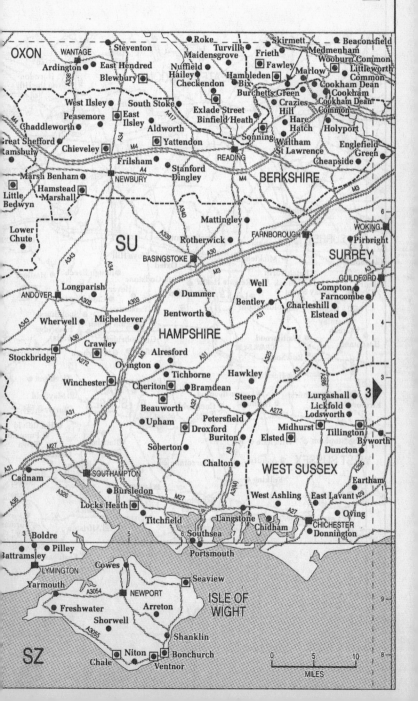

OXON
WANTAGE
Steventon
Roke
Turville
Skirmett
Beaconsfield
Ardington
East Hendred
Blewbury
Maidensgrove
Frieth
Medmenham
Wooburn Common
Nuffield
Fawley
Marlow
Littleworth
Common
Hailey
Hambleden
Bix
Cookham Dean
Checkendon
Burchetts Green
Cookham
West Isley
South Stoke
Exlade Street
Crazies
Hill
Cookham Dean
Common
Peasemore
East
Isley
Binfield Heath
Hare
Hatch
Holyport
Chaddleworth
Aldworth
Sonning
Waltham
St Lawrence
reat Shefford
Chieveley
Yattendon
Englefield
Green
amsbury
READING
Cheapside
Frilsham
Stanford
Dingley
BERKSHIRE
Marsh Benham
NEWBURY
Little
Bedwyn
Hamstead
Marshall
6
Lower
Chute
Mattingley
Rotherwick
FARNBOROUGH
WOKING
Pirbright
SU
BASINGSTOKE
A30
SURREY
GUILDFORD
Longparish
Dummer
Well
Compton
Farncombe
ANDOVER
Bentley
Charleshill
Elstead
5
Wherwell
Micheldever
Bentworth
HAMPSHIRE
4
Crawley
Alresford
Hawkley
Stockbridge
Ovington
Tichborne
Lurgashall
Lickfold
Winchester
Cheriton
Bramdean
Steep
Lodsworth
Beauworth
Petersfield
Midhurst
Tillington
3
Upham
Droxford
Buriton
Elsted
Byworth
Soberton
Duncton
Chalton
WEST SUSSEX
Cadnam
SOUTHAMPTON
Eartham
Bursledon
West Ashling
East Lavant
1
Locks Heath
Langstone
Oving
Titchfield
Chidham
CHICHESTER
Boldre
Pilley
Southsea
Donnington
attramsley
Portsmouth
LYMINGTON
Cowes
Yarmouth
Seaview
NEWPORT
Freshwater
Arreton
ISLE OF
WIGHT
9
Shorwell
Shanklin
SZ
Niton
Bonchurch
Chale
Ventnor
8

0   5   10
MILES

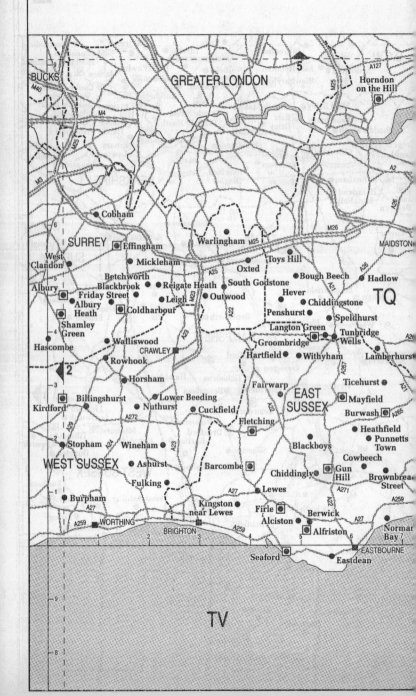

3

BUCKS

GREATER LONDON

Horndon
on the Hill

Cobham

SURREY

Effingham

Warlingham

MAIDSTON

West
Clandon

Mickleham

Oxted

Toys Hill

Bough Beech

Hadlow

Albury

Betchworth
Blackbrook

Reigate Heath

South Godstone

Hever

Chiddingstone

TQ

Friday Street

Leigh

Outwood

Penshurst

Speldhurst

Albury
Heath

Coldharbour

Langton Green

Tunbridge
Wells

Shamley
Green

Groombridge

Hascombe

Walliswood

CRAWLEY

Hartfield

Withyham

Lamberhurst

Rowhook

Fairwarp

Ticehurst

2

Horsham

Lower Beeding

EAST
SUSSEX

Mayfield

Billingshurst

Nuthurst

Cuckfield

Burwash

Kirdford

Fletching

Heathfield

Stopham

Wineham

Blackboys

Punnetts
Town

WEST SUSSEX

Ashurst

Barcombe

Chiddingly

Cowbeech

Gun
Hill

Fulking

Kingston
near Lewes

Lewes

Firle

Berwick

Brownbrea
Street

Burpham

Alciston

Alfriston

WORTHING

BRIGHTON

Seaford

Eastdean

EASTBOURNE

Normar
Bay

TV

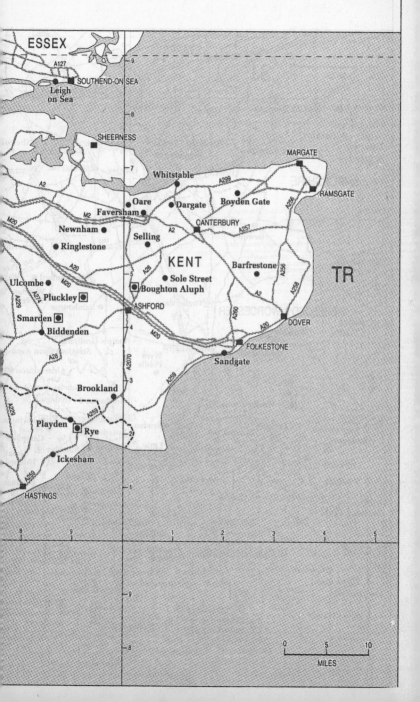

3

ESSEX

A127

SOUTHEND-ON-SEA

Leigh
on Sea

SHEERNESS

MARGATE

Whitstable

A299

RAMSGATE

A2

Oare

Dargate

Boyden Gate

A256

Faversham

M2

Newnham

CANTERBURY

A257

Ringlestone

Selling

A2

M20

A20

KENT

Barfrestone

A256

A28

Sole Street

A2

A259

Ulcombe

M20

Boughton Aluph

A274

Pluckley

TR

ASHFORD

A260

DOVER

Smarden

M20

A20

Biddenden

A2070

FOLKESTONE

A28

Sandgate

A259

Brookland

A259

A229

Playden

Rye

Ickesham

A259

HASTINGS

0   5   10
MILES

TR

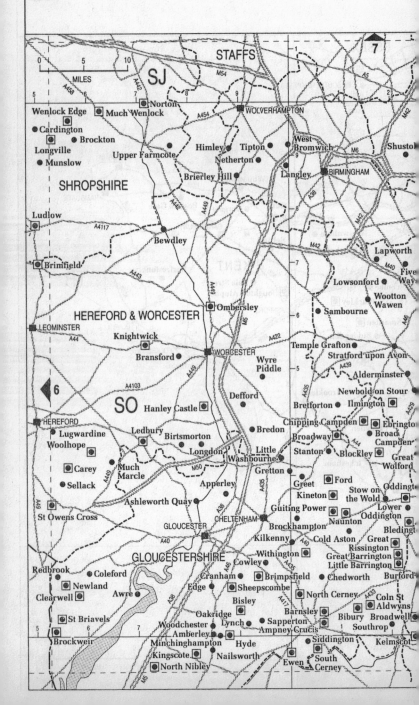

4

STAFFS

SJ

MILES

0   5   10

A458

M54

A5

A454   WOLVERHAMPTON

M6

Wenlock Edge   ● Much Wenlock   ● Norton

● Cardington

● Brockton

Longville   Upper Farmcote   Himley   ● Tipton   West Bromwich   Shusto

● Munslow   Netherton   Langley   BIRMINGHAM

SHROPSHIRE   Brierley Hill   A38

A442

Ludlow   A449   A38

A4117   Lapworth

Bewdley   M40   Five Way

● Brimfield   A443   Lowsonford   Wootton Wawen

HEREFORD & WORCESTER   A46

● LEOMINSTER   ● Ombersley   Sambourne

A44   M5   A22

Knightwick   Temple Grafton

Bransford   WORCESTER   Stratford upon Avon

A4103   Wyre Piddle   A439   Alderminster

6   SO   A435   Newbold on Stour

HEREFORD   Hanley Castle   Defford   Bretforton   Ilmington

Lugwardine   Ledbury   Bredon   Chipping Campden   Ebrington

Woolhope   Birtsmorton   Broadway   Broad Campden

Longdon   Little   Stanton   Blockley

Carey   Much Marcle   Washbourne   Great Wolford

Sellack   Gretton   Greet   Ford   Stow on the Wold   Oddingt

Apperley   Kineton   Lower

Ashleworth Quay   M50   Guiting Power   Naunton   Oddington

St Owens Cross   A38   Brockhampton   Bledingt

GLOUCESTER   CHELTENHAM   Great Rissington

A40   Kilkenny   Cold Aston   Great Barrington

GLOUCESTERSHIRE   Cowley   Little Barrington   Burford

Withington   Chedworth

Redbrook   ● Coleford   Cranham   Brimpsfield   Coln St Aldwyns

Newland   Edge   Sheepscombe   North Cerney   Bibury   Broadwell

Clearwell   Awre   Bisley   Barnsley   Southrop

St Briavels   Oakridge   Lynch   Sapperton   Ampney Crucis   Siddington   Kelmscot

Woodchester   Hyde   Ewen   South Cerney

Brockweir   Minchinghampton

Kingscote   Nailsworth

North Nibley

6

A49

A38

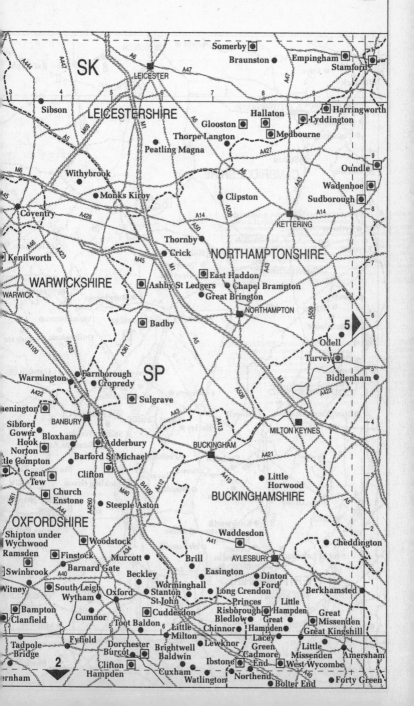

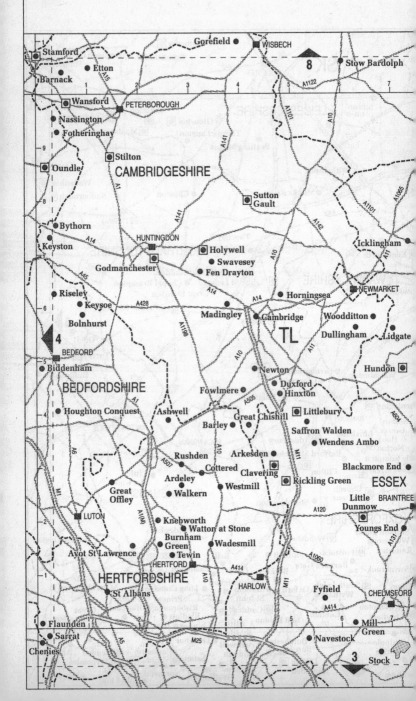

5

Gorefield ●   ■ WISBECH

Stamford ◉   ▲ 8   ● Stow Bardolph

● Etton

Barnack ●

◉ Wansford   ■ PETERBOROUGH

● Nassington

● Fotheringhay

◉ Stilton

◉ Oundle   **CAMBRIDGESHIRE**

◉ Sutton Gault

● Bythorn

Keyston ●   ■ HUNTINGDON   ● Holywell   ● Icklingham

Godmanchester ●   ● Swavesey

● Fen Drayton

● Horningsea   ● NEWMARKET

● Riseley

● Keysoe   ● Madingley   ◉ Cambridge   ● Woodditton

● Bolnhurst   **TL**   ● Dullingham   ● Lidgate

▲ 4   ■ BEDFORD   ● Hundon ◉

● Biddenham   ● Newton

BEDFORDSHIRE   ● Fowlmere   ● Duxford

● Hinxton

● Houghton Conquest   ● Ashwell   ● Great Chishill   ● Littlebury

● Barley   ● Saffron Walden

● Wendens Ambo

● Rushden   ● Arkesden   ● Blackmore End

● Cottered   ● Clavering   **ESSEX**

● Ardeley   ◉ Rickling Green

Great Offley   ● Walkern   ● Westmill   Little Dunmow ●   **BRAINTREE** ■

■ LUTON   ● Knebworth   ● Youngs End

● Watton at Stone

Burnham Green ●   ● Wadesmill

Ayot St Lawrence ●   ● Tewin

■ HERTFORD

HERTFORDSHIRE   ■ HARLOW   ● Fyfield   ■ CHELMSFORD

● St Albans

● Flaunden   ● Mill Green

● Sarrat   ● Navestock

Chenies ●   ▼ 3   ● Stock

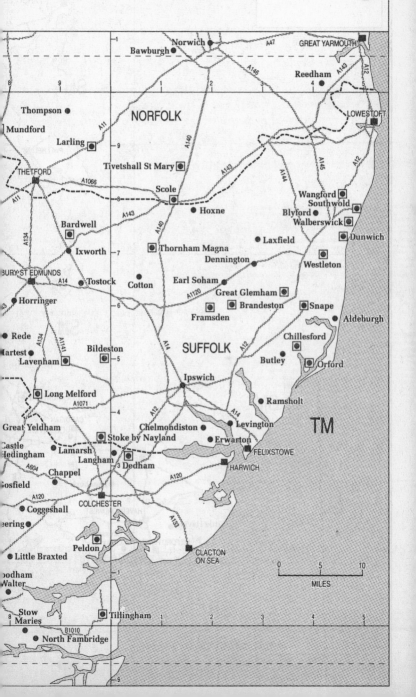

NORFOLK

Norwich ● Bawburgh ● GREAT YARMOUTH ■

A47 A146 A143 A12

Reedham ●

Thompson ● Mundford ● Larling ■ LOWESTOFT ■

A11 A140 A12

Tivetshall St Mary ■

THETFORD ■ A1066 Scole ■ A143 A144 A45 A12

Wangford ■ Southwold ● Blyford ● Walberswick ●

A11 Hoxne ● A143 A140 Dunwich ■

Bardwell ■ Thornham Magna ● Laxfield ● Westleton ■

Ixworth ● Dennington ●

A134 A14 Tostock ● Cotton ●

BURY ST EDMUNDS ■ Earl Soham ● Great Glemham ■

Horringer ● A1120 Brandeston ● Snape ■

Framsden ● Aldeburgh ●

Rede ● Bildeston ■ **SUFFOLK** Chillesford ●

A134 A1141 Lavenham ■ A14 Butley ● Orford ■

Martest ●

Ipswich ■ A12 Ramsholt ●

Long Melford ■ A1071 Levington ● **TM**

Great Yeldham ● A12 A14

Chelmondiston ● Erwarton ● FELIXSTOWE ■

Castle Hedingham ● Stoke by Nayland ■ Lamarsh ● HARWICH ■

A604 Langham ● Dedham ● A120

Chappel ●

Gosfield ● A120

Coggeshall ● COLCHESTER ■

Feering ● A133

Little Braxted ● CLACTON ON SEA ■

Woodham Walter ●

0   5   10

MILES

Stow Maries ● Tillingham ●

B1010

North Fambridge ●

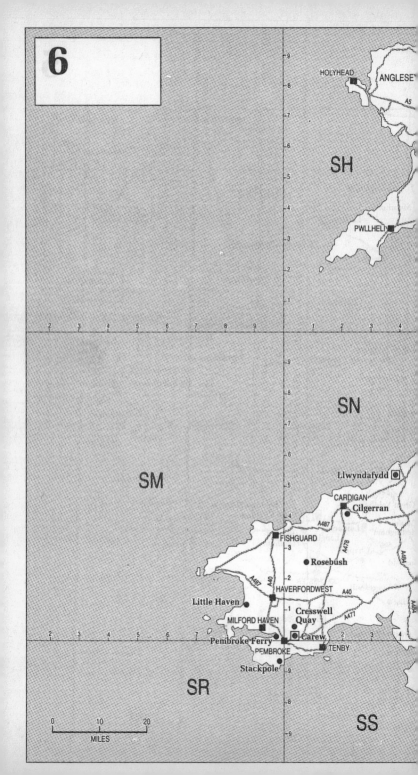

6

HOLYHEAD
ANGLESE
A5

SH

PWLLHELI

SN

SM

Llwyndafydd
CARDIGAN
Cilgerran
A487
FISHGUARD
A478
A48
Rosebush
A487
A40
HAVERFORDWEST
A40
Little Haven
Cresswell
Quay
A477
A48
MILFORD HAVEN
Pembroke Ferry
Carew
PEMBROKE
TENBY
Stackpole

SR

0   10   20
MILES

SS

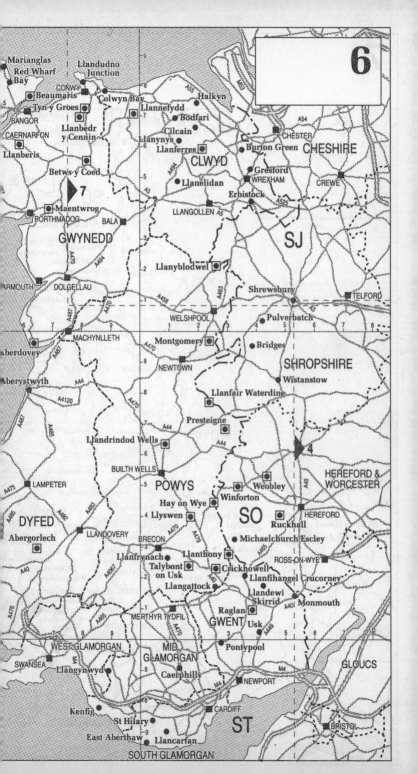

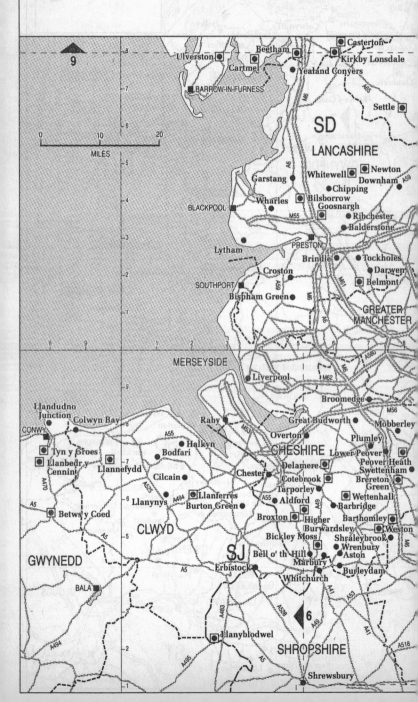

9

0   10   20
MILES

Casterton
Beetham
Ulverston
Kirkby Lonsdale
Cartmel
Yealand Conyers

BARROW-IN-FURNESS

Settle

SD

LANCASHIRE

Whitewell   Newton
Garstang   Downham
Chipping
Wharles   Bilsborrow
BLACKPOOL   Goosnargh
Ribchester
M55   Balderstone

Lytham   PRESTON

Brindle   Tockholes
Croston   Darwen
SOUTHPORT   A59   Belmont
Bispham Green
GREATER
MANCHESTER

MERSEYSIDE

Liverpool   M62
Broomedge

Llandudno   Raby   Great Budworth   Mobberley
Junction   Colwyn Bay
CONWY   Overton   Plumley
Tyn y Groes   Halkyn   CHESHIRE   Lower Peover
Llanbedr y   Bodfari   Peover Heath
Cennin   Llannefydd   Delamere   Swettenham
Chester   Cotebrook   Brereton
Cilcain   Tarporley   Green
Llanferres   Aldford   Wettenhall
Llanynys   Burton Green   Barbridge
Betws y Coed   Broxton   Higher   Barthomley
CLWYD   Burwardsley   Weston
Bickley Moss   Shraleybrook
Bell o' th' Hill   Wrenbury
GWYNEDD   Aston
Marbury
BALA   Erbistock   Burleydam
Whitchurch

6

Llanyblodwel

SHROPSHIRE

Shrewsbury

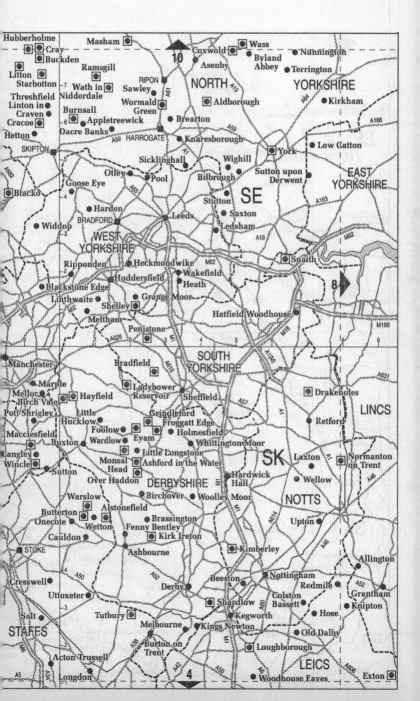

Hubberholme
Cray
Buckden
Litton
Starbotton
Threshfield
Linton in
Craven
Cracoe
Hetton
SKIPTON

Masham
Coxwold
Wass
Nunnington
Asenby
Byland
Abbey
Terrington

10
Ramsgill
Wath in
Nidderdale
RIPON
Sawley
Wormald
Green
NORTH
YORKSHIRE
Kirkham

Burnsall
Appletreewick
Dacre Banks
Aldborough
Brearton
HARROGATE
Knaresborough
Low Catton
York

SE
Sicklinghall
Wighill
Otley
Pool
Bilbrough
Sutton upon
Derwent
EAST
YORKSHIRE

Goose Eye
Blacko
Harden
BRADFORD
Stutton
Leeds
Saxton
Ledsham

WEST
YORKSHIRE
Widdop

Ripponden
Heckmondwike
Wakefield
Snaith
Blackstone Edge
Huddersfield
Heath
Linthwaite
Shelley
Grange Moor
Meltham
Hatfield Woodhouse
Penistone

8

Manchester
Bradfield
SOUTH
YORKSHIRE
Marple
Mellor
Birch Vale
Ladybower
Reservoir
Hayfield
Sheffield
Drakeholes
LINCS
Pott Shrigley
Little
Hucklow
Grindleford
Retford
Macclesfield
Foolow
Froggatt Edge
Buxton
Wardlow
Eyam
Holmesfield
Whittington Moor
SK
Cangley
Wincle
Little Longstone
Monsal
Head
Ashford in the Water
Laxton
Normanton
on Trent
Sutton
Over Haddon
Hardwick
Hall
DERBYSHIRE
Wellow
Warslow
Birchover
Woolley Moor
NOTTS
Butterton
Alstonefield
Onecote
Wetton
Brassington
Fenny Bentley
Upton
Cauldon
Kirk Ireton
STOKE
Ashbourne
Kimberley
Allington
Cresswell
Beeston
Nottingham
Uttoxeter
Derby
Redmile
Salt
Shardlow
Colston
Bassett
Grantham
Tutbury
Kegworth
Hose
Knipton
STAFFS
Melbourne
Kings Newton
Old Dalby
Acton Trussell
Burton on
Trent
Loughborough
Longdon
4
Woodhouse Eaves
LEICS
Exton

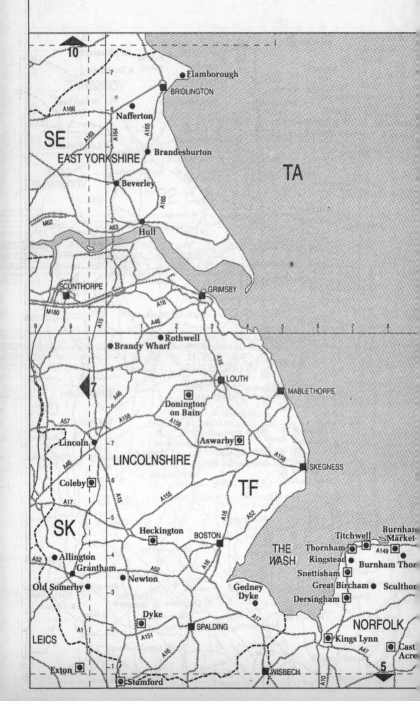

10

Flamborough
BRIDLINGTON

A166

Nafferton

SE
EAST YORKSHIRE

A165
A164
A165

Brandesburton

Beverley

A165

M62

A63

Hull

TA

SCUNTHORPE

M180

A18

A15

A46

GRIMSBY

Rothwell

Brandy Wharf

7

A46

A19

LOUTH

MABLETHORPE

Donington
on Bain

A158
A158

A57

Lincoln

Aswarby

A158

SKEGNESS

LINCOLNSHIRE

A46

Coleby

A15

A155

A16

A52

TF

A17

SK

Heckington

BOSTON

Titchwell

Burnham
Market

A52

Allington

Grantham

A52

Newton

A16

THE
WASH

Thornham
Ringstead

A149

Burnham Thor

Old Somerby

Snettisham

Great Bircham

Sculthor

Gedney
Dyke

Dersingham

A1

Dyke

A151

SPALDING

A17

NORFOLK

LEICS

A16

Kings Lynn

Cast
Acre

Exton

A10

A47

Stamford

WISBECH

5

8

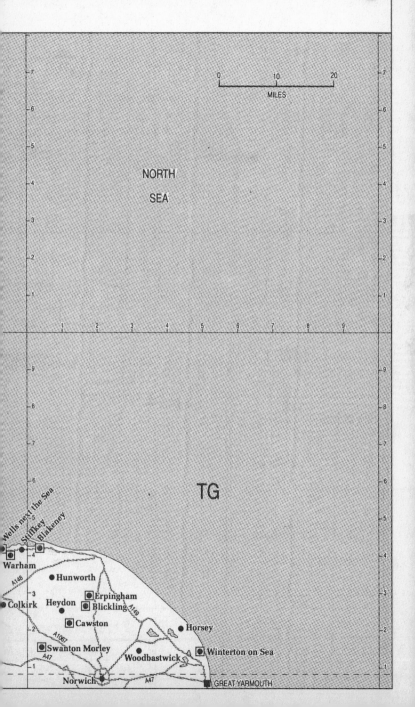

MILES

0   10   20

NORTH

SEA

TG

Wells next the Sea

Stiffkey

Blakeney

Warham

A148

Hunworth

Colkirk

Heydon

Erpingham

Blickling

A149

Cawston

Horsey

A1067

Swanton Morley

A47

Woodbastwick

Winterton on Sea

Norwich

A47

GREAT YARMOUTH

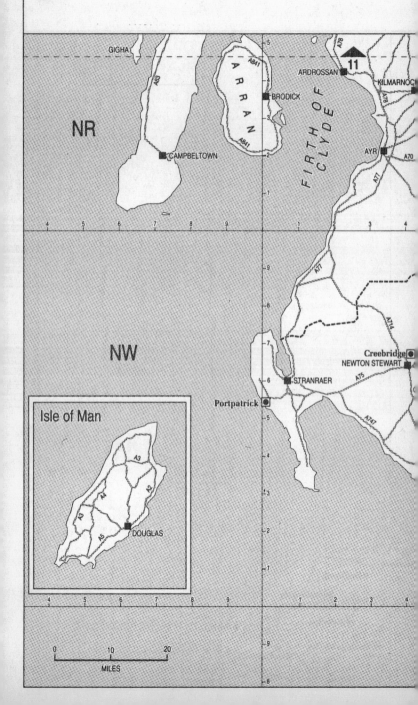

GIGHA

ARRAN

A841

BRODICK

ARDROSSAN

11

KILMARNOC

A63

FIRTH OF CLYDE

NR

A78

A71

CAMPBELTOWN

A841

AYR

A70

A77

NW

A77

A714

Creebridge

NEWTON STEWART

7

STRANRAER

A75

Portpatrick

A747

Isle of Man

A3

A2

A4

A5

A5

DOUGLAS

0   10   20
MILES

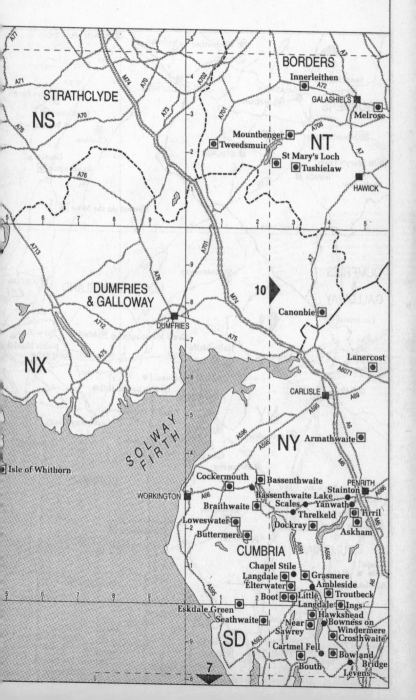

09

STRATHCLYDE

NS

BORDERS

NT

Innerleithen

GALASHIELS

Melrose

Mountbenger
Tweedsmuir

St Mary's Loch
Tushielaw

HAWICK

DUMFRIES & GALLOWAY

10

Canonbie

DUMFRIES

NX

Lanercost

CARLISLE

Isle of Whithorn

SOLWAY FIRTH

NY

Armathwaite

Cockermouth

Bassenthwaite

PENRITH

Bassenthwaite Lake

Stainton

WORKINGTON

Braithwaite

Scales

Yanwath

Threlkeld

Tirril

Loweswater

Dockray

Askham

Buttermere

CUMBRIA

Chapel Stile

Langdale
Elterwater

Grasmere
Ambleside

Boot

Little
Langdale

Troutbeck

Ings

Eskdale Green

Hawkshead

Seathwaite

Near
Sawrey

Bowness on
Windermere
Crosthwaite

SD

Cartmel Fell

Bouth

Bowland
Bridge
Levens

7

10

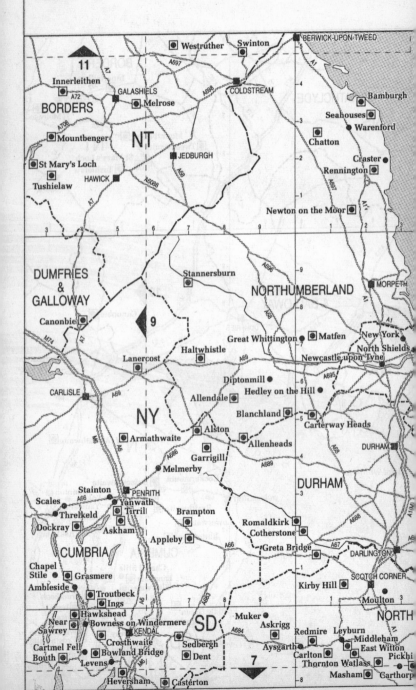

BERWICK-UPON-TWEED

Westruther Swinton

Innerleithen A697

BORDERS GALASHIELS Melrose COLDSTREAM

Mountbenger NT Bamburgh

Seahouses Warenford

St Mary's Loch JEDBURGH Chatton

Tushielaw HAWICK Craster Rennington

Newton on the Moor

DUMFRIES & GALLOWAY Stannersburn NORTHUMBERLAND

MORPETH

Canonbie 9 Great Whittington Matfen New York

Haltwhistle North Shields

Lanercost Newcastle upon Tyne

CARLISLE Diptonmill A695

NY Allendale Hedley on the Hill

Blanchland Carterway Heads

Armathwaite Alston Allenheads DURHAM

Garrigill

Melmerby A689

DURHAM

Stainton PENRITH

Scales Yanwath Romaldkirk SCOTCH CORNER

Threlkeld Tirril Brampton Cotherstone

Dockray Askham Greta Bridge DARLINGTON

Appleby A66

CUMBRIA Kirby Hill Moulton

Chapel Stile Grasmere NORTH

Ambleside Muker

Troutbeck Askrigg

Ings Redmire Leyburn

Near Sawrey Hawkshead SD Middleham

Bowness on Windermere KENDAL Aysgarth East Witton Pickhi

Cartmel Fell Crosthwaite Sedbergh Carlton Thornton Watlass

Bouth Levens Bowland Bridge Dent Masham Garthorp

Heversham Casterton 7

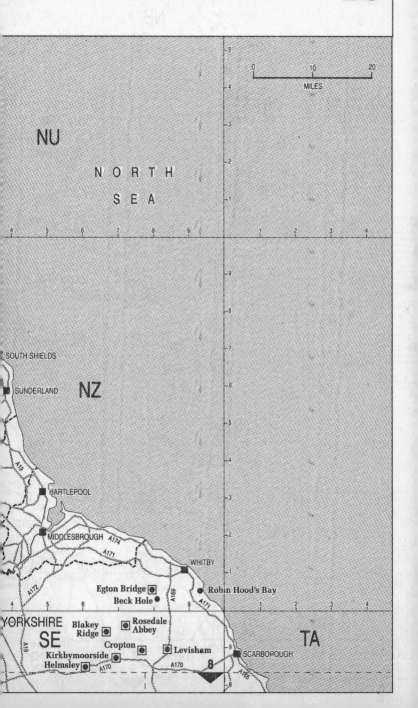

0   10   20
MILES

NU

N O R T H

S E A

5

4

3

2

1

4   5   6   7   8   9   1   2   3   4

9

8

7

SOUTH SHIELDS

SUNDERLAND   NZ   6

5

4

HARTLEPOOL   3

2

MIDDLESBROUGH   A174

A171   WHITBY   1

Egton Bridge   A169   Robin Hood's Bay
Beck Hole

A172   4   5   6   9   A171   1   2   3   4

YORKSHIRE   Blakey   Rosedale
SE   Ridge   Abbey   TA
Cropton
Kirkbymoorside   Levisham   9
Helmsley   A170   A170   SCARBOROUGH
8   A165
8

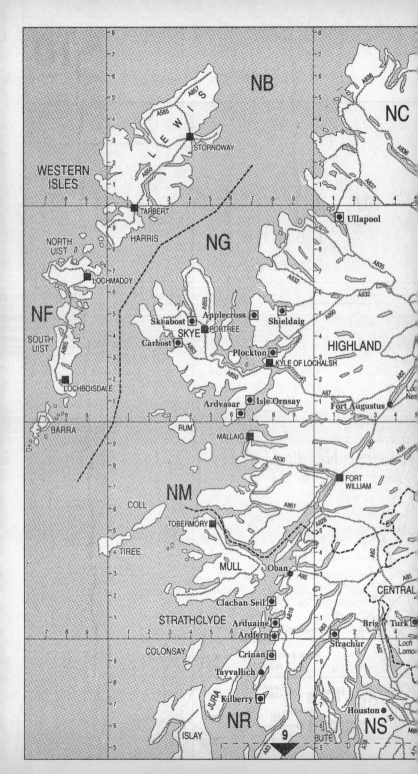

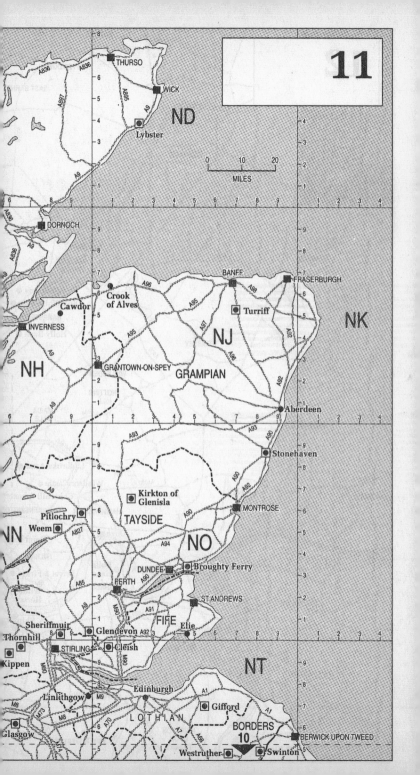

11

MILES
0   10   20

ND

THURSO
WICK
Lybster

DORNOCH

BANFF
FRASERBURGH
Crook
of Alves
Cawdor
Turriff
INVERNESS
NK
NJ
GRANTOWN-ON-SPEY
GRAMPIAN
NH
Aberdeen

Stonehaven

Kirkton of
Glenisla
Pitlochry
MONTROSE
Weem
TAYSIDE
NO
DUNDEE
Broughty Ferry
PERTH
Sheriffmuir
ST ANDREWS
Thornhill
Glendevon
Elie
FIFE
STIRLING
Cleish
Kippen
NT
Linlithgow
Edinburgh
Gifford
Glasgow
L O T H I A N
BORDERS
10
BERWICK UPON TWEED
Westruther
Swinton

NN

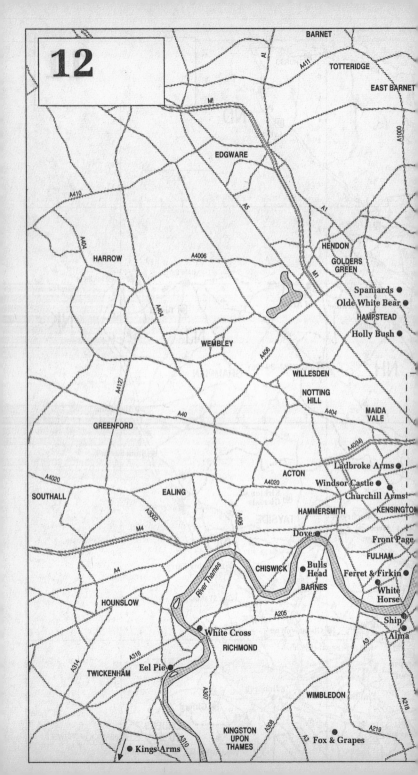

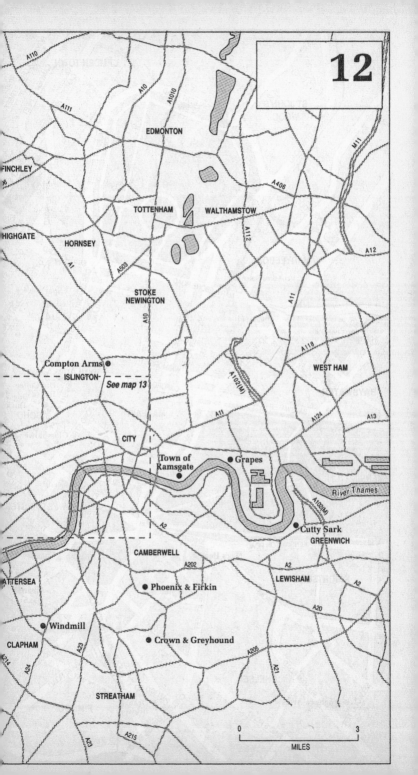

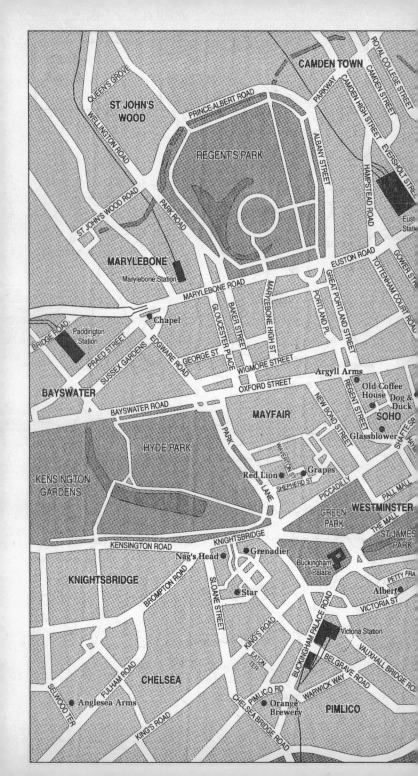

Report forms

Please report to us: you can use the tear-out forms on the following pages, the card in the middle of the book, or just plain paper – whichever's easiest for you. We need to know what you think of the pubs in this edition. We need to know about other pubs worthy of inclusion. We need to know about ones that should not be included.

The atmosphere and character of the pub are the most important features why it would, or would not, appeal to strangers, so please try and describe what is special about it. But the bar food and the drink are important too – please tell us about them.

If the food is really quite outstanding, tick the FOOD AWARD box on the form, and tell us about the special quality that makes it stand out – the more detail, the better. And if you have stayed there, tell us about the standard of accommodation – whether it was comfortable, pleasant, good value for money. Again, if the pub or inn place is worth special attention as a place to stay, tick the PLACE-TO-STAY AWARD box.

Please try to gauge whether a pub should be a main entry, or is best as a Lucky Dip (and tick the relevant box). In general, main entries need qualities that would make it worth other readers' while to travel some distance to them; Lucky Dips are the pubs that are worth knowing about if you are nearby. But if a pub is an entirely new recommendation, the Lucky Dip may be the best place for it to start its career in the *Guide* to encourage other readers to report on it, and gradually build up a dossier on it; it's very rare for a pub to jump straight into the main entries.

The more detail you can put into your description of a Lucky Dip pub that's only scantily decribed in the current edition (or not in at all), the better. This'll help not just us but also your fellow-readers gauge its appeal. A description of its character and even furnishings is a tremendous boon.

It helps enormously if you can give the full address for any new pub – one not yet a main entry, or without a full address in the Lucky Dip sections. In a town, we need the street name; in the country, if it's hard to find, we need directions. Without this, there's little chance of our being able to include the pub. And with any pub, it always helps to let us know about **prices** of food (and bedrooms, if there are any), and about any lunchtimes or evenings when food is **not** served. We'd also like to have your views on drinks quality – beer, wine, cider and so forth, even coffee and tea; and do let us know if it has bedrooms.

If you know that a Lucky Dip pub is open all day (or even late into the afternoon), please tell us – preferably saying which days.

When you go to a pub, don't tell them you're a reporter for the *Good Pub Guide*; we do make clear that all inspections are anonymous, and if you declare yourself as a reporter you risk getting special treatment – for better or for worse!

Sometimes pubs are dropped from the main entries simply because very few readers have written to us about them – and of course there's a risk that people may not write if they find the pub exactly as described in the entry. You can use the form at the front of the batch of report forms just to list pubs you've been to, found as described, and can recommend.

When you write to *The Good Pub Guide*, FREEPOST TN1569, WADHURST, East Sussex TN5 7BR, you don't need a stamp in the UK. We'll gladly send you more forms (free) if you wish.

Though we try to answer letters, there are just the four of us – and with other work to do, besides producing this *Guide*. So please understand if there's a delay. And from June till August, when we are fully extended getting the next edition to the printers, we put all letters and reports aside, not answering them until the rush is over (and after our post-press-day late summer holiday). The end of May is pretty much the cut-off date for reasoned consideration of reports for the next edition.